D1226413

Handbook *of* Health Psychology

Handbook *of* Health Psychology

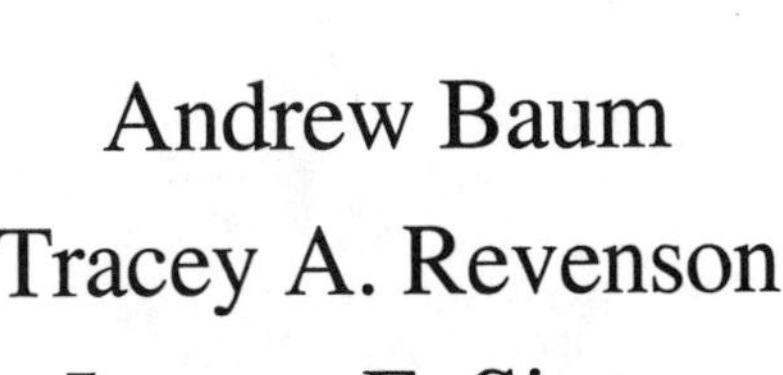

Andrew Baum

Tracey A. Revenson

Jerome E. Singer

LAWRENCE ERLBAUM ASSOCIATES, PUBLISHERS

2001 Mahwah, New Jersey London

Lawrence Erlbaum Associates, Inc., Publishers
10 Industrial Avenue
Mahwah, NJ 07430

Cover design by Kathryn Houghtaling Lacey

Library of Congress Cataloging-in-Publication Data

Handbook of health psychology / [edited by] Andrew Baum, Tracey A. Revenson, Jerome E. Singer.
p. cm.
Includes bibliographical references and index.
ISBN 0-8058-1495-7 (cloth : alk. paper)
1. Clinical health psychology—Handbooks, manuals, etc. 2. Medicine and psychology—Handbooks, manuals, etc. I. Baum, Andrew. II. Revenson, Tracey A. III. Singer, Jerome E.
[DNLM: 1. Behavioral Medicine. 2. Attitude to Health. 3. Disease—psychology. 4. Health Behavior. WB 103 H2363 2001]
R726.7 .H3645 2001
616'.001'9 —dc21 00-063628
CIP

Books published by Lawrence Erlbaum Associates are printed on acid-free paper, and their bindings are chosen for strength and durability.

Printed in the United States of America
10 9 8 7 6 5 4 3

To my mother, whose strength, love and boundless good will are a continuing inspiration, and to my wife Carrie and my children Jesse and Callie, who sustain me and make so much possible.

— A.B.

To my husband, Ed Seidman, for his unconditional love, to my daughter, Molly, my beloved principessa, and to the memory of my father, who believed I could become anything I wanted.

—T.A.R.

To Stanley Schachter, teacher, mentor, and friend.

—J.E.S.

Contents

Preface xiii

Introduction xv
Tracey A. Revenson and Andrew Baum

Part I. Basic Processes

1 Factors Influencing Behavior and Behavior Change 3
Martin Fishbein, Harry C. Triandis, Frederick H. Kanfer, Marshall Becker, Susan E. Middlestadt, and Anita Eichler

2 Representations, Procedures, and Affect in Illness Self-Regulation: A Perceptual-Cognitive Model 19
Howard Leventhal, Elaine A. Leventhal, and Linda Cameron

3 Conceptualization and Operationalization of Perceived Control 49
Kenneth A. Wallston

4 On Who Gets Sick and Why: The Role of Personality and Stress 59
Richard J. Contrada and Max Guyll

5 Visceral Learning 85
Bernard T. Engel

6 Biofeedback and Self-Regulation of Physiological Activity: A Major Adjunctive Treatment Modality in Health Psychology 95
Robert J. Gatchel

7 Behavioral Conditioning of the Immune System 105
Alexander W. Kusnecov

8 Physiological and Psychological Bases of Pain 117
Dennis C. Turk

9 Personality Traits as Risk Factors for Physical Illness 139
Timothy W. Smith and Linda C. Gallo

10 Personality's Role in the Protection and Enhancement of Health: Where the Research Has Been, Where It Is Stuck, How It Might Move 175
Suzanne C. Ouellette and Joanne DiPlacido

11 Social Comparison Processes in the Physical Health Domain 195
Jerry Suls and Réne Martin

12 Social Networks and Social Support 209
Thomas Ashby Wills and Marnie Filer

13 Self-Efficacy and Health 235
Brenda M. DeVellis and Robert F. DeVellis

14 The Psychobiology of Nicotine Self-Administration 249
Neil E. Grunberg, Martha M. Faraday, and Matthew A. Rahman

15 Obesity 263
Rena R. Wing and Betsy A. Polley

16 Alcohol Use and Misuse 280
Mark D. Wood, Daniel C. Vinson, and Kenneth J. Sher

Part II. Crosscutting Issues

17 Stress, Health, and Illness 321
Angela Liegey Dougall and Andrew Baum

18 What Are the Health Effects of Disclosure? 339
Joshua M. Smyth and James W. Pennebaker

19 Preventive Management of Work Stress: Current Themes and Future Challenges 349
Debra L. Nelson, James Campbell Quick, and Bret L. Simmons

20 Environmental Stress and Health 365
Gary W. Evans

21 Adjustment to Chronic Illness: Theory and Research 387
Annette L. Stanton, Charlotte A. Collins, and Lisa Sworowski

22 Recall Biases and Cognitive Errors in Retrospective Self-Reports: A Call for Momentary Assessments 405
Amy A. Gorin and Arthur A. Stone

23 Burnout and Health 415
Michael P. Leiter and Christina Maslach

24 Sociocultural Influences on Health 427
Caroline A. Macera, Cheryl A. Armstead, and Norman B. Anderson

25 The Multiple Contexts of Chronic Illness: Diabetic Adolescents and Community Characteristics 441
Dawn A. Obeidallah, Stuart T. Hauser, and Alan M. Jacobson

26 Childhood Health Issues Across the Life Span 449
Barbara G. Melamed, Barrie Roth, and Joshua Fogel

27 Social Influences in Etiology and Prevention of Smoking and Other Health Threatening Behaviors in Children and Adolescents 459
Richard I. Evans

28 Health, Behavior, and Aging 469
Ilene C. Siegler, Lori A. Bastian, and Hayden B. Bosworth

29 Informal Caregiving to Older Adults: Health Effects of Providing and Receiving Care 477
Lynn M. Martire and Richard Schulz

30 Stress Processes in Pregnancy and Birth: Psychological, Biological, and Sociocultural Influences 495
Christine Dunkel-Schetter, Regan A. R. Gurung, Marci Lobel, and Pathik D. Wadhwa

31 Women's Health Promotion 519
Barbara K. Rimer, Colleen M. McBride, and Carolyn Crump

32 Male Partner Violence: Relevance to Health Care Providers 541
Mary P. Koss, Maia Ingram, and Sara L. Pepper

33 Confronting Fertility Problems: Current Research and Future Challenges 559
Lauri A. Pasch

34 Patient Adherence to Treatment Regimen 571
Jacqueline Dunbar-Jacob and Elizabeth Schlenk

35 Rehabilitation 581
Robert G. Frank

36 Community Intervention 591
David G. Altman and Robert M. Goodman

37 Citizen Participation and Health: Toward a Psychology of Improving Health Through Individual, Organizational, and Community Involvement 613
Frances Butterfoss, Abraham Wandersman, and Robert M. Goodman

38 The Effects of Physical Activity on Physical and Psychological Health 627
Wayne T. Phillips, Michaela Kiernan, and Abby C. King

III. Applications to the Study of Disease

39 Hostility (and Other Psychosocial Risk Factors): Effects on Health and the Potential for Successful Behavioral Approaches to Prevention and Treatment 661
Redford B. Williams

40 Stress and Silent Ischemia 669
Willem J. Kop, John S. Gottdiener, and David S. Krantz

41 Stress, Immunity, and Susceptibility to Infectious Disease 683
Anna L. Marsland, Elizabeth A. Bachen, Sheldon Cohen, and Stephen B. Manuck

42 Nonpharmacological Treatment of Hypertension 697
Alvin P. Shapiro

43 Cancer 709
Barbara L. Andersen, Deanna M. Golden-Kreutz, and Vicki DiLillo

44 Subjective Risk and Helath Protective Behavior: Cancer Screening and Cancer Prevention 727
Leona S. Aiken, Mary A. Gerend, and Kristina M. Jackson

45 Stress and Breast Cancer 747
Douglas L. Delahanty and Andrew Baum

46 Behavioral Intervention in Comprehensive Cancer Care 757
William H. Redd and Paul Jacobsen

47 Frontiers in the Behavioral Epidemiology of HIV/STDs 777
Joseph A. Catania, Diane Binson, M. Margaret Dolcini, Judith Tedlie Moskowitz, and Ariane van der Straten

48 HIV Disease in Ethnic Minorities: Implications of Racial/Ethnic Differences in Disease Susceptibility and Drug Dosage Response for HIV Infection and Treatment 801
Vickie M. Mays, Bennett T. So, Susan D. Cochran, Roger Detels, Rotem Benjamin, Erica Allen, and Susan Kwon

49 Women and AIDS: A Contextual Analysis 817
Jeannette R. Ickovics, Beatrice Thayaparan, and Kathleen A. Ethier

50 Living with HIV Disease 841
Sheryl L. Catz and Jeffrey A. Kelly

51 Cultural Diversity and Health Psychology 851
Hope Landrine and Elizabeth A. Klonoff

Author Index 893

Subject Index 961

Preface

This volume was conceived during the waning stages of initial, rapid growth of health psychology. In the preceding years the field had defined itself, identified important contributions and targets of opportunity, and had achieved a remarkable degree of influence within its parent field as well as the larger behavioral medicine arena. Behavioral treatments and adjunctive treatments for palliation and cure were developed, prevention that relied on behavior and behavior change was expanded, and psychological variables were more routinely included in models of the etiology of disease and promotion or maintenance of good health. Public health conceptions of air-borne or water-borne diseases or disease vectors had been supplemented by "lifestyle-borne diseases" and the expansion of medical psychology practice with patients and at-risk individuals had occurred. Clearly this was a time of great accomplishment that required a pause and an opportunity to reflect and integrate all that had been learned and done.

As with all Handbooks, preparation and finalization of chapters and contributions took longer than was initially expected, and the pause in the rapid growth of health psychology was brief (if, indeed, there was a pause). As the volume was being put together, important new research and theory in areas like cancer, women's health, and socioeconomic or sociocultural phenomena appeared and new emphases on community involvement, prevention, and survivorship evolved. The field was continuing to grow and mature at a rate that made it difficult to keep up. Consequently, this volume had to do more than summarize previous work and chart new directions. It also had to integrate new work often as related chapters were being completed. The Handbook has incorporated these new and breaking developments for the most part and represents a comprehensive summary and integration of current research and theory in health psychology. It should serve as a valuable resource for many years, containing the roots and seeds of future discoveries and accomplishments as well as the more established and enduring bases, applications, and implications of our work over the past 30 years.

There are many people who have contributed to the development of health psychology and to this book over the years, far too many to thank in this preface. One who should be singled out, for his rare vision, wit, and patience, and for his support, friendship, and enthusiasm for health psychology is Larry Erlbaum. As a friend, colleague, publisher, and *mentsch* he has been and continues to be a pillar of the health psychology community. We would also like to thank Michele Hayward for her patience, outstanding organizational and editorial skills and stewardship of this project from its inception, and to production and editorial folks at LEA, most notably Art Lizza. Most of all, we thank the contributors to this volume and to the field of health psychology for their hard work, dedication, and vision.

International Advisory Board

Introduction

Tracey A. Revenson

Andrew Baum

The woods are lovely, dark and deep,
But I have promises to keep,
And miles to go before I sleep,
And miles to go before I sleep.
(Frost, 1923)

Over the past two decades, health psychology researchers have grappled with critical behavioral, biological, and social science questions: How do personality and behavior contribute to the pathophysiology of cardiovascular disease? What do women gain from screening mammography if it creates anxiety and avoidance of regular screening? Why do we expect individuals to take responsibility for condom use to prevent HIV transmission when using condoms is an interpersonal negotiation? When are social relationships supportive and when are they detrimental to health? Only some of these questions have been answered adequately, many findings have been refuted, and many questions have been reframed along the way. The chapters in this volume address the central questions (still) of interest for Health Psychology, and pose many more for the next decade of research and theory.

Although this is a first edition, one could argue that there are two precursors of this volume. In 1979, *Health Psychology—A Handbook,* edited by George Stone, Frances Cohen, and Nancy Adler, was published by Jossey-Bass, Inc. At that time the term *health psychology* was a fairly new one; only a handful of doctoral programs in psychology specifically trained health psychologists, and the Division of Health Psychology (Division 38) had just been established within the American Psychological Association (Wallston, 1997). In the mid–1980s, a series of five edited volumes were published by Lawrence Erlbaum Associates under the title, *Handbook of Psychology and Health* (Baum & Singer, 1982, 1987; Baum, Taylor, & Singer, 1984; Gatchel, Baum, & Singer, 1982; Krantz, Baum, & Singer, 1983). In contrast to the Stone et al. volume, the books in this series focused on specific topic areas, such as child and adolescent health, cardiovascular disorders, coping and stress, or on subdisciplines within psychology (clinical, social). This series was published over several years just as Health Psychology became firmly established in its own right. Although there has been a number of textbooks and edited volumes in the area of health psychology published since then, there has been no other comprehensive "handbook".[1] As there have been great advances in knowledge about health-behavior relationships in the past decade, the time seemed right for a handbook. Although many publications bear the designation of "handbook", the New Shorter Oxford English Dictionary offers the following definition, "A book containing concise in-

[1] There have been other handbooks in specialty areas, for example, *Handbook of Stress: Theoretical and Clinical Aspects* (Goldberger & Breznitz, 1983, second edition, 1993); *Behavioral Health: A Handbook of Health Enhancement and Disease Prevention* (Matarazzo et al., 1984); *Handbook of Behavioral Medicine* (Gentry, 1984)); *Health Psychology: A Psychobiological Perspective* (Feurestein, Labbe,& Kuczmierczyk, 1986); *Behavioral Medicine & Women: A Comprehensive Handbook* (Blechman & Brownell, 1988, revised 1998); and *Handbook of Diversity Issues in Health Psychology* (Kato & Mann, 1996).

formation on a particular subject; a guidebook" (1997, E 19). At nearly 900 pages, one could argue that this Handbook is not concise, but the chapters do synthesize current theory and knowledge on many substantive areas in the field, taking us through the development of a concept to its future directions.

The preface to Stone, Cohen, and Adler's handbook is just as fitting today as it was 21 years ago: "*In recent years there has been a growing concern about problems of health and illness and about the state and cost of the current health care delivery system. There has also been increasing awareness of the significance of psychological factors in the etiology, course, and treatment of disease and in the maintenance of health*" (1979, p. ix).

Let us use these two sentences as a springboard to report on the progress of health psychology, place current challenges in sociopolitical context, and guide our work for the future.

THE CURRENT SOCIOPOLITICAL CONTEXT OF HEALTH PSYCHOLOGY

An article published a decade ago in the *New England Journal of Medicine* illustrated one important aspect of the current health care crisis when it concluded that a black man in Harlem was less likely to reach 65 years of age than was a man in Bangladesh (McCord & Freeman, 1990). Americans spend more of their gross domestic product on health services than any other major industrialized country; in 1998, national health care expenditures totaled $1.15 trillion, or 13.5% of the gross domestic product (U.S. Health Care Financing Administration, 1999). Yet, the quality of healthcare and its availability to our citizens is more limited than in many nations that spend less. These enormous health expenditures do not assure better quality care or better health for all Americans. Despite overall declines in mortality, disparities among racial/ethnic groups in mortality and morbidity remain substantial: a White female child born in 1997 can expect to live 79.9 years, a black female child 74.7 years; the comparable figures for males are 74.3 and 67.2 (Hoyert, Kochanek, & Murphy, 1999). In 1997, overall mortality was 55 percent higher for Black Americans than for White Americans (National Center for Health Statistics, 1999). Many causes of mortality that may explain this differential include behaviorally-linked conditions, such as HIV infection, homicide, firearm-related deaths, unintentional injuries, and stroke. Stage-specific survival rates among women with breast cancer have increased overall in the past quarter-century, but the overall 5-year survival rates for women from 1989–1994 were 87% for White women and 71% for Black women (National Center for Health Statistics, 1999). Explanations for these disparities include the fact that, on average, white women receive prenatal care more often and earlier in their pregnancies, and seek medical care for breast cancer at an earlier stage of the disease.

Chronic diseases often affect those people who have the least access to health care and the fewest financial resources to pay for it. In 1998 an estimated 44.3 million Americans (16.3% of the population) were not covered by health insurance at any time during the year, and the percentage was double (32.3%) for poor people (National Center for Health Statistics, 1999). The uninsured rate among Hispanics was three times higher than that of non-Hispanic Whites (National Center for Health Statistics, 1999). Ethnic minority and elderly individuals, families living in poverty, and people living in rural areas or inner cities are often in the poorest health, have multiple risk factors for serious illness, receive the poorest health care, have little or no insurance coverage, and are less likely to receive preventive care. Despite medical progress in the past quarter-century that has led to reductions in the major causes of death (cancer, heart disease, and stroke), many underserved and ethnic minority groups are lagging behind (Macera, Armstead, & Anderson, chap. 24; Landrine & Klonoff, chap. 51). For example, the age-adjusted mortality rate (for all causes) for Blacks is approximately one and a half-times that of Whites (Macera et al., chap. 24). Approximately 31% of this excess mortality can be accounted for by six well-established risk factors related to behavior: smoking, alcohol intake, total serum cholesterol, blood pressure, obesity, and diabetes. An additional 38% can be accounted for by family income, despite the fact that income and the prevalence of risk factors co-vary. On a disease-specific level, coronary heart disease as a cause of death among Blacks far exceeds that of Whites, with both physiological factors (e.g, hypertension, cardiovascular reactivity) and social environmental factors (e.g., racial stress, socioeconomic status) playing a role. HIV/AIDS has disproportionately affected certain ethnic minority groups in this country as well as people in poverty, with behavioral mediating processes including intravenous drug injection and unprotected sex (Catania, Binson, Dolcini, Moskowitz, & van der Straten, chap. 47; Mays, So, Cochran, Detels, Benjamin, Allen, & Kwon, chap. 48). The research these examples reflect suggests we look more closely at the interaction of person, situation, and social-structural factors in understanding these health differentials. Important social structural factors include education and the economics of health care, which are mutually influential and which both influence health practices.

There are other factors that argue for the approach generally taken by health psychology and related disciplines like behavioral medicine, medical sociology, and medical anthropology. Perhaps the most important is that the medical model of disease and health that has dominated the prevention, treatment, and scientific study of these phenomena simply cannot account for nor explain the onset and progression of illness—who becomes ill, why people get particular diseases at a certain time in their life, and how these diseases respond to treatment. Where major diseases were once caused by microorganisms that could be controlled or eradicated with wonder drugs, improved sanitation, and other biological interventions, the diseases that dominate health care today are not. Rather, they are diseases of lifestyle, aging, or behavior interacting with genetic predisposition and biological changes. Most cardiovascular diseases have substantial genetic origins, reflect biological processes in their pathophysiology, and respond to medications and medical treatments. However, considerable variance in their development and course is explained by behavior: diet, exercise, tobacco use, and stress appear to contribute directly and indirectly to these diseases. Other major health threats in this modern era also appear to arise at least in part because of these factors, and cancer, diabetes, HIV disease, and other major diseases may be more readily controlled through thoughtful and systematic application of biobehavioral principles and the sociocultural context (e.g., Amaro, 1995). The confluence of the changing face of healthcare, the unequal burden of disease across our society, and the dominance of chronic diseases with substantial behavioral components has been key in the development of health psychology.

CURRENT APPROACHES IN HEALTH PSYCHOLOGY

At the time it was established, the discipline of health psychology brought together psychologists trained in traditional areas of psychology who shared a common interest in problems of health and illness and a common conceptual approach—but who brought their own disciplinary paradigms and methodologies to the table. Not surprisingly, this cacophony of scientific jargons, models, and approaches was confusing at times. It also brought a breadth and eclecticism to the study of health and behavior that has been partly responsible for its success.

The common approach was labeled the *biopsychosocial model* (Engel, 1977; Schwartz, 1982). In contrast to the biobehavioral model it replaced, this eponynymously named approach suggests a transaction of *psyche* and *soma*—that physiological, psychological *and* social factors are braided together in health and illness. The biopsychosocial model does not give primacy to biological indices; they are not the ultimate criteria for defining health and illness. Instead, the model argues, it is impossible to understand disease processes by knowing about only one component of the model. The biopsychosocial model was inclusive enough to be applied to risk estimates for particular diseases as well as health-promoting behaviors and environments, to disease progression as well as psychosocial adaptation to illness, and to individually-oriented therapeutic and behavior change interventions as well as broader community-based and media approaches. The biopsychosocial model stimulated more effective theories and research designs; facilitated multi-disciplinary thinking and, most importantly, suggested a multi-cause multi-effect approach to health and illness, rather than the limiting single-cause, single-effect approach.

Although the strength of experimental evidence is not consistent across all diseases or all psychological variables implicated in disease, research of the past 20 years strongly supports the biopsychosocial model. In a recent *Annual Review* chapter, Baum and Posluszny (1999) specify three pathways in which psychosocial or behavioral factors affect, and are affected by, health and illness: (1) direct biological changes that cause or are caused by emotional or behavioral processes; (2) behaviors that convey health risks; and (3) behaviors associated with illness or the possibility of becoming ill. Behavioral conditioning of the immune system (Kusnecov, chap. 7), pain processes (Turk, chap. 8), and the effects of stress on physiology (Dougall & Baum, chap. 17; G. Evans, chap. 20; Dunkel-Schetter, Gurung, Lobel, & Wadhwa, chap. 30; Kop, Gottdiener, & Krantz, chap. 40; Marsland, Bachen, Cohen, & Manuck, chap. 41; Delahanty & Baum, chap. 45) all exemplify direct influences—sometimes reciprocal, sometimes parallel—of psychological and physiological processes.

Many other phenomena of interest to health psychologists illustrate the second and third pathways: cognitive appraisals of control, abilities or others' situations (Fishbein, Triandis, Kanfer, Becker, Middlestadt, & Eichler, chap. 1; Leventhal, Leventhal, & Cameron, chap. 2; Wallston, chap. 3; Suls & Martin, chap. 11; DeVellis & DeVellis, chap. 13); personality (Contrada & Guyll, chap. 4; Smith & Gallo, chap. 9; Ouellette & DiPlacido, chap. 10; Williams, chap. 39); coping (Stanton, Collins, & Sworowski, chap. 21); interpersonal relationships (Wills & Filer, chap. 12; Smyth & Pennebaker, chap. 18; Evans, chap. 27) screening (Rimer, McBride, & Crump, chap. 31; Aiken, Gerend, & Jackson, chap. 44;) and adherence (Dunbar-Jacob & Schlenk, chap. 34). Well-established behavioral risk factors (pathway 2) include: smoking (Grunberg, Faraday, & Rahman, chap. 14,) alcohol intake (Wood, Vinson, & Sher, chap. 16), and weight control (Wing & Polley, chap. 15).

The role of biological, psychological and social factors in health and illness is not hard to accept. What has been more difficult to understand, and to translate into testable theories, is how health is affected by the *interplay* of those physiological, psychological, sociological and cultural factors. Previously, card-carrying health psychologists were trained in one of the more "traditional" areas of psychology (developmental, social, clinical, experimental) and, they tended to define problems through the paradigmatic lenses of that area. More recently, the field has seen a concerted attempt to blend approaches, conduct "translational" research, and develop more synergistic models. For example, the area of psychoneuroimmunology not only connects areas *within* psychology, but links them to a subdiscipline of biology/medicine (Andersen, Golden-Kreutz, & DiLillo, chap. 43; Andersen, Kiecolt-Glaser, & Glaser, 1994). A recent focus in cancer control and prevention examines how the presence of disease biomarkers affects treatment choices, screening behavior, and mental health (Lerman, 1997). In 1995, this emphasis on multidisciplinary knowledge found "legs" in the creation of the Office of Behavioral and Social Science Research at NIH in 1995. The mission of this office is, "to enhance and accelerate scientific advances in the understanding, treatment, and prevention of disease by greater attention to behavioral and social factors and their interaction with biomedical variables" (Anderson, 1999).

Other notable changes have occurred in the way health-behavior processes are studied. First, we have seen more and more research set in the world of everyday experience, linked to the social problems we face. For example, the pressing problems of violence against women (Koss, Ingram, & Pepper, chap. 32), alcohol and drug use (Grunberg et al., chap. 14; Wing & Polley, chap. 15); and workplace stress (Nelson, Quick, & Simmons, chap. 19;

Leiter & Maslach, chap. 23) fall under the rubric of health psychology because of their health-damaging consequences.

Second, health psychology (like its mother-field) has gone beyond individual-level processes to examine phenomena within social systems: the family (Martire & Schulz, chap. 29; Pasch, chap. 33); workplace (Nelson et al., chap. 19); school (G. Evans, chap. 20) and community (Obeidallah, Hauser, & Jacobson, chap. 25; Altman & Goodman, chap. 36; Butterfoss, Wandersman, & Goodman, chap. 37). Ecological approaches that examine the transactional relationships among individuals and the environments they live in, as well as inter-relationships among these settings, have received much theoretical attention and offer promise for understanding disease processes within cultural groups and for designing effective interventions (Anderson & McNeilly, 1991; Revenson, 1990; Smith & Anderson, 1986; Taylor, Repetti, & Seeman, 1997; Winnett, King, & Altman, 1989). These models have been applied to understanding health phenomena such as the effects of environmental stress (G. Evans, chap. 20), HIV infection among women (Amaro, 1995; Ickovics, Thayaparan, & Ethier, chap. 49); and social inequalities in health outcomes (Anderson, 1995; Macera et al., chap. 24). An ecological approach also recognizes the fact that health-behavior processes are developmental, and that we must understand the specific linkages at different stages of the life cycle (Melamed, Roth, & Fogel, chap. 26; Siegler, Bastian, & Bosworth, chap. 28; Martire & Schulz, chap. 29; Pasch, chap. 33; Ickovics et al., chap. 49).

Third, health psychologists look to health-promoting behaviors as well as health-damaging ones (Rimer et al., chap. 31). Health is clearly more than the absence of the signs and symptoms of physical disease. The inclusive definition offered by the World Health Organization defines health as a state of complete physical, mental and social well-being, and not as the mere absence of disease and infirmity (symptoms). For example, regular exercise may be one of the most powerful determinants of overall health, as well as a deterrent for many diseases (Phillips, Kiernan, & King, chap. 38). Early detection of breast and cervical cancers (as well as many other cancers) has resulted in lowered mortality rates among women of all ages (Rimer et al., chap. 31; Aiken et al., chap. 44).

All three of these changes have been shadowed by a call to bring cultural differences in health front and center when understanding the behavioral and social factors in health and illness (Amaro, 1995; Landrine & Klonoff, chap. 51). This may be the area where health psychology has had the least success but has the potential for the greatest contribution. Although it has been a central tenet of medical sociology and epidemiology for years, only recently have psychologists acknowledged the strong direct and indirect influences of socioeconomic status on health (e.g., Adler et al., 1994), whether conceptualized in terms of income, education or social class. For example, people with less than a high school education have death rates that are twice those for people with education beyond high school (National Center for Health Statistics, 1999). In a similar fashion, health psychology has increased attention to within group health-behavior processes for women (Stanton & Gallant, 1995), people of color (Anderson, 1995; Anderson & Eisner, 1997); and older persons (Manuck, Jennings, & Baum, 2000; Resnick & Rozensky, 1996).

Finally, there has been a willingness to blur the boundaries between what is termed "basic" and "applied" science, and to work to integrate knowledge and practice. Exemplars of this work are described in the chapters in the third section of this volume, as scholars translate research findings into effective and cost-effective techniques for individual treatment (Shapiro, chap. 42; Redd, & Jacobsen, chap. 46) and community-based interventions (Altman & Goodman, chap. 36; Butterfoos et al., chap. 37).

TRANSLATING HEATH PSYCHOLOGY RESEARCH INTO PRACTICE AND POLICY

With the exception of AIDS, the nature and patterns of disease over this century have changed from acute, infectious, and often fatal diseases to chronic disabling illnesses.

Heart disease, cancer, and stroke account for the greatest number of deaths in the United States, for both men and women, and, with other chronic conditions, account for increased disability, hospitalization days, and lowered quality of life. Much of this illness and disability—the preventable portion—has been linked to behavioral or lifestyle factors (Healthy People 2000, 1990; Matarazzo et al., 1994). A prime example is cigarette smoking, which has been implicated in the development of lung cancer, stroke, coronary artery disease, and low-birthweight babies.

The dramatic drop in mortality from infectious diseases such as tuberculosis, diphtheria, and polio over the past century was largely a result of advances in public health, accomplished by changes in the physical environment or through the use of preventive or therapeutic measures such as vaccines and antibiotics. No single exposure preventive interventions comparable to vaccines can "remove" the behavioral and lifestyle factors that are involved in the onset and progression of chronic disease. And, although recent emphases on disease prevention and health promotion among the medical and public health sectors provide a welcome contrast to the traditional biomedical model, most disease prevention efforts have been defined and practiced by the medical community in ways that seriously limit their utility.

Health psychology's contribution to decreasing the prevalence of illness has revolved primarily around individual behavior change, consistent with the foundations and history of the discipline. Similarly, most research in health psychology (translated into practice by its cousin, behavioral medicine) has been directed toward individual or group differences in health status indicators, risk factors, and habits (Rodin & Salovey, 1989). While recognizing the importance of primary prevention, health psychologists have concentrated their efforts on secondary prevention at the individual or small group level, to increase early detection of disease (for example, by encouraging routine screening for cancer). The successes of secondary prevention can be seen clearly in the area of cancer prevention and control—for example, the ability of mammography to identify breast cancer at an early stage improves the opportunity for effective treatment and survival (Aiken et al., chap. 44;

MMWR, 2000). Psychological interventions such as support groups and information hotlines have minimized the incidence of mental health problems as a consequence of illness (Stanton et al., chap. 21; Wills & Filer, chap. 12).

Most behavioral interventions focus on the individual as the target of change (or on aggregates of individuals). In contrast, Stokols (1992), among others, urges us "to provide environmental resources and interventions that promote enhanced well-being among occupants of an area" (1992, pp. 6–7). We are only beginning to understand the effects of living in neighborhoods that lack basic environmental resources—neighborhoods with extreme poverty, high crime rates, inadequate housing, public transportation or schools—on health and well-being (Fullilove, 1999). The case study detailed by Butterfoss et al. (chap. 37) in this handbook provides a blueprint for how researchers and health educators allied with community coalitions can improve community health outcomes. Altman and Goodman (chap. 36) describe a broader range of community-wide or policy strategies that can lead to community-wide change in health behaviors, such as changing the community's social norms regarding health behaviors such as smoking, nutrition or exercise (see also Revenson & Schiaffino, 2000). They stress the importance of including community members in health-promoting programs from their inception, and devising culturally-sensitive health promotion strategies in order for health interventions to be incorporated by the community once researchers have moved on. Clearly, "translating" our knowledge of biobehavioral mechanisms in health and illness to more widespread efforts will be a challenge for the next decade of community psychology.

CONCLUSION

The exponential growth in brain and behavioral sciences over the past decade is mirrored in the field of health psychology. But rapid growth also begets growing pains. Health psychologists have taken stock, many times, to assess our progress and our pitfalls (Coyne, 1997; Landrine & Klonoff, 1992; Taylor, 1984; 1987; 1990). As recently as March, 2000, when APA's division of Health Psychology sponsored a conference on the future of health psychology, a unified definition or vision for the field still did not exist. Despite this—or perhaps as a result of it—health psychologists have managed to make great progress in our understanding of the cognitive, behavioral, cognitive-behavioral, physiological, social, environmental, social environmental, personality, and developmental factors underlying health and illness processes over the past quarter-century. But there are many miles to go before we sleep.

REFERENCES

Adler, N. E., Boyce, T., Chesney, M. A., Cohen, S., Folkman, S., Kahn, R. L., & Syme, S. L. (1994). Socioeconomic status and health: The challenge of the gradient. *American Psychologist, 49*, 15–24.

Amaro, H. (1995). Love, sex and power: Considering women's realities in HIV prevention. *American Psychologist, 50*, 437–447.

Andersen, B. L., Kiecolt-Glaser, J. K., & Glaser, R. (1994). A biobehavioral model of cancer stress and disease course. *American Psychologist, 49*, 389–404.

Anderson, N. B. (1999). A definition of behavioral and social sciences research for the National Institutes of Health. Available: <http://www1.od.nih.gov/obssr/def.htm>

Anderson, N. B. (Ed.) (1995). Behavioral and sociocultural perspectives on ethnicity and health. [Special Issue]. *Health Psychology, 14*(7), 589–591.

Anderson, N. B., & Eisler, R. M. (Eds.).(1997). Research Issues on Minority Health. *Journal of Gender, Culture, and Health*, [Special Issue]. *2*(2).

Anderson, N. B. & McNeilly, M. (1991). Age, gender, and ethnicity as variables in psychophysiological assessment: Sociodemographics in context. *Psychological Assessment, 3*, 376–384.

Baum, A., & Posluszny, D. M. (1999). Health psychology: Mapping biobehavioral contributions to health and illness. *Annual Review of Psychology, 50*, 137–163.

Baum, A., & Singer, J .E. (1982). *Issues in child health and adolescent health.* Handbook of psychology and health series, Vol. 2. Hillsdale, NJ: Lawrence Erlbaum Associates.

Baum, A., & Singer, J. E. (1987). *Stress.* Handbook of psychology and health series, Vol. 5. Hillsdale, NJ: Lawrence Erlbaum Associates.

Baum, A., Taylor, S. E., & Singer, J. E. (1984). *Psychological aspects of health.* Handbook of psychology and health series, Vol. 4. Hillsdale, NJ: Lawrence Erlbaum Associates.

Blechman, E., & Brownell, K. (Eds.) (1998) *Behavioral medicine & women: A Comprehensive handbook.* New York: Guilford.

Coyne, J. C. (1997). Improving coping research: Raze the slum before any more building. *Journal of Health Psychology, 2*, 153–155.

Engel, G. (1977). The need for a new medical model: A challenge for biomedicine. *Science, 196*, 129–136.

Feuerstein, M., Labbe, E. E., & Kuczmierczyk, A. R. (1986). *Health psychology: A psychobiological perspective.* New York: Plenum.

Fullilove, M.T., (1999). *The house of Joshua: Meditations on family and place.* Omaha, NE: University of Nebraska Press.

Frost, R. (1923). "Stopping by woods on a snowy evening". In *New Hampshire.* New York: Henry Holt.

Gatchel, R. J., Baum, A, & Singer, J. E. (1982). *Clinical psychology and behavioral medicine: Overlapping disciplines.* Handbook of psychology and health series, Vol. 1. Hillsdale, NJ: Lawrence Erlbaum Associates.

Gentry, W. D (Ed.) (1984). *Handbook of Behavioral Medicine.* New York: Guilford.

Goldberger, L., & Breznitz, S. (Eds.) (1993). *Handbook of stress: Theoretical and clinical aspects* (2nd ed.) New York: Free Press.

Handbook. New Shorter Oxford English Dictionary (1997). [CD-ROM version] New York: Oxford University Press.

Healthy People 2000: National health promotion and disease prevention objectives. [DHHS Publication No. (PHS) 91–50212]. Washington, DC: U.S. Government Printing Office.

Hoyert, D. L., Kochanek, K. D., & Murphy, S. L. (1999). Deaths: Final data for 1997. *National Vital Statistics Reports, 47*(19), 1–104.

Kato, P. M. & Mann, T. (1996). *Handbook of diversity issues in health psychology.* New York: Plenum.

Krantz, D. S., Baum, A., & Singer, J. E. (1983). *Cardiovascular disorders and behavior.* Handbook of psychology and health series, Vol. 3. Hillsdale, NJ: Lawrence Erlbaum Associates.

Landrine, H., & Klonoff, E. A. (1992). Culture and health-related schemas: A review and proposal for interdisciplinary integration. *Health Psychology, 11*, 267–276.

Lerman, C. (1997). Psychological aspects of genetic testing: Introduction to the special issue. *Health Psychology, 16*(1), 3–7.

Manuck, S. B., Jennings, R., & Baum, A. (2000). *Behavior, health, and aging*. Mahwah, NJ: Lawrence Erlbaum Associates.

Matarrazo, J., Weiss, S. M., Herd, J. A., Miller, N. E., & Weiss, S. M. (1984). *Behavioral health: A handbook of health enhancement and disease prevention*. New York: Wiley-Interscience.

McCord, C., & Freeman, H. P. (1990). Excess mortality in Harlem. *New England Journal of Medicine, 322*(3), 173–177.

MMWR. (March 31, 2000). Implementing recommendations for the early detection of breast and cervical cancer among low-income women. *49*/No. RR–2.

National Center for Health Statistics. (1999). Health Insurance Coverage, 1998. Available: <http://www.census.gov/hhes/hlthins/hlthin98/hlt98asc.html>

Resnick, R. J., & Rozensky, R. H. (Eds.). (1996). *Health psychology through the life span: Practice and research opportunities*. Washington, DC: APA Books.

Revenson, T. A. (1990). All other things are *not* equal: An ecological perspective on the relation between personality and disease. In H. S. Friedman (Ed.), *Personality and Disease* (pp. 65–94). New York: John Wiley.

Revenson, T. A., & Schiaffino, K. M. (2000). Community-based health interventions. In J. Rappaport & E. Seidman (Eds.), *Handbook of community psychology* (pp. 471–493). New York: Kluwer Academic/Plenum.

Rodin, J., & Salovey, P. (1989). Health Psychology. *Annual Review of Psychology, 40*, 533–579.

Schwartz, G. (1982). Testing the biopsychosocial model: The ultimate challenge facing behavioral medicine? *Journal of Consulting and Clinical Psychology, 50*, 1040–1053.

Smith, T. W., & Anderson, N. B. (1986). Models of personality and disease: An interactional approach to Type A behavior and cardiovascular risk. *Journal of Personality and Social Psychology, 50*, 1166–1173.

Stanton, A., & Gallant, S. (Eds.) (1995). *The psychology of women's health*. Washington, DC: APA Books.

Stokols, D. (1992). Establishing and maintaining healthy environments. *American Psychologist, 47*(1), 6–22.

Stone, G., Cohen, F., & Adler, N. E. (1979). *Health psychology—A handbook*. San Francisco, CA: Jossey-Bass.

Taylor, S. E. (1984). Some issues in the study of coping: Response. *Cancer, 53*, 2313–2315.

Taylor, S. E. (1987). The progress and prospects of Health Psychology: Tasks of a maturing discipline. *Health Psychology, 6*, 73–87.

Taylor, S. E. (1990). Health Psychology: The science and the field. *American Psychologist, 45*, 40–50.

Taylor, S. E., Repetti, R. L., & Seeman, T. E. (1997). Health psychology: What is an unhealthy environment and how does it get under the skin? *Annual Review of Psychology, 48*, 411–447.

U.S. Health Care Financing Administration. (1999). National health expenditures, 1998. *Health Care Financing Review, 20*(1), Publication 03412.

Wallston, K. A. (1997). A history of Division 38 (Health Psychology): Healthy, wealthy, and Weiss. In D. A. Dewsbury (Ed.), *Unification through division: Histories of the divisions of the American Psychological Association*, volume 2. Washington, DC: APA Books.

Winnett, R. A., King, A. C., & Altman, D. G. (1989). *Health psychology and public health*. New York: Pergamon Press.

Handbook *of* Health Psychology

I

Basic Processes

1

Factors Influencing Behavior and Behavior Change

Martin Fishbein
Annenberg Public Policy Center, University of Pennsylvania

Harry C. Triandis
University of Illinois, Champaign-Urbana

Frederick H Kanfer
University of Illinois, Champaign-Urbana

Marshall Becker
University of Michigan, Ann Arbor

Susan E. Middlestadt
Academy for Educational Development

Anita Eichler
NIMH Office on AIDS

We are now nearing the end of the second decade of the AIDS epidemic. Although major advances in treatment have prolonged and improved the quality of life of those infected with HIV, there is still no cure for, or a vaccine to prevent, this deadly disease. Perhaps most important, it has become increasingly clear that primary prevention must focus on behavior and behavior change. AIDS is first and foremost a consequence of behavior. It is not who people are, but what people do that determines whether or not they expose themselves or others to HIV, the virus that causes AIDS. As Kelly, Murphy, Sikkema, and Kalichman (1993) pointed out, the task confronting the behavioral sciences is to develop theory-based intervention programs to reduce "risky" behaviors and increase "healthy" behaviors.

In order to change behavior, however, it is first necessary to understand why people behave the way they do. The more that is known about the variables underlying a person's decision to perform or not to perform a given behavior, the more likely it is that successful behavioral intervention programs can be developed. Given the severity of the AIDS epidemic, it seemed appropriate to bring together the developers and/or leading proponents of five major behavioral theories in order to identify a finite set of variables to be considered in any behavioral analysis. To this end, the National Institute of Mental Health (NIMH) organized a theorists workshop.

The participants at the workshop were Albert Bandura (social cognitive theory), Marshall Becker (health belief model), Martin Fishbein (reasoned action), Frederick Kanfer (self-regulation, self-control), and Harry Triandis (Subjective Culture and Interpersonal Relations). Anita Eichler, of the NIMH AIDS program, served as chairperson, and Susan Middlestadt, research director of the Academy of Educational Development's AIDSCOM program served as AIDS research consultant. On Day 1 of the conference, each participant described his theory and discussed how it could be applied to an understanding of AIDS-related behaviors. On Day 2, the participants identified a set of key variables. On Day 3, the focus was on operationally defining the variables identified on Day 2. This chapter briefly describes the five theories; discusses some main points of consensus, including the identification of eight key variables that appear to serve as the primary determinants of any given behavior; illustrates how these variables can be assessed; and considers some unresolved issues.

THEORIES OF BEHAVIOR AND BEHAVIOR CHANGE

Although there are a number of theories of behavior and behavior change available in the literature, there are three theories that have had a major impact on much of the behavioral research in the AIDS area: the health belief model (e.g., Becker, 1974, 1988; Janz & Becker, 1984; Montgomery et al., 1989), social cognitive theory (e.g., Bandura, 1986, 1992, 1994) and the theory of reasoned action (e.g., Ajzen & Fishbein, 1980; Fishbein, 1980; Fishbein & Ajzen, 1975; Fishbein, Middlestadt, & Hitchcock, 1991).

According to the health belief model, two major factors influence the likelihood that a person will adopt a recommended health protective behavior. First, individuals must feel personally threatened by the disease (i.e., they must feel personally susceptible to a disease with serious or severe consequences). Second, they must believe the benefits of taking the preventive action outweigh the perceived barriers to (and/or costs of) preventive action.

From the perspective of social cognitive theory, the initiation and persistence of an adaptive behavior depends on beliefs of self-efficacy and outcome expectancies. That is, in order to perform a given behavior individuals must believe in their capability to perform the behavior in question under different circumstances and they must have an incentive to do so (i.e., expected positive outcomes of performing the behavior must outweigh expected negative outcomes). Incentives may involve physical outcomes, social outcomes, or self-sanctions.

According to the theory of reasoned action, performance or nonperformance of a given behavior is primarily a function of the person's intention to perform (or to not perform) that behavior. The intention is, in turn, viewed as a function of two primary determinants—the individual's attitude toward performing the behavior (based on their beliefs about the consequences of performing the behavior, i.e., beliefs about the costs and benefits of performing the behavior) and their perception of the social (or normative) pressure exerted on them to perform the behavior.

The aforementioned three theories represent a public health, a clinical, and a social psychological approach to the prediction and understanding of behavior. Although there is no real competitor to the health belief model in the public health domain, there are other, well-established, clinical and social psychological behavioral theories. For example, in the clinical domain, the theory of self-regulation and self-control (e.g., F. H. Kanfer, 1970; F. H. Kanfer & Schefft, 1988; R. Kanfer & F. H. Kanfer, 1991), has received considerable attention. And, within social psychology, the theory of subjective culture and interpersonal relations (e.g., Triandis, 1972, 1977, 1980) is often viewed as a major competitor to the theory of reasoned action.

The theory of self-regulation and self-control describes how self-regulatory processes (i.e., self-observation, self-evaluation, and self-reinforcement) lead to satisfaction with behavioral performance and continuation of the behavior, or to dissatisfaction and either self-corrective action or termination of the behavior. Although more of a process than a predictive model, the theory identifies goal-setting (or intentions), self-efficacy, outcome expectancies, skills, and affective states (e.g., mood and emotion) as important determinants of behavior.

According to the theory of subjective culture and interpersonal relations, the likelihood of performing a given behavior is determined by intentions, habits, and facilitating factors. Intentions are, in turn, viewed as a function of perceived consequences of performing the behavior (i.e., outcome expectancies), social influences (including norms, roles and the self-concept), and emotions.

Among them, the five theories, briefly described above, have developed or contain almost all of the variables that have been utilized in attempts to understand and change a wide variety of human behaviors.

MAIN POINTS OF CONSENSUS

Early on, it became very clear that a distinction must be made between theories of behavioral prediction and theories of behavioral change. Whereas models of behavioral prediction focus on variables (or factors) that "determine" the performance or nonperformance of any behavior at a given point in time, models of behavior change focus on "states" of the organism or "stages" individuals may go through in their attempt to change behavior.

Generally speaking, there was agreement that people will continue to behave as they have in the past until some internal or external stimulus (e.g., a symptom, a mass media message) interrupts this "normal" flow of behavior. Behavioral prediction models attempt to identify variables that serve as determinants of ongoing behaviors. That is, these models focus on those variables that help to explain why some members of a given population are performing a given behavior while other members of the same population are not. In contrast, behavior change models focus first on the stimuli that "disrupt" ongoing behavior and then on the processes individuals may utilize in moving from one state or stage to another in their attempt to eliminate old or adopt new behaviors.

For example, a TV ad that informs the public about AIDS transmission (i.e., a "cue to action") may be an important first step in getting someone to consider behavior change. But whether a person is or is not exposed to such an ad may not be a determinant (and in fact may be a very poor predictor) of whether the person is or is not performing any given AIDS protective behavior (e.g., using a condom). Similarly, recognition that people's behavior is putting them at risk for AIDS may be, at least for some, a necessary step in a change process. Nevertheless, perceived risk may be unrelated to (and not be a determinant of) whether individuals are or are not performing a given AIDS-protective behavior.

Although behavioral prediction and behavior change theories often have different foci, they are quite complementary. Indeed, the intensity and direction of the variables identified in behavioral prediction theories often serve as markers or indicators of a state of the organism or a stage of change. For example, as is described later, there was general consensus that the intention to perform a given behavior is one of the immediate determinants of that behavior. The stronger the intention to perform a given behavior, the greater the likelihood that the person will, in fact, perform that behavior. By recognizing that intention is a continuous variable (ranging from strong intention not to perform a behavior through uncertainty to strong intentions to perform the behavior), it can be argued that the strength of a person's intention may serve as an index of a given state of the organism or of a stage in a change process. Thus, as people move from strong negative through neutral through weak positive intentions, they may be moving from what Prochaska and DiClemente (1983, 1986) called the precontemplative to the contemplative stage. Similarly, as individuals move from weak to strong positive intentions, they may be moving from what F. H. Kanfer and Schefft (1988) called an intentional state through a decisional state to a state of commitment.

Although process models of behavioral change are important, as a first step it is helpful to explain why people behave the way they do. Thus, the focus of the workshop was on identifying key variables that would enable the prediction and understanding of behavior. Clearly, if a limited number of variables that serve as potential determinants of any given behavior can be identified, it should be possible to measure these variables and examine the strength of the associations among them as well as the strength of the associations between each of these variables and the behavior in question. These analyses should lead to the identification of the one or two variables that most strongly influence the decision to perform (or not perform) a given behavior in a given population. Once identified, these variables should then serve as the primary focus of an intervention.

Variables Underlying Behavioral Performance

After a consideration of each of the five theories, a set of eight variables was identified that appear to account for most of the variance in any given deliberate behavior: intention, environmental constraints, skills, anticipated outcomes (or attitude), norms, self-standards, emotion, and self-efficacy. For a person to perform a given behavior, one or more of the following must be true:

1. The person has formed a strong positive intention (or made a commitment) to perform the behavior.
2. There are no environmental constraints that make it impossible for the behavior to occur.
3. The person has the skills necessary to perform the behavior.
4. The person believes that the advantages (benefits, anticipated positive outcomes) of performing the behavior outweigh the disadvantages (costs, anticipated negative outcomes); in other words, the person has a positive attitude toward performing the behavior.
5. The person perceives more social (normative) pressure to perform the behavior than to not perform the behavior.
6. The person perceives that performance of the behavior is more consistent than inconsistent with his or her self-image, or that its performance does not violate personal standards that activate negative self-sanctions.
7. The person's emotional reaction to performing the behavior is more positive than negative.
8. The person perceives that he or she has the capabilities to perform the behavior under a number of different circumstances; in other words, the person has perceived self-efficacy to execute the behavior in question.

Generally speaking, the first three factors are viewed as necessary and sufficient for producing any behavior. That is, for behavior to occur, a person must have a strong positive intention (i.e., have a commitment) to perform the behavior in question; the individual must have the skills necessary to carry out the behavior; and the environment must provide a context of opportunity, or be free of constraints, such that the behavior can occur. Thus, for example, if a male injecting drug user (IDU) is committed to using bleach every time he shares injection equipment, has bleach available, and has the skills necessary to use the bleach, the probability is close to 1.0 that he will bleach before sharing. Similarly, if this same person has formed a strong intention to always use a condom for vaginal sex with his spouse, has a condom available, does not experience strong resistance to condom use from his spouse, and has the necessary skills to use the condom, the probability will again be close to 1.0 that he will use a condom when he engages in vaginal sex with his spouse.

The remaining five variables are viewed as influencing the strength and direction of intention. For example, it can be argued that individuals will not form a strong intention to perform a behavior unless they first believe that behavioral performance will lead to more positive than negative outcomes and/or they believe that they have the skills and abilities necessary to perform that behavior (i.e., they believe that they can perform the behavior). In other words, attitudes and/or self-efficacy may influence the strength of a person's intention. It is important to recognize however, that one or more of these variables may also have a direct influence on behavior. Thus, for example, by influencing the amount of effort someone expends, and by influencing an individual's persistence in the face of barriers, self-efficacy may also have a direct impact on behavior.

It should also be recognized that behavioral performance can influence one or more of these five variables. Individuals may form a positive intention to perform, and may in fact perform a given behavior, at least in part because they believe that performance of the behavior will lead to a positively valued outcome. When individuals perform the behavior, however, this outcome may not occur. Clearly, this information will influence the person's behavioral beliefs (or outcome expectations), which may in turn influence intentions and future behavioral performances.

MEASUREMENT CONSIDERATIONS

Having identified eight variables (or factors) that are assumed to underlie the performance (or nonperformance) of any behavior, it is necessary to consider how each of these variables can be assessed. First, however, it is important to distinguish between variables that have "fixed" contents and those that have "variable" contents. To a certain extent, this distinction parallels the distinction between *etic* (i.e., universal) and *emic* (i.e., population specific) considerations. That is, for some variables (e.g., intention), item content is "fixed" and the assessment question is not "what" to measure, but how to best measure the construct in a given population. For other variables, however (e.g., behavioral beliefs or outcome expectancies), item content depends on the population being considered, and it is necessary to first go to a representative sample (and/or trained observers) of the population being studied in order to determine item content.

Thus, prior to attempting to develop any fixed item assessment instrument, the use of standardized elicitation procedures (see Ajzen & Fishbein, 1980) are recommended to identify four broad classes of variables: perceived outcomes of performing the behavior; relevant referents (either individuals or groups) vis-à-vis the behavior; perceived facilitators of, and barriers to, behavioral performance; and characteristics, qualities, and attributes of people who do and do not perform the behavior. In addition, it is sometimes necessary to consider a fifth class of variables, namely, action alternatives.

As becomes clear later, outcomes are necessary for developing measures of behavioral beliefs or outcome expectancies; relevant referents are necessary for developing normative measures; barriers and facilitator are necessary for assessing both environmental constraints and self-efficacy; and personal characteristics are necessary for assessing self-image and violations of self-standards. Action alternatives help one to identify relevant behaviors that either define a behavioral category (e.g., safe sex) or identify skills or courses of action necessary for goal attainment.

Clearly, however, outcomes, referents, barriers, facilitators, personal characteristics, and action alternatives will vary from behavior to behavior as well as from population to population. Thus, it is essential that open-ended elicitation questions be asked with respect to the specific behavior under consideration. Unfortunately, selecting this behavior is often more difficult than may first appear. Consider, for example, a situation in which a heterosexual male resists using a condom for vaginal sex with a casual partner. If the goal is to try to increase condom use in this situation, should the focus be on increasing the likelihood that the male will use a condom or on increasing the likelihood that the female will get her partner to use a condom? Although it can be argued that getting a partner to use a condom is no less a performance attainment than putting on a condom, it can also be argued that getting a partner to use a condom is a goal that may be attained only by performing one or more behaviors, such as "telling one's partner to use a condom," "refusing to have sex unless one's partner uses a condom," or "negotiating condom use with one's partner." Thus, it could also be argued that in an attempt to increase condom use in this situation, the focus should be on increasing the likelihood that the woman will perform one or more of these behaviors. Note, however, that in contrast to "telling one's partner to use a condom" or "refusing to have sex," "negotiating condom use" is not a single behavior but a behavioral category involving a number of different behaviors.

This distinction between goals (e.g., avoiding AIDS, getting a partner to use a condom), behavioral categories (e.g, practicing safe sex, negotiating condom use), and behaviors (e.g., using a condom, telling one's partner to use a condom) is discussed in more detail later. At this point, however, it is sufficient to point out that, with relatively few exceptions, the assessment of the eight variables is essentially identical whether the focus is on a goal, a behavioral category, or a specific behavior. Perhaps the major difference is that when the focus is on a behavioral category or a goal, it is also necessary to identify the behaviors comprising the category or the behaviors to be performed in the attempt to attain the goal. Given the primary concern with behavior, for illustrative purposes this chapter focuses on a specific behavior, namely, the likelihood that males will always use a condom for vaginal sex with their wives (or their main sexual partners). In addition, when appropriate, ways in which assessment procedures can be adapted for consideration of a behavioral category or a goal are illustrated. Generally speaking, however, in the examples, phrases such as "getting my husband (or main sexual partner) to always use a condom for vaginal sex," "engaging in safe sex," or "negotiating condom use for vaginal sex with my husband (or main sexual partner)," can be substituted for the phrase "always using a condom for vaginal sex with my spouse (or main sexual partner)."

Identifying Variable (Population-Specific) Content

As already indicated, the first stage in developing fixed-format assessment instruments is to identify salient outcomes, referents, facilitators, barriers, and personal characteristics with respect to the behavior in question. In addition, if the focus is on a behavioral category or a goal, it is necessary to identify the action alternatives that comprise the behavioral category and/or that lead to goal attainment. In order to obtain this information, it is necessary to ask a representative sample of the population a series of open-ended questions.

Perceived Outcomes. Anticipated outcomes or behavioral beliefs are viewed as one of the key variables underlying behavioral performance. To identify salient outcomes associated with a male's use of condoms for vaginal sex with his spouse (or main sexual partner), a representative sample of men could be asked questions such as the following:

1. What do you see as the advantages (positive outcomes of, benefits of, good things that would happen) of your always using a condom for vaginal sex with your spouse or main sexual partner?

2. What do you see as the disadvantages (negative outcomes, costs, bad things that would happen) of your always using a condom for vaginal sex with your spouse or main sexual partner?

3. What else comes to mind when you think about always using a condom for vaginal sex with your spouse or main partner? For example, how would always using a condom for vaginal sex with your wife (or main sexual partner) make you feel? How would it make others feel? How would they react?

Content analyses of the open-ended responses to these questions should allow the identification of a set of salient (frequently mentioned) outcomes or consequences. It is important to recognize that the same outcome may be seen as an advantage by some members of the population and as a disadvantage by others. For example, some people might see "preventing pregnancy" as a "good" thing whereas others may view this same outcome negatively. The content analysis should attempt to identify salient "outcomes" irrespective of their perceived value. Once this list is developed, the set of outcomes can be categorized in any number of ways. For example, a researcher might want to distinguish "costs" from "benefits," or might want to distinguish between "long-term" and "short-term" outcomes. Similarly, it may be useful to distinguish between "physical" outcomes (e.g., will protect me from AIDS), "social" outcomes (e.g., will make my partner angry), and "self-sanctions" (e.g., would make me feel dirty). Irrespective of the particular category system used, the important point is to identify the set of outcomes or consequences that the people in the population under study are most likely to consider when they think about performing the behavior in question.

Relevant Referents. Perceived normative pressure is also expected to influence behavioral performance. It is thus necessary to identify those individuals or groups that the individual perceives as potential sources of social influence. More specifically, it is important to identify those individuals or groups who are perceived to be putting pressure on the individual to perform or not perform the behavior in question. In order to obtain this information, the representative sample of men should also be asked questions, such as:

1. Please list those individuals or groups who would support or approve of your always using a condom for vaginal sex with your spouse or main sexual partner.

2. Please list those individuals or groups who would oppose or disapprove of your always using a condom for vaginal sex with your spouse or main sexual partner.

3. Please list any other individuals or groups that come to mind when you think about always using a condom for vaginal sex with your spouse or main sexual partner.

Content analyses can be conducted to identify the most frequently mentioned referents. Once again, it is important to recognize that a given referent (e.g., friends, spouse) may be listed by some as a person who would approve of the behavior and by others as a person who would disapprove of the behavior. The purpose of the content analysis should be to identify the referents mentioned most frequently by the population, irrespective of their perceived positions.

Barriers and Facilitator. In order to identify environmental constraints as well as other internal and external circumstances that may influence behavioral performance, questions such as the following can be asked:

1. What makes it difficult or impossible for you to always use a condom for vaginal sex with your wife? (Probe: Can you think of any other barriers or circumstances that would prevent you from, or make it hard for you to always use a condom for vaginal sex with your wife or main sexual partner?)

2. What helps you or makes it easier for you to always use a condom for vaginal sex with your wife? (Probe: Can you think of anything else that would facilitate or increase the likelihood that you will always use a condom for vaginal sex with your spouse or main sexual partner?)

Content analyses of responses to these items should allow identification of a set of "circumstances" that increase or reduce the likelihood of the behavior occurring. In contrast to "outcomes" and "referents," it is unlikely that the same circumstance will be seen as a facilitator by some respondents and as a barrier by others. Nevertheless, some people may mention the presence of a given factor or circumstance as a barrier whereas others may mention its absence as a facilitator. For example, some respondents may indicate that it is "harder" for them to always use a condom with their wives if they have been drinking or using drugs, and others may say it is "easier" for them to always use a condom if they have not been drinking or using drugs. Thus, once again, attempts should be made to develop a single set of circumstances whose presence or absence may facilitate or prevent the performance of the behavior in question.

It is important to note that the purpose is to identify circumstances that influence behavioral performance, and not outcomes of that performance and/or strategies that may help a person perform the behavior. Thus, for example, if a respondent says that one of the things that makes it more difficult for him to always use a condom with his wife is that "it will make my wife angry," then he is reporting a perceived outcome rather than a circumstance. Similarly, if the individual says it would be easier to always use a condom with my wife "if I had talked to her beforehand," then he is reporting a strategy that may be used to increase the likelihood of condom use, rather than a circumstance that can facilitate or hinder performance. Although a researcher may wish to retain a list of "strategies" (to be used in developing action alternatives and/or in identifying skills), these responses should be excluded from the analysis of barriers and facilitators. Similarly, outcomes should also be excluded in developing the set of circumstances that influence the behavior in question. However, if a respondent lists outcomes that he had not previously mentioned in response to the outcome questions, these responses should be included in the content analysis of outcomes.

In addition to asking a representative sample of the population to identify circumstances that may increase or decrease the likelihood of behavioral performance, it is often useful (and sometimes necessary) to also ask trained observers (or people familiar with the population) to identify factors that may facilitate or inhibit the behavior. As Nisbett and Ross (1980) pointed out, people are often quite inaccurate in identifying factors that influence their own behaviors. Thus, the obtained list of respondent-elicited circumstances should be supplemented with circumstances identified by independent observers.[1]

Once the set of circumstances influencing behavior has been identified, it can be categorized, like the set of perceived outcomes, in a number of different ways. Most obviously, a distinction can be made between facilitators and barriers. In addition and perhaps more important, each circumstance can be categorized as one that is "internal" or "external" to the individual. As is seen later, external circumstances are used to assess environmental constraints, and the full set of circumstances contribute to the development of self-efficacy items.

Personal Characteristics. In order to determine whether performance of the behavior in question is consistent or inconsistent with individual's self-image or self-standards, it is necessary to know how they perceive people who do and do not perform the behavior in question. Thus, the respondents can be asked questions such as:

1. How would you describe a man who ALWAYS or ALMOST ALWAYS uses a condom for vaginal sex with his wife (or main sexual partner)? That is, what do you believe are the characteristics, qualities, or attributes of such a person?

2. How would you describe a man who NEVER or ALMOST NEVER uses a condom for vaginal sex with his wife (or main sexual partner)? Once again, please list what you believe to be the characteristics, qualities, and attributes of such a person.

[1]The extent to which the circumstances identified by the trained observers match those identified by the sample of respondents is itself useful information that may indicate a number of internal mechanisms such as rationalizations, defenses, and so on.

Content analyses of responses to these items should allow researchers to arrive at a single set of frequently mentioned characteristics or "traits" of men who do or do not perform the behavior in question.

Action Alternatives. Although the aforementioned questions are sufficient for obtaining information necessary for developing fixed-format items to assess each of the potential variable content determinants of a given behavior, it is necessary to obtain additional information if the focus is on a behavioral category or a goal. More specifically, as already indicated, if the focus is on a behavioral category (e.g., safe sex, negotiating condom use), then it is necessary to identify those behaviors that comprise the behavioral category. Similarly, if the focus is on a goal or outcome (e.g., getting my partner to use a condom, avoiding AIDS), then it is necessary to identify the behaviors (or courses of action) that may increase the likelihood that the person will attain that goal. Note, however, that a given individual's perception of what behaviors define a behavioral category and/or of what behaviors will lead to goal attainment, may be very different from those held by a group of experts. For example, epidemiologists may include a very different set of behaviors in their definition of safe sex than will a layperson. Similarly, a clinician may see a different set of behaviors leading to goal attainment than will the patient. Thus, in identifying action alternatives, information should be obtained from knowledgeable experts as well as from a representative sample of the population under investigation.

For example, if the goal of an intervention was to increase the likelihood that women will engage in a behavioral category, such as practicing safe sex with their husbands (or main sexual partners), then a representative sample of women could be asked questions such as: What do you consider to be safe sex with your husband? That is, what sexual behaviors are safe? What sexual behaviors are dangerous?

Content analyses of responses to these types of questions should allow the identification of the behaviors that the population sees as comprising the behavioral category. In addition, they should help form an understanding of what respondents mean when they respond to questions about "safe sex" or other behavioral categories. A similar set of questions could be asked of a small sample of "experts." By looking at differences between the behaviors identified by the population and those identified by experts, an investigator can clarify and explicitly define (for the respondent) what is meant by the behavioral category. In addition, once a complete list of behaviors comprising a behavioral category is developed, one may wish to focus on one or more specific behaviors that could be studied in their own right and/or that could serve as the focus of an intervention.

Similarly, if there is interest in increasing the likelihood that women will attain a specific goal (e.g., get their husbands or main sexual partners to always use a condom for vaginal sex), a representative sample of women (as well as a small group of "experts") could be asked questions such as: What is involved in getting your husband (or main sexual partner) to always use a condom for vaginal sex? That is what would you have to do or say to get your husband to always use a condom for vaginal sex? What other behaviors could you perform to increase the likelihood that he will use a condom for vaginal sex?

Content analysis of responses to this set of questions again identifies a more specific set of behaviors that a respondent may use to attain the behavioral goal in question. Discrepancies between action alternatives identified by the population and those identified by experts provide important information. Moreover, responses to these questions provide insight into skills that may be required to attain that goal. In addition, this information, along with information on circumstances described earlier, provides the basis for developing self-efficacy items.[2]

As mentioned earlier, it is important to recognize that the salient sets of outcomes, referents, circumstances, and traits (as well as action alternatives) are expected to vary as a function of both the behavior under consideration and the population of interest. Clearly, the outcomes of using a condom for vaginal sex with a spouse (or main sexual partner) may be very different from those associated with using a condom for vaginal sex with a new or occasional partner. Similarly, heterosexual males may see different consequences of using a condom for vaginal sex with their wives (or main sexual partners) than do bisexual males or men with hemophilia. Moreover, Black males may perceive different outcomes and have different referents than White or Hispanic males. Thus, to fully understand the determinants of a given behavior in a given population, it is necessary to elicit outcomes, referents, circumstances and traits vis-à-vis that behavior in that population. This information can then be used to develop closed-format assessment items.

Suggestions for Assessing Each of the Eight Key Variables

In order to illustrate how the previous information may be used to develop fixed alternative assessment items, and to illustrate how variables with "fixed" content can be assessed, the focus continues to be on men's use of condoms for vaginal sex with their wives (or main sexual partners). Once again, however, it is important to note that the same set of procedures and types of items would be developed for investigations of behavioral categories or goal attainment.

Intentions to Perform the Behavior. As described earlier, there is general consensus that men who intend to "always use a condom for vaginal sex with my main partner" are significantly more likely to use a condom every time they have vaginal sex with their main partners than are men who do not have this intention. Moreover, the stronger the person's intention to "always use a condom for vaginal sex with my main partner," the more likely he is to carry out this behavior.

Unfortunately, the term *intention* has been used in different ways. For some, an intention is simply a weak statement of a wish or desire to perform a given behavior; for others, intentions have been viewed as a commitment or a self-instruction to carry out the behavior. The problem is a distinction between treating "intention" as an on/off variable (i.e., the person either intends or does not intend to act) and treating intention as a continuous variable varying in strength or intensity.

In the field of social psychology, where the concept of intention has been used most widely, the concept is viewed as a continuous variable, and it is usually measured with one or more of the following scales:

I will always use a condom for vaginal sex with my main partner

likely___:___:___:___:___:___:___unlikely

I intend to always use a condom for vaginal sex with my main partner

likely___:___:___:___:___:___:___unlikely

I will try to always use a condom for vaginal sex with my main partner

likely___:___:___:___:___:___:___unlikely

These scales assess respondents' subjective probability or subjective likelihood that they will perform (or will try to perform) the behavior in question.[3] Because probability or likelihood may be a difficult concept in some cultures, it is possible to substitute such scales as "agree–disagree," "certain–uncertain," or "true–false" for "likely–unlikely."

Similarly, there may be concern that respondents cannot handle 7-point (or 5-point or 9-point) scales. In these cases, this information can be obtained with a two-part question: Do you think it is likely or unlikely that you will always use a condom for vaginal sex with your main partner?

Responses of "I don't know," "neither," or "it's as likely as it is unlikely" are taken as indications that the respondent is at the midpoint of the scale. Those answering likely (or unlikely), should then be asked the following: And would you say that it was extremely likely (unlikely), quite likely (unlikely), or only slightly likely (unlikely)?

Once again, it should be recognized that both the judgment scale (i.e., Do you agree or disagree that ...) and the descriptive adverbs (do you agree strongly, moderately, or only slightly) can be changed. Needless to say, exactly how the question is asked should depend on the population being con-

[2]It is important to note that very often what will be obtained are behavioral categories rather than explicit behaviors in response to questions concerning paths to goal attainment. For example, "negotiate condom use" is a frequent response to a question such as "What would you have to do to get your spouse to always use a condom for vaginal sex?" When this is the case, it is important to identify the behaviors comprising the response category. Thus, for example, questions such as the following could be posed: What is involved in your negotiating condom use for vaginal sex with your spouse? That is, how would you negotiate condom use? What behaviors would you perform? What would you do or say as a part of this negotiation?

[3]For those who view intention as self-instruction, an additional scale, such as the following should also be developed:

When I am about to have vaginal sex with my spouse or main partner, I say to myself "Use a Condom."

Always____:____:____:____:____:____:____Never

sidered. However, for the question to assess intention as it is used here, it is necessary to arrive at a continuous measure that indicates the likelihood that a person will (or the strength of the individual's commitment to) perform or try to perform the behavior in question.

Environmental Constraints Preventing Behavioral Performance. Although often overlooked, there may be a number of environmental constraints that make performance of the behavior virtually impossible. With respect to condom use for vaginal sex with a spouse or main sexual partner, one environmental constraint that would prevent this behavior is the absence of condoms. Clearly, if a condom is not available, or the person does not have the money to buy one, this behavior cannot occur. Similarly, if a spouse (or main sexual partner) refuses to have vaginal sex if the individual uses a condom, then condom use is quite unlikely. Note that the concern here is with circumstances or factors that are external to the individual.

Unfortunately, there is no standardized procedure for assessing the degree to which such environmental constraints are present. However, it seems reasonable to assume that such a measure could be developed by considering the set of external circumstances identified during the elicitation phase of the research. That is, a measure could be developed by considering those "external" circumstances that serve as barriers to behavioral performance. For example, respondents could be asked questions, such as the following, to indicate the extent to which each external circumstance was usually present or absent:

When you are about to have vaginal sex with your spouse (or main sexual partner), how often do each of the following occur?

Each item could be scored from 1(Never) to 5(Always), and the sum of the items could serve as an index of the degree to which environmental constraints were present.[4]

1. Condoms are NOT available

______	______	______	______	______
Never	Almost Never	Sometimes	Almost Always	Always

2. Your spouse (or main sexual partner) resists your use of condoms

______	______	______	______	______
Never	Almost Never	Sometimes	Almost Always	Always

Skills Necessary for Behavioral Performance. It is becoming increasingly clear that those interested in understanding behavioral performance must pay attention to skill dimensions. With respect to a male's use of a condom for vaginal sex with his spouse or main sexual partner, the skills involved are those related to buying (or otherwise obtaining) and using a condom. Clearly, if the person does not know what a condom is, where to get it, or how to use it, then one will not be used. Moreover, as already described, if a partner is opposed to, or resists, condom use, additional skills, such as those involved in negotiating condom use, may also be necessary. Needless to say, such social negotiation skills become particularly relevant and important when the focus is on a woman's attempt to get her partner to use a condom.

It is therefore necessary to develop skill measures. Fortunately, some measures are already available. For example, Cleghorn et al. (1991) developed a highly reliable, observational test of condom use skills. More specifically, respondents are given a packaged condom and are asked to put the condom on a dildo. Trained observers then record the extent to which the person does or does not perform a number of specific actions such as "unrolling the condom," "holding the tip of the condom," and "covering 100% of the shaft of the penis."

With respect to negotiation skills, Kelly, St. Lawrence, Hood, and Brasfield (1989) constructed a set of eight role-play scenes following standard paradigms for assertion assessment (cf. Eisler, Miller, & Hersen, 1973; Hersen & Bellack, 1976). Each role play consisted of a scene narration in which a sexual partner attempts to pressure subjects to engage in a high risk practice or another person proposes a sexual encounter. The narrations were presented on audiotape, with each narration being followed by three prompts delivered live by a trained assistant who simulated the verbal conduct of the coercive partner. Subjects' responses were audiotape recorded and were later coded for overall effectiveness (on a scale from 1 = very ineffective to 7 = very effective), as well as for discrete components of skill. For example, in scenes depicting coercions to engage in high risk behavior, respondents were coded for acknowledging the partner's request, specifically refusing the high risk behavior, providing the reason for the refusal, noting the need to be safer, and suggesting a specific low risk alternative.

Generally speaking, the set of action alternatives identified during the elicitation phase of the research should provide guidelines and serve as the basis for developing skill measures. More specifically, by knowing the actions a person would have to perform to reach a given goal and/or by knowing what behaviors are included in a behavioral category, it should be possible to develop skill measures.

Behavioral Beliefs, Outcome Expectancies, Costs and Benefits, Perceived Consequences. In almost every behavioral theory, there is some recognition of the proposition that people will not perform a given behavior unless they believe (or anticipate) that the advantages (benefits, positive outcomes) of performing the behavior outweigh the disadvantages (costs, negative outcomes). That is, all theories agree that, at some level, people consider the possible outcomes of behavioral performance. Moreover, there is general consensus that it is not possible to simply generate a set of outcomes or consequences, but rather it is necessary to go to the population of interest and find out what the individuals believe to be the outcomes or consequences of engaging in a given behavior.

[4]Alternatively, a group of trained observers could be asked to indicate the degree to which each of these circumstances were present or absent for the population being considered.

The previous section described procedures for identifying a set of salient outcomes with respect to the performance of a given behavior in a given population. This set of salient outcomes can then serve as the basis for developing fixed alternative assessment items.

The assessment instrument should contain two questions for each outcome: One assessing the respondent's belief that performing the behavior will lead to the outcome; and another assessing the value the respondent places on the outcome. For example, among men, two frequently mentioned outcomes of using a condom for vaginal sex with a spouse (or main sexual partner) are that this behavior will "prevent pregnancy" and "reduce my sexual pleasure." Given these outcomes, item pairs such as the following can be developed:

(1a) My always using a condom for vaginal sex with my main partner will prevent her from becoming pregnant.

likely___:___:___:___:___:___:___unlikely

(1b) Preventing my main partner from becoming pregnant is:

good___:___:___:___:___:___:___bad

(2a) My always using a condom for vaginal sex with my main partner will reduce my sexual pleasure.

likely___:___:___:___:___:___:___unlikely

(2b) Reducing my sexual pleasure is:

good___:___:___:___:___:___:___bad

Individuals are positively motivated when they believe that behavioral performance leads to positive outcomes or prevents negative ones. They are negatively motivated (i.e., motivated not to engage in the behavior) when they believe that behavioral performance leads to negative outcomes or prevents positive ones. In order to capture the psychologic of the "double negative" (i.e., in order to insure that the prevention of a bad outcome will be seen as a positive motivator), it is essential to score both beliefs and outcome evaluations in a bipolar fashion (i.e., from –3 to +3). When this scoring system is used, it is possible to determine whether a given belief is serving as a positive or negative motivator (for performance of the behavior in question) by multiplying each belief (1a) by its corresponding outcome evaluation (1b). These products can then be summed algebraically across the set of salient outcomes to arrive at a single score that can be seen as an index of propensity or motivation to perform (or not perform) the behavior in question.

Within social psychology, such a cost–benefit or expectancy-value index has often been viewed as an indirect measure of the respondent's attitude toward performing the behavior in question (see, e.g., Fishbein & Ajzen, 1975). More specifically, the process already described uses a compensatory expectancy-value model to arrive at an indirect assessment of attitude.[5] The recognition that "outcome expectancy scores," "perceived consequent scores" and "cost–benefit analyses" are related to (or underlie) attitudes toward performing the behavior in question, suggests that, in addition to utilizing such an indirect estimate, it is also possible to measure the relevant attitude more directly.

Most people would agree that attitude is indexed along a biploar evaluative (good/bad) or affective (I like/I dislike) dimension. It is important to note, however, that when a person evaluates something as "good" or says "I like something," that person can mean one or more of the following:

1. The behavior is "wise," "beneficial" and "safe."
2. The behavior is "pleasant," "enjoyable" and "easy."
3. The behavior is "moral," "correct," and "appropriate."

Thus, it is important that a direct measure of attitude capture these potentially different meanings of the attitude concept. In order to do this, a semantic differential measure of attitude is recommended. The *semantic differential* is, by far, the most widely used attitude measurement instrument, and when properly constructed, there is considerable evidence to support its reliability and validity. Generally speaking, the process begins with a large number of bipolar adjective scales, relevant to the concept (or behavior) under consideration. By using factor analyses or other standardized item selection procedures, it is possible to identify the set of items that are the best indicants of the underlying attitudinal dimension. In order to insure that the three potential meanings of attitude are represented, items such as the following can be used:

My always using a condom for vaginal sex with my spouse or main partner

wise___:___:___:___:___:___:___foolish

pleasant___:___:___:___:___:___:___unpleasant

correct___:___:___:___:___:___:___incorrect

easy___:___:___:___:___:___:___difficult

safe___:___:___:___:___:___:___dangerous

enjoyable___:___:___:___:___:___:___unenjoyable

moral___:___:___:___:___:___:___immoral

beneficial___:___:___:___:___:___:___harmful

I like___:___:___:___:___:___:___I dislike

good___:___:___:___:___:___:___bad

A preliminary "attitude" score can be obtained by summing responses (scored from +3 [wise, enjoyable, good] to –3 [foolish, unenjoyable, bad]) on each bipolar adjective scale. Item total correlations can then be computed and used to eliminate scales unrelated to the underlying attitude dimension. The final set of items can then serve as a relatively direct measure of atti-

[5]As described earlier, there are a number of ways in which a set of outcomes can be categorized. More specifically, it might be desirable to distinguish between short- and long-term outcomes or between physical outcomes, social outcomes, and self-sanctions. Consistent with this, it may be useful to disaggregrate the overall expectancy-value score into a number of subscores. From a social-psychological perspective, however, the individual's attitude toward performing a given behavior is based on all of their salient outcome expectancies or behavioral beliefs.

tude. The sum over these scales is the attitude score. The higher the score, the more favorable the respondent's attitude toward performing the behavior in question. This direct measure should be highly correlated with, and may be used to validate, the indirect expectancy-value estimate.

Perceived Normative Pressure. As described earlier, some outcomes of performing a given behavior may be "social" in nature (e.g., My using a condom for vaginal sex with my spouse will make her think I don't trust her; will make her angry). Like other outcomes, these social outcomes enter into expectancy-value considerations and thus should be included in the analysis of outcome expectancies. It is important to recognize, however, that norms can influence behavior independent of outcome expectancies. That is, there is considerable evidence that individuals and groups may influence behavior even when they are not perceived as sources of positive or negative reinforcements. As Fishbein and Ajzen (1975) pointed out, people may often perform a behavior because they believe that an important other thinks they should perform that behavior, even though the important other may never know whether they have or have not performed the behavior. To fully understand why a person does or does not perform a given behavior, it is necessary to assess the extent to which the individual perceives social pressure to perform or not perform the behavior in question.

The first step in developing a measure of social pressure is to identify those individuals or groups that may be exerting pressure on the individual to perform or not perform the behavior. Once again, this cannot be done by simply making up a list of potential referents, but instead, as described earlier, it is necessary to go to the population of interest to identify a set of relevant individuals or groups. Thus, for example, when males are asked to list individuals or groups who would approve or disapprove of their always using condoms for vaginal sex with their wives or main sexual partners, two frequently mentioned referents are "my wife (or main sexual partner)" and "my friends." Although individuals may believe that a given referent thinks they should (or should not) perform a given behavior, this belief may have little impact on behavior unless they are motivated to comply with that referent. Note that that concern is with assessing the degree to which a person is motivated to comply with a given referent rather than the degree to which the person is motivated to comply with the specific behavioral proscription of that referent. Recognize, however, that a given referent may exert social pressure in some behavioral domains but not in others. Thus, in order to assess the social pressure exerted by a given referent, item pairs such as the following are necessary:

(1a) My wife (or main sexual partner) thinks

I should___:___:___:___:___:___:___I should not always use a condom when we have vaginal sex

(1b) When it comes to AIDS prevention,

I want to do___:___:___:___:___:___:___I do not want to do what my wife thinks I should do

(2a) Most of my friends think:

I should___:___:___:___:___:___:___I should not always use a condom when I have vaginal sex with my spouse (or main partner)

(2b) When it comes to AIDS prevention,

I want to do___:___:___:___:___:___:___I do not want to do what most of my friends think I should do

In order to capture the normative pressure exerted by a given referent, each normative belief should be weighted (i.e., multiplied) by people's motivation to comply with the referent. In contrast to an expectancy-value estimate, however, the psychologic of the "double negative" does not apply to social influence. That is, when individuals say they are not motivated to comply with a given referent, this does not imply that they perceive social pressure to do the opposite of what that referent thinks they should do. Thus, although normative beliefs (i.e., items 1a and 2a) may be scored from –3 to +3, motivation to comply (i.e., items 1b and 2b) should be scored from 1 (I do not want to do what the referent thinks I should do) to 7 (I want to do what the referent thinks I should do). Summing these products across all relevant referents leads to an index of perceived normative pressure.

A more direct assessment of perceived social pressure can be obtained by using measures such as the following:

(1) Most people who are important to me think

I should___:___:___:___:___:___:___I should not always use a condom when I have vaginal sex with my spouse (or main partner)

(2) People I respect and admire

want me to___:___:___:___:___:___:___do not want me to always use a condom when I have vaginal sex with my spouse (or main partner)

This direct measure should be highly correlated with, and may be used to validate, the indirect index of perceived social pressure to perform (or not perform) the behavior in question.

In addition to the social pressure created by individuals' perceptions (or beliefs) that specific referents think they should or should not perform a given behavior, their behavior is often also influenced by the behavior of others. For example, although parents often tell their children to "do what I say, not what I do," children often emulate their parents' behaviors. That is, parents often serve as "models" for their children's behaviors. As French and Raven (1959) pointed out, people often behave like others not because they believe that their behavior will "please" or "displease" the referent, or because they believe that the referent will "reward" or "punish" them, but because they want to be like the referent. Although there is no known standardized procedure for assessing this aspect of normative pressure, it seems reasonable to assume that an instrument analogous to the one already described could be developed. For example, it might be useful to employ item pairs such as the following:

(1a) Most of my friends always use a condom when they have vaginal sex with their wives (or main sexual partners)

likely___:___:___:___:___:___:___unlikely

(1b) When it comes to AIDS prevention,

I want to be___:___:___:___:___:___:___I do not want to be like most of my friends

In addition, this aspect of social pressure could be directly assessed with items such as:

(1) Most of the people who are important to me always use a condom when they have vaginal sex with their wives (or main sexual partners)

likely___:___:___:___:___:___:___unlikely

(2) Most of the people I respect and admire

Always___:___:___:___:___:___:___never
Use a condom when they have vaginal sex with their wives (or main sexual partners)

Self-Standards and Sanctions. As Bandura (1986) and Kanfer (1970) pointed out, although people may respond to social pressures, they do not constantly shift their behavior to conform to whatever others might want. Rather, they adopt certain standards of behavior for themselves; they do things that give them a sense of self-pride and they refrain from behaving in ways that violate their self-standards. Indeed, as described earlier, some outcome expectancies may refer to feelings of self-worth and self-censure (e.g., My always using a condom for vaginal sex with my wife or main sexual partner is the responsible thing to do, makes me feel dirty). Like other outcome expectancies, these positive and negative self-sanctions enter into expectancy-value considerations, and thus they should be included in the analysis of outcome expectancies.[6]

It is important to recognize, however, that perceptions of the self may influence behavior even in the absence of explicit outcome expectancies. That is, individuals may not consider whether performing (or not performing) a given behavior will make them feel "good" or "bad" about themselves, but rather, they may simply consider whether performance of the behavior is consistent or inconsistent with their self-image. As Triandis (1977) argued, the more individuals perceive that they are the type of person who would perform the behavior in question, the more likely they are to intend to, and to actually perform that behavior. Thus, to fully understand why people do or do not perform a given behavior, it is necessary to consider the degree to which performance of the behavior is consistent with their self-image. For example, an item, such as the following could be used:

I'm the kind of person who always uses a condom when I have vaginal sex with my wife (or main partner).

agree___:___:___:___:___:___:___disagree

Alternatively, a more indirect measure could be developed. As already described, a set of characteristics or traits can be identified that are associated with performance and nonperformance of the behavior. Then either an adjective check list or a semantic differential format could be used to assess the discrepancy between a person's self-image and his or her perception of a person who does (or does not) perform the behavior in question. For example, the following characteristics or traits are often mentioned when men are asked to describe men who do and do not always use condoms for vaginal sex with their wives or main sexual partners: cautious, responsible, caring, macho, foolish.

Respondents could first be asked to rate themselves on scales such as the following:

I am

cautious___:___:___:___:___:___:___a risk taker

responsible___:___:___:___:___:___:___irresponsible

caring___:___:___:___:___:___:___self-centered

macho___:___:___:___:___:___:___wimpy

wise___:___:___:___:___:___:___foolish

Respondents could then be asked to rate "A man who always uses a condom when he has vaginal sex with his wife (or main sexual partner)" on the same set of scales. An absolute discrepancy score could be calculated for each item, and the sum of the discrepancies would then serve as an index of the degree to which people's self-image deviated from their perception of a man who performed the behavior in question. The larger the discrepancy, the more the behavior is inconsistent with a person's self-image. This indirect measure should be highly correlated with the more direct measure suggested earlier.

Emotional Reactions. As already described, a behavioral performance that is consistent or inconsistent with a person's self-image may lead to feelings of pride or shame. Behavioral performance may also result in strong emotional reactions, such as feelings of elation, depression, delight, disgust, fear, anxiety, and repulsion. Again, when anticipating these positive and negative self-sanctions, they are best viewed as outcome expectancies and should be included in expectancy-value or cost–benefit analyses. In addition, however, people may experience emotional reactions when they

---

[6]Within the social cognitive framework, positive and negative self-sanctions are measured by having subjects rate their reactions to their own conduct on a scale ranging from highly self-satisfied, through neutral, to highly self-dissatisfied. For example:
How would you feel about always using a condom for vaginal sex with your spouse (or main sexual partner)?

−3	−2	−1	0	+1	+2	+3
Highly Self-Disatisfied			Neutral			Highly Self-Satisfied

merely think about performing the behavior. Emotional reactions of this type may also influence a person's decision to perform or not perform a given behavior.

It is important to distinguish between these emotional reactions and what was earlier described as affective feelings vis-à-vis the behavior in question. Although clearly related to "affect," this concept is conceptualized as a much stronger, classically conditioned positive or negative "gut" reaction to the "thought" of performing the behavior in question. Although no standardized set of items has been developed to assess emotional response, it appears that a semantic differential such as the following could be used to assess one's emotional reactions to a given behavior:

When I think about always using a condom for vaginal sex with my spouse (or main sexual partner), I feel

delighted___:___:___:___:___:___:___disgusted

happy___:___:___:___:___:___:___angry

joyful___:___:___:___:___:___:___depressed

anxious___:___:___:___:___:___:___calm

nauseated___:___:___:___:___:___:___exhilarated

frightened___:___:___:___:___:___:___relaxed

Self-Efficacy. The concept of perceived self-efficacy refers to individuals' beliefs in their capability to perform the behavior in question under different circumstances. The stronger the perceived self-efficacy, the stronger the intention to perform the behavior, and the greater the likelihood that a person will perform the behavior, given some incentive to do so.

Perceived self-efficacy with respect to a given behavior (or behavioral category, or a course of action directed at goal attainment) is always measured in relation to task demands that vary in difficulty, threat, complexity, or some other type of challenge or obstacle. In short, measurement of perceived self-efficacy demands gradations of challenge. In addition, people should be asked to judge their perceived self-efficacy as of now, and not for some future time. To put this somewhat differently, efficacy items should measure current perceived capabilities and not future hypothetical capabilities. Finally, items should measure individuals' efficacy to perform the behavior regularly or always. It is often easy to perform a behavior (e.g., using a condom for vaginal sex with a spouse) occasionally but difficult to perform this same behavior routinely or regularly, unless the behavior becomes habitual or automatic.

In devising self-efficacy items, the first step is to identify internal or external conditions that make performance difficult. Procedures for arriving at such a set of conditions or circumstances vis-à-vis any given behavior (or set of behaviors) were described earlier. With respect to the behavior of "always using a condom for vaginal sex with my spouse (or main sexual partner)," internal challenges may include high sexual arousal, and being high on alcohol or drugs. External challenges might include not having a condom available, or they might describe difficult circumstances such as having a resistant partner who is argumentative, inebriated, or high on drugs. If the focus is shifted from a male's condom use to a female's attempt to get her partner to use a condom, then circumstances in which a partner is abusive, threatening, and/or coercive one must also be considered. Based on this information, a scale such as the following may be constructed to assess a male's self-efficacy with respect to using a condom for vaginal sex with his spouse (or main sexual partner):[7]

Rate how confident you are that you can regularly do the things described below. Rate your degree of confidence as of now by recording a number from 0 to 100 using the scale given below:

0 10 20 30 40 50 60 70 80 90 100

Cannot do at all — Moderately certain can do — Certain can do

____ I can use a condom for vaginal sex with my wife (or main sexual partner) while under the influence of alcohol or drugs.

____ If my wife (or main sexual partner) didn't want me to use a condom for vaginal sex, I can convince her that it is necessary for me to do so.

____ I can delay vaginal sex with my wife (or main sexual partner) if a condom is not available.

____ I can use a condom for vaginal sex with my wife (or main sexual partner) while I am very sexually aroused.

The estimate of self-efficacy is obtained by summing responses (from 0 to 100) over the set of items. The higher the score, the greater the perceived self-efficacy.

SOME UNRESOLVED ISSUES

Although there is consensus that the previous eight variables serve as the major determinants of behavior, at present there is no consensus concerning the causal model linking these variables to behavior. Indeed, each of the theorists have essentially proposed an explicit causal ordering of some (or all) of these variables in their theories and there was no agreement on the strength of interrelationships among these variables or on where each variable would be located in a causal chain. For example, although some see considerable theoretical and/or empirical overlap between some variables (e.g., intention and self-efficacy; attitude and emotion), others would argue that these concepts are relatively independent. As another example, some see perceived normative pressure as directly influencing intention, and others argue that norms only have force when they lead to (or are backed up by) anticipated consequences. A third example of disagreement concerns the mediating role of intention. That is, whereas some would argue

[7]Studies that try to measure numerous variables place constraints on the number of items that can be used to measure any one of them. Researchers, therefore, have to sacrifice wide gradations of challenge and try to pick optimal levels of challenge for the population being studied.

that some variables (e.g., attitude, perceived norms) influence behavior only indirectly (i.e., through their influence on intention), others would argue for both a direct and an indirect effect of a given variable on behavior.

In general, however, there is agreement that intentions are most proximal to behavior, and the other seven variables may best be seen as either influencing the formation and strength of intentions and/or as influencing the likelihood that people will act on their intentions.

One implication of this is that it points out the necessity of measuring intentions prior to developing an intervention. Clearly, very different interventions will be necessary if a person (or group) has not yet developed a strong intention (or made a commitment) to perform a given behavior, than if the person has formed a strong intention, but is unable to act upon it.

Recall that we assume that a person will perform a given behavior if (a) he or she has a strong intention to do so, (b) he or she has the necessary skills to perform the behavior, and (c) there are no environmental constraints (or "external" barriers) to prevent behavioral performance. Thus, if one has formed a strong intention to perform a given behavior but is not acting upon that intention, the intervention should probably be focused upon improving skills and/or removing or helping one to overcome environmental constraints.

In contrast, if a person has not yet formed a strong intention to perform a given behavior, the goal of the intervention should be to strengthen the person's intention to perform that behavior. And, as indicated above, this could be accomplished by changing self-efficacy, outcome expectancies (or attitudes), perceived norms, self-standards, or emotions vis-à-vis that behavior. But what intentions should such interventions address?

Clearly, it is possible to try to change people's intentions to reach goals (e.g., to avoid AIDS), to engage in a category of behaviors (e.g., to practice safe sex), or to perform a given behavior (e.g., to always use a condom for vaginal sex with my spouse). Since there was general agreement that intentions to reach goals are often poor predictors of goal attainment or of the behaviors individuals may perform in their attempt to reach the goal, it was agreed that interventions should focus on behaviors rather than on goals or outcomes. For example, it was agreed that although little would be accomplished by strengthening someone's intention to "avoid AIDS," it would be appropriate to direct an intervention at strengthening a woman's intention to tell her partner to use a condom or at increasing a male's intention to use a condom. What was less clear, however, was whether it was appropriate to direct interventions at intentions to engage in behavioral categories such as "practicing safe sex," or "negotiating condom use with my partner." Unfortunately, intentions to engage in behavioral categories are not always good predictors (or determinants) of whether a person will (or will not) perform a given behavior within that category. For example, a young man may form a strong intention to engage in "safe sex," yet he may have little or no intention to "always use a condom." Similarly, a young woman may form a strong intention to "negotiate condom use with my partner," yet she may have little or no intention to "tell my partner to use a condom." Thus, if there is an interest in increasing the likelihood that men will use condoms or the likelihood that women will tell their partners to use condoms, it may be better to change intentions to use condoms and intentions to tell a partner to use condoms than to change intentions to practice "safe sex" or intentions to "negotiate condom use with my partner."

To complicate the issue even further, although condom use is a behavior for men, it is a goal for women. Women do not use condoms; at best, a woman can try to get her partner to use a condom. But is "getting my partner to use a condom" a goal or a behavioral category? As has been pointed out, in order to get a partner to use a condom, an individual may perform several specific behaviors (e.g., telling one's partner to use a condom, refusing to have sex unless one's partner uses a condom), at least some of which may reflect the behavioral category of "negotiating condom use with one's partner." Thus, once again, there is the question of whether it is more appropriate to try to increase a woman's intention to "get my partner to use a condom" or to increase her intention to perform one or more specific behaviors whose performance might increase the likelihood that a partner will use a condom. The way an individual answers this question has important implications for identifying the intention that the intervention should address. The question of what is or is not a goal, a behavior or a behavioral category, and the parallel question of what are appropriate intentions for interventions to address, are unresolved issues that require further attention.

Generally speaking, however, interventions that are not directed at increasing skills or removing environmental constraints should attempt to reinforce and strengthen intentions to engage in "desirable" (e.g., safe, healthy) behaviors and/or to weaken intentions to engage in "undesirable" (e.g., dangerous, unhealthy) behaviors.

By utilizing measures such as those already described, each of the eight potential determinants of behavior can be assessed and this information can be used to empirically identify the one or two variables that most strongly influence intentions to perform, and actual performance of, a given behavior in a given population. These empirically determined variables should then serve as the primary focus of an intervention.

For example, if norms are found to be most highly related to intentions and behavior, the intervention should focus on increasing perceived normative pressure to perform the behavior in question. In contrast, if self-efficacy is found to be most highly related to intentions and behavior, then the intervention should focus on increasing the person's self-efficacy with respect to that behavior. Because it is recognized that the relative importance of a given variable as a determinant of intention and/or behavior will depend on both the behavior under consideration and the population being studied, interventions should be based on empirical research. Little will be accomplished by directing an intervention at a given variable (e.g., outcome expectancies, norms, or self-standards) if the variable is unrelated (or only weakly related) to the behavior that needs to be changed. Given the limited resources available for prevention and change programs, it is essential that interventions focus on changing those variables that have the greatest probability of influencing the likelihood that members of a given population will engage in the behavior in question.[8]

ACKNOWLEDGMENTS

This chapter is dedicated to Marshall Becker, a true pioneer in health psychology. His contributions and humanity will be greatly missed. The chapter is a slightly revised version of M. Fishbein, A. Bandura, H. C. Triandis, F. H. Kanfer, M. H. Becker, S. E. Middlestadt, & A. Eichler (1992), *Factors Influencing Behavior and Behavior Change: Final Report—Theorist's Workshop.* Bethesda: NIMH. We are greatful to Dr. Bandura for his input on social cognitive theory, and in particular, for the definition, description and assessment of self-efficacy. Because of his strong belief that science is best advanced by developing a single theory (rather than by integrating parts of different theories), Dr. Bandura chose not to be a coauthor of the present chapter.

REFERENCES

Ajzen, I., & Fishbein, M. (1980). *Understanding attitudes and predicting social behavior.* Englewood Cliffs, NJ: Prentice-Hall.

Bandura, A. (1986). *Social foundations of thought and action: A social cognitive theory.* Englewood Cliffs, NJ: Prentice-Hall.

Bandura, A. (1992). Exercise of personal agency through the self-efficacy mechanism. In R. Schwarzer (Ed.), *Self-efficacy: Thought control of action* (pp. 3–38). Washington, DC: Hemisphere.

Bandura, A. (1994). Social cognitive theory and exercise of control over HIV infection. In R. J. DiClemente & J. L. Peterson (Eds.), *Preventing AIDS: Theories and methods of behavioral interventions* (pp. 1–20). New York: Plenum.

Becker, M. H. (1974). The health belief model and personal health behavior. *Health Education Monographs, 2,* 324–508.

Becker, M. H. (1988). AIDS and behavior change. *Public Health Reviews, 16,* 1–11.

CDC AIDS Community Demonstartion Projects Research Group. (1999). Community-level HIV intervention in 5 cities: Final outcome data from the CDC AIDS Community Demonstartion Projects. *AJPH, 89*(3), 1–10.

Cleghorn, F., Weller, P., Helquist, M., Woods, W., Rohde, F., & Middlestadt, S. E. (1991). *Improving the reliability of an observation instrument to assess condom skills.* Paper presented at the U.S.A.I.D. AIDS Prevention Conference, Rosslyn, VA.

[8]The theorists workshop that produced this paper was held in 1991. At that time, most AIDS psychosocial research was directed at identifying factors that put people at risk for acquiring or transmitting AIDS or at understanding the determinants of "safer" or "riskier" behaviors. There were few, if any, theory-based behavioral interventions to prevent the acquisition or transmission of HIV. Since that time, many of the ideas presented in this paper have served as the theoretical underpinnings for a number of successful behavior change interventions. For illustrations of how the concepts and measures described in the paper have been used to design, implement, and evaluate multi-site behavior change interventions at both the community and individual level, see Fishbein et al. (1996), the CDC AIDS Community Demonstartion Projects Research Group (1999), and Kamb et al. (1998).

Eisler, R. M., Miller, P. M., & Hersen, M. (1973). Components of Assertive Behavior. *Journal of Clinical Psychology, 29,* 259–299.

Fishbein, M. (1980). A theory of reasoned action: Some applications and implications. In H. Howe & M. Page (Eds.), *Nebraska Symposium on Motivation, 1979* (pp. 65–116). Lincoln: University of Nebraska Press.

Fishbein, M., & Ajzen, I. (1975). *Belief, attitude, intention and behavior: An introduction to theory and research.* Boston: Addison-Wesley.

Fishbein, M., Guenther-Grey, C., Johnson, W. D., Wolitski, R. J., McAlister, A., Rietmeijer, C. A., O'Reilly, K., & The AIDS Community Demonstration Projects. (1996). Using a theory-based community intervention to reduce AIDS risk behaviors: The CDC's AIDS Community Demonstartion Projects. In S. Oskamp & S. C. Thompson (Eds.), *Understanding and preventing HIV risk behavior: Safer sex and drug use* (pp. 177–206). Thousand Oaks, CA: Sage.

Fishbein, M., Middlestadt, S. E., & Hitchcock, P. J. (1991). Using information to change sexually transmitted disease-related behaviors: An analysis based on the theory of reasoned action. In J. N. Wasserheit, S. O. Aral, & K. K. Holmes (Eds.), *Research issues in human behavior and sexually transmitted diseases in the AIDS era* (pp. 243–257). Washington, DC: American Society for Microbiology.

French, J. R. P., Jr., & Raven, B. H. (1959). The basis of social power. In D. Cartwright (Ed.), *Studies in social power* (pp. 150–167). Ann Arbor: University of Michigan Press.

Hersen, M., & Bellack, A. S. (1976). Social skills training for chronic psychiatric patients: Rationale, research findings, and future directions. *Comprehensive Psychiatry, 17,* 559–780.

Janz, N. K., & Becker, M. H. (1984). The health belief model: A decade later. *Health Education Quarterly, 11,* 1–47.

Kamb, M. L., Fishbein, M., Douglas, J. M., Rhodes, F., Rogers, J., Bolan, G., Zenilman, J., Hoxworth, T., Mallotte, C. K., Iatesta, M., Kent, C., Lentz, A., Graziano, S., Byers, R. H., Peterman, T. A., & The Project RESPECT Study Group. (1998). HIV/STD prevention counselling for high-risk behaviors: Results from a multicenter, randomized controlled trial. *Journal of the American Medical Association, 280*(13), 1161–1167.

Kanfer, F. H. (1970). Self-regulation: Research, issues and speculations. In C. Neuringir & J. L. Michael (Eds.), *Behavior modification in clinical psychology* (pp. 178–220). New York: Appleton-Century-Crofts.

Kanfer, F. H., & Shefft, B. K. (1988). *Guiding the process of therapeutic change.* Champaign, IL: Research Press.

Kanfer, R., & Kanfer, F. H. (1991). Goals and self regulation: Applications of theory to work settings. In M. L. Maehr & P. R. Pintrich (Eds.), *Advances in motivation and achievement* (Vol. 7, pp. 287–326). Greenwich, CT: JAI Press.

Kelly, J. A., Murphy, D. A., Sikkema, K. J., & Kalichman, S. C. (1993). Psychological interventions to prevent HIV infection are urgently needed: New priorities for behavioral research in the second decade of AIDS. *American Psychologist, 48*(10), 1023–1034.

Kelly, J. A., St. Lawrence, J. S., Hood, H. V., & Brasfield, T. L. (1989). Behavioral intervention to reduce AIDS risk activities. *Journal of Consulting and Clinical Psychology, 57,* 60–67.

Montgomery, S. B., Joseph, J. G., Becker, M. H., Ostrow, D. G., Kessler, R. C., & Kirscht, J. P. (1989). The health belief model in understanding compliance with preventive recommendations for AIDS: How useful? *AIDS Education and Prevention, 1,* 303–323.

Nisbett, R. E., & Ross, L. (1980). *Human inference: Strategies and shortcomings of social judgment.* Englewood Cliffs, NJ: Prentice-Hall.

Prochaska, J. O., & DiClemente, C. C. (1983). Stages and processes of self-change in smoking: Towards an integrative model of change. *Journal of Consulting and Clinical Psychology, 51,* 390–395.

Prochaska, J. O., & DiClemente, C. C. (1986). Toward a comprehensive model of change. In W. Miller & N. Heather (Eds.), *Treating addictive behaviors.* New York: Plenum.

Triandis, H. C. (1972). *The analysis of subjective culture.* New York: Wiley.

Triandis, H. C. (1977). *Interpersonal behavior.* Monterey, CA: Brooks-Cole.

Triandis, H. C. (1980). Values, attitudes and interpersonal behavior. In H. Howe & M. Page (Eds.), *Nebraska Symposium on Motivation, 1979* (pp. 197–259). Lincoln: University of Nebraska Press.

2

Representations, Procedures, and Affect in Illness Self-Regulation: A Perceptual-Cognitive Model

Howard Leventhal
Rutgers University

Elaine A. Leventhal
Robert Wood Johnson School of Medicine

Linda Cameron
University of Auckland

The explosion of research in health psychology over the past 40 years has been accompanied by the proliferation of a variety of theoretical models to help find a better understanding of the reciprocal relations between health and behavior. One set of models that has been used for the analysis of behaviors to promote health and treat and adapt to disease (e.g., utility theories and social learning models) has focused on five types of variables: The cognitive processes involved in the perceptions of vulnerability to disease (Becker, 1974; Hochbaum, 1958; Janz & Becker, 1984; Rogers, 1983; Rosenstock, 1966); the availability of actions to manage threat and/or emotional reactions to it (Lazarus & Launier, 1978); intentions to act based on the perceptions of the barriers and benefits of particular actions for threat avoidance (Fishbein & Ajzen, 1974; Janz & Becker, 1984; Rosenstock, 1966); the views held by valued others respecting specific healthy and risky behaviors (Fishbein & Ajzen, 1974); and perceptions of self-competence or self-efficacy to perform these actions (Ajzen, 1988; Bandura, 1977; Clark & Zimmerman, 1990). To a substantial degree, these constructs are the inventions of the investigators (see Krasnegor, Epstein, Bennett-Johnson, & Yaffe, 1993; Leventhal & Cameron, 1987; Leventhal, Zimmerman, & Gutmann, 1984). This contrasts with a second set of models with names such as "self-regulation and adaptation" (Kanfer, 1977), "illness cognition" (Croyle & Barger, 1993), "mental representation in health and illness" (Skelton & Croyle, 1991), and "common-sense representation of illness danger" (Leventhal, Meyer, & Nerenz, 1980). These models, the focus of this chapter, make extensive use of constructs generated by their subjects (i.e., they incorporate the subjects' phenomenology into their scientific vocabulary). The approach reflects a long-standing tradition in social and personality psychology (e.g., Kelly, 1955; Lewin, 1935), and in studies of "folk illness" by medical anthropologists (e.g., Chrisman, 1977; Kleinman, 1980; Pachter, 1993; Simons, 1993). The variation in their names reflects differential emphasis on various features of self-regulation in acting to prevent, treat, cure, or adjust to acute or chronic illnesses. All of the models are driven by three fundamental themes:

1. Individuals are conceptualized as active problem solvers trying to make sense of potential or existent changes in

their somatic state and to act to avoid or control those changes perceived as signs of illness or physical disorder; in effect, individuals are self-regulating systems. In this framework, adaptation is a product of a problem-solving process in which decisions to take specific actions reflect the understanding (representation) of an illness threat, the availability of procedures for its management, and experience with the outcomes (costs and benefits) of specific procedures.

2. The adaptive process is based on common sense beliefs and appraisals. That is, the representation of a disease threat, the coping procedures selected for its management, and the appraisal of outcomes is a product of the individual's understanding and skills. Thus, these representations and procedures may not reflect the objective, biomedical nature of the threat or the medical procedures optimal for its control.

3. The notion of "folk-illness," which distinguishes the biomedical concept of disease from its social concept of illness, emphasizes the role of the sociocultural environment in shaping the self-regulation process. Thus, the individuals' representation of a threat and their selection and evaluation of coping procedures will reflect their perceptions (i.e., representation) of the attitudes and beliefs of their social and cultural environment. This environment includes family, friends, health practitioners (biomedical and traditional), mass media, socially defined roles (such as the passive versus active patient), and the linguistic terms used to label and describe specific diseases and treatments. Each of these factors constrains and shapes the substance and behavior of the self-regulation system. Because a wide range of factors shape the content (or "software") of the self-regulatory behavioral system, assessments across persons within a common socio-cultural domain, and assessments across cultural domains, will reveal both common and unique features of illness representations, coping strategies, and appraisals.

The first of the following sections describes the *commonsense model of self-regulation,* which was designed to capture both the common and the unique features of the adaptation process. This section defines the actor's phenomenological view of health threats and the procedures for their management; in effect, it describes both the *structure* and the *content* of the problem- solving system. The second section describes the *system dynamics,* or the processes involved in self-regulation. The focus here is on the rules governing the interactions among the system's perceptual, cognitive, and affective components as individuals construct representations of threats and procedures for threat control. The self system is central to the discussion of system dynamics as the meaning of specific illness episodes arises from their impact on the self. The third section focuses on the role of the social context in shaping behavior during illness episodes. The views exposed here concerning the ways in which the self and social environment influence health-related problem solving differ in important respects from the views espoused by utility and social learning approaches. The fourth section gives special attention to comparisons between self-regulation approaches and the utility and social learning models of the first set. The citations are designed to integrate the diverse literature relevant to the self-regulation approach here adopted. Exhaustive reviews are available elsewhere (Petrie & Weinman, 1997; Skelton & Croyle, 1991).

THE STRUCTURE AND CONTENT OF THE COMMONSENSE MODEL OF SELF-REGULATION

A psychological model of the processes involved in coping with specific episodes of illness and/or illness threats must depict the structure of the problem-solving system and its content (the cognitive and emotional material within it). Social-psychological research often considers the identification of mental contents as a task that is, at best, of secondary concern. Content is ignored, however, at the researcher's peril because it affects both structure and process. The content (e.g., ideas about the indicators, duration, causes, and ways of preventing and curing specific diseases) is the software or commonsense feature of the system as it reflects the declarative and procedural knowledge of the people under study. The categories in which these commonsense ideas are cast (e.g., the attributes of illness representations, the procedures in implicit memory, as well as the various rules governing the behavior of the system) are constructions of the investigator (Leventhal & Nerenz, 1985).

Although there is considerable diversity among self-regulation models of adaptation to health threats (e.g., Carver & Scheier, 1981, 1982, 1990, 1998; Lazarus & Folkman, 1984; Leventhal, 1970; Miller, Shoda, & Hurley, 1996; Prochaska, DiClemente, & Norcross, 1992), all share the following, specific features. First, the ongoing self-regulation process, or *episodic, problem solving,* is their primary focus. Second, the problem-solving process involves at least three sets of factors: (a) The individual actor's view, or *representation,* of the status of the health problem during the current, ongoing episode; (b) the actor's *procedures,* or plans and tactics, for the control of the threat; and (c) the actor's *appraisal* of the consequences of the coping efforts. The separation of the representation of the health threat from the procedures for threat management is a critical feature of the parallel model first presented in 1970 (see Fig. 2.1). The separation emerged from the repeated findings that messages about health threats did not lead to behavior unless they were combined with information depicting a plan for action. Whether it was the simple act of taking a tetanus shot (Leventhal, Singer, & Jones, 1965; Leventhal, Jones, & Trembly, 1966), or the more complex act of quitting smoking (Leventhal, Watts, & Pagano, 1967), the data showed that concrete information that defined a plan for action was necessary for the occurrence and maintenance of behavior. Although action plans did not generate behaviors by themselves, they were essential for connecting attitudes to behavior. These three factors—*representations, procedures for action, and appraisals*—along with feedback, are the basic constituents of a TOTE (test-operate-test-exit) unit in control theory (Carver & Scheier, 1981, 1982, 1990; Miller, Galanter, & Pribram, 1960; see Fig. 2.2). The TOTE representation suggests that the three components may be closely interrelated and less independent of one another than suggested by the stages represented in the parallel model (Fig. 2.1). This issue is discussed in more detail during the discussion of dynamics.

Figure 2.1 shows that health threats are processed as two parallel arms; the processing of information for *controlling danger*, upper arm, and the processing of information for *controlling the emotional responses* elicited by the danger, lower arm. The independence of the processing of danger and the processing of affect was seen in early studies of people's response to fear arousing communications. These studies showed that messages depicting the threat of diseases such as lung cancer or tetanus had three effects: They aroused fear, changed attitudes, and at times, influenced overt behavior. But neither the presence of fear nor its level had a consistent relation to behavioral outcomes. For example, messages arousing high levels of fear, in comparison to those arousing low levels, did not increase the frequency of behaviors such as taking tetanus inoculations (Leventhal et al., 1966; Leventhal et al., 1965). Outcome measures showed that fear had two, characteristic effects: It was temporary, and it produced attitudinal and behavioral "avoidance." Thus, intentions to drive safely (Leventhal & Trembly, 1968) and reports of decreases in cigarette smoking were enhanced by fear (Leventhal et al., 1967), whereas acts that could increase fear (e.g., taking a chest x-ray and discovering, perhaps lung cancer) were inhibited by fear (Leventhal & Watts, 1966). Recent studies support the hypothesis that fear facilitates behaviors to prevent disease and inhibits behaviors to detect or approach disease (Millar & Millar, 1996). The temporary quality of fear effects—they were visible for only 1 or 2 days following exposure to threat messages—contrasted with the promotion of health protective actions that lasted over weeks and sometimes months for subjects exposed to communications combining either a strong or weak threat message with action plans. This contrast created a problem for conceptualizing the effects of threat messages. Specifically, if the presence of an active state of fear or the intensity of this state was irrelevant for converting action plans into behavior, some type of "cognitive" change induced by the threat messages must be responsible for moving plans into action. These factors were labeled as the *representation* of the health threat, and the label defined a specific task, namely, identifying the content and structure of "representations."

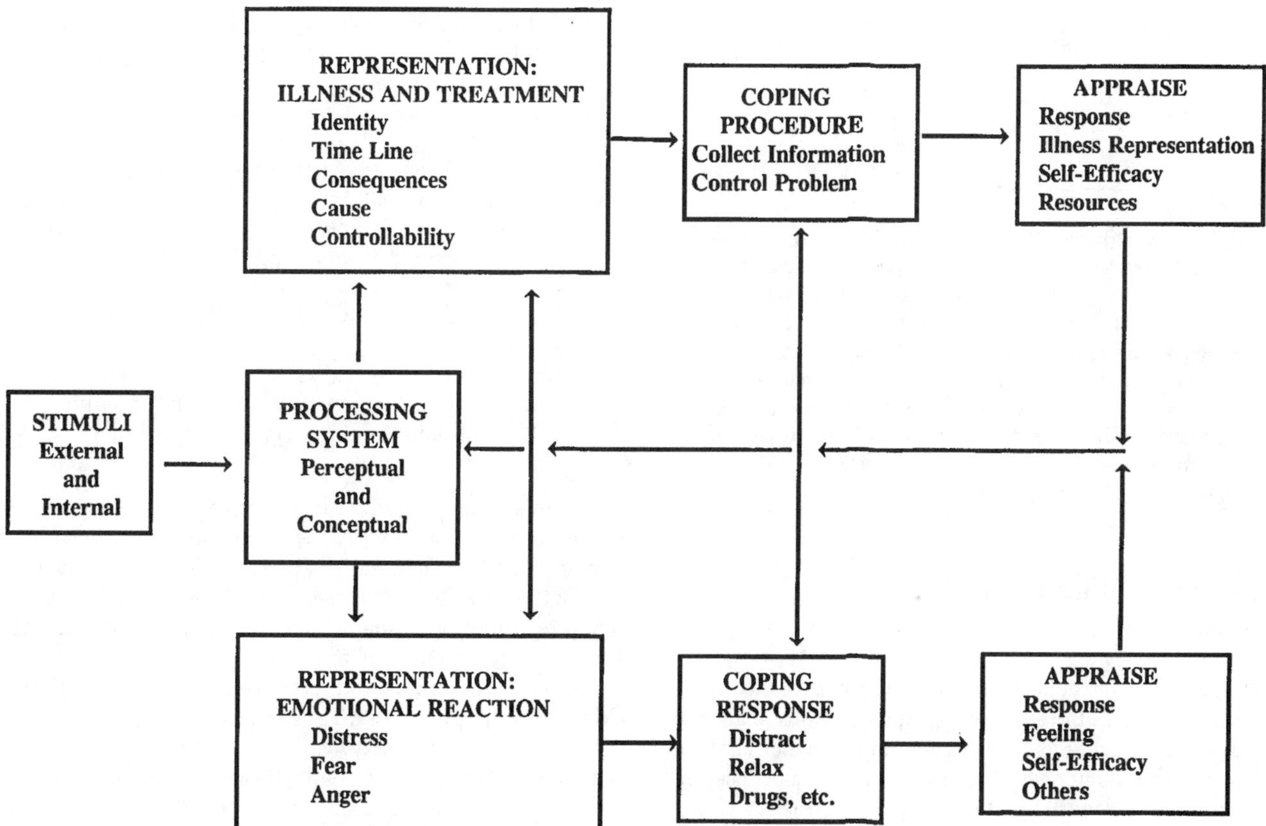

FIG. 2.1. The top arm of the parallel response model depicts the processing of the individual's phenomenal reality, or the representation of somatic experience and the plans, procedures, and outcome appraisals generated by the representation. A similar sequence for the emotional processes is represented by the lower arm. Arrows represent feedback and interactions among the processing levels (from Leventhal, Leventhal, & Schaefer, 1991).

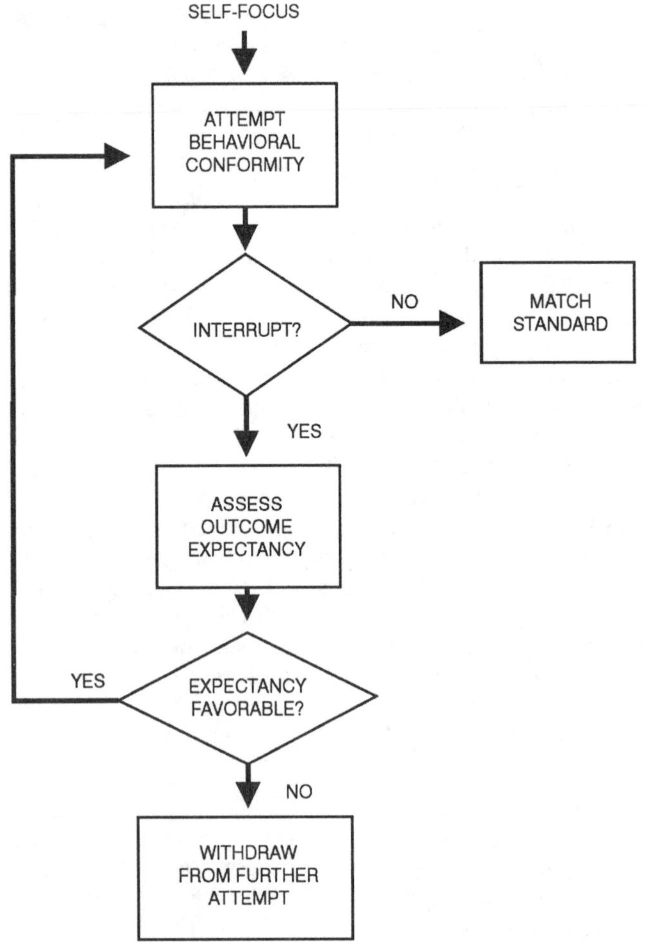

FIG. 2.2. A schematic depiction of a feedback loop, the basic unit of cybernetic control. In such a loop a sensed value is compared to a reference value or standard, and adjustments are made in an output function (if necessary) to shift the sensed value in the direction of the standard. Loops of this type may be arranged in parallel, hierarchies, the upper level loops in a hierarchy providing reference values for lower level ones, and loops in adjacent hierarchies providing reference values useful for shifting the ongoing process in new directions when obstructions are encountered (courtesy of Carver & Scheier, 1998).

The Problem-Solving Episodes: Illness Representations

The approach to the identification of the content of the illness representation (i.e., the substance that establishes goals and creates plans and actions for goal attainment and criteria for appraising action outcomes) was influenced by a decision to study illness behavior. In illness behavior (Kasl & Cobb, 1966), the *problem-solving episodes* are initiated by somatic stimuli (i.e., changes produced by a disease) or by disease labels. The objective was defined, therefore, as the investigation of the ways in which people understood and/or interpreted somatic symptoms and how they represented and coped with disease threats (Leventhal & Leventhal, 1993; Leventhal, Nerenz, & Strauss, 1982). It was assumed, incorrectly perhaps, that it would be possible to identify the same features of the representation of health threats whether by studying how people interpreted somatic symptoms or by studing health-related actions that are undertaken by persons who are asymptomatic or healthy.

The Content of Illness Representations. Data generated by open- and close-ended interviews with patients, and data from studies using multidimensional scaling of illness labels with undergraduates, identified five sets of attributes of illness representations (Fig. 2.1):

1. The *identity* of the threat, or the symptoms and labels that define it (Dempsey, Dracup, & Moser, 1995; Lau, Bernard, & Hartmann, 1989; Meyer, Leventhal, & Gutmann, 1985).
2. The *time line,* which can include beliefs regarding the time lines for development and duration of a disease, the point in time to use a treatment regimen, the time needed for cure or control, and the time from disease onset to death when no treatment is possible (Heidrich, Forsthoff, & Ward, 1994; Klohn & Rogers, 1991; Meyer et al., 1985).
3. The *causes* of the threat, which may involve external agents (e.g., bacteria, virus, job stress, or even bewitchment), internal susceptibilities (e.g., genetic factors), and behavioral causes (e.g., a bump causing breast cancer; Baumann, Cameron, Zimmerman, & Leventhal, 1989).
4. The anticipated and experienced *consequences* of the disease, which may involve physical, emotional, social, and economic outcomes (Cella, Tulsky, Gray, et al., 1993; Croyle & Jemmott, 1991; Klohn & Rogers, 1991; Leventhal, Easterling, Coons, Luchterhand, & Love, 1986; McGee, O'Boyle, Hickey, O'Malley, & Joyce, 1991).
5. Its *controllability,* which pertains to the anticipated and perceived responsiveness of the condition to self-treatment and expert intervention (Lau & Hartmann, 1983).

These representational attributes form the basis of lay models of illness as they have been described from the time of Hippocrates and Galen to the present (Schober & Lacroix, 1991); they are the attributes that guide the selection of coping procedures and shape their execution. For example, symptoms represented as a coronary threat typically stimulate rapid care-seeking and the cessation of other activities (Matthews, Siegel, Kuller, Thompson, & Varat, 1983); those of a possible cancer may lead to care-seeking if they fall within the set of symptoms typically attributed to cancer (e.g., a lump in the breast; Facione, 1993), or to a "wait and see" strategy to determine whether they are getting worse (Cameron, Leventhal, & Leventhal, 1993; Hackett & Cassem, 1969). The symptoms of a common cold may stimulate self-care procedures such as getting extra sleep, taking aspirins, taking vitamin C, and drinking fluids.

Illness Representations Have Structure. Representations also have structure. Structure is of two types: The attributes of representations are represented in both abstract and concrete form (e.g., identity is represented as the disease label and its symptoms, and time-line is represented as conceptual, clock time and perceptual, "felt" time). And representations are constructed from underlying schemata or patterns of attributes that may reflect beliefs about specific diseases or specific classes of disease.

The bilevel nature of attributes is critical for behavior as it is the concrete, symptomatic level of illness that is a consistent and powerful predictor of utilization of health care (Berkanovic, Hurwicz, & Landsverk, 1988; Berkanovic, Telesky, & Reeder, 1981; McKinlay & Dutton, 1974; Pescosolido, 1992). The more interesting examples of the abstract and concrete nature of representations are those in which knowledge of both abstract and concrete cognition is necessary for understanding behavior. For example, Yoder and Hornik (1996) examined mothers' use of oral rehydration treatment of infant diarrhea from six large surveys conducted in Africa and Asia, and found that the mothers' observation of concrete symptoms (vomiting, fever, reduced play) predicted use of treatment after controls were entered for the mothers' judgments of the severity of the child's illness. Thus, concrete experience had direct as well as indirect (mediated by severity judgments) effects on behavior. More dramatic evidence appears when abstract and concrete levels of processing generate conflicting goals and different criteria for appraising coping efficacy. Diabetes and hypertension provide well-studied examples. Diabetic patients rely on symptoms to vary their insulin and food intake to avoid hypoglycemia even though they are trained and active users of far more accurate, objective devices for assessment of blood glucose levels; subjective cues win out over the procedures guided by abstract knowledge (Gonder-Frederick & Cox, 1986, 1991). Hypertensive patients behave similarly. Meyer, Leventhal, and Gutmann (1985) found that 80% of the patients in their study who were in ongoing treatment for hypertension agreed with the statement that "People can't tell when their blood pressure is elevated." These patients agreed with this statement because their doctors told them that elevated base levels of blood pressure, the numbers that define chronic hypertension, are silent or asymptomatic. Later in the same interview, however, 90% of these patients reported they could tell whether their blood pressure was elevated on the basis of a variety of somatic cues such as heart palpitations, warm face, and headache. More importantly, patients were compliant and had better blood pressure control if they believed their medications were reducing their symptoms: If the medications were seen as ineffective in controlling symptoms, both adherence and blood pressure control were poor.

The belief that hypertension is symptomatic is unsurprising on three counts. First, the label, hypertension, suggests that specific somatic experiences accompany elevated blood pressure (Blumhagen, 1980). Second, unlike basal blood pressure levels, acute or phasic shifts in blood pressure induced by intense exertion (e.g., exercise) produce palpable somatic change (Pennebaker & Watson, 1988). Third, medical practitioners may inadvertently suggest that hypertension is symptomatic when they conduct a review of systems, the "head to toe" symptom based inquiry designed to detect comorbidities and/or unfavorable sequelae of hypertension. While these three factors play an important role in linking specific symptoms to the hypertension label, that they do so is likely a reflections of a fourth, more fundamental factor: the tendency of the cognitive system to connect or to define abstractions with concrete instances (Quinn & Eimas, 1997; Rosch, Mervis, Gray, Johnson, & Boyes-Braem, 1976). This linkage reflects what we have called the *symmetry rule*: the experience of symptoms will lead to a search for labels and the presence of labels will lead to a search for symptoms. The effect of symptoms on the search for labels is demonstrated by Schachter and Singer's (1962) classic study of emotional contagion. The search for symptoms given the presence of labels, is seen in studies where false feedback on elevations in blood pressure lead to increases in the reporting of symptoms identical to those reported by hypertensives (Baumann, Cameron, Zimmerman, & Leventhal, 1989; Croyle, 1990).

These matching of symptoms and labels to form disease representations reflects the integration of somatic sensations with underlying disease *schemata* or disease *prototypes*. The integration gives the self-diagnosis its implicit cause, time line, anticipated consequences, assumptions about controllability, and associated affective reactions. At any point in time, however, the individual may be conscious of only some of these factors. Investigators differ, however, concerning whether the process of matching a somatic input to memory involves a match to a prototype or a match to a specific, episodic memory (Croyle & Barger, 1993). This issue is dealt with in greater detail during a discussion of system dynamics.

Problem-Solving Episodes: Coping Procedures and Appraisals

Sensing a threat, the individual is faced with the problem of defining and controlling it, that is, preventing, curing, and/or halting its progression (Cioffi, 1991). The representation plays a central role in the selection, performance, and maintenance of procedures. A key proposition of our model is that "the representation of the disease affects the plausibility or choice of a procedure for threat control, defines a goal for the procedure, and sustains the performance of the procedure until the threat is removed" (Leventhal, Diefenbach, & Leventhal, 1992). In more familiar terms, the representations of the illness and the selected procedure create outcome expectations and a time frame for goal attainment. For example, individuals suffering from a runny nose and a headache may assume that they have an acute cold (identity and symptoms) that will last for a day or two (time frame), is uncomfortable but not life threatening (minimal consequences), and whose symptoms can be managed (control). The procedure for control, taking an over-the-counter medication such as aspirin or tylenol, has an identity, a label and expected somatic "side effects" (removal of headache and if aspirin, possible stomach acid), an expected time frame for efficacy (half hour to an hour to work with duration of 4 to 6 hours), with no serious consequences, expected control of any of its side effects (take an antacid with the aspirin), and so on.

The variety of coping procedures is enormous. They range from short-term actions such as using one or another of the vast number of over-the-counter medications, to participation in one of many procedures for the prevention or early detection of cancer or cardiovascular disease, to repetitive and longer term actions such as obtaining an annual check-up, adopting a low-fat diet, avoiding risk by quitting smoking, or adopting any of the wide variety of procedures used for months and years to minimize dysfunction and live with an incurable, chronic condition. It seems likely that the extraordinary variety of coping procedures is due in part to the perception that different, specific procedures are needed to deal with particular threats. For example, topical antibacterial agents are used for wounds but not for gastric distress.

In addition to their enormous variety and specificity, procedures for controlling threat have multiple objectives, and the very same procedure may have different objectives at varying points in time. For example, social comparison, one of a larger set of procedures defined by a search for information, may be useful for self-diagnosis of the *identity* of a symptom and simultaneously, for the reduction of fear. For example, if both you and a friend suffer from stomach pains, vomiting, and diarrhea 12 hours after eating the same dessert at lunch, it is more plausible to assume that you are both suffering from food poisoning rather than an ulcer or stomach cancer (Leventhal, Hudson, & Robitaille, 1997). Thus, a procedure may be used for both problem solution and emotion control at the very same point in time. Indeed, coping procedures have complex meanings. Unlike utility and social-learning frameworks, which assign two attributes to coping procedures, *response efficacy,* or the effectiveness of the response in meeting its goal, and *self-efficacy,* or the individual's ability to perform the response (Bandura, 1977), self-regulation models posit complex, multiattribute representations for procedures. Horne and his associates (Horne, 1997) revealed that individuals possess a range of strongly held beliefs regarding the identity, potential consequences, causes or modes of operation, and timelines for medications. For example, people hold specific beliefs about the risks of medications (e.g., that they can be addictive and have harmful as well as beneficial consequences). Thus, response efficacies include a causal route and a time line for efficacy, somatic effects in addition to symptom removal (identity or side effects), and a variety of consequences in addition to cure and/or control of disease. Procedures can be viewed within the same framework as illnesses: Their representations possess a full set of attributes and they reliably predict adherence to medication regimens (Horne, 1997). The variety, flexibility, and variation in functional utility of specific procedures belies the value of factorially derived classifications of coping responses as problem focused or emotion focused (Lazarus & Launier, 1978; H. Leventhal, 1970).

The contrast formed between the complexity of procedures when observed at the episodic level and the simplicity resulting from factorial studies of coping has led investigators to propose hierarchical models (Krohne, 1993; Leventhal, Suls, & Leventhal, 1993), with generalized strategies defining commonalities across broad classes of coping responses (e.g., risk aversion and energy conservation [Leventhal & Crouch, 1997; Leventhal, Leventhal, & Schaefer, 1991]), middle-level strategies for timing problem-solving responses and controlling emotional reactions (e.g., monitoring or blunting; Miller, 1996; Miller, Combs, & Kruus, 1993; Miller & Mangan, 1983), and specific, lower level procedures such as taking aspirins, exercise, and/or seeking medical care to manage or ward off particular somatic conditions (Klohn & Rogers, 1991; Stoller, 1993, 1997). The modest predictive power of currently used coping instruments, the inconsistent outcomes from study to study, and the failure of coping theory as a basis for interventions to improve adherence to preventive and treatment behaviors reflects the absence of solid empirical data on different levels of analysis. Exceptions are mentioned later (see Stone, Helder, & Schneider, 1988; Stone & Neale, 1984).

Although conscious deliberation enters into the planning and performance of many coping procedures, a substantial number of coping reactions are performed automatically. In fact, automatic behaviors for controlling a health threat may occur at all levels of coping. Consider, for example, a woman who thinks she may have a lump under her right arm. She may automatically and unintentionally execute specific coping tactics, such as searching for parallel, somatic features by touching and exploring the area under her left arm to determine whether a parallel feature is present, suggesting perhaps that both are permanent parts of herself rather than something caused by disease. Automaticity adds to the difficulty of investigating the coping process.

The Episode and Affective Reactions

A wide range of emotional responses appear at various points and in varying intensities in response to warnings, diagnoses, and treatment for disease threats. Examples abound: (a) Exposure to vivid motion pictures depicting the consequences of automotive accidents provokes a mixture of fear, anger, and depression (Leventhal & Trembly, 1968); (b) Exposure to vivid images of lung cancer surgery evokes fear responses and avoidance of chest x-rays (Leventhal & Watts, 1966); (c) Anecdotal reports often describe the diagnosis of breast cancer as equivalent to a "blow on the head"; (d) Diagnoses of recurrent gynecological cancer may arouse a sense of devastation (Andersen, 1999); (e) Emotional distress, characterized as anxiety and fear, fluctuate during hospitalization for medical treatment, rising as the day of surgery nears, peaking following recovery from anesthesia, and gradually declining over the days to discharge (Johnston, 1980); (f) Patients differ in the number of symptoms and level of distress reported in response to the "same" pharmacological agents during cancer chemotherapy (Love, Leventhal, Easterling, & Nerenz, 1989; Manne et al., 1994); (g) Anxiety and distress change with repeated treatment. Some patients show reductions of distress over chemotherapy cycles as they become increasingly familiar with the procedure and show fewer emotional responses (Nerenz, Leventhal, Easterling, & Love, 1986), whereas others show dramatic increases when a later treatment produces unexpected effects that high levels of uncertainty (Nerenz, Leventhal, & Love, 1982); 8) Associative learning may sustain nausea and anxiety over treatment trials, condition to formerly neutral cues, and contribute to a steady rise in distress levels over the course of treatment (Andrykowski, 1990; Bovbjerg et al., 1992; Leventhal, Easterling, Nerenz, & Love, 1988).

Bidirectionality of Emotion and Representations. The variation in emotional distress between persons and over time within the same person, in response to warnings of health threats and during medical treatment, indicates that affective reactions are highly dependent on the meaning individuals assign them. It appears that the affective tail is wagged by the cognitive dog (Lazarus, 1982, 1984). "Meaning" is an amalgam of the representation of the danger and its treatment, the perceived availability of resources to manage the consequences of both, and the outcome of these management efforts (Folkman, 1984; Lazarus, 1966; Lazarus & Folkman, 1984; Scherer, 1984, 1993).

The interplay between emotional reactions and cognition is not, however, uniformly from cognition to affect: It is bidirectional and affective reactions can precede or follow, and in either case, influence both cognition and behavior (Leventhal & Scherer, 1987). Physiological changes induced by exercise (Clark, 1982), sexual excitement or anger (Zillman, 1979), and physical illness can elicit a range of emotional states (Aneshensel, Frerichs, & Huba, 1984), and exacerbate fears of illness and death. Physical illnesses elicit emotional reactions through multiple indirect paths, such as their meaning or threat value or their impact on physical function (Brown, 1990; Zeiss, Lewinsohn, Rhode, & Seeley, 1996), and through a variety of direct paths. For example, the body's immune defenses have direct effects on the central nervous system (Hart, 1988) and diseases can cause cell death and/or depletion of neurotransmitter leading to depressed affect (Cummings, 1992; Leventhal, Patrick-Miller, Leventhal, & Burns, 1997).

The complexity of links between emotion and cognitive representations of illness is precisely what should be expected given that both emotion and cognition involve complex mental and physiological systems; they are not simple entities. Thus, it is expected that emotional reactions, and the individual's success in regulating these reactions, will have multiple effects on the cognitive side of the equation. Emotions can affect illness representations and coping by generating and/or amplifying somatic sensations, increasing feelings of vulnerability (Johnson & Tversky, 1983), or enhancing or minimizing perceptions of illness severity (Ditto, Jemmott, & Darley, 1988), by paralyzing action and lowering expectations of successful outcomes, and by damaging perceptions of self-efficacy (Leventhal, 1970; Seligman, 1975). These issues focus on process and are discussed in the following section.

THE DYNAMICS OF COMMON-SENSE SELF-REGULATION

The processes underlying the construction of illness representations, the selection and execution of coping procedures and their interaction with affective processes, represent the dynamics of self-regulation. These processes are at work in the evolution of episodes for both the prevention and management of illness. This constructive process takes place in the context of the self, that is, the individual's actual and (self) perceived characteristics (cognitive and emotional). A theme that is raised and repeated throughout this section is that coping procedures are guided by questions concerning the implications of illness for the self-system (Hooker & Kaus, 1994; Marcus & Nurius, 1986). Farmer and Good (1991) articulated a similar approach in medical anthropology. The meaning of cancer or cardiovascular disease for an individual emerges from an interaction of the individual's representations of the disease, its treatment and prevention, with the individual's self and with his or her daily function. People act on disease threats, and these actions provide important information about the threat as well as their resources and ability to regulate and protect their physical and psychological integrity.

Theoretical constructions of this interactive process can be made at multiple levels. The moment-by-moment problem-solving processes taking place during ongoing illness episodes involve interactions of concrete and abstract features of illness representations with concrete and abstract features of the self. At the concrete level, the symptomatic identity of the disease, anticipated symptoms, or somatic experiences of treatment, and experienced duration specific treatment side effects derive meaning from interactions with concrete aspects of the self, that is, with the "working" or functional self (e.g., energy to complete treatment, perception about one's ability to tolerate the pain and injury of treatment, etc.). Abstract components of the representation (e.g., beliefs about time until death, expectations regarding possible injury from aversive treatments such as surgery, chemotherapy, etc.) interact with higher order factors of the self-system such as optimism–pessimism or feelings of vulnerability to harm, and self-efficacy at performing specific self-treatment regimens. These meanings generated from the interaction of these higher order variables are presumed to be important for initiating and sustaining goal-directed, episodic behaviors. For example, feelings of vulnerability to a life-threatening disease creates motivation to adopt procedures for prevention (avoidance of death), and willingness to adopt and endure noxious medical treatments is generated by beliefs about the efficacy of the treatment, the intensity and duration of its noxious effects, and beliefs about the self such as perceiving oneself as able to endure distress and possessing an optimistic outlook on the likelihood of cure.

The procedures used to control threat elucidate the interactions among the illness models and representations of the self. For example, identification of somatic sensations as symptoms of risk involve questions such as, "How do I know if this lump is part of my normal self or a product of a threatening disease?" "Are my sensory experiences signs of illness or signs of stress?" When an individual performs a procedure such as taking an aspirin to control a headache, the expected outcome (i.e., the removal of the headache in a defined time frame for a defined period of relief) is a product of the underlying model of the illness and a model of the self's prior response to such treatment (e.g., headaches caused by stress are cured, headaches from nasal-respiratory inflammation recur after 3 or 4 hours, etc.). The response to treatment facilitates the identification of its source, and labeling its source spells out the implications of the headache episode for the self. Defining the questions raised in efforts to define the meaning and establish goals during illness episodes, and identifying the schemata underlying them, will be a major objective of self-regulation theory.

The discussion begins at a more atomistic level (i.e., the interaction of somatic sensations with memory structures in the construction of representations). It moves to questions involved in the dynamics of coping and to interactions of representations and coping procedures with affective processes. Interactions of these factors with the social environment are deferred to the following section.

Constructing Illness Representations

Figure 2.1 suggests that the self-regulation process is linear (i.e., that somatic or external stimuli generate illness representations that are followed by coping procedures and their appraisal). Although the backward pointing arrows in Fig. 2.1 indicate that a loop is created by postappraisal feedback, and feedback can alter any or all of the prior components including the stimulus inputs, these arrows do not overcome the overall linear view implied by the figure. It is worth stating, therefore, that procedures can create stimuli that generate representations as can affective responses. For example, the physically expected cardiac acceleration associated with physical or sexual exertion can generate the representation of coronary disease in vigilant persons. The discussion, however, follows a linear order and begins with the processes involved in the conversion of somatic stimuli to symptoms and health representations, and moves from there to the role of procedures in disambiguating stimuli (i.e., in converting ambiguous somatic sensations into health threats). The ability to distinguish nonself from self (i.e., pathogenic processes from normal and nonthreatening departures from baseline) is an integral part of this process. The interaction of affective processes, representations, coping, and the self-system are discussed last.

Converting Sensations to Symptoms: The Matching Process. Lazarus (1966) labeled the interpretive step of translating somatic sensations into symptoms, "primary appraisal." Use of the word "appraisal" is unfortunate, however, because it implies that decoding is a conscious process when it is known that much of the decoding process takes place outside awareness. The bilevel nature of the attributes of representations described earlier (e.g., identity as label symptoms, time lines as clock time and felt time) are consistent with the suggestion that the knowledge base used to transform a somatic sensation into a symptom includes both semantic memories (e.g., memories of labels such as heart disease, cancer, and colds) and concrete, perceptual memories of personal somatic experiences (e.g., memory of painful sensations in specific parts of the body during specific illness episodes; Millstein & Irwin, 1987). The semantic structures appear to be heavily involved in guiding how people think and talk about symptoms and in structuring long-term strategies or plans for symptom management. Perceptual memories of specific episodes, on the other hand, appear to generate an immediate, sensory link to appraisals of health status and treatment efficacy and they play a central role in the elicitation and maintenance of emotional reactions and automatic procedures for emotional control (Cameron & Leventhal, 1995; Easterling & Leventhal, 1989; Johnson, 1975).

As somatic sensations activate both types of process more or less simultaneously, the representation and procedures will reflect both types of memory store, as seen in the symmetry of symptoms and labels. In the majority of instances, representations and procedures are generated by matching of a set of somatic events rather than a single somatic sensation to an underlying schema. Bishop (1991) used a variety of clustering techniques to identify sets of symptoms that generate specific representations (see also, D'Andrade, Quinn, Nerlove, & Romney, 1972). For example, (a) headache, face flushing and chest pain; (b) hard or tender growths in various parts of the body accompanied by fatigue and general malaise; and (c) coughs, running noses, and fatigue, may lead to self-diagnoses of heart attack, cancer, and flu, respectively (Bishop, 1991; Bishop & Converse, 1986). The specificity of the interpretive process has considerable practical importance as multiple studies show that the nature of symptoms are related to delay in care seeking. For example, in her review of delay in care seeking by women with breast cancer, Facione (1993) noted that seven of nine studies showed longer delays for symptoms other than a lump in the breast (e.g., pain, bleeding or discharge, dimpling, etc.). Delay is understandable as symptoms are inherently ambiguous (i.e., they do not advertise their cause). Not surprisingly, delay is also common among primary care providers (Facione, 1993).

Croyle and Barger (1993) pointed out that two views of this matching process have been suggested by different investigators. Bishop and Converse (1986) viewed the process as matching a set of symptoms to a generalized prototype. This interpretation is supported by data showing that a set of symptoms is more quickly labeled and more likely to be recalled if it is constructed to match a prototype than if it is constructed randomly. On the other hand, Leventhal and colleagues (Leventhal, 1982, 1986; Leventhal & Diefenbach, 1991) described the process as an integration of current symptoms with the schema of specific illness episodes. The initial formulation of the hypothesis that an episode specific memory schema could underlie the decoding of somatic sensations and the formation of illness representations was based on clinical reports of phantom pain. Phantoms are most often reported following limb amputation, and the pain embedded in the phantom is typically identical to that experienced in an episode immediately prior to amputation (Melzack, 1973). The somatic sensations of limb and pain appear to be stored in perceptual memory (Melzack, 1992), and the complexity of the memory is highlighted by the manner in which the pain can ebb and flow as the phantom limb changes its apparent position. Observations congruent with the episodic hypothesis include reports that coronary patients may misdiagnose chest pains and delay care seeking in response to a second coronary attack because the symptomatology is not identical to that of their first episode. Croyle and Barger's (1993) suggestion that "only frequently experienced illness, such as the flu, stimulate the development of prototypes" and that "severe or unusual episodes, however, may serve as a direct basis for comparison" (p. 34) appears a reasonable resolution of these two viewpoints.

Person and Situation Factors Facilitate the Matching Process. Both person and environmental factors can enhance the availability of disease-specific schemata and enhance the likelihood of illness interpretation of symptoms. A compelling example of a personal factor is seen in a study of women who had been successfully treated for breast cancer (Easterling & Leventhal, 1989). Some of these women felt highly vulnerable to recurrence, and they expressed high levels of worry about cancer (an indicant of the activation of the representation of cancer) if they were experiencing vague, noncancer specific, symptoms (e.g., fatigue). Women who believed recurrence was unlikely did not express worry in response to these ambiguous symptoms. Similarly, a recent study of women who volunteered for a clinical trial on the effects of tamoxifen on blood lipids and bone density, revealed that symptom reports were associated with increased worry about breast cancer up to 6 months after entering the trial, even though the symptomatic side effects (e.g., hot flashes and vaginal irritation) were recognized as induced by the chemoprevention therapy and not by disease recurrence (Cameron, Leventhal, & Love, 1998). Not only did the tamoxifen side effects appear to generate worry about cancer, they also prompted increases in breast self-examinations to detect the possible appearance of new lumps. Importantly, a control group of placebo users did not exhibit these increases in cancer worry or breast self-examination use over time. In both studies, breast cancer representations (and, in the latter study, protective action) were activated by symptoms associated with the breast cancer experience even though these symptoms were not interpreted as signs of illness. Person factors have important consequences for the use of medical care, as data show that factors such as "hypochondriacal" attitudes are strong predictors of total utilization after accounting for the contribution of total number of illness conditions and the presence of symptoms (Barsky, Wyshak, & Klerman, 1986).

Situational factors have a similar effect in sensitizing illness schemata and facilitating a match to symptoms. For example, Salovey and Birnbaum (1989) found that the induction of negative moods increased feelings of vulnerability to serious diseases for subjects who were well; mood had no effect on vulnerability judgments by subjects who were ill. Thus, everyday illnesses activated illness schemata and stimulated feelings of vulnerability to more serious illness, overriding any additional sense of vulnerability that might be created by negative moods. The activation of illness schemata by the induction of negative mood and its associated increase in feelings of vulnerability to serious illness was visible, however, in healthy subjects. These laboratory data are consistent with field observations such as the flood of phone calls for cancer check ups that follow mass media reports of cancer in highly visible public personalities and the high rates of genetic testing for breast cancer among women who report a history of breast cancer among close family members (Chaliki et al., 1995).

The Interdependence of Representations and Coping Procedures. The initial formulation of the self-regulation model defined separate representation and procedural stages (Leventhal, 1970). The separation was consistent with the data showing that different types of information influenced representations and coping. More recent data point to a more integral or Gestalt-like relation between representations and procedures (Garner, 1962). The integral nature of the relation reflects findings showing that representations shape procedures (i.e., procedures that "fit" the presumed physical and physiological nature of the threat are preferred; Lacroix, Martin, Avendano, & Goldstein, 1991). For example, drinking liquid to treat gastric distress is integral because it fits the locus and nature of the stimulus, just as applying a soothing liquid or creams is integral to the treatment of surface irritations. The concrete component of the representation plays a central role in the selection and maintenance of procedures (Palatano & Seifert, 1997). The temporal expectations for these highly available procedures are also extremely clear. One should experience change instantaneously.

Anthropological studies provide numerous examples of the integrality of representations and coping procedures. Weller, Pachter, Trotter, and Baer (1993) described the symptoms of *empacho,* (vomiting, stomach pain, and swollen stomach), its presumed causes (intestinal obstructions caused by "eating too much, the wrong type or poorly prepared food, or eating at the wrong time"), and the procedures for its treatment. The procedures include "massage, rolling an egg on the stomach, ingesting olive oil or tea, etc.," all of which are designed to dislodge the presumed obstruction. Kaye (1993) provided a similarly graphic description of integrality for a disease called *mollera caida.* Symptoms of *mollera caida* include a sunken fontanelle (from which it derives its name), diarrhea, and sunken eyes, resulting from dehydration caused by gastroenteritis that can lead to infant death. Folk beliefs attribute it to falls or the abrupt withdrawal of the nipple during nursing, and treat it by holding the infant by the heels, sucking on the fontanelle or pressing on the soft palate, procedures designed to force the fontanelle to its original position. The treatments for both illnesses are integrally related to their symptoms and perceived cause.

Both *empacho* and *molera caida* illustrate that commonsense, cultural constructions build on observable indicators of a biologically definable condition. As the biology of a disease such as *molera caida* is constant over time and cultures, its key symptoms can shape similar treatments over hundreds of years, for example, from the time of the early Greeks and Romans, through the middle ages, to the Renaissance and 16th-century Aztec writing that blend European and new world views of the condition (Kaye, 1993). It would be a mistake, however, to assign such behaviors as anomalies of less developed cultures, as similar practices are readily identified in the United States in the few studies searching for them. For example, the self-care procedures reported for women with symptoms of breast cancer range from use of antibiotic ointments to cure ulcerations, washing to clear secretions, rubbing to soften tissue, applying heat and pulling to change the physical contour of the breast (Facione, 1993). The need to redefine a symptom emerges when such procedures fail to affect their target.

If–Then Rules and Questions for the Self. The proposed integrality of representational beliefs and coping procedures led us to borrow the formulation of cognitive theorists that representations and procedure are bound together as "if–then" rules (Anderson, 1983, 1993; Miller et al., 1996; Mischel & Shoda, 1995). The "if" refers to the cognitive definition of the stimulus pattern, the "then" to associated cognition regarding expected consequences and behavioral responses appropriate for its control. "If–then" rules are also activated by feedback from the outcomes of action. In the latter case, "if" refers to the stimulus pattern generated by the coping procedure and "then" corresponds to modifications in representational beliefs.

The questions initiating and sustaining a sequence of if–then rules emerge from the implications of illness for the self-system. Representations of illness, the timelines, anticipated physical indicators (symptoms and functional), as well as social and economic consequences, and beliefs about control, have important implications for the physical, emotional, and functional integrity of the self, and the time frame (i.e., existence) of the self. This has been described as a literal "collision" of illness and self-representations (Leventhal, Leventhal, & Carr, in press). A recent study by Heidrich, Forsthoff, and Ward (1994) illustrated how this impact affects emotional and interpersonal adjustment of women with breast cancer. Two major aspects of the representation of breast cancer, a chronic time line and physical dysfunction, had negative impact on emotional adjustment and anticipated satisfaction in close, interpersonal relationships. These effects were mediated, however, by the discrepancies created between the individual's current, cancer impacted self, and desired self characteristics. To move from a general proposition (i.e., that "if–then rules emerge from the collision of illness and self representations") to specific theoretical hypotheses, it is essential to identify the specific types of questions that emerge from this "collision."

Two Examples of If–Then Rules. Investigators have identified two, specific, schema-related questions that underlie "if–then" rules: the *stress-illness* question and the *aging-illness* question. The stress-illness question is resolved by what appear to be automatic, environmental searches designed to discriminate underlying, implicit schemata of illness and stress (Pennebaker, 1982). A search of individuals' life situation permit them to attribute ambiguous somatic symptoms (e.g., fatigue, headache, joint pains.) to current stressors or to illness. For example, when students were given a list of ambiguous symptoms and asked whether they would believe they were ill or stressed if they experienced them when awakening the next morning, they endorsed a stress attribution if a midterm was scheduled for the following day, and they endorsed an illness attribution if the question was asked the day before a class-free weekend. Symptoms that defined a clear picture of a known, physical illness were attributed to illness for both the exam and weekend days (Baumann et al., 1989). A similar effect appeared in the analysis of care seeking by a sample of elderly adults. When symptoms presented a clear sign of a health problem, life stressors had no effect on seeking medical care (Cameron, Leventhal, & Leventhal, 1995). Ambiguous symptoms, however, were attributed to stress and did not lead to use of medical care if they appeared soon after the occurrence of a new (less then a month) life stressor. If, however, the life stressor was old, respondents sought care for ambiguous symptoms, presumably because they believed that long-lasting stressors could cause illness (Cameron et al., 1995). Thus, commonsense has a "1-month rule" or temporal criterion for answering the stress-illness question and disambiguating a symptom set. It is interesting to note that the "1-month rule" matches the data on the relation of stressor duration for contracting colds following viral exposure (Cohen et al., 1998).

Where the stress-illness question appears to involve a quick, implicit search of the individual's life situation, the aging-illness question evokes searches of the properties of symptoms and the individual's physical self (Alonzo, 1980). Symptoms that are slow to appear and slow to change, and advanced chronological age of the person experiencing them, can encourage attributions of somatic changes to age rather than to illness (Prohaska, Keller, Leventhal, & Leventhal, 1987), although these effects can change due to historical conditions that alter people's perceptions of the risk and/or curability of different diseases (Facione, 1993). It seems unlikely that a great deal of conscious cogitation is necessary to answer the stress-illness or age-illness questions. In many, if not most, instances, the criteria or rules are applied automatically with little thought. Both cases, however, involve more than an underlying schemata of illness: The stress-illness question clearly involves emotion schemata (Pennebaker, 1982), and the age-illness question involves a schema of the physical self (Epstein, 1973). The attachment of affect to the self schema—for example, negative views of the body are more common among women than men (Muth & Cash, 1997)—may differ with age, and is likely to interact with disease-specific representations and to affect willingness to seek care for diseases that threaten changes in body image. It is also likely that a stress response to the stress-illness question addresses beliefs about the vulnerability of the self to emotional distress, and in particular, the ability to control distress.

Such beliefs may minimize illness attributions in response to ambiguous symptoms.

Just as there are stereotypes or beliefs about age, so too are there stereotypes about the victims of disease. These stereotypes then influence the processes of symptom labeling and attribution. For example, Martin, Gordon, and Lounsbury (1998) explored the impact of gender-related stereotypes regarding heart disease on the interpretation of cardiac-related symptoms. In samples of undergraduates, community dwelling adults, and physicians, they found that cardiac symptoms were discounted or minimized—not for women in general—but specifically for female victims who reported concurrent life stressors. Thus, a stereotype linking female gender to stress leads to the discounting of life threatening symptoms.

Differentiation of Illness Representations. Representations change as disease episodes unfold. For example, as their treatments go forward, patients with hypertension and patients with metastatic breast cancer show a shift from acute to chronic time lines in their illness representations (Leventhal et al., 1986; Meyer et al., 1985). Ongoing involvement with a chronic disease can generate important changes in the representation of specific disease attributes, and these changes can have important effects for adjustment and self-regulation. A change that has proven of special importance in predicting adjustment is breaking the symmetry of disease identity, that is, separating the label (concept of the underlying disease) from the symptoms that jointly define its identity.

The evidence is most clear in studies of adaptation to rheumatoid arthritis. Data show increasingly depressive mood over time for patients with rheumatoid arthritis (Affleck, Tennen, Pfeiffer, & Fifield, 1987; Brown, 1990; Zeiss et al., 1996). This increase is mediated by disruptions in physical function (Zeiss et al., 1996). The physical disruption appears to reflect losses to the self (e.g., arthritis "makes me feel that I am falling apart," and "When I think of myself, pain comes to mind"). These appraisals of loss of personal control (Felton & Revenson, 1984) reflect feelings of helplessness with regard to controlling the illness and its manifestations. Some patients, however, differentiate the underlying disease (its label and chronic time line) from its symptomatic manifestations (Schiaffino & Revenson, 1992). Having done so, they can focus their coping and outcome appraisals on their success in controlling the duration of episodes of symptom-induced dysfunction rather than their success in eliminating disease (Schiaffino, Shawaryn, & Blum, 1998). A positive correlation is found between coping and positive mood for patients who have made the differentiation and are coping with symptoms, but a negative correlation between coping and adjustment has been found for patients who have not made the differentiation; patients in the latter group experience failure as they appraise their coping with respect to their ability to control the underlying disease (Affleck et al., 1987). Pimm (1997) reviewed these data and described ongoing trials in which he and his collaborators hoped to confirm the finding that patients who differentiate their chronic rheumatoid condition from its symptoms of stiffness and pain, and made use of procedures (stretching and exercise) that allow them to lead more active and less dysfunctional lives, regardless of the degree of physical disease. The separation of the underlying, chronic (time line) condition from its manifestations (symptoms with variable, episodic time-lines) and engaging in coping reactions that produce positive effects in the controllable manifestations of the disease (e.g., reducing the extent and duration of symptom induced dysfunction) appears to be the key to self- management that generates a sense of control and positive affect (Schiaffino & Revenson, 1992). In sum, the alteration in the representation, which may be stored as a prototype or episodic image, focuses attention and procedures on controllable symptomatology. Propositional, if–then questions are framed by and test the validity of the underlying illness schema.

Updating Representations and Procedures. Appraisals of self-selected and medically prescribed diagnostic and treatment procedures are constantly modifying and updating illness representations. For example, a middle-aged male may experience a burning pain in the esophagus that can be represented either as gastric distress or cardiac pain. If the gastric distress interpretation holds sway, the choice of coping might be one or another home remedy such as drinking extra fluid, taking an antacid, or resting. If the coronary interpretation holds sway, then the choice of coping procedures might be the cessation of activities and consultation with a physician. The feedback from each of these procedures will serve to validate or invalidate its efficacy and update the representation. If the gastric distress diminishes following use of antacid, it confirms the initial self-diagnosis; if it does not, it opens new questions, the answers to which will be sought depending on factors such as the severity and duration of the symptoms and the affective responses elicited by alternative hypotheses.

A representation may be updated incorrectly regardless of whether a procedure is performed consciously or automatically. At least four different factors may contribute to error. First, the feedback may be ambiguous and open to a variety of conflicting interpretations. Second, the feedback may be familiar (e.g., change in gastric distress) and validate the most available hypothesis rather than that which is correct. Third, the threat associated with the correct interpretation may activate defensive minimization (e.g., is far more comfortable to think one has gastric upset than a life threatening coronary event; Ditto et al., 1988). Fourth, the desirable change in somatic activity may be incorrectly attributed to the most salient component of a complex procedure (e.g., drinking tea) rather than to a less salient and effective component (e.g., sitting and resting, which reduced the demand for cardiac output and reduced the esophageal pain).

Emotions, Representations, Procedures and Symptoms

Having separated the processing of cognitive and emotional experiences (See also Epstein, 1994; LeDoux, 1993), it is essential to address how the two interact. As stated earlier, both factors in this equation (i.e., emotional reactions and cognitive representations of illness) reflect the action of complex systems. It is impossible, therefore, to address all facets of this interaction because chapters can be written on the ways in which different patterns of physiological activity evoke episodic memories, and others on how matches of the cognitive or mood components at learning and recall affect memory retrievals (Bower, 1981). The focus here is on two, simpler issues. The first concerns how health and illness behaviors are affected by "hot" emotion (states) as distinct from "hot cognition." The second concerns how the processes involved in "hot emotion" and "hot cognition" differ from those in "cold" cognition. In addressing each of these issues, emotion is treated as a unified construct (i.e., as a factor in experience) and the many complexities of the system generating it are ignored.

Affect and Illness Cognition: Separate Process and Inseparable Outcomes

Although reasonably clear distinctions can be drawn between "hot emotion," "hot cognition," and "cold cognition," it is important to recognize that the boundaries separating them are fuzzy (Abelson, Kinder, Peters, & Fiske, 1982). "Hot emotion" refers, as might be expected, to states of emotional activation, to those times when a person is experiencing affect (i.e., is afraid, angry, or depressed) is having affect related thoughts, is showing facial and bodily expressions of affect, and is showing emotionally relevant somatic activation. "Hot cognition" refers to perceptions, images, and thoughts with emotional significance, that is, cognitive material associated with and capable of arousing emotion.

Hot Emotion and the Inhibition of Action. The disruption of coping (i.e., the inhibition of action) is the aspect of active fear emotion most frequently documented in the domain of health and illness behaviors. Numerous examples of coping inhibition were presented in the first section of the chapter, which reviewed the importance of studies of fear communication for the formulation of the parallel response model (Leventhal, 1970). Active levels of fear inhibited taking of chest x-rays (Leventhal & Watts, 1966) produced a 1-day delay by low esteem subjects in taking inoculations to protect against tetanus (Kornzweig, 1967; reviewed in Leventhal, 1970), and facilitated reports of short-term efforts to quit smoking (Leventhal et al., 1967). The conclusion merits repeating: Fear encourages avoidance of stimuli capable of increasing emotional activation by inhibiting approach behaviors. The consequence may be failure to engage in a threatening, but health-protective behavior (e.g., failure to take chest x-rays), or the facilitation of a health-promoting behavior (e.g., inhibition of cigarette smoking). In both cases, however, the effects of hot emotion are confined to the period during which emotion is activated (i.e., emotion must be present to produce inhibitory effects). These results and the self-regulatory model representing them, suggest that emotional distress has its greatest impact on the procedural component of the problem-solving process, and has little impact on the representation of the threat. Fear and its somatic sequelae (e.g., feeling shaky or down) communicate to individuals experiencing it that he or she may lack the competence to manage a danger (Leventhal, 1970; Leventhal & Mosbach, 1983), yet these reductions in feelings of self-competence may last only as long as the fear is present (see also Rescorla & Solomon, 1967).

Although fear, such as the fear of surgical treatment, may inhibit autonomous, health promotive actions, such as seeking diagnosis for symptoms of breast cancer, the very same state of fear can activate external resources and thereby overcome barriers created by the breakdown of autonomous action. Active fear encourages affiliation (Schachter, 1959) and creates an impulse to communicate and seek help to cope with both the emotion and its source (Shaver, Schwartz, Kirson, & O'Conner, 1987). Seeking out others activates social support and the support network is likely to compensate for the breakdown in internal resources by creating external pressures and assistance for care seeking (Cameron et al., 1993). Failure to consider the role of supportive others in the presence of threat, and failure to consider whether the behavior at issue approaches or avoids the source of threat, are likely responsible for the substantial inconsistency noted in studies relating fear to seeking diagnosis and care for risks of cancer (Croyle & Lerman, 1999; Facione, 1993). On the other hand, when fear is combined with the need to present oneself as strong and unconcerned with danger, it may encourage a rigid level of avoidance that threatens personal well-being by delaying interpersonal contacts essential for threat control.

Hot Cognition: Affect Integrated With Illness Cognition. Associative processes can create a tight link between affective and cognitive processes, the two acting as a single, integral unit (Leventhal, 1984). When cancer or heart disease are described as "dreaded and feared diseases," people are recognizing that they are not only negatively evaluated and perceived as painful, and a lethal threat, but that the cognitive elements defining them are powerful stimuli for fear. Thus, cancer and cardiovascular disease represent *hot cognition* (i.e., the cognition defining them are tightly linked with fear and signs of either disease must be avoided to prevent being overwhelmed by fear). A recent study by Cameron and Leventhal (1995) provided evidence for differentiating "hot emotion" from hot cognition. Young adults who perceived themselves as highly vulnerable to heart disease showed no increase in intentions to engage in regular exercise to protect their cardiovascular system when they were exposed to either a highly threatening message about heart disease or an exercise task that induced somatic sensations of cardiac arousal. By contrast, a reassuring "wellness" message about heart disease had an immediate enhancing effect on exercise intentions. But whereas the threat messages and somatic experience of cardiovascular arousal failed to produce an immediate effect, participants in both of these groups as well as participants in the wellness groups reported increases in exercise rates over the long term in comparison to a control group unexposed to threat or wellness information. The temporary inhibition of intended action by the threatening health information is consistent with inhibition by an active state of fear, but the improvement in exercise over the longer term (i.e., after the state of fear had declined) suggests that the cognitive representation of cardiovascular risk was imbued with motivating potential—that is, that the cognition of cause, (insufficient exercise), identity (what the disease will do functionally and experientially), time line (its effects are lasting), and consequences (it can kill) were imbued with motivational potential: These cognitions were "hot."

Forgas (1995) proposed that emotions "infuse" cognitive processes and influence how individuals reason about and draw conclusions respecting the people around them. He reviewed data suggesting that the effects of emotions on cognition are pronounced when the cognitive, evaluative process is lengthy and drawn out rather than instantaneous. Such schema are especially likely to form either when dealing with prolonged or chronic diseases that allow for considerable rumination, providing ample opportunity to link disease imagery with affective processes. If the rumination includes active procedures for threat management, the resulting cognition will likely motivate effective, problem-focused coping. On the other hand, in situations in which exposure to a disease threat provokes very high levels of fear and procedures to control the fear or the threat are unavailable, the continuous stimulation of ruminative processes by unresolved fear will lead to the formation of well-structured cognitive-affective memories lacking problem-focused coping procedures. These conditions are similar to those for the formation of posttraumatic stress syndrome (van der Kolk, 1987). Disease schemata formed under such conditions become catastrophic as they integrate ultimate threats, loss of control, and powerful affective expectations: "Cancer can and will destroy me, there is nothing that I or anyone else can do about it, and I will suffer enormous pain and distress." It may be necessary to disassemble such threat–fear–avoidance schemata to encourage individuals to take the steps needed for early detection of highly threatening diseases.

The need to distinguish the effects of learned, affective associations from the direct effects of emotional arousal is a familiar issue in domains such as learned helplessness (Maier & Jackson, 1979) and the treatment of fear-based phobias (Lang, Cuthbert, & Melamed, 1986). For example, when learned helplessness is involved, it is necessary to disconfirm old expectations that action in this context cannot reduce threat or avert failure, and to create new expectations that action can lead to protection or success. If a momentary state of fear or an automatic depletion of central neurotransmitter were responsible for the behavioral inhibition (Weiss, Glazer, Pohorecky, & Miller, 1975), then there would be no need for relearning because behavior would resume when fear dissipated and the neurotransmitter were replenished. Similarly, promoting adaptive behavior in response to prolonged health threats, for which individuals will have formed stable representations, requires attention both to the immediate impact of emotional arousal on disease representational attributes and to the reformulation of the cognitive and emotional associations established within the representational schemata.

A substantial number of studies have identified a variety of procedures for the regulation of emotional reactions during exposure to threatening circumstances (Carver, Scheier, & Weintraub, 1989; Lazarus & Folkman, 1984; Miller, 1996; Miller, Shoda, & Hurley, 1996). These efforts appear to have concentrated on the identification of coping traits or actions commonly used to cope with difficult life problems, and have generated a substantial amount of data suggesting that coping with feelings by means of tactics such as wishful thinking, avoidance, or mentally rehearsing painful or catastrophic outcomes are related to poorer adjustment (Lazarus & Folkman, 1984). The failure to distinguish the role of coping with respect to "affective states" versus "hot-cognition" may be the source of one of their more serious limitations (i.e., the failure to assess what actually transpires during problem solving episodes; E. A. Leventhal et al., 1993). Thus, both traitlike measures and problem-specific measures are ambiguous as to whether and when a particular response was actually performed during a threat episode, whether it was the only response performed, which responses were the most salient or most successful, and whether a response was performed to reduce a state of affective distress or to avoid thoughts or cues to affective distress. Failure to assess the ongoing sequence of procedures that unfold in the management of both the objective features of a health threat and the emotions provoked by that threat, ignores the contingencies among coping strategies and the possibility of a positive role for affectively focused coping. For example, effective management of a painful and potentially dangerous health threat that provokes intense and relatively prolonged active fear states might require periods of "time out" to allow one to recoup resources for problem management. When and how this "time out" is spent could be critical for adaptation. If it is spent in ruminative thought that amplifies emotional distress and forms hot cognition that encourages avoidance of problem solving, the time out will fail to contribute to a positive adaptation. On the other hand, if it is spent in a supportive social interchange or in distractive "rumination" designed to provide temporary surcease (e.g., engaging in a favorite hobby), which allows the individual to recover, creates a sense of control over self, and avoids the formation of cognition of uncontrollable and unapproachable dangers, then the individual can return to planning for problem management.

Suls and Fletcher (1985) postulated that this process of "dosing" is important for avoiding system breakdown and is consistent with the evidence just reviewed, suggesting that action to bring fear under control does not necessarily preclude effective problem management over the long term (Cameron & Leventhal, 1995; Leventhal & Watts, 1966). An assumption that underlies the "dosing" hypothesis is that emotions contain information about the status of information-processing and behavioral systems, that is, they can tell whether or not individuals have the energy, ability to concentrate, and skills needed to perform specific, self-protective procedures over protracted time frames, and that individuals can make conscious use of this information (Leventhal, 1970; Leventhal & Mosbach, 1983). As such, emotions serve as highly useful guides to coping efforts, as cues for an affective rule (i.e., *If* I am calm *Then* I can act, *If* I am anxious, *Then* I'd better wait before trying). Coping measures that fail to assess the dynamics of emotional regulation and problem solving, or that simply construe all "emotion-focused" and "avoidance" coping efforts as maladaptive, are likely to miss important information about effective and ineffective adaptation.

Negative Emotions and Symptoms

An issue that has received a great deal of attention in the past decade is whether negative affect, as a stable trait and as an episodic state, will encourage the development of illness representations by focusing attention inward and increasing the awareness of symptoms in ways that bias somatic perceptions and lead to tendencies to overreport illness (Costa & McCrae, 1987; Watson & Pennebaker, 1989). This thesis is based on observations of a modest-sized relation between negative affect and symptom reports (most correlations are in the .25 to .35 range) that is consistently reported in cross-sectional data (Watson & Pennebaker, 1989). Experimental studies support several aspects of this formulation. Higher levels of symptom reporting are found in environments lacking external cues to attract attention (Pennebaker & Brittingham, 1982). Experimental induction of negative affect results in higher levels of symptom reporting in both healthy (Croyle & Uretsky, 1987) and ill participants (Salovey & Birnbaum, 1989). It is important to note, however, that it is arbitrary to state that it is the high- rather than the low-reporting group that is biased in symptom reporting. Indeed, the available data suggests that negative affect interacts with cognitive processes in three ways: It activates somatic vigilance and increases accurate symptom reporting; it activates illness representations encouraging attribution to illness of vague symptoms that are not specific indicators of illness; and it may increase susceptibility to pathogens and other symptom generating events. These conclusions are derived from longitudinal studies, the more recent of which provide some degree of control over somatic experience.

Observations over long time frames are inconsistent with the hypothesis that negative affectivity is associated with inaccurate, overreporting of symptoms. In their study of a large sample of middle-aged males, Spiro, Aldwin, Levenson, and Busse (1990) confirmed the typical cross sectional relation between neurotic anxiety and symptom reporting, but no relation between emotional traits and increases in reports of physical or psychological symptoms over a 20-year time frame. Using a far shorter time frame in a situation with substantial control over somatic events, Diefenbach, Leventhal, Leventhal, and Patrick-Miller (1996) compared changes in symptom reports by elderly participants in a design where one group completed their reports before inoculation and 1 and 4 days after inoculation with vaccines for flu and tetanus, and completed them again in identical fashion before and after placebo inoculations. A second group went through the very same procedures in reverse order (i.e., placebo first and active inoculant second). Analyses comparing subjects divided into high and low scores on measures of both trait and state anxiety and trait and state depression showed baseline to postinoculation increases of local symptoms (sore arm, redness) after the active inoculations but not after the placebo inoculations. Reports of vague, flu-like symptoms declined after both active and placebo inoculation. The data showed the expected cross-sectional association of the negative affect measures with symptom reporting, but no differences between subjects scoring high on depression and/or anxiety (either trait or state) and those with low scores, with respect to increased reports of local symptoms or decreased reports of systemic, flu like symptoms. Thus, all subjects, regardless of their trait or state affects, were sensitive to increases in distinctive changes in somatic experience (redness and soreness of the arm) when these somatic changes are present, and all subjects gave less attention to somatic sensations that were vague and indifferent when they were expecting and searching for the distinctive symptoms and visible signs of vaccination.

A recent study of symptomatic side effects reported by women in a double-blind clinical trial of tamoxifen chemoprevention therapy provides strong evidence that negative affectivity is associated with greater symptom sensitivity and accurate symptom reports (Cameron et al., 1998). Postmenopausal women with breast cancer in remission were randomly assigned to take tamoxifen, a drug that induces hot flashes and other hormonally related side effects, or a placebo for a 2-year period. Assessments of symptom reports revealed that trait anxiety was associated with increases in reports of hormonally related symptoms during the first 3 months of the trial, but only among tamoxifen users and not among placebo users. Moreover, high anxiety was not associated with increases in reports of symptoms that were unrelated to tamoxifen use in either drug condition. Not only was high trait anxiety associated with greater sensitivity to symptoms, but low anxious placebo users exhibited tendencies to inaccurately underreport symptoms over the course of the trial in that their symptom reports decreased significantly over the first 6 months. Consequently, cross-sectional differences in symptom reports between high and low anxious groups may reflect a combination of greater sensitivity by high anxious individuals and inaccurate underreporting of symptoms by low anxious individuals.

These data are consistent with the hypothesis that negative affectivity is associated with an increased focus of attention to somatic activity, or a vigilance rule: *If* it is an unexpected somatic change, *then* anticipate and test for illness danger. This enhanced focus need not, however, lead to inaccurate symptom reports. Cameron et al. (1998) proposed that this increased vigilance is due to the activation of illness-related representations among high anxious individuals. The hypothesis is consistent with the data showing that high trait anxiety subjects given tamoxifen were more worried and ruminated more about breast cancer and exhibited a marked increase in breast self-examinations over the course of the trial, clear indications of the activation of a cancer representation. On the other hand, the vigilance generated by illness representations may bias symptom attributions even when it does not necessarily bias the quantity of symptoms reported. Wiebe and her associates (Wiebe, Alderfer, Palmer, Lindsay, & Jarrett,

1994) reported that their diabetic patients high in trait anxiety were more likely to attribute nondiabetes-related symptoms to changes in blood glucose.

Attribution and Direct Effects on Illness

The data generated in a clinical trial examining the development of colds in subjects exposed to respiratory virus produced evidence supporting the hypothesis that trait negative affect influenced symptom attribution, very likely by the activation of illness schemata, whereas state negative affect has a direct effect on illness severity (Cohen et al., 1995). These investigators found that, in comparison to subjects low in trait negative affect, subjects high on this measure reported a small but statistically reliable greater increase in reports of symptoms post viral exposure (.83 symptom). Trait negative affect was not related, however, to an "objective" postexposure measure of illness (weight of mucous discharge), which suggests that subjects high on trait negative affect reported more flu-like symptoms regardless of their level of illness. A measure of state negative affect (emotional mood at the start of the investigation) was related to the "objective" measure of illness (mucous discharge) which was related, in turn, to post-infection symptom levels. Concordant with others (Cameron et al., 1998; Wiebe et al., 1994), Cohen et al. (1995) suggested that subjects high in trait negative affect report more symptoms because they do not distinguish symptoms of flu from symptoms of emotional upset and/or irritability created by being sick. Second, they suggested that state negative mood affects symptom reporting because of its effect on disease (mucous discharge). Thus, the state measure may reflect the influence of current levels of life stress on susceptibility to illness and, therefore, to symptom reporting. This indirect path accounts, however, for only 9% of the postexposure increase in symptoms.

The studies reviewed so far suggest that trait negative affects have at best very small effects on symptom reporting when reporting is examined over time. Second, the effect seems to reflect two processes: Greater somatic attention and more accurate reporting of symptoms, and the activation of illness representations resulting in the attribution of vague (sensitive but nonspecific) symptoms to illness. This does not exhaust, however, the various paths by which negative affect can influence illness representations. Croyle and Uretsky's (1987) finding that induced negative emotion may alter the meaning of symptoms by increasing their judged severity may have more important implications for the role of affect in illness representations than that of merely increasing the number of symptoms reported. For example, Clark and Ehlers (1993) postulated that catastrophic interpretations of somatic symptoms represent the critical path for the development of panic disorders. Such interpretations heighten anxiety, intensify attention to the body and detection of somatic cues, and encourages the representations of these cues as signs of a physical catastrophe (e.g., "I'm having a heart attack" or "I'm about to faint"). These interpretations encourage the performance of self-protective procedures such as sitting and resting or leaning against the wall (Salkovskis, 1990, cited in Clark & Ehlers, 1993), and these actions may provide the illusion of control over catastrophic outcomes and reinforce and maintain the inappropriate interpretation of the somatic event by disallowing disconfirming feedback (i.e., not having a heart attack and not fainting). There may be an *emotion-severity* rule at play: *If* I am so upset, *then* it (the somatic sign) must be very serious and require immediate action.

Clark and Ehlers (1993) made two additional and extremely important points. First, catastrophic interpretations are specific to somatic sensations: Individuals with panic disorder do not seem to apply negative or catastrophic interpretations to ambiguous events that are not somatic. Consistent with the bilevel processing feature of the model, the perceptual nature (visual and/or palpable) of such cues appears to lie at the base of their motivating power (Klohn & Rogers, 1991). Second, and consistent with findings in the tamoxifen symptoms study, individuals suffering from panic disorders are more accurate perceivers of their somatic reactions (judging heart rates) than other types of phobic or normal subjects. The accuracy finding suggests why it may be so difficult to find anxious individuals reporting more symptoms in response to known somatic changes, relative to the symptom reports of nonanxious persons. When anxious persons report more symptoms than their nonanxious peers, it may simply reflect that the nonanxious are less accurate and underreporting.

A final issue to consider here is the possibility that different negative emotions may have different effects on somatic health and differ, therefore, in their effects on symptom reporting. The data reported by Cohen et al. (1995) suggested that mood state can affect susceptibility to upper-respiratory infections and produce a small increase in symptoms. Data showing relations between high levels of depression and poorer responses on tests of immune function (Cohen & Williamson, 1991; Patrick-Miller, 1994) suggest a mechanism that may underlie the relationship of negative affect to increased symptom reporting for infectious illnesses. It is not clear, however, whether it is depression per se or the feeling of loss of control over daily events that is the critical factor in increasing susceptibility to infectious illness and symptom reporting (Cohen, Tyrell, & Smith, 1991). It also seems unlikely that a specific emotional process, such as depression, will have the same effect on all diseases and, therefore, on reports of all types of symptoms. Diseases differ greatly from one another in their meaning as well as in their biology, and one specific affect, such as angry hostility, may increase the risk of cardiac disease (e.g., Smith, 1992), cardiac symptom reporting, and swift responding to cardiac symptoms (see Matthews et al., 1983) and yet have little impact on susceptibility to, reporting of symptoms, or seeking treatment for infectious disease.

Life Stressors and Distress Can Facilitate or Deter Illness Decisions

Studies examining the relation of life stress, and presumably of negative affect, to the decision that a person is ill and in need of professional care show that life stress increases health care utilization (Piliusik, Boylan, & Acredelo, 1987; Tessler, Mechanic, & Dimond, 1976). This finding is consistent with the attribution of symptoms to illness in the studies focused on negative affect and symptom reporting. Other studies, however, show no effect (Berkanovic et al., 1988; Sarason, Sarason, Potter, & Antoni, 1985). For example, in a carefully conducted study, Watson (1988) reported the usual modest association of negative affect to symptom reports for his college student subjects; the correlations held when computed across subjects and within subjects over time. There was, however, no association of negative affect with the use of health services. These findings, and others showing that negative affect is related to symptoms but not to medical care use or to objective disease indices, led Watson and Pennebaker (1989) to suggest that negative affect may be a confounding or nuisance factor in the study of the stress-illness relation.

The inconsistent relation between emotional stress and decisions to seek health care could reflect two sets of factors: inadequate conceptual analysis of the stress-decision process and methodological deficits contingent upon them. For example, Eckenrode and Gore (1981) found no effect of life stress on mothers' decisions to seek pediatric services for their symptomatic children when they used traditional cross-sectional methods of analysis that compared stressed to nonstressed mother–child pairs. An effect was visible, however, when the data were examined on a day-by-day basis, such that pediatric care seeking was more likely for symptomatic children the day following a stressful life event. The main conceptual deficit, however, is the unwarranted assumption that life stress will produce a simple main effect, such that high levels of stress increase decisions to seek medical care (Cohen & Williamson, 1991; Mechanic, 1979). The inadequacies of this model was made abundantly clear in the study by Cameron, Leventhal, and Leventhal (1995). Life stressors had quite different effects on care seeking depending on the nature of the individual's symptoms and the duration of the stressor. Symptoms that were clear and distinct signs of physical illness, such as a fever or a visible rash, led to care seeking regardless of whether a life stressor was present or absent. Care seeking increased for vague and ambiguous symptoms only when the stressor was of several weeks duration; when the stressor onset was recent, care seeking was minimal as the symptoms were attributed to stress rather than to illness. Emotional processes, in the form of rules (e.g., the stress-illness rule and the upset-serious rule) alter the meaning or representation of somatic events and the procedures generated by them.

Appetite, Impulse and Loss of Control

Positive affects have been ignored throughout this discussion, yet positive affects and appetitive states associated with them can have important effects on health and risk behaviors. This omission seems reasonable if there is agreement with the proposal that in comparison to positive affects, negative affects such as fear are far more potent determinants of behavior (Taylor, 1991). Taylor's (1991) proposal seems reasonable if the comparison is of negative states of fear and/or anger in comparison to the everyday positive states accompanying good food, joys of friendship, humor, and so forth. The steep gradient and rapid rise of negative affects, as well as their peak levels, does indeed create the experience of intensity. The proposal seems less reasonable, however, when the passions and addictive states involved with sexuality and substance use are considered. These affectively charged states regularly override cognitive controls, although it is unclear whether they are positive states or sequences of negative and positive affect (Solomon, 1980). The point at issue is that "hot affect," both negative and positive, can override "rational" cognitive controls and generate ample justification for doing so.

THE SOCIAL-INSTITUTIONAL CONTEXT OF ILLNESS EPISODES

Illness *episodes* are nested within a larger personal, social, and cultural context. Thus, the individual's life experiences, institutional affiliations and roles, and cultural context can influence the representation of symptoms (e.g., perceived identity, causes, time-lines, consequences and control), the affective reactions they evoke, the procedures used to manage the symptoms and affects, and the criteria for appraising outcomes. Thus, the effects of contextual factors on behavioral outcomes can be mediated by any one or any number of these components (see Fig. 2.3).

Interpersonal and Personal History

No life is exempt from illness, and the individual's illness history is a major determinant of the meanings, procedures, and appraisals evoked during a specific illness episode. Seasonal upper-respiratory illnesses, occasional or recurrent headaches, and gastrointestinal upsets generate a set of "acute" illnes prototypes that form the core of people's illness knowledge. These prototypes (e.g., the symptoms and labels, time lines, mild consequences, expectation for control, treatment procedures and associated affective distress) generate the most immediate and compelling interpretations and management strategies for the majority of people's illness episodes. The acute prototype is also consistent with people's need to sustain optimistic expectations (Taylor, 1983, 1991). For example, 40% of the women entering chemotherapy treatment for metastatic breast cancer believed their disease was equivalent to an acute, curable illness (Leventhal et al., 1986). The elderly experience an array of chronic musculoskeletal sensations, muscle aches and injuries, stiff and swollen joints, and chronic gastrointestinal problems, which add new prototypes and generate new rules (age-illness rule) for self-appraisal.

Repetitive, somatic experience is only one of the factors involved in prototype formation; social factors are another (Suls, Martin, & Leventhal, 1997). The social context gives meaning to undefined somatic experiences by suggesting labels, causes, time lines, procedures for self-management, and rules for treatment evaluation. For example, a parent's labeling, treatment procedures, and emotional reactions dur-

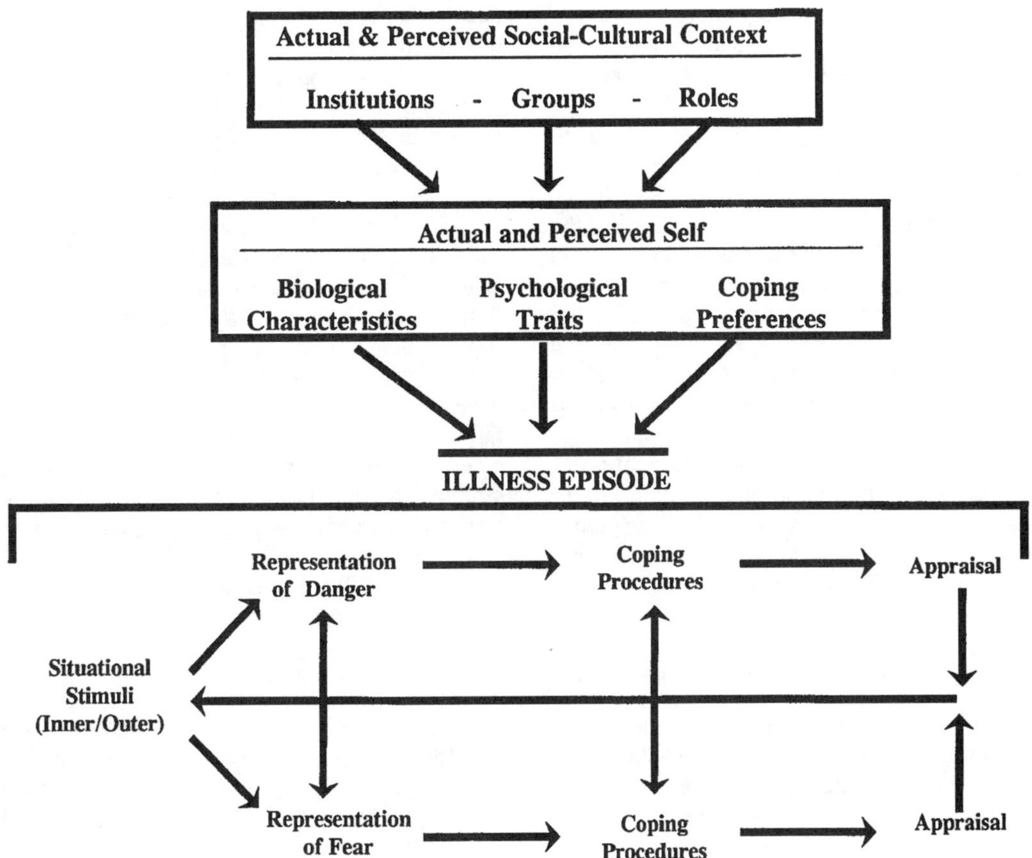

FIG. 2.3. Parallel response model set in context. The effect of contextual factors on response outcomes can be mediated by factors in any of the major components activated at the cognitive (e.g., time line, control) or affective (e.g., affect identity, procedures for control) level during an illness or health promotion episode.

ing a child's illness episodes can be more salient and more central a set of features of a child's illness prototypes than the somatic experiences initiating these episodes. The attentive, anxious parent questioning children about their symptoms and administering family remedies is (often inadvertently) shaping the children's perception of the importance of symptoms, the threat posed by them, and the possibility for their control. When a prototype or schema is activated by future symptoms, it will bring to life the meanings, emotions, coping procedures, and social expectations embedded in it (Mechanic, 1979). Little wonder, then, that "mature" and highly educated individuals (including medical specialists) feel helpless, frightened, and in need of "mothering" when severely ill (Mandel & Spiro, 1987).

The social factors shaping illness schemata extend well beyond the immediate family. Observation of sickness in others, media reports of disease and death, reports of medical advances, and discussions of the causes and consequences of illness all serve to add new labels, images, and affects to the schemata generated by personal somatic experiences. These varied social influences act throughout the life span and can play a critical role in shaping adaptation to somatic change. Imagine, for example, the experience of typical patients who are told by their doctor that they "have" hypertension. The label, hypertension, suggests that high blood pressure is caused by tension and states of hyperactivity (Blumhagen, 1980). The appropriate treatment requires medication and follow-up visits to monitor the effects of the medication on blood pressure. At each follow-up visit, the patient is greeted by the usual, "Hello! How are you feeling?" and a review of systems, that is, a step-by-step series of questions respecting symptoms in different areas of the body, to identify medication side effects and/or comorbid conditions (e.g., "Have you had any symptoms or problems with your eyes? With your ears? Any chest pains? Any problems breathing?"). Although the opening greeting, "How are you feeling?" is unlikely to be sufficient to create the impression that hypertension is symptomatic, it in combination with the review of systems, is more than enough to imply that individuals should feel something if they "have" hypertension. As few physicians are likely to explain why they are conducting the review of systems, nothing is said to contradict this inference. In short, it is eminently reasonable for patients to assume that hypertension is symptomatic, and their suspicions are readily confirmed if their blood pressure is not fully controlled and they check it whenever they feel any symptoms (e.g., a warm face, headache, and/or tension). As patients' are unlikely to check their blood pressure when they are asymptomatic, they will not generate evidence to disconfirm the association. In short, the medical interaction can create the conditions for biased self-assessments.

Meyer, Leventhal, and Gutmann (1985) supported the hypothesis that the doctor–patient exchange can influence patients to represent hypertension as a symptomatic condition. In addition to the data mentioned earlier (i.e., that 90% of the patients in a continuous treatment group believed they could tell when their blood pressure was elevated), a separate sample of patients showed a substantial increase in the belief that they could use symptoms to monitor their blood pressure from the time of their initial treatment until 6 months later after several visits: The proportion changed from 71% at the initial treatment to over 90% at the later point in time. Tape recordings of the patients' interactions with the practitioners were in accord with the interpretation that the medical encounter caused the change in beliefs as the bulk of the practitioners' questions were focused on symptoms and strongly implied that symptoms were possible indicators of blood pressure.

The Consequences of Unshared Representations

Patients' beliefs that they can use symptoms to monitor their hypertension is clearly at variance both with the practitioners' models of this disease and with data on the accuracy of people's ability to estimate their basal blood pressure levels. With regard to the accuracy issue, it is noteworthy that the average within-subject correlations of blood pressure with symptom reports of insurance company employees was only .14 (Baumann & Leventhal, 1985). The same average within-subject correlation was higher (.3) in a study that included an episode of vigorous activity (Pennebaker & Watson, 1988), although excluding this data point reduced the correlation to .14 (Pennebaker & Watson, 1988). Vigorous activity enhances accuracy as it introduces phasic cues, both external and internal, (increased rate of breathing, fatigue, etc.), related to pressure change, stable (i.e., tonic blood pressure does not).

The combination of the belief that individuals can monitor blood pressure has serious implications, however, within the context of the medical encounter. Patients who believe their blood pressure is symptomatic are in conflict with their practitioner's view that symptoms cannot be used to monitor base level blood pressure. Should they believe the explicit, medical model that hypertension is an asymptomatic disorder, or should they believe their implicit model that they can feel whether they are or are not "sick"? The Meyer et al. (1985) data showed that newly treated patients who believed they could monitor their blood pressure were more likely to drop out of treatment 6 months later than patients who concurred with the medical model. And fully 61% of the newly treated patients quit treatment 6 months later if during the first visit they told their physician they believed they could monitor their pressure. Only 24% had quit treatment among those who either did not believe they could monitor their pressure or did not tell the doctor about their belief. Open communication appears to have established the groundwork for conflict and quitting treatment.

Problems arising from sharing or not sharing disease models are not restricted to hypertension. Practitioner–patient disagreements have been documented among diabetics and doctors (Hampson, 1997), mothers and pediatricians (Becker et al., 1977), and the severely mentally ill and their psychiatrists (Jamison, 1995). Differences in the underlying schema of a disease held by patients and medical practitioners encourage different procedures for validating experience, that is, different if–then rules confirm the validity of contrasting models and the result in many instances is nonadherence to needed treatment. Greater discrepancies between patient and medical models have also been related to poorer function in daily living (e.g., failure to return to work; Lacroix et al., 1991). Under carefully controlled conditions, patients can be taught to use symptom monitoring to regulate use of medication if there are valid associations between symptoms and fluctuations in the underlying biological condition. Kovatchev, Cox, Gonder-Frederick, and Schlundt (1998) provided an exceptional example of this approach with diabetic patients.

Social Observation–Comparison

As the meaning of symptom and effectiveness of treatments are often ambiguous, it was natural for investigators to make use of social comparison theory (Festinger, 1954; Schachter, 1959; Schachter & Singer, 1962; Suls & Miller, 1977; Suls & Wills, 1991) in their efforts to understand behavior during illness episodes (Buunk & Gibbons, 1997). Motivation for social comparison is powerful when somatic experience is ambiguous, as seen in Schachter's (1959) studies of affiliation under conditions of threat. Motivation to affiliate was so strong that Schachter's participants opted to be with others in the same situation, rather than to be alone or with others in a different situation. This effect appeared even though subjects were prohibited from talking. As neither verbal or nonverbal communication are prohibited during most illness episodes or medical treatments, the opportunity and utility of social comparison during illness is far greater than that allowed Schachter's subjects. Social comparison, or better, social influence, can vary from seeking advice or information from another about a symptom or treatment, through responses to people's expressions of anxiety in response to illness, to receiving comments about their appearance (Zola, 1973). Comparison with others in similar or dissimilar circumstances to share information about symptoms and medications, is commonplace among the elderly (e.g., Brody & Kleban, 1983).

To understand the function of social information during illness episodes, it is essential to identify the goal(s) satisfied by the comparison process. For example, Kulik and Mahler (1987) found that preoperative coronary bypass patients who were in the same room with postoperative patients were less anxious prior to their operations and recovered faster after the operation compared to patients who were assigned roommates who were also awaiting surgery. Interestingly, the outcome was the same whether the roommate was undergoing a similar or different type of operation. Thus, unlike the laboratory setting where participants preferred and appeared to benefit from affiliation with similar others (Schachter, 1959), the data suggest that affiliation among individuals anticipating the threat of surgery sustains or even reinforces feelings of threat and fails to provide examples of successful, postoperative recovery. Kulik and Mahler (1997) suggested that social observation fulfills several important functions, such as providing reassurance and reducing fear of death and disfigurement by seeing that someone has "made it through," observing someone having lower postoperative levels of anxiety and pain than expected, and receiving information about the experiences of surgery and specific tips for coping. Thus, a recovering roommate may enable patients to model a view of themselves from the "outside," to envision themselves looking better than expected and improving from day to day, and not merely from the "inside" as fearful and pained. The meanings derived from these observations may increase feelings of control and prepare patients to direct their coping efforts more effectively. The apparently effortless nature of social comparison in the case examined by Kulik and Mahler contrasts with social comparisons involving substantial effort, the latter is typical of situations where practice is necessary for the acquisition of behavioral skills (Tennen & Affleck, 1997). Tennen and Affleck (1997) believed the presence of effort is a necessary criteria for the presence of social comparison, and that effort is likely essential to acquire the skills needed to manage chronic pain. Whether effort is or is not necessary, however, depends on the objective of social comparison. The identification of objectives within the self-regulation framework (e.g., Is social comparison producing information to clarify causes, consequences, and time lines, to define criteria for the appraisal of coping procedures, or to add procedures to the coping repertory?) will clarify when effort is and is not a necessary component of the social comparison process.

Culture and Language

Personal illness history and ongoing, interpersonal exchanges with illness take place within an extended cultural matrix, and representations, procedures for disease regulation, and appraisal criteria can be expected to reflect this context. Indeed, cultural beliefs and language impact virtually every attribute of the self-regulatory system. For example, the label "hypertension" suggests that physical and mental hyperactivity and tension are both signs and causes of elevated blood pressure (Blumhagen, 1980). Cultural beliefs about such causes of disease can discourage adherence to medically oriented treatment (Heurtin-Roberts & Reisin, 1992) and encourage adherence to culturally accepted treatment from traditional healers (Weller, 1984). The effects of culture-wide beliefs, both secular and religious, are both direct and indirect, and the indirect effects may be more common and less readily recognized. For example, religious beliefs regarding possession and retribution can create a background in which possession and wrongdoing can be seen as causes of disease, and atonement and good works seen as appropriate means of cure. Similarly, secular beliefs in the power of mechanical causation and scientific cure can lead to the minimization of the role of lifestyle in disease causation and to excessive reliance on medical "magic bullets."

The relation between culture and disease representations is, however, reciprocal. Both the biology of disease and beliefs about disease shape the medical care system, and the system in turn shapes and maintains these beliefs. For example, the representation of infectious illness as communicable, symptomatic, time limited and curable, created a care system oriented toward brief encounters with medical practitioners in a "fee for service" framework (Saward, 1977). Once in place, this service framework has encouraged and sustained the representation and treatment of both infectious and chronic illness within a common, acute disease model. It took a crisis in which chronic, life-threatening illnesses in an aging population overwhelmed the health care system and forced recognition that the acute illness model created significant problems for treatment (Knowles, 1977; White, 1973). The crisis made clear the need to revise the cultural model.

Transitions Over Illness Episodes and Over the Life Span

The one constancy in biological and behavioral systems is change. Illness episodes, both acute and chronic, are in constant flux. Symptoms vary in type, intensity, and duration, thoughts about cause and consequences dance across the stage of consciousness, and a variety of procedures are undertaken—some of which meet and others of which fail to meet hoped for outcomes. Change is the motif during any given episode and across the life span. Not only do different illnesses assail people as they age, the very same illnesses present with different symptoms in the old and young (Goodstein, 1985). A viable model of the behavioral adaptation to illness must capture this variation.

From Concrete to Abstract Representations: The Adolescent Transition. Aging adds substantially to our repertory of knowledge and skills in the health domain. This knowledge can be explicit (i.e., part of a verbalizeable set of propositions and facts) and implicit (i.e., part of a set of concepts and skills that shape perception and performance, even if they cannot be accessed in consciousness; Leventhal, 1982). Disease representations and procedures for disease management fall in both classes, and with age, greater differentiation can be anticipated among diseases, and between illness and health, and movement from use of concrete, episode specific representations to the inclusion of more abstract, prototypic features (Leventhal & Crouch, 1997). Millstein and Irwin (1987) illustrated how representations may change during the adolescent transition and provides strong support for the symptomatic nature of illness representations. When asked how they would define illness, nearly all (94%) participants, both the youngest (age 11–12) and oldest (age 15–16), mentioned one or more physical symptoms. A similar effect occurred when asked how they would define health: The absence of symptoms was mentioned by 54% of participants and a substantial number also mentioned disease prevention behaviors. The difference between the representation of illness and the representation of health was more clear among the older children. Of the younger children, 38% mentioned the absence of symptoms for health as compared to 18% of the older adolescents; the older group defined health in terms of functional ability and preventive behaviors. In short, the older adolescents differentiated the concepts of illness and health to a greater degree than the younger adolescents, and the differentiation was reflected in increased reporting of preventive action.

From Delay to Swift Care Seeking: A Later Life Transition. The differences between chronic and acute disease can generate major psychological discontinuities for an ill person. As has been suggested throughout this chapter, lifelong experience with the common cold builds prototypes of illness as short-term, self-limited affairs lacking serious consequences for the self. Expectations regarding source and type of treatment (e.g., aspirins that are self-prescribed or antibiotics given by a practitioner) and anticipated outcomes of these treatments are part of the prototype. As prototypes can operate automatically (i.e., without thought) they can facilitate adaptation to subsequent illness episodes that fit the prototype, and they can disrupt adaptation to episodes inconsistent with the prototype. The time frame and causes of chronic illness, their life threatening consequences and need for lifelong procedures for control, are inconsistent with both the explicit and implicit features of our prototypes of acute, infectious illness. The difficulty in resolving these inconsistencies was brought out by the data on patients with hypertension (only 28% of the patients new to treatment thought their disease was chronic, whereas 40% thought the problem was acute; Meyer et al., 1985), and the data on patients with metastatic breast cancer (29% believed their condition was acute at the start of chemotherapy treatment, which dropped to 11% 6 months later; Leventhal et al., 1986). Hypertensive patients holding an acute model were much more likely to drop out of treatment than those holding a chronic view. Thoughts of quitting paralleled the hypertensive data for cancer patients, but the life threat of the disease insured behavioral adherence.

A basic change appears to take place in people's views of their somatic and psychological system as they move into retirement age. This shift appears to be responsible for a change in the strategies used for avoiding and managing health threats and to reflect recognition that chronic illnesses are increasingly likely with advanced age and that physical and psychological resources are in decline. Specifically, older persons express greater interest and involvement in health promotive action (e.g., adherence to balanced diet, use of nutritional supplements, and are more adherent to treatment regimens; Prohaska et al., 1987). Older persons also report feeling substantially younger than their years and are optimistic about their ability to avoid deadly chronic illness. The pattern suggests that older persons are averse to taking health risks and eager to do what is necessary to maintain their resources (Baltes & Baltes, 1990; Carstensen, 1992; Leventhal & Crouch, 1997).

The risk aversion of the elderly is seen most clearly when we compare speed of care seeking for everyday symptoms by study participants who are over age 65 to participants who are middle aged (i.e., age 45–55). Estimates of the time elapsing from first noticing a symptom until calling for care show that both groups are quicker to seek care for symptoms they regard as serious when first noticed, and both are slower to seek care for those they regard as mild, although the elderly group delays less overall (Leventhal, Leventhal, Schaefer, & Easterling, 1993). Risk aversion is most visible when the time from first noticing to seeking care into two stages, an appraisal stage, or the duration from first noticing a symptom until deciding one is sick, and an illness stage, the duration from deciding one is sick until calling for care (E. A. Leventhal et al., 1993; Leventhal, Easterling, Leventhal, & Cameron, 1995). Compared to the middle aged, the elderly spend less time in appraisal, indicating that they are less willing to take chances with an event of uncertain implication. The elderly and the middle aged also differ once they decide they are ill. In this instance, the difference is moderated by the evaluation of symptom severity: For symptoms evaluated as very severe at onset, both groups spend little time before calling for expert advice, and for symptoms that are mild both groups are equally slow. But for symptoms that are judged possibly severe, the middle aged delay virtually six times longer than do the elderly; in fact, the middle aged actually take longer to call for an evaluation of these possibly serious symptoms than they do for their mild symptoms. Additional data suggest that lengthy illness delays by middle-aged respondents reflect avoidance, or fear of finding out they may have a life threatening illness (E. A. Leventhal et al., 1993). In summary, whereas these "stages" should not be thought of as sharply bounded periods, they do provide insight into the process underlying age difference in speed of response and support the hypothesis that older persons do adopt a help seeking strategy designed to avoid risk and conserve limited, physical resources.

Aging-related increases in physical frailty and declines in psychological function are likely to create a sense of fragility and vulnerability of the physical and psychological self and to set the stage for the formation of chronic disease prototypes (i.e., schemata in which diseases have extended time lines, stable symptoms, reduced possibility of cure and pose a threat to life and function). The underlying sense of vulnerability and its associated, chronic disease schemata should generate clearer images of the way chronic diseases can impact the self, giving the elderly a concrete view of the way disease can affect physical and cognitive function. These changes can lead to higher order, risk-averse, strategies, (e.g., Why take chances? Go to the doctor; Leventhal & Crouch, 1997), and to images of loss that are experienced as a diminished self (i.e., a self-deprived of work and social roles), or in terms of the disease taking over the self (Nerenz & Leventhal, 1983), and the individual living the life of a cancer or cardiac patient. Diseases that are seen to encompass and usurp the self will be imaged as intruders that create loss of hope and depression (Clemmey & Nicassio, 1997), leading to multiple negative consequences including poor adherence to treatment (Carney, Freedland, Eisen, Rich, & Jaffe, 1995). As such losses are highly aversive (Kahnemann &

Tversky, 1984), they likely encourage health promotive behavior among the elderly.

REPRESENTATIONAL MEANINGS DETERMINE HEALTH OUTCOMES

Implicit in the commonsense model of self-regulation is the assumption that illness representations, by directing coping procedures and appraisals, will be critically responsible for health-related outcomes that are at least partially influenced by behavior. Research by Weinman, Petrie and their associates (Petrie, Moss-Morris, & Weinman, 1995; Petrie, Weinman, Sharpe, & Buckley, 1996) demonstrated the potential impact of representations on important illness outcomes. For example, a recent study of patients diagnosed with Chronic Fatigue Syndrome (CFS) revealed that perceptions of illness consequences significantly predicted disability status. Patients who believed that "pushing themselves" beyond their present physical stamina would lead to catastrophic consequences (e.g., "I'd probably have a stroke and die") were more disabled in terms of work activities, household responsibilities, and recreational activities in relation to patients who believed that overexertion would lead to noncatastrophic consequences (Petrie et al., 1995). These group differences in disability did not appear to be due to differences in illness severity or psychological adjustment, because the two groups were virtually identical in terms of the time since illness onset, experiences of CFS symptoms and non-CFS symptoms, number of medical visits for CFS in the recent past, and mental health scores.

Further evidence that representational beliefs influence health outcomes is provided by a study revealing that illness perceptions reported by patients hospitalized for their first myocardial infarction predicted behavioral aspects of recovery during the next 6 months, even after controlling for illness severity and psychological adjustment (Petrie et al., 1996). Beliefs that heart disease is controllable or curable were found to be associated with a greater likelihood of regularly attending a rehabilitation course, whereas beliefs that heart disease is of relatively short duration were associated with a shorter delay in returning to work. Moreover, beliefs that the disease posed serious consequences were associated with a longer time until resuming work, household, recreational, and social activities. Taken together, these studies highlight the impact of representational beliefs on critical aspects of functioning and recovery from serious illness and suggest the potential efficacy of identifying and changing maladaptive beliefs at an early stage of illness in order to facilitate adaptation and recovery.

PROMOTING HEALTHY ACTION: A COMPARISON WITH OTHER BEHAVIORAL APPROACHES

Three Traditional Approaches

Most studies of the determinants of health behavior have been guided by the health belief model (Janz & Becker, 1984; Rosenstock, 1966), the "theory" of reasoned action (Fishbein & Ajzen, 1974) or its more recent embodiment as the "theory" of planned behavior (Ajzen, 1988), and social learning theory (Bandura, 1977). These models are in accord with the self-regulation position here presented in that all three postulate that health and illness behaviors are the product of: *motivational factors,* or cognitive-perceptual factors such as attitudes toward a health threat, perceived evaluation of the action by others in the social context ("social norms"), vulnerability perceptions, or perceptions regarding the magnitude of a health threat; and *action components,* such as an intention to act (Ajzen, 1988) or perceptions of self-efficacy, defined as the perceived ability to manage the action (Bandura, 1977; Rogers, 1983). Furthermore, the motivational and action components are regarded as integrally linked, such that intentions to perform a health promotive action (e.g., quitting smoking, reducing dietary fat, or practicing safe sex) are construed as products of the attitudes and perceptions regarding the action. The models also assume that self-efficacy is a cognitive-perceptual factor that taps an underlying willingness or motivation to engage in the action (Ajzen, 1988; Bandura, 1977; Rogers, 1983). However, many of the studies assessing self-efficacy and behavioral intentions fail to distinguish (conceptually and empirically) two uses of these constructs (i.e., as predictors of behavioral outcomes and as additional sources of motivation for action).

Differences With Traditional Theories

The self-regulation model provides a more detailed view of both the cognitive-perceptual factors affecting motivation and the connection between motivation and action in comparison to prior models. For example, whereas the other models emphasize attitudes or vulnerability perceptions as sources of motivation, the present model points to two parallel factors, emotional states and the representation of the threat. Second, the current model specifies specific components of the representation as determinants of action. Because the commonsense model identifies and assesses the representational features of threat (symptoms, labels, causes, control, timeline) from the point of view of the respondent and does not force the respondent to integrate these into a probability statement to satisfy the needs of a formal decision model, it provides a clearer set of guidelines for interventions designed to engage and modify the actor's perceptions and thoughts about a health threat. In short, the model provides a more detailed view of the actor's immediate goal representation, the cues that evoke action, and the rationale for selecting particular acts over others. The attitudes defined and assessed by the other theoretical approaches typically are not stored in memory structures; instead, individuals must access their representation of the relevant health threat in order to formulate the required attitudes that will enable them to respond to the study questions (e.g., "I am in favor of getting a mammogram").

Second, the self-regulation model contrasts with the other theories in that it differentiates between the abstract and concrete emotional features of illness representations, and the role of abstract and concrete factors in the generation of emotional reactions. By differentiating abstract and concrete levels of processing, the current version of self-regulation theory allows for conflict among goals and procedures; that is, the abstract and concrete facets of representations may differ in their criteria for response selection and outcome success. The current model argues that the concrete or perceptual level of representations is the basis for the formulation of abstractions and that level is often the most powerful prod to action (Palatano & Seifert, 1997). The multilevel feature of the model is critical for the analysis and understanding of the influence of emotion on illness-related perceptions, appraisals, and behaviors.

Third, the self-regulation model differs from the traditional theories by giving heavy emphasis to process; that is, it focuses on the continual interactions among the variables active during behavioral episodes to prevent and or control illness and to the updating and transitions that occur over time. The model also deals with changes in the representation of health threats from that of an acute to that of a chronic threat, and the need to revise procedures, outcome expectations, and outcome appraisals as a function of changes in the illness representation. The integrality hypothesis and the "if–then" rules expressing the relation of representation and coping merit special attention because they provide a vehicle for understanding and predicting the conditions for an individual's selection and appraisal of specific coping procedures. The contrast between the self-regulation perspective and the health belief and the reasoned (planned) action models is sharpest in this area, as neither of the latter provide a detailed view of process. Health belief variables, such as vulnerability and severity beliefs and the perceived costs and benefits of action, are beliefs at a moment. Neither these concepts nor those of intention, perceived norms, or attitudes suggest ways of engaging and changing individual cognition.

Social learning theory and similar cognitive-behavioral models (Rachman, 1997; Teasdale, 1997), share a focus on process with the self-regulation model. There are potentially important differences, however. First, the cognitive behavioral models have not presented a substantively detailed picture of illness representations. Second, cognitive-behavioral models have not yet focused on the *integral* nature of the relation of coping procedures to representations and the complexity of the representation of procedures (i.e., that procedures have labels and concrete representations, time lines, requirements for their performance or control—self and expert efficacy), and causal paths for their desired and undesired consequences. It is hard to imagine efficacy expectations for any procedure in the absence of a time line. Everyone wants to know, "How long will it take" to cure symptoms or block further progression. They also want to know "How much" or "How often" the procedure can be performed to insure efficacy without risk. If the objective is to insure adherence to treatment on the part of patients entering treatment for diseases such as hypertension or diabetes, or to reduce the distress of patients in chemotherapy treatment for cancer, or to encourage adherence to rehabilitation subsequent to coronary bypass surgery, the threat as perceived or misperceived by the patient must be addressed, these misperceptions must be corrected, and the problem representation must be linked to unbiased procedures for self-management. Thus, although many of the details of cognitive-behavioral therapy and the transactional systems approach developed by Lazarus (1966; Lazarus & Folkman, 1984) are similar to the current self-regulation model, their models lack the level of detail needed both for prediction and educational interventions. Finally, whereas all of the models identify social information as a critical determinant of action, only the self-regulation model asks whether social influence acts upon one or more features of the representation, plans, expectancies, skills for specific coping tactics, or the appraisal of coping outcomes. The self-regulation model also illustrates the effects of social influence on emotional processes (i.e., on both the type of affect experienced and the direction it provides to motivation).

Three factors have been responsible for the differences between the self-regulation model and cognitive-behavioral theories as they are applied to health problems. First, social learning and cognitive-behavioral theory developed within the framework of learning theory, which emphasized the acquisition of behaviors that were specified a priori by the investigator. Second, behavioral investigators accepted the behavioral goals specified by medical and public health authorities (e.g., stopping smoking, using safety belts, reducing dietary fat). Because the learning theory approach meshed with the acceptance of public health recommendations for the prevention and control of disease, investigators failed to examine the way their participants viewed these various health problems and health behaviors. By overlooking the ethology of health behavior, investigators have failed to recognize the large set of behaviors perceived as relevant for controlling health threats, the commonsense and cultural justifications for choosing one or another action for controlling risk, and the multiple goals creating motivation for action (Carver & Scheier, 1998). Third, unlike their academic counterparts, health researchers are under pressure to produce results that are of clinically significant magnitude. Behavioral intentions and self-efficacy expectations meet this demand because they are quick and easy to assess, they are good predictors of behavior, and they are likely to produce publishable findings.

The self-regulation model was developed from a social psychological framework that is attentive to the phenomenal world of the actor (Lewin, 1935), and was influenced by a range of themes in cognitive psychology (e.g., Anderson, 1983, 1993; Bruner, Goodnow, & Austin, 1956; Garner, 1962; Kahneman & Tversky, 1982; Nisbett & Ross, 1980). The model was also influenced at each step of its development by clinical practice. Thus, our studies have always reflected the needs of the clinician to understand the patient's perspective and to engage and involve the patient in self-management in seeking and using medical treatment (Johnson, 1975; Leventhal et al., 1991). Our self-regulation model has defined its concepts to represent the frame within which both patient and clinician operate.

Illness Cognition, Self-Regulation, and Practice

An important next step for the self-regulation model is to demonstrate its utility for the development and empirical testing of educational and therapeutic interventions. These interventions should be based on the concepts defining illness representations and should incorporate ideas as to how representations shape coping procedures. The presentations should make use of concrete (i.e., perceptual) as well as abstract material in order to fully engage participants' underlying schemata of illness and procedural strategies and tactics. The material must be skillfully designed to appeal to these cognitive structures and to meld them with the ecological and biological realities of potential or actual health threats. The participant in self-management has to learn how to determine whether specific, somatic symptoms and declines in feelings of vigor or pleasure define the presence of illness, and they must learn when to seek professional assistance in clarifying their perceived cause and meaning. Kovatchev, Cox, Gonder-Frederick and Schlundt (1998) offered a path to interventions in their analysis of the transitions involved in diabetic's use of symptoms to achieve control over blood sugar levels. When in treatment, patients must learn how to share information and develop realistic expectations about the consequences of disease and specific treatments, and they must learn how to be sensitive to the meaning of "side effects" and the time lines for effective outcomes. Professional or self-care procedures for the management of disease threats may change subjective experience and lead to increasing differentiation of the representation of a disease, (as with the separation of the symptoms from the underlying disease by patients with rheumatoid arthritis), and the differentiation of the positive and negative effects of treatment. A critical question is whether the model can be used to help patients shape these changes to enhance their ability to minimize the destructive impact of disease on their physical, emotional, and social well being; that is, can people be helped to live with chronic disease rather than be overwhelmed by it? If the self-regulation model adds to our understanding of the processes involved in avoiding and adapting to health threats and assists us in facilitating effective adaptations, it will vindicate the effort and time spent in its development.

ACKNOWLEDGMENTS

Preparation of this chapter was supported by grants AG 03501 and AG12072.

REFERENCES

Abelson, R. P., Kinder, D. R., Peters, M. D., & Fiske, S. T. (1982). Affective and semantic components in political person perception. *Journal of Personality and Social Psychology, 42*(4), 619–630.

Affleck, G., Tennen, H., Pfeiffer, C., & Fifield, J. (1987). Appraisals of control and predictability in adapting to a chronic disease. *Journal of Personality and Social Psychology, 53,* 273–279.

Ajzen, I. (1988). *Attitudes, personality, and behavior.* Homewood, IL: Dorsey Press.

Alonzo, A. A. (1980). Acute illness behavior: A conceptual exploration and specification. *Social Science and Medicine, 14,* 515–526.

Andersen, B. L. (1999, August). *Bio-behavioral aspects of cancer recurrence.* In M. A. Andrykowski and A. Baum (Chairs), Presidential Mini-convention on Cancer-State of the art research programs in cancer. American Psychological Association Annual Meeting, Boston.

Anderson, J. L. (1983). *The architecture of cognition.* Cambridge, MA: Harvard University Press.

Anderson, J. L. (1993). *The adaptive character of thought.* Hillsdale, NJ: Lawrence Erlbaum Associates.

Andrykowski, M. A. (1990). The role of anxiety in the development of anticipatory nausea in cancer chemotherapy: A review and synthesis. *Psychosomatic Medicine, 52,* 458–475.

Aneshensel, C. S., Frerichs, R. R., & Huba, G. J. (1984). Depression and physical illness: A multiwave, nonrecursive causal model. *Journal of Health and Social Behavior, 25,* 350–371.

Baltes, P. B., & Baltes, M. M. (1990). Psychological perspectives on successful aging: The model of selective optimization with compensation. In P. B. Baltes & M. M. Baltes (Eds.), *Successful aging: Perspectives from the behavioral sciences* (pp. 1–34). New York: Cambridge University Press.

Bandura, A. (1977). Self-efficacy: Toward a unifying theory of behavioral change. *Psychological Review, 84,* 191–215.

Barsky, A. J., Wyshak, G., & Klerman, G. L. (1986). Medical and psychiatric determinants of outpatient medical utilization. *Medical Care, 24,* 548–560.

Baumann, L., Cameron, L. D., Zimmerman, R., & Leventhal, H. (1989). Illness representations and matching labels with symptoms. *Health Psychology, 8,* 449–469.

Baumann, L. J., & Leventhal, H. (1985). "I can tell when my blood pressure is up, can't I?". *Health Psychology, 4,* 203–218.

Becker, M. D., Haefner, D. P., Kasl, S. V., Kirscht, J. P., Maiman, L. A., & Rosenstock, I. M. (1977). Selected psychosocial models and correlates of individual health-related behaviors. *Medical Care, 15*(5), 27–46.

Becker, M. H. (1974). The health belief model and personal health behavior. *Health Education Monographs, 2,* 326–473.

Berkanovic, E., Hurwicz, M., & Landsverk, J. (1988). Psychological distress and the decision to seek medical care. *Social Science & Medicine, 27*(11), 1215–1221.

Berkanovic, E., Telesky, C., & Reeder, S. (1981). Structural and psychological factors in the decision to seek medical care for symptoms. *Medical Care, 19,* 693–709.

Bishop, G. D. (1991). Understanding the understanding of illness: Lay disease representations. In J. A. Skelton & R. T. Croyle (Eds.), *Mental representation in health and illness.* (pp. 32–59). New York: Springer-Verlag.

Bishop, G. D., & Converse, S. A. (1986). Illness representations: A prototype approach. *Health Psychology, 5*(2), 95–114.

Blumhagen, D. (1980). Hyper-tension: A folk illness with a medical name. *Culture, Medicine, and Psychiatry, 4,* 197–227.

Bovbjerg, D. H., Redd, W. H., Jacobsen, P. B., Manne, S. L., Taylor, K. L., Surbonem, A., Crown, J. P., Norton, L., Gilewski, T. A., & Hudis, C. A. (1992). An experimental analysis of classically conditioned nausea during cancer chemotherapy. *Psychosomatic Medicine, 54,* 623–637.

Bower, G. H. (1981). Mood and memory. *American Psychologist, 36,* 129–148.

Brody, E. M., & Kleban, M. H. (1983). Day-to-day mental and physical health symptoms of older people: A report on health logs. *The Gerontologist, 23,* 75–85.

Brown, G. K. (1990). A causal analysis of chronic pain and depression. *Journal of Abnormal Psychology, 99,* 127–137.

Bruner, J. S., Goodnow, J. A., & Austin, G. A. (1956). *A study of thinking.* New York: Wiley.

Buunk, B. & Gibbons, F. X., (1997). *Social comparisons, health, and coping.* Hillsdale, NJ: Lawrence Erlbaum Associates.

Cameron, L. C, Leventhal, E. A., & Leventhal, H. (1993). Symptom representations and affect as determinants of care seeking in a community dwelling adult sample population. *Health Psychology, 12,* 171–179.

Cameron, L. C., Leventhal, E. A., & Leventhal, H. (1995). Seeking medical care in response to symptoms and life stress. *Psychosomatic Medicine, 57,* 37–47.

Cameron, L. C., & Leventhal, H. (1995). Vulnerability beliefs, symptoms experiences, and the processing of health threat information. *Journal of Applied Social Psychology, 25,* 1859–1883.

Cameron, L. C., Leventhal, H., Love, R. (1998). Trait anxiety, symptom perceptions, and illness-related responses among women in a Tamoxifen clinical trial. *Health Psychology, 17,* 459–469.

Carney, R. M., Freedland, K. E., Eisen, S. A., Rich, M. W., & Jaffe, A. S. (1995). Major depression and medication adherence in elderly patients with coronary artery disease. *Health Psychology, 14*(1), 88–90.

Carstensen, L. L. (1992). Social and emotional patterns in adulthood: Support for socioemotional selectivity theory. *Psychology and Aging, 7,* 331–338.

Carver, C. S., & Scheier, M. F. (1981). *Attention and self-regulation: A control-theory approach to human behavior.* New York: Springer-Verlag.

Carver, C. S., & Scheier, M. F. (1982). Control theory: A useful conceptual framework for personality-social, clinical, and health psychology. *Psychological Bulletin, 92*(1), 111–135.

Carver, C. S., & Scheier, M. F. (1990). Principles in self-regulation: Action and emotion. In E. T. Higgins & R. M. Sorrentino (Eds.), *Handbook of motivation and cognition: Foundations of social behavior* (Vol. 2, pp. 3–52). New York: Guilford.

Carver, C. S., & Scheier, M. F. (1998). *On the self regulation of behavior.* New York: Cambridge University Press.

Carver, C. S., Scheier, M. F., & Weintraub, J. K. (1989). Assessing coping strategies: A theoretically based approach. *Journal of Personality and Social Psychology, 56*(2), 267–283.

Cella, D. F., Tulsky, D. S., Gray, G., Sarafian, B., Linn, E., Bonomi, A., Siberman, M., Yellen, S. B., Winicour, P., & Brannon, J. (1993). The Functional Assessment of Cancer Therapy Scale: Development and validation of the general measure. *Journal of Clinical Oncology, 11*(3), 570–579.

Chaliki, H., Loader, S., Levenkron, J. C., Logan-Young, W., Hall, W. J., & Rowley, P. (1995). Women's receptivity to testing for a genetic susceptibility to breast cancer. *American Journal of Public Health, 85*(8), 1133–1135.

Chrisman, N. J. (1977). The health seeking process: An approach to the natural history of illness. *Culture, Medicine, and Psychiatry, 1,* 351–377.

Cioffi, D. (1991). Beyond attentional strategies: A cognitive-perceptual model of somatic interpretation. *Psychological Bulletin, 109*(1), 25–41.

Clark, D. M., & Ehlers, A. (1993). An overview of the cognitive theory and treatment of panic disorder. *Applied and Preventive Psychology, 2*(3), 131–139.

Clark, M. S. (1982). A role of arousal in the link between feeling states, judgments, and behavior. In M. S. Clark & S. T. Fiske (Eds.), *Affect and cognition: The seventeenth annual Carnegie symposium on cognition.* (pp. 263–289). Hillsdale, NJ: Lawrence Erlbaum Associates.

Clark, N., & Zimmerman, B. J. (1990). A social cognitive view of self-regulated learning about health. *Health Education Research: Theory & Practice, 5,* 371–379.

Clemmey, P. A., & Nicassio, P. M. (1997). Illness self-schemas in depressed and nondepressed rheumatoid arthritis patients. *Journal of Behavioral Medicine, 20,* 273–290.

Cohen, S., Doyle, W. J., Skoner, D. P., Fireman, P., Gwaltney, J. M., Jr., & Newsom, J. T. (1995). State and trait negative affect as predictors of objective and subjective symptoms of respiratory viral infections. *Journal of Personality and Social Psychology, 68,* 159–169.

Cohen, S., Frank, E., Doyle, W. J., Skoner, D. P., Rabin, B. S., & Gwaltney, J. M., Jr. (1998). Types of stressful life events that increase susceptibility to the common cold. *Health Psychology, 17*(3), 214–223.

Cohen, S., Tyrrell, D.A.J., & Smith, A. P. (1991). Psychological stress and susceptibility to the common cold. *New England Journal of Medicine, 325,* 606–612.

Cohen, S., & Williamson, G. M. (1991). Stress and infectious disease in humans. *Psychological Bulletin, 109,* 5–24.

Costa, P. T., & McRae, R. R. (1987). Neuroticism,somatic complaints and disease: Is the bark worse than the bite? *Journal of Personality, 55,* 299–315.

Croyle, R. T. (1990). Biased appraisal of high blood pressure. *Preventive Medicine, 19,* 40–44.

Croyle, R. T., & Barger, S. D. (1993). Illness cognition. In S. Maes, H. Leventhal, & M. Johnston (Eds.), *International review of health psychology* (Vol. 2, pp. 29–49). Chichester, UK: Wiley.

Croyle, R. T., & Jemmott, J. B., III (1991). Psychological reactions to risk factor testing. In J. A. Skelton & R. T. Croyle, (Eds.), *Mental representation in health and illness* (pp. 85–107). New York: Springer-Verlag.

Croyle, R. T., & Lerman, C. (1999). Risk communication in genetic testing for cancer susceptibility. *Journal of the National Cancer Institute Monographs, 25,* 59–66.

Croyle, R. T., & Uretsky, N. B. (1987). Effects of mood on self-appraisal of health status. *Health Psychology, 6,* 239–254.

Cummings, J. L. (1992). Depression and Parkinson's disease: A review. *American Journal of Psychiatry, 149,* 443–454.

D'Andrade, R. G., Quinn, N. R., Nerlove, S. B., & Romney, A. K. (1972) Categories of disease in American-English and Mexican-Spanish. In A. K. Romney, R. N. Shepard, & S. B. Nerlove (Eds.), *Multidimensional scaling: Theory and applications in the behavioral sciences: Volume 2. Applications* (2nd ed., pp. 11–53). New York: Seminar.

Dempsey, S. J., Dracup, K., & Moser, D. K. (1995). Women's decision to seek care for symptoms of acute myocardial infarction. *Heart and Lung, 24,* 444–456.

Diefenbach, M., Leventhal, E. A., Leventhal, H., & Patrick-Miller, L. (1996). Negative affect relates to cross-sectional but not longitudinal symptom reporting: Data from elderly adults. *Health Psychology, 15*(4), 282–288.

Ditto, P. H., Jemmott, J. B., III, & Darley, J. M. (1988). Appraising the threat of illness: A mental representational approach. *Health Psychology, 7,* 183–201.

Easterling, D. V., & Leventhal, H. (1989). The contribution of concrete cognition to emotion: Neutral symptoms as elicitors of worry about cancer. *Journal of Applied Psychology, 74,* 787–796.

Eckenrode, J., & Gore, S. (1981). Stressful events and social supports: The significance of context. In B. H. Gottlieb (Ed.), *Social networks and social supports* (pp. 43–68). Beverly Hills, CA: Sage.

Epstein, S. (1973). The self-concept: Or, a theory of a theory. *American Psychologist, 28,* 404–416.

Epstein, S. (1994). Integration of the cognitive and the psychodynamic unconscious. *American Psychologist, 49,* 709–724.

Facione, N. C. (1993). Delay versus help seeking for breast cancer syptoms: A critical review of the literature on patient and provider delay. *Social Science & Medicine, 376,* 1521–1534.

Farmer, P., & Good, B. J. (1991). Illness representations in medical anthropology: A critical review and a case study of the representation of AIDS in Haiti. In J. A. Skelton & R. T. Croyle, R. T. (Eds.), *Mental representation in health and illness* (pp. 132–162). New York: Springer-Verlag.

Felton, B. J., & Revenson, T. A. (1984). Coping with chronic illness: A study of illness controllability and the influence of coping strategies on psychological adjustment. *Journal of Consulting & Clinical Psychology, 52,* 343–353.

Festinger, L. (1954). A theory of social comparison processes. *Human Relations, 1,* 117–140.

Fishbein, M., & Ajzen, I., (1974). Attitudes towards objects as predictors of single and multiple behavioral criteria. *Psychological Review, 81,* 59–74.

Folkman, S. (1984). Personal control and stress and coping processes: A theoretical analysis. *Journal of Personality & Social Psychology, 46,* 839–852.

Forgas, J. P. (1995). Strange couples: Mood effects on judgments and memory about prototypical and atypical relationships. *Personality and Social Psychology Bulletin, 21*(7), 747–765.

Garner, W. R. (1962). *Uncertainty and structure as psychological concepts.* New York: Wiley.

Gonder-Frederick, L. A., & Cox, D. J. (1991). Symptom perception, symptom beliefs, and blood glucose discrimination in the self-treatment of insulin-dependent diabetes. In J. A. Skelton & R. T. Croyle (Eds.), *Mental representation in health and illness* (pp. 220–246). New York: Springer-Verlag.

Gonder-Frederick, L. A., & Cox, D. J. (1986). Behavioral responses to perceived hypoglycemic symptoms: A report and some suggestions. *Diabetes Educator, 12,* 105–109.

Goodstein, R. K. (1985). Common clinical problems in the elderly. *Psychiatric Annals, 15,* 299–312.

Hackett, T. P., & Cassem, N. H. (1969). Factors contributing to delay in responding to the signs and symptoms of acute myocardial infarction. *The American Journal of Cardiology, 24,* 651–658.

Hampson, S. E. (1997). Illness representations and the self-management of diabetes. In J. Weinman, & K. Petrie (Eds.), *Perceptions of health and illness* (pp. 323–347). London: Harwood Academic.

Hart, B. L. (1988). Biological basis of the behavior of sick animals. *Neuroscience & Biobehavioral Reviews, 12,* 123–137.

Heidrich, S. M., Forsthoff, C. A., & Ward, S. E. (1994). Psychological adjustment in adults with cancer: The self as mediator. *Health Psychology, 13,* 346–353.

Heurtin-Roberts, S., & Reisin, E. (1992). The relation of culturally influenced lay models of hypertension to compliance with treatment. *American Journal of Hypertension, 5,* 787–792.

Hochbaum, G. (1958). *Public Participation in Medical Screening Programs: A Socio-Psychological Study.* Public Health Service Publication no. 572, U.S. Government Printing Office.

Hooker, K., & Kaus, C. (1994) Health-related possible selves in young and middles adulthood. *Psychology and Aging, 9*(1), 126–133.

Horne, R. (1997). Representations of medication and treatment: Advances in theory and measurement. In K. J. Petrie & J. A. Wienman (Eds.), *Perceptions of health and illness: Current research and applications* (pp. 155–188). London: Harwood Academic.

Jamison, K. R. (1995). *An unquiet mind.* New York: Knopf.

Janz, N. K., & Becker, M. H. (1984). The health belief model: A decade later. *Health Education Quarterly, 11,* 1–42.

Johnson, E. J., & Tversky, A. (1983). Affect, generalization, and the perception of risk. *Journal of Personality and Social Psychology, 45,* 20–31.

Johnson, J. E. (1975). Stress reduction through sensation information. In I. C. Sarason & C. O. Speilberger (Eds.), *Stress anxiety* (Vol. 2, pp. 361–373). Washington: Hemisphere.

Johnston, M. (1980). Anxiety in surgical patients. *Psychological Medicine, 10,* 145–152.

Kahnemann, D., & Tversky, A. (1982). The simulation heuristic. In D. Kahnemann, P. Slovic, & A. Tversky (Eds.), *Judgment under uncertainty: Heuristics and biases* (pp. 201–208). New York: Cambridge University Press.

Kahnemann, D., & Tversky, A. (1984). Choices, values and frames. *American Pshychologist, 39,* 341–350.

Kanfer, F. H. (1977). The many faces of self-control, or behavior modification changes its focus. In R. B. Stuart (Ed.), *Behavioral self-management: Strategies, techniques, and outcomes.* New York: Brunner/Mazel.

Kasl, S. V., & Cobb, J. (1966) Health behavior, illness behavior and sick-role behavior. *Archives of Environmental Health, 12,* 531–541.

Kaye, M. A. (1993). Fallen fontanelle: Cultural-bound or cross- cultural? *Medical Anthropology: Cross-Cultural Studies in Health and Illness, 15,* 137–156.

Kelly, G. (1955). *The psychology of personal constructs. Vol. 1. A theory of personality.* New York: Norton.

Kleinman, A. (1980). *Patients and healers in the context of culture: An exploration of the borderland between antrhopology, medicine, and psychiatry.* Los Angeles: University of California Press.

Klohn, L. S., & Rogers, R. W. (1991). Dimensions of the severity of a health threat: The persuasive effects of visibility, time of onset, and rate of onset on young women's intentions to prevent osteoporosis. *Health Psychology, 10,* 323–329.

Knowles, J. H. (1977). The responsibility of the individual. In J. H. Knowles (Ed.), *Doing better and feeling worse* (pp. 57–80). New York: Norton.

Kornzweig, N. D. (1967). *Behavior change as a function of fear arousal and personality.* Unpublished doctoral dissertation, Yale University.

Kovatchev, B., Cox, D., Gonder-Frederick, L., & Schlundt, D. (1998). Stochastic model of self-regulation decision making exemplified by decisions concerning hypoglycemia. *Health Psychology, 17,* 227–284.

Krasnegor, N. A., Epstein, L., Bennett-Johnson, S., & Yaffe, S. J. (1993). *Developmental aspects of health compliance behavior* (pp. 91–124). Hillsdale, NJ: Lawrence Erlbaum Associates.

Krohne, H. W. (1993). Vigilance and cognitive avoidance as concepts in coping research. In H. W. Krohne (Ed.), *Attention and avoidance* (pp. 19–46). Seattle, WA: Hogrefe & Huber.

Kulik, J. A., & Mahler, H.I.M. (1987). The effects of preoperative roommate assignment on preoperative anxiety and postoperative recovery from bypass surgery. *Health Psychology, 6,* 525–543.

Kulik, J. A., & Mahler, H.I.M. (1997). Social comparison, Affiliation, and coping with acute medical threats. In B. P. Buunk & F. X. Gibbons (Eds.), *Health, coping, and well-being: Perspectives from social comparison theory* (pp. 227–261). Mahwah, NJ: Lawrence Erlbaum Associates.

Lacroix, J. M., Martin, B., Avendano, M., & Goldstein, R. (1991). Symptom schemata in chronic respiratory patients. *Health Psychology, 10,* 268–273.

Lang, P. Cuthbert, B., & Melamed, B. (1986). Cognition, emotion and illness. In S. McHugh & T. M. Vallis (Eds.), *Illness behav-*

ior: A multidisciplinary model (pp. 239–252) New York: Plenum.

Lau, R. R., Bernard, T. M., & Hartman, K. A. (1989). Further explorations of common sense representations of common illnesses. *Health Psychology, 8,* 195–219.

Lau, R. R., & Hartman, K. A. (1983). Common sense representations of common illnesses. *Health Psychology, 2*(2), 167–185.

Lazarus, R. S. (1966). *Psychological stress and the coping process.* New York: McGraw-Hill.

Lazarus, R. S. (1982). Thoughts on the relations between emotion and cognition. *American Psychologist, 37,* 1019–1024.

Lazarus, R. S. (1984). On the primacy of cognition. *American Psychologist, 39,* 124–129.

Lazarus, R. S., & Folkman, S. (1984). *Stress, appraisal, and coping.* New York: Springer.

Lazarus, R. S., & Launier, R. (1978). Stress related transactions between person and environment. In L. A. Pervin & M. Lewis (Eds.), *Perspectives in interactional psychology.* (pp. 287–327). New York: Plenum.

LeDoux, J. (1993). Emotional networks in the brain. In M. Lewis & J. M. Haviland (Eds.), *Handbook of emotions* (pp. 109–118). New York: Guilford.

Leventhal, E. A., & Crouch, M. (1997). Are there differences in perceptions of illness across the lifespan? In K. J. Petrie & J. A. Wienman (Eds.), *Perceptions of health and illness: Current research and applications* (pp. 77–102). London: Harwood Academic.

Leventhal, E. A., Easterling, D. V., Leventhal, H., & Cameron, L. D. (1995). Conservation of energy, uncertainty reduction, and swift utilization of medical care among the elderly: Study II. *Medical Care, 33*(10), 988–1000.

Leventhal, E. A., Leventhal, H., Schaefer, P., & Easterling, D. V. (1993). Conservation of energy, uncertainty reduction, and swift utilization of medical care among the elderly. *Journal of Gerontology, 48,* 78–86.

Leventhal, E. A., Suls, J., & Leventhal, H. (1993). Hierarchical analysis of coping: Evidence from life-span studies. In H. W. Krohne (Ed.), *Attention and avoidance: Strategies in coping with aversiveness* (pp. 71–99). Seattle, WA: Hogrefe & Huber.

Leventhal, H. (1970). Findings and theory in the study of fear communications. *Advances in Experimental Social Psychology, 5,* 119–186.

Leventhal, H. (1982). The integration of emotion and cognition: A view from the perceptual-motor theory of emotion. In M. Clark & S. Fiske (Eds.), *Affect and cognition: The 17th annual Carnegie symposium on cognition* (pp. 121–156). Hillsdale, NJ: Lawrence Erlbaum Associates.

Leventhal, H. (1984). A perceptual-motor theory of emotion. In L. Berkowitz (Ed.), *Advances in experimental social psychology* (pp. 117–182). Orlando, FL: Academic Press.

Leventhal, H. (1986). Symptom reporting: A focus on process. In S. McHugh & T. M. Vallis (Eds.), *Illness behavior: A multi- disciplinary model* (pp. 219–237). New York: Plenum.

Leventhal, H., & Cameron, L. D. (1987). Behavioral theories and the problem of compliance. *Patient Education and Counseling, 10,* 117–138.

Leventhal, H., & Diefenbach, M. (1991). The active side of illness cognition. In J. A. Skelton & R. T. Croyle (Eds.), *Mental representation in health and illness* (pp. 247–272). New York: Springer-Verlag.

Leventhal, H., Diefenbach, M., & Leventhal, E. A. (1992). Illness cognition: Using common sense to understand treatment adherence and affect cognition interactions. *Cognitive Therapy and Research, 16,* 143–163.

Leventhal, H., Easterling, D. V., Coons, H., Luchterhand, C., & Love, R. R. (1986). Adaptation to chemotherapy treatments. In B. Andersen (Ed.), *Women with cancer* (pp. 172–203). New York: Springer-Verlag.

Leventhal, H., Easterling, D. V., Nerenz, D., & Love, R. (1988). The role of motion sickness in predicting anticipatory nausea. *Journal of Behavioral Medicine, 11,* 117–130.

Leventhal, H., Hudson, S., & Robitaille, C. (1997). Social comparison and health: A process model. In B. Buunk & F. X. Gibbons (Eds.), *Health, coping and well being: Perspectives from social comparison theory* (pp. 411–432). Mahwah, NJ: Lawrence Erlbaum Associates.

Leventhal, H., Jones, S., & Trembly, G. (1966). Sex differences in attitude and behavior change under conditions of fear and specific instructions. *Journal of Experimental Social Psychology, 2,* 387–399.

Leventhal, H., & Leventhal, E. A. (1993). Affect, cognition and symptom reporting. In C. R. Chapman & K. M. Foley (Eds.), *Current and emerging issues in cancer pain: Research and practice* (pp. 153–173). New York: Raven.

Leventhal, H., Leventhal, E. A., & Carr, S. (in press). Behavioral research and cancer: Potential for the development of theory and practice.

Leventhal, H., Leventhal, E. A., & Schaefer, P. (1991). Vigilant coping and health behavior: A life span problem. In M. Ory & R. Abeles (Eds.), *Aging, health, and behavior* (pp. 109–140). Baltimore: Johns Hopkins.

Leventhal, H., Meyer, D., & Nerenz, D. (1980). The common sense representation of illness danger. In S. Rachman (Ed.), *Medical psychology* (pp. 7–30). New York: Pergamon.

Leventhal, H., & Mosbach, P. A. (1983). The perceptual-motor theory of emotion. In J. Cacioppo & R. Petty (Eds.), *Social psychophysiology* (pp. 353–388). New York: Guilford.

Leventhal, H., & Nerenz, D. (1985). The assessment of illness cognition. In P. Karoly (Ed.), *Measurement strategies in health* (pp. 517–554). New York: Wiley.

Leventhal, H., Nerenz, D., & Strauss, A. (1982). Self-regulation and the mechanisms for symptom appraisal. In D. Mechanic (Ed.), *Monograph series in psychosocial epidemiology 3: Symptoms, illness behavior, and help-seeking* (pp. 55–86). New York: Neale Watson.

Leventhal, H., Patrick-Miller, L., Leventhal, E. A., Burns, E. A. (1997). Does stress-emotion cause illness in elderly people? In W. Schaie & P. Lawton (Eds), *Emotion and adult development, Annual Review of Gerontology and Geriatrics, 17,* 138–184.

Leventhal, H., Singer, R., & Jones, S. (1965). Effects of fear and specificity of recommendations upon attitudes and behavior. *Journal of Personality and Social Psychology, 2,* 20–29.

Leventhal, H., & Scherer, K. R. (1987). The relationship of emotion to cognition: A functional approach to semantic controversy. *Cognition and Emotion, 1,* 3–28.

Leventhal, H., & Trembly, G. (1968). Negative emotions and persuasion. *Journal of Personality, 36,* 154–168.

Leventhal, H., & Watts, J. C. (1966). Sources of resistance to fear-arousing communications on smoking and lung cancer. *Journal of Personality, 34,* 155–175.

Leventhal, H., Watts, J. C., & Pagano, F. (1967). Effects of fear and instructions on how to cope with danger. *Journal of Personality and Social Psychology, 6,* 313–321.

Leventhal, H., Zimmerman, R., & Gutmann, M. (1984). Compliance: A self-regulation perspective. In W. D. Gentry (Ed.), *Handbook of behavioral medicine* (pp. 369–436). New York: Guilford.

Lewin, K. (1935). *A dynamic theory of personality.* New York: McGraw-Hill.

Love, R. R., Leventhal, H., Easterling, D., & Nerenz, D. (1989). Side effects and emotional distress during cancer chemotherapy. *Cancer, 63,* 604–612.

Maier, S. F., & Jackson, R. L. (1979). Learned helplessness: All of us were right (and wrong): Inescapable shock has multiple effects. In G. Bower (Ed.), *The psychology of learning and motivation* (pp. 155–218). New York: Academic Press.

Mandel, H., & Spiro, H. (1987). *When doctors get sick.* New York: Plenum.

Manne, S. L., Sabbioni, M., Bovbjerg, D. H., Jacobsen, P. B., Taylor, K. L., & Redd, W. H. (1994). Coping with chemotherapy for breast cancer. *Journal of Behavioral Medicine, 17*(1), 41–55.

Marcus, H., & Nurius, P. (1986). Possible selves. *American Psychologist, 41,* 954–969.

Martin, R., Gordon, E. E. I., & Lounsbury, P. (1998). Gender disparities in the interpretation of cardiac-related symptoms: The contribution of common sense models of illness. *Health Psychology, 17,* 346–357.

Matthews, K. A., Siegel, J. M., Kuller, L. H., Thompson, M., & Varat, M. (1983). Determinants of decision to seek medical treatment by patients with acute myocardial infarction symptoms. *Journal of Personality and Social Psychology, 44,* 1144–1156.

McGee, H. M., O'Boyle, C. A., Hickey, A., O'Malley, K., & Joyce, C.R.B. (1991). Assessing the quality of life of the individual: The SEIQuality of life with a healthy and a gastroenterology unit population. *Psychological Medicine, 21,* 749–759.

McKinlay, J. B., & Dutton, D. B. (1974). Social-psychological factors affecting health service utilization. In S. J. Mushkin (Ed.), *Consumer incentives for health care* (pp. 251–303). New York: Prodist.

Mechanic, D. (1979) The stability of health and illness behavior: Results from a 16–year follow up. *American Journal of Public Health, 69,* 1142–1145.

Melzack, R. (1973). *The puzzle of pain.* New York: Basic Books.

Melzack, R. (1992). Phantom limbs. *Scientific American, 226*(4), 120–126.

Meyer, D., Leventhal, H., & Gutmann, M. (1985). Common-sense models of illness: The example of hypertension. *Health Psychology, 4,* 115–135.

Millar, M. G., & Millar, K. (1996). The effects of anxiety on response times to disease detection and health promotion behaviors. *Journal of Behavioral Medicine, 19,* 401–413.

Miller, G. A., Galanter, E., & Pribram, K. H. (1960). Plans and the structure of behavior. New York: Henry Hold.

Miller, S. M. (1996). Monitoring and blunting of threatening information: Cognitive interference and facilitation in the coping process. In I. Sarason, B. Sarason, & G. R. Pierce (Eds.), *Cognitive interference: Theories, models and findings* (pp. 175–190). NJ: Lawrence Erlbaum Associates.

Miller, S. M., Combs, C., & Kruus, L. (1993). Tuning in and tuning out: Confronting the effects of confrontation. In H. W. Krohne (Ed.), *Attention and avoidance: Strategies in coping with aversiveness* (pp. 51–69). Seattle, WA: Hogrefe & Huber.

Miller, S. M., & Mangan, C. E. (1983). The interacting effects of information and coping style in adapting to gynecologic stress: Should the doctor tell all? *Journal of Personality and Social Psychology, 45,* 223–236.

Miller, S. M., Shoda, Y., & Hurley, K. (1996). Applying cognitive-social theory to health-protective behavior: Breast self-examination in cancer screening. *Psychological Bulletin, 119*(1), 70–94.

Millstein, S. G., & Irwin, C. E. (1987). Concepts of health and illness: Different constructs or variations on a theme? *Health Psychology, 6*(6), 515–524.

Mischel, W., & Shoda, Y. (1995). A cognitive-affective system theory of personality: Reconceptualizing situation, disposition, dynamics, and invarience in personality. *Psychological Review, 102,* 246–248.

Muth, J. L., & Cash, T. F., (1997). Body-image atttiudes: What difference does gender make? *Journal of Applied Social Psychology, 27,* 1438–1452.

Nerenz, D. R., & Leventhal, H. (1983). Self-regulation theory in chronic illness. In T. G. Burish & L. A. Bradley (Eds.), *Coping with chronic disease: Research and applications* (pp. 13–37). New York: Academic Press.

Nerenz, D. R., Leventhal, H., Easterling, D. V., & Love, R. R. (1986). Anxiety and drug taste as predictors of anticipatory nausea in cancer chemotherapy. *Journal of Clinical Oncology, 4,* 224–233.

Nerenz, D. R., Leventhal, H., & Love, R. R. (1982). Factors contributing to emotional distress during cancer chemotherapy. *Cancer, 50,* 1020–1027.

Nisbett, R., & Ross, L. (1980). *Human inference: Strategies and shortcomings of social judgment.* Englewood Cliffs, NJ: Prentice- Hall.

Pachter, L. M. (1993). Latino folk illnesses: Methodological considerations. *Medical Anthropology, 15,* 103–108.

Palatano, A. L., & Seifert, C. M. (1997). Opportunistic planning: Being reminded of pending goals. *Cognitive Psychology, 34,* 1–36.

Patrick-Miller, L. (1994). *Response to immunological challenge: The relationships amongst affect, age and immunity.* Unpublished masters thesis, Rutgers University, New Brunswick, NJ.

Pennebaker, J. W. (1982). *The psychology of physical symptoms.* New York: Springer-Verlag.

Pennebaker, J. W., & Brittingham, G. L. (1982). Environmental and sensory cues affecting the perception of physical symptoms. In A. Baum & J. E. Singer (Eds.), *Advances in environmental psychology: Vol. 4. Environment and health* (pp. 115–136). Hillsdale, NJ: Lawrence Erlbaum Associates.

Pennebaker, J. W., & Watson, D. (1988). Blood pressure estimation and beliefs among normotensives and hypertensives. *Health Psychology, 7,* 309–328.

Pescosolido, B. A. (1992). Beyond rational choice: The social dynamics of how people seek help. *American Journal of Sociology, 97*(4), 1096–1138.

Petrie, K. J., Weinman, J., Sharpe, N., & Buckley, J. (1996). Role of patients' views of their illness in predicting return to work and functioning after myocardial infarction: Longitudinal study. *British Medical Journal, 312,* 1191–1194.

Petrie, K. J., & Weinman, J. A. (1997). *Perception of health and illness: Current research and applications.* London: Harwood Academic.

Petrie, K. J., Moss-Morris, R., & Weinman, J. (1995). Catastrophic beliefs and their implications in the chronic fatigue syndrome. *Journal of Psychosomatic Research, 39,* 31–37.

Piliusik, M., Boylan,R., & Acredelo, C. (1987). Social support, life stress,and subsequent medical care utilization. *Health Psychology, 6,* 279–282.

Pimm, T. J. (1997). Self-regulation and psycho-educational interventions for rheumatic disease. In K. J. Petrie & J. A. Weinman (Eds.), *Perceptions of health and illness: Current research and applications* (pp. 349–377). Amsterdam: Harwood Academic.

Prochaska, J. O., DiClemente, C. C., & Norcross, J. C. (1992). In search of how people change: Applications to addictive behaviors. *American Psychologist, 47,* 156–163.

Prohaska, T. R., Keller, M. L., Leventhal, E. A., & Leventhal, H. (1987). Impact of symptoms and aging attribution on emotions and coping. *Health Psychology, 6,* 495–514.

Quinn, P. C., & Eimas, P. D. (1997). A reexamination of the perceptual-to-conceptual shift in mental representations. *Review of General Psychology, 1,* 271–287.

Rachman, S. (1997). The evolution of cognitive behaviour theory. In D. M. Clark & C. G. Fairburn (Eds.), *Science and practice of cognitive behaviour therapy* (pp. 3–26). New York: Oxford University Press.

Rescorla, R. A., & Solomon, R. L. (1967). Two-process learning theory: Relationships between Pavlovian conditioning and instrumental learning. *Psychological Review, 74,* 151–182.

Rogers, R. W. (1983). Cognitive and physiological processes in fear appeals and attitude change: A revised theory of protection motivation. In J. T. Caccioppo & R. E. Petty (Eds.), *Social psychophysiology: A source book* (pp. 153–176). New York: Guilford.

Rosch, E., Mervis, C. B., Gray, W. D., Johnson, D. M., & Boyes-Braem, P. (1976). Basic objective in natural categories. *Cognitive Psychology, 8,* 382–439.

Rosenstock, I. M. (1966). Why people use health services. *Milbank Memorial Fund Quarterly, 44,* 94ff.

Salkovskis, P. M. (1990). *The nature of, and interaction between, cognitive and physiological factors in panic attacks and their treatment.* Unpublished doctoral dissertation, University of Reading.

Salovey, P., & Birnbaum, D. (1989). Influence of mood on health-relevant cognitions. *Journal of Personality and Social Psychology, 57,* 539–551.

Sarason, I. B., Sarason, B. R., Potter, E. H., & Antoni, M. H. (1985). Life events, social support, and illness. *Psychosomatic Medicine, 47,* 156–163.

Saward, E. W. (1977). Institutional organizations, incentives and change. In J. H. Knowles (Ed.), *Doing better and feeling worse* (pp. 193–202). New York: Norton.

Schachter, S. (1959). *The psychology of affiliation: Experimental studies of the sources of gregariousness.* Stanford, CA: Stanford University Press.

Schachter, S., & Singer, J. E. (1962). Cognitive, social, and physiological determinants of emotional state. *Psychological Review, 69,* 379–399.

Scherer, K. R. (1984). On the nature and function of emotion: A component process approach. In K. R. Scherer & P. Ekman (Eds.), *Approaches to emotion* (pp. 293–317). Hillsdale, NJ: Lawrence Erlbaum Associates.

Scherer, K. R. (1993). Studying the emotion-antecedent appraisal process: An expert system approach. *Cognition and Emotion, 7,* 325–355.

Schiaffino, K. M., & Revenson, T. A. (1992). The role of perceived self-efficay, perceived control and causal attributions in adaptation to rheumatoid arthritis: distinguishing mediator from moderator effects. *Personality and Social Psychology Bulletin, 18,* 709–718.

Schiaffino, K. M., Shawaryn, M. A., & Blum, D. (1998). Examining the impact of illness representations on psychological adjustment to chronic illnesses. *Health Psychology, 17,* 262–268.

Schober, R., & Lacroix, J. M. (1991). Lay illness models in the enlightenment and the 20th century: Some historical lessons. In J. A. Skelton & R. T. Croyle (Eds.), *Mental representation in health and illness* (pp. 10–31). New York: Springer-Verlag.

Seligman, M.E.P. (1975). *Helplessness: On depression, development, and death.* San Francisco: Freeman.

Shaver, P., Schwartz, J., Kirson, D., & O'Conner, C. (1987). Emotion knowledge: Further exploration of a prototype approach. *Journal of Personality and Social Psychology, 52,* 1061–1086.

Simons, R. C. (1993). A simple defense of Western biomedical explanatory schemata. *Medical Anthropology, 15,* 201–208.

Smith, T. (1992). Hostility and health: Current status of a psychosomatic hypothesis. *Health Psychology, 11,* 139–150.

Skelton, J. A., & Croyle, R. T., (1991). *Mental representation in health and illness.* New York: Springer-Verlag.

Solomon, R. (1980). The opponent-process theory of acquired motivation: The costs of pleasure and the benefits of pain. *American Psychologist, 35,* 691–712.

Spiro, A., Aldwin, C. M., Levenson, M. R., & Busse, R. (1990). Longitudinal findings from the normative aging study: II. Do emotionality and extraversion predict symptom change? *Journal of Gerontology: Psychological Sciences, 45,* 136–144.

Stoller, E. (1993). Interpretations of symptoms by older people: A health diary study of illness behavior. *Journal of Aging and Health, 5,* 58–81.

Stoller, E. P. (1997). Medical self care: Lay management of symptoms by elderly people. In M. G. Ory & G. DeFries (Eds.), *Self-care in later life: Research, program, and policy issues* (pp. 24–61). New York: Springer.

Stone, A. A., Helder, L., & Schneider, M. S., (1988). Coping with stressful life events. In L. H. Cohen (Ed.), *Research on stressful life events: Theoretical and methodological issues* (pp. 182–210). Beverly Hills, CA: Sage.

Stone, A. A., & Neale, J. M. (1984). New measure of daily coping: Development and preliminary results. *Journal of Personality and Social Psychology, 46,* 892–906.

Suls, J., & Fletcher, B. (1985). The relative efficacy of avoidant and nonavoidant coping strategies: A meta-analysis. *Health Psychology, 4,* 469–481.

Suls, J., Martin, R., & Leventhal, H. (1997). Social comparison, lay referral, and the decision to seek medical care. In B. P. Buunk & R. X. Gibbons (Eds.), *Health, coping, and well-being: Perspectives from social comparison theory* (pp. 195–226). Mahwah, NJ: Lawrence Erlbaum Associates.

Suls, J., & Miller, R. L. (1997). *Social comparison processes: theoretical and empirical perspectives.* Washington, DC: Hemisphere.

Suls, J., & Wills, T. A. (1991). *Social comparison: contemporary theory and research.* Hillsdale, NJ: Lawrence Erlbaum Associates.

Taylor, S. (1983, November). Adjustment to threatening events: A theory of cognitive adaptation. *American Psychologist,* 1161–1173.

Taylor, S. (1991). Asymmetrical effects of positive and negative events: The mobilization-minimization hypothesis. *Psychological Bulletin, 110,* 67–85.

Teasdale, J. D. (1997). The relationship between cognition and emotion: The mind-in-place in mood disorders. In D. M. Clark & C. G. Fairburn (Eds.), *Science and practice of cognitive behaviour therapy* (pp. 67–117). New York: Oxford University Press.

Tennen, H., & Affleck, G. (1997). Social comparison as a coping process: A critical review and application to chronic pain disorders. In B. Buunk & F. X. Gibbons (Eds.), *Social comparisons, health, and coping* (pp. 263–298). Hillsdale, NJ: Lawrence Erlbaum Associates.

Tessler, R., Mechanic, D., & Dimond, M. (1976). The effects of psychological distress on physician utilization: A prospective study. *Journal of Health and Social Behavior, 17,* 353–364.

van der Kolk, B. A. (1987). *Psychological trauma.* Washington, DC: American Psychiatric Press.

Watson, D. (1988). Intraindividual and interindividual analyses of positive and negative affect: Their relation to health complaints, perceived stress, and daily activities. *Journal of Personality and Social Psychology, 54,* 1020–1030.

Watson, D., & Pennebaker, J. W. (1989). Health complaints, stress, and distress: Exploring the central role of negative affectivity. *Psychological Review, 96,* 234–254.

Weiss, J. M., Glazer, H. I., Pohorecky, L. A., & Miller, N. E. (1975). Effects of chronic exposure to stressors on avoidance-escape behavior and on brain norepinepherine. *Psychosomatic Medicine, 37,* 522–534.

Weller, S. C. (1984). Cross cultural concepts of illness: Variables and validation. *American Anthropologist, 86,* 341–351.

Weller, S. C., Pachter, L. M., Trotter, R. T., II, & Baer, R. D. (1993). Empacho in four Latino groups: A study of intra- and inter-cultural variation in beliefs. *Medical Anthropology, 15,* 109–136.

White, K. L. (1973). Life and death and medicine. *Scientific America, 229,* 23–33.

Wiebe, D. J., Alderfer, M. A., Palmer, S. C., Lindsay, R., & Jarrett, L. (1994). Behavioral self-regulation in adolescents with type I diabetes: Negative affectivity and blood glucose symptom perception. *Journal of Consulting and Clinical Psychology, 62*(6), 1204–1212.

Yoder, P. S., & Hornik, R. C. (1996). Symptoms and perceived severity of illness as predictive of treatment for diarrhea in six Asian and African sites. *Social Science and Medicine, 43*(4), 429–439.

Zeiss, A. M., Lewinsohn, P. M., Rhode, P., & Seeley, J. R. (1996). Relationship of physical disease and functional impairment to depression in older people. *Psychology & Aging, 11,* 572–581.

Zillman, D. (1979). *Hostility and aggression.* New York: Wiley.

Zola, I. (1973). Pathways to the doctor: From person to patient. *Science and Medicine, 7,* 677–689.

3

Conceptualization and Operationalization of Perceived Control

Kenneth A. Wallston
Vanderbilt University

> Personal control is being increasingly recognized as a central concept in the understanding of the relationships between stressful experience, behaviours and health. Experimental investigations indicate that control over aversive stimulation has profound effects on autonomic, endocrine and immunological responses, and may influence the pathological processes implicated in the development of cardiovascular disease, tumour rejection and proliferation, and the acquisition of gastrointestinal lesions. Clinically, control and lack of control have been identified as relevant to the experience of pain, anxiety and depression. In the field of psychosocial epidemiology, interesting observations are emerging that relate health to control over job parameters and other aspects of people's lives. (Steptoe & Appels, 1989, p. ix)

The construct of personal (or perceived) control plays an important, central role in health psychology. As exemplified by the previous quotation, it is relevant to stress-related situations and contributes to health-related behavior in individuals who are not experiencing stress. What is less clear is the way the construct of perceived control should be conceptualized and operationalized in health psychology research. This chapter first defines the construct conceptually. After pointing out a number of issues in the study of perceived control, the various ways in which health psychologists have operationalized the construct in their research are reviewed. The final section covers moderators of perceived control, thus illustrating the complex nature of the mechanisms by which perceived control operates to influence health behavior and health status.

CONCEPTUAL DEFINITIONS OF PERCEIVED CONTROL

Thompson (1981) defined personal control as "the belief that one has at one's disposal a response that can influence the aversiveness of an event" (p. 89). Perceived control (used synonymously in this chapter with *personal* control) has been defined as "the belief that one can determine one's own internal states and behavior, influence one's environment, and/or bring about desired outcomes" (K. A. Wallston, B. S. Wallston, S. Smith, & Dobbins, 1987, p. 5). "Most authors ... view control as a belief or cognition, reflecting the extent to which people think they can influence the situation, either by altering it, by changing its meaning or by regulating their own behavioral or emotional reactions" (Ormel & Sanderman, 1992, p. 196).

The fact that perceived control is a *belief* is critical. The perception may, or may not, be based on reality (Averill, 1973). When perceived control is based on reality, it is referred to as veridical or actual control; when it is patently not based on reality, it is sometimes referred to as illusory control (see Langer, 1975; Taylor, 1989). In most instances, the truth lies somewhere in between. Veridicality is not necessary or sufficient to bring about the perception of control, although the perception of control, however illusory, may have a profound effect on the individual.

Primary Versus Secondary Control

There are are least two separate ways by which a perception or feeling of control can be accomplished (Rothbaum, Weisz, & Snyder, 1982). In primary control, individuals enhance their rewards or achieve their objectives by influencing existing realities (e.g., other people, circumstances, symptoms, or behavior problems). In secondary control, individuals enhance their outcomes by accommodating to existing realities and maximizing satisfaction or goodness of fit with things as they are.

Targets of Control

Control is almost always directed at one or more *targets.* These targets include internal states, behavior, the environment (including behaviors of other people), and outcomes. The likelihood of multiple targets suggests that any conceptualization (and operationalization) of perceived control must be multifaceted. For example, individuals may perceive control over their own behaviors but not over others' behavior. They also may believe they have control over one aspect of their behavior (e.g., the ability to understand the words in a sentence) but not over other aspects of their behavior (e.g., the ability to understand the meaning of a sentence). Not only do targets differ, but control perceptions for targets differ over time. As a result, any attempt to treat the construct of perceived control simplistically is misguided.

In health psychology, the three most prevalent targets of control are health status, health behavior, and health care treatment. These are not the only targets of interest to health psychologists, however. For instance, Baum, Cohen, and Hall (1993) discussed control over environmental stressors such as hurricanes, earthquakes, tornados, explosions, and technological support services. Brownell (1991), on the other hand, focused on control over individuals' bodies. Anything that may impact on the individual is a potential target for control.

Appraisal

In Lazarus and Folkman's (1984) theory of stress and coping, primary appraisal refers to a judgment of the threat value of a stressor, whereas secondary appraisal refers to a judgment of available resources to deal with the threat. Perceptions of control affect and are affected by the process of secondary appraisal; the more resources available, the greater the perception of control and the better the ability to cope with the stressor. Some theoreticians in this area equate perceived control with "coping potential" (Craig Smith, personal communication, 1993); the greater the perceived control, the more likely the individual will cope successfully. Perceptions of control, therefore, can be thought of as personal coping resources.

ISSUES IN THE STUDY OF PERCEIVED CONTROL

Manipulated Versus Measured Control

The overwhelming majority of research on perceived control treats it as an individual difference construct that can be assessed by self-reports, usually with a paper-and-pencil instrument and sometimes by interview. In a smaller body of experimental research (e.g., Langer & Rodin, 1976; Mills & Krantz; 1979; Schulz, 1976), perceived control over some aspect of the environment, such as the health care delivery system, is manipulated in order to study the effects of perceived control on outcomes. For example, Langer and Rodin (1976) gave residents in a nursing home choice over which night they viewed a movie and whether the residents or the nursing staff had responsibility for watering plants. The investigators offered these choices to determine the effects that even a minimal amount of control has on mental and physical health.

The experimental research approach, rooted in social psychology, treats perceived control as an intervening variable. In these studies, some aspect of the situation is manipulated by the experimenter. Theoretically, the manipulation affects the subject's perception of control, which in turn helps determine the person's response to the situation (i.e., the outcome). An assumption in this type of research is that perceptions of control can be influenced by experiences.

In a series of field experiments conducted in the 1980s, Wallston and colleagues (see B. S. Wallston et al., 1987; K. A. Wallston, 1989; K. A. Wallston et al., 1991, for details) attempted to manipulate patients' perceptions of control over their health care situations by giving them enhanced choices and/or information to increase the predictability within the situations. The researchers expected that the patients' increased sense of control would lead to reduced feelings of distress and greater compliance with their medical regimens. No main effects for the control enhancing manipulations were found. Instead, the outcomes were determined by a complex interaction of the experimental conditions and patients' desire for control in those situations. The importance of taking into account individual differences such as desire for control are addressed later in this chapter.

In the aforementioned Wallston et al. studies, measures of perceived control administered after the experimental manipulations served both as an "outcome" of the manipulated independent variable (choice and/or predictability information) and as an "indicator" of the psychological process that intervened between the independent and the dependent variables. A separate set of questions served as the manipulation check in these studies. Among other things, these latter questions asked if the subject remembered being given a choice and/or predictability information. It is critical when conducting experimental manipulations of control to include both explicit manipulation checks as well as measures of perceived control as an outcome (or intervening) variable.

Levels of Specificity/Generalizability

In psychology in general, and health psychology in particular, perceived control has been assessed at three levels: *general,* cutting across many behaviors and situations faced by individuals; *midlevel,* pertaining to a given domain in people's lives (e.g., work, health, interpersonal relationships) but cutting across behaviors and situations within that domain; and *specific* to a given behavior and/or situation. Assessments at a general level are usually treated as stable personality traits, not easily amenable to change.

Caution should be exercised in assuming that mid- or specific-level assessments of perceived control remain stable over time because beliefs can change with each new experience. Investigators must choose a level of measurement that best suits their purposes. For example, the administration of a measure designed to assess perceived control over life in general should not be used to evaluate the effectiveness of a communication designed to convince diabetics they are in control of their own condition. Instead, a measure specific to health, or even one specific to diabetes, would be a better choice. When measuring perceived control after a deliberate manipulation of control, the instrument needs to be sensitive to change over time. Situation-specific measures are preferable in this instance.

Perceived Control as an Independent Versus Dependent Variable

In most of the work done to date, perceived control beliefs are treated as independent variables or causal agents, having some effect on an outcome or criterion variable. Work also has been done on the determinants of perceived control beliefs. In those instances, perceived control is treated as a dependent variable. The more perceived control is viewed as a stable attribute of the person or situation, the more likely it would be treated as an independent variable. In experiments in which the investigator manipulates the level of perceived control, the construct is treated as an independent variable. However, in doing a check of the manipulation, perceived control is typically analyzed as a dependent variable. Investigators need to be clear about whether control is an independent or dependent variable (or both) in their analyses.

The following section presents a number of ways in which perceived control has been operationalized in health psychology research. Almost all of these involve some sort of paper-and-pencil measures of beliefs, utilizing either single-item scales or, more usually, multi-item summated belief scales.

OPERATIONALIZATIONS OF PERCEIVED CONTROL

Locus of Control

Historically, most of the work linking perceived control and health evolved from Rotter's (1966) construct of *locus of control,* a generalized expectancy within his version of social learning theory (Rotter, 1954; 1982; Rotter, Chance, & Phares, 1972). *Locus,* the Latin word for "place," was dichotomized by Rotter into *internal* and *external.* A person with an internal locus of control orientation was conceptualized as someone who believes that valued reinforcements (or outcomes) occur as a direct consequence of personal actions or, perhaps, as a result of who or what the person is. An internal locus of control orientation is generally equated with perceived personal control. In contrast, an external orientation signifies a belief that reinforcements or outcomes are the result of other people's behaviors or, perhaps, random occurrences, not influenced by anything other than fate, luck, or chance. An external orientation typically is thought to signify a lack of perceived personal control.

Rotter (1966) developed the I–E scale as a means for assessing where along the internal–external continuum people's belief systems lay. The I–E scale is an example of assessment of perceived control at a general level. Generalized expectancies are developed through multiple experiences in varied situations (Rotter, 1954). By the time a person reaches adulthood and has experienced a wide range of situations, generalized expectancies have usually stabilized. Therefore, most investigators (e.g., Phares, 1976) have treated locus of control orientation as a personality trait. High I–E scores are reflective of externality and low I–E scores signify internality. I–E scale scores in late adolescents or adults are thought to be indicative of a relatively enduring characteristic of the individual, only changeable given profound new experiences or deliberate psychotherapy.

Health Locus of Control and Its Measurement

The I–E scale quickly became one of the most frequently used individual difference measures in psychology (cf. Rotter, 1975). Scores from Rotter's scale were applied to a wide variety of phenomena, including health. (See Strickland, 1978, and B. S. Wallston & K. A. Wallston, 1978, for reviews of early research linking I–E scores to health-related behaviors.) In 1973, the Wallstons became interested in applying the locus of control construct to health-related phenomena. Rotter (1975) stipulated that the predictability of behavior in a specific domain was more a function of expectancies related to that domain than generalized. Consequently, the Wallstons developed a midlevel, health domain-related locus of control scale, reasoning that such a measure would be general enough to cover a wide range of health-related behaviors and health-related circumstances while, at the same time, being specific enough to increase the predictability of health-related phenomena.

The first health locus of control (HLC) scale developed by B. S. Wallston, K. A. Wallston, Kaplan, and Maides (1976) was loosely modeled after Rotter's measure. Like the I–E scale, the original HLC scale was considered unidimensional, with high scores signifying increased externality. However, the HLC used a Likert response format rather than the forced-choice format employed by Rotter. The initial studies with the new scale (B. S. Wallston et al., 1976; K. A. Wallston, Maides, & B. S. Wallston, 1976) demonstrated its discriminant validity when compared to the I–E scale. The HLC scale predicted health outcomes and health-related information seeking better than the I–E scale, particularly among people for whom good health held high reinforcement value.

Multidimensionality of Locus of Control

A few investigators (e.g., Collins, 1974) used factor analysis to demonstrate that the I–E scale was multidimensional rather than unidimensional. Levenson (1973, 1974) posited that internality and externality were different dimensions rather than opposite ends of the same dimension. Levenson also suggested that externality itself was multidimensional. She developed the I, P, and C scales (Levenson, 1973, 1974, 1981) in which "powerful others externality" (P) was assessed separately from "chance externality" (C), and both of these were separate from "internality" (I).

Multidimensional Health Locus of Control

The separateness of internality and externality was supported by further investigation by the Wallstons, who noted that the internal consistency reliability of the HLC scale was considerably lower in subsequent samples than it had been in the sample used to develop the instrument. The correlations between the five internally worded HLC items and the six externally worded items was essentially zero, confirming the multidimensional nature of the measure. They agreed with Levenson's decision to split externality into two distinct dimensions, while recognizing that the relatively high correlation between Levenson's P and C scales ($r \sim .60$) was not ideal.

The multidimensional health locus of control (MHLC) scales (K. A. Wallston, B. S. Wallston, & DeVellis, 1978) were developed to more fully capture the different dimensions of locus of control. Modeled explicitly after Levenson's generalized I, P, and C scales, the MHLC scales consist of two "equivalent" forms (A & B), each of which have three six-item subscales: *internal health locus of control* (IHLC), or the belief that personal behavior influences health status; *powerful others health locus of control* (PHLC), or the belief that health status is influenced by the actions of powerful others, such as family, friends, and health professionals; and *chance health locus of control* (CHLC), or the belief that health status is strictly a function of fate, luck, or chance. The two alternative forms were developed for researchers who wanted to administer a measure of health locus of control beliefs before and after an intervention designed to alter such beliefs.[1]

The three subscales of the MHLC typically are orthogonal to (uncorrelated with) one another (K. A. Wallston et al., 1978; Wallston & Wallston, 1981). In most populations, IHLC and PHLC scores are uncorrelated. On occasion, however, a small positive association is found between IHLC and PHLC, particularly among older, less well-educated, or chronically ill samples. In most samples, IHLC and CHLC are usually somewhat negatively correlated, although the correlation seldom exceeds $r = -.25$. The two external dimensions, PHLC and CHLC, often correlate as high as $r = .30$. Nevertheless, this means that less than 10% of the variance in one external dimension is explained by its association with the other. This is in contrast to Levenson's P and C scales, which shared over 35% common variance. Because the MHLC subscales are orthogonal to one another, it is inappropriate to combine the subscales to compute a total MHLC scale score.

Form A or Form B of the MHLC have been administered in over 1,000 studies in the United States and other countries. The scales have been used to examine every conceivable health-related phenomenon (see Wallston & Wallston, 1981; K. A. Wallston & B. S. Wallston, 1982, for reviews of some of the early work with the MHLC), but in no way do the results of these studies present a coherent pattern. Once the MHLC scales were developed, the Wallstons withdrew their support of the original HLC scale; the new measure did everything the old measure did—and then some.

Because the MHLC was modeled after Levenson's I, P, and C scales, no attempt was made to include "negatively" worded items. This was criticized by Lau and Ware (1981), who indicated that having all the items keyed in the same "positive" direction (i.e., agreement on each item contributes to a high subscale score) diminishes the validity of the scales for those respondents with a "yea-saying" or "nay-saying" response set (Campbell, Siegman, & Rees, 1967). Lau and Ware (1981) subsequently developed a multidimensional health locus of control scale in which negatively worded items were included. Three of the four dimensions in the Lau and Ware instrument mimicked the three MHLC dimensions. Lau and Ware's fourth dimension, labeled "general health threat," assesses motivation to control health, a distinctly different construct from locus of control beliefs.[2]

Condition-Specific Control: A New Approach

In the years since the MHLC was published, several other researchers developed disease-specific or health-relat- ed-domain specific versions of the measure (see K. A. Wallston, Stein, & C. A. Smith, 1994, for references). Each time someone developed a version of the instrument, however, they chose a different set of items from the MHLC. As a result, scores from one scale were not equivalent to scores from another, thus making it impossible to compare scale scores across studies.

Part of the rationale for developing these more specific instruments paralleled the original reason for constructing the HLC scale: to increase predictability within a specific domain. Another reason was that some patients with an existing

[1]If the pretest and posttest were to be done in relatively close temporal proximity to one another, then having equivalent forms would minimize the chance that subjects taking the posttest would answer exactly as they had on the pretest. However, Forms A and B of the MHLC are only somewhat equivalent; they are not identical and do not yield identical normative scores (see K. A. Wallston et al., 1978). Therefore, when these measures are used in this fashion, a random half of the sample should be pretested with Form A and the other half with Form B, and then the alternative form should be given as a posttest. Otherwise, it might spuriously be concluded that the intervention affected HLC beliefs when, in actuality, the change in mean scores might only be due to a change in the form of the measuring instrument.

[2]Subsequently, there have been a couple of studies (e.g., Marshall, Collins, & Crooks, 1990) that have used statistical modeling techniques to pit the Lau and Ware scales against the MHLC scales. These studies have generally supported the three dimensions used in the MHLC rather than the four dimensions in the Lau and Ware (1981) measure.

medical diagnosis had difficulties responding to certain items such as, "I can pretty much stay healthy by taking good care of myself." It is difficult to respond to this item when you do not think of yourself as "healthy." The solution to the proliferation of nonequivalent disease-specific measures was to develop a generic version of the MHLC, labeled Form C (K. A. Wallston et al., 1994). Form C contains four, rather than three, dimensions. Factor analyses (K. A. Wallston et al., 1994) demonstrated that the "powerful others" items in Form C break down into two orthogonal dimensions, "control by doctors" (what Lau & Ware, 1981, called "provider control") and "control by others" (e.g., family or friends). Form C can be made specific to any medical condition by changing one word ("condition") in each item.

Form C appeals to many researchers investigating perceived control in persons with chronic diseases or other medical conditions. However, it must be remembered that Form C assesses beliefs in control over a particular condition (e.g., cancer or arthritis), not health locus of control, per se. These two types of beliefs (i.e., domain-specific and situation-specific) seldom intercorrelate higher than .60 (cf. K. A. Wallston et al., 1994). Just because individuals perceive control over their diagnosed condition does not necessarily mean they perceive control over their health in general, and vice versa. Thus, researchers using Form C may also wish to use Form A or Form B, if adding 18 items does not substantially increase subjects' burden. The advantage of administering both Form A/B and Form C is that this provides both a midlevel and a condition-specific assessment of locus of control beliefs, increasing the likelihood of discovering important relations with other constructs.

Limitations of the Locus of Control Construct

A limitation of the construct *locus of control* is its relation to only one of the targets of control: outcomes (or, in social learning terms, reinforcements). This is a problem because locus of control is an *outcome expectancy.* For instance, high scores on the IHLC scale signify individuals believe there is a relation between their behavior and their health status. What is not known, however, is the person's *behavioral expectancies*: Does the person feel capable of producing the behavior when it is called for? An outcome expectancy without a concomitant behavioral expectancy may not indicate much about perceptions of control. For example, a woman might feel the food she eats influences her weight and she might also think that her weight influences her health, but unless she also believes she is capable of limiting her caloric intake, she will not perceive much control over her weight or her health. Feeling "responsible" for an outcome is not exactly the same thing as being in control of that outcome.

Another shortcoming of locus of control as a means of conceptualizing perceived control is that just because a person believes other people play a role in determining outcomes does not necessary imply a lack of perceived control. This is especially true in the context of health outcomes, particularly when the "powerful others" are highly skilled health professionals. Many patients truly believe that transferring control to a benevolent, competent health care provider is, in fact, a means of gaining control over health. Similarly, individuals who blame themselves for their poor health but do not feel responsible for their good health could score highly on a measure of internal health locus of control without feeling in control of their health.

Marshall (1991) used covariance structure modeling with a sample of medical outpatients to conduct a multidimensional analysis of health-related personal control perceptions. As Marshall hypothesized, the structure of personal health control included four dimensions: response-outcome expectancies about illness prevention; response-outcome expectancies about illness management; self-blame for negative health outcomes; and perceived self-mastery over health outcomes. Only the latter dimension, perceived self-mastery over health outcomes, was uniquely associated with physical well-being. The constructs and measures to be described—specifically, self-efficacy, mastery, and competence—relate directly to Marshall's finding.

Self-Efficacy. Bandura, whose version of social learning theory (now called social cognitive theory) has eclipsed Rotter's, led the way in distinguishing between outcome and behavioral expectancies (Bandura, 1977, 1982). The most salient behavioral expectancy, labeled by Bandura (1977) as *self-efficacy,* is the individuals' confidence in their ability to carry out a specific behavior in a specific situation. Measures of self-efficacy have proven to be much better predictors of health behavior than measures of health locus of control beliefs (Bandura, 1997; O'Leary, 1992; Schwarzer, 1992; Wallston, 1992).

Self-efficacy relates to control of a different target—behavior—than locus of control that targets outcomes or reinforcements (K. A. Wallston et al., 1987). Most current social psychological theories of health behavior incorporate self-efficacy beliefs as a major explanatory construct. For example, Ajzen's Theory of Planned Behavior (Ajzen, 1985) has a construct labeled "perceived behavioral control," which is closely akin to self-efficacy. Even the venerable Health Belief Model (Rosenstock, 1966) has been reformulated to include self-efficacy as a separate mediator of health behavior (Rosenstock, Strecher, & Becker, 1988).

The difficulty for health researchers wanting to measure self-efficacy is that Bandura initially conceived of these beliefs as being highly behavior and situation specific. Thus, each new health behavior or health-related situation calls for a new and different measure of self-efficacy. Fortunately, there are now enough examples of self-efficacy measures in the literature (e.g., Condiotte & Lichtenstein, 1982; Schwarzer, 1993) that researchers can adapt to fit their own particular needs. This latter strategy is commonplace, although it is not without peril. Any new or adapted instrument should be thoroughly pilot tested before use, and a psychometric analysis should be done once the data have been collected to assess the reliability and validity of the new measure (DeVellis, 1991).

Generalized Self-Efficacy, Mastery, and Competence. Some psychologists take exception to Bandura's original notion of strict situational specificity. They believe self-efficacy can be generalized across behaviors and situations and thus can be assessed as a stable individual difference. For example, Schwarzer and colleagues developed measures of *generalized self-efficacy* and applied them successfully to health-related phenomena (Schwarzer, 1992, 1993). Sherer and Maddux (1985) also developed a generalized self-efficacy scale, and others used Pearlin and Schooler's (1978) Mastery scale to assess individual differences in personal control over the environment and the future (Hobfoll & Lerman, 1989; Hobfoll, Shoham, & Ritter, 1991).

Wallston and colleagues developed a similar generalized measure, the Perceived Competence (PC) scale, which has been applied to health-related situations. For example, C. A. Smith, Dobbins, and K. A. Wallston (1991) showed that perceived competence mediates depression and life satisfaction in persons with rheumatoid arthritis. Pender, Walker, Sechrist, and Frank-Stromborg (1990) used this same instrument (which they referred to as the Personal Competence Rating scale) in a study of health behavior in six employer-sponsored health promotion programs. In the Pender et al. study, the PC scale predicted more variance in the measurement of health-promoting lifestyle behavior than any other measure, including the MHLC. It also contributed significant variance after controlling for all other constructs in their model.

There now exists a midlevel instrument for health researchers who do not want or need to assess self-efficacy at highly specific levels, but who also do not want to operate at a general level. The Perceived Health Competence scale (PHCS; M. S. Smith, K. A. Wallston, & C. A. Smith, 1995) measures essentially the same construct as Marshall's (1991) perceived self-mastery over health outcomes, and can easily be made even more outcome specific (e.g., pain, weight loss). This eight-item, psychometrically sound measure of perceived control of health is unidimensional, and combines behavioral and outcome expectancies in a single measure.

Situation-Specific Perceived Control Scales. In addition to utilizing already established measures of perceived control of health (e.g., locus of control, self-efficacy, mastery, and competence), many health psychologists ask just one or two questions about perceptions of control, often making those questions relevant to the situation under investigation. For example, Affleck, Tennen, Pfeiffer, and Fifield (1987) assessed rheumatoid arthritis patients' beliefs about personal control over daily symptoms, course of disease, medical care, and treatment. For all patients, regardless of severity of condition, the belief in personal control over medical care and treatment was associated with positive psychological outcomes. For patients with mild symptoms, perceiving personal control over symptoms was unrelated to outcomes. For those with moderate or severe symptoms, however, the more they perceived control over their symptoms, the more positive was their mood. Perceiving personal control over the course of their arthritis was marginally associated with positive mood in patients with mild disease, but was negatively associated with positive mood in patients with more severe disease.[3]

Taylor, Helgeson, Reed, and Skokan (1991) conducted a longitudinal study of control and adjustment among a group of patients with severe coronary heart disease. At three points in time, participants were asked to respond to two control-related questions using 7-point rating scales: (a) "Regarding your heart problem, how much in control do you feel?" and (b) "Regarding your heart problem, how helpless do you feel?" Because the questions were highly correlated at each point in time, the investigators chose to combine them into an index (after reversing the second item) rather than to treat them separately. This strategy enhances the reliability of the measure.

In a study of gay men with AIDS, Taylor and colleagues (Reed, Taylor, & Kemeny, 1993) used a different measurement approach. In interviews in the subjects' homes, ratings (on 5-point scales) of personal control were obtained through three questions: (a) "How much control do you feel you have over the amount of fatigue, pain, or other symptoms you may experience on a daily basis?"; (b) "How much control do you feel you have over maintaining or improving your health, for example by influencing your immune system or by preventing AIDS-related conditions from occurring, getting worse, or coming back?"; and (3) "How much control do you feel you have over the medical care and treatment of your illness?" Like the study by Affleck et al. (1987), this study illustrates ways to assess the multiple targets of control.

In the series of field experiments by Wallston and colleagues, referred to earlier, in which patients' perceptions of control were manipulated in specific health care settings by providing choices and/or enhanced information (see K. A. Wallston, 1989, for a synopsis of these studies), the PCON scale (for perceived control) was used to assess the key intervening variable. PCON assesses control over actual health care delivery situations, not control over outcomes or behaviors. Although the general form of the PCON scale remained the same from situation to situation (e.g., outpatients receiving a barium enema or cancer chemotherapy; hospitalized patients postsurgery), the wording of the instructions and items were altered to fit the specifics of the situation. This type of easily adaptable measure is useful for health services researchers interested in patients' perceptions or those wishing to assess the effectiveness of control-enhancing interventions.

Learned Helplessness

When individuals learn over repeated trials that the things that happen to them are not contingent on their own actions, they develop learned helplessness (cf. Seligman, 1975). Learned helplessness is the obverse of perceived control; the greater the learned helplessness, the less the perceived control. Because of this, health psychologists can assess perceived con-

[3]Not only does this study by Affleck et al. (1987) illustrate the value of assessing multiple targets of control, it also reinforces the importance of including disease severity as a moderator variable in one's analyses.

trol at a mid- or specific-level by measuring the extent to which patients hold beliefs consistent with learned helplessness and/or exhibit behavioral/motivational deficits indicative of helplessness. A good example of this is the helplessness subscale from the Arthritis Helplessness Index (AHI; DeVellis & Callahan, 1994; Stein, K. A. Wallston, & Nicassio, 1989).

MODERATORS OF PERCEIVED CONTROL: THE ACTION IS IN THE INTERACTION

The major outcome measure in Rotter's (1954) social learning theory is "behavior potential"—the likelihood of a particular behavior (or set of functionally related behaviors) occurring in a given situation. According to Rotter's theory, measures of expectancy (such as locus of control beliefs) are supposed to work in conjunction with measures of reinforcement value to predict behavior potential in specific situations (Rotter, 1954).[4] In other words, reinforcement value moderates the relation between locus of control beliefs and behavior. For high levels of reinforcement value, internal locus of control beliefs should be predictive of behavior; for low levels, locus of control should be uncorrelated with behavior.

Within the health domain, the most relevant reinforcer of health behavior is good health. Consequently, researchers attempting to predict health behavior using measures of health locus of control beliefs (or any expectancy measure) should also assess the reinforcement value of health (K. A. Wallston, 1991; K. A. Wallston et al., 1976), especially among relatively healthy populations. Although considerably less attention has been paid to the assessment of health value, there are a number of techniques that have been developed to do so (M. S. Smith & K. A. Wallston, 1992). When studying populations whose health statuses are already compromised by illness or disease, or when health value cannot be assessed directly, an alternative approach is to use a measure of disease severity as a proxy. In general, when health is threatened, its value is higher than when it is not (M. S. Smith & K. A. Wallston, 1992).

Behavioral expectancies (such as self-efficacy beliefs—the individuals' confidence in thier ability to carry out the behaviors) have been suggested as the primary predictors of health behavior. These specific expectancies, in turn, are moderated by locus of control orientation and health value (K. A. Wallston, 1992). In other words, health behavior can be predicted by self-efficacy expectations only among individuals who value their health and who have an internal orientation toward their health. This calls for examining the three-way interactions among behavioral expectancies, outcome expectancies, and outcome value when attempting to predict health behavior.

Health psychologists, however, are interested in more than predicting health behavior. For many researchers, health status is the outcome they are attempting to explain. Theoretically, at least, expectancies about control (e.g., health locus of control or self-efficacy beliefs) should be related only to health status when the control expectancy predicts health behavior and the health behavior predicts health status. Conceptually, the relation between perceived control and subsequent health status is mediated by health behavior. This relation (between perceived control and health status) is also subject to moderation by individual and situational variables.

A good example of how perceived control beliefs interact with personal and situational variables can be found in a study of end-stage renal disease patients (Christensen, Turner, T. W. Smith, Holman, & Gregory, 1991). In this study, depressive symptomatology was the outcome and whether or not the patient had previously experienced a failed liver transplant was the situational factor. Christensen et al. predicted that the negative psychological effects of a transplant failure would be greater for those who had strong beliefs in the controllability of their illness, whether through their own efforts or through those of their health care providers. It was also predicted that among those patients who had not experienced a transplant failure, those with stronger beliefs in control would have more favorable psychological outcomes. Christensen et al. also predicted that disease severity would moderate the interaction, such that the more severe the disease, the stronger the interaction.

The results of the study were as predicted. Within the group of patients with lower disease severity, the two-way interaction between perceived control and transplant outcome was not significant. The predicted interaction was seen for those with higher disease severity, however. In the failed transplant group, the greater the perception of control, the more depressed the patient. Among the patients who never experienced a failed transplant, the results were just the opposite (Christensen et al., 1991).

The study of rheumatoid arthritis patients by Affleck et al. (1987) provides another example of the importance of examining interactions of perceived control with disease severity when predicting health status outcomes. Another study by the same team of investigators (Tennen, Affleck, Urrows, Higgens, & Mendola, 1992) found an even more complicated, but clinically important, set of interactional effects. Those patients who believed at the outset of the study that they had more control over their pain experienced less daily pain. With increased levels of pain, however, greater control was associated with less positive mood.

Indicators of disease severity are not the only potential moderators of the relation between control beliefs and health outcomes. For example, Kaplan and associates (Strawbridge et al., 1993; Wallhagen et al., 1994) found that internal health locus of control strongly predicted 6-year change in physical functioning for elderly women. Elderly men, on the other hand, were affected only if they had lower functioning at baseline. In these analyses, both gender and level of baseline functioning were treated as moderator variables. Other potential moderators (of the relation between perceived control and

[4]The phrase "in conjunction with" is best interpreted as "in interaction with" rather than "in addition to." Thus, measures of locus of control need to be multiplied by or crossed with reinforcement value to predict behavior (cf. B. S. Wallston & K. A. Wallston, 1984; K. A. Wallston, 1991).

health outcomes) are age, social class, social support, and availability of medical treatments. The important message from these studies is that variance in health status is poorly explained by direct (main) effects of perceived control. The action is in the interaction, and the challenge is to find the right moderators for each situation.

FUTURE DIRECTIONS

Other than predicting that perceived control will remain a central and important construct in health psychology well into the 21st century, it is not easy to speculate about the way the construct will be operationalized and utilized in the future. One thing is for certain: New and improved methods of measurement will be developed. These will probably occur in two diametrically opposite directions: a focus on perceived control of health as a unitary dimension; and an attempt to discover other important dimensions or loci of control, such as the influence of the environment and/or a "higher power" on one's health status.[5] As health psychologists become more aware of and comfortable with alternative ways of assessment —such as using computers or qualitative methods—less and less reliance will be placed on traditional paper-and-pencil measures. Method triangulation, such as combining quantitative and qualitative assessments, will become the norm rather than the exception.

K. A. Wallston (1992) pointed out that "the focus isn't strictly on locus," which did not stem the tide of research using the MHLC scale, but slowed it down some. The challenge for health psychologists is to select the most appropriate ways of measuring perceived control and to develop analytic strategies that examine interactions amoung these methods as well as with other constructs.

CONCLUSIONS

This chapter described the development of measures of perceived control of health as well as the ways in which the construct of perceived personal control has been conceptualized and operationalized by health psychologists. The complexity and the multidimensionality of the construct has been emphasized. Different levels of specificity in operationalizing the construct were presented, concentrating on the mid- and situationally specific levels. It was stressed that although measures of health locus of control may play a role in explaining variance in health behaviors and health status, these measures should optimally be used in conjunction with other indicators of perceived control of health (e.g., perceived health competence or other efficacy measures). Also stressed was the notion that the action is in the interaction. Perceptions of control moderate, or are moderated by, many other constructs, among them individual differences in demographic characteristics, background experiences, situational factors, and value orientations. Without adopting an interactionist perspective, health psychologists and other investigators in behavioral medicine will fail to discover the full explanatory power of perceived control.

[5]In fact, a God Locus of Health Control (GLHC) subscale has been developed that can be used by itself or in conjunction with the MHLC to assess the belief that God is the locus of control of a person's health (see K. A. Wallston, Malcarne, Flores, et al., 1999).

REFERENCES

Affleck, G., Tennen, H., Pfieiffer, C., & Fifield, J. (1987). Appraisals of control and predictability in adapting to chronic disease. *Journal of Personality and Social Psychology, 53*(2), 273–279.

Ajzen, I. (1985). The theory of planned behavior. *Organizational Behavior and Human Decision Processes, 50,* 179–211.

Averill, J. R. (1973). Personal control over aversive stimuli and its relationship to stress. *Psychological Bulletin, 80,* 286–303.

Bandura, A. (1977). Self-efficacy: Toward a unifying theory of behavior change. *Psychological Review, 84,* 191–215.

Bandura, A. (1982). Self-efficacy in human agency. *American Psychologist, 37,* 122– 147.

Bandura, A. (1997). *Self-efficacy: The exercise of control.* New York: Freeman.

Baum, A., Cohen, L., & Hall, M. (1993). Control and intrusive memories as possible determinants of chronic stress. *Psychosomatic Medicine, 55*(3), 274–286.

Brownell, K. D. (1991). Personal responsibility and control over our bodies: When expectation exceeds reality. *Health Psychology, 10* (5), 303–310.

Campbell, D. T., Siegman, C., & Rees, M. B. (1967). Direction-of-wording effects in the relationships between scales. *Psychological Bulletin, 68,* 293–303.

Christensen, A. J., Turner, C. W., Smith, T. W., Holman, J. M., & Gregory, M. C. (1991). Health locus of control and depression in end stage renal disease. *Journal of Consulting and Clinical Psychology, 53*(3), 419–424.

Collins, B. E. (1974). Four separate components of the Rotter I–E scale: Belief in a different world, a just world, a predictable world, and a politically responsive world. *Journal of Personality and Social Psychology, 29,* 281–391.

Condiotte, M. M., & Lichtenstein, E. (1982). Self-efficacy and relapse in smoking cessation programs. *Journal of Consulting and Clinical Psychology, 49,* 648–658.

DeVellis, R. F. (1991). *Scale development.* Newbury Park, CA: Sage.

DeVellis, R. F., & Callahan, L. F. (1994). A brief measure of helplessness in rheumatic disease: The helplessness subscale of the Rheumatology Attitudes Index. *Journal of Rheumatology, 20,* 866–869.

Hobfoll, S. E., & Lerman, M. (1989). Predicting receipt of social support: A longitudinal study of parents' reactions to their child's illness. *Health Psychology, 8*(1), 61–77.

Hobfoll, S. E., Shoham, S. B., & Ritter, C. (1991). Women's satisfaction with social support and their receipt of aid. *Journal of Personality and Social Psychology, 62*(2), 332–341.

Langer, E. J. (1975). The illusion of control. *Journal of Personality and Social Psychology, 32,* 311–328.

Langer, E. J., & Rodin, J. (1976). Effects of choice and enhanced personal responsibility for the aged. *Journal of Personality and Social Psychology, 34,* 191–198.

Lau, R. R., & Ware, J. E. (1981). Refinements in the measurement of health specific locus of control beliefs. *Medical Care, 19,* 1147–1148.

Lazarus, R. S., & Folkman, S. (1984). *Stress, appraisal, and coping.* New York: Springer.

Levenson, H. (1973). Multidimensional locus of control in psychiatric patients. *Journal of Consulting and Clinical Psychology, 41,* 397–404.

Levenson, H. (1974). Activism and powerful others: Distinctions within the concept of internal/external control. *Journal of Personality Assessment, 38,* 377–383.

Levenson, H. (1981). Differentiating among internality, powerful others, and chance. In H. Lefcourt (Ed.), *Research with the locus of control construct.* (Vol. 1, pp. 15–63). New York: Academic Press.

Marshall, G. N. (1991). A multidimensional analysis of internal health locus of control beliefs: Separating the wheat from the chaff. *Journal of Personality and Social Psychology, 61* (3), 483–491.

Marshall, G. N., Collins, B. E., & Crooks, V. C. (1990). A comparison of 2 multidimensional health locus of control instruments. *Journal of Personality Assessment, 54*(1–2), 181–190.

Mills, T., & Krantz, D. S. (1979). Information, choice, and reactions to stress: A field experiment in a blood bank with laboratory analogue. *Journal of Personality and Social Psychology, 37,* 608–620.

O'Leary, A. (1992). Self-efficacy and health: Behavioral stress—psychological mediation. Special issue: Cognitive perspectives in health psychology. *Cognitive Therapy and Research, 16*(2), 229–245.

Ormel, J., & Sanderman, R. (1992). Life events, personal control and depression. In A. Steptoe, & A. Appel (Eds.), *Stress, personal control and health* (pp. 193–213). Brussels, Luxembourg: Wiley.

Pearlin, L. I., & Schooler, C. (1978). The structure of coping. *Journal of Health and Social Behavior, 19*(1), 2–21.

Pender, N. J., Walker, S. N., Sechrist, K. R., & Frank-Stromborg, M. (1990). Predicting health promoting lifestyles in the workplace. *Nursing Research, 39*(6), 326–332.

Phares, E. J. (1976). *Locus of control in personality.* Morristown, NJ: General Learning Press.

Reed, G. M., Taylor, S. E., & Kemeny, M. E. (1993). Perceived control and psychological adjustment in gay men with AIDS. *Journal of Applied Social Psychology, 23*(10), 791–824.

Rosenstock, I. M. (1966). Why people use health services. *Milbank Memorial Fund Quarterly, 74,* 94–124.

Rosenstock, I. M., Strecher, V. J., & Becker, M. H. (1988). Social learning theory and the health belief model. *Health Education Quarterly, 15,* 175–183.

Rothbaum, F. M., Weisz, J. R., & Snyder, S. S. (1981). Changing the world and changing the self: A two-process model of perceived control. *Journal of Personality and Social Psychology, 42,* 5–37.

Rotter, J. B. (1954). *Social learning and clinical psychology.* Englewood Cliffs, NJ: Prentice-Hall.

Rotter, J. B. (1966). Generalized expectancies for internal vs. external control of reinforcement. *Psychological Monographs, 80,* 1–28.

Rotter, J. B. (1975). Some problems with misconceptions related to the construct of internal vs. external control of reinforcement. *Journal of Consulting and Clinical Psychology, 43,* 56–67.

Rotter, J. B. (1982). *The development and application of social learning theory: Selected papers.* Brattleboro, VT: Praeger.

Rotter, J. B., Chance, J., & Phares, E. J. (Eds.). (1972). *Application of social learning theory of personality.* New York: Holt, Rinehart & Winston.

Schultz, R. (1976). The effects of control and predictability on the physical and psychological well-being of the institutionalized aged. *Journal of Personality and Social Psychology, 33,* 563–573.

Schwarzer, R. (1992). *Self–efficacy: Thought control of action.* Washington DC: Hemisphere.

Schwarzer, R. (1993). *Measurement of perceived self-efficacy: Psychometric scales for cross-cultural research.* Berlin: Frie Universitat.

Seligman, M.E.P. (1975). *Helplessness: On depression, development and death.* San Francisco: Freeman.

Sherer, M., & Maddux, J. E. (1985). The self-efficacy scale: Construction and validation. *Psychological Reports, 51,* 663–671.

Smith, C. A., Dobbins, C. J., & Wallston, K. A. (1991). The mediational role of perceived competence in psychological adjustment to rheumatoid arthritis. *Journal of Applied Social Psychology, 21,* 1218–1247.

Smith, M. S., & Wallston, K. A. (1992). How to measure the value of health. *Health Education Research: Theory and Practice, 7,* 129–135.

Smith, M. S., Wallston, K. A., & Smith, C. A. (1995). The development and validation of the Perceived Health Competence Scale. *Health Education Research: Theory and Practice, 10,* 51–64.

Stein, M. J., Wallston, K. A., & Nicassio, P. M. (1988). Factor structure of the Arthritis Helplessness Index. *Journal of Rheumatology, 15,* 427–432.

Steptoe, A., & Appels, A. (Eds.). (1989). *Stress, personal control and health.* Brussels, Luxembourg: Wiley.

Strawbridge, W. J., Camacho, T. C., Cohen, R. D., & Kaplan, G. A. (1993). Gender differences in factors associated with changes in physical functioning in old age: A six year longitudinal study. *Gerontologist, 33*(5), 603–609.

Strickland, B. R. (1978). Internal–external expectancies and health-related behaviors. *Journal of Consulting and Clinical Psychology, 46,* 1192–1211.

Taylor, S. E. (1989). *Positive illusions: Creative self-deception and the healthy mind.* New York: BasicBooks.

Taylor, S. E., Helgeson, V. S., Reed, G. M., & Skokan, L. A. (1991). Self generated feelings of control and adjustment to physical illness. *Journal of Social Issues, 47*(4), 91–109.

Tennen, H., Affleck, G., Urrows, S., Higgens, P., & Mendola, R. (1992). Perceiving control, construing benefits, and daily processes in rheumatoid arthritis. Special Issue: The psychology of control. *Canadian Journal of Behavioral Science, 24*(2), 186–203.

Thompson, S. C. (1981). Will it hurt if I can control it? A complex answer to a simple question. *Psychological Bulletin, 90,* 89–101.

Wallhagen, M. I., Strawbridge, W. J., Kaplan, G. A., & Cohen, R. D. (1994). Impact of internal health locus of control on health outcomes for older men and women: A longitudinal perspective. *Gerontologist, 34*(3), 299–306.

Wallston, B. S., & Wallston, K. A. (1978). Locus of control and health: A review of the literature. *Health Education Monographs, 6,* 107–117.

Wallston, B. S., & Wallston, K. A. (1981). Health locus of control scales. In H. Lefcourt (Ed.), *Research with the locus of control construct* (Vol. 1, pp. 189–243). New York: Academic Press.

Wallston, B. S., & Wallston, K. A. (1984). Social psychological models of health behavior: An examination and integration. In A. Baum, S. Taylor, & J. E. Singer (Eds.), *Handbook of psychology and health. Vol. 4: Social aspects of health* (pp. 23–53). Hillsdale, NJ: Lawrence Erlbaum Associates.

Wallston, B. S., Wallston, K. A., Kaplan, G. D., & Maides, S. A. (1976). The development and evaluation of the health related locus of control (HLC) scale. *Journal of Consulting and Clinical Psychology, 44,* 580–585.

Wallston, B. S, Wallston, K. A., Smith, R. A., King, J. E., Rye, P. D., & Heim, C. R. (1987). Choice and predictability in the preparation for barium enemas: A person-by-situation approach. *Research in Nursing and Health, 10,* 13–22.

Wallston, K. A. (1989). Assessment of control in health care settings. In S. Steptoe & A. Appels (Eds.), *Stress, personal control and health* (pp. 85–105). Chicester, England: Wiley.

Wallston, K. A. (1991). The importance of placing measures of health locus of control beliefs in a theoretical context. *Health Education Research, Theory, and Practice, 6,* 251–252.

Wallston, K. A. (1992). Hocus-pocus, the focus isn't strictly on locus: Rotter's social learning theory modified for health. *Cognitive Therapy and Research, 16,* 183–199.

Wallston, K. A., Maides, S. A., & Wallston, B. S. (1976). Health related information seeking as a function of health related locus of control and health value. *Journal of Research in Personality, 10,* 215–222.

Wallston, K. A., Malcarne, V. L., Flores, L., Hansdottir, I., Smith, C. A., Stein, M. J., Weisman, M. H., & Clements, P. J. (1999). Does God determine your health? The God Locus of Health Control scale. *Cognitive Therapy and Research, 23,* 131–142.

Wallston, K. A., Smith, R.A.P., King, J. E., Smith, M. S., Rye, P., & Burish, T. G. (1991). Desire for control and choice of antiemetic treatment for cancer chemotherapy. *Western Journal of Nursing Research, 13,* 12–29.

Wallston, K. A., Stein, M. J., & Smith, C. A. (1994). Form C of the MHLS scales: A condition-specific measure of locus of control. *Journals of Personality Assessment, 63,* 534–553.

Wallston, K. A., & Wallston, B. S. (1982). Who is responsible for your health: The construct of health locus of control. In G. Sanders & J. Suls (Eds.), *Social psychology of health and illness* (pp. 65–95). Hillsdale, NJ: Lawrence Erlbaum Associates.

Wallston, K. A., Wallston, B. S., & DeVellis, R. (1978). Development of the Multidimensional Health Locus of Control (MHLC) scales. *Health Education Monographs, 6,* 160–170.

Wallston, K. A., Wallston, B. S., Smith, S., & Dobbins, C. (1987). Perceived control and health. *Current Psychological Research and Reviews, 6,* 5–25.

4

On Who Gets Sick and Why: The Role of Personality and Stress

Richard J. Contrada
Max Guyll
Rutgers, The State University of New Jersey

It has long been thought that personality and physical health are related. From ancient theories of temperament, through early clinical descriptions of physical disorders, prescientific thinking drew a close association between personality attributes and various somatic disorders. Several threads of systematic theory and research on the topic emerged following the birth of psychology and psychosomatic medicine. Since the middle of the 20th century, interest in personality and health has intensified considerably. It now represents a major focus of psychosocial research concerned with physical disease (Friedman, 1990).

Potential points of contact between the personality and physical health domains are numerous. Each, by itself, is a large and complex area of inquiry. The personality field has undergone considerable expansion and differentiation over the past 50 years. During the latter portion of that time period, there has been tension between two major pursuits: construction of a taxonomy of personality descriptors and development of an understanding of personality process (Cervone, 1991; Mischel & Shoda, 1994; Pervin, 1990). This debate reflects an important component of variation in assumptions and approaches within the personality field. However, there are also wide differences in the views of investigators within each camp, and many issues in personality research that have implications for understanding physical health do not map neatly onto the description/process dichotomy.

As this handbook will attest, the study of physical health and disease is a vast and diverse enterprise. Many physical conditions contribute to morbidity, mortality, and poor quality of life, and any one condition poses several subproblems, including diagnosis, epidemiology, etiology, prevention, treatment, and rehabilitation. As a result, the study of physical health and disease is a multidisciplinary endeavor, potentially involving investigators from several health-related fields, including psychologists interested in personality (Schwartz & Weiss, 1977).

This chapter is concerned with one portion of the personality–health interface, namely, that involving personality attributes that are thought to have health-damaging consequences because they increase psychological stress or exacerbate its effects. Like personality, stress has long been suspected of contributing to physical health problems. Moreover, the personality and stress constructs complement one another in that each provides a means of explaining and elaborating the other's role in shaping human adaptation. The concept of stress points to social and environmental factors outside the person that influence psychological well-being and physical health, and to psychological and physiological processes that mediate those effects. The study of personality points to dispositions within the person that can account for individual differences in responses to a stressor, and to attributes and processes that explain temporal and cross-situational consistency in stress-related response patterns. Thus, research that draws from both the personality and stress domains is more likely to provide a comprehensive understanding of psychosocial influences on physical health than does work in which one of these constructs is utilized to the exclusion of the other.

This chapter provides a discussion of conceptual issues, empirical findings, and methodological concerns that bear on the relations among personality, stress, and health. It examines personality as a psychosocial risk factor for disease and as a moderator of psychological stress. The review is selective in emphasizing research that supports associations between certain personality dispositions and both measures of physical disorder and markers of disease-related processes. The focus is primarily on the relation between personality and disease promoting processes that involve direct, psychophysiological effects of stress. However, some consideration is also given to behavioral factors that may mediate the health effects of stress-related personality attributes independently of, or in interaction with, psychophysiologic mechanisms. Issues and problems that emerge from this discussion are highlighted in a final section that takes stock of available theory and empirical findings and points to some potentially fruitful directions for further study.

WHO GETS SICK? PERSONALITY AS A RISK FACTOR

"Who gets sick?" is an epidemiological question that can only be answered by programmatic, prospective, multivariate research in which putative risk factors are evaluated with respect to their ability to predict objectively verified disease endpoints independently of potential confounds (Adler & Matthews, 1994). Personality represents but one of several psychosocial domains in which risk factors for physical disease have been sought, with other salient examples including psychological stress, social relationships, and health-related behaviors. However, the conceptual and methodological principles that arise from a consideration of the health effects of personality are relevant to a wide range of possible psychosocial risk factors, and there is reason to believe that personality and other psychosocial factors related to health often interact with one another rather than operating independently.

This section begins by describing major conceptual features that distinguish personality from other psychological constructs, and by discussing the implications of these features for framing the question, "Who gets sick?" An overview is then provided of the numerous personality attributes that have been implicated as possibly influencing vulnerability to physical disease. This section concludes with a discussion of those personality attributes for which the epidemiological evidence makes the strongest case for risk factor status.

Conceptual Elements of Personality

The question of how best to define *personality* and related terms such as *personology* has received extensive consideration (for classic discussions see Allport, 1937, and Murray, 1938; for more recent treatments, see Mischel, 1968, and Pervin, 1990). These analyses are not reviewed here. Instead, the discussion draws on previous work to provide a heuristic overview of some of the major conceptual elements of personality psychology. This discussion is necessarily cursory, however, and the reader is urged to consult the sources already cited for more comprehensive coverage of these issues.

Individual Differences

Individual differences refer to between-person variations in behavior. In this context, "behavior" may be construed narrowly in terms of a single domain of psychological activity, or it may be defined broadly to include cognition, affect, motivation, overt action, and neurobiological activity. Personality psychologists do not share a single view of the nature of individual differences per se, or of the importance of any one domain of individual differences in particular. Moreover, not all individual differences involve personality. Nonetheless, in a general sense, personality and the study of individual differences are intimately related.

The relevance of individual difference dimensions to the development and course of physical health problems depends on their association with mechanisms involved in the etiology and pathogenesis of disease, or with processes that affect the detection, control, and outcome of physical disorders. A rather wide range of individual difference constructs have been implicated as possible risk factors for physical illness. The field is narrowed, somewhat, when it is limited to those areas of individual differences that involve personality.

Patterning in Behavior

Much personality research may be distinguished from other areas of psychology by virtue of its focus on two specific forms of *patterning in behavior,* namely, temporal and cross-situational consistency. It is the observed or hypothesized stability of individual differences over time and in different contexts that provides a rationale for inferring drives, motives, traits, cognitive styles, and other dispositional constructs employed in personality psychology. Temporal and cross-situational consistency set personality attributes apart from other person factors, such as transient cognitive or emotional states, or highly situation-specific behavioral tendencies. Of course, psychological states and individual behaviors can be reflective of enduring personality attributes, and may have significant effects on physical health regardless of such an association. However, the nature of those effects and the mechanisms whereby they are mediated may at times differ from those involving personality (Cohen, Doyle, Skoner, Gwaltney, & Newsom, 1995; Scheier & Bridges, 1995).

Personality is not the sole source of temporal and cross-situational consistency in behavior. Enduring factors that exist outside individuals—such as occupation, economic conditions, and relations between ethnic groups—also may contribute to regularities in a person's behavior. Moreover, as argued from the standpoint of transactional theoretical orientations, the explanation of temporal and cross-situational consistency in behavior may defy a simple, analysis of variance like partitioning of person, situation, and person-by-situation interaction (Lazarus & Folkman, 1984). Instead, person and environment factors may reinforce and sustain one another in ways that make efforts to disentangle their independent contributions difficult or arbitrary. Notwithstanding these complexities, the involvement of personality attributes in behavioral patterning has major implications for specifying the role of personality as a risk factor for physical disease.

The two forms of behavioral patterning associated with personality factors provide a theoretical basis for linkages to health damaging processes. Temporal stability in a suspected personality risk factor may indicate a relationship to disease promoting mechanisms that develop gradually over time. For example, as an enduring disposition, hostility may be associated with repeated activation of physiologic activity that contributes to slowly progressing disorders such as atherosclerosis (T. W. Smith, 1992). Cross-situational consistency may operate in a similar manner. Consider conscientiousness, a trait that may be related to good health (Friedman et al., 1995). To the degree that conscientiousness involves a pattern of careful, prudent behavior that is displayed in a wide range of situations, the opportunity for the accumulation of risk reducing actions is increased. Thus, the two forms of behavioral patterning that define personality attributes as distinct from other psychological factors are also important for their implications regarding associations with disease promoting processes.

Recent studies involving naturalistic observations have provided evidence of a third form of behavioral patterning that may have interesting implications for the interface between personality and health. Mischel and colleagues (Mischel & Shoda, 1995; Shoda, Mischel, & Wright, 1994) demonstrated that individuals show consistent patterns of variability in their behavior across different situations. For example, children in a residential summer camp reliably displayed higher levels of particular behaviors (e.g., verbal aggression) in some situations (e.g., being teased by a peer, being approached by a peer) than in others (e.g., being warned by an adult, being punished by an adult). These situation behavior profiles consist of stable, meaningful variations in behavior, but are treated as random error in the more traditional focus in personality, where behavior often is aggregated across situations that may not always be psychologically equivalent. There may be similar consistencies in patterns of variation in behaviors that individuals display in situations that involve exposure to health risk.

Organization

The term *organization* is frequently used by personality psychologists, although with more than one meaning. In one usage, organization refers to the idea that personality is pervasive, involving the whole person as a unified, although highly complex, system. This notion is similar in certain respects to self- regulation perspectives employed in health psychology and behavioral medicine (e.g., Carver & Scheier, 1981; Schwartz, 1979). A systems view of the person is integral to the multilevel, bio–psycho–social model of health and disease (Engel, 1977), and also provides a framework within which to conceptualize processes whereby cognitive, affective, and other psychological systems may influence disease promoting mechanisms, a topic discussed later in this chapter.

In another usage, personality organization refers to the structure of interrelationships of personality descriptors. Multivariate methods have generated evidence of hierarchical organization in which relatively specific tendencies (e.g., being talkative, enjoying parties) cluster together to form more general dispositions (e.g., sociability, sensation seeking), which in turn cluster together to form still more general dispositions (e.g., extraversion; Eysenck, 1967). There is growing consensus that at a certain level of abstraction personality organization may be described in terms of a taxonomy of five personality factors that have been labeled extraversion, agreeableness, conscientiousness, neuroticism, and openness to experience (McCrae & Costa, 1985). This five-factor model provides a general framework for characterizing major dimensions of individual differences in personality.

Some of the traits that form the five-factor model, such as conscientiousness (Friedman et al., 1995) and neuroticism (Bolger & Zuckerman, 1995), have been investigated in relation to stress and health. However, many personality variables of interest to health psychologists—such as Type A behavior (Matthews, 1982), hostility (Barefoot, Dodge, Peterson, Dahlstrom, & R. Williams, 1989), optimism (Scheier & Carver, 1985), hardiness (Kobasa, 1979), and repressive coping (Weinberger, Schwartz, & Davidson, 1979)—involve facets of more than one of the five-factor traits, or are defined in terms of attributes whose location within the five-factor taxonomy has yet to be determined. Thus, the five-factor model remains to be more fully explored as a framework for organizing health-related personality attributes (T. W. Smith & P. G. Williams, 1992).

Personality Structure

Structure refers to neurobiological and/or psychological entities that are real and exist beneath the person's skin. Personality structures must be distinguished from the individual difference patterns from which they are typically inferred. A particular pattern of consistency in behavior across time and context may reflect an underlying personality structure, but the personality structure and the behavior pattern are conceptually distinct, with the former a putative cause of the latter. The concept of psychological structure is illustrated by the notion that hostile behavior reflects a set of underlying attitudes characterized by cynicism and distrust (T. W. Smith, 1992). An example of neurobiological structure may be found in Krantz and Durel's (1983) proposal that the overt display of Type A behavior is, in part, a reflection of activity of the sympathetic nervous system.

Consideration of the notion of personality structure suggests that, with respect to the role of personality, the question "Who gets sick?" is really asking "What personality structures lead to disease?" The interviews, questionnaires, and other assessment tools used to measure personality necessarily provide only an indirect indication of the presence, content, and form of the underlying psychological structure that presumably gives rise to both the observable manifestations of the personality attribute and to the risk for physical disorders. Moreover, the disease promoting structure for which the assessment device provides a marker may operate through mechanisms that do not involve all observable manifestations of the personality attribute. For example, it may be that cynical, distrusting attitudes need not be expressed in hostile behavior in order to increase coronary risk; it may suffice for those attitudes to operate through more subtle behavioral expressions to undermine the person's ability to develop and to maintain a supportive social network (T. W. Smith, 1992). Similarly, an underlying tendency toward hyperactivity of the sympathetic nervous system may be toxic to the coronary arteries regardless of whether it promotes the overt display of Type A behavior (Contrada, Krantz, & Hill, 1988). Although this problem is but a specific instance of the usual, third variable alternative to causal hypotheses, it is often overlooked in research concerning personality and health.

Context

Context refers to factors outside the skin that may influence behavior. Context is a multilevel concept. Revenson (1990) referred to four broad contextual dimensions: situational (immediate stimulus configuration), interpersonal (social relationships, group affiliations), sociocultural (socioeconomic status, reference group), and temporal (life stage). Of particular relevance to health problems are situational factors whose interaction with personality gives rise to stress and influences the coping process (Lazarus, 1966). These interactions must be viewed within the framework of interpersonal relationships from which stressful situations may emanate and to which the individual may turn for coping assistance (Thoits, 1986). The situational and interpersonal context is, in turn, shaped by larger sociocultural systems in which the origins of both stressors and coping resources frequently may be found and whose norms and conventions define the meaning of stress, coping, personality, illness, and health care (Kleinman, 1986). In the life of an individual, the foregoing elements of context are moderated by the temporal dimension within which development and maturation occur and shape personality, stress, coping, and physiological functioning.

As noted earlier, the relationship between context and behavior is not a one-way affair. Much has been written about processes whereby person and environment shape one another (Bandura, 1978; D. M. Buss, 1987; Lazarus & Folkman, 1984; Plomin, Lichenstein, Pedersen, McClearn, & Nesselroade, 1990; Scarr & McCartney, 1983). Theory concerning bidirectional pathways of influence between person and environment has far outrun its application in the study of personality and health. Much of the epidemiologic literature on psychosocial risk factors for physical disorders involves studies in which either person or environmental factors, but not both, have been examined in relation to disease outcomes. Thus, for example, even the relatively simple and familiar notion that Type A individuals show pathogenic physiological responses when confronted by "appropriately challenging and/or stressful situations" has not been given rigorous test in prospective epidemiological studies, which would require measurement of Type A behavior, environmental stressors, and coronary disease (Glass, 1977). It is not surprising, therefore, that there has been little empirical work addressing more difficult questions concerning the health consequences of personality that may involve bidirectional influences between person and context.

Process

The notions of individual differences, patterning, organization, and structure imply numerous psychological *processes*. Broad questions of general interest to the larger field of personality concern personality development, expression, and change. Of special relevance to the personality–stress interface are those processes whereby psychological structures become activated, influence construal of the social and physical environment, and regulate the individual's response to those construals (Mischel & Shoda, 1995). We will return to this in a later section of this chapter when the stress construct is discussed.

Possible Personality Risk factors

Many personality attributes have been implicated as possible contributors to physical disease. Table 4.1 describes a number of personality characteristics that have been investigated in research involving measures of health or markers for potentially health-related processes. The list is meant to be illustrative rather than exhaustive. For some of the entries, there is a suggestive empirical basis for a physical health linkage in the form of associations with measures of disease endpoints, but much of the work is cross-sectional. As a consequence, although this research may be useful in generating hypotheses regarding possible risk factors, it does not permit evaluation of those hypotheses (Matthews, 1988). Moreover, in many studies, whether cross-sectional or prospective, other methodological problems may be operating, such as selection biases (Suls, Wan, & Costa, 1995), or reliance on "soft" disease measures that are susceptible to confounding (Watson & Pennebaker, 1989), thereby undermining conclusions regarding personality–disease associations.

In many cases, the association between personality and disease is conceptual, rather than empirical, in that it is suggested by research or theory implying an association between the personality attribute and physiological responses to psychological stress. This sort of hypothetical relationship to disease is strongest where the stress response measure itself has been linked to disease-promoting processes. For example, Type A behaviors are reliably associated with physiological responses to stress that are related theoretically to atherogenic processes (Krantz & Manuck, 1984; Schneiderman, 1983), and have been associated empirically with coronary atherosclerosis in animals (Manuck, Kaplan, & Clarkson, 1983) and with recurrent myocardial infarction and stroke in humans (Manuck, Olsson, Hjemdalh, & Rehnqvist, 1992). A case for health relevance is obviously weaker if based on an association between the suspected personality factor and stress mea-

TABLE 4.1

Illustrative Selection of Personality Variables That Have Been Linked to Disease Through Associations With Stress Responses, Health-Damaging Behaviors, and/or Reactions to Illness

Person variable	Definition	Stress	Health behavior	Reaction to illness
Alexithymia (Henry et al., 1992)	Inability to understand or describe one's emotional state	✓	✓	
Anger control (Czajkowski et al., 1990	Resistance to becoming angry and/or controlling the experience of anger	✓		
Anger in (Czajkowski et al., 1990)	The experience of angry feelings without their expression	✓		
Anger out (Czajkowski et al., 1990)	Engaging in aggressive behaviors motivated by angry feelings	✓		
Antagonistic interpersonal style (Suarez & R. B. Williams, 1990)	Tendency to be disagreeable and to express anger towards others			
Attachment style (Feeney & Ryan, 1994)	Quality of the mental representation of the relationship of self to an attachment figure	✓		
Avoidance coping (Dunkel-Schetter et al., 1992)	Diversion of attention from the source and/or effects of stress	✓	✓	
Conflict, ambivalence of emotional expression (King & Emmons, 1990)	Discrepancy between one's style of emotional expression and emotional behavior encouraged by relevant social norms or goals	✓		
Conscientiousness, social dependability (Friedman et al., 1993)	Disposition characterized by prudence, forethought, conscientiousness, truthfulness, and freedom from vanity and egotism	✓	✓	
Defensive anger (S. B. Miller, 1993)	Conscious and/or unconscious disavowal of the experience and/or expression of anger	✓		
Defensive hostility (Helmers et al., 1995)	Hostility accompanied by a disinclination to report socially undesirable aspects of oneself	✓		
Defensiveness (Esterling et al., 1993)	Conscious and/or unconscious disinclination to report socially undesirable aspects of oneself	✓		
Denial (Esteve et al., 1992)	Conscious disavowal of reality	✓	✓	
Depression (Weisse, 1992)	Dysphoric mood characterized by intense sadness, helplessness, worthlessness, loneliness, and guilt	✓	✓	✓
Emotion focused coping (DeGenova et al., 1994)	Efforts to regulate emotional experience	✓	✓	✓
Emotional suppression (Gross & Levenson, 1993)	Conscious inhibition of emotional expressive behavior	✓		
Energy and activity (Keltikangas-Jarvinen & Raikkonen, 1993)	Tendency to engage in physical activity	✓	✓	✓
Extroversion (Siegler et al., 1995)	Syndrome characterized by sociability, emotional expressiveness, and novelty seeking	✓		
Femininity (vs. Masculinity) (Helgeson, 1991)	Exhibition of characteristics associated with the female (vs. male) gender role	✓	✓	✓
Goal representations, motivational correlates (Karoly & Lecci, 1993)	Mental representation of personally meaningful aspirations	✓	✓	✓

continued on next page

Person variable	Definition	Stress	Health behavior	Reaction to illness
Hardiness (Wiebe, 1991)	Syndrome Consisting of Challenge (vs. Threat), Internal (vs. External) Locus of Control, and Commitment (vs. Alienation)	✓		✓
Harm avoidance (Freedland et al., 1991)	Awareness and avoidance of aversive stimuli	✓	✓	
Helplessness (T. W. Smith et al., 1990)	Belief that one cannot alter the occurrence of expected, highly aversive outcomes	✓		✓
Hostility (T. W. Smith, 1992)	Cynical attitudes that increase proneness to anger	✓	✓	✓
Hysteria (MMPI) (Gatchel et al., 1995)	Syndrome characterized by naivety, self-centeredness, and a general malaise regarding medical conditions		✓	
John Henryism (James, 1994)	Persistent use of problem-focused coping and emotional stoicism despite environmental conditions of extreme and chronic stress	✓		
Locus of control (Schneider et al., 1991)	Generalized beliefs as to whether outcomes are internally or externally controlled	✓	✓	
Mania (MMPI) (Lipkus et al., 1994)	Syndrome characterized by impulsivity, sensation seeking, and sociability		✓	
Monitoring (vs. Blunting) (Schwartz et al., 1995)	Scanning for (vs. Avoiding) threat-relevant information	✓	✓	
Negative affectivity (Brief et al., 1993)	Tendency to experience unpleasant emotional states	✓		
Neuroticism (Siegler & Costa, 1994)	Tendency to experience emotional lability and anxiety		✓	
Novelty seeking (Freedland et al., 1991)	Responding with excitement to novel stimuli and reinforcement cues		✓	
Optimism (Carver et al., 1993)	Generalized expectation for positive outcomes	✓		
Other deception (Newton & Contrada, 1992)	Deliberate deception of others for purposes of impression management or goal achievement	✓		
Pessimistic explanatory style (Kamen-Siegel et al., 1991)	Belief that negative events are caused by internal, stable, and global factors, and that positive events are caused by external, unstable, and specific factors	✓	✓	✓
Positive emotionality (Depue et al., 1994)	Emotional experience that is activated by, and motivates one to approach rewarding stimuli	✓		
Problem focused coping (DeGenova et al., 1994)	Efforts to address the source of stress	✓	✓	✓
Psychopathic deviance (MMPI) (Lipkus et al., 1994)	Syndrome characterized by rebelliousness, impulsivity, and nonconformity			
Realistic acceptance (Reed et al., 1994)	Resignation to the prospect of death, associated with a tired, peaceful, but not necessarily pleasant affective state			✓
Repressed hostility (Helmers et al., 1995)	Unconscious denial of one's own hostility	✓		
Repression (Wallbott & Scherer, 1991)	Unconscious process serving to decrease awareness of distressing thoughts	✓		
Resiliency (vs. Vulnerability) (R. E. Smith et al., 1990)	Exhibition of well-being (vs. distress) following exposure to stressors	✓		✓
Reward dependence (Freedland et al., 1991)	Increased awareness of reward cues, and persistence in behaviors associated with reward		✓	

Person variable	Definition	Stress	Health behavior	Reaction to illness
Risk-taking, sensation-seeking (M. R. Levenson, 1990)	Purposive activity entailing novelty or danger sufficient to create anxiety in most people		✓	
Self-deception (Linden et al., 1993)	Unconscious process serving to protect self-esteem	✓		
Self-discrepancy (Strauman et al., 1991)	Perceived discrepancy between the actual self and a standard for self-evaluation	✓		
Self-efficacy (Wiedenfeld et al., 1990)	Perceived ability to cope successfully with a stressor	✓	✓	✓
Shyness (Bell et al., 1990)	Behavioral inhibition when with others in unfamiliar situations, subjectively experienced as unpleasant	✓		
Social introversion (MMPI) (Lipkus et al., 1994)	Syndrome characterized by the lack of a preference to engage in social interaction	✓		
Somatization (Miranda et al., 1991)	Tendency to attribute stress-produced bodily symptoms to physical causes and, consequently, to seek unneeded medical services		✓	
Trait anger (Suls et al., 1995)	Tendency to experience anger			
Trait anxiety (Kohn et al., 1991)	Tendency to experience unwarranted apprehension	✓	✓	
Trait humor (Rotton, 1992)	Coping mechanism moderating the relationship between stressful events and well-being	✓		
Type A Behavior Pattern (Dimsdale, 1993)	Competitive achievement-striving, hostility, time-urgency, and vigorous speech and motor mannerisms	✓	✓	✓
Unrealistic optimism (Taylor & Brown, 1994)	Unwarranted expectation of positive outcomes and/or exaggerated feelings of invulnerability		✓	

sures for which there is neither theory nor evidence to suggest a relationship to disease promoting processes.

A conceptual basis for a personality–disease linkage can also be inferred from research demonstrating an association between personality and certain behaviors. The latter may involve behavioral risk factors for disease, such as cigarette smoking or unsafe sex, or behavioral reactions to disease, such as treatment delay or noncompliance with medical regimens. As in the case of physiologic responses to stress, measures of health-related behaviors vary in the strength of their association with disease and, whatever the strength of that relationship, behaviors cannot be taken as proxies for the presence of physical disorders. At best, the existence of linkages to health damaging behaviors, like cross-sectional associations with disease, can only suggest hypotheses regarding the possible risk factor status of personality attributes.

Promising Personality Risk Factors

As noted earlier, epidemiological principles require that a set of relatively stringent criteria be satisfied before a variable may be elevated to risk factor status (Siegel, 1984). Among these are: (a) prospective research designs, which avoid many of the interpretive problems associated with cross-sectional research; (b) objective disease indicators, which reduce the effects of reporting biases and other confounding factors; (c) evidence of a consistent association, that is, replication of the personality–disease relation across diverse study populations and measures; (d) evidence of a strong association, such that the magnitude of the relationship is of practical significance; (e) biological plausibility, or the existence of theory and evidence of pathogenic mechanisms that can explain the personality–disease association. Application of these criteria severely shortens the list of contending personality attributes.

The following sections discuss three sets of personality dispositions: anger/hostility, emotional suppression/repression, and disengagement. Although they are not considered well-established risk factors, each appears promising as a potential risk factor for physical disease (Contrada, H. Leventhal, & O'Leary, 1990; Scheier & Bridges, 1995). Anger-related characteristics have for quite some time been subject to attention as possible contributors to somatic disorders (for a review, see Siegman, 1994), as has the suppression or repression of anger and of other negative emotions (e.g., Alexander, 1930). The term *disengagement* was recently suggested by Scheier and Bridges (1995) to refer collectively to helplessness/hopelessness, pessimism, fatalism, and depression, each of which has been linked to negative health outcomes.

Anger/Hostility

Anger, hostility, and aggressiveness are salient features of personality attributes that show promise as possible risk factors for physical disease. These three terms can be used to refer, respectively, to affective, cognitive, and behavioral constructs, and each may be conceived as either a state or trait (Spielberger et al., 1985). Factor analyses of relevant trait measures have generated findings consistent with this tripartite approach. Several studies have identified anger experience and anger expression factors (also referred to as neurotic and antagonistic hostility), which to some extent correspond to affective and behavioral dimensions (Musante, MacDougall, Dembroski, & Costa, 1989; Suarez & R. B. Williams, 1990). A third factor, found in at least one study, was labeled suspicion-guilt (Musante et al., 1989), and appears to be a cognitive-attitudinal dimension.

However, data calling into question the psychometric structure of some of the more frequently used scales for measuring anger-related attributes (e.g., Contrada & Jussim, 1992; Spielberger et al., 1985) pose problems for the three-factor structure of total scale scores. Moreover, an item-level factor analysis conducted by A. H. Buss and Perry (1992) generated evidence of four distinguishable anger-related attributes, and a recent, population-based study yielded evidence of eight separate dimensions (T. Q. Miller, Jenkins, Kaplan, & Salonen, 1995). Given the need for further clarification of these issues, the terms *anger/hostility* or *anger-related* are used here to refer collectively to the full set of characteristics in this domain, recognizing that the number and nature of its distinct elements remain to be determined.

The idea that anger-related attributes may contribute to physical disease has a long prescientific history (Siegman, 1994). Scientific interest in this hypothesis accelerated rapidly following the emergence of evidence suggesting that anger and hostility may reflect the "toxic" elements of the Type A, coronary-prone behavior pattern (Matthews, Glass, Rosenman, & Bortner, 1977). Currently available evidence provides fairly consistent support for this notion, pointing to a possible prospective association between anger/hostility and coronary heart disease (CHD; e.g., Barefoot, Dahlstrom, & R. B. Williams, 1983; Barefoot, Dodge, Peterson, Dahlstrom, & R. Williams, 1989; see reviews by Helmers, Posluszny, & Krantz, 1994; Scheier & Bridges, 1995; T. W. Smith, 1992).

In addition to studies of coronary disease, there is research suggesting that anger-related personality traits may contribute to traditional coronary risk factors. For example, Siegler (1994) reviewed evidence indicating possible associations between trait hostility and cigarette smoking, serum lipid levels, and obesity. In addition, Suls et al. (1995) reported a meta-analysis that provides some support for a relationship between trait anger and essential hypertension. However, inconsistencies across studies, and methodological problems in studies reporting positive findings, argue against drawing firm conclusions at the present time regarding the association between anger/hostility and coronary risk factors. It would seem that, for the most part, relationships between hostility and coronary disease are mediated by mechanisms not reflected in measures of traditional risk factors, such as may be associated with physiologic responses to stress.

Support for an association between anger/hostility and health outcomes other than coronary disease is limited (Scheier & Bridges, 1995). However, there is evidence to suggest a significant relationship between hostility and non-CHD mortality (Almada et al., 1991; Shekelle, Gale, Ostfeld, & Paul, 1983). In addition, other prospective studies suggest an association between hostility and cancer mortality (Carmelli et al., 1991), general health (Adams, 1994; Cartwright, Wink, & Kmetz, 1995), and suicide, attempted suicide, and nontraffic accidents and deaths (Romanov et al., 1994). Cross-sectional studies have reported associations between hostility and such non-CHD health outcomes such as asthma severity (Silverglade, Tosi, Wise, & D'Costa, 1994) and disorders of endocrine function (Fava, 1994). Although these findings suggest that anger/hostility may contribute to several sources of morbidity and mortality, the data on coronary disease appear more consistent and robust than those for other outcomes (Scheier & Bridges, 1995).

Emotional Suppression/Repression

To an even greater degree than is the case for anger/hostility, "emotional suppression/ repression" is a collection of seemingly conceptually related attributes whose number and nature have yet to be determined. Among the various distinctions that have been made within this domain are several that concern the emotion portion of the construct, for example, whether it is negative emotion in general, or anxiety or anger in particular, that is involved. Other distinctions concern that portion of the construct that has to do with the individual's coping response to or orientation toward negative emotion. For example, the term *repression* has sometimes been used in the technical, psychoanalytic sense to refer to an ego-defensive process whereby negative affect and associated thoughts are automatically removed from consciousness. By contrast, the term *suppression* has been used to refer to the deliberate, conscious, and effortful inhibition of negative affect and/or its expression. Other relevant constructs include denial (Lazarus, 1983), alexithymia (G. J. Taylor, 1984), conflict over emotional expression (King & Emmons, 1990), and inhibited power motivation (Jemmott, 1987). Although these attributes are in many cases conceptually distinct, and do not always show expected interrelationships (e.g., Newton & Contrada, 1994), the designation "emotional suppression/repression" is used as a general rubric in the discussion that follows except where greater specificity is required.

The notion that emotional suppression/repression may promote physical disease is contained in very early writings (see Siegman, 1994, for an overview). This idea overlaps with interest in anger/hostility in the form of the psychosomatic hypothesis linking anger suppression to essential hypertension (Alexander, 1930). A recent evaluation provided a degree of support for this hypothesis. In the Suls et al. (1995) meta-analysis cited earlier, the strongest evidence for an association between anger and resting blood pressure came from studies examining anger-related traits that involve not only a tendency to experience anger, but also a reluctance to express such feelings. There is also evidence from the Framingham Heart study indicating that the tendency to suppress anger may operate as a CHD risk factor for women, though not for men (Haynes, Feinleib, Kannel, 1980).

In addition to work in the cardiovascular area, emotional suppression/repression has been examined in relation to cancer. Indeed, low emotional expressiveness is a key feature of a "Type C" behavior pattern that has been suggested as a possible cancer risk factor (Temoshok, 1987). Support for this notion has been obtained in quasi-prospective studies indicating less frequent expression of anger in breast biopsy patients later found to have malignancies (Greer & Morris, 1975; Jansen & Muenz, 1984). However, negative results also have been obtained in this area (e.g., Greer, Morris, & Pettingale, 1979), and there is some evidence linking increased expression of emotion to breast cancer (Greer & Morris, 1975). Other findings indicate a possible prospective association between emotional inexpressiveness and cancer incidence (e.g., Grossarth-Maticek, Kanazir, Schmidt, & Vetter, 1982), but methodological considerations argue that this conclusion should be viewed guardedly, at best (Fox, 1978; Scheier & Bridges, 1995).

Disengagement

As noted earlier, Scheier and Bridges (1995) suggested that the term *disengagement* be used to refer collectively to a set of conceptually related attributes that include helplessness/hopelessness, pessimism, fatalism, and depression. Not all of these constructs are personality dispositions in the strict sense. Depending on how they are operationalized, they may show only modest levels of temporal stability, and often are measured in relation to specific situations. However, such context-specific person factors may reflect personality and, in any case, need to be taken into consideration to provide a more comprehensive theoretical account of psychosocial influences on physical disease.

One attribute that falls into this category is the pessimistic explanatory style, a tendency to attribute negative life events to internal, stable, and global causes. This construct was developed as a means of accounting for individual differences in the severity, generality, and duration of human responses to uncontrollable stressors (Peterson & Seligman, 1984). Pessimistic explanatory style has been linked to illness as reflected in self-report measures of health (Peterson, 1988), physician health ratings (Peterson, Seligman, & Vaillant, 1988), and shorter survival time in patients with coronary disease (Buchanan, 1995) and breast cancer (Levy, Morrow, Bagley, & Lippman, 1988).

Fatalism, like pessimism, involves negative expectations about future outcomes (Scheier & Bridges, 1995). These constructs bear a resemblance to helplessness/hopelessness, a passive orientation toward psychological stress that has been linked to poor cancer prognosis (Greer et al., 1979; Greer & Haybittle, 1990; Pettingale, Morris, & Greer, 1985). Scheier and Bridges (1995) suggested that "fatalism" may be a better label for a "realistic acceptance" construct that was implicated as a factor producing shorter survival time among individuals with AIDS in a study reported by Reed, Kemeny, Taylor, Wang, and Visscher (1994). There is also evidence of an association between pessimism/fatalism and enhanced risk of complications from coronary artery bypass graft surgery (CABG; Scheier et al., 1989).

The term *depression* has been used to refer to depressive symptomatology, that is, self-reports of low self-satisfaction, psychological distress, vegetative symptoms, and somatic complaints, which should be distinguished from a formally diagnosed clinical disorder (Coyne, 1994). There is evidence linking depression to cardiovascular events such as myocardial infarction (MI), CABG, and stroke (Carney, Freedland, & Lustman, 1994; Wassertheil-Smoller et al., 1994), and depression may operate as an independent risk factor for death following an MI (Frasure-Smith, Lesperance, & Talajic, 1993; Ladwig, Kieser, & Konig, 1991). Research examining depression in relation to the progression of AIDS has yielded mixed findings, however, and studies attempting to demonstrate a relationship between depression and cancer have yielded predominantly negative results (Scheier & Bridges, 1995).

WHY DO CERTAIN INDIVIDUALS GET SICK?: PERSONALITY AND STRESS

Research reviewed in the previous section provides promising clues concerning the personality attributes of individuals who may be expected to become sick. Those attributes—tendencies toward anger/hostility, emotional suppression/repression, and disengagement—provide a tentative and partial answer to what is essentially an empirical question: "Who gets sick?" The question, "Why do individuals with certain personality attributes get sick?" addresses the issue of causal process. This chapter is concerned with health damaging processes associated with psychological stress.

Health-related processes most closely associated with stress involve pathogenic changes that are produced as a result of direct, *psychophysiological* responses to environmental events or conditions. Research conducted in the past few decades has shed considerable light on the psychophysiology of stress. Building on Cannon's (1925) seminal research on the sympathetic-adrenomedullary system, and that of Selye (1956) on the pituitary-adrenocortical system, there now exist fairly detailed models describing the effects of stress on neuroendocrine, cardiovascular, immunological, and other biological systems. There has also been substantial progress in the identification of pathways whereby these physiological effects may influence mechanisms involved in the etiology and pathogenesis of physical disorders (e.g., Herbert & Cohen, 1993; Krantz & Manuck, 1984). To the degree that personality influences the frequency, intensity, and/or duration of stress, the psychophysiological correlates of stress constitute a plausible mediator of the effects of personality on health.

It was noted earlier that, in addition to direct, psychophysiological influences on disease mechanisms, personality may promote disease through its effects on health behaviors, and on reactions to illness. Health behaviors are those actions and inactions that affect the likelihood of injury or disease and include factors such as physical risk taking, diet, exercise, substance use, and the practice of unprotected sex. Reactions to illness are actions and inactions that occur in response to injury and sickness, and include factors such as the detection and interpretation of physical symptoms, the decision to seek medical treatment, adherence to medical regimens, responses to invasive medical procedures, recovery from acute illness, and adjustment to chronic disease. Whether psychological stress provides an explanation for observed associations between personality and either health behaviors or reactions to illness is often an open question in a given piece of research. However, health behaviors such as cigarette smoking and alcohol use have been conceptualized in terms of coping processes (e.g., Abrams & Niaura, 1987), as have the processes involved in monitoring the signs and symptoms of disease and managing illness (Contrada, E. Leventhal, & Anderson, 1994; Miller, Shoda, & Hurley, 1996). In addition, both health behaviors and reactions to illness often must be considered as alternative explanations for personality disease linkages that appear to involve the direct physiological effects of psychological stress (Watson & Pennebaker, 1989). Thus, for both theoretical and methodological reasons, findings that bear on the behavioral pathways to illness are highly germane to the present discussion.

This section begins by describing the major constructs involved in psychological stress theory. This sets the stage for an analysis of the pathways whereby personality may promote stress and its health damaging effects. The section concludes with a discussion of some of the evidence linking anger/hostility, emotional suppression/repression, and disengagement to measures that may reflect health damaging processes associated with psychological stress.

Conceptual Elements of Psychological Stress and Coping

As in the case of personality, conceptual issues surrounding the stress construct have been subject to considerable discussion and debate (Lazarus, 1966; Lazarus & Folkman, 1984; Mason, 1975; Selye, 1975). Concerns about the scientific status of the stress concept have led to suggestions that the term *stress* be abandoned or limited to a nontechnical usage to refer to a general topic or area of study. Nonetheless, scientific interest in stress has endured, and the concept obviously serves a useful purpose, albeit often at a rather general level of analysis. The following discussion focuses on major conceptual categories rather than attempting to present a detailed review of issues and controversies.

Stressors

Stressors are events or conditions that are demanding, challenging, or constraining in some way. Among types of stressors that have received intensive study are calamitous events such as natural and technological disasters (e.g., Baum, Cohen, & Hall, 1993); major life changes such as marriage, divorce, and bereavement (Holmes & Rahe, 1967); minor events such as the daily "hassles" of living (Kanner, Coyne, Schaefer, & Lazarus, 1981); and chronic conditions such as occupational stress (Karasek, Baker, Marxer, Ahlbom, & Theorell, 1981), crowding (Baum & Valins, 1977), and marital conflict (Kiecolt-Glaser et al., 1987). The designation of events and conditions as stressors is probabilistic in the sense that their occurrence may or may not precipitate a stress response. Whether or not this occurs is thought to reflect the operation of psychological processes discussed next.

Appraisal

The concept of *cognitive appraisal* has been discussed at length by Lazarus (1966; Lazarus & Folkman, 1984). It refers to an automatic, cognitive-evaluative process whereby events and conditions are judged with respect to their relevance to physical and psychological well-being. Primary appraisal involves an evaluation of harm or loss that has already been sustained or is threatened. Secondary appraisal involves an evaluation of available strategies and resources for managing the problem and its effects on the person. Stressful appraisals include harm/loss (damage has already been sustained), threat (damage appears likely), and challenge (threat accompanied by the possibility of growth or gain). They arise when individuals perceive that circumstances tax or exceed their adaptive resources (Lazarus & Folkman, 1984).

Problem Representation

Leventhal and associates (e.g., H. Leventhal, Meyer, & Nerenz, 1980) used the term *problem representation* to describe the initiating psychological event in the stress process. Closely related to the notion of cognitive appraisal, problem representation refers to the creation of a mental structure that characterizes the stressor in terms of specific attributes. For example, a physical symptom constitutes a health threat depending on how it is construed by the person. Relevant attributes include its label (e.g., cancer), causes (e.g., smoking), consequences (e.g., death), and time line (e.g., slowly worsening), and form part of a conceptual problem space that defines the health threat. Other features of the problem space include propositions representing specific actions that may cure the disorder or minimize potential damage, such as health care seeking or self-medication. This sort of feature analysis presumably accompanies and follows the appraisal process (Lazarus, 1966). Thus, the concept of problem representation may be used to refer broadly to the set of psychological processes whereby the individual encodes a stressor by developing a cognitive-affective structure. That structure includes features corresponding to attributes of the stressor and of possible coping strategies, and is associated with an appraisal of the significance of the stressor for physical and/or psychological well-being.

Details of appraisal and problem representation have at least two major consequences for subsequent phases of the stress process: They influence the quality and intensity of the ensuing emotional response, and guide the selection of procedures for coping with the stressor (Lazarus, 1991). For example, depending on specific features of perceived threat, harm, or loss, the individual may experience anger, fright, or sadness. In addition, it is the stressor as perceived by the individual, and the emotional reaction that arises from that perception, that influence the subsequent selection of coping procedures aimed at managing the situation. Because emotional and behavioral responses to stressors are accompanied by potentially pathogenic physiological changes, can involve disease promoting behaviors, and may affect the interpretation and response to physical symptoms and illness, it follows that the processes of cognitive appraisal and problem representation that mediate those responses are critically involved in the putative health damaging effects of stress.

Response Generation: Coping and Automatic Self-Regulation

Coping refers to effortful cognitive and behavioral activity that is aimed at managing either the stressor or its effects on the person (Lazarus & Folkman, 1984). Numerous coping strategies have been identified in stress research, and a broad distinction has been drawn between two forms of coping that have come to be referred to as *problem focused* and *emotion focused* (Lazarus, 1966; Mechanic, 1962). Problem-focused coping involves strategies aimed at altering the situation that gave rise to the stress appraisal, such as planning, information-seeking, and efforts at mastery. Emotion-focused coping involves strategies aimed at managing subjective responses to stressors, such as suppression of negative affect, distraction, and minimization. Alternative coping classifications also have been suggested in which additional, major classes of coping activity are distinguished from problem- and emotion-focused coping, such as avoidance strategies (Dunkel-Schetter, Feinstein, Taylor, & Falke, 1992) and relationship-focused coping (Coyne & Downey, 1991).

Not all cognitive and behavioral responses to stressors reflect coping. Lazarus and Folkman (1984) used the term coping to refer to activity that is conscious, deliberate, and effortful. Exposure to stress may elicit other, more automatic responses that, like coping, may play a role in determining how the stressful encounter is resolved. Examples of such automatic responses include motor patterns involved in the expression of emotion though facial movements (Tomkins, 1962) or vocal tone (Scherer, 1986), processes involved in the inhibition of communication between brain centers involved in emotion and language (Davidson, 1984), and ego-defense mechanisms such as repression (Haan, 1977). Rather than a categorical distinction, the difference between coping, and what might be referred to as more *automatic self-regulation,* may be conceptualized in terms of a continuum involving differences in the degree to which the activity is mediated by verbal-propositional cognition as opposed to schematic cognitive processing, or, at a more rudimentary level, reflex circuits.

The Stress Response

Stress may be manifested in many ways. Coping and the more automatic self-regulatory responses already discussed represent one set of stress manifestations. However, the term *stress response* is usually used to refer to indicators that reflect the negative impact or adaptive cost of stressful transactions. These responses may be characterized as falling within several broad domains, namely, subjective experience, cognitive functioning, emotional expression, physiological activity, and instrumental behavior (Baum, Grunberg, & Singer, 1982).

The stress response also may be viewed at a social level of analysis. Psychological stress can cause strain and conflict in interpersonal relationships, undermine group cohesion, and disrupt the functioning of organizations and institutions. Transactional approaches to stress point to the potential importance of the interplay between individual and social level stress processes. An individual may employ coping strategies whose effects on the social and physical environment have implications for future stress. Coping activity may eliminate, moderate, create, maintain, or exacerbate social level stressors (T. W. Smith, 1989), or it may enhance or diminish the social resources available to support subsequent coping efforts (Hobfoll, 1989).

The Personality–Stress Interface

The diagram in Fig. 4.1 depicts a framework that integrates the key conceptual elements implied by the personality and stress constructs. This chapter is concerned with the four major pathways whereby personality structure may influence the stress process. The reader is referred elsewhere for discussion of other aspects of the model (Contrada, 1994; Contrada et al., 1990) and of self-regulation principles on which the model is based (e.g., Carver & Scheier, 1981).

Stressor Exposure

There are several processes whereby personality may influence exposure to stressors. Three general mechanisms through which individuals determine the amount of contact they have with particular types of environmental settings were referred to by D. M. Buss (1987) as selection, evocation, and manipulation. Selection involves choosing whether or not to enter particular environments. By contrast, evocation and manipulation refer to the person's impact on the environment once it has been entered. In the case of evocation, attributes of the person elicit or provoke responses from the physical or social environment unintentionally, whereas manipulation entails intentional efforts to alter, create, or otherwise modify the environment. A fourth way a person can influence exposure to stressors is to prolong or shorten the length of stay in demanding situations.

Several personality attributes may promote disease, at least in part, by increasing exposure to stressful situations. There is evidence, for example, that Type A individuals hold demanding achievement-related goals for themselves, which may encourage them to take on difficult tasks (Matthews, 1982; Snow, 1978). Type As also prolong exposure to uncontrollable stressors they cannot master rather than relinquishing control to more competent others (S. M. Miller, Lack, & Asroff, 1985). Depressives elicit negative reactions from others (Coyne, 1976), and a similar process may work to increase the amount of interpersonal stress experienced by hostile individuals (T. W. Smith, 1989). There is also evidence that neuroticism increases exposure to life stressors (Bolger & Schilling, 1991; Bolger & Zuckerman, 1995). Beyond exerting an influence on the amount of stress a person experiences, the regulation of environmental exposures may reinforce and sustain the underlying personality structure, and reduce the availability of coping resources such as social support (T. W. Smith, 1989), thereby transforming both the person and the environment in a health damaging way.

Appraisal and Problem Representation

The notion that personality shapes the perception of potentially stressful situations is an important component of the theory surrounding most personality attributes suspected of influencing susceptibility to disease. Given exposure to a particular environmental demand or constraint, psychological structures associated with health protecting personality characteristics presumably operate so as to decrease the probability of a stress appraisal and, under the same conditions, health damaging attributes would be expected to increase the probability of a stress appraisal. Effects on stressor appraisal may account for a significant portion of the influence of personality on individual differences in the stress response.

Certain health-related personality traits are explicitly conceptualized in terms that point to linkages to appraisal and problem representation. For example, one component of hardiness (Kobasa, 1979) is a tendency to perceive life change as a challenge rather than a threat. Another component, internal locus of control, involves the belief that factors influencing the outcomes an individual experiences reside within the person, and are therefore at least potentially controllable. Thus, these dispositions show close conceptual relations to the appraisal process. Similarly, it is reasonable to posit an association between the generalized expectation for positive outcomes that characterizes optimistic individuals and a tendency to form stress dampening appraisals of demanding situations (Scheier & Carver, 1985). With respect to health damaging attributes, the pessimistic attribution style is likely to promote negative appraisals of life events (Peterson, 1988), and the cynical beliefs of hostile individuals are plausibly associated with stress inducing appraisals in the interpersonal domain (T. W. Smith, 1992).

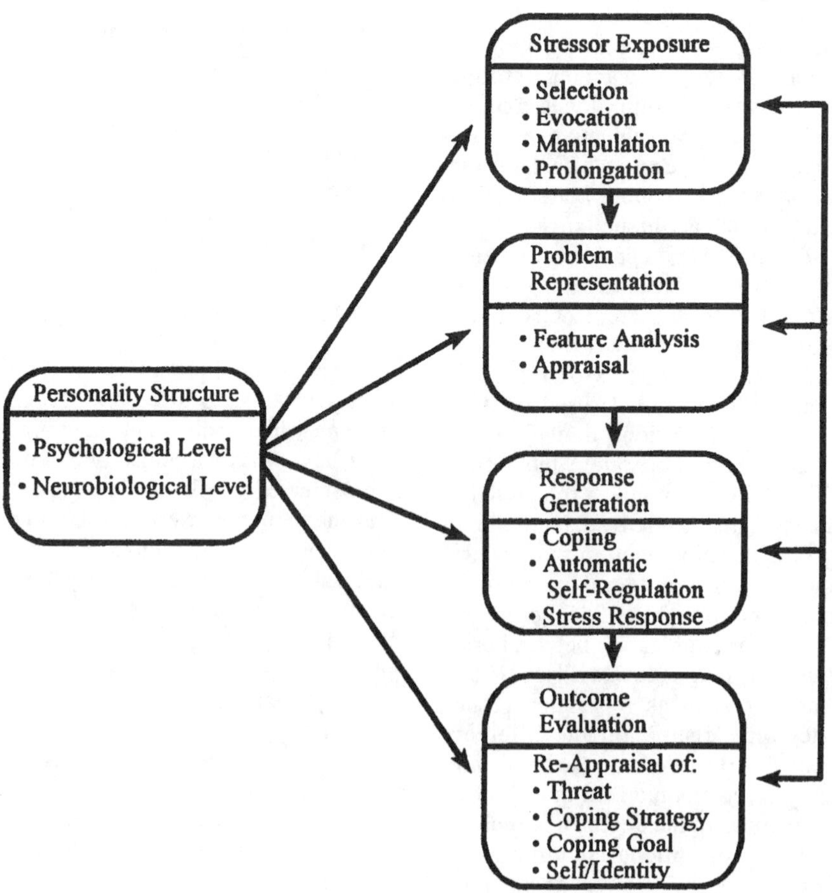

FIG. 4.1. Personality structures may influence each of four main elements of the stress process.

For other health-related attributes, associations with factors involved in the generation of emotional responses are less obvious. For example, the Type A behavior pattern was originally defined in terms of overt behavior, with little explicit reference to the appraisal process. However, subsequent analyses have suggested cognitive elements likely to influence the perception of stressors (e.g., Watkins, Fisher, Southard, Ward, & Schechtman, 1989). For certain emotion-related personality characteristics, such as the repressive coping style, it has been suggested that negative emotional reactions are themselves a source of threat in stressful circumstances (Newton & Contrada, 1992). In other words, after an environmental challenge or demand initiates a stress response, the repressive individual becomes anxious or upset, and this emotional reaction generates an additional threat appraisal because it conflicts with a desire to maintain emotional self-control.

Response Generation

Several health-related personality attributes have been explicitly conceptualized as coping styles, that is, characteristic tendencies to employ certain coping strategies in response to certain types of stressors. For example, according to Glass' (1977) uncontrollability model, the Type A, coronary-prone behavior pattern reflects vigorous efforts to master potentially uncontrollable stressors. Similarly, John Henryism, a possible risk factor for hypertension, has been defined as a tendency to cope actively with psychological stressors (James, 1994). At the level of definition, Type A behavior and John Henryism involve problem-focused coping styles, although both also appear to entail elements of stoicism that may influence emotion-focused coping. By contrast, other potentially health-related personality attributes are explicitly identified with emotion-focused coping, such as the cancer prone, Type C behavior pattern (Temoshok, 1987), anger-in (Spielberger et al., 1985), and repressive coping (Weinberger et al., 1979). Note that despite use of the term *coping* in the designations of several of these personality dispositions, it is in most cases an open question as to whether they involve coping in the sense of conscious, effortful, and deliberate activity, as opposed to more automatic responses to stressors.

Other health-related personality attributes are not defined as coping styles, but have been linked to coping styles. For example, as a belief structure, optimism cannot be equated with coping, but it has been shown to correlate with the use of particular coping strategies (e.g., Scheier et al., 1989). Similarly, trait hostility, which is also thought to involve a cognitive-affective structure, as distinct from being a coping style per se, has been associated with an antagonistic style of coping with interpersonal stressors (T. W. Smith, 1992).

Outcome Evaluation

Because outcome evaluation is a critical component of self-regulation (Carver & Scheier, 1981), it likely to be useful for understanding the effects of health-related personality characteristics. As the person responds to a stressor and engages in coping activity, information becomes available that may provide a basis for modifying the problem representation. There may be changes in the perceived severity of the threat, the expected efficacy of the initial coping strategy, coping goals (e.g., managing the problem vs. managing subjective reactions), and self-perception. The relationship between personality and outcome evaluation has received less explicit attention than the exposure, appraisal, and coping pathways depicted in Fig. 4.1.

Outcome evaluation does play a role in several models of Type A behavior. For example, Matthews (1982) hypothesized that the excessive achievement striving of Type A individuals might reflect their efforts to satisfy very demanding and ambiguous evaluative standards. Scherwitz, Berton, and H. Leventhal (1978) also discussed the possibility that certain aspects of Type A behavior might reflect heightened attention to discrepancies between their accomplishments and achievement-related goals. In a somewhat different approach, Strube (1987) suggested that the behavior of Type A individuals may reflect not so much a desire to satisfy high evaluative standards, but a desire to generate diagnostic information that would clarify their performance levels vis-à-vis those standards.

Outcome evaluation has also been implicated in theoretical models involving personality attributes other than Type A behavior. Scheier and Carver (1985) discussed the role dispositional optimism may play in the feedback process whereby individuals evaluate their progress toward important goals, and have outlined the consequences of this process for the degree to which they remain actively engaged in the coping process. It is also possible that cynical attitudes associated with trait hostility increase stress by influencing the evaluation of coping outcomes in the interpersonal domain (Contrada, 1994; T. W. Smith, 1992). The hostile individual may cope with potential interpersonal conflict by scrutinizing the behavior of others in order to determine their intentions. The hostile person's cynical attitudes may subsequently bias the interpretation of those behaviors, leading to the false conclusion that vigilance has successfully uncovered hostile motives, when other, more benign motives may actually be operating. Cynical interpretations might also lead the hostile individual to express anger in the form of communication style or overt aggression, which may be reciprocated in kind, thereby providing further "confirmation" of initial inferences about hostile motives. Thus, positive evaluations of coping strategies that are premised on false assumptions regarding the motives of others may be an important element of processes whereby hostility increases interpersonal stress.

Promising Personality Risk Factors and Health Damaging Processes

Earlier it was noted that both epidemiologic and process-oriented research will be required to develop and strengthen the case for a causal connections between personality and health. This section discusses the three promising personality risk factors—namely, anger/hostility, emotional suppression/repression, and disengagement—in relation to markers for stress-related, disease promoting processes. In each instance, the personality disposition is discussed first in relation to stress-related, potentially pathogenic psychophysiological activity, and then in relation to health- and illness-related behavior.

Anger/Hostility

Physiological Responses to Stressors. Cardiovascular and hormonal concomitants of anger and aggression have been the subject of study for quite some time (e.g., Ax, 1953; Funkenstein, 1956). Early research in this area was thought to have significance for understanding the development of essential hypertension and coronary disease, but the empirical observations that resulted were not highly consistent and the work was characterized by a number of conceptual and methodological problems (for a review and critique, see Diamond, 1982). More recently, this literature has come to exhibit some degree of coherence and methodological rigor, as well as a grounding in epidemiological findings, largely as a consequence of research on Type A behavior.

At the time that early psychophysiologic studies of Type A were conducted, hostility was thought to be but one facet of a larger, coronary prone behavior pattern that also involved competitiveness, achievement striving, and time urgency. As a result, for many studies, it is not possible to determine whether anger-related or nonanger-related attributes were responsible for associations between global Type A assessments and physiologic responses to stressors. In other cases, it is unclear whether anger-instigation was the active ingredient in the stressors that were employed (for a detailed review of these studies, see Wright, Contrada, & Glass, 1985). More recent epidemiologic findings pointing to hostility as the most health damaging component of Type A behavior now make it clear that it would be of use to be able to distinguish the specific contribution of anger-related attributes and stressors in these earlier studies. Nonetheless, it is of interest to note that there does appear to be a reliable association between global Type A behavior and cardiovascular responses to laboratory stressors that may be related to processes involved in the etiology and pathogenesis of coronary disease (Lyness, 1993).

A more specific linkage between anger-related attributes and cardiovascular reactivity to stressors developed out of two research strategies employed in early Type A studies. One involved the use of experimental manipulations designed to isolate anger-instigation from other demands and challenges (Glass et al., 1980). The other involved the use of assessment tools, most notably component analysis of Type A structured interviews, which make it possible to differentiate psychophysiologic correlates of anger-related and nonanger-related personality attributes (Dembroski, MacDougall, Shields, Petitto, & Lushene, 1978). There subsequently emerged a convergence between findings generated by epidemiological and psychophysiological research: Anger-related attributes that appeared to account for enhanced coronary risk among Type A individuals (e.g., Williams et al., 1980) also appeared most strongly associated with cardiovascular and other physiologic responses to stressors, which could account for the epidemiologic findings (e.g., Houston, 1988).

Currently available findings continue to support the hypothesis that anger-related personality attributes are associated with heightened cardiovascular responses to laboratory stressors. Based on a meta-analysis, Suls and Wan (1993) concluded that an antagonistic interpersonal style appears related to enhanced systolic and diastolic blood pressure responses to stressors containing elements likely to provoke anger. There was also evidence, albeit less consistent, suggesting that cynical hostility is associated with heightened diastolic blood pressure responses to anger provocation. These findings accord with results of a programmatic series of studies involving an animal model of coronary disease. Cynomolgus monkeys that exhibit heightened cardiac responses to psychosocial stressors have been found to be more behaviorally aggressive than less reactive animals, and research involving pharmacological blockade suggests that cardiac activity may mediate the relationship between aggressiveness and coronary disease in these monkeys (Manuck, Marsland, Kaplan, & J. K. Williams, 1995).

Thus, a convergence of findings from epidemiological and psychophysiological research strongly suggests that anger-related attributes increase risk for coronary atherosclerosis through effects on stress-related physiological processes. There is also reason to suspect that anger-related personality attributes are related to stress-related reductions in immune competence, which may increase risk for noncardiovascular diseases. Kiecolt-Glaser et al. (1993) demonstrated that, relative to other married couples, married couples who were hostile or negative during a discussion of marital problems showed greater reductions on four measures of immune function. Other findings indicated that the same couples had diminished immunological control of the Epstein–Barr virus.

Behavioral Responses to Stressors. It was noted earlier that there are some suggestions of a linkage between trait hostility and CHD risk factors that either are behaviors or are partially behaviorally determined, such as cigarette smoking, serum lipid levels, and obesity (Siegler, 1994). Other health-related behaviors associated with trait hostility include low levels of physical activity, poor dental hygiene, poor sleep habits (Koskenvou et al., 1988; Leiker & Hailey, 1988), and greater alcohol use (Houston & Vavak, 1991; Koskenvou et al., 1988; Leiker & Hailey, 1988; Shekelle et al., 1983). As T. W. Smith (1992) pointed out, however, these findings are mainly descriptive in nature. Although they suggest that hostility may endanger health as a consequence of its behavioral correlates, they do not indicate whether these behaviors reflect coping efforts, are in some other way related to psychological stress, or come about entirely as a consequence of nonstress-related processes.

The situation is similar with respect to health-related behaviors that represent reactions to illness. Findings have been reported that suggest an association between trait hostility and noncompliance with chemotherapy among breast cancer patients (Ayres, Hoon, Franzoni, Matheny, & Contach, 1994), with use of medication among hypertensives (Lee et al., 1992), and with an exercise rehabilitation program among cardiac patients (Digenio, Padayachee, & Groeneveld, 1992). Hostility also has been linked to slower recovery from physical trauma (K. E. Glancy et al., 1992) and a greater likelihood of experiencing cardiac symptoms among patients recovering from cardiac surgery (Jenkins, Stanton, & Jono, 1994). Further research is needed to determine whether these findings are best conceptualized as reflecting responses to stressors associated with being sick and undergoing treatment, involve stress not directly related to illness, or represent aspects of anger-related personality attributes that are unrelated to stress.

Emotional Suppression/Repression

Physiological Responses to Stressors. The psychophysiologic literature on personality attributes involving suppression, repression, and other avoidant orientations toward emotion has not yielded a highly consistent pattern of findings. In part, this reflects the fact that research in this area is rather heterogeneous with respect to conceptual orientation and measurement approach. For example, in the cardiovascular area, suppression/repression typically has been studied in relation to anger. By contrast, in other applications, suppression/repression has been conceptualized in relation to anxiety, distress, or other negative emotions and impulses. In addition to this distinction, there are various other methodological factors that make it difficult to evaluate evidence concerning style of emotional expression and physiologic responsivity to stress (Diamond, 1982; Engebretson, Matthews, & Scheier, 1989; Suls & Wan, 1993).

Despite conceptual and methodological difficulties, some tentative empirical generalizations in this area may be suggested. One is that nonexpression of anger and other negative emotions may be associated with heightened physiologic reactivity to stressors. Note that this evidence is not based on self-report measures such as the Anger-Expression scale (Spielberger et al., 1985), in which respondents are explicitly asked whether they tend to keep anger in (Houston, 1994; Siegman, 1994). Rather, research suggesting that failure to express anger may be associated with disease promoting physiologic responses has involved variations on an indirect measurement strategy introduced by Weinberger et al. (1979) as a means of assessing what they referred to as a repressive coping style. Repressive copers are identified as individuals with low scores on a measure of trait anxiety, such as the J. A. Taylor (1953) Manifest Anxiety Scale, and high scores on a disguised measure of defensiveness, the Marlowe–Crowne social desirability scale (Crowne & Marlowe, 1964; for a discussion of the rationale and construct validity of this assessment approach, see Weinberger, 1990). A series of studies employing this assessment approach has demonstrated that repressive copers show high levels of autonomic reactivity to various laboratory stressors (Asendorpf & Scherer, 1983; Kohlmann, Singer, & Krohne, 1989; Newton & Contrada, 1992; Weinberger et al., 1979).

Procedures for measuring repressive coping have been adapted by researchers interested in the cardiovascular effects of the suppression/repression of anger. Siegman, Anderson, and Boyle (1991) found that subjects with low trait anger scores and high Marlowe–Crowne scores exhibited greater heart rate responses to a serial subtraction task accompanied by harassment than "truly" low anger subjects with low scores on both measures. Using a somewhat different approach, Jamner, Shapiro, Goldstein, and Hug (1991) administered the Cook–Medley hostility scale (Cook & Medley, 1954) and Marlowe–Crowne social desirability scale to paramedics who underwent ambulatory blood pressure monitoring during the course of their workday. By contrast with the Siegman et al. (1991) study, Jamner et al. found that the combination of defensiveness (as reflected by high Marlowe–Crowne scores) and *high* levels of the anger-related trait, in this case, Cook–Medley hostility, was associated with cardiovascular responsiveness. The same conclusion is supported by results of a laboratory study reported by Helmers and Krantz (1994). High scores on both the Marlowe–Crowne and Cook–Medley scales, a pattern labeled "defensive hostility," identified men showing greater systolic and diastolic blood pressure responses to two laboratory stressors.

Recently, Helmers et al. (1995) utilized the defensive hostility construct in a study of individuals with coronary artery disease. It was found that patients characterized by this personality pattern showed more severe myocardial ischemia in response to an exercise test, more frequent ischemic episodes during daily life activities, and more severe ischemia in response to two laboratory stressors, by comparison with patients with other personality score combinations. Taken together with results reported by Jamner et al. (1991) and Helmers and Krantz (1994), the Helmers et al. (1995) findings suggest that cardiovascular responsiveness to stressors may exacerbate ischemic heart disease in coronary patients high in defensive hostility.

Other research suggests that the *expression* of anger is associated with heightened physiological reactivity. It was noted earlier that, in the meta-analysis conducted by Suls and Wan (1993), an antagonistic interpersonal style was found to be reliably associated with heightened blood pressure reactivity to anger provocation. Because antagonistic interpersonal style reflects the overt display of hostility during a structured interview (Dembroski et al., 1978), these results suggest that anger expression is associated with physiologic responses to interpersonal stressors that may promote cardiovascular disease. More recently, Siegman (1994) came to a similar conclusion, based both on correlational research involving trait measures of the expression of anger and experimental studies involving manipulations of paraverbal behaviors (e.g., loud and rapid speech) associated with the expression of anger.

Thus, both the suppression/repression and expression of anger/hostility have been implicated as correlates of stress-induced physiological responses that may promote cardiovascular disease. A detailed consideration of the conceptual and methodological factors that might reconcile these seemingly contradictory findings is beyond the purview of this chapter (for relevant discussions, see Houston, 1994, and Siegman, 1994). However, it is worth noting briefly the results of a study by Engebretson et al. (1989) in which some of these issues were addressed. Support was obtained for a matching hypothesis according to which it is not the person's anger-expression style per se that determines the intensity of cardiovascular responsiveness, but the degree of match between the person's preferred mode of anger expression and the opportunity to employ that mode of expression in the anger provoking situation. Subjects who characteristically hold their anger in showed decreased cardiovascular reactivity when required to write a positive evaluation of an annoying confederate, but not when required to write a negative evaluation. Subjects who characteristically express their anger showed the opposite pattern of response. These findings suggest that, among other factors that may account for inconsistencies regarding the cardiovascular correlates of anger expression, the degree of fit between anger-expression style and situational demands and constraints warrants further study.

Before leaving the topic of physiological correlates of anger suppression/repression, some findings involving measures of immune function should be mentioned. There is evidence linking trait measures of repression or defensiveness to low monocyte counts (Jamner, Schwartz, & Leigh, 1988) and to low immunological control of latent Epstein–Barr virus (Esterling, Antoni, Kumar, & Schneiderman, 1990, 1993). There is also evidence to suggest that individuals who show low levels of emotional disclosure during the course of writing about traumatic life experiences also show lower levels of immune competence (Esterling et al., 1990; Pennebaker, Kiecolt-Glaser, & Glaser, 1988). These findings argue for further efforts to determine whether stress-induced immunosuppression may be a pathway linking suppressed/repressed emotion to negative health outcomes.

Behavioral Responses to Stressors. There is little research directly examining the possibility that emotional suppression/repression is associated with health damaging behavioral responses to stressors. It is possible that linkages between trait anger/hostility and health damaging behaviors reviewed earlier (e.g., Siegler, 1994) reflect or are qualified by the manner or degree of anger expression, but anger-related measures used in this research do not allow such a determination. It is also possible that the tendency to suppress or to repress anger and other negative affects is part of a more general, avoidant coping style in which threatening events and associated emotional responses are minimized. If so, emotional suppression/repression may promote disease through behavioral processes that involve failure to seek information about health threats, failure to cope with them by taking direct action, or both (S. M. Miller et al., 1996; Suls & Fletcher, 1985). However, here again, there is a need for measurement-oriented research to clarify the behavioral correlates of personality attributes involving the degree and manner of emotional expression.

Disengagement

Physiological Responses to Stressors. Attributes falling in the disengagement cluster have been linked to biological measures that may reflect responses to psychological stress. For example, there is evidence that clinical depression is associated with elevations in both pituitary-adrenocortical and sympathetic-adrenomedullary activity (Esler et al., 1982; Siever & Davis, 1985; Roy, Pickar, De Jong, Karoum, & Linnoila, 1988). In addition, parasympathetic (vagal) tone, which can modulate the cardiovascular effects of sympathetic activation, is lower in depressed individuals (Balogh, Fitzpatrick, Hendricks, & Paige, 1993; Carney et al., 1988). Thus, it is possible that depression exerts a health damaging effect, particularly with respect to heart disease, as a consequence of stress-related physiological mechanisms (Carney, Freedland, Rich, & Jaffe, 1995).

There is also reason to believe that disengagement can influence health through effects on the immune system. Kamen-Siegel, Rodin, Seligman, and Dwyer (1991) reported an association between the pessimistic attributional style and lower cell-mediated immunity. More recently, Herbert and Cohen (1993) conducted a meta-analysis that provides evidence of a strong and consistent relation between clinically significant depression and three parameters of immune competence, namely, lower proliferative response of lymphocytes to mitogens, lower natural killer cell activity, and alterations in numbers of several types of white blood cells. There was also evidence that depressed mood in nonclinical populations is associated with lower functional immunity. The meta-analysis did not address the mechanisms that account for the linkage between depression and immunity. One set of plausible mechanisms discussed by Herbert and Cohen (1993) involves the link between depression and neuroendocrine mechanisms mentioned earlier.

Behavioral Responses to Stressors. Attributes falling in the disengagement cluster may produce health damaging effects as a consequence of behavioral responses to psychological stress. For example, the pessimistic explanatory style has been associated with poor health habits, such as cigarette smoking, excessive alcohol use, and low exercise levels (Peterson, 1988), and with behaviors reflecting poor management of illness, such as failure to increase fluid intake and to get adequate bed rest (Peterson, Colvin, & Lin, 1992). Herbert and Cohen (1993) noted that altered immune function in depressives might reflect behavioral correlates of depression, such as inadequate sleep, low levels of exercise, poor diet, cigarette smoking, and alcohol and drug use. Depression also has been associated with low levels of compliance with various medical regimens (e.g., Blumenthal, R. S. Williams, Wallace, R. B. Williams, & Needles, 1982; Eisen, Hanpeter, Kreuger, & Gard, 1987; Guiry, Conroy, Hickey, & Mulcahy, 1987). As with anger/hostility and emotional suppression/repression, it is not clear whether these behaviors are best conceptualized as a reflection of stress-related processes.

CONCEPTUAL AND METHODOLOGICAL ISSUES

Research reviewed in this chapter suggests possible relationships between personality attributes falling in three domains

—anger/hostility, emotional suppression/repression, and disengagement—and both physiological and behavioral pathways to physical disease that may involve responses to psychological stress. However, support for this hypothesis is not entirely consistent. Even with the focus in this chapter on research reporting positive associations, methodological problems and the small numbers of available studies provide reason to view the findings with caution. Perhaps the most appropriate overall conclusion to draw at the present time is that the evidence supports the plausibility of the personality–stress–disease hypothesis.

Research on personality, stress, or health poses many conceptual and methodological difficulties. The additional challenges that emerge from efforts to establish linkages across these three domains can be daunting. This section discusses some of the more salient issues and attempts to identify theoretical perspectives and methodological strategies that may prove fruitful in this endeavor. These issues are grouped into two general categories, namely, those concerned with units of analysis in personality, and those concerned with establishing linkages with health-related processes.

Units of Analysis in Personality and Their Measurement

Research suggests a number of observations regarding personality units that appear to warrant further examination as possible risk factors for physical disease. The following are three of the more salient observations:

1. *Content*: The tendency to experience negative emotions is strongly implicated as a personality domain that is relevant to stress and health.
2. *Structure*: The breadth and complexity of the behavior patterns associated with promising personality attributes remain unresolved.
3. *Context relevance*: Relations between health-related personality attributes and relevant factors in the social and physical environment have yet to be adequately explored.

Content

Perhaps the clearest theme to emerge from this chapter is that all three promising personality risk factors involve negative emotion. Thus, as pointed out previously (e.g., Contrada et al., 1990), descriptions of health damaging personality attributes have changed little since the theory of temperaments was put forth by Hippocrates and Galen. This observation agrees with conclusions based on previous reviews (e.g., Friedman & Booth-Kewley, 1987), and it is, perhaps, unsurprising, given long-standing and well-documented linkages between negative emotions and biological responses to stressors that have been implicated in the production of disease (Cannon, 1925; Mason, 1975). Several implications may be drawn from this observation.

One implication of the central role of emotion in health-related personality attributes is that it underscores the need for greater clarification of the statistical structure of affective trait measures. This issue, and the related issue of statistical structure of state affect measures, have received considerable attention, but a consensus has yet to emerge. The matter is often framed as a choice between two alternatives, one pointing to a set of five to seven qualitatively distinct affects (e.g., Ekman, 1992), and another to a two-factor space involving separable dimensions of positive and negative affect (e.g., Watson, Clark, & Tellegen, 1984). A structural model of affect also has been described that integrates these two perspectives (e.g., Diener & Fujita, 1995). Many of the studies reviewed here involved a single measure of a particular emotional trait; less frequently, a nonspecific measure (e.g., "neuroticism") was used. Both approaches permit only limited inferences regarding the contribution of emotion-related personality to health outcomes. It would seem useful for future studies examining the relation between emotional traits and physical health to include measures representing both dimensional and discrete emotions perspectives.

Another suggestion that might be taken from the salience of emotion in health-related personality attributes, and one that appears to be promising, is the potential utility of working backward from experienced and overtly manifested emotion to the personality structures and processes that might constitute its determinants. As noted earlier, many theories of emotion (e.g., Lazarus, 1991) emphasize cognitive processes, such as appraisal and problem representation, in the production of emotional states. Of the personality attributes discussed in this chapter, the concept of pessimistic explanatory style is arguably most explicit in attending to cognitive process, given its focus on the attributions that individuals generate to account for negative experiences. Cognitive factors also have received extensive examination in accounts of depression (e.g., Coyne & Gotlib, 1983), and Scheier and Bridges (1995) discussed the potential for processes involved in setting and evaluating progress toward goals to account for behavioral and emotional responses in individuals characterized by depression, fatalism, and pessimism. Similar analyses of anger/hostility (Contrada et al., 1990) and emotional suppression (Newton & Contrada, 1992) also have been described. A better understanding of the cognitive structures and processes underlying emotion-related dispositions should lead to improvements in the measurement of those constructs and to more detailed models of the interface between personality and stress.

Whatever the structure of emotional traits and the cognitive determinants of personality-related emotional reactions, there is ample evidence to indicate that expressive behaviors play a major role in the subjective experience (Izard, 1990), physiologic concomitants (Siegman, 1994), and interpersonal consequences (Gottman & Levenson, 1986) of emotion. However, although the items on conventional trait measures of negative emotions tap into expressive and interpersonal aspects of emotion, they do not necessarily provide optimal assessments of those factors. Conceptual analyses and multivariate methods have only recently begun to identify coherent facets of emotional traits such as anger/hostility (Barefoot et al., 1989; A. H. Buss & Perry, 1992; Contrada &

Jussim, 1992; T. Q. Miller et al., 1995), a step that is prerequisite to efforts to establish the relative contributions of experiential versus expressive components. It remains to be seen whether paper-and-pencil measures will be adequate to the task, or whether it will be necessary to supplement these with direct observations of vocal, facial, and other behavioral responses to actual, emotion provoking situations (e.g., Dembroski et al., 1978; Seigman, 1994).

Still another implication of the central role of emotion in health-related personality characteristics is the potential for confounding that arises in research that involves subjective measures of physical health (Watson & Pennebaker, 1989). Negative affectivity, or neuroticism—a tendency to experience and to express distressing emotions and other negative states—may contribute both to scores on emotion-related personality attributes, and to responses on symptom checklists, use of health care, and medical diagnoses that reflect patient complaints. The result may be a correlation that is spurious in the sense that it does not reflect a direct, physiologically mediated association between personality and the etiology or progression of a disease process. On the other hand, such an association may be of considerable substantive interest as an instance in which personality contributes to illness or illness management through behaviorally mediated processes involving symptom detection and control. Thus, further examination of negative affectivity in producing associations between personality and health should be directed toward elucidating the mechanisms, both artifactual and substantive, that may bring about such linkages (T. W. Smith & P. G. Williams, 1992).

Structure

The study of personality and health has at different times and for different purposes focused on both broadly and narrowly defined personality attributes. This is well illustrated by the history of research in the Type A area. What began as a multifaceted but coherent pattern consisting of competitiveness, achievement striving, time urgency, hostility, and vigorous speech and motor mannerisms was dissected into its constituent elements (Dembroski et al., 1978). One of those elements—hostility—was then identified as the most promising predictor of coronary disease. Subsequently there have been efforts to resolve hostility into still more circumscribed facets. Several componential schemes of hostility have been proposed, including one distinguishing between antagonistic interpersonal style, hostile content, and anger-in (Suls & Wan, 1993), and one involving cynicism, hostile affect, and hostile attributional style (Barefoot et al., 1989). Conversely, attempts also have been made to weave these components together into broader dimensions, such as anger experience and anger expression (e.g., Musante et al., 1989). At the same time, meta-analysis has been used to infer a generic, "disease-prone" personality that is broad and nonspecific in subsuming tendencies to experience other negative emotions in addition to anger (Friedman & Booth-Kewley, 1987).

Although factor analysis, component analysis, and meta-analysis of existing measures will likely continue to prove useful tools, efforts to determine the appropriate level of generality for describing health-related attributes might also benefit from alternative approaches derived from social-cognitive approaches to personality (Cantor & Zirkel, 1990; Mischel & Shoda, 1995). Rather than seeking personality units solely within the structure of items and scales for measuring traits, various "middle-level" personality constructs have been defined in terms of their relevance to the individual's identity, goals, and life concerns. Ewart and Kolodner (1991) followed such an approach in demonstrating the utility of a social competence interview for psychophysiological research. An interview protocol that required subjects to describe and to re-experience a recurring life goal or challenge provided a means of eliciting cardiovascular activity that may reflect disease promoting processes. Another example of an alternative to traditional structured personality tests is the assessment of self-discrepancies, or negative self-evaluations, the activation of which may provoke negative emotion states and associated reductions in immune competence (e.g., Strauman, Lemieux, & Coe, 1993). Personality structures reflected in life goals and standards for self-evaluation may lie closer to the personality–stress interface than more traditional, traitlike dispositions because their contents are defined by the individual, rather than by the investigator, and may have more explicit links to the social-environmental context from which stressors often emanate. At the same time, it should be possible to establish associations between these cognitive-motivational units and more traditional personality constructs, especially where the latter are well-established, major dimensions of personality, or are firmly tied to health or to health-related processes (T. W. Smith & P. G. Williams, 1992).

An issue related to the question of breadth concerns the structural complexity of health-related personality attributes. Type A, Type C, and hardiness are explicitly multifaceted but, at least in some formulations, the facets were thought to be highly interrelated, yielding single, albeit broad constructs. By contrast, the study of emotional suppression/repression suggests that it may be profitable to conceptualize health-related personality attributes as combinations of two or more relatively distinct dispositions. Both the repressive coping construct (Weinberger et al., 1979), and the concept of defensive hostility (Helmers et al., 1995; Jamner et al., 1991) are defined in terms of two, substantially independent personality factors, an emotional trait (anxiety or hostility) and a defensive or avoidant orientation toward negative emotion (as reflected in Marlowe–Crowne social desirability scores). Another example is the inhibited power motivation construct, which involves high power motivation, low affiliation motivation, and high activity inhibition (Jemmott, 1987). Beyond these few examples, very little is known about the health implications of particular combinations of distinctive personality attributes, and multicomponent models of personality dispositions raise conceptual and analytic issues that have yet to be resolved (Carver, 1989).

Context Relevance

Personality measures that have proved useful in identifying health damaging attributes differ in the way they represent contextual factors. Instruments such as the Cook–Medley Hostility scale, the Marlowe–Crowne Social Desirability scale, and the Life Orientation Test (a measure of trait optimism) (Scheier & Carver, 1985) contain items that refer to or imply general types of situations, for example, occasions that might stimulate anger or aggression, situations that raise questions about the respondents' or others' pro-social motives, or possible future scenarios involving positive or negative outcomes. By contrast, the attributional style questionnaire (a measure of pessimistic explanatory style) (Peterson, 1988) presents the subject with specific but hypothetical situations involving various negative events. The Structured Interview (used to assess global Type A and various anger-related attributes) (Dembroski et al., 1978) also contains questions that refer to hypothetical situations, but differs from questionnaire approaches in that it primarily is used to create a real situation in which to observe directly the respondent's behavioral response to social challenge. To the degree that the display of personality dispositions is contingent on the presence of conceptually congruent situation factors (Mischel & Shoda, 1995), the measurement of health-related personality attributes might benefit from more systematic attention to situational parameters contained in assessment devices.

The issue of context extends beyond the content of questionnaires and interviews. Very little is known about the manifestations of many health-related personality dispositions in naturalistic settings, although technological developments may stimulate efforts to address this gap in knowledge (Stone & Shiffman, 1994). Naturalistic research efforts guided by Mischel and Shoda's (1995) notion of situation–behavior relations might reveal individual consistencies in the use of certain coping strategies to manage some types of types of stressors, but not others, or to engage in health damaging behaviors under certain psychological conditions, but not others. The generalizability of personality–health associations across social and cultural categories also warrants much more attention. Findings involving even the fairly well-studied anger/hostility constructs have raised questions about gender differences in the pathogenicity of attributes falling in this domain (Stoney & Engebretson, 1994). Much remains to be explored concerning the interplay between health-related personality attributes and gender, ethnicity, and socioeconomic status (Anderson & Armstead, 1995).

Personality and Health-Damaging Processes

Research reviewed above also suggests a number of observations regarding the causal analysis of personality–disease linkages. Two of these are discussed below: (1) *Psychophysiological advances*: Technological advances permit more penetrating examinations of mechanisms linking personality to stress-related physiological activity than are available in the published literature; (2) *Health-related behavior*: Although direct, psychophysiological pathways to illness may be thought of as more closely associated with the health effects of personality and stress, behavioral pathways may warrant greater consideration.

Psychophysiological Advances

The application of more sophisticated psychophysiological methods would advance knowledge concerning personality and health in a number of ways. Within the laboratory, the availability of techniques such as spectral analysis, which distinguishes between sympathetic and parasympathetic nervous system influences on cardiac activity, makes possible a more fine-grained analysis of the autonomic control of cardiac responses to stressors (e.g., Kamada, Miyake, Kumashiro, Monou, & Inoue, 1992). Similarly, impedance cardiography can be used to determine the relative contributions of myocardial and vascular processes to stress-related blood pressure elevations (Kamarck, Jennings, Pogue-Geile, & Manuck, 1994). Refinements in these and other psychophysiologic methods permit the examination of neurogenic and hemodynamic mechanisms operating in healthy individuals. Still other techniques have become available to measure stress-induced physiological changes in coronary patients, such as myocardial ischemia and abnormalities in myocardial contraction (e.g., Helmers et al., 1995). Thus, in addition to focusing on psychophysiologic processes thought to be involved in the development of cardiovascular disorders, it is now possible to examine personality and stress in relation to psychophysiologic processes that may be responsible for the precipitation of clinical disease states at later stages of those disorders.

Outside the laboratory, the availability of instruments for the ambulatory monitoring of physiologic activity can generate evidence bearing on the relationship between personality and stress-related cardiovascular responses in the naturalistic setting (e.g., Jamner et al., 1991). As with laboratory methods, ambulatory methods also permit the assessment of clinically relevant events in patients with disease (Helmers et al., 1995). Evidence of this sort—involving associations linking personality, stress, and disease in naturalistic settings—is critical to arguments that psychophysiologic correlates of personality dispositions are relevant to processes that culminate in physical disease (Krantz & Manuck, 1984).

In addition to the foregoing examples from cardiovascular psychophysiology, it is possible to point to increasing sophistication in methods for assessing a range of parameters that reflect biological responses to psychological stress, including various measures of immunity, neuroendocrine activity, neurotransmitter and peptide receptor function, and metabolism (e.g., Herbert & Cohen, 1993; Schneiderman, Weiss, & Kaufman, 1989). Future research examining personality in relation to physiologic aspects of the stress response must exploit these developments if it is to add detail to current models concerning the psychosocial causation of physical disease and generate data that increase confidence in the validity of those models. If so, it will be possible to hold the next generation of studies in this area to a criterion of persuasiveness, rather than mere biological plausibility.

Personality and Health-Related Behavior

Although the focus in this chapter has been on personality factors thought to influence health directly, through psychophysiological pathways, there appears to be a sufficient basis for examining these attributes in relation to behavioral pathways as well. In some instances, evidence for associations between suspected personality risk factors and pathogenic behaviors was generated through efforts to introduce statistical controls for factors that might confound personality–disease relations deriving from physiological mechanisms. In other cases, the examination of associations between personality and health damaging behaviors appears to have been exploratory, or based on the general negative or maladaptive connotation of a personality descriptor. Research based on explicit theory linking personality attributes to health behavior or reactions to illness (e.g., S. M. Miller et al., 1996) might be expected to yield more consistent and robust findings.

In addition to the benefits of a more theoretical approach to work in this area, it may be useful to give greater consideration to the proper role of personality in this research. Some research appears to reflect a premature focus on one particular personality disposition, to the exclusion of others, and to rely too heavily on it alone in attempting to predict measures of health-related behavioral processes. Other research is based on a normative health behavior model in which personality is included in a list of relevant background variables in the absence of a systematic examination of potential points of connection between personality and the key elements of the behavioral model. If research guided by psychophysiological models has provided any lesson at all for more behavioral approaches, it is that personality is neither an overriding factor in physical illness nor an inconsequential one.

CONCLUSIONS

The major constructs and research approaches used in the study of personality, stress, and disease have evolved only to a modest degree in recent years. Current concerns about lack of theory, measurement problems, and other issues do not differ dramatically from those raised in reviews published decades ago. Nonetheless, although the robustness of beliefs in the importance of stress-related personality attributes is not always matched by effect sizes or theoretical sophistication, research in this area has progressed. Assertions that once were based on a single, prospective epidemiologic investigation, or on a handful of psychophysiologic experiments, are now based on consistent patterns of findings from large numbers of studies. There is a greater tendency to select for study types of stressors that appear psychologically relevant to the particular personality attribute under investigation. Personality factors that were once vaguely conceptualized as capable of exacerbating stress responses are now embedded in detailed theoretical frameworks positing specific stress promoting processes. In short, it would seem that the study of personality, stress, and disease is alive and reasonably well.

ACKNOWLEDGMENTS

We thank Michael Diefenbach and Ann O'Leary for their helpful comments on an earlier draft of this chapter. Thanks also to Jennifer Betancourt for her help in preparing the manuscript.

REFERENCES

Abrams, D. B., & Niaura, R. S. (1987). Social learning theory. In H. T. Blane & K. E. Leonard (Eds.), *Psychological theories of drinking and alcoholism* (pp. 131–178). New York: Guilford.

Adams, S. H. (1994). Role of hostility in women's health during midlife: A longitudinal study. *Health Psychology, 13,* 488–495.

Adler, N., & Matthews, K. (1994). Health psychology: Why do some people get sick and some stay well? *Annual Review of Psychology, 45,* 229–259.

Alexander, F. G. (1930). Emotional factors in essential hypertension. Presentation of a tentative hypothesis. *Psychosomatic Medicine, 1,* 175–179.

Allport, G. W. (1937). *Personality: A psychological interpretation.* New York: Holt, Rinehart & Winston.

Almada, S. J., Zonderman, A. B., Shekelle, R. B., Dyer, A. R., Daviglus, M. L., Costa, P. T., & Stamler, J. (1991). Neuroticism and cynicism and risk of death in middle-aged men: The Western Electric Study. *Psychosomatic Medicine, 53,* 165–175.

Anderson, N. B., & Armstead, C. A. (1995). Toward understanding the association of socioeconomic status and health: A new challenge for the biopsychosocial approach. *Psychosomatic Medicine, 57,* 213–225.

Asendorpf, J. B., & Scherer, K. R. (1983). The discrepant repressor: Differentiation between low anxiety, high anxiety, and repression of anxiety by autonomic-facial-verbal patterns of behavior. *Journal of Personality and Social Psychology, 45,* 1334–1346.

Ax, A. F. (1953). The physiological differentiation between anger and fear. *Psychosomatic Medicine, 15,* 433–442.

Ayres, A., Hoon, P. W., Franzoni, J. B., Matheny, K. B., & Cotanch, P. H. (1994). Influence of mood and adjustment to cancer on compliance with chemotherapy among breast cancer patients. *Journal of Psychosomatic Research, 38,* 393–402.

Balogh, S., Fitzpatrick, D. F., Hendricks, S. E., & Paige, S. R. (1993). Increases in heart rate variability with successful treatment in patients with major depressive disorder. *Psychopharmacology Bulletin, 29,* 201–206.

Bandura, A. (1978). The self system in reciprocal determinism. *American Psychologist, 33,* 344–358.

Barefoot, J., Dodge, K., Peterson, B., Dahlstrom, G., & Williams, R. (1989). The Cook–Medley hostility scale: Item content and ability to predict survival. *Psychosomatic Medicine, 51,* 46–57.

Barefoot, J. C., Dahlstrom, G., & Williams, R. B. (1983). Hostility, CHD incidence, and total mortality: A 25-year follow-up study of 255 physicians. *Psychosomatic medicine, 45,* 59–63.

Baum, A., Cohen, L., & Hall, M. (1993). Control and intrusive memories as possible determinants of chronic stress. *Psychosomatic Medicine, 55,* 274–286.

Baum, A., Grunberg, N. A., & Singer, J. E. (1982). The use of psychological and neuroendocrinological measurements in the study of stress. *Health Psychology, 1,* 217–236.

Baum, A., & Valins, S. (1977). *Architecture and social behavior: Psychological studies of social density.* Hillsdale, NJ: Lawrence Erlbaum Associates.

Bell, I. R., Jasnoski, M. L., Kagan, J., & King, D. S. (1990). Is allergic rhinitis more frequent in young adults with extreme shyness? A preliminary survey. *Psychosomatic Medicine, 52,* 517–525.

Blumenthal, J. A., Williams, R. S., Wallace, A. G., Williams, R. B., & Needles, T. L. (1982). Physiological and psychological variables predict compliance to prescribed exercise therapy in patients recovering from myocardial infarction. *Psychosomatic Medicine, 44,* 519–527.

Bolger, N., & Schilling, E. A. (1991). Personality and the problems of everyday life: The role of neuroticism in exposure and reactivity to daily stressors. *Journal of Personality, 59,* 525–537.

Bolger, N., & Zuckerman, A. (1995). A framework for studying personality in the stress process. *Journal of Personality and Social Psychology, 69,* 890–902.

Brief, A. P., Butcher, A. H., George, J. M., & Link, K. E. (1993). Integrating bottom-up and top-down theories of subjective well-being: The case of health. *Journal of Personality and Social Psychology, 64,* 646–653.

Buchanan, G. (1995). Explanatory style and cardiac disease. In G. Buchanan & M.E.P. Seligman (Eds.), *Explanatory style* (pp. 225–232). Hillsdale, NJ: Lawrence Erlbaum Associates.

Buss, A. H., & Perry, M. (1992). The aggression questionnaire. *Journal of personality and Social Psychology, 63,* 452–459.

Buss, D. M. (1987). Selection, evocation, and manipulation. *Journal of Personality and Social Psychology, 53,* 1214–1221.

Cannon, W. B. (1925). *Bodily changes in pain, hunger, fear, and rage.* Boston: Branford.

Cantor, N., & Zirkel, S. (1990). Personality, cognition, and purposive behavior. In L. A. Pervin (Ed.), *Handbook of personality theory and research* (pp. 135–164). New York: Guilford.

Carmelli, D., Halpern, J., Swan, G. E., Dame, A., McElroy, M., Gelb, A. B., & Rosenman, R. H. (1991). Twenty-seven-year mortality in the Western Collaborative Group Study: Construction of risk groups by recursive partitioning. *Journal of Clinical Epidemiology, 44,* 1341–1351.

Carney, R. M., Freedland, K. E., & Lustman, P. J. (1994). Depression and coronary disease in diabetic patients: 10–year follow-up (Abstract). *Psychosomatic Medicine, 56,* 149.

Carney, R. M., Freedland, K. E., Rich, M. W., & Jaffe, A. S. (1995). Depression as a risk factor for cardiac events in established coronary heart disease: A review of possible mechanisms. *Annals of Behavioral Medicine, 17,* 142–149.

Carney, R. M., Rich, M. W., TeVelde, A., Saini, J., Clark, K., & Freedland, K. E. (1988). The relationship between heart rate, heart rate variability and depression in patients with coronary artery disease. *Journal of Psychosomatic Research, 32,* 159–164.

Cartwright, L. K., Wink, P., & Kmetz, C. (1995). What leads to good health in midlife women physicians? Some clues from a longitudinal study. *Psychosomatic Medicine, 57,* 284–292.

Carver, C. S. (1989). How should multifaceted personality constructs be tested? Issues illustrated by self-monitoring, attributional style, and hardiness. *Journal of Personality and Social Psychology, 56,* 577–585.

Carver, C. S., Pozo, C., Harris, S. D., Noriega, V., Scheier, M. F., Robinson, D. S., Ketcham, A. S., Moffat, F. L., Jr., & Clark, K. C. (1993). How coping mediates the effect of optimism on distress: A study of women with early stage breast cancer. *Journal of Personality and Social Psychology, 65,* 375–390.

Carver, C. S., & Scheier, M. F. (1981). *Attention and self- regulation: A control-theory approach to human behavior.* New York: Springer-Verlag.

Cervone, D. (1991). The two disciplines of personality psychology. *Psychological Science, 2,* 371–377.

Cohen, S., Doyle, W. J., Skoner, D. P., Gwaltney, J. M., & Newsom, J. T. (1995). State and trait negative affect as predictors of objective and subjective symptoms of respiratory viral infections. *Journal of Personality and Social Psychology, 68,* 159–169.

Contrada, R. J. (1994). Personality and anger in cardiovascular disease: Toward a psychological model. In A. W. Siegman & T. W. Smith (Eds.), *Anger, hostility and the heart* (pp. 149–179). Hillsdale, NJ: Lawrence Erlbaum Associates.

Contrada, R. J., & Jussim, L. (1992). What does the Cook–Medley hostility scale measure? In search of an adequate measurement model. *Journal of Applied Social Psychology, 22,* 615–627.

Contrada, R. J., Krantz, D. S., & Hill, D. R. (1988). Type A behavior, emotion, and psychophysiologic reactivity: Psychological and biological interactions. In B. K. Houston & C. R. Snyder (Eds.), *Type A behavior pattern: Research, theory, and intervention* (pp. 254–274). New York: Wiley.

Contrada, R. J., Leventhal, E. A., & Anderson, J. R. (1994). Psychological preparation for surgery: Marshalling individual and social resources to optimize self-regulation. In S. Maes, H. Leventhal, & M. Johnston (Eds.), *International review of health psychology* (Vol. 3, pp. 220–266). New York: Wiley.

Contrada, R. J., Leventhal, H., & O'Leary, A. (1990). Personality and health. In L. A. Pervin (Ed.), *Handbook of personality theory and research* (pp. 638–669). New York: Guilford.

Cook, W., & Medley, D. (1954). Proposed hostility and pharisaic-virtue scales for the MMPI. *Journal of Applied Psychology, 38,* 414–418.

Coyne, J. C. (1976). Depression and the response of others. *Journal of Abnormal Psychology, 85,* 186–193.

Coyne, J. C. (1994). Self-reported distress: Analog or ersatz depression? *Psychological Bulletin, 116,* 29–45.

Coyne, J. C., & Downey, G. (1991). Social factors and psychopathology: Stress, social support, and coping processes. *Annual Review of Psychology, 42,* 401–425.

Coyne, J. C., & Gotlib, I. H. (1983). The role of cognition in depression: A critical appraisal. *Psychological Bulletin, 94,* 472–505.

Crowne, D. P., & Marlowe, D. (1964). *The approval motive: Studies in evaluative dependence.* New York: Wiley.

Czajkowski, S. M., Hindelang, R. D., Dembroski, T. M., Mayerson, S. E., Parks, E. B., & Holland, J. C. (1990). Aerobic fitness, psychological characteristics, and cardiovascular reactivity to stress. *Health Psychology, 9,* 676–692.

Davidson, R. J. (1984). Affect, cognition, and hemispheric specialization. In C. E. Izard, J. Kagan, & R. B. Zajonc (Eds.), *Emotions, cognition and behavior* (pp. 320–365). New York: Cambridge University Press.

DeGenova, M. K., Patton, D. M., Jurich, J. A., & MacDermid, S. M. (1994). Ways of coping among HIV-infected individuals. *Journal of Social Psychology, 134,* 655–663.

Dembroski, T. M., MacDougall, J. M., Shields, J. L., Petitto, J., & Lushene, R. (1978). Components of the Type A coronary-prone behavior pattern and cardiovascular responses to psychomotor challenge. *Journal of Behavioral Medicine, 1,* 159–176.

Depue, R. A., Luciana, M., Arbisi, P., Collins, P., & Leon, A. (1994). Dopamine and the structure of personality: Relation of agonist-induced dopamine activity to positive emotionality. *Journal of Personality and Social Psychology, 67,* 485–498.

Diamond, E. (1982). The role of anger and hostility in essential hypertension and coronary heart disease. *Psychological Bulletin, 92,* 410–433.

Diener, E., & Fujita, F. (1995). The personality structure of affect. *Journal of Personality and Social Psychology, 69,* 130–141.

Digenio, A. G., Padayachee, N., & Groeneveld, H. (1992). Multivariate models for compliance with phase 3 cardiac rehabilitation services in Johannesburg. *Annals of the Academy of Medicine, Singapore, 21,* 121–127.

Dimsdale, J. E. (1993). Coronary heart disease in women: Personality and stress-induced biological differences. *Annals of Behavioral Medicine, 15,* 119–123.

Dunkel-Schetter, C., Feinstein, L. G., Taylor, S. E., & Falke, R. L. (1992). Patterns of coping with cancer. *Health Psychology, 11,* 79–87.

Eisen, S. A., Hanpeter, J. A., Kreuger, L. W., & Gard, M. (1987). Monitoring medication compliance: Description of a new device. *Journal of Compliance in Health Care, 2,* 131–142.

Ekman, P. (1992). Are there basic emotions? *Psychological Review, 99,* 550–553.

Engebretson, T. O., Matthews, K. A., & Scheier, M. F. (1989). Relations between anger expression and cardiovascular reactivity:

Reconciling inconsistent findings through a matching hypothesis. *Journal of Personality and Social Psychology, 57,* 513–521.

Engel, G. L. (1977). The need for a new medical model: A challenge for biomedicine. *Science, 196,* 129–136.

Esler, M., Turbott, J., Schwarz, R., Leonard, P., Bobik, A., Skews, H., & Jackman, G. (1982). The peripheral kinetics of norepinephrine in depressive illness. *Archives of General Psychiatry, 39,* 285–300.

Esterling, B. A., Antoni, M. H., Kumar, M., & Schneiderman, N. (1993). Defensiveness, trait anxiety, and Epstein–Barr viral capsid antigen antibody titers in healthy college students. *Health Psychology, 12,* 132–139.

Esterling, B. A., Antoni, M. H., Kumar, M., & Schneiderman, N. (1990). Emotional repression, stress disclosure responses, and Epstein–Barr viral capsid antigen titers. *Psychosomatic Medicine, 52,* 397–410.

Esteve, L. G., Valdes, M., Riesco, N., Jodar, I., & de Flores, T. (1992). Denial mechanisms in myocardial infarction: Their relations with psychological variables and short-term outcome. *Journal of Psychosomatic Research, 36,* 491–496.

Ewart, C. K., & Kolodner, K. B. (1991). Social competence interview for assessing physiological reactivity in adolescents. *Psychosomatic Medicine, 53,* 289–304.

Eysenck, H. J. (1967). *The biological bases of personality.* Springfield, IL: Thomas.

Fava, G. A. (1994). Affective disorders and endocrine disease: New insights from psychosomatic studies. *Psychosomatics, 35,* 341–353.

Feeney, J. A., & Ryan, S. M. (1994). Attachment style and affect regulation: Relationships with health behavior and family experiences of illness in a student sample. *Health Psychology, 13,* 334–345.

Fox, B. H. (1978). Premorbid psychological factors as related to cancer incidence. *Journal of Behavioral Medicine, 1,* 45–133.

Frasure-Smith, N., Lesperance, F., & Talajic, M. (1993). Depression following myocardial infarction. *Journal of the American Medical Association, 270,* 1819–1825.

Friedman, H. S. (Ed.). (1990). *Personality and disease.* New York: Wiley.

Freedland, K. E., Carney, R. M., Krone, R. J., Smith, L. J., Rich, M. W., Eisenkramer, G., & Fischer, K. C. (1991). Psychological factors in silent myocardial ischemia. *Psychosomatic Medicine, 53,* 13–24.

Friedman, H. S., & Booth-Kewley, S. (1987). The "disease-prone personality": A meta-analytic review of the construct. *American Psychologist, 42,* 539–555.

Friedman, H. S., Tucker, J. S., Schwartz, J. E., Martin, L. R., Tomlinson-Keasey, C., Wingard, D. L., & Criqui, M. H. (1995). Childhood conscientiousness and longevity: Health behaviors and cause of death. *Journal of Personality and Social Psychology, 68,* 696–703.

Friedman, H. S., Tucker, J. S., Tomlinson-Keasey, C., Schwartz, J. E., Wingard, D. L., & Criqui, M. H. (1993). Does childhood personality predict longevity? *Journal of Personality and Social Psychology, 65,* 176–185.

Funkenstein, D. H. (1956). Nor-epinephrine-like and epinephrine-like substances in relation to human behavior. *Journal of Nervous and Mental Disease, 124,* 58–68.

Gatchel, R. J., Polatin, P. B., & Kinney, R. K. (1995). Predicting outcome of chronic back pain using clinical predictors of psychopathology: A prospective analysis. *Health Psychology, 14,* 415–420.

Glancy, K. E., Glancy, C. J., Lucke, J. F., Mahurin, K., Rhodes, M., & Tinkoff, G. H. (1992). A study of recovery in trauma patients. *Journal of Trauma, 33,* 602–609.

Glass, D. C. (1977). *Behavior patterns, stress, and coronary disease.* Hillsdale, NJ: Lawrence Erlbaum Associates.

Glass, D. C., Krakoff, L. R., Contrada, R. J., Hilton, W. F., Kehoe, K., Mannucci, E., Collins, C., Snow, B., & Elting, E. (1980). Effect of harassment and competition upon cardiovascular and plasma catecholamine responses in Type A and B individuals. *Psychophysiology, 17,* 453–463.

Gottman, J. M., & Levenson, R. W. (1986). Assessing the role of emotion in marriage. *Behavioral Assessment, 8,* 31–48.

Greer, S., & Morris, T. (1975). Psychological attributes of women who develop breast cancer: A controlled study. *Journal of Psychosomatic Research, 19,* 147–153.

Greer, S., Morris, T., & Pettingale, K. W. (1979). Psychological response to breast cancer: Effect on outcome. *Lancet, 2,* 785–787.

Greer, S., Morris, T., Pettingale, K. W., & Haybittle, J. L. (1990). Psychological response to breast cancer and 15–year outcome. *Lancet, 1,* 49–50.

Gross, J. J., & Levenson, R. W. (1993). Emotional suppression: Physiology, self-report, and expressive behavior. *Journal of Personality and Social Psychology, 64,* 970–986.

Grossarth-Maticek, R., Kanazir, D. T., Schmidt, P., & Vetter, H. (1982). Psychosomatic factors in the process of carcinogenesis. *Psychotherapy and Psychosomatics, 38,* 284–302.

Guiry, E., Conroy, R. M., Hickey, N., & Mulcahy, R. (1987). Psychological response to an acute coronary event and its effect on subsequent rehabilitation and lifestyle change. *Clinical Cardiology, 10,* 256–260.

Haan, N. (1977). *Coping and defending: Processes of self- environment organization.* New York: Academic Press.

Haynes, S. G., Feinleib, M., & Kannel, W. B. (1980). The relationship of psychosocial factors to coronary heart disease in the Framingham Study. *American Journal of Epidemiology, 111,* 37–58.

Helgeson, V. S. (1991). The effects of masculinity and social support on recovery from myocardial infarction. *Psychosomatic Medicine, 53,* 621–633.

Helmers, K. F., & Krantz, D. S. (1994). Defensive hostility and cardiovascular responses to stress: Effects of gender (Abstract). *Psychosomatic Medicine, 56,* 159.

Helmers, K. F., Krantz, D. S., Merz, C.N.B., Klein, J., Kop, W. J., Gottdiener, J. S., & Rozanski, A. (1995). Defensive hostility: Relationship to multiple markers of cardiac ischemia in patients with coronary disease. *Health Psychology, 14,* 202–209.

Helmers, K. F., Posluszny, D. M., & Krantz, D. S. (1994). Associations of hostility and coronary artery disease: A review of studies. In A. W. Siegman & T. W. Smith (Eds.), *Anger, hostility, and the heart* (pp. 67–96). Hillsdale, NJ: Lawrence Erlbaum Associates.

Henry, J. P., Haviland, M. G., Cummings, M. A., Anderson, D. L., Nelson, J. C., MacMurray, J. P., McGhee, W. H., & Hubbard, R. W. (1992). Shared neuroendocrine patterns of post-traumatic stress disorder and alexithymia. *Psychosomatic Medicine, 54,* 407–415.

Herbert, T. B., & Cohen, S. (1993). Depression and immunity: A meta-analytic review. *Psychological Bulletin, 113,* 472–486.

Hobfoll, S. E. (1989). Conservation of resources: A new attempt at conceptualizing stress. *American Psychologist, 44,* 513–524.

Holmes, T. H., & Rahe, R. H. (1967). The social readjustment rating scale. *Journal of Psychosomatic Research, 11,* 213–218.

Houston, B. K. (1988). Cardiovascular and neuroendocrine reactivity, global Type A, and components of Type A behavior. In B. K. Houston & C. R. Snyder (Eds.), *Type A behavior pattern: Research, theory, and intervention* (pp. 212–253). New York: Wiley.

Houston, B. K. (1994). Anger, hostility, and psychophysiological reactivity. In A. W. Siegman & T. W. Smith (Eds.), *Anger, hos-*

tility and the heart (pp. 97–115). Hillsdale, NJ: Lawrence Erlbaum Associates.

Houston, B. K., & Vavak, C. R. (1991). Hostility: Developmental factors, psychosocial correlates, and health behaviors. *Health Psychology, 10,* 9–17.

Izard, C. E. (1990). Facial expressions and the regulation of emotions. *Journal of Personality and Social Psychology, 58,* 487–498.

James, S. A. (1994). John Henryism and the health of African-Americans. *Culture, Medicine and Psychiatry, 18,* 163–182.

Jamner, L. D., Schwartz, G. E., & Leigh, H. (1988). The relationship between repressive and defensive coping styles and monocyte, eosinophile, and serum glucose levels: Support for the opioid peptide hypothesis of repression. *Psychosomatic Medicine, 50,* 567–575.

Jamner, L. D., Shapiro, D., Goldstein, I. B., & Hug, R. (1991). Ambulatory blood pressure and heart rate in paramedics: Effects of cynical hostility and defensiveness. *Psychosomatic Medicine, 53,* 393–406.

Jansen, M. A., & Muenz, L. R. (1984). A retrospective study of personality variables associated with fibrocystic disease and breast cancer. *Journal of Psychosomatic Research, 28,* 35–42.

Jemmott, J. B. (1987). Social motives and susceptibility to disease: Stalking individual differences in health risk. *Journal of Personality, 55,* 267–298.

Jenkins, C. D., Stanton, B. A., & Jono, R. T. (1994). Quantifying and predicting recovery after heart surgery. *Psychosomatic Medicine, 56,* 203–212.

Kamada, T., Miyake, S., Kumashiro, M., Monou, H., & Inoue, K. (1992). Power spectral analysis of heart rate variability in Type As and Type Bs during mental workload. *Psychosomatic Medicine, 54,* 462–470.

Kamarck, T. W., Jennings, J. R., Pogue-Geile, M., & Manuck, S. B. (1994). A multidimensional measurement model for cardiovascular reactivity: Stability and cross-validation in two adult samples. *Health Psychology, 13,* 471–478.

Kamen-Siegel, L., Rodin, J., Seligman, M.E.P., & Dwyer, J. (1991). Explanatory style and cell-mediated immunity in elderly men and women. *Health Psychology, 10,* 229–235.

Kanner, A. D., Coyne, J. C., Schaeffer, C., & Lazarus, R. S. (1981). Comparison of two modes of stress measurement: daily hassles and uplifts versus major life events. *Journal of Behavioral Medicine, 4,* 1–39.

Karasek, R., Baker, D., Marxer, F., Ahlbom, A., & Theorell, T. (1981). Job decision latitude, job demands, and cardiovascular disease: A prospective study. *American Journal of Public Health, 71,* 694–705.

Karoly, P., & Lecci, L. (1993). Hypochondriasis and somatization in college women: A personal projects analysis. *Health Psychology, 12,* 103–109.

Keltikangas-Jarvinen, L., & Raikkonen, K. (1993). Dependence between apolipoprotein E phenotypes and temperament in children, adolescents, and young adults. *Psychosomatic Medicine, 55,* 155–163.

Kiecolt-Glaser, J. K., Fisher, L. D., Ogrocki, P., Stout, J. C., Speicher, C. E., & Glaser, R. (1987). Marital quality, marital disruption, and immune function. *Psychosomatic Medicine, 49,* 13–34.

Kiecolt-Glaser, J. K., Malarkey, W. B., Chee, M., Newton, T., Cacioppo, J. T., Mao, H-Y., & Glaser, R. (1993). Negative behavior during marital conflict is associated with immunological down-regulation. *Psychosomatic Medicine, 55,* 395–409.

King, L. A., & Emmons, R. A. (1990). Conflict over emotional expression: Psychological and physical correlates. *Journal of Personality and Social Psychology, 58,* 864–877.

Kleinman, A. (1986). *Social origins of distress and disease.* New Haven, CT: Yale University Press.

Kobasa, S. C. (1979). Stressful life events, personality, and health: An inquiry into hardiness. *Journal of Personality and Social Psychology, 37,* 1–11.

Kohlmann, C. W., Singer, P., & Krohne, H. W. (1989). Coping disposition, actual coping, and the discrepancy between subjective and physiological stress reactions. In P. F. Lovibond & P. Wilson (Eds.), *Proceedings of the 24th International Congress of Psychology* (Vol. 9, pp. 67–78). Amsterdam: Elsevier.

Kohn, P. M., Lafreniere, K., & Gurevich, M. (1991). Hassles, health, and personality. *Journal of Personality and Social Psychology, 61,* 478–482.

Koskenvou, M., Kapiro, J., Rose, R. J., Kesnaiemi. A., Sarnaa, S., Heikkila, K., & Langinvanio, H. (1988). Hostility as a risk factor for mortality and ischemic heart disease in men. *Psychosomatic Medicine, 50,* 330–340.

Krantz, D. S., & Durel, L. A. (1983). Psychobiological substrates of the Type A behavior pattern. *Health Psychology, 2,* 393–411.

Krantz, D. S., & Manuck, S. B. (1984). Acute psychophysiologic reactivity and risk of cardiovascular disease: A review and methodological critique. *Psychological Bulletin, 96,* 435–464.

Ladwig, K. H., Kieser, M., & Konig, J. (1991). Affective disorders and survival after acute myocardial infarction. *European Heart Journal, 12,* 959–964.

Lazarus, R. S. (1966). *Psychological stress and the coping process.* New York: McGraw-Hill.

Lazarus, R. S. (1983). The coasts and benefits of denial. In S. Breznitz (Ed.), *The denial of stress* (pp. 1–30). New York: International Universities Press.

Lazarus, R. S. (1991). *Emotion and adaptation.* New York: Oxford University Press.

Lazarus, R. S., & Folkman, S. (1984). *Stress, appraisal, and coping.* New York: Springer.

Lee, D., Mendes de Leon, C. F., Jenkins, C. D., Croog, S. H., Levine, S., & Sudilovsky, A. (1992). Relation of hostility to medication adherence, symptom complaints, and blood pressure reduction in a clinical field trial of antihypertensive medication. *Journal of Psychosomatic Research, 36,* 181–190.

Leiker, M., & Hailey, B. J. (1988). A link between hostility and disease: Poor health habits? *Behavioral Medicine, 3,* 129–133.

Levenson, M. R. (1990). Risk taking and personality. *Journal of Personality and Social Psychology, 58,* 1073–1080.

Leventhal, H., Meyer, D., & Nerenz, D. (1980). The common sense representation of illness danger. In S. Rachman (Ed.), *Medical psychology* (Vol. 2, pp. 7–30). New York: Pergamon.

Levy, S., Morrow, L., Bagley, C., & Lippman, M. (1988). Survival hazards analysis in first recurrent breast cancer patients: Seven-year follow-up. *Psychosomatic Medicine, 50,* 520–528.

Linden, W., Chambers, L., Maurice, J., & Lenz, J. W. (1993). Sex differences in social support, self-deception, hostility, and ambulatory cardiovascular activity. *Health Psychology, 12,* 376–380.

Lipkus, I. M., Barefoot, J. C., Williams, R. B., & Siegler, I. C. (1994). Personality measures as predictors of smoking initiation and cessation in the UNC Alumni Heart Study. *Health Psychology, 13,* 149–155.

Lyness, S. A. (1993). Predictors of differences between Type A and B individuals in heart rate and blood pressure reactivity. *Psychological Bulletin, 114,* 266–295.

Manuck, S. B., Kaplan, J. R., & Clarkson, R. B. (1983). Behaviorally induced heart rate reactivity and atherosclerosis in cynomolgus monkeys. *Psychosomatic Medicine, 45,* 95–108.

Manuck, S. B., Marsland, A. L., Kaplan, J. R., & Williams, J. K. (1995). The pathogenicity of behavior and its neuroendocrine mediation: An example from coronary artery disease. *Psychosomatic Medicine, 57,* 275–283.

Manuck, S. B., Olsson, G., Hjemdalh, P., & Rehnqvist, N. (1992). Does cardiovascular reactivity to mental stress have prognostic value in postinfarction patients? A pilot study. *Psychosomatic Medicine, 54,* 102–108.

Mason, J. W. (1975). A historical view of the stress field. *Journal of Human Stress, 1,* 6–12, 22–36.

Matthews, K. (1988). CHD and Type A behaviors: Update on and alternative to the Booth-Kewley and Friedman quantitative review. *Psychological Bulletin, 104,* 373–380.

Matthews, K. A. (1982). Psychological perspectives on the Type A behavior pattern. *Psychological Bulletin, 91,* 293–323.

Matthews, K. A., Glass, D. C., Rosenman, R. H., & Bortner, R. W. (1977). Competitive drive, Pattern A, and coronary heart disease: A further analysis of some data from the Western Collaborative Group Study. *Journal of Chronic Diseases, 30,* 489–498.

McCrae, R. R., & Costa, P. T. (1985). Updating Norman's adequate taxonomy: Intelligence and personality dimensions in natural language and in questionnaires. *Journal of Personality and Social Psychology, 49,* 710–721.

Mechanic, D. (1962). *Students under stress: A study in the social psychology of adaptation.* New York: The Free Press.

Meyer, D., Leventhal, H., & Gutmann, M. (1985). Common-sense models of illness: The example of hypertension. *Health Psychology, 4,* 115–135.

Miller, S. B. (1993). Cardiovascular reactivity in anger-defensive individuals: The influence of task demands. *Psychosomatic Medicine, 55,* 78–85.

Miller, S. M., Shoda, Y., & Hurley, K. (1996). Applying cognitive-social theory to health-protecting behavior: Breast self-examination in cancer screening. *Psychological Bulletin, 119,* 70–94.

Miller, S. M., Lack, E. R., & Astroff, S. (1985). Preference for control and the coronary-prone behavior pattern: "I'd rather do it myself." *Journal of Personality and Social Psychology, 49,* 492–499.

Miller, T. Q., Jenkins, C. D., Kaplan, G. A., & Salonen, J. T. (1995). Are all hostility scales alike? Factor structure and covariation among measures of hostility. *Journal of Applied Social Psychology, 25,* 1142–1168.

Miranda, J., Perez-Stable, E. J., Munoz, R. F., Hargreaves, W., & Henke, C. J. (1991). Somatization, psychiatric disorder, and stress in utilization of ambulatory medical services. *Health Psychology, 10,* 46–51.

Mischel, W. (1968). *Personality assessment.* New York: Wiley.

Mischel, W., & Shoda, Y. (1994). Psychology has two goals: Must it be two fields? *Psychological Inquiry, 5,* 156–158.

Mischel, W., & Shoda, Y. (1995). A cognitive-affective system theory of personality: Reconceptualizing situations, dispositions, dynamics, and invariance in personality structure. *Psychological Review, 102,* 246–268.

Murray, H. A. (1938). *Explorations in personality.* New York: Oxford University Press.

Musante, L., MacDougall, J., Dembroski, T., & Costa, P. (1989). Potential for hostility and dimensions of anger. *Health Psychology, 8,* 343–354.

Newton, T. L, & Contrada, R. J. (1992). Repressive coping and verbal-autonomic response dissociation: The influence of social context. *Journal of Personality and Social Psychology, 62,* 159–167.

Newton, T. L., & Contrada, R. J. (1994). Alexithymia and repression: Contrasting emotion-focused coping styles. *Psychosomatic Medicine, 56,* 457–462.

Pennebaker, J. W., Kiecolt-Glaser, J., & Glaser, R. (1988). Disclosure of traumas and immune function: Health implications for psychotherapy. *Journal of Consulting and Clinical Psychology, 56,* 239–245.

Pervin, L. A. (1990). A brief history of modern personality theory. In L. A. Pervin (Ed.), *Handbook of personality theory and research* (pp. 3–18). New York: Guilford.

Peterson, C. (1988). Explanatory style as a risk factor for illness. *Cognitive Therapy and Research, 12,* 117–130.

Peterson, C., Colvin, D., & Lin, E. H. (1992). Explanatory style and helplessness. *Social Behavior and Personality, 20,* 1–14.

Peterson, C., & Seligman, M.E.P. (1984). Causal explanations as a risk factor for depression: Theory and evidence. *Psychological Review, 91,* 347–374.

Peterson, C., & Seligman, M.E.P., & Vaillant, G. E. (1988). Pessimistic explanatory style is a risk factor for physical illness: A thirty-five year longitudinal study. *Journal of Personality and Social Psychology, 55,* 23–27.

Pettingale, K. W., Morris, T., & Greer, S. (1985). Mental attitudes to cancer: An additional prognostic factor. *Lancet, 1,* 750.

Plomin, R., Lichtenstein, P., Pedersen, N. L., McClearn, G. E., & Nesselroade, J. R. (1990). Genetic influence on life events. *Psychology and Aging, 5,* 25–30.

Reed, G. M., Kemeny, M. E., Taylor, S. E., Wang, H-Y, J., & Visscher, B. R. (1994). Realistic acceptance as a predictor of decreased survival time in gay men with AIDS. *Health Psychology, 13,* 299–307.

Revenson, T. A. (1990). All things are *not* equal: An ecological perspective on the relation between personality and disease. In H. S. Friedman (Ed.), *Personality and disease* (pp. 65–94). New York: Wiley.

Romonov, K., Hatakka, M., Heskinen, E., Laaksonen, H., Kaprio, J., Rose, R., & Koskenvuo, M. (1994). Self-reported hostility and suicidal acts, accidents, and accidental deaths: A prospective study of 21,443 adults aged 25 to 59. *Psychosomatic Medicine, 56,* 328–336.

Rotton, J. (1992). Trait humor and longevity: Do comics have the last laugh? *Health Psychology, 11,* 262–266.

Roy, A., Pickar, D., De Jong, J., Karoum, F., & Linnoila, M. (1988). Norepinephrine and its metabolites in cerebrospinal fluid, plasma, and urine. *Archives of General Psychiatry, 45,* 849–857.

Scarr, S., & McCartney, K. (1983). How people make their own environments: A theory of genotype-environment effects. *Child Development, 54,* 424–435.

Scheier, M. F., & Bridges, M. W. (1995). Person variables and health: Personality predispositions and acute psychological states as shared determinants for disease. *Psychosomatic Medicine, 57,* 255–268.

Scheier, M. F., & Carver, C. S. (1985). Optimism, coping, and health: Assessment and implications of generalized outcome expectancies. *Health Psychology, 4,* 219–247.

Scheier, M. F., Matthews, K. A., Owens, J. F., Magovern, G. J., Lefebve, R. C., Abbott, R. A., & Carver, C. S. (1989). Dispositional optimism and recovery from coronary artery bypass surgery: The beneficial effects on physical and psychological well-being. *Journal of Personality and Social Psychology, 57,* 1024–1040.

Scherer, K. (1986). Vocal affect expression: A review and a model for future research. *Psychological Bulletin, 99,* 143–165.

Scherwitz, L., Berton, K., & Leventhal, H. (1978). Type A behavior, self-involvement, and cardiovascular response. *Psychosomatic Medicine, 40,* 593–609.

Schneider, M. S., Friend, R., Whitaker, P., & Wadhwa, N. K. (1991). Fluid noncompliance and symptomatology in end-stage renal disease: Cognitive and emotional variables. *Health Psychology, 10,* 209–215.

Schneiderman, N. (1983). Animal models of coronary disease. In D. S. Krantz, A. Baum, & J. E. Singer (Eds.), *Handbook of psychology and health: Vol. 3. Cardiovascular disorders* (pp. 19–56). Hillsdale, NJ: Lawrence Erlbaum Associates.

Schneiderman, N., Weiss, S. M., & Kaufman, P. G. (1989). *Handbook of research methods in cardiovascular behavioral medicine.* New York: Plenum.

Schwartz, G. E. (1979). The brain as a health care system. In G. C. Stone, F. Cohen, & N. E. Adler (Eds.), *Health psychology—A handbook* (pp. 549–571). San Francisco: Jossey-Bass.

Schwartz, G. E., & Weiss, S. M. (1977). What is behavioral medicine? *Psychosomatic Medicine, 39,* 377–381.

Schwartz, M. D., Lerman, C., Miller, S. M., Daly, M., & Masny, A. (1995). Coping disposition, perceived risk, and psychological distress among women at increased risk for ovarian cancer. *Health Psychology, 14,* 232–235.

Selye, H. (1956). *The stress of life.* New York: McGraw-Hill.

Selye, H. (1975). Confusion and controversy in the stress field. *Journal of Human Stress, 1,* 37–44.

Shekelle, R. B., Gale, M., Ostfeld, A. M., & Paul, O. (1983). Hostility, risk of coronary heart disease, and mortality. *Psychosomatic Medicine, 45,* 109–114.

Shoda, Y., Mischel, W., & Wright, J. C. (1994). Intra-individual stability in the organization and patterning of behavior: Incorporating psychological situations into the idiographic analysis of personality. *Journal of Personality and Social Psychology, 67,* 1023–1035.

Siegel, J. M. (1984). Type A behavior: Epidemiologic foundations and public health implications. *Annual Review of Public Health, 5,* 343–367.

Siegler, I. C. (1994). Hostility and risk: Demographic and lifestyle variables. In A. W. Siegman & T. W. Smith (Eds.), *Anger, hostility, and the heart* (pp. 199–214). Hillsdale, NJ: Lawrence Erlbaum Associates.

Siegler, I. C., & Costa, P. T., Jr. (1994). Personality and breast cancer screening behaviors. *Annals of Behavioral Medicine, 16,* 347–351.

Siegler, I. C., Feaganes, J. R., & Rimer, B. K. (1995). Predictors of adoption of mammography in women under age 50. *Health Psychology, 14,* 274–278.

Siegman, A. W. (1994). From Type A to hostility to anger: Reflections on the history of coronary-prone behavior. In A. W. Siegman & T. W. Smith (Eds.), *Anger, hostility, and the heart* (pp. 1–21). Hillsdale, NJ: Lawrence Erlbaum Associates.

Siegman, A. W., Anderson, R. W., & Boyle, S. (1991, March). *Repression, impression management, trait anxiety, and cardiovascular reactivity in men and women.* Paper presented at the annual meeting of the Society for Behavioral Medicine, Washington, DC.

Siever, L., & Davis, K. (1985). Overview: Toward a dysregulation hypothesis of depression. *American Journal of Psychiatry, 142,* 1017–1031.

Silverglade, L., Tosi, D. J., Wise, P. S., & D'Costa, A. (1994). Irrational beliefs and emotionality in adolescents with and without bronchial asthma. *Journal of General Psychology, 121,* 199–207.

Smith, R. E., Smoll, F. L., & Ptacek, J. T. (1990). Conjunctive moderator variables in vulnerability and resiliency research: Life stress, social support and coping skills, and adolescent sport injuries. *Journal of Personality and Social Psychology, 58,* 360–370.

Smith, T. W. (1989). Interactions, transactions, and the Type A pattern: Additional avenues in the search for coronary-prone behavior. In A. W. Siegman & T. M. Dembroski (Eds.), *In search of coronary-prone behavior* (pp. 91–116). Hillsdale, NJ: Lawrence Erlbaum Associates.

Smith, T. W. (1992). Hostility and health: Current status of a psychosomatic hypothesis. *Health Psychology, 11,* 139–150.

Smith, T. W., Peck, J. R., & Ward, J. R. (1990). Helplessness and depression in rheumatoid arthritis. *Health Psychology, 9,* 377–389.

Smith, T. W., & Williams, P. G. (1992). Personality and health: Advantages and limitations of the five-factor model. *Journal of Personality, 60,* 395–423.

Snow, B. (1978). Level of aspiration in coronary-prone and non-coronary-prone adults. *Personality and Social Psychology Bulletin, 4,* 416–419.

Spielberger, C. D., Johnson, E. H., Russell, S. F., Crane, R. J., Jacobs, G. A., & Worden, T. J. (1985). The experience and expression of anger: Construction and validation of an anger expression scale. In M. A. Chesney & R. H. Rosenman (Eds.), *Anger and hostility in cardiovascular and behavioral disorders* (pp. 5–30). Washington, DC: Hemisphere.

Stone, A. A., & Shiffman, S. (1994). Ecological momentary assessment (EMA) in behavioral medicine. *Annals of Behavioral Medicine, 16,* 199–202.

Stoney, C. M., & Engebretson, T. O. (1994). Anger and hostility: Potential mediators of the gender difference in coronary heart disease. In A. W. Siegman & T. W. Smith (Eds.), *Anger, hostility, and the heart* (pp. 215–237). Hillsdale, NJ: Lawrence Erlbaum Associates.

Strauman, T. J., Lemieux, A. M., & Coe, C. L. (1993). Self-discrepancy and natural killer cell activity: Immunological consequences of negative self-evaluation. *Journal of Personality and Social Psychology, 64,* 1042–1052.

Strauman, T. J., Vookles, J., Berenstein, V., Chaiken, S., & Higgins, E. T. (1991). Self-discrepancies and vulnerability to body dissatisfaction and disordered eating. *Journal of Personality and Social Psychology, 61,* 946–956.

Strube, M. J. (1987). A self-appraisal model of the Type A behavior pattern. In R. Hogan & W. H. Jones (Eds.), *Perspectives in personality: Theory, measurement and interpersonal dynamics* (pp. 201–250). Greenwich, CT: JAI Press.

Suarez, E. C., & Williams, R. B., Jr. (1990). The relationship between dimensions of hostility and cardiovascular reactivity as a function of task characteristics. *Psychosomatic Medicine, 52,* 558–570.

Suls, J., & Fletcher, B. (1985). The relative efficacy of avoidant and nonavoidant coping strategies: A meta-analysis. *Health Psychology, 4,* 249–288.

Suls, J., & Wan, C. K. (1993). The relationship between trait hostility and cardiovascular reactivity: A quantitative review and analysis. *Psychophysiology, 30,* 615–626.

Suls, J., Wan, C. K., & Costa, P. T., Jr. (1995). Relationship of trait anger to resting blood pressure: A meta-analysis. *Health Psychology, 14,* 444–456.

Taylor, G. J. (1984). Alexithymia: Concept, measurement, and implications for treatment. *American Journal of Psychiatry, 141,* 725–732.

Taylor, J. A. (1953). A personality scale of manifest anxiety. *Journal of Abnormal and Social Psychology, 48,* 285–290.

Taylor, S. E., & Brown, J. D. (1994). Positive illusions and well-being revisited: Separating fact from fiction. *Psychological Bulletin, 116,* 21–27.

Temoshok, L. (1987). Personality, coping style, emotion, and cancer: Towards an integrative model. *Cancer Surveys, 6,* 545–567.

Thoits, P. A. (1986). Social support as coping assistance. *Journal of Consulting and Clinical Psychology, 54,* 416–423.

Tomkins, S. (1962). *Affect, imagery, consciousness: Vol. 1. The positive affects.* New York: Springer.

Wallbott, H. G., & Scherer, K. R. (1991). Stress specificities: Differential effects of coping style, gender, and type of stressor on autonomic arousal, facial expression, and subjective feeling. *Journal of Personality and Social Psychology, 61,* 147–156.

Wassertheil-Smoller, S., for the SHEP Cooperative Research Group. (1994, March). *Change in depression as a precursor of cardiovascular events.* Paper presented at the Conference on Cardiovascular Disease, Epidemiology and Prevention, Tampa, FL.

Watkins, P. L., Fisher, E. B., Southard, D. R., Ward, C. H., & Schechtman, K. B. (1989). Assessing the relationship of Type A beliefs to cardiovascular disease and psychosocial stress. *Journal of Psychopathology and Behavioral Assessment, 11,* 113–125.

Watson, D., Clark, L. A., & Tellegen, A. (1984). Cross-cultural convergence in the structure of mood: A Japanese replication and a comparison with U. S. findings. *Journal of Personality and Social Psychology, 47,* 127–144.

Watson, D., & Pennebaker, J. W. (1989). Health complaints, stress, and distress: Exploring the central role of negative affectivity. *Psychological Review, 96,* 234–254.

Weinberger, D. A. (1990). The construct validity of the repressive coping style. In J. L. Singer (Ed.), *Repression and dissociation* (pp. 337–386). Chicago: University of Chicago Press.

Weinberger, D. A., Schwartz, G. E., & Davidson, R. J. (1979). Low-anxious, high-anxious, and repressive coping styles: Psychometric patterns and behavioral and physiological responses to stress. *Journal of Abnormal Psychology, 88,* 369–380.

Weisse, C. S. (1992). Depression and immunocompetence: A review of the literature. *Psychological Bulletin, 111,* 475–489.

Wiebe, D. J. (1991). Hardiness and stress moderation: A test of proposed mechanisms. *Journal of Personality and Social Psychology, 1,* 89–99.

Wiedenfeld, S. A., O'Leary, A., Bandura, A., Brown, S., Levine, S., & Raska, K. (1990). Impact of perceived self-efficacy in coping with stressors on components of the immune system. *Journal of Personality and Social Psychology, 59,* 1082–1094.

Williams, R. B., Jr., Haney, T. L., Lee, K. L., Blumenthal, J. A., & Whalen, R. E. (1980). Type A behavior, hostility, and coronary atherosclerosis. *Psychosomatic Medicine, 42,* 539–549.

Wright, R. A., Contrada, R. J., & Glass, D. C. (1985). Psychophysiologic correlates of Type A behavior. In E. S. Katkin & S. B. Manuck (Eds.), *Advances in behavioral medicine* (pp. 39–88). Greenwich, CT: JAI Press.

5

Visceral Learning

Bernard T. Engel
Department of Psychiatry and Behavioral Sciences, Duke University Medical Center

This chapter includes three sections. The first part is an overview of the historical discoveries and evolution of concepts about the autonomic nervous system. The second part is a selective review of the experimental findings on operant conditioning of visceral function. The third part is a theoretical consideration of the significance of the findings that visceral responses can be brought under stimulus control. The chapter leans heavily on the writings of Sheehan (1936) for the review of the history of findings and concepts about the autonomic nervous system. It also examines the overviews by Kuntz (1953) and Pick (1970); however, it became clear that they also used Sheehan as a primary source. Thus, whereas specific citations to Sheehan are not included in the first part, his work is followed in detail and anyone who wishes to get closer to the original sources should read the original. The second part includes a review of a number of issues relevant to the topic of visceral learning. Therefore, the chapter considers not only studies of operant conditioning of autonomic responses, but also studies on visceral perception. Although it trys to address the salient issues, no effort is made to provide a complete survey of the literature. However, it does try to provide interested readers with enough guidelines to enable them to find that literature. The third part tries to give some conceptual meaning to the findings reported in the previous part, and attempts are made to fit those concepts into the concepts introduced in the history section.

1800 YEARS IN LESS THAN 10 PAGES

Throughout most of recorded history little or no differentiation was made between the physiological nature of the autonomic nervous system and the functional significance of its actions. Furthermore, much of the speculation about function was part of the broader question of the way the nervous system worked, in general. Galen's hypothesis that "animal spirits" were generated by the brain and conveyed to the endorgans dominated thinking for more than one millennium. He proposed that the brain was the organ primarily responsible for regulating performance by communicating "sympathy" or "consent" among the different parts of the body. He also identified seven pairs of cranial nerves, among which the sixth had three main branches: the superior, recurrent laryngeal and costal. Thus, Galen included the vagus nerve and the sympathetic trunk as part of an anatomical and physiological unit. It is noteworthy that he felt that it was through these nerves that the viscera received "an 'exquisite' sensitivity from the brain, and a motor power from the spinal cord" (Sheehan, 1936, p. 1083). The "'exquisite' sensitivity" of the brain in the control of visceral function lies at the heart of the nature of visceral conditioning as that concept is understood today. It was not until the 17th century that Galen's model of the autonomic nervous system—a designation that did not appear until the late 19th century—began to be refined and eventually modified. Willis made several important anatomical and physiological observations and psychological speculations. He was the first to describe the spinal accessory nerve and the vagus nerve (which was referred to by him and others as the eighth nerve). He also was the first to note that stimulation of the vagal branch arising from the aortic arch (which is now called the depressor nerve) caused the heart to slow. He erred in perpetuating the view that the "intercostal" nerve originated in the brain. Willis was also among the first to introduce the concepts of voluntary and involuntary movement. According to Willis, the involuntary animal spirits flowed from the cerebellum to the body through the vagus and intercostal nerves: The voluntary spirits emanated from the brain and spinal cord. The nature of these concepts, and the galenic concept of sensitivity of the brain can be seen in Willis' notion that although thoracic and abdominal sensations were typically unconscious, they could become conscious if they were strong enough. Likewise, the cerebrum could voluntarily act (through the cerebellum) on visceral structures; for example, the exercise of the will over breathing. Thus, Willis believed that the intercostal and wandering (vagus) nerves served two functions: the origination of voluntary movements and the communication of sympathy among the various parts of the body.

Whytt, who followed Willis by about 100 years, introduced a very fundamental concept to explain involuntary movements. He proposed that there were local stimuli that were responsible for eliciting involuntary movements. Thus, he anticipated the existence of reflex pathways long before any evidence for these existed, and he recognized the importance of local stimuli in understanding the nature of visceral sensation. I believe that even today, the significance of adequate (local) stimuli is not fully appreciated. Whytt also elaborated greatly on the concept of sympathy by pointing out that sympathy required afferent feedback. For example, it was well known in his day that vomiting and nausea were associated with headaches, that the pupil of one eye would contract when light was shone in the opposite eye, and that the sight or smell of food provoked the flow of saliva. He argued that such sympathies presuppose feeling, and there must be sensory nerves that caused these perceptions.

Du Petit's studies in the early 18th century showed conclusively that the intercostal nerve did not originate in the brain. This finding raised a number of questions about the way in which voluntary and involuntary movements might interact: These questions are still not fully answered. However, for 18th century anatomists and physiologists, the predominant question was structural: How does information get to and from the brain and viscera? Winslow proposed that the sympathetic ganglia were independent neural control centers. Johnstone, who followed Winslow, proposed that the ganglia intercepted and prevented determinations of the will from reaching certain parts of the body. However, both models were inadequate because they did not explain Willis' observation that "strong" sensations could become conscious, and Whytt's argument about the existence of adequate stimuli and their roles in mediating sympathies. Nevertheless, there is one important implication of Winslow's and Johnstone's models that does require further consideration; namely, that the existence of autonomous control centers (Winslow) or sensory filters (Johnstone) means that there can be specific visceral effects as well as sympathies: Specificity is a necessary condition for visceral learning.

Bichat, who flourished in the early 19th century, introduced the concepts of organic and animal life (*la vie organique* and *la vie animale*). These concepts exist today in the notions of visceral and somatic functions, respectively. Bichat took this formulation further, ascribing the regulation of the continuous processes of organic life to the various nerve clusters that comprise the sympathetic ganglia; and, the intermittent, interactive (behavioral?) functions of animal life to the brain. He also argued that there was no such thing as a sympathetic nerve. Rather, there were multiple communications among the disseminated ganglia, which function independently and in concert with one another. Nevertheless, he left some room for Willis' strong sensations by suggesting that the sympathetic rami somehow enabled the animal life with its center in the brain to communicate with the organic life with its centers in the ganglia: how, and under what conditions was unclear. Reil, a contemporary of Bichat, accepted the notion that the ganglia were independent control centers; however, he also elaborated on the role of the white rami, suggesting that these were filters that normally prevented visceral sensations from reaching the brain except in certain diseases when visceral sensations could become conscious. Thus, a recurrent theme that still persists: Visceral sensations are involuntary and unconscious, except when they are not!

Throughout the first half of the 19th century there was a great deal of work directed at understanding how animal spirits and organic spirits interacted. Much of this took the form of anatomic and physiologic studies of the function of the sympathetic rami. One view was that they were the origin of the sympathetic nerves; a second view was that they were pathways for sympathetic nerves that arose in the ganglia; and the third was that they were regions where animal and organic fibers interacted. The latter view, which was championed by Remak and Müller, prevailed. What is especially noteworthy about this model is that it reflected an effort on the part of anatomists and physiologists to correlate structure and function, an effort that still goes on (e.g., Prechtl & Powley, 1990). There was a prevailing belief that it is possible to reliably differentiate between the animal and organic fibers on the basis of their structures. Students of the history of physiological psychology will recognize the similarity between this effort to correlate structure with function, and the position of the advocates of localization of brain function *vis-à-vis* the mass action theorists. Experimental psychologists also should recognize the similarity between Bichat's dichotomy between animal and organic spirits and the point of view still held by some that the distinction between operantly and classically conditionable responses has an anatomic basis; for example, according to Roberts (1986): "The [somato-]motor system (including perceptual processing) is the system by which organisms interact with an environment whose demands and particular features are unique to each member of the species" (p. 301).

Technological developments that occurred throughout the 19th century (and which are beyond the scope of this overview) led to great advances in neurophysiology and neuroanatomy. Bernard set out to understand how the nervous system mediated thermoregulation. In the process, he discovered the vasomotor nerves. Within a few years, he and others not only demonstrated the existence of vasoconstrictor and vasodilator fibers but also showed that vasomotor effects were mediated, at least in part, from brain stem structures. Also in the 19th century, Hall defined the basic principles of the reflex arc, and Cyon and Ludwig described the main features of the baroreflex. Thus, it was well-known and widely accepted that the sympathetic system included afferent as well as motor fibers. Because autonomic afferent activity was generally not perceived, these afferent, sympathetic fibers were regarded as elements in reflex arcs. Nevertheless, the possibility that these ordinarily insensible events could become sensible under poorly defined conditions was still troublesome and required special consideration.

By the end of the 19th and beginning of the 20th century, anatomical, physiological, and behavioral analyses of the autonomic nervous system began to diverge. Following a series of elegant anatomical studies, Gaskell defined the "involuntary nervous system" and its three major central, neural outflow pathways: the bulbar, thoracolumbar, and sacral divisions. He emphasized that these outflow pathways mediated two, antagonistic sets of nerves, which controlled the involuntary muscles and glands, one excitatory and the other inhibitory, and that they subserved catabolic and anabolic organic functions. Langley, his younger contemporary, greatly extended the analysis of the nature and structure of the two nervous systems through the use of pharmacologic tracing agents (e.g., nicotine, epinephrine, and pilocarpine). Langley also introduced the terms, autonomic nervous system and parasympathetic nervous system, to the literature. Conceptually, Langley had a major impact on 20th century thinking because he excluded visceral afferents from the autonomic nervous system: "the autonomic nervous system consists of the nerve cells and nerve fibres, by means of which efferent impulses pass to tissues other than the multinuclear striated muscle" (1921, p. 1).

Langley's exclusion of afferent fibers from the autonomic nervous system (ANS) has been very troublesome for physiologists. Pick (1970) characterized it as a "limited concept [that] subsequently gave rise to the widespread but erroneous notion concerning the lack of visceral afferent fibers" (p. 23). Contemporary physiologists largely ignore Langley's definition although anatomists still take it seriously (e.g., Prechtl & Powley, 1990). In addition to the "deafferentation" of the ANS, there was another related problem that evolved in the first 60 years or so of this century: It is the notion that the sympathetic nervous system responds en masse. Even though Whytt pointed out more than 200 years ago that there must be specificity in autonomic responding, the exclusion of afferent fibers, coupled with the clinical observation that visceral organs are relatively insensitive unless they are distended, has encouraged the view that the sympathetic nervous system is monolithic in its response because without feedback there is no mechanism for specificity. Several examples should illustrate the kinds of problems that result from this attribution. Bernard's emphasis on the relative constancy of the *mileau interior* and Cannon's concept of homeostasis are especially obvious because it is impossible to conceptualize the degree of regulation they intended in the absence of afferent feedback and specificity of action. Cardiovascular physiologists who have given their attention to blood pressure regulation (baroreflexes, chemoreflexes and renal control of blood pressure) also have found it necessary to include afferent feedback and specificity as factors in the regulation of the cardiovascular system. Exercise physiologists have built their models of cardiopulmonary regulation, and the interaction between cardiovascular and sudomotor regulation during exercise around the existence of highly specific, afferent, feedback mechanisms. Finally, physiologists who study thermoregulation have emphasized that the interaction between heat conservation (vasomotor regulation) and heat production (a- and b-adrenergic regulation of heat production in brown adipose tissues, and muscle activity, including shivering), depend greatly on feedback from peripheral, and feedforward from central neural receptors. The impact of Langley's definitions can be seen as recently as 1977, when Wurster found it necessary to write that "the monolithic view of mass sympathetic discharge has fallen" (p. 239).

Wurster (1977) also added that "much of the past and present sympathetic neurophysiology has been studied under anesthetized and paralyzed conditions. Almost all concepts of sympathetic control require testing in the unanesthetized, instrumented animal" (p. 239). Obviously, behavioral studies of autonomic function have always been carried out in unanesthetized animals. Classical conditioning methodology has been used extensively to demonstrate the integrative function of central, neural control of visceral efferent action, and even more importantly, the extent to which visceral afferent activity can serve as a conditional signal for efferent responses (the works of Bykov, 1957, Chernigovsky, 1967, and Adam, 1967, 1998 are especially noteworthy). Another important area of investigation has been the study of the autonomic concomitants of emotional behaviors (Cannon, 1929; Turpin, 1983). Also of special interest here is the research in exercise physiology. Despite the fact that Johansson (1895), and Krogh and Lindhard (1913) showed that some aspects of the cardio-pulmonary adjustments to exercise are emitted behaviors, namely, "central commands," exercise physiologists have generally attempted to explain all of the cardiopulmonary adjustments to exercise in terms of peripherally mediated reflexes (e.g., Rowell, 1980).

CONDITIONING OF VISCERAL RESPONSES

In 1938, Skinner wrote:

> Any given skeletal respondent may be duplicated with operants and hence may also be conditioned according to Type R. Whether this is also true of the autonomic part is questionable. There is little reason to expect conditioning of Type R in an autonomic response, since it does not as a rule naturally act upon the environment in a way that will produce a reinforcement. (p. 112)

Although he went on to cite anecdotal evidence for an autonomic operant that does "act naturally upon the environment"—the well-known disposition of young children to emit tears to obtain reinforcement—it was the negative statement cited earlier, coupled with the general eschewal of physiology among most experimental psychologists of the time, that became the dominant view in Western psychology over the next 30 years. Thus, behavioral scientists, who were the persons most likely to address the role of learning in autonomic regulation in conscious animals, were simply not interested.

The renaissance of the experimental analysis of operant autonomic conditioning began in the 1950s with studies of electrodermal conditioning by Kimmel and Hill (1960). Later Shearn (1961) wrote a review with a provocative question as its title: "Does the Heart Learn?" However, his answer was equivocal. Within a few years a few positive papers appeared: for example, Engel and Hansen (1966), Miller and Carmona (1967), followed by a extraordinarily large number of reports and reviews—mostly positive, many negative, many critical, and many excessive. Consider the spectrum of articles reprinted in Barber et al., (1971), and the large number of claims for clinical efficacy that provoked a largely critical rebuke from Orne (1979). The interested readers can examine these articles for themselves, so they are not reiterated here. Rather, the remainder of this section, addresses three, specific questions: Are the viscera sensitive? Are there any studies that have demonstrated autonomic conditioning under conditions in which somatomotor effects have been excluded? And, irrespective of the mechanism of action of visceral conditioning, does visceral conditioning have clinical significance?

Visceral Afferents

The existence of visceral afferents clearly is a necessary condition for the occurrence of operant visceral conditioning. If Langley's definition of the autonomic nervous system is valid, then it would be impossible to understand how contingent reinforcement could modulate visceral responses directly. Thus, the demonstration of visceral afferents, and the presence of central neural feedback from these afferents is a first step in addressing the existence of visceral learning. Several techniques have been exploited to evaluate the extent and importance of visceral afferents. Most of the traditional, Western physiological studies have focused on intrinsic effects, that is, direct recording of reflex reactions to adequate stimuli. Eastern European physiologists have made extensive use of classical conditioning methodology—so called, interoceptive conditioning—to demonstrate the existence of visceral sensation. American psychologists (mostly) have used traditional psychometric methods to demonstrate sensibility. Rather than review all of these studies, each is illustrated and then a few salient articles are cited from which the interested reader can educe further information.

Evidence for the Existence of Visceral Afferents. Langley (1921), of course, knew about the existence of afferent nerves; however, his justification for classifying all autonomic nerves as motor was that "the afferent nerves accompanying [the efferent, autonomic nerves] were not as a whole distinguishable from the other afferent nerves" (p. 9). Although it is not clear what Langley meant by "as a whole distinguishable," it is clear that there is evidence for the existence of visceral afferents in all vertebrates (Nilsson, 1983), and that these afferents perform in a way that makes them integral to the overall function of the visceral organs they serve in that they are sensitive to the kinds of stimuli that these organs are likely to experience. Thus, separating the afferent from the efferent function of the autonomic nervous system makes little sense. For example, there are both mechanorceptors and chemoreceptors in the heart, lung, and blood vessels (Armour, 1977) that provide important mechanisms for integrating cardiac function with systemic and pulmonary vascular function. There is also an extensive literature on the input from these receptors to brain stem foci (e.g., Langhorst, Schulz & Lambertz, 1983), which integrate cardiovascular function systemically. Similar principles apply to the regulation of other visceral organs such as the gut system and the urinary bladder.

Visceral Perception. It should be apparent that there has been an enduring interest in the nature of visceral perception. Abdominal sensations are often the earliest indicators of inflammation or obstruction (viz. Willis' "strong" sensations). The James theory of emotion—usually inappropriately called the James-Lange theory—appears in almost every introductory psychology text. According to the James (1890) theory, the perception of bodily changes is emotion. One of the earliest studies of visceral perception was the report by Cannon and Washburn (1912) in which they correlated hunger pangs with gastric contractions. It has also been reported that many patients can detect the occurrence of premature ventricular contractions (Kline & Bidder, 1946). This finding is especially interesting because it is one of the few examples of a sensible visceral response that does not involve either significant stretch in a viscus or the introduction of a chemical agent such as CO_2. The recognition that it is possible to operantly condition visceral responses has enhanced the interest in studies of visceral perception. Brener (1974) proposed that afferent feedback from a visceral response enables a subject to "calibrate" their performance relative to a response image that they have previously acquired and that is elicited by an external stimulus; and that "activation of the [response image] leads to a state of nervous system imbalance resulting in the response specified by the image" (p. 368). In 1977, Whitehead, Drescher, and Heyman (1977) described a psychometric method for measuring heart rate perception, and reported that there was no relation between the ability of subjects to learn to control their heart rates, and their ability to perceive their heart beats. There are several interpretations to this finding. The most obvious, of course, is that the finding shows that it is not possible to sense heart beats directly; however, that interpretation requires the elimination of alternative possibilities. One such possibility is that perception measured psychometrically is an inaccurate index of afferent neural activity from the heart; that is, the signal to which the subjects responded in the Whitehead et al. (1977) study is not mediated by receptors in the heart. For example, the signal to which the subjects responded in the Whitehead et al. (1977) study could have originated from stretch receptors in the ventricle or aorta responding to ventricular contraction and/or aortic stretch following the rise in blood pressure. It is common experience that people often report feeling their hearts "pounding" and that these sensations are the result of the pressure generated by the heart beat. As previously noted there is evidence that some patients can detect the occurrence of premature ventricular beats (Kline & Bidder, 1946). This study also showed that the patients detected the premature beat itself—which is relatively weak because the ventricle has not filled normally, and not the beat following the premature beat, which is relatively strong because the ventricle is especially distended. Another possibility for the Whitehead et al. (1977) finding is that the relation between detection and performance is not appropriately assessed using linear correlation methodology; for example, direction of change but not magnitude of response may be perceived. Since the report by Whitehead et al. (1977), there have been recurrent reports of the ability of human subjects to sense their heart beats, mostly appearing in PSYCHOPHYSIOLOGY. The reports have been largely preoccupied with methodological issues; however, most have in common the finding that people can detect their heart beats.

Interoceptive Conditioning. Probably most readers of this chapter will have a greater interest in conditioning studies than they will in perceptual or psychometric experiments. The classic works of Bykov (1957), Chernigovsky (1967) and Adam (1967) have already been cited. A study from Adam's laboratory illustrates the kinds of findings these experiments have yielded. Bardos (1989) studied the effect of intestinal distension on taste aversion in rats. He found that pairing a novel tasting solution with aversive, intestinal distension resulted in suppression of consumption of the novel solution on a subsequent test, during which there was no distention. He also tested the effect of the distending stimulus on a variety of behaviors: he compared distension with a fluid-filled balloon and an isovolumic, air-filled balloon. Because the fluid-filled balloon was nondistensible, and the air-filled balloon could be compressed, the fluid-filled balloon caused greater stretch in the gut wall. He found that consumption of a neutral, saccharine solution was similar in the two conditions, but the greater degree of stretch caused by the fluid-filled balloon suppressed other behaviors such as grooming and rearing. Thus, these studies showed evidence for interoceptive conditioning, and showed further that the gut manifested stimulus specificity (NB, Whytt's, adequate stimulus). In addition to the laboratory studies cited here, there also is evidence that taste aversion classical conditioning can mediate clinically significant effects. Bovbjerg et al. (1992) reported a controlled study of conditioned nausea in women receiving chemotherapy for breast cancer. Patients receiving a fruit-flavored drink, paired with infusion of a chemotherapeutic agent, reported significantly more nausea to the fruit drink in postchemotherapy trials than did control subjects in whom the fruit drink was not paired with infusion.

Operant Conditioning of Visceral Responses. Skinner (1938) raised the two major conceptual problems that need to be addressed in studies of operant conditioning of visceral responses: One is to demonstrate that visceral responses can "act upon the environment in any way that will produce a reinforcement," and the second is that, "the respondent may be chained to an operant." The majority of studies with people have tried to deal with the first issue by showing that the autonomic response in question can be modified so as to increase the probability of positive or negative reinforcement. However, studies with human subjects have not addressed the chaining question well; probably, because most experimental attempts to deal with this question call for surgical or pharmacological interventions that are difficult or impossible to implement in people. This section reviews a number of studies—mostly in animals—that seem to address Skinner's concerns. The reader who wishes to pore through the extensive literature published during the 1970s will find useful the collections of reprints useful published by Aldine under the title "Biofeedback and Self-Control" (Barber et al., 1971; Stoyva et al., 1972; Miller et al., 1974; Shapiro et al., 1973; DiCara et al., 1975; Barber et al., 1976; Kamiya et al., 1977; Stoyva et al., 1979) and "Biofeedback and Behavioral Medicine" (Shapiro et al., 1981). Those who want to avail themselves of bibliographic searches to review the literature after 1980, may find that the term *biofeedback* is more useful than the terms, *visceral conditioning* or *operant conditioning of visceral responses.*

The evidence that visceral responses can "act upon the environment in a way that will produce a reinforcement" is extensive. There are a multitude of studies that have shown that contingent reinforcement will change the rate of emission of visceral responses. The number of successful studies, mostly with people, included in the reviews cited here are very great. In addition, the studies with patients that are summarized later also are convincing. Animal studies are far fewer; however, these also show that visceral responses (in particular, cardiovascular responses) can be operantly conditioned (Engel, 1986). The reader should be warned that in evaluating the validity of such studies, it is important to separate habituation from conditioning. Multiple session experiments are the best way to control for habituation. The studies by Plumlee (1969), Harris, Gilliam, Findley, and Brady (1973), and Bardos, Talan, and Engel (1989), who taught monkeys to modify their blood pressures, and Engel and Gottlieb (1970), who successfully conditioned the same monkeys to increase and decrease their heart rates, showed that these autonomic responses could be operantly conditioned and that habituation was not a likely mechanism for the observed changes. In addition, the studies by Bardos et al. (1989) and Engel and Gottlieb (1970) are based on differential conditioning of a response within the same subject, a procedure that is a more robust test of visceral learning than is unidirectional conditioning. There are also anecdotal examples from common experience that indicate it is possible to emit a visceral response in order to obtain reinforcement. One example is the one that Skinner cited: "the ability of young children to cry 'real tears' to produce a reinforcing stimulus" (1938, pp. 112-113). A second example is the common experience (especially noteworthy in dogs) of salivation at the sight of food. And a third example is the ability that most people acquire to inhibit urinary bladder contractions—except under appropriate conditions. Also noteworthy is the capacity that many mammals (e.g., dogs, rodents) have to urinate repeatedly in order to mark their territories. The evidence that autonomically mediated responses can interact with the environment to obtain contingent reinforcement is unequivocal. However, to properly evaluate this interaction, the nature of the reinforcing stimulus must be considered. In Whytt's terms, the interaction will occur when the stimulus is adequate.

Skinner's second argument "that the respondent may be chained to an operant" is much more difficult to refute. There are two problems: First, the fact that a correlation can be demonstrated between a somatomotor response and an autonomically, mediated response does not necessarily mean that the "respondent is chained to the operant." The converse could also be true; for example, B. R. Dworkin, Filewich, Miller, Craigmyle, and Pickering (1979) showed that an acute rise in blood pressure will reduce the distance rats will run on a treadmill to escape a noxious stimulus. Second, even if one or another somatomotor response was experimentally ruled out, this does not necessarily mean that all somatomotor responses are ruled out. With regard to the last point, it is also important to recognize that even if the somatomotor system was paralyzed, the existence of chaining would not have unequivocally been excluded because paralysis prevents only the expression of the response but not its central neural mediation. As a matter of fact, the dichotomy between operants and respondents is physiologically naive because somatomotor and autonomic responses are necessarily integrated; for example, it is impossible to sustain striate muscle action without adequate blood flow. In any case, there have been several attempts to exclude somatomotor mediation as a factor in operant autonomic conditioning. One is by selecting responses that are not somatically mediated; for example, contraction of the urinary bladder (Lapides, Sweet, & Lewis, 1957). A second is to use pharmacological blockade to elucidate autonomic control mechanisms. Black (1967) carried out a series of studies of cardiac conditioning in dogs using curarization to block somatomotor responses. His general conclusion was that "heart rate can be changed by operant conditioning procedures. Secondly, these changes in heart rate are associated with skeletal movement. They are not necessarily associated with overt skeletal movement, but at least with central proceses involved in the initiation and maintenance of movement." (p. 20). Nevertheless, he also took pains to point out that his studies were "far from conclusive" (p. 20). The studies of Miller and his colleagues using curare to control movement in cardiac conditioning studies of rodents should be well-known and should not need detailed review. What is important, however, is the recognition reported by Miller and B. R. Dworkin (1974) that curarization is a complex technical procedure, and that the earlier reports using this methodology were faulted and not definitive. Nevertheless, after many years of effort, B. R. Dworkin and S. I. Dworkin addressed and overcame these problems (1990). Hopefully, in the near future, they will be able to clarify the role of somatomotor activity in cardiac conditioning in this model.

Several autonomic responses have been studied that are emitted independent of any somatomotor control: Many of these studies have been done with patients. This section considers only the behavioral and physiological aspects rather than the clinical implications. Weiss and Engel (1971) studied a series of patients who were trained to increase and decrease the prevalence of premature ventricular contractions of the heart. There is no evidence that these intracardiac effects have somatomotor correlates. Most of the patients were able to perform reliably. One patient was especially interesting because she reported a great deal of anxiety and distress when the frequency of her premature beats diminished. An interview revealed that she had found the presence of these aberrant beats reinforcing, and when they began to disappear, she feared that her heart had stopped beating! Clearly, this is further evidence for the reinforcing property of visceral sensation. Bleecker and Engel (1973b) studied a group of patients with atrial fibrillation. In these patients, the normal cardiac rate control mechanism—modulation of the depolarization of the atrial pacemaker—is absent. Thus, the ability of these patients to regulate their heart rates must have occurred either at the level of the arterio-ventricular node or at the ventricle, itself. Neither of these mechanisms has ever been shown to be affected by somatomotor activity. Burgio, Whitehead, and Engel (1985), and Burgio, Stutzman, and Engel (1989) trained patients with so-called, uninhibited urinary bladder contractions to inhibit these contractions (see, Burgio, Whitehead, & Engel, 1985; Fig. 3). Because the urinary bladder has only autonomic innervation, the ability to emit these responses could only occur through direct autonomic action.

The "chaining" issue has been addressed in other ways. First, the interaction between an operantly conditioned autonomic response (heart rate) under conditions where heart rate and blood pressure responses were elicited by another stimulus has been studied. In particular, two conditions have been studied: classical conditioning and exercise. In the first study, monkeys were alternately trained in a classical conditioning paradigm and in operant, heart rate slowing or speeding, training schedules (Ainslie & Engel, 1974). In all cases, the classical, unconditional stimulus (tail shock) was identical to the operant punisher. After operant training, the heart rate responses to the classical, conditional stimulus was modified in the direction of the operant heart rate response suggesting that the classical, unconditional stimulus may actually be an operant reinforcer. One other interesting aspect of this study was that although the classically conditioned heart rate response was altered as a result of the operant heart rate training, the blood pressure responses that were never under stimulus control did not change. This latter finding is a further demonstration of the degree of specificity to which autonomically mediated responses can be emitted.

Second, attempts were made to show that the cardiac response to exercise can be emitted independently of any reflexes. Bolme and Novotny (1969) demonstrated that if dogs are classically conditioned to exercise by walking on a treadmill, an increase in leg blood flow can be observed which occurs in response to the conditional stimulus, (i.e., prior to the onset of the exercise itself). Furthermore, if the animals are trained to discriminate between two conditional signals, one indicating a higher level of exercise than the other, then the animal will emit a greater blood flow response during the fore-period of the higher level cue. This study showed that the anticipatory responses to exercise (both somatomotor and cardiovascular) can be conditioned. However, it did not address the question of the role of conditioning in the regulation of the cardiovascular responses during exercise. Talan and Engel (1986) and Engel and Talan (1991b) built on this model. First, they operantly conditioned monkeys to exercise (lift weights) to avoid a tail shock. Then, they operantly conditioned them to slow their heart rates to avoid the identical shock. The two behavioral contingencies were signaled by different sets of cues. When the animals were performing the two behaviors reliably—training took place over months—they then taught them to perform both tasks at the same time. Thus, the animals had to lift weights to avoid tail shock, and they had to attenuate the tachycardia of exercise to avoid tail shock. In a typical experimental day, an animal performed in four experimental sessions: two that were exercise only and two that were combined heart rate slowing and exercise. In both studies, all animals learned the contingencies and performed highly reliably. In fact, some animals were able to attenuate the tachycardia of exercise in the combined sessions even while lifting the weights more often then in the exercise only sessions. These experiments showed that the heart rate response during exercise could beome an operant; however, there was still the possibility that some undefined somatomotor reflex could have mediated the cardiac response, although it is unclear how such a reflex could result in a slower heart rate during greater exercise. In order to address this last question, Engel and Talan (1991a) repeated these studies with three of the same animals at times when the animals were receiving any of three autonomically active drugs: (a) *atenolol*, which is a cardiac- specific β-blocker; (b) *atenolol* and *prazosin,* the latter being an α-adrenergic blocker; or (c) *methyl-atropine,* which is a vagal blocker that does not cross the blood-brain barrier. Thus, these drugs completely blocked one or another efferent component of the autonomic nervous system. If the heart rate response, during the combined session, was the result of a reflex response, then this intervention should have eliminated the animals' abilities to perform reliably because the drugs blocked one or another arm of the putative reflex, and it should have extinguished the reflex. In fact, none of the drugs interfered with performance. No matter which drug the animals received, they were able to consistently and reliably attenuate the tachycardia of exercise. In a later experiment from this laboratory (Chefer, Talan, & Engel, 1997) the investigators identified several brain areas that played a role in mediating conditioned attenuation of the tachycardia of exercise. This series of experiments would seem to answer Skinner's questions: animals can learn to attenuate the tachycardia of exercise to avoid shock, and an operantly conditioned heart rate response is not necessarily the result of a somatomotor mediated reflex.

CLINICAL FINDINGS

There are a great many studies of the clinical application of operant conditioning technology to the regulation of aberrant physiological responses, such as EEG activity in children with attention deficit disorders (Lubar, 1991), or anal (Engel, Nikoomanesh & Shuster, 1974) or urinary (Burgio, Robinson & Engel, 1986) sphincter training in incontinent patients. However, the responses brought under stimulus control in these studies were not autonomically mediated and are not considered here. Relatively wide-ranging reviews of many such clinical applications can be found in Hatch, Fisher and Rugh (1987), and Basmajian (1989).

The previous section, reviewed some of the evidence to support the hypothesis that autonomically, mediated responses can "act upon the environment in [a] way that will produce a reinforcement" and that "the [autonomic response need not] be chained to an operant." It should be clear that whereas these theoretical questions are important, they are secondary to the question of the clinical applicability of visceral conditioning. If visceral learning can occur, then it may be useful no matter what the underlying behavioral and physiological mechanisms are. This section reviews a number of studies that have shown that visceral responses can be operantly trained, and this training will result in clinically beneficial outcomes. It should be emphasized that not every study with patients is necessarily designed with a clinical endpoint in mind. For example, some studies already cited with patients were designed to enable a better understanding of the mediating mechanisms rather than to reveal a therapeutic benefit. In addition, readers should recognize that just because an outcome is clinically beneficial, it does not necessarily follow that it is optimal because that is determined by a variety of factors such as cost, ease of application, likelihood of patient compliance, and practitioner competence.

Operant training of autonomic responses has been applied clinically in two ways: (a) to train subjects to emit an operant, autonomic response; for example, skin vasodilatation, in the expectation that this behavior will result in a generalized reduction in sympathetic nervous activity and thus will facilitate relaxation; and (b) to train subjects to emit an operant autonomic response because the response itself is aberrant. There is very little physiological evidence to support the notion of generalized activation or reduction in sympathetic nervous activity. Given the extensive evidence for specificity within the autonomic nervous system already cited, there is very little reason to believe that any particular, sympathetically mediated response will represent all sympathetically mediated responses. Furthermore, in the case of skin vasodilatation, which is always implemented by teaching subjects to warm their hands or feet, there is strong evidence that the vasodilation is not under direct, sympathetic, nervous control (Freedman et al., 1988). Therefore, this section will limit its review to a few studies that have provided evidence that an aberrant, autonomic response can be altered to a degree sufficient to produce a clinically significant effect.

There have been a number of reports of successful outcomes using operant conditioning methodology to train patients with abnormal, autonomically mediated responses to gain or regain control of their aberrant responses. Two reports have been published that describe successful clinical outcomes in patients with cardiac arrhythmias: Weiss and Engel (1971) showed that some patients could learn to diminish the prevalence of ectopic ventricular beats; and Bleecker and Engel (1973a) showed that it was possible to teach a patient with Wolf-Parkinson-White syndrome to modulate her aberrantly conducted heart beats. Several studies have shown that it is possible to teach hypertensive patients to lower their blood pressures reliably in the laboratory (Benson, Shapiro, Tursky, & Schwartz, 1971; Kristt & Engel, 1975), and at home (Glasgow, Gaarder, & Engel, 1982; Glasgow, Engel, & D'Lugoff 1989; Pearce, Engel, & Burton, 1989). Finally, Burgio et al. (1985), and Burgio et al. (1989), have reported highly successful results in treating urinary incontinence in patients with uninhibited bladder dysfunction and Burgio et. al. (1998) have shown that behavioral treatments, including operant conditioning of bladder control, were significantly more effective than drugs in reducing urge urinary incontinence. Freedman, Ianni, and Wenig (1983) reported success in reducing the prevalence and severity of vasospastic responses in patients with Raynaud's disease by teaching them to warm their hands; however, as noted earlier, it is likely that the effect of such training is not mediated by the sympathetic fibers innervating the blood vessels in the skin.

CONCLUSIONS

My assessment of the history of research and conceptualization about the autonomic nervous system suggests that it is characterized by discovery and denial. The main point of the discoveries is that the nervous system is integrative and regulatory. Galen's basic notion that the brain communicates a sympathy among the parts of the body is true, and the rest is detail, however profound and complex. The denial comes largely from philosophical traditions that impute special properties to human function, even in the face of contradictory evidence. The imputation is that behavior can be conveniently dichotomized into voluntary and involuntary, conscious or unconscious. The hallmark of such dichotomies rests heavily on the apparent inability of human subjects to characterize their visceral sensations verbally. When evidence arises, which does not neatly fit into these dichotomies, it is dealt with as a special case (e.g., Willis' "strong" sensations), it is defined out of existence (e.g., Winslow's notion of the sympathetic ganglia as autonomous nerve centers; Johnstone's notion that the ganglia serve as filters to prevent visceral information from becoming conscious; Langley's extraordinary definition excluding afferent fibers from the autonomic nervous system; and Skinner's concern that autonomically mediated responses do not "naturally" act on the environment), or the data are simply ignored (e.g., the well-known ability of mammals to inhibit or induce bladder contractions and the experimental evidence of visceral sensation). There is a modern counterpart to this cartesian disposition to dichotomize. Within psychiatry the concept of psychosomatic medicine evolved as a dualistic model that separated putative, physical from mental, conscious from unconscious and voluntary from involuntary events (e.g., Alexander & French, 1948; Dunbar, 1954). Behavioral medicine evolved, in part, as a reaction to this dualism. However, as argued elsewhere (Engel, 1994), it failed to meet the challenge. Instead, it maintained the differentiation between physical and mental illness. The failure of behavioral medicine to deal with dualism in its manifold forms is clearly evident in the contemporary neologism, *biobehavioral.* Biobehavioral is simply a euphemism for psychosomatic.

In order to understand why the term, *biobehavioral,* needed to be invented, it is first necessary to understand how psychologists define behavior. *The Dictionary of Behavioral Science* defines behavior as the interaction of an organism with its physical and social environments (Wolman, 1989). The term, *organism,* is interpreted, literally, to mean the whole animal or person, and the term, *environment,* refers to the external environment. Thus, an autonomically, mediated response (or for that matter, a somatomotorically, mediated response!) and an interoceptive stimulus are excluded from the domain of behavior. Because behavior is limited to organisms rather than effectors, and because contemporary research has shown that motor responses, however mediated, are capable of interacting with the environment, it is necessary either to redefine behavior or to deny, once again, the implications of the data reviewed here. Obviously, contemporary proponents of behavioral medicine have chosen the latter course. It is clear that the definition of behavior is inadequate, and the host of dichotomies that infest the literature are inhibiting progress. Accordingly, behavior should be redefined to mean the interaction of an effector system with the environment. The effector system could be an organism, muscle contraction, glandular secretion, or immune response: The environment could be external or internal. When a response interacts with the environment, the process is behavior. The essence of the current definition, and of the definition proposed here, is that behavior is an *interaction* between a response and a stimulus; however, the definition proposed permits the investigator to define both the relevant stimuli and the appropriate unit of response. Within the framework of the proposed definition it will no longer be necessary to invoke dualistic notions. Anyone who wants to invoke dualistic processes, such as conscious/unconscious, voluntary/involuntary, or mental/physical should be expected to define the process and then empirically justify its autonomous existence. The bias is that if this level of rigor is implemented, none of these dualistic concepts will survive empirical test.

There is another feature to the proposed redefinition of behavior that is especially salient to students of visceral conditioning, namely, the interrelation between behavior and physiology. *Physiology* is defined as the science that treats of living organisms or their parts (Hoerr & Osol, 1956). *Behavior,* as defined here, is the interaction of an organism's effectors with the environmental contingencies (and the organism's learning history). Thus, physiology, as a science, focuses on organ function, whereas behavioral science is concerned with how that function serves the nearterm survival (coping) of the organism. Clearly, a comprehensive biological science (viz. the science of life) needs both. Integrative physiologists who are especially concerned with the ways in which organs interrelate, and behavioral scientists should recognize that their interests overlap greatly. An understanding of the ways organs work is fundamental to an understanding of the capacities for visceral learning: A knowledge of the extent to which visceral adaptations to environmental contingencies occur is fundamental to an understanding of the ways organs function.

REFERENCES

Adam, G. (1967). *Interoception and behavior.* Budapest: Akademiai Kiado.

Adam, G. (1998). *Visceral perception. Understanding internal cognition.* New York: Plenum.

Ainslie, G. W., & Engel, B. T. (1974). Alteration of classically conditioned heart rate by operant reinforcement in monkeys. *Journal of Comparative and Physiological Psychology, 87,* 373–382.

Alexander, F., & French, T. M. (1948). *Studies in psychosomatic medicine.* New York: The Roland Press.

Armour, J. A. (1977). Thoracic cardiovascular afferent nerves (Chap. 5). In W. C. Randall (Ed.), *Neural regulation of the heart* (pp. 131–156). New York: Oxford University Press.

Barber, T., DiCara, L. V., Kamiya, J., Miller, N. E., Shapiro, D., & Stoyva, J. (1971). *Biofeedback and self-control, 1970.* Chicago: Aldine-Atherton.

Barber, T., DiCara, L. V., Kamiya, J., Miller, N. E., Shapiro, D., & Stoyva, J. (1976). *Biofeedback and self-control, 1975/76.* Chicago: Aldine.

Bardos, G. (1989). Behavioral consequences of intestinal distension: Aversitivity and discomfort. *Physiology and Behavior, 45,* 79–85.

Bardos, G., Talan, M. I., & Engel, B. T. (1989). Learned control of systolic blood pressure raising and lowering in rhesus monkeys. *Acta Physiologica Hungarica, 73,* 433–446.

Basmajian, J. V. (Ed.). (1989). *Biofeedback: Principles and practice for clinicians* (3rd ed.). Baltimore: Williams & Wilkins.

Benson, H., Shapiro, D., Tursky, B., & Schwartz, G. E. (1971). Decreased systolic blood pressure through operant conditioning techniques in patients with essential hypertension. *Science, 173,* 740–742.

Black, A. H. (1967, October). *Operant conditioning of heart rate under curare.* (Tech. Rep. No. 12). Hamilton, Ontario: McMaster University, Department of Psychology.

Bleecker, E. R., & Engel, B. T. (1973a). Learned control of cardiac rate and cardiac conduction in the WolffParkinsonWhite syndrome. *New England Journal of Medicine, 288,* 560–562.

Bleecker, E. R., & Engel, B. T. (1973b). Learned control of ventricular rate in patients with atrial fibrillation. *Psychosomatic Medicine, 35,* 161–175.

Bolme, P., & Novotny, J. (1969). Conditional reflex activation of the sympathetic cholinergic vasodilator nerves in the dog. *Acta Physiologica Scandinavica, 77,* 58–67.

Bovbjerg, D. H., Redd, W. H., Jacobsen, P. B., et al. (1992). An experimental analysis of classically conditioned nausea during cancer chemotherapy. *Psychosomatic Medicine, 54,* 623–637.

Brener, J. (1974). A general model of voluntary control applied to the phenomena of learned cardiovascular change. In P. A. Obrist, A. H. Black, J. Brener, & L. V. DiCara (Eds.), *Cardiovascular psychophysiology* (pp. 365–391). Chicago: Aldine.

Burgio, K. L., Robinson, J. C., & Engel, B. T. (1986). The role of biofeedback in Kegel exercise training for stress urinary incontinence. *American Journal of Obstetrics and Gynecology, 154,* 58–64.

Burgio, K. L., Stutzman, R. E., & Engel, B. T. (1989). Behavioral training for postprostatectomy urinary incontinence. *Journal of Urology, 141,* 303–306.

Burgio, K. L., Whitehead, W. E., & Engel, B. T. (1985). Urinary incontinence in the elderly: Bladder-sphincter biofeedback and toileting skills training. *Annals of Internal Medicine, 103,* 507–515.

Burgio, K. L., Locher, J. L., Goode, P. S., Hardin, J. M., McDowell, B. J., Dombrowski, M., & Condib, D. (1998). Behavioral vs drug treatment for urge incontinence in older women: A randomized controlled trial. *Journal of the American Medical Asociation. 280,* 1995–2000.

Bykov, K. M. (1957). *The cerebral cortex and the internal organs.* New York: Chemical.

Cannon, W. B. (1929). *Bodily changes in pain, hunger, fear, and rage.* New York: Appleton-Century.

Cannon W. B., & Washburn, A. L. (1912). An explanation of hunger. *American Journal of Physiology, 29,* 441–454.

Chefer, S. I., Talan, M. I., & Engel, B. T. (1997). Central neural correlates of learned heart rate control during exercise: central command demystified. *Journal of Applied Physiology. 83,* 1448-1453.

Chernigovsky, V. N. (1967). *Interoceptors* (D. B. Lindsley, Ed; G. Onischenko, Trans.). Washington, DC: American Psychological Association.

DiCara, L. V., Barber, T. X., Kamiya, J., Miller, N. E., Shapiro, D., & Stovya, J. (1975). *Biofeedback & self-control, 1974.* Chicago: Aldine.

Dunbar, F. (1954). *Emotions and bodily changes. A survey of the literature on psychosomatic relationships, 1910–1953* (4th ed.). New York: Columbia University Press.

Dworkin, B. R., & Dworkin, S. I. (1990). Habituation, sensitization and classical conditioning. *Behavioral Neuroscience, 104,* 298–319.

Dworkin, B. R., Filewich, R. J., Miller, N. E., Craigmyle, N., & Pickering, T. G. (1979). Baroreceptor activation reduces reactivity to noxious stimulation: Implications for hypertension. *Science, 205,* 1299–1301.

Engel, B. T. (1994). A behaviorist's view of behavioral medicine. In T. Kikuchi, Sakuma, H., Saito, I., Tsuboi, K. (Eds.), *Biobehavioral Self-Regulation and Health* (pp. 355–361). Tokyo: Springer-Verlag-Tokyo.

Engel, B. T. (1986). An essay on the circulation as behavior. *Behavioral and Brain Science, 9,* 285–318.

Engel, B. T., & Gottlieb, S. H. (1970). Differential operant conditioning of heart rate in the restrained monkey. *Journal of Comparative and Physiological Psychology, 73,* 217–225.

Engel, B. T., & Hansen, S. (1966). Operant conditioning of heart rate slowing. *Psychophysiology, 3,* 176–187.

Engel, B. T., Nikoomanesh, P., & Shuster, M. M. (1974). Operant conditioning of rectosphincteric responses in the treatment of fecal incontinence. *New England Journal of Medicine, 290,* 646–649.

Engel, B. T., & Talan, M. I. (1991a). Autonomic blockade does not prevent learned heart rate attenuation during exercise. *Physiology & Behavior, 49,* 373–382.

Engel, B. T., & Talan, M. I. (1991b). Hemodynamic and respiratory concomitants of learned heart rate control during exercise. *Psychophysiology, 28,* 225–230.

Freedman, R. R., Ianni, P., & Wenig, P. (1983). Behavioral treatment of Raynaud's disease. *Journal of Consulting and Clinical Psychology, 151,* 539–549.

Freedman, R. R., Sabharwal, S. C., Ianni, P., Desai, N., Wenig, P., & Mayes, M. (1988). Nonneural beta-adrenergic vasodilating mechanism in temperature biofeedback. *Psychosomatic Medicine, 50,* 394–401.

Glasgow, M. S., Engel, B. T., & D'Lugoff, B. C. (1989). A controlled study of a standardized behavioral stepped treatment for hypertension. *Psychosomatic Medicine, 51,* 10–26.

Glasgow, M. S., Gaarder, K. R., & Engel, B. T. (1982). Behavioral treatment of high blood pressure. II. Acute and sustained effects of relaxation and systolic blood pressure biofeedback. *Psychosomatic Medicine, 44,* 155–170.

Harris, A. H., Gilliam, W. J., Findley, J. D., & Brady, J. V. (1973). Instrumental conditioning of large-magnitude, daily, 12–hour blood pressure elevations in the baboon. *Science, 182,* 175–177.

Hatch, J. P., Fisher, J. G. & Rugh, J. D. (1987). *Biofeedback: Studies in clinical efficacy.* New York: Plenum.

Hoerr, N. L., & Osol, A. (Eds.). (1956). *Blakiston's new Gould medical dictionary* (2nd ed.). New York: McGraw Hill.

James, W. (1890). *Principles ofpsychology.* New York: Henry Holt.

Johansson, J. E. (1895). The influence of muscular activity on breathing and cardiac action. *Skandinavisches Archiv fur Physiologie, 5,* 20–66.

Kamiya, J. Barber, T., Miller, N. E., Shapiro, D., & J. Stoyva. (1977). *Biofeedback and self-control, 1976/77.* Chicago: Aldine.

Kimmel, H. D., & Hill, F. A. (1960). Operant conditioning of the GSR. *Psychological Reports, 7,* 555–562.

Kline, E. M., & Bidder, G. B. (1946). A study of the subjective sensations associated with extrasystoles. *American Heart Journal, 31,* 254–259.

Kristt, D. A., & Engel, B. T. (1975). Learned control of blood pressure in patients with high blood pressure. *Circulation, 51,* 370–378.

Krogh, A., & Lindhard, J. (1913). The regulation of respiration and circulation during the initial stages of muscular work. *Journal of Physiology (London), 47,* 112–136.

Kuntz, A. (1953). *The autonomic nervous system.* Philadelphia: Lea & Febiger.

Langhorst, P., Shulz, G., & Lambertz, M. (1983). Integrative control mechanisms for cardiorespiratory and somatomotor functions in the reticular formation of the lower brain stem. In P. Grossman, K.H.L. Janssen, & D. Vaitl (Eds.), *Cardiorespiratory and cardiosomatic psychophysiology* (pp. 9–39). New York: Plenum.

Langley, J. N. (1921). *The autonomic nervous system* (Pt. 1). Cambridge: Heffer.

Lapides, J., Sweet, R. B., & Lewis, L. W. (1957). Role of striated muscle in urination. *Journal of Urology, 77,* 247–250.

Lubar, J. F. (1991). Discourse on the development of EEG diagnostics and biofeedback for attention-deficit/hyperactivity disorders. *Biofeedback and Self-Regulation, 16,* 201–225.

Miller, N. E., Barber, T. X., DiCara, L. V., Kamiya, J., Shapiro, D., & Stoyva, J. (1974). *Biofeedback and self-control, 1973.* Chicago: Aldine.

Miller, N. E., & Carmona, A. (1967). Modification of a visceral response, salivation in thirsty dogs, by instrumental training with water reward. *Journal of Comparative and Physiological Psychology, 63,* 1–6.

Miller, N. E., & Dworkin B. R. (1974). Visceral learning (Chap. 16). In P. A. Obrist, A. H. Black, J. Brener & L. V. DiCara (Eds.), *Cardiovascular psychophysiology* (pp. 312–331), Chicago: Aldine.

Nilsson, S. (1983). *Autonomic nerve function in the vertebrates.* New York: Springer-Verlag.

Orne, M. T. (1979). The efficacy of biofeedback therapy. *Annual Review of Medicine, 30,* 489–503.

Pearce, K. L., Engel, B. T., & Burton, J. R. (1989). Behavioral treatment of isolated systolic hypertension in the elderly. *Biofeedback and Self-Regulation, 14,* 207–217.

Pick, J. (1970). *The autonomic nervous system.* Philadelphia: Lippincott.

Plumlee, L. A. (1969). Operant conditioning of increases in blood pressure. *Psychophysiology, 6,* 283–290.

Prechtl, J. C., & Powley, T. L. . (1990). B-afferents: A fundamental division of the nervous system mediating homeostasis? *Behavioral and Brain Sciences, 13,* 289–329.

Roberts, L. E. (1986). Evidence for instrumental plasticity in the cardiovascular system is circumstantial. *Behavioral and Brain Sciences, 9,* 301–302.

Rowell, L. B. (1980). What signals govern the cardiovascular responses to exercise? *Medicine and Science in Sports and Exercise, 12,* 307–315.

Shapiro, D., Barber, T. X., DiCara, L. V. Kamiya, J., Miller, N. E., & Stoyva, J. (1973). *Biofeedback and self-control, 1972.* Chicago: Aldine.

Shapiro, D., Stoyva, J., Kamiya, J., Barber, T. X., Miller, N. E., & Schwartz, G. E. (1981). *Biofeedback and Behavioral Medicine, 1979/80.* New York: Aldine.

Shearn, D. (1961). Does the heart learn? *Psychological Bulletin, 58,* 452–458.

Sheehan, D. (1936). Discovery of the autonomic nervous system. *Archives of Neurology and Psychiatry, 35,* 1081–1115.

Skinner, B. F. (1938). *The behavior of organisms.* New York: Appleton-Century-Crofts.

Stoyva, J., Barber, T., DiCara, L. V., Kamiya, J., Miller, N. E., & Shapiro, D. (1972) *Biofeedback and Self-Regulation, 1971.* Chicago: Aldine.

Stoyva, J., Kamiya, J., Barber, T. X., Miller, N. E., & Shapiro, D. (1979). *Biofeedback and self-control, 1977/78.* Chicago: Aldine.

Talan, M. I., & Engel, B. T. (1986). Learned control of heart rate during dynamic exercise in nonhuman primates. *Journal of Applied Physiology, 61,* 545–553.

Turpin, G. (1983). Unconditioned reflexes and the autonomic nervous system In D. Siddle (Ed.), *Orienting and habituation: Perspectives in human research* (pp. 1–70). London: Wiley.

Weiss, T., & Engel, B. T. (1971). Operant conditioning of heart rate in patients with premature ventricular contractions. *Psychosomatic Medicine, 33,* 301–321.

Whitehead, W. E., Drescher, V. M., & Heyman, P. (1977). Relation of heart rate control to heartbeat perception. *Biofeedback and Self-Regulation, 2,* 371–392.

Wolman, B. B. (Ed.). (1989). *Dictionary of behavioral science* (2nd ed.). New York: Academic Press.

Wurster, R. D. (1977). Spinal sympathetic control of the heart (Chap. 9). In W. C. Randall (Ed.), *Neural regulation of the heart* (pp. 211–246). New York: Oxford University Press.

6

Biofeedback and Self-Regulation of Physiological Activity: A Major Adjunctive Treatment Modality in Health Psychology

Robert J. Gatchel
University of Texas Southwestern Medical Center at Dallas

> Before Harry Houdini performed one of his famous escapes, a skeptical committee would search his clothes and body. When the members of the committee were satisfied that the Great Houdini was concealing no keys, they would put chains, padlocks and handcuffs on him. ... Of course, not even Houdini could open a padlock without a key, and when he was safely behind a curtain, he would cough one up. He could hold a key suspended in his throat and regurgitate it when he was unobserved. ... The trick behind many of Houdini's escapes was in some ways just as amazing as the escape in itself. Ordinarily, when an object is stuck in a person's throat he will start to gag. He can't help it—it's an unlearned automatic reflux. But Houdini had learned to control his gag reflex by practicing hours with a small piece of potato tied to a string. (Lang, 1970, p. 2)

Through the years, there have been other unusual instances of the exercise of voluntary control over physiological functions noted in the scientific literature. Such was the case of a middle-aged male who had the ability to control the eruption of hairs over the entire surface of his body (Lindsley & Sassaman, 1938), or the case of an individual who could willfully produce complete cardiac arrest for periods of several seconds at a time (McClure, 1959). Numerous instances of voluntary acceleration of pulse rate were reported by Ogden and Shock (1939). Luria (1958) described a mnemonist who had obtained remarkable control of his heart rate and skin temperature. This individual could abruptly alter his heart rate by 40 beats per minute. He could also raise the skin temperature of one hand while simultaneously lowering the temperature of the other hand.

The modification of physiological activities such as those described has been the subject of practice and investigation by mystics and scientists for a considerable period of time. The goal of such control of physiological functions has been pursued for at least three reasons:

1. To achieve spiritual enlightment. Yogis and other mystics of the Eastern tradition have shown that through certain physical exercises or by shear act of will they are capable of producing tremendous physiochemical changes in their bodies resulting in perceived pleasant states of consciousness (Bagchi, 1959; Bagchi & Wenger, 1957).
2. To test theories of learning. Within psychology, learning theorists have long debated the issue of whether autonomic responses could be operantly conditioned.

3. As a clinical treatment procedure for modifying psychological and medical disorders.

This chapter focuses on this third category of how volitional control of physiological activity has been used as a clinical treatment modality for medically related disorders. This area has contributed significantly to the growing field of behavioral medicine and health psychology.

THE DEVELOPMENT OF BIOFEEDBACK TECHNIQUES

The previously reviewed acts of unusual physiological bodily control were traditionally viewed as rare feats that only certain extraordinarily gifted individuals could accomplish. However, starting in the 1960s, behavioral scientists began to develop techniques and empirically demonstrate that the "average person on the street" could learn a significant degree of control over physiological responding. The primary training method developed and utilized in this learning process has been labeled *biofeedback.* This initial research activity began to stimulate more interest, among both the scientific community and the general public, in the area of biofeedback because of its' many potentially important clinical and medical applications. For example, it would be therapeutically valuable if it was possible to teach patients with hypertension how to lower their blood pressure, or to teach patients with headaches how to control the vasodilation process involved in the pain phenomenon. Indeed, Birk (1973) was the individual who coined the term *behavioral medicine* to describe the application of a behavioral treatment technique (biofeedback) that could be applied to medicine or medical problems (e.g., headache pain).

The biofeedback technique itself is based on the fundamental learning principle that people learn to perform a particular response when they receive feedback or information about the consequences of that response, and then make the appropriate compensatory behavior adjustments. This is how individuals have learned to perform the wide variety of skills and behaviors utilized in everyday life. For instance, people learn how to drive a car by receiving continuous feedback concerning how much to turn the steering wheel in order to turn the car a certain distance, and how much pressure must be applied to the accelerator in order to make the car move at a certain speed. If this feedback is denied, for example by being blindfolded, individuals would never receive information about the consequences of their driving responses. They would therefore never be able to learn the proper adjustments needed in order to perform a successful driving maneuver. Accurate information feedback is thus fundamental to the learning of visual-motor skills. Indeed, Annent (1969) initially reviewed numerous experimental studies demonstrating the importance of feedback in the learning and performance of a wide variety of motor skills.

The availability of feedback is also of utmost importance in learning how to control internal physiological responses. However, much biological behavior is concerned with maintaining a constant internal "homeostasis" and is not readily accessible to conscious awareness. Indeed, people do not consciously experience some interoceptive awareness of internal biological activity, such as muscle tension or their pulse, because there is normally adaptive advantage to not having to consciously attend or control these activities on a continuous basis. Moreover, interoceptors do not normally have the extensive afferent representation at the cortical level that is needed for a high degree of perceptual acuity or the fine descriminability characteristics of audition or vision.

People do not normally receive feedback of these internal events in day-to-day situations, so they cannot be expected to control them. However, if individuals are provided biofeedback of, say, blood pressure via a visual display monitor, they can become more aware of the consequences of blood pressure changes and the ways adjustments can be made to modify and eventually control it. Receiving feedback serves to remove the "blindfold," enabling individuals to voluntarily control a response. The development of sensitive physiological recording devices and digital-logic technology has made it possible to detect small changes in visceral events and provide subjects with immediate feedback of these biological responses.

Today, biofeedback is broadly, and loosely, defined as a procedure for transforming some aspects of physiological behavior into electrical signals that are made accessible to exteroception or awareness (usually vision or audition). Sometimes, the feedback signal is combined with a tangible reward such as money or the opportunity to view attractive pictures in an attempt to motivate the individual and strengthen the effect of the targeted physiological response. In other instances, the clinician provides verbal praise for success in addition to feedback. These latter practices are also forms of biofeedback, because they too convey information to learners about their biological performance. In most instances, however, response-contingent lights or tones alone can be shown to augment voluntary control of physiological activity.

Borrowing heavily from operant conditioning techniques, the early biofeedback investigators during the 1960s and 1970s demonstrated some degree of operant or voluntary control in a wide variety of visceral, central nervous system, and somatomotor functions. Gatchel and Price (1979) provided an early review of this research that demonstrated learned control by human subjects of a wide variety of "involuntary responses": cardiac ventricular rate, systolic and diastolic blood pressure, peripheral vascular responses, electrodermal activity, gastric motility, skin temperature, penile tumescence, and various brain wave rhythms.

Encouraged by these early successes demonstrating voluntary control of normal physiological activity, medical and psychological clinicians soon began to question whether pathophysiological activity could also be controlled with the goal of restoring health or preventing illness. This stimulated a rapid growth of the scientific literature evaluating the clinical effectiveness of biofeedback. This research has been reviewed in a number of different sources (e.g., Hatch, Fisher, & Rugh, 1987). There is also a journal (*Biofeedback and Self Regulation*), and a professional society specializing in biofeedback and self-regulation (Association for Applied Psychophysiology and Biofeedback) that celebrated its 25th anniversary year in 1994. There are also a number of useful practitioner guides that have been published (e.g., Basmajian, 1989; Schwartz, 1987).

To date, the research literature has amply demonstrated that some degree of self-control is possible over behaviors long assumed to be completely involuntary. It has also been shown that, with biofeedback, it is possible to extend voluntary control to pathophysiological responding in order to modify the maladaptive behavior in the direction of health. Table 6.1 summarizes the various disorders for which biofeedback has been applied.

As can be seen in Table 6.1, many of the results produced are highly significant achievements. However, as reviewed elsewhere (Gatchel, 1997), many important questions still remain concerning the extent to which biofeedback and other physiological self-control techniques will be medically effective. Unfortunately, research evaluating therapeutic effectiveness of these procedures has been plagued by a number of problems. For example, to date, there are very few well-controlled clinical outcome studies that have been conducted using large numbers of patients having well-confirmed medical diagnoses. Moreover, the few comparative outcome studies that have been performed compare the relative effectiveness of biofeedback to various other behavioral techniques (e.g., simple relaxation training that is discussed later in this chapter). It would be extremely helpful to also compare biofeedback techniques with more traditional medical treatments, some of which have fairly well-established success rates. Combinations of medical and behavioral techniques should also be explored and evaluated.

It should also be noted that, unfortunately, there have been claims for the therapeutic efficacy of biofeedback that had been grossly exaggerated and even wrong. Overall, it is justified to conclude that relevant and encouraging data do exist, but at the present time the value of clinical training and biofeedback still has to be questioned in some areas. Moreover, terms such as *biofeedback therapists* and *biofeedback clinic,* which are now regularly encountered in may medical centers, are difficult to justify. They imply that a form of treatment exists that is more or less generally applicable to a variety of ills. Worse yet, they imply, at least in the minds of some, that biofeedback is a new alternative treatment modality. Currently, in the majority of areas in which it is applied, biofeedback should be viewed merely as an *adjunctive* treatment modality.

OTHER SELF-REGULATION METHODS FOR PRODUCING VOLITIONAL CONTROL OF PHYSIOLOGICAL ACTIVITY

Controlled Breathing

Many forms of yoga and meditation have traditionally viewed breathing as fundamentally linked to relaxation and good health. Indeed, one type of yoga—*Pranayama Yoga* (or the Science of Breath)—is totally devoted to the study of the effects of breathing exercises on mental and physical health.

The relaxation methods discussed in the next section begin with a focus on correct breathing. Deep, relaxed breathing involves allowing the air to flow easily to the bottom of the lungs with each inhalation (expanding the diaphragm and moving the stomach gently out) and slowly exhaling as the stomach moves gently in. The shoulders and chest remain still and relaxed during this process. Such deep, relaxed breathing serves as an effective distressor. In contrast, strained, shallow breathing and stress go hand in hand. Often, individuals who have breathed incorrectly for years (shallow breathing with their chests) are unaware of these effects until they experience correct, controlled breathing.

Muscle Relaxation Training

Systematic desensitization is a technique originally developed by Wolpe (1958) as a means of alleviating fear and anxiety. Wolpe based this procedure on the principle of *counterconditioning,* in which an attempt is made to substitute relaxation (an adaptive behavior), through learning, for anxiety (the deviant or maladaptive behavior) in response to a particular fear-producing object or situation. The procedure typically involves the pairing of deep muscle relaxation, which is taught by a progressive muscle relaxation technique originally developed by Jacobson (1938), with imagined scenes depicting situations or objects associated with fear or anxiety. Wolpe had his patients imagine the anxiety-related objects or situations because many of the fears treated were abstract in nature (e.g., fear of rejection by a loved one) and, therefore, could not be presented *in vivo* (in real life). However, even when the objects and situations can be presented in real life (e.g., fear of a specific object such as a bug), *in vitro* systematic desensitization is often employed. The effectiveness of systematic desensitization has been well documented (Gatchel, Baum, & Krantz, 1989).

Progressive muscle relaxation, which is an important component of the systematic desensitization treatment method, often can serve as a powerful therapeutic technique in its own right. Clinicians now frequently use it by itself to treat a wide variety of disorders, including generalized anxiety, insomnia, headache, and mild forms of agitated depression. Moreover, unlike the extensive training initially advocated by Jacobson, which took many months, many abbreviated forms taking only a few sessions have been developed. Overall, the technique is based on the premise that muscle tension is closely related to stress and anxiety, and that an individual will feel a significant reduction in experienced anxiety when tensed muscles can be made to relax.

Autogenic Training

At the time that Jacobson was developing the technique of progressive relaxation in the United States, Schultz was developing a relaxation technique called *autogenic training* in Europe. This work was subsequently published in this country (Schultz & Luthe, 1959). The technique was based on the clinical observation that hypnotized subjects often report sensations such as heaviness and warmth. These sensations, in

TABLE 6.1

Summary of Disorder/Problem Behavior for Which Physiological Self-Regulation Techniques Have Been Applied

Disorder	Summary of Findings
Anxiety	Studies have found that heart rate biofeedback may be useful for inhibiting cardiac acceleration and self-reported anxiety during acute stress. There is no conclusive evidence that biofeedback of other physiological responses such as electromyogram (EMG) is any more effective than simple muscle relaxation training. Research has also demonstrated the important role that placebo factors play in producing and maintaining fear reduction in a biofeedback treatment program.
Asthma	Although clinical studies have suggested the effectiveness of EMG biofeedback for asthma reduction, there have been a number of methodological problems associated with such studies. Nonspecific placebo factors may play an important role in asthma reduction.
Cancer Chemotherapy Side-Effects	Relaxation techniques have been effectively used in reducing the side effects (e.g., nausea and anticipation anxiety) often associated with cancer chemotherapy.
Cardiac Arrhythmias	The few cases available indicate that heart rate biofeedback seems to be effective in the treatment of cardiac arrhythmias such as sinus tachycardia, atrial fibrillation, and premature ventricular contractions. However, judgment must be withheld with regard to therapeutic value of biofeedback for such disorders generally until more research is conducted.
Depression	There are a number of studies indicating that mild forms of agitated depression can be treated with biofeedback and relaxation techniques. However, methodological problems with such studies, such as nonstandard methods employed in evaluating depression, make it difficult to interpret results across studies.
Dermatological Disorders	Although there have been some case studies suggesting the therapeutic effectiveness of biofeedback-assisted behavioral treatment techniques, there have been no well-controlled studies conducted to date. Moreover, there are various forms of dermatological disorders that may be differentially responsive to such treatment.
Dyskinesias	Biofeedback techniques have been used to treat a number of different dyskinesias, including spasmatic torticollis, Parkinson's disease, tardive dyskinesia, and Huntington's disease. Individual and multiple case reports suggest a possible use of EMG in the treatment of these disorders. However, the role of biofeedback is unclear because controls were not used.
Epileptic Seizures	At this time, the amount of control group research concerning possible therapeutic effects of EEG biofeedback for the treatment of epileptic seizures is limited, and all but the most speculative conclusions are premature. Positive results have been reported that are encouraging and it would seem to justify additional research.
Essential Hypertension	Research has shown some degree of success in reducing the symptoms of essential hypertension with biofeedback. Blood pressure can be effectively reduced using biofeedback. However, biofeedback is still an experimental form of treatment for hypertension, with little known about the exact physiological mechanisms involved in the process. Thus, it cannot be considered an alternative to pharmacological treatment at this time. Biofeedback is often used as one component in a more comprehensive behavioral intervention.
Gastrointestinal Disorders	Research results of the biofeedback-assisted modification of gastrointestinal behaviors are encouraging. Biofeedback by means of rectal or anal devices is currently the treatment of choice for many types of fecal incontinence. Moreover, it is likely to become a preferred treatment method for patients with constipation related to the inability to relax the striated pelvic floor muscles during defecation. In addition, thermal-biofeedback, as part of a comprehensive behavioral treatment program, is a promising approach to the treatment of irritable bowel syndrome.
Insomnia	There is a great deal of evidence indicating that biofeedback and relaxation techniques, as components of a more comprehensive behavioral treatment program, are effective in the treatment of insomnia.
Lower Motor Neuron Dysfunctions	The case studies reporting the successful application of biofeedback in the treatment of lower motor neuron dysfunction (EEG, peripheral nerve injury, Bell's Palsy) must currently be interpreted with some caution, given the lack of control procedures.
Migraine Headache	Research suggests that temperature biofeedback, combined with autogenic training, is more effective than no treatment and possibly superior to placebo treatments. Thus, such an approach is warranted for the treatment of migraine.
Muscle Contraction Headaches	The effects of EMG biofeedback exceed those for medication placebo, biofeedback placebo, and psychotherapy procedures. In addition, although research suggests that biofeedback and relaxation produce similar levels of improvement, biofeedback may offer greater benefits to a subset of patients.

Muscular Pain	Although tentative results are promising with regard to the biofeedback treatment of pain, the role of placebo factors is probably a potent one. As they are in many other pain syndromes, such factors need to be more carefully evaluated. It should also be recognized that the etiology of many muscular pain disorders, such as low back pain and myofascial pain, remains a mystery, and therefore, it is difficult to determine what specific physiological response to assess and modify.
Postural Hypotension	There is no effective treatment for this disorder, and severely affected patients must remain in the supine position. Although control group studies are not yet available, several good case studies have demonstrated that systolic blood pressure biofeedback training has enabled some patients to sit upright or to stand with crutches, which prior to training produced fainting.
Premenstrual Syndromes	There have been some studies suggesting the effectiveness of relaxation training for premenstrual symptoms, especially for severe symptoms. However, because of the current limited understanding of the syndrome (or syndromes), as well as the high rates of placebo responding, more research is needed.
Raynaud's Disease	Recent controlled research studies involving over 160 patients have shown that behavioral treatment, with biofeedback as a key modality, can be very effective, equalling the best clinical effects of many medical and surgical interventions. In light of the limitations of current medical and surgical treatments for Raynaud's disease, behavioral interventions appear to have much to offer for these patients.
Sexual Dysfunctions	Although genital responses have been shown to be responsive to both instructional control and biofeedback, there is no evidence that the direct conditioning of genital responses through biofeedback has therapeutic value. However, biofeedback may have a role to play in guiding the development of erotic and nonerotic fantasy, which can, in turn, have significant therapeutic value.
Temporolmandibular Disorders (TMD)	A considerable number of studies indicate that EMG biofeedback training, often accompanied by relaxation training or general stress management training, is an effective treatment modality for TMD. However, the mechanism by which such treatment works is not clearly understood.
Tinnitus	There have been a few case studies indicating the effectiveness of biofeedback and relaxation methods in reducing the severity of tinnitus symptoms.
Upper Motor Neuron Dysfunctions	A number of well-designed individual and multiple case studies has suggested the therapeutic effectiveness of biofeedback in the treatment of upper motor neuron disorders such as paresis, cerebral palsy, and incomplete spinal cord lesion. However, an appropriate number of control group experiments is still lacking except in the biofeedback treatment of paresis, where results are negative or ambiguous.

turn, appear to correspond to a state of deep relaxation. Schultz demonstrated that these sensations of relaxation can be created voluntarily, without hypnosis, when an individual passively repeats verbal statements focusing on these sensations (e.g., "my hands are heavy and warm"). The training is called *autogenic,* because patients repeat the verbal "formula" to themselves.

Autogenic training was referred to by Schultz and Luthe as *psychophysiologic psychotherapy* because of their perspective that mental and bodily processes occur simultaneously and interactively. This, of course, is similar to the current perspective of many therapies that emphasize the integrated training of mind and body. Although the early training program involved several months of training, therapists today have developed abbreviated training exercises that can be taught in one or two sessions.

The Relaxation Response

Transcendental meditation was initially developed by Maharishi Mahesh Yogi in India as a streamlined form of meditation to produce increased tranquility and spiritual growth. Maharishi believed that through the practice of his simple meditation methods, individuals could experience inner quietness and increased consciousness that would have positive health consequences. The meditation was called *transcendental* because it was believed that the mind would "transcend" ordinary thinking because the mind has a natural tendency to expand its boundaries under appropriate circumstances.

In 1968, Benson was asked by practitioners of transcendental meditation to evaluate its effects on physiological processes. At this time, during the 1960s, transcendental meditation was becoming very popular in the United States as a relatively simple method for experiencing increased awareness and inner tranquility. Indeed, during the 1960s and 1970s, many alternative forms of self-awareness (some involving drugs) were being experimented with by the lay public.

Benson and colleagues conducted a series of studies demonstrating that transcendental meditation did produce significant physiological changes, such as reduced oxygen consumption, metabolic rate, and cardiovascular responses, leading to a highly relaxed state associated with decreased sympathetic nervous system activity. Moreover, similar to the therapists in this country who shortened progressive relaxation and autogenic training methods, Benson embarked on creating a shortened, more Westernized version of the basic elements of transcendental meditation. He called his technique the *relaxation response* because it produces physiological effects eliciting a relaxation response. In evaluating transcendental meditation and other meditation techniques, Benson delineated four basic elements in these techniques: a quiet environment in which to practice; a word or object of meditation on which to focus (e.g., the "mantra"); a positive attitude of just letting go or just "let it happen;" and a comfortable sitting position that does not lead to sleep. Benson originally recommended practicing the relaxation response technique daily for about 20 minutes. His research (Benson, 1975) found that the relaxation response will produce significant physiological changes, especially decreases in sympathetic nervous system activity.

The Quieting Reflex

The Quieting Reflex is another type of relaxation method initially developed by Stroebel. Stroebel, after suffering with headaches for a long period of time, decided that stress and accompanying muscle tension were the primary cause of the excruciating headaches. In an attempt to reduce tension, he tried different techniques such as transcendental meditation and biofeedback. After receiving relief from the headaches using these techniques, he became convinced that the major method of reducing stress is learning to have a quiet body and an active mind. Moreover, he thought it was important to develop a technique that did not demand too much time from the hectic schedule that might prompt nonadherence. He sought a technique that had simplicity and would not take too much time so that a person could consistently practice it enough to make it a learned response or habit. He therefore developed the Quieting Reflex (Stroebel, 1983), with training directed at mastering a technique that eventually can be produced reflexibly. This technique is often taught for several sessions in conjunction with biofeedback training, which helps to increase experiences of heaviness and warmth through relaxation. Again, the goal is to produce a reduced state of physiological activation.

STRESS, HEALTH AND VOLITIONAL CONTROL

During the 1960s and 1970s, various self-management or self-control techniques were being developed for people to use in making healthy lifestyle changes such as diet control, exercise, smoking cessation, and so on. Physiological self-regulation methods were a natural extension of the trend. Moreover, volitional control techniques such as biofeedback and muscle relaxation became even more popular during the 1970s when results from the burgeoning field of stress research started to appear in the scientific literature. This research began to clearly document a close link between stress and health/illness. Stress has been shown to be a major behavioral/psychological link to illness (Gatchel et al., 1989). Chronic stressors can cause neural and endocrine change that alters the normal functioning of the organism (e.g., change in cardiovascular activity or immune system functioning). This physiological response to stress is also accompanied by behavioral responses as well. Stress and the subsequent behavioral response to it can affect health and facilitate, if not cause, some illnesses.

Stress has direct physiological effects on the body, and the cumulative wear and tear on the system caused by recurring stress can eventually cause damage to the system. Indeed, there is abundant evidence that stress can cause a number of physiological and biochemical changes. There is also a growing literature indicating that some of these changes can be linked directly to illness (Gatchel, 1994; Gatchel et al., 1988). Moreover, there are data to suggest that self-regulation methods to reduce stress (such as relaxation) may have beneficial health effects. For example, in a study of elderly nursing home residents who received a series of relaxation training sessions, it was found that there was an enhancement of natural killer cell activity (an indice of immune system functioning) at the end of training relative to pre-training levels (Kiecolt-Glaser et al., 1985).

With the realization of the relation between stress and maladaptive physiological activity, there has been an increased interest in attempts to develop *stress management techniques* in order to help individuals directly deal with stress and avoid negative psychophysiological consequences. Biofeedback and other volitional self-control techniques are integral parts of such stress management programs. Moreover, during the past decade, health psychologists have paid great attention to developing techniques of stress management that can be taught to large groups of people. This is because stress-related disorders appear to account for as much as $17 billion per year in lost productivity, with some estimates placing the annual cost of stress-related illnesses at $60 billion (Adams, 1978). This has caused increased motivation on the part of businesses and organizations to help their workers identify and cope more effectively with a variety of stressful events experienced on the job.

It is beyond the scope of this chapter to review the major components and types of stress management programs. There is a rapidly growing literature on this topic (Gatchel, 1994; Gatchel, Baum & Krantz, 1989). It should be noted, however, that these stress management programs have been developed and utilized extensively with populations that already suffer from a stress-related illness or are at high risk for a stress-related illness. Thus, individuals with psychophysiological disorders—such as essential hypertension, headache, and gastrointestinal problems—have been treated with such techniques (Gatchel & Blanchard, 1993; Gatchel et al., 1989). Moreover, stress management techniques have also been developed as a means of modifying Type A behavior associated with increased risk of coronary disease (e.g., Roskies et al., 1986). These programs have been documented to be helpful, and results demonstrating a decrease in physiological symptomatology again point to the close link between stress, behavior, and illness/health.

PERCEIVED VOLITIONAL CONTROL

The direct control of physiological responding can have significant implications for the modification of many psychological and physical disorders. Besides the direct effects on physiological functioning that these different methods of volitional control and stress management techniques, in general, produce, there has also been an interest in delineating important concomitant psychological factors that contribute to therapeutic efficacy. One such factor shown to be important is *perceived control.* Evidence has been reviewed elsewhere (Gatchel, 1980), indicating that individuals react differently to emotionally stressful events they perceive to be personally controllable relative to those perceived to be not in their control. This dimension of perceived controllability/uncontrollability of an emotional stressor has been shown to significantly affect self-report, behavioral, and physiological components of emotional stress.

There have also been studies demonstrating that many stress- reducing effects can be produced merely by creating the belief in subjects that they can control the amount of stress, even though they actually cannot do so. The first widely cited study that experimentally manipulated the perception of control over a stressor, where there actually was none, was conducted by Geer, Davison, and Gatchel (1970). There were two separate parts of this study. In the first part, all subjects were instructed to press a microswitch at the onset of a 6-second, painful electric shock so that their reaction time could be measured. Following 10 such trials, half of the subjects (perceived-control group) were told that by decreasing their reaction times during the second part of the experiment, which would also consist of 10 trials, they could reduce shock duration by half. These subjects were thus led to believe that they could actually exert control during the next 10 stressful trials. The other group of subjects were not led to believe that they could do anything to control the shock (perceived no-control group). All subjects, however, regardless of group assignment or reaction time speed, received 3-second shocks on all 10 pain trials during the second part of the experiment. Thus, the actual amount of aversive stimulation was held constant across the two groups. A major finding of this study was that the perceived no-control group subjects had a significantly greater frequency of spontaneous skin conductance fluctuations (an indication of heightened emotional stress) during the second half of the study relative to the perceived-control group subjects. These results therefore demonstrated that the perception of effective control, even if not veridical, can significantly decrease the electrodermal component of autonomic arousal produced by an aversive situation. Thus, there is little doubt that the perception of control, whether or not veridical, can significantly reduce the impact of emotionally stressful events. There are other studies documenting the stress-reducing effects of perceived control (Gatchel, 1980).

There is also research demonstrating the importance of the perception of the control in the context of studies in which subjects are taught self-control of physiological responses. For example, in an experiment by Gatchel, Hatch, Watson, Smith, and Gaas (1977), the relative effectiveness of heart rate biofeedback, false heart rate biofeedback, muscle relaxation, and combined heart rate biofeedback/muscle relaxation training in reducing anxiety in speech anxious subjects was evaluated. Subjects in the false biofeedback placebo group were led to believe that they were successfully learning to decrease heart rate voluntarily (even though they were actually not), which would later serve as an effective means of alleviating anxiety. Results of this study indicated that all four experimental groups showed a decrease in a self-report component of public speaking anxiety as a result of the treatment they received. There were no significant differences among the four groups. The fact that the false biofeedback placebo group demonstrated as much improvement as the active treatment group indicates the powerful impact of a false biofeedback false placebo condition. The perception by the group that they had active control over an anxiety competing response (heart rate deceleration), even when they in fact had none, significantly influenced their self-report of anxiety.

Although there were no significant differences found among groups on the self-report measure of anxiety, an evaluation of physiological indices yielded some interestingly different findings. Results indicated that the three active physiological self-control treatment groups showed significantly smaller heart rate and skin conductance level increases during a posttreatment assessment of anxiety, in comparison to the false biofeedback group. Thus, direct control over physiological activity translated into significant reduction in the overall psychophysiological indices of stress and anxiety.

The Placebo Effect

Research clearly demonstrates the important impact that the placebo effect has in biofeedback and other physiological self-control techniques directed at eliminating emotional stress. The placebo effect itself was originally shown to be an important factor in medical research when it was found that inert chemical drugs, which had no direct effect on physical events underlying various medical disorders, were often found to produce symptom reduction. An extensive literature on the placebo effect in medicine undeniably demonstrates that a patient's belief that a prescribed medication is active, even if it is in fact chemically inert, often leads to significant symptom reduction (e.g., Honigfeld, 1964; Shapiro, 1971). Indeed, Shapiro (1959) noted that "the history of medical treatment until relatively recently is the history of the placebo effect" (p. 303). Even response to a chemically active drug to some degree depends on a belief in the drug's actions and the faith in the doctor prescribing it.

The placebo effect has also been found to be an active ingredient in psychotherapy (e.g., Wilkens, 1973), especially when anxiety is being treated. Although the placebo effect is a "multidetermined phenomenon" that is not yet completely understood, one important psychological factor contributing to the placebo effect that has been shown to affect the outcome of psychotherapy is generalized expectancy of improvement (Wilkens, 1973). This can be produced merely by creating the belief in patients that they can control some degree of emotional stress.

The Placebo Effect and Perceived Control

How does perceived control relate to the placebo effect? Merely the expectancy or belief that a treatment is going to be therapeutic and effective, and that it is going to provide a means of coping with a stressful symptom or array of symptoms, will often lead to that very state of affair of symptom reduction. People suffering from a significant amount of stress and tension often feel at the mercy of this aversive emotional state, with no effective means of alleviating or personally controlling it. One of the chief attractions of tranquilizers, besides the reduction of the physiological components of stress, is that they allow individuals the comforting perception that they have a means of actively controlling the ingestion of a drug.

Indeed, this same perception of control factor can be seen in nonpharmacological treatments. For example, Goldfried and Trier (1974) demonstrated the effectiveness of muscle relaxation training in reducing anxiety when presented as an active self-control coping skill. This self-control concept has been reviewed as an important component of behavioral treatment techniques (e.g., Goldfried & Merbaum, 1973). Goldfried and Trier found that subjects who were given relaxation training presented as an active coping skill over which they exerted personal control demonstrated a significantly greater reduction in anxiety than subjects who were given identical muscle relaxation training, but that was presented as an "automatic" procedure for passively reducing anxiety.

Of course, the concept of personal or perceived control is not the entire reason why techniques such as muscle relaxation and biofeedback work. The techniques are still effective when relaxation is passively induced. There is little doubt, however, that the psychological or cognitive factor of perceived controllability plays a significant role in the stress reduction process. Indeed, the concept of *self-efficacy* in the treatment of maladaptive or emotional behavior has been emphasized (e.g., Bandura, 1986). A sense of self-efficacy greatly contributes to the reduction of emotional distress. Thus, direct volitional control of physiology may not only impact on the physiological component of stress, but may also simultaneously affect the other more psychological concomitants of this complex psychophysiological process.

CONCLUSIONS

Physiological self-regulation techniques such as biofeedback have an important place in the rapidly growing field of health psychology. To date, there is a great deal of research demonstrating the efficacy of these techniques in helping to manage a wide array of medically related disorders. It should again be emphasized, however, that more controlled research is needed to unequivocally document effectiveness for many of the disorders. Moreover, these techniques should be viewed merely as important *adjunctive* treatment modalities to be used as part of a more comprehensive treatment program. Many disorders are far too complex psychophysiologically, and will not be totally responsive to a single treatment modality. Finally, the therapeutic effects of these techniques are not only due to the direct link to physiological activity, but also the psychological process of perceived control. The further investigation of the complex psychophysiological mechanisms underlying the therapeutic efficacy of self-regulation techniques should lead to a greater refinement of training methods and a resultant more effective overall treatment strategy.

ACKNOWLEDGMENT

Some research reported in this chapter was supported by grants from the National Institutes of Health (MH46452, MH01107, and DE10713).

REFERENCES

Adams, J. D. (1978). Improving stress management: A action-research based OD intervention. In W. W. Burke (Ed.). *The cutting edge* (pp. 51–78). La Jolla, CA: University Associates.

Annent, J. (1969). *Feedback and human behavior.* Baltimore: Penguin.

Bagchi, B. K. (1959). Mysticism and mist in India. *Journal of the Denver Society of Psychosomatic Dentistry and Medicine, 16,* 1–32.

Bagchi, B. K., & Wenger, M. A. (1957). Electro-physiological correlates of some yogi exercises. *Electroencephalography and Clinical Neurophysiology* (Suppl. 7), 132–149.

Bandura, A. (1986). *The social foundations of thought and action.* Englewood Cliffs, NJ: Prentice-Hall.

Basmajian, J. V. (Ed.). (1989). *Biofeedback: Principles and practice for clinicians.* Baltimore: Williams & Wilkins.

Benson, H. (1975). *The relaxation response.* New York: Morrow.

Birk, L. (Ed.). (1973). *Biofeedback: Behavioral medicine.* New York: Grune & Stratton.

Gatchel, R.J. (1980). Perceived control: A review and evaluation of therapeutic implications. In A. Baum & J. E. Singer (Eds.), *Advances in environmental psychology* (pp. 1–22). Hillsdale, NJ: Lawrence Erlbaum Associates.

Gatchel, R. J. (1994). Stress and coping. In A. M. Colman (Ed.), *Companion encyclopedia of psychology* (pp. 560–579). London: Routledge.

Gatchel, R. J. (1997). Biofeedback. In A. Baum, C. McManus, S. Newman, J. Weinman, & R. West (Eds.). *Cambridge handbook of psychology, health and medicine* (pp. 197–199). London: Cambridge University Press.

Gatchel, R. J., Baum, A., & Krantz, D. (1989). *An introduction to health psychology* (2nd ed.). New York: McGraw-Hill.

Gatchel, R. J., & Blanchard, E. B. (Eds). (1993). *Psychophysiological disorders: Research clinical applications.* Washington, DC: American Psychological Association.

Gatchel, R. J., & Price, K. P. (1979). Biofeedback: An introduction and historical overview. In R. J. Gatchel & K. P. Price (Eds.), *Clinical applications of biofeedback: Appraisal and status* (pp. 1–11). Elmsford, NY: Pergamon.

Gatchel, R. J., Hatch, J. P., Watson, P. J., Smith, D., & Gaas, E. (1977). Comparative effectiveness of voluntary heart-rate control and muscular relaxation as active coping skills for reducing speech anxiety. *Journal of Consulting and Clinical Psychology, 45,* 1093–1100.

Geer, J. H., Davison, G. C., & Gatchel, R. J. (1970). Reduction of stress in humans through nonveridical perceived control of aversive stimulation. *Journal of Personality and Social Psychology, 16,* 731–738.

Goldfried, M. R., & Merbaum, M. (Eds). (1973). *Behavior change through self-control.* New York: Holt, Rinehart & Winston.

Goldfried, M. R., & Trier, C. S. (1974). Effectiveness of relaxation as an active coping skill. *Journal of Abnormal Psychology, 83,* 348–355.

Hatch, J. P., Fisher, J. G., & Rugh, J. D. (Eds.). (1987). *Biofeedback: Studies in clinical efficacy.* New York: Plenum.

Honigfeld, G. (1964). Non-specific factors in treatment: I. Review of placebo reactions and placebo reactors. *Diseases of the Nervous Systems, 25,* 145–156.

Jacobson, E. (1938). *Progressive relaxation.* Chicago: University of Chicago Press.

Kiecolt-Glaser, J. K., Glaser, R., Williger, D., Stout, J., Messick, G., & Sheppard, S. (1985). Psychosocial enhancement of immunocompetence in a geriatric population. *Health Psychology, 4,* 25–41.

Lang, P. J. (1970). Autonomic control or learning to play in internal organs. *Psychology Today,* pp. 11–16, October.

Lindsley, D. B., & Sassaman, W. H. (1938). Autonomic activity and brain potentials associated with "voluntary" control of pilomotors. *Journal of Neurophysiology, 1,* 342–349.

Luria, A. R. (1958). *The mind of a mnemonist* (L. Solotaroff, Trans.). New York: Basic Books.

McClure, C. M. (1959). Cardiac arrest through volition. *California Medicine, 90,* 440–448.

Ogden, E., & Shock, N.W. (1939). Voluntary hypercirculation. *American Journal of the Medical Sciences, 198,* 329–342.

Roskies E., Seraganian, P., Oseasohn, R., Martin, N., Smilga, C., & Hanley, J. A. (1986). The Montreal Type A intervention Project: Mayer findings. *Health Psychology, 1,* 45–60.

Schultz, J. H., & Luthe, W. (1959). *Autogenic training: A psychophysiologic approach in psychotherapy.* New York: Grune & Stratton.

Schwartz, M. S. (1987). *Biofeedback: A practitioner's guide.* New York: Guilford.

Shapiro, A. K. (1959). The placebo effect in the history of medical treatment-implications for psychiatry. *American Journal of Psychiatry, 116,* 298–304.

Shapiro, A. K. (1971). Placebo effects in medicine, psychotherapy, and psychoanalysis. In A. E. Bergen & S. L. Garfield (Eds.), *Handbook of psychotherapy and behavior change* (pp. 439–473). New York: Wiley.

Stroebel, C. (1983). *OR: The quieting reflex.* New York: Berkeley Books.

Wilkens, W. (1973). Expectancy of therapeutic gain: An empirical and conceptual critique. *Journal of Consulting and Clinical Psychology, 40,* 69–77.

Wolpe, J. (1958). *Psychotherapy and reciprocal inhibitions.* Palo Alto, CA: Stanford University Press.

7

Behavioral Conditioning of the Immune System

Alexander W. Kusnecov
Rutgers, The State University of New Jersey

The past two decades have witnessed the growth of a multidisciplinary research area centered around the notion that the brain, through the neuroendocrine system, modulates the immune system, while the immune system in turn modulates the brain. The various converging lines of evidence supporting this concept have been summarized elsewhere (Ader, Felten, & Cohen, 1991). However, serving as the basis for the present chapter is one of the most compelling demonstrations of brain–immune system interactions: behaviorally conditioned immunomodulation. This phenomenon is based on the observation that alterations of immune function can be linked in a learned manner to a conditioning stimulus (CS), such that the CS attains the power to reenlist the immunological change with which it had previously been associated. In the terminology of the conditioning literature, the inducer (e.g., immunosuppressive drug) of the immunological alteration may be viewed as the unconditioned stimulus (UCS), whereas the reenlisted immunological alteration after reexposure to the CS is a conditioned response (CR). Thus, not unlike the traditional Pavlovian conditioning of the salivary response in hungry dogs, the activity of the immune system can also be manipulated by conditioning.

Not surprisingly, the concept of conditioning the immune system first emerged from the former Soviet Union during the first half of the 20th century. Conducting research in laboratory animals, and examining the modulation or elicitation of specific and nonspecific host defenses within classical Pavlovian conditioning paradigms, results were obtained that suggested the immune system could be classically conditioned. Unfortunately, many of the studies were poorly reported and badly controlled (for a detailed review of these studies see Ader, 1981). More recently, Ader and Cohen (1975) demonstrated a conditioned immunopharmacologic effect on the antibody response in rats, and initiated the modern era of research on conditioning of the immune system. In doing so, they suggested in almost heretical fashion a possibly "learned" functional alteration in a biological system—the immune system—that presumably had been thought to function independently of the central nervous system (CNS). This implication was received with considerable skepticism, but spurred by a rapid accumulation of knowledge in the brain, behavioral, and immunological disciplines, it has gained general acceptance (Ader et al., 1991; Kusnecov & Rabin, 1994).

Much of the literature on behavioral conditioning of the immune system has been reviewed in detail elsewhere, with considerable emphasis on such issues as the generality of conditioning paradigms, conditioned and unconditioned stimuli, and immunological measures (Ader & Cohen, 1991; Kusnecov, Husband, & King, 1988). Therefore, this chapter tries to avoid detailed descriptions of studies already reviewed, and focuses more on recent and clinically applicable observations. A brief overview of the immune system is provided in the next section for those readers unfamiliar with immunology.

OVERVIEW OF THE IMMUNE SYSTEM

The immune system is a diffuse collection of specialized cells that function to protect the body (the *host*) from infection caused by foreign (or nonself) microorganisms, such as bacteria and viruses. Although it consists of well-circumscribed anatomic regions, the immune system is constantly in motion, its cells circulating throughout the body to maintain surveillance against potential pathogens breaching the skin and mucosal surfaces (e.g., upper respiratory, gastrointestinal, and urogenital tracts). Protection from infection is accomplished through two interdependent processes referred to as *natural* (i.e., *innate*) and *acquired* (i.e., *learned* or *adaptive*) immunity. Innate immunity is achieved by established nonspecific mechanisms that do not discriminate between the different types of infectious agents. The major cells of the innate immune response are the phagocytic cells, chief among which is the macrophage. Macrophages can be found in almost every tissue of the body (for this reason, they are also referred to as *tissue macrophages*).

Acquired immunity involves stimulation of a unique population of cells called lymphocytes, which are committed to respond against specific microorganisms. This type of immunity is a learning (or cognitive) process that is retained (memorized) by the immune system, and will recur again only to the same foreign substance. In contrast, the performance of innate defenses does not improve with repeated exposure to the same infectious microorganism.

The foreign substance against which an acquired immune response occurs is called an *antigen.* In a more restricted sense, an antigen is a specific molecular configuration against which only a small subset of lymphocytes will respond. There are potentially many antigens on a single bacterial cell or virus, such that within the subgroup of lymphocytes that react against a particular bacterial cell, different lymphocytes will react against different parts of the bacterial cell.

In contrast to innate immunity, then, the acquired immune response is distinguished by a number of hallmark characteristics:

1. *Specificity*: Each distinct antigen elicits only one immune response; that is, multiple immune responses may take place to several antigens present at the same time (e.g., different antigens present on the same bacterial cell).

2. *Diversity*: Each antigen is recognized by only one set of precommitted lymphocytes (i.e., different lymphocytes will recognize different antigens).

3. *Memory*: Each lymphocyte that responds to a specific antigen will do so again at a later time with greater speed and intensity; the first response is called a primary response, and subsequent responses on reexposure to the same antigen are called secondary, tertiary, and so on.

4. *Self-Limitation*: Responding lymphocytes can be downregulated so that the immune response need not persist after the antigen is removed from the body.

5. *Self/Nonself Discrimination*: Lymphocytes possess the ability to discriminate between molecules derived from the host (self) and those that appear from outside the organism (nonself); this is immunological tolerance, and it is a particularly critical function that prevents lymphocytes from attacking host tissue and causing autoimmune disease.

When a lymphocyte responds to an antigen it progresses through three distinct phases. Initial binding and recognition of antigen is the *inductive* phase, which initiates intracellular processes that progress to the *activation* phase, in which lymphocytes divide and multiply (or proliferate) and then differentiate (i.e., change form and function). Differentiation leads to the final *effector* phase. In this phase, lymphocytes are now effector cells, secreting various soluble products, such as cytokines and antibody, which promote the recruitment and expansion of more lymphocytes (and other types of cells) and the neutralization and elimination of antigen either through cytotoxic or antibody-mediated functions.

Although lymphocytes are not stationary and circulate throughout the body, they do localize in well-defined and widely distributed organs called lymph nodes. In addition, there are the *peyer's patches,* which are small lymphoid nodules that traverse the small intestine. And finally, there is the spleen (located beneath the liver), a heavily vascularized and the most commonly used lymphoid organ in experimental animal studies.

The cells of the immune system are hematopoietic (i.e., blood borne), and therefore, their formation is part of a continuing blood cell generating process known as *hematopoiesis.* This takes place in the bone marrow. Although in the bone marrow and another organ, the thymus, lymphocytes, macrophages, and other cells of the immune system are said to be immature, and cannot emigrate until they have differentiated into the "mature" state necessary to perform their specific functions. To emphasize this distinction, the bone marrow and thymus are referred to as *primary lymphoid organs,* whereas the spleen, lymph nodes, and gut-associated lymphoid tissue are called the *secondary lymphoid organs.*

Because they mediate the antigen-specific acquired immune response, lymphocytes are the preeminent cells of the immune system. All other cells (e.g., monocytes/macrophages, dendritic cells, granulocytes) that interact with lymphocytes serve either to present antigen to lymphocytes or to eliminate antigen in a nonspecific, innate manner. There are two major types of lymphocytes: **T** and **B** lymphocytes (interchangeable with the terms "T"-cells and "B"-cells).

In mammals, the B lymphocyte (so-called because of its discovery in the bursa of chickens, although there is no bursal equivalent in mammals) is derived from a common progenitor hematopoietic stem cell, and matures during fetal life in the liver and then in the adult bone marrow. The major function of B lymphocytes is the production of immunoglobulin molecules (abbreviated Ig). Structurally, there are five major classes or isotypes of immunoglobulin molecules: IgA, IgD, IgE, IgM, and IgG. When an immunoglobulin molecule is produced to specifically bind an antigen it is called an antibody. The production of antibodies against an antigen is called the humoral immune response.

B-cell induction occurs via binding of antigenic determinants to the B-cell receptor, which is commonly an IgM or IgG molecule. The receptor mediated recognition of antigen results in the B-cell undergoing clonal expansion. This type of activation can either be T lymphocyte dependent (i.e., helped by T-cells) or independent (i.e., direct interaction of antigen with

B-cells results in activation and antibody production without any co-stimulatory signals from T-cells). Ultimately, B-cell activation leads to differentiation into a bigger plasma cell, which produces and secretes antibodies. A plasma cell is more commonly referred to as an antibody forming cell (AFC), which in certain types of B-cell assays, is synonymous with a plaque forming cell (PFC).

Although most classes of antibody molecule are produced during the primary response, IgM production predominates. Once memory B-cells have formed during the effector stage of the primary response, their reactivation in a secondary immune response to the antigen that they are specific for results in predominantly IgG production systemically (e.g., in blood and spleen) and IgA mucosally (e.g., in the small intestines or upper respiratory tract).

T lymphocytes (or T-cells) are so-called because of their maturation in the thymus gland. Within the thymus, T-cells mature into cells that express various distinct molecules (e.g., CD4, CD8, and a T-cell receptor, TCR) that mediate important T-cell functions. Maturation in the thymus is essentially a selection process based on whether T-cells possess close affinity for molecules expressed by the major histocompatibility complex (MHC; see later), and the absence of reactivity to molecules (other than the MHC encoded molecules) expressed on self tissue. This latter criterion is the basis of self-tolerance, or absence of autoaggressive responses. A mature T-cell, therefore, will not react against non-MHC self antigens, but will strongly recognize MHC encoded molecules. This capability optimizes T-cell recognition of foreign antigens, which are presented to the T-cell in association with MHC encoded molecules. This is the molecular basis of antigen presentation to T-cells by macrophages, B-cells, and dendritic cells.

All T-cells emigrating from the thymus express a TCR, the purpose of which is to recognize specific antigenic peptides and initiate intracellular signals that will result in cell division (mitosis) and differentiation. However, T lymphocytes also differentially express molecules (CD4 and CD8), which is the basis of their segregation into two major functional subtypes. Hence, mature T-cells are designated as either $CD4^+$ or $CD8^+$. The CD4 T-cell helps or promotes antigen-specific B-cell responses, and is called a T-helper cell; CD8 T-cells mediate cytotoxic responses against foreign cells or host cells infected with viruses, and are therefore called cytotoxic T-cells.

Induction of a CD4 or CD8 T-cell response requires a recognition step in which antigen specifically binds to the TCR. The recognition step between antigen and TCR involves a physical interaction between the T-cell and another (non-T) host cell that presents the antigen in the molecular "clutches," as it were, of one of the proteins encoded by the MHC. This latter non-T-cell is called an antigen presenting cell (APC). For example, after performing their innate function of indiscriminately ingesting a large foreign substance by phagocytosis or endocytosis, macrophages will digest this substance into peptide fragments that are then loaded onto the MHC Class II molecule (see later) and transported to the cell surface. Induction of an immune response will then take place through the recognition of the MHC-bound foreign peptide by the appropriate T-cell that expresses a TCR "fitting" in a complementary manner the molecular configuration of the peptide antigen.

To understand this more fully it is necessary to consider the nature and function of the MHC more closely. The MHC is a set (*complex*) of genes found in all vertebrate mammals and located on distinct chromosomes (e.g., chromosome 6 in humans; chromosome 17 in the mouse). These genes code for protein molecules that are expressed on the cell membrane and, as described earlier, play a critical role in the presentation of antigen to T-cells. The main protein molecules encoded by the MHC are the Class I and Class II molecules. Class I MHC molecules are expressed on most cells in the body (i.e., cells of the immune system and cells not of the immune system). Expression of Class II MHC molecules is more restricted, occurring on B-cells, macrophages, dendritic cells, epidermal langerhans cells (found in skin), and thymic epithelial cells. These latter cells are said to be professional APC.

The major function of MHC encoded Class I and II molecules is the binding and presentation of antigenic peptides to T-cells whose receptors are capable of recognizing the peptide + MHC protein complex. In general, $CD4^+$ T-cells recognize antigen when it is bound by a MHC Class II molecule; $CD8^+$ T-cells recognize antigen when it is presented by a MHC Class I molecule. Thus, because of their dependence on MHC Class I and II expression, immune responses mediated by CD4 and CD8 T-cells are said to be MHC restricted.

It should be noted that there is another class of cytotoxic lymphocyte, known as a large granular lymphocyte, which does not appear to respond in a MHC-restricted and antigen-specific manner. These cells spontaneously lyse bacterial, viral, and tumor cells, and are known as natural killer (NK) cells. These lymphocytes, therefore, may be viewed as part of the innate, nonspecific immune response.

Much of the effector function of the acquired immune response involves the production of soluble substances (i.e., nonparticulate molecular products) that promote the elimination of antigen. Antibody molecules produced by B-cells represent one class of soluble effector mediators. However, another important class of molecules, and the most intensively studied, are the cytokines. Cytokines are protein molecules synthesized and secreted by cells (hence the cyto-) to serve as autocrine/paracrine signaling and growth and differentiation factors. Fibroblasts and endothelial cells secrete cytokines, but so do cells of the immune system. T lymphocytes, monocytes, and macrophages all secrete cytokines. There are some reports that B lymphocytes can also secrete cytokines.

The term *cytokines* is a generic term. Cytokines produced by T- cells are called lymphokines. Cytokines produced by monocytes and macrophages are called monokines. However, for convenience, and the fact that some monokines are also lymphokines, these products are referred to generically as cytokines, whether derived from T-cells or monocytes/macrophages. (To add to the confusion, many cytokines are called interleukins, i.e., to reflect the observation that they act "between leukocytes," and are abbreviated, IL. Many interleukins are produced by T lymphocytes.)

The major characteristics of cytokines are as follows: (a) They are generally not constitutively expressed and need to be induced. (b) Their actions are mediated through a specific receptor synthesized by the target cell. (c) Many cytokines have overlapping functions (i.e., they are pleiotropic, affecting more than one cell type), which allows for some redundancy. The latter characteristic is extremely germane to the present chapter, because cytokines both affect and are produced in the CNS.

In closing this section, it should be stated that the distinction between two major types of immunity—innate and acquired immunity—is largely a matter of convenience, because neither process functions independently of the other during immune defence. That is, the immune response against an infectious agent involves both the cells of the innate immune system (e.g., monocytes, macrophages, and neutrophils) and the lymphocytes of the acquired immune response. To provide a simple scenario, invasion of the host by bacterial cells results in their immediate ingestion by tissue macrophages. The ingested bacteria are fragmented by degradative enzymes into various peptide fragments and bacterial elimination is then further facilitated by a sensitization process in which the peptide fragments are presented by MHC Class II molecules to B and T lymphocytes. The specific lymphocytes recognizing the presented antigen are then activated and expanded into a population of effector cells that secrete antibodies and cytokines. The antibodies bind to any noningested bacterial cells and facilitate their destruction by other phagocytic cells. Cytokine production promotes this process by influencing B-cell antibody production, various T-cell functions (e.g., proliferation, cytotoxic activity, and cytokine production), and the bacterial killing functions of macrophages. Hence, innate and acquired immune responses are ongoing simultaneously through a sophisticated network of cellular and cytokine interactions.

For readers wanting to know more about the immune system, the introductory textbooks by Abbas, Lichtman, and Pober (1994) and Roitt, Brostoff, and Male (1989) are a particularly good place to start.

BEHAVIORAL CONDITIONING OF THE IMMUNE SYSTEM

There is now no question that immune function is under significant neuroendocrine and autonomic nervous system (ANS) control. Because the activities of the ANS and neuroendocrine system fluctuate in relation to behavior (e.g., stress), optimal protection from infectious disease may be determined by specific modes of behavior. The relation of psychosocial factors to immune function is reviewed elsewhere in this handbook, and represents one significant example of how behavior can modulate immune function. This section considers additional evidence demonstrating that the immune system may actually influence behavior in a learned manner. Because of space limitations, it is assumed that the reader is familiar with the general notions and terminology of learning theory.

As stated in the introduction, the first formal and exquisitely controlled demonstration of behaviorally conditioned modulation of an immune response was provided by Ader and Cohen (1975). This study is described in considerable detail because it is the prototype of the many studies that were conducted subsequently in other laboratories. Based on some serendipitous observations, Ader and Cohen (1975) hypothesized that an immunologic alteration could be reenlisted in a learned or conditioned manner by an environmental stimulus or stimuli previously associated with an immunomodulatory event. To test this, they utilized the conditioned taste aversion (CTA) paradigm in which a novel tasting solution (CS) is paired with an illness inducing drug (UCS), the result being that subsequent CS reexposure elicits enhanced neophobia or aversion. Behaviorally this is measured as reduced ingestion of the CS. Thus, in Ader and Cohen's experiment, the UCS was cyclophosphamide, a cytotoxic drug commonly used to destroy tumor cells in cancer patients, but that also has noxious and immunosuppressive side effects. The immune measure that was used in this experiment was the primary antibody response to sheep red blood cells (SRBC).

Thus, rats received a learning trial consisting of a paired presentation of the CS (saccharin solution) and an injection of cyclophosphamide. Three and/or 6 days later, these now conditioned animals were either reexposed to the CS, not given the CS (received water), or were injected again with the UCS. Thirty minutes after these treatments on Day 3, all groups were immunized with SRBC. Additional control groups were included to eliminate any placebo effects. Although a nonconditioned group was included (received water and UCS on the conditioning day), this was not a noncontingent control group. Later studies from Ader and Cohen's laboratory (and that of others) included this necessary control group without any change in the interpretation of the results. Measurement of the antibody response 6 days after immunization revealed the following pattern of results. As expected, animals that did not receive the immunosuppressive UCS had the highest antibody response, whereas those that received the UCS on the learning day and on the test day, just prior to immunization, had the lowest response. Between these two extremes, the remaining groups showed the pattern of results that had been predicted. The critical control group consisted of animals that were conditioned, but received the SRBC in the absence of the CS. As predicted, the antibody response of this group was significantly higher than the conditioned group that had been reexposed to the CS 30 minutes prior to immunization.

These results were interpreted as demonstrating a behaviorally conditioned immunosuppression. Subsequent confirmation of these results, using essentially the same paradigm and antigen (Rogers, Reich, Strom, & Carpenter, 1976; Wayner, Flannery, & Singer, 1978), served to establish the reliability of this phenomenon. In the ensuing years, numerous laboratories have extended these observations, seeking to characterize the parameters, behavioral and immunological, which allow for the expression or manifestation of this phenomenon. The phenomonenon is not species specific, having been demonstrated in rats, mice, guinea pigs, and (as is discussed here) in humans. Further, it is not restricted to the taste aversion paradigm: novel odors, discrete sounds, environmental contexts, as well as tactile stimulation, have all proven to be effective conditioning stimuli for demonstrating BCI (for reviews see Ader & Cohen, 1991, and Kusnecov, Husband, & King, 1988). Although cyclophosphamide has been the most commonly used UCS, other compounds with immunomosuppressive properties have been tested. For example, behaviorally conditioned immunosuppression has been demonstrated using methotrexate (Ader & Cohen, 1981), cyclosporine A (Grochowicz et al., 1991; Klosterhalfen & Klosterhalfen, 1990), antilymphocyte serum (Kusnecov et al., 1983), and morphine (Coussons-Read, Dykstra, & Lysle, 1994). Moreover, the phenomenon is not confined to demonstrations of conditioned immunosuppression, with numerous studies showing a conditioned enhancement of antigen-specific and nonspecific immune responses (Bovbjerg, Cohen, & Ader, 1987; Husband, King, & Brown, 1986–1987; Russell et al., 1984; Solvason, Ghanta, & Hiramoto, 1988).

The range of immune parameters amenable to conditioning is quite impressive. The antibody response to SRBC has been the most popular antigen-specific measure tested (Ader & Cohen, 1991; Gorczynski, 1991), although conditioned suppression of immunoglobulin responses to protein antigens, as well as to nonspecific mitogens, such as pokeweed mitogen (Kusnecov et al., 1988) have been successfully used. In addition to humoral immune responses, *in vitro* T-cell proliferative responses (Kusnecov et al., 1988) and T-cell mediated responses such as the graft-versus-host response (Bovbjerg, Ader, & Cohen, 1984), delayed-type hypersensitivity (Roudebush & Bryant, 1991), and tissue transplant rejection have been shown to be conditioned (Gorczynski, 1990; Grochowicz et al., 1991). Indeed, the latter demonstrates the potential clinical applicability of conditioned immunosuppression. Patients that have received organ transplants are maintained on immunosuppressive drug treatment to prevent rejection of transplanted tissue by mature T-cells intolerant of specific antigens expressed by the new organ. In two separate studies in mice, it was shown that rejection of foreign skin or cardiac tissue could be delayed by a CS that had been paired with either cyclophosphamide or cyclosporine, a potent T-cell immunosuppressant (Gorczynski, 1990; Grochowicz et al., 1991). In a clinical situation, therefore, it may be possible to enhance the immunosuppressive effects of drugs, such as cyclosporine, without increasing dosage, which carries the risk of deleterious side effects.

This applies to most clinical situations where drug therapy is provided for the specific purpose of suppressing the immune system. Autoimmune disease is a condition in which there has been a failure of self-tolerance by the immune system, resulting in T and B lymphocytes attacking either specific organs or any tissue expressing the self antigen that is being responded against. Patients with autoimmune disease receive a wide range of immunosuppressive treatments, including cyclosporine and cyclophosphamide. It has been demonstrated in animal models of autoimmune disease that the therapeutic use of either of these drugs can be enhanced by introducing a conditioning component into the regimen of drug treatment (Ader & Cohen, 1982; Klosterhalfen & Klosterhalfen, 1990; Klosterhalfen & Klosterhalfen, 1983). For example, Ader and Cohen used mice that spontaneously develop systemic lupus erythematosus and eventually die. Prior to onset of mortality, there is increased proteinuria, which can be delayed by treating mice with intermittent doses of cyclophosphamide. Ader and Cohen showed that if drug treatment was specifically paired with a novel saccharine solution, which served as a CS, proteinuria and mortality were significantly delayed in comparison to a control group of animals that had received saccharin on alternate days to that of drug treatment. Klosterhalfen & Klosterhalfen (1990) obtained similar results in rats with an experimentally induced autoimmune arthritis. They found that rats receiving paired presentations of cyclosporine and a novel chocolate milk solution developed less arthritic paw swelling, than nonconditioned animals receiving the same drug regimen. Thus, introducing a conditioning component into an ongoing therapeutic drug regimen may enhance the therapeutic efficacy of drug treatment.

Human Studies of Conditioning

Animal studies can suggest the plausibility of applying behaviorally conditioning paradigms in clinical settings requiring immunotherapy, but additional information is required to show that immune responses can be conditioned in humans. Demonstrations of conditioned immunomodulation in human subjects have been reported, although these are few in number. Gauci, Husband, Saxarra, and King (1994) investigated whether conditioning could modulate the allergic response in humans with perennial allergic rhinitis. Subjects received a single paired presentation of a novel drinking solution with exposure to a house dust mite allergen. Subsequent reexposure to the drinking solution alone revealed that mast cells from conditioned subjects contained increased levels of tryptase. This indicated increased mast cell degranulation, which constitutes part of the allergic response. Hence, consistent with previously held notions about the conditionability of allergic reactions, this finding provided experimental support that allergic responses may in part be influenced by conditioning stimuli.

Additional evidence for conditioning of a specific cellular immune response to antigen was provided by G. R. Smith and McDaniels (1983). In a study where subjects served as their own controls, it was shown that when an antigen (the purified protein derivative of tuberculin) was administered from a colored vial that consistently had been associated with saline (i.e., subjects received intradermal injections of saline, which not unexpectedly failed to elicit the classical swelling and redness associated with an immediate hypersensitivity response), the expected hypersensitivity reaction was significantly diminished. Although this study has not been repeated, it offers a reverse spin on the placebo literature in that expectations of a null response may actually drive a natural immune response in a similar direction.

In a more recent study, Buske-Kirschbaum, Kirschbaum, Stierle, Lehnert, and Hellhammer (1992) demonstrated a classical enhancement of the natural killer cell response in humans. Natural killer cells have long been considered an important surveillance mechanism against tumor cells. Consequently, upregulation of their function is of considerable clinical importance. Prior to this study, it had already been shown that NK cell activity can be both suppressed and enhanced by conditioning in rats and mice (O'Reilly & Exon, 1986; Solvason et al., 1988). In Buske-Kirschbaum et al.'s (1992) study, college students received paired presentations of a novel taste (a sherbet sweet) and an intravenous injection of epinephrine. The unconditioned response (the natural effect of exogenous epinephrine) was increased NK cell activity in the peripheral blood. Similarly, when conditioned subjects were reexposed to the CS some days later, the same effect was observed relative to conditioned subjects not reexposed to the CS. Hence, in human subjects it is possible to reenlist the NK cell enhancing effects of epinephrine using a taste CS. An additional follow-up study by the same group (Buske-Kirschbaum, Kirschbaum, Stierle, Jabaij, & Hellhammer, 1994) replicated these initial findings using a discriminative conditioning paradigm. This involved the presentation of a compound stimulus (CS^+: consisting of a novel sherbet sweet taste combined with white noise) together with epinephrine, whereas a second, different compound stimulus (CS^-: also taste + noise) was not associated with epinephrine. On subsequent testing, presentation of the CS^+ elicited a conditioned increase in NK cell activity, whereas the CS^- had no effect. These findings suggest that it may be possible to enhance the activity of NK cells using a conditioning approach. The advantage of increasing NK cell activity is most relevant in the treatment of cancer. However, additional studies using clinical populations are needed to test whether this is possible.

Conditioned Chemotherapeutic Effects. It is known that cancer patients receiving radiotherapy and chemotherapy experience conditioned anticipatory nausea. Not unlike the conditioned taste aversion paradigm, which itself reflects a biological predisposition to avoid toxic foods, a high percentage of cancer patients associate the nausea and illness induced by their therapy with aspects of the clinical setting, such as the staff, building, rooms, and so on. Bovbjerg et al. (1990) tested whether such a conditioned psychological reaction translates into immunological changes. The subject population for their study consisted of people with ovarian cancer, and who were receiving a schedule of chemotherapeutic treatment that was given every 4 weeks. Testing for a conditioned immunomodulation was conducted after at least three visits to the clinic, with patients arriving the evening prior to their next dose of chemotherapy. A baseline blood sample was obtained at home 3 to 8 days prior to the hospital visit, and a second blood sample was obtained just prior to drug infusion. Comparison of baseline and hospital blood samples did not reveal any differences in NK cell activity or percentages of lymphocyte subsets (Bovbjerg et al., 1990). However, the proliferative function of lymphocytes assayed with various T-cell mitogens was significantly reduced in the hospital. Behavioral assessments revealed that patients reported experiencing greater anxiety and nausea in the hospital.

In contrast to this latter study, Frederikson, Furst, Lekander, Rotstein, and Blomgren (1993) failed to observe any changes in mitogenic function of peripheral blood lymphocytes from breast cancer patients that had previously received several regimens of chemotherapeutic treatment and were tested prior to an additional drug treatment. Measures of anxiety and nausea were obtained, but were not related to immune changes. However, it should be noted that several methodological differences exist between this and Bovbjerg et al.'s (1990) study. Patients in the latter study received a more severe chemotherapeutic treatment, and, perhaps more importantly, 80% of patients requested sedative treatment during their hospital stay. In addition to differences in the cancerous condition (ovarian vs. breast cancer) of the two subject populations, it is unlikely that the two studies can be adequately compared.

An inherent problem in assessing conditioning effects in cancer patients is the sensitivity of the circumstances. The level of anxiety and concern about physical well-being naturally serves as a deterrent against establishing experimental designs of the type observed in animal studies, or the human studies cited earlier (e.g., Buske-Kirschbaum et al., 1992, 1994). A critical control in such studies is always a previously conditioned group that does not receive CS reexposure. This group represents a measure of residual immunomodulation during the learning trial(s). However, such a group appears to be difficult to obtain among cancer patients undergoing chemotherapy. To obtain such a group, it would be necessary to include a group that would have to skip a scheduled visit to the hospital, but still receive a blood draw at home. The experimental group would be patients who go in for their scheduled visit and are sampled in the hospital. Clearly, such a situation is unrealistic.

Alternatively, it is possible to establish designs in which a specific stimulus (e.g., taste) is paired with drug treatment. This stimulus can then be introduced in a neutral setting and should serve as a CS that elicits memories of the hospital experience. Baseline blood draws and CS reexposures could all be performed away from the hospital, and different groups can be included in which some are given the CS whereas others are either given no CS or a different CS not associated with the hospital and drug treatment. Indeed, Bovbjerg et al. (1992) demonstrated in breast cancer patients that the pairing of a distinctive beverage with drug treatment produced a conditioned nausea reaction to the beverage, compared to patients that had not received the beverage with chemotherapy. Thus, in light of this experimental demonstration of conditioned nausea, it may be possible to establish designs that may more adequately assess whether there are conditioned immunomodulatory changes in cancer patients. The importance of this information is more than academic, because conditioned suppression of important immune parameters may alter the effectiveness of immune surveillance against immunogenic tumors.

Is Conditioned Immunomodulation a Stress Artifact?

Despite abundant evidence for behaviorally conditioned immunomodulation, a persisting question is whether the CS is reenlisting the immunological effects of the UCS in a learned manner, or whether the CS is reenlisiting the stressor component of an aversive UCS. Because many of the agents used to modify the immune system—in particular, cyclophosphamide—have aversive properties independent of their direct immunological effects (e.g., illness), it is possible that these additional indirect effects are linked to the CS, resulting in a conditioned stress response. Indeed, Lysle and colleagues used a conditioned fear paradigm to show that when rats are reexposed to a context associated with prior delivery of electric footshock (viz. the shock chamber), there is an immediate suppression of lymphocyte proliferative activity in the spleen and in blood (Lysle, Cunnick, Fowler, & Rabin, 1988). This is also the same effect that the UCS itself exerts. Others have reported similar data for the antibody response of mice to SRBC (Zalcman, Richter, & Anisman, 1989).

Unconditioned stressors activate a variety of hormonal and neurotransmitter systems, many of which have been shown to modulate immune function (Kusnecov & Rabin, 1994), so it is reasonable to argue that conditioning paradigms using a UCS that in and of itself has a stressor component, are conditioning the stress reaction and not the actual immuno-biologi- cal changes it engenders. On the other hand, because the immunobiological alteration itself is a component of the cascade of responses to a specific stressor, it is possible that the immunologic change is linked to the CNS in a learned manner. Lysle, Cunnick, and Maslonek (1991) assessed this by blocking, during the learning trial, the immunological effects of a shock UCS with the beta adrenergic receptor blocker propranolol. When animals were subsequently reexposed to the CS, the immunosuppressive effects were still evident. Clearly, the animals learned to fear the context CS independent of whether there was blockade of the immunological alteration during learning. This can be interpreted as showing that what the animal learns is fear of the context CS. Therefore, the results are consistent with the abundant evidence for stress effects on immune function (Kusnecov & Rabin, 1994), and pose serious problems for the interpretation of conditioned immunomodulatory effects in conditioning paradigms involving the use of an inherently aversive UCS.

On the other hand, there are examples of a disparity between the presence of a conditioned behavioral response and immunological alteration due to CS reexposure. For instance, a robust conditioned taste aversion can exist up to 10 days after conditioning with cyclophosphamide, although evidence for a conditioned suppressive effect on spleen cell mitogenic activity and IgM production was observed only when the CS was represented 2 days after the conditioning trial (Kusnecov et al., 1988). Because rat spleen cell mitogenic function is an immune measure shown to be very sensitive to stressor-induced modulation (Lysle et al., 1988), the inability of a robust conditioned taste aversion response to alter mitogenic function at later times following conditioning with cyclophosphamide is inconsistent with a stress-mediated interpretation of conditioning data. Other examples of where conditioned immune alterations take place in the absence of conditioned taste aversion responses are provided elsewhere (Ader & Cohen, 1991).

If there is a learned interaction between the CNS and the immune system, it may require direct immunological perturbation through mechanisms that bypass initial CNS processing. For instance, in the case of CNS-initiated immune alteration, the necessity for a cognitive interaction between the brain and the immune system may be minimal, because the immune system already is likely to be sensitized to fluctuations in the concentration of various circulating stress-related hormones (e.g., catecholamines and glucocorticoids). Hence, any perturbation of the immune system due to a hormonal fluctuation that results from CNS arousal may not require a specific learned association between neural detection of an external stressor stimulus and the altered component of the immune system. On the other hand, learned associations more likely may take place if the immune system is altered independently of the CNS. Under these cir cumstances, the changes within the immune system serve as an interoceptive stimulus to the CNS. The processing of this information by the CNS may then be linked to parallel processing of any other exteroceptive information that could then be linked in a meaningful way to the immunologic perturbation. This type of analysis makes more biological sense if, as has been suggested (see Blalock, 1984), the immune system is viewed as a sensory organ that detects stimuli existing below the threshold of detection by conventional sensory modalities mediated by the CNS (e.g., touch, sight, etc.).

The use of immunopharmacologic agents that possess indirect aversive properties is unequivocally a confounding element in the interpretation of conditioning results. It has even led to some argument in relation to a theory proposed by Eikelboom and Stewart (1982) concerning the direction conditioned biologic responses should take relative to whether the UCS is acting on the afferent or efferent side of the CNS. If, for example, the UCS perturbs the immune system (the perturbation being the unconditioned response) without first acting through the CNS, then the CNS will attempt to restore homeostasis by correcting the perturbation; and it is this process of restoration that is conditioned. Therefore, in the case of immunosuppression due to a direct action on the immune system by a pharmacologic agent, efferent signals from the CNS function to overcome this suppression by enhancing immune function. Consequently, any CS linked with direct immunosuppression should actually be associated with the CNS processes that are compensating for this suppression, and therefore, the effect of CS reexposure should be a conditioned immunoenhancement. However, the predictions of this theory for conditioned immunomodulatory effects are generally outweighed by evidence to the contrary. Of course, there are cases where data can and have been interpreted in terms of this theory (Krank & MacQueen, 1988), but by and large, most conditioned immunomodulation studies, and in particular those using cyclophosphamide as the UCS, do not seem to conform to this theoretical perspective.

Activation of the Immune System as a UCS

The most profitable approach to elucidating whether the immune system and the CNS interact in a learned manner is likely to be through studies that utilize activation of the immune system as a UCS. This is predicated on an overwhelming body of evidence showing that activation of the immune system induces functional changes in the CNS (Besedovsky & Del Rey, 1992). Thus, it has been reported that immune activation alters sleep and feeding behaviors, increases the production of pituitary hormones, increases the synthesis and release of catecholamines peripherally and centrally, and increases neuronal firing in the hypothalamus (Besedovsky & Del Rey, 1992). Although these effects can be evoked by injection of antigens, they are also observed following treatment with cytokines, in particular, the proinflammatory cytokines IL-1, IL-6, and TNF (Schobitz, De Kloet, & Holsboer, 1994). The study of CNS activation by inflammatory cytokines is dominated by two experimental approaches: exogenous administration of recombinant cytokines, and challenge with the lipopolysaccharide (LPS) endotoxin of gram negative bacteria such as *E. Coli* (Tilders et al., 1994). Many of these studies are concerned with the characterization of behavioral and/or neuroendocrine changes, as well as the mode of cytokine action and specific target regions within the CNS.

Given the impact of cytokines and infection on illness-related behaviors, it is fitting that contemporary studies of conditioned immunomodulation began with the use of the conditioned taste aversion paradigm. Obviously, the ability to learn the physiological consequences of ingestion is fundamental to survival, and a functional link between this and the immune system should not be surprising. Indeed, conditioned taste aversion has been demonstrated using IL-1 and endotoxin administration as UCSs, indicating that these agents will signal illness centers in the brain (Tazi, Dantzer, Crestani, & Le Moal, 1988). Indeed, several reports now implicate the subdiaphragmatic vagus nerve as mediating the behavioral and physiological effects of endotoxin and IL-1 (which is induced by endotoxin; Bret-Dibat, Bluthe, Kent, Kelley, & Dantzer, 1995; Fleshner et al., 1995; Gaykema, Dijkstra, & Tilders, 1995). Because the subdiaphragmatic vagus is involved in regulating feeding behavior (G. P. Smith, Jerone, & Norgren, 1985), and because the gastrointestinal tract is the main portal of entry for potential pathogens, it should not be surprising that the mucosal immune system serves not only to eliminate pathogens, but also to initiate adaptive behaviors. Hence, it is well recognized that injection of animals with endotoxin, IL-1 and TNF will reduce food intake and physical activity, and prolong sleep (for review see Schobitz et al., 1994). The same behaviors are observed during infection. This evidence suggests that the immune system communicates local information to the CNS for the purpose of initiating appropriate behaviors that either promote recovery or maintain health.

The conditioned taste aversion paradigm demonstrates that organisms will retain information about gustatory stimuli associated with illness, especially that due to infection. In fact, recent studies have demonstrated that the behavioral and metabolic effects associated with endotoxin administration can be conditioned. Fever is a centrally regulated reaction to infectious illness, and is believed to optimize the immune response against bacterial infection. In a single trial conditioned taste aversion paradigm in which rats received a pairing of saccharin solution and an injection of endotoxin, it was shown that the initial (first few hours) hypothermic and subsequent hyperthermic effects of endotoxin could be reenlisted 7 days after the learning trial by reexposure to the CS alone (Bull, Brown, King, & Husband, 1991; Exton, Bull, King, & Husband, 1995). Other studies have similarly demonstrated conditioning of temperature alterations using nonantigenic stimuli, such as polyinosinic:poly-cytidylic acid (Poly I:C), which is a synthetic double-stranded RNA polynucleotide used to mimic double-stranded RNA viral infection (Dyck & Greenberg, 1991).

In addition to temperature, the endotoxin-induced increase in slow wave sleep has also been shown to be conditioned, implying that environmental cues may potentially influence the behavioral effects of infection (Exton, Bull, King, & Husband, 1995). Endotoxin is most notably recognized as a strong inducer of proinflammatory cytokines (eg., IL-1, TNF) produced by macrophages (Tilders et al., 1994), thus it is conceivable that these conditioned effects reflect an association between conditioning cues and cytokine effects on the CNS. For example, administration of IL-1 elicits many of the same thermogenic, anorectic, and sleep inducing effects of endotoxin (Schobitz et al., 1994). Indeed, conditioned taste aversion can take place using IL-1 as the UCS (Tazi et al., 1988), and this can result in the conditioned reenlistment of the thermogenic and adrenocortical activities of IL-1 (Dyck & Greenberg, 1991).

Endotoxin is not strictly speaking an antigen, and it activates primarily innate immune processes, so these studies demonstrate conditioning of the physiological effects of indiscriminate immune activation. Hence, there remains the question of whether antigenic stimulation can serve as a UCS. Unlike substances like endotoxin, injection with foreign proteins rarely results in a rapid and significant build up of circulating proinflammatory cytokines. The response to antigen is more selective, recruits less immune cells, and is usually anatomically confined to lymph nodes that drain the site where antigen entered the body. This relatively "low key" handling of antigen is due to the small fraction (1:50,000–1:100,000) of lymphocytes that is committed to any particular antigenic configuration potentially present in the world and that mammals are likely to encounter. It has been shown that recruitment of cytotoxic T-cells can be conditioned if engraftment of foreign skin tissue serves as a UCS in mice (Gorczynski, Macrae, & Kennedy, 1982). Foreign tissue contains a large number of antigens, and therefore the UCS in this case was immunological activation by an assembly of different antigens. More recently, two studies have been conducted that have used a single protein antigen as a UCS. In the first, repeated injections of egg albumin were administered to rats in association with audiovisual contextual cues (MacQueen, Marshall, Perdue, Siegel, & Bienenstock, 1989). Reexposure to the CS alone resulted in increased production of an enzyme (protease II) produced by rat mast cells that colonize the gastrointestinal tract. It remains to be determined whether this enzyme release was due to actions mediated by antigen-sensitized lymphocytes activated by the CS.

In the second study, Ader, Kelly, Moynihan, Grota, and Cohen (1993) exposed mice to repeated injections of a low, "physiologic" dose of the protein antigen keyhole limpet hemocyanin (KLH). These repeated injections were always paired with a novel gustatory CS, chocolate milk. Measures of serum IgG antibody produced specifically against KLH revealed enhanced production of antibody when these animals were reexposed, on the test day, to the CS and a low suboptimal dose of antigen. This low dose of antigen only marginally elevated residual levels of KLH-specific IgG in conditioned animals that did not receive the CS; but in the presence of CS reexposure, it resulted in a marked stimulation of KLH-specific antibody production. Presentation of the CS in the absence of a low "booster" dose of KLH did not increase antigen-specific IgG, indicating that the CS alone does not have the capacity to induce B cells to produce antibody in the absence of actual antigen.

These latter results by Ader et al. (1993) demonstrate a conditioned enhancement of the antibody response of memory B lymphocytes to a specific antigen. The mechanisms underlying this effect have yet to be dissected but, as alluded to earlier, may include the various cytokines produced in response to immunogenic stimulation. In the case of antigen-stimulated cytokine production, it is possible that locally produced cytokines within regionally distinct lymph nodes may activate the CNS via afferent neuronal pathways, thereby forming the link between immune activation and perception of unique environmental cues.

CONCLUSIONS

This chapter has reviewed evidence showing that the inherent link between the immune system and the brain can be exploited through conditioning techniques. As discussed earlier, conditioning studies using immunosuppressive drugs suggest clinical applicability in situations where autoimmune diseases or clinical suppression of transplanted tissue is the desired goal. This is especially pertinent in light of the aversive properties of immunosuppressive therapy. Given what it is understood about the impact of stress on immune function (see Glaser & Kiecolt-Glaser, 1994), it is important to minimize the physical side effects of drug treatment. This will undoubtedly also reduce the psychological reaction to such side effects, and any further harm this may have on disease outcome.

The few studies demonstrating direct conditioning of the immune response using immunological stimulation as the UCS suggest possibilities for the optimization of the immunological effects of vaccines that are routinely given to ward off infectious illnesses (e.g., polio, tetanus, etc.). This can be done through the alignment of vaccination regimens with behavioral conditioning procedures. Alternatively, if further studies are carried out to understand the physiological mechanisms underlying direct conditioning of the immune response to antigen, it may be possible to manipulate these systems to optimize the development of immunological memory against various vaccines.

Finally, given that cytokines have been shown to modulate CNS function, it is important to learn how they may be involved in the development of conditioned antigen-specific immune responses. Moreover, the use of cytokines has been tested clinically on cancer patients, with some serious side effects, including neuroendocrine and neuropsychological alterations (Denicoff et al., 1989). Given that cytokines represent a potentially powerful tool for the treatment of cancer, it may be important to introduce behavioral strategies that can optimize the immunobiological effects of cytokine therapy while minimizing the physical and psychological side effects. However, further research is required to confirm its utility as an adjunct to traditional medical therapy.

ACKNOWLEDGMENT

This work was supported by PHS grant 51051 and the Pathology Education and Research Foundation.

REFERENCES

Abbas, A. K., Lichtman, A. H., & Pober, J. S. (1194). *Cellular and molecular immunology* (2nd ed.). Philadelphia: W. B. Saunders.

Ader, R. (1981). A historical account of conditioned immunobiologic responses. In R. Ader (Ed.), *Psychoneuroimmunology* (pp. 321–352). New York: Academic Press.

Ader, R., & Cohen, N. (1975). Behaviorally conditioned immunosuppression. *Psychosomatic Medicine, 37,* 333–340.

Ader, R., & Cohen, N. (1981). Conditioned immunopharmacologic responses. In R. Ader (Ed.), *Psychoneuroimmunology* (pp. 185–228). New York: Academic Press.

Ader, R., & Cohen, N. (1982). Behaviorally conditioned immunosuppression and murine systemic lupus erythematosus. *Science, 214,* 1534–1536.

Ader, R., & Cohen, N. (1991). The influence of conditioning on immune responses. In R. Ader, D. L. Felten, & N. Cohen (Eds.), *Psychoneuroimmunology* (2nd ed., pp. 611–646). San Diego: Academic Press.

Ader, R., Felten, D. L., & Cohen, N. (1991). *Psychoneuroimmunology* (2nd ed.). San Diego: Academic Press.

Ader, R., Kelly, K., Moynihan, J. A., Grota, L. J., & Cohen, N. (1993). Conditioned enhancement of antibody production using antigen as the unconditioned stimulus. *Brain, Behavior and Immunity, 7,* 334–343.

Besedovsky, H. O., & Del Rey, A. (1992). Immune-endocrine networks. *Frontiers in Neuroendocrinology, 13,* 61–94.

Blalock, J. E. (1984). The immune system as a sensory organ. *Journal of Immunology, 132,* 1067–1070.

Bovbjerg, D., Ader, R., & Cohen, N. (1984). Acquisition and extinction of conditioned suppression of a graft-vs-host response. *Proceedings of the National Academy of Sciences of the United States of America, 79,* 583–585.

Bovbjerg, D., Cohen, N., & Ader, R. (1987). Behaviorally conditioned enhancement of delayed-type hypersensitivity in the mouse. *Brain, Behavior and Immunity, 1,* 64–71.

Bovbjerg, D., Redd, W. H., Jacobson, P. B., Manne, S. L., Taylor, K. L., Surbone, A., Crown, J. P., Norton, L., Gilewski, T. A., Hudis, C. A., Reichman, B. S., Kaufman, R. J., Currie, V. E., & Hakes, T. B. (1992). An experimental analysis of classically conditioned nausea during cancer chemotherapy. *Psychosomatic Medicine, 54,* 623–637.

Bovbjerg, D. H., Redd, W. H., Maier, L. A., Holland, J. C., Lesko, L. M., Niedzwiecki, D., Rubin, S. C., & Hakes, T. B. (1990). Anticipatory immune suppression and nausea in women receiving cyclic chemotherapy for ovarian cancer. *Journal of Consulting and Clinical Psychology, 58,* 153–157.

Bret-Dibat, J. L., Bluthe, R. M., Kent, S., Kelley, K. W., & Dantzer, R. (1995). Lipopolysaccharide and interleukin-1 depress food-motivated behavior in mice by a vagal-mediated mechanism. Brain, *Behavior and Immunity, 9,* 242–246.

Bull, D. F., Brown, R., King, M. G., & Husband, A. J. (1991). Modulation of body temperature through taste aversion conditioning. *Physiology and Behavior, 49,* 1229–1233.

Buske-Kirschbaum, A., Kirschbaum, C., Stierle, H., Jabaij, L., & Hellhammer, D. (1994). Conditioned manipulation of natural killer (NK) cells in humans using a discriminative learning protocol. *Biological Psychology, 38,* 143–155.

Buske-Kirschbaum, A., Kirschbaum, C., Stierle, H., Lehnert, H., & Hellhammer, D. (1992). Conditioned increase of natural killer cell activity (NKCA) in humans. *Psychosomatic Medicine, 54,* 123–32.

Coussons-Read, M. E., Dykstra, L. A., & Lysle, D. T. (1994). Pavlovian conditioning of morphine-induced alterations of immune status: Evidence for opioid receptor involvement. *Journal of Neuroimmunology, 55,* 135–142.

Denicoff, K. D., Durkin, T. M., Lotze, M. T., Quinlan, P. E., Davis, C. L., Listwak, S. J., Rosenberg, S. A., & Rubinow, D. R. (1989). The neuroendocrine effects of interleukin-2 treatment. *Journal of Clinical Endocrinology and Metabolism, 69,* 402–410.

Dyck, D. G., & Greenberg, A. H. (1991). Immunopharmacological tolerance as a conditioned response: Dissecting the brain-immune pathways. In R. Ader, D. L. Felten, & N. Cohen (Eds.), *Psychoneuroimmunology* (2nd ed., pp. 663–684). San Diego: Academic Press.

Eikelboom, R., & Stewart, J. (1982). Conditioning of drug-induced physiological responses. *Psychological Reviews, 89,* 507–528.

Exton, M. S., Bull, D. F., King, M. G., & Husband, A. J. (1995). Behavioral conditioning of endotoxin-induced plasma iron alterations. *Pharmacology, Biochemistry and Behavior, 50,* 675–679.

Exton, M. S., Bull, D. F., King, M. G., & Husband, A. J. (1995). Modification of body temperature and sleep state using behavioral conditioning. *Physiology and Behavior, 57,* 723–729.

Fleshner, M., Goehler, L. E., Hermann, J., Relton, J. K., Maier, S. F., & Watkins, L. R. (1995). Interleukin-1b induced corticosterone elevation and hypothalamic NE depletion is vagally mediated. *Brain Research Bulletin, 37,* 605–610.

Frederikson, M., Furst, C. J., Lekander, M., Rotstein, S., & Blomgren, H. (1993). Trait anxiety and anticipatory immune reactions in women receiving adjuvant chemotherapy for breast cancer. *Brain, Behavior and Immunity, 7,* 79–90.

Gauci, M., Husband, A. J., Saxarra, H., & King, M. G. (1994). Pavlovian conditioning of nasal tryptase release in human subjects with allergic rhinitis. *Physiology and Behavior, 55,* 823–825.

Gaykema, R.P.A., Dijkstra, I., & Tilders, F.J.H. (1995). Subdiaphragmatic vagotomy suppresses endotoxin-induced activation of hypothalamic corticotropin-releasing hormone neurons and ACTH secretion. *Endocrinology, 136,* 4717–4720.

Glaser, R., & Kiecolt-Glaser, J. (1994). *Handbook of human stress and immunity.* San Diego: Academic Press.

Gorczynski, R. M. (1990). Conditioned enhancement of skin allografts in mice. *Brain, Behavior and Immunity, 4,* 85–92.

Gorczynski, R. M. (1991). Conditioned immunosuppression: Analysis of lymphocytes and host environment of young and aged mice. In R. Ader, D. L. Felten, & N. Cohen (Eds.), *Psychoneuroimmunology* (2nd ed., pp. 647–662). San Diego: Academic Press.

Gorczynski, R. M., Macrae, S., & Kennedy, M. (1982). Conditioned immune response associated with allogeneic skin grafts in mice. *Journal of Immunology, 129,* 704–709.

Grochowicz, P. M., Schedlowski, M., Husband, A. J., King, M. G., Hibberd, A. D., & Bowen, K. M. (1991). Behavioral conditioning prolongs heart allograft survival in rats. *Brain, Behavior and Immunity, 5,* 349–356.

Husband, A. J., King, M. G., & Brown, R. (1986–1987). Behaviorally conditioned modification of T cell subset ratios in rats. *Immunology Letters, 14,* 91–94.

Klosterhalfen S., & Klosterhalfen, W. (1990). Conditioned cyclosporine effects but not conditioned taste aversion in immunized rats. *Behavioral Neuroscience, 104,* 716–724.

Klosterhalfen, W., & Klosterhalfen, S. (1983). Pavlovian conditioning of immunosuppression modifies adjuvant arthritis in rats. *Behavioral Neuroscience, 4,* 663–666.

Krank, M. D., & MacQueen, G. M. (1988). Conditioned compensatory responses elicited by environmental signals for cyclophosphamide-induced suppression of antibody production in mice. *Psychobiology, 16,* 229–235.

Kusnecov, A. W., Husband, A. J., & King, M. G. (1988). Behaviorally conditioned suppression of mitogen-induced proliferation and immunoglobulin production: Effect of time span between conditioning and reexposure to the conditioned stimulus. *Brain, Behavior and Immunity, 2,* 198–211.

Kusnecov, A. W., & Rabin, B. S. (1994). Stressor-induced alterations of immune function: Mechanisms and issues. *International Archives of Allergy and Immunology, 105,* 107–121.

Kusnecov, A. W., Sivyer, M., King, M. G., Husband, A. J., Cripps, A. W., & Clancy, R. L. (1983). Behaviorally conditioned suppression of the immune response by antilymphocyte serum. *Journal of Immunology, 130,* 2117–2120.

Lysle, D. T., Cunnick, J. E., Fowles, H., & Rabin, B. S. (1988). pavlovian conditioning of shock-induced suppression of lymphocyte reactivity: Acquisition, extinction, and pre-exposure effects. *Life Sciences, 42*(22), 2185–2194.

Lysle, D. T., Cunnick, J. E., & Maslonek, K. A. (1991). Pharmacological manipulation of immune alterations induced by an aversive conditioned stimulus: Evidence for a b-adrenergic receptor-mediated pavlovian conditioning process. *Behavioral Neuroscience, 105,* 443–449.

Macqueen, G. M., Marshall, J., Perdue, M., Siegel, S., & Bienenstock, J. (1989). Pavlovian conditioning of rat mucosal mast cells to secrete mast cell protease II. *Science, 243,* 83–85.

O'Reilley, C. A., & Exon, J. H. (1986). Cyclophosphamide-conditioned suppression of the natural killer cell response in rats. *Physiology and Behavior, 37,* 759–764.

Rogers, M. P., Reich, P., Strom, T. B., & Carpenter, C. B. (1976). Behaviorally conditioned immunosuppression: Replication of a recent study. *Psychosomatic Medicine, 38,* 447–452.

Roitt, I. M., Brostoff, J., & Male, D. K. (1989). *Immunology* (2nd ed.). London: Gower Medical.

Roudebush, R. E., & Bryant, H. U. (1991). Conditioned immunosuppression of a murine delayed type hypersensitivity response: Dissociation from corticosterone elevation. *Brain, Behavior and Immunity, 5,* 308–317.

Russell, M., Dark, K. A., Cummins, R. W., Ellman, G., Callaway, E., & Peeke, H.V.S. (1984). Learned histamine release. *Science, 225,* 733–734.

Schobitz, B., De Kloet, E. R., Holsboer, F. (1994). Gene expression and function of interleukin 1, interleukin 6 and tumor necrosis factor. *Progress in Neurobiology, 44,* 397–432.

Smith, G. R., & McDaniels, S. M. (1983). Psychologically mediated effect on the delayed hypersensitivity reaction to tuberculin in humans. *Psychosomatic Medicine, 45,* 65–70.

Smith, G. P., Jerone, C., & Norgren, R. (1985). Afferent axons in abdominal vagus mediate satiety effect of cholecystokinin in rats. *American Journal of Physiology, 249,* R638–R641.

Solvason, H. B., Ghanta, V. K., & Hiramoto, R. N. (1988). Conditioned augmentation of natural killer cell activity. Independence from nociceptive effects and dependence on interferon-b. *Journal of Immunology, 140,* 661–665.

Tazi, A., Dantzer, R., Crestani, F., & Le Moal, M. (1988). Interleukin-1 induces conditioned taste aversion in rats: A possible explanation for its pituitary-adrenal stimulating activity. *Brain Research, 473,* 369–371.

Tilders, F.J.H., DeRijk, R. H., Van Dam, A-M., Vincent, V.A.M., Schotanus, K., & Persoons, J.H.A. (1994). Activation of the hypothalamus-pituitary-adrenal axis by bacterial endotoxins: Routes and intermediate signals. *Psychoneuroendocrinology, 19,* 209–232.

Wayner, E. A., Flannery, G. R., & Singer, G. (1978). The effects of taste aversion conditioning on the primary antibody response to sheep red blood cells and Brucella abortus in the albino rat. *Physiology and Behavior, 21,* 995–1000.

Zalcman, S., Richter, M., & Anisman, H. (1989). Alterations of immune functioning following exposure to stressor-related cues. *Brain, Behavior and Immunity, 3,* 99–109.

8

Physiological and Psychological Bases of Pain

Dennis C. Turk
University of Washington

Pain has existed since time in memoriam. Perhaps the first documented mention of pain was in the Ebers papyrus dating back to the fourth century B.C. that indicated the use of opium for the treatment of headaches. Since that time, pain has been the focus of philosophical speculation and scientific attention, yet it continues to remain a challenging problem for the sufferer, health care providers, and society.

Pain has been classified in a number of different ways, including the use of a single temporal dimension ranging from acute (momentary pain or pain extending from several hours, days, and weeks) to chronic (persisting over periods of months) to single categorical systems, such as presumed etiology (e.g., neuropathic, somatic, psychogenic), to more multiaxial diagnoses in which multiple factors are included in the classification (e.g., location, system involved, temporal characteristics and pattern of occurrence, intensity, and etiology; Merskey, 1986). For simplicity, this chapter uses a categorical approach referring to four categories of pain: *acute, acute recurrent* (e.g., migraine headache), *chronic noncancer pain* (e.g., low back pain), and *pain associated with a malignant disease process* (i.e., cancer).

Pain is essential for survival because of its alarm function. In acute pain states, nociception (activation of sensory transduction in nerve fibers that convey information about tissue damage) has a definite purpose, it acts as a warning signal that requires immediate attention, reflexive withdrawal, and other actions in order to prevent further damage and to facilitate the healing process. In chronic pain states, this adaptive function plays a significantly smaller role and can often no longer be discerned. In the case of recurrent acute pain diagnoses, such as migraine headaches, the role of pain is even less clear because there is no protective action that can be taken or any tissue damage that can be prevented. Pain associated with neoplastic disease has some features in common with acute pain in that it may be a warning signal; whereas in others it is more like chronic pain because the pain may serve no purpose.

Pain is a common symptom in people who seek medical assistance accounting for over 70 million office visits to physicians each year (National Center for Health Statistics, 1986). Each of the four pain categories are extremely prevalent. Consider a sample of some available statistics. Over 23 million surgical procedures were performed in the United States in 1989 (Peebles & Schneidman, 1991) and most of these involved acute pain. Acute recurrent and chronic pain affect over 70 million Americans, with over 10% reporting the presence of pain over 100 days/year (Osterweis, Kleinman, & Mechanic, 1987). Estimates suggest that over 11 million Americans suffer from recurring episodes of migraine headaches (Stewart, Lipton, Celentano, & Reed, 1991), over 30 million experience chronic or recurrent back pain (Holbrook, Grazier, Kelsey, & Staufer, 1984), and 37 million have pain associated with arthritis (Lawrence et al., 1989). Approximately 3.5 million people in the United States have cancer (Raj, 1990). Bonica (1979) estimated that moderate to severe pain is reported by from 40% to 45% of patients initially following the diagnosis, from 35% to 45% at the intermediate states of the disease, and from 60% to 85% in advanced states of the cancer.

Given the lengthy history of pain and the statistics on its prevalence, it might be assumed that pain is well understood and readily treated. Despite advances in the understanding of anatomy and physiological processes and innovative and technically sophisticated pharmacological, medical, and surgical treatments, pain continues to be a perplexing puzzle for health care providers and a source of significant distress for individual pain sufferers. Moreover, pain is an extremely costly problem for society in health care expenditures, indemnity costs, and lost productivity. It has been estimated that chronic pain alone costs the American people approximately $65 billion a year (Bonica, 1986).

With such astronomical figures, it is all too easy to lose sight of the incalculable human suffering accompanying pain for both individuals and their family. Chronic pain, recurrent acute pain, as well as pain associated with cancer extend over long periods of time. The average duration of pain noted for patients treated at pain clinics exceeds 7 years with durations of from 20 to 30 years not uncommon (Flor, Fydrich, & Turk, 1992).

The emotional distress that is prevalent in a majority of pain patients may be attributed to a variety of factors, including fear, inadequate or maladaptive support systems and other coping resources, iatrogenic complications, overuse of tranquilizers and narcotic medication, inability to work, financial difficulties, prolonged litigation, disruption of usual activities, and sleep disturbance. Moreover, the experience of "medical limbo"—the presence of a painful condition that eludes diagnosis and that carry the implication of either psychiatric causation, malingering, on the one hand, or an undiagnosed life threatening disease—is itself a source of stress and can initiate psychological distress or aggravate a premorbid psychiatric condition. In the case of cancer, the stress of pain is superimposed on the general fear of living and possibly dying from a potentially lethal disease.

People with persistent pain complaints become enmeshed in the medical community as they go from doctor to doctor and test to test in a continuing search to have pain diagnosed and treated. For many, the pain becomes the central focus of their lives. As pain sufferers withdraw from society, they lose their jobs, alienate family and friends, and become isolated. In this ongoing and often elusive quest for relief, it is hardly surprising that they experience feelings of demoralization, helplessness, hopelessness, and outright depression.

In sum, the different forms of persistent pain create a demoralizing situation that confronts the individual not only with the stress created by pain but with a cascade of ongoing stressors that compromise all aspects of their lives. Living with persistent pain conditions requires considerable emotional resilience and tends to deplete people's emotional reserve, and taxes not only the individual but also the capacity of family, friends, coworkers, and employers to provide support.

It is reasonable to ask questions concerning how a problem as prevalent and costly as pain can be so poorly understood and managed. The primary intention of this chapter is to address the factors that contribute to the current unsatisfactory state of affairs regarding the treatment of pain. This survey begins with a review of the most common conceptualizations of pain and then examines the role of psychological factors in the etiology and exacerbation of pain and disability. This is followed by a description of several attempts to integrate physiological and psychological variables in comprehensive conceptual models. Finally, the current understanding of the physical, anatomical, and chemical bases of pain is reviewed, illustrating the physiological bases of both sensory and psychological components of pain.

CONCEPTUALIZATIONS OF PAIN

The concept of pain has undergone multiple transformations. In the past quarter century there has been a significant paradigm shift in thinking about pain that was ushered in by the gate control theory (Melzack & Wall, 1965). The gate control theory is examined later. First, it is helpful to examine the traditional unidimensional conceptualization that has been dominant since it was formally proposed by Descartes in the 15th century (although it dates back to the ancient Greeks; Melzack & Wall, 1982).

Unidimensional Sensory Model

Historically, pain has been understood from the perspective of Cartesian mind–body dualism in which pain was viewed as a sensory experience dependent on the degrees of noxious sensory stimuli impinging on the individual. From this perspective, there are two ends of a pain pathway just as there are two ends of a direct communication line where sensory stimulation at one end (at the periphery) has a direct stimulatory effect at the other end (the brain). From this view, stimulation at the periphery inevitably results in stimulation at the other, as if pulling one end of a string pulls a bell located somewhere in the brain.

Unidimensional models of pain adhere to a specificity concept postulating that pain is a specific sensation and that pain intensity is directly proportional to the amount of peripheral nociceptive input related to tissue damage (Melzack & Wall, 1982). From this model, the production of pain is traced to peripheral pain receptors at the site of the injury. It is assumed that some form of tissue damage will excite receptors that are specific, responding exclusively to nociceptive stimuli, initiating pain-specific nerve impulses that were transmitted along specific afferent pain pathways to specific pain centers localized in the brain where the experience of pain will motivate actions to avoid further harm.

The core of sensory-physiological models is that the amount of pain is a direct result of the amount, degree, or nature of sensory input or physical damage and is explained in terms of specific physiological mechanisms. Clinically, it is expected that the report of pain will be directly proportional to physical pathology.

This sensory model has prevailed largely unchanged despite its inability to account for a number of observations. For example, patients with objectively determined, equivalent degrees and types of tissue pathology vary widely in their reports of pain severity. The surgical procedures designed to inhibit pain transmission by severing neurological pathways that are believed to be subserving the reported pain may fail to alleviate it, and patients with equivalent degrees of tissue pathology treated with identical treatments respond in widely different ways (Turk & Nash, 1996).

Psychogenic Perspectives

As is frequently the case in medicine, when physical explanations prove inadequate to explain symptoms, psychological alternatives are invoked. If the pain reported is disproportionate to objectively determined physical pathology, or if the complaint is recalcitrant to "appropriate" treatment, then it is assumed that psychological factors must be involved, even if not causal.

Several variants of psychogenic etiologic models have been proposed. For example, a model of a "pain-prone" personality that predisposes individuals to experience persistent pain was originally described by Engel (1959) and extended by Blumer and Heilbronn (1981, 1982). According to Blumer and Heilbronn, the pain-prone disorder is characterized by denial of emotional and interpersonal problems, inactivity, anhedonia, depressed mood, guilt, inability to deal with anger and hostility, insomnia, craving for affection and dependency, lack of initiative, and a family history of depression, alcoholism, and chronic pain. People who can be characterized in this way are considered by Blumer and Heilbronn to be a homogeneous diagnostically unique group that can be considered part of the "depressive spectrum." Engel proposed that once the psychic organization necessary for pain has evolved, the experience of pain no longer requires peripheral stimulation.

Turk and Salovey (1984) critically examined both the hypothesis of a pain-prone personality and the empirical support for it marshaled by Blumer and Heilbronn (1982). Turk and Salovey found the hypothesized pain-prone disorder to be flawed conceptually, circular in reasoning with the definition itself tautological, and the explanatory model lacking in parsimony. In addition, the purported empirical support was criticized as being retrospective and based on small sample sizes. Moreover, the data used to support the existence of a pain-prone personality was judged to be analyzed by inappropriate statistical methods and the results subject to alternative and simpler explanations.

Beutler, Engle, Oro'-Beutler, Daldrup, and Meredith (1986) proposed a model that was conceptually similarly to Blumer and Heilbronn (1982). They suggested that difficulty expressing anger and controlling intense emotions in general are the predisposing factors linking chronic pain and the experience of negative affect. They viewed the experience of chronic pain and depression as similar disturbances or failures to process intensively emotional information (e.g., prolonged blocking or inhibition of intense interpersonal anger).

Recently, the American Psychiatric Association (1994) created two psychiatric diagnoses, pain associated with psychological factors either with or without a diagnosed medical condition. The specific diagnosis of "Pain Disorder Associated with Psychological Factors and a General Medical Condition" (307.89) is characterized by the fact that psychological and a general medical condition both have important roles in the onset, severity, exacerbation, and maintenance of pain. This set of diagnoses is so broadly defined, however, that virtually all patients who have persistent pain are likely to be viewed as suffering from a psychiatric problem.

The somatogenic–psychogenic dichotomy forms the basis for the distinction underlying attempts to identify "functional" versus "organic" groups, as well as references to a "functional overlay" (Leavitt & Garron, 1979; McCreary, Turner, & Dawson, 1977). It is also found in a residual manner in other current concepts linking "nonorganic" findings with psychological manifestations of pain and related "abnormal illness behavior" (Pilowsky, 1970; Pilowsky & Spence, 1975; Waddell, Main, Morris, DiPaola, & Gray, 1984; Waddell, McCulloch, Kummel, & Venner, 1980).

These psychogenic views are posed as alternatives to purely physiological models. Put simply, dichotomous reasoning is invoked. If the report of pain occurs in the absence of or is "disproportionate" to objective physical pathology, ipso facto, the pain has a psychological component.

Motivational View

A variation of the dichotomous somatic-psychogenic views is a conceptualization that is ascribed to by many third-party payers. They suggest that if there is insufficient physical pathology to justify the report of pain, the complaint is invalid, the result of symptom exaggeration or outright malingering. The assumption is that reports of pain without adequate biomedical evidence are motivated primarily by financial gain. This belief has resulted in a number of attempts to "catch" malingers using surreptitious observation methods and the use of sophisticated biomechanical machines geared toward identifying inconsistencies in functional performance. There are, however, no studies that have demonstrated dramatic improvement in pain reports subsequent to receiving disability awards. Yet, Koplow (1990) suggested that it is fear of malingering that drives the entire Social Security Disability System.

Although there appears to be little question that psychological factors play an important role in pain perception and response, the aforementioned models view physical and psychological factors as largely independent. Before examining models that attempt to integrate psychological factors with somatic factors, it is useful to examine the nature of the psychological factors involved in detail.

PSYCHOLOGICAL CONTRIBUTORS TO PAIN

Psychologists have made important contributions to understanding pain by demonstrating the importance of psychosocial and behavioral factors in the etiology, severity, exacerbation, and maintenance of pain. Several effective treatments have been developed based on these factors.

Operant Learning Mechanisms

As long ago as the early part of the 20th century, Collie (1913) discussed the effects of environmental factors in shaping the experience of people suffering with pain. A new era in thinking about pain began with Fordyce's (1976) description of the role of operant factors in chronic pain. The operant approach stands in marked contrast to the biomedical model of pain described earlier.

In the operant formulation, behavioral manifestations of pain rather than pain per se are central. It is suggested that when a person is exposed to a stimulus that causes tissue damage, their immediate response is withdrawal and attempts to escape from noxious sensations. This may be accomplished by avoidance of activity believed to cause or exacerbate pain, help seeking to reduce symptoms, and so forth. These behaviors are observable and, consequently, subject to the principles of operant conditioning.

The operant view proposes that acute "pain behaviors" (e.g., limping to protect a wounded limb from producing additional nociceptive input) may come under the control of external contingencies of reinforcement and thus develop into a chronic pain problem. Pain behaviors may be positively reinforced directly, for example, by attention from a spouse or health care providers. Pain behaviors may also be maintained by the escape from noxious stimulation by the use of drugs or rest, or the avoidance of undesirable activities such as work. In addition, "well behaviors" (e.g., activity, working) may not be sufficiently reinforcing, and therefore pain behaviors may be maintained because they are more rewarding. The pain behavior originally elicited by organic factors may come to occur, totally or in part, in response to reinforcing environmental events. Because of the consequences of specific behavioral responses, it is proposed that pain behaviors may persist long after the initial cause of the pain is resolved or greatly reduced.

The operant conditioning model does not concern itself with the initial cause of pain. Rather, it considers pain an internal subjective experience that may be maintained even after an initial physical basis of pain has resolved. The operant conditioning model focuses on overt manifestations of pain and suffering expressed as pain behaviors such as limping, moaning, and avoiding activity. Emphasis is placed on the communicative function of these behaviors. Thus, in one sense, the operant conditioning model can be viewed as analogous to the psychogenic models already described. That is, psychological factors are treated as secondary reactions to sensory stimulation, rather than directly involved in the perception of pain per se.

Several studies have provided evidence that supports the underlying assumptions of operant conditioning. For example, Cairns and Pasino (1977) and Doleys, Crocker, and Patton (1982) showed that pain behaviors (specifically, inactivity) can be decreased and well behaviors (i.e., activity) can be increased by verbal reinforcement with or without feedback and the setting of exercise quotas. Block, Kremer, and Gaylor (1980) demonstrated that pain patients reported differential levels of pain in an experimental situation depending on whether they knew they were being observed by their spouses or ward clerks. Pain patients with nonsolicitous spouses reported more pain when a neutral observer was present than when the spouse was present. When solicitous spouses were present, pain patients reported more pain than in the neutral observer condition. Two additional studies (Flor, Kerns, & Turk, 1987; Turk, Kerns, & Rosenberg, 1992) found that chronic pain patients reported more intense pain and less activity when they indicated their spouses were solicitous. These later studies suggest that spouses can serve as discriminative stimuli for the display of pain behaviors by chronic pain patients, including their reports of pain severity.

The operant view has also generated what has proven to be an effective treatment for select samples of chronic pain patients (see Keefe, Dunsmore, & Burnett, 1992; Keefe & Williams, 1989). Treatment focuses on extinction of pain behaviors and positive reinforcement of well behaviors.

Although operant factors undoubtedly play a role in the maintenance of disability, exclusive reliance on the operant conditioning model to explain the experience of pain has, however, been criticized for its exclusive focus on motor pain behaviors, failure to consider the emotional and cognitive aspects of pain (A. Schmidt, 1985a, 1985b; A. Schmidt, Gierlings, & Peters, 1989; Turk & Flor, 1987), and failure to treat the subjective experience of pain (Kotarba, 1983). The applicability of this model is problematic for pain associated with cancer because stoic behaviors and the inhibition of such pain behaviors as talking about pain and requesting medication are encouraged and even essential to inform health care providers regarding disease progress (Wilkie, Keefe, Dodd, & Copp, 1992).

A fundamental problem with the operant approach in practice is the emphasis on pain behavior rather than pain per se because behaviors that are observed are then used as the basis to infer something about the internal state of the individual—that the behaviors are communications of pain (Turk & Matyas, 1992). This is an indirect method and there is no way of determining from the behavior whether it results from pain or from a structural abnormality. Limping, for example, from the operant perspective is viewed as a pain behavior; however, this is an inference. It is quite possible that limping may result from physical pathology and has no direct association with pain, distress, or suffering. In the latter case, attempts to extinguish the putative pain behaviors will be fruitless and inappropriate.

To underscore the distinction between pain behavior as a communication and as a result of physical perturbation, two studies reported by Keefe et al. (1990a, 1990b) can be examined. These investigators failed to find a reduction of pain behavior in osteoarthritic knee pain patients following a coping skills program; however, the program did produce a reduction in pain and disability. Alteration of specific behaviors that result from structural pathology are not likely to result from coping skills training. Thus, calling these behaviors "pain behaviors" is open to question (Turk & Matyas, 1992).

A related concern about the pain behavior construct is captured by the emphasis on the communicative role of these behaviors. Several attempts to operationalize the pain behavior construct have broadened to the point that any behavior can be subsumed under the rubric of pain behaviors. For example, Vlaeyen, Van Eck, Groenman, and Schuerman (1987) asked nurses to observe pain patients and to enumerate behaviors that they felt communicated pain. Some of the behaviors identified included the failure of the patient to take initiative, insomnia, falling asleep during the day, querulousness, and boredom. Philips and Jahanshahi (1986) created a "pain behavior checklist" that included "self-help" strategies and "distraction."

Boredom, querulousness, fatigue, distraction, or other self-help strategies can readily be imagined to have causes and effects other than communication of pain. Boredom can result from an unstimulating environment, querulousness may be a premorbid characteristic of the individual, fatigue may be a consequence of vigorous exercise, and lying down during the day might indicate compliance with recommendations to practice relaxation exercises or to practice appropriate pacing behaviors. Importantly, distraction and other self-help strategies can clearly have adaptive functions above and beyond any communicative function.

Respondent Learning Mechanisms

Factors contributing to chronicity that have previously been conceptualized in terms of operant learning may also be initiated and maintained by respondent conditioning (Gentry & Bernal, 1977). Fordyce, Shelton, and Dundore (1982) hypothesized that avoidance behavior does not necessarily require intermittent sensory stimulation from the site of bodily damage, environmental reinforcement, or successful avoidance of aversive social activity to account for the maintenance of protective movements. Avoidance of activities has been shown to be related more to anxiety about pain than to actual reinforcement (Linton, 1985).

Lenthem, Slade, Troup, and Bentley (1983) and Linton, Melin, and Götestam (1985) suggested that once an acute pain problem exists, fear of motor activities that the patient expects to result in pain may develop and motivate avoidance of activity. Nonoccurrence of pain is a powerful reinforcer for reduction of activity and thus the original respondent conditioning may be followed by an operant learning process whereby the nociceptive stimuli and the associated responses need no longer be present for the avoidance behavior to occur. In acute pain states it may be useful to reduce movement, and consequently avoiding pain, to accelerate the healing process. Over time, however, anticipatory anxiety related to activity may develop and act as a conditioned stimulus (CS) for sympathetic activation (conditioned response, CR) that may be maintained after the original unconditioned stimulus (US, e.g., injury) and unconditioned response (UR, pain and sympathetic activation) have subsided (Lenthem et al., 1983; Linton et al., 1985; Philips, 1987a).

Pain related to sustained muscle contractions might, however, also be conceptualized as a US in the case where no acute injury was present and sympathetic activation and tension increases might be viewed as UR that may elicit more pain, and conditioning might proceed in the same fashion as already outlined. Thus, although the original association between pain and pain-related stimuli results in anxiety regarding these stimuli, with time the expectation of pain related to activity may lead to avoidance of adaptive behaviors even if the nociceptive stimuli and the related sympathetic activation are no longer present. (See Seligman & Johnson, 1973, on the role of expectation in learning processes.)

In acute pain, many activities that are neutral or pleasurable may elicit or exacerbate pain and are thus experienced as aversive and avoided. Over time, more and more activities may be seen as eliciting or exacerbating pain and will be avoided (stimulus generalization). Fear of pain may become conditioned to an expanding number of situations. Avoided activities may involve simple motor behaviors, but also work, leisure, and sexual activity (Philips, 1987a). In addition to the avoidance learning, pain may be exacerbated and maintained in these encounters with potentially pain increasing situations due to the anxiety-related sympathetic activation and muscle tension increases that may occur in anticipation of pain and also as a consequence of pain (Flor, Birbaumer, & Turk, 1990). Thus, psychological factors may directly affect nociceptive stimulation and need not be viewed as only reactions to pain.

The persistence of avoidance of specific activities reduces disconfirmations that are followed by corrected predictions (Rachman & Arntz, 1991). The prediction of pain promotes pain avoidance behavior and overpredictions of pain promote excessive avoidance behavior as demonstrated in the A. Schmidt (1985a, 1985b) studies. Insofar as pain avoidance succeeds in preserving the overpredictions from repeated disconfirmation, they will continue unchanged (Rachman & Lopatka, 1988). By contrast, repeatedly engaging in behavior that produces significantly less pain than was predicted is followed by adjustments in subsequent predictions, which also become more accurate. These increasingly accurate predictions are followed by increasingly appropriate avoidance behavior, even to elimination of all avoidance if that is appropriate. These observations add support to the importance of physical therapy, with patients progressively increasing their activity levels despite fear of injury and discomfort associated with renewed use of deconditioned muscles.

Thus, from a conditioning perspective, the patient may have learned to associate increases in pain with all kinds of stimuli that were originally associated with nociceptive stimulation (stimulus generalization). Sitting, walking, engaging in cognitively demanding work or social interaction, sexual activity, or even thoughts about these activities may increase anticipatory anxiety and concomitant physiological and biochemical changes (Philips, 1987a). Subsequently, patients may display maladaptive responses to many stimuli and reduce the frequency of performance of many activities other than those that initially induced pain. The physical abnormalities often observed in chronic pain patients (such as distorted gait, decreased range of motion, muscular fatigue) may thus actually be secondary to changes initiated in behavior through learning. As the pain symptoms persist, more and more situations may elicit anxiety and anticipatory pain and depression because of the low rate of reinforcement obtained, when behavior is much reduced (cf., Lenthem et al., 1983). With chronic pain, the anticipation of suffering or prevention of suffering may be sufficient for the long-term maintenance of avoidance behaviors.

Social Learning Mechanisms

Social learning has received some attention in the development and maintenance of chronic pain states. From this perspective, the acquisition of pain behaviors may occur by means of observational learning and modeling processes. That is, individuals can acquire responses that were not previously in their behavioral repertoire by the observation of others performing these activities. Bandura (1969) described and documented the important role of observational learning in many areas of human functioning. Children acquire attitudes about health and health care, the perception and interpretation of symptoms and physiological processes from their parents and social environment, as well as appropriate responses to injury and disease and thus may be more or less likely to ignore or overrespond to symptoms they experience (Pennebaker, 1982). The culturally acquired perception and interpretations of symptoms determines how people deal with illness (Nerenz & Leventhal, 1983). The observation of others in pain is an event that captivates attention. This attention may have survival value, may help to avoid experiencing more pain, and may help to learn what to do about acute pain. There is ample experimental evidence of the role of social learning from controlled, laboratory pain studies (Craig, 1986, 1988) and some evidence based on observations of patients behaviors in naturalistic and clinical settings (Christensen & Mortensen, 1975; Fagerhaugh, 1975). For example, Vaughan and Lanzetta (1980, 1981) demonstrated that physiological responses to pain stimuli may be vicariously conditioned during observation of others in pain. Richard (1988) found that children of chronic pain patients chose more pain-related responses to scenarios presented to them and were more external in their health locus of control responses than were children with healthy or diabetic parents. Moreover, teachers rated the pain patients' children as displaying more illness behaviors (e.g., complaining, whining, days absent, visit to school nurse) than children of healthy controls.

Expectancies and actual behavioral responses to nociceptive stimulation are based, at least partially, on prior leaning history. This may contribute to the marked variability in response to objectively similar degrees of physical pathology noted by health care providers.

Role of Cognitive Factors in Pain

A great deal of research has been directed toward identifying cognitive factors that contribute to pain and disability (Jensen, Turner, Romano, & Karoly, 1991; Turk & Rudy, 1986, 1992). These studies have consistently demonstrated that patients' attitudes, beliefs, expectancies about their plight, themselves, their coping resources, and the health care system affect the reports of pain, activity, disability, and response to treatment (Flor & Turk, 1988; Jensen, Turner, & Romano, 1994; Tota-Faucette, Gil, Williams, & Goli, 1993).

Beliefs About Pain. Clinicians working with chronic pain patients are aware that patients having similar pain histories and reports of pain may differ greatly in their beliefs about their pain. The cognitive-behavioral perspective (Turk, Meichenbaum, & Genest, 1983) suggests that behavior and emotions are influenced by interpretations of events, rather than solely by objective characteristics of the event itself. Thus, pain, when interpreted as signifying ongoing tissue damage, is likely to produce considerably more suffering and behavioral dysfunction than if it is viewed as being the result of a stable problem that may improve, although the amount of nociceptive input in the two cases may be equivalent (Spiegel & Bloom, 1983).

Certain beliefs may lead to maladaptive coping, increased suffering, and greater disability. Patients who believe their pain is likely to persist may be quite passive in their coping efforts and fail to make use of cognitive strategies or behavioral strategies to cope with pain. Patients who consider their pain to be an unexplainable mystery may negatively evaluate their own abilities to control or decrease pain, and are less likely to rate their coping strategies as effective in controlling and decreasing pain (Williams & Keefe, 1991; Williams & Thorn, 1989). People's cognitions (beliefs, appraisals, expectancies) regarding the consequences of an event and their ability are hypothesized to impact functioning in two ways. They may have a direct influence on mood and an indirect one through their impact on coping efforts.

A. Schmidt (1985a, 1985b) found evidence demonstrating that low back pain patients showed poor behavioral persistence in various exercise tasks and although their performance on these tasks was independent of physical exertion or actual self-reports of pain, it was related to previous pain reports. These patients appear to have a negative view of their abilities and expected increased pain if they performed physical exercises. Thus, the rationale for their avoidance of exercise was not the presence of pain but their learned expectation of heightened pain and the accompanying physical arousal that might exacerbate pain and reinforce their beliefs regarding the pervasiveness of their disability. These results are consistent with the respondent learning factors described earlier. A. Schmidt postulated that these negative perceptions of their capabilities for physical performance form a vicious circle, with the failure to perform activities reinforcing the perception of helplessness and incapacity.

A cognitive schema that views disability as a necessary aspect of pain, that activity despite pain is dangerous, and that pain is an acceptable excuse for neglecting responsibilities is likely to increase disability (Smith, Follick, Ahern, & Adams, 1986). Jensen, Turner, Romano, and Lawler (1994) demonstrated that patients' beliefs that emotions affect pain, that others should be solicitous when the patient experiences pain, and that one is disabled by pain were positively associated with psychosocial dysfunction. Patients who believed they were disabled by pain and that activity should be avoided because pain signified damage were more likely to reveal physical disability compared to patients who did not hold these beliefs. Similarly, Slater, Hall, Atkinson, and Garfin (1991) reported that patients' beliefs about their pain and disability were significantly related to actual measures of disability but not to physicians' ratings of disease severity.

The presence of pain may change the way people process pain-related and other information. For example, the presence of chronic pain may focus attention on all types of bodily signals. Chronic pain patients have been shown to complain about a multitude of bodily symptoms in addition to pain (A. Schmidt et al., 1989). Patients may interpret pain symptoms as indicative of an underlying disease and they may do everything to avoid pain exacerbations, most often by resorting to inactivity. For example, in acute pain states bed rest is often prescribed to relieve pressure on the spine. Patients ascribe to a belief that any movement of the back may worsen their condition and may still maintain this belief in the chronic state when their inaction is unnecessary as well as harmful.

Pennebaker, Gonder-Frederick, Cox, and Hoover (1985) showed that once cognitive structures (based on memories and meaning) about a disease are formed, they become stable and are very difficult to modify. People tend to avoid experiences that could invalidate their beliefs and they guide their behavior in accordance with these beliefs even in situations where the belief is no longer valid. Consequently, as noted, when the role of respondent conditioning was described, they do not receive corrective feedback.

In addition to beliefs about capabilities to function despite pain, beliefs about pain per se appear to be of importance in understanding response to treatment, compliance, and disability. For example, Schwartz, DeGood, and Shutty (1985) presented patients with information about the role of cognitive, affective, and behavioral factors and their own role in the rehabilitation process. They found that patients who rated the information as applicable to their pain condition had much better treatment outcomes. Those who disagreed with the concepts presented were found at follow-up to have higher levels of pain, lower levels of activity, and a high degree of dissatisfaction.

The results of several studies suggest that when successful rehabilitation occurs there appears to be an important cognitive shift from beliefs about helplessness and passivity to resourcefulness and ability to function regardless of pain. Consistent with the central role of a cognitive shift in rehabilitation, Herman and Baptiste (1981) noted that successes and failures in their treatment program could be distinguished most prominently on the basis of changes versus unchanged thought patterns relative to the prospect of living useful lives despite pain. Williams and Thorn (1989) found that chronic pain patients who believed that their pain was an "unexplained mystery" reported high levels of psychological distress and pain and also showed poorer treatment compliance than patients who believed they understood their pain.

In an innovative process study designed to evaluate the direct association between patients' beliefs and pain symptoms, Newton and Barbaree (1987) used a modified thought-sampling procedure to evaluate the nature of patients' thoughts during and immediately following headache both prior to and following treatment. Results indicated significant changes in certain aspects of headache-related thinking in the treated groups compared to the control group. Reduction in negative appraisal and increase in positive appraisal (e.g., "It's getting worse," "There is nothing I can do") revealed a significant shift in the thoughts of treated subjects in comparison with untreated subjects, indicating that treated subjects were evaluating headaches in a more positive fashion. Treated patients reported experiencing significantly fewer headache days per week and lower intensity of pain than untreated controls. Correlational analyses suggested that complaints of more intense pain were associated with more negative appraisals of headache episodes. Similar results were reported by Flor and Turk (1988) in which back pain and RA patients' negative thoughts predicted pain, disability, and physician visits. Newton and Barbaree noted that patients who reported the largest positive shift in appraisal also reported the greatest reduction in headache intensity.

The results of the Newton and Barbaree (1987) study support the argument that changes in cognitive reactions to headache might underlie headache improvement (see also, Blanchard, 1987; Holroyd & Andrasik, 1982). There appears to be strong evidence pointing toward a reduction in negative appraisal as representing the potential change mechanism in many pain treatment outcome studies. In considering the efficacy of biofeedback for back pain patients, Nouwen and Solinger (1979) concluded that "simultaneous accomplishment of muscle tension reduction and lowering reported pain convinced patients that muscle tension, and subsequently pain, could be controlled. ... As self-control could not be demonstrated in most patients, it seems plausible that the feeling of self-control, rather than actual control of physiological functions or events is crucial for further reductions" (p. 110). In other words, it appears that the extent to which voluntary control over muscles has been achieved dictate the outcome, which is not necessarily accompanied by lasting reductions in muscular reactivity.

Similar to Nouwen and Solinger (1979) interpretation, Blanchard (1987) speculated that, for headache patients, the maintenance of treatment effects endures in spite of almost universal cessation of regular home practice of biofeedback because the self-perpetuating cycle of chronic headache has been broken. The experience of headache serves as a stressor to cause, in part, a future headache. It may also serve to maintain improper analgesic medication consumption, the cessation of which can also lead to "rebound headache." By the end of treatment when the patient has experienced noticeable headache relief, it is as if patients redefine themselves as someone able to cope with headaches. As a consequence, one source of stress is removed and the person copes with recurrences more adaptively. The experience of headache serves as a stressor to cause, in part, a future headache.

Clearly, it appears essential for patients with chronic and recurrent acute pain to develop adaptive beliefs about the relation among impairment, pain, suffering and disability, and to deemphasize the role of experienced pain in their regulation of functioning. In fact, results from numerous treatment outcome studies have shown that changes in pain level do not parallel changes in other variables of interest, including activity level, medication use, return to work, rated ability to cope with pain, and pursuit of further treatment (see the meta-analysis reported by Flor et al., 1992).

Arntz and A. Schmidt (1989) suggested that the processing of internal information may become disturbed in chronic pain patients. It is possible that pain patients become preoccupied with and overemphasize physical symptoms and interpret them as painful stimulation, although they may be less able then healthy controls to differentiate threshold levels. Studies with diverse populations (e.g., irritable bowel syndrome: Whitehead, 1980; fibromyalgia: Tunks, Crook, Norman, &

Kalaher, 1988; angina pectoris: Droste & Roskamm, 1983; headaches: Borgeat, Hade, Elie, & Larouche, 1984) of pain patients have supported the presence of what appears to be a hypersensitivity characterized by a lowered threshold for labeling stimuli as noxious.

Even in nonmuscular pain states, the interpretation of painful stimulation may be important. For example, Spiegel and Bloom (1983) reported that the pain severity ratings of cancer patients could be predicted by the use of analgesics, the patients' affective state, but also the *interpretations of pain.* Patients who attribute their pain to a worsening of their underlying disease experienced more pain despite the same level of disease progression as compared to patients with more benign interpretations.

Beliefs About Controllability. There is evidence that the explicit expectation of uncontrollable pain stimulation may make the following nociceptive input be perceived as more intense (Leventhal & Everhart, 1979). Thus, people who have associated activity with pain may expect heightened levels of pain when they attempt to get involved in activity and then actually perceive higher levels of pain or avoid activity altogether. There are many laboratory studies demonstrating that controllability of aversive stimulation reduces it impact (cf. Averill, 1973; Thompson, 1981).

In chronic pain patients, lack of personal control is typically perceived and likely relates to the ongoing but unsuccessful efforts to control their pain. A large proportion of chronic pain patients tend to believe that they have limited ability to exert control over their pain (Turk & Rudy, 1988). Such negative, maladaptive appraisals about the situation and personal efficacy may reinforce the experience of demoralization, inactivity, and overreaction to nociceptive stimulation commonly observed in chronic pain patients (Biederman, McGhie, Monga, & Shanks, 1987). Furthermore, uncontrollability has been shown to augment the perception of pain intensity in laboratory studies (Miller, 1981).

The relation between perceived controllability and pain has been demonstrated in a variety of chronic pain syndromes. Mizener, Thomas, and Billings (1988) demonstrated that successfully treated migraine headache patients reported correlations between reduction in headache activity and increases in perceived control over physiological activity and their health in general. Flor and Turk (1988) examined the relation between general and situation-specific pain-related thoughts, conceptions of personal control, pain severity, and disability levels in chronic low back pain patients and rheumatoid arthritics. The general and situation-specific convictions of uncontrollability and helplessness were more highly related to pain and disability than disease-related variables for both samples. The combination of both situation-specific and general cognitive variables explained 32% and 60% of the variance in pain and disability, respectively. The addition of disease-related variables improved the predictions only marginally. Jensen and Karoly (1991) showed an association between patients' beliefs about the extent to which they can control their pain and outcome variables, including medication use, activity levels, and psychological functioning.

Self-Efficacy. Closely related to the sense of control over aversive stimulation is the concept of self-efficacy. A self-efficacy expectation is defined as a personal conviction that one can successfully execute a course of action (perform required behaviors) to produce a desired outcome in a given situation. This construct has been demonstrated as a major mediator of therapeutic change.

Bandura (1977) suggested that given sufficient motivation to engage in a behavior, it is a person's self-efficacy beliefs that determine the choice of activities that the person will initiate, the amount of effort that will be expended, and how long the person will persist in the face of obstacles and aversive experiences. Efficacy judgments are based on the following four sources of information regarding peoples' capabilities, in descending order of impact: (a) their own past performance at the task or similar tasks; (b) the performance accomplishments of others who are perceived to be similar to themselves; (c) verbal persuasion by others that they are capable; and (d) perception of their own state of physiological arousal, which is in turn partly determined by prior efficacy estimation. Performance mastery experience can be created by encouraging patients to undertake subtasks that are increasingly difficult or close to the desired behavioral repertoire. From this perspective, the occurrence of coping behaviors is conceptualized as being mediated by the person's beliefs that situation demands do not exceed their coping resources.

Dolce, Crocker, Moletteire, and Doleys (1986) and Litt (1988) reported that low self-efficacy ratings regarding pain control are related to low pain tolerance, and they are better predictors of tolerance than pain levels. Several studies also obtained self-efficacy ratings from pain patients and related them to patients' ability to control pain. For example, Manning and Wright (1983) obtained self-efficacy ratings from primipara concerning their ability to have a medication-free childbirth. These ratings were good predictors of medication use and time in labor without medication. Similarly, Council, Ahern, Follick, and Kline (1988) had patients rate their self-efficacy as well as expectancy of pain related to the performance of movement tasks. Patients' performance levels were highly related to their self-efficacy expectations, which in turn appeared to be determined by patients' expectancies of pain levels.

Converging lines of evidence from investigations of both laboratory and clinical pain indicate that perceived self-efficacy operates as an important cognitive factors in the control of pain (e.g., Bandura, O'Leary, Taylor, Gauthier, & Gossard, 1987; Lorig, Chastain, Ung, Shoor, & Holman, 1989), adaptive psychological functioning (e.g., Lorig et al., 1989; Rosensteil & Keefe, 1983; Spinhoven, Ter Kuile, Linssen, & Gazendam, 1989), disability (e.g., Dolce, Crocker, & Doleys, 1986; Lorig et al., 1989), impairment (e.g., Lorig et al., 1989), and treatment outcome (e.g., O'Leary, Shoor, Lorig, & Holman, 1988; Philips, 1987b). What are the mechanisms that account for the observed association between self-efficacy and behavioral outcome? Cioffi (1991) suggested at least four psychological processes could be responsible: (a) As perceived self-efficacy decreases anxiety and its concomitant physiological arousal, the patient may approach the task with less potentially distressing physical information to begin with; (b) the efficacious person is able to willfully distract attention from potentially threatening physiological sensations; (c) the efficacious person perceives and is distressed by physical sensations but simply persists in the face of them (stoicism); and (d) physical sensations are neither ignored nor necessarily distressing but rather are relatively free to take on a broad distributions of meanings (change interpretations).

Bandura (1977) suggested that those techniques that enhance mastery experiences the most will be the most powerful tools for bringing about behavior change. He proposed that cognitive variables are the primary determinants of behavior, but that these variables are most effectively influenced by performance accomplishments. The studies on headache, back pain, and rheumatoid arthritis cited above appear to support Bandura's prediction.

Cognitive Errors. In addition to specific efficacy beliefs, a number of investigators have suggested that a common set of cognitive errors will effect perceptions of pain and disability. A cognitive error may be defined as a negatively distorted belief about oneself or one's situation.

Lefebvre (1981) developed a Cognitive Errors Questionnaire (CEQ) to assess cognitive distortion in back pain patients. He found that chronic low back pain patients were particularly prone to cognitive errors such as "catastrophizing" (self-statements, thoughts, and images anticipating negative outcomes or aversive aspects of an experience or misinterpreting the outcome of an event to be extremely negative; characterized by lack of confidence and control and an expectation of negative outcome), "overgeneralization" (assuming that the outcome of one event necessarily applied to the outcome of future or similar events), "personalization" (interpreting negative events as reflecting personal meaning or responsibility), and "selective abstraction" (selectively attending to negative aspects of experience). Dufton (1989) reported that persons experiencing chronic pain had a tendency to make cognitive errors related to the emotional difficulties associated with living with pain, rather than the pain intensity alone, and those who made such errors were more depressed.

As was the case with self-efficacy, specific cognitive errors and distortions have been linked consistently to depression (e.g., Gil, Williams, Keefe, & Beckham, 1990; Lefebvre, 1981; Slater et al., 1991), self-reported pain severity (e.g., Gil et al., 1990; Keefe & Williams, 1989), and disability (e.g., Flor & Turk, 1988; Smith, Follick, et al., 1986b) in chronic pain patients. Such negative thoughts predict long-term adjustment to chronic pain, may mediate a portion of the relation between disease severity and adjustment, and make a unique contribution (over and above other cognitive factors) to the prediction of adjustment (Smith, Peck, & Ward, 1990).

Catastrophizing. Catastrophizing appears to be a particularly potent way of thinking that greatly influences pain and disability. Several lines of research (including experimental laboratory studies) of acute pain with normal volunteers and field studies with clinical patients suffering clinical pain have indicated that "catastrophizing"—extremely negative thoughts about one's plight—and adaptive coping strategies are important in determining people's reaction to pain. Two findings from laboratory studies are particularly important. Individuals who spontaneously utilize less catastrophizing self-statements and/or more adaptive coping strategies rated experimentally induced pain as lower and tolerated painful stimuli longer that those who indicate they engaged in more catastrophizing thoughts (Heyneman, Fremouw, Gano, Kirkland, & Heiden, 1990; Spanos, Horton, & Chaves, 1975).

People who spontaneously utilize less catastrophizing self-statements reported more pain in several acute and chronic pain studies (Butler, Damarin, Beaulieu, Schwebel, & Thorn, 1989; Martin, Nathan, Milech, & Van Keppel, 1989; Turner & Clancy, 1986). Moreover, Rosensteil and Keefe (1983) found that cognitive coping and suppression (adaptive strategies) and catastrophizing were predictive of adjustment.

Butler et al. (1989) demonstrated that in the case of post-surgical pain, cognitive coping strategies and catastrophizing thoughts correlated significantly with medication, pain reports, and nurses' judgments of patients' pain tolerance. Turner and Clancy (1986) showed that during cognitive-behavioral treatment reductions in catastrophizing were significantly related to reductions in pain tolerance and physical and psychosocial impairment. They showed that reducing in catastrophizing following cognitive-behavioral treatment related to reduction in pain intensity and physical impairment. Flor and Turk (1988) found that in low back pain sufferers and arthritis patients between 32% and 60% of the variance in pain and disability, respectively, was accounted for by cognitive factors that they labeled catastrophizing, helplessness, coping, and resourcefulness. In both the low back pain and the arthritis groups, the cognitive variables of catastrophizing and adaptive coping had substantially more explanatory power than did disease variables impairment. Finally, Keefe, Brown, Wallston, and Caldwell (1989) found that rheumatoid arthritis patients who reported high levels of pain, physical disability, and depression indicated excessive catastrophizing ideation reported on questionnaires administered 6 months earlier.

Some concerns with viewing catastrophizing as an independent cognitive variable have recently been raised. Sullivan and D'Eon (1990) reported significant association between catastrophizing and depression, suggesting that catastro- phizing indexes the cognitive and affective components of dysphoria rather than measuring distinct aspects of pain-related cognition. In other words, catstrophizing is conceptually and operationally confounded with depression. They suggested that depression might entirely explain the relation between the use of coping strategies and disability. Additional research is needed to directly address the links between catastrophizing and depression.

Coping. Self-regulation of pain and its impact depends on the person's specific ways of dealing with pain, adjusting to pain, and reducing or minimizing pain and distress caused by pain—that is, their coping strategies. Coping is assumed to be manifested by spontaneously employed purposeful and intentional acts, and it can be assessed in terms of overt and covert behaviors. *Overt* behavioral coping strategies include rest, medication, and use of relaxation. *Covert* coping strategies include various means of distracting oneself from pain, reassuring oneself that the pain will diminish, seeking information, and problem solving. These need not always be adaptive or maladaptive. Coping strategies are thought to act to alter both the perception of intensity of pain and a person's ability to manage or tolerate pain and to continue everyday activities (Turk et al., 1983).

Studies have found active coping strategies (efforts to function in spite of pain or to distract oneself from pain such as activity, ignoring pain) to be associated with adaptive functioning, and passive coping strategies (depending on others for help in pain control and restricted activities) to be related to greater pain and depression (Brown & Nicassio, 1987; Brown, Nicassio, & Wallston, 1989; Lawson, Reesor, Keefe, & Turner, 1990; Tota-Faucette et al., 1993). However, beyond this, there is no evidence supporting the greater effectiveness of one active coping strategy compared to any other (Fernandez & Turk, 1989). It seems more likely that different strategies will be more effective than others for some individuals at some times but not necessarily for all individuals all of the time.

A number of studies has demonstrated that if instructed in the use of adaptive coping strategies, the rating of intensity of pain decreases and tolerance of pain increases (for a review see Fernandez & Turk, 1989). The most important factor in poor coping appears to be the presence of catastrophizing rather than differences in the nature of specific adaptive coping strategies (e.g., Heyneman et al., 1990; Martin et al., 1989). Turk et al. (1983) concluded that "what appears to distinguish low from high pain tolerant individuals in their cognitive processing, catastrophizing thoughts and feelings that precede, accompany, and follow aversive stimulation" (p. 197).

EFFECTS OF PSYCHOLOGICAL FACTORS ON PHYSIOLOGICAL PARAMETERS ASSOCIATED WITH PAIN

Psychological factors may act indirectly on pain and disability by reducing physical activity, and consequently reducing muscle flexibility, strength, tone, and endurance. Fear of reinjury, fear of loss of disability compensation, and job dissatisfaction can also influence return to work. Several studies have suggested that cognitive factors may actually have a direct effect of physiological parameters associated more directly with the production or exacerbation of nociception. Cognitive interpretations and affective arousal may have a direct effect on physiology by increasing autonomic sympathetic nervous system arousal (Bandura, Taylor, Williams, Meffort, & Barchas, 1985), endogenous opioid (endorphins) production (Bandura et al., 1987), and elevated levels of muscle tension (Flor et al., 1985; Flor, Birbaumer, Schugens, & Lutzenberger, 1992a).

Effects of Thoughts on Sympathetic Arousal

Circumstances that are appraised as potentially threatening to safety or comfort are likely to generate strong physiological reactions. For example, Rimm and Litvak (1969) demonstrated that subjects exhibit physiological arousal when they only think about or imagine a painful stimuli. Barber and Hahn (1962) showed that subjects' self-reported discomfort and physiological responses (frontalis electromyographic activity, EMG; heart rate; skin conductance) were similar when they imagined taking part in a cold pressor test as compared to actually participating in it. In patients suffering from recurrent migraine headaches, Jamner and Tursky (1987) observed increase in skin conductance related to the processing of words describing migraine headaches.

Chronic increases in sympathetic nervous system activation, known as increased skeletal muscle tone, may set the stage for hyperactive muscle contraction and possibly for the persistence of a contraction following conscious muscle activation. Excessive sympathetic arousal and maladaptive behaviors are viewed as the immediate precursors of muscle hypertonicity, hyperactivity, and persistence. These in turn are the proximate causes of chronic muscle spasm and pain. It is not usual for someone in pain to exaggerate or amplify the significance of their problem and needlessly "turn on" their sympathetic nervous system (Ciccone & Grzesiak, 1984). In this way, cognitive processes may influence sympathetic arousal and thereby predispose the individual to further injury or otherwise complicate the process of recovery.

Several studies support the direct effect of cognitive factors on muscle tension. For example, Flor et al. (1985) demonstrated that discussing stressful events and pain produced elevated levels of EMG activity localized to the site of back patients' pain. The extent of abnormal muscular reactivity was best predicted by depression and cognitive coping style rather than pain demographic variables (e.g., number of surgeries or duration of pain). Flor et al. (1992a) replicated these results and extended them to patients with temporomandibular disorders. For this group, imagery reconstruction of episodes and pain produced elevated muscle tension in the facial muscles.

Although "causal," pain eliciting psychophysiological mechanisms (e.g., elevated EMG) may exist, only one longitudinal study has been reported that directly tested the causal relation and it found no consistent muscle hyperactivity during headache attacks compared to pain-free baseline, no differences in EMG activity between tension-type headache patients and controls, and EMG did not covary with stress, negative affect, or pain (Hatch et al., 1991). Moreover, the natural evolution and course of many chronic pain syndromes is unknown. At the present time, it is probably more appropriate to refer to abnormal psychophysiological patterns as antecedents of chronic pain states or to view them as consequences of chronic pain that subsequently maintain or exacerbate the symptoms rather than to assign them any direct etiological significance.

Effects of Thinking on Biochemistry

Bandura and his colleagues (1987) directly examined the role of central opioid activity in cognitive control of pain. They provided training in psychological control of pain where subjects received instructions and practice in using different coping strategies for alleviating pain, including attention diversion from pain sensations to other matters, vivification of engrossing imagery, dissociation of the limb in pain from the rest of the body, transformation of pain as nonpain sensations, and self-encouragement of coping efforts. They demonstrated that self-efficacy increased with cognitive training, self-efficacy predicted pain tolerance, and naloxone (an opioid antagonist) blocked the effects of cognitive control. The latter result directly implicates the direct effects of thoughts on the endogenous opioids. Bandura et al. (1987) concluded that the physical mechanism by which self-efficacy influences pain perception may at least be partially mediated by the endogenous opioid system. This conclusion fits well with the data from Maier, Dugan, Grau, and Hyson (1984), who showed that the uncontrollability of the stressor elicits opioid-mediated hypoalgesia. Opioid release is closely related to psychological factors, specifically subject's sense of control.

O'Leary et al. (1988) provided cognitive-behavioral stress management treatment to rheumatoid arthritis (RA) patients. RA is an autoimmune disease that may result from impaired functioning of the suppressor T-cell system. Degree of self-efficacy (expectations about the ability to control pain and disability) enhancement was correlated with treatment effectiveness. Those with higher self-efficacy and greater self-efficacy enhancement displayed greater numbers of suppressor T-cells (a direct effect of self-efficacy on physiology). Significant effects were also obtained for self-efficacy, pain, and joint impairment. Increased self-efficacy for functioning was associated with decreased disability and joint impairment.

Much more research is required before there can be confidence in the direct role of thoughts on physical mechanisms inducing nociception. However, the large body of research in psychoneuorimmunology attests to the direct role of psychological factors on the body's immune system. Based on the results of a handful of studies, it would seem that greater research efforts examining the direct effects of thoughts on the physiology known to be associated with pain—namely, sympathetic nervous system activity and the endorphins —would be a fruitful endeavor.

INTEGRATIVE MODELS

An integrative model of pain and chronic pain and acute recurrent pain, in particular, needs to incorporate the mutual interrelations among physical, psychosocial, and behavior factors and the changes that occur among these relations over time (Flor et al., 1990; Turk & Rudy, 1991). A model focusing on only one of these three core sets of factors will inevitably be incomplete.

Several sets of investigators have proposed integrative models of pain. Each with somewhat different emphasis but each of them attempts to integrate physiological and psychological variables in the etiology, severity, exacerbation, and maintenance of pain. The physiological model proposed by Melzack and Wall (1965) can be contrasted with the more psychological model of Turk et al. (1983) and the diathesis-stress model of Flor et al. (1989). Melzack and Wall focused primarily on the basic anatomy and physiology of pain, whereas Turk et al. and Flor et al. emphasised the influence of psychological processes on physical factors subserving the experience of pain.

Gate Control Theory

The first attempt to develop an integrative model designed to address the problems created by unidimensional models and to integrate physiological and psychological factors was the gate control theory proposed by Melzack and his colleagues (Melzack & Casey, 1968; Melzack & Wall, 1965). Perhaps the most important contribution of the gate control theory is the way it changed thinking about pain perception. Melzack and Casey (1968) differentiated three systems related to the processing of nociceptive stimulation—sensory-discriminative, motivational-affective, and cognitive-evaluative—which are all thought to contribute to the subjective experience of pain. Thus, the gate control theory specifically includes psychological factors as an integral aspect of the pain experience. It emphasized the central nervous system (CNS) mechanisms and provides a physiological basis for the role of psychological factors in chronic pain.

The gate control theory proposes that a mechanism in the dorsal horn substantia gelatinosa of the spinal cord acts as a spinal gating mechanism that inhibits or facilitates transmission of nerve impulses from the body to the brain on the basis of the diameters of the active peripheral fibers as well as the dynamic action of brain processes. It was postulated that the spinal gating mechanism was influenced by the relative amount of excitatory activity in afferent, large diameter (myelinated) and small diameter (unmyelinated nociceptors) fibers converging in the dorsal horns. It was further proposed that activity in A-beta (large diameter) fibers tend to inhibit transmission of nociceptive signals (closes the gate), whereas A-delta and c (small diameter fibers) primary afferent activity tends to facilitate transmission (open the gate). The hypothetical gate is proposed to be located in the dorsal horn and it is at this point that sensory input is modulated by the balance of activity of small diameter (A-delta and c) and large diameter (A-beta) fibers.

Melzack and Wall (1965) postulated further that spinal gating mechanism is influenced not only by peripheral afferent activity but also by efferent neural impulses that descend from the brain. They proposed that a specialized system of large diameter, rapidly conducting fibers (the central control trigger) activate selective cognitive processes that then influence, by way of descending fibers, the modulating properties of the spinal gating mechanism. They suggested that the brain stem reticular formation functions as a central biasing mechanism inhibiting the transmission of pain signals at multiple synaptic levels of the somatosensory system.

The gate control theory maintains that the large diameter fibers play an important role in pain by inhibiting synaptic transmission in dorsal horn cells. When large fiber input is decreased, mild stimuli, which are not typically painful, trigger severe pain. Loss of sensory input to this complex neural system—such as occurs in neuropathies, causalgia, and phantom limb pain—tend to weaken inhibition and lead to persistent pain. Herniated disc material, tumors, and other factors that exert pressure on these neural structures may operate through this mechanism. Emotional stress and medication that affect the reticular formation may also alter the biasing mechanisms and thus intensity of pain.

From the gate control perspective, the experience of pain is an ongoing sequence of activities, largely reflexive in nature at the outset, but modifiable even in the earliest stages by a variety of excitatory and inhibitory influences, as well as the integration of ascending and descending nervous system activity. The process results in overt expressions communicating pain and strategies by the person to terminate the pain. In addition, considerable potential for shaping of the pain experience is implied, because the gate control theory invokes continuous interaction of multiple systems (sensory-physiological, affect, cognition, and ultimately, behavior).

The gate control model describes the integration of peripheral stimuli with cortical variables, such as mood and anxiety, in the perception of pain. This model contradicts the notion that pain is either somatic or psychogenic and instead postulates that both factors have either potentiating or moderating effects on pain perception. In this model, for example, pain is not understood to be the result of depression or vice versa, but rather the two are seen as evolving simultaneously. Any significant change in mood or pain will necessarily alter the others.

The theory's emphasis on the modulation of inputs in the dorsal horns and the dynamic role of the brain in pain processes and perception resulted in psychological variables such as past experience, attention, and other cognitive activities being integrated into current research and therapy on pain. Prior to this formulation, psychological processes were largely dismissed as reactions to pain. This new model suggested that cutting nerves and pathways was inadequate as a host of other factors modulated the input. Perhaps the major contribution of the gate control theory was that it highlighted the central nervous system as an essential component in pain processes and perception.

The physiological details of the gate control model have been challenged and it has been suggested that the model is incomplete (Nathan, 1976; Price, 1987; R. F. Schmidt, 1972). As additional knowledge has been gathered since the original formulation in 1965, specific points of posited mechanisms have been disputed and have required revision and reformulation (Nathan, 1976; Wall, 1989). Overall, however, the gate control theory has proved remarkably resilient and flexible in the face of accumulating scientific data and challenges to it, and still provides a "powerful summary of the phenomena observed in the spinal cord and brain, and has the capacity to explain many of the most mysterious and puzzling problems encountered in the clinic" (Melzack & Wall, 1982, p. 261). This theory has had enormous heuristic value in stimulating further research in the basic science of pain mechanisms as well as in spurring new clinical treatments (Abram, 1993).

The gate control theory can be credited as a source of inspiration for diverse clinical applications to control or manage pain, including neurophysiologically based procedures (e.g., neural stimulation techniques, from peripheral nerves and collateral processes in the dorsal columns of the spinal cord, North, 1989), pharmacological advances (Abram, 1993), behavioral treatments (Fordyce, Roberts, & Sternbach, 1985), and those interventions targeting modification of attentional and perceptual processes involved in the pain experience (Turk et al., 1983). After the gate control theory was proposed in 1965, no one could try to explain pain exclusively in terms of peripheral factors.

Although the gate control theory provided a physical basis for the role of psychological factors in pain, it does not address the nature of the psychological factors in depth. That is, it does not incorporate many of the specific psychological variables reviewed here. The two models to be described, the diathesis-stress and cognitive-behavioral models, offer more conceptual models of the role of operant, respondent, social learning, and cognitive factors already described. These models, however, emphasize psychological factors adding little to the physiological factors postulated in the gate control theory.

Diathesis-Stress Model

Although everyone experiences acute pain, only a small percentage of people develop chronic pain syndromes. Flor et al. (1990) suggested that neither somatogenic nor psychogenic factors by themselves were sufficient to explain the development of chronic pain. They proposed that preconditions for chronic pain, including predisposing factors, precipitating stimuli, precipitating responses, and maintaining processes, were all required to explain the processes involved. The existence of a physiological predisposition or diathesis involving a specific body system is the first component of this model. This predisposition consists of a reduced threshold for nociceptive activation that may be related to genetic variables, previous trauma, or social learning experiences and results in a physiological response stereotypy of the specific body system. The existence of persistent aversive external and internal stimuli (pain-related or other stressors) with negative meaning activate the sympathetic nervous system and/or muscular processes (e.g., various aversive emotional stimuli such as familial conflicts or pressures related to employment) as unconditioned and conditioned stimuli and motivate avoidance responses. Aversive stimuli may be characterized by "excessive" intensity, duration, or frequency of an external or internal stimulus. "Inadequate" or "maladaptive" behavioral, cognitive, or physiological repertoire of the individual reduce the impact of these aversive environmental or internal stimuli.

Flor et al. (1990) suggested that an important role is played by the cognitive processing of external or internal stimuli related to the experience of stress and pain: for example, increased perception, preoccupation, and overinterpretation of physical symptoms or inadequate perception of internal stimuli such as muscle tension levels. Moreover, this suggests that the nature of the coping response (active avoidance, passive tolerance, or depressive withdrawal) may determine the type of problem that develops as well as the course of the illness. The diathesis-stress model proposes further that subsequent maladaptive physiological responding such as increased and persistent sympathetic arousal and increased and persistent muscular reactivity may induce or exacerbate pain episodes. The authors suggested that learning processes in the form of respondent conditioning of fear of activity (including social, motor, and cognitive activities) and operant learning of pain behaviors—but also operant conditioning of pain-related covert and physiological responses as described earlier—make a contribution to chronicity.

In short, the diathesis-stress model places greatest emphasis on the role of learning factors in the onset, exacerbation, and maintenance of pain for those people with persistent pain problems. Flor et al. (1990) suggested that a range of factors predispose individuals to develop chronic or recurrent acute pain; however, the predisposition is necessary but not sufficient. Conditioning and individual differences are central to this model.

Cognitive-Behavioral Model

The diathesis-stress model previously described tends to give priority to conditioning. The cognitive-behavioral model incorporates many of the same constructs as the diathesis-stress model (viz. anticipation, avoidance, and contingencies of reinforcement), but suggests that cognitive factors, and in particular expectations rather than conditioning factors, are of central importance (cf. Brewer, 1974). It suggests that so-called conditioned reactions are largely self-activated on the basis of learned expectations rather than automatically evoked. The critical factor for the cognitive-behavioral model, therefore, is not that events occur together in time, but that people learn to "predict them and to summon appropriate reactions" (Turk et al., 1983). It is the individual patient's processing of information that results in anticipatory anxiety and avoidance behaviors.

From the cognitive-behavioral model, people with pain are viewed as having negative expectations about their own ability to control certain motor skills without pain. Moreover, pain patients tend to believe they have limited ability to exert any control over their pain. Such negative, maladaptive appraisals about the situation and personal efficacy may reinforce the experience of demoralization, inactivity, and overreaction to nociceptive stimulation (Biederman et al., 1987; Brown & Nicassio, 1987). These cognitive appraisals and expectations are postulated as having an effect on behavior leading to reduced efforts and activity that may contribute to increased psychological distress (helplessness) and subsequently physical limitations.

If it is accepted that pain is a complex, subjective phenomenon that is uniquely experienced by each person, then knowledge about idiosyncratic beliefs, appraisals, and coping repertoires become critical for optimal treatment planning and for accurately evaluating treatment outcome. This view is nicely demonstrated in Reesor and Craig (1988). They showed that the primary difference between chronic low back pain patients who were referred because of the presence of many "medically incongruent" signs and those who did not display these signs was *maladaptive thoughts.* Interestingly there were no significant differences between these groups on the number of surgeries, compensation, litigation status, or employment status. These maladaptive cognitive processes may amplify or distort patients' experiences of pain and suffering. Thus, the cognitive activity of chronic pain patients may contribute to the exacerbation, attenuation, or maintenance of pain, pain behavior, affective distress, and dysfunctional adjustment to chronic pain (Turk & Rudy, 1986, 1992).

Biomedical factors that may have initiated the original report of pain play less and less of a role in disability over time, although secondary problems associated with deconditioning may exacerbate and serve to maintain the problem. Inactivity leads to increased focus on and preoccupation with the body and pain and these cognitive-attentional changes increase the likelihood of misinterpreting symptoms, overemphasis on symptoms, and the perception of oneself as being disabled. Reduction of activity, fear of reinjury, pain, loss of compensation, and an environment that perhaps unwittingly supports the "pain patient role" can impede alleviation of pain, successful rehabilitation, reduction of disability, and improvement in adjustment. As has been noted, cognitive factors may not only affect patients' behavior and indirectly their pain, but may actually have a direct effect of physiological factors believed to be associated with the experience of pain.

People respond to medical conditions in part based on their subjective representations of illness and symptoms (schema). When confronted with new stimuli, people engage in a "meaning analysis" that is guided by the schema that best match the attributes of the stimulus (Cioffi, 1991). It is on the basis of the person's idiosyncratic schema that incoming stimuli are interpreted, labeled, and acted on.

People build fairly elaborate representations of their physical state, and these representations provide the basis for action plans and coping (Nerenz & Leventhal, 1983; Turk, Rudy, & Salovey, 1986). Beliefs about the meaning of pain and people's ability to function despite discomfort are important aspects of the cognitive schema about pain (Slater et al., 1991). These representations are used to construct causal, covariational, and consequential information from their symptoms. For example, a cognitive schema that a person has a serious debilitating condition, that disability is a necessary aspect of pain, that activity is dangerous, and that pain is an acceptable excuse for neglecting responsibilities will likely result in maladaptive responses (Jensen et al., 1994; Schwartz et al., 1985; Williams & Thorn, 1989). Similarly, if people believe they have a serous condition that is quite fragile and a high risk for reinjury, they may fear engaging in physical activities (Philips, 1987a). Through a process of stimulus generalization, patients may avoid more and more activities, become more physically deconditioned, and consequently more disabled.

Patients' beliefs, appraisals, and expectations about their pain, their ability to cope, their social supports, their disorder, the medicolegal system, the health care system, and their employers are all important as they may facilitate or disrupt the patient's sense of control and ability to manage pain. These factors also influence peoples' investment in treatment, acceptance of responsibility, perceptions of disability, adherence to treatment recommendations, support from significant others, expectancies for treatment, and acceptance of treatment rationale (Slater et al., 1991; Turk & Rudy, 1991).

Cognitive interpretations also will affect how patients present symptoms to significant others, including health care providers and employers. Overt communication of pain, suffering, and distress will enlist responses that may reinforce the pain behaviors (overt communications of pain such as limping, moaning, ambulating in a guarded or distorted fashion) and impressions about the seriousness, severity, and uncontrollability of the pain. That is, complaints of pain may lead physicians to prescribe more potent medications, order additional diagnostic tests, and in some cases perform surgery. Family members may express sympathy, excuse the patient from usual responsibilities, and encourage passivity thereby fostering further physical deconditioning. It should be obvious that the cognitive-behavioral perspective integrates the operant conditioning emphasis on external reinforcement and respondent view of learned avoidance within the framework of information processing.

From the cognitive-behavioral perspective, people with chronic pain, as is true for all people, are viewed as active processors of information. They have negative expectations about their own ability and responsibility to exert any control over their pain. Moveover, they often view themselves as helpless. Such negative, maladaptive appraisals about their condition, situation, and their personal efficacy in controlling their pain and problems associated with pain serve to reinforce the experience of demoralization, inactivity, and the overreaction to nociceptive stimulation. These cognitive appraisals are posed as having an effect on behavior, leading to reduced effort, reduced perseverance in the face of difficulty, and activity and increased psychological distress.

The specific thoughts and feelings that people experienced prior to exacerbations of pain, during an exacerbation or intense episode of pain, as well as following a pain episode, can greatly influence the experience of pain and subsequent pain episodes (Newton & Barbaree, 1987). Moreover, the methods people use to control their emotional arousal and symptoms have been shown to be important predictors of both cognitive and behavioral responses (Flor & Turk, 1988; Reesor & Craig, 1988). As described previously, interrelated sets of cognitive variables include thoughts about the controllability of pain, attributions about the person's own ability to use specific pain coping responses, expectations concerning the possible outcomes of various coping efforts, and common erroneous beliefs about pain and disability.

The primary focus of the cognitive-behavioral model, similar to the diathesis-stress model, is on the person, rather than symptoms and pathophysiology. Unlike the diathesis-stress model, however, the cognitive-behavioral model places emphasis on the person's thoughts and feelings because these will influence behavior. Conversely, the cognitive-behavioral model acknowledges that environmental factors can also influence behavior and behavior can affect patients' thoughts and feelings. Bandura (1978) referred to this as a process of reciprocal determinism. From this perspective, assessment of and consequently treatment of the person with persistent pain requires a broader strategy then those based on the previous dichotomous models described, which examined and addressed the entire range of psychosocial, behavioral, and biomedical factors (Turk & Rudy, 1989, 1991).

Because of the emphasis placed on cognitive factors, cognitive-behavioral theorists sometimes read as if cognition is the most salient constituent of the pain experience; however, there is generally an attempt to temper this impression by emphasizing the continuously interactive nature of the pain experience, thereby rendering it pointless to attempt to identify any one constituent of the experience as more important than any others (Turk & Rudy, 1986, 1992).

The cognitive-behavioral perspective on pain management focuses on providing patients with techniques to gain a sense of control over the effects of pain on their life, as well as actually modifying the affective, behavioral, cognitive, and sensory facets of the experience. Behavioral experiences help to show people that they are capable of more than they assumed, increasing their sense of personal competence. Cognitive techniques help to place affective, behavioral, cognitive, and sensory responses under the patient's control. The assumption is that long-term maintenance of behavioral changes will occur only if patients have learned to attribute success to their own efforts. There are suggestions that these treatments can result in changes of beliefs about pain, coping style, and reported pain severity, as well as direct behavior changes (Dolce et al., 1986; Turner & Clancy, 1986, 1988). Further, treatment that results in increases in perceived control over pain and decreased catastrophizing also are associated with decreases in pain severity ratings and functional disability (Jensen et al., 1991; Turner, 1991).

The chapter now turns from these integrative conceptual models to specific anatomy, physiology, and chemical bases of pain. The models that have been described need to incorporate current understanding of the physical mechanisms of pain.

ANATOMICAL, PHYSIOLOGICAL, AND CHEMICAL BASES OF PAIN

Between the stimulus of tissue injury and the subjective experience of pain is a series of complex electrical and chemical events. In considering pain it is important to have a conceptual understanding of the physiological processes involved as well as the anatomical structures that are believed to be important. It is equally important to be aware that the understanding of pain is far from complete and thus what is described in this section must be viewed as a puzzle with many pieces missing and some in the wrong place.

Four distinct physiological processes have been identified in pain: transduction, transmission, modulation, and perception (Fields, 1987). Consideration of these processes will guide the review of anatomical, physiological, and chemical bases subserving the experience of pain.

Transduction

Embedded in the various tissues are nerve endings that respond best to noxious stimuli. Transduction or receptor activation is the process where one form of energy (chemical, mechanical, or thermal) is converted into another, in this case, the electrochemical nerve impulse in the primary afferents. By this process, information about a stimulus is converted to a form that is accessible to the brain. Information is coded by the frequency of impulses in the primary afferents activated by the stimulus. Noxious stimuli lead to electrical activity in the appropriate sensory nerve endings.

Transmission

Transmission refers to the process by which coded information is relayed to those structures of the central nervous system (CNS) whose activity produces the sensation of pain. The first stage of transmission is the conduction of impulses in primary afferents to the spinal cord. At the spinal cord, activity in the primary afferents activates spinal neurons that relay the pain message to the brain. This message elicits a variety of responses ranging from withdrawal reflexes to the subjective perceptual events ("It hurts!"). Once the noxious stimulus has been coded by the impulses in the peripheral nerve, the sensations that result are determined by the neurons of the pain transmission system.

There are three major neural components of the pain transmission system: the peripheral sensory nerves, which transmit impulses from the site of transduction to their terminals in the spinal cord; a network of relay neurons that ascend the spinal cord to brainstem and thalamus; and reciprocal connections between the thalamus and cortex. CNS neurons receive convergent input from numerous primary afferents, often of different types, including both nociceptive and non-nociceptive neurons that have spatially extensive receptive fields, which in some cases include the entire body surface. In addition, the responses of CNS neurons to noxious stimuli are variable because they are subject to inhibitory influences elicited by peripheral stimulation or originating within the brain itself.

The neurons activated by noxious stimuli and their pattern of activity is thus a complex function of the primary afferent barrage that arrives at the spinal cord and the inhibitory influences that are active at the time. The primary afferent nociceptors terminate in the dorsal horn of the spinal cord. The axons of spinal neurons activated by these afferent nociceptors cross to the anterolateral quadrant on the side opposite to the activated nociceptors. The message then ascends to the brainstem and via the thalamus to the cortex.

Melzack and Casey (1968) proposed that the paramedian pathway, with its diffuse projection to the limbic system and to the frontal lobe, primarily subserves the affective-motivational aspects of pain. Consistent with this idea is the well-established role of the brainstem reticular formation in behavioral arousal and in cortical arousal produced by a variety of sensory stimuli. In addition to producing arousal, the paramedian reticular formation plays an important role in escape behavior.

Noxious stimuli activate peripheral ending of the primary afferent nociceptor by the process of transduction. The message is then transmitted over the peripheral nerve to the spinal cord where it synapses with cells of origin of the two major ascending pain pathways, the spinothalamic and spinoreticulothalamic. The message is relayed in the thalamus to both the frontal and the somatosensory cortex, tracing the pain message along neural pathways from peripheral receptors to the cortex. It would appear that the relations among stimulus intensity, activity in pain transmission cells, and the perceived intensity of pain are simple and reproducible. This has an appealing simplicity, however, clinical observations indicate that the correlation between stimulus intensity and reported pain is actually unusual. In fact, the severity of reported pain may range from minimal to unbearable in different individuals with apparently similar injuries, and it is obvious that the subjectively experienced intensity of pain not only depends on the stimulus intensity but to a very large extent on psychological factors as described previously.

Modulation

Modulation refers to the neural activity leading to control of the pain transmission pathway. Input from the frontal cortex and hypothalamus activate cells in the midbrain, which control spinal pain transmission cells by means of cells in the medulla. The activity of this modulatory system is one reason why people with apparently severe injuries may deny significant levels of pain (Beecher, 1959; Wall, 1979).

Although we are far from understanding all the complexities of the human mind, we know that there are specific pathways in the CNS that control pain transmission, and there is evidence that these pathways can be activated by the psychological factors described earlier. The midbrain, periaqueductal gray matter, and adjacent reticular formation that project to the spinal cord via the rostroventral medulla, are all involved in the modulation of nociceptive signals (Fields, 1987). This pathway inhibits spinal neurons that respond to noxious stimuli. There is also a pain modulating pathway from the dorsolateral pons to the cord. The pathway from the rostral medulla to the cord is partly serotonergic, whereas that from the dorsolateral pons is at least noradrenergic.

In addition to the biogenic amine containing neurons, endogenous opioid peptides are present in all the regions implicated in pain modulation. The opioid-mediated analgesia system can be activated by electrical stimulation or by opiate drugs such as morphine. It can also be activated by pain, stress, and suggestion. Opioids produce analgesia by direct action on the CNS and activate the nociceptive modulating system. Opioid receptors have two distinct functions: chemical recognition and biological action. Researchers reasoned that the brain itself ought to synthesize molecules that would act at these highly specific receptor sites. Endogenous opioid peptides, namely, leucine-enkephalin, methionine-enkephalin, beta-endorphin, dynorphin, alpha-neoendorphin pharmacologically similar to morphine reversed by opioid antagonists (e.g., naloxone) have all been identified.

Perception

The final physiological process involved with pain is perception. Somehow, the neural activity of the pain transmission neurons produces a subjective experience. How this comes about is obscure, and it is not even clear in which brain structures the activity occurs that produces the perceptual event. The question remains, "How do objectively observable neural events produce subjective experience?" Because pain is fundamentally a subjective experience, there are inherent limitations to understanding it.

Pain responses cannot be predicted with certainty because there is great subjective variability. In some people, innocuous stimuli produce excruciating pain. In other situations, patients with severe injuries deny any significant pain. This variability presents a conundrum to health care providers and patients alike.

To understand the variability in individual experiences, it is useful to distinguish between pain detection threshold and pain tolerance. Pain threshold is a property of the sensory system that depends on the stimulus. It is highly reproducible in different people and in the same person at different times. In contrast to this reproducability, pain tolerance is highly variable. No two people react to pain in quite the same way. This distinction helps to understand the variability of pain. Pain tolerance is a manifestation of a person's reaction to pain and is highly dependent on psychological variables, described earlier. Not only does it vary between different people in the same situation, but the same individual may react differently in different situations.

There are several reasons for the variability: There may be an injury to the pain transmission system activity of the modulatory system that lowers pain intensity. There may be abnormal neural activity that may produce hypersensitivity that can result from self-sustaining processes set in motion by an injury but that may persist beyond the time it takes for the original injury to heal. This self-sustaining process may even create a situation where pain is present without the noxious stimulus produced by an active tissue damaging process (neuropathic pain, causalgia), Finally, the psychological processes and factors previously described may affect normal pain intensity creating unpredictable responses.

If pain were simply a sensation, these neural pain mechanisms would probably be sufficient to explain most of the clinically observed variability. However, pain is more than a sensation. The close association of the pain sensory system with the function of protection of the body from damage is unique among sensory systems. It is essential for understanding pain patients that the desire to escape from or terminate the sensation be considered. If it is not unpleasant, then it is not pain.

As noted in the discussions of the diathesis-stress and cognitive-behavioral models earlier, the meaning of pain is one important factor in determining pain tolerance. Different people have learned different ways of coping with pain; some minimize it and some overreact. Thus, for many people it may be as important to know what they think their pain means as it is to know its cause. Because of the importance of the person's interpretation, it is imperative, especially for persistent or recurrent pain, to make some inquiry about this issue for treatment.

Physical Factors Subserving Pain

Next some of the specific physical factors involved in pain are examined. When a stimulus of sufficient intensity to be tissue damaging (i.e., noxious) is applied to a sensitive part of the body such as the skin, somatic (musculoskeletal), and visceral structures, a chain of events is set in motion that eventually results in a sensation identifiable as painful. The capacity of tissues to elicit pain when noxious stimuli are applied to them depends on their innervation of nociceptors. Nociceptors are primary afferent nerves with peripheral terminals that can respond specifically and differentially to noxious stimuli. The peripheral terminals of the nociceptive afferents (pain receptors or nociceptors) are directly sensitive to brief intense thermal, mechanical, and chemical stimuli. Some of the chemicals that excite the nociceptors include kinins, histamine, and K^+ and H^+ ions that usually result from inflammation.

By the complex cascade of events described earlier, nociceptor activity produces several results. On the peripheral side there is prolongation of pain long after the termination of the stimulus and the development of hyperalgesia (stimuli above normal pain threshold perceived as more intense than in uninjured areas). In the peripheral tissues, the activity in nociceptors acts synergistically with the other processes initiated by tissue damage to produce increased blood flow and edema.

In addition to transient responses to these brief stimuli, nociceptors show relatively long-lasting increases in sensitivity when noxious stimuli are repeatedly applied. Long-lasting enhancement of nociceptor activity can be produced by a variety of diffusible substances that activate (potassium, serotonin, bradykinin, histamine) or sensitize the primary afferent (prostaglandins, leukotrienes, substance P) synthesized.

Of the afferent sensory fibers, A-delta and C-fibers, readily found in skin, muscle, and fascia, are slow conducting small diameter fibers that carry nociception, whereas A-beta fibers are activated by touch and pressure. The nociceptive fibers, which utilize substance P as a neurotransmitter, synapse at the dorsal horn, cross to the other side, and ascent via the spinothalamic tract. This tract transmits connecting fibers to the reticular formation of the brain stem and thalamic nuclei before ending in the somatosensory cortex. Although the cortex does not play an essential role in pain perception, it integrates the cognitive and behavioral aspects of pain.

The important endogenous pain inhibitory system involves descending analgesic pathways from the periaqueductal grey areas of midbrain to spinal dorsal horn via raphe magnus nucleus of the pons; local enkephalinergic interneurons in the spinal cord; and peripheral A-beta sensory fibers that presynaptically inhibit A-delta and C-fibers at the dorsal horn. The inhibitory system utilizes several neurotransmitters including serotonin, enkephalin, norepinephrine gamma aminobutyric acid (GABA), and somatostatin. The periaqueductal grey receives neuronal fibers from cortex, hypothalamus, and the limbic system, probably explaining the interaction of cognitive and emotional elements with pain perception and inhibition. Given the same noxious stimuli, the pain perception between two people may vary according to the phenomenon of attention or inhibition, both of which are probably modulated by various descending neurons. Emotion, attention, and motivation may all influence pain perception, probably through a complex network of reticular, limbic, and cortical fibers.

CONCLUSIONS

From the patient's point of view, the pain complaint connotes distress and is a plea for assistance. The subjective experience includes an urge to escape from the cause or, if that is not possible, to obtain relief. It is the overwhelming desire to terminate it that gives pain its power. Pain can produce fear, and if it persists, depression, and ultimately it can take away the will to live.

It has become abundantly clear that no isomorphic relation exists between tissue damage and pain report. The more recent conceptualizations discussed view pain as a perceptual process resulting from the nociceptive input and modulation on a number of different levels in the CNS and not as directly proportional to nociceptive input.

Pain is a subjective, perceptual experience, and one characteristic differentiating it from pure sensation is its affective quality. Thus, pain appears to have two defining properties: bodily sensation and an aversive affect (Fernandez & Turk, 1992; Melzack & Casey, 1968). Quintessentially, pain is experienced at a physical levels and an affective level. As underscored by the International Association for the Study of Pain (Merskey, 1986), "it [pain] is unquestionably a sensation in a part or parts of the body but it is also always unpleasant and therefore also an emotional experience" (p. S217).

In this chapter, conceptual models were presented to explain the subjective experience of pain. Current state of knowledge suggests that pain must be viewed as a complex phenomenon that incorporates physical, psychosocial, and behavioral factors. Failure to incorporate each of these factors will lead to an incomplete understanding. The range of psychological variables that have been identified as being of central importance in pain along with current understanding of the physiological basis of pain were reviewed. Several integrative models were described that try to incorporate the available research and clinical information. Pain has become a vigorous research area and the virtual explosion of information will surely lead to refinements in understanding of pain and advances in clinical management.

REFERENCES

Abram, S. E. (1993). Advances in chronic pain management since gate control. *Regional Anesthesia, 18,* 66–81.

American Psychiatric Association. (1994). *Diagnostic and statistical manual* (4th ed.). Washington, DC: American Psychiatric Association.

Arntz, A., & Schmidt, A.J.M. (1989). Perceived control and the experience of pain. In A. Steptoe & A. Appels (Eds.), *Stress, personal control and health* (pp. 131–162). Brussles- Luxembourg: Wiley.

Averill, J. R. (1973). Personal control over aversive stimuli and its relationship to stress. *Psychological Bulletin, 80,* 286–303.

Bandura, A. (1969). *Principles of behavior modification.* New York: Holt, Rinehart, & Winston.

Bandura, A. (1977). Self-efficacy: Toward a unifying theory of behavior change. *Psychological Review, 84,* 191–215.

Bandura, A. (1978). The self-system in reciprocal determinism. *American Psychologist, 33,* 344–359.

Bandura, A., O'Leary, A., Taylor, C. B., Gauthier, J., & Gossard, D. (1987). Perceived self-efficacy and pain control: Opioid and nonopioid mechanisms. *Journal of Personality and Social Psychology, 53,* 563–571.

Bandura, A., Taylor, C. B., Williams, S. L., Mefford, I. N., & Barchas, J. D. (1985). Catecholamine secretion as a function of perceived coping self-efficacy. *Journal of Consulting and Clinical Psychology, 53,* 406–414.

Barber, T., & Hahn, K. W. (1962). Physiological and subjective responses to pain producing stimulation under hypnotically-suggested and waking-imagined "analgesia." *Journal of Abnormal and Social Psychology, 65,* 411–418.

Beecher, H. K. (1959). *Measurement of subjective responses: Quantitative effects of drugs.* New York: Oxford University Press.

Beutler, L. E., Engle, D., Oro'-Beutler, M. E., Daldrup, R., & Meredith, K. (1986). Inability to express intense affect: A common link between depression and Pain? *Journal of Consulting and Clinical Psychology, 54,* 752–759.

Biedermann, H. J., McGhie, A., Monga, T. N., & Shanks, G. L. (1987). Perceived and actual control in EMG treatment of back pain. *Behaviour Research and Therapy, 25,* 137–147.

Blanchard, E. B. (1987). Long-term effects of behavioral treatment of chronic headache. *Behavior Therapy, 18,* 375–385.

Blumer, D., & Heilbronn, M. (1981). The pain-prone patients: A clinical and psychological profile. *Psychosomatics, 22,* 395–402.

Blumer, D., & Heilbronn, M. (1982). Chronic pain as a variant of depressive disease: The pain-prone disorder. *Journal of Nervous and Mental Disease, 170,* 381–406.

Block, A. R., Kremer, E. F., & Gaylor, M. (1980). Behavioral treatment of chronic pain: Variables affecting treatment efficacy. *Pain, 8,* 367–375.

Bonica, J. J. (1979). Caner pain: Importance of the problem. In J. J. Bonica & V. Ventafridda (Eds.), *Advances in pain research and therapy* (Vol. 2, pp. 1–12). New York: Raven.

Bonica, J. J. (1986) *The management of pain* (2nd ed.). Philadelphia: Lea & Febiger.

Borgeat, F., Hade, B., Elie, R., & Larouche L. M. (1984). Effects of voluntary muscle tension increases in tension headache. *Headache, 24,* 199–202.

Brewer, W. (1974). There is no convincing evidence for operant or classical conditioning in adult humans. In W. Weimer & D. Palermo (Eds.), *Cognition and the symbolic processes* (pp. 115–138). New York: Halstead.

Brown, G. K., & Nicassio, P. M. (1987). Development of a questionnaire for the assessment of active and passive coping strategies in chronic pain patients. *Pain, 31,* 53–62.

Brown, G. K., Nicassio, P. M., & Wallston, K. A. (1989). Pain coping strategies and depression in rheumatoid arthritis. *Journal of Consulting and Clinical Psychology, 57,* 652–657.

Butler, R., Damarin, F., Beaulieu, C., Schwebel, A., & Thorn, B. E. (1989). Assessing cognitive coping strategies for acute post-surgical pain. *Psychological Assessment: A Journal of Consulting and Clinical Psychology, 1,* 41–45.

Cairns, D., & Pasino, J. (1977). Comparison of verbal reinforcement and feedback in the operant treatment of disability of chronic low back pain. *Behavior Therapy, 8,* 621–630.

Christensen, M. F., & Mortensen, O. (1975). Long-term prognosis in children with recurrent abdominal pain. *Archives of Diseases of Children, 501,* 10–114.

Cioffi, D. (1991). Beyond attentional strategies: A cognitive-perceptual model of somatic interpretation. *Psychological Bulletin, 109,* 25–41.

Ciccione, D. S., & Grzesiak, R. C. (1984). Cognitive dimensions of chronic pain. *Social Science and Medicine, 19,* 1339–1345.

Collie, J. (1913). *Malingering and feigned sickness.* London: Edward Arnold.

Council, J. R., Ahern, D. K., Follick, M. J., & Kline, C. L. (1988). Expectancies and functional impairment in chronic low back pain. *Pain, 33,* 323–331.

Craig, K. D. (1986). Social modeling influences: Pain in context. In R.A. Sternbach (Ed.), *The psychology of pain* (2nd ed., pp. 67–95). New York: Raven.

Craig, K. D. (1988). Consequences of caring: Pain in human context. *Canadian Psychologist, 28,* 311–321.

Dolce, J. J., Crocker, M. F., & Doleys, D. M. (1986). Prediction of outcome among chronic pain patients. *Behavior Research and Therapy, 24,* 313–319.

Dolce, J. J., Crocker, M. F., Moletteire, C., & Doleys, D. M. (1986). Exercise quotas, anticipatory concern and self-efficacy expectancies in chronic pain: A preliminary report. *Pain, 24,* 365–375.

Doleys, D. M., Crocker, M., & Patton, D. (1982). Response of patients with chronic pain to exercise quotas. *Physical Therapy, 62,* 1112–1115.

Droste, C., & Roskamm, H. (1983). Experimental pain measurement inpatients with asymptomatic myocardial ischemia. *Journal of the American College of Cardiology, 1,* 940–945.

Dufton, B. D. (1989). Cognitive failure and chronic pain. *International Journal of Psychiatry in Medicine, 19,* 291–297.

Engel, G. L. (1959). "Psychogenic" pain and the pain-prone patient. *American Journal of Medicine, 26,* 899–918.

Fagerhaugh, S. (1975). Pain expression and control on a burn care unit. *Nursing Outlook, 22,* 645–650.

Fernandez, E., & Turk, D. C. (1989). The utility of cognitive coping strategies for altering perception of pain: A meta- analysis. *Pain, 38,* 123–135.

Fernandez, E., & Turk, D. C. (1992). Sensory and affective components of pain: Separation and synthesis. *Psychological Bulletin, 112,* 205–217.

Fields, H. L. (1987). *Pain.* New York: McGraw-Hill.

Flor, H., Birbaumer, N., Schugens, M. M., & Lutzenberger, W. (1992a). Symptom-specific psychophysiological responses in chronic pain patients. *Psychophysiology, 29,* 452–460.

Flor, H., Birbaumer, N., & Turk, D. C. (1990). The psychobiology of chronic pain. *Advances in Behaviour Research and Therapy, 12,* 47–84.

Flor, H., Fydrich, T., & Turk, D. C. (1992). Efficacy of multidisciplinary pain treatment centers: A meta-analytic review. *Pain, 49,* 221–230.

Flor, H., Kerns, R. D., & Turk, D. C. (1987). The role of spouse reinforcement, perceived pain, and activity levels of chronic pain patients. *Journal of Psychosomatic Research, 31,* 251–259.

Flor, H., & Turk, D. C. (1988). Chronic back pain and rheumatoid arthritis: Predicting pain and disability from cognitive variables. *Journal of Behavioral Medicine, 11,* 251–265.

Flor, H., Turk, D. C., & Birbaumer, N. (1985). Assessment of stress-related psychophisiological reactions in chronic back pain patients. *Journal of Consulting and Clinical Psychology, 53,* 354–364.

Flor, H., Turk, D. C., & Rudy, T. E. (1989). Relationship f pain impact and significant other reinforcement of pain behaviors: The mediating role of gender, marital status, and marital satisfaction. *Pain, 38,* 45–50.

Fordyce, W. E. (1976). *Behavioral methods for chronic pain and illness.* St. Louis, MO: C.V. Mosby.

Fordyce, W. E., Roberts, A. H., & Sternbach, R. A. (1985). The behavioral management of chronic pain: A response to critics. *Pain, 22,* 113–125.

Fordyce, W. E., Shelton, J., & Dundore, D. (1982). The modification of avoidance learning pain behaviors. *Journal of Behavioral Medicine, 4,* 405–414.

Gentry, W. D., & Bernal, G.A.A. (1977). Chronic pain. In R. Williams & W. D. Gentry (Eds.), *Behavioral approaches to medical treatment* (pp. 171–182). Cambridge, MA: Ballinger.

Gil, K. M., Williams, D. A., Keefe, F. J., & Beckham, J. C. (1990). The relationship of negative thoughts to pain and psychological distress. *Behavior Therapy, 21,* 349–352.

Hatch, J. P., Prihoda, T. J., Moore, P. J., Cyr-Provost, M., Borcherding, S., Boutros, N. N., & Seleshi, E. (1991). A naturalistic study of the relationship among electromyographic activity, psychological stress, and pain in ambulatory tension-type headache patients and headache-free controls. *Psychosomatic Medicine, 53,* 576–584.

Herman, E., & Baptiste, S. (1981). Pain control: Mastery through group experience. *Pain, 10,* 79–86.

Heyneman, N. E., Fremouw, W. J., Gano, D., Kirkland, F., & Heiden, L. (1990). Individual differences in the effectiveness of different coping strategies. *Cognitive Therapy and Research, 14,* 63–77.

Holbrook, T. L., Grazier, K., Kelsey, J. L., & Staufer, R. N. (1984). *The frequency of occurrence, impact and cost of selected musculoskeletal conditions in the United States.* Park Ridge, IL: American Academy of Orthopaedic Surgeons.

Holroyd, K. A., & Andrasik, F. (1982). Do the effects of cognitive therapy endure? A two-year follow-up of tension headache sufferers treated with cognitive therapy or biofeedback. *Cognitive Therapy and Research, 6,* 325–333.

Jamner, L. D., & Tursky, B. (1987). Syndrome-specific descriptor profiling: A psychophysiological and psychophysical approach. *Health Psychology, 6,* 417–430.

Jensen, M. P., & Karoly, P. (1991). Control beliefs, coping effort, and adjustment to chronic pain. *Journal of Consulting and Clinical Psychology, 59,* 431–438.

Jensen, M. P., Turner, J. A., & Romano, J. M. (1994). Correlates of improvement in multidisciplinary treatment of chronic pain. *Journal of Consulting and Clinical Psychology, 62,* 172–179.

Jensen, M. P., Turner, J. A., Romano, J. M., & Karoly, P. (1991). Coping with chronic pain: A critical review of the literature. *Pain, 47,* 249–283.

Jensen, M. P., Turner, J. A., Romano, J. M., & Lawler, B. K. (1994). Relationship of pain-specific beliefs to chronic pain adjustment. *Pain, 57,* 301–309.

Keefe, F. J., Brown, G. K., Wallston, K. S., & Caldwell, D. S. (1989). Coping with rheumatoid arthritis pain. Catastrophizing as a maladaptive strategy. *Pain, 37,* 51–56.

Keefe, F. J., Caldwell, D. S., Williams, D. A., Gil, K. M., Mitchell, D., Robertson, C., Martinez, S., Nunley, J., Beckham, J. C., Crisson, J. E., & Helms, M. (1990a). Pain coping skills training in the management of osteoarthritis knee pain: A comparative approach. *Behavior Therapy, 21,* 49–62.

Keefe, F. J., Caldwell, D. S., Williams, D. A., Gil, K. M., Mitchell, D., Robertson, C., Martinez, S., Nunley, J., Beckham, J. C., Crisson, J. E., & Helms, M. (1990b). Pain coping skills training in the management of osteoarthritis knee pain: II. Follow-up results. *Behavior Therapy, 21,* 435–447.

Keefe, F. J., Dunsmore, J., & Burnett, R. (1992). Behavioral and cognitive-behavioral approaches to chronic pain: Recent advances and future directions. *Journal of Consulting and Clinical Psychology, 60,* 528–536.

Keefe, F. J., & Williams, D. A. (1989). New directions in pain assessment and treatment. *Clinical Psychology Review, 9,* 549–568.

Koplow, D. A. (1990, November). *Legal issues.* Paper presented at the annual scientific session of the American Academy of Disability Evaluating Physicians, Las Vegas, NV.

Kotarba, J. A. (1983). *Chronic pain: Its social dimensions.* Beverly Hills, CA: Sage.

Lawrence, R. C., Hochberg, M. C., Kelsey, J. L., McDuffie, F. C., Medsger, T. A., Felts, W. R., & Shulman, L. E. (1989). Estimates of the prevalence of selected arthritis and musculo-skeletal diseases in the U.S. *Journal of Rheumatology, 16,* 427–441.

Lawson, K., Reesor, K. A., Keefe, F. J., & Turner, J. A. (1990). Dimensions of pain-related cognitive coping: Cross validation of the factor structure of the Coping Strategies Questionnaire. *Pain, 43,* 195–204.

Leavitt, F., & Garron, D. C. (1979). The detection of psychological disturbance in patients with low back pain. *Journal of Psychosomatic Research, 23,* 149–154.

Lefebvre, M. F. (1981). Cognitive distortion and cognitive errors in depressed psychiatric low back pian patients. *Journal of Consulting and Clinical Psychology, 49,* 517–525.

Lenthem, J., Slade, P. O., Troup, J.P.G., & Bentley, G. (1983). Outline of a fear-avoidance model of exaggerated pain perception. *Behaviour Research and Therapy, 21,* 401–408.

Leventhal, H., & Everhart, D. (1979). Emotion, pain and physical illness. In C. E. Izard (Ed.), *Emotion and psychopathology* (pp. 263–299). New York: Plenum.

Linton, S. (1985). The relationship between activity and chronic back pain. *Pain, 21,* 289–294.

Linton, S. J., Melin, L., & Götestam, K. G. (1985). Behavioral analysis of chronic pain and its management. In M. Hersen, R. Eisler, & P. Miller (Eds.), *Progress in behavior modification* (Vol. 7, pp. 1–38). New York: Academic Press.

Litt, M. D. (1988). Self-efficacy and perceived control: Cognitive mediators of pain tolerance. *Journal of Personality and Social Psychology, 54,* 149–160.

Lorig, K., Chastain, R. L., Ung, E., Shoor, S., & Holman, H. R. (1989). Development and evaluation of a scale to measure perceived self-efficacy in people with arthritis. *Arthritis and Rheumatism, 32,* 37–44.

Maier, S. F., Dugan, J. W., Grau, R., & Hyson, A. S. (1984). Learned helplessness, pain inhibition and the endogenous opioids. In M. Zeiler & P. Harzem (Eds.), *Advances in the analysis of behavior* (Vol. 7, pp. 102–114). New York: Wiley.

Manning, M. M., & Wright, T. L. (1983). Self-efficacy expectancies, outcome expectancies, and the persistence of pain control in childbirth. *Journal of Personality and Social Psychology, 45,* 421–431.

Martin, P. R., Nathan, P., Milech, D., & Van Keppel, M. (1989). Cognitive therapy vs. self-management training in the treatment of chronic headaches. *British Journal of Clinical Psychology, 28,* 347–361.

McCreary, C., Turner, J., & Dawson, E. (1977). Differences between functional versus organic low back pain. *Pain, 4,* 73–78.

Melzack, R., & Casey, K. L. (1968). Sensory, motivational and central control determinants of pain: A new conceptual model. In D. Kenshalo (Ed.), *The skin senses* (pp. 423–443). Springfield, IL: Thomas.

Melzack, R., & Wall, P. D. (1965). Pain mechanisms: A new theory. *Science, 50,* 971–979.

Melzack, R., & Wall, P. D. (1982). *The challenge of pain.* New York: Basic Books.

Merskey, H. (1986). Classification of chronic pain. Descriptions of chronic pain syndromes and definitions of pain terms. *Pain,* Suppl. 3, S1–S225.

Miller, S. M. (1981). Controllability and human stress: Method, evidence, and theory. *Behavior Research and Therapy, 17,* 287–304.

Mizener, D., Thomas, M., & Billings, R. (1988). Cognitive changes of migraineurs receiving biofeedback training. *Headache, 28,* 339–343.

Nathan, P. W. (1976). The gate control theory of pain: A critical review. *Brain, 99,* 123–158.

National Center for Health Statistics, Koch, H. (1986). The management of chronic pain in office-based ambulatory care: National Ambulatory Care Survey. In *Advanced Data from Vital and Health Statistics* (No. 123, DHHS Publication No. PHS 86–1250). Hyattsville, MD: Public Health Service.

Newton, C. R., & Barbaree, H. E. (1987). Cognitive changes accompanying headache treatment: The use of a thought-sampling procedure. *Cognitive Therapy and Research, 11,* 635–652.

Nerenz, D. R., & Leventhal H. (1983). Self-regulation theory in chronic illness. In T. Burish & L. A. Bradley (Eds.), *Coping with chronic illness* (pp. 13–37). Orlando, FL: Academic Press.

North, R. B. (1989). Neural stimulation techniques. In C. D. Tollison (Ed.), *Handbook of chronic pain management* (pp. 136–146). Baltimore, MD: Williams & Wilkins.

Nouwen, A., & Solinger, J. W. (1979). The effectiveness of EMG biofeedback training in low back pain. *Biofeedback and Self-Regulation, 4,* 103–111.

O'Leary, A., Shoor, S., Lorig, K., & Holman, H. R. (1988). A cognitive-behavioral treatment for rheumatoid arthritis. *Health Psychology, 7,* 527–544.

Osterweis, M., Kleinman, A., & Mechanic, D. (1987). *Pain and disability: Clinical, behavioral, and public policy perspectives.* Washington, DC: National Academy Press.

Peebles, R. J., & Schneidman, D. S. (1991). *Socio-economic factbook for surgery, 1991–1992.* Chicago: American College of Surgeons.

Pennebaker, J. W. (1982). *The psychology of physical symptoms.* New York: Springer-Verlag.

Pennebaker, J. W., Gonder-Frederick, L., Cox, D. J., & Hoover, C. W. (1985). The perception of general versus specific visceral activity and the regulation of health-related behavior. *Advances in Behavioral Medicine, 1,* 165–198.

Philips, H. C. (1987a). Avoidance behaviour and its role in sustaining chronic pain. *Behaviour Research and Therapy, 25,* 273–279.

Philips, H. C. (1987b). The effects of behavioural treatment on chronic pain. *Behaviour Research and Therapy, 25,* 365–377.

Philips, H. C., & Jahanshahi, M. (1986). Validating a new technique for the assessment of pain behavior. *Behaviour Research and Therapy, 24,* 35–42.

Pilowsky, I. (1970) Primary and secondary hypochondriasis. *Acta Psychiatrica Scandinavica, 46,* 273–285.

Pilowsky, I., & Spence, N. D. (1975). Patterns of illness behaviour in patient with intractable pain. *Journal of Psychosomatic Research, 19,* 279–287.

Price, D. D. (1987). *Psychological and neural mechanisms of pain.* New York: Raven.

Rachman, S., & Arntz, A. (1991). The overprediction and underprediction of pain. *Clinical Psychology Review, 11,* 339–356.

Rachman, S., & Lopatka, C. (1988). Accurate and inaccurate predictions of pain. *Behaviour Research and Therapy, 26,* 291–296.

Raj, P. P. (1990). Pain relief: Fact or fancy? *Regional Anesthesia, 15,* 157–169.

Reesor, K. A., & Craig, K. (1988). Medically incongruent chronic pain: Physical limitations, suffering and ineffective coping. *Pain, 32,* 35–45.

Richard, K. (1988). The occurrence of maladaptive health-related behaviors and teacher-related conduct problems in children of chronic low back pain patients. *Journal of Behavioral Medicine, 11,* 107–116.

Rimm, D. C., & Litvak, S. B. (1969). Self-verbalizations and emotional arousal. *Journal of Abnormal Psychology, 74,* 181–187.

Rosensteil, A. K., & Keefe, F. J. (1983). The use of coping strategies in chronic low back pain patients: Relationship to patient characteristics and current adjustment. *Pain, 17,* 33–44.

Schmidt, A.J.M. (1985a). Cognitive factors in the performance of chronic low back pain patients. *Journal of Psychosomatic Research, 29,* 183–189.

Schmidt, A.J.M. (1985b). Performance level of chronic low back pain patients in different treadmill test conditions. *Journal of Psychosomatic Research, 29,* 639–646.

Schmidt, A.J.M., Gierlings, R.E.H., & Peters, M. L. (1989). Environment and interoceptive influences on chronic low back pain behavior. *Pain, 38,* 137–143.

Schmidt, R. F. (1972). The gate control theory of pain: An unlikely hypothesis. In R. Jansen, W. D. Keidel, A. Herz, C. Streichele, J. P. Payne, & R.A.P. Burt (Eds.), *Pain: Basic principles, pharmacology, therapy* (pp. 57–71). Stuttgart, Germany: Thieme.

Schwartz, D. P., DeGood, D. E., & Shutty, M. S. (1985). Direct assessment of beliefs and attitudes of chronic pain patients. *Archives of Physical Medicine and Rehabilitation, 66,* 806–809.

Seligman, M.E.P., & Johnston, J. C. (1973). A cognitive theory of avoidance learning. In F. J. McGuigan & D. B. Lumsden (Eds.), *Contemporary approaches to conditioning and learning* (pp. 69–110). Washington, DC: Winston.

Slater, M. A., Hall, H. F., Atkinson, J. H., & Garfin, S. R. (1991). Pain and impairment beliefs in chronic low back pain: Validation of the Pain and Impairment Relationship Scale (PAIRS). *Pain, 44,* 51–56.

Smith, T. W., Follick, M. J., Ahern, D. L., & Adams, A. (1986). Cognitive distortion and disability in chronic low back pain. *Cognitive Therapy and Research,* 10, 201–210.

Smith, T. W., Peck, J. R., & Ward, J. R. (1990). Helplessness and depression in rheumatoid arthritis. *Health Psychology, 9,* 377–389.

Spanos, N. P., Horton, C., & Chaves, J. F. (1975). The effect of two cognitive strategies on pain threshold. *Journal of Abnormal Psychology, 84,* 677–681.

Spiegel, D., & Bloom, J. R. (1983). Pain in metastatic breast cancer. *Cancer, 52,* 341–345.

Spinhoven, P., Ter Kuile, M. M., Linssen, A.C.G., & Gazendam, B. (1989). Pain coping strategies in a Dutch population of chronic low back pain patients. *Pain, 37,* 77–83.

Stewart, W. F., Lipton, R. B., Celentano, D. D., & Reed, M. L. (1991). Prevalence of migraine headache in the United States. Relation to age, income, race, and other sociodemographic factors. *Journal of the American Medical Association, 267,* 64–69.

Sullivan, M.J.L., & D'Eon, J. L. (1990). Relation between catastrophizing and depression in chronic pain patients. *Journal of Abnormal Psychology, 99,* 260–263.

Thompson, S. C. (1981). Will it hurt less if I can control it? A complex answer to a simple question. *Psychological Bulletin, 90,* 89–101.

Tota-Faucette, M. E., Gil, K. M., Williams, F. J., & Goli, V. (1993): Predictors of response to pain management treatment. The role of family environment and changes in cognitive processes. *Clinical Journal of Pain, 9,* 115–123.

Tunks, E., Crook, J., Norman, G., & Kalaher, S. (1988). Tender points in fibromyalgia. *Pain, 34,* 11–19.

Turk, D. C., & Flor, H. (1987). Pain > pain behaviors: The utility and limitations of the pain behavior construct. *Pain, 31,* 277–295.

Turk, D. C., Kerns, R. D., & Rosenberg, R. (1992). Effects of marital interaction on chronic pain and disability: Examining the down-side of social support. *Rehabilitation Psychology, 37,* 259–274.

Turk, D. C., & Matyas, T. A. (1992). Pain-related behaviors > communications of pain. *American Pain Society Journal, 1,* 109–111.

Turk, D. C., Meichenbaum, D., & Genest, M. (1983). *Pain and behavioral medicine: A cognitive-behavioral perspective.* New York: Guilford.

Turk, D. C., & Nash, J. M. (1996). Psychological issues in chronic pain. In R. K. Portenoy, K. Foley, & R. Kanner (Eds.), *Contemporary neurology* (pp. 245–260). Philadelphia: Davis.

Turk, D. C., & Rudy, T. E. (1986). Assessment of cognitive factors in chronic pain: A worthwhile enterprise? *Journal of Consulting and Clinical Psychology, 54,* 760–768.

Turk, D. C., & Rudy, T. E. (1988). Toward an empirically derived taxonomy of chronic pain patients: Integration of psychological assessment data. *Journal of Consulting and Clinical Psychology, 56,* 233–238.

Turk, D. C., & Rudy, T. E. (1989). An integrated approach to pain treatment: Beyond the scalpel and syringe. In C. D. Tollison (Ed.), *Handbook of chronic pain management* (pp. 222–237). Baltimore, MD: Williams & Wilkins.

Turk, D. C., & Rudy, T. E. (1991). Persistent pain and the injured worker: Integrating biomedical, psychosocial, and behavioral factors. *Journal of Occupational Rehabilitation, 1,* 159–179.

Turk, D. C., & Rudy, T. E. (1992). Cognitive factors and persistent pain: A glimpse into Pandora's box. *Cognitive Therapy and Research, 16,* 99–112.

Turk, D. C., Rudy, T. E., & Salovey, P. (1986). Implicit models of illness: Description and validation. *Journal of Behavioral Medicine, 9,* 453–474.

Turk, D. C., & Salovey, P. (1984). "Chronic pain as a variant of depressive disease": A critical reappraisal. *Journal of Nervous and Mental Disease, 172,* 398–404.

Turner, J. A. (1991). Coping and chronic pain. In M.R. Bond, J.E. Charlton, & C.J. Woolf (Eds.), *Proceedings of the Sixth World Congress on Pain* (pp. 219–227). Amsterdam: Elsevier.

Turner, J. A., & Clancy, S. (1986). Strategies for coping with chronic low back pain: Relationship to pain and disability. *Pain, 24,* 355–363.

Turner, J. A., & Clancy, S. (1988). Comparison of operant behavioral and cognitive-behavioral group treatment for chronic low back pain. *Journal of Consulting and Clinical Psychology, 56,* 261–266.

Vaughan, K. B., & Lanzetta, J. T. (1980). Vicarious instigation and conditioning of facial expressive and autonomic responses to a model's expressive display of pain. *Journal of Personality and Social Psychology, 38,* 909–923.

Vaughan, K. B., & Lanzetta, J. T. (1981). The effect of modification of expressive displays on vicarious emotional arousal. *Journal of Experimental Social Psychology, 17,* 16–30.

Vlaeyen, J.W.S., Van Eek, H., Groenman, N. H., & Schuerman, J. A. (1987). Dimensions and components of observed chronic pain behavior. *Pain, 31,* 66–75.

Waddell, G., Main, C. J., Morris, E. W., DiPaola, M., & Gray, I. C. (1984). Chronic low-back pain, psychologic distress, and illness behavior. *Spine, 9,* 209–213.

Waddell, G., McCulloch, J. A., Kummel, E., & Venner, R. M. (1980). Nonorganic physical signs in low back pain. *Spine, 5,* 117–125.

Wall, P. D. (1979). On the relationship of injury to pain. *Pain, 6,* 63–264.

Wall, P. D. (1989). The dorsal horn. In P. D. Wall & R. Melzack (Eds.), *Textbook of pain* (2nd ed., pp. 102–111). New York: Churchill-Livingstone.

Whitehead, W. E. (1980). Interoception. In R. Hölzl and W. E. Whitehead (Eds.), *Psychophysiology of the gastrointestinal tract* (pp. 145–161). New York: Plenum.

Wilkie, D. J., Keefe, F. J., Dodd, M. J., & Copp, L. A. (1992). Behavior of patients with lung cancer: Description and associations with oncologic and pain variables. *Pain, 51,* 231–240.

Williams, D. A., & Keefe, F. J. (1991). Pain beliefs and the use of cognitive-behavioral coping strategies. *Pain, 46,* 185–190.

Williams, D. A., & Thorn, B. E. (1989). An empirical assessment of pain beliefs. *Pain, 36,* 251–258.

9

Personality Traits as Risk Factors for Physical Illness

Timothy W. Smith
Linda C. Gallo
University of Utah

The belief that stable patterns of thought, emotion, and behavior contribute to the development of physical illness has been present throughout the history of medicine (McMahon, 1976). Hippocrates, for example, argued that four basic temperaments or personality types reflected excesses of specific humors and caused corresponding medical disorders. Many centuries later, Sir William Osler (1892) suggested that coronary heart disease befell "not the neurotic, delicate person ... but the robust, the vigorous in mind and body, the keen and ambitious man, the indicator of whose engine is always at full speed ahead" (p. 839). The descriptions of personality, disease, and the nature of their relation have varied widely, but the essence of this psychosomatic hypothesis has remained unchanged.

Earlier in this century, the hypothesis was refined by the psychoanalytic school in psychosomatic medicine (Alexander, 1950; Dunbar, 1943). These models assigned a pathophysiological role to unconscious personality dynamics, and suggested a correspondence between specific emotional conflicts and medical conditions. Unlike previous psychoanalytic formulations of hysteria or hypochondriasis (Freud, 1933), these models identified causes for actual disease, rather than unfounded physical symptoms. For example, an unconscious conflict between aggressive impulses and anxiety concerning the consequences of their expression was described as a cause of essential hypertension. Although a weak scientific foundation limited the impact of this approach on the mainstream of either medicine or psychology (Surwit, R. B. Williams, & Shapiro, 1982), it set the stage for current research on personality and illness.

During the same period, developments in the physiology of stress provided an essential, scientifically credible set of mechanisms connecting personality and disease (Ax, 1953; Cannon, 1939; Seyle, 1936, 1952; Wolff, 1950). Not surprisingly, the psychophysiology of stress and emotion remains an integral component of this research area (Contrada, Leventhal, & O'Leary, 1990). The immediate predecessor of the current interest in the issue is undoubtedly the seminal work of M. Friedman and Rosenman (1959) on the Type A coronary prone behavior pattern. Although M. Friedman and Rosenman actively avoided describing their work in the language of personality traits, their work is now recognized as involving personality characteristics (Suls & Rittenhouse, 1987). Friedman and Rosenman's version of the centuries-old psychosomatic hypothesis was a major force in the early development of the larger fields of behavioral medicine and health psychology (G. C. Stone, F. Cohen, & Adler, 1979; Weiss, Herd, & Fox, 1981).

An often overlooked forerunner to current research on personality traits as risk factors for illness are early studies that used psychometrically sound measures of personality in large, prospective designs (e.g., Ostfeld, Lebovits, Shekelle, & Paul, 1964). Effects of personality variables on subsequent disease were examined while attempting to control statistically the possible confounding medical or demographic variables. Studies of this type provided important evidence of the merit of the hypothesis and the outlines of a methodology for constructing a credible epidemiological foundation for the field.

The current state of research on the hypothesis that personality traits can influence physical health comprises notable achievements and clear limitations. On the one hand, several literatures have matured to the point that the evidence is compelling; specific personality characteristics are indeed associated with increased risk of serious illness and premature death (e.g., T. Q. Miller, T. W. Smith, Turner, Guijarro, & Hallet, 1996). Further, plausible mechanisms accounting for this association have been articulated and evaluated, at least in a preliminary manner (S. Cohen & Herbert, 1996; Manuck, 1994). On the other hand, a steady climate of skepticism persists in much of the medical community (e.g., Angel, 1985), and the empirical support for the health relevance of some personality traits discussed in this literature is quite limited. Further, the implications of this work for the treatment and prevention of illness are largely unknown. Fortunately, conceptual, methodological, and analytic tools in personality psychology and behavioral medicine have evolved to the point where future studies will address these limitations in an increasingly compelling manner.

This chapter provides an overview and critique of the literature concerning personality traits as risk factors for physical disease. It begins by addressing some basic issues regarding the nature of personality, disease, and their potential association. After reviewing models of this association, it turns to theory and research on the major personality attributes in the field. Finally, it concludes with a critical evaluation of the state of the literature and issues to be addressed in its future.

BASIC ISSUES

What Is Personality?

Allport (1937) succinctly argued that "personality *is* something and personality *does* something" (p. 48, emphasis added). Personality traits are stable patterns of thought, emotion, and behavior that characterize an individual across time and situations. Traits are presumed to be based in psychological and/or biological structures within the individual, and they form a dimensional basis for comparing individuals. For example, some people are generally friendly and warm, whereas others are cold and disagreeable, presumably because of differences in their biologic and/or psychologic "make-up." Thus, from this perspective, personality *traits* are things that people "have" (Cantor, 1990).

In Allport's other, more active meaning, personality refers to the *processes* through which an individual's thoughts, emotions, and behavior cohere into meaningful patterns over time and across situations. These processes include the ways in which individuals select and interpret the contexts and situations of their lives, the goals they pursue, the strategies and tactics they employ in doing so, and the ways in which they evaluate and react to the outcome of these activities. These more circumscribed and dynamic psychological processes are closely associated with the stable patterns of thought, emotion, and behavior that are indicators of traits. Yet, this other sense of personality is obviously much more concerned with how traits operate, rather than their description. Thus, the study of personality as "doing" rather than having (Cantor, 1990) focuses on describing both the psychological mechanisms underpinning more broadly defined, static personality traits and the ways in which these "middle units" of personality are dynamically interrelated and expressed.

Current personality psychology reflects both of Allport's meanings, and recent developments of both types have the potential to make enormously valuable contributions to the study of personality and health (T. W. Smith & P. G. Williams, 1992). In the classic trait perspective, a far-reaching development is the emergence of the five-factor model of personality as an adequate taxonomy of basic personality characteristics (Digman, 1990; John, 1990; McCrae & John, 1992). Although descriptions vary across versions of this model, and despite several notable critics (e.g., Block, 1995), there is general consensus regarding the traits listed in Table 9.1—Extraversion, Agreeableness, Conscientiousness, Neuroticism, and Openness to Experience. These traits have been recovered in factor analyses of self- and other- ratings, and several reliable and valid measures of these broad dimensions and their subcomponents have been developed (Digman, 1990; John, 1990).

The validity and potential impact of this taxonomy are evident in the fact that these traits are clearly not simple mental abstractions or linguistic conveniences used by raters (e.g., Funder & Colvin, 1991; Moskowitz, 1990). Rather, they reflect verifiable, general dimensions of individual functioning. Further, these broadly defined traits are stable (McCrae & Costa, 1990), show patterns of variability consistent with genetic influences (Bouchard, Lylkken, McGue, Segal, & Tellegen, 1990), and predict behavior in many circumstances (Kendrick & Funder, 1988).

The elements of this taxonomy can provide a useful guide for organizing the growing array of otherwise conceptually isolated traits suggested as risk factors for physical illness (Costa & McCrae, 1987b; Marshall, Wortman, Vickers, Kusulas, & Hervig, 1994; T. W. Smith & P. G. Williams, 1992). Traits studied as risk factors are often described and studied individually, without attention to their overlap or even redundancy with other traits. One important application of the five-factor taxonomy is the conceptual and empirical description of traits suggested as potential risk factors. This use of the five-factor taxonomy might reveal similarities and differences among otherwise isolated traits. In addition, the five traits themselves might be viable candidates as risk factors (e.g., Costa, McCrae, & Dembroski, 1989). In either of these applications of the model, the well-validated assessment devices are likely to be useful to health researchers.

One important variation on the five-factor model substitutes the dimensions of Friendliness versus Hostility and Dominance versus Submissiveness for Agreeableness and Extraversion, respectively (Trapnell & Wiggins, 1990). This permits the integration of the five-factor approach with the interpersonal approach to personality (Carson, 1969; Kiesler, 1983; Leary, 1957; Wiggins, 1979). As depicted in Fig. 9.1, the dimensions of dominance and friendliness define a

TABLE 9.1
Elements of the Five-Factor Model of Personality

Trait	Opposite Pole	Facets or Components
Neuroticism	Emotional Stability	Anxiety, depression, angry hostility, self-consciousness, vulnerability, impulsiveness
Agreeableness	Antagonism	Trust, altruism, modesty, straight forwardness, compliance, tender mindedness
Extraversion	Introversion	Warmth, gregariousness, assertiveness, activity, excitement seeking, positive emotions
Conscientiousness	Unreliability	Competence, order, self-discipline, dutifulness, achievement striving, deliberation
Openness to Experience	Closed Mindedness	Fantasy, aesthetics, introspection, curiosity, novelty seeking, low dogmatism

Note. Adapted from Costa & McCrae, 1990.

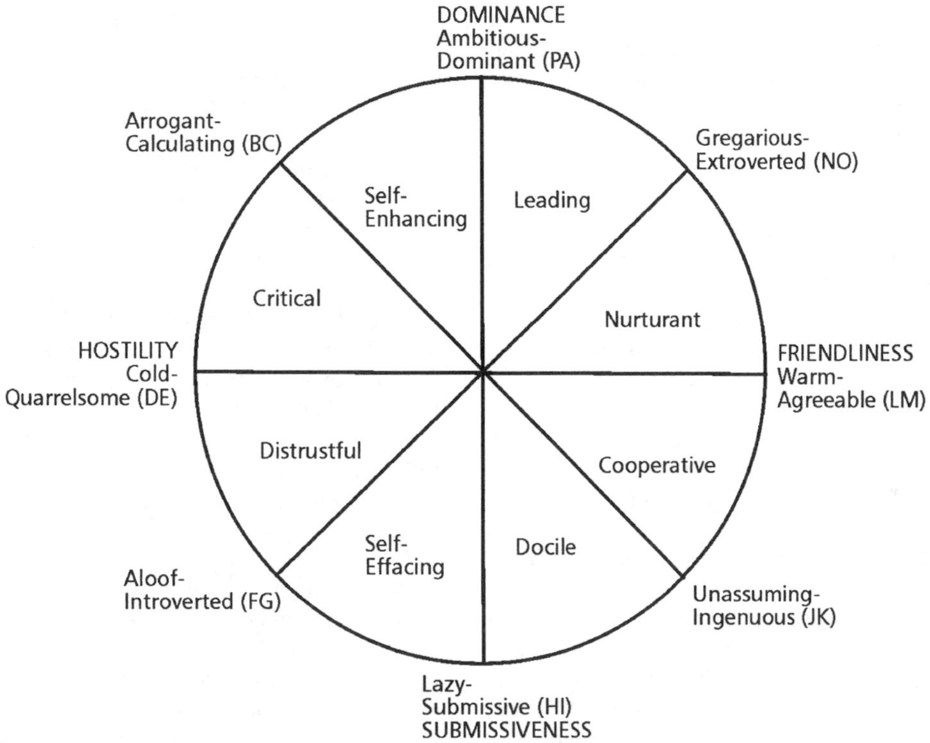

FIG. 9.1 The interpersonal circumplex.

two-dimensional space, or circumplex. The circumplex model has been used, conceptually and empirically, to describe a variety of personality characteristics, interactional behaviors, and social stimuli (Kiesler, 1991; Wiggins, 1991; Wiggins & Broughton, 1991). As a result, it has considerable potential for facilitating the integration of personality and social risk factors for disease (Gallo & Smith, 1998; T. W. Smith, Gallo, Goble, Ngu, & Stark, 1998; T. W. Smith, Limon, Gallo, & Ngu, 1996). That is, personality traits and aspects of the social environment can be described and even assessed through a common framework.

Although the five-factor model and its variants are potentially invaluable in identifying and organizing traits in the study of personality and health, they have less to say about the mechanisms through which traits influence behavior, emotion, and ultimately health. It is here that the second major emphasis in personality psychology is of use. Unfortunately, less agreement exists regarding an adequate taxonomy of the "middle units" of personality processes (Cantor, 1990). However, several overlapping sets have been articulated, and clear themes have emerged in the related research. These approaches follow from the cognitive social learning tradition in personality psychology (Kelly, 1955; Mischel, 1973; Rotter, 1954), and they share many conceptual similarities to interpersonal approaches in personality and clinical psychology (Kiesler, 1996; Westen, 1991). Examples of the constructs described in this literature are mental representations (i.e., schemas) of the self, others, relationships, and social interaction sequences (i.e., scripts); life tasks, motives, and goals; appraisals, values, and beliefs; strategies, tactics, and competencies in goal-directed behavior; and coping styles and behaviors (Cantor, 1990; McAdams, 1995; Mischel & Shoda, 1995, 1998; Oglevie & Rose, 1995; Westen, 1995).

An underlying premise in this tradition is that characteristics of the person are reciprocally related to the social environment. Intentionally or not, people choose to enter some situations and not others, and their actions and overt expressions of emotion elicit responses from their interaction partners in ways that reflect their personality traits (Asendorpf & Wilpers, 1998). These selected, evoked, and intentionally manipulated features of the individual's social environment in turn influence the individual (Bandura, 1977; Buss, 1987; Ickes, Snyder, & Garcia, 1997). Thus, an individual's thoughts, emotions, and behavior are seen as highly responsive to characteristics of the specific situation, and many situations are modified by the individual's actions. Through these recurring, reciprocal patterns, individuals foster social environments that maintain central features of their personalities over time (Caspi et al., 1989; Kiesler, 1996; Wachtel, 1994; Wagner, Kiesler, & Schmidt, 1995). A further implication of this view is that personality processes are best understood in the *contexts* that comprise and surround these reciprocal interactions between people and social environments (Revenson, 1990), such as characteristics of the physical environment, subculture, and socioeconomic factors. Personality descriptions are likely to be more accurate and informative to the extent that they consider individuals, their recurring social circumstances, and the context in which they are embedded.

Current versions of the cognitive-social approach to personality offer the potential for a comprehensive description of broad traitlike characteristics and recurring patterns of situationally specific responding (e.g., Mischel & Shoda, 1995, 1998). That is, the approach has the potential to describe the mechanisms through which traits, such as those in the five-factor taxonomy, influence thought, emotion, and behavior in interaction with social situations. Another important advantage of the cognitive-social perspective is its overlap with current stress and coping theory, given their mutual emphasis on cognitive appraisal processes, self-regulation of emotional responses, and strategies for managing situational threats and demands (Contrada, 1994). The general stress and coping model (e.g., Lazarus & Folkman, 1984; Lazarus, 1991) has become a cornerstone of health psychology and behavioral medicine, and it provides an important conceptual and empirical connection to the psychophysiological responses hypothesized to link personality traits and subsequent disease.

Another benefit of the cognitive-social approach is its relevance for interventions. Although the general trait approach is useful in identifying the personality characteristics that might be useful foci in interventions intended to prevent or manage illness, it has less to say about specific targets for change. With its increased attention to specific psychological mechanisms and dynamic patterns, the cognitive-social approach is likely to aid in the articulation and refinement of intervention techniques. For example, whereas the five-factor taxonomy might identify neuroticism and (low) agreeableness as useful targets for change, the cognitive-social perspective could suggest specific patterns of appraisals, beliefs, interaction tactics, and coping behaviors to be included in such interventions.

What Are the Appropriate Indications of Illness?

A revolutionary difference between psychoanalytic writing on hysteria and hypochondriasis as opposed to the later work of Alexander, Dunbar, and their colleagues lies in the nature of the health endpoint under consideration—abnormal illness behavior versus actual illness. This distinction was clearly drawn more recently in conceptual discussions of the potential effects of personality on health (e.g., F. Cohen, 1979). Outcomes such as symptom reports, utilization of health care resources (e.g., physician visits), taking medication, or receiving other treatments typically reflect the presence of illness, but are fallible indicators. In evaluating the role of personality in physical illness, care must be taken to avoid mistaking an association between personality traits and illness behavior for an association with actual illness. The former may or may not reflect the latter.

Despite the early and clear articulation of this issue, many influential empirical reports on the association between personality and physical illness relied heavily on these less definitive indices (e.g., Haynes, Feinleib, & Kannel, 1980; Kobasa, 1979; Scheier & Carver, 1985). Similarly, several important reviews of this literature (e.g., H. S. Friedman & Booth- Kewley, 1987) have been criticized for the potential misinterpretation of associations between personality traits and illness behaviors—especially somatic complaints—as reflecting the effects of personality on actual physical health (e.g., Matthews, 1988; Stone & Costa, 1990; T. W. Smith & Rhodewalt, 1991).

In the most notable example of this issue, several investigators have demonstrated that neuroticism is consistently related to somatic complaints, even in the absence of actual illness (Costa & McCrae, 1985a, 1987; Watson & Pennebaker, 1989). If the personality characteristic under consideration is associated with neuroticism and if the disease endpoint studied wholly or even partly reflects illness behavior rather than objectively documented disease, then this interpretive ambiguity arises; the association observed might involve personality traits and actual illness, or personality and illness behavior. Given this concern and its potential negative impact on the identification of robust causal influences on actual illness, symptom reports and other illness behaviors are no longer considered an acceptable operational definition of illness. Although illness behaviors are important topics for research, cumulative progress in the study of personality traits as risk factors requires less ambiguous methodologies.

A second major development in this literature is the recognition that the pathophysiology of the major diseases studied varies considerably across their progression. For example, the beginning stage of coronary heart disease (CHD) is characterized by microscopic injuries to the endothelial lining of the coronary arteries. The potential psychophysiological influences on this process might differ from those of the next stage—the slow progressive buildup of fatty deposits at the injury sites. Further, the factors that precipitate the emergence of overt symptoms of CHD (i.e., angina, myocardial infarction, sudden cardiac death) may differ still from those that hasten the progression of previously asymptomatic coronary artery disease (CAD; S. Cohen, J. R. Kaplan, & Manuck, 1994; Kamarck & Jennings, 1991). The natural histories of many forms of cancer and the course of HIV infection and AIDS include similar possibilities for heterogeneous psychophysiological influences over time. This poses two challenges for researchers in the area. First, biologically plausible mechanisms linking personality and disease must be articulated, and second, mechanisms must be tied to identifiable points in the etiology of the illness.

How Do We Evaluate the Personality–Disease Hypothesis?

In order to reach valid conclusions about the presence or absence of a hypothesized relation between a personality trait and illness, several common methodological issues must be addressed. These can be grouped into the classic, four categories of validity in research design specified by Cook and Campbell (1979)—statistical conclusion validity, internal validity, construct validity, and external validity (or generalizability).

Statistical associations between personality traits and illness are generally small, at least by the standards typical in behavioral research (J. Cohen, 1990). These effects are often at least as large as those involving more conventional risk factors for disease. Given the prevalence and cost of the diseases studied, even small effects can have important public health implications. However, small effects, multifactorial etiologies, and changing influences across the course of disease can make it difficult to detect significant covariation between personality characteristics and disease. As a result, large epidemiological studies and quantitative combination of independent results (i.e., meta-analysis) are essential in the development and evaluation of this literature. The results of individual studies must be considered with caution, especially if they employ small, select samples. T. Q. Miller and his colleagues (1991) demonstrated that the use of high risk samples and the associated restriction of range in disease prevalence and severity (i.e., disease-based spectrum bias) can mask the statistical association of personality traits and other risk factors with disease.

Given that personality characteristics are rarely manipulated experimentally, the issue of internal validity is central in this literature. A common strategy in early stages of investigation of a risk factor is the concurrent case control design, in which individuals with the disease (or more severe disease) are compared with controls on the trait of interest. However, given the many possible consequences of serious illness, the alternative interpretation that cognitive, emotional, and behavioral correlates of a disease might reflect consequences rather than causes of the condition often seems equally plausible(S. Cohen & Rodriguez, 1995). Prospective designs eliminate this ambiguity to a large extent, but because of their cost are often underrepresented in the literature on specific traits. Further, the possibility of unmeasured third variables accounting for statistical associations between personality and disease remains as a threat to internal validity even in prospective designs. Biologic, psychologic, and sociodemographic variables could exert simultaneous effects on personality and health, thereby producing a noncausal association.

As previously noted, many studies have relied on symptom reports or diagnoses in which somatic complaints are primary criteria (e.g., angina to operationalize CHD). This poses the threat to construct validity described earlier; the statistical associations might involve illness behavior rather than illness itself. The field has shown an increasing recognition of this concern over time.

However, the construct validity of the personality variables studied as predictors of illness is still often underemphasized. Scales are sometimes specifically developed to assess an individual trait described in a newly proposed model of personality and health. Sometimes such scales are employed prior to thorough construct validation. As a result, it is often uncertain if the statistical associations examined actually involve the personality trait(s) under study, as opposed to some other characteristic(s) assessed unintentionally. Similarly, the distinct versus overlapping nature of the growing array of traits in the field is largely neglected (H. S. Friedman et al., 1995). Thus, it is often unknown whether or not scales intended to assess similar characteristics actually do so (i.e., convergent validity), and whether or not scales with dissimilar names and conceptual descriptions actually assess distinct traits (i.e., discriminant or divergent validity). Careful attention to the issue, possibly using the five-factor model as an integrative tool and source of validated indicators (Gallo & Smith, 1998; Marshall et al., 1994; T. W. Smith & P. G. Williams, 1992), could improve the quality of this literature considerably.

Finally, as with much medical research, the literature on personality traits as risk factors can be rightfully criticized as employing samples that are disproportionately White, middle-class, and male (N. B. Anderson, 1989; N. B. Anderson & Armstead, 1995; Stanton, 1995). Thus, the generalizability of effects across sexes, races, and socioeconomic status is often unknown. Once apparently robust relationships are identified, their generalizability to more diverse groups should be examined. Given that many of these personality traits vary systematically as a function of age, race, sex, and socioeconomic status (e.g., Siegler, 1994), and that these demographic characteristics are themselves risk factors, the issue is likely to be important in the future of the research area.

MODELS OF THE ASSOCIATION BETWEEN PERSONALITY AND DISEASE

Even if reliable and valid associations between personality traits and subsequent illness can be established, the processes or mechanisms that underlie these effects have yet to be determined. Several models have been proposed to describe the association of personality characteristics and subsequent health (F. Cohen, 1979; S. Cohen & Rodriquez, 1995; Krantz & Glass, 1984; Suls & Sanders, 1989). The interactional and transactional *stress moderation models* suggest that physiological reactivity is the critical link underlying this statistical association. Likewise, the *constitutional vulnerability* model posits a physiological influence on disease, but identifies personality as a noncausal correlate or epiphenomenon of this responsivity. The *health behavior model* suggests that personality influences health by affecting health practices. Finally, the *illness behavior model* indicates that personality impacts the subjective experience of illness and the behavioral responses to perceived symptoms. The subsequent section elaborates on each of these models. It is important to note that they are not necessarily mutually exclusive, and that for any given personality characteristic, several models may explain health effects in a complementary manner.

Stress Moderation Models

Stress moderation models are based on the premise that stress is a fundamental component of the relation between personality and disease (e.g., F. Cohen, 1979; S. Cohen & Rodriquez, 1995; Contrada, Leventhal, & O'Leary, 1990; Houston, 1989; Suls & Rittenhouse, 1987). To explain the historically modest association of stress and illness (Rabkin & Struening, 1976), the interactional stress moderation model goes beyond a direct or main effect model by suggesting that individuals will differ in their degree of vulnerability to the detrimental effects of stress, as a consequence (in part) of their personality characteristics. Thus, personality traits are seen as moderators (Baron & Kenney, 1986) of the stress—illness relation, in that illness is more accurately predicted by the statistical interaction of environmental stress and personality traits. Further, the interactive effect of stress and personality on illness is, in turn, seen as mediated by differential psychophysiological responses to stressors as a function of an individual's standing on the personality dimension(s).

Given its central role in this model, it is important to describe the current status of the hypothesis that the psychophysiology of stress can influence disease. The prevailing theory suggests that psychological stress elicits increases in activity in the sympathetic adrenomedullary and hypothalamic, pituitary adrenocortical axes. Over time, pronounced, repetitive, or prolonged physiological responses are thought to contribute to the etiology of illness. Cardiovascular illnesses (e.g., CHD, hypertension, stroke) are believed to be fostered by activation of neuroendocrine (e.g., catecholamines, cortisol) and cardiovascular (e.g., blood pressure) responses (Barnett, Spence, Manuck, & Jennings, 1997; Kamarck & Jennings, 1991; Manuck, 1994; Markovitz, Raczynski, Wallace, Chettur, & Chesney, 1998). Infectious illnesses and cancer are presumed to be influenced by the effects of stress on the immune system (Herbert & S. Cohen, 1993; Kiecolt-Glaser & Glaser, 1995). Although definitive evidence is lacking, these pathways are biologically plausible and the research to date provides considerable, albeit preliminary, support for their role in pathophysiology.

Personality may serve to attenuate or exacerbate (i.e., moderate) the connection between stress and pathophysiology at several places in the stress and coping sequence (see Fig. 9.2). First, the degree to which a given event will be experienced as stressful depends on an individual's subjective appraisal of harm or loss, as well as the resources believed to be available for managing the situation (Lazarus & Folkman, 1984). Certain personality characteristics are thought to influence this subjective appraisal. For example, Type A individuals frequently appraise situations as involving more threat or demand than do Type B persons—a tendency thought to link TABP to cardiovascular disease (Houston, 1989). In contrast, hardy individuals are believed to perceive life events to be challenging, rather than threatening, which may decrease their vulnerability to disease (e.g., Kobasa, 1979). Through these appraisals, personality influences the emotional and motivational responses to events (Houston, 1992), and emotions and aroused motives influence psychophysiological response (Wright, 1996). Second, personality may influence the coping mechanisms that the individual applies in managing the stressor. Specific coping mechanisms probably cannot be categorically regarded as adaptive or maladaptive (e.g., Lazarus, 1990). However, personality may influence the likelihood that the individual will employ strategies that are adaptive in a given circumstance (Bolger & Zuckerman, 1995).

Although the succinctness of the interactional stress moderation approach is appealing, the model is somewhat limited. Fundamentally, it is a model of individual differences in responses to potentially stressful circumstances. These responses are viewed as the result of the static or statistical interaction of personality traits and aspects of the situation. Several researchers have advocated a more process-oriented approach (e.g., Bolger, 1990; Contrada et al., 1990, Houston, 1989; Lazarus, 1990; Revenson, 1990) that emphasizes the ongoing interplay between personality, coping, and contextual factors. Such models move beyond the static or statistical interactional approach by acknowledging the type of reciprocal transactions between persons and their environments typical of the cognitive-social learning and interpersonal models of personality already described. Thus, transactional views of the stress moderation process emphasize the ways in which people influence the objective features of their environments by actively choosing situations and subsequently responding to them in characteristic ways (Bandura, 1977; Buss, 1987; Cantor, 1990; Mischel, 1973). For example, because of their antagonistic interactional style, hostile persons are likely to evoke frequent interpersonal strain. Such conflicts probably confirm hostile expectations and increase the likelihood of future antagonistic behavior (Wagner et al., 1995).

The transactional approach submits that personality influences the stress/illness relation at three points in the stress and coping cycle (see Fig. 9.3). As in the interactional stress moderation approach, personality is thought to alter the appraisal of events and to influence the choice of coping responses. In addition, personality is thought to affect exposure to stressful events, through the individual's selection, evocation, and intentional provocation of characteristics of the situations they encounter (Buss, 1987). Personality characteristics that expose the individual to increased stress through these processes will also elicit the increased psychophysiological reactivity and subsequent potential for disease discussed earlier. Thus, from this perspective, psychosomatic processes are not simple consequences of specific personality characteristics, but reflect a dynamic process emerging from the recurring transactions between people and the social contexts they inhabit (Revenson, 1990; T. W. Smith, 1995).

Health Behavior Model

The stress moderation and transactional models rest on the assumption that the physiological components of stress mediate the association between personality and disease. In contrast, the health behavior model posits that the effects of personality traits on health are indirect, mediated by the intervening effects of health practices (see Contrada et al., 1990; F. Cohen, 1979). (See Fig. 9.4). This model is derived from research suggesting that certain behaviors (e.g., smoking, leading a sedentary lifestyle, and practicing poor nutrition habits) are reliably associated with disease risk (e.g., Blair et al., 1989; Holroyd & Coyne, 1987; Paffenbarger & Hale, 1975). Further, the model draws on research suggesting that personality traits, including hardiness (Wiebe & McCallum, 1986), neuroticism (Costa & McCrae, 1987a; McCrae, Costa, & Bosse, 1978), and hostility (Leiker & Hailey, 1988; Siegler, 1994) affect the likelihood that one will practice negative health habits.

Personality might influence the choice of health practices in several ways. First, psychological factors presumed to guide lifestyle choices may be components or correlates of personality constructs. Examples include variables such as locus of control, health beliefs and values, and self-efficacy (Bandura, 1989; Lau, 1988; Strickland, 1978). Alternatively, negative health practices may reflect ineffectual coping practices. That is, personality characteristics, such as hostility, may not only increase the likelihood that subjective stress will be experienced, but also that maladaptive behaviors, such as smoking or substance use, will be utilized as emotion-focused coping strategies. Research suggesting that individuals often adopt more negative health habits when exposed to stress is consistent with this hypothesis (Horowitz et al., 1979;

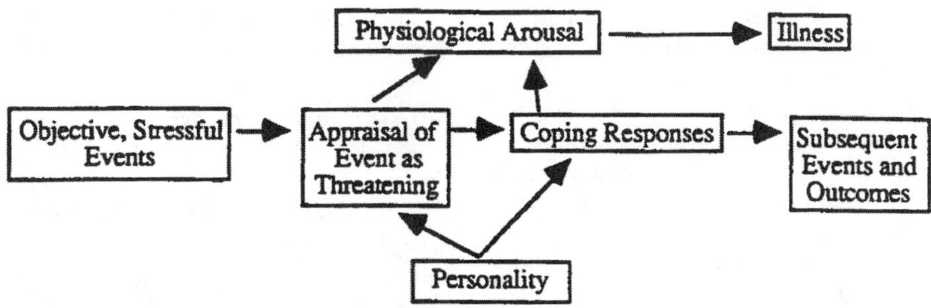

FIG. 9.2 The interactional stress moderation model.

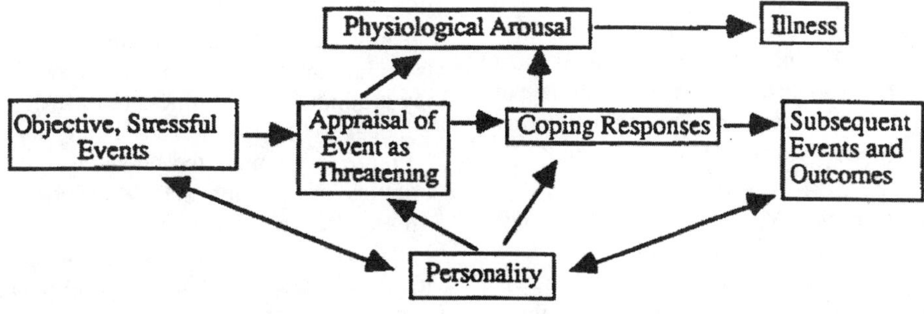

FIG. 9.3 The transactional stress moderation model.

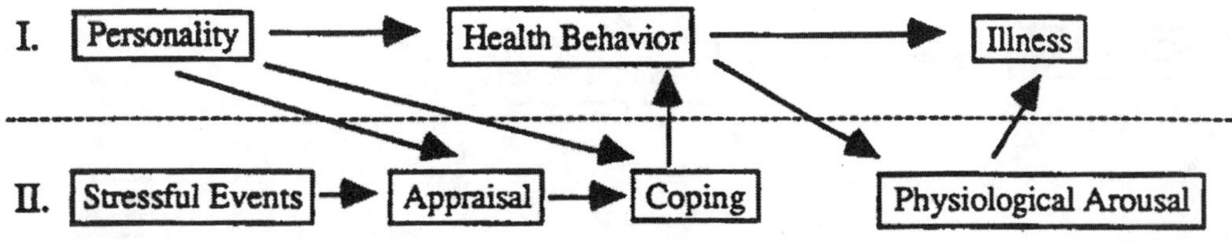

FIG. 9.4 The health behavior model.

Langlie, 1977; Shachter, Silverstein, Kozlowski, Herman, & Liebling, 1977).

As noted earlier, the health behavior model does not suggest that a direct physiological pathway connects personality to health. However, there may be physiological correlates of health behaviors that operate through the set of psychophysiological responses described in the stress moderation models. As portrayed in the lower panel of Fig. 9.4, many health practices produce physiological changes similar to those generated by stress. For example, stress-related alterations in nutrition or sleep habits appear to attenuate immune functioning (Hall et al., 1998; O'Leary, 1990). Furthermore, certain health practices, such as smoking, leading a sedentary lifestyle, and consuming caffeine, appear to intensify laboratory-induced stress responses (e.g., Blumenthal et al., 1990; MacDougall, Musante, Castillo, & Acevedo, 1988; M. D. Davis & Matthews, 1990). Thus, it is possible that the effects of stress on health behaviors produce pathophysiological responses similar to those described in the stress moderation models.

The health behavior model suggests that the common practice of controlling traditional risk factors (e.g., smoking, exercise, etc.) in epidemiological research might lead to an underestimate of the effects of personality on illness, as some of the impact of personality traits on health may occur through unhealthy lifestyles. Contrada et al. (1990) described several other methodological concerns with evaluations of this model. In particular, they emphasized the problems associated with utilizing self-report indices to assess health practices. Methodological artifacts such as social desirability may be particularly problematic in these studies, given the widespread publicity about the detrimental effects of health practices like smoking. In addition, Contrada and colleagues noted that the health behaviors commonly assessed in this research often exhibit only modest intercorrelations (e.g., Leventhal, Prochaska, & Hirshman, 1985; Norris, 1997), and that health behaviors appear to be inconsistent over time (Mechanic, 1979). Failure to recognize the limitations of most measures of health behavior could lead to an underestimate of their role as a mediator of the association between personality traits and subsequent illness.

Constitutional Predisposition Model

Regardless of whether or not the connection is direct, via psychophysiological responses, or indirect, via intervening effects on health behavior, the stress moderation and health behavior models share the common assumption that the statistical association between personality and health reflects a causal relation. Several researchers have suggested that it may not be causal, but instead may reflect the existence of a third variable (Krantz & Durel, 1983; Suls & Sanders, 1989; R. B. Williams, 1994). As depicted in Fig. 9.5, this model proposes that an underlying constitutional vulnerability causes a predisposition for autonomic lability, which subsequently influences both personality processes (e.g., emotional responses, etc.) and health problems. Thus, this model considers statistical associations between personality and subsequent health to be artifacts resulting from the existence of a biologic third variable.

Given the growing body of evidence suggesting that certain personality factors and physiological stress responses may be at least partially determined by genetic factors (Bouchard et al., 1990; Smith et al., 1987; Turner & Hewitt, 1992), this model may be particularly important. This approach has been applied to the relation of Type A behavior and coronary heart disease (Krantz & Durel, 1983), and more recently, to the association of hostility and disease (R. B. Williams, 1994). Future research is necessary to clarify possible genetic influences on other personality–disease relations.

Illness Behavior Model

In contrast to the previous models, the illness behavior approach suggests that personality does not actually affect illness, but that it influences behaviors related to the subjective perception of physical health. This model is derived from evidence indicating that objective health versus illness does not fully explain illness behaviors such as health care utilization, symptom reporting, work absenteeism, and self-medication (e.g., G. A. Kaplan & Camacho, 1983; Kaplan & Kotler, 1985; Maddox & Douglas, 1973). On the contrary, psychological variables strongly affect the likelihood that individuals will attend to physiological sensations and perceive that they are indicative of illness (Cioffi, 1991; F. Cohen, 1979; Pennebaker, 1982; Watson & Pennebaker, 1989).

Figure 9.6 depicts the potential effects of psychological variables on various manifestations of illness behavior. Symptom reports, which are reliably but weakly predictive of objective health outcomes (Idler, Kasl, & Lemke, 1990), provide the clearest example of the less than perfect relation between illness behaviors and disease. Self-reports of physical

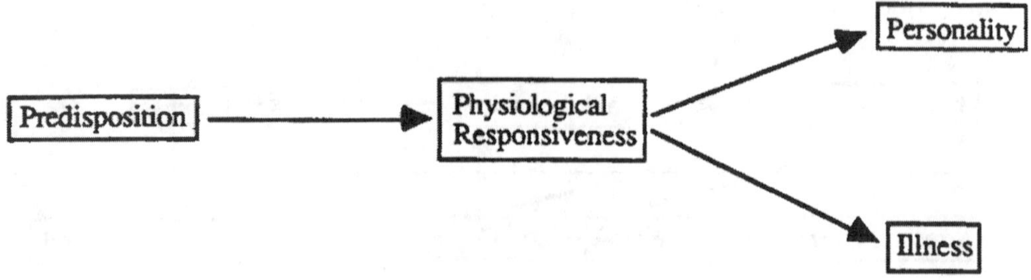

FIG. 9.5 The constitutional vulnerability model.

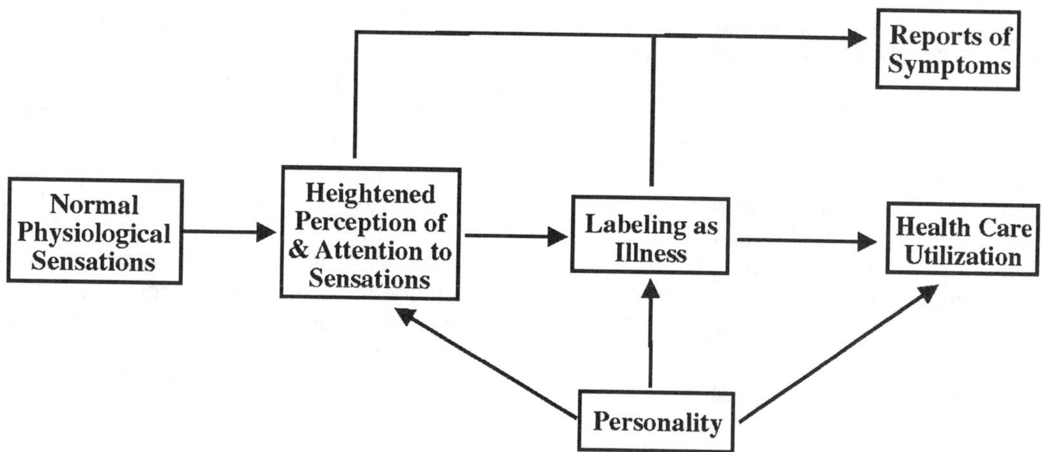

FIG. 9.6 The illness behavior model.

symptoms are influenced by various psychological factors, including health beliefs and differences in focus of attention (Pennebaker, 1982). For example, individuals higher in neuroticism are more likely to be concerned with somatic sensations, and subsequently, to report symptoms (Costa & McCrae, 1985a, 1987; Watson & Pennebaker, 1989). Furthermore, behavioral health indices such as health care visits may be influenced by somatic perceptions and other psychological processes. This phenomenon may be particularly relevant to studies comparing samples selected through medical clinics to control groups solicited from the community. These samples may be biased by psychological characteristics that relate to self-selection into health care settings. Any observed association between a targeted personality trait and illness may be confounded by the relation of the trait to health care utilization behaviors.

The preceding discussion illustrates the distinction between actual illness and illness behavior, and suggests the necessity of carefully evaluating the methodology utilized in studying personality and disease. As discussed previously in the section on validity threats, before the mechanism(s) by which personality contributes to disease can be clarified, the research must demonstrate that illness—and not simply illness behavior—is influenced by personality.

TRAITS LINKED TO HEALTH

The following sections review literature regarding several specific personality traits studied as risk factors. The list is not exhaustive; some traits discussed in this literature are not included. The criteria for including traits are that research published in refereed outlets shows considerable evidence of a prospective association of the trait with objective indicators of serious illness, or that despite the lack of such evidence, the trait is widely studied in the field. For each trait, a description of its usual measurement, the findings linking it to illness outcomes, and theory and research regarding the processes underlying this association are presented.

Type A Behavior

As noted earlier, the Type A behavior pattern (TABP) occupies a central place not only in the modern literature on personality and health, but also in the evolution of the larger fields of behavioral medicine and health psychology. The recent history of research on the topic illustrates most of the central conceptual and methodological issues in this area of research.

Assessment. Following M. Friedman and Rosenman's (1959) description of an "action-emotion complex" consisting of achievement striving, competitiveness, excessive job involvement, time urgency, and easily provoked hostility, two assessment procedures quickly achieved widespread use. The Structured Interview (SI; Rosenman, 1978) is a semistandardized interview intended to elicit a behavioral sample of the behaviors comprising the TABP, or their relative absence (i.e., the Type B pattern). With sufficient training in administration and scoring, reliable ratings can be achieved. A variety of studies indicate that valid ratings can be made with the procedure, with the caveat that the style of administration can affect the quality of ratings (Scherwitz, 1988). The second principal measure is the Jenkins Activity Survey (JAS; Jenkins, Rosenman, & Zyzanski, 1974). This self-report measure primarily assesses achievement striving, competitiveness, job involvement, and hard-driving behavior. Unlike the SI, it does not adequately sample individual differences in hostility. However, many years of research with various versions of the JAS have indicated that it is a reliable and valid measure of the other aspects of the TABP (Rhodewalt & T. W. Smith, 1991).

Because of its availability in a large, prospective study of coronary risk, the Framingham Type A scale (Haynes et al., 1980) is also recognized as a potentially important measure. However, it is poorly correlated with the SI and is more closely associated with both neuroticism and symptom reporting than either the SI or JAS (T. W. Smith, O'Keeffe, &

Allred, 1989; Suls & Marco, 1990). Thus, some of the association between the FTAS and illness endpoints involving symptom reports (e.g., angina vs. myocardial infarction or cardiac death) might involve the association between neuroticism and symptom reports already described.

Notably, the convergence among the three principal measures is more modest than would be expected if they are to be interpreted as reflecting a single construct. Thus, a basic measurement concern—poor convergent validity—limits much of the literature on the TABP (Rhodewalt & T. W. Smith, 1991).

Association With Disease. After nearly 20 years of cross-sectional and prospective research, a panel of experts convened by the American Heart Association concluded that the TABP was a robust risk factor for CHD (Cooper, Detre, & Weiss, 1981), with Type As having about a twofold greater risk than Type Bs. Several notable failures to replicate this relation appeared soon after the expert panel's conclusion. These included not only several prospective, multicenter studies (Shekelle, Gale, & Norusis, 1985; Shekelle, Hulley, et al., 1985), but a long-term follow-up from the original prospective study of the TABP (Ragland & Brand, 1988).

These and other negative findings (e.g., Barefoot, Peterson, et al., 1989) called into question the status of the TABP as a risk factor, and prompted a more fine-grained analysis of the broadly defined pattern. The negative reports also prompted skepticism in both the medical and popular health literature. However, skepticism about the TABP may have been both premature and too general. In a carefully rendered quantitative review of this literature, T. Q. Miller and his colleagues (1991) demonstrated that when it is assessed via the SI as opposed to self-report methods, the TABP is indeed a reliable risk factor for the subsequent development of CHD, even when the illness is defined in terms of objectively verified events (i.e., MI and SCD). This conclusion echoed the results of a previous quantitative review by Matthews (1988).

Additional analyses by T. Q. Miller et al. (1991) indicated that the historical trend toward more frequent negative findings was probably related to a shift over time in the types of populations studied. Whereas early studies included large proportions of initially healthy, low risk subjects, the later studies included a greater proportion of high risk subjects. The resulting overrepresentation of Type As in the samples and the restriction of range in the disease endpoint (i.e., disease-based spectrum bias) is likely to have reduced the statistical power for finding the association between the TABP and CHD.

The potential clinical importance of the TABP was suggested by the results of the Recurrent Coronary Prevention Project (RCPP; M. Friedmann et al., 1984). In this clinical trial, group therapy not only reduced Type A behavior in CHD patients, but also successfully reduced the rate of recurrent coronary events by nearly 50% (M. Friedman et al., 1984). Among patients with a mild previous infarction, treatment reduced the occurrence of cardiac death (Powell & Thoresen, 1988). Thus, in one of a very few attempts to experimentally alter a personality risk factor for serious illness, the results were quite encouraging.

Models of Association. Each model of the mechanisms linking the TABP to CHD has been based on a specific description of the psychological underpinnings of the pattern. For example, Glass (1977) suggested that these overt behaviors reflect a heightened motivation to exert control over environmental events, a low threshold for perceiving potential threats to this control, and an aggressive style in reasserting it. Powell (1992) elaborated this view, arguing that Type As see external events and other people as the primary cause of their difficulties and distress. When combined with the Type As' exaggerated belief in their ability to control others and the view that exerting control is the only coping strategy available to them, this external attribution leads Type As to engage in vigorous attempts to exert control and manage the events of their lives.

Price (1982) argued that a set of core beliefs is the foundation of the overt behavior pattern. For example, Type As are seen as believing that individuals must constantly prove themselves worthy through continual achievement, resources and opportunities for such achievements are limited, and no universal moral principles exist to ensure that people will be fair. As a result, Type As are engaged in an ongoing struggle to bolster their tentative sense of self-worth through what they perceive as a competition with potentially ruthless adversaries.

In all three models, appraisals of environmental threat and engagement in effortful coping are seen as activating psychophysiological reactivity—the final common pathway between the TABP and CHD. In the dozens of studies examining differences between Type As and Bs in their cardiovascular and neuroendocrine responses to threat and challenge, the majority have supported the basic prediction that Type As are more reactive (Harbin, 1989; Houston, 1988). These effects are most reliable when the SI is used to assess the TABP, and when the situation is at least mildly provoking or challenging. Thus, the results are generally consistent with the interactional stress moderation model discussed earlier.

A transaction model of the association between the TABP and CHD has also been outlined (T. W. Smith & N. B. Anderson, 1986; T. W. Smith & Rhodewalt, 1986). From this perspective, Type As are seen not only as overresponding to environmental stressors, but also as creating more frequent, severe, and enduring stressors. Thus, the increased psychophysiological responsiveness believed to link the pattern to disease comes from two sources: the stressors that most individuals experience, and the additional stressors Type As create for themselves through their stress engendering behavior. Examples of Type A stress engendering behaviors include selection of more demanding tasks, appraisal of tasks as requiring a greater level of achievement, eliciting or provoking competitive and disagreeable behavior from others, and evaluating their own performances harshly. Such cognitive and overt behaviors would increase the cumulative amount of exposure to threat and demand, increase psychophysiological responses, and perpetuate the Type A style itself (T. W. Smith & N. B. Anderson, 1986; T. W. Smith & Rhodewalt, 1986).

Another important view of the association between the TABP and illness takes the form of a constitutional predisposition model. From this perspective, overt Type A behaviors are seen as the consequence—rather than cause—of heightened sympathetic nervous system responsivity (Krantz & Durel, 1893). Likewise, this underlying biologic responsivity is thought eventually to cause disease. Thus, the statistical association between the TABP and CHD is a noncausal one, as both are influenced by a third variable. Some evidence suggests that there may be genetic influences on the TABP (Matthews, Rosenman, Dembroski, Harris, & MacDougall, 1984), as well as basic physiologic differences between Type As and Bs (R. B. Williams, Suarez, Kuhn, Schanberg, & Zimmermann, 1991). However, even if an underlying biologic substrate does account for the phenotypic behavioral differences between As and Bs, these overt behaviors are likely to remain important in the development of disease. For example, as described in the transactional view, biologically vulnerable Type As would be prone to exposing themselves to additional stressors. Such increased exposure to threats and demands would exert a negative effect on health, especially among individuals who are constitutionally hyperreactive.

Hostility as the Toxic Component of Type A

Concern about the inconsistent findings regarding the health effects of the TABP has had one invaluable effect on subsequent work in the field; it prompted the examination of the individual elements or components within the pattern. Beginning with a seminal paper by Matthews, Glass, Rosenman, and Bortner (1977), efforts to isolate a "toxic" component of the TABP quickly converged on hostility (Dembroski, MacDougall, Costa, & Grandits, 1989; Hecker, Chesney, Black, & Frautchi, 1988). This development sparked a resurgence of interest in the centuries-old hypothesis that chronic anger and hostility contribute to the development of CHD (Dembroski et al., 1989; Siegman, 1994).

Assessment. Although this area of research is usually identified by the label of hostility, that term is more accurately reserved for one of three closely related constructs (T. W. Smith, 1994). Anger refers to an unpleasant emotion, varying in intensity from mild irritation to rage. It can be construed as either a transitory state or a more enduring disposition (i.e., trait). Closely related emotions include contempt and resentment. In contrast, hostility refers to a cognitive phenomenon. In part, it refers to a negative attitude about others, consisting of enmity, denigration, and ill will. Cynicism—the belief that others are motivated by selfish concerns—and mistrust are closely related cognitive processes. Aggression refers to verbal behavior and physical actions that are destructive or hurtful. Although these three broad constructs are clearly related and often co-occur, they are distinct.

As with the TABP, two assessment procedures have become central indices of this trait (Barefoot & Lipkus, 1994; T. W. Smith, 1992). Several different behavioral rating systems have been developed, primarily in the context of systems for scoring individual components of the TABP (Dembroski et al., 1989; Hecker et al., 1988). The most thoroughly developed and validated of these is the Interpersonal Hostility Assessment Technique (IHAT; Barefoot & Lipkus, 1994; Haney et al., 1996). This rating system scores four specific aspects or manifestations of hostility in the Structured Interview—direct challenges or confrontations with the interviewer, hostile or uncooperative evasions of questions, indirect challenges, and expression of irritation. These ratings can be made reliably, and have been found to correlate with angiographically documented coronary artery disease (Barefoot et al., 1994; Haney et al., 1996).

The second widely used measure is the Cook and Medley Hostility (Ho) Scale (W. Cook & Medley, 1954). It consists of 50 true–false items, selected from the Minnesota Multiphasic Personality Inventory (MMPI) based on their ability to discriminate between teachers with good versus poor rapport with students (W. Cook & Medley, 1954). Subsequent research with the scale has shown that it correlates highly with other self-report measures of hostility, and correlates significantly, but less closely, with measures of other negative affects (e.g., Pope, T. W. Smith, & Rhodewalt, 1990; T. W. Smith & Frohm, 1985). The scale has also been found to be reliably associated with other affective, cognitive, and behavioral indicators of hostility (Allred & T. W. Smith, 1991; Pope et al., 1990; Rosenberg et al., 1998; T. W. Smith, Sanders, & Alexander, 1990).

One troublesome psychometric characteristic of the scale is its poorly defined internal structure (Contrada & Jussim, 1992). This has led some investigators to explore various approaches to identifying more homogeneous subsets of items (e.g., Barefoot, Dodge, et al., 1989; Costa, Zonderman, McCrae, & R. B. Williams, 1986). The scale's poor internal structure and its correlation with characteristics other than anger and hostility are clear limitations of the scale. However, the availability of large MMPI data sets in which previously established cohorts can be reevaluated regarding health status has permitted the rapid development of an epidemiological database on the health consequences of hostility, albeit with a somewhat flawed measure of the construct.

As in the case of the TABP, the primary behavioral and self-report measures of the construct are only modestly intercorrelated (Dembroski, MacDougall, R. B. Williams, Haney, & Blumenthal, 1985). Thus, the questionable convergence of these measures raises a concern about the nature of the construct(s) under study. There are a variety of other self-report and rating scale measures of anger, hostility, and aggressive behavior used in this literature (for a review, see Barefoot & Lipkus, 1994; T. W. Smith, 1992), but only a few of these have been used in large, follow-up studies of objective health outcomes (e.g., Barefoot et al., 1987).

Association With Disease. The initial studies of the prospective association between behavioral ratings of hostility and subsequent CHD all suggested that hostility was indeed an important risk factor (Dembroski et al., 1989; Hecker et al., 1988; Matthews et al., 1977). Similarly, several early studies suggested that self-reported hostility as measured by the Ho scale also predicted CHD and premature mortality (e.g., Barefoot, Dahlstrom, & R. B. Williams, 1983; Shekelle, Gale, Ostfeld, & Paul, 1983). However, several failures to replicate the latter effect soon appeared in the literature (Hearn, Murray, & Leupker, 1989; Leon, Finn, Murray, & Bailey, 1988), again raising concerns about the consistency and importance of the risk associated with this trait.

A recent meta-analysis of the literature on hostility and health supports the basic conclusion that this characteristic is associated with increased risk of serious illness and early death (T. Q. Miller et al., 1996). For example, behavioral measures of hostility were significantly associated with objectively defined CHD (i.e., MI, coronary death), as was the Ho scale. Interestingly, the association between the Ho scale and subsequent CHD was small, suggesting that negative findings in some studies may be due to limitations in sample size and the resulting low statistical power. The Ho scale and other measures of cognitive aspects of hostility were also reliable—and stronger—predictors of all-cause mortality. This suggests that there may be pathways between hostile attitudes and beliefs and serious illness that are outside the pathophysiology of CHD.

Mechanisms of Association. Several models of the association between hostility and health have been presented in the literature (T. W. Smith, 1992, 1994). Similar to the process described in the interactional stress moderation model and in the description of psychophysiological correlates of the TABP, R. B. Williams, Barefoot, and Shekelle (1985) suggested that hostile persons are likely to respond to everyday stressors with exaggerated cardiovascular and neuroendocrine responses. Further, heightened reactivity could facilitate the development of CVD. Some initial studies of the psychophysiological correlates of hostility suggested that this trait was not associated with greater reactivity to standard laboratory stressors, such as mental arithmetic (e.g., Sallis, Johnson, Trevorrow, Kaplan, & Hovell, 1987; M. A. Smith & Houston, 1987). However, subsequent studies have indicated that interpersonal stressors (e.g., harassment, conflict, self-disclosure) elicit reliably larger psychophysiological responses from hostile than nonhostile persons (Christensen & T. W. Smith, 1993; Hardy & T. W. Smith, 1988; S. B. Miller et al., 1998; Powch & Houston, 1996; T. W. Smith & Gallo, 1999; Suarez & R. B. Williams, 1989; Suarez, Kuhn, Schanberg, R. B. Williams, & Zimmermann, 1998). This literature generally supports the conclusion that hostility is associated with psychophysiological reactivity to interpersonal, but not nonsocial, stressors (Houston, 1994; Suls & Wan, 1993). In an interesting extension of this pattern, Lepore (1995) found that the provision of social support attenuated cardiovascular reactivity in nonhostile persons. Hostile subjects did not benefit from the availability of support. Thus, hostility may be associated with both heightened reactivity to social stressors and decreased psychophysiological benefit from social resources.

Hostility has also been linked to physiological stress responses in the natural environment. For example, Pope and T. W. Smith (1991) demonstrated that hostility is associated with larger daily excretion of cortisol, and Jamner, Shapiro, Goldstein, and Hug (1991) found that hostility is associated with larger ambulatory blood pressure responses to interpersonally stressful situations. Several ambulatory studies have indicated that hostility is associated with higher levels of blood pressure and/or heart rate during daily activities (Benotsch, Christensen, & McKelvey, 1997; Linden, Chambers, Maurice, & Lenz, 1993; Guyll & Contrada, 1998). Recent research has also shown that hostility is associated with stress-induced changes in immune responses, perhaps suggesting a mechanism through which this trait might influence noncardiovascular illnesses (Christensen, Edwards, Wiebe, Benotsch, & McKelvey, 1996).

Anger and hostility, considered either as individual difference variables or as transient, situationally evoked responses, have also been linked to the precipitation of myocardial ischemia among patients with significant coronary artery disease. The arousal of anger, irritation and frustration can precipitate ischemic changes during laboratory tasks (Ironson et al., 1992) and during routine daily activity, as assessed with ambulatory monitoring (Gabbay et al., 1996; Gullette, Blumenthal, & Babyak, 1997). Episodes of anger have also been found to precipitate acute myocardial infarctions (Mittleman et al., 1995). Further, ischemic changes have been found to be more pronounced among hostile patients, both in response to laboratory stessors (Burg, Jain, Soufer, Kerns, & Zaret, 1993), and during the course of daily activities (Helmers et al., 1993). One study suggested that the combination of high hostility and defensiveness as measured by the Marlowe–Crown Social Desirability Scale, was associated with greater ischemia among heart patients both in response to laboratory stressors and during ambulatory monitoring (Helmers et al., 1995). Thus, regardless of whether or not hostility can initiate and hasten the development of CAD, it is likely to contribute to CHD through the precipitation of ischemic events. Behavioral ratings of hostility have also been found to predict more rapid restenosis following coronary angioplasty (Goodman, Quigley, Moran, Meilman, & Sherman, 1996).

In addition to these direct psychophysiological connections between hostility and disease, research has addressed behavioral links. For example, hostility has been found to be consistently associated with increased experience of stressful life circumstances and decreased levels of social support, a pattern described as *psychosocial vulnerability* (T. W. Smith & Frohm, 1985; T. W. Smith, Pope, Sanders, Allred, & O'Keeffe, 1988). Compared with their more agreeable counterparts, hostile persons report more major life stressors and minor events (i.e., daily hassles), and fewer and less satisfactory social supports (Barefoot et al, 1983; Houston & Kelly, 1989; Scherwitz, Perkins, Chesney, & Hughes, 1991; T. W. Smith et al., 1988; Suls, Martin, & David, 1998). Hostility is also associated with self-reports and behavioral displays of marital conflict (Houston & Kelly, 1989; T. W. Smith, Sanders, & Alexander, 1990). This pattern of high conflict and low support also appears in hostile persons' descriptions of their work environments (T. W. Smith et al., 1988) and families of origin (Houston & Vavak, 1991; McGonigle, T. W. Smith, Benjamin, & Turner, 1993; T. W. Smith et al., 1988).

Although most of this research on psychosocial vulnerability has relied on cross-sectional or even retrospective methodologies, recent studies found evidence of a prospective association between hostility and subsequent increases in marital conflict (T. Q. Miller, Marksides, Chiriboga, & Ray, 1995; Newton & Kiecolt-Glaser, 1995). So, in addition to the heightened reactivity to interpersonal stressors described in the psychophysiological reactivity model, the psychosocial vulnerability model suggests that the risk associated with hostility might also reflect a greater degree of exposure to such situations and a concurrent lack of resources or buffers in facing them.

The transactional approach has also been applied to hostility (T. W. Smith, 1995; T. W. Smith & Pope, 1990). From this perspective, the heightened interpersonal conflict and reduced support experienced by hostile persons reflects a reciprocal relation between their actions and the responses of others. Through their expectations of mistreatment and outwardly disagreeable behavior, hostile persons are likely to create conflict, undermine cooperation and support, and foster opposition from others (T. W. Smith, 1995; T. W. Smith & Pope, 1990). Once created, such an environment would likely be interpreted as confirming the accuracy of the hostile person's interpersonal "world view," as well as the apparent necessity of an antagonistic behavioral style in dealing with others. Such dynamic patterns are likely to be seen in momentary interactions lasting a few minutes, in more enduring relations, and in repeating patterns over many years (Caspi et al., 1989; Henry, 1996; Kiesler, 1991; Wachtel, 1994).

Another psychological connection between hostility and health is consistent with the health behavior model. Several studies have indicated that hostile persons engage in unhealthy practices, such as smoking and excessive alcohol use (Siegler, 1994). Epidemiological studies attempting to control statistically the possible role of such health practices have suggested that the health behavior model does not account for the health consequences of this trait (T. Q. Miller et al., 1996). However, as noted earlier, compelling tests of such mediational models are extremely difficult to conduct (Contrada et al., 1990), and some studies do support the health behavior model of the effects of hostility on health (Evenson et al., 1997).

Constitutional models of the health consequences of hostility have also been presented. For example, R. B. Williams (1994) argued that low brain levels of serotonin could underlie the affective and behavioral features of hostility (cf. Coccaro, Kavoussi, Cooper, & Hauger, 1997), the autonomic lability identified as a psychophysiologic mechanism linking hostility and health, and unhealthy behaviors associated with this trait (e.g., smoking, alcohol consumption, excessive calorie and fat intake). Thus, a single central deficit—reduced brain levels of a specific neurotransmitter—is seen as responsible for this cluster of biobehavioral characteristics and the statistical association between hostility and health. J. R. Kaplan, Botchin, and Manuck (1994) similarly suggested that reduced central serotonergic drive might be the basis of the associations between aggressive behavior and related affect, physiological responsivity, and CHD in animal models.

Unlike the early literature on the global TABP, descriptions of these mechanisms linking hostility and health have not included detailed discussion of the psychological underpinnings of hostility. Certainly, hostile behavior can be seen as a strategy for exercising interpersonal control (Averill, 1982) or attempting to secure desired outcomes during competitive struggles (Bandura, 1973). Further, hostility is associated with endorsement of the beliefs related to the TABP (P. L. Watkins, Ward, Southard, & Fisher, 1992). Thus, the psychological perspectives on coronary prone behavior proposed by Glass (1977), Powell (1992), and Price (1982) described earlier are also relevant to hostility. However, other perspectives from outside traditional health psychology and behavioral medicine are relevant as well. For example, developmental models (Crick & Dodge, 1994; Lemerise & Dodge, 1993) suggest that chronic anger and aggressiveness arise in children from the tendency to attribute harmful intent to the actions of others, to overestimate the perceived appropriateness and effectiveness of aggression as a problem-solving strategy, and a lack of alternative prosocial strategies. Related work in developmental psychology suggests that reduced empathy contributes to aggressive behavior (P. A. Miller & Eisenberg, 1988).

Many of these developmental models of anger, hostility, and aggressive behavior suggest that social learning experiences in the family context during childhood are contributing factors (e.g., Lyons-Ruth, 1996). Central themes in these models are that hostility arises from a pattern of low positive involvement with parents, hostile and coercive parental behavior, and observations of dysfunctional marital interactions (Davies & Cummings, 1994; Patterson, 1985). Consistent with this view, hostile persons describe their early family environment as including low levels of affection and high levels of hostility and coercion (Houston & Vavak, 1991; McGonigle et al., 1993; T. W. Smith et al., 1988, 1996; Woodall & Matthews, 1989). Further, Matthews, Woodall, Kenyon, and Jacob (1996) reported that behaviorally rated family conflict predicted increases in hostility among adolescent males. Thus, the negative expectations, mistrust, and antagonistic social strategies of hostile adults seem likely to have been forged in a similar family context. Interestingly, young adults' perceptions of their parents as uncaring have been found to predict poor health in midlife (Russek & Schwartz, 1997).

This view of the effects of early experience on adult hostility reflects the psychological processes of identification and internalization (Henry, 1994). Identification (i.e., modeling) refers to the process through which individuals enact behavior they previously observed in significant others, such as observations of maladaptive interactions between parents (Davies & Cummings, 1994). Internalization refers to the development of abstract representations of others and relationships (i.e., schemas and scripts), which in turn form the basis for more generalized interpersonal expectancies (Westen, 1991). In this process, individuals come to view others and themselves in a manner consistent with recurring family patterns during childhood. That is, hostile persons would have acquired generalized expectations that others are neglectful, coercive, and blaming, similar to the treatment received from parents.

A third social learning process—introjection—provides additional insight into the likely psychological underpinnings of hostility. Introjection refers to the process through which individuals learn to respond to themselves in a manner similar to the treatment received from parents or other significant caregivers during development (Benjamin, 1994; Henry, 1996). Thus, hostile neglect and coercion from parents should result in low self-esteem and pointed self-criticism. Interestingly, despite the obvious external focus of anger and hostility, research suggests that these traits indeed have a self-directed component as well. Several investigators have found that individual differences in anger and hostility are correlated with vulnerable self-esteem, harsh self-evaluation, and the tendency to experience shame (Kernis, Grannemann, & Barclay, 1989; T. W. Smith, McGonigle, & Benjamin, 1998; Tangney, Wagner, Hill-Barlow, Marschall, & Gramzow, 1996). This pattern may lead hostile persons to be emotionally and behaviorally overresponsive to perceived mistreatment and criticism from others. Thus, the psychological underpinnings of hostility may include several central elements within current cognitive-social views of personality, such as negative working models of self, others, and relationships, goals of defending against others' attempts to take advantage of or dominate the individual, and a reliance on antagonistic social problem-solving strategies.

Are There Other Coronary Prone Characteristics? Research on the health consequences of hostility was largely motivated by the hypothesis that it was the "toxic" element within the TABP. However, some evidence suggests that at least one other characteristic might be worth pursuing in future research. In an important reanalysis of the original prospective study linking the TABP to subsequent CHD (i.e., the Western Collaborative Group Study), Houston, Chesney, Black, Cates, and Hecker (1992) identified several distinct groups of subjects through cluster analyses of individual behavioral characteristics (e.g., hostility, speech rate and volume, etc.). Not surprisingly, they found one cluster of subjects, defined by high levels of hostility, to be at significantly greater risk of subsequent CHD. Importantly, they identified a second group at increased risk: This one is identified by loud, rapid speech and the tendency to "talk over" the interviewer. The investigators suggested that this pattern reflected socially dominant or controlling behavior during the interview, raising the possibility that both hostility and social dominance are coronary prone behaviors. In additional analyses of this data, social dominance was significantly associated with all-cause mortality (Houston, Babyak, Chesney, Black, & Ragland, 1997), and a similar prospective association between self-reported dominance (i.e., low submissiveness) and incidence of myocardial infarction has been demonstrated in a large sample of men and women (Whiteman, Deary, Lee, & Fowkes, 1997).

Some previous research has suggested that the TABP is associated with interpersonal dominance (Yarnold & Grimm, 1986). Interestingly, individual differences in social dominance are a well-established risk factor for CAD in a nonhuman primate model of psychosocial risk (J. R. Kaplan et al., 1994; J. R. Kaplan & Manuck, 1998). Further, consistent with the psychophysiological reactivity perspective, the act of influencing or controlling others elicits heightened cardiovascular reactivity (T. W. Smith, Allred, Morrison, & Carlson, 1989; T. W. Smith, Baldwin, & Christensen, 1990; T. W. Smith et al., 1996). Thus, before accepting the conclusion that hostility is the lone risk factor within the TABP, researchers should consider the second primary axis of the interpersonal circumplex (see Fig. 9.1).

Neuroticism and Negative Affectivity

Negative emotions such as fear and sadness figured prominently in the early psychoanalytic formulations regarding the effects of personality processes on health (Alexander, 1950; Dunbar, 1943), as they did in early and continuing research on the psychophysiology of stress and emotion (Ax, 1953). Current interest in this general trait involves two distinct issues—the role of dispositional emotional distress or instability in the development of actual disease and the contribution of this trait to artifactual associations between personality and illness.

Although conceptualizations and definitions of this construct vary to some extent, it can be generally seen as "individual differences in the tendency to experience distress, and in the cognitive and behavioral styles that follow from this tendency" (McCrae & John, 1992, p. 195). High levels of neuroticism, emotional instability, or negative affectivity (Watson & Clark, 1984) are associated with chronic negative affect (including anxiety, tension, sadness, guilt, frustration, and irritability), as well as related characteristics (such as low self-esteem, impulsiveness, and self-consciousness). Individuals with low levels of this trait are characterized as calm, relaxed, and stable.

It is important to distinguish between elevations on this dimension that are within the range of normal variation and clinically significant conditions involving one or more negative affects (i.e., mood or anxiety disorders). Individuals with such disorders certainly are characterized by high levels of neuroticism or negative affectivity (Clark, Watson, & Mineka, 1994), and high levels of this trait pose an increased risk of developing a related clinical disorder (e.g., Hirschfeld et al., 1989; Zonderman, Herbst, Schmidt, Costa, & McCrae, 1993). Given this overlap, associations between the related clinical conditions and subsequent illness might actually reflect the health consequences of neuroticism. Therefore, the following section reviews research with both types of predictors: normal trait variation and presence of a diagnosable emotional disorder. However, because of the many potential differences between normal personality variation and pathological extremes, the parallels between these two types of research must be interpreted with caution (S. Cohen & Rodriguez, 1995; Coyne, 1994; T. W. Smith & Rhodewalt, 1991; Watson, Clark, & Harkness, 1994).

Assessment. Neuroticism and its components or facets are assessed by a great variety of self-report and observer rating scales (Gotlib & Cane, 1989; McCrae & John, 1992; Watson et al., 1994). These scales assess either the broad dimension, or one or more of its components. Similarly, the symptoms comprising diagnosable anxiety and mood disorders can be assessed by a variety of inventories and structured interviews (Clark, 1989). A review of the available measures is beyond the scope of this chapter. However, it is important to note two measurement issues. First, as discussed earlier, the overlapping yet distinct quality of neuroticism and diagnosable emotional disorders poses a difficult interpretive challenge. Findings obtained with measures of either type might reflect—wholly or in part—the effects of the other. Second, scales purporting to measure a single component of this broader dimension (e.g., anxiety, depression, low self-esteem) are likely to correlate closely with the higher order dimension and other components. Thus, scale names often imply more specificity and discriminant validity than is actually present. Yet, the individual components within this broad trait are conceptually and empirically distinguishable, and it is quite possible that they are differentially related to illness (Carver, 1989).

Neuroticism and Somatization. A large body of literature demonstrates that neuroticism is reliably associated with self-reports of illness (Costa & McCrae, 1985a, 1987; Watson & Pennebaker, 1989). As previously noted, the correlation between self-reports of physical symptoms and actual illness is significant but small. This raises the question as to whether the association between neuroticism and self-reported illness involves the component of variance in self-reports that overlaps with actual health or the component that is independent (i.e., illness behavior in the absence of illness).

Most of the literature on the association between neuroticism and self-reported illness does not include the independent measures of objective health that would answer this question. However, some evidence suggests neuroticism or negative affectivity accounts for discrepancies between objective indicators of disease and symptom reports. The correlation between neuroticism and the extent of CAD among patients undergoing diagnostic coronary angiography provides one such example. Despite the invasiveness of the procedure and the fact that it is usually reserved for cases in which there are at least some clear indications of the presence of CAD, a significant minority of coronary angiography patients is found to have normal arteries (T. W. Smith & Leon, 1992). These patients have much better prognoses than patients with documented disease, essentially equivalent to normal individuals. Yet, they continue to complain of anginalike chest pain (Bass & Wade, 1984; Lantinga et al., 1988; Ockene, Shay, Alpert, Weiner, & Dalen, 1980; Wielgosz & Earp, 1986).

Importantly, angiography patients without clinically significant CAD have been found to report higher levels of neuroticism or negative affectivity than do patients with CAD (Bass & Wade, 1984; Elias, Robbins, Blow, Rice, & Edgecomb, 1982; Lantinga, Spafkin, McCroskery, 1988; Wielgosz & Earp, 1986). This has prompted the interpretation that physically healthy but high N/NA individuals complain about noncardiac chest pain with sufficient intensity to undergo angiography in the absence of the usual medical indications for the procedure (Costa & McCrae, 1987a). Consistent with this interpretation, the tendency to complain about physical symptoms, as measured by the MMPI Hypochondriasis scale, is positively associated with longevity among angiography patients (Shekelle, Vernon, & Ostfeld, 1991). That is, the physically healthy somaticizing patients live longer than do the emotionally stable patients with significant coronary occlusions.

When such findings are combined with the results of prospective studies in which measures of N/NA do not predict premature death or the development of objectively verified illness (e.g., Almada, Zonderman, & Shekelle, 1991; Costa & McCrae, 1987a; G. A. Kaplan & Reynolds, 1988), it is quite possible that N/NA is a robust predictor of somatic complaints but not actual illness (Costa & McCrae, 1987a; Watson & Pennebaker, 1989). Some investigators have suggested that the association between N/NA and somatic complaints is so robust that somatic distress should be considered a component rather than correlate of the broader dimension (Watson & Pennebaker, 1989). Given the pervasive association of N/NA with a variety of measures of personality traits, virtually any correlation between a personality characteristic and an illness outcome influenced by illness behavior might be open to this alternative interpretation; rather than reflecting a link between psychological traits and actual illness, such correlations could reflect an association between neuroticism and illness behavior.

Neuroticism and Actual Illness. Several recent studies have challenged the broad conclusion that N/NA is related to illness behavior but not actual illness. In prospective designs with statistical controls for potential confounding factors, neuroticism and/or its components have been found to predict objectively verified physical morbidity or premature death. Similarly, diagnosable anxiety and mood disorders have been found to predict such objective health outcomes.

For example, individual differences in self-reported fear, anxiety, and depression have been found to predict increases in resting blood pressure levels and the incidence of essential hypertension (Jonas, Franks, & Ingram, 1997; Markovitz, Matthews, & Kannel, 1993; Markovitz, Matthews, Wing, Kuller, & Meilahn, 1991; Spiro, Aldwin, Ward, & Mroczek, 1995). Among individuals with essential hypertension, symptoms of depression are associated with increased risk of stroke and CVD-related death (Simonsick, Wallace, Blazer, & Gerkman, 1995). Similarly, self-reports of anxiety, tension, depression, and stress have been found to predict the development of CHD in initially healthy samples (Anda et al., 1993; Barefoot & Schroll, 1996; Eaker, Pinsky, & Castelli, 1992; Ford et al., 1998; Haines, Imeson, & Meade, 1987; Kawachi, Colditz, et al., 1994; Kawachi, Sparrow, Vokonas, & Weiss, 1994; Kubzansky et al., 1997; Rosengren, Tibblin, & Wilhelmsen, 1991). Emotional distress and maladjustment have also been prospectively linked to premature mortality (Herrmann et al., 1998; Martin et al., 1995; Somervell et al., 1989). Among patients with CHD, symptoms of anxiety and depression, as well as depressive disorders, have been found to predict length of survival and recurrent morbid events (Ahern et al., 1990; Barefoot et al., 1996; Carney, Rich, & Freedland, 1988; Denollet, Sys, &

Brutsaert, 1995; Follick et al., 1988; Frasure-Smith, Lesperance, & Taljic, 1993, 1995a, 1995b; Moser & Dracup, 1996). Finally, depressive and other symptoms of emotional distress have been found to predict more rapid immunological deterioration in HIV+ patients (Burack, Barrett, & Stall, 1993; Vedhara et al., 1997), although similar studies have failed to replicate this effect (Lyketsos, Hoover, & Guccione, 1993; Perry, Fishman, & Jacobsberg, 1992). Thus, contrary to earlier views, N/NA, its components, and related clinical conditions might indeed confer risk for the onset of serious illness and a poor prognosis.

It is important to note that the literature cited is selective; well-controlled studies employing large samples exist in which N/NA or its components do not predict the development or course of serious illness (e.g., G. A. Kaplan & Reynolds, 1988; Shekelle et al., 1991; Zonderman, Costa, & McCrae, 1989). Nonetheless, the effects of this trait on health clearly go beyond the well- documented association with illness behavior. Previous reviews of the evidence regarding the health effects of N/NA concluded that chronic emotional distress constituted a disease prone personality style (H. S. Friedman & Booth-Kewley, 1987), but were appropriately criticized for basing this conclusion, at least in part, on studies actually demonstrating an association between emotional distress and somatic complaints (Stone & Costa, 1990). The research reviewed here suggests that emotionally distressed persons may indeed be disease prone, but the two types of associations must be carefully distinguished.

Several approaches to resolving this ambiguity have appeared in recent years, each of which suggests that large, multifaceted personality constructs pose difficult challenges for research (Briggs, 1992; Carver, 1989). For example, Barefoot, Beckham, Peterson, Haney, and R. B. Williams (1992) found that among angiography patients, only the somaticizing component of N/NA was inversely related to CAD severity. Despite their significant correlations with somaticizing, measures of anxiety or global neuroticism were not independently correlated with objectively verified CAD. Thus, perhaps it is a specific facet of N/NA that contributes to the artifactual association with illness behavior.

The difference between transient versus stable aspects of negative emotions might also be an important distinction in this regard. S. Cohen and his colleagues (1995) found that both state and trait NA were associated with increased symptom reports following exposure to a respiratory virus. However, only the correlation of state NA with symptom reports could be explained as reflecting the development of more severe infections. The association between trait NA and symptoms was independent of objective measures of disease severity. In a related study (S. Cohen, Tyrell, & A. Smith, 1991), state but not trait NA was associated with increased risk of developing a verified respiratory infection following viral exposure. These findings raise the possibility that the actual arousal of negative emotions could influence health, but that some other feature(s) of the stable personality trait of neuroticism or the negative affectivity characteristic might be responsible for somatic complaints in the absence of disease. This interpretation again underscores the importance of examining the independent contributions of the facets or components of this broad trait (Carver, 1989).

Mechanisms of Association. The mechanisms possibly underlying the effects of N/NA on illness behavior have been detailed elsewhere (Cioffi, 1991; Watson & Pennebaker, 1989). Briefly, these include increased perception of somatic sensations, appraisals of benign sensations as possibly reflecting illness, and a corresponding lower threshold for seeking medical care.

Explanations for the possible association between N/NA and actual illness have primarily focused on the interactional stress moderation model (Cohen & Rodriguez, 1995). For example, a variety of studies indicate that stress and negative emotions can contribute to the suppression of immune responses (S. Cohen & Williamson, 1991; Herbert & S. Cohen, 1993; Kiecolt-Glaser & Glaser, 1995), thereby increasing vulnerability to infectious disease and cancer. In the case of fear, anxiety, and depression, cardiovascular psychophysiological mechanisms have been proposed. For example, both anxiety and depression have been found to be associated with reduced cardiovascular parasympathetic responsiveness and increased sympathetic reactivity (Carney, Freedland, Rich, & Jaffe, 1995; Hoehn-Saric & McCleod, 1988; Watkins, Grossman, Krishnan, & Sherwood, 1998). These mechanisms could contribute to the initiation and progression of CAD (Manuck, Marsland, Kaplan, & J. K. Williams, 1995), as well as the precipitation of acute cardiac events among individuals with advanced disease (Kamarck & Jennings, 1991). Thus, individuals high in N/NA would be expected to respond to potential stressors with more pronounced increases in negative emotions, with corresponding effects on pathophysiology.

Although rarely discussed in the literature on the health consequences of anxiety, depression, and other aspects of N/NA, the transactional stress moderation approach may also be relevant. For example, it is well established that depression is not only a consequence of stressful life experiences, but a cause of such events as well (Coyne, Burchill, & Stiles, 1991; Daley et al., 1997; Davila, Bradbury, Cohan, & Tochluk, 1997; Fincham, Beach, Harold, & Osborne, 1997; Hammen, 1991; Johnson & Jacob, 1997; Potthoff, Holahan, & Joiner, 1995). Through negative expectations regarding others and ineffective social skills, depressed persons are likely to engender resentment, conflict, and rejection in their social relations (Coyne et al., 1991). This environment would not only tend to maintain or exacerbate depression, but also would contribute to the psychophysiological stress responses believed to foster disease. Bolger and his colleagues (Bolger & Schilling, 1991; Bolger & Zuckerman, 1995) reported that neuroticism is related not only to greater emotional reactivity to negative events, but to greater exposure to such events as well, especially interpersonal conflicts. Thus, the stress engendering aspects of the various facets of N/NA are worthy of additional consideration.

Health behavior mechanisms connecting N/NA and illness have also been suggested (Cohen & Rodriguez, 1995). For example, this trait and its components have been found to be associated with reduced exercise, poor diet, smoking, alcohol consumption, poor adherence to medical regimens, and poor self-care (Booth-Kewley & Vickers, 1994; Carney et al., 1995; Wiebe, Alderfer, Palmer, Lindsay, & Jarrett, 1994). However, at least some studies have found that health behaviors do not account for the statistical association between N/NA and illness (Martin et al., 1995). Although this result might question the accuracy of the health behavior model in this instance, limitations in the assessment of health behaviors might result in an underestimate of its impact as a mediating variable.

Research on the potential health effects of N/NA and its components has primarily been directed toward the description of these associations. As a result, less attention has been paid to the psychological underpinnings of this trait, as compared to the literatures on the TABP and hostility. However, should the epidemiological research support the importance of these characteristics, then the large literatures in personality and clinical psychology on the nature of N/NA and related disorders will prove valuable in explicating the nature of their effects on health and identifying potential targets for change in intervention efforts (Clark et al., 1994; Coyne et al., 1991; Kendall & Ingram, 1989; Rehm, 1989; Watson et al., 1994).

Dispositional Optimism/Pessimism

The notion that optimistic expectations contribute to good health has long been a part of cultural beliefs regarding psychological effects on illness. In the past decade, this hypothesis has also played an important role in the current resurgence of interest in personality traits as risk factors. From distinct theoretical perspectives, two independent teams of investigators have examined the health consequences of optimism versus pessimism (Peterson & Seligman, 1987; Scheier & Carver, 1992). Although the implications of the resulting literature have been the source of some controversy, this trait has emerged as a major focus in current research.

Assessment. The Life Orientation Test (LOT; Scheier & Carver, 1985) is a widely used measure of optimism versus pessimism. The LOT is intended to assess generalized "expectations that good things will happen" (Scheier & Carver, 1985, p. 223). The LOT is hypothesized to assess individual differences at a critical junction in the process of self-regulation during encounters with potentially stressful events—the point at which expectations determine the pursuit of active, problem-focused coping efforts as opposed to withdrawal and passive coping (Scheier & Carver, 1985, 1992).

Although this self-report scale has adequate internal consistency (Scheier & Carver, 1985; Scheier, Carver, & Bridges, 1994), there is some debate as to whether it assesses a single dimension or separate (although highly correlated) optimism and pessimism factors (Marshall, Wortman, Kusulas, Hervig, & Vickers, 1992; Scheier et al., 1994). The scale correlates significantly with measures of similar constructs (e.g., hopelessness), but in some instances these correlations are not significantly larger than its correlations with other, conceptually distinct traits (T. W. Smith, Pope, Rhodewalt, & Poulton, 1989).

This issue is especially relevant in regard to the trait of neuroticism. For example, in an early study of this problem, T. W. Smith et al. (1989) found that the LOT was as closely correlated with measures of trait anxiety as it was with a second measure of generalized expectancies for positive outcomes (Fibel & Hale, 1978). This limited discriminant validity relative to neuroticism creates the interpretive ambiguities noted earlier. For example, previously reported correlations between optimism as measured by the LOT and physical symptom reports have been consistently shown to be largely (if not completely) attributable to this shared variance with neuroticism (Mroczek, Spiro, Aldwin, Ozer, & Bosse, 1993; Robbins, Spence, & Clark, 1991; Scheier et al., 1994; Smith et al., 1989). Although subsequent research has demonstrated that many correlations between the LOT and other outcomes (e.g., coping behavior, health practices) cannot be attributed to an overlap with neuroticism (Mroczek et al., 1993; Robbins et al., 1991; Scheier et al., 1994; T. W. Smith, Pope, Rhodewalt, & Poulton, 1989; S. E. Taylor et al., 1992), one important finding that served as an initial demonstration of the scale's utility in studying health (i.e., Scheier & Carver, 1985) does appear consequential to this methodological limitation.

A second approach to the assessment of pessimism is based on the attributional reformulation of the learned helplessness model of depression (Peterson & Seligman, 1987). In that model, the tendency to attribute negative events to internal, stable, and global causes (e.g., low ability) is seen as a contributing cause for depression. In contrast, the tendency to attribute such events to external, unstable, and specific causes is hypothesized to confer some resistance to the development of emotional distress. This attributional style can be assessed through either a structured, self-report inventory or a content coding scheme (Peterson & Seligman, 1987). Both techniques have been found to be reliable, although evidence of their convergent and discriminant validity is limited. Other measures of optimism, pessimism, and closely related constructs (e.g., fatalism, hopelessness) have been employed in studies of health, but they have been used less frequently.

Association With Objective Health Outcomes. As noted previously, correlations between optimism–pessimism and self-reports of illness or even physician visits might reflect the effects of shared variance with N/NA. There have been some studies using more objective indices, however. For example, Scheier et al. (1989) found that optimism was associated with a reduced likelihood of intraoperative myocardial infarction in a small sample of patients undergoing coronary artery bypass surgery. In a recent, larger replication (Scheier et al., 1999), optimism was associated with reduced likelihood of rehospitalization after bypass surgery. Peterson and his colleagues (1988) found that ratings of pessimistic attributional style predicted subsequent physician ratings of physical health in a sample of 99 initially healthy men who were followed for more than 35 years. Importantly, these effects remained significant even when initial ratings of physical and mental health were controlled. Jensen (1987) reported that hopelessness, as measured by the Millon Behavioral Health Inventory (Millon, Green, & Meaher, 1979) was associated with metastasis and earlier death in a sample of 50 women diagnosed with breast cancer. In a study of patients undergoing radiation treatment for cancer, pessimism as measured by the LOT was associated with increased risk of death over an 8-month follow-up. Interestingly, optimism scores were not related to survival (Schulz, Bookwala, Knapp, Scheier, & Williamson, 1996). Similarly, Reed, Kemeny, S. Taylor, Wang, and Visscher (1994) found that in a sample of 74 men diagnosed with AIDS, self-reports of "realistic acceptance" of their prognosis (i.e., pessimism or resignation) predicted significantly shorter survival times during a 4-year follow-up.

One limitation of the studies described here is their reliance on small samples. Other prospective studies have examined the effects of optimism–pessimism in larger samples. Everson and her colleagues (1996) reported that a two-item self-report hopelessness scale predicted increased risk of early mortality, as well as the incidence of myocardial infarction and cancer in a study of more than 2,000 men. Importantly, these effects were significant even in analyses controlling for medical risk factors and self-reported depression. Recently, their measure of hopelessness predicted the progression of atherosclerosis; men with high hopelessness scores showed larger increases in carotid artery disease over a 4-year period, compared with less hopeless subjects (Everson, G. A. Kaplan, Goldberg, R. Salonen, & J. T. Salonen, 1997). Anda and colleagues (1993) found that a single item hopelessness scale significantly predicted fatal and nonfatal CHD in a sample of 2,800 initially healthy men and women. The single item scale was a better predictor of CHD events than items measuring other depressive symptoms. In analyses of an archival sample of 1,100 men and women, Peterson, Seligman, Yurko, Martin, and Friedman (1998) found that ratings of one element of pessimistic attributional style—global attributions for negative events—predicted mortality over a 50-year follow-up. The association was particularly strong for accidental and violent deaths.

These studies suggest that individual differences in optimism versus pessimism might be related to health. However, other studies have failed to find such effects (e.g., Cassileth, Lusk, & D. S. Miller, 1985), and the number of studies with positive results is small when compared with the literature on the TABP, hostility, and N/NA. Further, one recent study found that parental ratings of optimism and cheerfulness were inversely related to longevity in a sample of more than 1,000 children followed for 60 years (H. S. Friedman et al., 1993). Given the small number of independent effects, the inconsistent results, small sample sizes in some cases, and unknown psychometric properties of the scales used in the larger studies, conclusions about the apparent health consequences of this trait should be tentative.

Mechanisms of Association. The mechanisms posited as linking optimism and health have included elements of both the stress moderation and health behavior models (Peterson & Seligman, 1987; Scheier & Carver, 1992). For example, Scheier and Carver (1985, 1992) argued that this generalized expectancy leads individuals to cope with potential stressors in distinct ways. For example, optimists are expected to persist in difficult situations and to rely on adaptive, active, and problem-solving coping strategies, as opposed to the passive and maladaptive strategies employed by pessimists. Research has supported this view, and the results apparently are not simply due to the confounding effects of other personality traits (e.g., Carver et al., 1993; Stanton & Snider, 1993; S. E. Taylor et al., 1992). These coping correlates of optimism accounted—at least in part—for an association between LOT scores and immune functioning (Segerstrom, S. E. Taylor, Kemeny, & Fahey, 1998). Pessimism has also been found to be associated with higher ambulatory blood pressure levels (Raikkonen et al., 1999). However, other psychophysiological mechanisms have not been studied in the context of optimism research.

Pessimistic individuals also appear to engage in unhealthy behaviors, such as noncompliance with medical treatment and less active self-care in response to illness (Lin & Peterson, 1990; Strack, Carver, & Blaney, 1987). The interpersonal impact of individual differences in optimism–pessimism are largely unknown. However, related research on depression (Coyne et al., 1991) would suggest that this central element of the transactional model might be useful in future studies of the potential impact of this trait on health.

Repressive Coping Style

Psychodynamic formulations of defense mechanisms, such as repression, figured prominently in the early psychosomatic theories (Alexander, 1950; Dunbar, 1943). The current period of interest in the health consequences of personality traits includes attention to a closely related construct: repressive coping. Interest in repressive coping dates to work by Weinberger, Schwartz, and Davison (1979). These investigators examined repressive coping as a potential explanation for the low correspondence between self-reports and physiological measures of anxiety and stress. The construct is generally defined as a tendency to avoid attention to and awareness of threatening events and related negative affects (Weinberger, 1990). This individual difference has been described not only as an explanation for desynchrony among channels of emotional response, but also as a risk factor for physical illness.

Assessment. The prevailing assessment procedure in this area involves the classification of subjects on the basis of two self-report instruments, the Taylor Manifest Anxiety Scale (TMAS; J. A. Taylor, 1953) and the Marlowe–Crowne Social Desirability Scale (M–CSDS; Crowne & Marlowe, 1964). Repressive copers are those individuals with low trait anxiety scores but high M–CSDS scores. These individuals are generally contrasted with groups described as low anxious (i.e., low TMAS, low M–CSDS) and high anxious (i.e., high TMAS, low M–CSDS). Some, but not all, studies include the fourth possible combination (i.e., high TMAS, high M–CSDS), described as defensive high anxious. Several studies attest to the validity of this classification system. For example, Weinberger et al. (1979) found that repressive coping was associated with reduced self-reports of state anxiety but heightened physiological reactivity in response to a laboratory stressor. This group also displayed behavioral indications of the expected avoidant cognitive style. Subsequent studies have indicated that repressive coping is associated with the predicted pattern of high autonomic responsiveness but low self-reports of distress (Asendorpf & Scherer, 1983), and restricted recall of emotionally threatening events (P. J. Davis, 1987; R. D. Hansen & C. H. Hansen, 1988).

One recently recognized ambiguity in the assessment of this construct is the multidimensional nature of the M–CSDS. This measure includes one component that is clearly consistent with the conceptual definition of repressive coping—self-deception. However, the scale also includes a second component that apparently reflects the tendency to present oneself in a positive light to others (i.e., impression management; Paulhus, 1984). This raises the question of the target or intent of the repressive coping; are these efforts directed inwardly as a way to manage unpleasant emotional experiences, or are they directed toward the social presentation of emotional adjustment? Some recent evidence suggests that the intrapsychic versus interpersonal nature of this coping style is an important question (Barger, Kircher, & Croyle, 1997; Newton & Contrada, 1992).

The current psychosomatic literature includes a closely related construct—alexithymia (Sifneos, 1973). This personality type involves the inability to recognize or verbalize emotional experience, or to use it constructively. Such individuals are also described as restricted in other aspects of inner experience (e.g., body awareness, day dreaming, etc.). Related conceptualizations suggest that alexithymia might be involved in abnormal illness behavior (i.e., somatization) and psychological influences on actual disease. Thus, in contrast to the efforts to minimize emotional experience described in conceptualizations of repressive coping, alexithymia is seen as a basic deficit in emotional experience and related processes. Despite the availability of reliable and valid assessment devices, alexithymia has not been studied in the type of large, prospective studies that would permit evaluation of its effect on subsequent health (Linden, Wen, & Paulhus, 1995).

Association With Illness. Repressive coping has primarily been studied as a potential risk factor for cancer. Using a follow-up case-control design, Dattore and his colleagues (1980) found that veterans subsequently diagnosed with cancer ($n = 75$) differed from controls ($n = 125$) on the basis of high scores on an MMPI measure of repression and low depression scores. Subjects had completed the psychological assessment at least two years prior to the diagnosis of cancer.

Repressive coping has also been linked to more rapid disease progression among cancer patients. Jensen (1987) found that the repressive style, as assessed by the TMAS/M–CSDS typology, was associated with subsequent metastasis and earlier death in a sample of 52 women previously diagnoses with breast cancer. This effect was significant even when controlling possible confounding medical variables (e.g., disease staging) and the previously described effects of hopelessness. An apparent replication of the effects of repressive coping on cancer incidence was reported in two European samples (Grossarth-Maticek, Siegrist, & Vetter, 1982). However, an unvalidated measure of emotional suppression was employed, and other features of the methods preclude firm conclusions (Scheier & Bridges, 1995). Additional evidence suggests that, consistent with the older psychosomatic view (Alexander, 1950), suppression of anger and aggressive impulses accelerates the development of essential hypertension (Perini, Muller, & Buhler, 1991) and cartoid artery atherosclerosis (Matthews et al., 1998). However, other evidence suggests that high levels of either anger suppression *or* anger expression are associated with increased risk of developing hypertension (Everson et al., 1998). Helmers and her colleagues (1995) found that the combination of high hostility scores on the Cook and Medley (1954) Ho scale and high scores on the M–CSDS were associated with greater levels of ischemia in CAD patients, both in response to laboratory stressors and during ambulatory monitoring. These findings could reflect general consequences of hostility or anger, rather than repressive coping or supression per se.

A related finding involves gay men who conceal their homosexual identity. Although not involving assessment of repressive coping per se, "closeted" HIV seronegative gay men have been found to be at increased risk of developing cancer and serious infectious illness over a 5-year follow-up period (Cole, Kemeny, S. E. Taylor, & Visscher, 1996). Among HIV seropositive gay men, concealment is associated with more rapid progression of the illness (Cole, Kemeny, S. E. Taylor, Visscher, & Fahey, 1996). Thus, concealment of information that could have potentially serious social ramifications posed a threat to health.

Mechanisms of Association. The prevailing view of mechanisms linking repressive coping and subsequent illness is an interactional stress moderational model. Several studies have supported the basic prediction that repressive coping is associated with greater autonomic reactivity during stressful situations (Aspendorpf & Scherer, 1983; Barger et al., 1997; Brown et al., 1996; Newton & Contrada, 1992).

An interesting finding consistent with this view involves the physiological effects of disclosure of previously undisclosed traumatic events. Failure to disclose such events has been linked to subsequent illness (e.g., Pennebaker & Beall, 1986). Further, disclosure through writing or discussion appears to have salubrious effects on several physiological mechanisms (e.g., Pennebaker, Kiecolt-Glaser, & Glaser, 1988; Smyth, 1998).

Jamner, Schwartz, and Leigh (1988) suggested that the autonomic responsivity associated with repressive coping is mediated by enhanced central endogenous opioid activity, consistent with a constitutional predisposition approach. Finally, health behavior mechanisms have also been discussed. For example, avoidant coping strategies might interfere with the appropriate recognition of and response to early symptoms of illness. The resulting delays in receipt of needed care could have deleterious consequences (Jensen, 1987; Weinberger, 1990). To date, the interpersonal impact of the repressive style has not been discussed at length in this literature. If subsequent epidemiological research suggests that this trait indeed contributes to illness, then transactional stress moderation mechanisms (such as the interpersonal correlates of repressive coping) might be explored.

Other Traits

Several other personality characteristics have figured prominently in the recent research in this area. However, the corresponding literatures lack the degree of epidemiological evidence regarding their health relevance that exists for the traits reviewed thus far. Clearly, Kobasa's (1979) description of psychological hardiness was a major impetus in the resurgence of interest in personality and health (Suls & Rittenhouse, 1987). In her framework, individuals characterized by an internal locus of control, a tendency to view major life changes as challenges rather than threats, and a sense of commitment in the major activities of their lives were hypothesized to be more resilient when exposed to stressful life circumstances.

Several studies found predicted associations among self-report measures of hardiness, life stress, and symptom reports (see Funk, 1992, for a review). Further, several studies demonstrated the predicted stress moderation effect on psychophysiological responses to laboratory stressors (Allred & T. W. Smith, 1989; Contrada, 1989; Wiebe, 1991). Other studies found evidence of effects of hardiness on self-reported health that were mediated by health behavior (Wiebe & McCallum, 1986). However, the degree of overlap between measures of hardiness and N/NA raised questions about the extent to which an association between emotional distress and somatic complaints accounted for much of the relevant findings (Funk, 1992; Funk & Houston, 1987), and some evidence has been consistent with this view (e.g., P. G. Williams, Weibe, & T. W. Smith, 1992). Thus, although the conceptual impact of this model on the developing field has been considerable, compelling evidence that hardiness influences actual physical health is scarce.

Power motivation is another trait studied as a potential risk factor (Jemmott, 1987). Defined as the desire to have an impact on others by controlling, influencing, or even helping them (McClleland, 1979), power motivation has been found to be concurrently associated with high blood pressure, and to predict the later development of essential hypertension in a 20-year prospective study of 79 initially healthy young men (McClelland, 1979). This trait, assessed by responses to the Thematic Apperception Test (Jemmott, 1987), has also been linked to reports of illness and immunosuppression (Jemmott et al., 1983; Jemmott et al., 1990; McClelland, Alexander, & Marks, 1982; McClelland, Floor, Davidson, & Saron, 1980; McClelland & Jemmott, 1980).

As previously discussed, individual differences in social dominance have been found to be related to the development of CHD in both human (Houston et al., 1992) and animal research (Manuck et al., 1995). Further, attempts to influence or control others elicit the type of cardiovascular reactivity hypothesized to contribute to CHD (T. W. Smith, Allred, Morrison, & Carlson, 1989; T. W. Smith et al., 1996; T. W. Smith, Nealey, Kircher, & Limon, 1997). Thus, the limited yet provocative research on power motivation might be seen as another indication of the potential usefulness of further study of the vertical axis of the interpersonal circumplex as an influence on health.

Finally, although most of the research related to the health consequences of traits in the current prevailing personality taxonomies has focused on hostility, emotional distress, and to a lesser extent dominance, recent evidence suggests that conscientiousness and openness to experience may be important as well. In an additional analysis of childhood predictors of longevity, H. S. Friedman and his colleagues (1993) reported that conscientiousness, as rated by parents and teachers, was associated with greater longevity. Subsequent research indicated that although conscientiousness is associated with positive health behaviors (Booth-Kewley & Vickers, 1994), the beneficial effects of this trait on longevity could not be accounted for by the mediating effects of health behaviors, including reduced alcohol consumption, nonsmoking status, prudent diet, or avoidance of accidents and violence (H. S. Friedman, Tucker, Reise, 1995). Curiosity—a component of openness to experience—has been found to predict increased survival over a 5-year follow-up of older adults, a result that could not be attributed to other known medical or behavioral risk factors (Swan & Carmelli, 1996).

CONCLUSIONS AND FUTURE DIRECTIONS

As noted at the outset of this chapter, the literature on personality and health contains some areas of cumulative progress but some unresolved problems as well. These concluding sections summarize the emerging findings, outline the limitations, and suggest some directions for maximizing the yield of future studies.

Do Personality Traits Predict Subsequent Illness?

Despite the conclusions of previous critiques of research in this area (e.g., Angel, 1985), there is clear evidence that personality traits do indeed predict objective health outcomes. Quantitative and qualitative reviews have summarized evidence that hostility and the TABP are associated with "hard" signs of CHD (i.e., MI and SCD) and reduced longevity (Adler & Matthews, 1994; T. Q. Miller et. al., 1991, 1996). These effects are statistically small, but given the scope and impact of the health outcomes examined, they are important contributions to an understanding of threats to public health. The results of several large, prospective studies examining objective health outcomes suggest that this relation does not reflect the effects of personality traits on simple illness behavior, and it does not reflect the effects of illness on personality.

The literature on the health effects of neuroticism or negative affectivity is more complex than it was even a few years ago. Although chronic negative emotions, such as anxiety and depression, are clearly associated with illness behavior in the absence of disease (Stone & Costa, 1990; Watson & Pennebaker, 1989), recent evidence suggests a more substantial role as well. Considered either as an individual difference within the range of normal variation, or as a diagnosable emotional disorder, chronic negative affect has been found to predict objective health outcomes in initially healthy samples and among patients with established disease. This area of research might benefit from an updated quantitative review to examine the level of inconsistency and possible causes among the independent studies available. The tentative review suggests that this trait is a potentially important influence on health. However, there are negative results from large, well-controlled prospective studies. Further, the circumstances under which N/NA contributes to illness behavior as opposed to actual illness remain to be identified (C. Smith, Wallston, & Dwyer, 1995).

The evidence that pessimism influences health is intriguing and suggestive, but is somewhat more limited than is the case for hostility or negative affectivity. The clarification of methodological issues in previous research on this trait should pave the way for more definitive studies, and the accumulating evidence suggests that such studies would be worthwhile. Finally, despite its central place in the personality and health literature, the evidence that repressive coping contributes to illness is limited to a small number of studies, and some of them used personality measures of undocumented validity. Repressive coping with anger (i.e., anger suppression or "anger-in") may be unhealthy, but this might reflect more general consequences of trait anger. Thus, conclusions about the effect of repressive coping on health will require several additional, methodologically sophisticated studies.

Although there is clear evidence of a reliable association between some personality traits and illness, several interpretive ambiguities remain even in the areas with consistent results. The degree of information about the personality trait(s) actually assessed by the measures used in this research varies considerably. As a result, it is sometimes unclear as to the specific psychological characteristic(s) involved in the effect. Second, given the correlational nature of even the prospective designs, the possibility that biologic, psychologic, or socioeconomic third variables account for the observed covariation between personality traits and disease must be acknowledged. Finally, even if it is assumed that the observed associations indicate causal effects of personality traits on health, the mechanisms through which these influences might operate are only tentatively identified (Krantz & Hedges, 1987). Importantly, animal models permit more direct evaluation of some of the central causal hypotheses and specified mechanisms, and the results of that work support the models already outlined (e.g., J. R. Kaplan et al., 1994; Manuck et al., 1995).

Is There a Disease Prone Personality?

An influential review of the personality and health literature suggested that individuals characterized by chronic negative affect displayed a disease prone personality (H. S. Friedman & Booth-Kewley, 1987). Although the basis of that conclusion was criticized appropriately on methodological grounds (Matthews, 1988; Stone & Costa, 1990), the subsequent research has indicated that the conclusion might have merit.

However, the evidence regarding the unhealthy effects of chronic hostility, anger, and disagreeable behavior is more compelling. Therefore, the earlier description of a disease prone personality underemphasized an important personality trait—agreeableness versus antagonism in the five-factor model, or friendliness versus hostility in the interpersonal variation of this taxonomy. Neuroticism and antagonism are independent traits, but obviously co-occur such that people with high levels of both characteristics are described not only as distressed, cold, and hostile, but selfish and intolerant as well (Saucier, 1992). Thus, this combination of chronic distress and disagreeable social behavior might constitute a disease prone personality.

Are There Other Personality Risk Factors?

The five-factor model and the interpersonal variation of this taxonomy suggest that the current research on personality risk factors might be expanded. The provocative findings in which conscientiousness and openness to experience predicted longevity (H. S. Friedman et al., 1993; Swan & Carmelli, 1996) were discussed earlier. These dimensions should be pursued in additional research. Similarly, some evidence from epidemiological studies suggests that social dominance might be a second facet of the TABP that confers risk of CHD and measure mortality (Houston et al., 1992, 1997), and this finding has an important parallel in nonhuman primate research on psychosocial influences on CAD (Manuck et al., 1995). Thus, the vertical axis of the interpersonal circumplex should also be examined in future research.

There are two dimensions that do not fall clearly within the current personality taxonomies that might be useful in future studies. The first dimension, discussed from several perspectives, involves social and emotional competence. The concept of *social intelligence* (Cantor & Kihlstrom, 1987) lies at the intersection of personality and traditional definitions of intelligence. This construct refers to the "declarative and procedural knowledge that individuals bring to bear in interpreting events and making plans in everyday life situations" (Cantor & Kihlstrom, 1987, p. 3). Consistent with the cognitive-social approach to personality described earlier (Cantor, 1990; Mischel & Shoda, 1995), this model emphasizes the processes underlying individuals' construal of situations, the goals they pursue, and the flexibility and effectiveness of the strategies they employ in those pursuits. Further, individuals vary in their social "expertise" in specific contexts, such as vocational achievement or personal relationships. *Emotional intelligence* (Mayer & Salovey, 1995) is a somewhat more circumscribed construct, referring to competence in identifying and regulating emotions in oneself and others. Another closely related concept with greater similarity to traditional descriptions and assessments of personality traits is *ego-resiliency* (Block & Kremen, 1996; Klohnen, 1996).

Although broad individual differences in social and emotional competence are difficult to describe and measure, it is apparent that persons differ in the extent to which they have the skills or competence to succeed in important life tasks. A further implication is that many life tasks will be particularly difficult for individuals with less expertise, with the likely result of increased stress. Consistent with the general view of the psychophysiology of stress as a link between personality traits and illness, limitations in social intelligence or competence could confer vulnerability to disease. Thus, the study of personality traits as risk factors might be expanded to include increased attention to skill and adaptive competencies, especially in emotional and social domains (Ewart, 1991; 1994).

The second health relevant dimension that falls outside traditional taxonomies is *social support*. Social support is clearly associated with reduced risk of physical illness and increased longevity (Adler & Matthews, 1994; Berkman, 1995; S. Cohen, Doyle, Skoner, Rabin, & Gwaltney, 1997; Hazuda, 1994; Orth-Gomer, 1994). Further, low support is associated with the pathophysiological mechanisms believed to link psychosocial processes to illness (Uchino et al., 1996). Although the traditional view of this construct is that it represents characteristics of the social environment (S. Cohen & Wills, 1985), recent evidence suggests that social support might be more accurately conceptualized as a characteristic of the person. For example, social support is closely related to other stable personality characteristics including shyness, neuroticism, anxiety, and depression (e.g., B. Sarason, Shearin, Pierce, & I. G. Sarason, 1987; I. G. Sarason, Levine, Basham, & B. Sarason, 1983). Further, perceptions of social support appear to be stable over time (Newcomb, 1990; I. G. Sarason, B. Sarason, & Shearin, 1986), and to remain consistent across settings (Lakey & Lewis, 1994). Finally, perceptions of social support seem to be heritable to some extent, with genetic factors accounting for as much as half or more of variance in support perceptions (Kendler, 1997; Plomin, Reiss, Heatherington, & Howe, 1994). Thus, rather than conceptualizing and studying social support as something distinct from the personality traits identified as risk factors, a person-focused alternative view of social support might be useful (Pierce, Lakey, I. G. Sarason, B. Sarason, & Joseph, 1997). Better still, models and methodological strategies that integrate social and personality characteristics hold particular promise.

It may be that low social support and limitations in social intelligence or competence can be described, at least in part, through combinations of traits in the current personality taxonomies (e.g., low agreeableness, high neuroticism). However, related research and theory suggest that these processes probably cannot be simply reduced to those variables. As a result, a somewhat broader view of the array of health relevant individual differences could add to the understanding of the ways in which personality can influence health.

Can We Make Better Use of Personality Psychology?

The discussion thus far illustrates how consideration of current personality taxonomies such as the five-factor model can provide much needed conceptual organization to this area of research. These taxonomies also point to some traits that might have been neglected in the area. Further, the related assessment devices and the psychometric tradition in which they are embedded can facilitate the evaluation and refinement of key measures of traits studied as predictors (Costa & McCrae, 1987a; H. S. Friedman et al., 1995; Marshall et al., 1994; T. W. Smith & P. G. Williams, 1992).

The second major emphasis in current personality psychology—the cognitive-social and interpersonal perspectives—also could make a major contribution to the study of personality traits as risk factors. As discussed earlier, these perspectives can be useful in identifying the mechanisms underlying the broad elements in trait taxonomies (e.g., Graziano, Jensen-Campbell, & Hair, 1996), as well as the psychological processes through which traits influence pathophysiology. Further, the constructs identified in these models (e.g., appraisal, coping strategies, social competencies, etc.) can be easily incorporated in the design of interventions.

However, perhaps a more far-reaching implication of the cognitive-social and interpersonal conceptualizations of personality is the blurring of the commonly held distinction between risk factors considered characteristics of the person (e.g., hostility) and those that are traditionally considered characteristics of the social environment (e.g., social support). The reciprocal relation between persons and social circumstances is a fundamental assumption of these models (Wagner et al., 1995), as is the assumption that these reciprocal patterns are evident over periods of many years (e.g., Caspi et al., 1989) and in specific, time-limited interactions (T. W. Smith, 1995). These assumptions pose a challenge to conceptualize risk without simple distinctions between personality and the social environment.

From this dynamic interactional perspective, risk is conferred not through specific personality traits, but through recurring transactions between persons and social environments (Revenson, 1990; T. W. Smith, 1995), such as the model of how hostility influences health presented in Fig. 9.7. In this elaboration of the previously discussed transactional model, hostile persons recurrently construct social circumstances that are both unhealthy (i.e., low in support and high in strain), and that maintain their own hostile interactional style. Hostility can be accurately described through the traits in personality taxonomies (i.e., low agreeableness and high neuroticism), but the "active ingredients" through which hostile persons create such an environment consist of the cognitive and behavioral processes identified in cognitive-social models of personality. Clearly, the description of the risk process linking hostility and health is incomplete without attention to the social context of hostility. In addition, the understanding of low support and high social strain as risk factors would be incomplete without attention to the ways in which individuals create and maintain those circumstances.

The interpersonal perspective in personality and clinical psychology may be of particular use in this reconceptualization of psychosocial risk. The interpersonal circumplex (see Fig. 9.1) provides a common conceptual and measurement framework for describing personality characteristics, social stimuli, and interactional behaviors (Benjamin, 1994; Kiesler, 1991; Wiggins, 1991). For example, both the personality trait of hostility and the environmen-

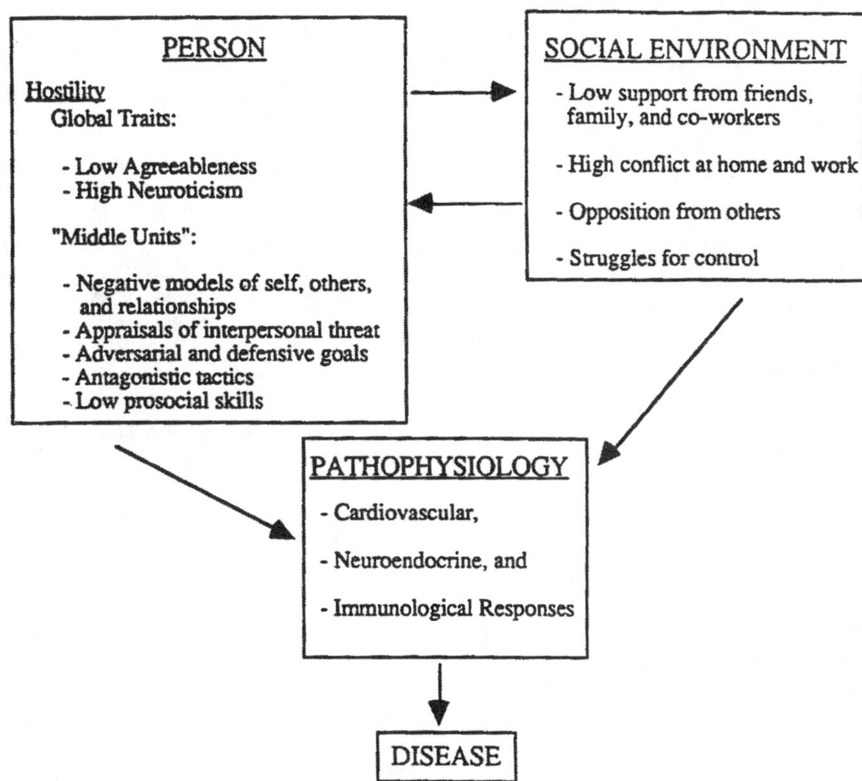

FIG. 9.7 The transactional model of the effects of hostility and the social environment on illness.

tal variable of social support can be located along the horizontal axis of the circumplex. Further, this perspective provides detailed models and assessments of the transactional processes linking persons and social contexts (Benjamin, 1994; Kiesler, 1996; Wagner et al., 1995).

Although the conceptual and perhaps treatment implications of the transactional view are clear, the implications of this model for epidemiological research are less obvious. Evidence from large prospective studies of personality and subsequent health is a critical component of research in this area. Simply put, nobody would pursue research on the traits without evidence that they predict objective health outcomes. Yet, typical analytic strategies in psychosocial epidemiology do not accommodate this reciprocal view of personality and social risk factors. Current practice in epidemiological studies of psychosocial risk factors reflects the traditional strategy of evaluating independent predictive utility, such as determining if smoking and blood pressure have statistically independent effects on CHD. Given that the causal processes through which psychosocial factors influence health may involve substantive relations among psychosocial characteristics, the practice of forcing statistical independence on naturally confounded variables seems likely to provide an inaccurate assessment of risk. That is, the traditional approach of examining statistically independent risk factors removes personality traits from essential elements of the surrounding social context (Revenson, 1990). Yet, in the transactional view, it is precisely this dynamic interaction of traits with contextual factors that influence the pathophysiology of disease.

An alternative analytic strategy would classify individuals in terms of naturally occurring patterns of personality and environmental characteristics, thereby providing a closer correspondence between specific statistical hypotheses and the transactional conceptual hypotheses about risk (Gallo & T. W. Smith, 1999). That is, multiple features of the hypothesized recurring cycles of personality—social environment transaction could be assessed and used to identify high and low risk groups (Wagner et al., 1995). For example, the global personality traits or even middle units of personality listed in Fig. 9.7 could be assessed along with the social environmental characteristics to which they are reciprocally related. Cluster analytic techniques could then be used to describe specific patterns of personality and social risk (Gallo & T. W. Smith, 1999), and included as predictors of subsequent health in prospective studies. Such naturally occurring groupings might reflect common adaptive and maladaptive interactional styles.

Are There Applications of Personality–Health Research?

The potential health benefits of modifying personality traits identified as risk factors are illustrated by the results of the

RCPP described earlier (M. Friedman et al., 1984; Powell & Thoresen, 1988). Enduring personality characteristics can be modified, and at least in that instance seemed to have had important consequences for subsequent health. Anger and hostility are amenable to treatment (Deffenbacher, 1994), as are other negative affects such as anxiety and depression (Chambless & Gillis, 1993; Hollon, Shelton, & Davis, 1993). Further, preliminary studies suggest such treatments may have positive effects on health (Gidron, Davidson, & Bata, 1999). Given the status of the related literatures, larger controlled trials examining the health benefits of interventions addressing these characteristics are justified, especially in high risk populations such as postinfarction patients.

The personality and health literature also has implications for primary prevention efforts. If traits such as (low) agreeableness and high neuroticism contribute to illness, then development of social and emotional adjustment and competencies should reduce risk. Attempts to prevent emotional disorders, antisocial behavior, and substance abuse in children and adolescents often focus on traits and processes that are similar to those discussed in models of the personality characteristics that confer risk of physical illness (Blechman, 1996; Blechman, Prinz, & Dumas, 1995; Caplan et al., 1992; Greenberg, Kusche, Cook, & Quamma, 1995; Tolan, Guerra, & Kendall, 1995). These prevention programs attempt to foster emotional self-regulation and social interaction competencies through educational methods. These interventions generally produce improved emotional adjustment, peer relations, and conflict resolution skills.

Although targeted toward mental health, this primary prevention technology may have beneficial effects on physical health as well. Thus, a final conclusion from the current research on personality traits as risk factors for physical illness is that the existing literature on primary prevention in the domain of social and emotional health may have valuable implications for the prevention of physical illness. Efforts to maximize the emotional and social adjustment of children and adolescents may contribute to their later physical health as adults.

REFERENCES

Adler, N., & Matthews, K. (1994). Health psychology: Why do some people get sick and some stay well? *Annual Review of Psychology, 45,* 229–259.

Ahern, D. K., Gorkin, L., Anderson, J. L., Tierney, C., Hallstrom, A., Ewart, C., Capone, R. J., Schron, E., Kornfeld, D., Herd, J. A., Richardson, D. W., & Follick, M. J. (1990). Biobehavioral variables and mortality or cardiac arrest in the Cardiac Arrythmia Pilot Study (CAPS). *American Journal of Cardiology, 66,* 59–62.

Alexander, F. (1950). *Psychosomatic medicine.* New York: Norton.

Allport, G. W. (1937). *Personality: A psychological interpretation.* New York: Holt.

Allred, K. D., & Smith, T. W. (1989). The hardy personality: Cognitive and physiological responses to evaluative treatments. *Journal of Personality and Social Psychology, 56,* 257–266.

Allred, K. D., & Smith, T. W. (1991). Social cognition in cynical hostility. *Cognitive Therapy and Research, 15,* 399–412.

Almada, S. J., Zonderman, A. B., & Shekelle, R. B. (1991). Neuroticism and cynicism and risk of death in middle-aged men: The Western Electric study. *Psychosomatic Medicine, 53,* 165–175.

Anda, R., Williamson, D., Jones, D., Macera, C., Eaker, E., Glassman, A., & Marks, J. (1993). Depressed affect, hopelessness, and the risk of ischemic heart disease in a cohort of U. S. adults. *Epidemiology, 4,* 285–294.

Anderson, N. B. (1989). Racial differences in stress-induced cardiovascular reactivity and hypertension: Current status and substantive issues. *Psychological Bulletin, 105,* 89–105.

Anderson, N. B., & Armstead, C. A. (1995). Toward understanding the association of socioeconomic status and health: A new challenge for the biopsychosocial approach. *Psychosomatic Medicine, 57,* 213–225.

Angel, M. (1985). Disease as a reflection of the psyche. *New England Journal of Medicine, 312,* 1570–1572.

Asendorpf, J. B., & Scherer, K. R. (1983). The discrepant repressor: Differentiation between low anxiety, high anxiety, and repression of anxiety by autonomic-facial-verbal patterns of behavior. *Journal of Personality and Social Psychology, 45,* 1334–1336.

Asendorpf, J. B., & Wilpers, S. (1998). Personality effects on social relationships. *Journal of Personality and Social Psychology, 74,* 1531–1544.

Averill, J. R. (1982). *Anger and aggression: An essay on emotion.* New York: Springer-Verlag.

Ax, A. R. (1953). The physiological differentiation between fear and anger in humans. *Psychosomatic Medicine, 15,* 433–442.

Bandura, A. (1973). *Aggression: A social learning analysis.* Englewood Cliffs, NJ: Prentice-Hall.

Bandura, A. (1977). *Social learning theory.* Englewood Cliffs, NJ: Prentice-Hall.

Bandura, A. (1978). The self-system in reciprocal determinism. *American Psychologist, 33,* 344–358.

Bandura, A. (1989). Human agency in social cognitive theory. *American Psychologist, 44,* 1175–1184.

Barefoot, J. C., Beckham, J., Peterson, B., Haney, T., & Williams, R. B. (1992). Measures of neuroticism and disease status in coronary angiography patients. *Journal of Consulting and Clinical Psychology, 60,* 127–132.

Barefoot, J. C., Dahlstrom, W. G., & Williams, R. B. (1983). Hostility, CHD incidence, and total mortality: A 25-year follow-up study of 255 physicians. *Psychosomatic Medicine, 45,* 59–63.

Barefoot, J. C., Dodge, K. A., Peterson, B. L., Dahlstrom, W. G., & Williams, R. B., Jr. (1989). The Cook–Medley hostility scale: Item content and ability to predict survival. *Psychosomatic Medicine, 51,* 46–57.

Barefoot, J. C., Helms, M. S., Mark, D. B., Blumenthal, J. A., Califf, R. M., Haney, T. L., O'Connor, C. M., Siegler, I. C., & Williams, R. B. (1996). Depression and long term mortality risk in patients with coronary artery disease. *American Journal of Cardiology, 78,* 613–617.

Barefoot, J. C., & Lipkus, I. M. (1994). The assessment of anger and hostility. In A. W. Siegman & T. W. Smith (Eds.), *Anger, hostility, and the heart* (pp. 43–66). Hillsdale, NJ: Lawrence Erlbaum Associates.

Barefoot, J. C., Patterson, J. C., Haney, T. L., Cayton, T., Hickman, J., & Williams, R. B., Jr. (1994). Hostility in asymptomatic men with angiographically confirmed coronary artery disease. *American Journal of Cardiology, 74,* 439–442.

Barefoot, J. C., Peterson, B. L., Harrell, F. E., Hlatky, M. A., Pryor, D. B., Haney, T. L., Blumenthal, J. A., Siegler, I. C., & Williams, R. B., Jr. (1989). Type A behavior and survival: A follow-up study of 1,467 patients with coronary artery disease. *American Journal of Cardiology, 64,* 427–431.

Barefoot, J.C., & Schroll, M. (1996). Symptoms of depression, acute myocardial infarction, and total mortality in a community sample. *Circulation, 93,* 1976–1980.

Barefoot, J. C., Siegler, I. C., Nowlin, J. B., Peterson, B. L., Haney, T. L., & Williams, R. B., Jr. (1987). Suspiciousness, health, and mortality: A follow-up study of 500 older adults. *Psychosomatic Medicine, 49,* 450–457.

Barger, S. D., Kircher, J. C., & Croyle, R. T. (1997). The effects of social context and deception on the physiological responses of repressive copers. *Journal of Personality and Social Psychology, 73,* 1118–1128.

Barnett, P. A., Spence, J. D., Manuck, S. B., & Jennings, J. R. (1997). Psychological stress and the progression of carotid artery disease. *Journal of Hypertension, 15,* 49–55.

Baron, R. M., & Kenney, D. A. (1986). The moderator-mediator variable distinction in social psychological research: Conceptual, strategic, and statistical considerations. *Journal of Personality and Social Psychology, 51,* 1173–1182.

Bass, C., & Wade, C. (1984). Chest pain with normal coronary arteries: A comparative study of psychiatric and social morbidity. *Psychological Medicine, 14,* 51–61.

Benjamin, L. S. (1994). SASB: A bridge between personality theory and clinical psychology. *Psychological Inquiry, 5,* 273–316.

Benotsch, E. G., Christensen, A. J., & McKelvey, L. (1997). Hostility, social support and ambulatory cardiovascular activity. *Journal of Behavioral Medicine, 20,* 163–176.

Berkman, L. F. (1995). The role of social relations in health promotion. *Psychosomatic Medicine, 57,* 245–254.

Blair, S. H., Kohl, H. W., Paffenbarger, R. S., Clark, M. S., Cooper, K. H., & Gibbons, L. W. (1989). Physical fitness and all-cause mortality: A prospective study of healthy men and women. *Journal of the American Medical Association, 262,* 2395–2401.

Blechman, E. A. (1996). Coping, competence, and aggression prevention: Part 2. Universal school-based prevention. *Applied and Preventive Psychology, 5,* 19–36.

Blechman, E. A., Prinz, R. J., & Dumas, J. E. (1995). Coping, competence, and aggression prevention: Part 1. Developmental model. *Applied & Preventative Psychology, 4,* 211–232.

Block, J. (1995). A contrarian view of the five-factor approach to personality description. *Psychological Bulletin, 117,* 182–215.

Block, J., & Kremen, A. M. (1996). IQ and ego-resiliency: Conceptual and empirical connections and separateness. *Journal of Personality and Social Psychology, 70,* 349–361.

Blumenthal, J. A., Fredrikson, M., Kuhn, C. M., Ulmer, R. A. Walsh-Riddle, S., & Appelbaum, M. (1990). Aerobic exercise reduces levels of cardiovascular and sympathoadrenal responses to mental stress in subjects without prior evidence of myocardial ischemia. *American Journal of Cardiology, 65,* 93–98.

Bolger, N. (1990). Coping as a personality process: A prospective study. *Journal of Personality and Social Psychology, 59,* 525–537.

Bolger, N., & Schilling, E. A. (1991). Personality and the problems of everyday life: The role of neuroticism in exposure and reactivity to daily stressors. *Journal of Personality, 59,* 355–386.

Bolger, N., & Zuckerman, A. (1995). A framework for studying personality in the stress process. *Journal of Personality and Social Psychology, 69,* 890–902.

Booth-Kewley, S., & Vickers, R. R. (1994). Associations between major domains of personality and health behavior. *Journal of Personality, 62,* 281–298.

Bouchard, T. J., Jr., Lylkken, D. T., McGue, M., Segal, B. L., & Tellegen, A. (1990). Sources of human psychological differences: The Minnesota study of twins reared apart. *Science, 250,* 223–228.

Briggs, S. R. (1992). Assessing the five-factor model of personality description. *Journal of Personality, 60,* 253–293.

Brown, L. L., Tomarken, A. J., Orth, D. N., Loosen, P. T., Kalin, N. H., & Davidson, R. J. (1996). Individual differences in repressive-defensiveness predict basal salivary cortisol levels. *Journal of Personality and Social Psychology, 70,* 362–371.

Burack, J. H., Barrett, D. C., & Stall, R. D. (1993). Depressive symptoms and CD4 lymphocyte decline among HIV-infected men. *Journal of the American Medical Association, 270,* 2568–2573.

Burg, M. M., Jain, D., Soufer, R., Kerns, R. D., & Zaret, B. L. (1993). Role of behavioral and psychological factors in mental stress-induced silent left ventricular dysfunction in coronary artery disease. *Journal of the American College of Cardiology, 22,* 440–448.

Buss, D. M. (1987). Selection, evocation, and manipulation. *Journal of Personality and Social Psychology, 53,* 1214–1221.

Cannon, W. B. (1939). *The wisdom of the body* (2nd ed.). New York: Norton.

Cantor, N. (1990). From thought to behavior: "Having" and "doing" in the study of personality and cognition. *American Psychologist, 45,* 735–750.

Cantor, N., & Kihlstrom, J. F. (1987). *Personality and social intelligence.* Englewood Cliffs, NJ: Prentice-Hall.

Caplan, M., Weissberg, R. P., Grober, J. S., Sivo, P. J., Grady, K., & Jacoby, C. (1992). Social competence promotion with inner-city and suburban young adolescents: Effects on social adjustment and alcohol use. *Journal of Consulting and Clinical Psychology, 60,* 56–63.

Carney, R. M., Freedland, K., Rich, M., & Jaffe, A. S. (1995). Depression as a risk factor for cardiac events in established coronary heart disease: A review of possible mechanisms. *Annals of Behavioral Medicine, 17,* 142–149.

Carney, R. M., Rich, M. W., & Freedland, K. E. (1988). Major depressive disorder predicts cardiac events in patients with coronary artery disease. *Psychosomatic Medicine, 50,* 627–633.

Carson, R. C. (1969). *Interaction concepts in personality.* Chicago: Aldine.

Carver, C. S. (1989). How should multifaceted personality constructs be tested? Issues illustrated by self-monitoring, attributional style, and hardiness. *Journal of Personality and Social Psychology, 56,* 577–585.

Carver, C. S., Pozo, C., Harris, S. D., Noriega, V., Scheier, M. F., Robinson, D. S., Ketcham, A. S., Moffat, F. L., & Clark, K. C. (1993). How coping mediates the effects of optimism on distress: A study of women with early stage breast cancer. *Journal of Personality and Social Psychology, 65,* 375–391.

Caspi, A., Bem, D. J., & Elder, G. H. (1989). Continuities and consequences of interactional styles across the life course. *Journal of Personality, 57,* 375–406.

Cassileth, B. R., Lusk, E. J., & Miller, D. S. (1985). Psychosocial correlates of survival in advanced malignant disease. *New England Journal of Medicine, 312,* 1551–1555.

Chambless, D. L., & Gillis, M. M. (1993). Cognitive therapy of anxiety disorders. *Journal of Consulting and Clinical Psychology, 61,* 248–260.

Christensen, A. J., Edwards, D. L., Wiebe, J. S., Benotsch, E. G., & McKelvey, L. (1996). Effect of verbal self-disclosure on NK cell activity: Moderating influence of cynical hostility. *Psychosomatic Medicine, 58,* 150–155.

Christensen, A. J., & Smith, T. W. (1993). Cynical hostility and cardiovascular response during self-disclosure. *Psychosomatic Medicine, 55,* 193–202.

Cioffi, D. (1991). Beyond attentional strategies: A cognitive-perceptual model of somatic interpretation. *Psychological Bulletin, 109,* 25–41.

Clark, L. A. (1989). The anxiety and depressive disorders: Descriptive psychopathology and differential diagnosis. In P. C. Kendall & D. Watson (Eds.), *Anxiety and depression: Districtive and overlapping features* (pp. 83–130). New York: Academic.

Clark, L. A., Watson, D., & Mineka, S. (1994). Temperament, personality, and the mood and anxiety disorders. *Journal of Abnormal Psychology, 103,* 103–116.

Coccaro, E. F., Kavoussi, R. J., Cooper, T. B., & Hauger, R. L. (1997). Central serotonin activity and aggression. *American Journal of Psychiatry, 154,* 1430–1435.

Cohen, F. (1979). Personality, stress, and the development of physical illness. In G. C. Stone, F. Cohen, & N. E. Adler (Eds.), *Health psychology: A handbook* (pp. 77–111). San Francisco: Jossey-Bass.

Cohen, J. (1990). Things I have learned (so far). *American Psychologist, 45,* 1304–1312.

Cohen, S., Doyle, W. J., Skoner, D. P., Fireman, P., Gwaltney, J. M., & Newsom, J. T. (1995). State and trait negative affect as predictors of objective and subjective symptoms of respiratory viral infections. *Journal of Personality and Social Psychology, 68,* 159–169.

Cohen, S., Doyle, W. J., Skoner, D. P., Rabin, B. S., Gwaltney, J. M. (1997). Social ties and susceptibility to the common cold. *New England Journal of Medicine, 277,* 1940–1944.

Cohen, S., & Herbert, T. (1996). Health psychology: Psychological factors and disease from the perspective of human psychoneuro-immunology. *Annual Review of Psychology, 47,* 113–142.

Cohen, S., Kaplan, J. R., & Manuck, S. B. (1994). Social support and coronary heart disease: Underlying psychological and biological mechanisms. In S. A. Schumaker & S. M. Czajkowski (Eds.), *Social support and cardiovascular disease* (pp. 195–222). New York: Plenum.

Cohen, S., & Rodriguez, M. (1995). Pathways linking affective disturbances and physical disorders. *Health Psychology, 14,* 374–380.

Cohen, S., Tyrell, D., & Smith, A. (1991). Psychological stress and susceptibility to the common cold. *New England Journal of Medicine, 325,* 606–612.

Cohen, S., & Williamson, G. (1991). Stress and infectious disease in humans. *Psychological Bulletin, 109,* 5–24.

Cohen, S., & Wills, T. A. (1985). Stress, social support, and the buffering hypothesis. *Psychological Bulletin, 98,* 310–357.

Cole, S. W., Kemeny, M. E., Taylor, S. E., & Visscher, B. R. (1996). Elevated physical health risk among gay men who conceal their homosexual identity. *Health Psychology, 15,* 243–251.

Cole, S. W., Kemeny, M. E., Taylor, S. E., Visscher, B. R., & Fahey, J. (1996). Accelerated course of human immunodeficiency virus infection in gay men who conceal their homosexual identity. *Psychosomatic Medicine, 58,* 219–231.

Contrada, R. J. (1989). Type A behavior, hardiness, and cardiovascular response to stress. *Journal of Personality and Social Psychology, 57,* 895–903.

Contrada, R. J. (1994). Personality and anger in cardiovascular disease: Toward a psychological model. In A. W. Siegman & T. W. Smith (Eds.), *Anger, hostility, and the heart* (pp. 149–172). Hillsdale, NJ: Lawrence Erlbaum Associates.

Contrada, R. J., & Jussim, L. (1992). What does the Cook and Medley hostility scale measure? In search of an adequate measurement model. *Journal of Applied Social Psychology, 22,* 615–627.

Contrada, R. J., Leventhal, H., & O'Leary, A. (1990). Personality and health. In L.A. Pervin (Ed.), *Handbook of personality: Theory and research* (pp. 638–669). New York: Guilford.

Cook, T. D., & Campbell, D. T. (1979). *Quasi-experimentation: Design and analysis issues for field settings.* Chicago: Rand McNally.

Cook, W., & Medley, D. (1954). Proposed hostility and pharisaic virtue scales for the MMPI. *Journal of Applied Psychology, 38,* 414–418.

Cooper, T., Detre, T., & Weiss, S. M. (1981). Coronary-prone behavior and coronary heart disease: A critical review. *Circulation, 63,* 1199–1215.

Costa, P. T., Jr., & McCrae, R. R. (1985). *The NEO Personality Inventory Manual.* Odessa, FL: Psychological Assessment Resources.

Costa, P. T., Jr., & McCrae, R. R. (1987a). Neuroticism, somatic complaints, and disease: Is the bark worse than the bite? *Journal of Personality, 55,* 299–316.

Costa, P. T., Jr., & McCrae, R. R. (1987b). Personality assessment in psychosomatic medicine. In T. M. Wise (Ed.), *Advances in psychosomatic medicine* (pp. 71–82). Basel, Switzerland: Karger.

Costa, P. T., McCrae, R. R., & Dembroski, T. M. (1989). Agreeableness versus antagonism: Explication of a potential risk factor for CHD. In A. W. Siegman & T. M. Dembroski (Eds.), *In search of coronary-prone behavior: Beyond Type A* (pp. 41–63). Hillsdale, NJ: Lawrence Erlbaum Associates.

Costa, P. T., Zonderman, A., McCrae, R. R., & Williams, R. B., Jr. (1986). Cynicism and paranoid alienation in the Cook and Medley hostility scale. *Psychosomatic Medicine, 48,* 283–285.

Coyne, J. C. (1994). Self-reported distress: Analog or ersatz depression? *Psychological Bulletin, 116,* 29–45.

Coyne, J. C., Burchill, S., & Stiles, W. (1991). An interactive perspective on depression. In C. R. Snyder & D. R. Forsyth (Eds.), *Handbook of social and clinical psychology* (pp. 327–349). New York: Guilford.

Crick, N. R., & Dodge, K. A. (1994). A review and reformulation of social information-processing mechanisms in children's social adjustment. *Psychological Bulletin, 115,* 74–101.

Crowne, D., & Marlowe, D. (1964). *The approval motive: Studies in evaluative dependence.* New York: Wiley.

Daley, S. E., Hammen, C., Burge, D., Davila, J., Paley, B., Linberg, N., & Herzberg, D. S. (1997). Predictors of the generation of episodic stress: A longitudinal study of late adolescent women. *Journal of Abnormal Psychology, 106,* 251–259.

Dattore, P. J., Shontz, F. C., & Coyne, L. (1980). Premorbid personality differentiation of cancer and noncancer groups: A test of the hypothesis of cancer proneness. *Journal of Consulting and Clinical Psychology, 48,* 388–394.

Davies, P. T., & Cummings, E. M. (1994). Marital conflict and child adjustment: An emotional security hypothesis. *Psychological Bulletin, 116,* 387–411.

Davila, J., Bradbury, T. N., Cohan, C. L., & Tochluk, S. (1997). Marital functions and depressive symptoms: Evidence for a stress generation model. *Journal of Personality and Social Psychology, 73,* 849–861.

Davis, M. D., & Matthews, K. A. (1990). Cigarette smoking and oral contraceptive use influence women's lipid, lipoprotein, and cardiovascular responses during stress. *Health Psychology, 9,* 717–736.

Davis, P. J. (1987). Repression and the inaccessibility of affective memories. *Journal of Personality and Social Psychology, 53,* 585–593.

Deffenbacher, J. L. (1994). Anger reduction: Issues, assessment, and intervention strategies. In A. W. Siegman & T. W. Smith (Eds.), *Anger, hostility, and the heart* (pp. 239–270). Hillsdale, NJ: Lawrence Erlbaum Associates.

Dembroski, T. M., MacDougall, J. M., Costa, P. T., Jr., & Grandits, G. A. (1989). Components of hostility as predictors of sudden death and myocardial infarction in the Multiple Risk Factor Intervention Trial. *Psychosomatic Medicine, 51,* 514–522.

Dembroski, T. M., MacDougall, J. M., Williams, R. B., Haney, T. L., & Blumenthal, J. A. (1985). Components of Type A, hostility and anger-in: Relationship to angiographic findings. *Psychosomatic Medicine, 47,* 219–233.

Denollet, J., Sys, S., & Brutsaert, D. L. (1995). Personality and mortality after myocardial infarction. *Psychosomatic Medicine, 57,* 582–591.

Digman, J. M. (1990). Personality structure: Emergence of the five-factor model. *Annual Review of Psychology, 41,* 417–440.

Dunbar, H. F. (1943). *Psychosomatic diagnosis.* New York: Hoeber.

Eaker, E. D., Pinsky, J., & Castelli, W. P. (1992). Myocardial infarction and coronary death among women: Psychosocial predictors from a 20-year follow-up of women in the Framingham study. *American Journal of Epidemiology, 135,* 854–864.

Elias, M. F., Robbins, M. A., Blow, F. C., Rice, A. P., & Edgecomb, J. L. (1982). Symptom reporting, anxiety pain patients. *Experimental Aging Research, 8,* 45–51.

Everson, S. A., Goldberg, D. E., Kaplan, G. A., Cohen, R. D., Pukkala, E., Tuomilehto, J., & Salonen, J. T. (1996). Hopelessness and risk of mortality and incidence of myocardial infarction and cancer. *Psychosomatic Medicine, 58,* 113–121.

Everson, S. A., Kaplan, G. A., Goldberg, D. E., Julkunen, J., & Salonen, J. T. (1998). Anger expression and incident hypertension. *Psychosomatic Medicine, 60,* 730–735.

Everson, S. A., Kaplan, G. A., Goldberg, D. E., Salonen, R., & Salonen, J. T. (1997). Hopelessness and 4-year progression of carotid atherosclerosis. *Arteriosclerosis, Thrombosis, and Vascular Biology, 17,* 1490–1495.

Everson, S. A., Kauhanen, J., Kaplan, G., Goldberg, D., Julkunen, J., Tuomilehto, J., Salonen, J. T. (1997). Hostility and increased risk of mortality and myocardial infarction: The mediating role of behavioral risk factors. *American Journal of Epidemiology, 146,* 142–152.

Ewart, C. K. (1991). Familial transmission of essential hypertension: Genes, environments, and chronic anger. *Annals of Behavioral Medicine, 13*(1), 40–47.

Ewart, C. K. (1994). Nonshared environments and heart disease risk: Concepts and data for a model of coronary-prone behavior. In E. Hetherington, D. Reiss, & Y. R. Plomin (Eds.), *The separate social worlds of siblings* (pp. 175–204). Hillsdale, NJ: Lawrence Erlbaum Associates.

Fibel, B., & Hale, W. D. (1978). The Generalized Expectancy for Success Scale—a new measure. *Journal of Consulting and Clinical Psychology, 46,* 924–931.

Fincham, F. D., Beach, S. R., Harold, G. T., & Osborne, L. N. (1997). Marital satisfaction and depression: Different causal relationships for men and women? *Psychological Science, 8,* 351–357.

Follick, M. J., Gorkin, L., Capone, R. J., Smith, T. W., Ahern, D. K., Stablein, D., Niaura, R., & Visco, J. (1988). Psychological distress as a predictor of ventricular arrhythmias in a post-myocardial infarction population. *American Heart Journal, 116,* 32–36.

Ford, D. E., Mead, L. A., Chang, P. P., Cooper-Patrick, L., Wang, N., & Klag, M. J. (1998). Depression is a risk factor for coronary artery disease in men. *Archives of Internal Medicine, 158,* 1422–1426.

Frasure-Smith, N., Lesperance, F., & Taljic, M. (1993). Depression following myocardial infarction. *Journal of the American Medical Association, 270,* 1819–1825.

Frasure-Smith, N., Lesperance, F., & Talajic, M. (1995a). Depression and 18–month prognosis after myocardial infarction. *Circulation, 91,* 999–1005.

Frasure-Smith, N., Lesperance, F., & Taljic, M. (1995b). The impact of negative emotions on prognosis following myocardial infarction: Is it more than depression? *Health Psychology, 14,* 388–398.

Friedman, H. S., & Booth-Kewley, S. (1987). The "disease-prone personality": A meta-analytic view of the construct. *American Psychologist, 42,* 539–555.

Friedman, H. S., Tucker, J. S., Schwartz, J. E., Martin, L. R., Tomlinson-Keasey, C., Wingard, D. L., & Criqui, M. H. (1995). Childhood conscientiousness and longevity: Health behaviors and cause of death. *Journal of Personality and Social Psychology, 68,* 696–703.

Friedman, H. S., Tucker, J. S., & Reise, S. P. (1995). Personality dimensions and measures potentially relevant to health: A focus on hostility. *Annals of Behavioral Medicine, 17,* 245–251.

Friedman, H. S., Tucker, J. S., Schwartz, J. E., Tomlinson-Keasey, C., Martin, L. R., Wingard, D. L., & Criqui, M. H. (1995). Psychosocial and behavioral predictors of longevity: The aging and death of the "Termites." *American Psychologist, 50,* 69–78.

Friedman, H. S., Tucker, J. S., Tomlinson-Keasey, C., Schwartz, J. E., Wingard, D. L., & Criqui, M. H. (1993). Does childhood personality predict longevity? *Journal of Personality and Social Psychology, 65,* 176–185.

Friedman, M., & Rosenman, R. H. (1959). Association of a specific overt behavior pattern with increases in blood cholesterol, blood clotting time, incidence of arcus senilis and clinical coronary artery disease. *Journal of the American Medical Association, 169,* 1286–1296.

Friedman, M., Thoresen, C. E., Gill, J. J., Powell, L. H., Ulmer, D., Thompson, L., Price, V. A., Rakin, D., Breall, W., Dixon, T., Levy, R., & Bourg, E. (1984). Alteration of Type A behavior and reduction in cardiac recurrences in post-myocardial infarction patients. *American Heart Journal, 108,* 237–248.

Freud, S. (1933). *A new series of introductory lectures on psychoanalysis.* New York: Norton.

Funder, D. C., & Colvin, C. R. (1991). Explorations in behavioral consistency: Properties of persons, situations, and behaviors. *Journal of Personality and Social Psychology, 60,* 773–794.

Funk, S. (1992). Hardiness: A review of theory and research. *Health Psychology, 11,* 335–345.

Funk, S., & Houston, B. K. (1987). A critical analysis of the Hardiness Scale's validity and utility. *Journal of Personality and Social Psychology, 53,* 572–578.

Gabbay, F. H., Krantz, D. S., Kop, W., Hedges, S., Klein, J., Gottdiener, J., & Rozanski, A. (1996). Triggers of myocardial ischemia during daily life in patients with coronary artery disease: Physical and mental activities, anger, and smoking. *Journal of the American College of Cardiology, 27,* 585–592.

Gallo, L. C., & Smith, T. W. (1998). Construct validation of health-relevant personality traits: Interpersonal circumplex and five-factor model analyses of the Aggression Questionnaire. *International Journal of Behavioral Medicine, 5,* 129–147.

Gallo, L. C., & Smith, T. W. (1999). Patterns of hostility and social support: Conceptualizing psychosocial risk as a characteristic of the person *and* the environment. *Journal of Research in Personality, 33,* 281–310.

Gidron, Y., Davidson, K., & Bata, I. (1999). The short-term effects of a hostility–reduction intervention on male coronary heart disease patients. *Health Psychology, 18,* 416–420.

Glass, D. C. (1977). *Behavior patterns, stress, and coronary disease.* Hillsdale, NJ: Lawrence Erlbaum Associates.

Goodman, M., Quigley, J., Moran, G., Meilman, H., & Sherman, M. (1996). Hostility predicts resentosis after percutaneous transluminal coronary angioplasty. *Mayo Clinic Proceedings, 71,* 729–734.

Gotlib, J. H., & Cane, D. G. (1989). Self-report assessment of depression and anxiety. In P. C. Kendall & D. Watson (Eds.), *Anxi-*

ety and depression: Distinctive and overlapping features (pp. 131–170). New York: Academic Press.

Graziano, W. G., Jensen-Campbell, L. A., & Hair, E. C. (1996). Perceiving interpersonal conflict and reacting to it: The case for agreeableness. *Journal of Personality and Social Psychology, 70,* 820–835.

Greenberg, M. T., Kusche, C. A., Cook, E. T., & Quamma, J. P. (1995). Promoting emotional competence in school-aged children: The effects of the PATHS curriculum. *Development and Psychopathology, 7,* 117–136.

Grossarth-Maticek, R., Siegrist, J., & Vetter, H. (1982). Interpersonal repression as a predictor of cancer. *Social Science and Medicine, 16,* 493–498.

Gullette, E., Blumenthal, J., & Babyak, M. (1997). Mental stress triggers myocardial ischemia during daily life. *Journal of the American Medical Association, 277,* 1521–1526.

Guyll, M., & Contrada, R. J. (1998). Trait hostility and ambulatory cardiovascular activity: Responses to social interaction. *Health Psychology, 17,* 30–39.

Haines, A. P., Imeson, J. D., & Meade, T. W. (1987). Phobic anxiety and ischaemic heart disease. *British Medical Journal, 295,* 297–299.

Hall, M., Baum, A., Buysse, D. J., Prigerson, H. G., Kupfer, D. J., & Reynolds, C. F. (1998). Sleep as a mediator of the stress-immune relationship. *Psychosomatic Medicine, 60,* 48–61.

Hammen, C. (1991). Generation of stress in the course of unipolar depression. *Journal of Abnormal Psychology, 100,* 55–561.

Haney, T. L., Maynard, K. E., Houseworth, S. J., Scherwitz, L. W., Williams, R. B., & Barefoot, J. C. (1996). Interpersonal hostility assessment technique: Description and validation against the criterion of coronary artery disease. *Journal of Personality Assessment, 66,* 386–401.

Hansen, R. D., & Hansen, C. H. (1988). Repression of emotionally tagged memories: The architecture of less complex emotions. *Journal of Personality and Social Psychology, 55,* 811–818.

Harbin, T. J. (1989). The relationship between Type A behavior pattern and physiological responsivity: A quantitative review. *Psychophysiology, 26,* 110–119.

Hardy, J. D., & Smith T. W. (1988). Cynical hostility and vulnerability to disease: Social support, life stress, and physiological response to conflict. *Health Psychology, 7,* 447–459.

Haynes, S. G., Feinleib, M., & Kannel, W. B. (1980). The relationship of psychosocial factors to coronary heart disease in the Framingham Study: III. Eight-year incidence of coronary heart disease. *American Journal of Epidemiology, 111,* 37–58.

Hazuda, H. P. (1994). A critical evaluation of U.S. epidemiological evidence and ethnic variation. In S. A. Schumaker & S. M. Czajkowski (Eds.), *Social support and cardiovascular disease* (pp. 119–144). New York: Plenum.

Hearn, M. D., Murray, D. M., & Leupker, R. V. (1989). Hostility coronary heart disease, and total mortality: A 33-year follow-up study of university students. *Journal of Behavioral Medicine, 12,* 105–121.

Hecker, M.H.L., Chesney, M. A., Black, G. W., & Frautchi, N. (1988). Coronary-prone behaviors in the Western Collaborative Group Study. *Psychosomatic Medicine, 50,* 153–164.

Helmers, K. F., Krantz, D. S., Howell, R., Klein, J., Bairey, N., & Rozanski, A. (1993). Hostility and myocardial ischemia in coronary artery disease patients: Evaluation by gender and ischemic index. *Psychosomatic Medicine, 50,* 29–36.

Helmers, K. F., Krantz, D. S., Mertz, C., Klein, J., Kop, W., Gottdiener, J., & Rozanski, A. (1995). Defensive hostility: Relationship to multiple markers of cardiac ischemia in patients with coronary disease. *Health Psychology, 14,* 202–209.

Henry, W. P. (1994). Differentiating normal and abnormal personality: An interpersonal approach based on the structural analysis of social behavior. In S. Strack & M. Lorr (Eds.), *Differentiating normal and abnormal personality* (pp. 316–340). New York: Springer.

Henry, W. P. (1996). The structural analysis of social behavior as a common metric for programmatic psychopathology and psychotherapy research. *Journal of Consulting and Clinical Psychology, 64,* 1263–1275.

Herbert, T. B., & Cohen, S. (1993). Depression and immunity: A meta-analytic review. *Psychological Bulletin, 113,* 472–486.

Herrmann, C., Brano-Driehorst, S., Kaminsky, B., Leibring, E., Staats, H., & Ruger, U. (1998). Diagnostic groups and depressed mood as predictors of 22–month mortality in medical inpatients. *Psychosomatic Medicine, 60,* 570–577.

Hirschfeld, R., Klerman, G., Lavori, P., Keller, M., Griffith, P., & Coryell, W. (1989). Premorbid personality assessments of first onset of major depression. *Archives of General Psychiatry, 46,* 345–350.

Hoehn-Saric, R., & McCleod, D. R. (1988). The peripheral sympathetic nervous system: Role in normal and pathophysiologic anxiety. *Psychiatric Clinics of North America, 11,* 375–386.

Hollon, S. D., Shelton, R. C., & Davis, D. D. (1993). Cognitive therapy for depression: Conceptual issues and clinical efficacy. *Journal of Consulting and Clinical Psychology, 61,* 270–275.

Holroyd, K. A., & Coyne, J. (1987). Personality and health in the 1980s: Psychosomatic medicine revisited? *Journal of Personality, 55,* 360–375.

Horowitz, M. J., Berfari, R., Hulley, S., Blair, S., Alvarez, W., Borhani, N., Reynolds, A., & Simon, N. (1979). Life events, risk factors, and coronary disease. *Psychosomatics, 20,* 586–592.

Houston, B. K. (1988). Cardiovascular and neuroendocrine reactivity, global Type A, and components of Type A behavior. In B. K. Houston & C. R. Snyder (Eds.), *Type A behavior pattern: Research, theory, and intervention* (pp. 212–253). New York: Wiley.

Houston, B. K. (1989). Personality dimensions in reactivity and cardiovascular disease. In N. Schneiderman, S. M. Weiss, & P. G. Kaufman (Eds.), *Handbook of research methods in cardiovascular behavioral medicine* (pp. 495–509). New York: Plenum.

Houston, B. K. (1992). Personality characteristics, reactivity, and cardiovascular disease. In J. R. Turner, A. Sherwood, & K. C. Light (Eds.), *Individual differences in cardiovascular response to stress* (pp. 103–124). New York: Plenum.

Houston, B. K. (1994). Anger, hostility, and psychophysiological reactivity. In A. W. Siegman & T. W. Smith (Eds.), *Anger, hostility, and the heart* (pp. 97–115). Hillsdale, NJ: Lawrence Erlbaum Associates.

Houston, B. K., Babyak, M. A., Chesney, M. A., Black, G., & Ragland, D. R. (1997). Social dominance and 22-year all-cause mortality in men. *Psychosomatic Medicine, 59,* 5–12.

Houston, B. K., Chesney, M. A., Black, G. W., Cates, D. S., & Hecker, M. L. (1992). Behavioral clusters and coronary heart disease risk. *Psychosomatic Medicine, 54,* 447–461.

Houston, B. K., & Kelly, K. E. (1989). Hostility in employed women: Relation to work and marital experiences, social support, stress, and anger expression. *Personality and Social Psychology Bulletin, 15,* 175–182.

Houston, B. K., & Vavak, C. R. (1991). Cynical hostility: Developmental factors, psychosocial correlates, and health behaviors. *Health Psychology, 10,* 9–17.

Ickes, W., Snyder, M., & Garcia, S. (1997). Personality influence on the choice of situations. In R. Hogan, J. Johnson, & S. Briggs (Eds.), *Handbook of personality psychology* (pp. 165–195). San Diego: Academic Press.

Idler, E. L., Kasl, S. V., & Lemke, J. H. (1990). Self-evaluated health and mortality among the elderly in New Haven, Connecticut and Iowa and Washington Counties, Iowa, 1982–1986. *American Journal of Epidemiology, 131,* 91–103.

Ironson, G., Taylor, C. B., Boltwood, M., Bartzokis, T., Dennis, C., Chesney, M., Spitzer, S., & Segall, G. M. (1992). Effects of anger on left ventricle ejection fraction in coronary artery disease. *American Journal of Cardiology, 70,* 281–285.

Jamner, L. D., Schwartz, G. E., & Leigh, H. (1988). The relationship between repressive and defensive coping styles and monocyte, eosinophile, and serum glucose levels: Support for the opiod peptide hypothesis of repression. *Psychosomatic Medicine, 50,* 567–575.

Jamner, L. D., Shapiro, D., Goldstein, I. B., & Hug, R. (1991). Ambulatory blood pressure and heart rate in paramedics: Effects of cynical hostility and defensiveness. *Psychosomatic Medicine, 53,* 393–406.

Jemmott, J. B., III. (1987). Social motives and susceptibility to disease: Stalking individual differences in health risks. *Journal of Personality, 55,* 267–298.

Jemmott, J. B., III, Borysenko, J., Borysenko, M., McClelland, D., Chapman, R., Meyer, D., & Benson, H. (1983). Academic stress, power motivation, and decrease in salivary secretory immunoglobulin A secretion rate. *Lancet, 1,* 1400–1402.

Jemmott, J. B., III, Hellman, L., McClelland, D. C., Locke, S. E., Kraus, L., Williams, R. M., & Valeri, C. R. (1990). Motivational syndromes associated with natural killer cell activity. *Journal of Behavioral Medicine, 13,* 53–73.

Jenkins, C. D., Rosenman, R. H., & Zyzanski, S. J. (1974). Prediction of clinical coronary heart disease by a test for the coronary-prone behavior pattern. *New England Journal of Medicine, 23,* 1271–1275.

Jensen, M. R. (1987). Psychobiological factors predicting the course of breast cancer. *Journal of Personality, 55,* 317–342.

John, O. P. (1990). The "Big Five" factor taxonomy: Dimensions of personality in the natural language and in questionnaires. In L. Pervin (Eds.), *Handbook of personality: Theory and research* (pp. 66–100). New York: Guilford.

Johnson, S. L., & Jacob, T. (1997). Marital interactions of depressed men and women. *Journal of Consulting and Clinical Psychology, 65,* 15–23.

Jonas, B. S., Franks, P., Ingram, D. D. (1997). Are symptoms of anxiety and depression risk factors for hypertension? *Archives of Family Medicine, 6,* 43–49.

Kamarck, T. W., & Jennings, J. R. (1991). Biobehavioral factors in sudden cardiac death. *Psychological Bulletin, 109,* 42–75.

Kaplan, G. A., & Camacho, T. (1983). Perceived health and mortality: A nine-year follow-up of the Human Population Laboratory cohort. *American Journal of Epidemiology, 117,* 292–304.

Kaplan, G. A., & Kotler, P. L. (1985). Self-reports predictive of mortality from ischemic heart disease: A nine-year follow-up of the Human Population Laboratory cohort. *Journal of Chronic Diseases, 38,* 195–201.

Kaplan, G. A., & Reynolds, P. (1988). Depression and cancer mortality and morbidity: Prospective evidence from the Alameda County study. *Journal of Behavioral Medicine, 11,* 1–13.

Kaplan, J. R., Botchin, M. B., & Manuck, S. B. (1994). Animal models of aggression and cardiovascular disease. In A. W. Siegman & T. W. Smith (Eds.), *Anger, hostility, and the heart* (pp. 127–148). Hillsdale, NJ: Lawrence Erlbaum Associates.

Kaplan, J. R., & Manuck, S. B. (1998). Monkeys, aggression, and the pathobiology of atherosclerosis. *Aggressive Behavior, 24,* 323–334.

Kawachi, I., Colditz, G. A., Ascherio, A., Rimm, E. B., Giovannucci, E., Stampfer, M. J., & Willett, W. C. (1994). Prospective study of phobic anxiety and risk of coronary heart disease in men. *Circulation, 89,* 1992–1997.

Kawachi, I., Sparrow, D., Vokonas, P. S., & Weiss, S. T. (1994). Symptoms of anxiety and risk of coronary heart disease: The normative aging study. *Circulation, 90,* 2225–2229.

Kelly, G. (1955). *The psychology of personal constructs.* New York: Norton.

Kendall, P. C., & Ingram, R. E. (1989). Cognitive-behavioral perspectives: Theory and research on depression and anxiety. In P. C. Kendall & D. Watson (Eds.), *Anxiety and depression: Distinctive and overlapping features* (pp. 27–54). New York: Academic Press.

Kendler, K. S. (1997). Social support: A genetic-epidemiologic analysis. *American Journal of Psychiatry, 154,* 1398–1404.

Kendrick, D. T., & Funder, D. C. (1988). Profiting from controversy: Lessons from the personality-situation debate. *American Psychologist, 43,* 23–34.

Kernis, M. H., Grannemann, B. D., & Barclay, L. C. (1989). Stability and level of self-esteem as predictors of anger arousal and hostility. *Journal of Personality and Social Psychology, 56,* 1013–1022.

Kiecolt-Glaser, J. K., & Glaser, R. (1995). Psychoneuroimmunology and health consequences: Data and shared mechanisms. *Psychosomatic Medicine, 57,* 269–274.

Kiesler, D. J. (1983). The 1982 interpersonal circle: A taxonomy for complementarity in human transactions. *Psychological Review, 90,* 185–214.

Kiesler, D. J. (1991). Interpersonal methods of assessment and diagnosis. In C. R. Snyder & D. R. Forsyth (Eds.), *Handbook of social and clinical psychology: The health perspective* (pp. 438–468). Elmsford, NY: Pergamon.

Kiesler, D. J. (1996). *Contemporary interpersonal theory and research: Personality, psychopathology, and psychotherapy.* New York: Wiley.

Klohnen, E. C. (1996). Conceptual analysis and measurement of the construct of ego-resiliency. *Journal of Personality and Social Psychology, 70,* 1067–1079.

Kobasa, S. C. (1979). Stressful life events, personality and health: An inquiry into hardiness. *Journal of Personality and Social Psychology, 37,* 1–11.

Krantz, D. S., & Durel, L. A. (1983). Psychobiological substrates of the Type A behavior pattern. *Health Psychology, 2,* 393–411.

Krantz, D. S., & Glass, D. C. (1984). Personality, behavior patterns, and physical illness: Conceptual and methodological issues. In W. D. Gentry (Ed.), *Handbook of behavioral medicine* (pp. 38–86). New York: Guilford.

Krantz, D. S., & Hedges, S. M. (1987). Some cautions for research on personality and health. *Journal of Personality, 55,* 351–357.

Kubzansky, L. D., Kawachi, I., Spiro, A., Weiss, S. T., Vokonas, P. S., & Sparrow, D. (1997). Is worrying bad for your heart? A prospective study of worry and coronary heart disease in the Normative Aging Study. *Circulation, 95,* 818–824.

Lakey, B., & Lewis, D. (1994). Antecedents of perceived support: Is perceived family environment generalized to new social relationships? *Cognitive Therapy and Research, 18,* 39–53.

Langlie, J. K. (1977). Social networks, health beliefs, and preventive health behavior. *Journal of Health and Social Behavior, 18,* 244–260.

Lantinga, L. J., Spafkin, R. P., & McCroskery, J. H. (1988). One year psychosocial follow-up of patients with chest pain and angiographically normal coronary arteries. *American Journal of Cardiology, 62,* 209–213.

Lau, R. R. (1988). Beliefs about control and health behavior. In D. S. Gochman (Ed.), *Health behavior: Emerging research perspectives* (pp. 43–63). New York: Plenum.

Lazarus, R. S. (1990). Stress, coping, and illness. In H. S. Friedman (Ed.), *Personality and disease* (pp. 97–120). New York: Wiley.

Lazarus, R. S. (1991). *Emotion and adaptation.* New York: Oxford University Press.

Lazarus, R. S., & Folkman, S. (1984). *Stress, appraisal, and coping.* New York: Springer.

Leary, T. (1957). *Interpersonal diagnosis of personality.* New York: Ronald.

Leiker, M., & Hailey, B. J. (1988). A link between hostility and disease: Poor health habits? *Behavioral Medicine, 3,* 129–133.

Leon, G. R., Finn, S. E., Murray, D., & Bailey, J. M. (1988). The inability to predict cardiovascular disease from hostility scores or MMPI items related to Type A behavior. *Journal of Consulting and Clinical Psychology, 56,* 597–600.

Lemerise, E. A., & Dodge, K. A.(1993). The development of anger and hostile interactions. In M. Lewis & J. M. Haviland (Eds.), *Handbook of emotions* (pp. 537–546). New York: Guilford.

Lepore, S. J. (1995). Cynicism, social support, and cardiovascular reactivity. *Health Psychology, 14,* 210–216.

Leventhal, H., Prohaska, T. R., & Hirshman, R. S. (1985). Preventive health behavior across the life span. In J. C. Rosen & L. J. Solomon (Eds.), *Prevention in Health Psychology, 8,* 199–235.

Lin, E. H., & Peterson, C. (1990). Pessimistic explanatory style and response to illness. *Behavior Research and Therapy, 28,* 243–248.

Linden, W., Chambers, L., Maurice, J., & Lenz, J. W. (1993). Sex differences in social support, self-deception, hostility, and ambulatory cardiovascular activity. *Health Psychology, 12,* 376–380.

Linden, W., Wen, F., & Paulhus, D. L. (1995). Measuring alexithymia, reliability, validity, and prevalence. In P. McRenolds, J. C. Rosen, & G. L. Chelune (Eds.), *Advances in personality assessment* (Vol. 10, pp. 51–95). New York: Plenum.

Lyketsos, C. G., Hoover, D. R., & Guccione, M. (1993). Depressive symptoms as predictors of medical outcomes in HIV infection. *Journal of the American Medical Association, 270,* 2563–2567.

Lyons-Ruth, K. (1996). Attachment relationships among children with aggressive behavior problems: The role of disorganized early attachment patterns. *Journal of Consulting and Clinical Psychology, 64,* 64–73.

MacDougall, J. M., Musante, L., Castillo, S., & Acevedo, M. C. (1988). Smoking, caffeine, and stress: Effects on blood pressure and heart rate in male and female college students. *Health Psychology, 7,* 461–478.

Maddox, G. L., & Douglas, E. B. (1973). Self-assessment and health: A longitudinal study of elderly subjects. *Journal of Health and Social Behavior, 14,* 87–93.

Manuck, S. B. (1994). Cardiovascular reactivity in cardiovascular disease: "Once more unto the breach." *International Journal of Behavioral Medicine, 1,* 4–31.

Manuck, S. B., Marsland, A. L., Kaplan, J. R., & Williams, J. K. (1995). The pathogenicity of behavior and its neuroendocrine mediation: An example from coronary artery disease. *Psychosomatic Medicine, 57,* 275–283.

Markovitz, J. H., Matthews, K. A., & Kannel, W. B. (1993). Psychological predictors of hypertension in Framingham Study: Is there tension in hypertension? *Journal of the American Medical Association, 270,* 2439–2443.

Markovitz, J. H., Matthews, K. A., Wing, R. R., Kuller, L. H., & Meilahn, E. N. (1991). Psychological, biological, and health behavior predictors of blood pressure change in middle-aged women. *Journal of Hypertension, 9,* 399–406.

Markovitz, J. H., Raczynski, J. M., Wallace, D., Chettur, V., & Chesney, M. (1998). Cardiovascular reactivity to video game predicts subsequent blood pressure increases in young men: The CARDIA Study. *Psychosomatic Medicine, 60,* 186–191.

Marshall, G. N., Wortman, C. B., Kusulas, J. W., Hervig, L. K., & Vickers, R. R., Jr. (1992). Distinguishing optimism from pessimism: Relations to fundamental dimensions of mood and personality. *Journal of Personality and Social Psychology, 62,* 1067–1074.

Marshall, G. N., Wortman, C. B., Vickers, R. R., Kusulas, J. W., & Hervig, L. K. (1994). The five-factor model of personality as a framework for personality–health research. *Journal of Personality and Social Psychology, 67,* 278–286.

Martin, L. R., Friedman, H. S., Tucker, J. S., Schwartz, J. E., Criqui, M. H., Wingard, D. L., & Tomlinson-Keasey, C. (1995). An archival prospective study of mental health and longevity. *Health Psychology, 14,* 381–387.

Matthews, K. A. (1988). CHD and Type A behaviors: Update on an alternative to the Booth–Kewley and Friedman quantitative review. *Psychological Bulletin, 104,* 373–380.

Matthews, K. A., Glass, D. C., Rosenman, R. H., & Bortner, R. W. (1977). Competitive drive, Pattern A, and coronary disease: A further analysis of some data from the Western Collaborative Group Study. *Journal of Personality and Social Psychology, 42,* 303–313.

Matthews, K. A., Owens, J. F., Kuller, L. H., Sutton-Tyrrell, K., & Jansen-McWilliams, L. (1998). Are hostility and anxiety associated with cartoid atherosclerosis in healthy post-menopausal women? *Psychosomatic Medicine, 60,* 633–638.

Matthews, K. A., Rosenman, R. H., Dembroski, T. M., Harris, E. L., & MacDougall, J. M. (1984). Familial resemblance in the components of the Type A behavior pattern: A reanalysis of the California Type A Twin Study. *Psychosomatic Medicine, 46,* 512–522.

Matthews, K. A., Woodall, K. L., Kenyon, K., & Jacob, T. (1996). Negative family environment as a predictor of boys' future status on measures of hostile attitudes, interview behavior, and anger expression. *Health Psychology, 15,* 30–37.

Mayer, J. D., & Salovey, P. (1995). Emotional intelligence and the construction and regulation of feelings. *Applied & Preventative Psychology, 4,* 197–208.

McAdams, D. P. (1995). What do we know when we know a person? *Journal of Personality, 63,* 365–396.

McClelland, D. C. (1979). Inhibited power motivation and high blood pressure in men. *Journal of Abnormal Psychology, 88,* 182–190.

McClelland, D. C., Alexander, C., & Marks, E. (1982). The need for power, stress, immune function, and illness among male prisoners. *Journal of Abnormal Psychology, 91,* 61–70.

McClelland, D. C., Floor, E., Davidson, R. J., & Saron, C. (1980). Stressed power motivation, sympathetic activation, immune function, and illness. *Journal of Human Stress, 6*(4), 6–15.

McClelland, D. C., & Jemmott, J. B. (1980). Power motivation, stress, and physical illness. *Journal of Human Stress, 6*(4), 6–15.

McCrae, R. R., & Costa, P. T. (1990). *Personality in adulthood.* New York: Guilford.

McCrae, R. R., Costa, P. T., Jr., & Bosse, R. (1978). Anxiety, extraversion, and smoking. *British Journal of Social and Clinical Psychology, 17,* 269–273.

McCrae, R. R., & John, O. P. (1992). An introduction to the Five-Factor Model and its applications. *Journal of Personality, 60,* 175–216.

McGonigle, M. M., Smith, T. W., Benjamin, L. S., & Turner, C. W. (1993). Hostility and nonshared family environment: A study of monozygotic twins. *Journal of Research in Personality, 27,* 23–34.

McMahon, C. E. (1976). The role of imagination in the disease process: Pre-Cartesian medical history. *Psychological Medicine, 6,* 179–184.

Mechanic, D. (1979). The stability of health and illness behavior: Results from a 16-year follow-up. *American Journal of Public Health, 69,* 1142–1145.

Miller, P. A., & Eisenberg, N. (1988). The relation of empathy to aggressive and externalizing/antisocial behavior. *Psychological Bulletin, 103,* 324–344.

Miller, S. B., Friese, M., Dolgoy, L., Sita, A., Lavoie, K., & Campbell, T. (1998). Hostility, sodium consumption, and cardiovascular response to interpersonal stress. *Psychosomatic Medicine, 60,* 71–77.

Miller, T. Q., Turner, C. W., Tindale, R. S., Posavac, E. J., & Dugoni, B. L. (1991). Reasons for the trend toward null findings in research on Type A behavior. *Psychological Bulletin, 110,* 469–485.

Miller, T. Q., Marksides, K. S., Chiriboga, D. A., & Ray, L. A. (1995). A test of the psychosocial vulnerability and health behavior models of hostility: Results from an 11-year follow-up study of Mexican Americans. *Psychosomatic Medicine, 57,* 572–581.

Miller, T. Q., Smith, T. W., Turner, C. W., Guijarro, M. L., & Hallet, A. J. (1996). A meta-analytic review of research on hostility and physical health. *Psychological Bulletin, 119,* 322–348.

Millon, T., Green, C. J., & Meaher, R. B. (1979). The MBHI: A new inventory for the psychodiagnostician in medical settings. *Professional Psychology, 10,* 529–539.

Mischel, W. (1973). Toward a cognitive social learning reconceptualization of personality. *Psychological Review, 80,* 252–283.

Mischel, W., & Shoda, Y. (1995). A cognitive-affective system theory of personality: Reconceptualizing situations, dispositions, dynamic, and invariance in personality structure. *Psychological Review, 102,* 246–268.

Mischel, W., & Shoda, Y. (1998). Reconciling processing dynamics and personality dispositions. *Annual Review of Psychology, 49,* 229–258.

Mittleman, M. A., Maclure, M., Sherwood, J. B., Mulry, R. P., Tofler, G. H., Jacobs, S. C., Friedman, R., Benson, H., & Muller, J. E. (1995). Triggering of acute myocardial infarction onset by episodes of anger. *Circulation, 92,* 1720–1725.

Moser, D. K., & Dracup, K. (1996). Is anxiety early after myocardial infarction associated with subsequent ischemic and arrhythmic events? *Psychosomatic Medicine, 58,* 395–401.

Moskowitz, D. S. (1990). Convergence of self-reports and independent observers: Dominance and friendliness. *Journal of Personality and Social Psychology, 59,* 1096–1106.

Mroczek, D. K., Spiro, A., Aldwin, C. M., Ozer, D. J., & Bosse, R. (1993). Construct validation of optimism and pessimism in older men: Findings from the normative aging study. *Health Psychology, 12,* 406–409.

Newcomb, M. D. (1990). Social support and personal characteristics: A developmental and interactional perspective. *Journal of Social and Clinical Psychology, 9,* 54–68.

Newton, T. L., & Contrada, R. J. (1992). Repressive coping and verbal autonomic response dissociation: The influence of social context. *Journal of Personality and Social Psychology, 62,* 159–167.

Newton, T. L., & Kiecolt-Glaser, J. K. (1995). Hostility and erosion of marital quality during early marriage. *Journal of Behavioral Medicine, 18,* 601–619.

Norris, F. H. (1997). Frequency and structure of precautionary behavior in the domains of hazard preparedness, crime prevention, vehicular safety, and health maintenance. *Health Psychology, 16,* 566–575.

Ockene, I. S., Shay, M. J., Alpert, J. S., Weiner, B. H., & Dalen, J. E. (1980). Unexplained chest pains in patients with normal coronary arteriograms: A follow-up study of functional status. *New England Journal of Medicine, 303,* 1249–1252.

Oglevie, D. M., & Rose, K. M. (1995). Self-with-other representations and a taxonomy of motives: Two approaches to studying persons. *Journal of Personality, 63,* 643–680.

O'Leary, A. (1990). Stress, emotion, and human immune function. *Psychological Bulletin, 108,* 363–382.

Orth-Gomer, K. (1994). International epidemiological evidence for a relationship between social support and cardiovascular disease. In S. A. Shumaker & S. M. Czajkowski (Eds.), *Social support and cardiovascular disease* (pp. 97–118). New York: Plenum.

Osler, W. (1892). The Lumelin Lectures on angina pectoris. *Lancet, 1,* 839–844.

Ostfeld, A. M., Lebovits, B. Z., Shekelle, R. B., & Paul, O. (1964). A prospective study of the relationship between personality and coronary heart disease. *Journal of Chronic Diseases, 17,* 265–276.

Paffenbarger, R. S., & Hale, W. E. (1975). Work activity and coronary heart mortality. *New England Journal of Medicine, 292,* 545–550.

Patterson, G. R. (1985). A microsocial analysis of anger and irritable behavior. In M. A. Chesney & R. H. Rosenman (Eds.), *Anger and hostility in cardiovascular and behavioral disorders* (pp. 83–102). New York: Hemisphere.

Paulhus, D. L. (1984). Two component models of socially desirable responding. *Journal of Personality and Social Psychology, 46,* 598–609.

Pennebaker, J. W. (1982). *The psychology of physical symptoms.* New York: Springer-Verlag.

Pennebaker, J. W., & Beall, S. K. (1986). Confronting a traumatic event: Toward an understanding of inhibition and disease. *Journal of Abnormal Psychology, 95,* 274–281.

Pennebaker, J. W., Kiecolt-Glaser, J., & Glaser, R. (1988). Disclosure of traumas and immune function: Health implications for psychotherapy. *Journal of Consulting and Clinical Psychology, 56,* 239–245.

Perini, C., Muller, F. B., & Buhler, F. R. (1991). Suppressed aggression accelerates early development of essential hypertension. *Journal of Hypertension, 9,* 399–406.

Perry, S., Fishman, B., & Jacobsberg, L. (1992). Relationships over 1 year between lymphocyte subsets and psychosocial variables among adults with infection by human immunodeficiency virus. *Archives of General Psychiatry, 49,* 396–401.

Peterson, C., & Seligman, M. (1987). Explanatory style and illness. *Journal of Personality, 55,* 237–265.

Peterson, C., Seligman, M., & Vaillant, G. E. (1988). Pessimistic explanatory style is a risk factor for physical illness: A thirty-five-year longitudinal study. *Journal of Personality and Social Psychology, 55,* 23–27.

Peterson, C., Seligman, M., Yurko, K., Martin, L. R., & Friedman, H. (1998). Catastrophizing and untimely death. *Psychological Science, 9,* 127–130.

Pierce, G. R., Lakey, B., Sarason, I. G., Sarason, B. R., & Joseph, H. (1997). Personality and social support processes: A conceptual overview. In G. R. Pierce, B. Lakey, I. G. Sarason, & B. R. Sarason (Eds.), *Sourcebook of social support and personality* (pp. 3–18). New York: Plenum.

Plomin, R., Reiss, D., Heatherington, E. M., & Howe, G. W. (1994). Nature and nurture: Genetic contributions to measures of the family environment. *Developmental Psychology, 30,* 32–43.

Pope, M. K., & Smith, T. W. (1991). Cortisol excretion in high and low cynically hostile men. *Psychosomatic Medicine, 53,* 386–392.

Pope, M. K., Smith, T. W., & Rhodewalt, F. (1990). Cognitive, behavioral, and affective correlates of the Cook and Medley Ho Scale. *Journal of Personality Assessment, 54,* 501–514.

Potthoff, J. G., Holahan, C. J., & Joiner, T. E. (1995). Reassurance seeking, stress generation, and depressive symptoms: An integrative model. *Journal of Personality and Social Psychology, 68,* 664–670.

Powch, I. G., & Houston, B. K. (1996). Hostility, anger-in, and cardiovascular reactivity in white women. *Health Psychology, 15,* 200–208.

Powell, L. H. (1992). The cognitive underpinnings of coronary-prone behaviors. *Cognitive Therapy and Research, 16,* 123–142.

Powell, L. H., & Thoresen, C. E. (1988). Effects of Type A behavioral counseling and severity of prior acute myocardial infarction on survival. *American Journal of Cardiology, 62,* 1159–1163.

Price, V. A. (1982). *Type A behavior pattern: A model for research and practice.* New York: Academic Press.

Rabkin, J. G., & Struening, E. H. (1976). Life events, stress, and illness. *Science, 194,* 1013–1020.

Ragland, D. R., & Brand, R. J. (1988). Type A behavior and mortality from coronary heart disease. *New England Journal of Medicine, 318,* 65–69.

Raikkonen, K., Matthews, K. A., Flory, J. D., Owens, J. F., & Gump, B. (1999). Effects of optimism, pessimism, and trait anxiety on ambulatory blood pressure and mood during everyday life. *Journal of Personality and Social Psychology, 76,* 104–113.

Reed, G. M., Kemeny, M., Taylor, S., Wang, H., & Visscher, B. (1994). Realistic acceptance as a predictor of decreased survival time in gay men with AIDS. *Health Psychology, 13,* 299–307.

Rehm, L. P. (1989). Behavioral models of anxiety and depression. In P. C. Kendall & D. Watson (Eds.), *Anxiety and depression: Distinctive and overlapping features* (pp. 55–82). New York: Academic Press.

Revenson, T. A. (1990). All other things are not equal: An ecological approach to personality and disease. In H. S. Freidman (Ed.), *Personality and disease* (pp. 65–96). New York: Wiley.

Rhodewalt, F., & Smith, T. W. (1991). Current issues in Type A behavior, coronary proneness, and coronary heart disease. In C. R. Snyder & D. R. Forsyth (Eds.), *Handbook of social and clinical psychology* (pp. 197–220). New York: Pergamon.

Robbins, A. S., Spence, J. T., & Clark, H. (1991). Psychological determinants of health and performance: The tangled web of desirable and undesirable characteristics. *Journal of Personality and Social Psychology, 61,* 755–765.

Rosenberg, E. L., Ekman, P., & Blumenthal, J. A. (1998). Facial expression and the affective component of cynical hostility in male coronary heart disease patients. *Health Psychology, 17,* 376–380.

Rosengren, A., Tibblin, G., & Wilhelmsen, L. (1991). Self-perceived psychological stress and incidence of coronary artery disease in middle-aged men. *American Journal of Cardiology, 68,* 1171–1175.

Rosenman, R. H. (1978). The interview method of assessment of the coronary-prone behavior pattern. In T. M. Dembroski, S. M. Weiss, J. L. Shields, S. G. Haynes, & M. Feinleig (Eds.), *Coronary-prone behavior* (pp. 55–70). New York: Springer-Verlag.

Rotter, J. B. (1954). *Social learning and clinical psychology.* Englewood Cliffs, NJ: Prentice-Hall.

Russek, L. G., & Schwartz, G. E. (1997). Perceptions of parental caring predict health status in midlife: A 35-year follow-up of the Harvard Mastery of Stress Study. *Psychosomatic Medicine, 59,* 144–149.

Sallis, J. F., Johnson, C. C., Trevorrow, T. R., Kaplan, R. M., & Hovell, M. F. (1987). The relationship between cynical hostility and blood pressure reactivity. *Journal of Psychosomatic Research, 31,* 111–116.

Sarason, B., Shearin, E. N., Pierce, G. R., & Sarason, I. G. (1987). Interrelations of social support measures: Theoretical and practical implications. *Journal of Personality and Social Psychology, 4,* 813–832.

Sarason, I. G., Levine, H. M., Basham, R. B., & Sarason, B. R. (1983). Assessing social support: The Social Support Questionnaire. *Journal of Personality and Social Psychology, 44,* 127–139.

Sarason, I. G., Sarason, B. R., & Shearin, E. N. (1986). Social support as an individual difference variable: Its stability, origins, and relational aspects. *Journal of Personality and Social Psychology, 4,* 813–832.

Saucier, G. (1992). Benchmarks: Integrating affective and interpersonal circles with the big-five personality factors. *Journal of Personality and Social Psychology, 62,* 1025–1035.

Schachter, S., Silverstein, B., Kozlowski, L. T., Herman, C. P., & Liebling, B. (1977). Effects of stress on cigarette smoking and urinary pH. *Journal of Experimental Psychology: General, 106,* 24–30.

Scheier, M. F., & Bridges, M. W. (1995). Person variables and health: Personality predispositions and acute psychological states as shared determinants for disease. *Psychosomatic Medicine, 57,* 255–268.

Scheier, M. F., & Carver, C. S. (1985). Optimism, coping, and health: Assessment and implications of generalized outcome expectancies. *Health Psychology, 4,* 219–247.

Scheier, M. F., & Carver, C. S. (1992). Effects of optimism on psychological and physical well-being: Theoretical overview and empirical update. *Cognitive Therapy and Research, 16,* 201–228.

Scheier, M. F., Carver, C. S., & Bridges, M. W. (1994). Distinguishing optimism from neuroticism (and trait anxiety, self-mastery, and self-esteem): A reevaluation of the Life Orientation Test. *Journal of Personality and Social Psychology, 67,* 1063–1078.

Scheier, M. F., Matthews, K. A., Owens, J., Magovern, G., Lefebure, R., Abbott, R., & Carver, C. (1989). Dispositional optimism and recovery from coronary artery bypass surgery: The beneficial effects of physical and psychological well-being. *Journal of Personality and Social Psychology, 57,* 1024–1040.

Scheier, M. F., Matthews, K. A., Owens, J. F., Schulz, R., Bridges, M. W., Magovern, G. J., & Carver, C. S. (1999). Optimism and rehospitalization after coronary artery bypass graft surgery. *Archives of Internal Medicine, 159,* 829–835.

Scherwitz, L. (1988). Interviewer behaviors in the Western Collaborative Group Study and the Multiple Risk Factor Intervention Trial Structured Interviews. In B. K. Houston & C. R. Synder (Eds.), *Type A behavior pattern: Research, theory, and intervention* (pp. 32–50). New York: Wiley.

Scherwitz, L., Perkins, L., Chesney, M., & Hughes, G. (1991). Cook–Medley hostility scales and subsets: Relationship to demographic and psychosocial characteristics in young adults in the cardia study. *Psychosomatic Medicine, 53,* 36–49.

Schulz, R., Bookwala, J., Knapp, J. E., Scheier, M., & Williamson, G. M. (1996). Pessimism, age, and cancer mortality. *Psychology and Aging, 11,* 304–309.

Segerstrom, S. C., Taylor, S. E., Kemeny, M. E., & Fahey, J. L. (1998). Optimism is associated with mood, coping, and immune change in response to stress. *Journal of Personality and Social Psychology, 74,* 1646–1655.

Seyle, H. (1936). A syndrome produced by diverse noxious agents. *Nature, 138,* 32.

Seyle, H. (1952). *The story of the adaptation syndrome.* Montreal: Acta.

Shekelle, R. B., Gale, M., & Norusis, M. (1985). Type A score (Jenkins Activity Survey) and risk of recurrent coronary heart disease in the Aspirin Myocardial Infarction Study. *American Journal of Cardiology, 56,* 221–225.

Shekelle, R. B., Gale, M., Ostfeld, A. M., & Paul, O. (1983). Hostility, risk of coronary heart disease, and mortality. *Psychosomatic Medicine, 45,* 109–114.

Shekelle, R. B., Hulley, S., Neaton, J., Billings, J., Borhani, N., Gerace, T., Jacobs, D., Lasser, N., Mittlemark, M., & Stamler, J. (1985). MRFIT Research Group: The MRFIT behavior pattern study II. Type A behavior pattern and incidence of coronary heart disease. *American Journal of Epidemiology, 122,* 559–570.

Shekelle, R. B., Vernon, S. W., & Ostfeld, A. M. (1991). Personality and coronary heart disease. *Psychosomatic Medicine, 53,* 176–184.

Siegler, I. C. (1994). Hostility and risk: Demographic and lifestyle variables. In A. W. Siegman & T. W. Smith (Eds.), *Anger, hostility, and the heart* (pp. 199–214). Hillsdale, NJ: Lawrence Erlbaum Associates.

Siegman, A. W. (1994). From Type A to hostility to anger: Reflections on the history of coronary-prone behavior. In A. W. Siegman & T. W. Smith (Eds.), *Anger, hostility and the heart* (pp. 1–22). Hillsdale, NJ: Lawrence Erlbaum Associates.

Sifneos, P. E. (1973). The prevalence of "alexithymic" characteristics in psychosomatic patients. *Psychotherapy and Psychosomatics, 22,* 255–262.

Simonsick, E. M., Wallace, R. B., Blazer, D. G., & Gerkman, L. F. (1995). Depressive symptomatology and hypertension-associated morbidity and morality in older adults. *Psychosomatic Medicine, 57,* 427–435.

Smith, C. A., Wallston, K. A., & Dwyer, K. A. (1995). On babies and bathwater: Disease impact and negative affectivity in the self-reports of persons with rheumatoid arthritis. *Health Psychology, 14,* 64–73.

Smith, M. A., & Houston, B. K. (1987). Hostility, anger expression, cardiovascular responsivity, and social support. *Biological Psychology, 24,* 39–48.

Smith, T. W. (1992). Hostility and health: Current status of a psychosomatic hypothesis. *Health Psychology, 11,* 139–150.

Smith, T. W. (1994). Concepts and methods in the study of anger, hostility, and health. In A. W. Siegman & T. W. Smith (Eds.), *Anger, hostility and the heart* (pp. 23–42). Hillsdale, NJ: Lawrence Erlbaum Associates.

Smith, T. W. (1995). Assessment and modification of coronary-prone behavior: A transactional view of the person in social context. In A. J. Goreczny (Ed.), *Handbook of health and rehabilitation psychology* (pp. 197–217). New York: Plenum.

Smith, T. W., Allred, K. D., Morrison, C., & Carlson, S. (1989). Cardiovascular reactivity and interpersonal influence: Active coping in a social context. *Journal of Personality and Social Psychology, 56,* 209–218.

Smith, T. W., & Anderson, N. B. (1986). Models of personality and disease: An interactional approach to Type A behavior and cardiovascular risk. *Journal of Personality and Social Psychology, 50,* 1166–1173.

Smith, T. W., Baldwin, M., & Christensen, A. (1990). Interpersonal influence as active coping: Effects of task difficulty on cardiovascular reactivity. *Psychophysiology, 27,* 429–437.

Smith, T. W., & Frohm, K. D. (1985). What's so unhealthy about hostility? Construct validity and psychosocial correlates of the Cook and Medley Ho Scale. *Health Psychology, 4,* 503–520.

Smith, T. W., & Gallo, L. C. (1999). Hostility and cardiovascular reactivity during marital interaction. *Psychosomatic Medicine, 61,* 436–445.

Smith, T. W., Gallo, L. C., Goble, L., Ngu, L., & Stark, K. (1998). Agency, communion, and cardiovascular reactivity during marital interaction. *Health Psychology, 17,* 537–545.

Smith, T. W., & Leon, A. S. (1992). *Coronary heart disease: A behavioral perspective.* Champaign-Urbana, IL: Research Press.

Smith, T. W., Limon, J. P., Gallo, L. C., & Ngu, L. Q. (1996). Interpersonal control and cardiovascular reactivity: Goals, behavioral expression, and the moderating effects of sex. *Journal of Personality and Social Psychology, 70,* 1012–1024.

Smith, T. W., McGonigle, M., & Benjamin, L. (1998). Sibling interactions, self-regulation, and cynical hostility in adult male twins. *Journal of Behavioral Medicine, 21,* 337–349.

Smith, T. W., Nealey, J. B., Kircher, J. C., & Limon, J. P. (1997). Social determinants of cardiovascular reactivity: Effects of incentive to exert influence and evaluative threat. *Psychophysiology, 34,* 65–73.

Smith, T. W., O'Keeffe, J. L., & Allred, K. D. (1989). Neuroticism, symptom reports, and Type A behavior: Interpretive cautions for the Framingham scale. *Journal of Behavioral Medicine, 12,* 1–11.

Smith, T. W., & Pope, M. K. (1990). Cynical hostility as a health risk: Current status and future directions. *Journal of Social Behavior and Personality, 5,* 77–88.

Smith, T. W., Pope, M. K., Rhodewalt, F., & Poulton, J. L. (1989). Optimism, neuroticism, coping, and symptom reports: An alternative interpretation of the Life Orientation Test. *Journal of Personality and Social Psychology, 56,* 640–648.

Smith, T. W., Pope, M. K., Sanders, J. D., Allred, K. D., & O'Keeffe, J. L. (1988). Cynical hostility at home and work: Psychosocial vulnerability across domains. *Journal of Research in Personality, 22,* 525–548.

Smith, T. W., & Rhodewalt, F. (1986). On states, traits, and processes: A transactional alternative to individual difference assumptions in Type A behavior and physiological reactivity. *Journal of Research in Personality, 20,* 229–251.

Smith, T. W., & Rhodewalt, F. (1991). Methodological challenges at the social/clinical interface. In C. R. Snyder & D. F. Forsyth (Eds.), *Handbook of social and clinical psychology* (pp. 739–756). New York: Pergamon.

Smith, T. W., Sanders, J. D., & Alexander, J. F. (1990). What does the Cook and Medley Hostility Scale measure? Affect, behavior, and attributions in the marital context. *Journal of Personality and Social Psychology, 58,* 699–708.

Smith, T. W., Turner, C. W., Ford, M., Hunt, S., Barlow, G., Stults, B., & Williams, R. (1987). Blood pressure reactivity in adult male twins. *Health Psychology, 6,* 209–220.

Smith, T. W., & Williams, P. G. (1992). Personality and health: Advantages and limitations of the five factor model. *Journal of Personality, 60,* 395–423.

Smyth, J. M. (1998). Written emotional expresion: Effect sizes, outcome types, and moderating variables. *Journal of Consulting and Clinical Psychology, 66,* 174–184.

Somervell, P. D., Kaplan, B. H., Heiss, G., Tyroler, H. A., Kleinbaum, D. G., & Obrist, P. A. (1989). Psychologic distress as a predictor of mortality. *American Journal of Epidemiology, 130,* 1013–1023.

Spiro, A., Aldwin, C. M., Ward, K. D., & Mroczek, D. K. (1995). Personality and the incidence of hypertension among older men: Longitudinal findings from the normative aging study. *Health Psychology, 14,* 563–569.

Stanton, A. L. (1995). Psychology of women's health: Barriers and pathways to knowledge. In A. L. Stanton & S. J. Gallant (Eds.), *The psychology of women's health: Progress and challenges in research and application* (pp. 3–21). Washington, DC: American Psychological Association.

Stanton, A. L., & Snider, P. R. (1993). Coping with breast cancer diagnosis: A prospective study. *Health Psychology, 12,* 16–23.

Stone, G. C., Cohen, F., & Adler, N. E. (1979). *Health psychology.* San Francisco: Jossey-Bass.

Stone, S. V., & Costa, P. T., Jr. (1990). Disease-prone personality or distress-prone personality? The role of neuroticism in coronary heart disease. In H. S. Friedman (Ed.), *Personality and disease* (pp. 178–200). New York: Wiley.

Strack, S., Carver, C., & Blaney, P. (1987). Predicting successful completion of an aftercare program following treatment for alcoholism: The role of dispositional optimism. *Journal of Personality and Social Psychology, 53,* 579–584.

Strickland, B. R. (1978). Internal-external expectancies and health-related behaviors. *Journal of Consulting and Clinical Psychology, 46,* 1192–1211.

Suarez, E. C., Kuhn, C. M., Schanberg, S. M., Williams, R. B., & Zimmermann, E. A. (1998). Neuroendocrine, cardiovascular, and emotional responses of hostile men: The role of interpersonal challenge. *Psychosomatic Medicine, 60,* 78–88.

Suarez, E. C., & Williams, R. B., Jr. (1989). Situational determinants of cardiovascular and emotional reactivity in high and low hostile men. *Psychosomatic Medicine, 51,* 404–418.

Suls, J., & Marco, C. A. (1990). Relationship between JAS- and FTAS-Type A behavior and non-CHD illnesses: A prospective study controlling for negative affectivity. *Health Psychology, 9,* 479–492.

Suls, J., Martin, R., & David, J. P. (1998). Person–environment fit and its limits: Agreeableness, neuroticism, and emotional reactivity to interpersonal conflict. *Personality and Social Psychology Bulletin, 24,* 88–98.

Suls, J., & Rittenhouse, J. D. (1987). Personality and health: An introduction. *Journal of Personality, 55,* 155–167.

Suls, J., & Sanders, G. S. (1989). Why do some behavioral styles place people at coronary risk? In A. W. Siegman & T. M. Dembroski (Eds.), *In search of coronary-prone behavior* (pp. 1–20). Hillsdale, NJ: Lawrence Erlbaum Associates.

Suls, J., & Wan, C. K. (1993). The relationship between trait hostility and cardiovascular reactivity: A quantitative review and analysis. *Psychophysiology, 30,* 615–626.

Surwit, R. S., Williams, R. B., & Shapiro, D. (1982). *Behavioral approaches to cardiovascular disease.* New York: Academic Press.

Swan, G. E., & Carmelli, D. (1996). Curiosity and mortality in aging adults: A five-year follow-up of the Western Collaborative Group Study. *Psychology and Aging, 11,* 449–453.

Tangney, J. P., Wagner, P. E., Hill-Barlow, D., Marschall, D. E., & Gramzow, R. (1996). Relation of shame and guilt to constructive versus destructive responses to anger across the lifespan. *Journal of Personality and Social Psychology, 70,* 797–809.

Taylor, J. A. (1953). A personality scale of manifest anxiety. *Journal of Abnormal and Social Psychology, 48,* 285–290.

Taylor, S. E., Kemeny, M. E., Aspinwall, L., Schneider, S. G., Rodriquez, R., & Herbert, M. (1992). Optimism, coping, psychological distress, and high risk sexual behavior among men at risk for Acquired Immunodeficiency Syndrome (AIDS). *Journal of Personality and Social Psychology, 63,* 460–473.

Tolan, P. H., Guerra, N., & Kendall, P. C. (1995). A developmental-ecological perspective on antisocial behavior in children and adolescents: Toward a unified risk and intervention framework. *Journal of Consulting and Clinical Psychology, 63,* 579–584.

Trapnell, P. D., & Wiggins, J. S. (1990). Extension of the Interpersonal Adjective Scales to include the big five dimensions of personality. *Journal of Personality and Social Psychology, 59,* 781–790.

Turner, J. R., & Hewitt, J. K. (1992). Twin studies of cardiovascular response to psychological challenge: A review and suggested future directions. *Annals of Behavioral Medicine, 14,* 12–20.

Uchino, B. N., Cacioppo, J. T., & Kiecolt-Glaser, J. K. (1996). The relationship between social support and physiological processes: A review with emphasis on underlying mechanisms and implications for health. *Psychological Bulletin, 119,* 488–531.

Vedhara, K., Nott, K. H., Bradbeer, C. S., Davidson, E.A.F., Ong, E.L.C., Snow, M.H.M., Palmer, D., & Nayagam, A. T. (1997). Greater emotional distress is associated with accelerated CD4+ Cell decline in HIV infection. *Journal of Psychosomatic Research, 42,* 379–390.

Wachtel, P. (1994). Cyclical processes in personality and psychopathology. *Journal of Abnormal Psychology, 103,* 51–66.

Wagner, C. C., Kiesler, D. J., & Schmidt, J. A. (1995). Assessing the interpersonal transaction cycle: Convergence of action and reaction interpersonal circumplex measures. *Journal of Personality and Social Psychology, 69,* 938–949.

Watkins, L. L., Grossman, P., Krishnan, R., & Sherwood, A. (1998). Anxiety and vagal control of heart rate. *Psychosomatic Medicine, 60,* 498–502.

Watkins, P. L., Ward, C. H., Southard, D. R., & Fisher, E. B., Jr. (1992). The type A belief system: Relationships to hostility, social support, and life stress. *Behavioral Medicine, 18,* 27–32.

Watson, D., & Clark, L. A. (1984). Negative affectivity: The disposition to experience aversive emotional states. *Psychological Bulletin, 96,* 465–490.

Watson, D., Clark, L. A., & Harkness, A. R. (1994). Structures of personality and their relevance to psychopathology. *Journal of Abnormal Psychology, 103,* 18–31.

Watson, D., & Pennebaker, J. W. (1989). Health complaints, stress, and distress: Exploring the central role of negative affectivity. *Psychological Review, 96,* 234–254.

Weinberger, D. A. (1990). The construct validity of the repressive coping style. In J. L. Singer (Ed.), *Repression and dissociation* (pp. 337–386). Chicago, IL: University of Chicago Press.

Weinberger, D. A., Schwartz, G. E., & Davison, R. J. (1979). Low anxious, high anxious, and repressive coping styles: Psychometric patterns and behavioral and physiological responses to stress. *Journal of Abnormal Psychology, 58,* 369–380.

Weiss, S. M., Herd, J. A., & Fox, B. H. (1981). *Perspectives on behavioral medicine.* New York: Academic Press.

Westen, D. (1991). Social cognition and object relations. *Psychological Bulletin, 109,* 429–455.

Westen, D. (1995). A clinical-empirical model of personality: Life after the Mischelian ice age and the Neolithic era. *Journal of Personality, 63,* 495–524.

Whiteman, M. C., Deary, I. J., Lee, A. J., & Fowkes, F.G.R. (1997). Submissiveness and protection from coronary heart disease in the general population: Edinburgh Artery Study. *Lancet, 350,* 541–545.

Wiebe, D. J. (1991). Hardiness and stress moderation: A test of proposed mechanisms. *Journal of Personality and Social Psychology, 60,* 89–99.

Wiebe, D. J., Alderfer, M. A., Palmer, S. C., Lindsay, R., & Jarrett, L. (1994). Behavioral self-regulation in adolescents with Type I diabetes: Negative affectivity and blood glucose symptom perception. *Journal of Consulting and Clinical Psychology, 62,* 1204–1212.

Wiebe, D. J., & McCallum, D. M. (1986). Health practices and hardiness as mediators in the stress–illness relationship. *Health Psychology, 5,* 425–438.

Wielgosz, A. T., & Earp, J. (1986). Perceived vulnerability to serious heart disease and persistent pain in patients with minimal or no coronary disease. *Psychosomatic Medicine, 48,* 118–124.

Wiggins, J. S. (1979). A psychological taxonomy of trait-descriptive terms: The interpersonal domain. *Journal of Personality and Social Psychology, 37,* 395–412.

Wiggins, J. S. (1991). Agency and communion as conceptual coordinates for the understanding and measurement of interpersonal behavior. In D. Cicchetti & W. Grove (Eds.), *Thinking clearly in psychology: Essays in honor of Paul Everett Meehl* (pp. 89–113). Minneapolis: University of Minnesota Press.

Wiggins, J. S., & Broughton, R. (1991). A geometric taxonomy of personality scales. *European Journal of Personality, 5,* 343–365.

Williams, P. G., Wiebe, D. J., & Smith, T. W. (1992). Coping processes as mediators of the relationship between hardiness and health. *Journal of Behavioral Medicine, 15,* 237–255.

Williams, R. B., Jr. (1994). Basic biological mechanisms. In A. W. Seigman & T. W. Smith (Eds.), *Anger, hostility, and the heart* (pp. 117–125). Hillsdale, NJ: Lawrence Erlbaum Associates.

Williams, R. B., Jr., Barefoot, J. C., & Shekelle, R. B. (1985). The health consequences of hostility. In M. A. Chesney & R. H. Rosenman (Eds.), *Anger and hostility in cardiovascular and behavioral disorders* (pp. 173–185). New York: Hemisphere.

Williams, R. B., Suarez, E. C., Kuhn, C. M., Schanberg, S. M., & Zimmermann, E. (1991). Biobehavioral basis of coronary-prone behavior in middle-aged men: Part I. Evidence for chronic sympathetic nervous system activation in Type As. *Psychosomatic Medicine, 53,* 517–527.

Wolff, H. G. (1950). Life stress and cardiovascular disorders. *Circulation, 1,* 187–203.

Woodall, K. L., & Matthews, K. A. (1989). Familial environment associated with Type A behaviors and psychophysiological responses to stress in children. *Health Psychology, 8,* 403–426.

Wright, R. A. (1996). Brehm's theory of motivation as a model of effort and cardiovascular response. In P. M. Gollwitzer & J. A. Bargh (Eds.), *The psychology of action: Linking cognition and motivation to behavior* (pp. 424–453). New York: Guilford.

Yarnold, P. R., & Grimm, L. G. (1986). Interpersonal dominance and coronary-prone behavior. *Journal of Research in Personality, 20,* 420–433.

Zonderman, A. B., Costa, P. T., & McCrae, R. R. (1989). Depression as a risk for cancer morbidity and mortality in a nationally representative sample. *Journal of the American Medical Association, 262,* 1191–1215.

Zonderman, A. B., Herbst, J., Schmidt, C., Costa, P., & McCrae, R. R. (1993). Depressive symptoms as a non-specific graded risk for psychiatric diagnoses. *Journal of Abnormal Psychology, 102,* 544–552.

10

Personality's Role in the Protection and Enhancement of Health: Where the Research Has Been, Where It Is Stuck, How It Might Move

Suzanne C. Ouellette
The City University of New York

Joanne DiPlacido
Central Connecticut State College

There is something engaging about research on positive health outcomes. Research that seeks to explain why some people thrive, or at least remain physically and psychologically intact in the face of arduous circumstances, catches on quickly. Whether it is called a sense of coherence, hardiness, optimism, resilience, or any one of a growing number of such terms, it is the personality characteristic that promises health in spite of hardship and inspires both scientists and ordinary folk. This chapter provides an overview of such research and offers encouraging yet cautionary advice about its future. Along with the gains of research on health protective personality characteristics, both specific conceptual and methodological shortcomings within and across work are pointed out on a number of different constructs. Also noted are more general ideological concerns about why and how such personality and health research is conducted. To address both the specific and the general critique, the chapter turns to contemporary trends within personality and the broader field of psychology for ideas about future personality and health research.

The first section contains summaries of work with some of the key constructs used in health research on positive outcomes. As a unit of personality, each of these constructs represents a distinguishing characteristic in people's system of behavior and experience that is thought to be relatively long standing and expressed through their thoughts, feelings, and/or actions across the various areas of their life. The chapter reviews sense of coherence, hardiness, a set of control-related notions (including dispositional optimism, explanatory style, health locus of control, and self-efficacy), and affiliative trust. These personality constructs have been found to do one or more of the following: correlate directly with health; correlate with health-related behaviors; and minimize persons' likelihood of getting sick or sicker in the wake of stressors, including stressors that consist of acute and chronic illness conditions. For each of the personality constructs, there are basic definitions and a sketch of the theoretical background, measurement strategies, key findings, and a statement on unresolved issues.

The second section pulls back from the particular constructs to raise questions that apply to the whole research enterprise on personality and positive health outcomes. These have to do with gaps in the literature and ideological assumptions that emerge from but are typically not addressed in published research reports. The ideological concerns are raised in the form of two dilemmas, a pair of "yes ... but" remarks. One involves assumptions about the relation between individuals and social structures, and the other involves assumptions about what constitutes the "good" that is implicit in the research. The call to tread carefully that is made here might indeed be issued for many health psychology topics, but it is particularly apt for research into positive outcomes. Findings from personality and health studies make their way into the popular media (e.g., Locke & Colligan, 1987) with great speed and the whole enterprise elicits remarkably high enthusiasm from new researchers. The quick popularity is encouraging, but researchers should remain wary.[1]

The final section of the chapter seeks ways of addressing both the specific and general questions that have been raised. Recent discussions are consulted in the general personality psychology literature and insights about the historical and ideological dimensions of all psychological research are provided by feminist and critical psychology. To encourage investigators about the viability of research on personality and positive health outcomes that is inspired by general personality, feminist, and critical sources, examples of especially promising new empirical work relevant to health psychology are cited.

WHAT'S IN THE LITERATURE ON POSITIVE HEALTH OUTCOMES?

The seven constructs described here have all received considerable research attention and continue to appear in the literature. Some constructs that may be familiar to the reader such as Type A Behavior Pattern and trait hostility have been left out because they are covered elsewhere in this volume. More important, these constructs have more to do with why people get sick than with the ways personality functions to maintain or improve their health. This chapter attempts to keep the focus on the latter. Nonetheless, as is described in what follows, personality characteristics that are presented as protectors and enhancers of health are most frequently cast in measurement efforts simply as those that correlate with lack of illness, that is, low illness scores.

A selective set of studies for each construct that is thought to be representative of the typical empirical approach to that construct is presented here. The results illustrate the now long available discussion of the three basic models in which personality gets linked to health (F. Cohen, 1979). In one, a direct connection is posited between personality and actual physiological, biological, and/or neurological states that are in turn related to health status; here, for example, investigators correlate personality scores with cardiovascular activity or immunological function. A second model portrays personality in its influence on health-related behaviors; in this scheme, personality is linked with matters such as whether people exercise, how they eat, and the extent to which they engage in high risk behaviors like smoking.

A third model portrays the stress buffering role of personality. It guides investigations that seek to determine the ways that personality influences peoples' response to the occurrence of stress (i.e., the ways it minimizes or maximizes the likelihood that a person will become ill, or more ill, following an encounter with a stressful situation). It has become standard practice to claim personality as a stress buffer when a significant statistical interaction is found between the stress and personality variables. Also, at this stage of the research, this model typically displays personality in relation with stress appraisal, coping strategies, and other mechanisms thought to be relevant to the stress process. Along with theoretical overviews and statements of issues awaiting resolution, the discussion indicates the extent to which data on each of the constructs fill out one or more of these models.

Sense of Coherence

Sense of coherence represents the individuals' ability to believe that what happens in their life is *comprehensible, manageable,* and *meaningful* (Antonovsky, 1993, 1987, 1979). Antonovsky (1987) referred to his construct as a generalized dispositional orientation toward the world:

> The sense of coherence is a global orientation that expresses the extent to which one has a pervasive, enduring though dynamic feeling of confidence that (1) the stimuli deriving from one's internal and external environments in the course of living are structured, predictable, and explicable [comprehensibility]; (2) the resources are available to one to meet the demands posed by these stimuli [manageability]; and (3) these demands are challenges, worthy of investment and engagement [meaningfulness]. (p. 19)

With his focus on salutogenic strengths, Antonovsky switched the emphasis from stress and its negative health consequences to a discussion of positive or adaptive coping in re-

[1]For one of us, there is more than a little ambivalence about those still almost weekly requests for a scale to measure hardiness, nearly 20 years after the first hardiness article and 10 years after the first of a series of articles sharply critical of hardiness measurement (cf. Ouellette, 1993). There is almost always a question about the relevance of the scale and even the construct for the group the investigator is seeking to study. A questionnaire designed for middle-aged, middle-class, male executives may not indeed work with a group of homeless children. Also, it is important that new researchers see the link between the latest wave of interest in thriving and resilience work with some older constructs like hardiness, but one also wishes for some new strategies for assessing these phenomena. The other of us approaches the audience of those interested in personality and health from the perspective of one in the early stages of a project on stress, stress resistance, and lesbian health. She is eager to publish findings on how personality (and other situation and structural) factors protect the health of lesbian women, but also keenly aware of the care with which these findings will need to be approached. Given the many unresolved methodological challenges in her chosen research area and even more important, a cultural and political climate in which discrimination against gays and lesbians remains prevalent, whatever results there are on links between individual lesbians' personalities and their health will need carefully be interpreted. Without capturing personality findings through the lens of the broad sociocultural context in which they sit, she risks provoking more stigmatization and neglect of social causes of poor health.

sponse to stress. Antonovsky, a sociologist, was interested in both personality dispositions that foster health and their structural sources, particularly the sociocultural and historical contexts in which these dispositions are embedded (Antonovsky, 1991). He saw institutionalized roles, cultural values, and norms as influences on all of the following: the processes through which people deal with stressors, the actual occurrence of stressors, and the resulting outcomes of the stress process (Antonovsky, 1991).

Antonovsky's theory states that a greater sense of coherence leads to a person's effective coping with a multitude of stressors and thereby positive health outcomes. The sense of coherence construct was predicted to be a stress buffer: Under stressful circumstances, those individuals with a strong sense of coherence—in contrast to those with a lower sense of coherence—would be better copers, more likely to draw on their own resources (i.e., ego strength) and those of others (i.e., social support), and as a result enjoy better health and well-being.

Antonovsky designed a scale to measure sense of coherence (the Orientation to Life Questionnaire, OLQ). The full OLQ scale includes 29 items and a shorter 13-item scale is also available. Adequate reliability and validity of this scale has been reported (Antonovsky, 1993, 1987; Frenz, Carey, & Jorgensen, 1993). The results obtained through use of the OLQ scale provide support for only parts of the stress buffer model. Only direct relations (correlations) between sense of coherence and health promoting variables, and mainly self-reported health outcomes have been empirically demonstrated. And much of this work on the salutogenic effects of sense of coherence has focused on psychological rather than physical health.

A prospective study with a repeated measures multivariate analysis of variance (MANOVA) design found main effects for hassles and sense of coherence on depression and anxiety (R. B. Flannery & G. J. Flannery, 1990). A greater number of hassles led to greater distress, and a greater sense of coherence led to lower distress among students from adult evening classes. There were, however, no significant interactions between hassles and sense of coherence to indicate sense of coherence's stress buffering role. Similarly, greater sense of coherence was related to lower psychological distress among adult Cambodians in New Zealand, but did not moderate the relation between life events and postmigration stressors and psychological distress (Cheung & Spears, 1995). In a sample of homeless women and low income housed women, higher levels of sense of coherence were related to less psychological distress among homeless women but not low income housed women (Ingram, Corning, & Schmidt, 1996).

Less published work relates sense of coherence to physical health outcomes, and most of what exists relies on self-reports of symptoms. In a study of kibbutz members, sense of coherence was negatively related to reported physical symptoms in the previous month, as well as reported limitations in daily activities due to health problems (Anson, Carmel, Levenson, Bonneh, & Maoz, 1993). A study conducted by Bowman (1996) found sense of coherence to be negatively related to self-reported physical symptoms in both Anglo-American and Native American undergraduates. Bowman noted that this study supported a fundamental assumption made by Antonovsky that people from different cultures may attain similar levels of sense of coherence, despite socioeconomic differences. It should be noted, however, that only college students from these two cultures were included in this study.

At least two studies have examined the salutogenic effect of sense of coherence among medical patients; specifically, individuals in recovery from elective surgery for joint replacement and patients living with the chronic illness of rheumatoid arthritis. At a 6-week follow-up of surgery patients, sense of coherence was positively related to life satisfaction, well-being, and self-rated health; sense of coherence was negatively related to psychological distress and pain (Chamberlain, Petrie, & Azariah, 1992). In a cross-sectional study of 828 patients with rheumatoid arthritis, lower sense of coherence scores were significantly related to more difficulty in performing daily living activities, more overall pain, and poorer global health status (Callahan & Pincus, 1995).

The mechanisms through which sense of coherence is related to health outcomes have also been examined. As predicted by theory, sense of coherence has been positively related to health enhancing behaviors such as use of social skills among Israeli adolescents (Margalit & Eysenck, 1990); social support availability among minority, homeless women in the United States (Nyamathi, 1991); and problem-focused coping among Swedish factory supervisors (Larsson & Setterlind, 1990). Sense of coherence was also negatively related to emotion-focused coping among Swedish factory supervisors (Larsson & Setterlind, 1990); HIV risk behaviors among U.S. minority homeless women (Nyamathi, 1991); and alcohol problems among older adults (Midanik, Soghikian, Ransom, & Polen, 1992). In addition to this review, the reader is referred to Antonovsky (1993) for a thorough review of the cross-cultural studies that examine the salutogenic effect of sense of coherence.

As can be seen from the aforementioned results, what is missing is solid empirical support for the stress moderating role of sense of coherence, and evidence for the complete mediational model linking sense of coherence and coping, social skills, health behaviors, or social support with actual physiological and biological health processes. Either these relationships for which Antonovsky provided an elaborate theoretical justification have not yet been tested, or obtained negative findings have not met the published page.

Hardiness

Hardiness, as conceptualized by Kobasa (later known as Ouellette), Maddi, and their colleagues (Kobasa, 1979, 1982; Kobasa, Maddi, & Kahn, 1982; Maddi, 1990; Ouellette, 1993), is a construct drawn from existential personality theory and is intended to represent a person's distinctive way of understanding self, world, and the interaction between self and world. Existentialism, both in its European forms and in the American version found in some of William James' work, disputes a view of the person as simply a passive victim of life's stresses and requires all investigation to begin with persons' subjective experience of life's demands. Drawing on the existential notion of authenticity, as well as the psychological literature on adult development and on the notion of control (Kobasa, 1979), the originators of the construct said that people's hardiness is reflected in the extent to which they are able to express commitment, control, and challenge in their actions, thoughts, and feelings. Commitment refers to individuals' engagement in life and view of their activities and experiences as meaningful, purposeful, and interesting. Control has to do with individuals' recognition that they have some influence over what life brings. Challenge indicates an orientation toward change as an inevitable and even rewarding part of life that is matched by an ability to be cognitively flexible and tolerant of ambiguity. The dynamic interplay of all three in people's basic stance toward life is theorized to promote stress resistance and to enhance psychological and physical health (Kobasa et al., 1982). Hardiness is said to lessen the negative effects of stress by its influence on the perception and interpretation of stressful events and its promotion of actions that minimize the toxicity of those events.

There are several different scales designed to measure hardiness. Some are results of efforts to shorten and psychometrically strengthen the original hardiness measure (e.g., Bartone, 1989), whereas others (e.g., Pollock & Duffy, 1990), although interesting in their own right, have only weak connection to the original conceptualization of hardiness. The most frequently cited measures are the original five-scale composite test of hardiness (Kobasa et al., 1982), and the 36- and 20-item abridged versions (Allred & T. W. Smith, 1989; F. Rhodewalt & Agustsdottir, 1984; R. Rhodewalt & Zone, 1989). The reader is referred to Maddi (1990) and Ouellette (1993) for reviews of the existing hardiness scales and attempts to organize at least some of the hardiness measurement story. Key critiques of the measures are Funk and Houston (1987) and Funk (1992).

The original hardiness scales have been criticized for their lack of balance of positive and negative items, that may lead to acquiescent response biases, and their facilitation of a confounding of hardiness with neuroticism. In addition, in some studies, low internal reliability among the challenge items, and low correlations between challenge and the other two scales (control and commitment) have been reported. There have also been questions about whether a total unitary hardiness score should be used, or separate scale scores reflecting the three hardiness components. Factor analyses have not been able definitively to answer this question because some researchers have found evidence for a unitary single dimension, and others have found two- or three-factor structures (Ouellette, 1993).

These criticisms have led to a more recent, not as yet widely used, measure of hardiness called the Personal Views Survey (cf. Maddi, 1990). Findings with this newer test appear to be more promising (e.g., Florian, Mikulincer, & Taubman, 1995). These reports emphasize the need for investigators to check the structure and psychometric properties of the hardiness measure within their own samples, and to make use of newer statistical strategies, such as structural equation modeling, to examine the structure of hardiness. Nonetheless, one of the originators of the hardiness concept (Ouellette, 1993, 1999) strongly calls for the serious consideration of measures other than simple self-report as alternative or additional methods of capturing hardiness with all its complexities. Use of a breadth of measurement approaches is especially important given the need to address hardiness in contexts different from those populated by the largely male, White, and middle-class executives on which the original measurement efforts were based.

The majority of studies on hardiness have provided evidence for a general relation between hardiness and psychological or physical health—the higher the hardiness, the fewer the symptoms. Wiebe and Williams (1992) reported that the most consistent finding in the hardiness literature is the lower reported levels of both concurrent and subsequent physical symptoms among individuals high in hardiness compared to those who score low in hardiness. Fewer studies, following the initial prospective demonstration of a stress and hardiness interaction among business executives (Kobasa et al., 1982), have actually confirmed the specific stress buffering role of hardiness (for reviews see Funk, 1992; Maddi, 1990; Orr & Westman, 1990; Ouellette, 1993).

Like sense of coherence, hardiness has been examined in a variety of groups, many of which are contending with what most would agree would be high levels of stress. Nurses, for example, have applied the construct of hardiness not only to patients but also to themselves in their high stress work settings. The nursing research has found links between hardiness and burnout for nurses involved in various kinds of nursing care (Keane, Ducette, & Adler, 1985; McCranie, V. A. Lambert, & C. E. Lambert, 1987; V. L. Rich & A. R. Rich, 1987; Topf, 1989); the influence of hardiness on student nurses' positive appraisal of their first medical-surgical experience (Pagana, 1990); and the relation between hardiness and activity levels in the elderly (Magnani, 1990). Other researchers have found hardiness to be related to less burnout among elementary school teachers (Holt, Fine, & Tollefson, 1987); positive indicators of both objective and perceived health status for women living with rheumatoid arthritis (R. Rhodewalt & Zone, 1989); fewer negative health changes among disaster workers responding to a major air transport tragedy (Bartone, Ursona, Wright, & Ingraham, 1989); and more effective performance among recruits in rigorous training for the Israeli army (Westman, 1990).

Hardiness studies have also included demonstrations of possible mechanisms through which this personality construct may have its health promoting effects. Findings show that the higher individuals score on hardiness, the less likely they are to appraise events pessimistically as stressful and threatening (Allred & T. W. Smith, 1989; Wiebe, 1991). Links have also been reported between the components of hardiness and the use of particular coping strategies (Westman, 1990; Williams, Wiebe, & T. W. Smith, 1992). Importantly, Florian et al. (1995) recently demonstrated in a longitudinal study that the different components of hardiness, at least among Israeli army recruits, have different appraisal and coping consequences. The commitment dimension reduced threat appraisal and emotion-focused coping while it increased their sense that they could respond effectively to the stress. The control dimension also reduced the appraisal of threat and increased sense of effectiveness, whereas it distinctively increased problem-solving coping and support-seeking strategies.

There is also some evidence that hardiness indirectly effects health status through its relation with health-related behaviors (e.g., Wiebe & McCallum, 1986). Less clear are the physiological and biological mediators and outcomes of hardiness. Investigators have examined a number of these, including arousal (Allred & T. W. Smith, 1989; Contrada, 1989; Wiebe, 1991) and immune function (e.g., Dillon & Totten, 1989), but results are few and not consistent.

There are clearly a number of points in the hardiness research endeavor at which an investigator could enter to make significant contributions. The lack of a consistent demonstration of a stress buffering effect needs to be approached in terms of measurement and conceptualization. With regard to the former, there are calls for both improvement in self-report scales and for other, in Robert White's terminology, longer ways of assessing hardiness (cf. Ouellette, 1999). With regard to conceptualization, there are a number of tasks needing attention. Given recent critiques and findings, what the originators of the concept called the dynamic constellation of commitment, control, and challenge needs to be better specified (Carver, 1989; Florian et al., 1995): What constitutes a constellation? Are high levels of all three components required for stress buffering, or can high levels of one compensate for low levels of another? A better specification is also needed of how people are to think about the ways hardiness operates in context in social settings (Wiebe & Williams, 1992). Kobasa (1982) reported differences between occupational groups in how hardiness relates to the health of the members of those occupations. Nonetheless, hardiness theory has yet to be elaborated sufficiently to explain these group differences. Finally, in drawing on existential approaches, the originators of hardiness had in mind an approach that would recognize the person and not just the variable (cf. Allport, 1961; Carlson, 1984; Ouellette Kobasa, 1990). The necessary idiographic, developmental, and historical work with hardiness awaits.

Dispositional Optimism

Scheier and Carver (1985, 1987, 1992) defined dispositional optimism as individuals' stable, generalized expectation that they will experience good things in life. Key in this theory is the principle that people's behaviors are strongly influenced by their beliefs about the probable outcomes of those behaviors. Outcome expectancies determine whether a person continues striving for a goal or gives up and turns away (Scheier & Carver, 1987). Optimistic outcome expectancies are theorized to lead an individual to engage in active behavior to attain a goal. Pessimistic outcome expectancies, on the other hand, are thought to lead an individual to give up and not engage in behaviors to attain the goal. With regard to optimism's role in influencing health, it has been hypothesized that optimism leads to more adaptive coping with stress. In general, optimists who believe they will most likely experience positive outcomes will engage actively in more problem-solving coping, whereas pessimists who expect bad outcomes will tend to engage in more avoidant coping.

Dispositional optimism is assessed with the Life Orientation Task (Lot; Scheier & Carver, 1985), a brief self-report questionnaire. Evidence for its sound reliability and validity can be found in Scheier and Carver's (1987) review. Dispositional optimism has been found to be related to better physical health outcomes and its positive role has been documented in many different samples. Among college students in the final weeks of the semester (a stressful time with final exams and final papers), optimists reported significantly less physical symptoms during the course of those weeks (Scheier & Carver, 1985). These same researchers have also gone beyond a reliance on self-reports of health status to find that among coronary artery bypass surgery patients, optimists when compared to pessimists were significantly less likely than pessimists to develop perioperative physiologic reactions that are considered markers for myocardial infarction (i.e., less Q-waves on EKGs and release of the enzyme AST), and were more likely to recover faster from surgery (Scheier et al., 1989).

In terms of mechanisms through which optimism influences health, a great deal of research has examined optimism's relation with coping. Among different populations, such as college students and men at risk for AIDS, optimists were found to be more active copers, whereas pessimists were more prone to engage in avoidant coping (see Scheier & Carver, 1987, 1992; T. W. Smith & Williams, 1992, for extensive reviews of this research). Fry (1995) found that, among female executives, higher optimism was associated with greater reliance on social support as a coping mechanism. Further, Aspinwall and Taylor (1992) found support for a mediational model, whereby optimism was related to coping, which in turn influenced both psychological and physical well-being among college students. Scheier et al. (1989) also found evidence for the mediational role of coping through which coping links optimism and physical health among coronary artery bypass patients. The reader can consult Schwarzer's (1994) review for more discussion of these and other studies on optimism and health outcomes.

Optimism has also been found to influence health through its relation with health habits. For example, among coronary artery bypass patients, optimists were more likely to take vitamins (Scheier et al., 1990, cited in Scheier & Carver, 1992); and among heart patients in a cardiac rehabilitation program, optimists were more successful in lowering their coronary risk through exercise and by lowering levels of saturated fat and body fat (Shepperd, Maroto, & Pbert, 1996). Among nonclinical samples, similar beneficial results with health habits emerge. Among college students, optimism was related to health enhancing behaviors (Robbins, Spence, & Clark, 1991), and among HIV seronegative men, optimists in comparison to pessimists had fewer anonymous sexual partners (Taylor et al., 1992, cited in Scheier & Carver, 1992). In another study examining safer sexual behavior patterns among heterosexual women, Morrill, Ickovics, Golubchikov, Beren, and Rodin (1996) found that women higher in optimism were four times more likely to adopt safer sexual practices at a 3-month follow-up than those lower in optimism.

Although many studies suggest that optimism is beneficial for physical well-being, inconsistent findings have been reported. There is room for additional support and clarification. In a study of patients recovering from elective joint replacement surgery (Chamberlain et al., 1992), optimism was positively correlated with measures of life satisfaction, and positive well-being, and negatively correlated with psychological distress and self-reported pain 6 months postoperatively; however, after controlling for presurgery levels of these variables, investigators found that optimism no longer significantly predicted health outcomes after surgery. In addition, like with hardiness, there have been serious questions about optimism's discriminant validity with neuroticism (T. W. Smith, Pope, Rhodewalt, & Poulton, 1989). Other critics have raised the important possibility that too much optimism (e.g., unrealistic optimism) could be related to negative health outcomes through people's unrealistic high expectations that good things will always happen (e.g, Schwarzer, 1994; Tennen & Affleck, 1987; Wallston, 1994). In this vein, Davidson and Prkachin's (1997) results highlighted how constructs of optimism (i.e., dispositional optimism and unrealistic optimism) are jointly important in predicting health promoting behaviors.

Explanatory Style

Explanatory style describes the causal attributions that individuals habitually make for the positive and negative events that happen in their life. An optimistic explanatory style is characterized by external, unstable, and specific attributions for negative events, and internal, stable, global attributions for positive events. A pessimistic explanatory style has the opposite pattern of causal attributions. Explanatory style, with its combination of cognitive and learning principles, is a construct with conceptual roots in American psychology similar to those of dispositional optimism. More specifically, explanatory style is a reformulation of learned helplessness theory, a theory proposed to account for individual differences in responses to uncontrollable events (Abramson, Seligman, & Teasdale, 1978). Researchers of explanatory style focus on the causal explanations for bad (or good) events rather than the causes of uncontrollable events. "A person who explains such events [bad] with stable, global, and internal causes shows more severe helplessness deficits than a person who explains them with unstable, specific, and external causes" (C. Peterson, Seligman, & Valliant, 1988, p. 24). Most of the research focuses on pessimistic explanatory style, and specifically one's attributions for negative events. Investigators have suggested, however, the importance of also focusing on attributions of positive events on well-being (e.g., Abramson, Dykman, & Needles, 1991; Anderson & Deuser, 1991; Gotlib, 1991). See C. Peterson and Seligman (1984, 1987) for an extensive review of the research on explanatory style and well-being, as well as its conceptual and methodological background.

Explanatory style, unlike most other personality constructs reviewed in this chapter that rely solely on self-report scales, can be measured through two very different modes of measurement. The first and most popular method is the Attributional Style Questionnaire (ASQ), a self-report questionnaire that lists hypothetical events. Respondents are asked to imagine that each of the events has happened to them, and then to write down one major cause of the event. They then rate each cause along each of the three dimensions (internal–external, stable–unstable, global–specific) on a 7-point scale. Ratings are added within type of event and across dimensions to get a composite score. Reliability and construct validity has been found to be satisfactory (C. Peterson, 1991a, 1991b, 1991c; C. Peterson & Seligman, 1987).

The second technique is a content analysis procedure referred to as the CAVE (content analysis of verbatim explanation) technique (C. Peterson, Schulman, Castellon, & Seligman, 1992). This technique was developed in order to capture nonhypothetical events and more spontaneous causes of events. The CAVE technique examines verbal material (e.g., interviews, biographies, letters, diaries) for events and causal explanations of the events. Investigators search for and identify these causal explanations in the text and then score them along the dimensions of internality, stability, and globality. The CAVE technique's reliability and validity has been established (C. Peterson, Maier, & Seligman, 1993). More recently, C. Peterson and Ulrey (1994) successfully measured explanatory style with a projective technique that identified causal explanations in TAT protocols.

Research on explanatory style has mainly examined direct relations with physical and psychological health outcomes. For example, a pessimistic explanatory style has been found to be related to increased depression (C. Peterson & Seligman, 1984) and immunosuppression—ratio of helper cells to suppressor cells (Kamen-Siegel, Rodin, Seligman, & Dwyer, 1991). Several studies have been prospective in design. In a study of college students, a pessimistic explanatory style was related to greater reported illness symptoms after 1 month and doctor visits 1 year later (C. Peterson & Seligman, 1987). In another study of college students, Dykema, Bergbower, and C. Peterson (1995) found the report of hassles to mediate the relation between explanatory style and illness. A pessimistic explanatory style led to increased reports of hassles, which led students to appraise major life events as having more negative impact on their lives, which in turn led to more illness 1 month later. Illness was represented by a composite score that included the number of times students were reported ill, doctor visits, missed classes, and a self-reported health rating.

A link between explanatory style and health has been impressively found in a 35-year prospective study using the CAVE technique (C. Peterson et al., 1988). In this study, explanations for bad events were extracted from interviews with Harvard University graduates from the classes of 1942 through 1944, done when respondents were age 25. The interviews were scored using the CAVE technique. At various ages, throughout a 35-year time period, respondents' health was rated by a research internist based on an extensive physical exam. Men with a pessimistic explanatory style at age 25 were rated as less healthy later in life compared to men with an optimistic explanatory style; these findings were most robust when the men were at age 45.

C. Peterson and Seligman (1987) suggested that explanatory style is related to health through coping. Preliminary data from a cross-sectional study indicated that a pessimistic explanatory style as represented on the stability and globality dimensions was related to low self-efficacy, unhealthy health habits, and stressful life events—variables that were, in turn, related to reported illness symptoms and number of doctor visits. Keep in mind, however, that these mediating variables are not commonly reported as measures of coping, and in the case of self-efficacy and stressful life events, the variables are most often considered to be predictors of coping. Another possible mechanism linking explanatory style and health is perception of health problems. C. Peterson and De Avila (1995) found that perceived preventability of health problems mediated the relation between explanatory style and risk perception among a community sample of adults. Their findings suggested that an optimistic explanatory style entails more perceived control over health problems, and thereby leads individuals to engage in positive health behaviors and ultimately enjoy better health.

More longitudinal research on the mediational role of health behaviors, and coping, as measured with reliable and valid measures, needs to be conducted in order to better understand the path that links explanatory style to health. The investigator eager to advance the work on explanatory style and health also need note that in most of the research conducted to date only the stability and globality dimensions of explanatory style have predicted health and well-being. This raises important questions about the role of the internality dimension. C. Peterson and Seligman (1987) reported that internality is the least reliable dimension and shows the most inconsistent associations with other variables. As with hardiness, the multifaceted nature of explanatory style raises particular conceptual and measurement challenges (cf. Carver, 1989). Although many different correlates of explanatory style have been found, there continues to be serious questioning of its meaning and of how best it is to be measured (C. Peterson, 1991a, 1991b). To help researchers contend with all the questionning, an important tool for those seeking to enter this challenging domain is a 1991 issue of *Psychological Inquiry,* which includes a target article by Peterson in which an overview on the explanatory style construct is presented, and commentaries and reactions to his statement by experts in the field.

Health Locus of Control and Self-Efficacy

Health locus of control and self-efficacy are somewhat hesitantly included in a chapter on personality and health. K. A. Wallston (1992) made clear that health locus beliefs were never conceptualized to be as stable as generalized locus of control beliefs. Thus, it was not considered to be a personality construct; rather, it was conceptualized as "a disposition to act in a certain manner in health-related situations" (p. 185). Similarly, Bandura and his colleagues repeatedly emphasized the specificity of the self-efficacy notion: The person's intended behavior needs to be specific to a particular situation in order for expectations of self-efficacy to predict whether that person engages in the behavior. A review of the research, however, revealed threads of "personality" in empirical work with both constructs that are relevant to this chapter.

Health locus of control (HLC) refers to individuals' beliefs about where control over their health is located, in internal sources such as a person's own behavior or external sources such as powerful others. The introduction of HLC (B. S. Wallston, K. A. Wallston, Kaplan, & Maides, 1976) was an attempt to apply Rotter's social learning theory to health-related behaviors. Rotter's expectancy value theory of behavior stated that the potential for individuals to engage in certain behaviors in a given situation was a function of people's expectancy about whether or not their engagement in a particular behavior would lead to a particular outcome in a given situation, and the value they place on that outcome. Accordingly, early work showed that HLC scores only predicted health-related behaviors when respondents in the research said they highly valued health (B. S. Wallston et al., 1976; K. A. Wallston, Maides, & B. S. Wallston, 1976). The focus on the values of health outcomes brings the investigator closer to the domain of personality (cf. Lazarus & Folkman, 1984).

With regard to measurement efforts, there has been an emphasis on the multidimensionality of HLC beliefs (K. A. Wallston, 1989; K. A. Wallston, B. S. Wallston, & DeVellis, 1978). The Multidimensionality Health Locus of Control Scale (MHLOC) measures internal beliefs about health, and external beliefs that are made up of two dimensions, chance and powerful others (K. A. Wallston, 1989; K. A. Wallston, B. S. Wallston, & DeVellis, 1978). The internal dimension measures people's belief that health is affected by their own behavior; the powerful others dimension measures beliefs that powerful others affect health; and the chance dimension measures beliefs that luck, chance, or fate influence health.

Results generated by the HLC construct have been mixed. The majority of studies have examined the influence of health locus of control on health behaviors or habits, with the assumption that greater HLC would be related to more positive health behaviors. When reviewing the vast literature on HLC, some studies do indeed find that a more internal locus of control (belief that one's health is controllable) is related to health promoting behaviors (e.g., exercise, eating healthy), which in turn leads to better health. However, there seems to be just as many studies that do not find an association between HLC and health behaviors. The reader is referred to K. A. Wallston (1992) for a good review of the theoretical underpinnings of the HLC construct, as well as results linking HLC to health behaviors.

K. A. Wallston (1991, 1992) discussed possible reasons for the lack of consistent findings in the literature and recalled the theoretical roots of social learning theory. Wallston is grappling with the need for a more elaborated view of what is happening in the health-related behavioral episode, and thereby, personality. Wallston noted that most of the research on HLC does not include a measure of health value. Value of the outcome was an important component of Rotter's original social learning theory. In support of Wallston's argument, one study found that value placed on participation of health promoting behaviors was more important in predicting health protective behaviors than locus of control; moreover, those who were high in health value and had an internal health locus of control were the most likely to perform health protective behaviors (Weiss & Larsen, 1990). Unfortunately, this type of research comprises a minority of the studies examining HLC.

In spite of the lack of consistent results, the health locus of control construct has not been entirely abandoned. K. A. Wallston (1992) noted that HLC beliefs were never expected to predict a large amount of the variance of measures of health behaviors. He emphasized the need for "more complex and inclusive theoretical models" (p. 252) to better predict and explain health-related behaviors. In that vein, Wallston pointed out the important additional role that self-efficacy can play in explaining health-related behaviors. Importantly, it was a generalized self-efficacy—indicative of what is considered to be a personality construct—to which he refered. To capture this, Wallston's research team has developed a perceived competence scale to measure generalized self-efficacy (K. A. Wallston, 1989).

Self-efficacy, in its own right, has become a very popular and formidable social cognitive construct for many health researchers. Based on Bandura's (1977) social learning theory, self-efficacy represents the degree to which individuals believe that they have the capability to perform an intended behavior: The more people believe they can perform the behavior, the more likely they will be to engage in the particular behavior. Reviews of the self-efficacy and health literature have found in general that self-efficacy predicts a vast number of health behaviors (Holden, 1991; A. O'Leary, 1992; Schwarzer, 1994). Schwarzer (1994) reported that self-efficacy has predicted physical exercise behavior, smoking behavior, weight control, and sexual risk behaviors.

Self-efficacy has been measured with many different scales. Due to the behavior–situation specificity theorized by Bandura, many researchers have developed their own scales designed to measure self-efficacy in specific situations. More recently, however, other researchers have developed more traitlike versions of self-efficacy. These conceptualizations can be considered dispositional or generalized self-efficacy (Shwarzer, 1994). Refer to Schwarzer (1994) for a good review of these generalized self-efficacy constructs. Schwarzer discussed Snyder, Irving, and Anderson's (1991) construct of hope, C. A. Smith, Dobbins, and K. A. Wallston's (1991) perceived competence construct, and Jerusalem and Schwarzer's (1992) generalized self-efficacy construct as all measuring this dispositional or generalized self-efficacy. These authors believe, similar to Bandura, that specific behaviors are best predicted by specific behaviors. However, when trying to make predictions across a variety of different situations, general self-efficacy scales are thought to be better predictors (Schwarzer, 1994).

Motives—Affiliative Trust

The work on motive strength and health by McClelland and his collaborators offered the only contemporary approach to understanding how people's personal dispositions lead to better physical health that gave serious consideration to unconscious processes. In this approach, motives are measured by the content analysis of TAT stories. Much of this work on motives has focused on the negative health affects of the stressed power motive syndrome (see McClelland, 1989, for a review of this work). However, Affiliative Trust–Mistrust —an object relations construct—found in stories of positive rather than cynical relations has been related to better immune function and fewer reported illnesses (McKay, 1991).

McKay (1991) was interested in examining whether internal representations of relations (i.e., object relations) would be associated with immune function. Respondents were asked to write stories in response to TAT pictures, and their stories were scored for Affilative Trust–Mistrust. Affiliative mistrust represents malevolent, or negative internal representations of relations which lead an individual to constantly experience loss, rejection, or disappointment. McKay theorized that "the fear that one will be abandoned or mistreated by others could have an immunosuppression effect through the same mechanisms that are involved in the connection between actual loss and decreased immune function" (p. 641). Benevolent, or trustful representations of relations, in contrast, could have an immunoenhancing effect.

Interrater reliability for the Trust–Mistrust scale showed good agreement between coders. Internal and test–retest reliability were moderate. The Mistrust subscale showed good construct validity, as did the Trust–Mistrust index, although to a lesser degree (the Trust–Mistrust index represented a composite of the Trust and Mistrust subscales). The Trust subscale, however, showed very little evidence of construct validity. See McKay (1991) for a full discussion of reliability and validity for the Trust–Mistrust scale.

Results indicated that greater Mistrust (representing malevolent object relations) was negatively related to helper-to-suppressor T-cell ratios (T4:T8), indicative of lower immune function. Greater mistrust was also related to greater reporting of all types of illnesses, including respiratory tract illnesses in the preceding year. Benevolent object relations indicated by high Trust–Mistrust scores were positively associated with better immune function (i.e., greater helper-to-suppressor T-cell ratios), and negatively related to reports of all illnesses and respiratory tract illnesses.

Unlike the other personality constructs discussed in this chapter, most of the research on motives and health has focused on physiological processes. It seems that this direct link with physiological processes would have stimulated a great deal of excitement. On the contrary, this work has been met with much skepticism. A possible bias against projective techniques as reliable and valid measures of personality within the field of health psychology has possibly prevented further testing of these provocative findings. Moreover, there have been serious methodological questions raised about McClelland and colleagues' reliance on S-IgA concentration (salivation) as a reliable and valid indicator of immune function (Valdimarsdottir & Stone, 1997). McKay's (1991) study using the more stable helper-to-suppressor T-cell ratios as a measure of immune function is an important response to the criticism.

CRITIQUE: STRENGTHS, WEAKNESSES, AND DILEMMAS

In the process of looking across and seeking to integrate the research on the reviewed personality constructs, a new investigator encounters a number of questions about the arena of personality and health that require attention. In addition, as the investigator considers where the field has been and where it can go next, there are two dilemmas to be confronted. These are depicted here in order to make the point that indeed something has been learned through a research focus on personality as a health promoting and enhancing factor and that learning has consequences beyond the simple accumulation of facts. There are policy-related and ideological implications to this work that investigators need to recognize and bring to a decision about whether to continue "business as usual" or consider some new ways of working with personality in health psychology.

To reduce the risk that this section of the chapter would become a litany of problems that does little more than discourage the eager new investigator, bore more seasoned readers, and dizzy everyone, the sources and intentions must be clarified. The checklist and dilemmas are inspired by available personality and health literature and a more general reading of contemporary psychology.

A CHECKLIST OF CONCERNS

What, Exactly, Is the Link Between Personality and Health?

Investigators need to be exact and modest about what it is that they are looking at when they speak of a link between personality and health. In the empirical knowledge now available, the amount of work illustrating the model linking personality to health behaviors and that portraying personality as a stress buffer vastly outweighs work supporting the model of a direct connection between personality and biological and physiological processes, especially if it is required that more than self-reports of health processes be measured. Much more is known about the strictly behavioral domain and psychological processes (i.e., about how personality relates to behaviors thought relevant to the maintenance of health and how it presents itself along side of stress in persons' lives), than is known about the biomedical aspects that accompany the psychological. Studies (Gruen, Silva, Ehrlich, Schweitzer, & Friedhoff, 1997) like one of women exposed to a stressful induced-failure task in which the personality attribute of self-criticism was found to be related to changes in plasma homovanillic acid (the metabolite of dopamine), as well as self-reports of stress and changes in mood, are relatively rare.

This is not pointed out to diminish the importance of the first two kinds of endeavors—they are potentially useful for health interventions (Brownell & L. R. Cohen, 1995; Cockburn et al., 1991; Rakowski, Wells, Lasater, & Carleton, 1991), risk reduction efforts (Morrill et al., 1996; Wulfert, Wan, & Backus, 1996), and counseling and clinical applications (Spalding, 1995). Rather, the intent is to encourage a recognition of all that is waiting for attention, and the need for interdisciplinary work involving social scientists and those trained in the biological and medical sciences to fill in the many undeserved gaps that still exist in the literature.

There are also limitations to the notion of personality as a stress buffer. Although they work with conceptual frameworks that strongly support the prediction of a stress-buffering role for personality, investigators have met serious difficulties in actually statistically demonstrating interactions between stress and personality variables, and thereby, the buffering function of personality. Although this has been made most specific about hardiness (Funk, 1992; Orr & Westman, 1990), the problem also troubles other constructs. The demonstration of the main effects of personality constructs on psychological and physical health indicators, at least through self-report assessments, are plentiful in the literature; but a significant interaction (stress × personality) term, the result taken to be the hallmark of buffering, is relatively rare. In the majority of studies that present themselves as about personality and health protection or enhancement, the interaction is simply not tested for; in other studies, it is sought and sometimes, but not always, found.

How Does One Assess Health as a Positive Outcome?

Given the kinds of measures that are typically employed, it may be concluded that it is much easier to assess health conceived of as the absence of illness than health as a distinct way of being that involves more than just not being sick. From the earliest days of formal discussion of personality, stress, and health issues, it has been assumed that outcomes would come in at least three independent forms: no change in health, negative changes in health, or positive changes in health (what Dohrenwend termed "growth"; Dohrenwend, 1978). Antonovsky introduced the term *salutogenesis* to emphasize that he was after more than the absence of illness, Kobasa and her colleagues wrote about hardiness and executives who not only do not get sick but thrive under stress. Nonetheless, in the research, it is most often symptom checklists that are relied on to represent all of the outcomes. High symptom scores are taken to represent illness and low scores stand in for health. As a number of researchers have recently noted, there are both conceptual and measurement challenges needing attention with regard to how convincingly to approach a distinctive notion of health and thriving in empirical research (V. E. O'Leary & Ickovics, 1995; Park, L. H. Cohen, & Murch, 1996; Tedeschi & Calhoun, 1996).

How to Choose Among the Constructs?

The new investigator needs seriously to take both similarities and differences between the constructs available for personality and health research. For example, although most of the variables studied involve some element of perceived control over the environment (e.g., C. Peterson & Stunkard, 1989), there are serious differences between theorists in what they say about control. Antonovsky's position stands out as the most distinctive. In each of his major statements on the theory of sense of coherence, Antonovsky (1979, 1987, 1991; Ouellette, 1998) detailed his differences with promoters of an internal locus of control. For him, work on locus of control and its emphasis on control as that which resides in the hands of autonomous, isolated individuals who perceive and enjoy a direct link between their voluntary actions and the outcomes they seek bore a strong cultural bias. In sense of coherence, he sought something other than a Western, capitalistic, and enterpreneurial perspective on human capability—something that could capture the ways in which a person experiences control as a result of trust and sense of community with others, something that could be experienced within a broad variety of cultures and socioeconomic circumstances. Another difference is represented by the notion of challenge. It is this component of hardiness that most distinguishes it from the other constructs reviewed. In fact, it has provoked a debate between Antonovsky (1979, 1987, 1991) and Ouellette (1998), whose theories overlap in many respects, about what keeps people healthy under stress. A third specific example of difference is easily illustrated through the affiliative trust construct. Here, there is an emphasis on unconscious aspects of the human experience. This stands in sharp constrast to cognitive social learning notions such as optimism and self-efficacy that emphasize what is in awareness and highly rational and deemphasize what is implicitly motivational and emotional (cf. McClelland, Koestner, & Wenberger, 1989).

Speaking more generally, it must be recognized that personality and health investigators have differed substantially in their essential theoretical commitments and have made, thereby, fundamentally very different assumptions about what constitutes personality. They differ on such matters as the complexity of personality and the degree to which it needs to be understood as that which emerges in and through social structures (cf. Antonovsky, 1991; Ouellette Kobasa, 1990). The new investigator is encouraged to look closely within the theoretical statements that support each of the constructs. It is within those statements, and not the scales where items across constructs often look remarkably the same or within recent adaptations of the construct in which confusingly radical redefinitions of constructs can emerge (e.g., Younkin & Betz, 1996), that one can find both the distinctiveness of the constructs and insights that have yet to be brought to empirical test (Gladden & Ouellette, 1997).

Is It All Neuroticism?

For a number of the personality constructs reviewed here, investigators have claimed a threat to construct validity because of the relation between those constructs and neuroticism (also sometimes referred to as negative affect; e.g., Funk, 1992). The most popular form of the claim goes as follows: If the personality construct under study does not continue to have an effect on health outcomes after the variance associated with neuroticism has been removed, then that personality construct is redundant. Most of the pursuit of this idea has been empirical, with investigators relying on exploratory and confirmatory factor analysis and/or multivariate regression strategies. The results of these studies have been mixed. For example, some have shown that a construct like hardiness loses its effect once neuroticism is entered into the regression equation (Allred & T. W. Smith, 1989); others show the effect remains (e.g., Florian et al., 1995). The ambiguity also emerged in work that took a number of constructs into account. Some studies demonstrated that all of the constructs similar to those of this chapter load on one large factor that can be labeled "health proneness" (Bernard, Hutchison, Lavin, & Pennington, 1996); others argued for the independence of constructs. A study by Robbins et al. (1991), for example, showed there is no single master personality construct like neuroticism that is more successful than any other at predicting health outcomes. They demonstrated that if the aim is to sort out the effects of personality on actual health complaints and beliefs about the maintenance of health, it is necessary to include several different kinds of personality contructs in the research.

A conceptual approach also needs to be taken to the question about neuroticism and redundancy. As Lazarus (1990) put it, it is all a matter of the theory that the investigator favors:

> The presumption by Ben-Porath and Tellegen, Costa and McCrae, and Watson is that negative affectivity (or neuroticism) is *the* basic factor in the claimed confounding. However, the argument could just as logically, and perhaps more fruitfully, be turned around so that appraisal of coping styles are treated as key variables in the relationship between negative affectivity (or neuroticism) and subjective distress or complaints about dysfunction. (p. 44)

Scheier, Carver, and Bridges (1994) suggested that optimism–pessimism can be understood, not as a variable better replaced by neuroticism, but as a subfactor within the broader dimension of neuroticism; and, in its role in coping and health, independent of other possible subfactors of this broader trait of neuroticism. Maddi and Khoshaba (1994) provided empirical support for Maddi's (1990) argument that the relation between hardiness and neuroticism is not the basis for the dismissal of hardiness, but that which was indeed predicted by the original hardiness theory. Hardiness was conceptualized as related to strain, and strain is that which is assessed through most measures of neuroticism.

There is much yet to be learned by taking seriously the variety in personality constructs that have been linked with health. Given the current emphasis on the five-factor model approach to personality (neuroticism is one of the five) and its use as a kind of gold standard in personality study (cf. Ouellette, 1999; Suls, David, & Harvey, 1996), however, there is fear that there will be pressure put on new investigators to see neuroticism as the simple answer to it all. Granted some form of negative emotion plays some role in illness processes. However, it is necessary to understand more about staying healthy than that it represents a lack of negative feelings.

To Whom Does the Link Between Personality and Health Apply and Does It Apply in the Same Way?

Although a remarkable diversity of respondent groups emerges in a look across the personality and health studies, there has been relatively little explicit concern in this literature for matters of race, ethnicity, class, sexual orientation, and other markers of diversity. This gap is especially striking because much of the basic literature has had to do with personality in interaction with stress and many of the markers of diversity have been themselves documented to be serious structural sources of stress in our society (Krieger, 1999; Meyer, 1995). Also, there are suggestions in the literature that the link between personality and health may hold for some groups, but not for others; and that the link may emerge in different ways for different groups. For example, Ingram et al. (1996) found that sense of coherence was related to distress among homeless women but not low income housed women. Kobasa (1982) found that the challenge dimension of hardiness was correlated with better reported health among business executives and lawyers but that former Vietnam army officers on their way to ROTC assignments reported more health complaints, the more they reported an orientation toward challenge. Others have noted that many of the hardiness results found in groups of men have not generalized to women (e.g., Schmied & Lawler, 1986).

The theories that support the sense of coherence and hardiness allow for and encourage the investigator systematically to look for such differences between groups. Note Kobasa and Maddi's early phenomenological emphasis on how individuals see their world. From an existential perspective, how individuals see the world is constituted by what they have at hand in their immediate and distant environments; and issues such as race, ethnicity, and job situation are part of this way of being in the world. Antonovsky defined sense of coherence as that which is shaped by the social structures in which people are socialized. Nonethess, the research has yet to be done that explicitly features diversity, especially with regard to the issues noted earlier. New investigations are in order so that an understanding of personality can inform the resolution of long-standing questions such as: Why is it that members of minority groups in society are often in greater risk of poorer health than members of the majority group?

DILEMMAS TO THINK ABOUT

"Yes ... But" 1: Can There Be Agency Without Blame? Can There Be Structures and Persons?

"Yes": A focus on personality as health promoting and enhancing has expanded the biomedical model and enabled a recognition of health (as well as illness), the importance of psychological factors, and the person as an active agent.

"But": This focus on the individuals' role in their staying healthy has led to blame being placed on those who get sick and a neglect of the social, cultural, and political causes of distress and lack of health.

The Yes. In what might be called the founding ideas behind the personality constructs reviewed, there is an emphasis on the search to understand the factors responsible for health in very trying circumstances. Antonovsky (1979) used the term *salutogenesis* to encompass data collected from persons who had survived the Holocaust and those in less profound but still troubling situations. The initial hardiness study (Kobasa, 1979) was done with business executives undergoing a major organizational change, the divestiture of American Telephone and Telegraph (AT&T). This company was "Ma Bell." Most of the executives had gone to work there, 20 plus years earlier, assured of a stable and predictable work environment. They never expected the break up that occurred. In contrast to then-popular emphasis in airline magazines and other media on the terrible effects of stress in peoples' lives, especially those of American icons like business executives, the empirical study showed that significant numbers of the executives were doing quite well in spite of their high stress levels at work and in other parts of their lives. Later, Kuo and Tsai (1986) used a hardiness, stress, and health framework to react against a literature on immigration that is filled with references to the bad things that occur when people come to a new country, such as identity crises. They provided documentation of immigrants who were doing quite well. Other examples of what is now popularly called resilience in the face of adversity can be found from research on adults living with a chronic illness and persons working in education and service provision (cf. Ouellette, 1993).

In a similar spirit is the formidable and still-growing literature based primarily in the developmental psychology literature on children who have remained resilient in a variety of circumstances, including serious childhood illness, homes with parents suffering physical and mental debilitation, poverty and other class-related problems (Anthony, 1987; Masten et al., 1999). O'Leary and Ickovics (1995) documented findings on what they called thriving from various research arenas and issued a call for more such investigations and particular attention to the many examples of women's ability to thrive in the face of strenuous circumstances.

To explain why it is that some persons stay healthy while others fall ill, researchers focused on personality. In choosing the kind of personality variables that were to be examined alongside of health, health-related behaviors, and stress, researchers were making a claim for a particular view of what it means to be a person. In their selection of constructs, they were emphasizing the extent to which persons are to be recognized as not simply passive recipients of what happens to them but active shapers of their worlds, including those situations relevant to their health. Their conceptual stance was clearly opposed to a strict behavioristic view that left no room for matters like personal choice and a psychodynamic one that associated the determination of behavior with unconscious patterns set early in an individual's life. As people see especially clearly in sense of coherence, hardiness, and all of the control constructs, their interest was in understanding agency and the person as a source of change.

The But. For several years now, one of us has taught graduate students who represent diverse ethnic, racial, cultural, and economic backgrounds and who are committed to use social science tools to do something about serious social problems like racism, homophobia, sexism, and the stigmatizing of those living with serious illnesses like AIDS. With such an audience, she has come to know very well that look of wariness that comes over students' faces as she gives the lecture on sense of coherence, hardiness, self-efficacy, and related constructs. They fear the consequences of the focus placed on characteristics of individuals, especially characteristics that represent agency. They question what will come of those who do not stay healthy under stress: Will they be blamed for the distress and illnesses they experience? They also worry that the spotlight placed on individuals serves to keep in the dark those social structures likely to be responsible for the stresses: Might not the emphasis on some individuals' resilience and thriving distract those who are willing and able to change the social structures and processes that make up racism, homophobia, sexism, and stigmatization? Is it just the excuse those folks who are determined not to see any of this change happen are seeking?

And it is not only graduate students who raise these questions. Ryan (1971) elaborated on how easy it is for those in power to attribute problems to defects in individuals rather than to unjust social systems. He included policymakers, liberal-minded reformers, and academics among those in power and showed how all participated in this way of thinking. His critique of victim blaming ideology was profoundly influential and is still found useful by those seeking to address the variety of forms in which inequality persists in society (cf. Lykes, Banuazizi, R. Liem, & Morris, 1996). There is also the compelling work of Sontag (1978, 1988) on illness and its metaphors. She made clear the pain caused to people living with a serious illness by research that seems to say: "If only you had this or that personality or attitude toward life, you would be fine." She also made the important point that constructs about personality are metaphors that serve to neutralize and make manageable distressing realities like suffering and death. From her perspective, psychologists and social scientists of health provide a kind of opiate for the pain that is an essential part of the human condition. Thereby, she claimed, social scientists engage in a kind of social denial (cf. Ouellette Kobasa, 1989)

Yes and But. The extent to which the juxtaposition of the personality and health research and the positions of Ryan, Sontag, and many graduate students represents a dilemma is well expressed in R. Liem and J. H. Liem (1996). They cited a good deal of research, including their own, that demonstrates the health damaging and other serious consequences of unemployment; and they displayed the inadequacy of the image of the unemployed victim that this research creates. They presented examples of unemployed individuals who contest the victim image and actively engage in resistance against the many threats to their welfare that are brought on by unemployment.

"Yes ... But" 2: Health as a Moral Value

"Yes": Research on personality as health promoting and enhancing recognizes the importance of structures and suggests some ways of changing them so that all can enjoy lower risk of illness and enhanced well-being.

"But": Underlying the effort to improve peoples' health are insufficiently examined assumptions about what health is and ideological commitments that are themselves shaped by social, cultural, and political forces.

The Yes. Many researchers interested in personality and health called for a view of personality that incorporates the social, cultural, and political stuctures through which personality is expressed. They have discussed how changes required for the enhancement of certain personality characteristics, and thereby, health would need to be instituted on both individual and group levels. For example, much of Antonovsky's last work was taken up with the consideration of how structural changes might be instituted that would increase sense of coherence as it is experienced both by individuals and groups; Bandura's (1995) most recent statement on self-efficacy and related agency constructs made clear their connection to broader social forces; and Ouellette Kobasa (1991) discussed how to foster particular environmental settings (i.e., community-based health advocacy organizations) that serve as special physical and social spaces for the expression of hardiness. All based their calls for change in the assumption that these changes will lead to the improvement in persons' health, an unquestionnably worthy goal for all. Who could question it?

The But. Several recent commentators on the science of linking psychological and social factors to biomedical phenomena have pointed out the essentially value-laden nature of the enterprise. In this discussion, seemingly universal and invariant notions like that of health are revealed to be socially and culturally constructed, as are theories about personality and the links between personality and health (cf. Marcus et al, 1996). What they said about the intricacies of how negative health outcomes are defined also holds for the positive outcomes that have been simply assumed as good and desirable throughout this chapter. One needs to ask, however: Positive and enhancing according to whom, in what circumstances, and when? Massey, Cameron, Ouellette, and Fine (1998) caution that what some investigators claim to be unquestionning indicators of having been resilient—of having successfully coped with life's stresses, such as staying in school or not getting pregnant, may be resilience from the perspective of the researcher, but not from the perspective of those being studied. A study by Green (1994) also underscores the danger of assuming what the good is. In a very provocative study of Central American women who have survived the horrors of war and oppression, Green showed how the experience of poor physical health—what many personality and health researchers would seek to help them minimize—is actually something they desire. Their symptoms are a way for these women to retain ties with their now-lost communities. To be healthy would be to lose all contact with the many who have died.

Yes and But. The claim that research on personality and health is infused with value judgments and shaped by social and cultural forces is not to be denied. The call here is for the discussion of values to be made more explicit and prominent in the literature. For example, why has more not been said by health psychologists about the fact that those variables identified by Western psychologists as what keeps people healthy—feeling in control, being committed, approaching the world optimistically, and so on—are also, in themselves, thought to be good ways of being in society. It is the socially undesirable variables like anger and hostility that make people sick. The job is not to make the research enterprise value free but rather to find ways to keep researchers ever-cognizant of the value judgments that are being made. Many of those who enter the arena of personality and health are those who are indeed seeking to use scientific tools for good ends, to find new ways of intervening in biomedical phenomena to relieve peoples' sufferings. The aim is not to discourage them but to have them recognize the complexity of all aspects of their work.

THE FUTURE FOR RESEARCH ON PERSONALITY AND HEALTH

The following is the basic message for future work: Key to the resolution of current concerns and dilemmas is the willingness of health researchers to take better advantage of the theoretical and methodological tools now available to them within the enterprise of personality psychology and the insights about the ideological and historical dimensions of their work provided by feminist (e.g., Stewart, 1994) and critical (e.g., Fox & Prilleltensky, 1997; Prilleltensky, 1997) psychology. This willingness will help ensure that more of the contributions and fewer of the limitations of research on personality as a health protective and enhancing factor will be realized. To support this message, the remaining pages are used to identify three interrelated ideas from the more general endeavors in psychology: the multifaceted nature of personality and personality psychology, the importance of transactions, and the usefullness of quantitative and qualitative research within local contexts. Key sources of these ideas are cited, some ways they can be connected to the concerns and dilemmas in health research are suggested, and some examples of their representation in empirical work are provided.

The Multifaceted Nature of Personality or There Is More to Personality than Traits

Much of health psychology seems to equate personality with traits and to be excessively preoccupied with the potential promise of descriptive approaches such as the five-factor model (e.g., T. W. Smith & Williams, 1992; Suls et al., 1996; cf. Ouellette, 1999). This limited view is in contrast to the concerns of the general field. Several recent statements strongly make the point that personality can be seen, given available conceptual schemes and measurement strategies, as constituted by several different units of analysis. It is not all just traits. McAdams (1996), for example, reviewed personality research to illustrate three levels on which personality operates. Beyond traits or what McAdams called the "psychology of the stranger," there is what he called the "personal concerns" level of analysis on which he placed constructs such as Little's (1993) personal projects and Emmons' personal strivings (Emmons & McAdams, 1991). On the third level, McAdams placed personality conceived of as a matter of identity and life stories. Here, the emphasis is on those personality processes involved in meaning making (Bruner, 1990), narratives about the self through the life course (Cohler, 1991), and the dialogical self (Hermans, Rijks, & Kempen, 1993).

As discussed elsewhere, the presence of all three levels has serious implications for the ways personality and health research is done (Ouellette, 1999). The variety of ways of conceiving of personality provide important options for a response to the specific concerns raised about how investigators think about outcomes, the choice between constructs, the generalizability of personality and health findings, and both dilemmas. For example, the second and third levels allow the researcher seriously to take the structures in which personality resides. The best of the research on these levels shows that persons have concerns in particular settings (e.g., Ogilvie & Rose, 1995) and stories about self are told in historical and cultural space (Franz & Stewart, 1994). This broader view of personality in context enables researchers to assess and seek to understand how it is that personality works similarly or differently across different groups to protect and enhance health. It also helps in addressing the dilemma around dealing with structures and individual agency.

The personality constructs reviewed in the first part of this chapter unfortunately have too often been approached simply as personality traits. There are solid grounds, however, within the theories that support each construct for understanding them as having to do with other ways of thinking about personality. Each reflects aspects of all three of McAdams' levels. In taking the broader view of these constructs, the move is away from a simple descriptive or McAdams' stranger approach to personality and toward an understanding of personality processes at play in such events as a person's actual facilitation, perception, and response to stressors in the environment.

But how can researchers do personality and health research taking advantage of the many levels? The case for the usefulness of these other units or ways of understanding personality for health psychology research was well made by Contrada, Leventhal, and O'Leary (1990) in their review of Type A research. They integrated a great many findings through use of a conceptual model framed around self processes. Contrada and his coauthors effectively brought together the work of Glass, Matthews, Price, and others by showing that for each of these investigators, personality has fundamentally to do with particular cognitive structures or belief systems about self and world. Rapkin and his colleagues (Rapkin et al., 1994) provided another good example. They developed what they called the Idiographic Functional Status Assessment for the systematic observation of others' goals. This interview strategy enables researchers as well as clinicians to take into account the ways individuals and subsamples within samples differ in terms of what determines their quality of life. In a study of 224 people living with AIDS, what people said about such things as the difficulty in their pursuit of their distinctive goals related significantly to their well-being and other health outcomes.

It Is About Transactions and Not Just Interactions

A second important insight that goes back in psychology's history at least as far as to Dewey and Bentley (1949), but that has been recently proposed with renewed vigor in a number of areas of psychology, is the notion that when investigators study aspects of persons in their environment, they are not studying elements that can be understood as independent, isolated, or separable from each other; but rather, they are looking at dynamic units that are synergistically related to each other—persons are defined in terms of the environments in which they participate and environments only become meaningful as they are taken up by and made relevant to the persons and other organisms that reside within them.

This idea has particular importance to that elusive stress buffer effect that has been attributed to personality. In most of the research to date, researchers have worked with statistical models requiring the construct representing it to be independent of the stress variable if personality is to be a buffer or moderator of stress. A transactional approach, however, makes clear how self-defeating such a requirement is. The complaint being voiced here about multiple regression is similar to that raised 13 years ago by Lazarus and Folkman (1984) when they argued that the processes of stress and coping would never be understood through an analysis of variance strategy that put person, situation, and person by situation interaction into separate, independent cells. More recently, Coyne and Gottlieb (1996) claimed that researchers' failure to seriously take the Lazarus and Folkman point about transactions has led to hundreds of misleading and inconsequential coping checklist studies. A stance should be maintained in the research that recognizes that people and what happens to them in forms such as stressful life events are inseparable and essentially related.

Moving to an empirical level, there are studies that are beginning to move in the direction suggested by Dewey and Bentley. There are studies demonstrating the important ways that personality not only correlates with how people respond to stress but also shapes the actual likelihood of stress occurrence (Bolger & Zuckerman, 1995; T. W. Smith & Anderson, 1986; T. W. Smith & Rhodewalt, 1986). In a daily diary study of 94 students, Bolger and Zuckerman demonstrated that the personality characteristic of neuroticism determined both how persons reacted to stress and their exposure to stressors. In their framework, a trait and process approach to personality are combined. Such work suggests not that researchers should give up on personality as a stress buffer, but rather that it is necessary to develop new ways of thinking about personality as that which goes beyond static traits. These new personality units of analysis must simultaneously represent what situations afford to persons and what persons make of situations (cf. Mischel & Shoda, 1995).

The perspective of transactions when used in a critical psychology framework also provides a way of addressing the debate over individuals and agency versus structures and social determinations (e.g., Prilleltensky, 1997). A transactional look at notions such as resilience and empowerment forces a recognition of personality constructs and persons in context. Health is never simply a matter of the success and rights of individuals in isolation but rather the integration and responsibilities of individuals in communities. A critical psychology perspective would find Antonovsky's critique of an internal locus of control and Antonovsky's interest in the promotion of coherent social structures as conducive to its aims for psychology (cf. Ouellette, 1998).

People in Local Contexts Have Much to Say About Their Health, Especially if One Gets Close Enough to Listen

Recent work has effectively and usefully taken the investigation of the relation between minority stress and health, from strict comparison studies that pit minority groups members against those in the majority, to studies within the minority groups themselves (examples include James, 1994; J. L. Peterson, Folkman, & Bakeman, 1996). These studies represent serious attempts at understanding both the distinctive stressors that result from minority status, and the unique and important ways in which these stressors combine with other psychosocial resources, including personality, to protect and enhance health. DiPlacido (1998) and Meyer (1995) examined these issues in the context of individuals' sexual minority status. Meyer (1995), as part of an attempt to understand why it is that in large-scale epidemiological studies gay men score no lower on mental health than do straight men in spite of the former's greater exposure to social stressors, found individual difference in mental health within a group of gay men. These differences were in turn related to discrimination, experiences of negative treatment in society, and internalized homophobia; the greater the degree of exposure to stressors associated with living a gay life in this society and the higher the internal state of self-rejection and shame, the greater the mental health problems.

Similarly, DiPlacido, in a pilot study, found what she called "internal stressors" (i.e., self-concealment of sexual orientation, and internalized homophobia), both resulting from heterosexism and homophobia, to be related to greater distress among lesbian and bisexual women. DiPlacido's work on lesbian and bisexual women (i.e., women who partner/have sex with women) marks an attempt at understanding stressors which result from having a double minority status (as both women and women who partner/have sex with other women), and in some cases a triple minority status (lesbian/bisexual women from racial and ethnic minority groups). DiPlacido underscored the multiple levels of stressors and their effects on well-being among minority women who live in a social context of sexism, racism, heterosexism, and homophobia. Moreover, these multiple levels of stressors remain very much in focus as this researcher examines the social and personality influences that buffer the negative effects of minority stress on health outcomes. Many of these sexual minority women do indeed lead healthy, productive lives; but these lives go on within a negative sociocultural climate of hate and stigmatization.

Although these largely quantitative research efforts have produced important findings, the point here is to encourage the use of qualitative data collection and analysis strategies as researchers move closer to local contexts in personality and health research. Feminist and critical approaches in psychology have led psychologists finally to recognize what sociologists, anthropologists, and our other fellow social scientists have known for years; that is, there is much to be gained through the application of phenomenological and qualitative approaches and a close look at the contexts in which stressors are experienced. Their relevance is especially clear as investigators seek to resolve the ideological and value dilemmas noted earlier. For example, Burton, Obeidallah, and Allison (1996) summarized descriptive data from several ethnographic accounts based in the inner-city communities in which African American teens live. They made clear why and how researchers need radically to rethink the assumptions made about what are and are not normative adolescent stresses and adaptative and nonadaptive outcomes for adolescents. For many of the research participants, there really are no childhoods or adolescences as they have come to be known in certain segments of society. Notions like the innocence of childhood and the moratorium of adolescence make little sense in lives in which 8-year-old girls are staying home from school to be the primary care takers of infant siblings, 12-year-old girls are dating the same men that their mothers are dating, and 13-year-old boys who have experienced extraordinary violence do not worry about what they will do when they get older because getting older does not strike them as much of a possibility. The message from these data is not that there are no grounds for evaluating positive outcomes. But rather, the advice is that the researcher needs to entertain the possiblity of a diversity of outcomes and use the insights of members of the local context in the construction of the lists of outcomes that can be called desirable. For example, spiritual development and involvement in religious activities—for which African American adolescents are rarely given credit and which the research literature typically portrays as a simple coping strategy (if it considers it at all)—is seen by community participants in the Burton work as the most important outcome or indicator of positive adjustment to stressors among teens.

Sabat and Harré (1992, 1994; Sabat, 1994) also demonstrated the effectiveness of phenomenological and qualitative approaches in health research, and the dangers of relying strictly on researchers' and formal and informal caregivers definition of healthy functioning. Using records of conversations with persons living with Alzheimer's disease, both in treatment centers and at their homes, interviews with caregivers, and interviews conducted by social workers with Alzheimer's sufferers together with their caregiver, they used discourse analysis to reveal much about the experience of living with Alzheimer's and the construction of that experience. For example, their interviews revealed a higher level of cognitive functioning, one that includes a subjective experience of self, than has ever been recorded through standardized psychometric measures. In addition, they demonstrated how it is that professional and family caregivers shape the social self that the person with Alzheimer's presents to the world. That self is often minimized by those others in ways that lower self-esteem and contribute to the general loss of personhood often seen with Alzheimer's disease. The Sabat and Harré work demonstrated that a subjectively experienced sense of self, a key component of personality, is both present in those living with Alzheimer's and highly valued by those persons.

CONCLUSION

Twenty years ago, when the research literature said that not everyone falls ill in the wake of stressors and that a person's personality actually serves to promote and enhance health, it said something new. Now, such a remark is old hat. A lengthy list of personality constructs have been proposed and shown to be related to health variables. At this time, a good deal is known about how personality has its effect through mechanisms such as the appraisal of stressors and the use of particular coping strategies. The endeavor has reached a point at which researchers are no longer primarily debating whether personality is related to health, but rather, which personality construct is the most powerful one and how little one needs to know about personality to make health predictions. Hopefully, this chapter serves to celebrate what has been learned but also warns against the enterprise becoming too smug and too narrow. Serious concerns remain about how personality is related to health and what is to be made of the relation. New researchers are encouraged to continue the struggle after understanding and, in so doing, to take good advantage of what the broader fields of psychology, including its critical elements, have to say.

ACKNOWLEDGMENTS

Work on this chapter was facilitated by a National Research Award in Health Psychology from NIMH 11532 to Joanne DiPlacido.

REFERENCES

Abramson, L. Y., Dykman, B. M., & Needles, D. J. (1991). Attributional style and theory: Let no one tear them asunder. *Psychological Inquiry, 2,* 11–13.

Abramson, L. Y., Seligman, M.E.P., & Teasdale, J. D. (1978). Learned helplessness in humans: Critique and reformulation. *Journal of Abnormal Psychology, 87,* 49–74.

Allport, G. W. (1961). *Pattern and growth in personality.* New York: Holt, Rinehart & Winston.

Allred, K. D., & Smith, T. W. (1989). The hardy personality: Cognitive and physiological responses to evaluative threat. *Journal of Personality and Social Psychology, 56,* 257–266.

Anderson, C. A., & Deuser, W. E. (1991). Science and the reformulated learned-helplessness model of depression. *Psychological Inquiry, 2,* 14–19.

Anson, O., Carmel, S., Levenson, A., Bonneh, D. Y., & Maoz, B. (1993). Coping with recent life events: The interplay of personal and collective resources. *Behavioral Medicine, 18,* 159–166.

Anthony, E. J. (1987). Children at high risk for psychosis growing up successfully. In E. J. Anthony & B. J. Cohler (Eds.), *The invulnerable child* (pp. 147–184). New York: Guilford.

Antonovsky, A. (1979). *Health, stress and coping.* San Francisco: Jossey-Bass.

Antonovsky, A. (1987). *Unraveling the mystery of health.* San Francisco: Jossey-Bass.

Antonovsky, A. (1991). The structural sources of salutogenic strengths. In C. I. Cooper & R. Payne (Eds.), *Personality and stress: Individual differences in the stress process* (pp. 67–104). New York: Wiley.

Antonovsky, A. (1993). The structure and properties of the sense of coherence scale. *Social Science and Medicine, 36,* 725–733.

Aspinwall, L. G., & Taylor, S. E. (1992). Modeling cognitive adaptation: A longitudinal investigation of the impact of individual differences and coping on college adjustment and performance. *Journal of Personality and Social Psychology, 63,* 989–1003.

Bandura, A. (1977). Self-efficacy: Toward a unifying theory of behavior change. *Psychological Review, 84,* 191–215.

Bandura, A. (Ed.). (1995). *Self-efficacy in changing societies.* New York: Cambridge University Press.

Bartone, P. T. (1989). Predictors of stress-related illness in city bus drivers. *Journal of Occupational Medicine, 31,* 857–863.

Bartone, P. T., Ursano, R. J., Wright, K. M., & Ingraham, L. H. (1989). The impact of a military air disaster on the health of assistance workers: A prospective study. *Journal of Nervous and Mental Disease, 177,* 317–328.

Bernard, L. C., Hutchison, S., Lavin, A., & Pennington, P. (1996). Ego-strength, hardiness, self-esteem, self-efficacy, optimism, and maladjustment: Health-related personality constructs and the "Big Five" model of personality. *Assessment, 3,* 115–131.

Bolger, N., & Zuckerman, A. (1995). A framework for studying personality in the stress process. *Journal of Personality and Social Psychology, 69,* 890–902.

Bowman, B. J. (1996). Cross-cultural validation of Antonovsky's Sense of Coherence Scale. *Journal of Clinical Psychology, 52,* 547–549.

Brownell, K. D., & Cohen, L. R. (1995). Adherence to dietary regimens: 1. An overview of research. *Behavioral Medicine, 20,* 149–154.

Bruner, J. (1990). *Acts of meaning.* Cambridge, MA: Harvard University Press.

Burton, L. M., Obeidallah, D. A., & Allison, K. (1996). Ethnographic insights on social context and adolescent development among inner-city African-American teens. In R. Jessor, A. Colby, & R. A. Shweder (Eds.), *Ethnography and human development: Context and meaning in social inquiry* (pp. 395–418). Chicago: University of Chicago Press.

Callahan, L. F., & Pincus, T. (1995). The Sense of Coherence Scale in patients with rheumatoid arthritis. *Arthritis Care & Research, 8,* 28–35.

Carlson, R. (1984). What's social about social psychology? Where's the person in personality research? *Journal of Personality and Social Psychology, 47,* 1304–1309.

Carver, C. S. (1989). How should multifaceted personality constructs be tested? Issues illustrated by self-monitoring, attributional style, and hardiness. *Journal of Personality and Social Psychology, 56,* 577–585.

Chamberlain, K., Petrie, K., & Azariah, R. (1992). The role of optimism and sense of coherence in predicting recovery from surgery. *Psychology and Health, 7,* 301–310.

Cheung, P., & Spears, G. (1995). Psychiatric morbidity among New Zealand Cambodians: The role of psychosocial factors. *Social Psychiatry & Psychiatric Epidemiology, 30,* 92–97.

Cockburn, J., Murphy, B., Schofield, P., Hill, D. J., & Borland, R. (1991). Development of a strategy to encourage attendance for screening mammography. *Health Education Research, 6,* 279–290.

Cohen, F. (1979). Personality, stress, and the development of physical illness. In G. C. Stone, F. Cohen, N. E. Adler, & Associates (Eds.), *Health psychology: A handbook* (pp. 77–112). San Francisco: Jossey-Bass.

Cohler, B. J. (1991). The life story and the study of resilience and response to adversity. *Journal of Narrative and Life History, 1,* 169–200.

Contrada, R. J. (1989). Type A behavior, personality hardiness, and cardiovascular responses to stress. *Journal of Personality and Social Psychology, 57,* 895–903.

Contrada, R. J., Leventhal, H., & O'Leary, A. (1990). Personality and health. In L. A. Pervin (Ed.), *Handbook of personality theory and research* (pp. 638–669). New York: Guilford.

Coyne, J. C., & Gottlieb, B. H. (1996). The mismeasure of coping by checklist. *Journal of Personality, 64,* 959–991.

Davidson, K., & Prkachin, K. (1997). Optimism and unrealistic optimism have an interacting impact on health-promoting behavior and knowledge changes. *Personality and Social Psychology Bulletin, 23,* 617–625.

Dewey, J., & Bentley, A. F. (1949). *Knowing and the known.* Boston: Beacon.

Dillon, K. M., & Totten, M. C. (1989). Psychological factors, immunocompetence, and health of breast-feeding mothers and their infants. *Journal of Genetic Psychology, 150,* 155–162.

DiPlacido, J. (1998). Minority stress among lesbians, gay men, and bisexuals: A consequence of heterosexism, homophobia, and stigmatization. In G. M. Herek (Ed.), *Stigma, prejudice, and violence against lesbians and gay men* (pp. 138–159). Newbury Park, CA: Sage.

Dohrenwend, B. S. (1978). Social stress and community psychology. *American Journal of Community Psychology, 6,* 1–14.

Dykema, J., Bergbower, K., & Peterson, C. (1995). Pessimistic explanatory style, stress, and illness. *Journal of Social and Clinical Psychology, 14,* 357–371.

Emmons, R. A., & McAdams, D. P. (1991). Personal strivings and motive dispositions: Exploring the links. *Personality and Social Psychology Bulletin, 17,* 648–654.

Flannery, R. B., & Flannery, G. J. (1990). Sense of coherence, life stress, and psychological distress: A prospective methodological inquiry. *Journal of Clinical Psychology, 46,* 415–420.

Florian, V., Mikulincer, M., & Taubman, O. (1995). Does hardiness contribute to mental health during a stressful real-life situation? The roles of appraisal and coping. *Journal of Personality and Social Psychology, 68,* 687–695.

Fox, D., & Prilleltensky, I. (Eds.). (1997). *Critical psychology: An introduction.* Thousand Oaks, CA: Sage.

Franz, C. E., & Stewart, A. J. (Eds.). (1994). *Women creating lives: Identities, resilience, & resistance.* San Francisco: Westview.

Frenz, A., Carey, M. P., & Jorgensen, R. S. (1993). Psychometric evaluation of Antonovsky's Sense of Coherence Scale. *Psychological Assessment, 5,* 145–153.

Fry, P. S. (1995). Perfectionism, humor, and optimism as moderators of health outcomes and determinants of coping styles of women executives. *Genetic, Social, & General Psychology Monographs, 121,* 211–245.

Funk, S. C. (1992). Hardiness: A review of theory and research. *Health Psychology, 11,* 335–345.

Funk, S. C., & Houston, B. K. (1987). A critical analysis of the hardiness scales' validity and utility. *Journal of Personality and Social Psychology, 53,* 572–578.

Gladden, R. M., & Ouellette, S. C. (1997). *Hardiness, social dominance orientation, and health.* Unpublished manuscript, The City University of New York.

Gotlib, I. H. (1991). Explanatory style: A question of balance. *Psychological Inquiry, 2,* 27–30.

Green, L. (1994). Fear as a way of life. *Cultural Anthropology, 9,* 227–256.

Gruen, R. J., Silva, R., Ehrlich, J., Schweitzer, J. W., & Friedhoff, A. J. (1997). Vulnerability to stress: Self-criticism and stress-induced changes in biochemistry. *Journal of Personality, 65,* 33–47.

Hermans, H.J.M., Rijks, T. I., & Kempen, H.J.G. (1993). Imaginal dialogues in the self: Theory and method. *Journal of Personality, 61,* 207–236.

Holden, G. (1991). The relationship of self-efficacy appraisals to subsequent health related outcomes: A meta-analysis. *Social Work in Health Care, 16,* 53–93.

Holt, P., Fine, M. J., & Tollefson, N. (1987). Mediating stress: Survival of the hardy. *Psychology in the Schools, 24,* 51–58.

Ingram, K. M., Corning, A. F., & Schmidt, L. D. (1996). The relationship of victimization experiences to psychological well-being among homeless women and low-income housed women. *Journal of Counseling Psychology, 43,* 218–227.

James, S. A. (1994). John Henryism and the health of African-Americans. *Culture, Medicine, and Psychiatry, 18,* 163–182.

Jerusalem, M., & Schwarzer, R. (1992). Self-efficacy as a resource factor in stress appraisal processes. In R. Schwarzer (Ed.), *Self-efficacy: Thought control of action* (pp. 195–213). Washington, DC: Hemisphere.

Kamen-Siegel, L., Rodin, J., Seligman, M.E.P., & Dwyer, J. (1991). Explanatory style and cell-mediated immunity in elderly men and women. *Health Psychology, 10,* 229–235.

Keane, A., Ducette, J., & Adler, D. (1985). Stress in ICU and non-ICU nurses. *Nursing Research, 34,* 231–236.

Kobasa, S. C. (1979). Stressful life events, personality, and health: An inquiry into hardiness. *Journal of Personality and Social Psychology, 37,* 1–11.

Kobasa, S. C. (1982). The hardy personality: Toward a social psychology of stress and health. In G. Sanders & J. Suls (Eds.), *Social psychology of health and illness* (pp. 3–33). Hillsdale, NJ: Lawrence Erlbaum Associates.

Kobasa, S. C., Maddi, S. R., & Kahn, S. (1982). Hardiness and health: A prospective study. *Journal of Personality and Social Psychology, 42,* 168–177.

Krieger, N. (1999). Embodying inequality: A review of concepts, measures, and methods for studying health consequences of discrimination. *International Journal of Health Services, 29,* 295–352.

Kuo, W. H., & Tsai, Y. (1986). Social networking, hardiness, and immigrants' mental health. *Journal of Health and Social Behavior, 27,* 133–149.

Larsson, G., & Setterlind, S. (1990). Work load/work control and health: Moderating effects of heredity, self-image, coping and health behavior. *International Journal of Health Sciences, 1,* 79–88.

Lazarus, R. S. (1990). "Theory based stress measurement": Response. *Psychological Inquiry, 1,* 41–51.

Lazarus, R. S., & Folkman, S. (1984). *Stress, appraisal, and coping.* New York: Springer.

Liem, R., & Liem, J. H. (1996). Mental health and unemployment: The making and unmaking of psychological casualities. In B. B. Lykes, A. Banuazizi, R. Liem, & M. Morris (Eds.), *Myths about the powerless: Contesting social inequalities* (pp. 105–127). Philadelphia: Temple University Press.

Little, B. R. (1993). Personal projects and the distributed self: Aspects of a conative psychology. In M. J. Suls (Ed.), *The self in social perspective: Vol. 4. Psychological perspectives on the self* (pp. 157–185). Hillsdale, NJ: Lawrence Erlbaum Associates.

Locke, S., & Colligan, D. (1987). *The healer within: The new medicine of mind and body.* New York: Penguin.

Lykes, B. B., Banuazizi, A., Liem, R., & Morris, M. (Eds.). (1996). *Myths about the powerless: Contesting social inequalities.* Philadelphia: Temple University Press.

Maddi, S. R. (1990). Issues and interventions in stress mastery. In H. S. Friedman (Ed.), *Personality and disease* (pp. 121–154). New York: Wiley.

Maddi, S. R., & Khoshaba, D. M. (1994). Hardiness and mental helalth. *Journal of Personality Assessment, 63,* 265–274.

Magnani, L. E. (1990). Hardiness, self-perceived health, and activity among independently functioning older adults. *Scholarly Inquiry for Nursing Practice: An International Journal, 4,* 171–184.

Marcus, H. R., Kitayama, S., & Heiman, R. J. (1996). Culture and "basic" psychological principles. In E. T. Higgins & A. W. Kruglanski (Eds.), *Social psychology: Handbook of basic principles* (pp. 857–913). New York: Guilford.

Margalit, M., & Eysenck, S. (1990). Prediction of coherence in adolescence: Gender differences in social skills, personality, and family climate. *Journal of Research in Personality, 24,* 510–521.

Massey, S., Cameron, A., Ouellette, S. C., & Fine, M. (1998). Qualitative approaches to the study of thriving: What can be learned? *Journal of Social Issues, 54,* 337–355.

Masten, A. S., Hubbard, J. J., Gest, S. D., Tellegen, A., Garmezy, N., & Ramirez, M. (1999). Competence in the context of adversity: Pathways to resilience and maladaptation from childhood to late adolescence. *Developmental Psychopathology, 11,* 143–169.

McAdams, D. P. (1996). Personality, modernity, and the stories self: A contemporary framework for studying persons. *Psychological Review, 96,* 690–702.

McClelland, D. C. (1989). Motivational factors in health and disease. *American Psychologist, 44,* 675–683.

McClelland, D. C., Koestner, R., & Weinberger, J. (1989). How do self-attributed and implicit motives differ? *Psychological Review, 96,* 690–702.

McCranie, E. W., Lambert, V. A., & Lambert, C. E. (1987). Work stress, hardiness, and burnout among hospital staff nurses. *Nursing Research, 36,* 374–378.

McKay, J. R. (1991). Assessing aspects of object relations associated with immune function: Development of the affiliative trust-mistrust coding system. *Psychological Assessment: A Journal of Consulting and Clinical Psychology, 3,* 641–647.

Meyer, I. H. (1995). Minority stress and mental health in gay men. *Journal of Health and Social Behavior, 7,* 9–25.

Midanik, L. T., Soghikian, K., Ransom, L. J., & Polen, M. R. (1992). Alcohol problems and sense of coherence among older adults. *Social Science and Medicine, 34,* 43–48.

Mischel, W., & Shoda, Y. (1995). A cognitive-affective system theory of personality: Reconceptualizing situations, dispositions, dynamics, and invariance in personality structure. *Psychological Review, 102,* 246–268.

Morrill, A. C., Ickovics, J. R., Golubchikov, V. V., Beren, S. E., & Rodin, J. (1996). Safer sex: Social and psychological predictors of behavioral maintenance and change among heterosexual women. *Journal of Consulting and Clinical Psychology, 64,* 819–828.

Nyamathi, A. M. (1991). Relationship of resources to emotional distress, somatic complaints, and high risk behaviors in drug recovery and homeless minority women. *Research in Nursing and Health, 14,* 269–277.

Ogilvie, D. R., & Rose, K. M. (1995). Self-with-others representations and a taxonomy of motives: Two approaches to studying persons. *Journal of Personality, 63,* 643–679.

O'Leary, A. (1992). Self-efficacy and health: Behavioral and stress-physiological mediation. *Cognitive Therapy and Research, 16,* 229–245.

O'Leary, V. E., & Ickovics, J. R. (1995). Resilience and thriving in response to challenge: An opportunity for a paradigm shift in women's health. *Women's Health: Research on Gender, Behavior, and Policy, 2,* 121–142.

Orr, E., & Westman, M. (1990). Does hardiness moderate stress, and how? A review. In M. Rosenbaum (Ed.), *On coping skills, self-control, and adaptive behavior* (pp. 64–94). New York: Springer.

Ouellette, S. C. (1993). Inquiries into hardiness. In L. Goldberger & S. Breznitz (Eds.), *Handbook of stress: Theoretical and clinical aspects* (2nd ed.). New York: The Free Press.

Ouellette, S. C. (1998). Remembering Aaron Antonovsky: A conversation cherished and one missed. *Megamot: Behavioral Sciences Quarterly, 39,* 19–30.

Ouellette, S. C. (1999). Self, social identity, and personality influences on health. In R. J. Contrada & R. D. Ashmore (Eds.), *Self, social identity, and physical health: Interdisciplinary explorations* (pp. 125–154). New York: Oxford University Press.

Ouellette Kobasa, S. C. (1989). Sontag on AIDS. *Social Policy, 19,* 60–63.

Ouellette Kobasa, S. C. (1990). Lessons from history: How to find the person in health psychology. In H. S. Friedman (Ed.), *Personality and disease* (pp. 14–37). New York: Wiley.

Ouellette Kobasa, S. C. (1991). AIDS volunteering: Links to the past and future prospects. In D. Nelkin, D. P. Willis, & S. V. Parris (Eds.), *A disease of society: Cultural and institutional responses to AIDS* (pp. 172–188). New York: Cambrige University Press.

Pagana, K. D. (1990). The relationship of hardiness and social support to student appraisal of stress in an initial clinical nursing situation. *Journal of Nursing Education, 29,* 255–261.

Park, C. L., Cohen, L. H., & Murch, R. L. (1996). Assessment and prediction of stress-related growth. *Journal of Personality, 64,* 71–105.

Peterson, C. (1991a). Further thoughts on explanatory style. *Psychological Inquiry, 2,* 50–57.

Peterson, C. (1991b). The meaning and measurement of explanatory style. *Psychological Inquiry, 2,* 1–10.

Peterson, C. (1991c). On shortening the Expanded Attributional Style Questionnaire. *Journal of Personality Assessment, 56,* 179–183.

Peterson, C., & De Avila, M. E. (1995). Optimistic explanatory style and the perception of health problems. *Journal of Clinical Psychology, 51,* 128–132.

Peterson, C., Maier, S. F., & Seligman, M.E.P. (1993). *Learned helplessness: A theory for the age of personal control.* New York: Oxford University Press.

Peterson, C., Schulman, P., Castellon, C., & Seligman, M.E.P. (1992). CAVE: Content analysis of verbatim explanations. In. C. P. Smith (Ed.), *Motivation and personality: Handbook of thematic content analysis* (pp. 383–392). New York: Cambridge University Press.

Peterson, C., & Seligman, M.E.P. (1984). Causal explanations as a risk factor for depression: Theory and evidence. *Psychological Review, 91,* 347–374.

Peterson, C., & Seligman, M.E.P. (1987). Explanatory style and illness. *Journal of Personality, 55,* 238–265.

Peterson, C., Seligman, M.E.P., & Valliant, G. E. (1988). Pessimistic explanatory style is a risk factor for physical illness: A thirty-five year longitudinal study. *Journal of Personality and Social Psychology, 55,* 23–27.

Peterson, C., & Stunkard, A. J. (1989). Personal control and health promotion. *Social Science and Medicine, 28,* 819–828.

Peterson, C., & Ulrey, L. M. (1994). Can explanatory style be scored from TAT protocols? *Personality and Social Psychology Bulletin, 20,* 102–106.

Peterson J. L., Folkman S., & Bakeman R. (1996). Stress, coping, HIV status, psychosocial resources, and depressive mood in African American gay, bisexual, and heterosexual men. *American Journal of Community Psychology, 24,* 461–487.

Pollock, S. E., & Duffy, M. E. (1990). The health-related hardiness scale: Development and psychometric analysis. *Nursing Research, 39,* 218–222.

Prilleltensky, I. (1997). Values, assumptions, and practices: Assessing the moral implications of psychological discourse and action. *American Psychologist, 52,* 517–535.

Rakowski, W., Wells, B. L., Lasater, T. M., & Carleton, R. A. (1991). Correlates of expected success at health habit change and its role as a predictor in health behavior research. *American Journal of Preventative Medicine, 7,* 89–94.

Rapkin, B. D., Smith, M. Y., Dumont, K., Correa, A., Palmer, S., & Cohen, S. (1994). Development of the idiographic functional status assessment: A measure of the personal goals and goal attainment activities of people with AIDS. *Psychology and Health, 9,* 111–129.

Rich, V. L., & Rich, A. R. (1987). Personality and burnout in female staff nurses. *Image, 19,* 63–66.

Rhodewalt, F., & Agustsdottir, S. (1984). On the relationship of hardiness to the type A behavior pattern: Perception of life events versus coping with life events. *Journal of Research in Personality, 18,* 211–223.

Rhodewalt, R., & Zone, J. B. (1989). Appraisal of life change, depression, and illness in hardy and non-hardy women. *Journal of Personality and Social Psychology, 56,* 81–88.

Robbins, A. S., Spence, J. T., & Clark, H. (1991). Psychological determinants of health and performance: The tangled web of desirable and undesirable characteristics. *Journal of Personality and Social Psychology, 61,* 755–765.

Ryan, W. (1971). *Blaiming the victim.* New York: Pantheon.

Sabat, S. R. (1994). Excess disability and malignant social psychology: A case study of Alzheimer's disease. *Journal of Community and Applied Social Psychology, 4,* 157–166.

Sabat, S. R., & Harré, R. (1992). The construction and deconstruction of self in Alzheimer's disease. *Aging and Society, 12,* 443–461.

Sabat, S. R., & Harré, R. (1994). The Alzheimer's disease sufferer as a semiotic subject. *PPP, 1,* 145–160.

Scheier, M. F., & Carver, C. S. (1985). Optimism, coping, and health: Assessment and implications of generalized outcome expectancies. *Health Psychology, 4,* 219–247.

Scheier, M. F., & Carver, C. S. (1987). Dispositional optimism and physical well-being: The influence of generalized outcome expectancies on health. *Journal of Personality, 55,* 169–210.

Scheier, M. F., & Carver, C. S. (1992). Effects of optimism on psychological and physical well-being: Theoretical overview and empirical update. *Cognitive Therapy and Research, 16,* 201–228.

Scheier, M. F., Carver, C. S., & Bridges, M. W. (1994). Distinguishing optimism from neuroticism (and trait anxiety, self-mastery, and self-esteem): A reevaluation of the Life Orientation Test. *Journal of Personality and Social Psychology, 67,* 1063–1078.

Scheier, M. F., Matthews, K. A., Owens, J. F., Magovern, G. J., Lefebre, R. C., Abbott, R. A., & Carver, C. S. (1989). Dispositional optimism and recovery from coronary artery bypass surgery: The beneficial effects on physical and psychological well-being. *Journal of Personality and Social Psychology, 57,* 1024–1040.

Schmied, L. A., & Lawler, K. A. (1986). Hardiness, Type A behavior, and the stress-illness relation in working women. *Journal of Personality and Social Psychology, 51,* 1218–1223.

Schwarzer, R. (1994). Optimism, vulnerability, and self-beliefs as health-related cognitions: A systematic overview. *Psychology and Health, 9,* 161–180.

Shepperd, J. A., Maroto, J. J., & Pbert, L. A. (1996). Dispositional optimism as a predictor of health changes among cardiac patients. *Journal of Research in Personality, 30,* 517–134.

Smith, C. A., Dobbins, C., & Wallston, K. A. (1991). The mediational role of perceived competence in adaptation to rheumatoid arthritis. *Journal of Applied Social Psychology, 21,* 1218–1247.

Smith, T. W., & Anderson, N. B. (1986). Models of personality and disease: An interactional approach to Type A behavior and cardiovascular risk. *Journal of Personality and Social Psychology, 50,* 1166–1173.

Smith, T. W., Pope, M. K., Rhodewalt, F., & Poulton, J. F. (1989). Optimism, neuroticism, coping, and symptom reports: An alternative interpretation of the Life Orientation Test. *Journal of Personality and Social Psychology, 56,* 640–648.

Smith, T. W., & Rhodewalt, F. (1986). On states, traits, and processes: A transactional alternative to the individual difference assumptions in Type A behavior and physiological reactivity. *Journal of Research in Personality, 20,* 229–251.

Smith, T. W., & Williams, P. G. (1992). Personality and health: Advantages and limitations of the five-factor model. *Journal of Personality, 60,* 395–423.

Snyder, C. R., Irving, L. M., & Anderson, J. (1991). Hope and health. In C. R. Snyder & D. R. Forsyth (Eds.), *Handbook of social and clinical psychology: The health perspective* (pp. 285–305). Elmsford, NY: Pergamon.

Sontag, S. (1978). *Illness as metaphor.* New York: Farrar, Straus, and Giroux.

Sontag, S. (1988). *AIDS and its metaphors.* New York: Farrar, Straus, and Giroux.

Spalding, A. D. (1995). Racial minorities and other high-risk groups HIV and AIDS at increased risk for psychological adjustment problems in association with health locus of control orientation. *Social Work in Health Care, 21,* 81–114.

Stewart, A. J. (1994). Toward a feminist strategy for studying women's lives. In C. E. Franz & A. J. Stewart (Eds.), *Women creating lives: Identities, resilience, and resistance* (pp. 3–35). San Francisco: Westview.

Suls, J., David, J. P., & Harvey, J. H. (1996). Personality and coping: Three generations of research. *Journal of Personality, 64,* 711–736.

Taylor, S. E., Kemeny, M. E., Aspinwall, L. G., Schneider, S. G., Rodriguez, R., & Herbert, M. (1992). Optimism, coping, psychological distress, and high-risk sexual behavior among men at risk for acquired immunodeficency syndrome (AIDS). *Journal of Personality and Social Psychology, 63,* 460–473.

Tedeschi, R. G., & Calhoun, L. G. (1996). The posttraumatic growth inventory: Measuring the positive legacy of traume. *Journal of Traumatic Stress, 9,* 455–471.

Tennen, H., & Affleck, G. (1987). The costs and benefits of optimistic explantions and dispositional optimism. *Journal of Personality, 55,* 377–393.

Topf, M. (1989). Personality hardiness, occupational stress, and burnout in critical care nurses. *Research in Nursing & Health, 12,* 179–186.

Valdimarsdottir, H. B., & Stone, A. A. (1997). Psychosocial factors and secretory immunoglobulin A. *Critical Reviews in Oral Biology and Medicine, 8,* 461–474.

Wallston, B. S., Wallston, K. A., Kaplan, G. D., & Maides, S. A. (1976). The development and validation of the health related locus of control (HLC) scale. *Journal of Consulting and Clinical Psychology, 44,* 580–585.

Wallston, K. A. (1989). Assessment of control in health-care settings. In A. Steptoe & A. Appels (Eds.), *Stress, personal control, and health* (pp. 85–105). Chicester, England: Wiley.

Wallston, K. A. (1991). The importance of placing measures of health locus of control beliefs in a theoretical context. *Health Education Research, 6,* 251–252.

Wallston, K. A. (1992). Hocus-pocus, the focus isn't strictly on locus: Rotter's social learning theory modified for health. *Cognitive Therapy and Research, 16,* 183–199.

Wallston, K. A. (1994). Cautious optimism vs. cockeyed optimism. *Psychology and Health, 9,* 201–203.

Wallston, K. A., Maides, S. A., & Wallston, B. S. (1976). Health related information seeking as a function of health related locus of control and health value. *Journal of Research in Personality, 10,* 215–222.

Wallston, K. A., Wallston, B. S., & DeVellis, R. (1978). Development of the multidimensional health locus of control (MHLC) scales. *Health Education Monographs, 6,* 160–170.

Weiss, G. L., & Larsen, D. L. (1990). Health value, health locus of control, and the prediction of health protective behaviors. *Social Behavior and Personality, 18,* 121–135.

Westman, M. (1990). The relationship between stress and performance: The moderating effect of hardiness. *Human Performance, 3,* 141–155.

Wiebe, D. J. (1991). Hardiness and stress moderation: A test of proposed mechanisms. *Journal of Personality and Social Psychology, 60,* 89–99.

Wiebe, D. J., & McCallum, D. M. (1986). Health practices and hardiness as mediators in the stress–illness relationship. *Health Psychology, 5,* 425–438.

Wiebe, D. J., & Williams, P. G. (1992). Hardiness and health: A social psychophysiological perspective on stress and adaptation. *Journal of Social and Clinical Psychology, 11,* 238–262.

Williams, P. G., Wiebe, D. J., & Smith, T. W. (1992). Coping processes and mediators of the relationship between hardiness and health. *Journal of Behavioral Medicine, 15,* 237–255.

Wulfert, E., Wan, C. K., & Backus, C. A. (1996). Gay men's safer sex behavior: An integration of three models. *Journal of Behavioral Medicine, 19,* 345–366.

Younkin, S. L., & Betz, N. E. (1996). Psychological hardiness: A reconceptualization and measurement. In T. W. Miller (Ed.), *Theory and assessment of stressful life events* (pp. 161–178). Madison, CT: International Universities Press, Inc.

11

Social Comparison Processes in the Physical Health Domain

Jerry Suls

René Martin
University of Iowa

The famous 19th-century medical pathologist Rudolf Virchow argued that medicine is a social science. Virchow was thinking mainly of the role of socioeconomic factors and social conventions in the etiology of disease, but this chapter argues that even more fundamental interpersonal processes play an essential role in understanding why people become ill, how people decide they are ill, whether they seek formal medical attention, and how they cope with illness. This chapter focuses on how people's health-related thoughts, feelings, and behaviors are influenced by comparisons with other people. It begins with a brief survey of classic social comparison theory and recent extensions and then considers four areas of health psychology, researched over the past 25 years, in which social comparison has been strongly implicated.

A BRIEF SURVEY OF SOCIAL COMPARISON THEORY

Festinger (1954) provided the first systematic theory of comparison processes. He noted that people have the need to evaluate the correctness of their opinions and gauge their capabilities for action. In the absence of physical objective standards, people engage in comparisons with others to establish their standing. Festinger proposed that people prefer similar others for gauging the correctness of their opinions and adequacy of their abilities.

Since the initial presentation of the theory, it has undergone several extensions and reinterpretations (Latané, 1966; Olson, Herman, & Zanna, 1986; Singer, 1966; Suls & R. L. Miller, 1977; Suls & Wills, 1991; Wheeler, Martin, & Suls, 1997). Schachter and Singer (1962) showed how social comparison extends to the interpretation of emotional states, a domain of clear relevance to the physical health domain where physical symptoms and trauma covary with affect. Mechanic (1972) emphasized how social comparisons with others play an important role in the interpretation of physical symptoms and health care seeking behavior.

Besides these extensions of the theory to domains beyond ability and opinion evaluation, the basic elements of the theory have also undergone refinement. From the inception of Festinger's theory, questions have been raised about how similarity of a comparison other should be best conceptualized. Goethals and Darley (1977) argued that comparisons are preferred with others who are similar by virtue of sharing attributes thought to be related to performance on the ability or opinion under evaluation. For example, for individuals to gauge their swimming performance ("How good am I?"), they should prefer to compare themselves with someone who is similar in body build, swimming experience, and level of motivation (Gastorf & Suls, 1978; Zanna, Goethals, & Hill, 1975). For individuals to predict whether they will be able to achieve a given performance ("Can I do X?"), they should want to learn the outcome of someone else who has already attempted the same goal and who has performed comparably to themselves in the past on a similar or related task (Wheeler et al., 1997).

The comparison of opinions is also more complex than Festinger proposed. Value-type opinions are personally relevant and lack an objectively correct answer. Because of their personal relevance, the views of others who share an individual's general perspective or background are most useful. On the other hand, beliefs refer to empirically verifiable facts. In this case, persons who are dissimilar on related attributes may provide a kind of "triangulation," so as to get a better "fix," or more objective view, by learning how someone with a different perspective thinks about the issue. Hence, value-type opinion comparison may be best served by comparisons with people who share related attributes (i.e., similar others), but belief-type opinion comparison may be preferred with persons who come at the issue from a different angle (Goethals & Darley, 1977; Gorenflo & Crano, 1989).

Thus far, the dynamics of social comparison for *self-evaluation* (i.e, the accurate rendering of abilities or opinions) have been considered. This was the main motivation served by social comparison according to Festinger. However, in recent years, there has been increasing recognition that comparison may also serve *self-enhancing* or *self-protective* motives (Goethals & Darley, 1977; Wills, 1981; Wood, 1989). Initial thinking suggested that the self-enhancement motivation for people who were experiencing a threat to self-esteem would be best served by comparing with others who were worse off (i.e., downward comparisons, to increase their self-esteem; Wills, 1981; Wood, Taylor, & Lichtman, 1985). More recently, this argument has been refined with the recognition that both upward and downward comparisons may increase self-esteem depending on the dimension under evaluation (Buunk, Collins, Taylor, Van Yperen, & Dakof, 1990; Collins, 1996; Major, Testa, & Bylsma, 1991; Taylor & Lobel, 1989). A third motive, *self-improvement,* has been also identified (Wood, 1989). In this case, people may prefer comparisons with persons who are doing better to inspire hope that their situation will improve or to learn information that will help them to improve themselves.

The impact of explicit comparisons made with others has been considered. However, recent research also indicates that people engage in implict projections of opinion and personal attributes (Gerard & Orive, 1987). Goethals, Messick, and Allison (1991) called this "constructive social comparison," referring to "in the head" estimates about the nature of social reality, such as the distribution of abilities and particular opinions. Suls (1986) proposed that these self-generated estimates may actually short circuit actual social comparisons. Fabricated or constructed comparison information may take the form of the well-known phenomenon of attributed projection, or false consensus where a person's own opinion or behavior is also attributed to others (Mullen et al., 1985; Ross, Greene, & House, 1977). Such constructions also may be biased in self-enhancing directions because they carry fewer constraints of reality. In some cases, however, constructions about norms may have to suffice because it is impossible for the individual (short of systematic polling) to gather all of the necessary information to obtain an accurate rendering of the norm. Regardless of the source of these constructed norms, it appears that they possess a self-perpetuating nature, and people may treat the constructed norm as veridical and behave in accord with them.

Three basic aspects of the study of social comparison processes have been described: the self-evaluation of abilities and opinions, the recognition that such motives as self-enhancement and self-improvement may also direct the comparison process, and the construction of fabricated comparison norms. Since the foundation of the group dynamics tradition (Lewin, 1958), social psychologists have sought to both identify basic social processes, such as interpersonal comparison, and illustrate how they have influence in real-world settings (Festinger, Schachter, & Back, 1950). The physical health arena is one such setting. The remainder of this chapter describes how study of the comparison process, particularly the three aspects of the process already surveyed, has enriched understanding in several areas of health psychology.

CONSTRUAL OF SOCIAL NORMS CONCERNING HEALTH-RELEVANT PRACTICES

A wide-range of lifestyle behaviors—such as smoking, alcohol, overeating, and seat belt use—have been associated with early mortality and morbidity. A major task of health psychologists has been to develop interventions to decrease the frequency of unhealthy behaviors and increase the frequency of healthy behaviors. Virtually all theoretical accounts of health-related practices posit that normative expectations about specific practices play a role in whether the behaviors are adopted. For example, Ajzen and Fishbein's (1980) theory of reasoned action posits that behavior is a function of the person's attitudes about the behavior and their perceptions of the subjective norm (i.e., others' opinions regarding the appropriateness of the behavior).

Evidence for social influence processes in health behaviors comes from many sources. For example, one of the most consistent predictors of alcohol and cigarette use among high school and college students is the students' perception of alcohol and cigarette use by their peers (e.g., Gerrard, Gibbons, Benthin, & Hessling, 1996; Graham, Marks, & Hansen, 1991; Kandel, 1980; Stein, Newcomb, & Bentler, 1988). Laboratory experiments and field studies indicate that people will move closer to the group's consensual position when they note a discrepancy between themselves and the group (Asch, 1956; Crandall, 1988; Schachter, 1951). For social influence to occur, of course, the individual must have identified (or think they have identified) the social norm. The general societal or cultural sentiments about a particular opinion or practice may be easily discerned (e.g., the general opinion about the unhealthy effects of smoking are well-known through the media). But the specifics of social norms regarding healthy and unhealthy practices may be harder to determine. Although society does not condone heavy drinking of alcohol, for example, there is no readily available definition of "drinking to excess." In the absence of comprehensive information about average use and the range of use, it is virtually impossible for individuals to obtain a precise idea of how much drinking other people, besides their closest companions, do. Each person has available only a narrow slice of the population from whom to infer the norms about the larger group. In addition, there is an awareness that public behavior may not represent people's private views (Deutsch & Gerard, 1955). All of these considerations make identification of social norms concerning health behavior a difficult undertaking for lay people.

False Consensus Effect

The complexity of identifying social norms forces people to depend on simpler rules of thumb, or heuristics, to infer social norms. One rule of thumb is the availability heuristic (Kahneman & Tversky, 1973), which evaluates the frequency or likelihood of an event or behavior on the basis of how easily instances or associations come to mind. Hence, when a behavior is easy to recall, it tends to be perceived as common. This implies that particularly memorable or accessible instances of a behavior will inflate estimates of the general probability of such behavior. Because people's own behavior is probably most available or accessible, people are likely to distort the norm in the direction of their own behavior. This is demonstrated in the well-known false consensus effect (FCE; Ross et al., 1977), or people's tendency to overestimate their similarity to others. Specifically, people ratings of their own behavior tend to be positively correlated with their estimates of others' behavior.

The FCE represents a form of social projection, or a constructed social comparison norm, as described in the introduction. This self-generated social consensus provides the individual with a justification for their behavior. Evidence of the false consensus effect has been demonstrated in several health domains (e.g., Graham et al., 1991). Chassin and associates (Chassin, Presson, Sherman, Corty, & Olshavsky, 1984) found that adolescents' ratings of their friends' use of alcohol, cigarettes, and marijuana were positively correlated with their own current use. Suls, Wan, and Sanders (1988) found a FCE for a wide range of health relevant practices (e.g., substance use, seat belts, etc.) among college students. For example, smokers believed that more of their peers smoked cigarettes than did the nonsmokers (See Fig. 11.1a).

Above Average Effect

By itself, the FCE cannot fully account for normative pressures for performing health relevant behaviors. For example, entry into college is usually associated with a shift toward college-wide norms encouraging increased alcohol consumption (e.g., Friend & Koushki, 1984). But, if the individual used themselves as the anchor for the norm, as the FCE suggests, then no such shift should be exhibited. To understand this, false consensus must be distinguished from other social perceptual processes. FCE represents a positive correlation (usually of modest to moderate size) between ratings of self and ratings of others. Where individuals place their standing (above, below, or at the same level) on the relevant dimension in relation to others is a separate issue. Survey studies of junior high school students' self-ratings and estimates of others' alcohol and cigarette use reveal that, although relative standing regarding cigarette smoking and alcohol use is correlated with the standing of peers (i.e., FCE), students consistently overestimated the degree to which their peers smoke cigarettes. This *overestimation* of friends' and peer use of unhealthy practices, such as smoking and alcohol use, is a highly reliable finding (Graham et al., 1991; Hansen & Graham, 1991) also found among college students and community-residing adults (Suls & Green, 1996). This perceptual bias has its complement; people also *underestimate* the degree to which others engage in healthy practices (Suls & Wan, 1987; Suls et al., 1988; see Fig. 11.1b). So, whereas people see themselves as sharing the same general perspective on particular practices (i.e., FCE), they also differentiate their position from others, seeing their behavior in a more desirable light (Taylor & Brown, 1988) ("above average").[1]

What would lead people to infer that others engage in unhealthy practices more than themselves but engage less in desirable healthy behaviors? Witnessing others engage in excessive drinking or suffering the consequences of alcohol overindulgence should be much more salient than the absence of such behavior. Consequently, extreme instances of such behavior are more likely to be highly available and probably receive inordinate weight in estimating the social norm. Such memorable instances may be even more accessible than an individual's own behavior. More than accessibility is probably involved, however, because people also tend to underestimate the frequency of healthy practices on the part of others compared to the self. The overestimation of unhealthy practices and the underestimation of healthy practices may both be manifestations of the "above average effect," whereby people perceive that they hold a more desirable position than do most other people (Taylor & Brown, 1988). Logically, of course, it is impossible for everyone to be better than average (unless the distribution is positively skewed; Krueger, 1998), so this perception appears to represent the result of a self-enhancing motivation to be perceived as distinctive and superior.

The impact of the FCE and above average effect on health behavior may be substantial. Perceiving social support for one's behavior (FCE) may permit one to feel at least somewhat secure with unhealthy practices. At the same time, the above average effect provides individuals with false reassurance that they are not acting as irresponsibly as some others. This may also provide an explanation for the illusion of invulnerability (Weinstein,1982), whereby people think they are at less risk of incurring disease than are their peers.

[1]The above average effect represents a comparison of an individual's estimate of own behavior versus his/her estimate of other people's behavior. Another way to establish the existence of a self-enhancing bias is to compare the individuals' estimates of others' behavior with the actual norm in the sample (e.g., how much alcohol they consume on average during a specific period of time). Such comparisons with the actual norms reveal a false uniqueness effect (Suls & Wan, 1987; Suls, Wan, Barlow, & Heimberg, 1990; Suls, Wan, & Sanders, 1988); that is, people underestimate the actual number of others performing desirable practices and overestimate the actual number performing undesirable practices. Unlike the above average effect, "false uniqueness" is identified by comparing estimates of the norm to the actual norm; however, both biases appear to be connected to the same self-enhancing dynamic.

People believe that if others drink more excessively, use their seat belts less, and ingest more red meat, then that means they are probably at lower risk than them.

Pluralistic Ignorance

Reliance on simple heuristics and self-serving motivation may contribute to normative perceptions that do not reflect reality. But even if such psychological factors were not in evidence, social norms would still be difficult to identify with accuracy because public behavior may not be an accurate reflection of private belief. This fact leads to still another psychological phenomenon with strong implications for health norm perception. Pluralistic ignorance is a psychological state characterized by the belief that individuals' private attitudes and judgments are different from those of others, even though their public behavior is identical (Allport, 1924; D. T. Miller & McFarland, 1987). In essence, people take a public position on a social issue that misrepresents their private position. One classic example is described by Schanck (1932), who studied a small rural community in which virtually all of the members condemned use of alcohol and card playing publicly because it was part of church dogma, but did not hold such extreme views privately. In this case, public behavior was used to identify the social norm, but because everyone mistakenly assumed that public behavior reflected private sentiment, they drew incorrect conclusions about others' feelings. Interestingly, because of pluralistic ignorance, the status quo is perpetuated because "even if no one believes ... everyone believes that everyone else believes" (D. T. Miller & McFarland, 1991, pp. 287–288). What causes people to maintain the public behavior? One explanation is the fear of being different or deviant. Another is people's desire to behave in accord with the norms of their valued social group. Because everyone is publicly behaving in the same way (and such comparison information suggests there is consensus favoring the public behavior), individuals assume that people agree with the prevailing sentiment and fail to recognize that social embarrassment or concern about not fitting in may also govern others' public behavior.

The role of pluralistic ignorance in college drinking practices has been studied recently (Prentice & D. T. Miller, 1993). Alcohol use by college undergraduates has become a major issue of concern because excessive drinking is a common practice on many college campuses and is associated with low academic performance, legal infractions, alcohol-related car accidents, and other negative consequences. Furthermore, entry into college is associated with an increase in alcohol consumption (Friend & Koushki, 1984). What accounts for the apparent peer support for excessive rather than moderate drinking? Many experts identify drinking as an important part of the identities of many college students and their social life. Despite the strong public norms favoring drinking on campus, Prentice and Miller noted students may privately hold misgivings about alcohol practices as they obtain firsthand exposure to sick roommates and inappropriate behavior associated with drinking. Students may privately have great misgivings about alcohol, but, believing that others are still comfortable with alcohol, they may perpetuate the norm by hiding their own concern. According to this reasoning, there may be pluralistic ignorance about students' concern with alcohol use on campus.

Indeed, undergraduate students at Princeton University who were surveyed about their own level of concern about drinking practices and their estimate of the level of concern of the average student or friends demonstrated evidence of pluralistic ignorance. Whether rating a peer or a friend, the students believed others were more comfortable with drinking than they were (see Fig. 11.1c). Prentice and D. T. Miller (1993) proposed that "individuals assume that other's outward display of comfort and ease reflects their actual feelings,

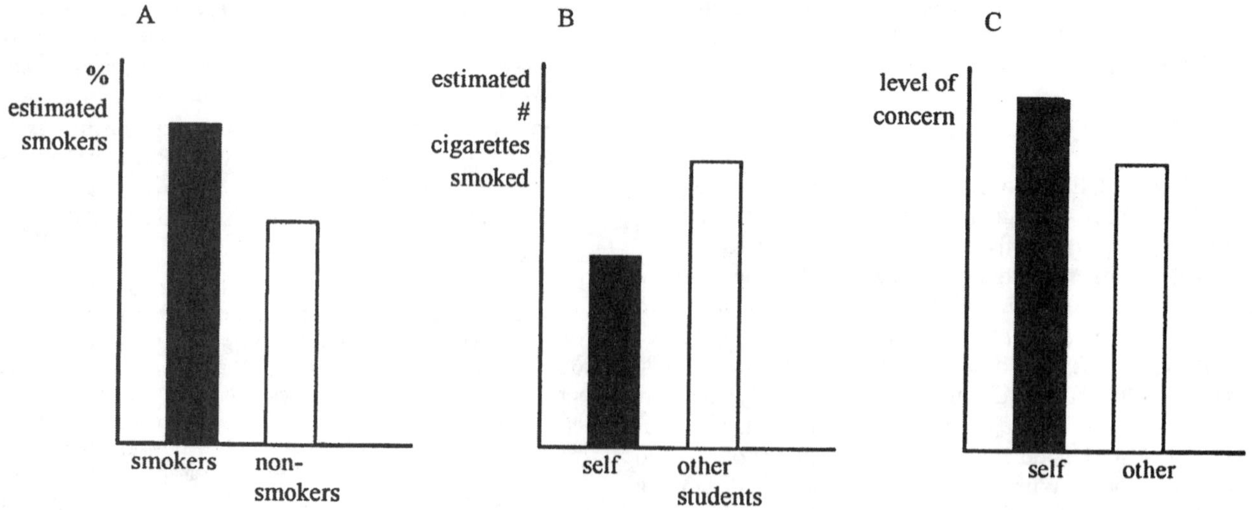

FIG. 11.1 False consensus (A), above average effect (B), and pluralistic ignorance (C).

even though those individuals' own identical behavior is somewhat at odds with their internal states" (p. 247).

In subsequent research, the relation between pluralistic ignorance and changes in drinking behavior on campus was assessed (Prentice & D. T. Miller, 1993, study 3). Both college men and women showed the pluralistic ignorance effect at the beginning of the academic year. Also, students' own level of drinking was uncorrelated with others' (projected) attitudes about drinking, suggesting that they were not complying with what they thought was the college norm favoring excessive drinking. However, by the end of the term, the college men reported the same low level of concern as their peers and the correlation between their own drinking and the perceived drinking norm had increased. This pattern of results suggested that the college men responded to their deviance from the perceived (and erroneous) norm by increasing their alcohol consumption. Women, on the other hand, showed no change in attitudes over time; they continued to perceive themselves as being more uncomfortable with campus drinking practices than were their peers and showed no correlation between their drinking behavior and others' atttitudes. There are several reasons why the females may not have demonstrated the social influence shown by the men, but for reasons of brevity they are not considered here. Some data, however, may help shed some light on this interesting gender difference.

More on the Social Construction of Norms Concerning Health Relevant Practices

In several studies, Suls and Green (1996) examined the degree to which pluralistic ignorance extended to other health relevant practices. They wondered whether college students were privately very concerned about the level of illegal drug use, cigarette smoking, and unsafe sex practices on campus, but interpreted the nonchalance of their peers in a way that perpetuated erroneous social norms. They also wanted to examine the degree to which false consensus and the above-average effect characterized the socially constructed norms concerning a wide range of important health practices. Finally, they wanted to explore some initial data suggesting that gender differences in misestimations of social norms may have a significant impact on health behavior.

Nearly 1,000 college students enrolled at a large midwestern university completed surveys about the degree to which each engaged in certain practices and the degree to which they were concerned about the practices on campus. They were also asked about the degree they thought their friends and the average student engaged in these practices and were concerned about the practices on campus. Inquiries were made about alcohol use, driving while drunk, marijuana, cigarette smoking, bulemia, and condom use. Across all behaviors, students reported being more concerned about negligent behavior than they thought other students were. In other words, students misperceived the norm by thinking that others were less concerned than they were.

What accounts for this erroneous construal of the norm? The self-perceptions and estimates of others' frequency of engaging in the various health relevant practices are informative about this question. Across practices, students perceived that they engaged in the unhealthy practices less frequently than did their peers. This provides additional evidence of the above average effect. Comparisons of students' estimates of other people's behavior with the actual reported behavior norms (taken from the same sample) also showed that students consistently overestimated the degree to which others engaged in unhealthy practices (i.e., false uniqueness; see footnote 1). These results suggest that Prentice and D. T. Miller's (1993) notion that everyone is observing identical behavior, which leads to the misestimation of the norm, requires revision. Suls and Green's health perception data indicate that students did not think they were behaving identically to others. Indeed, individual respondents perceived that they drank and engaged in all of the other negligent practices less than their friends. Obviously, everyone cannot be drinking less than their friends. Hence, some aspect of pluralistic ignorance is driven by a self-enhancing overestimation of how much others engage in undesirable practices. A few extreme cases also may be so vivid they lead to inflated estimates. Ironically, the erroneous representation of the social norm might acquire a life of its own and cause the individual to engage in unhealthy practices subsequently.

Gender Differences in Norm Estimation

In initial studies, Suls and Green (1996) found that, although both male and female college students exhibited pluralistic ignorance, the males reported somewhat lower levels of concern than did females. In subsequent studies, students were asked to answer about themselves and also to estimate the frequency and level of concern about several health relevant practices for male and female peers separately. For most health behaviors, male college students consistently rated their own level of concern as higher than other males and closer to their estimate of female students' level of concern. Males' self-reported frequency of undesirable behavior fell between their estimate of male behavior and female friends. Thus, surprisingly, there was evidence that males identified themselves with their perception of female norms, rather than with male norms. Female students also showed pluralistic ignorance and the above average effect with regard to their same-sex peers; however, they showed no identification with male attitudes or behavior (see Table 11.1).

TABLE 11.1
Level of Concern Regarding Unsafe Sex (i.e., failure to use condom) Among College Students

Target	Male Subject	Female Subject
Self	5.6	6.9
Average Male	4.0	4.4
Average Female	6.1	6.3

Note. Level of concern was measured on an 11-point scale, ranging from 0 ("doesn't bother me/them at all") to 10 ("bothers me/them very much").

This gender difference in norm perception has several potential implications. Male college students think their same-sex peers are less concerned and act more inappropriately than they do. Furthermore, males assume their concerns are frequently closer to those of females. This might create considerable sex-role conflict for males, particularly those concerned about maintaining a masculine image. There is speculation that concerns about maintaining a "macho" image may prompt male students to act in ways to reduce the (erroneous) discrepancy they perceive between themselves and their same-sex peers. This might explain why males in Prentice and Miller's study showed a decrease in concern and an increase in alcohol use. Although more research is needed, understanding gender stereotypes for health behaviors might help suggest ways to reduce unhealthy practices.

Normative Perceptions and Behavior Change

The knowledge gained from studying the perception of social norms regarding health practices has implications for health prevention programs. Misperception of peer substance use and other unhealthy practices functions as a passive form of social influence (Graham et al., 1991). Researchers have developed prevention programs in which erroneous normative perceptions about prevalence and acceptability of drug use among peers are corrected. In a study with junior high school students, Hansen and Graham (1991) found that normative education, which tried to correct the misestimation of drug use norms, was effective in reducing alcohol, marijuana, and tobacco use over a year's time. A comparison group treatment, involving resistance training to peer influence, was ineffective. Hansen and Graham observed that resistance training may fail because instruction in techniques to resist peer pressure communicates first that peer pressure exists and implies that most adolescents perceive substance use as common and acceptable.

Prentice and D. T. Miller (1993) strongly advocate group interventions. They noted that programs targeting the individual may not be fully successful because private attitudes may be changed, but social norms and public behaviors may be unaffected. Encouraging students to speak openly about their private atttitudes within the group may, however, expose pluralistic ignorance. As social and health psychologists learn more about how people construe and misconstrue social norms, better interventions may be developed to encourage healthy and discourage unhealthy practices.

SYMPTOM INTERPRETATION, LAY REFERRAL, AND THE DECISION TO SEEK MEDICAL CARE

Social comparison processes also play a role in appraisal of symptoms and the decision to seek medical attention (Safar, Tharps, Jackson, & H. Leventhal, 1979; Sanders, 1982). Physical signs and symptoms occur frequently and most are ambiguous (e.g., a nagging headache, a bruise, heart palpitations). How do people decide when somatic sensations are indicative of illness and whether to go for treatment? In addition to using commonsense models (H. Leventhal, Meyer, & Nerenz, 1980), past experience, and assessing the severity and likelihood that the symptoms are significant (Pennebaker, 1982), people also rely on members of their lay referral network for advice and social comparison (Friedson, 1961). Close to 70% of patients experiencing symptoms talk to at least one layperson about the symptoms and discuss what action should be taken (M. H. Miller, 1973; Suchman, 1965). Some aspects of this information seeking appears to involve direct social comparisons. Just as Schachter and Singer (1962) found that people label ambiguous physiological states by comparison with the emotions exhibited by others, people experiencing physical symptoms also may compare with others to determine if they are experiencing the same thing and how these sensations should be interpreted (Mechanic, 1972). Sometimes these comparisons are explicit, as when a person experiencing ambiguous physical symptoms asks friends if they are experiencing or have experienced the same sensations in the past. On other occasions, these comparisons appear to be made at a nonconscious level.

Suls, Martin, and H. Leventhal (1997) presented a model recently that integrates the literature on basic social comparison processes with the medical literature on lay referral. Three scenarios seem to cover most instances of comparison used in lay referral for symptom appraisal and the decision to seek formal care. The first scenario, called *symptom-induced social comparison* refers to cases when the individual experiences physical symptoms, forms a tentative opinion about them, and seeks out others with whom to compare that assessment (see Fig. 11.2a). In essence, this scenario involves the dynamics, described in the introduction, concerning social comparisons of opinions. Recall that the selection of a comparison other depends on whether the opinion is a belief or a value. However, symptom appraisal has elements of both beliefs and values. The individual wants to know whether the symptoms represent a definable medical condition (i.e., a potentially veridical entity). For belief-type opinions, dissimilar others provide valuable information because of the triangulation process, described earlier. In addition, someone with medical or health expertise should be most informative. Not only do they have a dissimilar perspective, but they also possess some expertise that may be considered objective. Recall that, according to Festinger (1954), objective or physical standards were the preferred source of information to reduce uncertainty; social comparisons were sought only when objective information was unavailable. In lieu of a physician or health care professional, the opinion of a lay expert (e.g., a neighbor who works part-time as a nursing assistant) will be useful. Hence, people may seek comparison with dissimilar others, especially those who have some kind of expertise, even if limited.

Value considerations also can figure in symptom-induced comparison. An illness may be manifested differently across people and many questions about illness are not answered by expert diagnosis, but rather with reference to a particular person's situation and life responsibilities. Someone with a similar physical constitution and background may provide a benchmark for interpreting one's symptoms.

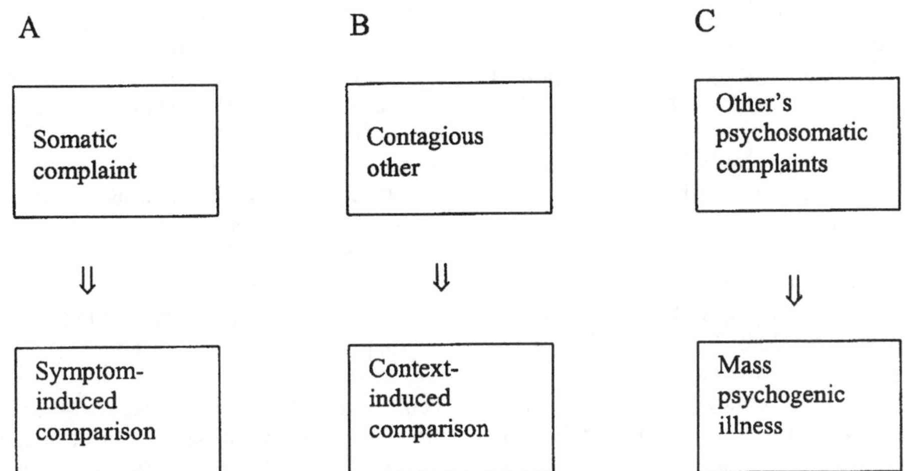

FIG. 11.2 Three scenarios for lay referral for health care.

Hence, symptom-induced comparison has elements of belief ("Are these symptoms indicative of a disease?") and value ("Am I the kind of person who contracts this disorder?" and "How will these symptoms affect my lifestyle?"). As a result, both similar and dissimilar others may be sought as comparison others. Suls et al. (1997) reasoned that dissimilar experts should have favored status because they have the additional virtue of providing "objective" or expert criteria. In best of all possible situations, the "lay expert" would be someone of similar age, experience, and physical history, thereby satisfying value and belief concerns. Recent evidence involving surveys and interviews with young adults and senior citizens provided some empirical evidence for these predictions (Cameron, E. A. Leventhal, & H. Leventhal, 1993; Suls & Martin, 1995).

Context-Induced Social Comparison

The second scenario involves a situation in which the individual has had contact with someone who becomes verifiably ill with some contagious disorder or toxin. The awareness, via social comparison, of exposure to contagious or toxic elements induces symptom vigilance to ascertain whether signs and symptoms experienced match those presented by the ill target. In this scenario, comparison is prompted by the other person who is ill, rather than the initial manifestation of symptoms as described in the first scenario (see Fig. 11.2b).

The context-induced scenario resembles the comparison of abilities. There need be no exhange of opinions; merely being exposed to someone who is physically ill may prompt self-monitoring of relevant sensations in the same way that exposure to someone of superior ability may induce a comparison and consequent self-evaluation. In context-induced evaluations, comparers consider whether they have a particular set of physical symptoms, the meaning of which is provided by the proximity of a contagious other.

The choice of an appropriate comparison other depends partly on the nature of the health threat. For common contagious illnesses, almost any person with whom an individual has had contact or shared exposure is probably considered a relevant and similar comparison other. For certain illnesses, similiarity may be defined by other factors. Exposure to someone with chicken pox may not induce symptom vigilance if individuals have had chicken pox in the past, because they know they now are immune to future episodes. Other disorders may involve environmental exposure to various toxins, so that relevant comparison with others who induce self-monitoring would have to share similar attributes and worksite exposure.

Context-induced comparison shares features of ability social comparison, but there is a notable difference. In the ability domain, comparison is prompted by people's initial uncertainty about their standing. However, in the symptom evaluation domain, the illness of another person with whom they have shared contact or exposure creates the uncertainty regarding their own physical status and induces symptom monitoring.

Mass Psychogenic Illness

The third scenario involves widespread symptom perception among a group of individuals, even though there is no objective evidence of physical illness based on medical tests (see Fig. 11.2c). Such episodes tend to occur most commonly during stressful periods. Typically, the "illness" spreads among people with whom individuals work closely or know personally (Colligan, Pennebaker, & Murphy, 1982). The classic case is the so-called June Bug episode studied by Kerckhoff and Back (1968), which occured in an industrial plant. Victims (about 25% of the employees) reported nausea and feverishness, which sent some to the hospital, although no objective evidence of illness was found. The conclusion of health inspectors and Kerckhoff and Back was that the people who became ill showed a pattern of hysterical contagion in which psychosomatic symptoms of stress were mislabeled as markers of physical illness.

Like context-induced comparison, a social comparison process is induced by the social context, but here the symptoms are not really indicative of physical disease. Typically, in psychogenic episodes, people are already fatigued, anxious, and experiencing ambiguous symptoms (e.g., the June Bug episode occurred during a busy time at the plant). If others claim to have contracted a flu or been bitten by a bug, then this becomes a plausible illness label for another person's ambiguous state. As in the context-induced scenario, the information search preceding mass psychogenic episodes resembles the way in which people make ability comparisons. Similarity of environment and exposure of the comparison other with the "illness" are critical. Further, if the other has similar constitutional attributes, then this probably facilitates the attribution of illness in oneself because similarity may suggest a comparable level of vulnerability. Indeed, available evidence suggests that mass psychogenic illness tends to occur among persons who share personal attributes (Stahl & Lebedun, 1974).

Illness Delay. These three scenarios apply both to symptom appraisal, as described earlier, and the decision to seek medical attention ("Should I go to a physician?"). The framework provided may also explain why there is no straightforward conclusion about whether lay referral encourages or delays seeking medical attention. In the current scene of managed care, this is an important issue for theoretical and practice reasons. Sanders' (1982) review suggested that members of the lay network generally encourage seeking professional advice, but some empirical studies (Cameron et al., 1993) report that patients were advised by their relatives or friends to seek medical attention only about one half of the time.

Delay can arise from several features of comparison in lay referral. Experimental and anthropological research indicates that people rate disorders as less serious if they are more common (Clark, 1959; Jemmott, Ditto, & Croyle, 1986). Hence, symptoms that are prevalent among members of an individual's social network tend to be perceived as minor and less deserving of medical attention. In these cases, comparing with others who share the symptoms may delay seeking of medical attention.

In the mass psychogenic illness episode, however, if comparison others present so-called symptoms, others also may refer themselves for medical care. Sanders (1981) also found that, even if an objective test carried out by the individual suggested nothing was wrong, people were more apt to seek medical attention if members of their social network advised that they should do so. One interpretation of these results is that people are more likely to seek medical attention if peers give permission for them to assume the sick role.

The complex comparison dynamics involved in lay referral may explain why only about one third of people with physical symptoms needing attention refer themselves for medical consultation (Ingham & P. Miller, 1979; G. Scrambler & A. Scrambler, 1985). At the same time, a large proportion of people who do report symptoms to a health care provider have no demonstrable disease (Costa & McCrae, 1987). Both under- and overutilization of health care resources may occur as a function of social comparison processes operating in the lay referral network. More examination of these processes by health psychologists may be able to encourage appropriate self-referral for medical care.

AFFILIATION, COMPARISON, AND COPING WITH MEDICAL THREATS

Thus far, the chapter has considered the role that comparison processes play in the instigation of health-related practices and symptom appraisal. Interpersonal comparisons also play a role when people are actively coping with acute medical threats such as when they are awaiting medical procedures. People may affiliate and compare with others in their attempts to cope with impending medical threats, such as surgery.

Research on this topic was instigated by Schachter's (1959) pioneering laboratory studies on the effects of fear on affiliation (see Cottrell & Epley, 1977; Rofe, 1984, for reviews). Several experiments showed that people facing novel threats, such as electric shock, preferred to affiliate with others currently anticipating the same threat as themselves rather than alone or with others facing a different threat. These results are consistent with social comparison theory: People were experiencing uncertainty about the novel threat and were motivated to affiliate with similar others because they provided the best gauge for evaluating the appropriateness of their emotional state. For Schachter, emotional self-evaluation via social comparison was served by affiliating with others awaiting the same threat (i.e., a similar other). He acknowledged, however, that people might also want cognitive clarity about the impending threat to reduce uncertainty about the nature and dangers associated with the situation. Schachter differentiated cognitive clarity from emotional comparison even though both seem to involve social comparison. Seeking cognitive clarity was thought of in nonsocial terms by Schachter and focused on threat relevant information seeking. Emotional comparison processes were considered to be inherently interpersonal and focused on evaluating people's feelings.

The results of an early experiment by Schachter (1959) suggested that the need for cognitive clarity did not account for affiliation under stress (see Kulik, Mahler, & Moore, 1996). Also, Zimbardo and Formica (1963) found that high compared to low threat (of electric shock) subjects indicated a greater preference for awaiting threat in the presence of someone also facing the same threat than someone who had already experienced the threat. If cognitive clarity were the motive for affiliation, it would seem to be best served by someone who just experienced the threat. The conclusion drawn by Zimbardo and Formica was that emotional comparison was the primary motive. This and later research seemed to reinforce that people prefer to affiliate and exchange information with other persons facing the same threats. Indeed, social support groups are frequently assumed to be so popular and, presumably effective, because they allow people who have the same problem to share their feelings.

Subsequent research (R. L. Miller & Suls, 1977; Rofe, 1984) has found that affiliation preferences are not necessarily as straightforward as Schachter contended. Although emotional comparison seems to explain Zimbardo and Formica's results, the experimenter in their study told subjects they could not talk with the potential affiliate. Hence, cognitive clarity may not have been a motive in the experiment because it was essentially blocked by the experimenter's instructions (see Kulik & Mahler's 1997 critique). In real-world contexts, however, communication is unlikely to be prohibited, so cognitive clarity may be an important motivation for social comparison under threat. There are several reasons why cognitive clarity may be an important consideration. Problem-focused efforts would be enhanced by talking to others who had more experience with the threat, had some expertise or skill, or simply served as successful role models. Several studies of ability-related affiliation (R. L. Miller & Suls, 1977; Nosanchuk & Erickson, 1985) demonstrated that individuals preferred more talented associates to work with on challenging tasks, presumably because of the clarity they could provide.

Kulik and his associates reported a series of studies reexamining affiliation under threat in real-world medical settings that explore the emotional comparison versus cognitive clarity question. In one study, Kulik and Mahler (1989) asked men hospitalized for coronary bypass procedures whether they would prefer assignment to a roommate who was awaiting bypass surgery (like themselves), a roommate who was back on the main ward recovering after bypass surgery, or whether they had no preference. Contrary to the emotional comparison notion, patients most often preferred a roommate who was already recovering from the surgery. Presumably, this was because such an individual could provide more cognitive clarity about the procedure and its sequalae. Indeed, comments from patients confirmed this interpretation ("It's more helpful for me to talk to someone who's already had it, because the guy that's waiting doesn't know anything about it, only what he's told"; Kulik & Mahler, 1997, p. 231). Laboratory research also confirms that cognitive clarity seems more critical for affiliation than emotional comparison. For example, individuals awaiting cold pressor pain spent more time watching and discussing the threat with someone who was threat experienced (had already undergone the cold pressor) than with someone who was threat inexperienced (Kulik, Mahler, & Earnest, 1994).

An important question for health care providers concerns what types of affiliations influence hospital recovery. If cognitive clarity is more important than emotional comparison, then assignment to a postoperative roommate should promote better adaptation than a fellow preoperative roommate. An initial study by Kulik and Mahler (1987) found that coronary bypass patients reported less anxiety prior to surgery, walked more after surgery, and had a shorter hospital stay if assigned preoperatively to a roommate who was postoperative, rather than preoperative (Kulik & Mahler, 1987). A recent extension (Kulik et al., 1996) compared patients who waited alone with patients assigned to a roommate who was similar or dissimilar in type of operation (cardiac vs. low threat noncardiac) and either similar or dissimilar in operative status (preoperative vs. postoperative). In this study, the patient adapted better if a roommate had a similar (i.e., cardiac) problem. Also, patients were less anxious prior to surgery and had shorter postoperative stays if assigned to a roommate who was postoperative. In short, a roommate who presumably provided the greatest cognitive clarity (a postoperative cardiac roommate) was associated with the fastest recovery and the situation with the lowest cognitive clarity (no roommate) was associated with the slowest recovery. Although patients made some emotional comparisons (e.g., discussing their emotions about surgery prior to surgery), roommates talked about many irrelevant topics so emotional comparison was not the predominant preoccupation that Schachter's theory would predict. Second, although patients made more emotional comparisons under high than low threat with a roommate facing the same surgery, the rate of comparison did not vary as a function of the type of surgery, a finding contrary to the emotional comparison hypothesis. There was evidence of some emotional contagion; patients became more alike in their level of anxiety regardless of the similarity of the roommate' problem (Kulik, Moore, & Mahler, 1993). Emotional comparison theory would anticipate this should occur in accord with the similarity of the patients. Since this did not occur, Kulik and Mahler (1997) believed the results may best be seen as evidence for a primitive emotional contagion (Hatfield, Cacioppo, & Rapson, 1993). Although this contagion could be the result of comparison, it may also reflect a more general mimicry of facial expressions, vocalizations, posture, and body movements.

The processes that underlie the affiliation preferences and health outcomes of awaiting medical procedures with others remain to be disentangled. At the least, however, the findings suggest that information seeking via comparison may be more important to patients waiting for surgery than gauging their emotions. In this regard, and contrary to Schachter's hypothesis, fellow patients who have already recovered from surgery may create better adaptation and shorter hospital stays for the preoperative patient than assignment to preoperative patients. Further, assignment to roomates of preoperative patients may create an emotional contagion that is deleterious to patients and staff. Research to date suggests that comparison for cognitive clarity may be more critical than comparison of emotions. Hence, this may be a case where problem-focused coping on the part of the patient can be encouraged in an attempt to adapt to acute medical threats. More research needs to be conducted, however, to ascertain whether all types of postoperative patients are of equal benefit. Cognitive clarity may be undermined if a postoperative patient is a neurotic complainer or suffering postoperative complications. In any case, for health psychologists, roommate assignment is an intriguing and potentially cost-effective measure to facilitate comparison in the interests of cognitive clarity and encourage adjustment in hospital.

COPING WITH CHRONIC MEDICAL THREATS VIA SOCIAL COMPARISON

Some medical threats are not acute but involve long-term adaptation to serious, and even life-threatening illnesses. Since the mid-1980s, health psychologists have actively studied the use of social comparison as a coping strategy by patients adapting to chronic health problems. One of the major inspirations for these efforts was Wills's (1981) theory that people who are threatened make downward comparisons; that is, they compare themselves with others who are worse off in order to feel better. Thus, for Wills (1987), downward comparison was an emotion-focused coping strategy (see also Gibbons & Gerrard, 1991). These ideas received support in a seminal study of women with breast cancer conducted by Wood et al. (1985). When asked how well they were adapting, nearly 80% of breast cancer patients reported adjusting somewhat better or much better than others. Among patients who did not know another woman who was in worse condition, they chose to imagine others who were adapting poorly (Taylor, Wood, Lichtman, 1983), a result reminiscent of the fabricated or constructed social comparisons discussed earlier in the section on "Norm Construction."

Since the publication of this research, there have been scores of studies assessing comparisons made by persons suffering from a variety of medical or other problems, including parents of medically fragile infants (Affleck & Tennen, 1991), patients with rheumatoid arthritis (Affleck, Tennen, Pfeiffer, & Fifield, 1988; Blalock, B. M. DeVellis, & R. F. DeVellis, 1989), physical disability (Buunk, 1995), persons trying to quit smoking (Gibbons, Gerrard, Lando, & McGovern, 1991), cardiac patients (Helgeson & Taylor, 1993), as well as cancer patients (Buunk et al., 1990; Molleman, Pruyn, & van Knippenberg, 1986). The general outcome has been that persons undergoing such health threats report a high degree of downward comparison; also, downward comparisons tend to be associated with higher emotional well-being, a result consistent with downward comparison theory. For example, arthritis patients mentioned more downward than upward comparisons (Affleck & Tennen, 1991).

However, Taylor and Lobel (1989) identified contradictory findings that did not support the predictions of downward comparison theory. In some reports (e.g., Molleman et al., 1986), medical patients under threat appeared to compare or desire affiliation with people doing better than themselves. To explain this discrepancy, Taylor and Lobel proposed that people may engage in upward affiliation to facilitate problem-focused coping by gaining information or finding hopeful or inspiring examples for identification. Downward comparisons (which need not involve actual contact), in contrast, serve as an emotion-focused strategy that improve affective well-being. This perspective seemed atttactive because some empirical evidence indicates that people rate themselves as superior to others on comparative ratings scales, but choose to affiliate and seek information from others who are superior (see Wood, 1989, for a review; also R. L. Miller & Suls, 1977; Nosanchuk & Erickson, 1985). Thus, Taylor and Lobel argued for a distinction between self-enhancement, which is served by downward comparisons, and self-improvement, which is served by affiliation with persons better off.

Not all of the evidence supports Taylor and Lobel's (1989) perspective, however (see Buunk, 1994). For example, persons in support groups for eating disorders and smoking show a preference for having others in their group who suffer more serious problems (Gibbons & Gerrard, 1991). These results suggest that sometimes people do prefer downward contacts, consistent with Will's downward comparison theory.

Recently, Wood and VanderZee (1997) proposed a reconciliation of downward comparison and Taylor and Lobel's theories. According to Wood and VanderZee, whether patients react positively or negatively to upward and downward comparisons depends on whether they believe they will improve or decline on the dimension of comparison (see Major et al., 1991). If patients believe their status will improve, upward comparison or contact will be pleasing, but if they believe they are unlikely to improve, then upward comparison should engender negative emotions. Conversely, if patients believe their condition will not decline, then downward comparison should be self-enhancing. However, patients who believe they are likely to worsen should find downward comparisons highly threatening. Hence, in this conception, both upward and downward comparisons can have either positive or negative effects. The patient's expectations of prognosis determine which outcome is most likely. Wood and VanderZee conducted a review of the available empirical evidence for their model with regard to cancer patients. Although some evidence is consistent with the model, they noted that too few studies provide a direct index of the perceived expectancy, the critical moderator.

Another related perspective on comparison and coping with chronic health threats has been presented by Buunk et al. (1990). Buunk et al., like Wood and VanderZee, also proposed that upward and downward comparisons can have negative or positive effects. They observed that when individuals learn that someone is worse off (i.e., downward comparisons), this may imply that they are not as bad off *or* that it is possible to get worse. When individuals learn that another is better off, this may imply that they are not doing as well as some others *or* it is possible to improve. In studies of cancer patients and couples experiencing martial distress, Buunk et al. found that persons high in self-esteem were better able to focus on the positive implications of both upward and downward comparisons. People with low self-esteem, in contrast, tended to draw conclusions from both upward and downward comparisons that were discouraging. People with high self-esteem tend to more optimistic, so the findings are consistent with Wood and VanderZee's analysis.

Before the relative merits of the theoretical approaches to comparison and coping can be determined, another problem needs to be resolved. Virtually all of the evidence regarding comparisons and well-being in medical populations is based on cross-sectional, correlational methodologies. Hence, inferences about causation, confounding, and possible third variable explanations cannot be ruled out. In addition to noting this methodological problem, Tennen and Affleck (1997) argued that reports of relative standing or scores from comparative rating scales do not necessarily represent the result of downward coping efforts, but merely comparison conclusions. These conclusions may be accurate, rather than biased, because some patients will be doing well and will be veridically "better off" than others (Affleck et al., 1988). Although Tennen and Affleck are correct that longititudinal studies are needed to distinguish between comparisons and outcomes, all comparisons need not be effortful or intentional to be helpful. Patients may contemplate that "things could be worse" without intending anything beforehand; nonetheless, once patients have the thought they may seize on it for comfort.

Similarly, constructed norms may bouy a patient's spirits even if they are based on no concrete explicit comparisons. For example, Suls, Marco, and Tobin (1991) interviewed a sample of 100 senior citizens, many of whom were coping with serious chronic illnesses. After rating their health on a 4-point scale (excellent, good, fair, poor), respondents were asked to "report about the kinds of information that 'came to mind' in thinking about their overall level of health," such as whether they thought about how their health compared to someone else, to a group, with their health some time in the past, or based on direct feedback information from someone else. Sixty-seven percent of the sample reported that their health was "good" or "excellent," a result consistent with larger survey studies of elderly self-assessments of health (Levkoff, Cleary, & Wetle, 1987; B. S. Linn & M. W. Linn, 1980). Interestingly, mention of social comparison was unrelated to health ratings. Temporal comparisons were related to ratings, but in a negative direction (i.e., mentioning temporal comparison was associated with lower self-ratings of health). Because no specific, explicit social or temporal comparisons were related to the positive self-ratings, it was not obvious what factors accounted for the overwhelmingly positive health assessments. Suls et al. proposed that rather than being based on specific comparisons, the health assessments were based on implicit comparisons with a fabricated, generalized other and a stereotypical notion that most of the elderly population is quite frail and ill. Although many of the elderly respondents had serious diseases, they evaluated themselves positively because of their general stereotypes rather than a specific comparison other.

In any case, longitudinal studies are needed that include intensive assessments of the prospective relation between comparison coping efforts and subsequent outcomes (Tennen & Affleck, 1997). In this way, researchers can obtain more direct evidence of the causal relation between comparison efforts and adaptational outcomes. In addition, measures of expectancy, in accord with Wood and VanderZee's model, should be included. More attention also needs to be paid to identification of specific evaluative questions served by a given comparison (Suls, 1999). Patients diagnosed with cancer might initially ask "Will I survive this?" Upward contact with a longtime survivor may be useful and inspiring. But other questions are more specific ("Will I become nauseous or lose my hair after radiation therapy?") and probably are best answered by people who are closer in standing to themselves. Some important concerns are in the form of "Can I do X?" In such instances, individuals might compare themselves with someone who is similar in background attributes (age, gender) who has recently gone through the procedure (Wheeler et al., 1997). Available research has conceptualized upward and downward comparisons in global terms (better vs. worse). Patients, however, probably make finer distinctions among potential comparison others both with regard to background factors and current adaptation to disease.

Although the study of comparison processes among chronically ill patients has identified an important area of coping, health psychologists still do not know what social comparison opportunities should be made available to patients and how they should be implemented. Perhaps Kulik and his associates' efforts with regard to acute medical threats (reviewed earlier) may offer suggestions in this regard. Also, more attention to the specific day-to-day evaluative questions and concerns pressing on patients and members of their support network may facilitate this active line of health psychological research.

CONCLUSIONS

This chapter has reviewed four areas of health psychology in which the role of social comparison has been strongly implicated. Classic and contemporary social psychological comparison theories and research shed light on some important medical and public health phenomena, and also provide suggestions for possible interventions. There is good reason to believe that social comparison processes will be implicated in other health psychology domains because comparison is such a fundamental aspect of social behavior. Just as advances in cellular biology and medical technology have contributed significantly to medical science and health care, it is clear that Virchow's 19th-century observation was correct—medical science is grounded in a social field.

REFERENCES

Affleck, G., & Tennen, H. (1991). Social comparison and coping with major medical disorders. In J. Suls & T. A. Wills (Eds.), *Social comparison: Contemporary theory and research* (pp. 369–393). Hillsdale, NJ: Lawrence Erlbaum Associates.

Affleck, G., Tennen, H., Pfeiffer, C., & Fifield, J. (1988). Social comparisons in rheumatoid arthritis: Accuracy and adaptational significance. *Journal of Social and Clinical Psychology, 6,* 219–234.

Allport, F. H. (1924) *Social psychology.* Boston: Houghton Mifflin.

Asch, S. (1956). Studies in independence and conformity: A minority of one against a unanimous majority. *Psychological Monographs, 70,* 1–70.

Ajzen, I., & Fishbein, M. (1980). *Understanding attitudes and predicting social behavior.* Englewood Cliffs, NJ: Prentice-Hall.

Blalock, S. J., DeVellis, B. M., & DeVellis, R. F. (1989). Social comparison among individuals with rheumatoid arthritis. *Journal of Applied Social Psychology, 19,* 665–680.

Buunk, B. P. (1994). Social comparison processes under stress: Towards an integration of classic and recent perspectives. In W. Stroebe & M. Hewstone (Eds.), *European Review of Social Psychology* (Vol. 5, pp. 211–241). London: Wiley.

Buunk, B. P. (1995). Comparison direction and comparison dimension among disabled individuals: Toward a refined conceptualization of social comparison under stress. *Personality and Social Psychology Bulletin, 21,* 316–330.

Buunk, B. P., Collins, R. L., Taylor, S. E., Van Yperen, N., & Dakof, G. A. (1990). The affective consequences of social comparison: Either direction has its ups and downs. *Journal of Personality and Social Psychology, 59,* 1238–1249.

Cameron, L., Leventhal, E. A., & Leventhal, H. (1993). Symptom representation and affect as determinants of care seeking in a community-dwelling, adult sample population. *Health Psychology, 12,* 171–179.

Chassin, L., Presson, C., Sherman, J., Corty, E., & Olshavsky, R. (1984). Predicting the onset of cigarette smoking in adolescents: A longitudinal study. *Journal of Applied Social Psychology, 14,* 224–243.

Clark, M. (1959). *Health in the Mexican-American culture.* Berkeley, CA: University of California Press.

Colligan, M., Pennebaker, J., & Murphy, L. (Eds.). (1982). *Mass psychogenic illess: A social psychological analysis.* Hillsdale, NJ: Lawrence Erlbaum Associates.

Collins, R. L. (1996). For better or worse: The impact of upward comparisons on self-evaluations. *Psychological Bulletin, 119,*51–69.

Costa, P. T., Jr., & McCrae, R. (1987). Neuroticism, somatic complaints, and disease: Is the bark worse than the bite? *Journal of Personality, 55,* 297–316.

Cottrell, N. B., & Epley, S. W. (1977). Affiliation, social comparison, and socially mediated stress reduction. In J. Suls & R. L. Miller (Eds.), *Social comparison processes: Theoretical and empirical perspectives* (pp. 43–68). Washington, DC: Hemisphere.

Crandall, C. S. (1988). Social contagion of binge eating. *Journal of Personality and Social Psychology, 55,* 588–598.

Deutsch, M., & Gerard, H. (1955). A study of normative and informational social influences upon individual judgment. *Journal of Abnormal and Social Psychology, 51,* 629–636.

Festinger, L. (1954). A theory of social comparison processes. *Human Relations, 1,* 117–140.

Festinger, L., Schachter, S., & Back, K. (1950). *Social pressures in informal groups: A study of human factors in housing.* New York: Harper.

Freidson, E. (1961). *Patients' views of medical practice.* New York: Russell Sage.

Friend, K. E., & Koushki, P. A. (1984). Student substance abuse: Stability and change across college years. *Public Opinion Quarterly, 40,* 427–448.

Gastorf, J. W., & Suls, J. (1978). Performance evaluation via social comparison: Performance similarity versus related attribute similarity. *Social Psychology Quarterly, 41,* 297–305.

Gerard, H. B., & Orive, R. (1987). The dynamics of opinion formation. In L. Berkowitz (Ed.), *Advances in experimental social psychology* (Vol. 20, pp. 171–202). New York: Academic Press.

Gerrard, M., Gibbons, F. X., Benthin, A. C., & Hessling, R. M. (1996). A longitudinal study of the reciprocal nature of risk behaviors and cognitions in adolescents: What you do shapes what you think and vice versa. *Health Psychology, 15,* 344–354.

Gibbons, F. X., & Gerrard, M. (1991). Downward comparison and coping with threat. In J. Suls & T. A. Wills (Eds.), *Social comparison: Contemporary theory and research* (pp. 317–346). Hillsdale, NJ: Lawrence Erlbaum Associates.

Gibbons, F. X., Gerrard, M., Lando, H., & McGovern, P. G. (1991). Social comparison and smoking cesssation: The role of the "typical smoker." *Journal of Experimental Social Psychology, 27,* 239–258.

Goethals, G. R., & Darley, J. (1977). Social comparison theory: An attributional approach. In J. Suls & R. L. Miller (Eds.), *Social comparison processes: Theoretical and empirical perspectives* (pp. 259–278). Washington, DC: Hemisphere.

Goethals, G. R., Messick, D. M., & Allison, S. T. (1991). The uniqueness bias: Studies of constructive social comparison. In J. Suls & T. A. Wills (Eds.), *Social comparison: Contemporary theory and research* (pp. 317–346). Hillsdale, NJ: Lawrence Erlbaum Associates.

Gorenflo, D. W., & Crano, W. D. (1989). Judgmental subjectivity/objectivity and locus of choice in social comparison. *Journal of Personality and Social Psychology, 57,* 605–614.

Graham, J. W., Marks, G., & Hansen, W. B. (1991). Social influence processes affecting adolescent substance use. *Journal of Applied Psychology, 76,* 291–298.

Hansen, W. B., & Graham, J. W. (1991). Preventing alcohol, marijuana, and cigarette use among adolescents: Peer resistance training versus establishing conservative norms. *Preventative Medicine, 20,* 414–430.

Hatfield, E., Cacioppo, J. T., & Rapson, R. L. (1993). Emotional contagion. *Current Directions in Psychological Science, 2,* 96–99.

Helgeson, V. S., & Taylor, S. E. (1993). Social comparisons and adjustment among cardiac patients. *Journal of Applied Social Psychology, 23,* 1171–1195.

Ingham, I., & Miller, P. (1979). Symptom prevalence and severity in a general practice. *Journal of Epidemiology and Community Health, 33,* 191–198.

Jemmott, J. B., III, Ditto, P. H., & Croyle, R. T. (1986). Judging health status: Effects of perceived prevalence and personal relevance. *Journal of Personality and Social Psychology, 50,* 899–905.

Kandel, D. B. (1980). Drug and drinking behavior among youth. In A. Inkeles, N. J. Smelser, & R. Turner (Eds.), *Annual review of sociology* (Vol. 6, pp. 235–286). Palo Alto, CA: Annual Reviews.

Kahneman, D., & Tversky, A. (1973). On the psychology of prediction. *Psychological Review, 80,* 237–251.

Kerckhoff, A. C., & Back, K. W. (1968). *The June Bug: A study of hysterical contagion.* New York: Appleton-Century-Crofts.

Krueger, J. (1998). Enhancement bias in descriptions of self and others. *Personality and Social Psychology Bulletin, 24,* 505–516.

Kulik, J. A., & Mahler, H. L. (1987). Effects of preoperative roommate assignment on preoperative anxiety and postoperative recovery from coronary bypass surgery. *Health Psychology, 6,* 525–543.

Kulik, J. A., & Mahler, H. L. (1989). Stress and affiliation in a hospital setting: Preoperative roommate preferences. *Personality and Social Psychogy Bulletin, 15,* 183–193.

Kulik, J. A., & Mahler, H. L. (1997). Social comparison, affiliation, and coping with acute medical threats. In B. P. Buunk & F. X. Gibbons (Eds.), *Health and coping: Perspectives from social comparison theory* (pp. 227–261). Mahwah, NJ: Lawrence Erlbaum Associates.

Kulik, J. A., Mahler, H. L., & Earnest, A. (1994). Social comparison and affiliation under threat: Going beyond the affiliation-choice paradigm. *Journal of Personality and Social Psychology, 66,* 301–309.

Kulik, J. A., Mahler, H. L., & Moore, P. (1996). Social comparison and affiliation under threat: Effects on recovery from major surgery. *Journal of Personality and Social Psychology, 71,* 967–979.

Kulik, J. A., Moore, P., & Mahler, H. L. (1993). Stress and affiliation: Hospital roommate effects on preoperative anxiety and social interaction. *Health Psychology, 12,* 119–125.

Latané, B. (Ed.). (1966). Studies in social comparison. *Journal of Experimental Social Psychology* (Suppl. 1).

Leventhal, H., Meyer, D., & Nerenz, D. (1980). The common sense representation of illness danger. In S. Rachman (Ed.), *Contributions to medical psychology* (Vol. 2, pp. 7–30). New York: Pergamon.

Levkoff, S. E., Cleary, P. D., & Wetle, T. (1987). Differences in the appraisal of health between aged and middle-aged adults. *Journal of Gerontology, 42,* 114–120.

Lewin, K. (1958). Group decision and social change. In E. Maccoby, T. M. Newcomb, & E. L. Hartley (Eds.), *Readings in social psychology* (3rd ed., pp. 183–196). New York: Holt.

Linn, B. S., & Linn, M. W. (1980). Objective and self-assessed health in the old and very old. *Social Science and Medicine, 14a,* 311–315.

Major, B., Testa, M., & Bylsma, W. (1991). Responses to upward and downward social comparisons: The impact of esteem-relevance and perceived control. In J. Suls & T. Wills (Eds.), *Social comparison: Contemporary theory and research.* (pp. 237–260). Hillsdale, NJ: Lawrence Erlbaum Associates.

Mechanic, D. (1972). Social psychological factors affecting the presentation of bodily complaints. *New England Journal of Medicine, 286,* 1132–1139.

Miller, D. T., & McFarland, C. (1987). Pluralistic ignorance: When similarity is interpreted as dissimilarity. *Journal of Personality and Social Psychology, 53,* 298–305.

Miller, D. T., & McFarland, C. (1991). When social comparison goes awry: The case of pluralistic ignorance. In J. Suls & T. A. Wills (Eds.), *Social comparison: Contemporary theory and research* (pp. 287–313). Hillsdale, NJ: Lawrence Erlbaum Associates.

Miller, M. H. (1973). Seeking advice for cancer symptoms. *American Journal of Public Health, 63,* 955–961.

Miller, R. L., & Suls, J. (1977). Affiliation preferences as a function of attitude and ability similarity. In J. Suls & R.L. Miller (Eds.), *Social comparison processes: Theoretical and empirical perspectives* (pp. 103–124). Washington, DC: Hemisphere.

Molleman, E., Pruyn, J., & van Knippenberg, A. (1986). Social comparison processes among cancer patients. *British Journal of Social Psychology, 25,* 1–13.

Mullen, B., Atkins, J., Champion, D., Edwards, C., Hardy, D., Story, J., & Vanderklok, M. (1985). The false consensus effect: A meta-analysis of 115 hypothesis tests. *Journal of Experimental Social Psychology, 21,* 262–283.

Nosanchuk, T. A., & Erickson, B. (1985). How high is up? Calibrating social comparison in the real world. *Journal of Personality and Social Psychology, 25,* 1–13.

Olson, J. M., Herman, C. P., & Zanna, M. (Eds.). (1986). *Relative deprivation and social comparison* (Vol. 4). Hillsdale, NJ: Lawrence Erlbaum Associates.

Pennebaker, J. W. (1982). *The psychology of physical symptoms.* New York: Springer-Verlag.

Prentice, D. A., & Miller, D. T. (1993). Pluralistic ignorance and alcohol use on campus: Some consequences of misperceiving the social norm. *Journal of Personality and Social Psychology, 64,* 243–256.

Rofe, Y. (1984). Stress and affiliation: A utility theory. *Psychological Review, 91,* 235–250.

Ross, L., Greene, D., & House, P. (1977). The "false consensus effect": An egocentric bias in social perception and attributional processes. *Journal of Experimental Social Psychology, 13,* 279–301.

Safer, M., Tharps, Q., Jackson, T., & Leventhal, H. (1979). Determinants of three stages of delay in seeking care at a medical care clinic. *Medical Care, 17,* 11–29.

Sanders, G. S. (1981). The interactive effect of social comparison and objective information on the decision to see a doctor. *Journal of Applied Social Psychology, 11,* 390–400.

Sanders, G. S. (1982). Social comparison and perceptions of health and illness. In G. S. Sanders & J. Suls (Eds.), *Social psychology of health and illness* (pp. 129–157). Hillsdale NJ: Lawrence Erlbaum Associates.

Scambler, G., & Scambler, A. (1985). The illness iceberg and aspects of consulting behavior. In R. Fitzpatrick & J. Hinton (Eds.), *The experience of illness* (pp. 32–50). London: Tavistock.

Schachter, S. (1951). Deviation, rejection, and communication. *Journal of Abnormal and Social Psychology, 46,* 190–207.

Schachter, S. (1959). *The psychology of affiliation.* Stanford, CA: Stanford University Press.

Schachter, S., & Singer, J. E. (1962). Cognitive, social, and physiological determinants of emotional state. *Psychological Review, 69,* 379–399.

Schanck, R. L. (1932). A study of community and its group institutions conceived of as behavior of individuals. *Psychological Monographs, 43*(2), 1–133.

Singer, J. E. (1966). Social comparison—progress and issues. *Journal of Experimental Social Psychology, Suppl. 1,* 103–110.

Stahl, S. M., & Lebedun, M. (1974). Mystery gas: An analysis of mass hysteria. *Journal of Health and Social Behavior, 15,* 44–50.

Stein, J. A., Newcomb, M. D., & Bentler, P. M. (1987). An 8-year study of multiple influences on drug use and drug use consequences. *Journal of Personality and Social Psychology, 53,* 1094–1105.

Suchman, E. A. (1965). States of illness and medical care. *Journal of Health and Social Behavior, 6,* 114–128.

Suls, J. (1986). Notes on the occasion of social comparison theory's thirtieth birthday. *Personality and Social Psycholgy Bulletin, 12,* 289–296.

Suls, J. (1999). The importance of the question in motivated cognition and social comparison. *Psychological Inquiry, 10,* 73–75.

Suls, J., & Green, P. (1996) *Misconstrual of social norms about health-relevant practices in college students: False consensus, pluralistic ignorance, and the above-average effect.* Unpublished manuscript, University of Iowa.

Suls, J., Marco, C., & Tobin, S. (1991). The role of temporal comparison, social comparison, and direct appraisal in the elderly's self-evaluations of health. *Journal of Applied Social Psychology, 21,* 1125–1144.

Suls, J., & Martin, R. (1995). *A study of reasons given for lay referral in cases of physical symptoms and injury in young adults.* Unpublished manuscript, University of Iowa.

Suls, J., Martin, R., & Leventhal, H. (1997). Social comparison, lay referral, and the decision to seek medical care. In B. P. Buunk & F. X. Gibbons (Eds.), *Health and coping: Perspectives from social comparison theory* (pp. 195–226). Mahwah, NJ: Lawrence Erlbaum Associates.

Suls, J., & Miller, R. L. (Eds.). (1977). *Social comparison processes: Theoretical and empirical perspectives.* Washington, DC: Hemisphere.

Suls, J., & Wan, C. K. (1987). In search of the false uniqueness phenomenon: Fear and estimates of social consensus. *Journal of Personality and Social Psychology, 52,* 211–217.

Suls, J., Wan, C. K., Barlow, D., & Heimberg, R. (1990). The fallacy of uniqueness: Social consensus perceptions of anxiety disorder patients and community residents. *Journal of Research in Personality, 24,* 415–432.

Suls, J., Wan, C., & Sanders, G. (1988). False consensus and false uniqueness in estimating the prevalence of health-protective behaviors. *Journal of Applied Social Psychology, 18,* 66–79.

Suls, J., & Wills, T. A. (Eds.). (1991). *Social comparison: Contemporary theory and research.* Hillsdale, NJ: Lawrence Erlbaum Associates.

Taylor, S. E., & Brown, J. D. (1988). Illusion and mental health: A social psychological perspective. *Psychological Bulletin, 103,* 193–210.

Taylor, S. E., & Lobel, M. (1989). Social comparison activity under threat: Downward evaluation and upward contacts. *Psychological Review, 96,* 569–575.

Taylor, S. E., Wood, J. V., & Lichtman, R. (1983). It could be worse: Selective evaluation as a response to victimization. *Journal of Social Issues, 39,* 19–40.

Tennen, H., & Affleck, G. (1997). Social comparison as a coping process: A critical review and application to chronic pain disorders. In B. P. Buunk & F. X. Gibbons (Eds.). *Health and coping: Perspectives from social comparison theory* (pp. 263–298). Mahwah, NJ: Lawrence Erlbaum Associates.

Weinstein, N. (1982). Unrealistic optimism about susceptibility to health problems and future life events. *Journal of Behavioral Medicine 5,* 441–460.

Wheeler, L. (1966). Motivation as a determinant of upward comparison. *Journal of Experimental Social Psychology,* 2 (Suppl. 1), 27–31.

Wheeler, L., Martin, R., & Suls, J. (1997). The Proxy social comparison model for self-assessment of ability. *Personality and Social Psychology Review, 1,* 54–61.

Wills, T. A. (1981). Downward comparison principles in social psychology. *Psychological Bulletin, 90,* 245–271.

Wills, T. A. (1987). Downward comparison as a coping mechanism. In C. R. Snyder & C. E. Ford (Eds.), *Coping with negative life events: Clinical and social psychological perspectives* (pp. 243–268). New York: Plenum.

Wood, J. V. (1989). Theory and research concerning social comparisons of personal attributes. *Psychological Bulletin, 106,* 231–248.

Wood, J. V., Taylor, S. E., & Lichtman, R. (1985). Social comparison in adjustment to breast cancer. *Journal of Personality and Social Psychology, 49,* 1169–1183.

Wood, J. V., & VanderZee, K. (1997). Social comparison among cancer patients: Under what conditions are comparisons upward or downward? In B. P. Buunk & F. X. Gibbons (Eds.), *Health and coping: Perspectives from social comparison theory* (pp. 299–328). Mahwah, NJ: Lawrence Erlbaum Associates.

Zanna, M., Goethals, G., & Hill, S. (1975). Evaluating sex-related ability Social comparison with similar others and standard setters. *Journal of Experimental Social Psychology, 11,* 86–93.

Zimbardo, P., & Formica, R. (1963). Emotional comparison and self-esteem as determinants of affiliation. *Journal of Personality, 31,* 141–162.

12

Social Networks and Social Support

Thomas Ashby Wills
Marnie Filer Fegan
Ferkauf Graduate School of Psychology and Albert Einstein College of Medicine

This chapter considers how social support is related to physical health, including research on mortality, morbidity, and recovery from illness. During the past 10 years there has been a large amount of research showing measures of social network structure, or measures of available supportive functions, to be related to various outcomes (Belle, 1989; S. Cohen & Syme, 1985; I. G. Sarason, B. R. Sarason, & Pierce, 1990; Pierce, B. R. Sarason, & I. G. Sarason, 1996; Vaux, 1988; Wills, 1990b). During this time, there have been substantial advances in recognizing how beneficial social support can be; at the same time, this research has raised intriguing questions about how social support works.

The theme of the chapter is how social support works, because at present this question is less understood. A number of different mechanisms have been suggested as the basis for which an abstract social variable, social support, is related to objective physiological intermediaries (e.g., blood pressure) and to disease endpoints (e.g., mortality from myocardial infarction). These suggested mechanisms are most interesting from the standpoint of health psychology because they represent an interface between psychological theories of stress, coping, and affect, as well as physiological models of disease processes. Although a plethora of mechanisms has been suggested, the current evidence on the mechanism of support effects is mixed and sometimes fragmentary, so at present there is no consensus for seeing one particular mechanism as most likely. Hence the goal here is to survey the range of evidence available on social support and to suggest the relevance of possible mechanisms where they are indicated by the evidence.

This chapter is organized first by concepts about social support and then by areas of research. It first defines basic concepts and discusses conceptual issues where debate is still occurring. Then it describes the nature of five groups of mechanisms that have been postulated to account for the relationship between social support and health, and discusses briefly the approach for testing each mechanism. The chapter then covers evidence from several areas of social support research. It begins by surveying epidemiologic studies of morbidity and all-cause mortality, and then considers research on social support effects for three specific disease conditions: cancer, diabetes, and renal failure. The chapter then considers specific topics, such as social support effects among children and adolescents, social support effects during pregnancy, and social support effects in elderly populations. A final section summarizes the current findings and discusses some questions for further research.

CONCEPTS IN SOCIAL SUPPORT RESEARCH

Social support is broadly defined as resources and interactions provided by others that may be useful for helping a person to cope with a problem. Under this broad definition, however, several different perspectives on social support are encompassed, and these are reflected in different assessment approaches and research designs. One point of divergence is whether support is conceptualized as the number of persons an individual knows, or whether support should be conceptualized as the amount of effective resources available to an individual, irrespective of the absolute number of friends and acquaintances. Another area of divergence is whether it is adequate to obtain a global assessment of a person's support, or whether it is necessary to measure specific dimensions of support provided by persons from different life domains, including spouse, friends, and workmates. The broad definition also does not guarantee that social support is only effective for persons with many problems, because it is also possible that support is effective across the board, such that persons with relatively few problems show just as much benefit as persons with many problems. Finally, the "may" in the broad definition allows the possibility that interactions regarded as supportive by the deliverer may not always be so perceived by the recipient (Coriell & S. Cohen, 1995; Rook, 1990). These varying perspectives on social support have produced several different research approaches, each with its own advantages and limitations. Although we see some approaches as more useful than others, attention is given to all of these perspectives in the course of the chapter. The following sections discuss some basic terms and concepts in detail.

Structural Versus Functional Measures

First is the distinction between *structural* and *functional* aspects of support. Structural and functional measures involve different theoretical assumptions about the basis for effects of support, with structural measures giving emphasis to the total number of linkages people have in their community. Structural measures assume it is the quantity of established, regular social connections that is important, and that the range of connections with different parts of the community may also be informative. Structural measures include items asking about the existence of primary social relationships, such as being married or having relatives and children who live nearby. They also tap frequency of visiting with neighbors and talking with friends, either in person or on the telephone (or, these days, by Internet). Other items in typical structural measures tap the existence of normative social roles, such as being employed and belonging to community organizations. These items can be combined to produce indices for the total size of a person's network, the number of different social roles a person occupies, and other indices such as the percent of kin in the network or the number of network members who know each other (Hall & Wellman, 1985). The goal of such indices is to provide a quantitative measure of the number of social network connections. Analyses for structural measures are typically based on the total score for social connections, but investigators have sometimes performed separate tests for component indices to determine whether particular types of social connections might be differentially beneficial for men and women (e.g., Berkman & Syme, 1979; House, Robbins, & Metzner, 1982). It should be noted that a structural measure does not ask about the quality of the existing relationships, nor does it ask about what resources the network members provide.

Functional measures are based on the assumption that it is the quality of available resources that is most important, hence these measures aim to assess the extent to which supportive functions are available to an individual (Wills, 1985). In contrast to structural inventories, functional measures ask about the availability of a particular function (e.g., ability to confide with somebody about problems and worries). They do not necessarily determine who the support comes from (although some inventories do assess availability of emotional support from different sources), but rather focus on whether support is available if needed.

Functional inventories typically include multi-item scales to assess the perceived availability of each of several supportive functions. Scales for *emotional support* (also termed appraisal, confiding, ventilation, or esteem support) have items that ask whether there are persons with whom you can share fears and worries, persons with whom you can talk about problems freely, and persons who make you feel understood and accepted. Scales for *instrumental support* (also termed tangible, material, or practical support) ask whether there are persons who could provide assistance with financial problems (i.e., lending money), transportation, repairs, housework, or child care. Scales for *informational support* (also termed advice, guidance, or feedback) include items asking whether there are persons available who can provide useful information and can make suggestions about relevant resources and alternative courses of action. Scales for *companionship support* (also termed belonging) include items that ask whether there are persons available for companionship with various kinds of leisure activities, such as going to movies, sporting events, theaters or museums, hiking, or boating. From these scales, subjects would receive a total score for emotional support, for example, based on their cumulative responses to the availability of different aspects of this function. It is typical to find scores for the different dimensions of functional support substantially correlated; for example, individuals with higher scores for emotional support also tend to have higher scores for instrumental and informational support. Whether this is attributable to perceptual factors, personality influences, or individual differences in the ability to recruit supporters has not been entirely worked out (see S. Cohen, Sherrod, & Clark, 1986; Coble, Gantt, & Mallinckrodt, 1996); for this reason, investigators often test unique effects of different dimensions as well as the total functional support score.

There are two interesting facts about structural and functional measures: They are not highly correlated, and they are both related to health outcomes. The first fact is initially puzzling to some, who assume that the more persons an individual knows then the more support they must have available. The probable explanation for the low correlation of structural and functional measures is that the existence of a relationship does not provide much information about the quality of that relationship (Wills, 1991); it is possible that people with a relatively small social network may still have available a large amount of esteem support, instrumental support, and so on, because of the nature of their relationships. The fact that both structural and functional measures are related to health outcomes is still not well understood. There are reasons to believe that structural and functional support contribute to health status through different mechanisms, but this question has not been entirely explicated.

Main Effects Versus Buffering Effects

A second issue in social support research is whether social support is primarily useful to persons experiencing a high level of life stress, or whether support is useful irrespective of a person's stress level. The issue is a basic one for social support researchers because it directs attention to the question of what kind of process is involved in the operation of support. This question has been examined in studies that include both a measure of social support and a measure of life stress, and therefore can test for whether effects of support are dependent on stress level (S. Cohen & Wills, 1985).

The first possibility is usually termed the *main effect model* because it is demonstrated by a statistical main effect, indicating that support is equally beneficial to persons with low or high stress. The second possibility, termed the *buffering model,* is demonstrated by a Stress × Support interaction effect, indicating that the effect of support is much greater for persons at a high level of stress. The terminology derives from the portrayal of support as a buffer that protects a person from the potentially adverse impact of negative events. Whereas buffering effects have frequently been observed in studies that used good functional measures and sizable samples, main effects are more typical for structural measures, and a main effect model has been observed in some other conditions (S. Cohen & Wills, 1985; Wills, 1991; Wills, Mariani, & Filer, 1996).

Matching of Functional Support to Needs

A theoretical issue that has been prominent in research on functional measures is what is known as the *matching hypothesis* (S. Cohen & McKay, 1984; Cutrona & Russell, 1990). Given the definition that support functions are useful for helping persons to cope with problems, the question arises concerning whether particular functions are best matched with specific needs; if so, then the availability of specific functional dimensions would be particularly helpful for persons who had a specific need. For example, a subgroup of persons within the general population might have adequate self-esteem but experience high financial stress because of unemployment, low income, and so on. In this case, it might be hypothesized that the availability of instrumental support, including financial aid or in-kind services, would be the primary (or only) useful function for these persons. Situations can be imagined in which functions such as emotional or informational support would be most useful, and the effectiveness of the available support would depend on the match between the functions provided by individuals' relationships and the needs evoked by their problem.

The status of the matching hypothesis remains an intriguing question for research. There have been some studies showing that buffering effects occur only for situations predicted by the matching hypothesis (e.g., Peirce, Frone, Russell, & Cooper, 1996). However, studies with functional inventories typically find emotional support to be a broadly useful function (Wills, 1991), even in situations where it might not be expected to be particularly useful (e.g., Krause, 1987). Current research is trying to extend this work through delineating the support needs evoked by particular kinds of life events, and through developing and testing theory on how functional support actually works.

Where Support Acts in the Disease Process

A question of particular importance is where in the disease process social support acts. Does it act primarily to prevent development of risk factors among those who are healthy? Does it act to retard the onset of a clinical disease episode among persons who have accumulated risk factors? Or, does it reduce disease severity and speed recovery among those who have suffered a disease episode? Each of these models is important from a health standpoint, but would represent quite different modes of operation (Cohen, 1988).

An answer to the question depends on several types of findings. If support were strongly related to incident disease (onset of new illness among those initially healthy), this would imply that the protective effect of support occurs early in the disease process. If support were more strongly related to prevalent disease (cases of existing illness), this would imply that effects of support occur later in the disease process, either through reducing the severity of disease among those originally affected or by enhancing recovery from disease.

The question of where support acts in the disease process is not easily answered, because chronic diseases such as CHD have onset periods that span a decade or more, whereas infectious diseases like as upper respiratory infection have a period of a few days from exposure to infection to recovery. Long-term prospective research and short-term intensive studies each have advantages and disadvantages, and accordingly the question cannot be completely answered by any single study. A full understanding of the question requires cumulated findings from many sources, and is only beginning to emerge. The most recent evidence has shown social support strongly related to recovery from disease, but there is also some evidence for protective effects of support at earlier points in disease processes. This issue is discussed at several points in the chapter.

THEORETICAL MECHANISMS AND MODELS OF ANALYSIS

How is support related to health? In theory, social support could be related to physical health through several different mechanisms. These are not mutually exclusive but are discussed in terms of three general categories. In addition, alternative theoretical mechanisms are appropriately analyzed through different statistical models. The following section first describes two statistical issues relevant for testing different types of theoretical mechanisms, and then discusses theoretical mechanisms through which social support is currently believed to operate.

Statistical Models: Buffering Effect Versus Main Effect

As noted earlier, support could be beneficial to persons irrespective of their stress level, or alternatively, support could be most useful to persons currrently experiencing a high level of stressful events. Evaluating these modes of operation requires a study that includes reliable measures of life stress and social support, has adequate variability in both of these predictors, and has a reasonable criterion measure of health status. Testing the statistical models can be done with analysis of variance using dichotomized predictors and testing the Stress × Support interaction effect, or in multiple regression using continuous predictors and testing the cross-product term for stress and support. The latter procedure is preferable because it typically increases statistical power (J. Cohen & P. Cohen, 1983).

Examples of a pure main effect, a partial buffering effect, and a complete buffering effect are presented in Fig. 12.1, which shows possible effects of social support at different levels of stress. If support operates as a main effect relationship, then persons with higher support have more favorable health status, and the effect of support is comparable at low stress and at high stress (Fig. 12.1A). If support operates as a buffering effect, then the impact of life stress on symptomatology is reduced for persons who have high social support. A partial buffering effect is presented in Fig. 12.1B. Here, high support reduces the impact of stress but there is still a significant effect for stress; that is, persons with high stress and high support still have significantly more symptomatology than persons with low stress and high support. A complete buffering effect is presented in Fig. 12.1B; here, support completely eliminates the effect of life stress so that persons with high stress and high support are not significantly different from those with low stress and high support.

Note that detection of most interaction effects has greater power requirements than detection of main effects (Aiken & West, 1991). For this reason, it is desirable for a study testing buffering effects to have a sizable sample in order to have adequate power for detecting this type of interaction (McClelland & Judd, 1993). It is still not uncommon to see studies that found no significant interaction effect, and then rejected the buffering hypothesis, in situations where the sample was so small that power was inadequate for detecting this type of interaction.

Statistical Models: Direct Versus Indirect Effects

Another statistical issue is the distinction between direct and indirect effects (Baron & Kenny, 1986). It is possible that support acts directly on variables relevant for health status, such as blood pressure; in this case, support has a *direct effect* on the criterion. Alternatively, it is possible that beneficial effects of support are transmitted through an intermediary variable; for example, support could be related to more effective preventive health behaviors and this would result in sustained reduction in blood pressure. In this case, support has an *indirect effect* on the criterion, mediated through preventive behavior. Evaluating these modes of operation requires a study that includes measures of variables believed to be possible mediators of the effect of support. Testing for the existence of direct and indirect effects can be analyzed in procedures such as path analysis or structural modeling (B. M. Baron & Kenny, 1986; Wills & Cleary, 1996, 1999).

The distinction between direct and indirect effects is diagramed in Fig. 12.2 with respect to hypothetical variables: a support predictor S, one or more possible mediators (Ms), and an outcome measure O. It is important to recall that social support is related to better health status in both cases. However, in a direct effect model, the support predictor S is related to the outcome O and its mode of action does not involve any intermediate variable (Fig. 12.2A). In an indirect effect model, the support predictor S is related to an intermediate variable M, which in turn is causally related to the outcome O;

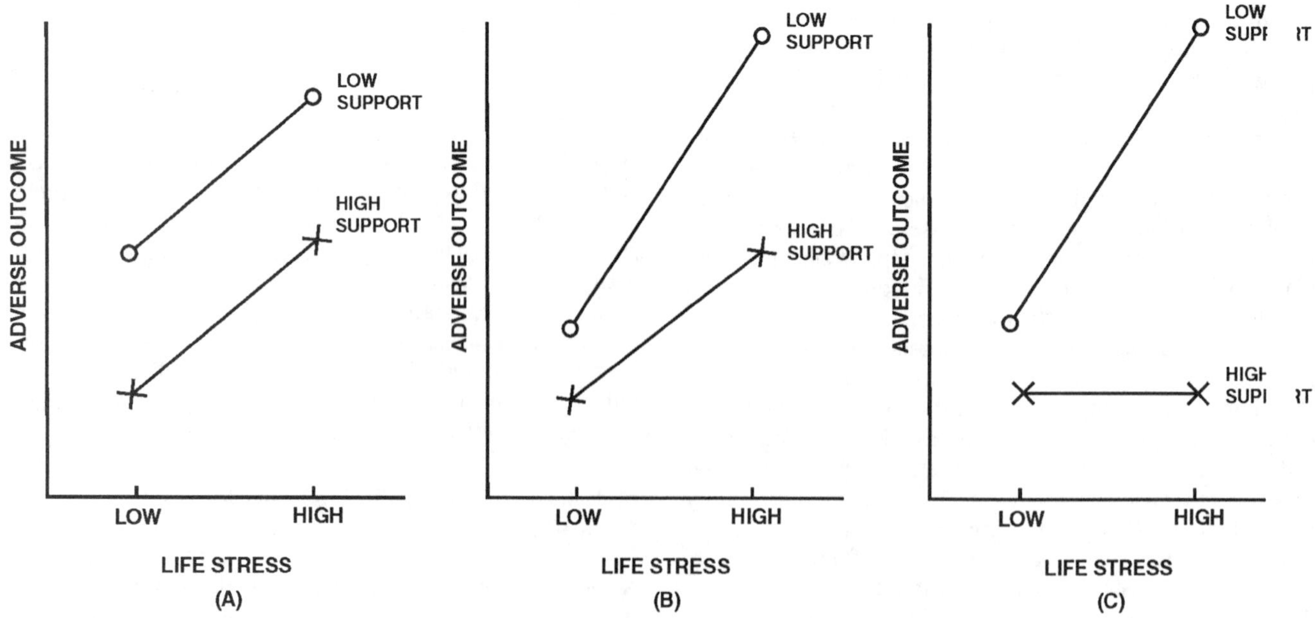

FIG. 12.1. Illustrations of main-effect vs. buffering results for persons with low vs. high stress and low vs. high support: (A) main effect result, (B) partial buffering result, (C) complete buffering result.

this is sometimes termed a *mediated relationship* because the effect of social support is transmitted through the mediator (FIg. 12.2B). Mixed models are possible, in which support has an indirect effect and also a significant direct effect (for more discussion see Wills & Cleary, 1996; Wills, McNamara, & Vaccaro, 1995).

Physiological Mechanisms

Seven mechanisms, which are illustrated graphically in various parts of Fig. 12.3, are described with respect to theoretical mechanisms. Two variant mechanisms posit that support acts directly on physiological variables. One mechanism posits that the presence of other persons has a calming effect that is essentially innate because of evolutionary processes for social species. Other things being equal, individuals would be more relaxed and in a more positive affective state when other persons were around, compared with when they were alone or isolated from others. This could be construed as a direct effect in that relaxed states and positive affect could be related to a range of physical variables conducive to health (Fig. 12.3A).

The second mechanism posits that good support is related to better immune system functioning (e.g., more proliferative T4 cells or natural killer cells) through reducing levels of depression and anxiety in times of stress. This would really be construed as an indirect effect because support acts on anxiety/depression which in turn acts on the immune system. To analyze this mechanism it is necessary to show that support is related to lower depression, which in turn is related to better immune system function, which in turn is related to lower likelihood of infectious or other disease (Fig. 12.3B).

Appraisal and Reactivity Mechanisms

For the appraisal mechanism, it is posited that the knowledge that support is available to cope with problems makes persons appraise stressors as less severe. Because of the less severe threat appraisal, persons then would be less depressed/anxious when subjected to life stressors. This mechanism would be analyzed by measuring individuals' cognitive appraisals of stress and showing that these appraisals were linked to anxiety/depression. This would be construed as an indirect effect because the buffering effect of support occurs through altering the cognitive appraisal (Fig. 12.3C).

For the reactivity mechanism, it is posited that having support available makes persons less physiologically reactive (i.e., less change in heart rate and blood pressure) when subjected to acute stressors, and hence makes them less prone to disease conditions that are linked to cardiovascular reactivity, such as hypertension. Unlike the direct calming effect, this mechanism should be relevant only in times of stress, and would be analyzed by showing physiological reactivity was moderated by the availability of social support (Fig. 12.3D).

Behavioral Mechanisms

Linkage to Fewer Harmful Behaviors. One type of behavioral mechanism posits that high social support is re-

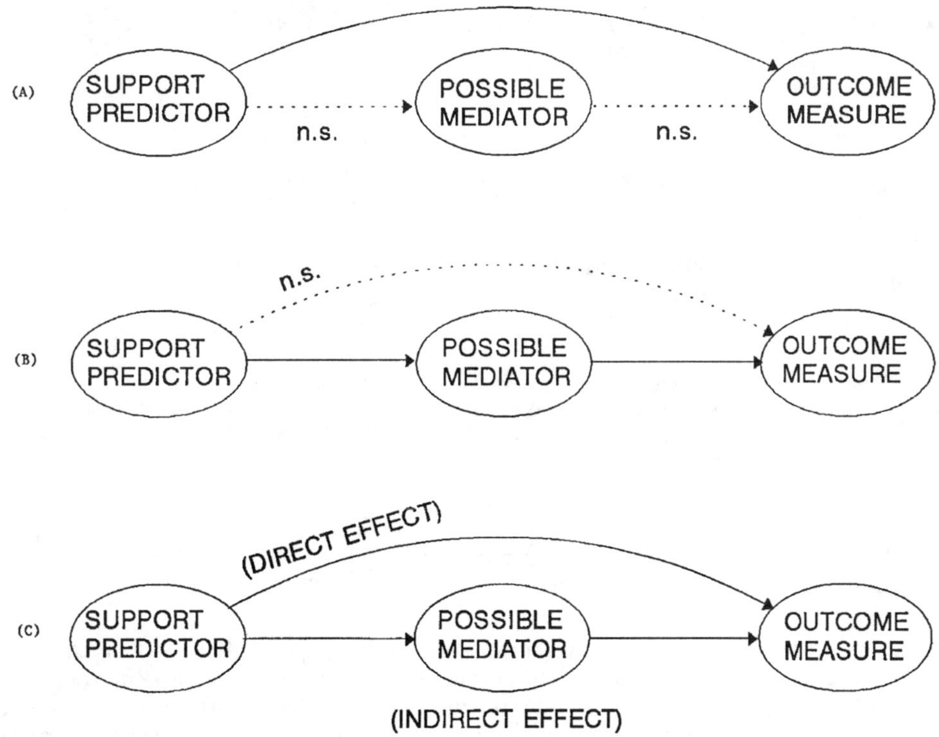

FIG. 12.2. Illustration of types of relationships between social support and health outcomes. (A) Direct effect. (B) Fully mediated effect. (C) Partially mediated effect.

lated to lower levels of harmful behaviors that are relevant for health risk (Fig. 12.3E). For example, persons with high support could be less likely to smoke cigarettes, or less likely to engage in heavy alcohol consumption and/or binge drinking (Wills, 1990a). In analyzing this mechanism it would be shown that support is related to lower levels of smoking and alcohol use, and that substance use is the primary causal factor in relation to subsequent adverse health outcomes.

Linkage to More Protective Behaviors. Two variant mechanisms posit that social support is linked to patterns of behavior that lead to better health outcomes. In one mechanism (Fig. 12.3F), it is posited that support is related to more help seeking in times of stress and greater access to preventive services in the community (e.g., cancer screening, regular physician visits). This would be expected to reduce mortality rates. In analyzing this mechanism it would be shown that support was related to more help seeking and medical service utilization, and the latter was related to physical health status (Wills & DePaulo, 1991). The second mechanism (Fig. 12.3G) posits that having good social support enables persons to cope more effectively with problems and hence reduces anxiety/depression in times of stress (Thoits, 1986). This mechanism would be analyzed by showing that support is related to patterns of coping with problems, and coping in turn was related to less anxiety/depression and better physical health.

EPIDEMIOLOGIC STUDIES

Research with large samples from the general population initially drew wide attention to social support through demonstrations that support was prospectively related to lower mortality (Berkman & Syme, 1979; House et al., 1982). Subsequent studies broadened the base for the field through demonstration of similar effects across age groups and national populations.

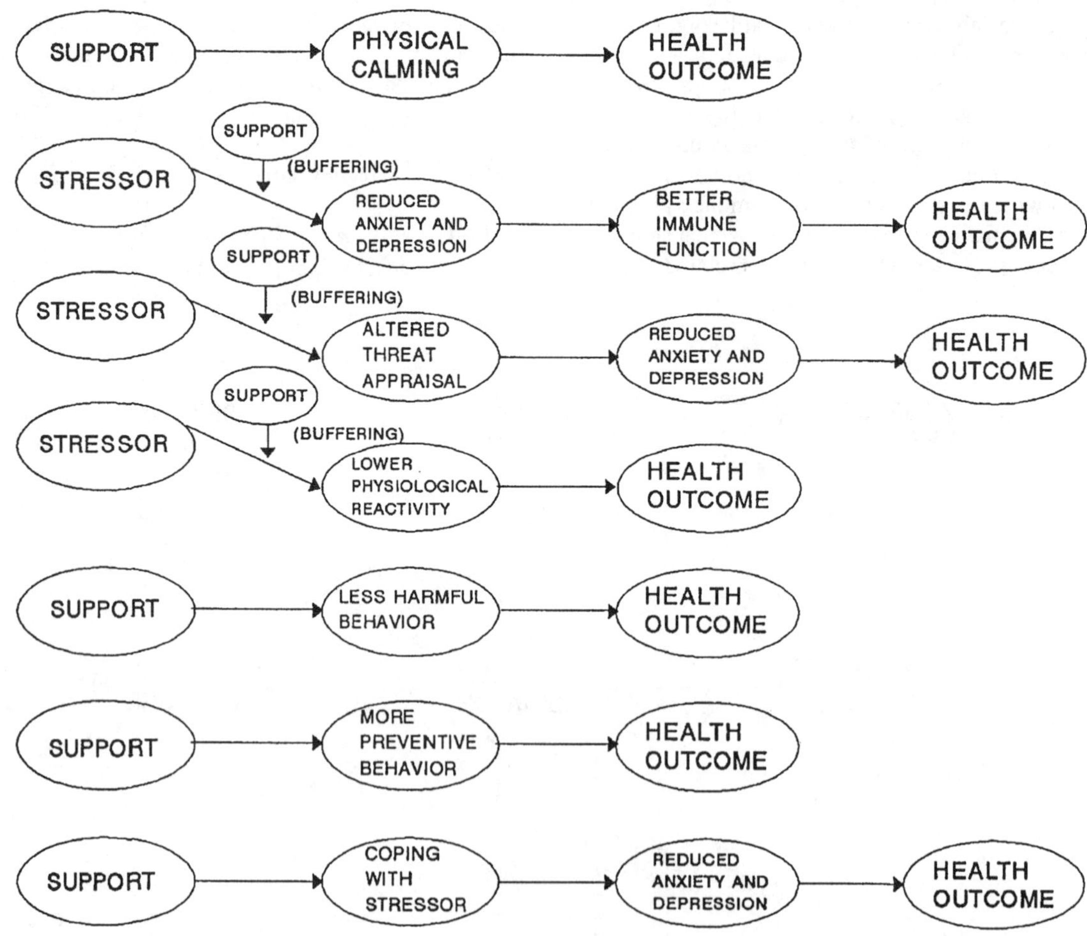

FIG. 12.3. Illustration of possible theoretical mechanisms of support–health relationships. (A) Support acts directly on physiological variable. (B) Support has an indirect effect on immune function, mediated through anxiety/depression. (C) Support has an indirect effect on anxiety/depression, mediated through cognitive appraisal of stressors; anxiety/depression is then related to health outcome. (D) Support reduces physiological reactivity when a stressor is encountered; reactivity is then related to health outcome. (E) Support is indirectly related to health status through a relation to health-harmful behavior, which is then related to the health outcome. (F) Support is indirectly related to health status through a relation to preventive behavior, which is then related to the health outcome. (G) Support is indirectly related through influencing coping, which then affects level of anxiety/depression.

These studies are discussed in some detail because they are essential for understanding the epidemiologic evidence on social support and health (House, Landis, & Umberson, 1988). The focus is on prospective studies in which a sample of participants is examined at a baseline measurement; the sample is then followed for a period of several years, and the health status of the participants at the follow-up point is determined. The studies typically include measures for demographics and baseline health status, used as control variables to test the possibility that low support at baseline is attributable to a demographic third factor (e.g., low income) or is a consequence of preexisting illness. Significant effects of social support are commonly found with control for possible confounders, so all this evidence is not discussed in detail. This section first discusses studies of prevalent disease conducted with general population samples and samples of elderly persons, and then discusses studies on incident disease and recovery from illness.

Social Networks and Mortality in General Populations

A number of prospective studies using social network measures have been conducted, with follow-up periods ranging from 5 to 9 years (Berkman & Syme, 1979; Blazer, 1982; B. S. Hanson, J. T. Isacsson, Janzon, & Lindell, 1989; House et al., 1982; G. A. Kaplan et al., 1988; Orth-Gomer & Johnson, 1987; Schoenbach, B. H. Kaplan, Fredman, & Kleinbaum, 1986; Welin et al., 1985; Welin, Larsson, Svärdsudd, B. Tibblin, & G. Tibblin, 1992). The social network measures indexed the existence of a range of social connections as described previously. The outcome was mortality status at follow-up as verified through death certificates, usually with close to 100% ascertainment. The results consistently showed number of social connections to be inversely related to mortality rate, and although results tend to be stronger for men than for women, significant effects have been observed for both genders. In some cases, the investigators analyzed the network measure as a total scale (e.g., G. A. Kaplan et al., 1988; Orth-Gomer & Johnson, 1987), whereas in other studies analyses were performed both for the total network score and for each of the component items (Berkman & Syme, 1979; House et al., 1982). Most component items show significant relationships to mortality, indicating that effects are not simply driven by a particular aspect of social networks.

Researchers have examined the question of whether the effect of social networks represents a *gradient effect,* with progressive reduction in mortality for each higher level of social connections, or a *threshold effect,* such that elevated mortality is found only for persons with few social connections and no effects are observed at higher levels. The studies are somewhat divided on this, with some investigators reporting results that resemble a threshold effect (e.g., House et al., 1982). However, other studies have shown a clear gradient effect, with a continous reduction in mortality rates across increasing levels of social connections (e.g., Berkman & Syme, 1979; G. A. Kaplan et al., 1988; Welin et al., 1985), and some studies have found gradient effects for specific causes of death (e.g., cardiovascular disease) occurring together with threshold effects for mortality from cancer (Welin et al., 1992). The repeated findings of gradient effects suggest that the protective effect of social network does not occur just for a small group of socially isolated persons.

Functional Support and Mortality

Although the initial research in the area predominantly used structural measures, some studies have tested whether functional measures have value for predicting mortality. Blazer's (1982) study of a U.S. elderly sample included both structural and functional measures; results indicated that a measure of perceived support (e.g., availability of a confidant, availability of instrumental assistance) was a strong inverse predictor of mortality, independent of a variety of demographic and biomedical controls. Here the structural measures were nonsignificant when tested with the functional measure, suggestive of an indirect effect, with social connections contributing to greater emotional and instrumental support and the latter being proximal protective factors. These findings were extended in European studies. B. S. Hanson, J. T. Isacsson, Janzon, and Lindell (1989) included scales for the perceived availability and adequacy of emotional support and of instrumental/informational support. They found a significant effect for the former measure: Men with low emotional support had 2.5 times the risk of mortality over the study period, controlling for demographic status and a variety of biomedical variables.

Buffering effects were analyzed with data for male participants from the Malmö study (Falk, B. S. Hanson, Isacsson, & Ostergren, 1992). Both structural and functional measures were tested as possible buffers in relation to a measure of stress from job strain. The job stress measure itself showed a significant relationship to higher risk of mortality. Results for the support measures showed a relative risk of 3.6 for men with high stress and low emotional support, and 1.2 for those with high stress and high emotional support; thus a buffering effect was demonstrated. An analogous effect was found for the structural measure (termed *social participation*; from B. S. Hanson et al., 1989), with risks of 2.6 and 1.3, respectively. Hence, in this study, both the structural measure and the functional measure showed evidence of buffering effects, although the measures were not analyzed together.

A recent analysis from the Gothenburg study also tested for buffering effects with an all-male sample (Rosengren, Orth-Gomer, Wedel, & Wilhelmsen, 1993). A measure of 10 negative life events was obtained at a baseline assessment together with an interview designed to assess the availability of emotional support from close relationships and from a variety of peripheral social relationships (termed *social integration,* but not directly analogous to a social network measure). Over four levels of life events the range of mortality rates was 15.1 for men with low emotional support and 1.2 for men with high emotional support; hence these data indicate a buffering effect of emotional support with respect to mortality. For the social integration measure, no buffering effect was found.

Support and Health in Elderly Samples

Research focusing on health in samples of older persons is of additional importance because the burden of chronic illness is greater among these persons. Research conducted in recent years has corroborated the relevance of social network measures for the health status of elderly persons. For example, Seeman, G. A. Kaplan, Knusden, R. Cohen, and Guralnik (1987) analyzed data from a 17.5 year follow-up of subjects from the Alameda County study who were age 38 or older at baseline. They found that the overall social network index was inversely related to mortality for both men and women. A study conducted in an urban area in Finland (Jylhä & Arö, 1989) followed an urban sample and obtained multi-item scales for social contacts (i.e., frequency of visiting) and outside-home social participation (similar to Welin's scale for outside-home activities) in addition to single-item measures for marriage, children, and loneliness. A continuous score for social participation was inversely related to mortality, again with significant results for both men and women. A study with a U.S. national sample (Steinbach, 1992) found a social participation index prospectively related to lower likelihood of both institutionalization and mortality, and these findings were obtained with control for demographic characteristics and health status at baseline. Persons with higher social participation were half as likely to experience an adverse outcome. Another study focusing on a sample of rural elderly in France (Grand, Grosclaude, Bucquet, Pous, & Albarede, 1990) observed protective effects for a social network scale indexing membership in community groups; a scale for close relationships (marriage and children) was marginally significant, but this was probably attributable to a sample size that was relatively small in comparison to other studies.

Beneficial effects of social support have also been indicated in research conducted with Asian populations. For example, Ho (1991) conducted a 2-year follow-up with a sample in Hong Kong age 70 or older. Measures were obtained for marital status, social contacts, community integration, participation in family and community events, and instrumental support. All of the social network indices were inversely related to mortality, but the instrumental support measure was nonsignificant. A study based on a representative national sample of Japanese elderly (Sugisawa, Liang, & Liu, 1994) is of interest because the investigators tested for both direct and indirect effects of support. This study used structural measures, including scales termed *social contact* (average frequency of visiting with children, relatives, and friends) and *social participation* (organizational membership and attendance), and also obtained a brief functional scale indexing the availability of caring and confiding. The investigators tested whether support measures were related to health status through intermediate variables including functional disability and cigarette smoking. Some evidence for indirect effects was observed; for example, social contacts and social participation were inversely related to functional disability, and being married was inversely related to cigarette smoking. The social participation scale showed a direct effect, that is, it was inversely related to mortality independent of all the intermediate variables (and of demographic and biomedical controls). These analyses suggest indirect effects for marriage and social contacts, operating through different pathways than the direct effect for social participation.

Social Support and Incident Disease

The previous section covered studies that showed a relation between social support and prevalent disease (i.e., mortality from cardiovascular disease, cancer, or other causes). What evidence is there that social support is relevant for disease onset? This question is addressed by studies of incident disease, examining (in longitudinal research) whether social support predicts onset of new disease among those who were initially healthy.

The number of studies on incident disease is still relatively small. One is a study conducted in Honolulu, Hawaii, in which a cohort of males of Japanese ancestry was followed over 7 years (Reed, McGee, Yano, & Feinlieb, 1983). A nine-item structural scale assessed social connections with relatives, coworkers, and religious and social organizations. The social network score was significantly inversely related to existing disease at baseline (i.e., prevalent disease) and this was true for several types of disease including myocardial infarction and angina. Analyses for 7-year onset of heart disease among those initially disease free showed social network to be inversely related to new disease, but analyses with biomedical controls reduced this effect to nonsignificance. In contrast to this are findings from a study in Gothenburg, Sweden (Orth-Gomer, Rosengren, & Wilhelmsen, 1993), where the study group was 736 men who were ascertained to be disease free at baseline and were followed up 6 years later. Both a score for emotional support and a score for social integration were significantly inversely related to incident heart disease, analyzed with biomedical controls. The marginal results in the Honolulu study may have been attributable to the fact that heart disease is less common in Japanese populations, so the lower rates make it difficult to detect the smaller number of disease onset events.

A study examining both prevalence, incidence, and survival from illness was conducted by Vogt, Mullooly, Ernst, Pope, and Hollis (1992), who followed a sample of HMO members over a 15-year interval and used medical records to determine both prevalent and incident disease, including cardiovascular disease (ischemic heart disease, hypertension, stroke) and cancer. A 26-item inventory administered at baseline assessed social connections with family, friend, and community networks, and was scored for three indices termed network size, network scope, and frequency of interaction. Health measures and outcomes were assessed through search of HMO records and state vital statistics. The network scores were independent predictors of 15-year mortality; the strongest effect was for network scope, with a relative risk of 6.7 for those in the lower versus upper thirds of the distribution. However, incidence analyses, predicting 15-year disease hazard among those disease free at baseline, were largely nonsignificant; only network scope was related to significantly lower incidence for one disease. These investigators were also able to analyze predictors of survival through examining the subsequent experience of persons with a new disease episode. Findings indicated that higher network scores predicted increased survival; this was found for heart disease, cancer, and stroke. The contrast between results for incidence and survival analyses drew attention to a possible role of social support for enhancing recovery from illness.

Support and Recovery from Illness

Because evidence showing social support inversely related to mortality is strikingly consistent but evidence for a relation of support to disease onset is minimal, the question of social support and recovery from illness assumes particular theoretical importance for understanding the way support operates. Evidence on this question is available from several previous studies and has been a focus of recent research. In studies of recovery, the participants typically are patients recruited at the time of hospitalization for a disease episode; the criterion variable is degree of recovery from disease or survival time after an initial disease episode. The available studies vary considerably in characteristics such as sample size, length of follow-up, and nature of the support measures. Here emphasis is given to studies with larger samples and longer follow-up times, although some attention is given to other studies that illustrate interesting points.

A study with strong design characteristics was conducted by Williams et al. (1992). The investigators followed a large sample of patients for an average of 9 years after intake. At intake all the participants had significant coronary artery disease, as indicated by angiography findings showing greater than 75% stenosis of at least one major artery. The support indices included being married, having a confidant, and visiting with friends and relatives. The predictive analyses focused on survival time after intake and included a medical risk score composed from 10 physical variables measured at intake and shown empirically to be significant predictors of survival. Results showed that patients who were unmarried and without a confidant had a significantly lower survival rate (50%) compared with those having high support (82%); control analyses showed this result was independent of medical risk and of the patient's economic resources. The findings of Williams et al. (1992) were consistent with a study of an all-male sample followed for 3 years (Ruberman, Weinblatt, Goldberg, & Chaudhary, 1984), which found elevated mortality for persons with a high score on life stress and a low score for social networks (based on visiting friends and relatives, and belonging to a social club, fraternal organization, church, or temple). This latter result suggests a stress buffering effect for social networks, but Ruberman et al. (1984) did not conduct a formal test for interaction. Other studies have used a specific indicator, marital status, and have indicated that survival times after myocardial infarction are longer for married individuals (Chandra, Szklo, Goldberg, & Tonascia, 1983; Wiklund et al., 1988). It is noteworthy that several of these studies found significant protective effects of support for both men and women.

A report by Berkman, Leo-Summers, and Horwitz (1992) from their study of elderly persons is of interest because it is based on a community sample followed over time (as in Vogt et al., 1992). These investigators focused on a group of 165 participants who were hospitalized for acute myocardial infarction during the ongoing study. A noteworthy aspect is that the support measures were from an interview conducted prior to the illness episode, unlike other studies where support measures were typically obtained after hospitalization; so these data are truly prospective. Support measures included a social network index and a three-level functional index reflecting the number of persons who were available to talk about problems. Results showed that persons with greater emotional support were more likely to survive over a 6-month period, and emotional support was related to survival at all points during the follow-up interval. Persons with high support were about three times as likely to survive compared to those with low support, an effect size comparable to effects for several medical risk factors measured in the study. A similar trend was noted for the social network index but was not significant.

Several studies have obtained criterion measures directly assessing the patient's extent of recovery from heart disease, such as physical activity limitations and recurrent symptomatology. King, Reis, Porter, and Norsen (1993) measured different aspects of functional support in a sample of coronary artery surgery patients followed for 1 year after the operation. Predictive analyses showed esteem and companionship support most consistently related to outcomes (i.e., greater well-being, less functional disability, fewer angina symptoms); some effects were also observed for instrumental support. Helgeson (1991) obtained structural and functional measures with a sample of myocardial infarction patients followed for 3 months to 1 year after the illness. A functional measure (emotional support from spouse) was inversely related to angina symptoms and rehospitalization and positively related to perceived health; the structural measure was not significantly related to any criterion. A series of reports by Kulik and Mahler (1987, 1989, 1993) was based on a sample of patients recovering from coronary bypass surgery. The investigators obtained a measure of general emotional support from spouse through a rating of marital satisfaction and a recording of the proportion of days the spouse visited the patient in the hospital. Results showed that the combination of good marital relationship and high visiting was related to less pain medication usage after surgery and faster release from the hospital. Data from 13-month follow-up indicated emotional support predicted better quality of life, more ambulation, and less cigarette smoking at follow-up. Marital status was not significant in these analyses when its correlation with emotional support was statistically controlled, suggesting an indirect effect. It should be noted that functional support is also related to recovery from mental illness, with or without concomitant psychotherapy (see, e.g., Billings & Moos, 1985; Cross, Sheehan, & Khan, 1980; Dadds & McHugh, 1992; Moos, Finney, & Cronkite, 1990), but there is relatively little research on this topic.

Research on social support and recovery from cancer is more complex (see Helgeson, S. Cohen, & Fritz, 1998; Reifman, 1995). The epidemiologic research in this area has been dominated by studies of marital status, which is at best a proxy for functional support. The literature includes a study of 1,262 persons followed for a 10-year period, which found marriage related to longer survival time for breast cancer (Neale, Tilley, & Vernon, 1986), and a study of 25,706 cases with various types of cancers (J. S. Goodwin, Hunt, Key, & Samet, 1987), which found a survival advantage for married persons, controlling for the fact that married persons were likely to be diagnosed at an earlier stage of cancer (which suggests a behavioral mechanism). However, several studies have found no significant survival effect for marital status (e.g., Cassileth et al., 1985; LeMarchand, Kolonel, & Nomura, 1984), and although these tend to be with smaller samples with more severe disease and shorter follow-ups, they indicate some inconsistency in the literature.

Marital status is only one index of social connections, so it is important to discuss studies that have obtained more extensive measures of social networks. Two studies have found social network measures related to longer survival time, one with a sample of 208 patients followed for 20 years (Funch & Marshall, 1983) and one with a community-based sample of 339 cancer cases followed for 17 years (Reynolds & G. A. Kaplan, 1990). This research is augmented by evidence from studies with smaller samples and follow-ups, which show cancer survival time related to measures of social participation (Hislop et al., 1987), contacts with friends (Waxler-Morrison, Hislop, Mears, & Kan, 1991), and social integration (Ell, Nishimoto, Mediansky, Mantell, & Hamovitch, 1992). These studies found social network measures predicted survival time with control for demographics and for medical variables such as stage at diagnosis. The minimal evidence for support effects on cancer incidence (Helgeson & Cohen, 1996) contrasts with the general robustness of findings on survival time, and indicates this as a promising area for investigation.

SPECIFIC AREAS OF RESEARCH

The following sections discuss some specific areas of research on social support. The aim of this section is both to show the scope of research efforts and to give consideration to the mechanisms of how support works.

Specific Disease Conditions

Social Support and Adjustment to Cancer. The potential role of social support for helping persons with cancer has been a significant focus of research. This has been true both because of the severity of the disease and because adjustment involves both issues of coping with emotional distress and of dealing with interpersonal relationships. Research on how social support facilitates adjustment to cancer has included studies on specific support functions as well as several intervention studies with peer support groups (see Helgeson & S. Cohen, 1996).

Several studies have examined how supportive functions from family members and medical professionals may be relevant for persons with cancer. These studies concur in finding that emotional support is the function desired from family members, particularly with respect to discussing fears and concerns about the disease (Dakof & Taylor, 1990; Dunkel-Schetter, 1984; Rose, 1990). In contrast, patients want informational support from medical professionals but do not want it from family members. An important aspect of this research has been the finding that emotional support may be inhibited in family settings through a reluctance of family members to talk about the disease, because of fear that it will be upsetting to the patient; but it is exactly this aspect of support that patients themselves say they find most helpful. Probably for this reason, the patients in these studies rate emotional support from family members as helpful but sometimes inadequate, and report they may keep their thoughts and feelings to themselves because other people do not want to hear them.

Social support has been shown related to indices of better adjustment to illness, such as reduced anxiety, increased self-esteem, or better functional ability. Emotional support has been found related to better adjustment in breast cancer patients in both concurrent studies (e.g., Zemore & Shepel, 1989) and longitudinal research (e.g., Northouse, 1988). In the few studies that compared different support functions, emotional support is typically shown to be related to adjustment but effects for instrumental support are sometimes nonsignificant (e.g., Primomo, Yates, & Woods, 1990). It should be noted that there has been little research using multidimensional functional inventories with good psychometric properties, and conclusions about the differential effects of support functions accordingly are somewhat qualified. Investigators have suggested that effects of emotional support on adjustment to illness are mediated through reduced emotional distress and improved coping (cf. Ell et al., 1992). Although this inference is plausible, explicit mediation tests of these mechanisms have not been conducted.

The evidence showing support measures related to reduced emotional distress and increased survival has motivated several intervention studies designed to enhance the well-being of cancer patients. Methodological characteristics in this literature are quite variable and several studies used brief interventions or lacked reasonable control groups (see Helgeson & S. Cohen, 1996). Two studies with true randomized designs and intensive interventions have shown positive results. A notable study by Spiegel, Bloom, Kramer, and Gottheil (1989) involved a peer support group conducted over a 1-year period for patients with advanced breast cancer. The group sessions were facilitated by a professional leader and were intended to provide emotional support through frank sharing of feelings and experiences, as well as expressions of reassurance and caring. A 10-year follow-up of the sample found that support group participants had significantly increased survival time compared with control participants. Analyses were conducted to test whether the survival advantage was attributable to reduced emotional distress, but these results were inconclusive.

A randomized study by F. I. Fawzy et al. (1990, 1993) was conducted for patients with melanoma. The patients received education about the disease, received instruction from staff members about stress reduction and coping strategies, and participated in group discussion with other patients and a group facilitator. Results indicated that patients who received the intervention showed reduced psychological distress, enhanced immune system function (e.g., natural killer cell activity), and increased survival at 6 years. Similar to the Spiegel et al. (1989) study, this research involved a true randomized design, and the results of these two studies together have been provocative.

This discussion is not meant to minimize the impact of educational interventions, which focus on providing information about the disease and its treatment. These have been shown to have a significant effect on treatment compliance and survival time in cancer patients (e.g., Richardson et al., 1987; Richardson, Shelton, Krailo, & Levine, 1990). Some studies included group educational experiences (Helgeson & S. Cohen, 1996) and a study by Helgeson, Cohen, Schulz, and Yasko (1999) found a group education condition had more beneficial effects than a peer support condition.

Social Support and Adjustment to Arthritis. Arthritis is a chronic disease that involves unpredictability and interference with daily activities as well as recurrent pain. Supportive relationships, particularly with spouses, may be relevant for facilitating adjustment to the disease (Melamed & Brenner, 1990; Revenson, 1994). As in studies of cancer patients, investigators have examined what types of interactions with spouses or friends are perceived as supportive or nonsupportive. For example, Lanza, Cameron, and Revenson (1995) interviewed arthritis patients about perceptions of recent support episodes. Coding of responses indicated that instrumental support was most frequently reported as helpful (e.g., "friend came and cleaned my whole house"); emotional support was second (e.g., "Spouse understood how I felt"). In the category of unhelpful episodes, lack of instrumental support was mentioned most often (e.g., "Husband expected me to do the laundry which I couldn't"), whereas critical remarks and lack of understanding were mentioned less often. Comparable to other studies, spouses were mentioned as most often providing helpful emotional support and physicians as providing helpful instrumental support.

Studies of the contributions of support to adjustment among arthritis patients have included several types of outcomes. Functional measures are shown to be related to higher self-esteem (Fitzpatrick, Newman, Lamb, & Shipley, 1988), more positive affect (Affleck, Pfeiffer, Tennen, & Fifield, 1988), and greater life satisfaction (Smith, Dobbins, & Wallston, 1991). In addition, longitudinal studies have shown social support related to decreased depression over time (Brown, Wallston, & Nicassio, 1989; Fitzpatrick, Newman, Archer, & Shipley, 1991; Smith & Wallston, 1992). Goodenow, Reisine, and Grady (1990) compared a social network measure with a composite functional measure for predicting several outcomes. They found that the functional measure was related to better adjustment in home and family domains. For predicting depression, the social network index was inversely related to depression in zero-order correlations, but this effect disappeared when the functional measure was added; this implies that the effect for the structural measure was mediated through greater functional support.

In a somewhat different design, Revenson and Majerovitz (1991) studied spouses of arthritis patients, comparing a measure of received support from the spouse with a measure of received support from network members. The study tested buffering effects of support measures for the stressor of disease severity. Results showed a buffering effect for network support but not for spouse support. In this case, the measures were for received support (not perceived availability of support) and the support provider was ill, so it is not clear whether these data are contradictory to the other study. A related study (Revenson, Schiaffino, Majerovitz, & Gibofsky, 1991) showed independent, opposite effects for supportive behaviors (positively related to adjustment) and problematic interaction behaviors, negatively related to adjustment. This study also found an interaction, with depressive symptoms particularly elevated among persons receiving less supportive behaviors and more problematic behaviors.

Indirect effects were tested by Manne and Zautra (1989), who investigated mediational effects for different aspects of support. These investigators obtained a measure for a 10-item composite of emotional and instrumental responses presumed to be helpful for persons with arthritis, together with an index of responses predicted to be unhelpful, namely, the number of critical remarks made by the spouse during an interview. Analyses indicated independent and opposite contributions for the two scales; support was related to better adjustment and criticism was related to worse adjustment. The authors tested for mediation and found that the support score was related to more cognitive coping (which was related to better adjustment) whereas criticism was related to more avoidant coping (which was related to worse adjustment). Thus mediation of support effects through coping was demonstrated and different pathways were demonstrated for supportive and unsupportive behaviors.

Social Support and Adjustment to Diabetes. Diabetes is a chronic illness in which extensive self-care efforts are necessary, and failure to comply with the daily preventive regimen may lead to adverse physical complications. Because glucose metabolism may be upset by negative emotional states and the preventive regimen for diabetes involves continued interactions with other persons, social support may be of considerable relevance for adjustment to this disease condition.

A study by Littlefield, Rodin, Murray, and Craven (1990) examined buffering effects of social support on depression among a sample of individuals with Type I diabetes, using a measure of stress from disease-related disability. Marital status was used as the structural measure. A functional index was obtained through an inventory for emotional and instrumental support; this was analyzed as a difference score assessing the discrepancy between the amount of support patients desired and the amount of support they received. The majority of respondents (70%) thought they received as much support as they needed, or more; hence the discrepancy score distribution was cut into a group with a positive discrepancy score (labeled as adequate support) and a group with a negative discrepancy score (labeled as inadequate support). Multiple regression analysis indicated a Support × Disability interaction effect: Disability was strongly related to depression among persons with inadequate support, but the effect of disability was considerably reduced for persons with adequate support. These results show a buffering effect of functional support.

Krause (1995) set out to examine the association of social support, stress, and diabetes mellitus. Interviews were conducted with a community sample of individuals age 65 or older; of this sample, 143 indicated they currently had diabetes. Stress was assessed in terms of the stressful life events in the preceding year that occurred in connection either with highly valued social roles (e.g., spouse, parent) or in less valued roles. Social support was indexed through a measure assessing how often emotional support was received. Findings from logistic regression models, with control for demographic variables and obesity, a risk factor for Type II diabetes, indicated the risk of having diabetes increased with number of undesirable life events but emotional support reduced this effect. The buffering effect of emotional support was found to be significant for stress from highly valued social roles. Krause hypothesized that support could be acting in part to restore individuals' perceptions of control in their important social roles, although perceived control was not directly measured in this study.

A study by Griffith, Field, and Lustman (1990) tested the association of social support, stressful life events, and glucose control. A sample of adult subjects (40 insulin dependent and 40 non-insulin dependent) was randomly drawn from a central registry. Social support was indexed by a visual analogue scale assessing the degree of satisfaction with support received from "those people important to you." Blood samples drawn as part of an annual evaluation were analyzed to determine glycosylated hemoglobin (HbA1c) level, which provides an index of glucose control during the past 6 to 8 weeks. Analysis of variance showed a buffering effect of social support: Under high stress, individuals with high levels of support satisfaction had better glucose control, but this did not occur under low levels of stress.

A related study with adolescents was conducted by C. L. Hanson, Henggeler, and Burghen (1987) to test the relation of family support to adherence with the diabetic regimen. Interviews were conducted with adolescents with Type I diabetes and their mothers. Parental support was indexed through the adolescent's perception of parental behaviors that are supportive of the diabetic treatment, and adolescents also completed a competence scale assessing four domains: cognitive, social, physical, and self-esteem. Stress was indexed by the adolescent's perception of life changes in the family and their own lives during the past year, and metabolic control was assessed by averaging the patient's HbA1c levels at the time of the clinic visit and at some point during the year prior. Self-report and observational methods assessed five areas of adherence behavior (e.g., diet, glucose testing, foot care). Findings from multiple regression showed that low stress and high adherence were independently associated with better metabolic control. Parental support was correlated with better adherence, which in turn was correlated with better metabolic control; this pattern is suggestive of an indirect effect for support, although mediation was not specifically tested. An interaction effect on metabolic control was not found for parental support, but a buffering effect was found for peer social competence. Parental support is believed to help the adolescent in a main effect manner through continuous monitoring and supervising of their regimen, which increases the likelihood of adherence. The buffering effect of peer competence was attributed to the fact that interference with the diabetic regimen may derive from peer activities (e.g., going out for a hamburger and Coke), hence well-developed social skills may enable adolescents to cope better with these kinds of temptations.

Some complexity of results was found by R. M. Kaplan and Hartwell (1987) in analysis of longitudinal data from an intervention study on diabetes control involving a sample of individuals with Type II diabetes. Individuals were assigned to one of four group intervention programs (diet, exercise, diet plus exercise, and diabetes education). Support indices were obtained from Sarason's Social Support Questionnaire, which provided scores for both network size and for satisfaction with functional support. Results generally indicated opposite predictive effects of support for men and women. At baseline, support satisfaction among men was associated with less worry about diabetes and worse glucose control, but among women support satisfaction was associated with more worry and better control. A different pattern was noted for participation in the treatment program; for women, larger network size was related to less participation whereas no correlation was observed for men. Outcome was indexed by change scores reflecting differences between values for baseline and follow-up variables. Support satisfaction was not related to outcome, but network size was. Among men, larger network size was related to less change in glucose control and blood lipids; among women, these effects were smaller and generally nonsignificant. It was suggested that large networks may involve obligations that interfere with successful management of health behaviors.

Social Support and Hemodialysis. The health status of patients with kidney failure may be sustained through renal dialysis. The procedure is a demanding one because it involves continued effort by the patient, as well as strict compliance to dietary changes necessary to maintain electrolyte balance. Therefore, social support may be relevant for helping patients to meet the demands of this treatment regimen. The role of family support in renal dialysis has been studied by several investigators. Devins et al. (1990) administered Berkman's social network index and other structural measures to a sample of dialysis patients and analyzed relationships to survival over an average 46-month follow-up. Most support indices were nonsignificant, although an index of leisure activities was related to greater survival time.

In contrast, significant results were found by Christensen and colleagues (Christensen et al., 1992; Christensen, Wiebe, Smith, & Turner, 1994) in studying the role of a functional measure of family support in a sample of hemodialysis patients followed over an average 44-month period. Estimated 5-year mortality rates were 18% for the high support group and 52%

for the low support group. The authors considered whether the survival advantage was attributable to support effects on depression or on treatment adherence. Though both mechanisms were plausible and Christensen et al. (1992) had previously shown support related to better adherence, neither depression nor adherence predicted survival in this study, hence the researchers were not able to conduct mediation analysis to suggest inferences about the causality of the effect.

Social Support and Adjustment to HIV Infection. Social support has recently been investigated in relation to adjustment to HIV status, including psychological outcomes and physiological variables. Nott and Power (1995) studied the relationship between social support and various affect and coping measures in a 6-month longitudinal investigation with a sample of HIV-positive men. Support was assessed using the Significant Others Scale, which measures actual and ideal levels of emotional and instrumental support. A Medical Coping Modes questionnaire was also given to participants to examine the ways in which individuals coped with their illness. The data indicated that individuals received levels of support that were average to moderately high, relative to expectation. Results showed that support was related to higher levels of self-esteem and coping efficacy, and to lower levels of depressive symptomatology and perceived stress.

Pakenham, Dadds, and Terry (1994) studied the relationship of social support to coping and adjustment in a sample of 96 HIV-positive gay or bisexual men and a comparison group of 33 seronegative gay/bisexual men. Stress was operationalized as the number of HIV-related problems the subject had experienced, and a problem checklist was given to assess daily stressors in his life. A version of Vaux's Social Support Resources Scale was used to assess several structural indices (e.g., partner present vs. absent, network size, frequency of contact), and scores were obtained for the proportion of network members who provided emotional or instrumental support in relation to coping with being HIV-infected (or coping with the AIDS epidemic, for controls). Analyses controlling for stage of infection showed that greater emotional support and frequency of contact with network members were related to unfavorable outcome (lower CD4 count), whereas larger network size and proportion of close friends were associated with higher CD4 count, a favorable outcome. The researchers tested for interactions of support measures with the stress index, but little evidence for buffering was found. It was not clear how to account for the discrepant results, and replication of the findings was recommended.

Two studies have focused on social support in relation to progression of HIV infection. Theorell et al. (1995) studied a sample of HIV-positive males representing all infected cases with moderately severe or severe hemophilia in Sweden. Participants were initially studied in 1985, approximately a year after they had learned of their HIV status, and were followed through 1990. Support was measured with a version of Henderson's schedule assessing confidant support from close relationships, and progression of HIV infection over a 5-year period was indexed with CD4 cell counts. Results indicated that persons with higher support showed slower disease progression. The researchers related the findings to other studies showing more rapid disease progression for persons with negative emotional states (e.g., anxiety or depression), but these variables were not measured directly in the study, hence no test of mediation effects was performed.

Several dimensions of social relationships were measured in a study that invited participation from all known HIV-infected homosexual men in the city of Malmo, Sweden and obtained completed data from 69% of this population (Persson, Gullberg, Hanson, Moestrup, & Ostergren, 1994). The outcome measure was the mean CD4 cell count from readings obtained during the study period (median = 3, range = 1–7). Indices of network size, anchorage, and social participation were based on measures used in the original Malmo study of social support (B. S. Hanson et al., 1989). Analyses predicting CD4 count with control for age and medical treatment showed that individuals with more favorable outcomes had higher scores on one structural measure (social integration) and on one functional measure (instrumental support). Thus there is evidence that both structural and functional aspects of social networks may serve a protective role for HIV infection.

Support Effects for Children and Adolescents

The effects of social support among children and adolescents have recently been studied (see Sandler, Miller, Short, & Wolchik, 1989; Wills, 1990c). This body of literature contains more research using functional measures, which typically index a combination of emotional and informational support from parents, sometimes with parallel measures for support for peers. Some investigators have studied the effect of support on mental health outcomes (depression/anxiety symptoms or behavioral adjustment problems); others have studied effects of support in relation to adolescents' substance use. Research on social support at younger ages becomes theoretically more complex because individuals participate simultaneously in two different types of social networks—the family network and the peer network—and in some cases these different networks have opposite effects on outcomes (Wills, 1990c; Wills, Mariani, & Filer, 1996).

Studies with mental health outcomes have generally shown protective effects for parental support, sometimes including stress buffering effects, whereas effects for peer support are often not significant. Greenberg, Siegel, and Leitch (1983) tested contributions of parent and peer emotional support to indices of positive mental health (self-esteem and life satisfaction) in adolescents; they found that parental support showed stress buffering effects, such that the impact of negative life events was reduced for adolescents with high parental support. For peer support, the main effect was significant but smaller in magnitude and no buffering effect was observed. Dubow and Tisak (1989; Dubow, Tisak, Causey, Hryshko, & Reid, 1991) demonstrated a similar effect in a sample of younger children, with teacher-rated school adjustment and behavior problems as criterion variables. It was suggested that parental support was related to more active coping, which itself had a stress buffering effect, but no explicit mediation test was performed.

A long-term prospective study by Newcomb and Bentler (1988) related a composite support index (primarily parental support) measured in middle adolescence to a range of outcomes measured 8 years later in young adulthood. Their results, obtained from structural modeling analyses, indicated support was a protective factor in relation to a variety of mental health and behavioral outcomes. The range of effects observed was surprising even to the investigators, who emphasized that the impact of support on adolescents is not restricted to a narrow domain. A 7-month prospective study by DuBois, Felner, Meares, and Krier (1994), conducted in early adolescence, showed a functional measure for family support related concurrently to higher grade point average and less conduct problems, psychological distress, and substance use; most of these effects remained significant in prospective analyses. This study tested what was essentially a three-way interaction among socioeconomic disadvantage, stress, and social support. The interaction results were consistent with buffering effects, as support had stronger relationships to criterion variables among the high disadvantage group, compared with the low disadvantage group. Buffering effects were found for support from school personnel as well as for support from family members, so this study demonstrates buffering effects for support that occurs outside of primary relationships.

Independent effects of social support and social conflict were demonstrated by Barrera, Chassin, and Rogosch (1993). Support from parents was related to higher self-esteem and fewer externalizing behavior problems, whereas support from friends was not consistently related to these criteria in multivariate analyses. Conversely, conflict with parents was related to lower self-esteem and more behavior problems (cf. Matthews, Woodall, Kenyon, & Jacob, 1996). Another study (Forehand et al., 1991) showed that support from a parent buffered the impact of family-related stressors, such as divorce or parental depression, on adolescents' mental health. A 1-year longitudinal study with a community sample of 13- to 16-year-olds (Farrell, Barnes, & Banerjee, 1995) examined the effect of family cohesion for buffering the effect of a particular stressor, father's problem drinking. Results showed prospective buffering effects. Father's drinking was related to increases in psychological distress, antisocial behavior, and heavy drinking over time for adolescents in families with low cohesion, but these effects did not occur for adolescents in families with high cohesion.

An interesting study of help seeking in adolescence was based on an Australian sample of secondary school students (Rickwood & Braithwaite, 1994). A functional measure assessed the availability of confiding relationships. The dependent measures asked whether the respondent had sought any help for a psychological problem in the previous 3 months and if so, whether it had been from informal networks or from a professional helping agent (doctor, school counselor, or mental health service). Results indicated that adolescents were more likely to seek help from informal networks than from professional sources (cf. Wills & DePaulo, 1991). Logistic regression analyses indicated that high symptom level and female gender were predictors of help seeking, and confidant support was related to more help seeking, controlling for gender and symptom level. Thus, this study provides some evidence for a behavioral mechanism of how social support operates for emotional problems.

The relation of parental or peer support to adolescent substance use has also received attention. Functional measures, typically indexing good communication and emotional supportiveness from parents, have been shown in several studies to be a strong protective factor, related to lower likelihood of substance use (e.g., J. S. Brook, D. W. Brook, Gordon, Whiteman, P. Cohen, 1990; Dishion, Reid, & Patterson, 1988). Studies with measures of parental emotional support have indicated that parental support is inversely related to adolescent substance use and has stress buffering effects, such that the relation between life stress and substance use is considerably reduced among adolescents with higher parental support (Barrera et al., 1993; Wills et al., 1992; Wills & Vaughan, 1989). Peer support, in contrast, typically is unrelated to substance use and sometimes is positively related (Wills & Vaughan, 1989). Fondacaro and Heller (1983) showed that a protective effect of parental emotional support was observable in a college student sample, whereas social network indices were positively related to heavy drinking, probably because they reflected frequency of socializing and "partying." It should be noted that the predictors of adolescent substance use are quite similar to the predictors of HIV risk (Donovan & Jessor, 1985; Stein, Newcomb, & Bentler, 1994). This suggests that many of the effects reported here are likely to be relevant also for HIV risk (Leigh & Stall, 1993), but there has been little research on adolescent risk behavior with a focus on social support.

Mediation tests to indicate how social support works in adolescence were conducted in two studies that used different measures and samples. A study by Wills, DuHamel, and Vaccaro (1995) was based on a sample of adolescents surveyed at age 12.5. This study focused on a temperament model of substance use and also obtained a 4-item scale for parental emotional support. Structural modeling analysis indicated parental support was related to more behavioral coping and self-control, and to fewer deviant peer affiliations. These effects largely mediated the relationship between support and adolescent substance use, but an inverse effect for support going directly to substance use (net of all other variables in the model) was also observed.

A mediational analysis by Wills and Cleary (1996) used data from a sample of adolescents who were assessed on three occasions between age 12 and 15. In this study, support was measured with a 12-item scale that assessed emotional and instrumental support from parents, and a measure of major negative life events was included. Regression analyses showed Stress × Support interactions for adolescents' tobacco, alcohol, and marijuana use at all three assessment points, consistent in form with buffering effects. Structural modeling analyses indicated the effect of parental support was mediated through multiple pathways, including effects on more adaptive coping, higher academic competence, less deviance prone attitudes, and fewer deviant peer affiliations. Mediation through relations of support to more adaptive coping was an important pathway that was consistent with previous theory on resiliency effects (Thoits, 1986; Wills, Blechman, & McNamara, 1996). Interaction analyses in structural modeling showed that buffering occurred through two different processes: one in which support reduced the impact of risk factors (e.g., negative life events) and another in which support increased the impact of protective factors (e.g., behavioral coping). The results show that the effects of social support are mediated through multiple pathways to both risk and protective factors.

Social Support and Substance Use in Adults

A number of studies have examined how social network and social support measures are related to substance use among adults. Most studies show functional support measures to be protective in that they are related to lower likelihood of substance use or amount of use (e.g., less heavy alcohol consumption). The distinction between onset and maintenance of substance use becomes somewhat blurred in this literature because most studies do not show clearly whether support acts to prevent onset of use, reduces level of habitual use, or increases the likelihood of quitting. A theoretically interesting aspect of this research, however, is that the precise composition of the social network is quite important, because opposite effects may be observed depending on whether or not the network includes substance users (see Wills, 1990a).

Studies of general populations have suggested a protective effect for both structural and functional indices. A study of a national probability sample by Umberson (1987) found that persons who were married and/or had children showed lower rates of substance abuse as well as higher levels of some health protective behaviors (cf. Kirscht, 1983). These findings are consistent with data from several studies showing structural indices related to lower prevalence of cigarette smoking (Sugisawa et al., 1994; Waldron & Lye, 1989), and with data showing marriage and functional support related to lower levels of alcohol and tranquilizer use (Brennan & Moos, 1990; Timmer, Veroff, & Colten, 1985). A study of an urban African American sample (Romano, Bloom, & Syme, 1991) found interactions with gender such that a social network index was inversely related to smoking among women, whereas a 1-item emotional support measure was positively related to smoking among men. (In the latter case, it was suggested that the construct validity of the measure was in question.) This study also showed that a measure of perceived control over health was inversely related to smoking (cf. Wills, 1994), but Romano et al. did not explicitly test whether the effect of social networks was mediated through perceived control.

A test of the matching hypothesis for buffering effects was conducted by Peirce et al. (1996) with a community sample, using scales for emotional, instrumental, and companionship support. These were tested as buffering agents for indices of stress from financial problems, with change in alcohol use over a 3-year period as the criterion. For indices of problem drinking, instrumental support was indicated as a buffer because it reduced the relationship between stress and problem drinking. The results were interpreted as consistent with the matching hypothesis in that instrumental support showed a buffering effect with respect to this financial stressor, whereas emotional support and companionship support did not.

Jenninson (1992) conducted a test of the buffering hypothesis for life stress and alcohol use in a sample of individuals age 60 and over. Life stress was indexed through questions pertaining to role loss (divorce, unemployment, etc.). Structural indices included marital status, group membership and church attendance, and presence of siblings and other family members. Findings indicated an increase in drinking among individuals experiencing traumatic life events such as unemployment, loss of spouse, or hospitalization of a relative. Several social network variables were found to reduce the relationship between life stress and excessive drinking; these included church attendance, quality of marital relationship, number of close friends and kin in the network, and support from siblings. These findings are similar to a recent analysis of data for elderly men from the Malmö study (B. L. Hanson, 1994). This analysis found that men who engaged in heavy drinking had less support from spouse, lower scores for community integration, and less frequent contact with friends and relatives. Hanson's (1994) study, however, did not test for buffering effects.

Several studies have identified social support as a factor that facilitates cessation of substance use or continued abstinence after cessation. This process was originally studied with both community-based samples and clinical samples of alcoholics; findings indicated that persons with greater emotional support from friends and family were more likely to stop drinking and remained abstinent for longer periods of time (Billings & Moos, 1983; Rosenberg, 1983). Similar results were shown in studies of opiate addicts, which found that individuals with greater emotional support from friends or relatives showed lower levels of illicit drug use and fewer adverse consequences, such as overdose (Rhoads, 1983; Tucker, 1985). The Tucker (1985) study also showed a buffering effect, such that negative life events did not lead to increase in drug use over time for persons who had high emotional support. In these studies, social network measures typically do not show significant protective effects. In fact, the studies by Rhoads (1983) and Tucker (1985) both found increased adverse outcomes among persons who had more close friends, if the friends were substance users.

The effect of social support in smoking cessation has received the most detailed study. The researchers recruit samples of smokers who are either committed to quitting on their own or are enrolled in formal smoking cessation programs; subjects are followed after the quit attempt so that effects of social factors on cessation can be determined (e.g., Coppotelli & Orleans, 1985; Mermelstein, S. Cohen, Lichtenstein, Kamarck, & Baer, 1986). For example, Mermelstein et al. (1986) followed persons during a clinic-based smoking cessation program and for 1 year afterward. They found that emotional support from spouse and friends was related to successful quitting and to abstinence during the first 3 months after cessation. However, the only predictor of long-term abstinence was the spouse's smoking status: Persons were more likely to relapse if the spouse was a smoker. This finding is comparable to data from a study of long-term cessation in a community sample (B. S. Hanson et al., 1990). Participants were more likely to have quit smoking if they were married and their spouse was a nonsmoker, as compared to participants who lived alone. However, married men with smoking spouses had the lowest quit rate of all groups. This study also tested various structural measures and found that a measure reflecting formal and informal group memberships was related to a higher rate of quitting smoking; but a measure reflecting frequency of social contact showed the opposite effect, possibly because men with high rates of socializing were more likely to encounter smokers (cf. Fondacaro & Heller, 1983).

A comparative study by Havassey, Hall, and Wasserman (1991) investigated the relation of a range of structural and functional indices to relatively short-term (3-month) relapse status with three different samples from treatment programs: cigarette smokers, alcohol abusers, and opiate users. General functional measures tapped emotional support, instrumental support, and interpersonal conflict; specific measures indexed abstinence-specific support from a partner. Structural measures included both a social network index and a drug-specific structural measure that indexed how many persons in their network (spouse, friends, and/or household members) were users of the participant's problem drug. Results indicated that high social integration was a protective factor, related to lower likelihood of relapse, as was having a partner (vs. none). Abstinence-specific functional support also showed a significant protective effect, but the general functional indices were all nonsignificant. Drug use by network members was a significant risk factor, related to greater likelihood of relapse. Analogous results were found in follow-ups of participants in alcoholism treatment programs (Gordon & Zrull, 1991; Longabaugh, Beattie, Noel, Stout, & Malloy, 1993), which showed that abstinence-specific support enhanced recovery whereas perceived approval for drinking among network members undermined the recovery process.

Support and Pregnancy

Studies with somewhat different designs have examined the effects of social support during pregnancy. This research has included medical outcome measures such as pregnancy complications and infant's birthweight, both of which are of prognostic significance for the infant's health and development. Such research provides a valuable opportunity to bridge the social and physical domains during a period that is of crucial importance for the health status of both mother and infant (Lobel, Dunkel-Schetter, & Scrimshaw, 1992).

Collins, Dunkel-Schetter, Loebel, and Scrimshaw (1993) investigated the role of social support in a sample of economically disadvantaged women (65% Latina and 20% African American). Interviews were conducted on several occasions during pregnancy, and medical charts were reviewed after delivery to assess outcome measures. A structural index was derived from items on number of kin in network, number of close friends, and whether the subject was living with the baby's father. A composite functional index was based on receipt of emotional, instrumental, and informational support during pregnancy; separate scores were also obtained for support from the baby's father and for support from health care providers. An inventory of stressful life events during pregnancy was obtained together with assessments of depression. Structural modeling analyses tested main effects of support on birth outcomes with control for two indices of medical risk. Results indicated the structural index was related to higher birthweight, the functional index was related to fewer labor complications and better infant developmental status at birth (Apgar score), and the indices of support from father and health care providers were related to better developmental status. A buffering effect was found for functional support in relation to infant's birthweight: Support was positively related to birthweight for women experiencing a high level of stressful life events but was unrelated to birthweight among women with low stress. An analogous buffering effect was also found for maternal depression. It should be noted that the results for structural and functional measures were independent effects, so these findings represent different ways in which social relationships contribute to improved birth outcomes.

The effects of social support in teenage pregnancy were investigated by Turner, Grindstaff, and Phillips (1990), with the rationale that additional stressors face adolescents during pregnancy and their risk for certain birth complications is increased. A sample of adolescent mothers was interviewed on two occasions, the first after confirmation of pregnancy and the second 4 weeks after the birth. Support was assessed with a composite functional measure assessing emotional, instrumental, and companionship support; separate scores were obtained for support from parents, partner, and friends. Birth outcomes were assessed in terms of birthweight and maternal depressive symptomatology. Multiple regression analysis, with control for medical risk factors, showed parental support to be positively related to infant birthweight and inversely related to depression. For prediction of maternal depression, two other variables (living with parents and friends' support) were also inversely related to depression. Turner et al. performed different tests for buffering effects and found a buffering effect for maternal depression among higher SES mothers, whereas for lower SES mothers, main effects of support were observed for both birthweight and depression.

A behavioral mechanism for relationships between social support and pregnancy outcomes was examined by St. Clair, Smeriglio, Alexander, and Celentano (1989) in a study of the association between social network structure and prenatal care utilization. The investigators conducted postpartum interviews with low income, inner-city women in an area in which many women failed to receive prenatal care. Social network structure was characterized by questions assessing three sectors: household, relatives, and friends. Analyses indicated that utilizers of prenatal care had a larger number of relatives in the network, were more likely to have frequent contact with friends (by telephone or visiting), and had fewer children in the household. In contrast, an index of emotional intimacy indicated that mothers who had high emotional intimacy with relatives were less likely to utilize care. Findings are reminiscent of other studies testing whether persons with dense, kin-centered networks are less likely to use preventive medical services (Broadhead, Gehlbach, DeGruy, & Kaplan, 1989; McKinlay, 1973).

Thinking about the role of social support for pregnant women has led to investigations assessing the impact of support interventions. A well-known Guatemalan study conducted by Sosa, Kennell, Klaus, Robertson, and Urrutia (1980) studied the effects of a supportive lay woman ("doula") who was present during labor and delivery. Participants were randomly assigned to either an experimental group or a control group. The experimental condition consisted of receiving constant support from the doula from admission through delivery in the form of physical contact, interpersonal interaction, and the presence of a friendly and sympathetic companion, whereas the control group received routine prenatal care. Outcome measures consisted of the length of labor, the presence or absence of birth complications, and the nature of maternal–infant interactions observed following delivery. Findings indicated that women with a doula had significantly shorter labor periods and fewer delivery problems; also, these women stroked, smiled, and talked to their infants more during interactions following birth. The authors suggested that the effects of the supportive companion may be physiological in nature; reduced maternal anxiety leads to lower levels of catecholamines, which facilitates uterine contractility (Zuspan, Cibils, & Pose, 1962) hence reducing delivery complications. These findings were replicated in a study by Kennell, Klaus, McGrath, Robertson, and Hinkley (1991) with a sample of low income women in Texas, including a condition with a person who observed the delivery but did not interact with the patient. Results showed beneficial effects of having a doula, and even participants with only an observer showed better outcomes in comparison to controls. The doula group used oxytocin less often to augment labor, received less epidural anesthesia, and had significantly shorter labor durations and fewer caesarian and forceps deliveries. In terms of infant outcomes, the newborns of the doula group remained in the hospital the least amount of time.

A nonreplication was reported by Villar et al. (1992) in a study conducted with women in four urban sites in Latin America (Argentina, Brazil, Cuba, and Mexico). The participants were women with one or more risk factors for delivering a low birthweight baby; they were randomly assigned to an intervention group consisting of 4 to 6 home visits from a nurse or social worker, in addition to routine prenatal care, or to a control group that received routine care. The home visits focused on health education by the visitor, who also suggested that the mother involve a support person (husband, mother, sister, friend, or neighbor) in the intervention activities—although such involvement was not documented. Outcome analyses indicated the groups did not differ significantly on variables such as preterm delivery; infants of experimental group mothers were somewhat heavier, but the differences were not statistically significant. The reasons for the nonreplication remain unclear; they could include the timing or nature of the intervention, the focus on cognitive education, or the higher-than-average risk status of the mothers.

Support Effects in Elderly Populations

Paralleling the epidemiologic research on social support and health in the elderly is research investigating specific support effects among elderly individuals. These studies have involved a variety of support and stress measures. For example, Silverstein and Bengtson (1991) focused on intergenerational family relationships using 14-year longitudinal data from three generations in 328 families. Self-administered questionnaires focused on perceived emotional supportiveness for grandparents from their children (now adults), and support effects were tested in relation to stressors such as age-related physical decline and social losses. Logistic regression analyses suggested a buffering effect, showing that intimate ties to offspring were related to an increased longevity and decreased distress only among persons who had lost a family member or spouse. Silverstein and Bengtson suggested intergenerational relations help persons cope with disruptions in family memberships and partially compensate for the loss of support from other sources. Another analysis of data from the same sample (Silverstein & Bengtson, 1994) found interaction terms indicating that emotional support moderated the decline in well-being caused by health problems. Among widowed parents, instrumental support from children also moderated the decline in positive well-being associated with health problems and the decline in well-being associated with being widowed.

Several studies have examined effects of support in relation to specific stressors of the elderly. Cutrona, Russell, and Rose (1986) conducted a 6-month longitudinal study with a sample of 50 community-dwelling elderly. Support was measured with a multidimensional functional inventory, and life stress with a geriatric life events scale. Prospective analyses indicated support was related to improvement in physical health and reduction in depressive symptomatology. A buffer interaction was found for the mental health criterion, with support inversely related to depression only among persons who had experienced a high level of life events. Emotional support was the function most strongly related to physical health, whereas emotional and informational support both were related to less depression. A related prospective study by Phifer and Murrell (1986) also found a buffering effect, with the association between loss events and depression onset reduced among persons with more emotional and instrumental support.

The stressor of chronic financial strain was examined by Krause (1987) in a community sample of older adults. The stress measure assessed whether the individual had enough money for basic needs (i.e., food, clothing, etc.). Social support was indexed through the dimensions of emotional, instrumental, tangible help, and support provided to others. Regression analysis found that the stressor of chronic financial strain exerted a significant effect on depression, somatic symptoms, and positive affect. Several effects of social support were found for buffering the impact of financial strain. In particular, effects of financial strain on depressed affect and somatic scores were reduced among individuals who received high levels of informational support. Emotional support also served as a buffer of financial strain in terms of the positive affect measure (i.e., less decrease in positive affect for those with higher support).

Effects of structural and functional support indices in relation to depression onset following a particular stressor were investigated by Tompkins, Schulz, and Rau (1988) in a sample of stroke patients and their support persons, interviewed three times over a 14-month period after the stroke. Functional measures included assessment of emotional, instrumental, or informational support, plus a global rating of satisfaction with the quality and quantity of social contacts with people in general. Structural indices included network size, frequency of contact, and gender composition. Patients were classified into depressed versus nondepressed groups on the basis of a cut of symptomatology scores at Time 2 and Time 3, respectively. Patients who became depressed were discriminated at baseline by having fewer members in the intimate network and being less satisfied with their contacts with people in general. Measures of post-stroke functional support did not predict depression, so it appears that a more broadly based support network is essential for enhancing adjustment in this population.

Potts, Hurwicz, Goldstein, and Berkanovic (1992) investigated effects of social support in a longitudinal study on preventive health behaviors among the elderly, using data from a survey of health care utilization among persons in an HMO. Health-related preventive and risk behaviors were measured by asking how frequently the respondent engaged in each behavior (e.g., exercising, consuming red meat, smoking, taking vitamins). Support was assessed with a mixed structural/functional scale that included frequency of contact with friends and family as well as items on availability of confidant relationships. Findings indicated that respondents with higher support scores were more likely to endorse health promotive attitudes and also were more likely to engage in six of eight preventive behaviors assessed. Thus this study provides some evidence for a behavioral mechanism of support effects.

Support and Physiological Variables

A number of studies have investigated how social support is related to physiological variables. These include measures of cardiovascular parameters (e.g., heart rate, blood pressure), sympathetic nervous system activity (e.g., catecholamines), and immune system function (e.g., proliferation of T-cells or NK cells). All of these variables have a plausible status as risk factors and accordingly provide a perspective on the mechanism of how social support is related to health (see S. Cohen & Herbert, 1996; Seeman, Berkman, Blazer, & Rowe, 1994; Uchino, Cacioppo, & Kiecolt-Glaser, 1996). The studies typically include statistical controls for demographic factors that could be correlated with both support and physiological variables, and sometimes demonstrate that the effect of support is independent of medical variables. Although this body of literature contains great diversity in the support measures used and the physiological indices studied, some consistencies have been observed.

One consistent finding is that social support is related to better cardiovascular regulation, particularly lower blood pressure. This has been observed in diverse populations and for both men and women (e.g., Dressler, Mata, Chavez, Viteri, & Gallagher, 1986; B. S. Hanson, S. O. Isacsson, Janzon, Lindell, & Rastam, 1988; Kasl & Cobb, 1980; Knox, Theorell, Svensson, & Waller, 1985; Livingston, Levine, & Moore, 1991). Functional support measures typically have tapped support from spouse or family, but also include other sources such as coworkers or supervisors. Of the studies that indexed functional support from family and included a stress measure, all found significant stress buffering effects for family support. Interestingly, structural and functional measures both have been found inversely related to blood pressure (Uchino et al., 1996). Some studies have found support measures related to endocrine measures such as epinephrine or norepinephrine (Ely & Mostardi, 1986; Knox et al., 1985); the latter study used path analysis to suggest that the effect of support on blood pressure was mediated through lower heart rate.

A different paradigm is used in laboratory studies in which participants are exposed to mildly stressful conditions and social support is experimentally manipulated, typically with measures of reactivity in heart rate and blood pressure as the criterion. Results indicate participants who receive support show less cardiovascular reactivity (e.g., Gerin, Pieper, Levy, & Pickering, 1992; Lepore, 1995). In addition, buffering effects are found when subjects receive support from a friend or family member, but are not found when the support comes from a stranger (Gerin, Milner, Chawla, & Pickering, 1995; Kamarck, Annunziato, & Amateau, 1995). Because high reactivity is suggested as a risk factor for cardiovascular disease, these studies indicate a mechanism through which support could reduce risk for heart disease. Several investigators have examined whether the protective effect is mediated through reductions in perceived stress, but have found little support for this hypothesis (e.g., Lepore, 1995). It is worth noting that persons show lower blood pressure when in the presence of a family member in naturalistic conditions (Spitzer, Llabre, Ironson, Gelllman, & Schneiderman, 1992), so a direct effect mechanism is not implausible.

Measures of social support have also been correlated with levels of three stress-related hormones: epinephrine, norepinephrine, and cortisol. Although the number of studies is small and designs are diverse, several studies have found functional measures related to lower catecholamine levels. Fleming, Baum, Gisriel, and Gatchel (1982) studied residents in the Three Mile Island area after a power plant accident and found that persons with high emotional support had lower levels of norepinephrine; a buffering effect was observed, with the impact of residential status (close to vs. far away from the plant) on catecholamine levels being reduced for persons with high emotional support. Seeman et al. (1994) studied a community-based sample of elderly persons who were screened to be in the top third of their age group on physical and cognitive ability. Results indicated that women with higher scores for social ties showed lower levels of norepinephrine. Results for functional measures were significant for men: Those with high emotional support had lower levels of epinephrine, norepinephrine, and cortisol; results for instrumental support were in the same direction but were of smaller magnitude.

Relationships between social support and indices of immune system function represent another research area in which designs and measures are diverse, and this research is often conducted with highly stressed populations (e.g., caregivers for an ill family member). The greater variance of immune system assays combined with typically smaller sample sizes for the studies (attributable to the high cost of the assays) may be responsible for a higher proportion of studies with null results. Nonetheless, meta-analysis showed a significant effect for social support over the range of immune-system indices studied (Uchino et al., 1996). The support measures vary but typically index confiding and emotional support from close relationships. Studies with positive findings include studies of healthy subjects (Thomas, J. M. Goodwin, & J. S. Goodwin, 1985), spouses of cancer patients (Baron et al., 1990) and cancer patients themselves (Levy et al., 1990), and caregivers for Alzheimer's patients (Esterling, Kiecolt-Glaser, Bodnar, & Glaser, 1994; Kiecolt-Glaser, Dura, Speicher, Trask, & Glaser, 1991). As noted previously, two studies of patients with HIV have found social support related to less decline in CD4 cell counts (Persson et al., 1994; Theorell et al., 1995). Kiecolt-Glaser et al. (1991) found a stress buffering effect, with more longitudinal decline in immune function for caregivers with high chronic stress and low emotional support. Esterling et al. (1994) reported evidence for a mediation effect: Caregivers with poor immune system function (in this case, lower natural killer cell activity) made more visits to physicians for infectious illnesses, which suggests a linkage of social support to illness through alterations in immune system function. It should be noted that several studies have tested whether effects of social support on immune system parameters were mediated through changes in depression or perceived stress, and all these tests were negative. Although the tests were conservative ones because of small sample sizes, failure to find mediation through psychological distress suggests that alternative mechanisms may be more plausible.

CONCLUSIONS

This chapter has tried to provide a comprehensive picture of research on social support and health, being selective to some extent but trying to convey the "big picture" of what this work means to the researcher and clinician. The one single conclusion most relevant to all audiences is that social support is consistently shown to be related to better physical health. The evidence supporting this conclusion is persuasive because social support has been shown to predict lower mortality rate. This has been found in prospective studies where the sample was followed for long periods of time after the initial assessment; the effect is shown with statistical control for a wide range of variables that could be correlated with social support; and the protective effect of social support has been shown to occur for both men and women in a variety of national populations, including North America, Europe, and Asia. A more subtle—but important—point is that the effect sizes found for social support measures are sometimes comparable to effects found for medical risk factors. Whereas some persons tend to assume that risk factors such as cholesterol and blood pressure reflect true physical risk and must be many times more powerful than social factors, this is not always the case. A number of the studies discussed have obtained indices for support measures and biomedical risk factors, and have noted comparable effect sizes.

Is it Network Structure or Functional Support That Is Really Related to Physical Health? Recent research has blurred what previously seemed like a sharp distinction between the effects of structural indices and functional measures. Although early studies consistently reported that higher social network scores were related to lower risk of mortality, recent research has shown functional measures to be significant predictors of mortality as well, and several studies have shown stress buffering effects for functional measures with physical health as the outcome. The research continues to show social integration (i.e., through marriage, children, friends, relatives, formal group memberships, and informal group memberships) as a predictor of mortality, but evidence is building for measures of functional support as showing similar effects. In addition, the few studies that have addressed this question have suggested that the effect of social networks is mediated through the availability of functional support. This conclusion is tentative because of the indirect methods currently used to analyze the question, but on the evidence it cannot be dismissed.

Is Any Support Function Particularly Important? The evidence is clear that emotional support is the function most widely useful for adjustment and health. Across a wide range of methods, measures, and health conditions, it has been found that emotional support is related to better outcomes. This has been found even in conditions where other functions would be expected to be more relevant, such as elderly persons coping with financial stress, arthritis patients coping with physical limitations on daily activities, or cancer patients coping with threats to survival. The only qualification to this conclusion is that studies have tended to place the most emphasis on emotional support, and in a number of cases have made only minimal efforts to measure other functions. Yet, in the few studies with multidimensional inventories, the evidence clearly favors emotional support as the most useful function across a wide range of situations. This fact has profound implications for the understanding of supportive relationships.

Do Stress-Buffering Effects Really Exist? Buffering effects of social support have been found for a wide variety of stressors including job strain, financial stress, and disease severity. Moreover, buffering effects have been demonstrated not only for depression but for outcomes including substance use, glucose levels, catecholamine levels, and infant birthweight. Given the volume of the evidence, it seems less relevant to question whether buffering effects exist and more relevant to determine how they occur.

Is Social Support Only Relevant for the Most Isolated? The evidence is not completely definitive on this question; a few studies have reported findings consistent with a threshold effect, but several studies have shown a graded effect of support on mortality across the levels of support measured. This evidence argues strongly against the existence of an effect of support only for the most isolated. In the studies with threshold effects, the evidence is itself internally inconsistent, with both graded effects and threshold effects sometimes observed in the same study. The conservative conclusion is that social integration has beneficial effects for persons across different levels of support, and we think this conclusion should be maintained unless it can be clearly rejected.

Is Social Support Only Relevant for Middle-Aged Men? The research considered here shows beneficial effects of social support over the range from age 10 to 80. A number of studies have been discussed that show comparable effects of social support for men and women, hence sufficient evidence has not been encountered to suggest that beneficial effects of support are a gender-linked phenomenon. The evidence contains suggestive indications of emotional support and confiding as being more relevant for women and a looser network of reliable alliances and companionship activities as being more relevant for men (Berkman, Vaccarino, & Seeman, 1993; Wills, 1998). However, there are enough exceptions to this pattern that sharp gender distinctions cannot be made with much confidence.

What About Negative Effects of Social Networks? It has been noted that social relationships involve strains and conflicts and that persons may not always receive as much support as they expect. From these observations, some investigators have suggested that effects of social networks may be largely negative ones. This suggestion ignores two basic facts that recur in research on social support. One fact is that persons typically rate their support networks in quite favorable terms, indicating that they perceive a high level of supportive functions to be available and that they generally receive about as much support as they need. The second fact is the consistent finding that support is inversely related to mortality (and to several other indices of physical and mental health status) in large representative samples. Whatever the mix of supportive and conflictual aspects that exists in typical social networks, the evidence indicates that in the prevailing conditions of the natural environment the balance of effects of social networks is a positive one. While negative aspects in networks exist, effects of positive aspects seem greater.

Where in the Disease Process Does Social Support Act? This is the most frustrating question in social support research. Obtaining a clear answer is most difficult from a methodological standpoint and current evidence is only suggestive. The striking aspect of current research is the dearth of evidence showing relationships of social support to disease onset together with a fair amount of evidence showing social support related to recovery from disease. It is tempting to conclude that support might primarily act at this stage of the disease process, and this aspect of the evidence is compelling from an applied standpoint because it shows the substantial benefits of having good support after a disease episode. However, a conclusion that supports only acts at this stage could well be illusory, as methodological issues make it considerably more difficult to detect effects for disease incidence, and there is considerable evidence showing social support related to risk factors that must ultimately be related to disease onset. Thus further research on the role of support in disease onset may be an important area.

Have We Learned Anything About How Support Acts? On this front there is both good news and bad news. The good news is that a substantial amount of research has been conducted during the last 10 years, and the research has provided evidence consistent with several different mechanisms. Social support has been related to measures of stress hormones and cardiovascular reactivity, which are relevant to risk for heart disease; to cigarette smoking and heavy alcohol use, which are known risk factors for heart disease and several types of cancer; to indices of help seeking and health service utilization that are of broad significance for prevention of physical and mental illness; and to indices of immune system function, which have been linked to infectious diseases and chronic illness. The bad news is that there have been relatively few tests of whether support effects are mediated through these mechanisms, and a few studies testing for mediation through emotional distress or perceived stress have produced generally negative results. This evidence is not damaging, partly because some studies with null results have had methodological limitations and partly because a few studies have clearly shown mediational effects. This is an area where much progress probably will be made in the next decade.

Have All the Interesting Questions About Social Support Already Been Answered? The answer is "Hardly so." This chapter has addressed only a part of the developing research on social support, and many of the most interesting questions remain to be studied. There are surprisingly few studies that have obtained comprehensive measures for both social networks and functional social support, and more research is needed to compare the respective contributions of structural and functional constructs. Studies specifically designed for studying how the effect of social support is mediated will be of considerable value, and contributions will likely occur through studies that include measures of plausible psychological mediators, such as coping processes and perceived control, as well as measures of neuroendocrine hormones or immune system parameters that have been linked to disease endpoints. Support effects for health of specific populations, such as children, have received only minimal attention in current research. Disease conditions where social support has important effects for both patients and caregivers, such as stroke (Tompkins et al., 1988) and Alzheimer's disease (Kiecolt-Glaser et al., 1991), have barely been considered in the present chapter, and represent areas where good research will continue to be informative. The effects of support for extreme stressors such as warfare have been little studied (see, e.g., Solomon, Mikulincer, & Hobfoll, 1987) and represent an area where social support effects could be even more significant than has been found for the kinds of stressors that have been studied in previous research. Intervention studies to enhance social support for persons with physical illness appear to have promise at this time, and further efforts in this area are greatly needed. Findings from support intervention research may be applied to helping persons who have been victimized through child abuse or crime (cf. Pynoos, Sorenson, & Steinberg, 1993), and similar efforts may have value for helping persons deal with stressors of international migration (Shuval, 1993) or natural disasters (Weisäth, 1993), which are areas likely to be of increasing importance in the current world.

ACKNOWLEDGMENTS

Preparation of this chapter was supported by a Research Scientist Development Award K02-DA00252 and grant R01-DA08880 from the National Institute on Drug Abuse.

REFERENCES

Aiken, L. S., & West, S. G. (1991). *Multiple regression: Testing and interpreting interactions.* Newbury Park, CA: Sage.

Affleck, G., Pfeiffer, C., Tennen, H., & Fifield, H. (1988). Social support and psychosocial adjustment to rheumatoid arthritis. *Arthritis Care and Research, 1,* 71–77.

Barerra, M., Jr., Chassin, L., & Rogosch, F. (1993). Effects of social support and conflict on adolescent children. *Journal of Personality and Social Psychology, 64,* 602–612.

Baron, R. M., & Kenny, D. A. (1986). The moderator-mediator distinction in social-psychological research: Conceptual, strategic, and statistical considerations. *Journal of Personality and Social Psychology, 51,* 1173-1182.

Baron, R. S., Cutrona, C. E., Hicklin, D., Russell, D. W., & Lubaroff, D. M. (1990). Social support and immune function among spouses of cancer patients. *Journal of Personality and Social Psychology, 59,* 344–352.

Belle, D. (Ed.). (1989). *Children's social networks and social supports.* New York: Wiley.

Berkman, L. F., Leo-Summers, L., & Horwitz, R. I. (1992). Emotional support and survival after myocardial infarction: A prospective, population-based study of the elderly. *Annals of Internal Medicine, 117,* 1003–1009.

Berkman, L., & Syme, S. L. (1979). Social networks, host resistance, and mortality: A nine-year follow-up study of Alameda County residents. *American Journal of Epidemiology, 109,* 186-204.

Berkman, L. F., Vaccarino, V., & Seeman, T. (1993). Gender differences in cardiovascular morbidity and mortality: The contribution of social networks and social support. *Annals of Behavioral Medicine, 15,* 112–118.

Billings, A. G., & Moos, R. H. (1983). Psychosocial processes of recovery among alcoholics and their families. *Addictive Behaviors, 8,* 205-218.

Billings, A. G., & Moos, R. H. (1985). Life stressors and social resources affect posttreatment outcomes among depressed patients. *Journal of Abnormal Psychology, 94,* 140–153.

Blazer, D. G. (1982). Social support and mortality in an elderly community population. *American Journal of Epidemiology, 115,* 684-694.

Brennan, P. L., & Moos, R. H. (1990). Life stressors, social resources, and late-life problem drinking. *Psychology and Aging, 5,* 491–501.

Broadhead, W. E., Gehlbach, S. H., DeGruy, F. C., & Kaplan, B. H. (1989). Functional versus structural social support and health care utilization in a family medicine outpatient practice. *Medical Care, 27,* 221–233.

Brook, J. S., Brook, D. W., Gordon, A. S., Whiteman, M., & Cohen, P. (1990). The psychosocial etiology of adolescent drug use: A family interactional approach. *Genetic, Social, and General Psychology Monographs, 116,* 111–267.

Brown, G. K., Wallston, K. A., & Nicassio, P. M. (1989). Social support and depression in rheumatoid arthritis: A one-year prospective study. *Journal of Applied Social Psychology, 19,* 1164–1181.

Cassileth, B. R., Lusk, E. J., Miller, D. S., Brown, L. L., & Miller, C. (1985). Psychosocial correlates of survival in advanced malignant disease? *New England Journal of Medicine, 312,* 1551–1555.

Chandra, V., Szklo, M., Goldberg, R., & Tonascia, J. (1983). The impact of marital status on survival after an acute myocardial infarction: A population-based study. *American Journal of Epidemiology, 117,* 320–325.

Christensen, A. J., Smith, T. W., Turner, C. W., Holman, J. M., Gregory, M. C., & Rich, M. A. (1992). Social support and adherence in dialysis: An examination of main and buffering effects. *Journal of Behavioral Medicine, 15,* 313–325.

Christensen, A. J., Wiebe, J. S., Smith, T. W., & Turner, C. W. (1994). Predictors of survival among hemodialysis patients: Effect of perceived family support. *Health Psychology, 13,* 521–525.

Coble, H. M., Gantt, D. L., & Mallinckrodt, B. (1996). Attachment, social competency, and the capacity to use social support. In G. R. Pierce, B. R. Sarason, & I. G. Sarason (Eds.), *Handbook of social support and the family* (pp. 141–172). New York: Plenum.

Cohen, J., & Cohen, P. (1983). *Applied multiple regression/correlation analysis for the behavioral sciences* (2nd ed.). Hillsdale, NJ: Lawrence Erlbaum Associates.

Cohen, S. (1988). Psychosocial models of the role of social support in the etiology of physical disease. *Health Psychology, 7,* 269-297.

Cohen, S., & Herbert, T. B. (1996). Health psychology: Psychological factors and physical disease from the perspective of human psychoneuroimmunology. *Annual Review of Psychology, 47,* 113–142.

Cohen, S., & McKay, G. (1984). Social support, stress, and the buffering hypothesis: A theoretical analysis. In A. Baum, J. E. Singer, & S. E. Taylor (Eds.), *Handbook of psychology and health* (Vol. 4, pp. 253–267). Hillsdale, NJ: Lawrence Erlbaum Associates.

Cohen, S., Sherrod, D. R., & Clark, M. S. (1986). Social skills and the stress-protective role of social support. *Journal of Personality and Social Psychology, 50,* 963-973.

Cohen, S., & Syme, S. L. (Eds.). (1985). *Social support and health.* Orlando, FL: Academic Press.

Cohen, S., & Wills, T. A. (1985). Stress, social support, and the buffering hypothesis. *Psychological Bulletin, 98,* 310-357.

Collins, N. L., Dunkel-Schetter, C., Loebel, M., & Scrimshaw, S. C. M. (1993). Social support correlates of birth outcomes and postpartum depression. *Journal of Personality and Social Psychology, 65,* 1243–1258.

Coppotelli, H., & Orleans, C. T. (1985). Partner support and other determinants of smoking cessation and maintenance in women. *Journal of Consulting and Clinical Psychology, 53,* 455–460.

Coriell, M., & Cohen, S. (1995). Concordance in the face of a stressful event: When do members agree that one supported the other? *Journal of Personality and Social Psychology, 69,* 289–299.

Cross, D. G., Sheehan, P. W., & Khan, J. A. (1980). Alternative advice and counsel in psychotherapy. *Journal of Consulting and Clinical Psychology, 48,* 615–625.

Cutrona, C., Russell, D., & Rose, J. (1986). Social support and adaptation to stress by the elderly. *Psychology and Aging, 1,* 47–54.

Cutrona, C. E., & Russell, D. (1990). Type of social support and specific stress: Toward a theory of optimal matching. In B. R. Sarason, I. G. Sarason, & G. R. Pierce (Eds.), *Social support: An interactional view* (pp. 319–366). New York: Wiley.

Dadds, M. R., & McHugh, T. A. (1992). Social support and treatment outcome in behavioral family therapy for child conduct problems. *Journal of Consulting and Clinical Psychology, 60,* 252–269.

Dakof, G. A., & Taylor, S. E. (1990). Victims' perceptions of social support: What is helpful from whom? *Journal of Personality and Social Psychology, 58,* 80–89.

Devins, G. M., Mann, J., Mandin, H., Paul, L. C., Hons, R. B., Burgess, E. D., Taub, K., Schorr, S., Letourneau, P. K., & Buckle, S. (1990). Psychosocial predictors of survival in end-stage renal disease. *Journal of Nervous and Mental Disease, 178,* 127–133.

Dishion, T. J., Reid, J. B., & Patterson, G. R. (1988). Empirical guidelines for a family intervention for adolescent drug use. In R. H. Coombs (Ed.), *The family context of adolescent drug use* (pp. 189-224). New York: Haworth.

Donovan, J., & Jessor, R. (1985). Structure of problem behavior in adolescence and young adulthood. *Journal of Consulting and Clinical Psychology,* 53, 890-904.

Dressler, W. W., Mata, A., Chavez, A., Viteri, F. E., & Gallagher, P. (1986). Social support and arterial blood pressure in a central Mexican community. *Psychosomatic Medicine, 48,* 338–350.

DuBois, D. L., Felner, R. D., Meares, H., & Krier, M. (1994). Prospective investigation of the effects of socioeconomic disadvantage, life stress, and social support on early adolescent adjustment. *Journal of Abnormal Psychology, 103,* 511–522.

Dubow, E. F., & Tisak, J. (1989). The relation between stressful life events and adjustment in elementary school children: The role of social support and problem-solving skills. *Child Development, 60,* 1412-1423.

Dubow, E. F., Tisak, J., Causey, D., Hryshko, A., & Reid, G. (1991). A two-year longitudinal study of stressful life events, social support, and problem-solving skills: Contributions to children's behavioral and academic adjustment. *Child Development, 62,* 583–599.

Dunkel-Schetter, C. (1984). Social support and cancer: Findings based on patient interviews. *Journal of Social Issues, 40,* 77–98.

Ell, K., Nishimoto, R., Mediansky, L., Mantell, J., & Hamovitch, M. (1992). Social relationships, social support and survival among patients with cancer. *Journal of Psychosomatic Research, 36,* 531–541.

Ely, D. L., & Mostardi, R. A., (1986). Effects of life stress and temperament pattern on cardiovascular risk factors in police officers. *Journal of Human Stress, 12,* 77–91.

Esterling, B. A., Kiecolt-Glaser, J. K., Bodnar, J. C., & Glaser, R. (1994). Chronic stress, social support, and persistent alterations in the natural killer cell response to cytokines in older adults. *Health Psychology, 13,* 291–299.

Falk, A., Hanson, B. S., Isacsson, S-O., & Ostergren, P-O. (1992). Job strain and mortality in elderly men: Social network, support, and influence as buffers. *American Journal of Public Health, 82,* 1136–1139.

Farrell, M. P., Barnes, G. M., & Banerjee, S. (1995). Family cohesion as a buffer against the effects of problem-drinking fathers on psychological distress, deviant behavior, and heavy drinking in adolescents. *Journal of Health and Social Behavior, 36,* 377–385.

Fawzy, F. I., Cousins, N., Fawzy, N. W., Kemeny, M. E., Elashoff, R., & Morton, D. (1990). A structured psychiatric intervention for cancer patients: I. Changes over time in methods of coping and affective disturbance. *Cancer Intervention, 47,* 720–725.

Fawzy, F. I., Fawzy, N. W., Hyun, C. S., Elashoff, R., Guthrie, D., Fahey, J. L., & Morton, D. L. (1993). Malignant melanoma: Effects of an early structured psychiatric intervention, coping, and affective state on recurrence and survival 6 years later. *Archives of General Psychiatry, 50,* 681–689.

Fitzpatrick, R., Newman, S., Lamb, R., & Shipley, M. (1988). Social relationships and psychological well-being in rheumatoid arthritis. *Social Science and Medicine, 27,* 399–403.

Fitzpatrick, R., Newman, S., Archer, R., & Shipley, M. (1991). Social support, disability and depression: A longitudinal study of rheumatoid arthritis. *Social Science and Medicine, 33,* 605–611.

Fleming, R., Baum, A., Gisriel, M. M., & Gatchel, R. J. (1982). Mediating influences of social support on stress at Three Mile Island. *Journal of Human Stress, 8,* 14–22.

Fondacaro, M. R., & Heller, K. (1983). Social support factors and drinking among college student males. *Journal of Youth and Adolescence, 10,* 363-383.

Forehand, R., Wierson, M., Thomas, A., Armistead, L., Kempton, T., & Neighbors, B. (1991). The role of family stressors and parent relationships on adolescent functioning. *Journal of the American Academy of Child and Adolescent Psychiatry, 30,* 316–322.

Funch, D. P., & Marshall, J. (1983). The role of stress, social support, and age in survival from breast cancer. *Journal of Psychosomatic Research, 27,* 77–83.

Gerin, W., Pieper, C., Levy, R., & Pickering, T. G. (1992). Social support in social interaction: A moderator of cardiovascular reactivity. *Psychosomatic Medicine, 54,* 324–336.

Gerin, W., Milner, D., Chawla, S., & Pickering, T. G. (1995). Social support as a moderator of cardiovascular reactivity in women: A test of the direct effect and buffering hypotheses. *Psychosomatic Medicine, 57,* 16–22.

Goodenow, C., Reisine, S. T., & Grady, K. E. (1990). Quality of social support and associated social and psychological functioning in women with rheumatoid arthritis. *Health Psychology, 9,* 266–284.

Goodwin, J. S., Hunt, W. C., Key, C. R., & Samet, J. M. (1987). The effect of marital status on stage, treatment, and survival of cancer patients. *Journal of the American Medical Association, 258,* 3125–3130.

Gordon, A. J., & Zrull, M. (1991). Social networks and recovery: One year after inpatient treatment. *Journal of Substance Abuse Treatment, 8,* 143–152.

Grand, A., Grosclaude, P., Bucquet, H., Pous, J., & Albarede, J. L. (1990). Psychosocial factors and mortality among the elderly in a rural French population. *Journal of Clinical Epidemiology, 43,* 773–782.

Greenberg, M. T., Siegel, J. M., & Leitch, C. J. (1983). The nature and importance of attachment relationships to parents and peers during adolescence. *Journal of Youth and Adolescence, 12,* 373-386.

Griffith, L. S., Field, B. J., & Lustman, P. J. (1990). Life stress and social support in diabetes: Association with glycemic control. *International Journal of Psychiatry in Medicine, 20,* 365–372.

Hall, A., & Wellman, B. (1985). Social networks and social support. In S. Cohen & S. L. Syme (Eds.), *Social support and health* (pp. 23-42). Orlando, FL: Academic Press.

Hanson, B. L. (1994). Social network, social support and heavy drinking in elderly men: A population study of men born in 1914, Malmö, Sweden. *Addiction, 89,* 725–732.

Hanson, B. S., Isacsson, J. T., Janzon, L., & Lindell, S-E. (1989). Social network and social support influence mortality in elderly men: Prospective population study of men born in 1914 in Malmö, Sweden. *American Journal of Epidemiology, 130,* 100–111.

Hanson, B. S., Isacsson, S. O., Janzon, L., Lindell, S. E., & Rastam, L. (1988). Social anchorage and blood pressure in elderly men. *Journal of Hypertension, 6,* 503–510.

Hanson, B. S., Isacsson, S. O., Janzon, L., & Lindell, S-E. (1990). Social support and quitting smoking for good. Is there an association? Results from the population study "Men born in 1914," Malmö, Sweden. *Addictive Behaviors, 15,* 221–233.

Hanson, C. L., Henggeler, S. W., & Burghen, G. A. (1987). Social competence and parental support as mediators of the link between stress and metabolic control in adolescents with insulin-dependent diabetes mellitus. *Journal of Consulting and Clinical Psychology, 55,* 529-533.

Havassey, B. E., Hall, S. M., & Wasserman, D. A. (1991). Social support and relapse: Commonalities among alcoholics, opiate users, and cigarette smokers. *Addictive Behaviors, 16,* 235–246.

Helgeson, V. S. (1991). The effects of masculinity and social support on recovery from myocardial infarction. *Psychosomatic Medicine, 53,* 621–633.

Helgeson, V. S., & Cohen, S. (1996). Social support and adjustment to cancer: Reconciling descriptive, correlational, and intervention research. *Health Psychology, 15,* 135–148.

Helgeson, V. S., Cohen, S., & Fritz, H. L. (1998). Social ties and the onset and progression of cancer. In J. C. Holland & W. Breitbart (Eds.), *Psycho-oncology* (pp. 99–109). New York: Oxford.

Helgeson, V. S., Cohen, S., Schulz, R., & Yasko, J. (1999). Education and peer discussion group interventions and adjustment to breast cancer. *Archives of General Psychiatry, 56,* 340–347.

Hislop, T. G., Waxler, N. E., Coldman A. J., Elwood, J. M., & Kan, L. (1987). The prognostic significance of psychosocial factors in women with breast cancer. *Journal of Chronic Diseases, 40,* 729–735.

Ho, S. C. (1991). Health and social predictors of mortality in an elderly Chinese cohort. *American Journal of Epidemiology, 133,* 907–921.

House, J. S., Landis, K. R., & Umberson, D. (1988). Social relationships and health. *Science, 241,* 540-545.

House, J. S., Robbins, C., & Metzner, H. L. (1982). The association of social relationships and activities with mortality. *American Journal of Epidemiology, 116,* 123-140.

Jennison, K. M. (1992). The impact of stressful life events and social support on drinking among older adults: A general population survey. *International Journal of Aging and Human Development, 35,* 99–123.

Jylhä, M., & Arö, S. (1989). Social ties and survival among the elderly in Tampere, Finland. *International Journal of Epidemiology, 18,* 158–164.

Kamarck, T. W., Annunziato, B., & Amateau, L. M. (1995). Affiliation moderates the effects of social threat on stress-related cardiovascular responses. *Psychosomatic Medicine, 57,* 183–194.

Kaplan, G. A., Salonen, J. T., Cohen, R. D., Brand, R. J., Syme, S. L., & Puska, P. (1988). Social connections and mortality: Prospective evidence from Finland. *American Journal of Epidemiology, 128,* 370-380.

Kaplan, R. M., & Hartwell, S. L. (1987). Diferential effects of social support and social network on physiological and social outcomes in men and women with Type II diabetes mellitus. *Health Psychology, 6,* 387–398.

Kasl, S. V., & Cobb, S. (1980). The experience of losing a job: Some effects on cardiovascular functioning. *Psychotherapy and Psychosomatics, 34,* 88–109.

Kennell, J., Klaus, M., McGrath, S., Robertson, S., & Hinkley, C. (1991). Continuous emotional support during labor in a US hospital. *Journal of the American Medical Association, 265,* 2197–2201.

Kiecolt-Glaser, J. K., Dura, J. R., Speicher, C. E., Trask, O. J., & Glaser, R. G. (1991). Spousal caregivers of dementia victims: Longitudinal changes in immunity and health. *Psychosomatic Medicine, 53,* 345–362.

King, K. B., Reis, H. T., Porter, L. A., & Norsen, L. H. (1993). Social support and long-term recovery from coronary artery surgery: Effects on patients and spouses. *Health Psychology, 12,* 56–63.

Kirscht, J. (1983). Preventive health behavior: A review. *Health Psychology, 2,* 277-301.

Knox, S. S., Theorell, T., Svensson, J. C., & Waller, D. (1985). The relation of social support and working environment to medical variables associated with blood pressure in young males: A structural model. *Social Science and Medicine, 21,* 525–531.

Krause, N. (1987). Chronic financial strain, social support, and depressive symptoms among older adults. *Psychology and Aging, 2,* 185-192.

Krause, N. (1995). Stress and diabetes mellitus in later life. *International Journal of Aging and Human Development, 40,* 125–1433.

Kulik, J. A., & Mahler, H.I.M. (1987). The effects of preoperative roommate assignment on pre-operative anxiety and recovery from coronary artery bypass surgery. *Health Psychology, 6,* 525–543.

Kulik, J. A., & Mahler, H.I.M. (1989). Social support and recovery from surgery. *Health Psychology, 8,* 221–238.

Kulik, J. A., & Mahler, H.I.M. (1993). Emotional support as a moderator of adjustment and compliance after coronary artery bypass surgery: A longitudinal study. *Journal of Behavioral Medicine, 16,* 45–63.

Lanza, A. F., Cameron, A. E., & Revenson, T. A. (1995). Perceptions of helpful and unhelpful support among married individuals with rheumatic diseases. *Psychology and Health, 10,* 449–462.

Leigh, B. C., & Stall, R. (1993). Substance use and risky sexual behavior for exposure to HIV. *American Psychologist,* 48, 1035-1045.

LeMarchand, L., Kolonel, L. N., & Nomura, A.M.Y. (1984). Relationship of ethnicity and other prognostic factors to breast cancer survival patterns in Hawaii. *Journal of the National Cancer Institute, 73,* 1259–1265.

Lepore, S. J. (1995). Cynicism, social support, and cardiovascular reactivity. *Health Psychology, 14,* 210–216.

Levy, S. M., Herberman, R. B., Whiteside, T., Sanzo, K., Lee, J., & Kirkwood, J. (1990). Perceived social support and tumor estrogen/progesterone receptor status as predictors of natural killer cell activity in breast cancer patients. *Psychosomatic Medicine, 52,* 73–85.

Littlefield, C. H., Rodin, G. M., Murray, M. A., & Craven, J. L. (1990). Influence of functional impairment and social support on depressive symptoms in persons with diabetes. *Health Psychology, 9,* 737-749.

Livingston, I. L., Levine, D. M., & Moore, R. D. (1991). Social integration and Black intraracial variations in blood pressure. *Ethnicity and Disease, 1,* 135–149.

Lobel, M., Dunkel-Schetter, C., & Scrimshaw, S.C.M. (1992). Prenatal maternal stress and prematurity: A prospective study of socioeconomically disadvantaged women. *Health Psychology, 11,* 32-40.

Longabaugh, R., Beattie, M., Noel, N., Stout, R., & Malloy, P. (1993). The effect of social investment on treatment outcome. *Journal of Studies on Alcohol, 54,* 465–478.

Marshall, J. R., & Funch, D. P. (1983). Social environment and breast cancer: A cohort analysis of patient survival. *Cancer, 52,* 1546–1550.

Manne, S., & Zautra, A. (1989). Spouse criticism and support: Their association with coping and psychological adjustment among women with rheumatoid arthritis. *Journal of Personality and Social Psychology, 56,* 608-617.

Matthews, K. A., Woodall, K. L., Kenyon, K., & Jacob, T. (1996). Negative family environent as a predictors of boys' future status on measures of hostile attitudes, and anger expression. *Health Psychology, 15,* 30–37.

McClelland, G. H., & Judd, C. M. (1993). Statistical difficulties of detecting interactions and moderator effects. *Psychological Bulletin, 114,* 376–390.

McKinlay, J. B. (1973). Social networks, lay consultation and help seeking behavior. *Social Forces, 51,* 275–292.

Melamed, B. G., & Brenner, G. F. (1990). Social support and chronic medical illness: An interaction-based approach. *Journal of Social and Clinical Psychology, 9,* 104–117.

Mermelstein, R., Cohen, S., Lichtenstein, E., Kamarck, T., & Baer, J. S. (1986). Social support and smoking cessation and maintenance. *Journal of Consulting and Clinical Psychology, 54,* 447-453.

Moos, R. H., Finney, J., & Cronkite, R. (1990). *Alcoholism treatment: Context, process, and outcome.* New York: Oxford University Press.

Neale, A. V., Tilley, B. C., & Vernon, S. W. (1986). Marital status, delay in seeking treatment, and survival from breast cancer. *Social Science and Medicine, 23,* 305–312.

Newcomb, M. D., & Bentler, P. M. (1988). Impact of adolescent drug use and social support on problems of young adults: A longitudinal study. *Journal of Abnormal Psychology, 97,* 64-75.

Northouse, A. L. (1988). Social support in patients' and husbands' adjustment to breast cancer. *Nursing Research, 37,* 91–95.

Nott, K. H., & Power, M. J. (1995). The role of social support in HIV infection. *Psychological Medicine, 25,* 971–983.

Orth-Gomer, K., & Johnson, J. V. (1987). Social network interaction and mortality: A 6-year follow-up study of a random sample of the Swedish population. *Journal of Chronic Disease, 40,* 949-957.

Orth-Gomer, K., Rosengren, A., & Wilhelmsen, L. (1993). Lack of social support and incidence of coronary heart disease in middle-aged Swedish men. *Psychosomatic Medicine, 55,* 37–43.

Pakenham, K. I., Dadds, M. R., & Terry, D. J. (1994). Relationships between adjustment to HIV and both social support and coping. *Journal of Consulting and Clinical Psychology, 62,* 1194–1203.

Persson, L., Gullberg, B., Hanson, B. S., Moestrup, T., & Ostergren, P. O. (1994). HIV infection: Social network, social support, and CD4 lymphocyte values in infected homosexual men in Malmo, Sweden. *Journal of Epidemiology and Community Health, 48,* 580–585.

Peirce, R. S., Frone, M. R., Russell, M., & Cooper, M. L. (1996). Financial stress, social support, and alcohol involvement: A longitudinal test of the buffering hypothesis in a general population survey. *Health Psychology, 15,* 38–47.

Pierce, G. R., Sarason, B. R., & Sarason, I. G. (Eds.). (1996). *Handbook of social support and the family.* New York: Plenum.

Phifer, J. F., & Murrell, S. A. (1986). Etiologic factors in the onset of depression symptoms in older adults. *Journal of Abnormal Psychology, 95,* 282–291.

Potts, M. K., Hurwicz, M., Goldstein, M. S., & Berkanovic, E. (1992). Social support, health-promotive beliefs, and preventive health behaviors among the elderly. *Journal of Applied Gerontology, 11,* 425–440.

Primomo, J., Yates, B. C., & Woods, N. F. (1990). Social support for women during chronic illness: The relationships among sources and types of adjustment. *Research in Nursing and Health, 13,* 153–161.

Pynoos, R. S., Sorenson, S. B., & Steinberg, A. M. (1993). Interpersonal violence and traumatic stress reactions. In L. Goldberger & S. Breznitz (Eds.), *Handbook of stress: Theoretical and clinical aspects* (pp. 573–590). New York: The Free Press.

Reed, D., McGee, D., Yano, K., & Feinlieb, M. (1983). Social networks and coronary heart disease among Japanese men in Hawaii. *American Journal of Epidemiology, 117,* 384–396.

Reifman, A. (1995). Social relationships and recovery from illness: A literature review. *Annals of Behavioral Medicine, 17,* 124–131.

Revenson, T. A. (1994). Social support and marital coping with chronic illness. *Annals of Behavioral Medicine, 16,* 122–130.

Revenson, T. A., & Majerovitz, S. D. (1991). The effects of chronic illness on the spouse: Social resources as stress buffers. *Arthritis Care and Research, 4,* 63–72.

Revenson, T. A., Schiaffino, K. M., Majerovitz, S. D., & Gibofsky, A. (1991). The relation of positive and problematic support to depression among rheumatoid arthritis patients. *Social Science and Medicine, 33,* 807–813.

Reynolds, P., & Kaplan, G. A. (1990). Social connections and risk for cancer: Prospective evidence from the Alameda County study. *Journal of Behavioral Medicine, 16,* 101–110.

Rhoads, D. L. (1983). A longitudinal study of life stress and social support among drug abusers. *International Journal of the Addictions, 18,* 195-222.

Richardson, J. L., Marks, G., Johnson, C. A., Graham, J. W., Chan, K. K., Selser, J. N., Kishbaugh, C,. Barranday, Y., & Levine, A. M. (1987). Path model of multidimensional compliance with cancer therapy. *Health Psychology, 6,* 183-207.

Richardson, J. L., Shelton, D. R., Krailo, M., & Levine, A. M. (1990). The effect of compliance with treatment on survival among patients with hematologic malignancies. *Journal of Clinical Oncology, 8,* 356–364.

Rickwood, D. J., & Braithwaite, V. A. (1994). Social-psychological factors affecting help-seeking for emotional problems. *Social Science and Medicine, 39,* 563–572.

Romano, P. S., Bloom, J., & Syme, S. L. (1991). Smoking, social support, and hassles in an urban African-American community. *American Journal of Public Health, 81,* 1415–1422.

Rook, K. S. (1990). Parallels in the study of social support and social strain. *Journal of Social and Clinical Psychology, 9,* 118–132.

Rose, J. H. (1990). Social support and cancer: Adult patients' desire for support from family, friends, and health professionals. *American Journal of Community Psychology, 18,* 439–464.

Rosenberg, H. (1983). Relapsed versus non-relapsed alcohol abusers: Coping skills, life events, and social support. *Addictive Behaviors, 8,* 183-186.

Rosengren, A., Orth-Gomer, K., Wedel, H., & Wilhelmsen, L. (1993). Stressful life events, social support, and mortality in men born in 1933. *British Medical Journal, 307,* 102-105.

Ruberman, W., Weinblatt, E., Goldberg, J. D., & Chaudhary, B. S. (1984). Psychosocial influences on mortality after myocardial infarction. *New England Journal of Medicine, 311,* 552–559.

Sandler, I. N., Miller, P., Short, J., & Wolchik, S. A. (1989). Social support as a protective factor for children in stress. In D. Belle (Ed.), *Children's social networks and social supports* (pp. 277-307). New York: Wiley.

Sarason, I. G., Sarason, B. R., & Pierce, G. R. (Eds.). (1990). *Social support: An interactional view.* New York: Wiley.

Schoenbach, V. J., Kaplan, B. H., Fredman, L., & Kleinbaum, D. G. (1986). Social ties and mortality in Evans County, Georgia. *American Journal of Epidemiology, 123,* 577-591.

Seeman, T. E., Berkman, L. F., Blazer, D., & Rowe, J. W. (1994). Social support and neuroendocrine function. *Annals of Behavioral Medicine, 16,* 95–106.

Seeman, T. E., Kaplan, G. A., Knusden, L., Cohen, R., & Guralnik, J. (1987). Social network ties and mortality among the elderly in the Alameda County study. *American Journal of Epidemiology, 126,* 714–723.

Shuval, J. T. (1993). Migration and stress. In L. Goldberger & S. Breznitz (Eds.), *Handbook of stress: Theoretical and clinical aspects* (pp. 641–657). New York: The Free Press.

Silverstein, M., & Bengtson, V. L. (1991). Do close parent–child relations reduce the mortality risk of older parents? *Journal of Health and Social Behavior, 32,* 382–395.

Silverstein, M., & Bengtson, V. L. (1994). Does intergenerational social support influence the psychological well-being of older parents? The contingencies of declining health and widowhood. *Social Science and Medicine, 38,* 943–957.

Smith, C. A., Dobbins, C. J., & Wallston, K. A. (1991). The mediational role of perceived competence in psychological adjustment to rheumatoid arthritis. *Journal of Applied Social Psychology, 21,* 1218–1247.

Smith, C. A., & Wallston, K. A. (1992). Adaptation in patients with chronic rheumatoid arthritis: Application of a general model. *Health Psychology, 11,* 151-162.

Solomon, Z., Mikulincer, M., & Hobfoll, S. E. (1987). Objective versus subjective measurement of stress and social support: Combat-related reactions. *Journal of Consulting and Clinical Psychology, 55,* 577-583.

Sosa, R., Kennell, J., Klaus, M., Robertson, S., & Urrutia, J. (1980). The effect of a supportive companion on perinatal problems, length of labor, and mother–infant interaction. *New England Journal of Medicine, 303,* 597–600.

Spiegel, D., Bloom, J., Kramer, H., & Gottheil, E. (1989). Effect of psychosocial treatment on survival of patients with metastatic breast cancer. *Lancet, ii,* 888–891.

Spitzer, S. B., Llabre, M. M., Ironson, G. H., Gellman, M. D., & Schneiderman, N. (1992). The influence of social situations on ambulatory blood pressure. *Psychosomatic Medicine, 54,* 79–86.

St. Clair, P. A., Smeriglio, V. L., Alexander, C. S., & Celentano, D. D. (1989). Social network structure and prenatal care utilization. *Medical Care, 27,* 823–831.

Stein, J. A., Newcomb, M. D., & Bentler, P. M. (1994). Psychosocial correlates and predictors of AIDS risk behaviors, abortion and drug use among a community sample of young adult women. *Health Psychology, 13,* 308–318.

Steinbach, U. (1992). Social networks, institutionalization, and mortality among elderly people in the United States. *Journal of Gerontology: Social Sciences, 47,* S183–S190.

Sugisawa, H., Liang, J., & Liu, X. (1994). Social networks, social support, and mortality among older people in Japan. *Journal of Gerontology: Social Sciences, 49,* S3–S13.

Theorell, T., Blomkvist, V., Jonsson, H., Schulman, S., Berntorp, E., & Stigendel, L. (1995). Social support and the development of immune function in human immunodeficiency virus infection. *Psychosomatic Medicine, 57,* 32–36.

Thoits, P. A. (1986). Social support as coping assistance. *Journal of Consulting and Clinical Psychology, 54,* 416-423.

Thomas, P. D., Goodwin, J. M., & Goodwin, J. S. (1985). Effects of social support on stress-related changes in cholesterol level, uric acid level, and immune function in an elderly sample. *American Journal of Psychiatry, 142,* 735–737.

Timmer, S. G., Veroff, J., & Colten, M. E. (1985). Life stress, helplessness, and use of alcohol and drugs to cope. In S. Shiffman & T. A. Wills (Eds.), *Coping and substance use* (pp. 171-198). Orlando, FL: Academic Press.

Tompkins, C. A., Schulz, R., & Rau, M. T. (1988). Post-stroke depression in primary support persons: Predicting those at risk. *Journal of Consulting and Clinical Psychology, 56,* 502-508.

Tucker, M. B. (1985). Coping and drug use among heroin-addicted women and men. In S. Shiffman & T. A. Wills (Eds.), *Coping and substance use* (pp. 147–170). Orlando, FL: Academic Press.

Turner, R. J., Grindstaff, C. F., & Phillips, N. (1990). Social support and outcome in teenage pregnancy. *Journal of Health and Social Behavior, 31,* 43–57.

Uchino, B. N., Cacioppo, J. T., & Kiecolt-Glaser, J. K. (1996). The relationship between social support and physiological processes: A review with emphasis on underlying mechanisms and implications for health. *Psychological Bulletin, 119,* 488–531.

Umberson, D. (1987). Family status and health behaviors: Social control as a dimension of social integration. *Journal of Health and Social Behavior, 28,* 306-319.

Vaux, A. (1988). *Social support: Theory, research, and intervention.* New York: Praeger.

Villar, J., Farnot, U., Barros, F., Victora, C., Langer, A., & Belizan, J. M. (1992). A randomized trial of psychosocial support during high-risk pregnancies. *New England Journal of Medicine, 327,* 1266–1271.

Vogt, T. M., Mullooly, J. P., Ernst, D., Pope, C. R., & Hollis, J. F. (1992). Social networks as predictors of ischemic heart disease, cancer, stroke and hypertension: Incidence, survival and mortality. *Journal of Clinical Epidemiology, 45,* 659–666.

Waldron, I., & Lye, D. (1989). Family roles and smoking. *American Journal of Preventive Medicine, 5,* 136–141.

Waxler-Morrison, N., Hislop, T.G., Mears, B., & Kan, L. (1991). Effects of social relationships on survival for women with breast cancer: A prospective study. *Social Science and Medicine, 33,* 177–183.

Weisäth, L. (1993). Disasters: Psychological and psychiatric aspects. In L. Goldberger & S. Breznitz (Eds.), *Handbook of stress: Theoretical and clinical aspects* (pp. 591–616). New York: The Free Press.

Welin, L., Larsson, B., Svärdsudd, K., Tibblin, B., & Tibblin, G. (1992). Social network and activities in relation to mortality from cardiovascular disease, cancer and other causes: A 12–year follow-up of the Study of Men Born in 1913 and 1923. *Journal of Epidemiology and Community Health, 46,* 217–132.

Welin, L., Tibblin, G., Svärdsudd, K., Tibblin, B., Ander-Peciva, S., Larsson, B., & Wilhelmsen, L. (1985). Prospective study of social influences on mortality. *Lancet, i,* 915-920.

Wiklund, I., Oden, A., Sanne, H., Ulvenstam, G., Wilhelmsson, C., & Wilhelmsen, J. (1988). Prognostic importance of somatic and psychosocial variables after a first myocardial infarction. *American Journal of Epidemiology, 128,* 786–795.

Williams, R. B., Barefoot, J. C., Califf, R. M., Haney, T. L., Saunders, W. B., Pryor, D. B., Hlatky, M. A., Siegler, I. C., & Mark, D. B. (1992). Prognostic importance of social resources among patients with CAD. *Journal of the American Medical Association, 267,* 520-524.

Wills, T. A. (1985). Supportive functions of interpersonal relationships. In S. Cohen & S. L. Syme (Eds.), *Social support and health* (pp. 61-82). Orlando, FL: Academic Press.

Wills, T. A. (1990a). Multiple networks and substance use. *Journal of Social and Clinical Psychology, 9,* 78-90.

Wills, T. A. (Ed.). (1990b). Social support. Special issue of *Journal of Social and Clinical Psychology.* New York: Guilford.

Wills, T. A. (1990c). Social support and the family. In E. Blechman (Ed.), *Emotions and the family* (pp. 75-98). Hillsdale, NJ: Lawrence Erlbaum Associates.

Wills, T. A. (1991). Social support and interpersonal relationships. In M. S. Clark (Ed.), *Review of personality and social psychology* (Vol. 12, pp. 265-289). Newbury Park, CA: Sage.

Wills, T. A. (1994). Self-esteem and perceived control in adolescent substance use: Comparative tests in concurrent and prospective analyses. *Psychology of Addictive Behaviors, 8,* 223–234.

Wills, T. A. (1998). Social support and health in women. In E. Blechman & K. Brownell (Eds.), *Behavioral medicine and women: A comprehensive handbook* (pp. 118–123). New York: Guilford.

Wills, T. A., Blechman, E. A., & McNamara, G. (1996). Family support, coping and competence. In E. M. Hetherington & E. A. Blechman (Eds.), *Stress, coping, and resiliency in children and the family* (pp. 107–133). Hillsdale, NJ: Lawrence Erlbaum Associates.

Wills, T. A., & Cleary, S. D. (1996). How are social support effects mediated: A test for parental support and adolescent substance use. *Journal of Personality and Social Psychology, 71,* 937–952.

Wills, T. A., & Cleary, S. D. (1999). Theoretical models and frameworks for child health research. In D. Drotar (Ed.), *Handbook of research in pediatric and clinical child psychology* (pp. 21-49). New York: Kluwer Academic/Plenum Publishers.

Wills, T. A., & DePaulo, B. M. (1991). Interpersonal analysis of the help-seeking process. In C. R. Snyder & D. R. Forsyth (Eds.), *Handbook of social and clinical psychology* (pp. 350-375). Elmsford, NY: Pergamon.

Wills, T. A., DuHamel, K., & Vaccaro, D. (1995). Activity and mood temperament as predictors of adolescent substance use: Test of a self-regulation mediational model. *Journal of Personality and Social Psychology, 68,* 901–916.

Wills, T. A., Mariani, J., & Filer, M. (1996). The role of family and peer relationships in adolescent substance use. In G. R. Pierce, B. R. Sarason, & I. G. Sarason (Eds.), *Handbook of social support and the family* (pp. 521–549). New York: Plenum.

Wills, T. A., McNamara, G., & Vaccaro, D. (1995). Parental education related to adolescent stress-coping and substance use. *Health Psychology, 14,* 464–478.

Wills, T. A., Vaccaro, D., & McNamara, G. (1992). The role of life events, family support, and competence in adolescent substance use: A test of vulnerability and protective factors. *American Journal of Community Psychology, 20,* 349-374.

Wills, T. A., & Vaughan, R. (1989). Social support and substance use in early adolescence. *Journal of Behavioral Medicine, 12,* 321-339.

Zemore, R., & Shepel, L. F. (1989). Effects of breast cancer and mastectomy on emotional support and adjustment. *Social Science and Medicine, 28,* 19–27.

Zuspan, F. P., Cibils, L. A., & Pose, S. V. (1962). Myometrial and cardiovascular responses to alterations in plasma epinephrine and norepinephrine. *American Journal of Obstetrics and Gynecology, 84,* 841–851.

13

Self-Efficacy and Health

Brenda M. DeVellis

Robert F. DeVellis
University of North Carolina at Chapel Hill

Kate Lorig, a health educator at Stanford University, tells a story about encouraging people with arthritis to begin exercise programs. Often, she explains, they believe that exercise would be beneficial but they also believe that embarking on a successful exercise program is not something that they can personally do. She will ask them, "Could you exercise for 15 minutes a day?" If they say they cannot, then she asks them if they would be able to exercise for 10 minutes? (Or 5? Or 1?) Eventually, virtually everyone admits to being able to exercise at some minimal level. If individuals agree they could exercise for 1 minute, then she might ask them if they could exercise for 1 minute on five separate occasions during the day. If they agree, then she points out that what they have agreed they can do amounts to more than 30 minutes of exercise per week. From this beginning, people often progress quickly to achieving the 15 minutes of exercise per day that they initially felt incapable of doing. What has allowed them to progress from a state of inaction to a modest but significant change in their health behavior? Arguably, the critical factor is the perception that people have the ability to initiate and execute an exercise program. That is, they have a sense of self-efficacy.

In the quest to understand and regulate health behavior, few theoretical constructs have been enlisted as enthusiastically as self-efficacy. The concept has been discussed both as one of the major components of social cognitive theory and as a theory in its own right. Whichever approach is taken, it is clear that self-efficacy has generated a substantial amount of research and has been applied to understanding, predicting, and changing a vast range of human behavior —including behavior related to health and illness. Since its promulgation in the 1970s, self-efficacy has become progressively more visible in the health literature. Entering the text word "self-efficacy" into the MEDLINE database reveals no citations between 1966 and 1975, 9 between 1976 and 1980, 75 between 1881 and 1986, 343 between 1987 and 1992, and 552 between 1993 and July 1997. Thus, it is clear that self-efficacy is a preeminent concept in contemporary health psychology.

Bandura (1995a, 1995b, 1997), the creator of self-efficacy and social cognitive theory, published two major books on self-efficacy that cover much of the research done in the area prior to 1997. In addition, Maddux (1995) published an edited book on self-efficacy containing reviews of self-efficacy in a number of domains, as well as a spirited interchange between Bandura and Kirsch about the relation between efficacy and outcome expectations. Another recent review of self-efficacy has been done by Schwarzer and Fuchs (1995) and, finally, Maibach and Murphy (1995) wrote a very helpful, user friendly article on measuring self-efficacy.

This chapter draws heavily on the aforementioned books and articles. It begins by discussing how self-efficacy has emerged from earlier social learning theory concepts and its present status as a pivotal aspect of social cognitive theory. Next, it discusses processes that mediate the influence of self-efficacy on behavior. This is followed by differentiating self-efficacy from other psychological constructs. It then examines factors that contribute to a sense of self-efficacy and summarizes issues related to its measurement. Finally, it presents a brief overview of studies examining self-efficacy and health.

ORIGINS OF THE SELF-EFFICACY CONSTRUCT

The concept of self-efficacy grew out of social learning theory, which in turn grew out of principles of operant conditioning. According to these principles, behavior is determined by the consequences (i.e., reinforcing, neutral, or punishing stimuli) it produces. Rotter's social learning theory carried the ideas underlying these principles into the realm of more complex, cognitively influenced, social behavior. Two critical determinants of behavior, according to social learning theory, are the value individuals place on a specific outcome and the expectancy that the behavior in question will produce that outcome. Thus, at the core of Rotter's theory is the individual's belief about what will result from a given action. If someone expects good things to result from a given action, that action has a higher likelihood of occurring than if the expectation is for a bad outcome. This is stated a bit more formally in Rotter's (1954) own words: "The occurrence of a behavior of a person is determined not only by the nature or importance of goals or reinforcements but also by the person's anticipation or expectancy that these goals will occur" (p. 102). In other words, people will behave if they believe their behavior will produce a desired effect. Within this framework, outcome expectancies are essentially beliefs about the way the world works, that is, about how contingencies are arranged or the relationships between actions and their consequences.

Rotter later introduced the idea of locus of control, which refers to the generalized belief that the occurrence of outcomes is under the control of oneself (i.e., internal locus of control) or outside of the self (i.e., external locus of control). Controlling forces outside of the self also included control of one's outcomes by chance and/or powerful other people. This idea was subsequently adapted specifically for health-related outcomes (B. S. Wallston, K. A. Wallston, Kaplan, & Maides, 1976; K. A. Wallston, B. S. Wallston, & R. DeVellis, 1978) Although the notion of locus of control recognized that individual perceptions of influence over actions were determinants of action, the perceptions in question still concerned outcome expectancies. Locus of control, like the earlier conceptualizations of outcome expectancies, primarily assessed beliefs about how the world works. The idea that "I make a difference in how the world works" was imbedded in the locus of control concept, but the emphasis on personal agency was not yet fully developed.

Bandura developed a separate social learning theory largely independently from Rotter (Woodward, 1982). Notable additions in Bandura's theory were imitation as a process through which behavior could be acquired and, later, the concept of self-efficacy. Bandura (1986) changed the name of his theory from social learning theory to social cognitive theory. This change reflected the broader scope of his theory and the central contribution of thought processes to motivation, action, and affect (Bandura, 1986). An extremely important conceptual advancement was Bandura's explicit distinction between outcome expectancy and what he termed *self-efficacy*. He reasoned that individuals may believe that their own behavior would result in a certain desired outcome (thus, having a high outcome expectancy and an internal locus of control) but might feel incapable of performing that behavior. Such a perceived incapacity was described as weak self-efficacy with respect to the particular behavior. In contrast, if the belief that they are capable of performing a particular behavior is strong, then self-efficacy for the behavior in question is strong. Thus, Bandura's model made a distinction between beliefs regarding how the world works (i.e., outcome expectancies) and beliefs about what they are capable of doing (i.e., self-efficacy).

Why wasn't this distinction recognized earlier? Outcome expectancies alone may have appeared to be all that was needed. Asking "What do you think will happen if you do X," seemingly assumes that the ability to do X is not at issue, and for many behaviors this may be the case. But depending on how the question was asked and interpreted, and on what the behavior was, outcome expectancies might or might not capture the idea of self-efficacy. Thus, asking "If you stop smoking, will your health improve?" might evoke different answers depending on how it is interpreted. One person might reason, "well, I *can't* stop, so the answer is 'no,'" whereas another reasons, "well, if I *could,* I guess I *would,*" and answer, "yes." Bandura's work revealed that recognizing self-efficacy as a distinct and essential determinant of behavior avoids ambiguity and thus has obvious utility. People who respond affirmatively when asked about whether quitting smoking will result in better health may give an answer that takes into consideration whether or not they feel able to quit. But, asking separately about whether quitting would result in better health (outcome expectancy) and whether individuals believe they can quit (self-efficacy) greatly reduces the chances for ambiguity or confusion. The extensive use of the concept of self-efficacy by clinical and research psychologists since its introduction attests to the recognized utility of distinguishing self-efficacy from outcome expectancies.

DEFINITIONS: SELF-EFFICACY AND OUTCOME EXPECTATIONS

Over the years, Bandura's definition of self-efficacy and discussion of its relation to outcome expectations has been elaborated and applied to increasingly diverse arenas of behavior. At one point, Bandura (1977b) defined outcome expectations as "a person's estimate that a given behavior will lead to certain outcomes" (p. 79). He then defined self-efficacy as "the conviction that one can successfully execute the behavior required to produce the outcomes" (p. 79). By 1986, the definition of self-efficacy was stated more broadly as "people's judgments of their capabilities to organize and execute courses of action required to attain designated types of performances" (Bandura, 1986, p. 391). Over the same period of time, however, Bandura's definition of outcome expectations remained essentially unchanged as "a judgment of the likely consequence such behavior will produce" (Bandura, 1986, p. 391). Although his basic definition of outcome expectations had not changed, Bandura tried to clarify what he meant by "outcome expectations" because he thought people were misinterpreting both what he meant by "self-efficacy" and the relation between self-efficacy expectations and outcome expectations. Of particular concern was the boundary between behavior and the outcomes it produces. To clarify his position on this issue, Bandura gave the example of an athlete who is confident that he can jump 6 feet. The strength of the athlete's confidence that he can jump 6 feet, he argued, is the efficacy expectation, and the outcome of "jumping 6 feet" is the praise and self-satisfaction the athlete receives on completing the act. Thus, according to Bandura, self-efficacy in this case would not be merely how confident the person felt about the ability to execute the multiple behaviors and subskills that go into a successful jump (e.g., the speed of running during the approach; the velocity of the push off from the ground). This is so because the sequence of subskills does not constitute the relevant behavior. Rather, the attainment of jumping 6 feet is the behavior. The successful performance of this athletic act is then rewarded by the outcomes of praise, admiration, and/or the satisfaction of doing something well. As Bandura (1986) wrote, "If an act is defined as a six-foot leap, then a six foot leap is the realization of that act, not a consequence of it" (p. 392). Bandura also emphasized that possession of skills alone does not guarantee successful execution of the act because competent functioning requires the ability to use those skills in appropriate combinations under diverse sets of circumstances.

As another example, a person prescribed a complex medication regimen may possess all the requisite skills to count out a week's worth of multiple medicines and cluster them into "morning," "noon," "dinner," and "before sleep" doses for each day. The person also may have seen pill boxes in drug stores that allow pills to be arranged in this way. Someone lacking the ability to apply skills in the appropriate combinations and contexts, however, may not recognize that a means of accomplishing their goal of taking the medicines as prescribed is to use these pill boxes. A more efficacious person, according to Bandura's definition, would be able to make the connection between their basic skills of pill counting and pill sorting and the availability of special pill boxes to achieve a system that greatly facilitates their medication adherence.

The example just described illustrates that mere possession of the requisite skills and the existence of external resources do not guarantee successful performance. Individuals' belief that they can coordinate the skills into an orchestrated behavioral sequence is also an important part of the equation.

In fact this belief that people can cope with the complexities of a complicated medication regimen operates partially independently of underlying skills (Bandura 1986, p. 391). Why? Because if people have low self-efficacy, they may never try a new approach to the problem, even though it would succeed if attempted. In contrast, people with high self-efficacy but fewer skills may have a resilient belief in their ability to achieve their goal. This may motivate them to persist in trying various alternative solutions until they eventually stumble onto one that works.

Bandura's (1997) discussion of self-efficacy reinforces the idea that the concept should be applied to coordinated behavioral sequences rather than subskills. He defined perceived self-efficacy as "beliefs in one's capabilities to organize and execute the courses of action required to produce given attainments" (p. 3). In addition, Bandura (1997) noted that the definition of self-efficacy encompasses not only the execution of behaviors and behavioral attainments, but also the perceived strength of individuals' ability to regulate motivation, thought processes, affective states, and the social and physical environment (Maibach & Murphy, 1995).

SELF-EFFICACY AS AN INTEGRAL PART OF SOCIAL COGNITIVE THEORY

Bandura asserted that to understand the impact of self-efficacy beliefs correctly and fully, they must be examined within the context of social cognitive theory, which includes three elements: the person, the person's behavior, and the environment. Each can influence the others in a process that Bandura referred to as "reciprocal causation." Characteristics of the person component include cognitive, affective, and biological factors, whereas behaviors include all the things that people say and do. Finally, the environment represents all factors outside of the person, including the social structure. This notion of reciprocal causation among the person, the person's behavior, and the environment leads to an examination of not just the ways people's environments influence their thoughts and/or behavior but the ways people's thoughts and/or behavior influence their environments.

Because self-efficacy is a belief, it is aligned most closely with the "person" component of Bandura's tripartite social cognitive theory; he viewed self-efficacy as the preeminent "person" attribute. Nevertheless, self-efficacy must be conceptualized in relation to relevant contexts, which can include elements of the person's behavior, their environment, and/or other aspects of the person. For example, 6 months after giving up cigarettes, individuals may have a strong sense of efficacy to refrain from smoking cigarettes if in a "no smoking restaurant" with friends who do not smoke. They may have a weaker sense of efficacy for refraining from smoking if in a bar drinking a soft drink with friends who are smoking. Efficacy might be further weakened if they have two alcoholic drinks in that same bar with those same smoking friends. Finally, efficacy would be weaker still if the person additionally had a terrible day at work and was feeling "down in the dumps." Thus, this emphasis on viewing self-efficacy within specific contexts anchors it to the individuals' environment (a smoking permitted bar vs. a smoking prohibited restaurant), the individuals' behavior (drinking alcoholic vs. a nonalcoholic drink), and other aspects of the individuals themselves (e.g., mood). In this example, the strength of self-efficacy to refrain from smoking varied according to levels of social influence, the physical environment, cues about the acceptability of smoking, and mood.

PROCESSES THAT MEDIATE THE INFLUENCE OF SELF-EFFICACY ON BEHAVIOR

According to Bandura (1997), self-efficacy is a powerful predictor of the kinds of activities people do, how long and how intensively they persist in doing them, and the amount of distress or satisfaction they experience in the face of life's opportunities, challenges, and hardships. Furthermore, self-efficacy even affects whether or not different people perceive the same event as an opportunity, challenge, or hardship. For example, someone who has high self-efficacy for successfully completing gross motor tasks requiring strength and coordination may view a recommended exercise regimen as a challenge to be faced with enthusiasm and strong expectations for success. A person with lower self-efficacy for this type of activity may view the same situation with dread, anticipating failure and embarrassment.

Bandura (1997) described four processes through which self-efficacy achieves its effects: cognition, motivation, affect, and selection. Each of these four processes can operate alone, but they usually "operate in concert, rather than isolation" (p. 116), and the mechanisms underlying each of the four overlap considerably.

Cognition

Self-efficacy is itself a cognition. However, other cognitions can mediate between self-efficacy and behavior. Self-efficacy thus can influence the way that people understand or interpret situations. For example, people who believe that they cannot solve a problem may come to believe the problem is inherently unsolvable. As a result, even if circumstances change, this interpretation may preclude effective action.

Motivational Processes

Motivational processes constitute the second major group of factors that mediate the influence of self-efficacy on performance. Bandura acknowledged, however, that motivational processes in humans involve a substantial cognitive component. Thus, beliefs about causal sequences can enhance or attenuate individuals' motivation to pursue a given behavior. He went on to describe cognitive activities associated with theories other than social cognitive theory that have motivational implications. These include attributions, outcome expectancies, and goal setting.

Attributions concern the causes that people ascribe for events that have already happened to them. For example, imagine that a woman who has not exercised in years finishes a 10-minute bicycle ride and experiences mild "windedness" and tightness in her calf muscles. Someone with a strong sense of efficacy for exercising more regularly might attribute these symptoms to beneficial health changes (e.g., "I'm exercising enough for an aerobic benefit and my legs are getting a good workout"), whereas someone with a weak sense of efficacy might attribute them to inherent weakness (e.g., "I'm too out of shape to do this"). As a consequence, the former woman might continue to ride her bike regularly while the latter desists.

The second type of cognitive motivator is outcome expectancies. The outcomes that people anticipate from implementing a course of action should have motivational value. Bandura (1997), however, believed that outcome expectancies do not add much to the prediction of behavior over and above the contribution of self-efficacy because "efficacy beliefs affect the extent to which people act on their outcome expectations" (p. 126). Of course, a sense of self-efficacy is unlikely to lead to action if people believe that the action will not produce the desired outcome.

Goal setting, in the context of self-regulation, is the third motivator that mediates the influence of self-efficacy on behavior. Self-regulation refers to the "automatic and deliberate processes by which people control and direct their cognitions, emotions, and behaviors in the pursuit of their goals" (Barone, Maddux, & Snyder, 1997, p. 303). Self-efficacy can influence self-regulation in four ways (Bandura, 1997). First, self-efficacy influences what goals people set for themselves. Those people with higher self-efficacy in a particular domain of achievement will set higher goals than those with lower self-efficacy. Second, self-efficacy affects people's reactions to perceived discrepancies between their goals and actual performance (Barone et al., 1997). People with a high sense of self-efficacy will work harder and persist longer to attain their goals than people with low self-efficacy. Third, "self-efficacy in solving problems and making decisions influences the efficiency and effectiveness of problem solving and decision making" (Bandura, 1997, p. 291). Finally, self-efficacy influences whether or not a person will choose to enter goal-relevant situations.

Affective Processes

The third major group of processes that mediate the influence of self-efficacy are affective and consist of exercising control over thought, affect, and action (Bandura, 1997). First, with respect to thought, efficacy beliefs influence what stimuli people attend to (e.g., an elevator may go unnoticed by most people but not by someone with an elevator phobia), how people appraise situations cognitively (e.g., as a threat in the case of low self-efficacy and a challenge when efficacy beliefs are high), and whether past situations (e.g., a medical appointment) are remembered in positive, neutral, or negative terms. With respect to affect, efficacy beliefs influence "perceived cognitive abilities to control perturbing trains of thought when they intrude on the flow of consciousness" (p. 137) Thus, in essence, affective states may enhance or undermine self-efficacy through their cuing, motivational, and reinforcing properties. One of the objectives of self-regulation is fostering affective states conducive to the successful completion of desired actions. Finally, actions also can mediate the influence of self-efficacy on emotions. In essence, efficacy beliefs influence the types of actions that people take. The consequences of taking more effective courses of action will differ from those of less effective alternatives. Thus, actions are a mechanism through which efficacy beliefs influence emotions. And these emotions, in turn, can mediate between self-efficacy and subsequent actions.

Selection Processes

The fourth major group of processes that mediate the influence of self-efficacy involve selection processes, that is, choosing environments into which people put themselves. These choices are heavily influenced by people's sense of efficacy to function in specific environments. People will avoid environments they believe exceed their capabilities and will gravitate toward environments they feel they can handle. People with higher self-efficacy are more likely to place themselves in challenging situations and persist in gaining mastery over those situations once they are in them. Moreover, these choices may have enduring consequences. Bandura (1997) noted that choices that often seem insignificant at the time end up, in hindsight, being crucial turning points in a person's life with major effects on people's life paths. An example of this is an adult who feels inefficacious with respect to classroom settings who thus fails to attend a lecture at a local school about cancer screening and neglects to recognize an important warning sign.

Thoughts on Mediational Processes

Bandura's point in discussing mediators of self-efficacy is to illustrate how various processes help to translate a given level of self-efficacy into a given behavioral performance. It is worth noting that factors other than self-efficacy will also influence cognitive, motivational, affective, and selective processes related to behavior. Thus, a full understanding of self-efficacy alone is unlikely to yield a full understanding of how each of these processes influences behavior. Moreover, characterizing these processes as mediators between self-efficacy and behavior amounts to acknowledging them as more immediate (although not necessarily more comprehensive) determinants of behavior. Thus, do not interpret the inclusion of concepts from other theories in the preceding sections as suggesting that social cognitive theory fully supplants the theories from which those concepts are derived.

HOW SELF-EFFICACY DIFFERS FROM OTHER CONSTRUCTS AND CONCEPTS

Bandura (1997) viewed personal efficacy beliefs as the preeminent factor in human agency. He briefly described a number of other person characteristics (e.g., locus of control, self-esteem, self-confidence) with the dual goals of showing how they differ from the construct of self-efficacy and demonstrating that they are not as powerful as self-efficacy in explaining, predicting, or intervening on human behavior. As noted earlier, the vast number of studies that have examined self-efficacy and the growing number of interventions that have self-efficacy as a cornerstone testify to its importance. Other evidence of the power of the self-efficacy construct has been its addition to major models of behavior that had existed for a relatively long time without self-efficacy in them (e.g., the health belief model; Strecher & Rosenstock, 1977; theory of reasoned action; Montano, Kasprzk & Taplin, 1997) and the inclusion of self-efficacy in more recently developed theories of behavior such as Social Action Theory (Ewart, 1991) and the Cognitive-Social Health Information Processing (C-SHIP) Model (Miller & Diefenbach, 1998).

There are a number of constructs that have been mistakenly equated with self-efficacy. This has led to confusion at both the conceptual and operational levels. This confusion occurs, in part, because the personality traits, states, and processes that these concepts represent can both influence and be influenced by self-efficacy. This does not mean, however, that any of these concepts are equivalent to self-efficacy (Strecher, B. DeVellis, Becker, & Rosenstock, 1986).

Health Locus of Control

Health locus of control refers to a generalized expectation about where control for a person's health resides. Thus, health locus of control concerns the extent to which people think their health is controlled by their own actions and efforts, by the actions of others (e.g., physicians and nurses), or by fate or chance. In this scheme, health is an outcome and locus of control is concerned with the *perceived relation between actions and outcomes* (Maibach & Murphy, 1995). Self-efficacy, on the other hand, is concerned with the extent to which people feel capable of undertaking the specific behavior(s) that may or may not lead to a desired outcome. For example, individuals may firmly believe their health status (outcome) is influenced by what they eat (behavior) and thus that if they ate less fat they would live a longer and healthier life. They might, however, also feel incapable of restricting their consumption of fatty foods. Thus, people can view their own health as determined by their own actions (internal locus of control) but feel unable to carry out the actions that will lead to better health. The person caught in this dilemma has an internal locus of control but low self-efficacy when it comes to restricting fat consumption.

Self-Esteem

Self-esteem refers to "the overall affective evaluation of one's own worth, value, or importance" (Blascovich & Tomaka, 1991, p. 115). Blascovich and Tomaka further described self-esteem as part of the broader construct of self-concept. The latter includes both cognitive and behavioral as well as emotional aspects of people's self-representation. They also pointed out that self-esteem, especially when measured globally, tends to be quite stable across time and contexts. Although both self-esteem and self-efficacy concern an assessment of some aspect of oneself, the preceding definition highlights several key distinctions. Whereas self-efficacy has strong cognitive components, self-esteem is more evaluative and affective. It is, in essence, how individuals feel about themselves in a global sense. This "global sense" is the second key difference between self-esteem and self-efficacy. Although the latter is specific to time and context, self-esteem is traitlike (i.e., relatively invariant). Despite these important differences, the two are not entirely independent. Perceiving oneself as efficacious in a variety of contexts is likely, over time, to exert a positive influence on self-esteem. Similarly, high self-esteem seems more likely than its opposite to engender a strong sense of self-efficacy in a novel situation. It seems unlikely, however, that either of these two variables will be determined primarily by the other in most circumstances. Thus, although it is possible to describe mechanisms that link the two, their differences are clear and the terms are by no means interchangeable. Bandura highlighted the distinction between the two concepts by pointing out that high self-efficacy for some tasks (e.g., being able to brush one's teeth well) will do little to enhance self-esteem and that low self-efficacy for others (e.g., not being able to ride a unicycle) will not compromise how individuals evaluate themselves globally.

Coping

Lazarus and Folkman (1984) articulated a comprehensive model of coping that shares some assumptions with the construct of self-efficacy and interfaces with it at several points. According to the Lazarus and Folkman model, two types of cognitive appraisal—primary appraisal and secondary appraisal—influence coping. *Primary appraisal* refers to categorizing a situation in terms of its meaning and significance for an individual's well-being. It involves formulating an answer to the question, "Am I in trouble or being benefitted now or in the future and in what way?" (p. 31). As a result of primary appraisal, a situation can be viewed as stressful, benign-positive, or irrelevant. There are three types of stressful primary appraisals: harm/loss, threat, and challenge. Secondary appraisal refers to an assessment of what might be, and can be, done when people conclude that either a threat or an opportunity exists. Self-efficacy is relevant for both primary and secondary appraisal. High self-efficacy for a situation can lead to a primary appraisal of that situation as benign, positive, or as irrelevant, but not as stressful. If a situation is appraised as stressful, then self-efficacy becomes a major, if not the major, component of secondary appraisal. Bandura (1997) noted that instilling a sense of or increasing a sense of self-efficacy can transform threatening situations into safe ones.

Self-confidence

Self-confidence describes "an overall evaluation of ability rather than an evaluation of capability with regard to certain tasks" (Maibach & Murphy, 1995, p. 40). According to Bandura (1997), although confidence refers to strength of a belief, it does not necessarily specify the cause of the certainty. For example, people can be extremely confident that they will live to age 90 based on the knowledge that all of their grandparents lived to this age. Thus, their confidence may have nothing to do with their beliefs about their behavioral capabilities. Perceived self-efficacy, on the other hand, refers to the belief in individuals' power to attain given levels of performance. A self-efficacy assessment, therefore, includes both the affirmation of capability and the strength of that belief. Finally, self-confidence is a colloquial expression used in everyday language. Bandura cautioned readers to keep the term *self-confidence* in everyday language but to not equate it with self-efficacy, which is more precisely defined. Some of the confusion about the relation of self-confidence to self-efficacy probably arises from the fact that one way of measuring self-efficacy is to ask people to rate how confident they feel in their ability to do a specified activity. Although expressing self-efficacy in terms of confidence may be a useful means for researchers to communicate with respondents who are not theoreticians, it should not, Bandura asserted, be treated as a synonym for self-efficacy in formal discussions of the concept.

Generalized Self-Efficacy

Generalized self-efficacy refers to a "sense of efficacy that operates across all situations and domains of functioning" (Maibach & Murphy, 1995, p. 40). Maibach and Murphy (1995) noted that conceptualizing self-efficacy in this way is antithetical to the way Bandura defined self-efficacy because in social cognitive theory, self-efficacy must be tied to specific domains of functioning and specific contexts. Maibach and Murphy believed that this misguided idea of generalized self-efficacy evolved out of a misinterpretation of how the term *generality* is used in discussions of the three measurement dimensions of self-efficacy (i.e., level, strength, generality). As an example, individuals whose efficacy beliefs are high in generality may feel efficacious with respect to performing a behavior, such as avoiding high fat foods, in a variety of different settings. This is not the same, however, as feeling efficacious across multiple domains of behavior, such as dietary regulation, exercise, and avoidance of stress.

SOURCES OF SELF-EFFICACY

Beliefs about personal efficacy are learned from five major sources: enactive mastery or learning through personal experience; vicarious experience, which includes learning through the observation of events and/or other people; verbal persuasion; physiological state; and affective state.

Enactive Mastery

Bandura (1997) stated that enactive mastery experiences are the most potent source of efficacy information because they provide the most authentic evidence that individuals can do what it takes to succeed. Furthermore, Bandura noted, successive mastery over tasks required to engage in a behavior helps people develop and refine skills. In addition, it fosters development of a repertoire of coping mechanisms to deal with problems encountered. There is no one-to-one correspondence between performance and perceived self-efficacy, however (Bandura, 1997). Both successful and unsuccessful experiences are cognitively processed and the way each experience is attended to, weighted, and interpreted will influence its impact on self-efficacy. Thus the extent that personal experience will alter people's perceived efficacy "depends on their preconceptions of their capabilities, the perceived difficulty of the tasks, the amount of effort they expend, the amount of external aid they receive, the circumstances under which they perform, the temporal pattern of their successes and failures, and the way these enactive experiences are cognitively organized and reconstructed in memory" (Bandura, 1997, p. 81). People with low self-efficacy in a particular domain may discount their successes as "flukes," whereas people with high preexisting self-efficacy may discount their failures as "flukes." All other things being equal, however, direct mastery experiences are the most potent source of efficacy information.

Vicarious or Observational Experience

Fortunately, people do not have to learn everything through direct experience but can learn from observing events and/or the behaviors of others in conjunction with the consequences that follow those events or behaviors. These events/people are referred to as "models." Bandura (1997) considered vicarious experience and modeling as the second most powerful source of self-efficacy information and, under some circumstances, vicarious experience and modeling can surpass the influence of enactive experiences.

There are four processes that influence the impact of observational learning: attention, retention, behavioral production, and motivational processes. First, an observer needs to attend to the model and Bandura cited a number of factors related to attributes of the observer (e.g., perceptual set, cognitive capabilities and preconceptions, arousal level, acquired preferences) and attributes of the event (e.g., salience, affective valence, complexity, prevalence, accessibility, functional value) that can influence what, if anything, receives attention. Next the person must retain the information that has been observed. This involves an active process of transforming information from discrete ideas into organized, symbolic form, such as general principles that can govern action in multiple situations. Behavioral production involves the translation into behavior of the principles that arose from attention and retention processes. The observer's physical capabilities and the number and complexity of subskills required to execute the behavior affect whether, and how well, individuals perform the modeled behavior. In addition, observers go through a self-regulation process whereby they monitor their skill at doing the behavior in light of their conception of how, and how well, the behavior should be done and then attempt to modify their behavior so that it better matches their conception of how it should be done. Finally, motivational processes influence the effect of modeling on the observer's self-efficacy. For example, people who are highly motivated to achieve a very high standard of performance may suffer a loss of self-efficacy if the performance of a model they view as comparable to them in ability falls short of this standard.

Verbal Persuasion and Social Evaluations

Verbal persuasion is the third source of efficacy information. If all other factors are equal, then verbal persuasion alone is a less powerful source of efficacy information than either enactive or vicarious experience. The right kind of verbal feedback from a credible source can significantly facilitate self-change efforts, however. Thus, positive feedback that is "within realistic bounds," focuses on achieved progress, highlights personal capabilities, and is delivered by a credible person can lead a person to try harder and persist longer. If a person is given the wrong kind of feedback, however, the results can be devastating. For example, feedback framed as a gain (e.g., you have progressed toward your goal by 75%) can enhance self-efficacy, whereas the same feedback framed as a deficit (e.g., you are short of your goal by 25%) can cause self-efficacy to plummet. Likewise, feedback that is overinflated will be discounted when individuals try out the new behavior and fall short of their goal. Bandura (1997) noted that it is easier to undermine people's efficacy through destructive feedback than it is to bolster self-efficacy through constructive feedback. Furthermore, he noted, that much of the feedback given in society is deficit oriented and destructive to a sense of efficacy. Finally, verbal persuasion works best in tandem with the other forms of efficacy enhancement (i.e., enactive experience, vicarious experience, and physiological and affective states).

Physiological State

People's physiological state can influence self-efficacy. Bandura noted that people are more apt to expect failure if they are highly physiologically aroused. This expectation occurs as a result of previous associations of physical arousal with impaired performance. People who experience sweaty palms and trembling knees as they are about to give a talk often find that their efficacy for public speaking plummets and their performance then may, in fact, be impaired. The presence of such arousal, however, does not automatically result in impaired performance. People who view their arousal not as a sign of incompetence at public speaking but as a sign of positive energy and heightened interest may find that their heightened arousal facilitates rather then impairs self-efficacy and may also result in a more dynamic presentation. Likewise, a sedentary person just starting an exercise program can interpret transient fatigue and mild aches as a sign of physical vulnerability and stop or they may see it as diagnostic of a neuromuscular system that is "coming alive."

Affective States

People's moods can affect their sense of self-efficacy. Positive mood states contribute to a heightened sense of self-efficacy and negative mood states contribute to a poorer sense of self-efficacy. When in negative moods people are more apt to recall and focus on past failures and shortcomings, whereas people experiencing a positive mood are more apt to recall and focus on past success experiences. This mood relevant recall and focus has been shown to occur when a person is experiencing a naturally occurring mood state or is experiencing a mood that has been induced by an investigator in a research setting.

MEASURING SELF-EFFICACY

The measurement of self-efficacy has many features in common with the measurement of other psychological constructs and a few that are more specific. The general features include the avoidance of ambiguously worded items, use of multiple rather than single indicators, attainment of acceptable reliability, and demonstration of the validity of the measurement procedure. These are not discussed here. Readers may consult other sources (e.g., DeVellis, 1991; Nunnally & Bernstein, 1994) for a more general discussion of these and other technical measurement issues. The remainder of this section focuses on conceptual issues that have particular relevance to measuring self-efficacy.

Measurement in psychology typically involves obtaining some indication of the state of a construct that is not self-evident. The validity of the measurement process is the extent to which the manifestation obtained corresponds to the true state of the variable in question. One requirement for valid measurement, therefore, is that the data gathered correspond very closely to the concept they represent. This, in turn, requires that the concept be sufficiently clear to guide the development or selection of the measurement strategy.

Behaviors Versus Attainments

Should self-efficacy assess the person's confidence in doing something or achieving something? Although the early discussions of self-efficacy emphasized its impact on specific behaviors (Bandura, 1977a), self-efficacy is not restricted to overt, discrete actions. Self-efficacy with respect to goals, behavioral attainments, and self-regulation (i.e., thoughts, feelings, perceptions, and motivations as well as behavior) are an integral part of the most recent descriptions of the phenomenon (Bandura, 1997; Maibach & Murphy, 1995). The choice of measuring a specific behavior, behavioral attainment, or self-regulation should be based on the nature of the phenomenon under investigation. If the objective is to predict a specific action, then the self-efficacy assessment should probably correspond to the completion of that action. If the behavior in question is most reasonably defined in terms of a performance attainment (e.g., weight loss), then the attainment may serve as a marker for the behavior when assessing self-efficacy. In this case, self-efficacy would be assessed in relation to the goal of losing 8 pounds in 4 weeks and the outcome expectancy might include receiving complements on appearance, fitting into preferred clothes, and self-satisfaction about having achieved the goal.

Time Frame

Generally, self-efficacy assessments should focus on the present. Bandura (1997) highlighted the importance of asking about what people believe they can do rather than will do. He noted that the former assesses self-efficacy and the latter assesses behavioral intention. Implicit in the "can do" wording is the notion of doing the behavior in question now. Confidence in a person's ability to act at an unspecified future time runs the risk of confusing self-efficacy and intention. One exception that Bandura (1997) acknowledged is a circumstance requiring sustained action over time, such as refraining from smoking. There is little utility in determining whether someone can refrain from smoking at a specific instant, as opposed to over some time interval. Thus, Bandura advocated wording self-efficacy items to assess confidence with respect to a specified time interval (e.g., not smoking for a week), when the attainment in question involves a sustained pattern of behavior.

Specificity

Self-efficacy is not a unitary attribute but a class of attributes. That is, self-efficacy will vary within the same individual across domains (e.g., self-efficacy for getting a new job vs. self-efficacy for refraining from smoking) and contexts (e.g., given different amounts of time to prepare a response or acting in familiar vs. strange physical settings). Before attempting to measure self-efficacy in a specific circumstance, that circumstance should be understood and explicated as fully as possible. Is the goal of the specific assessment to understand self-efficacy under relatively broad or relatively narrow conditions?

Specificity and breadth are both desirable aspects of assessment. Typically, one is achieved at the expense of the other and their relative merits will depend on the measurement goal. As a practical matter, little is likely to be gained by operationalizing self-efficacy at either extreme of this continuum. Extremes aside, greater specificity is usually preferable.

One potentially useful approach is to specify the domain of interest (e.g., adherence to a recommendation to avoid dietary saturated fats) and then to consider what types of situational factors might reasonably be expected to influence self-efficacy within that domain. Both Bandura (1997) and Maibach and Murphy (1995) recommended using a variety of methods, including open-ended questionnaires and elicitation interviews as a means of understanding the types of circumstances and performance demands that individuals may face. In thinking about situational influences, the criterion for inclusion should be what is reasonable or likely rather than what is possible. Thus, assessing efficacy under circumstances that pose real-world challenges to the respondent (e.g., eating in a restaurant with a limited menu, being a dinner guest when a high fat meal is served) is likely to be useful. Possible but unlikely scenarios (e.g., having someone offer you $100 to eat a pepperoni pizza) are less likely to correspond to the circumstances the respondent will actually face and, thus, will lower the validity of the assessment procedure.

Measurement Models

The preceding sections have suggested that how self-efficacy is measured should correspond with the reasons for measuring it. Similarly, how the data yielded by measurement processes are treated should correspond with the assumptions underlying measurement procedures. An issue that is often overlooked in self-efficacy assessment is the correspondence between measurement procedures and measurement models. As an example, consider two different measurement strategies. In the first strategy, the purpose of having multiple items is primarily as a way of reducing error that might be associated with each individual item. The items themselves, however, are intended to get at essentially the same information. Three items that all gather similar information about self-efficacy for quitting smoking might be: "I am able to quit smoking successfully," "Giving up cigarettes is something I am able to do," and "I will be successful in my attempts to stop smoking cigarettes." Each asserts the same idea but in a slightly different way. Thus, it can be presumed (and could be empirically tested) that the items are equally sensitive detectors of self-efficacy for quitting smoking. An alternative perspective is to think about different items as tapping different levels of self-efficacy. For example, successive items might ask about confidence to refrain from smoking during a 2-hour movie in a theater, during a 2-hour meal with nonsmokers, and during a 2-hour meal during which all the other diners were smoking. In this case, the items represent a progression of challenges or barriers to the successful attainment of the behavioral goal. The investigator would probably expect the items to reveal different degrees of self-efficacy, in inverse proportion to the difficulty of the situation the item describes. Summing or averaging the items may not be the best means of capturing the information they can provide. Bandura stated a preference for items of the latter type, asserting that "to achieve explanatory and predictive power, measures of personal efficacy must be tailored to domains of functioning *and must represent gradations of task demands within those domains*" (Bandura, 1997, p. 42, emphasis added).

These two strategies for developing self-efficacy items reflect quite different measurement models. The first example corresponds fairly well to classical measurement theory based on an assumption of parallel, equally weighted items. The second is more like a Guttman scale (see Nunnally & Bernstein, 1994, pp. 72–75, for a brief description and discussion of limitations) or instruments based on item response theory (IRT; see Hambleton, Swaminathan, & Rogers, 1991, for a good general introduction). Methods for developing, validating, and reporting scales from these different models are not equivalent. On one hand, self-efficacy at a conceptual level seems well suited to psychometric methods derived from item response theory. That is, it seems reasonable to assume that, within a given domain of self-efficacy, there should exist items that are sensitive to progressively higher levels of the construct. On the other hand, these methods are fairly demanding and require large sample sizes. Nunnally and Bernstein (1994, p. 396), for example, recommended samples of from 200 to 500 for applying IRT, even with very short scales. Treating items that represent progressively higher levels of an attribute as if they all reflected the attribute equivalently introduces its own logical and technical difficulties. Although this issue cannot be resolved here, it is worth considering when choosing how to measure self-efficacy.

Maibach and Murphy (1995) provided several examples of measurement strategies. These usually include a description of a situation or a scenario that establishes the context of the behavior and a response scale. The latter begins with a statement that respondents are to indicate a degree of certainty that they can do each of the things indicated by statements that follow the response option scale. Immediately after this statement is a scale that typically has 11 numerical values (e.g., the numbers 0 through 10) accompanied by three verbal labels: "cannot do at all," "moderately certain can do," and "certain can do" located, respectively under the extreme left, midpoint, and extreme right of the row of numerical values. Maibach and Murphy's examples then list multiple items describing behaviors or behavioral attainments. For each of these, respondents are required to provide a number from the numerical scale, thus indicating their confidence in doing whatever the item states. A hypothetical tool for assessing smoking abstinence, developed on the basis of examples provided by Maibach and Murphy (1995), appears as Table 13.1.

Note that in this example, the behavior (refraining from smoking) has a specified duration (an hour). Also, self-efficacy is assessed in the context of three activities (having a snack, a cup of coffee, or a beer) that may differentially impact self-efficacy. In addition, these behaviors are described as occurring in different settings and social contexts. Thus, the self-efficacy assessments gathered are context specific and the contexts represent different degrees of how difficult it might be to refrain from smoking.

OVERVIEW OF STUDIES EXAMINING SELF-EFFICACY AND HEALTH

As mentioned at the beginning of this chapter, there has been an enormous amount of research in the area of self-efficacy and health and many of these studies have been summarized in detailed reviews that have appeared since 1985 (e.g., Bandura, 1995, 1997; O'Leary, 1985; Schwarzer, 1992; Strecher et al., 1986). Bandura (1997) devoted over 60 pages of his 600-page book to summarizing health functioning in relation to the biological effects of self-efficacy, including pain tolerance and biological markers of distress, the role of self-efficacy in health promoting behavior, and the role of self-efficacy beliefs in recovery from heart attacks. In the same book, he devoted another 40 pages to the health-related topic of athletic functioning and 40 more pages to a chapter that covers anxiety and phobic dysfunctions, depression, eating disorders, and alcohol abuse. Maddux (1995) included chapters on self-efficacy in relation to health behavior (Maddux, Brawley, & Boykin, 1995), physiological stress responses (O'Leary & Brown, 1995), recovery from heart attack (Ewart, 1995), addictive behaviors (DiClemente, Fairhurst, & Piotrowski, 1995), anxiety disorders (Williams, 1995), and depression (Maddux & Meier, 1995).

The overall conclusion emerging from these and other sources is that self-efficacy is an important variable for both health research and health interventions. The results of many

TABLE 13.1
Example of a Hypothetical Self-Efficacy Measure

Below are a series of situations. For each one, please indicate how confident you are that you could **refrain from smoking** for the entire time if you were to face that situation immediately after leaving this session today. Assume that each situation lasts for about one hour. Indicate your certainty by writing a number from 0 to 10 in the space following the description of each situation.

0	1	2	3	4	5	6	7	8	9	10
Cannot do at all					**Moderately certain can do**					**Certain can do**

	Confidence Rating
1. I am at home alone having a snack.	______
2. I am at home alone having a cup of coffee.	______
3. I am at home alone having a beer.	______
4. I am at home with nonsmoking friends having a snack.	______
5. I am at home with nonsmoking friends having a cup of coffee.	______
6. I am at home with nonsmoking friends having a beer.	______
7. I am at home with smoking friends having a snack.	______
8. I am at home with smoking friends having a cup of coffee.	______
9. I am at home with smoking friends having a beer.	______
10. I am at a restaurant with nonsmoking friends having a meal.	______
11. I am at a coffee shop with nonsmoking friends having a cup of coffee.	______
12. I am at a bar with nonsmoking friends having a beer.	______
13. I am at a restaurant with smoking friends having a meal.	______
14. I am at a coffee shop with smoking friends having a cup of coffee.	______
15. I am at a bar with smoking friends having a beer.	______

interventions and cross-sectional studies suggest a link between self-efficacy and the adoption of health promotive and disease preventive behaviors. Bandura's (1992) review of studies on coping with chronic health conditions concluded that the impact of therapeutic interventions on health behavior was at least partly, if not completely, mediated by self-efficacy. He drew the same conclusion when focusing on the personal change efforts among people who want to prevent illness and promote their own health. He viewed self-efficacy as critical at all three stages of health promoting behavior change: the initiation of change, generalized use of the change under different circumstances, and maintenance of the behavior change. More recently, Bandura (1997, pp. 279–313) cited an array of studies suggesting that greater self-efficacy increases the likelihood of initiating actions aimed at improving health, enhances people's responsiveness to health communications urging regulation of health behaviors, augments adherence to habit change programs and other forms of health promoting behavior, and reduces relapse to addictive behaviors.

Self-efficacy has also been shown to influence the extent of recovery following an illness episode and level of functioning among people with chronic illnesses. Ewart (1995) described a line of research focused on recovery following acute myocardial infarction (AMI). He reported that post-AMI men often have inaccurate self-appraisals of their physical capacities, leading to fear and underactivity that impede successful rehabilitation. Ewart found a number of ways to increase patients' self-efficacy for activity, which in turn lead to increased activity. For example, as these people took their treadmill test 3 weeks post-AMI, self-efficacy for physical activity was enhanced by having nurses and physicians provide reassurance and appropriate interpretations of internal bodily sensations. Self-efficacy was also enhanced through enactive mastery, whereby patients first identified the activities they feared and then were guided through those activities in small increments. Vicarious learning was promoted by having participants in the study observe other patients similar to themselves successfully performing the treadmill test. Ewart observed that changes in jogging self-efficacy following the treadmill test were more predictive of activity level over the following week than was actual biological condition. He further noted that "self-efficacy appraisals are superior to functional exercise evaluation in predicting adherence to rehabilitative exercise regimens" (p. 208). He also found that people can have self-efficacy that is too high. Of those people in the top one third of the distribution on jogging self-efficacy, 57% were exercising beyond the recommended regimen and were therefore endangering their lives.

Another intervention based on self-efficacy and aimed at people with chronic illness was referred to at the beginning of this chapter: Lorig's Arthritis Self-Management Program (Lorig & Gonzalez, 1992). The goal of this group intervention is to improve the self-management and coping skills of people who have arthritis. The group leaders, many of whom have arthritis themselves, help participants set reasonable and achievable goals for behavior change. Goals are broken into small steps and participants are allowed to undertake only those behaviors for which their self-efficacy exceeds 70, on a scale with 0 being totally inefficacious and 100 being totally efficacious. In this way, participants are guaranteed success in enacting the behavior. The program capitalizes on modeling, furthermore, by having people who are coping well with arthritis as group leaders. Participants can also look to other group members for positive coping models. Verbal persuasion efforts by the group leader and other group members are also an important source of efficacy information in these groups. Finally, the group leaders help participants to examine and reinterpret the attributions they are making for their physical symptoms. For example, they are taught that some of the fatigue they attribute to their illness is, in fact, attributable to a lack of activity and that the remedy for fatigue is not inactivity.

Although self-efficacy can affect health outcomes via its influence on health behavior, it may also contribute to improved health in other ways. Bandura (1997, pp. 262–279) described correlational and experimental studies, suggesting that high self-efficacy mitigates psychological states such as stress that increase susceptibility to disease, dampens autonomic arousal in the presence of feared stimuli, correlates with alterations in catecholamine activation over the course of phobics' mastery of feared stimuli, reduces the production of opioids in response to pain (presumably, by attenuating the psychological distress resulting from the pain), and predicts greater pain tolerance following pain management training.

In a recent study, Benight et al. (1997) investigated the possibility that coping self-efficacy would buffer psychological and physiological disturbances in HIV-infected men following a natural disaster (Hurricane Andrew in Florida). A total of 36 HIV-positive men were assessed 6 months after the hurricane. Their psychological and physical status was compared to that of an age equivalent group of healthy men who had similar exposure to the natural disaster. They found that greater levels of self-efficacy for coping with the demands of hurricane recovery were related to less emotional distress and less posttraumatic stress disorder in both groups of men. Among the men who were HIV-positive, higher levels of coping self-efficacy were associated with better physiological responses as measured by lower norepinephrine to cortisol ratios (NE/C).

Wiedenfeld et al. (1990) examined the immune system impact of experimentally manipulated perceived self-efficacy to control a stressor. People with severe snake phobia were assessed during three phases of mastery development: baseline, an efficacy acquisition phase (during which they gained an increasing sense of coping efficacy through guided mastery), and a maximal efficacy phase. Participants who acquired coping skills more rapidly during the second phase showed immunoenhancement, whereas the small subset of people who acquired a sense of coping self-efficacy more slowly during the second phase showed immunosupression. The authors concluded from this study that the development of skills to manage stress can enhance immunologic functioning.

It is an oversimplification, however, to characterize various biological processes as consistently health conducive or health disruptive. Heightened activity of the immune system, for example, may be a good thing or a bad thing, depending on the specific circumstances an individual confronts. Nonetheless, it is fair to say that the biological changes and states associated with greater self-efficacy often appear to be beneficial.

It would be inaccurate to suggest that all studies examining self-efficacy confirm its importance for understanding health and health behavior. One recent article, for example, found that self-efficacy did not mediate the effects of modeling on the ability to endure pain (Symbaluk, Heth, Cameron, & Pierce, 1997). Furthermore, subtleties and complexities underlying the operation of efficacy beliefs continue to emerge. Zautra, Hoffman, and Reich (1997) reported, for example, that efficacy beliefs for making positive events happen and for coping with negative events operate independently. Also, as noted earlier, it is possible for self-efficacy to encourage unhealthy behaviors, such as exercising too much during the recovery phase of an illness (Ewart, 1995). It is not difficult to imagine other circumstances where a high sense of self-efficacy for completing a risky behavior, such as handling venomous snakes, could compromise a person's well-being.

CONCLUSIONS

The bulk of evidence clearly establishes self-efficacy as a preeminent concept worthy of the theoretical and empirical attention it has received. Several characteristics of the construct justify this conclusion. First, it has emerged from a rich theoretical context. Thus, its similarities to and differences from other constructs can be more clearly understood. Its role in a cascade of events culminating in a specific behavior can also be more clearly understood because of its strong linkages to theory. Second, self-efficacy has undergone extensive empirical scrutiny. There are multiple examples of investigations intended to clarify the nature of the construct as well as reports demonstrating its utility in applied contexts. These latter studies also reveal a third important characteristic of self-efficacy: Unlike some other theoretically related constructs, such as locus of control, self-efficacy provides an excellent basis not only for understanding but also for devising interventions to change health-related behaviors. A fourth, related, characteristic contributing to the importance of self-efficacy is its specificity. As the vignette at the opening of this chapter illustrated, the specificity of self-efficacy perceptions enables manageable intermediate goals to be established, further enhancing its utility to interveners. Finally, although its specificity mitigates against a single, universally accepted measure of self-efficacy, researchers and practitioners have found it relatively easy to devise methods of assessing the construct in ways that appear satisfactory.

Despite its clear utility, self-efficacy should not be expected to do everything. The proportion of variance in health behavior not explained by self-efficacy will often be considerable. Although the effects of some other constructs in health psychology on health behavior will be mediated by self-efficacy, others will not. Suggestions that self-efficacy fully captures the effects of outcome expectations, for example, seem forced. Broadening the definition of self-efficacy to subsume other constructs seems to contradict its inherent specificity, one of its most attractive features. These issues notwithstanding, self-efficacy remains a concept that will continue to find widespread utility in health psychology.

REFERENCES

Bandura, A. (1977a). Self-efficacy: Toward a unifying theory of behavioral change. *Psychological Review, 84,* 191–215.

Bandura, A. (1977b). *Social learning theory.* Englewood Cliffs, NJ: Prentice-Hall.

Bandura, A. (1986). *Social foundations of thought and action: A social cognitive approach.* Englewood Cliffs, NJ: Prentice-Hall.

Bandura, A. (1992). Exercise of personal agency through the self-efficacy mechanism, In R. Schwarzer (Ed.), *Self-efficacy: Thought control of action* (pp. 3–38). Washington, DC: Hemisphere.

Bandura, A. (1995a). On rectifying conceptual ecumenism. In J. E. Maddux (Ed.), *self-efficacy, adaptation, and adjustment: Theory, research, and application* (pp. 347–375). New York: Plenum.

Bandura, A. (1995b). *Self-efficacy in changing societies.* USA: Cambridge University Press.

Bandura, A. (1997). *Self-efficacy: The exercise of control.* New York: Freeman.

Barone, D. F., Maddux, J. E., & Snyder, C. R. (1997). *Social cognitive psychology.* New York: Plenum.

Benight, C. C., Antoni, M. H., Kilbourn, K., Ironson, G., Kumar, M. A., Fletcher, M. A., Redwine, L., Baum, A., & Schneiderman, N. (1997). Coping self-efficacy buffers psychological and physiological disturbances in HIV-infected men following a natural disaster. *Health Psychology, 16,* 248–255.

Blascovich, J., & Tomaka, J. (1991). Measures of self-esteem. In J. R. Robinson, P. R. Shaver, & L. S. Wrightsman (Eds.), *Measures of personality and social psychological attitudes* (pp. 115–160). San Diego: Academic Press.

DeVellis, R. F. (1991). *Scale development: Theory and applications.* Newbury Park, CA: Sage.

DiClemente, C. C., Fairhurst, S. K., & Piotrowski, N. A. (1995). Self-efficacy and addictive behaviors. In J. E. Maddux (Ed.), *Self-efficacy, adaptation, and adjustment: Theory, research and application* (pp. 109–141). New York: Plenum.

Ewart, C. K. (1991). Social action theory for a public health psychology. *American Psychologist, 46,* 931–946.

Ewart, C. K. (1995). Self-efficacy and recovery from heart attack: Implications for a social cognitive analysis of exercise and emotion. In J. E. Maddux (Ed.), *Self-efficacy, adaptation, and adjustment: Theory, research and application* (pp. 203–226). New York: Plenum.

Hambleton, R. K., Swaminathan, H., & Rogers, H. J. (1991). *Fundamentals of item response theory.* Newbury Park, CA: Sage.

Lazarus, R. S., & Folkman, S. (1984). *Stress, appraisal, and coping.* New York: Springer.

Lorig, K., & Gonzalez, V. (1992). The integration of theory with practice: A 12–year case study. *Health Education Quarterly, 19,* 355–368.

Maddux, J. E. (1995). *Self-efficacy, adaptation, and adjustment: Theory, research and application.* New York: Plenum.

Maddux, J. E., Brawley, L., & Boykin, A. (1995). Self-efficacy and healthy behavior: Prevention, promotion, and detection. In J. E. Maddux (Ed.), *Self-efficacy, adaptation, and adjustment: Theory, research and application* (pp. 173–202). New York: Plenum.

Maddux, J. E., & Meier, L. J. (1995). Self-efficacy and depression. In J. E. Maddux (Ed.), *Self-efficacy, adaptation, and adjustment: Theory, research and application* (pp. 143–169). New York: Plenum.

Maibach, E., & Murphy, D. A. (1995). Self-efficacy in health promotion research and practice: Conceptualization and measurement. *Health Education Research, 10,* 37–50.

Miller, S. M., & Diefenbach, M. A. (1998). The Cognitive-Social Health Information Processing (C-SHIP) Model: A theoretical framework for research in behavioral oncology. In D. S. Krantz & A. Baum (Eds.), *Technology and methods in behavioral medicine* (pp. 219–244). Mahwah, NJ: Lawrence Erlbaum Associates.

Montano, D. E., Kasprzyk, D., & Taplin, S. H. (1997). The theory of reasoned action and theory of planned behavior. In K. Glanz, F. M. Lewis, & B. K. Rimer (Eds.), *Health behavior and health education: Theory, research, and practice* (pp. 85–112). San Francisco: Jossey-Bass.

Nunnally, J. C., & Bernstein, I. H. (1994). *Psychometric theory* (3rd ed.). New York: McGraw-Hill.

O'Leary, A. (1985). Self-efficacy and health. *British Research in Therapy, 23,* 437–451.

O'Leary, A., & Brown, S. (1995). Self-efficacy and the physiological stress response. In J. E. Maddux (Ed.), *Self- efficacy, adaptation, and adjustment: Theory, research and application* (pp. 227–246). New York: Plenum.

Rotter, J. B. (1954). *Social learning theory and clinical psychology.* Englewood Cliffs, NJ: Prentice-Hall.

Schwarzer, R. (1992). Self-efficacy in the adoption and maintenance of health behaviors: Theoretical approaches and a new model. In R. Schwarzer (Ed.), *Self-efficacy: Thought control and action* (pp. 217–243). Washington, DC: Hemisphere.

Schwarzer, R., & Fuchs, R. (1995). Changing risk behaviors and adopting health behaviors: The role of self-efficacy. In A Bandura (Ed.), *Self-efficacy in changing societies* (pp. 259–288). USA: Cambridge University Press.

Strecher, V., DeVellis, B., Becker, M., & Rosenstock, R. (1986). The role of self-efficacy in achieving health behavior change. *Health Education Quarterly, 13,* 73–92.

Strecher, V., & Rosenstock, R. (1997). The Health Belief Model. In K. Glanz, F. M. Lewis, & B. K. Rimer (Eds.) *Health behavior and health education: Theory, research, and practice* (pp. 41–59). San Francisco: Jossey-Bass.

Symbaluk, D. G., Heth, C. D., Cameron, J., & Pierce, W. D. (1997). Social modeling, monetary incentives, and pain endurance: The role of self-efficacy and pain perception. *Personality and Social Psychology Bulletin, 23,* 258–269.

Wallston, B. S., Wallston, K. A., Kaplan, G. D., & Maides, S. A. (1976). Development and validation of the health locus of control (HLC) scale. *Journal of Consulting and Clinical and Clinical Psychology, 44,* 580–585.

Wallston, K. A., Wallston, B. S., & DeVellis, R. F. (1978). Development of the Multidimensional Health Locus of Control (MHLC) Scales. *Health Education Monographs, 6,* 161–170.

Wiedenfeld, S. A., O'Leary, A., Bandura, A., Brown, S., Levine, S., & Raska, K. (1990). Impact of perceived self-efficacy in coping with stressors on components of the immune system. *Journal of Personality and Social Psychology, 59,* 1082–1094.

Williams, S. L. (1995). Self-efficacy and anxiety and phobic disorders. In J. E. Maddux (Ed.), *Self-efficacy, adaptation, and adjustment: Theory, research and application* (pp. 69–107). New York: Plenum.

Woodward, W. R. (1982). The "discovery" of social behaviorism and social learning theory, 1870–1980. *American Psychologist, 37,* 396–410.

Zautra, A. J., Hoffman, J., & Reich, J. W. (1997). The role of two kinds of efficacy beliefs in maintaining the well-being of chronically stressed older adults. In B. Gottlieb (Ed.), *Coping with chronic stress* (pp. 269–290). New York: Plenum Press.

14

The Psychobiology of Nicotine Self-Administration

Neil E. Grunberg

Martha M. Faraday

Matthew A. Rahman

Uniformed Services University of the Health Sciences

Knowledge and perceptions of cigarette smoking and tobacco use have changed dramatically since health psychology began (i.e., over the past 25 to 50 years). A short half century ago, tobacco use was considered to be a behavior of choice and was commonplace in society. Most men smoked in public, some women smoked in public, and more women smoked in private. In the middle of this century, smoking was not considered by the general public to be a health hazard and was touted by tobacco companies and celebrities as an enhancer of good health. By the mid 1970s, the health care community's attitudes toward tobacco use had turned negative, but tobacco use still was common among men, was increasing among women, and was erroneously viewed by the public and by many health care professionals as a matter of free choice. During the last quarter of this century, the story of tobacco use has undergone a Dr. Jekyll to Mr. Hyde transformation. It has gone from the standard behavior of gentlemen and some ladies to the monstrosity of a shunned suicidal behavior that pollutes the environment and everyone near the smoker. Since the 1970s, it has become unquestionably clear that the behavior of tobacco use is the single greatest cause of death and illness in the world. Tobacco use results in cardiovascular diseases, many cancers, chronic obstructive lung diseases, increased morbidity, and immunosuppression. Since the 1980s, it has become well-known that tobacco use involves addiction to nicotine, that the use and abuse of tobacco also is a result of behavioral and biological actions of nicotine in addition to nicotine dependence per se, and that psychological and situational variables become associated with tobacco use and thereby contribute to the use and abuse of deadly tobacco products.

This chapter discusses those psychobiologic phenomena that are central to why people smoke and why it is so difficult to quit. The psychobiology of nicotine self-administration includes behaviors (e.g., self-administering nicotine) that are directly relevant to tobacco use; psychological and behavioral effects of nicotine that contribute to tobacco use (e.g., euphoria, mood regulation, attentional effects; changes in eating behavior and appetite); psychological phenomena that come to elicit nicotinelike effects (e.g., classical conditioning, operant conditioning, paired associations); and psychological consequences of nicotine abstinence (craving, increased appetite and feeding, irritability, sleep disturbances). As such, this chapter in the tobacco story is the domain of psychologists who are interested in behaviors that affect health and psychologists who study interactions of psychology and biology as they relate to health.

The first section presents evidence that humans and animals self-administer nicotine. The second section explains that nicotine self-administration is established by principles of reinforcement. The third section reviews effects of nicotine on the body that are believed to underlie the euphoric and dependence effects of nicotine. The fourth section explains how several principles of learning theory interact with pharmacologic actions of nicotine to cement the addictive behavior. The fifth section reviews additional psychobiologic effects of nicotine that reinforce nicotine self-administration and that may help to explain individual differences in tobacco use. The sixth and final section discusses clinical implications of these findings and future directions for research regarding the psychobiology of nicotine self-administration.

HUMANS AND ANIMALS SELF-ADMINISTER NICOTINE

The most basic evidence for drug addiction is self-administration of the drug. With regard to nicotine, it is clear that humans and animals self-administer nicotine. The fact that people smoke cigarettes and use other tobacco products (e.g., cigars, chewing tobacco, snuff) is consistent with the interpretation that nicotine is the substance that exerts addictive and psychobiologic effects that maintain self-administration, but these behaviors do not necessarily mean that nicotine per se exerts these effects. In fact, tobacco contains roughly 500 chemicals and tobacco smoke contains roughly 4,000 chemicals in addition to nicotine (Dube & Green, 1982). Therefore, careful empirical studies have been conducted to determine that nicotine per se is self-administered. These studies include investigations with human and animal subjects. The advantage of human subjects is that they offer face valid evidence that humans indeed self-administer nicotine. The advantage of animal subjects is that investigators can isolate variables to focus on nicotine without the potential confound of attitudes, opinions, beliefs, biases, and so on. The additional advantage of animal investigations is that true experiments can be conducted (i.e., random assignment and manipulation of treatment groups; something that is unethical to do with addictive drugs in human subjects and with minors). Another advantage of animal investigations is that invasive analyses are possible, including brain dissection and neurochemical and molecular biologic assays of specific brain regions.

There are several types of human nicotine self-administration studies (Ashton & Watson, 1970; Deneau & Inoki, 1967; Goldberg & Henningfield, 1988; Goldfarb, Jarvik, & Glick, 1970; Henningfield, 1984; Henningfield & Goldberg, 1983, 1988; Henningfield, Miyasato, & Jasinski, 1983; Henningfield, Yingling, Griffiths, & Pickens, 1980; Jarvik, Glick, & Nakamura, 1970; Pomerleau, Fertig, & Shanhan, 1983; Russell, Wilson, Patel, Feyerabend, & Cole, 1975; Schachter, 1978; Schachter, Kozlowski, & Silverstein, 1977; Schachter, Silverstein, & Perlick, 1977):

1. Studies of humans smoking cigarettes in laboratory settings in which the smoking topography (e.g., number of cigarettes, number of puffs per cigarettes) and the nicotine yield of the cigarettes (i.e., based on published data) are used to determine the extent to which nicotine was self-administered and the extent to which that self-administration reflects nicotine titration.
2. Studies of humans smoking cigarettes in natural settings in which the smoking topography is measured but the cigarettes have a manipulated amount of nicotine and the manipulated amount changes between groups or over time.
3. Studies of humans smoking cigarettes in laboratory settings with commercially available cigarettes in which the smoking behavior and topography is carefully observed and the nicotine yield is used to determine nicotine self-administration.
4. Human studies in laboratory settings where the smoking is measured by a machine (e.g., subjects smoke on a cigarette that is connected to a machine that measures number of puffs, duration of puff, interpuff interval, depth of inhalation) and the nicotine yield is known or manipulated.
5. Human studies in laboratory settings where smoking behavior is carefully measured, nicotine yield of cigarettes is known, and additional nicotine is administered (e.g., by intravenous infusion, oral ingestion, transdermal administration) to determine how nicotine self-administration and smoking are affected by nicotine administration via a separate source.
6. Human studies in laboratory settings where smoking behavior is carefully measured, nicotine yield of cigarettes is known, and nicotine excretion from the body is manipulated (e.g., by manipulation of urinary pH) to determine how nicotine self-administration and smoking are affected by nicotine availability.
7. Human studies in laboratory settings in which nicotine is self-administered intravenously.

There also are several types of animal laboratory studies of nicotine self-administration (Clarke & Kumar, 1984; Corrigall & Coen, 1989, 1991; Cox, Goldstein, & Nelson, 1984; Donny, Caggiula, Knopf, & Brown, 1995; Glick, Visker, & Maisonneuve, 1996; S. R. Goldberg, Spealman, & D. M. Goldberg, 1981; Hanson, Ivester, & Morton, 1979; Rose & Corrigall, 1997; Shoaib, Schindler, & S. R. Goldberg, 1997; Yanagita, Ando, Kato, & Takado, 1983): intravenous nicotine self-administration, intracranial nicotine self-administration, and inhalation of tobacco smoke.

The research has revealed that humans and animals self-administer nicotine, humans and animals titrate nicotine self-administration (i.e., the more nicotine is available in the body, the less is self-administered; the less the nicotine that is available in the body, the more is self-administered), and humans and animals increase nicotine self-administration over time demonstrating tolerance to this drug.

All of these studies indicate that nicotine is self-administered, but they do not reveal the underlying psychobiological mechanisms. To uncover these mechanisms, it is relevant to consider basic principles of reinforcement.

NICOTINE SELF-ADMINISTRATION IS ESTABLISHED BY POSITIVE AND NEGATIVE REINFORCEMENT

Humans and animals self-administer nicotine as a result of the consequences of this behavior following well-established principles of psychology (Hull, 1943; Skinner, 1938; Thorndike, 1911; Watson, 1924). *Reinforcement* occurs because nicotine has effects that result in continued and increased self-administration of nicotine. *Positive reinforcement* operates in that nicotine results in specific effects that are found to be desirable and thereby maintain and increase nicotine self-administration. These positive reinforcing actions include specific neurochemical changes that result in the following: euphoria, neuroendocrine changes that modulate reward and regulate physiologic processes, control of appetite and body weight, alterations in attentional processes, and psychosocial rewards (e.g., imitation of role models, acceptance of peers, etc.). *Negative reinforcement* operates in that nicotine offsets specific actions that are found to be undesirable and thereby maintain and increase nicotine self-administration. These negative reinforcing effects of nicotine self-administration include offsetting the unpleasantness of classic withdrawal symptoms (e.g., craving, irritability) as a result of nicotine abstinence and offsetting other undesired effects of nicotine abstinence (e.g., body weight gain, attentional difficulties, sleep disturbances). The psychobiologic reinforcing effects of nicotine that contribute to nicotine self-administration are discussed in the next three sections of this chapter.

NICOTINE'S CENTRAL NERVOUS SYSTEM (CNS) ACTIONS PRODUCE EUPHORIA AND DEPENDENCE

Tobacco smoking is a means to self-administer the addictive drug, nicotine. Similar to other addictive drug-taking behaviors, tobacco use is characterized primarily by highly controlled or compulsive use, psychoactive effects, and drug-reinforced behavior. In addition, addiction consists of stereotypic patterns of substance use, use despite harmful effects, relapse following abstinence, and recurrent drug cravings. Addicted individuals also may experience tolerance (i.e., over time the dosage necessary to obtain a desired effect increases), physical dependence (i.e., the substance is necessary in order for normal physiological functioning to occur), and euphoriant drug effects (U.S. Department of Health and Human Services, USDHHS, 1988). Addiction to nicotine is a process that occurs over time and requires the individual to initiate and maintain self-administration. Reasons for initiating and maintaining nicotine self-administration via tobacco product use include biological actions of the drug as well as psychological and behavioral drug actions. This section reviews the biological mechanisms and neurobiological underpinnings of nicotine addiction.

Nicotinic Cholinergic Receptors

The self-administration of nicotine via puffs on a tobacco containing product results in nicotine entering the body and reaching the brain within 15 seconds (USDHHS, 1988). Once in the body, nicotine has a half-life of about 2 hours. The drug acts throughout the body at nicotinic cholinergic receptors (nAChRs) at muscle end plates and in autonomic ganglia, and in the brain at nAChRs that regulate and modulate many neurotransmitter and neuroendocrine systems. It is thought that nAChRs in the brain are primarily responsible for biologic rewarding effects of nicotine (Balfour, 1994; Kellar, Schwartz, & Martino, 1987). Stimulation of nAChRs in the lung or at other peripheral cites also may contribute to rewarding effects of nicotine (Ginzel, 1987; Ginzel & Lucas, 1980).

The nAChRs all are similar in basic physical structure. They consist of five subunits arranged in a circle to form a channel. When an appropriate agonist binds to the receptor, the channel opens and allows the flow of positively charged ions (e.g., Ca^{2+} or Na^{+} or other cations, depending on the receptor subtype). The five subunits consist of different types. The α-subunits (ranging from α2 to α9) contain sites where agonists (i.e., acetylcholine, nicotine) bind. The β subunits (β2 to β4) are believed to be primarily structural in function. These nAChRs are distributed presynaptically in certain regions of the brain, including the ventral tegmental area (VTA), nucleus accumbens (Nacc), medial habenula, interpenduncular nucleus, hypothalamus, and hippocampus.

There are several subgroups of nAChRs that differ in structure, binding affinity for nicotine, and function. The subgroups are defined according to subunit composition. Most binding sites in the mammalian brain consist of the $(\alpha 4)_3(\beta 2)_2$ nAChR subset (Lindstrom, Anand, Peng, & Gerzanich, 1995). These receptors are found presynaptically and modulate neurotransmitter release (Lindstrom et al., 1995; Nakayama, Okuda, & Nakashima, 1994). A small percentage of brain nAChRs are composed in part of α7 and α8 subunits. This subset of nAChRs appears to act as agonist-gated ion channels that allow calcium to enter the cell and initiate various second messenger cascades (Lindstrom et al., 1995). The function of many of these combinations is not yet known.

The fact that nicotine's effects in humans and animals on a variety of psychological states and behaviors vary with individuals and environments may be partially explained by the fact that each subunit combination results in a distinct pattern of sensitivity to nicotinic agonists. This structural and functional diversity allows nAChRs to mediate different effects in different tissues, with nicotine sometimes enhancing activity and sometimes antagonizing activity (Nakayama et al., 1994). In addition, studies in mice of different genotypes indicate that nAChR densities may underlie the extent to which nicotine exerts behavioral effects (Collins, Miner, & Marks, 1988; Marks, Romm, Campbell, & Collins, 1989; Marks, Romm, Gaffney, & Collins, 1986). As Balfour (1994) wrote, "Each smoker probably uses tobacco in a way which maximizes the properties that he/she finds most rewarding. These may reflect both stimulation and desensitization of the heterogenous population of nicotinic receptors now known to be present in the brain" (p. 1422).

Nicotine's Effects on Neurotransmitter Systems

Via actions at presynaptic $(\alpha4)_3(\beta2)_2$ nAChRs, nicotine alters activity of many different neurotransmitter systems, including those of dopamine, norepinephrine, endogenous opioids, and serotonin. Most of the work done on mechanisms underlying nicotine addiction has focused on the dopaminergic system (Corrigall, 1991) because enhancement of dopamine neurotransmission in specific brain areas is believed to be fundamental to drug reward or euphoriant effects (Di Chiara, Acquas, Tanda, & Cadoni, 1993; Koob, 1992; Nestler, 1992), including effects of cocaine, heroin, amphetamines, and alcohol. In addition, cellular and molecular changes that occur in these brain areas as a result of repeated drug self-administration may contribute to drug dependence and addiction (Balfour, 1994; Koob & Bloom, 1988; Koob & Swerdlow, 1988). Regions of the brain that mediate reward effects are phylogenetically old and respond to natural stimuli, addictive drugs, and electrical stimulation. The natural stimuli that evoke dopamine release by neurons that originate in the VTA and terminate in the NAcc are associated with behaviors essential to the survival of the individual and the species such as feeding, sexual behavior, birth, care of offspring, and some social behaviors (e.g., mutual grooming) (Salamone, 1994).

Tolerance to nicotine's effects is, in part, mediated by increased numbers of nAChRs (Lindstrom et al., 1995) and also depends on cellular changes in the mesolimbic dopamine system that occur with repeated nicotine self-administration (Flores, Rogers, Pabreza, Wolfe, & Kellar, 1992). These changes are similar to those that occur in response to other drugs of abuse and may include increased synthesis of the enzyme tyrosine hydroxylase (the rate-limiting step in dopamine manufacture), increased rates of spontaneous firing activity in VTA neurons, and changes in the structure of cell bodies, dendrites, and axons (Balfour, 1994; Beitner-Johnson, Guitart, & Nestler, 1992; Gold & Miller, 1992; Koob & Bloom, 1988; Nestler, 1992; Ritz & Kuhar, 1993; Rosecrans & Karan, 1993). In the NAcc, chronic addictive drug use alters G-protein levels and second messenger cascades, biochemicals that control rates of neurotransmitter synthesis and release. These neuronal-level changes reflect the fact the mesolimbic dopaminergic neurons adjust to the repeated presence of nicotine in a compensatory way by developing tolerance. Normal physiologic functioning now occurs in the presence of the drug (i.e., "physical dependence"). However, once the drug is removed (e.g., by overnight abstinence from smoking or by abrupt smoking cessation), dopamine release in the NAcc virtually disappears and the individual experiences unpleasant withdrawal symptoms. It is important to note that classical drug reward effects from nicotine are a short-lived phenomenon. In the tolerant human or animal, nicotine is necessary to maintain normal functioning and to prevent withdrawal. Subjective reward effects per se largely disappear with chronic nicotine administration.

Nicotine also affects the production and release of the endogenous opioid peptides beta-endorphin and enkephalins (Bacher, Wang, & Hollt, 1995; USDHHS, 1988). Some of nicotine's early reward effects may be regulated through these systems. In addition, these systems also may regulate nicotine's long-term maintenance effects (Bozarth, 1994; Corrigall, 1991).

Serotonin, which is implicated in the addiction process of other drugs of abuse (Grunberg, 1994), is also released by nicotine administration (USDHHS, 1988). The nAChRs have been found on a wide variety of presynaptic serotonin neurons located in sites at which nicotine has been shown to have an effect (Rosecrans & Karan, 1993; Yu & Weckler, 1994). Specifically, the serotonin receptor subtype $5HT_3$ seems to be a principal player in this process, and may play a role in nicotine's effects on mood (Carmody, 1993; Kaplan, Sadock, & Grebb, 1994; Ribeiro, Bettiker, Bogdanov, & Wurtman, 1993), attentional processes (Carmody, 1993), and modulation of the dopamine reward process (Di Chiara et al., 1993; Montgomery, Rose, & Herberg, 1993). These actions may contribute to nicotine addiction. Upon nicotine abstinence (e.g., when quitting smoking), changes in serotonin levels may alter mood and attentional processes in ways that the individual finds aversive. For example, these altered serotonin levels may be manifested as depressed or anxious mood and inability to focus attention—commonly reported sequelae of smoking cessation. The individual's desire to alleviate these unpleasant symptoms may motivate the individual to resume smoking.

Norepinephrine (NE) also is released by nicotine (USDHHS, 1988). In addition, nicotine administration increases the activity of tyrosine hydroxylase, the rate-limiting step in NE formation, principally in the locus coeruleus (Mitchell, Smith, Joseph, & Gray, 1992). NE in the locus coeruleus functions to focus attention (Hodges et al., 1992). NE also interacts with serotonin in mood disorders (Kaplan et al., 1994). Some of nicotine's addictive characteristics may be mediated by interactions of the NE system with other biochemical systems as well (Mitchell et al., 1992).

Nicotine's Effects on Neuroendocrine Systems

Nicotine affects the hypothalamic-pituitary-adrenal axis (Stolerman, 1991; USDHHS, 1988). Increased levels of prolactin, corticotropin-releasing hormone, the pro-opiomelanocortin group of hormones (beta-endorphin, beta-lipoprotein, melanocyte-stimulating hormone), adrenocorticotropin hormone, growth hormone, vasopressin, and neurophysin I have been found after acute and chronic administration of nicotine in humans and animals. Nicotine also directly stimulates the release of corticosteroids from the adrenal cortex by direct activation of nAChRs on autonomic ganglia terminating on the adrenal glands. Nicotine also affects levels of plasma and hypothalamic insulin. All of these hormones play important regulatory roles throughout the body and brain and may interact with neurotransmitter systems in the addiction process of nicotine.

CLASSICAL CONDITIONING, OPERANT CONDITIONING, AND PAIRED ASSOCIATIONS ALL CONTRIBUTE TO NICOTINE SELF-ADMINISTRATION

The powerful effects of nicotine to control behavior are evident in nicotine self-administration and the central effects of this extraordinary drug. Yet, this information does not completely capture the full extent of the hold that nicotine-containing products have on the nicotine addict. In addition to nicotine's direct effects to develop drug dependence and self-administration, nicotine self-administration is accompanied by psychological phenomena that reinforce the effects of the drug by becoming intertwined with the direct pharmacologic actions of nicotine. As a result, psychological, behavioral, and environmental conditions that become associated with nicotine self-administration come to elicit the same biological actions of nicotine itself. This result makes treatment of nicotine addiction even more complex and mandates the incorporation of psychological as well as pharmacologic strategies to treatment.

The major psychological phenomena that become associated with nicotine self-administration operate through classical conditioning, operant conditioning, and paired associations. *Classical,* or *Pavlovian, conditioning* refers to the phenomenon in which stimuli that initially do not elicit a given response (neutral stimuli, NS) eventually come to elicit those responses (conditional or conditioned responses, CR) when paired repeatedly with a stimulus that normally elicits the given response (the unconditional or unconditioned stimulus, US). In Pavlov's classic studies of digestive physiology in dogs, a tone (NS) was repeatedly paired with food (US) until eventually the presentation of the tone alone (now a conditional or conditioned stimulus, CS) resulted in salivation (CR; Pavlov, 1927). *Operant* or *instrumental* or *Skinnerian conditioning* refers to the phenomenon by which consequences of a behavior come to increase or decrease the likelihood of that behavior (Skinner, 1938; Watson, 1924). For example, a given behavior or stimulus that is followed by the provision of food (particularly to a food-deprived subject) is rewarded. A behavior or stimulus that is followed by an electric shock is punished. *Paired associationism* was a concept studied by Gestaltist psychologists that referred to the phenomenon by which stimuli "associated" in time or in space (e.g., experienced close together chronologically or spatially) come to be psychologically joined and bound together (Koffka, 1935; Köhler, 1929). For example, the co-occurrence of visual stimuli near each other results in a perception and memory of these stimuli "together."

All three psychological principles operate to reinforce and strengthen nicotine self-administration by binding together a wide range of stimuli and consequences of tobacco use with biologic actions of nicotine. In the case of nicotine self-administration, environmental (e.g., a bar, the sight of an ashtray or cigarette), psychological (e.g., stress, anxiety, dysphoria), situational (e.g., on a break, when resting, when partying), and social (e.g., with friends) variables and stimuli can become conditioned stimuli that come to elicit the same biologically based responses as does nicotine itself. As a result of conditioning to tobacco use cues, efforts to abstain from nicotine become increasingly difficult as these psychological principles of learning continue to elicit positive and negative nicotine-related effects. These psychological effects help to explain why treatment of nicotine dependence only with nicotine replacement products (e.g., nicotine gum, patch, nasal spray) is not as effective as many people expect when they know that nicotine is an addictive drug. Actually, it is the fact that nicotine is a powerful and addictive drug with powerful biological and psychological effects that increases the likelihood that psychological conditioning occurs. Treatment of nicotine dependence must include ways to offset and extinguish the conditioning effects of nicotine and that requires psychological and behavioral strategies.

OTHER PSYCHOLOGICAL AND BEHAVIORAL EFFECTS OF NICOTINE CONTRIBUTE TO NICOTINE SELF-ADMINISTRATION

In addition to nicotine's "classic" addictive properties, the drug's effects to alter many psychological states and behaviors contribute significantly to its self-administration and to individual differences in reported effects of nicotine-containing products. The multiplicity of these effects is reflected by the variety of reasons people report for smoking: to control appetite and reduce body weight; to alter attentional processes; to manage negative moods such as anxiety, depression, and feelings of hostility; to relax; to relieve boredom; and to alleviate and cope with stress (USDHHS, 1988). Research on these consequences of smoking indicates that nicotine is the agent exerting these effects. In addition, these effects have been demonstrated in experimental settings with human and animal subjects.

In addition, failure to maintain successful cessation is related to unwanted alterations in psychological states and behaviors that occur apart from feelings of craving nicotine. Specifically, individuals report relapsing because of body weight gain; alterations in attention; feelings of anxiety, depression, and irritability; and inability to cope with stress (Hughes, Higgins, & Hatsukami, 1990; Shiffman, 1979, 1982, 1985, 1986; Shiffman & Jarvik, 1976; USDHHS, 1988). Many of these effects also have been demonstrated in animals. The following sections review key work regarding effects of nicotine and effects of nicotine cessation on appetite control and body weight regulation, alterations in attentional processes, and interactions with stress. In addition, these sections highlight the role of individual differences such as gender and genotype in these effects. These sections include a more detailed review of specific empirical findings because these psychobiologic effects of nicotine that contribute to nicotine self-administration currently are receiving active research attention and because these psychobiologic effects illustrate complex multivariate interactions among genotype, gender, environment, physiology, behavior, and cognition.

Appetite Control and Body Weight Regulation

For hundreds of years people have known that tobacco smoking reduces body weight, with the average smoker weighing approximately 7 pounds less than the average nonsmoker (USDHHS, 1988). Many smokers, especially adult women and adolescent girls, cite smoking's appetite and body weight-controlling effects as major reasons for initiating and continuing to smoke, despite the well-publicized health hazards, and report unwanted weight gain after cessation as a reason for relapse to smoking (Grunberg, Winders, & Wewers, 1991; R. C. Klesges, Elliot, & Robinson, 1997; R. C. Klesges & L. M. Klesges, 1988; R. C. Klesges, Meyers, L. M. Klesges, & La Vasque, 1989). Animal studies indicate that these effects are the result of nicotine and that cessation from nicotine results in increased weight gain (e.g., Grunberg, 1982, 1986). Further, there are sex differences in these effects with female humans and rats exhibiting greater weight changes as a result of nicotine administration than males, and greater weight rebounds in cessation than males (Grunberg, Bowen, & Morse, 1984; Grunberg et al., 1991; Grunberg, Popp, & Winders, 1988; Grunberg, Winders, & Popp, 1987). The underlying mechanisms for effects of nicotine and of nicotine cessation on body weight are related to alterations in food consumption, activity level, and metabolism. Of these three processes, food consumption exerts the greatest influence over nicotine-related body weight changes.

Food Consumption. Nicotine decreases consumption of sweet-tasting, high carbohydrate foods without altering consumption of other foods (e.g., salty, bland) (Grunberg, 1982; Grunberg et al., 1984; Grunberg, Bowen, Maycock, & Nespor, 1985; Grunberg, Popp, & Winders, 1988). When only bland food (e.g., standard laboratory chow) is available, male rats administered nicotine do not decrease feeding but female rats still exhibit decreased consumption, indicating that nicotine's effects to alter feeding are more potent in females (Grunberg et al., 1987). Studies of nicotine's effects on biochemical responses that mediate energy utilization indicate that chronic nicotine decreases peripheral insulin levels (Grunberg, Popp, Bowen, et al., 1988). Decreases in insulin result in increased fat, protein, and glycogen utilization; decreased fat storage; and may account for a decrease in preference for and consumption of sweet-tasting foods (Rodin, Wack, Ferrannini, & DeFronzo, 1985). Changes in feeding patterns also may be accounted for by the fact that nicotine increases insulin levels in the brain, specifically in the hypothalamus (Grunberg & Raygada, 1991). Increases in brain insulin have been implicated in food intake and body weight regulation (Woods & Porte, 1983).

Sex differences in feeding and body weight also are apparent in effects of nicotine cessation. When only bland food is available, male rats previously administered nicotine resume normal rates of body weight gain (i.e., increasing body weight over time as the animal gets older), but absolute body weight remains lower relative to saline control animals (Grunberg et al., 1987). In contrast, when only bland food is available to females, rates of body weight gain and absolute body weight values of animals previously administered nicotine become indistinguishable from controls within weeks of cessation (Grunberg et al., 1987). When a variety of foods is available in cessation, including sweet-tasting, high carbohydrate foods, body weight of males previously administered nicotine remains decreased when compared to controls even though males increase consumption of sweet-tasting foods (Grunberg, Popp, & Winders, 1988). For females exposed to nicotine, however, access to sweet-tasting, high carbohydrate foods in cessation results in increased rates of body weight gain as well as absolute body weight increases compared to controls (Grunberg, Popp, & Winders, 1988).

The mechanisms for changes in feeding and body weight in cessation also may be related to changes in peripheral and central insulin levels. These mechanisms have been investigated in male rats, but not in females. Specifically, in cessation peripheral insulin levels increase and hypothalamic insulin levels decrease (Grunberg & Raygada, 1991). These changes are consistent with the observed effects of cessation in males on body weight (i.e., to return rates of body weight gain to normal) and feeding (i.e., to increase consumption when sweet-tasting foods are available).

Taken together, these findings suggest that the reason women are more likely to report using smoking as a means of controlling body weight and avoiding quitting to prevent body weight gain may in part be a consequence of greater female sensitivity to these nicotine effects. With regard to clinical implications, these results indicate that adolescent and adult women may need to learn alternative strategies for body weight and appetite control (e.g., exercise) to prevent initiation of smoking, and in cessation women should avoid consumption of sweet-tasting, high carbohydrate foods in order to prevent excessive body weight gain (e.g., by consuming low calorie, sweet-tasting foods; Grunberg et al., 1985).

Activity Level. Nicotine's effects on body weight also are in part the result of alterations in activity level. These effects are complex, and depend on sex and genotype (i.e., rat strain) of subject as well as on the subject's environment (Bowen, Eury, & Grunberg, 1986; Faraday, Rahman, Scheufele, & Grunberg, 1996; Grunberg & Bowen, 1985). In male Sprague–Dawley rats (an albino strain), chronic nicotine administration increased activity levels (Grunberg, 1982; Grunberg & Bowen, 1985; others) and in male Long–Evans rats (a nonalbino strain) nicotine administration decreased activity (Faraday et al., 1996). These effects in Sprague–Dawley males are consistent with nicotine's body weight reducing effects (i.e., increased activity levels results in increased calorie expenditure). Effects of chronic nicotine administration in female rats are similar across strains and are not consistent with nicotine's body weight-reducing effects (Bowen et al., 1986; Faraday et al., 1996).

These effects also may depend on subjects' environment. When subjects were housed in same-sex groups, chronic nicotine increased activity of Long–Evans males and females (Faraday et al., 1996). The finding that drug effects in rats vary depending on the context in which nicotine is administered is consistent with smokers' reports that nicotine can have opposite effects on arousal (e.g., calming, as well as invigorating, energizing, and relieving boredom). Importantly, regardless of sex, strain, or environment, nicotine administration reduced body weight, indicating that apart from and in spite of qualitative activity effects, the net result of nicotine administration is body weight reduction.

Effects of nicotine cessation on activity also depend on subjects' strain and sex. For males, strain is an important variable. Sprague–Dawley males decreased activity in cessation (Grunberg & Bowen, 1985), but Long–Evans males did not change activity levels (Faraday et al., 1996). As with effects of nicotine, females responded similarly across strains, and did not change activity levels in cessation (Bowen et al., 1986; Faraday et al., 1996). Again, these changes are consistent with increased body weight in cessation for Sprague–Dawley males only.

Taken together, these findings suggest that the extent to which changes in activity levels contribute to body weight effects of nicotine and nicotine cessation depend on the individual's sex and genotype, with genotype more important for males, and possibly on the environment in which nicotine-containing products are used. These results also underscore the special vulnerability that females may have to nicotine's body weight effects.

Metabolic Effects. Nicotine's body weight reducing effects in part are the result of changes in metabolism probably mediated by the actions of peripheral insulin. The effects of nicotine administration and cessation on body composition have been examined in male rats. Nicotine reduces body fat stores without altering body protein or body water when compared to controls and in nicotine cessation these proportions return to control levels (Winders & Grunberg, 1990).

Attentional Processes

Many smokers report that smoking enhances attentional abilities (USDHHS, 1988). In humans, empirical studies indicate that nicotine's attentional effects vary. Whether nicotine enhances, impairs, or has no effect on attention depends on many factors, including the complexity of the task, the timing of testing, the route of nicotine administration, and the nature of the subject pool. With regard to subject selection, results differ substantially depending on whether study participants were smokers who were in withdrawal (e.g., after a required overnight cigarette abstinence), smokers who were not in withdrawal, or nonsmokers. With smokers in withdrawal, tasks that index focused, selective, divided, and sustained attention generally indicate that nicotine administration returns performance to predeprivation baseline levels (for review, see Heishman, Taylor, & Henningfield, 1994). With nondeprived smokers and nonsmokers, nicotine enhances motor responding (e.g., quickness with which a subject depresses a key measuring reaction time) in tests of focused and divided attention (Heishman et al., 1994). With a complex task (simulated driving in the context of a computerized game), nondeprived smokers performed more poorly (e.g., had more rear-end collisions) than deprived smokers and nonsmokers (Spilich, June, & Renner, 1992). Overall, these studies suggest that in the smoker nicotine ameliorates attentional deficits on simple task performance that occur with withdrawal and in the nondeprived smoker or nonsmoker there is little absolute enhancement of performance. On complex tasks, nicotine may actually impair performance in smokers.

The fact that individuals vary considerably in these responses suggests that nicotine's effects on attentional processes may be an example of the extent to which different individuals use nicotine to obtain different desired effects. That is, the extent to which nicotine's attentional effects contribute to self-administration and relapse from cessation may depend on the individual smoker. Studies with rats indicate that these individual differences in attentional responses to nicotine may be biologically based (e.g., mediated by genotype, including sex) and also may depend on subjects' environment.

Behavioral indices that reflect processes believed to underlie information processing (Swerdlow, Caine, Braff, & Geyer, 1992) and possibly attention (Acri, 1994; Acri, Brown, Saah, & Grunberg, 1995; Acri, Grunberg, & Morse, 1991; Acri, Morse, Popke, & Grunberg, 1994) in humans and in rats have been used to examine nicotine's effects. These indices consist of the acoustic startle reflex (ASR) and pre-pulse inhibition (PPI) of the ASR. The acoustic startle reflex is a characteristic sequence of involuntary, muscular responses elicited by a sudden, intense acoustic stimulus (Davis, 1984). Jumping in response to an unexpected car backfire is an everyday example of the startle reflex. The reflex is present in all mammals, including humans and rats, and is considered an index of reactivity to external acoustic stimuli. Because the reflex can be elicited using the same stimuli across species (Swerdlow, Braff, Taaid, & Geyer, 1994), the paradigm has face validity for generalizing from an animal model to human issues.

Pre-pulse inhibition (PPI) of the acoustic startle reflex (ASR) occurs when the startling stimulus is preceded by a nonstartling acoustic stimulus by a short interval (about 100 msec). The presence of the pre-pulse results in measurably reduced startle amplitude (Braff et al., 1978; Graham, 1975). In the example of a car backfire, the ability of this loud noise to startle would be reduced if the listener also heard the engine sounds immediately preceding the backfire. This reduction in startle amplitude is pre-pulse inhibition of the ASR. As with the ASR, the phenomenon of pre-pulse inhibition occurs in humans and in rats. Pre-pulse inhibition is believed to index an innate sensory-cognitive-motor "gating" mechanism that operates at a nonvolitional level and underlies the organism's ability to select relevant stimuli from the environment while screening out irrelevant information (Swerdlow et al., 1992). PPI also has been interpreted to reflect processes associated with attention (Acri, 1994; Acri et al., 1994; Acri, Grunberg, & Morse, 1991), and in humans PPI is negatively correlated with distractibility (Karper et al., 1996).

The effects of nicotine on ASR and PPI are qualitatively different in various rat strains. In Sprague–Dawley rats, nicotine administration enhances startle and PPI (Acri, 1994; Acri et al., 1991, 1994, 1995; Faraday, O'Donoghue, & Grunberg, 1999). This enhancement has been interpreted as analogous to the attentional enhancement reported by some human smokers when they smoke (Acri, 1994; Acri et al., 1994). Within the Sprague–Dawley strain, there are large individual differences in the magnitude of this enhancement, with some subjects exhibiting large increases and others exhibiting relatively small increases (Acri, 1994). In contrast, for Long–Evans rats, nicotine decreases startle and impairs pre-pulse inhibition, suggesting that for these subjects nicotine hampers information processing and attention (Faraday, Rahman, Scheufele, & Grunberg, 1998; Faraday et al., 1999). These varying responses within and across strains of rats are consistent with the variance of attentional responses to nicotine in the human literature. To the extent that these differences are biologically based, the mechanisms for the varying behavioral responses to nicotine are likely differences in central tissue sensitivity (e.g., differences in density, distribution, and/or affinity of nicotinic cholinergic receptors in the brain). Variations in receptor density have been implicated in similar behavioral differences in strains of mice, with the greatest nicotine effects associated with the largest numbers of nAchRs (Collins et al., 1988; Marks et al., 1986, 1989; Marks, Stitzel, & Collins, 1989), but similar studies have not been performed across rat strains. With the advent of progressively more sophisticated and noninvasive imaging technology in humans and in rats (e.g., positron emission tomography with receptor-specific radioactive labels, functional magnetic resonance imaging, and so on), it soon may be possible to document differential nicotinic cholinergic activity in living, behaving humans and animals.

Environment and sex of subject also influence whether the net effect of nicotine is an enhancement or an impairment of startle and sensory-gating. When Long–Evans rats are housed either singly or in same-sex groups, nicotine administration impairs sensory-gating for females regardless of housing condition (Faraday et al., 1998). For males, however, nicotine's effects depend on housing with impairment of singly housed subjects' PPI but enhancement of group-housed subjects' PPI. Again, these differential nicotine effects depending on the environment in which the drug is administered are consistent with the diversity of human uses of nicotine.

Overall, the human and animal literatures on nicotine and attention suggest that nicotine's psychological effects are highly individual. It is possible, therefore, that some smokers smoke to enhance attention, some smoke in spite of impaired attention because nicotine exerts other desired effects (e.g., body weight and appetite control), and still others smoke in order to blunt attention (i.e., to ameliorate hyperreactive or hypervigilant states). These individual differences are relevant in the context of prevention. Specifically, if individuals differentially experience attentional effects of nicotine, then the extent to which nicotine exerts desired attentional effects (e.g., enhancement or blunting) may make initiation of tobacco use more or less likely.

In cessation from nicotine, some smokers report impaired attentional processes (Shiffman, 1979, 1982, 1986; USDHHS, 1988). Animal studies indicate that effects of nicotine cessation depend to some extent on rat strain. In Sprague–Dawley male rats, cessation results in startle responses similar to pre-drug baselines but reduced pre-pulse inhibition (Acri, 1994; Acri et al., 1991). This result in Sprague–Dawley males is consistent with human reports of impaired attention in cessation. In Long–Evans males and females, ASR and PPI responses return to baseline levels in cessation (Faraday et al., 1998). Because nicotine impairs attentional processes in Long–Evans rats, this return to baseline reflects a net improvement. As with the nicotine and attention literature, the nicotine cessation and attention literature also suggests that responses are individual-specific. This specificity may have important clinical implications. That is, for effective cessation, individuals who use nicotine to obtain particular attentional effects may need to learn alternative strategies to obtain similar effects without nicotine (e.g., learning to cope with distractions, learning to use relaxation techniques to attenuate hypervigilance). This custom-tailored approach to cessation may enhance success rates (Grunberg, 1995).

Interactions With Stress

It is well-established that stress and the use of addictive substances, including nicotine, are positively correlated. Epidemiologic studies and laboratory experiments indicate that under stress, smokers smoke more than when not under stress (Epstein & Collins, 1977; Rose, Ananda, & Jarvik, 1983; Schachter, Silverstein, et al., 1977; Shiffman, 1982, 1985; USDHHS, 1988). These reports may seem to be paradoxical given that nicotine, a sympathomimetic, increases physiological (e.g., heart rate, blood pressure) and biochemical stress responses (e.g., cortisol) in humans and in animals (Morse, 1989; USDHHS, 1988). Several explanations have been proposed for this dissociation between subjective experience and biologic responses known as Nesbitt's paradox (e.g., Parrot, 1998; Schachter, 1973): (a) Stress speeds nicotine excretion so that the smoker must self-administer more nicotine in order to obtain desired behavioral and psychological effects similar to those experienced in the nonstressed state; (b) nicotine's behavioral and psychological effects are different in the stressed state than in the nonstressed state; (c) nicotine alleviates the unpleasant subjective experience of stress (e.g., feelings of anxiety or irritability, inability to concentrate); and (d) individuals misattribute the symptoms of stress for symptoms of withdrawal (Grunberg & Baum, 1985; Grunberg, Morse, & Barrett, 1983; Schachter, Silverstein, et al., 1977; USDHHS, 1988). These explanations are not mutually exclusive and together probably account for why people smoke more under stress, and why different individuals are more or less vulnerable to increased smoking under stress.

The interaction of stress with nicotine's effects on attentional processes (as indexed by the ASR and PPI paradigm) in an animal model provides a useful exemplar for how these processes might occur. Importantly, there are sex and genotypic differences in these effects. Specifically, ASR and PPI responses in rats are altered by brief exposure to a mild physical stressor—immobilization for 20 minutes. The stressor is administered by placing the rat in a device that holds it firmly without pinching or causing pain. The stressful nature of the procedure appears to result from rodents' instinctual aversion to being unable to move freely. This stress procedure produces reliable peripheral biochemical changes in the form of elevated adrenocorticotropin hormone (ACTH), beta-endorphins, and corticosterone consistent with a stress response (e.g., Acri, 1994; Kant et al., 1983; Raygada, Shaham, Nespor, Kant, & Grunberg, 1992). These biochemical stress responses do not diminish with repeated exposure to the stressor and are similar in males and females (Kant et al., 1983).

In Sprague–Dawley males, exposure to this stressor increases startle and PPI (Acri, 1994; Faraday et al., 1999). In Sprague–Dawley females and Long–Evans males and females, however, immobilization has no consistent effects on startle and PPI (Faraday et al., 1999). These findings suggest that stress alone enhances information processing and possibly attention in Sprague–Dawley males and does not alter these processes in other subjects. When subjects are administered nicotine concurrent with the stress experience, however, there are dramatic changes in this pattern.

Specifically, in stressed Sprague–Dawley males administered a low dosage of chronic nicotine (6 mg/kg/day), stress and nicotine have additive effects on ASR and PPI (Acri, 1994). That is, these subjects exhibit more startle and more sensory-gating than nonstressed low dose nicotine-treated subjects (for which nicotine enhances startle and PPI) and saline-treated stressed subjects (for which stress increases ASR and PPI). In stressed Sprague–Dawley males administered a higher nicotine dosage (12 mg/kg/day), the effects of nicotine and stress cancel one another, and ASR and PPI responses are indistinguishable from nonstressed saline controls (Acri, 1994; Faraday et al., 1999).

This pattern of responses to the stress and nicotine interaction is consistent with several of the proposed explanations for why smokers increase smoking under stress. For example, if stress speeds nicotine metabolism, then behavioral responses to a nicotine dosage (12 mg/kg/day) that increases attention in a nonstressed subject might be attenuated when the subject experiences stress because of reduced nicotine bioavailability. These data also suggest that nicotine's actions under stress may be different than its actions in the nonstressed state. Specifically, nicotine is known to act on behavioral and biologic indices according to an inverted-U shaped function (i.e., at low dosages nicotine increases these indices and at higher dosages it decreases them). If stress also increases these indices (e.g., attentional processes), then low dosages of nicotine plus stress are likely to have additive effects but high dosages of nicotine plus stress are likely to push the organism over the top of the inverted U-shaped curve and result in reduced or normal responses. To the extent that increased reactivity and sensory-gating as a result of stress are experienced as unpleasant (e.g., as hyperreactive or hypervigilant states), then these data also are consistent with the idea that individuals self-administer nicotine in order to alleviate these effects.

For stressed Sprague–Dawley females administered nicotine, a different picture emerges. Specifically, stress by itself does not affect ASR and PPI in these subjects and nicotine alone enhances these responses. Together, stress and nicotine administration exert additive effects on ASR and PPI at both low and high nicotine dosages (Faraday et al., 1999). Therefore, for Sprague–Dawley females, stress in the presence of nicotine increases reactivity and sensory-gating above levels that result from nicotine administration alone. This sex difference in behavioral effects of the nicotine × stress interaction suggests that, for Sprague–Dawley females, stress may even slow the metabolism of nicotine, resulting in enhanced effects of the same drug dosage when compared to nonstressed subjects who are administered nicotine. These results also are consistent with the idea that nicotine's effects under stress are different than in the nonstressed state.

In contrast, for Long–Evans males and females, concurrent stress and nicotine administration do not produce ASR and PPI patterns substantially different from effects of nicotine alone (Faraday et al., under review). These findings suggest that for this rat strain stress does not alter nicotine metabolism and that ASR and PPI effects of nicotine are similar during stress or not during stress. To the extent that interoceptive, subjectively experienced effects of nicotine (e.g., changes in attentional processes) serve as cues to the individual that a particular drug action is occurring, these results suggest that for some people the lack of stress-induced changes in these cues might result in the individual not experiencing stress. That is, these individuals would not perceive that nicotine's effects were altered when in a challenging or threatening situation and therefore would not be likely to increase nicotine self-administration. It is also possible that these subjects represent a subset of smokers for whom the effects of nicotine are powerful enough to make any effects of stress irrelevant.

Overall, human and animal reports indicate that stress may interact with smoking behavior in several different ways, and that there are sex and possibly other genotypic differences in these effects. This interaction is particularly relevant for effective cessation. Understanding the extent to which stress alters various psychobiologic processes that also are altered by nicotine is important to determining the individual's propensity for relapse to smoking under stress. For example, an ex-smoker who under stress increases food consumption, becomes hyperreactive, and feels anxious may be more vulnerable to smoking relapse because of nicotine's capacity to ameliorate these effects than an individual for whom these responses do not occur.

TOBACCO ABUSE CAN BEST BE TREATED BY UNDERSTANDING THE ROLE OF NICOTINE AND THERE IS A LOT OF NICOTINE PSYCHOBIOLOGIC RESEARCH TO DO

It is now clear that tobacco use is a form of nicotine self-administration and that psychological and biological variables interact to maintain this behavior. Overwhelming evidence that nicotine is addicting, however, does not mean that nicotine replacement alone will serve as a magic bullet to stop tobacco use. In light of the many psychobiologic interactions that are involved in tobacco use, psychological and pharmacologic strategies should be used together to treat tobacco dependence. Simply prescribing a nicotine replacement product without treating the behavioral and psychological variables involved in maintaining nicotine self-administration usually fails. Treatments that consider the multivariate aspects of tobacco use are likely to be more successful. In light of emerging evidence that individual differences (including sex and other genotypic differences) are most pronounced in some of the psychological effects of nicotine that contribute to nicotine self-administration, it is these psychobiologic effects that must be studied and considered in detail to develop the most effective treatments and prevention strategies to avoid tobacco use.

CONCLUSIONS

This volume provides examples of great progress in health psychology over the past 25 years. Understanding of tobacco use and the interaction of psychological and biological variables in nicotine self-administration is a particularly clear example of how multivariate focus on health and behavior problems has resulted in substantial progress that can result in improved health.

ACKNOWLEDGMENTS

The opinions or assertions contained herein are the private ones of the authors and are not to be construed as official or reflecting the views of the Department of Defense or the Uniformed Services University of the Health Sciences.

REFERENCES

Acri, J. B. (1994). Nicotine modulates effects of stress on acoustic startle reflexes in rats: Dependence on dose, stressor and initial reactivity. *Psychopharmacology, 116*(3), 255–265.

Acri, J. B., Brown, K. J., Saah, M. I., & Grunberg, N. E. (1995). Strain and age differences in acoustic startle responses and effects of nicotine in rats. *Pharmacology Biochemistry and Behavior, 50*(2), 191–198.

Acri, J. B., Grunberg, N. E., & Morse, D. E. (1991). Effects of nicotine on the acoustic startle reflex amplitude in rats. *Psychopharmacology, 104*(2), 244–248.

Acri, J. B., Morse, D. E., Popke, E. J., & Grunberg, N. E. (1994). Nicotine increases sensory gating measured as inhibition of the acoustic startle reflex in rats. *Psychopharmacology, 114*(2), 369–374.

Ashton, H., & Watson, D. W. (1970). Puffing frequency and nicotine intake in cigarette smokers. *British Medical Journal, 3*(5724), 679–681.

Bacher, B., Wang, X., & Hollt, V. (1995). Regulation of proenkephalin gene expression in bovine adrenal medullary chromaffin cells by nicotine. In P.B.S. Clarke, M. Quick, F. Adlkofer, & Thurau (Eds.), *Effects of nicotine on biological systems II* (pp. 167–172). Basel, Switzerland: Birkhauser Verlag.

Balfour, D.J.K. (1994). Neural mechanisms underlying nicotine dependence. *Addiction, 89,* 1419–1423.

Beitner-Johnson, D., Guitart, X., & Nestler, E. J. (1992). Common intracellular actions of chronic morphine and cocaine in dopaminergic brain reward regions. In P. W. Kalivas & H. H. Samson (Eds.), *The neurobiology of drug and alcohol addiction, annals of the New York Academy of Sciences, 654,* (pp. 70–87). New York: New York Academy of Science.

Bowen, D. J., Eury, S. E., & Grunberg, N. E. (1986). Nicotine's effects on female rats' body weight: Caloric intake and physical activity. *Pharmacology Biochemistry and Behavior, 25,* 1131–1136.

Bozarth, M. A. (1994). Opiate reinforcement processes: Re-assembling multiple mechanisms. *Addiction, 89,* 1425–1434.

Braff, D., Stone, C., Callaway, E., Geyer, M., Glick, I., & Bali, L. (1978). Prestimulus effects on human startle reflex in normals and schizophrenics. *Psychophysiology, 15*(4), 339–343.

Carmody, T. P. (1993). Affect regulation, nicotine addiction, and smoking cessation. *Journal of Psychoactive Drugs, 24,* 111–122.

Clarke, P.B.S., & Kumar, R. (1984). Effects of nicotine and d-amphetamine on intracranial self-stimulation in a shuttle box test in rats. *Psychopharmacology, 84*(1), 109–114.

Collins, A. C., Miner, L. L., & Marks, M. J. (1988). Genetic influences on acute responses to nicotine and nicotine tolerance in the mouse. *Pharmacology Biochemistry & Behavior, 30,* 269–278.

Corrigall, W. A. (1991). Understanding brain mechanisms in nicotine reinforcement. *British Journal of Addiction, 86,* 507–10.

Corrigall, W. A., & Coen, K. M. (1989). Nicotine maintains robust self-administration in rats on a limited-access schedule. *Psychopharmacology, 99*(4), 473–478.

Corrigall, W. A., & Coen, K. M. (1991). Selective dopamine antagonists reduce nicotine self-administration. *Psychopharmacology, 104*(2), 171–176.

Cox, B. M., Goldstein, A., & Nelson, W. T. (1984). Nicotine self-administration in rats. *British Journal of Pharmacology, 83*(1), 49–55.

Davis, M. (1984). The mammalian startle response. In R. Eaton (Ed.), *Neural mechanisms of startle behavior* (pp. 287–351). New York: Plenum.

Deneau, G. A., & Inoki, R. (1967). Nicotine self-administration in monkeys. *Annals of the New York Academy of Science, 142*(article 1), 277–279.

Di Chiara, G., Acquas, E., Tanda, G., & Cadoni, C. (1993). Drugs of abuse: Biochemical surrogates of specific aspects of neural reward? In Wonnacott, S. (Ed.), *Neurochemistry of drug dependence* (Series: Biochemical Society Symposium, Vol. 59, pp. 65–81). London: Portland Press.

Donny, E. C., Caggiula, A. R., Knopf, S., & Brown, C. (1995). Nicotine self-administration in rats. *Psychopharmacology, 122*(4), 390–394.

Dube, M. F., & Green, C. R. (1982). Methods of collection of smoke for analytical purposes. *Recent Advances in Tobacco Science, 8,* 42–102.

Epstein, L., & Collins, F. (1977). The measurement of situational influences of smoking. *Addictive Behaviors, 2,* 47–53.

Faraday, M. M., O'Donoghue, V., & Grunberg, N. E. (1999). Effects of nicotine and of stress on startle and sensory-gating depend on rat strain and sex. *Pharmacology Biochemistry & Behavior, 62*(2), 273–284.

Faraday, M. M., Rahman, M. A., Scheufele, P. M., & Grunberg, N. E. (1998). Nicotine impairs sensory-gating in Long-Evans rats. *Pharmacology Biochemistry & Behavior, 61*(3), 281–289.

Faraday, M. M., Rahman, M. A., Scheufele, P. M., & Grunberg, N. E. (1996, March). *Effects of nicotine on locomotor activity of Long–Evans rats.* Paper presented at the Society for Research on Nicotine and Tobacco, Washington, DC.

Flores, C. M., Rogers, S. W., Pabreza, L. A., Wolfe, B. B., & Kellar, K. J. (1992). A subtype of nicotinic cholinergic receptor in rat brain is composed of alpha 4 and beta 2 subunits and is up-regulated by chronic nicotine treatment. *Molecular Pharmacology, 41*(1), 31–37.

Ginzel, K. H. (1987). The lungs as sites of origin of nicotine-induced skeletomotor relaxation and behavioral and electrocortical arousal in the cat. In *Proceedings of the International Symposium on Nicotine* (pp. 269–292). Goldcoast, Australia: ICSU Press.

Ginzel, K. H., & Lucas, E. A. (1980). Electrocortical and behavioral arousal from various regions of the arterial tree. *Sleep Research, 9,* 29.

Glick, S. D., Visker, K. E., & Maisonneuve, I. M. (1996). An oral self-administration model of nicotine preference in rats: Effects of mecamylamine. *Psychopharmacology, 128*(4), 426–431.

Gold, M. S., & Miller, N. S. (1992). Seeking drugs/alcohol and avoiding withdrawal: The neuroanatomy of drive states and withdrawal. *Psychiatric Annals, 22,* 430–435.

Goldberg, S. R., & Henningfield, J. E. (1988). Reinforcing effects of nicotine in humans and experimental animals responding under intermittent schedules of i.v. drug injection. *Pharmacology Biochemistry & Behavior, 30*(1), 227–234.

Goldberg, S. R., Spealman, R. D., & Goldberg, D. M. (1981). Persistent behavior at high rates maintained by intravenous self-administration of nicotine. *Science, 214*(4520), 573–575.

Goldfarb, T. L., Jarvik, M. E., & Glick, S. D. (1970). Cigarette nicotine content as a determinant of human smoking behavior. *Psychopharmacologia, 17*(1), 89–93.

Graham, F. K. (1975). The more or less startling effects of weak prestimuli. *Psychophysiology, 12,* 238–248.

Grunberg, N. E. (1982). The effects of nicotine and cigarette smoking on food consumption and taste preferences. *Addictive Behaviors, 7,* 317–331.

Grunberg, N. E. (1986). Behavioral and biological factors in the relationship between tobacco use and body weight. In E. S. Katkin & S. B. Manuck (Eds.), *Advances in Behavioral Medicine* (Vol. 2, pp. 97–129). Greenwich, CT: JAI Press.

Grunberg, N. E. (1994). Overview: Biological processes relevant to drugs of dependence. *Addiction, 89,* 1443–1446.

Grunberg, N. E. (1995). A custom-tailored approach to smoking cessation. *International Journal of Smoking Cessation, 4*(1), 2–5.

Grunberg, N. E., & Baum, A. (1985). Biological commonalities of stress and substance abuse. In S. Shiffman & T. A. Wills (Eds.), *Coping and substance use* (pp. 25–62). New York: Academic Press.

Grunberg, N. E., & Bowen, D. J. (1985). The role of physical activity in nicotine's effects on body weight. *Pharmacology Biochemistry & Behavior, 23,* 851–854.

Grunberg, N. E., Bowen, D. J., & Morse, D. E. (1984). Effects of nicotine on body weight and food consumption in rats. *Psychopharmacology, 83,* 93–98.

Grunberg, N. E., Bowen, D. J., Maycock, V. A., & Nespor, S. M. (1985). The importance of sweet taste and caloric content in the effects of nicotine on specific food consumption. *Psychopharmacology, 87,* 198–203.

Grunberg, N. E., Morse, D. E., & Barrett, J. E. (1983). Effects of urinary pH on the behavioral responses of squirrel monkeys to nicotine. *Pharmacology Biochemistry & Behavior, 19,* 553–557.

Grunberg, N. E., Popp, K. A., Bowen, D. J., Nespor, S. M., Winders, S. E., & Eury, S. E. (1988). Effects of chronic nicotine administration on insulin, glucose, epinephrine, and norepinephrine. *Life Sciences, 42,* 161–170.

Grunberg, N. E., Popp, K. A., & Winders, S. E. (1988). Effects of nicotine on body weight in rats with access to "junk" foods. *Psychopharmacology, 94,* 536–539.

Grunberg, N. E., & Raygada, M. (1991). Effects of nicotine on insulin: Actions and implications. In *Advances in pharmacological sciences: Effects of nicotine on biological systems* (pp. 131–142). Basel, Switzerland: Birkhauser Verlag.

Grunberg, N. E., Winders, S. E., & Popp, K. A. (1987). Sex differences in nicotine's effects on consummatory behavior and body weight in rats. *Psychopharmacology, 91,* 221–225.

Grunberg, N. E., Winders, S. E., & Wewers, M. E. (1991). Gender differences in tobacco use. *Health Psychology, 10*(2), 143–153.

Hanson, H. M., Ivester, C. A., & Morton, B. R. (1979). Nicotine self-administration in rats. In N. A. Krasnegor (Ed.), *Cigarette Smoking as a dependence Process* (NIDA Research Monograph 23, DHEW Publication No. ADM 74–800, pp. 70–90). U.S. Department of Health, Education, and Welfare, Public Health Service, Alcohol, Drug Abuse, and Mental Health Administration, National Institute on Drug Abuse.

Heishman, S. J., Taylor, R. C., & Henningfield, J. E. (1994). Nicotine and smoking: A review of effects on human performance. *Experimental and Clinical Psychopharmacology, 2*(4), 345–395.

Henningfield, J. E. (1984). Behavioral pharmacology of cigarette smoking. In T. Thompson, P. B. Dews, & J. E. Barrett (Eds.), *Advances in behavioral pharmacology* (Vol. 4, pp. 131–210). Orlando, FL: Academic Press.

Henningfield, J. E., & Goldberg, S. R. (1983). Nicotine as a reinforcer in human subjects and laboratory animals. *Pharmacology Biochemistry & Behavior, 19*(6), 989–992.

Henningfield, J. E., & Goldberg, S. R. (1988). Pharmacologic determinants of tobacco self-administration by humans. *Pharmacology Biochemistry & Behavior, 30*(1), 221–226.

Henningfield, J. E., Miyasato, K., & Jasinski, D. R. (1983). Abuse liability and pharmacodynamic characteristics of intravenous and inhaled nicotine. Journal of Pharmacology and *Experimental Therapeutics, 234*(1), 1–12.

Henningfield, J. E., Yingling, J., Griffiths, R. R., & Pickens, R. (1980). An inexpensive portable device for measuring puffing behavior by cigarette smokers. *Pharmacology Biochemistry & Behavior, 12*(5), 811–813.

Hodges, H., Sinden, J., Turner, J. J., Netto, C. A., Sowinski, P., & Gray, J. A. (1992). Nicotine as a tool to characterise the role of the forebrain cholinergic projection system in cognition. In P. M. Lippiello, A. C. Collins, J. A. Gray, & J. H. Robinson (Eds.), *The biology of nicotine: Current research issues* (pp. 157–182). New York: Raven.

Hughes, J. R., Higgins, S. T., & Hatsukami, D. (1990). Effects of abstinence from tobacco: A critical review. In L. T. Kozlowski, H. Annis, H. D. Cappell, F. Glaser, M. Goodstadt, Y. Israel, H. Kalant, E. M. Sellers, & E. Vingilis (Eds.), *Research advances in alcohol and drug problems* (Vol. 10, pp. 317–398). New York: Plenum.

Hull, C. L. (1943). *Principles of behavior: An introduction to behavior theory.* New York: Appleton-Century-Crofts.

Jarvik, M. E., Glick, S. D., & Nakamura, R. K. (1970). Inhibition of cigarette smoking by orally administered nicotine. *Clinical Pharmacology and Therapeutics, 11*(4), 574–576.

Kant, G. J., Lenox, R. H., Bunnell, B. N., Mougey, E. H., Pennington, L. L., & Meyerhoff, J. L. (1983). Comparison of the stress response in male and female rats: Pituitary cyclic AMP and plasma prolactin, growth hormone and corticosterone. *Psychoneuroendocrinology, 8,* 421–428.

Kaplan, H. I., Sadock, B. J., & Grebb, J. A. (1994). *Kaplan and Sadock's synopsis of psychiatry: Behavioral sciences, clinical psychiatry* (7th ed.). Baltimore, MD: Williams & Wilkins.

Karper, L. P., Freeman, G., Grillon, C., Morgan, C., Charney, D., & Krystal, J. (1996). Preliminary evidence of an association between sensorimotor gating and distractibility in psychosis. *Journal of Neuropsychiatry and Clinical Neuroscience, 8*(1), 60–66.

Kellar, K. J., Schwartz, R. D., & Martino, A. M. (1987). Nicotinic cholinergic receptor recognition sites in brain. In W. R. Martin, G. R. Van Loon, E. T. Iwamoto, & L. T. Davis (Eds.), *Tobacco smoking and nicotine. A neurobiological approach* (pp. 467–480). New York: Plenum.

Klesges, R. C., Elliot, V. E., & Robinson, L. A. (1997). Chronic dieting and the belief that smoking controls body weight in a biracial, population-based adolescent sample. *Tobacco Control, 6*(2), 89–94.

Klesges, R. C., & Klesges, L. M. (1988). Cigarette smoking as a dietary strategy in a university population. *International Journal of Eating Disorders, 7,* 413–419.

Klesges, R. C., Meyers, A. W., Klesges, L. M., & La Vasque, M. E. (1989). Smoking, body weight, and their effects on smoking behavior: A comprehensive review of the literature. *Psychological Bulletin, 106,* 1–27.

Koffka, K. (1935). *Principles of Gestalt psychology.* New York: Harcourt, Brace.

Köhler, W. (1929). *Gestalt psychology.* New York: Liveright.

Koob, G. F. (1992). Drugs of abuse: anatomy, pharmacology and function of reward pathways. *Trends in Pharmacologic Science, 13*(5), 177–184.

Koob, G. F., & Bloom, F. E. (1988). Cellular and molecular mechanisms of drug dependence. *Science, 242*(4879), 715–723.

Koob, G. F., & Swerdlow, N. R. (1988). The functional output of the mesolimbic dopamine system. *Annals of the New York Academy of Science, 537,* 216–227.

Lindstrom, J., Anand, R., Peng, X., & Gerzanich, V. (1995). Neuronal nicotinic receptor structure and function. In P.B.S. Clarke, M. Quick, F. Adlkofer, & Thurau (Eds.), *Effects of nicotine on biological systems II* (pp. 45–52). Basel, Switzerland: Birkhauser Verlag.

Marks, M. J., Romm, E., Campbell, S. M., & Collins, A. C. (1989). Variation of nicotinic binding sites among inbred strains. *Pharmacology Biochemistry & Behavior, 33,* 679–689.

Marks, M. J., Romm, E., Gaffney, D. K., & Collins, A. C. (1986). Nicotine-induced tolerance and receptor changes in four mouse strains. *Journal of Pharmacology and Experimental Therapeutics, 237*(3), 809–819.

Marks, M. J., Stitzel, J. A., & Collins, A. C. (1989). Genetic influences on nicotine responses. *Pharmacology Biochemistry & Behavior, 33*(3), 667–678.

Mitchell, S. N., Smith, K. M., Joseph, M. H., & Gray, J. A. (1992). Acute and chronic effects of nicotine on catecholamine synthesis and release in the rat central nervous system. In P. M. Lippiello, A. C. Collins, J. A. Gray, & J. H. Robinson (Eds.), *The biology of nicotine: Current research issues* (pp. 97–120). New York: Raven.

Montgomery, A.M.J., Rose, I. C., & Herberg, A. J. (1993). The effect of a 5–HT3 receptor antagonist, ondansetron, on brain-stimulation reward and its interaction with direct and indirect stimulants of central dopaminergic transmission. *Journal of Neural Transmission-General Action, 91,* 1–11.

Morse, D. E. (1989). Neuroendocrine responses to nicotine and stress: Enhancement of peripheral stress responses by the administration of nicotine. *Psychopharmacology, 98,* 539–543.

Nakayama, H., Okuda, H., & Nakashima, T. (1994). Molecular diversity and properties of brain nicotinic acetylcholine receptor. *Nippon Yakurigaku Zassi, 104,* 241–249.

Nestler, E. J. (1992). Molecular mechanisms of drug addiction. *Journal of Neuroscience, 12,* 2439–2450.

Parrott, A. C. (1998). Nesbitt's paradox resolved? Stress and arousal modulation during cigarette smoking. *Addiction, 93,* 317–320.

Pavlov, I. (1927). *Conditioned reflexes.* New York: Oxford University Press.

Pomerleau, O. F., Fertig, J., & Shanhan, S. (1983). Nicotine dependence in cigarette smoking: An empirically based, multivariate model. *Pharmacology Biochemistry & Behavior, 19*(2), 291–299.

Raygada, M., Shaham, Y., Nespor, S. M., Kant, G. J., & Grunberg, N. E. (1992). Effect of stress on hypothalamic insulin in rats. *Brain Research Bulletin, 29,* 129–134.

Ribeiro, E. B., Bettiker, R. L., Bogdanov, M., & Wurtman, R. J. (1993). Effects of systemic nicotine on serotonin release in rat brain. *Brain Research, 621*(2), 311–318.

Ritz, M. C., & Kuhar, M. J. (1993). Psychostimulant drugs and a dopamine hypothesis regarding addiction: Update on recent research. *Biochemical Society Symposium, 59,* 51–64.

Rodin, J., Wack, J., Ferrannini, E., & Defronzo, R. A. (1985). Effect of insulin and glucose on feeding behavior. *Metabolism, 34*(9), 826–831.

Rose, J. E., Ananda, S., & Jarvik, M. E. (1983). Cigarette smoking during anxiety-provoking and monotonous tasks. *Addictive Behaviors, 8*(4), 353–359.

Rose, J. E., & Corrigall, W. A. (1997). Nicotine self-administration in animals and humans: Similarities and differences. *Psychopharmacology, 130*(1), 28–40.

Rosecrans, J. A., & Karan, L. (1993). Neurobehavioral mechanisms of nicotine action: Role in the initiation and maintenance of tobacco dependence. *Journal of Substance Abuse Treatment, 10,* 161–170.

Russell, M. A., Wilson, C., Patel, U. A., Feyerabend, C., & Cole, P. V. (1975). Plasma nicotine levels after smoking cigarettes with high, medium, and low nicotine yields. *British Medical Journal, 2*(5968), 414–416.

Salamone, J. D. (1994). The involvement of nucleus accumbens dopamine in appetitive and aversive motivation. *Behavioural Brain Research, 61,* 117–133.

Schachter, S. (1973). Nesbitt's paradox. In W. L. Dunn, Jr. (Ed.), *Smoking behavior: Motives and incentives* (pp. 147–155). Washington, DC: Winston.

Schachter, S. (1978). Pharmacological and psychological determinants of smoking. *Annals of Internal Medicine, 88*(1), 104–114.

Schachter, S., Kozlowski, L. T., & Silverstein, B. (1977). Studies on the Interaction of Psychological and Pharmacological Determinants of Smoking. The effects of urinary pH on cigarette smoking. *Journal of Experimental Psychology, 106*(1), 13–19.

Schachter, S., Silverstein, B., & Perlick, D. (1977). Psychological and pharmacological explanations of smoking under stress. *Journal of Experimental Psychology, 106*(1), 31–40.

Shiffman, S. (1979). The tobacco withdrawal syndrome. In N. A. Krasnegor (Ed.), *Cigarette smoking as a dependence process* (NIDA Research Monograph 23, DHEW Publication No.

79–800, pp. 158–184). U.S. Department of Health, Education, and Welfare, Public Health Service, Alcohol, Drug Abuse, and Mental Health Administration, National Institute on Drug Abuse.

Shiffman, S. (1982). Relapse following smoking cessation: A situational analysis. *Journal of Consulting and Clinical Psychology, 50*(1), 71–86.

Shiffman, S. (1985). Coping with temptations to smoke. In S. Shiffman & T. A. Wills (Eds.), *Coping and substance use* (pp. 223–240). New York: Academic Press.

Shiffman, S. (1986). A cluster-analytic classification of smoking relapse episodes. *Addictive Behaviors, 11*(3), 295–307.

Shiffman, S., & Jarvik, M. (1976). Smoking withdrawal symptoms in two weeks of abstinence. *Psychopharmacology, 50,* 35–39.

Shoaib, M., Schindler, C. W., & Goldberg, S. R. (1997). Nicotine self-administration in rats: Strain and nicotine pre-exposure effects on acquisition. *Psychopharmacology, 129*(1), 34–43.

Skinner, B. F. (1938). *The behavior of organisms: An experimental analysis.* New York: Appleton-Century-Crofts.

Spilich, G. J., June, L., & Renner, J. (1992). Cigarette smoking and cognitive performance. *British Journal of Addiction, 87,* 1313–1326.

Stolerman, I. P. (1991). Behavioural pharmacology of nicotine: Multiple mechanisms. *British Journal of Addiction, 86,* 533–536.

Swerdlow, N. R., Braff, D. L., Taaid, N., & Geyer, M. A. (1994). Assessing the validity of an animal model of deficient sensorimotor gating in schizophrenic patients. *Archives of General Psychiatry, 51,* 139–154.

Swerdlow, N. R., Caine, S. B., Braff, D. L., & Geyer, M. A. (1992). The neural substrates of sensorimotor gating of the startle reflex: A review of recent findings and their implications. *Journal of Psychopharmacology, 6*(2), 176–190.

Thorndike, E. L. (1911). *Animal intelligence.* New York: MacMillan.

U.S. Department of Health and Human Services. (1988). *The health consequences of smoking: Nicotine addiction, a report of the surgeon general* (DHHS Publication No. CDC 88-8406). Washington, DC: U.S. Government Printing Office.

Watson, J. B. (1924). *Behaviorism.* Chicago: University of Chicago Press.

Winders, S. E., & Grunberg, N. E. (1990). Effects of nicotine on body weight, food consumption and body composition in male rats. *Life Sciences, 46,* 1523–1530.

Woods, S. C., & Porte, D. (1983). The role of insulin as a satiety factor in the cetral nervous system. *Advances in Metabolic Disorders, 10,* 457–468.

Yanagita, T., Ando, K., Kato, S., & Takada, K. (1983). Psychopharmacological studies on nicotine and tobacco smoking in rhesus monkeys. *Psychopharmacology Bulletin, 19*(3), 409–412.

Yu, Z. J., & Weckler, L. (1994). Chronic nicotine administration differentially affects neurotransmitter release from rat striatal slices. *Journal of Neurochemistry, 63,* 186–194.

15

Obesity

Rena R. Wing

Betsy A. Polley

University of Pittsburgh School of Medicine

Obesity is a significant health problem in the United States. One out of every two Americans is either overweight or obese (Flegal, Carroll, Kuczmarski, & Johnson, 1998). Obesity is a major cause of morbidity and mortality, both independently and through its association with hypertension, diabetes, and hyperlipidemia. Although genetic factors clearly play a role in obesity, the dramatic increases that are occurring in the prevalence of obesity are the result of changes in lifestyle, including changes in both intake and exercise. This chapter briefly discusses epidemiological aspects of obesity and the health and psychosocial consequences of this disease. However, it focuses primarily on the behavioral factors associated with the development of obesity and lifestyle interventions that have been developed for prevention and treatment of this major health problem.

DEFINING OBESITY

Obesity technically means an excess of body fat, and is distinct from "overweight," which means an excess of body weight. However, except in rare situations, such as body builders (who may be overweight but not overfat), the two are highly related and consequently the terms are often used interchangeably.

Obesity is most commonly quantified using the Body Mass Index (BMI), which is weight in kg divided by height in meters squared. Although this measure does not actually assess body fatness, it generally is highly correlated with measures of body fat. A BMI of 25–29.9 is used to define overweight and a BMI > 30 is used to define obese (Table 15.1).

Other measures of body fatness are used primarily in research settings. These include measuring skinfold thickness with calipers, using underwater weighing to measure body density, and using dual x-ray absorptiometry to measure lean body mass (Lohman, 1992).

PREVALENCE

Obesity is a major health problem in the United States, due to its prevalence and its association with morbidity and mortality. It is estimated that one of every two Americans is overweight or obese (Flegal, et al., 1998). Obesity increases with age, peaking at about age 50, and occurs more commonly in women than in men, especially in minority women. Approximately 55% to 60% of African American women and Mexican American women, from age 40 to 60, are overweight (see Fig. 15.1).

Despite all of the recent attention to obesity, the increased public interest in exercise, and the development of new low fat products, the prevalence of obesity is increasing, not decreasing (Kuczmarski, Flegal, Campbell, & Johnson, 1994). In studies conducted between 1960 and 1980, approximately 25% of Americans were overweight. Now, 33% of Americans are overweight. The exact cause of this increased obesity is unclear. It appears that dietary intake has not increased over this period (and intake of fat has decreased), raising the possibility that the increased prevalence of obesity is due to decreases in physical activity (Heini & Weinsier, 1997).

TABLE 15.1

Body Weights in Pounds According to Height and Body Mass Index

	Body Mass Index (kg/m²)													
	19	20	21	22	23	24	25	26	27	28	29	30	35	40
Height (in)	**Body Weight (lb)**													
58	91	96	100	105	110	115	119	124	129	134	138	143	167	191
59	94	99	104	109	114	119	124	128	133	138	143	148	173	198
60	97	102	107	112	118	123	128	133	138	143	148	153	158	185
61	100	106	111	116	122	127	132	137	143	148	153	179	204	211
62	104	109	115	120	126	131	136	142	147	153	158	164	191	218
63	107	113	118	124	130	135	141	146	152	158	163	169	197	225
64	110	116	122	128	134	140	145	151	157	163	169	174	204	232
65	114	120	126	132	138	144	150	156	162	168	174	180	210	240
66	118	124	130	136	142	148	155	161	167	173	179	186	216	247
67	121	127	134	140	146	153	159	166	172	178	185	191	223	255
68	125	131	138	144	151	158	164	171	177	184	190	197	230	262
69	128	135	142	149	155	162	169	176	182	189	196	203	236	270
70	132	139	146	153	160	167	174	181	188	195	202	207	243	278
71	136	143	150	157	165	172	179	186	193	200	208	215	250	286
72	140	147	154	162	169	177	184	191	199	206	213	221	258	294
73	144	151	159	166	174	182	189	197	204	212	219	227	265	302
74	148	155	163	171	179	186	194	202	210	218	225	233	272	311
75	152	160	168	176	184	192	200	208	216	224	232	240	279	319
76	156	164	172	180	189	197	205	213	221	230	238	246	287	328

Note. Each entry gives the body weight in pounds (lb) for a person of a given height and body mass index. Pounds have been rounded off. To use the table, find the appropriate height in the lefthand column. Move across the row to a given weight. The number at the top of the column id the body mass index for the height and weight.

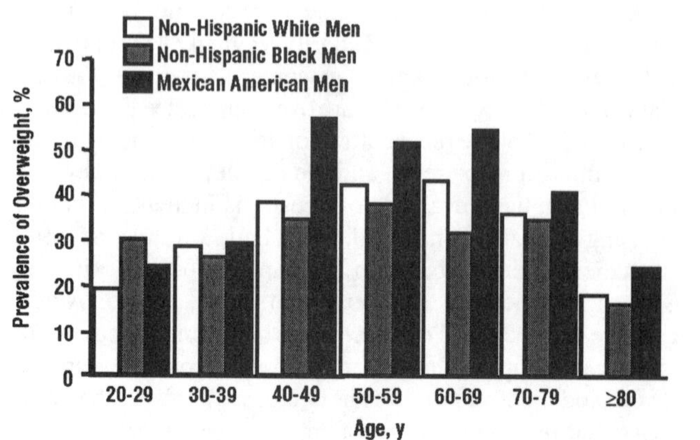

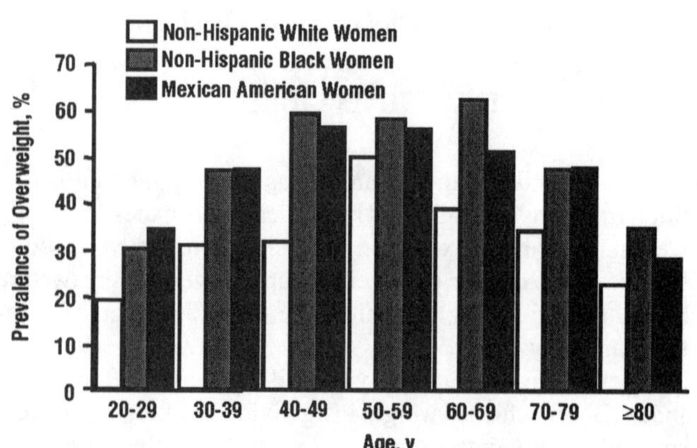

FIG. 15.1. Unadjusted prevalence of overweight by age and race/ethnicity for men and women, U.S. population age 20 or older, from 1988 to 1991. Reprinted from Kuczmarski, Fiegal, Campbell, & Johnson (1994).

There has also been an increase in the prevalence of obesity in children. Currently, approximately 27% of children (age 6–11) and 22% of adolescents (age 12–18) are obese (Gortmaker, Dietz, Sobol, & Wehler, 1987). This high prevalence of obesity in children is of particular concern, because overweight children typically become overweight adults (Epstein, 1993).

CONSEQUENCES OF OBESITY

Impact of Obesity on Morbidity and Mortality

Obesity increases the risk of developing coronary heart disease, diabetes, hypertension, and some forms of cancer. These risks of obesity are particularly strong in individuals under age 40 (Van Itallie, 1985). Several prospective studies, following large cohorts of subjects, have shown that individuals who are even modestly overweight have a greater risk of developing coronary heart disease (Garrisson & Castelli, 1985; Hubert, Feinleib, McNamara, & Castelli, 1983; Willett et al., 1995). In addition, gaining weight in adulthood increases the risk of coronary heart disease (Willett et al., 1995). Similarly, for diabetes, both current weight and weight gain since age 18 are strongly related to the chance of developing this disease (Colditz et al., 1990; Colditz, Willett, Rotnitzky, & Manson, 1995). In the National Health and Nutrition Examination Survey (NHANES II), overweight adults were about three times as likely to develop diabetes as nonoverweight adults; the risk of developing hypertension was also increased threefold in overweight adults (Van Itallie, 1985).

What is less recognized by many is the fact that obesity also increases the risk of certain forms of cancer, particularly hormone-dependent cancers (endometrial, ovarian, breast, cervical, prostate) and gastrointestinal/hepatic/renal cancers (colorectal, gallbladder, pancreatic; Manson et al., 1995; Pi-Sunyer, 1991).

The relation between obesity and mortality is complex and different studies reach different conclusions (Van Itallie & Lew, 1992). Some of the discrepancies between these studies are due to methodological problems, such as the failure to control for smoking (smokers are thinner and die earlier; thus, low body weight may appear to be a risk factor for mortality, whereas it is really smoking that is the risk factor). In the strongest studies, there appears to be an almost linear, continuous relation between BMI and mortality. For example, the Nurses Health Study followed over 115,000 women, from age 30 to 55 at study entry, for 16 years (Manson et al., 1995). The lowest mortality rates were seen in women with a BMI of 19 to 21 (equivalent to 15% below the U.S. average for women of similar age). Among women with a BMI of 32 or greater, the relative risk of death from cardiovascular disease was 4.1 and the risk of death from cancer was 2.1 compared to women with a BMI of < 19 (Manson et al., 1995). Weight gain of 10 kg since age 18 was also associated with increased mortality.

Effect of Body Fat Distribution on Health Consequences of Obesity

It has become increasingly clear that body fat distribution, as well as total body fat, contributes to the health consequences of obesity (J. Vague, Bjorntorp, Guy-Grand, Rebuffe-Scrive, & P. Vague, 1985). Abdominal obesity, where a disproportionate amount of fat is found in the abdominal areas, is associated with increased risk of hypertension, diabetes, coronary heart disease, and mortality (Pi-Sunyer, 1991). Abdominal obesity is seen most commonly in men, in those who are heavier, and also appears to be associated with high dietary fat intake, low exercise, and smoking; there also appears to be a genetic contribution to body fat distribution (Kaye, Folsom, Prineas, Potter, & Gapstur, 1990; Wing, Matthews, Kuller, Meilahn, & Plantinga, 1991a).

The most accurate way to determine the amount of fat in the abdominal area is to use sophisticated techniques such as computed tomography (CT scans) or magnetic resonance imaging (MRI). However, a very simple way of estimating abdominal obesity is to measure the circumference of the waist. A waist circumference of > 95 cm suggests high abdominal obesity (Lemieux, Prud'Homme, Bouchard, Tremblay, & Despres, 1996). Recent studies suggest that weight loss and increased exercise may each contribute independently to reducing abdominal obesity (Despres et al., 1991; Wadden et al., 1988).

Psychosocial Consequences of Obesity

Overweight individuals are exposed to significant prejudice and discrimination. Children as young as age 6 rate overweight children as lazy, stupid, dirty, and prefer not to play with overweight peers (Wadden & Stunkard, 1993). These prejudices exist throughout society, extending even to physicians who prefer not to treat overweight patients.

Gortmaker, Must, Perrin, Sobol, and Dietz (1993) documented important social and economic consequences of obesity that were greater than those seen with many other chronic physical conditions. A sample of over 10,000 individuals were studied first at age 16 to 24, and then followed prospectively for the next 7 years. Women who were overweight at age 16 to 24 were found, 7 years later, to have completed less schooling, to be 20% less likely to be married, and to have lower household income, independent of baseline socioeconomic status or aptitude test scores. Men who were overweight at age 16 to 24 were 11% less likely to be married. In contrast, the young people who had asthma, musculoskeletal abnormalities, and other chronic health conditions at baseline did not show any of these negative consequences. Although this study did not directly measure discrimination, it is likely that the stigma and discrimination associated with being overweight explain these results.

Given these findings of prejudice and discrimination against the obese, it might be expected that the obese would have higher rates of depression and psychological disturbances. However, in population-based studies, no significant differences in psychological measures between obese and lean subjects have been reported (Wadden & Stunkard, 1993). The only psychological effects seem to be very specific to obesity, with greater dissatisfaction with body shape among the obese and greater problems with binge eating. Binge eating disorder (BED), which was included in the appendix of *DSM–IV* and is characterized by periods of eating large amounts of food and a feeling of loss of control, occurs in less than 10% of individuals with BMI of < 30 but in over 40% of those with BMI > 34 (Marcus, 1993; Spitzer et al., 1992).

Benefits of Weight Loss

As already discussed, obesity clearly increases morbidity and mortality. To date there has not been a major clinical trial to show that weight loss decreases mortality, but there is extensive evidence that weight loss will lower blood pressure, reduce total and LDL cholesterol, increase HDL cholesterol, decrease triglycerides, and improve glycemic control (Kanders & Blackburn, 1992; Olefsky, Reaven, & Farquhar, 1974; Wing et al., 1987). Many of these positive effects may be related to the fact that weight loss improves insulin sensitivity, which is in turn associated with blood pressure, lipids, and glycemic control. Moreover, each of these changes occur after just modest weight losses of approximately 10% of initial body weight. Although larger weight losses produce greater benefits, small weight losses in even very overweight persons will produce significant improvement in these health parameters. Thus, individuals who are markedly overweight do not need to reduce to ideal body weight to experience health benefits; rather, such individuals should be encouraged to lose 10% of their weight (20 lb in a 200 lb person) and then maintain this weight loss as a way of improving their health.

There are also positive effects of weight loss on psychosocial variables. Behavioral weight control programs that assess mood before, during, and after participation in treatment show reductions in depression and anxiety over the course of the program (Wadden & Stunkard, 1993; Wing, Epstein, Marcus, & Kupfer, 1984). Although subsequent to treatment there is some worsening in mood, these measures usually remain below baseline levels.

Unfortunately, many individuals who try to lose weight will experience initial success followed subsequently by weight regain. Thus, researchers have been trying to determine whether such yo-yo dieting, or weight cycling, has negative physiological or psychological effects. The most recent prospective studies on this topic suggest that there are no negative effects of such voluntary weight cycles (National Task Force on the Prevention and Treatment of Obesity, 1994). When overweight individuals lose weight and then subsequently return to baseline, their lipids and blood pressure also return to baseline, but do not overshoot baseline. Weight cycling also does not negatively affect resting metabolic rate, the ease/difficulty of future weight loss efforts, or body fat distribution. Fewer studies have assessed psychological parameters, but these too do not appear to differ consistently between weight cyclers and nonweight cyclers (Foster, Wadden, Kendall, Stunkard, & Vogt, 1996; Venditti, Wing, Jakicic, Butler, & Marcus, 1996).

In several epidemiological studies, it was observed that weight cycling increased the risk of all cause mortality, and particularly cardiovascular deaths (Blair, Shaten, Brownell, Collins, & Lissner, 1993; Lissner et al., 1991; National Task Force on the Prevention and Treatment of Obesity, 1994). However, more detailed analyses of these data suggest that these negative effects occur primarily in association with involuntary weight loss, and that voluntary weight losses may, in contrast, be related to improved health and decreased risk of mortality (Williamson et al., 1995).

CAUSES OF OBESITY

Genetics

Twin studies and adoption studies have consistently shown a strong genetic component to obesity (Bouchard, 1995; Stunkard et al., 1986; Stunkard, Harris, Pedersen, & McClearn, 1990). Although there continues to be discussion regarding the proportion of the variability in obesity that is attributable to genetics versus environment, many conclude that it is probably close to 50:50.

Bouchard and colleagues showed that genetic variation interacts with environmental manipulations in determining weight change (Bouchard et al., 1990). These investigators overfed 12 pairs of monozygotic twins 1,000 kcal/day extra for 100 days. They found marked variability between twin pairs in the amount of weight gained with overfeeding, but a high degree of concordance within twin pairs; thus, weight gain in one twin predicted weight gain in the other. Similar findings were observed with exercise (Bouchard et al., 1994), suggesting that the effect of these behavior changes on body weight may be mediated by genetic factors.

The recent discovery of the genes responsible for obesity in several animal models (specifically the ob gene, which codes for leptin, and the gene for the leptin receptor) has dramatically energized this field and led to a burgeoning of research on the regulation of body weight (Campfield, Smith, & Burn, 1996). A number of genes that may be related to human obesity are currently being examined. However, the importance of these genetic factors must be kept in perspective. The recent marked increases in the prevalence of obesity are not due to changes in genes, but clearly arise from changes in the environment. Similarly, as native populations become Westernized, their risk of obesity rises dramatically. These changes are due to adoption of a Western diet (sometime referred to as "Coca-Cola-nization") and decreased physical activity. This is well illustrated by a recent study comparing Pima Indians who live in the United States with a group of recently identified Pimas, from the same genetic background, who live in a rural area of Mexico (Ravussin, Valencia, Esparza, Bennett, & Schulz, 1994). These Mexican Pimas, who have no electricity, maintain an agrarian lifestyle and consume a traditional Pima diet. Whereas 50% of American Pimas are overweight, with a mean BMI of 35.5, the Mexican Pimas have an average BMI of only 25.1. Such data suggest that genetic background may predispose some individuals to obesity or leanness, but environmental factors determine whether these predispositions will be manifested.

Environmental and Behavioral Factors

Body weight is regulated by the amount of energy taken in through eating and the amount of energy expended. When these two are in balance, weight is maintained. Energy imbalance will result in weight change. When there is an increase in eating or a decrease in expenditure, weight gain occurs; with decreased eating and/or increased expenditure, weight loss occurs. Each of these behaviors is briefly reviewed next.

Eating Behavior. Until recently it has been difficult to demonstrate that overweight individuals eat more than normal weight individuals. This is due to the fact that the only way of determining intake has been to ask people to self-report what they eat, a notoriously unreliable approach. Recent studies using the doubly labeled water technique to more objectively determine energy expenditure have allowed researchers to back track to estimate energy intake (Schoeller et al., 1986). (Because individuals who are weight stable must be in energy balance, there must be a balance between what is eaten and what is being expended.) With this more precise measure, it has become clear that overweight individuals eat more than normal weight, as would be expected for their heavier weight. In addition, studies with overweight persons who consider themselves "light-eaters" have shown that these individuals actually have much higher intake than they recognize (Bandini, Schoeller, Cyr, & Dietz, 1990; Lichtman et al., 1992).

There is also evidence that overweight individuals consume greater amounts of dietary fat than do leaner individuals (Rolls & Shide, 1992; Tucker & Kano, 1992). Fat has 9 calories per gram, whereas carbohydrates and protein each have 4 calories per gram. Thus, it is easy to overeat fat. In addition, several investigators have shown that overweight individuals prefer food stimuli with higher fat intake (Drewnowski, Brunzell, Sande, Iverius, & Greenwood, 1985; Drewnowski, Kurth, & Rahaim, 1991). This may be particularly true of overweight individuals who repeatedly lose and regain weight (Mela & Sacchetti, 1991). In addition, children's preferences for high fat foods appear to be determined not only by the child's own fatness but also by the fatness of their mother (Johnson & Birch, 1994), suggesting that one aspect of genetic vulnerability to obesity may be through increased preference for high fat foods. Other studies also provide evidence that genetic factors may influence taste preferences and percent energy derived from carbohydrates and fat (although genetic factors do not seem to play a large role in determining total energy intake).

Eating behavior is a complex phenomenon, controlled by many physiological processes, learning history, and sociocultural factors. One of the strongest determinants of food intake is preference; people eat what they like. Preferences may to some extent be innately programmed. Humans innately prefer sweet taste and may also exhibit an innate preference for meat, for dietary fat, or both (Institute of Medicine, 1991). However, learning history and sociocultural factors also play a major role in determining food preferences. Rozin and Schiller (1980) showed that 6- to 7-year-old Mexican children will select a spicy hot snack over a sweet one when given a choice, despite the fact that there appears to be an innate aversion to chilis and a liking for sweets. Familiarity is also an important determinant of food preference, and it is possible to change food preferences by increasing familiarity with a previously novel food item (Birch & Fisher, 1996). Pairing foods with positive social contexts can also affect preferences such that foods served at holidays or used as rewards become preferred. In contrast, when children are coerced to eat a food, their preference for that food decreases. Thus learning history is an important determinant of food preferences.

Whether it is necessary to change food preferences in adults in order to change intake or how best to do so, is unclear. Studies with low sodium diets have shown that after repeated exposure to low sodium foods there is a change in salt preference in favor of lower sodium content. Thus, changing the behavior eventually changes the preferences (not the reverse). Whether this occurs with fat preferences is unclear.

Other factors that influence intake include the social environment, the foods available, and their prices. People eat more when in the company of others, and will model the consumption of their peers. Experimental studies have shown that intake of a subject can be increased by having a confederate consume more cookies from a buffet table (Wing & Jeffery, 1979). Variety of foods also affect the amount eaten. If only one type of food is available at a meal, people will eat some of this item and then gradually cease eating. However, if a new type of food is then introduced, consumption of the new food will increase, demonstrating a phenomenon called "sensory specific satiety" (Hetherington & Rolls, 1996). Thus one way to limit intake may be to limit the choices available at a given meal. A recent study has shown that increasing the variety of fruits available at a cafeteria and decreasing the costs of these foods leads to increased fruit consumption (Jeffery, French, Raether, & Baxter, 1994). Thus, cost, availability, and variety all influence intake without modifying preferences. Given the goal of improving eating habits of the American public as a whole, it is interesting to consider whether by making healthier foods more available and less expensive it would be possible to increase consumption of these foods and consequently preferences, rather than first trying to influence food preferences.

Energy Expenditure. There are several components to energy expenditure. Resting metabolic rate (RMR) is the energy expended when resting in bed in order to maintain various body systems, such as body temperature. RMR accounts for approximately 60% to 70% of total energy expenditure in sedentary individuals and is primarily determined by the amount of lean body mass. Overweight individuals have more lean body mass, as well as more fat mass, thus these individuals tend to have higher RMR than less overweight individuals.

The second component of energy expenditure (accounting for about 10% of expenditure) is the thermic effect of food, or the energy cost involved in metabolizing food. There is inconsistency regarding differences between obese and lean in this component of energy expenditure, but even if differences do occur they are small and represent an unlikely explanation for marked obesity.

The third component is voluntary physical activity. This component is the most variable. Although it accounts for 20% to 30% of total energy expenditure in sedentary individuals, it represents a larger component in those who are more active. A number of studies have shown that overweight individuals are less active than normal weight individuals, although not all studies are consistent (Pi-Sunyer, 1992). Recent studies suggest that overweight individuals not only spend less time doing physical activity, but they also spend more time doing inactive pursuits (such as watching TV; Ching et al., 1996). A number of studies have shown a direct association between hours of TV/day and prevalence of obesity (Gortmaker et al., 1996). This third component is clearly the most easily modified aspect of energy expenditure, and is a primary target of lifestyle interventions for prevention and treatment of obesity.

PREVENTION

As previously described, the problem of obesity is increasing in the United States. One approach to this problem is to try to prevent weight gain and the development of obesity by focusing either on entire populations or on selected individuals. In the public health approach, researchers have attempted to prevent weight gain in entire populations by providing education about nutrition, exercise, and weight; improving access to healthy foods and exercise; or offering incentives for healthy behavior to all individuals in a given community (Taylor et al., 1991), worksite (Hennrikus & Jeffery, 1996), or school (Simons-Morton, Parcel, Baranowski, Forthofer, & O'Hara, 1991). Other programs are able to offer more intensive weight gain prevention interventions by focusing on selected individuals rather than large populations. For example, Jeffery conducted two randomized, controlled prevention trials. In the first study of 219 normal weight subjects, the intervention was provided via a monthly newsletter for 1 year (Forster, Jeffery, Schmid, & Kramer, 1988). Subjects were also asked to report their weight each month on a postcard, and received financial incentives for weight maintenance. The treatment was effective for men, but not for women: Men in the intervention group lost 4.7 lb and controls lost 1.4 lb; for women, the weight losses were 1.0 lb and 0.1 lb. The second study used a similar treatment, but included 1,226 normal weight and overweight subjects (Jeffery & French, 1997), and specifically included a sample of lower SES women. Over 1 year there were no group differences in weight gain, although there was a trend for men and higher SES women in the control group to gain more weight than those in the treated group (but among lower SES women, there was a trend for higher weight gain in the treated group).

A more cost effective approach may be to identify individuals who are at particularly high risk for weight gain, and tailor the intervention to their specific situation. Several groups at high risk for weight gain include young adults, women in the menopausal transition, and recent ex-smokers. Weight gain prevention may also be particularly cost effective in groups for whom weight gain carries particularly adverse health risks, such as those at risk for developing diabetes. Before discussing these specific approaches, several methodological points are of interest. First, it is important to assess both acceptability and effectiveness of prevention interventions. Individuals who do not yet have a weight problem may be less willing to participate in interventions to prevent weight gain; the ideal time for weight gain prevention interventions would be when individuals are at high risk for weight gain, and are willing to make changes to prevent the problem.

Second, most prevention studies have analyzed group differences in mean weight gain, which is the analysis strategy commonly used in weight loss programs. However, prevention studies are not intended to produce large weight losses, but rather to prevent relatively small weight gains. Therefore there may be relatively small differences between groups in mean weight change. It may thus be more instructive to compare the treatment and control group on the percentage of subjects who maintain their baseline weight rather than comparing mean weight changes. However, few studies have used this analysis strategy.

YOUNG ADULTS

The risk of large weight gains is greatest during the young adult years. One study looked at the 10-year incidence of major weight gain in adults, defined as a weight gain of at least 5 BMI units, or about 30 lb, in 10 years (Williamson, Kahn, Remington, & Anda, 1990). Such major weight gains occurred most commonly in those from age 25 to 34, affecting 8.4% of women and 3.9% of men in this age group. In addition, the Dormont High School study found that between age 17 and 34, women gained 17 lb and men gained 38 lb (Yong, Kuller, Rutan, & Bunker, 1993).

There has been no research on why young adults gain weight, but this time period clearly encompasses many life changes that could influence eating and exercise habits. For example, most people make the transition from being students to being employed, and they often have dramatic changes in their living situations, either establishing their own residence or getting married and living with a spouse. Many individuals begin a family and are engaged in childrearing. Because they are busy in their new adult roles, they may have less time available for meal planning and food preparation and may also spend less time in organized sports activities.

There are no published studies to prevent weight gain in young adults, but a recent pilot study to prevent weight gain in normal weight women from age 25 to 35 compared weekly group meetings or a correspondence course to a no-treatment control group (Klem & Wing, 1997). At the end of the 10-week treatment, the women who attended weekly meetings had lost 4.7 lb, the correspondence group had lost 1.8 lb, and the control group had lost 0.8 lb. However, women appeared to be more likely to participate in the correspondence course than the weekly meetings; 86% of women randomized to the correspondence group attended the initial orientation and enrolled in the study, compared to only 50% of women assigned to group meetings. These results suggest that from a public health perspective the correspondence approach may be as or more effective than the group meetings.

A similar study to prevent weight gain in young adult men focused on increasing their physical activity through weekly meetings and group exercise sessions or a correspondence intervention. After 4 months of treatment, men in the group program and the correspondence program had lost similar amounts of weight (1.9 vs. 1.3 kg, respectively), and those in the control group gained 0.22 kg (Leermakers, Jakicic, & Wing, unpublished study). Fitness changes were also somewhat better in the two interventions than in the control group, with no differences between the interventions. Further research is needed to determine what type of intervention will be most acceptable and effective in preventing weight gain in men and women in this high risk age group.

PREGNANCY

One life event common in the young adult years is pregnancy; difficulty in losing the weight gained during pregnancy may contribute to the development of obesity in young adult women. The recommended weight gain during pregnancy is 25 lb to 35 lb for normal weight women, with a higher range for underweight women and a lower range for overweight women (National Academy of Sciences Institute of Medicine, 1990). Most women lose this weight after the baby is born, and have a permanent weight gain of only 1 or 2 pounds. However, a subset of women retain far more weight, with the strongest predictor of permanent weight retention being excessive weight gain during pregnancy. For example, one study found that women who gained more than recommended during their pregnancy were 17.0 lb over their pre-pregnancy weights 6 months after delivery, and 31% were classified as overweight; in contrast, those who gained within the guidelines were only 8.4 lb above their pre-pregnancy weight and only 14% were overweight (Scholl, Hediger, Schall, Ances, & Smith, 1995).

The majority of studies that have attempted to prevent excessive weight gain during pregnancy have been in women who have comorbid health problems, particularly gestational diabetes. In women who develop diabetes during pregnancy, levels of glucose in the blood are no longer appropriately regulated by the body; therefore strict attention to diet and exercise are necessary to control blood glucose levels. Studies that have examined the use of a calorie-restricted diet to improve glucose levels in pregnant women with diabetes have also found that the rate of weight gain was reduced during the period of calorie restriction (Algert, Shragg, & Hollingswroth, 1985), suggesting that weight gain during pregnancy can be limited with calorie restriction with no adverse effects. Only one study has examined the use of calorie restriction, exercise, and feedback about weight gain to prevent excessive weight gain in nondiabetic pregnant women. In this study, 61 normal weight women and 49 overweight women were randomly assigned to receive either standard pregnancy counseling or an individualized behavioral intervention designed to prevent excessive weight gain during pregnancy. Preliminary results show that the intervention reduced the number of normal weight women with excessive weight gain from 58% to 33%; however, the intervention was not effective for women who were already overweight before becoming pregnant (Polley, Wing, Meier, Sims, & DeBranski, 1997).

SMOKING CESSATION

Another key time for weight gain prevention efforts may be in the period following smoking cessation. Individuals who smoke weigh about 7 lb less than nonsmokers and smoking cessation is associated with about a 6 lb weight gain (Klesges, Meyers, Winders, & French, 1989). Concern about weight gain is thought to interfere with smoking cessation, especially in women; thus, some researchers have attempted to prevent this weight gain by offering weight control interventions in conjunction with smoking cessation interventions (Gritz, Klesges, & Meyers, 1989; Perkins, 1994). For example, Hall and colleagues (Hall, Tunstall, Vila, & Duffy, 1992) offered a 2-week smoking cessation program, then randomly assigned the 165 participants who completed the program to a control group, a support group for weight issues, and a more intensive individualized behavioral program to prevent weight gain. In the behavioral intervention, individuals monitored their weight daily, and restricted their calories in response to weight gain. They were also given an exercise prescription and taught behavioral strategies. At 6 weeks and 52 weeks, weight gains in the two prevention groups were no different from weight gain in the control group, but participants in the two prevention groups were more likely to return to smoking. Similar results were found by Pirie (Pirie et al., 1992), who provided weight control counseling at the same time as the smoking cessation intervention. Thus, efforts to combine smoking cessation programs with weight gain prevention programs have been unsuccessful in preventing weight gain, and appear to increase smoking relapse rates. Better results may be obtained by focusing on exercise, rather than weight loss, in the period surrounding smoking cessation (Marcus, Albrecht, Niaura, Abrams, & Thompson, 1991).

MENOPAUSAL TRANSITION

A high risk period for weight gain in women is the period surrounding menopause; women gain on average 1–2 lb/year between age 40 and 55. It was once thought that menopause itself caused weight gain, but recent studies show that weight gain occurs in this age group regardless of menopausal status or use of hormone replacement therapy (Wing, Matthews, Kuller, Meilahn, & Plantinga, 1991b), and is best correlated with changes in physical activity level (Owens, Matthews, Wing, & Kuller, 1992). It is particularly important to prevent weight gain in this age group because of the high risk of cardiovascular disease that occurs in postmenopausal women. In the ongoing Women's Healthy Lifestyle Project, healthy perimenopausal women participated in a 20-week behavioral program that focused on reducing dietary fat intake and increasing moderate intensity activities, such as walking. They were also encouraged to lose modest amounts of weight (5–15 lb, depending on baseline weight status). Participants will be followed for 5 years, but 6-month results are now available (Simkin-Silverman et al., 1995). After 6 months, women in the prevention group had lost 10 lb on average, versus 0.5 lb in the control group. Women attended 11 of 15 sessions, and demonstrated improvements in risk factors such as diet and exercise habits, lipid profiles, and blood pressure. The researchers have not reported the percentage of women who gained weight in each group, but the dramatic differences in average weight change suggest that an intensive prevention program is well-accepted and successful, at least in the short term, for this group of women.

OVERWEIGHT CHILDREN

Finally, another approach to preventing obesity is to treat children and adolescents who are already developing weight problems. About a quarter of children in the United States are overweight, and a recent review found that about half of obese school-age children become obese adults, a risk four to seven times higher than that of their normal weight peers (Serdula et al., 1993). Thus, efforts to treat obesity in childhood may prevent adult obesity. Behavior change may be more effective in children because parents still have some degree of control over the children's eating, and can be trained to provide appropriate modeling and contingencies. Epstein and colleagues conducted a series of family-based behavioral treatment programs for overweight children, with remarkably good results, both short and long term (Epstein, 1996). In Epstein's programs, both parents and children attend weekly group meetings, and weight loss is promoted through: (a) a simple diet plan, the "stoplight diet," that promotes healthy food choices by categorizing foods as red, yellow, or green; (b) an exercise program; and (c) instruction in the use of behavioral techniques such as self-monitoring, social reinforcement, and modeling. As long as 10 years after these 6- to 12-month programs, treated children have decreased their percent overweight by approximately 8% to 15%, and untreated controls have increased their percent overweight by 8% to 12%, depending on the study (Epstein, Valoski, Wing, & McCurley, 1994). Children are most successful in these programs when they are treated with their overweight parents (and both are targeted for weight loss), and children tend to be more successful than their parents (Epstein, 1996).

OTHER HIGH RISK GROUPS

Several other groups are known to be at high risk for obesity, but there have been no systematic studies to prevent weight gain in these individuals. One well-documented group is the offspring of mothers with gestational diabetes. These infants are often overweight at birth, and although their weight may normalize in early childhood, they are at increased risk of becoming overweight in later childhood and adolescence (Pettitt et al., 1991; Silverman et al., 1991). For example, Silverman and colleagues found that by age 8, 50% of the offspring of diabetic mothers had weights greater than the 90th percentile (Silverman et al., 1991). Prevention efforts would be particularly beneficial in the children of diabetic mothers because both having a diabetic mother and obesity are risk factors for the development of NIDDM.

Because obesity is a strong risk factor for NIDDM, it might also be beneficial to prevent the development of diabetes by treating or preventing weight gain in those at risk for NIDDM, including those with a family history of NIDDM and/or impaired glucose tolerance. Several studies have shown that individuals with multiple risk factors for NIDDM can reduce their risk of developing NIDDM by losing weight (Pan et al., 1997; Torjesen et al., 1997). For example, a recent study offered a 2-year behavioral weight loss program to overweight, middle-aged individuals with a family history of diabetes (Wing et al., 1998). A no-treatment control group was compared to groups given diet only, exercise only, or diet plus exercise. Initial weight losses were better in the groups given diet instruction, but unfortunately, at 2 years there were no group differences in weight loss. However, in each of the groups a 10 lb weight loss reduced the risk of developing diabetes over 2 years by about 30%. Thus again even modest weight losses can have a dramatic impact on health.

In summary, it is quite possible to identify groups that are at high risk for becoming obese, but there has been very little research in the prevention of weight gain in these groups. Initial results suggest that this may be a promising area for research.

TREATMENT

Since the 1970s, behavioral approaches have been the treatment of choice for mild to moderate obesity. The goal of behavioral approaches is to help patients change their eating and exercise behaviors by teaching them to rearrange the antecedents (cues) and consequences (reinforcers) that control these behaviors. Behavioral programs are typically delivered in a closed group format, with weekly meetings for approximately 6 months, followed by less frequent contact. At each meeting, participants are weighed individually, self-monitoring records are collected and reviewed, and a lecture/discussion is presented. Topics include nutrition and exercise information (e.g., low fat eating, eating in restaurants, exercise in different weather conditions) and behavioral topics (e.g., self-monitoring of eating and exercise behavior, stimulus control, assertiveness).

The weight losses obtained during the initial phase of behavioral treatment programs have improved over the past 25 years, as documented by several reviews of this literature (Brownell & Jeffery, 1987; Wadden, 1993). Summarizing studies published between 1990 and 1995, Wing (1997) concluded that, on average, participants in behavioral programs will lose 9.7 kg over 26 weeks of treatment (Table 15.2).

However, in contrast to improved short-term results, long-term results have remained fairly constant. With current treatments, patients maintain a weight loss of 5.2 kg at 1 year follow-up (Wing, 1997), or about 61% of their initial weight loss (Wing, 1997). Few studies have provided data for 3 to 5 years of treatment, but it appears that there is continued weight regain in these longer studies (Kramer, Jeffery, Forster, & Snell, 1989; Wadden, Sternberg, Letizia, Stunkard, & Foster, 1989). Consequently, behavioral researchers have been focusing on improving long-term weight loss and maintenance. The basic behavioral techniques used in standard behavioral weight control programs are described, and new approaches being used to produce longer lasting changes in diet, exercise, and body weight are highlighted.

BEHAVIORAL TECHNIQUES

Participants in behavioral weight loss programs are given calorie, fat, and exercise goals designed to produce a weight loss of about 2 lb per week. To determine an appropriate calorie goal for weight loss, current intake is estimated by assuming that the individual consumes 12 kcal/lb of body weight. Thus a 200 lb person would be estimated to be eating 2400 kcal/day to maintain their weight. In order to promote a weight loss of 2 lb/week, this intake must be reduced by 1,000 kcal/day or 7,000 kcal/week. Typically, behavioral programs use calorie goals of 1,000 to 1,500 kcal/day, with the higher goal reserved for individuals who weigh more than 200 lb. The fat goal may range from 20% to 30% of calories from fat, and is usually prescribed to participants in grams/day to facilitate self-monitoring. If an individual was assigned a 1,000 kcal goal with 20% as fat, then 200 calories would be from fat; because one gram of fat has 9 calories, the participant would be given a fat gram goal of 22 grams of fat. The exercise goal has traditionally been set at about 1,000 kcal/week over current activity levels. Walking is the preferred type of exercise because it is easy and requires minimal equipment. A good rule of thumb is that 1 mile of walking expends 100 calories; thus, 1,000 kcals can be expended by walking 2 miles on 5 days each week. More detailed energy expenditure charts that take into account current body weight and indicate calories expended in a variety of other activities are often used in behavioral programs.

TABLE 15.2
Summary of Results (Mean + SD) of 14 Behavioral Treatment Studies 1990–1995

	Total
Studies	N = 14
Treatment Groups	N = 34
Subjects/Group at Entry	N = 33 ± 12
Initial Wt (kg)	92.8 ± 7.9
Duration Treatment (wks)	27 ± 13
% Completing Treatment	83 ± 13%
Weight Loss during Treatment (kg)	9.7 ± 4.1
Weight Loss/Week (kg/wk)	0.39 ± 0.15
Duration of Follow-up (Pre to Follow-up) (wks)	64 ± 17
Duration of Follow-up from Post Treatment (wks)	40 ± 11
# of Contacts during Follow-up	6.3 ± 5.0
% Completing Follow-up	76 ± 13%
Weight Loss (Pre to Follow-up) (kg)	5.6 ± 3.0
% of Initial Weight Loss Retained	60.3 ± 21.7

Note. Excluding no treatment control groups, computer only treatment programs, and exercise only conditions. Adapted from "Behavioral Approaches to the Treatment of Obesity" by R. R. Wing. In G. Bray, C. Bouchard, & P. T. James (Eds.), *Handbook of Obesity*, New York: Marcel Dekker.

The cornerstone of behavior change is self-monitoring, in which patients track their progress toward calorie, fat, and exercise goals. Patients are asked to keep a diary of their eating and exercise behaviors, which is to be filled out throughout the day (rather than retrospectively). They are instructed to list everything they eat and drink, using food labels or a book of food composition to estimate calories and/or fat. Each type of exercise is also listed, including time spent exercising, and the number of calories expended. For each diary entry they are also encouraged to note the time of day and circumstances. The patient is then taught to use the diary to evaluate their current behavior, identify problems, and select specific behaviors to target for change.

After identifying a target behavior, goal setting is used to specify the desired change. Although the overall goals for weight loss are quite general (e.g., eat 1,500 kcal/day, < 20% from fat, and exercise 1,000 kcal/week), the use of specific goals breaks the behavior change into small, achievable steps. Thus, a person whose diary shows they are exceeding their fat goal is more likely to succeed if they set a small, specific goal (e.g., "use jam instead of margarine on toast at breakfast"), rather than a general goal, such as "continue to lower fat intake."

Stimulus control techniques are a powerful tool for reorganizing the environment to support the desired behaviors. Patients are taught that it is difficult to consistently make good eating and exercise choices in an environment that does not support the desired behavior. Thus, they are instructed to reduce (or eliminate) cues that encourage overeating/high fat eating (e.g., "do not allow chips, desserts, or other tempting foods in the house"), and to make it as easy as possible to make good choices (e.g., "leave exercise equipment in a highly visible area," "have low-fat snacks readily available in refrigerator").

Finally, participants are also asked to change the environmental consequences of their behavior using positive reinforcers, such as positive feedback or financial contingencies to reward behavior changes.

DIET

Initially, behavioral treatment programs focused primarily on calorie restriction. More recently, participants have been given goals for calorie and fat, and asked to monitor and modify both aspects of their behavior. This change is due in part to the evidence that overweight individuals have higher consumption of fat (Rolls & Shide, 1992; Tucker & Kano, 1992).

Moreover, fat is energy dense compared to other macro nutrients (i.e., fat has 9 kcal/gram and carbohydrate and protein have only 4 kcal/gram), and thus it is easy to overeat when consuming a high-fat diet. In fact, several studies have shown that individuals who are asked simply to restrict fat, but are not asked to count or restrict calories, reduce both their fat and calorie intake and consequently lose weight (Insull et al., 1990; Kendall, Levitsky, Strupp, & Lissner, 1991)—although this may be a temporary phenomena. To determine whether calorie restriction is more or less effective than fat restriction, Jeffery and colleagues compared weight losses achieved by women who were given either a calorie goal only or a fat gram goal only (Jeffery, Hellerstedt, French, & Baxter, 1995). No differences in weight loss were observed over 18 months. However, two other studies (Pascale, Wing, Butler, Mullen, & Bononi, 1995; Schlundt et al., 1993) found evidence that better weight losses are achieved when subjects are given goals for both calories and fat. Thus, this is the strategy now used in most behavioral treatment programs. Fat modified foods (e.g., fat substitutes) have been recently developed and are now widely marketed. It has not yet been determined how the use of fat modified foods affects body weight and weight loss efforts.

Structured Diets: VLCDs and Balanced Structured Eating

Whereas most behavioral weight loss programs recommend balanced diets of from 1,000 to 1,500 kcal/day, some studies have included periods of very low calorie diets (VLCDs). VLCDs are diets of < 800 kcal/day, usually consumed as liquid formula. The simplicity of drinking several cans of liquid each day, and removing food entirely from the diet, makes such regimens effective for some individuals. In fact, VLCDs have been shown to produce weight losses of approximately 20 lb in 12 weeks (Wadden, Stunkard, & Brownell, 1983). However, the problem has been that the weight is often regained when foods are reintroduced to the diet. Wadden and Wing (Wadden, Foster, & Letizia, 1994; Wadden et al., 1989; Wing, Blair, Marcus, Epstein, & Harvey, 1994; Wing, Marcus, Salata, et al., 1991) have tried, in several randomized controlled studies, to develop strategies that would increase the long-term effectiveness of VLCD regimens. These investigators have used VLCD's within the context of long-term behavioral program (Wadden et al., 1994; Wing et al., 1994), continuing to see patients frequently after food intake resumed. However, despite continued contact and the fact that the initial weight losses are improved with the VLCD, in the long term (1–5 years later), patients treated with behavioral programs that included use of VLCD have weight loss comparable to those who were treated in behavioral programs with balanced 1,000 to 1,500 kcal/day diets throughout.

Wing and colleagues also tried to use VLCDs intermittently, alternating 12 weeks of VLCDs with 12 weeks of low calorie diet (Wing et al., 1994). They found that adherence to the second VLCD, and consequently weight loss during the second VLCD, was very poor (Smith & Wing, 1991). Thus, again, overall the VLCDs added little to the low calorie approach.

Behavioral researchers continue to be intrigued with VLCDs because they are successful at helping patients achieve initial weight loss. Recent findings that liquid diets of 400, 600, and 800 kcal/day all produce identical weight loss (Foster et al., 1992) suggest that the advantage of these regimens may be in their simplicity and structure, not the very low calorie intake recommended. Behavioral researchers have thus tried to maintain the simplicity and structure of these regimens, but use higher calorie goals (900 or 1,000) to make these diets safer and allow their use over longer periods of time. Wadden and colleagues (1997) recently utilized a 900 kcal/day diet that consisted of 4 servings daily of liquid meal replacement (150 kcal each) and a prepackaged dinner entree (280–300 kcal) with salad. Subjects utilizing this diet as part of an intensive behavioral program lost 14.5 kg after 17 weeks and maintained the weight loss at 1 year. Similarly, subjects participating in a 10-center clinical trial of cardiovascular risk factor management who were given prepackaged foods lost more weight over 10 weeks than subjects who were allowed to select their own diets according to the American Heart Association (AHA) Step 1 and Step 2 guidelines (4.5 vs. 3.5 kg for men; 4.8 vs. 2.8 kg for women; McCarron et al., 1997).

Jeffery, Wing, and colleagues also showed that providing subjects with the food they are to eat or prescribing a meal-by-meal eating plan may improve weight losses (Jeffery et al., 1993; Wing, Jeffery, Burton, et al., 1996). In their first study on this topic (Jeffery et al., 1993), these investigators randomly assigned 202 overweight adults to either a no-treatment control group, a standard behavioral treatment (SBT), a SBT with food provision, a SBT with financial incentives, or a SBT with food provision and financial incentives. Subjects in the food provision conditions were given a box of food each week for 18 months. This food provision markedly improved weight losses. Subjects in the SBT condition lost 7.7, 4.5, and 4.1 kg at 6, 12, and 18 months, whereas those given food lost 10.1, 9.1, and 6.4 kg at these three time points (see Fig. 15.2). Thus, at 12 months, food provision actually doubled the weight losses. No effect of financial incentives was observed. These positive effects of food provision were replicated in a second study by these investigators. In addition, they found that simply telling patients exactly what to eat for each meal and providing them with a grocery list to purchase these foods was as effective as giving patients the food (Wing, Jeffery, Burton, et al., 1996). It appeared that subjects given meal plans plus grocery lists, as well as those actually given the food, changed the types of food stored in the home and reported a more regular pattern of meal eating and less difficulty with estimating portion size, finding time to plan meals, and controlling eating when not hungry.

All of these studies suggest that patients may find it helpful to be given some structure as they begin to learn new eating and exercise habits. Merely telling patients to consume 1,000 kcal/day with 20% as fat may be more difficult than providing examples of specific meal plans and eating patterns that satisfy these goals.

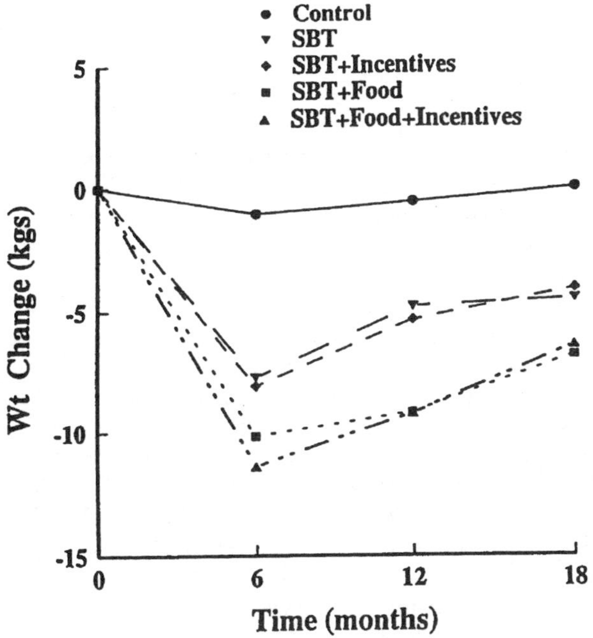

FIG. 15.2. Weight change at 6, 12, and 18 months by treatment group (SBT = standard behavioral treatment). Reprinted from Jeffery et al. (1993).

EXERCISE

The single best predictor of long-term maintenance of weight loss is exercise, and randomized trials consistently show better long-term results for the combination of diet plus exercise than for either intervention alone (Pronk & Wing, 1994). Exercise may improve long-term weight loss by both psychological and physiological mechanisms. Exercise increases caloric expenditure, and may also minimize loss of lean body mass, thereby lessening the reduction in resting energy expenditure observed with weight loss. In addition, exercise has been shown to influence mood state and may maintain or even suppress appetite, thereby making it easier for patients to adhere to their diet in the long term.

The benefits of exercise are observed most consistently in weight loss programs with moderate calorie restriction (diets of 1,000–1,500 kcal/day). Previous studies with very low calorie diets have often failed to show benefits of exercise, perhaps because of the large weight losses achieved with the diet alone. For example, Wadden and colleagues (1997) randomly assigned 128 overweight women to year-long programs focused on diet only (diet of 900–925 kcal), or diet combined with resistance training, aerobic training, or the combination of resistance and aerobic training. Weight losses across the four conditions were 16.5 kg at 24 weeks and 15.1 kg at 48 weeks; no differences were seen between conditions in weight, body composition, mood, or appetite.

Exercise predicts maintenance of weight loss, so the issue becomes how best to encourage overweight individuals to adopt and maintain a higher level of physical activity. One approach may be to encourage more flexible exercise routines. In working with overweight children, Epstein, Wing, Koeske, and Valoski (1985) found that a lifestyle exercise program, where children could choose the type of exercise and the time at which they exercised, was more effective than programmed exercise, where the same exercise had to be done on preset days and times. Jakicic, Wing, Butler, and Robertson (1995) extended this reasoning to adults and hypothesized that encouraging overweight women to exercise in several 10-minute bouts might be more effective than the usual 30- to 40-minute bout prescription. In this study, all women received the same diet, the same behavioral program, and the same exercise goals. However, the long bout group did their exercise in one 40-minute bout, whereas the short bout group was instructed to exercise in four 10-minute bouts. Thus, the short bout group could take a brief walk after each meal, or whenever they found a free 10 minutes. The short bout exercise prescription led to better exercise adherence; these subjects were more likely to exercise on any given day and completed more minutes of exercise over the course of the program (see Fig. 15.3). Their weight losses were also somewhat better. Interestingly, the short and long bout group had comparable improvements in cardiovascular fitness.

Another way to improve exercise adherence is to focus more on the environmental cues and reinforcers for this behavior. Wing and Jeffery, therefore, compared a standard behavioral group that was given diet and exercise goals but encouraged to exercise on their own, with a group given supervised exercise, or supervised exercise with a personal trainer to cue exercise, supervised exercise with financial incentives for attending sessions, or supervised exercise with a trainer and incentives (Wing, Jeffery, Pronk, & Hellerstedt, 1996). The personal trainer and the incentives both were effective in improving attendance at the supervised sessions and the best attendance occurred when both interventions were combined. However, despite better attendance at walk sessions, there were no differences in overall self-reported physical activity. Surprisingly, the best weight loses occurred in the group given diet and exercise goals and encouraged to exercise on their own. Whether this result derives from the benefits of home-based versus group (supervised) exercise (King, Haskell, Taylor, Kraemer, & DeBusk, 1991; Perri, Martin, Leermakers, Sears, & Notelovitz, 1997) or suggests that emphasizing exercise too much may detract from diet remains unclear.

Epstein and colleagues, in their work with overweight children, compared the effectiveness of increasing physical activity (as done in the aforementioned studies) with the effectiveness of decreasing sedentary activities (e.g., TV and computers). A treatment focusing on decreasing sedentary activities was found to produce greater weight losses, better dietary adherence, and increased liking for high intensity activities (Epstein et al., 1995).

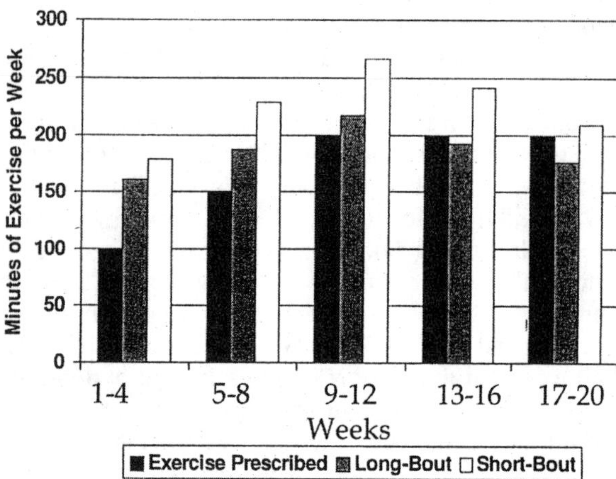

FIG. 15.3. Comparison of exercise adherence rates in overweight women during a 20-week behavioral weight loss program with exercise prescribed in long bouts versus short bouts. Adapted from data published in Jakicic, Wing, Butler, & Robertson (1995).

SOCIAL SUPPORT

Social support has also been investigated as a factor in changing eating and exercise behavior. Friends and family members not only provide social support, but also may model appropriate (or inappropriate) eating and exercise behaviors and serve as a "cue" for these behaviors. Thus, one common strategy is to ask spouses to participate in the weight loss program along with the participant, and to make the same changes in eating and exercise behavior. A recent meta-analysis showed a small positive effect of spouse involvement (Black, Gleser, & Kooyers, 1990), but results have been inconsistent. In a study of patients with type 2 diabetes treated with or without their spouses, Wing found a significant gender effect; women lost more weight when treated with their spouses, but men lost more weight when treated alone (Wing, Marcus, Epstein, & Jawad, 1991).

Other researchers have begun to investigate nonspouse support, including coworkers, other participants, or friends. Jeffery (Hennrikus & Jeffery, 1996) found that worksite interventions, including team competitions, improve long-term weight loss. Wing and Jeffery found that a "personal trainer" increased exercise adherence (Wing, Jeffery, Pronk, & Hellerstedt, 1996); the personal trainer was not a trained exercise physiologist, but a "paid" support person, who reminded the participant of exercise appointments and then walked with the participant. Wing and Jeffery (1999) recently conducted a pilot study to examine the effects of an intervention designed to increase social support through team building activities and group competitions, using participants who were recruited either as individuals or in groups of four acquaintances. They found the best weight losses in those individuals who were recruited with friends and provided with the social support intervention.

These data suggest that efforts to increase social support may be effective in both improving initial and long-term weight losses.

PHARMACOTHERAPY

In recent years, there has been tremendous interest in the pharmacologic treatment of obesity (National Task Force on the Prevention and Treatment of Obesity, 1996). This interest is spurred by the fact that long-term results of behavioral programs continue to be disappointing. There is also increased recognition that obesity is a chronic problem, requiring chronic ongoing therapy. Thus, investigators are beginning to consider long-term (perhaps lifelong) drug treatment for obesity, as would occur with hypertension or other chronic diseases. As part of this change in attitudes about weight loss drugs, the Food and Drug Administration (FDA) in 1996 approved dexfenfluramine for extended use in the treatment of obesity. Dexfenfluramine, which increases serotonin levels by stimulating the release and inhibiting the reuptake of central serotonin, became one of the most widely used drugs. In addition, the combination of fenfluramine (a serotonergic drug) and phentermine (a catecholaminergic drug) became extremely popular for the treatment of obesity. However, evidence suggesting that dexfenfluramine and fenfluramine might be associated with cardiac disease led to their rapid withdrawal from the market.

Despite this adverse experience with pharmacologic treatment of obesity, there continues to be great interest in developing a new drug for this disease. Several other drugs have recently been approved, including orlistat, which is a pancreatic lipase inhibitor, and sibutramine, which is a norepineph- rine and serotonin reuptake inhibitor. These drugs appear to be modestly effective and have fewer risks. At present all that can be concluded is that there must be careful consideration of the risk–benefit ratio of each drug for each individual patient. Moreover, because these medications are typically considered adjuncts to behavioral lifestyle interventions, it will be important to determine how best to combine these two approaches.

MAINTENANCE

Given the major difficulty in producing long-term weight loss, researchers have specifically focused on questions related to the maintenance process. Based on Marlett and Gordon's relapse prevention model (Marlatt & Gordon, 1985), an effort has been made to identify specific situations that might pose problems for dieters and to determine whether coping skills are related to success in dealing with such relapse crises.

Researchers have identified three types of situations where dieters are at risk for overeating. These include situations involving food cues (e.g., being in a restaurant; family meal), situations involving affective cues (e.g., anger, depression) and situations involving boredom or transition (e.g., watching TV). These three high risk situations are quite similar to those identified by smokers.

Moreover, performance of a coping response appears to be related to surviving the relapse crisis. When subjects were asked if they had used any behavioral and/or coping strategies to keep them from overeating, the main difference between lapses that were successfully survived versus those that were not was the performance of any coping responses. Grilo, Shiffman, and Wing (1989) showed that behavioral coping strategies (such as leaving the room) and cognitive coping responses (devaluing the food) are equally effective in preventing lapses, but that the combination of a behavioral and cognitive strategy is the most effective response.

Given this, it is interesting to ask whether the ability to generate coping responses to hypothetical high risk situations would be related to success at long-term weight loss. The answer appears to be "yes." In a study by Drapkin, Wing, and Shiffman (1995), dieters were asked at the beginning of a weight loss program to listen to four scenarios describing high risk situations (i.e., family celebration with food, TV, anger, frustration at work). They rated the difficulty of each of these situations and generated as many coping responses to each scenario as they could. Participants who were able to generate more coping responses to the hypothetical situation subsequently lost more weight. Moreover, participants were able to accurately anticipate which situation would be most difficult for them. Participants who noted the negative affect situation as most difficult were later most likely to lapse in situations involving negative affect. These results suggest the possibility of individually tailoring treatment and teaching patients to deal with those situations that cause them personally the greatest difficulty.

Perri and colleagues have done the most systematic research on the maintenance process (Perri, Nezu, & Viegner, 1992). They showed, for example, that relapse prevention training followed by continued therapist contact improves long-term weight maintenance (Perri, Shapiro, Ludwig, Twentyman, & McAdoo, 1984). Relapse prevention training was provided to one group during the last 6 weeks of the treatment program; these participants were taught about the process of relapse, and practiced skills needed to identify and cope with high risk situations and to recover from acute lapses. Then, during the first 6 months after treatment, half of the participants were asked to maintain weekly contact with therapists by mailing in postcards with information about their progress, which was followed by a telephone call from the therapist. The group that received both relapse prevention training and continued therapist contact had significantly better weight maintenance than any other group, losing an additional 1.6 lb over the year of follow-up (compared to weight regains of 12.3 lb with relapse training only, and 6.5 lb with contact only).

Because so few participants in clinical weight loss programs go on to successfully maintain their weight loss, some researchers have begun to recruit and study individuals who have successfully lost weight and maintained the weight loss. Wing, at the University of Pittsburgh, and Hill, at the University of Colorado, developed a national registry of individuals who have successfully lost 30 lb (regardless of method) and maintained the loss for at least a year; registry members are recruited primarily through media coverage (i.e., magazine, radio, newspaper). Although this is not a representative sample of all successful losers, it provides a rare opportunity to study weight maintenance. The initial cohort of 784 individuals in the registry reported an average weight loss of 66 lb, which they had kept off for 5 years. Nearly all of the registry members used both diet and exercise to lose weight and to maintain their weight loss (Klem, Wing, McGuire, Seagle, & Hill, 1997b). Reported calorie and fat intake were low (averaging 1,380 kcal/day with 24% as fat) and exercise levels were very high (2,800 kcal/week). These data suggest the continued importance of these two behavioral strategies for long-term weight control.

CONCLUSIONS

This chapter has broadly reviewed obesity, with a focus on areas relevant to health psychology. Obesity has long been a focus of health psychologists because behavior plays such an important role in the etiology and treatment of this highly prevalent disorder, which is associated with poor health outcomes, including heart disease and diabetes. Several areas of obesity research offer exciting new areas for research, including:

1. The interaction between genes, such as the ob and leptin receptor genes, and behavior in the etiology of obesity.
2. The determinants of food choice, including availability, cost, and preference.
3. Prevention of weight gain, both in the general population and in identified high risk groups.
4. The effect of low fat and fat modified foods on weight.
5. The use of exercise in weight control and weight maintenance (e.g., appropriate levels, how best to facilitate the adoption of exercise habits, decreasing sedentary activity).
6. The combination of behavior therapy with pharmacological agents.
7. Maintenance of weight loss.

Advances in genetic research and pharmacotherapy have heightened interest in obesity research, and it is vitally important that health psychologists continue to work with scientists and practitioners in these fields, using a multidisciplinary approach to further understand the determinants of obesity, and how best to prevent and treat this condition.

REFERENCES

Algert, S., Shragg, P., & Hollingswroth, D. R. (1985). Moderate caloric restriction in obese women with gestational diabetes. *Obstetrics and Gynecology, 65,* 487–491.

Bandini, L. G., Schoeller, D. A., Cyr, H. N., & Dietz, W. H. (1990). Validity of reported energy intake in obese and nonobese adolescents. *American Journal of Clinical Nutrition, 52,* 421–425.

Birch, L. L., & Fisher, J. A. (1996). The role of experience in the development of children's eating behavior. In E. D. Capaldi (Ed.), *Why we eat what we eat: The psychology of eating* (pp. 113–141). Washington, DC: American Psychological Association.

Black, D. R., Gleser, L. J., & Kooyers, K. J. (1990). A meta-analytic evaluation of couples weight-loss programs. *Health Psychology, 9,* 330–347.

Blair, S. N., Shaten, J., Brownell, K., Collins, G., & Lissner, L. (1993). Body weight change, all-cause and cause-specific mortality in the Multiple Risk Factor Intervention Trial. *Annals of Internal Medicine, 119*(7, P. 2), 749–757.

Bouchard, C. (1995). Genetics and the metabolic syndrome. *International Journal of Obesity, 19,* S52–S59.

Bouchard, C., Tremblay, A., Despres, J. P., Nadeau, A., Lupien, P., Theriault, G., Dussault, J., Moorjani, S., Pinault, S., & Fournier, G. (1990). The response to long-term overfeeding in identical twins. *New England Journal of Medicine, 322,* 1477–1482.

Bouchard, C., Tremblay, A., Despres, J. P., Theriault, G., Nadeau, A., Lupien, P. J., Moorjani, S., Prudhomme, D., & Fournier, G. (1994). The response to exercise with constant energy intake in identical twins. *Obesity Research, 2,* 400–410.

Brownell, K. D., & Jeffery, R. W. (1987). Improving long-term weight loss: Pushing the limits of treatment. *Behavior Therapy, 18,* 353–374.

Campfield, L. A., Smith, F. J., & Burn, P. (1996). The OB protein (leptin) pathway—a link between adipose tissue mass and central neural networks. *Hormone and Metabolic Research, 28,* 619–632.

Ching, P.I.Y.H., Willett, W. C., Rimm, E. B., Colditz, G. A., Gortmaker, S. L., & Stampfer, M. J. (1996). Activity level and risk of overweight in male health professionals. *American Journal of Public Health, 86*(1), 25–30.

Colditz, G. A., Willett, W. C., Rotnitzky, A., & Manson, J. E. (1995). Weight gain as a risk factor for clinical diabetes mellitus in women. *Annals of Internal Medicine, 122,* 481–486.

Colditz, G. A., Willett, W. C., Stampfer, M. J., Manson, J. E., Hennekens, C. H., Arky, R. A., & Speizer, F. E. (1990). Weight as a risk factor for clinical diabetes in women. *American Journal of Epidemiology, 132,* 501–513.

Despres, J. P., Pouliot, M. C., Moorjani, S., Nadeau, A., Tremblay, A., Lupien, P. J., Theriault, G., & Bouchard, C. (1991). Loss of abdominal fat and metabolic response to exercise training in obese women. *American Journal of Physiology, 261,* E159–E167.

Drapkin, R. G., Wing, R. R., & Shiffman, S. (1995). Responses to hypothetical high risk situations: Do they predict weight loss in a behavioral treatment program or the context of dietary lapses? *Health Psychology, 14,* 427–434.

Drewnowski, A., Brunzell, J. D., Sande, K. J., Iverius, P. H., & Greenwood, M.R.C. (1985). Sweet tooth reconsidered: Taste responsiveness in human obesity. *Physiology of Behavior, 35,* 617–622.

Drewnowski, A., Kurth, C. L., & Rahaim, J. E. (1991). Taste preferences in human obesity: Environmental and familial factors. *American Journal of Clinical Nutrition, 54,* 635–641.

Epstein, L. H. (1993). New developments in childhood obesity. In A. J. Stunkard & T. A. Wadden (Eds.), *Obesity: Theory and therapy* (pp. 301–312). New York: Raven.

Epstein, L. H. (1996). Family-based behavioural intervention for obese children. *International Journal of Obesity, 20*(Suppl. 1), S14–S21.

Epstein, L. H., Valoski, A. M., Vara, L. S., McCurley, J., Wisniewski, L., Kalarchian, M. A., Klein, K. R., & Shrager, L. R. (1995). Effects of decreasing sedentary behavior and increasing activity on weight change in obese children. *Health Psychology, 14,* 109–115.

Epstein, L. H., Valoski, A., Wing, R. R., & McCurley, J. (1994). Ten year outcomes of behavioral family based treatment for childhood obesity. *Health Psychology, 13,* 373–383.

Epstein, L. H., Wing, R. R., Koeske, R., & Valoski, A. (1985). A comparison of lifestyle exercise, aerobic exercise, and calisthenics on weight loss in obese children. *Behavior Therapy, 16,* 345–356.

Flegal, K. M., Carroll, M. D., Kuczmarski, R. J., & Johnson, C. L. (1998). Overweight and obesity in the United States: Prevalence and trends, 1960–1994. *International Journal of Obesity, 22,* 39–47.

Forster, J. L., Jeffery, R. W., Schmid, T. L., & Kramer, M. (1988). Preventing weight gain in adults: A pound of prevention. *Health Psychology, 7,* 515–525.

Foster, G. D., Wadden, T. A., Kendall, P. C., Stunkard, A. J., & Vogt, R. A. (1996). Psychological effects of weight loss and regain: A prospective evaluation. *Journal of Consulting and Clinical Psychology, 64*(4), 752–757.

Foster, G. D., Wadden, T. A., Peterson, F. J., Letizia, K. A., Bartlett, S. J., & Conill, A. M. (1992). A controlled comparison of three very-low-calorie diets: Effects on weight, body composition, and symptoms. *American Journal of Clinical Nutrition, 55,* 811–817.

Garrisson, R. J., & Castelli, W. P. (1985). Weight and thirty-year mortality of men in the Framingham Study. *Annals of Internal Medicine, 103,* 1006–1009.

Gortmaker, S. L., Dietz, W. H., Sobol, A. M., & Wehler, C. A. (1987). Increasing pediatric obesity in the United States. *American Journal of Diseases in Children , 141,* 535–540.

Gortmaker, S. L., Must, A., Perrin, J. M., Sobol, A. M., & Dietz, W. H. (1993). Social and economic consequences of overweight in adolescence and young adulthood. *New England Journal of Medicine, 329,* 1008–1012.

Gortmaker, S. L., Must, A., Sobol, A. M., Peterson, K., Colditz, G. A., & Dietz, W. H. (1996). Television viewing as a cause of increasing obesity among children in the United States, 1986–1990. *Archives of Pediatrics & Adolescent Medicine, 150,* 356–362.

Grilo, C. M., Shiffman, S., & Wing, R. R. (1989). Relapse crises and coping among dieters. *Journal of Consulting and Clinical Psychology, 57(4),* 488–495.

Gritz, E. R., Klesges, R. C., & Meyers, A. W. (1989). The smoking and body weight relationship: Implications for intervention and postcessation weight control. *Annals of Behavioral Medicine, 11,* 144–153.

Hall, S. M., Tunstall, C. D., Vila, K. L., & Duffy, J. (1992). Weight gain prevention and smoking cessation: Cautionary findings. *American Journal of Public Health, 82,* 799–803.

Heini, A. F., & Weinsier, R. L. (1997). Divergent trends in obesity and fat intake patterns: The American paradox. *American Journal of Medicine, 102,* 259–264.

Hennrikus, D. J., & Jeffery, R. W. (1996). Worksite intervention for weight control: A review of the literature. *American Journal of Health Promotion, 10*(6), 471–498.

Hetherington, M. M., & Rolls, B. J. (1996). Sensory-specific satiety: Theoretical frameworks and central characteristics. In E. D. Capaldi (Ed.), *Why we eat what we eat: The psychology of eating* (pp. 267–290). Washington, DC: American Psychological Association.

Hubert, H. B., Feinleib, M., McNamara, P. M., & Castelli, W. P. (1983). Obesity as an independent risk factor for cardiovascular disease: A 26–year follow-up of participants in the Framingham Heart Study. *Circulation, 67,* 968–977.

Institute of Medicine. (1991). *Improving America's diet and health: From recommendations to action.* Washington, DC: National Academy Press.

Insull, W., Henderson, M. M., Prentice, R. L., Thompson, D. J., Clifford, C., Goldman, S., Gorbach, S., Moskowitz, M., Thompson, R., & Woods, M. (1990). Results of a randomized feasibility study of a low-fat diet. *Archives of Internal Medicine, 150,* 421–427.

Jakicic, J. M., Wing, R. R., Butler, B. A., & Robertson, R. J. (1995). Prescribing exercise in multiple short bouts versus one continuous bout: Effects on adherence, cardiorespiratory fitness, and weight loss in overweight women. *International Journal of Obesity, 19,* 893–901.

Jeffery, R. W., & French, S. A. (1997). Preventing weight gain in adults–design, methods and one-year results from the Pound of Prevention study. *International Journal of Obesity, 21,* 457–464.

Jeffery, R. W., French, S. A., Raether, C., & Baxter, J. E. (1994). An environmental intervention to increase fruit and salad purchases in a cafeteria. *Preventive Medicine, 23,* 788–792.

Jeffery, R. W., Hellerstedt, W. L., French, S. A., & Baxter, J. E. (1995). A randomized trial of counseling for fat restriction versus calorie restriction in the treatment of obesity. *International Journal of Obesity, 19,* 132–137.

Jeffery, R. W., Wing, R. R., Thorson, C., Burton, L. R., Raether, C., Harvey, J., & Mullen, M. (1993). Strengthening behavioral interventions for weight loss: A randomized trial of food provision and monetary incentives. *Journal of Consulting and Clinical Psychology, 61,* 1038–1045.

Johnson, S. L., & Birch, L. L. (1994). Parents' and children's adiposity and eating style. *Pediatrics, 94*(5), 653–661.

Kanders, B. S., & Blackburn, G. L. (1992). Reducing primary risk factors by therapeutic weight loss. In T. A. Wadden & T. B. Van Itallie (Eds.), *Treatment of the seriously obsese patient* (pp. 213–230). New York: Guilford.

Kaye, S. A., Folsom, A. R., Prineas, R. J., Potter, J. D., & Gapstur, S. M. (1990). The association of body fat distribution with lifestyle and reproductive factors in a population study of postmenopausal women. *International Journal of Obesity, 14,* 583–591.

Kendall, A., Levitsky, D. A., Strupp, B. J., & Lissner, L. (1991). Weight loss on a low-fat diet: Consequence of the imprecision of the control of food intake in humans. *American Journal of Clinical Nutrition, 53,* 1124–1129.

King, A. C., Haskell, W. L., Taylor, C. B., Kraemer, H. C., & DeBusk, R. F. (1991). Group- vs home-based exercise training in healthy older men and women: A community-based clinical trial. *Journal of the American Medical Association, 266,* 1535–1542.

Klem, M. L., & Wing, R. R. (1997). The acceptability of primary prevention of weight gain in women aged 25 through 34 (Abstract). *Annals of Behavioral Medicine, 19 (Supp.),* S100.

Klem, M. L., Wing, R. R., McGuire, M. T., Seagle, H. M., & Hill, J. O. (1997). A descriptive study of individuals successful at long-term maintenance of substantial weight loss. *American Journal of Clinical Nutrition, 66,* 239–246.

Klesges, R. C., Meyers, A. W., Winders, S. E., & French, S. N. (1989). Determining the reasons for weight gain following smoking cessation: Current findings, methodological issues, and future directions for research. *Annals of Behavioral Medicine, 1,* 134–143.

Kramer, F. M., Jeffery, R. W., Forster, J. L., & Snell, M. K. (1989). Long-term follow-up of behavioral treatment for obesity: Patterns of weight regain among men and women. *International Journal of Obesity, 13,* 123–136.

Kuczmarski, R. J., Flegal, K. M., Campbell, S. M., & Johnson, C. L. (1994). Increasing prevalence of overweight among U.S. adults. The National Health and Nutrition Examination Surveys, 1960 to 1991. *Journal of the American Medical Association, 272,* 205–211.

Lemieux, S., Prud'Homme, D., Bouchard, C., Tremblay, A., & Despres, J. (1996). A single threshold value of waist girth identifies normal-weight and overweight subjects with excess visceral adipose tissue. *American Journal of Clinical Nutrition, 64,* 685–693.

Lichtman, S. W., Pisarska, K., Berman, E. R., Pestone, M., Dowling, H., Offenbacher, E., Weisel, H., Heshka, S., Matthews, D. E., & Heymsfield, S. B. (1992). Discrepancy between self-reported and actual caloric intake and exercise in obese subjects. *New England Journal of Medicine, 327,* 1893–1898.

Lissner, L., Odell, P. M., D'Agostino, R. B., Stokes, J., Kreger, B. E., Belanger, A. J., & Brownell, K. D. (1991). Variability of body weight and health outcomes in the Framingham population. *New England Journal of Medicine, 324,* 1839–1844.

Lohman, T. G. (1992). *Advances in Body Composition Assessment.* Champaign, IL: Human Kinetics Publishers.

Manson, J. E., Willett, W. C., Stampfer, M. J., Colditz, G. A., Hunter, D. J., Hankinson, S. E., Hennekens, C. H., & Speizer, F. E. (1995). Body weight and mortality among women. *New England Journal of Medicine, 333*(11), 677–685.

Marcus, B. H., Albrecht, A. E., Niaura, R. S., Abrams, D. B., & Thompson, P. D. (1991). Usefulness of physical exercise for maintaining smoking cessation in women. *American Journal of Cardiology,* 68, 406–407

Marcus, M. D. (1993). Binge eating in obesity. In C. G. Fairburn & G. T. Wilson (Eds.), *Binge eating: Nature, assessment, and treatment* (pp. 77–96). New York: Guilford.

Marlatt, G. A., & Gordon, J. R. (1985). *Relapse prevention: Maintenance strategies in addictive behavior change.* New York: Guilford.

McCarron, D. A., Oparil, S., Chait, A., Haynes, R. B., Kris-Etherton, P., Stern, J. S., Resnick, L. M., Clark, S., Morris, C. D., Hatton, D. C., Metz, J. A., McMahon, M., Holcomb, S., Synder, G. W., & Pi-Sunyer, F. X. (1997). Nutritional management of cardiovascular risk factors: a randomized clinical trial. *Archives of Internal Medicine, 157,* 169–177.

Mela, D. J., & Sacchetti, D. A. (1991). Sensory preferences for fats: Relationships with diet and body composition. *American Journal of Clinical Nutrition, 53,* 908–915.

National Academy of Sciences Institute of Medicine. (1990). *Nutrition during pregnancy.* Washington, DC: National Academy Press.

National Task Force on the Prevention and Treatment of Obesity. (1994). Weight cycling. *Journal of the American Medical Association, 272,* 1196–1202.

National Task Force on the Prevention and Treatment of Obesity. (1996). Long-term pharmacotherapy in the management of obesity. *Journal of the American Medical Association, 276*(23), 1907–1915.

Olefsky, J., Reaven, G. M., & Farquhar, J. W. (1974). Effects of weight reduction on obesity: Studies of lipid and carbohydrate metabolism in normal and hyperlipoproteinemic subjects. *Journal of Clinical Investigation, 53,* 64–77.

Owens, J. F., Matthews, K. A., Wing, R. R., & Kuller, L. H. (1992). Can physical activity mitigate the effects of aging in middle-aged women? *Circulation, 85,* 1265–1270.

Pan, X. R., Li, G. W., Hu, Y. H., Wang, J. X., Yang, W. Y., An, Z. X., Hu, Z. X., Lin, J., Xiao, J. Z., Cao, H. B., Liu, P. A., Jiang, X. G., Jiang, Y. Y., Wang, J. P., Zheng, H., Zhang, H., Bennett, P. H., & Howard, B. V. (1997). Effects of diet and exercise in preventing NIDDM in people with impaired glucose tolerance. *Diabetes Care, 20*(4), 537–544.

Pascale, R. W., Wing, R. R., Butler, B. A., Mullen, M., & Bononi, P. (1995). Effects of a behavioral weight loss program stressing calorie restriction versus calorie plus fat restriction in obese individuals with NIDDM or a family history of diabetes. *Diabetes Care, 18(9),* 1241–1248.

Perkins, K. A. (1994). Issues in the prevention of weight gain after smoking cessation. *Annals of Behavioral Medicine, 16,* 46–52.

Perri, M. G., Martin, A. D., Leermakers, E. A., Sears, S. F., & Notelovitz, M. (1997). Effects of group- versus home-based exercise in the treatment of obesity. *Journal of Consulting and Clinical Psychology, 65,* 278–285.

Perri, M. G., Nezu, A. M., & Viegener, B. J. (1992). *Improving the long-term management of obesity.* New York: Wiley.

Perri, M. G., Shapiro, R. M., Ludwig, W. W., Twentyman, C. T., & McAdoo, W. G. (1984). Maintenance strategies for the treatment of obesity: an evaluation of relapse prevention training and posttreatment contact by mail and telephone. *Journal of Consulting and Clinical Psychology, 52,* 404–413.

Pettitt, D. J., Bennett, P. H., Saad, M. F., Charles, M. A., Nelson, R. G., & Knowler, W. C. (1991). Abnormal glucose tolerance during pregnancy in Pima Indian women: Long-term effects on offspring. *Diabetes, 40*(Suppl. 2), 126–130.

Pirie, P. L., McBride, C. M., Hellerstedt, W. L., Jeffery, R. W., Hatsukami, D., Allen, S., & Lando, H. (1992). Smoking cessation in women concerned about weight. *American Journal of Public Health, 82,* 1238–1243.

Pi-Sunyer, F. X. (1991). Health implications of obesity. *American Journal of Clinical Nutrition, 53,* 1595S-1603S.

Pi-Sunyer, F. X. (1992). The effects of increased physical activity on food intake, metabolic rate, and health risks in obese individuals. In T. A. Wadden & T. B. Van Itallie (Eds.), *Treatment of the seriously obese patient* (pp. 190–210). New York: Guilford.

Polley, B. A., Wing, R. R., Meier, A., Sims, C., & DeBranski, C. (1997). Preventing excessive weight gain during pregnancy in overweight and normal weight women (Abstract). *Annals of Behavioral Medicine, 19*(Suppl.), S071.

Pronk, N. P., & Wing, R. R. (1994). Physical activity and long-term maintenance of weight loss. *Obesity Research, 2,* 587–599.

Ravussin, E., Valencia, M. E., Esparza, J., Bennett, P. H., & Schulz, L. O. (1994). Effects of a traditional lifestyle on obesity in Pima Indians. *Diabetes Care, 17,* 1067–1074.

Rolls, B. J., & Shide, D. J. (1992). The influence of dietary fat on food intake and body weight. *Nutrition Reviews, 50*(10), 283–290.

Rozin, P., & Schiller, D. (1980). The nature and acquisition of a preference of chili pepper by humans. *Motivation and Emotion, 4,* 77–101.

Schlundt, D. G., Hill, J. O., Pope-Cordle, J., Arnold, D., Virts, K. L., & Katahn, M. (1993). Randomized evaluation of a low fat ad libitum carbohydrate diet for weight reduction. *International Journal of Obesity, 17,* 623–629.

Schoeller, D. A., Ravussin, E., Schutz, Y., Acheson, K. J., Baertschi, P., & Jequier, E. (1986). Energy expenditure by doubly labeled water: Validation in humans and proposed calculation. *American Journal of Physiology, 250,* R823–R830.

Scholl, T. O., Hediger, M. L., Schall, J. I., Ances, I. G., & Smith, W. K. (1995). Gestational weight gain, pregnancy outcome, and postpartum weight retention. *Obstetrics and Gynecology, 86,* 423–427.

Serdula, M. K., Ivery, D., Coates, R. J., Freedman, D. S., Williamson, D. F., & Byers, T. (1993). Do obese children become obese adults? A review of the literature. *Preventive Medicine, 22,* 167–177.

Silverman, B. L., Rizzo, T., Green, O. C., Cho, N. H., Winter, R. J., Ogata, E. S., Richards, G. E., & Metzger, B. E. (1991). Long-term prospective evaluation of offspring of diabetic mothers. *Diabetes, 40*(Suppl. 2), 121–125.

Simkin-Silverman, L., Wing, R. R., Hansen, D. H., Klem, M. L., Pasagian-Macaulay, A., Meilahn, E. N., & Kuller, L. H. (1995). Prevention of cardiovascular risk factor elevations in healthy premenopausal women. *Preventive Medicine, 24,* 509–517.

Simons-Morton, B. G., Parcel, G. S., Baranowski, T., Forthofer, R., & O'Hara, N. M. (1991). Promoting physical activity and a heathful diet among children: Results of a school-based intervention study. *American Journal of Public Health, 81,* 986–991.

Smith, D. E., & Wing, R. R. (1991). Diminished weight loss and behavioral compliance during repeated diets in obese patients with Type II diabetes. *Health Psychology, 10,* 378–383.

Spitzer, R. L., Devlin, M., Walsh, B. T., Hasin, D., Wing, R., Marcus, M., Stunkard, A., Yanovski, S., Agras, S., Mitchell, J., & Nonas, C. (1992). Binge eating disorder: A multisite field trial of the diagnostic criteria. *International Journal of Eating Disorders, 11,* 191–203.

Stunkard, A. J., Harris, J. R., Pedersen, N. L., & McClearn, G. E. (1990). The body-mass index of twins who have been reared apart. *New England Journal Medicine, 322,* 1483–1487.

Stunkard, A. J., Sorensen, T. I. A., Hanis, C., Teasdale, T. W., Chakraborty, R., Schull, W. J., & Schulsinger, F. (1986). An adoption study of human obesity. *New England Journal Medicine, 314,* 193–198.

Taylor, C. B., Fortmann, S. P., Flora, J., Kayman, S., Barrett, D. C., Jatulis, D., & Farquhar, J. W. (1991). Effects of long-term community health education on body mass index: The Stanford Five-City Project. *American Journal of Epidemiology, 134,* 235–249.

Torjesen, P. A., Birkeland, K. I., Anderssen, S. A., Hjermann, I., Holme, I., & Urdal, P. (1997). Lifestyle changes may reverse development of the insulin resistance syndrome; The Oslo Diet and Exercise Study: A randomized trial. *Diabetes Care, 20,* 26–31.

Tucker, L. A., & Kano, M. J. (1992). Dietary fat and body fat: A multivariate study of 205 adult females. *American Journal of Clinical Nutrition, 56,* 616–622.

Vague, J., Bjorntorp, P., Guy-Grand, B., Rebuffe-Scrive, M., & Vague, P. (1985). *Metabolic complications of human obesities.* Amsterdam, The Netherlands: Elsevier Science.

Van Itallie, T. B. (1985). Health implications of overweight and obesity in the United States. *Annals of Internal Medicine, 103,* 983–988.

Van Itallie, T. B., & Lew, E. A. (1992). Assessment of morbidity and mortality risk in the overweight patient. In T. A. Wadden & T. B. Van Itallie (Eds.), *Treatment of the seriously obese patient* (pp. 3–32). New York: Guilford.

Venditti, E. M., Wing, R. R., Jakicic, J. M., Butler, B. A., & Marcus, M. D. (1996). Weight cycling, psychological health, and binge eating in obese females. *Journal of Consulting and Clinical Psychology, 64,* 400–405.

Wadden, T. A. (1993). The treatment of obesity: An overview. In A. J. Stunkard & T. A. Wadden (Eds.), *Obesity theory and therapy* (pp. 197–218). New York: Raven.

Wadden, T. A., Foster, G. D., & Letizia, K. A. (1994). One-year behavioral treatment of obesity: Comparison of moderate and severe caloric restriction and the effects of weight maintenance therapy. *Journal of Consulting and Clinical Psychology, 62,* 165–171.

Wadden, T. A., Sternberg, J. A., Letizia, K. A., Stunkard, A. J., & Foster, G. D. (1989). Treatment of obesity by very low calorie diet, behaviour therapy, and their combination: A five-year perspective. *International Journal of Obesity, 13,* 39–46.

Wadden, T. A., & Stunkard, A. J. (1993). Psychosocial consequences of obesity and dieting. Research and clinical findings. In A. J. Stunkard & T. A. Wadden (Eds.), *Obesity: Theory and therapy* (pp. 163–177). New York: Raven.

Wadden, T. A., Stunkard, A. J., & Brownell, K. D. (1983). Very low calorie diets: Their efficacy, safety, and future. *Annals of Internal Medicine, 99,* 675–684.

Wadden, T. A., Stunkard, A. J., Johnston, F. E., Wang, J., Pierson, R. N., Van Itallie, T. B., Costello, E., & Pena, M. (1988). Body fat deposition in adult obese women: II. Change in fat distribution accompanying weight reduction. *American Journal of Clinical Nutrition, 47,* 229–234.

Wadden, T. A., Vogt, R. A., Andersen, R. E., Bartlett, S. J., Foster, G. D., Kuehnel, R. H., Wilk, J., Weinstock, R., Buckenmeyer, P., Berkowitz, R. I., & Steen, S. N. (1997). Exercise in the treatment of obesity: Effects of four interventions on body composition, resting energy expenditure, appetite, and mood. *Journal of Consulting and Clinical Psychology, 65,* 269–277.

Willett, W. C., Manson, J. E., Stampfer, M. J., Colditz, G. A., Rosner, B., Spiezer, F. E., & Hennekens, C. H. (1995). Weight, weight change, and coronary heart disease in women. *Journal of the American Medical Association, 273,* 461–465.

Williamson, D. F., Kahn, H. S., Remington, P. L., & Anda, R. F. (1990). The 10–year incidence of overweight and major weight gain in US adults. *Archives of Internal Medicine, 150,* 665–672.

Williamson, D. F., Pamuk, E., Thun, M., Flanders, D., Byers, T., & Heath, C. (1995). Prospective study of intentional weight loss and mortality in never-smoking overweight US white women aged 40–64 years. *American Journal of Epidemiology, 141*(12), 1128–1141.

Wing, R. R. (1997). Behavioral approaches to the treatment of obesity. In G. Bray, C. Bouchard, & P. T. James (Eds.), *Handbook of obesity* (pp. 855–873). New York: Marcel Dekker.

Wing, R. R., Blair, E., Marcus, M., Epstein, L. H., & Harvey, J. (1994). Year-long weight loss treatment for obese patients with Type II diabetes: Does inclusion of an intermittent very low calorie diet improve outcome? *The American Journal of Medicine, 97,* 354–362.

Wing, R. R., Epstein, L. H., Marcus, M. D., & Kupfer, D. J. (1984). Mood changes in behavioral weight loss programs. *Journal of Psychosomatic Research, 28*(3), 189–196.

Wing, R. R., & Jeffery, R. W. (1979). The effect of two behavioral techniques and social context on food consumption. *Addictive Behaviors, 4,* 71–74.

Wing, R. R., & Jeffrey, R. W. (1999). Benefit of recruiting participants with friends and increasing social support for weight loss and maintenance. *Journal of Consulting and Clinical Psychology, 67,* 132–138.

Wing, R. R., Jeffery, R. W., Burton, L. R., Thorson, C., Sperber Nissinoff, K., & Baxter, J. E. (1996). Food provision vs. structured meal plans in the behavioral treatment of obesity. *International Journal of Obesity, 20,* 56–62.

Wing, R. R., Jeffery, R. W., Pronk, N., & Hellerstedt, W. L. (1996). Effects of a personal trainer and financial incentives on exercise adherence in overweight women in a behavioral weight loss program. *Obesity Research, 4,* 457–462.

Wing, R. R., Koeske, R., Epstein, L. H., Nowalk, M. P., Gooding, W., & Becker, D. (1987). Long-term effects of modest weight loss in Type II diabetic patients. *Archives of Internal Medicine, 147,* 1749–1753.

Wing, R. R., Marcus, M. D., Epstein, L. H., & Jawad, A. (1991). A "family-based" approach to the treatment of obese Type II diabetic patients. *Journal of Consulting and Clinical Psychology, 59,* 156–162.

Wing, R. R., Marcus, M. D., Salata, R., Epstein, L. H., Miaskiewicz, S., & Blair, E. H. (1991). Effects of a very-low-calorie diet on long-term glycemic control in obese Type 2 diabetic subjects. *Archives of Internal Medicine, 151,* 1334–1340.

Wing, R. R., Matthews, K. A., Kuller, L. H., Meilahn, E. N., & Plantinga, P. (1991a). Waist to hip ratio in middle-aged women: Associations with behavioral and psychosocial factors and with changes in cardiovascular risk factors. *Arteriosclerosis and Thrombosis, 11,* 1250–1257.

Wing, R. R., Matthews, K. A., Kuller, L. H., Meilahn, E. N., & Plantinga, P. L. (1991b). Weight gain at the time of menopause. *Archives of Internal Medicine, 151,* 97–102.

Wing, R. R., Venditti, E. M., Jakicic, J. M., Polley, B. A., & Lang, W. (1998). Lifestyle intervention in overweight individuals with a family history of diabetes. *Diabetes Care, 21,* 350–359.

Yong, L. C., Kuller, L. H., Rutan, G., & Bunker, C. (1993). Longitudinal study of blood pressure: Changes and determinants from adolescence to middle age. The Dormont High School follow-up study, 1957–1963 to 1989–1990. *American Journal of Epidemiology, 138,* 973–983.

16

Alcohol Use and Misuse

Mark D. Wood
University of Rhode Island

Daniel C. Vinson

Kenneth J. Sher
University of Missouri-Columbia

Alcohol consumption is a complex, multifaceted phenomenon related to both objective drinking topographies such as quantity, frequency, and patterns of use, and to accompanying physiological, psychological, and social consequences. Adverse consequences from drinking may occur as a result of chronic misuse (e.g., pancreatitis, liver disease), or from single episodes of hazardous use (e.g., alcohol-related motor vehicle crashes). Although alcohol abuse and dependence often tend to be the focal points for discussion of alcohol-related problems, a burgeoning literature on the association between hazardous drinking (e.g., intoxication, heavy drinking) and various types of bodily trauma highlights the importance of recognizing that even "nonproblem" drinkers are placed at substantially increased risk as a function of alcohol consumption (Klatsky, Friedman, & Siegelaub, 1981; National Institute on Alcohol Abuse and Alcoholism, [NIAAA], 1997). In this chapter we use the term *alcohol use* to describe any alcohol consumption, and group hazardous drinking, alcohol abuse, and alcohol dependence under the label *alcohol misuse.*

The *Diagnostic and Statistical Manual of Mental Disorders,* Fourth Edition (*DSM–IV*; American Psychiatric Association, APA, 1994) defines two major categories of alcohol use disorders: alcohol abuse and alcohol dependence. *Alcohol abuse,* or nondependent problem drinking, is characterized by one or more of the following as a result of alcohol use: (a) failure to fulfill major role obligations; (b) recurrent physically hazardous use; (c) recurrent alcohol-related legal problems; or (d) continued use despite persistent alcohol-related social or interpersonal problems. *Alcohol dependence* is characterized by three (or more) of the following symptoms occurring at any time in a 12-month period: (a) tolerance; (b) withdrawal; (c) alcohol consumption frequently in larger amounts or over a longer period than was intended; (d) persistent desire to reduce intake or unsuccessful attempts to control alcohol use; (e) a great deal of time engaging in activities to obtain alcohol or to recover from its effects; (f) limiting or suspending important social, occupational, or recreational activities because of alcohol use; and (g) continued use despite persistent alcohol-related physical or psychological problems. Alcohol dependence is further subtyped as occurring with or without physical dependence (i.e., tolerance and withdrawal).

EPIDEMIOLOGY OF ALCOHOL USE, ABUSE, AND DEPENDENCE

Alcohol Use

There are two predominant methods for measuring alcohol consumption. Production and distribution statistics (e.g., tax records of total beverage sales) are analyzed to estimate per capita consumption at the population level, and surveys are used to examine consumption patterns among both the general population and various targeted subpopulations. Apparent per capita consumption represents an estimate of consumption calculated to include all individuals age 14 and older and can be adjusted for the proportion of abstainers to yield a per drinker estimate of consumption (Williams, Stinson, Sanchez, & Dufour, 1998). Apparent per capita estimates do not include illicit or home production, tax-free personal imports or alcohol that is purchased but not consumed, and they do not they provide information about the distribution of consumption patterns. Nonetheless, they provide valuable information about patterns of drinking by geography, time, and beverage type. For example, apparent per capita consumption decreased 20.7% from 2.76 gallons in 1980–1981 to 2.19 gallons of pure alcohol in 1996 (Williams et al., 1998). These levels are still considerably higher than the consistent per capita consumption levels near 2.0 gallons observed throughout the 1950s. Beer is the alcoholic beverage of choice in the U.S., accounting for 57.1% of per capita consumption, followed by spirits (29.2%) and wine (13.7%; Williams et al., 1998). The downward trend in consumption seen in the U.S. also has been documented in other countries (Smart, 1989).

Population-based surveys substantially augment information derived from aggregate statistics by providing information about sociodemographic variations in patterns of consumption, as well as incidence and prevalence rates of alcohol abuse and dependence. Survey data mirror aggregate statistics, with significant downward trends in consumption, proportions of current drinkers, weekly drinkers, and frequent heavy drinking (e.g., those reporting five or more drinks per occasion as often as once per week; Midanik & Clark, 1994; Williams & Debakey, 1992). However, these trends appear to vary as a function of ethnicity. For example, using data from national probability samples collected in 1984 and 1995, Caetano and Clark (1998) found significant decreases in frequent heavy drinking among White men, but relatively stable rates of frequent heavy drinking among Black and Hispanic men. Trends in drinking patterns among women showed less variability by ethnicity than those of men in this study. Despite encouraging trends overall, prevalence rates for frequent heavy drinking, alcohol abuse or dependence diagnoses, and alcohol-related morbidity and mortality remain high, and the social costs associated with alcohol use and misuse are staggering. For example, Midanik and Room (1992) noted that nine percent of adult men reported drinking five or more drinks at least one day a week while four percent reported eight or more drinks a day at least once a week. These numbers, potentially indicative of heightened risk for various negative outcomes at the low end, and of both negative consequences and alcohol dependence symptoms at the high end, were nearly twice as high among 18- to 29-year-old men.

Alcohol Abuse and Dependence

The prevalence of alcohol abuse and dependence in the general population has been examined in three studies: the Epidemiologic Catchment Area Study (ECA; Robins & Regier, 1991); the 1988 Alcohol Supplement to the National Health Interview Survey (NHIS; Grant et al., 1991); and the National Longitudinal Alcohol Epidemiologic Survey (NLAES; Grant et al., 1994). Past year prevalence for either *DSM–IV* alcohol abuse or dependence was 7.41% in the NLAES sample, representing approximately 13.8 million people (Grant et al., 1994). Across the three studies, alcohol abuse or dependence diagnoses were between 2.5 to 5 times higher in men than women, with past year prevalence rates of *DSM–IV* abuse or dependence of 11.0% for men and 4.08% for women in the most recent of these studies (Grant et al., 1994). Grant et al. (1991) noted that gender differences were least pronounced in younger cohorts (age 18–29) and interpreted these findings as suggestive of increasing alcohol use disorders in women. Grant et al. (1994) observed the same convergence for men and women in the younger cohort, but more fine-grained analyses indicated that the pattern held only for non-Black women. There is also a large amount of variation in the prevalence of alcohol use disorders across the life span, with patterns differing across ethnic groups (Caetano, 1991; Helzer, Burnam, & McEvoy, 1991; NIAAA, 1993). These differences have implications for the high levels of alcohol-related morbidity and mortality exhibited among African Americans (Herd, 1991).

ECONOMIC COST OF ALCOHOL ABUSE

Two prevalent methods of estimating the economic cost of alcohol abuse[1] are the cost-of-illness method (e.g., Rice, Kelman, Miller, & Dunmeyer, 1990) and the external costs method (e.g., Heien & Pittman, 1993; Manning, Keeler, Newhouse, Sloss, & Wasserman, 1989). The cost-of-illness method includes estimates of: (a) medical consequences of alcohol consumption, treatment of alcohol use disorders, (b) morbidity costs (e.g., the value of lost productivity as a result of alcohol misuse), (c) mortality costs (e.g., premature deaths due to alcohol consumption) (NIAAA, 1993). In 1985, these costs totaled over $70 billion (Rice et al., 1990). Others have suggested that estimates of external costs, that is the cost that alcohol abusers impose on the nonabusing population, represent a more useful approach because these estimates can be weighed against revenue generated from alcohol excise and sales taxes (Heien & Pittman, 1993; Manning et al., 1989). Heien and Pittman (1993) estimated the external costs of alcohol abuse in 1985 at $9.5 billion. These estimates include: (a) $6.62 billion for medical costs, morbidity, and mortality for victims (excluding passengers) of auto crashes caused by drinking drivers; (b) $1.98 billion for victims of other accidents (e.g., fires, firearm accidents, falls, etc.); and (c) $0.91 billion for property damage caused by alcohol abusing individuals and government costs for DWI enforcement and administration of the social welfare system. Manning et al. (1989) concluded that excise taxes accounted for only about half of the external costs of abuse. Despite increases in excise taxes on alcohol, there is still a considerable disparity between external cost estimates and revenue generated from excise and sales taxes on alcoholic beverages (NIAAA, 1993).

[1]In this case the term "alcohol abuse" refers to any cost generating aspect of alcohol use or misuse and is not consistent with the clinical diagnostic criteria detailed earlier.

SCOPE OF COVERAGE

The remainder of the chapter focuses on health-related consequences of alcohol use, abuse, and dependence, as well as putative etiologic factors for alcohol use and misuse. First, a range of psychological, physiological, and social consequences of alcohol use and misuse are reviewed. Second, biological, psychological, and social-developmental factors related to alcohol use, as well as those implicated in the development of alcohol use disorders, are discussed.

HEALTH-RELATED CONSEQUENCES OF ALCOHOL USE AND MISUSE

Psychological Aspects of Alcohol Use and Misuse

Individuals with alcohol use disorders are more than twice as likely to exhibit another psychiatric disorder than are persons without an alcohol abuse/dependence diagnosis (Regier et al., 1990), but the nature of these beyond-chance associations are difficult to assess. Several possible states of nature exist, including: (a) alcohol disorder secondary to psychiatric disorder; (b) psychiatric disorder secondary to alcohol disorder; (c) common diathesis; (d) bidirectional influence; and (e) overlapping diagnostic criteria (Clark, Watson, & Reynolds, 1995; Schuckit, Irwin, & S. Brown, 1990). Comorbidity rates vary according to the population sampled, diagnostic approach, specific disorder, gender, and extent of other drug use (Ross, Glaser, & Stiasny, 1988; NIAAA, 1993). Our review of psychiatric comorbidity draws on data from clinical samples, the ECA Survey, and the National Comorbidity Survey (NCS; Kessler et al., 1994).

Comorbidity of Alcohol Use Disorders and Axis I Disorders

Anxiety Disorders. Among Axis I disorders, in both the ECA and NCS samples, anxiety disorders had the greatest rate of co-occurrence with alcohol use disorders (Kessler et al., 1997; Regier et al., 1990). It should be noted that the high levels of comorbidity between alcohol use and anxiety disorders are, in part, due to the relatively high population base rates of anxiety disorders. Because of these high population base rates, when expressed as an odds ratio[2] anxiety disorders demonstrate a modest association with alcohol use disorders (1.5; NIAAA, 1993). For individuals who met *DSM–III–R* alcohol abuse criteria, a recent NCS report noted lifetime prevalence rates for any anxiety disorder of 22.7% for men and 48.8% for women, with much higher lifetime prevalence rates of 35.8% and 60.7% in alcohol dependent men and women respectively (Kessler et al., 1997). In a recent prospective study, Kushner, Sher, and Erickson (1999) presented strong evidence for reciprocal causal influences between anxiety disorders and alcohol dependence. Specifically, they found that having an anxiety disorder at Years 1 or 4 of their study quadrupled the risk for a new onset of alcohol dependence in Year 7. Conversely, they also found that alcohol dependence at Years 1 or 4 increased the risk for a new onset of anxiety disorders in Year 7 by three to five times.

Kushner, Sher, and Beitman (1990), in a review of comorbidity between specific anxiety disorders and alcohol use disorders, noted that while agoraphobia and social phobia co-occurred at roughly twice the community sample base rate for either disorder, the association between simple phobias and alcohol use disorders does not appear to exceed expected levels in the community. Further, although generalized anxiety disorder and panic disorder appear at greater than chance levels in alcohol-dependent samples, alcohol use disorders do not appear to be overrepresented in psychiatric samples of generalized anxiety disorder and panic patients, suggesting that the increased association in alcohol dependent patient samples is, in part, a function of alcohol withdrawal. Differential referral patterns may also account for the differences in comorbidity rates across different treatment settings. Schuckit and Hesselbrock (1994), examined studies published since 1975 on the relation between anxiety disorders and alcohol dependence. They concluded that although alcohol dependent individuals undoubtedly manifest more anxiety symptoms than individuals in the general population, evidence is equivocal and methodologically suspect with respect to the demonstration of significant levels of comorbidity for alcohol use and anxiety disorders (see Kushner, 1996, for an alternative perspective).

With respect to order of onset, Kushner et al. (1990) reported that phobias (simple, social, and agoraphobia) typically, but not invariably, antedate the onset of alcohol use disorders. However, for panic disorder, generalized anxiety disorders, and obsessive-compulsive disorders, they noted that no clear pattern emerges.

Although most commonly studied with respect to combat-related stress, post-traumatic stress disorder (PTSD) may occur as a result of exposure to a wide-range of traumatic stressors (e.g., robbery, physical assault, injury, accident), with different types of stressors carrying different implications for PTSD rates, severity, and comorbidity (Breslau, Davis, Adreski, & Peterson, 1991; P. Brown & Wolfe, 1994). Comorbidity rates among male veterans and female civilians presenting for substance abuse treatment have ranged from 35% to 46% (P. Brown & Wolfe, 1994; Kovach, 1986; McFall, Mackay, & Donovan, 1991). Helzer, Robins, and McEvoy (1987) using data from the St. Louis site of the ECA survey, noted that men with PTSD were almost twice as likely to meet *DSM–III* substance abuse disorder criteria, while women with PTSD were at nearly three times greater risk for *DSM–III* substance abuse disorders than women without PTSD. In an analysis, again using ECA data from the St. Louis site, Cottler, Compton, Mager, Spitznagel, and Janca (1992) found that the onset of drug and alcohol problems typically preceded the onset of PTSD symptoms. These data sug-

[2]An odds ratio depicts the relative risk of a comorbid disorder, given the presence of an alcohol use disorder, as compared with the risk of the comorbid disorder occurring in the entire population. A comorbidity proportion illustrates the number of cases of a comorbidity disorder per 100 cases of individuals with an index diagnosis.

gest a potential vulnerability to PTSD among substance users, perhaps due to a tendency to deal with stress through the use of ineffective coping strategies (e.g., substance use; P. Brown & Wolfe, 1994), although a common diathesis (e.g., risk-taking) cannot be ruled out.

Affective disorders. Individuals who met criteria for either alcohol abuse or dependence diagnoses exhibited 1.9 times greater risk for an affective disorder in the ECA study, while the proportion of respondents with an alcohol use disorder diagnosis with a comorbid affective diagnosis (13.4%) was nearly identical to the proportion of alcohol use disorders in the total ECA community sample (Regier et al., 1990). In the NCS sample, lifetime co-occurrence of alcohol abuse with any affective disorder was 10.2% for men and 34.5% for women. For alcohol dependence the comorbidity of these two disorders was even higher at 28.1% for men and 53.5% for women (Kessler et al., 1997). Additionally, alcohol use disorder and affective disorder comorbidity vary a good deal by specific disorder, with higher prevalence rates among individuals diagnosed with depression as compared to those with either dysthymia or mania diagnoses. In the NCS sample, in terms of relative risk, for alcohol abuse odds ratios for any affective disorder were lower than those observed in the ECA study (0.64 for men and 1.78 for women). However, for alcohol dependence, risks for an affective disorder were much more pronounced, with odds ratios of 3.16 for men and 4.36 for women (Kessler et al., 1997). Among clinical samples of those seeking alcohol treatment, major depression prevalence has ranged from 8% to 65% (Merikangas & Gelernter, 1990; Ross, Glaser, & Germanson, 1988). Order of onset appears to be moderated by gender, with depressive disorder preceding alcohol use disorders for 65% of women, and 41% of men (Hesselbrock, Meyer, & Keener, 1985).

Although the lifetime prevalence rate for bipolar disorder is much lower in the general population than the rate for major depression (0.8% versus 4.9% respectively), those with bipolar disorder in the ECA study were 4.6 times more likely to diagnose with alcohol dependence than those without a mood disorder, the highest odds ratio of comorbidity for any Axis 1 disorder (Regier et al., 1990). Evidence from clinical samples appears to reflect similar patterns (Hesselbrock et al., 1985; Ross, Glaser, & Germanson, 1988), although other research suggests that bipolar disorders are more prevalent among those meeting drug abuse or dependence diagnoses than alcohol abuse or dependent individuals (Brady & Lydiard, 1992).

Schizophrenia. An important feature of the ECA study is the inclusion of institutionalized individuals in sufficient numbers to examine comorbidity between substance use and more severe psychiatric disorders. Over 33% of schizophrenic individuals in the ECA study met criteria for alcohol abuse or dependence, compared to a community prevalence rate of 13.5% (Regier et al., 1990). Lifetime prevalence rates of substance use disorders in samples of schizophrenic patients have ranged from 10% to 65%, with demographic (e.g., age, S.E.S) and methodological (e.g., sampling and ascertainment bias) differences across studies making more precise estimates difficult (Mueser, Bellack, & Blanchard, 1992).

Psychosexual Disorders. Psychosexual dysfunction is a common comorbid disorder, affecting 30% of those with alcohol use disorders in an alcohol treatment seeking sample (Ross, Glaser, & Germanson, 1988). Although few studies have examined gender differences for comorbidity of alcohol and psychosexual disorders, it appears that these disorders tend to co-occur more frequently in women than men (Ross, Glaser, & Stiasny, 1988).

Other Substance Use Disorders. Helzer et al. (1991) noted that much of the overall comorbidity between alcohol use and other psychiatric disorders is accounted for by the co-occurrence of alcohol and other drug use disorders. In the ECA study, 18% of individuals with a lifetime alcohol abuse or dependence diagnosis met lifetime criteria for drug abuse or dependence compared to only 3.5% of those without a lifetime alcohol use disorder. Similarly, in the NCS sample, for both men and women, the largest odds ratios of alcohol use disorders were with drug use disorders (Kessler et al., 1997). The risk for a psychiatric disorder is also substantially higher among those abusing multiple substances, as compared to either alcohol-dependent individuals or those in the general community (Helzer & Przybeck, 1988; Ross, Glaser, & Germanson, 1988).

A strong association between tobacco and alcohol use has been widely noted, prompting examination of the prevalence of comorbid alcohol and tobacco use disorder diagnoses in both alcoholic and general population samples. Among individuals with alcohol use disorders, it is estimated that smoking prevalence ranges from 75% to 90% (NIAAA, 1997). In a general population survey of young adults, Breslau, Kilbey, and Andreski (1991), noted that individuals with moderate nicotine dependence were 3.2 times more likely to meet criteria for lifetime alcohol dependence than were those without nicotine dependence. In a recent prospective, high-risk study, Sher, Gotham, Erickson, and P. Wood (1996) used structured diagnostic interviews to examine relations between alcohol use disorders and tobacco dependence over a three-year period during young adulthood. Among the study's most notable findings were cross-sectional and prospective relations between family history of alcoholism and both alcohol and tobacco use disorders, as well as significant reciprocal relations between alcohol use disorders and tobacco dependence.

Comorbidity of Alcohol Use Disorders and Axis II (Personality) Disorders

According to the *DSM–IV*, a personality disorder is "an enduring pattern of inner experience and behavior that deviates markedly from the expectations of the individual's culture, is pervasive and inflexible, has an onset in adolescence or early adulthood, is stable over time, and leads to distress or impairment" (APA, 1994, p. 629). It appears that personality disorders from the anxious-fearful (avoidant, dependent, obsessive-compulsive, and passive-aggressive) and dramatic-emotional (borderline, narcissistic, histrionic, and antisocial) clusters predominate in alcoholic samples (Alnaes & Torgersen, 1988; Poldrugo & Forti, 1988). Because of the very high rates of comorbidity between antisocial personality disorder (APD) and alcohol use disorders, APD is considered separately, and then the co-occurrence of alcohol abuse/dependence and other personality disorders is summarized.

Antisocial Personality Disorder. Alcohol use disorders are highly comorbid with APD in general population (e.g., Helzer & Przybeck, 1988; Kessler et al., 1997), clinical (e.g., Hesselbrock et al., 1985), and criminal (e.g., Lewis, Cloninger, & Pais, 1983) samples, even when overlapping diagnostic criteria are eliminated (Lewis, 1984). Prevalence of APD in alcohol dependent samples has ranged from 16% to 49% (Meyer & Kranzler, 1990). Prospective studies indicate, for men (and probably for women), that early conduct problems predict subsequent alcohol and drug disorders and APD (Hawkins, Catalano, & Miller, 1992; Nathan, 1988; Zucker & Gomberg, 1986).

Other Axis II Disorders. The overwhelming majority of studies of alcoholism and personality disorders have relied on clinical samples and thus are likely to overestimate comorbidity because patients with multiple diagnoses are more likely to be found in treatment settings (i.e., Berkson's fallacy, see Cohen & Cohen, 1984). However, the few studies that have examined comorbidity between alcohol use disorders and Axis II disorders also indicate extensive comorbidity (e.g., Drake, Adler, & Vaillant, 1988; Drake & Vaillant, 1985; Tausignant & Kovess, 1989; Zimmerman & Coryell, 1989). For example, in a series of reports, Drake, Vaillant, and colleagues reported prevalence rates of *DSM–III* personality disorders in a community sample of middle-aged men. Drake and Vaillant (1985) reported that 37% of the 62 men who met lifetime *DSM–III* criteria for alcohol abuse/dependence received a personality disorder diagnosis at age 47. Comorbid diagnoses of passive-aggressive, histrionic, and dependent personality were most common (all greater than 10% of the alcoholic sample; Drake et al., 1988). Furthermore, antisocial, borderline, histrionic, narcissistic, dependent, and passive-aggressive personality disorders were all more common among alcoholics than nonalcoholics in this community sample (Drake et al., 1988).

Relations Between Comorbid Diagnoses, Disorder Severity and Treatment Outcome

Generally, across both Axis I and Axis II disorders, the co-occurrence of alcohol and another psychiatric disorder or symptomatology is associated with a more severe alcohol disorder course and poorer treatment outcome (Hesselbrock et al., 1985; Litt, Babor, DelBoca, Kadden, & Cooney, 1992; Rounsaville, Dolinsky, Babor, & Meyer, 1987). Individuals with co-occurring alcohol use and antisocial personality disorders, for example, demonstrate earlier onset, more severe course, higher relapse rates, greater treatment attrition, poorer overall prognosis, and deficits in occupational and social functioning compared to individuals with an alcohol use disorder only (Hesselbrock, Meyer, & Hesselbrock, 1992). However, some studies have found no differences in treatment outcomes among groups with multiple versus single disorders (Booth, Yates, Petty, & K. Brown, 1991; Brower, Blow, Hill, & Mudd, 1994; Powell et al., 1992).

It is important to recognize that comorbid individuals represent a heterogeneous group for which traditional treatment programs may be ill-suited. Treatment for a comorbid disorder also presupposes that psychiatric comorbidity is being recognized, which, particularly among individuals with affective or anxiety disorders, may not be the case. There is evidence supporting a model of bi-directional influence, which would suggest the need to treat both disorders simultaneously. Consistent with this notion, there are a few treatment outcome studies that suggest that addressing anxiety disorders in conjunction with alcohol treatment is efficacious in reducing symptomatology for both disorders (R. Brown, Evans, I. Miller, Burgess, & Mueller, 1997; Fals-Stewart & Schafer, 1992; Tollefson et al., 1992). With more severe psychopathology (e.g., schizophrenia), it has been suggested that increased attention needs to be focused on the psychiatric disorder itself. For example, efforts to alter aspects of the environment, such as living situations, as well as increases in family and social support could reap substantial dividends in the maintenance of treatment gains (Mueser et al., 1992).

ALCOHOL'S EFFECT ON PHYSICAL HEALTH AND ORGAN SYSTEMS

Alcohol abuse and dependence have adverse effects on almost all physical illness. Even in disease not directly caused by alcohol, alcohol abuse and dependence complicate the illness because of accompanying social and psychological problems, including noncompliance with medical treatment and follow-up. In this section, we focus on those biomedical diseases with which alcohol use is causally associated, either increasing or decreasing the risk of disease. We recognize, however, that the relationship between alcohol use and physical health is complex and that the social and psychological factors can be removed from the following discussion only artificially.

It's also important to note that alcohol's negative effects on morbidity can be ameliorated with relatively simple interventions over short periods of time. For example, in a recent clinical trial, alcoholic patients scheduled for elective surgery were randomly assigned to a control group, who received usual care, or an intervention group who received disulfiram 800 mg twice a week for four weeks prior to surgery. Postoperative complications were reduced from 74% to 31% (Tonnesen, Rosenberg, Nielsen, Rasmussen, & Hauge, 1999).

Alcohol Use and the Overall Risk of Mortality

By its direct adverse effects on health, alcohol accounts for over 100,000 deaths per year making it the third leading cause of death in the United States (McGinnis & Foege, 1993; Shultz, Rice, & Parker, 1990; Stinson & De Bakey, 1992). About 15% to 20% of these alcohol-related deaths were ascribed directly to alcohol on the death certificate, with diagnoses such as alcoholic cirrhosis and alcohol poisoning. The rest of the deaths were due to diseases (about 40% of the 100,000 total) or injuries (about 45%) for which there is a quantifiable link with alcohol consumption. The assumptions underlying the calculations are debatable in several diseases, as we will review later. More important for clinicians caring for individuals, these calculations do not always provide enough information to allow an individual to calculate precisely how their use of alcohol affects their risk of sickness, injury, or death.

A complex relationship between alcohol use and the overall risk of mortality has been demonstrated in several prospective longitudinal studies (Ashley, Ferrence, Room, Rankin, & Single, 1994; Fuchs et al., 1995; Thun et al., 1997). The relative risk of overall mortality was lowest in light drinkers, those who consumed about one drink per day, and was slightly greater both in those who abstained and in heavier drinkers (Thun et al., 1997).

The effect of alcohol on mortality varies by gender and age. Women who drink face a lower risk of cardiovascular death than abstainers, but an increased risk of breast cancer death. Overall mortality is lowest around one drink a day, but primarily in women at highest risk of cardiovascular death (Fuchs et al., 1995). Because young adults have a lower basal risk of cardiovascular death and an increased risk of alcohol-related injury death, their overall mortality risk increases with alcohol consumption; among older adults, light to moderate drinking is associated with lower overall mortality risk (Scragg, 1995).

The reasons for the higher mortality risk for abstainers remain uncertain. It is not explained by confounding by smoking or other known risk factors for mortality (Gronbaek et al., 1994; Klatsky, Armstrong, & Friedman, 1992). In theory, it could be due to ex-drinkers and lifelong abstainers being classified together as non-drinkers, and there are some data supporting that hypothesis (Lazarus, Kaplan, Cohen, & Leu, 1991). However, other studies that analyzed lifelong abstainers and ex-drinkers separately found both groups at higher risk of coronary heart disease mortality (Klatsky, Armstrong, & Friedman, 1990) or total mortality (Boffetta & Garfinkel, 1990; Scherr et al., 1992). The issue continues to be unsettled with some recent cohort studies finding no cardioprotective benefit of light drinking (Hart, G. D. Smith, Hole, & Hawthorne, 1999), while another recent study indicates that risk of death from sudden cardiac death is reduced as a result of moderate alcohol consumption (Albert et al., 1999).

Mortality risk may vary by type of alcoholic beverage, with reduction of risk among wine drinkers, but not among drinkers of spirits (Gronbaek et al., 1995). The apparent benefit of wine consumption may be due to confounding by other lifestyle variables (Wannamethee & Shaper, 1999).

The previous studies all employed a longitudinal observational design, and may have found an association between light drinking and reduced overall mortality risk because of unmeasured confounding variables. It is hazardous to extrapolate from their findings and advise current abstainers to start drinking. These studies do, however, raise important questions about whether and how light drinking affects cardiovascular disease risk, and about how clinicians and patients can assess and weigh those benefits against the health risks of drinking.

Alcohol and Heart Disease

Many studies have demonstrated an association between abstinence from alcohol and an increased risk of coronary artery disease, including myocardial infarction (heart attack) and sudden cardiac death. A meta-analytic study by Maclure (1993), found an L-shaped curve in which two drinks per week reduced the risk of coronary disease as much as higher doses. At two drinks per week, the risk of coronary disease relative to abstainers was 0.88 (95% confidence interval 0.83 to 0.92). Above that level, the curve was flat; even at seven or more drinks per day, the relative risk was 0.95 (95% CI 0.83 to 1.09). Maclure considered and excluded multiple possible spurious causes for the association. Furthermore, the higher risk for non-drinkers is not due to an increased risk of coronary disease among ex-drinkers, who might have stopped drinking because of illness, obscuring a decreased risk among life-long abstainers (Klatsky, Armstrong, & Friedman, 1990). Most studies published since Maclure's meta-analysis continue to confirm these conclusions (Albert et al., 1999; Doll, Peto, Hall, Wheatley, & Gray, 1994; Goldbert, Burchfiel, Reed, Wergowske, & Chiu, 1994). Others raise doubts about whether light or infrequent drinking confers any cardiovascular benefit relative to lifelong abstention (Hanna, Chou, & Grant, 1997; Hart, G. D. Smith, Hole, & Hawthorne, 1999).

The mechanism by which low-level alcohol consumption might lead to a decreased risk of coronary disease is uncertain. There is considerable evidence that the effect is mediated by alcohol's effects on high density lipoprotein (HDL; Gaziano et al. 1993; NIAAA, 1997). Furthermore, alcohol's effect on plasma concentrations of endogenous tissue-type plasminogen activator (t-PA) may promote lysis of intravascular clots (Hendriks, Veenstra, Velthuis-te Wierik, Schaafsma, & Kluft, 1994; Ridker, Vaughan, Stampfer, Glynn, & Hennekens, 1994). Still other factors may be involved. In addition to possible long-term benefits, one case-control study found evidence for a short-term benefit, with the risk of a heart attack being reduced by consuming one or two drinks in the previous 24 hours (McElduff & Dobson, 1997).

Not all of alcohol's effects on the heart are beneficial (Moushmoush & Abi-Mansour, 1991; Preedy, Atkinson, Richardson, & Peters, 1993; Zakhari, 1991). Ethanol is toxic to cardiac muscle, and drinking over about six drinks per day substantially increases the risk of developing cardiomyopathy and congestive heart failure (Richardson, Wodak, Atkinson, Saunders, & Jewitt, 1986). The risk is greater in men than in women (Wu, Sudhakar, Jaferi, Ahmed, & Regan, 1976), and even smaller amounts of alcohol may damage cardiac muscle over time (Kupari & Koskinen, 1993). The mechanism of the injury and what makes the disease progress from a reversible condition to a permanent one are unclear (Preedy, Atkinson, Richardson, & Peters, 1993).

Alcohol and Hypertension

Alcohol is associated with increased blood pressure (Marmot et al., 1994). In the Intersalt study, consumption of three to four drinks or more per day was associated with significantly higher systolic and diastolic blood pressure, two to five millimeters of mercury (mm Hg), in both men and women (J. Stamler et al., 1989). These results persisted after statistically adjusting for 24-hour sodium and potassium excretion, body mass index, and smoking. In both Japanese men (Wakabayashi, Nakamura, Kono, Shinchi, & Imanishi, 1994), and African American men and women (Strogatz et al., 1991), alcohol was associated with significantly higher blood pressure even at levels of consumption as low as one drink per day (Wakabayashi et al., 1994) or less (Strogatz et al., 1991), suggesting no readily identifiable threshold exists in the relation between alcohol and blood pressure.

Blood pressure may be more closely related to the frequency of drinking than the quantity (Russell, Cooper, Frone, & Welte, 1991), suggesting that studies that report only average consumption per day may obscure more complex relationships between alcohol drinking and blood pressure. The relationship between pattern of drinking and blood pressure, however, is not a simple one. Greater day to day variability in consumption was associated with higher blood pressure in the Intersalt study (Marmot et al., 1994), and a British study found drinking in the previous three days had more effect on blood pressure than more remote drinking (Maheswaran, Gill, Davies, & Beevers, 1991).

Randomized crossover trials in both hypertensive (Ueshima et al., 1993) and normotensive (Howes, 1994; Puddey, Beilin, Vandongen, Rouse, & Rogers, 1985) men and women have demonstrated a short-term pressor effect of heavy drinking. When drinking is reduced from three drinks per day or more to either abstinence or light drinking, blood pressure in these studies dropped by four to twelve mm Hg in four days to three weeks (Howes, 1994; Puddey, Beilin, Vandongen, Rouse, & Rogers, 1985; Ueshima et al., 1993). In a randomized clinical trial that focused on alcohol consumption (in addition to providing antihypertensive medication, which both intervention and control groups received), systolic blood pressure was significantly lower in the intervention group (11.9 compared with 4.6 mmHg in the control group; Lang, Nicaud, Darne, Rueff, & WALPA group members, 1995).

A reduction in blood pressure of this magnitude, although statistically significant, is small when one is considering any given individual. However, because hypertension is a highly prevalent condition and because of its association with stroke and ischemic heart disease, a reduction in blood pressure of this magnitude throughout a population would be associated with a 9% reduction in coronary heart disease mortality and a 14% reduction in stroke mortality (J. Stamler et al., 1989; R. Stamler, 1991). As reviewed by MacMahon (1987), approximately 5% to 7% of hypertension can be attributed to heavy alcohol drinking, more in men (11%) and little (perhaps as little as 1%) in women. Drinking three to four drinks per day (for men) or two to three drinks per day (for women) increases the risk of having hypertension by about 40% to 50%, while six or seven drinks per day doubles the risk for both men and women (MacMahon, 1987; Witteman et al., 1990).

Alcohol and Stroke

Cerebrovascular accidents are of two kinds, *ischemic* strokes, in which blood flow to a part of the brain is stopped by a clot within an artery, and *hemorrhagic* strokes, in which bleeding in or around the brain occurs. The effects of alcohol drinking on these two types of strokes differ. The association between alcohol and ischemic stroke risk appears to be J-shaped. In a case-control study in New York City, consumption of up to 2 drinks per day was protective against ischemic stroke (odds ratio 0.55, 95% confidence interval 0.42–0.72). Results varied little by age, gender, and ethnicity (Sacco et al., 1999).

In contrast to ischemic stroke, the risk of hemorrhagic stroke increases monotonically with increasing alcohol consumption (Carmargo, Jr. 1989; Gorelick, 1989; Klatsky, Armstrong, & Friedman, 1989). The relationship appears to be linear rather than J-shaped, with increased risk at even low levels of consumption, although the magnitude of risk at low consumption levels is uncertain. At higher levels of drinking (five or more drinks per day), alcohol is associated with a four-fold increase in the risk of hemorrhagic stroke (NIAAA, 1997).

Alcohol and Cancer

Alcohol is associated with an increased risk of total cancer mortality, beginning at consumption levels of 3 or more drinks per day (Blot, 1992). At five drinks per day, the risk is 50% greater than for non-drinkers (Boffetta & Garfinkel, 1990).

In cohort studies, alcohol appears to increase the risk of breast cancer by approximately 9% per 10 g of alcohol (about 0.75 to 1 drink) per day (95% confidence interval 4% to 13%; Smith-Warner et al., 1998). One older meta-analysis found that the risk estimates were biased by the source of control patients, with studies that recruited controls from the community showing no effect (Roth, Levy, Shi, & Post, 1994). However, Longnecker and colleagues, considered this and other sources of bias and concluded that they were not sufficient to explain the findings (Giovannucci et al. 1993; Longnecker, 1994). Therefore, the association appears to be valid.

Because breast cancer and alcohol exposure are common, an association between the two is important. But as Schatzkin and Longnecker point out, "causality has not been established" (1994, p. 1101). A review by Rosenberg, Metzger, and Palmer (1993) also concluded that the evidence linking alcohol and breast cancer is weak and quite possibly due to confounding. The mechanism(s) underlying the association has not been found, and much work remains to be done. It is worth noting that the reduction in the risk of coronary disease (12% for a drink twice a week, 9% for one drink per day; Maclure, 1993) is of about the same magnitude as the increase in the risk of breast cancer (9% for a drink a day; Longnecker, 1994).

For several types of cancer, an association with alcohol is either absent or unclear. Even among alcoholics, no increased risk of several kinds of cancer was observed, including cancer of the stomach and bladder (Adami et al., 1992). For ovarian cancer, one study found heavy drinkers at decreased risk (Gwinn et al., 1986), while another found a significant overall trend of increased risk (La Vecchia et al., 1992).

For other types of cancer, the association with alcohol use is less controversial (Thun et al., 1997). The relative risk for oral and pharyngeal cancer, adjusted for smoking, increases from 1.2 with one to four drinks per week to 1.7 at five to 14 drinks per week to 8.8 at 30 or more drinks per week (Blot et al., 1988). Relative risks for laryngeal and esophageal cancer are similarly increased by moderate to heavy drinking (Steinberg & Tenner, 1994). An association with rectal cancer, particularly for beer, has been found, but is still considered speculative (Blot, 1992). Heavy alcohol drinking is related to cirrhosis and cirrhosis is related to hepatocellular carcinoma, but the relationship between heavy drinking and primary liver cancer is less clear (Naccarato & Farinati, 1991). Alcohol may act as a co-carcinogen in liver cancer along with other agents, possibly Hepatitis B virus or chemical carcinogens (Naccarato & Farinati, 1991).

Alcohol and Peptic Ulcer

Alcohol drinking is commonly assumed to increase the risk of gastritis and other inflammatory conditions of the upper gastrointestinal track mucosa, including peptic ulcer of the stomach or duodenum. Examination of the 1988 National Health Interview Study, however, revealed that much of that association is due to confounding with cigarette smoking; moreover, smoking is a modifier of the risk due to alcohol. Among non-smokers, each ounce of alcohol consumed per day was associated with a 13% increase in the risk of ulcer disease; among smokers, the increase was only 7% and was no longer statistically significant (Chou, 1994).

Alcohol and Liver Disease

The association between alcohol and liver disease is well established (Crabb, 1993). The spectrum of alcohol-related liver disease extends from acute fatty liver (a transient and reversible increase in the amount of fat within the liver) to alcoholic hepatitis (acute inflammation of the liver) to cirrhosis (permanent and often progressive scarring). While most people who consume large quantities of alcohol will develop acute fatty liver, only about 15% to 30% will develop cirrhosis (NIAAA, 1997). Why only certain individuals develop cirrhosis is unclear. While race does not appear to be a factor (Parrish, Dufour, Stinson, & Harford, 1993), risks of developing cirrhosis may vary by gender (Grant, Dufour, & Harford, 1988; Lieber, 1994), although see Klatsky and Armstrong (1992). If present, the gender difference may be due to variation in alcohol metabolism, including differences in gastric alcohol dehydrogenase activity and first-pass metabolism, both lower in women (Frezza et al., 1990). In addition, women have less body water per kilogram of body weight and, therefore, attain higher blood alcohol levels for a given dose per kilogram (Lieber, 1994).

Generally, the risk of cirrhosis for women begins to rise at 20 grams of ethanol per day (1.67 drinks), but only at 60 grams per day for men (5 drinks; Grant, Dufour, & Harford, 1988; Lieber, 1994). Lower doses, however, may increase risk. In a longitudinal study of over 128,000 adults over three to ten years, Klatsky and Armstrong found that those who drank one to two drinks per day at baseline had an almost eight-fold increase in cirrhosis risk, rising to a 33-fold risk with six or more drinks per day. Usual beverage choice had no apparent effect on the risk (Klatsky & Armstrong, 1992).

The mechanism of hepatic injury remains uncertain. As reviewed by Lieber (1994), alcohol is metabolized to acetaldehyde by three intracellular systems. Both acetaldehyde and other by-products of the three metabolic pathways are toxic to hepatic cells. Malnutrition, while not a sufficient cause of cirrhosis in alcoholics, probably plays an important role in the progression of the disease (Grant, Dufour, & Harford, 1988; Lieber, 1994). Interactions with viruses (such as Hepatitis C virus) may be involved (Lieber, 1994). Genetic predisposition may also play a role (NIAAA, 1997) but cirrhosis is found across cultures and correlates with average per capita alcohol consumption (Grant, Dufour, & Harford, 1988; Parrish, Higuchi, & Dufour, 1991), suggesting that cultural and ethnic differences (and, by extrapolation, genetic differences) are not overriding.

Alcohol and Pancreatitis

Pancreatitis is an acute inflammation of the pancreas. It is often severe, with a complicated course. Heavy alcohol drinking is considered to be responsible for approximately 35% of the cases of acute pancreatitis, although that percentage varies widely by the population studied (Steinberg & Tenner, 1994); most of the remaining cases are associated with gallstone disorders. As with cirrhosis of the liver, which develops in only a minority of those who drink heavily, only 5% of alcoholics develop acute pancreatitis, for reasons as yet unknown (Singh & Simsek, 1990; Steinberg & Tenner, 1994). The relationship between the quantity and frequency of drinking and the risk of pancreatitis appears to be direct (Singh & Simsek, 1990), but the duration of alcohol abuse and quantity of consumption required before the risk of pancreatitis increases are uncertain. One study of patients presenting with a first episode of acute pancreatitis found that those who had drunk more than 1,000 grams of alcohol in the preceding week were more likely to develop complications (50% vs. 21%) and more likely to die (16% vs. none; Jaakkola, Sillanaukee, Lof, Koivula, & Nordback, 1994). This study, however, does not help define a drinking threshold at which risk of pancreatitis begins to increase.

As is true for hepatic cirrhosis, the mechanism of alcohol-induced pancreatitis is uncertain. Several mechanisms have been proposed and studied in animals and humans, including reflux of duodenal or biliary secretions into the pancreatic duct, blockage of the pancreatic duct by inflammation or other factors, and a direct toxic effect of alcohol (Singh &

Simsek, 1990). Nutrition may also play a role, although studies have reached conflicting conclusions about what that role might be. Studies in animals suggest that a diet high in protein or dietary fat increases the likelihood of pancreatitis (Singh & Simsek, 1990), but studies in humans have found no evidence of high protein or fat intake in patients with a history of alcoholic pancreatitis (Mezey, Kolman, Diehl, Mitchell, & Herlong, 1988; Wilson et al., 1985).

Alcohol and Hormonal Changes

Hormonal systems are complex in their regulation by internal and external stimuli and in their effects on other organs and functions. Alcohol's effects on hormonal systems are likewise complex. Much is known, primarily by animal studies, but the clinical implications and applications of this extensive knowledge are uncertain (NIAAA, 1997).

Long-term alcohol abuse is associated with changes in the hypothalamic–pituitary–gonadal (HPG) axis in both men (Emanuele et al., 1993) and women (Mello, Mendelson, & Teoh, 1993). Measurable effects have been seen in short-term studies in men, with increases in prolactin and decreases in testosterone levels (Ida et al., 1992). In a controlled clinical trial, women drinking two standard drinks per day had small but significant increases in estrogens at several points in the menstrual cycle (Reichman et al., 1993), but chronic heavy alcohol drinking is associated with decreases in estrogens, increases in prolactin, and disruption of the menstrual cycle (Mello, Mendelson, & Teoh, 1993).

Thyroid function can also be disrupted by alcohol abuse, with decreased levels of triiodothyronine (T_3, the metabolically more active form of circulating thyroid hormone), possibly related to malnutrition or liver disease as much as to direct effects of alcohol itself (Jackson, 1993).

Alcohol and Cognitive Disorders

Acutely, alcohol has obvious effects on the brain (Peterson, Rothfleisch, Zelazo, & Pihl, 1990), among which are its effects on memory. Intoxication can cause a "blackout," a period of time when recollection is impaired. Blackouts are a type of anterograde amnesia similar to that caused by some benzodiazepines (Vinson, 1989). It has been assumed that an alcoholic blackout is an important early sign of alcoholism, but it is not infallible. In a 10-year longitudinal study of 230 young men, one or more blackouts at baseline had a sensitivity of 48% and a specificity of 81% in predicting the future development of alcohol dependence or abuse (Anthenelli, Klein, Tsuang, T. Smith, & Schuckit, 1994). Moreover, alcohol-induced blackouts are relatively common occurrences, particularly among some segments of the population. For example, in a recent national study, 26.7% of college students reported one or more alcohol-induced blackouts since the beginning of the current school year (Wechsler, Dowdall, Maenner, Gledhill-Hoyt, & Lee, 1998).

Following acute intoxication, after breath alcohol levels have returned to zero, there is little evidence of any lingering impairment in neuropsychological tests (Lemon, Chesher, Fox, Greeley, & Nabke, 1993). In more complex tasks, such as piloting an aircraft, there may be more of a lingering effect (Yesavage, Dolhert, & Taylor, 1994).

Drinking moderately over many years may be associated with deterioration in cognitive function (Parsons, 1994), but possible effects are usually modest (Parsons, 1986). In one long-term cohort study, those who drank heavily (28 or more drinks per week) performed worse on cognitive tests and failed to improve on tests of verbal ability, whereas light and moderate drinkers did; but in neuropsychological tests, controlling for baseline performance, measures of drinking had little effect (Arbuckle, Chaikelson, & Gold, 1994). The effect of the quantity of drinking may be conditional on the frequency of drinking, with little effect among those who drink less often than three times a week (Parker, Parker, & Harford, 1991). Among community dwelling elderly, there appears to be little effect of light to moderate alcohol consumption (Hebert et al., 1993).

Alcoholism is associated with chronic brain diseases, especially Wernicke encephalopathy and Korsakoff psychosis (Victor, 1992, 1993). Wernicke encephalopathy is characterized by neurological signs such as ataxia, nystagmus, and confusion. Korsakoff psychosis is a combination of retrograde amnesia (an inability to recall remote memories) and anterograde amnesia (an inability to lay down new memories). Wernicke and Korsakoff syndromes usually occur together in varying degrees, and are probably due to nutritional deficiency and less to direct toxic effects of alcohol itself (Victor, 1993). Although it has been assumed that Korsakoff syndrome is preceded by Wernicke encephalopathy, there is evidence to the contrary (Blansjaar & Van Dijk, 1992). Improved nutrition, with vitamin replacement and abstinence from alcohol, is helpful and some of the signs of Wernicke–Korsakoff syndrome will resolve acutely (Victor, 1993). However, the amnesia (classic Korsakoff syndrome) will resolve in only about 20% of patients (Victor, 1993), and predicting which patients with Wernicke–Korsakoff syndrome will improve is difficult (Berglund, 1991).

Alcohol and Fetal Effects

Alcohol is a leading cause of preventable birth defects (NIAAA, 1997). Fetal alcohol syndrome (FAS) is defined by the presence of growth retardation, specific craniofacial anomalies, and behavioral and cognitive abnormalities. Neuropsychological abnormalities include attention deficits, impulsivity (Streissguth et al., 1994), and mental retardation (Spohr, Willms, & Steinhausen, 1993; Steinhausen, Willms, & Spohr, 1993). Alcohol's effects on fetal development vary by dose, the pattern of drinking, and the timing of exposure during pregnancy relative to stages of development of different parts of the fetal brain and other organ systems. Lesser degrees of involvement are called fetal alcohol effects (FAE; American Academy of Pediatrics Committee on Substance Abuse and Committee on Children with Disabilities, 1993; NIAAA, 1997).

The true prevalence of FAS and FAE are uncertain (NIAAA, 1997). The characteristic facial features can be readily recognized by trained observers in the newborn period (Abel, Martier, Kruger, Ager, & Sokol, 1993), but many affected infants probably go unrecognized. Some of the abnormalities tend to resolve with time, but the effects on mental function have been shown to persist for more than a decade (NIAAA, 1997; Spohr, Willms, & Steinhausen, 1993; Steinhausen, Willms, & Spohr, 1993; Streissguth et al., 1994).

Because of the variety of abnormalities seen in fetal alcohol syndrome and the resulting heterogeneity in clinical samples, the threshold of drinking that causes them is uncertain. Approximately two drinks per day is known to be associated with FAE, although some infants exposed to higher alcohol doses in utero show no apparent effects (NIAAA, 1997; Streissguth et al., 1994a). Studies in mono- and dizygotic twins have shown greater concordance among identical twins, suggesting that genetic factors may play a role (Streissguth & Dehaene, 1993), but all races studied are about equally susceptible (Jacobson, Jacobson, Sokol, Martier, & Ager, 1993).

Alcohol and Injury

Alcohol use is frequently associated with injury. Blood samples are positive for alcohol in about one half of traffic and fire fatalities as well as a substantial proportion of other traumatic deaths (Hingson & Howland, 1993; NIAAA, 1997; G. S. Smith, Branas, & Miller, 1999). Injury deaths account for approximately 45% of all alcohol-related deaths and for 80% of alcohol-related years of productive life lost (McGinnis & Foege, 1993; Shultz, Rice, & Parker, 1990). In addition, alcohol is frequently cited as a factor in non-fatal injuries as well (NIAAA, 1997).

Unintended Injuries. Observational longitudinal studies have provided information about the risks of fatal injury associated with varying amounts of alcohol consumption. Two studies specifically examined deaths due to injuries and found that drinking more than an average of five or six drinks per day at baseline approximately doubled the risk of dying in the following eight or nine years, relative to people who drank fewer than five drinks per occasion (Anda, Williamson, & Remington, 1988) or lifelong abstainers (Klatsky & Armstrong, 1993). Both studies showed that lesser quantities of average drinking did not significantly increase the risk of fatal injury, but injury risk may be more related to peak rather than average alcohol consumption. Both reports acknowledged that subjects reporting light average drinking at baseline may have consumed significantly more alcohol before their injury, and that this could have spuriously led to an underestimate of alcohol's association with injury (Anda et al., 1988; Klatsky & Armstrong, 1993). Supporting this contention, a study from Finland found the risk of a fatal injury was lowest among men who drank only once or twice a year, and the risk in men with daily drinking was over three times as great as for non-drinkers. Differences in women were not significant (Vartiainen et al., 1994).

Case-control studies have yielded conflicting estimates of the association between alcohol and injury risk, particularly in studies of hip fracture risk. Some studies have shown that alcohol use increases the risk of hip fracture starting at a threshold of seven or more drinks per week (Grisso et al., 1994) or two or more drinks per day (Hernandez-Avila et al., 1991). Others found no association (Cumming & Klineberg, 1994; Kreiger, Gross, & Hunter, 1992; LaVecchia, Negri, Levi, & Baron, 1991; Nelson, Sattin, Langlois, DeVito, & Stevens, 1992), and one found that daily drinking reduced the risk of a fall among elderly persons (O'Loughlin, Robitaille, Boivin, & Suissa, 1993). All these studies measured subjects' average alcohol consumption rather than consumption on the day of injury. Two case-control studies have assessed alcohol levels at or shortly after the time of injury. Honkanen et al. (1983), studying falls in a public place, and Zador (1991), studying fatal motor vehicle accidents, recruited control subjects at comparable times and locations as the case subjects' accidents. Both studies found that the risk of injury rose exponentially as blood alcohol level rose, with odds ratios of sixty (Honkanen et al., 1983) to several hundred (Zador, 1991) at blood alcohol levels over 0.15 grams per 100 ml blood.

The amount of alcohol that increases the risk of injury may be low, with measurable decrements in driving performance at levels as low as 0.01 g/100 ml (Roehrs, Beare, Zorick, & Roth, 1994). Yesavage et al. (1994) found pilot performance in a flight simulator was impaired even eight hours after inducing a blood alcohol level of 0.1 g/100 ml, when alcohol levels had presumably returned to zero. Data from a national survey also provide evidence that injury risk increases at an average consumption of one drink a day for both men and women, and with consumption of 5 or more drinks on one occasion as infrequently as twice a year (Cherpitel, Tam, Midanik, Caetano, & Greenfield, 1995).

A recent case-control study of skiing injuries found evidence that a hangover effect may be a more important risk factor for injury than acute intoxication (Cherpitel, Meyers, & Perrine, 1998). In addition, data from the National Alcohol Survey suggest that risk-taking disposition may also be more important than alcohol use (Cherpitel, 1999). Studies employing a case-crossover analysis, in which injured persons are compared to themselves on previous days (Maclure, 1991) may shed light on this issue (Vinson et al., 1995). In sum, the relationship between alcohol and injury is likely a complex one.

Intended Injuries. Some injuries are the result of interpersonal violence. The relationship between alcohol drinking and physical aggression is complex, but laboratory experiments show a dose-response effect that varies by individuals' predispositions to aggression (Taylor & Chermack, 1993). Epidemiologically, drinking and being a victim of violent crime are associated, but the nature of the association is unclear (Abbey, 1991; Amaro, Fried, Cabral, & Zuckerman, 1990; Muscat & Huncharek, 1991).

Suicide was unrelated to alcohol consumption in one longitudinal study (Paffenbarger, Jr., Lee, & Leung, 1994), but drinking more than three drinks a day was associated with a 3.5-fold increase in suicide risk in another (Ross, Bernstein, Trent, Henderson, & Paganini-Hill, 1990). In a study of 5,412 formerly hospitalized psychiatric patients, suicide risk among men and women who met alcohol or drug use disorder criteria was 11.9 and 60 times higher respectively than would be expected in a control population (Black, Warrack, & Winokur, 1985). It appears that recent heavy alcohol use, suicidal intent, lack of social support, depression, and medical problems all moderate the risk of suicide among alcoholics (Murphy, Wetzel, Robins, & McEvoy, 1992).

Social Consequences of Alcohol Use and Misuse

In addition to physical illness and injury, alcohol misuse has substantial negative consequences across social, occupational, and criminal justice spheres, ranging from consequences experienced by the abusing individual, his or her family, intimate others, co-workers and colleagues, to larger institutions such as the health care and legal systems. Further, these negative social consequences are important diagnostic determinants of alcohol abuse and dependence. Accordingly, next we summarize some of these consequences by examining relations between alcohol misuse and: (a) role performance in school and the work place; (b) family interaction, performance as a parent, and familial violence; (c) high risk behaviors; and (d) crime.

Alcohol and Role Performance

Well-publicized, reports of alcohol use among college students highlight significant, negative correlations between alcohol use and academic grade point average (Center on Addiction and Substance Abuse at Columbia University, 1994; Presley, Meilman, & Lyerla, 1993; Wechsler, Davenport, Dowdall, Moeykens, & Castillo, 1994; Wechsler et al., 1998). However, research in this area is typically cross-sectional and statistically univariate. Hence, little is known about direction of causality, or whether the observed relations between alcohol involvement and poor academic outcomes remain when examined in conjunction with other known predictors of academic failure (which might covary with alcohol involvement). In a longitudinal study, Cook and Moore (1993), found that frequent high-school drinkers (more than one drinking occasion per week) completed, on average, 2.3 fewer years of college than those who were not frequent drinkers. P. Wood, Sher, Erickson, & DeBord (1997), in a five-year longitudinal study, examined relations between academic problems, *freshmen year* alcohol involvement, deviance, academic investment, campus involvement, and academic ability. Analyses indicated that modest bivariate prospective associations between freshmen year alcohol involvement and academic failure over the next six years were not observed when subsequent analyses controlled for, among other things, a history of conduct problems, intellectual ability and illicit drug use. More recently, M. Wood, Sher, and McGowan (in press), replicated and extended these results by prospectively examining relations between alcohol involvement *assessed throughout the college years* and early adult educational and occupational attainment. Consistent with the earlier study, when background variables and other known predictors of early adult role attainment were included in analyses, significant prospective relations between alcohol involvement and educational attainment were reduced. In contrast to the earlier study, significant, albeit modest, prospective relations remained between college years' alcohol use and abuse and educational attainment after controlling for the effects of parental education levels, and individual differences associated with gender, family history of alcoholism status, and high school academic achievement and aptitude. Additionally, moderational analyses indicated that individuals who were successful in high school were more negatively affected by collegiate alcohol abuse than those with more marginal pre-college academic performance. While less consistent prospective relations were observed between college years' alcohol involvement and early adult occupational attainment, significant, prospective associations between college years' alcohol dependence and occupational attainment were observed in both bivariate and multivariate analyses. Taken together, results from these two studies suggest that alcohol use is but one of a range of psychosocial variables that researchers and institutional programs need to consider in order to better understand and ameliorate poor academic outcomes.

Alcohol misuse has demonstrated consistent positive associations with work place injury and absenteeism (Holder & Blose, 1991; Marmot, North, Feeney, & Head, 1993; Webb et al., 1994). Although there is limited evidence suggesting similar patterns for moderate-to-high levels of alcohol use (Gill, 1994; Jenkins, Harvey, Butler, & Thomas, 1992), at least one other study found no significant differences between work injuries and absences and high alcohol consumption (Webb et al., 1994).

There also appears to be an association between alcohol abuse or dependence and income, which is moderated by age. Mullahy and Sindelar (1992) found that young adults (ages 22–29) who met abuse or dependence criteria had slightly higher incomes than their nonabusing/dependent peers, with marked differences (in the opposite direction) appearing between age 30 and 59. These differences may be due to educational attrition among heavier drinkers (e.g., Cooke & Moore, 1993), followed by entry into the work force at an earlier age than lighter drinkers, whose income catches up and surpasses that of their alcoholic counterparts by age 30.

In sum, studies in the area suggest that whereas relations between moderate alcohol use and work place injury and absence are unclear, there is ample evidence to conclude that early identification and referral of problem drinkers could reduce work time lost due to accidents and absences, and could potentially benefit work place productivity. Further, the research by Mullahy and Sindelar (1992), and Cook and Moore (1993), suggests that a large amount of the impact of alcohol abuse or dependence on income may be due to its effects on educational attainment.

Alcohol and the Family

Sher (1991), reviewing the literature on alcoholism and family interaction, noted that some tentative conclusions are warranted. First, alcoholic families, compared to nonalcoholic control families, report greater conflict, less family cohesion, expressiveness, independence, intellectual-cultural orientation, and active-recreational orientation. Importantly, it appears that these differences may persist only in the active phases of a parent's drinking, as they have not been found in studies comparing the family environment of recovered alcoholics with controls (e.g., Moos & Billing, 1982). Second, drawing most heavily on the work of Steinglass and associates, Sher (1991) concluded that it appears that alcohol can serve a variety of adaptive functions in the family (e.g., inhibition or expression of certain behaviors), and that there is a great deal of heterogeneity among the interaction patterns of alcoholic families.

An increased risk of injury is also seen among all ages of children whose parents are problem drinkers (Bijur, Kurzon, Overpeck, & Scheidt, 1992). Relative to children of nondrinking mothers, children whose mothers were classified as problem drinkers were 2.1 times as likely to have received injuries in the previous 12 months that required medical treatment or led to missing time from school. If the child's father was also a problem drinker, the relative risk increased to 2.7; but if only the father was a problem drinker, the child's injury risk appeared to be unaffected. These data suggest that some problem drinkers are deficient in providing adequate supervision to children under their care.

Alcohol misuse is a consistent correlate of familial violence, although as reviews of this literature have noted, a number of methodological problems preclude conclusions about alcohol's causal role in partner and child abuse (Collins & Messerschmidt, 1993; Hamilton & Collins, 1985; Miller, 1990; Steinglass & Robertson, 1983; Widom, 1993). Data on the relation between alcohol and family violence mainly come from three sources: (a) official records; (b) clinical samples; and (c) survey data; with each approach having particular strengths, weaknesses, and potential sources of bias.

A range of factors is important in understanding spouse/partner abuse, including both victim's and perpetrator's alcohol and drug abuse, marital conflict, and hostility (Leonard & Senchak, 1993, 1996; B. Miller et al., 1990). Cross-sectional research has also supported the role of men's aggression-related alcohol expectancies as a predictor of marital violence (Leonard & Senchak, 1993), but more recent longitudinal research with the same sample did not support hypothesized relations between men's alcohol-related aggressive expectancies and severe marital violence (Quigley & Leonard, 1999). When alcohol is present in a spousal violence situation, the most common pattern is drinking by both perpetrator and victim (Collins & Messerschmidt, 1993). Studies from the National Family Violence Surveys (Coleman & Straus, 1983; Kantor & Straus, 1987, 1989) have found consistent associations between frequency of husband's drunkenness and wife abuse. However, from these and other studies, it appears that the relation is curvilinear, with episodic drunkenness more strongly associated with both violence perpetration and victimization than infrequent, continuous, or near continuous drunkenness (Coleman & Straus, 1983; Hamilton & Collins, 1985).

In a review of the literature on alcohol and child abuse, Widom (1993) noted that despite the improved methodologies of more recent studies, the basic conclusions of earlier reviewers (e.g., Hamilton & Collins, 1985; Orme & Rimmer, 1981) remain unaltered. That is, the pattern of findings in this area are contradictory and methodological problems continue to hinder conclusions regarding the association between parent alcohol misuse and child victimization. Nonetheless, taken as a whole, results suggest that there is a link. Famularo, Kinscherff, and Fenton (1992), in analyses of randomly selected court records, found that parental alcohol abuse was significantly related to physical, but not sexual, abuse of offspring. In a case control study using ECA data, Kelleher, Chaffin, Hollenberg, and Fischer (1994) noted that parents who met alcohol abuse or dependence criteria exhibited levels of physical abuse and neglect 2.5 and 3.3 times higher than those of abuse or dependence criteria compared to sociodemographically matched controls. More generally, parents with any type of substance use disorder were 2.7 and 3.1 times more likely to have reported abusing their children than matched controls, after further controlling for other psychopathology (depression and antisocial personality disorder), number in household, and social support. The relation between alcoholism and child abuse also appears to be stronger than that of child abuse with other psychopathology (Famularo, Stone, Barnum, & Wharton, 1986).

Less is known about the prevalence of parental alcohol misuse among incest or extrafamilial sexual abuse victims. Russell, Henderson, and Blume (1985) reviewed several studies that reported very high rates of alcoholism among parents of incest victims. Hernandez (1992) compared incest and extrafamilial sexual abuse among adolescents with and without a family history of alcohol problems and noted that sexually abused adolescents were significantly more likely to have a substance abusing parent than adolescents who had not experienced abuse. Consistent with these findings, Sher, Gershuny, Peterson, and Raskin (1997) observed significantly higher levels across a number of specific types of sexual abuse among offspring of alcoholics as compared to controls. Additionally, Sher et al. (1997) found that many of a number of mild to severe childhood stressors more commonly experienced by children of alcoholics were related to alcohol use disorders in adulthood. At least for women, other studies also support the etiological significance of childhood physical and/or sexual abuse in the development of alcohol problems (B. Miller et al., 1990; B. Miller, Downs, & Testa, 1993).

In sum, research on the effects of alcohol misuse on the family is fraught with methodological limitations that make it difficult to discern the extent of a causal association between alcohol and family problems. Prospective studies using standardized diagnostic measures and multivariate analyses are needed to characterize more fully the temporal sequence of the association and to identify important mediators and moderators of relations between alcohol and family violence.

Alcohol and High Risk Behaviors

Risky Sex. Alcohol's disinhibiting effects on behavior have long been noted, as have its deleterious effects on judgment and decision-making processes. Anecdotal associations between alcohol consumption and sexual behavior pervade our culture, and are not without empirical support, although it appears that expectations regarding alcohol's effect on sexuality are more powerful (at least at lower doses) than are pharmacological effects (Crowe & George, 1989). Across adolescent, young adult heterosexual, and adult homosexual samples, cross-sectional data show that those who drink more heavily are more likely to engage in risky sexual practices (Erickson & Trocki, 1992; McEwan, McCallum, Bhopal, & Madhok, 1992; Meilman, 1993; Stall, McKusick, Wiley, Coates, & Ostrow, 1986; Strunin & Hingson, 1992; Wechsler et al., 1994; Wechsler et al., 1998). Risky sex is defined here as unprotected vaginal or anal intercourse outside the context of an ongoing monogamous relationship. In contrast to cross-sectional results, one longitudinal study found that drinking was correlated with the frequency of risky sex only in between-subjects analysis and not in within-subjects analysis (Leigh, 1993). The association, therefore, may be due to confounding by other variables, such as generalized risk taking. Methodological limitations, and the inherent difficulty of conducting research in this area, make causal inferences regarding alcohol's role in risky sex extremely difficult. Leigh and Stall (1993), in a comprehensive review of the literature on alcohol and risky sex, noted that studies are limited by a necessary reliance on self-reports, introducing attributional, social desirability, and memory biases for both substance use and sexual activity that may be worsened when the two are examined in combination. They also noted that sampling characteristics such as time of data collection, geographic location, age, sexual orientation, and gender may influence the relation between alcohol use and risky sex. Leigh and Stall (1993) concluded that there is good reason to suspect that third variable explanations (e.g., sensation seeking or impulsive personality traits and situational factors) mediate much of the relation between alcohol consumption and high risk sexual behaviors, noting that studies have observed strong correlations between tobacco use (which is not typically ascribed causal status) and risky sex. Additionally, those studies that have controlled for extraneous variables have observed much attenuated or nonsignificant relations between alcohol use and high risk sexual behavior. They also caution that health education messages that assume a causal role for alcohol may be harmful because they potentially provide a means to avoid personal responsibility by "blaming the booze" (Critchlow, 1983).

In summary, empirical ambiguity surrounding a causal role for alcohol in the initiation of risky sex should not be taken to imply that messages about alcohol's deleterious effects on cognition and judgment should not be incorporated in prevention efforts. Instead, the association could be noted while attempting to minimize the acceptability of using intoxication as a means of excusing dangerous behavior (Leigh & Stall, 1993). Alternatively, as Leigh and Stall (1993) also noted, alcohol and drug abuse also may be viewed as potential markers of risky sexual behaviors in lieu of any demonstrated causal relationship.

Drinking and Driving. Data from the Fatality Analysis Reporting System (FARS), a database of over 800,000 fatal motor vehicle crashes over a 20-year period indicate that between 1977 and 1996 there has been a 22% decrease in alcohol-related fatal motor vehicle crashes (Yi, Stinson, Williams, & Bertolucci, 1998). Despite these encouraging decreases, alcohol was still involved in 32.4% of all fatal car crashes in 1996. Moreover, after a 47% reduction between 1982 and 1995 in alcohol-related fatalities among the youngest cohort of drivers (ages 16–20), there was a slight (5%) increase in alcohol-related fatalities for this age group in 1996 (Yi et al., 1998). Examination of future FARS data will be necessary to determine whether the increase is merely a fluctuation or signals the beginning of a new trend.

Fell (1990) and Yi et al. (1998) suggested several possible explanations for the observed decreases in drinking and driving including: (a) increased public awareness of the problem; (b) media-covered implementation of stricter and swifter enforcement measures; (c) changes in drinking and driving laws (i.e., increases in the legal drinking age in 35 states between 1982 and 1988, zero tolerance laws in 43 states and the District of Columbia for drivers under 21, decreases in allowable BAC levels to less than .08 in 13 states by 1998); (d) prevention and intervention efforts that feature alternatives to legal deterrents (e.g., server training, designated driver programs); (e) a decrease in the population of young drivers; (f) an overall decrease in per capita alcohol consumption; and (g) overall safety improvements for vehicles and roadways, as well as increased use of seat belt and passive restraint systems. Further, a growing body of literature indicates that a number of factors other than alcohol use and alcohol problems distinguish drinking drivers from those who do not drink and drive, including personality traits (e.g., impulsivity, sensation seeking, hostility, social responsibility), and other individual differences such as alcohol outcome expectancies and driving-related aggression (McMillen, Pang, Wells-Parker, & Anderson, 1992; Stacy, Newcomb, & Bentler, 1991b). Additionally, there is a great deal of heterogeneity among drinking drivers along dimensions such as alcohol dependence, psychiatric severity, non-alcohol related traffic violations, and social instability (Wieczorek & Miller, 1992). Interventions tailored to these differences might lead to lower rates of recidivism for DWI/DUI offenders than has been seen to date.

Alcohol and Crime

The relation between alcohol and crime is complex, involving consideration of alcohol's anticipated and actual effects on the individual (e.g., expectations of increased aggression, impaired judgment, decision-making, and interpersonal skills), situational correlates (e.g., locale, time of day or night), and cultural factors (e.g., SES, widespread notions regarding alcohol's disinhibitory effects and its social cue properties). Alcohol involvement in crime is typically studied by event analysis (e.g., police or medical records or reports), or from the retrospective accounts of incarcerated offenders. Each approach has disadvantages, most notably incomplete or inaccurate records for the former method, and sampling and recall biases for the latter. The current state of knowledge is not such that causal inferences regarding alcohol and crime can be made.

Estimates of alcohol involvement prior to the commission of homicide have ranged from 7% to 85%, with most studies indicating greater than 60% of offenders had consumed alcohol prior to the offense (Collins, 1991; Collins & Messerschmidt, 1993; Murdoch, Pihl, & Ross, 1990; Pernanen, 1991; Roizen, 1997). For assault, Murdoch et al. (1990) summarized results from seven studies, noting that from 24% to 82% of offenders were intoxicated when the crimes were committed. Cordilia (1985) suggested that alcohol's association with the perpetration of property crimes differs according to whether the crimes are premeditated or opportunistic in nature.

Increasingly, researchers and prevention specialists are calling attention to alcohol's involvement in sexual assault. Koss, Gidycz, and Wisniewski (1987) examined the prevalence of sexual victimization in a national sample of college students and observed that 53.7% of women respondents had experienced some degree of sexual victimization (ranging from unwanted petting to rape), while 12.1% and 15.4% reported attempted rape and rape respectively. In another study from the same data set, Koss and Dinero (1989) found that respondent's alcohol use was one of four variables demonstrating predictive power for rape vulnerability, although as noted by Roizen (1997), the relationship between alcohol use and rape in this sample was not a strong one. Muelenhard and Linton (1987) in a survey of college men and women, noted that 55% of the men who reported they had committed sexual assault on a date indicated that they were either intoxicated or "mildly buzzed" at the time of the incident. Although methodological limitations, such as small and biased samples and reliance on retrospective accounts, preclude causal inferences, several explanations for the relation between alcohol consumption and sexual assault have been proposed. With respect to men who commit sexual assault, these include: (a) expectations of increased power and sexuality associated with drinking; (b) misattribution of a woman's friendly interaction as indicative of sexual interest; and (c) the tendency to use intoxication as a means of diminishing personal responsibility for behavior (Abbey, 1991). Because alcohol use, particularly heavy drinking, has marked deleterious effects on psychomotor and cognitive functioning, sexual assault victims are probably less capable of either physically or verbally thwarting an attack. Further, there are data indicating that a drinking woman is perceived as more sexually available (George, Gournic, & McAfee, 1988) and that bar victimization of women appears to be a frequent occurrence, with 32.6% of women surveyed in recent study reporting either attempted or completed rape associated with drinking in a bar (Parks & Miller, 1997). Research on sexual assault typically has been retrospective and most surveys have not assessed whether assailants and victims had consumed alcohol prior to the assault (Abbey, 1991; Roizen, 1997). Prospective and case control studies are needed to clarify alcohol's influence on sexual assault in order to guide education efforts as well as to better identify those at greatest risk.

Summary of Health Related Consequences of Alcohol Use and Misuse

Alcohol misuse is highly prevalent in the United States (and many other cultures) and is associated with a broad range of adverse health and psychosocial outcomes. Excessive alcohol consumption and alcohol use disorders have been shown to have deleterious effects on most organ systems, to be a major cause of fatal and nonfatal injury, and to contribute to a range of psychological and social problems (NIAAA, 1993, 1997). Against this backdrop of many deleterious consequences of alcohol misuse, there is some evidence for possible health benefits of light or moderate drinking (Albert et al., 1999; Friedman & Klatsky, 1993).

It is becoming increasingly clear that the relative risks and benefits of alcohol consumption are likely to vary across the life span. During adolescence and early adulthood, motor vehicle crashes represent the most serious consequences of alcohol use as well as the leading cause of mortality for this age group (NIAAA, 1993). Given the steep monotonic relationship between blood alcohol level and impaired driving, it is difficult to believe that any drinking during this period of life, no matter how socially normative, is likely to have positive benefits on overall health. On the other hand, CHD is the leading cause of mortality in middle age, and as discussed earlier, it appears that moderate alcohol consumption reduces CHD, presumably because of its effects on HDL and/or platelet function. The effects of alcohol on these two important health problems highlight several important issues with respect to alcohol and health: (a) the relation between alcohol consumption and various consequences is dose dependent, (b) the shapes of dose-response curves vary as a function of the health-related outcome under consideration and are not necessarily monotonic, and (c) the health consequences of alcohol consumption need to be viewed in a life-span develop- mental context.

Clearly, although a considerable amount is known concerning the effects of alcohol on health broadly defined, much more needs to be known with respect to elucidating the mechanisms underlying the consequences of alcohol use and misuse. Interpretation of many associations is complicated by a variety of third variables and unmeasured confounders and vulnerability factors that are important determinants of alcohol effects. Alcohol use is often accompanied by other "risky" or outright health-damaging behaviors and isolating unique effects of alcohol is frequently difficult. Similarly, as previously noted, many individuals who tend to misuse alcohol probably also tend to experience other psychological and social problems, and associations between alcohol consumption and many adverse psychosocial outcomes (e.g., disrupted family life, impaired work performance, crime, psychological disorders) are difficult to disentangle. Thus, clinicians are often limited in their ability to ascribe a causal role to alcohol.

PUTATIVE ETIOLOGIC FACTORS

Overview

An understanding of the prevalence and distribution of alcohol misuse in both the general population and at-risk subpopulations, as well as increased knowledge of alcohol's effects on physical and mental health are vital steps toward ameliorating human suffering and reducing the myriad negative health and social consequences of alcohol misuse. Contemporary alcohol researchers are also working to identify the biological, psychological, and social determinants of maladaptive drinking patterns. Next, each of these broad areas is addressed in turn while recognizing that most contemporary theories view alcohol use and misuse as being caused, maintained, and exacerbated by a combination of biological, psychological, and social factors.

Biological/Genetic Influences on Alcohol Use and Misuse

The observation that alcohol abuse and dependence tend to run in families has prompted a great deal of research aimed at identifying genetic mechanisms underlying alcohol use and the pathogenesis of alcohol use disorders. Studies utilizing behavior-genetic approaches in human samples, as well as animal studies, have amassed considerable evidence for genetic influences on alcohol use and misuse.

Behavior-Genetic Studies of Alcohol Use and Misuse

Behavior-genetic research can be loosely classified into five categories: (a) family studies; (b) twin studies; (c) adoption studies; (d) genetic marker studies; and (e) vulnerability studies. Family and vulnerability studies are not truly behavior-genetic in that they are not capable of separating genetic and environmental influences. The following summary of findings from behavior-genetic studies borrows heavily from more comprehensive recent reviews of this body of research (e.g., Ball & Murray, 1994; McGue, 1994; 1999; Merikangas, 1990).

Family Studies. Family studies have confirmed the long-standing clinical observation that alcohol use disorders tend to run in families (see Cotton, 1979; Merikangas, 1990 for reviews). For example, Dawson, Harford, and Grant (1992) noted that individuals who reported alcoholism in a first-degree relative (i.e., parent, sibling, or children) were at 86% greater risk for alcohol dependence than those without a family history of alcoholism.

True behavior-genetic studies attempt to explain behavior by partitioning variation in behavior according to genetic and environmental sources. In the simplest behavior-genetic model, the phenotype under study can be disaggregated into three components: (a) genetic effects; (b) shared environmental effects (e.g., parental SES); and (c) nonshared or unique environmental effects (e.g., peer influences).

Twin Studies. Twin studies are an important methodology for examining genetic and environmental influences for both alcohol use and alcohol use disorders. To the extent that alcohol use and misuse are genetically influenced, monozygotic (MZ) twins, who share 100% of their genetic makeup, would be expected to show higher concordance (agreement rates) for both alcohol use and alcohol use disorders as compared to dizygotic (DZ) twins, who are no more genetically alike than any pair of siblings. A number of assumptions need to be met in order to draw strong inferences from these studies. Nevertheless, studies are generally consistent in showing higher MZ concordance for both alcohol consumption and alcohol use disorders (Ball & Murray, 1994; McGue, 1994). In men, heritability estimates for alcoholism are consistent across studies and range from 50% to 60% (McGue, 1999). The studies differ somewhat in the extent to which genetic effects are generalizable to women, although shared environmental effects have been demonstrated consistently for both men and women (McGue, 1994). For men, by and large across the major twin studies, genetic effects have accounted for a greater share of the variance in alcohol abuse or dependence than shared environmental influences (McGue, 1994).

In contrast to some earlier studies, results from two more recent population-based studies suggest heritability for women is equal to that of men (Heath et al., 1997; Kendler, Heath, Neale, Kessler, & Eaves, 1992). In comparing their results with earlier findings, Kendler et al. (1992) suggested that previous female twin study participants, who were typically ascertained while seeking alcohol treatment, may not be representative of alcoholics in the entire population. McGue (1999) asserts, that taken as a whole, the literature supports the inference of genetic influence on alcoholism among women, but precise estimates of heritability risk cannot be drawn from existing data.

Adoption Studies. Adoption studies represent a powerful methodology for disentangling the genetic and environmental determinants of alcohol use and misuse. In a typical cross-fostering design, alcoholism in the adoptive home and alcoholism in the biological parents are orthogonally crossed. Adoption studies generally show an important role for genetics in the transmission of alcoholism in men, with more ambiguous findings with respect to alcoholism in women. Moreover, some of these studies have suggested genetic heterogeneity of at least two different types in the genetic predisposition to alcoholism (e.g., Cadoret, Yates, Troughton, Woodworth, & Stewart, 1995; Cloninger, Bohman, & Sigvardsson, 1981).

Studies conducted in Denmark, Sweden, and the United States all have found significantly higher rates of alcohol use disorders in adopted-away offspring of alcoholics. Goodwin, Schulsinger, Hermansen, Guze, and Winokur (1973) noted that male adoptees with an alcoholic biological parent were at almost four times greater risk for alcoholism than a control group (18% vs. 5%) comprised of adoptees with either no family history of psychopathology, or of psychopathology other than alcoholism. Cloninger et al. (1981) found that alcohol abuse (at least one temperance board registration) was significantly higher among family history positive compared to family history negative adoptees (22.8% vs. 14.7%). Cadoret et al. (1995) noted direct genetic effects from biological parents to adopted-away offspring for drug abuse and dependency. Moreover, Cadoret and colleagues are the only investigators to observe an effect of adoptive parent alcoholism on offspring alcoholism, and have obtained these findings in men and women across multiple studies (McGue, 1994).

The interplay between genetic and environmental influences can be expressed with reference to two behavior-genetic processes: (a) gene-environment (G-E) correlations; and (b) G-E interactions. G-E *correlations* can be classified as *passive, reactive,* and *active* (Plomin, DeFries, & Loehlin, 1977). Passive G-E correlations reflect the degree to which environmental influences are not independent of inherited genes. Reactive, or evocative, G-E correlations refer to the differential reactions elicited from others by different genotypes. Active G-E correlations relate to the tendency for individuals to seek environments that complement their genotype. Each type of G-E correlation may play a role in the etiology of alcohol misuse, and could, presumably, relate to alcohol use more generally (Searles, 1988). G-E *interactions* are potentially important in the etiology of alcohol use and misuse as well. Cloninger et al.'s (1981) Type I alcoholism is an example of a G-E interaction. According to Cloninger and colleagues, environmental factors determine whether one type of genetic predisposition will result in alcoholism.

Taken together, twin and adoption studies have provided very strong evidence for the role of both genetic and environmental factors in the pathogenesis of alcohol use and misuse. Nevertheless, these methodologies also have been criticized with respect to issues such as poor measurement of environmental influences, and for inattention to nonshared environmental effects and indirect genetic effects such as G-E correlations and interactions (Reiss, Plomin, & Hetherington, 1991; Searles, 1988).

Genetic Linkage and Association Studies. The demonstration of major single gene effects for diseases such as Huntingon's and muscular dystrophy has motivated a great deal of genetic research aimed at identifying specific markers for psychiatric disorders, including alcohol abuse and dependence (see McClearn, Plomin, Gora-Maslak, & Crabbe, 1991). A particular subtype of alcohol dehydrogenase (ADH) isoenzyme (the ß subunit) has been found to vary in different ethnic groups and is associated with differential sensitivity to alcohol. For example, individuals with the $ß_2$ subunit (approximately 65% of the Asian population) appear to oxidize alcohol faster than those with the $ß_1$ subunit (most Caucasians) resulting in higher levels of acetaldehyde (alcohol's initial metabolite) which may lead to tissue damage (NIAAA, 1993). Genetic and ethnic variation in acetaldehyde dehydrogenase (ALDH) isoenzymes also exist, and these are thought to be more important with respect to alcoholism. More specifically, it appears that Asian alcoholics have substantially lower rates of the ALDH isoenzyme (ALDH2) than Asian nonalcoholics, suggesting that this type of isoenzyme serves some protective function against the development of alcoholism (McGue, 1994, 1999).

Early reports of an association with the A1 allele of the dopamine DRD2 receptor gene and severe alcoholism (Blum et al., 1990) led to an intense concentration of research effort and some controversy in the field of genetics (see Holden, 1994). Uhl, Persico, and S. Smith (1992), in a meta-analysis of seven DRD2 studies, concluded that there appeared to be sufficient evidence to support an association between DRD2 alleles and substance abuse (on the basis of odds ratios averaged across studies). In contrast, Gelernter, Goldman, and Risch (1993) conducted a meta-analysis of all DRD2 studies subsequent to Blum et al. (1990), and found no significant differences between alcoholic and control groups on comparison of allele frequencies. They concluded that sampling error and/or ethnic variation between alcoholic and control groups are the most likely explanation in those studies demonstrating positive results. At this time it appears that the association between DRD2 A1 allele and alcoholism is not supported either with respect to the pattern of positive findings, or through identification of a physiological mechanism supporting its role in the etiology of alcoholism (McGue, 1999).

Genetic linkage studies attempt to identify within-family associations between a genetic marker and a particular disorder, which would suggest the existence of a disorder-susceptibility locus in close proximity to the marker site. Rising methodological concerns with regard to association studies have led to an increased focus on genetic linkage methods (McGue, 1999). The ongoing Collaborative Study on the Genetics of Alcoholism (COGA; Begleiter et al., 1995) is a systematic attempt to use linkage methods to identify specific genes contributing to the risk of alcohol use disorders. Reich et al. (1998) reported that several chromosomal regions showed suggestions of linkages with alcoholism. The strongest evidence of linkage was found on chromosomes 1 and 7, with more modest evidence on chromosome 2. Interestingly, there was suggestive evidence for linkage on chromosome 4 near the site of the alcohol dehydrogenase genes (ADH), which, as previously noted, appear to exert protective effects against alcoholism among some Asians. In another recent linkage study, Long et al. (1998) reported highly suggestive evidence for linkage at chromosome 11, with good (but more modest) evidence for linkage with alcoholism at chromosome 4, with the findings for the latter region partially overlapping the region identified by Reich et al. (1998). These studies have identified genetic regions that can be targeted in future replication attempts and are viewed as important first steps in the identification of genes that contribute to the risk for alcohol use disorders (McGue, 1999).

Vulnerability Studies. Vulnerability studies attempt to identify specific mechanisms of risk for alcohol misuse. Offspring of alcoholics are often utilized because they are known to be at increased risk for alcohol use disorders, and can be examined prior to the age of risk for alcohol use or misuse. Numerous studies have found differences between children of alcoholics (COAs) and children of nonalcoholics (nonCOAs) in terms of their responses to alcohol, as well as across a range of cognitive, behavioral, neurophysiological, and biochemical measures (Sher, 1991).

A number of studies have compared the neurophysiological characteristics of COAs and nonCOAs. With respect to spontaneous electroencephalographic (EEG) activity in sober COAs, there have been some positive findings (e.g., Ehlers & Schuckit, 1991; Gabrielli et al., 1982), but taken as a whole, results have been equivocal for variation in EEG activity as a function of family history (Sher, 1991).

Event-related potentials (ERPs) are discrete waveforms elicited by direct sensory stimulation of a participant (e.g., a brief flash of light) or by engagement in a cognitive task (e.g., making judgments regarding the properties of a stimulus). COA/nonCOA differences have been demonstrated in the latter paradigm. Most notably, male COAs have been shown to have reduced P3 (a positive wave occurring approximately 300 msec after stimulus onset) amplitude compared to controls in both visual and auditory tasks. The P3 is thought to index cognitive processes such as stimulus evaluation, attentional resources, or memory updating processes, with its generators thought to be localized in the hippocampal region of the CNS. Polich, Pollock, and Bloom (1994), in a meta-analysis, found that COAs consistently demonstrated significantly decreased P3 amplitudes relative to controls. Age, task difficulty, and stimulus modality were all significant moderators of this effect. Although the P3 appears to reliably differentiate COAs from nonCOAs, it also appears to distinguish between individuals suffering from, or at risk for, a wide-range of psychiatric disorders, including schizophrenia and affective disorders. Thus, Polich et al. (1994) concluded that it is unlikely that the P3 is a *specific* biological marker for alcoholism.

In a review of vulnerability studies examining cognitive/neuropsychological functioning, Sher (1991) concluded that available data suggest differences in the cognitive functioning of COAs and nonCOAs, particularly relating to deficits in verbal ability and abstraction/conceptual reasoning among COAs. Studies conducted since this review have also suggested reliable differences in visuospatial learning related to temporal organization, attention, and informational encoding (Harden & Pihl, 1995; Schandler, Cohen, & Antick, 1992; Schandler et al., 1988). The etiologic significance of these observed differences is presently unclear, although several plausible hypotheses can be forwarded. For example, impaired verbal and problem-solving abilities may contribute to school failure, consequent loss of self-esteem, and adoption of a deviant role. Findings of impaired educational achievement among COAs are consistent with this notion. A second hypothesis is that cognitive deficits may lead to reduced coping abilities with consequent use of alcohol as a coping strategy. Another possibility is that alcohol consumption subjectively improves cognitive performance in some COAs and is thus reinforcing. This hypothesis is supported by results from several researchers who have reported that adolescent COAs tend to believe that alcohol improves cognitive and motor performance (S. Brown, Creamer, & Stetson, 1987; Chassin, Mann, & Sher, 1988; Sher, Walitzer, P. Wood, & Brent, 1991).

In the search for a biochemical marker for alcohol use disorders, monoamine oxidase (MAO) has received the most empirical attention to date. MAO is an important enzyme in the breakdown of dopamine, norepinephrine and serotonin. In most studies, the human blood platelet is the source of MAO and is usually assumed to be an index of brain MAO activity. In studies comparing MAO activity levels in COA and nonCOA groups, there is general support for the hypothesis that low MAO activity may represent a predisposition for alcoholism. Research by von Knorring and colleagues (von Knorring, Bohman, von Knorring, & Oreland, 1985; von Knorring, Oreland, & von Knorring, 1987) suggests that low MAO activity may characterize only one form of alcoholism (the Type II alcoholism identified in the Swedish adoption studies). This hypothesis is also consistent with research demonstrating that low platelet MAO activity is associated with behavioral undercontrol traits such as sensation seeking and impulsivity (e.g., Fowler, von Knorring, & Oreland, 1980; Murphy et al., 1977; Perris et al., 1980; Sher, Bylund, Walitzer, Hartmann, & Ray-Prenger, 1994). However, results from a recent study indicate that MAO activity is associated with a range of factors such as cigarette and other drug use, other psychopathology, medical illness, metabolic factors, and, as noted above, personality traits (Anthenelli et al., 1998). Thus, MAO activity may be a consequence of alcohol or other drug use or a non-specific indicator of a range of disorders related to disinhibition and impulsivity (NIAAA, 1997).

The general hypothesis that differences in responses to alcohol may underlie COA vulnerability to alcohol misuse has been examined for alcohol metabolism, subjective intoxication, autonomic, electromyographic (EMG), and EEG activity. Differential sensitivity indexed by these measures could be related to both the negative (e.g., relief of negative affect) or positive (e.g., sensitivity to alcohol's euphoric effects) reinforcement properties of alcohol, or to decreased sensitivity to alcohol's aversive effects. For ethical reasons, it is desirable to exclude abstainers and naive drinkers from alcohol consumption studies. Thus, most studies cannot distinguish whether obtained differences are the result of initial sensitivity or acquired (e.g., tolerance) sensitivity. Taken as a whole, existing data suggest that there are no differences between COAs and nonCOAs with respect to absorption or elimination of alcohol (Sher, 1991).

The extant literature is equivocal regarding COA/nonCOA differences on alcohol's subjective effects. At least five studies have reported reduced subjective intoxication in COAs (Moss, Yao, & Maddock, 1989; O'Malley & Maisto, 1985; Pollock, Teasdale, Gabrielli, & Knop, 1986; Schuckit, 1980, 1984), while others have reported either no differences, or greater subjective intoxication in COAs compared to nonCOAs (de Wit & McCracken, 1990; Kaplan, Hesselbrock, O'Connor, & DePalma, 1988; Nagoshi & Wilson, 1987; Sher, Walitzer, Bylund, & Hartmann, 1989; Vogel-Sprott & Chipperfield, 1987). Newlin and Thomson (1990) have proposed that the seemingly contradictory literature on the direction of

COA/nonCOA differences in alcohol effects can be reconciled by considering the time course of intoxication. They have suggested that COAs are more sensitive to the effects associated with the ascending limb of the blood alcohol curve (when blood alcohol levels are rising), and less sensitive to the effects associated with the descending limb of the blood alcohol curve.

COA/nonCOA differences have been observed for indices of CNS (e.g., EEG) and peripheral nervous system (e.g. heart rate) functioning following alcohol consumption. Pollock et al. (1983) reported higher levels of fast alpha EEG activity (associated with self-reports of well-being) in intoxicated COAs compared to controls. Several studies have documented increased heart rate in COAs, compared to nonCOAs, subsequent to alcohol consumption, and it has been postulated that these increases might index an increased incentive value for alcohol (Finn & Pihl, 1987; Finn, Zeitouni, & Pihl, 1990; Nagoshi & Wilson, 1988). Generally, there is little evidence of COA/nonCOA differences following alcohol consumption on other autonomic measures such as finger pulse amplitude, blood pressure, and electrodermal activity (Sher, 1991).

Individual differences in the ability of alcohol to dampen autonomic responses to discrete stressors have been suggested as etiologically significant for the development of drinking problems. For example, persons for whom alcohol is particularly efficient in dampening stress responses may be more likely to drink alcohol in greater quantities (Sher, 1987). At least three studies have found that COAs demonstrate less heart rate reactivity to a stressor after alcohol consumption than nonCOAs (Finn & Pihl, 1987; Finn et al., 1990; Levenson, Oyama, & Meek, 1987). These findings are consistent with the notion that individuals with a positive family history of alcoholism receive greater reinforcement from alcohol consumption.

In summary, although no specific marker for vulnerability for the development of alcohol use disorders has yet emerged, there are encouraging findings. The cognitive processes indexed by the P3 may be etiologically important in the development of alcoholism even though reduced amplitude of the P3 is not specific to those at-risk for alcoholism. To the extent that the P3 indexes aspects of attention or memory updating, it could figure prominently in information-processing theories of alcoholism. MAO may represent a variable that distinguishes COAs and nonCOAs. The potential etiologic significance of MAO remains promising due to: (a) its association with alcohol abuse and dependence; (b) its link to neurotransmitters that appear to be associated with the development of alcoholism; and (c) its relation to traits predictive of alcoholism (e.g., aggression and impulsivity).

Sher (1991) noted, that two areas of consistency seem to emerge from studies of differential responses between COAs and nonCOAs. First, it appears that COAs are *less sensitive* to subjective intoxicating effects of alcohol, which may lead them to drink greater amounts of alcohol. Consistent with this notion, Schuckit (1994) reported that lower subjective responses to alcohol and less body sway in a baseline alcohol challenge study were associated with a fourfold increase in alcoholism 10 years later. Second, it appears, in seeming contradiction of the first conclusion, that COAs are *more sensitive* to some of alcohol's effects, such as stress response dampening and hyperreactivity to the stimulant properties of alcohol (e.g., Finn et al., 1990). Although these effects may seem incompatible, alcohol is known to have widely varying effects, and it is conceivable that the effects on subjective intoxication (in a nonstressed state) and autonomic stress responses are relatively independent. Newlin and Thomson's (1990) hypothesis that COA/nonCOA differences in alcohol effects can be resolved by consideration of the limb of the blood alcohol curve is intriguing, and if valid would suggest that COAs are doubly vulnerable to alcohol's effects. That is, their greater sensitivity to the reinforcing effects of alcohol, and decreased sensitivity to the negative effects of alcohol could lead to greater amounts of consumption with relatively fewer aversive side effects. Finally, the lack of specificity observed for measures such as P3 or MAO should not be taken to preclude their utility in understanding the etiology of alcoholism. Alcohol abuse and dependence are quite heterogeneous and, as reviewed earlier, frequently co-occur with other psychiatric disorders.

Animal Studies. Behavior-genetic studies with rodents have demonstrated a number of phenomena that may be important in understanding the determinants of alcohol-seeking behavior and the effects of alcohol in humans. The primary advantages of genetic animal models of alcohol abuse are related to experimental control, ethics, and cost. The major disadvantages stem from the difficulty in modeling important environmental antecedents of human alcoholism, and the fact that genetic animal models are, at best, only partial models of alcoholism (Crabbe & Phillips, 1990).

Selective breeding techniques have been used in the development of over a dozen rodent models of alcohol consumption and effects. For example, rats have been selectively bred for high and low preference for alcohol containing solutions (Crabbe, 1989; Li, Lumeng, McBride, & Murphy, 1992), with alcohol preferring strains often achieving high blood alcohol levels and expending considerable effort to obtain alcohol. Also, rats and mice have been bred for a variety of responses to alcohol, including sensitivity to stimulant and sedative effects and dependence-related phenomena such as tolerance and withdrawal sensitivity (Crabbe, Belknap, & Buck, 1994). These models, in addition to demonstrating how various aspects of alcohol-related behavior can be under genetic control, also offer the opportunity to study environmental effects on different genotypes and permit intrusive methods to assess neuropharmacological and neurophysiological correlates of these genetically mediated differences. For example, differences between alcohol preferring and nonalcohol preferring rats in monoaminergic and opioid functioning have been demonstrated using a range of techniques to study regionalized neuropharmacological functioning (Froelich, Zweifel, Harts, Lumeng, & Li, 1991; McBride, Murphy, Lumeng, & Li, 1990).

McGue (1999) suggested that animal models will likely make their greatest contribution to alcoholism etiology by helping to identify and characterize specific genes that influence individual differences in alcohol-related behaviors. For example, in recent years, a number of advances have been made in identifying variations in quantitative trait loci (QTL) for alcohol-related phenotypes in mice, many of which have homologues in the human genome that can be targeted in human genetic research (for reviews see NIAAA, 1997, and McGue, 1999). Additionally, transgenic approaches, which utilize genetically engineered animals to over- or under-express specific gene products, are increasingly being used to isolate the effects of individual genes on alcohol-related behaviors (Homanics, Quinlan, Mihalek, & Firestone, 1998; McGue, 1999; Wehner & Bowers, 1995).

Neurochemical Mediators of Alcohol's Effects. Several neurotransmitter systems—including the monoamines (e.g., dopamine, serotonin), neuropeptides (e.g., endorphins, enkephalins), and amino acids (e.g., gamma-aminobutyric acid [GABA] and glutamate)—all appear to be affected by alcohol. Further, each of these neurotransmitters binds with multiple receptor subtypes, which may themselves be differentially affected by alcohol.

The monoamines, as well as GABA and the endogenous opiates, are thought to be associated with alcohol's reinforcing effects. Alcohol preferring rats have been found to have lower levels of dopamine and serotonin than alcohol nonpreferring rats in certain brain regions (Hwang, Lumeng, Wu, & Li, 1990; Li et al., 1992). In humans, individuals with alcohol use disorders have been found to have lower levels of serotonin metabolites (Gorelick, 1989; Roy Virkkunen, & Linnoila, 1990), and an inverse relationship between these metabolites and length of abstinence also has been noted (Banki, 1981). These findings have led some researchers to suggest that alcohol consumption may serve to increase alcoholic's serotonin to "normal" levels (Kranzler & Anton, 1994). Further, dopamine and serotonin agonists and antagonists have been shown to alter alcohol intake in rats and humans in predictable ways (Kranzler & Anton, 1994; Li et al., 1992; McBride et al., 1990). The relations between the monoaminergic neurotransmitters and alcohol's reinforcing effects are obviously complex and are not as yet totally understood. Nonetheless, the finding that decreased levels of serotonin and its primary metabolites are associated with alcohol use and problems is provocative given serotonin's association with mood and impulse control, both of which have been implicated as important aspects of proposed alcoholism typologies (e.g., Cloninger, 1987).

GABA is the major inhibitory neurotransmitter in the mammalian central nervous system, providing the brain with a means to control neuronal excitation. Alcohol's effects on the $GABA_A$ receptor may be a mechanism for alcohol's anxiolytic, sedative, and motor impairment effects as demonstrated by GABA antagonists' ability to offset these effects (Korpi, 1994). The finding that an experimental drug (Ro 15-4513) counteracts ethanol's motor impairment effects elicited intense research efforts to define the parameters of the drug's effects and to identify other drugs that block alcohol's effects. Across several experiments, Ro 15-4513 has not been found to consistently affect the psychomotor stimulant, hypothermia, or lethal effects of alcohol, suggesting multiple mechanisms for alcohol's effects (Korpi, 1994).

Glutamate, the central nervous system's major excitatory neurotransmitter, is implicated in alcohol's cognitive and motor impairment and amnesic effects through its action on two receptor sites: N-methyl-D-aspartate (NMDA) and α amino-3-hydroxy-5-methyl-4-isoxazole propionic acid (AMPA; Lovinger, White, & Weight, 1989; NIAAA, 1993). Ethanol has been shown to inhibit NMDA receptor activation in neurons taken from several mice CNS regions, including the hippocampus, spinal cord, and neocortex (Lovinger et al., 1989). Alcohol's effects on AMPA receptors have been studied less frequently than NMDA receptors, but they appear to be less sensitive to alcohol and are thought to be involved in the decreased respiration and general anesthesia effects that occur as a result of extremely heavy alcohol consumption (NIAAA, 1993).

In a review of the literature on alcohol and glutamatergic transmission, Tsai, Gastfriend, and Coyle (1995) proposed a glutamatergic basis for alcoholism. They noted that, in addition to cognitive and motor impairment effects, many of alcohol's chronic and neurotoxic effects are the result of disturbances in glutamatergic neurotransmission. For example, they suggested that up-regulation of NMDA receptors, in response to chronic inhibition by ethanol, mediates withdrawal, the cognitive deficits associated with alcohol dementia and Wernicke–Korsakoff syndrome, and leads to cell death through chronic augmentation of postsynaptic neurons (an effect known as excitotoxicity). They also proposed that *decreased* (or down-regulated) glutamate receptor density occurring in the developing fetus in response to intrauterine alcohol exposure is a mechanism for fetal alcohol syndrome.

Converging evidence suggests that the endogenous opiates are an important mechanism for alcohol's reinforcing effects. Kranzler and Anton (1994) pointed to the following findings in summarizing the evidence for a role for endogenous opiates in alcohol use and alcohol use disorders: (a) lower basal levels of plasma and cerebral-spinal fluid beta-endorphins have been observed in alcoholics compared to nonalcoholics; (b) alcohol preferring mice have demonstrated lower levels of endogenous opiates prior to alcohol consumption; (c) basal beta-endorphin levels were found to be comparable for asymptomatic offspring of alcoholics and abstinent alcoholics, and were significantly lower in those with a family history of alcoholism than individuals without a family history of alcoholism; (d) after consuming alcohol, asymptomatic offspring of alcoholics exhibited a significantly greater increase in beta-endorphin levels, resulting in levels comparable to those demonstrated following alcohol ingestion by adult offspring of nonalcoholics; and (e) opioid antagonists (e.g., naltrexone) have been shown to reduce alcohol consumption, craving, and risk for relapse. It appears that the delta opioid receptor is an important receptor for alcohol's reinforcing effects (Froelich et al., 1991). Based on findings from controlled clinical trials that showed naltrexone in conjunction with therapy effectively decreased alcohol use and problems (O'Malley et al., 1992; Volpicelli, Alterman, Hayashida, & O'Brien, 1992), this opioid antagonist was approved for the pharmacological treatment of alcohol dependence (as part of a comprehensive treatment program) by the U.S. Food and Drug Administration.

Several of the neurotransmitters discussed earlier, as well as others, are implicated in withdrawal and tolerance from chronic alcohol consumption. Increases in excitatory neurotransmitters, as well as reduced input by inhibitory neurotransmitters, are associated with alcohol withdrawal (see Glue & Nutt, 1990, for a review). Alcohol tolerance is thought to be at least partially the result of neuronal adaptation to the acute effects of alcohol (NIAAA, 1993). The down-regulation of GABA receptors appears to be important in both withdrawal and tolerance, as research has shown that sensitivity to GABA agonists decreases with chronic alcohol exposure (Dietrich, 1987). Adenosine, norepinephrine, and vasopressin are also implicated in the development and maintenance of tolerance (NIAAA, 1993).

PSYCHOLOGICAL ETIOLOGIC FACTORS

Psychological approaches to the study of alcohol use and misuse can be broadly classified into four categories: (a) personality theories; (b) cognitive/social learning theories; (c) psychopharmacological approaches; and (d) social interactional or developmental theories (Blane & Leonard, 1987; Leonard & Blane, 1999). The first three of these broad perspectives are summarized here and the last is reviewed in the subsequent section on putative social-developmental etiologic factors.

Personality Theories

Personality traits have maintained a near ubiquitous presence in psychologically based theories of alcoholism. Despite the apparent conceptual appeal of an "addictive personality," decades of empirical research have failed to identify a unique constellation of personality traits that characterize alcoholics. Nevertheless, there is convergent evidence for the etiologic significance of specific, broad-based personality constructs for alcohol abuse and dependence, particularly within the context of larger psychosocial models (see Sher, Trull, Bartholow, & Vieth, 1999, for a review).

There are a number of conceptual and methodological issues relating to the study of personality and alcohol that limit the confidence with which the results of given studies can be interpreted. For example, there is general consensus that alcoholism is both clinically and etiologically heterogeneous, and failure to consider relevant subtypes may mask possible relations. As noted earlier, individuals with alcohol use disorders are at increased risk for other psychopathology, making unambiguous attribution of personality characteristics to a particular disorder problematic. Additionally, ambiguity has often been more the exception than the rule with respect to operationalizing personality (see Nathan, 1988).

Relations between alcohol abuse or dependence and personality may be artifactually influenced by factors such as content overlap between purported personality measures and diagnostic criteria (e.g., drinking-related behavior) or by "third variables" (e.g., gender, developmental stage; Sher et al., 1999). With respect to study designs, cross-sectional studies, the most frequently used methodology in the study of personality and alcoholism, are incapable of resolving whether personality factors are antecedents to, or consequences of, alcohol use disorders. Prospective designs, although useful with respect to the resolution of temporal precedence, are not immune to third variable alternative explanations.

Consistent with a more comprehensive review of this topic (Sher & Trull, 1994), this discussion is limited to three broad-band personality dimensions (i.e., neuroticism/emotionality, impulsivity/disinhibition, and extraversion/sociability), each of which have been found to be associated with alcohol abuse and dependence. Empirical support for this classification scheme comes from a study that factor analyzed 46 scales that purportedly measure basic dimensions of personality (Zuckerman, Kuhlman, & Camac, 1988). Others, notably Tarter (1988) and Cloninger (1987), used different, plausible, three-factor classification schemes, and we note also that the five factor model of personality may have utility in the prediction of alcohol use disorders (see Martin & Sher, 1994, and Sher et al., 1999).

There is consistent empirical evidence that alcoholics exhibit significant elevations on measures of neuroticism/emotionality (Barnes, 1979, 1983; Sher et al., 1999). The frequent co-occurrence of anxiety and alcohol use disorders also is consistent with a relationship between negative affect and alcohol use disorders (Kessler et al., 1997; Kushner et al., 1990). Findings from cross-sectional studies of COAs have been mixed, with some studies noting differences in measures of neuroticism/emotionality between high risk and low risk individuals (e.g., Finn & Pihl, 1987; Sher et al., 1991), whereas at least one other study found no differences (Schuckit, 1983). Additionally, another cross-sectional study found that harm avoidance, a measure conceptually similar to neuroticism, predicted negative alcohol consequences and alcohol dependence symptoms, but not quantity-frequency indices (Sher, M. Wood, Crews, & Vandiver, 1995). Historically, there has been less evidence from prospective studies regarding the importance of neuroticism/emotionality in predicting alcohol abuse or dependence, at least in men (e.g., Jones, 1968; Robins, Bates, & O'Neal, 1962; Vaillant & Milofsky, 1982). However, more recent prospective studies have found neuroticism/ emotionality to be predictive of subsequent alcohol involvement (Caspi et al., 1997; Chassin, Curran, Hussong, & Colder, 1996; Clonginer, Sigvardsson, & Bohman, 1988; Labouvie, Pandina, White, & Johnson, 1990; Sieber, 1981). In sum, particularly when drawing on the relatively sparse existing database of prospective studies, the etiological relevance of neuroticism/emotionality remains unresolved. Enhanced understanding of the role of neuroticism/ emotionality in alcohol use disorders may be achieved by consideration of potential moderators of this relation (Sher et al., 1999). For example, there is some evidence that neurotic traits may be particularly etiologically significant for alcohol abuse and dependence among women (e.g., Jones, 1971).

Impulsive/disinhibited traits appear to be the most etiologically significant personality dimensions for alcohol use and misuse. This taxonomy includes such constructs as sensation seeking, aggressiveness, impulsivity, psychoticism, and novelty seeking (Sher & Trull, 1994). The high degree of comorbidity between alcohol use and antisocial personality disorders noted earlier is consistent with the high level of impulsivity and antisociality often exhibited by alcoholics (Regier et al., 1990). In cross-sectional high risk studies, COAs consistently differ from nonCOAs on indices of impulsivity, novelty seeking, antisociality, and aggression (Alterman et al., 1998; Sher et al., 1995). Most critically, prospective studies consistently indicate that traits such as aggression, conduct problems, impulsivity, unconventionality, and novelty seeking strongly portend the development of alcohol misuse, as well as other forms of substance misuse (Bates & Labouvie, 1995; Caspi et al., 1997; Cloninger et al., 1988; Hawkins et al., 1992; Pederson, 1991; Schuckit, 1998; Zucker Fitzgerald, & Moses, 1995; Zucker & Gomberg, 1986).

It should be noted that whether or not these personality dimensions constitute motivational traits or behavior has been the subject of some debate. Nathan (1988) suggested that it is primarily behavior that is etiologically significant for substance abuse and concluded that the evidence for the prognostic importance of personality traits more narrowly defined is largely nonexistent. Others (e.g., Zucker & Gomberg, 1986) have claimed that "antisocial personality is part of personality and it plays a significant etiological role" (p. 785). As Sher and Trull (1994) noted, the debate is largely centered on the question of how personality is operationalized.

Reviews of the literature suggest that extraversion/sociability does not tend to distinguish alcoholic and nonalcoholic individuals (Barnes, 1983; Cox, 1985; Lang, 1983). Further, high-risk, cross-sectional studies have not consistently demonstrated COA/nonCOA differences on measures of extraversion/sociability (Sher, 1991), although one study did find that sociability predicted substance use among adolescent COAs but not controls (Molina, Chassin, & Curran, 1994). However, there is some evidence from longitudinal studies to suggest that extraversion/sociability predict subsequent alcohol misuse (Jones, 1968; Kilbey, Downey, & Breslau, 1998; Sieber, 1981). Sher et al. (1999) suggest that the seeming paradox between the null findings in alcoholic samples and the positive findings in non-clinical samples may be resolved by consideration of the course of the disorder. Specifically, extraversion/sociability may be important risk factors for the *development* of alcohol problems, but there is evidence suggesting that this trait becomes increasingly "masked" as alcohol dependence increases (Kammeier, Hoffman, & Loper, 1973).

In summary, the existing literature indicates that impulsivity/disinhibition, and possibly neuroticism/emotionality, appear to be etiologically important for alcohol misuse. The role of extraversion/sociability is less certain, but there is some evidence supporting this trait as etiologically relevant in the development of alcohol problems. However, demonstration of significant correlations between personality dimensions and alcohol use disorders does little to establish their importance in the etiology of alcohol use disorders. Current theorizing has evolved to the point where personality traits are typically viewed as important mediating or moderating variables within larger psychosocial etiologic models (e.g., Cloninger, 1987; Jessor & Jessor, 1977; Rogosch, Chassin, & Sher, 1990; Sher, 1991; Sher & Trull, 1994; Zucker, 1987; Zucker & Gomberg, 1986).

Cognitive/Social Learning Theories

The following section briefly summarizes recent research examining cognitive factors of putative etiological relevance in the development and maintenance of alcohol use and misuse. For a more comprehensive review of social learning theory approaches as applied to alcohol use and alcoholism, see Maisto, Carey, and Bradizza (1999).

Over the past 20 years, alcohol outcome expectancies, have figured prominently in the search for the psychosocial correlates and determinants of alcohol use and misuse. An outgrowth of learning theory and social learning approaches, alcohol outcome expectancies can be defined as beliefs that people have about the behavioral, cognitive, and emotional effects of drinking alcohol (Goldman, S. Brown, & Christiansen, 1987). A great many cross-sectional studies have found alcohol outcome expectancies to be strong correlates of both alcohol use and misuse for adolescents, college students, and adults, across drinking patterns ranging from abstention to alcoholism (e.g., S. Brown, Goldman, & Christiansen, 1985; Connors, O'Farrell, Cutter, & Thompson, 1986; Fromme, Stroot, & Kaplan, 1993; Leigh, 1987; Leigh & Stacy, 1993; Mann, Chassin, & Sher, 1987; M. Wood, Nagoshi, & Dennis, 1992). Although more research has focused on positive rather than negative outcome expectancies, there is sufficient evidence to suggest that the latter also may be important predictors of alcohol use and misuse (Adams & McNeil, 1991; Leigh, 1989). Nevertheless, in studies involving direct comparison of these two types of expectancies, positive outcome expectancies have wielded greater prediction on indices of use and problems (Fromme et al., 1993; Leigh & Stacy, 1993; Stacy, Widaman, & Marlatt, 1990).

Researchers also have begun to examine outcome expectancies as mediators (Sher et al., 1991) and moderators (Cooper, Russell, Skinner, Frone, & Mudar, 1992; Kushner, Sher, M. Wood, & P. Wood, 1994) of relations between alcohol use and misuse and other psychosocial constructs. Studies of adolescents and children have supported the hypothesis that alcohol outcome expectancies play a role in the initiation of drinking in that they are present, presumably via vicarious learning, prior to personal drinking experience and predict subsequent alcohol use (Christiansen, G. T. Smith, Roehling, & Goldman, 1989; P. Miller, G. T. Smith, & Goldman, 1990; G. T. Smith, Goldman, Greenbaum, & Christiansen, 1995).

Comparatively few prospective studies examining relations between alcohol outcome expectancies and alcohol use and misuse have been conducted. Nonetheless, the small body of existing literature supports a role for outcome expectancies in the etiology of alcohol use, and perhaps in the escalation of drinking to problematic levels. Outcome expec- tancies have been identified in children as young as age 8, become more homogeneous in older age groups, and, at least for early adolescents, increase over time (Miller et al., 1990; G. T. Smith et al., 1995). In contrast to these findings, a four-year prospective study of college students, observed significant decreases in alcohol outcome expectancies during young adulthood (Sher, M. Wood, P. Wood, & Raskin, 1996). Combining this study with those described above, the literature suggests that outcome expectancies are initially formed through vicarious learning, are augmented by early alcohol use (as well as numerous other social influences), and then are subsequently tempered by more substantial experience with alcohol. Prospective studies also have provided empirical evidence regarding reciprocal influence between alcohol outcome expectancies and alcohol use (Bauman, Fisher, Bryan, & Chenowith, 1985; Sher et al., 1996; G. T. Smith et al., 1995), suggesting a potential role for outcome expectancies in the escalation of drinking to problematic levels. Alternatively, at least one other study (Stacy, Newcomb, & Bentler, 1991a) did not find evidence for reciprocal influence, perhaps due to a substantially longer follow-up interval. Thus, it appears that alcohol outcome expectancies play a role in the initiation of alcohol use, and alcohol use in turn strengthens outcome expectancies.

Additionally, researchers are beginning to apply contemporary cognitive theory and methodology to the study of alcohol outcome expectancies (see Goldman, DelBoca, & Darkes, 1999 for a review). Rather, Goldman, Roehrich, & Brannick (1992), in an application of semantic network theory, used multidimensional scaling techniques to categorize expectancies along dimensions of social/positive to antisocial/negative and sedative versus arousing effects. They found that for light drinkers, the most highly endorsed effects were related to sedation, whereas heavy drinkers endorsed more arousing effects. They also noted that negative expectancies seemed to be less frequently accessed, suggesting they are further along the activation network and thus are presumably less likely to influence drinking behavior.

In sum, alcohol outcome expectancies appear to be etiologically significant for alcohol use and misuse. Research and theory in this area has begun to move beyond static descriptions of relations between outcome expectancies and drinking behavior, and instead examine the role of alcohol outcome expectancies within the context of larger psychosocial models. For example, Sher (1991) suggested that outcome expectancies may be etiologically important as either mediators (e.g., of individual differences in alcohol sensitivity), or moderators (e.g., of relations between more distal psychosocial variables such as negative mood states and drinking behavior). Finally, the modification of outcome expectancies has potential implications with respect to prevention and intervention efforts. To this end, Darkes and Goldman (1993, 1998) provided evidence for the effectiveness of an intervention challenging social and sexual outcome expectancies in decreasing drinking levels over brief (2-week) follow-ups.

Drawing from motivational models of alcohol use and misuse (e.g., Cox & Klinger, 1988), psychosocial research has examined cross-sectional associations between particular types of drinking motives and alcohol use and problems in adolescent, college student, and adult samples (Carey & Correia, 1997; Cooper, 1994; Cooper, Frone, Russell, & Mudar, 1995). In a college student sample, Carey and Correia (1997) found that negative reinforcement motives demonstrated stronger associations with alcohol problems than did positive reinforcement motives. Cooper (1994) found support for a four-factor measure of drinking motives derived from the model proposed by Cox & Klinger (1988), with subsequent analyses indicating that both negative (coping) and positive (mood enhancement) motives were associated with adolescent alcohol use and problems. Cooper et al. (1995) extended the earlier study by examining relations between mood enhancement and coping motives and patterns of alcohol use and problems in both an adolescent and adult sample. Consistent with the hypothesis that negative reinforcement motives would be more predictive of pathological drinking patterns, in both samples coping motives were related to both alcohol use and problems, while enhancement motives were related to alcohol use but not directly related to problems.

Coping skills also have been identified as an important psychosocial determinant of alcohol use and misuse. From a social learning perspective, alcohol misuse may occur when environmental stressors overwhelm coping abilities, particularly in conjunction with higher levels of positive alcohol outcome expectancies (Abrams & Niaura, 1987). Wills (1986) noted an inverse relation between perceived coping skills and alcohol use among adolescents in both cross-sectional and longitudinal analyses. Further, he found that coping moderated life stress-alcohol use relations, with a strong relation demonstrated at lower levels of coping and weaker relations at higher levels of coping. Cooper, Russell, and George (1988) found that positive alcohol outcome expectancies moderated the relation between coping strategies and alcohol use, such that individuals with high outcome expectancies who used avoidant styles of coping with negative affect were most likely to cope by using alcohol. These results have also been replicated in a college student sample (Evans & Dunn, 1995).

Psychopharmacological Approaches to Alcohol Use and Misuse

Motivation to drink can result from either the positive or negative reinforcement properties of alcohol. The tension-reduction hypothesis (TRH; Cappell & Greeley, 1987; Greeley & Oei, 1999) is the most prominent example of the latter class of negative reinforcement approaches to understanding alcohol use and misuse. Basically, the TRH postulates that: (a) alcohol is tension reducing and (b) in stressful situations individuals will be motivated to drink. Empirical evidence for the TRH is mixed, at least in part due to differences in operationalization of key variables (e.g., tension), and methodologies (e.g., cross-sectional vs. prospective, experimental vs. correlational; Pohorecky, 1991).

Contemporary refinements of the TRH have focused on examinations of relations between experimentally elicited stress and alcohol consumption, and have more explicitly incorporated the notion that the stress reducing effects of alcohol are centrally (e.g., CNS) mediated (Sayette, 1993; Sher, 1987). In the following we summarize the stress response dampening model (Levenson, Sher, Grossman, Newman, & Newlin, 1980; Sher, 1987), as well as two other psychopharmacological models that draw heavily on information-processing explanations of alcohol's effects—the attention-allocation model (Steele & Josephs, 1988; 1990), and the attention-disruption model (Sayette, 1993).

Sher (1987) noted that the stress response dampening (SRD) model is essentially a scaled down TRH, in which alcohol is hypothesized to reduce responsivity to a stressor and thus is particularly reinforcing in certain stressful situations. SRD effects have been most consistently demonstrated with respect to cardiovascular response, but have been observed with other physiological, self-report, and behavioral measures as well (Sayette, 1993; Sher, 1987). Evidence for the etiologic significance of stress response dampening comes from studies that have found that individual differences in susceptibility to alcohol use disorders (i.e., behavioral undercontrol personality traits, family history of alcoholism) are associated with increased sensitivity to alcohol's stress dampening effects (Finn & Pihl, 1987; Levenson et al., 1987; Sher & Levenson, 1982; Sher et al., 1994). Although the mechanism(s) of the SRD effect are unclear and critical tests of the model have not been conducted, it has been suggested, consistent with many of the findings reviewed under neurochemical mediators of alcohol's effects, that GABA and possibly norepinephrine are implicated in alcohol's tension reducing effects (Sher, 1987).

Steele and Josephs (1988, 1990) proposed that whether alcohol is stress reducing or stress inducing is contingent on both alcohol's effects on information processing and environmental factors. They labeled the phenomenon "alcohol myopia" and described it as a narrowing in the ability to retrieve a range of perceptual cues to those most immediate and salient in a given situation. While questions remain with regard to specific aspects of the theory, empirical tests of the model have typically yielded positive results (Sayette, 1999). Steele and colleagues consistently demonstrated that in conjunction with moderate doses of alcohol, pleasant or neutral distraction (e.g., rating slides of famous paintings) leads to reductions in self-reports of state anxiety during a countdown period to a self-disclosing speech. Demonstration of alcohol's anxiogenic effects in lieu of distraction has been less consistent, but nonetheless has been noted (Steele & Josephs, 1990). The attention-allocation model is more comprehensive than previous models in that it proposes an explanation for both the anxiolytic and anxiogenic effects of alcohol, but does not explain demonstrated SRD effects in the absence of distracting activity (Sayette, 1993). Nevertheless, given the positive results to date, future research that investigates relations between this construct and other risk factors for alcohol misuse could yield valuable information on the etiology of alcohol use and misuse.

Sayette (1993) proposed a model hypothesizing that SRD effects are mediated by disruption in the appraisal of stressful information and accompanying impairment in the ability to integrate it with related information from long-term memory. Sayette argued that if a stressor is sufficiently appraised, alcohol's effects will be anxiogenic; but if encoding of the stressor is disrupted, alcohol will be anxiolytic. Direct tests of the model have yet to be conducted (e.g., measurement of disruption of cognitive appraisal in conjunction with SRD). Nonetheless, the model appears to resolve some existing discrepancies in the literature by consideration of a range of factors, including the temporal ordering of alcohol administration and stress manipulations, the implications of dosage and stressor differences, and alcohol's known deleterious effects on the encoding of information.

There is a fairly large body of human and animal research examining the latter postulate of the TRH—that stressful situations will result in increased alcohol consumption. Cappell and Greeley (1987) noted that in both humans and animals, experimentally-induced *conflict* has typically resulted in increases in alcohol consumption, while more ecologically valid laboratory paradigms (e.g., social anxiety stressors) have yielded less consistent results. Sher (1987) concluded that the likelihood that stress will lead to alcohol consumption is qualified by a number of psychological and social factors, particularly the availability of alternative means of coping and the consideration of the potentially negative consequences of alcohol consumption.

Two studies have reported results supportive of the stress-induced drinking aspect of the TRH for men. Lang, Pelham, Johnston, and Gelernter (1989) examined subjective distress and alcohol consumption among participants who interacted with children trained to behave in both "normal" and "deviant" (Attention Deficit Disordered/Conduct Disordered) styles. Both men and women exhibited significantly higher levels of subjective distress as a function of interacting with the "deviant" child, but only men drank significantly more alcohol in this situation. Stasiewicz and Lisman (1989) randomly assigned undergraduate men to be exposed to either an infant crying or a smoke alarm, followed by a taste-testing task. Participants who heard the infant crying reported higher levels of distress and consumed significantly more alcohol than those exposed to the smoke alarm.

Neither the original tension reduction hypothesis, nor the subsequent models of alcohol consumption were proposed as comprehensive models of alcohol use and misuse. Nonetheless, they have been important in understanding some of the conditions under which alcohol consumption can be reinforcing and in linking these reinforcing effects with putative vulnerability factors.

SOCIAL-DEVELOPMENTAL PUTATIVE ETIOLOGIC FACTORS

Theories on the initiation, maintenance, and escalation of alcohol and substance use have included social factors as both direct and indirect influences (Jessor & Jessor, 1977; Flay & Petraitis, 1994; Kandel, 1973; Kaplan, 1980; Zucker & Gomberg, 1986). In large part due to the observation that alcoholism tends to run in families, studies of family environment and interaction comprise the largest area of inquiry in this domain. However, other social variables, most notably peer and mass media influences, have been linked to alcohol use and misuse.

Familial Influences on Alcohol Use and Misuse

The family, as a primary and initial agent of socialization, obviously exerts a myriad of direct and indirect influences on the developing individual. A range of familial factors have been found to relate to either the intergenerational transmission of alcohol use and misuse, or to poor adolescent or adult adjustment more generally. These include parental monitoring, communication, cohesiveness, social support, parent and sibling attitudes toward alcohol use, familial conflict, parental loss through divorce or separation, disruption of family rituals, unfair and harsh disciplinary practices, and parent and sibling modeling (Barnes, 1990; Barrera, Chassin, & Rogosch, 1993; Bennett, & Wolin, 1990; Catalano et al., 1992; Duncan, Duncan, & Hops, 1994; Harburg, Davis, & Caplan, 1982; Holmes & Robins, 1987; Isohanni, Oja, Moilanen, & Koiranen, 1994; Kandel & Andrews, 1987; Zucker, 1976).

Essentially, each of the factors listed can be classified as related to either parental nurturance, control, or modeling (either directly through imitation of behaviors or indirectly through the adoption of attitudes, expectations, or family rituals; Barnes, 1990; Jacob & Leonard, 1994). Researchers have begun to conduct more fine-grained analyses to examine potential mediators and moderators of relations between family factors and alcohol use, and have extended these investigations to racially heterogeneous samples.

Chassin, Barrera, and colleagues, in a programmatic series of studies, have examined mediational and moderational factors in relations between family history of alcoholism and adolescent substance use and psychological symptomatology. Chassin, Rogosch, and Barrera (1991) found higher levels of both substance abuse and psychological symptomatology among offspring of current alcoholics compared to controls. Barrera et al. (1993) examined the effects of social support and social conflict conjointly and found that their effects were largely independent. Lack of social support from parents was predictive of substance use, whereas conflict predicted general externalizing behavior, but not substance use. Chassin, Pillow, Curran, Molina, and Barrera (1993) demonstrated that decreased parental monitoring and environmental stress-negative affect appear to underlie the link between a family history of alcoholism and adolescent substance use. They also observed a direct effect, consistent with a modeling interpretation, from mothers' alcohol use to adolescent substance use. Taken together, these findings suggest multiple pathways for substance use in at-risk individuals. Parental alcohol abuse appears to be related to offspring substance use directly by social learning, and indirectly by decreased parental monitoring and environmental stress, both of which serve to increase the likelihood of affiliation with drug-using peers. This affiliation is, in turn, strongly associated with drug use by offspring. Molina et al. (1994), examined whether the observed relations between parent monitoring and stress-negative affect were moderated by family history status. They found no evidence for differential relations, instead noting significant relations between these factors regardless of family history status, suggesting prevention efforts would equally apply to those with and without a family history of alcoholism.

Sher and colleagues, utilizing data from an ongoing longitudinal study of young adults at low and high risk for the development of alcoholism, examined potential mediators of the family history-substance use disorder relation in two recent studies. Sher et al., (1997) found that retrospectively assessed childhood stressors (e.g., verbal, emotional, physical and sexual abuse) demonstrated consistent and often robust relations with family history status. This study also observed significant associations between several childhood stressors (most notably embarrassment, emotional, physical, and sexual abuse of the participant, exposure to verbal abuse of other family members) and lifetime alcohol use disorder diagnoses. Additional analyses indicated that childhood stressors partially mediated the family history—alcohol use disorder relation, although the magnitude of the mediational effect was not large. Erickson, Sher, and P. Wood (1997) used state-trait analyses to prospectively examine alcohol expectancies, childhood stressors, and a vulnerability index (comprised of broad-band "constitutional" predictors of family history status) as mediators of the family history—substance use disorder relation. They found consistent evidence for a mediational role of alcohol expectancies and the vulnerability index across alcohol, other drug, and tobacco dependence, while childhood stressors mediated relations between family history of alcoholism status and tobacco dependence.

Overwhelmingly, research to date on familial influences on alcohol use and misuse has been conducted using predominantly White samples. As noted earlier, descriptive statistics regarding alcohol use, misuse, morbidity, and mortality among minority populations are available from the epidemiological literature, but until relatively recently little has been known about whether observed social influence factors generalize to minority populations. Barnes and colleagues, utilizing a general population sample that oversampled Blacks, reported on familial influences on alcohol use and misuse among black and white adolescents. In both cross-sectional and longitudinal analyses, they observed that high parental monitoring and social support were important protective factors for adolescent alcohol abuse and deviant behaviors more generally (Barnes & Farrell, 1992; Barnes, Farrell, & Banerjee, 1994). Although for the most part the lack of higher order interactions observed by Barnes et al. (1994) suggests that familial influences are similar for Black and White adolescents, some interesting interactions did emerge. Specifically, religiosity may insulate Black adolescents from abuse, and peer drinking appears to be a stronger influence for deviant behaviors among White rather than Black adolescents. Catalano et al. (1992), noted that patterns of drug use *initiation* differed among ethnic groups and sexes, even after controlling for socioeconomic factors. They also noted that family factors appear to exert the greatest protective influence for Black youths and the least protective for Whites.

Imitative modeling of parent or sibling drinking behavior is one of the most straightforward hypotheses regarding the intergenerational transmission of alcohol misuse. Whereas there is evidence to suggest its importance for the initiation of alcohol and other substance use (e.g., Chassin et al., 1993; Kandel & Andrews, 1987), it also appears that relations between parent and offspring drinking habits vary systematically. For example, Harburg and colleagues, in a series of studies, found evidence for imitative modeling effects associated with abstaining and light drinking parents, and "fall-off" (i.e., negative modeling or nonimitative) effects associated with heavy drinking parents (Harburg et al., 1982; Harburg, DiFranceisco, Webster, Gleiberman, & Schork, 1990; Harburg, Gleiberman, DiFranceisco, Schork, & Weissfeld, 1990; Webster, Harburg, Gleiberman, Schork, & DiFranceisco, 1989). Additionally, McCord (1988) demonstrated that father-son transmission of alcoholism was more likely when the alcoholic father was held in high esteem by the mother.

Studies examining the moderating role of family interactions on the later expression of alcoholism among offspring of alcoholics have uncovered some provocative findings. Wolin and colleagues, using semistructured interviews with both parents and adult offspring, assessed the extent to which "family rituals" (e.g., celebrating holidays, taking vacations) were disrupted by an alcoholic parent's drinking. Families were classified as either "distinctive" (little or no family ritual disruption) or "subsumptive" (family rituals subsumed by an alcoholic parent's drinking). Wolin and colleagues (Wolin, Bennett, & Noonan, 1979; Wolin, Bennett, Noonan, & Teitelbaum, 1980) found that subsumptive families and, to a lesser extent intermediate families, tended to produce alcoholic offspring whereas distinctive families did not. An additional study reported that offspring of alcoholics who exhibited high levels of "deliberateness" in establishing and maintaining rituals in their own families were less likely to experience alcohol problems themselves (Bennett, Wolin, Reiss, & Teitelbaum, 1987). As Sher (1991) previously noted, these findings are compelling, but await replication in larger samples with systematic attempts to eliminate potential third-variable explanations. Additionally, prospective studies are needed to more clearly elucidate the temporal ordering of effects.

Peer, Social Network, and Broader Sociocultural Influences. In a review of family and peer influences on adolescent alcohol use, Jacob and Leonard (1994) noted that the study of peer influences has, in large part, received its impetus from observed associations between: (a) early peer rejection and the development of delinquent behavior in childhood and adolescence; and (b) adolescent alcohol involvement and association with deviant peers. They also noted that although there is little doubt that substance use by friends, particularly close friends (e.g., Morgan & Grube, 1991), is among the strongest predictors of adolescent substance use, the question of whether the mechanism for these effects is one of self-selection versus peer influence remains unresolved. Toward this end, two recent studies (Curran, Stice, & Chassin, 1997; Wills & Cleary, 1999) examined selection versus socialization (peer influence) mechanisms in adolescent substance use. In both studies consistent evidence was observed for peer influences mechanisms, with more modest evidence for selection effects observed in one study (Curran et al., 1997), but not the other.

Joint investigations of peer and family influences have indicated that there are multiple pathways to adolescent alcohol use and misuse, and that the importance of these pathways is likely to vary at different developmental stages (Chassin et al., 1993; Duncan et al., 1994; Gerrard, Gibbons, Zhao, Russell, & Reis-Bergan, 1999; Kandel & Andrews, 1987). Kandel and Andrews (1987) compared the influences of parents and peers on adolescent drinking and drug use and concluded that peer influences were much more important with respect to adolescent frequency of drinking. Alternatively, for the initiation of alcohol use, parent factors played a larger role than peer influences, although the total amount of variance explained was quite small (7%), making inferences regarding the substantive importance of these findings difficult. Kandel and Andrews also noted, consistent with Chassin et al. (1993), that closeness to parents was a protective factor, both directly through alcohol use and indirectly through decreased likelihood of affiliating with drug-using peers. Ary, Tildesley, Hops, and Andrews (1993) observed that both parent and peer attitudes and drinking behaviors were prospective predictors of adolescent alcohol use. Duncan et al. (1994) suggested that the relation between family influence and childhood/adolescent alcohol use may be curvilinear, waxing in late childhood and middle-to-late adolescence, and waning in early adolescence when peer influences assume greater importance.

Social influence factors of another sort have been noted in research with college students. Baer, Stacy, and Larimer (1991) found that college students' misperceptions regarding drinking norms exist across several reference groups including best friends, immediate living group, and for students in general. They noted a strong tendency for individuals to nearly always perceive close friends and members of social reference groups as consuming alcohol more frequently than themselves. Although the particular mechanisms related to this effect are not clear, the findings suggest that these misperceptions could influence heavier drinking or insulate individuals or groups against recognition of hazardous drinking.

Mass Media Effects on Alcohol Use and Misuse. Alcohol commercials and portrayals of alcohol consumption are extremely prevalent features of the mass media landscape. For example, in 1990 and 1991, average alcohol advertisements per television hour ranged from 5.7 during major professional sports events to 0.22 during situation comedies, with an average of over 6 drinking acts per hour of prime time television (Grube, 1993). Content analyses of commercials and prime-time fictional television programs indicate that drinkers tend to be characterized as attractive, affluent, sociable, have high social status, typically experience positive and seldom experience negative consequences (Grube, 1993; Wallack, Grube, Madden, & Breed, 1990). One survey indicated that 73% of the general public agreed that alcohol advertising was a major influence on underage drinking (Grube & Wallack, 1994).

Empirically, much less is known about the effects of high levels of exposure to alcohol advertising and alcohol portrayals on actual alcohol consumption, drinking norms, and alcohol outcome expectancies. Smart (1988) reviewed the affects of alcohol advertising on overall alcohol consumption by examining: (a) advertising bans and restrictions; (b) correlational studies of exposure to advertisements; (c) econometric studies (correlations of advertising expenditures with aggregate measures of alcohol consumption); and (d) experimental studies. He noted that methodological problems severely limited the interpretability of findings, but generally concluded that there was little evidence to suggest any more than weak associations between advertising and alcohol consumption. Nonetheless, he suggested that more carefully designed econometric, experimental, and prospective studies would be useful additions to the extant literature.

Typically, researchers in the area have tacitly assumed that mere exposure to alcohol ads or portrayals (often indirectly assessed) is sufficient to elicit attitudinal and behavioral changes. Grube and Wallack (1994) suggested, in accordance with information processing theory, that advertisements may only affect attitudes and behaviors when they are attended to and remembered. To this end, they investigated relations between awareness of television beer advertising, drinking knowledge, alcohol outcome expectancies, and intentions to drink as adults among a group of 10- to 14-year-old youths. In conservative analyses, they demonstrated: (a) awareness of alcohol advertising was significantly associated with increased knowledge of brands and slogans and with positive beliefs about drinking; (b) alcohol outcome expectancies mediated the relation between alcohol advertising and intentions to drink as an adult; and (c) awareness of ads was *not* significantly related to negative beliefs about alcohol. These findings indicate that cognitive variables (e.g., alcohol outcome expectancies) may be an important mechanism of influence for mass media effects, and suggest prevention efforts should not ignore alcohol advertising as a potential source of social influence.

CONCLUSIONS

In reviewing etiological factors in alcohol use and misuse, several important issues need to be highlighted. First, alcohol is a drug that affects most of the neurotransmitter systems that have been identified as playing key roles in motivating and regulating human behavior. The neuropharmacological consequences of alcohol consumption are likely to play a key role in both alcohol-seeking behavior and determining the amount an individual consumes on a given occasion. Second, there are large individual differences in the likelihood that persons will misuse alcohol. Many of these individual differences are probably determined by genetic factors. However, the mechanisms describing how heredity exerts its effects are currently unknown. Although available research suggests that vulnerability is associated with differential sensitivity to alcohol effects, other genetically mediated mechanisms that do not rely on individual differences in ethanol sensitivity are also quite plausible (Sher, 1991). Third, at present, the strongest correlates (both cross-sectionally and prospectively) of alcohol use and misuse are psychological constructs including certain behavior patterns (especially those characterized by impulsivity) and alcohol outcome expectancies. Fourth, social influences ranging from the family, to peers, to mass media and other cultural and political variables all appear to exert important influences on alcohol use. A comprehensive understanding of the etiology of alcohol misuse will require an understanding of how these diverse factors influence alcohol consumption both independently and in combination.

The broad range of biopsychosocial determinants of alcohol consumption and problems have important implications for development of techniques for preventing and treating alcohol misuse. Although intervention in alcohol problems is discussed elsewhere in this volume (see Altman & Goodman, chap. 36), it is worth noting here that interventions have been developed that target biological, psychological, and social variables. For example, at the biological level, there appears to be therapeutic benefit to employing pharmacologic agents that reduce craving and antagonize some of the reinforcing effects of alcohol (O'Malley et al., 1992; Volpicelli et al., 1992). At the psychological level, attempts to modify individually held beliefs about the consequences of alcohol consumption (i.e., alcohol outcome expectancies), although preliminary, show promise (e.g., Darkes & Goldman, 1993; 1998). At the social level, interventions that attempt to change perceived drinking norms appear to be an important component of multi-component prevention programs (e.g., Baer, 1993; Marlatt et al., 1998) and have demonstrated efficacy in universal prevention efforts with college students (Haines & Spear, 1996). Against this background of efforts targeted at individuals, social policy interventions (e.g., increasing the drinking age, decreasing permissible blood alcohol levels for drivers, stricter enforcement and harsher penalties of drinking and driving laws) have been shown to be particularly important in reducing certain alcohol-related problems (e.g., alcohol-related motor vehicle crashes). Thus, it seems likely that the effective prevention and treatment of alcohol misuse will involve interventions at each level of biopsychosocial organization.

ACKNOWLEDGMENTS

Preparation of this chapter was supported in part by a grant from the Alcoholic Beverage Medical Research Foundation and Grant R29 AA12241 from the National Institute on Alcohol Abuse and Alcoholism to Mark D. Wood, Grant R37 AA7231 from the National Institute on Alcohol Abuse and Alcoholism to Kenneth J. Sher and by an award from the Generalist Physician Faculty Scholars Program of the Robert Wood Johnson Foundation to Daniel C. Vinson.

We gratefully acknowledge Heather Gotham and Matt Kushner, who provided valuable comments on an earlier draft.

REFERENCES

Abbey, A. (1991). Acquaintance rape and alcohol consumption on college campuses: How are they linked? *Journal of American College Health, 39,* 165–169.

Abel, E. L., Martier, S., Kruger, M., Ager, J., & Sokol, R. J. (1993). Ratings of fetal alcohol syndrome facial features by medical providers and biomedical scientists. *Alcohol: Clinical and Experimental Research, 17*(3), 717–721.

Abrams, D. B., & Niaura, R. S. (1987). Social learning theory. In H. T. Blane & K. E. Leonard (Eds.), *Psychological theories of drinking and alcoholism* (pp. 131–178). New York: Guilford.

Adami, H., McLaughlin, J. K., Hsing, A. W., Wolk, A., Ekbom, A., Holmberg, L., & Persson, I. (1992). Alcoholism and cancer risk: A population-based cohort study. *Cancer Causes Control, 3,* 419–425.

Adams, S. L., & McNeil, D. W. (1991). Negative alcohol expectancies reconsidered. *Psychology of Addictive Behaviors, 5,* 9–14.

Albert, C. M., Manson, J. E., Cook, N. R., Ajani, U. A., Gaziano, J. M., & Hennekens, C. E. (1999). Moderate alcohol consumption and the risk of sudden cardiac death among U.S. male physicians. *Circulation, 100,* 944–950.

Alnaes, R., & Torgersen, S. (1988). The relationship between *DSM–III* symptom disorders (Axis I) and personality disorders (Axis II) in an outpatient population. *Acta Psychiatica Scandinavica, 78,* 485–492.

Alterman, A. I., Bedrick, J., Cacciola, J. S., Rutherford, M. J., Searles, J. S., McKay, J. R., & Cook, T. G. (1998). Personality pathology and drinking in young men at high and low risk familial risk for alcoholism. *Journal of Studies on Alcohol, 59,* 495–502.

Amaro, H., Fried, L. E., Cabral, H., & Zuckerman, B. (1990). Violence during pregnancy and substance use. *American Journal of Public Health, 80*(5), 575–590.

American Academy of Pediatrics Committee on Substance Abuse and Committee on Children with Disabilities. (1993). Fetal alcohol syndrome and fetal alcohol effects. *Pediatrics, 91*(5), 1004–1006.

American Psychiatric Association. (1994). *Diagnostic and statistical manual of mental disorders* (4th ed.). Washington, DC: Author.

Anda, R. F., Williamson, D. F., & Remington, P. L. (1988). Alcohol and fatal injuries among U.S. adults: Findings from the NHANES I Epidemiologic Follow-Up Study. *Journal of the American Medical Association, 260,* 2529–2532.

Anthenelli, R. M., Klein, J. L., Tsuang, J. W., Smith, T. L., & Schuckit, M. A. (1994, May). The prognostic importance of blackouts in young men. *Journal of Studies on Alcoholism,* 290–295.

Anthenelli, R. M., Tipp, J., Li, T.-K., Magnes, L., Schuckit, M. A., Rice, J., Warwick, D., & Nurnberger, J. I. (1998). Platelet monoamine oxidase (MAO) activity in subgroups of alcoholics and controls: Results from the COGA study. *Alcoholism: Clinical and Experimental Research, 22,* 598–604.

Arbuckle, T. Y., Chaikelson, J. S., & Gold, D. P. (1994). Social drinking and cognitive functioning revisited: the role of intellectual endowment and psychological distress. *Journal of Studies on Alcoholism, 55,* 352–361.

Ary, D. V., Tildesley, E., Hops, H., & Andrews, J. (1993). The influence of parent, sibling, and peer modeling and attitudes on adolescent use of alcohol. *The International Journal of the Addictions, 28,* 853–880.

Ashley, M. J., Ferrence, R., Room, R., Rankin, J., & Single. E. (1994). Moderate drinking a health: Report of an international symposium. *Canadian Medical Association Journal, 151,* 809–824.

Baer, J. S. (1993). Etiology and secondary prevention of alcohol problems with young adults. In J. S. Baer, G. A. Marlatt, & R. J. McMahon (Eds.), *Addictive behaviors across the lifespan: Prevention, treatment, and policy issues* (pp. 111–137). Newbury Park, CA: Sage.

Baer, J. S., Stacy, A., & Larimer, M. (1991). Biases in the perception of drinking norms among college students. *Journal of Studies on Alcohol, 52,* 580–586.

Ball, D. M., & Murray, R. M. (1994). Genetics of alcohol misuse. *British Medical Bulletin, 50,* 18–35.

Banki, C. J. (1981). Factors influencing monoamine metabolites and tryptophan in patients with alcohol dependence. *Journal of Neural Transmission, 50,* 98–101.

Barnes, G. E. (1979). The alcoholic personality: A reanalysis of the literature. *Journal of Studies on Alcohol, 40,* 571–633.

Barnes, G. M. (1983). Clinical and prealcoholic personality characteristics. In B. Kissin, & H. Begleiter (Eds.), *The pathogenesis of alcoholism: Psychosocial factors* (Vol 6, pp. 113–196). New York: Plenum.

Barnes, G. M. (1990). Impact of the family on adolescent drinking patterns. In R. L. Collins, K. E. Leonard, and J. S. Searles (Eds.), *Alcohol and the family: Research and clinical perspectives* (pp. 137–161). New York: Guilford.

Barnes, G. M., & Farrell, M. P. (1992). Parental support and control as predictors of adolescent drinking, delinquency, and related problem behaviors. *Journal of Marriage and the Family, 54,* 763–776.

Barnes, G. M., & Farrell, M. P., & Banerjee, S. (1994). Family influences on alcohol abuse and other problem behaviors among black and white adolescents in a general population sample. *Journal of Research on Adolescence, 4,* 183–201.

Barrera, M., Chassin, L., & Rogosch, F. (1993). Effects of social support and conflict on adolescent children of alcoholics and nonalcoholic fathers. *Journal of Personality and Social Psychology, 64,* 602–612.

Bates, M. E., & Labouvie, E. W. (1995). Personality-environment correlations and alcohol use: A process-oriented study of intraindividual change during adolescence. *Psychology of Addictive Behaviors, 9,* 23–35.

Bauman, K. E., Fisher, L. A., Bryan, E. S., & Chenowith, R. L. (1985). Relationship between subjective expected utility and behavior: A longitudinal study of adolescent drinking behavior. *Journal of Studies on Alcohol, 46,* 32–38.

Begleiter, H., Reich, T, Hesselbrock, V., Porjesz, B, Li, T.-K, Schuckit, M. A., Edenberg, H. J., & Rice, J. P. (1995). The Collaborative Study on the Genetics of Alcoholism. *Alcohol, Health and Research World, 19,* 228–236.

Bennett, L. A., & Wolin, S. J. (1990). Family culture and alcoholism transmission. In R. L. Collins, K. E. Leonard, and J. S. Searles (Eds.), *Alcohol and the family: Research and clinical perspectives* (pp. 194–219). New York: Guilford.

Bennett, L. A., Wolin, S. J., Reiss, D., & Teitelbaum, M. A. (1987). Couples at risk for transmission of alcoholism: Protective influences. *Family Process, 26,* 111–129.

Berglund, M. (1991). Clinical and physiological implications and correlations. *Alcohol and Alcoholism, 1,* S399–402.

Bijur, P. E., Kurzon, M., Overpeck, M. D., & Scheidt P. C., (1992). Parental alcohol use, problem drinking, and children's injuries. *Journal of the American Medical Association, 267*(23), 3166–3171.

Black, J. D. W., Warrack, G., & Winokur, G. (1985). The Iowa record-linkage study. I. Suicides and accidental deaths among psychiatric patients. *Archives of General Psychiatry, 42,* 71–75.

Blane, H. T., & Leonard, K. E. (Eds.). (1987). *Psychological theories of drinking and alcoholism.* New York: Guilford.

Blansjaar, B. A., & Van Dijk, J. G. (1992). Korsakoff minus Wernicke syndrome. *Alcohol and Alcoholism, 27*(4), 435–437.

Blot, W. J. (1992). Alcohol and cancer. *Cancer Research, 52,* S2119–S2123.

Blot, W. J., McLaughlin, J. K., Winn, d. M., Austin, D. F., Greenberg, R. S., Preston-Martin, S., Beernstein, L., Schoenberg, J. B., Stemhagen, A., Fraumeni, J. F. (1988). Smoking and drinking in relation to oral and pharyngeal cancer. *Cancer Research, 48,* 3282–3287.

Blum, K., Noble, E., Sheridan, P. J., Montgomery, A., Ritchie, T., Jagadeeswaran, P., Nogami, H., Briggs, A. H., & Cohen, J. B. (1990). Allelic association of human dopamine D_2 receptor gene in alcoholism. *Journal of the American Medical Association, 263,* 2055–2060.

Boffetta, P., & Garfinkel, L. (1990). Alcohol drinking and mortality among men enrolled in an American Cancer Society prospective study. *Epidemiology, l,* 342–348.

Booth, B. M., Yates, W. R., Petty, F., & Brown, K. (1991). Patient factors predicting early alcohol-related readmissions for alcoholics: role of alcoholism severity and psychiatric co-morbidity. *Journal of Studies on Alcohol, 52,* 37–43.

Brady, K. T., & Lydiard, R. B. (1992). Bipolar affective disorder and substance abuse. *Journal of Clinical Psychopharmacology, 12,* 17–22.

Breslau, N., Davis, G. C., Andreski, P., & Peterson, E. (1991). Traumatic events and post-traumatic stress disorder in an urban population of young adults. *Archives of General Psychiatry, 48,* 216–222.

Breslau, N., Kilbey, M. M., & Andreski, P. (1991). Nicotine dependence, major depression, and anxiety in young adults. *Archives of General Psychiatry, 48,* 1069–1074.

Brower, K. J., Blow, F. C., Hill, E. M., & Mudd, S. A. (1994). Treatment outcome of alcoholics with and without cocaine disorders. *Alcoholism: Clinical and Experimental Research, 18,* 734–739.

Brown, P. J., & Wolfe, J. (1994). Substance abuse and posttraumatic stress disorder comorbidity. *Drug and Alcohol Dependence, 35,* 51–59.

Brown, R. A., Evans, D. M., Miller, I. W., Burgess, E. S., & Mueller, T. I. (1997). Cognitive-behavioral treatment for depression in alcoholism. *Journal of Consulting and Clinical Psychology, 65,* 715–726.

Brown, S. A., Creamer, V. A., & Stetson, B. A. (1987). Adolescent alcohol expectancies in relation to personal and parental drinking patterns. *Journal of Abnormal Psychology, 96,* 117–121.

Brown, S. A., Goldman, M. S., & Christiansen, B. A. (1985). Do alcohol expectancies mediate drinking patterns of adults? *Journal of Consulting and Clinical Psychology, 53,* 512–519.

Cadoret, R. J., Yates, M. D., Troughton, E., Woodworth, G., & Stewart, M. A. (1995). Adoption study demonstrating two genetic pathways to drug abuse. *Archives of General Psychiatry, 52,* 42–52.

Caetano, R. (1991). Findings from the 1984 National Survey of Alcohol Use among U.S. Hispanics. In W. B. Clark & M. E. Hilton (Eds.), *Alcohol in America: Drinking practices and problems* (pp 293–307). Albany: State University of New York Press.

Caetano, R., & Clark, C. L. (1998). Trends in alcohol consumption patterns among Whites, Blacks, and Hispanics: 1984 and 1995. *Journal of Studies on Alcohol, 59,* 659–668.

Cappell, H., & Greeley, J. (1987). Alcohol and tension reduction: An update on research and theory. In H. T. Blane & K. E. Leonard (Eds.), *Psychological theories of drinking and alcoholism* (pp 15–50). New York: Guilford.

Carmargo, C. A., Jr. (1989). Moderate alcohol consumption and stroke. *Stroke, 20*(12), 1611–1626.

Carey, K. B., & Correia, C. J. (1997). Drinking motives predict alcohol problems in college students. *Journal of Studies on Alcohol, 58,* 100–105.

Caspi, A., Begg, D., Dickson, N., Harrington, H.-L., Langley, J., Moffitt, T. E., & Silva, P. A. (1997). Personality differences predict health-risk behaviors in adulthood: Evidence from a longitudinal study. *Journal of Personality and Social Psychology, 73,* 1052–1063.

Catalano, R. F., Morrison, D. M., Wells, E. A., Gillmore, M. R., Iritani, B., & Hawkins, J. D. (1992). Ethnic differences in family factors related to early drug initiation. *Journal of Studies on Alcohol, 53,* 208–217.

Center on Addiction and Substance Abuse at Columbia University. (1994, June). *Rethinking rites of passage: Substance abuse on America's campuses.* New York: Columbia University.

Chassin, L., Curran, P. J., Hussong, A. M., & Colder, C. R. (1996). The relation of parent alcoholism to adolescent substance use: A longitudinal follow-up study. *Journal of Abnormal Psychology, 105,* 70–80.

Chassin, L., Mann, L. M., & Sher, K. J. (1988). Self-awareness theory, family history of alcoholism, and adolescent alcohol involvement. *Journal of Abnormal Psychology, 97,* 206–217.

Chassin, L., Pillow, D. R., Curran, P. J., Molina, B. S. G., & Barrera, M. (1993). Relation of parental alcoholism to early adolescent substance use: A test of three mediating mechanisms. *Journal of Abnormal Psychology, 102,* 3–19.

Chassin, L., Rogosch, F., & Barrera, M. (1991). Substance use and symptomatology among adolescent children of alcoholics. *Journal of Abnormal Psychology, 100,* 449–463.

Cherpitel, C. J. (1999). Substance use, injury, and risk-taking dispositions in the general population. *Alcoholism: Clinical and Experimental Research, 23,* 121–126.

Cherpitel, C. J., Meyers, A. R., & Perrine, M. W. (1998). Alcohol consumption, sensation seeking and ski injury: A case-control study. *Journal of Studies on Alcohol, 59,* 216–221.

Cherpitel, C. J., Tam, T., Midanik, L., Caetano, R., & Greenfield, T. (1995). Alcohol and non-fatal injury in the U.S. general population: A risk function analysis. *Accident Analysis and Prevention, 27,* 651–661.

Chou, S. P. (1994). An examination of the alcohol consumption and peptic ulcer association—results of a national survey. *Alcohol: Clinical and Experimental Research, 18*(1), 149–153.

Christiansen, B. A., Smith, G. T., Roehling, P. V., & Goldman, M. S. (1989). Using alcohol expectancies to predict adolescent drinking behavior after one year. *Journal of Consulting and Clinical Psychology, 57,* 93–99.

Clark, L. A., Watson, D., & Reynolds, S. (1995). Diagnosis and classification of psychopathology: Challenges to the system and future directions. In J. T. Spence, J. M. Darley, & D. J. Foss (Eds.), *The Annual Review of Psychology, 46,* (pp 121–153). Palo Alto, CA: Annual Reviews Inc.

Cloninger, C. R. (1987). Neurogenetic adaptive mechanisms in alcoholism. *Science, 236,* 410–416.

Cloninger, C. R., Bohman, M., & Sigvardsson, S. (1981). Inheritance of alcohol abuse: Cross-fostering analysis of adopted men. *Archives of General Psychiatry, 38,* 861–868.

Cloninger, C. R., Sigvardsson, S., & Bohman, M. (1988). Childhood personality predicts alcohol abuse in young adults. *Alcoholism: Clinical and Experimental Research, 12,* 494–505.

Cohen, P., & Cohen, J. (1984). The clinician's illusion. *Archives of General Psychiatry, 41,* 1178–1182.

Coleman, D. H., & Straus, M. A. (1983). Alcohol abuse and family violence. In E. Gootheil, K. A. Druley, T. E., Skoloda, & H. M. Waxman (Eds.), *Alcohol, drug abuse, and aggression* (pp. 104–124). Springfield, IL: Thomas.

Collins, J. J. (1991). Drinking and violations of the criminal law. In D. J. Pittman & H. Raskin White (Eds.), *Society, culture, and drinking patterns reexamined* (Alcohol, culture, and social control monograph series, pp. 650–660). New Brunswick, NJ: Rutgers Center of Alcohol Studies.

Collins, J. J., & Messerschmidt, P. M. (1993). Epidemiology of alcohol-related violence. *Alcohol, Health, and Research World, 17,* 93–100.

Connors, G. J., O'Farrell, T. J., Cutter, H. S. G., & Thompson, D. L. (1986). Alcohol expectancies among male alcoholics, problem drinkers, and nonproblem drinkers. *Alcoholism: Clinical and Experimental Research, 10,* 667–671.

Cook, P. J., & Moore, M. J. (1993). Drinking and schooling. *Journal of Health Economics, 12,* 411–429.

Cooper, M. L. (1994). Motivations for alcohol use among adolescents: Development and validation of a four-factor model. *Psychological Assessment, 6,* 117–128.

Cooper, M. L., Frone, M. R., Russell, M., & Mudar, P. (1995). Drinking to regulate positive and negative emotions: A motivational model of alcohol use. *Journal of Personality and Social Psychology, 69,* 990–1005.

Cooper, M. L., Russell, M., & George, W. H. (1988). Coping, expectancies, and alcohol abuse: A test of social learning formulations. *Journal of Abnormal Psychology, 97,* 218–230.

Cooper, M. L., Russell, M., Skinner, J. B., Frone, M. R., & Mudar, P. (1992). Stress and alcohol use: Moderating effects of gender, coping, and alcohol expectancies. *Journal of Abnormal Psychology, 101,* 139–152.

Cordilia, A. (1985). Alcohol and property crime: Exploring the causal nexus. *Journal of Studies on Alcohol, 46,* 161–171.

Cottler, L. B., Compton, W. M., Mager, D., Spitznagel, E. L., Janca, A. (1992). Posttraumatic stress disorder among substance users from the general population. *American Journal of Psychiatry, 149,* 664–670.

Cotton, N. S. (1979). The familial incidence of alcoholism. *Journal of Studies on Alcohol, 40,* 89–116.

Cox, W. M. (1985). Personality correlates of substance abuse. In M. Galizio & S. A. Maisto (Eds.), *Determinants of substance abuse* (pp. 209–246). New York: Plenum.

Cox, W. M., & Klinger, E. (1988). A motivational model of alcohol use. *Journal of Abnormal Psychology, 97,* 168–180.

Crabb, D. W. (1993). The liver. In M. Galanter (Ed), *Recent developments in alcoholism, Vol 11: Ten years of progress* (pp. 207–230). New York: Plenum.

Crabbe, J. C. (1989). Genetic animal models in the study of alcoholism. *Alcoholism: Clinical and Experimental Research, 13,* 120–127.

Crabbe, J. C., Belknap, J. K., & Buck, K. J. (1994). Genetic animal models of alcohol and drug abuse. *Science, 264,* 1715–1723.

Crabbe, J. C., & Phillips, T. C. (1990). Genetic animal models. *Alcohol, Health, and Research World, 14,* 179–186.

Critchlow, B. (1983). Blaming the booze: The attribution of responsibility for drunken behavior. *Personality and Social Psychology Bulletin, 9,* 451–473.

Crowe, L. C., & George, W. H. (1989). Alcohol and human sexuality: Review and integration. *Psychological Bulletin, 105,* 374–386.

Cumming, R. G., & Klineberg, R. J. (1994). Case-control study of risk factors for hip fractures in the elderly. *American Journal of Epidemiology, 139*(5), 493–503.

Curran, P. J., Stice, E., & Chassin, L. (1997). The relation between adolescent alcohol use and peer alcohol use: A longitudinal random coefficients model. *Journal of Consulting and Clinical Psychology, 65,* 130–140.

Darkes, J., & Goldman, M. S. (1993). Expectancy challenge and drinking reduction: Experimental evidence for a mediational process. *Journal of Consulting and Clinical Psychology, 61,* 344–353.

Darkes, J., & Goldman, M. S. (1998). Expectancy challenge and drinking reduction: Process and structure in the alcohol expectancy network. *Experimental and Clinical Psychopharmacology, 6,* 64–76.

Dawson, D. A., Harford, T. C., & Grant, B. F. (1992). Family history as a predictor of alcohol dependence. *Alcoholism: Clinical and Experimental Research, 16,* 572–575.

de Wit, H., & McCracken, S. G. (1990). Ethanol self-administration in males with and without an alcoholic first-degree relative. *Alcoholism: Clinical and Experimental Research, 14,* 63–70.

Dietrich, R. A. (1987). Interaction of ethanol with other drugs. In M. Galanter (Ed.), *Recent developments in alcoholism* (Vol. 5, pp. 283–301). New York: Plenum.

Doll, R., Peto, R., Hall, E., Wheatley, K., & Gray, R. (1994). Mortality in relation to consumption of alcohol: 13 years' observations on male British doctors. *British Medical Journal, 309,* 911–918.

Drake, R. E., Adler, D. A., & Vaillant, G. E. (1988). Antecedents of personality disorders in a community sample of men. *Journal of Personality Disorders, 2,* 60–68.

Drake, R. E., & Vaillant, G. E. (1985). A validity study of axis II of *DSM–III. American Journal of Psychiatry, 142,* 553–558.

Duncan, T. E., Duncan, S. C., & Hops, H. (1994). The effects of family cohesiveness and peer encouragement on the development of adolescent alcohol use: A cohort sequential approach to the analysis of longitudinal data. *Journal of Studies on Alcohol, 55,* 588–599.

Ehlers, C. L., & Schuckit, M. A. (1991). Evaluation of EEG alpha activity in sons of alcoholics. *Neuropsychopharmacology, 4,* 199–205.

Emanuele, M. A., Halloran, M. M., Uddin, S., Tentler, J., J., Emanuele, N. V., Lawrence, A. M., & Kelley, M. R. (1993). The effects of alcohol on the neuroendocrine control of reproduction. In S. Zakhari (Ed.), *Alcohol and the endocrine system* (pp. 89–116). Bethesda, MD: National Institute on Alcohol Abuse and Alcoholism.

Ericksen, K. P., & Trocki, K. F. (1992). Behavioral risk factors for sexually transmitted diseases in American households. *Social Science and Medicine, 34,* 843–853.

Erickson, D. J., Sher, K. J., & Wood, P. K. (1997, June). *A prospective state-trait analysis of potential mediators of the family history/substance abuse relation.* Poster presented at the annual meeting of the Research Society on Alcoholism, July 19–24, San Francisco, CA.

Evans, D. M., & Dunn, N. J. (1995). Alcohol expectancies, coping responses and self-efficacy judgements: A replication and extension of Cooper et al.'s 1988 study in a college sample. *Journal of Studies on Alcohol, 56,* 186–193.

Fals-Stewart, W., & Schafer, J. (1992). The treatment of substance abusers diagnosed with obsessive-compulsive disorder: An outcome study. *Journal of Substance Abuse Treatment, 9,* 365–370.

Famularo, R., Kinscherff, R., & Fenton, T. (1992). Parental substance abuse and the nature of child maltreatment. *Child Abuse and Neglect, 16,* 475–483.

Famularo, R., Stone, K., Barnum, R., & Wharton, R. (1986). Alcoholism and severe child maltreatment. *American Journal of Orthopsychiatry, 56,* 481–485.

Fell, J. C. (1990). Drinking and driving in America: Disturbing facts—encouraging reductions. *Alcohol, Health, and Research World, 14,* 18–25.

Finn, P. R., & Pihl, R. O. (1987). Men at high risk for alcoholism: The effect of alcohol on cardiovascular response to unavoidable shock. *Journal of Abnormal Psychology, 96,* 230–236.

Finn, P. R., Zeitouni, N. C., & Pihl, R. O. (1990). Effects of alcohol on psychophysiological hyperreactivity to nonaversive and aversive stimuli in men at high risk for alcoholism. *Journal of Abnormal Psychology, 99,* 79–85.

Flay, B. R., & Petraitis, J. (1994). The theory of triadic influence: A new theory of health behavior with implications for preventive interventions. In *Advances in medical sociology: A reconsideration of health behavior change models* (Vol. 4, pp. 19–44). Greenwich, CT: JAI.

Fowler, C. J., von Knorring, L., & Oreland, L. (1980). Platelet monoamine oxidase activity in sensation seekers. *Psychiatry Research, 3,* 273–279.

Frezza, M., Di Padova, C., Pozzato, G., Terpin, M., Baraona, M., & Lieber, C. S. (1990). High blood alcohol levels in women: The role of decreased gastric alcohol dehydrogenase activity and first-pass metabolism. *New England Journal of Medicine, 322,* 95–99.

Friedman, G. D., & Klatsky, A. L. (1993). Is alcohol good for your health? *New England Journal of Medicine, 329,* 1882–1883.

Froelich, J. C., Zweifel, M., Harts, J., Lumeng, L., & Li, T. K. (1991). Importance of delta opioid receptors in maintaining high alcohol drinking. *Psychopharmacology, 103,* 467–472.

Fromme, K., Stroot, E., & Kaplan, D. (1993). Comprehensive effects of alcohol: Development and psychometric assessment of a new expectancy questionnaire. *Psychological Assessment, 5,* 19–27.

Fuchs, C. S., Stampfer, M. J., Colditz, G. A., Giovannucci, E. L., Manson, J. E., Kawachi, I., Hunter, D. J., Hankinson, S. E., Hennekens, C. H., Rosner, B., Speizer, F. E., & Willett, W. C. (1995). Alcohol consumption and mortality among women. *New England Journal of Medicine, 332(19),* 1245–1250.

Gabrielli, W. F., Jr., Mednick, S. A., Volavka, J., Pollock, V. E., Schulsinger, F., & Itil, T. M. (1982). Electroencephalograms in children of alcoholic fathers. *Psychophysiology, 19,* 404–407.

Gaziano, J. M., Buring, J. E., Breslow, J. L., Goldhaber, S. Z., Rosner B., VanDenburgh, M., Willett, W., & Hennekens, C. H. (1993). Moderate alcohol intake increased levels of high-density lipoprotein and its subfractions, and decreased risk of myocardial infarction. *New England Journal of Medicine, 329,* 1829–1834.

Gelernter, J., Goldman, D., & Risch, N. (1993). The A1 Allele at the D_2 Dopamine Receptor Gene and Alcoholism: A Reappraisal. *Journal of the American Medical Association, 269,* 1673–1677.

George, W. H., Gournic, S. J., McAfee, M. P. (1988). Perceptions of postdrinking female sexuality: Effects of gender, beverage choice, and drink payment. *Journal of Applied Social Psychology, 18,* 1295–1317.

Gerrard, M., Gibbons, F. X., Zhao, L., Russell, D. W., & Reis-Bergan, M. (1999). The effect of peers' alcohol consumption on parental influence: A cognitive mediation model. *Journal of Studies on Alcohol,* Supplement No. 13, 32–44.

Gill, J. (1994). Alcohol problems in employment: epidemiology and response. *Alcohol and Alcoholism, 29,* 233–248.

Giovannucci, E., Stampfer, M. J., Colditz, G. A., et al. (1993). Recall and selection bias in reporting past alcohol consumption among breast cancer cases. *Cancer Causes Control, 4,* 441–448.

Glue, P., & Nutt, D. (1990). Overexcitement and disinhibition: Dynamic neurotransmitter interactions in alcohol withdrawal. *British Journal of Psychiatry, 157,* 491–499.

Goldbert, R. J., Burchfiel, C. M., Reed, D. M., Wergowske, G., & Chiu, D. (1994). A prospective study of the health effects of alcohol consumption in middle-aged and elderly men. *Circulation, 89*(2), 651–659.

Goldman, M. S., Brown, S. A., & Christiansen, B. A. (1987). Expectancy theory: Thinking about drinking. In H. T. Blane & K. E. Leonard (Eds.), *Psychological theories of drinking and alcoholism* (pp. 181–226). New York: Guilford.

Goldman, M. S., Del Boca, F. K., & Darkes, J. (1999). Alcohol expectancy theory: The application of cognitive neuroscience. In K. E. Leonard & H. T. Blane (Eds.), *Psychological theories of drinking and alcoholism* (2nd ed., pp. 203–246). New York: Guilford.

Goodwin, D. W., Schulsinger, F., Hermansen, L., Guze, S. B., & Winokur, G. (1973). Alcohol problems in adoptees raised apart from alcoholic biological parents. *Archives of General Psychiatry 28,* 238–243.

Gorelick, P. B. (1989). The status of alcohol as a risk factor for stroke. *Stroke, 20*(12), 1607–1610.

Grant, B. F., Dufour, M. C., & Harford, T. C. (1988). Epidemiology of alcoholic liver disease. *Seminar on Liver Diseases, 8*(1), 12–25.

Grant, B. F., Harford, T. C., Chou, P., Pickering, R., Dawson, D. A., Stinson, F. S., & Noble, J. (1991). Prevalence of *DSM–III–R* alcohol abuse and dependence, United States, 1988. *Alcohol, Health, and Research World, 15,* 91–96.

Grant, B. F., Harford, T. C., Dawson, D. A., Chou, P., Dufour, M., & Pickering, R. (1994). Prevalence of *DSM–IV* Alcohol Abuse and Dependence: United States, 1992. *Alcohol, Health, & Research World, 18,* 243–248.

Greeley, J., & Oei, T. (1999). Alcohol and tension reduction. In K. E. Leonard & H. T. Blane (Eds.), *Psychological theories of drinking and alcoholism* (2nd ed., pp. 14–53). New York: Guilford.

Grisso, J. A., Kelsey, J. L., Strom, B. L., O'Brien, L. A., Maislin, G., LaPann, K., Samelson, L., & Hoffman, S. (1994). Risk factors for hip fracture in black women. *New England Journal of Medicine, 330*(22), 1555–1559.

Gronbaek, M., Deis, A., Sorensen, T. I. A., Becker, U., Schnohr, P., & Jensen, G. (1995). Mortality associated with moderate intakes of wine, beer, or spirits. *British Medical Journal, 310,* 1165–1169.

Gronbaek, M., Deis, A., Sorensen, T. I. A., Becker, U., Borch-Johnsen, K., Müller, C., Schnohr, P., & Jensen, G. (1994). Influence of sex, age, body mass index, and smoking on alcohol intake and mortality. *British Medical Journal, 308,* 302–306.

Grube, J. W. (1993). Alcohol portrayals and alcohol advertising on television: Content and effects on children and adolescents. *Alcohol, Health, & Research World, 17,* 61–66.

Grube, J. W., & Wallack, L. (1994). Television beer advertising and drinking knowledge, beliefs, and intentions among schoolchildren. *American Journal of Public Health, 84,* 254–259.

Gwinn, M. L., Webster, L. A., Lee, N. C., Layde, P. M., & Rubin, G. L. (1986). The Cancer and Steroid Hormone Study Group: Alcohol consumption and ovarian cancer risk. *American Journal of Epidemiology, 123*(5), 759–766.

Haines, M., & Spears, S. (1996). Changing the perception of the norm: A strategy to decrease binge drinking among college students. *Journal of American College Health, 45,* 134–140.

Hamilton, C. J., & Collins, J. J., Jr. (1985). The role of alcohol in wife beating and child abuse: A review of the literature. In J. J. Collins, (Ed.) *Drinking and crime: Perspectives on the relationship between alcohol consumption and criminal behavior* (pp. 253–287). New York: Guilford.

Hanna, E. Z., Chou, S. P., & Grant, B. F. (1997). The relationship between drinking and heart disease morbidity in the United States: Results from the national health interview survey. *Alcoholism: Clinical and Experimental Research, 21,* 111–118.

Harburg, E., Davis, D. R., & Caplan, R. (1982). Parent and offspring alcohol use: Imitative and aversive transmission. *Journal of Studies on Alcohol, 43,* 497–516.

Harburg, E., DiFranceisco, W., Webster, D. W., Gleiberman, L., & Schork, A. (1990). Familial transmission of alcohol use: II. Imitation of and aversion to parent drinking (1960) by adult offspring (1971)Tecumseh, Michigan. *Journal of Studies on Alcohol, 51,* 245–256.

Harburg, E., Gleiberman, L., DiFranceisco, W., Schork, A, & Weissfeld, L. (1990). Familial transmission of alcohol use, III. Impact of imitation/non-imitation of parent alcohol use (1960) on the sensible/problem drinking of their offspring (1977). *British Journal of Addiction, 85,* 1141–1155.

Harden, P. W., & Pihl, R. O. (1995). Cognitive function, cardiovascular reactivity, and behavior in boys at high risk for alcoholism. *Journal of Abnormal Psychology, 104,* 94–103.

Hart, C. L., Smith, G. D., Hole, D. J., & Hawthorne, V. M. (1999). Alcohol consumption and mortality from all causes, coronary heart disease, and stroke: Results from a prospective cohort study of Scottish men with 21 years of follow up. *British Medical Journal, 318,* 1725–1729.

Hawkins, J. D., Catalano, R. F., & Miller, Y. (1992). Risk and protective factors for alcohol and other drug problems in adolescence and early adulthood: Implications for substance abuse prevention. *Psychological Bulletin, 112,* 64–105.

Heath, A. C., Bucholz, K. K., Madden, P. A. F., Dinwiddie, S. H., Slutske, W. S., Bierut, L J., Statham, D. J., Dunne, M. P., Whitfield, J. B., & Martin, N. G. (1997). Genetic and environmental contributions to alcohol dependence risk in a national twin sample: Consistency of findings in women and men. *Psychological Medicine, 27,* 1381–1391.

Hebert, L. E., Scherr, P. A., Beckett, L. A., Albert, M. S., Rosner, B., Taylor, J. O., & Evans, D. A. (1993). Relation of smoking and low-to-moderate alcohol consumption to change in cognitive function: A longitudinal study in a defined community of older persons. *American Journal of Epidemiology, 137*(8), 881–891.

Heien, D. M., & Pittman, D. J. (1993). The external costs of alcohol abuse. *Journal of Studies on Alcohol, 54,* 302–307.

Helzer, J. E., Burnam, A., & McEvoy, L. T. (1991). Alcohol abuse and dependence. In L. N. Robins and D. A. Regier (Eds.), *Psychiatric disorders in America: The epidemiologic catchment area study* (pp. 81–115). New York: The Free Press.

Helzer, J. E., & Przybeck, T. R. (1988). Co-occurrence of alcoholism with other psychiatric disorders in the general population and its impact on treatment. *Journal of Studies on Alcohol, 49,* 219–224.

Helzer, J. E., Robins, L. N., & McEvoy, L. (1987). Post-traumatic stress disorder in the general population: Findings of the epidemiologic catchment area survey. *New England Journal of Medicine, 317,* 1630–1634.

Hendriks, H. F., Veenstra, J., Velthuis-te Wierik, E. J., Schaafsma, G., & Kluft, C. (1994). Effect of moderate dose of alcohol with evening meal on fibrinolytic factors. *British Medical Journal, 308,* 1003–1006.

Herd, D. (1991). Drinking patterns in the Black population. In W. B. Clark & M. E. Hilton (Eds.), *Alcohol in America: Drinking practices and problems* (pp. 308–328). Albany: State University of New York Press.

Hernandez, J. T. (1992). Substance abuse among sexually abused adolescents and their families. *Journal of Adolescent Health, 13,* 658–662.

Hernandez-Avila, M., Colditz, G. A., Stampfer, M. J., Rosner, B., Speizer, F. E., & Willett, W. C. (1991). Caffeine, moderate alcohol intake, and risk of fractures of the hip and forearm in middle-aged women. *American Journal of Clinical Nutrition, 54,* 157–163.

Hesselbrock, V., Meyer, R. E., & Hesselbrock, M. N. (1992). Psychopathology and addictive disorders: The specific case of antisocial personality disorder. In C. P. O'Brien & J. H. Jaffe (Eds). *Addictive states* (pp. 179–191). New York: Raven.

Hesselbrock, M. N., Meyer, R. E., & Keener, J. J. (1985). Psychopathology in hospitalized alcoholics. *Archives of General Psychiatry, 42,* 1050–1055.

Hingson, R., & Howland, J. (1993). Alcohol and non-traffic unintended injuries. *Addiction, 88,* 877–883.

Holden, C. (1994). A cautionary genetic tale: The sobering story of D_2. *Science, 264,* 1696–1697.

Holder, H. D., & Blose, J. O. (1991). A comparison of occupational and nonoccupational disability payments and work absences for alcoholics and nonalcoholics. *Journal of Occupational Medicine, 33,* 453–457.

Holmes, S. J., & Robins, L. N. (1987). The influence of childhood disciplinary experience on the development of alcoholism and depression. *Journal of Child Psychology and Psychiatry, 28,* 399–415.

Homanics, G., E., Quinlan, J. J., Mihalek, R. M., & Firestone, L. L. (1998). Alcohol and anesthetic mechanisms in genetically engineered mice. *Frontiers in Bioscience, 3,* D548–558.

Honkanen, R., Ertama, L., Kuosmanen, P., Linnoila, M., Alha, A., & Visuri, T. (1983). The role of alcohol in accidental falls. *Journal of Studies on Alcohol, 44,* 231–245.

Howes, L. G. (1994). Pressor effect of alcohol (letter). *Lancet, 2,* 835.

Hwang, H. B., Lumeng, L., Wu, J. Y., & Li, T. K. (1990). Increased number of GABAergic terminals in the nucleus accumbens is associated with alcohol preference in rats. *Alcoholism: Clinical and Experimental Research, 14,* 503–507.

Ida, Y., Tsujimaru, S., Nakamura, K., Shirao, I., Mukasa, H., Egami, H., & Nakazawa, Y. (1992). Effects of acute and repeated alcohol ingestion on hypothalamic–pituitary–gonadal and hypothalamic–pituitary–adrenal functioning in normal males. *Drug and Alcohol Dependency, 31,* 57–64.

Isohanni, M., Oja, H., Moilanen, I., Koiranen, M. (1994). Teenage alcohol drinking and non-standard family background. *Social Science and Medicine, 38,* 1565–1574.

Jaakkola, M., Sillanaukee, P., Lof, K., Koivula, T., & Nordback, I. (1994). Amount of alcohol is an important determinant of the severity of acute alcoholic pancreatitis. *Surgery, 115,* 31–38.

Jackson, I. M. D. (1993). Regulation of the hypothalamic-pituitary-thyroid axis and the effects of alcohol. In S. Zakhari (Ed.), *Alcohol and the endocrine system* (pp. 283–291). Bethesda, MD: National Institute on Alcohol Abuse and Alcoholism.

Jacob, T., & Leonard, K. (1994). Family and peer influences on the development of adolescent alcohol abuse. In *The development of alcohol problems: Exploring the biopsychosocial matrix of risk.* National Institute on Alcohol Abuse and Alcoholism Research Monograph 26, pp. 123–155. Washington, DC: N.I.H. Publication No. 94-3495.

Jacobson, J. L., Jacobson, S. W., Sokol, R. J., Martier, S. S., & Ager, J. W. (1993). Teratogenic effects of alcohol on infant development. *Alcoholism, 17*(1), 174–183.

Jenkins, R., Harvey, S., Butler, T., & Thomas, R. L. (1992). A six year longitudinal study of the occupational consequences of drinking over "safe limits" of alcohol. *British Journal of Industrial Medicine, 49,* 369–374.

Jessor, R., & Jessor, S. L. (1977). Problem behavior and psychosocial development: A longitudinal study of youth. San Diego, CA: Academic Press.

Jones, M. C. (1968). Personality correlates and antecedents of drinking patterns in adult males. *Journal of Consulting and Clinical Psychology, 32,* 2–12.

Jones, M. C. (1971). Personality correlates and antecedents in women. *Journal of Consulting and Clinical Psychology, 36,* 61–69.

Kammeier, M. L., Hoffman, H., & Loper, R. G. (1973). Personality characteristics of alcoholics as college freshmen and at time of treatment. *Quarterly Journal of Studies on Alcohol, 34,* 390–399.

Kandel, D. B. (1973). Adolescent marihuana use: Role of parents and peers. *Science, 181,* 1067–1070.

Kandel, D. B., & Andrews, K. (1987). Processes of adolescent socialization by parents and peers. *The International Journal of the Addictions, 22,* 319–342.

Kantor, G. K., & Straus, M. A. (1989). Substance abuse as a precipitant of wife abuse victimizations. *American Journal of Drug and Alcohol Abuse, 15,* 173–189.

Kaplan, H. B. (1980). *Deviant behavior in defense of self.* New York: Academic Press.

Kaplan, R. F., Hesselbrock, V. M., O'Connor, S., & DePalma, N. (1988). Behavioral and EEG responses to alcohol in nonalcoholic men with a family history of alcoholism. *Progress in Neuro-Psychopharmacology and Biological Psychiatry, 12,* 873–885.

Kelleher, K., Chaffin, M., Hollenberg, J., & Fischer, E. (1994). Alcohol and drug disorders among physically abusive and neglectful parents in a community-based sample. *American Journal of Public Health, 84,* 1586–1590.

Kendler, K. S., Heath, A. C., Neale, M. C., Kessler, R. C., & Eaves, L. J. (1992). A population-based twin study of alcoholism in women. *Journal of American Medical Association, 268,* 1877–1882.

Kessler, R. C., Crum, R. M., Warner, L. A., Nelson, C. B., Schulenberg, J., & Anthony, J. C. (1997). Lifetime co-occurrence of *DSM–III–R* alcohol abuse and dependence with other psychiatric disorders in the National Comorbidity Survey. *Archives of General Psychiatry, 54,* 313–321.

Kessler, R. C., McGonagle, K. A., Zhao, S., Nelson, C. B., Hughes, M., Eshleman, S., Wittchen, H. U., Kendler, K. S. (1994). Lifetime and 12–month prevalence of *DSM–III–R* psychiatric disorders in the United States: Results from the National Comorbidity Survey. *Archives of General Psychiatry, 51,* 8–19.

Kilbey, M. M., Downey, K., & Breslau, N. (1988). Predicting the emergence and persistence of alcohol dependence in young adults: The role of expectancy and other risk factors. *Experimental and Clinical Psychopathology, 6,* 149–156.

Klatsky, A. L., & Armstrong, M. A. (1992). Alcohol, smoking, coffee, and cirrhosis. *American Journal of Epidemiology, 136,* 1248–1257.

Klatsky, A. L., & Armstrong, M. A. (1993). Alcohol use, other traits, and risk of unnatural death: A prospective study. *Alcohol: Clinical and Experimental Research, 17,* 1156–1162.

Klatsky, A. L., Armstrong, M. A., & Friedman, G. D. (1989). Alcohol use and subsequent cerebrovascular disease hospitalizations. *Stroke, 20*(6), 741–746.

Klatsky, A. L., Armstrong, M. A., & Friedman, G. D. (1990). Risk of cardiovascular mortality in alcohol drinkers, ex-drinkers and nondrinkers. *American Journal of Cardiology, 66,* 1237–1242.

Klatsky, A. L., Armstrong, M. A., & Friedman, G. D. (1992). Alcohol and mortality. *Annals of Internal Medicine, 117,* 646–654.

Klatsky, A. L., Friedman, G. D., & Siegelaub, A. B. (1981). Alcohol and mortality: A ten-year Kaiser-Permanente experience. *Annals of Internal Medicine, 95,* 139–145.

Korpi, E. R. (1994). Role of $GABA_A$ receptors in the actions of alcohol and in alcoholism: Recent advances. *Alcohol and Alcoholism, 29,* 115–129.

Koss, M. P., & Dinero, T. E. (1989). Discriminant analysis of risk factors for sexual victimization among a national sample of college women. *Journal of Consulting and Clinical Psychology, 57,* 242–250.

Koss, M. P., Gidycz, C. A., & Wisniewski, N. (1987). The scope of rape: Incidence and prevalence of sexual aggression and victimization in a national sample of higher education students. *Journal of Consulting and Clinical Psychology, 55,* 162–170.

Kovach, J. (1986). Incest as a treatment issue for alcoholic women. *Alcohol Treatment Quarterly, 3,* 1–15.

Kranzler, H. R., & Anton, R. F. (1994). Implications of recent neuropsychopharmacologic research for understanding the etiology and development of alcoholism. *Journal of Consulting and Clinical Psychology, 62,* 1116–1126.

Kreiger, N., Gross, A., & Hunter, G. (1992). Dietary factors and fracture in postmenopausal women: a case-control study. *International Journal of Epidemiology, 21*(5), 953–958.

Kupari, M., & Koskinen, P. (1993). Relation of left ventricular function to habitual alcohol consumption. *American Journal of Cardiology, 72,* 1418–1424.

Kushner, M. G. (1996). Relationship between alcohol problems and anxiety disorders. *American Journal of Psychiatry, 153,* 139.

Kushner, M. G., Sher, K. J., & Beitman, B. D. (1990). The relation between alcohol problems and the anxiety disorders. *American Journal of Psychiatry, 147,* 685–695.

Kushner, M. G., Sher, K. J., & Erickson, D. J. (1999). Prospective analysis of the relation between *DSM–III* anxiety disorders and alcohol use disorders. *American Journal of Psychiatry, 156,* 723–732.

Kushner, M. G., Sher, K. J., Wood, M. D., & Wood, P. K. (1994). Anxiety and drinking behavior: Moderating effects of tension-reduction alcohol outcome expectancies. *Alcoholism: Clinical and Experimental Research, 18,* 852–860.

Labouvie, W., W., Panidna, R. J., White, H. R., & Johnson, V. (1990). Risk factors of adolescent drug use: An affect-based interpretation. *Journal of Substance Abuse, 2,* 265–285.

La Vecchia, C., Negri, E., Franceschi, S., Parazzini, F., Gentile, A., & Fasoli, M. (1992). Alcohol and epithelial ovarian cancer. *Journal of Clinical Epidemiology, 45*(9), 1025–1030.

La Vecchia, C., Negri, E., Levi, F., & Baron, J. A. (1991). Cigarette smoking, body mass and other risk factors for fractures of the hip in women. *International Journal of Epidemiology, 20*(3), 671–677.

Lang, A. R. (1983). Addictive personality: A viable construct? In P. K. Levison, D. R. Gerstein, & D. R. Maloff (Eds.), *Commonalities in substance abuse and habitual behavior* (pp. 157–235. Lexington, MA: Lexington Books.

Lang, A. R., Pelham, W. E., Johnston, C., & Gelernter, S. (1989). Levels of adult alcohol consumption induced by interactions with child confederates exhibiting normal versus externalizing behaviors. *Journal of Abnormal Psychology, 98,* 294–299.

Lang, T., Nicaud, V., Darne, B., Rueff, B., & WALPA group members. (1995). Improving hypertension control among excessive alcohol drinkers: a randomised controlled trial in France. *Journal of Epidemiology and Community Health, 49,* 610–616.

Lazarus, N., Kaplan, G., Cohen, R., & Leu, D. (1991). Change in alcohol consumption and risk of death from all causes and from ischaemic heart disease. *British Medical Journal, 303,* 553–556.

Leigh, B. C. (1987). Beliefs about the effects of alcohol on self and others. *Journal of Studies on Alcohol, 48,* 567–475.

Leigh, B. C. (1989). In search of the seven dwarves: Issues of measurement and meaning in alcohol expectancy research. *Psychological Bulletin, 105,* 361–373.

Leigh, B. C. (1993). Alcohol consumption and sexual activity as reported with a diary technique. *Journal of Abnormal Psychology, 102*(3), 490–493.

Leigh, B. C., & Stacy, A. W. (1993). Alcohol outcome expectancies: Scale construction and predictive utility in higher order confirmatory models. *Psychological Assessment, 5,* 216–229.

Leigh, B. C., & Stall, R. (1993). Substance use and risky sexual behavior for exposure to HIV: Issues in methodology, interpretation, and prevention. *American Psychologist, 48,* 1035–1045.

Lemon, J., Chesher, G., Fox, A., Greeley, J., & Nabke, C. (1993). Investigation of the "hangover" effects of an acute dose of alcohol on psychomotor performance. *Alcohol: Clinical and Experimental Research, 17*(3), 665–668.

Leonard, K. E., & Blane, H. T. (Eds.). (1999). *Psychological theories of drinking and alcoholism* (2nd ed.). New York: Guilford.

Leonard, K. E., & Senchak, M. (1996). Prospective prediction of husband marital aggression within newlywed couples. *Journal of Abnormal Psychology, 105,* 369–380.

Leonard, K. E., & Senchak, M. (1993). Alcohol and premarital aggression among newlywed couples. *Journal of Studies on Alcohol, Supplement 11,* 96–108.

Levenson, R. W., Oyama, O. N., & Meek, P. S. (1987). Greater reinforcement from alcohol for those at risk: Parental risk, personality risk, and gender. *Journal of Abnormal Psychology, 96,* 242–253.

Levenson, R. W., Sher, K. J., Grossman, L., Newman, J., & Newlin, D. (1980). Alcohol and stress response dampening: Pharmacological effects, expectancy, and tension reduction. *Journal of Abnormal Psychology, 89,* 528–538.

Lewis, , C. E. (1984). Alcoholism, antisocial personality, narcotic addiction: An integrative approach. *Psychiatric Developments, 3,* 223–235.

Lewis, C. E., Cloninger, C. R., & Pais, J. (1983). Alcoholism, antisocial personality and drug use in a criminal population. *Alcohol and Alcoholism, 18,* 53–60.

Li, T. K., Lumeng, L., McBride, W. J., & Murphy, J. M. (1992). An experimental approach to understanding the genetic and neurobiological basis of alcoholism. *Transactions of the American clinical and climatological association, 104,* 61–72.

Lieber, C. S. (1994). Alcohol and the liver: 1994 update. *Gastroenterology 106,* 1085–1105.

Litt, M. D., Babor, T. F., DelBoca, F. K., Kadden, R. M., & Cooney, N. L. (1992). Types of alcoholics, II: Application of an empirically derived typology to treatment matching. *Archives of General Psychiatry, 49,* 609–614.

Long, J. C., Knowler, W. C., Hanson, R. L., Robin, R. W., Urbanek, M., Moore, E., Bennet, P. H., & Goldman, D. (1998). Evidence for genetic linkage to alcohol dependence on chromosomes 4 and 11 from an autosome-wide scan in an American Indian population. *American Journal of Medical Genetics (Neuropsychiatric Genetics), 81,* 216–221.

Longnecker, M. P. (1994). Alcoholic beverage consumption in relation to risk of breast cancer: Meta-analysis and review. *Cancer Causes Control, 5,* 73–82.

Lovinger, D., M., White, G., & Weight, F. F. (1989). Ethanol inhibits NMDA-activated ion current in hippocampal neurons. *Science, 243,* 1721–1724.

Maclure, M. (1991). The case-crossover design: a method for studying transient effects on the risk of acute events. *American Journal of Epidemiology, 133,* 144–153.

Maclure, M. (1993). Demonstration of deductive meta-analysis: ethanol intake and risk of myocardial infarction. *Epidemiology Review, 15*(2), 328–351.

MacMahon, S. (1987). Alcohol consumption and hypertension. *Hypertension 9*(2), 111–119.

Maheswaran, R., Gill, J. S., Davies, P., & Beevers, D. G. (1991). High blood pressure due to alcohol: A rapidly reversible effect. *Hypertension, 17,* 787–792.

Maisto, S. L., Carey, K. B., & Bradizza, C. M. (1999). Social learning theory. In K. E. Leonard and H. T. Blane (Eds.), *Psychological theories of drinking and alcoholism* (2nd ed., pp. 106–163). New York: Guilford.

Mann, L. M., Chassin, L., & Sher, K. J. (1987). Alcohol expectancies and the risk for alcoholism. *Journal of Consulting and Clinical Psychology, 55,* 411–417.

Manning, W. G., Keeler, E. B., Newhouse, J. P., Sloss, E. M., & Wasserman, J. (1989). The taxes of sin: Do smokers and drinkers pay their way? *Journal of the American Medical Association, 261,* 1604–1609.

Marlatt, G. A., Baer, J. S., Kivlahan, D. R., Dimeff, L. A., Larimer, M. E., Quigley, L. A., Somers, J. M., & Williams, E. (1998). Screening and brief intervention for high-risk college student drinkers: Results from a 2–year follow-up assessment. *Journal of Consulting and Clinical Psychology, 66,* 604–615.

Marmot, M. G., Elliott, P., Shipley, M. J., Dyer, A. R., Ueshima, H., Beevers, D. G., Stamler, R., Kesteloot, H., Rose, G., & Stamler, J. (1994). Alcohol and blood pressure: The INTERSALT study. *British Medical Journal, 308,* 1263–1267.

Marmot, M. G., North, F., Feeney, A., & Head, J. (1993). Alcohol consumption and sickness absence: From the Whitehall II study. *Addiction, 88,* 369–382.

Martin, E. D., & Sher, K. J. (1994). Family history of alcoholism, alcohol use disorders and the five-factor model of personality. *Journal of Studies on Alcohol, 55,* 81–90.

McBride, W. J., Murphy, J. M., Lumeng, L., & Li, T. K. (1990). Serotonin, dopamine, and GABA involvement in alcohol drinking of selectively bred rats. *Alcohol, 7,* 199–205.

McClearn, G. E., Plomin, R., Gora-Maslak, G., & Crabbe, J. C. (1991). The gene chase in behavioral science. *Psychological Science, 2,* 222–229.

McCord, J. (1988). Identifying developmental paradigms leading to alcoholism. *Journal of Studies on Alcohol, 49,* 357–362.

McElduff, P., & Dobson, A. J. (1997). How much alcohol and how often? population based case-control study of alcohol consumption and risk of a major coronary event. *British Medical Journal, 314,* 1159–1163.

McEwan, R. T., McCallum, A., Bhopal, R. S., & Madhok, R. (1992). Sex and the risk of HIV infection: The role of alcohol. *British Journal of Addiction, 87,* 577–584.

McFall, M. E., Mackay, P. W., & Donovan, D. M. (1991). Combat-related post-traumatic stress disorder and severity of substance abuse in Vietnam veterans. *Journal of Studies on Alcohol, 53,* 357–362.

McGinnis, J. M., & Foege, W. H. (1993). Actual causes of death in the United States. *Journal of the American Medical Association, 270,* 2207–2212.

McGue, M. (1994). Genes, environment, and the etiology of alcoholism. In *The development of alcohol problems: Exploring the biopsychosocial matrix of risk.* National Institute on Alcohol Abuse and Alcoholism Research Monograph 26, pp. 1–40. Washington, DC: N.I.H. Publication No. 94-3495.

McGue, M. (1999). Behavioral genetic models of alcoholism and drinking. In K. E. Leonard & H. T. Blane (Eds.), *Psychological theories of drinking and alcoholism* (2nd ed., pp. 372–421). New York: Guilford.

McMillen, D. L., Pang, M. G., Wells-Parker, E., & Anderson, B. J. (1992). Alcohol, personality traits, and high risk driving: A comparison of young, drinking driver groups. *Addictive Behaviors, 17,* 525–532.

Meilman, P. W. (1993). Alcohol-induced sexual behavior on campus. *Journal of American College Health, 42,* 27–31.

Mello, N. K., Mendelson, J. H., & Teoh, S. K. (1993). An overview of the effects of alcohol on neuroendocrine function in women. In S. Zakhari (Ed), *Alcohol and the endocrine system* (pp. 139–169). Bethesda, MD: National Institute on Alcohol Abuse and Alcoholism.

Merikangas, K. R. (1990). The genetic epidemiology of alcoholism. *Psychological Medicine, 20,* 11–22.

Merikangas, K. R., & Gelernter, C. S. (1990). Comorbidity for alcoholism and depression. *Psychiatric Clinics of North America, 13,* 613–630.

Meyer, R. E., & Kranzler, H. R. (1990). Alcohol abuse/dependence and comorbid anxiety and depression. In C. R. Cloninger & J. D. Maser (Eds.), *Comorbidity of mood and anxiety disorders* (pp. 283–292). Washington, DC: American Psychiatric Press.

Mezey, E., Kolman, C. J., Diehl, A. M., Mitchell, M. C., & Herlong, H. F. (1988). Alcohol and dietary intake in the development of chronic pancreatitis and liver disease in alcoholism. *American Journal Clinical Nutrition, 48,* 148–151.

Midanik, L. T., & Clark, W. B. (1994). The demographic distribution of U.S. drinking patterns in 1990: Description and trends from 1984. *American Journal of Public Health, 84,* 1218–1222.

Midanik, L. T., & Room, R. (1992). The epidemiology of alcohol consumption. *Alcohol, Health, and Research World, 16,* 183–190.

Miller, B. A. (1990). The interrelationships between alcohol and drugs and family violence. *National Institute on Drug Abuse Research Monograph, 103,* 177–207.

Miller, B. A., Downs, W. R., & Testa, M. (1993). Interrelationships between victimization experiences and women's alcohol use. *Journal of Studies on Alcohol, Supplement 11,* 109–117.

Miller, B. A., Nochajski, T. H., Leonard, K. E., Blane, H. T., Gondoli, D. M., & Bowers, P. M. (1990). Spousal violence and alcohol/drug problems among parolees and their spouses. *Women and Criminal Justice, 1,* 55–72.

Miller, P. M., Smith, G. T., & Goldman, M. S. (1990). Emergence of alcohol expectancies in childhood: A possible critical period. *Journal of Studies on Alcohol, 51,* 343–349.

Molina, B.S.G., Chassin, L., & Curran, P. J. (1994). A comparison of mechanisms underling substance abuse for early adolescent children of alcoholics and controls. *Journal of Studies on Alcohol, 55,* 269–275.

Moos, R. H., & Billings, A. G. (1982). Children of alcoholics during the recovery process: Alcoholic and matched control families. *Addictive Behaviors, 7,* 155–164.

Morgan, M., & Grube, J. W. (1991). Closeness and peer group influences. *The British Journal of Social Psychology, 30,* 159–169.

Moss, H. B., Yao, J. K., & Maddock, J. M. (1989). Responses by sons of alcoholic fathers to alcoholic and placebo drinks: Perceived mood, intoxication, and plasma prolactin. *Alcoholism: Clinical and Experimental Research, 13,* 252–257.

Moushmoush, B., & Abi-Mansour, P. (1991). Alcohol and the heart: the long-term effects of alcohol on the cardiovascular system. *Archives of Internal Medicine, 151,* 36–42.

Muehlenhard, C. L., & Linton, M. A. (1987). Date rape and sexual aggression in dating situations: Incidence and risk factors. *Journal of Counseling Psychology, 34,* 186–196.

Mueser, K. T., Bellack, A. S., & Blanchard, J. J. (1992). Comorbidity of schizophrenia and substance abuse: Implications for treatment. *Journal of Consulting and Clinical Psychology, 60,* 845–856.

Mullahy, J., & Sindelar, J. L. (1992). Effects of alcohol on labor market success: Income earnings, labor supply, and occupation. *Alcohol, Health, and Research World, 16,* 134–139.

Murdoch, D., Pihl, R. O., & Ross, D. (1990). Alcohol and crimes of violence: Present issues. *The International Journal of the Addictions, 25,* 1065–1081.

Murphy, D. L., Belamker, R. H., Buchsbaum, M., Marin, N. F., Ciarnello, R., & Wyatt, R. J. (1977). Biogenic amine related enzymes and personality variations in normals. *Psychological Medicine, 7,* 149–157.

Murphy, G. E., Wetzel, R. D., Robins, E., & McEvoy, L. (1992). Multiple risk factors predict suicide in alcoholism. *Archives of General Psychiatry, 49,* 459–463.

Muscat, J. E., & Huncharek, M. D. (1991). Firearms and adult, domestic homicides: the role of alcohol and the victim. *American Journal of Forensic Medical Pathology, 12*(2), 105–110.

Naccarato, R., & Farinati, F. (1991). Hepatocellular carcinoma, alcohol, and cirrhosis: Facts and hypotheses. *Digestive Diseases and Sciences, 36,* 1137–1142.

Nagoshi, C. T., & Wilson, J. R. (1987). Influence of family alcoholism history on alcohol metabolism, sensitivity, and tolerance. *Alcoholism: Clinical and Experimental Research, 11,* 392–398.

Nagoshi, C. T., & Wilson, J. R. (1988). One-month repeatability of emotional responses to alcohol. *Alcoholism: Clinical and Experimental Research, 12,* 691–697.

Nathan, P. E. (1988). The addictive personality is the behavior of the addict. *Journal of Consulting and Clinical Psychology, 56,* 183–188.

National Institute on Alcohol Abuse and Alcoholism. (1993). *Eighth special report to the U.S. Congress on alcohol and health* (N.I.H. Publication No. 94-3699). Washington, DC: Author.

National Institute on Alcohol Abuse and Alcoholism. (1997). *Ninth special report to the U.S. Congress on alcohol and health* (N.I.H. Publication No. 97-4017). Washington, DC: Author.

Nelson, D. E., Sattin, R. W., Langlois, J. A., DeVito, C. A., & Stevens, J. A. (1992). Alcohol as a risk factor for fall injury events among elderly persons living in the community. *Journal of the American Geriatric Society, 40*(7), 658–661.

Newlin, D. B., & Thomson, J. B. (1990). Alcohol challenge with sons of alcoholics: A critical review and analysis. *Psychological Bulletin, 108,* 383–402.

O'Loughlin, J. L., Robitaille, Y., Boivin, J., & Suissa, S. (1993). Incidence of and risk factors for falls and injurious falls among the community-dwelling elderly. *American Journal of Epidemiology, 137,* 342–354.

O'Malley, S. S., Jaffe, A. J., Chang, G., Schottenfeld, R. S., Meyer, R. E., & Rounsaville, B. (1992). Naltrexone in the treatment of alcohol dependence. *Archives of General Psychiatry, 49,* 881–887.

O'Malley, S. S., & Maisto, S. A. (1985). Effects of family drinking history and expectancies on responses to alcohol in men. *Journal of Studies on Alcohol, 46,* 289–297.

Orme, T., & Rimmer, J. (1981). Alcoholism and child abuse: A review. *Journal of Studies on Alcohol, 42,* 273–287.

Paffenbarger, R. S., Jr., Lee, I. M., & Leung, R. (1994). Physical activity and personal characteristics associated with depression and suicide in American college men. *Acta Psychiatrica Scandinavica, 377,* 16–22.

Parker, E. S., Parker, D. A., & Harford, T. C. (1991). Specifying the relationship between alcohol use and cognitive loss: the effects of frequency of consumption and psychological distress. *Journal of Studies on Alcoholism, 52*(4), 366–373.

Parks, K. A., & Miller, B. A. (1997). Bar victimization of women. *Psychology of Women Quarterly, 21,* 509–525.

Parrish, K. M., Dufour, M. C., Stinson, F. S., & Harford, T. C. (1993). Average daily alcohol consumption during adult life among decedents with and without cirrhosis: The 1986 National Mortality Followback Survey. *Journal of Studies on Alcohol, 54,* 450–456.

Parrish, K. M., Higuchi, S., & Dufour, M. C. (1991). Alcohol consumption and the risk of developing liver cirrhosis: Implications for future research. *Journal of Substance Abuse, 3*(3), 325–335.

Parsons, O. A. (1986). Cognitive functioning in sober social drinkers: A review and critique. *Journal of Studies on Alcoholism, 47,* 101–114.

Parsons, O. A. (1994). Determinants of cognitive deficits in alcoholics: The search continues. *Clinical Neuropsychologist, 8*(1), 39–58.

Pederson, W. (1991). Mental health, sensation seeking, and drug use patterns: A longitudinal study. *British Journal of Addiction, 86,* 195–204.

Pernanen, K. (1991). *Alcohol in human violence.* New York: Guilford.

Perris, C., Jacobson, L, von Knorring, L., Oreland, L., Perris, H., & Ross, S. B. (1980). Enzymes related to biogenic amine metabolism and personality characteristics in depressed patients. *Acta Psychiatrica Scandinavica, 61,* 477–484.

Peterson, J. B., Rothfleisch, J., Zelazo, P. D., & Pihl, R. O. (1990). Acute alcohol intoxication and cognitive functioning. *Journal of Studies on Alcohol, 51*(2), 114–122.

Plomin, R., DeFries, J. C., & Loehlin, J. C. (1977). Genotype-environment interaction and correlation in the analyses of human behavior. *Psychological Bulletin, 84,* 309–322.

Pohorecky, L. A. (1991). Stress and alcohol interaction: An update of human research. *Alcoholism: Clinical and Experimental Research, 15,* 438–459.

Poldrugo, F., & Forti, B. (1988). Personality disorders and alcoholism treatment outcome. *Drug and Alcohol Dependence, 21,* 171–176.

Polich, J., Pollock, V. E., & Bloom, F. E. (1994). Meta-analysis of P300 amplitude from males at risk for alcoholism. *Psychological Bulletin, 115,* 55–73.

Pollock, V. E., Teasdale, T. W., Gabrielli, W. F., & Knop, J. (1986). Subjective and objective measures of response to alcohol among young men at risk for alcoholism. *Journal of Studies on Alcohol, 47,* 297–304.

Pollock, V. E., Volavka, J., Goodwin, D. W., Mednick, S. A., Gabrielli, W. F., Knop, J., & Schulsinger, F. (1983). The EEG after alcohol administration in men at risk for alcoholism. *Archives of General Psychiatry, 40,* 857–861.

Powell, B. J., Penick, E. C., Nickel, E. J., Liskow, B. I., Riesenmy, K. D., Campion, S. L., & Brown, E. F. (1992). Outcomes of co-morbid alcoholic men: A 1-year follow-up. *Alcoholism: Clinical and Experimental Research, 16,* 131–138.

Preedy, V. R., Atkinson, L. M., Richardson, P. J., & Peters, T. J. (1993). Mechanism of ethanol-induced cardiac damage. *British Heart Journal, 69,* 197–200.

Presley, C. A., Meilman, P. W., & Lyerla, M. S. (1993, January). *Alcohol and drugs on American college campuses: Use, consequences, and perceptions of the campus environment, Vol. 1.* Carbondale, IL: Core Institute.

Puddey, I. B., Beilin, L. J., Vandongen, R., Rouse, I. L., & Rogers, P. (1985). Evidence for a direct effect of alcohol consumption on blood pressure in normotensive men. *Hypertension, 7*(5), 707–713.

Quigley, B. M., & Leonard, K. E. (1999). Husband alcohol expectancies, drinking, and marital-conflict styles as predictors of severe marital violence among newlywed couples. *Psychology of Addictive Behaviors, 13,* 49–59.

Rather, B. C., Goldman, M. S., Roehrich, L., & Brannick, M. (1992). Empirical modeling of an alcohol expectancy memory network using multidimensional scaling. *Journal of Abnormal Psychology, 101,* 174–183.

Regier, D. A., Farmer, M. E., Rae, D. S., Locke, B. Z., Keith, S. J. Judd, L. L., & Goodwin, F. K. (1990). Comorbidity of mental disorders with alcohol and other drug abuse. *Journal of the American Medical Association, 264,* 2511–2518.

Rehm, J. (1993). Methodological approaches and problems in research into alcohol-related accidents and injuries. *Addiction, 88,* 885–896.

Reich, T., Edenberge, H. J., Goate, A., William, J. T., Rice, J. P., Van Eerdewegh, P., Foroud, T., Hesselbrock, V., Schuckit, M. A., Bucholz, K., Porjesz, B., Li, T.-K., Conneally, P. M., Nurnberge, J. J. Jr., Tischfield, J. A., Crowe, R. R., Clonger, C. R., Wu, W., Shears, S., Carr, K., Crose, C., Willig, C., & Begleiter, H. (1998). Genome-wide search for genes affecting risk for alcohol dependence. *American Journal of Medical Genetics (Neuropsychiatric Genetics), 81,* 206–215.

Reichman, M. E., Judd, J. T., Longcope, C., Schatzkin, A., Clevidence, B. A., Nair, P. P., Campbell, W. S., & Taylor, P. R. (1993). Effects of alcohol consumption on plasma and urinary hormone concentrations in premenopausal women. *Journal of the National Cancer Institute, 85*(9), 722–727.

Reiss, D., Plomin, R., & Hetherington, E. M. (1991). Genetics and psychiatry: An unheralded window on the environment. *American Journal of Psychiatry, 148,* 283–291.

Rice, D. P., Kelman, S, Miller, L. S., & Dunmeyer, S. (1990). *The economic costs of alcohol and drug abuse and mental illness: 1985.* Reported submitted to the Office of Financing and Coverage Policy of the Alcohol, Drug Abuse, and Mental Health Administration, U.S. Department of Health and Human Services. San Francisco, CA. Institute for Health and Aging, University of California.

Richardson, P. J., Wodak, A. D., Atkinson, L., Saunders, J. B., & Jewitt, D. E. (1986). Relation between alcohol intake, myocardial enzyme activity, and myocardial function in dilated cardiomyopathy: Evidence for the concept of alcohol induced heart muscle disease. *British Heart Journal, 56,* 165–170.

Ridker, P. M., Vaughan, D. E., Stampfer, M. J., Glynn, R. J., & Hennekens, C. H. (1994). Association of moderate alcohol consumption and plasma concentration of endogenous tissue-type plasminogen activator. *Journal of the American Medical Association, 272*(12), 929–933.

Robins, L. N., Bates, W., & O'Neal, P. (1962). Adult drinking patterns of former problem children. In D. Pittman & C. R. Snyder (Eds.), *Society, culture, and drinking patterns* (pp. 395–412). New York: Wiley.

Robins, L. N., & Regier, D. A. (1991). *Psychiatric disorders in America: The epidemiologic catchment area study.* New York: The Free Press.

Roehrs, T., Beare, D., Zorick, F., & Roth, T. (1994). Sleepiness and ethanol effects on simulated driving. *Alcoholism: Clinical and Experimental Research, 18*(1), 154–158.

Rogosch, F., Chassin, L., & Sher, K. J. (1990). Personality variables as mediators and moderators of family history risk for alcoholism: Conceptual and methodological issues. *Journal of Studies on Alcohol, 51,* 310–318.

Roizen, J. (1997). Epidemiological issues in alcohol-related violence. In M. Galanter (Ed.), *Recent developments in alcoyholism* (Vol. 13, pp. 7–40). New York: Plenum.

Rosenberg, L., Metzger, L. S., & Palmer, J. R. (1993). Alcohol consumption and risk of breast cancer: A review of the epidemiologic evidence. *Epidemiological Review, 15*(1), 133–144.

Ross, H. E., Glaser, F. B., & Stiasny, S. (1988). Sex differences in the prevalence of psychiatric disorders in patients with alcohol and drug problems. *British Journal of Addiction, 83,* 1179–1192.

Ross, H. E., Glaser, F. B., & Germanson, T. (1988). The prevalence of psychiatric disorders in patients with alcohol and other drug problems. *Archives of General Psychiatry, 45,* 1023–1031.

Ross, R. K., Bernstein, L., Trent, L., Henderson, B. E., & Paganini-Hill, A. (1990). A prospective study of risk factors for traumatic deaths in a retirement community. *Preventive Medicine, 19*(3), 323–334.

Roth, H. D., Levy, P. S., Shi, L., & Post, E. (1994). Alcoholic beverages and breast cancer: Some observations on published case-control studies. *Journal of Clinical Epidemiology, 47*(2), 207–216.

Rounsaville, B. J., Dolinsky, Z. S., Babor, T. F., & Meyer, R. E. (1987). Psychopathology as a predictor of treatment outcome in alcoholics. *Archives of General Psychiatry, 44,* 505–513.

Roy, A., Virkkunen, M., & Linnoila, M. (1990). Serotonin in suicide, violence, and alcoholism. In E. F. Coccaro & D. L. Murphy (Eds.), *Serotonin in major psychiatric disorders* (pp. 187–208). Washington, DC: American Psychiatric Press.

Russell, M., Cooper, M. L., Frone, M. R., & Welte, J. W. (1991). Alcohol drinking patterns and blood pressure. *American Journal of Public Health, 81,* 452–457.

Russell, M., Henderson, C., & Blume, S. (1985). *Children of alcoholics: A review of the literature.* New York: Children of Alcoholics Foundation.

Sayette, M. A. (1993). An appraisal-disruption model of alcohol's effects on stress responses in social drinkers. *Psychological Bulletin, 114,* 459–476.

Sayette, M. A. (1999). Cognitive theory and research. In K. E. Leonard & H. T. Blane (Eds.), *Psychological theories of drinking and alcoholism* (2nd ed., pp. 247–291). New York: Guilford.

Schandler, S. L., Brannock, J. C., Cohen, M. J., Antick, J., & Caine, K. (1988). Visuospatial learning in elementary school children with and without a family history of alcoholism. *Journal of Studies on Alcohol, 49,* 538–545.

Schandler, S. L., Cohen, M. J., & Antick, J. R. (1992). Activation, attention, and visuospatial learning in adults with and without a family history of alcoholism. *Alcoholism: Clinical and Experimental Research, 16,* 566–571.

Schatzkin, A., & Longnecker, M. P. (1994). Alcohol and breast cancer. *Cancer, 74*(3), S1101–S1110.

Scherr, P. A., LaCroix, A. Z., Wallace, R. B., Berkman, L., Curb, J. D., Cornoni-Huntley, J., Evans, D. A., & Hennekens, C. H. (1992). Light to moderate alcohol consumption and mortality in the elderly. *Journal of the American Geriatric Society, 40*(7), 651–657.

Schuckit, M. A. (1980). Self-ratings of alcohol intoxication by young men with and without family histories of alcoholism. *Journal of Studies on Alcohol, 41,* 242–249.

Schuckit, M. A. (1983). Extroversion and neuroticism in young men at higher or lower risk for alcoholism. *American Journal of Psychiatry, 140,* 1223–1224.

Schuckit, M. A. (1984). Subjective responses to alcohol in sons of alcoholics and control subjects. *Archives of General Psychiatry, 41,* 879–884.

Schuckit, M. A. (1994). Low level of response to alcohol as a predictor of future alcoholism. *American Journal of Psychiatry, 151,* 184–189.

Schuckit, M. A. (1998). Biological, psychological, and environmental predictors of alcoholism risk: A longitudinal study. *Journal of Studies on Alcohol, 59,* 485–494.

Schuckit, M. A., & Hesselbrock, V. (1994). Alcohol dependence and anxiety disorders: What is the relationship? *American Journal of Psychiatry, 151,* 1723–1734.

Schuckit, M. A., Irwin, M., & Brown, S. A. (1990). The history of anxiety symptoms among 171 primary alcoholics. *Journal of Studies on Alcohol, 51,* 34–41.

Scragg, R. (1995). A quantification of alcohol-related mortality in New Zealand. *Australian and New Zealand Journal of Medicine, 25,* 5–11.

Searles, J. S. (1988). The role of genetics in the pathogenesis of alcoholism. *Journal of Abnormal Psychology, 97,* 153–167.

Sher, K. J. (1987). Stress response dampening. In H. T. Blane & K. E. Leonard, (Eds.), *Psychological theories of drinking and alcoholism* (pp. 227–271). New York: Guilford.

Sher, K. J. (1991). *Children of alcoholics: A critical appraisal of theory and research.* Chicago: University of Chicago Press.

Sher, K. J., Bylund, D. B., Walitzer, K. S., Hartmann, J., & Ray-Prenger, C. (1994). Platelet monoamine oxidase (MAO) activity: Personality, substance use, and the stress-response dampening effect of alcohol. *Experimental and Clinical Psychopharmacology, 2,* 53–81.

Sher, K. J., Gershuny, B. S., Peterson, L., & Raskin, G. (1997). The role of childhood stressors in the intergenerational transmission of alcohol use disorders. *Journal of Studies on Alcohol, 58,* 414–427.

Sher, K. J., Gotham, H. J., Erickson, D. J., & Wood, P. K. (1996). A prospective, high-risk study of the relationship between tobacco dependence and alcohol use disorders. *Alcoholism: Clinical and Experimental Research, 20,* 485–492.

Sher, K. J., & Levenson, R. W. (1982). Risk for alcoholism and individual differences in the stress-response dampening effect of alcohol. *Journal of Abnormal Psychology, 91,* 350–368.

Sher, K. J., & Trull, T. J. (1994). Personality and disinhibitory psychopathology: Alcoholism and antisocial personality disorder. *Journal of Abnormal Psychology, 103,* 92–102.

Sher, K. J., Trull, T. J., Bartholow, B. D., & Vieth, A. (1999). Personality and alcoholism: Issues, methods, and etiological processes. In K. E. Leonard & H. T. Blane (Eds.), *Psychological theories of drinking and alcoholism* (2nd ed., pp. 54–105). New York: Guilford.

Sher, K. J., Walitzer, K. S., Bylund, D. B., & Hartmannn, J. (1989). Alcohol, stress, and family history of alcoholism. *Alcoholism: clinical and Experimental Research, 13,* 337.

Sher, K. J., Walitzer, K. S., Wood, P. K., & Brent, E. E. (1991). Characteristics of children of alcoholics: Putative risk factors, substance use and abuse, and psychopathology. *Journal of Abnormal Psychology, 100,* 427–448.

Sher, K. J., Wood, M. D., Crews, T. M., & Vandiver, P. A. (1995). The tridimensional personality questionnaire: Reliability and validity studies and derivation of a short form. *Psychological Assessment, 7,* 195–208.

Sher, K. J., Wood, M. D., Wood, P. K., & Raskin, G. (1996). Alcohol outcome expectancies and alcohol use: A latent variable cross-lagged panel study. *Journal of Abnormal Psychology, 105,* 561–574.

Shultz, J. M., Rice, D. P., & Parker, D. L. (1990). Alcohol-related mortality and years of potential life lost: United States, 1987. *Morbidity and Mortality Weekly Report, 39,* 173–178.

Sieber, M. F. (1981). Personality scores and licit and illicit substance use. *Personality and Individual Differences, 2,* 235–241.

Singh, M., & Simsek, H. (1990). Ethanol and the pancreas. *Gastroenterology, 98,* 1051–1062.

Smart, R. G. (1988). Does alcohol advertising affect overall consumption? A review of empirical studies. *Journal of Studies on Alcohol, 49,* 314–323.

Smart, R. G. (1989). Is the postwar drinking binge ending? Cross-national trends in per capita alcohol consumption. *British Journal of Addiction, 84,* 743–748.

Smith, G. S., Branas, C. C., & Miller, T. R. (1999). Fatal nontraffic injuries involving alcohol: A metaanalysis. *Annals of Emergency Medicine, 33,* 659–668.

Smith, G. T., Goldman, M. S., Greenbaum, P. E., & Christiansen, B. A. (1995). Expectancy for social facilitation from drinking: The divergent paths of high-expectancy and low-expectancy adolescents. *Journal of Abnormal Psychology, 104,* 32–40.

Smith-Warner, S. A., Spiegelman, D., Yaun, S., van den Brandt, P. A., Folsom, A. R., Goldbohm, R. A., Graham, S., Holmberg, L., Howe, G. R., Marshall, J. R., Miller, A. B., Potter, J. D., Speizer, F. E., Willett, W. C., Wolk, A., & Hunter, D. J. (1998). Alcohol and breast cancer in women: A pooled analysis of cohort studies. *Journal of the American Medical Association, 279,* 535–540.

Spohr, H. L,, Willms, J., & Steinhausen, H. C. (1993). Prenatal alcohol exposure and long-term developmental consequences. *Lancet, 341*(8850), 907–910.

Stacy, A. W., Newcomb, M. D., & Bentler, P. M. (1991a). Cognitive motivation and drug use: A 9–year longitudinal study. *Journal of Abnormal Psychology, 100,* 502–515.

Stacy, A. W., Newcomb, M. D., & Bentler, P. M. (1991b). Personality, problem drinking, and drunk driving: Mediating, moderating, and direct-effect models. *Journal of Personality and Social Psychology, 60,* 795–811.

Stacy, A. W., Widaman, K. F., & Marlatt, G. A. (1990). Expectancy models of alcohol use. *Journal of Personality and Social Psychology, 58,* 918–928.

Stall, R., McKusick, L., Wiley, J., Coates, T., & Ostrow, D. (1986). Alcohol and drug use during sexual activity and compliance with safe sex guidelines for AIDS: The AIDS Behavioral Research Project. *Health Education Quarterly, 13,* 359–371.

Stamler, J., Rose, G., Stamler, R., Elliott, E., Dyer, A., & Marmot, M. (1989). INTERSALT study findings: Public health and medical care implications. *Hypertension, 14*(5), 570–577.

Stamler, R. (1991). Implications of the INTERSALT study. *Hypertension, 17*(1), S I-16–S I-20.

Stasiewicz, P. R., & Lisman, S. A. (1989). Effects of infant cries on alcohol consumption in college males at risk for child abuse. *Child Abuse and Neglect, 13,* 463–470.

Steele, C. M., & Josephs, R. A. (1988). Drinking your troubles away II: An attention-allocation model of alcohol's effect on psychological stress. *Journal of Abnormal Psychology, 97,* 196–205.

Steele, C. M., & Josephs, R. A. (1990). Alcohol myopia: Its prized and dangerous effects. *American Psychologist, 45,* 921–933.

Steinberg, W., & Tenner, S. (1994). Acute pancreatitis. *New England Journal of Medicine, 330*(17), 1198–1210.

Steinglass, P., & Robertson, A. (1983). The alcoholic family. In B. Kissin, & H. Begleiter (Eds.), *The pathogenesis of alcoholism: Psychosocial factors* (pp. 243–307). New York: Plenum.

Steinhausen, H. C., Willms, J., & Spohr H. L. (1993). Long-term psychopathological and cognitive outcome of children with fetal alcohol syndrome. *Journal of the American Academy of Child Adolescent Psychiatry, 32,* 990–994.

Stinson, F. S., & DeBakey, S. F. (1992). Alcohol-related mortality in the United States, 1979–1988. *British Journal of Addiction, 87,* 777–783.

Streissguth, A. P., & Dehaene, P. (1993). Fetal alcohol syndrome in twins of alcoholic mothers: Concordance of diagnosis and IQ. *American Journal of Medical Genetics, 47,* 857–861.

Streissguth, A. P., Sampson, P. D., Olson, H. C., Bookstein, F. L., Barr, H. M., Scott, M., Feldman, J., & Mirsky, A. F. (1994). Maternal drinking during pregnancy: Attention and short-term memory in 14–year old offspring-a longitudinal prospective study. *Alcohol: Clinical and Experimental Research, 19*(1), 202–218.

Strogatz, D. S., James, S. A., Haines, P. S., Elmer, P. J., Gerber, A. M., Browning, S. R., Ammerman, A. S., & Keenan, N. L. (1991). Alcohol consumption and blood pressure in black adults: The Pitt County study. *American Journal of Epidemiology, 133,* 442–450.

Strunin, L., & Hingson, R. (1992). Alcohol, drugs, and adolescent sexual behavior. *The International Journal of the Addictions, 27,* 129–146.

Tarter, R. (1988). Are there inherited behavioral traits that predispose to substance abuse? *Journal of Consulting and Clinical Psychology, 56,* 189–196.

Tausignant, M., & Kovess, V. (1989). Borderline traits among community alcoholics and problem drinkers: Rural-urban differences. *Canadian Journal of Psychiatry, 34,* 796–799.

Taylor, S. P., & Chermack, S. T. (1993). Alcohol, drugs and human physical aggression. *Journal of Studies on Alcohol, Supplement 11,* 78–88.

Thun, M. J., Peto, R., Lopez, A. D., Monaco, J. H., Henley, J., Heath, C. W., Jr., & Doll, R. (1997). Alcohol consumption and mortality among middle-aged and elderly U.S. adults. *New England Journal of Medicine,*

Tollefson, G. D., Montague-Clouse, J., & Tollefson, S. L. (1992). Treatment of comorbid generalized anxiety in a recently detoxified alcoholic population with a selective serotonergic drug (buspirone). *Journal of Clinical Psychopharmacology, 12,* 19–26.

Tonnesen, H., Rosenberg, J., Nielsen, H. J., Rasmussen, V., & Hauge, C. (1999). Effect of preoperative abstinence on poor postoperative outcome in alcohol misusers: Randomised controlled trial. *British Medical Journal, 318,* 1311–1316.

Tsai, G., Gastfriend, D. R., & Coyle, J. T. (1995). The glutamatergic basis of human alcoholism. *American Journal of Psychiatry, 152,* 332–340.

Ueshima, H., Mikawa, K., Baba, S., Sasaki, S., Ozawa, H., Tsushima, M., Kawaguchi, A., Omae, T., Katayama, Y., & Kayamori, Y. (1993). Effect of reduced alcohol consumption on blood pressure in untreated hypertensive men. *Hypertension, 21,* 248–252.

Uhl, G. R., Persico, A. M., & Smith, S. S. (1992). Current excitement with D_2 dopamine receptor gene alleles in substance abuse. *Archives of General Psychiatry, 49,* 157–160.

Vaillant, G. E., & Milofsky, E. S. (1982). The etiology of alcoholism: A prospective viewpoint. *American Psychologist, 37,* 494–503

Vartiainen, E., Puska, P., Pekkanen, J., Tuomilehto, J., Lonnqvist, J., & Ehnholm, C. (1994). Serum cholesterol concentration and mortality from accidents, suicide, and other violent causes. *British Medical Journal, 309,* 445–447.

Victor, M. (1992). Alcoholic dementia. *Canadian Journal of Neurological Science, 21*(2), 88–99.

Victor, M. (1993). Persistent altered mentation due to ethanol. *Neurolology Clinic, 11*(3), 639–661.

Vinson, D. C. (1989). Acute transient memory loss. *American Family Physician, 39,* 249–254.

Vinson, D. C., Mabe, N., Leonard, L. L., Alexander, J., Becker, J., Boyer, J., & Moll, J. (1995). Alcohol and injury: A case-crossover study. *Archives of Family Medicine, 4(6),* 505–511.

Vogel-Sprott, M., & Chipperfield, B. (1987). Family history of problem drinking among male social drinkers: Behavioral effects of alcohol. *Journal of Studies on Alcohol, 48,* 430–436.

Volpicelli, J. R., Alterman, A. I., Hayashida, M., & O'Brien, C. P. (1992). Naltrexone in the treatment of alcohol dependence. *Archives of General Psychiatry, 49,* 876–880.

von Knorring, A-L., Bohman, M., von Knorring, L., & Oreland, L. (1985). Platelet MAO activity as a biological maker ins subgroups of alcoholism. *Acta Psychiatrica Scandanavica, 72,* 51–58.

von Knorring, L., Oreland, L., & von Knorring A-L. (1987). Personality traits and platelet MAO activity in alcohol and drug abusing teenage boys. *Acta Psychiatrica Scandanavica, 75,* 307–314.

Wakabayashi, K., Nakamura, K., Kono, S., Shinchi, K., & Imanishi, K. (1994). Alcohol consumption and blood pressure: An extended study of self-defence officials in Japan. *International Journal of Epidemiology, 23,* 307–311.

Wallack, L., Grube, J. W., Madden, P. A., & Breed, W. (1990). Portrayals of alcohol on prime-time television. *Journal of Studies on Alcohol, 51,* 428–437.

Wannamethee, S. G., & Shaper, A. G. (1999). Type of alcoholic drink and risk of major coronary heart disease events and all-cause mortality. *American Journal of Public Health, 89,* 685–690.

Webb, G. R., Redman, S., Hennrikus, D. J., Kelman, G. R., Gibberd, R. W., & Sanson-Fisher, R. W. (1994). The relationships between high-risk and problem drinking and the occurrence of work injuries and related absences. *Journal of Studies on Alcohol, 55,* 434–446.

Webster, D. W., Harburg, E., Gleiberman, L., Schork, A., & DiFranceisco, W. (1989). Familial transmission of alcohol use: I. Parent and adult offspring alcohol use over 17 years—Tecumseh, Michigan. *Journal of Studies on Alcohol, 50,* 557–566.

Wechsler, H., Davenport, A., Dowdall, G., Moeykens, B., & Castillo, S. (1994). Health and behavioral consequences of binge drinking in college. *Journal of the American Medical Association, 272*(21), 1672–1677.

Wechsler, H., Dowdall, G. W., Maenner, G., Gledhill-Hoyt, J. & Lee, H. (1998). Changes in binge drinking and related problems among American college students between 1993 and 1997: Results of the Harvard School of Public Health College Alcohol Study. *Journal of American College Health, 47,* 57–68.

Wehner, J. M., & Bowers, B. J. (1995). Use of transgenics, null mutants, and antisense approaches to study ethanol's actions. *Alcoholism: Clinical and Experimental Research, 19,* 811–820.

Widom, C. S. (1993). Child abuse and alcohol use and abuse. In *Alcohol and interpersonal violence: Fostering multidisciplinary perspectives.* National Institute on Alcohol Abuse and Alcoholism Research Monograph 24, pp. 291–314. Washington, DC: N.I.H. Publication no. 93-3496.

Wieczorek, W. F., & Miller, B. A. (1992). Preliminary typology designed for treatment matching of driving-while-intoxicated offenders. *Journal of Consulting and Clinical Psychology, 60,* 757–765.

Williams, G. D., Stinson, F. S., Sanchez, L. L., & Dufour, M. C. (1998, December). *Apparent per capita alcohol consumption: National, state, and regional trends, 1977–1996.* NIAAA Surveillance Report No. 47. Washington, DC: U.S. Government Printing Office.

Williams, G. D., & Debakey, S. F. (1992). Changes in levels of alcohol consumption: United States, 1983–1988. *British Journal of Addiction, 87,* 643–648.

Wills, T. A. (1986). Stress and coping in early adolescence: Relationships to substance use in urban school samples. *Health Psychology, 5,* 503–529.

Wills, T. A., & Cleary, S. D. (1999). Peer and adolescent substance use among 6–9th graders: Latent growth analyses of influence versus selection mechanisms. *Health Psychology, 18,* 453–463.

Wilson, J. S., Bernstein, L., McDonald, C., Tait, A., McNeil, D., & Pirola, R. C. (1985). Diet and drinking habits in relation to the development of alcoholic pancreatitis. *Gut, 26,* 882–887.

Witteman, J. C. M., Willett, W. C., Stampfer, M. J., Colditz, G. A., Kok, F. J., Sacks, F. M., Speizer, F. E., Rosner, B., Hennekens, C. H. (1990). Relation of moderate alcohol consumption and risk of systemic hypertension in women. *American Journal of Cardiology, 65,* 633–637.

Wolin, S. J., Bennett, L. A., & Noonan, D. L. (1979). Family rituals and the reoccurrence of alcoholism over generations. *American Journal of Psychiatry, 136,* 589–593.

Wolin, S. J., Bennett, L. A., Noonan, D. L., & Teitelbaum, M. A. (1980). Disrupted family rituals: A factor in the intergenerational transmission of alcoholism. *Journal of Studies on Alcohol, 41,* 199–214.

Wood, M. D., Nagoshi, C. T., & Dennis, D. A. (1992). Alcohol use norms and expectations as predictors of alcohol use and problems in a college student sample. *American Journal of Drug and Alcohol Abuse, 18,* 461–476.

Wood, M. D., Sher, K. J., & McGowan, A. K. (in press). Collegiate alcohol involvement and role attainment in early adulthood: Findings from a prospective high-risk study. *Journal of Studies on Alcohol.*

Wood, P. K., Sher, K. J., Erickson, D. J., & DeBord, K. A. (1997). Predicting academic problems in college from freshman alcohol involvement. *Journal of Studies on Alcohol, 58,* 200–210.

Wu, C. F., Sudhakar, M., Jaferi, G., Ahmed, S. S., & Regan, T. J. (1976). Preclinical cardiomyopathy in chronic alcoholics: a sex difference. *American Heart Journal, 91*(3), 281–286.

Yesavage, J. A., Dolhert, N., & Taylor, J. L. (1994). Flight simulator performance of younger and older aircraft pilots: Effects of age and alcohol. *Journal of the American Geriatric Society, 42,* 577–582.

Yi, H., Stinson, F. S., Williams, G. D., & Bertolucci, D. (1998, December). Trends in alcohol-related fatal traffic crashes, United States: 1975–1996 (Surveillance Report # 46, National Institute on Alcohol Abuse and Alcoholism). Washington, DC: U.S. Department of Health and Human Services.

Zador, P. L. (1991). Alcohol-related relative risk of fatal driver injuries in relation to driver age and sex. *Journal of Studies on Alcohol, 52,* 302–310.

Zakhari, S. (1991). Vulnerability to cardiac disease. In M. Galanter (Ed.), *Recent developments in alcoholism* (pp. 225–262). New York: Plenum.

Zimmerman, M., & Coryell, W. (1989). *DSM–III* personality disorder diagnoses in a nonpatient sample: Demographic correlates and comorbidity. *Archives of General Psychiatry, 46,* 682–689.

Zucker, R. A. (1976). Parental influences upon drinking patterns of their children. In M. Greenblatt and M. A. Schuckit, (Eds.), *Alcoholism and problems in women and children* (pp. 211–238). New York: Grune & Stratton.

Zucker, R. A. (1987). The four alcoholisms: A developmental account of the etiologic process. In P. C. Rivers & N. B. Lincoln (Eds.), *Alcohol and addictive behavior* (pp. 27–83). Lincoln: University of Nebraska Press.

Zucker, R. A., Fitzgerald, H. E., & Moses, H. D. (1995). Emergence of alcohol problems and the several alcoholisms: A developmental perspective on etiologic theory and life course trajectory. In D. Cicchetti & D. J. Cohen (Eds.), *Developmental psychopathology: Vol. 2. Risk, disorder, and adaptation* (pp. 677–711). New York: John Wiley & Sons.

Zucker, R. A., & Gomberg, E.S.L. (1986). Etiology of alcoholism reconsidered: The case for a biopsychosocial process. *American Psychologist, 41,* 783–793.

Zuckerman, M., Kuhlman, D. M., & Camac, C. (1988). What lies beyond E and N? Factor analyses of scales believed to measure basic dimensions of personality. *Journal of Personality and Social Psychology, 54,* 96–107.

II

Crosscutting Issues

17

Stress, Health, and Illness

Angela Liegey Dougall
Andrew Baum
University of Pittsburgh Cancer Institute

The customary introduction to stress suggests that it is still a matter of scientific debate, despite the fact that it is a common and influential state. It shares aspects of mind and body, representing a good instance of more holistic integration of these constructs. It is also a crosscutting process, influencing a wide array of illnesses, health behaviors, and aspects of health and well-being. Despite the general lack of a consensus on a precise definition of stress or the best approach to measuring it, there is considerable evidence to suggest that stress has important effects on physical and mental states, pathophysiology of disease, and performance (for reviews see Baba, Jamal, & Tourigny, 1998; Biondi & Zannino, 1997; S. Cohen & Williamson, 1991; McEwen & Stellar, 1993). This chapter considers conceptual models of stress, the broad array of behaviors and bodily systems involved in the stress response, and the impact of stress on chronic disease processes. Differences in the consequences of acute and chronic stress, as well as the implications of observed differences between them are also explored.

THE STRESS CONSTRUCT

Perhaps the most difficult aspect of studying stress is deriving a widely accepted definition of it. Most theorists agree that stress is (or can be) adaptive, that it is associated with threatening or harmful events, and that it is typically characterized by aversive or unpleasant feelings and mood. Beyond this, there are few areas of universal agreement. Some theorists have argued that stress can be positive, but others have insisted that it is a fundamentally aversive state (e.g., Baum, 1990; Selye, 1956/1984). Some have pointed out apparently simultaneous biological and psychological activation, suggesting that stress is an emotion, and some have described stress as a general state of arousal associated with taking strong action or dealing with a strong stimulus (e.g., Baum, 1990; Mason, 1971). Stress has been variously defined as a stimulus, as a response, and as a process involving both. It has been described as both specific and nonspecific responses to danger with little evidence to support one or another contention. However, it appears to be a fundamental component of adjustment and adaptation to environmental change, and as such has assumed a critical role in theories of human evolution. From these many notions have come a few major theories of stress that reflect integration and synthesis of prior theories and that describe a pattern of responses to threat, harm, or loss.

Biological Theories of Stress

A history of the stress concept could begin with early philosophers, but modern stress theory really began with Cannon's work early in the 20th century. Cannon (1914) was interested in the effects of stress on the sympathetic nervous system (SNS) and with application of the concept of homeostasis to interaction with the environment. Stressful events elicited negative emotions associated with SNS activation and disequilibrium in bodily systems. This activation was associated with the release of sympathetic adrenal hormones (i.e., epinephrine, norepinephrine), which prepared the organism to respond to the danger posed, characteristically by fighting or fleeing. This early description of stress did not consider the measures of activation or persistence, focusing solely on SNS arousal and release of sympathetic hormones.

Selye (1956/1984) focused his attention solely on the activation of the hypothalamic-pituitary-adrenal cortical (HPA) axis. Initially interested in the effects of hormonal extracts, Selye (1956/1984) discovered a "universal" response to stressful events that included adrenal hypertrophy, lymphoid involution, and ulceration of the digestive tract. He characterized stress as a nonspecific physiological response to a variety of noxious events and argued that, regardless of the stressor presented, the same response was seen, driven by activation of the HPA axis.

In contrast to these more focused approaches, Mason (1971) argued that stress affected many biological systems and that responses were based on the type of stressor presented. He concluded that stress was a unified catabolic response with the primary purpose of maintaining high levels of circulating blood glucose and providing the organism with energy to sustain resistance. Although he viewed emotional reactions as nonspecific, he maintained that responses in endocrine pathways followed response patterns that were specific to the stressor.

Whereas these early biological models of stress were typically narrow in focus and ignored or only hinted at important psychological aspects of stress, their importance can be illustrated in several ways. The systems that received most attention in these early theories were the SNS and the HPA axis. Both are arguably principal drivers of stress responding and persist today as focal points in studies of physiological responses during and after stress. Work by Cannon and Selye accurately identified these systems as integral parts of the stress response and focused attention on consequences of prolonged or excessive activation of these systems as primary consequences of stress. Mason recognized the integrated nature of these responses as well as the broad panoply of responses characterizing stress. Sympathetic arousal and activation of the HPA axis are hallmarks of the stress response and have been used as manipulation checks for stressors and explored as mechanisms underlying stress effects on the body.

These theories of biological activity offered some insights into psychological aspects of stress. Cannon's (1914) notion of critical stress levels suggested that organisms had thresholds, or limits, on normal or nonpathogenic responses to threat and his discussion of emotional stress suggested that emotional stimuli and responses were important in stress as well. In addition, stressors were stimuli that had to be recognized as a threat in order to elicit a response. Selye (1956/1984) argued that adaptive energy or the capacity to adapt to stressors is limited and depletion of adaptive reserves can have consequences, an idea consistent with notions of life change, stressful life events, and aftereffects of stress (e.g., S. Cohen, 1980; Holmes & Rahe, 1967; Rahe, 1987).

As critical as they are for understanding bodily responses to threat or challenge, these theories were also important because they introduced the notion that the nervous and endocrine systems jointly produced the arousal state characteristic of stress. Cannon incorporated emotional activation in his physiological model of stress, but Selye did not consider more psychologically relevant events or dynamics directly. Despite this, Selye was responsible for popularizing the construct and made stress theory more accessible and readily integrated into independent and parallel theories in the psychological literature on stress.

Psychological Theories

Psychological theories of stress that developed largely independent of work on its biological bases, focused on variability of response to stressors. Lazarus (1966) emphasized the contribution of the individual to the interaction with an environmental stressor. Like Mason, Lazarus argued that people actively perceived and reacted to stressors and there was considerable individual variation in this experience. The occurrence of an event alone was not sufficient to induce stress. Instead, the notion of appraisal, or cognitive interpretation of the stressor, was introduced and integrated into a trans- actional model. For stress to be experienced, it was necessary for an individual to appraise the event as threatening or harmful. Stress appraisals then elicited negative emotions, but unlike other models, it was the appraisal of the event, and not the emotional reaction, that determined subsequent physiological and behavioral responses. Additional appraisal processes were used by the individual to determine what available coping strategies could be used to deal with the situation and whether the problem should be attacked or accommodated.

The primary appraisals and perceived stress in this theory were important because they suggested that psychological variables or CNS activity mediate the relation between stressful events and bodily reactions. Rather than an unidirectional process originating from the occurrence of a stressor, Lazarus conceptualized stress as a dynamic process in which an individual was constantly reappraising the situation as new information was obtained. Lazarus and Folkman (1984) later expanded on this model and defined stress as the "particular relationship between the person and the environment that is appraised by the person as taxing or exceeding his or her resources and endangering his or her well-being" (p. 19). Central to this model were the processes of cognitive appraisals and coping, both of which mediated this relation and determined stress-related outcomes.

The model of stress proposed first by Lazarus (1966) and then by Lazarus and Folkman (1984) focused on the transactional process between the individual and the environment. However, Hobfoll (1989) argued that such a definition was circular in nature and hard to test. In order to make the stress relation more specific, he based his conceptualization of stress on a model of conservation of resources. Individuals actively sought to gain and maintain resources, and stress occurred in response to the actual loss, threat of loss, or lack of gain of these resources. Individuals reacted to either real or perceived loss of resources by trying to minimize the amount of loss experienced. Although this model was more parsimonious than the Lazarus and Folkman (1984) model, it was still consistent with their general framework of appraisals of loss or threat leading to stress.

Defining Stress

A unifying theme in many of these theories is adaptation and adjustment to changes in a person's environment. Selye (1956/1984) argued that life involves constant change and adaptation. Much of this is minor and hardly noticed, not unlike the continual adjustments a person makes to the steering wheel of a car while driving it. The grooves and bumps in the road represent an uneven environment that requires small changes in steering to maintain a straight path not unlike minor or routine stressors that are encountered every day. Major stressors present dangers more similar to oncoming cars; they require more dramatic and memorable efforts to avoid collision or driving off the road. Each adjustment involves a specific response (e.g., the minor adjustment of the wheel or more effortful maneuvering to avoid other cars). Each also appears to have a nonspecific component, composed largely of SNS and HPA arousal and bodily "support" for cognitive or behavioral adjustments. When these adjustments are more substantial or sudden, they may also affect mood and behavior. Regardless, this nonspecific arousal both motivates and supports coping, making it faster, "stronger," and more effective in accomplishing the adjustments needed to adapt. Collectively, the specific coping directed at threatening, harmful, or otherwise upsetting situations and the nonspecific activation supporting these responses may be considered "stress."

There remains considerable variability in the way stress is defined or conceptualized. Consistent with the previous emphasis on adjustment and adaptation, stress can be described as "a negative emotional experience accompanied by predictable biochemical, physiological, and behavioral changes that are directed toward adaptation either by manipulating the situation to alter the stressor or by accommodating its effects" (Baum, 1990, p. 653). When challenged or threatened, both specific adjustments and supportive nonspecific activation are likely and both continue until the source of stress is eliminated or the individual has successfully accommodated its effects. In this context, stress is an adaptive process with the goal of either altering a stressful situation or adjusting to and minimizing its negative effects. When confronted with a stressor, the body responds in ways consistent with a catabolic fight or flight reaction. Negative health effects occur when these emergency responses are extreme or prolonged. Additionally, variability in the stress process occurs through the influence of factors that affect appraisal of stressors and coping efforts.

Methodological Approaches

Although these general and more specific models of stress models have guided many studies, individual researchers' operational definitions of stress have varied. Historically there has been an emphasis on the stimulus or stressor end of the model, often either measuring outcomes after an organism confronts a particular stressor or counting the number of accumulating life events. Other researchers focus on the emotional, physiological, or behavioral responses to stressors and use these responses to predict physical and mental health. More researchers are beginning to integrate these two elements and incorporate measures of person characteristics, such as appraisal and coping, to more accurately predict who is more resilient or more vulnerable to stress.

Stimulus-based approaches often compare groups of organisms either exposed or not exposed to a particular stressor. Acute stress is often manipulated in the laboratory using administered stimuli such as noise, immobilization, and electric shock (in animals) and challenging mental tasks or threatening situations (in humans). Naturally occurring events are also examined, such as residential crowding, ambient noise, natural disasters, or life threatening accidents. Differences across levels of exposure allow researchers to determine the impact of the stressor on physical and mental health outcomes. Another common approach is to ask participants to indicate which of a list of events occurred within a given time frame (e.g., 6–12 months). Participants can also rate each event on the amount of adjustment required to adapt to the stressor. The relations observed between life event measures and outcomes were consistent but usually modest, with life events generally accounting for less than 9% of the variance in outcome measures (for reviews see Rahe, 1972; Sarason, de Monchaux, & Hunt, 1975; Zimmerman, 1983).

Substantial improvements have been made in the prediction of outcomes through the use of personal interviews, such as the Life Events and Difficulties Schedule (LEDS; G. W. Brown & Harris, 1989). Through the use of interview techniques, specific information regarding the actual event and its context can be gathered and rated by objective reviewers. Therefore, many of the response errors and sources of bias inherent in self-report measures can be minimized. Unfortunately, extensive training of interviewers and raters, as well as costs associated with lengthy individual visits with study participants, limit the feasibility of this approach. However, the incorporation of the contextual meaning of the events rather than just the occurrence of the event has increased the magnitude of the relations found between life stress and outcomes. Using this method, researchers have demonstrated that life events and chronic difficulties contribute to the risk of developing many mental and physical conditions, such as depression, schizophrenia, anxiety, myocardial infarction, multiple sclerosis, abdominal pain, and menstrual disorders (for a review, see G. W. Brown & Harris, 1989). More recently, chronic stress measured in this way has been linked to susceptibility to viral infection (S. Cohen et al., 1998). Clearly, identification of objective predictors of mental and physical health outcomes is valuable for the prediction of stress consequences. However, such an approach reveals little about the way stress works or why it has these effects.

Other theories and measures of stress focus more intently on responses, arguing that it is the response that is most closely linked to outcomes or consequences and the extent to which the event is experienced as stressful is a better metric than is the event itself. In controlled laboratory settings or in naturalistic environments, researchers can measure cognitive, behavioral, and physiological changes before, during, and/or after a stressor. Changes in these response systems can then be correlated with physical and mental health outcomes.

Individual difference variables or other factors affecting how stressful events are experienced are also important predictors of both responses and outcomes. Situational factors affecting appraisals of stressors and a person's ability to resist them, as well as individual differences in appraisal or response, are critical determinants of outcomes.

There are many important intervening variables that affect interactions of the perceiver and the situation and affect appraisals of severity or the likelihood of successful adaptation. Among the more frequently studied stress mediators are perceptions of control, predictability, coping, and the availability of social support (Aldwin & Revenson, 1987; S. Cohen & Wills, 1985; Glass & Singer, 1972; Lazarus & Folkman, 1984; Skinner, 1995; Uchino, Cacioppo, & Kiecolt-Glaser, 1996). Individuals with greater perceptions of control and more social support, as well as situations characterized by appraisals of greater predictability, typically produce less stress and better outcomes. One reason for these differential effects may be the availability of and the types of coping strategies used to deal with the event. When individuals perceive that they can control the event, it may promote the use of more problem-focused techniques or greater acceptance, thereby alleviating much of the distress experienced. Additionally, greater predictability of the event allows individuals to prepare in the time before the event to deal effectively with the situation. Similarly, perceptions of available social support may serve to enhance the coping resources of individuals through offers of tangible aid or advice.

ACUTE AND CHRONIC STRESS

Not all exposures to stressors are equal and it can probably be assumed that more or worse exposures have more impact than fewer or less severe exposures. Stressor intensity and duration likely interact to produce a range of potential effects. The most common distinction between acute and chronic stress is based on the duration of the stressor. However, as already noted, there is inter- and intraindividual variability in stress responding even to the same stressor. Therefore, acute and chronic stress may best be conceptualized by examining the interactions among the duration of the event itself (acute or chronic), the duration of threat perception (acute or chronic), and the duration of psychological, physiological, or behavioral responses (acute or chronic; Baum, O'Keeffe, & Davidson, 1990).

A "perfect acute" stress situation would refer to a situation characterized by an acute stressor duration, short-lived threat perception, and an acute response, typical of most laboratory stress situations. A subject in a laboratory study of stress is normally exposed to a brief (5–30 minutes) stressor (or combination of stressors), views it as stressful for as long as it is present, and recovers rapidly after termination of the stressor. Chronic stress, however, is more complex. A "perfect chronic" situation would refer to a chronic event, chronic threat, and chronic responding. In reality, most stressful experiences consist of combinations of acute and chronic durations of the event, threat, and response, and this characterization may not be stable. For instance, following a hurricane (an acute event), an individual may continue to experience perceived threat or harm and may exhibit chronic responding—such as elevations in norepinephrine (NE), epinephrine (EPI), cortisol, heart rate (HR), and blood pressure (BP)—and reductions in immune system functions. However, over time the individual may start to habituate to the chronic threat and show decreased stress responding (i.e., chronic threat with short-lived responding). The goal for stress reduction is for the individual to adapt to the stress situation and no longer perceive the chronic threat or respond to it. Unfortunately, not all individuals habituate or adapt to a stressor, and chronic stress persists or can even sensitize people to new stressors.

The alterations seen in the physiological, cognitive, and behavioral response systems are generally the same in both acute and chronic stress situations, but where acute stress occurs continuously, chronic stress does not appear to be a steady-state phenomenon. Rather, responding appears to be episodic, occurring repeatedly throughout the day as reminders or unwanted intrusions accost an individual. This appears to be the case whether the stressor is still present or long past. It is unlikely that an individual is conscious of a stressor 24 hours a day, 7 days a week, 365 days a year. Instead, it seems more likely that people experience good and bad days and good and bad moments within each day. Episodes of stress may be triggered by exposures to the event, reminders of the event, or anticipation of the event. Most models of stress fail to consider the impact of this repetitive activation of stress response systems, or the possibility that the experience of chronic stress may be best characterized as acute episodes of stress related to an overarching stressor.

The episodic nature of chronic stress is supported by evidence that although certain populations report higher levels of distress than comparison groups, there is considerable day-to-day and within-day variations among individuals within the group (Dougall, Baum, & Jenkins, 1998; Stone, Reed, & Neale, 1987). These variations average to consistent high levels over longer time frames. In addition to these daily fluctuations, the response systems themselves do not always covary. Each system has it own circadian or activity-based pattern of ups and downs, as well as different reactivity and recovery times (e.g., Mason, 1968; Nesse et al., 1985). For example, EPI and NE show immediate increases in response to an acute stressor, whereas cortisol responses are delayed and last much longer. Therefore, single assessments limit an individuals view of the stress process.

It is not hard to understand why an individual faced with daily stressors (e.g., hectic commutes to work or longtime care giving to a sick relative) experiences stress or excessive demand when dealing with them. Persistence of chronic stress responding after an event is long over is harder to explain and is an important question for stress researchers to tackle. It has been suggested that one important element in understanding chronic stress is the occurrence of stressor-related intrusive thoughts, especially in the absence of an ongoing stressor (Baum, L. Cohen, & Hall, 1993; Baum, Schooler, & Dougall, 1998; Craig, Heisler, & Baum, 1996). Plenty of evidence suggests that stressor-related intrusive thoughts are a common symptom following threatening events (e.g., Baider & De-Nour, 1997; Delahanty, Dougall, Craig, Jenkins, & Baum, 1997; Delahanty, Herberman, et al., 1997; Ironson et al., 1997). Intrusive thoughts are thought to be part of ongoing cognitive processing of the event (Creamer, Burgess, & Pattison, 1992; Greenberg, 1995; Horowitz, 1986). They help an individual work through the situation. Indeed, as individuals recover, they report fewer stressor-related intrusions (e.g., Delahanty, Dougall et al., 1997). However, intrusive thoughts tend to be unwanted, unbidden, and uncontrollable, which are characteristics common to many other types of stressors. In at least some cases, these characteristics of intrusive thoughts may make them more stressful and are related to greater chronic stress (e.g., Dougall, Craig, & Baum, 1999). Rather than being exclusively adaptive, these thoughts may serve as stressors in their own right, possibly sensitizing individuals to other reminiscent stimuli. Intrusions combined with other environmental event-related stimuli may serve to perpetuate chronic stress by eliciting the acute episodes described earlier.

Trauma and Chronic Stress

Intrusive thoughts are most prevalent following extreme stressors. However, they do occur following less severe events and even after benign and positive events that occur in everyday life (Berntsen, 1996). Although positive and neutral intrusions also occur, intrusive thoughts with negative valences are implicated in chronic stress and are probably one of the most salient hallmark symptoms of posttraumatic stress disorder (PTSD; American Psychiatric Association, 1994). Posttraumatic stress disorder is a special case of extreme stress responding following life threatening or extreme stressors. It has broad base effects across all domains of functioning, impairing an individual's ability to function normally. Victims experience the persistent recurrence of three categories of symptoms: reexperiencing or reliving the event, emotional numbing and avoidance of trauma-related stimuli, and heightened physiological arousal (APA, 1994). In addition to intrusive thoughts, victims experience other common symptoms such as recurrent and disruptive dreams, sleep disturbances, emotional withdrawal, anxiety, dissociation, aggressiveness, hyperarousal, and an exaggerated startle response (APA, 1994).

Posttraumatic stress disorder is also characterized by unusual physiological response profiles. When victims are reminded of the trauma, cardiovascular, respiratory, and negative emotional responses are typically more exaggerated compared with reactivity to unrelated stimuli. As in chronic stress situations, circulating levels of EPI, NE, and their metabolites are elevated (Kosten, Mason, Giller, Ostroff, & Harkness, 1987; Mason, Giller, Kosten, & Harkness, 1988; Mason, Giller, Kosten, Ostroff, & Podd, 1986; Yehuda, Southwick, Giller, Ma, & Mason, 1992). This chronic adrenergic activation is accompanied by down regulation of noradrenergic receptors, thereby helping to sustain the increased output (Lerer, Gur, Bleich, & Newman, 1994; Murburg, Ashleigh, Hommer, & Veith, 1994; Yatham, Sacamano, & Kusumakar, 1996). In contrast, the alterations in the functioning of the HPA axis appear to result in suppressed release of glucocorticoids (i.e., cortisol in humans; Kosten et al., 1987; Yehuda, Boisoneau, Mason, & Giller, 1993; Yehuda et al., 1990). This dysregulation appears to be the result of a blunted pituitary adrenocorticotropic hormone (ACTH) response to corticotropin releasing factor (CRF) from the hypothalamus (Yehuda, Giller, Levengood, Southwick, & Siever, 1995; Yehuda, Resnick, Kahana, & Giller, 1993). ACTH travels to the adrenal cortex where it stimulates release of cortisol. Because less ACTH is released, less cortisol is elicited. In addition to these alterations, there is an up regulation of glucocorticoid receptors on lymphocytes, probably due to the low circulating levels of glucocorticoids (Yehuda, Boisoneau, Lowy, & Giller, 1995; Yehuda, Lowy, Southwick, Shaffer, & Giller, 1991). The presence of large numbers of receptors may also regulate the transient hypersecretion of cortisol seen in PTSD patients in response to a novel stressor or acute symptomatology (Yehuda et al., 1990; Yehuda, Resnick, et al., 1993).

The experience of trauma is not limited by the physical presence of the precipitating event. Despite the often acute nature of traumatic events, responding may last for months or years. Additionally, time of onset is not limited to the time of exposure, and episodes of acute and chronic PTSD have been defined based on whether or not symptoms last less than or more than 3 months (APA, 1994). Although individual symptoms of PTSD predict subsequent diagnosis, not all of the symptoms need to be present for a diagnosis to occur. Additionally, many of these same symptoms are exaggerations of normal stress reactions to an overwhelming event and may in fact serve to promote adaptation to such a situation. This is consistent with the pervasive finding that a majority of trauma victims do not develop PTSD, but there are still a significant number of victims (approximately 25%) who are affected (Green, 1994).

These considerations suggest that it is important to identify factors in the environment or in the individual that affect whether or not an individual experiences symptoms of posttraumatic stress or ultimately develops PTSD. Several vulnerability factors have been identified, such as a genetic predisposition to heightened autonomic arousal and a history of psychopathology (e.g., Foy, Resnick, Sipprelle, & Carroll, 1987; Goldberg, True, Eisen, & Henderson, 1990; True et al., 1993), as well as factors that influence normal stress responses such as gender, social class, social support, perceived control, and coping (for reviews see Gibbs, 1989; Green, 1994; Vitaliano, Maiuro, Bolton, & Armsden, 1987).

STRESS RESPONSES AND CONSEQUENCES

Emerging models of stress consider a range of responses and consequences of stress that bear on productivity, health, and well-being. Stress affects mood, behavior, and problem solving, changes individuals' motivation to achieve goals or engage in self-protective behavior, and appears to lessen restraints against harmful behaviors. Stress affects the whole body. The effects of stress on the SNS and the HPA axis were documented in the seminal work of Selye (1956/1984) and

Cannon (1914). These systems contribute to stimulation of others and exert direct and indirect effects on metabolism and arousal. Changes in these response systems are thought to account for some of the effects of stress on health, but are consistent with a mobilization of energy, and as such are inherently adaptive. Increases in heart rate and blood pressure, as well as increases in the release of neuroendocrines such as EPI, NE, ACTH, glucocorticoids, and prolactin prepare an individual to face a stressor and fight or to flee from the scene. Additionally, stress-related decreases in several markers of immune system functioning have been observed (for reviews see Herbert & S. Cohen, 1993; O'Leary, 1990). These changes could be adaptive, in that when an organism is injured in battle, the swelling, fever, and other characteristics of an immune response are delayed and therefore do not interfere with the actions of the organism. However, prolonged suppression of a variety of functions could open windows of heightened vulnerability to infection or progression of neoplastic disease.

In addition to physiological changes, stress can increase negative emotions such as depression, anxiety, anger, fear, and overall symptom reporting. Unwanted or uncontrollable thoughts and memories about a stressor may also be experienced (Baider & De-Nour, 1997; Delahanty, Dougall, et al., 1997; Delahanty, Herberman, et al., 1997; Ironson et al., 1997). These stressor-related intrusions are both a symptom of stress and a stressor in their own right. Painful event-related images and thoughts may elicit their own stress response and may help to perpetuate chronic stress responding by repeatedly exposing an individual to the stressor.

Stress also affects performance. Because attention is typically focused on dealing with stressors when they are present, people may have problems attending to more mundane tasks, such as balancing a checking account, monitoring computer screens, or assembling a product (for reviews see Baba et al., 1998; Cooper, 1988; Kompier & DiMartino, 1995; Krueger, 1989; McNally, 1997). Unfortunately, many of these tasks may be work or safety related (e.g., writing a report or driving an automobile) and could have severe consequences if done improperly. Further, exposure to even a brief laboratory stressor has been shown to induce transient performance deficits in tasks given during the stressor or after it (Glass & Singer, 1972). These negative aftereffects occur even though physiological and emotional responding has decreased and the individual appears to have adapted to the acute stressor. Other consequences of stress include deterioration of sleep quality and quantity, increases in aggressive behaviors, and changes in appetitive behaviors such as eating, drinking, and smoking (e.g., Conway, Vickers, Weid, & Rahe, 1981; Ganley, 1989; Grunberg & Baum, 1985; Mellman, 1997; Sadeh, 1996; Spaccarelli, Bowden, Coatsworth, & Kim, 1997). These wide-reaching effects of stress illustrate the importance of examining the effects of stress on the whole organism rather than focusing on one system such as the SNS, reports of depression, or alcohol use. Responses across all systems work in concert to help the individual adapt by either altering the situation or accommodating its effects. Whereas these biological, cognitive, and behavioral alterations may be adaptive in the short-term, chronic activation of these response systems results in wear and tear on the organism and may make the organism more susceptible to negative mental and physical health outcomes.

Stress and Health

Stress can affect health as well as intervene at any point in the disease process: in disease etiology, progression, treatment, recovery, or recurrence. Stress exerts these effects in three basic ways: as direct physiological changes resulting from stress-related arousal (e.g., immunosuppression, damage to blood vessels), as cognitive and behavioral changes that convey physiological changes (e.g., intrusive thoughts, smoking, drug use), and as physiological, cognitive, and behavioral changes associated with an individual's illness that affect exposure or treatment (e.g., viral exposure, drug metabolism, treatment adherence, seeking medical help). As discussed later, stress has important implications for the onset, progression, and treatment of almost every known major disease.

Although often difficult to measure, stress appears to affect pathogenic processes that contribute to the onset of disease. One of the most salient mechanisms through which stress can promote disease is through chronic, sustained, and/or exaggerated responses, making them pathological. Prolonged feelings of depression or anxiety can interrupt normal functioning and result in the development of clinical disorders, whereas transient alterations in mood are considerably less harmful (e.g., Kendler et al., 1995; Terrazas, Gutierrez, & Lopez, 1987). Continued self-medication or use of licit or illicit drugs may lead to addiction, and eating disorders may develop from extreme alterations in eating behaviors (e.g., Grunberg & Baum, 1985; Meyer, 1997; Sharpe, Ryst, Hinshaw, & Steiner, 1997). Prolonged or often-repeated elevations in blood pressure may result in permanent changes contributing to hypertension and elevated circulating levels of stress hormones may contribute to atherosclerosis and heart disease (Markovitz & Matthews, 1991). Chronic immune system suppression appears to interfere with the ability to ward off pathogens making individuals more susceptible to infectious diseases such as colds, flu, and Human Immunodeficiency Virus (HIV) disease (for reviews see Dorian & Garfinkel, 1987; O'Leary, 1990). Stress also appears to affect tumor suppression and progression of cancer (e.g., Ben-Eliyahu, Yirmiya, Liebeskind, Taylor, & Gale, 1991; Bohus, Koolhaas, de Ruiter, & Heijnen, 1992; Stefanski & Ben-Eliyahu, 1996). Although exhaustive evaluations of the direct role of stress in disease etiology are hard to conduct, recent evidence from studies of controlled viral challenges and wound healing confirm the clinically relevant impact of stress on health and disease (e.g., Cohen et al., 1998; Kiecolt-Glaser, Marucha, Malarkey, Mercado, & Glaser, 1995; Marucha, Kiecolt-Glaser, & Favagehi, 1998; Stone et al., 1992).

Behavioral and cognitive deficits seen during stress can also affect disease by increasing an individual's chance of exposure to pathogenic agents. Individuals under stress are more likely to engage in high risk behaviors like unprotected sex and intravenous drug use (Demas, Schoenbaum, Wills, Doll, & Klein, 1995; Harvey & Spigner, 1995; Hastings, Anderson, & Hemphill, 1997). These activities increase the likelihood that an individual will be exposed to an infectious disease or experience unplanned consequences such as pregnancy. As already discussed, decrements in performance can result in dismissal from work or injury and death as a result of inattention and lack of concentration while engaging in important activities, such as driving a car or operating machinery (for reviews see Baba et al., 1998; Cooper, 1988; Kompier & DiMartino, 1995; Krueger, 1989; McNally, 1997). Stress-related behaviors such as smoking, alcohol use, and sedentary lifestyles may also contribute to etiology of serious health problems (R. M. Kaplan, Sallis, & Patterson, 1993).

Disease progression and treatment are also affected by stress. New feelings of depression or anxiety may interfere with treatment of preexisting disorders and can increase the likelihood of acute disease events such as heart attacks (e.g., Frasure-Smith, Lesperance, & Talajic, 1995; Kamarck & Jennings, 1991; Tennant, 1985). Individuals in treatment for psychiatric disorders (e.g., schizophrenia, depression, substance use, or eating disorders) may relapse and experience a return of their symptoms or return to their abusive behaviors (e.g., Belsher & Costello, 1988; Brewer, Catalano, Haggerty, Gainey, & Fleming, 1998; S. A. Brown, Vik, Patterson, Grant, & Schuckit, 1995; Shiffman et al., 1996; Tennant, 1985). Physiological changes may also interfere with the metabolism of prescription drugs (Katzung, 1992; Zorzet, Perissin, Rapozzi, & Giraldi, 1998), and behavioral and cognitive stress effects may impair treatment, reducing the likelihood that patients comply with instructions, prescriptions, and recommendations given by their medical teams (e.g., Brickman & Yount, 1996; Mehta, Moore, & Graham, 1997). Additionally, transient stressors, especially those producing strong emotions such as depression, anxiety, or outward expressions of anger, can promote platelet aggregation, contributing to the underlying cardiovascular disease state, or can trigger acute cardiac events such as myocardial infarction and sudden cardiac death (e.g., Frasure-Smith et al., 1995; Mendes de Leon, 1992; Wenneberg et al., 1997).

Stress can also retard the speed of recovery, make adjustment to diseases and injuries harder, and increase the rates of disease recurrence. Patients who report more stress have a harder time recovering from and adjusting to illnesses or injuries than individuals who report less stress (e.g., Grassi & Rosti, 1996; Kiecolt-Glaser, Stephens, Lipetz, Speicher, & Glaser, 1995; Marucha et al., 1998; Mullins, Chaney, Pace, & Hartman, 1997). Additionally, stress management interventions given prior to surgery or other medical procedures have improved healing and rehabilitation afterward (e.g., Enqvist & Fischer, 1997; Ross & Berger, 1996). Stress may also make patients in remission more vulnerable to recurrence of their disease; among people with latent viruses (e.g., HSV, EBV), stress has been linked to reactivation of the viruses and disease symptoms (e.g., Jenkins & Baum, 1995; Kiecolt-Glaser, Fisher et al., 1987; Kiecolt-Glaser, Glaser et al., 1987; Kiecolt-Glaser et al., 1988). Stress has also been linked with recurrence of cancer, which is possibly a result of its immunosuppressive effects (Baltrusch, Stangel, & Titze, 1991).

Most of these health effects are linked with episodes of long-term or chronic stress. However, acute stressors may also affect health by making an individual more vulnerable during a time of exposure to an infectious agent or by triggering acute events such as heart attacks (as discussed earlier). The difference between acute and chronic stress is not always clearly defined, and most of the models already discussed fail to make a distinction between the two. Closer examination of the meaning and implications of short- and long-term stress needs to be addressed before examining the relation between stress and disease more closely.

STRESS AND DISEASE

Although stress affects everyday functioning and well-being, its more profound consequences are manifest as influences on disease processes. Whereas the effects of stress on the immune system are one putative mechanism for explaining the relation between stress and disease, other stress response systems affect disease processes as well. Further, these effects are apparent at several levels and stages of ill health. By examining the effects of stress on some major diseases, the importance of stress in the disease process as well as the integration of whole body responses are highlighted.

In addition to the effects of stress on the onset, management, and recovery from disease, there is evidence to suggest that people with chronic diseases experience more stress, that is, that these illnesses (or aspects of their management) can cause stress. Patients tend to report more social problems and psychological symptoms than people in the general population and more psychiatric morbidity has been associated with poorer disease management (e.g., Dougall et al., 1998; Irvine, B. Brown, Crooks, Roberts, & Browne, 1991; Mayou, Peveler, Davies, Mann, & Fairburn, 1991; Mullins et al., 1997). This bidirectional relation between stress and disease has lead researchers to propose that in some cases a vicious cycle develops, in which chronic diseases predispose individuals to psychiatric symptoms and social problems that then impair self-care and result in poor disease management. Disease flare-ups, recurrence, or increases in symptoms then further exacerbate psychiatric symptoms and social problems (e.g., Mayou et al., 1991).

Stress and Immune-Mediated Disease

One of the most salient mechanisms through which stress can make an individual more vulnerable to disease is the link between stress and immune functioning. Both acute and chronic stress have been linked with decreases in immune system activity (for reviews see Herbert & S. Cohen, 1993; O'Leary, 1990). These instances of immunosuppression could render the body less able to fight off pathogens or recover from injuries. Researchers have documented consistent decreases in the ability of lymphocytes to proliferate when challenged with a known pathogen (Bachen et al., 1992; Delahanty et al., 1996; Kiecolt-Glaser, Fisher, et al., 1987; Zakowski, L. Cohen, Hall,

Wollman, & Baum, 1994). These decreases in lymphocyte functioning are seen in both acute and chronic stress situations.

Researchers have also examined alterations in the functioning of immune cells involved in faster acting natural immunity. Natural killer (NK) cells are large granular lymphocytes that act quickly to destroy viral and cancer cells (Moretta, Ciccone, Mingari, Biassoni, & Moretta, 1994), but are affected differently by acute and chronic stress. Decreases in the number and capacity of NK cells to lyse tumor cells in vitro have been observed in populations exposed to chronic stress (e.g., Esterling, Kiecolt-Glaser, Bodnar, & Glaser, 1994; Ironson et al., 1997). However, alterations in NK cell activity in response to acute stress are more dynamic. Initially there appears to be an increase in NK cell activity, followed by a rebound decrease and then recovery to baseline (Delahanty et al., 1996; Schedlowski et al., 1993). Additionally, stress can interfere with seroconversion following Hepatitis B vaccination, decreasing the amount of protection normally afforded (Glaser et al., 1992).

These immune system alterations appear to be related to SNS activation (i.e., increases in heart rate, blood pressure, and catecholamines). Greater SNS activation has been associated with larger alterations in immune functioning (for reviews see Cacioppo, 1994; Esquifino & Cardinali, 1994). Changes in immune system parameters, such as numbers of lymphocytes and their ability to proliferate or lyse other cells, have been correlated with changes in cardiovascular arousal (specifically, changes in blood pressure and heart rate) and plasma catecholamine levels (L. Cohen, Delahanty, Schmitz, Jenkins, & Baum, 1993; Delahanty et al., 1996; Schedlowski et al., 1993; Zakowski et al., 1994). Additionally, adrenergic blockade before challenge has been shown to ameliorate immune system changes to a laboratory stressor (Bachen et al., 1995), and cardiovascular reactivity to a stressful task has been used to examine differences in stress-related immune responses (Caggiula et al., 1995; Herbert et al., 1994; Manuck, S. Cohen, Rabin, Muldoon, & Bachen, 1991; Zakowski, McAllister, Deal, & Baum, 1992). Measured as changes in blood pressure and heart rate associated with a stressor, people who exhibit higher reactivity to a laboratory challenge also exhibit larger immune changes. Psychological variables such as control, predictability, social support, and availability of a behavioral response have also been shown to mediate immune system alterations associated with stress. In general, uncontrollable or unpredictable stressors or situations affording little social support produce greater immunosuppression (e.g., Baron, Cutrona, Hicklin, Russell, & Lubaroff, 1990; Kennedy, Kiecolt-Glaser, & Glaser, 1988; Sieber, Rodin, Larson, Ortega, & Cummings, 1992; Wiedenfeld et al., 1990; Zakowski, 1995).

Infectious Illness. Infectious illness refers to diseases caused by pathogens (e.g., virus, bacteria) that is communicable between two or more individuals. Primary defenses against these illnesses are immune system activity that seeks to control and destroy infectious agents. Because stress is associated with periods of lowered immune activity, it should also be associated with less resistance to infectious illnesses. Research in both controlled and natural settings provides support for the contention that stress is associated with vulnerability to infectious illness (for reviews see Biondi & Zannino, 1997; S. Cohen & Williamson, 1991; Kiecolt-Glaser & Glaser, 1995; McEwen & Stellar, 1993). In natural environments, increases in stress often precede the onset of illnesses (Kasl, Evans, & Niederman, 1979; Rahe, 1972; Stone et al., 1987). Additionally, physiological reactivity moderates the effects of stress on illness, with high reactors developing more respiratory infections than low reactors (Boyce et al., 1995). Reactivations of latent viral infections such as herpes simplex virus (HSV) and Epstein–Barr virus (EBV) also appear more likely when individuals are experiencing ongoing stress (Kiecolt-Glaser, Fisher et al., 1987; Kiecolt-Glaser, Glaser et al., 1987; Kiecolt-Glaser et al., 1988).

In addition to these correlational studies, recent advances in measurement procedures have made it possible to conduct studies in controlled environments, confirming that individuals with high levels of life stress are more likely to become infected and display symptoms when exposed to cold viruses (S. Cohen et al., 1998; Stone et al., 1992). In these studies, healthy participants are typically exposed to known amounts of a cold virus and then quarantined in a hotel room for 5 or more days. There are two major disease outcomes that are examined. One outcome is the rate of viral infection, typically ranging from 69% to 100% of the sample exposed to the virus, and the other is the actual incidence of cold symptoms, ranging from 19% to 71% of the sample (S. Cohen et al., 1998; S. Cohen, Tyrrell, & Smith, 1991; Stone et al., 1992). Although individuals cannot have cold symptoms without being infected, they can be infected without showing signs of a cold. Rates of both viral infection and cold symptoms increase in a dose–response fashion with the amount of life stress the participants report (S. Cohen et al., 1991, 1998; Stone et al., 1992). More severe and chronic stressors tend to have a greater impact on disease development than less severe or acute stressors (S. Cohen et al., 1998).

Cancer. The relations among stress, immunity, and cancer appear to be more complex than those underlying the pathophysiology of infectious diseases. In part, this is due to the chronic nature of cancer and the more acute time frames of most infections. In addition, immune activity has an unknown role in controlling initial mutations or in the process from benign to malignant neoplastic growth and a suspected but underexplored role in resistance to tumor growth and metastatic spread. There is better general evidence that stress is associated with cancer progression and may be linked to survival as well as general susceptibility, risk, and quality of life. Again, problems related to the chronic nature of cancer development and treatment have made studies of stress and cancer incidence difficult, and research on disease course, recurrence, survival, and so on share similar problems.

These problems have often left the literature linking stress and cancer weak and open to alternative explanations. Inconsistent findings are also an issue, with studies reporting significant and nonsignificant association of depression and cancer (e.g., Hahn & Petitti, 1988; G. A. Kaplan & Reynolds,

1988; Shekelle et al., 1981; Zonderman, Costa, & McCrae, 1989) and few relations between bereavement or other major stressors and the development of cancer (e.g., Jones & Goldblatt, 1986; Keehn, Goldberg, & Beebe, 1974). Significant loss in a 6-year prodromal period predicted breast cancer in one study (Forsen, 1991), but overall there is little evidence of direct stress effects in the development of cancer (e.g., Fox, 1978, 1983). Again, problems of timing and tracking of disease-related events makes this research difficult and uncontrolled. Tumors develop over years or decades and grow irregularly. Further, several different mutagenic events are needed to produce malignancy, suggesting several points at which stress could affect initial development. Mechanisms such as cellular DNA repair have been proposed and some studies have linked stress to poorer DNA repair capabilities (e.g., Kiecolt-Glaser et al., 1985), but in general there is no evidence of stress-related repair suppression as a component of cancer onset.

There is better evidence of stress-related modulation of cancer course and some of immune system involvement, focusing principally on NK cell numbers and activity. Retrospective studies of life stress and cancer have suggested that stressful events are associated with shorter survival, fatigue, distress, and recurrence of breast cancer (Funch & Marshall, 1983; Ramirez et al., 1989). Some investigators have not found evidence of life stress associations with cancer course (Ell, Nishimoto, Mediansky, Mantell, & Hamovitch, 1992; Greer, Morris, & Pettingale, 1979; Hislop, Waxler, Coldman, Elwood, & Kan, 1987; Jamison, Burish, & Wallston, 1987). Studies have not consistently studied the impact of cancer-related stress on disease course, nor has systematic consideration of stressor timing issues, coping, or social assets been characteristic of this work. However, coping, social support, and other stress mediators are associated with length of survival among cancer patients (Dean & Surtees, 1989; Goodwin, Hunt, Key, & Samet, 1987; Greer et al., 1979; Hislop et al., 1987; Levy et al., 1990; Neale, Tilley, & Vernon, 1986).

Stress has considerable influence on the number and activity of NK cells, presumably through stimulation and inhibition associated with neuroendocrine activity during stress (e.g., Kiecolt-Glaser & Glaser, 1992; O'Leary, 1990; Schedlowski et al., 1993; Schneiderman & Baum, 1992). Further studies have found that stress, social support, and fatigue or depression are related to NK activity in cancer patients and differences in NK activity appear to be related to prognostic risk (Levy, Herberman, Lippman, & D'Angelo, 1987; Levy, Herberman, Lippman, D'Angelo, & Lee, 1991; Levy, Herberman, Maluish, Schlien, & Lippman, 1985). Aparicio-Pages, Verspaget, Pena, Jansen, and Lamers (1991) found evidence of NK activity predicting disease course in GI cancer, but only among patients who exhibited NK activity in normal ranges.

Perhaps the best evidence for stress effects on cancer course are results of stress-reducing psychological interventions for cancer patients. These interventions appear to have the capacity to extend survival and bolster immune system activity. These issues are dealt with in greater detail elsewhere in this Handbook (see chap. 46, this volume). It is sufficient to conclude here that the evidence that stress affects cancer course is suggestive and encouraging but far from definitive or complete.

Stress and Heart Disease

Stress can be implicated throughout the natural history of coronary heart disease (CHD), in its formation, progression, and in triggering a cardiac event. Stress affects CHD mainly through its influences on behavioral factors and activation of the autonomic nervous system (ANS; Kamarck & Jennings, 1991). In particular, stress activates the SNS resulting in increases in epinephrine and norepinephrine that lead to increased beta and alpha receptor activity (Kamarck & Jennings, 1991; Markovitz & Matthews, 1991). Briefly, beta activation increases heart rate and heart contractility, therefore increasing cardiac output and blood pressure (Guyton, 1991). Alpha activation causes vasoconstriction of the arteries and veins and causes increases in total peripheral resistance and venous return, both of which increase blood pressure (Guyton, 1991). All of these physiological events may contribute to CHD. For example, with an increase in blood flow, shear stress on the arteries is increased causing cells in the blood to be damaged and plaque to form and/or rupture (Traub & Berk, 1998). This, along with sharp increases in epinephrine, stimulates platelet activation and the sequelae that follow (Markovitz & Matthews, 1991; Wenneberg et al., 1997). Activation of the parasympathetic nervous system (PNS) can have opposite effects on the heart and blood vessels, and extensive PNS activation can also lead to cardiac events (Lane, Adcock, & Burnett, 1992; Podrid, 1984).

Stress can contribute to atherosclerosis and other underlying CHD processes by increasing heart rate and decreasing diastolic and washout periods in recirculation zones leading to increased contact of the blood constituents and vessel walls (Markovitz & Matthews, 1991; Traub & Berk, 1998). Platelet aggregation, along with coronary vasoconstriction and plaque rupture, can lead to other priming processes such as thrombosis, ischemia, and acute myocardial infarction. As discussed earlier, stress and its related emotional indices (e.g., hostility) increase platelet aggregation through induction of the ANS (Kamarck & Jennings, 1991; Markovitz & Matthews, 1991; Wenneberg et al., 1997).

Psychological stress is also associated with transient changes in coronary circulation and metabolism along with the other coronary changes discussed earlier. Stress may reduce oxygen delivery to the heart and thereby lower the threshold for myocardial ischemia or may trigger acute arrhythmic events through activation of the ANS, making myocardial infarction more likely (e.g., Frasure-Smith et al., 1995; Jiang et al., 1996; Kaufmann et al., 1998; Natelson & Chang, 1993; Podrid, 1984; Saini & Verrier, 1989). Recent evidence has also suggested that mental stress-induced ischemic episodes are good indicators of 5-year rates of cardiac events (Jiang et al., 1996). Additionally, stress-induced silent ischemia (ischemia without angina) occurs much more frequently than is detectable by some clinical measures (see

Kop, Gottdiener, & Krantz, chap. 41, in this volume). There is also evidence that acute stress events, such as public speaking and anger provoking situations, can disrupt cardiac electrical potential and lead to arrhythmias and possibly to myocardial infarction (Mendes de Leon, 1992; Natelson & Chang, 1993; Saini & Verrier, 1989). These arrhythmic disturbances may also be linked to an individual's prevailing psychological state. For example, increased incidences of arrhythmias are associated with anxiety and depressive disorders, Type A/competitiveness, and postinfarction distress (Cameron, 1996; Frasure-Smith et al., 1995; Moser & Dracup, 1996; Rosenman, 1996; Tennant, 1987).

Stress and Diabetes

Just about every neuroendocrine system responds to stress. Hormonal control is essential for individuals with endocrine disorders, and if this control is upset by stress, the hormonal balance is lost and disease symptoms worsen. In addition to direct effects of stress on hormonal levels, stress affects many of the risk factors associated with disease onset and flare-ups, such as diet, licit and illicit drug intake, and compliance with treatment regimens.

One of the most common neuroendocrine disorders is diabetes mellitus, affecting approximately 6%, or 1 in 17, of the U.S. population (American Diabetes Association, 1997). There are two primary types of diabetes mellitus, insulin-dependent or Type I and insulin independent or Type II. Both disorders are the result of high blood glucose levels and are characterized by symptoms such as blurred vision, unexplained fatigue, and increases in thirst and urination. A primary fuel for all body cells, circulating glucose enters cells to be used through the action of another hormone called insulin. In Type I diabetes, the immune system attacks the insulin-producing cells in the pancreas slowing insulin production and decreasing the amount of glucose that can be used by cells (Bosi & Sarugeri, 1998; Schranz & Lernmark, 1998). The onset of Type I diabetes usually occurs before age 40 (more than 50% develop Type I before age 20) and is more common among Whites than other racial groups (ADA, 1997).

In contrast, Type II diabetes typically occurs later in life, with 11% of the U.S. population between age 65 and 74 having the disease (ADA, 1997). Additionally, Mexican Americans, Puerto Rican Americans, African Americans, and Native Americans have higher incidence rates than Cuban Americans and Whites. Type II diabetes develops gradually over time as the cells in the body become resistant to the effects of insulin, thereby decreasing the amount of glucose that can enter the cells to be used. Although both Type I and Type II diabetes are more prevalent when there is a family history of the disease and appear to have genetic links (Bosi & Sarugeri, 1998; Krolewski, Fogarty, & Warram, 1998; Schranz & Lernmark, 1998), Type II diabetes is also associated with several other behavioral and physiological risk factors. The most common Type II risk factors, are older age, ethnicity, being overweight, being a smoker, having high blood pressure, having high levels of fat in the blood, and being a woman who had gestational diabetes (Bloomgarden, 1998; Danne, Kordonouri, Enders, Hovener, & Weber, 1998; Ryan, 1998; Sanchez-Thorin, 1998).

Stress does not directly cause diabetes, but it may make individuals more susceptible to diabetes onset (ADA, 1997; Ionescu-Tirgoviste, Simion, Mariana, Dan, & Iulian, 1987). For example, part of the stress response is oriented toward liberation of large quantities of glucose for cells to use for energy. In Type I diabetes, stress may overwhelm the pancreas' ability to produce insulin and, as a result, unmask the diabetes sooner than the onset would normally occur. Similarly, in Type II diabetes, stress hormones interfere with insulin use in an already compromised system resulting in earlier detection of diabetic symptoms. Furthermore, stress plays a role in the risk factors associated with diabetes onset (e.g., obesity and high blood pressure) and can impact treatment by interfering with glycemic control (K. S. Aikens, J. E. Aikens, Wallander, & Hunt, 1997; J. E. Aikens, Kiolbasa, & Sobel, 1997; Murphy, Thompson, & Morris, 1997). Stress-related behaviors (e.g., eating, alcohol use, cigarette smoking, inactivity, and forgetting to take medications) can impair self-care and result in abnormal glucose levels.

Stress can also have direct effects on symptoms and disease management. As mentioned earlier, stress increases blood glucose levels. In Type I diabetes, the body does not produce enough insulin to handle the high blood glucose levels and in Type II diabetes, the body cells are resistant to insulin so blood glucose levels remain high. Therefore, high blood glucose levels associated with stress cannot be properly handled by the body (Surwit & Wiliams, 1996). Untreated high glucose levels are dangerous and can lead to ketoacidosis and diabetic coma (Guyton, 1991).

Stress and Rheumatoid Arthritis

Rheumatoid arthritis (RA) is a debilitating chronic disease that afflicts 70,000 people a year in the United States (Janeway & Travers, 1994). Most cases are a result of a T-cell (CD4) mediated autoimmunity that results in joint inflammation and destruction (Janeway & Travers, 1994). Some cases also involve the production of autoantibodies called rheumatoid factor. As with other chronic diseases, people with RA experience many limitations and disease-related stressors. The most frequent stressors patients report are taking care of their disease, their lack of control over the disease, and the resultant fatigue, pain, and functional impairment (Katz, 1998; Melanson & Downe-Wamboldt, 1995).

In addition to the inherent stressfulness of RA, disease activity and symptoms are exacerbated by the occurrence of daily stressors (Affleck et al., 1997; Zautra et al., 1997, 1998). Similar to the stress and disease relations observed in diabetes and other chronic diseases, a cyclic pattern can develop in which RA leads to increases in stress which in turn exacerbates RA symptoms. However, the relation between stress and disease activity is not clear-cut. The type of stressful event as well as important psychosocial factors, such as spousal support, can alter the relation between stress and RA (Zautra et al., 1998). Minor types of stressors appear to affect RA disease activity and symptoms differently than major life events such as the death of a loved one. Although daily stress has been linked to exacerbation of RA, major life events have actually been associated with decreases in disease activity (Potter & Zautra, 1997). This finding is supported by differences in immunological responses in RA patients to minor and major stressors. Some have suggested that acute, minor stressors are generally associated with increases in immune system activity, whereas major stressors are generally associated with decreases in the same immune parameters (Huyser & Parker, 1998; Zautra et al., 1989). As already mentioned, T-cells, especially CD4 cells, and autoantibodies from B-cells are responsible for the joint inflammation and destruction seen in RA. Therefore, increases in the activity of these cells in response to minor stress should be associated with increases in disease activity. Likewise, the decreases in immune system activity following major stressors should be associated with less disease activity (Huyser & Parker, 1998; Potter & Zautra, 1997).

These differential effects appear to be mediated by the release of catecholamines and cortisol (Huyser & Parker, 1998). Rheumatoid arthritis is typically characterized by decreases in HPA axis activity (i.e., cortisol) and increases in SNS activity (i.e., epinephrine and norepinephrine). Each of these systems have opposing effects on RA management and symptoms. Cortisol has important anti-inflammatory actions that decrease RA activity by reducing the chemical activators of the inflammation process and by suppressing the immune system (Guyton, 1991). Consequently, corticosteroids are often prescribed to RA patients to help manage their symptoms. In contrast, SNS activation has been associated with changes in immune activity and RA symptoms (Huyser & Parker, 1998). Additionally, RA patients have heightened SNS reactivity to minor stressors (Zautra et al., 1998). Although both cate- cholamine and cortisol levels increase in response to stress, it has been proposed that the heightened SNS reactivity to minor stressors counteracts any anti-inflammatory effects of HPA axis activation and cortisol release and results in exacerbations of RA activity and symptoms (Huyser & Parker, 1998). In contrast, RA patients who report major life events may experience dramatic increases in HPA axis activation and cortisol release, which in turn may result in decreases in disease activity (Huyser & Parker, 1998; McFarlane & Brooks, 1990).

Although stress can have a profound impact on the etiology and course of RA, there is a subset of RA patients who appear to be immune to its effects. In these patients genetic and etiological influences appear to be more influential in determining RA symptoms (Rimon & Laakso, 1985). Two subgroups of RA patients have been identified based on whether or not RA patients are seropositive for the autoantibody rheumatoid factor. In patients who are seronegative, the occurrence of negative life events are associated not only with increases in disease activity but also with the onset of the disease. In contrast, in people who are seropositive, no such relations exist (Stewart, Knight, Palmer, & Highton, 1994), suggesting that vulnerability to stress is linked to the physiology of the disease process.

CONCLUSIONS

Stress is a critical crosscutting process that is basic to research, theory, and application in health psychology. It represents modifiable variance in the etiology of disease, affects nearly every behavior that contributes to good or bad health outcomes, and has direct effects on all or most bodily systems and can thereby contribute to developing health problems as well. Stress is basic to the commerce between organisms and their environments, motivating them to take action against stressors or to insulate themselves from stress effects. It also produces nonspecific catabolic arousal, driven primarily by neural-endocrine regulatory loops that supports adaptive capabilities such as fight or flight. More specific aspect of stress responding, tied more closely to the stressful situation and its interaction with the organism's resources and abilities, are reflected in emotional responding and coping as well as in cognitive appraisal processes and memory.

Most people are able to adapt to stressful situations and even in the most extreme cases, it would be expected that most people would be able to cope effectively and move on to new challenges. The multiple changes that occur during stress facilitate adaptation. However, there are negative effects of stress that have been observed, including aspects of the pathophysiology of cardiovascular disorders, infectious illnesses (including HIV disease and hepatitis), cancer, diabetes, and autoimmune diseases like rheumatoid arthritis. These effects appear most often when stress responses are extremely intense or abnormally prolonged. They can also become manifest when resources and coping are not able to immediately overcome or displace stressful conditions. Uncontrollable stress appears to be more difficult to resist than controllable and predictable periods of threat or demand.

Quantification of contributions of stress to disease etiology and personal susceptibility to major health problems has been a slow project, but has been increasingly successful in measuring harmful and beneficial effects of stress. Similarly, the ability to intervene and modify lifestyle, coping, social resources, and appraisals of major chronic illnesses, stressors, and associated conditions has continued to improve. Research during the next 10 years should continue framing the extent and limits of stress effects on health and disease and designing ways to minimize unnecessary risk.

REFERENCES

Affleck, G., Urrows, S., Tennen, H., Higgins, P., Pav, D., & Aloisi, R. (1997). A dual pathway model of daily stressor effects on rheumatoid arthritis. *Annals of Behavioral Medicine, 19,* 161–170.

Aikens, J. E., Kiolbasa, T. A., & Sobel, R. (1997). Psychological predictors of glycemic change with relaxation training in non-insulin-dependent diabetes mellitus. *Psychotherapy and Psychosomatics, 66,* 302–306.

Aikens, K. S., Aikens, J. E., Wallander, J. L., & Hunt, S. (1997). Daily activity level buffers stress-glycemia associations in older sedentary NIDDM patients. *Journal of Behavioral Medicine, 20,* 379–390.

Aldwin, C. M., & Revenson, T. A. (1987). Does coping help? A re-examination of the relation between coping and mental health. *Journal of Personality and Social Psychology, 53,* 337–348.

American Diabetes Association. (1997). *American Diabetes Association complete guide to diabetes.* Alexandria, VA: Author.

American Psychiatric Association. (1994). *Diagnostic and statistical manual of mental disorders* (4th ed.). Washington, DC: Author.

Aparicio-Pages, M. N., Verspaget, H. W., Pena, A. S., Jansen, J.B.M.J., & Lamers, C.B.H.W. (1991). Natural killer cell activity in patients with neuroendocrine tumors of the gastrointestinal tract: Relation with circulating gastrointestinal hormones. *Neuropeptides, 20,* 1–7.

Baba, V. V., Jamal, M., & Tourigny, L. (1998). Work and mental health: A decade in Canadian research. *Canadian Psychology, 39,* 94–107.

Bachen, E. A., Manuck, S. B., Cohen, S., Muldoon, M. F., Raible, R., Herbert, T. B., & Rabin, B. S. (1995). Adrenergic blockade ameliorates cellular immune responses to mental stress in humans. *Psychosomatic Medicine, 57,* 366–372.

Bachen, E. A., Manuck, S. B., Marsland, A. L., Cohen, S., Malkoff, S. B., Muldoon, M. F., & Rabin, B. S. (1992). Lymphocyte subset and cellular immune response to a brief experimental stressor. *Psychosomatic Medicine, 54,* 673–679.

Baider, L., & De-Nour, A. K. (1997). Psychological distress and intrusive thoughts in cancer patients. *Journal of Nervous and Mental Disease, 185,* 346–348.

Baltrusch, H. J., Stangel, W., & Titze, I. (1991). Stress, cancer, and immunity. New developments in biopsychosocial and psychoneuroimmunologic research. *Acta Neurologica, 13,* 315–327.

Baron, R. S., Cutrona, C. E., Hicklin, D., Russell, D. W., & Lubaroff, D. M. (1990). Social support and immune function among spouses of cancer patients. *Journal of Personality and Social Psychology, 59,* 344–352.

Baum, A. (1990). Stress, intrusive imagery, and chronic distress. *Health Psychology, 9*(6), 653–675.

Baum, A., Cohen, L., & Hall, M. (1993). Control and intrusive memories as possible determinants of chronic stress. *Psychosomatic Medicine, 55,* 274–286.

Baum, A., O'Keeffe, M. K., & Davidson, L. M. (1990). Acute stressors and chronic response: The case of traumatic stress. *Journal of Applied Social Psychology, 20,* 1643–1654.

Baum, A., Schooler, T. Y., & Dougall, A. L. (1998). The role of experience in acute and chronic stress. Manuscript submitted for publication.

Belsher, G., & Costello, C. G. (1988). Relapse after recovery from unipolar depression: A critical review. *Psychological Bulletin, 104,* 84–96.

Ben-Eliyahu, S., Yirmiya, R., Liebeskind, J., Taylor, A., & Gale, R. (1991). Stress increases metastatic spread of a mammary tumor in rats: Evidence for mediation by the immune system. *Brain, Behavior, and Immunity, 5,* 193–205.

Berntsen, D. (1996). Involuntary autobiographical memories. *Applied Cognitive Psychology, 10,* 435–454.

Biondi, M., & Zannino, L. (1997). Psychological stress, neuroimmunomodulation, and susceptibility to infectious diseases in animals and man: A review. *Psychotherapy and Psychosomatics, 66,* 3–26.

Bloomgarden, Z. T. (1998). Insulin resistance: Current concepts. *Clinical Therapeutics, 20,* 216–231.

Bohus, B., Koolhaas, J. M., de Ruiter, A.J.H., & Heijnen, C. J. (1992). Psycho-social stress: Differential alterations in immune system functions and tumor growth. In R. Kvetnansky, R. McCarty, & J. Axelrod (Eds.), *Stress: Neuroendocrine and molecular approaches* (Vols. 1–2, pp. 607–621). Philadelphia: Gordon & Breach.

Bosi, E., & Sarugeri, E. (1998). Advances and controversies in etiopathogenesis of Type 1 (insulin-dependent) diabetes mellitus. *Journal of Pediatric Endocrinology and Metabolism, 11*(Suppl 2), 293–305.

Boyce, W. T., Chesney, M., Alkon, A., Tschann, J. M., Adams, S., Chesterman, B., Cohen, F., Kaiser, P., Folkman, S., & Wara, D. (1995). Psychobiologic reactivity to stress and childhood respiratory illnesses: Results of two prospective studies. *Psychosomatic Medicine, 57,* 411–422.

Brewer, D. D., Catalano, R. F., Haggerty, K., Gainey, R. R., & Fleming, C. B. (1998). A meta-analysis of predictors of continued drug use during and after treatment for opiate addiction. *Addiction, 93,* 73–92.

Brickman, A. L., & Yount, S. E. (1996). Noncompliance in end-stage renal disease: A threat to quality of care and cost containment. *Journal of Clinical Psychology in Medical Settings, 3,* 399–412.

Brown, G. W., & Harris, T. O. (Eds.). (1989). *Life events and illness.* New York: Guilford.

Brown, S. A., Vik, P. W., Patterson, T. L., Grant, I., & Schuckit, M. A. (1995). Stress, vulnerability and adult alcohol relapse. *Journal of Studies on Alcohol, 56,* 538–545.

Cacioppo, J. T. (1994). Social neuroscience: Autonomic, neuroendocrine, and immune responses to stress. *Psychophysiology, 31,* 113–128.

Caggiula, A., McAllister, C. G., Matthews, K. A., Berga, S. L., Owens, J. F., & Miller, A. L. (1995). Psychological stress and immunological responsiveness in normally cycling, follicular-stage women. *Journal of Neuroimmunology, 59,* 103–111.

Cameron, O. (1996). Depression increases post-MI mortality: How? *Psychosomatic Medicine, 58,* 111–112.

Cannon, W. B. (1914). The interrelations of emotions as suggested by recent physiological researches. *American Journal of Physiology, 25,* 256–282.

Cohen, L., Delahanty, D. L., Schmitz, J. B., Jenkins, F. J., & Baum, A. (1993). The effects of stress on natural killer cell activity in healthy men. *Journal of Applied Biobehavioral Research, 1,* 120–132.

Cohen, S. (1980). Aftereffects of stress on human performance and social behavior: A review of research and theory. *Psychological Bulletin, 88,* 82–108.

Cohen, S., Frank, E., Doyle, W. J., Skoner, D. P., Rabin, B. S., & Gawltney, J. M., Jr. (1998). Types of stressors that increase susceptibility to the common cold in healthy adults. *Health Psychology, 17,* 214–223.

Cohen, S., Tyrrell, D.A.J., & Smith, A. P. (1991). Psychological stress and susceptibility to the common cold. *New England Journal of Medicine, 325,* 606–612.

Cohen, S., & Williamson, G. M. (1991). Stress and infectious disease in humans. *Psychological Bulletin, 109,* 5–24.

Cohen, S., & Wills, T. A. (1985). Stress, social support, and the buffering hypothesis. *Psychological Bulletin, 98,* 310–357.

Conway, T. L., Vickers, R. R., Weid, H. W., & Rahe, R. (1981). Occupational stress and variation in cigarette, coffee, and alcohol consumption. *Journal of Health and Social Behavior, 22,* 155–165.

Cooper, C. (1988). Predicting susceptibility to short-term stress with the defence mechanism test. *Work and Stress, 2,* 49–58.

Craig, K. J., Heisler, J. A., & Baum, A. (1996). Intrusive thoughts and the maintenance of chronic stress. In I. G. Sarason, G. R. Pierce, & B. R. Sarason (Eds.), *Cognitive Interference: Theories, methods, and findings. The LEA series in personality and clinical psychology,* (pp. 397–413). Mahwah, NJ: Lawrence Erlbaum Associates.

Creamer, M., Burgess, P., & Pattison, P. (1992). Reaction to trauma: A cognitive processing model. *Journal of Abnormal Psychology, 101,* 452–459.

Danne, T., Kordonouri, O., Enders, I., Hovener, G., & Weber, B. (1998). Factors modifying the effect of hyperglycemia on the development of retinopathy in adolescents with diabetes. Results of the Berlin Retinopathy Study. *Hormone Research, 50*(Suppl. 1), 28–32.

Dean, C., & Surtees, P. G. (1989). Do psychological factors predict survival in breast cancer? *Journal of Psychosomatic Research, 33,* 561–569.

Delahanty, D. L., Dougall, A. L., Craig, K. J., Jenkins, F. J., & Baum, A. (1997). Chronic stress and natural killer cell activity following exposure to traumatic death. *Psychosomatic Medicine, 59,* 467–476.

Delahanty, D. L., Dougall, A. L., Hawken, L., Trakowski, J. H., Schmitz, J. B., Jenkins, F. J., & Baum, A. (1996). Time course of natural killer cell activity and lymphocyte proliferation in response to two acute stressors. *Health Psychology, 15,* 48–55.

Delahanty, D. L., Herberman, H. B., Craig, K. J., Hayward, M. C., Fullerton, C. S., Ursano, R. J., & Baum, A. (1997). Acute and chronic distress and posttraumatic stress disorder as a function of responsibility for serious motor vehicle accidents. *Journal of Consulting and Clinical Psychology, 65,* 560–567.

Demas, P., Schoenbaum, E. E., Wills, T. A., Doll, L. S., & Klein, R. S. (1995). Stress, coping, and attitudes toward HIV treatment in injecting drug users: A qualitative study. *AIDS Education and Prevention, 7,* 429–442.

Dorian, B., & Garfinkel, P. E. (1987). Stress, immunity, amd illness: A review. *Psychological Medicine, 17,* 393–407.

Dougall A. L., Baum, A., & Jenkins, F. J. (1998). Daily fluctuation in chronic fatigue syndrome severity and symptoms. *Journal of Applied Biobehavioral Research, 3,* 12–28.

Dougall, A. L., Craig, K. J., & Baum, A. (1999). Assessment of characteristics of intrusive thoughts and their impact on distress among victims of traumatic events. *Psychosomatic Medicine, 61,* 38–48.

Ell, K., Nishimoto, R., Mediansky, L., Mantell, J., & Hamovitch, M. (1992). Social relations, social support and survival among patients with cancer. *Journal of Psychosomatic Research, 36,* 531–541.

Enqvist, B., & Fischer, K. (1997). Preoperative hypnotic techniques reduce consumption of analgesics after surgical removal of third mandibular molars: A brief communication. *International Journal of Clinical and Experimental Hypnosis, 45,* 102–108.

Esquifino, A. I., & Cardinali, D. P. (1994). Local regulation of the immune response by the autonomic nervous system. *Neuroimmunomodulation, 1,* 265–273.

Esterling, B. A., Kiecolt-Glaser, J. K., Bodnar, J. C., & Glaser, R. (1994). Chronic stress, social support, and persistent alterations in the natural killer cell response to cytokines in older adults. *Health Psychology, 13,* 291–298.

Forsen, A. (1991). Psychosocial stress as a risk for breast cancer. *Psychotherapy and Psychosomatics, 55,* 176–185.

Fox, B. H. (1978). Premorbid psychological factors as related to cancer incidence. *Journal of Behavioral Medicine, 1,* 45–133.

Fox, B. H. (1983). Current theory of psychogenic effects on cancer incidence and prognosis. *Journal of Psychosocial Oncology, 1,* 17–31.

Foy, D. W., Resnick, H. S., Sipprelle, R. C., & Carroll, E. M. (1987). Premilitary, military, and postmilitary factors in the development of combat-related posttraumatic stress disorder. *The Behavior Therapist, 10,* 3–9.

Frasure-Smith, N., Lesperance, F., & Talajic, M. (1995). The impact of negative emotions on prognosis following myocardial infarction: Is it more than depression? *Health Psychology, 14,* 388–398.

Funch, D. P., & Marshall, J. (1983). The role of stress, social support and age in survival from breast cancer. *Journal of Psychosomatic Research, 27,* 77–83.

Ganley, R. M. (1989). Emotion and eating in obesity: A review of the literature. *International Journal of Eating Disorders, 8,* 343–361.

Gibbs, M. S. (1989). Factors in the victim that mediate between disaster and psychopathology: A review. *Journal of Traumatic Stress, 2,* 489–514.

Glaser, R., Kiecolt-Glaser, J. K., Bonneau, R. H., Malarkey, W., Kennedy, S., & Hughes, J. (1992). Stress-induced modulation of the immune response to recombinant hepatitis B vaccine. *Psychosomatic Medicine, 54,* 22–29.

Glass, D. C., & Singer, J. E. (1972). *Urban stress: Experiments on noise and social stressors.* New York: Academic Press.

Goldberg, J., True, W. R., Eisen, S. A., & Henderson, W. G. (1990). A twin study of the effects of the Vietnam war on posttraumatic stress disorder. *Journal of the American Medical Association, 263,* 1227–1232.

Goodwin, J. S., Hunt, W. C., Key, C. R., & Samet, J. M. (1987). The effect of marital status on stage, treatment, and survival of cancer patients. *Journal of the American Medical Association, 258,* 3125–3130.

Grassi, L., & Rosti, G. (1996). Psychosocial morbidity and adjustment to illness among long-term cancer survivors: A six-year-follow-up study. *Psychosomatics, 37,* 523–532.

Green, B. L. (1994). Psychosocial research in traumatic stress: An update. *Journal of Traumatic Stress, 7,* 341–362.

Greenberg, M. A. (1995). Cognitive processing of traumas: The role of intrusive thoughts and reappraisals. *Journal of Applied Social Psychology, 25,* 1262–1296.

Greer, S., Morris, T., & Pettingale, K.W. (1979). Psychological response to breast cancer: Effect on outcome. *Lancet, 2,* 785–787.

Grunberg, N. E., & Baum, A. (1985). Biological commonalities of stress and substance abuse. In S. Shiffman & T. A. Wills (Eds.), *Coping and substance use* (pp. 25–62). Orlando, FL: Academic Press.

Guyton, A. C. (1991). *Textbook of medical physiology* (8th ed.). Philadelphia: Saunders.

Hahn, R. C., & Petitti, D. B. (1988). Minnesota Multiphasic Personality Inventory—rated depression and the incidence of breast cancer. *Cancer, 61,* 845–848.

Harvey, S. M., & Spigner, C. (1995). Factors associated with sexual behavior among adolescents: A multivariate analysis. *Adolescence, 30,* 253–264.

Hastings, T., Anderson, S. J., & Hemphill, P. (1997). Comparisons of daily stress, coping, problem behavior, and cognitive distortions in adolescent sexual offenders and conduct-disordered youth. *Sexual Abuse: Journal of Research and Treatment, 9,* 29–42.

Herbert, T. B., & Cohen, S. (1993). Stress and immunity in humans: A meta-analytic review. *Psychosomatic Medicine, 55,* 364–379.

Herbert, T. B., Cohen, S., Marsland, A. L., Bachen, E. A., Rabin, B. S., Muldoon, M. F., & Manuck, S. B. (1994). Cardiovascular reactivity and the course of immune response to an acute psychological stressor. *Psychosomatic Medicine, 56,* 337–344.

Hislop, T. G., Waxler, N. E., Coldman, A. J., Elwood, J. M., & Kan, L. (1987). The prognostic significance of psychosocial factors in women with breast cancer. *Journal of Chronic Diseases, 40,* 729–735.

Hobfoll, S. E. (1989). Conservation of resources. *American Psychologist, 44,* 513–524.

Holmes, T. H., & Rahe, R. H. (1967). The Social Readjustment Rating Scale. *Journal of Psychosomatic Research, 11,* 213–218.

Horowitz, M. J. (1986). *Stress response syndromes* (2nd ed.). New York: Jason Aronson.

Huyser, B., & Parker, J. C. (1998). Stress and rheumatoid arthritis: An integrative review. *Arthritis Care and Research, 11,* 135–145.

Ionescu-Tirgoviste, C., Simion, P., Mariana, C., Dan, C. M., & Iulian, M. (1987). The signification of stress in the aetiopathogenesis of Type-sub-2 diabetes mellitus. *Stress Medicine, 3,* 277–284.

Ironson, G., Wynings, C., Schneiderman, N., Baum, A., Rodriguez, M., Greenwood, D., Benight, C. C., Antoni, M., LaPerriere, A., Huang, H., Klimas, N., & Fletcher, M. A. (1997). Post traumatic stress symptoms, intrusive thoughts, loss and immune function after Hurricane Andrew. *Psychosomatic Medicine, 59,* 128–141.

Irvine, D., Brown, B., Crooks, D., Roberts, J., & Browne, G. (1991). Psychosocial adjustment in women with breast cancer. *Cancer, 67,* 1097–1117.

Jamison, R. B., Burish, T. G., & Wallston, K. A. (1987). Psychogenic factors in predicting survival of breast cancer patients. *Journal of Clinical Oncology, 5,* 768–772.

Janeway, C. A., Jr., & Travers, P. (1994). *Immunobiology: The immune system in health and disease.* New York: Garland.

Jenkins, F. J., & Baum, A. (1995). Stress and reactivation of latent herpes simplex virus: A fusion of behavioral medicine and molecular biology. *Annals of Behavioral Medicine, 17,* 116–123.

Jiang, W., Babyak, M., Krantz, D. S., Waugh, R. A., Coleman, R. E., Hanson, M. M., Frid, D. J., McNulty, S., Morris, J. J., O'Connor, C. M., & Blumenthal, J. A. (1996). Mental stress-induced myocardial ischemia and cardiac events. *Journal of the American Medical Association, 275,* 1651–1656.

Jones, D. R., & Goldblatt, P. O. (1986). Cabcer mortality following widow(er)hood: Some further results from the OPCS longitudinal study. *Stress Medicine, 2,* 129–140.

Kamarck, T., & Jennings, J. R. (1991). Biobehavioral factors in sudden cardiac death. *Psychological Bulletin, 109,* 42–75.

Kaplan, G. A., & Reynolds, P. (1988). Depression and cancer mortality and morbidity: Prospective evidence from the Alameda County study. *Journal of Behavioral Medicine, 11,* 1–13.

Kaplan, R. M., Sallis, J. F., Jr., & Patterson, T. L. (1993). *Health and human behavior.* New York: McGraw-Hill.

Kasl, S. V., Evans, A. S., & Niederman, J. C. (1979). Psychosocial risk factors in the development of infectious mononucleosis. *Psychosomatic Medicine, 41,* 445–466.

Katz, P. P. (1998). The stresses of rheumatoid arthritis: Appraisals of perceived impact and coping efficacy. *Arthritis Care and Research, 11,* 9–22.

Katzung, B. G. (1992). Introduction to autonomic pharmacology. In B. G. Katzung (Ed.), *Basic and clinical pharmacology* (5th ed., pp. 69–81). Norwalk, CT: Appleton & Lange.

Kaufmann, P. G., McMahon, R. P., Becker, L. C., Bertolet, B., Bonsall, R., Chaitman, B., Cohen, J. D., Forman, S., Goldberg, A. D., Freedland, K., Ketterer, M. W., Krantz, D. S., Pepine, C. J., Raczynski, J., Stone, P. H., Taylor, H., Knatterud, G. L., & Sheps, D. S. (1998). The Psychophysiological Investigations of Myocardial Ischemia (PIMI) study: Objective, methods, and variablity of measures. *Psychosomatic Medicine, 60,* 56–63.

Keehn, R. J., Goldberg, L. D., & Beebe, G. W. (1974). Twenty-four year mortality follow-up of army veterans with disability separations for psychoneurosis in 1944. *Psychosomatic Medicine, 36,* 27–46.

Kendler, K. S., Kessler, R. C., Walters, E. E., MacLean, C., Neale, M. C., Heath, A. C., & Eaves, L. J. (1995). Stressful life events, genetic liability, and onset of an episode of major depression in women. *American Journal of Psychiatry, 152,* 833–842.

Kennedy, S., Kiecolt-Glaser, J. K., & Glaser, R. (1988). Immunological consequences of acute and chronic stressors: Mediating role of interpersonal relationships. *British Journal of Medical Psychology, 61,* 77–85.

Kiecolt-Glaser, J. K., Fisher, L. D., Ogrocki, P., Stout, J. C., Speicher, C. E., & Glaser, R. (1987). Marital quality, marital disruption, and immune function. *Psychosomatic Medicine, 49*(1), 13–34.

Kiecolt-Glaser, J. K., & Glaser, R. (1992). Psychoneuroimmunology: Can psychological interventions modulate immunity. *Journal of Consulting and Clinical Psychology, 60,* 569–575.

Kiecolt-Glaser, J. K., & Glaser, R. (1995). Psychoneuroimmunology and health consequences: Data and shared mechanisms. *Psychosomatic Medicine, 57,* 269–274.

Kiecolt-Glaser, J. K., Glaser, R., Shuttleworth, E. C., Dyer, C. S., Ogrocki, P., & Speicher, C. E. (1987). Chronic stress and immunity in family caregivers of Alzheimer's disease victims. *Psychosomatic Medicine, 49,* 523–535.

Kiecolt-Glaser, J. K., Kennedy, S., Malkoff, S., Fisher, L., Speicher, C. E., & Glaser, R. (1988). Marital discord and immunity in males. *Psychosomatic Medicine, 50,* 213–229.

Kiecolt-Glaser, J. K., Marucha, P. T., Malarkey, W. B., Mercado, A. M., & Glaser, R. (1995). Slowing of wound healing by psychological stress. *Lancet, 346,* 1194–1196.

Kiecolt-Glaser, J. K., Stephens, R. E., Lipetz, P. D., Speicher, C. E., & Glaser, R. (1985). Distress and DNA repair in human lymphocytes. *Journal of Behavioral Medicine, 8,* 311–320.

Kompier, M. A., & DiMartino, V. (1995). Review of bus drivers' occupational stress and stress prevention. *Stress Medicine, 11,* 253–262.

Koston, T. R., Mason, J. W., Giller, E. L., Ostroff, R. B., & Harkness, L. (1987). Sustained urinary norepinephrine and epinephrine elevation in post-traumatic stress disorder. *Psychoneuroendocrinology, 12,* 13–20.

Krolewski, A. S., Fogarty, D. G., & Warram, J. H. (1998). Hypertension and nephropathy in diabetes mellitus: What is inherited and what is acquired? *Diabetes Research and Clinical Practice, 39*(Suppl.), S1–S14.

Krueger, G. P. (1989). Sustained work, fatigue, sleep loss and performance: A review of the issues. *Work and Stress, 3,* 129–141.

Lane, J. D., Adcock, R. A., & Burnett, R. E. (1992). Respiratory sinus arrhythmia and cardiovascular responses to stress. *Psychophysiology, 29,* 461–470.

Lazarus, R. S. (1966). *Psychological stress and the coping process.* New York: McGraw-Hill.

Lazarus, R. S., & Folkman, S. (1984). *Stress, appraisal, and coping.* New York: Springer.

Lerer, B., Gur, E., Bleich, A., & Newman, M. (1994). Peripheral adrenergic receptors in PTSD. In M. M. Murburg (Ed.), *Catecholamine function in posttraumatic stress disorder: Emerging concepts. Progress in psychiatry* (No. 42, pp. 257–276). Washington, DC: American Psychiatric Press.

Levy, S., Herberman, R., Lippman, M., & D'Angelo, T. (1987). Correlation of stress factors with sustained depression of natural killer cell activity and predicted prognosis in patients with breast cancer. *Journal of Clinical Oncology, 5,* 348–353.

Levy, S., Herberman, R., Lippman, M., D'Angelo, T., & Lee, J. (1991). Immunologic and psychosocial predictors of disease recurrence in patients with early stage breast cancer. *Behavioral Medicine, Summer,* 67–75.

Levy, S. M., Herberman, R. B., Maluish, A. M., Schlien, B., & Lippman, M. (1985). Prognostic risk assessment in primary breast cancer by behavioral and immunological parameters. *Health Psychology, 4,* 99–113.

Levy, S. M., Herberman, R. B., Whiteside, T., Sanzo, K., Lee, J., & Kirkwood, J. (1990). Perceived social support and tumor estrogen/progesterone receptor status as predictors of natural killer cell activity in breast cancer patients. *Psychosomatic Medicine, 52,* 73–85.

Manuck, S. B., Cohen, S., Rabin, B. S., Muldoon, M. F., & Bachen, E. A. (1991). Individual differences in cellular immune response to stress. *Psychological Science, 2,* 111–115.

Markovitz, J. H., & Matthews, K. A. (1991). Platelets and coronary heart disease: Potential psychophysiologic mechanisms. *Psychosomatic Medicine, 53,* 643–668.

Marucha, P. T., Kiecolt-Glaser, J. K., & Favagehi, M. (1998). Mucosal wound healing is impaired by examination stress. *Psychosomatic Medicine, 60,* 362–365.

Mason, J. W. (1968). Organization of psychoendocrine mechanisms. *Psychosomatic Medicine, 30,* 565–808.

Mason, J. W. (1971). A re-evaluation of the concept of "non-specificity" in stress theory. *Journal of Psychiatric Research, 8,* 323–333.

Mason, J. W., Giller, E. L., Kosten, T. R., & Harkness, L. (1988). Elevation of urinary norepinephrine/cortisol ratio in posttraumatic stress disorder. *Journal of Nervous and Mental Disease, 176,* 1498–1502.

Mason, J. W., Giller, E. L., Kosten, T. R., Ostroff, R. B., & Podd, L. (1986). Urinary free-cortisol levels in posttraumatic stress disorder patients. *Journal of Nervous and Mental Disease, 174,* 145–149.

Mayou, R., Peveler, R., Davies, B., Mann, J., & Fairburn, C. (1991). Psychiatric morbidity in young adults with insulin-dependent diabetes mellitus. *Psychological Medicine, 21,* 639–645.

McEwen, B. S., & Stellar, E. (1993). Stress and the individual: Mechanisms leading to disease. *Archives of Internal Medicine, 153,* 2093–2101.

McFarlane, A. C., & Brooks, P. M. (1990). Psychoimmunology and rheumatoid arthritis: Concepts and methodologies. *International Journal of Psychiatry in medicine, 20,* 307–322.

McNally, R. J. (1997). Implicit and explicit memory for trauma-related information in PTSD. In R. Yehuda & A. C. McFarlane (Eds.), *Psychobiology of posttraumatic stress disorder. Annals of the New York Academy of Science* (Vol. 821, pp. 219–224). New York: New York Academy of Sciences.

Mehta, S., Moore, R. D., & Graham, N. M. H. (1997). Potential factors affecting adherence with HIV therapy. *AIDS, 11,* 1665–1670.

Melanson, P. M., & Downe-Wamboldt, B. (1995). The stress of life with rheumatoid arthritis as perceived by older adults. *Activities, Adaptation, and Aging, 19,* 33–47.

Mellman, T. A. (1997). Psychobiology of sleep disturbances in posttraumatic stress disorder. In R. Yehuda & A. C. McFarlane (Eds.), *Psychobiology of posttraumatic stress disorder. Annals of the New York Academy of Sciences* (Vol. 821, pp. 142–149). New York: New York Academy of Sciences.

Mendes de Leon, C. F. (1992). Anger and impatience/irritability in patients of low socioeconomic status with acute coronary heart disease. *Journal of Behavioral Medicine, 15,* 273–284.

Meyer, D. F. (1997). Codependency as a mediator between stressful events and eating disorders. *Journal of Clinical Psychology, 53,* 107–116.

Moretta, L., Ciccone, E., Mingari, M. C., Biassoni, R., & Moretta, A. (1994). Human natural killer cells: Origin, clonality, specificity, and receptors. *Advances in Immunology, 55,* 341–380.

Moser, D. K., & Dracup, K. (1996). Is anxiety early after myocardial infarction associated with subsequent ischemic and arrhythmic events? *Psychosomatic Medicine, 58,* 395–401.

Mullins, L. L., Chaney, J. M., Pace, T. M., & Hartman, V. L. (1997). Illness uncertainty, attributional style, and psychological adjustment in older adolescents and young adults with asthma. *Journal of Pediatric Psychology, 22,* 871–880.

Murburg, M. M., Ashleigh, E. A., Hommer, D. W., & Veith, R. C. (1994). Biology of catecholaminergic systems and their relevance to PTSD. In M. M. Murburg (Ed.), *Catecholamine function in posttraumatic stress disorder: Emerging concepts. Progress in psychiatry* (No. 42, pp. 3–15). Washington, DC: American Psychiatric Press.

Murphy, L. M. B., Thompson, R. J., Jr., & Morris, M. A. (1997). Adherence behavior among adolescents with Type 1 Insulin-dependent diabetes mellitus: The role of cognitive appraisal processes. *Journal of Pediatric Psychology, 22,* 811–825.

Natelson, B. H., & Chang, Q. (1993). Sudden death: A neurocardiologic phenomenon. *Neurologic Clinics, 11,* 293–308.

Neale, A.V., Tilley, B.C., & Vernon, S.W. (1986). Marital status, delay in seeking treatment and survival from breast cancer. *Social Science and Medicine, 23,* 305–312.

Nesse, R. M., Curtis, G. C., Thyer, B. A., McCann, D. S., Huber-Smith, M. J., & Knopf, R. F. (1985). Endocrine and cardiovascular responses during phobic anxiety. *Psychosomatic Medicine, 47,* 320–332.

O'Leary, A. (1990). Stress, emotion, and human immune function. *Psychological Bulletin, 108,* 363–382.

Podrid, P. J. (1984). Role of higher nervous activity in ventricular arrhythmia and sudden cardiac death: Implications for alternative antiarrhythmic therapy. *Annals of the New York Academy of Sciences, 432,* 296–313.

Potter, P. T., & Zautra, A. J. (1997). Stressful life events' effects on rheumatoid arthritis disease activity. *Journal of Consulting and Clinical Psychology, 65,* 319–323.

Rahe, R. H. (1972). Subjects' recent life changes and their near future illness reports. *Annals of Clinical Research, 4,* 250–265.

Rahe, R. H. (1987). Recent life changes, emotions, and behaviors in coronary heart disease. In A. Baum & J. E. Singer (Eds.), *Handbook of psychology and health: Stress* (Vol. 5, pp. 229–254). Hillsdale, NJ: Lawrence Erlbaum Associates.

Ramirez, A. J., Craig, T.K.J., Watson, J. P., Fentiman, I. S., North, W.R.S., & Rubens, R. D. (1989). Stress and relapse of breast cancer. *British Medical Journal, 298,* 291–293.

Rimon, R., & Laakso, R. (1985). Life stress and rheumatoid arthritis: A 15-year follow-up study. *Psychotherapy and Psychosomatics, 43,* 38–43.

Rosenman, R. H. (1996). Personality, behavior patterns, and heart disease. In C. L. Cooper (Ed.), *Handbook of stress, medicine, and health* (pp. 217–231). Boca Raton, FL: CRC Press.

Ross, M. J., & Berger, R. S. (1996). Effects of stress inoculation training on athletes' postsurgical pain and rehabilitation after orthopedic injury. *Journal of Consulting & Clinical Psychology, 64,* 406–410.

Ryan, E. A. (1998). Pregnancy in diabetes. *Medical Clinics of North America, 82,* 823–845.

Sadeh, A. (1996). Stress, trauma, and sleep in children. *Child and Adolescent Psychiatric Clinics of North America, 5,* 685–700.

Saini, V. & Verrier, R. L. (1989). The experimental study of behaviorally induced arrhythmias. In N. Schneiderman, S. M. Weiss, & P. G. Kaufmann (Eds.), *Handbook of research methods in cardiovascular behavioral medicine. Plenum series in behavioral psychophysiology and medicine* (pp. 51–67). New York: Plenum.

Sanchez-Thorin, J. C. (1998). The epidemiology of diabetes mellitus and diabetic retinopathy. *International Ophthalmology Clinics, 38,* 11–18.

Sarason, I. G., de Monchaux, C., & Hunt, T. (1975). Methodolical issues in the assessment of life stress. In L. Levi (Ed.), *Emotions: Their parameters and measurement* (pp. 499–509). New York: Raven.

Schedlowski, M., Jacobs, R., Stratmann, G., Richter, S., Hädicke, A., Tewes, U., Wagner, T.O.F., & Schmidt, R. E. (1993). Changes of natural killer cells during acute psychological stress. *Journal of Clinical Immunology, 13*(2), 119–126.

Schneiderman, L., & Baum, A. (1992). Acute and chronic stress and the immune system. In N. Schneiderman, P. McCabe, & A. Baum (Eds.), *Perspectives in behavioral medicine: Stress and disease processes* (pp. 1–25). Hillsdale, NJ: Lawrence Erlbaum Associates.

Schranz, D. B., & Lernmark, A. (1998). Immunology in diabetes: An update. *Diabetes-Metabolism Reviews, 14,* 3–29.

Selye, H. (1984). *The stress of life* (rev. ed.). New York: McGraw-Hill. (Original work published in 1956)

Sharpe, T. M., Ryst, E., Hinshaw, S. P., & Steiner, H. (1997). Reports of stress: A comparison between eating disordered and non-eating disordered adolescents. *Child Psychiatry and Human Development, 28,* 117–132.

Shekelle, R. B., Raynor, W. J., Ostfeld, A. M., Garron, D. C., Bieliauskas, L. A., Liu, S. C., Maliza, C., & Paul O. (1981). Psychological depression and 17–year risk of death from cancer. *Psychosomatic Medicine, 43,* 117–125.

Shiffman, S., Hickcox, M., Paty, J. A., Gnys, M., Kassel, J. D., & Richards, T. J. (1996). Progression from a smoking lapse to relapse: Prediction from abstinence violation effects, nicotine dependence, and lapse characteristics. *Journal of Consulting and Clinical Psychology, 64,* 993–1002.

Sieber, W. J., Rodin, J., Larson, L., Ortega, S., & Cummings, N. (1992). Modulation of human natural killer cell activity by exposure to uncontrollable stress. *Brain, Behavior, and Immunity, 6,* 141–156.

Skinner, E. A. (1995). *Perceived control, motivation, and coping. Sage series on individual differences and development* (Vol. 8). Thousand Oaks, CA: Sage.

Spaccarelli, S., Bowden, B., Coatsworth, J. D., & Kim, S. (1997). Psychosocial correlates of male sexual aggression in a chronic delinquent sample. *Criminal Justice and Behavior, 24,* 71–95.

Stefanski, V., & Ben-Eliyahu, S. (1996). Social confrontation and tumor metastasis in rats: Defeat and beta-adrenergic mechanisms. *Physiology and Behavior, 60,* 277–282.

Stewart, M. W., Knight, R. G., Palmer, D. G., & Highton, J. (1994). Differential relationships between stress and disease activity for immunologically distinct subgroups of people with rheumatoid arthritis. *Journal of Abnormal Psychology, 103,* 251–258.

Stone, A. A., Bovbjerg, D. H., Neale, J. M., Napoli, A., Valdimarsdottir, H., Cox, D., Hayden, F. G., & Gawltney, J. M. (1992). Development of common cold symptoms following experimental rhinovirus infection is related to prior stressful life events. *Behavioral Medicine, 18,* 115–120.

Stone, A. A., Reed, B. R., & Neale, J. M. (1987). Changes in daily event frequency precede episodes of physical symptoms. *Journal of Human Stress, 13,* 70–74.

Surwit, R. S., & Williams, P. G. (1996). Animal models provide insight into psychosomatic factors in diabetes. *Psychosomatic Medicine, 58,* 582–589.

Tennant, C. C. (1985). Stress and schizophrenia: A review. *Integrative Psychiatry, 3,* 248–255.

Tennant, C. C. (1987). Stress and coronary heart disease. *Australian and New Zealand Journal of Psychiatry, 21,* 276–282.

Terrazas, E. E., Gutierrez, J.L.A., & Lopez, A. G. (1987). Psychosocial factors and episode number in depression. *Journal of Affective Disorders, 12,* 135–138.

Traub, O., & Berk, B. C. (1998). Laminar shear stress: Mechanisms by which endothelial cells transduce an atheroprotective force. *Arteriosclerosis, Thrombosis, and Vascular Biology, 18,* 677–685.

True, W. R., Rice, J., Eisen, S. A., Heath, A. C., Goldberg, J., Lyons, M. J., & Nowak, J. (1993). A twin study of genetic and environmental contributions to liability for posttraumatic stress symptoms. *Archives of General Psychiatry, 50,* 257–264.

Uchino, B. N., Cacioppo, J. T., & Kiecolt-Glaser, J. K. (1996). The relationship between social support and physiological processes: A review with emphasis on underlying mechanisms and implications for health. *Psychological Bulletin, 119,* 488–531.

Vitaliano, P. P., Maiuro, R. D., Bolton, P. A., & Armsden, G. C. (1987). A psychoepidemiologic aproach to the study of disaster. *Journal of Community Psychology, 15,* 99–122.

Wenneberg, S. R., Schneider, R. H., Walton, K. G., MacLean, C.R.K., Levitsky, D. K., Mandarino, J. V., Waziri, R., & Wallace, R. K. (1997). Anger expression correlates with platelet aggregation. *Behavioral Medicine, 22,* 174–177.

Wiedenfeld, S. A., O'Leary, A., Bandura, A., Brown, S., Levine, S., & Raska, K. (1990). Impact of perceived self-efficacy in coping with stressors on components of the immune system. *Journal of Personality and Social Psychology, 59,* 1082–1094.

Yatham, L. N., Sacamano, J., & Kusumakar, V. (1996). Assessment of noradrenergic functioning in patients with non-combat-related posttraumatic stress disorder: A study with desmethylimipramine and orthostatic challenge. *Psychiatry Research, 63,* 1–6.

Yehuda, R., Boisoneau, D., Lowy, M. T., & Giller, E. L., Jr. (1995). Dose–response changes in plasma cortisol and lymphocyte glucocorticoid receptors following dexamethasone administration in combat veterans with and without posttraumatic stress disorder. *Archives in General Psychiatry, 52,* 583–593.

Yehuda, R., Boisoneau, D., Mason, J. W., & Giller, E. L. (1993). Relationship between lymphocyte glucocorticoid receptor number and urinary-free cortisol excretion in mood, anxiety, and psychotic disorder. *Biological Psychiatry, 34,* 18–25.

Yehuda, R., Giller, E. L., Levengood, R. A., Southwick, S. M., & Siever, L. J. (1995). Hypothalamic-pituitary-adrenal functioning in post-traumatic stress disorder: Expanding the concept of the stress response spectrum. In M. J. Friedman, D. S. Charney, & A. Y. Deutch (Eds.), *Neurobiological and clinical consequences of stress: From normal adaptation to PTSD* (pp. 351–365). Philadelphia: Lippincott-Raven.

Yehuda, R., Lowy, M. T., Southwick, S. M., Shaffer, D., & Giller, E. L. (1991). Lymphocyte glucocorticoid receptor number in posttraumatic stress disorder. *American Journal of Psychiatry, 148,* 499–504.

Yehuda, R., Resnick, H., Kahana, B., & Giller, E. L. (1993). Long-lasting hormonal alterations to extreme stress in humans: Normative or maladaptive. *Psychosomatic Medicine, 55,* 287–297.

Yehuda, R., Southwick, S., Giller, E. L., Ma, X., & Mason, J. W. (1992). Urinary catecholamine excretion and severity of PTSD symptoms in Vietnam combat veterans. *Journal of Nervous and Mental Disease, 180,* 321–325.

Yehuda, R., Southwick, S. M., Nussbaum, G., Wahby, V., Giller, E. L., & Mason, J. (1990). Low urinary cortisol excretion in patients with post-traumatic stress disorder. *Journal of Nervous and Mental Disease, 178,* 366–369.

Zakowski, S. G. (1995). The effects of stressor predictability on lymphocyte proliferation in humans. *Psychology and Health, 10,* 409–425.

Zakowski, S. G., Cohen, L., Hall, M. H., Wollman, K., & Baum, A. (1994). Differential effects of active and passive laboratory stressors on immune function in healthy men. *International Journal of Behavioral Medicine, 1*(2), 163–184.

Zakowski, S. G., McAllister, C. G., Deal, M., & Baum, A. (1992). Stress, reactivity, and immune function in healthy men. *Health Psychology, 11*(4), 223–232.

Zautra, A. J., Hoffman, J. M., Matt, K. S., Yocum, D., Potter, P. T., Castro, W. L., & Roth, S. (1998). An examination of individual differences in the relationship between interpersonal stress and disease activity among women with rheumatoid arthritis. *Arthritis Care and Research, 11,* 271–279.

Zautra, A. J., Hoffman, J., Potter, P., Matt, K. S., Yocum, D., & Castro, L. (1997). Examination of changes in interpersonal stress as a factor in disease exacerbations among women with rheumatoid arthritis. *Annals of Behavioral Medicine, 19,* 279–286.

Zautra, A. J., Okun, M. A., Robinson, S. E., Lee, D., Roth, S. H., & Emmanual, J. (1989). Life stress and lymphocyte alterations among patients with rheumatoid arthritis. *Health Psychology, 8,* 1–14.

Zimmerman, M. (1983). Methodological issues in the assessment of life events: A review of issues and research. *Clinical Psychology Review, 3,* 339–370.

Zonderman, A. B., Costa, P. T., & McCrae, R. R. (1989). Depression as a risk factor for cancer morbidity and mortality in a nationally representative sample. *Journal of the American Medical Association, 262,* 1191–1195.

Zorzet, S., Perissin, L., Rapozzi, V., & Giraldi, T. (1998). Restraint stress reduces the antitumor efficacy of cyclophosphamide in tumor-bearing mice. *Brain, Behavior, and Immunity, 12,* 23–33.

18

What Are the Health Effects of Disclosure?

Joshua M. Smyth
North Dakota State University

James W. Pennebaker
University of Texas

Across history and cultures, people seek to disclose their personal experiences. Confession constitutes an important aspect of healing rituals in a variety of cultures. Indeed, self-disclosure is integral to the majority of psychotherapeutic orientations. Cross-cultural studies indicate that people everywhere are inclined to share their emotions with others and even the darkest secrets—once told to one person in confidence—spread quickly to others (Rimé, 1995). Such social sharing is thought to be part of the process by which people avoid the negative consequences of stressful life events. Metaphorical language for disclosure suggests that emotions are harbored in the body until disclosed. Individuals "get things off their chest" or "get it out of their system" when disclosing. They "blow off steam." Others may worry if friends are "bottling up" their emotions.

There is abundant evidence, however, that individuals do not always disclose their emotions surrounding a major life event to those around them. Although people may have an intense desire to express or discuss negative events, social constraints may force them not to do so (Lepore, Silver, Wortman, & Wayment, 1996; Pennebaker & Harber, 1993). Some negative life events, such as rape or abuse, may have a social stigma attached to them. Some people may not have access to sympathetic or supportive listeners. Others may have access to a support network, but receive support that is perceived as inappropriate or insensitive. For instance, a support provider may not know how to respond to a traumatized individual and either minimize the event or resort to glib responses (e.g., "it could be worse"; Wortman & Silver, 1989). To avoid hearing such unhelpful and painful responses, many individuals will choose not to disclose the trauma. Similarly, revealing struggles tends to elicit more rejection from others than acting as if you are coping well. Finally, some individuals may be abandoned by their social network during times of crisis. This is especially true in cases of "irrevocable" stressors, such as death or terminal illness, where support providers feel especially helpless (Lehman, Wortman, & Williams, 1987).

Talk therapy (including psychoanalysis, behavioral, and cognitive therapies) provides individuals a safe environment to disclose, and has been shown to reduce distress and to promote physical and mental well-being (Mumford, Schlesinger, & Glass, 1983; Smith, Glass, & Miller, 1980). A process common to most therapies is the labeling of the problem and a discussion of its causes and consequences. Further, participating in therapy presupposes that the individual acknowledges the existence of a problem and openly discusses it with another. Emotional writing also provides individuals with the chance to disclose without fear of negative social consequences. As is discussed in this chapter, the mere act of disclosure is a powerful therapeutic agent that may account for a substantial portion of the healing process.

It is important to briefly highlight the differences between emotional expression and emotional disclosure. Emotional expression refers to the natural venting of feelings, often in nonverbal ways: crying, laughter, screams of rage. Emotional disclosure, on the other hand, requires the translation of feelings into language and, thus, is a more self-reflective process.

Raw emotional expression—without self-reflection and language—may be unhealthy. A number of studies have now linked the persistent tendencies to express negative emotion with increased stress and health problems (Pennebaker & Beall, 1986; Watson, 1988; Watson & Pennebaker, 1989), depression (Nolen-Hoeksema, 1987), and hopelessness (Keltner, Ellsworth, & Edwards, 1993). It may not be emotional expression itself that is helpful, but rather when emotional and cognitive components are facilitated into an improved understanding or worldview (Bowlby, 1980; Parkes & Weiss, 1983; Shuchter & Zisook, 1993). Emotional disclosure, then, represents the willful expression of emotional material coupled with the self-reflection and language processes necessary for improvement. Nonverbal emotional expression (or disclosure) may be less effective than verbal or written disclosure, as it lacks the organizing principles of the transduction of emotional experience into language (see Berry & Pennebaker, 1993).

Over the last decade, researchers have been exploring the value of talking or writing about emotional experiences by both inducing disclosure in the laboratory and examining disclosure in individuals' day-to-day lives. Disclosing about deeply personal issues has been found to promote physical health, subjective well-being, and certain adaptive behaviors. There is increasing empirical evidence that emotions and attitudes affect physical health (see Dienstfrey, 1991; Locke & Colligan, 1987). Severe and minor naturalistic stressors, for instance, have been associated with both symptoms and illness (Antoni, 1985; Brantley & Jones, 1993; Cohen, Tyrell, & Smith, 1991, 1993; Pennebaker & Susman, 1988; Stone, Reed, & Neale, 1987). This chapter focuses specifically on emotional disclosure about stressful events and how this process may influence health.

There are now several studies that have found comparable beneficial emotional, cognitive, and physiological effects from writing (while alone), speaking into a tape recorder, and speaking to a therapist (Donnelly & Murray, 1991; Esterling, Antoni, Fletcher, Margulies, & Schneiderman, 1994; Murray, Lamnin, & Carver, 1989). Both writing and speaking about emotional experiences produce greater improvements than writing about superficial topics. It is important to note, however, that all of these cases are dissimilar from the normal daily exchanges individuals may have with their friends. These are actual or implied interactions where no feedback is given, thus eliminating the possibility of social punishment. Hence, examining disclosure in this fashion allows a relatively "pure" view of the effects of disclosure uncontaminated by social feedback/stigma processes. This section discusses the general findings and limitations of disclosure paradigms. Whereas a few studies have asked individuals to disclose personal experiences through talking, most involve writing.

Although Pennebaker and others have investigated the effects of written disclosure (described in detail later), emotional disclosure more generally has been shown to have a variety of positive effects. Disclosure to a receptive audience may help people make sense of traumatic events (Silver, Boon, & Stones, 1983), and/or gain coping strategies or enhanced control over their emotions (Clark, 1993). Ornish and colleagues (e.g., 1990), for example, demonstrated that improvement of coronary atherosclerosis may occur as a result of comprehensive lifestyle changes, and suggest that emotional disclosure and support are vital components of this improvement.

Although beyond the scope of this chapter to review, emotional expression and emotional disclosure seem to play an important role in many illnesses (see Davison & Pennebaker, 1996; Friedman & Booth-Kewley, 1987). Similarly, there is considerable historical evidence that the repression or denial of emotions is linked to the development of a variety of disorders (see Singer, 1990).

One area producing accumulating support for the important role of emotional disclosure is cancer research. Temoshok and colleagues (1985) found that the tendency to suppress negative emotions was associated with unfavorable outcomes in malignant melanoma (skin cancer) patients (part of the "Type C" personality style). Expressing emotion, however, was positively related to lymphocytes at tumor base—a response related to favorable outcomes (Temoshok, 1985). Temoshok concluded that emotional expression variables may be the more active components of the type C personality. Reviews consistently support the hypothesis that emotional disclosure is involved in the onset and progression of a variety of cancers (e.g., Gross, 1989; Meyer & Mark, 1995).

Several studies have attempted to manipulate the degree of social support and emotional disclosure in cancer patients. Spiegel, Bloom, Kraemer, and Gottheil (1989) found that women suffering from advanced breast cancer who were randomly assigned to nonspecific group therapy (a context that allowed them to talk over their day-to-day troubles in a supportive setting) lived, on average, one and a half years longer that those in an information-only control group. A subsequent study (Classen, Koopman, Angell, & Spiegel, 1996) suggested that inhibiting emotional expression was associated with poorer adjustment to advanced breast cancer. Although social support is a broad concept with many components, certainly the opportunity to disclose to others is one of them. To what degree the therapeutic effects of social support are due to disclosure is not yet clear; at least for some groups or circumstances, however, it may be substantial (e.g., Caplan, 1990).

Pennebaker and colleagues conducted several surveys in attempts to understand the link between disclosure and more general health. Pennebaker and O'Heeron (1984) found that in spouses of suicide or accidental death victims, talking about the death was associated with fewer self-report health problems and ruminations in the year following the death. Three larger surveys were conducted by Pennebaker. In the first, over 700 female undergraduates completed a questionnaire assessing current health history, trauma history, and additional related variables. Three groups of participants had experienced sexual trauma ($n = 58$), death of a parent ($n = 41$), parents' divorce ($n = 81$), and another was a group of controls ($n = 536$). Of these four groups, those having experienced sexual trauma were most likely to report all physical symptoms, and groups that had experienced parental death or divorce reported more symptoms than the control group (Pennebaker, 1985). This finding was partially replicated in a survey published in *Psychology Today* that received over 24,000 responses. A random sample of just over 2,000 of these responses revealed that responders who reported sexual trauma prior to age 17 were more likely to report nearly every physical or emotional health problem than all other respondents. Finally, in a survey of 115 medical students, those students who had experienced a trauma and had not disclosed about it had more self-reported health provider visits, diseases, symptoms, and nonprescription medication use than the other participants.

These and related studies supported a link between the experience of trauma and subsequent self-reported health, and suggested the salutary role of disclosure in this relation. Although promising, they relied on correlational designs that attempted to demonstrate the potential value of confiding in others or, the converse, the health risks of not talking. In order to isolate some of the causal mechanisms, a group of studies was conducted whereby participants were encouraged to either disclose or not disclose emotional experiences that they had experienced earlier in their lives.

Although studies involving both talking and writing have been conducted in examining the effects of disclosure, most of the stronger ones have relied on writing. The remainder of the chapter focuses on written disclosure for several reasons. First, this is a relatively recent and exciting area of experimental research that has shown promising results across a variety of outcomes. Second, as mentioned earlier, written disclosure allows the investigation of the health effects of disclosure "uncontaminated" by stigma processes. Writing may thus ultimately prove more useful than interpersonally based disclosure procedures. Third, written disclosure has received a relatively large amount of media coverage and is likely high in public awareness. *American Health,* for instance, published articles entitled "Writing your wrongs" (Pennebaker, 1991) and "Writing off the unemployment blues" (Wilenski, 1993), both lauding the benefits of emotional writing. Numerous articles on written disclosure have appeared in *USA Today* and *Psychology Today.*

The standard laboratory writing technique has involved randomly assigning participants to one of two (or more) groups: an experimental group that discloses emotional material, and a control group that does not. Both groups are asked to write about assigned topics for 3 to 5 consecutive days, for 15 to 30 minutes each day. Writing is generally done in the laboratory with no feedback given. Those assigned to the control conditions are typically asked to write about superficial topics, such as how they use their time. The standard instructions for those assigned to the experimental group are a variation on the following:

> For the next (three) days, I would like for you to write about your very deepest thoughts and feeling about an extremely important emotional issue that has affected you and your life. In your writing, I'd like you to really let go and explore your very deepest emotions and thoughts. You might tie your topic to your relationships with others, including parents, lovers, friends, or relatives, to your past, your present, or your future, or to who you have been, who you would like to be, or who you are now. You may write about the same general issues or experiences on all days of writing or on different topics each day. All of your writing will be completely confidential. Don't worry about spelling, sentence structure, or grammar. The only rule is that once you begin writing, continue to do so until your time is up.

This writing process seems exceptionally powerful at producing emotional disclosure. Participants—from children to the elderly, from honor students to maximum security prisoners—disclose a remarkable range and depth of traumatic experiences. Examples of the various writing topics include (from Greenberg & Stone, 1992): death of a loved one (15%); divorce-separation (4%); serious problems of close other (13%); family problems (9%); problems with friends or peers (7%); physical or sexual abuse-attack (actual or threatened, not including mild physical punishment; 5%); problems concerning sexuality or intimacy (26%); frightening or dangerous nonpersonal event (e.g., car accident, injury-illness of self; 7%); admitting to doing something bad, shameful, or stupid (5%); and difficulties involving school or job (5%). Lost loves, deaths, sexual and physical abuse incidents, and tragic failures are all common themes in studies. If nothing else, the writing paradigm demonstrates that when individuals are given the opportunity to disclose deeply personal aspects of their lives, they readily do so. Even though a large number of participants report crying or being deeply upset by the experience, the overwhelming majority report that the writing experience was valuable and meaningful in their lives.

EFFECTS OF DISCLOSURE ON OUTCOME MEASURES

Researchers have relied on a variety of physical and mental health measures to evaluate the effect of writing: those pertaining to health reports and visits to health professionals, emotional and well-being measures, employment/academic functioning outcomes (e.g., reemployment and academic achievement), immunological outcomes associated with the writing procedure, and assessments of short-term effects. Although more complete reviews may be found elsewhere (Pennebaker, 1993; Smyth, 1998), studies from each category are discussed later. The health reports are considered first.

Written Disclosure and Health Reports

Pennebaker and Beall (1986) showed that college students who disclosed had significantly fewer visits to health services, as compared to control subjects, for 6 months following the experiment. Greenberg and Stone (1992) found a decrease in physician visits for college students who wrote about deeply traumatic events as opposed to subjects who wrote about relatively mild traumatic events or superficial topics. Richards, Pennebaker, and Beall (1995) found that among 95 maximum security prison inmates, those assigned to write about past traumas showed a drop in illness visits after writing (compared to controls). Some studies have altered the instructions to subjects regarding what to write about in attempts to ascertain both the mechanism and parameters of these expression effects. Pennebaker and his colleagues (Pennebaker, 1991; Pennebaker, Colder, & Sharp, 1990; Pennebaker & Francis, 1996) had college freshman write about their deepest thoughts and feelings about coming to college, while control subjects wrote about superficial topics. These studies found that experimental subjects had improved physical health (as measured by visits to health providers) relative to control subjects for the 2 to 4 months following writing. In sum, these self-report symptom studies have revealed beneficial effects from written expression on reported health.

Written Disclosure and Affective/Well-Being Measures

Distress, negative moods, and depression have each been improved in several disclosure studies (Greenberg & Stone, 1992; Greenberg, Stone, & Wortman, 1996; Murray & Segal, 1994; Rimé, 1995; Schoutrop, Lange, Brosschot, & Everaerd, 1996; Spera, Buhrfeind, & Pennebaker, 1994). Several studies have also failed to find hypothesized improvements in self-reported well-being and affect (Pennebaker & Beall, 1986; Pennebaker & Francis, 1996; Pennebaker, Kiecolt-Glaser, & Glaser, 1988; Petrie, Booth, Pennebaker, Davison, & Thomas, 1995). Although such equivocal results exist, a meta-analysis of well-being and affect measures in written disclosure studies found an overall significant positive effect (see Smyth, 1998). Inconsistent results may be due to procedural or measurement differences between studies, or to moderating variables that influence the magnitude of the effect of written disclosure on psychological well-being (Smyth, 1998).

Written Emotional Expression and Employment or Academic Functioning

Some studies have examined outcomes related to employment and academic functioning. Francis and Pennebaker (1992) found that in a group of university employees, experimental subjects writing once a week for 4 weeks showed a reduction in absentee rates relative to control subjects for the 2 months subsequent to writing about upsetting experiences. Spera et al. (1994) found that among 63 recently unemployed professionals, those assigned to write about the thoughts and emotions surrounding their job loss were reemployed more quickly than those who wrote about nontraumatic topics. Pennebaker and colleagues (Pennebaker, 1991; Pennebaker et al., 1990) found that college students assigned to the experimental group performed better than control subjects on measures of academic achievement, such as grade point average, even after controlling for academic history (SAT scores and prior GPA).

Written Disclosure and Immune Function

Other studies have examined the immunological effects of written disclosure. Pennebaker et al. (1988) showed that students assigned to the experimental condition exhibited improved immune function relative to control subjects after the last day of writing. Francis and Pennebaker (1992) found that experimental subjects (university employees) writing once a week for 4 weeks had improved liver enzyme function relative to control subjects for the 2 months subsequent to writing about upsetting experiences. Esterling, Antoni, Kumar, and Schneiderman (1990) found that college student subjects with the highest proportion of emotion-focused words in their essays (interpreted as high disclosers) evidenced more efficient immune function than those subjects whose essays conveyed less emotion. Esterling et al. (1994) showed that college students assigned to write about traumatic topics had significantly better cellular immune control over a latent herpes virus (Epstein–Barr) than did controls. Finally, Petrie et al. (1995) assigned subjects who tested negative to Hepatitis B antibodies to write about traumatic or neutral events immediately prior to receiving their first Hepatitis B vaccine (with booster injections at 1 and 4 months). Subjects in the emotional expression group showed significantly higher antibody levels against Hepatitis B at 4 and 6 month follow-up periods. Overall, subjects assigned to write about traumatic events consistently show improvements in immunological function when compared to subjects assigned to write about neutral topics.

Short-Term Effects of Written Emotional Disclosure

Subjects' mood is also influenced by the writing procedure. During the procedure, subjects writing about traumas have a distinct shift to more negative moods; no changes in affect are observed for subjects writing about innocuous topics. Similarly, experimental subjects show marked increases on measures on autonomic arousal, such as blood pressure and skin conductance. This is interesting because the effect of the writing task several weeks later is the opposite: Subjects who wrote about traumas typically have more positive affect and less negative affect than control subjects. In the absence of intervening coping strategies, this is contrary to the prediction of stress and coping theory, which would suggest that the short-term stress produced by writing about past trauma would result in negative long-term outcomes (both in terms of mood and health). This implies that the negative state initially engendered by writing must reverse or be alleviated at some point following writing, yet prior to measurement of (improved) health outcomes. Clearly, additional information on factors contributing to this shift is important to understanding the manner in which disclosure is producing health benefits.

Are Outcomes Related?

Although presented in isolation, it is also recognized that these various outcome types are likely related. For example, the impact of writing on academic/employment functioning outcomes may be mediated by changes in well-being, reported health, and physiological function. Reemployment, for example, may be more likely for individuals with improved well-being (who may be more pleasant), whereas grade point average will be higher for those who are healthier (who do not miss classes). This is partially supported by

Pennebaker, Mayne, and Francis (1997), who found that outcomes included in the academic/employment functioning category (grade point average and reemployment) were consistently associated with physical health outcomes. It should also be noted that the relation among these outcome types is likely quite dynamic. Changes in mood (possibly resulting from changes in well-being), for example, are known to impact the immune system (Knapp, 1990). Improved health is likely to result in improved well-being, and so forth.

PROCEDURAL DIFFERENCES THAT AFFECT THE DISCLOSURE EFFECTS

Writing about emotional experiences clearly influences measures of physical and mental health. In recent years, several investigators have attempted to define the boundary conditions of the disclosure effect. Some of the most important findings are as follows:

1. Writing versus talking about traumas. Most studies comparing writing alone versus talking either into a tape recorder (Esterling et al., 1994) or to a therapist (Murray et al., 1989; Donnelly & Murray, 1991) find comparable biological, mood, and cognitive effects. Talking and writing about emotional experiences are both superior to writing about superficial topics.

2. Topic of disclosure. Whereas two studies have found that health effects only occur among individuals who write about particularly traumatic experiences (Greenberg & Stone, 1992; Lutgendorf, Antoni, Kumar, & Scheiderman, 1994), most studies have found that disclosure is more broadly beneficial. Choice of topic, however, may selectively influence the outcome. For beginning college students, for example, writing about emotional issues about coming to college influences grades more than writing about traumatic experiences (Pennebaker & Beall, 1986; Pennebaker, Colder, & Sharp, 1990).

3. Length or days of writing. Different experiments have variously asked participants to write from 1 to 5 days, ranging from consecutive days to sessions separated by a week, ranging from 15 to 30 minutes for each writing session. In Smyth's (1998) meta-analysis, a promising trend was found, suggesting that the more days over which the experiment lapses, the stronger the effects. This suggests that writing once each week over a month may be more effective than writing four times within a single week. Self-reports of the value of writing do not distinguish shorter writing from longer writing sessions.

4. Actual or implied social factors. Unlike psychotherapy, the writing paradigm does not employ feedback to the participant. Rather, after individuals write about their own experiences, they are asked to place their essays into an anonymous-looking box with the promise that their writing will not be linked to their name. In one study comparing the effects of having students either write on paper that would be handed in to the experimenter versus write on a "magic pad" (wherein the writing disappears when the person lifts the plastic writing cover), no autonomic or self-report differences were found (Czajka, 1987).

5. Individual differences. No consistent personality or individual difference measures have distinguished who does versus does not benefit from writing. Most commonly examined variables unrelated to outcomes include age, anxiety (or negative affectivity), and inhibition or constraint. The one study that preselected participants on hostility found that those high in hostility benefited more from writing than those low in hostility (Christensen et al., 1996). Additionally, the recent meta-analysis by Smyth (1998) suggests that males may benefit from written disclosure more than females (although both benefit overall).

6. Educational, linguistic, or cultural effects. Within the United States, the disclosure paradigm has benefited senior professionals with advanced degrees at rates comparable to maximum security prisoners with 6th-grade educations (Richards et al., 1995; Spera et al., 1994). Among college students, no differences have been found as a function of the students' ethnicity or native language. The disclosure paradigm has produced consistently positive results among French-speaking Belgians (Rimé, 1995), Spanish-speaking residents of Mexico City (Dominguez et al., 1995), multiple samples of adults and students in The Netherlands (Schoutrop et al., 1996), and even English-speaking New Zealand medical students (Petrie et al., 1995).

7. Writing in clinical samples. There is some evidence that writing may not work by itself in samples that may have disordered cognitive processing or relatively severe depression. For instance, a recent large-scale study by M. Stroebe and W. Stroebe (1996) on recently bereaved older adults failed to find benefits of writing. Similarly, Gidron and colleagues (1996) found that in a group of 14 posttraumatic stress syndrome (PTSD) patients, the half assigned to write and orally expand about their traumas seemed to get worse (compared to controls). The authors suggest that writing may not benefit PTSD patients in the absence of cognitive and/or coping skills training. Although this study has several limitations (small sample size, confounding of oral elaboration with written disclosure), it nonetheless sounds a cautionary note for the use of written disclosure in clinically at-risk populations. Additionally, Richards and colleagues (1995) found that men imprisoned for sexual crimes benefited from writing, whereas men imprisoned for other reasons did not benefit. These studies collectively suggest that care must be taken to evaluate the effect of written disclosure in varying populations prior to its potential therapeutic application.

Overall, the effects of written disclosure appear generalizable across age, gender, race/ethnicity, social class, and a variety of other demographic variables. Although several moderating variables were found in the recent meta-analysis (Smyth, 1998), these were the exception, not the rule. One clear caveat must be repeated: Beneficial effects have only been clearly demonstrated in subjects that are both psychologically and physically healthy.

WHAT IS THE CLINICAL BENEFIT OF EMOTIONAL WRITING ABOUT TRAUMATIC OR STRESSFUL EVENTS?

The results of a recent meta-analysis demonstrate that emotional writing about traumatic or stressful events produces significant health benefits in healthy subjects (Smyth, 1998). Thirteen experimental studies, comprising over 800 individuals, were included in this analysis. It is important to note that all of the participants in these studies were psychologically and physically healthy. The binomial effect size display (BESD) is a method of showing the practical importance of an effect size, and is presented as the difference in outcome rates between experimental and control groups (Rosenthal & Rubin, 1982). The overall effect size of writing about trauma ($d = .47$), in terms of a BESD, is a 23% improvement in the experimental group over the control group. For example, illness rates decreasing from 75% in the control group to 52% in the experimental group, or experimental subjects being 23% more likely to find reemployment after layoffs.

When evaluating clinical relevance, it may be more illustrative to compare this writing task to other psychological, behavioral, or educational treatments. (For ease in comparison, all effect size estimates have been translated into BESD.) In a landmark meta-analysis of psychotherapy outcomes, Smith and Glass (1977) reported an average 32% improvement for those receiving psychotherapy over those who do not. Although their analyses of subgroups (i.e., particular psychotherapeutic orientations) has been challenged, the overall effect size is comparable, albeit somewhat larger, to that achieved by writing (a 23% improvement). More recent analyses of psychological, behavioral, or educational interventions have reported similar or smaller effect sizes than the writing task. Wells-Parker, Bangert-Drowns, McMillen, and Williams (1995), in an examination of the effects of remediation with drinking/driving offenders, found an average reduction of from 8% to 9% over controls (no remediation), as compared to the 23% difference between experimental and control conditions in the emotional writing task. A research synthesis of the effects of psychosocial interventions with adult cancer patients found improvement ranging from 9% to 14% across various outcome measures, again somewhat lower than the improvement produced by writing (Meyer & Mark, 1995). Lipsey and Wilson (1993) examined effect sizes from 302 meta-analyses of behavioral and educational interventions, and reported very similar average improvements for randomized experiments (23%). It is not possible to strictly compare effect sizes between studies when the outcome measures are dissimilar, But these findings support the view that the effect produced by the writing task is clinically significant and similar to that found in other quantitative analyses of psychological interventions.

Summary

When healthy individuals write or talk about personally upsetting experiences in the laboratory, consistent and significant health improvements are found. The effects include both subjective and objective markers of health and well-being, and are of clinically relevant magnitude. The effects produced by disclosure appear to generalize across settings, most individual differences, many Western cultures, and are independent of social feedback.

WHY DOES DISCLOSURE WORK?

Most of the research on disclosure has been devoted to demonstrating its effectiveness rather than on identifying the underlying mechanisms. The following are general models that attempt to explain the value of disclosure.

Inhibition and Disclosure

The original theory that motivated the first studies on disclosure was based on the assumption that not talking about important psychological phenomena was a form of inhibition. Disclosure (via writing or otherwise) was conceptualized as allowing individuals to confront upsetting topics, reducing the constraints or inhibitions associated with not talking about the event. Drawing on existing animal and psychophysiological literatures, it was asserted that active inhibition was a form of physiological work. This inhibitory work, reflected in autonomic and central nervous system arousal, was viewed as a chronic low level stressor. This prolonged stress response could then cause or exacerbate psychosomatic processes, increasing the risk of illness and other stress-related problems. Just as constraining thoughts, feelings, or behaviors linked to a stressful or traumatic event was stressful, disclosing thoughts and feelings about these experiences should, in theory, reduce the stress of inhibition.

Findings to support the inhibition model of psychosomatics are growing. Individuals who conceal their gay status (Cole, Kemeny, Taylor, & Visscher, in press), traumatic experiences in their past (Pennebaker, 1993), or who are considered inhibited or shy by others (Kagan, Reznick, & Snidman, 1988), exhibit more health problems than those less inhibited. Although inhibition seems to contribute to long-term health problems, the idea that disclosure reduces inhibition and should therefore improve health is not as well supported. Greenberg and Stone (1992) found that individuals benefited equally from writing about traumas about which they had told others as about traumas that they had kept secret. Self-reports of inhibition before and after disclosure have not consistently related to health benefits. At this point, the role of inhibition in promoting health within the paradigm of emotional disclosure is not fully understood.

It should also be noted that it is not clear how inhibition and disclosure are related: Are they distinct constructs or opposite ends of a continuum? Several factor analyses have suggested that, in fact, inhibition and disclosure are distinct constructs (Larson & Chastain, 1990; Malatesta & Culver, 1993). In both cases, self-concealment (viz. inhibition) was correlated with physical symptoms, whereas self-disclosure was unrelated to symptoms. Finally, self-concealment predicted physical and psychological symptomatology even after statistically controlling for trauma level, trauma distress, trauma disclosure, social support variables, and general disclosure tendencies.

Cognitive and Linguistic Changes Associated With Writing

In recent years, researchers have begun analyzing the language that individuals use in writing about emotional topics. A first strategy was to have independent raters evaluate the essays' overall contents to see if it was possible to predict who would benefit most from writing. Interestingly, judges noted that essays of people who benefit from writing appeared to be "smarter," "more thoughtful," and "more emotional" (Pennebaker, 1993). However, the relatively poor interjudge reliability led to the development of a computerized text analysis system.

In 1991, a computer program called Linguistic Inquiry and Word Count (LIWC) was created that analyzed essays in text format. LIWC had been developed by having groups of judges evaluate the degree to which about 2,000 words or word stems were related to each of several dozen categories (for a full description, see Pennebaker & Francis, 1996). The categories included negative emotion words (sad, angry), positive emotion words (happy, laugh), causal words (because, reason), and insight words (understand, realize). For each essay that a person wrote, it was possible to quickly compute the percentage of total words that these and other linguistic categories represented.

Analyzing the experimental subjects' data from six writing studies, three linguistic factors reliably predict improved physical health. First, the more that individuals use positive emotion words, the better their subsequent health. Second, a moderate number of negative emotion words predicts health. Both very high and very low levels of negative emotion word use correlate with poorer health. Third, and most important, an increase in both causal and insight words over the course of writing is strongly associated with improved health (Pennebaker, Mayne, & Francis, 1997). Indeed, this increase in cognitive words covaries with judges' evaluations of the construction of a story or narrative. That is, people who benefit from writing begin with a poorly organized description and progress to a coherent story by the last day of writing.

The language analyses are particularly promising in that they suggest that certain features of essays predict long-term physical health. Further, these features are congruent with current views on narratives in psychology. The next issue that is currently being addressed is the degree to which cohesive stories or narratives predict changes in real-world cognitive processes. That is, does a coherent story about a trauma produce improvements in health by reducing ruminations or flashbacks? Does a story ultimately result in the assimilation of an unexplained experience that allows the person to get on with life? To what degree does the use and integration of emotion language affect the narrative and, ultimately, health (see also, Lee & Beattie, 1996)? These are the theoretical questions that psychologists must address.

Traumatic Memory Research

Additional information can be drawn from traumatic stress and memory research. Traumatic stress research has often noted the distinction between memories for ordinary events and memories for traumatic events; memories for traumatic events seem immutable, and are more emotional and perceptual than declarative in nature (Terr, 1994). Memories for traumatic events are often initially experienced as sensory fragments of the original event. Visual, olfactory, auditory, or even kinesthetic sensations, as well as intense feelings thought to represent those sensations at the time of the traumatic event, are typically reported (van der Kolk & van der Hart, 1991). Memories for traumatic events are also encoded differently, perhaps due to restricted attentional focus or altered hippocampal memory function due to extreme arousal (van der Kolk, 1994).

When an individual is upset about a traumatic event, memories cannot be integrated into a personal narrative, resulting in the memory being stored as sensory perceptions, obsessional ruminations, or behavioral reenactments (Janet, 1909; van der Kolk & van der Hart, 1991). McFarlane and others have noted that it is the persistence of intrusive and distressing symptoms, avoidance, and hyperarousal, not the traumatic memory itself, that result in observed psychological and biological dysfunction (e.g., McFarlane, 1992). Traumatized individuals often, for example, narrow their attentional focus to be "on guard" for sources of potential threat. This creates a state of chronic physiological overarousal. Such hyperarousal promotes state-dependent recall of traumatic memories and involuntary intrusions of the trauma, leading in turn to further increased arousal.

One goal in treating traumatic memories is thus to facilitate the processing of traumatic memory (Foa, Rothbaum, & Molnar, 1995). Foa and Riggs (1994) noted that traumatic memories are more disorganized than other memories, and treatments aimed at organizing memory should thus be particularly effective (as more organized memories should be easier to integrate into existing memory). This is supported by work in both clinical and healthy populations. DiSavino and colleagues (1993) analyzed victims' trauma-related narratives during exposure and found that evidence of decreasing disorganization over time was associated with improvement. Similarly, increases in linguistic indicators of coherence and evidence of a narrative becoming more focused over writing sessions is associated with increased improvement (Pennebaker et al., 1997). Van der Kolk and Fisler (1995) found traumatized individuals initially had no narrative memories of traumatic events, and developed a narrative over time only as they became aware of more elements of the traumatic experience.

The primary problem with processing, organizing, and integrating traumatic memories may be that they lack any verbal component, and therefore cannot be effectively communicated or organized. Rauch and colleagues (1996) found that during the provocation of traumatic memories there was a decrease in activation of Broca's area (the area most involved in the transduction of subjective experience into speech), and a simultaneous increase of activation in areas of the right hemisphere that are thought to process intense emotions and visual images. It seems the lack of a linguistic representation interferes with the development of a personal narrative and the assimilation of traumatic memories. Disclosing about the traumatic event (through writing or speech) may force the transduction of the memories from sensory/affective components into an organized, linguistic format (Pennebaker et al., 1997). Disclosure about traumatic events may thus facilitate several processes considered central in the treatment of traumatic memory, specifically: the deconditioning of memories related to the traumatic event from affective/physiological responses, and restructuring of dissociated traumatic memories from intrusive reexperiencing of feelings and sensations into a personal, integrated narrative (Foa & Kozak, 1986). Written or verbal disclosure may be necessary as deconditioning of traumatic memories and responses will not occur merely through reexperiencing fragments of the trauma (e.g., intrusions, ruminations), as affective and sensory elements of the trauma remain separate from the rest of memory. This prevents the creation of an integrated memory that is no longer a trigger for conditioned (fear) responses.

The process of disclosure about traumatic or stressful events may produce positive effects by initially forcing the encoding of the traumatic memory into narrative language. Although initially increasing distress, it should allow a modification of the fear structure associated with the trauma, in turn facilitating the integration of the traumatic memory. A more integrated memory should lead to a reduction in intrusive reexperiencing and the attenuation of conditioned fear responses. Reductions in intrusive remembering and fear responses should ameliorate chronic hyperarousal and ultimately lead to the reduction of both psychological and physiological symptomatology.

CONCLUSIONS

Both subjective and quantitative evaluations of the evidence support the conclusion that written disclosure about traumatic or stressful events produces health benefits in both somatic and psychological domains. Several theoretical explanations of how these changes may occur were presented, focusing primarily on how disclosure may promote the formation of a structured narrative out of previously unstructured sensory fragments. This new structure should lead to the cognitive assimilation of traumatic memories and subsequent biological alterations. Developments in relating linguistic parameters to health outcomes offer exciting insight into this process. It should be noted that, although plausible, these models are speculative and must be tested in future research. The degree to which individuals improve after writing was related to several factors, suggesting that existing research cannot be easily generalized to subgroups of individuals not well-represented in existing research. As the health benefits of written disclosure in healthy people seems clear, future research needs to explore the theoretical basis of disclosure and evaluate emotional writing as a supplemental treatment for individuals who have experienced traumatic events.

REFERENCES

Antoni, M. H. (1985). Temporal relationship between life events and two illness measures: A cross-lagged panel analysis. *Journal of Human Stress, 11*(1), 21–26.

Berry, D., & Pennebaker, J. (1993). Nonverbal and verbal emotional expression and health. *Psychotherapy and Psychsomatics, 59,* 11–19.

Bowlby, J. (1980). *Loss: Sadness and depression: Vol. 3, Attachment and loss.* New York: Basic Books.

Brantley, P., & Jones, G. (1993). Daily stress and stress-related disorders. *Annals of Behavioral Medicine, 15,* 17–25.

Caplan, G. (1990). Loss, stress, and Mental health. *Community Mental Health Journal, 26,* 27–48.

Christensen, A., Edwards, D., Wiebe, J., Benotsch, E., McKelby, J., Andrews, M., & Lubaroff, D. (1996). Effect of verbal self-disclosure on natural killer cell activity: Moderating influences of cynical hostility. *Psychosomatic Medicine, 58,* 150–155.

Clark, L. (1993). Stress and the cognitive-conversational benefits of social interaction. *Journal of Social and Clinical Personality, 12,* 25–55.

Classen, C., Koopman, C., Angell, K., & Spiegel, D. (1996). Coping styles associated with adjustment to advanced breast cancer. *Health Psychology, 15,* 434–437.

Cohen, S., Tyrell, D., & Smith, A. (1991). Psychological stress and susceptibility to the common cold. *New England Journal of Medicine, 425,* 738.

Cohen, S., Tyrell, D., & Smith, A. (1993). Negative life events, perceived stress, negative affect, and susceptibility to the common cold. *Journal of Personality and Social Psychology, 64,* 141–149.

Cole, S. W., Kemeny, M. W., Taylor, S. E., & Visscher, B. R. (in press). Elevated health risk among gay men who conceal their homosexuality. *Health Psychology.*

Czajka, J. A. (1987). *Behavioral inhibition and short term physiological responses.* Unpublished master's thesis, Southern Methodist University.

Davison, K., & Pennebaker, J. (1996). Social psychosomatics. In E. Higgins & A. Kruglanski, et al. (Eds.), *Social psychology: Handbook of basic principles* (pp. 102–120). New York: Guilford.

Dienstfrey, H. (1991). *Where the mind meets the body.* New York: Harper Collins.

DiSavino, P., Turk, E. Massie, E. Riggs, D. Penkower, D., Molnar, C., & Foa, E. (1993). *The content of traumatic memories: Evaluating treatment efficacy by analysis of verbatim descriptions of the rape scene.* Paper presented at the 27th annual meeting of the Association for the Advancement of Behavior Therapy, Atlanta, Georgia.

Dominguez, B., Valderrama, P., Meza, M. A., Perez, S. L., Silva, A., Martinez, G., Mendez, V. M., & Olvera, Y. (1995). The roles of emotional reversal and disclosure in clinical practice. In J. W. Pennebaker (Ed.), *Emotion, disclosure, and health* (pp. 255–270). Washington, DC: American Psychological Association.

Donnelly, D. A., & Murray, E. J. (1991). Cognitive and emotional changes in written essays and therapy interviews. *Journal of Social and Clinical Psychology, 10,* 334–350.

Esterling, B., Antoni, M., Kumar, M., & Schneiderman, N. (1990). Emotional repression, stress disclosure responses, and Epstein–Barr capsid antigen titers. *Psychosomatic Medicine, 52,* 397–410.

Esterling, B. A., Antoni, M. H., Fletcher, M. A., Margulies, S., & Schneiderman, N. (1994). Emotional disclosure through writing or speaking modulates latent Epstein–Barr virus reactivation. *Journal of Consulting and Clinical Psychology, 62,* 130–140.

Foa, E., & Kozak, M. (1986). Emotional processing of fear: Exposure to corrective information. *Psychological Bulletin, 99,* 20–35.

Foa, E., & Riggs, D. (1994). Posttramatic stress disorder and rape victims. In R. Pynoos (Ed.), *Posttraumatic stress disorder: A clinical review* (pp. 133–163). Lutherville, MD: Sidran Press.

Foa, E., Rothbaum, B., & Molnar, C. (1995). Cognitive-behavioral treatment of posttraumatic stress disorder. In M. Friedman, D. Charney, & A. Deutch (Eds.), *Neurobiological and clinical consequences of stress: From normal adaptation to posttraumatic stress disorder* (pp. 483–494). Philadelphia: Lippincott-Raven.

Francis, M. E., & Pennebaker, J. W. (1992). Putting stress into words: Writing about personal upheavals and health. *American Journal of Health Promotion, 6,* 280–287.

Friedman, H. S., & Booth-Kewley, S. (1987). The "disease-prone personality": A meta-analytic view of the construct. *American Psychologist, 42,* 539–555.

Gidron, Y., Peri, T., Connolly, J. F., & Shalev, A. Y. (1996). Written disclosure in posttraumatic stress disorder: Is it benficial for the patient? *Journal ofNervous and Mental Disease, 184,* 505–507.

Greenberg, M. A., & Stone, A. A. (1992). Writing about disclosed versus undisclosed traumas: Immediate and long-term effects on mood and health. *Journal of Personality and Social Psychology, 63,* 75–84.

Greenberg, M. A., Stone, A. A., & Wortman, C. B. (1996). Health and psychological effects of emotional disclosure: A test of the inhibition-confrontation approach. *Journal of Personality and Social Psychology, 71,* 588–602.

Gross, J. (1989). Emotional expression in cancer onset and progression. *Social Science and Medicine, 28,* 1239–1248.

Janet, P. (1909). *Les nervoses.* Paris.

Kagan, J., Reznick, J. S., & Snidman, N. (1988). Biological bases of childhood shyness. *Science, 240,* 167–171.

Keltner, D., Ellsworth, P., & Edwards, K. (1993). Beyond simple pessimism: Effects of sadness and anger on social perception. *Journal of Personality and Social Psychology, 64,* 740–752.

Knapp, P. (1990). Short-term immunological effect of induced emotion. *Psychosomatic Medicine, 52,* 246–252.

Larson, D., & Chastain, R. (1990). Self-concealment: Conceptualization, measurement, and health implications. *Journal of Social and Clinical Psychology, 9*(4), 439–455.

Lee, V., & Beattie, G. (1996). The rhetorical organization of verbal and non-verbal behaviour in emotion talk: A conversation analytic approach. Paper presented at the (Non) Expression of Emotions and Health and Disease Conference, Tilburg, The Netherlands.

Lehman, D., Wortman, C., & Williams, A. (1987). Long-term effects of losing a spouse or child in a motor vehicle crash. *Journal of Personality and Social Psychology, 52,* 218–231.

Lepore, S., Silver, R., Wortman, C., & Wayment, H. (1996). Social constraints, intrusive thoughts, and depressive symptoms among bereaved mothers. *Journal of Personality and Social Psychology, 70,* 271–282.

Lipsey, M., & Wilson, D. (1993). The efficacy of psychological, educational, and behavioral treatment. Confirmation from meta-analysis. *American Psychologist, 48,* 1181–1209.

Locke, S. E., & Colligan, D. (1987). *The healer within: The new medicine of mind and body.* New York: NAL-Dutton.

Lutgendorf, S. K., Antoni, M. H., Kumar, M., & Schneiderman, N. (1994). Changes in cognitive coping strategies predict EBV-antibody titre change following a stressor disclosure induction. *Journal of Psychosomatic Research, 38,* 63–78.

Malatesta, C., & Culver, C. (1993). Gendered health: Differences between men and women in the relation between physical symptoms and emotion expression behaviors. In H. C. Trane & J. Pennebaker (Eds.), *Emotional inhibition and health* (pp. 116–144). Goettingen, Germany: Hogrefe and Huber.

McFarlane, A. (1992). Avoidance and intrusion in posttraumatic stress disorder. *Journal of Nervous and Mental Disease, 180,* 439–445.

Meyer, T., & Mark, M. (1995). Effects of psychosocial interventions with adult cancer patients: A meta-analysis of randomized experiments. *Health Psychology, 14,* 101–108.

Mumford, E., Schlesinger, H. J., & Glass, G. V. (1983). Reducing medical costs through mental health treatment: Research problems and recommendations. In A. Broskowski, E. Marks, & S. H. Budman (Eds.), *Linking health and mental health* (pp. 257–273). Beverly Hills, CA: Sage.

Murray, E. J., Lamnin, A. D., & Carver, C. S. (1989). Emotional expression in written essays and psychotherapy. *Journal of Social and Clinical Psychology, 8,* 414–429.

Murray, E., & Segal, D. (1994). Emotional processing in vocal and written expression of feelings about traumatic experiences. *Journal of Traumatic Stress, 7,* 391–405.

Nolen-Hoeksema, S. (1987). Sex differences in unipolar depression: Evidence and theory. *Psychological Bulletin, 101,* 259–282.

Ornish, D., Brown, S., Scherwitz, L., Billings, J., Armstrong, W., Ports, T., McLanahan, S., Kirkeeide, R., Brand, R., & Gould, K. (1990). Can lifestyle changes reverse coronary heart disease? The Lifestyle Heart trial. *Lancet, 336,* 129–133.

Parkes, C. M., & Weiss, R. S. (1983). *Recovery from bereavement.* New York: Basic Books.

Pennebaker, J. (1985). Traumatic experience and psychosomatic disease: Exploring the roles of behavioural inhibition, obsession, and confiding. *Canadian Psychology, 26,* 82–95.

Pennebaker, J. W. (1991, Jan./Feb.). Writing your wrongs. *American Health, 10,* 64–67.

Pennebaker, J. W. (1993). Putting stress into words: Health, linguistic, and therapeutic implications. *Behaviour Research and Therapy, 31,* 539–548.

Pennebaker, J. W., & Beall, S. K. (1986). Confronting a traumatic event: Toward an understanding of inhibition and disease. *Journal of Abnormal Psychology, 95,* 274–281.

Pennebaker, J. W., Colder, M., & Sharp, L. K. (1990). Accelerating the coping process. *Journal of Personality and Social Psychology, 58,* 528–537.

Pennebaker, J. W., & Francis, M. E. (1996). Cognitive, emotional, and language processes in disclosure. *Cognition and Emotion, 10,* 601–626.

Pennebaker, J. W., & Harber, K. (1993). A social stage model of collective coping: The Loma Prieta earthquake and the Persian Gulf war. *Journal of Social Issues, 49*(4), 125–146.

Pennebaker, J. W., Kiecolt-Glaser, J., & Glaser, R. (1988). Disclosure of traumas and immune function: Health implications for psychotherapy. *Journal of Consulting and Clinical Psychology, 56,* 239–245.

Pennebaker, J. W., Mayne, T. J., & Francis, M. E. (1997). Linguistic predictors of adaptive bereavement. *Journal of Personality and Social Psychology, 72,* 863–871.

Pennebaker, J., & O'Heeron, R. (1984). Confiding in others and illness rate among spouses of suicide and accidental death victims. *Journal of Abnormal Psychology, 93,* 473–476.

Pennebaker, J., & Susman, J. (1988). Disclosure of traumas and psychosomatic processes. *Social Science and Medicine, 26,* 327–333.

Petrie, K. J., Booth, R., Pennebaker, J. W., Davison, K. P., & Thomas, M. (1995). Disclosure of trauma and immune response to Hepatitis B vaccination program. *Journal of Consulting and Clinical Psychology, 63,* 787–792.

Rauch, S., van der Kolk, B., Fisler, R., & Alpert, N. (1996). A symptom provocation study of posttraumatic stress disorder using positron emission tomography and script driven imagery. *Archives of General Psychiatry, 53,* 380–387.

Richards, J. M., Pennebaker, J. W., & Beall, W. E. (1995). *The effects of criminal offense and disclosure of trauma on anxiety and illness in prison inmates.* Paper presented the Midwest Psychological Association, Chicago.

Rimé, B. (1995). Mental rumination, social sharing, and the recover from emotional exposure. In J. W. Pennebaker (Ed.), *Emotion, disclosure, and health* (pp. 271–292). Washington, DC: American Psychological Association.

Rosenthal, R., & Rubin, D. (1982). A simple, general purpose display of magnitude of experimental effect. *Journal of Educational Psychology, 74,* 166–199.

Schoutrop, M. J. A., Lange, A., Brosschot, J., & Everaerd, W. (1996, June). *The effects of writing assignments on reprocessing traumatic events: Three experimental studies.* Paper presented at The (Non) Expression of Emotions and Health and Disease Conference, Tilburg, The Netherlands.

Schuchter, S., & Zisook, S. (1993). The course of normal grief. In M. Stroebe, W. Stroebe, & R. Hansson (Eds.), *Handbook of bereavement: Theory, research, and intervention* (pp. 23–43). Cambridge, England: Cambridge University Press.

Silver, R., Boon, C., & Stones, M. (1983). Searching for meaning in misfortune: Making sense of incest. *Journal of Social Issues, 39,* 81–101.

Singer, J. L. (1990). *Repression and dissociation.* Chicago: University of Chicago Press.

Smith, M., & Glass, G. (1977). Meta-analysis of psychotherapy outcome studies. *American Psychologist, 32,* 752–760.

Smith, M. L., Glass, G. V., & Miller, R. L. (1980). *The benefits of psychotherapy.* Baltimore: Johns Hopkins University Press.

Smyth, J. M. (1998). Written emotional expression: Effect sizes, outcome types, and moderating variables. *Journal of Consulting and Clinical Psychology, 66,* 174–184.

Spera, S. P., Buhrfeind, E. D., & Pennebaker, J. W. (1994). Expressive writing and coping with job loss. *Academy of Management Journal, 37,* 722–733.

Spiegel, D., Bloom, J., Kraemer, H., & Gottheil, E. (1989). Effects of psychosocial treatment of patients with metastatic breast cancer. *Lancet, 2,* 888–891.

Stone, A., Reed, B., & Neale, J. (1987). Changes in daily event frequency precede episodes of physical symptoms. *Journal of Human Stress, 13,* 70–74.

Stroebe, M., & Stroebe, W. (1996, June). *Writing assignments and grief.* Paper presented at the (Non) Expression of Emotions and Health and Disease Conference, Tilburg, The Netherlands.

Temoshok, L. (1985). Biopsychosocial studies on cutaneous malignant melanoma: Psychosocial factors associated with prognostic indicators, progression, psychophysiology, and tumor–host response. *Social Science and Medicine, 20,* 833–840.

Temoshok, L., Heller, B., Sagebiel, R., Blois, M., Sweet, D., Di Clemente, R., & Gold, M. (1985). The relationship of psychosocial factors to prognostic indicators in cutaneous malignant melanoma. *Journal of Psychosomatic Research, 29,* 139–154.

Terr, L. (1994). *Unchained memories.* New York: Basicbooks, Inc.

van der Kolk, B. (1994). The body keeps the score: Memory and the evolving pyschobiology of posttraumatic stress. *Harvard Review of Psychiatry, 1,* 253–265.

van der Kolk, B., & Fisler, R. (1995). Dissociation and the fragmentary nature of traumatic memories: Review and experimental confirmation. *Journal of Traumatic Stress, 8,* 505–525.

van der Kolk, B., & van der Hart, O. (1991). The intrusive past: The flexibility of memory and the engraving of trauma. *American Imago, 48,* 425–454.

Watson, D. (1988). Intraindividual and interindividual anlyses of positive and negative affect: Their relation to health complaints, perceived stress, and daily activities. *Journal of Personality and Social Psychology, 54,* 1020–1030.

Watson, D., & Pennebaker, J. (1989). Health complaints, stress, and distress. *Psychological Review, 96,* 324–354.

Wilenski, D. (1993, June). Writing off the unemployment blues. *American Health, 12,* 35.

Wortman, C., & Silver, R. (1989). The myths of coping with loss. *Journal of Consulting and Clinical Psychology, 57,* 349–357.

Wells-Parker, E., Bangert-Drowns, R., McMillen, R., & Williams, M. (1995). Final results from a meta-analysis of remedial interventions with drunk-driving offenders. *Addiction, 90,* 907–926.

19

Preventive Management of Work Stress: Current Themes and Future Challenges

Debra L. Nelson
Oklahoma State University

James Campbell Quick
The University of Texas at Arlington

Bret L. Simmons
Oklahoma State University

Work stress may be defined, in broader though parallel fashion to job stress (J. C. Quick & Nelson, 1997), as the mind–body arousal resulting from physical and/or psychological demands associated with work. Work stress may lead to enhanced work performance up to an optimum level of stress. Conversely, it may place an employee at risk of distress if the work stress is too intense, frequent, chronic, unremitting, or employees do not possess necessary skills to meet the work demands and manage their stress response. Work stress underload may also lead to potential problems associated with boredom, lack of attention, and other less than desirable psychological outcomes due to unused capacity within the employee. Understanding work stress is important so as to reduce strain, distress, and dysfunction for employees in working environments. Health psychology and occupational health psychology become important in the context of work stress research and practice to the extent that they are central to: assessing risk factors for strain, distress, and dysfunction and designing preventive management programs to enhance healthy work stress. The aims of the latter may be either to reduce, to increase, and/or to modify the amount, focus, and direction of stress in the work environment.

A BRIEF HISTORICAL OVERVIEW

The concern of psychology with work stress may be arguably traced to Hugo Münsterberg's efforts to study industrial accidents and human safety in the early 20th century (Offermann & Gowing, 1990), as indicated in Fig. 19.1. The figure includes key historical events during the 20th century related to work stress. In the extreme, industrial accidents can become full-blown crises in which the human, organizational, and technological elements of the system are overwhelmed, such as occurred in Union Carbide's plant in Bhopal (J. C. Quick, 1997; Shrivastava, 1987). This chapter focuses on the less extreme yet more frequently occurring forms of work stress, strain, and distress that occur in organizations.

Kahn, Wolfe, Quinn, Snoek, and Rosenthal's (1964) studies in role conflict and ambiguity drew attention to the organizational stress problem of role taking in large industrial organizations. Kahn et al. (1964) used social psychology as their conceptual and theoretical point of departure. Prior to this seminal program of research, the primary focus in stress research has been its physiological origins and medical consequences, neither with particular attention to the work or organizational context. Kahn et al.'s (1964) research drew attention to the sources of role stress as a subset of work stress, to the adverse interpersonal and psychological consequences of role stress, and to some of the strategies for achieving a better fit between the person and the work environment. This line of investigation emphasized the psychosocial work environment and attributed the source of the stress to various aspects of individual's interpersonal environment at work in contrast to Münsterberg's attention to the physical environment and safety.

Levinson (1963, 1975) took a different approach to understanding the psychological dimensions of work stress. Whereas his focus was on executives, his basic psychological model does not differ across organizational levels or between functions. His psychoanalytic model draws attention to the role of psychodynamics and the individual's responsibility in the stress process. Although Kahn focused on the interpersonal environment, Levinson emphasized the intrapersonal psychological processes related to stress and strain for executives at work. The two key intrapersonal concepts in Levinson's psychoanalytic model for executive stress are the ego-ideal and the self-image. The conflict between these two is the root of stress for the individual within the psychoanalytic model. Intense conflict between the ego-ideal and self-image may lead to extreme stress and self-destructive behavior, as in executive suicide (Levinson, 1963).

Shortly after Kahn et al. (1964) and Levinson (1963, 1975) were formulating their approaches to work and executive stress, as noted in Fig. 19.1, Gardell (1971) was in the midst of evolving his framework for understanding work environment psychology. Developed within the Swedish cultural and intellectual tradition, Gardell's (1987) approach emphasized *workload* and *self- determination* as the two independent constructs necessary to understand work stress and strain. Karasek (1979), an American who brought these concepts concerning work environment psychology to the United States, relabeled the dimensions *job demands* and *job decision latitude.*

Work stress and occupational health psychology became matters of serious public concern in the United States with the passage of public law 91-596 (Occupational Safety and Health Act, 1970; J. C. Quick, Camara, et al., 1997). By the early 1980s, work-related psychological disorders and distress were among the top 10 occupational health risks identified by the National Institute for Occupational Safety and Health (Ordin, 1992; see Fig. 19.1). At about the same time, J. C. Quick and J. D. Quick (1984) were translating the public health notions of prevention and preventive medicine into an organizational stress context (also noted in Fig. 19.1).

MAJOR THEORETICAL FRAMEWORKS

There is a major theoretical framework in the domain of work stress and health psychology associated with each of the unfolding events in the brief historical time line included in Fig. 19.1. Each theoretical framework has associated with it a conceptual model as the basis for the theory. In addition, Cooper (1998) collected the theories of organizational stress in one

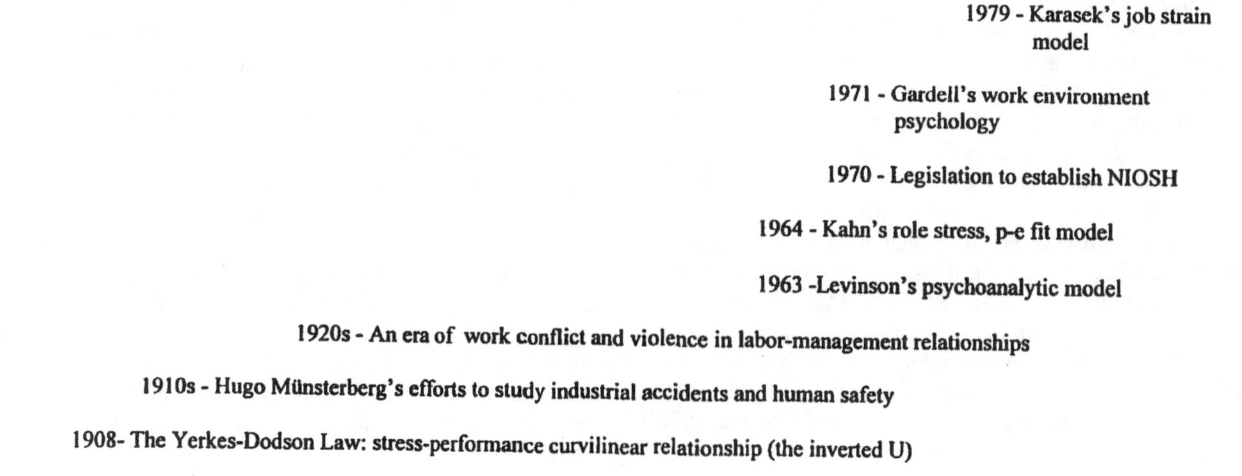

1900 1910 1920 1930 1940 1950 1960 1970 1980 1990 2000

Work-related psychological disorders and distress: Top 10 occupational health risks

1984 - Quick & Quick's prevention model

1979 - Karasek's job strain model

1971 - Gardell's work environment psychology

1970 - Legislation to establish NIOSH

1964 - Kahn's role stress, p-e fit model

1963 -Levinson's psychoanalytic model

1920s - An era of work conflict and violence in labor-management relationships

1910s - Hugo Münsterberg's efforts to study industrial accidents and human safety

1908- The Yerkes-Dodson Law: stress-performance curvilinear relationship (the inverted U)

FIG. 19.1. A brief historical overview of work stress and health psychology.

volume, which goes beyond the relatively brief treatment of theoretical frameworks and conceptual models in this section. There is some overlap of theories in the domain of work stress and there is a differential impact of these theories in the field.

The Role Stress/Person–Environment Fit Model

Kahn et al. (1964) used a role set framework as the basis for examining role stress in organizations. The role set may refer either to the variety of social roles a person engages at different times (e.g., researcher, father, and coach) or to the aggregation of role senders (e.g., supervisors, peers, and customers) who communicate expectations to an employee in a focal role (Merton, 1957). When these expectations are ambiguous, conflicting, and/or excessive, they create role stress for the focal person. Sutton and Kahn (1987) subsequently focused attention on uncertainty and lack of control as major sources of stress in the psychosocial organization, suggesting that prediction, understanding, and control are antidotes for organizational stress.

The evolution of this theoretical framework led to an examination of the person's fit within the psychosocial environment; that is, the individual's expectational fit within the role set. The person–environment fit approach to organizational stress took Kahn's original role stress approach one step further (Edwards & Cooper, 1990). The person–environment fit approach was later expanded to consider competing versions of the approach (Edwards, 1996). Specifically, the Supplies–Values (S–V) fit approach considers environmental supplies and employee values and the Demands–Abilities (D–A) fit approach considers environmental demands and employee abilities. This framework continues within a social psychological context.

The Psychoanalytic Framework

Levinson's (1963, 1975) stress framework was developed in the context of psychoanalytic theory. The two key personality elements or concepts within the theory were defined in a psychoanalytic context. The first concept is the ego-ideal, defined as the internalized image of an individual's idealized self or perfected self. The ego-ideal is the standard toward which an individual strives over time. The second concept is the self-image, defined as the set of one's positive and negative attributes. The self-image is that which the individual strives to remake in the image of the ego-ideal. The degree of discrepancy between these two elements of the personality is a measure of the amount of stress a person experiences at a given point in time.

Schwartz (1990) extended this psychoanalytic model to examine the processes of corporate decay within the National Aeronautics and Space Administration (NASA) and within General Motors Corporation (GMC). His research indicated that although narcissism and fantasy may reduce momentary stress associated with external reality, these psychological processes may have serious adverse consequences for individual and organizational well-being.

The Demand–Control Model

The core of the demand–control, or job strain, model suggested that increasing work demands lead to a linear increase in job stress and the combination of increasing work demands and restricted work environment control leads to a linear increase in unresolved strain. Hence, this framework makes a rather clear distinction between job stress and job strain: The former does not carry a pejorative or negative denotation, whereas the latter does. This is consistent with the Yerkes–Dodson law's positive performance implications of increasing stress up to some optimum point on the inverted-U.

The negative effects of job strain, or job distress, are manifested in a variety of behavioral, psychological, and medical consequences (J. C. Quick, J. D. Quick, Nelson, & Hurrell, 1997). Common forms of psychological distress include depression, job burnout, anger, and job dissatisfaction (Karasek, 1979). Common forms of medical distress are backaches and headaches, ulcer disease and cardiovascular problems (Theorell & Karasek, 1996). Common forms of behavioral distress are workplace violence, accident proneness, and substance abuse (Mack, Shannon, J. D. Quick, & J. C. Quick, 1998). High strain jobs, characterized by high job demands and low employee control, have significantly higher incidence rates of distress in the forms of exhaustion, dissatisfaction, illness days, pill (i.e., tranquilizers and sleeping pills) consumption, and even myocardial infarctions (Karasek et al., 1988).

The Effort–Reward Imbalance Model

Siegrist (1996) proposed a third theoretical framework and conceptual model to assess adverse health effects of stressful experience at work that is an addition to the person–environment fit model and the demand–control model. The effort–reward imbalance model uses a sociological backdrop, as opposed to a psychological one, and focuses on reciprocity of exchange in occupational life where high cost/low gain conditions are considered particularly stressful. This model considers both extrinsic (work pressures and obligations) and intrinsic (personal coping patterns) effort variables, as well as extrinsic (money and social status) and intrinsic (self-esteem) reward variables. A prospective study and a cross-sectional study of blue collar men ($n_1 = 416$; $n_2 = 179$) provided support for the effort–reward imbalance model when new cardiovascular events is used as the strain indicator.

The Preventive Stress Management Model

The preventive stress management model evolved from the translation of the public health notions of prevention and preventive medicine into an organizational stress context (J. C. Quick & J. D. Quick, 1984). The core of the model is a stress process framework that proposes that organizational demands and stressors (i.e., physical, task specific, role, and interpersonal demands) trigger the stress response within individuals. This stress response may lead to enhanced health and performance on the job (eustress) or may lead to reduced health and performance on the job (distress). Organizations are concerned with work stress because of the organizational costs that may accrue from employees' psychological, medical, and behavioral distress (J. C. Quick, J. D. Quick, et al., 1997). The direct organizational costs of job strain take the form of turnover and absenteeism, performance problems on the job, and compensation awards. In addition, there are indirect organizational costs of job strain that may be reflected in low morale, low job satisfaction, faulty decision making, and distrust in working relationships.

The preventive intervention and treatment components of the preventive stress management model center on the public health and preventive medicine stages of primary, secondary, and tertiary prevention. Primary prevention aims to change the environment and manage organizational demands and stressors. Secondary prevention aims to change the employees and alter their responses to necessary and inevitable demands in the work environment. Tertiary prevention aims to heal individuals and/or organizations in distress. These three stages of prevention afford organizations a platform for leadership and managerial action and intervention for the purpose of creating healthy, high performance organizations. In addition to the stages of prevention as a basis for translation, public health and preventive medicine also offer the notions of surveillance, monitoring, and screening for use in an organizational stress context (Ordin, 1992).

INTERNATIONAL NATURE OF RESEARCH

These theoretical frameworks and conceptual models are crafted by a range of international scholars and researchers. The international nature of research related to work stress and occupational health psychology is reflected in diversity of 50 scholars from Europe, North America, and Israel who wrote the section on psychosocial and organizational factors of health hazards on the job for the *Encyclopaedia of Occupational Health and Safety* (Sauter, Murphy, Hurrell, & Levi, 1997). What emerges from these and similar efforts is an appreciation for the cultural diversity associated with what is defined as stressful at work and value differences regarding healthy interventions.

The preceding historical overview described the early foundations of work stress research. The next section discusses the contemporary research, identifying major themes and important issues that have evolved.

CURRENT THEMES AND RESEARCH ISSUES

Research on work stress has burgeoned in the recent past, and the literature reflects the interdisciplinary nature of this line of inquiry. The early studies were conducted in the tradition of the major theoretical approaches described in the preceding section. Role stress, the job control model, and the identification of stress-related outcomes were dominant themes. The contemporary literature has continued somewhat in these traditions; however, there are emerging themes that have evolved and flourished. Three of these themes are the changing nature of work and organizations, individual differences in the stress experience, and the role of social support.

The Changing Nature of Work

Change is the order of the day in organizations. Although the world of work has always been a dynamic one, today's changes come at a frantic pace. Globalization, new technologies, increased workforce diversity, and the accompanying changes in organizational environments have placed increased pressure on individuals. The reengineering of business processes, smaller companies that employ fewer people, the shift from making a product to providing a service, and the increasing disappearance of the job as a fixed collection of tasks have changed the nature of work and the workplace (Cascio, 1995). Although the common stressors of role conflict and role ambiguity, time pressures, and interpersonal demands abound, there are some stressors that are of particular concern in organizations facing massive change in such short time frames.

The work of Staw, Sandelands, and Dutton (1981) identified the tendency for change to be perceived as a threat by individuals, groups, and organizations. The response to this threat is rigidity, including a restriction of information flow and a constriction of control. These actions may well be counterproductive, because they are not responsive to the types of change characteristic of today's work environment. Some of the stressors emanating from the environment are working with computers, electronic performance monitoring, violence, job insecurity, interactive demands, work/home conflicts, teamwork, and workforce diversity.

The physical and psychological stressors that emanate from working with computers are realities for many workers. Many companies are paying the price: U.S. West directory assistance operators were diagnosed as suffering from cumulative trauma disorder, costing the company $5 million (Fernberg, 1990). The social isolation that sometimes stems from jobs high in computer use may prove stressful as well. Particularly vulnerable to lack of social contact are those individuals who work in virtual offices or who telecommute. Whereas telecommuting was once an option initiated by employees who wanted to balance work and family concerns, companies are now trying to reduce real estate costs through offering telecommuting.

Electronic performance monitoring (EPM) has grown along with the increase in computerization of work. Although EPM facilitates managerial knowledge of detailed performance of employees, it may feel to workers like omnipresent and camouflaged surveillance. Mounting evidence indicates that electronically monitored workers experience more stress than their nonmonitored coworkers (Aiello & Kolb, 1995). EPM can also lead to deteriorated quality of working relationships with supervisors and peers.

There has been a dramatic increase in violence in the workplace. Assaults and violent actions are the second leading cause of death in the U.S. workplace, following transportation accidents (Bureau of Labor Statistics, 1995). Almost

7,600 workers were murdered on the job in the United States during the 1980s (Harvey & Cosier, 1995).

As a result of the massive restructuring of the 1990s, job insecurity abounds. More than 7 million permanent layoffs have been announced since 1987 in the United States (Cascio, 1995). As organizational retrenchment and restructuring continue, global job loss is expected to persist throughout the 1990s (Haugen & Meisenheimer, 1991). These changes create fears of job loss and worries about whether people will be able to fit into the "new" organizational arrangement. Survivors of restructuring may have feelings of guilt, and resent the loss of valued relationships at work. At the least, survivors suffer from work overload, as the organization attempts to accomplish more work with a smaller workforce.

The very notion of the career has evolved from one in which the model was one of working for one, or a very few, organizations and advancing up the organizational hierarchy. The premium is now on employability rather than employment, on taking charge of one's own career by developing portable skills, and on adding value to the organization.

The expansion of the service sector has resulted in an increase in jobs characterized by interactive demands; that is, jobs that require interaction with a wide variety of constituencies. Service jobs are inherently stressful, due to the requirement to give quality service to sometimes demanding and often irate customers (Singh, Goolsby, & Rhoads, 1994). Service jobs are often characterized by emotional labor, defined by Hochschild (1983) as "the management of feeling to create a publicly observable facial and bodily display" (p. 7). Emotional labor has been linked to substance abuse, headaches, absenteeism, and other forms of psychological distress. Often, what must be displayed to others is at odds with what is really felt, which creates dissonance and alienation from one's own emotions. Preliminary evidence indicates that this dissonance between feelings and expression may be the prime source of distress (Adelmann, 1995).

Work–home demands are a source of chronic stress. Over 75% of all families are characterized by dual careers (Guinn, 1989). Some companies are attempting to accommodate employees with flexible work arrangements and child-care assistance, but many workers are not privy to these amenities. The potential for overload from balancing multiple expectations is high. Parenting has an additive effect on work–home conflict.

Teamwork is the order of the day in most organizations. Teams, although sometimes the source of satisfaction, can also place a premium on the individual's interpersonal skills. Members that violate behavioral norms are often harshly sanctioned. As self-directed teams take on the work that was once reserved for managers, role ambiguity and role conflict may result.

The workforce is much more diverse than ever. Although this has obvious advantages, many employees find that working with those who are different from themselves can be stressful. Members of minority groups may experience distress from conflict, confusion, and denigration. A major contributing factor to this distress is the prevalence of ethnocentric attitudes among employees (Marsella, 1994).

Individual Differences

Another theme in the current research literature is that of the role of individual differences in the stress process. Past studies have focused on Type A behavior and locus of control as personality influences, among others, accumulating substantial knowledge. The contemporary literature has seen an emphasis on identifying other personologic variables that affect the stress-strain relation. The focus is on three emerging individual differences: hardiness, self-reliance, and negative affect. These dispositional factors hold potential for strongly affecting the stress–strain connection, with implications for designing interventions in organizations.

Hardiness. Hardiness is a personality disposition that influences how people interact with others and with the environment (Maddi, 1998). It is defined as the individuals' view of their place in the world that simultaneously expresses commitment, control, and challenge (Kobasa, 1979; Kobasa, Maddi, & Kahn, 1982). Commitment, as a dimension of hardiness, is a tendency to be involved in whatever one encounters. Individuals who are committed find the persons, events, and things in their environments to be meaningful. Control reflects a tendency to feel, think, and act as if one is influential, rather than helpless, in affecting life (Ouellette, 1997). Challenge is the belief that change is normal, and that changes are opportunities for growth rather than threats.

Hardiness is learned rather than inherited, and is presumed to decrease the likelihood of stress-related illnesses and performance problems. It achieves these effects through transformational coping, the search for social support to supplement this coping, and beneficial health practices (Maddi, 1998). Early evidence on hardiness was accumulated from retrospective and longitudinal studies at a large Midwestern telephone company. Executives were tracked for a 5-year period using questionnaires. Results indicated that executives who were hardy were less likely to report physical illness than those who were low on hardiness. In addition, hardiness was independent of education, age, managerial level, and marital status (Maddi, 1998; Ouellette, 1997).

Subsequent research has examined the effects of hardiness in a variety of samples and settings. Strategies have ranged from qualitative investigations to controlled experiments (for reviews, see Maddi, 1990; Ouellette, 1993). The majority of the studies have confirmed the relation between hardiness and health. Some studies have examined the relation between hardiness and performance. A study of military officer training candidates in Israel indicated that hardiness was related to successful completion of training (Westman, 1990). Hardiness was also found to be related to basketball performance throughout the season in a study of male high school athletes (Maddi & Hess, 1992).

The measurement of hardiness was originally achieved with an instrument containing a combination of true–false, forced-choice, and rating scale items. The original measure was criticized for the finding that the challenge dimension was unrelated to the other two dimensions in several samples

(Funk & Houston, 1987; Hull, Van Treuren, & Virnelli, 1987). The PVS–II, a second generation hardiness measure, was developed to avoid these difficulties. The 50-item measure has been shown to possess commitment, control, and challenge scores that are internally consistent, moderately intercorrelated, and strongly correlated with overall hardiness score (Maddi, 1997). Some problems, however, seem to persist, including a low internal reliability for the challenge dimension (Ouellette, 1997). This raises questions as to whether hardiness is unidimensional, or should be conceived of as multidimensional, with the dimensions showing separate relations with health.

Most of the research on hardiness has utilized data gathered by self-report measures. Cohen and Edwards (1988) viewed the evidence linking hardiness and improved well-being as equivocal. Because hardiness is proposed to be a disposition, coping efforts related to hardiness should be stable over time and across situations. Cohen and Edwards (1988) considered this evidence to be contradictory.

Despite its criticisms, hardiness remains an intriguing dispositional factor with potential to influence the stress-strain relation. Preliminary evidence in small groups indicates the efficacy of using focusing, situational reconstruction, and compensatory self-improvement techniques for enhancing hardiness among individuals (Maddi, 1994).

Self-reliance. Self-reliance is an individual difference reflected by the development of healthy, secure, interdependent relationships with others. Its roots are in Ainsworth and Bowlby's (1991) early studies of personality that resulted in attachment theory. Bowlby suggested that attachment is a biological imperative, controlled by the central nervous system, thus contributing to the survival of the human species. Ainsworth, Blehar, Waters, and Wall's (1978) studies identified three dominant patterns of attachment in infants: secure (called self-reliant by Bowlby, 1982, 1988), avoidant, and anxious-ambivalent. These early experiences become internal working models of self and other, and influence the individual's beliefs about the availability and responsiveness of attachment figures (Lopez, 1995).

Recent research suggests that attachment orientations extend into adult years and across the life span (Hazan & Shaver, 1987). Hazan and Shaver (1990) proposed that adulthood attachments are essential for effectiveness and satisfaction at work. Ainsworth's three patterns of attachment are labeled in the management literature as self-reliant (secure), counterdependent (avoidant), and overdependent (anxious-ambivalent; Nelson, J. C. Quick, & Joplin, 1991; J. C. Quick, Nelson, & J. D. Quick, 1990).

Self-reliance is an orientation characterized by a reciprocity and flexibility in relationships, and a pattern of interdependence. It is based on the belief that others will be available in stressful and anxious times of need. Adults who are self-reliant form secure, supportive relationships at work and at home. At work, interdependence is evidenced by close relationships with a variety of colleagues both inside and outside the organization. Self-reliance may be a critical factor in newcomer adjustment to organizations (Nelson & J. C. Quick, 1991). An attrition analysis of military officer candidates and basic trainees indicated that candidates who were self-reliant were better able to develop the social support necessary for successful completion of training (J. C. Quick, Joplin, Nelson, Manglesdorff, & Fiedler, 1996).

Counterdependence is an orientation rooted in the belief that no one will be available in situations of distress. Counterdependent individuals frequently overinvest in work activities, preferring to complete tasks themselves rather than ask for assistance. They may resist offers of support from others, and isolate themselves in the workplace.

Overdependence is an orientation based on a belief that others may not be available when needed. The overdependent individual seeks out and relies on more supports than are necessary or appropriate for the situation. Overdependence frequently leads to an individual relinquishing responsibility for personal well-being. Individuals who use an overdependent orientation may "drain" their social support relationships by their clingy nature and their failure to reciprocate.

Self-reliant individuals possess a sense of felt security, derived from internal working models that view others as available and responsive. They report fewer symptoms of distress (J. C. Quick, Joplin, Nelson, & J. D. Quick, 1992). Counterdependent and overdependent individuals report more physical symptoms (Hazan & Shaver, 1990) and higher levels of distress (Mikulincer, Florian, & Weller, 1993). Self-reliance may moderate the stress–distress relation. Future research should examine the relations between quality and quantity of social support relationships and the three attachment orientations.

Negative Affect. Negative affect is a stable disposition that contributes to dysphoric mood that permeates an individual's attitudes and behavior (Watson & Clark, 1984). Individuals high on negative affect (NA) possess more negative perceptions and appraisals than individuals low on NA. It is possible that individuals high on NA report more distress because they are more sensitive to stressors, or because they create the stressors they experience due to their negative world views (McCrae & Costa, 1994).

Because individuals high on negative affect (NA) possess negative views of themselves and the world around them, NA is likely to strengthen the relation between self-reported job stressors and psychological outcomes (Watson, Pennebaker, & Folger, 1987). Evidence provided by Brief, Burke, George, Robinson, and Webster (1988) indicated that NA was confounded with measures of self-reported work and nonwork stressors and distress in the form of job dissatisfaction, somatic complaints, life dissatisfaction, and depressive symptoms; thus, correlations between self-reports of stressors and distress may be inflated by NA. Other researchers have found that controlling for NA diminished the relation between stressors and somatic complaints, but not between stressors and other forms of distress (Chen & Spector, 1991).

Many of the studies of NA are cross-sectional in nature. In an attempt to improve on existing designs and measures, Schonfeld (1996) conducted a longitudinal study of teachers that included measures taken during preemployment and from 4 to 5 months on the new job. Three "neutrally worded" stressor measures were constructed in an attempt to minimize reference to distress. The stressors were moderately related to postemployment depressive symptoms and job satisfaction, and to motivation among Whites (but not among Blacks and Hispanics). Correlation and regression coefficients were largely unchanged when NA and psychophysiologic symptoms, measured at preemployment, were controlled.

Complicating the comparison of studies is the fact that various measures of NA have been utilized. These include measures of anxiety, psychasthenia, repression-sensitization, neuroticism, and others (Watson & Clark, 1984). Brief et al. (1988) used the Taylor Manifest Anxiety Scale (Taylor, 1953) and Schonfeld (1996) utilized the Center for Epidemiologic Studies Depression Scale (Radloff, 1977) and a psychophysi- ologic symptoms measure; both state measures with time frames of 1 week.

Despite these complications, NA appears to be an important dispositional variable in work stress research. It may be a methodological "nuisance" variable, or it may be a cause of work stressors. Future studies that are longitudinal, utilizing objective measures of stressors and strains, and are conducted using a variety of samples and settings will enhance knowledge in this regard.

Social Support

The past decade has witnessed a dramatic increase in the literature on social support and work stress. House's (1981) framework identified four dimensions of support related to work stress, including emotional (empathy and caring), informational (suggestions for problem solving), appraisal (feedback on behavior), and instrumental (direct aid) forms of support. He noted the importance of support from the supervisor and coworkers, and argued that organizations can be barriers to social support or facilitators of it. According to House, social supports allow individuals to extend their repertoires of skills and knowledge by drawing on the resources of support providers.

House, Landis, and Umberson (1988) conducted a meta-analysis that indicated that individuals with lower social support levels possessed significantly higher morbidity and mortality. Although lower levels of support are associated with higher distress, the mechanisms whereby this association occurs have not been adequately identified. A long-standing debate surrounding this issue centers on the question of whether social support has a main effect or buffering effect on health. Social support can have a main effect on health by promoting better health (Corneil, 1997) or lack of social support can cause ill health (Cohen & Syme, 1985). The buffering hypothesis suggests that social support intervenes between the stressor and distress to reduce its deleterious effects. There seems to be evidence in support of both hypotheses. Cohen and Wills (1985) found evidence for both main effects and buffering effects. Workplace social support was added to the job strain model, and a buffering of the effects of job strain by social support was found in three of four studies on cardiovascular disease (Landsbergis, Schnall, Schwartz, Warren, & Pickering, 1995). Ganster (1995) concluded that the evidence regarding the buffering hypothesis is mixed at best.

Uchino, Cacioppo, and Kiecolt-Glaser (1996) examined the research on social support and physiological processes using meta-analysis and qualitative procedures. Their review indicated that social support was related to positive effects on the cardiovascular, immune, and endocrine systems. Health-related behaviors did not appear to be responsible for the associations between social support and health. Further, they found evidence for the buffering effect in some studies.

A study of 92 newcomers in organizations indicated that the availability of social support was associated with positive newcomer adjustment (Nelson & J. C. Quick, 1991). Recent evidence also indicates that it is the perception of social support that is most closely related to adjustment and health (J. G. Sarason, B. R. Sarason, Brock, & Pierce, 1996). If this is the case, then it is possible that another variable, potentially an individual difference/personality factor, is affecting both stress and social support. Self-reliance, or attachment orientation, is one such variable.

In summary, the changing nature of work, individual differences, and social support are three themes common to the current work stress literature. The next section turns to potential challenges and opportunities for those researchers who study work stress.

FUTURE CHALLENGES FOR RESEARCH

The challenge for future researchers in occupational health psychology is to advance the creation of "healthy" organizations. A healthy organization is one in which all people have the opportunity to achieve high performance, high satisfaction, and well-being (Quick, Quick, Nelson, & Hurrell, 1997). Through enhanced emphasis on the root causes of both health and distress in the workplace, healthy organizations should experience diminishing reliance on secondary and tertiary preventive interventions (Cooper & Cartwright, 1994). The challenge for researchers and practitioners alike is that the discovery of some of these root causes may require a fundamentally new, or at least an expanded, frame of reference. Three particularly challenging areas of future opportunity are research into eustress and positive affect (PA), diversity issues, and nonrecursive relations.

Eustress and Positive Affect

Eustress has been defined as "a positive discrepancy between and individual's perceived state and desired state, provided that the presence of this discrepancy is considered important by the individual" (Edwards & Cooper, 1988, p. 1448). Eustress is analogous with an overall, general state of happiness or subjective well-being (Brebner & Martin, 1995). Characterizing eustress as the stress of fulfillment, Kahn and Byosiere (1992) advocated that because the stress of life cannot be avoided, people should seek to maximize the eustress component. Engaging work and the generation of frequent positive events are two possible paths to eustress.

Eustress was identified earlier in this chapter as the type of stress that may lead to enhanced health and performance on the job. Edwards and Cooper (1988) posited that eustress may improve health not only by decreasing the rate of development of degenerative diseases but also by actually reversing the development of disease. They described the ways eustress may improve health directly through hormonal and biochemical changes or indirectly by facilitating attempts to cope with existing stress.

A longitudinal study of air traffic controllers (ATCs) provides an exceptional example of healthy stress (Rose, 1987). Over a 3-year period, the cortisol values of 201 men were measured every 20 minutes for 5 hours on 3 or more days and compared to both objective and subjective assessments of workload. Whereas the increases in cortisol for all levels of workload were slight, the men who showed the highest increase in cortisol to increased work reported themselves as more satisfied and were regarded by peers as more competent. These high cortisol responders also showed less frequent illness than those with lower cortisol levels, who for any given level of work tended to have more minor health problems. Rose described the men whose cortisol increased in response to challenging work as *engaged* rather than stressed. Elsewhere, the happiness derived from engagement in mindful challenge has been termed "flow" (Csikszentmihalyi, 1990). In their review of Rose's study, Ganster and Schaubroeck (1991) described the healthy state of physiological arousal experienced by the engaged workers as eustress.

Although there is a paucity of research on eustress in the workplace, recent reviews on health psychology concur that evidence supports the suggestion that positive daily events and positive cognitions may directly contribute to physical health outcomes (Adler & Matthews, 1994; Cohen & Herbert, 1996). Indirectly, both trait positive affect (PA) and eustress-induced state PA may facilitate coping through social support by improving social interactions (Edwards & Cooper, 1988). Studies have shown that PA is positively related to both frequency (Watson, Clark, McIntyre, & Hamaker, 1992) and quality (Berry & Hansen, 1996) of social interaction.

The personality trait PA reflects an individual's predisposition to experience positive emotional states (Burke, Brief, & George, 1993). It is well established that NA and PA are independent constructs (Burke et al., 1993; George & Brief, 1992). Similar to eustress, PA has received relatively little attention from occupational stress researchers. Although negative affect (NA) influences self-reports of stressors and strains, it is not expected to exert a strong influence on self-reports of positive experiences at work; however, PA is expected to be very influential in this regard (Burke et al., 1993). Positive affect may exert more general and longer lasting effects than negative affect, and even modest and temporary shifts in affect can improve patterns of social interaction in the workplace (Baron, 1993).

In a recent study of both state PA and state NA in Canadian workers, Brown and Moskowitz (1997) determined that individuals who reported state PA reported less subjective experiences of physical illness. Using daily event-sampling methodology to minimize problems with retrospection, they found that unpleasant affective state (NA) alone influenced occurrence of minor illness with no contribution from trait neuroticism. Interestingly, participants in their study reported more than twice as many occurrences of pleasant as unpleasant affect.

A similar bias for the positive was found in a study of stress reactions on and off the job for employees of Volvo in Sweden (Frankenhaeuser et al., 1989). Both managers and clerical workers experienced more positive stress (effort involvement) than negative stress (work overload). Female clerical workers self-reported positive stress twice as often as negative stress.

In fact, recent studies suggest that most people are reasonably happy most of the time (E. Diener & C. Diener, 1996; Lykken & Tellegen, 1996). E. Diener and C. Diener (1996) posited that this may indicate a positive baseline for affect in humans. Individual differences in this happiness baseline may be determined by traits (e.g., optimism, extroversion, and self-esteem), supportive personal relationships, religious faith, a culture that offers positive interpretations for most daily events, and engaging work and leisure (Myers & E. Diener, 1995).

Individuals with a positive orientation to life seem to be more engaged in their lives and make the best of both work and nonwork situations. These optimistic individuals manage challenging and stressful events with less subjective distress and less adverse impact on their physical well-being (Scheier & Carver, 1992).

A growing body of research suggests that the way people habitually explain to themselves why events happen influences their expectations for controlling future events, which may in turn affect their well-being (Seligman, 1991). Compared to pessimists, people with an optimistic style of explaining bad events tend to experience better health (Peterson, 1995). Similar to the underdeveloped knowledge of eustress and PA, less is known about the significance of explanatory style for good events (Peterson, Buchanan, & Seligman, 1995). Because an optimistic explanatory style can be learned (Seligman, 1991), this knowledge could help organizations that discern the value of generating eustress and PA through purposeful attention to positive events to maximize their effort and investment.

The growing evidence that happiness is healthy, and that most people are happy, suggests that a shift in focus to the positive from the negative in occupational stress research merits strong consideration. In as much as the subjective well-being purposed by the study of occupational health psychology results from the complex interaction of both frequent positive and infrequent negative stress outcomes, the optimal research agenda implores balance. The creation of healthy workplaces implies that processes designed to generate eustress are at least as important as processes designed to prevent distress.

Five principles guide the preventive stress management philosophy (J. C. Quick & J. D. Quick, 1984):

1. Individual and organizational health are interdependent.
2. Management has a responsibility for individual and organizational health.
3. Individual and organizational distress are not inevitable.
4. Each individual and organization reacts uniquely to stress.

5. Organizations are dynamic, ever-changing entities.

The lack of knowledge about eustress suggests that researchers have equated individual and organizational health with the absence of distress. Because eustress and distress are independent constructs, a better understanding of the sources and healthy consequences of engaging work experiences is in order. Practitioners, then, could have enhanced confidence in the value of providing engaging work and consistently generating small positive events in the workplace.

Diversity Issues in Occupational Stress Research

The experience of eustress and distress in the workplace will vary according to an individual's culture, gender, age, and the interaction between the these variables. For example, an extensive review of social support reveals that it is a multidimensional construct across the spectrum of diversity variables (Uchino et al., 1996). Although social support predicts better cardiovascular regulation in both men and women, sex differences appear to determine the importance of type of social support. Because the association between social support and cardiovascular function may vary across cultures, Uchino et al. (1996) emphasized the importance of proper operationalization of social relationships within a specific cultural context. Their review also suggested that whereas social support has beneficial effects on physiological processes across all age groups, it may be more important to the health of older adults. They even suggested that individuals with high social support may biologically age at a slower rate.

Understanding the particular stresses experienced by females, ethnic minorities, and aging workers is improving but still insufficient. Keita and Hurrell (1994) offered a collection of studies on diversity and family issues that represents important progress in this area. There is considerable opportunity to increase the understanding of cross-national as well as cross-cultural objective stressors, coping processes, and approaches to research (Cooper & Payne, 1992).

H. F. Myers (1996) stated that despite the heterogeneity of American society, the theorizing and research of health psychology reflects the mainstream bias of psychology and medicine, focused primarily on White, heterosexual, middle-class American men. This is problematic because if research samples are not adequately diverse, then false conclusions about particular groups could subsequently lead to providing them with ineffective health care interventions (Mann & Kato, 1996). If there are to be genuinely healthy organizations, then the challenge in occupational health psychology must be to generate opportunities for engagement and prevent sources of distress for all people in these organizations.

To do so requires recognizing the heterogeneity that exists within groups and incorporating it into the design of studies. For example, although it is important to understand the differences in stress and health that exist between Whites and Hispanics (Gutierres, Saenz, & Green, 1994), researchers should appreciate that Mexicans, Cubans, and Puerto Ricans may themselves differ with regard to perception of and response to stress (Krause & Goldenhar, 1992). An exploratory study of stressors for professional women found that Mexican American women reported experiencing less racism at work than Puerto Rican and African American women and less sexism than Anglo-American women (Walcott-McQuigg, 1994). These within-group differences should also exist for Asian Americans, and within all groups should be most apparent among more recent immigrants.

Sex and gender issues present especially important challenges. Most researchers confuse the terms *sex* and *gender* by using the two interchangeably. Unfortunately, Jick and Mitz's (1985) observation that "virtually all of the research dealing with sex differences in the stress process makes the implicit assumption that sex and sex-role identity are equivalent" (p. 415) is still true today. Enhanced understanding of *sex differences* in occupational stress is very important, but this term should be reserved for reference to biological distinctions between males and females.

Conversely, the term *gender differences* should be reserved for differential role behaviors that are learned as appropriate for either males or females (Mann, 1996). Gays, lesbians, and single fathers are all invisible in the study of occupational stress and health. Accordingly, a fundamental rethinking of the value of capturing the within-group variance of gender differences is in order (Matuszek, Nelson, & J. C. Quick, 1995). Although the few studies that attempt to address gender differences and such things as work–family conflict are encouraging (Frone, Russell, & Barnes, 1996), the challenge remains to explore ways to operationalize gender beyond "0 = male and 1 = female."

It is important to remember that the purpose for studying the aforementioned cultural and gender differences is in order to better target interventions and promote health for all people (Mann & Kato, 1996). Women's work roles, family composition, the allocation of family responsibilities, and the cultural diversity of the workplace will all continue to evolve. A balanced preventive and generative approach to occupational stress and health suggests that researchers become increasingly anticipatory of these changes.

Nonrecursive Relationships Among Variables

A methodological challenge for future occupational stress researchers is the examination of nonrecursive relations among variables. A nonrecursive relation is one in which two (or more) variables are involved in two-way causation (Bentler & Chou, 1987). Although few current structural models in occupational stress research incorporate nonrecursive models, reciprocal causation among variables may be especially important to consider when studying chronic stress and chronic ill health.

When individuals consistently experience both role-related stress and health problems, it may be difficult to determine which came first. In order to obtain an unbiased estimate of the effect of stress on health requires the researcher to partial out the reciprocal effect of health on stress (Kessler, Magee, & Nelson, 1996). Nonrecursive models may also be required in other situations where the temporal order between cause and effect is ambiguous.

Nonrecursive relations require that instrumental variables be incorporated into the model. Instrumental variables are theoretically related to only one of the antecedent variables in the reciprocal relation (Bentler & Chou, 1987). Frone, Russell, and Cooper's (1992) specification of a nonrecursive model in their study of stress and work–family conflict (WFC) provides a very good example of proper methodology. In their cross-sectional study, job distress and family distress functioned as the instrumental variables in the nonrecursive model of work–family conflict. Their results support the concept that the conflict relations between work and family are reciprocal.

Nonrecursive models require careful a priori theorization and research design to allow estimation of the structural equation model (SEM). The use of SEM is advantageous because it allows simultaneous examination of reciprocal relations between several variables (Williams & Podsakoff, 1989). The use of nonrecursive models should contribute additional support for causal inference as stress researchers increase their use of longitudinal designs.

THE RESEARCH–PRACTICE DIALOGUE

Perhaps the greatest challenge for the future of preventive stress management lies in establishing and maintaining an effective dialogue between researchers and practitioners. Communication between the two groups has increased in recent years, but there still remains a perceptible division between them. Undoubtedly there are successful workplace interventions that go unpublished, and there is knowledge gleaned by researchers that fails to be translated into application by practitioners. For several decades, scholars have called for more rigorous evaluation studies of workplace interventions. A review of recent literature suggests that there may be reasons for cautious optimism.

Workplace Interventions

One of the guiding principles of preventive stress management is that individuals and organizations are responsible for health and well-being. Accordingly, workplace interventions can be classified as focusing on the individual or on the organization. Most interventions at the individual level, typically referred to as "stress management interventions," consist of secondary prevention efforts that help individuals alter the ways they respond to job stressors. In contrast, most organizational interventions are primary prevention programs aimed at changing the nature of job and/or organizational stressors. A review of the literature on interventions indicates substantial progress in the knowledge of individual level interventions, with comparably less progress in the knowledge of organizational interventions.

The increase in published studies of stress management interventions is evidenced by two reviews by Murphy (1984, 1996). Murphy (1984) contained only one third as many studies as Murphy (1996). Stress management interventions are typically offered as a single session focusing on techniques for helping individuals identify and manage symptoms of stress (Hurrell & Murphy, 1996). Common techniques for such programs include muscle relaxation, meditation, cognitive-behavioral skills, biofeedback, or a combination of these. Most interventions use a combination of techniques.

Murphy (1996) reviewed 64 studies that were published in peer-reviewed literature and evaluated a health outcome. Almost 90% of the studies used reliable and valid outcome measures, including physiologic/biochemical markers or validated self-report measures. Most of the studies were preventive, and were offered to all employees on a voluntary basis. The effectiveness of the techniques varied. Cognitive-behavioral methods were more effective for psychological outcomes, whereas muscle relaxation was more effective for physiologic outcomes. Biofeedback was the least frequently used technique and the least effective. Meditation was the sole technique that showed significant effects on all outcome measures, although it was used in only three studies. Interventions that used a combination of techniques produced more consistent results across all outcomes.

This review indicated considerable progress in evaluating the efficacy of individual-level interventions. Along with the progress in terms of the number of published studies came a wider range of outcome measures. Three studies evaluated biochemical changes after training (e.g., catecholamines, angiotensin, renin, and aldosterone) with positive results. In addition, three studies assessed health care costs following stress management interventions and reported impressive results.

Kahn and Byosiere (1992) noted a surge in practitioner interventions that focus on the effects of stress and target individuals, and indicated that most of these efforts have not been evaluated in terms of serious research. Although cautioning that research evidence is meager and methodological problems abound, they concluded that evaluation studies show that stress management interventions produced significant reductions in subjective distress and psychophysiological indicators.

Turning to those programs that focus on the organizational level and seek to alter, reduce, or eliminate stressors, the evidence is sparse. Several case studies have been documented. Terra (1995), for example, recounted a case study of a participatory approach to job redesign and implementation of self-managing teams in the Dutch metal can industry. Murphy (1996) reported that a few empirical studies have demonstrated the reductions in strain associated with flexible work schedules (Pierce & Newstrom, 1983), increased employee participation in decision making (Jackson, 1983), and increased worker autonomy (Wall & Clegg, 1981). Each of these methods has the net effect of increasing employee control over work.

Karasek and Theorell (1990) posited the thesis that the design of workplaces may be more important than individual coping responses in creating ill health. Their research at the Karolinska Institute of Sweden suggested that redesign efforts should focus on increasing worker control and social support in order to enhance individual health.

Kompier (1996) reviewed five theoretical approaches to job design to isolate the factors that affect stress, psychological well-being, and job satisfaction. The approaches examined included the job characteristics model (JCM), the Michigan organizational stress model (MOS), the job demands/job control model (JD-JC), the sociotechnical approach, and the action-theoretical approach with its roots in German work psychology. Kompier concluded that there is remarkable similarity in the approaches. The factors that appear to affect motivation and enjoyment of work are control, meaningfulness and feedback, and cooperation at the workplace. Kompier concluded that the answer is "no" to the question of whether stress prevention programs utilize this knowledge and emphasize job redesign.

Ganster (1995) examined three theoretical bases for interventions. The job demands–job control model, he argued, has sufficient empirical evidence to warrant job redesign interventions to improve employee well-being. He cautioned that Type A and other personality factors need to be considered when implementing these interventions. Evidence suggests that social support can play a key role in enhancing employee well-being, yet there is little research on how or if social support can be augmented in organizations. Role clarification is another intervention that warrants evaluation. Ganster lamented the lack of controlled evaluations of interventions, and argued that the absence of published studies does not mean that too little is known to recommend such interventions.

Given that such knowledge exists, why is it not implemented in organizational interventions? Part of the reason may be due to a lack of communication between researchers and practitioners. Another contributing factor may be the differing perspectives of managers and employees. Managers may view stress as primarily caused by individual factors, and thus the responsibility of the employee. They may view stress management programs as "quick fixes" requiring less effort than interventions directed at changing the job or the organization. On the other hand, employees view stress as caused mainly by organizational and job conditions. Such differing views do not lend themselves to effective approaches to prevention.

Ultimately, comprehensive interventions that encompass both the individual worker and the organization will be needed to address the prevention and amelioration of distress. Current themes in the stress literature point to interventions focusing on contemporary sources of distress, increasing individual hardiness and self-reliance, and improving social support at work as promising avenues. Individual adaptation and organizational change need to be integrated. Individual interventions must not be used as temporary measures to pacify employees while distressful organizational conditions go untreated. The effective implementation of work stress interventions requires organizational stress diagnosis, planning for prevention, organizational and individual intervention, and careful evaluation of the outcomes of the intervention (J. C. Quick, J. D. Quick, et al., 1997). Given the dynamic nature of the stress experience, this is of necessity an iterative, ongoing process.

Participatory action research has been cited by a number of authors (cf. Hurrell & Murphy, 1996; Landsbergis et al., 1995) as a preferred approach for evaluating comprehensive interventions. This approach involves researchers and organization members joining in all aspects of the intervention, from needs assessment to evaluation. Worker involvement in all phases of the change process is critical for sustained change. In addition, both qualitative and quantitative methods are needed, along with assessments of both the process and the outcomes of the intervention.

Bridging the Research–Practice Gap

The notion of the "healthy company" has received increased attention in the literature (Cooper & Williams, 1994). This notion suggests an expanded definition of organizational effectiveness that goes beyond profitability. Healthy organizations create health and well-being for employees and other constituents (Jaffe, 1995).

To accomplish the aim of creating and maintaining healthy organizations, the gap between research and practice must be bridged. There are two avenues for accomplishing this goal. First, an exchange program can be set up for researchers and practitioners, similar to those programs in place in organizations and universities. Such an exchange would allow both parties to experience the world of the other party. Researchers would see the reality of organizational constraints like budgets and politics, and practitioners, removed from their element, might be able to explore a wider range of alternatives for intervention. Another advantage of such exchanges would be to establish a common medium for dialogue between the two groups. This would work to eliminate the common feeling that researchers and practitioners each have their own languages, and that there is often little common ground.

Second, venues should be created to facilitate increased interaction between researchers and practitioners. Such venues allow individuals to meet on neutral ground, away from their workplaces, to work on the overarching goal of increasing individual and organizational health. Some laudable efforts are already underway. The National Institute for Occupational Safety and Health (NIOSH) and the American Psychological Association (APA) formed a partnership to refine and implement strategies for the prevention of work-related psychological disorders. The partnership has resulted in three conferences: "Work and Well-Being: An Agenda for the 1990s" (1990), "Stress in the '90s: A Changing Workforce in a Changing Workplace" (1992), and "Work Stress and Health '95: Creating Healthier Workplaces." The three conferences drew a wealth of international researchers and practitioners and produced a series of books, with several contributions devoted to work stress interventions.

Another venture of note is that of the International Stress Management Association, which held its Sixth International Congress on Stress and Health in Australia in 1996. The Congress attendees were an impressive mix of researchers and practitioners, with many sessions focusing on organizational and individual interventions.

Exchange programs and venues for establishing dialogues are ways of promoting joint ventures between researchers and practitioners. The evaluation of workplace interventions requires such partnerships, particularly given the calls for action research as a preferred approach. Effective interventions demand attention to both individuals and organizations, and they demand the best efforts of researchers and practitioners in collaboration.

REFERENCES

Adelmann, P. K. (1995). Emotional labor as a potential source of job stress. In S. L. Sauter & L. R. Murphy (Eds.), *Organizational risk factors for job stress* (pp. 371–382). Washington, DC: American Psychological Association.

Adler, N., & Matthews, K. (1994). Health psychology: Why do some people get sick and some stay well? In L. W. Porter & M. R. Rosenzweig (Eds.), *Annual review of psychology* (Vol. 45, pp. 229–259). Palo Alto, CA: Annual Reviews.

Aiello, J. R., & Kolb, K. J. (1995). Electronic performance monitoring: A risk factor for workplace stress. In S. L. Sauter & L. R. Murphy (Eds.), *Organizational risk factors for job stress* (pp. 163–180). Washington, DC: American Psychological Association.

Ainsworth, M.D.S., Blehar, M. C., Waters, E., & Wall, S. (1978). *Patterns of attachment: A psychological analysis of the strange situation.* Hillsdale, NJ: Lawrence Erlbaum Associates.

Ainsworth, M.D.S., & Bowlby, J. (1991). An ethological approach to personality. *American Psychologist, 46,* 333–341.

Baron, R. A. (1993). Affect and organizational behavior: When and why feeling good (or bad) matters. In J. K. Murnighan (Ed.), *Social psychology in organizations: Advances in theory and research* (pp. 65–88). Englewood Cliffs, NJ: Prentice-Hall.

Bentler, P. M., & Chou, C. P. (1987). Practical issues in structural modeling. *Sociological Methods and Research, 16,* 78–117.

Berry, D. S., & Hansen, J. S. (1996). Positive affect, negative affect, and social interaction. *Journal of Personality and Social Psychology, 71,* 796–809.

Bowlby, J. (1982). *Attachment* (2nd ed.). New York: Basic Books.

Bowlby, J. (1988). *A secure base.* New York: Basic Books.

Brebner, J., & Martin, M. (1995). Testing for stress and happiness: The role of personality factors. In C. D. Spielberger & I. G. Sarason (Eds.), *Stress and emotion: Anxiety, anger, and curiosity* (Vol. 15, pp. 139–172). Washington, DC: Taylor & Francis.

Brief, A. P., Burke, M. J., George, J. M., Robinson, B. S., & Webster, J. (1988). Should negative affectivity remain an unmeasured variable in the study of job stress? *Journal of Applied Psychology, 73,* 193–198.

Brown, K. W., & Moskowitz, D. S. (1997). Does unhappiness make you sick? The role of affect and neuroticism in the experience of common physical symptoms. *Journal of Personality and Social Psychology, 72,* 907–917.

Bureau of Labor Statistics. (1995). *National census of fatal occupational injuries.* (Publication No. USDL-96-315). Washington, DC: Author.

Burke, M. J., Brief, A. P., & George, J. M. (1993). The role of negative affectivity in understanding relations between self-reports of stressors and strains: A comment on the applied psychology literature. *Journal of Applied Psychology, 78,* 402–412.

Cascio, W. F. (1995). Whither industrial and organizational psychology in a changing world of work? *American Psychologist, 50,* 929–939.

Chen, P. Y., & Spector, P. E. (1991). Negative affectivity as the underlying cause of correlations between stressors and strains. *Journal of Applied Psychology, 76,* 398–407.

Cohen, S., & Edwards, J. R. (1988). Personality characteristics as moderators of the relationship between stress and disorder. In W. J. Neufeld (Ed.), *Advances in the investigation of psychological stress* (pp. 235–283). New York: Wiley.

Cohen, S., & Herbert, T. B. (1996). Health psychology: Psychological factors and physical disease from the perspective of human psychoneuroimmunology. In J. T. Spence, J. M. Darley, & D. J. Foss (Eds.), *Annual review of psychology* (Vol. 47, pp. 113–142). Palo Alto, CA: Annual Reviews.

Cohen, S., & Syme, S. L. (1985). *Social support and health.* New York: Academic Books.

Cohen, S., & Wills, T. A. (1985). Stress, social support, and the buffering hypothesis. *Psychological Bulletin, 98,* 310–357.

Cooper, C. L. (1998). *Theories of organizational stress.* Cambridge, England: Oxford University Press.

Cooper, C. L., & Cartwright, S. (1994). Healthy mind, healthy organization—A proactive approach to occupational stress. *Human Relations, 47,* 455–471.

Cooper, C. L., & Payne, R. L. (1992). International perspectives on research into work, well-being, and stress management. In J. C. Quick, L. R. Murphey, & J. J. Hurrell, Jr. (Eds.), *Stress and well-being at work: Assessments and interventions for occupational mental health* (pp. 348–368). Washington, DC: American Psychological Association.

Cooper, C. L., & Williams, S. (1994). *Creating healthy work organizations.* Chichester, England: Wiley.

Corneil, D. W. (1997). Social support. In J. Stellman (Ed.), *Encyclopaedia of Occupational Health and Safety* (sect. 34.48). Geneva, Switzerland: International Labour Office.

Csikszentmihalyi, M. (1990). *Flow: The psychology of optimal experience.* New York: Harper & Row.

Diener, E., & Diener, C. (1996). Most people are happy. *Psychological Science, 7,* 181–185.

Edwards, J. R. (1996). An examination of competing versions of the person–environment fit approach to stress. *Academy of Management Journal, 39,* 292–339.

Edwards, J. R., & Cooper, C. L. (1988). The impacts of positive psychological states on physical health: A review and theoretical framework. *Social Science Medicine, 27,* 1447–1459.

Edwards, J. R., & Cooper, C. L. (1990). The person–environment fit approach to stress: Recurring problems and some suggested solutions. *Journal of Organizational Behavior, 11,* 293–307.

Fernberg, P. M. (1990). Why "white collar" doesn't mean "danger-free." *Modern Office Technology, 35,* 49–52.

Frankenhaeuser, M., Lundberg, U., Frederikson, M., Melin, B., Tuomisto, M., Myrsten, A., Hedman, M., Bergman-Losman, B., & Wallin, L. (1989). Stress on and off the job as related to sex and occupational status in white-collar workers. *Journal of Organizational Behavior, 10,* 321–346.

Frone, M. R., Russell, M., & Barnes, G. M. (1996). Work-family conflict, gender, and health-related outcomes: A study of employed parents in two community samples. *Journal of Occupational Health Psychology, 1,* 57–69.

Frone, M. R., Russell, M., & Cooper, M. L. (1992). Antecedents and outcomes of work–family conflict: Testing a model of the work–family interface. *Journal of Applied Psychology, 77,* 65–78.

Funk, S. C., & Houston, B. K. (1987). A critical analysis of the hardiness scales' validity and utility. *Journal of Personality and Social Psychology, 53,* 572–578.

Ganster, D. C. (1995). Interventions for building healthy organizations: Suggestions from the stress research literature. In L. R. Murphy, S. L. Sauter, & G. P. Keita, (Eds.), *Job stress interventions* (pp. 323–336). Washington, DC: American Psychological Association.

Ganster, D. C., & Schaubroeck, J. (1991). Work stress and employee health. *Journal of Management, 17,* 235–271.

Gardell, B. (1971). *Production technology and job satisfaction: A social psychological study of industrial work.* Stockholm: Personnel Administration Board. (Original in Swedish)

Gardell, B. (1987). Efficiency and health hazards in mechanized work. In J. C. Quick, R. S. Bhagat, J. E. Dalton, & J. D. Quick (Eds.), *Work stress: Health care systems in the workplace* (pp. 50–71). New York: Praeger Scientific.

George, J. M., & Brief, A. P. (1992). Feeling good-doing good: A conceptual analysis of the mood at work-organizational spontaneity relationship. *Psychological Bulletin, 112,* 310–329.

Guinn, S. L. (1989). The changing workforce. *Training & Development Journal, 43,* 36–39.

Gutierres, S. E., Saenz, D. S., & Green, B. L. (1994). Job stress and health outcomes among White and Hispanic employees: A test of the person–environment fit model. In G. P. Kieta & J. J. Hurrell, Jr. (Eds.), *Job stress in a changing workforce: Investigating gender, diversity, and family* (pp. 107–125). Washington, DC: American Psychological Association.

Harvey, M. G., & Cosier, R. A. (1995). Homicides in the workplace: Crisis or false alarm? *Business Horizons, 38,* 11-20.

Haugen, S. E., & Meisenheimer, J. R., II. (1991). U. S. labor market weakened in 1990. *Monthly Labor Review, 114,* 3–16.

Hazan, C., & Shaver, P. R. (1987). Romantic love conceptualized as an attachment process. *Journal of Personality and Social Psychology, 52,* 511–524.

Hazan, C., & Shaver, P. R. (1990). Love and work: An attachment-theoretical perspective. *Journal of Personality and Social Psychology, 59,* 270–280.

Hochschild, A. R. (1983). *The managed heart: Commercialization of human feeling.* Berkeley: University of California Press.

House, J. S. (1981). *Work stress and social support.* Reading, MA: Addison-Wesley.

House, J. S., Landis, K. R., & Umberson, D. (1988). Social relationships and health. *Science, 241,* 540–545.

Hull, J. G., Van Treuren, R. R., & Virnelli, S. (1987). Hardiness and health: A critique and alternative approach. *Journal of Personality and Social Psychology, 53,* 518–530.

Hurrell, J. J., Jr., & Murphy, L. R. (1996). Occupational stress intervention. *American Journal of Industrial Medicine, 29,* 338–341.

Jackson, S. E. (1983). Participation in decision making as a strategy for reducing job-related strain. *Journal of Applied Psychology, 68,* 3–19.

Jaffe, D. T. (1995). The healthy company: Research paradigms for personal and organizational health. In S. L. Sauter & L. R. Murphy (Eds.), *Organizational risk factors for job stress* (pp. 13–40). Washington, DC: American Psychological Association.

Jick, T. D., & Mitz, L. F. (1985). Sex differences in work stress. *Academy of Management Review, 10,* 408–420.

Kahn, R. L., & Byosiere, P. (1992). Stress in organizations. In M. D. Dunnette & L. M. Hough (Eds.), *Handbook of industrial and organizational psychology* (2nd ed., Vol. 3, pp. 517–650). Palo Alto, CA: Consulting Psychologists Press.

Kahn, R. L., Wolfe, D. M., Quinn, R. P., Snoek, J. D., & Rosenthal, R. A. (1964). *Organizational stress: Studies in role conflict and ambiguity.* New York: Wiley.

Karasek, R. A. (1979). Job demands, job decision latitude, and mental strain: Implication for job design. *Administrative Science Quarterly, 24,* 285–308.

Karasek, R. A., Theorell, T., Schwartz, J. E., Schnall, P. L., Pieper, C. F., & Michela, J. L. (1988). Job characteristics in relation to the prevalence of myocardial infarction in the US health examination survey (HES) and the health and nutrition examination survey (HANES). *American Journal of Public Health, 78,* 910–918.

Karasek, R., & Theorell, T. (1990). *Healthy work: Stress, productivity, and the reconstruction of working life.* New York: Basic Books.

Keita, G. P., & Hurrell, J. J., Jr. (1994). Introduction. In G. P. Keita & J. J. Hurrell, Jr. (Eds.), *Job stress in a changing workforce: Investigating gender, diversity, and family* (pp. xiii–xiv). Washington, DC: American Psychological Association.

Kessler, R. C., Magee, W. J., & Nelson, C. B. (1996). Analysis of psychosocial stress. In H. B Kaplan (Ed.), *Psychosocial stress: Perspectives on structure, theory, life-course, and methods* (pp. 333–366). San Diego, CA: Academic Press, Inc.

Kobasa, S. C. (1979). Stressful life events, personality and health: An inquiry into hardiness. *Journal of Personality and Social Psychology, 37,* 1–11.

Kobasa, S. C., Maddi, S. R., & Kahn, S. (1982). Hardiness and health: A prospective study. *Journal of Personality and Social Psychology, 42,* 168–177.

Kompier, M.A.J. (1996). Job design and well-being. In M. J. Schabracq, J.A.M. Winnubst, & C. L. Cooper (Eds.), *Handbook of work and health psychology* (pp. 329–368). Chichester, England: Wiley.

Krause, N., & Goldenhar, L. M. (1992). Acculturation and psychological distress in three groups of elderly Hispanics. *Journal of Gerontology: Social Sciences, 47,* S279–S288.

Landsbergis, P. A., Schnall, P. L., Schwartz, J. E., Warren, K., & Pickering, T. G. (1995). Job strain, hypertension, and cardiovascular disease: Empirical evidence, methodological issues, and recommendations for future research. In S. L. Sauter & L. R. Murphy (Eds.), *Organizational risk factors for job stress* (pp. 97–112). Washington, DC: American Psychological Association.

Levinson, H. (1963). What killed Bob Lyons? *Harvard Business Review, 41,* 127–143.

Levinson, H. (1975). *Executive stress* (rev. ed.). New York: Mentor Books.

Lopez, F. G. (1995). Contemporary attachment theory: An introduction with implications for counseling psychology. *The Counseling Psychologist, 23,* 395–415.

Lykken, D., & Tellegen, A. (1996). Happiness is a stochastic phenomenon. *Psychological Science, 7,* 186–189.

Mack, D. A., Shannon, C., Quick, J. D., & Quick, J. C. (1998). Stress, prevention, and workplace violence. In R. W. Griffin, A. O'Leary-Kelly, & J. Collins (Eds.), *Dysfunctional behavior in organizations: Vol. 1. Violent behavior in organizations* (pp. 119–141). Greenwich, CT: JAI Press.

Maddi, S. (1990). Issues and interventions in stress mastery. In H. S. Friedman (Ed.), *Personality and disease* (pp. 122–154). New York: Wiley.

Maddi, S. (1994). The hardiness enhancing lifestyle program (HELP) for improving physical, mental, and social wellness. *Health net wellness lecture series.* Irvine, CA: University of California.

Maddi, S. (1997). Personal views survey II: A measure of dispositional hardiness. In C. P. Zalaquett & R. J. Woods (Eds.), *Evaluating stress: A book of resources.* Lanham, MD & London: The Scarecrow Press.

Maddi, S. (1998). Hardiness in health and effectiveness. In H. S. Friedman (Ed.), *Encyclopedia of mental health* (Vol. 2, pp. 323–335). San Diego, CA: Academic Press.

Maddi, S., & Hess, M. J. (1992). Personality hardiness and success in basketball. *International Journal of Sport Psychology, 23,* 360–368.

Mann, T. (1996). Health psychology of gender or sexual orientation. In P. M. Kato & T. Mann (Eds.), *Handbook of diversity issues in health psychology* (pp. 187–198). New York: Plenum.

Mann, T., & Kato, P. M. (1996). Diversity issues in health psychology. In P. M. Kato & T. Mann (Eds.), *Handbook of diversity issues in health psychology* (pp. 3–18). New York: Plenum.

Marsella, A. J. (1994). Work and well-being in an ethnoculturally pluralistic society: Conceptual and methodological issues. In G. B. Keita & J. J. Hurrell, Jr. (Eds.), *Job stress in a changing workforce* (pp. 147–160). Washington, DC: American Psychological Association.

Matuszek, P.A.C., Nelson, D. L., & Quick, J. C. (1995). Gender differences in distress: Are we asking the right questions? *Journal of Social Behavior and Personality, 10,* 99–120.

McCrae, R. R., & Costa, P. T., Jr. (1994). The stability of personality: Observations and evaluations. *Current Directions in Psychological Science, 3,* 173–175.

Merton, R. K. (1957). The role set. *British Journal of Sociology, 8,* 106–120.

Mikulincer, M., Florian, V., & Weller, A. (1993). Attachment styles, coping strategies and post-traumatic psychological distress: Impact of the Gulf War in Israel. *Journal of Personality and Social Psychology, 64,* 817–826.

Murphy, L. R. (1984). Occupational stress management: A review and appraisal. *Journal of Occupational Psychology, 57,* 1–15.

Murphy, L. R. (1996). Stress management in work settings: A critical review of the health effects. *American Journal of Health Promotion, 11,* 112–135.

Myers, D. G., & Diener, E. (1995). Who is happy? *Psychological Science, 6,* 10–19.

Myers, H. F. (1996). Foreword. In P. M. Kato & T. Mann (Eds.), *Handbook of diversity issues in health psychology* (pp. xi–xiv). New York: Plenum.

Nelson, D. L., & Quick, J. C. (1991). Social support and newcomer adjustment in organizations: Attachment theory at work? *Journal of Organizational Behavior, 12,* 543–554.

Nelson, D. L., Quick, J. C., & Joplin, J. R. (1991). Psychological contracting and newcomer socialization: An attachment theory foundation. *Journal of Social Behavior and Personality, 6,* 55–72.

Occupational Safety and Health Act of 1970. Pub. L. No. 91–596, 84 Stat. 1590 (1970).

Offermann, L. R., & Gowing, M. K. (1990). Organizations of the future: Changes and challenges. *American Psychologist, 45,* 95–108.

Ordin, D. L. (1992). Surveillance, monitoring, and screening in occupational health. In J. Last & R. B. Wallace (Eds.), *Maxcy–Rosenau–Last public health and preventive medicine* (13th ed., pp. 551–558). Norwalk, CT: Appleton & Lange.

Ouellette, S. (1993). Inquiries into hardiness. In L. Goldberger & S. Breznitz (Eds.), *Handbook of stress: Theoretical and clinical aspects* (pp. 202–240). New York: The Free Press.

Ouellette, S. (1997). Hardiness. In J. M. Stellman (Ed.), *ILO encyclopaedia of occupational health and safety* (p. 34.42). Chicago: Rand McNally.

Peterson, C. (1995). Explanatory style and health. In G. M. Buchanan & M.E.P. Seligman (Eds.), *Explanatory Style* (pp. 233–246). Hillsdale, NJ: Lawrence Erlbaum Associates.

Peterson, C., Buchanan, G., & Seligman, M.E.P. (1995). Explanatory style: History and evolution of the field. In G. M. Buchanan & M.E.P. Seligman (Eds.), *Explanatory Style* (pp. 1–20). Hillsdale, NJ: Lawrence Erlbaum Associates.

Pierce, J. L., & Newstrom, J. W. (1983). The design of flexible work schedules and employee responses: Relationships and processes. *Journal of Occupational Behavior, 4,* 247–262.

Quick, J. C. (1997). Idiographic research in organizational behavior. In C. L. Cooper & S. E. Jackson (Eds.), *Creating tomorrow's organizations: A handbook for future research in organizational behavior* (pp. 475–492). Chichester, England: Wiley.

Quick, J. C., Camara, W. J., Hurrell, J. J., Jr., Johnson, J. V., Piotrkowski, C. S., Sauter, S. L., & Spielberger, C. D. (1997). Introduction and historical overview. *Journal of Occupational Health Psychology, 2,* 3–6.

Quick, J. C., Joplin, J. R., Nelson, D. L., Mangelsdorff, A. D., & Fiedler, E. (1996). Self-reliance and military service training outcomes. *Journal of Military Psychology, 8,* 279–293.

Quick, J. C., Joplin, J. R., Nelson, D. L., & Quick, J. D. (1992). Behavioral responses to anxiety: Self-reliance, counterdependence, and overdependence. *Anxiety, Stress, and Coping, 5,* 41–54.

Quick, J. C., & Nelson, D. L. (1997). Job stress. In L. H. Peters, S. A. Youngblood, & C. R. Greer (Eds.), *The Blackwell dictionary of human resource management.* In C. Argyris & C. L. Cooper (Eds.), *The Blackwell encyclopedia of management* (pp. 193–194). Oxford, England: Basil Blackwell.

Quick, J. C., Nelson, D. L., & Quick, J. D. (1990). *Stress and challenge at the top: The paradox of the successful executive.* Chichester, England: Wiley.

Quick, J. C., & Quick, J. D. (1984). *Organizational stress and preventive management.* New York: McGraw-Hill.

Quick, J. C., Quick, J. D., Nelson, D. L., & Hurrell, J. J., Jr. (1997). *Preventive stress management in organizations.* Washington, DC: American Psychological Association.

Radloff, L. S. (1977). The CES–D scale: A self-report depression scale for research in the general population. *Applied Psychological Measurement, 1,* 385–401.

Rose, R. M. (1987). Neuroendocrine effects of work stress. In J. C. Quick, R. S. Bhagal, J. E. Dalton, & J. D. Quick (Eds.), *Work stress: Health care systems in the workplace* (pp. 130–147). New York: Praeger.

Sarason, I. G., Sarason, B. R., Brock, D. M., & Pierce, G. R. (1996). Social support: Current status, current issues. In C. D. Spielberger & I. G. Sarason (Eds.), *Stress and emotion: Anxiety, anger and curiosity* (pp. 3–27). Washington, DC: Taylor & Francis.

Sauter, S. L., Murphy, L. R., Hurrell, J. J., & Levi, L. (Eds.). (1997). Part I. Hazards on the job/ Section 34: Psychosocial and organizational factors. In J. M. Stellman (Ed.), *ILO encyclopaedia of occupational health and safety* (pp. 34.1–34.77). Chicago: Rand McNally.

Scheier, M. F., & Carver, C. S. (1992). Effects of optimism on psychological and physical well-being: Theoretical overview and empirical update. *Cognitive Therapy and Research, 16,* 201–228.

Schonfeld, I. S. (1996). Relation of negative affectivity to self-reports of job stressors and psychological outcomes. *Journal of Occupational Health Psychology, l,* 397–345.

Schwartz, H. S. (1990). *Narcissistic process and corporate decay: The theory of the organizational ideal.* New York: NYU Press.

Seligman, M.E.P. (1991). *Learned optimism.* New York: Knopf.

Shrivastava, P. (1987) *Bhopal: Anatomy of a crisis.* Cambridge, MA: Ballinger.

Siegrist, J. (1996). Adverse health effects of high-effort/low-reward conditions. *Journal of Occupational Health Psychology, 1,* 27–41.

Singh, J., Goolsby, J. R., & Rhoads, G. K. (1994). Behavioral and psychological consequences of boundary spanning burnout for customer service representatives. *Journal of Marketing Research, 31,* 558–569.

Staw, B. M., Sandelands, L. E., & Dutton, J. E. (1981). Threat-rigidity effects in organizational behavior: A multilevel analysis. *Administrative Science Quarterly, 26,* 501–524.

Sutton, R. I., & Kahn, R. L. (1987). Prediction, understanding, and control as antidotes to organizational stress. In J. W. Lorsch (Ed.), *Handbook of organizational behavior* (pp. 272–285). Englewood Cliffs, NJ: Prentice-Hall.

Taylor, J. A. (1953). A personality scale of manifest anxiety. *Journal of Abnormal and Social Psychology, 48,* 285–290.

Terra, N. (1995). The prevention of job stress by redesigning jobs and implementing self-regulating teams. In L. R. Murphy, S. L. Sauter,

& G. P. Keita, (Eds.), *Job stress interventions* (pp. 265–282). Washington, DC: American Psychological Association.

Theorell, T., & Karasek, R. A. (1996). Current issues relating to psychosocial job strain and cardiovascular disease research. *Journal of Occupational Health Psychology, 1,* 9–26.

Uchino, B. N., Cacioppo, J. T., & Kiecolt-Glaser, J. K. (1996). The relationship between social support and physiological processes: A review with emphasis on underlying mechanisms and implications for health. *Psychological Bulletin, 119,* 488–531.

Walcott-McQuigg, J. A. (1994). Worksite stress: Gender and cultural diversity issues. *AAOHN Journal, 42,* 528–533.

Wall, T. D., & Clegg, C. W. (1981). A longitudinal study of group work redesign. *Journal of Occupational Behavior, 2,* 31–49.

Watson, D., & Clark, L. A. (1984). Negative affectivity: The disposition to experience aversive emotional states. *Psychological Bulletin, 96,* 465–490.

Watson, D., Clark, L. A., McIntyre, C. W., & Hamaker, S. (1992). Affect, personality and social activity. *Journal of Personality and Social Psychology, 63,* 1011–1025.

Watson, D., Pennebaker, J. W., & Folger, R. (1987). Beyond negative affectivity: Measuring stress and satisfaction in the workplace. *Journal of Organizational Behavior Management, 8,* 141–152.

Westman, M. (1990). The relationship between stress and performance: The moderating effect of hardiness. *Human Performance, 3,* 141–155.

Williams, L., & Podsakoff, P. (1989). Longitudinal field methods for studying reciprocal relationships in organizational behavior research: Toward improved causal analysis. In L. Cummings & B. Staw (Eds.), *Research in organizational behavior, 11,* 247–292.

20

Environmental Stress and Health

Gary W. Evans
Cornell University

Although environmental conditions play a prominent role in health and psychological processes, antecedent factors in these processes have largely been neglected within health psychology. Instead, the focus has been on various markers of health, with considerable attention to stress-related mechanisms, interceding between the environment and health. Another focus within health psychology that has directed attention away from environmental factors has been coping resources, with the examination of either social support, personality, or coping strategies that potentially alter the impact of environmental demands on health. But what characteristics of the environment itself are likely to impinge on health and psychological processes? When this question has been addressed within health psychology, environment has been operationalized primarily in social terms. Family and work social climates, as well as sociocultural and economic conditions, predominate in the few environmental studies in health psychology. This chapter intends to draw greater attention to the potential role of the physical environment in health and psychological processes.

Why might the physical environment be important to health psychology? For one reason, the physical environment clearly impacts health. Adverse physical conditions can cause toxicological reactions, challenge homeostatic balance, produce physical trauma, or function as vectors bearing pathogens. Physical factors can also be a source of environmental demands that pressure coping resources.

A second reason the physical environment is worthy of scrutiny within health psychology is because the environment can be modified and thus becomes a potential intervention target to improve health and well-being. Third, environmental conditions are objective and thus can be measured more readily in reliable and valid ways. For example, researchers can system- atically monitor density or noise levels in precise, accurate ways that can then be examined as possible causal factors in health. Fourth, physical environmental conditions tend to be stable. Increasingly, research suggests that chronic environmental demands are most likely to have negative impacts on health (Lepore, 1995). Finally, the concept of psychological stress that is central to several formulations of health, behavior, and disease (see chap. 17, this volume) has been utilized to broaden understanding of how physical features of the environment can influence human health and well-being.

There are at least three major ways in which the physical environment might operate as a psychological stressor, straining human adaptive capacities. First, this can occur when a stressor directly loads, or pressures, the system. Both crowding and noise, for example, create a surfeit of stimulation that can directly overload the system, causing discomfort, negative affect, and under some circumstances, the marshaling of adaptive resources. Both negative affect and adaptive responses to challenge or threat in turn directly affect neuroendocrine and cardiovascular functioning. Physical stressors can also interact with psychosocial conditions to exacerbate negative affect and/or psychophysiologic mobilization. For example, noise plus high workload demands leads to more serious health outcomes than workload levels alone. Noise and crowding frequently covary with other psychosocial risk factors (e.g., poverty, inadequate working conditions), and thus have the potential to contribute to multiple risk situations.

A second manner in which the physical environment can contribute to stress is by damaging or ameliorating coping resources themselves. People rarely respond to suboptimal physical or psychosocial conditions passively; instead, they invoke various coping strategies to reestablish some modicum of balance between environmental demands and personal resources. Evidence is presented herein, for example, that crowding interferes with the development and maintenance of socially supportive relationships in the residential environment. Both chronic noise and chronic crowding appear to contribute to learned helplessness, adversely affecting self-efficacy and related motivational processes.

The third way in which physical conditions can operate as stressors is to elicit coping strategies that in turn lead to poor health. Studies of noise, for example, reveal that increases in substance abuse occur under noisy working conditions.

Another aspect of research on psychological stress and health relevant to this chapter on environmental stressors are the concepts of vulnerability and resilience (Cohen, Kessler, & Gordon, 1995; Rutter, 1983). Just as certain personal or situational characteristics can render individuals more or less vulnerable to social stressors, there is evidence of vulnerable subgroups among the population who appear more adversely affected by noise and by crowding, respectively.Thus throughout both direct, main effects and associations between environmental stressors and health, as well as occasions with vulnerable subgroups, are noted.

The field of environmental stress (Cohen, Evans, Stokols, & Krantz, 1986; Evans, 1982; Evans & Cohen, 1987) is sufficiently developed such that exhaustive coverage is impossible. A small amount of environmental stress research has examined climatic conditions as potential psychological stressors influencing human stress responses (Bell & Greene, 1982; Evans, 1994). Research on housing conditions as a possible stressor have also been undertaken (Freeman, 1984). The focus of this chapter is on the two most studied environmental stressors, crowding and noise. Health outcomes include physical health and psychological health. Moreover, the chapter examines underlying psychosocial and psychophysiological processes that may help explain the linkages between noise and crowding and major physical and psychological health outcomes. Psychophysiological mechanisms, immune function, social resources, coping strategies, and motivational processes are examined.

CROWDING

The element of crowding that relates most strongly to physical and psychological health is people per room. Traffic congestion may also prove to be a potent stressor. Area measures of crowding, such as people per acre, generally have little or no relation to health. Although some studies of crowding separate group size effects from density effects, the vast majority of studies have confounded these two factors, manipulating or measuring density as it covaries with group size. Therefore, some of the effects attributed to crowding may be due to group size rather than the amount of space per person. At the same time, when attempts have been made to distinguish between these related concepts, density and group size, the impacts of density typically persist.

Physical Health

Early interest in crowding in the public health field emanated from concerns about the spread of disease among crowded populations (Cox, Paulus, McCain, & Karlovac, 1982). There is a large literature on this topic. Physical health has been operationalized in this literature as rates of illness based on archival data, visits to infirmary, physical development among children, and self-reports of somatic symptoms. Archival evidence for positive associations between crowding and ill health come from studies in prisons (McCain, Cox, & Paulus, 1976; Paulus, 1988), refugee camps (Arnow, Hierholzer, Higbee, & Harris, 1977), and schools (Essen, Fogelman, & Head, 1978; Koopman, 1978). The Arnow et al. (1977) study is noteworthy because they demonstrated good correlation over time between Vietnamese refugee camp population fluctuations with changes in a highly contagious disease (acute conjunctivitis). There is also evidence that crowded residential conditions are linked to disease both among children (Booth & Johnson, 1975; Jacobson, Chester, & Fraser, 1977) and among adults (Levy & Herzog, 1978; McGlashen, 1977; Menton & Meyers, 1977; Sims, Downham, McQuillin, & Gardner, 1976; Wyndham, Gonin, & Reid, 1978; Yarnell, 1979). Yodfat, Fidel, Cohen, and Eliakim (1979) found that linkages among residential crowding and asthma were due to number of children rather than density per se. Booth (1976) found that male adults, but not women, had greater levels of disease in crowded homes. Traffic congestion levels among commuters is also associated with illness-related absenteeism from work (Novaco, Stokols, & Milanesi, 1990).

Several studies of residential crowding find little or no correlates with disease (Brett & Benjamin, 1957; Collette & Webb, 1974; Mackintosh, 1934; McKinlay & Truelove, 1947; Quinn, Lowry, & Zwaag, 1978), and Winsborough (1965) uncovered an inverse relation between areal density and tuberculosis. Schmitt and colleagues also found no relation between residential density and disease rates, but found small, positive correlations with areal density (people per acre) measures (Schmitt, 1966; Schmitt, Zane, & Nishi, 1978). Similar trends have been uncovered by Levy and Herzog (1974). Kellett (1984) made the important point that certain diseases should be expected a priori to correlate with crowding more so than others. Kellett examined mortality patterns for specific diseases in London for a 5-year period. As in prior work, persons per room rather than people per acre appeared more useful in predicting mortality. Second, diseases wherein a major stress component is believed to be operative (e.g., hypertension, myocardial infarction, vascular disorders, asthma) were related to household crowding whereas many other diseases (e.g., various forms of cancer) were not.

Freedman and colleagues challenged many of these studies of crowding and disease, noting that poor or nonexisting controls for other variables such as socioeconomic status are common in the crowding and epidemiological literature. They found in a well-controlled epidemiological analysis that residential crowding was not a significant predictor of disease (Freedman, Heshka, & Levy, 1975). However, the prison studies and a few of the residential studies (e.g., Menton & Meyers, 1977) do have good controls for SES. Furthermore, there are trends in the data indicating that when individual levels of exposure to density and individual indices of health are compared rather than aggregated population statistics, such as used by Freedman and colleagues, stronger results occur. Nonetheless, Freedman and colleagues' cautious perspective on crowding and disease is well taken. Overall findings are suggestive but not rigorously or consistently supportive of a crowding–disease link. It would be useful to include, in the same individual-based study, disease rates for disorders that ought to vary with stress exposure plus inclusion of immunological measures.

A handful of studies in institutional contexts have examined crowding and infirmary visits. These studies converge on positive associations between levels of crowding and infirmary visits among shipboard military personnel (Dean, Pugh, & Gunderson, 1975, 1978), college campus residents (Baron, Mandel, Adams, & Griffen, 1976; Stokols, Ohlig, & Resnik, 1978), and prisoners (Paulus, 1988). The prison effects were most noticeable among inmates forced to live under dormitory-like conditions rather than in single cells. Trends also indicated that the associations in prisons were somewhat stronger for men than women and for African American in comparison to Anglo prisoners (Paulus, 1988). Wener and Keys (1988) found that increases in density (doubling up cell mates) markedly elevated (nearly 50%) sick call rates among prison inmates.

A few studies have examined physical development among crowded children, uncovering evidence of negative associations between household density and physical stature (Booth, 1976; Essen et al., 1978; Goduka, Poole, & Aotaki-Phenice, 1992). Crowded children, particularly boys, are shorter. Shapiro (1974) also found that boys, but not girls, motoric development appeared to be inhibited in crowded homes. Moreover, this effect was amplified among children of less educated mothers. More recently, Widmayer and colleagues (1990) found delayed psychomotor development among infants as a function of household density, controlling for socioeconomic status (SES).

Self-reported levels of physical illness are positively associated with crowding in prisons (Cox, Paulus, & McCain, 1984; McCain et al., 1976), among college dormitory women but not men (Karlin, Epstein, & Aiello, 1978), and among crowded home settings (Gove & Hughes, 1983)—although Booth (1976) found this association among men, but not women, in crowded homes. Giel and Ormel (1977) and Baldassare (1979) failed to replicate the association between home crowding levels and self-reported illness. The validity of all the self-report data on illness and crowding is suspect given retrospective self-report indices. On the other hand, Cox et al. (1984) found a dose–response function between number of inmates per cell and self-reported illness levels among male prisoners. Of additional interest, Gove and Hughes (1983) provided some evidence that heightened illness levels associated with crowded residences are related to lack of sleep and lower resistance when exposed to other sick family members (all self-reported).

There is evidence that some of the association between crowded living conditions and self-reported health symptoms is mediated by loss of perceived control over the living environment. Ruback and associates found that both female and male prisoners' reports of ill health in association with crowding were also negatively related to perceived control (Ruback & Carr, 1984; Ruback, Carr, & Hopper, 1986). Another way in which environmental stressors like crowding can impinge on health is through injuries. Rhesus monkeys when crowded, for example, show a 5-fold increase in incidents of injuries (Boyce, O'Neill-Wagner, Price, Haines, & Suomi, 1998).

Psychophysiological

Several studies have examined the relation between crowding and blood pressure in people. Laboratory studies with random assignment to density levels have found small but significant elevations among crowded versus uncrowded participants (Epstein, Lehrer, & Woolfolk, 1978; Evans, 1979). Field studies of prisoners (D'Atri, 1975; Paulus, McCain, & Cox, 1978) and automobile commuters (Novaco, D. Stokols, Campbell, & J. Stokols, 1979; Schaeffer, Street, Singer, & Baum, 1988; Stokols et al., 1978) have also revealed correlational evidence for elevated blood pressure under more crowded or congested living or commuting conditions. The commuting studies have found that the effects are stronger for car poolers rather than solo drivers, for Type B rather than Type A drivers, among external versus internal locus of control drivers, and among drivers with less residential choice. One field study found no relations between chronic residential crowding and blood pressure or neuroendocrine indices among adults (Booth, 1976), although small, statistically significant elevations in serum cholesterol were noted among crowded men. No such correlation was noted among women. Booth's sample did not vary much in density, which may have weakened his findings. Evans, Lepore, Shejwal, and Palsane (1998) found elevated blood pressure among crowded boys, but not girls, among working-class families in India.

Another cardiovascular function, blood pressure reactivity, has been related to chronic crowding in adults. Residents of more crowded neighborhoods had higher reactivity (increase from baseline in blood pressure levels) and took longer to return to resting baseline levels (Fleming, Baum, Davidson, Rectanus, & McArdle, 1987). Both heightened reactivity and protracted recovery to baseline are potentially important precursors to the development of coronary heart disease.

Neuroendocrine markers of stress, typically urinary catecholamines and cortisol, have been noted in several studies of crowded commuters (Lundberg, 1976; Singer, Lundberg & Frankenhaeuser, 1978) and among bus drivers operating under more congested driving conditions (Evans & Carrere, 1991).

Pedestrian exposure to more crowded urban areas elevates neuroendocrine activity, at least for males (Heshka & Pylypuk, 1975), and residence in neighborhoods perceived as more crowded because of commercial establishments and more people on the street is associated with increased urinary catecholamine levels (Fleming, Baum, & Weiss, 1987). Dormitory crowding, however, had no apparent effects on neuroendocrine activity among college students (Karlin et al., 1978). A small sample size may have rendered low power. These authors did find, however, that uncrowded residents' neuroendocrine indices dropped over the course of the semester, whereas crowded residents' neuroendocrine levels increased over the same time period. Schaeffer, Baum, Paulus, and Gaes (1988) found that prisoners housed in more open, unpartitioned dormitories felt more crowded and experienced elevated chronic catecholamine levels in comparison to prisoners living in smaller groups.

The critical role of control has been implicated in some of these psychophysiological crowding studies. Lundberg (1976) and his colleagues found that passengers with greater choice over seating were less negatively impacted by congested commuting. Evans and Carrere (1991) found that the neuroendocrine effects of traffic congestion on bus drivers were largely mediated by perceived control on the job. On the other hand, perceived control did not mediate the positive relation between prison crowding and neuroendocrine elevations (Schaeffer, Baum, Paulus, & Gaes, 1988).

A few laboratory studies have also utilized skin conductance as an index of psychophysiologic stress, generally finding elevations among more crowded participants (Aiello, Epstein, & Kalin, 1975; Aiello, Nicosia, & Thompson, 1979; Bergman, 1971; Nicosia, Hyman, Karlin, Epstein, & Aiello, 1979). Studies of crowding and skin conductance are evenly split on gender differences, with some studies finding more pronounced effects among males than females and other studies finding no sex differences. There is also evidence that skin conductance may be more strongly affected by crowding when physical touching occurs. McCallum, Rusbult, Hong, Walden, and Schopler (1979) found that acute crowding elevated palmar sweat but only when experimental subjects were motivated to maintain high levels of group performance. When performance was permitted to deteriorate under crowding, no physiological elevations were noted. Finally, in a field study, Cox, Paulus, McCain, and Schkade (1979) found a significant positive correlation between the palmar sweat index and crowding among prison inmates.

Although indirect, some findings by Hutt and Vaizey (1966) may shed some light on psychophysiological mechanisms associated with crowding and psychophysiologic responses. Chronically overaroused children responded to high density laboratory conditions by extreme social and physical withdrawal; whereas chronically underaroused children and children without arousal disturbance reacted in the opposite direction, becoming more engaged and aggressive with other children.

Many animal studies have examined endocrine activity among crowded species both under laboratory and field conditions (see Evans, 1978, for a review). Generally, this research indicates support for a population regulation feedback mechanism whereby crowded animals' fertility declines. This occurs more markedly among subordinate rather than dominant animals and appears to be mediated by adrenal cortical activity. Attempts to link crowding with population regulation among human beings have proven futile.

Immune Function

Animal but not human work has examined immunological processes as a function of crowding, generally finding evidence of compromised immune functioning among more crowded animals (Christian, 1963; E. A. Edwards & Dean, 1977; Thiessen & Rodgers, 1961). These effects appear to be stronger among subordinate rather than dominant animals and among animals without a history of crowded living conditions (Cassel, 1971). Cassel (1974) pointed out, however, that compromised immune function alone cannot account for changes in morbidity among crowded animals because both infectious and noninfectious diseases are elevated among crowded animals.

Psychological Health

Ever since 1962 when Calhoun published his famous *Scientific American* study of pathology among overpopulated rats, researchers and policymakers alike have wondered about the potential role of crowded living conditions on mental health. The chapter first reviews research on linkages between density and psychological distress and then turns its attention to recent work examining possible underlying mechanisms for this linkage.

Many studies have uncovered positive relations between residential density and self-reported psychological distress (Edwards, Fuller, Sermsri, & Vorakitphokatorn, 1990; Evans, Palsane, Lepore, & Martin, 1989; Gabe & Williams, 1987; Gove & Hughes, 1983; Hassen, 1977; Jain, 1987; Lakey, 1989; Marsella, Escudero, & Gordon, 1970). Mitchell (1971) found greater worrying among crowded families but only if they were also poor. Crowding in Mitchell's study was unrelated, however, to more serious indices of psychiatric illness. Lepore, Evans, and Schneider (1991) found evidence that residential crowding causes psychological distress in a prospective, longitudinal study of crowding and mental health. Controlling for educational levels and income, they found that crowded residents did not differ from uncrowded residents in psychological distress symptoms during initial occupancy ($r = .12$), but after 2 months and 8 months the associations became significant ($r = .21$; $r = .27$). This is the only prospective study of crowding and health. Webb and Collette (1975) found an association between residential density and use of prescription hypnotics.

Booth (1976), Baldassare (1979), and Giel and Ormel (1977) failed to find a positive association between residential crowding and psychological distress. These studies had little variance in density. Moreover, Baldassare relied on mental health indices of questionable sensitivity (one dichotomous item in one case, and three dichotomous items in a second case). Two studies of neighborhood crowding levels have also found linkages to psychological distress (Collette & Webb, 1974; Fleming, Baum, & Weiss, 1987).

Studies utilizing archival indices such as psychiatric admissions or suicide rates generally find very weak or insignificant associations between crowding and pathology when measured in the aggregate (Freedman et al., 1975; Gove &

Hughes, 1980; Schmitt, 1966; Schmitt et al., 1978). In some studies negative associations between density and psychiatric admissions have been uncovered, probably created by the association of living alone and mental disorder (Galle, Gove, & McPherson, 1972; Levy & Herzog, 1974, 1978). One exception to these generally negative trends in archival indices of mental health and crowding is notable. Several prison studies have found clear, strong associations between the total population size of prison populations and indices of psychiatric illness (Paulus, 1988).

Quite a number of studies have examined psychological symptoms among children living in crowded homes. Plant (1937) described several case studies noting a pattern of low self-sufficiency and little idealism among children from crowded homes. He attributed these patterns to mental strain associated from always having to get along with others and to exposure to adults under close quarters that made it difficult to look up to or idealize grownups. Crowded children have increased levels of various symptoms of psychological distress (Booth, 1976; Gasparini, 1973; Murray, 1974; Saegert, 1982; Wachs, 1987). Parents in more crowded homes report relief when their children are outside (Gove & Hughes, 1983), have more difficulty supervising their children (Mitchell, 1971), and are generally less responsive and involved with their children (Bradley & Caldwell, 1984; Evans, Maxwell, & Hart, 1999; Wachs & Camli, 1991) in comparison to uncrowded parents of comparable social class. These trends appear to be exacerbated in the presence of other risk factors, particularly poverty (Baldassare, 1981; Bradley et al., 1994).

Psychosocial Resources

Some of the relation between high residential density and psychological distress in children may be linked to family interactions, which have been found to be more contentious under crowded living conditions (Booth, 1976; Gasparini, 1973; Saegert, 1982). There may also be greater incidence of physical punishment and open expression of anger between parents and children in crowded homes (Booth & Edwards, 1976; Light, 1973), although Gove and Hughes' (1983) study did not support this finding.

Another factor that may help explain the link between high residential crowding and symptoms of psychological distress in children is withdrawal. Aiello, Thompson, and Baum (1985) reviewed several field and laboratory studies documenting increased social withdrawal under crowded conditions among young children. Similar trends exist in the adult literature, indicating that crowded adults interact with housemates less (Baum & Valins, 1977, 1979; Proshansky, Ittelson, & Rivlin, 1970); are less friendly with their neighbors (McCarthy & Saegert, 1978), and have impaired social support with those they live with (Evans et al., 1989; Lakey, 1989; Lepore et al., 1991). Baldassare (1979) did not replicate linkages between residential crowding and neighboring. People under crowded conditions also tend to be less affiliative in their behaviors toward others (R. L. Munroe & R. H. Munroe, 1972) and view others in more negative or suspicious terms (Bickman et al., 1973; Griffit & Veitch, 1971; McCarthy & Saegert, 1978). There is also evidence that crowded working conditions lead to greater social withdrawal from coworkers (Oldham & Fried, 1987). Finally, as already noted, parents in crowded homes are less responsive to their children (Bradley & Caldwell, 1984; Wachs & Camli, 1991). Furthermore, this relative unresponsiveness partially accounts for less complex parent to child verbalizations to infants and toddlers (Evans, et al., 1999).

Evidence that social withdrawal and impaired social relationships are a primary mechanism accounting for the relation between crowding and psychological distress has been documented in some detail by two research programs. Baum and colleagues found that more crowded dorm residents report more unwanted social interaction in their dorms. These same crowded residents also evidence greater behavioral indices of withdrawal outside of the dorm. They sit farther away from other research participants and withdraw more in group interaction games (Baum & Valins, 1977, 1979). Residential exposure to high levels of street traffic is also associated with less neighboring (Appleyard & Lintell, 1972; Halpern, 1995). Evans and Lepore showed direct evidence for a similar pattern. They found both cross-sectionally (Evans et al., 1989) and in a prospective, longitudinal design (Lepore et al., 1991) that the negative effects of residential crowding on psychological distress (with controls for social class) are mediated by social support. Similar patterns also appear to occur among children in crowded residences (Evans, et al., 1998).

Evans and Lepore (1993a) also found that crowded relative to uncrowded residents were less likely to offer support to a confederate under stress in an uncrowded laboratory setting. Of additional interest, crowded residents in comparison to uncrowded residents were also less responsive to offers of social support during a stressful situation (see Fig. 20.1). *Ignored* meant that the subject did not look at or made no verbal acknowledgment of the confederate; *acknowledgment* meant some brief comment or a head nod was given in response to offers of support; and *accepted* meant the subject was very re-

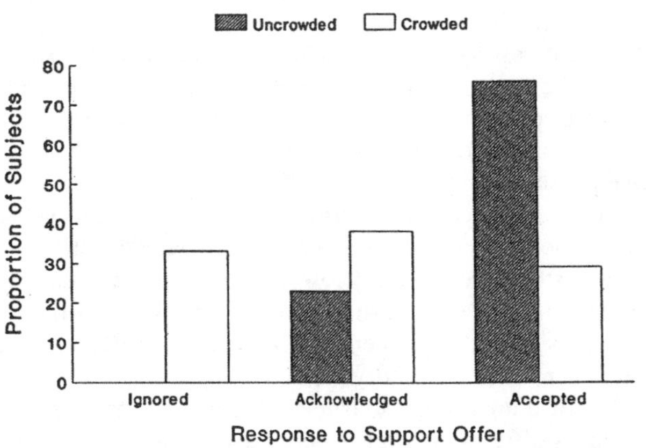

FIG. 20.1

sponsive to the confederate's offers of support, elaborating or embellishing on their offers of support.

Motivation

Many theorists have postulated that a prime reason why crowding can have negative impacts on psychological health is because of reduced behavioral options and greater difficulty in regulating social interaction (Altman, 1975; Baron & Rodin, 1978; Schmidt & Keating, 1979). An important psychological consequence of prolonged exposure to an aversive, uncontrollable stressor, such as crowding, may be learned helplessness. Persons chronically exposed to crowding report feeling a greater sense of powerlessness over their living environments than their less crowded counterparts (Baum & Valins, 1977, 1979; Baron et al., 1976; Carr, Hopper & Ruback, 1986; Saegert, 1978). Sherrod (1976), Aiello, DeRisi, Epstein, and Karlin (1977), Evans (1979), Nicosia et al. (1979), and Dooley (1978) all found negative aftereffects immediately following laboratory exposure to crowded conditions. Sherrod, Evans, and Nicosia and colleagues each utilized the Glass and Singer (1972) aftereffects paradigm that measures persistence on challenging puzzles. Giving up sooner in the face of challenge in an achievement context may be indicative of greater helplessness (Cohen, 1980; Glass & Singer, 1972). Dooley (1978) incorporated proofreading performance as her aftereffects measure. Saegert, Mackintosh, and West (1975) reported that crowded train stations produced negative aftereffects in women only. Nicosia's data also indicated more severe aftereffects of crowding among women.

Parallel trends to the laboratory work have been noted in studies of more chronic, crowded living conditions, finding less persistence on difficult puzzles among persons living in more crowded neighborhoods (Fleming, Baum, & Weiss, 1987). Moreover, perception of control over social interactions largely accounted for the main effect of neighborhood crowding on the helplessness indicator. Residents of crowded dorms feel less control over social interaction than their uncrowded counterparts (Baum & Valins, 1977, 1979) and exhibit behavioral strategies in a group prisoners' dilemma game consistent with helplessness (Baum, Aiello, & Calesnick, 1978; Baum, Gatchel, Aiello, & Thompson, 1981). Interestingly, the development of helplessness strategies in the game over the course of the initial semester under crowded conditions was mirrored by residents growing external attributions for problems in the dormitory over this same time period (Baum et al., 1981). Uncrowded residents generally felt self-efficacy over problems in their dormitory over the course of the semester and these internal attributions remained stable over time. Crowded dormitory residents are also less likely to seek clarification when given ambiguous instructions about an impending laboratory procedure than were uncrowded dormitory residents.

Traffic congestion also is related to motivational deficits. Greater traffic congestion levels have been related to decreased task motivation on challenging puzzles and proofreading (Novaco et al., 1979; Schaeffer et al., 1988; D. Stokols, et al., 1978).

The most direct evidence for helplessness induced by crowding comes from a pair of studies on residential crowding and children by Rodin (1976). Matched on socioeconomic indicators, elementary-aged schoolchildren living in more crowded public housing were less likely to control the administration of outcomes in an operant conditioning paradigm in comparison to their less crowded counterparts. In a second study, helplessness was induced in adolescents by a classic helplessness paradigm, pretreatment with an insoluble versus a soluble puzzle. Helplessness was monitored on a second challenging but solvable puzzle. The main effect of pretreatment solvability (the helplessness induction) was significantly moderated by residential crowding with heightened vulnerability to the induction of helplessness among the more crowded children. In their study of children in India, Evans, et al., (1998) replicated Rodin's effects (but for girls only). Saegert (1982), however, did not replicate these findings examining a sample of children from public housing projects in New York City.

Summary

Residential crowding has little impact on physical morbidity among the general population. Residential crowding may be linked, however, to ill health among vulnerable subgroups of the populations, particularly young children and extremely crowded, captive populations (e.g., prisons, refugee camps). Evidence linking high density exposure either under controlled conditions or in the field to elevated cardiovascular functioning is quite strong. Neuroendocrine functioning also appears elevated, although less data are available. The potential clinical implications of these two data patterns has not been explored in the crowding literature.

Psychological distress is increased by residential crowding. Individual but not aggregate level analyses continue to uncover a positive association between crowded living conditions and poorer psychological health. Several studies have excellent controls for sociodemographic factors and one is a prospective, longitudinal analysis. Psychological distress associated with residential crowding may be caused by a typical coping strategy for dealing with chronic high density living conditions—social withdrawal. An unintended consequence of this social withdrawal may be a breakdown in socially supportive relationships. There is not strong evidence, however, that human crowding is associated with more extreme forms of psychopathology characterized in some animal studies as a behavioral sink.

There is also evidence that crowding may lead to the development of motivational deficits, particularly among children in achievement-related contexts. There is indirect evidence suggesting that these motivational deficits are related to learned helplessness from diminished perceived control over the environment.

NOISE

Noise, which is defined as unwanted sound, is typically measured in decibels. Decibels is a logarithmic scale with a change in 10 decibels perceived as approximately twice as loud. There is considerably more research on noise and health in comparison to research on crowding and health. The bulk of the noise and health research has occurred in industrial settings. More recently, studies of noise and health have also focused on people living in airport impact zones or near to road traffic noise. Prolonged exposure to high levels of noise is clearly linked to hearing damage (Kryter, 1994). Because the thrust of this chapter is on environmental stress, the noise-related hearing damage literature is not discussed.

Physical Health

Studies have examined exposure to either occupational noise or community noise and disease. Outside of cardiovascular problems, there appears to be little relation between noise exposure and physical disease. In industrial settings, noise has been associated with increased risk for myocardial infarction (Ising, Babisch, & Günther, 1999), reductions in cardiorespiratory efficiency (Semczuk & Gorny, 1971), difficulties in peripheral circulation and cardiac problems generally (Jansen, 1961), electrocardiogram abnormalities suggestive of coronary heart disease (Cuesdan et al., 1977), general sickness- related absenteeism (Cohen, 1973), and self-reported fatigue (Carlestam, Karlsson & Levi, 1973; Melamed & Bruhis, 1996). Several industrial studies have found no associations between occupational noise exposure and rates of coronary heart disease (Lees, Romeril, & Wetherall, 1980) or rates of total illness (Lees et al., 1980).

Community airport noise studies have shown that higher levels of noise exposure are associated with greater contact with physicians for coronary-related problems (Knipschild, 1977a) and, for women only, use of drugs to treat hypertension (Knipschild & Oudshoorn, 1977; Koszarny, Maziarka, & Szata, 1981). These studies also show an association with greater physician contact in general (Knipschild, 1977b), rates of colds (Ising et al., 1990), as well as total health symptoms (Pulles & Stewart, 1990), and higher levels of coronary heart disease symptoms among women but not men (Koszarny et al., 1981). Graeven (1974) and Hiramatsu, Tamamoto, Taira, Ito, and Nakasone (1993), however, found no differences in self-reported health symptoms between persons living in airport impact zones versus citizens in quiet neighborhoods.

Turning to road traffic noise, Cameron, Robertson, and Zaks (1972) found little relation between community noise levels (self-reported) and illness rates. Babisch, Elwood, Ising, and Kruppa (1993) found slight elevated risk (1.2 odds ratio) in noisier traffic areas in three different sites for men residing in areas above 65 dBA Leq. However, when comparing across different noise levels varying from > 50 dBA Leq to 70, they uncovered no linear relation.

Another area of physical health worthy of note in the noise literature is birth defects and other abnormalities during pregnancy. Not surprisingly, findings in this area are highly controversial and not at all definitive. Jones and Tauscher (1978) found higher rates of birth defects in high airport noise impact zones relative to quieter areas, but Edmonds, Layde, and Erickson (1979) could not replicate the findings. Several rodent studies have found abnormal fetal development following noise exposure (Welch, 1973). There is evidence that women working under very noisy conditions, particularly if subjected to additional stressors like shiftwork, have more pregnancy complications such as vaginal bleeding and pregnancy-induced hypertension (Nurminen & Kurppa, 1989). Babies born in areas with high noise impact have lower birth weights (Ando & Hattori, 1977; Knipschild et al. (1981) with controls for socioeconomic status. Ando (1987) also found an increase in low birth weight babies following the opening of a new airport. Schell (1981) also noted that female infants, but not males, had significantly shorter gestation periods in high airport noise impact zones. Moreover, Ando and Hattori (1977) showed diminished levels of human placental lactogen levels in mothers living in high noise airport impact zones. Finally, Schell and Ando (1991) found a dose–response function relating airport noise levels and 3-year-olds' physical stature (but not weight) in a large epidemiological study. The data on possible linkages between noise and early development are sobering to consider in light of environmental surveys of neonatal, intensive care units that are often populated by premature babies. Levels of noise match or exceed recommended standards for ambient traffic exposure and health (Lawson, Daum, & Turkewitz, 1977).

Psychophysiological

Although previous reviews of noise indicate that cardiovascular responses (typically blood pressure or pulse) to noise under acute exposures rapidly habituate (Glass & Singer, 1972; Kryter, 1994), more careful scrutiny of this literature indicates important exceptions. Persons who are noise sensitive do not easily habituate (Conrad, 1973; Stansfeld & Shine, 1993), nor do individuals who are hypertensive (von Eiff, Friedrich, & Neus, 1982). Short-term habituation is blocked when people perform demanding cognitive tasks under noise (Carter & Beh, 1989; Conrad, 1973; Mosskov & Ettema, 1977). Evans et al. (1996) also showed that noise significantly increases blood pressure over a 20-minute period without habituation, if it follows exposure to a psychological stressor (i.e., giving a speech, taking a final examination).

Other psychophysiological indices examined under acute noise have included electrodermal activity, ECG, EEG, and neuroendocrine activity. Results parallel the cardiovascular data, indicating rapid habituation (Finkle & Poppen, 1948; Fruhstorfer & Hensel, 1980). Recent findings suggest, however, that when short-term exposure to loud noise is accompanied by demanding tasks, habituation may be blocked (Frankenhaeuser & Lundberg, 1977; Ising, Rebentisch, Poustka, & Curio, 1990; Lundberg & Frankenhaeuser, 1978). Work by Tafalla and Evans (1997) indicated a central role of effort in the performance/physiological activation tradeoff. Performance can be maintained, at least under many circumstances (e.g., short-term tasks that do not demand large amounts of attention or memory), by additional cognitive effort. Such maintenance of performance, however, appears to exact a cost of greater psychophysiological activation. It is noteworthy that McCallum et al. (1979) found a very similar pattern for performance under crowded laboratory conditions.

There is also evidence indicating that habituation is interfered with by calling attention to the potential negative impacts of noise on the person (Vera, Vila, & Godoy, 1992). This latter finding might explain why noise sensitive persons apparently do not readily habituate to repeated exposures of acute noise in the laboratory. Perhaps they are more threatened or concerned about potential harmful effects of the noise.

Field research on noise and psychophysiologic outcomes has occurred primarily in industrial settings. The occupational noise and psychophysiologic literature is too large to review exhaustively herein. Several reviews of this literature (Kryter, 1994; Thompson, 1981, 1993; Welch, 1979) have characterized the findings similarly. Unfortunately, nonexperimental designs have frequently been employed in the occupational noise and health literature with poor or nonexisting controls, and many studies have relied on poor estimates of noise exposure. Furthermore, blood pressure is often poorly measured. Many of the industrial studies have relied on one or two measures of blood pressure taken during a physical at work by medical personnel. Moreover, annual medical examinations or other medical screenings may seriously bias estimates since some workers become excluded.

Thompson concluded from her two reviews that workers with adequate hearing protection are unlikely to show much effect of noise on the cardiovascular system. Kryter (1994) reflected greater concern but also remained skeptical, noting the paucity of well-designed research studies; Welch (1979) sounded a considerably greater sense of alarm about cardiovascular health risks from chronic, occupational exposure to noise. Interestingly, Welch's review is based primarily on Eastern European literature that includes worksites with generally very high levels of occupational noise exposure, often coupled with a paucity of hearing protection programs. The bulk of the literature in the other major reviews is based on North American and Western European studies where occupational noise levels tend to be lower and hearing protection programs more common.

Difficulties in exposure estimation in industrial studies of noise and cardiovascular functioning are illustrated by one of the most thorough investigations (Talbott et al., 1985). Although these investigators found no significant differences in blood pressure readings that were carefully administered to men from noisy and from quiet manufacturing plants, they also uncovered a clear, consistent positive link between elevated diastolic blood pressure and severe hearing loss in the noisy plant. Moreover, looking at the subset of men who had worked for at least 15 years in the two respective manufacturing plants, occupational noise exposure did significantly relate to both systolic and diastolic blood pressure (Talbott et al., 1990). See Lercher (1996) for an in-depth discussion of noise exposure estimation and health outcomes.

It is also conceivable that subsets of workers may be particularly vulnerable to the chronic effects of noise exposure on their cardiovascular systems. For example, Tarter and Robins (1990) found that male, African American automobile plant workers suffered increased blood pressure, whereas their Anglo counterparts, who were exposed to comparable levels of high noise at work, did not show this relation. Tarter and Robins speculated that perhaps racial differences in propensity for hypertension might explain these findings. Given the fact that individual differences in noise sensitivity interfere with habituation to acute noise exposure as reviewed earlier, it might be hypothesized that noise sensitivity creates vulnerable subgroups within occupationally noise-exposed groups. This idea has not been tested, although mixed support of such a pattern has been uncovered in community studies of aircraft noise (Neus, Ruddel, & Schulte, 1983; Stansfeld, 1993).

A few longitudinal studies of noise and cardiovascular functioning in industrial settings have been conducted. By comparing the same worker in quiet and noisy periods, some of the weaknesses most endemic to cross-sectional studies (e.g., selection bias) are reduced. The U.S. Raytheon (1975) study, for example, found a significant reduction in medical problems after the implementation of a hearing conservation program in the plant. No changes in similar health indices occurred over the same time period among workers in quiet plant areas. Moreover, the greater the level of compliance observed (e.g., wearing hearing protection), the greater the apparent health benefit. Hypertension and cardiovascular disease were included in the overall health records monitored but could not be singled out because of insufficient sample size. Antonova (1971) compared miners before and after their workshifts in either noisy or quiet areas of the mine. Noise significantly elevated mean arterial pressure with no changes in the quiet group pre and post work. Systolic blood pressure was significantly elevated among brewery workers when they did not wear ear plugs in comparison to days in which they did (Ising & Melchert, 1980). Cortisol fluctuations were also shown to be dependent on the use of earplugs in a similar design (Melamed & Bruhis, 1996).

Another more rigorous approach to studying industrial noise exposure and psychophysiological responses is to simulate occupational noise exposure under experimental conditions with random assigment to noise conditions. Three-hour exposure to jet turbines significantly elevated blood pressure over resting levels among workers in a jet assembly plant (Ortiz, Arguelles, Crespin, Sposari, & Villafane, 1974). Mosskov and Ettema (1977) and Rovekamp (1983) found elevations in blood pressure in 2- to 3-hour noise exposures but at much lower intensities of noise than employed by Ortiz and colleagues. Cartwright and Thompson (1975) found no effects, however, of a 1-hour exposure to loud noise, but Carter and Beh (1989) were able to significantly elevate cardiovascular parameters from 1 hour of exposure, as long as participants simultaneously worked at a difficult task.

This latter finding, along with other experimental findings reviewed earlier on the multiplicative effects of noise and task demands on cardiovascular and neuroendocrine functioning, is interesting to consider in light of a small number of occupational noise studies that have also incorporated additional measures of working conditions. A Russian industrial study reviewed by Welch (1979) found elevated cardiovascular functioning in a noisy manufacturing plant among workers with higher levels of workload demands. Workers with low workloads did not reveal any cardiovascular correlates of occupational noise exposure. Parallel results were recently uncovered in a longitudinal study (Melamed, Boneh-Kristal, & Froom, 1999). Cottington, Matthews, Talbott, and Kuller (1983) also reported a significant interaction of job stress and noise on diastolic blood pressure. Job stress was associated with higher blood pressure in a noisy manufacturing plant but not a quiet one with good controls for SES and cardiovascular risk. Similarly, Lercher, Hortnagl, and Kofler (1993) found that annoyance with noise at work had a small positive association with diastolic blood pressure. This relation was significantly amplified, however, among workers who also reported job dissatisfaction and low levels of social support on the job. Occupational exposure to noise levels may also interact with shift work. Ottmann, Rutenfranz, Neidhart, and Boucsein (1987) and Cesana et al. (1982) both found elevated catecholamine levels related to noise levels at work but only among workers on rotating shifts. Nonshift workers in noisy work areas did not reveal these associations. Lercher et al. (1993) also found higher levels of blood pressure among workers annoyed by noise who also engaged in shiftwork relative to nonshiftwork employees.

There has been a small number of industrial studies or simulation studies with prolonged noise exposure that have examined neuroendocrine and other biochemical markers of stress rather than cardiovascular functioning. Mixed results have been uncovered with no relation between noise exposure and cholesterol (Brown, Thompson, & Folk, 1975), cortisol (Brandenberger, Follenius, & Tremolieres, 1977; Cavatorta et al., 1987; Slob, Wink, & Radder, 1973), and with one or more catecholamines (Carlestam et al., 1973; J. Osguthorpe, Mills, & N. Osguthorpe, 1983; Paulocci, 1975; Slob et al., 1973). Other studies have uncovered significant, although typically small, associations between noise levels on the job or from simulated exposures and various psychophysiologic indicators, such as reduced urine volume and 17-ketosteroid levels (Gibbons, Lewis, & Lord, 1975), elevated fatty acids (Ortiz et al., 1974; Proniewska et al., 1972), higher levels of cholesterol (Cantrell, 1974; Ortiz et al., 1974; Rai, Singh, Upadkyay, Patil, & Nayer, 1981), increased epinephrine levels (Cavatorta et al., 1987; Ortiz et al., 1974; Slob et al., 1973), elevated cortisol (Cantrell, 1974; J. Osguthorpe et al., 1983; Rai et al., 1981), and increased levels of ACTH and oxytocin (Fruhstorfer & Hensel, 1980). Although there are more published positive findings, it is important to keep in mind that most of these noise and biochemical studies find small changes, and null results are more difficult to get published. On the other hand, there is also a large animal literature generally consistent with significant biochemical outcomes from acute noise exposure under controlled conditions (B. Welch & A. Welch, 1970).

Increasingly, researchers have turned their attention to community studies of noise and psychophysiologic parameters, particularly blood pressure. Traffic noise levels appear to have no relation to blood pressure in community samples (Elwood, Ising, & Babisch, 1993; Lercher & Kofler, 1993; Knipschild & Salle, 1979) or show a small positive association (von Eiff, Friedrich, & Neus, 1982; Neus, Ruddel, Schulte, & von Eiff, 1983, Wu, Chiang, Huang, & Chang, 1993). Regecova and Kellcrova (1995) found that traffic noise both at home and at school was associated with elevated blood pressure among 3- to 7-year-olds. Interestingly, there were multiplicative effects as well of school and home noise. The Neus study is noteworthy because it is longitudinal. The Wu study bears mention as well since they found that traffic noise elevated young children's blood pressure as a function of hearing status. Congenitally deaf children were unaffected by road noise, whereas their able-hearing counterparts suffered small elevations. Herbold, Hense, and Keil (1974) noted a small positive relation between traffic noise levels and hypertension prevalence among adults and Babisch, Fromme, Beyer, and Ising (1996) found elevated overnight neuroendocrine stress hormones. Simulated exposure to traffic noise under controlled conditions elevates both cardiovascular and neuroendocrine activity as a function of sound intensity (Ising, Dienel, & Markert, 1980; Osada, Ogawa, Hirokawa, & Haruta, 1973). Ising's study is particularly interesting because, as in several of the acute noise exposure studies noted earlier, he found that exposure to simulated traffic noise while working had significant effects on both cardiovascular and neuroendocrine levels, especially when mental loads were higher. In one of the more rigorous tests of ambient noise exposure and cardiovascular health, Peterson, J. S. Augenstein, Tanis, and D. G. Augenstein (1981) were able to produce sustained, elevated arterial blood pressure in monkeys exposed for long periods of time to simulated recordings of aircraft and traffic noise played at typical ambient levels (Leq = 78). Their work also showed that these monkeys sustained no hearing damage.

Studies of airport noise, which is typically louder and less predictable than road traffic noise, generally find stronger associations between noise exposure and elevated cardiovascular functioning in comparison to the road traffic noise studies. Most studies have focused on children rather than adults, which might also explain the generally more consistent, positive results than those uncovered in the road traffic noise literature.

Knipschild (1977a) found a dose–response relation between community airport noise exposure and hypertension among adult residents in Amsterdam. Two studies of simulated, military aircraft flights at low altitude have shown significant increases in blood pressure among elderly residents (Michalak, Ising & Rebentisch, 1990) and in catecholamines among middle-aged adults (Maschke, Breinl, Grimm, & Ising, 1992). Several studies have found significant relations between exposure to aircraft noise and elevated blood pressure in children (Cohen, Evans, Krantz, & Stokols, 1980; Cohen et al., 1986; Evans, Hygge & Bullinger, 1995; Ising et al., 1990; Karagodina, Soldatkina, Vinokur, & Klimukhin, 1969; Karsdorf & Klappach, 1968; Schmeck & Poustka, 1993). Several of these studies have very thorough statistical controls for socioeconomic status. One study has found no relation between airport noise levels and blood pressure (Cohen, Evans, Krantz, Stokols, & Kelly, 1981), but these data were explained by selective attrition (persons in noisy areas with the highest levels of blood pressure left the area). Roche, Chumlea, and Siervogel (1982) found no association between ambient noise exposure in suburban communities with no nearby airports or major highways. This study is flawed because of unreliable blood pressure measurement procedures and use of self-reports for noise exposure estimation.

Evans and colleagues (1995) also investigated reactivity to a noise source, as well as chronic neuroendocrine activity levels as a function of community airport noise exposure. As shown in Table 20.1, they found evidence of elevated catecholamine activity, but no shifts in cortisol among elementary schoolchildren living in the flight path of a major international airport. Of further interest, children chronically exposed to noise appeared less reactive to an acute noise source while reading.

Ising and his colleagues found parallel trends for epinephrine, but not norepinephrine, and also found elevated cortisol in two sets of studies with adults that simulated exposure to night-time aircraft operations (Maschke, Ising, & Arndt, 1995). Of additional interest, in one study they generated a dose–response function between elevated overnight hormonal levels and sound intensity levels. Finally, Evans, Bullinger, and Hygge (1998) replicated their cross-sectional aircraft noise and young children's health findings in a prospective, longitudinal study of children living in the vicinity of the new, Munich international airport.

Immune Function

A large number of animal studies have utilized noise as a stressor to investigate altered immune function. The results, like those of the few human studies are quite mixed (Bly, Goodard, & McLean, 1993). Sieber et al. (1992), for example, found that uncontrollable but not controllable noise significantly decreased natural killer cells among healthy male subjects; Weisse et al. (1990) found the opposite pattern with controllable noise causing lymphocyte resistance to mitogens to drop.

Coping Behaviors

An alternative pathway by which noise and other environmental stressors may impact physical health is the exacerbation of substance abuse. Cigarette smoking and alcohol consumption both increase under stress (Cohen et al., 1986). In the presence of loud noise, nicotine ingestion reduces muscle tension (Hutchinson & Emley, 1973) and accelerates habituation (Friedman, Horvath, & Meares, 1974). In a particularly interesting study, Cherek (1985) demonstrated a dose–response function between cigarette smoking (objective, experimental measures) and controlled exposures to varying noise levels (60–90 dBA).

TABLE 20.1
Twelve-Hour, Overnight Neuroendocrine Measures

Variable	Quiet	Noisy
Epinephrine	368.62 ng/hr	526.36 ng/hr
Norepinephrine	766.22 ng/hr	1,108.82 ng/hr
Cortisol	3.62 ug/hr	3.75 ug/hr

Psychological Health

Several different types of studies have examined chronic noise exposure and mental health. The first set of studies explored possible relations between psychiatric admissions and aircraft noise exposure with decidedly mixed results. Several studies have found positive correlations between admission rates and high noise exposure (Abey-Wickrama, A'Brook, Gattioni, & Herridge, 1969; Herridge & Chin, 1972; Jenkins, Tarnopolsky, & Hand, 1981; Meecham & Smith, 1977). Nonsignificant relations have been found by Gattoni and Tarnopolsky (1973), and Jenkins, Tarnopolsky, Hand, and Barker (1979) found an inverse relation between noise levels and psychiatric admissions in the same region (Heathrow, to the West of London) utilized by Abey-Wickrama and by Jenkins et al. (1981). Kryter (1990), in a further analysis of some of Jenkins' data, discovered large ethnic differences that might have explained Jenkins' puzzling findings. Many of these studies have poor controls for social class and all are cross-sectional.

Self-reports of psychological distress were unrelated to road traffic noise levels in two cross-sectional studies (Tarnopolsky & Morton-Williams, 1980; Tarnopolsky, Watkins, & Hand, 1980) and in a prospective, longitudinal study (Stansfeld, 1993). The absence of support for a link between road traffic noise exposure and psychological health could be due, in part, to noise measurement. Halpern (1995) found that peak noise levels predicted several indices of psychological health, controlling for socioeconomic status of residents. Mean levels of traffic noise had no mental health correlates. Physician treatment for psychological problems, as well as use of hypnotic drugs, was associated with aircraft noise around Amsterdam (Knipschild, 1977b). Koszarny et al. (1981) demonstrated a similar relation, but only among women. Knipschild and Oudshoorn (1977) also found a clear relation among prescription rates for tranquilizers and aircraft noise over a 7-year period. Moreover, these authors found longitudinal trends in use of hypnotic pharmaceuticals that tracked changes in noise levels in airport impact zones. At the same time, they noted lower and consistently similar utilization rates among quiet neighborhoods of comparable socioeconomic composition. Grandjean, Graf, Lauber, Meier, and Muller (1976) found a dose–response function linking airport noise exposure to self-reported use of sleeping pills and tranquilizers. Watkins, Ttarnopolsky, and Jenkins (1981), however, could not replicate the linkages between drug usage and aircraft noise exposure. One study has also uncovered a coarse dose–response function between occupational noise exposure and psychological symptoms among blue-collar workers (McDonald, 1989). Interestingly, in light of earlier work on crowding, social support and psychological health, Mc Donald also noted that impaired interpersonal relationships at work appeared to play a role in the mental health–noise links.

Motivation

Interestingly, the initial study of helplessness and human beings utilized inescapable noise as the induction stimulus. Hiroto (1974) demonstrated that short-term exposure to inescapable noise induces helplessness. Adults were exposed to noise or quiet during an initial phase of an experiment. Half of the noise subjects could avoid the noise by learning an avoidance response. For the other half of the noise subjects, the noise was inescapable. The groups were then tested in a similar situation where noise could easily be avoided by a simple manual response. A second series of experiments replicated Hiroto's findings and also demonstrated that the helplessness induced by inescapable noise generalized to persistence on subsequent task performance (Hiroto & Seligman, 1975). Subjects exposed to inescapable noise exhibited significantly greater helplessness in the second testing phase, regardless of the similarity of the helplessness induction and testing phase (Hiroto & Seligman, 1975). Furthermore, the helplessness effects of inescapable noise were greater for external locus of control individuals (Hiroto, 1974). Krantz, Glkass, and Snyder (1974) found similar results in two studies of inescapable versus escapable noise. One final detail of Hiroto and Seligman's work worthy of note is that the learned helplessness effects of inescapable noise were quite similar to the induction of helplessness produced by exposing subjects to insoluble concept formation problems.

A large number of studies, initiated by Glass and Singer's pioneering work on perceived control and stress (1972) have examined performance aftereffects, immediately following exposure to uncontrollable noise. The basic paradigm includes exposing participants to noise while working on a cognitive task for a period of about 30 minutes. The participant then leaves the room and is asked to do another, apparently unrelated task where noise is no longer present (see Cohen, 1980, for an overview of this paradigm). Uncontrollable noise causes deficits in task persistence on puzzles (Gardner, 1978; Glass & Singer, 1972; Glass, Singer, and Friedman, 1969; Percival & Loeb, 1980; Sherrod, Hage, Halpern, & Moore, 1977; Wohlwill, Nasar, DeJoy, & Foruzani, 1976). Work by Glass and Singer (1972) also showed that the controllability, and to a lesser extent the predictability, of the noise is a critical component of these aftereffects. In a test of the external validity of the initial Glass and Singer findings, Moran and Loeb (1977) utilized tape-recorded aircraft noise and found, unexpectedly, that such noise did not appear to induce aftereffects in the laboratory. Percival and Loeb (1980) reasoned that perhaps airport noise, because of its temporal qualities, is rather predictable. Thus, they replicated the original Moran and Loeb finding utilizing the same stimuli, but of particular interest, found that when the aircraft noise bursts were sudden rather than the typical slow onset pattern of an approaching aircraft, negative aftereffects could be reliably produced. Rotton, Olszewski, Charleton, and Soler (1978) also showed that meaningful speech rather than noise could induce the same negative aftereffect. Evans et al. (1996) indicated that these negative aftereffects are amplified if exposure to uncontrollable noise occurs among subjects already under psychological stress. Finally, Glass and Singer (1972) found that uncontrollable noise interferes with subsequent proofreading accuracy.

A small number of studies has also examined possible relations between chronic noise exposure and susceptibility to helplessness. Evans et al. (1995) adapted the Glass and Singer aftereffects puzzle for young children. They found that children living in high airport noise zones were less likely to persist at solving line tracing puzzles than their quiet community counterparts. Cohen and colleagues (Cohen et al., 1980, 1981) found that aircraft noise-exposed children were significantly less likely to solve a difficult, challenging puzzle than quiet comparison groups. Of particular interest, noise-impacted children were also more likely to simply give up on the puzzle before the allotted 4 minutes had passed. Fifteen percent of children from noisy schools failed the puzzle by giving up in comparison to only 2% of children from quiet schools. It is worth noting that the puzzles were designed and pretested to be fun and engaging to elementary-aged schoolchildren. These effects were replicated by Cohen and colleagues and similar trends were also found for home noise levels (Cohen et al., 1986). Both the Evans and Cohen studies had well-matched SES comparison groups. Moch-Sibony (1984) found very similar results in kindergarten children exposed to higher levels of aircraft noise in Paris. Wachs (1987) also showed that infants exposed to more noise at home manifest less mastery-oriented play as indexed by a standardized observation instrument. Of additional interest, teachers in noisy schools frequently report more difficulties motivating students than do teachers from quiet schools (see Evans & Lepore, 1973b, for a review). Finally, Cohen et al. (1986) uncovered a relation between children's willingness to relinquish choice and chronic noise exposure. Children from noisy schools relative to quiet schools were significantly more likely to allow an experimenter to choose a reward at the conclusion of their experiments rather than make their own choice.

Summary

Both industrial and community studies find no clear, consistent pattern of data on noise and morbidity. Similarly, data on acute noise exposure and altered immune functions are mixed. Although not plentiful, there is a confluence of findings suggestive of noise impacts on in utero development that warrant followup. Several studies point to noise as a factor in elevated smoking.

Acute noise produces short-lived elevations in cardiovascular and neuroendocrine functioning. Recent research suggests, however, that individuals sensitive to noise as well as situations with high workload demands can diminish and perhaps even block such habituation. A plethora of methodologically weak, occupational noise and health studies reveal decidedly mixed findings on noise and blood pressure. Some longitudinal studies indicate small, positive associations between occupational noise exposure and blood pressure elevations. Road traffic noise appears to have no significant impact on blood pressure of community residents, but persons living in the proximity of airports, particularly children, are at risk for elevated blood pressure. The clinical significance of these elevations is unknown at this time.

Data on noise and psychological health are unclear. The preponderance of poorly designed studies links community noise levels to rates of psychiatric illness. There are better studies indicating some link between community noise exposure and utilization of pharmaceutical hypnotics. Both laboratory and field studies reveal that noise, particularly uncontrollable noise, can contribute to diminished motivation related to learned helplessness. Children chronically exposed to noise may be particularly susceptible to this phenomenon.

DISCUSSION

Application of the construct of psychological stress to examine the role of the physical environment in human health has proven useful in the case of crowding and noise. The primary contributions to date have been the identification of stress-related outcome measures likely to be related to environmental stressors and the preliminary development of a conceptual model for thinking about how and under what conditions noise, crowding, and other environmental stressors might adversely impact human well-being.

Conceptual Issues

A central deficiency has been an inattention to the role of underlying psychophysiological processes or social resources in the environmental stressor–disease link. In searching for answers to the question, why does crowding or noise cause disease?, there are very little data that has tested mechanisms like elevated cardiovascular functioning or diminished self-efficacy. What the data generally show, as depicted in Fig. 20.2, is a broad set of outcome measures independently assessed.

More studies are needed that simultaneously investigate physical or psychological health outcomes and one or more underlying processes in the same sample of individuals. For example, Evans and Lepore (Evans et al., 1989; Evans & Lepore, 1993a; Lepore et al., 1991) showed evidence for the model shown in Fig. 20.3—namely, that high residential density causes deterioration in social support resources, which in turn accounts for the linkage between density and psychological ill health.

There are an unbelievably large number of studies of noise and cardiovascular functioning (principally blood pressure) that have not also looked at some disease endpoint. Similarly, no studies have examined crowding, immune function, and physical morbidity.

Several psychophysiologic mechanisms are prime candidates for more in-depth scrutiny as intervening processes that could link environmental conditions to ill health. Alterations in neuroendocrine functioning affect cardiovascular activity, primarily via adrenomedullary action as well as alter immune functioning via adrenocortical pathways (Baum & Grunberg, 1995).

Cardiovascular reactivity is another process warranting analysis. Two viable, competing hypotheses exist. Sustained, chronic exposure to uncontrollable, environmental stressors like crowding or noise may deplete the organism's ability to respond adequately to challenge with cardiovascular mobilization (Dienstbier, 1989). Alternatively, heightened sensitivity and vigilance from chronic stressor exposure might exacerbate reactivity (Krantz & Manuck, 1984).

Learned helplessness and other motivational processes related to chronic environmental stressor exposure have not been adequately developed. It seems clear that one of the potentially most injurious aspects of chronic environmental stressors is their intractability. Several aspects of motivation and chronic environmental stress warrant additional research. The role of attributional processes, which is well documented in the helplessness literature, has not been applied to environmental stress research. It is clear that attributional processes are salient to environmental stressors like noise and crowding. Noise annoyance is strongly affected by attributions about the origins of noise stimuli, as well as their perceived health impacts (Koelega, 1987). Feelings of arousal induced by personal space invasions (Worchel & Teddlie, 1976), expectancies (Schmidt & Keating, 1979), or informational cues (Langer & Saegert, 1977; Paulus & Matthews, 1980) can all be attributed to crowding or other environmental conditions with varying consequences. The potential interplay among environmental stressors and uncontrollability, helplessness, and negative health outcomes (such as depression) is an area ripe for further study. Motivation or effort to maintain task performance or productivity under suboptimal conditions may be a salient factor, as well, in determining the long-term health consequences of chronic exposure to adverse environmental conditions. Several noise studies both in the laboratory and the field, as well as one crowding study indicate that task performance can be sustained under adverse conditions but at a "cost" of psychophysiological activation. The long-term health consequences of people expending additional effort to do their job when the environment is not optimal is an important and unresearched topic.

Studies of underlying psychosocial processes, such as social support or control, also raise provocative conceptual issues about environment, stress, and coping. Social support and control have each traditionally been conceptualized as exogenous factors that moderate stressor–outcome relations. As can be seen herein, however, chronic exposure to crowding or to noise directly effects social support and control processes, respectively. These psychosocial processes mediate rather than moderate the impacts of these chronic environmental demands. Other chronic stressors may have similar effects on coping resources.

In considering hypothetical mechanisms, it is also prudent to carefully scrutinize the traditional practice of statistically controlling risk factors in environmental epidemiology. For example, several noise and coronary heart disease investigations control for smoking levels. However, what if noise exposure increases smoking as a coping device, as suggested by some studies already reviewed? By statistically partialling out a "risk" factor, a psychologically relevant process that may underlie the noise–health link has been eliminated.

At a more abstract level, the construct validity implications of statistical controls or the practice of random assign-

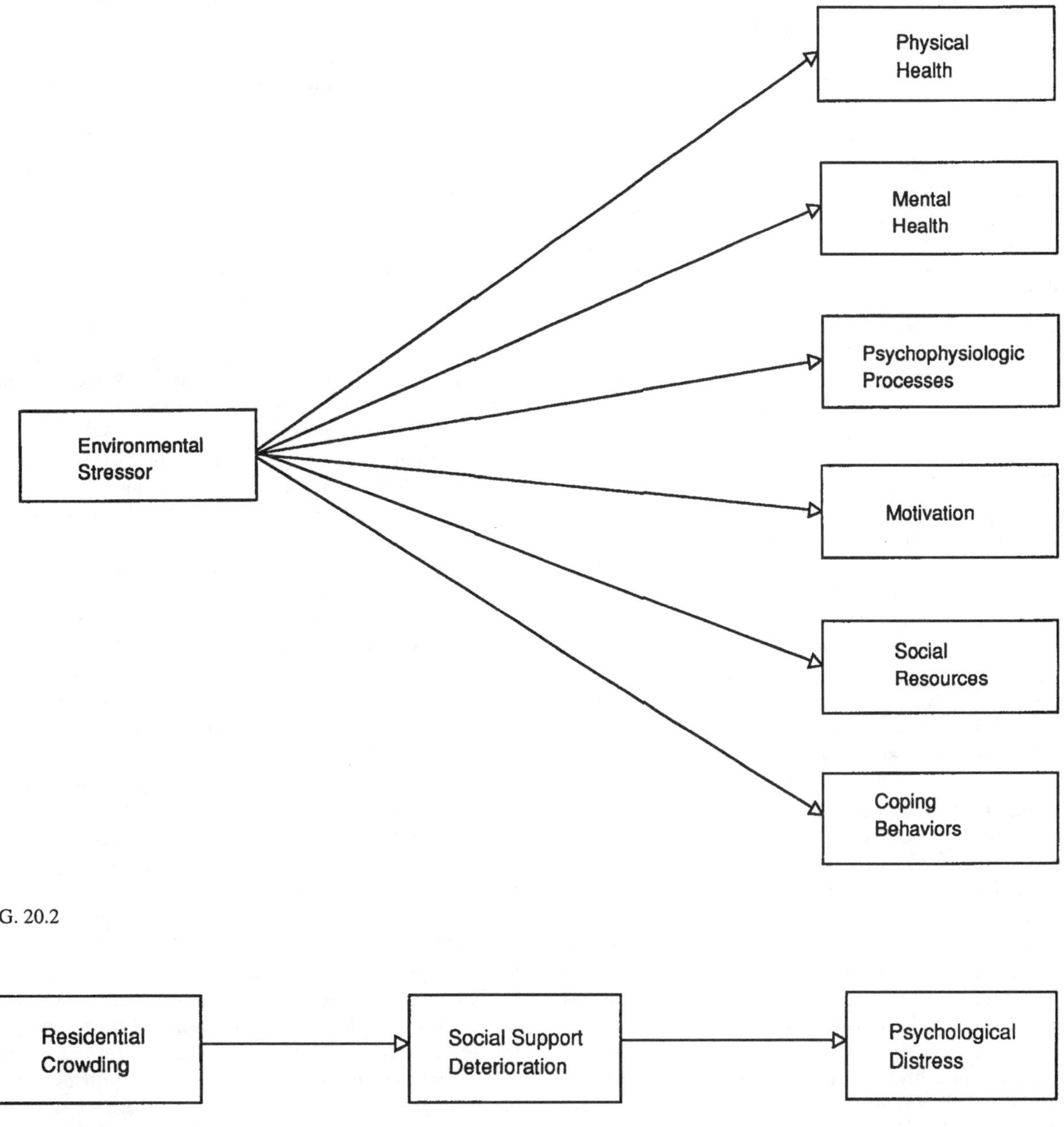

FIG. 20.2

FIG. 20.3

ment in experimental studies of stress and health should be carefully considered. By removing environmental stressors from their natural context (i.e., poverty, other suboptimal environmental factors) for the purposes of study, ecological validity of the stressor–health relation may be distorted. Perhaps crowding and poverty together or noise and certain job requirements together, respectively, lead to pathology. By isolating one independent variable either through statistical or experimental design means for purposes of causal modeling, the actual incidence of adverse outcomes from suboptimal environmental conditions may be dramatically underestimated (Lepore & Evans, 1996).

It might also be valuable to conceptualize the physical environment not only as a source of stress but also as a source of coping resources (Becker, 1990). Research on coping, like stress, tends to overly focus on intrapsychic mechanisms, missing the potential role of the social and physical environment to promote or interfere with health. For example, research on crowding suggests that floorplan layouts that incorporate greater intervening, hierarchically arranged spaces, buffer the negative effects of residential crowding on psychological distress (Evans, Lepore, & Schroeder, 1996). Similarly, children in crowded homes who have a place where they can spend some time by themselves appear to suffer fewer negative outcomes (Wachs & Gruen, 1982).

Although children exposed to multiple risk factors are more likely to suffer adverse physical and mental health outcomes, some children are more resilient than others (Rutter, 1987). Bradley and colleagues (1994) found that low residential density was a significant, independent, protective factor among poor, low birth weight babies tested 1 and 3 years later on a wide array of physical and psychological health measures.

Methodological Issues

In addition to some of the conceptual issues associated with statistically controlling for risk factors, statistical approaches that partial out variables in order to "control" for possible confounding effects are also fraught with analytic problems. Statistical models that partial or covary out variables are based on the assumption of no interaction between the independent variable and the potential control variable on the outcome. Controlling for social class, for example, presupposes that noise or crowding do not interact with social class to affect health or well-being. The same statistical problem may occur with controls for certain risk factors, such as family history of coronary heart disease, hypertension status, or age, to name some common examples. Utilization of analysis of covariance or its regression equivalents assumes that the slopes of the respective regression lines between the outcome variable and the independent variable and the covariate (partial b) are parallel (i.e., no statistical interaction). Researchers should not employ covariance or analogous regression procedures to control for risk factors or contextual factors, such as socioeconomic status, without first assessing this basic statistical assumption.

Another analytic issue concerns effect size considerations. When the correlation coefficient between noise exposure and blood pressure, for example, is squared, not a lot of variance is explained. But this is also true if the same is done for cigarette smoking and lung cancer. It is also true that the variance explained in mental health by crowding is on the same order of magnitude as the variance explained by income (Evans et al., 1998; Gove & Hughes, 1983). Critics of the apparently small role of the physical environment in health need to grapple with this issue more in comparative, rather than in absolute, terms.

There is critical need for prospective, longitudinal designs in the field. There is only one crowding study incorporating such a design (Lepore et al., 1991) and just a handful of industrial studies of noise and health that incorporate a longitudinal component. Self-selection into noisy or crowded environments, as well as possible spuriousness, loom as major threats to internal validity in most of the field studies reviewed herein. Too many cross-sectional field studies exist. Furthermore, not enough integrated research programs have examined the same environmental stressor and health in the lab and in the field. The value of integrating lab and field work is illustrated by Cohen and colleagues' work on aircraft noise and children where laboratory-based concepts and measures were brought to bear on the study of chronic, community noise exposure (Cohen et al., 1986).

Caution is needed in generalizing from aggregate level, epidemiological studies to individual health responses to the physical environment. Several examples of this ecological fallacy were previously reviewed, particularly in crowding field studies, where people per room as indexed by census tract did not yield the same pattern of results as when individual health measures were assessed. Parallel trends were noted in the noise and health literature (Lercher, 1996). One reason aggregate-level comparisons can be misleading is related to exposure estimation. Large degrees of variance in exposure are truncated into a single estimate of exposure when aggregate level data are examined. Furthermore, the actual environment as experienced is even further removed from the exposure metric in comparison to individual residential or work environment assessments.

The problems of exposure estimation and adequate representation of physical stressors in studies are common in the environmental stress literature. Many studies have only gross estimates of actual exposure to the physical stressor. Crowding and noise are typically estimated indirectly and do not account for individual movement throughout the day across settings. One indication of the importance of this issue is found in the noise literature where several studies on industrial noise show that duration of exposure is a critical variable. Similarly, utilization of hearing protection affects noises and health findings in industrial settings. Residential room location can also impact noise exposure (Lercher, 1996). An interesting example of the importance of exposure estimation comes from a recent study by Maxwell (1996) of crowding in preschoolchildren. Children in more crowded day-care centers had greater behavioral and emotional problems only if they also lived in crowded homes.

Moreover, the range of environmental variables in many studies is often truncated and/or the distribution of environmental exposures is badly skewed. Both of these problems strain the general linear model that forms the underlying statistical basis employed in most studies of the physical environment, stress, and health. For example, many studies of crowding have hardly any people in homes with more than 1.5 persons per room. Most laboratory studies expose people to quiet or noise and several community noise studies transform continuous data into a noise/quiet dichotomy. Badly skewed data, as well as use of dichotomous categories, reduce statistical power.

Furthermore, there is some indication of threshold effects for noise and crowding health effects. Recall for example some recent evidence that traffic noise above 65 dBA Leq appears necessary before cardiovascular risk elevates. This nonlinearity also adversely affects statistical power. Studies of traffic congestion and health outcomes indicate that log transformations (Halpern, 1995), or use of indices such as percentage of time at high congestion levels (Evans & Carrere, 1991), predict outcomes significantly better than do mean levels of exposure. This nonlinearity can also appear at the opposite end of the environmental exposure spectrum. Living alone is associated with psychological impairment as well as low social support (Gabe & Williams, 1987; Galle et al., 1972). Crowding studies that calculate persons per room as the density metric that include people living alone distort the estimate of association between crowding and health outcomes.

Outcome measures are also wanting. Several studies of psychological health employed one item or scales of unknown psychometric properties. Studies of health sorely need standardized, sensitive indicators. Immune function would be a particularly valuable adjunct to environmental morbidity studies. Several studies of blood pressure incorporated one or two readings, often taken in a medical setting. Such data are unreliable and of questionable validity.

Health psychology has demonstrated that individual, biological, and personological characteristics are central to understanding health and disease. A smaller body of work within health psychology has also examined the potential role of sociocultural factors in human health. Hopefully, this chapter has directed attention to the potential direct, indirect, and interactive roles the physical environment can play in health and human behavior.

ACKNOWLEDGMENTS

Preparation of this chapter was partially supported by grants from the National Institutes of Health (1 RO1 HL47325-01) the National Science Foundation (BNS-8920483) and the U.S. Department of Agriculture (Hatch-NY 327407). I am grateful to Jana Cooperman and Tamir Ebbin for bibliographic assistance. I thank Steve Lepore, Paul Paulus, and Shirley Thompson for critical feedback on earlier drafts.

REFERENCES

Abey-Wikrama, I., A'Brook, M. F., Gattioni, F.E.G., & Herridge, C. F. (1969). Mental-hospital admissions and aircraft noise. *The Lancet, 633,* 1275–1277.

Aiello, J. R., Epstein, Y. M., & Karlin, R. A. (1975). *Field experimental research on human crowding.* paper presented at the Eastern Psychological Association Convention, New York.

Aiello, J. R., DeRisi, D. T., Epstein, Y. M., & Karlin, R. A. (1977). Crowding and the role of interpersonal distance preference. *Sociometry, 40,* 271–282.

Aiello, J. R., Nicosia, G., & Thompson, D. E. (1979). Physiological, social, and behavioral consequences of crowding on children and adolescents. *Child Development, 50,* 195–202.

Aiello, J. R., Thompson, D. E., & Baum, A. (1985). Children, crowding, and control: Effects of environmental stress on social behavior. In J. F. Wohwill & W. van Vliet (Eds.), *Habitats for children* (pp. 97–124). Hillsdale, NJ: Lawrence Erlbaum Associates.

Altman, I. (1975). *The environment and social behavior.* Monterey, CA: Brooks-Cole.

Ando, Y. (1987). Effects of daily dose on the fetus and cerebral hemispheric specialization of children. *Inter-Noise '87, 2,* 941–944.

Ando, Y., & Hattori, H. (1977). Effects of noise on human placental lactogen (HPL) levels in maternal plasma. *British Journal of Obstetrics and Gynaecology, 84,* 115–118.

Antonova, K. (197 1). Effects of general vibration on equipment operators in ore-dressing plants. *Hygiene and Sanitation, 36,* 457–460.

Appleyard, D., & Lintell, M. (1972). The environmental quality of city streets. *Journal of the American Institute of Planners, 38,* 84–101.

Arnow, P. M., Hierholzer, J. C., Higbee, J., & Harris, D. H. (1977). Acute hemorrhagic conjunctivitis: A mixed virus outbreak among Vietnamese refugees on Guam. *America Journal of Epidemiology, 105,* 68–74.

Babisch, W., Elwood, P., Ising, H., & Kruppa, B. (1993). Traffic noise as a risk factor for myocardial infarction. In H. Ising & B. Kruppa (Eds.), *Noise and disease* (pp. 158–166). New York: Verlag.

Babisch, W., Fromme, H., Beyer, A., & Ising, H. (1996). Elevated catecholamine levels in urine in traffic noise exposed subjects. *Proceedings on Internoise 96, 4,* 2153–2158. Liverpool, UK.

Baldassare, M. (1979). *Residential crowding in urban America.* Berkeley, CA: University of California Press.

Baldassare, M. (1981). The effects of household density on subgroups. *American Sociological Review, 46,* 110–118.

Baron, R. M., Mandel, D. R., Adams, C. A., & Griffen, L. M. (1976). Effects of social density in university residential environments. *Journal of Personality and Social Psychology, 34,* 434–446.

Baron, R. M., & Rodin, J. (1978). Personal control as a mediator of crowding. In A. Baum, J. E. Singer, & S. Valins (Eds.), *Advances in environmental psychology* (Vol. 1). Hillsdale, NJ: Lawrence Erlbaum Associates.

Baum, A., Aiello, J. R., & Calesnick, L. E. (1978). Crowding and personal control: Social density and the development of learned helplessness. *Journal of Personality and Social Psychology, 36,* 1000–1011.

Baum, A., Gatchel, R. J., Aiello, J. R., & Thompson, D. (1981). Cognitive mediation of environmental stress. In J. H. Harvey (Ed.), *Cognition, social behavior, and the environment* (pp. 513–533). Hillsdale, NJ: Lawrence Erlbaum Associates.

Baum, A., & Grunberg, N. (1995). Measurement of stress hormones. In S. Cohen, R. C. Kessler, & L. Gordon (Eds.), *Measuring stress* (pp. 175–192). New York: Oxford University Press.

Baum, A., & Valins, S. (1977). *Architecture and social behavior: Psychological studies of social density.* Hillsdale, NJ: Lawrence Erlbaum Associates.

Baum, A., & Valins, S. (1979). Crowding and the regulation of social contact. In L. Berkowitz (Ed.), Advances in experimental social psychology (Vol. 12, pp. 131–175). New York: Academic Press.

Becker, F. (1990). *The total workplace.* New York: Van Nostrand-Reinhold.

Bell, P., & Greene, T. (1982). Thermal stress: Physiological comfort, performance, and social effects of hot and cold environments. In G. W. Evans (Ed.), *Environmental stress* (pp. 75–104). New York: Cambridge University Press.

Bergman, B. A. (1971). The effects of group size, personal space, and success-failure upon physiological arousal, test performance, and questionnaire response. *Dissertation Abstract International, 2319,* 3419-A–3420-A.

Bickman, L., Teger, A., Gabriele, T., McLaughlin, C., Berger, M., & Sunaday, E. (1973). Dormitory density and helping behavior. *Environment and Behavior, 5,* 456–490.

Bly, S., Goodard, M., & McLean, J. (1993). A review of the effects of noise on the immune system. In M. Vallet (Ed.), *Noise as a public health problem: Proceedings of the 6th international congress* (Vol. 2, pp. 509–512). Cedex, France: INRETS.

Booth, A. (1976). *Urban crowding and its consequences.* New York: Praeger.

Booth, A., & Edwards, J. N. (1976). Crowding and family relations. *American Sociological Review, 41,* 308–321.

Booth, A., & Johnson, D. R. (1975). The effect of crowding on child health and development. *American Behavioral Scientist, 18,* 736–749.

Boyce, W. T., O'Neill-Wagner, P., Price, C., Haines, M., Soumi, S. (1998). Crowding stress and violent injuries among behaviorally inhibited rhesus macaques. *Health Psychology, 17,* 285–289.

Bradley, R. H., & Caldwell, B. (1984). The home inventory and family demographics. *Developmental Psychology, 20,* 315–320.

Bradley, R. H., Whiteside, L., Mundfrom, D. J., Casey, P. H., Kelleher, K. J., & Pope, S. K. (1994). Early indications of resilience and their relation to experiences in the home environments of low birthweight, premature children living in poverty. *Child Development, 65,* 346–360.

Brandenberger, G., Follenius, M., & Tremolieres, C. (1977). Failure of noise exposure to modify temporal patterns of plasma cortisol in man. *European Journal of Applied Physiology, 36,* 239–246.

Brett, G., & Benjamin, B. (1957). Housing and tuberculosis in a mass radiography survey. *British Journal of Preventative Social Medicine, 11,* 7–9.

Brown, J., Thompson, R., & Folk, F. (1975). Certain nonauditory physiological responses to noise. *Journal of the American Hygiene Association, 36,* 285–291.

Calhoun, J. B. (1962). Population density and social pathology. *Scientific American, 206,* 139–148.

Cameron, P., Robertson, D., & Zaks, J. (1972). Sound pollution, noise pollution and health: Community parameters. *Journal of Applied Psychology, 56,* 67–74.

Cantrell, R. (1974). Prolonged exposure to intermittent noise: Audiometric, biochemical, motor, psychological, and sleep effects. *Laryngoscope, 84,* 1–55.

Carlestam, G., Karlsson, C., & Levi, L. (1973). Stress and disease in response to exposure to noise—A review. In W. Ward (Ed.), *Proceedings of the 2nd International Congress o Noise as a Public Health Problem* (Rep. No. 550/9-73-008, pp. 479–486). Washington, DC: EPA.

Carr, T. S., Hopper, C. H., & Ruback, R. B. (1986). Perceived control in prison: Its relation to reported crowding, stress, and symptoms. *Journal of Applied Social Psychology, 16,* 375–386.

Carter, N. L., & Beh, H. C. (1989). The effect of intermittent noise on cardiovascular functioning during vigilance task performance. *Psychophysiology, 26,* 548–559.

Cartwright, L., & Thompson, R. (1975). The effects of broadband noise on the cardiovascular system in normal resting adults. *Journal of the American Industrial Hygiene Association, 36,* 653–658.

Cassel, J. (1971). Health consequences of population density and crowding. In National Academy of Sciences. *Rapid population growth: Consequences and policy implications* (pp. 250–265). Baltimore, MD: Johns Hopkins University Press.

Cassel, J. (1974). An epidemiological perspective of psycho-social factors in disease etiology. *American Journal of Physiological Health, 64,* 1040–1043.

Cavatorta, A., Falzoi, M., Ronamelli, A., Cigala, F., Ricco, M., Bruschi, G., Franchini, L., & Borghetti, A. (1987). Adrenal response in the pathogenesis of arterial hypertension in workers exposed to high noise levels. *Journal of Hypertension, 5,* 463–466.

Cesana, G. C., Ferrario, M., Curti, R., Zanettini, R., Cyfieco, A., Sega, R., Palermo, A., Mara, G., Libretti, A., & Alegefi, S. (1982). Work-stress and urinary catecholamines excretion in shift workers exposed to noise: I. Epinepherine (E) and norepinepherine (NE). *La Medicina del Lavoro, 2,* 99–109.

Cherek, D. R. (1985). Effects of acute exposure to increased levels of background industrial noise on cigarette smoking behavior. *International Archives of Occupational and Environmental Health, 56,* 23–30.

Christian, J. (1963). The pathology of overpopulation. *Military Medicine, 128,* 571–603.

Cohen, A. (1973). Industrial noise and medical, absence, and accident record data on exposed workers. In W. Ward (Ed.), Proceedings of the 2nd International Congress on Noise as a Public Health Problem (Report No. EPA 550/973-008, pp. 451–454). Washington, DC: EPA.

Cohen, S. (1980). After effects of stress on human performance and social behavior: A review of research and theory. *Psychological Bulletin, 88,* 82–108.

Cohen, S., Evans, G. W., Krantz, D. S., & Stokols, D. (1980). Physiological, motivational, and cognitive effects of aircraft noise on children. *American Psychologist, 35,* 231–243.

Cohen, S., Evans, G. W., Krantz, D. S., Stokols, D., & Kelly, S. (1981). Aircraft noise and children: Longitudinal and cross-sectional evidence on adaptation to noise and the effectiveness of noise abatement. *Journal of Personality and Social Psychology, 40,* 331–345.

Cohen, S., Evans, G. W., Stokols, D., & Krantz, D. S. (1986). *Behavior, health, and environmental stress.* New York: Plenum.

Cohen, S., Kessler, R. C., & Gordon, L. (1995). Strategies for measuring stress in studies of psychiatric and physical disorders. In S. Cohen, R. C. Kessler, & L. Gordon (Eds.), *Measuring stress* (pp. 3–28). New York: Oxford University Press.

Collette, J., & Webb, S. (1974). *Urban density, crowding and stress reactions.* Paper presented at the Pacific Sociological Association Meeting, San Jose, CA.

Conrad, D. W. (1973). The effects of intermittent noise on human serial decoding performance and physiological response. *Ergonomics, 16,* 739–747.

Cottington, E. M., Matthews, K. A., Talbott, E., & Kuller. (1983). *Occupational stress and diastolic pressure in a blue- collar population: The Pittsburgh noise-hypertension project.* Paper presented at the Annual Meeting for the Society for Epidemiology, Winnipeg, Manitoba.

Cox, V. C., Paulus, P. B., & McCain, G. (1984), Prison crowding research: The relevance for prison housing standards and a general approach regarding crowding phenomena. *American Psychologist, 39,* 1148–1160.

Cox, V. C., Paulus, P. B., McCain, G., & Karlovac, M. (1982). The relationship between crowding and health. In A. Baum & J. E. Singer (Eds.), *Advances in environmental psychology* (Vol. 4, pp. 271–294). Hillsdale, NJ: Lawrence Erlbaum Associates.

Cox, V. C., Paulus, P. B., McCain, G., & Schkade, J. (1979). Field research on the effects of crowding in prisons and on offshore drilling platforms. In J. Aiello & A. Baum (Eds.), *Residential crowding and design* (pp. 95–106). NY: Plenum.

Cuesdan, L., Teganeanu, S., Tutu, C., Raiciu, M., Carp, C., & Coatu, S. (1977). Study of cardiovascular and auditory pathophysiological implications in a group of operatives working in noisy industrial settings. *Psychophysiology, 14,* 53–61.

D'Atri, D. A. (1975). Psychophysiological responses to crowding. *Environment and Behavior, 7,* 237–250.

Dean, L. M., Pugh, U. M., & Gunderson, E.K.E. (1975). Spatial and perceptual components of crowding: Effects on health and satisfaction. *Environment and Behavior, 7,* 335–336.

Dean, L. M., Pugh, U. M., & Gunderson, E.K.E. (1978). The behavioral effects of crowding. *Environment and Behavior, 10,* 419–432.

Dienstbier, R. (1989). Arousal and physiological toughness: Implications for mental and physical health. *Psychological Review, 96,* 84–100.

Dooley, B. B. (1978). Effects of social density on men with "close" or "far" personal distance. *Journal of Population, 71,* 251–265.

Edmonds, L., Layde, & Erickson, J. (1979). *Airport noise and teratogenesis.* Unpublished manuscript.

Edwards, E. A., & Dean, L. M. (1977). Effects of crowding of mice on humoral antibody formation and protection to lethal antigenic challenge. *Psychosomatic Medicine, 39,* 19–24.

Edwards, J. N., Fuller, T. D., Sermsri, S., & Vorakitphokatorn, S. (1990). *Chronic stress and psychological well-being: Evidence from Thailand on housing crowding.* Paper presented at the World Congress of Sociology, Madrid, Spain.

Elwood, P., Ising, H. R., & Babisch, W. (1993). Traffic noise and cardiovascular disease: The Caerphilly and Speedwell studies. In H. Ising & B. Kruppa (Eds.), *Noise and disease* (pp. 128–134). New York: Verlag.

Epstein, Y. M., Lehrer, P., & Woolfolk, R. L. (1978). *Physiological, cognitive, and behavioral effects of repeated exposure to crowding.* Washington, DC: American Psychological Association.

Essen, J., Fogelman, K., & Head, J. (1978). Children's housing and their health and physical development. *Childcare and Health Development, 4,* 357–369.

Evans, G. W. (1978). Crowding and the developmental process. In A. Baum & Y. Epstein (Eds.), *Human responses to crowding* (pp. 117–140). Hillsdale, NJ: Lawrence Erlbaum Associates.

Evans, G. W. (1979). Behavioral and physiological consequences of crowding in humans. *Journal of Applied Social Psychology, 9,* 27–46.

Evans, G. W. (Ed.). (1982). *Environmental stress.* New York: Cambridge University Press.

Evans, G. W. (1994). The psychological costs of chronic exposure to ambient air pollution. In R. L. Isaacson & K. F. Jensen (Eds.), *The vulnerable brain and environmental risks: Vol. 3. Toxins in air and water* (pp. 167–182). New York: Plenum.

Evans, G. W., Allen, K., Tafalla, R., & O'Meara, T. (1996). Multiple stressors. *Journal of Environmental Psychology, 16,* 147–154,

Evans, G. W., Bullinger, M., & Hygge, S. (1998). Chronic noise exposure and physiological response: A prospective, longitudinal study of children under environmental stress. *Psychological Science, 9,* 75–77.

Evans, G. W., & Carrere, S. (1991). Traffic congestion, perceived control, and psychophysiological stress among urban bus drivers. *Journal of Applied Psychology, 76,* 658–663.

Evans, G. W., & Cohen, S. (1987). Environmental stress. In D. Stokols & I. Altman (Eds.), *Handbook of environmental psychology* (pp. 571–610). New York: Wiley.

Evans, G. W., Hygge, S., & Bullinger, M. (1995). Chronic noise and psychological stress. *Psychological Science, 6,* 333–338.

Evans, G. W., & Lepore, S. J. (1993a). Household crowding and social support: A quasi-experimental analysis. *Journal of Personality and Social Psychology, 65,* 308–316.

Evans, G. W., & Lepore, S. J. (1993b). Nonauditory effects of noise on children: A critical review. *Children's Environments, 10,* 31–51.

Evans, G. W., Lepore, S. J., & Schroeder, A. (1996). The role of architecture in human responses to crowding. *Journal of Personality and Social Psychology, 70,* 41–46.

Evans, G. W., Lepore, S. J., Shejwal, B., & Palsane, M. N. (1998). Chronic residential crowding and children's well being: An ecological perspective. *Child Development, 69,* 1514–1523.

Evans, G. W., Maxwell, L. E., & Hart, B. (1999). Parental language and verbal responsiveness to children in crowded homes. *Developmental Psychology, 35,* 1020–1023.

Evans, G. W., Palsane, M. N., Lepore, S. J., & Martin, J. (1989). Residential density and psychological health: The mediating effects of social support. *Journal of Personality and Social Psychology, 57,* 994–999.

Finkle, A., & Poppen, J. (1948). Clinical effects of noise and mechanical vibrations of a turbo-jet engine on man. *Journal of Applied Physiology, 1,* 183–204.

Fleming, I., Baum, A., Davidson, L., Rectanus, E., & McArdle, S. (1987). Chronic stress as a reactivity factor in physiologic reactivity to challenge. *Health Psychology, 11,* 221–237.

Fleming, I., Baum, A., & Weiss, L. (1987). Social density and perceived control as mediators of crowding stress in high-density residential neighborhoods. *Journal of Personality and Social Psychology, 52,* 899–906.

Freedman, J. L., Heshka, S., & Levy, A. (1975). Population density and Pathology: Is there a relationship? *Journal of Experimental and Social Psychology, 11,* 539–552.

Freeman, H. L. (1984). Housing. In H. L. Freeman (Ed.), *Mental health and the environment* (pp. 197–225). London: Churchill Livingston.

Frankenhaeuser, M., & Lundberg, U. (1977). The influence of cognitive set on performance and arousal under different noise loads. *Motivation and Emotion, 1,* 139–149.

Friedman, J., Horvath, T., & Meares, R. (1974). Tobacco smoking and the stimulus barrier. *Nature, 248,* 455–456.

Fruhstorfer, B., & Hensel, H. (1980). Extra auditory responses to long term intermittent noise stimulation in humans. *Journal of Applied Physiology, 49,* 985–993.

Gabe, J., & Williams, P. (1987). Women, housing and mental health. *International Journal of Health Services, 17,* 667–679.

Galle, O. R., Gove, W. R., & McPherson, J. M. (1972). Population density and pathology: What are the relations for man? *Science, 176,* 23–30.

Gardner, G. T. (1978). Effects of federal human subjects regulations on data obtained in environmental stressor research. *Journal of Personality and Social Psychology, 36,* 628–634.

Gasparini, A. (1973). Influence of the dwelling on family life: A sociological survey in Modena, Italy. *Ekestics, 216,* 344–348.

Gattoni, F., & Tarnopolsky, A. (1973). Aircraft noise and psychiatric morbidity. *Psychological Medicine, 3,* 516–520.

Gibbons, S., Lewis, A., & Lord, P. (1975). Noise and vibration on board ship. *Journal of Sound and Vibration, 43,* 253–261.

Giel, R., & Ormel, J. (1977). Crowding and subjective health in the Netherlands. *Social Psychiatry, 12,* 37–42.

Glass, D. C., & Singer, J. E. (1972). *Urban stress: Experience on noise and social stressors.* New York: Academic Press.

Glass, D. C., Singer, J. E., & Friedman, E. (1969). Psychic cost of adaptation to an environmental stressor. *Journal of Personality and Social Psychology, 41,* 200–210.

Goduka, I. N., Poole, D., & Aotaki-Phenice, L. (1992). A comparative study of black South African children from three different contexts. *Child Development, 63,* 509–525

Gove, W. R., & Hughes, M. (1983). *Overcrowding in the household.* New York: Academic Press.

Graeven, D. B. (1974). The effects of airplane noise on health: An examination of three hypotheses. *Journal of Health and Social Behavior, 15,* 336–343.

Grandjean, E., Graf, P. Lauber, A., Meier, H., & Muller, R. (1976). Survey on the effects of noise around three civil airports in Switzerland. In R. Kerlin (Ed.), *Internoise '76* (pp. 85–90). Washington, DC: Institute of Noise Control Engineers.

Griffitt, W., & Veitch, R. (1971). Influences of population density on interpersonal affective behavior. *Journal of Personality and Social Psychology, 17,* 92–98.

Halpern, D. (1995). *Mental health and the built environment.* London: Taylor & Francis.

Hassen, R. (1977). Social and psychological implications of high population density. *Civilisations, 27,* 230–236.

Herbold, M., Hense, H. W., & Keil, U. (1974). Effects of road traffic noise on prevalence of hypertension in men: Results of the Luebeck blood pressure study. *Social and Preventative Medicine, 34,* 19–23.

Herridge, C., & Chin, B. (1972). Aircraft noise and mental hospital admissions. *Sound, 6,* 32–36.

Heshka, S., & Pylypuk, A. (1975). *Human crowding and adrenocortical activity.* Paper presented at the Canadian Psychological Association Convention, June, Quebec City, Canada.

Hiramatsu, K., Tamamoto, T., Taira, K., Ito, A., & Nakasone, T. (1993). Response to questionnaire on health around a military airport. In M. Vallet (Ed.), *Proceedings of the 6th International Congress on Noise as Public Health problem* (Vol. 2, pp. 473–476). Cedex, France: INRETS.

Hiroto, D. (1974). Locus of control and learned helplessness. *Journal of Experimental Psychology, 102,* 187–193.

Hiroto, D. S., & Seligman, M.E.P. (1975). Generality of learned helplessness in man. *Journal of Personality and Social Psychology, 31,* 311–327.

Hutchinson, R., & Emley, G. (1973). Effects of nicotine on avoidance, conditioned suppression and aggression response measures in animals and man. In W. Dunn (Ed.), *Smoking behavior: Motives and incentives* (pp. 171–196). New York: Wiley.

Hutt, C., & Vaizey, M. J. (1966). Differential effects of group density on social behaviour. *Nature, 209,* 1371–1372.

Ising, H., Babisch, W., & Günther, T. (1999). Work noise as a factor in myocardial infarction. *Journal of Clinical and Basic Cardiology, 2,* 64–68.

Ising, H., Dienel, D., & Markert, B. (1980). Health effects of traffic noise. *International Archives of Occupational and Environmental Health, 47,* 179–190.

Ising, H., & Melchert, H. (1980). Endocrine and cardiovascular effects of noise. In J. Tobias, G. Jansen, & W. Ward (Eds.), *Proceedings of the 3rd International Congress on Noise as a Public Health Problem* (pp. 241–245). Rockville, MD: American Speech Language and Hearing Association.

Ising, H., Rebentisch, E., Babisch, W., Curio, I., Sharp, D., & Baumgartner, H. (1990). Medically relevant effects of noise from low-altitude flights—results of an interdisciplinary pilot study. *Environmental International, 16,* 411–423.

Ising, H., Rebentisch, E., Poustka, F., & Curio, I. (1990). Annoyance and health risk caused by military low-altitude flight noise. *International Archives of Occupational and Environmental Health, 62,* 357–363.

Jacobson, J. A., Chester, T. J., & Fraser, D. W. (1977). An epidemic of disease due to serogroup B *neisseria meningitidis* in Alabama: Report of an investigation and community wide prophylaxis with a sulfonamide. *Journal of Infectious Diseases, 136,* 104–108.

Jain, U. (1987). *The psychological consequences of crowding.* New Delhi: Sage.

Jansen, G. (1961). Adverse effects of noise on iron and steel workers. *Stahl Eisen, 81,* 217–220.

Jenkins, L., Tarnopolsky, A., & Hand, D. (1981). Psychiatric admissions and aircraft noise from London airport: Four-year, three hospitals' study. *Psychological Medicine, 11,* 765–782.

Jenkins, L., Tarnopolsky, A., Hand, D., & Barker, S. (1979). Comparison of three studies of aircraft noise and psychiatric admissions conducted in the same area. *Psychologic Medicine, 9,* 681–693.

Jones, F. N., & Tauscher, J. (1978). Residence under an airport landing pattern as a factor in teratism. *Archives of Environmental Health, 33,* 10–12.

Karagodina, I. L., Soldatkina, S. A., Vinokur, I. L., & Klimukhin, A. A. (1969). Effect of aircraft noise on the population near airports. *Hygiene and Sanitation, 34,* 182–187.

Karlin, R., Epstein, Y., & Aiello, J. (1978). Strategies for the investigation of crowding. In A. H. Esser & B. G. Greenbie (Eds.), *Design for commonality and privacy* (pp. 71–88). New York: Plenum.

Karsdorf, G., & Klappach, H. (1968). The influence of traffic noise in the health and performance of secondary school students in a large city. *Zeitschrift fur die gesamte Hygiene, 14,* 52–54.

Kellett, J. (1984). Crowding and territoriality: A psychiatric view. In H. L. Freeman (Ed.), *Mental health and the environment* (pp. 71–96). London: Churchill Livingstone.

Knipschild, P. (1977a). V. Medical effects of aircraft noise: Community cardiovascular survey. *International Archives of Occupational and Environmental Health, 40,* 185–190.

Knipschild, P. (1977b). VI. Medical effects of aircraft noise: General practice survey. *International Archives of Occupational and Environmental Health, 40,* 191–196.

Knipschild, P., Meijer, H., & Salle, H. (1981). Aircraft noise and birthweight. *International Archives of Occupational and Environmental Health, 48,* 131–136.

Knipschild, P., & Oudshoorn, N. (1977). VII. Medical effects of aircraft noise: Drug survey. *International Archives of Occupational and Environmental Health, 40,* 197–200.

Knipschild, P., & Salle, H. (1979). Road traffic noise and cardiovascular disease. *International Archives of Occupational and Environmental Health, 44,* 55–59.

Koelega, H. (Ed.). (1987). *Environmental annoyance.* Amsterdam: Elsevier.

Koopman, J. S. (1978). Diarrhea and school toilet hygiene in Cali, Colombia. *American Journal of Epidemiology, 107,* 412–420.

Koszamy, Z., Maziarka, S., & Szata, W. (1981). *The effect of airplane noise on the inhabitants of areas near the Okecie airport in Warsaw.* Washington, DC: National Aeronautics and Space Administration.

Krantz, D. S., Glass, D. C., & Snyder, M. (1974). Helplessness, stress level, and the coronary-prone behavior pattern. *Journal of Experimental Social Psychology, 10,* 284–300.

Krantz, D. S., & Manuck, S. (1984). Acute physical reactivity and risk for coronary heart disease: A review and methodologic critique. *Psychological Bulletin, 96,* 435–464.

Kryter, K. (1990). Aircraft noise and social factors in psychiatric hospital admission rates: A re-examination of some data. *Psychological Medicine, 20,* 395–411.

Kryter, K. (1994). *The handbook of hearing and the effects of noise.* New York: Academic.

Lakey, B. (1989). Personal and environmental antecedents of perceived social support developed at college. *American Journal of Community Psychology, 17,* 503–519.

Langer, E., & Saegert, S. (1977). Crowding and cognitive control. *Journal of Personality and Social Psychology, 35,* 175–182.

Lawson, K., Daum, C., & Turkewitz, G. (1977). Environmental characteristics of a neonatal intensive-care unit. *Child Development, 48,* 1633–1639.

Lees, R. E., Romeril, C. S., & Wetherall, L. D. (1980). A study of stress indicators in workers exposed to industrial noise. *Canadian Journal of Public Health, 71,* 261–265.

Lepore, S. J. (1995). Measurement of chronic stressors. In S. Cohen, R. C. Kessler, & L. Gordon (Eds.), *Measuring stress* (pp. 102–121). New York: Oxford University Press.

Lepore, S. J., & Evans, G. W. (1996). Coping with multiple stressors in the environment. In M. Zeidner & N. Endler (Eds.), *Handbook of coping* (pp. 350–377). New York: Wiley.

Lepore, S. J., Evans, G. W., & Schneider, M. (1991). The dynamic role of social support in the link between chronic stress and psychological distress. *Journal of Personality and Social Psychology, 61,* 899–909.

Lercher, P. (1996). Environmental noise and health: An integrated research perspective. *Environment International, 22,* 117–128.

Lercher, P., Hortnagl, J., & Kofler, W. W. (1993). Work noise annoyance and blood pressure: Combined effects with stressful working conditions. *International Archives of Occupational and Environmental Health, 65,* 23–28.

Lercher, P., & Kofler, W. (1993). Adaptive behavior to road traffic noise, blood pressure, and cholesterol. In M. Vallet (Ed.), *Proceedings of the 6th International Congress on Noise as a Public Health Problem* (pp. 465–468). Cedex, France: INRETS.

Levy, L., & Herzog, A. N. (1974). Effects of population density and crowding on health and social adaptation in the Netherlands. *Journal of Health and Social Behavior, 15,* 228–240.

Levy, L., & Herzog, A. (1978). Effects of crowding on health and social adaptation in the city of Chicago. *Urban Ecology, 3,* 327–354.

Light, R. (1973). Abused and neglected children in America: A study of alternative policies. *Harvard Educational Review, 43,* 556–598.

Lundberg, U. (1976). Urban commuting. Crowdedness and catecholamine excretion. *Journal of Human Stress, 2,* 26–34.

Lundberg, U., & Frankenhaeuser, M. (1978). Psychophysiological reactions to noise as modified by personal control over noise intensity. *Biological Psychology, 6,* 51–60.

Mackintosh, J. (1934). Housing and tuberculosis. *British Journal of Tuberculosis, 28,* 67–70.

Marsella, A. J., Escudero, M., & Gordon, P. (1970). The effects of dwelling density on mental disorders in Filipino men. *Journal of Health and Social Behavior, 11,* 288–294.

Maschke, C., Breinl, S., Grimm, R., & Ising, H. (1992). Der eirfflub von nachtfluglarm auf den schlaf und die katecholaminausscheidung [The effect of night time aircraft noise exposure on sleep and catecholamine excretion]. *Bundesgesundheitsblatt, 35,* 119–125.

Maschke, C., Ising, H., & Arndt, D. (1995). Nachtlicher verkehrslarm und gesundheit: Ergebnisse von labor- und feldstudien [Night time traffic noise exposure and health: Results from laboratory and field studies]. *Bundesgesundheitsblatt, 38,* 130–136.

Maxwell, L. (1996). Multiple effects of home and day care crowding. *Environment and Behavior, 28,* 494–511.

McCain, G., Cox, V., & Paulus, P. B. (1976). The relationship between illness complaints and degree of crowding in a prison environment. *Environment and Behavior, 8,* 283–290

McCallum, R., Rusbult, C., Hong, G., Walden, T., & Schopler, J. (1979). Effects of resource availability and importance of behavior on the experience of crowding. *Journal of Personality and Social Psychology, 37,* 1304–1313.

McCarthy, D., & Saegert, S. (1978). Residential density, social overload, and social withdrawal. In J. Aiello & A. Baum (Eds.), *Residential crowding and design* (pp. 55–76). New York: Plenum.

McDonald, N. (1989). Jobs and their environment: The psychological impact of work in noise. *Irish Journal of Psychology, 10,* 39–55.

McGlashen, N. (1977). Viral hepatitis in Tasmania. *Social Science and Medicine, 11,* 731–744.

McKinlay, P., & Truelove, S. (1947). Epidemiology of infective hepatitis among allied troops in Italy. *British Journal of Social Medicine, 1,* 33–50.

Meecham, W. C., & Smith, H. G. (1977). Effect of jet aircraft noise on mental hospital admissions. *British Journal of Audiology, 11,* 81–85.

Melamed, S., Boneh-Kristal, E., & Froom, P. (1999). Industrial noise exposure and risk factors for cardiovascular disease. *Noise and Health, 4,* 49–56.

Melamed, S., & Bruhis, S. (1996). The effects of chronic industrial noise exposure on urinary cortisol, fatigue, and irritability. *Journal of Occupational and Environmental Medicine, 38,* 252–256.

Menton, K. G., & Myers, G. C. (1977). The structure of urban mortality. A methodological study of Hannover, Germany. Part II. *International Journal of Epidemiology, 6,* 213–223.

Michalak, R., Ising, H., & Rebentisch, E. (1990). Acute circulatory effects of military low-altitude flight noise. *International Archives of Occupational and Environmental Health, 62,* 365–372.

Mitchell, R. E. (1971). Some social implications of high density housing. *American Sociological Review, 36,* 18–29.

Moch-Sibony, A. (1984). Study of the effects of noise on the personality and certain psychomotor and intellectual aspects of children, after a prolonged exposure. *Travail Humane, 47,* 155–165.

Moran, S.L.V., & Loeb, M. (1977). Annoyance and behavior aftereffects following interfering and non-interfering aircraft noise. *Journal of Personality and Social Psychology, 62,* 719–726.

Mosskov, J. I., & Ettema, J. H. (1977). II. Extra-auditory effects in short-term exposure to aircraft and traffic noise. *International Archives of Occupational and Environmental Health 40,* 165–173.

Munroe, R. L., & Munroe, R. H. (1972). Population density and affective relationships in three East African societies. *Journal of Social Psychology, 88,* 15–20.

Murray, R. (1974). The influence of crowding on children's behavior. In D. Canter & T. Lee (Eds.), *Psychology and the built environment* (pp. 112–117). New York: Wiley.

Neus, H., Ruddel, H., & Schulte, W. (1983). Traffic noise and hypertension: An epidemiological study of the role of subjective reactions. *International Archives of Occupational and Environmental Health, 51,* 223–229.

Neus, H., Ruddel, H., Schulte, W., & von Eiff, A. W. (1983). The long term effect of noise on blood pressure. *Journal of Hypertension, 1,* 251–253.

Nicosia, G., Hyman, D., Karlin, R. A., Epstein, Y. M., & Aiello, J. R. (1979). Effects of bodily contact on reactions to crowding. *Journal of Applied Social Psychology, 9,* 508–523.

Novaco, R., Stokols, D., Campbell, J., & Stokols, J. (1979). Transportation, stress, and community psychology. *American Journal of Community Psychology, 7,* 361–380.

Novaco, R., Stokols, D., & Milanesi, L. (1990). Objective and subjective dimensions of travel impedance as determinants of commuting stress. *American Journal of Community Psychology, 18,* 231–257.

Nurminen, T., & Kurppa, K. (1989). Occupational noise exposure and course of pregnancy. *Scandinavian Journal of Work and Environmental Health, 15,* 117–124.

Oldham, G., & Fried, Y. (1987). Employee reactions to workspace characteristics. *Journal of Applied Psychology, 72,* 75–80.

Ortiz, G. A., Arguelles, A. E., Crespin, H. A., Sposari, G., & Villafane, C. T. (1974). Modifications of epinepherine, norepinepherine, blood lipid fractions and the cardiovascular system produced by noise in an industrial medium. *Hormone Research, 5,* 57–64.

Osada, Y., Ogawa, S., Hirokawa, A., & Haruta, K. (1973). Physiological effects of long-term exposure to low level noise. *Bulletin of Institutional Public Health, 22,* 61–67.

Osguthorpe, J., Mills, J., & Osguthorpe, N. (1983). Non-auditory effects of low frequency noise. In G. Rossi (Ed.), *Proceedings of the 4th International Congress as a Public Health Problem* (pp. 699–702). Milano, Italy: Centro Ricerche E Studi Amplifon.

Ottman, W., Rutenfranz, J., Neidhart, B., & Boucsein, W. (1987). Combining effects of shiftwork and noise on catecholamine excretion and electrodermal activity. In A. Oginski, J. Pokorski, & J. Rutenfranz (Eds.), *Contemporary advances in shiftwork research* (pp. 64–75). Krakow, Poland: Medical Academy.

Paolucci, G. (1975). Influence of noise on catecholamine excretion. In M. Whitcomb (Ed.), *Effects of long duration noise exposure on hearing and health* (C9-1–C9-2). (Report No. AGARD-CP-171). Neuilly sur Seine, France: European Space Agency.

Paulus, P. B. (1988). *Prison crowding: A psychological perspective.* New York: Springer-Verlag.

Paulus, P. B., & Matthews, R. (1980). Crowding attribution and task performance. *Basic and Applied Social Psychology, 1,* 3–14.

Paulus, P. B., McCain, G., & Cox, V. C. (1978). Death rates, psychiatric commitments, blood pressure, and perceived crowding as a function of institutional crowding. *Environmental Psychology and Nonverbal Behavior, 3,* 107–116.

Percival, L., & Loeb, M. (1980). Influence of noise characteristics on behavioral aftereffects. *Human Factors, 22,* 341–352.

Peterson, E. A., Augenstein, J. S., Tanis, D. C., & Augenstein, D. G. (1981). Noise raises blood pressure without impairing auditory sensitivity. *Science, 211,* 1450–1452.

Plant, J. S. (1937). Family living space and personality development. In *Personality and the cultural pattern* (pp. 510–520). Cambridge, MA: Harvard University Press.

Proniewska, W., Kalincinski, I., Kinalska, I., Korecki, R., Pawlicka, E., & Swianiewica, W. (1972). Effect of noise on the lipid components of blood. *Acta Physiological Polonica, 23,* 705–710.

Proshansky, H., Ittelson, W. H., & Rivlin, L. (1970). Freedom of choice and behavior in a physical setting. In H. Proshansky, W. Ittelson, & L. Rivlin (Eds.), *Environmental psychology* (pp. 173– 182). New York: Holt, Rinehart & Winston.

Pulles, M.P.J., & Stewart, R. (1990). Adverse effects of environmental noise on health: An interdisciplinary approach. *Environmental International, 16,* 437–445.

Quinn, R. W., Lowry, P. N,, & Zwaag, R. V. (1978). Significance of hemolytic streptococci for Nashville school children: Clinical and serologic observations. *Southern Medical Journal, 71,* 242–246.

Rai, R. M., Singh, A. P., Upadhyay, T. N., Patil, S.K.B., & Nayer, H. S. (1981). Biochemical effects of chronic exposure to noise in man. *International Archives of Occupational and Environmental Health, 48,* 331–337.

Rege[illegible]va, V., & Kellcrova, E. (1995). Effects of urban noise pollution on blood pressure and heart rate in school children. *Journal of Hypertension, 13,* 405–412.

Roche, A., Chumlea, W., & Siervogel, R. (1982). Longitudinal study of human hearing: Its relationship to noise and other factors III. Results from the first five years. *Air Force Aerospace Medical Research Laboratory,* AFAMRL TR 82–68.

Rodin, J. (1976). Density, perceived choice and response to controllable and uncontrollable outcomes. *Journal of Experimental Social Psychology, 12,* 564–578.

Rotton, J., Olszewski, D., Charleton, M., & Soler, E. (1978). Loud speech, conglomerate noise, and behavioral aftereffects. *Journal of Applied Psychology, 63,* 360–365.

Rovekamp, A. (1983). Physiological effects of environmental noise on normal and more sound sensitive human beings. In G. Rossi (Ed.), *Proceedings of the 4th International Congress on Noise as a Public Health Problem* (pp. 605–614). Milano, Italy: Centro Riche E Studi Amplifoni.

Ruback, B., & Carr, T. (1984). Crowding in a women's prison: Attitudinal and behavioral effects. *Journal of Applied Social Psychology, 14,* 57–68.

Ruback, B., Carr, T., & Hopper, C. (1986). Perceived control in prisons: Its relation to reported crowding, stress, and symptoms. *Journal of Applied Social Psychology, 16,* 375–386.

Rutter, M. (1983). Stress, coping and development. In N. Garmezy & M. Rutter (Eds.), *Stress, coping, and development in children* (pp. 1–43). New York: McGraw-Hill.

Rutter, M. (1987). Psychosocial resilience and protective mechanisms. *American Journal of Orthopsychiatry, 57,* 316–331.

Saegert, S. (1978). High density environments: Their personal and social consequences. In A. Baum & Y. Epstein (Eds.), *Human response to crowding* (pp. 259–282). Hillsdale, NJ: Lawrence Erlbaum Associates.

Saegert, S. (1982). Environment and children's mental health: Residential density and low income children. In A. Baum & J. E. Singer (Eds.), *Handbook of psychology and health* (pp. 247–271). Hillsdale, NJ: Lawrence Erlbaum Associates.

Saegert, S., Mackintosh, E., & West, S. (1975). Two studies of crowding in urban public spaces. *Environment and Behavior, 7,* 159–184.

Schaeffer, M, A., Baum, A., Paulus, P. B., & Gaes, G. G. (1988). Architecturally mediated effects of social density in prison. *Environment and Behavior, 20,* 3–19.

Schaeffer, M. A., Street, S., Singer, J. E., & Baum, A. (1988). Effects of control on the stress reactions of commuters. *Journal of Applied Social Psychology, 11,* 944–957.

Schell, L. (1981). Environmental noise and prenatal growth. *American Journal of Physical Anthropology, 56,* 63–70.

Schell, L. M., & Ando, Y. (1991). Postnatal growth of children in relation to noise from Osaka international airport. *Journal of Sound and Vibration, 151,* 371–382.

Schmeck, K., & Poustka, F. (1993). Psychiatric and psychophysiological disorders in children living in a military jetfighter training area. In M. Vallet (Ed.), *Proceedings of the 6th International Congress on Noise as a Public Health Problem* (pp. 477–480).

Schmidt, D., & Keating, J. (1979). Human crowding and personal control. *Psychological Bulletin, 86,* 680–700.

Schmitt, R. C. (1966). Density, health and social disorganization. *Journal of the American Institute of Planners, 32,* 38–40.

Schmitt, R. C., Zane, L. Y. S., & Nishi, S. (1978). Density, health, and social disorganization revisited. *Journal of American Planning Association, 44,* 209–211.

Semczuk, B., & Gorny, H. (1971). Studies on the effect of noise on cardiorespiratory efficiency. *Polish Medical Journal, 10,* 594–599.

Shapiro, A. H. (1974). Effects of family density and mothers' education on preschoolers' motor skills. *Perceptual and Motor Skills, 38,* 79–86.

Sherrod, D. R. (1976). Crowding, perceived control, and behavioral aftereffects. *Journal of Applied Social Psychology, 4,* 171–186.

Sherrod, D. R., Hage, J. N., Halpern, P. L., & Moore, B. S. (1977). Effects of personal causation and perceived control on responses to an aversive environment: The more control, the better. *Journal of Experimental Psychology, 13,* 14–27.

Sieber, W., Rodin, J., Larson, L., Ortega, S., Cummings, N., Levy, S., Whiteside, T., & Herberman, R. (1992). Modulation of human natural killer cell activity by exposure to uncontrollable stress. *Brain, Behavior and Immunity, 6,* 141–156.

Sims, D. G., Downham, M.A.P.S., McQuillin, J., & Gardner, P. S. (1976). Respiratory syncytial virus infection in north-east England. *British Medical Journal, 2,* 1095–1098.

Singer, J., Lundberg, U., & Frankenhaeuser, M. (1978). Stress on the train: A study of urban commuting. In A. Baum, J. Singer, & S. Valins (Eds.), *Advances in environmental psychology* (Vol. 1, pp. 41–56). Hillsdale, NJ: Lawrence Erlbaum Associates.

Slob, A., Wink. A., & Radder, J. (1973). The effects of acute noise exposure on the excretion of corticosteroids, adrenalin and noradrenalin in man. *International Archives of Arbeitsmedicine, 31,* 225–235.

Stansfeld, S. A., & Shine, P. (1993). Noise sensitivity and psychophysiological responses to noise in the laboratory. In M.

Vallet (Ed.), *Proceedings of the 6th International Congress On Noise as a Public Health Problem* (pp. 481–484). Cedex, France: INRETS.

Stansfield, S. A. (1993). Noise, noise sensitivity and psychiatric disorder: Epidemiological and psychophysiological studies. *Psychological Medicine, Monograph Supplement, 22,* 1–44.

Stokols, D., Novaco, R., Campbell, J., & Stokols, J. (1978). Traffic congestion, Type-A behavior, and stress. *Journal of Applied Psychology, 63,* 467–480.

Stokols, D., Ohlig, W., & Resnik, S. (1978). Perception of residential crowding, classroom experiences, and student health. In A. Esser & B. Greenbie (Eds.), *Design for communality and privacy* (pp. 89–111). New York: Plenum.

Tafalla, R. J., & Evans, G. W. (1997). Noise, physiology and human performance: The potential role of effort. *Journal of Occupational Health Psychology, 2,* 148–155.

Talbott, E. O., Findlay, R. C., Kuller, L. H., Lenkner, L. A., Matthews, K. A., Day, R. D., & Ishii, E. K. (1990). Noise-induced hearing loss and high blood pressure. *Journal of Occupational Medicine, 32,* 690–697.

Talbott, E., Helmkamp, J., Matthews, K., Kuller, L., Cottington, E., & Redmond, G. (1985). Occupational noise exposure, noise-induced hearing loss, and the epidemiology of high blood pressure. *American Journal of Epidemiology, 121,* 501–514.

Tarnopolsky, A., & Morton-Williams, J. (1980). *Aircraft noise and prevalence of psychiatric disorders: Research report.* Social and Community Planning Research, 35 Northampton Square, London, EC1. Cited in Stansfeld, S. (1993). Noise, noise sensitivity and psychiatric disorder: Epidemiological and psychophysiological studies. *Psychological Medicine, Monograph Supplement, 22,* 1–44.

Tarnopolsky, A., Watkins, G., & Hand, D. J., (1980). Aircraft noise and mental health: I. Prevalence of individual symptoms. *Psychological Medicine, 10,* 683–698.

Tarter, S. K., & Robins, T. G. (1990). Chronic noise exposure, high frequency hearing loss, and hypertension among automotive assembly workers. *Journal of Occupational Medicine, 32,* 685–689.

Thiessen, D., & Rodgers, D. (1961). Population density and endocrine function. *Psychological Bulletin, 58,* 441–451.

Thompson, S. J. (1981). *Epidemiology feasibility study: Effects of noise on the cardiovascular system* (Report No. 550/9-81-103). Washington, DC: Environmental Protection Agency.

Thompson, S. J. (1993). Review: Extraaural health effects of chronic noise exposure in humans. In H. Ising & B. Kruppa (Eds.), *Larm und krankheit* [Noise and disease] (pp. 107–117). New York: Verlag.

U.S. Raytheon Company. (1975). *The effects of a company hearing conservation program on extra-auditory disturbances in workers.* NIOSH (Contract No. CDC-99-74-28). Cited in Thompson, S. (1981). *Epidemiology feasibility study: Effects of noise on the cardiovascular system* (Report No. 550/9-81-103). Washington, DC: Environmental Protection Agency.

Vera, M. N., Vila, J., & Godoy, J. F. (1992). Physiological and subjective effects of traffic noise: The role of negative self-statements. *International Journal of Psychophysiology, 12,* 267–279.

Von Eiff, A. W., Friedrich, G., & Neus, H. (1982). Traffic noise, a factor in the pathogenesis of essential hypertension. *Controlled Nephrology, 30,* 82–86.

Wachs, T. D. (1987). Specificity of environmental action as manifest in environmental correlates of infant's mastery motivation. *Developmental Psychology, 23,* 782–790.

Wachs, T. D., & Camli, O. (1991). Do ecological or individual characteristics mediate the influence of the physical environment upon maternal behavior. *Journal of Environmental Psychology, 11,* 249–264.

Wachs, T., & Gruen, G. (1982). *Early experience and human development.* New York: Plenum.

Watkins, G., Tarnopolsky, A., & Jenkins, L. (1981). Use of medicines and health care services. *Psychological Medicine, 11,* 155–168.

Webb, S. D., & Collette, J. (1975). Urban ecological and household correlates of stress-alleviative drug use. *American Behavioral Scientist, 18,* 750–770.

Weisse, C., Pato, C., McAllister, C., Littman, R. Paul, S., & Baum, A. (1990). Differential effects of controllable and uncontrollable acute stress on lymphocyte proliferation and lecocyte percentages in humans. *Brain, Behavior, and Immunity, 4,* 339–351.

Welch, B. L. (1973). Physiological effects of noise. *Federation Proceedings, 32,* 2091–2120.

Welch, B. L. (1979). *Extra-auditory health effects of industrial noise: Survey of foreign literature* (AHRL-TR-79-41). Aerospace Medical Research Laboratory, Wright Patterson Air Force Base.

Welch, B. L., & Welch, A. S. (1970). *Physiological effects of noise.* New York: Plenum.

Wener, R., & Keys, C. (1988). The effects of changes in jail population densities on crowding, sick call, and spatial behavior. *Journal of Applied Social Psychology, 18,* 852–866.

Widmayer, S., Peterson, L., Larner, M., Carnahan, S., Calderon, A., Wingerd, J., & Marshall, R. (1990). Predictors of Haitian-American infant development at twelve months. *Child Development, 61,* 410–415.

Winsborough, H. H. (1965). The social consequences of high population density. *Law and Contemporary Problems, 30,* 120–126.

Wohlwill, J. F., Nasar, J. L., DeJoy, D. M., & Foruzani, H. H. (1976). Behavioral effects of a noisy environment: Task involvement versus passive exposure. *Journal of Applied Psychology, 61,* 67–74.

Worchel, S., & Teddlie, C. (1976). Factors affecting the experience of crowding: A two-factor theory. *Journal of Personality and Social Psychology, 34,* 30–40.

Wu, T., Chiang, H., Huang, J., & Chang, P. (1993). Comparison of blood pressure in deaf-mute children and children with normal hearing: Association between noise and blood pressure. *International Archives of Occupational and Environmental Health, 65,* 119–123.

Wyndham, C. H., Gonin, R., & Reid, R. D. (1978). Seasonal variation in acute respiratory diseases and meningitis in Black miners living in hostels. *South African Medical Journal, 54,* 353–358.

Yarnell, J.W.G. (1979). Do housing conditions influence respiratory morbidity and mortality in children? A study of hospital admissions and respiratory deaths in seven districts in South Whales. *Public Health, 93,* 157–162.

Yodfat, Y., Fidel, J., Cohen, C., & Eliakim, M. (1979). Chronic bronchitis and bronchial asthma in a rural community in Israel: Relation to socioenvironmental factors. *Israel Journal of Medical Sciences, 15,* 573–578.

21

Adjustment to Chronic Illness: Theory and Research

Annette L. Stanton
Charlotte A. Collins
Lisa A. Sworowski
University of Kansas

There are only two health outcomes that are of importance. First, there is life expectancy. Second, there is function or quality of life during the years that people are alive.
—Kaplan (1990, p. 1218)

Most people confront chronic disease, if not in themselves then in those they love. Indeed, more than 50% of deaths in the United States are attributable to cardiovascular disease and malignant neoplasms alone. In addition to their interest in decreasing mortality, health psychologists are dedicated to aiding those who live with chronic disease maintain fulfilling lives. Health psychologists and others have devoted intense energy to identifying psychosocial and behavioral contributors to and consequences of chronic disease. This chapter provides an analysis of current knowledge regarding psychological adjustment to chronic conditions.

Researchers have conducted hundreds of empirical studies to enhance understanding of adaptation to chronic illness. The present literature review focused on pertinent studies of adults with cancer, cardiovascular disease, diabetes, rheumatic diseases (particularly rheumatoid arthritis), and acquired immune deficiency syndrome (AIDS), which are conditions that comprise significant causes of mortality and morbidity and have received substantial empirical attention by researchers in health psychology and related fields. The aim is not to review this voluminous literature in detail. Rather, the focus is on crosscutting issues in the conceptualization of adjustment to these conditions, as well as extant theories and empirical findings regarding determinants of adjustment to chronic illness. Further, the discussion concentrates on individual adult adjustment, and the reader is referred to relevant literatures on adjustment to chronic disease in children (e.g., Roberts, 1995), intimate partners (e.g., Revenson, 1994), and families (e.g., Kerns, 1995).

CONCEPTUALIZING ADJUSTMENT TO CHRONIC DISEASE

Sometimes when I wake up in the morning, I forget for a moment that I have cancer. Then it hits me like a ton of bricks and I think, "Will I live to see my little girl graduate from college?" Who wouldn't have these fears?

The doctor brought the psychologist with him when I got my diagnosis. He thought I would fall apart at my third diagnosis of cancer. I figure I'll get rid of it and go on, just like I've done the last two times.

So much positive has come from my experience with cancer. But I've also never been so scared or angry or sad in my life.

I have cancer but it doesn't have me.

These reflections from individuals with cancer[1] represent a sampling of the array of reactions that accompany a diagnosis of chronic disease. These individuals viewed themselves as adjusting well to their disease. What constitutes positive adjustment to chronic illness? Researchers have advanced various conceptualizations of adaptive functioning or health-related quality of life (QOL). Although many researchers explicitly outline their framework for conceptualizing positive functioning, others' definitions are implicit, revealed by their choice of outcome measures in their studies of adjustment to chronic disease. The literature reveals at least five conceptualizations of positive adjustment: successful performance of various adaptive tasks that accompany chronic disease, absence of psychological disorder, relatively low experience of negative affect and/or high experience of positive affect, behavioral/functional status, and appraisals of satisfaction or well-being in various life domains.

Some theorists have defined adaptive tasks in chronic illness, the mastery of which signals successful adjustment. For example, Moos and Schaefer (1984) outlined the illness-related tasks of managing pain and other symptoms, dealing with the hospital environment and treatment, and preserving adequate relationships with medical personnel. More general tasks involve sustaining a "reasonable emotional balance" (p. 10), a sound self-image, and relationships with close others, while preparing for an uncertain future. Taylor (1983), in her theory of cognitive adaptation to threatening events, provided evidence from her study of breast cancer patients that successful adjustment requires adequate resolution of a search for meaning, the ability to retain mastery over one's life, and enhancement of self-esteem. N. M. Clark et al. (1991) suggested that successful self-management of chronic disease requires sufficient knowledge about the disease and its treatment to make informed decisions about health care, the performance of activities to manage the disease, and the application of skills to preserve adequate psychosocial functioning. Relatedly, many researchers focus on the individual's experience of disease- and treatment-related symptoms as indicative of adjustment. For example, the experience of greater fatigue, pain, or nausea compared with others undergoing similar treatments would reflect less positive adjustment.

Researchers also have been interested in documenting the prevalence of psychological disorders (e.g., Cordova et al., 1995; Derogatis et al., 1983; Rosenberger et al., 1993), particularly adjustment disorders, depression, and anxiety disorders in individuals with chronic illness. In these conceptualizations, the relative absence of symptoms is taken as an indicator of good adjustment. It also should be noted that assessment of some relevant symptoms of psychological disorder is complicated by their overlap with symptoms of the chronic disease or its treatment (e.g., D. A. Clark, Cook, & Snow, 1998). For example, fatigue is both a symptom of depression and a common side effect of treatments for cancer; several other somatic symptoms of psychological disorder also are concomitants of chronic disease.

The literature also reveals a focus on affective experience as central to adjustment. Maintenance of relatively low levels of negative affect and, in some studies, high levels of positive affect defines optimal adjustment in these studies. Both general (e.g., state anxiety, global distress) and disease-specific (e.g., fear of cancer recurrence) measures are used. Reviewing the literature on coping with rheumatoid arthritis, Zautra and Manne (1992) found that most studies relied on the absence of negative affect to indicate adequate adjustment. This finding is consistent with the adjustment literature across several chronic diseases.

Functional status and role-related behaviors also can indicate adjustment. Return to work has been used as an adjustment index in many studies of those undergoing cardiac events, for example. Other examples of functional status include mobility, completion of physical rehabilitation, and ability to adhere to medical treatment regimens.

Many researchers view the individual's appraisals of satisfaction in various life domains as the crux of positive adjustment. Some are interested in overall appraisals of life satisfaction, whereas others focus on satisfaction in specific domains. Both general and disease-specific conceptualizations are evident. Often examined are satisfaction or well-being in physical, functional, emotional, and social domains (e.g., Lutgendorf, Antoni, Schneiderman, Ironson, & Fletcher, 1995; Nayfield, Ganz, Moinpour, Cella, & Hailey, 1992).

Several points emerge from the examination of the array of conceptualizations of adjustment to chronic illness. First, adjustment to chronic illness is multidimensional, including both intra- and interpersonal dimensions. Within these realms, intraindividual adjustment comprises cognitive (e.g., intrusive thoughts, self-evaluations), emotional (e.g., depression, anxiety), behavioral (e.g., return to work), and physical (e.g., symptom reports) functioning. Interpersonal adjustment often is relevant with regard to both personal relationships (e.g., family, friends) and relationships with health care providers. Further, the dimensions are interrelated. For example, negative emotional reactions (e.g., anxiety) can contribute to functional status (e.g., poor glycemic control) in individuals with diabetes (Lustman, 1988).

Second, consensus exists regarding the centrality of individuals' appraisal of their adjustment. Although other sources of information (e.g., physician report, work functioning) are valuable, they cannot substitute for the individual's own perception of QOL. A complicating factor for researchers in this area is the potential for response shift in individuals' QOL perceptions (e.g., Sprangers, 1996). That is, patients' internalized standards of measurement for QOL may change as they undergo treatment or compare themselves to others who are similarly diagnosed. For example, rather than gauging QOL against premorbid functioning, individuals may shift their standard, concluding, "I'm doing well for someone going through chemotherapy, especially compared to that man in clinic yesterday."

Third, although psychological and physical dysfunctions are central adaptive outcomes, it is important to note that positive adjustment is not simply the absence of pathology. Positive and negative affect, often used as indicators of adjustment

[1]All quotes from individuals with cancer in the chapter are from the first author's research program.

to chronic disease, represent two fairly independent dimensions (e.g., Diener & Larsen, 1993). Thus, using only depressive symptoms to indicate QOL will yield only a partial picture of adjustment. A disease that robs life of some of its joys will not necessarily foster intensely negative emotions. In addition to experiencing positive affect, finding positive meaning in the disease experience or attaining personal or spiritual growth also comprise important adaptive outcomes. Further, contributors to positive functioning may not be identical to determinants of negative experience.

Fourth, it is important to consider not only the valences of adjustment dimensions, but also their duration and interference with one's functioning and goal pursuits. Individuals' acute feelings of anxiety and loss on learning that they have a chronic disease may not compromise adjustment, for example, unless these feelings interfere markedly with the ability to make important treatment decisions or they persist long after diagnosis.

Clearly, adjustment to chronic disease is a complex phenomenon. It is recommended that researchers carefully consider their assumptions with regard to what constitutes positive adjustment, tailor their assessments to the theoretical question of interest, recognize that any particular assessment is likely to provide only a snapshot of circumscribed dimensions of functioning, and limit their conclusions regarding adjustment accordingly. Only through accrual of research tapping multiple dimensions of adjustment can a comprehensive portrait of adaptation to chronic disease be achieved.

EMPIRICAL STUDIES OF ADJUSTMENT

How do people with chronic disease fare with regard to psychological adjustment? Both in the psychological and medical literatures, a plethora of studies and reviews address this question. Indeed, Wood-Dauphinee (1996), citing a MEDLINE search of surgical studies from 1989 to 1995, found that abstracts containing the words "quality of life" and reporting standardized measures had increased from 27.4% in 1989 to 1990 to 48.3% in 1993 to 1995. Here, the discussion relies on empirical and meta-analytic reviews of studies addressing adjustment for the five chronic diseases targeted in this chapter, as well as single studies that describe adjustment across patients with different conditions.

van't Spijker, Trijsburg, and Duivenvoorden (1997) conducted a meta-analytic review of 58 studies performed from 1980 to 1994 of psychological sequelae of cancer diagnosis. Focusing on studies that included validated instruments, the authors found that from 0% to 46% of patients qualified for depressive disorder and from .9% to 49% qualified for anxiety disorder across the various studies. Compared to published reference norms for the general population, cancer patients were significantly more depressed (although the effect size was not significant for samples in studies published after 1987), but not significantly more anxious or globally distressed. People with cancer were significantly less distressed, depressed, and anxious than were reference psychiatric patients, and they were less anxious than other medical patient groups.

Several other reviewers of the adjustment literature also conclude that those with chronic illness in general maintain adequate psychological functioning, although a significant minority of patients may be at risk for persistent decrement in function in specific domains. For example, Katz, Rodin, and Devins (1995) reviewed studies of self-esteem in cancer patients. No differences emerged between cancer patients and controls on global self-esteem, but body esteem was impaired in cancer patients who had disfiguring surgery (e.g., head and neck cancer). Reviewing the research on adjustment to coronary events, Ell and Dunkel-Schetter (1994) suggested that the majority of myocardial infarction patients evidence no long-term psychological impairment, although approximately one third may demonstrate long-term impairment in overall psychosocial functioning and quality of life, and a minority experience persistent depressive symptoms. Cox and Gonder-Frederick (1992), in their review of behavioral diabetes research, drew similar conclusions. They suggested that both children and adults diagnosed with diabetes report psychological disturbance following diagnosis, but that adjustment returns to premorbid levels after approximately a year. However, they also reported studies revealing higher rates of psychological disorder (particularly depression and anxiety) in diabetic patients than in the general population. In her review, DeVellis (1995) found that depressive symptoms appear more prevalent in those with rheumatic disease than in people with no chronic illness, although most individuals with rheumatic conditions do not report significant depressive symptoms. Reviewing studies on the psychological impact of HIV/AIDS, Chesney and Folkman (1994) reported an apparent decrease in documented adverse psychological responses to HIV/AIDS over the time the virus has been studied, perhaps owing to advances in medical treatment, counseling interventions, and public awareness. However, they found that disease progression has an important impact on psychological response, with asymptomatic individuals evidencing no clear elevation in anxiety and depressive symptoms, and symptomatic or AIDS-diagnosed individuals evidencing more pronounced distress. Furthermore, women with HIV may experience more depressive symptoms than men with HIV (Ickovics et al., 1999).

Several studies have examined individuals' adjustment across multiple chronic conditions. For example, Cassileth et al. (1984) examined 758 patients with arthritis, diabetes, cancer, renal disease, dermatologic disorders, or depression versus the general public on the Mental Health Index. Psychological status was comparable across patients with different physical diseases and between patients and the comparison group. Patients with chronic disease had more favorable psychological status than did depressed outpatients. Stewart et al. (1989) assessed 9,385 adults at physician office visits in three U.S. cities. Fifty-four percent had at least one of nine chronic conditions (i.e., hypertension, myocardial infarction, congestive heart failure, angina, arthritis, chronic lung problems, back problems, gastrointestinal complaints, diabetes). For eight of nine conditions, patients demonstrated lower functioning in physical, social, and role-related domains, as well as mental health, health perceptions, and bodily pain, compared with those with no chronic disease. However, mental health was the domain least affected by chronic condition, and the majority of variance in functioning and well-being was not explained by the presence of these chronic conditions.

Two broad conclusions extend from the descriptive literature on adjustment to chronic illness. First, most individuals appear to adjust well to chronic illness, often resulting in psychological adjustment indicators comparable to or slightly below general population norms and more positive than individuals who carry psychological diagnoses. Given that chronic illness presents numerous potential stressors, how can we account for this apparent positive psychological adaptation? Several explanations are possible. Perhaps most individuals are able to muster sufficient internal and external resources in the face of chronic illness to maintain high QOL. These contributors to adjustment are discussed in a subsequent section. Another compatible possibility is that chronic diseases carry the potential for positive as well as negative consequences and that people's ability to extract positive meanings from their disease experience balances any negative consequences. For example, Folkman, Moskowitz, Ozer, and Park (1997), in a study of HIV+ and HIV– caregiving partners of men with AIDS, found that although study participants reported high levels of depressive symptoms, they also evinced positive morale and positive states of mind comparable to general population norms, and they reported experiencing positive meaningful events. A third possibility is that, as mentioned previously, individuals shift their comparison standards as they adapt to disease, so that they evaluate their own adjustment vis à vis their status as a person with arthritis rather than as a healthy person, and they compare themselves to others with arthritis rather than healthy others. Thus, owing to pervasive human tendencies toward positive self-evaluation (e.g., Taylor & Brown, 1988) and toward comparing themselves favorably to others who are under similar threats (e.g., Stanton, Danoff-Burg, Cameron, Snider, & Kirk, 1999; Taylor & Lobel, 1989), they are likely to evaluate themselves as doing very well for "an arthritis patient." Another potential explanation for the apparently positive adjustment to chronic illness is that, rather than potentiating global maladjustment, chronic disease carries more circumscribed impact for most people. For example, Andersen (e.g., B. L. Andersen, B. Anderson, & deProsse, 1989a, 1989b; B. L. Andersen, Woods, & Copeland, 1997), in her studies of women with cancer, observed that experience with cancer is more likely to produce "islands" of life disruption in specific realms and at specific points in the disease trajectory than to confer substantial risk for global dysfunction. If only global adjustment is assessed, researchers may miss meaningful points of impact of the disease on psychosocial function.

A second conclusion is that considerable variability is apparent in psychological adjustment, both across studies and across individuals within single studies. Across-study variability is not surprising, given that researchers have used a wide range of measures with samples that vary considerably in demographic attributes and points in the disease trajectory. Moreover, individual variability in reaction to chronic illness certainly is to be expected, given that any particular disease represents multiple stressors (e.g., pain, threat to life, ambiguity regarding the future, appearance and functional changes, interpersonal challenges, financial strain), each of which may or may not be pertinent to a specific individual. Such stressors will carry differential relevance, depending on such factors as the individual's goal structure, psychological and contextual resources, and specific coping strategies. For example, individuals whose experience with serious disease saps already scarce environmental and personal resources may be at substantial risk for pronounced life disruption and distress. The next section presents a theoretical and empirical analysis of such factors that may support or hinder individuals as they face chronic illness and thus render them differentially vulnerable to adjustment difficulties.

THEORETICAL PERSPECTIVES ON CONTRIBUTORS TO ADJUSTMENT TO CHRONIC ILLNESS

Many theories of adjustment to chronic illness derive from more general conceptual frameworks regarding adjustment to stressful or traumatic experiences. One of the most prominent among these general theories is that of Lazarus and colleagues (e.g., Lazarus & Folkman, 1984). According to Lazarus, central determinants of adaptive outcomes include personal resources, attributes of the situation, cognitive appraisals, and coping strategies. Although Lazarus and Folkman (1984) discussed preexisting resources and situational attributes, they were more interested in processes initiated by the individual that unfold over the course of the stressful encounter. These include individuals' cognitive appraisals of the potential for harm (i.e., threat appraisal) and benefit (i.e., challenge appraisals) arising from the encounter (i.e., primary appraisals), as well as appraisals of their ability to control or manage the situation's demands (i.e., secondary appraisal). The process of appraisal catalyzes the initiation of coping strategies, which are "cognitive and behavioral efforts to manage specific external and/or internal demands that are appraised as taxing or exceeding the resources of the person" (p. 141). According to Lazarus and Folkman (1984), these cognitive appraisals and coping strategies engaged in response to a stressor substantially determine adaptive outcomes in emotional, social, and somatic realms. Similarly, Moos and colleagues (e.g., Moos & Schaefer, 1993) included in their conceptual model of stress and coping the influences of the environmental system (e.g., life stressors, social resources), the personal system (e.g., demographic and personal attributes), life crises and transitions (i.e., event-related factors), and cognitive appraisals and coping processes on each other and on health and well-being.

Specific theories on adjustment to chronic illness expand on such general conceptual frames. An example is the model of Maes, Leventhal, and de Ridder (1996). They expanded on the Lazarus and Folkman (1984) theory by emphasizing the potentially important roles of contextual factors (e.g., other life events, demographic attributes, cultural and social environment), characteristics of the specific disease situation (e.g., asthma in general versus a specific asthmatic attack), and associated disease representations (e.g, appraisals of the identity, controllability, duration, causes, and consequences of the disease and symptoms; Leventhal & Nerenz, 1983) in determining coping and adaptation.

As have other theorists, Maes et al. also focused on the influence of individuals' life goals on disease representations and coping processes. The more individuals' central goals in life are threatened by the disease, the more stressful the situation, and the more their appraisals, coping processes, and internal and external resources are challenged. Perceived goal blockage is likely to engender distress and an attempt to cope. In his cognitive-motivational-relational theory of emotion, Lazarus (1991a) revised the conceptualization of primary appraisal to include dimensions of goal relevance, goal congruence, and type of ego involvement. As one woman with advanced cancer stated, "Every time there's a big shift in what I can do, like when I couldn't drive anymore, I get really upset for awhile. I usually try to write out my anger and sadness. Then I eventually start to focus on what I can still do and who I still am, and I'm okay until the next slide and plateau." Thus, coping can be conceived as a goal-directed process. As Lazarus stated (1991a):

> The connection between coping and intentions or goals has not been of interest to those working on the coping process. Yet how the person copes depends not only on the coping possibilities and how they are appraised but also on what a person wants to accomplish in the encounter. Moreover, new agendas arise from the ongoing flow of events in the adaptational encounter. More than one goal is apt to be involved in each encounter, and these are apt to change in primacy and salience. (p. 115)

Coping processes can be understood as lower order goals (e.g., express emotions about having cancer) that serve as a path to achieving higher order goals (e.g., maintain emotional balance, live a fulfilling life) (Lazarus, 1991b).

Also relevant with regard to the importance of goals in coping and adaptation is the self-regulation theory of Carver and Scheier (e.g., 1981, 1990, 1998), which they have applied to coping with illness (Scheier & Bridges, 1995). In their view, "illness represents one general and significant class of events that can interfere with the pursuit of life's activities and goals, both those that are health related and those that are not. ... [Illness] can interfere, to a lesser or greater extent, with the general set of plans and activities that give a person's life its form and meaning" (Scheier & Bridges, 1995, pp. 261–262). To the extent that an individual expects to continue successful goal pursuit in the face of having a chronic disease, then initiation of approach-oriented coping strategies are likely. However, if a person expects unremitting goal blockage, then disengagement may ensue. For example, assume that maintaining close family ties is an important goal for Dionne, who has AIDS. If Dionne expects that goal attainment is possible, she is likely to seek support actively from family members, in the best case resulting in the receipt of such aid and consequent feelings of security and caring. However, if she believes that her family sees AIDS as a shameful condition, Dionne may avoid interactions with family or she may not disclose her status to them, leaving her feeling isolated and depressed. Of course, another possibility is that Dionne may shift her goals, such that she focuses more on maintaining close relationships in general than on family ties specifically. This example illustrates how goals and goal-related appraisals may determine the nature of the coping process and influence adaptation (see also Affleck et al., 1998).

Both general theories of human functioning and those specific to coping with stressful experiences and chronic disease in particular can serve to guide researchers in their attempt to understand determinants of adjustment to chronic illness. Theoretically grounded approaches, such as those that use the Lazarus and Folkman framework (see, e.g., Smith & Wallston, 1992, on rheumatoid arthritis; Stanton & Snider, 1993, on breast cancer; Pakenham, Dadds, & Terry, 1994, on AIDS), will yield more systematic and substantial advances than will research that is solely empirically driven, just as they will allow researchers not to reinvent the wheel in devising "new" models where established theory already exists. For example, attempts to identify contributors to depression in chronic disease may take as a starting point general theories regarding determinants of depression, as well as extant stress and coping theories. The literature on adjustment to chronic illness would benefit from careful delineation of the central conceptual points at which general and disease-specific theories diverge in their utility for specifying contributors to positive adaptation, meaningful differences among chronic diseases with regard to their impact on adjustment, and how competing theories fare with regard to their differential and combined utility in specifying the most significant influences on adaptation to chronic illness. What follows is an analysis of the state of the empirical literature on determinants of adjustment. The broad conceptual categories in stress and coping theories (e.g., Lazarus & Folkman, 1984; Maes et al., 1996) are used as an organizing framework for this discussion.

EMPIRICAL RESEARCH ON CONTRIBUTORS TO ADJUSTMENT TO CHRONIC ILLNESS

This section aims to provide a sketch of factors that help and hinder individuals as they confront chronic illness. A working model is depicted in Fig. 21.1 (see also Maes et al., 1996; Taylor & Aspinwall, 1996). It should be noted that, to increase readability, not all potential causal paths are displayed, and recursive relations are likely. The contextual factors of the disease itself and the environment are addressed first, followed by consideration of the personal context, including demographic and personality attributes. Cognitive appraisal and coping processes then receive attention.

The Disease- and Treatment-Related Context

> Losing my hair, that was the worst part. The nausea wasn't much fun either. They were constant reminders that I didn't have control over my body.

Chronic diseases vary along numerous conceptual dimensions, including controllability, predictability, and severity

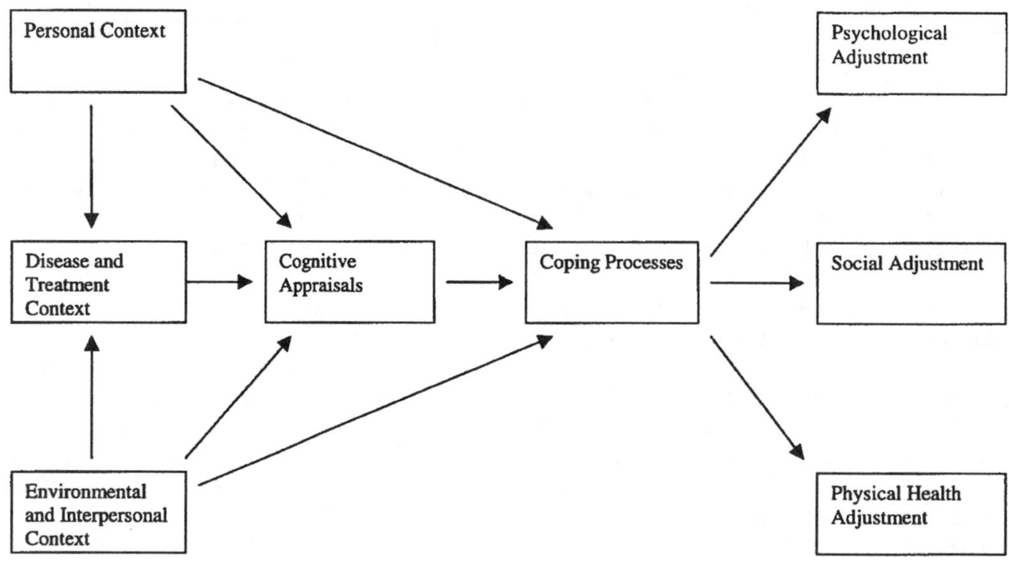

FIG. 21.1. Model of influences on adjustment to chronic illness.

(e.g., lethality, life disruption). Disease- and treatment-specific variables can be mapped at least partially onto these conceptual dimensions. For example, disease course (e.g., progressive or remitting), prognosis, lifestyle change required, side effect-related toxicity and life disruption, and degree of associated pain and disability all vary in controllability, predictability, and severity across different chronic diseases. Even within disease category, it would be a mistake to assume homogeneity. For example, different cancers carry dramatically different prognoses. Adding further to across- and within-disease variability is the fact that, although the disease process itself accounts for much variance in these dimensions, several also are substantially determined by individual factors. What is one person's significant pain may be another person's annoyance. Chemotherapy-induced hair loss may prompt a "Hair by Chemo" t-shirt purchase for one individual and painful social isolation for another. Thus, although disease- and treatment-related factors often are considered exogenous variables in models of adjustment, their existence and impact actually may be influenced significantly by individuals' external and internal resources. Further, individual characteristics and behaviors may interact with disease-related factors to influence adaptive outcomes. Problem-focused coping may be effective only for controllable aspects of a disease, for example.

In light of this complexity, it is a general observation that, when disease- and treatment-specific factors (e.g., prognosis, treatment toxicity, pain) are demonstrated to be related to adaptive outcomes, they often reflect relations of low controllability, low predictability, and high severity with poorer adjustment. Note that many studies do not reveal significant relations of disease-related factors with adjustment. For example, disease stage is related inconsistently across studies to adjustment to cancer (van't Spijker et al., 1997). Such inconsistent relations between disease-related factors and adjustment may result from the use of small samples and thus insufficient statistical power to detect relations, or from restricted ranges on disease-specific factors, such as low frequency of advanced cancers in a sample. Inconsistent relations also may reflect variability in study participants' experience of or meanings attributed to disease stage. Large-scale and meta-analytic (e.g., Moyer, 1997) studies are necessary to examine the influences of disease- and treatment-related factors on psychosocial outcomes.

Complexity in the determinants and impact of disease-related factors carries several implications for research. First, studies comparing outcomes across diseases will be useful to the extent that they can disentangle mechanisms for obtained effects. For example, the finding that rheumatoid arthritis and systemic blood cancer patients reported more negative affect, less positive affect, and less acceptance of their illness than patients with hypertension or diabetes (Felton & Revenson, 1984; Felton, Revenson, & Hinrichsen, 1984) may reflect differences in perceived controllability or severity of consequences among those diseases. Second, many researchers treat disease-related variables as covariates in analyses. Although this is a reasonable approach, some investigators do not report the magnitude of the relations between the covariates and outcomes, with the result that nothing is learned about the potential impact of disease variables. Investigators also often do not report first testing for interactions of disease-related variables with other predictors before including the variables as covariates. Not only is prior testing of such interactions a statistical requirement of covariance analysis, but it also may yield important findings. For example, disease trajectory may interact with coping processes, such that problem-focused coping may be more effective during diagnosis and treatment planning than after treatment termination.

Finally, although researchers in adjustment to chronic disease typically have included disease characteristics as predictors of adaptive outcomes, it is clear that these factors also can be conceptualized usefully as dependent variables. For example, identification of factors that contribute to the likelihood of experiencing treatment-related side effects (e.g., the finding that high anxiety and treatment context predict the development of anticipatory nausea during chemotherapy; Redd, 1990) has important applied implications.

The Environmental and Interpersonal Context

> I come to this support group because it's the only place that I don't have to put on my "strong" face. People here know what it's like to have a really bad day with cancer.
>
> My husband lost his job and had to take a new one in [another city]. I can't afford to lose my insurance because of the cancer, so I can't quit my job. We have to live apart. He was my mainstay during chemotherapy; I don't know how I'll do without him.

A person lives with chronic disease within an environmental, cultural, and interpersonal context. Such contextual factors have received relatively little empirical attention, with the exception of social support. Even social support typically has been examined from the perspective of the individual (Felton & Shinn, 1992). Although the individual's perspective may be centrally important, examination of the interpersonal context also may yield rich data on adjustment processes. Given their relative emphases in the literature, the focus is on social support and the intimate interpersonal context, although the larger environmental and cultural contexts are mentioned and exemplary references are provided.

The Environmental and Cultural Context. As poignantly illustrated in the quotation from the cancer survivor experiencing job lock, the environmental context (e.g., concurrent life events, chronic strains) may influence adjustment to chronic disease. For example, Evers, Kraaimaat, Geenen, and Bijlsma (1997) found that having more stressful life events was associated with higher anxiety shortly after diagnosis in rheumatoid arthritis patients, but not with distress a year later. Lepore and Evans (1996) argued that coping with one stressor can affect individuals' ability to adapt to a subsequent stressor through interference with their appraisals (e.g., higher evaluation of threat), resources, or motivation to cope with the subsequent stressor. Both stressors external to the chronic disease, such as death of a loved one, and those related to it, such as resultant financial strain, are likely to affect adaptation.

Taylor, Repetti, and Seeman (1997) reviewed characteristics across multiple environments (e.g., community, family, work) that contribute to adverse health outcomes. They concluded that "unhealthy environments are those that threaten safety, that undermine the creation of social ties, and that are conflictual, abusive, or violent" (p. 411). It is reasonable to suggest that these attributes also would provoke adjustment difficulties in those already contending with chronic disease. In addition to these major chronic environmental strains, it is likely that seemingly more benign environments might prove daunting to the individual with chronic disease. A work environment that was negotiated facilely prior to illness may be impossible when a person's concentration and energy level are impaired by medical treatment. As Mechanic (1995) noted, disease-related disability results from "a lack of fit between the capacities of individuals and the environment in which they must function" (p. 1209).

Theoretical and empirical reviews reveal that ethnic and cultural factors also influence illness vulnerability, attention to and interpretation of somatic and emotional changes, a person's actions regarding symptoms, and subsequent interpretations and adaptation (e.g., Angel & Thoits, 1987; Kato & Mann, 1996; Landrine & Klonoff, 1992; K. Young & Zane, 1995). For example, Angel and Cleary (1984) found that Mexican Americans low in acculturation reported more symptoms than non-Hispanic Whites; however, they were less likely to seek care for those symptoms. High concealment of homosexual identity predicted faster progression in HIV-seropositive gay men (Cole, Kemeny, Taylor, Visscher, & Fahey, 1996). Such concealment may reflect an adopted strategy for avoiding social rejection and stigmatization or a marker of inhibited temperament (Cole et al., 1996). Particularly in light of the high mortality rates for chronic diseases in some ethnic and cultural groups (e.g., greater age-adjusted mortality rates in African Americans than Whites for heart and cerebrovascular disease, diabetes and kidney disease, AIDS, and cancer; National Center for Health Statistics, 1996), greater empirical attention to ethnic and cultural influences on causes and adaptive consequences of disease is essential (see Landrine & Klonoff, this volume).

The Interpersonal Context and Social Support. Social support can be conceived as involving interpersonal transactions that offer emotional comfort, information, concrete aid, or enhanced self-regard (Wills, this volume). Many useful papers are available on the conceptualization and measurement of social support (e.g., Cohen & Wills, 1985; Hobfoll & Vaux, 1993; Pierce, J. G. Sarason, & B. R. Sarason, 1996), as well as the influence of social relationships on physical health outcomes (e.g., Cohen & Syme, 1985; Reifman, 1995; Uchino, Cacioppo, & Kiecolt-Glaser, 1996). Although the findings are not without exception (e.g., Bolger, Foster, Vinokur, & Ng, 1996; Revenson, Wollman, & Felton, 1983), reviews of the relation between social support and psychological adjustment to chronic illness suggest that social support in general is related to positive adaptation to several chronic diseases, including rheumatic diseases (DeVellis, Revenson, & Blalock, 1997), cancer (Blanchard, Albrecht, Ruckdeschel, Grant, & Hemmick, 1995; Helgeson & Cohen, 1996), and cardiovascular disease (Shumaker & Czajkowski, 1994). For example, Duits, Boeke, Taams, Passchier, and Erdman (1997) reviewed 17 prospective studies of adjustment to coronary artery bypass graft surgery (CABG). They found that higher preoperative social support predicted more positive postoperative adjustment. Individual studies demonstrate that the impact of social support may vary as a function of attributes of the provider and recipient, as well as the nature and timing of the support provided. Mechanisms by which social support achieves its effects also are receiving increased attention (e.g., Uchino et al., 1996).

Conceptualizations of social support include its use as a coping strategy, as a coping resource in the environment, and as dependent on personality attributes and coping of the individual (Schreurs & de Ridder, 1997). In their review of studies assessing coping and social support in chronic disease, Schreurs and de Ridder (1997) found that prospective studies consistently revealed that a mechanism by which social support promotes positive well-being is through its effect on approach-oriented coping, thus supporting the beneficial effects of social support as a coping resource. For example, in a 4-year prospective study of cardiac patients, Holahan, Moos, Holahan, and Brennan (1997) demonstrated that higher social support and lower stress in familial and extrafamilial domains predicted greater cognitive and behavioral approach-oriented coping, which in turn contributed to lower depressive symptoms.

It also is clear that the receipt and effectiveness of social support is partially dependent on personal attributes of the recipient and the reactions of others. A role-playing experimental study by Silver, Wortman, and Crofton (1990) demonstrated that cancer patients who reported some distress but maintained a positive attitude received more support from peers than did highly distressed or very well-adjusted patients. In a prospective investigation of rheumatoid arthritis patients, Smith and Wallston (1992) reported that higher helplessness appraisals were associated with passive coping in patients, which in turn was related to lower perceived quality of emotional support, and greater psychosocial impairment and declining self-reported health over time.

Recently, a burgeoning interest in negative aspects of social relationships is apparent in the literature. Behaviors from close others that are insensitive, critical, conflictual, withdrawing, or unreceptive can potentiate adjustment difficulties in chronically ill individuals (e.g., Herbert & Dunkel-Schetter, 1992; Holahan et al., 1997; Lepore & Helgeson, 1998; Manne, Taylor, Dougherty, & Kemeny, 1997), as can the ill individual's perceived inability to live up to the expectations of important others (Hatchett, Friend, Symister, & Wadhwa, 1997). Inadequate relationships with medical staff also can be detrimental to health and well-being. Lerman et al. (1993) reported that 83% of 97 breast cancer patients cited communication difficulties with the medical team and that communication problems predicted heightened distress 3 months later. Even well-intentioned support attempts may provoke negative outcomes in some cases. Support attempts that lead to dependence, obligation, patronization, lack of control, or reinforcement of maladaptive behaviors (e.g., pain behaviors) may impair adjustment in the chronically ill person (e.g., Coyne, Ellard, & Smith, 1990; Kerns, 1995; Revenson, 1994; Romano et al., 1992). Whereas some researchers have found that both positive and negative aspects of support make unique contributions to adjustment to chronic illness (e.g., Holahan et al., 1997; Revenson, Schiaffino, Majerovitz, & Gibofsky, 1991), others have suggested that the potential harmful effects of negative reactions from the social environment outweigh the benefits of positive support (e.g., Manne et al., 1997).

In addition to considering the potentially positive and negative aspects of social support, researchers point to the importance of the match between what the individual needs over the illness course and what is offered by the social milieu in influencing adjustment (e.g., Cutrona, 1996; Mechanic, 1995; Taylor & Aspinwall, 1990). For example, informational support generally is valued from an expert, either a medical professional or a person who has adjusted well to the same disease, whereas emotional support is valued from family members and friends, as well as from health care providers (e.g., Helgeson & Cohen, 1996; Taylor & Aspinwall, 1990). Even for self-reliant individuals, the rising demands of progressive illness may render instrumental and emotional social support increasingly important, although such demands also may contribute to the erosion of support over time (e.g., Zich & Temoshok, 1990).

Clearly, specific facets of interpersonal relationships can both aid and hinder adjustment to chronic illness, depending on the nature of the support attempt, attributes of the provider and recipient, and demands of the illness. Although the conceptual and data analytic complexities can be daunting, intimate relationships provide rich ground for delineating the complex interplay of factors influencing adaptation for couples (e.g., Revenson, 1994) and families (e.g., Kerns, 1995) within the larger social and environmental sphere (e.g., Lepore, 1997).

The Personal Context

> Cancer is not the worst thing that could happen. Things always have turned out well for me, and I think this will, too. Even if the surgery doesn't work, I'm old, I've had a good life. Things will be okay.

Numerous personality and other individual difference characteristics have been tested for predictive utility in adjustment to chronic disease. There are several paths by which stable individual difference variables might affect adjustment (Bolger & Zuckerman, 1995; Costa, Somerfield, & McCrae, 1996; Hewitt & Flett, 1996). An additive model assumes that personality (or other individual differences characteristics) and coping (or appraisal) have independent, direct effects on adjustment. A mediational model involves coping as a mediator between personality and outcomes, such that people high on neuroticism are more likely to cope through avoidance, which in turn predicts poor adjustment, for example. An interactive model implies that personality and coping interact, such that avoidant coping is effective for those low in neuroticism but maladaptive for those high in neuroticism, for example. Here, select demographic and personality attributes that are promising are examined as risk or protective factors in adjustment.

Demographic and Background Attributes. Although not often a focus of studies on adjustment to chronic illness, demographic and other stable premorbid characteristics often are included as covariates or otherwise examined in relation to adaptation. Examples of consistent findings are that younger cancer patients are more likely to be distressed than older patients (van't Spijker et al., 1997); that women report lower quality of life after myocardial infarction (MI) and are less likely to participate and remain in cardiac rehabilitation programs than men (Brezinka & Kittel, 1995; Shumaker et al., 1997); that higher educational attainment is associated with lower disability from rheumatoid arthritis, particularly among men (Leigh & Fries, 1991); and that a premorbid history of psychological disorder confers risk for poor emotional and behavioral outcomes (e.g; return to work) across several chronic illnesses (Taylor & Aspinwall, 1990).

Methodologically sound research in this area examines potential confounding factors (e.g., women are older and sicker upon first MI than men; Shumaker et al., 1997) and compares findings on the variables of interest to those from the general population (e.g., higher rates of depression in women than men). An important direction for research is to examine mechanisms for obtained results, in order to target interventions productively. For example, are older adults with cancer less distressed than younger adults because they experience less violation of cognitive schemas, they engage in more positive downward social comparisons, and they perceive less attendant blockage of central goals, or is the age difference an epiphenomenon of younger adults' propensity to report greater distress in general?

Personality Characteristics. The five basic factors of personality (i.e., neuroticism, extraversion, openness to experience, agreeableness, conscientiousness) have garnered attention in the broader coping literature (e.g., Bolger, 1990; Costa et al., 1996). For example, neuroticism's association with maladjustment appears to be mediated through use of greater avoidant and less approach-oriented coping (e.g., social support, problem-focused coping; see Costa et al., 1996; Hewitt & Flett, 1996, for reviews). An interactive model of effects of neuroticism and coping on adjustment also has received support (Bolger, 1990). These personality factors have received less attention with regard to adjustment to chronic disease. In a 7-year longitudinal study of adjustment to rheumatoid arthritis, Smith, Wallston, and Dwyer (1995) found that negative affectivity (typically considered equivalent to neuroticism) was empirically distinct from disease impact variables (i.e., pain, functional impairment). Further, controlling for negative affectivity, disease impact was associated uniquely with several components of sick-role behavior (e.g.; information seeking, use of medical treatments) and with some adjustment indices (e.g., life satisfaction, fatigue) but not others (e.g.; depressive symptoms). In another longitudinal study, Affleck, Tennen, Urrows, and Higgins (1992) found that catastrophizing coping partially mediated the relation between neuroticism and chronic negative mood and pain in arthritis patients. Although neuroticism may be an important precursor of coping and other adjustment-related variables, it does not appear to account for the lion's share of the variance in predicting adjustment. Thus, coping is not "just" neuroticism. Rather than being considered merely a nuisance variable in research, however, high neuroticism might be viewed as an immediately identifiable risk factor in those who confront chronic disease, whereupon early intervention can be instituted to diminish maladjustment. The personality factor of conscientiousness also deserves more attention in research on adjustment to chronic disease, as it appears to predict positive physical health outcomes in healthy samples (Friedman et al., 1995).

Dispositional optimism (Scheier & Carver, 1985), a construct reflecting generalized expectancies for favorable outcomes, appears to be a promising predictor of positive adjustment to illness. Moderately negatively correlated with neuroticism but demonstrating discriminant validity (see Carver et al., 1993), optimism has been studied in longitudinal investigations of cancer, coronary heart disease, and HIV. Carver et al. (1993) examined optimism as a prospective predictor of well-being in women undergoing breast cancer surgery. Assessed prior to surgery, optimism was associated positively with approach-oriented coping (e.g., active coping, planning, realistic acceptance) and negatively with avoidant coping (e.g., denial, behavioral disengagement). Controlling for prior distress, optimism predicted lower distress at 3, 6, and 12 months after surgery, relations that were partially mediated through coping strategy use, particularly acceptance, denial, and behavioral disengagement. Stanton and Snider (1993) also found that coping (i.e., cognitive avoidance, positive focus) partially mediated the effect of optimism on distress and vigor prior to surgery for breast cancer, but that optimism did not prospectively predict distress following surgery. Assessed prior to CABG surgery, dispositional optimism correlated positively with problem-focused coping and negatively with denial (Scheier et al., 1989). Moreover, optimism predicted faster in-hospital recovery and faster return to normal life activities 6 months later. In a sample of HIV+ and HIV– men, Lutgendorf et al. (1995) found optimism to be associated with the use of active coping strategies and with lower psychological distress (see also Taylor et al., 1992). These findings suggest that optimism may be an important protective factor in those adjusting to chronic disease, at least in part via promotion of actively engaged coping strategies.

As the foregoing illustrates, investigation of these and other individual difference characteristics (e.g., self-esteem: Katz et al., 1995, and Druley & Townsend, 1998; locus of control: Reich, Zautra, & Manne, 1993; Type A behavior pattern: Denollet & De Potter, 1992) can illuminate risk and protective factors in adjustment to illness. Such factors often can be assessed easily in the earliest phases of diagnosis and treatment. Because interventions are not readily available to modify stable personal dispositions, however, the examination of mechanisms (e.g., coping, appraisal) by which these attributes have their effects also is essential.

Cognitive Appraisals

> The most frustrating part is the loss of control, from not being able to work right now to not knowing if the cancer will come back, and not being able to do a lot to prevent it. I hate feeling out of control.

Researchers have studied many sorts of cognitive appraisals in relation to chronic disease (e.g., disease representation; Leventhal & Nerenz, 1983). Here, the focus is on those subsumed in the Lazarus and Folkman (1984) framework.

Primary Appraisal. Primary appraisal, involving the individual's determination of a potentially stressful encounter's significance for well-being through assessments of threat/harm and challenge/benefit in the encounter, plays a pivotal role in stress and coping theory (Lazarus & Folkman, 1984). However, primary appraisal processes have received little empirical attention relative to coping processes, owing in part to lack of consensus regarding conceptualization and measurement. Studies reveal that individuals with chronic medical conditions see the potential for both harm and benefit from their experience (e.g., Stanton, 1991; Stanton & Snider, 1993). For example, a woman diagnosed with breast cancer might judge her experience as involving loss, whereby she must give up a body part; threat, in that her life expectancy and goals for work and family roles may be curtailed; and challenge, as her diagnosis represents an opportunity to reorder priorities and draw closer to her partner. Waltz, Badura, Pfaff, and Schott (1988) found that primary appraisals of threat and harm/loss were important predictors of subsequent anxiety and depression in 372 male cardiac patients. Stanton and Snider (1993) found that, prior to biopsy for breast cancer, women who perceived greater threat to a number of life realms from the potential diagnosis were more distressed. Prebiopsy threat and challenge appraisals did not predict subsequent negative and positive affect on diagnosis or surgery, however. With continued refinement of the primary appraisal construct (e.g., Lazarus, 1991a), it may prove a valuable tool for understanding individuals' goal structures and their assessment of how chronic disease may impede or further central aims.

Secondary Appraisal. In secondary appraisal, the following question may be posed, "What, if anything, can I do about this situation?" Thus, an individual's capacity to manage or change the situation is assessed. Smith and Lazarus (1990) refined the secondary appraisal construct to include cognitive evaluations of accountability for blame/credit, potential for problem- and emotion-directed coping attempts, and expectancies regarding potential for change in the situation. Underlying secondary appraisal, and garnering substantial attention by researchers, is the question of what people can and cannot control in their experience. A central quality of chronic disease is that control over progression and ultimate outcome of the disease is not guaranteed, despite individuals' intense efforts to pursue medical care and implement lifestyle modifications. Thus, the success of primary control attempts (Rothbaum, Weisz, & Snyder, 1982) is uncertain, although a person may generate the perception of substantial control (e.g., Taylor, Lichtman, & Wood, 1984). Further, across several chronic diseases, individuals are likely to discover controllable aspects of their experience, perceiving greater control over the consequences of their disease (e.g., symptoms, daily management) than over the course of their disease (e.g., rheumatoid arthritis: Affleck, Tennen, Pfeiffer, & Fifield, 1987; AIDS: Thompson, Nanni, & Levine, 1994; cancer: Thompson, Sobolew-Shubin, Galbraith, Schwankovsky, & Cruzen, 1993).

Research demonstrates that control appraisals can influence both the choice of coping strategies and adjustment across time. Findings from the general literature on stress, appraisal, and coping, in which situations of relatively high controllability are associated with more problem-focused coping attempts and low control situations with use of emotion-focused coping (e.g., Folkman & Lazarus, 1980), are mirrored in the chronic disease literature. For example, Folkman, Chesney, Pollack, and Coates (1993), in a longitudinal study of 425 HIV+ and HIV– gay men, found that high perceived control over a self-selected stressful situation was associated with greater approach-oriented coping (i.e., problem solving, information seeking, positive reappraisal), which in turn predicted decreased depressed mood after controlling for prior depressed mood and HIV symptoms.

Another observation from the chronic disease literature is that the specific control domain matters with regard to predicting adaptive outcomes. Several studies have revealed that perceived control over disease consequences (e.g., symptoms) is associated more strongly with positive adaptation than is appraised control over disease course (e.g., Affleck et al., 1987; Thompson et al., 1993, 1994). Further, perceptions of control in specific domains interact with other aspects of the disease to influence adjustment. For example, Affleck and colleagues (1987) found that, in the context of severe rheumatic disease, those who perceived more control over disease course evidenced more mood disturbance, whereas those who perceived more control over disease symptoms reported less mood disturbance. Thus, high control appraisals may be adaptive when the severe threat is controllable but may hinder adjustment when the threat is realistically uncontrollable (see also Helgeson, 1992).

It is clear that control appraisals regarding disease are multidimensional. In adapting to disease, individuals are likely to shift attention from uncontrollable dimensions to aspects of the illness that carry the potential for control and perhaps to additional controllable life goals. Belief that an individual has control in realms that in fact are responsive to control attempts may bolster adaptation. Such findings suggest the importance of differentiating empirically among various potential control domains and of examining precursors of control appraisals.

Coping Processes

> I do a bunch of things. I talk to my wife. I get as much information as I can about treatments and the latest research. I rely on my faith. I try to live each day as I want to.

Faced with a chronic disease, most individuals initiate a variety of attempts to manage the associated stressors. Broadly, coping attempts may be directed toward solving the problem at hand (i.e., problem-focused coping) or managing emotions associated with the stressor (i.e., emotion-focused coping) (Folkman & Lazarus, 1980). Thus, a person with AIDS may initiate a complex medical treatment regimen, as well as garnering comfort from friends. Several conceptual and empirical limitations accompany this distinction (e.g., Stanton, Danoff-Burg, Cameron, & Ellis, 1994), however, and researchers have demonstrated that the problem- and emotion-focused coping categories can be subsumed under the higher order classification of approach- versus avoidance-oriented coping mechanisms (e.g., Tobin, Holroyd, Reynolds, & Wigal, 1989). Examples of approach-oriented strategies are coping through seeking social support, active positive reframing, information seeking, problem solving, and emotional expression. Avoidant strategies include denial, distraction, cognitive avoidance, and behavioral disengagement. Yet other processes, such as religious coping, potentially can serve either approach-oriented or avoidant goals.

Reviews of the general literature (Roth & Cohen, 1986; Suls & Fletcher, 1985) suggest that avoidant and approach strategies vary in effectiveness as a function of the temporal sequence and characteristics of stressors. Avoidant strategies temporarily may reduce the effects of acute, severe stressors because they prevent one from becoming overwhelmed when emotional resources are limited. As stress persists, however, approach strategies afford opportunities for actions that may alleviate the stressor or its emotional concomitants.

By definition, chronic disease is a long-term stressor, for which the coping demands and their efficacy may vary over time. Although avoidant coping has been demonstrated useful at circumscribed points, its general untoward impact on adjustment is evident in numerous studies. For example, Levine et al. (1987) found that male cardiac patients high on denial of their illness spent fewer days in the coronary care unit and had fewer indications of cardiac dysfunction during hospitalization than did nondeniers. However, deniers were less compliant with exercise training and had more days of rehospitalization during the year following discharge. Stanton and Snider (1993) found that greater use of cognitive avoidance coping prior to breast biopsy predicted more distress at that point, after cancer diagnosis and after surgery (with initial levels of distress controlled; see also Carver et al., 1993). Reviewers of the chronic disease literature demonstrate consensus in the conclusion that avoidant coping is maladaptive over the long term (e.g., DeVellis et al., 1997, for rheumatic disease; Folkman, 1993, for HIV). Reviewing the literature across several diseases, Maes et al. (1996) concluded that "avoidant emotion-focused coping strategies are related to poor psychological adjustment and poor adherence to medical advice ..." (p. 235). Why is avoidant coping maladaptive? Certainly, avoiding the reality of disease will impair both active problem-focused and emotion-focused coping attempts. Avoidant coping itself may take maladaptive paths, such as excessive drinking or drug use. Further, cognitive avoidance paradoxically may prompt intrusion of the threatening material (Horowitz, 1986; Wegner & Pennebaker, 1992), in turn amplifying distress.

In general, research also suggests a complementary advantage for approach-oriented coping strategies in bolstering adjustment to chronic disease (e.g., Fleishman & Fogel, 1994; Holahan et al., 1997). For example, L. D. Young (1992) reviewed the literature on rheumatoid arthritis, concluding, "active, problem-focused coping attempts (e.g., information seeking, cognitive restructuring, pain control, and rational thinking) were consistently associated with positive affect, better psychological adjustment, and decreased depression" (p. 621). However, this chapter concurs with the conclusion of Maes et al. (1996) that the findings for the association of approach-oriented strategies and better adjustment are not as consistent as those for the relation of avoidant coping and poorer adjustment. This difference may occur because approach-oriented strategies (particularly problem-focused approach) may not be effective in the case of uncontrollable aspects of disease, because the utility of approach-oriented strategies is outweighed by the disutility of avoidant strategies when both are examined, or because adjustment indices used typically assess negative (e.g., depression) rather than positive (e.g., life satisfaction) adaptation, which may have differential relations with approach-oriented and avoidant coping (e.g., Blalock, DeVellis, & Giorgino, 1995; Stanton, 1991).

Beyond these associations of higher order coping approaches with adjustment, consistent relations of adjustment with any particular coping strategy are more difficult to discern. However, intensive research on specific coping mechanisms is beginning to prove fruitful, for example, that on social comparison (Buunk & Gibbons, 1997; Taylor & Lobel, 1989), focusing on benefit (Affleck & Tennen, 1996), and emotional processing and expression (Kelley, Lumley, & Leisen, 1997; Stanton et al., 1994, 1997; Stanton & Franz, 1999). Theoretically grounded longitudinal and experimental research that takes into account such factors as the specific problem with which the individual is coping and the relevant adaptive outcomes (e.g., Blalock et al., 1995), the intentionality of the coping effort (Compas, Connor, Osowiecki, & Welch, 1997), the larger interpersonal and environmental context (e.g., Revenson, 1994), and measurement issues in the assessment of coping (Coyne & Gottlieb, 1996) will advance understanding of the process of coping with chronic illness.

FUTURE DIRECTIONS IN RESEARCH ON ADJUSTMENT TO CHRONIC ILLNESS

Obviously, the factors that influence adjustment to chronic illness have been painted in broad strokes, focusing on promising constructs and crosscutting themes. Although this chapter has attempted to provide a modicum of critical analysis of this literature, readers are encouraged to pursue the cited references for deeper examination of issues of particular interest. In addition, the categories of predictors on which this chapter has focused also have been suggested to influence disease onset, progression, and survival (e.g., Epping-Jordan, Compas, &

Howell, 1994; Ickovics et al., 1999; Mulder, Antoni, Duivenvoorden, Kauffmann, & Goodkin, 1995; Scheier & Bridges, 1995). Thus, continued investigation is warranted for understanding factors that bolster and impede both quality of life and disease endpoints.

The review of the literature suggested considerable individual variability in response to chronic disease, within the context of generally positive adjustment. Several risk and protective factors were identified that predicted adjustment consistently across chronic diseases. However, few researchers have compared predictors of adjustment across diseases in single studies. Research identifying meaningful differences among diseases (e.g., degree of life threat, pain, required behavior change), their relations with adaptive outcomes, and mechanisms for differential relations across diseases is warranted. Further, much more is known about predictors of negative psychosocial outcomes than is known about contributors to positive functioning. The literature's prominent focus on negative affect as an outcome has yielded valuable findings. However, in limiting their attention to indicators of maladjustment, researchers may fail to uncover important contributors to positive functioning.

Development and testing of disease-specific theories, continued refinement of stress and coping theories, and comparison of the predictive utilities of competing theories are important venues for further research. Application of other established psychological and biological theories also are proving productive in enhancing our understanding of adjustment to chronic disease (e.g., Andersen, Kiecolt-Glaser, & Glaser, 1994; Andersen et al., 1997; Calfas, Ingram, & Kaplan, 1997; Glaser & Kiecolt-Glaser, 1994; Stanton et al., 1998). Longitudinal research in adaptation to chronic disease allows testing of links among psychosocial and biological variables within a biopsychosocial framework (e.g., Andersen et al., 1994). Theoretical grounding of research is essential in disentangling the complex relations of multiple influences on numerous adaptive outcomes in chronic disease.

The literature review revealed a number of methodologically and conceptually sophisticated studies, allowing for some degree of causal inference regarding determinants of adjustment to illness. It appears that things have moved beyond the point at which atheoretical, cross-sectional research is very useful in this area. Rather, theory-grounded, longitudinal, and experimental designs will illuminate important influences on adjustment, their interactions, and mechanisms by which they have their effects. For example, Reich et al. (1993) discovered significant interactions among demographic (patient age), personality (locus of control), and interpersonal (spouse encouragement of control) variables in predicting the psychological distress of rheumatoid arthritis patients. Another study with arthritis patients revealed interactions between pain level and daily coping strategies in predicting mood (Affleck, Urrows, Tennen, & Higgins, 1992). The Affleck et al. study also is notable in its microanalytic examination of coping processes, an approach especially appropriate for diseases for which coping demands occur on a daily basis (see also Porter & Stone, 1996; Tennen & Affleck, 1996). The complexity of such findings can be daunting, especially because the nature of chronic illness involves its presentation of multiple strains, which may constantly change shape. However, longitudinal and experimental research will allow more precise identification of contextual and individual factors that promote favorable adjustment and will point the way for tailored intervention.

What implications does research on adjustment to chronic illness carry for intervention? A good example of effective direct application of findings from stress and coping theory is Folkman and colleagues' (1991) coping effectiveness training. Effective in bolstering quality of life in HIV+ men, this approach includes: (a) appraisal training to disaggregate global stressors into specific coping tasks and to differentiate between alterable and immutable aspects of specific stressors; (b) coping training to tailor application of problem-focused and emotion-focused coping efforts to relevant stressors; and (c) social support training to increase effectiveness in selecting and maintaining supportive resources. Other effective psychosocial interventions exist for enhancing quality of life, improving medical regimen adherence, and potentially improving disease endpoints in individuals across several chronic diseases (e.g., Young, 1992, for rheumatoid arthritis; B. L. Andersen, 1992, and Meyer & Mark, 1995, for cancer; Cox & Gonder-Frederick, 1992, for diabetes; Bennett & Carroll, 1994, and Burell, 1996, for cardiovascular disease; Kelly & Murphy, 1992, and Lutgendorf et al., 1997, for HIV; Devins & Binik, 1996, for chronic diseases). Such interventions typically include an emotionally supportive context to address disease-specific worries, information regarding the disease and its treatment, and training in specific cognitive and behavioral coping strategies (B. L. Andersen, 1992). Extant theoretically grounded research on adjustment to chronic disease can refine such interventions through: pointing to effective targets for interventions (e.g., Coyne, 1995, on couple-oriented approaches; Thompson, 1991, for interventions to influence control appraisals; Lanza & Revenson, 1993, for issues in designing social support interventions); suggesting potential mechanisms by which interventions may gain their utility (e.g., through decreasing avoidant coping and increasing approach-oriented strategies); identifying at-risk patients for which interventions may be appropriate (e.g., patients low in optimism, younger cancer patients); and targeting intervention components for maximal effectiveness (e.g., selecting specific coping skills as a function of stressor controllability). Finally, both disease-specific and higher order conceptual dimensions (e.g., controllability) may be useful in understanding adjustment and developing interventions. For example, finding that people are likely to evidence a peak in distress at the point of diagnosis (e.g., Cassileth et al., 1984; Stanton & Snider, 1993) will allow us to know when to intervene. Specification of the underlying factors that confer risk for distress at that point (e.g., perceived low predictability, low control, high disease severity) will offer guidance in how to intervene.

The literature to date offers a foundation for understanding adjustment to chronic illness. However, there is still much to learn about complex determinants of adjustment trajectories and disease endpoints across time, across individuals, and across disease contexts. Such investigation accrues greater importance in light of the observation that individuals are surviving for many years after diagnosis of diseases once considered rapidly fatal. Ultimately, research conducted by health psychologists should enable more individuals living with chronic diseases to share the cancer patient's sentiment, "I have cancer but it doesn't have me."

ACKNOWLEDGMENT

The preparation of this chapter was supported in part by U.S. Army Medical Research and Materiel Command under DAMD-17-94-J-4244.

REFERENCES

Affleck, G., & Tennen, H. (1996). Construing benefits from adversity: Adaptational significance and dispositional underpinnings. *Journal of Personality, 64,* 899–922.

Affleck, G., Tennen, H., Pfeiffer, C., & Fifield, J. (1987). Appraisals of control and predictability in adapting to chronic disease. *Journal of Personality and Social Psychology, 53,* 273–279.

Affleck, G., Tennen, H., Urrows, S., & Higgins, P. (1992). Neuroticism and the pain-mood relation in rheumatoid arthritis: Insights from a prospective daily study. *Journal of Consulting and Clinical Psychology, 60,* 119–126.

Affleck, G., Tennen, H., Urrows, S., Higgins, P., Abeles, M., Hall, C., Karoly, P., & Newton, C. (1998). Fibromyalgia and women's pursuit of personal goals: A daily process analysis. *Health Psychology, 17,* 40–47.

Affleck, G., Urrows, S., Tennen, H., & Higgins, P. (1992). Daily coping with pain from rheumatoid arthritis: Patterns and correlates. *Pain, 51,* 221–229.

Andersen, B. L. (1992). Psychological interventions for cancer patients to enhance the quality of life. *Journal of Consulting and Clinical Psychology, 60,* 552–568.

Andersen, B. L., Anderson, B., & deProsse, C. (1989a). Controlled prospective longitudinal study of women with cancer: I. Sexual functioning outcomes. *Journal of Consulting and Clinical Psychology, 57,* 683–691.

Andersen, B. L., Anderson, B., & deProsse, C. (1989b). Controlled prospective longitudinal study of women with cancer: II. Psychological outcomes. *Journal of Consulting and Clinical Psychology, 57,* 692–697.

Andersen, B. L., Kiecolt-Glaser, J. K., & Glaser, R. (1994). A biobehavioral model of cancer stress and disease course. *American Psychologist, 49,* 389–404.

Andersen, B. L., Woods, X. A., & Copeland, L. J. (1997). Sexual self-schema and sexual morbidity among gynecologic cancer survivors. *Journal of Consulting and Clinical Psychology, 65,* 221–229.

Angel, R., & Cleary, P. D. (1984). The effects of social structure and culture on reported health. *Social Science Quarterly, 65,* 814–828.

Angel, R., & Thoits, P. (1987). The impact of culture on the cognitive structure of illness. *Culture, Medicine, and Psychiatry, 11,* 465–494.

Bennett, P., & Carroll, D. (1994). Cognitive-behavioural interventions in cardiac rehabilitation. *Journal of Psychosomatic Research, 38,* 169–182.

Blalock, S. J., DeVellis, B. M., & Giorgino, K. B. (1995). The relationship between coping and psychological well-being among people with osteoarthritis: A problem-specific approach. *Annals of Behavioral Medicine, 17,* 107–115.

Blanchard, C. G., Albrecht, T. L., Ruckdeschel, J. C., Grant, C. H., & Hemmick, R. M. (1995). The role of social support in adaptation to cancer and to survival. *Journal of Psychosocial Oncology, 13(1/2),* 75–95.

Bolger, N. (1990). Coping as a personality process: A prospective study. *Journal of Personality and Social Psychology, 59,* 525–537.

Bolger, N., Foster, M., Vinokur, A. D., & Ng, R. (1996). Close relationships and adjustment to a life crisis: The case of breast cancer. *Journal of Personality and Social Psychology, 70,* 283–294.

Bolger, N., & Zuckerman, A. (1995). A framework for studying personality in the stress process. *Journal of Personality and Social Psychology, 69,* 890–902.

Brezinka, V., & Kittel, F. (1995). Psychosocial factors of coronary heart disease in women: A review. *Social Science and Medicine, 42,* 1351–1365.

Burell, G. (1996). Behavioral medicine interventions in secondary prevention of coronary heart disease. In K. Orth-Gomér & N. Schneiderman (Eds.), *Behavioral medicine approaches to cardiovascular disease prevention* (pp. 227–236). Mahwah, NJ: Lawrence Erlbaum Associates.

Buunk, B. P., & Gibbons, F. X. (Eds.). (1997). *Health, coping, and well-being: Perspectives from social comparison theory.* Mahwah, NJ: Lawrence Erlbaum Associates.

Calfas, K. J., Ingram, R. E., & Kaplan, R. M. (1997). Information processing and affective distress in osteoarthritis. *Journal of Consulting and Clinical Psychology, 65,* 576–581.

Carver, C. S., Pozo, C., Harris, S. D., Noriega, V., Scheier, M. F., Robinson, D. S. Ketcham, A. S., Moffat, F. L., & Clark, K. C. (1993). How coping mediates the effect of optimism on distress: A study of women with early stage breast cancer. *Journal of Personality and Social Psychology, 65,* 375–390.

Carver, C. S., & Scheier, M. F. (1981). *Attention and self- regulation: A control-theory approach to human behavior.* New York: Springer-Verlag.

Carver, C. S., & Scheier, M. F. (1990). Origins and functions of positive and negative affect: A control-process view. *Psychological Review, 97,* 19–35.

Carver, C. S., & Scheier, M. F. (1998). *On the self-regulation of behavior.* New York: Cambridge University Press.

Cassileth, B. R., Lusk, E. J., Strouse, T. B., Miller, D. S., Brown, L. L., Cross, P. A., & Tenaglia, A. N. (1984). Psychosocial status in chronic illness: A comparative analysis of six diagnostic groups. *New England Journal of Medicine, 311,* 506–511.

Chesney, M. A., & Folkman, S. (1994). Psychological impact of HIV disease and implications for intervention. *Psychiatric Clinics of North America, 17,* 163–182.

Clark, D. A., Cook, A., & Snow, D. (1998). Depressive symptom differences in hospitalized, medically ill, depressed psychiatric inpatients and nonmedical controls. *Journal of Abnormal Psychology, 107,* 38–48.

Clark, N. M., Becker, M. H., Janz, N. K., Lorig, K., Rakowski, W., & Anderson, L. (1991). Self-management of chronic disease by older adults. *Journal of Aging and Health, 3,* 3–27.

Cohen, S., & Syme, S. L. (1985). *Social support and health.* New York: Academic Press.

Cohen, S., & Wills, T. A. (1985). Stress, social support, and the buffering hypothesis. *Psychological Bulletin, 98,* 310–357.

Cole, S. W., Kemeny, M. E., Taylor, S. E., Visscher, B. R., & Fahey, J. L. (1996). Accelerated course of human immunodeficiency virus infection in gay men who conceal their homosexual identity. *Psychosomatic Medicine, 58,* 219–231.

Compas, B. E., Connor, J., Osowiecki, D., & Welch, A. (1997). Effortful and involuntary responses to stress: Implications for coping with chronic stress. In B. H. Gottlieb (Ed.), *Coping with chronic stress* (pp. 105–130). New York: Plenum.

Cordova, M. J., Andrykowski, M. A., Kenady, D. E., McGrath, P. C., Sloan, D. A., & Redd, W. H. (1995). Frequency and correlates of posttraumatic-stress-disorder-like symptoms after treatment for breast cancer. *Journal of Consulting and Clinical Pychology, 63,* 981–986.

Costa, P. T., Somerfield, M. R., & McCrae, R. R. (1996). Personality and coping: A reconceptualization. In M. Zeidner & N. Endler (Eds.), *Handbook of coping: Theory, research, applications* (pp. 44–61). New York: Wiley.

Cox, D. J., & Gonder-Frederick, L. (1992). Major developments in behavioral diabetes research. *Journal of Consulting and Clinical Psychology, 60,* 628–638.

Coyne, J. C. (1995). Interventions in close relationships to improve coping with illness. In R. Lyon, P. Ritvo, & M. Sullivan (Eds.), *Close relationships through chronic illness and disability* (pp. 96–121). New York: Sage.

Coyne, J. C., Ellard, J. H., & Smith, D.A.F. (1990). Social support, interdependence, and the dilemmas of helping. In B. R. Sarason, I. G. Sarason, & G. R. Pierce (Eds.), *Social support: An interactional view* (pp. 129–149). New York: Wiley.

Coyne, J. C., & Gottlieb, B. H. (1996). The mismeasure of coping by checklist. *Journal of Personality, 64,* 959–991.

Cutrona, C. E. (1996). *Social support in couples.* Thousand Oaks, CA: Sage.

Denollet, J., & De Potter, B. (1992). Coping subtypes for men with coronary heart disease: Relationship to well-being, stress, and Type A behaviour. *Psychological Medicine, 22,* 667–684.

Derogatis, L. R., Morrow, G. R., Fetting, J., Penman, D., Piasetsky, S., Schmale, A. M., Henrichs, R., & Carnickle, C.L.M. (1983). The prevalence of psychiatric disorders among cancer patients. *Journal of the American Medical Association, 249,* 751–757.

DeVellis, B. M. (1995). Psychological impact of arthritis: Prevalence of depression. *Arthritis Care and Research, 8,* 284–289.

DeVellis, B. M., Revenson, T. A., & Blalock, S. J. (1997). Rheumatic disease and women's health. In S. J. Gallant, G. P. Keita, & R. Royak-Schaler (Eds.), *Health care for women: Psychological, social, and behavioral influences* (pp. 333–347). Washington, DC: American Psychological Association.

Devins, G. M., & Binik, Y. M. (1996). Facilitating coping with chronic physical illness. In M. Zeidner & N. Endler (Eds.), *Handbook of coping: Theory, research, applications* (pp. 640–696). New York: Wiley.

Diener, E., & Larsen, R. J. (1993). The experience of emotional well-being. In M. Lewis & J. M. Haviland (Eds.), *Handbook of emotions* (pp. 405–415). Hillsdale, NJ: Lawrence Erlbaum Associates.

Druley, J. A., & Townsend, A. L. (1998). Self-esteem as a mediator between spousal support and depressive symptoms: A comparison of healthy individuals and individuals coping with arthritis. *Health Psychology, 17,* 255–261.

Duits, A. A., Boeke, S., Taams, M. A., Passchier, J., & Erdman, R.A.M. (1997). Prediction of quality of life after coronary artery bypass graft surgery: A review and evaluation of multiple, recent studies. *Psychosomatic Medicine, 59,* 257–268.

Ell, K., & Dunkel-Schetter, C. (1994). Social support and adjustment to myocardial infarction, angioplasty, and coronary artery bypass surgery. In S. A. Shumaker & S. M. Czajkowski (Eds.), *Social support and cardiovascular disease* (pp. 301–332). New York: Plenum.

Epping-Jordan, J. E., Compas, B. E., & Howell, D. C. (1994). Predictors of cancer progression in young adult men and women: Avoidance, intrusive thoughts, and psychological symptoms. *Health Psychology, 13,* 539–547.

Evers, A. W. M., Kraaimaat, F. W., Geenen, R., & Bijlsma, J. W. J. (1997). Determinants of psychological distress and its course in the first year after diagnosis in rheumatoid arthritis patients. *Journal of Behavioral Medicine, 20,* 489–504.

Felton, B. J., & Revenson, T. A. (1984). Coping with chronic illness: A study of illness controllability and the influence of coping strategies on psychological adjustment. *Journal of Consulting and Clinical Psychology, 52,* 343–353.

Felton, B. J., Revenson, T. A., & Hinrichsen, G. A. (1984). Stress and coping in the explanation of psychological adjustment among chronically ill adults. *Social Science and Medicine, 18,* 889–898.

Felton, B. J., & Shinn, M. (1992). Social integration and social support: Moving "social support" beyond the individual level. *Journal of Community Psychology, 20,* 103–115.

Fleishman, J. A., & Fogel, B. (1994). Coping and depressive symptoms among people with AIDS. *Health Psychology, 13,* 156–169.

Folkman, S. (1993). Psychosocial effects of HIV infection. In L. Goldberger & S. Breznitz (Eds.), *Handbook of stress: Theoretical and clinical aspects* (2nd ed., pp. 658–681). New York: The Free Press.

Folkman, S., Chesney, M., McKusick, L., Ironson, G., Johnson, D. S., & Coates, T. J. (1991). Translating coping theory into intervention. In J. Eckenrode (Ed.), *The social context of coping* (pp. 239–259). New York: Plenum.

Folkman, S., Chesney, M., Pollack, L., & Coates, T. (1993). Stress, control, coping, and depressive mood in human immunodeficiency virus-positive and -negative gay men in San Francisco. *Journal of Nervous and Mental Disease, 181,* 409–416.

Folkman, S., & Lazarus, R. S. (1980). An analysis of coping in a middle-aged community sample. *Journal of Health and Social Behavior, 21,* 219–239.

Folkman, S., Moskowitz, J. T., Ozer, E. M., & Park, C. L. (1997). Positive meaningful events and coping in the context of HIV/AIDS. In B. H. Gottlieb (Ed.), *Coping with chronic stress* (pp. 293–314). New York: Plenum.

Friedman, H. S., Tucker, J. S., Schwartz, J. E., Tomlinson-Keasey, C., Martin, L. R., Wingard, D. L., & Criqui, M. H. (1995). Psychosocial and behavioral predictors of longevity: The aging and death of the "Termites." *American Psychologist, 50,* 69–78.

Glaser, R., & Kiecolt-Glaser, J. (Eds.). (1994). *Handbook of human stress and immunity.* San Diego: Academic Press.

Hatchett, L., Friend, R., Symister, P., & Wadhwa, N. (1997). Interpersonal expectations, social support, and adjustment to chronic illness. *Journal of Personality and Social Psychology, 73,* 560–573.

Helgeson, V. S. (1992). Moderators of the relation between perceived control and adjustment to chronic illness. *Journal of Personality and Social Psychology, 63,* 656–666.

Helgeson, V. S., & Cohen, S. (1996). Social support and adjustment to cancer: Reconciling descriptive, correlational, and intervention research. *Health Psychology, 15,* 135–148.

Herbert, T. B., & Dunkel-Schetter, C. (1992). Negative social reactions to victims: An overview of responses and their determinants. In L. Montada, S-H. Filipp, & M. J. Lerner (Eds.), *Life crises and experiences of loss in adulthood* (pp. 497–518). Hillsdale, NJ: Lawrence Erlbaum Associates.

Hewitt, P. L., & Flett, G. L. (1996). Personality traits and the coping process. In M. Zeidner & N. Endler (Eds.), *Handbook of coping: Theory, research, applications* (pp. 410–433). New York: Wiley.

Hobfoll, S. E., & Vaux, A. (1993). Social support. In L. Goldberger & S. Breznitz (Eds.), *Handbook of stress: Theoretical and clinical aspects* (2nd ed., pp. 685–705). New York: The Free Press.

Holahan, C. J., Moos, R. H., Holahan, C. K., & Brennan, P. L. (1997). Social context, coping strategies, and depressive symptoms: An expanded model with cardiac patients. *Journal of Personality and Social Psychology, 72,* 918–928.

Horowitz, M. J. (1986). *Stress response syndromes.* Northvale, NJ: Jason Aronson.

Ickovics, J. R., Hamburger, M., Vlahor, D., Schoenbaum, E., Schuman, P., Boland, B., Reid, A., & Moore, J. (1999, August). *Chronic depressive symptoms hasten mortality and CD4+ lymphocyte decline among women with HIV: Prospective longitudinal analyses from the HIV Epidemiological Research Study (HERS).* Paper presented at the annual convention of the American Psychological Association, Boston.

Kaplan, R. M. (1990). Behavior as the central outcome in health care. *American Psychologist, 45,* 1211–1220.

Kato, P. M., & Mann, T. (Eds.). (1996). *Handbook of diversity issues in health psychology.* New York: Plenum.

Katz, M. R., Rodin, G., & Devins, G. M. (1995). Self-esteem and cancer: Theory and research. *Canadian Journal of Psychiatry, 40,* 608–615.

Kelley, J. E., Lumley, M. A., & Leisen, J. C. C. (1997). Health effects of emotional disclosure in rheumatoid arthritis patients. *Health Psychology, 16,* 331–340.

Kelly, J. A., & Murphy, D. A. (1992). Psychological interventions with AIDS and HIV: Prevention and treatment. *Journal of Consulting and Clinical Psychology, 60,* 576–585.

Kerns, R. D. (1995). Family assessment and intervention. In P. M. Nicassio & T. W. Smith (Eds.), *Managing chronic illness: A biopsychosocial perspective* (pp. 207–244). Washington, DC: American Psychological Association.

Landrine, H., & Klonoff, E. A. (1992). Culture and health-related schemas: A review and proposal for interdisciplinary integration. *Health Psychology, 11,* 267–276.

Lanza, A. F., & Revenson, T. A. (1993). Social support interventions for rheumatoid arthritis: The cart before the horse? *Health Education Quarterly, 20,* 97–117.

Lazarus, R. S. (1991a). *Emotion and adaptation.* New York: Oxford University Press.

Lazarus, R. S. (1991b). Progress on a cognitive-motivational-relational theory of emotion. *American Psychologist, 46,* 819–834.

Lazarus, R. S., & Folkman, S. (1984). *Stress, appraisal, and coping.* New York: Springer.

Leigh, J. P., & Fries, J. F. (1991). Education level and rheumatoid arthritis: Evidence from five data centers. *Journal of Rheumatology, 18,* 24–34.

Lepore, S. J. (1997). Social-environmental influences on the chronic stress process. In B. H. Gottlieb (Ed.), *Coping with chronic stress* (pp. 133–160). New York: Plenum.

Lepore, S. J., & Evans, G. W. (1996). Coping with multiple stressors in the environment. In M. Zeidner & N. Endler (Eds.), *Handbook of coping: Theory, research, applications* (pp. 350–377). New York: Wiley.

Lepore, S. J., & Helgeson, V. S. (1998). Social constraints, intrusive thoughts, and mental health after prostate cancer. *Journal of Behavioral Medicine, 17,* 89–106.

Lerman, C., Daly, M., Walsh, W. P., Resch, M., Seay, J., Barsevick, A., Birenbaum, L., Hegan, T., & Martin, G. (1993). Communication between patients with breast cancer and health care providers. *Cancer, 72,* 2612–2620.

Leventhal, H., & Nerenz, D. R. (1983). A model for stress research with some implications for the control of stress disorders. In D. Meichenbaum & M. Jaremko (Eds.), *Stress reduction and prevention* (pp. 5–38). New York: Plenum.

Levine, J., Warrenburg, S., Kerns, R., Schwartz, G., Delaney, R., Fontana, A., Gradman, A., Smith, S., Allen, S., & Cascione, R. (1987). The role of denial in recovery from coronary heart disease. *Psychosomatic Medicine, 49,* 109–117.

Lustman, P. J. (1988). Anxiety disorders in adults with diabetes mellitus. *Psychiatric Clinics of North America, 11,* 419–432.

Lutgendorf, S. K., Antoni, M. H., Ironson, G., Klimas, N., Kumar, M., Starr, K., McCabe, P., Cleven, K., Fletcher, M. A., & Schneiderman, N. (1997). Cognitive-behavioral stress management decreases dysphoric mood and herpes simplex virus-Type 2 antibody titers in symptomatic HIV-seropositive gay men. *Journal of Consulting and Clinical Psychology, 64,* 31–43.

Lutgendorf, S., Antoni, M. H., Schneiderman, N., Ironson, G., & Fletcher, M. A. (1995). Psychosocial interventions and quality of life changes across the HIV spectrum. In J. E. Dimsdale & A. Baum (Eds.), *Quality of life in behavioral medicine research* (pp. 205–239). Hillsdale, NJ: Lawrence Erlbaum Associates.

Maes, S., Leventhal, H., & De Ridder, D.T.D. (1996). Coping with chronic diseases. In M. Zeidner & N. Endler (Eds.), *Handbook of coping: Theory, research, applications* (pp. 221–251). New York: Wiley.

Manne, S. L., Taylor, K. L., Dougherty, J., & Kemeny, N. (1997). Supportive and negative responses in the partner relationship: Their association with psychological adjustment among individuals with cancer. *Journal of Behavioral Medicine, 20,* 101–125.

Mechanic, D. (1995). Sociological dimensions of illness behavior. *Social Science and Medicine, 41,* 1207–1216.

Meyer, T. J., & Mark, M. M. (1995). Effects of psychosocial interventions with adult cancer patients: A meta-analysis of randomized experiments. *Health Psychology, 14,* 101–108.

Moos, R. H., & Schaefer, J. A. (1984). The crisis of physical illness. In R. Moos (Ed.), *Coping with physical illness* (pp. 3–26). New York: Plenum.

Moos, R. H., & Schaefer, J. A. (1993). Coping resources and processes: Current concepts and measures. In L. Goldberger & S. Breznitz (Eds.), *Handbook of stress: Theoretical and clinical aspects* (2nd ed., pp. 234–257). New York: The Free Press.

Moyer, A. (1997). Psychosocial outcomes of breast-conserving surgery versus mastectomy: A meta-analytic review. *Health Psychology, 16,* 284–298.

Mulder, C. L., Antoni, M. H., Duivenvoorden, H. J., Kauffmann, R. H., & Goodkin, K. (1995). Active confrontational coping predicts decreased clinical progression over a one-year period in HIV-infected homosexual men. *Journal of Psychosomatic Research, 39,* 957–965.

National Center for Health Statistics. (1996). *Health United States, 1995.* Hyattsville, MD: U.S. Public Health Service.

Nayfield, S. G., Ganz, P. A., Moinpour, C. M., Cella, D. F., & Hailey, B. J. (1992). Report from a National Cancer Institute (USA) workshop on quality of life assessment in cancer clinical trials. *Quality of Life Research, 1,* 203–210.

Pakenham, K. I., Dadds, M. R., & Terry, D. J. (1994). Relationships between adjustment to HIV and both social support and coping. *Journal of Consulting and Clinical Psychology, 62,* 1194–1203.

Pierce, G. R., Sarason, I. G., & Sarason, B. R. (1996). Coping and social support. In M. Zeidner & N. Endler (Eds.), *Handbook of coping: Theory, research, applications* (pp. 434–451). New York: Wiley.

Porter, L. S., & Stone, A. A. (1996). An approach to assessing daily coping. In M. Zeidner & N. Endler (Eds.), *Handbook of coping: Theory, research, applications* (pp. 133–150). New York: Wiley.

Redd, W. H. (1990). Management of anticipatory nausea and vomiting. In J. C. Holland & J. H. Rowland (Eds.), *Handbook of psychooncology* (pp. 369–382). New York: Oxford University Press.

Reich, J. W., Zautra, A. J., & Manne, S. (1993). How perceived control and congruent spouse support affect rheumatoid arthritis patients. *Journal of Social and Clinical Psychology, 12,* 148–163.

Reifman, A. (1995). Social relationships, recovery from illness, and survival: A literature review. *Annals of Behavioral Medicine, 17,* 124–131.

Revenson, T. A. (1994). Social support and marital coping with chronic illness. *Annals of Behavioral Medicine, 16,* 122–130.

Revenson, T. A., Schiaffino, K. M., Majerovitz, S. D., & Gibofsky, A. (1991). Social support as a doubled-edged sword: The relation of positive and problematic support to depression among rheumatoid arthritis patients. *Social Science and Medicine, 33,* 807–813.

Revenson, T. A., Wollman, C. A., & Felton, B. J. (1983). Social supports as stress buffers for adult cancer patients. *Psychosomatic Medicine, 45,* 321–333.

Roberts, M. A. (Ed.). (1995). *Handbook of pediatric psychology.* New York: Guilford.

Romano, J. M., Turner, J. A., Friedman, L. S., Bulcroft, R. A., Jensen, M. P., Hops, H., & Wright, S. F. (1992). Sequential analysis of chronic pain behaviors and spouse responses. *Journal of Consulting and Clinical Psychology, 60,* 777–782.

Rosenberger, P. H., Bornstein, R. A., Nasrallah, H. A., Para, M. F., Whitaker, C. C., Fass, R. J., & Rice, R. R. (1993). Psychopathology in human immunodeficiency virus infection: Lifetime and current assessment. *Comprehensive Psychiatry, 34,* 150–158.

Roth, S., & Cohen, L. J. (1986). Approach, avoidance, and coping with stress. *American Psychologist, 41,* 813–819.

Rothbaum, F., Weisz, J., & Snyder, S. (1982). Changing the world and changing the self: A two-process model of perceived control. *Journal of Personality and Social Psychology, 42,* 5–37.

Scheier, M. F., & Bridges, M. W. (1995). Person variables and health: Personality predispositions and acute psychological states as shared determinants for disease. *Psychosomatic Medicine, 57,* 255–268.

Scheier, M. F., & Carver, C. S. (1985). Optimism, coping, and health: Assessment and implications of generalized outcome expectancies. *Health Psychology, 4,* 219–247.

Scheier, M. F., Matthews, K. A., Owens, J. F., Magovern, G. J., Sr., Lefebvre, R. C., Abbott, R. A., & Carver, C. S. (1989). Dispositional optimism and recovery from coronary artery bypass surgery: The beneficial effects on physical and psychological well-being. *Journal of Personality and Social Psychology, 57,* 1024–1040.

Schreurs, K.M.G., & de Ridder, D.T.D. (1997). Integration of coping and social support perspectives: Implications for the study of adaptation to chronic diseases. *Clinical Psychology Review, 17,* 89–112.

Shumaker, S. A., Brooks, M. M., Schron, E. B., Hale, C., Kellen, J. C., Inkster, M., Wimbush, F. B., Wiklund, I., Morris, M., & CAST Investigators. (1997). Gender differences in health-related quality of life among postmyocardial infarction patients: Brief report. *Women's Health: Research on Gender, Behavior, and Policy, 3,* 53–60.

Shumaker, S. A., & Czajkowski, S. M. (Eds.). (1994). *Social support and cardiovascular disease.* New York: Plenum.

Silver, R. L., Wortman, C. B., & Crofton, C. (1990). The role of coping in support provision: The self-presentational dilemma of victims in life crises. In B. R. Sarason, I. G. Sarason, & G. R. Pierce (Eds.), *Social support: An interactional view* (pp. 397–426). New York: Wiley.

Smith, C. A., & Lazarus, R. S. (1990). Emotion and adaptation. In L. A. Pervin (Ed.), *Handbook of personality: Theory and research* (pp. 609–637). New York: Guilford.

Smith, C. A., & Wallston, K. A. (1992). Adaptation in patients with chronic rheumatoid arthritis: Application of a general model. *Health Psychology, 11,* 151–162.

Smith, C. A., Wallston, K. A., & Dwyer, K. A. (1995). On babies and bathwater: Disease impact and negative affectivity in the self-reports of persons with rheumatoid arthritis. *Health Psychology, 14,* 64–73.

Sprangers, M.A.G. (1996). Response-shift bias: A challenge to the assessment of patients' quality of life in cancer clinical trials. *Cancer Treatment Reviews, 22*(Suppl. A), 55–62.

Stanton, A. L. (1991). Cognitive appraisals, coping processes, and adjustment to infertility. In A. L. Stanton & C. Dunkel-Schetter (Eds.), *Infertility: Perspectives from stress and coping research* (pp. 87–108). New York: Plenum.

Stanton, A. L., Danoff-Burg, S., Cameron, C., Collins, C., Bishop, M., Kirk, S., Dinoff, B., Leibowitz, R., & Twillman, R. (1997, November). *Effects of coping through emotional processing and expression on quality of life in breast cancer patients.* Paper presented at the Department of Defense Breast Cancer Research Program Meeting, Washington, DC.

Stanton, A. L., Danoff-Burg, S., Cameron, C. L., & Ellis, A. P. (1994). Coping through emotional approach: Problems of conceptualization and confounding. *Journal of Personality and Social Psychology, 66,* 350–362.

Stanton, A. L., Danoff-Burg, S., Cameron, C. L., Snider, P., & Kirk, S. B. (1999). Social comparison and adjustment to breast cancer: An experimental examination of upward affiliation and downward evaluation. *Health Psychology, 18,* 151–158.

Stanton, A. L., Estes, M. A., Estes, N. C., Cameron, C. L., Danoff-Burg, S., & Irving, L. M. (1998). Treatment decision making and adjustment to breast cancer: A longitudinal study. *Journal of Consulting and Clinical Psychology, 66,* 313–322.

Stanton, A. L., & Franz, R. (1999). Focusing on emotion: An adaptive coping strategy? In C. R. Snyder (Ed.), *Coping: The psychology of what works* (pp. 90–118). New York: Oxford University Press.

Stanton, A. L., & Snider, P. R. (1993). Coping with a breast cancer diagnosis: A prospective study. *Health Psychology, 12,* 16–23.

Stewart, A. L., Greenfield, S., Hays, R. D., Wells, K., Rogers, W. H., Berry, S. D., McGlynn, E. A., & Ware, J. E. (1989). Functional status and well-being of patients with chronic conditions: Results from the Medical Outcomes Study. *Journal of the American Medical Association, 262,* 907–913.

Suls, J., & Fletcher, B. (1985). The relative efficacy of avoidant and nonavoidant coping strategies: A meta-analysis. *Health Psychology, 4,* 249–288.

Taylor, S. E. (1983). Adjustment to threatening events: A theory of cognitive adaptation. *American Psychologist, 38,* 1161–1173.

Taylor, S. E., & Aspinwall, L. G. (1990). Psychosocial aspects of chronic illness. In P. T. Costa & G. R. VandenBos (Eds.), *Psychological aspects of serious illness: Chronic conditions, fatal diseases, and clinical care* (pp. 7–60). Washington, DC: American Psychological Association.

Taylor, S. E., & Aspinwall, L. G. (1996). Mediating and moderating processes in psychosocial stress: Appraisal, coping, resistance, and vulnerability. In H. B. Kaplan (Ed.), *Psychosocial stress: Perspectives on structure, theory, life- course, and methods* (pp. 71–110). San Diego: Academic Press.

Taylor, S. E., & Brown, J. D. (1988). Illusion and well-being: A social psychological perspective on mental health. *Psychological Bulletin, 103,* 193–210.

Taylor, S. E., Kemeny, M. E., Aspinwall, L. G., Schneider, S. G., Rodriguez, R., & Herbert, M. (1992). Optimism, coping, psychological distress, and high-risk sexual behavior among men at risk for Acquired Immunodeficiency Syndrome (AIDS). *Journal of Personality and Social Psychology, 63,* 460–473.

Taylor, S. E., Lichtman, R. R., & Wood, J. V. (1984). Attributions, beliefs about control, and adjustment to breast cancer. *Journal of Personality and Social Psychology, 46,* 489–502.

Taylor, S. E., & Lobel, M. (1989). Social comparison activity under threat: Downward evaluation and upward contacts. *Psychological Review, 96,* 569–575.

Taylor, S. E., Repetti, R. L., & Seeman, T. (1997). Health psychology: What is an unhealthy environment and how does it get under the skin? *Annual Review of Psychology, 48,* 411–447.

Tennen, H., & Affleck, G. (1996). Daily processes in coping with chronic pain: Methods and analytic strategies. In M. Zeidner & N. Endler (Eds.), *Handbook of coping: Theory, research, applications* (pp. 151–177). New York: Wiley.

Thompson, S. C. (1991). Interventions to enhance perceptions of control. In C. R. Snyder & D. Forsyth (Eds.), *Handbook of social and clinical psychology* (pp. 607–623). New York: Pergamon.

Thompson, S. C., Nanni, C., & Levine, A. (1994). Primary versus secondary and central versus consequence-related control in HIV-positive men. *Journal of Personality and Social Psychology, 67,* 540–547.

Thompson, S. C., Sobolew-Shubin, A., Galbraith, M. E., Schwankovsky, L., & Cruzen, D. (1993). Maintaining perceptions of control: Finding perceived control in low-control circumstances. *Journal of Personality and Social Psychology, 64,* 293–304.

Tobin, D. L., Holroyd, K. A., Reynolds, R. V., & Wigal, J. K. (1989). The hierarchical factor structure of the Coping Strategies Inventory. *Cognitive Therapy and Research, 13,* 343–361.

Uchino, B. N., Cacioppo, J. T., & Kiecolt-Glaser, J. K. (1996). The relationship between social support and physiological processes: A review with emphasis on underlying mechanisms and implications for health. *Psychological Bulletin, 119,* 488–531.

van't Spijker, A., Trijsburg, R. W., & Duivenvoorden, H. J. (1997). Psychological sequelae of cancer diagnosis: A meta-analytical review of 58 studies after 1980. *Psychosomatic Medicine, 59,* 280–293.

Waltz, M., Badura, B., Pfaff, H., & Schott, T. (1988). Marriage and the psychological consequences of a heart attack: A longitudinal study of adaptation to chronic illness after 3 years. *Social Science and Medicine, 27,* 149–158.

Wegner, D., & Pennebaker, J. (Eds.). (1992). *Handbook of mental control.* New York: Prentice-Hall.

Wood-Dauphinee, S. (1996). Quality-of-life assessment: Recent trends in surgery. *Canadian Journal of Surgery, 39,* 368–372.

Young, K., & Zane, N. (1995). Ethnocultural influences in evaluation and management. In P. M. Nicassio & T. W. Smith (Eds.), *Managing chronic illness: A biopsychosocial perspective* (pp. 163–206). Washington, DC: American Psychological Association.

Young, L. D. (1992). Psychological factors in rheumatoid arthritis. *Journal of Consulting and Clinical Psychology, 60,* 619–627.

Zautra, A. J., & Manne, S. L. (1992). Coping with rheumatoid arthritis: A review of a decade of research. *Annals of Behavioral Medicine, 14,* 31–39.

Zich, J., & Temoshok, L. (1990). Perceptions of social support, distress, and hopelessness in men with AIDS and ARC: Clinical implications. In L. Temoshok & A. Baum (Eds.), *Psychosocial perspectives on AIDS: Etiology, prevention, and treatment* (pp. 201–227). Hillsdale, NJ: Lawrence Erlbaum Associates.

22

Recall Biases and Cognitive Errors in Retrospective Self-Reports: A Call for Momentary Assessments

Amy A. Gorin
Arthur A. Stone
State University of New York at Stony Brook

One of the primary means of obtaining information from participants in behavioral science research is through the use of retrospective self-reports. Research participants are often required to recall both qualitative and quantitative details about prior events, symptoms, behaviors, and psychological processes (Babor, J. Brown, & Del Boca, 1990). Retrospective self-reports also play an important role in clinical practice. Patients are commonly asked to provide information about their health histories, previous affective states, cognitions, symptoms, and health behaviors for use in assessment and treatment. The benefits of retrospective self-reports are numerous: They can be developed quickly, are easy to administer and to complete, tend to have strong face validity (Stone, Shiffman, & DeVries, 1999), and are very economical (Baker & Brandon, 1990).

Until recently, participants' confidence in their own reports was the primary indicator of the accuracy of retrospective recall. As participants are usually quite confident in their own recall, the validity of retrospective self-reports has generally been assumed to be high (Fienberg, Loftus, & Tanur, 1985; Read, Vokey, & Hammersley, 1990). However, research in the field of autobiographical memory questions this assumption. Specifically, a growing body of empirical studies indicates that instead of producing reliable and valid information as once assumed, retrospective self-reports are susceptible to numerous recall biases and cognitive errors (Jobe & Mingay, 1991; Jobe, White, Kelley, Mingay, & Sanchez, 1990; Thompson, Skowronski, Larsen, & Betz, 1996). According to Ross (1989, p. 342), retrospective recall appears to be "an active, constructive, schema-guided process," which at times is inaccurate. This is not to suggest that retrospective self-reports are meaningless—they undoubtedly provide valuable information about participants' general perceptions of past events and, perhaps, about their future actions. Rather, it appears necessary to recognize their limitations as tools for gathering accurate, detailed, autobiographical facts and to explore alternative means of obtaining such information.

Given researchers' and clinicians' heavy reliance on retrospective self-reports, this chapter has three goals. First, it reviews autobiographical memory processes involved in retrospective self-reporting such as personal memories and generic personal memory. Second, it provides a summary of the types of recall biases and cognitive errors that impact retrospective self-reports. Rather than reviewing all relevant studies in detail, one or two examples of each recall bias are used to highlight the sorts of errors that can occur. Third, it introduces a relatively new alternative to retrospective self-reports, namely, intensive momentary-based assessments, and discusses instances when this approach may be preferable to traditional self-report methods of collecting information.

AUTOBIOGRAPHICAL MEMORY

Autobiographical memory, also known as everyday or ecological memory, refers to memory and knowledge of personal information and experiences (Bruce, 1985; Robinson & Swanson, 1990). It is believed to be organized by a limited number of self-schemata that process personally relevant information in a meaningful fashion, producing a coherent view of the self that may or may not reflect reality. Schemata can center around specific traits (e.g., outgoing vs. shy, dependent vs. independent) or social roles (e.g., student, daughter, etc.) and are believed to be formed through the abstraction of information from past and present experiences (Barclay & Subramariam, 1987).

The types of information organized by self-schemata include *personal memories* (e.g., visual images of specific episodes from the past, such as remembering an argument with a coworker) and *generic personal memory* (e.g., knowledge about the types of instances individuals are likely to experience, such as knowing what it is like to be angry; Brewer, 1994). Recent, low frequency, and/or emotionally laden experiences are likely to be retained as personal memories (White, 1989), whereas other types of experiences tend to fade rather quickly (Engle & Lumpkin, 1992). In contrast to the episodic nature of personal memories, generic personal memory is formed gradually over time as a series of similar events is experienced (Menon, 1994). New and old experiences are automatically integrated (Hawkins & Hastie, 1990) creating a knowledge base that lacks specific time and location indicators (Means, Mingay, Nigam, & Zarrow, 1988).

The present understanding of autobiographical memory processes suggests that retrospective self-reports can be produced in several ways: They can be reproduced from personal memories, reconstructed from generic personal memory, or derived from a combination of reproduction and reconstruction. For example, a person may recall some details of an event from personal memories (e.g., a 30th birthday party) and fill in forgotten details with information from generic personal memory (e.g., general knowledge of what birthday parties entail). The choice of strategy depends in large part on the type of experience to be recalled. Memories of infrequently experienced and/or recent events are likely to be reproduced, whereas memories of events that are commonplace or have been experienced in the distant past are likely to be reconstructed (Blair & Burton, 1987). An exception to this pattern is temporal information (e.g., when an event occurred or how long it lasted), which regardless of retention interval or frequency of event occurrence is almost always reconstructed (Thompson et al., 1996).

Although it was once believed that reproduction was less prone to cognitive errors than reconstruction (see Sudman, Bradburn, & Schwarz, 1996), recent work indicates that both strategies are susceptible to systematic recall biases. In the following sections, the impact of these biases on three broad categories of self-report questions is examined. These categories include previous experiences (e.g., "How did you feel then?"), frequency rates (e.g., "How often have you … ?"), and temporal information (e.g., "When did it occur?"). Within each category, the types of reproduction and reconstruction errors that reduce recall accuracy are discussed.

RETROSPECTIVE RECALL BIASES AND COGNITIVE ERRORS

Previous Experience

Participants in behavioral science research are often asked to recall how they thought, felt, or behaved in the past. Questions can concern either a person's experience at a specific point in time (e.g., pretreatment pain level) or a summary estimate of typical experiences (e.g., average pain level over the past 6 months). Questions pertaining to a specific point in time appear to require participants to reproduce information from personal memories, whereas summary measures presumably require participants to base their answer on generic personal memory or cognitively compute an average of the experiences they reproduce (Stone et al., 1999). Although these types of questions are common in retrospective self-reports, results from numerous studies indicate that participants have difficulty providing accurate answers. For instance, a substantial discrepancy between real-time and retrospective reports was found in Stunkard and colleagues' examination of vomiting among postoperative gastric reduction patients (Stunkard, Foster, Glassman, & Rosato, 1985). Following surgery, patients recorded the number of times they vomited each day in weekly diaries for 6 months. At the end of the monitoring period, they were asked to recall the number of times they had vomited in the week following surgery. Results indicated that for the first postoperative week, patients retrospectively recalled vomiting an average of 12.1 times, whereas their real-time reports produced a much lower average of 3.4 times. This trend of retrospective overreporting continued throughout the 6-month period.

Discrepancies between retrospective and real-time reports have also been documented over shorter time frames. Over a 7-day period, for example, significant discrepancies have been found between retrospective and real-time reports of coping strategies (Ptacek, R. Smith, Epse, & Raffety, 1994) and pain severity (Stone, Broderick, Kaell, & Porter, 1995). Even over a limited 2-day period, retrospective recall of coping strategies has been shown to differ greatly from real-time reports (Stone et al., in press). At retrospective recall, 29% of participants experiencing work or marital stress failed to report a coping strategy they had endorsed during real-time reports recorded during the previous 48 hours.

Reproduction Errors. Why do participants err when retrospectively recalling previous experiences? If a memory is reproduced, recall is likely to be biased by the types of experiences retained as personal memories. The infrequent and/or emotionally laden events that are held in episodic form over time are, by definition, not representative of average experiences. When basing reports on these extreme instances from the past, errors are likely to occur. This bias was demonstrated in a study of emotional recall (Thomas & Diener, 1990) in which participants recorded their mood either four times a day for 3 weeks or at the end of the day for 6 weeks. Comparisons of summary self-reports completed after daily monitoring with daily mood assessments revealed that participants in both groups retrospectively overestimated the intensity of their positive and negative moods. The authors concluded that participants' responses were based on recall of key emotional events rather than recall of all relevant information. Similar errors have been found in studies of drug use (Hammersley, 1994) and pain severity (Stone, Broderick, Porter, & Kaell, 1997).

Recent events are also more likely to be stored episodically as personal memories than are distal events. Consequently, when participants base their answers on the personal memories they are able to reproduce, their reports are likely to be disproportionately influenced by recent experiences. A comparison of momentary and end-of-day assessments of mood, for instance, demonstrated that retrospective reports were biased toward the most recently experienced emotional state of the day, rather than representing the entire day's mood (Shiffman, 1995). This recency effect has also been observed in studies of pain (Redelemeir & Kahneman, 1996; Stone et al., 1997).

Reconstruction Errors. Similar to the reproduction of experiences from personal memory, reconstruction of information about previous experiences from generic personal memory is prone to error. As generic personal memory is constantly updated by new experiences, one source of information that is particularly salient and likely to bias recall is current state (Jobe & Mingay, 1991). Participants often reconstruct reports of previous experiences by surveying how they feel at the moment of recall. How this information affects retrospective reporting depends in large part on the self-schemata or implicit self-theories participants hold about the stability of their experiences over time (Barclay & Subramariam, 1987; Conway & Ross, 1984). If experiences are believed to remain relatively constant, then participants will likely overestimate the similarity between their current and past states. In contrast, if experiences are believed to change over time, then participants will likely exaggerate differences between current and previous states.

Researchers have found that of the implicit self-theories, beliefs of stability tend to be most common (Ross, 1989). As a result, participants frequently equate their previous experiences with the experiences they are having at the time of retrospective reporting (e.g., Eich, Reeves, Jaeger, & Graff-Radford, 1985; Singer, 1977). Although less common, implicit self-theories of change can also influence participants' reports, particularly when participants expect change due to some sort of intervention or treatment (e.g., Conway, 1989; Conway & Ross, 1984). In a study of hip replacement patients, for example, Mancuso and Charlson (1995) compared actual preoperative health reports with postoperative estimates of the same time period. Retrospectively, only 1% of patients accurately recalled their overall preoperative functioning: The majority of patients (65%) retrospectively rated their preoperation condition as worse than it actually was, exaggerating the amount of improvement they had made following surgery. A similar pattern of results has been found with chronic pain patients undergoing treatment (Linton & Melin, 1982) and patients recovering from prostate surgery and hysterectomies (Aseltine, Carlson, Fowler, & Barry, 1995).

In addition to current state, any other experiences that have occurred between the target event and the recall task are likely to be automatically integrated into generic personal memory. Consequently, participants' retrospective recall is based on both knowledge of past experiences and information about more recent experiences. One area where this poses a significant problem is in the measurement of stress and coping. If a stressful event is assessed after it is successfully dealt with, participants are likely to retrospectively minimize the event's initial stressfulness. This phenomenon, known as "effort after meaning," was first described by G. W. Brown and Harris (1978) and it can significantly bias retrospective reports of stress, coping, and other experiences.

In sum, people have great difficulty accurately recalling their previous experiences at either a specific point in the past or on a summary level. Estimates based on the reproduction of personal memories are likely to be biased by extreme and/or recent experiences. When reconstructing answers, reports are likely to be influenced by current state, implicit theories of stability, and the automatic integration of new and old experiences in generic personal memory.

Frequency Rates

Participants in behavioral science research are commonly asked to provide information about the frequency of various events and experiences. Participants' choice of recall strategy has been demonstrated to be a function of the overall frequency of an event: Information about infrequent events is likely to be reproduced, whereas information about frequent events is likely to be reconstructed (e.g., Blair & Burton, 1987; Menon, 1994). An examination of recall for medical visits by Means and Loftus (1991, Experiment 1) supports this assertion. In this study, participants were asked to recall how many times they had received medical attention in the previous 12 months for allergies, acute injuries, or dental work. After estimating frequency rates, they were asked to indicate how they derived their answers. When only one medical visit was reported, over 80% of participants endorsed reproducing the individual instance from memory as their primary recall strategy. In contrast, when three or more visits were reported, less than 50% of participants reported basing their answers on recall of distinct personal memories. Clearly, as the overall frequency rates increased, the reproduction of information from personal memories decreased. As with recall of previous functioning, the use of both reproductive and reconstructive strategies when answering frequency questions is prone to recall biases and these errors are considered in the following section.

Reproduction Errors. When participants provide frequency information about irregular or uncommon events (i.e., less than three instances within a given recall category), they typically reproduce the relevant instances from personal memories and then add them to derive their answers (Means, Swan, Jobe, & Esposito, 1994). One type of error that affects reproduction of frequency information is omission (Blair & Burton, 1987). Omission, or the failure to recall an event, is believed to be caused by several factors, most notably inadequate retrieval cues. For instance, Smith, Jobe, and Mingay (1991) asked participants the question, "Altogether, during the past month, about how many times would you say you have eaten (a specific food)?" Prior to answering the question, participants were instructed to either think and take notes about the most recent time they had eaten the food, to think about as many different occasions on which they had eaten the food, or they were given no instructions at all. Omission rates were significantly reduced for participants instructed to think of as many different occasions as possible, suggesting that frequency estimates are influenced by the cognitive context in which they are made.

Length of retention interval has also been shown to be a factor in omission rates. In a study by Mathiowetz (1988), only 2% of medical visits occurring during a week of retrospective reporting were omitted, and approximately 30% of medical visits occurring 6 weeks prior to retrospective reporting were omitted. Omission rates increased by more than 3% with each passing week, providing strong evidence of an association between omission and length of retention interval.

Although less common than omission, errors of commission, or the inappropriate inflation of frequency rates, also affect frequency information reproduced from personal memories (Cummings, Nevitt, & Kidd, 1988). The leading explanation for commission is a phenomenon known as forward telescoping, or the shifting of dates ahead in time (Thompson, Skowronski, & Lee, 1988). Forward telescoping results in overestimation of frequency rates when events are mistakenly imported into the time frame under study. (*Note*: Examples and explanations of telescoping errors are discussed in more detail in the temporal information section). Commission may also be due to source monitoring errors (Johnson, Hashtroudi, & Lindsay, 1993). That is, rate inflation may occur when participants confuse real occasions with instances in which an event was mentally reviewed or verbally discussed (Johnson & Raye, 1981).

Reconstruction Errors. When estimating rates of frequently occurring events (i.e., three or more instances within a given recall category), reconstructive rather than reproductive strategies are likely to be used. Perhaps the most common reconstructive strategy employed when generating frequency information is decomposition (Means & Loftus, 1991; Means et al., 1994). Decomposition involves breaking the time frame of interest into discrete segments, estimating the frequency rate for one segment, and then multiplying that rate by the total number of segments to derive the overall frequency. For example, if asked "How many times in the past month have you exercised?", a participant using decomposition might estimate the number of times they exercised in the past week and multiply that weekly value by four to arrive at a monthly total. To the degree that the event in question is stable over time, this strategy will produce accurate answers. However, for events that do not show temporal stability, the use of decomposition will produce errors. Returning to the exercise example, there could be many possible reasons why the number of times exercised in the past week may be exceptional and not representative of monthly exercise totals. Thus, depending on the circumstances, decomposition can lead to either accurate responses, overestimation, or underestimation.

Reconstruction of frequency rates can also be biased by normative expectations held in generic personal memory about how often a particular event should or typically occurs (Bradburn, Rips, & Shevell, 1987). For example, when Means and Loftus (1991) asked participants how they derived their frequency estimates of dental visits within the past 12 months, 41% of participants acknowledged basing their answers on the common rule of thumb that you should visit the dentist once or twice a year. Expectations such as this lead participants to anchor and adjust their estimates to ensure they fall within the normative range, consequently limiting the range of values participants are willing to provide as frequency rates.

Just as participants have normative expectations about frequency rates, they also have implicit beliefs about how memory works. One example of this is the common belief that infrequent events are difficult to remember and frequent events are easy to recall (Bradburn et al., 1987). Based on this belief, participants will gauge an event's frequency based on ease of retrieval. If they have difficulty remembering the event (e.g., cannot recall a specific instance or can remember only a few details), they are likely to report it as infrequent. Alternatively, if instances of events are easy to retrieve (e.g., instances come quickly to mind with vivid details), they are likely to be judged as having a higher rate of occurrence (Means et al., 1994). Although this assumption, commonly referred to as the availability heuristic (Tversky & Kahneman, 1974), leads to correct answers at times, equating the level of detail remembered with rate of occurrence can be problematic. A demonstration of this is that specific examples of plane crashes are easier to recall than car accidents, but car accidents occur much more frequently.

In sum, retrospective recall of frequency rates is often biased and inaccurate. If frequency rates are reproduced, they are prone to errors of omission and commission. If they are reconstructed, decomposition strategies, normative expectations, and the availability heuristic are likely to impact their validity.

Temporal Information

Temporal information refers to information about an event's date and/or duration and is often of interest to behavioral science researchers. Unlike previous experiences and frequency rates, temporal information is rarely held episodically in the form of personal memories (Burt & Kemp, 1991). Rather, three lines of evidence suggest that temporal information is almost entirely reconstructed from generic personal memory (Friedman, 1993). First, research participants are not particularly accurate when providing temporal information (Barclay & Wellman, 1986; Thompson, 1982). Cohen and Java (1995), for instance, found that only 50% of health events (e.g., vomiting, back pain, and toothaches) occurring within a 3-month interval were retrospectively dated within 2 weeks of their actual occurrence. Second, when given the opportunity, participants tend to shy away from providing exact dates. In a study by Huttenlocher and colleagues (1990), only 23% of participants asked to date a previous in-home interview were willing to venture a guess (Huttenlocher, Hedges, & Bradburn, 1990). Third, when Thompson, Skowronski, and Betz (1993) asked participants to indicate the recall strategies they used to date personal events, less than 18% endorsed reproducing the exact date from memory (Thompson et al., 1993). More frequently, participants reported reconstructing temporal information by relating the event of interest to a general reference period (e.g., summer), basing answers on general temporal schemata (e.g., event happened at work and I only work weekdays), or basing estimates on the clarity of the event memory (e.g., the clearer the memory of the event, the more recently it occurred).

Based on such evidence, a reconstructive model of temporal memory has been advanced, emphasizing the role of generic personal memory (Friedman, 1993; Skowronski, Betz, Thompson, & Shannon, 1991). The model holds that the reconstruction of temporal information is guided by time-related schemata that organize general temporal knowledge (Larsen & Thompson, 1995). One powerful temporal framework is day of the week (DOW) schema, which contains general knowledge about the types of activities a person is likely to be engaged in on a given day of the week (e.g., Monday through Friday work, Wednesday evening class, Saturday morning errands, etc.). Two sources of information indicate that when participants are asked to date an event, their DOW schemas are activated. First, participants consistently perform above chance when identifying which day of the week an event occurred (Skowronski & Thompson, 1990). This is particularly true for events in which contextual information is recalled, presumably because the vivid details facilitate links between events and the DOW schema (Larsen & Thompson, 1995). Second, the error pattern for dating events is unevenly distributed around multiples of seven—indicating that participants tend to err in terms of the given week an event occurred, rather than the day of the week (Huttenlocher, Hedges, & Prohaska, 1992; Skowronski et al., 1991). These two findings suggest that exact dates are not encoded in personal memories but rather are reconstructed from temporal schemas. In this section, a few of the more prominent biases and errors that come into play during temporal reconstruction are reviewed.

Telescoping. Although participants are often correct about the day of week a given event occurred, they can rarely identify an event's exact date. More often than not, an event is forward telescoped and given a date more recent than its actual occurrence (Cohen & Java, 1995; Thompson et al., 1988). This phenomenon has been observed for several types of events ranging from crime incidents (Loftus & Marburger, 1983) to entertainment outings (Huttenlocher, Hedges & Prohaska, 1988). Substantial telescoping was observed, for example, when participants estimated the dates of unique personal events occurring within a 3-month period (Thompson et al., 1988, Experiment 1). Upon recall, the dates of events occurring at the beginning of the study were shifted forward by an average of 7 days. Examples of reverse telescoping, or shifting an event back in time, are also found in the literature, but are less common (Means & Loftus, 1991; Rubin & Baddeley, 1989; Sudman & Bradburn, 1973). Together, forward and reverse telescoping affect the validity of not only temporal information but of frequency information as well.

The cognitive mechanisms behind telescoping are not well understood (Rubin & Baddeley, 1989). One hypothesis that has been proposed is that the clarity of the memory, or the amount of detail remembered about an event, affects the date it is given (Bradburn et al., 1987). This hypothesis, which appears to be the temporal equivalent of the availability heuristic, posits that when many details are remembered, an event will be dated as occurring recently, and when only a few details are remembered, an event will be dated as occurring in the past. Although one study found support for this hypothesis (N. R. Brown, Rips, & Shevell, 1985), other studies have demonstrated that the magnitude of the telescoping effect is not related to participants' reported clarity of memory or confidence in dating accuracy (Thompson et al., 1988). More work is needed to fully understand the factors contributing to telescoping errors.

Bounding and Rounding. Another interesting phenomenon observed when participants reconstruct dates is bounding. *Bounding* refers to the tendency to restrict estimates to a self-imposed, limited interval. This error was observed by Huttenlocher et al. (1990). When recalling the date of a prior in-home interview, participants tended to self-restrict their estimates to under 60 days, although in actuality several participants were interviewed outside of the bounded interval. The cause of the boundary effect is not clear, but may be due in part to participants' beliefs about what constitutes a reasonable time frame for a recall task.

Huttenlocher and colleagues also noted that when participants were asked to report their answers in terms of the amount of time passed since the interview (instead of giving the exact date), participants tended to respond in terms of prototypic answers, that is, they *rounded* (e.g., weeks or months, rather than exact number of days). Response patterns were unevenly distributed around the values of 7, 10, 14, 21, 30, and 60 days, reflecting a strong tendency to round estimates off to the number of weeks or months elapsed. These values accounted for 70% of participants' response, while in reality they represented less than 10% of the actual values. As with bounding, the source of rounding errors is not known, but may reflect participants' reliance on schemas when answering temporal related questions.

Duration Biases. A series of studies by Burt and colleagues highlights the reconstructive nature of duration estimates. Examinations of both personal and historical events revealed that having no memory for a given event did not significantly increase duration estimate errors (Burt, 1992; Burt & Kemp, 1991). Rather than basing duration estimates on recall of specific personal memories, participants appear to base their answers on generic personal memory about the event category in question (Burt & Kemp, 1991). For instance, if asked to estimate the length of a friend's visit that is not recalled from personal memories, participants will tend to base their answers on generic knowledge about the typical length of a guest visit. This reconstruction strategy results in errors when the event in question has an atypical duration (Burt, 1993).

In sum, recall of temporal information is almost entirely reconstructive in nature. Participants rely on DOW schemas, as well as general knowledge from generic personal memory, to guide their responses. As a result, temporal estimates are subject to errors such as telescoping, bounding, and rounding.

SUMMARY OF RETROSPECTIVE RECALL BIASES AND THEIR IMPACT

In light of recent work in the area of autobiographical memory, significant biases and errors appear to be inherent in retrospective recall. Both the reproduction of information from personal memories and the reconstruction of information from generic personal memory tend to be inaccurate. Reports based on reproductive strategies are likely to be based on extreme instances from the past and are subject to omission and commission errors. Reports based on reconstructive strategies are likely to be influenced by the integration of new and old information as well as current state, decomposition strategies, and normative expectations. Reports of temporal information are also almost entirely reconstructed, with participants relying on inexact generic knowledge such as DOW schemas to answer temporal questions.

The magnitude of these errors is significant, even over limited retention intervals (e.g., Shiffman, 1995; Stone et al., 1998). In a study of time usage, for instance, participants retrospectively recalled less than 60% of the activities they had engaged in during a 2-hour observation period the previous day (Engle & Lumpkin, 1992). Similar error rates are found in studies with extended retention intervals. Retrospective recall of medication usage over a period of 3 months, for example, revealed omission rates of 40%—an error that could result in potentially serious drug interactions (Cohen & Java, 1995). Recall is even more susceptible to biases and errors as retention intervals expand from months to years. For instance, when hospital CEOs were asked to retrospectively report the type of business strategy they employed 2 years ago, 58% were completely inaccurate (Golden, 1992). Taken together with the work already reviewed, these findings seriously question the ability of research participants or patients to accurately report previous experiences, frequency rates, and temporal information over short and long retention intervals.

Within the past two decades, survey developers have turned to autobiographical memory researchers in efforts to devise ways to minimize recall biases and improve the accuracy of retrospective self-reports (Huber & Power, 1985; Loftus, Fienberg, & Tanur, 1985). This collaborative work has produced several strategies, including instructing participants in the use of retrieval aids such as timeliness and landmarks (Loftus & Marburger, 1983; N. F. Smith, Jobe, & Mingay, 1991), providing participants with more time to respond to answers (Hammersley, 1994), using bounded-recall interviews (Babor et al., 1990), and increasing participant motivation by stressing confidentiality and giving performance feedback (Baker & Brandon, 1990). Although the effectiveness of many of these techniques has yet to be empirically demonstrated, research in this area suggests many promising ways to limit errors that occur during retrospective self-reporting (see Sudman et al., 1996, for extended discussion).

ECOLOGICAL MOMENTARY ASSESSMENT: AN ALTERNATIVE TO RETROSPECTIVE SELF-REPORTS

An alternative approach to dealing with recall biases has been to move to momentary-based assessment strategies eliminating the retrospective nature of reports. The experience sampling method (ESM) developed by Csikszentmihalyi and colleagues (Csikszentmihalyi & Larsen, 1987) was the first momentary-based assessment approach to focus on behaviors and mental states (for a detailed account of the historical antecedents of momentary assessments in behavioral science research, see Stone et al., 1999). Since the introduction of ESM, behavioral science researchers have used momentary assessment strategies not only to study psychological experiences but physiological variables as well. Stone and Shiffman (1994) coined the term *ecological momentary assessment* (EMA) to reflect the increasing scope of momentary-based assessment approaches. In this section, EMA is defined and a discussion of its strengths and weaknesses as a research tool is provided.

There are three defining characteristics of EMA that differentiate it from traditional self-report measures. First, as its name implies, EMA focuses on what is happening on a momentary basis. Instead of asking participants to summarize their functioning over several weeks, days, or even hours, participants in EMA studies usually record how they feel and what they are doing at the moment of the assessment. For instance, a typical EMA question would be, "On a scale from 1 to 7, please rate how fatigued you are *at this moment*." Unlike retrospective recall, which is often reconstructive, participants' answers to such questions are not likely to be based on generic personal memory. Rather, participants are simply required to report the experiences they are having at that moment.

Second, in contrast to the laboratory and clinical settings typical of retrospective self-report administration, EMA data are collected in the participants' usual environments. Participants carry signaling devices with them throughout their normal daily routine, including while at work and at home. By maximizing ecological validity, EMA minimizes the possibility that reports are an artifact of the testing situation (e.g., white coat hypertension, test anxiety) and, as a result, the data collected are more likely to be representative of participants' typical functioning (Stone & Shiffman, 1994).

Third, EMA differs from retrospective self-reports in terms of its sampling strategy. Although retrospective measures are typically administered only once at the convenience of the researcher or clinician, EMA involves numerous momentary collections per day over a series of several days or weeks. In a typical EMA study, the exact timing of reports are randomly selected in order to ensure a representative and unbiased view of the phenomenon of interest. Whereas random reports are essential for the study of rapidly changing psychological states, they are not the only sampling strategy available for use with EMA. Depending on the research question at hand, event-contingent (e.g., complete report every time a stressful situation occurs) and time-contingent (e.g., fill out report every 2 hours) strategies can be employed. These are appropriate for the study of relatively rare or infrequent events.

Advantages and Limitations of EMA

In addition to avoiding recall biases and providing a representative view of the phenomenon of interest, the intensive sampling strategy of EMA allows for a detailed analysis of within-subjects effects. Diurnal cycles and the impact of environmental and situational factors on participants' experiences can be explored with EMA data. For example, using an EMA design, diurnal cycles in rheumatoid arthritis patients' pain and fatigue levels have been examined, providing new insights into disease experience (Stone et al., 1997). Variations in outcomes due to environmental and social factors may prove to be an important factor to consider when assessing disease severity and treatment response. Although extremely useful for detailed within-subjects analyses, the multiple reports per person generated through use of an EMA design can also be aggregated across time to examine between-subjects effects. These momentary-based "trait" measures provide summaries of participants' experiences that are not subject to retrospective recall biases.

Although there are many advantages to using EMA, there are also a few notable limitations. Given the intensive nature of the assessment strategy, participant burden is a legitimate concern. Early indicators suggest that completion rates in EMA studies are quite high and missing data are not a significant problem (Ockenfels et al., 1995; Smyth et al., 1996; Stone et al., 1997), but assessments should be brief so as to not add to participants' work load. There also is some concern about possible reactive effects of momentary assessments on participants' daily experiences. By requiring participants to attend closely to their daily experiences, their perception of their own experiences may inadvertently change. Initial work in the area of pain indicates that EMA monitoring does not change participants' perceptions (Cruise, Broderick, Porter, Kaell, & Stone, 1996), however, more work needs to be done to understand the effects monitoring has on participants' daily lives.

In addition to challenging participants, EMA designs pose some problems for researchers. Statistically, the multiple reports per person generated through EMA assessment strategies violate the assumptions of traditional linear modeling. To side step this issue, alternative, and at times complex, methods of analyzing the data need to be employed (see Schwartz & Stone, 1997). EMA can also be financially taxing. Special equipment, including signaling devices (e.g., watches or palmtop computers) and computer programs, are necessary to complete EMA projects.

In sum, although EMA requires extra effort on both the part of researchers and participants, it improves on traditional retrospective self-reports measures in many respects. Most notably, recall biases and cognitive errors are eliminated. In addition, EMA data are suitable for the examination of individual differences and complex interactions between environmental and psychosocial factors. Given these strengths, EMA is a viable research tool for gathering accurate autobiographical facts.

CONCLUSIONS

This chapter reviews recall biases and cognitive errors that affect retrospective self-reports. The studies examined suggest that the magnitude of retrospective reporting errors are significant and can threaten the validity of information obtained from research participants. Within the past two decades, researchers have begun to develop means of improving participants' reports. These efforts have taken two general forms: improve the accuracy of retrospective reporting through methods such as memory aids and bounded recall, and eliminate the possibility of retrospective recall biases by moving to momentary-based assessment strategies. Both approaches offer ways to improve the accuracy of information gained from self-reports, however, momentary assessments have the additional advantages of maximizing ecological validity and allowing for examination of within-subjects effects such as diurnal cycles and associations between environmental and psychosocial factors. Although ideal for the study of rapidly changing states and frequently occurring events, momentary assessments are not well-suited for all research questions (e.g., studies of extremely rare events). Thus, in addition to the continued development of momentary-based assessment strategies, further research examining autobiographical memory processes contributing to retrospective recall biases is needed. Of particular use would be studies identifying instances when reporting errors are most likely to occur. More work is needed to fully understand the cognitive processes involved in both momentary and retrospective self-reports, but the implications of the existing research are clear: Momentary assessment strategies should be employed whenever possible, and in cases in which the use of EMA is not feasible, the impact of recall biases and cognitive errors on retrospective self-reports needs to be acknowledged.

REFERENCES

Aseltine, R. H., Carlson, K. J., Fowler, F. J., & Barry, M. J. (1995). Comparing prospective and retrospective measures of treatment outcomes. *Medical Care, 33*(4), AS67–AS76.

Babor, T. F., Brown, J., & Del Boca, F. K. (1990). Validity of self-reports in applied research on addictive behaviors: Fact or fiction? *Behavioral Assessment, 12,* 5–31.

Baker, T. B., & Brandon, T. H. (1990). Validity of self-reports in basic research. *Behavioral Assessment, 12,* 33–51.

Barclay, C. R., & Subramariam, G. (1987). Autobiographical memories and self-schemata. *Applied Cognitive Psychology, 1,* 169–182.

Barclay, C. R., & Wellman, H. M. (1986). Accuracies and inaccuracies in autobiographical memories. *Journal of Memory and Language, 25,* 93–103.

Blair, E., & Burton, S. (1987). Processes used in the formulation of behavioral frequency reports in surveys. *Proceedings of the Sec-*

tion on Survey Methods Research: American Statistical Association, 167–172.

Bradburn, N. M., Rips, L. J., & Shevell, S. K. (1987). Answering autobiographical questions: The impact of memory and inference on surveys. *Science, 236,* 157–161.

Brewer, W. F. (1994). Autobiographical memory and survey research. In N. Schwarz & S. Sudman (Eds.), *Autobiographical memory and the validity of retrospective reports* (pp. 11–20). New York: Springer-Verlag.

Brown, G. W., & Harris, T. (1978). *The social origins of depression: A study of psychiatric disorder in women.* New York: Springer-Verlag.

Brown, N. R., Rips, L. J., & Shevell, S. K. (1985). Subjective dates of natural events in very long-term memory. *Cognitive Psychology, 17,* 139–147.

Bruce, D. (1985). The how and why of ecological memory. *Journal of Experimental Psychology: General, 114*(1), 78–90.

Burt, C.D.B. (1992). Reconstruction of the duration of autobiographical events *Memory and Cognition, 20*(2), 124–132.

Burt, C.D.B. (1993). The effect of actual event duration and event memory on the reconstruction of duration information. *Applied Cognitive Psychology, 7,* 63–73.

Burt, C.D.B., & Kemp, S. (1991). Retrospective duration estimation of public events. *Memory and Cognition, 19*(3), 252–262.

Cohen, G., & Java, R. (1995). Memory for medical history: Accuracy of recall. *Applied Cognitive Psychology, 9,* 273–288.

Conway, M. (1989). On bias in autobiographical recall: Retrospective adjustments following disconfirmed expectations. *Journal of Social Psychology, 130*(2), 183–189.

Conway, M., & Ross, M. (1984). Getting what you want by revising what you had. *Journal of Personality and Social Psychology, 47*(4), 738–748.

Cruise, C. E., Broderick, J., Porter, L., Kaell, A. T., & Stone, A. A. (1996). Reactive effects of diary self-assessment in chronic pain patients. *Pain, 67,* 253–258.

Csikszentmihalyi, M., & Larson, R. (1987). Validity and reliability of the experience-sampling method. Special issue: Mental disorders in their natural settings: The application of time allocation and experience sampling techniques in psychiatry. *Journal of Nervous and Mental Disease, 175,* 526–536.

Cummings, S. R., Nevitt, M. C., & Kidd, S. (1988). Forgetting falls: The limited accuracy of recall of falls in the elderly. *Journal of the American Geriatrics Society, 36,* 613–616.

Eich, E., Reeves, J. L., Jaeger, B., & Graff-Radford, S. B. (1985). Memory for pain: Relation between past and present pain intensity. *Pain, 223,* 375–379.

Engle, P. L., & Lumpkin, J. B. (1992). How accurate are time-use reports? Effects of cognitive enhancement and cultural differences on recall accuracy. *Applied Cognitive Psychology, 6,* 141–159.

Fienberg, S. E., Loftus, E. F., & Tanur, J. M. (1985). Cognitive aspects of health survey methodology: An overview. *Milbank Memorial Fund Quarterly: Health and Society, 63*(3), 547–564.

Friedman, W. J. (1993). Memory for time of past events. *Psychological Bulletin, 113*(1), 44–66.

Golden, B. R. (1992). The past is the past—or is it? The use of retrospective accounts as indicators of past strategy. *Academy of Management Journal, 35*(4), 848–860.

Hammersley, R. (1994). A digest of memory phenomena for addiction research. *Addiction, 89,* 283–293.

Hawkins, S. A., & Hastie, R. (1990). Hindsight: Biased judgements of past events after the outcomes are known. *Psychological Bulletin, 107*(3), 311–327.

Huber, G. P., & Power, D. J. (1985). Retrospective reports of strategic level managers: Guidelines for increasing accuracy. *Strategic Management Journal, 6,* 171–180.

Huttenlocher, J., Hedges, L. V., & Bradburn, N. M. (1990). Reports of elapsed time: Bounding and rounding processes in estimation. *Journal of Experimental Psychology: Learning, Memory, and Cognition, 16*(2), 196–213.

Huttenlocher, J., Hedges, L. V., & Prohaska, V. (1988). Hierarchical organization in ordered domains: Estimating the dates of events. *Psychological Review, 95,* 471–484.

Huttenlocher, J., Hedges, L. V., & Prohaska, V. (1992). Memory for day of week: A 5 + 2 day cycle. *Journal of Experimental Psychology: General, 125*(3), 313–325.

Jobe, J. B., & Mingay, D. J. (1991). Cognition and survey measurement: History and overview. *Applied Cognitive Psychology, 5,* 172–192.

Jobe, J. B., White, A. A., Kelley, C. L., Mingay, D. J., & Sanchez, M. J. (1990). Recall strategies and memory for health care visits. *Milbank Quarterly, 68*(2), 171–189.

Johnson, M. K., Hashtroudi, S., & Lindsay, D. S. (1993). Source monitoring. *Psychological Bulletin, 114*(1), 3–28.

Johnson, M. K., & Raye (1981). Reality monitoring. *Psychological Review, 88,* 67–85.

Larsen, S. F., & Thompson, C. P. (1995). Reconstructive memory in the dating of personal and public news events. *Memory and Cognition, 23*(6), 780–790.

Linton, S. J., & Melin, L. (1982). The accuracy of remembering chronic pain. *Pain, 13,* 281–285.

Loftus, E. F., Fienberg, S. E., & Tanur, J. M. (1985). Cognitive psychology meets the national survey. *American Psychologist, 40*(2), 175–180.

Loftus, E. F., & Marburger, W. (1983). Since the eruption of Mt. St. Helens, has anyone beaten you us? Improving the accuracy of retrospective reports with landmark events. *Memory and Cognition, 11*(2), 114–120.

Mancuso, C. A., & Charlson, M. E. (1995). Does recollection error threaten the validity of cross-sectional studies of effectiveness. *Medical Care, 33*(4), AS77–AS88.

Mathiowetz, N. A. (1988). Forgetting events in autobiographical memory: Findings from a health care survey. *Proceedings of the Section on Survey Method Research: American Statistical Association,* 167–172.

Means, B., & Loftus, E. F. (1991). When personal history repeats itself: Decomposing memories for recurring events. *Applied Cognitive Psychology, 5,* 297–318.

Means, B., Mingay, D. J., Nigam, A., & Zarrow, M. (1988). A cognitive approach to enhancing health survey reports of medical visits. In M. M. Gruneberg, P. E. Morris, & R. N. Sykes (Eds.), *Practical aspects of memory: Current research and issues: Vol. 1. Memory for everyday life* (pp. 537–542). Chichester, England: Wiley.

Means, B., Swan, G., Jobe, J. B., & Esposito, J. (1994). The effect of estimation strategies on the accuracy of respondents reports of cigarette smoking. In N. Schwarz & S. Sudman (Eds.), *Autobiographical memory and the validity of retrospective reports* (pp. 161–172). New York: Springer-Verlag.

Menon, G. (1994). Judgements of behavioral frequencies: Memory search and retrieval strategies. In N. Schwarz & S. Sudman (Eds.), *Autobiographical memory and the validity of retrospective reports* (pp. 161–172). New York: Springer-Verlag.

Ockenfels, M. C., Porter, L., Smyth, J., Kirschbaum, C., Hellhammer, D. H., & Stone, A. A. (1995). Effect of chronic stress associated with unemployment on salivary cortisol: Overall cortisol levels, diurnal rhythm, and acute stress reactivity. *Psychosomatic Medicine, 57,* 460–467.

Ptacek, J., Smith, R., Epse, K., & Raffety, B. (1994). Limited correspondence between daily coping reports and retrospective coping recall. *Psychological Assessment, 6,* 41–49.

Read, J. D., Vokey, J. R., & Hammersley, R. H. (1990). Changing photos of faces: Effects of exposure duration and photo similarity on recognition and the accuracy–confidence relationship. *Journal of Experimental Psychology: Learning, Memory, and Cognition, 16,* 870–882.

Redelemeir, D., & Kahneman, D. (1996). Patients' memories of pain medical treatments: Real-time and retrospective evaluations of two minimally invasive procedures. *Pain, 66,* 3–8.

Robinson, J. A., & Swanson, K. L. (1990). Autobiographical memory: The next phase. *Applied Cognitive Psychology, 4,* 321–335.

Ross, M. (1989). Relation of implicit theories to the construction of personal histories. *Psychological Review, 96,* 341–357.

Rubin, D. C., & Baddeley, A. D. (1989). Telescoping is not time compression: A model of the dating of autobiographical events. *Memory and Cognition, 17,* 653–661.

Schwartz, J. E., & Stone, A. A. (1997). Data analysis for EMA studies. *Health Psychology, 17,* 6–16.

Shiffman, S. (1995, June). *Ecological momentary assessment: Collecting behavioral field data in real time.* Symposium conducted at the meeting of the Academy of Behavioral Medicine Research, Williamsburg, VA.

Singer, E. (1977). Subjective evaluations as indicators of change. *Journal of Health and Social Behavior, 18,* 84–90.

Skowronski, J. J., Betz, A. L., Thompson, C. P., & Shannon, L. (1991). Social memory in everyday life: Recall of self-events and other-events. *Journal of Personality and Social Psychology, 60*(6), 831–843.

Skowronski, J. J., & Thompson, C. P. (1990). Reconstructing the dates of personal events: Gender differences in accuracy. *Applied Cognitive Psychology, 4,* 371–381.

Smith, A. F., Jobe, J. B., & Mingay, D. J. (1991). Question induced cognitive biases in reports of dietary intake in college men and women. *Health Psychology, 10*(4), 244–257.

Smyth, J. M., Ockenfels, M. C., Gorin, A. A., Catley, D., Porter, L. S., Kirschbaum, C., Hellhammer, D. H., & Stone, A. A. (1996). Individual differences in the diurnal cycle of cortisol. *Psychoneuroendocrinology, 22*(2), 89–105.

Stone, A. A., Broderick, J. B., Kaell, A. T., & Porter, L. E. (1995). *Do retrospective reports of pain due to rheumatoid arthritis over seven days correspond to momentary reports of pain for the same period?* Unpublished manuscript.

Stone, A. A., Broderick, J. B., Porter, L. S., & Kaell, A. T. (1997). The experience of rheumatoid arthritis pain and fatigue: Examining momentary reports and correlates over one week. *Arthritis Care and Research, 10*(3), 185–193 .

Stone, A. A., Schwartz, J. E., Neale, J. M., Shiffman, S., Marco, C. A., Hickcox, M., Paty, J., Porter, L. S., & Cruise, L. J. (1998). A comparison of coping assessed by ecological momentary assessment and retrospective recall. *Journal of Personality and Social Psychology, 74,* 1670–1680.

Stone, A. A., & Shiffman, S. S. (1994). Ecological Momentary Assessment (EMA) in behavioral medicine. *Annals of Behavioral Medicine, 16,* 199–202.

Stone, A. A., Shiffman, S. S., & DeVries, M. (1999). Rethinking our self-report assessment methodologies: An argument for collecting ecologically valid momentary assessments. In D. Kahneman, E. Diener, & N. Schwarz (Eds.), *Understanding quality of life: Scientific perspectives on enjoyment and suffering* (pp. 26–39). New York: Russell Sage.

Stunkard, A., Foster, G., Glassman, J., & Rosato, E. (1985). Retrospective exaggeration of symptoms: Vomiting after gastric surgery for obesity. *Psychosomatic Medicine, 47*(2), 150–155.

Sudman, S., & Bradburn, N. M. (1973). Effects of time and memory factors on responses in surveys. *Journal of the American Statistical Association, 68,* 805–815.

Sudman, S., Bradburn, N. M., & Schwarz, N. (1996). *Thinking about answers: The application of cognitive processes to survey methodology.* San Francisco, CA: Jossey-Bass.

Thomas, D. L., & Diener, E. (1990). Memory accuracy in the recall of emotions. *Journal of Personality and Social Psychology, 59*(2), 291–297.

Thompson, C.P. (1982). Memory for unique personal events: The roommate study. *Memory and Cognition, 10,* 324–332.

Thompson, C. P., Skowronski, J. J., & Betz, A. L. (1993). The use of partial temporal information in dating personal events. *Memory and Cognition, 21*(3), 352–360.

Thompson, C. P., Skowronski, J. J., Larsen, S. F., & Betz, A. L. (1996). *Autobiographical memory: Remembering what and remembering when.* Mahwah, NJ: Lawrence Erlbaum Associates.

Thompson, C. P., Skowronski, J. J., & Lee, D. J. (1988). Telescoping in dating naturally occurring events. *Memory and Cognition, 16,* 461–468.

Tversky, A., & Kahneman, D. (1974). Judgement under uncertainty: Heuristics and biases. *Science, 185,* 1123–1131.

White, R. T. (1989). Recall of autobiographical events. *Applied Cognitive Psychology, 3,* 127–135.

23

Burnout and Health

Michael P. Leiter
Acadia University

Christina Maslach
University of California, Berkeley

Work plays a central role in people's physical and psychological well-being. Not only does it provide income and other tangible resources, but it is a source of status, social support, life satisfaction, and self-identity. However, work can also have adverse effects on the individual worker, especially with respect to health (Ilgen, 1990). The risks to physical well-being, in terms of injuries and diseases caused by the job, have long been the concern of the field of occupational health, but it is only recently that more attention has been given to job risk factors for psychological well-being (e.g., Sauter, Murphy, & Hurrell, 1990).

Much of this attention has focused on job stress, which is a general rubric referring to the impact of external job demands (stressors) on the worker's internal experience (stress response), and to the subsequent outcomes of this process. Stress impairs performance by reducing people's capacity for complex physical skills and by impairing cognitive functioning. Stress compromises the immune system, increasing the risk of viral and bacterial infections. The chronic tension associated with stress increases vulnerability to musculoskeletal problems. Empirical evidence has been found for the negative effects of job stress on physical health (especially cardiovascular problems), as well as on psychological well-being (e.g., job dissatisfaction, negative affect). Job stress is also predictive of various behavioral responses, such as lowered job performance, problems with family relationships, and self-damaging behaviors (see Kahn & Byosiere, 1992; Sauter & Murphy, 1995).

WHAT IS BURNOUT?

One type of job stress that has been studied in recent years is *burnout,* which involves a prolonged response to chronic interpersonal stressors on the job (Maslach, 1982; Maslach & Leiter, 1997). The three key dimensions of burnout are an overwhelming exhaustion; feelings of frustration, anger, and cynicism; and a sense of ineffectiveness and failure. The experience impairs both personal and social functioning. Whereas some people may quit the job as a result of burnout, others will stay on, but they will only do the bare minimum (rather than their very best). This decline in the quality of work and in both physical and psychological health can be very costly—not just for the individual worker, but for everyone affected by that person.

Burnout is recognized as a particular occupational hazard for various people-oriented professions, such as human services, education, and health care. The therapeutic relationships that such providers develop with their service recipients can be quite stressful because they demand an ongoing and intense level of personal, emotional contact. Within such occupations, the norms are clear, if not always stated explicitly: to be selfless and put others' needs first, to work long hours and do whatever it takes to help a client or patient or student, to go the extra mile and to give one's all. When such norms are combined with work settings that are high in demands and low in resources, then the risk for burnout is high (Maslach & Goldberg, 1998).

Not surprisingly, burnout has long been an issue of concern for health care occupations (Leiter & Harvie, 1996; Maslach, 1979, 1997; Maslach & Jackson, 1982; Maslach & Ozer, 1995). The caregiving relationship between health worker and patient involves significant emotional experiences. Some of these experiences are enormously rewarding and uplifting, as when patients recover because of the worker's efforts. However, other experiences are emotionally stressful for the health practitioner, such as working with difficult or unpleasant patients, having to give "bad news" to patients or their families, dealing with patient deaths, or having conflicts with coworkers or supervisors. These emotional strains are sometimes overwhelming and lead to emotional exhaustion.

To protect themselves against such disruptive feelings, health professionals may moderate their compassion for patients by distancing themselves psychologically, avoiding overinvolvement, and maintaining a more detached objectivity (a process known as "detached concern"; Lief & Fox, 1963). For example, if a patient has a condition that is upsetting to see or otherwise difficult to work with, it is easier for practitioners to provide the necessary care if they think of the patient as a particular "case" or "symptom" rather than as a human being who is suffering. However, the blend of compassion and emotional distance is difficult to achieve in actual practice, and too often the balance shifts toward a negative and depersonalized perception of patients. A derogatory and demeaning view of patients is likely to be matched by a decline in the quality of the care provided to them.

Many health professionals have not had sufficient preparation for the emotional reality of their work and its subsequent impact on their personal functioning. Thus, the experience of emotional turmoil on the job is likely to be interpreted as a failure to "be professional" (i.e., to be nonemotional, cool, and objective). Consequently, these health workers begin to question their own ability to work in a health career and to feel that their personal accomplishments are falling short of their expectations. These failures may be as much a function of the work setting as of any personal shortcomings; providing good health care may be difficult to accomplish in the context of staff shortages, poor training, or inadequate resources. Nevertheless, health workers may begin to develop a negative self-evaluation, which can impair their job performance or even lead them to quit the job altogether.

Thus, burnout appears to be an important factor in job turnover, absenteeism, and low morale. It is also correlated with various indices of personal and social dysfunction. But the most critical bottom line for burnout is its link to a deterioration in the quality of care or service provided to clients or patients.

A MULTIDIMENSIONAL MODEL OF BURNOUT

Unlike unidimensional models of stress, burnout is best conceptualized in terms of its three core components: emotional exhaustion, depersonalization, and reduced personal accomplishment (Maslach, 1993). According to this model, burnout is an individual stress experience embedded in a context of complex social relationships, and it involves the person's conception of both self and others.

Emotional exhaustion refers to feelings of being emotionally overextended and having depleted emotional resources. The major sources of this exhaustion are work overload and personal conflict at work. People feel drained and used up, without any source of replenishment. They lack enough energy to face another day or another person in need. The emotional exhaustion component represents the basic stress dimension of burnout.

Depersonalization refers to a negative, callous, or excessively detached response to other people, which often includes a loss of idealism. It usually develops in response to the overload of emotional exhaustion, and is self-protective at first—an emotional buffer of "detached concern." But the risk is that the detachment can turn into dehumanization. The depersonalization component represents the interpersonal dimension of burnout.

Reduced personal accomplishment refers to a decline in feelings of competence and productivity at work. This lowered sense of self-efficacy has been linked to depression and an inability to cope with the demands of the job, and it can be exacerbated by a lack of social support and of opportunities to develop professionally. Staff members experience a growing sense of inadequacy about their ability to help clients, and this may result in a self-imposed verdict of failure. The personal accomplishment component represents the self-evaluation dimension of burnout.

Conceptual Issues

The interrelations among the three components of burnout have been the subject of much theorizing and research. The only measure that assesses all three of these burnout components is the Maslach Burnout Inventory (MBI), so it is considered the standard tool for research in this field (Maslach & Jackson, 1981, 1986; Maslach, Jackson, & Leiter, 1996). There are now three versions of the MBI designed for use with different occupations, which reflects the developing interest in this phenomenon. The original version of the MBI (now known as the MBI–HSS) was designed for use with people working in the human services (including health care). It was in these occupations where the greatest continuing concern about burnout has been evident. A second version of the MBI (the MBI–ES) was developed for use by people working in educational settings. Given the increasing interest in burnout within occupations that are not so clearly people oriented, a third, general version of the MBI (the MBI–GS) has recently been developed. Here, the three components of the burnout construct are conceptualized in slightly broader terms, with respect to the general job, and not just to the personal relationships that may be a part of that job. Thus, the three components are exhaustion, cynicism (a distant attitude toward the job), and reduced professional efficacy (Maslach, Jackson, & Leiter, 1996).

The general version of the MBI was a significant departure from the established focus on the service relationship as the burnout concept was developed (Cherniss, 1980; Maslach,

1982). Almost from the original release of the MBI, researchers used the scale, modified or unmodified, with occupational groups other than public human service providers, including civil servants (Golembiewski & Munzenrider, 1988), military (Leiter, Clark, & Durup, 1994), computer programmers (Lee & Ashforth, 1993), police officers (Burke, 1987), managers (Lee & Ashforth, 1993), and entrepreneurs (Gryskiewicz & Buttner, 1992). These researchers saw that people in these occupations confronted crises in energy, involvement, and efficacy that shared core features with the experiences of human service workers, despite a less intense contact with people. The MBI–HSS did not fully assess burnout outside of human services because of the frequent reference to service recipients in the items; not only did these groups' scores on the MBI–HSS subscales differ from norms established with human service providers, but the factor structure for the MBI was not maintained across other occupational groups. The MBI–GS addressed this problem by developing a variation of the MBI that maintained a consistent factor structure across a variety of occupations including human service providers (nurses) along with a variety of managerial and technical occupations (Leiter & Schaufeli, 1996; Maslach, Jackson, & Leiter, 1996).

Exhaustion is the central quality of burnout and the most obvious manifestation of this complex syndrome. When people describe themselves or others as experiencing burnout, they are most often referring to the experience of exhaustion. In fact, nurses who responded to an advertisement about burnout scored much higher than the average on exhaustion but only moderately higher on the other two aspects of the syndrome (Pick & Leiter, 1991). Of the three aspects of burnout, exhaustion is the most widely reported and the most thoroughly analyzed. The strong identification of exhaustion with burnout has led some to argue that the other two aspects of the syndrome are incidental or unnecessary (Shirom, 1989). However, the fact that exhaustion is a necessary criterion for burnout does not mean it is a sufficient one.

Although exhaustion reflects the stress dimension of burnout, it fails to capture the critical aspects of the relation people have with their work. People do not simply feel exhausted when they experience a mismatch with their job. Exhaustion prompts people to attempt to distance themselves emotionally and cognitively from their work, as can be seen clearly in the human services. The emotional demands of this work exhaust a service provider's capacity to be involved with, and responsive to, the needs of service recipients. Depersonalization is people's attempt to put distance between themselves and service recipients by actively ignoring the qualities that make them unique and engaging people. Recipients' demands are more manageable when they are considered impersonal objects. Outside of the human services, people use cognitive distancing by developing an indifference or cynical attitude when they are exhausted and discouraged. Distancing is such an immediate reaction to exhaustion that a strong relation from exhaustion to depersonalization or cynicism is found consistently in burnout research, across a wide range of organizational and occupational settings (Maslach, Jackson, & Leiter, 1996).

The relation of reduced personal accomplishment to the other two aspects of burnout is somewhat more complex. In some instances, reduced personal accomplishment appears to be a function, to some degree, of either exhaustion, cynicism, or a combination of the two (Byrne, 1994; Lee & Ashforth, 1996). A work situation with chronic, overwhelming demands that contribute to exhaustion or cynicism is likely to erode an individual's sense of accomplishment or effectiveness. Further, the experience of exhaustion or depersonalization interferes with effectiveness: It is difficult for people to gain a sense of accomplishment when feeling exhausted or when helping people toward whom they are indifferent. However, in other settings, reduced accomplishment appears to develop in parallel with the other two burnout aspects, rather than sequentially (Leiter, 1993). Here the lack of efficacy seems to arise more clearly from a lack of relevant resources, whereas exhaustion and cynicism emerge from the presence of work overload and social conflict.

The inclusion of psychological distance in the construct of depersonalization or cynicism, along with professional inefficacy, make burnout much broader than established ideas of occupational stress. The stressful implications of emotional exhaustion are clearly tied to physical well-being, but the other two aspects of burnout are primarily related to psychological and social functioning. Together, the three aspects of burnout provide a rich and productive basis for examining psychological aspects of health in work organizations.

Personal Characteristics of Burnout

Burnout has been studied primarily in postindustrialized nations (United States, Canada, Europe, and Israel), although recently increased interest is being expressed in the syndrome by researchers in other nations. To date, most research on burnout has focused on human service occupations (Cordes & Dougherty, 1993; Leiter & Harvie, 1996; Maslach, Jackson, & Leiter, 1996), with the most frequent reports of burnout occuring among health care workers, teachers, and social workers. There are not substantial differences in burnout levels associated with gender, race, or age. As discussed later, burnout does vary with work conditions, and these may in turn be related to demographic characteristics. For example, in many organizations women have lower status positions relative to men, and they may also report more indicators of burnout due to a diminished quality of their work life. Human service workers in Europe tend to score lower on exhaustion and depersonalization/cynicism (Schaufeli, Maslach, & Marek, 1993; Van Yperen, Buunk, & Schaufeli, 1992). The absence of definite associations between burnout and personal characteristics has focused research and interventions on qualities of work settings.

Engagement With Work

Burnout is one end of a continuum in the relation people establish with their jobs. As a syndrome of exhaustion, cynicism, and ineffectiveness, it stands in contrast to the energetic, involved, and effective state of engagement with work. Recently, the multidimensional model of burnout has been expanded to this other end of the continuum (Leiter & Maslach, 1998). Engagement is defined in terms of the same three dimensions as burnout, but at the positive end of those dimensions rather than the negative. Thus, engagement consists of a state of high *energy* (rather than exhaustion), strong *involvement* (rather than cynicism), and a sense of *efficacy* (rather than a reduced sense of accomplishment).

This state is distinct from established constructs in organizational psychology such as organizational commitment, job satisfaction, or job involvement. Organizational commitment focuses on an employee's allegiance to the organization, which provides employment rather than to the work itself. The two concepts are related, but the focus of involvement differs. Organizational commitment focuses on the organization; engagement with work focuses on the work itself. Job satisfaction is the extent to which work is a source of need fulfillment and contentment, or a means of freeing employees from hassles or dissatisfiers; it does not encompass the person's relationship with the work itself. Job involvement is similar to the involvement aspect of engagement with work, but does not include the energy and effectiveness dimensions. Engagement with work provides a more complex and thorough perspective on an individual's relationship with work.

The extensive research on burnout has consistently found linear relations of workplace conditions across the full range of the MBI subscales. Just as high levels of personal conflict are associated with high levels of emotional exhaustion, low levels of conflict are strong predictors of low exhaustion. Conversely, high personal accomplishment is associated with supportive personal relationships, the enhancement of sophisticated skills at work, and active participation in shared decision making. These patterns indicate that the opposite of burnout is not a neutral state, but a definite state of mental health within the occupational domain. Whereas the burnout concept describes a syndrome of distress that may arise from enduring problems with work, engagement describes a positive state of fulfillment.

The concept of a burnout-to-engagement continuum enhances the understanding of how the organizational context of work can affect workers' well-being. It recognizes the variety of reactions that employees can have to the organizational environment, ranging from the intense involvement and satisfaction of engagement, through indifference, to the exhausted, distant, and discouraged state of burnout. One important implication of the burnout–engagement continuum is that strategies to promote engagement may be just as important for burnout prevention as strategies to reduce the risk of burnout. A work setting designed to support the positive development of the three core qualities of energy, involvement, and effectiveness should be successful in promoting the well-being and productivity of its employees.

SOURCES AND OUTCOMES OF BURNOUT

The empirical research on contributing factors has found that situational variables are more strongly predictive of burnout than are personal ones. In terms of antecedents of burnout, both job demands and a lack of key resources are particularly important. Work overload and personal conflict are the major demands, and the lack of such resources as control coping, social support, skill use, autonomy, and decision involvement seem to be especially critical. The consequences of burnout are seen most consistently in various forms of job withdrawal (decreased commitment, job dissatisfaction, turnover, and absenteeism), with the implication of a deterioration in the quality of care or service provided to clients or patients. Burnout is also linked to personal dysfunction, primarily in terms of impaired physical and mental health, although there is some evidence for increased substance abuse as well as marital and family conflicts. Figure 23.1 presents a diagrammatic summary of these major research findings, which have been discussed in a number of recent reviews (see Cordes & Dougherty, 1993; Leiter & Maslach, 1998; Maslach, Jackson, & Leiter, 1996; Schaufeli, Maslach, & Marek, 1993). This chapter concentrates on those findings having to do with health.

Unlike acute stress reactions, which develop in response to specific critical incidents, burnout is a cumulative stress reaction to ongoing occupational stressors. To put it in the terms of Selye's (1967) general adaptation syndrome, burnout is the exhaustion phase, following those of alarm and resistance. In this final phase, after prolonged exposure to stress, the physiological resources are depleted, and irreversible physical damage is caused to the organism. With burnout, the emphasis has been more on the process of psychological erosion, and the psychological and social outcomes of this chronic exposure, rather than just the physical ones. Because burnout is a prolonged response to chronic interpersonal stressors on the job, it tends to be fairly stable over time.

In a similar way, Brill (1984) conceptualized stress as an adaptation process that is temporary and is accompanied by mental and physical symptoms, whereas burnout refers to a breakdown in adaptation accompanied by chronic malfunctioning. This acute versus chronic temporal distinction implies that both concepts can only be discriminated retrospectively when the adaptation has been successfully performed (job stress) or when a breakdown in adaptation has occurred (burnout). In other words, stress and burnout are distinguished more in terms of process than specific physical symptoms (Maslach & Schaufeli, 1993).

Even though the stress literature provides a clear theoretical basis for a relation between burnout and health, such a relation has not been studied extensively. Of the three burnout components, emotional exhaustion is the closest to an orthodox stress variable, and thus it should be more predictive of stress-related health outcomes than the other two components. Exhaustion indicates a depletion of resources and personal energy. An exhausted individual is lacking the necessary resources for making an effective contribution at work as well as those needed to ward off disease and maintain physical well-being. However, the exhaustion may not be high enough to cause such severe debilitation that the person cannot function on the job, or is too sick to work.

Indeed, a consistent finding in burnout research is the correlation between the exhaustion component and various physical symptoms of stress: headaches, gastrointestinal dis-

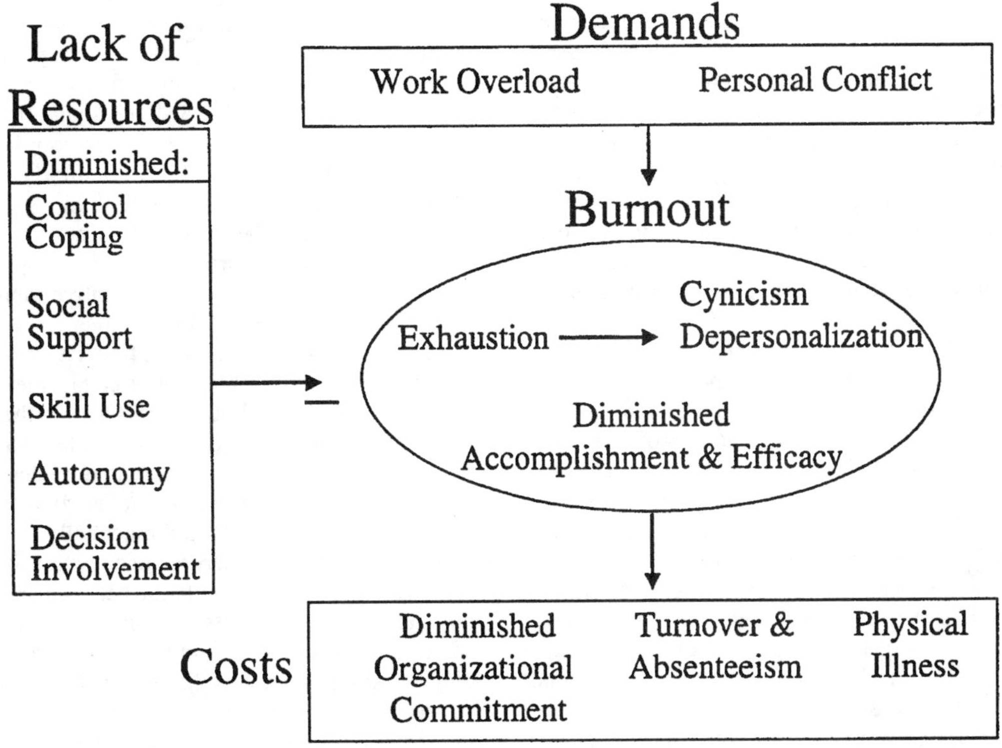

FIG. 23.1. Model of burnout. Modified and reproduced by special permission of the Publisher, Consulting Psychologists Press, Inc., Palo Alto, CA 94303 from the Maslach Burnout Inventory Manual by Christina Maslach, Susan E. Jackson, and Michael P. Leiter. Copyright 1996 by Consulting Psychologists Press, Inc. All rights reserved. Further reproduction is prohibited without the publisher's written consent.

orders, muscle tension, hypertension, cold/flu episodes, and sleep disturbances (Bhagat, Allie, & Ford, 1995; Burke & Deszca, 1986; Golembiewski & Munzenrider, 1988; Hendrix, Summers, Leap, & Steel, 1995; Jackson & Maslach, 1982; Kahill, 1988; Leiter, Clark, & Durup, 1994; Leiter & Harvie, 1996). One study found that emotional exhaustion and a work environment index predicted distinct patterns of health symptoms and behaviors, even after controlling for negative affect and demographic variables. Work environment was most predictive of symptoms and behaviors associated with muscle aches and pains, whereas the exhaustion component of burnout predicted health symptoms related to sleep disturbances and visits to the doctor for cardiovascular complaints (Maslach, Zedeck, Skitka, & Mosier, 1997).

Despite this link between burnout and stress-related health behaviors, there has not yet been any research on relevant health outcomes, such as the utilization of health care services or the filing of workman's compensation claims for stress. There has also been no theorizing to suggest that burnout has a connection to the development or progression of specific diseases, and consequently there is no empirical research on this issue.

In terms of mental, as opposed to physical, health, the link with burnout is much more complex. It has often been presumed that burnout may result in subsequent mental disabilities, and there has been some evidence in support of that view. For example, emotional exhaustion was found to be correlated with anxiety (Corrigan et al., 1994), and higher phases of burnout were associated with worsening scores on a mental health index (Golembiewski & Munzenrider, 1991).

However, an alternative interpretation of such correlations is that burnout is itself a form of mental illness, rather than a cause of it. Much of this discussion has focused on depression, and whether or not burnout is a distinctly different phenomenon. Research conducted during the development of the MBI found burnout to be distinct from, but related to, anxiety and depression (Maslach & Jackson, 1981, 1986). A subsequent analysis (Leiter & Durup, 1994) demonstrated the distinction between burnout and depression in a confirmatory factor analysis of the MBI and the Beck Depression Inventory. This analysis established that burnout is a problem specific to the work context, in contrast to depression that tends to pervade every domain of a person's life. These findings lent empirical support to earlier claims that burnout is job related and situation specific, as opposed to depression that is general and context-free (Freudenberger, 1983; Warr, 1987).

In their analysis of various conceptualizations of burnout, Maslach and Schaufeli (1993) noted five common elements with respect to mental health. First, there is a predominance of dysphoric symptoms such as mental or emotional exhaustion, fatigue, and depression. Second, the emphasis is on mental and behavioral symptoms more than physical ones. Third, burnout symptoms are work related. Fourth, the symptoms manifest themselves in "normal" persons who did not suffer from psychopathology before. Fifth, decreased effectiveness and work performance occur because of negative attitudes and behaviors.

Based on a similar analysis, Bibeau et al. (1989) proposed some diagnostic criteria for burnout. The principal subjective indicator is a general state of severe fatigue accompanied by loss of self-esteem resulting from a feeling of professional incompetence and job dissatisfaction; multiple physical symptoms of distress without an identifiable organic illness; and problems in concentration, irritability, and negativism. The principal objective indicator of burnout is a significant decrease in work performance over a period of several months, which has to be observable in relation to recipients (who receive services of lesser quality), supervisors (who observe a decreasing effectiveness, absenteeism, etc.), and colleagues (who observe a general loss of interest in work-related issues). Bibeau et al. (1989) also mentioned three criteria of exclusion that allow a differential diagnosis. These subjective and objective indicators of burnout should not result from sheer incompetence (i.e., the person has to have performed quite well in the job during a significant period), major psychopathology, or family-related problems. Also, severe fatigue resulting from monotonous work or a high work load is excluded because this is not necessarily accompanied by feelings of incompetence or lowered productivity. Although this is a provocative proposal for assessing burnout in clinical terms, there has not been any research to establish its validity. Moreover, there is not, as yet, any reliable method for diagnosing burnout at the individual level (Maslach & Schaufeli, 1993).

An issue that has received very little attention in the burnout literature is whether mental dysfunction is a cause, rather than an effect, of burnout. In other words, are people who are mentally healthy better able to cope with chronic stressors and thus less likely to experience burnout? Although not assessing burnout directly, one study addressed this question by analyzing archival longitudinal data of people who worked in interpersonally demanding jobs (Jenkins & Maslach, 1994). The results showed that people who were psychologically healthier in adolescence and early adulthood were more likely to enter, and remain in, such jobs, and they showed greater involvement and satisfaction with their work. Given this longitudinal data set, this study was better able to establish causal relations than is true for the typical correlational studies.

The issue of correlation and causality is familiar but often forgotten, and this is as true for burnout as for other research literatures. Just because one interpretation is plausible does not mean that it is the correct one. To illustrate this point, consider the research on burnout and coping styles, which often finds a correlation between the different components of burnout and specific coping techniques. For example, problem-focused coping (e.g., making a plan of action, finding compromise) has been correlated with greater personal accomplishment, whereas emotion-focused coping (e.g., ignoring problems, looking for a silver lining, reminding oneself that things could be worse) has been correlated with depersonalization (Bhagat et al., 1995). Similarly, nurses who used more palliative coping (wishful thinking, self-blame, denial/escape) had higher levels of burnout on all dimensions, and those who used more existential coping (finding a sense of meaning and coherence) or preventive coping (trying to reduce anticipated problems) had higher levels of engagement (Ogus, 1995). But which comes first, coping or burnout? Is it that the experience of burnout or engagement causes people to cope differently with stressors? Or, does the use of different coping styles lead them to be more or less burned out? Or, is there some critical third variable that mediates this relationship? The implications of these alternative answers are important both theoretically and practically.

A similar argument can be made with respect to the commonly found negative correlation between job satisfaction and burnout. The overall pattern of the research findings has led some researchers to conclude that, although burnout and job dissatisfaction are clearly linked, they are not identical constructs (Zedeck, Maslach, Mosier, & Skitka, 1988). However, the specific nature of that link is still a matter of speculation. Does burnout cause people to be dissatisfied with their job? Or, does a drop in satisfaction serve as the precursor to burnout? Alternatively, both burnout and job dissatisfaction may be caused by another factor, such as poor working conditions.

HOW DOES BURNOUT HAPPEN?

Inherent to the concept of stress is the problematic relation between the individual and the situation. In the case of job stress, the basic idea is that it is the result of a misfit between the person and the job. Some of the earliest models of organizational stress focused on this notion of job–person fit, and subsequent theorizing continues to highlight the importance of both individual and contextual factors (see Kahn & Byosiere, 1992).

As applied to burnout, this approach proposes that the greater the gap, or misfit, between the person and the job, the greater the likelihood of burnout. However, a new aspect of this approach is the specification of six areas in which this mismatch can take place (Maslach & Leiter, 1997). In each area, the nature of the job is not in harmony with the nature of people, and the result is the increased exhaustion, cynicism, and inefficacy of burnout. On the other hand, when better fit exists in these six areas, then engagement with work is the likely outcome.

The six areas in which mismatches can occur are workload, control, reward, community, fairness, and values (see Fig. 23.2). Each area of mismatch has a distinct relation with burnout and engagement, and an assessment of all six is necessary for a thorough consideration of the impact of the workplace on workers (see Maslach & Leiter, 1997, for a more extensive discussion of these issues).

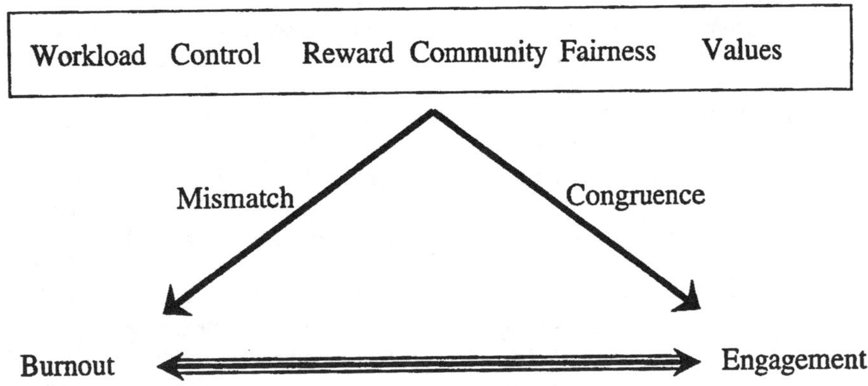

FIG. 23.2. Job–person fit.

Workload. The most obvious, and most commonly discussed, mismatch has to do with overload. Basically, job demands exceed human limits. People have to do too much in too little time with too few resources. They find it difficult to keep up with the rushed pace of work. In many of the human service professions, this kind of overload is a chronic job condition, not an occasional emergency, so there is little opportunity to rest, recover, and restore balance. The resulting burnout can lead to a deterioration in the quality of the work and a disruption of collegial relationships.

The obvious and straightforward relation of chronic work overload with exhaustion is consistently supported in the research as well as in the experience of working people. Both qualitative and quantitative work overload contribute to exhaustion by depleting the capacity of people to meet the demands of the job. The critical point occurs when people are unable to recover from work demands. That is, acute fatigue resulting from an especially demanding event at work—meeting a deadline or addressing a crisis—need not lead to burnout if people have an opportunity to recover during restful periods at work or at home (Shinn, Rosario, Morch, & Chestnut, 1984).

A sustainable workload, in contrast, provides opportunities to use and refine existing skills, as well as to become effective in new areas of activity (Landsbergis, 1988). It builds involvement by opening new opportunities, and by removing concern about work overwhelming personal capacity. A sustainable workload stops the cycle of exhaustion that is a driving force in the experience of burnout for many people.

Control. Another major mismatch occurs when people have little control over the work they do. As human beings, people have the ability to think and solve problems, and want to have the opportunity to make choices and decisions. In other words, they want to have some input into the process of achieving the outcomes for which they will be held accountable. A mismatch occurs when people are constrained by rigid policies and tight monitoring. They do not have much room to improve or customize or innovate—with the result that they do not feel efficacious or responsible for the outcomes.

In contrast, people are more committed to, and derive more satisfaction from, actions that they have freely chosen. The process of making a decision has an enduring impact on employees' experience of participating in organizational life and the responsibility they take for its outcomes. Participative decision making is a cornerstone of job enrichment strategies (Hackman, 1986) as much because of its power to engender commitment as for its capacity to make good use of knowledge and experience within a group of colleagues. Active participation in organizational decision making has been consistently found to be associated with higher levels of personal accomplishment and lower levels of exhaustion (Cherniss, 1980; Leiter, 1992).

Reward. A third type of job–person mismatch involves a lack of appropriate rewards for the work people do. This lack of recognition devalues both the work and the workers. Prominent among these rewards are external ones such as salary and benefits.

Intrinsic rewards (such as pride in doing something of importance and doing it well) can also be a critical part of this area of work life. What keeps work involving for most people is the pleasure they experience with the day-to-day flow of work that is going well (Leiter, 1992). When things are going very well, people experience intrinsic satisfaction continuously in their day-to-day work. An enjoyable workflow supports overall psychological well-being, and physical health as well. The more enjoyable and challenging aspects of work are often the source of recognition from professional colleagues outside of the immediate work setting. The more tedious aspects of work are not only dull in themselves, they crowd out opportunities for engaging in the creative activities that bring professional recognition and reward. Congruence between individuals and organizations regarding material rewards and opportunities for intrinsic satisfaction are an important part of a congruent workplace (Richardsen, Burke, & Leiter, 1992).

Community. The fourth job–person mismatch occurs when people lose a sense of positive connection with others in the workplace. People thrive in community and function best when they share praise, comfort, happiness, and humor with people they like and respect. Unfortunately, some jobs isolate people from each other, or make social contact impersonal. However, what is most destructive of community is chronic and unresolved conflict with others on the job. Such conflict produces constant negative feelings of frustration and hostility, and reduces the likelihood of social support.

Community is evident in social support that can take many forms at work. Generally, support from colleagues is more strongly related with effectiveness, whereas support from supervisors, especially instrumental support that assists people in managing their workload, is more closely associated with lower levels of exhaustion. Regardless of its specific form, social support has been found to be associated with greater engagement (Leiter & Maslach, 1988).

Fairness. A serious mismatch between the person and the job occurs when there is not perceived fairness in the workplace. Fairness communicates respect and confirms people's self-worth. Mutual respect between people is central to a shared sense of community. Unfairness can occur when there is inequity of workload or pay, or when there is cheating, or when evaluations and promotions are handled inappropriately. If procedures for grievance or dispute resolution do not allow for both parties to have voice, then those will be judged as unfair.

A lack of fairness undermines a person's engagement with work and exacerbates burnout in at least two ways. First, the experience of unfair treatment is exhausting. People react with anger, hurt, or anxiety when they are unfairly treated. They obsess on the offensive situation, trying to discover ways of influencing events or forcing another outcome. The personal antagonism toward those who treated one unfairly keeps the emotional upset alive. It can lead to sleep disturbance with the consequential fatigue. Complaining about unfair treatment is emotionally draining, time consuming, and rarely leads to meaningful action. Second, unfair decisions indicate a weak organizational culture in which the personal biases or ambitions of people with authority dominate the allocation of resources and the access to opportunities. It is a sign that neither the espoused values of a well-crafted mission statement nor the personal values of committed staff members drive organizational life.

Fairness in personal contacts with people at work and with the formal decision making and evaluation processes of an organization are critical to maintaining engagement with work. Fairness indicates that individuals and the organization have a common perspective on the work of the organization and the contribution of employees to its mission. Fairness builds the trust that is necessary to support productive involvement with work.

Values. The sixth area of job–person misfit occurs when there is a mismatch between the requirements of the job and people's personal principles. In some cases, people might feel constrained by the job to do things that are unethical and not in accord with their own values. For example, they might have to tell a lie or be otherwise deceptive or not forthcoming with the truth. In other instances, people may be caught between conflicting values of the organization, as when there is a discrepancy between the lofty mission statement and actual practice.

People become vulnerable to burnout when they experience incongruity between personal and organizational values (Leiter & Harvie, 1997). Sometimes these crises are the result of people realizing that they entered an occupation with mistaken expectations. Often, human service professionals encounter a collapse of the professional mystique in their first job (Cherniss, 1980; Leiter, 1991). They find that the autonomy, power, and satisfaction they anticipated from their careers on the basis of media images or idealistic professional training are unfounded. They encounter public social service organizations whose values are based more on institutional survival or social control than on a sense of community. The resulting value crisis often contributes to burnout.

Changes in the political and economic environments of social institutions in postindustrial societies have increased the frequency and intensity of burnout for people who are established in their careers (Leiter, 1999). In these transitions, the organizational values change abruptly while individuals remain committed to personal values of customer service that were previously supported by the organization. Often, the changes begin with mismatches in one of the other areas of organizational life, but their impact on burnout is most intense when these mismatches lead to value conflict.

Congruency between individual and organizational values build engagement by justifying the energy people put into highly demanding jobs, encouraging involvement, and building effectiveness. Contributing to a meaningful personal goal is a powerful incentive for individuals. When this work contributes as well to the organizational mission, people may be rewarded with additional opportunities for meaningful work. As such, value congruence produces a self-perpetuating dynamic that supports engagement with work.

An Interactive Approach. Problems in one of these six areas of organizational life tend to be associated with problems in other areas. For example, excessive workload often indicates problems in control and autonomy, because much of what people identify as excessive work demands are externally imposed tasks. Professors in research universities rarely complain about the long hours they choose to spend in their research labs, but often grumble about their assigned teaching responsibilities. Similarly, surgeons will freely choose to spend long days in the operating room, but complain bitterly about any new forms or reporting procedure imposed by the hospital.

The areas of community, fairness, and reward all encompass personal relationships among people to some degree. An organization that has a strong and vibrant sense of community is likely to provide recognition for employees' contributions to its success and to treat people fairly as well as with respect. Although it is productive to examine each of these three areas in terms of their unique focus on personal relationships, they are not entirely independent of one another. Currently, it is unclear if some job–person mismatches are more important than others, or if there is some minimum number that will be more likely to produce burnout, and future research will need to address these and related issues.

To varying degrees, values mediate the relations of the other five mismatches with burnout. At times, some mismatches may have direct implications for an employee's experience of one or more of the three dimensions of burnout. For example, as mentioned earlier, workload can be a direct predictor of exhaustion. In addition to their direct relations with energy, involvement, and effectiveness, the impact of the mismatches is often a function of value conflict. To focus on one potential mismatch, conflicts over control at work often occur when organizations put limits on the professional autonomy of staff members, as when teachers become frustrated with administrative policies that limit their approach to curriculum. These constraints have a much stronger personal impact if they conflict with the teachers' deeply held values about their professional role. For example, a teacher who valued arts education would be more strongly at odds with a back-to-basics policy than would a teacher who valued solid math and literacy skills primarily. Both teachers would be working within a system that constrained their professional autonomy, but only the first teacher would be experiencing value incongruity with the organization. This teacher would be much more susceptible to experiencing burnout.

The mismatches in these six critical areas of organizational life are not simply a list summarizing research findings from burnout studies. Rather, they provide a conceptual framework for the crises that disrupt the relations people develop with their work. This approach emphasizes the social quality of burnout—it has more to do with the organizational context of the job than with simply the unique characteristics of an individual.

ORGANIZATIONAL HEALTH

Burnout provides a perspective on individual mental health that reflects the health of the organizations in which people work. From this perspective, health is not limited to the physical or emotional well-being of individuals, but is evident in enduring patterns of social interactions among people. This is similar to the position of family therapists that it is often more productive to recast difficulties in a troubled family as a breakdown of a social system rather than as the problems of an individual whom the family has identified as the patient. A family problem is one for which each member shares a responsibility. They regain health when all members of the family change the way in which they interact with one another. In an organizational setting, some problems, such as burnout, are better cast as difficulties of the social context of work than as failings of individual employees.

Organizational health is evident throughout the social context in which people work. As with individuals, organizational health requires a reasonable balance of demands with appropriate coping resources. Periods of extreme demand that prompt an organization to work at peak levels are balanced with periods of rest and recuperation within an ongoing context of a readily manageable pace of activity. When this balance is exceeded for a prolonged period, members of the organization experience the strain on the organizational system: A stressed organization creates strain for its members. This resolution is contrary to the long-term viability and productivity of the organization in a manner similar to a breakdown of an individual's health: The whole individual suffers when any bodily system is under excessive strain. In contrast, engagement with work is associated with a sense of well-being for both individuals and organizations.

Social Versus Individual Perspectives on Burnout

Viewing burnout as a function of the social environment raises the question of individual variation within it. If the impact of the environment is so critical, should not everyone (or no one) in a particular social setting be experiencing burnout? The wide range of burnout responses in any large organization often prompts observers to explain burnout in terms of personal failings, faulty self-concepts, or personality attributes. However, there are other explanations for this variation. First, not everyone experiences the same social environment. Burnout varies according to people's occupational role or their status in an organization. Nurses report consistently higher exhaustion than physicians, although both work very hard in a hospital setting. Managers report a stronger sense of professional efficacy than frontline workers, even though the accomplishments of managerial life are often elusive (Leiter & Harvie, 1998).

Second, people have different values. They bring some of these differences to work with them in the first place. Other differences arise from the unique experiences people have at work or in their personal life. For example, caring for an elderly parent or a chronically ill child may have a profound impact on an individual's values concerning health care, despite many common experiences with colleagues at work. These are important variations in values and experience that could readily affect individuals' experience of burnout without necessarily implying anything about their personality.

Most of the recommended strategies to alleviate burnout have been individual ones—which is particularly paradoxical given that (as mentioned earlier) research has found that situational and organizational factors play a far bigger role in burnout than individual variables (Maslach & Goldberg, 1998). Moreover, there is not much persuasive evidence that these types of self-help, personal stress management techniques are effective—especially in the workplace, where people have much less control of stressors than in other domains of their life. Contrary to this individualistic perspective, any progress in dealing with burnout will depend on the development of strategies that focus on the job context and its impact on the people who work within it.

The close ties of burnout to its social environment point toward organizational interventions. Individually oriented approaches (developing effective coping skills or learning deep relaxation) may help individuals to alleviate exhaustion, but they do not really deal with the other two components of burnout. The use of the complete multidimensional model of burnout focuses attention on the relation between the person and the job situation, rather than either one or the other in isolation. This seems to be a more promising approach for dealing with individual burnout in its situational context. Moreover, a focus on what would promote engagement in the workplace could be a better framework for developing effective interventions than a focus simply on what would reduce stress. The former is more likely to change the job situation, and the latter leads to strategies of changing the person (Maslach & Goldberg, 1998).

Furthermore, the recognition of six areas of job–person mismatch expands the range of options for intervention. For example, rather than concentrating on the area of work overload for an intervention (such as teaching people how to cope with overload, or how to cut back on work, or how to relax), a focus on some of the other mismatches may be more effective. People may be able to tolerate greater workload if they value the work and feel they are doing something important, or if they feel well-rewarded for their efforts, and so an intervention could target these areas of value and reward.

Organizational Interventions

Organizational interventions rooted in ongoing management practices are the most effective and enduring route to alleviating or preventing burnout. They have three critical advantages over individual treatment that people may seek, either on their own initiative or through some sort of employee assistance program. First, organizational interventions have a wider scope. They improve the quality of the work environment for a large number of people, in contrast with the individual focus of most therapy programs. Second, organizational interventions are not solely oriented toward eliminating a problem; they are directed toward improving the effectiveness of the work setting. This quality of organizational interventions increases their duration because they are not an ongoing cost for an organization, but a means of furthering organizational goals of service provision or productivity. Third, organizational interventions focus directly on the work environment rather than implicitly blaming the victims for experiencing problems. That is, they approach burnout as a management problem, not as an individual failing. This perspective shifts responsibility for action to a more powerful sector with greater resources for effecting change in organizational life.

An organizational approach to burnout (Maslach & Leiter, 1997) is much more demanding than individual treatment. For one, many more people must reach agreement on the nature of the problem and the urgency in addressing it than is the case with individual treatment. Often important stakeholders in an organization are committed to opposing perspectives on a problem and its solution, as is evident in many conflicts between management and unions or among professional groups. Second, the information required for cooperative action is not readily available. The staff survey process that assesses burnout, engagement with work, and the six areas of organizational life demands considerable time, collaboration, and sophisticated analysis (see Maslach & Leiter, 1997, for a more extensive discussion of this process).

Designing and implementing interventions that have a lasting impact on burnout and its consequences for health are a major challenge in large organizations. The six mismatch framework indicates the range of organizational problems related to burnout. The web of relationships among these six areas of organizational life captures the complexity inherent in an organization. The capacity to make effective interventions will grow with increased knowledge about organizational dynamics and their impact on the thoughts and feelings of the people who make up large organizations.

CONCLUSIONS

Burnout is a syndrome of exhaustion, depersonalization, and reduced personal accomplishment in contrast to engagement with work that is characterized by energy, involvement, and effectiveness. Although the sources and immediate consequences of burnout lie within the work environment, burnout compromises the physical health and psychological well-being of people at work and at home. Alleviating and preventing burnout requires an understanding of six critical areas of work environments: workload, control, reward, community, fairness, and values. These six areas of organizational life have a variety of consequences for the way people feel about their work. This interactive view of burnout provides a rich and dynamic approach to understanding the impact of a critical life arena—the work environment—on health.

REFERENCES

Bhagat, R. S., Allie, S. M., & Ford, Jr., D. L. (1995). Coping with stressful life events: An empirical analysis. In R. Crandall & P. L. Perrewe (Eds.), *Occupational stress: A handbook* (pp. 93–112). Washington, DC: Taylor & Francis.

Bibeau, G., Dussault, G., Larouche, L. M., Lippel, K., Saucier, J. F., Vezina, M., & Vidal, J. M. (1989). *Certains aspects culturels, diagnostiques et juridiques de burnout* [Some cultural diagnostic and juridical aspects of burnout]. Montreal: Confederation des Syndicats Nationaux.

Brill, P. L. (1984). The need for an operational definition of burnout. *Family & Community Health, 6,* 12–24.

Burke, R. J. (1987). Burnout in police work: An examination of the Cherniss model. *Group and Organization Studies, 12*(2), 174–188.

Burke, R. J., & Deszca, E. (1986). Correlates of psychological burnout phases among police officers. *Human Relations, 39,* 487–502.

Byrne, B. M. (1994). Burnout: Testing for the validity, replication, and invariance of causal structure across elementary, intermediate, and secondary teachers. *American Educational Research Journal, 31,* 645–673.

Cherniss, C. (1980). *Professional burnout in human service organizations.* New York: Praeger.

Cordes, C. L., & Dougherty, T. W. (1993) A review and an integration of research on job burnout. *Academy of Management Review, 18,* 621–656.

Corrigan, P. W., Holmes, P. E., Luchins, D., Buican, B., Basit, A., & Parks, J. J. (1994). Staff burnout in a psychiatric hospital: A cross-lagged panel design. *Journal of Organizational Behavior, 15,* 65–74.

Freudenberger, H. J. (1983). Burnout: Contemporary issues, trends, and concerns. In B. A. Farber (Ed.), *Stress and burnout in the human service professions* (pp. 23–28). New York: Pergamon.

Golembiewski, R. T., & Munzenrider, R. (1988). *Phases of burnout: Developments in concepts and applications.* New York: Praeger.

Golembiewski, R. T., & Munzenrider, R. (1991). Burnout and mental health: A pilot study. *Organization Development Journal, 9,* 51–57.

Gryskiewicz, N., & Buttner, E. H. (1992). Testing the robustness of the progressive phase burnout model for a sample of entrepreneurs. *Educational and Psychological Measures, 52,* 747–751.

Hackman, J. R. (1986). The psychology of self-management in organizations. In M. S. Pallak & R. Perloff (Eds.), *Psychology and work: Productivity, change, and employment* (pp. 123–151). Washington, DC: American Psychological Association.

Hendrix, W. H., Summers, T. P., Leap, T. L., & Steel, R. P. (1995). Antecedents and organizational effectiveness outcomes of employee stress and health. In R. Crandall & P. L. Perrewe (Eds.), *Occupational stress: A handbook* (pp. 73–92). Washington, DC: Taylor & Francis.

Ilgen, D. R. (1990). Health issues at work. *American Psychologist, 45,* 273–283.

Jackson, S. E., & Maslach, C. (1982). After-effects of job-related stress: Families as victims. *Journal of Occupational Behaviour, 3,* 63–77.

Jenkins, S. R., & Maslach, C. (1994). Psychological health and involvement in interpersonally demanding occupations: A longitudinal perspective. *Journal of Organizational Behavior, 15,* 101–127.

Kahill, S. (1988). Symptoms of professional burnout: A review of the empirical evidence. *Canadian Psychology, 29,* 284–297.

Kahn, R. L., & Byosiere, P. (1992). Stress in organizations. In M. D. Dunnette & L. M. Hough (Eds), *Handbook of industrial and organizational psychology* (Vol. 3, pp. 571–650). Palo Alto, CA: Consulting Psychologists Press.

Landsbergis, P. A. (1988). Occupational stress among health care workers: A test of the job demands-control model. *Journal of Organizational Behavior, 9*(3), 217–239.

Lee, R. T., & Ashforth, B. E. (1993). A longitudinal study of burnout among supervisors and managers: Comparisons between the Leiter and Maslach (1988) and Golembiewski et al. (1986) models. *Organizational Behavior and Human Decision Processes, 54,* 369–398.

Lee, R. T., & Ashforth, B. E. (1996). A meta-analytic examination of the correlates of the three dimensions of job burnout. *Journal of Applied Psychology, 81,* 123–133.

Leiter, M. P. (1991). The dream denied: Professional burnout and the constraints of service organizations. *Canadian Psychology, 32,* 547–558.

Leiter, M. P. (1992). Burnout as a crisis in professional role structures: Measurement and conceptual issues. *Anxiety, Stress, & Coping, 5,* 79–93.

Leiter, M. P. (1993). Burnout as a developmental process: Consideration of models. In W. B. Schaufeli, C. Maslach, & T. Marek (Eds.), *Professional burnout: Recent developments in theory and research* (pp. 237–250). Washington, DC: Taylor & Francis.

Leiter, M. P. (1999). Burnout among teachers as a crisis in psychological contracts. In R. Vandenberghe & M. Huberman (Eds.), *Understanding and preventing teacher burnout: A sourcebook of international research and practice* (pp. 202–210). Cambridge, England: Cambridge University Press.

Leiter, M. P., Clark, D., & Durup, J. (1994). Distinct models of burnout and commitment among men and women in the military. *Journal of Applied Behavioral Science, 30,* 63–82.

Leiter, M. P., & Durup, J. (1994). The discriminant validity of burnout and depression: A confirmatory factor analytic study. *Anxiety, Stress, & Coping, 7,* 357–373.

Leiter, M. P., & Harvie, P. (1996). The correspondence of supervisor and subordinate perspectives on major organizational change. *Journal of Occupational Health Psychology, 2*(4), 1–10.

Leiter, M. P., & Harvie, P. (1997). Burnout among mental health workers: A review and a research agenda. *International Journal of Social Psychiatry, 42,* 90–101.

Leiter, M. P., & Harvie, P. (1998). Conditions for staff acceptance of organizational change: Burnout as a mediating construct. *Anxiety, Stress, & Coping, 11,* 1–25.

Leiter, M. P., & Maslach, C. (1988). The impact of interpersonal environment on burnout and organizational commitment. *Journal of Organizational Behavior, 9,* 297–308.

Leiter, M. P., & Maslach, C. (1998). Burnout. In H. Friedman (Ed.), *Encyclopedia of Mental Health* (pp. 347–357). San Diego, CA: Academic Press.

Leiter, M. P., & Schaufeli, W. B. (1996). Consistency of the burnout construct across occupations. *Anxiety, Stress, & Coping, 9,* 229–243.

Lief, H. I., & Fox, R. C. (1963). Training for "detached concern" in medical students. In H. I. Lief, V. F. Lief, & N. R. Lief (Eds.), *The psychological basis of medical practice* (pp. 12–35). New York: Harper & Row.

Maslach, C. (1979). The burnout syndrome and patient care. In C. A. Garfield (Ed.), *Stress and survival: The emotional realities of life-threatening illness* (pp. 111–120). St. Louis: Mosby.

Maslach, C. (1982). *Burnout: The cost of caring.* Englewood Cliffs, NJ: Prentice-Hall.

Maslach, C. (1993). Burnout: A multidimensional perspective. In W. B. Schaufeli, C. Maslach, & T. Marek (Eds.), *Professional burnout: Recent developments in theory and research* (pp. 19–32). Washington, DC: Taylor & Francis.

Maslach, C. (1997). Burnout in health professionals. In A. Baum, S. Newman, J. Weinman, R. West, & C. McManus (Eds.), *Cambridge handbook of psychology, health, and medicine* (pp. 275–278). Cambridge, England: Cambridge University Press.

Maslach, C., & Goldberg, J. (1998). Prevention of burnout: New perspectives. *Applied and Preventive Psychology, 7,* 63–74.

Maslach, C., & Jackson, S. E. (1981). *The Maslach Burnout Inventory* (research ed.). Palo Alto, CA: Consulting Psychologists Press.

Maslach, C., & Jackson, S. E. (1982). Burnout in health professions: A social psychological analysis. In G. Sanders & J. Suls (Eds.), *Social psychology of health and illness* (pp. 227–251). Hillsdale, NJ: Lawrence Erlbaum Associates.

Maslach, C., & Jackson, S. E. (1986). *The Maslach Burnout Inventory* (2nd ed.). Palo Alto, CA: Consulting Psychologists Press.

Maslach, C., Jackson, S. E., & Leiter, M. P. (1996). *The Maslach Burnout Inventory* (3rd ed.). Palo Alto, CA: Consulting Psychologists Press.

Maslach, C., & Leiter, M. P. (1997). *The truth about burnout.* San Francisco, CA: Jossey-Bass.

Maslach, C., & Ozer, E. (1995). Theoretical issues related to burnout in health workers. In L. Bennett, D. Miller, & M. Ross (Eds.), *Health workers and AIDS: Research, intervention and current issues in burnout and response* (pp. 1–14). London: Harwood Academic.

Maslach, C., & Schaufeli, W. B. (1993). Historical and conceptual development of burnout. In W. B. Schaufeli, C. Maslach, & T. Marek (Eds.), *Professional burnout: Recent developments in theory and research* (pp. 1–16). Washington, DC: Taylor & Francis.

Maslach, C., Zedeck, S., Skitka, L. J., & Mosier, K. (1997, April). *Health outcomes of job burnout.* Paper presented at the 18th Annual Scientific Sessions of the Society of Behavioral Medicine, San Francisco.

Ogus, E. D. (1995). Burnout and coping strategies: A comparative study of ward nurses. In R. Crandall & P. L. Perrewe (Eds.), *Occupational stress: A handbook* (pp. 249–261). Washington, DC: Taylor & Francis.

Pick, D., & Leiter, M. P. (1991). Nurses' perceptions of the nature and causes of burnout: A comparison of self-reports and standardized measures. *Canadian Journal of Nursing Research, 23*(3), 33–48.

Richardsen, A. M., Burke, R. J., & Leiter, M. P. (1992). Occupational demands, psychological burnout, and anxiety among hospital personnel in Norway. *Anxiety, Stress, & Coping, 5,* 62–78.

Sauter, S. L., & Murphy, L. R. (Eds.). (1995). *Organizational risk factors for job stress.* Washington, DC: American Psychological Association.

Sauter, S. L., Murphy, L. R., & Hurrell, J. J., Jr. (1990). Prevention of work-related psychological disorders: A national strategy proposed by the National Institute for Occupational Safety and Health (NIOSH). *American Psychologist, 45,* 1146–1158.

Schaufeli, W. B., Maslach, C., & Marek, T. (Eds.). (1993). *Professional burnout: Recent developments in theory and research.* Washington, DC: Taylor & Francis.

Selye, H. (1967). *Stress in health and disease.* Boston: Butterworth.

Shinn, M., Rosario, M., Morch, H., & Chestnut, D. E. (1984). Coping with job stress and burnout in the human services. *Journal of Personality and Social Psychology, 46,* 864–876.

Shirom, A. (1989). Burnout in work organizations. In C. L. Cooper & I. Robertson (Eds.), *International review of industrial and organizational psychology* (pp. 25–48). New York: Wiley.

Van Yperen, N. W., Buunk, B. P., & Schaufeli, W. B. (1992). Communal orientation and the burnout syndrome among nurses. *Journal of Applied Social Psychology, 22*(4), 173–189.

Warr, P. B. (1987). *Work, unemployment and mental health.* Oxford, England: Clarendon.

Zedeck, S., Maslach, C., Mosier, K., & Skitka, L. (1988). Affective response to work and quality of family life: Employee and spouse perspectives. *Journal of Social Behavior & Personality, 3,* 135–157.

24

Sociocultural Influences on Health

Caroline A. Macera
Centers for Disease Control and Prevention

Cheryl A. Armstead
University of South Carolina

Norman B. Anderson
National Institutes of Health

The health experience of Americans has improved enormously over the course of the 20th century. Communicable and infectious diseases, the major causes of premature death in the United States prior to 1930, have been replaced by chronic illnesses such as heart disease and cancer. Furthermore, age-adjusted mortality from heart disease has decreased from 307.2 per 100,000 in 1950 to 138.3 per 100,000 in 1995. Similarly, infant mortality has decreased from 12.6 per 1,000 live births in 1980 to 7.6 per 1,000 live births in 1995. These changes mean that a majority of people in this country can expect to live a long and productive life. In fact, a child born in 1995 could expect to live 75.8 years compared to 47.3 years for a child born in 1900 (National Center for Health Statistics, 1997).

Unfortunately, these astounding improvements in health status have not affected all Americans equally. Lagging behind are many of the underserved and minority populations (Kington & Smith, 1997; Liao & Cooper, 1995). The ethnic composition of the U.S. population has changed from being primarily White to include a large percentage of African Americans (or Blacks), Hispanics, and Asian and Pacific Islanders. This cultural diversity will continue to increase because of high immigration and birth rates among minority populations. Each ethnic group views health within its own cultural context, which complicates the decision to seek and continue treatment, and to use preventive measures. Additionally, social conditions may put minorities at higher risk for specific health problems. The purpose of this chapter is to first present basic demographic and health characteristics of the major ethnic groups in this country, and then to describe a contextual model of hypertension in Blacks as an example of how ethnic disparities in health status may occur and be understood.

DISTRIBUTION OF ETHNIC MINORITIES

Although there is a great deal of diversity within ethnic groups, this chapter uses the five general categories as collected and reported by the National Center for Health Statistics (1997): White, Black, American Indian or Native Alaskan, Asian and Pacific Islander, and Hispanic origin. When possible, data is presented by non-Hispanic White and non-Hispanic Black groups. Because there is no consistent agreement on terminology, this chapter uses African American and Black interchangeably throughout.

African Americans, or Blacks, the largest minority group in the United States, number almost 34 million and represent 12.8% of the population (U.S. Bureau of the Census, 1995). During 1994, the African American population grew at a faster rate than the White population (1.5% compared to only 0.8%), but not as fast as the Hispanic population (3.5%). Blacks are projected to be the second largest minority group in this country by 2025 (Fig. 24.1).

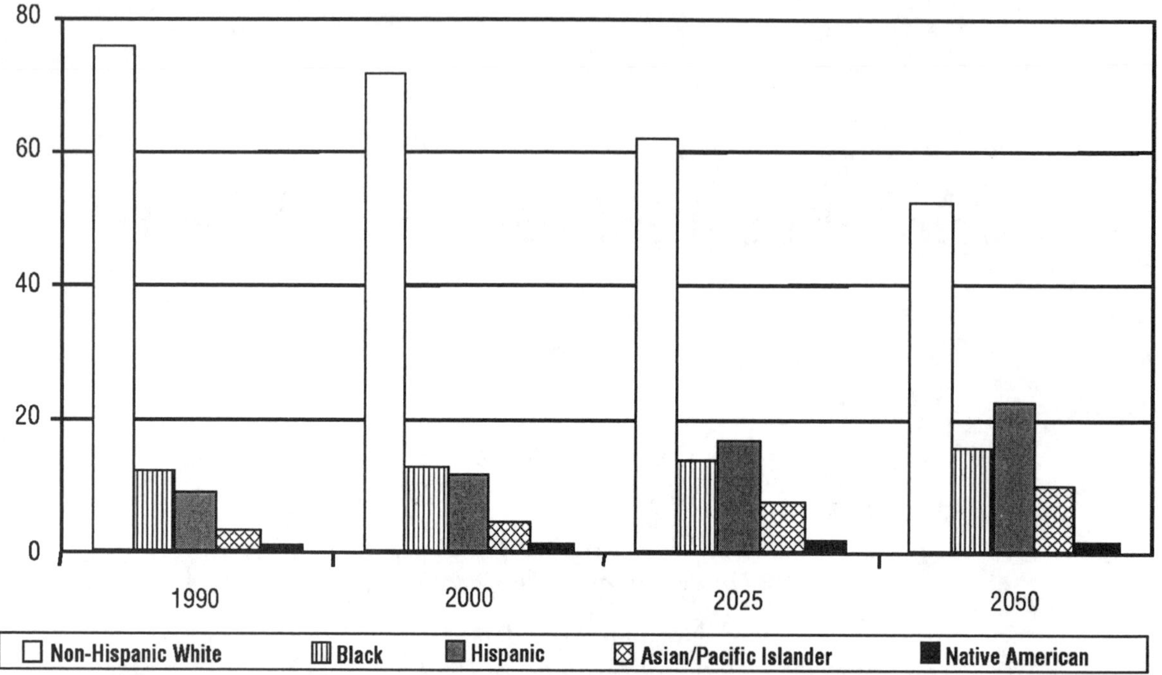

FIG. 24.1

The term *Hispanic* is used to summarize information about people of all races whose ancestry can be traced to Spain, Mexico, Puerto Rico, Cuba, or to any of the Spanish-speaking Latin American countries. The 1990 census enumerated 29.2 million Hispanics classified as Mexican Americans, Puerto Ricans, Cuban Americans, and about 30 additional Hispanic-origin groups aggregated as Other Hispanics (U.S. Bureau of the Census, 1995). Hispanics in the United States represent about 10.9% of the population and are the nation's second largest minority group. However, because of high immigration and birth rates, Hispanics are expected to replace African Americans as the largest ethnic minority group in the United States by 2025.

Asians and Pacific Islanders in the United States number about 10 million (representing 3.7% of the population), and speak more than 30 major languages or dialects (U.S. Bureau of the Census, 1995). The major groups in this category include Chinese, Filipinos, Japanese, Koreans, and Native Hawaiians. Furthermore, about two thirds of the persons in this population group speak their native language at home, and more than 60% of Southeast Asians (Vietnamese, Cambodian, Hmong, and Laotian) have limited proficiency in English. Although a small proportion of the U.S. population, this diverse minority group is expected to increase to more than five times its current size and represent 10.3% of the population by 2050 (U.S. Bureau of the Census, 1995).

Native Americans in the United States number about 2.3 million, just less than 1% of the population. Although this group is expected to grow steadily over the next 50 years, the percent of the population that is American Indian or Alaskan Native would only rise to 1.1% by 2050, remaining the smallest minority group in the United States (U.S. Bureau of the Census, 1995).

LIFE EXPECTANCY

One measure of the health of a population is its life expectancy, a value that heavily weights early mortality, but does not incorporate quality of life issues. Throughout the 20th century, African Americans experienced substantial improvements in life expectancy, but they still have an estimated life span of 6 to 8 years less than Whites (Table 24.1). For both Whites and African Americans, women live longer than men, resulting in a higher proportion of women alive, especially in the older age groups. The life expectancy at birth for African American men increased 2.2% (or 1.4 years) from 1980 to 1995 compared to a 3.8% (or 2.7 years) increase for White men. The increase in life expectancy for African American women during this same period was identical to that for White women, 1.9% (about 1.5 years; National Center for Health Statistics, 1997).

Although comparable national data are not available for the other ethnic groups, information on residents of Texas suggests that life expectancy at birth for Hispanics is the same as non-Hispanic Whites and higher than non-Hispanic Blacks (Centers for Disease Control and Prevention, 1994; Markides, 1989). Similarly, area-specific studies have found life expectancy for Asian and Pacific Islanders in the United States to be higher than that of Whites. However, data on life expectancy for Asians may be particularly subject to

TABLE 24.1
Life Expectancy at Birth in Years (1980 and 1995)

	White		African American	
Year	Men	Women	Men	Women
1980	70.7	78.1	63.8	72.5
1995	73.4	79.6	65.2	73.9
% change	+3.8	+1.9	+2.2	+1.9

Note: From National Center for Health Statistics (1997).

misclassification and underestimates of the number of deaths within ethnic groups (Gardner, 1994; Hahn, Truman, & Barker, 1996).

Life expectancy for Native Americans is lower than for Whites primarily because of the high death rate for persons under age 45. This higher rate is due to excess mortality from intentional and unintentional injuries rather than from chronic diseases. The death rates for Native Americans are based on death certificate identification of the decedent as a member of this minority group. Unfortunately, it has been demonstrated that many Native Americans have been classified as White on death certificates (Classification of American Indian race on birth and death certificates, 1993; Frost, Taylor, & Fries, 1992; Hahn et al., 1996; Sugarman & Lawson, 1993), thereby artificially reducing the death rate for persons in this group.

MAJOR CAUSES OF DEATH

As shown in Table 24.2, the highest death rate in 1995 is found for Black men (1,016.7 per 100,000). Although most men and women in all ethnic groups experienced a decline in overall mortality rate from 1985 to 1995, the largest decline was among White men (9.6%). Ethnic differences are apparent for mortality, but also for other health indicators such as preventable hospitalizations (Pappas, Hadden, Kozak, & Fisher, 1997).

By examining the top five causes of death (Table 24.3), it is clear that all ethnic groups share some common characteristics in spite of the differences in mortality rates. Among the leading causes of death for both men and women in most ethnic groups are diseases of the heart and cerebrovascular disease (stroke). A major chronic condition associated with these conditions is hypertension. After heart disease and stroke, the major contributors to the high mortality rate among Black men are HIV infection, violence, and unintentional injuries.

HEALTH STATUS

Unlike identifying the major causes of death, measuring good health is a complicated task. Often health status is simply defined as the absence of disease, even though a complex of physical, social, cognitive, and psychological factors are involved in determining overall health. This chapter uses high blood pressure, or hypertension, as a marker for health status because of its association with the major causes of death and disability for all ethnic groups. Hypertension is usually defined as having a systolic pressure of at least 140 mm Hg or a diastolic pressure of at least 90 mm Hg, or taking antihypertensive medication. About half the people who have hypertension are undiagnosed. Furthermore, only about one fourth of those who know they have the disease have it adequately controlled through lifestyle modification or medication (Havas et al., 1996). Uncontrolled hypertension increases the risk of circulatory diseases (particularly heart disease and stroke), and kidney disease (Burt et al., 1995).

Because it is an important marker of health, questions about hypertension are routinely included in national surveys, thus providing comparable estimates of the prevalence of hypertension for White, African American, and Mexican American subgroups. As shown in Fig. 24.2 and Table 24.4, African Americans have the highest prevalence of hypertension, almost 1.5 times that of Whites, whereas Mexican Americans have an intermediary prevalence (Burt et al., 1995; National Center for Health Statistics, 1997). The percentage of the population with hypertension has decreased between 1976 and 1980 and 1988 and 1994 for Whites and African Americans, but has remained constant for Mexican Americans: The decrease was over 40% among Whites, but less than 30% among Blacks. Consequently, Blacks will continue to experience disproportionately higher rates of morbidity and mortality from heart disease, stroke, and renal disease compared to the other ethnic groups.

TABLE 24.2
Age-Adjusted Mortality Rates Per 100,000 Population (1985 and 1995)

	White		African American		Hispanic		Asian and Pacific Islander		American Indian or Native Alaskan	
	Men	Women	Men	Women	Men	Women	Men	Women	Men	Women
1985	669.7	385.3	1,053.4	594.8	524.8	286.6	396.9	228.5	602.6	353.3
1995	605.7	366.4	1,016.7	571.0	515.0	274.4	384.4	231.4	580.4	368.0
% change	−9.6	−4.9	−3.5	−4.0	−1.9	−4.3	−3.2	+1.3	−3.7	+4.2

Note: From National Center for Health Statistics (1997).

TABLE 24.3
Five Leading Causes of Death in 1995

	White	African-American	Hispanic	Asian and Pacific Islander	American Indian or Native Alaskan
Men	1. Diseases of the heart	1. Diseases of the heart	1. Diseases of the heart	1. Diseases of the heart	1. Diseases of the heart
	2. Malignant neoplasms	2. Malignant neoplasms	2. Malignant neoplasms	2. Malignant neoplasms	2. Unintentional injuries
	3. Cerebrovascular diseases	3. HIV infection	3. Unintentional injuries	3. Cerebrovascular diseases	3. Malignant neoplasms
	4. Unintentional injuries	4. Homicide	4. HIV infection	4. Unintentional injury	4. Chronic liver diseases
	5. Chronic Obstructive Pulmonary Diseases	5. Unintentional injuries	5. Homicide	5. Pneumonia and influenza	5. Suicide
Women	1. Diseases of the heart	1. Diseases of the heart	1. Diseases of the heart	1. Malignant neoplasms	1. Diseases of the heart
	2. Malignant neoplasms	2. Malignant neoplasms	2. Malignant neoplasms	2. Diseases of the heart	2. Malignant neoplasms
	3. Cerebrovascular diseases	3. Cerebrovascular diseases	3. Cerebrovascular diseases	3. Cerebrovascular diseases	3. Unintentional injuries
	4. Chronic Obstructive Pulmonary Diseases	4. Diabetes mellitus	4. Diabetes mellitus	4. Unintentional injuries	4. Diabetes mellitus
	5. Pneumonia and influenza	5. HIV infection	5. Unintentional injuries	5. Pneumonia and influenza	5. Cerebrovascular diseases

Note: From National Center for Health Statistics (1997).

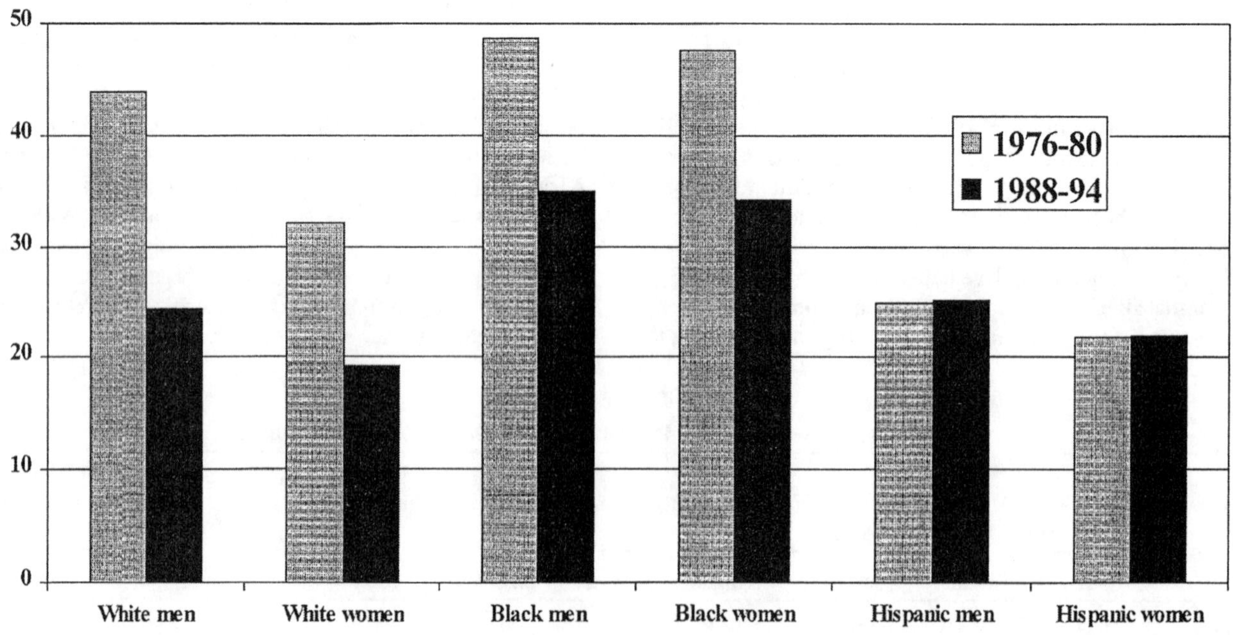

FIG. 24.2. Percent of population with hypertension among persons from age 20 to 74, in the United States from 1976 to 1980 and 1988 to 1994. (Hypertension is defined as either systolic pressure of at least 140 mm Hg or diastolic pressure of at least 90 mm Hg, or taking antihypertensive medication.) From National Center for Health Statistics (1997).

TABLE 24.4
Percent of Population with Hypertension Among Persons from Age 20 to 74 (1976–1980 and 1988–1994)

	White		African American		Mexican American	
Year	Men	Women	Men	Women	Men	Women
1976–1980	43.9	32.1	48.7	47.6	25.0	21.8
1988–1994	24.4	19.3	35.0	34.2	25.2	22.0
% change	–44.4	–39.9	–28.1	–28.2	+0.8	+0.8

Note: A person with hypertension is defined by either having elevated blood pressure (systolic pressure of at least 140 mmHg or diastolic pressure of at least 90 mmHg) or taking antihypertensive medication. From National Center for Health Statistics (1997).

For less than 10% of those with hypertension, there is a definite cause. However, for over 90% of people with hypertension, the cause is unknown and it is termed *essential* hypertension (Frohlich, 1994). Hypertension occurs more frequently among Blacks, older individuals, less educated individuals, those who are obese or have gained weight, those who are physically inactive, and those who use alcohol excessively. Additionally, some individuals with augmented sodium metabolism may develop hypertension (Frohlich, 1994). Because none of these risk factors alone explains a majority of the risk for developing hypertension, it is clear that this disease develops from multiple interacting mechanisms rather than from a single source (Calhoun & Oparil, 1995; Flack et al., 1995). Among the contributors to this disorder are genetic, biological, nutritional, behavioral, social, environmental, and psychological factors.

SOCIAL AND CULTURAL FACTORS RELATED TO HEALTH STATUS

Given the changing demographic makeup of the United States, it is necessary to examine subpopulations within the major ethnic groups that may be at high risk for disease. The rest of this chapter focuses on the development and description of a model that may explain how social and cultural influences interact to affect health status, using the example of hypertension in Blacks. Although this model focuses on Black/White differences in hypertension risk, many elements of the model may be generalizable to other ethnic subpopulations and other health problems.

Contextual Model of Hypertension in Blacks

The contextual model of hypertension in Blacks reflects the contribution of sociology, psychology, and the natural sciences in attempting to systematically understand the key determinants of ethnic differences in the development and maintenance of hypertension. The unacceptableness of unidimensional or strictly genetic accounts of the determinants of hypertension in Blacks is exemplified in the Report of the Secretary's Task Force on Blacks and Minority Health (1986):

> Black, in the United States is a sociological category. Some investigators have confused ethnic identity with genetic constitution, simplistically equating them. The heterogeneity of blood pressure levels and hypertension prevalence in Black populations in Africa, the Caribbean, and the Americas casts doubt on the proposition that genetic factors are primarily responsible for the blood pressure excess in U.S. Blacks. ... It becomes clear that any explanation of blood pressure differences between Black populations must take into explicitly account of environmental determinants and influences. (p. 27)

Within the contextual model, hypertension risk factors interact with ethnicity in the context of the environment and culture.

Cardiovascular Reactivity

In recent years, researchers in health psychology and behavioral medicine have explored the role of cardiovascular reactivity as a potential contributor to the high rates of hypertension. *Reactivity* is defined as the magnitude and pattern of acute changes in cardiovascular activity (reactivity) in response to behavioral, social, and environmental stressors. According to Krantz and Manuck (1984), the measurement of reactivity contributes unique information regarding the physiological functioning of the individual beyond that provided by resting or baseline levels alone. The reactivity hypothesis rests on the assumption that acute changes in cardiovascular reactivity to laboratory procedures are analogous to cardiovascular challenges encountered in daily life (Anderson, McNeilly, Armstead, Clark, & Pieper, 1993). Reactivity studies also suggest that exaggerated changes in cardiovascular parameters, which occur when individuals are exposed to behavioral, psychological, or physical challenges precede the development of sustained hypertension (Julius & Schork, 1971). Individuals at risk for hypertension show greater sympathetic nervous system reactivity to stressors. In animal as well as human research, groups at risk for hypertension have shown greater stress reactivity than groups with relatively lower risk. For example, "hyperreactivity" has been observed in Blacks as compared to Whites, in anxious versus nonanxious persons, in anger suppressors versus anger expressors, and in chronically stressed versus nonstressed individuals. Hyperreactivity is thought to be a risk marker for hypertensive risk and may be also directly implicated in the pathogenesis of hypertension.

There have been a substantial number of studies on Black–White differences in autonomic reactivity (Anderson, McNeilly, & Myers, 1992). These studies have been conducted with both children (Dysart, Treiber, Pflieger, Davis, & Strong, 1994; Murphy, Stoney, Alpert, & Walker, 1995) and adults (Anderson, 1989) and have utilized a wide variety of laboratory stressors, experimental designs, physiological measures, and population subgroups. Despite the diversity of approaches used, most studies have demonstrated that Blacks show a greater blood pressure reactivity to laboratory stressors as compared to Whites. Perhaps more important, is that the mechanisms responsible for producing the stress-induced blood pressure response may be different in Blacks than in Whites. Blacks have been found to exhibit greater blood pressure reactivity mediated by peripheral vasoconstriction (characteristic of the vascular pattern of reactivity; Girdler, Hinderliter, & Light, 1993; Terrell & Manuck, 1996), whereas the blood pressure response of Whites has shown a greater cardiac involvement (characteristic of the cardiac pattern of reactivity). These results, particularly the heightened peripheral vasoconstrictive responses in Blacks, have been observed among children, adults, normotensives, and borderline hypertensives. It has been most clearly seen in studies using stressors, such as the forehead cold pressor test, that are specifically designed to produce a predominantly vascular pattern of reactivity among Blacks. The studies have not consistently found greater reactivity in Black adults with a positive family history (Anderson, Lane, Taguchi, & Williams, 1989; Anderson, Lane, Taguchi, Williams, & Houseworth, 1989).

Augmented Reactivity in Blacks

Thus far, research using the reactivity paradigm has been largely concerned with describing racial differences in reactivity. The next logical step is to identify the variables that are predictive of heightened vascular reactivity among Blacks. Anderson et al. (1991) noted that physiological and psychophysiological responses obtained in an experimental laboratory are partly a function of the socioecological niche that the individual occupies at that time.

The principal tenet of the proposed contextual model is that the exaggerated peripheral vascular reactivity observed in many Blacks relative to Whites is a function of a number of biological, psychological, behavioral, environmental, and sociocultural factors. The model begins with the premise that in reactivity research, race should be viewed as a proxy for the effects of differential exposure to chronic social and environmental stressors rather than as a proxy for the effects of genetic differences. Black Americans, on average, are exposed to a wider array of chronic stressors than their White counterparts. These chronic stressors interact with nervous system activity, which in turn leads to the release of neuroendocrine substances, including norepinephrine and adrenocorticotrophin hormone (ACTH), augmented sodium retention, and enhanced vasoconstriction. The resulting higher levels of endogenous sodium and ACTH not only increase blood volume but also act to potentiate the vasoconstrictive effects of norepinephrine on the peripheral vasculature. Over time, the repeated stressor-induced episodes of vascular reactivity may lead to structural changes in the vascular wall (e.g., increased wall-to-lumen ratio), which further augments reactivity. If repeated frequently over a number of years, this process has the potential to lead to the development of sustained hypertension. The remainder of this chapter is devoted to describing each component of this model.

Chronic Stressors and the Social Environment

Many writers view race as a sociological designation that indicates exposure to common life experiences. According to the model presented here, one distinguishing feature of the life experiences between Black and White Americans is exposure to chronic life stressors. As a consequence of historical factors and the continued race consciousness of society, Blacks currently experience a greater array of chronic stressors relative to Whites. These chronic socioecological stressors include, among others, higher unemployment, higher poverty rates and lower income levels, lower status occupations and lower social status, residential crowding, and substandard housing (Bullard, 1994; Farley, 1984; Farley & Allen, 1989; Harris, 1982; McLoyd, 1990). Many of these chronic social and environmental stressors have been associated with hypertensive status among Blacks. For example, socioeconomic status shows a strong inverse relation with hypertension among Blacks (Adams-Campbell, Brambilla, & McKinlay, 1993).

Racial Stress. Racism represents one of the most pernicious forms of chronic psychosocial stress facing African Americans today. A burgeoning body of literature identifies racism as a macrosocial factor contributing to the vast racial disparity of health outcomes found among African Americans and Whites (Jackson et al., 1996; McNeilly et al., 1996). Racial stress has been found to be related to both blood pressure status (Krieger, 1990; Krieger & Sidney, 1996) and cardiovascular reactivity (Armstead, 1991; Armstead, K. A. Lawler, Gorden, Cross, & Gibbons, 1989; Jones, Harrell, Morris-Prather, Thomas, & Omowale, 1996; McNeilly et al., 1995; Morris-Prather et al., 1996).

Historically, African Americans often received severe punitive sanctions for expressing emotions they experienced when exposed to racism. Anger suppression may be a historical coping style that presently serves as a moderator of the interaction between racism and blood pressure status and reactivity. Gentry, Chesney, Gary, Hall, and Harburg (1982) found that males who are high in interracial hostility and who tend to keep anger suppressed have the highest mean diastolic pressure. Krieger (1990) found that Black women who reported usually accepting and keeping quite about racist treatment were 4.4 times more likely to report being hypertensive than were Blacks who talked to others. Among Whites, this relation did not hold true. In another study, Krieger and Sidney (1996) found that hypertension was significantly higher among working-class Blacks reporting that they typically "accepted" unfair treatment and had not experienced racial discrimination in one of seven situations relative to those reporting that they "challenged" unfair treatment and experienced racial discrimination. Among professional Black adults, systolic blood pressure was 9 to 10 mm Hg higher among those reporting a higher frequency of discrimination and those reporting that they "accepted" unfair treatment. Black–White differences in blood pressure were partially explained by incorporating variables for exposure and coping styles utilized with racial discrimination.

Armstead (1991) and Armstead et al. (1989) found that anger suppression was related to increased diastolic reactivity to racist stimuli and to a speech stressor. Vascular activation may be end products of chronic anger suppression as a result of coping with racism. Chronic exposure to racial stress may contribute to concomitant changes in the peripheral vasculature in ways similar to other chronic stressors. Anger kinetics may play a role in catecholamine release and subsequent hemodynamic changes associated with racial laboratory stressors.

Lower Socioeconomic Status. The health history of African Americans in the United States is filled with accounts of pervasive disease morbidity and mortality associated with social stratification (Anderson & Armstead, 1995). In U.S. society, social stratification occurs as a function of ethnicity, gender, or socioeconomic status. The term *socioeconomic status* (SES) is typically used to describe stratified inequality in ranking that exists in society. Educational attainment is also one of the strongest predictors of health outcomes in the United States. Higher educational attainment does not consistently bring comparable health benefits for minorities (Pappas, Queen, Hadden, & Fisher, 1993). For example, Blacks have significantly lower SES than Whites by every measure. What is often not recognized, however, is that at most levels of SES, morbidity and mortality rates are higher for Blacks than for Whites (Lillie-Blanton & Laveist, 1996; Williams, 1996).

At present, it is unclear how SES differentially influences hypertension risk behaviors or blood pressure-related knowledge, attitudes, and beliefs of minorities. Stratification and discrimination may directly and/or indirectly interact with socioeconomic status to create a highly vulnerable underclass of African American citizens with poorer overall health, poorer health behaviors, increased daily life stress, and lack of access to health care (Williams, 1992). Lower SES Blacks may not only receive more exposure to environmental risk factors, psychosocial risk factors, and deficits in medical care, but also may be more vulnerable to them. Dressler (1996) found diastolic blood pressure levels were associated with an interaction between lower socioeconomic status and increased exposure to stressful life events.

In the case of essential hypertension, a consistently strong gradient for SES exists, especially for African Americans. Among both Blacks and Whites, hypertension is higher at the lower end of the SES spectrum, yet the relation clearly reflects an interaction of gender, ethnic, and socioeconomic stratification (Adams-Campbell et al., 1993; Williams, 1992).

If SES is linked to hypertension in a causative way, it should be expected that it is also linked to physiological systems relevant to hypertension. One possible biological mediator of SES effects on hypertension effect is cardiovascular reactivity. Carroll, Davey-Smith, Sheffield, Shipley, and Marmot (1997) examined the relation of SES, hostility, and blood pressure reactions to mental stress in British men. They found that systolic pressure reactivity was positively associated with SES. Higher SES was associated with greater reactivity. Armstead, Anderson, and Lawler (1994) found an interaction between SES and ethnicity for laboratory reactivity to a speech stressor among African American and White women. Lower socioeconomic status Black women demonstrated greater reactivity than White women or higher SES Black women. This indicates that being Black and poor may physiologically predispose individuals to hyperreactivity, which may be a risk marker for essential hypertension.

SES is related to several factors known to enhance reactivity, such as emotional suppression (Armstead et al., 1989; Durel et al., 1989; Johnson, 1989), lower levels of social support (Kamarck, Manuck, & Jennings, 1990), and greater exposure to chronic stress (James & Kleinbaum, 1976). The contextual model of hypertension suggests that lower SES may be an index of exposure to these reactivity-enhancing factors, especially among Blacks, and may serve as a predictor of augmented cardiovascular responsivity in this group. If SES is related to reactivity, then ethnic group differences in SES might partially account for the mixed reactivity results among African Americans and Whites. Calhoun, Mutinga, Wyss, and Oparil (1994) suggest that SES-related stress may cause sympathetic nervous system hyperreactivity by vascular mechanisms.

Socioecological Stressors. Harburg et al. (1973) found that Detroit Blacks residing in neighborhoods high in socioecologic stress, characterized by low SES and high social instability (SIS; defined as high crime and divorce rates), exhibited significantly higher blood pressures than Blacks living in low SES but more stable neighborhoods. Among Whites, socioecologic stress did not influence blood pressure. Similarly, James and Kleinbaum (1976) found that for Black men from age 45 to 54, high stress counties (low SES, high SIS) of North Carolina were associated with significantly higher hypertension-related mortality (e.g., hypertensive heart disease and stroke) than low stress counties. As in Harburg's Detroit studies, no stress–mortality relation was found for White men. In a study of residential crowding, Fleming, Baum, and Weiss (1987) found that individuals living in densely populated neighborhoods had higher blood pressure and greater heart rate reactivity during a challenging behavioral task than those who lived in less crowded neighborhoods.

Family environment is a socioecological stressor that has been found to influence hemodynamic reactivity in children prospectively (Wright et al., 1993). For example, parental reports of greater conflict and control were associated with vascular reactivity among 6- to 8-year-old children at a 2-year follow-up. Thus, not only are Blacks exposed more frequently to chronic stressors, but these socioenvironmental factors may have greater health consequences for Blacks.

Chronic Stress and Vascular Reactivity: Physiologic Mediators

If the differential exposure to chronic stressors is related to acute cardiovascular reactivity as proposed, it should be possible to identify specific physiological mechanisms linking these phenomena in Blacks. It is proposed that exposure to chronic stressors enhances sympathetic nervous system activity that results in augmented sodium retention and catecholamine release. Augmented sodium retention and catecholamine release may, in addition to increasing blood volume, contribute to the greater vascular responses in Blacks.

Sympathetic Nervous System (SNS) Effects. Of critical importance is whether exposure to chronic stress is associated with this hypothesized physiological scenario. In support of this, research from animal and human studies has demonstrated that exposure to acute and chronic uncontrollable stress may augment resting SNS tone; enhance sympathetic reactivity to acute, novel stressors; elevate plasma levels of catecholamines, ACTH, and opioid peptides; and augment sodium retention (Baum, Gatchel, & Schaeffer, 1983; Davidson, Fleming, & Baum, 1987; Fleming, Baum, Davidson, Rectanus, & McArdle, 1987; Koepke & DiBona, 1985; Koepke, Light, & Obrist, 1983; J. E. Lawler, Naylor, & Abel, 1993; Lawler, Zheng, Li, Wang, & Edgemon, 1996; Light, Koepke, Obrist, & Willis, 1983; McCarty, Horwatt, & Konarska, 1988).

Studies of reactivity indicate that norepinephrine elicits elevations in blood pressure through vasoconstrictive effects on the peripheral vasculature (Goldstein, 1983). ACTH has been shown to potentiate norepinephrine's vasoconstrictive effects, particularly in humans and animals with reduced renal excretory capacity (Bassett, Strand, & Cairncross, 1978; Strand & Smith, 1980; Whitworth, Coghlan, Denton, Hardy, & Scoggins, 1979), and to augment norepinephrine-induced contractions of a striated muscle (Bassett et al., 1978; Strand & Smith, 1980). Importantly, ACTH also induces sodium and water retention (Lohmeier & Carroll, 1985).

In a series of studies at the University of North Carolina and the University of Iowa, investigators examined the role of stress and sodium retention in dogs and spontaneously hypertensive rats (Grignolo, Koepke, & Obrist, 1982; Koepke & DiBona, 1985; Koepke et al., 1983; Light, 1987). In these studies, animals who were exposed to chronic stress showed significant reductions in sodium and fluid excretion and an associated rise in blood pressure that was mediated by renal sympathetic nerves. In perhaps the first study of stress and sodium retention in humans, Light et al. (1983) discovered that a stressful laboratory task (competitive reaction time) led to decreased urinary sodium excretion in men with risk factors for hypertension (positive parental history of hypertension and/or borderline hypertension) but only if these men showed evidence of high SNS activity as indicated by above average heart rate increases. It has also been found that low intake of dietary potassium enhances vasopressor responses to cold stress in African Americans, but not in Whites (Sudhir et al., 1997). Ionic mediation of reactivity by sodium, calcium, and potassium interactions is implicated, but remains largely unstudied.

Sodium Effects. Several lines of research implicate sodium as a principal physiological mediator of heightened vascular reactivity in Blacks. First, considerable evidence exists that heightened sympathetic activity may induce sodium retention (Weinberger, Luft, & Henry, 1982). Although the dietary sodium intake of Blacks may not be significantly higher than that of Whites (Grim et al., 1980), Blacks excrete less sodium in urine and exhibit greater pressor response to sodium loading (Luft et al., 1979; Luft, Grim, & Weinberger, 1985). Thus, Blacks may be more susceptible to the blood pressure effects of sodium despite a similar dietary intake relative to Whites. Research suggests that sodium may augment cardiovascular reactivity in subjects at risk for hypertension (Ambrosioni et al., 1982; Ambrosioni, Costa, Montebugnoli, Borghi, & Magnani, 1981; Falkner, Onesti, & Angelakos, 1981). Finally, studies in both humans and spontaneously hypertensive rats indicate that sodium may exert its influence on blood pressure via heightened vasoconstriction rather than by increasing cardiac output (Nilsson, Ely, Friberg, Kalstrom, & Folkow, 1985). Therefore, given the influence of the SNS on sodium retention, the greater sodium sensitivity among Blacks, and the effects of sodium on both reactivity and vascular resistance, sodium may be the pivotal physiological mechanism responsible for the observed race differences in vascular reactivity.

How might sodium contribute to increased vascular resistance? Sodium may lead to heightened vascular resistance through its effects on plasma norepinephrine release and action. Although in normotensive individuals sodium loading has been shown to decrease plasma and urinary norepinephrine levels, the opposite effect has been observed for salt-sensitive and hypertensive individuals. In these individuals, sodium loading increases plasma and urinary norepinephrine levels, whereas sodium deprivation has the opposite effect (Koolen & Van Brummelen, 1984; Luft et al., 1979; Takeshita, Imaizumi, Ashihara, & Nakamura, 1982). Furthermore, high sodium intake has been shown to potentiate the effects of norepinephrine on the vasculature (Rankin, Luft, Henry, Gibbs, & Weinberger, 1981), and has also been associated with increased pressor responses to infused norepinephrine in Black hypertensives relative to White hypertensives (Dimsdale, Graham, Ziegler, Zusman, & Berry, 1987). Thus, if Blacks exhibit an exaggerated antinatriuresis, this may lead to an increased release vasoconstrictive action of plasma norepinephrine. This chain of events would increase peripheral vascular resistance in Blacks. Moreover, chronic stressors that stimulate the release of plasma norepinephrine would interact with higher prevailing sodium levels to further stimulate vascular reactivity (Henry, 1988). Deter et al. (1997) found that salt sensitivity was related to increased anger irritation levels and increased reactivity to an information-processing task. They suggested that salt sensitivity, psychosocial, and psychophysiological traits, such as reactivity, interact to play a role in the pathogenesis of hypertension. It is hypothesized that the heightened vascular reactivity observed in Blacks may ultimately result in structural changes (i.e., hypertrophy) in the peripheral vasculature, which in turn may further augment vascular hyperactivity (Folkow, 1982, 1987). A long-term consequence of this process could be sustained hypertension.

In summary, compelling evidence exists that Blacks in American society are systematically exposed to a wider array of chronic social stressors compared to their White counterparts. These stressors involve lower SES, higher rates of poverty, higher unemployment, lower status occupations, exposure to racism, and more crowded and ecologically stressful residential environments. Many have been related to elevated blood pressure and increased hypertension prevalence. Research with humans and animals suggests that exposure to chronic stress may increase tonic SNS activity, acute autonomic reactivity, and urinary sodium retention. Future studies may determine whether the types of stressors that many Blacks are exposed to on a daily basis are related to these potentially pathological sequelae.

Behavioral and Psychological Factors

It is conceivable that chronic social stressors may increase catecholamine release and sodium retention through specific behavioral or psychological factors. Early research demonstrated an association between, anger, Type A behavior, and higher levels of plasma norepinephrine and blood pressure among Whites (Friedman, Byers, Diamant, & Rosenman, 1975). To date, only one study has examined these relations in Blacks (Durel et al., 1989). Although this study yielded nonsignificant relations between norepinephrine and anger for both Blacks and Whites, it did demonstrate positive correlations between anger and cardiovascular reactivity in these individuals.

Several studies have shown that behavioral and psychological factors are linked to elevated blood pressure and hypertension among Blacks (Anderson, Myers, Pickering, & Jackson, 1989; James, 1985). For example, suppressed anger and hostility have been associated with elevated blood pressure and hypertension in both adolescents and adults (Harburg, Blakelock, & Roeper, 1979; Johnson, Schork, & Spielberger, 1987; Johnson, Spielberger, Worden, & Jacobs, 1987). In general, this literature has indicated that Blacks who frequently suppress their anger when provoked, or who express their anger without reflection, have higher resting blood pressure levels than those who routinely express their anger when provoked or who express it only after some reflection (Gentry et al., 1982). Recently, the experience of frequent anger has been related to higher ambulatory blood pressures among Black women while at work (Durel et al., 1989). At this time, research has not examined whether inhibited anger expression is related to sodium excretion or catecholamine release among Blacks.

Another behavioral factor associated with high blood pressure among Blacks is the "John Henryism" behavioral pattern of hard work and determination against overwhelming odds. James, Hartnett, and Kalsbeek (1983) speculated that Blacks who exhibit this type of determination, but who also have few resources to help them achieve their goals, may be at greatest risk for developing hypertension (James, LaCroix, Kleinbaum, & Strogatz, 1984). Furthermore, it has been found that low SES Blacks who are high in John Henryism have a higher percentage of hypertension than persons who are low in John Henryism or have a high SES (James, Strogatz, Wing, & Ramsey, 1987). Interestingly, no interaction of John Henryism with education or blood pressure has been found for Whites, suggesting, as James and colleagues (1983) noted, that this coping style may be particularly relevant to Black populations.

The behavior of individuals high in John Henryism may actually increase their exposure to stressful social and environmental circumstances. That is, these individuals may continually strive to gain control over their environment in spite of numerous barriers, thereby potentially exposing themselves more frequently to frustrating and stressful situations. Whether this exposure to behaviorally mediated chronic stress results in enhanced SNS and altered sodium regulation remains to be empirically determined. It has been reported, however, that active behavioral coping with acute laboratory stressors enhances sodium retention (Light et al., 1983). It is this active coping with real-life stressors that is the sine qua non of the John Henryism pattern.

Several studies support the notion of active coping as a moderating variable in laboratory reactivity and ambulatory monitoring situational effects. Saab et al. (1997) found that during a speech stressor (active coping), Black men responded with lower blood pressure, cardiac output, and heart rate changes than did White men, White women, or Black women. They also reported more inhibitory-passive coping, hostility, pessimism, and less social support than other groups. Light et al. (1995) found that high effort coping in addition to high job status predicted diastolic blood pressure at work and in the laboratory for both Black and Whites. Job strain coupled with lower status is also implicated in reactivity (K. A. Lawler & Schmied, 1992).

Chronic social stressors may also have other psychological and emotional effects that could potentially influence sodium retention and neuroendocrine release. For example, low income Blacks have been found to report more psychological distress than low or high income Whites and high income Blacks, perhaps due to the combined burden of poverty and racism (Kessler & Neighbors, 1986). Additionally, the stressful residential environments to which many Blacks are exposed (e.g., crowding and crime) are related to stress symptoms, such as anxiety, depression, somatic complaints, lower levels of perceived control, and enhanced sympathetic nervous system activity (Baum et al., 1983; Davidson et al., 1987; Fleming et al., 1987; Schaeffer & Baum, 1984). It has been suggested that urban Black youths have decreased quality and quantity of social support. In fact, African Americans residing in high poverty areas have a higher percentage of people who report being unmarried, having no current partner, and having no best friend compared with those living in nonpoverty areas. These findings on the relative lack of potentially supportive social relationships have also been observed in Whites (Belle, 1982). Social support has been found to have both direct and indirect stress buffering effects on resting blood pressure (Strogatz et al., 1997) and on cardiovascular reactivity (Gerin, Milner, Chawla, & Pickering, 1995; Kamarck, Manuck, & Jennings, 1990; McNeilly et al., 1995).

Biological and Genetic Factors

Although genetic variables have been identified as important in determining sodium excretion in both Blacks and Whites (Luft, Miller, Cohen, Fineberg, & Weinberger, 1988; Grim et al., 1984), epidemiologic evidence suggests that the association of parental history and risk for hypertension may not be as strong among Blacks relative to Whites (R. Stamler, J. Stamler, Riedlinger, Algera, & Roberts, 1979). In fact, no published studies have reported the expected relation between parental history of hypertension and cardiovascular reactivity among Black adults (Anderson et al., 1986; Anderson, Lane, Taguchi, & Williams, 1989; Anderson, Lane, Taguchi, Williams, & Houseworth, 1989; Rowlands et al., 1982), although this relation has been found fairly consistently among Whites (Fredrikson & Matthews, 1990). A possible explanation for these somewhat puzzling findings may be the substantial influence of psychosocial factors in the development of hypertension among Blacks. That is, psychosocial factors, such as chronic stress, may overshadow the influence of parental history such that risk for hypertension and hyperactivity are augmented even in persons with a negative parental history. This could result in a diminished ability to detect differences between parental history groups among Blacks.

Second, although sodium retention has a clear genetic component (Grim et al., 1984), it may also be stimulated by psychosocial stress. To the degree that Blacks, particularly low income Blacks, experience more psychological stress than do Whites or upper income Blacks (Kessler & Neighbors, 1986), they may consequently be more susceptible to inhibited sodium excretion.

Finally, the genetic distinction between Black and White Americans is, at best, ambiguous. It has been noted that the gene pool of American Blacks is comprised of a heterogeneous mixture of genes from genetically diverse populations in Africa (Hiernaux, 1975; Mourant, 1983) and the U.S. Caucasian population (Glass & Li, 1953; Pollitzer, 1958). In fact, Reed (1969) estimated that up to 505 of the genes of Black Americans are derived from Caucasian ancestors, whereas Lewontin and associates (Lewontin, 1973; Lewontin, Rose, & Kamin, 1984) reported that genetic differences between individuals within a race have a substantially greater impact on the total species genetic variation than genetic differences between races. Therefore, although genetic factors no doubt play a role in reactivity among Blacks, their influence on between-race differences is likely to be considerably less.

Coping Resources

Thus far, the chapter has been discussing the various physiologic, social, and behavioral factors that may contribute to the augmented sodium retention, greater vascular reactivity, and higher hypertension prevalence among Blacks as compared to Whites. It is important to note, however, that there may be factors inherent in the culture and traditions of Black Americans that may counteract the sympathetic and hypertensinogenic effects of chronic stress. A number of researchers have advocated the view that minorities share many characteristics (contextual, social, and behavioral) associated with unique intra- and interethnic stress coping mechanisms (Armstead, 1991; Dressler, 1993; Smyth & Yarandi, 1996; Williams, 1996).

According to the contextual model, certain cultural traditions such as strong kinship ties, unique forms of emotional expressiveness, social support, and spirituality could decrease the effects of stress and consequently the effects of stress on SNS activity, sodium retention, and blood pressure level. It has been found, for instance, that resting blood pressure levels among Whites who attend church regularly are lower than among those with less frequent attendance (Graham et al., 1978). It would be of interest to determine whether Blacks exposed to chronic life stressors (e.g., low income Blacks) but who also have a high cultural "buffer" (e.g., strong religious orientation, social support, or an extended family network) exhibit lower tonic SNS activity, lower sodium retention, and lower cardiovascular reactivity than those individuals less connected with cultural resources.

Because of the paucity of coping, stress, vulnerability, and resiliency measures, the complexity of behavior in this population is often misrepresented and misunderstood (Stevenson, 1997). It is important that researchers perform ethnographic studies of culture, stress, and coping in minority populations before making generalizations about psychosocial mediators of cardiovascular reactivity. Furthermore, studies of behavioral risk factors, adaptive behaviors, and maladaptive behaviors are warranted from a culturally sensitive perspective (Bagley, Angel, Dilworth-Anderson, Liu, & Schinke, 1995; Myers, Kagawa-Singer, Kumanyika, Lex, & Markides, 1995). It is imperative to understand how culture and ethnicity may interact with the laboratory environment, the perceptions of laboratory stressors, and the psychological and physiological coping responses to stressors.

TESTING THE CONTEXTUAL MODEL

Directions for Research

The contextual model presented here was designed to provide a stimulus for examining both the basis for racial differences in vascular reactivity as well as for exploring within-race variability in vascular responses among Blacks. Toward these ends, the model suggests a number of testable hypotheses and research questions. Various components of the model could be tested using either field or laboratory methodologies. For example, the model would predict that Blacks who are exposed to higher levels of chronic stress should have higher resting stress hormone levels (e.g., catecholamines, ACTH) and exaggerated responses to novel stimuli, suggesting increased SNS activity compared to Blacks experiencing lower levels of chronic stress. Second, chronic stress should also be positively associated with increased sodium retention (i.e., slower sodium excretion rates) and greater vascular reactivity in Blacks. Third, the combination of chronic stress exposure and behavioral and psychological factors, such as anger suppression and John Henryism, should be positively associated with both increased SNS activity and greater sodium retention. Dietary sodium loading (or saline infusions) should potentiate vascular reactivity in Blacks experiencing chronic stress. Furthermore, macrosocial phenomenon, such as lower SES, residence in socially unstable communities, and chronic exposure to racial stress should be positively associated with increased SNS activity and greater sodium retention. Finally, the contextual model would predict that Blacks with more coping resources (e.g., high social support, strong religious orientation, and racial identity) will show lower SNS activity and decreased sodium retention relative to those with fewer coping resources.

CONCLUSIONS

In summary, according to the proposed model, race is viewed as a sociocultural designation that denotes differential exposure to chronic social stressors. It is proposed that Black Americans are exposed to significantly more chronic social stressors than White Americans. Many of these chronic social stressors have been associated with hypertension prevalence in epidemiological studies. Furthermore, chronic stress has been shown to augment cardiovascular reactivity to acute stress in both animals and humans and to increase sodium retention in SHRs. Acute stress has also been demonstrated to increase sodium retention in humans. The essential element of this model is that chronic social stressors that are overrepresented within the Black American population due to historical factors are related to an increase in sodium retention and enhanced reactivity. This altered sodium metabolism and reactivity may be further augmented by biological, behavioral, and psychological risk factors for hypertension and modulated by stress coping resources. It is hoped that this model will serve as a stimulus for further research on the biopsychosocial aspects of autonomic reactivity and hypertension in minorities. Disparity in health status will remain a problem in this country until researchers begin to look at ethnic-specific pathways using this type of contextual modeling approach. This is a challenge directed at researchers to test the applicability of this model to other minority populations.

REFERENCES

Adams-Campbell, L. L., Brambilla, D. J., & McKinlay, S. M. (1993). Correlates of the prevalence of self-reported hypertension among African-American and white women. *Ethnicity & Disease, 3,* 119–125.

Ambrosioni, E., Costa, F. V., Borghi, C., Montebugnoli, L., Giordani, M. F., & Magnani, B. (1982). Effects of moderate salt restriction on intralymphocytic sodium and pressor response to stress in borderline hypertension. *Hypertension, 4,* 789–794.

Ambrosioni, E., Costa, F. V., Montebugnoli, L., Borghi, C., & Magnani, B. (1981). Intralymphocytic sodium concentration as an index of response to stress and exercise in young subjects with borderline hypertension. *Clinical Science, 61*(suppl. 7), 25s-27s.

Anderson, N. B. (1989). Racial differences in stress-induced cardiovascular reactivity and hypertension: Current status and substantive issues. *Psychological Bulletin, 105*(1), 89–105.

Anderson, N. B., & Armstead, C. A. (1995). Toward understanding the association of socioeconomic status and health: A new challenge for the biopsychosocial approach. *Psychosomatic Medicine, 57,* 213–225.

Anderson, N. B., Lane, J. D., Taguchi, F., & Williams, R. B., Jr. (1989). Patterns of cardiovascular responses to stress as a function of race and parental hypertension in men. *Health Psychology, 8,* 525–540.

Anderson, N. B., Lane, J. D., Taguchi, F., Williams, R. B., Jr., & Houseworth, S. J. (1989). Race, parental history of hypertension, and patterns of cardiovascular reactivity in women. *Psychophysiology, 26,* 39–47.

Anderson, N. B., McNeilly, M. D., Armstead, C., Clark, R., & Pieper, C. (1993). Assessment of cardiovascular reactivity: A methodological overview. *Ethnicity & Disease, 3*(Suppl.), S29–S37.

Anderson, N. B., McNeilly, M., & Myers, H. (1991). Autonomic reactivity and hypertension in Blacks: A review and proposed model. *Ethnicity & Disease, 1,* 154–170.

Anderson, N. B., McNeilly, M., & Myers, H. (1992). Toward understanding race difference in autonomic reactivity: A proposed conceptual model. In J. Rick Turner et al. (Eds.), *Individual differences in cardiovascular response to stress* (pp. 125–145). New York: Plenum.

Anderson, N. B., Myers, H. F., Pickering, T., & Jackson, J. S. (1989). Hypertension in Blacks: Psychosocial and biological perspectives. *Journal of Hypertension, 7,* 161–172.

Anderson, N. B., Williams, R. B., Jr., Lane, J. D., Haney, T., Simpson, S., & Houseworth, S. J. (1986). Type A behavior, family history of hypertension, and cardiovascular responses among Black women. *Health Psychology, 5,* 393–406.

Armstead, C. A. (1991). *The relationship between control, hostility, anger suppression, and cardiovascular reponsivity to racism, interpersonal, and active coping stressors among Black and White women.* Unpublished doctoral dissertation, University of Tennessee.

Armstead, C. A., Anderson, N. B., & Lawler, K. A. (1994). *The interactions of socioeconomic status, ethnicity, and cardiovascular reactivity among women.* Paper presented at the annual meeting of the American Psychosomatic Society, Boston.

Armstead, C. A., Lawler, K. A., Gorden, G., Cross, J., & Gibbons, J. (1989). Relationship of racial stressors to blood pressure responses and anger expression in Black college students. *Health Psychology, 8,* 541–556.

Bagley, S. P., Angel, R., Dilworth-Anderson, P., Liu, W., & Schinke, S. (1995). Adaptive health behaviors among ethnic minorities. *Health Psychology, 14,* 632–640.

Bassett, J. R., Strand, F. L., & Cairncross, K. D. (1978). Glucocorticoids, adrenocorticotropic hormone and related polypeptides on myocardial sensitivity to noradrenaline. *European Journal of Pharmacology, 49,* 243–249.

Baum, A., Gatchel, R. J., & Schaeffer, M. A. (1983). Emotional, behavioral, and physiological effects of chronic stress at Three Mile Island. *Journal of Consulting and Clinical Psychology, 51,* 565–572.

Belle, D. (1982). The impact of poverty on social networks and supports. *Marriage and Family Review, 5,* 89–103.

Bullard, R. D. (1994). *Dumping in Dixie: Race, class, and environmental quality.* Boulder, CO: Westview Press.

Burt, V. L., Whelton, P., Roccella, E. J., Brown, C., Cutler, J. A., Higgins, M., Horan, M. J., & Labarthe, D. (1995). Prevalence of hypertension in the U.S. adult population: Results from the Third National Health and Nutritional Examination Survey, 1988–1991. *Hypertension, 25,* 305–313.

Calhoun, D. A., Mutinga, M. L., Wyss, J. M., & Oparil, S. (1994). Muscle sympathetic nervous system activity in Black and Caucasian hypertensive subjects. *Journal of Hypertension, 12*(11), 1291–1296.

Calhoun, D. A., & Oparil, S. (1995). Racial differences in the pathogenesis of hypertension. *American Journal of the Medical Sciences, 310*(Suppl. 1), S86–S90.

Carroll, D., Davey-Smith, G., Sheffield, D., Shipley, M. H., & Marmot, M. G. (1997). The relationship between socioeconomic status, hostility, and blood pressure reactions to mental stress in men: Data from the Whitehall II study. *Health Psychology, 16,* 131–136.

Centers for Disease Control and Prevention. (1994). *Chronic disease in minority populations.* Atlanta: Author.

Classification of American Indian race on birth and death certificates—California and Montana. (1993). *Mortality Morbidity Weekly Report, 42,* 220–223.

Davidson, L. M., Fleming, R., & Baum, A. (1987). Chronic stress, catecholamines, and sleep disturbance at Three Mile Island. *Journal of Human Stress, 13,* 75–83.

Deter, H. C., Buchholz, K., Schorr, U., Schachinger, H., Turan, S., & Sharma, A. M. (1997). Psychophysiological reactivity of salt-sensitive normotensive subjects. *Journal of Hypertension, 15,* 839–844.

Dimsdale, J. E., Graham, R. M., Ziegler, M. G., Zusman, R. M., & Berry, C. C. (1987). Age, race, diagnosis, and sodium effects on the pressor response to infused norepinephrine. *Hypertension, 10,* 564–569.

Dressler, W. W. (1993). Type A behavior: Contextual effects within a southern Black community. *Social Science Medicine, 36,* 289–295.

Dressler, W. W. (1996). Hypertension in the African American community: Social, cultural, and psychological factors. *Seminars in Nephrology, 16,* 71–82.

Durel, L. A., Carver, C. S. Spitzer, S. B., Llabre, M. M., Weintraub, J. K., Saab, P. G., & Schneiderman, N. (1989). Associations of blood pressure with self-report measures of anger and hostility among Black and White men and women. *Health Psychology, 8,* 557–575.

Dysart, J. M., Treiber, F. A., Pflieger, K., Davis, H., & Strong, W. B. (1994). Ethnic differences in the myocardial and vascular reactivity to stress in normotensive girls. *American Journal of Hypertension, 7,* 15–22.

Falkner, B., Onesti, G., & Angelakos, E. T. (1981). Effect of salt loading on the cardiovascular response to stress in adolescents. *Hypertension, 3*(2), II195–II199.

Farley, R. (1984). *Blacks and Whites: Narrowing the gap?* Cambridge, MA: Harvard University Press.

Farley, R., & Allen W. R. (1989). *The color line and the quality of life in America.* New York: Oxford University Press.

Flack, J. M., Amaro, H., Jenkins, W., Kunitz, S., Levy, J., Mixon, M., & Yu, E. (1995). Epidemiology of minority health. *Health Psychology, 14,* 592–600.

Fleming, I., Baum, A., Davidson, L. M., Rectanus, E., & McArdle, S. (1987). Chronic stress as a factor in psychologic reactivity to challenge. *Health Psychology, 6,* 221–237.

Fleming, I., Baum, A., & Weiss, L. (1987). Social density and perceived control as mediators of crowding stress in high-density residential neighborhoods. *Journal of Personality and Social Psychology, 52,* 899–906.

Folkow, B. (1982). Physiological aspects of primary hypertension. *Psychological Reviews, 62,* 347–504.

Folkow, B. (1987). Psychosocial and central nervous influences in primary hypertension. *Circulation, 76*(1), I10–I19.

Fredrikson, M., & Matthews, K. A. (1990). Cardiovascular responses to behavioral stress and hypertension: A meta-analytic review. *Annals of Behavioral Medicine, 12,* 80–89.

Friedman, M., Byers, S. O., Diamant, J., & Rosenman, R. H. (1975). Plasma catecholamine response of coronary prone subjects (Type A) to a specific challenge. *Metabolism: Clinical & Experimental, 24,* 205–210.

Frohlich, E. D. (1994). Hypertension. In T. A. Pearson, M. H. Criqui, R. V. Luepker, A. Oberman, & M. Winston (Eds.), *Primer in Preventive Cardiology* (pp. 131–142). Dallas, TX: American Heart Association.

Frost, F., Taylor, V., & Fries, E. (1992). Race misclassification of Native Americans in a surveillance, epidemiology, and end results registry. *Journal of the National Cancer Institute, 84,* 957–962.

Gardner, R. W. (1994). Mortality. In N.W.S. Zane, D. T. Takeuchi, & K.N.J. Young (Eds.), *Confronting critical health issues of Asian and Pacific Islander Americans* (pp. 53–104). Thousand Oaks, CA: Sage.

Gentry, W. D., Chesney, A. P., Gary, H. E., Jr., Hall, R. P., & Harburg, E. (1982). Habitual anger-coping styles: I. Effect on mean blood pressure and risk for essential hypertension. *Psychosomatic Medicine, 44,* 195–202.

Gerin, W., Milner, D., Chawla, S., & Pickering, T. G. (1995). Social support as a moderator of cardiovascular reactivity in women: A test of the direct effects and buffering hypotheses. *Psychosomatic Medicine, 57,* 16–22.

Girdler, S. S., Hinderliter, A. L., & Light, K. C. (1993). Peripheral adrenergic receptor contributions to cardiovascular reactivity: Influence of race and gender. *Journal of Psychosomatic Research, 37,* 177–193.

Glass, B., & Li, C. C. (1953). The dynamics of racial intermixture: An analysis based on the American Negro. *American Journal of Human Genetics, 5,* 1–20.

Goldstein, D. S. (1983). Plasma catecholamines and essential hypertension: An analytical review. *Hypertension, 5,* 86–99.

Graham, T. W., Kaplan, B. H., Coroni-Huntley, J. C., James, S. A., Becker, C., Hames, C. G., & Heyden, S. (1978). Frequency of church attendance and blood pressure elevation. *Journal of Behavioral Medicine, 1,* 37–43.

Grignolo, A., Koepke, J. P., & Obrist, P. A. (1982). Renal function, heart rate and blood pressure during exercise and shock avoidance in dogs. *American Journal of Physiology, 242,* R482–R490.

Grim, C. E., Luft, F. C., Weinberger, M. H., Miller, J. Z., Rose, R. J., & Christian, J. C. (1984). Genetic, familial, and racial influences on blood pressure control systems in man. *Australian and New Zealand Journal of Medicine, 14,* 453–457.

Grim, C. E., Luft, F. C., Miller, J. Z., Meneely, G. R., Battarbee, H. D., Hames, C. G., & Dahl, L. K. (1980). Racial differences in blood pressure in Evans County, Georgia: Relationship to sodium and potassium intake and plasma renin activity. *Journal of Chronic Diseases, 33,* 87–94.

Hahn, R. A., Truman, B. I., & Barker, N. D. (1996). Identifying ancestry: The reliability of ancestral identification in the United States by self, proxy, interviewer, and funeral director. *Epidemiology, 7,* 75–80.

Harburg, E., Blakelock, E. H., Jr., & Roeper, P. R. (1979). Resentful and reflective coping with arbitrary authority and blood pressure: Detroit. *Psychosomatic Medicine, 41,* 189–202.

Harburg, E., Erfurt, J. C., Chape, C., Hauenstein, L. S., Schull, W. J., & Schork, M. A. (1973). Socioecological stressor areas and Black-White blood pressure: Detroit. *Journal of Chronic Diseases, 26,* 595–611.

Harris, W. H. (1982). *The harder we run: Black workers since the Civil War.* New York: Oxford University Press.

Havas, S., Fujimoto, W., Close, N., McCarter, R., Keller, J., & Sherwin, R. (1996). The NHLBI workshop on hypertension in Hispanic Americans, Native Americans, and Asian/Pacific Islander Americans. *Public Health Reports, 111,* 451–458.

Henry, J. P. (1988). Stress, salt, and hypertension. *Social Science and Medicine, 26,* 293–302.

Hiernaux, J. (1975). *The people of Africa.* New York: Scribner's.

Jackson, J. S., Brown, T. N., Williams, D. R., Torres, M., Sellers, S. L., & Brown, K. (1996). Racism and the physical and mental health status of African Americans: A thirteen year national panel study. *Ethnicity & Disease, 6,* 132–147.

James, S. A. (1985). Psychosocial and environmental factors in Black hypertension. In W. Hall, E. Saunders, & N. Schulman (Eds.), *Hypertension in Blacks: Epidemiology, pathophysiology and treatment* (pp. 132–143). Chicago: Year Book Publishers.

James, S. A., Hartnett, S. A., & Kalsbeek, W. D. (1983). John Henryism and blood pressure differences among Black men. *Journal of Behavioral Medicine, 6,* 259–278.

James, S. A., & Kleinbaum, D. G. (1976). Socioecological stress and hypertension-related mortality rates in North Carolina. *American Journal of Public Health, 66,* 354–358.

James, S. A., LaCroix, A. Z., Kleinbaum, D. G., & Strogatz, D. S. (1984). John Henryism and blood pressure differences among Black men: II. The role of occupational stressors. *Journal of Behavioral Medicine, 7,* 259–275.

James, S. A., Strogatz, D. S., Wing, S. B., & Ramsey, D. L. (1987). Socioeconomic status, John Henryism, and hypertension in Blacks and Whites. *American Journal of Epidemiology, 126,* 664–673.

Johnson, E. H. (1989). The role of the experience and expression of anger and anxiety in elevated blood pressure among Black and White adolescents. *Journal of the National Medical Association, 81,* 573–584.

Johnson, E. H., Schork, N. J., & Spielberger, C. D. (1987). Emotional and familial determinants of elevated blood pressure in Black and White adolescent females. *Journal of Psychosomatic Research, 31,* 731–741.

Johnson, E. H., Spielberger, C. D., Worden, T. J., & Jacobs, G. A. (1987). Emotional and familial determinants of elevated blood pressure in Black and White adolescent males. *Journal of Psychosomatic Research, 31,* 287–300.

Jones, D. R., Harrell, J. P., Morris-Prather, C. E., Thomas, J., & Omowale, N. (1996). Affective and physiological responses to racism: The roles of afrocentrism and mode of presentation. *Ethnicity & Disease, 6,* 109–122.

Julius, S., & Schork, M. A. (1971). Borderline hypertension—a critical review. *Journal of Chronic Disease, 23,* 723–754.

Kamarck, T. W., Manuck, S. B., & Jennings, J. R. (1990). Social support reduces cardiovascular reactivity to psychological challenge: A laboratory model. *Psychosomatic Medicine, 52,* 42–58.

Kessler, R. C., & Neighbors, H. W. (1986). A new perspective on the relationships among race, social class, and psychological distress. *Journal of Health and Social Behavior, 27,* 107–115.

Kington, R. S., & Smith, J. P. (1997). Socioeconomic status and racial and ethnic differences in functional status associated with chronic diseases. *American Journal of Public Health, 87,* 805–810.

Koepke, J. P., & DiBona, G. F. (1985). High sodium intake enhances renal nerve and antinatriuretic responses to stress in spontaneously hypertensive rats. *Hypertension, 7*(3, pt. 1), 357–363.

Koepke, J. P., Light, K. C., & Obrist, P. A. (1983). Neural control of renal excretory function during behavioral stress in conscious dogs. *American Journal of Physiology, 245,* R251–R258.

Koolen, M. I., & Van Brummelen, P. (1984). Adrenergic activity and peripheral hemodynamics in relation to sodium sensitivity in patients with essential hypertension. *Hypertension, 76,* 820–825.

Krantz, D. S., & Manuck, S. B. (1984). Acute psychophysiologic reactivity and risk of cardiovascular disease: A review and methodologic critique. *Psychological Bulletin, 96,* 435–464.

Krieger, N. (1990). Racial and gender discrimination: Risk factors for high blood pressure? *Social Science & Medicine, 30,* 1273–1281.

Krieger, N., & Sidney, S. (1996). Racial discrimination and blood pressure: The CARDIA study of young Black and White adults. *American Journal of Public Health, 86*(10), 1370–1378.

Lawler, J. E., Naylor, S. K., & Abel, M. M. (1993). Predictability of foot shock differentially affects the phasic blood pressure of SHR, BHR, and WKY rats. *Physiology & Behavior, 54,* 369–374.

Lawler, J. E., Zheng, G., Li, S., Wang, C. H., & Edgemon, I. P. (1996). Norepinephrine levels in discrete brain nuclei in borderline hypertensive rats exposed to compound stressors. *Brain Research Bulletin, 41,* 87–92.

Lawler, K. A., & Schmied, L. A. (1992). A prospective study of women's health: The effects of stress, hardiness, locus of control, Type A behavior, and physiological reactivity. *Women and Health. 19,* 27–41.

Lewontin, R. C. (1973). The appointment of human diversity. *Evolutionary Biology, 6,* 381–398.

Lewontin, R. C., Rose, S., & Kamin, L. J. (1984). *Not in our genes: Biology, ideology, and human nature.* New York: Pantheon.

Liao, Y., & Cooper, R. S. (1995). Continued adverse trends in coronary heart disease mortality among Blacks, 1980–91. *Public Health Reports, 111,* 572–579.

Light, K. C. (1987). Psychosocial precursors of hypertension: Experimental evidence. *Circulation, 76*(1), 167–176.

Light, K. C., Brownley, K. A., Turner, J. R., Hinderliter, A. L., Girdler, S. S., Sherwood, A., & Anderson, N. B. (1995). Job status and high-effort coping influence work blood pressure in women and Blacks. *Hypertension, 25,* 554–559.

Light, K. C., Koepke, J. P., Obrist, P. A., & Willis, P. W. (1983). Psychological stress induces sodium and fluid retention in men at high risk for hypertension. *Science, 220,* 429–431.

Lillie-Blanton, M., & Laveist, T. (1996). Race/ethnicity, the social environment, and health. *Social Science & Medicine, 43,* 83–91.

Lohmeier, T. E., & Carroll, R. G. (1985). Adrenocortical hormones and their interaction with angiotensin II and catecholamines in the production of hypertension. In F. Mantero, E. G. Biglieri, J. W. Funder, & B. A. Scoggins (Eds.), *The adrenal gland and hypertension* (Vol. 27, pp. 1159–176). New York: Raven.

Luft, F., Grim, C., & Weinberger, M. (1985). Electrolyte and volume homeostasis in Blacks. In W. Hall, E. Saunders, & N. Shulman (Eds.), *Hypertension in Blacks: Epidemiology, pathophysiology, and treatment* (pp. 115–131). Chicago: Yearbook Medical.

Luft, F. C., Miller, J. Z., Cohen, S. J., Fineburg, N. S., Weinberger, M. H. (1988). Heritable aspects of salt sensitivity. *American Journal of Cardiology, 61,* 1H–6H.

Luft, F. C., Rankin, L. I., Henry, D. P., Bloch, R., Grim, C. E., Weyman, A. E., Murray, R. H., & Weinberger, M. H. (1979). Plasma and urinary norepinephrine values at extremes of sodium intake in normal man. *Hypertension, 1,* 261–266.

Markides, K. S. (1989). Consequences of gender differentials in life expectancy for Black and Hispanic Americans. *International Journal of Aging & Human Development, 29,* 95–102.

McCarty, R., Horwatt, K., & Konarska, M. (1988). Chronic stress and sympathetic-adrenal medullary responsiveness. *Social Science in Medicine, 26,* 333–341.

McLoyd, V. C. (1990). The impact of economic hardship on Black families and children: Psychological distress, parenting, and socioemotional development. *Child Development, 61,* 341–346.

McNeilly, M. D., Anderson, N. B., Armstead, C. A., Clark, R., Corbett, M., Robinson, E. L., Pieper, C. F., & Lepisto, E. M. (1996). The perceived racism scale: A multidimensional assessment of the experience of White racism among African Americans. *Ethnicity & Disease, 6,* 154–166.

McNeilly, M., Robinson, E., Anderson, M., Pieper, C., Shan, A., Toth, P., Martin, P., Jackson, D., Saulter, T., White, C., Kuchibatla, M., Collado, S., & Gerin, W. (1995). Effects of racist provocation and social support on cardiovascular reactivity in African American women. *International Journal of Behavioral Medicine, 2,* 321–338.

Morris-Prather, C. E., Harrell, J. P., Collins, R., Leonard, K., L., Boss, M., & Lee, J. W. (1996). Gender differences in mood and cardiovascular responses to socially stressful stimuli. *Ethnicity and Disease, 6,* 123–131.

Mourant, A. E. (1983). *Blood relations: Blood groups and anthropology.* New York: Oxford University Press.

Murphy, J. K., Stoney, C. M., Alpert, B. S., & Walker, S. S. (1995). Gender and ethnicity in children's cardiovascular reactivity: 7 years of study. *Health Psychology, 14,* 48–55.

Myers, H. F., Kagawa-Singer, M., Kumanyika, S., K., Lex, B. W., & Markides, K. S. (1995). Behavioral risk factors related to chronic diseases in ethnic minorities. *Health Psychology, 14,* 613–621.

National Center for Health Statistics. (1997). *Health, United States, 1995–96.* Hyattsville, MD: Public Health Service.

Nilsson, H., Ely, D., Friberg, P., Kalstrom, G. E., & Folkow, B. (1985). Effects of high and low sodium diets on the resistance vessels and their adrenergic vasoconstrictor fibre control in normotensive (WKY) and hypertensive (SHR) rats. *Acta Physiologica Scandinavica, 125,* 323–334.

Pappas, G., Hadden, W., Kozak, L. J., & Fisher, G. (1997). Potentially avoidable hospitalizations: Inequalities in rates between U.S. socioeconomic groups. *American Journal of Public Health, 87,* 811–816.

Pappas, G., Queen, S., Hadden, W., & Fisher, G. (1993). The increasing disparity in mortality between socioeconomic groups in the United States, 1960 and 1986. *New England Journal of Medicine, 329,* 103–109.

Pollitzer, W. S. (1958). The Negroes of Charleston, SC: A study of hemoglobin types, serology, and morphology. *American Journal of Physical Anthropology, 16,* 241–263.

Rankin, L. I., Luft, F. C., Henry, D. P., Gibbs, P. S., & Weinberger, M. H. (1981). Sodium intake alters the effects of norepinephrine on blood pressure. *Hypertension, 3,* 650–656.

Reed, T. (1969). Caucasian genes in American Negroes. *Science, 165,* 762–768.

Report of the Secretary's Task Force on Black and Minority Health. (1986). *MMWR: Morbidity and Mortality Weekly Report, 35,* 109–112.

Rowlands, D. B., DeGiovanni, J., McLeay, R. A., Watson, R. D., Stallard, T. J., & Littler, W. A. (1982). Cardiovascular response in Black and White hypertensives. *Hypertension, 4,* 817–820.

Saab, P. G., Llabre, M. M., Schneiderman, N., Hurwitz, B. E. , McDonald, P. G., Evans, J., Wohlgemuth, W., Hawashi, P., & Klein, B. (1997). Influence of ethnicity and gender on cardiovascular responses to active coping and inhibitory-passive coping challenges. *Psychosomatic Medicine, 58,* 434–446.

Schaeffer, M. A., & Baum, A. (1984). Adrenal cortical response to stress at Three Mile Island. *Psychosomatic Medicine, 46,* 227–237.

Smyth, K., & Yarandi, H. N. (1996). Factor analysis of the Ways of Coping Questionnaire for African-American women. *Nursing Research, 45,* 25–29.

Stamler, R., Stamler, J., Riedlinger, W. F., Algera, G., & Roberts, R. H. (1979). Family (parental) history and prevalence of hypertension: Results of a nationwide screening program. *Journal of the American Medical Association, 241,* 43–46.

Stevenson, H. C., Jr. (1997). "Missed, dissed, and pissed": Making meaning of neighborhood risk, fear and anger management in urban Black youth. *Cultural Diversity and Mental Health, 3,* 37–52.

Strand, F. L., & Smith, C. M. (1980). LPH, ACTH, MSH and motor system. *Pharmacology & Therapeutics, 11,* 509–533.

Strogatz, D. S., Croft, J. B., James, S. A., Keenan, N. L., Browning, S. R., Garrett, J. M., & Curtis, A. B. (1997). Social support, stress, and blood pressure in Black adults. *Epidemiology, 8*(5), 482–487.

Sudhir, K., Forman, A., Yi, S. I., Sorof, J., Schmidlin, O., Sebastian, A., & Morris, R. C., Jr. (1997). Reduced dietary potassium reversibly enhances vasopressor response to stress in African Americans. *Hypertension, 28,* 1083–1090.

Sugarman, J. R., & Lawson, L. (1993). The effect of racial misclassification on estimates of end-stage renal disease among American Indians and Alaska Natives, Pacific Northwest, 1988–1990. *American Journal of Kidney Disease, 21,* 383–386.

Takeshita, A., Imaizumi, T., Ashihara, T., & Nakamura, M. (1982). Characteristics of responses to salt loading and deprivation in hypertensive subjects. *Circulation Research, 51,* 457–464.

Terrell, D. F., & Manuck, S. B. (1996). Interactive influences of ethnicity, gender and parental hypertension on hemodynamic responses to behavioral challenge. *Ethnicity & Disease, 6,* 286–300.

U.S. Bureau of the Census. (1995). Current Population Reports, Series P23–189, *Population profile of the United States: 1995.* Washington, DC: U.S. Government Printing Office.

Weinberger, M., Luft, F., & Henry, D. (1982). The role of the SNS in the modulation of sodium excretion. *Clinical Experimental Hypertension, A4,* 719–735.

Whitworth, J. A., Coghlan, J. P., Denton, D. A., Hardy, K. J., & Scoggins, B. A. (1979). Effect of sodium loading and ACTH on blood pressure of sheep with reduced renal mass. *Cardiovascular Research, 13,* 9–15.

Williams, D. R. (1992). Black–White differences in blood pressure: The role of social factors. *Ethnicity and Disease, 2,* 126–141.

Williams, D. R. (1996). Race/ethnicity and socioeconomic status: Measurement and methodological issues. *International Journal of Health Services, 26,* 483–505.

Wright, L. B., Treiber, F. A., Davis, H., Strong, W. B., Levy, M., Van Huss, E., & Batchelor, C. (1993). Relationship between family environment and children's hemodynamic responses to stress: A longitudinal evaluation. *Behavioral Medicine, 19,* 115–121.

25

The Multiple Contexts of Chronic Illness: Diabetic Adolescents and Community Characteristics

Dawn A. Obeidallah
Harvard School of Public Health

Stuart T. Hauser
Judge Baker Childrens' Center, Harvard Medical School, and Josling Diabetes Center

Alan M. Jacobson
Josling Diabetes Center and Harvard Medical School

Adolescents diagnosed with diabetes negotiate at least two worlds of competing demands simultaneously. First, as part of normative adolescent development, they navigate the challenges of individuation, development of behavioral and cognitive autonomy, and intensification of close relationships with friends. In contrast to this push toward independence and greater sense of freedom, successful treatment of diabetes involves changes in diet and exercise habits, monitoring of glucose levels, and administration of insulin (Hauser et al., 1986; Hauser et al., 1997). These paradoxical stressors of adolescence and of disease maintenance contribute to divergent behaviors and somewhat opposing goals for diabetic adolescents and their families.

The diagnosis of diabetes requires a substantial reorganization of families and complicates already nuanced aspects of childrearing (Anderson, 1995; Blechman & Delamater, 1993; Hauser & Solomon, 1985; Reiss, Steinglass, & Howe, 1998). Some families, in response to adolescents' diagnosis of diabetes, step up protection over them by excessively monitoring diet and activities with friends. Such responses may be at odds with the developmental challenges of adolescence and contribute to new tensions between newly diagnosed diabetic adolescents and their parents. In the context of this tension, other social supports, including neighbors and community resources, may take on substantial importance (Powers et al., 1985).

The chronic nature of diabetes, particularly when first occurring during the already complex transition to adulthood, paints a stressful picture for adolescents and their families (Jacobson, et al., 1997; Wertlieb et al., 1990). The burden of these multiple stressors may overtax families' ability to function adaptively. Families that are overtaxed sometimes reach outside the family for assistance, frequently turning to their communities for additional help and support (Powers et al., 1985; Stack & Burton, 1993). The majority of research on diabetic adolescents, however, focuses on the family as the sole social context (Hauser, Jacobson, Benes, & Anderson, 1997), excluding contexts of peers, schools, and most importantly for the purposes of this chapter, communities.

This work is in response to social scientists' calls for further investigations of diabetic individuals with respect to neighborhood and community influences (Glasgow & Anderson, 1995). The basic premise is that families in need, especially those with a child recently diagnosed with diabetes, can draw on the strength of their communities or be undermined by the negative aspects of their communities; or they can experience both strengths and vulnerabilities from the same community. This chapter sets out to discuss differences between families of diabetic and nondiabetic adolescents. In addition, it addresses the wealth of variability and potential sources of these individual differences within diabetic adolescents.

COMMUNITY CONTEXTS AND ADOLESCENTS

Drawing largely on an ecological-transactional model, the view presented here is that adolescents live within multiple layers of context, each layer influencing and interacting with other layers to create a synergistic force that shapes adolescent development (Bronfenbrenner, 1979; Lynch & Cicchetti, 1998). Specifically, adolescents exist in families embedded within communities functioning in the context of broader macrosystems (e.g., regional norms and values) that occur during certain historical times and periods (Bronfenbrenner, 1986; Dixon & Lerner, 1999; Elder, 1974). These contexts are interdependent and reciprocal: Not only do they contribute to adolescents' and families' experiences, but individuals shape each context. For instance, families of adolescents with diabetes may reach out to their community for help and support. Similarly, neighbors in communities that are more organized and supportive may attempt to reach out to help families in need.

The past two decades have witnessed a resurgence of social science interest in community influences on youth and families (Brooks-Gunn, Duncan, Klebanov, & Sealand, 1993; Burton, Obeidallah, & Allison, 1996; Sampson, 1993; Sampson, Raudenbush, & Earls, 1997; Simcha-Fagan & Schwartz, 1986). Multiple theoretical paradigms regarding community influences on residents' outcomes have been proposed, such as social disorganization theory (Sampson, 1993; Shaw & McKay, 1942), social capital theory (Coleman, 1994), collective efficacy (Sampson et al., 1997), and social control theory (Hirschi, 1969). Accumulating empirical evidence suggests a consistent pattern between characteristics of community social control and social organization, and youth outcomes: Communities with high levels of social control and organization are associated with optimal outcomes for youth. In communities with high levels of control and organization, neighbors look out for one another, anonymity is minimal, and concern for neighbors and the neighborhood is the accepted and practiced norm. Communities with these characteristics tend to boast lower rates of school drop out, teen pregnancy, violent behavior, and drug use.

Sampson (1993) showed that communities with higher levels of social organization and control had lower rates of juvenile delinquency than did less well organized neighborhoods. Interpretations of this link suggest that in communities with high levels of control, neighbors, in a collective and individual sense, organize to enforce the norms they deem valuable, such as low drug use and truancy. Similarly, Elliott and Huizinga (1990) reported that, even after controlling for socioeconomic status, rates of alcohol and drug use were lower in more organized communities. Other studies have shown that neighborhood characteristics have implications for the effectiveness of violence prevention initiatives as well. The positive effect of prevention programs has been found to be dampened in high risk neighborhoods (Aber, Jones, Brown, Chaudry, & Samples, 1998).

Studies of the neighborhood primarily examine economically challenged youth and communities, and within this circumscribed scope, attend largely to minority youth. This focus underscores the needs of minority youth in economically impoverished situations (Stack & Burton, 1993; Wilson, 1987), connecting these needs and their contexts to youths' functioning (Brooks-Gunn et al., 1993), giving rise to meaningful basic research and valuable policy initiatives. Yet, concentration largely on youth who are economically impoverished leads to a lack of information regarding youth who face other profound challenges. Adolescents confronting the challenges of chronic illness, whether in economically impoverished or more advantaged communities, may experience life in their communities in ways that are unique from their nonchronically ill counterparts. Adolescents with diabetes and their families represent a special challenge to communities, because their needs may be greater than those of other families living nearby. Diabetic adolescents may be more isolated than their neighboring peers, and need additional support from their community.

A recent literature search of key words community—neighborhood, and diabetic or chronically ill youth—was conducted across several databases (September, 1999; psychological abstracts, sociological abstracts, and medline abstracts). This search yielded only a handful of studies examining community influences on diabetic youth. Two studies are from the same research group (Turner-Henson and colleagues). Examining 10- to 12-year-olds with heart disease, asthma, and diabetes, Turner-Henson (1993) showed a relation between mothers' perceptions of neighborhood as resourceful and increased interactions with the community. These results are intuitively appealing and could be expanded on by an exploration of the specifics of what mothers of chronically ill youth found resourceful. In addition, Turner-Henson's work (Turner-Hensen, 1993; Holaday, Swan, & Turner-Hensen, 1997) included only pre- and young adolescents. As youth traverse adolescence, they interact in their neighborhoods with increasing frequency (Furstenberg, 1993). Consequently, it should be possible to discern more distinct patterns between individual adolescents with diabetes as they move through middle and later adolescent years. In another study, Powers et al. (1985) assessed diabetic, psychiatrically ill, and healthy preadolescents, early adolescents, and middle adolescents. Parents reported on whether their family turns to their community for assistance during difficult times. Results showed that above all other groups of adolescents (i.e., psychiatrically ill and healthy), families of diabetic youth were more active in seeking support from their neighbors and community resources (Powers et al., 1985). The emergent pattern across these studies suggest that families of diabetic youth turn to their neighbors and communities. In addition to parents' subjective reports, new research efforts along these lines could benefit by including adolescents' subjective reports, local health professionals' subjective reports, and objective indicators of neighborhood characteristics (e.g., U.S. Census Bureau reports, police records). Furthermore, future research should include adolescents and families from diverse ethnic groups in order to explore the influences of cultural values and relative neighborhood advantage or deprivation on diabetic families' use of communities. Explorations could also examine whether families' patterns of seeking community support vary by adolescents' age. In deepening knowledge of these connections, future studies could identify the conditions under which families of diabetic youth are likely to turn to communities, and under what conditions they are least likely to turn to communities for help. It would also be possible to determine whether families of diabetic children living in low resource communities differ in their patterns of use compared to their counterparts living in higher resource communities.

Because youth with chronic illness have not been systematically studied with respect to community influences, it is not clear whether neighborhood characteristics previously identified as promoting optimal outcomes (e.g., lower teen pregnancy, lower juvenile delinquency) would be the same for youth with diabetes. Given the lack of empirical studies in this area, there can only be speculation about the way that communities may be connected to youth with chronic illnesses. Systematic investigation of these links should include not only tests of traditional theories of neighborhood influence (e.g., social organization), but also more recent contemporary innovative theories regarding neighborhood connections (e.g., collective efficacy; Sampson et al., 1997). For instance, tests of collective efficacy could include measures of residents' perceptions of the potential for support from neighbors to determine whether youth with chronic illnesses perceive support differently than their non-ill counterparts. In addition, empirical investigations could assess whether chronically ill youth are more or less responsive to neighborhood support: Are youth with diabetes more or less likely to be influenced by dynamics in their neighborhood? Are diabetic youth more likely to fare better in terms of general adjustment in certain neighborhoods? Are diabetic youth more likely to be compliant with illness-related treatments in certain neighborhoods? How does gender influence these linkages with community support?

STAGE–ENVIRONMENT FIT MODEL AND COMMUNITIES

The thinking regarding the question of optimal community contexts for youth with chronic illness is guided by the stage–environment fit perspective, presented by Eccles and colleagues (Eccles, Midgley, Wigfield, et al., 1993; Eccles, Lord, & Roeser, 1996). The stage–environment fit model uses a developmental perspective (Hunt, 1975), which has at its center the notion that developmentally appropriate contexts promote optimal psychosocial growth. Specifically, this model suggests that positive outcomes result from a match (i.e., a good fit) between the adolescents' developmental stage and the demands of their social context. In contrast, negative outcomes are hypothesized to result from a developmental mismatch (i.e., a poor fit) between an adolescent's developmental stage and the demands of his or her social context (Eccles & Midgley, 1989). Although the stage–environment fit model was originally proposed to examine links between early adolescents' academic performance and the demands of their school environment (Eccles & Midgley, 1989; Eccles et al., 1993, Eccles et al., 1996), this paradigm has significant implications for understanding youth with chronic illness in context. With the exception of Obeidallah, Hauser, and Jacobson (1999), the majority of the research on the stage–environment fit model has focused exclusively on normative, nonclinical populations. Moreover, although schools and families have been explored as important settings for providing appropriate challenges for adolescents, communities have been all but overlooked.

Findings suggest that highly organized and cohesive communities contribute to better functioning among nonchronically ill youth. It is possible that highly organized and cohesive communities would be linked to better functioning among youth with diabetes. In such neighborhoods, neighboring parents and community leaders could work together to help diabetic adolescents cope with the management of their illness. In addition, in highly cohesive neighborhoods, parents may work collaboratively to prevent local nondiabetic adolescents from alienating or ridiculing youth with diabetes.

On the other hand, communities that are too cohesive may create a situation where diabetic adolescents feel singled-out as a function of their disease and the efforts required for its proper management. What constitutes a good match for adolescents without chronic illness may, then, in fact represent a poor fit for adolescents with diabetes. The complex dance that youth with diabetes engage in—balancing the demands of caring for their disease with the demands of normative adolescent development—may change the expected positive connections between community cohesiveness and adolescents' outcomes. The same community characteristics identified as promoting optimal outcomes among physically healthy adolescents may be the very ones that are deleterious for adolescents with diabetes.

Central to neighborhood's differential influence on diabetic adolescents are issues of control. Kyngas and Barlow (1995) suggest that adolescents who see their parents and the diabetes as controlling may be more inclined to rebel against both. Similarly, it can be argued that highly socially controlled communities act as another restrictive force for diabetic adolescents. Adolescents living in highly controlled and organized neighborhoods, who not only feel overregulated by their disease—and perhaps, by their families' response to their disease—may also feel as if the cohesiveness in their neighborhood is an additional restrictive force. High levels of community social control, which otherwise may be connected to youths' likelihood of experiencing better outcomes, could instead represent another force undermining diabetic adolescents' struggle for independence and autonomy.

It is possible that adolescents who live in highly cohesive neighborhoods would be associated with positive outcomes. Although moderately cohesive neighborhoods may represent the most optimal fit for diabetic adolescents, it is unlikely that neighborhoods characterized by anomie, disorganization, and utter disarray are better for such youth. In fact, it is likely that neighborhoods characterized by high levels of social disorganization would not be the most optimal environment for any adolescent (i.e., diabetic or otherwise). Often, families in neighborhoods with high levels of social disorganization find that they are isolated from other families and from local services. Unfortunately, isolated families may "face dilemmas in an ever-increasing spiral of difficulty, whereas a family who has supports may turn to others for help" (Palfrey, 1994, p. 29).

Instead of either end of the cohesiveness spectrum, we propose that the most developmentally and disease-sensitive communities are those that are reasonably cohesive, with moderate levels of social organization and control. Neighborhoods with moderate levels of organization and control provide a backdrop of solid connections between neighbors that are not overbearing or excessively controlling. Within a person-environment fit model (Hunt, 1975), it is in such community contexts that adolescents with diabetes have the highest likelihood of successfully negotiating the competing demands of their disease and those associated with normative adolescent development. Testing these ideas empirically involves comparing adjustment indices between youth with and without chronic illness. As predictors, it would be important to include direct objective measures of neighborhoods, such as those provided by U.S. census, local police records of criminal behavior, or other official reports. Optimally, these objective measures could be coupled with subjective reports from adolescents themselves and their family members, and local peers. Additional useful information may be gleaned from key individuals in the neighborhood, such as town leaders and local government officials. Using this multimethod, multireporter approach would facilitate the development of a measure of community cohesiveness and organization. This measure would ideally be continuous so that it would be possible to note whether and where community levels of cohesiveness become problematic for diabetic youth. This approach would not only help researchers understand the experiences of youth with diabetes better, but would also deepen the understanding of the way communities potentially influence nonchronically ill adolescents.

In order to capture developmental issues in context, it is important to assess youth with diabetes over time. Multiple assessments across adolescence could help identify different levels of risk associated with certain community characteristics. Determining whether patterns of risk across adolescence differed for diabetic versus nondiabetic youth would be an interesting and important endeavor. Assessments could begin during preadolescence and continue until early adulthood. Ways to measure developmental status include chronological age, pubertal status, and/or timing. Such developmental markers could be linked to developmental challenges (e.g., interpersonal relationships) and connected to other psychosocial outcomes.

DANGEROUS NEIGHBORHOODS AND FAMILIES WITH DIABETIC YOUTH

Previous research suggests that emotional stress, particularly from an uncontrollable source, may impede functioning at multiple levels (Allison et al., 1999; Dweck & Light, 1980; Seligman & Maier, 1967). Adolescents living in communities marked by high crime and violence are likely to be living in a stressful context. Stress and its influence on developing systems has particular relevance when considering the impact of dangerous communities on youth with chronic illness.

Concerns related to dangerous neighborhoods supersede issues of socioeconomic status. Neighborhood research has shown that socioeconomic disadvantage is not monolithically associated with community crime (Furstenberg, 1993) or other negative outcomes (Obeidallah, Burton, & Allison, 1999). In regard to adolescents with diabetes, studies examining socioeconomic status and outcomes revealed varied findings: Some research suggests that in lower socioeconomic households, family functioning is compromised after the diagnoses of diabetes is made (Northam et al., 1996), whereas other research indicates that there is no relation between diabetic control and socioeconomic status (Frey & Denyes, 1989; Marteau, Bloch, & Baum, 1987). These two streams of research converge to suggest that socioeconomic status is not necessarily a marker of negative outcomes; instead, other contextual factors, such as levels of community violence and crime, may be more meaningful predictors of outcomes for adolescents with diabetes. In fact, a growing body of research indicates relations between exposure to crime in neighborhoods and youths' development of posttraumatic stress symptoms (Fitzpatrick & Boldizar, 1993; Selner-O'Hagan et al., 1998). Given the dearth of research in this area, however, explorations of the direct effects of socioeconomic status, as well as the interaction between socioeconomic status and community contexts, are necessary in order to best determine these connections.

Despite the theoretical and practical importance of such studies, the relation between community danger and outcomes among youth with diabetes has not been systematically addressed. It is possible, indeed likely, that dangerous communities influence the well-being of adolescents with diabetes. In addition, dangerous communities contribute to the way that parents interact with adolescents. For example, in an effort to guard their young from harm, parents living in dangerous neighborhoods often dramatically increase their control over their children (Burton, 1993; Palfrey, 1994). At its extreme, increased control can take the form of lock-up strategies, wherein children are sent to their rooms immediately following school (Furstenberg, 1993). Families with diabetic adolescents, who may already be acting in overprotective ways in response to the disease, may feel particularly compelled to bolster their protection over their youth in dangerous neighborhoods.

Although tight control may be beneficial for adolescents' physical well-being and safety, it may exact a toll in terms of adolescents' attainment of important developmental needs. For example, the opportunities for development of interpersonal relationships with peers may be undermined among diabetic youth who live in overprotective families in dangerous neighborhoods. Further, this type of overcontrol may lay the planks for acting out or rebelling, possibly unintentionally increasing youths' likelihood of falling into harm's way. Gender also may play a strong role, with some families stepping-up their protective efforts for their adolescent daughters more so than for their sons. Such differential treatment based on gender may contribute to group differences between girls and boys who have diabetes.

In contrast, some families in dangerous neighborhoods may be overstressed, and in turn, may withdraw from actively working with adolescents in their development of adherence to treatment protocols. In both scenarios, families respond to stresses in their communities and then in turn directly influence adolescents' experiences. The extra complications associated with management of diabetes contributes to the hypothesis that the harmful effects of dangerous communities would be exacerbated among diabetic youth.

COMMUNITIES CONTEXTS, DIABETIC ADOLESCENTS, AND THEIR PEERS

Although the needs of youth with diabetes have been identified by the medical profession, little research has explored the community risks specific to diabetic adolescents. A central risk to youth with diabetes may be through peers in their community. Certainly, there has been a good deal of research exploring the links between diabetic adolescents and their peer groups. Jacobson and colleagues (Jacobson et al., 1990; Jacobson et al., 1997) found that 55% of adolescents did not talk to their friends about their diabetes. Even more striking, 35% of adolescents with diabetes thought they would be better liked if they did not have diabetes. Such a pattern belies adolescents' tendency to want to be similar to other peers, especially during early adolescence. Adolescents who depart from typical maturation may be at increased risk for isolation from peers, have poor self-concept, and experience lower self-esteem. Youth who are socially rejected are those most likely to engage in risky and problematic behavior (Coie et al., 1995; Kupersmidt et al., 1995). Diabetic youth who are excluded from peer groups may be accepted only by those youth who have also been socially rejected. A differential association model (Sullivan, 1996) suggests that adolescents who associate with delinquent peers have an increased vulnerability to engage in risk-taking behavior.

In addition to the individual level risk connected with deviant peers, community attributes may also play a role in increasing diabetic youths' vulnerability to deviant activities. Communities that are socially disorganized and exhibit low social control tend to have a higher proportion of deviant youth compared to neighborhoods that are less disorganized and controlled (Sampson et al., 1997; Simcha-Fagan & Schwartz, 1986). Diabetic adolescents, who may already be vulnerable to peer pressure, and who live in neighborhoods where they have more opportunity to associate with delinquent peers, may find it especially difficult to avoid risk-taking behaviors. Risk-taking behaviors, such as using drugs and smoking, have a far more deleterious effect on diabetic adolescents than their nondiabetic counterparts. This is so because such substances may interact with the disease as well as medication, predisposing these youth for even more significant troubles. Rates of morbidity and mortality show a sharp increase among drug-using diabetic adolescents compared to their nondrug-using diabetic counterparts and their nonchronically ill peers (Patterson & Garwick, 1998). Thus, community influences may differentially influence adolescents, dependent on their chronic illness status; chronically ill youth may be particularly vulnerable to peer pressure and may experience worse outcomes associated with risk-taking behaviors than their nonchronically ill counterparts.

Additional studies that measure diabetic adolescents' peer networks, including adolescents' perceptions of peers as well as direct assessments of peers themselves, would help close the gaps in an understanding of diabetic adolescents' peer relationships. Through the investigation of diabetic adolescents' peer groups in relation to community characteristics, it is possible to determine the mediating and moderating influences between peers and communities for diabetic adolescents. Peers may mediate connections between community characteristics and diabetic adolescents' experiences—for example, in socially disorganized communities, there may be more delinquent and deviant activity for youth to get involved in. In such contexts, diabetic adolescents who may be socially isolated, may have more opportunity to associate with delinquent peers and engage in delinquent activities. Thus, in the mediating model, the negative influence of troubled communities operates through peers. In a moderating model, delinquent peers would exert a deleterious influence on diabetic adolescents only in contexts where the neighborhood shows signs of disorganization. That is, moderately socially organized neighborhoods would buffer diabetic adolescents from becoming involved with delinquent peers and their activities.

CONCLUSIONS

This work takes an ecosystemic perspective in examining the multiple contexts that adolescents with diabetes traverse. The importance of person–environment match between adolescents, their families, and communities has been discussed. The discussion also has challenged the notion that highly cohesive neighborhoods are the best environments for adolescents with diabetes. It also has described potential pitfalls in dangerous neighborhoods for families and adolescents with diabetes. Finally, the idea has been explored that diabetic adolescents living in troubled neighborhoods may be more susceptible to engaging in risk-taking behaviors.

Underlying the idea of a good fit between communities and adolescents with diabetes is the assumption that adolescents with diabetes may experience their communities differently than do their nondiabetic peers. In particular, it is suggested that what may constitute a good match for nondiabetic youth and their communities may not necessarily include the same ingredients that create an optimal match for diabetic youth. Instead, the possibility is raised that, to the extent to which highly cohesive and organized neighborhoods represent a controlling force, they may be associated with more negative outcomes for diabetic adolescents. This concept is in accordance with earlier work by Reiss, Gonzalez, and Kramer (1984), which suggested that chronically ill family members who were in families with high levels of family integration and coordination were more likely to die earlier than their counterparts in families that were less cohesive. A moderate level of cohesion in communities would lead to the most optimal match between community characteristics and adolescents with diabetes.

In keeping with an ecosystemic perspective, communities do not simply impact adolescents directly. Instead, community characteristics influence families, and families in turn influence adolescents. In highly stressed communities, families may bolster efforts to protect adolescents from proximal dangers. This healthy wish to protect a child from danger, however, may be exacerbated in families that already engage in protective strategies surrounding the management and care of diabetes. Although increased protection may help adolescents' physical well-being to some extent, it may have the unfortunate consequence of undermining adolescents' attempts at individuation and attainment of other developmentally appropriate goals.

Previous research shows that in neighborhoods with low levels of social organization and control, adolescents' risk of engaging in deviant activity is increased (Furstenberg, 1993). The greater the prevalence of adolescents who engage in delinquent activity, the more opportunity for other adolescents to become associated with delinquent activity. It is suggested that such a situation presents a particularly risky situation for diabetic adolescents. Diabetic adolescents may be more susceptible to trying to "fit in" with peers (Thomas & Hauser, 1997), a situation that exposes them to the negative influence of peer pressure. If this is the case, then adolescents with diabetes who live in neighborhoods with low levels of social organization may be most vulnerable to engaging in delinquent activity. In other words, the relation between socially disorganized neighborhoods and delinquent adolescents may be intensified by diabetic adolescents' increased vulnerability to peer pressure.

Clearly, individual differences among diabetic adolescents exist, creating a mosaic of complex and diverse patterns within this special group. Individual differences occur at multiple layers. First of all, not all youth in the same community are exposed to the same level of community characteristics. Second, among those who are exposed to the same level of a community characteristic, not all will respond in the same way (Cicchetti & Aber, 1998). One line of inquiry relevant to researchers, health practitioners, and policymakers is to identify which community characteristics are associated with better or worse adherence to management of the disease. Within such identified high risk communities, what protects adolescents with diabetes from experiencing negative outcomes? How does gender figure into these models? Are girls or boys more sensitive to community characteristics in terms of their disease management? How would disease management interact with community characteristics to contribute to other outcomes (e.g., pregnancy status, school achievement, drug use)?

Currently, psychosocial predictors of diabetic youths' health status include a patients' adherence and stress (Johnson, 1995). This work suggests that in addition to these individual level predictors, medical health professionals consider the context in which diabetes will be managed. The full gamut of highly organized to highly chaotic and dangerous neighborhoods has implications for how adolescents manage their disease, as well as for how their families will cope with maintenance. Consideration of the neighborhood context with respect to diabetic adolescents should occur at multiple levels, including the medical level (e.g., pediatricians taking into account the contextual barriers to compliance), research level (e.g., social scientists exploring the potential role of community characteristics on diabetic adolescents' adherence, general well-being, and family processes), and the policy level (e.g., implementing social policy that moves toward creating optimal environments for all youth, with particular attention to those who are chronically ill).

The focus here has been primarily on the broader context of neighborhoods; other contexts, such as schools, also play a significant role in shaping diabetic adolescents' experiences (Delamater, Bubb, Warren-Boulton, & Fisher, 1984). A valuable line of future research is to consider these interlocking contexts in their contribution to diabetic adolescents' development.

Although the aim of this chapter has been to describe communities and adolescents with diabetes, the information presented may be used as a template to better understand those youth who are HIV-positive, have asthma, lupus, cystic fibrosis, hemophilia, or other chronic illness. Discovering convergent themes running through studies of various discrete chronic illnesses and community connections will help researchers ultimately to arrive at a place where new factors, in a new context, can be identified that can enhance adaptation of these special groups of adolescents.

ACKNOWLEDGMENTS

We gratefully acknowledge the scholarly help of Barbara Anderson and Timothy Davis in the preparation of this work.

REFERENCES

Aber, J. L., Jones, S. M., Brown, J. L., Chaudry, N., & Samples, F. (1998). Resolving conflict creatively: Evaluating the developmental effects of a school-based violence prevention program in neighborhood and classroom context. *Development & Psychopathology, 10,* 187–213.

Allison, K. W., Burton, L., Marshall, S., Perez-Febles, A., Yarrington, J., Kirsh, L. B., & Merriwether-DeVries, C. (1999). Life experiences among urban adolescents: Examining the role of context. *Child Development, 70,* 1017–1029.

Anderson, B. J. (1995). Childhood and adolescent psychological development in relation to diabetes mellitus. In C. Kelnar (Ed.), *Childhood and adolescent diabetes* (pp. 107–119). London: Chapman & Hall.

Blechman, E. A., & Delamater, A. M. (1993). Family communication and Type 1 diabetes: A window on the social environment of chronically ill children. In R. Cole & D. Reiss (Eds.), *How do families cope with chronic illness? Family research consortium: Advances in family research* (pp. 1–24). Hillsdale, NJ: Lawrence Erlbaum Associates.

Brooks-Gunn, J., Duncan, G. J., Klebanov, P. K., & Sealand, N. (1993). Do neighborhoods influence child and adolescent development? *American Journal of Sociology, 99,* 353–395.

Burton, L. M. (1993). Teenage childbearing as an alternative life-course strategy in multigeneration black families. In R. A. Pierce & M. Black (Eds.), *Life-span development: A diversity reader* (pp. 163–176). Dubuque, IA: Kendall/Hunt.

Burton, L. M., Obeidallah, D. A., & Allison, K. (1996). Ethnographic insights on social context and adolescent development among inner city, African-American teens. In R. Jessor, A. Colby, & R. Shweder (Eds.), *Ethnography and Human Development* (pp. 395–418). Chicago: The University of Chicago Press.

Bronfenbrenner, U. (1979). *The ecology of human development: Experiments by nature and design.* Cambridge MA: Harvard University Press.

Bronfenbrenner, U. (1986). *Ecology of the family as a context for human development.* Cambridge, MA: Harvard University Press.

Cicchetti, D., & Aber, L. (1998). Contextualism and developmental psychopathology. *Development and Psychopathology, 10,* 137–141.

Coie, J., Terry, R., Lenox, K., & Lochman, John. Childhood peer rejection and aggression as predictors of stable patterns of adolescent disorder. *Development & Psychopathology, 7,* 697–713.

Coleman, J. S. (1994). Social capital, human capital, and investment in youth. In A. C. Petersen & J. T. Mortimer (Eds.), *Youth unemployment and society* (pp. 34–50). New York: Cambridge University Press.

Delamater, A. M., Bubb, J., Warren-Boulton, E., & Fisher, E. B. (1984). Diabetes management in the school setting: The role of the school psychologist. *School Psychology Review, 13,* 192–203.

Dixon, R. A., Lerner, R. M. (1999). History and systems in developmental psychology. In M. H. Bornstein & M. E. Lamb (Eds.), *Developmental psychology: An advanced textbook* (pp. 3–45). Mahwah, NJ: Lawrence Erlbaum Associates.

Dweck, C. S., & Light, B. G. (1980). Learned helplessness and intellectual achievement. In J. Garber & M. E. Seligman (Eds.), *Human helplessness: Theory and applications* (pp. 197–221). New York: Academic Press.

Eccles, J., Lord, L., & Roester, R. (1996). Round holes, square pegs, rocky roads and sore feet: The impact of stage–environment fit on young adolescents' experiences in schools and families. In *Adolescence: Opportunities and Challenges, Rochester Symposium on Developmental Psychopathology* (Vol. 7).

Eccles, J., S., & Midgley, C. (1989). Stage-environment fit: Developmentally appropriate classrooms for early adolescents. In R. E. Ames & C. Ames (Eds.), *Research on motivation in education* (pp. 139–186). San Diego, CA: Academic Press.

Eccles, J. S., Midgley, C., Wigfield, A., Buchanan, C. M., Reuman, D., Flanagan, C., & MacIver, D. (1993). Development during adolescence: The impact of stage-environment fit on young adolescents' experiences in schools and in families. *American Psychologist, 48,* 90–101.

Elder, G. H., Jr. (1974). *Children of the great depression.* Chicago: University of Chicago Press.

Elliott, D. S., & Huizinga, D. (1990). The mediating effects of the social structure in high risk neighborhoods. Paper presented at the annual meeting of the American Sociological Association, Washington, DC.

Fitzpatrick, K. M., & Boldizar, J. P. (1993). The prevalence and consequences of exposure to violence among African-American youth. *Journal of the American Academy of Child & Adolescent Psychiatry, 32,* 424–430.

Frey, M. A., & Denyes, M. J. (1989). Health and illness self-care in adolescents with IDDM: A test of Orem's theory. *Advances in Nursing Science, 12,* 67–75.

Furstenberg, F. F. (1993). How families manage risk and opportunity in dangerous neighborhoods. In W. J. Wilson (Ed.) *Sociology and the public agenda* (pp. 231–258). Newbury Park, CA: Sage.

Glasgow, R. E., & Anderson, B. J. (1995). Future directions for research on pediatric chronic disease management: Lessons from diabetes. *Journal of Pediatric Psychology, 20,* 389–402.

Hauser, S. T., Jacobson, A. M., Benes, K. A., & Anderson, B. J. (1997). Psychosocial aspects of diabetes mellitus in children and adolescents: Implications and interventions.

Hauser, S. T., Jacobson, A. M., Lavori, P., Wolfsdorf, J. I., Herskowitz, R. D., Milley, J. E., Bliss, R., Wertlieb, D., & Stein, J. (1990). Adherence among children and adolescents with insulin-dependent diabetes mellitus over a four-year longitudinal follow-up: II. Immediate and long-term linkages with the family milieu. *Journal of Pediatric Psychology, 15,* 527–42.

Hauser, S. T., Jacobson, A. M., Wertlieb, D., Weiss-Perry, B., Follansbee, D., Wolfsdorf, J. I., Herskowitz, R. D., Houlihan, J., & Rajapark, D. C. (1986). Children with recently diagnosed diabetes: Interactions within their families. *Health Psychology, 5*(3), 273–296.

Hauser, S. T., & Solomon, M. (1985). Coping with diabetes: Views from the family. In P. Ahmed & M. Ahmed (Eds.), *Coping with diabetes* (pp. 234–266). Springfield, IL: Thomas.

Hirschi, T. (1969). *Causes of delinquency.* Berkeley: University of California Press.

Holaday, B., Swam, J. H., & Turner-Henson, A. (1997). Images of neighborhood and activity patterns of chronically ill schoolage children. *Environment and Behavior, 29,* 348–373.

Hunt, D. E.(1975). Person-environment interaction: A challenge found wanting before it was tried. *Review of Educational Research, 45,* 209–230.

Kupersmidt, J. B., Burchinal, M., & Patterson, C. J. (1995). Developmental patterns of childhood peer relations as predictors of externalizing behavior problems. *Development & Psychopa-t hology, 7,* 825–843.

Jacobson, A. M., Hauser, S. T., Cole, C., Willett, J. B., Wolfsdorf, J. I., Dvorak, R., Wolpert, H., Herman, L., & de Groot, M. (1997). Social relationships among young adults with insulin-dependent diabetes mellitus: Ten-year follow-up of an onset cohort. *Diabetic Medicine, 14,* 73–79.

Jacobson, A. M., Hauser, S. T., Lavori, P., & Wolfsdorf, J. I. (1990). Adherence among children and adolescents with insulin-dependent diabetes mellitus over a four-year longitudinal follow-up: I. The influence of patient coping and adjustment. *Journal of Pediatric Psychology, 15,* 511–526.

Johnson, S. B. (1995). Insulin-dependent diabetes mellitus in childhood. *Handbook of pediatric psychology* (pp. 265–285). New York: Guilford.

Kyngas, H., & Barlow, J. (1995). Diabetes: An adolescent's perspective. *Journal of Advanced Nursing 22*(5), 941–947.

Lynch, M., & Cicchetti, D. (1998). An ecological-transactional analysis of children and contexts: The longitudinal interplay among child maltreatment, community violence, and children's symptomatology. *Development & Psychopathology, 10,* 235–257.

Marteau, T. M., Bloch, S., & Baum, D. J. (1987). Family life and diabetic control. *Journal of Child Psychology & Psychiatry & Allied Disciplines, 28,* 823–833.

Northam, E., Anderson, P., Adler, R., Werther, G. et al. (1996). Psychosocial and family functioning in children with insulin-dependent diabetes at diagnosis and one year later. *Journal of Pediatric Psychology, 21,* 699–717.

Obeidallah, D. A., Burton, L. M., & Allison, K. A. (1999). *Context of vulnerability: Neighborhoods of pregnant and non pregnant urban adolescent girls.* Unpublished manuscript.

Obeidallah, D. A., Hauser, S. T., & Jacobson, A. M. (1999). The long-branch of phase-environment fit: Concurrent and longitudinal implications of match and mismatch among diabetic and non-diabetic youth. *Journal of Adolescent Research, 14,* 95–121.

Palfrey, J. S. (1994). *Community child health: An action plan for today.* Westport, CT: Praeger.

Patterson, J. M., & Garwick, A. W. (1998). Theoretical linkages: Family meanings and sense of coherence. In H. I. McCubbin & E. A. Thompson (Eds.), *Stress, coping, and health in families: Sense of coherence and resiliency. Resiliency in families series* (pp. 71–89). Thousand Oaks, CA: Sage.

Petersen, A. C., Compas, B. E., Brooks-Gunn, J., Stemmler, M., Ey, S., & Grant, K. E. (1993). Depression in adolescence. *American Psychologist, 48,* 155–168.

Powers, S. I. et al. (1985). Coping strategies of families of seriously ill adolescents. *Journal of Early Adolescence, 5,* 101–113.

Reiss, D., Gonzalez, S., & Kramer, N. (1984). Family process, chronic illness, and death. *Archives of General Psychiatry, 43,* 795–804.

Reiss, D., Steinglass, P., & Howe, G. (1998). The family's organization around the illness. In R. E. Cole & D. Reiss (Eds.), *How do families cope with chronic illness* (pp. 173–213). Hillsdale, NJ: Lawrence Erlbaum Associates.

Sampson, R. J. (1993). The community context of violent crime. In W. J. Wilson (Ed.), *Sociology and the public agenda* (pp. 259–286). Newbury Park, CA: Sage.

Sampson, R. J., Raudenbush, S. W., & Earls, F. (1997). Neighborhoods and violent crime: A multilevel study of collective efficacy. *Science, 227 (volume),* 918–224.

Seligman, M. E., & Maier, S. F. (1967). Failure to escape traumatic shock. *Journal of Experimental Psychology, 74,* 1–9.

Selner-O'Hagan, M., Kindlon, D. J., Buka, S. L., Raudenbush, S. W., & Earls, F. J. (1998). Assessing exposure to violence in urban youth. *Journal of Child Psychology & Psychiatry & Allied Disciplines, 39,* 215–224.

Shaw, C., & McKay, H. (1942). *Juvenile delinquency and urban areas.* Chicago: The University of Chicago.

Simcha-Fagan, O., & Schwartz, J. E. (1986). Neighborhood and delinquency: An assessment of contextual effects. *Crimonology, 24,* 667–703.

Stack, C. B., & Burton, L. M. (1993). Kinscripts. *Journal of Comparative Family Studies, 24,* 157–170.

Sullivan, M. L. (1996). Neighborhood social organization: A forgotten object of ethnographic study? In R. Jessor & A. Colby (Eds.), *Ethnography and human development: Context and meaning in social inquiry. The John D. and Catherine T. MacArthur Foundation series on mental health and development* (pp. 205–224). Chicago: University of Chicago Press.

Turner-Henson, A. (1993). Mothers of chronically ill children and perceptions of environmental variables. *Issues in Comprehensive Pediatric Nursing, 16,* 63–76.

Wertlieb, D., Jacobson, A. M., & Hauser, S. T. (1990). The child with diabetes: A developmental stress and coping perspective. In P. T. Costa & G. R. VandenBos (Eds.), *Psychological aspects of serious illness: Chronic conditions, fatal diseases and clinical care* (pp. 61–102). Washington, DC: American Psychological Association.

Wilson, W. J. (1987). *The truly disadvantaged: The inner-city, the underclass, and public policy.* Chicago: University of Chicago.

26

Childhood Health Issues Across the Life Span

Barbara G. Melamed
Barrie Kaplan
Joshua Fogel
Yeshiva University

Drotar et al. (1989) reviewed two decades of child health research and proclaimed the need for a developmental perspective to guide the focus of health promotion. This would also pinpoint where and by whom the site of delivery of services should occur. Some of the factors that make children likely to develop illness are genetic (family history of disease) and environmental (poverty, crowding, lack of nutrition). These factors are difficult to alter. In addition, the mental health of the parents and their level of functioning at the time of their child's incipient illness is likely to determine how soon a child receives access to health care treatment, and how effectively the recommended treatment program can be implemented. For instance, many parents either cannot afford or do not completely understand the concept of prolonged medication even when the symptoms have abated (i.e., antibiotic treatment). Even when parents are psychologically well adjusted there are numerous problems that can exacerbate stress, including:

1. Establishing relationships with medical personnel (Moos, 1977).
2. Coping with medical procedures associated with treatment.
3. Coping with symptoms associated with the condition (whether it is acute or chronic) (Moos, 1977).
4. Coping with the possible separation from parents, other family members, and friends.
5. Coping with the new social pressures such as being labeled as "ill" or having a medical problem.
6. Coping with the limitations that result from a change in lifestyle (e.g., diabetic children must change their diets, asthmatic children must exercise caution during physical activity).
7. Stress of missing school and acclimating during the return to school.
8. Coping with the added burden facing the entire family, including time and money.

Some protection for the child is afforded by certain policy regulations. Unfortunately, access to public health for immunization and inoculation against childhood illness is not as universal as school requirements. Once a child has been admitted to the public school system, further immunizations for new diseases may not be as successful as in the earlier years. In addition, environmentally induced problems exist. Asthma or lead poisoning are difficult to change in the absence of laws protecting children from environmental contaminants. Accidental deaths by falling from heights and seat belt wearing are often prevented only when the absence of window guards and wrong application or absence of seat belts are enforced by penalty. Even in these cases, new incidents of infant death by inappropriate inflation of automobile air bags may confuse parents about the proper precautions. Parents often misunderstand safety rule communication and do not provide children with a model of preventive habits.

This chapter focuses on three areas of research as representative of some of the issues that determine whether children can receive adequate care by retraining parents, health care professionals, and policymakers on the importance of prevention across the life span. Studies dealing with issues of illness onset in children diagnosed with asthma will hopefully illuminate issues in self-management across a wide range of chronic illnesses. The issue of organ transplantation has become a serious consideration and will continue to be prevalent in the 21st century. Therefore, it is used as a prototype to discuss issues of decision-making and treatment compliance issues that raise the ethical and practical concerns involved in having this choice. Finally, the issues of prevention of accident, injury, and recognition of the precursors of child abuse are discussed. The chapter attempts to set forth a functional analysis for use by health care professionals to help them see where to focus their efforts, whether it be on prevention, remediation, or teaching self-care behaviors. Future directions for research are specified.

DEVELOPMENTAL ASSESSMENT OF COPING

Differences in Conceptualization and Assessment of Coping

An understanding of coping requires knowing what the task demands of the situation involve, as well as what resources the family has to bring to problem solving. In addition, the mental age of the child must be considered to assess whether the illness problems overwhelm the developmental task of that life period. As others have pointed out, there are few reliable and valid instruments that measure children's coping (Ryan-Wenger, 1992, Wertlieb et al., 1987). The importance of assessment is to determine which coping strategies are most suitable for the numerous stressful events that children and adolescents confront. The difficulty of constructing such a scale and assessing coping mechanisms can be attributed to several causes. There is confusion about the difference between coping mechanisms and coping styles. The two are often used interchangeably, although they relate to different types of behavior. Coping mechanisms are the focus of this chapter and, according to Lazarus and Folkman (1984), the term refers to constantly changing cognitive and behavioral efforts to manage specific internal and external demands that are appraised as taxing or exceeding the resources of the person. Implicit in this definition is the ability to deliberately alter, modify, or adjust both behaviors and thoughts in an attempt to cope with a stressor. In contrast, a coping style is more stable over time and reflects personality characteristics (Lazarus & Folkman, 1984). The definition really demands that the "resources of the person" be considered. This must be applied individually because age as a proxy for developmental ability is known to be deceptive if used without also having knowledge of conceptual level of reasoning and physical maturation or limitations imposed by illness/accident or birth defects.

CHRONIC ILLNESS

Timing Considerations

It is often found that during a critical period at about 6 months to age 3, children separated from a parent due to death, illness, divorce, abandonment, and so on may suffer from attachment problems. This is particularly likely if the children are sick themselves and are in a hospital or another institution with a low staff: children ratio for extended times.

Adaptation to chronic illness is influenced by the rate at which improvements are being made in medical research. For example, adjustment to childhood cancer previously involved providing assistance to families who were anticipating a child's inevitable death. Better survival rates for certain childhood chronic illnesses, including cancer, cystic fibrosis, and AIDS, necessitate new models of continual adjustment to long-term changes in health status.

Despite significant medical advances, chronic illnesses still need to be conceptualized as long-term sources of stress for both children and their families. Long-term health disturbances involve repeated hospitalizations, discomfort, uncertain outcomes, multiple diagnostic procedures, and periodic medical evaluations. Financial resources may be severely strained in families with a chronically ill child, diverting funds from other pursuits. Childhood stress, in turn, may be increased without the additional resources for pursuing special needs educational programs and recreational activities.

Siblings may resent parent's increased attention toward a chronically ill child, especially because sibling conflicts tend to increase during middle childhood. Conflicts are affected by a combination of children's temperaments and parental behavior. Illness changes functioning and roles within the family.

Beliefs about Chronic Illness

Childhood chronic illnesses differ widely with regard to their complexity of medical management. Juvenile diabetes, for example, involves daily adherence to dietary restrictions, blood glucose testing, and insulin injections. Other diseases, such as juvenile rheumatoid arthritis and juvenile diabetes, may involve heightened levels of discomfort. A child may suffer in terms of feeling different from others, which is especially painful in middle childhood.

With their advancing cognitive abilities, children develop more sophisticated notions of cause-and-effect processes in illness development. The cause of illness shifts from being viewed as an external person or action, to an event located within the body. As children's cognitive development matures to include concrete operational thinking, illness representations are altered. Illness beliefs refer to lay understandings of the ways disease processes develop. Children between age 7 and 10 are initially likely to conceive illness in terms of contamination; this implies that an external person, object, or action is responsible for producing illness. Later, children begin to explain illness in terms of internalization. Children, however, have only vague understandings of disease processes at this point.

Additional advances in cognitive development introduce new understandings of the ways illness develops. At approximately age 11, children begin to understand how internal physiological processes are altered to produce disease. The cause of illness shifts from being viewed as an external person or action, to an event located within the body.

Asthma management is the focus of this section, as it is currently the fastest growing epidemic in the United States and is diagnosed in very young children.

ASTHMA

Asthma is the most common disease of childhood and a leading cause of morbidity in adults. Despite significant advances in medical treatment, asthma morbidity and mortality rates have risen dramatically over the past two decades, especially in minority and socioeconomically disadvantaged populations.

Asthma is a lung disease characterized by a variety of features, including airway obstruction or narrowing that is reversible either spontaneously or with treatment. Pathologically, it is characterized as a chronic inflammatory disease of the airways, with a granulocytic-lymphocytic submucosal infiltration, epithelial cell desquamation, and mucus gland hypertrophy and hyperplasia (Wamboldt & Gavin, 1991).

Prevalence

Asthma is the most common chronic disorder of childhood affecting from 4% to 9% of children (Geller, 1996). As many as 50% of the cases are diagnosed before the child reaches age 2. The highest incidence of asthma seems to be from birth to age 4. The estimated prevalence of asthma among children in the United States increased by almost 40% between 1981 and 1988 and is still on the rise. Although the increase occurred mainly among White children, the prevalence of asthma still remains higher in Black children than in White children. Factors that have been implicated in the current rise in asthma prevalence are outdoor air pollution, the decreasing quality of indoor environments as a result of exposure to maternal smoking, and the high levels of dust mites. Other genetic and environmental factors that contribute to the prevalence of childhood asthma are positive family history, male sex, low birth weight, maternal smoking and season of birth (Arshad, Stevens, & Hide, 1993). The increased prevalence of asthma may also be a manifestation of an increase in sensitization among children to inhaled allergens, such as those present in house dust, cat fur, and grass pollen.

Treatment

When asthma is managed properly, hospitalization is rarely necessary. However, about 43% of its economic impact is related to emergency department use, hospitalization, and death, all resulting from the failure of preventive treatment (Milgrom et al., 1996). Current goals of management of asthma are geared toward the relief of obstruction, restoration of oxygenation and ventilation, and prevention of complications. Antiasthma medications improve pulmonary function via three primary mechanisms: bronchodilation, protection of the airways from allergen or histamine challenge, and resolution of airway hyperresponsiveness through antiinflammatory properties. Selective beta agonists, corticosteroids, theophylline, and anticholinergic agents have become the most common of the pharmacologic treatments, and fall into the bronchodilator category. Inhalation is the preferred route because it offers rapid onset of action, delivery directly to the airways, fewer systematic side effects and smaller doses than would be required of oral or intravenous routes. In severe cases, intubation and mechanical ventilation are used.

Day-to-day management of symptoms of the illness utilize educational programs involving both the child and the parents. Physician involvement is recommended. Some of the programs include self-charting of symptoms and medication usage. These programs are aimed at increasing self-management knowledge and skills. The parents must understand the use of their children's inhaled drugs, and if they are being used to prevent episodes or relieve symptoms. Prevention by controlling cigarette smoking and dust mites might decrease the severity of symptoms.

Clinical success is determined by the extent to which people adhere to the complex medical regimen involved. Medical regimens for asthma care are particularly vulnerable to adherence problems because of their duration, the use of multiple medication on both routine and pro re nata (prn, as needed) schedules, and the periods of symptom remission (Rand & Wise, 1994). Medical compliance is defined as the extent to which the person's behavior, in terms of taking medications, following diets, or executing lifestyle changes, coincides with medical or health advice (Weinstein, 1995). Some factors that would contribute to a classification of noncompliance are complete failure to obtain or take the prescribed medication, improper taking of medication because of patient misunderstanding of correct dosage and schedule, omission of doses, increasing or reducing dosage or schedule of dosage, and discontinuing therapy before the end of the recommended period. Children are at a particular risk for nonadherence and noncompliance. It has been documented that only about 50% of inhaled medication is taken as prescribed and compliance does not improve with rising severity of illness (Milgrom et al., 1996). This number may be as high as 90% of pediatric asthmatics (Wamboldt & Gavin, 1991). A common problem among children and adolescents is nonadherence with anti-inflammatory inhalers, which are prophylactic and do not yield an immediate improvement in symptoms. Most children are not using proper inhaler techniques, and are not using an appropriate spaced device to maximize medication delivery to the conducting airways. The metered dose inhaler (MDI) is the most commonly used inhalation technique, however, considerable skill and coordination are needed to use it correctly. A study by Boccuti, Celano, Geller, and Phillips (1996) demonstrated that a significant proportion of children with moderate to severe asthma use poor techniques with from 14% to 26% making critical errors. Just because children use it correctly in front of a practitioner, does not mean they generalize it outside the office. Indirect and direct methods of obtaining information on accuracy are available. Indirect methods use clinical judgments, self-reports, and asthma diaries. Direct measures include biochemical assays that analyze blood or urine testing to objectively measure levels of medication or byproducts in the body. The downside of these methods is laboratory costs and delay in results. There are now electronic devices such as the MDI, which are attached to aerosol inhalers. These devices record the time at which the inhalers are used, and can track patterns of medication usage over a period of several months. In a study (Milgrom et al., 1996) attempting to evaluate adherence in children with asthma to regimens of inhaled corticosteroids and beta agonists, data were collected electronically by metered dose inhaler monitors and compared with traditional diary. There was a large discrepancy between the diary entries and chronologic records of children. Electronic monitoring demonstrated much lower adherence to prescribed therapy than was reported by patients on their diary cards. This important issue of compliance in children is the dependence on their parents for the knowledge and upkeep of their regimens. The parents of an asthmatic child are frequently faced with complex decisions that have to take into account the child's asthma as well as more general developmental needs (Schwam, 1987). Because parents of asthmatic children are under so much stress, it may be important to measure their quality of life and the quality of life of the children to assess adherence influences. Asthma specific scales for children include the Child Asthma Questionnaire and the Pediatric Asthma Quality of Life Questionnaire (Osman & Silverman, 1996). Other predictors of noncompliance may be the level of the stress of the parent (Parenting Stress Index, Abidin, 1986), and the level of depression in both parents and children. Poor symptom perception may undermine compliance (Wamboldt, 1998). Once stable predictors of noncompliance are uncovered, then practitioners can predict who is at risk. Reliable interventions can lower the chance of exacerbation of disease as well as reduce hospitalizations.

TRANSPLANTATION

Psychologists perform various roles in pediatric organ and bone marrow transplants. Usually, patient-centered consultation involves bedside consultation and other forms of patient contact. Indirect psychological consultation relies just on the referral source without any patient contact. Collaborative team consultation involves interaction with the patient, referral source, and other team members (Resnick & Kruczek, 1996).

The referral sources are usually the primary clinical personnel, such as physicians and nurses. The psychologist should balance the needs of both the patient and clinical personnel (Resnick & Kruczek, 1996). However, collaborative relationships with the referral sources are very important and the psychologist should not use a distant authoritarian manner. Satisfaction by the clinical personnel is strongly related to the diagnosis agreement between the referral source and the psychologist (Olson et al., 1988). Also, a collaborative relationship helps avoid issues of territoriality (Carpenter, 1989).

Transplantation consultation and liaison require special skills. The first skill is a knowledge of the biophysiologic components along with their associated psychosocial issues. The second skill is an understanding of the hospital culture along with a tolerance for professional ambiguity and intrusions imposed by medical priorities. The third skill is learning to deliver psychological services both formally and informally, with an understanding that patients and their visiting families do not automatically want psychological services. The fourth skill is the ability to translate and communicate psychological principles and interventions that others can understand and even perform (Carpenter, 1989).

Possible roles associated with transplantation patients involve pre- and posttransplant assessment of the patient and family, assisting with coping during and after the procedure, support for the emotional needs of staff members, and sometimes grief work with the family, sibling donor, or staff if the patient dies (Rappaport, 1988).

Behavioral intervention procedures for varying accompanying behavioral problems are often necessary. A chart listing various suggestions for improving behavioral problems is offered by Charlop, Parrish, Fenton, and Cataldo (1987, p. 494).

Stress

Pediatric organ transplantation (OT) can be classified into three phases. The first, or pretransplant, phase includes the weeks and months before admission where the decision for the transplant and then the search for the donor is made. The second, or acute, phase is the inpatient hospitalization, which typically lasts from 1 to 3 months. The third, or the posttransplant, phase is the time that is only relevant for transplant survivors. Posttransplant complication monitoring continues for a few months and medical and neuropsychological monitoring extends to a few years (Phipps, 1994).

Each phase has its own set of stressors. Some pretransplant phase stressors are the family stress of possible sibling donors, which sibling donor is more appropriate, the patient being indebted to the sibling, the waiting period, and the misconception that the patient will acquire the personality characteristics of the donor (Phipps, 1994).

Some acute phase stressors are patient isolation, sterilization, physical restrictions, sensory deprivation, and hospitalization (Andrykowski, 1994; Phipps, 1994; Phipps & DeCuir-Whalley, 1990).

Some posttransplant phase stressors are physical and social isolation, adjustment to society, the patient's appearance, medical procedures, hospitalization, returning to school, treatment-related side effects, extreme dependence on the medical staff, repeated infection, and the possibility of death (Andrykowski, 1994; Bradford & Tomlinson, 1990; Phipps, 1994; Phipps & DeCuir-Whalley, 1990).

A model of family stress in transplantation suggests that initially there is an adjustment phase to the news of the required transplantation. It is viewed as a stressor that interacts with the existing family resources and the perceptions of this stressor. This leads to the adaptation phase where initially they treat everything as a crisis. This leads to a "pile-up." Strategies to deal with this pile-up involve coping methods of perception of this pile-up and use of existing and new resources (Hare, Skinner, & Kliewer, 1989).

Various patient responses to these stressors are anxiety, depression, withdrawal, anger, hostility, survivor guilt, noncompliance, sleep difficulties, anorexia, paranoia, and acting out (Andrykowski, 1994).

During each of the three phases of OT, appropriate play techniques can ameliorate some patient stress. During the pretransplant phase, children are encouraged to bring their own materials or toys are given to them. During the acute phase, too demanding play activity might be considered intrusive. Instead, minimal participation activities such as reading a story, listening to an audiotape, and viewing a movie is enjoyed. During the posttransplant phase, play interactions can combat the sensory deprivation and social isolation. Tactile activities, such as finger painting or sand and glitter, are helpful. Fantasy play can help to cope with the isolation where the patient can now freely experiment with feelings and situations (Gottlieb & Portnoy, 1988).

Parental Stress. One study showed that mother's stress increased as they moved from the pretransplantation phase to the 1- and 6-month posttransplantation phases. Clinically significant stress was found in 20%, 56%, and 41% of mothers at pretransplantation, and 1-month and 6-month posttransplantation phases, respectively. A greater financial burden, disrupted planning, and caretaker burden stresses were greater at 1 month and 6 months posttransplantation than pretransplantation (Rodrigue et al., 1997).

Another study showed that fathers had lower parenting stress than mothers based on the Parenting Stress Index. This could be either because fathers coped better or fathers were not as involved as mothers. Fathers felt financial stress, disrupted planning of family activities, and increased family burden (e.g., travel restrictions, altering of their schedule to care for the ill child) (Rodrigue et al., 1996).

Posttraumatic Stress Disorder (PTSD). Symptoms of PTSD are common among pediatric OT patients. Denial and avoidance are very common. Reexperiencing of life threats is often not noticed unless the psychologist probes the patient (Stuber, Nader, Yasuda, Pynoos, & Cohen, 1991). Girls are more at risk than boys for PTSD (Wintgens, Boileau, & Robacy, 1997).

Social Support Family members often comprise the social support system. OT patients tend to have fewer friends and active peer experiences. Often the extensive parental social support leads to parental overprotection and patient dependency. Separation anxiety occurs when the patient is separated from the parent (Schweitzer & Hobbs, 1995; Stuber, 1993).

Sometimes social support is not beneficial. If the social support network is too supportive, some patients may feel uncomfortable because they lack control (Littlefield, 1992).

Parental Psychosocial Issues

Parents react to OT issues in different ways. Some parents act in a highly assertive manner that often presents problems to the OT team. Others act underorganized and do not become too involved (Bradford & Tomlinson, 1990).

Preoperative psychosocial issues begin with the initial hospital experience where there is a loss of control, denial of medical reality, and attempted trust building efforts with the hospital staff. The wait at home has concrete issues such as a financial burden with subsequent concerns about the need to get public involvement to raise funds. The parents feel guilt over issues such as the death of the donor, competition for limited organs, and the burden of the informed consent decision for the child. Anger is felt due to a loss of control and a feeling of being forgotten and abandoned (Slater, 1994).

Perioperative psychosocial issues begin with anxiety immediately after the operation. The first 2 weeks are viewed as a possible new beginning. The remainder of hospitalization is a roller coaster period due to the fear of rejection and infection, and the lack of control over the ultimate outcome (Slater, 1994).

Postoperative psychosocial issues begin with the return home where they adapt a new parental role concerning a fear of rejection and death, and a readjustment in family structure (Slater, 1994). One study of parents of bone marrow transplantation (BMT) patients done a year after surgery showed that 37% of the parents had financial concerns, 23% had child-related problems, and 19% had problems sleeping. Very few reported marital or social relationship problems (Sormanti, Dungan, & Rieker, 1994).

Coping

Children can cope with either problem-focused coping (e.g., problem solving, cognitive restructuring) or emotion-focused coping (e.g., social support, problem avoidance, religious belief) (Kronenberger et al., 1996).

One study of children waiting for BMT showed that avoidance and distraction coping were associated with more aggression, anxiety, withdrawal, and depression. Children who coped with religion were less withdrawn, more aggressive, and more depressed. Problem solving and cognitive restructuring were not related to better adjustment. This might be because the severity of BMT overwhelmed the children (Kronenberger et al., 1996).

Developmental Considerations

OT issues are pertinent to child development, especially after a successful transplant. During infancy, the parent should be careful about developing overprotectiveness for the child. Once the child is a toddler, autonomy should be encouraged. Play opportunities should exist with as little restriction as possible, although the parent might be concerned about the child's frailty. The school-age child should, as much as possible, have a school education to allow for peer interaction. The adolescent should be monitored for risk-taking independent behavior. This can be dangerous if the child forgets to take the immunosuppressant medications or observe the dietary restrictions (Sexson & Rubenow, 1992; Slater, 1994).

Cognitive Functioning

OT can affect cognitive functioning. A successful renal transplant may prevent a downward trend in cognitive functioning associated with end-stage renal disease. Some studies suggest that there are moderate gains (Hobbs & Sexson, 1993; Schweitzer & Hobbs, 1995; Stewart, Kennard, Waller, & Fixler, 1994).

Liver transplants have mixed results concerning cognitive functioning. Some claim there are improvements or no change (Hobbs & Sexson, 1993; Schweitzer & Hobbs, 1995) whereas others claim there are deficits (Stewart et al., 1994).

One study of heart transplant patients showed that they did not have greater cognitive deficits than a cardiac disease/open heart surgery control group (Stewart et al., 1994).

Quality of Life

One study showed that BMT child survivors had good quality of life (physical and psychosocial dimensions of functioning). However, the domains tested were for adults and are of questionable use for children (Powers, Vannatta, Noll, Cool, & Stehbens, 1995).

New measures for determining quality of life have been developed specifically for children. One is a 16-item multiple choice questionnaire in a self-report format using a Likert scale. It takes from 5 to 10 minutes to complete. The children should do it themselves because differences were noted when parents' responses were compared with the childrens' responses. Each question represents one health-related sphere (e.g., mobility, friends, vision). This test was validated on 12- to 15-year-old adolescents waiting for OT. The young adolescents rated the positive spheres of breathing, friends, mobility, and mental function as most important. They rated the negative sphere of death as the most important followed by unconsciousness as the next worst. These OT patients had more problems with breathing, eating, and elimination than the control group (Apajasalo, Sintonen, et al., 1996).

Another quality of life measure was developed for 8- to 11-year-old children surviving OT. It has 17 dimensions and is in the form of a structured interview. It takes from 20 to 30 minutes to complete. The OT patients had more problems eating, eliminating, and concentrating than the control group (Apajasalo, Rautonen, et al., 1996).

Adherence

Lack of adherence can cause a successful OT to fail. This issue is quite serious. One study showed no adherence problems for children under age 2. However, 73% of preschoolers (age 2–6), 82% of school-age children (age 7–12), and 40% of adolescents (age 12 and up) had adherence problems (Phipps & DeCuir-Whalley, 1990). Another study showed that 50% of adolescents do not always take their medication (Schweitzer & Hobbs, 1995).

Some factors associated with poor adherence are poor self-esteem, family conflict, and multiple family stressors (Wainwright & Gould, 1997). One study showed that informative support (advice or personal feedback) and emotional support (caring, sympathy, love) by fathers were negatively related to adherence to the immunosuppressant medications of azathioprine and cyclosporine. It is possible that this occurred either because the fathers only became involved due to the poor adherence or perhaps this occurred because this was the way the child was attempting to gain control (Foulkes, Boggs, Fennell, & Skibinski, 1993).

Future Directions

Many OT studies rely on small sample sizes (Schweitzer & Hobbs, 1995). Future research should focus on more prospective studies that use larger sample sizes. A possible solution is for multiple investigators in different hospitals to collaborate in their research. This will offer more concrete and valid information on the effects of OT on children.

INJURY PREVENTION

Injuries are an important health issue for children. Injury is the third leading cause of death in the United States and the leading cause for children, adolescents, and young adults (Irwin, Cataldo, Matheny, & Peterson, 1992). Previous research has presented confusing and conflicting results on the determinants of childhood injuries, particularly psychosocial predictors. In an analysis of 532 pediatric patients at a prepaid clinic during 12 months, it was found that four factors independently associated with the risk of at least one treated injury: high activity level, high rate of pediatric utilization for noninjury-related visits during the follow-up period, occurrence of a treated injury during the preceding year, and a negative attitude toward medical care providers by the child's mother. Mothers who work more than 15 hours a week outside the home and who have more life events in the preceding year are more likely to have children with serious injuries. Thus, Horwitz, Morgenstern, DiPietro, and Morrison (1988) concluded that these characteristics must be targeted for stressed families.

Adolescents

In a study (Kolbe, 1990) conducted by the Centers for Disease Control, the behaviors that contribute most to adverse health and social outcomes were grouped into six categories: behaviors that result in unintentional and intentional injury such as motor vehicle accidents, homicide, and suicide; drug and alcohol use; sexual behaviors that result in sexually transmitted diseases, including human immunodeficiency virus infection or unintended pregnancy; tobacco use; dietary behaviors that contribute to adult morbidity and mortality; and physical inactivity.

Adolescents are more prone to athletic injuries and suicide than children at other developmental periods. In a study (Baumert, Henderson, & Thompson, 1998) surveying high school students in grades 9 through 12, athletes and nonathletes were found to differ in specific health risk behaviors. Adolescent athletes appear less likely to smoke cigarettes or marijuana, more likely to engage in healthy dietary behaviors, and less likely to feel bored or hopeless.

Peterson and Brown (1994) reviewed the literature on unintentional injuries in children. They pointed out the similarities between factors predicting both unintentional injuries and child neglect. It was not until the 1980s that the focus shifted from the physical environment to sociocultural and personal factors, including the immediate environment and the skills and abilities of the parents. A deficit in problem solving and a failure to provide appropriate supervision appear to be difficult constructs to measure as both involve a lack of response. In coming up with a working model to encompass all of the etiological factors for child injury, they provide both caregiver-based and child-based variables. Several studies showed that stress contributes to risk of child injury. Thus, families who exist in poverty, chaos, crowding, and residence change have a higher chance of having a vulnerable child. Social isolation may increase caregiver stress, particularly in young single mothers. Maternal depression may be a particularly critical injury risk factor (Garbarino et al., 1991).

A recent study (Kramer, Warner, Olfson, Ebanks, Chaput, & Weissman, 1998) of the offspring of depressed parents found that there is an increased susceptibility to specific medical conditions and hospitalization relative to the depression status of both the parent and the offspring. The study revealed that the offspring depression status was associated with a history of general medical problems and hospital visits only among those offspring who also had a depressed parent. The association was demonstrated for genitourinary disorders, headaches, respiratory disorders, and hospitalizations. Parental depression without considering offspring depression was limited to a report of unconsciousness in the offspring and may be related to an increased prevalence of accidents resulting from inadequate parental monitoring among depressed parents. These findings were consistent with a longitudinal study of children of depressed parents (Billings & Moos, 1985). They found that the offspring of depressed parents had more general medical problems, more health risk factors (i.e., smoking, drinking, and drug use), and poorer functioning than children of nondepressed controls. It was further found that having a parent with a lifetime measurement of depression even if it had remitted, still presents a risk for medical problems. In the two-generation study, it was found that a history of depression in both the offspring and the parents was necessary to exhibit a significant association between depression and medical problems. However, these results may be due to either genetic or environmental influences or both. There is some association between allergies and depression, which may mean that both dysfunction in the adrenergic and cholinergic systems may predispose people to both atopic disorders (e.g., allergy and asthma) and some forms of depression. This may be passed on genetically, thus producing the medical comorbidity only among those with two generations of depression.

CONCLUSIONS

Thus, within each of the areas of research reviewed, it is important to consider the parents' state of stability, ongoing stressors in the home, and the childrens' developmental age in the assessment and treatment programming of the health care team. The first task of a functional analysis would be to view the problem within the framework of what developmental tasks need to be accomplished during the next 5 years of the child's life. Differences between independence struggles and age capacities will indicate how involved the parent should be in the implementing of the medical program. Often compliance can be improved by educational discussions and nonthreatening guidance of parents in more appropriate problem solving. In the case of adolescents, they may be encouraged to modify the program to fit in more with their life style and identification needs. Especially in the area of suspected child neglect when too many visits to the emergency room with accidents or asthmatic attacks occur, the parent needs to feel believed and not evaluated or blamed for the injury or failure of medical compliance. A team approach by the hospital staff and health consultants would allow better supervision and more constructive individualization of programs as multiple input will pinpoint strengths and weaknesses in each individual involved in the care of children. When parental depression is lifelong, it may be necessary to encourage an independent evaluation of the suffering parent so that medication and social support from the other spouse may be improved. In impoverished environments due to dysfunctional families, low access to health care, poverty, crowdedness, or environmental hazards, the school could serve as an entry point for mobilizing community resources.

REFERENCES

Abidin, R. R. (1986). *Parenting stress index* (2nd ed.). Charlottesville, VA: Pediatric Psychology Press.

Andrykowski, M. A. (1994). Psychiatric and psychosocial aspects of bone marrow transplantation. *Psychosomatics, 35,* 13–24.

Apajasalo, M., Rautonen, J., Holmberg, C., Sinkkonen, J., Aalberg, V., Pihko, H., Siimes, M. A., Kaitila, I., Makela, A., Erkkila, K., & Sintonen, H. (1996). Quality of life in pre-adolescence: A 17–dimensional health-related measure (17D). *Quality of Life Research, 5,* 532–538.

Apajasalo, M., Sintonen, H., Holmberg, C., Sinkkonen, J., Aalberg, V., Pihko, H., Siimes, M. A., Kaitila, I., Makela, A., Rantakari, K., Anttila, R., & Rautonen, J. (1996). Quality of life in early adolescence: A sixteen-dimensional health-related measure (16D). *Quality of Life Research, 5,* 205–211.

Arshad, S., Stevens, M., & Hide S. (1993) The effect of genetic and environmental factors on the prevalence of allergic disorders at the age of two years. *Clinical and Experimental Allergy, 23,* 504–511.

Baumert, P. W., Jr., Henderson, J. M., & Thompson, N. J. (1998). Health risk behaviors of adolescent participants in organized sports. *Journal of Adolescent Health, 22,* 460–465.

Billings, A. G., & Moos, R. H. (1985). Psychological processes of remission in unipolar depression: Comparing depressed patients with matched community controls. *Journal of Consulting & Clinical Psychology, 53,* 314–325.

Boccuti, L., Celano, M., Geller, R., & Phillips, K. (1996). Development of a scale to measure children's metered-sode inhaler and spacer technique. *Annals of Allergy, Asthma, & Immunology, 77,* 217–221.

Bradford, R., & Tomlinson, L. (1990). Psychological guidelines in the management of pediatric organ transplantation. *Archives of Disease in Childhood, 65,* 1000–1003.

Carpenter, P. J. (1989). Establishing the role of the pediatric psychologist in a university medical center-based oncology service. *Journal of Training and Practice in Professional Psychology, 3,* 21–28.

Charlop, M. H., Parrish, J. M., Fenton, L. R., & Cataldo, M. F. (1987). Evaluation of hospital-based outpatient pediatric psychology services. *Journal of Pediatric Psychology, 12,* 485–503.

Drotar, D., Johnson, S. B., Ianotti, R., Krasnegor, N., Matthews, K. A., & Melamed, B. G. (1987). Child health psychology. *Health Psychology, 8,* 781–784.

Drotar, D., Johnson, S. B., Ianotti, R., Krasnegor, N., Matthews, K. A., Melamed, B. G., Millstein, S., Peterson, R. A., Popiel, D., & Routh, D. K. (1989). Child health psychology. *Health Psychology, 8,* 781–784.

Fennell, R. S., Foulkes, L.-M., & Boggs, S. R. (1994). Family-based program to promote medication compliance in renal transplant children. *Transplantation Proceedings, 26,* 102–103.

Foulkes, L.-M., Boggs, S. R., Fennell, R. S., & Skibinski, K. (1993). Social support, family variables, and compliance in renal transplant children. *Pediatric Nephrology, 7,* 185–188.

Garabino, J., Koarwlny, K., & Dubrow, N. (1991). *No place to be growing up in a war zone.* Lexington, MA: Lexington Books.

Geller, M. (1996). Acute management of severe childhood asthma. *AACN Clinical Issues, 7,* 519–528.

Gottlieb, S. E., & Portnoy, S. (1988). The role of play in a pediatric bone marrow transplantation unit. *Children's Health Care, 16,* 177–181.

Hare, J., Skinner, D., & Kliewer, D. (1989). Family systems approach to pediatric bone marrow transplantation. *Children's Health Care, 18,* 30–36.

Hobbs, S. A., & Sexson, S. B. (1993). Cognitive development and learning in the pediatric organ transplant recipient. *Journal of Learning Disabilities, 26,* 104–113.

Horowitz, S. M., Morgenstern, H., DiPietro, L., & Morrison, C. L. (1988). Determinants of pediatric injuries. *American Journal of Diseases of Children, 146*(6), 605–611.

Irwin, C. E., Jr., Cataldo, M. F., Matheny, A. P., Jr., & Peterson, L. (1992). Health consequences of behaviors: Injury as a model. *Pediatrics, 90, 798–807.*

Kolbe, L. (1990). An epidemiology surveillance system to monitor the prevalence of youth behaviors that most affect health. *Health Education, 21,* 44–448.

Kramer, R. A., Warner, V., Olfson, M., Ebanks, C. M., Chaput, F., & Weissman, M. M. (1998). General medical problems among the offspring of depressed parents: A 10–year follow-up. *Journal of the American Academy of Child & Adolescent Psychiatry, 37,* 602–611.

Kronenberger, W. G., Carter, B. D., Stewart, J, Morrow, C., Martin, K., Gowan, D., & Sender, L. (1996). Psychological adjustment of children in the pretransplant phase of bone marrow transplantation: Relationships with parent distress, parent stress, and child coping. *Journal of Clinical Psychology in Medical Settings, 3,* 319–335.

Lazarus, R., & Folkman, S. (1984). *Stress, appraisal and coping.* New York: Springer.

Littlefield, C. (1992). Social support and organ transplantation. In J. Craven & G. M. Rodin (Eds.), *Psychiatric aspects of organ transplantation* (pp. 50–66). New York: Oxford University Press.

Milgrom, H., Bender, B., Ackerson, L., Bowry, P., Smith, B., & Rand, C. (1996). Noncompliance and treatment failure in children with asthma. *Journal of Allergy and Clinical Immunology, 98,* 1051–1057.

Moos, R. (1977). *Coping with physical illness.* New York: Plenum.

Olson, R. A., Holden, E. W., Friedman, A., Faust, J., Kenning, M., & Mason, P. J. (1988). Psychological consultation in a children's hospital: An evaluation of services. *Journal of Pediatric Psychology, 13,* 479–492.

Osman, L., & Silverman, M. (1996). Measuring quality of life for young children with asthma and their families. *European Respiratory Journal, 9,* 35–41.

Peterson, L., & Brown, D. (1994). *Integrating child injury and abuse-neglect research: Common histories, etiologies, and solutions.*

Phipps, S. (1994). Bone marrow transplantation. In D. J. Bearison & R. K. Mulhern (Eds.), *Pediatric psychooncology: Psychological perspectives on children with cancer* (pp. 143–170). New York: Oxford University Press.

Phipps, S., & DeCuir-Whalley, S. (1990). Adherence issues in pediatric bone marrow transplantation. *Journal of Pediatric Psychology, 15,* 459–475.

Powers, S. W., Vannatta, K., Noll, R. B., Cool, V. A., & Stehbens, J. A. (1995). Leukemia and other childhood cancers. In M. C. Roberts (Ed.), *Handbook of pediatric psychology* (2nd ed., pp. 310–326). New York: Guilford.

Rappaport, B. S. (1988). Evolution of consultation-liaison services in bone marrow transplantation. *General Hospital Psychiatry, 10,* 346–351.

Rand, C., & Wise, R. (1994). Measuring adherence to asthma medication regimens. *American Journal of Respiratory and Critical Care Medicine, 149,* S69–S76.

Resnick, R. J., & Kruczek, T. (1996). Pediatric consultation: New concepts in training. *Professional Psychology: Research and Practice, 27,* 194–197.

Rodrigue, J. R., MacNaughton, K., Hoffmann, R. G., III, Graham-Pole, J., Andres, J. M., Novak, D. A., & Fennell, R. S. (1996). Perceptions of parenting stress and family relations by fathers of children evaluated for organ transplantation. *Psychological Reports, 79,* 723–727.

Rodrigue, J. R., MacNaughton, K., Hoffmann, R. G., III, Graham-Pole, J., Andres, J. M., Novak, D. A., & Fennell, R. S. (1997). Transplantation in children: A longitudinal assessment of mother's stress, coping, and perceptions of family functioning. *Psychosomatics, 38,* 478–486.

Ryan-Wenger, N. M. (1992). A taxonomy of children's coping strategies: A step toward theory development. *American Journal of Orthopsychiatry, 62,* 256–263.

Ryan-Wenger, N. M., & Schwam, J. (1987). Assisting the parent of a child with asthma. *Journal of Asthma, 24,* 45–54.

Schwam, J. (1987). Assisting the parent of a child with asthma. *Journal of Asthma, 24,* 45–54.

Schweitzer, J. B., & Hobbs, S. A. (1995). Renal and liver disease: End-stage and transplantation issues. In M. C. Roberts (Ed.), *Handbook of pediatric psychology* (2nd ed., pp. 425–445). New York: Guilford.

Sexson, S., & Rubenow, J. (1992). Transplants in children and adolescents. In J. Craven & G. M. Rodin (Eds.), *Psychiatric aspects of organ transplantation* (pp. 33–49). New York: Oxford University Press.

Slater, J. A. (1994). Psychiatric aspects of organ transplantation in children and adolescents. *Child and Adolescent Psychiatric Clinics of North America, 3,* 557–598.

Sormanti, M., Dungan, S., & Rieker, P. P. (1994). Pediatric bone marrow transplantation: Psychosocial issues for parents after a child's hospitalization. *Journal of Psychosocial Oncology, 12*(4), 23–42.

Stewart, S. M., Kennard, B. D., Waller, D. A., & Fixler, D. (1994). Cognitive function in children who receive organ transplantation. *Health Psychology, 13,* 3–13.

Stuber, M. L. (1993). Psychiatric aspects of organ transplantation in children and adolescents. *Psychosomatics, 34,* 379–387.

Stuber, M. L., Nader, K., Yasuda, P., Pynoos, R. S., & Cohen, S. (1991). Stress responses after pediatric bone marrow transplantation: Preliminary results of a prospective longitudinal study. *Journal of the American Academy of Child and Adolescent Psychiatry, 30,* 952–957.

Wainwright, S. P., & Gould, D. (1997). Non-adherence with medications in organ transplant patients: A literature review. *Journal of Advanced Nursing, 26,* 968–977.

Wamboldt, M. Z. (1998). Wheeze by any other name is (not) the same: The role of symptom perception in asthma. *Journal of Asthma, 35,* 133–135.

Wamboldt, M., & Gavin, L. (1998). Pulmonary disorders. In R. Ammerman & J. V. Campo (Eds.), *Handbook of pediatric psychology and psychiatry, Vol. 2: Disease, injury, and illness* (pp. 266–297). Boston: Allyn & Bacon.

Weinstein, A. (1995). Clinical management strategies to maintain drug compliance in asthmatic children. *Annals of Allergy, Asthma, & Immunology, 74,* 304–310.

Wertlieb, D., Weigel, C., & Feldstein, M. (1987). Measuring children's coping. *American Journal of Orthopsychiatry, 57,* 548–560.

Wintgens, A., Boileau, B., & Robacy, P. (1997). Posttraumatic stress symptoms and medical procedures in children. *Canadian Journal of Psychiatry, 42,* 611–616.

27

Social Influences in Etiology and Prevention of Smoking and Other Health Threatening Behaviors in Children and Adolescents

Richard I. Evans
University of Houston

In his widely cited review of psychosocial approaches to smoking prevention, Flay (1985) commented on the brevity of the time line of prevention research:

> Four generations of research on psychosocial approaches to smoking prevention have been conducted within less than one half of a human generation (indeed, less than one decade). Given this, remarkable progress has been made in an important area of health psychology and public health. ... Research on smoking prevention ... has evolved more systematically and progressed further than most other areas of health promotion. (p. 482)

For more than four decades, it has been my privilege to be an active participant-observer in the research processes just described (Evans, 1998), and the present chapter presents an historical perspective from that frame of reference. There is growing evidence that the components of smoking prevention programs may also be applicable to addressing the prevention of use of alcohol and other drugs as described, for example, by Glynn, Leukefeld, and Ludford (1985), and may be, at least, a basis for AIDS prevention interventions as well.

In examining the history of smoking prevention efforts, one first encounters the approach of conventional wisdom that high fear arousal is perceived as the major device for discouraging children and youth from beginning to smoke. As Janis and Feshbach (1953) suggested in their now classic study, high fear arousal to encourage a health protective behavior (oral hygiene) does have some impact on short-term changes in such behavior but may not impact on truly long-term changes. For example, Marston (1970) reported that immediately after a heart attack (certainly high fear arousal), individuals may change their lifestyles to minimize high risk behaviors (e.g., diet, smoking) to avoid a recurrence, but, over time, may return to many of their original risk-taking behaviors. So, even under conditions of intense fear, as pointed out in earlier research by Evans (1979), permanent changes in health habits may not occur. In fact, in the most recent report on smoking rates among adolescents, Johnston, Bachman, and O'Malley (1995) reported that most students in 8th, 10th, and 12th grades perceive a "great risk" in smoking, even in the face of increasing prevalence of smoking among these students. Further discussion of this report is addressed later in this chapter.

Because of the persistence of conventional wisdom concerning the effectiveness of "scare tactics" to prevent health threatening behaviors, a more detailed examination of fear arousal as a mechanism for instituting modification of behaviors may be instructive at this point. In his extensive review of the fear arousal literature, Higbee (1969) pointed out that no blanket statement could be made concerning the value of fear arousal as a persuasive device. However, this review suggested a basis for several interesting hypotheses that relate to the effects of various levels of fear arousal from minimal to high, effects of fear-arousing communications over time, and combining fear arousal with other persuasive devices in targeted behavior modifications. The value of testing such hypotheses was supported by Janis (1967); Evans, Rozelle, Lasater, Dembroski, and Allen (1970); and Sutton (1982). Some studies that have examined some of these hypotheses concerning the role of fear arousal are used as examples in prevention of health threatening behaviors in adolescents.

As it became increasingly evident that fear arousal in itself, that is, simply emphasizing the negative effects of engaging in a particular health threatening behavior was not enough (Evans, 1979), investigators sought to expand their prevention strategies. Janis and Feshbach (1953), in the study mentioned earlier, reported that the combination of a minimal fear approach with general toothbrushing instructions was more effective in increasing the incidence of toothbrushing among adolescent subjects than a strong fear appeal alone. Subsequently, Leventhal, Singer, and Jones (1965) challenged the relative importance of fear arousal in itself as a motivator to change a health-related behavior. In a study involving persuasion to submit to tetanus inoculations, these researchers found that providing highly specific instructions on how to obtain such inoculations, without depending solely on the fear of contracting a life threatening disease, was more effective in motivating individuals to engage in this specific prevention behavior than the effects of fear alone.

Our University of Houston Social Psychology/Behavioral Medicine Research Group pursued the problem of the relative effectiveness of fear arousal in a series of basic studies in preventive dentistry with young adolescents (Evans et al., 1970). Results of these studies indicated that exposing the students on only one occasion to elaborated instructions and the modeling of specific oral hygiene behaviors (without fear or positive appeals) resulted in significantly more effective oral hygiene behavior. General oral hygiene instructions coupled with a positive appeal were almost as effective. Effective, but significantly less so, were fear appeals coupled with merely general oral hygiene instructions. Furthermore, it was found that simply testing subjects at irregular intervals, possibly perceived as monitoring, was almost as effective as the various persuasive messages. When the short-term study was extended over time, behavior changes were maintained (Evans, Rozelle, Noblitt, & Williams, 1975). In order to cross-validate self-reports of toothbrushing, a procedure not present in the Janis and Feshbach (1953) study, a chemical indicator of cleanliness of teeth, was employed (Evans, Rozelle, Lasater, Dembroski, & Allen, 1968). This cross-validation procedure was later generalized to smoking prevention studies as the research group developed the "pipeline procedure" to increase the validity of self-reports of cigarette smoking (Evans, Hansen, & Mittelmark, 1977). Incidentally, this was not a "bogus" pipeline, as often incorrectly stated in descriptions of this procedure. Actual, rather than bogus, measures of nicotine in blood assays were used.

Approaches to prevention of smoking, which incorporated some elements of fear arousal that have been used extensively, but with only limited success, include the information model and the affective model described by Edmundson, McAlister, Murray, Perry, and Lichenstein (1991). The information model is based on the assumption that providing adolescents with factual information about a potentially destructive behavior such as smoking or drug use, will prevent them from engaging in the behavior. Such information may be presented in a variety of ways such as didactic lectures by a classroom teacher, videotapes and films, posters and pamphlets, or guest speakers who are experts in the area. Despite evidence that indicates this approach to be largely ineffective (Goodstadt, 1978; Thompson, 1978), it remains the approach of choice of many school-based smoking prevention programs according to Murray, Davis-Hearn, Goldman, Pirie, and Luepker (1988). Programs based on the "affective model" stress more global attitude changes directed at such factors as enhanced self-esteem, improved decision making and goal-setting, and often do not include specific information about health risks of smoking (Glynn et al., 1985). Little evidence exists in support of the application of this model for effective prevention (Hansen, Johnson, Flay, Graham, & Sobel, 1988; Tobler, 1986).

The limited effectiveness of fear-arousing information, even in earlier investigations, led our Research Group to consider alternate conceptual foundations for prevention interventions. During the early 1970s, as a research component of the National Heart Center at Baylor College of Medicine, the research group was challenged by the notion that even without being directly exposed to any systematic prevention program, most young adolescents at that time were aware of the dangers of smoking, including long-term health consequences such as heart disease and cancer. As elementary schoolchildren, they often utilized such information in an attempt to persuade their parents to quit smoking. At about the time they entered junior high school, however, many began to smoke. Fear of the consequences induced by knowledge of the dangers of smoking appeared to be insufficient to prevent its onset among many young adolescents exposed to social pressures to engage in the behavior, as even currently appears to be the case as was suggested in the Johnston et al. (1995) report.

However, because of conventional wisdom related to the value of fear arousal as a persuasive device, it was not surprising that a survey of junior high school smoking prevention programs revealed that most programs focused almost completely on fear-arousing messages. They emphasized the long-term effects of smoking such as heart disease or cancer without consideration for the present-oriented rather than future-oriented time perspective of young adolescents (Mittelmark, 1978). The programs rarely reflected feedback from target groups in their designs and seemed to ignore previous research on the effective use of media. A critical problem was the lack of any form of systematic evaluation of these programs. A series of focused interviews was conducted with a large population of seventh-grade students (Evans, Raines, & Hanselka, 1984). These interviews suggested that various levels of peer pressure, models of smoking parents, and smoking-related messages in the mass media that featured attractive smokers, seemed for many adolescents to outweigh concerns about the dangers of smoking.

Inferences from this study suggest that three overall considerations may be important in examining the effect of social influence on the decision to smoke:

1. Sources of social influences: These may include peers or friends, siblings, parents, admired public figures, perceived social norms, and social climate.
2. Mechanisms of social influence: These may be overt (direct social pressure such as from peers) or covert (effects of modeling).
3. Susceptibility to social influences: These may include various intrapersonal characteristics (e.g., self-efficacy, risk-taking, optimism or pessimism) and social cognitions (perceptions).

A pilot study was conducted that supplemented messages addressing the health consequences of smoking with information concerning social pressures that might impact young adolescents to begin smoking, together with training in specific skills to resist these pressures (Evans et al., 1978). More recently, this has been described as "resistance skills training." Considering the results of this pilot study, a prevention program based on an incorporation of such social influences was developed and evaluated. The social inoculation model, as it was described, appears to have guided much of the prevention research for the past two decades. Referring to the work of the Houston Group (Evans, 1976, 1983, 1984; Evans et al., 1984; Evans et al., 1981; Evans & Raines, 1982), Edmundson et al. (1991) stated:

> The social influences model recognizes smoking in adolescents as primarily a social behavior. This model includes the following four components: (1) information on the negative social effects and short-term physiological consequences of tobacco use; (2) information on the social influences that encourage smoking among adolescents, particularly peer, parent, and mass media influences; (3) correction of inflated normative expectations of the prevalence of adolescent smoking; and (4) training, modeling, rehearsing, and reinforcing of methods to resist those influences and to communicate that resistance to others, particularly peers. (p. 154)

The evolution of social influences models has drawn on various concepts in psychology. Bandura's (1977) social learning theory was particularly relevant in early formulations of the social inoculation model. As applied to the initiation of smoking, the theory suggested that children might acquire expectations and learned behaviors vis-à-vis smoking through observation. They might learn vicariously that smoking appears to relieve tension or anxiety. Vicariously learned expectations of the positive and negative consequences of cigarette smoking could be important factors in the ultimate decision regarding smoking behavior. Bandura's (1982, 1989, 1995; Evans, 1989a) more recent development of the concept of self-efficacy, which further explicates this notion, has become central to some current models of smoking and drug use cessation such as the stage theories developed by DiClemente et al. (1991), although Bandura (1995) has some reservations concerning stage theories, even as they integrate the concept of self-efficacy. This social inoculation model, which involved inoculating adolescents with the knowledge and social skills to resist various social pressures to smoke, may be regarded as a behavioral application of McGuire's (1961) cognitive inoculation model. McGuire's (1968) communication-persuasion model, essentially an information-processing analysis, proved to be useful as a guide for the utilization of the social inoculation concept involved in the development and delivery of prevention programs.

To discuss more fully the components of the social inoculation model, it should be pointed out that it considered both the socioenvironmental and personality or intrapersonal determinants that contribute to the complex of influences that encourage the use of harmful substances. Implicit in the model was the conception that as children reach early adolescence, they experience greatly increased vulnerability to social pressures to engage in risk-taking behaviors, greater mobility, and greater freedom from adult authority figures. Experimentation with personal identity and lifestyle choices, which marks this period of development, could include use of tobacco or other harmful substances, and conflicting expectations could override both personal beliefs and parental or family values. This model identified smoking, or use of alcohol and other drugs, both as a form of rebellion against authority including risk-taking, and as part of a new and different lifestyle for adolescents during the early teenage years. For example, it might predict the initiation of smoking for children as young as age 10 or 11. In fact, it might be noted here that in the 1970s, as the original social inoculation studies (which addressed smoking) were being planned, smoking initiation reflected an upward trend from the elementary grades to high school (Johnston, Bachman, & O'Malley, 1979; Thompson, 1978), with a significant shift in rate of the initiation of smoking when entering junior high school. Thus, we chose to begin our prevention intervention with seventh-grade students. Even preliminary results from the current NIDA-supported Middle School Drug Prevention project (Evans, 1994) indicate that 31.8% of the subjects had initiated at least some cigarette smoking at or before they were 11 years old.

Variations of the social influences-based models that have been involved in the formation of prevention programs have appeared to be, at least initially, quite effective in preventing the use of harmful substances as reported by a number of investigators including Best et al. (1984); Biglan, Glasgow, et al. (1987); Biglan, Severson, et al. (1987); Ellickson, Bell, and McGuigan (1993); Flay, d'Avernas, Best, Kersell, and Ryan (1983); Flay et al. (1987); McAlister, Perry, and Maccoby (1979); McAlister, Perry, Killen, Slinkard, and Maccoby (1980); Pentz et al. (1989); and Perry, Killen, Slinkard, and McAlister (1989). The cognitive behavioral model, which expands the social influences model with additional problem-solving, decision-making, and self-control methods, has also been the basis for prevention programs that have produced initial positive results as reported by Kendall and Hollon (1979); Gilchrest, Schinke, and Blythe (1979); Schinke and Blythe (1981); and Schinke and Gilchrest (1983). The life skills model developed by Botvin and Eng

(1982) and Botvin, Eng, and Williams (1980) incorporates components of the social influences model and the cognitive behavioral model, with a particularly strong emphasis on training adolescents to cope with social challenges. This program also appears to have produced promising results.

Other possibly relevant conceptual areas in psychology that were described in the 1979 Surgeon General's Report on Smoking in Children and Adolescents (Evans, Henderson, Hill, & Raines, 1979) might be utilized in programs designed to prevent the use of harmful substances. Included here would be Festinger's (1957) theory of cognitive dissonance used in explorations of conflict between health beliefs and the initiation of health threatening behaviors such as smoking, and the Jessor and Jessor (1977) multideterminant conceptual structure of problem behavior, which had been successful in predicting age-graded problem behaviors that are considered to be acceptable in adults but not in adolescents. The latter model has been incorporated into several longitudinal research designs, for example, the work of Sherman, Chassin, and Presson (1979) and Sherman et al. (1982). These investigators attempted to explain the onset of smoking and the transition in status from nonsmoker to smoker. Ajzen and Fishbein (1970) and Fishbein and Ajzen (1975) proposed a framework for predicting behavioral intentions, which were assumed to mediate and thus predict subsequent overt behavior. For example, this model, which has been applied with some success in studies of alcohol use in adolescents (Schlegel, Crawford, & Sanford, 1977), also appears to lend itself to empirically testable hypotheses that could tease out important components of the development of smoking behavior. Henderson's (1979) small-scale study of smoking in a population of ninth-grade students, based on Fishbein's and Ajzen's (1975) model, provided a provocative basis from which more elaborate investigations employing such models could be pursued within structural equation or causal models (Dill, 1981). Subsequent investigators also developed interventions directed toward altering some of the situational and intrapersonal determinants of smoking (Botvin et al., 1980; Hurd et al., 1980). Other investigators began focusing on mediators of the initiation of the use of harmful substances such as modifying perceptions of social norms as well as directly addressing mediators such as peer pressure (Sussman, 1989).

In recent years, as researchers began working within the framework of structural equation modeling (SEM) and path analyses, they began to address the question of synergism. That is, to what degree does the initiation of use of one harmful substance trigger the initiation of use of another substance? A syndrome of problem behavior initiation may be present that includes the use of tobacco, alcohol, and illegal drugs together with other risk-taking behaviors (Elders, Perry, Ericksen, & Giovani, 1994). It appears that adolescents often engage in more than one risk behavior during this stage in their lives. Even though the specific risk behaviors may differ, the common thread for all adolescents may be exposure to such risk factors. Researchers in prevention began to recognize that all prevention programs, however different in focus (e.g., avoiding tobacco, illegal drugs, and alcohol; preventing pregnancy and sexually transmitted diseases; prevention of violence), may all be connected by the same set of factors that enhance adolescents' susceptibility to engage in high risk behaviors. Vega, Zimmerman, Warheit, Apospori, and Gil (1993) suggested that distribution of risk factors is similar among ethnic groups even if the susceptibility to those risk factors may differ. Risk taking may begin with one risk behavior such as cigarette smoking and progress to other more risky behaviors as the student gets older. Kandel and Yamaguchi (1993) suggested that cigarette smoking itself is a risk factor for illegal drug use and that there is a predictable pattern of engaging in harder and harder drugs. Such hypothesized synergism among the use of various drugs must be considered in prevention programs (Stall, McKusick, Wiley, Coates, & Ostrow, 1986). Another recently emerging area of problematic behavior is excessive gambling among adolescents (National Research Council, 1999), which also appears to be operative within the context of co-morbid substance use behaviors (Evans, 1999).

Longitudinal research designs employing confirmatory factor analysis and SEM, such as the research group and others are employing in current or past investigations, should help identify multiple indicator latent variables and possible causal relationships among the use of various substances and other health-risk behaviors. Drawing on preliminary findings from the NIDA-supported Middle School Drug Prevention Study currently underway (Evans, 1994), it has been noted that drug use profiles (by ethnicity and race) indicate that such profiles differ within a tri-ethnic sample in terms of the sequence of the use of various health threatening substances:

- Among middle school Whites: cigarettes, hallucinogens, inhalants and steroids.
- Among middle school African-Americans: intravenous (IV) drugs, marijuana, and smokeless tobacco.
- Among middle school Latinos: cigarettes, cocaine, inhalants, IV drugs, marijuana, and steroids.

These preliminary analyses suggest that the synergistic pattern involving the use of various substances may differ among ethnic and racial groups and should be considered in prevention programs. Such profiles add a level of complexity to the conceptualization of gateway substances. In particular, this research appears to suggest that there is no general gateway substance, but rather that gateway substances may differ among various individuals and groups.

At least three theoretical possibilities exist concerning synergism in the use of health threatening substances: (a) nonsynergism (i.e., there is no tendency for persons engaging in particular risk behaviors to be engaging in other such behaviors); (b) simple synergism that describes persons engaging in particular risk behaviors as tending to engage in other risk behaviors without a specific causal sequence in the initiation of such behaviors; and (c) gateway synergism, as demonstrated in the Kandel and Yamaguchi (1993) study in which persons engaging in particular risk behaviors tend to engage in other risks, with certain risk behaviors leading causally to the initiation of others. Although risk behavior synergism has been reported by some investigators who utilized cross-sectional data (Biglan et al., 1990; Hingston, Strunin, Berlin, &

Herren, 1990), the lack of data available from sound prospective investigations precludes distinguishing between simple and gateway synergism. So a general guideline is not clearly developed concerning whether interventions should focus on the prevention of the use of one harmful substance or should address various harmful substances simultaneously.

The issue of AIDS prevention must now be seriously considered within this context. Because of the current concern about risky sexual behavior, including exposure to HIV among adolescents, one could hardly undertake a drug use prevention investigation without recognizing the relation between drug use and sexual behavior. Teenage sexual activity within the context of drug use may well result in impairment of responsible decision making that would otherwise lead to the practice of "safer sex" (Adler, Kegeles, Irwin, & Wibbelsman, 1990).

According to Evans, Getz, and Raines (1991), this relation between HIV risk, drug use, and sexual behavior may be a complex, reciprocally reinforcing, biopsychosocial phenomenon. Despite their increasing knowledge of the dangers of drug use and unprotected sexual behaviors, as would be expected based on earlier studies of the use of harmful substances, many young adolescents still initiate such behaviors (Miller, Turner, & Moses, 1990; Morrison, 1985). When theory is marshaled to explain such phenomena, possible perspectives are reflected in some variant of Rational Choice Theory or Subjective Expected Utility Theory (Gilbert, Bauman, & Udry, 1986; Luker, 1975; Weisman et al., 1991). These theories could also be utilized to examine the decision-making process involving cost–benefit analyses of alternative behaviors. Another investigation currently being conducted by the research group employs a planned behavior–action control perspective that pays close attention to the role of social influences in the use of harmful substances as related to at-risk sexual behavior. Consistent with the discussion of sexual behavior presented by Weismann et al., it can be inferred that the initiation of drug use is best regarded as relationally determined, that is, not only does it require the presence of another person (at least for it to constitute an HIV risk), but the actions of that other person occur within a social context having impact on the quality of one's decision-making processes vis-à-vis drug use.

While suggesting that teenage sexual behavior can be interpreted as rational (Lowenstein & Furstenberg, 1991), it can be argued that sexual activity in the context of drug use can result in the derailing of a decision process that might otherwise lead to the practice of safer sex as described by Adler et al. (1990). If Dryfoos' (1990) estimate is correct, that 25% of the adolescent population is using alcohol or marijuana heavily and is engaging in unprotected sexual intercourse, we might infer that this same proportion is at high risk for contracting HIV. Her estimation that underprivileged African-American and Hispanic adolescents, particularly those who are falling short academically, are overrepresented in this high risk group is consistent with epidemiological data linking drug use, early sexual activity, race or ethnicity, and AIDS prevalence (Miller et al., 1990; Strassberg & Mahoney, 1988). These findings appear to be supported by early results from a current study dealing with a study population that fits the profile of adolescents at high risk for both substance abuse and HIV-risk sexual behavior.

A study by Kirby (1997), which assessed curricula used for preventing sexual risk behavior, suggests that AIDS prevention programs might be based on social learning or social influence models such as social inoculation, even as such models have been utilized in drug use prevention programs. Such AIDS prevention programs focus on reducing specific risk-taking behaviors. They are interactive, provide training for teachers who are taught about social influences such as peer pressure and the media, and finally, focus on specific group norms and behaviors.

Another significant problem that should be addressed is the at-risk status of minority youth. For example, in the NIDA supported study previously described, differences among minority groups in incidence of use of various substances represent critical information that must be considered. Prevention programs must be sensitive to the distinctions that are present when there is a focus on minority populations. For example, as indicated earlier, my research has demonstrated a correlation between the use of certain substances and particular ethnic or racial affiliation. As shown in Tables 27.1 and 27.2, data from the studies described earlier indicate some significant differences in use among three ethnic groups. For example, African-American adolescents tend to report smoking less than Whites and Hispanics, while some Hispanic populations report a more frequent use of inhalants than do other groups. A properly conducted prevention intervention program must be sensitive to such differences in frequency and patterns of use to ensure that the most effective indigenous message is presented to all groups. The value of "cookie cutter" programs merely based on data from primarily White subjects are clearly subject to question.

Although use of substances and the prevention of such use among members of the majority population have been widely studied (Bell & Battjes, 1985; Glynn et al., 1985), few large-scale studies have targeted minority populations. Among these are investigations conducted by Botvin (1986), Schinke et al., (1988) and Orlandi (1986). Minority and low socioeconomic status generally are considered important risk factors for substance abuse although the relationships are complex (Dryfoos, 1990; Pentz, Trebow, Hansen, MacKinnon, 1990).

A large number of the young African-American and Hispanic, as well as White, adolescents living in the target area of one of my current investigations, and those in investigations such as reported by Botvin (1986), are routinely confronted with high drug availability and may have limited skills to cope with explicit and implicit social influences to use these drugs. This type of environment may well exemplify the "drug abuse crisis" described in earlier research (Evans, 1989b), and most recently cited by the Columbia University Drug Addiction Center (Merrill, 1995) as the most critical problem faced by children and adolescents, and provides a strong rationale for implementing such investigations in such target areas.

Another issue confronting prevention researchers is that high dosage–high frequency, truly long-term prevention pro-

TABLE 27.1
Percentage Reporting Use of Various Drugs × Ethnicity Among Middle School Students in Grades 6 Through 8 (N = 2,446)

	Whites	African American	Mexican American
	(45%)	(36%)	(20%)
Alcohol	61%	42%	54%
Beer	58%	50%	60%
Cigarettes	48%	32%[a]	54%
Cocaine	3%	3%	5.3%
Downers	4%	2%	3%
Hallucinogens	7%	2%[a]	6%
Inhalants	17%	7%[a]	20%
IV drugs	2%	2%	2%
Marijuana	12%	18%	21%
Smokeless tobacco	21%	6%[a]	12%
Speed	5%	3%	7%
Steroids	4%	2%	1%
Ecstasy	2%	1%	2%

[a]Significantly less reported use than other ethnic groups.

TABLE 27.2
Percentage Reporting Use of Various Drugs × Ethnicity Among High School Students in Grades 9 Through 12 (N = 2,190)

	Whites	African-American	Mexican-American
	(49%)	(33%)	(16%)
Alcohol	84%	70%	78%
Beer	80%	69%	75%
Cigarettes	66%	40%[a]	65%
Cocaine	6%	2%	10%
Downers	6%	2%	5%
Hallucinogens	15%	2%a	15%
Inhalants	15%	4%[a]	18%
IV drugs	2%	1%	1%
Marijuana	30%	27%	40%
Smokeless tobacco	34%	5%[a]	20%
Speed	13%	1%[a]	8%
Steroids	3%	1%	2%
Ecstasy	6%	1%	5%

[a]Significantly less reported use than other ethnic groups.

grams and their benefits, in terms of cost-effectiveness, must be considered because the effects of short term interventions often wash out (Murray, Pirie, Luepker, & Pallonen, 1989). As indicated earlier, Johnston et al. (1995) reported an increase in smoking among 8th and 10th graders. Botvin, Schinke, and Orlandi (1995) elaborated on this point when they stated the following:

> Follow-up studies designed to provide data concerning the durability of the prevention effects produced by social influence approaches have reported positive behavioral effects lasting for up to 4 years (Elder et al., 1993; Luepker, Johnson, Murray, & Pechacek, 1983; McAlister et al., 1980; Murray et al., 1989; Telch, Killen, McAlister, Perry, & Maccoby, 1982). Efforts to establish the durability of prevention effects for longer than 3 or 4 years have been disappointing. Data from several longer term follow-up studies have shown that these effects gradually decay over time (Flay et al., 1989; Murray et al., 1988), suggesting the need for continuing intervention or booster sessions. Because little is known about the nature and timing of booster interventions or the extent to which social influence approaches may require further refinement, additional research is needed. (p. 171)

On this issue, Bandura (1995) suggests a possible prescription for higher dosage interventions:

> Researchers are applying promising prevention models in school settings under severe constraints well suited to undermine their effectiveness. The general conclusion is that these approaches work in the short run, but their effects dissipate over time. There are several problems with this indiscriminate verdict. Informative evaluation research requires assessment of quality of implementation. Otherwise, there is no way of knowing whether weak results reflect a deficient model, or deficient application of a good one. Outcome studies of school-based programs rarely provide data on adequacy of implementation. Journal editors should insist that outcome studies include sound data on quality of implementation. School-based applications are probably long on didactics, but short on personal enablement. By enablement I do not mean a stock set of refusal tactics. Rather, it involves equipping children with skills and efficacy beliefs that enable them to regulate their own behavior and manage the diverse pressures in interpersonal relationships for detrimental conduct. Meta-analyses show that the more children practice exercising regulatory control, the more successful they are in resisting detrimental health habits. (p. 10)

Although this "washing out" of the effects of many of the prevention programs may account for only some of the variance related to the increase in smoking among children and adolescents, this now challenges the overall effectiveness of prevention programs over the last several years. Johnston et al. (1995) speculated that one reason for this increase in smoking is that smokers attractive to teenagers are once again being frequently "modeled" in the media. It is also possible that, as has been discovered in recent years, schools have been less enthusiastic about smoking prevention programs because over all, substance abuse curricula are in place with little modification of their content despite the changing face of the psychosocial influences to which adolescents are exposed. Ellickson et al. (1993) pointed out, however, that even with equivocation concerning long-term effectiveness of prevention programs, any successful delay of engaging in high risk behavior results in a lowered risk of contracting an STD, being in a car wreck, or other consequences of high risk behavior that can result in poorer health and higher treatment costs. The longer onset is delayed, the more success will be gained in avoiding illness and psychosocial effects attached to high risk behavior. If initiation can be delayed long enough, will the adolescent's high risk avoidance behavior carry over into adult decision making about health choices? If success is achieved in changing social norms, these same messages must be communicated within the community as well as in the school or social setting where adolescents may initially be exposed to the messages. Considerable evidence of the value of this is apparent as more and more institutions and communities are committed to limiting exposure of nonsmokers to smokers.

Strategies for monitoring prevention programs with appropriate modification of their content over time would appear to be one major step that might be taken to address the alarming findings in the Johnston et al. (1995) report. In fact, we are currently exploring in our major longitudinal investigations the effect of high dosage prevention interventions throughout the tenure of prospective investigations. Other investigators are also responding to this problem of washing out of early effects of prevention programs in a similar manner. Future prevention research should consider:

1. Synergism among an array of health threatening behaviors.
2. Differences in frequency of patterns of use of harmful substances among various ethnic and racial groups.
3. The need for high dosage truly long-term continual prevention interventions.
4. Promote the involvement of school, communities, and mass media in modifying group norms and behaviors (including eliminating youth targeted content in cigarette ads), so that norms and displays of models of the use of cigarettes and use of other substances become an increasingly less effective stimulus for the initiation of such behaviors by adolescents.

ACKNOWLEDGMENTS

This research was supported in the context of the Psychology Research Training Grant 5 TI DE 138, National Institute of Dental Research; the Social Psychological Deterrents of Smoking in Schools Project, National Heart, Lung & Blood Institute Grant 17269, through the Baylor College of Medicine National Heart & Blood Vessel Research and Demonstration Center; the Minority Adolescent Drug Use Prevention, National Institute on Drug Abuse, 1 RO1 DA07024-01A3, Richard I. Evans, principal investigator; and AIDS Prevention Among Minority Adolescents, National Institute of Child Health and Human Development, 1 RO1 HD30638-01, Richard I. Evans, principal investigator.

REFERENCES

Adler, N. E., Kegeles, S. M., Irwin, C. E., & Wibbelsman, C. (1990). Adolescent contraceptive behavior: An assessment of decision processes. *Journal of Pediatrics, 116,* 463–471.

Ajzen, I., & Fishbein M. (1970). The prediction of behavior from attitudinal and normative variables. *Journal of Experimental Social Psychology, 6,* 466–487.

Bandura, A. (1977). *Social learning theory.* Englewood Cliffs, NJ: Prentice-Hall.

Bandura, A. (1982). Self-efficacy mechanisms in human agency. *American Psychology, 37,* 122–147.

Bandura, A. (1989). Self-efficacy: Toward a unifying theory of behavior chance. *Psychological Review, 84,* 919–925.

Bandura, A. (1995, March). *Moving into forward gear in health promotion and disease prevention.* Keynote address presented at the annual meeting of the Society of Behavioral Medicine, San Diego, CA.

Bell, C. S., & Battjes, R. (Eds.). (1985). *Prevention research: Deterring drug abuse among children and adolescents* (DHHS Publication No. ADM 87–1334 NIDA Research Monograph 63). Washington, DC: U.S. Government Printing Office.

Best, J. A., Flay, B. R., Towson, S. M., Ryan, K. B., Perry, C. L., Brown, K. S., Kersell, M. W., & d'Avernas, J. R. (1984). Smoking prevention and the concept of risk. *Journal of Applied Social Psychology, 14,* 257–273.

Biglan, A., Glasgow, R., Ary, D., Thompson, R., Severson, H., Lichtenstein, E., Weissman, W., Faller, C., & Gallison, C. (1987). How generalizable are the effects of smoking prevention programs? Refusal skills training and parent messages in a teacher-administered program. *Journal of Behavioral Medicine, 10,* 613–628.

Biglan, A., Metzler, C. W., Wirt, R., Ary, D., Noell, J., Ochs, L., French, C., & Hood, D. (1990). Social and behavioral factors associated with high-risk sexual behavior among adolescents. *Journal of Behavioral Medicine, 13,* 245–261.

Biglan, A., Severson, H., Ary, D., Faller, C., Gallison, C., Thompson, R., Glasgow, R., & Lichtenstein, E. (1987). Do smoking prevention programs really work? Attrition and the internal and external validity of an evaluation of a refusal skills training program. *Journal of Behavioral Medicine, 10,* 159–171.

Botvin, G. J. (1986). Substance abuse prevention research: Recent development and future directions. *Journal of School Health, 56,* 369–386.

Botvin, G. J., & Eng, A. (1982). The efficacy of a multicomponent approach to the prevention of cigarette smoking. *Preventive Medicine, 11,* 199–211.

Botvin, G. J., Eng, A., & Williams, C. L. (1980). Preventing the onset of cigarette smoking through life skills training. *Preventive Medicine, 9,* 135–143.

Botvin, G. J., Schinke, S., & Orlandi, M. A. (1995). School-based health promotion: Substance abuse and sexual behavior. *Applied & Preventive Psychology 4,* 167–184.

DiClemente, C. C., Fairhurst, S. K., Velasquez, M. M., Prochaska, J. O., Velicer, W. F., & Rossi, J. S. (1991). The process of smoking cessation: An analysis of precontemplation, contemplation and preparation stages of change. *Journal of Consulting and Clinical Psychology, 59,* 295–304.

Dill, C. A. (1981). *A decision theory approach to health related behaviors: A structural equation analysis.* Unpublished doctoral dissertation, University of Houston, Houston, TX.

Dryfoos, J. (1990). *Adolescents at risk.* New York: Oxford University Press.

Edmundson, E., McAlister, A., Murray, D., Perry, C., & Lichtenstein, E. (1991). Approaches directed to the individual. In D. R. Shopland, D. M. Burns, J. M. Samet, & E. R. Gritz (Eds.), *Strategies to control tobacco use in the United States: A blueprint for public health in the 1990s* (Publication No. 92–3316, pp. 147–199.) Washington, DC: National Institutes of Health.

Elder, J. P., Wildey, M., de Moor, C., Sallis, J. F., Eckhardt, L., Edwards, C., Erickson, A., Golbeck, A., Hovell, M., Johnston, D., Levitz, M. D., Molgaard, C., Young, R., Vito, D. & Woodruff, S. I. (1993). The long-term prevention of tobacco use among junior high school students: Classroom and telephone intervention. *American Journal of Public Health, 83*(9), 1239–1244.

Elders, J., Perry, C., Ericksen, M., & Giovani, G. (1994). Commentary: The report of the Surgeon General: Preventing tobacco use among young people. *American Journal of Public Health, 84,* 543–547.

Ellickson, P. L., Bell, R. M., & McGuigan, K. (1993). Preventing adolescent drug use: Long-term results of a junior high program. *American Journal of Public Health, 83,* 856–861.

Evans, R. I. (1976). Smoking in children: Developing a social psychological strategy of deterrence. *Preventive Medicine, 5,* 122–127.

Evans, R. I. (1979). Fear is not enough: Modification of behavior to prevent disease. *Postgraduate Medicine, 65,* 195–197.

Evans, R. I. (1983). Deterring smoking in adolescents: Evolution of a research program in applied social psychology. *International Journal of Applied Psychology, 32,* 71–83.

Evans, R. I. (1984). A social inoculation strategy to deter smoking in adolescents. In J. D. Matarazzo, S. M. Weiss, J. A. Herd, N. E. Miller, & S. M. Weiss (Eds.), *Behavioral health: A handbook of health enhancement and disease prevention* (pp. 765–774). New York: Wiley.

Evans, R. I. (1989a). *Albert Bandura: The man and his ideas.* New York: Praeger Press.

Evans, R. I. (1989b). The evolution of challenges to researchers in health psychology. *Health Psychology, 8,* 631–639.

Evans, R. I. (1994). *Minority adolescent drug use prevention: First Year Progress Report to NIDA.* (Grant No. R01 DA07024). Unpublished progress report to National Institute of Drug Abuse.

Evans, R. I. (1998). An historical perspective on effective prevention. In W. J. Bukoski & R. I. Evans (Eds.), National Institute on Drug Abuse Technical Research Monograph Series No. 176, *Cost Benefit/Cost Effectiveness Research on Drug Abuse Prevention: Implications for Programming and Policy.* NIH Publication No. 98-4021 (pp. 37–58). Washington, DC: U.S. Department of Health and Human Services, National Institutes of Health, Superintendent of Documents, U.S. Government Printing Office.

Evans, R. I. (1999). *Prevention of gambling among adolescents.* Unpublished manuscript commissioned by the National Research Council, University of Houston.

Evans, R. I., Getz, J. G., & Raines, B. E. (1991, August). *Theory-guided models in prevention of AIDS in adolescents.* Paper presented at Science Weekend, American Psychological Association Conference, San Francisco, CA.

Evans, R. I., Hansen, W. B., & Mittelmark, M. B. (1977). Increasing the validity of self-reports of smoking behavior in children. *Journal of Applied Psychology, 62*(4), 521–523.

Evans, R. I., Henderson, A. H., Hill, P. C., & Raines, B. E. (1979). Smoking in children and adolescent: Psychosocial determinants and prevention strategies. In the U. S. Public Health Services, *Smoking and Health: A Report of the Surgeon General.* Washington, DC: U. S. Department of Health, Education and Welfare.

Evans, R. I., & Raines, B. E. (1982). Control and prevention of smoking in adolescents: A psychosocial perspective. In T. J. Coates, A. C. Petersen, & C. Perry (Eds.), *Promoting adolescent health: A dialog on research and practice* (pp. 101–136). New York: Academic Press.

Evans, R. I., Raines, B. E., & Hanselka, L. L. (1984). Developing data-based communications in social psychological research: Adolescent smoking prevention. *Journal of Applied Social Psychology, 14,* 289–295.

Evans, R. I., Rozelle, R. M., Lasater, T. M., Dembroski, T. M., & Allen, B. P. (1968). New measure of effects of persuasive communications: A chemical indicator of toothbrushing behavior. *Psychological Report, 23,* 731–736.

Evans, R. I., Rozelle, R. M., Lasater, T. M., Dembroski, T. M., & Allen, B. P. (1970). Fear arousal, persuasion, and actual versus implied behavioral change: New perspective utilizing a real-life dental hygiene program. *Journal of Personality & Social Psychology, 16,* 220–227.

Evans, R. I., Rozelle, R. M., Maxwell, S. E., Raines, B. E., Dill, C. A., Guthrie, T. J., Henderson, A. H., & Hill, P. C. (1981). Social modeling films to deter smoking in adolescents: Results of a three-year field investigation. *Journal of Applied Psychology, 66,* 399–414.

Evans, R. I., Rozelle, R. M., Mittelmark, M. B., Hansen, W. B., Bane A. L., & Havis, J. (1978). Deterring the onset of smoking in children: Knowledge of immediate physiological effects and coping with peer pressure, media pressure and parent modeling. *Journal of Applied Social Psychology, 8,* 126–135.

Evans, R. I., Rozelle, R. M., Noblitt, R., & Williams, D. L. (1975). Explicit and implicit persuasive communication over time to initiate and maintain behavior change: A new perspective utilizing a real-life dental hygiene program. *Journal of Applied Social Psychology, 5,* 150–156.

Festinger, L. (1957). *A theory of cognitive dissonance.* Stanford, CA: Stanford University Press.

Fishbein, M., & Ajzen, I. (1975). *Belief, attitude, intention and behavior: An introduction to theory and research.* Reading, MA: Addison-Wesley.

Flay, B. R. (1985). Psychosocial approaches to smoking prevention: A review of findings. *Health Psychology, 4,* 449–488.

Flay, B. R., d'Avernas, J. R., Best, J. A., Kersell, M. W., & Ryan, K. B. (1983). Cigarette smoking: Why young people do it and ways of preventing it. In P. McGrath & P. Firestone (Eds.), *Pediatric and adolescent behavioral medicine.* New York: Springer-Verlag.

Flay, B. R., Hansen, W. B., Johnson, C. A., Collins, L. M., Dent, C. W., Dwyer, K. M., Hockstein, G., Grossman, L., Rauch, J., Sobol, D. F., Sobel, J. L., Sussman, S., & Ulene, A. (1987). Implementation effectiveness trial of a social influences smoking prevention program using schools and television. *Health Education Research, 2,* 385–400.

Flay, R., Keopke, D., Thomson, S. J., Santi, S., Best, J. A., & Brown, K. S. (1989). Long term follow-up of the first Waterloo smoking prevention trial. *American Journal of Public Health, 79*(10), 1371–1376.

Gilbert, M. A., Bauman, K. E., & Udry, J. R. (1986). A panel study of subjective expected utility for adolescent sexual behavior. *Journal of Applied Social Psychology, 16,* 745–756.

Gilchrest, L. D., Schinke, S. P., & Blythe, B. J. (1979). Primary prevention services for children and youth. *Children and Youth Services Review, 1,* 379–391.

Glynn, T. J., Leukefeld, C. G., & Ludford, J. P. (Eds.), (1985). *Preventing adolescent drug abuse: Intervention strategies* (NIDA Monograph No. 47, DHHS Publication No [ADM] 85-1280). Washington, DC: National Institutes of Health.

Goodstadt, M. S. (1978). Alcohol and drug education: Model and outcomes. *Health Education Monograph, 6,* 263–279.

Hansen, W. B., Johnson, C. A., Flay, B. R., Graham, J. W., & Sobel, J. (1988). Affective and social influences approaches to the prevention of multiple substance abuse among seventh grade students: Results from Project SMART. *Preventive Medicine, 17,* 135–154.

Henderson, A. H. (1979, August). *Adolescent smoking decisions: Role of health beliefs and social-psychological perceptions.* Paper presented at the meetings of the American Psychological Association, New York.

Higbee, K. L. (1969). Fifteen years of fear arousal: Research on threat appeals: 1953–1968. *Psychological Bulletin, 72,* 426–444.

Hingston, R. W., Strunin, L., Berlin, B. M., & Herren, T. (1990). Beliefs about AIDS, use of alcohol and drugs, and unprotected sex among Massachusetts adolescents. *American Journal of Public Health, 80,* 295–299.

Hurd, P. D., Johnson, C. A., Pechacek, T., Bast, L. P., Jacobs, D. R., & Luepker, R. V. (1980). Prevention of cigarette smoking in seventh grade students. *Journal of Behavioral Medicine, 3,* 15–28.

Janis, I. L. (1967). Effects of fear arousal on attitude: Recent developments in theory and experimental research. *Advances in Experimental Psychology, 4,* 166–224.

Janis, I. L., & Feshbach, S. (1953). Effects of fear-arousing communications. *Journal of Abnormal & Social Psychology, 48,* 78–92.

Jessor, R., & Jessor, S. L. (1977). *Problem behavior and psychosocial development: A longitudinal study of youth.* New York: Academic Press.

Johnston, L. D., Bachman, J. G., & O'Malley, P. M. (1979). *1979 highlights: Drugs and the nation's high school students: Five year national trends* (USDHEW PHS Publication No. [ADM] 80-930). Washington, DC: National Institutes of Health.

Johnston, L. D., Bachman, J. G., & O'Malley, P. M. (1995, July 20). Smoking rates climb among American teenagers, who find smoking increasingly acceptable and seriously underestimate the risks. *The University of Michigan News Release.*

Kandel, D., & Yamaguchi, K. (1993). From beer to crack: Developmental patterns of drug involvement. *American Journal of Public Health, 83,* 851–855.

Kendall, P. C., & Hollon, S. D. (1979). *Cognitive-behavioral interventions: Theory, research and practice.* New York: Academic Press.

Kirby, D. (1997). School-based programs to reduce sexual risk-taking behavior. *Children and Youth Services Review, 19,* 415–436.

Leventhal, H., Singer, R. P., & Jones, S. (1965). Effects of fear and specificity of recommendations upon attitudes and behavior. *Journal of Personality & Social Psychology, 2,* 20–29.

Lowenstein, G., & Furstenberg, F. (1991). Is teenage sexual behavior rational? *Journal of Applied Social Psychology, 21,* 957–986.

Luepker, R. V., Johnson, C. A., Murray, D. M., & Pechacek, T. F. (1983). Prevention of cigarette smoking: Three year follow-up of educational programs for youth. *Journal of Behavioral Medicine, 6,* 53–61.

Luker, K. (1975). *Taking chances: Abortion and the decision not to contracept.* Berkeley: University of California Press.

Marston, M. V. (1970). Compliance with medical regimens: A review of the literature. *Nursing Research, 19,* 312–323.

McAlister, A., Perry, C., Killen, J., Slinkard, L., & Maccoby, N. (1980). Pilot study of smoking, alcohol and drug abuse prevention. *American Journal of Public Health, 70,* 719–721.

McAlister, A., Perry, C., & Maccoby, N. (1979). Adolescent smoking: Onset and prevention. *Pediatrics, 63,* 650–658.

McGuire, W. J. (1961). The effectiveness of supportive refutational defenses in immunizing and restoring beliefs against persuasion. *Sociometry, 24,* 184–197.

McGuire, W. J. (1968). The nature of attitudes and attitude change. In G. Lindzey & E. Aronson (Eds.), *Handbook of social psychology* (pp. 136–314). Reading, MA: Addison-Wesley.

Merrill, J. (1995, August). *Can prevention research really be defensible in national health policy?* Paper presented at the 103rd convention of the American Psychological Association, New York.

Miller, H. G., Turner, C. G., & Moses, L. E. (Eds.). (1990). *HIV: The second decade.* Washington, DC: National Academy Press.

Mittelmark, M. B. (1978). *Information on imminent versus long term health consequences: Impact on children's smoking behavior, intentions, and knowledge.* Unpublished doctoral dissertation, University of Houston, Texas.

Morrison, D. M. (1985). Adolescent contraceptive behavior: A review. *Psychological Bulletin, 98,* 538–568.

Murray, D. M., Davis-Hearn, M., Goldman, A. I., Pirie, P., & Luepker, R. V. (1988). Four- and five-year follow-up results from four seventh-grade smoking prevention strategies. *Journal of Behavioral Medicine, 11*(4), 395–405.

Murray, D. M., Pirie, P., Luepker, R. V., & Pallonen, U. (1989). Five- and six-year follow-up results from four seventh-grade smoking prevention strategies. *Journal of Behavioral Medicine, 12*(2), 207–218.

National Research Council. (1999). *Pathological gambling: A critical review.* Washington, DC: National Academy Press.

Orlandi, M. A. (1986). Community-based health promotion: A multicultural approach. *Journal of School Health, 56,* 394–401.

Pentz, M. A., MacKinnon, D. P., Flay, B. R., Hansen, W. B., Johnson, C. A., & Dwyer, J. H. (1989). Primary prevention of chronic diseases in adolescence: Effects of the midwestern prevention project on tobacco use. *American Journal of Epidemiology, 130,* 713–724.

Pentz, M. A., Trebow, E. A., Hansen, W. B., & MacKinnon, D. P. (1990). Effects of program implementation on adolescent drug use behavior: The Midwestern Prevention Project. *Evaluation Review, 14,* 264–289.

Perry, C., Killen, J., Slinkard, L. A., & McAlister, A. L. (1989). Peer teaching and smoking prevention among junior high students. *Adolescence, 15,* 277–281.

Schinke, S. P., & Blythe, B. J. (1981). Cognitive-behavioral prevention of children's smoking. *Child Behavioral Therapy, 3,* 25–42.

Schinke, S. P., Botvin, G. J., Trimble, J. E., Orlandi, M. A., Gilchrest, L. D., & Locklear, V. S. (1988). Preventing substance abuse among American-Indian adolescents: A bicultural competence skills approach. *Journal of Counsel Psychology, 35,* 87–90.

Schinke, S. P., & Gilchrest, L. D. (1983). Primary prevention of tobacco smoking. *Journal of School Health, 53,* 416–419.

Schlegel, R. P., Crawford, C. A., & Sanford, M. D. (1977). Correspondence and mediational properties of the Fishbein model: An application to adolescent alcohol use. *Journal of Experimental Social Psychology, 13,* 421–430.

Sherman, S. J., Chassin, L., & Presson, C. C. (1979, September). *Social psychological factors in adolescent cigarette smoking.* Paper presented at the meeting of the American Psychological Association, New York.

Sherman, S. J., Presson, C. C., Chassin, L., Bensenberg, M., Corty, E., & Olschavsky, R. W. (1982). Smoking intentions in adolescents: Direct experience and predictability. *Personality and Social Psychology Bulletin, 8,* 376–383.

Stall, R., McKusick, L., Wiley, J., Coates, T. J., & Ostrow, D. G. (1986). Alcohol and drug use during sexual activity and compliance with safe-sex guidelines for AIDS: The AIDS behavioral research project. *Health Education Quarterly, 13,* 3–13.

Strassberg, D. L., & Mahoney, M. A. (1988). Correlates of the contraceptive behavior of adolescents and young adults. *Journal of Sex Research, 4,* 531–536.

Sussman, S. (1989). Two social influence perspectives of tobacco use development and prevention. *Journal of Behavioral Medicine, 5,* 1–8.

Sutton, S. R. (1982). Fear-arousing communications: A critical examination of theory and research. In J. R. Eiser (Ed.), *Social psychology and behavioral medicine* (pp. 303–337). Chichester: Wiley.

Telch, M. J., Killen, J. D., McAlister, A. L., Perry, C. L. & Maccoby, N. (1982). Long term follow up of a pilot project on smoking prevention with adolescents. *Journal of Behavioral Medicine, 5,* 1–8.

Thompson, E. L. (1978). Smoking education programs, 1960–1976. *American Journal of Public Health, 68,* 250–257.

Tobler, N. S. (1986). Meta-analysis of 143 adolescent drug prevention programs: Quantitative outcome results of program participants compared to a control or comparison group. *Journal of Drug Issues, 16,* 537–567.

Vega, W., Zimmerman, R., Warheit, G., Apospori, E., & Gil, A. (1993). Risk factors for early adolescent drug use in four ethnic and racial groups. *American Journal of Public Health, 83,* 185–189.

Weisman, C. S., Plichta, S., Nathanson, C. A., Chase, G. A., Ensminger, M. E., & Robinson, J. C. (1991). Adolescent women's contraceptive decision making. *Journal of Health Social Behavior, 32,* 130–144.

28

Health, Behavior, and Aging

Ilene C. Siegler
Lori A. Bastian
Hayden B. Bosworth
Duke University

Health psychology has always been sensitive to age as an important construct because the distributions of diseases by age are not random and are important in determining the psychological impact of different diseases. Epidemiology, on the other hand, studies age as a prominent risk factor for disease. Both are important in understanding the set of associations in health, behavior, and aging.

The psychology of adult development and aging looks at persons aging normally, some with and some without specific diseases, to examine the ways disease influences the aging process. Health psychology studies individuals with specific physical illnesses and seeks to understand how the aging process might modify the impact of that disease (Siegler & Vitaliano, 1998). The psychology of adult development and aging and health psychology are two subdisciplines of psychology that have multidisciplinary partners. The multidisciplinary aspects of studying aging are part of gerontology and limited to studying primarily the elderly, whereas the medical aspects of aging are studied as a postgraduate branch of medicine called geriatrics (Hazzard, Bierman, Blass, Ettinger, & Halter, 1994; Maddox et al., 1995). Behavioral medicine is a multidisciplinary approach to understanding problems in health psychology that interact with the same problems in psychosomatic medicine (Blechman & Brownell, 1998; Matthews, in press).

Handbooks are common in the psychology of adult development and aging. In each of the Handbooks there has been a "health psychology" chapter (Deeg, Kardaun, & Fozard, 1996; Eisdorfer & Wilkie, 1977; M. F. Elias, J. W. Elias, & P. K. Elias, 1990; Siegler & Costa, 1985). As a group, they provide excellent reviews of the relevant literature that need not be repeated here. As part of a set of master lectures on adult development and aging, Siegler (1989) was given the "health psychology" assignment and tried to conceptualize the intersection of health, behavior, and aging as developmental health psychology. This chapter reflects an updating of that initial effort and focuses on emergent findings in the past 10 years and aims to be illustrative rather than exhaustive.

Understanding the issues in health, behavior, and aging first requires discussing what has been a central question in the field: What is normal aging? Second, some important methodological ideas are reviewed from the psychology of adult development that will be useful in health psychology. The chapter then takes up the issue of a life-span developmental versus "phase" theory view of a developmental health psychology. It then considers some new data and thinking about women's and men's health in middle and later life, and reviews the findings from some recent empirical studies that show the excellent results from the synergy of developmental and health psychology.

WHAT IS NORMAL AGING AND HOW IS IT DIFFERENT FROM DISEASE?

This question drove the initial longitudinal studies of normal aging, such as the Duke Longitudinal Study (Busse et al., 1985). Shock's (see Shock et al., 1984) initial observations were essentially correct, that some, albeit rare, individuals age without the typical declines (as was shown by a careful testing of participants in the Baltimore Longitudinal Study of Aging, BLSA) and normal aging itself is a relatively benign set of processes (Williams, 1994). This is not to say that older persons do not have health problems or that the probability of health problems does not increase with age. But rather, when they do, they can be attributed to a particular disease process rather than just the passage of time. The resulting problems then could be considered the fault of a chronic disease process that is not rapidly fatal, but treated, and remains as a companion for the rest of life. Thus, it seems "unfair" to blame aging. It used to be that normal aging was accepted and disease treated. However, current cohorts raised on such slogans as "Better living through chemistry" are trying to treat normal aging as well.

A table taken from a recent NIA publication summarizes what the Baltimore Longitudinal Study of Aging (BLSA) teaches about normal aging (NIA, 1996).

Definitions of normal aging are a moving target and change as a function of individual's risk modification behavior and effective treatments. Thus, Table 28.1 is true today; but future research may point out changes for future cohorts. As new cohorts age, they may well be different from current middle-aged and elderly persons. As is discussed later, psychology of aging has spent considerable time understanding these shifting patterns of aging.

TABLE 28.1
What is Normal Aging?

Individuals age at extremely different rates. In fact, even within one person, organs and organ systems show different rates of decline. However, some generalities can be made, based on data from the Baltimore Longitudinal Study of Aging. It is important to remember that these statements do not apply to all people.

Heart. It grows slightly larger with age. Maximal oxygen consumption during exercise declines in men by about 10% with each decade of adult life and in women, by about 7.5%. However, cardiac output stays nearly the same as the heart pumps more efficiently.

Lungs. Maximum breathing (vital) capacity may decline by about 40% between age 20 and 70.

Brain. With age, the brain loses some cells (neurons) and others become damaged. However, it adapts by increasing the number of connections between cells—synapses—and by regrowing the branch-life extensions, dendrites, and axons that carry messages in the brain.

Kidneys. They gradually become less efficient at extracting wastes from the blood. Bladder capacity declines. Urinary incontinence, which may occur after tissues atrophy, can often be managed through exercise and behavioral techniques.

Body Fat. The body does not lose fat with age but redistributes it from just under the skin to deeper parts of the body. Women are more likely to store it in the lower body—hips and thighs—while men store it in the abdominal area.

Muscles. Without exercise, estimated muscle mass declines 22% for women and 23% for men between age 30 and 70. Exercise can prevent this loss.

Sight. Difficulty focusing close up may begin in the 40s; the ability to distinguish fine details may begin to decline in the 70s. From age 50 on, there is increased susceptibility to glare, greater difficulty in seeing at low levels of illumination, and more difficulty in detecting moving targets.

Hearing. It becomes more difficult to hear higher frequencies with age. Hearing declines more quickly in men than in women.

Personality. After about age 30 personality is stable. Sudden changes in personality sometimes suggest disease processes.

METHODOLOGICAL CONCERNS FROM PSYCHOLOGY OF AGING

Psychology of aging has made major contributions in the explication of the meanings of age, period, and cohort and important factors in understanding development (Baltes, 1968; Schaie, 1965; Schaie & Herzog, 1985). Here, the focus is on the implications of developmental designs for health psychology.

Period/Time Effects

The definition of a period, or time effect, is a societal or cultural change that may occur between two measurements that present plausible alternative rival explanations for the outcome of a study (Baltes, Reese, & Nesselroade, 1988; Schaie, 1977). In order to specifically describe a period, or time effect, in health and disease, these effects are described in terms of new diagnostic tools or medical therapies that present plausible alternative rival explanations for the outcome of a study.

The introduction of the prostate-specific antigen (PSA) test in 1987 is an example of the effects of period/time effects accounting for age-related changes in detecting prostate cancer. With the increased use of the PSA test as a diagnostic tool for prostate cancer, there is now an increasing number of prostate cancers being diagnosed among older adults that would not have been diagnosed based on previous diagnostic techniques (Amling et al., 1998). Because prostate cancer prevalence rates increase with age, researchers studying longitudinally the relation between age and onset of prostate cancer would have to account for the introduction of this relatively new diagnostic tool.

Information is becoming made available quicker and improvements in diagnostic techniques and treatments are increasing in frequency. This is a benefit for the population, but it makes research more difficult, particularly if an intervention is in process and new information or changes in medical procedure is being made and available to the public at-large. Subsequently, health psychologists are going to have to become more aware and flexible in the way they deal with these increasing period/time effects. An example of researchers adapting to historical or period effects has been the ongoing Women's Health Initiative study, in which information on estrogen use is being collected (Matthews et al., 1997). Since the design of this large observational and intervention study in the late 1980s (Roussow et al., 1995), there has been an increased number of data to suggest that the influence of estrogen is related to long-term benefits, such as preventing or delaying osteoporosis, heart disease, and Alzheimer's disease (Jacobs & Hillard, 1996). More recently, researchers have identified newer selective estrogen receptor modulators (i.e., Raloxifene and lower doses of conjugated estrogen (0.3 mg) that may be as effective as the more traditional 0.625 mg Premarin but with fewer side effects (Delmas et al., 1997; Bastian, Couchman, Nanda, & Siegler, 1998; Genant et al., 1997). The increase in awareness of the possible association of estrogen and diseases, such as Alzheimer's disease, and the addition of newer therapies may have altered women's perception and experiences with hormonal replacement medication and influence study observations.

Human immunodeficiency virus/acquired immunodeficiency syndrome (HIV/AIDS) information is being made readily available, which is quickly influencing treatment outcomes. AIDS and aging were once mutually exclusive conditions: The AIDS epidemic began in young adults and they died before they had time to age (Justice & Whalen, 1996). Much has happened since 1982, when the first Centers for Disease Control (CDC) definition of AIDS was published. Better therapies, specifically protease inhibitors, have changed HIV infection to be a chronic condition (Flexner, 1998; Hogg et al., 1998). Given the current success of these therapies, more HIV infected persons should be expected across the life span. It will be necessary to learn how to adjust management for specific populations, such as the elderly. More may be learned about the immune function and aging while treating HIV infection and AIDS in various age groups.

As researchers move from studying diseases cross-sectionally and move toward examining the disease path and as they continue to apply this acquired information to interventions, they will need to better understand period and time effects and the ways they may influence ongoing studies.

Is the Age at Disease Onset Important?

An area often neglected in the study of aging and disease is whether the development of a particular disease in young adults has the same etiology or recommendations for treatment, as among older adults. For example, a disease that is influenced by age of onset is prostate cancer. The risk of prostate cancer increases faster with age than any other form of cancer (National Cancer Institute, 1991). After age 50, both mortality and incidence rates from prostate cancer increase almost exponentially. Ninety-five percent of cases of prostate cancer are diagnosed in men between age 45 and age 89, with a median age at diagnosis of age 72 (Winkelstein & Ernster, 1979). There is widespread clinical impression among physicians treating prostate cancer that the disease is more virulent and rapidly progressive in younger men (Meikle & Smith, 1990) and as a result treatment options vary based on the age of onset. More invasive procedures are used for later stages at earlier age of onset than at comparable stages at later age of onset.

Depression is another example in which age of onset is an important factor in understanding the etiology and subsequent treatment. Depression in the elderly is a serious medical condition that is underdiagnosed and undertreated (NIH, 1992). A common approach to characterizing depression has been to study its risk factors and presentations according to age of first onset. This method dichotomizes depression into early-onset depression and late-onset depression, generally using the range from age 50 to 60 as a cut-off point (Steffens, Hays, George, Krishnan, & Blazer, 1996). Late-onset depression is more frequently associated with structural brain changes and cerebrovascular disease, and early-onset depression seems to be more influenced by family and genetic factors (Coffey, Figiel, Djang, & Weiner, 1990; Figiel et al., 1991). Clinically, patients with late-onset depression show more loss of interest, less pathological guilt, more psychosis, and more generalized anxiety (Krishnan, Hays, Tupler, George, & Blazer, 1995). There is also evidence that late-onset depressives may be more refractory to antidepressant treatment than patients with early-onset depression (Hickie, Scott, Wilhelm, & Brodaty, 1997) and suffer higher mortality rates (Philbert, Richards, Lynch, & Winokur, 1997).

Age of Disease Onset by Gender Interaction. Not only is age of disease onset an important issue to consider when examining the relation between aging, disease, and behavior, but the consideration of how gender interacts with age of disease onset is just as important. This is particularly the case for coronary heart disease because clinical manifestations of coronary heart disease (CHD) occurs among women on average 10 years later than for men, with the occurrence of myocardial infarction being almost 20 years later (Wenger, 1995).

An example of the importance of considering gender in terms of age of onset interaction is provided in the Framingham study, which is a 30-year follow-up examining a number of specific risk factors for CHD by age group and gender. Results from the study indicate that the majority of significant associations between risk factors and CHD apparent in younger men and women remain significant in older age groups, but not consistently in both sexes. Systolic blood pressure and vital capacity, for example, both demonstrate strong risk associations for CHD in younger men and women and the association increases for older men, but decreases for older women (age 65–94). The effects of diastolic blood pressure are strong risk associations for CHD in younger adults and the effects decrease in older adults, particularly among older women. The risk association for serum cholesterol, cigarettes, relative weight decreases the risk of CHD in older adults, whereas blood glucose increases the risk of CHD (Harris, Cook, Kannel, & Goldman, 1988).

Another gender interaction is diabetes. At all ages, but especially in premenopausal women, diabetes mellitus is a far more powerful risk factor of CHD for women than for men (Barrett-Connor, Cohn, Wingard, & Edelstein, 1991). Adult onset diabetes, in the Nurses' Health Study was associated with a three- to sevenfold increased risk of a cardiovascular event, with this risk amplified by associated risk factors (Manson et al., 1991). The mechanisms imparting risk among diabetic women are uncertain, but may include lipid abnormalities, hypertension, fibrinogen abnormalities, and the upper body obesity syndrome, all of which are common concomitants of diabetes mellitus. Further, after age 45, women are twice as likely as men to develop diabetes (Wenger, 1995).

Usefulness of a Life Span Perspective

In the psychology of adult development and aging, it is almost a matter of catechism that development needs to be understood in a life span perspective. Is this true in developmental health psychology as well? Two areas of research that have gotten attention in the past 10 years are the tremendous increase in the numbers of centenarians and the role of hormone replacement therapy (HRT) as an antidote to aging for women. Both research areas argue for lifespan development within particular phases, not as a continuous process.

Centenarians and the role of health and aging. Centenarian status is not easy to predict from earlier in the life cycle. It sounds trite to say that one must live until 80 or 90 to get to be 100; but it is not at all obvious from a group of very old people, who will be the rare person to get all the way to 100. This not only makes them very hard to locate and to study, but also to describe. In studies that require cognitive testing, centenarians are generally seen as expert survivors (Poon, Johnson, & Martin, 1997). When the full population of living centenarians is studied, the variances are extreme in both physical health and cognitive functioning (Forette, 1997).

HRT and the Logic of Estrogen-Related Disease

Until recently, women's health research has mainly focused on reproduction and cancers unique to women. Given that the incidence of chronic diseases in women increase after menopause (a marker of midlife), it is logical to use the terminology pre- and postmenopausal to describe adult women's health. The postmenopausal period extends beyond age 50 and can be divided into three additional phases based on the incidence of chronic diseases. As shown in Table 28.2, women's health can be described in four phases: Phase 1–premenopause; Phase 2—postmenopause (age 50–64) with the development of diseases such as breast cancer; Phase 3—postmenopause (age 65–79) with the development of diseases such as heart disease; and Phase 4—postmenopause (age 80 and up) with the long-term development of diseases such as osteoporosis and Alzheimer's dementia.

The terminology "estrogen-related diseases" can be used to organize and describe diseases associated with estrogen. Although some of these diseases, such as osteoporosis, heart disease, endometrial cancer, and breast cancer are well established to be associated with estrogen in women (Col et al., 1997; Colditz et al., 1995; Grady et al., 1992; Grady, Gebretsadik, Kerlikowske, Ernster, & Petitti, 1995; Newcomb & Storer, 1995), other diseases like Alzheimer's dementia and colon cancer have been reported to be associated with estrogen but are generally considered more controversial (Kawas et al., 1997; Nanda, Bastian, Hasselblad, & Simal, 1999; Paganini-Hill & Henderson, 1996; Potter, 1995). Estrogen-related diseases can be used as a shorthand to represent the potential HRT may have on the public health of women. A much better understanding of how estrogen is related to these and other diseases can be expected because of anticipated results from the Women's Health Initiative (WHI; Rossouw et al., 1995). Reported to be the largest study of women's health in the world, WHI researchers have compiled a battery of psychological measures in addition to the longitudinal assessment of disease incidence as outcome measures (Matthews et al., 1997).

Conversely, there is not a clear marker of midlife in men. However, there may be a role for discussing phases of diseases in men's health as well. Like estrogens, androgen levels decrease with age and have a broad range of effects on sexual organs and metabolic processes. Androgen deficiency in men older than age 65 leads to a decrease in muscle mass, osteoporosis, decrease in sexual activity, and changes in mood and cognitive function (Swerdloff & Wang, 1993) leading to speculation that there may be at least two phases of chronic diseases related to androgen levels in men. Whether men over age 65 would benefit from androgen replacement therapy is not known. Any potential benefits from this therapy would need to be weighed against the possible adverse effects on the prostate and cardiovascular system.

EMERGENT FINDINGS ON AGING AND HEALTH/DISEASE

The literature has matured in this area as investigators have started to ask important questions about how age interacts with other factors to try to look at the potential mechanisms that relate psychosocial factors to disease outcomes. Kop (1997) provided an interesting theoretical statement. He argued that psychosocial factors, such as hostility and socioeconomic status are important in understanding the risks of heart disease only under age 55. Whether this turns out to be true requires significantly more empirical verification. However, it is consistent with findings reported by House et al. (1992), suggesting from survey data that the number of chronic conditions

TABLE 28.2
Women's Health in Four Phases Based on Peak Incidence of Estrogen-Related Disease

	Phase 1 Premenopausal	Phase 2	Phase 3	Phase 4
Age	< 50	50–64	65–79	80 and older
Diseases	Reproductive concerns Breast cancer	Breast cancer Endometrial cancer	Heart disease Cerebrovascular disease	Osteoporosis Alzheimer's dementia

reported by individuals stratified by SES and age indicated that the average number of conditions for an older person, age 75+, in the upper social class was the same as for a middle-aged person (around age 45) in the lower social class strata.

Jennings et al. (1997) studied middle-aged men (age 46–64) from the Kuopio study to ask empirical questions about the role of age, disease (hypertension), and medication on cardiovascular reactivity and found that there are no simple answers. All three of the factors have effects of reactivity. Thus, the role of age in studies of health psychology needs to be determined paradigm by paradigm, and disease by disease.

Kaplan (1992) reported on data from the Alameda county study to ask if risk factor modification undertaken in later life has an impact on mortality—the answer is a definite yes. When those over age 70 in the Alameda county study were followed for 17 years, current smoking, physical inactivity, consuming more than 45 drinks per month, being more than 10% underweight or 30% overweight, and having a low social network index were associated with mortality, whereas marital status, race, and SES were not.

The Role of Health-Related Quality of Life

Clinicians and policymakers are recognizing the importance of measuring health-related quality of life to inform patient management and policy decisions, but researchers have been a little slower to examine this outcome. An understanding of what determines good health outcomes is highly valued by patients and is necessary in order to maintain function and, therefore, improve health-related quality of life (Stewart et al., 1989). One reason why researchers have chosen not to consider health-related quality of life as an outcome measure is that this concept misleadingly suggests an abstract philosophical approach, whereas most approaches used in the medical contexts do not attempt to include more general notions such as life satisfaction or living standards and instead concentrate on aspects of personal experience that might be directly related to health (Fitzpatrick et al., 1992). Nevertheless, despite the proliferation of instruments and the theoretical literature devoted to the measurement of health-related quality of life, no unified approach has been devised for its measurement, and little agreement has been attained on what it means (Bergner, 1989; Gill & Feinstein, 1994; Spilker, Molinek, Johnson, Simpson, & Tilson, 1990).

Although, health-related quality of life has not been clearly defined, it is important to begin to consider outcomes other than mortality and morbidity, particularly as life expectancy continues to increase and chronic diseases are becoming more prevalent. Health-related quality of life is important for measuring the impact of chronic disease (Patrick & Erickson, 1993). It will be interesting to see if Baby Boomers have the same patterns as earlier generations. Physiologic and clinical measures provide information to clinicians, but they often correlate poorly with functional capacity and well-being (Guyatt, Feeny, & Patrick, 1993). For example, in patients with chronic heart and lung disease, exercise capacity in the laboratory is only weakly related to exercise capacity in daily life (Guyatt et al., 1985). Another example of health-related quality of life instruments improving assessment is that these instruments have been shown to be better than conventional rheumatologic measures as predictors of long-term outcomes in rheumatoid arthritis in terms of both morbidity and mortality (Leigh & Fries, 1991; Wolfe & Cathey, 1991).

There is evidence of great individual variation in functional status and well-being that is not accounted for by age or disease condition (Sherbourne, Meredith, & Ware, 1992). The field of health psychology needs to consider health-related quality of life because a commonly observed phenomena that two patients with the same clinical criteria often have dramatically different responses. For example, two patients, with the same range of motion and even similar ratings of back pain, may have different role function and emotional well-being. Although some patients may continue to work without major depression, others may quit their jobs and have major depression. Thus, health-related quality of life is often a better index of the impact that health has on functioning than diagnostic or clinical criteria. It, however, does not have the same etiologic significance as a verified diagnosis according to standard criteria.

CONCLUSIONS

Aging has taken on a higher profile given the demographic revolution due to increased longevity (Qualls & Abeles, in press). Interest in aging issues is often due to a concern with the health, disease, and disability of the elderly population (Siegler, in press). As the demographic revolution occurs, it is important to note that the number of adults with diseases will continue to increase (prevalence), but because of improvements in diagnostic tools and treatments, will be able to live longer. However, despite the fact that there will be increasing numbers of people with chronic diseases, the incidence of certain diseases continues to decline. This demographic revolution, however, is spread unevenly around the world (Murray & Lopez, 1996).

The writing of this chapter has lead to three conclusions that summarize current thinking on health, behavior, and aging:

1. Gender and age interact in important ways during adult life and aging. This is especially true in terms of diseases such as AIDS, coronary artery disease, and cancers. In the last decade, gender differences in the etiology and treatment of diseases have been illuminated. These differences have provided the impetus to create a women's health medical specialty. Examples have been presented in this chapter of gender differences and similarities across the adult life span.

   Several studies have examined the issue of differences in health care use between men and women. Landmark studies identified a gender disparity in the diagnosis and treatment of chest pain and CHD (Tobin et al., 1987). This study has led to further studies demonstrating sex differences in the rates of cardiac catheterization and coronary artery bypass surgery (Ayanian & Epstein, 1991). These studies have changed the way medical students are taught about evaluating chest pain and have resulted in the reporting of other gender disparities on such topics as renal transplants (Held, Pauly, Bovbjerg, Newmann, & Salvatierra, 1988) and HIV/AIDS (Bastian et al., 1993). The recognition that there is a need to improve the training of clinicians in women's health, has led to the development of a new interdisciplinary specialty in women's health (Wallis, 1992). One consequence of the focus on women's health has been the widening of the definition of health to include social interactions, domestic issues, mental health, and reproductive function (Litt, 1997).

2. Life span development is theory, which at the present time, is not practical given the state of the science. Researchers are able to use data at one phase of the life cycle to inform them about developments in adjacent phases and periods approaching 40 years.
3. Survival as a quantity of life measure is different than quality of life measures. Although there is a growing emphasis to include health-related quality of life as an additional outcome measure other than morbidity and mortality for health-related interventions, and that health-related quality of life is a useful discriminator among different population segments, and is an important predictor of health and health behaviors, the field still needs to alleviate a number of measurement-related issues and difficulties. The continued efforts to identify those content areas and response dimensions that likely will provide the best discrimination among populations and the greatest sensitivity to change are essential to enable health psychologists to guide future health policy and resources.

ACKNOWLEDGMENTS

This work was supported by grants R01 AG12458 from National Institute on Aging and R01 HL55356 from National Heart Lung and Blood Institute. The third author was supported in part by the Department of Veterans Affairs, Veterans Health Administration, HSR&D Service, Program 824 Funds.

REFERENCES

Amling, C. L., Blute, M. L., Lerner, S. E., Bergstralh, E. J., Bostwick, D. G., & Zincke, H. (1998). Influence of prostate-specific antigen testing on the spectrum of patients with prostate cancer undergoing radical prostatectomy at a large referral practice. *Mayo Clinic Proceedings, 73,* 401–406.

Ayanian, J. Z., & Epstein, A. M. (1991). Differences in the use of procedures between women and men hospitalized for coronary heart disease. *New England Journal of Medicine, 325,* 221–225.

Baltes, P. B. (1968). Longitudinal and cross-sectional sequence in the study of age and generation effects. *Human Development, 11,* 145–171.

Baltes, P.B., Reese, H.W., & Nesselroade, J. R. (1988). *Introduction to research methods: Life-span developmental psychology.* Hillsdale, NJ: Lawrence Erlbaum Associates.

Barrett-Connor, E. L., Cohn, B. A., Wingard, D. L., & Edelstein, S. L. (1991). Why is diabetes mellitus a stronger risk factors for fatal ischemic heart disease in women than in men? The Rancho Bernado Study. *Journal of the American Medical Association, 265,* 627–631.

Bastian, L. A., Bennett, C. L., Adams, J., Waskin, H., Divine, G., & Edlin, B. R. (1993). Differences between men and women with HIV-related pneumocystis carinii pneumonia: Experience from 3,070 cases in New York City in 1987. *Journal of Acquired Immune Deficiency Syndromes, 6,* 617–623.

Bastian, L. A., Couchman, G. M., Nanda, K., & Siegler, I. C. (1998). Hormone replacement therapy: Benefits, risks and management. *Clinics Atlas of Office Procedures, 1,* 1–9.

Bergner, M. (1989). Quality of life, health status, and clinical research. *Medical Care, 27* (Suppl. 3), S148-S156.

Blechman, E. A., & Brownell, K. D. (Eds.). (1998). *Behavioral medicine and women: A comprehensive handbook.* New York: Guilford.

Busse, E. W., Maddox, G. L., Buckley, C. E., Burger, P. C., George, L. K., Marsh, G. R., Nebes, R. D, Nowlin, J. B., Palmore, E. B., Ramm, D., Siegler, I. C., Vogel, S. F., Wang, S. H, & Woodbury, M. A. (1985). *The Duke longitudinal studies of normal aging: 1955–1980.* New York: Springer.

Coffey, C. E., Figiel, G. S., Djang, W. T., & Weiner, R. D. (1990). Subcortical hyperintensity on MRI: A comparison of normal and depressed elderly subjects. *American Journal of Psychiatry, 147,* 187–189.

Col, N. F., Eckman, M. H., Karas, R. H., Pauker, S. G., Goldberg, R. J., Ross, E. M., Orr, R. K., & Wong, J. B. (1997). Patient-specific decisions about HRT in postmenopausal women. *Journal of the American Medical Association, 277,* 1140–1147.

Colditz, G. A., Hankinson, S. E., Hunter, D. J., Willett, W. C., Manson, J. E., Stampfer, M. J., Hennekens, C., Rosner, B., & Speizer, F. E. (1995). The use of estrogens and progestins and the risk of breast cancer in postmenopausal women. *New England Journal of Medicine, 332,* 1589–1593.

Deeg, D.H.J., Kardaun, J.W.P.F., & Fozard, J. L. (1996). Health, behavior & aging. In J. E. Birren & K. W. Schaie (Eds.), *Handbook of the psychology of aging* (4th ed., pp. 129–149). San Diego, CA: Academic Press.

Delmas, P. D., Bjarnason, N. H., Mitlak, B. H., Ravoux, A. C., Shah, A. S., Huster, W. J., Draper, M., & Christiansen, C. (1997). Effects of raloxifene on bone mineral density, serum cholesterol concentrations, and uterine endometrium in postmenopausal women. *New England Journal of Medicine, 337,* 1686–1687.

Eisdorfer, C., & Wilkie, F. W. (1977). Stress, disease, aging and behavior. In J. E. Birren & K. W. Schaie (Eds.), *Handbook of the psychology of aging* (pp. 251–275). New York: Van Nostrand Reinhold.

Elias, M. F., Elias, J. W., & Elias, P. K. (1990). Biological and health influences on behavior. In J. E. Birren & K. W. Schaie (Eds.), *Handbook of the psychology of aging* (3rd ed., pp. 79–102). San Diego, CA: Academic Press.

Figiel, G. S., Krishnan, K. R. R., Doriaswamy, P. S., Rao, V. P., Nemeroff, C. B., & Boyko, O. B. (1991). Subcortical hyperintensities on brain magnetic resonance imaging: A comparison between late age onset and early onset elderly depression subjects. *Neurobiology Aging, 245,* 245–247.

Fitzpatrick, R., Fletcher, A., Gore, S., Jones, D., Spiefelhalter, D., & Cox, D. (1992). Quality of life measure in health care: I. Applications and issues in assessment. *British Medical Journal, 305,* 1074–1077.

Flexner, C. (1998). HIV-protease inhibitors. *New England Journal of Medicine, 338,* 1281–1292.

Forette, B. (1997). Centenarians: Health and frailty. In J.-M. Robine, J. W. Vaupel, B. Jeune, & M. Allard (Eds.), *Longevity: To the limits and beyond* (pp. 105–112). New York: Springer-Verlag.

Genant, H. K., Lucas, J., Weiss, S., Akin, M., Emkey, R., McNaney-Flint, H., Downs, R., Mortola J., Watts, N., Yang, H. M., Banav, N., Brennan, J. J., & Nolan, J. C. (1997). Low-dose esterified estrogen therapy: Effects on bone, plasma estradiol concentrations, endometrium, and lipid levels. Estratab/osteoporosis study group. *Archives Internal Medicine, 157*(22), 2609–2615.

Gill, T. M., & Feinstein, A. R. (1994). A critical appraisal of the quality of quality-of-life measurements. *Journal of the American Medical Association, 272*(8), 619–626.

Grady, D., Rubin, S. M., Petitti, D. B., Fox, C. S., Black, D., Ettinger, B., Ernster, V. L., & Cummings, S. R. (1992). Hormone therapy to prevent disease and prolong life in postmenopausal women. *Annals of Internal Medicine, 117,* 1016–1037.

Grady, D., Gebretsadik, T., Kerlikowske, K., Ernster, V., & Petitti, D. (1995). Hormone replacement therapy and endometrial cancer: A meta-analysis. *Obstetrics and Gynecology, 85,* 304–313.

Guyatt, G. H., Thompson, P. J., Berman, L. B., Sullivan, M. J., Townsend M., Jones, N. L., & Pugsley, S. O. (1985). How should we measure function in patients with chronic heart and lung disease. *Journal of Chronic Disease, 38,* 517–524.

Guyatt, G. H, Feeny, D. H., & Patrick, D. L. (1993). Measuring health-related quality of life. *Annals Internal Medicine, 118,* 622–29.

Harris, T., Cook, E. F., Kannel, W. B., & Goldman, L. (1988). Proportional hazards analysis of risk factors for coronary heart disease in individuals 65 or older. The Framingham Heart Study. *Journal of the American Geriatrics Society, 36,* 1023–1028.

Hazzard, W. R., Bierman, E. L., Blass, J. P., Ettinger, W. H., Jr., & Halter, J. B. (Eds.). (1994). *Principles of geriatric medicine and gerontology* (3rd ed.). New York: McGraw-Hill.

Held, P. J., Pauly, M. V., Bovbjerg, R. R., Newmann, J., & Salvatierra, O., Jr. (1988). Access to kidney transplantation. *Archives of Internal Medicine, 148,* 2594–2600.

Hickie, I., Scott, E., Wilhelm, K., & Brodaty, H. (1997). Subcortical hyperintensities on magnetic resonance imaging in patients with severe depression—a longitudinal evaluation. *Biological Psychiatry, 42*(5), 367–374.

Hogg, R. S., Heath, K. V., Yip, B., Craib, K. J., O'Shaughnessy, M. V., Schechter, M. T., & Montaner, J. S. (1998). Improved survival among HIV-infected individuals. *Journal of the American Medical Association, 279,* 450–454.

House, J. S., Kessler, R. C., Herzog, A. R., Mero, R. P., Kinney, R. P., & Breslow, M. J. (1992). Social stratification, age and health. In K. W. Schaie, J. House, & D. G. Blazer (Eds.), *Aging, health behaviors and health outcomes* (pp. 1–32). Hillsdale, NJ: Lawrence Erlbaum Associates.

Jacobs, S., & Hillard, T. C. (1996). Hormone replacement therapy in the aged: A state of the art review. *Drugs Aging, 8,* 193–213.

Jennings, J. R., Kamarck, T., Manuck, S., Everson, S. A., Kaplan, G., & Salonen, J. T. (1997). Aging or disease? Cardiovascular reactivity in Finnish men over the middle years. *Psychology and Aging, 12,* 225–238.

Justice, A. C., & Whalen, C. (1996). Aging in AIDS; AIDS and aging. *Journal of General Internal Medicine, 11,* 645–647.

Kaplan, G. A. (1992). Health and aging in the Alameda County study. In K. W. Schaie, J. House, & D. G. Blazer (Eds.), *Aging, health behaviors and health outcomes* (pp. 69–88). Hillsdale, NJ: Lawrence Erlbaum Associates.

Kawas, C., Resnick, S., Morrison, A., Broakmeyer, R., Corrada, M., Zonderman, A., Bacal, C., Lingle, D. D., & Metter, E. (1997). A prospective study of estrogen replacement therapy and the risk of developing Alzheimer's disease: The Baltimore Longitudinal Study of aging. *Neurology, 48,* 1517–1521.

Kop, W. (1997). Acute and chronic psychological risk factors for coronary syndromes: Moderating effects of coronary artery disease severity. *Journal of Psychosomatic Research, 43,* 167–181.

Krishnan, K.R.R., Hays, J. C., Tupler, L. A., George, L. K., & Blazer, D. G. (1995). Clinical and phenomenological comparisons of late-onset and early-onset depression. *American Journal Psychiatry, 152,* 785–788.

Leigh, P., & Fries, J. (1991). Morality predictors among 263 patients with rheumatoid arthritis. *Journal of Rheumatology, 18,* 307–312.

Litt, I. F. (1997). *Taking our pulse: The health of America's women.* Stanford, CA: Stanford University Press.

Maddox, G. L., Atchley, R. C., Evans, J. G., Finch, C. E., Hultsch, D. F., Kane, R. A., Mezey, M.D., & Siegler, I. C. (Eds.). (1995). *Encyclopedia of aging: A comprehensive multidisciplinary review of gerontology and geriatrics* (2nd ed.). New York: Springer.

Manson, J. E., Colditz, G. A., Stampfer, M. J., Willett, C., Krolewski, A. S., Rosner, B., Arky, R. A., Speizer, F. E., & Hennekens, C. H. (1991). A prospective study of maturity-onset diabetes mellitus and risk of coronary heart disease and stroke in women. *Archives of Internal Medicine, 151,* 1141–1147.

Matthews, K. A. (in press). Aging from a behavioral medicine point of view. In S. H. Qualls & N. Abeles (Eds.), *Dialogues in psychology of aging.* Washington, DC: APA Press.

Matthews, K. A., Shumaker, S. A., Bowen, D. J., Langer, R. D., Hunt, J. R., Kaplan, R. M., Klesges, R. C., & Ritenbaugh, C. (1997). Women's Health Initiative. Why now? What is it? What's new? *American Psychologist, 52,* 101–116.

Meikle, A. W., & Smith, J. A., III. (1990). Epidemiology of prostate cancer. *Urologic Clinics of North America, 17,* 709–718.

Murray, C.L.G., & Lopez, A. D. (Eds.). (1996). *The global burden of disease.* Washington, DC: World Health Organization.

Nanda, K., Bastian, L. A., Hasselblad, V., & Simel, D. L. (1999). Hormone replacement therapy and the risk of colorectal cancer: A meta-analysis. *Obstetric and Gynecology, 93,* 880–888.

National Cancer Institute. (1991). National Cancer Institute round table on prostate cancer: Future research directions. Cancer Research, 51, 2498–2505.

National Institute on Aging. (1996). *In search of the secrets of aging.* (2nd ed.). Bethesda, MD: U.S. Government Printing Office.

National Institutes of Health. Consensus Development Panel on Depression in Late Life. (1992). Diagnosis and treatment of depression in late life. *Journal of the American Medical Association, 268,* 1018–1024.

Newcomb, P., & Storer, B. E. (1995). Postmenopausal hormone use and risk of large-bowel cancer. *Journal of National Cancer Institute, 87,* 1067–1071.

Paganini-Hill, A., & Henderson, V. W. (1996). Estrogen replacement therapy and risk of Alzheimer disease. *Archives of Internal Medicine, 156,* 1213–1217.

Patrick, D. I., & Erickson P. (1993). *Health status and health policy: Quality of life in health care evaluation and resources allocation.* New York: Oxford University Press.

Philbert, R. A., Richards, L., Lynch, C. F., & Winokur, G. (1997). The effect of gender and age at onset of depression on mortality. *Journal of Clinical Psychiatry, 58*(8), 355–360.

Poon, L. W., Johnson, M. A., & Martin, P. (1997). Looking into the crystal ball: Will we ever be able to accurately predict individual differences in longevity? In J. M. Robine, J. W. Vaupel, B. Jeune, & M. Allard (Eds.), *Longevity: To the limits and beyond* (pp. 113–119). New York: Springer-Verlag.

Potter, J. D. (1995). Hormones and colon cancer. *Journal of the National Cancer Institute, 87,* 1039–1040.

Qualls, S. H., & Abeles, N. (Eds.). (in press). *Dialogues on psychology and aging*. Washington, DC: American Psychological Association.

Rossouw, J. E., Finnegan, L. P., Harlan, W. R., Pinn, V. W., Clifford, C., & McGowan, J.A. (1995). The evolution of the Women's Health Initiative: Perspectives from the NIH. *Journal of the American Medical Women's Association, 50,* 50–55.

Schaie, K. W. (1965). A general model for the study of developmental problems. *Psychological Bulletin, 64,* 91–107.

Schaie K. W. (1977). Quasi-experimental designs in the psychology of aging. In J. E. Birren & K. W. Schaie (Eds.), *Handbook of the psychology of aging* (pp. 39–58). New York: Van Nostrand Reinhold.

Schaie K. W., & Herzog, C. (1985). Measurement in the psychology of adulthood and aging. In J. E. Birren & K. W. Schaie (Eds.), *Handbook of the psychology of aging* (2nd ed., pp. 61–92). New York: Van Nostrand Reinhold.

Sherbourne, C. D., Meredith, L. S., & Ware, J. E. (1992). Social support and stressful life events: Age differences in their effects on health-related quality of life among the chronically ill. *Quality of Life, 1,* 235–246.

Shock, N., Greulich, R. C., Costa, Jr., P. T., Andres, R., Lakatta, E. G., Arenberg, D., & Tobin, J. D. (Eds.). (1984). *Normal human aging: The Baltimore Longitudinal Study of Aging*. Washington, DC: U.S. Department of Health and Human Services.

Siegler, I. C. (1989). Developmental health psychology. In M. Storandt & G. R. Vanden Bos (Eds.), *The adult years: Continuity and change* (pp. 119–142). Washington, DC: American Psychological Association.

Siegler, I. C. (in press). Aging and health from the aging point of view. In S. H. Qualls & N. Abeles (Eds.), *Dialogues on psychology and aging*. Washington, DC: American Psychological Association.

Siegler, I. C., & Costa, P. T. (1985). Health behavior relationships. In J. E. Birren & K. W. Schaie (Eds.), *Handbook of the psychology of aging* (2nd ed., pp. 144–166). New York: Van Nostrand Reinhold.

Siegler, I. C., & Vitaliano, P. P. (1998). In search of a double paradigm: Introduction to a special issue of *Health Psychology* on Aging and Health. *Health Psychology, 17,* 6.

Spilker, B., Molinek, F. R., Jr., Johnson, K. A., Simpson, R. L., Jr., & Tilson, H. H. (1990). Quality of life bibliography and indexes. *Medical Care, 28*(Suppl. 12), DS1-DS77.

Steffens, D. C., Hays, J. C., George, L. K., Krishnan, K.R.R., & Blazer, D. G. (1996). Sociodemographic and clinical correlates of number of depressive episodes in the depression elderly. *Journal of Affective Disorders, 39,* 99–106.

Stewart, A. L., Greenfield, S., Hays, R. D., Wells, K., Rogers, W. H., Berry, S. D., McGlynn, E. A., & Ware, J. E. (1989). Functional status and well-being of patients with chronic conditions: Results from the Medical Outcomes Study. Journal of the American Medical Association, 262, 907–913.

Swerdloff, R. S., & Wang, C. (1993). Androgen deficiency and aging in men. *Western Journal of Medicine, 59,* 579–585.

Tobin, J. N., Wassertheil-Smoller, S., Wexler, J. P., Steingart, R. M., Budner, N., Lense, L., & Wachspress, J. (1987). Sex bias in considering coronary bypass surgery. *Annals of Internal Medicine, 107,* 19–25.

Wallis, L. A. (1992). Women's health: A specialty? Pros and cons. *Journal of Women's Health, 1,* 107–108.

Wenger, N. K. (1995). Hypertension and other cardiovascular risk factors in women. *American Journal of Hypertension, 8,* 94S-99S.

Williams, M. E. (1994) . Clinical management of the elderly patient. In W. R. Hazzard, E. L. Bierman, J. P. Blass, W. H. Ettinger, Jr., & J. B. Halter (Eds.), *Principles of geriatric medicine and gerontology* (3rd ed., pp. 195–201). New York: McGraw-Hill.

Winkelstein, W., Jr., & Ernster, V. L. (1979). Epidemiology and etiology. In G. P. Murphy (Ed.), *Prostatic cancer* (pp. 1–17). Littleton, MA: PSG.

Wolfe, F., & Cathey, M. (1991). The assessment and prediction of functional disability in rheumatoid arthritis. *Journal of Rheumatology, 18,* 1298–1306.

29

Informal Caregiving to Older Adults: Health Effects of Providing and Receiving Care

Lynn M. Martire
Richard Schulz
University of Pittsburgh

The provision of ongoing care to an impaired older friend or relative is often a stressful experience that impacts the mental and physical health of the caregiver. Because caregiving sometimes has severe consequences for the health of the caregiver, and because these individuals are an invaluable resource to the rapidly growing population of older adults, research on caregiving has burgeoned over the past two decades. The important role of health psychology in this area of research is demonstrated by the fact that many of the advances made in understanding the consequences of caregiving have resulted from the application of theoretical models and methodologies borrowed from this field.

This chapter first briefly describes the nature and prevalence of informal caregiving to impaired older adults. The second and third sections review the evidence for the effects of caregiving on the individual who provides care and the older adult who receives that care, respectively. The latter focus on the consequences of informal care for the older adult represents a relatively new direction in caregiving research that has important linkages to other literatures in social and health psychology. Because providing care to another person is not always bad for the caregiver, and receiving care is not always good for the care recipient, the second and third sections describe both the negative and positive consequences of providing care and receiving care. Finally, the chapter concludes by highlighting the interactive nature of helping and being helped and the need to address the perspectives of both the caregiver and care recipient in future descriptive and intervention research.

OVERVIEW OF INFORMAL CAREGIVING TO OLDER ADULTS

One unfortunate consequence of growing older is the increased difficulty in carrying out everyday activities such as driving, shopping, and preparing meals (instrumental activities of daily living, IADLs), or even personal care activities such as bathing and dressing (activities of daily living, ADLs). For many older adults, this difficulty stems from illnesses such as arthritis, heart disease, and diabetes, the most chronic health problems of older men and women (Benson & Marano, 1994). Such difficulty with everyday activities, often referred to as functional disability, eventually progresses to the point where the older adult needs assistance from others.

Although the likelihood of becoming disabled increases with age, the functional ability of the older adult population is actually characterized by much variability. Of the 95% of U.S. adults from age 65 to 74 who live in noninstitutionalized settings, only 11% are ADL or IADL impaired. This percentage rises to 27% for those from age 75 to 84, and 60% of those over age 85 experience some amount of disability (Manton, Corder, & Stallard, 1997). Investigations utilizing several different national data sets have shown that between 1982 and 1994, the proportion of the population age 65 and older that was disabled decreased slightly (Crimmins, Saito, & Reynolds, 1997; Manton et al., 1997). Despite the relatively low rates of disability before age 85 and the modest improvements in the physical functioning of older adults in general, the contrasting dramatic growth in the proportion of the population that is older will result in a predictable increase in the number of disabled older adults in the future. Thus, as the number of older adults continues to grow, so will the number of older adults who have difficulty with everyday activities and who need and receive assistance from informal caregivers.

Some amount of functional disability in the older adult population is due to cognitive impairment. Conservative estimates indicate that 2.1 million adults age 65 or older are cognitively impaired and this number is projected to rise to 3.2 million by the year 2015 (U.S. General Accounting Office, 1998). It is estimated that approximately 2.1 million of these individuals will need active assistance with personal care.

National household surveys show that the prevalence of informal caregiving is indeed high and has grown substantially in the past 10 years. Using a relatively restrictive definition of caregiving (i.e., helping an older adult with at least two IADLs or one ADL), a 1988 survey estimated that there were seven million caregiving households in the United States (American Association of Retired Persons [AARP] and the Travelers Foundation, 1988). Applying this same definition of caregiving, the number of caregivers in 1996 had grown to 21.3 million, or triple the number in 1988 (National Alliance for Caregiving and the AARP, 1997). It is likely that this number includes caregivers to older adults with acute health problems as well as caregivers to older adults with long-standing health conditions. Regardless, this number illustrates that caregiving is a growing national concern.

Given the prevalence of caregiving, a logical question to ask is: Who are the informal caregivers to older impaired adults? Most older adults receive assistance from their spouse. But, when the spouse is no longer alive or is unavailable to provide assistance, adult children usually step in to help. Adult daughters and daughters-in-law are more likely than sons and sons-in-law to provide routine assistance with household chores and personal care over long periods of time (e.g., Horowitz, 1985) and they also spend more hours per week in providing assistance (e.g., Montgomery, 1992). Although caregiving tasks are sometimes divided among several family members or friends, the more typical scenario is that the majority of care is provided by one family member.

DETRIMENTAL AND BENEFICIAL EFFECTS OF PROVIDING CARE TO AN IMPAIRED OLDER ADULT

Theoretical Models of the Effects of Caregiving

Caregiving is an activity that is rich in contextual variability because of the differences among caregivers in their personality attributes and life circumstances as well as among care recipients and their health conditions. The complexity of the context of caregiving mandates the use of theoretical models to guide the design and interpretation of studies in this area. One of the most basic ways to conceptualize the caregiving experience is in terms of a framework for interactions between the individual and the environment (Elliott & Eisdorfer, 1982). The three elements of this model include a potential activator or stressor, an individual's reaction to the activator, and the consequences of that reaction. In the context of caregiving, potential activators or stressors stem from the care-recipient's functional disability or cognitive impairment, whereas reactions are the transient physiological or psychosocial responses to specific activators (e.g., increased negative affect) and consequences are the prolonged or cumulative effects of these reactions (e.g., risk for infectious disease or clinical depression). This basic model has been elaborated and applied to a number of caregiving contexts, including caregivers of spinal cord injured persons, stroke victims, dementia patients, the chronically mentally ill, cardiac patients, and cancer patients (e.g., Aneshensel, Pearlin, Mullan, Zarit, & Whitlatch, 1995; Haley, Levine, Brown, & Bartolucci, 1987; Pearlin, Mullan, Semple, & Skaff, 1990; Schulz, Tompkins, & Rau, 1988).

One recent iteration of a stress-process model that links environmental demands to health outcomes may be particularly applicable to elder caregiving (Cohen, Kessler, & Gordon, 1995). This model has been modified for this chapter (see Fig. 29.1). As applied to elder caregiving, environmental demands include providing instrumental assistance and emotional support in response to the older adult's disability. If individuals perceive these demands as threatening and also view their coping resources as inadequate, they perceive themselves as under stress (e.g., Lazarus & Folkman, 1984). The appraisal of stress is presumed to trigger physiological, affective, behavioral, or cognitive responses that place the individual at increased risk for mental and physical health problems.

This model also allows for the possibility that individuals may feel they have the capacity to deal with caregiving demands and thus appraise these demands positively (Kramer, 1997; Lawton, Kleban, Moss, Rovine, & Glicksman, 1989). This appraisal may in turn lead to positive physiological, affective, behavioral, or cognitive responses, and decreased risk for mental and physical health problems. It is important to note that this second pathway has less empirical support than the first but has also received less attention.

Although the physiological, affective, behavioral, and cognitive responses to caregiving are important outcomes in their own right, Fig. 29.1 shows that they can also be conceptualized as mediators in this process because they help to explain how caregiving experiences are manifested in altered mental or physical health status. Examples of cognitive mediators of the relation between caregiving experiences and mental health include an enhanced or eroded sense of control or mastery over events occurring in life, and changes in self-esteem. For example, stressors encountered in providing assistance to an impaired older adult may result in symptoms of depression or anxiety by giving caregivers the sense that they cannot master challenges such as those posed by caregiving. Mediators of physical health outcomes are most likely to be physiological or behavioral and include altered immune response, cardiovascular reactivity, and changes in preventive health behaviors. To the extent that caregiving stress compromises immune or cardiac functioning or prohibits self-care activities, the caregiver is placed at increased risk for infectious and chronic illnesses.

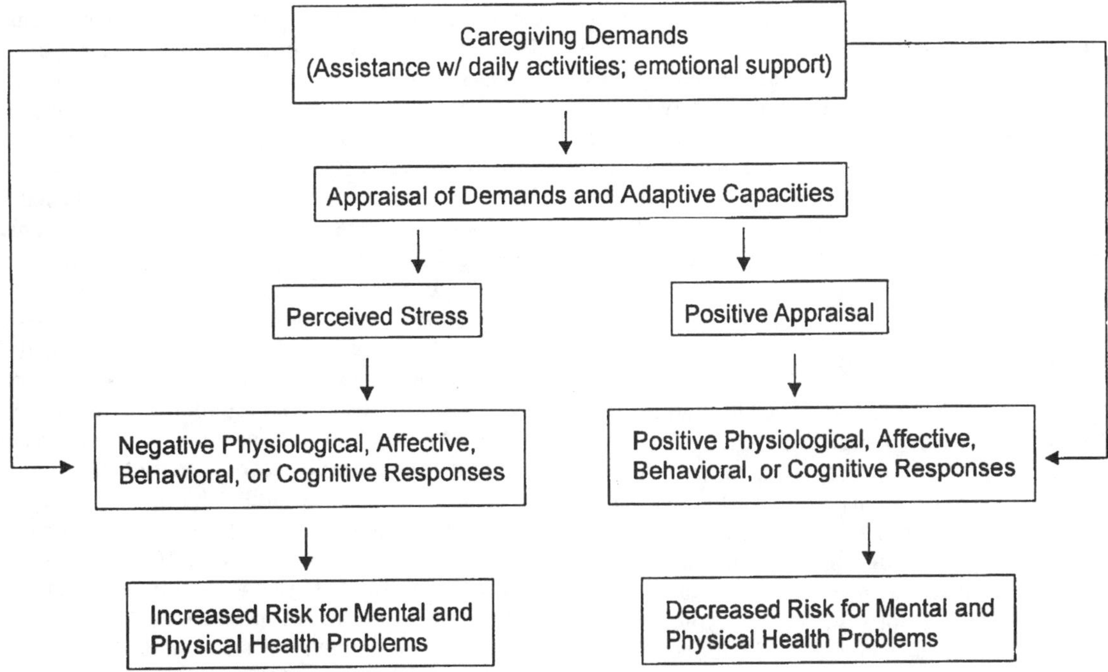

FIG. 29.1. A model of the health effects of elder caregiving. Adapted from Cohen et al. (1995).

Although not represented in this model, other factors have been identified as moderating or conditioning factors in the caregiving stress process. Moderators of caregiving stress indicate the conditions under which the negative impact of stress on health is likely to be strongest and thus aid in the identification of health risk factors. A search for moderators of caregiving stress has been motivated in part by the recognition that there is much variability in the way individuals respond to caregiving. For example, caregivers may experience negative mental and physical health effects that last for an extended period of time (e.g., after cessation of caregiving due to death or placement of the care-recipient) or, alternatively, may adapt to the stress of caregiving even while it persists.

One proposed moderator of caregiving stress is emotional or instrumental support to a caregiver from the spouse, other family members, or friends. It has been suggested that the effects of caregiving stress on mental and physical health are buffered (i.e., lessened) when caregivers receive high levels of support from others. Other proposed moderators or buffers of caregiving stress include the caregiver's use of adaptive coping strategies; a high quality relationship between caregiver and care-recipient; personality characteristics of the caregiver such as greater perceived control or mastery, optimism, and low neuroticism; and greater financial resources of the caregiver. It is important to note that several factors, such as perceived control or mastery and the quality of the relationship between caregiver and care-recipient, may explain how caregiving experiences affect mental and physical health as well as condition the effects of caregiving experiences on health (i.e., act as both mediators and moderators of caregiving experiences).

Three features of the model depicted in Fig. 29.1 are important to point out. One critical feature is that the appraisal of caregiving demands is not necessary in order for these demands to place the individual at increased or decreased risk for negative health outcomes. This is illustrated by the arrows directly linking demands to negative and positive responses. For example, caregivers may not feel burdened by caregiving but respond negatively by neglecting their own needs such as eating regularly or going to the doctor. The second feature concerns the existence of many possible feedback loops. Although the model as specified is primarily unidirectional, it is recognized that dealing with stressors is a complex, dynamic process in which responses at one stage of the model may subsequently feed back to earlier stages. Finally, the reciprocal nature of the relation between psychological problems and physical disorders (Cohen & Rodriguez, 1995) suggests that the effects of caregiving stress on physical health may be mediated by changes in mental health or vice versa (Hooker, Monahan, Bowman, Frazier, & Shifren, 1998; Wright, Clipp, & George, 1993).

Although this chapter focuses on the provision of care to older adults, it is important to note that much of the model presented in Fig. 29.1 is also applicable to caregivers of chronically ill individuals of other ages, such as a parent providing care to a child with cystic fibrosis or an individual providing care to a middle-aged adult with spinal cord injury. That is, there are many similarities across such caregiving situations in terms of caregiving stressors and rewards, mental and physical health outcomes, and mediating and moderating factors in these processes (Quittner, Glueckauf, & Jackson, 1990; Schulz & Quittner, 1998). However, each age group and patient population is likely to pose distinct caregiving demands as well as challenges for the caregiving researcher. For example, the factors of care-recipient age and kin relationship between caregiver and care-recipient are often confounded, making it difficult to disentangle the role that each of these factors might play in the type of help provided and in the mental and physical health outcomes experienced.

Detrimental Effects of Caregiving

Several different approaches have been used to examine the negative effects of elder caregiving. One strategy has been to compare caregivers to noncaregivers or to population-based norms. More commonly, investigators have focused solely on caregivers and examined the extent to which the care-recipient's level of disability, or the appraised stressfulness of providing assistance, affects such outcomes as the caregiver's health. Prior research has typically focused on the most stressful caregiving situations. Thus, many studies have focused on the effects of providing care to an older adult with Alzheimer's disease or other dementing illness. Dementia caregiving poses some of the most difficult challenges faced by caregivers because it involves watching the care-recipient become progressively intellectually impaired and requires managing a variety of unpredictable asocial and problematic behaviors.

Several reviews of the literature have been conducted recently in regard to caregiving to older adults who suffer from Alzheimer's disease or another type of dementia (e.g., Schulz, O'Brien, Bookwala, & Fleissner, 1995) and caregiving to older adults who are physically or cognitively disabled (e.g., Schulz, Visintainer, & Williamson, 1990; Wright et al., 1993). The remainder of this section reviews general conclusions from these articles, as well as findings from a select number of studies conducted since these articles were published. The most common sociodemographic and psychosocial correlates of health outcomes are described, and evidence is provided for a few factors that have been shown to function as moderating or mediating factors in the relation between caregiving stress and health. Findings are also reviewed from studies examining the effects of caregiving on individuals' work and leisure activities and their relationships with family members.

Mental Health Outcomes. Depressive symptoms have been the most frequently examined indicator of mental health in caregiving research. Depressive symptomatology has been assessed with self-report instruments such as the Center for Epidemiologic Studies-Depression Scale (CES–D; Radloff, 1977) and the Beck Depression Inventory (Beck, Ward, Mendelson, Mock, & Erbaugh, 1961), as well as through clinical interviews using measures such as the Hamilton Depression Rating Scale (Hamilton, 1967). Other mental health indicators that have been examined include anxiety, life satisfaction, and psychotropic medication use.

Overall, there is overwhelming evidence that caregiving is associated with poorer mental health (e.g., Schulz et al., 1995). Caregivers often have elevated levels of depressive symptomatology and higher prevalence rates for clinical depression and anxiety than population norms or noncaregivers. Not surprisingly, caregivers also use antidepressants and antianxiety medications more often than noncaregivers. The majority of the most recently published studies also provide evidence for poorer mental health among caregivers than noncaregivers (e.g., Haley et al., 1995; Jutras & Lavoie, 1995; Rose-Rego, Strauss, & Smyth, 1998).

It is important to note that these mental health consequences of caregiving have likely been overestimated to some extent due to the sampling strategies used in prior research. Caregivers have been most commonly recruited from support groups and social service agencies, resulting in samples that are likely to be more distressed than the general population of caregivers. Only a few studies have used population-based samples (e.g., Grafstrom, Fratiglioni, Sandman, & Winblad, 1992; Moritz, Kasl, & Ostfeld, 1992; Schulz et al., 1997). Based on their finding in a population-based sample that only slightly more than half of spousal caregivers reported experiencing mental or physical strain as a result of caregiving, Schulz and colleagues (1997) concluded that studies utilizing samples of distressed or strained caregivers may have overestimated the negative mental health effects of caregiving.

Several recent studies and reviews have examined differences in the mental and physical health effects of caregiving according to gender and ethnicity. Few gender or ethnicity differences have been found in regard to physical health. However, studies have generally shown that Black caregivers report less burden and depressive symptomatology and greater life satisfaction than White caregivers (e.g., Haley et al., 1995; Hinrichsen & Ramirez, 1992; Lawton, Rajagopal, Brody, & Kleban, 1992; Miller, Campbell, Farran, Kaufman, & Davis, 1995) and these differences in adjustment do not appear to be explained by greater severity of objective caregiving stressors or sociodemographic variables (Haley et al., 1995). In regard to gender differences in the mental health effects of caregiving, most studies have found that greater caregiving burden and emotional distress are reported by females than males (see review by Miller & Cafasso, 1992), even when there are no differences in functional impairment of the care-recipient or caregiver involvement in care. However, these findings raise the issue of whether these differences reflect the fact that women in general report higher levels of depressive symptomatology than do men. One recent study addressed this issue by comparing the well-being of husband and wife caregivers as well as noncaregiving husbands and wives. This study demonstrated that caregiving wives were more depressed than caregiving husbands but that there were no differences between noncaregiving husbands and wives, suggesting there is something specific to caregiving that leads to greater depression in women than in men (Rose-Rego et al., 1998).

Other correlates of poorer mental health include greater caregiving stress and poorer self-rated physical health of the caregiver. Problem behaviors of the older adult are often the most frequently endorsed stressor of dementia caregiving and there is evidence that this factor is more strongly related to caregivers' depression than provision of assistance with daily tasks (Schulz et al., 1995). Also, lower socioeconomic status, being a spouse, and sharing a residence with the older adult are caregiver characteristics consistently related to greater depressive symptoms (Meshefedjian, McCusker, Bellavance, & Baumgarten, 1998; Schulz et al., 1995; Wright et al., 1993). Caregivers who have higher levels of neuroticism and lower levels of mastery not only tend to have more depressive symptoms but also report that their care-recipient has greater difficulty with IADLs (Bookwala & Schulz, 1998).

Some attention has been given to identifying factors that mediate the relation between caregiving stress and mental health outcomes. There is evidence that the effects of stress on mental health may be explained by the caregiver's cognitive responses. That is, an eroded sense of mastery and self-esteem as a caregiver has been shown to explain the process by which caregiving stress results in more negative affect (Franks & Stephens, 1992). In addition, there is evidence from two recent studies that the quality of the relation between the caregiver and care-recipient can operate as an explanatory variable in the stress and depression relation. The first study showed that the presence of problem behaviors in the patient was associated with greater depression in the caregiver because such behaviors were detrimental to the quality of the relation between the patient and caregiver (Lawrence, Tennstedt, & Assmann, 1998). A second study of adult child caregivers demonstrated that the relation between the parent's cognitive impairment and the caregivers' depressive symptoms was explained by increased conflict between the parent and adult child (Townsend & Franks, 1995).

The factor that has most frequently been examined as a potential moderator of caregiving stress and mental health is social support to the caregiver; however, there are conflicting findings in regard to the benefits of such support. Emotional support from an adult daughter caregiver's social network has been shown to buffer the negative effects of behavior problems and assistance with daily activities on depressive symptoms (Li, Seltzer, & Greenberg, 1997), and instrumental support in the form of paid assistance to the care-recipient with personal care and household tasks has been shown to buffer the effects of problem behaviors on caregivers' depressive symptoms (Bass, Noelker, & Rechlin, 1996). However, neither emotional nor instrumental support buffered the negative effects of caregiving stress on emotional health in other investigations (e.g., Aneshensel et al., 1995; Franks & Stephens, 1996). The quality of experiences in noncaregiving domains has recently been shown to be a conditioning factor in the caregiving stress process. For adult daughter caregivers who are married, have children living at home, and are employed, high levels of stress in their experiences as mothers exacerbated the negative effects of caregiving stress on life satisfaction and high levels of rewards in the employee role buffered the negative effects of caregiving stress on depression (Stephens & Townsend, 1997). In addition, spousal and adult child caregivers who had a close relationship with their care-recipient prior to onset of Alzheimer's disease were shown to feel less burdened by caregiving than those whose relationship was not close (Williamson & Schulz, 1990). One recent study revealed that the caregiver's psychological resources are also beneficial in the context of caregiving stress, in that high levels of mastery in caregiving buffered the negative effects of the care-recipient's problem behaviors and functional disability on caregiver's depression (Miller et al., 1995).

Physical Health Outcomes. Although traditionally given less attention than mental health outcomes, research on the physical health effects of caregiving has been more common in the past several years. Evidence continues to accumulate that caregivers are at risk for physical health problems. Schulz and colleagues concluded that the most consistent evidence for the negative effects of caregiving on physical health has been found for self-reported global health, in that caregivers perceive their health to be worse than noncaregivers. At the time of that review, there was mixed evidence for differences in health care utilization between caregivers and noncaregivers and little evidence for differences in other health behaviors such as following a proper diet and exercising (Schulz et al., 1995). However, a recent study of a large population-based sample of mostly nondementia caregivers showed that individuals whose spouse was ADL impaired did not find time for exercise, had inadequate rest, did not take enough time to rest when sick, and forgot to take their medications, more often than noncaregivers (Burton, Newsom, Schulz, Hirsch, & German, 1997). These self-reports of global health, physical symptoms, and health behaviors should be viewed cautiously because emotional distress exerts a significant influence on such reports.

Research on the physical health effects of caregiving has advanced because of the recent focus on objective physiological indicators of health such as immune functioning (e.g., natural killer cell activity) and metabolic functioning (e.g., high density and low density lipoprotein, HDL and LDL, cholesterol and insulin levels). At the time of the review by Schulz and colleagues (1995), only a few studies had examined caregivers' immune functioning. Studies published since that review support the hypothesis that caregivers have compromised immune functioning (e.g., Castle, Wilkins, Heck, Tanzy, & Fahey, 1995; Esterling, Kiecolt-Glaser, Bodnar, & Glaser, 1994; Kiecolt-Glaser, Glaser, Gravenstein, Malarkey, & Sheridan, 1996; Kiecolt-Glaser, Marucha, Malarkey, Mercado, & Glaser, 1995). For example, caregivers of relatives with Alzheimer's disease have an impaired immune response to influenza virus vaccination relative to matched controls (Kiecolt-Glaser et al., 1996) and also show impaired wound healing relative to controls (Kiecolt-Glaser et al., 1995). In regard to metabolic functioning, one recent study of spousal caregivers revealed that older male caregivers had a significantly larger body mass index and were more obese than controls and female caregivers showed a greater increase in weight than controls over a 15- to 18-month period of time, putting them at risk for higher lipid levels, high blood pressure, cardiovascular disease, and arthritis in weight-bearing joints such as the hips and knees (Vitaliano, Russo, Scanlan, & Greeno, 1996). Nondiabetic spousal caregivers to dementia patients also have significantly higher insulin levels than gender-matched spouses of nondemented older adults (Vitaliano, Scanlan, Krenz, Schwartz, & Marcovina, 1996).

The effects of caregiving on physical health are not as consistent or as strong as those observed for mental health (Schulz et al., 1995; Vitaliano, Schulz, Kiecolt-Glaser, & Grant, 1997). One explanation for this discrepancy is that physical health effects may take longer to emerge and thus may not be as salient as mental health effects until the caregiving role has been occupied for a long duration or even until after this role has been relinquished. However, once the effects on physical health emerge, they may be long lasting, as demonstrated by studies showing altered immune response several years after cessation of caregiving due to bereavement (e.g., Esterling et al., 1994).

Common correlates of poorer physical health in dementia caregivers are more depressive symptoms, less social support, and greater cognitive impairment of the care-recipient (Schulz et al., 1995). In addition, caregiver characteristics such as lower socioeconomic status, being older, and sharing a residence with the care-recipient are fairly consistently related to poorer physical health for caregivers (Wright et al., 1993). In terms of mediating factors in the stress and physical health relation, indicators such as immune response and health behaviors may explain how caregiving stress results in illness conditions and symptoms; however, little attention has been paid to systematically testing such models in the context of caregiving.

There is recent evidence that perceived control conditions the effects of caregiving on preventive health behaviors. Spousal caregivers with a strong sense of control over events in life report getting more rest than caregivers with a weak sense of control (Burton et al., 1997). Instrumental support in the form of assistance with caregiving tasks has been shown to buffer the effects of caregiving stress on perceptions of global physical health and deterioration in health as a result of caregiving (Bass et al., 1996; Franks & Stephens, 1996). High levels of emotional and instrumental support also are associated with better immune responses for dementia caregivers, suggesting that support may buffer the negative effects of caregiving stress on immune response outcomes (Esterling, Kiecolt-Glaser, & Glaser, 1996).

Although mental and physical health are the main outcomes examined in research on the effects of caregiving, there are a variety of other consequences of caregiving. For most caregivers, this activity reflects just one aspect of their lives in that they have many other interests and demands outside of caregiving. Therefore, researchers have examined how caregiving affects other family and nonfamily domains of an individual's life. One particular line of research in this area has focused on adult daughter caregivers, prompted by the recognition that much informal care is provided by adult daughters and daughters-in-law and that these middle-aged women may be particularly burdened by caregiving because of competing demands for their time and energy. Due to demographic trends of the past few decades in delayed childbearing and increased workforce participation of women, many midlife women in the United States have children living at home and are also employed outside the home. Reflecting these trends, the results of a recent national survey showed that the typical caregiver is a married woman in her mid-forties who works full time, and 41% of caregivers have one or more children under age 18 living in their household (National Alliance for Caregiving and the AARP, 1997). In general, research findings indicate that other social roles occupied by caregivers such as spouse, parent, and employee have the potential to add to the caregiver's burden, but they also may provide crucial financial and psychosocial resources for sustaining the provision of care.

The following sections review findings from studies that have examined the effects of caregiving on work and leisure activities and relationships with family members. Such outcomes may be most usefully conceptualized as mediating factors in that they may explain how the burden or stress of caregiving is ultimately manifested in poorer mental and physical health for the caregiver. Much of the work reviewed here focuses on women caregivers who have multiple social roles.

Work and Leisure Activities. Results of a national survey show that 64% of caregivers are employed at least part time, and this percentage rises to 76% for caregivers between age 35 and 49 (National Alliance for Caregiving and the AARP, 1997). Early on, researchers interested in the consequences of combining caregiving and employment focused solely on occupancy of the employment role as a correlate of caregiver health outcomes. In general, these studies showed that employed caregivers experienced less caregiver strain and better mental health than those who were not employed (e.g., Giele, Mutschler, & Orodenker, 1987; Miller, 1989; Skaff & Pearlin, 1992), and this finding did not seem to be due to less provision of care by employed than nonemployed caregivers. This finding is probably explained by advantages that paid employment seems to have for all adults, such as greater financial resources, respite from family demands (including elder caregiving), and the greater social contact and social support that is gained in the workplace.

More recent research on employed caregivers has moved beyond role occupancy to focus on experiences in the workplace and in caregiving that may be important determinants of caregivers' health (e.g., Martire, Stephens, & Atienza, 1997). Several studies have shown that experiences in caregiving can negatively spill over into work (e.g., Barling, MacEwen, Kelloway, & Higginbottom, 1994; Neal, Chapman, Ingersoll-Dayton, & Emlen, 1993; Scharlach, 1994; Stephens, Franks, & Atienza, 1997). For example, employed caregivers report that due to caregiving responsibilities they are often exhausted at work or unable to concentrate, disrupted at work, or miss work. There is evidence that such negative spillover from caregiving to work is a mechanism that explains how the stress of caregiving becomes manifested in greater depressive symptomatology for the caregiver (Stephens et al., 1997).

Individuals who provide care to an impaired elder also experience changes in their leisure and social activities. Caregivers have been shown to be more restricted than noncaregivers in their ability to socialize with friends, participate in group or organized activities, exercise or participate in sports, and go out for dinner or a show (e.g., George & Gwyther, 1986; Haley, Levine, Brown, Berry, & Hughes, 1987), and studies have demonstrated that this restriction can be a direct result of the stress of caregiving (e.g., Kinney, Stephens, Franks, & Norris, 1995; Miller & Montgomery, 1990; Stull, Kosloski, & Kercher, 1994). Less social activity often means that caregivers have less opportunity to interact with, and obtain support and advice from, others. For some caregivers, such limitations in access to available social resources may explain how caregiving is harmful to mental health. A study of spousal caregivers of cancer patients found that the effect of caregiving stress on depressive symptomatology was explained by restriction in the caregiver's daily and social activities (e.g., going shopping and visiting friends; Williamson, Shaffer, & Schulz, 1998).

Relationships With Family Members. Providing ongoing care to an impaired elder puts a strain on relationships with others. The most obvious relationship affected by caregiving is the one between the caregiver and older adult. However, most of the research in this particular area has focused on the effects of caregiving on a marriage (e.g., Stephens & Franks, 1995; Suitor & Pillemer, 1992). Husbands are a crucial source of support to adult daughter caregivers, and thus the potential negative effects of caregiving on the caregiver's marriage are important to examine. In one study of married adult daughter caregivers, three quarters reported that caregiving prevented them from spending time with their husband and two thirds reported that worrying about caregiving responsibilities had interfered with their relationship with their husband (Stephens & Franks, 1995). Such negative spillover of caregiving into marriage was associated with greater depressive symptomatology for the caregiver.

Providing care to an older relative also has the potential to create problems with other family members such as siblings. Conflict with family members often centers around the caregiver's perceptions that he or she is not receiving enough assistance from siblings or that siblings do not appreciate the caregiver's efforts, and such conflict is related to greater depressive symptoms for the caregiver (e.g., Semple, 1992). Such family conflict may be especially likely for adult child caregivers and their siblings, who frequently disagree about how the parent should be taken care of and who will help with particular tasks. In fact, married caregiving daughters report that siblings are the greatest source of interpersonal stress in regard to caregiving (Suitor & Pillemer, 1996).

Beneficial Effects of Caregiving

The caregiving health effects model presented at the beginning of this section specified that the demands posed by caregiving may not always be appraised as stressful, allowing for the possibility of positive physiological, affective, behavioral, or cognitive responses to caregiving demands (Fig. 29.1). Unfortunately, the positive aspects of caregiving have received far less attention than the negative. Reflecting the novelty of this area of research, the majority of studies on the positive aspects of caregiving have been published in the past 10 years (Kramer, 1997). As noted by others, lack of attention to the positive aspects of caregiving may seriously skew perceptions of the caregiving experience and limit the ability to enhance theories of caregiver health (e.g., Kinney & Stephens, 1989; Kramer, 1997).

Caregivers often report positive experiences as a result of providing ongoing care to an older adult. When asked to describe the experience of caregiving, the majority of caregivers (57%) use positive words such as "rewarding," "happy," and "enjoyable" (National Alliance for Caregiving and the AARP, 1997). The specific rewards from caregiving that individuals refer to include the comfort of knowing that relatives are well cared-for and an increased sense of mastery from meeting the challenges of caregiving (e.g., Lawton et al., 1989; Miller, 1989; Stephens, Franks, & Townsend, 1994). One recent study provides indirect evidence that rewarding aspects of caregiving may benefit caregivers' mental health. A study of spousal caregivers of older adults who were in the early stages of physical disability showed that increased task assistance over time was related to decreased anxiety and depression for the caregiver, suggesting that being able to help a spouse may have beneficial effects for the caregiver when the recipient has low to moderate levels of disability (Beach, Schulz, & Jackson, 1997).

Providing care to a parent may also be an important part of an individual's identity. One recent study found that the majority of adult daughters and daughters-in-law reported that being a caregiver was highly central to how they saw themselves (Martire, Stephens, & Townsend, 1997). Through caregiving, spouses and adult children can also derive added meaning from life by perceiving caregiving as a positive experience in which a new perspective is gained and they become more resilient people (Noonan & Tennstedt, 1997).

Research on the positive aspects of caregiving has been advanced conceptually by the finding that positive or rewarding experiences of caregiving do not merely represent a lack of stressful or problematic experiences (e.g., Lawton et al., 1989; Riedel, Fredman, & Langenberg, 1998). That is, stressful and rewarding aspects of caregiving do not seem to represent opposite ends of a single continuum but rather reflect two distinct dimensions. In fact, caregiving rewards have been shown to predict mental health outcomes even after controlling for the effects of caregiving stress (Noonan & Tennstedt, 1997; Stephens et al., 1994). Despite the fact that positive and negative experiences are two distinct dimensions of caregiving, the effects of caregiving rewards or satisfaction on health do not seem to be as strong as the negative aspects of caregiving. In some instances, caregiving uplifts have not been shown to be related to better well-being (e.g., Kinney & Stephens, 1989, Sheehan & Nuttall, 1988), and in other studies such positive experiences have only been related to positive indicators of mental health such as life satisfaction (Martire et al., 1997; Stephens et al., 1994). These findings have prompted others to conclude that the positive aspects of caregiving are very important for many caregivers but do not result in significant containment of stress over time (e.g., Aneshensel et al., 1995). Contradicting this point, a recent study showed that greater caregiving rewards such as feeling needed and seeing that the care-recipient received high quality care buffered the effects of caregiving difficulties on perceived burden (Riedel et al., 1998).

To summarize this section on the health effects of caregiving, fairly strong negative effects of caregiving on mental health have been demonstrated in past research, whereas evidence for negative physical health effects of caregiving is sparse but accruing. Such research is critical because caregivers who are burdened are more likely to relinquish caregiving by placing their relative in a long-term care facility or passing on responsibility to another caregiver (e.g., Montgomery & Kosloski, 1994). Much of the responsibility for informal elder care falls to middle-aged family members who have other family and work responsibilities. Although much has been made of the burden that such individuals may feel, it is important to keep in mind that additional roles may also serve as psychosocial and financial resources that help to relieve the stress of caregiving and ensure that the caregiver can continue to provide care. Although frequently burdensome, providing care to an older adult can also be a fulfilling experience and the positive dimensions of caregiving may even offset the problematic aspects.

The health effects of caregiving may be less pronounced in studies that do not focus on highly distressed caregivers such as those individuals providing care to an older adult with Alzheimer's disease or another type of dementia. In addition, many of the effects of caregiving, particularly the physical health effects, may take years to emerge. Although studies on the effects of caregiving on health over time are becoming more common (e.g., Goode, Haley, Roth, & Ford, 1998; Schulz & Williamson, 1991; Vitaliano, Russo, et al., 1996), prospective studies are still very rare. Researchers need to study caregivers over longer periods of time and, more importantly, continue to follow them through important caregiving transitions such as institutionalization and death of the care-recipient (e.g., Skaff, Pearlin, & Mullan, 1996). It may be that individuals who have predisposing mental or physical health problems are at highest risk for experiencing health problems during caregiving (Redinbaugh, MacCallum, & Kiecolt-Glaser, 1995). This possibility makes it important to assess the caregiver's mental and physical health status prior to taking on the caregiving role.

BENEFICIAL AND DETRIMENTAL EFFECTS OF RECEIVING INFORMAL CARE

The extent to which an individual's health is affected by caregiving has direct implications for the amount and quality of assistance provided to the older adult. Thus, caregiving research has addressed the welfare of the care-recipient, albeit indirectly. However, it is critical to assess the more proximal effects of receiving care. Possibly one of the most important reasons for this focus is that the older adult's responses to assistance in turn affect the amount and quality of future care from friends and family members. To date, the effects of receiving care have been paid far less attention than the effects of providing care to an ill older adult and thus there is much to learn about the extent to which care is or is not well-received, and why. Recognizing this, researchers have broadened their investigations to focus on the effects of receiving as well as providing care (e.g., Newsom & Schulz, 1998).

The greater focus on the caregiver in past research is in part due to the fact that many studies have focused on caregiving to older adults who suffer from cognitive impairment due to Alzheimer's disease, stroke, or other dementing illnesses. Problems associated with assessing the perspective of cognitively impaired elders include difficulty in recruiting these individuals and obtaining valid and reliable information from them in regard to the care they receive and their level of distress (Cotrell & Schulz, 1993; Spencer, Tompkins, & Schulz, 1997). However, it is important to keep in mind that the majority of older adults who receive informal care are cognitively intact, and even individuals with mild to moderate cognitive impairment are often capable of articulating their feelings and concerns. Furthermore, for those care-recipients who are severely cognitively impaired, alternative research methods such as proxy reports can be used to obtain a picture of the care-recipient's views (e.g., Logsdon & Teri, 1995).

Theoretical Models of the Effects of Care Receiving

Little attention has been paid to developing or testing theoretical methods that specify how receipt of assistance with daily activities may lead to an impaired older adult's increased or decreased risk for additional mental and physical health problems and the mechanisms that explain how this process occurs. Is there variability in the extent to which assistance from others is viewed as helpful by the older adult? Does receiving assistance have significant effects on an older adult's mental and physical health beyond the effects of their present disability? Recent evidence suggests that the answers to these questions may be affirmative. In one study, 60% of stroke patients reported at least one unhelpful action by the spouse when an attempt was made to help with daily activities (Clark & Stephens, 1996). Another study found that 40% of older care-recipients reported emotional strain in response to help they received from their spouse and this strain predicted greater depressive symptomatology for the recipient 1 year later (Newsom & Schulz, 1998).

The concept of person–environment fit may be useful in understanding the health effects of receiving care. According to this framework, psychological adjustment is a function of the degree of fit between aspects of the environment and the individual's personal characteristics (e.g., E. Kahana, B. Kahana, & Riley, 1989). Although the concept of person–environment fit has typically been used in an attempt to understand how older adults adjust to different physical environments (e.g., Parmelee & Lawton, 1990), it may also be helpful in terms of thinking about how such individuals adjust to their social environment. The degree of fit between assistance provided and the older adult's needs or preferences for assistance may determine whether such assistance is perceived as helpful or unhelpful.

The caregiving health model presented earlier has been adapted as a first step toward developing a model of the health effects of care receiving (see Fig. 29.2). In this model, receipt of assistance with daily activities (i.e., instrumental support) and illness-specific emotional support are conceptualized as experiences that are appraised by the care-recipient as either helpful or unhelpful, depending on whether or not such support fits the recipient's needs or preferences. Similar to the caregiving model, the appraisal of assistance as unhelpful is presumed to result in negative physiological, affective, behavioral, or cognitive responses that place the older adult at increased risk for exacerbated or additional mental and physical health problems. Alternatively, assistance from others may be perceived as helpful and thus lead to positive responses associated with a decreased risk for exacerbated or additional mental and physical health problems.

A likely indicator of mental health to be affected by the quality of instrumental and emotional support from others is the recipient's experience of depressive symptoms (e.g., Cohen & Wills, 1985). It is well known that chronic illnesses, particularly those involving pain, put older adults at risk for depression (e.g., Williamson & Schulz, 1992). Responses to receiving support are likely to put a patient at a further increased or decreased risk for depression. One aspect of physical health that is likely to reflect the effects of receiving support is the older adult's level of functional disability. That is, the extent to which assistance is helpful or unhelpful is likely to affect older adults' future ability to carry out daily activities on their own or with minimal help from others (Baltes & Wahl, 1992).

Cognitive responses have been proposed as likely mediators of the relation between receipt of care and mental health problems such as depressive symptomatology. It has been suggested that emotional support and instrumental assistance contain self-relevant messages for recipients that may apply generally to their life or to coping with illness. Specifically, theorists have proposed that self-evaluations of domain-specific efficacy may explain the positive or negative effects of support to older adults on their mental health (Antonucci & Jackson, 1987; Bandura, 1997). Support from others also may cause recipients to feel more or less autonomous (i.e., self-governing) or competent (Ryan & Solky, 1996), which may in turn affect their mental health. Responses that may mediate the relation between receipt of care and disability are most likely to be cognitive or behavioral in nature and include following a proper diet, using assistive devices, and obtaining medical care. It seems particularly plausible that assistance received from informal caregivers has an impact on the extent to which older adults take care of their own health. As noted by others, family members often serve as a source of motivation and advice for the older adult who is attempting to develop or maintain self-care behaviors and are also very involved with interactions between the older adult and the medical care system (e.g., Prohaska, 1998).

Findings from the field of social psychology offer specific hypotheses in regard to moderating factors or conditions under which support does or does not fit an older adult's needs or preferences or has positive or negative effects on mental and physical health. Much of this evidence regarding recipients' reactions to help has been obtained in experimental studies with individuals who were not acquainted with each other, rather than more naturally occurring helping situations between close friends or family members. Researchers have demonstrated that a recipient's reactions to help received

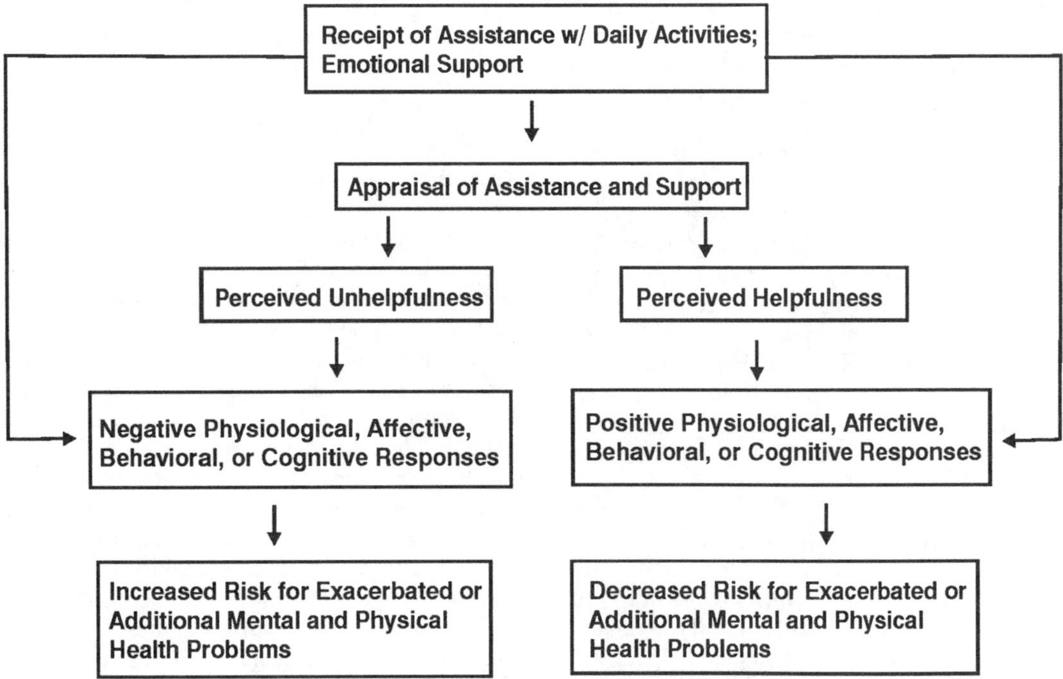

FIG. 29.2. A model of the health effects of elder care-receiving. Adapted from Cohen et al. (1995).

from others are often determined by multiple factors that fall under three general categories: characteristics of the support provider (i.e., the caregiver), characteristics of the support recipient (i.e., the care-recipient), and characteristics of the provided support (i.e., emotional support and assistance with activities of daily living; see reviews by Fisher, Nadler, & Whitcher-Alagna, 1982; Nadler & Fisher, 1986).

Applying this general framework to the impaired older care-recipient, one characteristic of caregivers that may be important in determining the recipient's reactions to support is their relationship to the older adult. For example, it may be more difficult for some older adults to accept support from an adult child than from a spouse. Characteristics of the recipient that may be important in determining the perceived helpfulness of emotional support and instrumental assistance include level of perceived control or desire for control, level of self-esteem, and the importance of carrying out tasks independently (e.g., Daubman, 1995; Nadler & Fisher, 1986). Characteristics of provided support that have received the most empirical attention as determinants of recipients' reactions to support include the type of support, the amount of support, and the timing of support (e.g., DePaulo, Brittingham, & Kaiser, 1983). To this list of potential moderating factors, a fourth must be added—the quality of the relationship between the caregiver and care-recipient. We believe that relationship quality is a factor that is likely to be important in determining the recipient's responses to assistance.

There are three specific points to be made about the model presented in Fig. 29.2. First, as is true for the literature on the health effects of caregiving, some research on recipients' reactions to assistance does not assume that task assistance and emotional support have to be appraised as helpful or unhelpful by the recipient in order for health effects to occur (see arrows directly linking task assistance and emotional support to negative and positive responses). Some studies examine the relation between the amount of received assistance and the care-recipient's well-being without assessing the perceived helpfulness of such assistance (e.g., Silverstein, Chen, & Heller, 1996). A second important feature of Fig. 29.2 relates to the possibility that receipt of care might be associated with positive mental health outcomes but negative physical health outcomes, or vice versa. For example, studies focusing on chronic pain patients and their families have demonstrated that assistance from family members is associated with more positive affect for the patient but also increased disability and pain behaviors (Kerns & Weiss, 1994). Finally, as was true for the caregiving health effects model presented earlier, much of the model presented in Fig. 29.2 is applicable to not only different patient populations but also to young and middle-aged care-recipients.

Beneficial Effects of Care Receiving

As noted at the beginning of this chapter, the benefits to older adults of receiving assistance from family members are many and include less assistance from paid helpers and delayed institutionalization. Simply put, assistance from family members enables older adults to live independently for a longer period of time. Most of the advantages of receiving care from family and friends are assumed and not examined empirically.

There are additional potential advantages to receiving informal care beyond reduced health care costs and delayed institutionalization. One benefit is the opportunity to become closer to family members. For older adults who are primarily receiving care from an adult child, this contact provides the opportunity for both individuals to gain a new appreciation of each other and the time they have left together (Walker, Martin, & Jones, 1992). The same principle is true for older adults who are primarily receiving care from a spouse. Moreover, when older husbands and wives both suffer from chronic illness, increased closeness may result from mutual assistance.

Several studies provide empirical evidence for the benefits of receiving care. Having instrumental support available if needed has been shown to prevent a decline in older adults' health-related feelings of self-efficacy (i.e., perceptions that staying healthy depends on factors under one's own control) over a 3-year period (McAvay, Seeman, & Rodin, 1996). Such feelings of efficacy are critical in terms of maintaining health and functional ability (Bandura, 1997). In addition, older adults receiving assistance from others with daily activities have been shown to be more likely to engage in self-care activities such as using assistive devices or special clothing and avoiding harmful activities (Norburn et al., 1995). The manner in which support is offered can also be beneficial to the care-recipient. One research program has looked at the extent to which family members provide autonomy support, defined as being able to take recipients' perspectives and encourage them to be more self-directed (Ryan & Solky, 1996). This approach has recently been applied to nursing home residents in a study showing that assistance from family members and nursing home staff that supported a sense of autonomy was related to greater life satisfaction for the care-recipient (Kasser & Ryan, in press).

Detrimental Effects of Care Receiving

An accumulating literature has documented the negative consequences that occur when an ill older adult's family members are critical or hostile in their actions or communications (e.g., Rook, 1984; Stephens, Kinney, Norris, & Ritchie, 1987) or even abusive (e.g., Pillemer & Suitor, 1992). However, actions or communications that are intended by the provider to be supportive may also backfire and have negative rather than positive effects on the recipient (Burg & Seeman, 1994). For the purposes of both description and intervention, it may be just as important to determine why well-intended actions are unhelpful as it is to examine correlates of hostile or critical actions by family members toward their ill older relatives.

For individuals dealing with a chronic illness, seemingly supportive efforts of significant others such as offering advice, avoiding discussion of the illness, and becoming highly involved in the patient's life, are often reported as unhelpful (Dunkel-Schetter, Blasband, Feinstein, & Herbert, 1992). In addition, patients agree that family and friends sometimes make suggestions that are unhelpful or upsetting, or find it hard to understand the way the patient feels (Revenson, Schiaffino, Majerovitz, & Gibofsky, 1991). Consistent with these findings, a recent study of older stroke patients and their spouses showed that the most frequently mentioned unhelpful actions were being critical of the patient's attempts at recovery, underestimating or overestimating the patient's abilities, and not providing assistance correctly (Clark & Stephens, 1996).

Mental Health Outcomes. As in the literature on the mental health effects of caregiving, studies on the mental health effects of receiving care have primarily focused on depressive symptoms as the outcome of greatest interest. Clark and Stephens (1996) examined the effects of both helpful actions (e.g., general assistance with activities such as cooking, housework, and transportation, and showing love or affection) and unhelpful actions and found that only the latter were predictive of the patient's greater depressive symptomatology, controlling for the patient's level of functional disability. Another study of older women with osteoarthritis and their husbands examined negative reactions to receiving instrumental or emotional support from the husband and how these reactions related to depressive symptoms and life satisfaction after controlling for the patient's level of functional disability and amount of instrumental or emotional support received (Martire et al., 1998). Patients who felt they had little control over the assistance they received from their husband or who felt less competent in carrying out tasks on their own as a result of this assistance experienced more depressive symptoms and less life satisfaction. Similarly, patients who felt more rejected (undermined or put down) as a result of their husband's attempts to be emotionally supportive experienced more depressive symptoms and less life satisfaction.

Much has been written about the potential problems that may emerge when a family member becomes overly involved in the welfare of a chronically ill patient (e.g., Coyne, Wortman, & Lehman, 1988). Several studies that focus on older adults (who may or may not have been disabled) have provided empirical evidence for these detrimental effects of overinvolvement. Older adults receiving high levels of emotional support have been shown to have a less internal locus of control at a later point in time, suggesting that too much support can erode feelings of control (Krause, 1987). In addition, emotional and instrumental support received from adult children was shown to be associated with less depressive symptomatology up to a threshold point, beyond which more support was associated with more depressive symptoms (Silverstein et al., 1996). This nonlinear effect of support on well-being was particularly pronounced for older adults who were unmarried and had low expectations for support from their children, suggesting that too much assistance is particularly problematic for older adults who may believe that adults should provide support to their children and not vice versa. In another study, receiving ADL assistance from adult children was positively related to older adults' depressive symptoms, even after controlling for health-related factors (Lee, Netzer, & Coward, 1995). In this study, older adults who gave more support to their children than they received were the least depressed.

Findings from a separate program of research suggest that the perception that one is being overhelped may be more important than the actual amount of overhelping (Thompson & Sobolew-Shubin, 1993; Thompson, Sobolew-Shubin, Graham, & Janigian, 1989). In this research on stroke patients, overprotection was assessed in terms of not letting the patient do things that could be done independently, taking over the patient's responsibilities unnecessarily, and shielding the patient from upsetting or frustrating situations or events. Patients who felt overprotected by their family caregivers for these reasons were found to be more depressed even after controlling for the severity of the stroke. Overprotection was not related to quantity of support, suggesting that overprotection was not simply the equivalent of providing too much assistance. Although it has often been suggested that overhelping or overprotection is detrimental to an older adult's mental health because it makes the recipient feel less efficacious, competent, or independent (e.g., Krause, 1995), investigators have yet to examine such explanatory or mediating mechanisms empirically.

The findings of several studies directly address the issue of person–environment fit. The common approach used in these studies is to examine the interaction between amount or nature of assistance and personality characteristics of the recipient. A recent study of spousal caregiving dyads focused on amount of assistance from the spouse, personal characteristics of the care-recipient, the extent to which care-recipients experienced mental or emotional strain from receiving assistance with ADLs and IADLs, and the care-recipient's level of depressive symptomatology. Recipients with lower self-esteem and lower mastery reported more strain as a result of receiving care, especially those who received high levels of ADL and IADL assistance from the spouse. Insufficient help was found to be associated with more care-receiving strain for those with low perceived control but was associated with less strain for those with high perceived control, suggesting that individuals with high levels of perceived control prefer lesser amounts of assistance (Newsom & Schulz, 1998). Moreover, greater care receiving strain predicted more depressive symptomatology for the recipient 1 year later.

As further evidence for person–environment fit, one study showed that older adults who have an internal locus of control (i.e., perceive that events in their lives are primarily under their control) and whose social network encourage them to be reliant on others for support experience poorer mental health, whereas individuals with an external locus of control experienced better mental health when receiving this same type of support (Reich & Zautra, 1991). Another study by the same investigators revealed that older adults who were encouraged to be self-reliant at a time when they had a significant increase in activity limitations experienced poorer mental health (Zautra, Reich, & Newsom, 1995). Finally, although not focused specifically on older adults, one study found that women who appraise rheumatoid arthritis as a challenge (rather than a threat) experience more depression when they receive high levels of instrumental, emotional, and informational support from their husband (Schiaffino & Revenson, 1995).

Physical Health Outcomes. Little attention has been paid to whether or not the receipt of care has negative effects on the older adult's physical health beyond their existing health condition, and virtually no attention has been paid to explanatory or conditioning factors in this process. One common suggestion is that the actions of others can be unsupportive in the sense that they can foster a sense of dependency or incompetency in the older adult that contributes to poorer physical functioning (Baltes, 1988). Evidence for this hypothesis has been found for older adults receiving assistance from nursing home staff as well as individuals receiving assistance from family members (Baltes & Wahl, 1992). Another study found that instrumental support in the form of assistance with tasks and provision of information was associated with increased risk for onset of new or recurrent disability in a sample of highly functioning older men, suggesting that receipt of support may have led to reduced confidence in the ability to carry out tasks independently and decreased effort in this regard (Seeman, Bruce, & McAvay, 1996).

Although not necessarily focusing on caregiving situations, the chronic pain literature has documented the impact that family members' actions can have on the functioning of an individual suffering from conditions such as low back pain, headaches, and osteoarthritis. A number of studies have shown that family members unintentionally reinforce pain behaviors and inactivity in chronic pain patients by acting solicitously toward the patient (i.e., providing assistance even when it may not be needed) (e.g., Romano et al., 1992; Turk, Kerns, & Rosenberg, 1992).

To summarize this section on the health effects of care receiving, the positive aspects of receiving care have for the most part been assumed and not evaluated empirically. However, there is evidence from several different literatures that emotional support and task assistance from informal caregivers, although usually well-intended, can sometimes backfire and have negative rather than positive effects on the older adult care-recipient. Less is known about the extent to which receiving care affects an older adult's mental and physical health beyond the effects of his or her preexisting disability. Studies have not yet begun to address the roles of gender and ethnicity in the mental and physical health effects of receiving care. Furthermore, although a fair number of studies reviewed here were prospective in nature, most focused on general samples of older adults receiving instrumental support as broadly defined (e.g., McAvay et al., 1996; Silverstein et al., 1996) rather than ill or disabled older adults receiving illness-specific emotional support or task assistance (e.g., Schiaffino & Revenson, 1995; Zautra et al., 1995). Prospective studies focusing on the latter group may be most useful in terms of exploring the ways the health effects of receiving care change as a result of such factors as health transitions of the care-recipient or a change of primary caregiver.

As noted at the beginning of this section, research on the effects of receiving care is important because the recipient's response to assistance is an important determinant of the quality of future care, as well as future help-seeking behavior and reciprocity (DePaulo et al., 1983). As is true for the caregiving literature, an interesting question is whether the negative or positive aspects of receiving assistance have a greater impact on health. Furthermore, what are the conditions under which an older adult is better off receiving care from formal (i.e., paid) caregivers than from family or friends?

CONCLUSIONS

This chapter demonstrated that the perspectives of both the caregiver and the older adult care-recipient are important to consider in investigations of the health effects of informal caregiving. Moreover, evidence was provided that there are negative and positive aspects to both caregiving and care receiving. However, by organizing the review to focus separately on the caregiver and care-recipient, it may be falsely concluded that health effects of caregiving and care receiving are best viewed in isolation from each other. Therefore, this chapter concludes with a discussion of the interactive nature of helping and being helped.

Table 29.1 depicts four mental and physical health effect scenarios for the elder caregiving dyad. As illustrated, both the caregiver and care-receiver may experience positive health effects (cell 1) or negative health effects (cell 4) from the provision and receipt of care. Obviously, the first scenario is the optimal situation, whereas the fourth cell represents a scenario which should be of particular concern to researchers and policymakers. The second cell represents a health "trade-off," whereby the caregiver experiences negative health effects but the care-recipient benefits from received assistance. This may be the most typical scenario of the four, and is illustrated by findings from a study of married men recovering from myocardial infarction (MI). In this study, the wife's protective buffering (i.e., protecting the spouse from upsetting events and taking over tasks and responsibilities) was associated with the husband's increased efficacy in recovering from an MI but was also associated with her increased distress (Coyne & Smith, 1991). The third cell of Table 29.1 depicts another possible tradeoff whereby the care-recipient's health suffers as a result of receiving assistance but the caregiver benefits from the provision of assistance. One way that this scenario may occur is when the caregiver underestimates the older adult's abilities and provides more assistance than needed, thereby making the caregiver feel positively about his or her efforts but also causing the older adult to be more dependent on the caregiver for assistance in the future (e.g., Clark & Stephens, 1996).

TABLE 29.1
Typology of Dyadic Mental and Physical Health Effects of Informal Caregiving

Health Effects on the Care-Recipient	Health Effects on the Caregiver	
	Positive	Negative
Positive	1	2
Negative	3	4

The health effects illustrated in Table 29.1 also serve to bring another issue to the forefront. Obviously, health effects experienced by the caregiver and care-recipient do not exist in isolation from each other. The mental and physical health of each member of the caregiving dyad likely affects the mental and physical health of the other individual, a phenomenon often referred to as contagion. Several recent studies have demonstrated that the mental health status (e.g., depressive symptomatology) of a married older adult has a significant impact on the mental health of their spouse, even after taking into account the spouse's physical health status (Bookwala & Schulz, 1996; Coyne et al., 1987; Tower & Kasl, 1995). This picture emerges over many years, making it difficult to determine the causal ordering of such effects.

Evidence for the negative effects of informal caregiving on both the caregiver and care-recipient suggests that psychosocial interventions that are designed to improve the caregiving situation should target both the caregiver and care-recipient. To date, interventions have primarily been targeted at lessening the burden and subsequent negative health effects of informal caregiving through such approaches as education, support groups, counseling or psychotherapy, in-home respite programs, and free-standing or institutional adult day-care programs. Other literatures examine the efficacy of psychosocial interventions for improving the quality of life of specific chronic illness populations, such as individuals with arthritis, visual impairment, terminal illness, and individuals recovering from stroke or myocardial infarction. To date, there are only a handful of studies evaluating the efficacy of psychosocial interventions targeted at both members of elder caregiving dyads, in the context of conditions such as visual impairment (e.g., Horowitz, November 1997), osteoarthritis (e.g., Keefe et al., 1996) and psychiatric illness (e.g., Sherrill, Frank, Geary, Stack, & Reynolds, 1997; Teri, Logsdon, Uomoto, & McCurry, 1997). Clearly, there is a need for research of this kind.

Psychosocial interventions should target caregivers through efforts to relieve their burden as well as education in regard to providing the best assistance and support to the older adult. Given the importance of autonomy and control issues to many older adults, interventions aimed at getting nursing home staff to be more autonomy-supportive may be usefully applied to informal caregivers (Baltes, Neumann, & Zank, 1994). Care-recipients can be targeted through efforts to help them find the best ways to communicate the need for help, and education in regard to how their illness affects their caregiver. Of course, the most thorough psychosocial intervention would also target the older adult's primary health care provider in an attempt to improve communication between this individual and both the patient and caregiver and subsequently improve the quality of care provided to the patient (Council on Scientific Affairs, American Medical Association, 1993). An added benefit of multitargeted psychosocial interventions in the context of informal caregiving is that findings from this research can inform models of the health effects of caregiving and care receiving by identifying mediating and conditioning factors in these processes.

ACKNOWLEDGMENTS

Preparation of this chapter was in part supported by grants from the National Institute of Mental Health (MH46015, MH52247, and MH19986), the National Institute on Aging (AG13305 and AG01532), and the National Cancer Institute (CA61303 and CA64711).

REFERENCES

American Association of Retired Persons and the Travelers Foundation. (1988). *National survey of caregivers: Summary of findings.* Washington, DC: Author.

Aneshensel, C. S., Pearlin, L. I., Mullan, J. T., Zarit, S. H., & Whitlatch, C. J. (1995). *Profiles in caregiving: The unexpected career.* San Diego, CA: Academic Press.

Antonucci, T. C., & Jackson, J. S. (1987). Social support, interpersonal efficacy, and health: A life course perspective. In L. L. Carstensen & B. A. Edelstein (Eds.), *Handbook of clinical gerontology* (pp. 291–311). New York: Pergamon.

Baltes, M. M. (1988). The etiology and maintenance of dependency in the elderly: Three phases of operant research. *Behavior Therapy, 19,* 301–319.

Baltes, M. M., Neumann, E., & Zank, S. (1994). Maintenance and rehabilitation of independence in old age: An intervention program for staff. *Psychology and Aging, 9,* 179–188.

Baltes, M. M., & Wahl, H. W. (1992). The dependency-support script in institutions: Generalization to community settings. *Psychology and Aging, 7,* 409–418.

Bandura, A. (1997). *Self-efficacy: The exercise of control.* New York: Freeman.

Barling, J., MacEwen, K. E., Kelloway, E. K., & Higginbottom, S. F. (1994). Predictors and outcomes of elder-care based interrole conflict. *Psychology and Aging, 9,* 391–397.

Bass, D. M., Noelker, L. S., & Rechlin, L. R. (1996). The moderating influence of service use on negative caregiving consequences. *Journal of Gerontology: Social Sciences, 51B,* S121–S131.

Beach, S. R., Schulz, R., & Jackson, S. (1997, November). *Changes in intensity of caregiving as a predictor of changes in caregiver physical and mental health and service utilization.* Paper presented at the 50th Annual Scientific Meeting of the Gerontological Society of America, Cincinnati, OH.

Beck, A. T., Ward, C. H., Mendelson, M., Mock, J., & Erbaugh, J. (1961). An inventory for measuring depression. *Archives of General Psychiatry, 4,* 561–571.

Benson, V., & Marano, M. A. (1994). Current estimates from the National Health Interview Survey, 1993. National Center for Health Statistics. *Vital and Health Statistics, 10(190).*

Bookwala, J., & Schulz, R. (1996). Spousal similarity in subjective well-being: The Cardiovascular Health Study. *Psychology and Aging, 11,* 582–590.

Bookwala, J., & Schulz, R. (1998). The role of neuroticism and mastery in spouse caregivers' assessment of and response to a contextual stressor. *Journal of Gerontology: Psychological Sciences, 53B,* P155–P164.

Burg, M. M., & Seeman, T. E. (1994). Families and health: The negative side of social ties. *Annals of Behavioral Medicine, 16,* 109–115.

Burton, L. C., Newsom, J. T., Schulz, R., Hirsch, C. H., & German, P. S. (1997). Preventive health behaviors among spousal caregivers. *Preventive Medicine, 26,* 162–169.

Castle, S., Wilkins, S., Heck, E., Tanzy, K., & Fahey, J. (1995). Depression in caregivers of demented patients is associated with altered immunity: Impaired proliferative capacity, increased CD8+, and a cytotoxicity marker (CD56+ CD8+). *Clinical Experimental Immunology, 101,* 487–493.

Clark, S. L., & Stephens, M.A.P. (1996). Stroke patients' well-being as a function of caregiving spouses' helpful and unhelpful actions. *Personal Relationships, 3,* 171–184.

Cohen, S., Kessler, R. C., & Gordon, L. U. (1995). Strategies for measuring stress in studies of psychiatric and physical disorders. In S. Cohen, R. C. Kessler, & L. U. Gordon (Eds.), *Measuring stress: A guide for health and social scientists* (pp. 3–26). New York: Oxford University Press.

Cohen, S., & Rodriguez, M. (1995). Pathways linking affective disturbances and physical disorders. *Health Psychology, 14,* 374–380.

Cohen, S., & Wills, T. A. (1985). Stress, social support, and the buffering hypothesis. *Psychological Bulletin, 98,* 310–357.

Cotrell, V., & Schulz, R. (1993). The perspective of the patient with Alzheimer's disease: A neglected dimension of dementia research. *The Gerontologist, 33,* 205–211.

Council on Scientific Affairs, American Medical Association. (1993). Physicians and family caregivers: A model for partnership. *Journal of the American Medical Association, 269,* 1282–1284.

Coyne, J. C., Kessler, R. C., Tal, M., Turnbull, J., Wortman, C. B., & Greden, J. (1987). Living with a depressed person. *Journal of Clinical and Consulting Psychology, 55,* 347–352.

Coyne, J. C., & Smith, D. A. (1991). Couples coping with myocardial infarction: A contextual perspective on wives' distress. *Journal of Personality and Social Psychology, 61,* 404–412.

Coyne, J. C., Wortman, C., & Lehman, D. (1988). The other side of support: Emotional overinvolvement and miscarried helping. In B. Gottlieb (Ed.), *Social support: Formats, processes, and effects* (pp. 305–330). Beverly Hills, CA: Sage.

Crimmins, E. M., Saito, Y., & Reynolds, S. L. (1997). Further evidence on recent trends in the prevalence and incidence of disability among older Americans from two sources: The LSOA and the NHIS. *Journal of Gerontology: Social Sciences, 52B,* S59–S71.

Daubman, K. A. (1995). Help which implies dependence: Effects on self-evaluations, motivation, and performance. *Journal of Social Behavior and Personality, 10,* 677–692.

DePaulo, B. M., Brittingham, G. L., & Kaiser, M. K. (1983). Receiving competence-relevant help: Effects on reciprocity, affect, and sensitivity to the helper's nonverbally expressed needs. *Journal of Personality and Social Psychology, 45,* 1045–1060.

Dunkel-Schetter, C., Blasband, D. E., Feinstein, L. G., & Herbert, T. B. (1992). Elements of supportive interactions: When are attempts to help effective? In S. Spacapan & S. Oskamp (Eds.), *Helping and being helped: Naturalistic studies* (pp. 83–114). Newbury Park, CA: Sage.

Elliott, G. R., & Eisdorfer, C. (Eds.). (1982). *Stress and human health: Analysis and implications of research; a study by the Institute of Medicine, National Academy of Sciences.* New York: Springer.

Esterling, B. A., Kiecolt-Glaser, J. K., Bodnar, J. C., & Glaser, R. (1994). Chronic stress, social support, and persistent alterations in the natural killer cell response to cytokines in older adults. *Health Psychology, 13,* 291–299.

Esterling, B. A., Kiecolt-Glaser, J. K., & Glaser, R. (1996). Psychosocial modulation of cytokine-induced natural killer cell activity in older adults. *Psychosomatic Medicine, 58,* 264–272.

Fisher, J. D., Nadler, A., & Whitcher-Alagna, S. (1982). Recipients' reactions to aid. *Psychological Bulletin, 91,* 27–54.

Franks, M. M., & Stephens, M.A.P. (1992). Multiple roles of middle-generation caregivers: Contextual effects and psychological mechanisms. *Journal of Gerontology: Social Sciences, 47,* S123–S129.

Franks, M. M., & Stephens, M.A.P. (1996). Social support in the context of caregiving: Husbands' provision of support to wives involved in parent care. *Journal of Gerontology: Psychological Sciences, 51B,* P43–P52.

George, L. K., & Gwyther, L. P. (1986). Caregiver well-being: A multidimensional examination of family caregivers of demented adults. *The Gerontologist, 26,* 253–259.

Giele, J. Z., Mutschler, P. H., & Orodenker, S. Z. (1987). *Stress and burdens of caregiving for the frail elderly.* Working paper no. 36, Brandeis University, Waltham, MA.

Goode, K. T., Haley, W. T., Roth, D. L., & Ford, G. R. (1998). Predicting longitudinal changes in caregiver physical and mental health: A stress process model. *Health Psychology, 17,* 190–198.

Grafstrom, M., Fratiglioni, L., Sandman, P.O., & Winblad, B. (1992). Health and social consequences for relatives of demented and non-demented elderly: A population-based study. *Journal of Clinical Epidemiology, 45,* 861–870.

Haley, W. E., Levine, E. G., Brown, S. L., & Bartolucci, A. A. (1987). Stress, appraisal, coping, and social support as predictors of adaptational outcome among dementia caregivers. *Psychology and Aging, 2,* 323–330.

Haley, W. E., Levine, E. G., Brown, S. L., Berry, J. W., & Hughes, G. H. (1987). Psychological, social, and health consequences of caring for a relative with senile dementia. *Journal of the American Geriatric Society, 35,* 405–411.

Haley, W. E., West, C.A.C., Wadley, V. G., Ford, G. R., Shite, F. A., Barrett, J. J., Harrell, L. E., & Roth, D. L. (1995). Psychological, social, and health impact of caregiving: A comparison of black and white dementia family caregivers and noncaregivers. *Psychology and Aging, 10,* 540–552.

Hamilton, M. (1967). Development of a rating scale for primary depressive illness. *British Journal of Social and Clinical Psychology, 6,* 278–296.

Hinrichsen, G. A., & Ramirez, M. (1992). Black and White dementia caregivers: A comparison of their adaptation, adjustment and service utilization. *The Gerontologist, 32,* 375–381.

Hooker, K., Monahan, D. J., Bowman, S. R., Frazier, L. D., & Shifren, K. (1998). Personality counts for a lot: Predictors of mental and physical health of spouse caregivers in two disease groups. *Journal of Gerontology: Psychological Sciences, 53B,* P73–P85.

Horowitz, A. (1985). Sons and daughters as caregivers to older parents: Differences in role performance and consequences. *The Gerontologist, 25,* 612–617.

Horowitz, A. (1997, November). Development of a family based program of rehabilitation: Understanding the reciprocal relationships between family and elder well-being. In A. Horowitz (Chair), *Beyond caregiving: Families as partners in geriatric rehabilitation.* Symposium conducted at the 50th Annual Scientific Meeting of the Gerontological Society of America, Cincinnati, OH.

Jutras, S., & Lavoie, J. P. (1995). Living with an impaired elderly person: The informal caregiver's physical and mental health. *Journal of Aging and Health, 7,* 46–73.

Kahana, E., Kahana, B., & Riley, K. (1989). Person–environment transactions relevant to control and helplessness in institutional settings. In P. S. Fry (Ed.), *Psychological perspectives of helplessness and control in the elderly* (pp. 121–146). New York: Elsevier North-Holland.

Kasser, V. G., & Ryan, R. M. (in press). The relation of psychological needs for autonomy and relatedness to vitality, well-being, and mortality in a nursing home. *Journal of Applied Social Psychology.*

Keefe, F. J., Caldwell, D. S., Baucom, D., Salley, A., Robinson, E., Timmons, K., Beaupre, P., Weisberg, J., & Helms, M. (1996). Spouse-assisted coping skills training in the management of osteoarthritic knee pain. *Arthritis Care and Research, 9,* 279–291.

Kerns, R. D., & Weiss, L. H. (1994). Family influences on the course of chronic illness: A cognitive-behavioral transactional model. *Annals of Behavioral Medicine, 16,* 116–121.

Kiecolt-Glaser, J. K., Glaser, R., Gravenstein, S, Malarkey, S. B., & Sheridan, J. (1996). Chronic stress alters the immune response to influenza virus vaccine in older adults. *Proceedings of the National Academy of Sciences, 93,* 3043–3047.

Kiecolt-Glaser, J. K., Marucha, P. T., Malarkey, W. B., Mercado, A. M., & Glaser, R. (1995). Slowing of wound healing by psychological stress. *Lancet, 346,* 1194–1196.

Kinney, J. M., & Stephens, M.A.P. (1989). Hassles and uplifts of giving care to a family member with dementia. *Psychology and Aging, 4,* 402–408.

Kinney, J. M., Stephens, M.A.P., Franks, M. M., & Norris, V. R. (1995). Stresses and satisfactions of family caregivers to older stroke patients. *Journal of Applied Gerontology, 14,* 3–21.

Kramer, B. J. (1997). Gain in the caregiving experience: Where are we? What next? *The Gerontolgoist, 37,* 218–232.

Krause, N. (1987). Understanding the stress process: Linking social support with locus of control beliefs. *Journal of Gerontology, 42,* 589–593.

Krause, N. (1995). Assessing stress-buffering effects: A cautionary note. *Psychology and Aging, 10,* 518–526.

Lawrence, R. H., Tennstedt, S. L., & Assmann, S. F. (1998). Quality of the caregiver–care recipient relationship: Does it offset negative consequences of caregiving for family caregivers? *Psychology and Aging, 13,* 150–158.

Lawton, M. P., Kleban, M. H., Moss, M., Rovine, M., & Glicksman, A. (1989). Measuring caregiving appraisal. *Journal of Gerontology: Psychological Sciences, 46,* P181–P189.

Lawton, M. P., Rajagopal, D., Brody, E., & Kleban, M. H. (1992). The dynamics of caregiving for a demented elder among Black and White families. *Journal of Gerontology: Social Sciences, 47,* S156–S164.

Lazarus, R. S., & Folkman, S. (1984). *Stress, appraisal, and coping.* New York: Springer.

Lee, G. R., Netzer, J. K., & Coward, R. T. (1995). Depression among older parents: The role of intergenerational exchange. *Journal of Marriage and the Family, 57,* 823–833.

Li, L. W., Seltzer, M. M., & Greenberg, J. S. (1997). Social support and depressive symptoms: Differential patterns in wife and daughter caregivers. *Journal of Gerontology: Social Sciences, 52B,* S200–S211.

Logsdon, R. G., & Teri, L. (1995). Depression in Alzheimer's disease patients: Caregivers as surrogate reporters. *Journal of American Geriatrics Society, 43,* 150–155.

Manton, K. G., Corder, L., & Stallard, E. (1997). Chronic disability trends in elderly United States populations: 1982–1994. *Proceedings of the National Academy of Sciences: Medical Sciences, 94,* 2593–2598.

Martire, L. M., Stephens, M.A.P., & Atienza, A. A. (1997). The interplay of work and caregiving: Relationships between role satisfaction, role involvement, and caregivers' well-being. *Journal of Gerontology: Social Sciences, 52B,* S279–S289.

Martire, L. M., Stephens, M.A.P., Druley, J. A., Berthoff, M. A., Fleisher, C. L., & Wojno, W. C. (1998, August). Older women coping with osteoarthritis: Negative reactions to spousal support. In J. Tucker (Chair), *Social relationships and health: An aging perspective.* Symposium conducted at the 106th Annual Convention of the American Psychological Association, San Francisco, CA.

Martire, L. M., Stephens, M.A.P., & Townsend, A. L. (1997, November). *The psychological centrality of women's multiple roles: Positive and negative effects on well-being.* Paper presented at the 50th Annual Scientific Meeting of the Gerontological Society of America, Cincinnati, OH.

McAvay, G. J., Seeman, T. E., & Rodin, J. (1996). A longitudinal study of change in domain-specific self-efficacy among older adults. *Journal of Gerontology: Psychological Sciences, 51B,* P243–P253.

Meshefedjian, G., McCusker, J., Bellavance, F., & Baumgarten, M. (1998). Factors associated with symptoms of depression among informal caregivers of demented elders in the community. *The Gerontologist, 38,* 247–253.

Miller, B. (1989). Adult children's perception of caregiver stress and satisfaction. *Journal of Applied Gerontology, 8,* 275–293.

Miller, B., & Cafasso, L. (1992). Gender differences in caregiving: Fact or artifact? *The Gerontologist, 32,* 498–507.

Miller, B., Campbell, R. T., Farran, C. J., Kaufman, J. E., & Davis, L. (1995). Race, control, mastery, and caregiver distress. *Journal of Gerontology: Social Sciences, 50B,* S374–S382.

Miller, B. H., & Montgomery, A. A. (1990). Family caregivers and limitations on social activities. *Research on Aging, 12,* 72–93.

Montgomery, R. J. (1992). Gender differences in patterns of child-parent caregiving relationships. In J. W. Dwyer & R. T. Coward (Eds.), *Gender, families, and elder care* (pp. 65–83). Newbury Park, CA: Sage.

Montgomery, R.J.V., & Kosloski, K. (1994). A longitudinal analysis of nursing home placement for dependent elders cared for by spouses vs adult children. *Journal of Gerontology: Social Sciences, 49,* S62–S74.

Moritz, D. J., Kasl, S. V., & Ostfeld, A. M. (1992). The health impact of living with a cognitively impaired elderly spouse. *Journal of Aging and Health, 4,* 244–267.

Nadler, A., & Fisher, J. D. (1986). The role of threat to self-esteem and perceived control in recipient reactions to help: Theory and development and empirical validation. *Advances in Experimental Social Psychology, 19,* 81–122.

National Alliance for Caregiving and the American Association of Retired Persons. (1997). *Family caregiving in the U.S.: Findings from a national survey.* Bethesda, MD: National Alliance for Caregiving.

Neal, M. B., Chapman, N. J., Ingersoll-Dayton, B., & Emlen, A. C. (1993). *Balancing work and caregiving for children, adults, and elders.* Newbury Park, CA: Sage.

Newsom, J. T., & Schulz, R. (1998). Caregiving from the recipient's perspective: Negative reactions to being helped. *Health Psychology, 17,* 172–181.

Noonan, A. E., & Tennstedt, S. L. (1997). Meaning in caregiving and its contribution to caregiver well-being. *The Gerontologist, 37,* 785–794.

Norburn, J.E.K., Bernard, S. L., Konrad, T. R., Woomert, A., DeFriese, G. H., Kalsbeek, W. D., Koch, G. G., & Ory, M. G. (1995). Self-care and assistance from others in coping with functional status limitations among a national sample of older adults. *Journal of Gerontology: Social Sciences, 50B,* S101–S109.

Parmelee, P. A., & Lawton, M. P. (1990). The design of special environments for the aged. In J. E. Birren & K. W. Schaie (Eds.), *Handbook of the psychology of aging* (pp. 464–488). San Diego, CA: Academic Press.

Pearlin, L. I., Mullan, J. T., Semple, S. J., & Skaff, M. M. (1990). Caregiving and the stress process: An overview of concepts and their measures. *The Gerontologist, 30,* 583–594.

Pillemer, K., & Suitor, J. J. (1992). Violence and violent feelings: What causes them among family caregivers? *Journal of Gerontology, 47,* 165–172.

Prohaska, T. (1998). The research basis for the design and implementation of self-care programs. In M. G. Ory & G. H. DeFriese (Eds.), *Self-care in later life: Research, program, and policy issues* (pp. 62–84). New York: Springer.

Quittner, A. L., Glueckauf, R. L., & Jackson, D. N. (1990). Chronic parenting stress: Moderating versus mediating effects of social support. *Journal of Personality and Social Psychology, 59,* 1266–1278.

Radloff, L. S. (1977). The CES–D scale: A self-report depression scale for research in the general population. *Applied Psychological Measurement, 1,* 385–401.

Redinbaugh, E. M., MacCallum, R. C., & Kiecolt-Glaser, J. K. (1995). Recurrent syndromal depression in caregivers. *Psychology and Aging, 10,* 358–368.

Reich, J. W., & Zautra, A. J. (1991). Experimental and measurement approaches to internal control in at-risk older adults. *Journal of Social Issues, 47,* 143–158.

Revenson, T. A., Schiaffino, K. M., Majerovitz, S. D., & Gibofsky, A. (1991). Social support as a double-edged sword: The relation of positive and problematic support to depression among rheumatoid arthritis patients. *Social Science and Medicine, 33,* 801–813.

Riedel, S. E., Fredman, L., & Langenberg, P. (1998). Associations among caregiving difficulties, burden, and rewards in caregivers to older post-rehabilitation patients. *Journal of Gerontology: Psychological Sciences, 53B,* P165–P174.

Romano, J. M., Turner, J. A., Friedman, L. S., Bulcroft, R. A., Jensen, M. P., Hops, H., & Wright, S. F. (1992). Sequential analysis of chronic pain behaviors and spouse responses. *Journal of Consulting and Clinical Psychology, 60,* 777–782.

Rook, K. S. (1984). The negative side of social interaction: Impact on psychological well-being. *Journal of Personality and Social Psychology, 46,* 1097–1108.

Rose-Rego, S. K., Straus, M. E., & Smyth, K. A. (1998). Differences in the perceived well-being of wives and husbands caring for persons with Alzheimer's disease. *The Gerontologist, 38,* 224–230.

Ryan, R. M., & Solky, J. A. (1996). What is supportive about social support? On the psychological needs for autonomy and relatedness. In G. R. Pierce, B. G. Sarason, & I. G. Sarason (Eds.), *Handbook of social support and the family* (pp. 249–267). New York: Plenum.

Scharlach, A. E. (1994). Caregiving and employment: Competing or complementary roles? *The Gerontologist, 34,* 378–385.

Schiaffino, K. M., & Revenson, T. A. (1995). Relative contributions of spousal support and illness appraisals to depressed mood in arthritis patients. *Arthritis Care and Research, 8,* 80–87.

Schulz, R., Newsom, J., Mittelmark, M., Burton, L., Hirsch, C., & Jackson, S. (1997). Health effects of caregiving: The Caregiver Health Effects Study: An ancillary study of the Cardiovascular Health Study. *Annals of Behavioral Medicine, 19,* 110–116.

Schulz, R., O'Brien, A. T., Bookwala, J., & Fleissner, K. (1995). Psychiatric and physical morbidity effects of dementia caregiving: Prevalence, correlates, and causes. *The Gerontologist, 35,* 771–791.

Schulz, R., & Quittner, A. L. (Ed.). (1998). Caregiving for children and adults with chronic conditions: A life span approach [Special issue]. *Health Psychology, 17*(2).

Schulz, R., Tompkins, C. A., & Rau, M. T. (1988). A longitudinal study of the psychosocial impact of stroke on primary support persons. *Psychology and Aging, 3,* 131–141.

Schulz, R., Visintainer, P., & Williamson, G. M. (1990). Psychiatric and physical morbidity effects of caregiving. *Journal of Gerontology: Psychological Sciences, 45,* P181–P191.

Schulz, R., & Williamson, G. M. (1991). A 2–year longitudinal study of depression among Alzheimer's caregivers. *Psychology and Aging, 6,* 569–578.

Seeman, T. E., Bruce, M. L., & McAvay, G. J. (1996). Social network characteristics and onset of ADL disability: MacArthur studies of successful aging. *Journal of Gerontology: Social Sciences, 51B,* S191–S200.

Semple, S. J. (1992). Conflict in Alzheimer's caregiving families: Its dimensions and consequences. *The Gerontologist, 32,* 648–655.

Sheehan, N. W., & Nuttall, P. (1988). Conflict, emotion, and personal strain among family caregivers. *Family Relations, 37,* 92–98.

Sherrill, J. T., Frank, E., Geary, M., Stack, J. A., & Reynolds, C. F. (1997). Psychoeducational workshops for elderly patients with recurrent major depression and their families. *Psychiatric Services, 48,* 76–81.

Silverstein, M., Chen, X., & Heller, K. (1996). Too much of a good thing? Intergenerational social support and the psychological well-being of older parents. *Journal of Marriage and the Family, 58,* 970–982.

Skaff, M. M., & Pearlin, L. I. (1992). Caregiving: Role engulfment and the loss of self. *The Gerontologist, 32,* 656–664.

Skaff, M. M., Pearlin, L. I., & Mullan, J. T. (1996). Transitions in the caregiving career: Effects on sense of mastery. *Psychology and Aging, 11,* 247–257.

Spencer, K. A., Tompkins, C. A., & Schulz, R. (1997). Assessment of depression in patients with brain pathology: The case of stroke. *Psychological Bulletin, 122,* 132–152.

Stephens, M.A.P., & Franks, M. M. (1995). Spillover between daughters' roles as caregiver and wife: Interference or enhancement? *Journal of Gerontology: Psychological Sciences, 50B,* P9–P17.

Stephens, M.A.P., Franks, M. M., & Atienza, A. A. (1997). Where two roles intersect: Spillover between parent care and employment. *Psychology and Aging, 12,* 30–37.

Stephens, M.A.P., Franks, M. M., & Townsend, A. L. (1994). Stress and rewards in women's multiple roles: The case of women in the middle. *Psychology and Aging, 9,* 45–52.

Stephens, M.A.P., Kinney, J. M., Norris, V. K., & Ritchie, S. W. (1987). Social networks as assets and liabilities in recovery from stroke by geriatric patients. *Psychology and Aging, 2,* 125–129.

Stephens, M.A.P., & Townsend, A. L. (1997). Stress of parent care: Positive and negative effects of women's other roles. *Psychology and Aging, 12,* 376–386.

Stull, D. E., Kosloski, K., & Kercher, K. (1994). Caregiver burden and generic well-being: Opposite sides of the same coin? *The Gerontologist, 34,* 88–94.

Suitor, J. J., & Pillemer, K. (1992). Status transitions and marital satisfaction: The case of adult children caring for elderly parents suffering from dementia. *Journal of Social and Personal Relationships, 9,* 549–562.

Suitor, J. J., & Pillemer, K. (1996). Sources of support and interpersonal stress in the networks of married caregiving daughters: Findings from a 2–year longitudinal study. *Journal of Gerontology: Social Sciences, 51B,* S297–S306.

Teri, L., Logsdon, R. G., Uomoto, J., & McCurry, S. M. (1997). Behavioral treatment of depression in dementia patients: A controlled clinical trial. *Journal of Gerontology: Psychological Sciences, 52B,* P159–P166.

Thompson, S. C., & Sobolew-Shubin, A. (1993). Overprotective relationships: A nonsupportive side of social networks. *Basic and Applied Social Psychology, 14,* 363–383.

Thompson, S. C., Sobolew-Shubin, A., Graham, M. A., & Janigian, A. S. (1989). Psychosocial adjustment following a stroke. *Social Science and Medicine, 28,* 239–247.

Tower, R. B., & Kasl, S. V. (1995). Depressive symptoms across older spouses and the moderating effect of marital closeness. *Psychology and Aging, 10,* 625–638.

Townsend, A. L., & Franks, M. M. (1995). Binding ties: Closeness and conflict in adult children's caregiving relationships. *Psychology and Aging, 10,* 343–351.

Turk, D. C., Kerns, R. D., & Rosenberg, R. (1992). Effects of marital interaction on chronic pain and disability: Examining the down side of social support. *Rehabilitation Psychology, 37,* 259–273.

U.S. General Accounting Office (Health, Education, and Human Services Division). (1998). *Alzheimer's disease: Estimates of prevalence in the United States* (GAO/HEHS-98-16). Washington, DC: GAO.

Vitaliano, P. P., Russo, J., Scanlan, J., & Greeno, K. (1996). Weight changes in caregivers of Alzheimer's care recipients: Psychobehavioral predictors. *Psychology and Aging, 11,* 155–163.

Vitaliano, P. P., Scanlan, J. M., Krenz, C., Schwartz, R. S., & Marcovina, S. M. (1996). Psychological distress, caregiving, and metabolic variables. *Journals of Gerontology: Psychological Sciences, 51B,* P290–P297.

Vitaliano, P. P., Schulz, R., Kiecolt-Glaser, J., & Grant, I. (1997). Research on physiological and physical concomitants of caregiving: Where do we go from here? *Annals of Behavioral Medicine, 19,* 117–123.

Walker, A. J., Martin, S. S., & Jones, L. L. (1992). The benefits and costs of caregiving and care receiving for daughters and mothers. *Journal of Gerontology: Social Sciences, 47,* S130–S139.

Williamson, G. M., & Schulz, R. (1990). Relationship orientation, quality of prior relationship, and distress among caregivers of Alzheimer's Patients. *Psychology and Aging, 5,* 502–509.

Williamson, G. M., & Schulz, R. (1992). Physical illness and symptoms of depression among elderly outpatients. *Psychology and Aging, 7,* 343–351.

Williamson, G. M., Shaffer, D. R., & Schulz, R. (1998). Activity restriction and prior relationship history as contributors to mental health outcomes among middle-aged and older spousal caregivers. *Health Psychology, 17,* 152–162.

Wright, L. K., Clipp, E. C., & George, L. K. (1993). Health consequences of caregiver stress. *Medicine, Exercise, Nutrition, and Health, 2,* 181–195.

Zautra, A. J., Reich, J. W., & Newsom, J. T. (1995). Autonomy and sense of control among older adults: An examination of their effects on mental health. In L. A. Bond, S. J. Cutler, & A. Grams (Eds.), *Promoting successful and productive aging* (pp. 153–170). Thousand Oaks, CA: Sage.

30

Stress Processes in Pregnancy and Birth: Psychological, Biological, and Sociocultural Influences

Christine Dunkel-Schetter
Regan A. R. Gurung
University of California, Los Angeles
Marci Lobel
State University of New York, Stony Brook
Pathik D. Wadhwa
University of Kentucky College of Medicine

From the time of its inception, health psychology has accumulated a strong record of research on psychological aspects of various diseases such as heart disease and cancer. In contrast, the field has not delved much into reproductive health. Research in nursing, public health, and medicine has been conducted on the biopsychosocial aspects of infertility, contraception, abortion, miscarriage and stillbirth, on prenatal genetic screening and health behaviors, on labor and delivery, and on maternal and infant health in general. Such issues are prime research topics for attention by health psychology, as any quick reading of the available literature indicates. This chapter focuses on pregnancy and birth specifically, although this is only one of a plethora of important underresearched topics in reproductive health.

A central event in most women's reproductive life cycles is the prenatal period culminated by the birth of a child. During these 9 months, numerous well-established changes in physiology take place. These changes are accompanied by psychological changes that are not as well documented, nor are the interrelations of the physiological changes to psychological factors well mapped out as yet. The effects of pregnancy on mood or affect, social resources, coping processes, and various behaviors are highly variable from woman to woman depending on her circumstances and her condition. To what extent are women anxious about having a first or a subsequent birth? Does prenatal anxiety vary as a function of her available coping resources? Do women with close relationships with the father of the baby have better health and well-being in pregnancy than women who do not have this relationship? Are certain personal characteristics such as self-esteem associated with positive prenatal health behavior? Does the way a woman perceives and copes with challenges in her pregnancy influence her emotional adjustment or her infant's health? What are the mechanisms accounting for relations of maternal psychosocial factors and maternal, fetal, and infant outcomes? These are the kinds of health psychology questions that can be considered in building a better understanding of pregnancy.

Pregnancy is an ideal condition for study by health psychologists for many reasons. First, it has a clear-cut and finite time frame. Second, millions of women experience it annually. Third, many of the issues such as the prevention of infant mortality are international in scope. Finally, evidence for interactions of mind and body are numerous. For example, it is known that having a companion present during labor to provide support has beneficial effects on labor outcomes (Kennell, Klaus, McGrath, Robertson, & Hinkley, 1991; Sosa, Kennell, Klaus, Robertson, & Urrutia, 1980). It is also well established that behaviors such as smoking, diet, and adherence to medical regimens have effects on fetal growth and infant health (McCormick et al., 1990). Emerging research also indicates that life stress and its emotional effects are risk factors for adverse birth outcomes for mother and infant. It is this latter topic—prenatal stress processes and effects on birth outcomes—that is the central focus in this chapter. By studying stress processes in pregnancy, the many interactions of psychological, sociocultural, and biological systems and their effects on birth outcomes can be examined. More specifically, the mechanisms accounting for the links between stress and birth outcomes are unknown, and can be probed within a broad-based stress framework.

PREGNANCY AND STRESS

Although biological perspectives sometimes view pregnancy as a physical stressor to the body, there are limitations of such models for studying pregnancy. For one, the human body has many adaptive mechanisms to ensure the health of mother and fetus (Amiel-Tison & Pettigrew, 1991). In fact, pregnancy is best conceptualized as a normative developmental transition involving changes of many kinds that may or may not be perceived as stressful. This may be especially true in a first pregnancy. A woman's social network may change, with her family and marital relationships growing stronger or more strained. She may develop new friendships with other expecting mothers or parents, and become less close with others who do not have children. Emotions may range over the course of pregnancy from happy to anxious, "blue," or sad. Behaviors such as abstinence from smoking, alcohol, and drug use, and regular prenatal care, healthy diet, and moderate exercise may differ markedly from prepregnancy behaviors. Variability in these issues among women is even greater in second, third, or further pregnancies, as a function of the experiences of earlier pregnancies and the conditions of the current one. Understanding the variability in responses to pregnancy and determining the factors that predict such variation is one goal of the research.

MULTILEVEL STRESS MODELS AS APPLIED TO PREGNANCY

Many factors at different levels of theoretical analysis influence the degree to which a woman experiences particular changes, emotional responses, and events in pregnancy. These levels include sociological, cultural, familial, dyadic, and individual. For example, maternal socioeconomic status has been shown to influence substance use, prenatal care utilization, and diet, as well as stress levels in pregnancy (Feldman, 1997; Gazmararian, Adams, & Pamuk, 1996; Kramer, 1998; Moore et al., 1991). Ethnic and cultural differences have been found in attitudes about a particular pregnancy, about pregnancy in general, and in health behaviors (Schaffer, Velie, Shaw, & Todoroff, 1998; Scrimshaw, Zambrana, & Dunkel-Schetter, 1997; Zambrana & Scrimshaw, 1997; Zambrana, Scrimshaw, N. Collins, & Dunkel-Schetter, 1997). Some of these factors—socioeconomic indicators, attitudes toward pregnancy, and health behaviors, in particular—have been shown in turn to influence rates of medical complications and outcomes such as prematurity and infant birthweight (J. W. Collins, Herman, & David, 1997; Gudmundsson, Bjorgvinsdottir, Molin, Gunnarsson, & Marsal, 1997; Safonova & Leparsky, 1998; Zimmer-Gembeck & Helfand, 1996). Age also plays a part, with teenage pregnancy creating a vulnerable group of women for whom prenatal changes are perhaps the most stressful and pose the most risk (McAnarney, 1987). For example, teens are at high risk for substance use and inadequate health care in pregnancy (Koshar, Lee, Goss, Heilemann, & Stinson, 1998). Marital status has also been found to be important to pregnancy processes and outcomes, with married women at lower risk of many adverse outcomes (Ahmed, 1990; Arntzen, Moum, Magnus, & Bakketeig, 1996; McIntosh, Roumayah, & Bottoms, 1995). Psychosocial mechanisms such as availability and receipt of support of all kinds are likely explanations for these marital effects.

At the individual level, a host of factors such as maternal personality, coping style, and coping resources influence the degree and rate of changes in pregnancy and outcomes. For example, women with high perceived control or mastery appear to have better pregnancy outcomes (Rini, Dunkel-Schetter, Sandman, & Wadhwa, 1999). Women who cope with challenges in pregnancy in certain ways (e.g., Yali & Lobel, 1999), and who have ample resources to cope (e.g., Dunkel-Schetter, Sagrestano, Feldman, & Killingsworth, 1996), also appear to fare much better. For example, naturally occurring social support has been associated with larger birth weight infants and with fewer labor complications (N. L. Collins, Dunkel-Schetter, Lobel, & Scrimshaw, 1993).

Variability in response to pregnancy may also be due to biological factors such as genetic predisposition, obstetrical and gynecological history, and state of prepregnancy health. Possible pathways between psychosocial factors and outcomes such as maternal complications or infant health include processes at many biological levels of analysis that range from systemic (endocrine and immune processes) to molecular (gene expression). Historically, pregnancy has been studied at only single levels of analysis, but current trends in perinatal research are toward multilevel analyses in which biological, psychological, and sociocultural factors are examined jointly.

In short, there are many factors at many different levels of analysis that influence exposure to stress in pregnancy, appraisals of stress, emotional responses to stressors, and effects of them on mental and physical health outcomes. Furthermore, these factors interact and work together in complex causal sequences in their effects on maternal, fetal, and infant outcomes. Thus, a broad biopsychosocial approach to understanding pregnancy and birth, similar to that found in much of health psychology, is appropriate in this context, and offers avenues for productive research.

This chapter overviews some of the biopsychosocial interrelationships in pregnancy and birth with special attention to stress processes. Stress processes are inherently biopsychosocial and provide a useful entry point to the broader arena of study. It begins with a review of the mainly descriptive research on the prevalence and variability of emotional responses in pregnancy. The next section lays out the array of potential pregnancy and birth outcomes that may be studied. Because of their significance as health issues, special attention is devoted to length of gestation, preterm delivery, and to low birth weight. To provide some groundwork for examining links between stress and these particular outcomes, the etiology of preterm delivery and low birthweight is also briefly discussed. Next, the chapter reviews recent evidence regarding stress as an independent risk factor for adverse outcomes. The next section is devoted to mechanisms or pathways that may account for stress–birth outcome effects. Two general mechanisms are discussed: physiological pathways and behavioral pathways. Following the discussion of mechanisms, two moderators of stress outcome effects are examined. These are coping processes and social support processes. Insomuch as there is very little research on coping, this topic is treated briefly. In contrast, there is both a solid existing research literature and a growing body of work on social support in pregnancy; thus this topic is covered in some depth. The section on social support provides a brief conceptual basis for the study of support in pregnancy, and then reviews research on the relation of social support to birth outcomes.

EMOTIONAL RESPONSES IN PREGNANCY

Some experts have suggested that heightened levels of estrogen and progesterone in pregnancy make pregnant women more emotionally vulnerable, although the impact of hormones on prenatal mood has not been established empirically (Leifer, 1980). For the most part, prenatal emotion has not been examined as a topic in its own right, but rather it has been described in the coverage of other topics, mainly in studies focusing on the impact of maternal emotion on birth outcomes or on postpartum adjustment (cf. Leifer, 1980). In these studies, mean levels of emotion are often not reported, and when reported, are not usually compared to population means, or otherwise given meaningful interpretation (e.g., Affonso, Mayberry, Lovett, & Paul, 1994; Brooke, Anderson, Bland, Peacock, & Stewart, 1989; Chalmers, 1983; Farber, Vaughn, & Egeland, 1981; Kalil, Gruber, Conley, & Syntiac, 1993). Furthermore, of the limited number of studies of women's emotional state during pregnancy, a fair portion were published 20 or more years ago. These studies may offer an inaccurate view of emotions in pregnant women of today due to important societal changes that are likely to have altered the experience of pregnancy. For example, more pregnant women are in the workforce now than in previous decades, which has affected societal views of pregnancy and the way pregnant women view themselves (Horgan, 1983; Lobel, 1998). Although the tendency to treat pregnancy as a sickness has receded over the last few decades (Seegmiller, 1993), pregnancy has been increasingly medicalized. Most women now routinely undergo prenatal tests such as ultrasonography, amniocentesis, chorionic villus sampling, and alphafetoprotein testing. There is conflicting evidence about whether such testing, and the greater availability of medical interventions, provides reassurance to pregnant women or focuses their attention on the number of things that can go wrong (Diaz & Lobel, 1998; Tunis & Golbus, 1991). Because of these changes, research must be fairly current to accurately represent the emotional state of pregnant women today.

Three types of studies comprise the research literature on prenatal emotion. One type, which includes many of the older studies, examines the prevalence of various indicators of psychopathology in pregnant women and compares these to population norms. Studies of psychosis, suicide, and admission to psychiatric hospitals have generally found that these are less common in pregnant than nonpregnant women, and in those who do experience psychiatric disorders, a history of disorder prior to pregnancy is often present (reviewed by Elliott, 1984; Leifer, 1980). A second type of study, comprised of qualitative interviews with pregnant women, is the primary source of data on positive emotions (e.g., Mercer, 1986) and on emotional fluctuations in pregnancy. The media and other popular sources often depict pregnant women as displaying what one best-selling women's health guide calls "dramatic emotional changes" (Carlson, Eisenstat, & Ziporyn, 1996). Qualitative reports suggest that a portion of women do experience emotional lability during pregnancy (Leifer, 1980; Mercer, 1986), but there appears to be high interindividual variation. Furthermore, it is unknown whether emotional lability is any more common in pregnant women than in other groups. More controlled studies with repeated measures over the course of pregnancy are needed to examine emotional states in pregnant women and appropriate comparison groups.

A third type of study has employed standard measures of emotion in pregnant women, occasionally comparing sample means to population norms. Studies of this type have focused almost exclusively on negative emotions, particularly anxiety and depression, although "distress" (e.g., Hedegaard, Henriksen, Sabroe, & Secher, 1993) and "tension" (e.g., Elliott, Rugg, Watson, & Brough, 1983; Mercer & Ferketich, 1988) have been measured in a few studies. These quantitative studies of prenatal state anxiety and prenatal depression yield information about normative levels of negative emotion in pregnant women and to some extent about stability and change in negative emotion over the course of pregnancy.

Prenatal State Anxiety

Studies using standardized measures such as the State–Trait Anxiety Inventory (STAI; Spielberger, 1983) have produced extremely similar estimates of prenatal levels of state anxiety, and the levels reported are close to published norms for these instruments for nonpregnant women (e.g., Crandon, 1979; Molfese, Bricker, Manion, Beadnell et al., 1987; Pagel, Smilkstein, Regen, & Montano, 1990;

Park, Moore, Turner, & Adler, 1997). Thus, on average, pregnant women in these studies do not appear to experience elevated anxiety. However, study participants have been mostly socioeconomically advantaged, White, and married or partnered. There is conflicting evidence about whether anxiety is greater in women of lower socioeconomic status or in other demographically at-risk groups (e.g., Norbeck & Anderson, 1989a; Pond & Kemp, 1992).

There is a high degree of interindividual variability in anxiety in these studies. For example, variation from the mean by approximately 10 or 11 points on the STAI appears to be common in samples of pregnant women, and is approximately equal to the standard deviation derived from population norms. Thus, levels of anxiety in both pregnant and nonpregnant women commonly range within a spread of approximately 20 points (10 points below the mean to 10 points above), which constitutes about a third of the entire STAI response range. In essence, these data indicate that there are fairly large differences in anxiety from woman to woman, whether pregnant or not.

A few studies have assessed anxiety at multiple time points, providing a way to examine whether prenatal anxiety is stable across the 9-month period. These studies also enable determination of whether using single assessments offers valid estimates of prenatal emotion. Although studies employing repeated measurement have utilized samples of quite different composition, there is an impressive convergence of evidence that state anxiety is fairly stable across pregnancy (Elliott et al., 1983; Lobel & Dunkel-Schetter, 1990; Norbeck & Anderson, 1989a; Perkin, Bland, Peacock, & Anderson, 1993; Zax, Sameroff, & Farnum, 1975). One of the most methodologically rigorous and comprehensive of these investigations was conducted among married, working-class urbanites in Britain (Elliott et al., 1983). For the sample as a whole, no significant change in anxiety was observed across pregnancy. However, the authors noted that variance in individual patterns of change was "striking." That is, some women did experience changes in anxious emotion, although as Elliott et al. cautioned, these patterns of change are difficult to interpret and individual variation across pregnancy was not associated with any particular maternal characteristics.

Three older studies have been cited frequently as demonstrating variation in anxiety levels during pregnancy, but on close examination, they offer little evidence to support this claim (Edwards & Jones, 1970; Gorsuch & Key, 1974; Lubin, Gardener, & Roth, 1975). For example, Lubin et al. found an exceptionally small (1.5 points out of a 21-point range), but statistically significant, difference between anxiety in the second trimester compared to the first or third trimesters using one measure. But they found no difference on a second standard measure of anxiety between trimesters. Furthermore, anxiety in this sample was low and comparable to population levels. The remaining two studies found small changes in anxiety over time, but neither study examined whether the changes were statistically significant. For participants in both of these studies, anxiety scores at virtually every time point were well within one standard deviation of the population norm.

To summarize, across samples with great variability in socioeconomic status, racial characteristics, marital status, medical risk, and parity, a consistent pattern of temporal variation in anxiety over the course of pregnancy does not appear to exist. Women experience normal levels of anxiety throughout their pregnancy, although a minority of women experience some changes over time. However, even for these women, there does not appear to be a consistent pattern of variation associated with the progression of pregnancy.

Prenatal Depression

As with data on anxiety during pregnancy, information about depression is available almost exclusively from investigations conducted for other purposes. These studies, less numerous than those of anxiety, concur that most women do not experience clinical levels of depression during pregnancy. The more recent studies indicate that mean scores on the Beck Depression Inventory, the most common measure used, are below cutoffs for mild depression (Cameron et al., 1996; Molfese, Bricker, Manion, Beadnell et al., 1987; O'Hara, Zekoski, Philipps, & Wright, 1990; Steer, Scholl, Hediger, & Fischer, 1992). Older studies (reviewed by Kaplan, 1986) and those using other depression measures (Elliott et al., 1983; Lubin et al., 1975; Mercer & Ferketich, 1988; Neter, Collins, Lobel, & Dunkel-Schetter, 1995; Perkin et al., 1993; Rofe, Lewin, & Padeh, 1981) also find that the majority of women do not report depression. Similarly, in the few studies examining prenatal depression at multiple time points, it appears to be fairly stable for the majority of women (Cameron et al., 1996; Chapman, Hobfoll, & Ritter, 1997; Elliott et al., 1983; Lubin et al., 1975; and see review by Kaplan, 1986), although there are notable exceptions (e.g., O'Hara et al., 1990).

O'Hara and colleagues (1990) have demonstrated the importance of distinguishing between major depression, minor depression, and depressive symptomatology or dysphoric mood in pregnant women. They found that pregnant women are not more likely to exhibit clinically notable levels of depression (minor or major) than nonpregnant women, but they do experience more depressive symptomatology, especially in late pregnancy. Thus, according to these results, pregnant women are likely to experience some emotional distress during the last trimester, but not at levels considered harmful or requiring clinical intervention.

The next section considers the specific pregnancy and birth outcomes that may be influenced by emotional state during pregnancy, as well as by the other psychosocial and psychobiological factors mentioned earlier.

PREGNANCY AND BIRTH OUTCOMES

The study of stress processes in pregnancy involves a wide continuum of possible variables and outcomes for study. These can be broadly classified by the time of their occurrence into *prenatal, labor and delivery,* and *postpartum* periods. This developmental continuum can be extended to include prepregnancy conditions such as infertility and, at the other end of the continuum, parenting and child development outcomes. Factors of interest during pregnancy can be further classified into maternal factors versus fetal and neonatal factors (see Table 30.1). *Maternal prenatal* variables include prenatal affect and well-being and maternal complications such as gestational diabetes and pregnancy-induced hypertension. *Maternal labor and delivery* outcomes include variables such as length of labor, mode of delivery, use of analgesia and anesthesia, and dysfunctions of labor. *Maternal postpartum* variables include postpartum depression, postpartum medical complications such as maternal hemorrhaging, and parenting variables such as difficulty in breastfeeding or caring for the infant. *Fetal variables* include growth and development parameters and fetal neurobehavioral maturation. *Infant outcomes* (at and after birth) include birth complications and infant health and behavior. Another important infant outcome is *birth weight,* which is described further later.

An outcome of special interest cuts across these categories because it involves both mother and fetus (i.e., the maternal–fetal unit), as well as pregnancy and delivery. This outcome is the *timing of delivery,* also referred to as *length of gestation. Preterm birth* (delivery before 37 weeks gestation) is one of the major causes of *low birth weight* (less than or equal to 2,500 grams). Fetuses with less time in utero have less time to grow and develop normally. Thus, infants born preterm, especially very preterm (under 35 weeks), are more likely to be low in birth weight. Low birth weight infants in turn are at risk for many complications medically and developmentally (Newnham, 1998; Thompson et al., 1997). Most notably, very low birth weight babies are at significantly higher risk for infant mortality. Preterm delivery and low birth weight are among the largest contributors to infant mortality (McCormick, 1985). Thus, infant mortality, low birth weight, and preterm delivery constitute important targets for programmatic public health efforts (Alexander, 1998; Berendes, Kessel, & Yaffe, 1991; Paneth, 1995; Shiono & Behrman, 1995).

Of special interest in studying pregnancy and birth in the United States is the nation's very high rate of low birth weight (and preterm delivery) relative to other industrialized nations. The United States compares unfavorably to 36 countries reporting infant mortality data to the World Health Organization (25th), with 8.4% of infants born at low birth weight in the United States each year. This rate has been climbing steadily over the past 10 years, and there are stable and important demographic differences with rates of low birth weight as high as 13% in non-Hispanic Blacks, 9.4% in Puerto Ricans living in the continental United States, and closer to 6% in other groups (David & Collins, 1997). Similarly, rates of preterm delivery are disproportionately high in non-Hispanic Blacks (Rowley, Hogue, Blackmore, Ferre, Hatfield-Timajchy, Branch, & Atrash, 1993).

Very low socioeconomic status is one contributor to risk of low birth weight in the United States, but it does not appear to account for all the variation among groups in the population (Frisbie, Biegler, deTurk, Forbes, & Pullum, 1997). Psychosocial factors have shown impressive power to predict variation in birth weight when demographic differences such as age, education, income, and race/ethnicity are controlled (Copper et al., 1996; Goldenberg et al., 1991; Herrera, Salmeron, & Hurtado, 1997; Paarlberg, Vingerhoets, Passchier, Dekker, & Van Geijn, 1995; Orr et al., 1996; Shiono, Rauh, Park, Lederman, & Zuskar, 1997; Zimmer-Gembeck & Helfand, 1996). Thus, biopsychosocial models of birth weight and preterm delivery are currently the most accepted and most researched models in this area, having edged out narrower biomedical models some time ago. Work has focused on the link

TABLE 30.1
Schema for the Clarification of Outcomes in Perinatal Research

Developmental Continuum	Maternal	Fetal and Infant
Prepregnancy	Ob-Gyn conditions (e.g., infertility)	(Not applicable)
Prenatal (prepartum)	Pregnancy loss Medical complications Neuroendocrine, immune, and hemodynamic parameters Affect and well-being Health behaviors	Fetal growth Neuroendocrine, immune, and hemodynamic parameters Fetal neurobehavioral development
Labor & Delivery (intrapartum)	Analgesia Mode of delivery Abnormal labor Gestational length and preterm delivery	Fetal distress Neonatal complications (respiration, asphyxia) Infant birthweight
Post-birth (postpartum and first years of life)	Medical complications Depression & "blues" Caregiving/parenting Breastfeeding	Infant health Infant development

between psychosocial factors (especially stress) and preterm delivery and low birth weight. These outcomes are the focus of the following review on stress and birth outcomes.

THE ETIOLOGY OF PRETERM DELIVERY AND LOW BIRTH WEIGHT

The etiology of preterm delivery is not well understood (Adams, Sarno, Harlass, Rawlings, & Read, 1995; Moore et al., 1994), although it is believed that early delivery may occur as a result of more than one disorder or pathway. There are at least two categories of preterm birth that appear to have somewhat different etiologies (Berkowitz, Blackmore-Prince, Lapinski, & Savitz, 1998; Meis, 1998). *Spontaneous preterm birth* appears to account for approximately three quarters of all preterm births and may be accompanied by preterm labor or preterm rupture of membranes (Klebanoff, 1998). Early labor or rupture of membranes may occur due to infection or other causes (Bryant-Greenwood, Millar, Yamamoto, Bogic, & Tashima, 1998). *Indicated preterm birth* accounts for the remaining one quarter of preterm births. These result from complications leading to mandated delivery by either Caesarian section or labor induction with or without Cesarean section. Studies of preterm delivery may look at whether the delivery occurred at less than 37 weeks, or they may use a more stringent criterion such as 35 weeks. Other research examines *gestational age* (also referred to as *gestational length*) in weeks (or days) as a continuous variable. Similarly, studies of *low birth weight* may examine infants of 2,500 grams or less, or may use the more stringent category of very *low birth weight* infants of 1,500 grams or less. They may also examine the continuous distribution of birth weight in grams.

At least two processes appear to be intertwined here. The length of gestation and the weight of the infant are highly correlated, typically sharing approximately 10% to 30% variance. This reflects the fact that the etiology of low birth weight involves processes that contribute to fetal growth and growth retardation independent of preterm delivery. In order to disentangle the processes leading to preterm delivery from those leading to fetal growth retardation, birth weight as an outcome variable must be examined after controlling for the length of gestation. Very little research has addressed this issue in analyses. Research on either of these two endpoints (PTD and LBW) is useful in understanding the possible contribution of stress to adverse outcomes of pregnancy and research that takes both length of gestation and birth weight into account is especially valuable.

STRESS AS AN INDEPENDENT RISK FACTOR FOR ADVERSE OUTCOMES

Since the 1970s, many empirical studies have been published addressing the role of stress in preterm delivery, infant birth weight, and related outcomes. Studies in the past 10 years have been the most sophisticated with larger samples, better measures, and more controlled analyses that address the issues of confounding and independence of any effects of stress. This is a very rapidly developing area of research with growing interest in medicine and public health.

However, differences in design and samples across investigations continue to make it difficult to compare results. For example, characteristics of samples vary in the nationality, ethnicity, social class, risk status, and parity (birth history) of pregnant women. The number and timing of prenatal assessments varies from single assessments at various times in gestation to repeated assessments, most often in the second or third trimester. Few studies conduct assessments in the first trimester, which may be a particularly vulnerable time for effects of stress on some birth outcomes (e.g., birth defects). At the same time, early prenatal assessment creates biases in sampling because socioeconomically disadvantaged women are much less likely to be in prenatal care at this point (Gazmararian et al., 1996). Most studies conduct prenatal assessments late in pregnancy with the advantage of lowering attrition and loss prior to collection of labor and delivery data. The disadvantage of this approach is that women delivering preterm can then be missing prenatal data by virtue of having already delivered their infants. Thus, the issues involved in selecting a research design are very complex and are important to consider in evaluating the research.

Conceptualizations of stress have been quite diverse in this literature, including assessments of stress exposure, emotional responses, and appraisals of stress (Lobel & Dunkel-Schetter, 1990). Self-report methods are the norm, due mainly to the difficulty of measuring stress more objectively, but there are also advantages of a phenomenological approach to studying stress (Cohen, Kessler, & Gordon, 1995; Lazarus & Folkman, 1984). Life events and state anxiety are the constructs most often assessed, but measures of depression and generalized distress also appear in the literature. In addition to these, quite a few studies have focused on occupational stress and physical strain or exertion (see Woo, 1997, for a review). This work is relevant but not as well developed as research on life stress. Nonetheless, distinguishing physical exertion from psychological stress is very important to understanding mechanisms. Adverse outcomes may result from physical strain in strenuous daily activities or from perceiving that the demands of life stressors exceed people's coping capacity. It is unlikely that physical strain and appraised stress have the same effects on physiology and outcomes of pregnancy.

Finally, many studies include other constructs such as mastery or self-esteem in approaches to understanding stress and birth outcomes. Sometimes these psychosocial variables are combined with stress variables into broader psychosocial risk indices (e.g., Nuckolls, Kaplan, & Cassel, 1992). It can be argued that this strategy maximizes empirical predictive power at the expense of theoretical clarity, which is only obtained by examining stress variables and related moderators and mediators separately.

Existing research has not yet focused on chronic stress and its effects on pregnancy, despite plausible mechanisms whereby chronic stress might influence both fetal growth and preterm labor and delivery. Some work has included an instrument assessing perceived stress (PSS; Cohen, Kamarck, & Mermelstein, 1983; Cohen & Williamson, 1988). Although not designed to assess chronic stress per se, this instrument appears to capture the extent to which a woman feels overwhelmed by stress from any and all sources, unable to cope with or control the stress, and emotionally distressed. This scale has been associated with both gestational length and birth weight (Lobel, Dunkel-Schetter, & Scrimshaw, 1992; Zambrana et al., 1997). Additional research incorporating direct approaches to the study of chronic stress in pregnancy (Lepore, 1995) would be very valuable.

Several review articles have been published, each addressing certain aspects of the literature on stress and birth outcomes (Istvan, 1986; R. P. Lederman, 1986; Levin & DeFrank, 1988; Lobel, 1994). Some address stress as a risk factor for low birth weight specifically (Brooks-Gunn, 1991; McAnarney & Stevens-Simon, 1990). In a comprehensive review on the determinants of low birth weight, Kramer (1987) concluded cautiously that "stress and anxiety may provoke pre-term labour in some susceptible women" (p. 684), and they are important risk factors to study along with physical activity, maternal employment, antenatal care, and genital tract infection.

Since the publication of this review, newer evidence strengthens the case that stress is a risk factor for preterm labor and delivery. Approximately 20 studies on stress and preterm delivery, most of which are well controlled, have appeared since 1986. For example, Nordentoft et al. (1996) studied 2,432 Danish women at 20 weeks gestation using the most sophisticated life events assessment methods available (i.e., those of Brown & Harris, 1978). They found that severity of life events was associated with preterm delivery after controlling for education, age, and cohabitation. Similarly, Hedegaard, Henriksen, Secher, Hatch, and Sabroe (1996) found that the presence of one or more highly stressful life events during pregnancy was associated with risk of preterm delivery in 5,873 Danish women studied prospectively. Together these studies and others provide fairly convincing evidence that life event exposure may pose a risk for preterm delivery, although the risk ratios were relatively small.

Other studies using measures of stress other than life events support the role of stress in the etiology of preterm delivery. In a multicenter study of 2,593 women in the United States who were assessed at approximately 26 weeks gestation, a two-item stress measure (part of a larger psychosocial risk index) was significantly associated with preterm delivery after controlling for race, age, marital status, insurance, education, and substance abuse (Copper et al., 1996). The two items were "There is a great deal of nervous strain associated with my daily activities" and "In general, I am very tense and nervous." The content of this measure raises the question of whether stress as a risk factor is based in environmental circumstances or is more reflective of personality predispositions of women. That is, the risk may lie either in the exposure to stressors or in the patterns of appraising and responding to stressors. Some contribution from each is expected within a transactional model of stress (Lazarus & Folkman, 1984). However, this issue has been addressed to some extent.

Lobel, Dunkel-Schetter, and Scrimshaw (1992) studied 130 pregnant women from early gestation throughout pregnancy with assessments at every prenatal visit. Multiple measures of stress (including life events, state anxiety, and perceived stress) were included in each assessment. Structural equation modeling methods were used to combine stress variables into a latent factor, providing the advantages of minimizing the effects of measurement error and using a common core of shared variance among stress measures as the predictor of outcomes (Lobel & Dunkel-Schetter, 1990). The best latent factor to represent stress was composed of state anxiety, perceived stress, and ratings of perceived distress from life events. The total number of life events (or exposure alone) did not correlate with the latent factor or with outcomes. However, the latent stress factor predicted both birth weight and gestational age at delivery after controlling for medical risk factors including smoking.

In a subsequent study, Wadhwa, Sandman, Porto, Dunkel-Schetter, and Garite (1993) included a more contextually based measure of stress in which anxiety and concerns about the pregnancy were assessed in questionnaires administered to 90 pregnant women. In contrast to more general stress or anxiety measures, a 5-item index assessing *pregnancy anxiety* was most significantly associated with risk of early labor and delivery. Recently, these results have been replicated in studies in which life events, state anxiety, perceived stress, and pregnancy anxiety were measured in structured interviews with two samples of pregnant women. In both samples, results indicate that pregnancy anxiety is an important component of stress in predicting preterm delivery (Dunkel-Schetter, 1998). For example, Rini et al. (1999) found that pregnancy anxiety and state anxiety were moderately intercorrelated. When modeled as a latent factor, this anxiety factor predicted length of gestation in a sample of 230 women (half Hispanic and half non-Hispanic White) after controlling for the effects of obstetric and sociodemographic risk factors.

In addition, this study distinguished psychosocial resources (i.e., self-esteem, mastery, and dispositional optimism) from stress variables by assessing the former with standard scales and combining the scores into a latent factor. Labeled *personal resources,* this factor significantly predicted birth weight. Thus, stress was associated with length of gestation and not with intrauterine growth, whereas personal resources (mastery, self-esteem, optimism) were associated with birth weight and not length of gestation. Prior studies reporting significant associations between stress and birth weight or intrauterine growth have not controlled for personality factors or personal resources such as these, nor have they addressed the issue of confounding of different psychosocial constructs in multivariate analyses (e.g. Goldenberg et al., 1991). Possible mechanisms explaining these effects are discussed in the next section, but briefly, it seems likely that different mechanisms are involved. Neuroendocrine and immune pathways are implicated in the stress–preterm findings in the literature, whereas behavioral pathways appear to be more promising in linking personality (or personal resources) and birth weight. As noted earlier, pinpointing the mechanisms responsible for links between psychosocial factors and birth outcomes is critical.

MECHANISMS OF STRESS–BIRTH OUTCOMES EFFECTS

There are two major classes of mechanisms through which psychosocial factors such as stress influence health in humans: a direct, physiological pathway mediated primarily by central and peripheral stress responses of the nervous, endocrine, and immune systems; and an indirect, behavioral pathway mediated by health-related behaviors such as smoking, alcohol and drug abuse, nutrition, exercise and physical activity, and reduced compliance or adherence to other aspects of health care. Each of these possible mechanisms is discussed in the context of the effects of maternal psychosocial factors on pregnancy outcomes.

Physiological Mechanisms

The responses of the nervous, endocrine, and immune systems to psychological stress are well-established (see, e.g., Axelrod & Reisine, 1984; Herbert & Cohen, 1993, for reviews) and have been proposed as central mechanisms linking psychosocial factors to health outcomes (Chrousos & Gold, 1992; McEwen, 1998). Several researchers have suggested that stress-related responses of the neuro-immuno-endocrine axis during pregnancy may contribute to adverse outcomes such as preterm birth, fetal growth restriction/low birth weight, and neurodevelopmental deficits. For instance, elevated levels of hypothalamic, pituitary, and placental stress hormones have been implicated in the initiation of preterm labor and delivery (Hobel, Dunkel-Schetter, & Roesch, 1998; McLean et al., 1995; Wadhwa, Porto, Garite, Chicz-DeMet, & Sandman, 1998). The immunosuppressive effects of stress and hypothalamic-pituitary-adrenal (HPA) activation may increase susceptibility to infection (DeSouza, 1993; Jemmot & Locke, 1984), which in turn plays a role in the etiology of premature rupture of membranes and preterm birth (Garite, 1994; Lockwood, 1994; Romero et al., 1994). Vasoconstriction and hypoxia in response to sympathetic-adrenal-medullary (SAM) activation decrease uteroplacental perfusion, and may thereby contribute to fetal growth restriction and low birth weight (Cosmi, Luzi, Gori, & Chiodi, 1990; Myers, 1975; Shepherd, Stanczyk, Bethea, & Novy, 1992).

Stress-related processes involving the nervous, endocrine, and immune systems may also play an important role in embryonic and fetal brain development (Glover, 1997). Normal brain development requires precise interactions between environmental signals and genes that regulate cell differentiation, migration, and circuit formation. Experimental studies using animal models have demonstrated that intrauterine environmental influences, including alterations in the biochemical milieu effected by stress, stress hormones, immune products, and vascular dynamics, can modulate cell fate choice and neuronal growth, with permanent consequences for cognitive, affective, and behavioral outcomes over the life span (Wadhwa, 1998).

To date, there have been very few systematic investigations of these physiological processes as potential mediators of the prenatal stress and pregnancy outcome link in humans. A few studies have examined the association between catecholamines and anxiety at the onset of labor (e.g., R. P. Lederman, E. Lederman, Work, & McCann, 1985), and between catecholamines and physical activity during pregnancy (e.g., Katz, Jenkins, Haley, & Bowes, 1991). In one study (Dorn, Susman, & Petersen, 1993), a sample of 40 pregnant adolescents was assessed during the middle and latter part of gestation and postpartum. Subjects with an increase in cortisol levels across a 40-minute period measured before 20 weeks gestation and again at 2 to 3 weeks postpartum had fewer symptoms of anxiety and depression than subjects with no cortisol increase. There was, however, no relation between cortisol and symptoms of anxiety or depression at the 34 to 36 week gestation assessment. In a sample of 54 adult pregnant women, maternal plasma levels of the principal pituitary-adrenal stress hormones (adrenocorticotropin hormone, ACTH; ß-endorphin. bE; and cortisol) measured at the beginning of the third trimester of pregnancy were significantly correlated with psychosocial factors. Subjects reporting higher levels of prenatal stress had higher plasma levels of ACTH and cortisol, whereas subjects reporting higher levels of social support had lower plasma levels of ACTH and cortisol. After controlling for the effects of factors known to influence hormone levels during pregnancy, including gestational age, circadian variation, and obstetric risk, a combination of maternal psychosocial and sociodemographic factors accounted for 36% of the variance in ACTH, 13% of the variance in cortisol, and 3% of the variance in bE (Wadhwa, Dunkel-Schetter, Chicz-DeMet, Porto, & Sandman, 1996). Another study addressed the link between maternal psychosocial factors and immune parameters. In a sample of 72 pregnant women, high levels of stress and low or inadequate social support were associated with depression of lymphocyte activity (Herrera, Alvarado, & Martinez, 1988).

With reference to fetal outcomes, again, a very small number of studies have examined the relations between maternal psychosocial factors and fetal physiology. Recently, a series of longitudinal studies were conducted by DiPietro and colleagues to study the functional development of the fetal central nervous system over the course of gestation and to identify risk factors for neurodevelopmental delays (DiPietro, Hodgson, Costigan, Hilton, & Johnson, 1996a, 1996b). In these studies, the sequence and characteristics of fetal neurobehavioral development and maturation (i.e., fetal autonomic, motoric, state, and interactive functioning) were assessed serially at six time points between 20 and 38 weeks gestation. Findings indicated that chronic maternal psycho logical distress was significantly associated with delayed and impaired neurobehavioral maturation of the fetus—that is, greater maternal stress was associated with reduced fetal heart rate variability and reduced coupling between fetal heart rate and movement (DiPietro et al., 1996a, 1996b). In another study of 37 women, maternal levels of trait anxiety were significantly associated with uteroplacental and fetal blood flow. Using measures of pulsatility index (PI) derived from doppler flow studies of the umbilical and fetal middle cerebral artery at from 37 to 40 weeks gestation, results indicated that fetuses of mothers with high trait anxiety had significantly higher PI values in the umbilical artery, significantly lower PI values in the fetal middle cerebral artery, and a significantly lower cerebro-umbilical PI ratio (signs of fetal hypoxia and compensatory redistribution of blood flow to the fetal brain; Sjostrom, Valentin, Thelin, & Marsal, 1997).

Finally, one study with a sample of 40 low risk pregnant women examined maternal blood pressure responses to a laboratory-based behavioral stressor (interactive arithmetic task) during pregnancy. Infant birth outcomes were subsequently obtained from medical records. Results indicated that mothers with greater psychophysiological stress reactivity (in this case, larger diastolic blood pressure responses to behavioral stress) delivered infants with significantly lower birth weights and decreased gestational age (McCubbin et al., 1996).

Two sets of issues warrant consideration when thinking about physiological mediators of the effects of maternal psychosocial factors in pregnancy. First, progressive changes that occur in maternal physiology over the course of gestation may produce changes in the typical pattern of biological responses to stress. For example, neuroendocrine alterations in pregnancy, which are characterized by the evolution of a transient endocrine unit, the placenta, and by modification of negative feedback mechanisms, result in a significant and progressive increase in plasma concentrations of HPA and placental hormones (corticotropin-releasing hormone, CRH; adrenocorticotropic hormone, ACTH; beta-endorphin, bE; cortisol; estrogens; progesterone) over the course of gestation (Petraglia, Florio, Nappi, & Genazzani, 1996). These increases of peripherally circulating hormones may exert inhibitory influences on the hypothalamus and pituitary, and thereby attenuate endocrine responsivity to exogenous stimuli (Goland, Conwell, Warren, & Wardlaw, 1992; Schulte, Weidner, & Allolio, 1990). Similarly, cardiovascular alterations in pregnancy, which include a progressive diminution of the sensitivity of baroreceptor reflex mechanisms and an increase in plasma volume with advancing gestation (Monga & Creasy, 1994), may result in a blunted sympathetic (noradrenergic) response to exogenous stimuli (Barron, Mujais, Zinaman, Bravo, & Lindheimer, 1986).

Consistent with this premise, studies of physiological reactivity in pregnancy have reported attenuated responses to exogenous challenges. For instance, pregnancy has been associated with blunted sympathetic-adrenal-medullary responses, including vascular responses to norepinephrine and epinephrine infusion (Nisell, Hjemdahl, & Linde, 1985); blunted heart rate and catecholamine responses to physical maneuvers such as standing, upright tilt, isometric handgrip, and cold pressor (Barron et al., 1986; Nisell, Hjemdahl, Linde, & Lunell, 1985a, 1985b); blunted plasma renin activity response to thermal stress (Vaha-Eskeli, Erkkola, Scheinin, & Seppanen, 1992); and blunted blood pressure responses to physical and mental challenges (Matthews & Rodin, 1992). Attenuated HPA responses have also been reported in late gestation, including ACTH and cortisol responses to administration of exogenous CRH in humans and baboons (Goland et al., 1992; Schulte et al., 1990). A recent preliminary study of maternal physiological responses to behavioral stress (speech/math task) at various gestational ages suggested, first, a progressive attenuation of the maternal psychophysiological stress response over the course of gestation, and second, that the degree of attenuation was accounted for in substantial part by maternal baseline stress hormone levels, namely, ACTH and cortisol (Wadhwa, Sandman, Chicz-DeMet, & Porto, 1997). At present, the function of these changes is not known, but these advances in stress pathophysiology research appear to be important to untangling the mechanisms involved in stress–outcome links.

The second set of issues relates to the ontogeny of fetal development. Fetal growth and development is a logarithmic process, with rapid mitosis at early stages and cellular hypertrophy and accumulation of fat, glycogen, and connective tissue later in gestation (Lockwood & Weiner, 1986). It is well-established that there are several sensitive or critical periods in development. The presence or absence of a particular experience at a critical period in the life cycle may exert an extraordinary and dramatic influence over structure and/or function well beyond that point in development. There may be critical periods during pregnancy when the developing fetus is especially vulnerable to pre- and perinatal insults (Bornstein, 1989; Dunkel-Schetter & Lobel, 1998). For example, the effects of hypoxia on the developing fetus not only depend on the severity and duration of hypoxia but also on the time period during gestation when hypoxia occurs. Although the effects of equivalent degrees of chronic hypoxia during early and late gestation on fetal growth restriction may appear to be similar in magnitude, hypoxia experienced early in gestation produces greater fetal nervous system disability than hypoxia experienced later in gestation, when mechanisms to evoke the brain-sparing effect have developed and are in place (Amiel-Tison & Pettigrew, 1991; Wadhwa, 1998). For these reasons, psychobiological interactions in models of pregnancy should not only incorporate explanations of mechanisms through which maternal signals are relayed to the placenta and/or fetus, but they should take into account alterations in maternal psychophysiological responses over the course of gestation and the fetal developmental time line.

Behavioral Mechanisms

The effects of prenatal health-related behaviors such as poor eating habits, smoking, alcohol, and drug abuse on fetal development are well-documented. An increased risk of spontaneous abortion, fetal growth restriction, preterm delivery, and cognitive and motor deficits of the central nervous system are among these (Abrams, 1994; Andres & Jones, 1994).

An emerging literature supports a significant role for psychosocial variables such as prenatal stress and depression in countertherapeutic health behaviors in pregnancy. For example, many studies between 1975 and 1997 examined the associations between maternal psychosocial factors and smoking, alcohol, or drug abuse in human pregnancy (Barnet, Duggan, Wilson, & Joffe, 1995; Borrelli, Bock, King, Pinto, & Marcus, 1996; Bresnahan, Zuckerman, & Cabral, 1992; Hutchins & DiPietro, 1997; McCormick et al., 1990; Pritchard, 1994; Zuckerman, Amaro, Bauchner, & Cabral, 1989). Most studies rely on self-reports of health behaviors, but a very small number include biological screens such as cotinine assays for smoking or toxicological assays for alcohol and other illicit drugs. Psychosocial factors examined in these studies include social support, depression, stress, maternal personality (self-esteem, locus of control, hostility, coping style), and whether the pregnancy was intended or unintended.

Approximately 80% of the studies reported significant associations between maternal psychosocial factors and prenatal health behaviors. Higher levels of prenatal stress or depression were associated with increased incidence of risk posing behaviors. Higher levels of social support were associated with decreased incidence of these behaviors. Among personality and individual difference variables, higher levels of self-esteem, locus of control, and an intended pregnancy were associated with decreased incidence, and higher levels of hostility and defensive coping style were associated with increased incidence of these behaviors, respectively. In addition to these correlational findings, emerging evidence suggests psychosocial factors such as stress, depression, and partner support may play an important role in the success of prenatal intervention programs to reduce the incidence of these behavioral practices (Ingersoll, Lu, & Haller, 1995; Wiemann & Berenson, 1998).

Overall, this literature provides strong support for the hypothesis that psychosocial factors are related to one or more of the risk posing behaviors in human pregnancy both because of the consistency of findings and because of methodological strengths of studies including the range of populations studied. The study samples were representative of the general population, and ranged from middle-class, married, Anglo women to low socioeconomic class, single, African American women and teenagers. The majority of the research is prospective and studies assess both psychosocial factors and health behaviors at one or more times during pregnancy.

MODERATORS OF STRESS–BIRTH OUTCOME EFFECTS

Not only is stress ubiquitous in the course of living, but pregnancy entails a number of changes that women may find stressful, as described earlier. However, the fact that pregnant women on average do not experience high levels of emotional distress suggests that intervening factors moderate the influences of prenatal stress on women's emotional state. These factors may account for individual differences among pregnant women in levels of prenatal anxiety and depression. Coping, or the way that women manage problems during pregnancy, is one likely factor. Social support is another commonly studied resource that may facilitate successful adaptation. Existing research on coping and social support in pregnancy is described next. It must be noted, however, that research on coping in pregnancy is in its infancy, whereas there is a considerable body of work on social support in pregnancy.

COPING IN PREGNANCY

A large number of studies substantiate that people who cope successfully with stressful situations are least likely to experience negative mood; conversely, maladaptive coping exacerbates or increases negative mood. The predominant view of coping is that it includes anything people do to manage problems or emotional responses, whether or not successful (Carver & Scheier, 1994; Lazarus & Folkman, 1984; Pearlin & Schooler, 1978). Despite a voluminous literature on coping within other health contexts, studies of coping in pregnancy have been rare.

Although this research is limited, the findings provide a fairly clear picture of the impact of the three most commonly studied types of coping: avoidance, problem solving, and positive appraisal. *Avoidant coping,* which involves behavioral or cognitive disengagement from problems, is associated with greater emotional distress in pregnancy (Hansell, 1993; Martinez, 1989; Perez, 1982; Spirito et al., 1991; Yali, 1998; Yali & Lobel, 1999). This corroborates a large body of work demonstrating the deleterious emotional impact of avoidant coping in a variety of populations (e.g., Aldwin & Revenson, 1987; Fleishman & Fogel, 1994; Stanton & Snider, 1993). Avoidance may exacerbate emotional distress in pregnant women because ironically, people often become preoccupied with the thoughts that they attempt to suppress, and because the inhibition of thoughts, feelings, and behaviors can cause autonomic arousal (cf. Lobel, Yali, Zhu, & DeVincent, 1998). Also, the use of avoidant coping requires sustained effort to screen out stressor-relevant cues (cf. Lazarus & Folkman, 1984); this can be taxing and is likely to deplete pregnant women's already limited physical energy. Avoidant coping may have harmful nonemotional consequences as well. For example, women who use avoidant coping may neglect to get appropriate assistance or necessary medical attention.

A second type of coping, labeled *problem solving, active coping,* or *approach-oriented coping,* tends to be effective in nonpregnant populations (e.g., Aspinwall & Taylor, 1992; Folkman, Lazarus, Dunkel-Schetter, DeLongis, & Gruen, 1986), but the evidence in pregnancy is mixed (see Hansell, 1993; Martinez, 1989; Spirito et al., 1991; Yali, 1998; Yali & Lobel, 1999). One reason is that active ways of coping may lead to an increased focus on problems, some of which may not be remediable in pregnancy. For example, Yali and Lobel (1999) found that women at high medical risk who coped by preparing for the baby (e.g., acquiring furniture and supplies) were emotionally worse off than women who did not cope in this way. They reasoned that this type of coping focuses attention on the baby, which is distressing among women whose pregnancy may not result in a healthy child. Although problem-focused coping strategies such as preparation are associated with positive outcomes in some stressful situations (Compas, Malcarne, & Fondacaro, 1988; Holahan & Moos, 1990, 1991; Roth & Cohen, 1986), they may not be efficacious for people facing imminent or severe threats (cf. Bolger, 1990; Carver & Scheier, 1994). Thus, coping through preparation and other types of problem solving may be more adaptive for pregnant women at low medical risk. This possibility has yet to be tested empirically.

Positive appraisal is the only type of coping that has consistently been associated with lower distress in pregnant women (Barth & Schinke, 1983; Perez, 1982; Spirito et al.,

1991; Yali, 1998; Yali & Lobel, 1999). This way of coping involves viewing a stressful situation positively, emphasizing what can be gained or what benefits might accrue from it. Positive appraisal has been shown to be an adaptive form of coping in a variety of populations undergoing stressful events (Dunkel-Schetter, Folkman, & Lazarus, 1987).

Issues of measurement are important considerations in research on prenatal coping. Standard versions of coping instruments such as the Ways of Coping, or the COPE (Carver, Scheier, & Weintraub, 1989; Folkman & Lazarus, 1985), may not be appropriate for use in pregnant women because they do not capture the situationally specific ways in which women may manage the strains and challenges of being pregnant and they contain some items inappropriate in the context of pregnancy. To address this issue, Lobel and colleagues developed a pregnancy-specific coping instrument that has been used in two samples of pregnant women of different socioeconomic, racial, and other composition (Lobel et al., 1998; Yali, 1998; Yali & Lobel, 1999). The Prenatal Coping Inventory (PCI) includes items from standard coping measures and items that pregnant women endorsed during open-ended interviews and pilot testing. Similar factors were derived from factor analyses of the PCI in both samples. These include factors reflecting preparation for motherhood, avoidance, positive appraisal, and prayer. The first three correspond to categories of coping that have been identified in the few previous studies of pregnant women. Prayer, a type of coping not examined previously, was the most frequently reported type of coping used by women in both of these studies. Unexpectedly, use of prayer was associated with increased emotional distress. The authors suggested that the type of prayer practiced by study participants may have been a form of rumination, which typically produces unfavorable emotional consequences (Nolen-Hoeksema, 1991; Nolen-Hoeksema & Morrow, 1993; Park & Cohen, 1993). The high reliance on prayer in these two studies in conjunction with its adverse impact highlight the value of further research on this coping strategy among pregnant women.

Although it serves as a useful starting point, several important questions about the impact of coping and the psychological mechanisms involved have yet to be addressed. For example, are pregnant women who cope with stress adaptively at lower risk for adverse birth outcomes? Conversely, does maladaptive coping with stress in pregnancy increase risk? What leads women to select and exercise particular ways of coping? Researchers have begun to look at the latter question by examining the role of disposition, or individual traits, and the role of appraisal, or the way that pregnant women evaluate their situation. They find that women who are dispositionally optimistic and those who view their pregnancy as controllable select more efficacious ways of coping, and thereby experience lower emotional distress (Yali, 1998). However, virtually nothing is known about how other types of dispositional characteristics or appraisal influence coping in pregnancy. Knowledge about these factors may help clinicians identify women at emotional risk in pregnancy and give us useful information about the sorts of coping training that might be effective for particular groups of women.

SOCIAL SUPPORT AND RELATIONSHIPS IN PREGNANCY

The birth of an infant is a major life event and transition for parents, and usually influences many others close to the baby's mother. By virtue of the ties of kinship, the extended families of both parents are often intricately involved in the pregnancy and may be major sources of support for the pregnant woman. Close interpersonal relationships and the social support derived from them influence how individuals cope with stress. Thus, these are important topics in the study of pregnancy (Berthiaume, David, Saucier, & Borgeat, 1998; Dunkel-Schetter et al., 1996; Elbourne & Oakley, 1991; Nuckolls et al., 1972). This chapter focuses primarily on the supportive aspects of close relationships and does not address other relationship issues such as marital satisfaction, intimacy, and commitment (for a review see Berscheid & Reis, 1998).

Although the association between social support and health has been well-documented (Cohen & Syme, 1985; House, 1987; B. R. Sarason, I. G. Sarason, & Gurung, 1997), research on the role of specific relationships and the mechanisms that might account for their association with healthier pregnancies has been limited. This section has reviewed correlational pregnancy research on global support, on specific sources or providers of support, on various functions or types of support, and on negative aspects of social relationships. The chapter concludes with a review of research on supportive interventions and on mechanisms whereby support may influence outcomes.

The term *social support* has been principally defined as either *available* or *perceived support,* or alternatively as *received* or *enacted support.* These terms differentiate between support individuals believe to be available if they should need it and the amount of support that they actually receive or report to have received (Barrera, 1986; Dunkel-Schetter & Bennett, 1990; Gottlieb, 1985). Beyond the distinction between perceived and received support, social support has been further categorized in many different (although not mutually exclusive) ways. For example, support can be distinguished by *function* or *type* of support (emotional, informational, instrumental). Other distinctions such as *global versus specific* support (support for general stressors or specific stressors) have also been used. Finally, categories may be created by focusing on who is providing the support (or *source of support*; e.g., spouse, family, friends, doctors, and medical staff). These different categories can be fit into a hierarchy with the general approach (received or perceived) as the primary dimension. Within each, the dimension of source of support can be distinguished and finally different types or functions of support can be embedded within each source (Schwarzer, Dunkel-Schetter, & Kemeny, 1994). For example, emotional support received from baby's father, or perceived emotional support from baby's father can be studied, and either received or perceived support can be studied with reference to family or friends.

As documented by a number of reviews (cf., Dunkel-Schetter et al., 1996; R. P. Lederman, 1995; Paarlberg et al., 1995; Scholl, Hediger, & Belsky, 1994), social support and close relationship processes play an important role in both the psychological well-being of pregnant women as well as in determining the course of labor and birth outcomes. A large number of correlational and experimental intervention studies have shown that, in general, social support is related to lower levels of stress, anxiety, and depression during pregnancy (Albrecht & Rankin, 1989; N. L. Collins et al., 1993; Clifford, Weaver, & Hays, 1989; Gurung, Dunkel-Schetter, Collins, & Hobel, 1998; MacDonald, Peacock, & Anderson, 1992; O' Hara, 1986; Thorpe, Dragonas, & Golding, 1992; Tilden, 1983; Zuckerman, Amaro, Bauchner, & Cabral, 1989). For example, Zuckerman et al. (1989) examined the effects of different types of support on depressive symptoms in a low income multiethnic sample and showed that total support was negatively related to reports of depressive symptoms. More recently, Berthiaume et al. (1998) interviewed 350 French Canadian women at the beginning of their second semester of pregnancy and found that satisfaction with social support was significantly related to lower levels of prepartum depression, as were employment and self-esteem.

In work on social support in pregnancy, several constructs have been conceptualized and measured and the best ways to combine these measures of social support have been investigated (e.g., N. L. Collins et al., 1993; Gurung et al., 1998). For example, Gurung et al. (1998) used structural equation modeling to compare competing models of support in pregnancy. Three main types of support (perceived, received, and network), two primary sources of support (friends/family and baby's father), and three major functions of support (tangible, informational, and advice) were measured. The best fitting model was one with two factors (one for each source of support), each with received and perceived support measures included and that collapsed across the type/function measures. The empirical validity of conceptualizing support primarily by source is also consistent with similar analyses of support measures and concepts in other contexts (e.g., men with HIV, Schwarzer et al., 1994).

SPECIFIC SOURCES OR PROVIDERS OF SOCIAL SUPPORT IN PREGNANCY

Past pregnancy research has both focused on different sources of support (Gurung et al., 1998; Davis, Rhodes, & Hamilton-Leaks, 1997; Sagrestano, Feldman, Rini, Woo, & Dunkel-Schetter, in press), and examined the positive and negative implications of perceiving or receiving social support from specific relationships or sources (Cramer & McDonald, 1996; Zimmermann-Tansella, Bertagni, Siani, & Micciolo, 1994). The major comparison is between support transactions at the level of a dyad (e.g., support provided to the baby's mother from the baby's father), versus at the level of a network or group (e.g., support provided by friends and family). Yet a different set of studies has focused on the impact of support from professional sources (e.g., nurses and doctors; Blondel, 1998).

The baby's father has been a critical focus of attention, and his role as a major source of support has been reported in a number of different studies (Casper & Hogan, 1990; N. L. Collins et al., 1993; Giblin, Poland, & Ager, 1990; Lantican & Corona, 1992; Zayas & Busch-Rossnagel, 1992). Social support from baby's father has been shown to significantly influence outcomes such as prenatal care utilization and emotional distress (e.g., Gurung et al., 1998; Hobfoll & Leiberman, 1987; Kalil et al., 1993; MacDonald et al., 1992; Norbeck & Anderson, 1989b; Norbeck, Lindsey, & Carrieri, 1981; Norbeck & Tilden, 1983; O'Hara, 1986; Tietjen & Bradley, 1985). For example, Sable, Stockbauer, Schramm, and Land (1990), in a sample of 1,464 women, showed that support from the baby's father was a stronger predictor of prenatal care than was support from others. Women who were at a greater risk for receiving inadequate prenatal care were African American, less educated, poor, had unwanted pregnancies, higher parity, and perhaps most importantly, were single (see also, Giblin et al., 1990).

Support from the baby's father has been found to be especially important among certain ethnic groups (e.g., Zambrana et al., 1997). For example, in a study of acculturation and psychosocial risk factors in pregnant Mexican American and Mexican immigrant women, Zambrana et al. (1997) found that support from the baby's father was associated with significantly less stress, less substance abuse, and more positive attitudes toward the pregnancy. These results further indicated that acculturation was a significant factor in relationship status, with Mexican-immigrant women being more likely to live with and be married to the baby's father than the more acculturated Mexican American women.

In contrast to the baby's father, support from the family does not seem to be as significant a predictor of pregnancy outcomes. Although the expected positive associations of family support with outcomes such as well-being and birth weight are seen, the relation with the initiation of health care, even among low income groups who might depend more on their families for material support, is not as uniform (Dunkel-Schetter et al., 1996; St. Clair, Smeriglio, Alexander, & Celantano, 1989; St. John & Winstin, 1989; Zambrana, Hernandez, Dunkel-Schetter, & Scrimshaw, 1991). However, this relation may vary depending on the age and ethnicity of the pregnant women. For example, Turner, Grindstaff, and Phillips (1990) found that family support is especially crucial for pregnant teenagers. Specifically, teenagers who reported higher levels of family support had babies with higher birth weights and experienced less postpartum depression. Similarly, Boyce, Schaefer, and Uitti (1985) showed that pregnant teenagers who perceived their family to be more helpful had fewer neonatal complications.

Studies of ethnic minority groups in the United States show that for some groups (e.g., African Americans, Latinas) the family is a critical source of support in pregnancy, particularly female relatives (Knouse, 1991; Zuniga, 1992). Mexican American families tend to live in close units with extensive bonds to other family units and the extended family serving as the primary source of support (Chilman, 1993, Keefe, Padilla, & Carlos, 1979). Similarly, the family is the most important source of support to African Americans (Cauce, Felner, & Primavera, 1982; Miller, 1992). In one of the most cited studies of ethnic differences in support, Norbeck and Anderson (1989b) measured life stress, social support, anxiety state, and substance use at mid- and late pregnancy in Hispanic, European American, and African American low income women. They found that none of the social support measures were significant predictors of gestational age, birth weight, or gestation and labor complications when the sample was analyzed as a whole. However, for African Americans, lack of social support from the woman's partner or mother was a significant predictor of gestational complications and of the likelihood of prolonged labor and cesarean section complications. For Whites, social support was significantly related to length of labor and to drug use, although high levels of social support were associated with longer labor. Similarly, White women with high stress and high support from relatives also had more delivery complications. None of the support measures were statistically significant predictors of complications or birth outcomes for the Hispanics.

In a direct test of ethnic differences in social support, Sagrestano et al. (in press) analyzed data from two multiethnic prospective studies of 246 and 504 African American, Latina, and non-Hispanic White pregnant women, and found strong ethnic differences in support from family and friends. Multivariate analyses of ethnic differences controlling for sociodemographic variables showed that African American women reported receiving the most support from family followed by Latinas and White women. However, White women reported more family members in their social networks than did Latinas. Furthermore, Latinas reported higher quality interactions with family.

How do the effects of support from different sources compare? In a recent study designed to answer this question, Gurung et al. (1998) compared the support received from the baby's father with that received from her friends and family in an ethnically diverse sample of 480 women (African American, Latin American, and non-Hispanic White). Various types of support measures were assessed at multiple time points before the birth, together with standard measures of depression and anxiety. Different sources of support were associated with different outcomes. Specifically, social support from the baby's father predicted significantly less anxiety but not significant differences in depressed mood. Support from the mother's friends and family were significant predictors of maternal depressed mood, but did not predict anxiety (cf. Kalil et al., 1993). Social support from the baby's father predicted maternal changes in anxiety independent of sociodemographic variables such as age, ethnicity, and SES and individual difference measures such as mastery and coping. This difference in support effects by source is consistent with the theory and some results in the social support literature indicating that support is most effective when there is a match between the type of support a person needs and the type provided (e.g., Cutrona, 1990) for support to be effective. Others discuss the existence of an optimal support provider for different specific needs (Cantor, 1979; Litwak, 1985).

Taken together, these results present a compelling set of findings for pregnancy researchers and health psychologists, suggesting that different sources of support cannot be thought of as interchangeable. Support from the baby's father has been shown to be significantly related to less stress, anxiety and depression, better utilization of prenatal care, and better birth outcomes even when other sources of support are available. Focusing on support from specific sources (e.g., partners and spouses) has greatly advanced the understanding of stress and coping with chronic and terminal illnesses like cancer and AIDS (e.g., Hays, Turner, & Coates, 1992; Helgeson & Cohen, 1996). Similarly, the documented positive impact of support from the baby's father on pregnancy outcomes opens up new avenues of research in which the father may be more central. Furthermore, studies with greater emphasis on close relationship processes and those that include both the pregnant mother and the baby's father in their designs, currently an uncommon procedure in prenatal research, will undoubtedly prove to be highly effective in advancing prediction of psychological, labor, and birth outcomes in pregnancy. In summary, whereas support from the baby's father seems generally effective, support from friends and family is only effective for certain samples, such as teenagers and certain ethnic groups (including African American and Latinas).

FUNCTIONS OR TYPES OF SOCIAL SUPPORT IN PREGNANCY

Three functional aspects of social support have been most commonly studied and primarily as received support: instrumental (tangible or material) support, informational (or advice) support, and emotional support. Some studies on pregnancy included analyses of several functions of support. For example, Norbeck and Tilden (1983) compared the different functions of support in a group of low risk pregnant women and found moderating effects of instrumental support and indirect effects of emotional and informational support on pregnancy outcomes. Low support was detrimental, although the effects varied as a function of stress level. Women who reported high stress during pregnancy and low levels of instrumental support experienced more infant and gestation complications (e.g., premature labor and poor infant status), whereas women who reported low tangible support in the context of low stress during pregnancy reported more labor and delivery problems (e.g., prolonged labor and cesarean delivery).

N. L. Collins et al. (1993) measured four types of social support (material aid, assistance with tasks, advice and information, and the amount of listening) and computed partial correlations between the four types and four outcomes (birth weight, abnormal labor, postpartum depression, and a 5-minute Apgar) controlling for many factors. Results indicated that a relation between greater support and higher Apgar scores was due to receipt of prenatal task and informational support rather than emotional support. Furthermore, the association of social support with labor progress was primarily a function of task and material support. Finally, although an overall index of the four types of support did not relate to depression, women who received more material support tended to be less depressed after childbirth.

In general, evidence suggests that different types of support are likely to be beneficial in pregnancy, although it is important to factor in the context and stressfulness of the situations in which it is offered (Dunkel-Schetter, Blasband, Feinstein, & Herbert, 1992).

NEGATIVE ASPECTS OF CLOSE RELATIONSHIPS IN PREGNANCY

A discussion of the association between close relationships and psychological well-being and health outcomes during pregnancy cannot be complete without a consideration of the negative aspects of relationships. Whereas a majority of past research has emphasized the health promoting effects of social support, there has been rising concern that the absence of negative social interactions may be even more important for mental health (Cutrona, 1996; Schuster, Kessler, & Aseltine, 1990). Emerging findings from research in the area of marital conflict and close relationships suggests that support from romantic partners and families can have negative as well as positive consequences (Pasch & Bradbury, 1998; Ramsey, Abell, & Baker, 1986; Rook, 1992). Cramer and McDonald (1996) interviewed 42 young low income mothers and found that although family assistance helps many teenagers who have to cope with the challenges of poverty and childrearing, such support was perceived to entail conflict, stress, frustration, and disappointment due to interpersonal tensions, conflicting interests, or relatives with limited ability to provide support. They also found a consistent discrepancy between the young mother's high expectations and her support network's lower performance. Rhodes and Woods (1995) found similar results in a study of 157 pregnant minority teenagers whose network members were the sources of interpersonal problems (including criticism, intrusiveness, conflict, and disappointment) and support. These studies illustrate the frequently noted dual nature of supportive relationships, that is, their capacity to be beneficial and harmful.

Evidence of the darker side of close personal relationships also comes from newer literature on violence during pregnancy (Ballard et al., 1998; McFarlane, Parker, & Soeken, 1996a). Although no pregnancy outcome was consistently found to be associated with violence during pregnancy in a review by Petersen, Gazmararian, Spitz, and Rowley (1997), one study (McFarlane, Parker, & Soeken, 1996b) found that abuse during pregnancy was a significant risk for low birth weight as well as maternal low weight gain, infections, anemia, smoking, and use of alcohol and drugs (see also Parker, McFarlane, & Soeken, 1994). Of greater importance is the fact that abuse and violence during pregnancy appear to be quite common. A review by Gazmararian et al. (1996) indicates that the prevalence of violence during pregnancy ranges from 9% to 20%. Similarly, McFarlane, Parker, and Soeken (1996b) found that the prevalence of physical or sexual abuse during pregnancy was high (16%). Estimates of violence in women in general are generally somewhat lower than these rates. In fact, family violence may be a more common problem for pregnant women than some conditions for which they are routinely screened and evaluated. One correlate of violence in pregnancy seems to be an unwanted pregnancy. Gazmararian et al. (1995) showed that women of all socioeconomic groups with unwanted pregnancies had 4.1 times the odds of experiencing physical violence compared to women with pregnancies that were wanted. In studying close relationships in pregnancy, and the potentially beneficial social support they can provide, pregnancy researchers must consider the negative sides of these relations as well.

SUPPORT INTERVENTIONS IN PREGNANCY AND OUTCOMES

In contrast to the correlational work on close relationships in pregnancy, the majority of studies assessing the influence of professional support are experimental, with interventions utilizing either nurses, social workers, midwives, or other trained medical practitioners. Three extensive reviews of the intervention literature (Blondel, 1998; Elbourne & Oakley, 1991; Elbourne, Oakley & Chalmers, 1989) agree that there was a trend toward better birth outcomes (e.g., lower preterm delivery), more positive affect, higher satisfaction with antenatal care, better communication with medical staff, and fewer gestation and labor complications in the intervention groups, although in general the reviews note considerable methodological problems in the literature despite many promising findings.

More recent studies are among the most rigorous and these are therefore mentioned briefly despite some remaining concerns with methodological issues. Studies assessing social support interventions have documented improvements in birth weight (e.g., Heins, Nance, McCarthy, & Efird, 1990; Oakley, Rajan, & Grant, 1990; Olds, Henderson, Tatelbaum, & Chamberlin, 1986), prenatal mortality (e.g., Sokol, Woolf, Rosen, & Weingarden, 1980) utilization of labor and delivery interventions (Oakley et al., 1990), and infant health (e.g., Olds et al., 1998). Norbeck, DeJoseph, and R. T. Smith (1996) used focus groups to develop culturally relevant standardized face-to-face interventions that provided the support usually provided by the participants' mother or male partners. One hundred and fourteen at-risk African American women were randomly assigned to the control group or the support group. The rate of low birth weight (LBW) was 9.1% in the social support intervention group compared to 22.4% in the control group. Similarly, Rogers, Peoples-Sheps, and Suchindran (1996) evaluated the impact of an intervention using paraprofessionals to provide social support to pregnant teenagers through home visits. The support focused on helping the teenagers better use the resources provided by network members, and also consisted of advice and the provision of emotional support. The intervention group consisted of 1,901 primiparous teenagers in intervention counties who were compared to 4,613 teenagers from counties in which the program was not offered. Results indicated that the intervention teenagers initiated prenatal care earlier and were less likely to have a preterm birth. Olds et al. (1998), conducted two randomized trials of prenatal and infancy home visitation using registered nurses and involving four prenatal visits. In contrast to women in a control group, nurse-visited women showed improved maternal caregiving and better health care behaviors. Furthermore, among women who smoked, those who were nurse-visited had 75% fewer preterm deliveries.

Interventions have also been shown to have some long-term effects. In one study, Oakley, Hickey, Rajan, and Rigby (1996) compared the health of 255 women who were offered a social support intervention provided by midwives during pregnancy with 254 controls who received normal care only. The participants were followed up at 6 weeks, 1 year, and 7 years. At the 7-year follow-up, factors such as child and mother health, child development, and health and welfare service use were assessed. Results showed that mothers and infants in the intervention group had significantly better physical and psychological health than those in the control groups 7 years after the intervention. The development of better social support interventions in pregnancy and methodologically rigorous evaluations of them is critical.

PATHWAYS BETWEEN PRENATAL SUPPORT AND BIRTH OUTCOMES

The general finding that social support and personal relationships have beneficial effects on the psychological well-being of the pregnant mother and on labor, delivery, and birth outcomes still leaves unanswered the question of the pathways or mechanisms of the social support effect. The two main models of support–outcome relations have been the *direct effects* model and the *stress buffering* model. If support truly was a moderator of stress effects on outcomes of pregnancy, then there should be evidence for the stress buffering model. However, most of the correlational studies provide fairly consistent evidence that prenatal social support has main effects on birth weight (Hoffman & Hatch, 1996; Molfese, Bricker, Manion, & Yaple, 1987; Norbeck & Tilden, 1983; Reeb, Graham, Zyzanski, & Kitson, 1987; Zacariah, 1996). For example, Turner et al. (1990) measured perceived social support from family, friends, and romantic partner in a study of 243 pregnant teenagers and found that family support had a significant direct effect on birth weight adjusted for length of gestation.

This support for main effects notwithstanding, theories have tended to emphasize the buffering model in which social support is protective primarily or solely for those in stressful circumstances (Norbeck & Anderson, 1989b; Norbeck & Tilden, 1983; Nuckolls et al., 1972). Nuckolls et al. (1972), for example, showed that life stress and social support interacted such that among high stress women, high social support was associated with fewer complications but there was no effect of social support in low stress women. The stress buffering process conceivably operates either during the appraisal process to reduce stress appraisals or, for events appraised as highly stressful, at the time of coping.

The absence of much comparison of the two models in prenatal social support research (i.e., main effect and buffering or interactions with stress) is due to two trends in this literature. First, comparisons of effects is hampered by the fact that studies testing for main effects of social support do not usually measure stress and test for buffering. Second, different conceptualizations of support make comparisons of findings across studies difficult. Although no clear patterns can be seen in the pregnancy literature, the social support literature on other health populations suggests that network measures of support tend to have direct effects whereas measures of emotional support tend to have buffering effects (Pierce, I. G. Sarason, & B. R. Sarason, 1996). This may be worth following up in pregnancy research.

In terms of mediators, there are many ways in which social support could promote positive pregnancy outcomes other than by buffering stress, including promoting adaptive health behaviors. To date, a few pregnancy studies have explored the relation between social support and health behaviors such as drinking, smoking, and substance use (Aaronson, 1989; Albrecht & Rankin, 1989; Ramsey, Abell, & Baker, 1986). For example, Giblin et al. (1990) in a sample of African American pregnant women and MacDonald et al. (1992) in a sample of British pregnant women, both found that social support reduced the incidence of maladaptive health behaviors such as smoking and alcohol consumption. Given the links between these maladaptive health behaviors and negative pregnancy outcomes (Archie, 1992), health behaviors appear to be important mediators of the effects of social support in pregnancy on outcomes.

The fact remains that social support in general benefits some people, in some situations, and under some conditions (Coyne & D. A. Smith, 1991; Dakof & Taylor, 1990; Sandler & Lakey, 1982), and the key for health psychologists is to identify which people do best under what conditions. The research on the effects of a companion during labor provide a good example of this issue. The presence of a supportive woman, or *doula,* during childbirth has been associated with significantly shorter labor and fewer complications during delivery (Kennel et al., 1991; Sosa et al., 1980). However, studies investigating the effects of the presence of the baby's father during delivery have been ambiguous (e.g., Henneborn & Cogan, 1975). Studies designed to pinpoint moderators of the effects of support in labor have revealed that the personality of the women in labor plays a major part in their distress during labor and delivery; the presence of the baby's father benefited only those women high in anxiety and who were more dependent (Keinan, Ezer, & Feigin, 1992; Keinan & Hobfoll, 1989). The inclusion of measures of constructs such as this can help to formulate new directions in pregnancy research.

CONCLUSIONS

The scope of this chapter is quite broad, but a unifying focus is the role of stress as an independent risk factor for adverse outcomes of pregnancy. In order to scientifically study this issue properly, there needs to be an appreciation of the multiple levels of analysis involved as both antecedents and consequences of stress, and also an understanding of the outcomes of interest and their etiology. Having covered these issues, albeit briefly, research on the pattern of emotions in pregnancy was reviewed. Such research is of descriptive use in and of itself, and it also sets the stage for considering the links between stress and birth outcomes, particularly because the predictive components of stress appear to be emotion-based. Research on stress and outcomes was reviewed. It was suggested that anxiety, and pregnancy anxiety, in particular may be the most risk-posing components of stress for preterm delivery. Mechanisms, both physiological and behavioral, were elaborated in light of current research findings. Two possible moderators of stress, coping behavior, and social support were covered in separate sections. Research on coping behavior in pregnancy is in its infancy, but promising new directions are emerging. Research on social support in pregnancy is much more developed, although support appears to operate more as a resource (with main effects on outcomes) than as a stress buffer (i.e., moderator). Understanding potential moderators is an important step in eventually intervening to improve maternal, fetal, and infant outcomes.

What are some promising directions for future research? Regarding stress as an independent risk factor for adverse outcomes of pregnancy (especially preterm delivery), the following directions merit attention: (a) What types of stress are most potent? A comparison of chronic and acute stressors is warranted and may be informed in part by emerging research on chronic stress and allostatic load (McEwen & Stellar, 1993) in which biopsychological mechanisms are proposed whereby chronic stress may lead to poor health outcomes. (b) To what extent is stress exposure, versus emotional responses to stress, responsible for risk in pregnancy? This is an open issue with important implications for understanding mechanisms. Some combination of the two may prove to be most detrimental. (c) When in pregnancy is stress most potent? The timing of stress in pregnancy is a key issue, and it is not yet known whether there are vulnerable periods for risk of preterm delivery or low birth weight, and it is not known whether a particular duration of exposure to stress is necessary for adverse effects (i.e., thresholds exist). If vulnerable periods or threshold levels of exposure exist, these might be different for various outcomes (e.g., preterm delivery, low birth weight). Understanding the precise timing of stress in predicting specific adverse effects is essential to planning any intervention efforts.

With respect to emotions in pregnancy, future research might focus on the following issues: the nature of the emotions studied; the confounding of emotion measures with somatic complaints common in pregnancy, and the distinction between mean levels of emotion and individual variation.

Few studies have distinguished traditional emotions from pregnancy-specific worries, concerns, or fears. Yet there is considerable theoretical and empirical value in measuring pregnancy-specific concerns (Elliott et al., 1983; Glazer, 1980; Levin, 1991; Rini et al., 1999; Roesch, Dunkel-Schetter, & Hobel, 1998; Wadhwa et al., 1993; Yali & Lobel, 1999). Women may experience a number of specific concerns about their pregnancies and babies, and these tend to change in content and strength across pregnancy. Better understanding of these contextually based emotions and their associations with traditional emotional states, such as anxiety, is an important issue for future research.

Regarding measures of emotion, many of the standard measures typically used contain somatic indicators of negative emotion, including fatigue, changes in appetite, decreased sexual interest, or sleep disturbance, which can produce inflated negative emotion scores because women usually experience these symptoms in the course of a normal pregnancy (cf. Kaplan, 1986). Some researchers have resolved this problem by removing items with somatic content from measures such as the Beck Depression Inventory (e.g., Chapman, Hobfoll, & Ritter, 1997; O'Hara, Zekoski, Philipps, & Wright, 1990), but a number of studies examining prenatal mood have not used corrected measures. The validity of standard depression measures in pregnancy and postpartum is unknown and should be addressed in future research.

The distinction between mean differences in emotion and individual variation over time in pregnancy is one of the most important issues raised by this body of research. As Elliott et al.'s (1983) work demonstrates, a sample of women might not differ in emotion on average—either over time or relative to a comparison group—although individual members of the sample might experience substantial changes in their emotions over the course of pregnancy, or might experience levels of emotion that are different from the comparison group. For this reason, it is useful for researchers to provide more detailed information than the standard tests of between-group differences. Ipsative approaches have rarely been used and may be quite useful in targeting women at risk. More research designs with repeated assessment of emotions and stress in pregnancy are also needed.

Regarding social support, an important goal for further study is to develop a better understanding of when support is beneficial and when it is not, and to specify the conditions under which each holds true. One direction is to consider various sociocultural milieus in which women experience pregnancy. In studies of predominantly Hispanic and African American pregnant women, some important differences have been observed between groups in support, as well as attitudes and behaviors in pregnancy (Sagrestano et al., in press; Zambrana et al., 1997; Zambrana, Dunkel-Schetter, Collins, & Scrimshaw, 1999). Furthermore, there is a relative dearth of research concerning support processes in pregnancy in Asian families. Like Hispanics, Asian Americans (Chinese, Japanese, Indian, Korean among others) are also known for their collectivist values and strong family orientations (Gaines, 1997; Gurung & Mehta, 1998). For example, in Indian families it is not uncommon for the pregnant women's mother-in-law, rather than her mother, to move into her son's home to help her daughter-in-law during gestation and to help take care of the baby after it is born. To what extent does this attenuate the stressfulness of pregnancy for Indian American women? Asians and Asian Americans of various origin raise new categories of empirical questions for further research. Moreover, the broader domain of sociocultural influences on stress processes in pregnancy is an exciting opportunity for interdisciplinary research.

Another issue in the support arena is the need to gain more than simply the pregnant woman's perspective on prenatal support conditions. By studying multiple perspectives, including that of the baby's father, researchers may gain a multifaceted and more accurate view of support relationships than by assessing the maternal perspective alone. This direction raises new questions: Do the pregnant woman and her partner agree about how much support he provides? What characteristics of fathers enable them to be better prenatal support providers? Do individual differences such as the mother's level of mastery, or relationship characteristics such as marital satisfaction, influence how much support is given by the baby's father during pregnancy? These questions can be optimally answered by involving both parents in research designs.

There are two further research directions that should be mentioned. Interestingly, they concern the generation before, and the generation after the pregnant mothers that are being studied today. With reference to earlier generations, newer research on intergenerational risk factors has developed in conjunction with research on ethnicity and socioeconomic status in pregnancy. For example, a recent study by Coutinho, David, and J. W. Collins (1997) examined a transgenerational data set of Illinois vital records to test whether parental birth weight was related to infant birth weight among African Americans and Whites born between 1989 and 1991. The authors found that parental birth weights were important risk factors for low birth weight (LBW) in both ethnic groups. However, the effects were particularly dramatic in African Americans for whom the rate of LBW among those born to LBW mothers was 17.9% compared to 10.8% among African Americans born of non-LBW mothers (rates for Whites were 8.5 and 4.8, respectively). Similarly, a Dutch study by Lumey and Stein (1997) of women born between 1944 and 1946 during a Dutch famine found evidence of long-term biologic effects of maternal intrauterine undernutrition, extending even into the next generation (Lumey & Stein, 1997). Emanuel (1997) highlighted some of the research directions suggested by these remarkable findings. A similar set of results is emerging with respect to preterm delivery. Porter, Fraser, Hunter, Ward, and Varner (1997) found that risk of preterm birth was higher among mothers who were themselves born before 37 weeks gestation. With respect to the focus of this chapter, these intergenerational effects suggest that a number of socioeconomic, cultural, and psychosocial factors may have long-term influences on maternal health and on the health of subsequent generations. Health psychology has much to bring to an understanding of these provocative and important issues.

A second future direction concerns the offspring of the pregnant women studied today. Work suggests that prenatal experience may have important consequences for the length of gestation and the growth of the fetus. Little research, however, has extended the paradigm to look at the influence of prenatal factors on infant health and well-being during infancy, childhood, adolescence, or adulthood. Hypotheses can be derived from current research concerning the consequences of prenatal stress for health and well-being of the offspring across the life span (Wadhwa, 1998). An evolving view is that the blueprint for brain development is not contained in genetic makeup alone, but is the result of a dynamic process involving interactions between genes and environment. The prenatal environment is the earliest setting in which such interactions may occur. Researchers working with animal and human models of pregnancy are discovering in numerous ways that the influence of the prenatal environment on brain and nervous system development may have far-reaching consequences for the cognitive and emotional functioning of the offspring later in life. These possibilities open up a new horizon for researchers interested in biopsychosocial models of pregnancy.

In conclusion, the study of stress in pregnancy and its many ramifications is a large research arena with numerous exciting frontiers. Biopsychosocial approaches to the study of pregnancy and birth are accepted across disciplines, and interdisciplinary research collaboration is essential. Health psychology is in a unique position to contribute to this endeavor in the next millenium.

ACKNOWLEDGMENTS

This chapter draws from the results of Christine Dunkel-Schetter's collaborative research with Curt Sandman, Ph.D., Calvin Hobel, M.D., and Pathik Wadhwa, Ph.D., M.D. This program of research has been supported by several joint grants (NIH R01 HD28413, NIH R01 HD28202, NIH R01 HD29553). During the development of this chapter, R. Gurung was supported as a postdoctoral fellow by the UCLA Training Grant in Health Psychology (MH 15750), P. Wadhwa was supported in part by NIH grant R29 HD33506, and M. Lobel was supported in part by NIH grant R29 NR03443. The authors would like to thank Christine Rini for her valuable comments on this chapter and Sarah Roper for her assistance in the preparation of the chapter. Dunkel-Schetter would also like to acknowledge the contributions of Nancy Collins, Ph.D., Pam Feldman, Ph.D., Susan Scrimshaw, Ph.D., Grace Woo, Ph.D., and Ruth Zambrana, Ph.D.

REFERENCES

Aaronson, L. S. (1989). Perceived and received support: Effects on health behavior during pregnancy. *Nursing Research, 38*(1), 4–9.

Abrams, B. (1994). Maternal nutrition. In R. K. Creasy & R. Resnik (Eds.), *Maternal–fetal medicine: Principles and practice* (3rd ed., pp. 162–170). Philadelphia: Saunders.

Adams, M. M., Sarno, A. P., Harlass, F. E., Rawlings, J. S., & Read, J. A. (1995). Risk factors for preterm delivery in a healthy cohort. *Epidemiology, 6*(5), 525–532.

Affonso, D. D., Mayberry, L. J., Lovett, S. M., & Paul, S. (1994). Cognitive adaptation to stressful events during pregnancy and postpartum: Development and testing of the CASE instrument. *Nursing Research, 43,* 338–343.

Ahmed, F. (1990). Unmarried mothers as a high-risk group for adverse pregnancy outcomes. *Journal of Community Health, 15*(1), 35–44.

Albrecht, S. A., & Rankin, M. (1989). Anxiety levels, health behaviors, and support systems of pregnant women. *Maternal-Child Nursing Journal, 18*(1), 49–60.

Aldwin, C. M., & Revenson, T. A. (1987). Does coping help? A reexamination of the relation between coping and mental health. *Journal of Personality and Social Psychology, 53,* 337–348.

Alexander, G. R. (1998). Preterm birth: Etiology, mechanisms and prevention. *Prenatal and Neonatal Medicine, 3,* 3–9.

Amiel-Tison, C. & Pettigrew, A. G. (1991). Adaptive changes in the developing brain during intrauterine stress. *Brain and Development, 13*(2), 67–76.

Andres, R. L., & Jones, K. L. (1994). Social and illicit drug use in pregnancy. In R. K. Creasy & R. Resnik (Eds.), *Maternal–fetal medicine: Principles and practice* (pp. 182–198). Philadelphia: Saunders.

Archie, C. (1992). Licit and illicit drug use in pregnancy. In N. Hacker & J. G. Moore (Eds.), *Essentials of obstetrics and gynecology* (2nd ed., pp. 189–196). Philadelphia: Saunders.

Arntzen, A., Moum, T., Magnus, P., & Bakketeig, L. S. (1996). Marital status as a risk factor for fetal and infant mortality. *International Journal of Epidemiology, 25*(3), 578–584.

Aspinwall, L. G., & Taylor, S. E. (1992). Modeling cognitive adaptation: A longitudinal investigation of the impact of individual differences and coping on college adjustment and performance. *Journal of Personality and Social Psychology, 63,* 989–1003.

Axelrod, J., & Reisine, T. D. (1984). Stress hormones: Their interaction and regulation. *Science, 224*(4648), 452–459.

Ballard, T. J., Saltzman, L. E., Gazmararian, J. A., Spitz, A. M., Lazorick, S., & Marks, J. S. (1998). Violence during pregnancy: Measurement issues. *American Journal of Public Health, 88*(2), 274–276.

Barnet, B., Duggan, A. K., Wilson, M. D., & Joffe, A. (1995). Association between postpartum substance use and depressive symptoms, stress, and social support in adolescent mothers. *Pediatrics, 96*(4, pt. 1), 659–666.

Barrera, M. (1986). Distinctions between social support concepts, measures, and models. *American Journal of Community Psychology, 14*(4), 413–445.

Barron, W. M., Mujais, S. K., Zinaman, M., Bravo, E. L., & Lindheimer, M. D. (1986). Plasma catecholamine responses to physiologic stimuli in normal human pregnancy. *American Journal of Obstetrics and Gynecology, 154*(1), 80–84.

Barth, R. P., & Schinke, S. P. (1983). Coping with daily strain among pregnant and parenting adolescents. *Journal of Social Service Research, 7,* 51–63.

Berendes, H. W., Kessel, S., & Yaffe, S. (1991). *Advances in the prevention of low birth weight. Proceedings of an international symposium.* Washington, DC: National Center for Education in Maternal and Child Health.

Berkowitz, G. S., Blackmore-Prince, C., Lapinski, H., & Savitz, D. A. (1998). Risk factors for preterm birth subtypes. *Epidemiology, 9*(3), 279–285.

Berscheid, E., & Reis, H. T. (1998). Attraction and close relationships. In D. T. Gilbert, S. T. Fiske, & L. Gardner (Eds.), *The handbook of social psychology* (Vol. 2, pp. 193–281). Boston: McGraw-Hill.

Berthiaume, M., David, H., Saucier, J-F., & Borgeat, F. (1998). Correlates of pre-partum depressive symptomatology: A multivariate analysis. *Journal of Reproductive & Infant Psychology, 16,* 45–56.

Blondel, B. (1998). Social and medical support during pregnancy: An overview of the randomized controlled trials. *Prenatal Neonatal Medicine, 3,* 141–144.

Bolger, N. (1990). Coping as a personality process: A prospective study. *Journal of Personality and Social Psychology, 59,* 525–537.

Bornstein, M. H. (1989). Sensitive periods in development: Structural characteristics and causal interpretations. *Psychological Bulletin, 105*(2), 179–197.

Borrelli, B., Bock, B., King, T., Pinto, B., & Marcus, B. H. (1996). The impact of depression on smoking cessation in women. *American Journal of Preventive Medicine, 12*(5), 378–387.

Boyce, W. T., Schaefer, C., & Uitti, C. (1985). Permanence and change: Psychological factors in the outcome of adolescent pregnancy. *Social Science & Medicine, 21,* 1279–1287.

Bresnahan, K., Zuckerman, B., & Cabral, H. (1992). Psychosocial correlates of drug and heavy alcohol use among pregnant women at risk for drug use. *Obstetrics and Gynecology, 80*(6), 976–980.

Brooke, O. G., Anderson, H. R., Bland, J. M., Peacock, J. L., & Stewart, C. M. (1989). Effects on birth weight of smoking, alcohol, caffeine, socioeconomic factors, and psychosocial stress. *British Medical Journal, 298,* 795–801.

Brooks-Gunn, J. (1991). Stress and support during pregnancy: What do they tell us about low birthweight. In H. Berendes, S. Kessel, & S. Yaffe (Eds.), *Advances in the prevention of low birth weight* (pp. 39–60). Washington, DC: National Center for Education in Maternal and Child Health.

Brown, G. W., & Harris, T. (1978). *Social origins of depression.* London: Tavistock.

Bryant-Greenwood, G. D., Millar, L. K., Yamamoto, S. Y., Bogic, L. V., & Tashima, L. (1998). Preterm birth: The premature rupture of the fetal membrane in the absence of infection. *Prenatal and Neonatal Medicine, 3,* 60–63.0

Cameron, R. P., Grabill, C. M., Hobfoll, S. E., Crowther, J. H. Ritter, C., & Lavin, J. (1996). Weight, self-esteem, ethnicity, and depressive symptomatology during pregnancy among inner-city women. *Health Psychology, 15*(4), 293–297.

Cantor, M. H. (1979). Neighbors and friends: An overlooked resource in the informal support system. *Research on Aging, 1,* 434–463.

Carlson, K., J., Eisenstat, S. A., & Ziporyn, T. (1996). *The Harvard guide to women's health.* Cambridge, MA: Harvard University Press.

Carver, C. S., & Scheier, M. F. (1994). Situational coping and coping dispositions in a stressful transaction. *Journal of Personality and Social Psychology, 66,* 184–195.

Carver, C. S., Scheier, M. F., & Weintraub, J. K. (1989). Assessing coping strategies: A theoretically based approach. *Journal of Personality and Social Psychology, 56,* 267–283.

Casper, L. M., & Hogan, D. P. (1990). Family networks in prenatal and postnatal health. *Social Biology, 37,* 84–101.

Cauce, A. M., Felner, R. D., & Primavera, J. (1982). Social support in high-risk adolescents: Structural components and adaptive impact. *American Journal of Community Psychology, 10*(4), 417–428.

Chalmers, B. (1983). Psychosocial factors and obstetric complications. *Psychological Medicine, 13,* 333–339.

Chapman, H. A., Hobfoll, S. E., & Ritter, C. (1997). Partners' stress underestimations lead to women's distress: A study of pregnant inner-city women. *Journal of Personality and Social Psychology, 73,* 418–425.

Chilman, C. S. (1993). Hispanic families in the United States. In H. P. Mc Adoo (Ed.), *Family ethnicity: Strength in diversity* (pp. 141–163). Newbury Park, CA: Sage.

Chrousos, G. P., & Gold, P. W. (1992). The concepts of stress and stress system disorders. Overview of physical and behavioral homeostasis. *Journal of the American Medical Association, 267*(9), 1244–1252.

Clifford, E., Weaver, S. M., & Hays, D. M. (1989). Stress and pregnancy complications: A prospective study. In F. J. McGuigan, W. E. Sime, & J. W. McDonald (Eds.), *Stress and tension control 3: Stress management* (pp. 217–228). New York: Plenum.

Cohen, S., & Syme, S. L. (1985). Issues in the study and application of social support. In S. Cohen & S. L. Syme (Eds.), *Social support and health* (pp. 3–22). San Diego: Academic Press.

Cohen, S., & Williamson, G. M. (1988). Perceived stress in a probability sample of the United States. In S. Spacapan & S. Oscamp (Eds.) *The social psychology of health* (pp. 31–67). Newbury Park, CA: Sage.

Cohen, S., Kamarck, T., Mermelstein, R. (1983). A global measure of perceived stress. *Journal of Health & Social Behavior, 24*(4), 385–396.

Cohen, S., Kessler, R. C., & Gordon, L. U. (1995). *Measuring stress.* New York: Oxford University Press.

Collins, J. W., Jr., Herman, A. A., & David, R. J. (1997). Very-low-birthweight infants and income incongruity among African American and White parents in Chicago. *American Journal of Public Health, 87*(3), 414–417.

Collins, N. L., Dunkel-Schetter, C., Lobel, M., & Scrimshaw, S.C.M. (1993). Social support in pregnancy: Psychosocial correlates of birth outcomes and postpartum depression. *Journal of Personality and Social Psychology, 65*(6), 1243–1258.

Compas, B. E., Malcarne, V. L., & Fondacaro, K. M. (1988). Coping with stressful events in older children and young adolescents. *Journal of Consulting and Clinical Psychology, 56,* 405–411.

Copper, R. L., Goldenberg, R. L., Das, A., Elder, N., Swain, M., Norman, G., Ramsey, R., Cotroneo, P., Collins, B. A., Johnson, F., Jones, P., & Meier, A. M. (1996). The preterm prediction study: Maternal stress is associated with spontaneous preterm birth at less than thirty-five weeks' gestation. *American Journal of Obstetrics and Gynecology, 175*(5), 1286–1292.

Cosmi, E. V., Luzi, G., Gori, F., & Chiodi, A. (1990). Response of utero-placental fetal blood flow to stress situation and drugs. *European Journal of Obstetrics, Gynecology, and Reproductive Biology, 36*(3), 239.

Coutinho, R., David, R. J., & Collins, J. W. (1997). Relation of parental birth weights to infant birth weight among African Americans and Whites in Illinois. *American Journal of Epidemiology, 146,* 804–809.

Coyne, J. C., & Smith, D. A. (1991). Couples coping with a myocardial infarction: A contextual perspective on wives' distress. *Journal of Personality & Social Psychology, 61*(3), 404–412.

Cramer, J. C., & McDonald, K. B. (1996). Kin support and family stress: Two sides to early childbearing and support networks. *Human Organization, 55,* 160–169.

Crandon, A. J. (1979). Maternal anxiety and obstetric complications. *Journal of Psychosomatic Research, 23,* 109–111.

Cutrona, C. E. (1990). Stress and social support: In search of optimal matching. *Journal of Social & Clinical Psychology, 9,* 3–14.

Cutrona, C. E. (1996). Social support as a determinant of marital quality: The interplay of negative and supportive behaviors. In G. R. Pierce, B. R. Sarason, & I. G. Sarason (Eds.), *Handbook of social support and the family. Plenum series on stress and coping* (pp. 173–194) New York: Plenum.

Dakof, G. A., & Taylor, S. E. (1990). Victims' perceptions of social support: What is helpful from whom? *Journal of Personality & Social Psychology, 58*(1), 80–89.

David, R. J., & Collins, J. W. (1997). Differing birth weight among infants of U. S.-born Blacks, African-born Blacks and U. S.-born Whites. *New England Journal of Medicine, 337*(17), 1209–1233.

Davis, A. A., Rhodes, J. E., & Hamilton-Leaks, J. (1997). When both parents may be a source of support and problems: An analysis of pregnant and parenting female African American adolescents' relationships with their mothers and fathers. *Journal of Research on Adolescence, 7,* 331–348.

DeSouza, E. B. (1993). Corticotropin-releasing factor and interleukin-1 receptors in the brain-endocrine-immune axis. Role in stress response and infection. *Annals of the New York Academy of Science, 697,* 9–27.

Dias, L., & Lobel, M. (1998, May). *Anxiety during prenatal testing: Impact of knowledge and satisfaction with information.* Presented at the meeting of the American Psychological Society, Washington, D.C.

DiPietro, J. A., Hodgson, D. M., Costigan, K. A., Hilton, S. C., & Johnson, T. R. (1996a). Development of fetal movement—fetal heart rate coupling from 20 weeks through term. *Early Human Development, 44*(2), 139–151.

DiPietro, J. A., Hodgson, D. M, Costigan, K. A., Hilton, S. C., & Johnson, T. R. (1996b). Fetal neurobehavioral development. *Child Development, 67*(5), 2553–2567.

Dorn, L. D., Susman, E. J., & Petersen, A. C. (1993). Cortisol reactivity and anxiety and depression in pregnant adolescents: A longitudinal perspective. *Psychoneuroendocrinology, 18*(3), 219–239.

Dunkel-Schetter, C. (1998). Maternal stress and preterm delivery. *Prenatal and Neonatal Medicine, 3,* 39–42.

Dunkel-Schetter, C., & Bennett, T. L. (1990). Differentiating the cognitive and behavioral aspects of social support. In B. R. Sarason, I. G Sarason, & G. R. Pierce (Eds.), *Social support: An interactional view* (pp. 267–296). New York: Wiley.

Dunkel-Schetter, C., Blasband, D., Feinstein, L. G., & Herbert, T. L. (1992). Elements of supportive interactions: When are attempts to help effective? In S. Spacapan & S. Oskamp (Eds.), *Helping and being helped in the real world* (pp. 83–114). Newbury Park, CA: Sage.

Dunkel-Schetter, C., Folkman, S., & Lazarus, R. S. (1987). Correlates of social support receipt. *Journal of Personality and Social Psychology, 53*(1), 71–80.

Dunkel-Schetter, C., & Lobel, M. (1998). Pregnancy and childbirth. In E. A. Blechman & K. D. Brownell (Eds.), *Behavioral medicine and women: A comprehensive handbook* (pp. 475–482). New York: Guilford.

Dunkel-Schetter, C., Sagrestano, L. M., Feldman, P., & Killingsworth, C. (1996). Social support and pregnancy: A comprehensive review focusing on ethnicity and culture. In G. R. Pierce, B. R. Sarason, & I. G. Sarason (Eds.), *Handbook of social support and the family. Plenum series on stress and coping* (pp. 375–412). New York: Plenum.

Edwards, K. R., & Jones, M. R. (1970). Personality changes related to pregnancy and obstetric complications. *Proceedings of the 78th Annual Convention of the American Psychological Association, 5,* 341–342.

Elbourne, D., & Oakley, A. (1991). An overview of trials of social support during pregnancy. In H. Berendes, S. Kessel, & S. Yaffee (Eds.), *Advances in the prevention of low birthweight: An international symposium* (pp. 203–223). Washington, DC: National Center for Education in Maternal and Child Health.

Elbourne, D., Oakley, A., & Chalmers, I. (1989). Social and psychological support during pregnancy. In I. Chalmers, M. Enkin, & M.J.N.C. Keirse (Eds.), *Effective care in pregnancy and childbirth: Vol. 1. Pregnancy* (pp. 221–236). Oxford, England: Oxford University Press.

Elliott, S. A. (1984). Pregnancy and after. In S. Rachman (Ed.), *Contributions to medical psychology* (pp. 93–116). Oxford, England: Pergamon.

Elliott, S. A., Rugg, A. J., Watson, J. P., & Brough, D. I. (1983). Mood changes during pregnancy and after the birth of a child. *British Journal of Clinical Psychology, 22,* 295–308.

Emanuel, I. (1997). Invited commentary: An assessment of maternal intergenerational factors in pregnancy outcome. *American Journal of Epidemiology, 146*(10), 820–825.

Farber, E. A., Vaughn, B., & Egeland, B. (1981). The relationship of prenatal maternal anxiety to infant behavior and mother–infant interaction during the first six months of life. *Early Human Development, 5,* 267–277.

Feldman, P. (1997). *The roles of socioeconomic status and ethnicity in psychosocial processes during pregnancy.* Unpublished doctoral dissertation, University of California, Los Angeles.

Fleishman, J. A., & Fogel, B. (1994). Coping and depressive symptoms among people with AIDS. *Health Psychology, 13,* 156–169.

Flores, K. S., Lobel, M., & Meyer, B. (1998). The impact of biomedical risk on levels and patterns of emotional distress in pregnancy. Under reveiw. *American Journal of Obstetrics and Gynecology.*

Folkman, S., & Lazarus, R. S. (1985). If it changes it must be process: Study of emotion and coping during three stages of a college examination. *Journal of Personality and Social Psychology, 48,* 150–170.

Folkman, S., Lazarus, R. S., Dunkel-Schetter, C., DeLongis, A., & Gruen, R. J. (1986). Dynamics of a stressful encounter: Cognitive appraisal, coping, and encounter outcomes. *Journal of Personality and Social Psychology, 50,* 992–1003.

Frisbie, W. P., Biegler, M., de Turk, P., Forbes, D., & Pullum, S. G. (1997). Racial and ethnic differences in determinants of intrauterine growth retardation and other compromised birth outcomes. *American Journal of Public Health, 87*(12), 1977–1983.

Gaines, R. (1997). Detachment and continuity: The two tasks of mourning. *Contemporary Psychoanalysis, 33*(4), 549–571.

Garite, T. J. (1994). Premature rupture of the membranes. In R. K. Creasy & R. Resnick (Eds.), *Maternal–fetal medicine: Principles and practice* (pp. 625–638). Philadelphia: Saunders.

Gazmararian, J. A., Adams, M. M., & Pamuk, E. R. (1996). Associations between measures of socioeconomic status and maternal health behavior. *American Journal of Preventive Medicine, 12*(2), 108–115.

Gazmararian, J. A., Adams, M. M., Saltzman, L. E., Johnson, C. H., Bruce, F. C., Marks, J. S., & Zahniser, S. C. (1995). The relationship between pregnancy intendedness and physical violence in mothers of newborns. The PRAMS Working Group. *Obstetrics and Gynecology, 85*(6), 1031–1038.

Gazmararian, J. A., Lazorick, S., Spitz, A. M., Ballard, T. J., Saltzman, L. E., & Marks, J. S. (1996). Prevalence of violence against women. *Journal of American Medical Association, 275*(24), 1915–1920.

Giblin, P. T., Poland, M. L., & Ager, J. W. (1990). Effects of social supports on attitudes, health behaviors and obtaining prenatal care. *Journal of Community Health, 15*(6), 357–368.

Glazer, G. (1980). Anxiety levels and concerns among pregnant women. *Research in Nursing and Health, 3,* 107–113.

Glover, V. (1997). Maternal stress or anxiety in pregnancy and emotional development of the child. *British Journal of Psychiatry, 171,* 105–106.

Goland, R. S., Conwell, I. M., Warren, W. B., & Wardlaw, S. L. (1992). Placental corticotropin-releasing hormone and pituitary-adrenal function during pregnancy. *Neuroendocrinology, 56*(5), 742–749.

Goldenberg, R. L., Cliver, S. P., Cutter, G. R., Hoffman, H. J., Copper, R. L., Gotlieb, S., & Davis, R. O. (1991). Maternal psychological characteristics and interauterine growth retardation. *Pre- and Peri-Natal Psychology Journal, 6*(2), 129–134.

Gorsuch, R. L., & Key, M. K. (1974). Abnormalities of pregnancy as a function of anxiety and life stress. *Psychosomatic Medicine, 36,* 352–362.

Gottlieb, B. H. (1985). Assessing and strengthening the impact of social support on mental health. *Social Work, 30*(4), 293–300.

Gudmundsson, S., Bjorgvinsdottir, L., Molin, J., Gunnarsson, G., & Marsal, K. (1997). Socioeconomic status and perinatal outcome according to residence area in the city of Malmo. *Acta Obstet Gyneco Scand, 76,* 318–323.

Gurung, R.A.R, Dunkel-Schetter, C., Collins, N., & Hobel, C. (1998). *Predicting social support and Adjustment during the course of a pregnancy.* Paper presented at the August 1998 meeting of the American Psychological Association, San Francisco.

Gurung, R.A.R., & Mehta, V. (1998). *Ethnic Identity, Self Concept, Well-Being and Beliefs in Asian-Indians.* Paper presented at the August 1998 meeting of the American Psychological Association, San Francisco.

Hansell, P.L.L. (1993). *Coping strategies in gynecological issues: The effect of loss, threat, and challenge appraisals.* Unpublished doctoral dissertation, University of Alabama.

Hays, R. B., Turner, H., & Coates, T. J. (1992). Social support, AIDS-related symptoms, and depression among gay men. *Journal of Consulting & Clinical Psychology, 60*(3), 463–469.

Hedegaard, M., Henriksen, T. B., Sabroe, S., & Secher, N. J. (1993). Psychological distress in pregnancy and preterm delivery. *British Medical Journal, 307,* 234–239.

Hedegaard, M., Henriksen, T. B., Secher, N. J., Hatch, M., & Sabroe, S. (1996). Do stressful life events affect duration of gestation and risk of preterm delivery. *American Journal of Epidemiology, 7,* 339–345.

Heins, H. C., Nance, N. W., McCarthy, B. J., & Efird, C. M. (1990). A randomized trial of nurse-midwifery prenatal care to reduce low birthweight. *Obstetrics and Gynecology, 75,* 341–345.

Helgeson, V. S., & Cohen, S. (1996). Social support and adjustment to cancer: Reconciling descriptive, correlational, and intervention research. *Health Psychology, 15*(2), 135–148.

Henneborn, W. J., & Cogan, R. (1975). The effect of husband participation on reported pain and probability of medication during labor and birth. *Journal of Psychosomatic Research, 19*(3), 215–222.

Herbert, T. B., & Cohen, S. (1993). Stress and immunity in humans: A meta-analytic review. *Psychosomatic Medicine, 55*(4), 654–679.

Herrera, J. A., Alvarado, J. P., & Martinez, J. E. (1988). The psychosocial environment and the cellular immunity in the pregnant patient. *Stress Medicine, 4*(1), 49–56.

Herrera, J. A., Salmeron, B., & Hurtado, A. (1997). Prenatal biopsychosocial risk assessment and low birth weight. *Social Science Medicine, 44*(8), 1107–1114.

Hobel, C. J., Dunkel-Schetter, C., & Roesch, S. (1998). Maternal stress as a signal to the fetus. *Prenatal Neonatal Medicine, 3,* 116–120.

Hobfoll, S. E., & Lieberman, J. R. (1987). Personality and social resources in immediate and continued stress resistance among women. *Journal of Personality and Social Psychology, 52*(1), 18–26.

Hoffman, S., & Hatch, M. C. (1996). Stress, social support and pregnancy outcome: a reassessment based on recent research. *Pediatric and Perinatal Epidemiology, 10*(4), 380–405.

Holahan, C. J., & Moos, R. H. (1990). Life stressors, resistance factors, psychological health: An extention of the stress-resistance paradigm. *Journal of Personality and Social Psychology, 58,* 909–917.

Holahan, C. J., & Moos, R. H. (1991). Life stressors, personal and social resources, and depression: A four year structural model. *Journal of Abnormal Psychology, 100,* 31–38.

Horgan, D. (1983). The pregnant woman's place and where to find it. *Sex Roles, 9,* 333–339.

House, J. S. (1987). Social support and social structure. *Sociological Forum, 2,* 135–146.

Hutchins, E., & DiPietro J. (1997). Psychosocial risk factors associated with cocaine use during pregnancy: A case-control study. *Obstetrics and Gynecology, 90*(1), 142–147.

Ingersoll, K. S., Lu, I. L., & Haller, D. L. (1995). Predictors of in-treatment relapse in perinatal substance abusers and impact on treatment retention: A perspective study. *Journal of Psychoactive Drugs, 27*(4), 375–387.

Istvan, J. (1986). Stress, anxiety, and birth outcomes: A critical review of the evidence. *Psychological Bulletin, 100*(3), 331–348.

Jemmot, J., & Locke, S. (1984). Psychosocial factors, immunologic meditation and human susceptibility to infectious diseases: How much do we know? *Psychological Bulletin, 95,* 78–108.

Kalil, K. M., Gruber, J. E., Conley, J., & Syntiac, M. (1993). Social and family pressures on anxiety and stress during pregnancy. *Pre and perinatal Psychology Journal, 8*(2), 113–118.

Kaplan, B. J. (1986). A psychobiological review of depression during pregnancy. *Psychology of Women Quarterly, 10,* 35–48.

Katz, V. L., Jenkins, T., Haley, L., & Bowes, W. A. (1991). Catecholamine levels in pregnant physicians and nurses: A pilot study of stress and pregnancy. *Obstetrics and Gynecology, 77*(3), 338–342.

Keefe, S. E., Padilla, A. M., & Carlos, M. L. (1979). The Mexican-American extended family as an emotional support system. *Human Organization, 38,* 144–152.

Keinan, G., Ezer, A., & Feigin, M. (1992). The influence of situational and personal variables on the effectiveness of social support during childbirth. *Anxiety Research, 4*(4), 325–337.

Keinan, G., & Hobfall, S. E. (1989). Stress, dependency, and social support: Who benefits from husband's presence in delivery? *Journal of Social and Clinical Psychology, 8,* 32–49.

Kennel, J. H., Klaus, M. (1979). Early mother-infant contact: Effects on the mother and the infant. *Bulletin of the Menninger Clinic, 43*(1), 69–78.

Kennell, J., Klaus, M., McGrath, S., Robertson, S., & Hinkley, C. (1991). Continuous emotional support during labor in a U. S. hospital. *Journal of the American Medical Association, 265,* 2197–2201.

Klebanoff, M. A. (1998). Conceptualizing categories of preterm birth. *Prenatal Neonatal Medicine, 3,* 13–15.

Knouse, S. B. (1991). Social support for Hispanics in the military. *International Journal of Intercultural Relations, 15,* 427–444.

Koshar, J. H., Lee, K. A., Goss, G., Heilemann, M. S., & Stinson, J. (1998). The Hispanic teen mother's origin of birth, use of prenatal care, and maternal and neonatal complications. *Journal of Pediatric Nursing, 13*(3), 151–157.

Kramer, M. S. (1987). Determinants of low birth weight: Methodological assessment and meta-analysis. *Bulletin of the World Health Organization, 65*(5), 663–737.

Kramer, M. S. (1998). Socioeconomic determinants of intrauterine growth retardation. *European Journal of Clinical Nutrition, 52*(1), S32–33.

Lantican, L. S. M., & Corona, D. F. (1992). Comparison of the social support networks of Filipino and Mexican-American primigravidas. *Health Care for Women International, 13,* 329–338.

Lazarus, R. S., & Folkman, S. (1984). *Stress, appraisal, and coping.* New York: Springer.

Lederman, R. P. (1986). Maternal anxiety in pregnancy: Relationship to fetal and newborn health status. *Annual Review of Nursing Research, 4,* 3–19.

Lederman, R. P. (1995). Relationship of anxiety, stress, and psychosocial development to reproductive health. *Behavioral Medicine, 21,* 101–112.

Lederman, R. P., Lederman, E., Work, B., Jr., & McCann, D. S. (1985). Anxiety and epinephrine in multiparous women in labor: Relationship to duration of labor and fetal heart rate pattern. *American Journal of Obstetrics and Gynecology, 153*(8), 870–877.

Leifer, M. (1980). *Psychological effects of motherhood: A study of first pregnancy.* New York: Praeger.

Levin, J. S. (1991). The factor structure of the pregnancy anxiety scale. *Journal of Health and Social Behavior, 32,* 368–381.

Levin, J. S., & DeFrank, R. S. (1988). Maternal stress and pregnancy outcomes: A review of the psychosocial literature. *Journal of Psychosomatic Obstetrics and Gynecology, 9,* 3–16.

Lepore, S. J. (1995). Measurement of Chronic Stressors. In S. Cohen, R. C. Kessler, & L. U. Gordon (Eds.), *Measuring stress: A guide for health and social scientists* (pp. 102–120). New York: Oxford University Press.

Litwak, E. (1985). *Helping the elderly: The complementary roles of informal networks and formal systems.* New York: Guilford.

Lobel, M. (1994). Conceptualizations, measurement, and effects of prenatal maternal stress on birth outcomes. *Journal of Behavioral Medicine, 17*(3), 225–272.

Lobel, M. (1998). Pregnancy and mental health. In H. Friedman (Ed.), *Encyclopedia of mental health* (pp. 229–238). San Diego, CA: Academic Press.

Lobel, M., & Dunkel-Schetter, C. (1990). Conceptualizing stress to study effects on health: Environmental, perceptual, and emotional components. *Anxiety Research, 3,* 213–230.

Lobel, M., Dunkel-Schetter, C., & Scrimshaw, S.C.M. (1992). Prenatal maternal stress and prematurity: A prospective study of socioeconomically disadvantaged women. *Health Psychology, 11*(1), 32–40.

Lobel, M., Yali, A. M., Zhu, W., & DeVincent, C. (1998). Emotional reactions to the stress of high-risk pregnancy: The role of optimism and coping (Abstract). *Annals of Behavioral Medicine, 20,* 29.

Lockwood, C. J. (1994). Recent advances in elucidating the pathogenesis of preterm delivery, the detection of patients at risk, and preventive therapies. *Current Opinion in Obstetrics and Gynecology, 6*(1), 7–18.

Lockwood, C. J., & Weiner, S. (1986). Assessment of fetal growth. *Clinics in Perinatology, 13*(1), 3–35.

Lubin, B., Gardener, S. H., & Roth, A. (1975). Mood and somatic symptoms during pregnancy. *Psychosomatic Medicine, 37,* 136–146.

Lumey, L. H., & Stein, A. D. (1997). Offspring birthweights after maternal intrauterine undernutrition: A comparison with sibships. *American Journal of Epidemiology, 146,* 810–819.

MacDonald, L. D., Peacock, J. L., & Anderson, H. R. (1992). Marital status: Association with social and economic circumstances, psychological state and outcomes of pregnancy. *Journal of Public Health Medicine, 14*(1), 26–34.

Martinez, M. (1989). *Stress, coping, and pregnancy health among immigrant Latino women.* Unpublished doctoral dissertation, University of California, Berkeley.

Matthews, K. A., & Rodin, J. (1992). Pregnancy alters blood pressure responses to psychological and physical challenges. *Psychophysiology, 29*(2), 232–240.

McAnarney, E. R. (1987). Young maternal age and adverse neonatal outcome. *American Journal of Disease of Children, 141*(10), 1053–1059.

McAnarney, E. R., & Stevens-Simon, C. (1990). Maternal psychological stress/depression and low birth weight. Is there a relationship? *American Journal of Diseases of Children, 144*(7), 789–792.

McCormick, M. C. (1985). The contribution of low birth weight to infant mortality and childhood morbidity. *New England Journal of Medicine, 312,* 82–89.

McCormick, M. C., Brooks-Gunn, J., Shorter, T., Holmes, J. H., Wallace, C. Y., & Heagarty, M. C. (1990). Factors associated with smoking in low-income pregnant women: Relationship to birth weight, stressful life events, social support, health behaviors and metal distress. *Journal of Clinical Epidemiology, 43*(5), 441–448.

McCubbin, J. A., Lawson, E. J., Cox, S., Sherman, J. J., Norton, J. A., & Read, J. A. (1996). Prenatal maternal blood pressure response to stress predicts birth weight and gestational age: A preliminary study. *American Journal of Obstetrics and Gynecology, 175*(3, pt. 1), 706–712.

McEwen, B. S. (1998). Protective and damaging effects of stress mediators. *New England Journal of Medicine, 338*(3), 171–179.

McEwen, B. S., & Steller, E. (1993). Stress and the individual: Mechanisms leading to disease. *Archives of Internal Medicine, 153,* 2093–2101.

McFarlane, J., Parker, B., & Soeken, K. (1996a). Abuse during pregnancy: Associations with maternal health and infant birth weight. *Nursing Research, 45*(1), 37–42.

McFarlane, J., Parker, B., & Soeken, K. (1996b). Physical abuse, smoking, and substance use during pregnancy: Prevalence, interrelationships, and effects on birth weight. *Journal of Obstetric, Gynecologic, and Neonatal Nursing, 25*(4), 313–320.

McIntosh, L. J., Roumayah, N. E., & Bottoms, S. F. (1995). Perinatal outcome of broken marriage in the inner city. *Obstetrics and Gynecology, 85*(2), 233–236.

McLean, M., Bisits, A., Davies, J., Woods, R., Lowry, P., & Smith, R. (1995). A placental clock controlling the length of human pregnancy. *Nature Medicine, 1*(5), 460–463.

Meis, P. J. (1998). Indicated preterm births: A review. *Prenatal Neonatal Medicine, 3,* 113–115.

Mercer, R. T. (1986). *First-time motherhood: Experiences from teens to forties.* New York: Springer.

Mercer, R. T., & Ferketich, S. L. (1988). Stress and social support as predictors of anxiety and depression during pregnancy. *Advances in Nursing Science, 10,* 26–39.

Miller, M. C. (1992). Winnicott unbound: The fiction of Philip Roth and the sharing of potential space. *International Review of Psycho-Analysis, 19*(4), 445–456.

Molfese, V. J., Bricker, M. C., Manion, L., Beadnell, B. et al. (1987). Anxiety, depression and stress in pregnancy: A multivariate model of intra-partum risks and pregnancy outcomes. *Journal of Psychosomatic Obstetrics and Gynaecology, 7,* 77–92.

Molfese, V. J., Bricker, M. C., Manion, L., Beadnell, B., & Yaple, K. (1987). Stress in pregnancy: The influence of psychological and social mediators in perinatal experiences. *Journal of Psychosomatic Obstetrics & Gynaecology, 6,* 33–42.

Monga, M., & Creasy, R. K. (1994). Cardiovascular and renal adaptation to pregnancy. In R. K. Creasy & R. Resnic (Eds.), *Maternal–fetal medicine: Principles and practice* (3rd ed., pp. 758–767). Philadelphia: Saunders.

Moore, M. L., Meis, P., Jeffries, S., Ernest, J. M., Buerkle. L., Swain, M., & Hill, C. (1991). A comparison of emotional state and support in women at high and low risk for preterm birth, with diabetes in pregnancy, and in non-pregnant professional women. *Pre- and Peri-Natal Psychology Journal, 6*(2), 109–127.

Moore, M. L., Michielutte, R., Meis, P. J., Ernest, J. M., Wells, H. B., Buescher, P. A. (1994). Etiology of low-birthweight: A population based study. *Preventative Medicine, 23,* 793–799.

Myers, R. E. (1975). Maternal psychological stress and fetal asphyxia: A study in the monkey. *American Journal of Obstetrics and Gynecology, 122*(1), 47–59.

Neter, E., Collins, N., Lobel, M., & Dunkel-Schetter, C. (1995). Psychosocial predictors of postpartum depressed mood among socioeconomically disadvantaged women. *Women's Health: Research on Gender, Behavior, and Policy, 1,* 51–75.

Newnham, J. (1998). Consequences of fetal growth restriction. *Current Opinion in Obstetrics and Gynecology, 10*(2), 145–149.

Nisell, H., Hjemdahl, P., & Linde, B. (1985). Cardiovascular responses to circulating catecholamines in normal pregnancy and in pregnancy-induced hypertension. *Clinical Physiology, 5*(5), 479–493.

Nisell, H., Hjemdahl, P., Linde, B., & Lunell, N. O. (1985a). Sympathoadrenal and carduivascular reactivity in pregnancy-induced hypertension: I. Responses to isometric exercise and a cold pressor test. *British Journal of Obstetrics an Gynecology, 92*(7), 772–731.

Nisell, H., Hjemdahl, P., Linde, B., & Lunell, N. O. (1985b). Sympathoadrenal and cardiovascular reactivity in pregnancy-induced hypertension: II. Response to tilting. *American Journal of Obstetrics and Gynecology, 152*(5), 554–560.

Nolen-Hoeksema, S. (1991). Responses to depression and their effects on the duration of depressive episodes. *Journal of Abnormal Psychology, 100,* 569–582.

Nolen-Hoeksema, S., & Morrow, J. (1993). Effects of rumination and distraction on naturally occurring depressed mood. *Cognition and Emotion, 7,* 561–570.

Norbeck, J. S., & Anderson, N. J. (1989a). Life stress, social support, and anxiety in mid- and late-pregnancy among low income women. *Research in Nursing and Health, 12,* 281–287.

Norbeck, J. S., & Anderson, N. J. (1989b). Psychosocial predictors of pregnancy outcomes in low-income Black, Hispanic, and White women. *Nursing Research, 38,* 204–209.

Norbeck, J. S., DeJoseph, J. F., & Smith, R. T. (1996). A randomized trial of an empirically-derived social support intervention to prevent low birthweight among African American women. *Social Science & Medicine, 43*(6), 947–954.

Norbeck, J. S., Lindsey, A. M., & Carrieri, V. L. (1981). The development of an instrument to measure social support. *Nursing Research, 30,* 264–269.

Norbeck, J. S., & Tilden, V. P. (1983). Life stress, social support, and emotional disequilibrium in complications of pregnancy: A prospective, multivariate study. *Journal of Health and Social Behavior, 24,* 30–46.

Nordentoft, M., Lou, H. C., Hansen, D., Nim J., Pryds, O., Rubin, P., & Hemmingsen, R. (1996). Intrauterine growth retardation and premature delivery: The influence of maternal smoking and psychosocial factors. *American Journal of Public Health, 86,* 347–354.

Nuckolls, K. B., Cassel, J., & Kaplan, B. H. (1972). Psychosocial assets, life crises, and the prognosis of pregnancy. *American Journal of Epidemiology, 95,* 431–441.

Oakley, A., Hickey, D., Rajan, L., Rigby, A. S. (1996). Social support in pregnancy: Does it have long-term effects? *Journal of Reproductive & Infant Psychology, 14*(1), 7–22.

Oakley, A., Rajan, L., & Grant, A. (1990). Social support and pregnancy outcome. *British Journal of Obstetrics and Gynecology, 97,* 155–162.

O'Hara, M. W. (1986). Social support, life events, and depression during pregnancy and the puerperium. *Archives of General Psychiatry, 43,* 569–573.

O'Hara, M. W., Zekoski, E. M., Philipps, L. H., & Wright, E. J. (1990). Controlled prospective study of postpartum mood disorders: Comparison of childbearing and nonchildbearing women. *Journal of Abnormal Psychology, 99,* 3–15.

Olds, D., Henderson, C., Kitzman, H., Eckenrode, J., Cole, R., & Tatelbaum, R. (1998). The promise of home visitation: Results of two randomized tests. *Journal of Community Psychology, 26,* 5–21.

Olds, D. L., Henderson, C. R., Tatelbaum, R., & Chamberlin, R. (1986). Improving the delivery of prenatal care and outcomes of pregnancy: A randomized trial of nurse home visitation. *Pediatrics, 77,* 16–28.

Orr, S. T., James, S. A., Miller, C. A., Barakat, B., Daikoku, N., Pupkin, M., Engstrom, K., & Huggins, G. (1996). Psychosocial stressors and low birthweight in an urban population. *American Journal of Preventive Medicine, 12*(6), 459–466.

Paarlberg, K. M., Vingerhoets, J.J.M., Passchier, J., Dekker, G. A., & Van Geijn, H. P. (1995). Psychosocial factors and pregnancy outcome: A review with emphasis on methodological issues. *Journal of Psychosomatic Research, 39*(5), 563–595.

Pagel, M. D., Smilkstein, G., Regen, H., & Montano, D. (1990). Psychosocial influences on new born outcomes: A controlled prospective study. *Social Science and Medicine, 30,* 597–604.

Paneth, N. S. (1995). The problem of low birth weight. *Future of Children, 5,* 35–56.

Park, C. L., & Cohen, L. H. (1993). Religious and nonreligious coping with the death of a friend. *Cognitive Therapy and Research, 17,* 561–577.

Park, C. L., Moore, P. J., Turner, R. A., & Adler, N. E. (1997). The roles of constructive thinking and optimism in psychological and behavioral adjustment during pregnancy. *Journal of Personality and Social Psychology, 73,* 584–592.

Parker, B., McFarlane, J., & Soeken, K. (1994). Abuse during pregnancy: Effects on maternal complications and birth weight in adult and teenage women. *Obstetrics and Gynecology, 84*(3), 323–328.

Pasch, L. A., & Bradbury, T. N. (1998). Social support, conflict, and the development of marital dysfunction. *Journal of Consulting & Clinical Psychology, 66*(2), 219–230.

Pearlin, L. I., & Schooler, C. (1978). The structure of coping. *Journal of Health and Social Behavior, 19,* 2–21.

Perez, R. G. (1982). *Stress and coping as determinants of adaptation to pregnancy in Hispanic women.* Unpublished doctoral dissertation, University of California, Los Angeles.

Perkin, M. R., Bland, J. M., Peacock, J. L., & Anderson, H. R. (1993). The effect of anxiety and depression during pregnancy on obstetric complications. *British Journal of Obstetrics and Gynaecology, 100,* 629–634.

Petersen, R., Gazmararian, J. A., Spitz, A. M., & Rowley, D. L. (1997). Violence and adverse pregnancy outcomes: A review of the literature and directions for future research. *American Journal of Preventive Medicine, 13*(5), 366–373.

Petraglia, F., Florio, P., Nappi, C., & Genazzani, A. R. (1996). Peptide signaling in human placenta and membranes: Autocrine, paracrine, and endocrine mechanisms. *Endocrine Reviews, 17*(2), 156–186.

Pierce, G. R., Sarason, I. G., & Sarason, B. R. (1996). Coping and social support. In M. Zeidner & N. S. Endler (Eds.), *Handbook of coping: Theory, research, applications* (pp. 434–451). New York: Wiley.

Pond, E. F., & Kemp, V. H. (1992). A comparison between adolescent and adult women on prenatal anxiety and self-confidence. *Maternal-Child Nursing Journal, 20,* 11–20.

Porter, T. F., Fraser, A. M., Hunter, C. Y., Ward, R. H., & Varner, M. W. (1997). The risk of preterm birth across generations. *Obstetrics & Gynecology, 90,* 63–67.

Pritchard, C. W. (1994). Depression and smoking in pregnancy in Scotland. *Journal of Epidemiology and Community Health, 48*(4), 377–382.

Ramsey, C. N., Abell, T. D., & Baker, L. C. (1986). The relationship between family functioning, life events, family structure, and the outcome of pregnancy. *Journal of Family Practice, 22,* 521–527.

Reeb, K. G., Graham, A. V., Zyzanski, S. J., & Kitson, G. C. (1987). Predicting low birthweight and complicated labor in urban Black women: A biopsychosocial perspective. *Social Science & Medicine, 25*(12), 1321–1327.

Rhodes, J. E., & Woods, M. (1995). Comfort and conflict in the relationships of pregnant, minority adolescents: Social support as a moderator of social strain. *Journal of Community Psychology, 23*(1), 74–84.

Rini, C. K., Dunkel-Schetter, C., Sandman, C. A., & Wadhwa, P. D. (1999). Psychological adaptation and birth outcome: The role of personal resources, stress and sociocultural context in pregnancy. *Health Psychology, 18*(4), 333–345.

Roesch, S. C., Dunkel-Schetter, C., & Hobel, C. J. (1998). Testing a latent trait-state model of stress and pregnancy (Abstract). *Annals of Behavioral Medicine, 20,* 29.

Rofe, Y., Lewin, I., & Padeh, B. (1981). Emotion during pregnancy and delivery as a function of repression-sensitization and number of childbirths. *Psychology of Women Quarterly, 6,* 163–173.

Rogers, M. M., Peoples-Sheps, M. D., & Suchindran, C. (1996). Impact of social support program on teenage prenatal care use and pregnancy outcomes. *Journal of Adolescent Health, 19*(2), 132–140.

Romero, R., Mazor, M., Munoz, H., Gomez, R., Galasso, M., & Sherer, D. M. (1994). The preterm labor syndrome. *Annals of the New York Academy of Sciences, 734,* 414–429.

Rook, K. S. (1992). Detrimental aspects of social relationships: Taking stock of an emerging literature. In H.O.F. Veiel & U. Baumann (Eds.), *The meaning and measurement of social support. The series in clinical and community psychology* (pp. 157–169). New York: Hemisphere.

Roth, S., & Cohen, L. J. (1986). Approach, avoidance, and coping with stress. *American Psychologist, 41,* 813–819.

Rowley, D. L., Hogue, C. J., Blackmore, C. A., Ferre, C. D., Hatfield-Timajchy, K., Branch, P., & Atrash, H. K. (1993). Preterm delivery among African-American women: A research strategy. *Racial Differences in Preterm Delivery, 9*(6), 1–6.

Sable, M. R., Stockbauer, J. W., Schramm, W. F., & Land, G. H. (1990). Differentiating the barriers to adequate prenatal care in Missouri, 1987–88. *Public Health Report, 105,* 549–555.

Safonova, T., & Leparsky, E. A. (1998). The unwanted child. *Child Abuse and Neglect, 22*(2), 155–157.

Sagrestano, L. M., Feldman, P., Rini, C., Woo, G., & Dunkel-Schetter, C. (in press). Ethnicity and social support during pregnancy. *American Journal of Community Psychology.*

Sandler, I. N., & Lakey, B. (1982). Locus of control as a stress moderator: The role of control perceptions and social support. *American Journal of Community Psychology, 10*(1), 65–80.

Sarason, B. R., Sarason, I. G., Gurung, R. A. R. (1997). Close personal relationships and health outcomes: A key to the role of social support. In S. Duck (Ed), *Handbook of personal relationships: Theory, research and interventions* (2nd ed., pp. 547–573). Chichester, England: Wiley.

Schaffer, D. M., Velie, E. M., Shaw, G. M., & Todoroff, K. P. (1998). Energy and nutrient intake and health practices of Latinal and white non-Latinal in the 3 months before pregnancy. *Journal of the American Dietetic Association, 98*(8), 876–884.

Scholl, T. O., Hediger, M. L., & Belsky, D. H. (1994). Prenatal care and maternal health during adolescent pregnancy: A review and meta-analysis. *Journal of Adolescent Health, 15*(6), 444–456.

Schulte, H. M., Weidner, D., & Allolio, B. (1990). The corticotrophin releasing hormone test in late pregnancy: Lack of adrenocorticotrophin and cortisol response. *Clinical Endocrinology, 33*(1), 99–106.

Schuster, T. L., Kessler, R. C., & Aseltine, R. H. (1990). Supportive interactions, negative interactions, and depressed mood. *American Journal of Community Psychology, 18*(n3), 423–438.

Schwarzer, R., Dunkel-Schetter, C., & Kemeny, M. (1994). The multidimensional nature of received social support in gay men at risk of HIV infection and AIDS. *American Journal of Community Psychology, 22*(3), 319–339.

Scrimshaw, S.C.M., Zambrana, R., & Dunkel-Schetter, C. (1997). Issues in Latino women's health: Myths and challenges. In S. B. Ruzek, V. L. Oleson, & A. E. Clarke (Eds.), *Women's health: Complexities and differences* (chap. 13). Ohio University Press.

Seegmiller, B. (1993). Pregnancy. In F. L. Denmark & M. A. Paludi (Eds.), *Psychology of women: A handbook of issues and theories* (pp. 437–474). Westport, CT: Greenwood Press.

Shepherd, R. W., Stanczyk, F. Z., Bethea, C. L., & Novy, M. J. (1992). Fetal and maternal endocrine responses to reduced uteroplacental blood flow. *Journal of Clinical Endocrinology and Metabolism, 75*(1), 301–307.

Shiono, P. H., & Behrman, R. E. (1995). Low birth weight: Analysis and recommendations. *Future of Children, 5,* 4–18.

Shiono, P. H., Rauh, V. A., Park, M., Lederman, S. A., & Zuskar, D. (1997). Ethnic differences in birthweight: The role of lifestyle and other factors. *American Journal of Public Health, 87,* 787–793.

Sjostrom, K., Valentin, L., Thelin, T., & Marsal, K. (1997). Maternal anxiety in late pregnancy and fetal hemodynamics. *European Journal of Obstetrics, Gynecology, and Reproductive Biology, 74*(2), 149–155.

Sokol, R. J., Woolf, R. B., Rosen, M. G., & Weingarden, K. (1980). Risk, antepartum care, and outcome: Impact of a maternity and infant care project. *Obstetrics and Gynecology, 56,* 150–156.

Sosa, R., Kennell, J., Klaus, M., Robertson, S., & Urrutia, J. (1980). The effect of a supportive companion on perinatal problems, length of labor, and mother–infant interaction. *New England Journal of Medicine, 303,* 597–600.

Spielberger, C. D. (1983). *Manual for the state-trait anxiety inventory.* Palo Alto, CA: Consulting Psychologists Press.

Spirito, A., Ruggiero, L., Bowen, A., McGarvey, S., Bond, A., & Coustan, D. (1991). Stress, coping, and social support as mediators of the emotional status of women with gestational diabetes. *Psychology and Health, 5,* 111–120.

St. Clair, P. A., Smeriglio, V. L., Alexander, C. S., & Celentano D. D. (1989). Social network structure and prenatal care utilization. *Medical Care, 27*(8), 823–831.

St. John, C., & Winston, T. J. (1989). The effect of social support on prenatal care. *Journal of Applied Behavioral Science, 25*(1), 79–98.

Stanton, A. L., & Snider, P. R. (1993). Coping with a breast cancer diagnosis: A prospective study. *Health Psychology, 12,* 16–23.

Steer, R. A., Scholl, T. O., Hediger, M. L., & Fischer, R. L. (1992). Self-reported depression and negative pregnancy outcomes. *Journal of Clinical Epidemiology, 45,* 1093–1099.

Thompson, R. J., Gustafson, K. E., Oehler, J. M., Catlett, A. T., Brazy, J. E., & Goldstein, R. F. (1997). Developmental outcome of very low birth weight infants at four years of age as a function of biological risk and psychosocial risk. *Developmental & Behavioral Pediatrics, 18*(2), 91–96.

Thorpe, K. J., Dragonas, T., & Golding, J. (1992). The effects of psychosocial factors on the emotional well-being of women during pregnancy: A cross-cultural study of Britain and Greece. *Journal of Reproductive and Infant Psychology, 10,* 191–204.

Tietjen, A. M., & Bradley, C. F. (1985). Social support and maternal psychosocial adjustment during the transition to parenthood. *Canadian Journal of Behavioural Science, 17*(2), 109–121.

Tilden, V. P. (1983). The relation of life stress and social support to emotional disequilibrium during pregnancy. *Research in Nursing and Health, 6,* 167–174

Tunis, S. L., & Golbus, M. S. (1991). Assessing mood states in pregnancy: Survey of the literature. *Obstetrical and Gynecological Survey, 46,* 340–345.

Turner, R. J., Grindstaff, C. F., & Phillips, N. (1990). Social support and outcome in teenage pregnancy. *Journal of Health and Social Behavior, 31,* 43–57.

Vaha-Eskeli, K. K., Erkkola, R. U., Scheinin, M., & Seppanen, A. (1992). Effects of short-term thermal stress on plasma catecholamine concentrations and plasma renin activity in pregnant and nonpregnant women. *American Journal of Obstetrics and Gynecology, 167*(3), 785–789.

Wadhwa, P. D. (1998). Prenatal stress and life-span development. In H. S. Friedman (Eds.), *Encyclopedia of mental health* (Vol. 3, pp. 265–280). San Diego: Academic Press.

Wadhwa, P. D., Dunkel-Schetter, C., Chicz-DeMet, A., Porto, M., & Sandman, C. A. (1996). Prenatal psychosocial factors and the neuroendocrine axis in human pregnancy. *Psychosomatic Medicine, 58*(5), 432–446.

Wadhwa, P. D., Porto, M., Garite, T. J., Chicz-DeMet, A., & Sandman, C. A. (1998). Maternal corticotropin-releasing hormone levels in the early third trimester predicts length of gestation in human pregnancy. *American Journal of Obstetrics and Gynecology, 179,* 1079–1085.

Wadhwa, P. D., Sandman, C. A., Chicz-DeMet, A., & Porto, M. (1997). Placental CRH modulates maternal pituitary adrenal function in human pregnancy. *Annals of the New York Academy of Science, 814,* 276–281.

Wadhwa, P. D., Sandman, C. A., Porto, M., Dunkel-Schetter, C., & Garite, T. J. (1993). The association between prenatal stress and infant birth weight and gestational age at birth: A prospective investigation. *American Journal of Obstetrics and Gynecology, 69*(4), 858–865.

Wiemann, C. M., & Berenson, A. B. (1998). Factors associated with recent and discontinued alcohol use by pregnant adolescents. *Journal of Adolescent Health, 22*(5), 417–423.

Woo, G. (1997). Daily demands during pregnancy, gestational age, and birthweight: Reviewing physical and psychological demands in employment and non-employment contexts. *Annals of Behavioral Medicine, 19*(4), 385–398.

Yali, A. M. (1998). *Stress-resistance resources and the coping process: The role of optimism, social support, and socioeconomic status in pregnancy.* Unpublished doctoral dissertation, State University of New York at Stony Brook.

Yali, A. M., & Lobel, M. (1999). Coping and distress in pregnancy: An investigation of medically high risk women. *Journal of Psychosomatic Obstetrics and Gynecology*, 20, 39–52.

Zachariah, R. (1996). Predictors of psychological well-being of women during pregnancy: Replication and extension. *Journal of Social Behavior & Personality, 11,* 127–140.

Zambrana, R. E., Dunkel-Schetter, C., Collins, N., & Scrimshaw, S. C. (1999). Mediators of ethnic-associated differences in infant birth weight. *Journal of Urban Health, 76,* 102–116.

Zambrana, R. E., Hernandez, M., Dunkel-Schetter, C., & Scrimshaw, S.C.M. (1991). Ethnic differences in the substance use patterns of low-income pregnant women. *Family and Community Health, 13*(4), 1–11.

Zambrana, R. E., & Scrimshaw, S. C. (1997). Maternal psychosocial factors associated with substance use in Mexican-origin and African American low-income pregnant women. *Pediatric Nursing, 23*(3), 253–259.

Zambrana, R. E., Scrimshaw, S. C., Collins, N., & Dunkel-Schetter, C. (1997). Prenatal health behaviors and psychosocial risk factors in pregnant women of Mexican origin: The role of acculturation. *American Journal of Public Health, 87*(6), 1022–1026.

Zax, M., Sameroff, A. J., & Farnum, J. E. (1975). Childbirth education, maternal attitudes, and delivery. *American Journal of Obstetrics and Gynecology, 123,* 185–190.

Zayas, L. H., & Busch-Rossnagel, N. A. (1992). Pregnant Hispanic women: A mental health study. *Families in Society, 73*(9), 515–521.

Zimmer-Gembeck, M. J., & Helfand, M. (1996). Low birthweight in a public prenatal care program: Behavioral and psychosocial risk factors and psychosocial intervention. *Social Science and Medicine, 43*(2), 187–197.

Zimmermann-Tansella, C., Bertagni, P., Siani, R., & Micciolo, R. (1994). Marital relationships and somatic and psychological symptoms in pregnancy. *Social Science & Medicine, 38,* 559–564.

Zuckerman, B., Amaro, H., Bauchner, H., & Cabral, H. (1989). Depressive symptoms during pregnancy: Relationship to poor health behaviors. *American Journal of Obstetrics and Gynecology, 160*(5), 1107–1111.

Zuniga, M. E. (1992). Families with Latino roots. In E. W. Lynch & M. J. Hanson (Eds.), *Developing cross-cultural competence: A guide for working with young children and their families* (pp. 151–179). Baltimore, MD: Brookes.

31

Women's Health Promotion

Barbara K. Rimer
National Cancer Institute, Rockville, MD
Colleen M. McBride
Duke University Medical Center
Carolyn Crump
University of North Carolina

Health promotion has been defined by Green and Kreuter (1990) as the combination of educational and environmental supports for actions and conditions of living conducive to health. Within this broad definition, health promotion includes such diverse health promoting behaviors as appropriate nutrition, smoking prevention and cessation, exercise, stress management, and screening for prevalent diseases (e.g., cancer). Because women can expect to live longer than ever before, their lifelong health habits will become more important. Fletcher (1995) observed, "Many of the deadliest conditions for women are stopped not only by knowing more molecular medicine but knowing better how to help our patients to shed unhealthy habits and adopt healthy ones."

It is important that health promotion for women not be seen as a set of isolated recommendations and activities but within an integrated framework (Rimer, 1995b) that addresses the potential synergistic effect of both good and bad health habits (Lane, Macera, Croft, & Meyer, 1996). As an example, quitting smoking reduces the risk of three major killers of women—cancer, heart disease, and stroke—as well as other conditions and diseases like the complications of diabetes. Decreasing dietary fat may not only decrease the risk of heart disease but also breast and colon cancers. And regular exercise may reduce not only the risk of heart disease and osteoporosis but also of breast and colon cancers. Health habits interact in other ways as well. For example, there is evidence that smokers may be less likely to get mammograms and regular exercise (Orleans, Rimer, Salmon, & Kozlowski, 1990; Rimer et al., 1990; McBride, Curry, Taplin, Anderman, & Grothaus, 1993), and women who practice more health promoting behaviors report a more favorable health status (Lane et al., 1996). Neither health behaviors nor their consequences exist in a vacuum.

An assessment of women's health habits and risk factors indicates that there is much room for improvement. Currently, nearly 25% (more than 22 million women) of women are current cigarette smokers, 20% have cholesterol of 240 mg/dl or greater, 20% have high blood pressure, and 35% are obese. Moreover, 73% of adult women do not report regular participation in aerobic exercise, and minority women and those with lower levels of education are the most likely to be sedentary. Most women still are not getting regular mammograms or colorectal cancer screening. Clearly, the need for effective women's health promotion has never been greater.

Solutions and programs must be appropriate for women, that is, reflect the psychological, social, economic and political realities of women's lives. Ruzek and Hill (1986) stressed the need for positive health information reflective of women's own experience of health and illness. Consequently, effective health promotion strategies must be drawn from a continuum of interventions that can be applied not only at the individual, family, and organizational levels but also at the community and policy levels (Chesney & Ozer, 1995). Interventions also must reflect life-span needs and concerns unique to women. Moreover, the health promotion agenda of younger women will be different from those who are peri- or postmenopausal.

This chapter focuses on the proven, accepted dimensions of health promotion, including diet, smoking, exercise, and cancer screening. Each section includes a brief epidemiologic overview summarizing relevant prevalence data and the rationale for the recommended behavior as well as a summary of the continuum of relevant intervention research targeted to women or that has special implications for women. The goal is to review briefly not only what health promoting behaviors are recommended for women but also to summarize the evidence for effective interventions that promote healthy behaviors for women. It becomes evident that far too little is known about how to influence health promotion, especially among certain categories of women (e.g., ethnic minorities and older women). Often, studies that include both men and women lack the power to reach firm conclusions about gender-specific efficacy. Moreover, unless programs are designed with women's needs as a foundation, they may not succeed. As Chesney and Ozer (1995) cautioned, women are not a homogeneous group. Strategies for health promotion should, but rarely do reflect the socioeconomic status (SES), racial, cultural, and age diversity of women.

The first half of this chapter examines health behavior changes (including reducing dietary fat, smoking cessation, and increasing physical activity) that are essential to promoting women's health. The second half of the chapter examines screening behavior in the areas of breast, cervical, and colon cancers.

DIET

Dietary Risk Factors for Women

Diet is an important risk factor in the development of cardiovascular disease and cancer. Consistent evidence suggests that a diet high in fat is positively associated with hypercholesterolemia, which is a key risk factor for heart disease. In particular, diets high in saturated fats increase levels of low density lipoproteins (LDLs) that appear to be most important in the development of atherosclerosis in both women and men (Rich-Edwards, Manson, Hennekens, & Buring, 1995). Women with blood cholesterol levels over 265 mg/dl have a two times greater risk of developing heart disease compared to those with levels under 200 mg/dl (Packard, 1985). Although cholesterol levels among Americans have been declining, 20% of adult women have cholesterol levels over 240. Moreover, during menopause women experience a steep increase in their average cholesterol level due in large part to their decreasing estrogen levels (Busch, Fried, & Barrett-Connor, 1988).

Dietary factors have a somewhat more complex association with cancer risk (Doll, 1996; Willett, 1995). Two large epidemiologic studies of women, the Nurses Health Study conducted with over 120,000 female nurses and the Iowa Women' s Study conducted with over 30,000 women, found that consumption of red and processed meat products (Willett et al., 1995) was associated with as much as a twofold increase in women' s risk of colon cancer. However, neither of these large studies of women or five other studies have found a relation between total dietary fat or saturated fat consumption and increased risk of breast cancer (Hunter et al., 1996). In contrast, the evidence of a protective effect of fruit and vegetable consumption is consistent and overwhelming, with more than 200 studies indicating significantly reduced risk of cancers of the breast, cervix, and colon among women (Block, Patterson, & Subar, 1992; Doll, 1996; Willett, 1995). Evidence for the protective role of fiber independent from that of fruits and vegetables is as yet inconclusive, with case control studies indicating stronger effects than prospective studies (Willett, 1995). Thus, reduction of dietary fat and increased consumption of fruits and vegetables are essential components of health promotion programs for women.

Diet and Overweight

Diet has an indirect effect on women's health through its influence on body weight. Eating a diet high in fat is positively associated with overweight and obesity (Romieu et al., 1988). Lifetime weight gain of as little as 5 to 8 kg after age 18 increases women's risk for coronary artery disease (Willett et al., 1995). It is encouraging that even modest weight loss, on the order of 10% of initial body weight, can improve blood pressure, lipid profiles, glucose, and insulin (Wing & Jeffery, 1995; Wood, Stefanick, Williams, & Haskell, 1991). Approximately, 35% of American women are overweight, defined as 20% above their ideal weight (Kuczmarski, Flegal, Campbell, & Johnson, 1994). Although the prevalence of overweight has increased for the American population as a whole (Kuczmarski et al., 1994), it is consistently highest among women, particularly African American and Hispanic women, and those with low socioeconomic status (Jeffery & French, 1996; Kuczmarski et al., 1994). Data from the most recent National Health and Nutrition Examination Survey (NHANES III) indicate that 33% of White women, 49% of African American women, and 48% of Mexican American women are obese, that is, they are 30% or more above ideal body weight (Manson & VanItallie, 1996). Being obese substantially increases women's risk of hypertension, hyperlipidemia, Type II diabetes, and coronary artery disease, as well as postmenopausal breast cancer, cancers of the endometrium, and gall bladder (Manson & VanItallie, 1996).

Consistent evidence demonstrates that the average American's weight increases steadily with age (Manson & VanItallie, 1996). For women, pregnancy has been suggested as an important determinant of this lifetime weight gain (Boardley, Sargent, Coker, Hussey, & Sharpe, 1995; D. E. Smith et al., 1994). In a large multisite coronary risk factor study of young adults, women who became pregnant experienced greater weight gains (2–3 kg) over a 5-year follow-up than women who remained nulliparous. African American women gained almost twice as much weight as did White women (D. E. Smith et al., 1994). Interventions that encourage women to maintain an optimal weight over the life span are a necessary component of health promotion efforts for women.

Dietary Practices

The average American consumes a diet consisting of approximately 36% of calories from fat (U.S. Department of Health and Human Services, USDHHS, 1991). Current recommendations are that dietary fat should be limited to 30% of total calories and that individuals should consume from 20 to 30 grams of fiber per day (USDHHS, 1991). Data from the Behavioral Risk Factor Survey indicate that fewer than one quarter of American women reported behaviors that comply with these national dietary guidelines (Serdula et al., 1995). For example, of the almost 14,000 women surveyed, about half reported eating only one to two servings of fruits and vegetables per day in contrast to the five recommended servings. Rates of consumption are even lower among African American (Serdula et al., 1995) and Hispanic women (Subar et al., 1995). Although many women are not in full compliance with current dietary recommendations, three quarters of the women who were surveyed in 114 worksites reported they were either preparing to, were active in or were maintaining dietary changes of decreased fat and increased fiber (Glanz et al., 1994). However, low income and less educated women were consistently less inclined to be considering or to have adopted healthy dietary practices than those with higher socioeconomic status (Balcazar, Castro, & Krull, 1995; Glanz et al., 1994; Jeffery & French, 1996).

Cultural factors have a complex influence on women's likelihood of adhering to dietary guidelines (Balcazar et al., 1995). Two studies have indicated that less acculturated Mexican American women were less likely to avoid foods high in fat and more likely to consume high calorie foods than highly acculturated women. However, these same less acculturated women consumed more fiber than highly acculturated women. The health promoting and health compromising components of different ethnic diets must be considered in health promotion activities.

It has been widely argued that for women, dietary practices are deeply enmeshed with their concerns about body weight (Brownell, 1991). Studies of adolescents in particular indicate that girls believe more strongly than boys in the benefits of a healthy diet for weight control and improving their appearance (Gracey, Stanley, Burke, Corti, & Beilin, 1996). Often, this translates into unhealthy dieting practices that in their most extreme form can lead to eating disorders, including anorexia and bulimia. More prevalent, however, is women's reported dissatisfaction with their weight (de Castro & Goldstein, 1995; Sobal, Nicolopoulos, & Lee, 1995), ongoing restriction of calorie intake (de Castro & Goldstein, 1995), and active dieting (Horm & Anderson, 1993) as compared to men. African American women, although heavier on average than women of other racial ethnic groups, do not appear to have the same level of weight concerns or a high prevalence of dieting (Horm & Anderson, 1993). Thus, the presence or absence of weight concerns, other personal motivators, as well as the cultural and socioeconomic environment, are important considerations in effecting dietary behavior change among women.

Barriers and Facilitators to Dietary Change

Factors that influence dietary change can be categorized as those that predispose and enable the initial adoption of behavior change and those that reinforce or maintain these changes (Green & Kreuter, 1990). Knowledge of the fat and fiber content of foods, beliefs in a diet–disease connection, being motivated, and perceiving benefits to dietary change all have been noted as factors that predispose individuals to reduce their dietary fat (Bowen, Fries, & Hopp, 1994; Glanz et al., 1994; Gracey et al., 1996; Kristal et al., 1995). Enabling factors, such as access to low fat food choices in community, school, and worksite settings, perceived norms, and social support favoring low fat diets have also been positively associated with reductions in dietary fat (Bowen et al., 1994; Kristal et al., 1995). Comparison of the relative contribution of these predisposing and enabling factors have shown that predisposing factors are better predictors of dietary intentions, self-efficacy, and likelihood of reducing dietary fat than are enabling factors (Kristal et al., 1995). Others have shown synergism between these factors with women's motivation to make dietary changes particularly enhanced if they have support for such changes from their friends (Kelsey et al., 1996).

In the longer term, factors such as feelings of wellness and a development of a distaste for fat that occur subsequent to dietary fat reduction have been positively associated with maintenance of fat reduction (Urban, White, Anderson, Curry, & Kristal, 1992). In contrast, feelings of deprivation with respect to food choices are important deterrents to maintenance. Moreover, women who have made dietary changes also cite increased time for meal planning, preparation, and costs of low fat menus as additional deterrents to long-term maintenance of dietary changes (Urban et al., 1992). Thus, interventions that enhance motivation, as well as the perceptions and experienced benefits of healthy dietary practices, have the greatest likelihood of success. Moreover, recommended dietary changes must be incorporable into women's daily lives, be within their economic means, and include foods that are accessible and palatable to multiethnic and low income communities.

Interventions to Promote Healthy Diets

Intensive health promotion interventions that target the individual for dietary change have had some success. The Women's Health Trial, a multicenter feasibility study to lower dietary fat among women, demonstrated that relatively dramatic reductions in dietary fat can be achieved among highly motivated women (Insull et al., 1990). A sample of 300 women from age 45 to 69 was randomized either to a control or intervention group. Women assigned to the intervention attended small group sessions over a period of a year. Sessions were led by a nutritionist who instructed women how to choose low fat foods, modify recipes, self-monitor fat intake, and develop individualized low fat eating plans. Women in the intervention group experienced a mean reduction in dietary fat from 39% at baseline to 21% at the 6-month follow-up. In contrast, women in the comparison group experienced a nonsignificant reduction in fat from 39% to 38%. Significant treatment effects were maintained over 24 months of follow-up.

Women's influence over the dietary practices of their families is also evidenced by results of the Women's Health Trial. Husbands of the women who participated in the trial experienced reductions in dietary fat that were comparable to those of their wives (White et al., 1991). Moreover, because women place more value on, and are at more advanced stages of readiness to adopt healthy eating patterns than men (M. K. Campbell et al., 1994; Curry, Kristal, & Bowen, 1992; Glanz et al., 1994; Gracey et al., 1996), they are likely to be the most receptive to dietary interventions. Family-focused dietary interventions that engage both children and their parents, primarily mothers, to participate in home-based nutrition education activities and increase physical activity also have had success (Crockett, 1987). These family-based interventions represent an important area for further research.

Tailored health education materials that provide the optimal characteristics of intensive and interactive interventions, but are relatively inexpensive and easily disseminable, hold promise for application to dietary interventions. Using standard questionnaires and computer algorithms, the content of written materials can be tailored to the factors most salient to a woman's dietary practices. Using these techniques, M. K. Campbell and colleagues (1994) evaluated a one-time mailed nutrition information packet with a sample of predominantly female family practice patients. Materials included in the nutrition information packet were tailored to the participant's stage of readiness, dietary intake, motivation, self-efficacy, and barriers to dietary changes. Those who received the tailored packet were significantly more likely to have used the materials, and reported significantly greater decreases in dietary fat intake than those who received nontailored and control materials (M. K. Campbell et al., 1994). In contrast, other targeted approaches that have not customized materials to psychosocial variables have had less success in influencing dietary fat reductions (Bowen et al., 1994).

Larger scale environmental and health marketing interventions that are characteristically less intensive but have broader reach have also been evaluated. Worksite-based interventions that encourage employees to implement changes in the worksite environment, such as increasing availability of low fat food items in vending machines, have had limited success (Glasgow, Terborg, Hollis, Severson, & Boles, 1995; Sorenson et al, 1998). However, initial results of the Working Well worksite trial have indicated a nonsignificant downward trend in dietary fat consumption and significant increases in fruit and vegetable consumption among intervention participants compared to those in the control worksites (Sorenson et al., 1996). Motivating employees to participate in intervention activities and to support each other's efforts to make dietary changes has been difficult (Glasgow et al., 1995). Sorenson and colleagues (1998) have extended the traditional worksite model to include a family involvement component. This intervention is being tested in 22 community health centers that employ a large proportion of low income women who live in the surrounding community. The family component includes a learn-at-home program, annual family newsletters, and family festivals to encourage a home environment that is supportive of worker's attempts to change their eating patterns. Preliminary results indicate that consumption of fruits and vegetables was positively associated with household support. This worksite project and eight other interventions to increase fruit and vegetable consumption are part of the national Five A Day program that is being funded by the National Cancer Institute (Havas et al., 1994). The program objective is to promote a simple, positive message: Eat five or more servings of fruit and vegetables daily as part of a low fat, high fiber diet (Heimendinger, Van Duyn, Chapelsky, Foerster, & Stables, 1996). The Five A Day program is being conducted n partnership with the food industry, including supermarkets, restaurants, food merchandisers, and suppliers. The retailers and their suppliers participate by displaying the Five A Day logo on eligible products, incorporating the program message in print and broadcast advertisements, and sponsoring taste tests and supermarket tours. The impact of these efforts is currently being evaluated.

Diet Summary

Adoption of healthy diets is a central tenet of health promotion for women. The combination of individual, family-based, and environmental interventions to promote decreased dietary fat, and increased fruit, vegetable, and fiber consumption, has shown promise. However, personal motivators and stage of readiness to adopt dietary changes, as well as the sociocultural contexts of minority and low income women must be considered in the design of dietary interventions. Recent advances in health communication strategies that enable tailoring message content to the needs of specific groups may help to expand the reach and appropriateness of dietary interventions to important demographic subgroups of women.

CIGARETTE SMOKING

Smoking is the leading preventable cause of death for women. It is estimated that 140,000 women die annually of smoking-related causes (Blumenthal, 1996). About 80% of female lung cancer and a comparable proportion of heart disease in the United States is attributable to cigarette smoking (Rich-Edwards et al., 1995; Shopland & Burns, 1993). Disturbing increases in rates of initiation among adolescent girls (USDHHS, 1994) and relatively low rates of cessation among adult women smokers, particularly heavy smokers, make understanding smoking behavior and identifying interventions that are most appropriate for women an important health promotion priority.

Health Effects of Smoking for Women

Smoking significantly increases women's risk of heart disease, stroke, chronic obstructive pulmonary disease, and cancers of the lung, bladder, nasopharynx, and esophagus (Rich-Edwards et al., 1995). Recent evidence suggests that dose for dose, women may be more susceptible to tobacco carcinogens than men (Zang & Wynder, 1996). Moreover, specific to women are the legion of negative reproductive health-related effects of smoking that include: infertility, which is measured as delay in time to conception (Daling, Weiss, Spadoni, Moore, & Voigt, 1987); ectopic pregnancy (Stergachis, Scholes, Daling, Weiss, & Chu, 1991); spontaneous abortion (USDHHS, 1989); pelvic inflammatory disease (Marchbanks, Lee, & Peterson, 1990); amenorrhea (Pettersson, Fries, & Nillius, 1973); earlier onset of menopause (Willett et al., 1983), which is a risk factor for osteoporotic fractures; as well as cancers of the endometrium and uterus (USDHHS, 1990). Moreover, smoking and use of oral contraceptives significantly increase the risk of myocardial infarctions among women over age 35 (USDHHS, 1990). There is also growing epidemiological evidence of the association between smoking and the development of cervical cancer. A review of 30 studies noted positive associations generally ranging from a two- to fourfold increase in risk (Winkelstein, 1990). Evidence of measurable levels of nicotine and cotinine in the cervical fluids of women smokers supports the biological plausibility of smoking as a risk factor for cervical cancer (Hellberg, Nilsson, Haley, Hoffman, & Wynder, 1988).

Physiological Effects of Nicotine on Women

At equivalent levels of nicotine intake, women metabolize nicotine more slowly than men (Fant, Everson, Dayton, Pickworth, & Henningfield, 1996) and therefore experience higher sustained blood levels of nicotine. This slower metabolism is thought to enhance the reinforcing properties of smoking (Fant et al., 1996). Moreover, evidence suggests that there are also racial differences in nicotine metabolism (Wagenknecht et al., 1990), which may further increase the dependence properties of nicotine for minority women. Clinical evidence of greater perceptions of muscle tension (Epstein, Dickson, McKenzie, Russell, 1984) and reaction time (Knott, 1991) that have been associated with nicotine deprivation in women compared to men suggest that women may derive greater physiologic benefits from nicotine. Although there appear to be no gender differences in the severity of symptoms experienced during nicotine withdrawal, it has been suggested that women experience withdrawal differently than men (Fant et al., 1996), with women reporting more depressive affect and cigarette craving than men (Svikis, Hatsukami, Hughes, Carroll, & Pickens, 1986).

There is consistent evidence that nicotine increases the metabolism of smokers as evidenced in smokers weighing less on average than nonsmokers (Perkins, 1994). The majority of smokers who quit gain from 5 to 10 pounds, with up to 15% of quitters gaining 25 or more pounds (Kawachi, Trois, Rotnitzky, Coakley, & Colditz, 1996; Williamson et al., 1991). The stronger metabolic effects of nicotine in women may place them at greater risk of gaining weight and cause them to gain more weight than their male counterparts (Perkins, 1994; Williamson et al., 1991). Moreover, a consistent dose-response relation has been observed with heavier smokers gaining more weight with cessation than lighter smokers (Kawachi et al., 1996; Williamson et al., 1991). Women who smoked 15 or more cigarettes per day were four times more likely than women who smoked less than 15 cigarettes to gain 13 kilograms or more after quitting (Williamson et al., 1991).

Patterns of Smoking Among Women

Despite widespread public awareness of the multiple health risks associated with smoking, one out of every four girls under age 18 is a smoker and more than 25 million American women smoke (Blumenthal, 1996). Whereas the last two decades have seen an overall decrease in smoking prevalence, the rate of smoking has declined much more slowly among women than among men (Husten, Chrismon, & Reddy, 1996). If current trends continue, smoking rates of women will overtake those of men by the year 2000. Smoking rates are highest, approaching 30%, among women of reproductive age (18–44 years; Husten et al., 1996). Rates of smoking are particularly high among young White women with a high school education or less and low income. Cessation rates are lower among African American women (30% have quit) compared to White women (43% have quit; Stotts, Glynn, & Baquet, 1991). Minority and young women who have low rates of self-initiated cessation are also underrepresented in formal smoking cessation programs. A greater proportion of women than men are precontemplators, that is, not considering quitting smoking within 6 months and have lower self-confidence that they could quit if they were to try (Schorling, 1995; Tessaro et al., 1997). However, the debate continues regarding whether or not women are less likely to be successful at quitting when they try than men, with some evidence suggesting that women are more likely than men to relapse (Nides et al., 1995) and others indicating no gender differences (Garvey, Bliss, Hitchcock, Heinold, & Rosner, 1992; Hill et al., 1994; Husten et al., 1996). Regardless, rates of relapse are very high, both among self-quitters (Garvey et al., 1994) and those who participate in formal cessation programs (Pirie et al., 1992).

Barriers to Smoking Cessation For Women

Weight concerns (i.e., a strong desire to stay thin and fear of weight gain) have been suggested to be key factors that influence women to take up smoking (Camp, Klesges, & Relyea, 1993; French, Perry, Leon, & Fulkerson, 1994) and keep them from quitting (Garvey et al., 1994; Klesges et al., 1988). Lack of awareness of the health effects of smoking has been indicated as an important barrier to cessation among African American women (Manfredi, Lacey, Warnecke, & Buis, 1992; Schorling, 1995). Fear of irritability and depression, loss of an important pleasure, and perceiving smoking to be beneficial for stress management also have been widely reported as barriers to cessation among both White (Sorensen & Pechacek, 1987) and minority women (Ahmed, D. R. Brown, Gary, & Saadatmand, 1994; Manfredi et al., 1992; Shervington, 1994; Tessaro et al., 1997). This is particularly true among low income women who report few available resources for dealing with the life stresses associated with economic disadvantage (Manfredi et al., 1992; Shervington, 1994). Living with other smokers or being married to a smoker is an important barrier to cessation for women (Garvey et al., 1992; Murray, Johnston, Dolce, Lee, & O'Hara, 1995). Moreover, the lack of a strong social network and living in a low income environment characterized by high rates of smoking and weak norms supporting smoking cessation reduce African American women's likelihood of and success at cessation (Manfredi et al., 1992). Confidence in ability to quit (Gritz, Berman, Bastani, & Wu, 1992; Hill et al., 1994), intrinsic motivators such as health concerns and desire for self-control (Curry, Wagner, & Grothaus, 1991), and social support from family, friends, coworkers, and spouses regardless of their smoking status (Cohen & Lichtenstein, 1990; Hill et al., 1994), have been positively associated with success at quitting.

Smoking Cessation Interventions for Women

Interventions specifically designed for women smokers have attempted to address the role of weight concerns as an inhibitor to cessation and long-term maintenance. A randomized trial tested nicotine gum or a behavioral weight control program each alone, or in combination as adjuncts to an intensive group cessation intervention for weight concerned women smokers (Pirie et al., 1992). The intervention integrated accepted cognitive and behavioral coping strategies for quitting smoking, changing eating behaviors, and developing a walking program. The weight gain prevention intervention was highly attractive to women smokers. Nicotine replacement reduced postcessation withdrawal symptoms (Hatsukami, McBride, Pirie, Hellersteadt, & Lando, 1991) and initially decreased postcessation weight gain (Pirie et al., 1992). However, the tested adjunctive components failed to increase cessation rates or long-term weight gain. Evaluation of a similar but more intensive intervention that included as part of the most intensive component an individualized aerobic exercise plan not only failed to increase cessation rates but had higher rates of relapse than the control condition (Hall, Tunstall, Vila, & Duffy, 1992).

Results of these two studies have led some to conclude that interventions requiring simultaneous changes in diet, smoking, and exercise may overburden individuals who are trying to quit smoking. Further, it is suggested that change in one behavior may undermine success in another behavior change. For example, calorie restriction may enhance the reinforcing properties of nicotine, thus, making cessation more difficult (Hall et al., 1992; Perkins, 1994). Recent evidence that women's weight gain is relatively small in the month after quitting (McBride, French, Pirie, & Jeffery, 1996) suggests that weight gain prevention adjuncts do not necessarily need to be provided coincident with cessation interventions in order to be effective. Moreover, weight concerns increase steadily during the 12 months after cessation (McBride et al., 1996). Thus, as has been suggested elsewhere (Gritz et al., 1992), weight-related adjuncts could be provided in the months after cessation.

Interventions designed to evaluate the benefit of physical activity for smoking cessation among women have also had mixed results. An earlier study found no advantage in decreasing relapse rates and actually increased reports of tension and anxiety among women quitters who participated in nine activity sessions that emphasized a walking/jogging activity plan as compared to two comparison groups (Russell, Epstein, Johnston, Block, & Blair, 1988). However, adherence to the intervention as indicated by posttreatment fitness levels appeared to be low. A more intensive intervention that required women to participate in multiple weekly sessions of aerobic activity for 3 weeks prior to their quit date reported more positive findings (B. H. Marcus, Albrect, et al., 1995). Although cessation rates were higher in the exercise group, achieving compliance with a comparable intensive intervention may be difficult in real-world settings given the results of the earlier trial (Russell et al., 1988). Recent data based on over 9,300 women smokers in the Nurses Health Study indicate that moderate levels of physical activity minimize postcessation weight gain for women (Kawachi et al., 1996). Thus, evaluations of interventions that promote less rigorous exercise regimens are needed.

In response to decreasing participation rates in group cessation programs and smokers' preferences for self-guided cessation interventions, several innovative randomized trials have evaluated minimal self-help cessation interventions provided in an outreach format to "nonvolunteer" smokers. Typically, these interventions have included some combination of written self-help guides (Gritz et al., 1992; Curry, McBride, Grothaus, Louie, & Wagner, 1995), personalized feedback (Curry et al., 1995), and outreach telephone counseling (Curry et al. 1995). Although these outreach approaches have been well-received by smokers, they have not resulted in uniformly higher quit rates than those observed in untreated control groups or than national secular trends. However, of the minimal strategies tested, telephone counseling has shown the greatest potential particularly among smokers who, prior to being called, were not thinking about quitting (Curry et al., 1995). It has been argued that the effectiveness of these proactive approaches might be enhanced if they were provided within the context of a meaningful health event or clinical context (Curry et al., 1995).

Women are higher utilizers of health services, particularly in their reproductive and childrearing years. Moreover, women's childbearing role creates unique physical, social, and clinical contexts for smoking cessation interventions. For example, social awareness of the health risks of smoking to the fetus makes pregnancy a "teachable moment" of enhanced motivation for smoking cessation (Floyd, Rimer, Giovino, Mullen, & Sullivan, 1993). Provision of minimal cessation interventions—such as self-help booklets, advice to quit from a health care provider, and counseling either face to face or via the telephone—have been shown to substantially increase rates of cessation during pregnancy, particularly in middle income women (Ershoff, Mullen, & Quinn, 1989; Sexton & Hebel, 1984). However, with a few exceptions (Windsor et al., 1985), clinic-based interventions with low income pregnant smokers have had far less favorable results (Kendrick et al., 1995).

Moreover, these interventions have had little or no impact on high postpartum relapse rates (Ershoff, Quinn, & Mullen, 1995). Several randomized trials testing relapse prevention interventions that include self-help guides and telephone counseling adjuncts in late pregnancy and early postpartum are currently underway (McBride, Curry, Lando, & Pirie, 1994). Cessation interventions based in pediatric, family planning, and WIC clinics that serve a high proportion of women of childbearing age (Secker-Walker, Chir, Solomon, Flynn, & Dana, 1994) have also been evaluated (Kendrick et al., 1995; Severson, Andrews, Lichtenstein, Wall, & Akers, 1997; Wall, Severson, Andrews, Flynn, & Dana, 1994). However, these clinical settings offer special challenges due to high patient volume and limited provider resources to implement cessation interventions (Kendrick et al., 1995; Wall et al., 1994).

Community-based smoking cessation interventions that have included quit contests, outreach recruitment to cessation services, and policy initiatives have been somewhat disappointing (COMMIT, 1995; Lando et al., 1995). These interventions have had the greatest impact on lighter smokers, who are also most likely to quit on their own (COMMIT, 1995). The fact that rates of cessation among heavy smokers have not been influenced by these approaches suggests that more intensive intervention programs may be necessary for this recalcitrant group of smokers.

Smoking Summary

High rates of smoking among women make the development and evaluation of effective smoking cessation interventions a health promotion priority. The unique barriers to quitting reported by women suggest that interventions must address weight concerns, stressful lifestyles, and more healthful ways to cope with negative moods and depression. More work is needed to design and evaluate interventions that encourage smoking cessation simultaneous with behavior changes (e.g., increasing exercise) that can enhance the potential for long-term maintenance of cessation.

Women's greater use of health services presents multiple opportunities for providing cessation interventions to women in clinical settings. However, organizational and system barriers to these interventions present major obstacles to widespread adoption of these approaches. Community-wide interventions could accelerate secular trends in cessation, particularly among light smokers. However, these approaches are likely to be ineffective for highly addicted smokers.

PHYSICAL ACTIVITY

Health Effects of Physical Activity

A sedentary lifestyle is associated with death from coronary heart disease, colon cancer, and diabetes (Powell, Thompson, Caspersen, & Kendrick, 1987; USDHHS, 1996); in contrast, a physically active lifestyle reduces morbidity associated with multiple chronic diseases and improves the quality of life (Bouchard, Shephard, & Stephens, 1994; Paffenbarger et al., 1986). Overall mortality for women was associated with low levels of cardiorespiratory fitness (RR = 5.35); however, there was no association between the two based on self-reported physical inactivity (Blair, Kohl, & Barlow, 1993). Other evidence suggests that increases in physical activity result in improved psychosocial status, functional status, and physical fitness (Minor & J. D. Brown, 1993).

Physical activity provides protection against osteoporosis, a major cause of morbidity and mortality of older women (NIH, 1985), by increasing peak bone mass at maturity, maintaining bone mass during the third and fourth decades, and by retarding the loss of bone mass in the fifth decade of life (Kohrt, Snead, Slatopolsky, & Birge, 1995; Sinaki & Offord, 1988). Some evidence suggests that resistance exercise, as compared to endurance activities, may result in greater gains in bone mass, and for postmenopausal women, greater gain in bone density occurs when exercise is combined with estrogen replacement therapy (Kohrt et al., 1995; USDHHS, 1996). Among the elderly, increased muscle strength and balance appears to reduce the potential for falls and maintain the independent living status of elderly women (Wolfson, Whipple, Derby, Judge, & King, 1996).

Evidence of associations between inactivity and other diseases such as breast, ovarian, endometrial, and uterine cancers is both limited and inconsistent (USDHHS, 1996). Nonetheless, there is some evidence that physical activity during adolescence and early adulthood may be protective against breast cancer (Bernstein, Henderson, Hanisch, Sullivan-Halley, & Ross, 1994; Mittendorf et al., 1995). Moreover, regular moderate exercise limits symptoms and improves function for chronic conditions, such as osteoarthritis and rheumatoid arthritis (Allegrante, Kovar, MacKenzie, Peterson, & Gutin, 1993; Fisher, Kame, Rouse, & Pendergast, 1994).

Negative affects of physical activity on women's health, such as training-induced amenorrhea, excessive activity associated with eating disorders, and the need for adaptations in activity during pregnancy, are relevant for only a few girls and women (Dubbert, 1995). Because these conditions are not prevalent, they are best addressed in clinical settings rather than through public health interventions.

Prevalence of Physical Activity Patterns of Women

Despite the established positive health benefits of physical activity, 25% of U.S. adults have sedentary lifestyles (i.e., no leisure time physical activity) and an additional 33% are insufficiently active to realize health benefits or maintain cardiorespiratory fitness (USDHHS, 1996). In spite of the "fitness movement" and programs to increase activity levels during the last two decades, physical inactivity levels remain high among all women (i.e., 59%) and, more so among minority women (i.e., 65%; King, Jeffery, et al., 1995; CDC, 1995). Fifty percent of adults who initiate an exercise program are likely to drop out within 6 months (Dishman & Sallis, 1994). Unfortunately, with only minimal declines in the proportion of women who are sedentary, limited progress has been made toward the Year 2000 objectives of increasing physical activity (Healthy people 2000, 1990; McGinnis & Lee, 1995).

Evidence indicates that inactivity levels increase with age, from 26% for women from age 18 to 34 as compared to 42% of women who are age 65 and older (Duelberg, 1992; Washburn, Kline, Lackland, & Wheeler, 1992). Physical inactivity is also associated with being overweight, having a history of being physically inactive, and smoking (Bild et al., 1993; Blair, Powell et al., 1993). In addition, smokers are more likely to drop out of exercise programs than nonsmokers (Dishman & Sallis, 1994).

Minority women are less likely than White women to engage in physical activity: only 29% of White women and 18% of African American women in the United States are physically active at a health enhancing level, according to data from the 1992 Behavioral Risk Factor Surveillance System (BRFS; CDC, 1995). A disproportionate number of minority women are also economically disadvantaged, have a lower level of education, and are overweight; each of those factors are independently related to low levels of physical activity (Caspersen & Merritt, 1995; Kanders et al., 1994). Thus, both African American and White women with less than a high school education were less likely to report regular activity (17%) than those women with a high school education (24%) and college graduates (34%). Women in the lowest income category were least likely to report physical activity (21%) as compared to women in the highest income category (35%).

Any discussion of patterns in women's physical activity must acknowledge that self-report measures used in national surveillance data may be less appropriate for women than men because they typically do not assess gendered activities such as housework, child and elder care, and occupational activity (Dubbert, 1995). In addition, some measures underestimate activity for those involved in multiple activities (Caspersen & Merritt, 1995).

Physical Activity Recommendations for Women

The substantial positive health benefits of physical activity have led the NIH consensus conference on physical activity (1995) to recommend that all Americans should engage in regular activity at a level appropriate to their ability. To this end, all children and adults should set and reach a goal of accumulating at least 30 minutes of moderate-intensity physical activity on most, preferably all days of the week. Those who currently meet these standards may derive additional health and fitness benefits by becoming more physically active or including more vigorous activity. Similarly, it has been shown that regular moderate intensity activity, such as walking and gardening, results in substantial health benefits (Pate et al., 1995; USDHHS, 1996).

Women can meet the daily goal of 30 minutes of moderate intensity exercise—enough to expend approximately 200 calories—by briskly walking 2 miles, bicycling 7 miles at a moderate pace (13 miles per hour), or swimming half-a-mile at a moderate pace (35 yards per minutes) (Cooper, 1982; Pate et al., 1995). Unfortunately, many women may find it difficult to set aside 30 minutes a day for exercise. For them, it is especially important to recognize that short bouts of activity lasting 8 to 10 minutes, such as walking up multiple flights of stairs, walking short distances, gardening, housework, and child care activities also have been shown to result in health benefits (Leon, Connett, Jacobs, & Rauramaa, 1987; Paffenbarger et al., 1986).

Compared with the health benefits, the risks of physical activity are low, so most women do not need medical consultation or pretesting prior to initiating a program of moderate-intensity physical activity (ACSM, 1995; USDHHS, 1996). A medical evaluation is suggested, however, for women over age 50 planning a vigorous program with known coronary heart disease (CHD) or who have multiple CHD risk factors. However, women who are currently not engaged in physical activity should gradually increase the time spent in a physical activity from an initial comfortable time period (e.g., 10 minutes) to the recommended time of 30 minutes. This may take 2 to 16 weeks, depending on the women's age, health, weight, and initial fitness level (ACSM, 1995; Cooper, 1982). Women with specific fitness goals beyond the health-related benefits of physical activity may need to obtain more specific recommendations, including the type of activities, level of intensity, frequency, duration, and information about strength and flexibility exercises (Pate et al., 1995).

Barriers and Facilitators to Physical Activity for Women

There is a dearth of research regarding the specific types of impediments that contribute to women's low participation in physical activity (Crawford, E. L. Jackson, & Godbey, 1991; B. H. Marcus, Dubbert, et al., 1995). However, the limited evidence suggests that barriers to physical activity differ by gender and among women, and vary by ethnic background, income level, and education (Dishman & Sallis, 1994).

Time is consistently the most frequently mentioned hindrance to initiating and sustaining a regular exercise program (Benedict, 1996; Johnson, Corrigen, Dubbert, & Gramling, 1990; Martin & Dubbert, 1982). Many women may not begin exercising or may drop out of physical activity programs if the time issue is not adequately addressed. It is not surprising, therefore, that having children is negatively associated with womens' participation in vigorous exercise (Verhoef, Love, & Rose, 1992), and that women with children under age 5 are least likely to report exercise participation (B. H. Marcus, Pinto, Simkin, Audrain, & Taylor, 1994).

Social-psychological and structural factors intervene between intention and actual participation, and consequently are important considerations in developing a program to increase womens' participation in physical activity (Dishman & Sallis, 1994; Jackson, Crawford, & Godbey, 1993; Kay & G. Jackson, 1991). Psychological dispositions such as social anxiety, self-consciousness, low will power, low self-efficacy, and perceived lack of coordination and fitness level can inhibit women's participation in physical activities, as can social factors such as a lack of companionship or a lack of role models (Benedict, 1996; Dishman & Sallis, 1994; Dubbert, 1995; Ebrahim & Rowland, 1996; B. H. Marcus, Dubbert et al., 1995; NIH, 1995; USDHHS, 1996). Womens' concern for safety and security are also important in their decision to participate in physical activities (Henderson, Stalnaker, & Taylor, 1988). Poor health is also a common barrier to consistent exercise for women (Kriska et al., 1986). When health-related conditions hinder womens' physical activity, it is important that their physicians be knowledgeable and interested in promoting their participation in physical activity (Ebrahim & Rowland, 1996; U.S. Preventive Services, 1996).

Women also report numerous structural barriers to physical activity, including limited financial resources, inhospitable climate, scheduling difficulties, lack of opportunity to participate (and knowledge of such opportunity), transportation problems, and negative reference group attitudes about the appropriateness of certain activities (A. C. King et al., 1992). Available information concerning structural barriers that are specific to minority women (Bild et al., 1993; J. Datillo, A. M. Datillo, Samdahl, & Kleiber, 1994; Shaw, Bonen, & McCabe, 1991) suggest that among low income minority women, responsibilities for family care, lack of finances, body image/health problems, and housework are factors that inhibit their physical activity. Minority women also place less value on fitness and thinness, and report fewer opportunities for leisure activities as compared to White women (Mayo, 1992).

In contrast, factors that facilitate physical activity include inexpensiveness of the activity, greater "accessibility" (Bild et al., 1993) that includes a convenient location and flexibility in scheduling (Stephens, Jacobs, & White, 1985). Moreover, different factors are associated with initiation of a physical activity program compared to those that encourage long-term maintenance of the program (B. H. Marcus, Dubbert et al., 1995). Due to changes in life circumstances, women often have a greater number of lapses in regular activity programs compared to men during an equivalent time period (Dubbert, Stetson, & Corrigan, 1991; Marcus, Dubbert et al., 1995; USHHS, 1996). As noted by A. C. King (1991), more information is needed to prevent the relapses typically occurring as women experience significant transitions: passage through puberty, attending college, becoming pregnant, raising children, going through menopause, and becoming involved in family caregiving.

In sum, many women must overcome barriers to engage in physical activity. Some of these barriers, such as perceived lack of coordination, may be related to gender stereotypes suggesting that strenuous activity is unfeminine. Other barriers—low self-efficacy, low will power—signify the important links between beliefs and behavior. However, many barriers reflect the contemporary reality of limited time, money, or adequate public space that is safe for physical activity. It is difficult to imagine how the many hindrances to physical activity can be overcome, without attention to the structural barriers imposed by policies and the environment.

Interventions to Increase Physical Activity

Most health behavior change programs related to physical activity are focused primarily on individual behavior change (Gottlieb & Green, 1987; Lewis et al., 1993). But successful interventions require multiple strategies that are focused on contextual factors (structural, organizational, environmental, and public policy determinants) and individual behavior (Stokols, 1992; Winkleby, 1994). Unfortunately, it is difficult to identify the most effective programs for women because most exercise intervention studies have involved a limited number of participants, have been of short duration, and have validated participants' self-reported activity; moreover, gender differences in response to interventions are often not reported (Dubbert, 1995; A. C. King et al., 1992). Very few interventions have been specifically designed to increase women's, and more particularly minority and older women's, levels of physical activity (B. H. Marcus, Dubbert, King, & Pinto, 1995).

Individual Behavior Change Approaches. Individual strategies focus on psychological barriers to physical activity that they seek to eliminate through reinforcement, goal setting, self-monitoring, feedback, decision making, skills training to prevent relapse, incentives and contests, behavioral counseling, and prompts and reminders (A. C. King et al., 1992; B. H. Marcus et al., 1995; USDHHS, 1996). Intervention studies demonstrating significant changes have involved programs that were convenient (A. King, Taylor, Haskell, & Debusk, 1988; A. King, Haskell, Young, Oka, & Stefanick, 1995) and based on social learning theory (McAuley, Courneya, Rudolph, & Lox, 1994). New developments in tailored messaging allow messages promoting physical activity to be individually tailored to stage of change and self-identified barriers.

Interventions in Health Care Settings. The U.S. Preventive Services Task Force (1996) identified "physical activity counseling" in their list of recommended clinical preventive services. But there are barriers to physician recommendations regarding physical activity, including lack of time, limited reimbursement for such services, and physician's lack of confidence in counseling patients (A. C. King et al., 1992). The recently developed Physician Assessment and Counseling for Exercise Program (PACE) is a protocol developed by Sallis and his colleagues (CDC, 1992; Wooten et al., 1991). The training program developed as part of the PACE project was successful in preparing providers to counsel patients in 5 minutes or less about exercise (Long et al., 1996). The PACE program was found efficacious in a controlled intervention study involving 255 patients, 84% female, from 17 physician offices (Calfas et al., 1996). The intervention group received 3 to 5 minutes of physical activity counseling from the physician and a telephone call 2 weeks later. At follow-up, 52% of intervention patients adopted regular activity as compared to only 12% of the controls and of the patients who were already active, the intervention patients reported walking more than controls (Calfas et al., 1996).

Worksite Interventions. Some employees benefit from working for organizations that provide facilities, equipment, or favorable policies (e.g., flextime) to promote physical activity. The 1992 survey of U.S. worksites reported that

33% of worksites with from 50 to 99 employees and 47% of worksites with from 100 to 249 employees provide exercise facilities. This represents a significant increase in worksites offering programs during the past 10 years. However, these figures may overestimate employee access to exercise facilities or equipment and health promotion programs because the majority of U.S. employees (56%) work for companies with fewer than 99 employees.

In recently completed worksite trials, the primary focus of the interventions was on individual behavior change strategies (Abrams et al., 1994; Glasgow et al., 1995). Worksite physical activity programs usually involve less than 20% of the eligible employees (Crump, Earp, Kozma, & Hertz-Picciotto, 1996). These programs often do not attract the sedentary, blue-collar, less educated employees, however there are some exceptions when a program uses multiple communication methods, offers incentives to encourage participation, and ensures that the program activities are offered at convenient times for shift employees (Heirich, Foote, Erfurt, & Konopka, 1993; A. King, Carl, Birkel, & Haskell, 1988). Programs that encourage peer support or train lay health advisors may have great potential in manufacturing worksites (Heirich et al., 1993; Tessaro, 1996).

Community Interventions. Community-wide interventions concentrate on producing population change rather than individual change. The three large health behavior trials conducted in the United States during the 1980s—Minnesota Heart Health Program (Luepker et al., 1994), Pawtucket Heart Health Program (Carleton et al., 1995), and the Stanford Five-City Project (Farquhar et al., 1990)—all included a physical activity component. It is difficult to compare results across these studies because the outcome measures of physical activity varied. Unfortunately, the results of these community-based trials have been disappointing. However, many of the strategies and approaches used were actually individually oriented. The recent focus on environmental and policy level changes may increase the chances of realizing community level change in physical activity levels.

Summary Physical Activity and Women

In contrast to improved lifestyle habits, reduction in dietary fat and smoking and control of high blood pressure and cholesterol, levels of physical inactivity have not improved in the United States during the last 10 years. The strong relation between physical inactivity and chronic disease demands a strong public health approach that includes a combination of environment, organization, and public policy strategies (A. C. King et al., 1992). A social ecological approach seeks to change policies, physical structures, and social norms, as well as individual factors (e.g., behavior and attitudes), that have an impact on physical activity (McLeroy, Bibeau, Steckler, & Glanz, 1988; Stokols, 1992). Interventions targeted at public and organizational policies are the next generation of community-based interventions and such interventions may have a greater impact on community levels of health behaviors than individual change programs (Winkleby, 1994).

CANCER SCREENING

Recommendations for cancer screening vary across the age spectrum and depending on what organization issues the advice. Most medical organizations (see Table 31.1) recommend Pap tests and clinical breast exams for women in their 20s and 30s, mammograms either in the 40s or starting at age 50, and screening for colorectal cancer with fecal occult blood tests (FOBTS) and sigmoidoscopy at age 50. Data indicate that there is widespread, but not universal, adherence to Pap test guidelines, but most women are not being screened appropriately for breast and colorectal cancer. Moreover, rates are lower for low SES and older women. Screening for breast, cervical, and colorectal cancers is discussed briefly.

Current Status of Breast Cancer Screening in the United States

In 2000, more than 182,000 women were diagnosed with breast cancer and 40,800 women died of the disease (American Cancer Society, 2000). Numerous studies have shown that regular mammograms with or without clinical breast exams can reduce mortality by about 30% for women from age 50 to 69 (Fletcher, Black, Harris, Rimer, & Shapiro, 1993). However, there is considerable debate about the benefits of mammography for women in their 40s (Fletcher et al., 1993; Rimer, 1995a; Smart, Hendrick, Rutledge, & R. A. Smith, 1995).

The proportion of American women who are receiving regular mammograms has increased dramatically since 1987, when one third of women had ever had a mammogram, and only 17% had one in the preceding year (Dawson & Thompson, 1990). By 1990, nearly two thirds of women age 40 and older reported having had at least one mammogram, although only 31% were following guidelines (Morbidity Mortality Weekly Report, MMWR, 1990). From 1987 to 1992, the proportion of women who reported recent mammograms increased at least twofold for women in every age and racial/ethnic group. Screening remained lower for women over age 70 (Breen & Kessler, 1995). The proportion of women who are getting regular mammograms has increased dramatically since 1987. In 1992, based on the NHIS, about 35% of women over age 40 had ever been screened; 35% of women in their 40s, 42% of women in their 50s, 29% of women in their 60s, and 31% of women 70+ reported a recent mammogram.

In 1987, the NHIS showed that underusers were more likely to be less educated, reside outside of metropolitan areas, and to be members of a minority. By 1990, the racial gap had been reduced on a national level, although it was still significant in many regions of the United States, such as the South. Currently, the most relevant demographic factors for predicting mammography use are lower income status and lower levels of education (Breen & Kessler, 1994), which transcend the impact of race alone.

Barriers and Facilitators to Breast Cancer Screening

The characteristics of women who do not get regular mammograms are generally consistent from study to study and are sim-

TABLE 31.1

Screening Guidelines for Breast, Colorectal, and Cervical Cancers for Selected Health Care Organizations

	American Cancer Society	American College of Obstetrics and Gynecology	U.S. Preventative Health Services Task Force (72)	National Cancer Institute's Patient Data Query (PDQ) System	American College of Radiology	American College of Family Physicians
Breast Cancer	Mammography and CBE yearly for women age 40 and older. CBE every three years ages 20-39; every year age 40 and older. Monthly BSE for all women age 20 and older.	Mammography should be performed every 1-2 years for women ages 40-49 and then annually thereafter.	Mammography every 1-2 years with or without CBE for women ages 50-69.	Mammography every 1-2 years for women age 40 and older. Women at higher risk should talk with their physicians re schedule.	Yearly mammographs for asymptomatic women age 40 and older. It is reasonable to institute screening mammography at an earlier age in women with high risk factors.	Counsel about potential risks and benefits of mammography and CBE for women ages 40-49. Offer mammography and CBE every 1-2 years for women ages 50-69.
Cervical Cancer	Pap test and pelvic exam yearly for all women who are, or have been, sexually active or who have reached age 18. After 3 consecutive normal smears, Pap test less often at the discretion of physician.	Pap test and pelvic exam yearly for all women who are, or have been, sexually active or who have reached age 18. After 3 consecutive normal smears, Pap test less often at the discretion of physician.	Pap test every 1-3 years for all women who are sexually active and/or who have a cervix. No evidence to support an upper limit, but age 65 can be defended in women with a history of normal and regular Pap tests.	Evidence strongly suggests a decrease in mortality for regular screening with Pap tests in women who are sexually active or who have reached age 18. The upper limit at which such screening ceases to be effective in unknown.	N/A	Offer Pap test at least every 3 years for women who have ever had sex and have a cervix.
Colorectal Cancer	One of the following schedules for men and women age 50 and over; FOBT yearly and sigmoidoscopy every 5 years; colonoscopy every 10 years; double-contrast barium enema every 5-10 years (DRE at time of screening except for FOBT). Those with high risk for colorectal cancer should begin screening earlier and/or more frequently.	After the age of 50 years, a DRE should accompany the pelvic examination and an annual FOBT should be performed; sigmoidoscopy should be performed every 3-5 years.	FOBT and/or sigmoidoscopy yearly at age 50 and older. There is insufficient evidence to determine which screening method is preferable or whether the combination produces greater benefit than either one alone.	FOBT either annually or biennially using rehydrated or nonrehydrated stool specimens in people ages 50-80 decreases mortality for colorectal cancer. Regular screening by sigmoidoscopy in people over age 50 may decrease mortality from colorectal cancer. There is insufficient evidence to determine the optimal interval for such screening.	N/A	Screen for colorectal cancer annually with FOBT, sigmoidoscopy, colonoscopy, or barium enema in adults age 50 and older.

Note. CBE, clinical breast examination; BSE, breast self-examination; DRE, digital rectal examination; FOBT, fecal occult blood test. Adapted from "Cancer Screening" by B. K. Rimer, J. M. Schildkraut, and Robert Hiatt in V. T. Devita, S. Hellman, and S. A. Rosenberg (Eds.), *Cancer: Principles and Practice of Oncology*, Philadelphia: Lippincott-Raven. Copyright 1997. Adapted by permission.

ilar to those for Pap tests (Rimer, 1994). The most important barrier is the lack of a recommendation by a woman's physician (Burg, Lane, & Polednak, 1990; Coleman & Feuer, 1992; Fox, Murata, & Stein, 1991; Rimer, Keintz, Keller, Engstrom, & Rosan, 1989; Siegler, Feaganes, & Rimer, 1995). Women who are older, African American, or Hispanic are less likely than middle-aged White women to report receiving such a recommendation. Other factors contributing to women's nonparticipation in mammography, according to their self-report, are an absence of breast problems or the belief that mammograms are unnecessary in the absence of symptoms.

Other barriers to mammography exist, but they account for much less of the variance in explaining the behavior. These barriers, which may be important for individual women or subgroups of women, include anxiety about the possibility of finding a problem and concern about radiation and pain (e.g., Fullerton, Kritz-Silverstein, Sadler, & Barrett-Connor, 1996). Pain, in fact, may be more of a problem than previously indicated (Kornguth, Keefe, & Conaway, 1996). These concerns may be important for individual women or subgroups of women. For example, African American and Hispanic women seem to be more concerned about pain and report more anxiety about the mammography experience. There is some evidence that older African American women are more fatalistic about cancer in general (Rimer, Ross, Cristinzio, & E. King, 1992), and unmarried women are less likely to have mammograms (Calle, Flanders, Thun, & Martin, 1993).

Access and environmental barriers also may inhibit mammography use. A study conducted in a health maintenance organization (HMO; McBride et al., 1993) found that nonparticipants had more difficulty getting to the facility, would have to travel farther, and were more likely to rate the facility as inconvenient. Women without health insurance are less likely to participate in mammography or Pap testing (Breen & Kessler, 1994). Women in managed care organizations are more likely to get mammograms and Pap tests (Collins & Simon, 1996).

However, studies show that even when the cost barrier is removed, other important psychological barriers remain (Rimer et al., 1989). If these barriers are not addressed, women still may not pursue regular mammograms. Although not a major barrier, cost has been reported as a barrier for some (e.g., women age 50 to 59 or Hispanic women; Fox et al., 1991).

Women are more likely to get mammograms when advised by their physicians (Dawson & Thompson, 1990; Rimer et al., 1989), when they know the recommended screening interval for their age, and when they are aware of the relation between age and breast cancer screening (Champion, 1991; Slenker & Grant, 1989). There also is evidence that women with more social ties are more likely to have mammograms (E. King et al., 1993). Having had a recent CBE also is related to having mammograms (Lane, Caplan, & Grimson, 1996). Finally, Fullerton et al. (1996) showed that regular mammography users were more likely to use estrogen, have a history of reproductive cancer, and rate their health as excellent.

In one of the few analyses to examine the relation of personality variables to mammography, Siegler et al. (1995) showed that among women in their 40s who were part of the UNC Alumnae Study, conscientiousness, extroversion, assertiveness, and low depression predicted mammography use.

Cervical Cancer Screening

In 2000, cervical cancer was diagnosed in 12,800 women, and 4,600 died of the disease (American Cancer Society, 2000). U.S. mortality from cervical cancer has not declined since the 1970s (Devsa, Young, Brinton, & Fraumeni, 1989; Eddy, 1990). This is unfortunate because deaths from cervical cancer are nearly 100% preventable. The Pap test is a widely accepted screening test to prevent mortality for cervical cancer. Although there never has been a randomized clinical trial (RCT) to evaluate the Pap test, and precise estimates of sensitivity and specificity are not known (Wong & Feussner, 1993b), cervical cancer is considered almost totally avoidable through regular Pap tests. The only real controversy about Pap test screening centers on the upper age for screening.

According to the 1987 NHIS, the percentages of women who reported never having had a Pap test were approximately 11% of women overall, 10% of White women, 11.9% of African American women, and 24.7% of Hispanic women. The proportion of women who reported having had a Pap test remained stable from 1987 to 1992 overall, but it increased slightly for Hispanic women and remained low for women over age 70 (Breen & Kessler, 1995). The 1992 NHIS data show that from 89% to 95% of women from age 18 to 69 report ever having had a Pap test, but the number is a bit lower (82%) for women age 70+. In addition, anywhere from 43% to 76% of women report having had a Pap test in the past year.

Barriers and Facilitators to Cervical Cancer Screening

Many of the barriers and facilitators to Pap tests are similar to those for breast cancer screening. Older women and women past childbearing age may not recognize that Pap tests are still necessary (Caplan, Wells, & Haynes, 1992), and some women and physicians believe that women who are not sexually active do not need Pap tests (Wilcox & Mosher, 1993). Most women who have not had Pap tests have had contact with the health care system, indicating that, as for mammography, the failure of women to receive Pap tests reflects a missed clinical opportunity (Harlan, Bernstein, & Kessler, 1991).

Knowledge and beliefs about cervical cancer screening vary by age and ethnicity. For example, Hispanic women are less likely to be aware of Pap tests and therefore may require education about the need for Pap tests. Most studies show a relation between a belief in the benefits of Pap tests and regular screenings (Rimer, 1995a). Women who are embarrassed about getting a Pap test and those who say they are too busy also are less likely to be screened (Cockburn, White, Hirst, & Hill, 1992). Women who do not participate in screening are more likely to cite procrastination or a belief that the test is unnecessary as reasons for not being screened (Harlan et al., 1991). As with mammography, women who do not get other preventive services are less likely to have Pap tests (Rimer,

1992, 1995a). Minority women seem to be more embarrassed than White women about getting Pap tests (Calle et al., 1993). Older Hispanic women are especially at risk for underusing both mammography and Pap testing. Some studies show that women who are more knowledgeable about Pap tests, including the recommended screening interval, are more likely to be tested (Howard, 1987).

Interventions to Increase Screening Adherence

More studies have been conducted to test interventions of increased screening for breast cancer than for other cancers. The literature shows that the best approach to screening is to use multiple interventions directed at patients, physicians, the health care system and, if possible, the community. Multistrategy interventions generally are more effective, although single approaches have been successful in some cases (Rimer, 1994). For example, a nurse practitioner in a hospital clinic was given the responsibility for identifying older, poor, African American women who were due for mammograms and then approaching them (Mandelblatt et al., 1993). This intervention resulted in a significant increase in the proportion of these women who received mammograms. Similarly, public health nurses and community health workers were used to increase cervical cancer screening among poor women in Chicago (Ansell, Lacey, Whitman, Chen, & Phillips, 1994). In another case, a video was created that highlighted a woman's internal attributions about her personal responsibility for getting mammograms (Rothman, 1992), which according to self-reports increased use of mammography.

In one study, women in an independent practice association model HMO were invited to participate in breast cancer screening (Rimer, Ross, Balshem, & Engstrom, 1993). Nonadherent women were sent reminders, which doubled adherence rates. For women who remained adherent, telephone counseling tripled the chances that woman would get a mammogram. During a brief counseling session that averaged 5 minutes, the counselor's goal was to identify and overcome a woman's personal barriers to mammography (A. C. King et al., 1994). These strategies have been tested in other settings with similar results (e.g. Davis et al., 1997), although in many other settings the effect of reminders has been more modest.

Costanza et al. (1992) conducted patient education in a community health center, and Fletcher et al. (1993) implemented a community-wide media campaign. Lane, Polednak, and Burg (1989) used community health education strategies, including a game (Burg et al., 1990). These studies also included free or low cost mammograms as part of the intervention package. Similar community-based approaches have been used to increase cervical cancer screening (Dignan, Michielutte, Wells, & Bahnson, 1994). This approach was effective among high risk women. Thus, these programs included strategies that were parent directed, physician directed, system directed, and sometimes community based.

Although less research has been conducted in cervical cancer screening compared with breast cancer screening, many of the same approaches appear to be effective. Outreach strategies led by community health workers can increase use of cervical cancer screening, and in reach interventions within community health centers also can be effective (Ansell et al., 1994; Lacey et al., 1993). Because most U.S. women are getting regular Pap tests, mass media approaches may not be effective or appropriate. Clinic-based approaches hold promise. Attempts to streamline the process of appointments and waiting time contribute to improved adherence (Harris, O'Malley, Fletcher, & Knight, 1990), and invitations from providers also increase cervical cancer screening (Creighton & Evans, 1992). The combination of health education and the immediate offer of a Pap test increased screening in one study (Cockburn, 1990).

Thus, as with breast cancer screening, the most effective behavior change investigations use a mix of intervention strategies directed at physicians, patients, and in some cases, the community (Costanza et al., 1992; Fletcher et al., 1993; Lane et al., 1989; Rimer et al., 1993; Vellozzi, Romans, & Rothenberg, 1996).

COLORECTAL CANCER SCREENING

Colorectal cancer is one of the leading causes of mortality in the Western world (Solomon & McLeod, 1993). In 1996, 66,800 U.S. women were diagnosed with colorectal cancer and 28,500 died from the disease. Five percent of Americans reaching age 50 will develop this disease by age 80; 2.5% will die from it (Wong & Feussner, 1993a). Well-established risk factors for colorectal cancer include familial polyposis syndromes, Crohn's disease, ulcerative colitis, age, family history, previous history of cancer (endometrial, ovarian, or breast), and Ashkenazi Jewish lineage (Oldenski & Flareau, 1992).

The long natural history of colorectal cancer makes it a good candidate for screening. And in recent years, studies have shown the efficacy of both fecal occult blood tests (FOBT) and sigmoidoscopy in reducing mortality from colorectal cancer (Ahlquist et al., 1993; Ransohoff & Lang, 1993; Selby, 1993; Selby, Friedman, Quesenberry, & Weiss, 1992). Recently, the U.S. Preventive Services Task Force (1996) upgraded its evidence for colorectal cancer with FOBTs and sigmoidoscopy, periodicity unspecified, and other organizations recommend more frequent screening (see Table 31.1). Colorectal cancer screening is especially important for women; women often think they are at lower risk than men for this disease. Yet, according to the 1992 NHIS, only 15% of women had a recent fecal occult blood test and 5% had a recent sigmoidoscopy.

Barriers to Colorectal Cancer Screening

Far less is known about adherence to colorectal cancer screening than to screening for breast and cervical cancer, and even less is known about barriers for women. There do appear to be barriers that are related to perceptions and concerns about the tests. The tests are seen as painful, embarrassing, and inconvenient. Many people do not know that colorectal cancer screening is needed (Myers et al., 1990). As with other cancer screening tests, people are more likely to be screened if their physician advises them to do so (Myers et al., 1991;

Myers, Balshem, Wolf, Ross, & Millner, 1993). There is some evidence that women may be less likely to be screened than men. For example, Borum (1996) found that 39% of female patients in a university clinic had an FOBT as compared to 59% of male patients. Efforts need to be made to encourage physicians to increase their use of CRC screening.

Blalock, DeVellis, Afifi, and Sandler (1990) and Hunter et al. (1990) also found that personal experience with cancers of relatives or friends increases participation in screening by FOBT and sigmoidoscopy. In addition, increasing age, not smoking, and higher education levels in populations who believe that cancer is curable are likely to be associated with greater participation in colorectal screening activities (Myers et al., 1990).

Interventions to Promote Colorectal Cancer Screening

There have been no reported studies designed to increase colorectal cancer screening among women specifically, and few have been developed for men and women. Those few interventions tested to date suggest that the same approaches that have been successful for enhancing breast and cervical cancer screening are likely to be effective for colorectal cancer. These include such techniques as reminder letters, postcards, and telephone calls (Thompson, Michnich, Gray, Friedlander, & Gilson, 1986; Myers et al., 1991). Because physicians have not yet accepted colorectal cancer screening, physician education is essential. There is a real need to extend what is known about screening for women's cancers to colorectal cancer. In view of the fact that perhaps one third or more of colon cancer deaths could be avoided by regular screening, the need for intervention research is urgent.

CONCLUSIONS

Over the past decade, significant progress has been made in understanding women's health and particularly health promotion. Significant progress has been made in identifying barriers to participation in screening for breast and cervical cancer, and successful interventions have been developed. Major challenges for the future are to increase screening for these cancers among the women who have not yet been reached, including some ethnic minorities and women with low levels of education. In addition, almost nothing is known about women's barriers to colorectal screening or how to overcome them.

As the previous sections have demonstrated, too few women are exercising, and far too many are overweight. Far too little is known about how to prevent smoking among girls or how to help women stop smoking. Gender-appropriate interventions are needed that fit into women's increasingly busy lifestyles. Time-intensive, centralized interventions are not likely to be the answer for most women; brief programs and tailored methods that can be delivered by telephone or mail should be investigated further. Special attention in program design and evaluation should be paid to those groups of women who are most likely to be out of step with health promotion recommendations. These include minority women, poor women, and those with less education. Instrumental help in reducing access barriers may be needed.

Finally, there should be more attention to the efficacy of multiple risk factor or, at least, phased risk factor reduction programs. Health promotion behaviors do not exist in isolation, and it is important to determine whether and how health promotion synergy can be achieved by focusing on more than one risk factor. Similarly, both the benefits and risks of behaviors and interventions need to be considered not just for a single disease, such as cancer, but for cancer and heart disease, for example. As women live longer, health promotion behaviors are a critical part of not just living but living well.

ACKNOWLEDGMENTS

Work on this chapter was supported by grants from the National Cancer Institute (1R01CA63782-03, 1R01CA59734-03, 5R01CA60141-02, 1P01CA72099) and the National Heart Lung and Blood Institute (5R01HL48121-04).

REFERENCES

Abrams, D. B., Boutwell, W. B., Grizzle, J., Heimendinger, J., Sorensen, G., & Varnes, J. (1994). Cancer control at the workplace: The working well trial. *Preventive Medicine, 23,* 15–27.

Ahlquist, D. A., Wieand, H. S., Moertel, C. G., McGill, D. B., et al. (1993). Accuracy of fecal occult blood screening for colorectal neoplasia. *Journal of the American Medical Association, 269,* 1262.

Ahmed, F., Brown, D. R., Gary, L. E., & Saadatmand, F. (1994). Religious predictors of cigarette smoking: Findings for African American women of childbearing age. *Behavioral Medicine, 20,* 34–43.

Allegrante, J., Kovar, P., MacKenzie, C., Peterson, M., & Gutin, B. (1993). A walking education program for patients with osteoarthritis of the knee: Theory and intervention strategies. *Health Education Quarterly, 20,* 63–81.

American Cancer Society (2000). *Cancer facts and figures.* New York: Author.

American College of Sports Medicine. (1995). *ACSM's guidelines for exercise testing and prescription* (5th ed.). Baltimore: Williams & Wilkins.

Ansell, D., Lacey, L., Whitman, S., Chen, E., & Phillips, C. (1994). A nurse-delivered intervention to reduce barriers to breast and cervical cancer screening in Chicago inner city clinics. *Public Health Reports, 109,* 104–111.

Balcazar, H., Castro, F. G., & Krull, J. L. (1995). Cancer risk reduction in Mexican American women: The role of acculturation, education, and health risk factors. *Health Education Quarterly, 22*(1), 61–84.

Benedict, S. (1996). *Barriers to women's healthy behavior.* Paper presented at the Behavioral Medicine Meeting, Washington, DC.

Bernstein, L., Henderson, B. E., Hanisch, R., Sullivan-Halley, J., & Ross, R. K. (1994). Physical exercise and reduced risk of breast cancer in young women. *Journal of the National Cancer Institute, 86,* 1403–1408.

Bild, D., Jacobs, D., Sidney, S., Haskell, W., Anderssen, N., & Oberman, A. (1993). Physical activity in young Black and White women: The CARDIA Study. *Annals of Epidemiology, 3,* 636–644.

Blair, S. N., Kohl, H.W., & Barlow, C. E. (1993). Physical activity, physical fitness, and all-cause mortality in women: Do women need to be active? *Journal of the American College of Nutrition, 12,* 368–371.

Blair, S. N., Powell, K. E., Bazzare, T. L., Early, J. L., Epstein, L. H., Green, L. W., Harris, S. S., Haskell, W. L., King, A. C., Koplan, J., Marcus, B. H., Paffenbarger, R. S., & Yeager, K. K. (1993). Physical inactivity workshop V. *Circulation, 88,* 1402–1405.

Blalock, S. J., DeVellis, B. M., Afifi, R. A., & Sandler, R. S. (1990). Risk perceptions and participation in colorectal cancer screening. *Health Psychology, 9,* 792–806.

Block, G., Patterson, B., & Subar, A. (1992). Fruit, vegetables, and cancer prevention: A review of the epidemiological evidence. *Nutrition and Cancer, 19,* 1–29.

Blumenthal, S. J. (1996). Smoking *v* Women's Health: The challenge ahead. *Journal of the American Medical Women's Association, 51,* 8.

Boardley, D. J., Sargent, R. G., Coker, A. L., Hussey, J. R., & Sharpe, P. A. (1995). The relationship between diet, activity, and other factors, and postpartum weight change by race. *Obstetrics & Gynecology, 86,* 834–838.

Borum, M. L. (1996). Patient and physician gender may influence colorectal cancer screening by resident physicians. *Journal of Women's Health, 5,* 363–368.

Bouchard, C., Shephard, R. J., & Stephens, T. (Eds.). (1994). The consensus statement: assessing the level and quality of evidence.. In C. Bouchard, R. J. Shephard, T. Stephens (Eds.), *Physical activity, fitness, and health: International proceedings and consensus statement* (pp. 9–76). Champaign, IL: Human Kinetics.

Bowen, D. J., Fries, E., & Hopp, H. P. (1994). Effects of dietary fat feedback on behavioral and psychological variables. *Journal of Behavioral Medicine, 17*(6), 589–604.

Breen, N., & Kessler, L. (1994). Changes in the use of screening mammography: Evidence from the 1987 and 1990 National Health Interview Surveys. *American Journal of Public Health, 84,* 62–67.

Breen, N., & Kessler, L. (1995). Trends in Cancer Screening—United States, 1987 and 1992. *Morbidity and Mortality Weekly Report, 45,* 57–61.

Brownell, K. D. (1991). Dieting and the search for the perfect body: Where physiology and culture collide. *Behavior Therapy, 22,* 1–12.

Burg, M., Lane, D., & Polednak, A. (1990). Age group differences in the use of breast cancer screening tests. *Journal of Aging and Health, 2,* 514–529.

Busch, T. L., Fried, L. P., & Barrett-Connor, E. (1988). Cholesterol, lipoproteins, and coronary heart disease in women. *Clinical Chemistry, 34,* B60–B70.

Calfas, K. J., Long, B. J., Sallis, J. F., Wooten, W. J., Pratt, M., & Patrick, K. (1996). A controlled trial of physician counseling to promote the adoption of physical activity. *Preventive Medicine, 25,* 225–233.

Calle, E. E., Flanders, W. D., Thun, M. J., & Martin, L. M. (1993). Demographic predictors of mammography and pap smear screening in U.S. women. *American Journal of Public Health, 33,* 51–60.

Camp, D. E., Klesges, R. C., & Relyea, G. (1993). The relationship between body weight concerns and adolescent smoking. *Health Psychology, 12*(1), 24–32.

Campbell, M. K., DeVellis, B. M., Strecher, V. J., Ammerman, A. S., DeVellis, R. F., & Sandler, R. S. (1994). Improving dietary behavior: The effectiveness of tailored messages in primary care settings. *American Journal of Public Health, 84,* 783–787.

Caplan, L. S., Wells, B. L., & Haynes, S. (1992). Breast cancer screening among older racial/ethnic minorities and Whites: Barriers to early detection. *Journal of Gerontology, 47,* 101–110.

Carleton, R., Lasater, T., Assaf, A., Feldman, H., McKinlay, S., & Pawtucket Heart Health Program Writing Group. (1995). The Pawtucket Heart Health Program: Community changes in cardiovascular risk factors and projected disease risk. *American Journal of Public Health, 85,* 777–785.

Caspersen, C. J., & Merritt, R. K. (1995). Physical activity trends among 26 states, 1986–1990. *Medicine and Science in Sports and Exercise, 27*(5), 713–720.

Centers for Disease Control and Prevention. (1992). *Project PACE: Physician's manual: Physician-based assessment and counseling exercise.* Atlanta, GA: Author.

Centers for Disease Control and Prevention. (1995). Prevalence of recommended levels of physical activity among women—behavioral risk factor surveillance system, 1992. *Morbidity and Mortality Weekly Report, 44,* 105–107.

Champion, V. L. (1991). The relationship of selected variables to breast cancer detection behaviors in women 35 and older. *Oncology Nursing Forum, 18,* 733–739.

Chesney, M. A., & Ozer, E. M. (1995). Women and health: In search of a paradigm. *Women's Health: Research on Gender, Behavior, and Policy, 1,* 3–26.

Cockburn, J., White, V. M., Hirst, S., & Hill, D. (1992). Barriers to cervical screening in older women. *Australian Family Physician, 21,* 973–978.

Cohen, S., & Lichtenstein, E. (1990). Partner behaviors that support quitting smoking. *Journal of Consulting and Clinical Psychology, 58,* 304–309

Coleman, E. A., Feuer, E. J., & NCI Breast Cancer Screening Consortium Members. (1992). Breast cancer screening among women from 65 to 74 years of age in 1987–88 and 1991. *Annals of Internal Medicine, 117,* 961–966.

Collins, K. S., & Simon, L. J. (1996). Women's health and managed care: Promises and challenges. *Women's Health Issues, 6,* 39–44.

COMMIT Research Group. (1995). Community Intervention Trial for Smoking Cessation (COMMIT): 1. Cohort results from a four-year community intervention. *American Journal of Public Health, 84,* 183–192.

Cooper, K. H. (1982). *The aerobics program for total well-being.* New York: Bantam.

Costanza, M. E., Annas, G. J., Brown, M. L., Cassel, C. K., Champion, V., Cohen, H. J., Frame, P. S., Glasse, L., Mor, V., & Pauker, S. J. (1992). Supporting statements and rationale. *Journal of Gerontology, 47,* 7–16.

Crawford, D., Jackson, E. L., & Godbey, G. (1991). A hierarchical model of leisure constraints. *Leisure Sciences, 13,* 320–390.

Creighton, P. A., & Evans, A. M. (1992). Audit of practice based cervical smear programme: Completion of the cycle. *British Medical Journal, 304,* 963–966.

Crockett, S. J. (1987). The family team approach to fitness: A proposal. *Public Health Reports, 102*(5), 546–551.

Crump, C. E., Earp, J. L., Kozma, C., & Hertz-Picciotto, I. (1996). Effect of organizational-level variables on differential employee participation in 10 federal worksite health promotion programs. *Health Education Quarterly, 23*(2), 204–223

Curry, S., Wagner, E. H., & Grothaus, L. C. (1991). Evaluation of intrinsic and extrinsic motivation interventions with a self-help smoking cessation program. *Journal of Consulting and Clinical Psychology, 59,* 318–324.

Curry, S. J., Kristal, A. R., & Bowen, D. J. (1992). An application of the stage model of behavior change to dietary fat reduction. *Health Education Research, 7,* 97–105.

Curry, S. J., McBride, C. M., Grothaus, L. C., Louie, D., & Wagner, E. H. (1995). A randomized trial of self-help materials, personalized feedback and telephone counseling with nonvolunteer smokers. *Journal of Consulting and Clinical Psychology, 63,* 1005–1014.

Daling, J., Weiss, N., Spadoni, L., Moore, D. E., & Voigt, L. (1987). Cigarette smoking and primary tubal infertility. In M. J. Rosenberg (Ed.), *Smoking and reproductive health* (pp. 40–46). Littleton, MA: PSG Publishing.

Datillo, J., Datillo, A. M., Samdahl, D., & Kleiber, D. (1994). Leisure orientations and self-esteem in women with low incomes who are overweight. *Journal of Leisure Research, 26,* 23–38.

Davis, N. A., Lewis, M. J., Rimer, B. K., Harvey, C. M., & Koplan, J. P. (1997). Evaluation of a phone intervention to promote mammography in a managed care plan. *American Journal of Health Promotion, 11,* 247–249.

Dawson, D. A., & Thompson, G. B. (1990). *Breast cancer risk factors and screening: United States, 1987* (DHHS Publication No. PHS 900-1500). Hyattsville, MD: U.S. Department of Health and Human Services.

Debusk, R., Stenestrand, U., Sheehan, M., & Haskell, W. (1990). Training effects of long versus short bouts of exercise in healthy subjects. *American Journal of Cardiology, 65,* 1010–1013.

de Castro, J. M., & Goldstein, S. J. (1995). Eating attitudes and behaviors of pre- and postpubertal females: Clues to the etiology of eating disorders. *Physiology & Behavior, 58,* 15–23.

Devsa, S. S., Young, J. L., Brinton, L. A., & Fraumeni, J. F. (1989). Recent trends in cervix uteri cancer. *Cancer, 64,* 2184.

Dignan, M., Michielutte, R., Wells, H. B., & Bahnson, J. (1994). The Forsyth County cervical cancer prevention project: Cervical cancer screening for Black women. *Health Education & Research, 9,* 411–420.

Dishman, R. K., & Sallis, J. F. (1994). Determinants and interventions for physical activity and exercise. In C. Bouchard, R.J. Shephard, & T. Stephens (Eds.), *Physical activity, fitness and health* (pp. 214–238). Champaign, IL: Human Kinetics Press.

Doll, S. R. (1996). Nature and nurture: Possibilities for cancer control. *Carcinogenesis, 17,* 177–184.

Dubbert, P. (1995). Physical activity in women. *Consensus development conference consensus statement about physical activity and cardiovascular health.* Bethesda, MD: NIH.

Dubbert, P. M., Stetson, B., & Corrigan, S. A. (1991, August). Predictors of exercise maintenance in community women. In B. H. Marcus & A. C. King (Chairs), *Women and exercise: Community and special populations.* Symposium conducted at the American Psychological Association Annual Convention, San Francisco.

Duelberg, S. (1992). Preventive health behavior among Black and White women in urban and rural areas. *Social Science and Medicine, 34*(2), 191–198.

Ebrahim, S., & Rowland, L. (1996). Towards a new strategy for health promotion for older women: Determinants of physical activity. *Psychology, Health & Medicine, 1,* 29–40.

Eddy, D. M. (1990). Screening for cervical cancer. *Annals of Internal Medicine, 113,* 214.

Epstein, L. H., Dickson, B. E., McKenzie, S., & Russell, P. O. (1984). The effects of smoking on perception of muscle tension. *Psychopharmocology, 83,* 173–178.

Ershoff, D. H., Mullen, P. D., & Quinn, V. P. (1989). A randomized trial of serialized self-help smoking cessation program for pregnant women in an HMO. *American Journal of Public Health, 79,* 2.

Ershoff, D. H., Quinn, V. P., & Mullen, P. D. (1995). Relapse prevention among women who stop smoking early in pregnancy: A randomized clinical trial of a self-help intervention. *American Journal of Preventive Medicine, 11,* 178–184.

Fant, R. V., Everson, D., Dayton, G., Pickworth, W. B., & Henningfield, J. E. (1996). Nicotine dependence in women. *Journal of the American Medical Women's Association, 51,* 19–24.

Farquhar, J., Foartmann, S., Flora, J., Taylor, C., Haskell, W., Williams, P., Maccoby, N., & Wood, P. (1990). Effects of communitywide education on cardiovascular disease risk factors: The Stanford Five-City Project. *Journal of the American Medical Association, 264,* 359–365.

Fisher, N. M., Kame, V. D., Rouse, L., & Pendergast, D. R. (1994). Quantitative evaluation of a home exercise program on muscle and functional capacity of patients with osteoarthritis. *American Journal of Physical Medicine and Rehabilitation, 73,* 413–420.

Fletcher, S. W. (1995, November). *Women and health in the 21st century: The Helmut Schumann lectureship in studies of healthful living.* Paper presented at Hitchcock Foundation, 12th Annual Helmut Schumann at Dartmouth-Hitchcock Medical Center.

Fletcher, S. W., Black, W., Harris, R., Rimer, B. K., & Shapiro, S. (1993). Report of the international workshop on screening for breast cancer. *Journal of the National Cancer Institute, 85,* 1644–1656.

Floyd, R. L., Rimer, B. K., Giovino, G. A., Mullen, P. D., & Sullivan, S. E. (1993). A review of smoking in pregnancy: Effects on pregnancy outcomes and cessation efforts. *Annual Review of Public Health, 14,* 379–411.

Fox, S. A., Murata, P. F., & Stein, J. A. (1991). The impact of physician compliance on screening mammography for older women. *Archives of Internal Medicine, 151,* 50–56.

French, S. A., Perry, C. L., Leon, G. R., & Fulkerson, J. A. (1994). Weight concern dieting behavior, and smoking initiation in adolescents: A prospective epidemiologic study. *American Journal of Public Health, 84,* 1818–1820.

Fullerton, J. T., Kritz-Silverstein, D., Sadler, G. R., & Barrett-Connor, E. (1996). Mammography usage in a community-based sample of older women. *Annals of Behavioral Medicine, 18,* 67–72.

Garvey, A. J., Bliss, R. E., Hitchcock, J. L., Heinold, J. W., & Rosner, B. (1992). Predictors of smoking relapse among self-quitters: A report from the normative aging study. *Addictive Behaviors, 17,* 367–377.

Glanz, K., Patterson, R. E., Kristal, A. R., DiClemente, C. C., Heimendinger, J., Linnan, L., & McLerran, D. F. (1994). Stages of change in adopting health diets: Fat, fiber, and correlates of nutrient intake. *Health Education Quarterly, 21,* 499–519.

Glasgow, R. E., Terborg, J. R., Hollis, J. F., Severson, H. H., & Boles, S. M. (1995). Take heart: Results from the initial phase of a work-site wellness program. *American Journal of Public Health, 85*(2), 209–216.

Gottlieb, N. H., & Green, L. W. (1987). Ethnicity and lifestyle health risk: Some possible mechanisms. *Journal of Health Promotion, 2*(1), 37–45, 51.

Gracey, D., Stanley, N., Burke, V., Corti, B., & Beilin, L. J. (1996). Nutritional knowledge, beliefs and behaviors in teenage school students. *Health Education Research, Theory & Practice, 11,* 187–204.

Green, L., & Kreuter, M. (1990). *Health promotion planning.* Palo Alto, CA: Mayfield.

Gritz, E. R., St. Jeor, S. T., Bennett, G., Biener, L., Blair, S. N., Bowen, D. J., Brunner, R. L., DeHorn, A., Foreyt, J. P., Haire-Joshu, D., Hall, S. M., Hill, D. R., Jensen, J., Kristeller, J., Marcus, B. H., Nides, M., Pirie, P. L., Solomon, L. J., Stillman, F., Ernst, J., & Mealer, C. Z. (1992). Task Force 3: Implications with respect to intervention and prevention. *Health Psychology, 11*(Suppl.), 17–25

Gritz, E. R., Berman, B. A., Bastani, R., & Wu, M. (1992). A randomized trial of a self-help smoking cessation intervention in a nonvolunteer female population: Testing the limits of the public health model. *Health Psychology, 11*(5), 280–289.

Hall, S. M., Tunstall, C. D., Vila, K. L., & Duffy, J. (1992). Weight gain prevention and smoking cessation: Cautionary findings. *American Journal of Public Health, 82,* 799–803.

Harlan, L. C., Bernstein, A. B., & Kessler, L. G. (1991). Cervical cancer screening: Who is not screened and why. *American Journal of Public Health, 81,* 885–891.

Harris, R. P., O'Malley, M. S., Fletcher, S. W., & Knight, B. P. (1990). Prompting physicians for preventive procedures: A five-year study of manual and computer reminders. *American Journal of Preventive Medicine, 6,* 145–152.

Hatsukami, D., McBride, C., Pirie, P., Hellerstedt, W., & Lando, H. (1991). Effects of nicotine gum on prevalence and severity of withdrawal in female cigarette smokers. *Journal of Substance Abuse, 3,* 427–440.

Havas, S., Heimendinger, J., Reynolds, K., et al. (1994). 5 a day for better health: A new research initiative. *Journal of the American Dietary Association, 94,* 32–36.

Healthy people 2000: National health promotion and disease prevention objectives. (1990). Washington, DC: Public Health Service, U.S. Department of Health and Human Services.

Heimendinger, J., Van Duyn, M. A., Chapelsky, D., Foerster, S., & Stables, G. (1996). The national 5 A Day for better health program: A large-scale nutrition intervention. *Journal of Public Health Management and Practice, 2,* 27–35.

Heirich, M., Foote, A., Erfurt, J., & Konopka, B., (1993). Work-site physical fitness programs: Comparing the impact of different program designs on cardiovascular risks. *Journal of Occupational Medicine, 35,* 510–517.

Hellberg, D., Nilsson, S., Haley, N. J., Hoffman, D., & Wynder, E. (1988). Smoking and cervical intraepithelial neoplasia: Nicotine and cotinine in serum and cervical mucus in smokers and nonsmokers. *American Journal of Obstetrics and Gynecology, 158,* 910–913.

Henderson, K. A., Stalnaker, D., & Taylor, G. (1988). The relationship between barriers to recreation and gender-role personality traits for women. *Journal of Leisure Research, 20,* 69–80.

Hill, H. A., Schoenbach, V. J., Kleinbaum, D. G., Strecher, V. J., Orleans, C. T., Gebski, V. J., & Kaplan, B. H. (1994). A longitudinal analysis of predictors of quitting smoking among participants in a self-help intervention trial. *Addictive Behaviors, 19*(2), 159–173.

Horm, J., & Anderson, K. (1993). Who in America is trying to lose weight? *Annals of Internal Medicine, 119,* 672–676.

Howard, J. (1987). Using mammography for cancer control: An unrealized potential. *CA: A Cancer Journal for Clinicians, 37,* 33–48.

Howe, G. R., Hirohata, T., Hislop, T. G., et al. (1990). Dietary factors and risk of breast cancer: Combined analysis of 12 case-control studies. *Journal of the National Cancer Institute, 82,* 561–569.

Hunter, D. J., Spiegelman, D., Adami, H. O., Beeson, L., vanden Brandt, P. A., Folsom, A. R., Fraser, G. F., Goldbohm, A., Graham, S., Howe, G. R., Kushi, L. H., Marshall, J. R., McDermott, A., Miller, A. B., Speizer, F. E., Wolk, A., Yuan, S. S., & Willett, W. (1996). Cohort studies of fat intake and the risk of breast cancer—A pooled analysis. *New England Journal of Medicine, 334,* 356–361.

Hunter, W., Farmer, A., Mant, D., Verne, J., Northover, J., & Fitzpatrick, R. (1990). The effect of self-administered fecal occult blood tests on compliance with screening for colorectal cancer: Results of a survey of those invited. *Family Practice, 8,* 367–372.

Husten, C. G., Chrismon, J. H., & Reddy, M. N. (1996). Trends and effects of cigarette smoking among girls and women in the United States, 1965–1993. *Journal of the American Medical Women's Association, 51,* 11–18.

Insull, W., Henderson, M. M., Prentice, R. L., et al. (1990). Results of a randomized feasibility study of a low-fat diet. *Archives of Internal Medicine, 150,* 421–427.

Jackson, E. L., Crawford, D. W., & Godbey, C. (1993). Negotiation of leisure constraints. *Leisure Sciences, 15,* 1–11.

Jeffery, R. W., & French, S. A. (1996). Socioeconomic status and weight control practices among 20- to 45-year-old women. *American Journal of Public Health, 86,* 1005–1010.

Johnson, C. A., Corrigan, S. A., Dubbert, P. M., & Gramling, S. E. (1990). Perceived barriers to exercise and weight control practices in community women. *Women & Health, 16,* 177–191.

Kanders, B. S., Ullmann-Joy, P., Foreyt, J. P., Heymsfield, S. B., Heber, D., Elashoff, R. M., Ashley, J. M., Reeves, R. S., & Blackburn, G. L. (1994). The Black American lifestyle intervention (BALI): The design of a weight loss program for working-class African-American women. *Journal of American Dietetic Association, 94*(3), 310–312.

Kawachi, I., Trois, R. J., Rotnitzky, A. G., Coakley, E. H., & Colditz, G. A. (1996). Can physical activity minimize weight gain in women after smoking cessation? *American Journal of Public Health, 86,* 999–1004.

Kay, T., & Jackson, G. (1991). Leisure despite constraint: The impact of leisure constraints on leisure participation. *Journal of Leisure Research, 23,* 301–313.

Kelsey, K. S., Kirkley, B. G., DeVellis, R. F., Earp, J. A., Ammerman, A. S., Keyserling, T. C., Shannon, J., & Simpson, Jr., R. J. (1996). Social support as a predictor of dietary change in a low-income population. *Health Education Research, 11,* 383–395.

Kendrick, J. S., Zahniser, S. C., Miller, N. et al. (1995). Integrating smoking cessation into routine public prenatal care: The smoking cessation in pregnancy project. *American Journal of Public Health, 85,* 217–222.

King, A. C. (1991). Community intervention for promotion of physical activity and fitness. *Exercise and Sport Sciences Reviews, 19,* 211–259.

King, A. C. (1994). Community and public health approaches to the promotion of physical activity. *Medicine and Science in Sports and Exercise, 26*(11), 1405–1412.

King, A., Carl, F., Birkel, L., & Haskell, W. (1988). Increasing exercise among blue-collar employees: The tailoring of worksite programs to meet specific needs. *Preventive Medicine, 17,* 357–365.

King, A. C., Blair, S. N., Bild, D. E., Dishman, R. K., Dubbert, P. M., Marcus, B. H., Oldridge, N. B., Paffenbarger Jr., R. S., Powell, K. E., & Yeager, K. (1992). Determinants of physical activity and interventions in adults. *Medicine and Science in Sports and Exercise, 24*(6), S221–S236.

King, A., Haskell, W., Young, D., Oka, R., & Stefanick, M. (1995). Long-term effects of varying intensities and formats of physical activity on participation rates, fitness, and lipoproteins in men and women aged 50 to 65 years. *Circulation, 91,* 2596–2604.

King, A. C., Jeffery, R. W., Fridinger, F., Dusenbury, L., Provence, S., Hedlund, S. A., & Spangler, K. (1995). Environmental and policy approaches to cardiovascular disease prevention through physical activity: Issues and opportunities. *Health Education Quarterly, 22,* 499–511.

King, A., Taylor, C., Haskell, W., & Debusk, R. (1988). Strategies for increasing early adherence to and long-term maintenance of home-based exercise training in healthy middle-aged men and women. *American Journal of Cardiology, 61,* 628–632.

King, E., Resch, N., Rimer, B. K., Lerman, C., Boyce, A., & McGovern-Gorchov, P. (1993). Breast cancer screening practices among retirement community women. *Preventive Medicine, 22,* 1–19.

Klesges, R. C., Brown, K., Pascale, R.W., et al. (1988). Factors associated with participation, attrition, and outcome in a smoking cessation program at the workplace. *Health Psychology, 7,* 575–589.

Knott, V. J. (1991). Neurophysiological aspects of smoking behavior: A neuroelectric perspective. *British Journal of Addiction, 86,* 511–515.

Kohrt, W. M., Snead, D. B., Slatopolsky, E., & Birge, S. J. (1995). Additive effects of weight-bearing exercise and estrogen on bone mineral density in older women. *Journal of Bone and Mineral Research, 10,* 1303–1311.

Kornguth, P. J., Keefe, F. J., & Conaway, M. R. (1996). Pain during mammography: Characteristics and relationship to demographic and medical variables. *Pain, 66,* 187–194.

Kriska, A. M., Bayless, C., Cauley, J. A., Laporte, R. E., Sandler, R. B., & Pambianco, G. (1986). A randomized exercise trail in older women: Increased activity over two years and the factors associated with compliance. *Medicine and Science in Sports and Exercise, 18,* 557–562.

Kristal, A. R., Patterson, R. E., Glanz, K., Heimendinger, J., Hebert, J. R., Feng, Z., & Probart, C. (1995). Psychosocial correlates of healthful diets: Baseline results from the working well study. *Preventive Medicine, 24,* 221–228.

Kuczmarski, R. J., Flegal, K. M., Campbell, S. M., & Johnson, C. L. (1994). Increasing prevalence of overweight among US adults. *Journal of the American Medical Association, 272,* 205–211.

Lacey, L., Whitfield, J., DeWhite, W., Ansell, D., Whitman, S., Chen, E., & Phillips, C. (1993). Referral adherence in an inner city breast and cervical cancer screening program. *Cancer, 72,* 950–955.

Lando, H. A., Pechacek, T. F., Pirie, P. L., Murray, D. M., Mittelmark, M. B., Lichtenstein, E., Nothwehr, F., & Gray, C. (1995). Changes in adult cigarette smoking in the Minnesota heart health program. *American Journal of Public Health, 85,* 201–208.

Lane, D. S., Polednak, A. P., & Burg, M. A. (1989). Measuring the impact of varied interventions on community-wide breast cancer screening. In P. N. Anderson, P. F. Engstrom, & L. E. Mortenson (Eds.), *Advances in cancer control: Innovations and research* (pp. 103–114). New York: Alan R. Liss.

Lane, D. S., Caplan, L. S., & Grimson, R. (1996). Trends in mammography use and their relation to physician and other factors. *Cancer Detection and Prevention, 20,* 332–341.

Lane, M. J., Macera, C. A., Croft, J. B., & Meyer, P.A. (1996). Preventive health practices and perceived health status among women over 50. *Women's Health Issues, 6,* 279–285.

Leon, A, Connett, J., Jacobs, D., & Rauramaa, R. (1987). Leisure-time physical activity levels and risk of coronary heart disease and death: The Multiple Risk Factor Intervention trial. *Journal of American Medical Association, 258,* 2388–2395.

Lewis, C. E., Raczynski, J. M., Heath, G. W., Levinson, R., Hilyer, J. C., & Cutter, G. R. (1993). Promoting physical activity in low-income African-American communities. *Ethnicity & Disease, 3,* 106–118.

Long, B. J., Calfas, K. J., Wooten, W., Sallis, J. F., Patrick, K., Goldstein, M., Marcus, B. H., Schwenk, T. L., Chenoweth, J., Carter, R., Torres, T., Palinkas, L. A., & Heath, G. (1996). A multi-site field test of the acceptability of physical activity counseling in primary care: Project PACE. *American Journal of Preventive Medicine, 12,* 73–81.

Luepker, R., Murray, D., Jacobs, D., Mittelmark, M., Bracht, N., Carlaw, R., et al. (1994). Community education for cardiovascular disease prevention: Risk factor changes in the Minnesota Heart Health Program. *American Journal of Public Health, 84,* 1383–1393.

Mandelblatt, J., Traxler, M., Lakin, P., Thomas, L., Chauhan, P., Matseoane, S., Kanetsky, P., & Harlem Study Team. (1993). A nurse practitioner intervention to increase breast and cervical cancer screening for poor, elderly Black women. *Journal of General Internal Medicine, 8,* 173–178.

Manfredi, C., Lacey, L., Warnecke, R., & Buis, M. (1992). Smoking-related behavior, beliefs, and social environment of young Black women in subsidized public housing in Chicago. *American Journal of Public Health, 82,* 267–272.

Manson, J. E., Colditz, G. A., Stampfer, M. J., et al. (1990). A prospective study of obesity and risk of coronary heart disease in women. *New England Journal of Medicine, 3222,* 882–889.

Manson, J. E., & VanItallie, T. B. (1996). America's obesity epidemic and women's health. *Journal of Women's Health, 5,* 329–334.

Marchbanks, P. A., Lee, N. C., & Peterson, H. B. (1990). Cigarette smoking as a risk factor for pelvic inflammatory disease. *American Journal of Obstetrics and Gynecology, 162,* 639– 644.

Marcus, B. H., Albrecht, A. E., Niaura, R. S., Taylor, E. R., Simkin, L. R., Feder, S. I., Abrams, D. B., & Thompson, P. D. (1995). Exercise enhances the maintenance of smoking cessation in women. *Addictive Behaviors, 21,* 87–92.

Marcus, B. H., Dubbert, P. M., King, A. C., & Pinto, B. M. (1995). Physical activity in women: Current status and future directions. In A. L. Stanton & S. J. Gallant (Eds.), *The psychology of women's health: Progress and challenges in research and application* (pp. 349–379). Washington, DC: American Psychological Association.

Marcus, B. H., Pinto, B., Simkin, L., Audrain, J., & Taylor, E. (1994). Application of theoretical models to exercise behavior among employed women. *American Journal of Health Promotion, 9,* 49–55.

Martin, J., & Dubbert, P. (1982). Exercise applications and promotion in behavioral medicine. Journal of Clinical Psychology, 50, 1004–1071.

Mayo, K. (1992). Physical activity practices among American Black working women. *Qualitative Health Research, 2*(3), 318–333.

McAuley, E., Courneya, K., Rudolph, D., & Lox, C. (1994). Enhancing exercise adherence in middle-aged males and females. *Preventive Medicine, 23,* 498–506.

McBride, C. M., Curry, S. J., Lando, H., & Pirie, P. L. (1994, October). *Project HOPP: Strategies to prevent relapse to smoking for pregnant and postpartum women.* Poster presented at the 9th World Conference on Tobacco and Health.

McBride, C. M., Curry, S. J., Taplin, S., Anderman, C., & Grothaus, L. (1993). Exploring environmental barriers to participation in mammography screening in an HMO. *Journal of Cancer Epidemiology, Biomarkers & Prevention, 2,* 599–605.

McBride, C. M., French, S. A., Pirie, P. L., & Jeffery, R. W. (1996). Changes over time in weight concerns among women smokers engaged in the cessation process. *Annals of Behavioral Medicine, 18,* 273–279.

McGinnis, J. M., & Lee, P. R. (1995). Healthy people 2000 at mid decade. *Journal of American Medical Association, 273*(14), 1123–1129.

McLeroy, K. R., Bibeau, D., Steckler, A., & Glanz, K. (1988). An ecological perspective on health promotion perspectives. *Health Education Quarterly, 15,* 351–377.

Minor, M. A., & Brown, J. D. (1993). Exercise maintenance of persons with arthritis after participation in a class experience. *Health Education Quarterly, 20,* 83–95.

Mittendorf, R. Longnecker, M. P., Newcomb, P. A., Dietz, A. T., Greenberg, E. R., Bogdan, G. F., et al. (1995). Strenuous physical activity in young adulthood and risk of breast cancer (United States). *Cancer Causes and Control, 6,* 347–353.

MMWR. (Ed). (1990). Use of mammography—United States, 1990 (Editorial Note). *Morbidity and Mortality Weekly Report, 39,* 621–630.

Murray, R. P., Johnston, J. J., Dolce, J. J., Lee, W. W., & O'Hara, P. (1995). Social support for smoking cessation and abstinence: The lung health study. *Addictive Behaviors, 20,* 159–170.

Myers, R. E., Balshem, A. M., Wolf, T. A., Ross, E. A., & Millner, L. (1993). Adherence to continuous screening for colorectal neoplasia. *Medical Care, 31,* 508–519.

Myers, R. E., Ross, E. A., Wolf, T. A., Balshem, A., Jepson, C., & Millner, L. (1991). Behavioral interventions to increase adherence in colorectal cancer screening. *Medical Care, 29,* 1039–1050.

Myers, R. E., Trock, B. J., Lerman, C., Wolf, T., Ross, E., & Engstrom, P. F. (1990). Adherence to colorectal cancer screening in an HMO population. *Preventive Medicine, 19,* 502–514.

National Institutes of Health. (1984). Consensus development conference: Osteoporosis. *Journal of American Medication Association, 252,* 799–802.

National Institutes of Health. (1995). *Consensus development conference consensus statement about physical activity and cardiovascular health.* Bethesda, MD: NIH.

Nides, M. A., Gonzales, D., Tashkin, D. P., Rakos, R. F., Murray, R. P., Bjornson-Benson, W. M., Lindgren, P., & Connett, J. E. (1995). Predictors of initial smoking cessation and relapse through the first 2 years of the lung health study. *Journal of Consulting and Clinical Psychology, 63*(1), 60–69.

Oldenski, R. J., & Flareau, B. J. (1992). Colorectal cancer screening. *Cancer Epidemiology, Prevention, and Screening, 19,* 621–635.

Orleans, C.T., Rimer, B. K., Salmon, M. A., & Kozlowski, L. (1990). Psychological and behavioral consequences and correlates of smoking cessation. In *The health benefits of smoking cessation—A report of the surgeon general* (pp. 521–578). Rockville, MD: U.S. Department of Health and Human Services.

Packard, B. A. (1985). Heart disease in women. In *Women's Health Report of the Public Health Service Task Force on Women's Health Issues* (Vol. 2, pp. 57–61).

Paffenbarger, R. S., Hyde, R. T., Wing, A. L., et. al. (1986). Physical activity, all-cause mortality, and longevity of college alumni. *New England Journal of Medicine, 314,* 605–613.

Pate, R. R., Pratt, M., Blair, S. N., Haskell, W. L., Macera, C. A., Bouchard, C., Buchner, D., Ettinger, W., Heath, G. W., King, A. C., Kriska, A., Leon, A. S., Marcus, B. H., Morris, J., Paffenbarger, R. S., Patrick, K., Pollock, M. L., Rippe, J. M., Sallis, J., & Wilmore, J. H. (1995). Physical activity and publich health: A recommendation from the Centers for Disease Control and Prevention and the American College of Sports Medicine. *Journal of the American Medical Association, 273,* 402–407.

Perkins, K. A. (1994). Issues in the prevention of weight gain after smoking cessation. *Annals of Behavioral Medicine, 16, 46–52.*

Pettersson, R., Fries, H., & Nillius, S. J. (1973). Epidemiology of secondary amenorrhea: I. Incidence and prevalence rates. *American Journal of Obstetrics and Gynecology, 117*(1), 80–86.

Pirie, P. L., McBride, C. M., Hellerstedt, W., Jeffery, R. W., Hatsukami, D., Allen, S., & Lando, H. (1992). Smoking cessation in women concerned about weight. *American Journal of Public Health, 83,* 1238–1243.

Powell, K. E., Thompson, P. D., Caspersen, C. J., & Kendrick, J. S. (1987). Physical activity and the incidence of coronary heart disease. *Annual Review Public Health, 8,* 253–287.

Ransohoff, D. F., & Lang, C. A. (1993). Sigmoidoscopic screening in the 1990s. *Journal of the American Medical Association, 269,* 1278.

Rich-Edwards, J. W., Manson, J. E., Hennekens, C. H., & Buring, J. E. (1995). The primary prevention of coronary heart disease in women. *New England Journal of Medicine, 332,* 1758–1766.

Rimer, B. K. (1992). Understanding the acceptance of mammography by women. *Annals of Behavioral Medicine, 14,* 197–2003.

Rimer, B. K. (1994). Interventions to increase mammography screening—lifespan and ethnicity issues. *Cancer, 74,* 323–328.

Rimer, B. K. (1995a). Mammography use in the U.S.: Trends and the impact of interventions. *Annals of Behavioral Medicine, 16,* 317–326.

Rimer, B. K. (1995b). *Towards an integrated framework of women's health.* Presented to Society of Behavioral Medicine, San Diego, CA.

Rimer, B. K., Keintz, M. K., Keller, H. B., Engstrom, P. F., & Rosan, J. R. (1989). Why women resist screening mammography: Patient-related barriers. *Radiology, 172,* 243–246.

Rimer, B. K., Ross, E., Balshem, A., & Engstrom, P. F. (1993). The effect of a comprehensive breast screening program on self-reported mammography use by primary care physicians and women in a health maintenance organization. *Journal of the American Board of Family Practice, 6,* 443–451.

Rimer, B. K., Ross, E., Cristinzio, C. S., & King, E. (1992). Older women's participation in breast screening. *Journal of Gerontology, 47,* 85–91.

Rimer, B. K., Trock, B., Balshem, A., Engstrom, P. F., Rosan, J., & Lerman, C. (1990). Breast screening practices among primary physicians: Reality and potential. *Journal of the American Board of Family Practice, 3,* 26–34.

Romieu, I., Willett, W. C., Stampfer, M. J., et al. (1988). Caloric intake and other determinants of relative weight. *American Journal of Clinical Nutrition, 47,* 406–412.

Russell, P. O., Epstein, L. H., Johnston, J. J., Block, D. R., & Blair, E. (1988). The effects of physical activity as maintenance for smoking cessation. *Addictive Behaviors, 13,* 215–218.

Ruzek, S. L., & Hill, J. (1986). Promoting women's health: Redefining the knowledge base and strategies for change. *Health Promotion, 1,* 301–309.

Schorling, J. B. (1995). The stages of change of rural African-American smokers. *American Journal of Preventive Medicine, 11,* 170–177.

Secker-Walker, R. H., Chir, B., Solomon, L. J., Flynn, B. S., & Dana, G. S. (1994). Comparisons of the smoking cessation counseling activities of six types of health professionals. *Preventive Medicine, 23,* 800–808.

Selby, J. V. (1993). How should we screen for colorectal cancer? *Journal of the American Medical Association, 269,* 1294.

Selby, J. V., Friedman, G. D., Quesenberry, C. P., Jr., & Weiss, N. S. (1992). A case-control study of screening sigmoidoscopy and mortality from colorectal cancer. *New England Journal of Medicine, 326,* 653.

Serdula, M. K., Coates, R. J., Byers, T., Simoes, E., Mokdad, A. H., & Subar, A. F. (1995). Fruit and vegetable intake among adults in 16 states: Results of a brief telephone survey. *American Journal of Public Health, 85,* 236–239.

Severson, H. H., Andrews, J. A., Lichtenstein, E., Wall, M., & Akers, L. (1997). Reducing maternal smoking and relapse: Long-term evaluation of a pediatric intervention. *Preventive Medicine, 26,* 120–130.

Sexton, M., & Hebel, J. R. (1984). A clinical trial of change in maternal smoking and its effect on birth weight. *Journal of the American Medical Association, 251,* 911–915.

Shaw, S. M., Bonen, A., & McCabe, J. (1991). Do more contraints mean less leisure? Examining the relationship between constraints and participation. *Journal of Leisure Research, 25,* 386–300.

Shervington, D. O. (1994). Attitudes and practices of African-American women regarding cigarette smoking: Implications for interventions. *Journal of the National Medical Association, 86,* 337–343.

Shopland, D. R., & Burns, D. M. (1993). Medical and public health implications of tobacco addiction. In C. T. Orleans & J. Slade (Eds.), *Nicotine addiction principles and management* (pp. 105–128). New York: Oxford University Press.

Siegler, I. C., Feaganes, J. R., & Rimer, B. K. (1995). Predictors of adoption of mammography in women under age 50. *Health Psychology, 14,* 274–278.

Sinaki, M., & Offord, K. P. (1988). Physical activity in postmenopausal women: Effect on back muscle strength and bone mineral density of the spine. *Archives of Physical Medicine and Rehabilitation, 69,* 277–280.

Slenker, S. E., & Grant, M. C. (1989). Attitudes, beliefs, and knowledge about mammography among women over forty years of age. *Journal of Cancer Education, 4,* 61–65.

Smart, C. R., Hendrick, R. E., Rutledge, J. H., & Smith, R. A. (1995). Benefit of mammography screening in women ages 40–49 years. Current evidence from randomized controlled trials. *Cancer, 75,* 1619–1626.

Smith, D. E., Lewis, C. E., Caveny, J. L., Perkins, L. L., Burke, G. L., & Bild, D. E. (1994). Longitudinal changes in adiposity associated with pregnancy. The CARDIA study. *Journal of the American Medical Association, 271,* 1747–1751.

Sobal, J., Nicolopoulos, V., & Lee, J. (1995). Attitudes about overweight and dating among secondary school students. *International Journal of Obesity, 19,* 376–381.

Solomon, M. J., & McLeod, R. S. (1993). Screening strategies for colorectal cancer. *Colorectal Cancer, 73,* 31–45.

Sorensen, G., Hunt, M. K., Cohen, N., Stoddard, A., Stein, E., Phillips, J., Baker, F., Combe, C., Hebert, J., & Palombo, R. (1998). Worksite and family education for dietary change: The treatwell 5–A-Day program. *Health Education Research, 13,* 577–591.

Sorensen, G., & Pechacek, T. F. (1987). Attitudes toward smoking cessation among men and women. *Journal of Behavioral Medicine, 19,* 129–137.

Sorensen, G., Thompson, B., Glanz, K., Feng, Z., Kinne, S., DiClemente, C., Emmons, K., Heimendinger, J., Probart, C., Lichtenstein, E., & the Working Well Trial. (1996). Work site-based cancer prevention: Primary results from the working well trial. *American Journal of Public Health, 86,* 939–947.

Stephens, T., Jacobs, D. R., & White, C. C. (1985). A descriptive epidemiology of leisure-time physical activity. *Public Health Reports, 100,* 147–158.

Stergachis, A. S., Scholes, D., Daling, J. R., Weiss, N. S., & Chu, J. (1991). Maternal cigarette smoking and the risk of ectopic pregnancy. *American Journal of Epidemiology, 133,* 332–337.

Stokols, D. (1992). Establishing and maintaining healthy environments: Toward a social ecology of health promotion. *American Psychology, 47,* 6–22.

Stotts, C. R., Glynn, T. J., & Baquet, C. R., (1991). Smoking cessation among Blacks. *Journal of Health Care for the Poor and Underserved, 2,* 307–319.

Subar, A. F., Heimendinger, J., Patterson, B. H., Krebs-Smith, S. M., Pivonka, E., & Kessler, R. (1995). Fruit and vegetable intake in the United States: The Baseline Survey of the Five A Day for Better Health Program. *American Journal of Health Promotion, 9,* 352–360.

Svikis, D., Hatsukami, D., Hughes, J., Carroll, K., & Pickens, R. (1986). Sex differences in tobacco withdrawal syndrome. *Addictive Behaviors, 11,* 459–462.

Tessaro, I. (1996, March). *Lay-health advisor program for women working in manufacturing firms.* Paper presented at the Society of Behavioral Medicine Meeting, Washington, DC.

Tessaro, I., Lyna, P. R., Rimer, B. K., Heisler, J., Woods-Powell, C. T., Yarnall, K.S.H., & Barber, L. T. (1997). Readiness to change smoking behavior in a community health center population. *Journal of Community Health, 22,* 15–31.

Thompson, R. S., Michnich, M. E., Gray, J., Friedlander, L., & Gilson, B. (1986). Maximizing compliance with hemoccult screening for colon cancer in clinical practice. *Medical Care, 24,* 904–914.

Urban, N., White, E., Anderson, G. L., Curry, S., & Kristal, A. R. (1992). Correlates of maintenance of a low-fat diet among women in the women's health trial. *Preventive Medicine, 21,* 279–291.

U.S. Department of Health and Human Services. (1989). *Reducing the health consequences of smoking. A report of the surgeon general.* U.S. Department of Health and Human Services, Public Health Service, Center for Disease Control, Center for Chronic Disease Prevention and Health Promotion, Office on Smoking and Health.

U.S. Department of Health and Human Services. (1990). *The health benefits of smoking cessation.* U.S. Department of Health and Human Services, Public Health Service, Center for Disease Control, Center for Chronic Disease Prevention and Health Promotion, Office on Smoking and Health. (DHHS Publication No. CDC 90-8416).

U.S. Department of Health and Human Services. (1991). *Healthy people 2000: National health promotion and disease prevention objectives.* U.S. Department of Health and Human Services, Public Health Service, Center for Disease Control, Center for Chronic Disease Prevention and Health Promotion.

U.S. Department of Health and Human Services. (1991). *Cervical cancer control: Status and Directions.* Rockville, MD: NIH.

U.S. Department of Health and Human Services. (1994). *Preventing tobacco use among young people: A report of the surgeon general.* Atlanta, GA: U.S. Department of Health and Human Services, Public Health Service, Centers for Disease Control and Prevention, National Center for Chronic Disease Prevention and Health Promotion, Office on Smoking and Health.

U.S. Department of Health and Human Services. (1996). *Physical activity and health: A report of the surgeon general.* Washington, DC: Superintendent of Documents.

U.S. Preventive Services Task Force. (1996). *Guide to clinical preventive services* (2nd ed.). Baltimore, MD: Williams & Wilkins.

Vellozzi, C. J., Romans, M., & Rothenberg, R. B. (1996). Delivering breast and cervical cancer screening services to underserved women: Part II. Implications for policy. *Women's Health Issues, 6,* 211–220.

Verhoef, M.J., Love, E.J., & Rose, M.S. (1992). Women's social roles and their exercise participation. *Women & Health, 4,* 15–29

Wagenknecht, L., Cutter, G., Haley, N., Sidney, S., Manolio, T., Hughes, G., & Jacobs, D. (1990). Racial differences in serum cotinine levels among smokers in the coronary artery risk development in (young) adults study. *American Journal of Public Health, 80,* 1053–1056.

Washburn, R., Kline, G., Lackland, D., & Wheeler, F. (1992). Leisure time physical activity: Are there Black/White differences? *Preventive Medicine, 21,* 127–135.

White, E., Hurlich, M., Thompson, R. S., Woods, M. N., Henderson, M. M., Urban, N., & Kristal, A. (1991). Dietary changes among husbands of participants in a low-fat dietary intervention. *American Journal of Preventive Medicine, 7,* 319–325.

Wilcox, L. S., & Mosher, W. D. (1993). Factors associated with obtaining health screening among women of reproductive age. *Public Health Reports, 108,* 76–86.

Willett, W. C. (1995). Diet, nutrition, and avoidable cancer. *Environmental Health Perspectives, 103*(Suppl. 8), 165–170.

Willett, W. C., Manson, J. E., Stampfer, M. J., Colditz, G. A., Rosner, B., Speizer, F. E., & Hennekens, C. H. (1995). Weight, weight change, and coronary heart disease in women. Risk within the "normal" weight range. *Journal of the American Medical Association, 273,* 461–465.

Willett, W., Stampfer, M. J., Bain, C., Lipnick, R., Speizer, F. E., Rosner, B., Cramer, D., & Hennekens, C. H. (1983). Cigarette smoking, relative weight, and menopause. *American Journal of Epidemiology, 117*(6), 945–957.

Williamson, D. F., Madans, J., Anda, R. F., Kleinman, J. C., Giovino, G. A., & Byers, T. (1991). Smoking cessation and severity of weight gain in a national cohort. *New England Journal of Medicine, 11,* 739–745.

Windsor, R. A., Cutter, G., Morris, J., Reese, Y., Manzella, B., Bartlett, E. E., Samuelson, C., & Spanos, D. (1985). The effectiveness of smoking cessation methods for smokers in public health maternity clinics: A randomized trial. *American Journal of Public Health, 75,* 1389–1392.

Wing, R. R., & Jeffery, R. W. (1995). Effect of modest weight loss on changes in cardiovascular risk factors: Are there differences between men and women or between weight loss and maintenance? *International Journal of Obesity, 19,* 67–73.

Winkleby, M. A. (1994). The future of community-based cardiovascular disease intervention studies. *American Journal of Public Health, 84*(9), 1369–1372.

Winkelstein, Jr., W. (1990). Smoking and cervical cancer—current status: A review. *American Journal of Epidemiology, 133,* 945–957.

Wolfson, L., Whipple, R., Derby, C., Judge, J., & King, M. (1996). Balance and strength training in older adults: Intervention gains and Tai Chi maintenance. *Journal of the American Geriatrics Society, 44,* 498–506.

Wong, J. G., & Feussner, J. R. (1993a). Screening for colon cancer: Is it worth the expense? *North Carolina Medical Journal, 54,* 634–638.

Wong, J. G., & Feussner, J. R. (1993b). Screening for cervical cancer: Pap smears can save lives. *North Carolina Medical Journal, 54,* 342–345.

Wood, P. D., Stefanick, M. L., Williams, P. T., & Haskell, W. L. (1991). The effects on plasma lipoproteins of a prudent weight-reducing diet, with or without exercise, in overweight men and women. *New England Journal of Medicine, 325,* 461–466.

Wooten, W., Long, B., Patrick, K., Sallis, J., Calfas, K., & VanCamp, S., (1991). Project P.A.C.E.: Physician-based activity assessment and counseling for exercise—the theoretical rationale. *Medicine Science and Sports in Exercise, 23,* S221–236.

Zang, E. A., & Wynder, E. L. (1996). Differences in lung cancer risk between men and women: Examination of the evidence. *Journal of the National Cancer Institute, 88,* 183–192.

32

Male Partner Violence: Relevance to Health Care Providers

Mary P. Koss
Maia Ingram
University of Arizona
Sara L. Pepper
Region 2 Consortium, Idaho

Since the 1970s, researchers and advocacy groups have documented the extent of partner violence, as well as the health and medical consequences of violence in women's lives. As a result, violence by male intimates is now recognized as one of the most prevalent and serious threats to the health of women. Despite gains in awareness and knowledge of the risk and outcomes of abuse, however, victims of partner violence have remained largely unrecognized in medical care settings. Yet, as efforts aimed at primary and secondary prevention of illness and injuries, as well as cost containment, become central to health care, partner violence is ever more clearly an issue of medical concern. To underscore the relevance of the problem to health care practitioners, this chapter reviews empirical evidence regarding both the prevalence and the impact of partner violence within the medical care system. The review covers three principal areas. First, the most frequent portals of entry, the consequences and medical presentations associated with abuse, and the disproportionately high rate of medical care utilization by victims are reviewed. Second, the rate and consequences of failure to identify and appropriately treat and refer victims in the medical setting are described. Third, the potential role of health care providers in the detection and referral of victims, as well as personal and systematic barriers to these actions are presented. The chapter concludes with a critique of the existing methodologies in the field and suggests avenues of future study to address the many gaps in existing knowledge.

TERMINOLOGY

Although the term *domestic violence* is often used to describe abusive adult relationships, the present discussion adopts the expression *male partner violence* to denote violence against women by male intimates. This alternative term reflects a need to clearly define the predominant pattern in violent relationships, as well as those most likely to result in physical harm. Although large scale studies have reported that men and women are about equally likely to be physically aggressive toward an intimate partner at least once (Straus & Gelles, 1990; Straus, Gelles, & Steinmetz, 1980), further analysis reveals that both the frequency and severity of assaults by men against female intimates are much greater than assaults perpetrated by women against male partners (R. A. Berk, S. F. Berk, Loseke, & Rauma, 1983; Brush, 1990; Bureau of Justice Statistics, 1994; M. P. Koss, Goodman, et al., 1994; Makepeace, 1989). Women are much more likely to be injured in assaults by a male intimate than are men by a female partner (R. A. Berk et. al., 1983; Brush, 1990; Bureau of Justice Statistics, 1995; Makepeace,

1989; Stets & Straus, 1990). Likewise, women are four times more likely to be stalked in their lifetime than men (8.2% vs. 2.3%; Tjaden & Thoennes, 1998b). Men are also more likely to kill an intimate partner than are women (Browne & Williams, 1989, 1993; Bureau of Justice Statistics, 1994; Campbell, 1992; Mercy & Saltzman, 1989).

In addition, the intention of violence perpetrated by male and female partners is found to differ. From interviews with 232 men and 67 women arrested for domestic violence under a mandatory arrest law, Hamberger, Lohr, and Bonge (1994) found that reasons for women's violence sorted into categories of retribution (i.e., "payback") and self-defense, whereas the intentions of violence perpetrated by men sorted into categories such as domination and punishment. Issues of ownership and control are also found to be primary factors involved in the lethal outcomes of men's violence against female partners (Campbell, 1992). An analysis of all homicides involving intimate partners during a 5-year time period in Dayton, Ohio, revealed that the largest category of male motive for murder of a female partner was jealousy, followed by those labeled "male dominance issues," such as one in which the woman refused to get the perpetrator more wine, and those in which the woman resisted the murderer's sexual advances. In contrast, in approximately 85% of female homicides of a male partner, the woman had a history of being battered by that man, and the murder was precipitated by his threatening with a weapon or actually striking the woman (Campbell, 1992).

The term *partner violence* is also descriptive of the assailants women most typically face. Women are at a greater risk of assault, including rape and homicide, by a current or former husband or boyfriend than they are by a casual acquaintance or stranger (Browne & Williams, 1989,1993; Campbell, 1992; Finkelhor & Yllo, 1985; Frieze, 1983; Russell, 1982). Assault by male intimates is more likely to be severe—involving punching, kicking, choking, and threats or use of a weapon—and to result in more severe injuries, than are assaults by others (Browne, 1993). In addition, the term highlights the fact that violence against women often occurs within relationships that are not, or are no longer, formal marriages. Women receiving treatment for battering-related injuries or health problems are more likely to be single, separated, or divorced than are nonbattered women (Berrios & Grady, 1991; Elliott & M. M. Johnson, 1995; Stark et al., 1981). Furthermore, violence in dating and courtship relationships is increasingly recognized as a significant problem (Browne & Williams, 1993; Makepeace, 1989).

Finally, use of the term male partner violence serves a practical purpose. It limits the focus of the present review to violence within adult relationships; the significant problems of childhood victimization and its sequelae are not specifically addressed here. Violence within same-sex couples is similarly not covered in this chapter (but see Kanuha, 1990; Lobel, 1986; Renzetti, 1992). Additional practical considerations limit the scope of the chapter to the consequences of abuse on the physical health of women. For discussion of psychiatric sequelae, see M. P. Koss, Goodman et al. (1994).

FORMAL DEFINITION OF PARTNER VIOLENCE

Male partner violence is generally broadly defined to be inclusive of the various types of behaviors that are used to coerce, control, and demean women. From an international perspective, the United Nations recognizes violence against women as "any act of gender-based violence that results in, or is likely to result in, physical, sexual, or psychological harm or suffering to women, including threats of such acts, coercion, or arbitrary deprivations of liberty, whether occurring in public or private life" (Economic and Social Council, 1992, p. 5). Specifically included in this definition are marital rape, sexual harassment, and threats or intimidation. Although discussion of the global health impact of violence against women is beyond the scope of this chapter, it is important to note that researchers and health care providers worldwide are singling out partner violence as a major public health threat to women. For a comprehensive review of the health burden of violence against women throughout the world, see Heise, Raikes, Watts, and Zwi (1994), Heise, Ellsburg, and Gottmoeller (1999), and M. P. Koss, Heise, and N. F. Russo (1994).

As defined by the American Medical Association, partner violence "is characterized as a pattern of coercive behaviors that may include repeated battering and injury, psychological abuse, sexual assault, progressive social isolation, deprivation, and intimidation. These behaviors are perpetrated by someone who is or was involved in an intimate relationship with the victim" (AMA, 1992, p. 40). The violence within an abusive relationship is characterized as a recurrent experience in which a woman is placed in physical danger or controlled by the threat or use of force. Included in the definition of physical abuse are pushing, slapping, punching, kicking, choking; assault with a weapon; tying down or restraining; leaving the woman in a dangerous place; and refusing to help when the woman is sick or injured. Partner violence may also involve emotional or psychological abuse, including physical and social isolation; extreme jealousy and possessiveness; deprivation, degradation, and humiliation; intimidation and threats of harm; intense criticizing, insulting, belittling, and ridiculing; and driving fast and recklessly to frighten the woman. Sexual abuse is also often part of violent relationships, and may include forced sexual acts or sexual degradation, such as trying to make her perform sexual acts against her will; hurting her during sex or assaulting her genitals, including use of objects intravaginally, orally, or anally; pursuing sex when she is not fully conscious or is afraid to say no; and coercing her to have sex without protection against pregnancy or sexually transmitted diseases (AMA, 1992).

In referring to the patterns of abusive relationships so defined, the AMA uses the terms *partner violence* and *domestic violence* interchangeably. For the reasons already cited, however, the term *male partner violence* is preferable. It more adequately conveys the broad range and classes of acts that define abusive relationships. Domestic violence more typically connotes battery, obscuring the other manifestations of abuse included in the definition. This use of the term *domestic violence* appears to put blinders on what researchers study. As this review reveals, other forms of abuse—such as isolation, psychological abuse, and threats—have been little studied or written about by the medical community. Empirical data is thus largely limited to the impact of physical and sexual violence on women's health and medical care utilization.

GENERAL PREVALENCE AND PATTERNS

Physical Assault

Limited surveillance techniques and widely acknowledged underreporting make reliable estimates of the prevalence of partner violence difficult. No nationwide system exists to collect and update data specifically on violence within intimate relationships, and no consistent procedures are employed for identification of victims. The National Crime Victimization Survey (NCVS), an annual general survey of crime, provides estimates that 572,000 women annually are victims of violent crimes by intimate partners, giving a rate of 5 per 1,000 population (Bureau of Justice Statistics, 1994). These estimates, however, are heavily criticized on the basis of serious methodological flaws in the data collection methods and questioning regarding intimate violence used in the NCVS (Browne, 1993; M. P. Koss, Goodman et al., 1994; Stark & Flitcraft, 1988). These statistics fall far below the range of generally accepted estimates based on large scale surveys of violence within couples. The National Family Violence Surveys, based on probability samples and telephone data collection, have estimated that each year nearly 2 million women, or more than 3 out of every 100, are severely physically assaulted by a male partner (Straus & Gelles, 1990; Straus et al., 1980). In a randomized telephone survey of 6,000 households, nearly one in eight husbands reported using physical aggression against their wives during the preceding 12 months (Straus & Gelles, 1990). A study of dating or courtship violence, conducted with women students at colleges and universities nationwide, found that 32% had experienced at least some degree of physical aggression in these types of relationships (White & M. P. Koss, 1991). The national estimates based on telephone surveys are likely to be conservative due to the exclusion of nonhouseholds from the sample frames. This omission means that several living situations are missed where women may be at high risk for violence, including prisons, psychiatric hospitals, the military, and colleges. Additionally, the method misses the homeless, those too poor to own a telephone, and women whose partners control their ability to freely receive calls. Overall, based on review of these data, experts have concluded that a true estimate would lie somewhere between 3 and 4 million women (8%–10%) annually, and between 21% and 34% of women in their lifetime, are victims of male partner violence (Browne & Williams, 1993; Stark & Flitcraft, 1988).

Demographically, studies of prevalence consistently find that younger women are at greater risk of abuse than are older (Gin, Rucker, Frayne, Cygan, & Hubbell, 1991; Grisso et al., 1991; McLeer & Anwar, 1989; Parker, McFarlane, & Soeken, 1994; Stark et al., 1981). In a study of women presenting for injuries at an urban emergency department, McLeer and Anwar (1989) found that 42% of injuries in the 18- to 20-year-old age goup were due to battering, compared to 35% in the 21- to 30-year-old age group, and 26% in the 31- to 40-year-old age group. Battering caused 18% of injuries among women age 61 and older. This pattern is also seen among women presenting for prenatal care, with teenagers and women in their early 20s more likely to be abused during pregnancy than are older women (Helton, McFarlane, & Anderson, 1987; Parker et al., 1994). Researchers have documented differences in rates of partner violence among ethnic groups, but suggest that these are confounded with social class, indicated by income, unemployment, and education (Lockhart, 1991). For example, the rates of partner violence are higher for low income Black women (144/1,000) than for higher income Black women (58/1,000; Hamptom & Gelles, 1994). Russo, Denious, Keita, and Koss (1997) reported similar results among the 439 Black women who participated in the Commonwealth Fund's national survey on women's health. The problem of male partner violence is found across all socioeconomic groups (Elliott & M. M. P. Johnson, 1995; Gin et al., 1991; Heise et al., 1994; McFarlane, Parker, Soeken, & Bullock, 1992; Stark & Flitcraft, 1988). Review of the data reveals that although low income women report higher rates of current partner violence (11%) than do middle income women (10%) or higher income women (8%), the difference in rates is fairly small (Stark & Flitcraft, 1988). In another aspect of the pattern, some evidence suggests that violence within a relationship may escalate over time. Of women killed by a male partner, 64% had been previously physically abused by that man (Campbell, 1992).

Marital Rape

Between 10% and 14% of women are raped and sexually assaulted within the context of marriage or cohabitation, applying the legal definitions (Finkelhor & Yllo, 1985; Frieze, 1983; Russell, 1982). Women who are victims of physical abuse are especially vulnerable to sexual abuse, with estimates of prevalence from various studies ranging between 26% and 52% of physically abused women also being raped by their husband or partner (Campbell, 1989; Finkelhor & Yllo, 1985; Frieze, 1983; Hanneke, Shields, & McCall, 1986; Russell, 1982; Shields & Hanneke, 1983). Marital rape in the absence of other forms of physical violence is rare (Campbell, 1989; Elliott & M. M. P. Johnson, 1995; Hanneke et al., 1986). Men who are both physically and sexually abusive are consistently found to perpetrate the most violent and severe assaults on their partner, with the majority of victims being repeatedly assaulted during the course of the relationship (Campbell, 1989; Finkelhor & Yllo, 1985; Frieze, 1983; Shields & Hanneke, 1983). Women who are victims of both physical and sexual violence are also at greater risk for abuse during pregnancy, as well as at greater risk of homicide (Campbell, 1989; Frieze, 1983). The occurrence of sexual assault in marriage is associated with greater trauma and more severe depression and low self-esteem than is found among victims of physical abuse alone (Campbell, 1989, Frieze, 1983)

Psychological Abuse

Limited data are available on the prevalence and impact of stalking and emotional or psychological abuse on health and health care utilization. Such nonphysical forms of control and character assassination may be more difficult to measure and relate to outcomes, as well as less apparent. Several attempts have been made to address the issue, however (Canadian Centre for Justice Statistics, 1994; Elliott & M. M. P. Johnson, 1995; O'Campo, Gielen, Faden, & Kass, 1994; Talley, Fett, Zinsmeister, & Melton, 1994; Tjaden & Thoennes, 1998b). The National Violence Against Women Survey collected data via telephone from 16,000 women nationally (Tjaden & Thoennes, 1998a). Results revealed that 8.1% of U.S. women have been stalked in their lifetime. Of these incidents, 60% involved current or ex-boyfriends, spouses, cohabiting partners, or dates. Just 21% of the stalking behavior was initiated before the relationship ended. The remainder occurred both before and after (36%), or just after the relationship ended (43%). The Canadian Centre for Justice Statistics' National Survey on Violence Against Women used five questions to measure prevalence of emotional abuse of women by male partners in that country, including questions on jealousy, limiting her contact with family or friends, belittling and insulting her, preventing access to family income, and insisting on knowing her whereabouts at all times. Approximately one third of ever-married women reported that their current or previous partner was emotionally abusive in at least one of the five ways. In the majority of cases, emotional abuse was concomitant with physical or sexual abuse; only 18% of women who reported no physical violence by a partner reported experiencing emotional abuse (Canadian Center for Justice Statistics, 1994). A U.S. population-based study found similar results (Talley et al., 1994). Talley and colleagues found that only 14% of reported emotional and verbal abuse occurred in the absence of either sexual or physical abuse.

Elliott and M. M. P. Johnson (1995) described the complex relation between the types of partner violence experienced by women patients seen in a primary care setting. In this sample, all women who were physically abused also reported experiencing emotional abuse in that relationship. Descriptions of the excessive control over emotional and social behavior that typified emotional abuse in this sample included being followed, made to feel guilty when she wanted to go out with friends, taking away or disabling her car, and constant threats of assault. Two thirds of the women who reported any type of partner violence experienced all categories of abuse used in the study, including severe battery and use of weapons (Elliott & M. M. P. Johnson, 1995).

PREVALENCE OF PARTNER VIOLENCE IN MEDICAL CARE SETTINGS

The American Medical Association recommends screening for partner violence in all portals of entry into the medical care system (AMA, 1992). For women, the most common entries are emergency, obstetric, and primary care services. The prevalence of victims in these settings, and the presentations most commonly associated as outcomes of abuse, are discussed in the material that follows.

Emergency Care

The overall prevalence of intimate partner abuse identified in surveys of 3,455 patients in 11 community emergency rooms was 14.4% for past year physical or sexual abuse (Dearwater et al., 1998). The lifetime prevalence of emotional or physical abuse was 36.8% (Dearwater et al., 1998). Approximately one in eight women patients, or more than one in four emergency department visits by women are related to assault by a male partner (Abbot, R. Johnson, Koziol-McLain, & Lowenstein, 1995; McLeer & Anwar, 1989; Stark et al., 1981). Male partner violence is the largest single cause of injury to women requiring emergency medical treatment, accounting for up to one half of all injuries to women seen there (Stark et al., 1981). Further results of the study by Stark and colleagues (1981) show that the pattern of injuries sustained in beatings can generally distinguish victims of violence from accident victims. Physically abused women compared to those involved in accidents are more likely to have injuries to multiple parts of the body, as well as more likely to have injuries to the face, head, neck, throat, breast, chest, or abdomen. Accidental injuries are likely to involve the extremities, particularly the elbow, knee, or hip area. The types of injuries seen also differ, with battered women likely to have abrasions and contusions, or pains for which no physiologic cause can be discovered. Accidental injuries are more likely to involve sprains or strains. Fractures, dislocations, and lacerations occur with about equal frequency to abused and nonabused women.

In a study of 218 women who had presented to an emergency department with injuries resulting from partner violence, Berrios and Grady (1991) found that as a result of the abusive episode, many women required significant medical intervention and testing. Forty-one percent of the women interviewed required radiographic studies, 25% required stitches or casting, and 27% received medications. Eleven percent had suffered loss of consciousness, and 5% had a permanent impairment, such as disfigurement, hearing loss, or visual impairment. Victims frequently had lacerations (39%), musculoskeletal injuries (25%), or internal injuries (13%), and many suffered choking or strangulation (23%). Twenty-eight percent of the sample had been admitted to the hospital, and 13% underwent major surgical intervention. In one third of all cases, a weapon had been used. Ten percent of the victims were pregnant at the time of the assault (Berrios & Grady, 1991).

Sexual assault victims often present with injuries from battery, as well as with genital injuries ranging from vulvar contusions to major vaginal tears (Geist, 1988). One third of rapes include anal or oral penetration in addition to vaginal contact, with anorectal injuries likely (Geist, 1988). In emergency department-based studies, nearly one third of rape victims had documented histories of battering; 58% of rape victims over age 30 were battered (Stark et al., 1981). The pattern of partner violence was very rarely identified as the context of rape, however.

One of the most troublesome aspects of the problem, the recurrent and perhaps escalating nature of partner violence, can clearly be seen in emergency care utilization (Berrios & Grady, 1991; Grisso et al., 1991; Stark et al., 1981). Nearly one in five abused women has presented for medical treatment of trauma more than 11 times; another 23% has been treated 6 to 10 times previously for injuries from abuse (Stark & Flitcraft, 1988). In a study of the incidence of injuries in women of Philadelphia, Grisso and colleagues (1991) found that the majority of women presenting for emergency care two or more times during the study year had been victims of violence. Of the women repeaters whose first injury was due to violence, nearly half of subsequent injuries were also due to violence (Grisso et al., 1991). Women positively identified as victims of partner violence had, on average, seven treatment episodes in the emergency service, compared with 4.89 for those identified as having a probable history of partner violence, 3.94 for women with histories suggestive of abuse, and 1.96 for nonbattered women (Stark et al., 1981). A medical response that appropriately identifies and treats victims of violence and addresses safety from continuing abuse is clearly needed.

Prenatal Care

Since young women in their most active childbearing years are among those at highest risk for abuse, the experience and outcomes of violence during pregnancy deserve special attention. The effect of the pregnancy on the risk of assault apparently differs across relationships. In a sample of 290 pregnant women, Helton and colleagues (1987) found that 15% reported physical battering by their current male partner prior to the present pregnancy, and 8% reported battering during the present pregnancy. Another 4% had been threatened with physical assault before and/or during the pregnancy. Of the women battered while pregnant, 88% had been abused before the pregnancy; one third of whom reported that battering increased since they were pregnant. One third of the women battered during pregnancy had sought medical care for injuries sustained in the attack. The most frequent sites of abuse were the head and face, the breasts, and the back and buttocks (Helton et al., 1987). Stewart (1995) also reported findings on the prevalence of abuse from a survey of 548 pregnant women. In this sample, 10% were physically abused by their partner prior to becoming pregnant, and 7% reported abuse during the current pregnancy. Nearly two thirds of those battered during pregnancy reported that the abuse increased during this time. Two thirds of those abused during pregnancy received medical treatment for the abuse (Stewart, 1995).

In a study of 691 Black, Hispanic, and White pregnant women in public prenatal care clinics in Houston and Baltimore, 17% reported physical or sexual abuse during the current pregnancy (McFarlane et al., 1992). Sixty percent of abused women in this sample reported two or more violent episodes, with White women experiencing the most frequent and severe assaults. These researchers also found that abuse is related to timing of entry into prenatal care. Compared to nonabused women in this sample, abused women were twice as likely to begin prenatal care in the third trimester (21% vs. 11%; McFarlane et al., 1992). In a comparison of the prevalence of abuse during pregnancy among 1,203 poor teenage and adult women, teenagers were found to have significantly higher rates of physical and sexual abuse (20.6%) than were adults in this sample (14.2%; Parker et al., 1994). Compared with teenagers, however, adult women experienced more severe physical and emotional abuse, and were more likely to be abused within an ongoing relationship with a significant partner. This study found no difference in timing of entry into prenatal care between teenage and adult women overall, but did find a significant association between abuse and late (third trimester) entry into prenatal care (Parker et al., 1994).

Women who experience violence during pregnancy are at increased risk for giving birth to premature as well as full-term low birth weight infants (Bullock & McFarlane, 1989; Parker et al., 1994; Satin, Hemsell, Stone, Theriot, & Wendel, 1991). This difference is especially pronounced among women giving birth at private hospitals, where 17.5% of infants born to battered women were of low birth weight (< 5 lb., 8 oz), compared to 4.2% of births to nonabused women (Bullock & McFarlane, 1989). Overall, of both public and private hospital births in this sample, twice as many low birth weight infants were born to battered women (12.5%) as were born to nonbattered women (6.6%). Compared with nonpregnant victims, sexual assault during pregnancy has been found to be associated with less severe genital and nongenital trauma, yet a high rate of preterm (16%) and low birth weight (24%) births (Satin et al., 1991).

Parker and colleagues (1994) also found physical or sexual abuse during pregnancy to be significantly associated with low birth weight. In addition, abuse was associated with the risk factors and maternal complications of low weight gain, infections, anemia, smoking, and alcohol or drug usage (Parker et al., 1994). Amaro, Fried, Cabral, and Zuckerman (1990), in a study of the relation between partner violence during pregnancy and drug use, found that victims as compared to nonvictims were more likely to be White, born in the United States, single, and to be on Medicaid. The two groups were similar in educational attainment, age, employment, and parity. On psychosocial measures, victims were more likely than nonvictims to report a history of depression, attempted suicide, and lack of support during their pregnancy. Women abused during pregnancy were at greater risk than those nonabused to be heavy users of alcohol and illicit drugs (Amaro et al., 1990). Thus abuse may itself be a risk factor for pregnancy complications, as well as contribute to other known risks, compounding the effect.

Primary Care

The health and medical impacts of violence against women extend well beyond the immediate risk of injuries and the need for emergency services. In fact, a majority of medical visits related to abuse take place in primary care offices (Stark et al., 1981; Stark & Flitcraft, 1988). At least one incident of criminal victimization, including noncontact crimes such as break-in, attempted robbery, and purse snatching, is a common experience among women primary care patients, affecting as many as 57% (M. P. Koss, Woodruff, & P. G. Koss, 1991). In this sample, 21.3% had experienced completed rape since age 14. Through further analysis, M. P. Koss and associates (M. P. Koss, P. G. Koss, & Wodruff, 1991; M. P. Koss, Woodruff, & P. G. Koss, 1991) revealed that victims of severe physical crimes such as rape and assault are especially likely to use medical care services up to 2 years following the attack. In a clinic-based study, Walsh and Broadhead (1992) found 48% of female patients at a combined family practice and university student health center reported having some type of contact sexual victimization in their lifetime; 25% of the patients in this setting reported experiences of rape or attempted rape. Women of all ages with a history of past or current partner abuse are found to be disproportionately represented among women receiving a variety of services in primary care settings. A study of the prevalence of partner violence among women patients in a midwestern family practice clinic found that 38% reported experiencing physical abuse (defined to include sexual abuse) by a partner during their lifetimes, and 12% reported current physical abuse (Elliott & M. M. P. Johnson, 1995). In a study conducted across three university-affiliated internal medicine clinics, 34% of women in the ethnically diverse sample had ever experienced partner violence, and 17% were currently victims of violence from a cohabiting male partner (Gin et al., 1991).

Elliott and M. M. P. Johnson (1995) compared the reasons for the medical appointments of women patients in a family practice clinic, and found group differences between women with no history of physical abuse, those with a past history, and those currently living in a physically abusive relationship. Of the women reporting no history of partner abuse, over half (52%) stated the purpose of their visit as routine health maintenance, such as a physical exam. Of those who had past experience with an abusive partner, 38% were being seen for routine examinations and 62% had specific complaints. Of the women reporting current physical abuse, none had appointments for routine exams; all visits were related to a specific complaint such as neck stiffness, the need to refill a prescription for antidepressant medication, a rash, migraine headaches, and an injured arm (Elliott & M. M. P. Johnson, 1995).

A history of sexual and physical abuse is associated with a variety of physical health complaints. Many studies on the physical health consequences of abuse have focused on childhood abuse and later medical problems in adult women (see Fry, 1993; E. A. Walker et al., 1992). Studies that address the health consequences of victimization by violence in adulthood generally include in their sample women with any history of abuse and so too include those abused as children (Drossman et al., 1990; Rapkin, Kames, Darke, Stampler, & Naliboff, 1990; Reiter, Shakerin, Gambone, & Milburn, 1991; E. A. Walker, A. N. Gelfand, M. D. Gelfand, M. P. Koss, & Katon, 1995; E. A. Walker, Katon, Roy-Byrne, Jemelka, & J. Russo, 1993; Walling et al., 1994). It is therefore difficult to separate the effects of these childhood and adulthood abuse experiences. The health problems most studied in relation to abuse are chronic conditions, most commonly pelvic pain and gastrointestinal disorders.

Chronic Pelvic Pain. Chronic pelvic pain, generally defined as noncyclic pelvic pain of greater than 6 months duration, accounts for approximately 10% of all gynecological visits, and is listed as the indication for up to 34% of diagnostic laparoscopies (Reiter, 1990; Reiter & Gambone, 1990). It is the third most frequent indication for hysterectomy, accounting for approximately 12% or 78,000 such surgeries annually (Lee, Dicker, Rubin, & Ory, 1984; Reiter et al., 1991). It is considered a frustrating syndrome to treat for both the patient and her physician, because in approximately 35% of cases no intrapelvic pathology is evident, diminishing hope for a medical cure (Reiter, 1990).

Research on correlates of chronic pelvic pain indicates that between 53% and 64% of patients referred to a specialty clinic for this condition have a history of physical and/or sexual abuse (Rapkin et al., 1990; Reiter & Gambone, 1990; Toomey, Hernandez, Gittleman, & Hulka, 1993; Walling et al., 1994). Rapkin and colleagues (1990) found a high prevalence of childhood abuse (52%) among a sample of chronic pelvic pain patients, whereas abuse during adulthood (since the 18th birthday) was reported by 16%. In this sample, physical abuse was more predictive of chronic pelvic pain than was sexual abuse. A similar study (Walling et al., 1994) distinguished between any sexual abuse (i.e., forced or coerced fondling through clothing, touching, kissing) and major sexual abuse (i.e., penetration or other direct contact with unclothed genitals). Using these criteria, in this sample 36% of 64 chronic pelvic pain patients experienced major sexual abuse before age 15, and 33% had experienced such abuse since their 15th birthday; some women had experienced both. Rates for "any" sexual abuse were even higher. In addition, 39% reported physical abuse before age 15, and 36% since that time (Walling et al., 1994). It should be noted that sexual abuse in these samples, as in the general population, generally was found to be concomitant with physical abuse.

Reiter and colleagues (1991) reported that rates of abuse are higher among chronic pelvic pain patients with no identifiable somatic abnormality than among patients with probable somatic pelvic pain. Of 52 women with "nonsomatic" pelvic pain, 67% had experienced sexual abuse or trauma before age 20, compared with 28% of 47 women with identified "somatic" pelvic pain reporting such abuse. The study by Rapkin and associates (1990) looked at women with chronic pelvic pain and found a significant difference in the proportions of those with and without identified pelvic pathology who had experienced physical abuse in adulthood. None of the 19 chronic pelvic pain patients with identified pathology had been victims of physical abuse as an adult, compared to 27% of 11 women with no identified pathology.

An abuse history also appears to be associated with other physical symptoms. Two studies of chronic pelvic pain each used two comparison groups: one of pain-free gynecology patients, and one of female chronic headache patients. The data suggest a general association between abuse and chronic pain, as well as a specific association between major sexual abuse and chronic pelvic pain (Rapkin et al., 1990; Walling et al., 1994). Women evaluated for chronic pelvic pain who have a positive history of abuse also report significantly more physical and psychological symptoms unrelated to pelvic pain than do women who have not been abused (Reiter et al., 1991; Reiter & Gambone, 1990; Toomey et al., 1993).

Gastrointestinal Disorders. Among the most common additional complaints of chronic pelvic pain patients are those consistent with gastrointestinal disorders, most particularly irritable bowel syndrome (IBS). Considerable overlap has been reported in diagnoses of the two disorders, with as many as 79% of chronic pelvic pain patients also meeting criteria for probable irritable bowel syndrome (Hogston, 1987; E. A. Walker et al., 1991). Both organically based and functional gastrointestinal disorders have also been researched for association with abuse history in women (Drossman et al., 1990; Talley et al., 1994; E. A. Walker et al., 1993, 1995). Functional gastrointestinal disorders, including IBS, nonulcer dyspepsia, and chronic abdominal pain make up about 35% of gastrointestinal disorder diagnoses, and occur more frequently in women (Drossman et al., 1990). These disorders have no known pathogenesis or established treatment, and are the most common chronic gastrointestinal conditions seen in primary care, as well as the most common reason for referral to gastroenterologists (Drossman et al., 1990; Talley et al., 1994).

In various clinical samples, between 44% and 59% of all female gastroenterology patients report a history of sexual abuse, and between 32% and 48% of female patients have experienced severe sexual trauma (Drossman et al., 1990, Walker et al., 1993, 1995). Thirty-six percent of 206 female patients in a study by Drossman and associates (1990) reported physical and/or sexual abuse since age 14. In this study, women with functional gastrointestinal disorders were more likely than those with organic disorders to report a history of severe sexual abuse and frequent physical abuse. However, another study of women gastroenterology patients with and without histories of severe sexual trauma found no significant difference between the two groups in terms of diagnostic category (functional or organic disorder; E. A. Walker et al., 1995). These authors found that a history of severe sexual trauma was significantly associated with physical abuse as an adult, however. Victims of severe sexual trauma also suffered from significantly more lifetime psychiatric disorders, and more medically unexplained physical symptoms, both including and excluding gastrointestinal symptoms, than women patients without a history of sexual trauma (E. A. Walker et al., 1995).

Other Chronic Pain. Other chronic pain, particularly chronic headache, is also found to be associated with physical and sexual abuse in women (Domino & Haber, 1987; Haber & Roos, 1985). Some evidence suggests that chronic headache may be a syndrome especially related to experience with male partner violence in adulthood. Of women referred to a pain center for chronic headaches unresponsive to headache medication regimens, 61% had experienced prior physical abuse, 11% had been sexually abused, and 28% had experienced both physical and sexual abuse (Domino & Haber, 1987). The abuse reported occurred primarily after age 20, with an average duration of abuse of approximately 8 years. Headache onset in all cases followed initiation of the abuse. A major difference in headache etiology was found between abused and nonabused women, with 75% of abused women developing headache pain after age 20, as compared to 86% of nonabused women developing headache problems before age 20.

Several studies have demonstrated that medical utilization increases following victimization experiences (Golding, 1994; Golding, Stein, Siegel, Burnam, & Sorenson, 1988; Kimerling & Calhoun, 1994; M. P. Koss, P. G. Koss, & Woodruff, 1991; Liebschutz, Mulvey, & Samet, 1997). One related factor may be that women who have experienced contact or noncontact crime rate their health significantly less well than women who have not been victimized (Kimerling & Calhoun, 1994; M. P. Koss, Woodruff, & P. G. Koss, 1991; M. P. Koss, P. G. Koss, & Woodruff, 1990). M. P. Koss, P. G. Koss, and Woodruff (1991) found that those women who had experienced severe crimes such as rape or repeated physical assault had the greatest number of health complaints and symptoms of emotional distress. In addition, this study found a positive linear relation between the level of victimization and both the mean number of outpatient visits in the year of the crime (index year), and the mean outpatient expenses during that time, as recorded in medical records. Medical record review indicated that medical care utilization of victims surpassed that of nonvictims only following the victimization. Whereas nonvictims' utilization in the index year increased only 2% over a 2-year baseline period, assault victims' physician visits increased 31% and those by rape victims increased 56% during the same time period. The rate of utilization among victims remained significantly higher than that of nonvictims in the last year of the study, 2 years following the crime. Kimerling and Calhoun (1994), controlling for all routine medical visits such as annual physicals and gynecological exams, as well as initial emergency room and other medical visits due to injuries sustained in the attack, found similar increased utilization with victims of sexual assault in a self- report study of medical usage.

Victims of abuse suffering from pelvic pain or gastrointestinal disorders appear to have higher rates of medical utilization than their nonabused counterparts (Schei, 1990; Talley et al., 1994). A study of pelvic pain conducted in Norway found that 48% of 63 women living in an abusive relationship within the past year had a history of pelvic pain, as compared to 21% of 114 women in a comparison group never abused by a male partner. The abused women were significantly more likely to have seen a physician for the condition (26%) than were the nonabused women (9%) (Schei, 1990). A population-based study with 30- to 49-year-old residents of a midwestern county, surveying gastrointestinal symptoms and self-reported abuse, found a similar result (Talley et al., 1994). There were significant associations between symptoms of functional gastrointestinal disorders and physical, sexual, and psychological abuse in childhood and adulthood. Fifty-two percent of abused subjects reported abuse as both children and adults. Of all respondents classified as having

IBS, 60% had seen a physician for their symptoms at some time in the past. Among respondents with gastrointestinal symptoms, significantly more visits were made to physicians by those patients who had experienced any abuse, those who had been abused in adulthood and childhood, by those with any history of sexual abuse, and by those with a history of frequent emotional or verbal abuse, as compared to nonabused respondents (Talley et al., 1994).

Increased health care utilization is not a unique attribute of women with a history of abuse, but rather is found among those people experiencing psychological distress and stressful life events in general (Katon, Ries, & Kleinman, 1984). Neither are the symptoms of those with psychosocial factors such as anxiety, stress, depression, and lack of social support necessarily more associated with functional, or "nonsomatic," disorders than with organic or medically explained disorders (Smith et al., 1990; E. A. Walker et al., 1995; Whitehead, Bosmajian, Zonderman, Costa, & Schuster, 1988). For example, Smith and associates (1990) found that psychosocial factors could not distinguish between patients with irritable bowel syndrome and those for whom an organic disease was found to explain the symptoms. Both groups of patients, however, had significantly more psychosocial difficulties than did a comparison group of patients with no gastrointestinal disorder. It was concluded that psychosocial criteria were determinants of health care seeking for the entire study group (Smith et al., 1990). Such somatization is regarded as highly prevalent in primary care. In a review, Katon et al. (1984) estimated that between 25% and 75% of primary care visits are primarily related to psychosocial distress, but that patients most often present with somatic complaints. As many as 60% of primary care patients present recurrently with physical symptoms that are related to psychosocial distress, a pattern that has been found to decrease significantly when the patient is referred to short-term psychotherapy (Katon et al., 1984).

Consistent with these findings, victims of partner violence experience higher levels of psychological distress than nonvictims (McCauley et al., 1995; Gelles & Harrop, 1989), yet somatic complaints are most often the problems bringing abused women into contact with the health care system. Victims are more likely to seek medical care than they are to use mental health services, social services, victim assistance, legal aid, or counseling from clergy (Kimerling & Calhoun, 1994; M. P. Koss, P. G. Koss, & Woodruff, 1991). Physicians and other health care practitioners are thus exceptionally well positioned to identify victims and to provide an opportunity to consider treatment options. Perhaps partially accounting for increased medical utilization is the finding that victimized women are more likely to engage in health risk and self-injurious behaviors such as smoking, alcohol use, and failure to use seatbelts (M. P. Koss, P. G. Koss, & Woodruff, 1991). Women with a history of abuse are also at a higher risk for exhibiting eating disorders than nonabused women (Root & Fallon, 1988). In addition, risk of suicide is increased among victims of partner violence compared with nonvictims (Amaro et al., 1990; Berrios & Grady, 1991; Stark et al., 1981).

IMPLICATIONS FOR MEDICAL CARE

The medical community has begun to recognize both the impact of partner violence and the role that health care providers can play in detecting and referring patients who have been physically abused. In 1992, the American Medical Association issued guidelines on the diagnosis and treatment of domestic violence, and the Joint Commission on Accreditation of Healthcare Organizations (JCAHO) began requiring that all accredited hospitals implement protocols in their treatment facilities for identifying, treating, and referring victims of abuse (AMA, 1992). The AMA Council on Ethical and Judicial Affairs has written that the principles of beneficence and nonmaleficence that guide medical practice require physicians to do more than treat only the injuries and symptoms of abuse (Council on Ethical and Judicial Affairs, 1992). These calls for involvement in the issue are prompted both by growing awareness of the health and financial costs associated with violence, and evidence for the appropriateness of screening for abuse due to the high likelihood that physicians and other practitioners will encounter victims in their practices (Council on Scientific Affairs, 1992). Despite these recommendations, the medical community has been reluctant to recognize its obligation in partner violence intervention. The majority of women favor routine physician inquiry about physical and sexual abuse and believe that physicians can be helpful (Friedman, Samet, Roberts, Hudlin, & Hans, 1992), but physicians in every medical setting neglect screening for partner violence among their patients. In fact, women report that among the services to which they turn for help in ending violence in their lives, such as the police, social service/counseling, lawyers, clergy, women's shelters, women's groups and district attorneys, medical professionals are least likely to be very or somewhat effective (Bowker & Maurer, 1987). Failure to identify victims as abused may lead to continued medical utilization for physical complaints, inappropriate diagnoses, and may contribute to her staying in a potentially life threatening situation.

Victims' Experience in the Medical Care System

The medical community is in a critical position to intervene in partner violence. Not only are victims of partner violence highly likely to present themselves to some type of health care setting, it may also be one of the only types of services with which they come in contact. Isolation characterizes the life of a woman experiencing partner violence. A violent partner attempts to minimize the contact that his victim has with outside organizations that he believes may jeopardize his control over her (Sassetti, 1993; L. Walker, 1979, 1984). Violent incidents may precipitate contact with law enforcement, but the likelihood that the victim will reach out for help in these high stress situations is slim. Experience with the criminal justice system has taught many women that the police can only hold her abuser for a limited period of time, and on release she will be unprotected. She is under extreme pressure to make decisions, and believes that the law cannot protect her (Bouza, 1991).

A victim of partner abuse can, however, justify trips to the doctor for routine examinations, prenatal care, or treatment of conditions that are not recognized as an outcome of the abuse. Medical attention following a violent explosion may also be necessary, although women often wait several days before presenting to a physician for fear that the abuse will be detected. Of 74 women surveyed in a woman's shelter in Michigan, over half revealed that they did not seek care immediately after an attack (Campbell, Pliska, Taylor, & Sheridan, 1994). A woman's abuser may refuse to allow his victim to seek medical treatment for fear of being detected, however it may become apparent in the following days that she must seek attention. At this point, the woman is calmer and more likely to have entered a stage of reconciliation with her abuser (L. Walker, 1984). Unless she is asked, she may prefer to mask the source of her injuries.

Lack of Detection

Emergency Departments. Emergency departments have been recognized as a portal of entry for victims of partner violence, but physicians in this setting have consistently failed to routinely screen their patients. Stark, Flitcraft, and Frazier (1979) conducted a retrospective study to determine the incidence of partner violence among women presenting in an emergency department during a 2-month period by evaluating medical records for evidence of abuse. Although physicians had identified less than 3% of the 481 female patients as victims of violence, the full medical histories revealed that at least 10% of the patients could positively be identified as victims and another 15% had case histories strongly indicative of abuse (Stark, Flitcraft, & Frazier, 1979). In a more recent study of 47 women (12% of total sample) who indicated on an anonymous survey that their present trip to the emergency department could be related to abuse by a current partner, only 4 were asked about partner violence by emergency department professionals (Abbot, R. Johnson, Koziol-McLain, & Lowenstein, 1995).

To better understand how clinicians respond to partner violence, Kurz (1987) conducted a participant observation study of health care providers in four emergency departments in Philadelphia. The staff in three departments had been informed of the study and referral cards were made available to them, but no additional information was given about partner violence. In the fourth setting, a formal documentation system was set up and one staff member actively educated herself on the characteristics of partner violence. Of the patients that met the observers' established criteria for suggested violence, 40% of cases in the first three departments received no response from medical staff, 49% received acknowledgment and a hotline number but staff involvement was brief and routine, and 11% received a positive response in which staff viewed the case as legitimate and deserving of time and attention, noted partner violence on the record, and spoke with the woman about safety issues. Women who were characterized as "true victims" were more likely to receive a positive response than those who were viewed as "troublesome," "evasive," or appeared under the influence of drugs or alcohol. These women were more often diagnosed as suffering from depression or substance abuse. Under the conditions of the fourth emergency department, 32% of cases still received no response and 21% only a partial response, however 47% received a positive response, due primarily to the efforts of eight of the staff members who saw intervention as part of their job. Reasons given for lack of response were similar to those found in the other three sites (Kurz, 1987).

Education is a key factor in facilitating the screening process, and has only recently begun to be incorporated into formal medical training (Baker, 1995). Of the California emergency departments responding to a survey, only 23% of the physician directors confirmed that their emergency department had conducted an educational session on the issue of spousal abuse (Morbidity & Mortality Weekly Report, 1992). This is unfortunate because even without protocol, education exerts a positive influence on the likelihood that a physician will suspect abuse (Tilden et al., 1994).

Having a formal protocol in place for the treatment of partner violence has a positive impact on the rate of screening in emergency departments. For example, McLeer, Anwar, Herman, and Macquiling (1989) conducted a retrospective study in the years before and after the establishment of protocol formalizing policies and procedures to identify victims of partner abuse in an emergency department in Philadelphia. Rates of identification jumped from 5.6% to 30.0% with the implementation of protocol. When the same emergency department was studied 10 years later to determine if screening continued in the absence of a protocol, identification had again fallen to 7.6%, despite little demographic alteration in the population seeking care at the hospital. This dramatic change was interpreted as employee turnover and due to new staff who had not been included in the training on partner abuse and who did not prioritize its identification (McLeer et al., 1989). A recent Morbidity and Mortality Weekly Report survey to assess the progress of emergency departments in California toward the year 2000 objectives found that as few as 29% had established written policies and procedures regarding suspected victims of partner abuse. Although 93% reported having referral lists, only 9% of those submitted were comprehensive, including information on domestic violence services, mental health and community agencies, criminal justice system agencies, social services agencies, and legal assistance agencies (Morbidity & Mortality Weekly Report, 1993).

Nevertheless, establishing protocol does not ensure that the recommended practices regarding victims of violence will be followed. Emergency department physicians neglect to fully carry out policies and procedures when administering rape examinations to victims of sexual assault. The National Victim Center reported that 60% of victims receiving examinations were never advised about pregnancy testing or how to prevent a pregnancy, 73% were not given information about testing for exposure to HIV/AIDS, and 34% were not given information about testing for exposure to sexually transmitted diseases (National Victim Center, 1992).

An underlying issue that must be addressed is that with or without protocol, physicians generally underestimate the likelihood that their patients are victims. A recent survey of emergency departments in Massachusetts revealed that half of the respondents estimated that 2% or less of their patients were victims of partner violence (Isaac & Sanchez, 1994). Compared with an established rate of from 20% to 30% (Flitcraft, 1990; Morbidity & Mortality Weekly Report, 1993), this appraisal seems improbable. It is more likely that a large percentage of victims go undetected and unaided.

Primary Care. Although primary care providers are more likely than emergency department physicians to attend victims of partner violence for a variety of presenting health issues, formal policies and procedures have been even slower to appear in primary care settings. Just as in emergency departments, without protocol physicians are extremely unlikely to question their patients about possible abuse. Moreover, many are unaware of the true prevalence of partner violence. A mail survey was sent to 221 health care providers asking about their attitudes toward partner violence among their patients. The majority of physicians believed that abuse was infrequent (Tilden et al., 1994). Of 164 female patients surveyed in both a private and public health care site, only 7% were ever asked about physical abuse, and just 6% were asked about sexual abuse (Friedman et al., 1992). There is evidence that protocol for screening for violence would be effective. Inclusion of a question regarding partner violence on a self-administered health history form resulted in 11.6% of women responding affirmatively as compared to 0% identified among the group not given the question (Freund, Bak, & Blackhall, 1996).

Prenatal Care. It has been established that pregnant women are at risk for partner violence (Gielen, O'Campo, Faden, Kass & Xue, 1994; Hamberger, Saunders & Hovey, 1992; Helton, 1989; Helton et al., 1987; Hillard, 1985; Morbidity & Mortality Weekly Report, 1994). Routine prenatal care, however, is limited to the assessment of risk factors such as hypertension, diabetes, and nutritional inadequacies that may predict pregnancy complications or poor birth outcomes. Although the American College of OB/GYN has recommended that routine screening for partner violence be included on the list of risk factors because it places women in immediate danger (American College of Obstetrics and Gynecology, 1989), screening in prenatal clinics is rare. Survey of 374 pregnant women seeking care at a community health care clinic during a 2-month period revealed that 23.7% of the respondents affirmed that they had experienced physical assault in the past year, but only 1.7% had been asked by their physician if they were a victim of abuse (Hamberger et al., 1992). The Helton et al. (1987) study of 290 women attending public and private prenatal clinics identified 8% as experiencing violence during their current pregnancy, none of whom had been assessed for partner violence by their physician (Helton et al., 1987).

Misdiagnosis

Failing to probe for the underlying cause of injuries or unexplainable somatic problems not only sends a woman back into a dangerous situation where she may suffer more serious injury, it also initiates an ongoing cycle of contacts with medical and mental health providers with increasingly severe sequelae for the patient (Council on Scientific Affairs, 1992). Treatment of chronic pelvic pain, a common presenting complaint among victims of partner violence, can be perplexing for the physician who cannot find an etiology for the pain, and is therefore unable to make a diagnosis. Hysterectomies are often recommended in the absence of a definitive etiology, in spite of significant morbidity and occasional mortality accompanying the operation and the frequent lack of desired therapeutic outcomes (Gambone & Reiter, 1990). A study of 152 chronic pelvic pain patients found that 30% had undergone a previous hysterectomy, only to experience a recurrence of the pain after the surgery (Slocumb, 1990).

Physicians looking for the physical etiology of a disease may become frustrated and decide that their patient's condition is mentally based. Physicians who fail to find an organic cause of the woman's complaints of headache, bowel disorders, muscle pains, or painful intercourse tend to label her as "somatizing," "hysteric," or as a "well-known patient with multiple vague complaints." Medical records confirm that 1 in 4 female victims of partner violence are diagnosed using pseudopsychiatric labels, as compared to 1 in 50 nonvictims (Stark et al., 1979). The likely response of the physician is to prescribe medication for the "somatizing" woman with the aim of calming her down and satisfying her need for some type of medical response to her problem. Nearly 1 in 4 victims receives a prescription for tranquilizers, as compared to 1 in 10 nonvictims (Stark et al., 1979).

Primary care physicians' use of labels to classify the physical complaints of victims of partner violence is based on misapplication of the terms *psychosomatic* and *somatization disorder* as defined by the psychiatric profession. Those patients suffering from somatization disorder are defined by the *Diagnostic and Statistical Manual of Mental Disorders* (3rd, rev. ed., *DSM–III–R*) as having a lifetime history of physical complaints and current experience of multiple (13 or more) somatic symptoms. Numerous medical problems manifested in victims of partner violence present with symptoms similar to those with somatization disorder, such as the psychologic components of anxiety, which is often expressed in abdominal pain, the vegetative symptoms of depression, and panic disorder (Smith, 1990). In the case of violence victims, however, these are in direct response to a life context that is producing the condition. "Psychosomatic" is often misused to refer to a somatic dysfunction for which psychological factors are believed to play a causal role, however the term actually refers to the inseparability and interdependence of psychosocial and biologic aspects of humankind, of which the immediate social context of the patient is an integral part (Lipowski, 1984). Proper clinical management cannot be achieved without correct diagnosis. If the complaint finally is found lacking medical explanation, screening for factors such as partner abuse is even more strongly indicated.

Retraumatization

A woman caught in a cycle of partner violence is in constant battle to control her situation and minimize the damage to herself and her family. She is the daily target of accusations that she is the cause of the problems in the relationship, and although she may suspect that this is another facet of her partner's abuse, her isolation makes this difficult to confirm. Because a slip on her part may lead to severe outcomes, she must carefully choose ways to reach out for help that will not put herself and her children at more danger. Lack of response to her efforts may drive her further into desperation and the belief that she is alone in a situation for which there is no escape. An outside perspective may view a woman's behavior as "helpless," however this is a misinterpretation of a victim's struggle for survival.

A victim of partner abuse may risk asking for a physician for help in resolving a violent predicament (Martins, Holzapfel, & Baker, 1992). But, rather than openly exposing herself and her situation, she is more likely to give strong clues to her physician that she is experiencing abuse (Warshaw, 1992). Affirmation that she is not responsible for the violence and information about options available to her may be all a woman requires in order to begin the process of ending the abuse. When the physician misses her underlying pleas for help, the woman's fears that she is without social support are verified.

Women seeking assistance from their physician by presenting with unexplainable complaints often find that it is their batterers who receive affirmation. Victims of male partner violence are frequently labeled with substance abuse problems or mental disturbances in order to explain the failure to identify a medical explanation for the illness (Flitcraft, 1993; Kurz, 1987; Stark et al., 1981). In this manner, the physician–patient relationship actually replicates the subjugation and name calling that a victim is currently experiencing with her partner. This results in an increased sense of despair and helplessness that may contribute to the sequelae she is already experiencing due to the violence (Warshaw, 1992). Medical labeling occurs at the height of a woman's vulnerability, encouraging her perception that her abusive relationship is the symptom of her own dependency and helplessness, and the impression that she, and not her partner, is sick. This intensifies her sense of confusion about the situation, as well as heightening fears that she cannot escape this dangerous relationship (Stark et al., 1979).

Physician Involvement in Patient Care

Many explanations have been offered to account for the low rate of victim identification among health care providers. Burge (1989) argued that the biomedical framework does not consider partner violence to be a health problem, and therefore physicians do not feel responsible for dealing with the issue. Candib (1990) pointed out that recognizing male partner violence against women is a challenge for the family physician who holds fundamental assumptions about the importance of the nuclear family for the health of all its members. Kurz (1987) suggested that among partner violence victims presenting in an emergency department, only those who appear to be "true victims," thus evoking the sympathy of the health care provider, will be identified. The fact that identification of victims is low across all types of medical care settings regardless of protocol indicates that screening will not take place unless physicians consider it part of their role as health care providers. Attitudes toward screening, however, constitute only one of the many impediments to victim identification.

Systemic Barriers. Physicians encounter myriad obstacles to diagnosing the existence of partner violence, from the type of training they receive to the systematic pressures of the medical setting. The biomedical framework in which physicians are trained does not prepare them to consider the social context in which the patient lives, but rather defines her problem in a physical, diagnostic category that can be cured and prevented from recurring. By looking at only physical body parts, physicians are actually reconstructing a false history, because they neglect to recognize the possibility that the real danger to her well-being comes not from the illness or injury that they are treating, but from returning to a situation of escalating violence (Warshaw, 1992).

Biomedical training also requires that physicians evaluate what is directly presented to them, including the immediate symptoms, the medical history of the patient, and the relevant physiological data. They are expected to fit this information into diagnostic categories that are linked to various treatments. This single process does not allow the physician to consider the social causes of the symptoms or factors that cannot be controlled by a medical solution (Stark et al., 1979).

The medical record provides evidence of the manner in which the woman's perspective is devalued in the patient–physician exchange. Inherent in the words "complains of" is the assertion that the woman's symptoms are not indicative of a real problem. By focusing on the physical character of these symptoms exclusive of the woman's life experience, she is further diminished, and the real etiology behind her "complaint" is obscured (Warshaw, 1993). The needs of the patient reaching out for assistance and the physician attempting to diagnose her are subsumed by the more powerful medical community.

Personal Barriers. Physicians, as well as patients, are operating within larger social contexts, and the implications of partner violence have resonance in their lives far beyond the point that the patient departs from their office. Just as in society as a whole, it is much more comfortable to underestimate the existence of this type of violence, which is frightening and incomprehensible. Depending on education and personal experience, a physician may undergo a range of emotional responses from believing that the woman must be doing something to provoke such violence to being extremely frustrated that any one would choose to stay in such a situation.

Attitudes Toward Women. Evidence of the sexism experienced by women in the medical field is well established. Women entering medical school are extremely likely to undergo an incident of gender-based discrimination or sexual harassment from supervisors and men of higher professional status during their years of study (Cotton, 1992; Grant, 1988; Komaromy, Bindman, Haber, & Sande, 1993), contributing to an overall hostile learning and work experience (Komaromy et al., 1993). Women also endure more subtle forms of discrimination from their supervisors, such as the questioning of their physical stamina and emotional stability, and being addressed in disparaging terms in front of colleagues (Grant, 1988). Although perhaps better able to control their environment as professionals, women physicians suffer discrimination in the form of lower salaries, regardless of their years spent in practice (Council on Ethical and Judicial Affairs, 1994).

Gender-based discrimination has recently been emerging as a concern facing the medical profession, however the slow pace of the community to confront the issue is further evidence of the entrenched state of the problem. It is inevitable that such attitudes be transferred to the care of female patients. Evidence suggests that gender bias plays an inappropriate role in clinical decision making. Physicians are more likely to attribute women's health complaints to emotional causes, and to characterize women's concerns about their health as overanxious (Council on Ethical and Judicial Affairs, 1994).

Societal beliefs also influence physician treatment of victims of male partner violence. Health care providers with more liberal attitudes are less likely to blame victims for the violence (Rose & Saunders, 1986), and victims are more likely to receive empathetic treatment from female practitioners (Rose & Saunders, 1986; Saunders & Kindy, 1993; Tilden et al., 1994).

Personal Fears. Sugg and Inui (1992) employed an ethnographic interview technique to discover barriers to partner violence screening, and determined several dominant themes among the 38 physicians interviewed. The responses, characterized by the analogy of opening Pandora's box, were broken down into several categories. In all, 38% expressed fears that seeing a patient as a victim was "too close for comfort," indicating that physician identification with their patients may preclude them from considering intimate violence in their differential diagnosis, especially when patients are from similar, typically White, middle-class backgrounds. A second category was "fear of offending" (55%), originating in the physician's discomfort with areas that are culturally defined as private. By overwhelming response the physicians faulted "the tyranny of the time schedule" for failing to screen, and voiced frustration with the expectations on the physician to address all of these problems. Finally, a major concern was that physicians felt "powerless" (50%) in their capacity to help a woman who disclosed an abusive relationship (Sugg & Inui, 1992).

Warshaw (1989) suggested that issues put forth by physicians, such as lack of time, are really masking feelings of being professionally overwhelmed. Because the expectation of health care providers is that they find out what is wrong and solve the problem, they find it difficult to enter areas that are unfamiliar and do not have a prescribed response. Personal bias may also impede physicians who feel their own personal safety at risk when someone whom they perceive as similar to themselves is also a victim of partner abuse (Warshaw, 1989).

To explore the constraints of the biomedical framework on partner violence intervention, Warshaw and Poirier (1991) reconstructed a videotaped interview between a physician and his patient who was suffering from extremely high blood pressure for which the etiology was unclear. The forms of treatment provided to the patient had all been unsuccessful. The physician was clearly frustrated as he limited himself to searching for an organic cause of his patient's condition. He finally broke out of the biomedical structure of the patient–physician interaction in order to inquire into the social context of her life and understand the larger and abusive context in which she lived for the past 25 years. Warshaw and Poirier argued that although the medical model may provide distance from disturbing realities by confining itself to objectivity, it also limits the physicians' ability to understand the etiology of the disease they are treating (Warshaw & Poirier, 1991).

CONCLUSIONS

The studies reviewed here document the extent of male partner violence, and in particular the prevalence of victims in the medical care system. Injuries resulting from partner violence are recognized as a major threat to the lives of women presenting in emergency departments. Although data confirming direct links between violence and health outcomes in primary and prenatal care is sparse, the high rate of medical utilization among victims as compared to nonvictims points to an association, if not a causal relation. Health care institutions have begun to respond to the problem by recommending policies and procedures with regard to identifying and treating victims, however this effort has not yet been adapted on an individual level, nor has the effect of this approach been evaluated. It is clear that more and better research is necessary in order to understand the full impact of violence on the health of women, and to reach appropriate conclusions about how best to treat the problem within the medical community.

Methodological Problems

Violence is a multifaceted phenomenon, and is manifested not only physically, but also psychologically and sexually. Studies to date reflect the attempts of investigators to understand the impact of different forms of violence on victims. However, the process is complicated by the complexity of the problem, as evidenced in the lack of consistent definitions across studies, difficulties around measuring health outcomes, and a lack of analysis of the multivariate nature of factors that may influence or compound the effects of violence.

The most widely used tool to define and measure violence between partners is the Conflict Tactics Scale (CTS), which assesses overall violence during the past year as well as incidents of severe violence. This scale has been criticized as a measurement of male partner abuse because it fails to reflect the inequality inherent in an abusive relationship and does not take into account issues of power and control. For example, women may consider threats to take the children more threatening than actual incidence of violence. Recent studies have utilized instruments that include elements of psychological abuse in their analysis, but as yet a more sensitive and reliable alternative has not been developed to replace the CTS. Such an instrument is necessary to provide a consistent measure of the occurrence of violence between partners.

A problem similarly exists with the lack of a standardized screening instrument to identify victims of partner violence in the medical setting. Studies and protocols employ varying definitions of any abuse, severe abuse, childhood versus adulthood abuse, and partner violence, for example. Estimates of prevalence and assessment of outcomes of abuse are made difficult by the use of inconsistent terminology. The development, testing, and use of a common screening tool could facilitate data collection, as well as more appropriate identification and referral of victims.

The health outcomes of partner violence are also difficult to measure due to the lack of routine documentation in medical charts. Currently, investigators must rely on self-report of partner violence and the recorded frequency of care. As long as health care providers fail to consider and document the relation between violence and the manifestations of illness in their patients, no reliable record will exist. Recommendations to establish protocol for screening victims need to be operationalized across medical settings in order to adequately assess the effects of partner violence on the health of women and improve treatment.

A related issue concerns the need to more clearly define and research symptoms associated with violence in order to establish etiology. For instance, it has been shown that patients suffering from either functional or organic gastrointestinal disorders are relatively likely to have a history of abuse, yet the pathogenesis has not been elucidated. In addition, the high overlap of chronic pelvic pain and gastrointestinal symptoms suggests perhaps a similarity in the experience of these disorders that needs further investigation.

A third problem with current research on partner violence is the lack of a methodological approach to deal with the interaction between different forms of violence and the resulting impact on health. There currently exist two bodies of literature addressing violence toward women, one focusing on physical aggression and the other on sexual assault. Often, however, these two forms of violence are part of the same phenomenon. Yet the health outcomes associated with rape may be overlooked for partner violence victims because the abuse is continuous and the assailant is not a stranger. Multivariate methodologies are needed to study the interactional nature of physical and sexual abuse, rather than continuing to view them in isolation.

A multivariate perspective is needed, too, in order to understand the relations and effects of other factors that may co-occur with partner violence. The interactions and cumulative effects of poverty, childhood experiences, witnessing violence, drug and alcohol misuse, and other social factors on health outcomes are unknown. The pathways of the various associations—for example, between alcohol misuse and gastrointestinal disorders, alcohol misuse and partner violence, and partner violence and gastrointestinal disorders—could be made clearer with multivariate approaches.

Finally, the majority of the research regarding the health impacts of male partner violence continues to be informed primarily by the medical model. Analysis focuses on the individual and fails to see the social context in which violence takes place. This process tends to dehumanize and decontextualize women, and obscures social factors that compound the health effects of violence and play a large role in their emotional and physical responses to the situation. Future research must include a gender analysis that legitimizes these responses to better elucidate the most appropriate form of treatment for the problem by the medical community.

Gaps in Knowledge

This chapter has suggested that in failing to diagnose the existence of partner violence in the lives of their patients, health care providers may actually be contributing to its maintenance. In order to better inform health care providers on the effects of violence among their patients and suggest approaches to treatment, several aspects of violence and its interaction with other social factors are recommended as a focus for further research. A prerequisite is the formation of a nationwide data collection system that will more accurately measure incidence and prevalence. The system should also help to develop and promote the use of consistent definitions of psychological, physical, and sexual violence against both children and adults. Breakdowns in terms of age, ethnicity, and socioeconomic status and the relation of these factors to forms and outcomes of violence will also provide valuable information.

Anthropological study of the meaning of violence among different groups within the general population is a second area for research. Too little empirical research examines the extent and nature of partner violence from a cultural context (for exceptions see Chester et al., 1994; Chrestman, Polacca, & Koss, 1999; Lefley, Scott, Llabre, & Hicks, 1993, 1997; Ramos, Koss, & Russo, 1999; Russo, Denious, Keita, & Koss, 1997). Hampton and Gelles (1994) suggested three reasons for the neglect of women of color in partner violence research. First, small sample sizes make it difficult to generalize findings to the minority population. Small sample sizes also hinder intragroup analyses of ethnic groups by further breaking them down based on established predictors of violence such as unemployment and education. Second are concerns that research findings will exacerbate already existing perceptions that violence is more prevalent within minority ethnic groups. Third is a general lack of interest in the impact of partner violence on women of color. Furthermore, existing research investigating ethnic differences suffers from methodological complications. Crenshaw (1993) pointed out that research measures are developed and validated in majority populations and they tend to ignore the social and cultural context of other ethnic groups. Current instrumentation reflects uniformity assumptions about family organization, lifestyle, place of residence, and beliefs about what is acceptable conduct within a relationship. Specifically, partner violence screening questions may assume a nuclear family when extended families are the norm in many cultures, may be written from a paternalistic family model that ill-suits matrilinear and matrilocal kin structure that is prevalent among American Indians as well as other groups, and are biased toward urban lifestyles, failing to consider that denying telephone or transportation may be frequent and serious forms of intimidation in rural areas.

Current instrumentation reflects the assumption that beliefs about what is acceptable conduct within a relationship and what constitutes violence are the same across cultural groups. Questions may emphasize behaviors that are less important within some cultures, while failing to elucidate others that could cause more damage to the physical and emotional safety of women. Research on the definitions of violence in different groups is necessary in order to develop an instrument that competently measures violence, as well as providing health care providers with cross-cultural information on the best ways to screen for victimization among their patients.

More descriptive research is also needed on women's experience in the medical system. As the chronic pelvic pain and irritable bowel syndrome literature is beginning to suggest, some women may be shunted through the system and treated according to the diagnosis they receive, while in fact their symptoms may overlap both, and may be related to an undisclosed history of abuse. The problem of inappropriate prescribing of tranquilizers and sedatives to victims of partner violence is another area in need of further research.

As in the case of physical violence and sexual assault, there is currently little understanding of how other factors may interact with partner abuse to result in the high utilization of health services. Current studies on health outcomes of victimization generally include women with any history of abuse thus failing to partial effects among cumulative violence a woman may have faced across her life span. A second area of investigation must be directed toward isolating the effect of partner violence, as well as attempting to identify and assess other components accompanying the abuse, such as substance abuse, poverty, and childhood experience that may either interact with partner violence or work in isolation to produce health effects.

A final area of research involves the provision of more information on the potential effects of screening in order to base recommendations regarding victim identification on reasonable conclusions. Although patient screening is currently being encouraged in all health care settings, there has been no evaluation of whether identification improves treatment or actually assists the victims in some way. Negative outcomes must also be assessed, such as the possible threat to confidentiality by institutions that may discriminate against the victim. It is also necessary to examine the impact of forcing physicians to screen while their attitudes regarding women and partner violence remain the same. If physicians do not agree with the underlying causes and effects of partner violence, then they may be less likely to make the referrals proposed by the protocol.

The research community has begun to respond to the need for more research in the area of women's health. However, the overwhelming impact of violence on the lives and health of women outlined here is not reflected in the allocation of resources. The research community must begin to make violence against women a priority in order to adequately address a major health concern of women and provide the medical community with an appropriate response.

REFERENCES

Abbot, J., Johnson, R., Koziol-McLain, J., & Lowenstein, S. R. (1995). Domestic violence against women: Incidence and prevalence in an emergency department population. *Journal of the American Medical Association, 273,* 1763–1767.

Amaro, H., Fried, L. E., Cabral, H., & Zuckerman, B. (1990). Violence during pregnancy and substance abuse. *American Journal of Public Health, 80,* 575–579.

American College of Obstetrics and Gynecology. (1989). The battered woman. *ACOG Technical Bulletin,* 124, whole.

American Medical Association. (1992). Diagnostic and treatment guidelines on domestic violence. *Archives of Family Medicine, 1,* 39–47.

Baker, N. J. (1995). Strategic footholds for medical education about domestic violence. *Academic Medicine, 70,* 982–985.

Berk, R. A., Berk, S. F., Loseke, D. R., & Rauma, D. (1983). Mutual combat and other family violence myths. In D. Finkelhor, R. J. Gelles, G. T. Hotaling, & M. A. Straus (Eds.), *The dark side of families: Current family violence research* (pp. 197–212). Beverly Hills, CA: Sage.

Berrios, D. C., & Grady, D. (1991). Domestic violence: Risk factors and outcomes. *Western Journal of Medicine, 155,* 133–135.

Bouza, A. (1991). Responding to domestic violence. In M. Steinman (Ed.), *Women battering: Policy responses* (pp. 191–202). Cincinnati, OH: Anderson.

Bowker, L., & Maurer, L. (1987). The medical treatment of battered wives. *Women and Health, 12,* 25–45.

Browne, A. (1993). Violence against women by male partners: Prevalence, outcomes, and policy implications. *American Psychologist. 48,* 1077–1087.

Browne, A., & Williams, K. R. (1989). Exploring the effect of resource availability and the likelihood of female-perpetrated homicides. *Law and Society Review, 23,* 75–94.

Browne, A., & Williams, K. R. (1993). Gender, intimacy, and lethal violence: Trends from 1976 through 1987. *Gender and Society, 7,* 78–98.

Brush, L. D. (1990). Violent acts and injurious outcomes in married couples: Methodological issues in the National Survey of Families and Households. *Gender and Society, 4,* 56–67.

Bullock, L., & McFarlane, J. (1989). The birth weight/battering connection. *American Journal of Nursing, 89,* 1153–1155.

Bureau of Justice Statistics. (1994). *Violence between intimates.* Office of Justice Programs. Washington, DC: U.S. Department of Justice.

Bureau of Justice Statistics. (1995). *Violence against women: Estimates from the redesigned survey.* Office of Justice Programs. Washington, DC: U.S. Department of Justice.

Burge, S. (1989). Violence against women as a health care issue. *Family Medicine, 21,* 368–373.

Campbell, J. C. (1989). Women's responses to sexual abuse in intimate relationships. *Health Care for Women International, 10,* 335–346.

Campbell, J. C. (1992). "If I can't have you, no one can": Power and control in homicide of female partners. In J. Radford & Diana E. H. Russell (Eds.), *Femicide: The politics of woman killing* (pp. 99–113). New York: Twayne.

Campbell, J., Pliska, M., Taylor, W., & Sheridan, D. (1994). Battered women's experiences in the emergency department. *Journal of Emergency Nursing, 20,* 280–288.

Canadian Centre for Justice Statistics. (1994). Wife assault: The findings of a national survey. *Juristat Service Bulletin,* 14.

Candib, L. (1990). Naming the contradiction: Family medicine's failure to face violence against women. *Family and Community Health, 13,* 47–57.

Chester, R., Robin, R. W., Koss, M. P., Lopez, J., & Goldman, D. (1994). Grandmother dishonored: Violence against women by male partners in American Indian communities. *Violence & Victims, 9,* 249–258.

Chrestman, K., Polacca, M., & Koss, M. P. (1999). Domestic violence. In J. M. Galloway, B. W. Goldberg, & J. S. Alperts (Eds.), *Primary care of Native Americans: Diagnosis, therapy, and epidemiology* (pp. 315–322). Boston: Butterworth, Heineman.

Cotton, P. (1992). Harassment hinders women's care and careers. *Journal of the American Medical Association, 267,* 778–783.

Council on Ethical and Scientific Affairs, American Medical Association. (1992). Violence against women: Relevance for medical practitioners. *Journal of the American Medical Association, 267*(23), 3184–3189.

Council on Ethical and Judicial Affairs, American Medical Association. (1992). Gender discrimination in the medical setting. *Women's Health International, 4,* 1–11.

Council on Scientific Affairs. (1992). Violence against women: Relevance for medical practitioners. *Journal of the American Medical Association, 2647*(23), 3184–3189.

Crenshaw, K. (1993). Mapping the margins: Intersectionally, identity politics, and violence against women of color. *Stanford Law Review, 42,* 1241–1299.

Domino, J. V., & Haber, J. D. (1987). Prior physical and sexual abuse in women with chronic headache: Clinical correlates. *Headache, 27,* 310–314.

Dearwater, S. R., Coben, J. H., Campbell, J. C., Nah, G., Glass, N., McLoughlin, E., & Bekemeier, B. (1998). Prevalence of intimate partner abuse in women treated at community hospital emergency departments. *Journal of the American Medical Association, 280* (5), 433–438.

Drossman, D. A., Leserman, J., Nachman, G., Li, Z., Gluck, H., Toomey, T. C., & Mitchell, M. (1990). Sexual and physical abuse in women with functional and organic gastrointestinal disorders. *Annals of Internal Medicine, 113,* 828–833.

Economic and Social Council. (1992). *Report to the working group on violence against women.* Vienna: United Nations. (E/CN.6/WG.21/1992/L.3)

Elliott, B. A., & Johnson, M.M.P. (1995). Domestic violence in a primary care setting. *Archives of Family Medicine, 4,* 113–119.

Finkelhor, D., & Yllo, K. (1985). *License to rape: Sexual abuse of wives.* New York: Holt, Rinehart & Winston.

Flitcraft, A. (1990). Battered women in your practice? *Patient Care, 24,* 107–110.

Flitcraft, A. (1993). Physicians and domestic violence: Challenges for prevention. *Health Affairs, Winter,* 154–161.

Freund, K. M., Bak, S. M., & Blackhall, L. (1996). Identifying domestic violence in primary care practice. *Journal of General Internal Medicine, 11,* 44–46.

Friedman, L., Samet, F., Roberts, M., Hudlin, M., & Hans, P. (1992). Inquiry about victimization experiences: A survey of patient preferences and physician practices. *Archives of Internal Medicine, 152,* 1186–1190.

Frieze, I. H. (1983). Investigating the causes and consequences of marital rape. *Signs: Journal of Women in Culture and Society, 8,* 532–553.

Fry, R. (1993). Adult physical illness and childhood sexual abuse. *Journal of Psychosomatic Research,* 37, 89–103.

Gambone, J. & Reiter, R. (1990). Nonsurgical management of chronic pelvic pain: A multidisciplinary approach. *Clinical Obstetrics and Gynecology, 33,* 205–211.

Geist, R. F. (1988). Sexually related trauma. *Emergency Medicine Clinic North America, 6,* 439–466.

Gelles, R. J., & Harrop, J. W. (1989). Violence, battering, and psychological distress among women. *Journal of Interpersonal Violence, 4,* 400–419.

Gielen, A., O'Campo, P., Faden, R., Kass, N., & Xue, X. (1994). Interpersonal conflict and physical violence during the childbearing year. *Social Science and Medicine, 39,* 781–787.

Gin, N. E., Rucker, L., Frayne, S., Cygan, R., & Hubbell, F. A. (1991). Prevalence of domestic violence among patients in three ambulatory care internal medicine clinics. *Journal of General Internal Medicine, 6,* 317–322.

Golding, J. M. (1994). Sexual assault history and physical health in randomly selected Los Angeles women. *Health Psychology, 13,* 130–138.

Golding, J. M., Stein, J. A., Siegal, J. M., Burnam, M. A., & Sorenson, S. B. (1988). Sexual assault history and use of health and mental health services. *American Journal of Community Psychology, 16,* 625–644.

Grant, L. (1988). The gender climate of medical school: Perspectives of women and men students. *Journal of the American Medical Women's Association, 4,* 109–110, 115–119.

Grisso, J. A., Wishner, A. R., Schwarz, D. F., Weene, B. A., Holmes, J. H., & Sutton, R. L. (1991). A population-based study of injuries in inner-city women. *American Journal of Epidemiology, 134,* 59–68.

Haber, J. D., & Roos, C. (1985). Effects of spouse and/or sexual abuse in the development and maintenance of chronic pain in women. In H. L. Fields, R. Dubner, & F. Cervero, (Eds.), *Advances in pain research and therapy* (Vol. 9, pp. 889–895). New York: Raven.

Hamberger, L. K., Lohr, J. M., & Bonge, D. (1994). The intended function of domestic violence is different for arrested male and female perpetrators. *Family Violence & Sexual Assault Bulletin, 10,* 40–44.

Hamberger, K., Saunders, D., & Hovey, M. (1992). Prevalence of domestic violence in community practice and rate of physician inquiry. *Family Medicine, 24,* 283–287.

Hampton, R. L., & Gelles, R. J. (1994) Violence toward Black women in a nationally representative sample of Black families. *Journal of Comparative Family Studies, 25,* 105–119.

Hanneke, C. R., Shields, N. M., & McCall, G. J. (1986). Assessing the prevalence of marital rape. *Journal of Interpersonal Violence, 1,* 350–361.

Heise, L., Ellsburg, M., & Gottemoeller, M. (1999). Ending Violence Against Women. *Population Reports, Issues in World Health,* Series L, Number 11, 1–43.

Heise, L. L., Raikes, A., Watts, C. H., & Zwi, A. B. (1994). Violence against women: A neglected public health issue in less developed countries. *Social Science and Medicine, 39,* 1165–1179.

Helton, A. (1989). Battering during pregnancy. *American Journal of Nursing, 86,* 910–913.

Helton, A., McFarlane, J., & Anderson, E. (1987). Battered and pregnant: A prevalence study. *American Journal of Public Health, 77,* 1337–1339.

Hillard, P. (1985). Physical abuse during pregnancy. *Obstetrics and Gynecology, 66,* 185–190.

Hogston, P. (1987). Irritable bowel syndrome as a cause of chronic pain in women attending a gynecology clinic. *British Medical Journal, 294,* 934–935.

Isaac, N., & Sanchez, R. (1994). Emergency department response to battered women in Massachusetts. *Annals of Emergency Medicine, 23,* 855–858.

Kanuha, V. (1990). Compounding the triple jeopardy: Battering in lesbian of color relationships. *Women and Therapy, 9,* 169–184.

Katon, W., Ries, R. K., & Kleinman, A. (1984). The prevalence of somatization in primary care. *Comprehensive Psychiatry, 25,* 208–215.

Kimerling, R., & Calhoun, K. S. (1994). Somatic symptoms, social support, and treatment seeking among sexual assault victims. *Journal of Consulting and Clinical Psychology, 62,* 333–340.

Komaromy, M., Bindman, A., Haber, R., & Sande, M. (1993). Sexual harassment in medical training. *New England Journal of Medicine, 328*(5), 322–326.

Koss, M. P., Goodman, L. A., Browne, A., Fitzgerald, L. F., Russo, N. F., & Keita, G. P. (1994). *No safe haven: Male violence against women at home, at work, and in the community.* Washington, DC: American Psychological Association.

Koss, M. P., Heise, L. L., & Russo, N. F. (1994). The global health burden of rape. *Psychology of Women Quarterly, 19,* 509.

Koss, M. P., & Heslet, L. (1992). Somatic consequences of violence against women. *Archives of Family Medicine, 1,* 53–59.

Koss, M. P., Koss, P. G., & Woodruff, W. J. (1991). Deleterious effects of criminal victimization on women's health and medical utilization. *Archives of Internal Medicine, 151,* 342–347.

Koss, M. P., Woodruff, W. J., & Koss, P. G. (1990). Relation of criminal victimization to health perceptions among women medical patients. *Journal of Consulting and Clinical Psychology, 58,* 147–152.

Koss, M. P., Woodruff, W. J., & Koss, P. G. (1991). Criminal victimization among primary care medical patients: Prevalence, incidence, and physician usage. *Behavioral Sciences and the Law, 9,* 85–96.

Kurz, D. (1987) Emergency Department responses to battered women: Resistance to medicalization, *Social Problems, 34,* 69–81.

Lee, N. C., Dicker, R. C., Rubin, G. L., & Ory, H. W. (1984). Confirmation of the preoperative diagnosis for hysterectomy. *American Journal of Obstetrics and Gynecology, 150,* 283–287.

Lefley, H. P., Scott, C. S., Llabre, M., & Hicks, D. (1993). Cultural beliefs about rape and victims' response in three ethnic groups. *American Journal of Orthopsychiatry, 63,* 623–632.

Liebschutz, J. M., Mulvey, K. P., & Samet, J. H. (1997). Victimization among substance-abusing women: Worse health outcomes. *Archives of Internal Medicine, 157,* 1093–1097.

Lipowski, Z. (1984) What does the word "psychosomatic" really mean? A historical and semantic inquiry. *Psychosomatic Medicine, 46,* 153–171.

Lobel, K. (Ed.). (1986). *Naming the violence: Speaking out about lesbian battering.* Seattle: Seal.

Lockhart, L. L. (1991) Spousal violence: A cross-racial perspective. In R. L. Hampton (Ed.), *Black family violence* (pp. 85–101). Lexington, MA: Lexington.

Makepeace, J. M. (1989). Dating, living together, and courtship violence. In M. A. Pirog-Good & J. Stets (Eds.), *Violence in dating relationships: Emerging social issues* (pp. 94–107). New York: Praeger.

McCauley, J., Kern, D. E., Kolodner, K., Dill, L. Schroeder, A. F., DeChant, H. K., Ryden, J., Bass, E. B., & Derogatis, L. R. (1995). The "Battering Syndrome": Prevalence and clinical characteristics of domestic violence in primary care internal medicine practices. *Annals of Internal Medicine, 123,* 737–746.

McFarlane, J., Parker, B., Soeken, K., & Bullock, L. (1992). Assessing for abuse during pregnancy: Severity and frequency of injuries associated with entry into prenatal care. *Journal of the American Medical Association, 2647*(23), 3176–3178.

McLeer, S. V., & Anwar, R. (1989). A study of battered women presenting in an emergency department. *American Journal of Public Health, 79,* 65–66.

McLeer, S. V., Anwar, R.A.H., Herman, S., & Macquiling, K. (1989). Education is not enough: A systems failure in protecting battered women. *Annals of Emergency Medicine, 18,* 651–653.

Mercy, J. A., & Saltzman, L. E. (1989). Fatal violence among spouses in the United States, 1976–85. *American Journal of Public Health, 79,* 595–599.

Morbidity and Mortality Weekly Report. (1993). Emergency department response to domestic violence: California, 1992. *Morbidity and Mortality Weekly Report, 42*(32), 617–619.

Morbidity and Mortality Weekly Report. (1994). Physical violence during the 12 months preceding childbirth: Alaska, Maine, Oklahoma, and West Virginia, 1990–91. *Morbidity and Mortality Weekly Report, 43*(8), 132–137

National Victim Center. (1992, August 23). *Rape in America: A report to the nation.* National Victim Center, Arlington, VA.

O'Campo, P., Gielen, A. C., Faden, R. R., & Kass, N. (1994). Verbal abuse and physical violence among a cohort of low-income pregnant women. *Women's Health Issues, 4,* 29–37.

Parker, B., McFarlane, J., & Soeken, K. (1994). Abuse during pregnancy: Effects on maternal complications and birthweight in adult and teenage women. *Obstetrics and Gynecology, 84,* 323–328.

Ramos, L. L., Koss, M. P., & Russo, N. F. (1999). Mexican American women's definitions of rape and sexual abuse. *Hispanic Journal of Behavioral Sciences, 21,* 236–265.

Rapkin, A. J., Kames, L. D., Darke, L. L., Stampler, F. M., & Naliboff, B. (1990). History of physical and sexual abuse in women with chronic pelvic pain. *Obstetrics and Gynecology, 76,* 92–96.

Reiter, R. C. (1990). A profile of women with chronic pelvic pain. *Clinical Obstetrics and Gynecology, 33,* 130–136.

Reiter, R. C., & Gambone, J. C. (1990). Demographic and historical variables in women with idiopathic chronic pelvic pain. *Obstetrics and Gynecology, 75,* 428–432.

Reiter, R. C., Shakerin, L. R., Gambone, J. C., & Milburn, A. K. (1991). Correlation between sexual abuse and somatization in women with somatic and nonsomatic chronic pelvic pain. *American Journal of Obstetrics and Gynecology, 165,* 104–109.

Renzetti, C. (1992). *Violent betrayal: Partner abuse in lesbian relationships.* Newbury Park, CA: Sage.

Root, M. P., & Fallon, P. (1988). The incidence of victimization experiences in a bulimic sample. *Journal of Interpersonal Violence, 3*(2), 161–173.

Rose, K., & Saunders, D. (1986). Nurses' and physicians' attitudes about women abuse: The effects of gender and professional role. *Health Care for Women International, 7,* 427–438.

Russell, D. (1982). *Rape in marriage.* New York: Macmillan.

Russo, N. F., Denious, J. Keita, G. P., & Koss, M. P. (1997). Intimate violence and Black women's health. *Women's Health: Research on Gender, Behavior, and Policy, 3,* 315–348.

Sassetti, M. (1993). Domestic violence. *Primary Care, 20,* 289–305.

Satin, A. J., Hemsell, D. L., Stone, I. C., Theriot, S., & Wendel, G. D. (1991). Sexual assault in pregnancy. *Obstetrics and Gynecology, 77,* 710–714.

Saunders, D., & Kindy, P. (1993). Predictors of physicians' response to woman abuse: The role of gender, background, and brief training. *Journal of General Internal Medicine, 8,* 606–609.

Schei, B. (1990). Psycho-social factors of pelvic pain: A controlled study of women living in physically abusive relationships. *Acta Obstetrics Gynecology Scandanavia, 69,* 67–71.

Shields, N. M., & Hanneke, C. R. (1983). Battered wives reactions to marital rape. In D. Finkelhor, R. J. Gelles, G. T. Hotaling, & M. A. Straus (Eds.), *The dark side of families: Current family violence research.* Beverly Hills, CA: Sage.

Slocumb, J. (1990). Operative management of chronic abdominal pelvic pain. *Clinical Obstetrics and Gynecology, 33,* 196–204.

Smith, R. (1990). *Somatization disorder in the medical setting.* USDHHS, Public Health Service, Alcohol, Drug Abuse, and Mental Health Administration.

Smith, R. C., Greenbaum, D. S., Vancouver, J. B., Henry, R. C., Reinhart, M. A., Greenbaum, R. B., Dean, H. A., & Mayle, J. E. (1990). Psychosocial factors are associated with health care seeking rather than diagnosis in irritable bowel syndrome. *Gastroenterology, 98,* 293–301.

Stark, E., & Flitcraft, A. (1988). Violence among intimates: An epidemiological review. In V. B. Van Hasselt, R. L. Morrison, A. S. Bellack, & M. Hersen (Eds.), *Handbook of family violence* (293–317). New York: Plenum.

Stark, E., Flitcraft, A., & Frazier, W. (1979). Medicine and patriarchal violence: A social construction of a "private event." *International Journal of Health Services, 9,* 461–488.

Stark, E., Flitcraft, A., Zuckerman, D., Grey, A., Robison, J., & Frazier, W. (1981). *Wife abuse in the medical setting: An introduction for health personnel. Monograph 7,* Rockville, MD: National Clearinghouse on Domestic Violence.

Stets, J. E., & Straus, M. A. (1990). The marriage license as a hitting license: A comparison of assaults in dating, cohabitating, and married couples. In M. A. Straus & R. J. Gelles (Eds.), *Physical violence in American families: Risk factors and adaptation to violence in 8,145 families* (pp. 33–52). New Brunswick, NJ: Transaction.

Stewart, D. (1995). Physical abuse in pregnancy. Selected abstracts of Women's Health: Key Research and Health Care Issues, a Women's Health Office National Multidisciplinary Conference. *Women's Health Issues, 5,* 45.

Straus, M. A., & Gelles, R. J. (1990). *Physical violence in American families: Risk factors and adaptation to violence in 8,145 families.* New Brunswick, NJ: Transaction.

Straus, M. A., Gelles, R. J., & Steinmetz, S. (1980). *Behind closed doors: Violence in the American* family. Garden City, NY: Anchor.

Sugg, N., & Inui, T. (1992). Primary care's physicians' response to domestic violence: Opening Pandora's box. *Journal of the American Medical Association, 267*(23), 3157–3160.

Talley, N. J., Fett, S. L., Zinsmeister, A. R., & Melton, J. (1994). Gastrointestinal tract symptoms and self-reported abuse: A population-based study. *Gastroenterology, 107,* 1040–1049.

Tilden, V., Schmidt, T., Limandri, B., Chiodo, G., Garland, M., & Loveless, P. (1994). Factors that influence clinicians' assessment and management of family violence. *American Jounal of Public Health, 84,* 628–633.

Tjaden, P., & Thoennes, N. (1998a). *Final report on prevalence, incidence, and consequences of violence against women.* National Institute of Justice and Centers for Disease Control and Prevention. Washington, DC: U.S. Department of Justice.

Tjaden, P., & Thoennes, N. (1998b). *Stalking in America: Findings from the National Violence Against Women Survey* (NCJ 169562). National Institute of Justice and Centers for Disease Control and Prevention. Washington, DC: U.S. Department of Justice.

Toomey, T. C., Hernandez, J. T., Gittleman, D. F., & Hulka, J. F. (1993). Relationship of sexual and physical abuse to pain and psychological assessment variables in chronic pain patients. *Pain, 53,* 105–109.

Walker, E. A., Gelfand, A. N., Gelfand, M. D., Koss, M. P., & Katon, W. J. (1995). Medical and psychiatric symptoms in female gastroenterology clinic patients with histories of sexual victimization. *General Hospital Psychiatry, 17,* 85–92.

Walker, E. A., Katon, W. J., Hansom, J., Harrop-Griffiths, J., Holm, L., Jones, M. L. (1992). Medical and psychiatric symptoms in women with childhood sexual abuse. *Psychosomatic Medicine, 54,* 658–664.

Walker, E. A., Katon, W. J., Jemelka, R., Alfrey, H., Bowers, M., & Stenchever, M. A. (1991). The prevalence of chronic pelvic pain and irritable bowel syndrome in two university clinics. *Journal of Psychosomatic Obstetrics and Gynaecology, 12*(Suppl.), 65–75.

Walker, E. A., Katon, W. J., Roy-Byrne, P. P., Jemelka, R. P., & Russo, J. (1993). Histories of sexual victimization in patients with irritable bowel syndrome or inflammatory bowel disease. *American Journal of Psychiatry, 150,* 1502–1506.

Walker, L. (1979). *The battered woman.* New York: Harper & Row.

Walker, L. (1984). *The battered woman syndrome.* New York: Springer.

Walling, M. K., Reiter, R. C., O'Hara, M. W., Milburn, A. K., Lilly, G., & Vincent, S. D. (1994). Abuse history and chronic pelvic pain in women: I. Prevalences of sexual abuse and physical abuse. *Obstetrics and Gynecology, 84,* 193–199.

Walsh, A. G., & Broadhead, W. G. (1992). Prevalence of lifetime sexual victimization among female patients. *Journal of Family Practice, 35,* 511–516.

Warshaw, C. (1989). Limitations of the medical model in the care of battered women. *Gender & Society, 3,* 506–517.

Warshaw, C. (1993). Domestic violence: Challenges to medical practice. *Journal of Women's Health, 2,* 73–80.

Warshaw, C., & Poirier, S. (1991). Case and commentary: Hidden stories of women. *Second Opinion, Oct.,* 48–59.

White, J. W., & Koss, M. P. (1991). Courtship violence: Incidence in a national sample of higher education sudents. *Violence and Victims, 6,* 247–256.

Whitehead, W. E., Bosmajian, L., Zonderman, A. B., Costa, P. T., & Schuster, M. M. (1988). Symptoms of psychologic distress associated with irritable bowel syndrome. *Gastroenterology, 95,* 709–714.

33

Confronting Fertility Problems: Current Research and Future Challenges

Lauri A. Pasch
University of California, San Francisco

The great majority of young adults intend to become parents at some point in their lives (Jacobson & Heaton, 1991). Couples who desire to have children usually assume that pregnancy will occur naturally over a period of months of not using contraceptive methods. For at least 8% of married couples in the United States in which the woman is of childbearing age, this period of anticipating pregnancy passes without success (Abma, Chandra, Mosher, Peterson, & Piccinino, 1997). For many of these couples, the life goal of having biologically related children is at least temporarily out of reach. Infertility is not a discrete event, but instead an unfolding process. The recognition that pregnancy is not occurring is often followed by attempts to increase the likelihood of pregnancy. Some couples decide to seek the assistance of a physician. If medical intervention is pursued, a protracted period of medical tests and treatment follows, with or without success. Eventually, unsuccessful couples consider other options, including adoption, surrogacy, or remaining without children. Some couples never seek medical treatment, perhaps as a result of financial, moral, cultural, or religious reasons. These couples may pursue other options to having children aside from biological parenthood, may continue to attempt conception by traditional methods, may seek nonmedical assistance (e.g., from religious leaders or alternative medicine providers), or may conclude that having children is simply not meant to be for them. Whatever the circumstances, each step in the process has the potential to be emotionally devastating.

This chapter provides an introduction to psychological issues associated with infertility and its treatment. Over the past two decades, there has been an explosion of technology available to treat infertility and a concomitant growth in public demand to use these so-called high tech treatments. These developments have made infertility and its treatment a topic of considerable public interest and concern. Unfortunately, medical advances are occurring faster than their individual, family, and societal implications can be anticipated or understood. Many misunderstandings and myths persist in popular culture about infertility and its treatment. This chapter presents what is currently known and what further information is needed.

The first section presents background information on infertility and introduces the complexity of the issues couples face. The second section examines the empirical literature pertaining to how fertility problems affect individuals and couples and discusses risk and protective factors for psychological adjustment. The third section focuses on psychological consequences of the use of assisted reproductive technologies when they are and are not successful. The fourth section turns to the question of how infertility can be prevented, which is a new area of interest for psychologists. Unfortunately, current knowledge in these areas is limited by the almost exclusive focus in research on White individuals of middle to upper socioeconomic status who seek medical treatment for their fertility problems. It is possible that the findings would be very different if the literature were more representative of all individuals facing infertility. The final section delineates challenges for future work that cut across the specific topic areas.

BACKGROUND

Infertility is medically defined as the inability of a couple to conceive after 12 months of sexual intercourse without contraception (Office of Technology Assessment, OTA, 1988). Impaired fecundity is a broader concept affecting substantially more couples, and includes difficulty or danger carrying a baby to term, as well as problems in conception. The medical definition of infertility is used to screen couples for fertility treatment, and is different from the more permanent condition of sterility. Indeed, estimates suggest that 50% of couples meeting the medical definition for infertile who seek medical treatment will eventually be successful in bearing a child, either through medical intervention or simply with the passage of time (OTA, 1988).

Media reports have suggested that there is an infertility epidemic in the United States. Unfortunately, there are few reliable sources of information regarding rates of infertility. However, the best source currently available, the National Survey of Family Growth (NSFG), has not found an overall increase in rates of infertility in recent years, although there have been increases among certain subpopulations (Mosher & Bachrach, 1996). Mosher and Bachrach (1996) concluded that the widespread perception of an "epidemic" of infertility is probably due to a combination of the aging of the "baby boom" cohort who often delayed childbearing and thus have faced difficulty conceiving, and the dramatic increase in high tech treatments for infertility and the resulting demand for infertility services. The NSFG found that of the 60.2 million women of reproductive age, 9.3 million had sought medical services related to fertility problems (Abma et al., 1997).

The last two decades have seen major advances in scientific understanding of the causes of infertility. These advances have improved understanding of the role of psychological factors. For example, two decades ago, it was commonly believed that psychological problems, particularly of the woman, were to blame for a significant number of cases of infertility (OTA, 1988). Now a biological explanation (i.e., hormonal problems, blockage in the fallopian tubes, low sperm count or sperm abnormalities) can be found for most cases of infertility. Psychogenesis models have been largely refuted by research (OTA, 1988). When psychological distress does occur in infertile couples it is now thought to be a result of the stress of infertility or its treatment, as opposed to a cause of the fertility problem itself. Nevertheless, remnants of psychogenesis models persist in popular culture. The common but usually unhelpful suggestion "Relax and you'll get pregnant" is an example of the lingering belief that a woman's psychological status is to blame for her fertility problem. These messages are painful for many infertile women, and may lead them to retreat from their social networks (Abbey, Andrews, & Halman, 1991).

The lack of evidence that psychological problems cause infertility does not mean that psychological issues never play a role. For example, there is now concern that the stress of infertility treatment itself may reduce the likelihood of success. For example, Boivin and Takefman (1995) found that women who reported more daily stress during an in vitro fertilization (IVF) cycle were less likely to become pregnant in that cycle than their less stressed counterparts. What is not clear from this or other similar studies is whether stress had a causal role in determining the success of treatment or if patients who had lower chance of success for medical reasons were simply more stressed before and during the process, knowing that they would probably have disappointing results. Clearly, the influence of stress on treatment success is an area in need of further inquiry because results would possibly suggest a need for radical changes in treatment practices.

Advances in scientific understanding of the causes of infertility have also led to a shift to thinking of infertility as a couple's issue not solely a women's issue. Fertility problems were previously attributed the woman, but the biological cause is now thought to be equally likely due to male factors as female factors, or due to joint problems (OTA, 1988). Therefore, from a medical point of view, infertility is now thought to characterize the couple who is attempting pregnancy, even though only one member of the couple may have the biological problem. From a psychological point of view, infertility is truly a couple's issue, not an individual issue, because regardless of which member of the couple has the biological problem, both partners are unable to achieve their goal of having children.

Even though infertility is a couples' issue, it remains a significant women's health issue as well. There is evidence that infertile women see having children as more important than men do, are more affected emotionally by the experience of infertility, and play a more central role in seeking treatment and making treatment decisions (see Berg, Wilson, & Weingartner, 1991; Leiblum, Kemmann, & Lane, 1987). The vast majority of treatments are aimed at the woman. Thus, women bear more of the physical and emotional costs of infertility treatment. They also suffer more of the stigma associated with the patient role than their partners and are at greater risk of being exploited by technological advances that do not take into account the potential impact on the individuals involved.

The last two decades have seen an explosion of advances in medical technologies aimed at increasing infertile couples' chances of pregnancy. The most publicized of the advances is IVF. IVF is a technique in which drugs are used to stimulate the maturation of oocytes, mature oocytes are removed from the ovary using ultrasound-guided aspiration, fertilization is attempted in the laboratory using the man's sperm, and the resulting embryos are transferred into the uterus. Other similar but less commonly used techniques include gamete intrafallopian transfer (GIFT) and zygote intrafallopian transfer (ZIFT). These treatments are collectively termed *assisted reproductive technologies* (ARTs). First used successfully in 1978, ARTs have evolved from being a cutting edge technology used by a small number of patients to a relatively mainstream procedure (Society for Assisted Reproductive Technology/American Society of Reproductive Medicine, 1998).

New infertility treatment options become available each year. For example, an important development in 1991 was a procedure called intracytoplasmic sperm injection. This procedure is used for couples with moderate to severe male factor infertility. A single sperm is chosen and injected into the egg to achieve fertilization. Another popular choice is the use of donor oocytes, which offers older couples the opportunity to experience pregnancy and to have a child who is genetically related to the father. The use of donor oocytes has increased most significant barrier to conception with advanced maternal age is deterioration of the older woman's oocytes as opposed to uterine factors (Sauer, Paulson, & Lobo, 1992). Oocytes from a younger donor are stimulated using drugs, retrieved from her ovary, fertilized in the laboratory with the recipient's partner's sperm, and then transferred to the recipient's uterus. The use of donor oocytes (and donor sperm, which has been available for many years) brings many challenges for couples, including how to choose a donor, and whether and what to tell the child and others about the child's genetic heritage.

Infertility treatment decisions are often made under conditions of extreme stress and vulnerability. Couples usually consider these high tech techniques after months or years of trying other, less invasive approaches. When many couples face these decisions, they feel they have no time to waste, because the chances of success fall as the woman ages (SART/ASRM, 1998). Treatment decision making also occurs within the broader context of the couple's life, which may involve securing jobs, reaching educational goals, changing careers, managing work stress, relocating, dealing with family problems, dealing with other medical problems, and so forth. Fertility problems can create barriers in this broader context. For example, individuals may put off changing jobs or going back to school to maintain their medical insurance. Couples may wait to relocate or buy a home until the children are born, and so forth.

THE PSYCHOLOGICAL IMPACT OF INFERTILITY

Psychological Reactions to Infertility

There is no doubt that infertility is deeply distressing for many people. Indeed, Freeman et al. (1987) found that half of their sample of women described infertility as the most upsetting experience of their lives. However, there is significant controversy in the literature regarding the extent of psychological distress among individuals who experience fertility problems. The clinical and anecdotal literature suggests that infertility almost invariably sparks a life crisis. However, methodologically rigorous quantitative research has generally not upheld this view (see Dunkel-Schetter & Lobel, 1991; Stanton & Danoff-Burg, 1995). Quantitative studies have compared the psychological adjustment of individuals experiencing fertility problems assessed using standard measures to either normative data for the general population or to a population of fertile individuals (i.e., Connolly, Edelmann, Cooke, & Robson, 1992). Overall, these studies have found that although the experience of infertility is emotionally upsetting and disruptive for many people, the majority do not experience clinically significant emotional reactions, loss of self-esteem, or adverse marital or sexual consequences.

What accounts for the discrepancy between clinical/anecdotal reports and quantitative research? A number of explanations have been offered including: lack of sensitivity of the global measures used in quantitative research, desire on the part of research participants to appear more healthy so that they will be considered good candidates for infertility treatment, and overgeneralization of the problems experienced by a small number of patients who seek mental health treatment to the infertility population in general (Dunkel-Schetter & Lobel, 1991). There is probably some truth to each of these explanations. However, as Dunkel-Schetter and Lobel (1991) concluded, perhaps the most compelling reason for the discrepancy is that there is substantial variability between individuals in their response to the infertility. No one set of responses characterize most people who experience infertility.

Infertility from a Stress and Coping Framework

In light of these findings, Stanton and Dunkel-Schetter (1991) proposed that psychological reactions to infertility be conceptualized using a stress and coping framework (i.e., Lazarus & Folkman, 1984). The use of this well-established theoretical model represents a major advance, in light of the atheoretical nature of most previous research on infertility. In this framework, psychological adjustment in response to stressful life events is thought to be a function of characteristics of the situation the individual is facing, cognitive appraisal, and coping resources (including social support). This framework is useful because it helps researchers to go beyond simply describing the psychological status of infertile couples or comparing them to other couples. Furthermore, the stress and coping framework is not based on the idea that infertility necessarily represents an emotional crisis for all individuals, which is an assumption of much of previous work. Instead, the framework points to factors that might impede or facilitate psychological adjustment. An overview of recent research organized using a stress and coping framework is presented next.

Characteristics of the Situation. The evaluation period prior to receiving a diagnosis is associated with particularly high levels of distress (Berg & Wilson, 1991; Connolly et al., 1992) and the longer this period lasts without progress, the more distress individuals experience (Connolly, Edelmann, & Cooke, 1987). There is also evidence that the greater the number of tests and treatment procedures attempted and the more money invested, the more distress individuals experience (Abbey, Halman, & Andrews, 1992).

The type of diagnosis (i.e., male factor, female factor, unexplained, or combined causes) may lead to differential levels of distress. Several studies have addressed this question but have shown conflicting results (see Connolly et al., 1992; Nachtigall, Becker, & Wozny, 1992). One finding that has emerged is that regardless of the type of diagnosis, women have been found to take more responsibility and blame for the couple's infertility (McEwan, Costello, & Taylor, 1987; Tennen, Affleck, & Mendola, 1991). This has been attributed to a desire to protect their husbands from stigma and may add to the psychological burden women experience (Stanton & Danoff-Burg, 1995).

Whether a couple is facing primary infertility, meaning they have no children, or secondary infertility, meaning they are experiencing difficulty having another child, may also lead to differential levels of distress. Leiblum et al. (1987) reported that initial childlessness was a significant predictor of depressive symptoms among women. Newton, Hearn, and Yuzpe (1990) reported that initial childlessness predicted anxiety but not depression for women, and for men, initial childlessness did not predict either depression or anxiety. Litt, Tennen, Affleck, and Klock (1992) did not find that childlessness was related to adjustment.

Individual Appraisal. There are a number of potentially important domains of cognitive appraisal regarding infertility, including meaning of the fertility problem with regard to threat to important life goals, causal attributions for the fertility problem, and perceived control over having a child. Each of these has received some attention in research, but most have used small sample sizes and/or mixed samples in terms of timing within the treatment trajectory, or nonstandardized measures, thus limiting their impact. Extent of threat to life goals has been studied in patients using ARTs but not among general infertile populations. For example, Newton, Hearn, Yuzpe, and Houle (1992) reported that women who thought having children was necessary for their gender role fulfillment were more depressed and anxious following ART failure than those who did not endorse such views. Causal attributions were examined in several studies showing that those who believed they were responsible for their fertility problem were more distressed (Morrow, Thoreson, & Penney, 1995; Stanton, 1991; Tennen et al., 1991). Regarding perceived control over an individual's ability to have a child, termed *infertility- specific control,* two studies have found that higher perceived control was adaptive (Campbell, Dunkel-Schetter, & Peplau, 1991; Tennen et al., 1991), whereas others have found no relation (Abbey & Halman, 1995), perhaps owing to differences in the nature of the samples studied with respect to the treatment trajectory.

Coping Resources. A number of studies have addressed the relation between coping and adjustment. Escape-avoidance coping (e.g., "I hoped a miracle would happen") appears to be associated with more distress (Band, Edelmann, Avery, & Brinsden, 1998; Morrow et al., 1995; Stanton, Tennen, Affleck, & Mendola, 1992). Finding positive aspects of infertility or using positive reappraisal as a coping strategy (e.g., "I focused on other fulfilling things I can do outside of parenting") and seeking support (e.g., "I talk to someone about my feelings") appear to be associated with less distress (Stanton, 1991).

These coping studies used cross-sectional designs with couples who were at various points in their treatment trajectory. An important unanswered question is whether particular coping strategies are more effective at different points in the treatment trajectory. Also, it is unclear from these studies whether these coping strategies play a role in determining the level of distress or are used as a result of the level of distress (i.e., those in great distress may feel they need to use escape-avoidance strategies to reduce distress). These two possibilities have different implications for intervention.

Social Environment. Support from one's spouse and good quality of the relationship with one's spouse appear to be associated with more positive adjustment to infertility (e.g., Connolly et al., 1992). The protective effects of relationships with family and friends are not well-understood because fear of insensitive remarks sometimes leads individuals with fertility problems to avoid discussing their problem with others (Abbey et al., 1991).

Conclusions Regarding Literature Using a Stress and Coping Framework

Research using a stress and coping framework to understand adjustment to infertility represents a major advance over previous work that was mainly descriptive, but it is clearly in its early stages. Although some potential risk and protective factors have been identified, the research is limited by the use of nonstandardized measures, small sample sizes, poor sampling methods, and the lack of longitudinal designs.

Research to date has also been limited by the individual nature of traditional stress and coping models. These models do not fully appreciate the dyadic context in which medical problems occur. Attention to the dyadic context is particularly important when studying infertility, which is even more of a "couples issue" than many other medical problems. Other medical problems clearly affect both partners, but basically characterize only the afflicted partner. A departure from the traditional individually based stress and coping framework is evident in a few studies that examine how the appraisal, coping, and adjustment of one partner may be related to the psychological adjustment of the other and how differences between partners in appraisal and coping may impact communication and the overall impact of the fertility problem on the relationship and each partner's adjustment. Stanton, Tennen, Affleck, and Mendola (1992) studied couples who were seeking treatment for infertility and found that the only variable of one partner that was related to the other's adjustment was coping through seeking support. As wives sought more support, their husbands reported less distress. Levin, Goldman, Sher, and Theodos (1997) found that husbands, but not wives, were more distressed to the extent that both partners were high in the use of emotional-oriented coping.

Pasch, Dunkel-Schetter, and Christensen (1995) developed a dyad-oriented conceptual model of individual and relationship adjustment in response to infertility. The model proposes that spouses make individual appraisals of the meaning and threat posed by the fertility problem and that each spouse has a tendency toward the use of certain coping strategies. Each spouse's appraisal and coping then impacts the couple's ability to communicate with each other regarding the fertility problem. Specifically, it was proposed that differences between partners in their appraisal and coping with infertility would increase the likelihood of communication problems. To study communication, partners were asked to participate in a communication task in which they discussed an aspect of their fertility problem that was a source of tension in their relationship (e.g., deciding which treatments to try). Briefly, it was found that destructive communication was more common in couples in which partners differed in their commitment to having children, and in their use of several coping strategies. For example, to the extent that husbands used distancing as a coping strategy to a greater degree than their wives did, communication was more destructive. Couples with more destructive communication reported more negative effects of the fertility problem on their marriage, and more adjustment problems. Although further testing is needed, this model can be applied to understanding the effects of other health problems that couples face and is intended to yield a more complete understanding of how stress and coping processes occur within the marital context.

PSYCHOLOGICAL CONSEQUENCES OF ART USE

Although ARTs offer the possibility of pregnancy and childbirth for infertile couples, there is little doubt that the use of ARTs is highly stressful and has the potential to lead to significant negative psychological consequences, particularly when they fail. The potential for negative psychological consequences of using these treatments is a major concern (see Leiblum, 1997).

Despite recent advances in the success of ARTs, the vast majority of ART attempts do not lead to achievement of the valued goal of a baby. Based on data from 1995 attempts, 18.2% of ART cycles lead to the birth of infants, 26% of ART cycles were incomplete, and 56% ended in complete cycles but negative pregnancy tests. Furthermore, at least 18% of ART pregnancies did not go to term and at least 3% ended in serious delivery or neonatal complications or death (SART/ASRM, 1998).

The potential for negative psychological consequences of ARTs is heightened by several critical changes that have occurred over the past 5 years. ARTs have evolved from being a cutting-edge technology used by a small number of patients to a relatively mainstream procedure (SART/ASRM, 1998). The routinization and spread of ART services has had the effect that patients no longer receive intensive individualized care, and may no longer feel like pioneers in trying the new technology. Negative psychological effects of failure may intensify as couples no longer experience the positive emotions that can be associated with being one of the few patients who have access to the latest technology (Milne, 1987) and as the individualized care and special attention given to patients using new technology is reduced.

In addition, patients are making multiple ART attempts in the face of repeated failure. When IVF first became available, it was common for patients to try it as a "last chance effort." Now patients are often told that they should expect to make multiple ART attempts to achieve pregnancy. Although making multiple attempts increases the overall likelihood of pregnancy, recent data suggest that from 40% to 60% of couples will still not be successful in achieving a pregnancy following six cycles (Alsalili et al., 1995). The negative psychological impact of repeated failed attempts may be substantially greater and more debilitating than those associated with one failed attempt. Also, the recommendation that couples make multiple attempts may also increase couples' difficulty in knowing when to stop treatment and may make it even more difficult, as time elapses, to explore other options (i.e., adoption; Leiblum, 1997).

The following section discusses the current research literature on the psychological consequences of ART failure and on factors associated with psychological adjustment to ART failure.

Research on Psychological Consequences of ART Failure

Although much concern has been voiced about how patients react to failed ART, strong research evidence is sparse. However, the few studies that used standard measures suggest that during the period from initial assessment for treatment to a few weeks after receiving negative pregnancy test results, the prevalence of mild to moderate depression increases substantially (Newton et al., 1990; Reading, Chang, & Kerin, 1989). Although women tend to be at higher risk for negative reactions to failure than are men, studies that have included men reveal they also experience increases in depression following failure (Newton et al., 1990).

Very few follow-up studies have addressed the longer term effects of ART failure. The evidence that has appeared on psychological effects beyond the few weeks following negative pregnancy test results is generally based on very small sample sizes, use of nonstandardized measures, and/or retrospective accounts. For example, Baram, Tourtelot, Muechler, and Huang (1988) studied 32 women and 14 men who, on average, had made their last IVF attempt 1.5 years prior to the study. A significant number of respondents (66% of the women, 40% of the men) reported depression following IVF failure, many noting multiple episodes, with an overall decrease in depressive symptoms over time. However, the number reporting on time periods over 6 months is far too small to allow conclusions to be drawn, and nonstandard measures of depression were used. Because prospective, longitudinal studies have not been conducted, there is very little information about the duration of depressive symptoms.

The psychological effects of repeated ART failures have received even less research attention. However, the few studies that do exist, albeit with significant research design limitations, suggest increasing negative effects with increasing numbers of failures. Thiering, Beaurepaire, Jones, Saunders, and Tennant (1993) compared cross-sectionally 113 first-time IVF patients (1 month prior to their first cycle) with 217 patients who had had one or more previous IVF attempts (on the first day of the subsequent cycle) and found that 25% of repeat patients met standard criteria for clinically elevated depression, whereas rates for first-time patients (15%) were similar to community norms (12%).

Research on Factors Associated With Psychological Adjustment to ART Failure

Mental health professionals who conduct pretreatment assessments with ART patients are in the position of needing to identify patients who might have significant adjustment problems. However, currently little is known about what predicts poor psychological outcomes in response to ART failure.

One important issue from both a theoretical and applied perspective is the role of pre-ART expectations regarding treatment success in determining distress in the event of failure. Several studies have shown that ART patients tend to overestimate their chances of success and believe they have control over whether they will become pregnant (Leiblum et al., 1987). There is controversy over the function of these unrealistically positive expectations in determining psychological outcomes in the event of failure. Concern has been raised that patients who have unrealistic expectations may experience severe distress in the event of failure (Callan & Hennessey, 1988). However, this concern has not been tested empirically. Collins, Freeman, Boxer, and Tureck (1992) found that women who made high estimates of the likelihood of success anticipated less distress in the event of failure, but the researchers did not investigate whether they actually were more distressed. Regarding optimism as a general trait, Litt et al. (1992) found that women who were high in trait optimism were less distressed postfailure than their more pessimistic counterparts, even after controlling for pre-ART distress. The finding that positive expectations are related to less distress is consistent with other psychological research. Specifically, cognitive adaptation theory (S. E. Taylor & Brown, 1988) suggests that unrealistically positive expectations and exaggerated perceptions of control (termed *positive illusions*), instead of being indicators of poor functioning, are actually adaptive reactions to threatening life events in many circumstances. Numerous studies of adjustment to health threats have supported this proposition (Leedham, Meyerowitz, Muirhead, & First, 1995). What is unclear is what happens when patients' expectations are clearly not met, as in the case of a failed ART attempt. Some have argued that in situations like ART in which patients have little control, positive illusions may be damaging (Tennen & Affleck, 1987). Others have argued that when positive illusions are disconfirmed, individuals are able to rethink the situation so that they can continue to see it in a positive light (e.g., S. E. Taylor & Armor, 1996). This theoretical puzzle remains unresolved. Based on cognitive adaptation theory, positive illusions in ART patients may actually prove to be a reasonable and adaptive stress management technique, given the intense demands of treatment, and would not be expected to lead to undue distress in the event of failure.

From a clinical practice point of view, the findings with respect to positive expectations will have important implications concerning how to prepare patients for treatment. The need for patients to have a clear understanding of the likelihood of success is critical because of the invasive nature of treatment, the high financial cost, the low likelihood of success, and the intense value patients place on achieving the goal of pregnancy. However, concern that patients' unrealistic expectations may lead to serious distress in the event of treatment failure has led some members of the field of reproductive medicine to conclude that patient expectations must be monitored throughout the process and patients must be repeatedly reminded of the low success rates, the risk for multiple births, and so forth (e.g., Callan & Hennessey, 1988). Although the need for informed consent at the time of the decision to embark on ART is clear, without evidence that later interventions would have the desired effect of reducing post-ART distress, it is premature to intervene with patient expectations once a decision to elect to use ART is made. If unrealistically positive expectations are actually a sign of adaptive coping, it may not be beneficial to undermine those expectations.

Prospective longitudinal research is needed that identifies factors present prior to ART that render a person or couple vulnerable to distress following failure. This research would be able to solve puzzles, such as the role of positive expectations in determining postfailure distress. More generally, it would provide an empirical basis to guide assessment protocols and supportive interventions.

Conclusions Regarding Psychological Consequences of ART Failure

Although there has been much concern about the psychological effects of ART treatment, the research literature contains more gaps than answers. The psychological effects of ART failure, and the effects of repeated failures are not yet known. Furthermore, most research has not addressed the entire range of possible ART failure experiences (i.e., patients who are not even able to complete a cycle, patients who experience miscarriages). The psychological effects of ART miscarriages may be substantial given that patients experience the happiness of receiving a positive pregnancy test after the stressful treatment experience only to find that the fetus did not survive. Ultimately, their sense of loss and concomitant distress may be greater than if they had not become pregnant.

Only a few of the studies are prospective and longitudinal (see Downey & McKinney, 1990). The few longitudinal studies that have been conducted have either used very small sample sizes, had poor sampling methods, or used nonstandardized measures. In the absence of prospective, longitudinal research, little is known about the psychological consequences of the possible paths couples take and of outcomes they encounter. Very little research has placed the experience of ART failure in the broader context of possible outcomes that infertile couples might experience (i.e., having a child through ART, choosing not to use ART, or adopting a child). Even patients who have success with ARTs may experience psychological distress. Such distress could be associated with having multiple gestations, preterm delivery, residual stress from previous failures, or simply having a new baby. There may also be psychological consequences of the decision not to try ARTs, as individuals may find themselves regretting the decision not to try everything possible. New advances in technology may intensify this problem, as individuals may feel obligated to revisit their decision as hopes for success are renewed. In order to facilitate informed decision making and policy, there is a clear need to identify the relative consequences of different choices and outcomes.

Finally, despite the importance of identifying those patients at highest risk for poor adjustment, very little research has investigated factors associated with adjustment to ART failure.

Research on Psychological Adjustment Among Families Created by ARTs

There has been initial concern about the psychological functioning of families created by ARTs. These concerns have included unrealistic expectations for the child, overprotectiveness, maternal depression, marital difficulties, and so forth (e.g., see McMahon, Ungerer, Beaupaire, Tennant, & Saunders, 1995). In the last several years, a number of studies have begun to evaluate whether parents, children, and families created by the use of ARTs differ from other families on a number of indicators of psychological adjustment. For example, Golombok, Cook, Bish, and Murray (1995) compared four types of families (IVF families, donor insemination families, families with a naturally conceived child, and adoptive families) with a child between age 4 and 8 on a host of standardized measures of family functioning and found relatively few differences, with the exception of quality of parenting, which was found to be superior in IVF and donor insemination families.

Although the sample sizes have been limited and sampling methods for control families need to be improved, thus far the existing studies suggest that early concerns were not warranted. In fact most differences favor assisted conception families, perhaps due to the fact that these children are always wanted and the parents tend to be older than the average parent and perhaps more prepared for becoming parents. However, research on ART families is clearly just beginning. Suggestions for advancing this area of research are discussed later.

PREVENTION OF INFERTILITY

Infertility prevention efforts could help some women and men to avoid the many psychological, social, economic, and health consequences associated with infertility. Infertility prevention is an important new area in need of psychological research. However, prevention of infertility is inherently complex. Although there are several known controllable and therefore preventable causes of infertility, many causes of infertility are not well-understood (e.g., abnormal sperm count), and some are not currently known to be amenable to prevention (e.g., endometriosis; OTA, 1998). Additionally, there are many potential causes of infertility that are difficult to avoid (e.g., environmental toxins). Thus for many couples who experience infertility, there was nothing known that could have been done to prevent it.

Emphasizing the idea that infertility can be prevented could send the destructive message that individuals are to blame if they do encounter fertility problems. There is evidence that women already tend to blame themselves for infertility, even in the case of male factor infertility. Therefore, a fine line must be walked between providing information about those aspects of infertility that are controllable, and inappropriately suggesting that those who experience infertility are to blame for it.

Two of the most prevalent preventable causes of infertility, sexually transmitted diseases and delayed childbearing, are discussed next.

Sexually Transmitted Diseases

One preventable cause of infertility is sexually transmitted diseases (STDs), primarily gonorrhea and chlamydia. Pelvic infections (i.e., pelvic inflammatory disease, PID), which are caused by STDs, cause blocked or scarred fallopian tubes. Tubal abnormalities caused by STDs account for at least 15% of infertility cases in the United States (Eng & Butler, 1997). The risk of infertility increases with the number of times a person has chlamydia or gonorrhea, the duration and severity of infection, and the time between infection and treatment. STD-related infertility is fully preventable if the STD infection is diagnosed and treated promptly. One of the major challenges in preventing infertility due to STDs is that the original STD infection is often asymptomatic, and thus undetected for many years. The resulting fertility problem may be discovered many years after acquiring the infection.

Adolescent and young adult women are at greatest risk for experiencing damage to their reproductive potential as a result of STDs. Women are at greater risk than men because STDs spread from men to women more easily than from women to men; STDs are more likely to be asymptomatic in women, and thus remain undetected, resulting in delayed treatment or no treatment; and STDs pose serious threats to women's reproductive capability, as well as cause potential harm to unborn children and breastfed infants, whereas STDs rarely cause harm to male reproductive organs (Eng & Butler, 1997). Adolescents and young adults are at risk because STDs are so common among their age group, they are more likely to have multiple partners, and given the same level of exposure, adolescent women may be biologically more susceptible to cervical infections than older women (Cates, 1990). Although it is well-known that adolescence is a particularly risky period for unwanted pregnancy, it is less well-known that adolescence is a reproductive life stage with potentially dire consequences for later reproductive life stages.

Currently there is very little knowledge of what adolescents and young adults know and believe about STDs other than HIV, and the extent to which health professionals convey this information to their patients. A study of African American adolescents at high risk for acquiring STDs showed that over 80% of boys and girls reported that having children was important to them, but that most thought it was best to postpone having children until their twenties or thirties (Levin, Pasch, Millstein, & Ellen, 1999). However, many were lacking in critical information that would assist them in protecting their reproductive potential for the future. The majority of adolescents thought that fertility problems were not preventable. More than one third did not know that STDs can be asymptomatic. Over half of the adolescents did not know that chlamydia, gonorrhea, and PID cause fertility problems, with boys having significantly less knowledge than girls. Importantly, among sexually active adolescents, those who knew that particular STDs cause infertility were more likely to have had an STD check-up in the last 6 months when they did not have symptoms than those who were not aware of the relationship.

These results and future research on what adolescents believe about STDs and infertility may have implications for improving existing STD prevention programs. Emphasizing to adolescents that screening and treatment of STDs can help them to protect their fertility may be an effective motivator because having children in the future is salient for most adolescents. Also, focusing on protecting a person's ability to achieve the valued goal of having children is more positive than traditional STD prevention messages, which emphasize abstinence and avoidance of disease and unwanted pregnancy. Future research is needed to address how to frame messages regarding protecting fertility, particularly those directed at young men, because the potential risk to their own reproductive potential is relatively low. In one STD prevention program targeting high risk adolescents, messages have been developed aimed at encouraging young men to seek STD screening in order to protect the reproductive potential of their current and future partners and their community in general (Ellen, McCright, & Davis, 1998).

The need for effective STD prevention programs is particularly great in light of recent dramatic increases in rates of chlamydia, particularly among ethnic minority adolescents (Centers for Disease Control and Prevention, 1996). Why ethnic minority adolescents tend to be more likely to contract STDs is not well-understood, but several reasons have been suggested, including lower socioeconomic resources, poor access to health care, and geographic location (CDC, 1996). Based on current STD rates, ethnic minority women will begin to constitute a greater proportion of the infertile population in the years to come, often without the financial resources needed to take advantage of high tech treatments.

Delayed Childbearing

Because a woman's reproductive life span is biologically circumscribed, delaying childbearing increases the likelihood of infertility. Fertility decreases somewhat after age 30, with a sharp drop around age 35, and falls substantially after age 40 (Speroff, Glass, & Kase, 1994). The longer a woman waits to attempt conception, the greater the likelihood that she will encounter difficulty becoming pregnant. With women's changing roles in society, delaying having a first child to the 30s and 40s has become increasingly common. Often women who have pursued careers and postponed starting a family are very disappointed to learn that the option of becoming a parent by traditional methods is no longer available to them.

Should women who want to have children be encouraged to do so when they are younger? This is a difficult question because, on the one hand, the optimal timing of reproduction can only be determined by the individuals involved and occurs in the context of sociocultural, developmental, and economic considerations. Also, emphasizing the importance of not waiting too long to have biologically related children assumes the primacy of biological parenthood, when for many people adoption or other ways to resolve infertility may be acceptable (see Revenson, 1997). Additionally, it is important to note that broad societal problems play an important role in leading women to delay childbearing (i.e., inadequate parental leave policies and childcare options; see Maranto, 1995). Nevertheless, young women may benefit from more complete information regarding the relation between age and fertility and from encouragement to consider formulating a life plan that allows adequate time for reaching reproductive goals—whatever those goals may be.

Future medical advances will likely change the meaning and implications of the "biological clock." As described earlier, recent evidence has revealed that it is the poor quality of older women's oocytes that causes them to be unable to conceive (Sauer et al., 1992). Advances in scientific understanding of oocyte microbiology suggest that in the next few decades, young women will have the option of freezing their oocytes to preserve their chances of biological motherhood later (Porcu et al., 1997). However, limits in the availability and costs of this technology will likely make it an option for a relatively small number of women, at least in the foreseeable future.

Conclusions Regarding Prevention of Infertility

Because of the social, personal, and economic costs of infertility, there is a need for research geared toward the development of infertility prevention programs targeting young men and women. The goal of these programs would be to facilitate young men and women in achieving their personal reproductive goals, both in terms of protecting their fertility from STDs and making reproductive choices that take into account the relation between age and fertility. Formative research is necessary because at present, little is known about the attitudes and beliefs underlying these behaviors. Established behavioral health decision-making models can be used to guide research and interventions in this domain.

For example, the Theory of Planned Behavior (TPB; Ajzen, 1985) can be applied to the behavior of delaying childbearing. The TPB has been previously applied successfully to decisions about contraceptive use in addition to a variety of other health behaviors (i.e., Adler, Kegeles, & Irwin, 1990). Briefly, the TPB contends that an individual's behavior is a function of his or her behavioral intention to perform that behavior. Behavioral intentions, in turn, are thought to be influenced by how favorable the individual is toward the behavior (attitude), and the perceived social pressure from significant others with respect to the behavior (subjective norm). Attitudes, in turn, are a function of the individual's beliefs concerning the likelihood that the behavior will be accompanied by certain outcomes, weighted by the evaluation of each outcome (how good or bad it would be if it were to occur). In this case, a woman may believe that delaying childbearing will have the positive consequences of allowing her to achieve career advances, increase financial status, and reach a sense of emotional maturity. She may also believe that it may have the negative consequence of increasing the likelihood that she would never be able to have children, but feel that the likelihood of that outcome is small relative to the likelihood of the positive outcomes she expects. The subjective norm is a function of the perception of whether significant others (in this case, perhaps the partner, doctor, friends, boss) think the individual should perform the behavior, weighted by motivation to comply with these wishes. The TPB also takes into account that not all behaviors are under the individual's control, and thus actual and perceived control are thought to influence behavioral intentions and the translation of intentions into behavior. In the case of delaying childbearing, a woman may not have the intention to delay childbearing, but may not have a suitable partner, or may encounter health problems that limit her ability to attempt conception. Additionally, sociocultural influences can be examined within the TPB framework as factors influencing both attitudes and subjective norms regarding childbearing. By concentrating on the rational and predictable nature of behavior, the use of the TPB or other established decision-making theories can identify important target areas and specific messages for educational and behavior change efforts that focus on the key considerations determining intention and behavior.

Finally, a note of caution is appropriate regarding the dissemination of information about infertility prevention. It is important that individuals be informed of the controllable causes of infertility because this knowledge will allow them, along with their partners, to make informed decisions and attempt to achieve their future reproductive goals. However, educational efforts must be framed carefully so as not to suggest that infertile individuals are to blame if they do encounter fertility problems. Women are the most likely victims of such destructive messages, because infertility has historically been attributed to them.

FUTURE CHALLENGES

Although the empirical base on psychological aspects of infertility is growing, it is evident that many questions remain. This section delineates several key challenges for future research that cut across specific content areas.

Attention to Nonrepresented Groups

Available research on psychological aspects of infertility is not representative of the general population of infertile individuals in the United States. There are several factors that reduce the generalizability of the findings. First, most research has been conducted on White women or couples. As described earlier, it is estimated that ethnic minority women, specifically African American women, will begin to constitute a greater proportion of the infertile population in the years to come, because they are contracting STDs at high rates. At this point almost nothing is known about the psychological meaning of infertility or its treatment for these populations. There is evidence from other areas of reproductive health research of racial and ethnic differences in preferences for the use of medical intervention (i.e., prenatal diagnostic testing; see Kupperman, Gates, & Washington, 1996). Understanding how cultural or ethnic issues may impact what it means to be unable to have biologically related children, decisions regarding whether and how to seek medical treatment, and the acceptability of various resolutions of infertility (i.e., adoption, living without children, assisted reproductive technologies) are important avenues for future research. Such research may provide medical professionals with information that could improve access to and comfort with medical treatment for the individuals of various cultural and ethnic groups.

Second, individuals from lower socioeconomic groups are underrepresented in research. An individual's ability to make use of infertility treatments is highly dependent on their financial resources, because most medical insurance does not cover infertility-related services. Because individuals from lower socioeconomic groups have not been participants in research, nothing is known about the psychological consequences of wanting to use fertility treatment and not being able to for economic reasons. Additionally, among those patients who do use infertility services, individuals from lower socioeconomic groups are far more likely to experience financial stress and strain. Couples may take out loans, take second mortgages on their homes, or put off taking vacations or making large purchases in order to pay for fertility treatment. Little is known about how this financial strain may impact couples. If treatment is successful, then couples may be left with residual financial problems as they enter the transition to parenthood. If they are not successful, then they may experience serious regret at having expended their life savings and still not have a baby.

Third, the majority of research has studied individuals who are seeking infertility treatment and mostly from infertility specialists. As a result, there is little information about the experience of couples with fertility problems who do not seek treatment at all, or those who terminate treatment. What factors do couples consider when deciding whether or not to pursue treatment? How does the relative value placed on having biologically related children determine whether and how long couples seek medical treatment? What barriers exist with regard to access to treatment?

Fourth, although there has been recent attention to the issues lesbian couples and single women face (see Jacob, 1997; Chan, Raboy, & Patterson, 1998), they have also been largely neglected. Although not facing infertility as medically defined, these women can face additional barriers in pursuing their reproductive goals within a sociopolitical system that questions their rights to procreate at all, and particularly to use reproductive technologies (see Golombok & Tasker, 1994).

All of the aforementioned problems concerning the representativeness of the current research literature stem from the sampling methods employed. Most research participants have been recruited through infertility specialists at the time when they were in the process of treatment, or shortly thereafter. Although the ease of this approach renders it an obvious first step in understanding the experience of infertile individuals, many infertile individuals never see an infertility specialist. It is now necessary to go further with sampling methods to include the broader array of possible paths. A number of methodologies can be used to address this goal. For example, large national surveys similar to the National Survey of Family Growth could include detailed investigation of when and why individuals sought or did not seek treatment. Another strategy would be to recruit research participants at earlier points in the treatment trajectory, such as from family practitioners or obstetrics and gynecology practices. Additionally, it will be important to conduct prospective studies that follow participants as they consider various options and experience various outcomes. Only in this way can we understand the natural history of the experience of infertility and its treatment, and those factors that predict who will experience significant adjustment problems. Increasing the representativeness of research will not only provide information about currently unstudied groups, it will also broaden understanding of the sociocultural construction of the importance of biological parenthood, the meaning of infertility, and various modes of resolution of it.

Incorporation of Theory and Knowledge From Psychology

As described, most research on psychological aspects of infertility has been atheoretical. The move toward the use of stress and coping models represents an important advance. However, there is a wealth of knowledge and theory within psychology that can be brought to bear on understanding infertility aside from theories of psychological adjustment.

For example, as discussed earlier, there has been concern about the psychological functioning of families conceived through ARTs. Early research has focused on the question of whether ART families are more poorly adjusted overall than other families. This focus on pathology may have developed because of remnants of the belief that infertile individuals are psychologically deficient in some way. Research should now move beyond comparing these families to others to tackle important challenges these families face. For example, one question that is beginning to be addressed is whether, what, and when to tell ART children about their origin. This question is particularly important with respect to children conceived through donor gametes, because these children not only are conceived using reproductive technology but also do not have genetic ties with one or both of their parents. Regarding the question of whether to tell the child, there is significant research on the effects of family secrets on children that can be usefully applied (e.g., Imber- Black, 1993). Regarding the questions of when and how to tell the child, there is basic research on children's cognitive development that might help in judging what types of information about their origin children can understand at particular ages (e.g., Springer, 1996). There are also many lessons to be learned from the literature on the psychology of adoption (e.g., Brodzinsky & Schechter, 1990). Making use of broad theory and knowledge will prevent research and clinicians working in the area of infertility from having to "reinvent the wheel" each time a new issue must be faced. In addition, there is the potential to advance the scope of the theory itself.

Attention to Applied Problems

In addition to incorporating theory, attention should be directed to addressing applied problems. Practicing psychologists and other mental health professionals working in the field of reproductive medicine are now faced with many challenges. They conduct pre-ART assessments with couples. These assessments often have multiple purposes, including identification of patients in need of additional support services during the ART process and sometimes to identify patients they think would not be good candidates for treatment for psychological reasons. They conduct assessments of potential oocyte donors to determine if they understand and are psychologically prepared for being a donor. They offer supportive interventions to patients who experience significant distress.

As the knowledge base advances, there is a need for development of research-based assessment, prevention, and intervention protocols for use with infertility patients (Adler, Keyes, & Robertson, 1991; Pasch & Dunkel-Schetter, 1997). Although there is widespread belief in the importance of psychological interventions, current procedures are based on an extremely limited empirical foundation. For example, research identifying the risk and protective factors present prior to ART that predict which individuals are likely to be in need of additional support would provide a much-needed empirical basis for pre-ART assessments. By identifying the factors associated with adjustment to ART failure, mental health professionals would be able to target psychological services to those patients at highest risk and thus prevent the development of serious negative outcomes.

Attention to the Constantly Changing Face of Infertility Treatment

The future is sure to bring many more technological developments, raising even more complex ethical, legal, and moral dilemmas. New treatments will continue to come into popular use before the psychological community can consider their potential risks to emotional adjustment and family development. Current treatments will become medically obsolete before their impact is fully understood. Because infertility treatment is a constantly moving target, psychologists who work in this area must remain abreast of new developments and employ the tools of the field to investigate and intervene as appropriate to assist patients, the medical community, and the community at large in understanding the psychological impact of these developments.

REFERENCES

Abbey, A., Andrews, F. M., & Halman, L. J. (1991). The importance of social relationships for infertile couples' well-being. In A. L.

Stanton & C. Dunkel-Schetter (Eds.), *Infertility: Perspectives from stress and coping research* (pp. 61–86). New York: Plenum.

Abbey, A., & Halman, L. J. (1995). The role of perceived control, attributions, and meaning in members' of infertile couples well-being. *Journal of Social and Clinical Psychology, 14*(3), 271–296.

Abbey, A., Halman, L. J., & Andrews, F. M. (1992). Psychosocial, treatment, and demographic predictors of the stress associated with infertility. *Fertility and Sterility, 57*(1), 122–128.

Abma, J., Chandra, A., Mosher, W. D., Peterson, L. S., & Piccinino, L. J. (1997). Fertility, family planning, and women's health: New data from the 1995 National Survey of Family Growth. *Vital and Health Statistics. Series 23: Data from the National Survey of Family Growth, 19,* 1–114.

Adler, N. E., Kegeles, S. M., & Irwin, C. E. (1990). The utility of multiple strategies for understanding complex behaviors. *American Journal of Public Health, 80,* 1180–1182.

Adler, N. E., Keyes, S., & Robertson, P. (1991). Psychological issues in reproductive technologies: Pregnancy-inducing technology and diagnostic screening. In J. Rodin & A. Collins (Eds.), *Women and new reproductive technologies: Medical, psychosocial, legal, and ethical dilemmas* (pp. 111–133). Hillsdale, NJ: Lawrence Erlbaum Associates.

Ajzen, I. (1985). From intentions to actions. In J.K.J. Beckman (Ed.), *Action control from cognition to behavior* (pp. 11–39). New York: Springer-Verlag.

Alsalili, M., Yuzpe, A., Tummon, I., Parker, J., Martin, J., Daniel, S., Rebel, M., & Nisker, J. (1995). Cumulative pregnancy rates and pregnancy outcome after in-vitro fertilization: > 5000 cycles at one centre. *Human Reproduction, 10*(2), 470–474.

Band, D. A., Edelmann, R. J., Avery, S., & Brinsden, P. R. (1998). Correlates of psychological distress in relation to male infertility. *British Journal of Health Psychology, 3,* 245–256.

Baram, D., Tourtelot, E., Muechler, E., & Huang, K. E. (1988). Psychosocial adjustment following unsuccessful in vitro fertilization. *Journal of Psychosomatic Obstetrics and Gynaecology, 9,* 181–190.

Berg, B. J., & Wilson, J. F. (1991). Psychological functioning across stages of treatment for infertility. *Journal of Behavioral Medicine, 14*(1), 11–26.

Berg, B. J., Wilson, J. F., & Weingartner, P. J. (1991). Psychological sequelae of infertility treatment: The role of gender and sex-role identification. *Social Science and Medicine, 33*(9), 1071–1080.

Boivin, J., & Takefman, J. (1995). Stress level across stages of in vitro fertilization in subsequently pregnant and nonpregnant women. *Fertility and Sterility, 64*(4), 802–810.

Brodzinsky, D. M., & Schechter, M. D. (Eds.). (1990). *Psychology of adoption.* New York: Oxford University Press.

Callan, V. J., & Hennessey, J. F. (1988). Emotional aspects and support in in vitro fertilization and embryo transfer programs. *Journal of In Vitro Fertilization and Embryo Transfer, 5*(5), 290–295.

Campbell, S. M., Dunkel-Schetter, C., & Peplau, L. A. (1991). Perceived control and adjustment to infertility among women undergoing in vitro fertilization. In A. L. Stanton & C. Dunkel-Schetter (Eds.), *Infertility: Perspectives from stress and coping research* (pp. 133–153). New York: Plenum.

Cates, W. J. (1990). Epidemiology and control of sexually transmitted diseases in adolescents. In M. Schydlower & M. Shafer (Eds.), *AIDS and other sexually transmitted diseases* (pp. 409–427). Philadelphia: Hanly & Belfus.

Centers for Disease Control and Prevention. (1996). *Sexually transmitted disease surveillance 1995.* U.S. Department of Health and Human Services, Public Health Service. Atlanta: Centers for Disease Control and Prevention.

Chan, R. W., Raboy, B., & Patterson, C. J. (1998). Psychosocial adjustment among children conceived via donor insemination by lesbian and heterosexual mothers. *Child Development, 69*(2), 443–457.

Collins, A., Freeman, E. W., Boxer, A. S., & Tureck, R. (1992). Perceptions of infertility and treatment stress in females as compared with males entering in vitro fertilization treatment. *Fertility and Sterility, 57*(2), 350–356.

Connolly, K. J., Edelmann, R. J., & Cooke, I. D. (1987). Distress and marital problems associated with infertility. *Journal of Reproductive and Infant Psychology, 5,* 49–57.

Connolly, K. J., Edelmann, R. J., Cooke, I. D., & Robson, J. (1992). The impact of infertility on psychological functioning. *Journal of Psychosomatic Research, 36*(5), 459–468.

Downey, J., & McKinney, M. (1990). Psychiatric research and the new reproductive technologies. In N. L. Stotland (Ed.), *Psychiatric aspects of reproductive technology* (pp. 155–168). Washington, DC: American Psychiatric Press.

Dunkel-Schetter, C., & Lobel, M. (1991). Psychological reactions to infertility. In A. L. Stanton & C. Dunkel-Schetter (Eds.), *Infertility: Perspectives from stress and coping research* (pp. 29–60). New York: Plenum.

Ellen, J. E., McCright, J., & Davis, E. (1998, December). *Youth United Through Health Education (The YUTHE Project): A community-based peer-led STD prevention program.* Paper presented at the National STD Prevention Conference, Dallas, Texas.

Eng, T. R., & Butler, W. T. (Eds.). (1997). *The hidden epidemic: Confronting sexually transmitted diseases.* Washington, DC: National Academy Press.

Freeman, E. W., Rickels, K., Tausig, J., Boxer, A., Mastroianni, L. J., & Tureck, R. W. (1987). Emotional and psychosocial factors in follow-up of women after IVF-ET treatment. *Acta Obstetricia et Gynecologica Scandinavica, 66,* 517–521.

Golombok, S., Cook, R., Bish, A., & Murray, C. (1995). Families created by the new reproductive technologies: Quality of parenting and social and emotional development of the children. *Child Development, 66,* 285–298.

Golombok, S., & Tasker, F. (1994). Donor insemination for single heterosexual and lesbian women: Issues concerning the welfare of the child. *Human Reproduction, 9,* 1972–1976.

Imber-Black, E. (Ed.). (1993). *Secrets in families and family therapy.* New York: Norton.

Jacob, M. C. (1997). Concerns of single women and lesbian couples considering conception through assisted reproduction. In S. R. Leiblum (Ed.), *Infertility: Psychological issues and counseling strategies* (pp. 189–206). New York: Wiley.

Jacobson, C. K., & Heaton, T. B. (1991). Voluntary childlessness among American men and women in the late 1980's. *Social Biology, 38*(1/2), 79–93.

Kuppermann, M., Gates, E., & Washington, A. E. (1996). Racial-ethnic differences in prenatal diagnostic test use and outcomes: Preferences, socioeconomics, or patient knowledge? *Obstetrics and Gynecology, 87*(5), 675–682.

Lazarus, R. S., & Folkman, S. (1984). *Stress, appraisal, and coping.* New York: Springer.

Leedham, B., Meyerowitz, B., Muirhead, J., & First, W. (1995). Positive expectations predict health after heart transplantation. *Health Psychology, 14*(1), 74–79.

Leiblum, S. R. (Ed). (1997). *Infertility: Psychological issues and counseling strategies.* New York: Wiley.

Leiblum, S. R., Kemmann, E., & Lane, M. K. (1987). The psychological concomitants of in vitro fertilization. *Journal of Psychosomatic Obstetrics and Gynecology, 6,* 165–178.

Levin, H., Pasch, L. A., Millstein, S. G., & Ellen, J. E. (1999). *Attitudes and beliefs about STDs and infertility among African-American adolescents.* Paper presented at the annual meeting of the American Psychological Association, Boston.

Levin, J. B., Goldman Sher, T., & Theodos, V. (1997). The effect of intracouple coping concordance on psychological and marital distress in infertility patients. *Journal of Clinical Psychology in Medical Settings, 4*(4), 361–372.

Litt, M. D., Tennen, H., Affleck, G., & Klock, S. (1992). Coping and cognitive factors in adaptation to in vitro fertilization failure. *Journal of Behavioral Medicine, 15*(2), 171–187.

Maranto, G. (1995). Delayed childbearing: How a woman's fertility declines with age. *Atlantic Monthly, 275*(6), 55–65.

McEwan, K. L., Costello, C. G., & Taylor, P. J. (1987). Adjustment to infertility. *Journal of Abnormal Psychology, 96*(2), 108–116.

McMahon, C., Ungerer, J., Beaupaire, J., Tennant, C., & Saunders, D. (1995). Psychosocial outcomes for parents and children after in vitro fertilization: A review. *Journal of Reproductive and Infant Psychology, 13,* 1–16.

Milne, B. J. (1987). Couples' experiences with in vitro fertilization. *Journal of Obstetric and Gynecological Neonatal Nursing, 17,* 347–352.

Morrow, K. A., Thoreson, R. W., & Penney, L. (1995). Predictors of psychological distress among infertility clinic patients. *Journal of Consulting and Clinical Psychology, 63*(1), 163–167.

Mosher, W. D., & Bachrach, C. A. (1996). Understanding U.S. Fertility: Continuity and change in the National Survey of Family Growth, 1988–1995. *Family Planning Perspectives, 28*(4), 4–12.

Nachtigall, R. D., Becker, G., & Wozny, M. (1992). The effects of gender-specific diagnosis on men's and women's response to infertility. *Fertility and Sterility, 57*(1), 113–121.

Newton, C. R., Hearn, M. T., & Yuzpe, A. A. (1990). Psychological assessment and follow-up after in vitro fertilization: Assessing the impact of failure. *Fertility and Sterility, 54*(5), 879–886.

Newton, C. R., Hearn, M. T., Yuzpe, A. A., & Houle, M. (1992). Motives for parenthood and response to failed in vitro fertilization: Implications for counseling. *Journal of Assisted Reproduction and Genetics, 9*(1), 24–31.

Office of Technology Assessment, U.S. Congress. (1988). *Infertility: Medical and social choices* (Publication No. OTA-BA-358). Washington, DC: U.S. Government Printing Office.

Pasch, L. A., & Dunkel-Schetter, C. (1997). Fertility problems: Complex issues for women and couples. In S. J. Gallant, G. P. Keita, & R. Royak-Schaler (Eds.), *Health care for women: Psychological, social, and behavioral influences.* (pp. 187–201). Washington, DC: American Psychological Association.

Pasch, L. A., Dunkel-Schetter, C., & Christensen, A. (1995, August). Communication in couples with fertility problems. In S. Manne (Chair), *Couples coping with severe medical problems.* Symposium presented at the annual meeting of the American Psychological Association, Los Angeles.

Porcu, E., Fabbri, R., Seracchioli, R., Ciotti, P., Magrini, O., & Flamigni, C. (1997). Birth of a healthy female after intracytoplasmic sperm injection of cryopreserved human oocytes. *Fertility and Sterility, 68*(4), 724–726.

Reading, A. E., Chang, L. C., & Kerin, J. F. (1989). Psychological state and coping styles across an IVF treatment cycle. *Journal of Reproductive and Infant Psychology, 7,* 95–103.

Revenson, T. A. (1997). Assisted reproductive technologies and feminism: Is reconciliation possible? In A. van Lenning, M. Bekker, & I. Vanwesenbeeck (Eds.), *Feminist utopias in a postmodern era* (pp. 101–119). Tilburg University Press.

Society for Assisted Reproductive Technology/American Society of Reproductive Medicine. (1998). Assisted reproductive technology in the United States and Canada: 1995 results generated from the American Society for Reproductive Medicine/Society for Assisted Reproductive Technology Registry. *Fertility and Sterility, 69*(3), 389–398.

Sauer, M. V., Paulson, R. J., & Lobo, R. A. (1992). Reversing the natural decline in human fertility. *Journal of the American Medical Association, 268,* 1275–1279.

Speroff, L., Glass, R., & Kase, N. (1994). *Clinical gynecologic endocrinology and infertility* (5th ed.). Baltimore: Williams & Wilkins.

Springer, K. (1996). Young children's understanding of a biological basis for parent–offspring relations. *Child Development, 67,* 2841–2856.

Stanton, A. L. (1991). Cognitive appraisals, coping processes, and adjustment to infertility. In A. L. Stanton & C. Dunkel-Schetter (Eds.), *Infertility: Perspectives from stress and coping research* (pp. 87–108). New York: Plenum.

Stanton, A. L., & Danoff-Burg, S. (1995). Selected issues in women's reproductive health: Psychological perspectives. In A. L. Stanton & S. J. Gallant (Eds.), *The psychology of women's health* (pp. 261–305). Washington, DC: American Psychological Association.

Stanton, A. L., & Dunkel-Schetter, C. (Eds.). (1991). *Infertility: Perspectives from stress and coping research.* New York: Plenum.

Stanton, A. L., Tennen, H., Affleck, G., & Mendola, R. (1992). Coping and adjustment to infertility. *Journal of Social and Clinical Psychology, 11*(1), 1–13.

Taylor, S. E., & Armor, D. A. (1996). Positive illusions and coping with adversity. *Journal of Personality, 64*(4), 873–898.

Taylor, S. E., & Brown, J. D. (1988). Illusion and well-being: A social psychological perspective on mental health. *Psychological Bulletin, 103*(2), 193–210.

Tennen, H., & Affleck, G. (1987). The costs and benefits of optimistic explanations and dispositional optimism. *Journal of Personality, 55*(2), 377–393.

Tennen, H., Affleck, G., & Mendola, R. (1991). Causal explanations for infertility: Their relation to control appraisals and psychological adjustment. In A. L. Stanton & C. Dunkel-Schetter (Eds.), *Infertility: Perspectives from stress and coping research* (pp. 109–131). New York: Plenum.

Thiering, P., Beaurepaire, J., Jones, M., Saunders, D., & Tennant, C. (1993). Mood state as a predictor of treatment outcome after in vitro fertilization/embryo transfer technology. *Journal of Psychosomatic Research, 37*(5), 481–491.

34

Patient Adherence to Treatment Regimen

Jacqueline Dunbar-Jacob
Elizabeth Schlenk
University of Pittsburgh

There is little doubt that a major contributor to health care costs is the failure of patients to adhere satisfactorily to treatment regimen. Indeed, the costs of nonadherence to pharmaceutical therapies alone has been estimated to exceed $100 billion a year (Grahl, 1994). The costs of nonadherence to other forms of treatment (e.g., diet, exercise, smoking cessation, and dialysis) have not been estimated, but given their contribution to disease management, they yield costs over and above those due to poor adherence to prescribed medication.

A portion of the costs of poor adherence lies in the necessity to further treat the complications or progression of varied diseases. For example, the person with hypertension who adheres poorly to treatment may progress to a stroke; the person with diabetes who adheres poorly may progress to limb loss, blindness, and/or cardiovascular disease. Both instances may lead to the necessity for rehabilitation and caretaking services as well as additional forms of treatment. Even in life threatening conditions, poor adherence has been observed. For example, poor adherence to treatment accounts for 25% of graft failures in organ transplantation (Rovelli et al., 1989). Even small deviations from the prescribed regimen can have significant clinical implications for the transplant patient. Indeed, poor adherence to treatment has been linked to unnecessary complications, as well as to disease progression in multiple diseases (Dunbar-Jacob & Schlenk, 1996).

More recently, poor adherence has been linked to the development of treatment-resistant organisms in infectious disease. The increase in tuberculosis in the past decade has been linked in part to variable adherence and/or to early cessation of antituberculosis medications (Bloom & Murray, 1992; Gibbons, 1992; Nolan, Aitken, Elarth, Anderson, & Miller, 1986). Similarly, poor adherence to antibiotic therapies has been associated with treatment resistance among children with otitis media (DeLalla, 1998) and has been suspected in a portion of disease-resistant staphylococcal and streptococcal infections (Schwarzmann, 1998). Most recently, there are indications that even slight deviations from prescribed antiretroviral medications may lead to the development of drug resistant strains of the HIV virus (Vanhove, Schapiro, Winters, Merigan, & Blaschke, 1996). Unfortunately, these drug resistant viruses are themselves transmissible.

The problems of poor adherence are also found in other conditions. For example, in primary prevention immunization rates are less than optimal in both the pediatric and geriatric groups. The failure to immunize leads to excess cases of such conditions as measles in childhood (Mason, 1992) and pneumonia among the elderly (Nichol, Margolis, Wuorenma, & VonSternberg, 1994). Poor adherence has also been a significant problem in rehabilitation where performance of therapeutic exercise looks similar to efforts to follow drug regimen (Dunbar-Jacob, 1998).

DEFINITIONS OF ADHERENCE

One factor that influences the degree of poor adherence found in research and clinical populations is the definition of adherence that is selected. Adherence can be defined in at least two general ways. The first is through the pattern of adherence problem expressed by the patient. The second is by the quantitative assessment that is made.

Patterns of Adherence

There are at least six behavior patterns that constitute problematic adherence. These consist of failure to adopt the regimen, early stoppage of treatment, reduction in levels of treatment, over treatment, variability in the conduct of the regimen, and dosage interval errors.

Adoption of the treatment regimen is the first step in adherence. Yet the problem of adoption is fairly significant. There are some data to suggest that as many as 20% of persons fail to fill medication prescriptions (Burns, Sneddon, Lovell, McLean, & B. J. Martin, 1992). The proportion of persons who simply fail to start dietary or exercise regimens has been less well studied but is estimated to be significant. These individuals are rarely described in studies of adherence.

For those who initiate treatment, there is the problem of early stoppage. These persons are often referred to as dropouts or as nonadherers. There is considerable variation in the proportion who drop out of treatment, with the lowest rates seen in clinical trials and the highest in exercise regimen. Indeed, 50% of persons who initiate exercise programs for cardiac rehabilitation are found to terminate early (Oldridge, 1984, 1988). In the clinical trials arena, the rates of dropout are estimated to average between 5% and 25% (Dunbar & Knoke, 1986). One of the difficulties in defining dropping out of treatment is that some portion of these persons may drop back in to treatment at a later point in time or with a different care provider.

For those individuals who stay in treatment, several patterns may be found. First among those is alterations in treatment dosing. This may include both reductions in the dose or in increases in the dose that has been prescribed. For example, the patient may reduce or increase the dose of medication that is taken or the number of exercise regimens performed per week. Underdosing may occur, for example, in response to side effects, to spacing out inadequate quantities of medication, or to a belief that a lower dose is preferable. Overdosing occurs in at least two ways. Patients may miss medication and "double up" to achieve the requisite number of doses. Or individuals may decide that extra doses are called for to combat symptoms. In either case, the risks of overdosing and of untoward side effects are high. Our research has found these patterns in patients with rheumatoid arthritis and for those with hyperlipidemia, symptomatic and asymptomatic disorders, respectively, as well as among posttransplant patients. Both patterns may be found within the same individual.

The second pattern found among those who stay in treatment is variability in adherence. This pattern may be the most common form of adherence problem found. In this instance, the individual follows medication, dietary, and/or exercise regimen to varying degrees over time. Typically, the regimen may be missed at episodic intervals. Whole days or specific doses may be missed for varying intervals. When the regimen is missed for a period of several days and then resumed seemingly spontaneously, the period is referred to as a "regimen holiday" (Urquhart & Chevalley, 1988).

The third type of problem found among those who stay in treatment is that of dosing interval errors. This pattern is particularly the case for medication taking, but also may be seen with exercise regimen. In the case of medication taking, individuals may consume doses too close together or too far apart. For example, asthma patients have been found to consume puffs of inhaled medication too close together to support efficacy (Berg, Dunbar-Jacob, & Rohay, 1995). Similarly, patients with rheumatoid arthritis have been found to take doses as close as 2 hours apart as well as more than 36 hours apart (Dunbar-Jacob et al., 1992).

There are, therefore, numerous patterns of poor adherence or nonadherence. Typically, these have been treated as equivalent in studies of adherence with the term *adherence* defined as the total dosage consumed divided by the total prescribed over some period of time. This obscures the nature of the adherence problem. Thus, the first consideration in defining poor adherence is the specification of the type of adherence problem or problems that are of interest.

Quantitative Assessment of Adherence

Another approach to defining poor adherence relates to the level of data used. The proportion of the prescribed regimen that is carried out can be examined. This yields a percentage adherence score. For a group, then, the average (mean or median) adherence is reported. Related to this, and often not clearly specified in the literature, is a report of the proportion of persons who meet some adherence criterion, that is, defining a group's adherence by the proportion of persons who achieve or fail to achieve some preestablished level of adherence. The convention has been 80% for most investigations since the landmark study of adherence to antihypertensive medications by Haynes et al. (1976). Although logic would suggest that the level of adherence set would be related to the level necessary to achieve therapeutic benefit, little data are available on the relation between level of adherence and achievement of clinical benefit. Other methods of defining adherence include a determination of the proportion of persons who have attained clinical benefit, a desired outcome of good adherence, but not the equivalent; the clinical judgment of level of adherence; and the level of attainment of performance of multiple components of a treatment regimen. Each of these definitions influences the rate of adherence reported.

MAGNITUDE OF THE PROBLEM

The problem of poor adherence to treatment regimen has a significant impact on the outcomes of care and subsequently on health care costs. Nonadherence to health care regimens is a prevalent problem that cuts across disorders, treatment regimens, ages, gender, and ethnic and socioeconomic groups (Burke & Dunbar-Jacob, 1995; Dunbar-Jacob, Burke, & Puczynski, 1995). There is some indication that persons with life threatening conditions may adhere somewhat better than others. But in these conditions (e.g., cancer, AIDS, and transplantation), there is a burgeoning body of evidence to suggest that even modest deviations have significant clinical impact (DeGeest, 1996). Additionally, there is some evidence that persons participating in clinical trials may also have better adherence (Schron et al., 1995). Even in these situations, adherence is far from perfect.

Nonadherence varies over the course of treatment with steeper declines in adherence noted earlier in treatment. For example, from 16% to 50% of patients with hypertension discontinue their medication within the first 12 months (Flack, Novikov, & Ferrario, 1996; Jones, Gorkin, Lian, Staffa, & Fletcher, 1995) and 50% of patients in cardiac rehabilitation programs drop out in the first 12 months (Oldridge, 1984). Over the long run, adherence continues to decrease but at a less marked rate than observed at the outset of treatment. For example, in the Lipid Research Clinic-Coronary Primary Prevention Trial (LRC–CPPT), reductions in dietary fat and cholesterol began to show reversals at 12 months that continued over the 7-year clinical trial (Lipid Research Clinics Program, 1984a, 1984b). Thus, interventions to promote adherence need to focus on initial adherence as well as maintenance of adherence.

Medication Adherence

Studies have shown that from 20% to 80% of persons do not adhere to medication prescriptions to the extent of gaining therapeutic benefit (Dunbar-Jacob et al., 1995). Among persons with chronic disorders, from 50% to 90% do not adhere to medication prescriptions (Cramer, Scheyer, & Mattson, 1990). Medication nonadherence rates vary depending on the method and time of measurement. A review of antihypertensive medication adherence found that adherence by self-report was 75%, whereas adherence by pill count was 52% (Dunbar-Jacob, Dwyer, & Dunning, 1991). Dunbar-Jacob, Burke et al. (1996) compared self-report, pill count, and electronic monitors in subjects taking a lipid-lowering drug and found poor correspondence among the measures with self-report by 7-day recall at 97%, pill count at 94%, and electronic monitors at 84%. Using electronic monitors in subjects with epilepsy, Cramer et al. (1990) reported mean adherence rates of 88% during the 5 days before the clinic visit, 86% during the 5 days after the clinic visit, and only 67% during a 5-day period 1 month later. Thus, electronic monitors seem to provide a more accurate measure of medication adherence compared to self-report and pill counts, and medication adherence appears to decline between clinic visits.

Dietary Adherence

Dietary recommendations often accompany medication prescriptions for chronic disorder regimens, for example hypertension, diabetes, and hyperlipidemia. Modifying long-standing dietary habits and maintaining newly established eating plans can be difficult. Adherence with low fat, low cholesterol diets ranges from 13% to 76% (Glanz, 1979), whereas long-term adherence with weight reducing diets is less than 50%, with few persons maintaining the weight loss (Glanz, 1979).

Exercise Adherence

Exercise adherence is a problem across healthy and chronic disorder populations with 50% dropping out of exercise during the first 3 to 6 months and a leveling off of the dropout rate between 55% and 75% by 1 year (Carmody, Senner, Malinow, & Matarazzo, 1980). An exercise regimen can be time consuming, inconvenient, and expensive, all of which are barriers to exercise adherence. For persons managing chronic disorders, additional exercise barriers exist, such as fatigue and pain. For example, in fibromyalgia, exercise nonadherence was high at 44%. Reasons reported for missing exercise included finding time when facing changes in routine (85.2%) and presence of fibromyalgia symptoms, such as fatigue and pain (44.4%; Schlenk, Okifuji, Dunbar-Jacob, & Turk, 1996).

In 1996, the U.S. surgeon general released a report on physical activity and health that recommended 30 minutes or more of moderate-intensity physical activity on all, or most, days of the week (U.S. Department of Health and Human Services, 1996). This physical activity can be accumulated during the course of the day (Pate et al., 1995). Despite this recommendation, over 60% of U.S. adults are not regularly active and 25% of U.S. adults are not active at all. Only 22% of U.S. adults engage in sustained physical activity of any intensity five times weekly for 30 minutes (U.S. Department of Health and Human Services, 1996).

PREDICTORS OF POOR ADHERENCE

In general, the literature over the past three decades has examined poor adherence as a solitary construct. Most predictors that have been identified have accounted for small proportions of variance in adherence and further have not been consistently supported in studies. Perhaps the most consistent predictors have included self-efficacy, initial adherence, complexity of the regimen, and disruptive schedules (e.g., Dunbar-Jacob, 1998; Dunbar-Jacob, Schlenk, Burke, & Matthews, 1998). Numerous other factors have been identified, but have not been consistently related to adherence across studies. These factors include age, social support, mood, income, system of care, clinician–patient communication, and beliefs (e.g., Dunbar-Jacob, Schlenk et al., 1998).

Predictor studies and intervention studies typically have not discriminated between the various patterns of poor adherence. Nor have the predictor studies distinguished between varying models of adherence. Yet poor adherence can take multiple forms. Thus, it makes intuitive sense that predictors and interventions might vary between these forms. There are a number of dimensions that would appear to separate adherence behaviors into independent categories or models, with the probability of identifying differing predictor variables and differing effectiveness in interventions. Two of these important dimensions include whether poor compliance is intentional or unintentional and whether it is a lack of capability. Unfortunately, the research on predictors of adherence has not separated out those factors that may predict a decision to not adhere versus unintentional nonadherence episodes versus a lack of capability to adhere.

Much of the literature on adherence treats adherence problems as intentional decisions or a failure of motivation on the part of patients. Thus, patients may make decisions based on numerous factors. One of these important factors is beliefs. These may be beliefs about treatment, about capability to carry out treatment, or about the effectiveness of treatment. Several theories have addressed adherence from this perspective, including Self-Efficacy Theory (Bandura, 1997), Health Belief Model (Janz & Becker, 1984; Rosenstock, 1974), Theory of Reasoned Action/Theory of Planned Behavior (Ajzen, 1991; M. Fishbein & Ajzen, 1975), and the Common Sense Model of Illness (Leventhal, Meyer, & Nerenz, 1980). A second factor, which relates to an intentional decision model of adherence, is the evaluation of the burden of adherence. In this case, factors such as the personal costs associated with care, the stigma that may be encountered from having treatment witnessed, the impact on quality of life, and the effort associated with managing treatment all may influence the decision to follow treatment.

An examination of the patient reports of poor adherence reveals that the most commonly reported reason is forgetting (Dunbar-Jacob, 1997). Research (Morell, Park, Kidder, & M. Martin, 1997) suggests that busy and/or disruptive schedules may also contribute to poor adherence. Forgetting and disruption would be related to nonintentional nonadherence episodes. Research has suggested that it is not unusual for patients to report intending to take a dose of medication but something interrupted them (a phone call, a visitor, etc.) and then they became distracted and forgot to return to the medication when the distraction ended. Similarly, patients who report business travel or vacations where daily schedules are disrupted also report higher missed doses of treatment (Dunbar-Jacob, 1997; Schlenk et al., 1996). Although such reports are offered by patients, there has been little systematic research in this area.

A third model of poor adherence addresses whether or not the patient has the capability to carry out the regimen. A variety of factors are at play here. These factors include whether the patient has adequate knowledge to carry out the treatment, whether the skills are present, and whether the patient has the cognitive and/or physical capability to engage in the treatment. Few studies have examined these factors. Studies identifying the proportion of poor adherence that was related to lack of adequate knowledge were conducted in the mid-1970s (e.g., Boyd, Covington, Stanaszek, & Coussons, 1974) but have not been examined more recently. Studies examining cognitive or physical capability have also been limited. Park, Willis, Morrow, Diehl, and Gaines (1994) suggested that those dimensions tapped by standard neuropsychological tests have not been associated with adherence. But much work remains to be done in this dimension.

In addition to the failure to examine determinants of or predictors of adherence from the perspective of either patterns of adherence or models of poor adherence, multiple methods of measurement of adherence have been used in these studies. As becomes evident later, different measures of adherence classify different persons as adherent or nonadherent. It is likely, therefore, that predictor variables will behave differently in different studies. Research supports this notion, suggesting that different measurement methods lead to different predictor variables in the same population on the same regimen (Dunbar-Jacob, Sereika, Rohay, Burke, & Kwoh, 1995).

MEASURES OF ADHERENCE

An examination of the research on adherence shows that multiple methods of assessment are used. These include such strategies as self-report (interview or questionnaire or daily diaries), clinician reports, pill counts, biological indicators, clinical outcome, and electronic event monitoring. Each yields somewhat different information about the patient's behavior with regard to their regimen as well as different reports of adherence. Thus, the selection of a strategy to measure adherence requires careful attention to the limitations of each method and ideally requires a well-specified definition of adherence. There is no gold standard for assessment of adherence (Cramer, Mattson, Prevey, Scheyer, & Ouellette, 1989), although electronic event monitors provide the most complete and timely data on adherence (Dunbar-Jacob, Sereika, Rohay, & Burke, 1998). Measures, in general, should provide accurate, relevant, specific, objective data that is economically feasible, practical, and easy to administer (Westfall, 1986).

One of the major differences between measurement methods is the difference in reported adherence that may be obtained between them, even when the same regimen in the same person is assessed. The variation in reported adherence by different measurement methods was first reported by Mattson and Friedman (1984) based on data from the Aspirin Myocardial Infarction Study. In this study, subjects were randomly assigned to aspirin or to placebo. Adherence was measured by pill count, platelet aggregation, and salicylate levels. Adherence ranged from 81% to 97% in the drug group and from 78% to 97% in the placebo group depending on the strategy examined, with adherence highest for the behavioral (pill count) method. These variations are likely dependent on characteristics of the measures. Salicylate levels would be fairly short lived and would reflect adherence just prior to the clinic visit. Work by a number of investigators indicates that adherence is at its peak just before and just after a clinic visit (Cramer et al., 1989; Kass, Meltzer, Gordon, Cooper, & Goldberg, 1986; Norell, 1981). Thus, the salicylate levels would reflect adherence just prior to the visit. Platelet aggregation would have a longer impact but would not provide information on the degree of adherence over time. Individual variations in drug metabolism and other related biological factors would impact on the level of platelet aggregation identified. The pill count, while estimating the amount of medication consumed over the measurement period, would also be affected by the willingness of the subjects to return all unused medication as well as their memory to do so.

Similar differences in adherence by measurement method have been reported by others (e.g., Burke et al., 1992; Dunbar, Dunning, Dwyer, Burke, & Snetselaar, 1991; Dunbar-Jacob, Burke et al., 1996; Dunbar-Jacob, Burke, Rohay, Sereika, & Muldoon, 1997; Hyman et al., 1982; Norell, 1981; Petitti, Friedman, & Kahn, 1981; Rand & Wise, 1994; Rudd, Ahmed,

Zachary, Barton, & Bonduelle, 1990; Wilson & Endres, 1986). Typically, self-report measures overestimate adherence when compared with other measures. This is not unexpected as the self-report measures, excluding daily diaries, rely on memory and willingness to report. Given the difficulties in remembering recurring behaviors, the tendency is to rely on recent events as indicators of longer term events. Coupled with peak adherence at the time of assessment at a clinic visit, this basis for estimation of adherence would lead to a personal overrating of longer term adherence behaviors. The diaries are more accurate than interviews or questionnaires, but also are limited by the willingness of the patient to record daily and accurately. Work suggests that group averages may approximate those seen with electronic monitoring, but sensitivity to poor adherence is low (Dunbar-Jacob, Sereika, & Burke, 1998).

The electronic measures tend to report the lowest levels of adherence. These methods record onto microprocessor chips the exact time and date that an event occurred. For a fuller discussion, see Dunbar-Jacob, Sereika, Rohay, and Burke (1998). Thus, patterns of poor adherence can be identified. Monitors are available for medication taking, exercise, and for cued diary entries. The major limitation is sensitivity to actual regimen conduct. Experience with electronic monitoring of medication taking over as much as a 12-month period suggests that the effort to manipulate the monitor at the prescribed time day after day without taking medication is an unlikely expenditure. Deception with the monitor may be estimated with the addition of relevant biological assays.

No matter the method of assessment, however, the distribution of adherence data for medication consumption and for appointment keeping appears to assume a J-curve, which is robust and resistant to transformation (Dunbar-Jacob, Sereika, Rohay, & Probstfield, 1994). Thus, the analysis of adherence data does not lend itself to traditional parametric approaches. Less information is available on the distribution of adherence data for exercise or for diet. Information on these distributions would be valuable.

IMPACT ON CLINICAL OUTCOME

Adherence is a mediator of clinical outcome. However, there is a paucity of knowledge about the amount of adherence to a prescribed treatment that is required to produce a desired clinical outcome. Only a few studies have investigated the amount of medication adherence required to produce a desired clinical outcome (DeGeest, 1996; Haynes et al., 1976). No studies have investigated the amount of adherence to behavioral treatment required for a desired clinical outcome.

The relations between the three adherence behaviors of medication taking, following a therapeutic diet, and following an exercise program and clinical outcomes are discussed. The clinical outcomes reported in the literature include relapse, sign and symptom relief, health status, hospitalization, morbidity, and mortality.

Medication Adherence and Clinical Outcomes

Most of the research on the relation between adherence and clinical outcomes has been conducted in the area of pharmacological treatment. Better medication adherence was related to prevention of relapse in tuberculosis (Dupon & Raynaud, 1992), epilepsy (Cramer et al., 1989; Reynolds, 1987), childhood leukemia (Klopovich & Trueworthy, 1985), schizophrenia (Leff et al., 1989; Mantonakis, Jemos, Christodoulou, & Lykouras, 1982), and alcoholism (Fawcett et al., 1984, 1987; Pisani, Fawcett, Clark, & McQuire, 1993). Interestingly, adherence to antibiotics for otitis media was not related to decreased reoccurrence based on urinary assay (Reed, Lutz, Zazove, & Ratcliffe, 1984). Perhaps adequate antibiotic was taken to fend off repeat infection.

Better medication adherence was related to sign and symptom relief in hypertension (Fletcher, Deliakis, Schoch, & Shapiro, 1979; Haynes, Gibson, D. W. Taylor, Bernholz, & Sackett, 1982; McKenny, Munroe, & Wright, 1992), peptic esophageal stenosis (Starlinger, Appel, Schemper, & Schiessel, 1985), chronic bronchitis (Dompeling et al., 1992), schizophrenia (Verghese et al., 1989), manic depression (Connelly, Davenport, & Nurnberger, 1982), and chronic pain (Berndt, Maier, & Schutz, 1993). Medication adherence was not related to symptom relief in asthma (Dompeling et al., 1992) or open angle glaucoma (Granstrom, 1985).

Better medication adherence was related to some dimensions of health status in a few studies. In hypertension, medication adherence was related to clinical health status and perceived health status but not functional status (B. Given, C. W. Given, & Simoni, 1979). In rheumatoid arthritis, self-reported medication adherence was not related to health status or functional status (Taal, Rasker, Seydel, & Weigman, 1993) but was related to reduced pain (Dunbar-Jacob, Kwoh et al., 1996). Because self-report tends to overestimate medication adherence, measurement errors may have obscured the relation between adherence and health status.

Medication nonadherence was related to higher rates of hospitalization in hypertension (Maronde et al.,1989), manic depression (Connelly et al., 1982), schizophrenia (Gaebel & Pietzcker, 1985), and alcoholism (Fawcett et al., 1987). Medication nonadherence was related to morbidity across acute and chronic disorders as well as preventive regimens. Adherence to antibiotics was related to resolution of acute urinary tract infections in the elderly (Cheung et al., 1988). In chronic bronchitis, medication nonadherence was related to poorer pulmonary function test results (Dompeling et al., 1992). In psychiatric disorders, such as depression in the elderly (Cole, 1985) and manic depression (Connelly et al., 1982), medication nonadherence was related to a worse clinical course. Medication nonadherence among renal transplant recipients resulted in return to dialysis (Kalil, Heim-Duthoy, & Kasiske, 1992), renal insufficiency during pregnancy (O'Donnell et al., 1985), and organ rejection (Rovelli et al., 1989; Schweizer et al., 1990). Similarly, heart transplant recipients who had minor departures in immunosuppressive medications showed organ rejection and other adverse occurrences (DeGeest, 1996). Nonadherence to medications taken for preventive purposes was related to higher morbidity as well. Nonadherence to antihypertensive medications was related to an increase risk for coronary heart disease (Psaty, Koepsell, Wagner, LoGerfo, & Inui, 1990). Similarly, nonadherence to preventive medications for tuberculosis (Nolan et al., 1986) and malaria (Wetsteyn & deGeus, 1993) was related to higher occurrence of these respective disorders.

Medication nonadherence was related to mortality in patients with epilepsy (Lip & Brodie, 1992), asthma (Robertson, Rubinfeld, & Bowes, 1992), and organ transplantation (Lanza, Cooper, Boyd, & Barnard, 1984; Schweizer et al., 1990). Similarly, medication adherence was related to survival among patients with hematologic malignancies (Richardson, Shelton, Krailo, & Levine, 1990).

In summary, nonadherence to prescribed medication has been associated with poorer clinical outcomes across a wide variety of disorders. The costs of nonadherence are high in terms of patient health, health care utilization, and even mortality.

Dietary Adherence and Clinical Outcomes

Nonadherence to low fat diets was related to mortality (R. B. Singh, Niaz, Ghosh, R. Singh, & Rastogi, 1993; Swank & Dugan, 1990) and cardiac events (R. B. Singh et al., 1993). Nonadherence to diabetic diets was related to diabetic ketoacidosis (Mulrow, Bailey, Sonksen, & Slavin, 1987; White, Kolman, Wexler, Polin, & Winter, 1984) and hospitalizations and emergent visits (H. A. Fishbein, 1985; White et al., 1984) but not to measures of diabetic control, such as weight and glycosylated hemoglobin (Mulrow et al., 1987). Given that multiple factors influence diabetic control in conjunction with medication adherence, it may be difficult to impact these specific clinical measures.

Exercise Adherence and Clinical Outcomes

Nonadherence to prescribed exercise in postsurgical patients was related to lower range of motion, joint extension, and functional status, and higher relapse (Hawkins, 1989; Hawkins & Switlyk, 1993; Rives, Gelberman, Smith, & Carney, 1992). In older women, adherence to group exercise improved change in sway (Lichtenstein, Shields, Shiavi, & Burger, 1989). In summary, exercise adherence improves clinical outcomes, in particular sign and symptom relief and prevention of relapse.

INTERVENTIONS TO PROMOTE ADHERENCE

Interventions to promote adherence across medication, dietary, and exercise regimens have tended to focus on behavioral strategies or education plus behavioral strategies. Whereas most of these interventions have been modestly successful in promoting adherence, few have been tested in randomized, controlled clinical trials. The strategies that have been shown to be successful in improving adherence include some combination of self-monitoring, counseling, stimulus control or cueing, positive reinforcement, self-efficacy enhancement, and social support enhancement.

Self-monitoring of blood pressure and/or medication taking (Edmonds et al., 1985; Haynes et al., 1976; Logan, Milne, Achber, Campbell, & Haynes, 1979) and exercise (Atkins, Kaplan, Timms, Reinsch, & Lofback, 1984; King, C. B. Taylor, Haskell, & DeBusk, 1988; Rogers et al., 1987) improved regimen adherence. Counseling promoted adherence with medication taking (Bailey et al., 1990; Colcher & Bass, 1972; Peterson, McLean, & Millingen, 1984), dietary management in large clinical trials (Dolecek et al., 1986; Glueck, Gordon, Nelson, Davis, & Tyroler, 1986; Simkin-Silverman et al., 1995), and exercise (Belisle, Roskies, & Levesque, 1987; King & Frederiksen, 1984; King et al., 1988). Stimulus control or cueing improved adherence to medication taking (Haynes et al., 1976; Logan et al., 1979) and exercise (Atkins et al., 1984; Keefe & Blumenthal, 1980). Positive reinforcement promoted adherence to medications (Bailey et al., 1990; Haynes et al., 1976; Logan et al., 1979) and exercise (Atkins et al., 1984; Keefe & Blumenthal, 1980). Self-efficacy enhancement is a newer strategy based on social cognitive theory (Bandura, 1997) that has been used successfully to promote dietary adherence (McCann, Follette, Driver, Brief, & Knopp, 1988). Social support enhancement promoted adherence to medication taking (J. P. Kirscht, J. L. Kirscht, & Rosenstock, 1981; Morisky et al., 1983) and dietary prescriptions (Barnard, Scherwitz, & Ornish, 1992; Bovbjerg et al., 1995).

In summary, these studies suggest that regimen adherence can be improved by behavioral interventions that are frequently complex. Future efforts should be focused on the development and testing of new treatments addressing specific patterns of poor adherence.

CONCLUSIONS

Adherence to a treatment regimen poses a significant problem in medical care both in terms of the patient's clinical status as well as financial burden. Efforts to intervene have been limited. Thus, there is minimal information that can be relied on with confidence in efforts to improve adherence within either a clinical or research setting. Clearly there is a need for randomized, controlled studies evaluating interventions.

In the research that has been carried out, limitations have existed due to the measurement and to the definitions of adherence that have been used. Each measure yields somewhat differing information about adherence. Differences in the rates of adherence and in the sensitivity to poor adherence exist leading to variations in reports of adherence among populations as well as within populations where more than one measure is used. These variations in sensitivity to poor adherence may lead to differences in the identification of predictors or determinants of adherence. Indeed, these variations may be contributing to the lack of consistency in the identification of adherence determinants.

The research that has been carried out has also tended to ignore the various patterns of adherence that may occur. These patterns range from failing to participate in the regimen altogether, to variability in regimen conduct, to timing errors, all of which can contribute to variations in clinical outcome. To move the understanding of adherence behaviors forward, the research needs to become more specific about the definition of adherence, its pattern, and the type of adherence problem being addressed. The use of electronic monitors and potentially diaries in the assessment of adherence will allow these subclassifications of poor adherence to be better identified and characterized.

As the clinical outcomes associated with poor adherence have become more salient and the costs have impact on a cost-conscious health care system, the interest in adherence has increased. The newer measurement technologies permit a more refined and specific assessment of adherence problems and patterns, which is contributing toward a finer understanding of this significant problem in health care. The limited studies detailing the problems of adherence, the paucity of intervention studies, as well as the variability created by the coarser view of adherence that has characterized research in the field all point to the need for further focused research in this difficult problem affecting all aspects of health care.

REFERENCES

Ajzen, I. (1991). The theory of planned behavior. *Organizational behavior and human decision processes, 50*(2), 179–211.

Atkins, C. J., Kaplan, R. M., Timms, R. M., Reinsch, S., & Lofback, K. (1984). Behavioral exercise programs in the management of chronic obstructive pulmonary disease. *Journal of Consulting and Clinical Psychology, 52*(4), 591–603.

Bailey, W. C., Richards, J. M., Jr., Brooks, C. M., Soong, S. J., Windsor, R. A., & Manzella, B. A. (1990). A randomized trial to improve self-management practices of adults with asthma. *Archives of Internal Medicine, 150*(8), 1664–1668.

Bandura, A. (1997). *Self-efficacy: The exercise of control.* New York: Freeman.

Barnard, N. D., Scherwitz, L. W., & Ornish, D. (1992). Adherence and acceptability of a low-fat, vegetarian diet among patients with cardiac disease. *Journal of Cardiopulmonary Rehabilitation, 12*(6), 423–431.

Belisle, M., Roskies, E., & Levesque, J. M. (1987). Improving adherence to physical activity. *Health Psychology, 6*(2), 159–172.

Berg, J., Dunbar-Jacob, J., & Rohay, J. (1995). Assessing inhaler medication adherence using an electronic monitoring device. *Annals of Behavioral Medicine, 17S.*

Berndt, S., Maier, C., & Schutz, H. W. (1993). Polymedication and medication compliance in patients with chronic non-malignant pain. *Pain, 52*(3), 331–339.

Bloom, B. R., & Murray, C. J. L. (1992). Tuberculosis: Commentary on a reemergent killer. *Science, 257*(5073), 1055–1064.

Boyd, J. R., Covington, T. R., Stanaszek, W. F., & Coussons, R. T. (1974). Drug defaulting: I. Determinants of compliance. *American Journal of Hospital Pharmacy, 31*(4), 362–367.

Bovbjerg, V. E., McCann, B. S., Brief, D. J., Follette, W. C., Retzlaff, B. M., Dowdy, A. A., Walden, C. E., & Knopp, R. H. (1995). Spouse support and long-term adherence to lipid-lowering diets. *American Journal of Epidemiology, 141*(5), 451–460.

Burke, L. E., & Dunbar-Jacob, J. (1995). Adherence to medication, diet, and activity recommendations: From assessment to maintenance. *Journal of Cardiovascular Nursing, 9*(2), 62–79.

Burke, L. E., Dunbar-Jacob, J., Glaister, C., McCall, M., Sereika, S., Dwyer, K., Kwoh, C. K., & Starz, T. W. (1992, May). *Influence of question type on self-reported medication compliance in rheumatoid arthritis patients.* Paper presented at the Sigma Theta Tau International Nursing Research Conference, Columbus, OH.

Burns, J. M., Sneddon, I., Lovell, M., McLean, A., & Martin, B. J. (1992). Elderly patients and their medication: A post-discharge follow-up study. *Age and Ageing, 21*(3), 178–181.

Carmody, T. P., Senner, J. W., Malinow, M. R.., & Matarazzo, J. D. (1980). Physical exercise rehabilitation: Long-term dropout rate in cardiac patients. *Journal of Behavioral Medicine, 3*(2), 163–168.

Cheung, R., Sullens, C. M., Seal, D., Dickins, J., Nicholson, P. W., Deshmukh, A. A., Denham, M. J., & Dobbs, S. M. (1988). The paradox of using a 7 day antibacterial course to treat urinary tract infections in the community. *British Journal of Clinical Pharmacology, 26*(4), 391–398.

Colcher, I. S., & Bass, J. W. (1972). Penicillin treatment of streptococcal pharyngitis: A comparison of schedules and the role of specific counseling. *Journal of the American Medical Association, 222*(6), 657–659.

Cole, M. G. (1985). The course of elderly depressed out-patients. *Canadian Journal of Psychiatry, 30*(3), 217–220.

Connelly, C. E., Davenport, Y. B., & Nurnberger, J. I., Jr. (1982). Adherence to treatment regimen in a lithium carbonate clinic. *Archives of General Psychiatry, 39*(5), 585–588.

Cramer, J. A., Mattson, R. H., Prevey, M. L., Scheyer, R. D., & Ouellette, V. L. (1989). How often is medication take as prescribed? A novel assessment technique. *Journal of the American Medical Association, 261*(22), 3273–3277.

Cramer, J. A., Scheyer, R. D., & Mattson, R. H. (1990). Compliance declines between clinic visits. *Archives of Internal Medicine, 150*(7), 1509–1510.

DeGeest, S. (1996, March). Assessment of adherence in heart transplant recipients. In J. Dunbar-Jacob (Chair), *Adherence in chronic disease.* Symposium presented at the fourth International Congress of Behavioral Medicine, Washington, DC.

DeLalla, F. (1998). Cefixime in the treatment of upper respiratory tract infections and otitis media. *Chemotherapy, 44*(Suppl. 1), 19–23.

Dolecek, T. A., Milas, N. C., Van Horn, L. V., Farrand, M. E., Gorder, D. D., Duchene, A. G., Dyer, J. R., Stone, P. A., & Randall, B. L. (1986). A long-term nutrition intervention experience: Lipid responses and dietary adherence patterns in the Multiple Risk Factor Intervention Trial. *Journal of the American Dietetic Association, 86*(6), 752–758.

Dompeling, E., Van Grunsven, P. M., Van Schayck, C. P., Folgering, H., Molema, J., & Van Weel, C. (1992). Treatment with inhaled steroids in asthma and chronic bronchitis: Long-term compliance and inhaler technique. *Family Practice, 9*(2), 161–166.

Dunbar, J., Dunning, E. J., Dwyer, K., Burke, L., & Snetselaar, L. (1991, March). *Influence of question type on self-reported compliance with dietary regimen.* Paper presented at the 12th annual meeting of Society of Behavioral Medicine, Washington, DC.

Dunbar, J., & Knoke, J. (1986, May). *Prediction of medication adherence at one year and seven years: Behavioral and psychological factors.* Paper presented at the Society for Clinical Trials Seventh Annual Conference, Montreal, Canada.

Dunbar-Jacob, J. (1997, November). *Understanding the reasons for patient's noncompliance and how these reasons impact therapeutic regimens and outcomes of care.* Paper presented at a workshop, Pharmaceutical Care Programs: Their Role in Medication Compliance by EMMG, Kansas City, KS.

Dunbar-Jacob, J. (1998, December). *Challenges in rehabilitation clinical trials: Adherence to intervention regimens.* Paper presented at the Workshop on Clinical Trials in Rehabilitation by the National Advisory Board on Medical Rehabilitation Research, Bethesda, MD.

Dunbar-Jacob, J., Burke, L. E., & Puczynski, S. (1995). Clinical assessment and management of adherence to medical regimens. In P. M. Nicassio & T. W. Smith (Eds.), *Managing chronic illness: A biopsychosocial perspective* (pp. 313–349). Washington, DC: American Psychological Association.

Dunbar-Jacob, J., Burke, L. E., Rohay, J. M., Sereika, S., & Muldoon, M. F. (1997, November). *How comparable are self-report, pill count, and electronically monitored adherence data*? Poster presented at the 70th Scientific Sessions of the American Heart Association, Orlando, FL.

Dunbar-Jacob, J., Burke, L. E., Rohay, J. M., Sereika, S., Schlenk, E. A., Lipello, A., & Muldoon, M. F. (1996). Comparability of self-report, pill count, and electronically monitored adherence data. *Controlled Clinical Trials, 17*(Suppl. 2), 80S.

Dunbar-Jacob, J., Dwyer, K., & Dunning, E. J. (1991). Compliance with antihypertensive regimen: A review of the research in the 1980s. *Annals of Behavioral Medicine, 13*(1), 31–39.

Dunbar-Jacob, J., Kwoh, C. K., Rohay, J. M., Burke, L. E., Sereika, S., & Starz, T. (1996, March). *Medication adherence and functional outcomes in rheumatoid arthritis.* Poster presented at the Fourth International Congress of Behavioral Medicine, Washington, DC.

Dunbar-Jacob, J., Kwoh, C. K., Starz, T. W., Sereika, S., McCall, M., Glaister, C., Burke, L. E., Dwyer, K., Rosella, J., & Holmes, J. (1992, July). *Adherence to arthritis medication.* Poster presented at the International Congress of Behavioral Medicine, Hamburg, Germany.

Dunbar-Jacob, J., & Schlenk, E. A. (1996). Treatment adherence and clinical outcome: Can we make a difference? In R. J. Resnick, & R. H. Rozensky (Eds.), *Health psychology through the life span: Practice and research opportunities* (pp. 323–343). Washington, DC: American Psychological Association.

Dunbar-Jacob, J., Schlenk, E. A., Burke, L. E., & Matthews, J. T. (1998). Predictors of patient adherence: Patient characteristics. In S. A. Shumaker, E. Schron, J. Ockene, & W. L. McBee (Eds.), *Handbook of health behavior change* (2nd ed., pp. 491–511). New York: Springer.

Dunbar-Jacob, J., Sereika, S., & Burke, L. E. (1998, August). *Use of daily diaries in assessing compliance.* Paper presented at the fifth International Congress of Behavioral Medicine, Copenhagen, Denmark.

Dunbar-Jacob, J., Sereika, S., Rohay, J., & Burke, L. E. (1998). Electronic methods in assessing adherence to medical regimens. In D. S. Kranz & A. Baum (Eds.), *Technology and methods in behavioral medicine* (pp. 95–113). Mahwah, NJ: Lawrence Erlbaum Associates.

Dunbar-Jacob, J., Sereika, S., Rohay, J. M., Burke, L. E., & Kwoh, C. K. (1995). Predictors of adherence: Differences by measurement method. *Annals of Behavioral Medicine, 17S*, S196.

Dunbar-Jacob, J., Sereika, S., Rohay, J. M., & Probstfield, J. (1994). J-shaped compliance distribution revisited. *Controlled Clinical Trials, 15*(3S), 120.

Dupon, M., & Raynaud, J. M. (1992). Tuberculosis in patients infected with Human Immunodeficiency Virus 1: A retrospective multicentre study of 123 cases in France. *Quarterly Journal of Medicine, 85*(306), 719–730.

Edmonds, D., Foester, E., Groth, H., Greminger, P., Siegenthaler, W., & Vetter, W. (1985). Does self-measurement of blood pressure improve patient compliance in hypertension? *Journal of Hypertension, 3*(Suppl. 1), S31–S34.

Fawcett, J., Clark, D. C., Aagesen, C. A., Pisani, V. D., Tilkin, J. M., Sellers, D., McGuire, M., & Gibbons, R. D. (1987). A double-blind, placebo-controlled trial of lithium carbonate therapy for alcoholism. *Archives of General Psychiatry, 44*(3), 248–256.

Fawcett, J., Clark, D. C., Gibbons, R. D., Aagesen, C. A., Pisani, V. D., Tilkin, J. M., Sellers, D., & Stutzman, D. (1984). Evaluation of lithium therapy for alcoholism. *Journal of Clinical Psychiatry, 45*(12), 494–499.

Fishbein, H. A. (1985). Precipitants of hospitalization in insulin-dependent diabetes mellitus (IDDM): A statewide perspective. *Diabetes Care, 8*(Suppl. 1), 61–64.

Fishbein, M., & Ajzen, I. (1975). *Belief, attitude, intention, and behavior: An introduction to theory and research.* Reading, MA: Addison-Wesley.

Flack, J. M., Novikov, S. V., & Ferrario, C. M. (1996). Benefits of adherence to antihypertensive drug therapy. *European Heart Journal, 17*(Suppl. A), 16–20.

Fletcher, S. W., Deliakis, J., Schoch, W. A., & Shapiro, S. H. (1979). Predicting blood pressure control in hypertensive patients: An approach to quality-of-care assessment. *Medical Care, 17*(3), 285–292.

Gaebel, W., & Pietzcker, A. (1985). One-year outcome of schizophrenic patients: The interaction of chronicity and neuroleptic treatment. *Pharmacopsychiatry, 18*(3), 235–239.

Gibbons, A. (1992). Exploring new strategies to fight drug-resistant microbes. *Science, 257*(5073), 1036–1038.

Given, B., Given, C. W., & Simoni, L. E. (1979). Relationships of processes of care to patient outcomes. *Nursing Research, 28*(2), 85–93.

Glanz, K. (1979). Dieticians' effectiveness and patient compliance with dietary regimens: A pilot study. *Journal of the American Dietetic Association, 75*(6), 631–636.

Glueck, C. J., Gordon, D. J., Nelson, J. J., Davis, C. E., & Tyroler, H. A. (1986). Dietary and other correlates of changes in total and low-density lipoprotein cholesterol in hypercholesterolemic men: The lipid research clinics coronary primary prevention trial. *American Journal of Clinical Nutrition, 44*(4), 489–500.

Grahl, C. (1994). Improving compliance: Solving a $100 billion problem. *Managed HealthCare*, S11–S13.

Granstrom, P. A. (1985). Progression of visual field deficits in glaucoma: Relation to compliance with pilocarpine therapy. *Archives of Ophthalmology, 103*(4), 529–531.

Hawkins, R. B. (1989). Arthroscopic stapling repair for shoulder instability: A retrospective study of 50 cases. *Arthroscopy: The Journal of Arthroscopic and Related Surgery, 5*(2), 122–128.

Hawkins, R. J., & Switlyk, P. (1993). Acute prosthetic replacement for severe fractures of the proximal humerus. *Clinical Orthopaedics and Related Research, 289*, 156–160.

Haynes, R. B., Gibson, E. S., Taylor, D. W., Bernholz, C. D., & Sackett, D. L. (1982). Process versus outcome in hypertension: A positive result. *Circulation, 65*(1), 28–33.

Haynes, R. B., Sackett, D. L., Gibson, E. S., Taylor, D. W., Hackett, B. C., Roberts, R. S., & Johnson, A. L. (1976). Improvement of medication compliance in uncontrolled hypertension. *Lancet 1*, 1265–1268.

Hyman, M. D., Insull, W. Jr., Palmer, R. H., O'Brien, J., Gordon, L., & Levine, B. (1982). Assessing methods for measuring compliance with a fat-controlled diet. *American Journal of Public Health, 72*(2), 152–160.

Janz, N. K., & Becker, M. H. (1984). The Health Belief Model: A decade later. *Health Education Quarterly, 11*(1), 1–47.

Jones, J. K., Gorkin, L., Lian, J. F., Staffa, J. A., & Fletcher, A. P. (1995). Discontinuation of and changes in treatment after start of new courses of antihypertensive drugs: A study of a United Kingdom population. *British Medical Journal, 311*(7000), 293–295.

Kalil, R.S.N., Heim-Duthoy, K. L., & Kasiske, B. L. (1992). Patients with a low income have reduced renal allograft survival. *American Journal of Kidney Diseases, 20*(1), 63–69.

Kass, M. A., Meltzer, D. W., Gordon, M., Cooper, D., & Goldberg, J. (1986). Compliance with topical pilocarpine treatment. *American Journal of Ophthalmology, 101*(5), 515–523.

Keefe, F. J., & Blumenthal, J. A. (1980). The life fitness program: A behavioral approach to making exercise a habit. *Journal of Behavior Therapy and Experimental Psychology, 11*(1), 31–34.

King, A. C., & Frederiksen, L. W. (1984). Low-cost strategies for increasing exercise behavior: Relapse preparation training and social support. *Behavior Modification, 8*(1), 3–21.

King, A. C., Taylor, C. B., Haskell, W. L., & DeBusk, R. F. (1988). Strategies for increasing early adherence to and long-term maintenance of home-based exercise training in healthy middle-aged men and women. *American Journal of Cardiology, 61*(8), 628–632.

Kirscht, J. P., Kirscht, J. L., & Rosenstock, I. M. (1981). A test of interventions to increase adherence to hypertensive medical regimens. *Health Education Quarterly, 8*(3), 261–272.

Klopovich, P. M., & Trueworthy, R. C. (1985). Adherence to chemotherapy regimens among children with cancer. *Topics in Clinical Nursing, 7*(1), 19–25.

Lanza, R. P., Cooper, D. K. C., Boyd, S. T., & Barnard, C. N. (1984). Comparison of patients with ischemic, myopathic, and rheumatic heart diseases as cardiac transplant recipients. *American Heart Journal, 107*(1), 8–12.

Leff, J., Berkowitz, R., Shavit, N., Strachan, A., Glass, I., & Vaughn, C. (1989). A trial of family therapy v. a relatives group for schizophrenia. *British Journal of Psychiatry, 154*, 58–66.

Leventhal, H., Meyer, D., & Nerenz, D. (1980). The common-sense representation of illness danger. In S. Rachman (Ed.), *Medical psychology* (pp. 7–30). New York: Pergamon.

Lichtenstein, M. J., Shields, S. L., Shiavi, R. G, & Burger, C. (1989). Exercise and balance in aged women: A pilot controlled clinical trial. *Archives of Physical Medicine and Rehabilitation, 70*(2), 138–143.

Lip, G.Y.H., & Brodie, M. J. (1992). Sudden death in epilepsy: An avoidable outcome? *Journal of the Royal Society of Medicine, 85*(10), 609–611.

Lipid Research Clinics Program. (1984a). The Lipid Research Clinics Coronary Primary Prevention Program Trial results: I. Reduction in incidence of coronary heart disease. *Journal of the American Medical Association, 251(3)*, 351–364.

Lipid Research Clinics Program. (1984b). The Lipid Research Clinics Coronary Primary Prevention Program Trial results: II. The relationship of reduction in incidence of coronary heart disease to cholesterol lowering. *Journal of the American Medical Association, 251(3)*, 365–374.

Logan, A. G., Milne, B. J., Achber, C., Campbell, W. P., & Haynes R. B. (1979). Work site treatment of hypertension by specially trained nurses. *Lancet, 2*(8153), 1175–1178.

Mantonakis, J. E., Jemos, J. J., Christodoulou, G. N., & Lykouras, E. P. (1982). Short-term social prognosis of schizophrenia. *Acta Psychiatrica Scandinavica, 66*(4), 306–310.

Maronde, R. F., Chan, L. S., Larsen, F. J., Strandberg, L. R., Laventurier, M. F., & Sullivan, S. R. (1989). Underutilization of antihypertensive drugs and associated hospitalization. *Medical Care, 27*(12), 1159–1166.

Mason, J. O. (1992). Addressing the measles epidemic. *Public Health Reports, 107*(3), 241–242.

Mattson, R. H., & Friedman, R. B. (1984). Medication adherence assessment in clinical trials. *Journal of Controlled Clinical Trials, 5*(4), 488–496.

McCann, B. S., Follette, W. C., Driver, J. L., Brief, D. J., & Knopp, R. H. (1988, August). *Self-efficacy and adherence in the dietary treatment of hyperlipidemia.* Paper presented at the American Psychological Association 96th Annual Convention, Atlanta, GA.

McKenney, J. M., Munroe, W. P., & Wright, J. T., Jr. (1992). Impact of an electronic medication compliance aid on long-term blood pressure control. *Journal of Clinical Pharmacology, 32*(3), 277–283.

Morisky, D. E., Levine, D. M., Green, L. W., Shapiro, S., Russell, R. P., & Smith, C. R. (1983). Five-year blood pressure control and mortality following health education for hypertensive patients. *American Journal of Public Health, 73*(2), 153–162.

Morell, R. W., Park, D. C., Kidder, D. P., & Martin, M. (1997). Adherence to antihypertensive medications across the life span. *The Gerontologist, 37*(5), 609–619.

Mulrow, C., Bailey, S., Sonksen, P. H., & Slavin, B. (1987). Evaluation of an Audiovisual Diabetes Education Program: Negative results of a randomized trial of patients with non-insulin-dependent diabetes mellitus. *Journal of General Internal Medicine,2*(4), 215–219.

Nichol, K. L., Margolis, K. L., Wuorenma, J., & VonSternberg, T. (1994). Efficacy and cost effectiveness of vaccination against influenza among elderly persons living in the community. *New England Journal of Medicine, 331*, 778–784.

Nolan, C. M., Aitken, M. L., Elarth, A. M., Anderson, K. M., & Miller, W. T. (1986). Active tuberculosis after isoniazid chemoprophylaxis of Southeast Asian refugees. *American Review of Respiratory Disease, 133*(3), 431–436.

Norell, S. E. (1981). Monitoring compliance with pilocarpine therapy. *American Journal of Ophthalmology, 92*(5), 727–731.

O'Donnell, D., Sevitz, H., Seggie, J. L., Meyers, A. M., Botha, J. R., & Myburgh, J. A. (1985). Pregnancy after renal transplantation. *Australian and New Zealand Journal of Medicine, 15*(3), 320–325.

Oldridge, N. B. (1984). Compliance and dropout in cardiac exercise rehabilitation. *Journal of Cardiac Rehabilitation, 4*(5), 166–177.

Oldridge, N. B. (1988). Cardiac rehabilitation exercise programme: Compliance and compliance-enhancing strategies. *Sports Medicine, 6*(1), 42–55.

Park, D. C., Willis, S. L., Morrow, D., Diehl, M., & Gaines, C. L. (1994). Cognitive function and medication usage in older adults. *Journal of Applied Gerontology, 13*(1), 39–57.

Pate, R. R., Pratt, M., Blair, S. N., Haskell, W. L., Macera, C. A., Bouchard, C., Buchner, D., Ettinger, W., Heath, G. W., King, A. C., Kriska, A., Leon, A. S., Marcus, B. H., Morris, J., Paffenbarger, R. S., Patrick, K., Pollock, M. L., Rippe, J. A., Sallis, J., & Wilmore, J. H. (1995). Physical activity and public health: A recommendation from the Centers for Disease Control and Prevention and the American College of Sports Medicine. *Journal of the American Medical Association, 273*(5), 402–407.

Peterson, G. M., McLean, S., & Millingen, K. S. (1984). A randomized trial of strategies to improve patient compliance with anticonvulsant therapy. *Epilepsia, 25*(4), 412–417.

Petitti, D. B., Friedman, G. D., & Kahn, W. (1981). Accuracy of information on smoking habits provided on self-administered research questionnaires. *American Journal of Public Health, 71*(3), 308–311.

Pisani, V. D., Fawcett, J., Clark, D. C., & McGuire, M. (1993). The relative contributions of medication adherence and AA meeting attendance to abstinent outcome for chronic alcoholics. *Journal of Studies on Alcohol, 54*(1), 115–119.

Psaty, B. M., Koepsell, T. D., Wagner, E. H., LoGerfo, J. P., & Inui, T. S. (1990). The relative risk of incident coronary heart disease associated with recently stopping the use of beta-blockers. *Journal of the American Medical Association, 263*(12),1653–1657.

Rand, C. S., & Wise, R. A. (1994). Measuring adherence to asthma medication regimens. *American Journal of Respiratory and Critical Care Medicine, 149*(2, P. 2), S69–S76.

Reed, B. D., Lutz, L. J., Zazove, P., & Ratcliffe, S. D. (1984). Compliance with acute otitis media treatment. *Journal of Family Practice, 19*(5), 627–632.

Reynolds, E. H. (1987). Early treatment and prognosis of epilepsy. *Epilepsia, 28*(2), 97–106.

Richardson, J. L., Shelton, D. R., Krailo, M., & Levine, A. M.. (1990). The effect of compliance with treatment on survival among patients with hematologic malignancies. *Journal of Clinical Oncology, 8*(2), 356–364.

Robertson, C. F., Rubinfeld, A. R., & Bowes, G. (1992). Pediatric asthma deaths in Victoria: The mild are at risk. *Pediatric Pulmonology, 13*(2), 95–100.

Rogers, F., Juneau, M., Taylor, C. B., Haskell, W. L., Kraemer, H. C., Ahn, D. K., & DeBusk, R. F. (1987). Assessment by a microprocessor of adherence to home-based moderate-intensity exercise training in healthy, sedentary middle-aged men and women. *American Journal of Cardiology, 60*(1), 71–75.

Rives, K., Gelberman, R., Smith, B., & Carney, K. (1992). Severe contractures of the proximal interphalangeal joint in Dupuytren's disease: Results of a prospective trial of operative correction and dynamic extension splinting. *Journal of Hand Surgery, 17*(6), 1153–1159.

Rosenstock, I. M. (1974). The historical origins of the health belief model. *Health Education Monographs, 2,* 328–335.

Rovelli, M., Palmeri, D., Vossler, E., Bartus, S., Hull, D., & Schweizer, R. (1989). Noncompliance in organ transplant recipients. *Transplantation Proceedings, 21*(1, P. 1), 833–834.

Rudd, P., Ahmed, S., Zachary, V. Barton, C., & Bonduelle, D. (1990). Improved compliance measures: Applications in an ambulatory hypertensive drug trial. *Clinical Pharmacology and Therapeutics, 48*(6), 676–685.

Schlenk, E. A., Okifuji, A., Dunbar-Jacob, J. M., & Turk, D. C. (1996). Exercise adherence in fibromyalgia. *Arthritis and Rheumatism, 39*(9, Suppl.), S221.

Schron, E. B., Hamilton, G., Rand, C., Friedman, R., Dunbar-Jacob, J., & Sereika, S. (1995, May). *Adherence in clinical trials: Ancillary studies of strategies to improve adherence.* Paper presented at a workshop at the 16th Annual Meeting of the Society for Clinical Trials, Seattle, WA.

Schwarzmann, S. W. (1998). Novel cost-effective approaches to the treatment of community-acquired infections. *Annals of Pharmacotherapy, 32*(1), S27–S30.

Schweizer, R. T., Rovelli, M., Palmeri, D., Vossler, E., Hull, D., & Bartus, S. (1990). Noncompliance in organ transplant recipients. *Transplantation, 49*(2), 374–377.

Simkin-Silverman, L., Wing, R. R., Hansen, D. H., Klem, M. L., Pasagian-Macaulay, A. P., Meilahn, E. N., & Kuller, L. H. (1995). Prevention of cardiovascular risk factor elevations in healthy premenopausal women. *Preventive Medicine, 24*(5), 509–517.

Singh, R. B., Niaz, M. A., Ghosh, S., Singh, R., & Rastogi, S. S. (1993). Effect on mortality and reinfarction of adding fruits and vegetables to a prudent diet in the Indian experiment of infarct survival (IEIS). *Journal of the American College of Nutrition, 12*(3), 255–261.

Starlinger, M., Appel, W. H., Schemper, M., & Schiessel, R. (1985). Long-term treatment of peptic esophageal stenosis with dilation and cimetidine: Factors influencing clinical result. *European Surgical Research, 17*(4), 207–214.

Swank, R. L., & Dugan, B. B. (1990). Effect of low saturated fat diet in early and late cases of multiple sclerosis. *Lancet, 336*(8706), 37–39.

Taal, E., Rasker, J. J., Seydel, E. R., & Weigman, O. (1993). Health status, adherence with health recommendations, self-efficacy and social support in patients with rheumatoid arthritis. *Patient Education and Counseling, 20*(2–3), 63–76.

Urquhart, J., & Chevalley, C. (1988). Impact of unrecognized dosing errors on the cost and effectiveness of pharmaceuticals. *Drug Information Journal, 22,* 363–378.

U.S. Department of Health and Human Services. (1996). *Physical activity and health: A report of the Surgeon General Executive Summary.* Rockville, MD: Author.

Vanhove, G. F., Schapiro, J. M., Winters, M. A., Merigan, T. C., & Blaschke, T. F. (1996). Patient compliance and drug failure in protease inhibitor monotherapy. *Journal of the American Medical Association, 276*(24), 1955–1956.

Verghese, A., John, J. K., Rajkumar, S., Richard, J., Sethi, B. B., & Trivedi, J. K. (1989). Factors associated with the course and outcome of schizophrenia in India: Results of a two-year multicentre follow-up study. *British Journal of Psychiatry, 154,* 499–503.

Westfall, U. E. (1986). Methods for assessing compliance. *Topics in Clinical Nursing, 7*(4), 23–30.

Wetsteyn, J. C. F. M., & deGeus, A. (1993). Comparison of three regimens for malaria prophylaxis in travelers to east, central, and southern Africa. *British Medical Journal, 307*(6911), 1041–1043.

White, K., Kolman, M. L., Wexler, P., Polin G., & Winter, R. J. (1984). Unstable diabetes and unstable families: A psychosocial evaluation of diabetic children with recurrent ketoacidosis. *Pediatrics, 73*(6), 749–755.

Wilson, D. P., & Endres, R. K. (1986). Compliance with blood glucose monitoring in children with type I diabetes mellitus. *Journal of Pediatrics, 108*(6), 1022–1024.

35

Rehabilitation

Robert G. Frank
University of Florida

Rehabilitation "is defined as the development of a person to the fullest physical, psychological, social, vocational, avocational, and educational potential consistent with his or her physiological or anatomical impairment and environmental limitations. Realistic goals are determined by the person and those concerned with the patient's care. Thus, one is working to obtain optimal function, despite residual disability, even if the impairment is caused by a pathological process, it cannot be reversed, even with the best of modern medical treatment" (DeLisa, Martin, & Currie, 1988, p. 3).

Rehabilitation is a broad, interdisciplinary field, composed of "health care teams." Rehabilitation teams utilize either a multidisciplinary or an interdisciplinary approach. In the *multidisciplinary approach,* individuals from a variety of disciplines work in parallel to improve an individual's function. In contrast, *interdisciplinary teams* use a coordinated, integrated approach to treatment with a common focus on outcomes. Intrinsic to both approaches, however, is an inherent emphasis on restoring individuals to their highest level of function in multiple realms. As noted in the previous definition, psychological functions are an important rehabilitation outcome. Psychological factors have a significant influence in all domains involved in rehabilitation: physical, social, vocational, avocational, and educational. Psychologists are well accepted as a integral member of rehabilitation teams.

Over the last two decades, rehabilitation has been one of the fastest growing areas of the health care industry (Frank, Gluck, & Buckelew, 1990). The growth in rehabilitation has been fueled by a number of factors. Recent advances in medical management have led to higher survival rates for accident victims. Although survivors of traumatic injuries benefit from technological advances, many are left with residual disability requiring treatment (Frank et al., 1990). Second, the "graying of America" has led to an increase in individuals who suffer from chronic conditions, many requiring rehabilitation. Chronic conditions engender significant health care costs. In the Medicare program, for example, 10% of the beneficiaries account for 70% of medical expenditures (Hoffman, Rice, & Sung, 1995). Individuals with limitations in activities due to chronic conditions account for only 17% of the population, but 47% of the medical expenditures. As many as 100 million Americans had chronic conditions in 1995, and per capita costs for these individuals are three times higher than individuals without chronic health care costs (Hoffman et al., 1995).

THE DEVELOPMENT OF REHABILITATION

Rehabilitation's growth has been tied to armed conflicts that have produced large numbers of disabled individuals. After World War I, improvements in battlefield management led to an increased number of veterans with residual disabilities. During World War II, dramatic improvements in battlefield management, and accompanying residual disability, led to the development of a medical specialty in the area of rehabilitation. The term *physiatrist,* originally used in 1938 to describe a physician specializing in rehabilitation, gained prominence. Until World War II, rehabilitation consisted of enabling individuals to ambulate to perform low energy activities. During World War II, Howard A. Rusk, a prominent early physiatrist, demonstrated that aggressive rehabilitation, including early ambulation after surgery, diverse recreational activities of varying intensity, and psychologically supported programs produced better outcomes (Frank et al., 1990).

Medicare is the primary payment source for rehabilitation programs. Almost half of all rehabilitation care is funded by Medicare and a quarter of all rehabilitation outpatient stays

(Frank et al., 1990). Changes in Medicare payment policy have enormous implications for rehabilitation and the post-acute care segment as these services were the fastest growing component of Medicare during the 1990s (MedPac, 1998).

In 1983, Congress amended the Social Security Act (PubL. No. 98-21) to create a prospective payment system for 467 diagnoses (or DRGs). Under this Prospective Payment System (PPS), a hospital was paid a fixed, determined amount for each diagnostic group. Free-standing rehabilitation units, psychiatric and pediatric units, and separate inpatient rehabilitation hospitals were exempted from the implementation of PPS. Rehabilitation's exemption from prospective payment led to a boom in rehabilitation hospitals and units. New models of care developed as a function of the change in payment methodologies. With the advent of prospective payment, care was divided into an acute and post-acute phase. Hospitals were rewarded for minimizing the acute treatment and moving patients rapidly to the rehabilitation or post-acute program, where payment limitations were less restrictive (Frank et al., 1990).

Exemption of rehabilitation from the prospective payment system led to an explosion in the number of post-acute care providers and the availability of services. The incentives to transfer patients from the acute to the post-acute environment led health care systems to develop methods of transferring much sicker patients to the post-acute environment. Financial incentives from Medicare that the payment policy created by the exemption from prospective payment for rehabilitation and post-acute services contributed to this surge of growth in rehabilitation. Within the post-acute environment, differentiation among providers emerged. Lower cost skilled nursing facilities (SNFs) began to compete with rehabilitation units and hospitals. The trend toward moving sicker patients to less intensive care settings extended to skilled nursing facilities. Patients that previously had been treated only in rehabilitation units were transferred to SNFs with no apparent decrement in the quality of their care. The growth in SNFs put substantial pressure on rehabilitation facilities. According to the language of the prospective payment exemption, rehabilitation facilities are limited to 10 specific conditions, most of which are musculoskeletal and neurological (MedPac, 1998).

In 1997, in the Balanced Budget Act, Congress modified the exemption from prospective payment. By expanding the definition of transfers, the breadth of the exemption from DRGs has narrowed substantially. Now, post-acute stays are more integrated into the payment for acute stays. This modification is creating another round of evolution in the post-acute sector. The benefit of transferring patients to post-acute stays has been reduced, and hospitals will no longer be incentivized to transfer to post-acute stays (MedPac, 1998).

Changes in payment methodology, as well as overall changes in health care delivery systems, portend rapid, continued evolvement of rehabilitation, as well as other health care delivery models. Historically, changes in payment methodology for clinical interventions in rehabilitation have preceded periods of rapid evolution in clinical delivery systems.

Within rehabilitation, there has been increased recognition of the parallels between primary care delivery models and the comprehensive care provided to individuals with disability in rehabilitation settings. Because disabling conditions also have pervasive effects across a spectrum of health needs, rehabilitation providers often provide comprehensive care to the individual with disability. Although technically a tertiary service, rehabilitation defies traditional classification. In contrast to traditional tertiary care providers, rehabilitation providers often focus across multiple organ systems addressing comprehensive health issues providing continuous care. This model of care, labeled the "cardinal symptom" approach, recognizes that a disabling condition can become the focus of health care. A disability may affect so many aspects of individuals' health care, that their health care is essentially defined by the condition. The consequences of a disability (e.g., spinal cord injury, MS, or brain injury) may interact pervasively to require that a typical tertiary care provider, such as a rehabilitation specialist, becomes the manager of all health care, much like a primary care clinician (Frank, 1997, 1999). In the "cardinal symptom" model, the rehabilitation provider uses primary care clinicians as consultants. This stands in contrast to the typical model in which the primary care clinician uses specialists as consultants.

Although psychologists have been integrated into rehabilitation care since the inception of the field, recognition of models of care (such as the cardinal symptom approach) creates unique opportunities for psychologists. Psychologists' skills readily exploit "cardinal symptom" management. Many psychologists working in rehabilitation settings provide continuous, comprehensive psychological services to their patients. In addition, psychologists often coordinate care and assure continuity of services from other providers. As psychologists' work with individuals attempting to reintegrate into their communities after experiencing a disabling condition, psychological factors often interact with medical outcomes and community limitations. As health care delivery systems evolve, alternative models of primary care (e.g., the cardinal symptom approach, in which specialists manage most aspects of care) using primary care providers as consultants will be more common. Psychologists working with individuals regarding adjustment to chronic symptoms will often coordinate other aspects of care. Undoubtedly, future psychologists practicing in rehabilitation settings will see substantial opportunities to coordinate care as cardinal symptom managers.

THE CONTEXT OF REHABILITATION

Three concepts—impairment, disability, and handicap—are critical to understanding rehabilitation. *Impairment* includes any loss or abnormality of psychological, physiological, or anatomical structure or function. Impairment is deviation from the norm that may be temporary or permanent. It may affect only one domain such as psychological, physiological, anatomical structure or function, or all areas. Impairment may reflect the active, ongoing activity of a pathological state or may be the consequence of a disease.

Disability is "in the context of health experience, a disability is any restriction or lack (resulting from an impairment) of ability to perform an activity in the manner within the range considered normal for the human being" (World Health Organization, 1980, p. 28). Whereas functional limitations derive from impairment, the synergistic effects of impairment on the person or body as a whole constitute disability. Disability relates to the integrated activities an individual would normally address. A disability is an aspect of an individual rather than a description of the person. For example, an individual has a disability in contrast to being disabled.

In contrast to impairment and disability, *handicap* refers to the individuals' perception and assessment of their abilities. An individual is handicapped relative to the activities of others. The values and attitudes of nonhandicapped individuals play a central role in defining the concept of "handicapped." Disadvantage from handicap develops as a result of an individual being unable to perform with expected norms (World Health Organization, 1980).

PSYCHOLOGICAL FUNCTIONING

A significant concern in rehabilitation is the adjustment of the individual to the change in functions. Whether the change begins after an acute injury with rapid onset or the change is a more gradual decline associated with the slow onset of a chronic condition, psychological adjustment is critical to the outcome. As noted in the World Health Organization's definitions of disability and impairment, the psychological perception, both in terms of the individual sustaining the disabling event and from the perception of the individual evaluating the person with a disability, is critical. In evaluating psychological response or coping with disability, two primary concerns are tantamount. First, what was the individual's psychological functioning prior to the onset of the disabling event? Second, after the onset of the disabling event, what psychological skills does the individual have to cope with the event?

Initial interest in psychological response to catastrophic injury increased after World War II when individuals began routinely surviving spinal cord injury (SCI). Adjustment to such a catastrophic change in life was of significant psychological interest. An array of models were posited to describe the psychological changes associated with SCI. Most frequent were variants of stage models in which individuals evolved through a series of fixed stages of psychological reactions to the SCI (Frank et al., 1987). Stage models were generally derived from psychoanalytic theory. All stage models, regardless of the unique variations, posited a "depressive" phase. The depression was viewed as therapeutic in aiding recovery. Indeed, in many early writings, it was common for authors to dogmatically assert the absence of a depressive phase as pathological. Implicit to most early models of adjustment—derived almost universally from adjustment to spinal cord injury—was the requirement that the injuring event was the most salient distinguishing feature and was viewed as a predictor of the individual's behavior (Elliott & Frank, 1996). Individual factors, personality, and coping were all viewed as less predictive of outcome than the occurrence and onset of the disabling event (e.g., SCI). Only in the last decade has this approach been viewed as inadequate (Elliott & Frank, 1996).

Research on spinal cord injury can serve as a template to understanding adjustment to both acute and chronic catastrophic injury or illness. Although there are many holes in the empirical literature, there is now adequate evidence to show that disorders associated with disability should be viewed as similar to other psychological disorders. Evaluation should include careful review of psychological, biological, and social factors. Each leg of this triangle represents a critical and interactive vector with the other two legs. Of particular importance in the arena of rehabilitation are biological factors. In many conditions treated in rehabilitation, profound alterations of the biology of the individual occur. For example, in SCI, there is reason to believe that the adrenal-cortical function is altered by injury. Frank, Kashani, Wonderlich, Lising, and Visot (1985) found a high rate of false positives among nondepressed individuals challenged in a dextamethanone suppression test. Such findings demonstrate the complexities of understanding the contribution of biological factors to psychological functioning and impairment after catastrophic injury or illness.

DEVELOPMENTAL FACTORS IN REHABILITATION

Within the realm of psychological response to injury or illness, there is a paucity of theory and empirical data. Clearly, development in late adolescence and early adulthood is critically important in understanding psychological response to catastrophic injury as, most often, catastrophic injury occurs during late adolescence. Younger adults show more pervasive psychopathology in response to catastrophic injury, such as SCI (Frank, Elliott, Buckelew, & Haut, 1988) or amputation (Frank et al., 1984), than older adults. Other psychological factors, such as locus of control, have been shown to have significant predictive value in determining psychological adjustment to catastrophic injury or illness. For example, Frank and Elliott (1989) found individuals who had higher internal attributions of control were less depressed than patients who attributed control to chance or health personnel. In contrast, Bulman and Wortman (1977) found that patients in rehabilitation who blame themselves for their injury were rated by nursing staff as coping more effectively, although this interpretation has been criticized (Frank et al., 1987).

PSYCHOLOGICAL FACTORS IN REHABILITATION

The majority of empirical and theoretical work on adjustment to catastrophic injury or illness has focused on psychopathological responses. A plethora of studies has examined depression as well as a few other responses (e.g., anxiety or adjustment disorders). Few studies have focused on what has sometimes been labeled the "positive emotions," such as hope or courage. Indeed, even within the realm of psychopathological responses, little is known of the discreet symptoms constituting mood disorders. Hopelessness is a frequently cited symptom of depression, yet little is known of the course of hopelessness after catastrophic injury or of the factors that mitigate the emotion. There is some evidence that cognitive affective symptoms such as dysphoric mood, acknowledgment of guilt, and suicide ideation are the most efficient predictors of the development of a major depressive disorder (Frank, Chaney, Clay, & Kay, 1991). Dysphoria appears to be a core symptom in the development of depression following chronic illness or catastrophic injury (Frank et al., 1992).

Cognitive factors are significant in predicting outcome to catastrophic injury or chronic illness. It appears individuals with greater personal psychological resources who have demonstrated better adjustment before injury or illness are less likely to display depressive or other psychopathological behaviors after the incident. Although there is little direct evidence for this hypothesis, there is significant indirect support (Elliott & Frank, 1996). Elliott and colleagues found that effective skills in problem solving and greater confidence in problem solving were significantly associated with lower scores of self-import depression among individuals with spinal cord injury. In other work, Elliott, Witty, Herrick, and Hoffman (1991) found that higher levels of hope and goal-directed energy are associated with less distress, regardless of time since injury onset. Social and cognitive characteristics (e.g., problem solving, hope, and locus of control) play significant roles in mediating the outcome of adjustment to catastrophic injury or illness (Elliott & Frank, 1996).

INTERPERSONAL ASPECTS OF ADJUSTMENT

Interpersonal dynamics also mediate adjustment to catastrophic illness or injury. Overall, psychopathological responses to catastrophic injury are overdiagnosed by staff in rehabilitation settings (Frank et al., 1987). The skill of rehabilitation staff in diagnosing depression varies considerably across disciplines (Caplan, 1983; Frank et al., 1987). Although rehabilitation staff overdiagnose depression, the presence of depressive symptoms also alters the interpersonal dynamic.

In a series of studies, Frank and colleagues (1987) demonstrated that individuals with catastrophic injury may receive more ingenuine feedback and support than depressed, noninjured persons. Consequently, many individuals with catastrophic injury or chronic illness may receive more complex, less clear responses from individuals around them. In addition, rehabilitation staff have been found to have more hostile and anxious feelings after listening to individuals with disabling conditions present as depressed. The stigma of disabling conditions pressures individuals with disabilities to monitor their demeanor and to maintain an optimistic and positive attitude. The manifestation of dysphoria or depression results in more punitive responses to the behavior of the individual with disability (Frank et al., 1987).

The role of families in the adjustment of individuals with disability is significant (Frank, 1994). The interaction between family function and the recovery of an individual with catastrophic injury or chronic illness is poorly understood. It is now clear that families with enhanced problem-solving and behavioral coping strategies are more facilitative to effective adjustment (Leach, Frank, Bouman, & Farmer, 1994). Assessment of family functioning and its contribution to individual outcome is complex. The domains of both the parent and child must be individually assessed, and the interaction of these relationships also must be reviewed (Frank et al., 1998).

Disease status may be independent of psychological perceptions and skills. Comprehensive assessment of individual adjustment to catastrophic injury or illness is now recognized as a multidimensional process. Individuals appear to adapt according to psychological skills and attributes, personality factors, biological factors, and environmental responses. Within these multiple domains, common adaption models can be articulated. In contrast to historic approaches that have attempted to define adjustment according to the impeding event (e.g., spinal cord injury, traumatic brain injury, rheumatoid arthritis), more recent approaches evaluate individual attributes, environmental factors, and the biology of the illness yielding cohorts presenting of common psychological responses. Frank and colleagues (1998) showed how common trajectories of adaption to chronic illness can be developed that classify individuals and their families. Critical to this approach is recognition that individuals and their families change continuously; factors such as the disabling condition, individual and family development, and psychological and environmental factors all modify the response.

THE SOCIAL PSYCHOLOGY OF DISABILITY

Research on attitudes of individuals toward persons with disabilities is more than half a century old. Nondisabled persons tend to hold an unfavorable attitude toward persons with disability, although some authors have suggested that societal opinion is more ambivalent than prejudicial (Dunn, in press). Individuals without disability often intentionally ignore people with disabilities to suppress emotional reactions. This creates an environment of rejection and isolation for individuals with a disability. Most often, the "just world" hypothesis (Lerner, 1980) has been invoked to describe the attitude of individuals without disability toward those with disability. The "just world" theory holds that people believe good things should happen to good people and bad things, such as disability, happen to bad individuals. To maintain this view, nondisabled people must devalue or castigate individuals with disability. Not all views of individuals with disability are negative in content. Individuals with disability can be viewed as coping with their impairment in an ennobling or otherwise outstanding manner. Such attitudes place undue emphasis on the disability, ignoring the individual's abilities (Yuker, 1994). Typically in social interactions, the disability becomes a pervasive characteristic of the individuals with little attention paid to their other attributes or abilities.

Individuals with disability can establish positive interactions by reducing the discomfort of the able-bodied individual. When individuals with disability recognize their disability, assertively request assistance, or express interest in other people and common topics, or display adaptive emotional adjustment to the disability, they are more accepted by individuals without disability (Dunn, in press).

Recently, increasing attention has been paid to the construct of reality negotiation as a useful organizing principle respecting the multiple perspectives applicable in rehabilitation (Dunn, in press). Reality negotiation occurs when individuals rely on cognitive strategies to promote favorable beliefs about the self and situations that threaten self-esteem and well-being (Elliott et al., 1991). Reality negotiation utilizes an array of important constructs that appear to have relevance to rehabilitation, including positive illusions (Taylor & Brown, 1988), dispositional optimism (Scheier, Carver, & Bridges, 1994), attributional style (Peterson, Maier, & Seligman, 1993), control (Heckhausen & Schultz, 1995), locus of control (Leftcourt & Davidson-Katz, 1991), and hope (Snyder, 1994). In practice, it is difficult to empirically evaluate the person–environment interaction when considering adjustment or reactions to disability (Dunn, in press).

DESCRIPTION OF REHABILITATION INTERVENTIONS

Rehabilitation has applications to a staggering array of health conditions. Most often, attention has been directed to acquired conditions that limit function. As noted earlier, spinal cord injury has been an area of interest for all disciplines involved in rehabilitation. More recently, as survival after traumatic brain injury has increased, much attention has been directed to that field. Although SCI piqued interest in the psychology of adjustment to catastrophic injury, the first catastrophic injury with a high survival rate was amputation. In the following section, each of these conditions is reviewed to provide perspective on rehabilitation psychology. Spinal cord injury is examined in greatest detail. The rehabilitation treatment issues elaborated here have relevance to all rehabilitation treatment. Congenital conditions or disabling conditions of childhood are not discussed.

Spinal Cord Injury

Treatment of spinal cord injury (SCI) has defined the development of rehabilitation psychology. Although rehabilitation psychology is much broader than this single condition, the work of rehabilitation psychologists in virtually every aspect of the treatment of individuals with SCI has defined the broader context of rehabilitation psychology. In SCI, the psychological treatment needs of the individual and family change through out the individual's life span. Although adjustment to disability is often the initial issue motivating referral to a psychologist, psychological treatments associated with SCI are diverse. Treatments may range from behavioral approaches to managing bladder dysfunction, to family or marital therapy, consultation with treating professionals regarding sadness arising from repeated exposure to profound loss, to psychological issues the individuals with injury encounter related to their disability.

The prevalence of spinal cord injury in the United States is about 906/1,000,000, yielding 230,000 living individuals with SCI in 1992 (Richards, Kewman, & Pierce, in press). More than half of all injuries occur in individuals from age 16 to 30, with men making up almost 80% of all spinal cord injury cases (Richards et al., in press).

Damage to the spinal cord may result in a complete or incomplete lesion. An incomplete lesion results in some sparing of neurologic function in the spinal cord. Complete lesions sever all function of the cord. Neurologic level refers to the lowest level of the spinal cord with intact sensory and/or motor function (although motor and sensory functions may have different neurological levels and may affect the sides of the body differently). Paraplegia results from loss of function in the thoracic, lumbar, or sacral portions of the spinal cord; arm and hand function are intact. Tetraplegia results from injury to the cervical portion of the spinal cord; arm and hand function are impaired.

Spinal cord injury creates a number of unique and vexing problems both in daily function and psychological adjustment. Substance abuse, related to both alcohol and drugs, is common among individuals with spinal cord injury. Substance abuse is frequently a factor in the injury. Many spinal cord rehabilitation programs address substance abuse. Sexuality can be profoundly impaired by spinal cord injury. Depending on the level of neurological deficit, males can experience impairment of "psychogenic erections" (i.e., erections solely triggered by mental or nontactile stimulation). Patients with complete upper motor neuron lesions are likely to have reflex erections (i.e., automatic erections typically stimulated by contact that can occur in the absence of arousal). These erections cannot reach adequate tumescence to allow sexual intercourse. Ejaculation in psychogenic erections are unlikely in this group.

In men with complete lower motor neuron lesions, about one in four is able to have a psychogenic erection and is less likely to have reflex erections. About one in five of these individuals is able to ejaculate. Even in those individuals able to ejaculate, fertility often is problematic, because sperm counts tend to be low (Richards et al., in press). Women with SCI are capable of achieving orgasm. A substantial portion of women post-SCI may be able to be taught manipulation techniques that could improve sexual response and experience. Hormonal and menstrual cycles in women are altered after spinal cord injury, and appropriate birth control counseling should be emphasized. The absence of stimulation often leads many women to the erroneous belief that they are not able to get pregnant.

Spinal cord injury is associated with a number of secondary complications that are preventable and costly. Psychological interventions have pertinence to the behavioral factors involved in the development of these complications. Two of the most common disabling, and costly, secondary complications are pressure ulcers and urinary tract infections. The occurrence of each of these secondary complications can be lessened if the individual with SCI utilizes effective and routine self-care methods.

Pressure ulcers result from restriction of blood flow to the skin that depletes available oxygen resulting in degeneration of tissue, lack of sensory input, and impaired mobility. The skin is sensitive to even moderate, persistent pressure. Atrophy, repetitive trauma, scarring, and/or secondary bacterial infection, shearing force, and reduced transcutaneous oxygen tension are major etiologic factors. Sites most prone to the development of pressure ulcers are bony prominence such as the sacrum, ischium, heels, ankles, and trochanter.

Pressure ulcers are one of the most common debilitating secondary complications of SCI, and severity of pressure ulcers varies. Treatments range from bed rest, or "down time," to surgery. Enormous cost is associated with surgical intervention. More than a decade ago, surgical intervention for a pressure ulcer cost more than $60,000 per case (Stover, Whiteneck, & DeLisa, 1995). Over time, most individuals with SCI will develop pressure ulcers.

Coping with spinal cord injury requires exacting self-care. Skin pressure must be relieved at least every 30 minutes, fluid consumption must be monitored, skin must be inspected daily, and a balanced diet must be maintained. A person's ability and motivation to follow this complex regiment can be affected by poor psychological adjustment to injury or the presence of overshadowing psychopathology or substance abuse. In addition, depressed individuals may be prone to self-neglect. Untreated or improperly treated pressure ulcers will not heal and tend to be potentially life threatening.

The incidence of renal failure secondary to recurrent urinary tract infections (UTI) in persons with physical disability has decreased markedly. Despite this decrease, UTI remains a common event after spinal cord injury, because a complex regimen is required to manage bladder function. The bladder must be managed to establish and maintain unrestricted urine flow from the kidneys and to maintain urine sterility and bladder continence, thereby preserving renal function. Neurologic damage that affects control of the bladder coupled with the need for catheters to facilitate emptying result in impairment of normal anatomic and physiological defense mechanisms responsible for eliminating bacteria and maintaining urine sterility. In the neurogenic bladder, stagnant residual urine allows bacteria to accumulate leading to bladder infections.

Psychological variables, personal hygiene, and the ability to understand and implement the treatment regiment are all prerequisites for effective management of bladder dysfunction associated with SCI. Similarly, the prevention of pressure ulcers requires a complex self-care regiment. Management of bladder dysfunction and prevention of pressure ulcers following spinal cord injury are two vivid examples of the high need for self-care following spinal cord injury. A number of psychological parameters interact with these treatment regiments altering health outcomes. Failure to follow these treatment regiments can result in serious medical complications, high cost hospitalizations, and impaired health for the individual with SCI. Although routine education regarding self-care and prevention often is provided by other professionals, rehabilitation psychologists have an important role in the educational process, scientific understanding of the behavioral aspects, and the treatment of poor regiment compliance. Relatively little attention has been directed to these important areas within the rehabilitation psychology literature and in the clinical literature. The opportunity to impact these important self-treatment skills through telemedicine interventions, better definition of risk factors, and better assessment of cognitive and behavioral skills required for effective self-care and the role of primary care giving is needed.

Psychological interventions with individuals who sustain SCI have been fairly common. Interestingly, although there has been a strong interest among psychologists in spinal cord injury, many of the individuals who sustain spinal cord injuries are not introspective individuals (Rohe & Krause, 1993). Consequently, a number of models of intervention have been developed for spinal cord rehabilitation units. Often, psychologists work with physicians and other staff to indirectly treat the individual. Psychological services can be packaged as part of the rehabilitation treatment. Routine referral to the psychology service can destigmatize the process and reduce resistance (Richards et al., in press). Increasingly, there has been an emphasis on educational approaches to psychological treatment. Group sessions are common, and information regarding areas such as coping, stress management, common psychological changes, and physiological changes after spinal cord injury are presented in a didactic model with discussion. Introduction of family members into treatment groups allows treatment of broader systems. An important aspect of these groups is the management of interpersonal reactions to spinal cord injury. Spinal cord injury is a stigmatizing condition that can result in excessive reactions from individuals lacking experience with persons with disabilities (Frank & Elliott, 1987). Individuals with spinal cord injury face strong pulls for cheerful and optimistic demeanor. The manifestation of depression or other aberrant psychological states results in rejection and alienation (Frank & Elliott, 1987). In addition, rehabilitation settings can demand "appropriate" psychological responses to injury such as grieving and depression. Individuals who fail to exhibit these responses may be pressured to respond according to more appropriate "norms" (Frank & Elliott, 1987).

Treatment of caregivers and families can be a critical part of rehabilitation after SCI. Caregiving requirements for persons with SCI can range dramatically. Individuals with high level tetraplegia can be entirely dependent, whereas low level paraplegics can be essentially independent. The adjustment of the individual with SCI has been studied frequently, but much less is known of the reaction of caregivers to SCI. It is known that individuals with SCI demand increases in emotional and physical duties of care providers, especially in the first year postinjury (Shewchuk, Richards, & Elliott, 1998). Also, it is known that, over time, SCI creates significant deterioration in functioning of families with a member with SCI (McGowan & Roth, 1986).

Elements of social support have been found to be associated with adjustments following spinal cord injury. Relationships that provide a sense of attachment and intimacy have been associated positively with more satisfying spare time activity (Elliott & Shewchuk, 1995). Physical symptoms and anxiety have been shown to be highly interdependent in a study of caregivers and individuals with spinal cord injuries. Anxiety was found to be a salient predictor of the initial levels of and rate of change in physical symptoms of the caregivers. Physical symptoms in younger patients received significantly predictive initial levels of anxiety. Physical symptoms and positive affect predicted initial levels of depressive behavior among caregivers. Expressive social support predicted the rate of change and anxiety in depressive behavior over time (Shewchuk et al., 1998). Finds such as this underscore the need for longitudinal assessment of family and dynamics after spinal cord injury.

Caregiver problem-solving ability is pertinent to the outcomes of the individual with spinal cord injury. In a recent study, depressive behavior at admission was significantly predictive of acceptance of disability at discharge. Caregiver tendencies to impulsively and carelessly problem solve are associated with lower acceptance of feelings at discharge. Moreover, caregiver impulsiveness/carelessness in problem-solving style was significantly predictive of pressure ulcer diagnosis at follow-up (Elliott, 1998). Overall, this finding suggests that caregiver problem-solving styles are associated with health outcomes following disability. Rehabilitation efforts need to be directed to the caregiver as well as to the individual with the disability during rehabilitation and following return to the community.

Traumatic Brain Injury

Over the last two decades, traumatic brain injury (TBI) has become one of the primary diagnostic entities treated in medical rehabilitation facilities. Traumatic brain injury comprises about 10% of the inpatient rehabilitation unit population. Overall, the incidence of TBIs is estimated to be 102.1/100,000 in the United States (Rosenthal & Ricker, in press). The pattern of behavioral cognitive and psychosocial disabilities resulting from TBI provides many opportunities for psychological interventions.

Damage to the brain from external mechanical forces, such as occurs in TBI, can result in a broad array of sequelae. Initial neurobehavioral response to injury typically is classified by the Glasgow Coma Scale (Teasdale & Jennette, 1974). The Glasgow Coma Scale assesses the patient's behavior response within the domains of eye movement, motor functions, and vocalization. The total score ranges from 3 to 15 with lower scores representing increased depth of unconsciousness. Scores of 8 or lower typically are considered severe brain injuries, whereas scores between 9 and 12 are classified as moderate injuries. The Glasgow is an excellent crude indicator of likely outcome, but it is far from a perfect predictor.

A traumatic brain injury generally is classified as a closed or open injury. A *closed brain injury* occurs when the brain, which is bathed with cerebral spinal fluid, is rapidly reaccelerated and then decelerated (most commonly in a motor vehicle accident or fall). Mechanical forces are applied to the brain in the acceleration and deceleration that produce shearing and tearing effects. The anterior aspects of the skull can become contused against the bony prominence as the brain is accelerated and decelerated. The posterior aspects of the brain meet the relatively smooth rear casing of the skull; consequently, contusions to the frontal areas of the brain, including the frontal lobes and temporal lobes, are common following TBI. Acceleration and deceleration injuries are accompanied by shearing and torquing effects as the brain rotates within the skull creating excessive pressure on the ascending and descending pathways. This widespread disruption of axonal tracks typically is referred to as diffuse axonal injury (DAI; Rosenthal & Ricker, in press). Diffuse axonal injury is a primary source of post-brain injury impairment, however, biochemical cascades occurring days to hours following the injury also are a significant factor in the residual impairment.

Open, or *penetrating, injuries* share many of the same characteristics as closed head injuries. In addition, a penetrating injury of the skull casing results in direct tissue destruction in the area of impact. Resulting mechanical changes in the brain may produce many of the same effects noted in an acceleration/deceleration injury.

Edema is a common secondary complication of most severe brain injuries and occurs when there is an increase of water concentration within the cells or between the cells or both. Edema leads to increased inner cranial pressure that may create further cerebral impairment. Following a traumatic brain injury there is an increase of the catecholamines, norepinephrine and epinephrine. This cascade of catecholamines can result in changes in glucose, cortisone, and thyroid hormones. Rosenthal and Ricker (in press) provided a more comprehensive description of biological factors associated with brain injury.

Predicting the specific deficits of TBI is difficult. Commonly, deficits in arousal, attention, memory, capacity for new learning, ability to initiate behavior, maintaining and organizing goal-directed behavior, self-awareness, language and communication, visual spatial, efficiency, agitation, aggression, decision in habitation, and oppression are observed. An individual may present one, all, or a combination of these symptoms.

Psychologists play an important role in the assessment and treatment of TBI. While an individual is on the acute (neurosurgery or medicine unit) unit, psychologists frequently are involved in assessing their recovery and gross domains of function. In addition, psychologists may work with hospital staff to develop behaviorally based treatment programs to manage difficult behaviors such as agitation, disinhibition, or aggression. Often, psychologists work with the family members of the injured individuals regarding their responses to the injury, helping family to understand the changed cognitive status of their loved ones.

Once injured individuals are transferred to the rehabilitation unit, the psychologist may become more involved in the management of their care. While continuing, in a more comprehensive manner, many of the activities in the acute unit, the psychologist also will begin more complex evaluations of the individual's cognitive and emotional functioning. This often includes a neuropsychological assessment focusing on the domains of intellectual functioning, cognitive functioning, memory, and problem solving. Although batteries utilized for this assessment vary according to practitioner preferences, a common emphasis in all batteries is the evaluation of stable cognitive skills, as well as more "fluid" areas that are more frequently affected by injury. In addition, continued involvement in behavior management is common for psychologists treating individuals with TBI. Often, behavior management programs are paired with psychopharmacological interventions designed to help modulate problem behaviors such as disinhibition or agitation. Psychologists must be knowledgeable about psychopharmacological interventions for these disorders and their effects on both the normal and impaired brain. Sensitivity to the power of the psychopharmacological effects is critical to the design of carefully titrated behavioral programs, which produce a joint treatment package that is most effective. Continued education of patients and their family regarding the issues they will face in recovery is critical to successful outcomes. Invariably, severe or moderate brain injury produces some sequelae that the individual and family must find ways to manage. Awareness of these disabilities and the ability to address these problems are critical to good outcome.

One of the more controversial areas of rehabilitation within TBI is the use of "cognitive rehabilitation." Cognitive rehabilitation emphasizes cognitive retraining to ameliorate deficits produced by injury. There are two general approaches to cognitive retraining: compensatory and restorative. The compensatory models are more congruent with general rehabilitation approaches, but place a much higher emphasis on cognitive intervention. Rosenthal and Ricker (in press) provided a more detailed description of these views. Whereas there is some promise for both types of rehabilitation, little empirical study has validated these approaches. It is likely that some specific skills, such as visual scanning, attention and concentration, and spatial organization are impacted by cognitive treatment. Such improvements are difficult to evaluate due to the lack of untreated controlled studies and difficulty developing sensitive measurement devices.

Following the rehabilitation phase, individuals are likely to return to their community for the *post-acute* phase of treatment. Post-acute refers to any treatment after rehabilitation hospitalization and may range from treatment in a sub-acute, high intensity skilled nursing facility, to treatment in the community and day treatment programs (Malec & Ponsford, in press). Many issues involved in post-acute rehabilitation are similar to those described in cognitive retraining. In addition to addressing basic cognitive deficits, post-acute programs emphasize community reintegration, the management of deficits, and the response of individuals in the communities to these deficits. Frequent emphasis is placed on the use of orthoses, or compensatory devices that can improve outcome (e.g., memory notebooks).

Like other community-based rehabilitation efforts, post-acute rehabilitation typically is managed with a transdisciplinary team. These teams are more focused on individual community integration than many other rehabilitation programs. In some countries such as Australia, there has been extensive development of community-based post-acute programs. Although such programs flourished briefly in the United States, lack of funding curtailed these programs. Post-acute programs serve individuals with a profound range of defects, ranging from gross memory and planning and motivation defects to minor levels of physical impairment. Some individuals return to work, and others are challenged by having any social activity. Moreover, the pattern of defects often is unique. The absence of a consistent outcome measure for describing post-acute outcome studies has clouded understanding of the efficacy of these programs. Generally, community integration programs appear to increase the number of individuals who can live independently in the community, but few individuals are totally independent and most continue to require some support. Community integration programs may need to provide rehabilitation interventions long after the onset of injury, perhaps for the entire life of the injured individual.

Amputation

Fifty years ago, the first study of adjusting to "misfortune among war veterans with amputations" marked the beginning of psychology's involvement in rehabilitation (Rybarczyk, Szymanski, & Nicholas, in press). Despite the early interest of psychologists in amputation, there have been relatively few studies of the psychological changes associated with this catastrophic limb loss.

The most common type of amputation is the removal of a lower extremity (90%). Men are more likely to have amputations than women, and the majority of amputations (75%) are performed in individuals over ager 65 (Rybarczyk et al., in press). Many individuals undergoing amputations have complex medical conditions leading to death for from 40% to 60% of lower extremity amputees within 2 years of the procedure. Individuals with amputation are at high risk for a second amputation in the contra-lateral leg. The common causes of amputation are vascular disease and infection, trauma, tumors, congenital deformities, or abnormalities. The majority of amputations results from vascular disease. In addition to the medical challenges associated with amputation, there are common psychological changes. As many as 62% of amputees experience dysphoria, 33% experience anxiety, 53% experience crying spells, and 47% experience insomnia (Shukla, Sahu, Tripathi, & Gupta, 1982). The incidence of depression ranges from 21% to 35% (Kashani, Frank, Kashani, Wonderlich, & Reid, 1983).

Despite these common emotional reactions, amputation can induce a wide spectrum of psychological responses. Responses range from viewing the amputation as a great personal tragedy to a "new lease on life" (Rybarczyk et al., in press). Careful assessment of psychological reactions, as well as medical comorbidities, is essential. Although conventional wisdom suggests individuals improve as a function of time from the point of amputation, there is little research to support this idea. There is little research to support systematic stages of reaction to catastrophic injury, and amputation is no exception.

Pain in the amputated limb, referred to as phantom limb pain, is a common experience after amputation, affecting from 60% to 90% of individuals (Rybarczyk et al., in press). Phantom limb pain can be continuous or episodic and most frequently is experienced shortly after surgery. About half the individuals experiencing amputation note a decrease in phantom limb pain, and the remainder experience no relief or an exacerbation of pain. The ideology of phantom limb pain is poorly understood, but appears to be higher in individuals who had amputation secondary to blood clots and in those who experienced more preamputation pain and pain in the stump following amputation.

Disability following amputation is believed to be greater for below-the-knee amputations than above-the-knee amputations. Little empirical data has been found to substantiate this belief.

CONCLUSIONS

The continuum of care for health conditions can be grossly divided into acute conditions and chronic conditions. Chronic conditions that require continuous intervention for the same medical problems include rehabilitation services. Rehabilitation is defined as goal oriented interventions designed to develop individuals to their fullest physical, psychological, social, vocational, and educational potential. Psychologists have significant opportunities in each of these domains. In addition, the evolving "post-acute" sector of care that focuses on the integration of an individual into the community following the disabling conditions offers many role opportunities for psychologist.

Rehabilitation requires a broad range of psychological skills ranging from the treatment of more common psychopathological disorders to health psychology intervention to family and marital treatment. System issues are of critical importance in rehabilitation. Both the treating milieu, including the reactions of the rehabilitation staff, the family, and the individual are critical in determining the outcome. Psychologists working in rehabilitation must be knowledgeable of systems interventions and proficient in understanding both the social psychology and the clinical psychology of disability. Increasingly, psychologists in rehabilitation are designing interventions that collate interventions at the individual, family, and community level. At the same time, these interventions also are often sensitive to the diminishment of health resources and to maintaining the individual at the highest level of individual function. Rehabilitation and the chronic sector of care offer an important paradigm for the delivery of psychological services as the number of individuals with disabilities increases in the United States. Delivery systems such as the "cardinal symptom approach" that focus on the most disabling health concerns offer psychologists opportunities to create primary care delivery roles in which they provide continuous, comprehensive, coordinated service to individuals. Although this model may defy traditional definitions of primary care, as health care delivery systems evolve to meet the needs of consumers, traditional definitions will fall by the wayside.

REFERENCES

Bulman, R. J., & Wortman, C. B. (1977). Attribution of blame and copying in the "real world": Severe accident victims react to their lot. *Journal of Personality and Social Psychology, 35,* 251–363.

Caplan, B. (1983). Staff and patient perception of patient mood. *Rehabilitation Psychology, 28,* 67–77.

DeLisa, J. A., Martin, G. M., & Currie, D. M. (1988). Rehabilitation medicine: Past, present, and future. In *Rehabilitation medicine: Principles and practice* (pp. 3–24). Philadelphia: Lippincott.

Dunn, D. S. (in press). Matters of perspective: Some social psychological issues in disability and rehabilitation. In R. G. Frank & T. R. Elliott (Eds.), *Handbook of rehabilitation psychology.* Washington, DC: American Psychological Association.

Elliott, T. R. (1998, August). *Caregiver problem solving abilities predict adjustment following SCI.* Paper presented at the convention of the Annual Convention of the American Psychological Association, San Francisco, CA.

Elliott, T. R., & Frank, R. G. (1996). Depression after spinal cord injury. *Archives of Physical Medicine and Rehabilitation, 77,* 816–823.

Elliott, T. R., & Shewchuk, R. (1995). Social support and leisure activities following severe physical disability: Testing the mediating effects of depression. *Basic Applied Social Psychology, 16,* 471–587.

Elliott, T. R., Witty, T. E., Herrick, S. E., & Hoffman, J. T. (1991). Negotiating reality after physical loss: Hope, depression, and disability. *Journal of Personality and Social Psychology, 61,* 608–613.

Frank, R. G. (1994). Families and rehabilitation. *Brain Injury, 8*(3), 193–195.

Frank, R. G. (1997). Changes in the post-acute health delivery system in the United States: International implications. *Proceedings of the 5th conference of the IATSBI and 20th conference of the Australian Society for the Study of Brain Impairment,* Melbourne, Australia, 498–502.

Frank, R. G. (1999). Organized delivery systems: Implications for clinical psychology services or we zigged when we should have zagged. *Rehabilitation Psychology, 44*(1), 36–51.

Frank, R. G., Chaney, J. M., Clay, D. L., & Kay, D. R. (1991). Depression in rheumatoid arthritis: A re-evaluation. *Rehabilitation Psychology, 36*(4), 219–230.

Frank, R. G., Chaney, J. M., Shutty, M. S., Clay, D. L., Beck, N. C., Kay, D. R., Elliott, T. R., & Gambling, S. (1992). Dysphoria: A major symptom factor in persons with disability or chronic illness. *Psychiatry Research, 43,* 231–241.

Frank, R. G., & Elliott, T. R. (1987). Life stress and psychological adjustment following spinal cord injury. *Archives of Physical Medicine and Rehabilitation, 68*(6), 344–347.

Frank, R. G., & Elliot, T. R. (1989). Spinal cord injury and health locus of control beliefs. *Paraplegia, 27*(4), 250–256.

Frank, R. G., Elliott, T. R., Buckelew, S. P., & Haut, A. E. (1988). Age as a factor in response to spinal cord injury. *American Journal of Physical Medicine and Rehabilitation, 67*(3), 128–131.

Frank, R. G., Elliott, T. R., Wonderlich, S. A., Corcoran, J. R., Umlauf, R. L., & Ashkanazi, G. S. (1987). Gender differences in interpersonal response to spinal cord injury. *Cognitive Therapy and Research, 11*(4), 437–448.

Frank, R. G., Gluck, J. P., & Buckelew, S. P. (1990). Rehabilitation: Psychology's greatest opportunity? *American Psychologist, 45*(6), 757–761.

Frank, R. G., Kashani, J. H., Kashani, S. R., Wonderlich, S. A., Umlauf, R. L., & Ashkanazi, G.S. (1984). Psychological response to amputation as a function of age and time since amputation. *British Journal of Psychiatry, 144,* 493–497.

Frank, R. G., Kashani, J. H., Wonderlich, S. A., Lising, A. A., & Visot, L. R. (1985). Depression and adrenal function in spinal cord injury. *American Journal of Psychiatry, 142*(2), 252–253.

Frank, R. G., Thayer, J. F., Hagglund, K. J., Vieth, A. Z., Schopp, L. H., Beck, N. C., Kashani, J. H., Goldstein, D. E., Cassidy, J. T., Chaney, J. M., Clay, D. L., Hewett, J. E. & Johnson, J. C. (1998). Trajectories of adaptation in pediatric chronic illness: The importance of the individual. *Journal of Consulting and Clinical Psychology, 66*(3), 521–532.

Heckhausen, J., & Schulz, R. (1995). A life-span theory of control. *Psychological Review, 102,* 284–304.

Hoffman, C., Rice, D., & Sung, H. Y. (1995). Persons with chronic conditions; Their prevalence and costs. *Journal of the American Medical Association, 276,* 1473–1479.

Kashani, J. H., Frank, R. G., Kashani, S. R., Wonderlich, S. A., & Reid, J.C. (1983). Depression among amputees. *Journal of Clinical Psychiatry, 44*(7), 256–258.

Leach, L. R., Frank, R. G., Bouman, D. E., & Farmer, J. E. (1994). Family functioning, social support, and depression after traumatic brain injury. *Brain Injury, 8*(7), 599–606.

Leftcourt, H. M., & Davidson-Katz, K. (1991). Locus of control and health. In C. R. Snyder & D. R. Forsyth (Eds.), *Handbook of social and clinical psychology: The health perspective* (pp. 246–266). Elmsford, NY: Pergamon.

Lerner, M. J. (1980). *The belief in a just world: A fundamental delusion.* New York: Plenum.

Malec, J. F., & Ponsford, J. L. (in press). Post-acute brain injury rehabilitation. In R. G. Frank & T. R. Elliott (Eds.), *Handbook of rehabilitation psychology.* Washington, DC: American Psychological Association.

McGowan, M. B., & Roth, R. S. (1986). Family satisfaction and functional independence in spinal cord injury adjustment. *Archives of Physical Medicine and Rehabilitation, 67,* 657.

MedPac. (June, 1998). *Report to the Congress: Context for a changing Medicare program.* Medicare Payment Advisory Commission.

Peterson, C., Maier, S., & Seligman, M.E.P. (1993). *Learned helplessness: A theory for the age of personal control.* New York: Oxford University Press.

Richards, J. S., Kewman, D. G., & Pierce, C. A. (in press). Spinal cord injury rehabilitation. In R. G. Frank & T. R. Elliott (Eds.), *Handbook of rehabilitation psychology.* Washington, DC: American Psychological Association.

Rohe, D. E., & Krause, J. S. (1993). *The five factor model of personality: Findings among males with spinal cord injury.* Paper presented at the annual convention of the American Psychological Association, Toronto, Ontario, Canada.

Rosenthal, M., & Ricker, J. (in press). Traumatic brain injury. In R. G. Frank & T. R. Elliott (Eds.), *Handbook of rehabilitation psychology.* Washington, DC: American Psychological Association.

Rybarczyk, B., Szymanski, J. J., & Nicholas, J.J. (in press). Psychological adjustment to a limb amputation. In R. G. Frank & T. R. Elliott (Eds.), *Handbook of rehabilitation psychology.* Washington, DC: American Psychological Association.

Scheier, M. F., Carver, C. S., & Bridges, M. W. (1994). Distinguishing optimism from neuroticism (and trait anxiety, self-mastery, and self-esteem): A re-evaluation of the Life Orientation Test. *Journal of Personality and Social Psychology, 67,* 1063–1078.

Shewchuk, R., Richards, J. S., & Elliott, T. (1998). Dynamic processes in the first year of a caregiver career. *Health Psychology, 17,* 125–129.

Shukla, G. D., Sahu, S. C., Tripathi, R. P., & Gupta, D. K. (1982). A psychiatric study of amputees. *British Journal of Psychiatry, 141,* 50–53.

Snyder, C. R. (1994). *The psychology of hope: You can get there from here.* New York: The Free Press.

Stover, S. L., Whiteneck, G. G., & DeLisa, J. A. (Eds.). (1995). *Spinal cord injury: Clinical outcomes from model systems.* Gatherburg: Aspen.

Taylor, S. E., & Brown, J. D. (1988). Illusion and well-being: A social psychological perspective on mental health. *Psychological Bulletin, 103,* 193–210.

Teasdale, G., & Jennette, B. (1974). Assessment of coma and impaired consciousness. *Lancet, 2,* 81–84.

World Health Organization. (1980). *International classification of impairments, disabilities and handicaps.*

Yuker, H. E. (1994). Variables that influence attitudes toward people with disabilities: Conclusions from the data. *Journal of Social Behavior and Personality, 9,* 3–22.

36

Community Intervention

David G. Altman
The Wake Forest University School of Medicine
Robert M. Goodman
Tulane University School of Public Health and Tropical Medicine

This chapter reviews community interventions to promote health and prevent disease. Community interventions typically emanate from a health promotion perspective, with health promotion defined as education, organizational, economic, environmental, and advocacy efforts that foster healthful behaviors and settings. The goals of community interventions can be quite diverse, ranging from decreasing morbidity or mortality, to increasing the practice of a healthy behavior, to securing passage of health policies. Community interventions typically employ an array of programmatic approaches. These include those steeped in informational, behavioral, organizational, community development, environmental, and policy perspectives. A distinction is sometimes made between community interventions (i.e., interventions that attempt to achieve small but widespread changes) and interventions in communities (i.e., interventions that seek large changes among targeted groups; Green & Kreuter, 1991). Issues surrounding both types of intervention are covered.

Because most community interventions employ a wide array of intervention approaches, from those focused on changing individual behavior to those that target policies that facilitate or impede individual behavior, the line between community interventions and individual interventions is drawn artificially. Instead, community interventions are viewed as a set of approaches that utilize a vast array of change strategies. As noted throughout this chapter, however, a community intervention does have features that distinguish it from interventions that only target individuals or small groups.

There is a long history of community intervention in the field of public health (Rosen, 1993). Contemporary approaches to community health promotion can be traced to the late 1800s (Minkler, 1990; Nyswander, 1967). Over the years, community interventionists have drawn on a variety of theoretical perspectives to guide community intervention, including those from psychology (Farquhar, Fortmann, Wood, & Haskell, 1983; Iscoe & Harris, 1984; Levine, Toro, & Perkins, 1993; Maccoby & Altman, 1988; Shea & Basch, 1990), health education, community development (Bracht & Kingsbury, 1990; Kinne, Thompson, Chrisman, & Hanley, 1989), social ecology (Binder, Stokols, & Catalano, 1975; Stokols, 1992), and policy (Bennis, Benne, & Chin, 1969; Elder, Schmid, Dower, & Hedlund, 1993; Freudenberg, 1984–1985; McAlister, 1991; McKnight, 1987; Milio, 1981; Sarason, 1983; Steckler, 1989).

Although public health professionals have utilized community interventions for many years, psychology has played a less prominent role in recent years, although the theoretical underpinnings of health education and health promotion were articulated by Lewin (1951; field theory) and Rosenstock (1974; Health Belief Model), to name two. As noted throughout this chapter, however, the knowledge, skills, and perspectives of modern-day psychology, especially community psychology, have great potential for contributing to this domain of work (Iscoe, 1982; Revenson & Schiaffino, 2000; Winett, King, & D. G. Altman, 1989).

The following case illustration of a partnership approach serves as an example of community interventions that are informed by many of the concepts in this chapter, particularly social ecology, which is defined after the illustration.

BRIEF CASE STUDY: COMMUNITY-BASED SUBSTANCE ABUSE PREVENTION

The use of alcohol, tobacco, and other drugs (ATOD) by young people remains a substantial threat to the nation's health, and the age of initial ATOD use appears to be dropping (Department of Health and Human Services, 1991; DuRant, Escobedo, & Heath, 1995). In the early 1990s, the Centers for Substance Abuse Prevention (CSAP) responded to the continuing threat to the nation's young by funding approximately 250 community partnerships, each for 5 years, with the goal of reducing the adverse health consequences that ATOD use can cause (Davis, 1991).

Figure 36.1 is a model of a CSAP partnership (Butterfoss, Goodman, & Wandersman, 1993). The model shows a formative stage for the partnership during which the agency that is granted the funding (lead agency) convenes an ad hoc committee of local community leaders. The ad hoc committee nominates influential citizens to serve on committees repre-

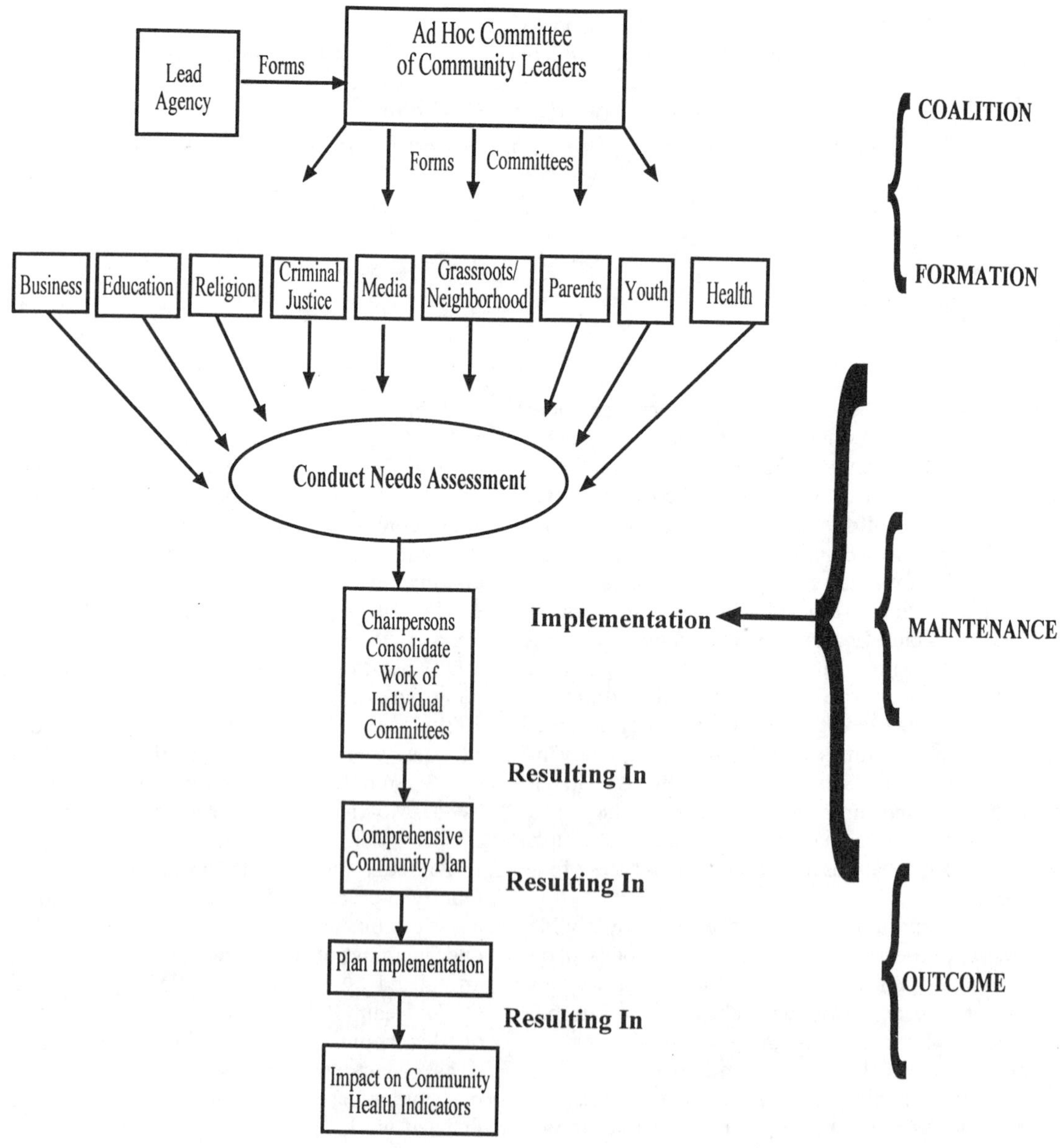

FIG. 36.1. A model for a community coalition to address alcohol, tobacco, and other drug abuse.

senting important sectors of the community. Once the committees are formed, the members are provided with background information of the seriousness of ATOD use among youth, and possible strategies for use reduction and prevention. The proposed strategies are directed at individual influences, such as degree of coping skills, self-esteem, and communication skills; family influences, such as family cohesiveness, parental modeling, and parenting skills; and community influences, such as the presence of supportive resources, sound economic conditions, and limited availability of potentially harmful substances.

Prior to deciding on which combination of strategies to adopt, each committee gathers information regarding ATOD use in its community, thus assessing the level of the problem locally. The availability of local resources to address ATOD use also is ascertained. Based on this assessment, the committees integrate their findings and develop a community-wide plan for addressing youth ATOD use. The plan consists of the selected strategies to be implemented, time lines for implementation, agencies and individuals designated to carry out the strategies, sources and amounts of funding for the effort, and the types of positive health outcomes anticipated if the strategies are effectively implemented. During implementation, the lead agency and highly committed volunteers from the community assure that the committees and their planned activities are monitored and maintained. The partnership uses professional evaluators to assess whether the desired outcomes result.

The example serves to illustrate a complex community intervention. It is characterized by active participation of multiple community sectors and constituencies. An advantage in working with such a pluralistic group is that members bring different talents and resources into play, thus facilitating the implementation of health promotion strategies that are applied simultaneously to influence individual youth, their family, the surrounding neighborhoods, the organizations that serve them, and local policy that influences community life. The use of multiple strategies that are directed at the "social fabric" of communities derives from a social ecological perspective.

THE SOCIAL ECOLOGY PERSPECTIVE FOR COMMUNITY INTERVENTION

The approach to community intervention discussed here is influenced by ecological and systems theories as well as by epidemiology. Disciplines concerned with the overall health of communities, such as community psychology and public health, are experiencing a shift in emphasis from social psychology to social ecology (Trickett, 1987, 1996). The traditional approach to community health development is grounded largely in social psychology where successes often are calibrated as changes in the risk producing behaviors of individuals (Hawkins & Catalano, 1992; McLeroy, Bibeau, Steckler, & Glanz, 1988; Steckler et al., 1995) or in the context of stages of change (DiClemente & Prochaska, 1985; Prochaska & DiClemente, 1983, 1984; Prochaska, Velicer, DiClemente, Guadgnoli, & Rossi, 1990). The "Just Say No" campaign championed by Nancy Reagan in the 1980s is one example of such a strategy. In contrast, the example in Fig. 36.1 focuses on community factors such as peer pressure, family home life, availability of unhealthy substances, and advertising that often make just saying no quite difficult.

Another prominent example in the 1970s and 1980s derives from several large scale community studies funded by the National Institutes of Health that extended from social psychology models. These included the Stanford Five-Community Project, the Minnesota Heart Health Project, and the Pawtucket Heart Health Project (Carleton, Lasater, Assaf, Feldman & McKinlay, 1995; Farquhar et al., 1983, 1990; Luepker et al., 1994). These projects used a combination of strategies directed at different segments of communities (often referred to as channels). The project evaluations were directed largely at behaviorally based outcomes such as weight reduction, modification of food buying habits and other diet-related risk behaviors, reduction in blood pressure, cholesterol, pulse rate, smoking, and coronary heart disease and mortality risk (Mittelmark, Hunt, Heath, & Schmid, 1993). Although reductions in risk-associated behaviors are essential outcomes of community interventions, these individual changes are influenced by, and often depend on, larger level social changes, or alterations in the social ecology of communities (Stokols, 1992; Winett, 1995).

From an ecological perspective, the potential to change individual risk behavior is considered within the social and cultural context in which it occurs. Interventions that are informed by this perspective are directed largely at social factors, such as community norms and the structure of community services, including their comprehensiveness, coordination, and linkages, in addition to individual motivations and attitudes. As others noted (Thompson & Kinne, 1990):

> The increasing focus on "community" in health promotion is due, at least in part, to growing recognition that behavior is greatly influenced by the environment in which people live. Proponents of community approaches to behavioral change recognize that local values, norms, and behavior patterns have a significant effect on shaping an individual's attitudes and behaviors. (p. 45)

In the Fig. 36.1 example, the use of key community influentials on committees, such as school principals, police chiefs, juvenile court justices, and editors of papers is directed at influencing local norms and consequently behavior. For instance, involving juvenile justices in the coalitions may influence the approaches to sentencing youth drug offenders to assure family involvement, mandatory drug counseling, and school attendance.

Ecological and systems theories view behavior as a function of the surrounding context. Articulation of an ecological approach has been provided by others writing in diverse disciplines (Binder et al., 1975; Bronfenbrenner, 1977; Kelly, 1966, 1968, 1988; McLeroy et al., 1988; Mills & Kelly, 1972; Moos, 1979; Rappaport, 1977; Revenson, 1990; Stokols, 1992, 1996; Trickett, Kelly, & Todd, 1972; Vincent & Trickett, 1983). At its most basic level, ecological theory posits that individuals and settings are mutually influential, this influence occurs in subsystems at multiple levels of analysis, and influence changes over time and settings. Central to this chapter are the implications of taking a social ecological perspective in the design and implementation of health promotion interventions. Thus, an interventionist committed to the ecological model would not typically take a reductionism approach. Rather, they would search for, as in the case of the ATOD partnership, points of leverage at multiple levels of analysis in the sociocultural context relevant to the topic at hand, and would use multiple approaches to achieving change.

Rapaport (1977) wrote an eloquent statement on the implications for interventionists adopting an ecological model:

> Interventions should be based on an understanding of local conditions and on a longitudinal assessment of the organization in the community; they should focus on anticipating effects of the intervention on all the members of a setting and use a wide variety of strategies and tactics for creating change. ... Accountability requires this orientation which focuses on a local situation and is concerned with its future side effects rather than short-term data analysis. ... Given the opportunity to develop and use its own resources a community will adapt to its environment, and often the job of community development will require interventionists to assist in the location and development of such resources. (p. 156)

From a social ecology perspective, individual change is understood within the social and cultural context in which it is to occur; the interventions that are suggested as efficacious, therefore, are more often directed at the social fabric rather than at individual motivations and attitudes. Mittelmark and colleagues (1993), for instance, suggested that the most effective NHLBI projects targeted a higher level of analysis: contests in work settings for producing weight reduction; church-based programs to reduce diet-related risk behaviors; school-based programs directed at smoking control, body fatness and food preferences; media programs that influence risk-related behaviors. Other evidence suggests that for comprehensive community strategies to be maximally effecting in reducing risk, sufficient resources are essential, especially the time allotted for interventions, the number of staff, and the level of staff expertise (Goodman, Steckler, Hoover, & Schwartz, 1993; Goodman, Wheeler, & Lee, 1995).

There are four overarching principles that best characterize an ecological systems approach, and each is described briefly here. The ecological purist may well object to the broad categories of the ecological paradigm used here. The discussion resorts to "lumping," rather than "splitting," in order to simplify the connection between the core components of an ecological approach and principles of health promotion strategy.

ECOLOGICAL PRINCIPLE 1: MULTIPLE LEVELS, COMPLEXITY, NEGATIVE ENTROPY

Multiple levels of analysis are perhaps the single most identifiable feature of an ecological approach. Levels have been defined differently by people, but in essence they relate to personal, interpersonal, organizational, and societal dimensions (see Fig. 36.1). An ecological model also assumes that these different levels relate to each other in a complex and embedded array of relations. Negative entropy is a concept taken from systems theory and thermodynamics and refers to the idea that systems have a tendency to strive for energy and complexity and away from simplicity. Certainly, community partnerships illustrate this complexity. As previously noted, the development of a community plan requires coordination across multisectorial committees. The plan strategies require integration of complementary approaches—for instance, school-based drug prevention education may be linked to policies restricting teachers and other school employees from smoking on school grounds; these strategies may be linked to the vigilant enforcement policies restricting the placement of vending machines selling tobacco that youth may access, or store sales of liquor to minors. Such strategies are not only complex, but also require a degree of energy and commitment that exceeds a "Just Say No" strategy.

ECOLOGICAL PRINCIPLE 2: INTERDEPENDENCE, HOLISM, CONTEXT

The combined strategies noted in the previous paragraph suggest holism as a second ecological principle. *Holism* refers to the idea that phenomena are more than the sum of their parts. Intervening on one part of a multilevel system, for example, will both affect other parts of the system and the system as a whole. Thus, the properties of interdependence and reciprocity suggest that to intervene on one aspect of a system, it is advisable to evaluate how other components in the system, and the system as a whole, might change as a result. Drawing attention to the context in which intervention occurs and the interrelations between levels within context, is one of the most important contributions that an ecological orientation makes to health promotion intervention. The CSAP partnership committees are one illustration of the interrelationship among levels. Effective committee operations were crucial to the organization of the partnership, because the committees conducted community needs assessments, formulated community plans, and spearheaded plan implementation. The success of the partnership was predicated on building a strong organizational infrastructure through a committee system. The formation of the infrastructure depended on good working relationships among committee members and staff. Thus, reinforcing good interpersonal interactions among committee members assured positive group functioning and increased the likelihood that the committees produced and implemented a workable community plan.

ECOLOGICAL PRINCIPLE 3: DYNAMIC EQUILIBRIUM, CYCLING OF RESOURCES

The principle of resource cycling orients the interventionist to the fact that systems are rich in resources that change over time. These resources are available to be marshaled by interventionists for the benefit of the people and environments in a setting. Dynamic equilibrium refers to systems and relations within systems being in motion, energetic, changing, and productive. In contrast to a static view of a context, a dynamic view focuses on the acquisition and utilization of resources by system components. The partnership approach demonstrates both dynamic equilibrium and cycling of resources that are in evidence when the partnership makes an effective transition across the stages of formation, implementation, maintenance, and outcomes (see Fig. 36.1). Each stage requires a different configuration of resources (e.g., implementation requires expertise in needs assessment and community interventions, or programmatic resources; maintenance requires ongoing commitments to funding and staffing, or political influence with funding organizations).

ECOLOGICAL PRINCIPLE 4: ADAPTATION, EQUIFINALITY, SUCCESSION

Underlying adaptation are the concepts of change and coping. Thus, adaptation refers to the components in systems, and the systems themselves, being in a constant stage of influence, flux, accommodation, and change. Equifinality is a concept taken from systems theory and refers to the idea that there are many paths to a final state. Succession refers to the notion that over time, forms of life change in a regular sequence. In addition, an ecological approach is oriented toward studying naturally occurring phenomena and contributing to improving or maintaining the functioning of biopsychosocial systems.

Ecological theory is guided by the principle that the whole is more than the sum of its parts and thus behavior and environment are viewed as interdependent rather than independent (Wicker, 1979). Furthermore, an ecological perspective considers different levels of analysis like the layers of an onion, each system nested within another with each system constrained both by the system it surrounds and the system that surrounds it (Wicker, 1979). Few studies of health behavior specify the sequence or causal linkages by which individuals influence, and are influenced by, the larger social context (D. G. Altman, 1986; Winett et al., 1989).

The ultimate goal of most health interventions, regardless of the level of analysis, is to improve the health status of individuals as individuals, not systems or environments, experience illness and health. In the case of a community intervention to reduce tobacco use, for example, the focus of macrolevel interventions (e.g., increasing the tax on cigarettes) may also influence the actions that individuals take (e.g., not purchasing cigarettes). Similarly, a goal of many microlevel interventions (e.g., teaching worksite employees how to quit smoking) may influence actions taken at higher levels of analysis (e.g., implementation of a worksite smoking policy). There are interactional and synergistic connections among levels of analysis. The means by which individuals are reached and influenced, however, can vary as a function of the level at which one intervenes. In more cases than not, there is a reciprocity of influence between levels of analysis (Winett et al., 1989). Furthermore, Green (1986) noted that individuals and systems are not "mutually exclusive or opposite ends of a political or theoretical continuum" (p. 29). Focusing on one level has concomitant costs and benefits. Curtailing and eventually eliminating smoking in the workplace may require changes in organizational policies that are mutually agreeable to management and labor, implementation of coworker support programs, and availability of cessation programs for individuals attempting to quit smoking.

OTHER THEORETICAL PERSPECTIVES ON COMMUNITY INTERVENTION

Although the use of ecological theory in community intervention has been advocated, the reality is that a variety of other theoretical and conceptual perspectives have guided many community intervention campaigns conducted to date (McAlister, 1991). These include the health belief model (Rosenstock, 1974), communication-persuasion model (McGuire, 1981), diffusion theory (E. M. Rogers, 1983), social cognitive theory (Bandura, 1986, 1997), the theory of reasoned action (Ajzen & Fishbein, 1980), and community development (Bracht et al., 1994; Bracht & Kingsbury, 1990; Bracht & Tsouros, 1990; Lefebvre, Lasater, Carleton, & Peterson, 1987).

The Stanford Three Community (TCS) and the Five City Projects (FCP), for example, used hybrids of these theoretical perspectives (Farquhar et al., 1983, 1990; Maccoby & D. G. Altman, 1988) as did many other large interventions (Puska, 1984; Shea & Basch, 1990) (Lefebvre et al., 1987). There have been several useful reviews (Bloom, 1996; Shea & Basch, 1990) of the theoretical perspectives underlying community intervention and primary prevention and thus this topic is only summarized here.

Social Cognitive Theory

Social cognitive theory has been a key approach guiding the development of many community health promotion interventions (Farquhar et al., 1983; Flora & Cassidy, 1990; Winett et al., 1989). There is a substantial empirical database of research on social cognitive theory (Bandura, 1986, 1997) and it is utilized in whole or part by many researchers and practitioners involved in community intervention work. Key variables in social cognitive theory include self-efficacy, outcome expectancies, and perceived incentive value. Self-efficacy refers to people's belief about how capable they are to perform a specific behavior (Bandura, 1986, 1997). Self-efficacy has been identified as one of the cornerstones of a person's willingness to participate in community change (Zimmerman & Rappaport, 1988). Self-efficacy plays a role in promoting the induction, generalization, and maintenance of a new behavior. Outcome expectancy refers to a person's belief that a behavior will result in a specific outcome (Bandura, 1986, 1997). It is unlikely that a person will expend time and effort to bring about a change if it is perceived that the change will not have the intended effect. Perceived incentive value refers to the relative importance placed on a possible outcome (Bandura, 1986, 1997). In general, people are more likely to engage in a behavior if they consider the behavior to be important (i.e., valuable).

Social Marketing

Social marketing has grown in popularity in recent years (Kotler & Roberto, 1989; Novelli, 1990) and now is incorporated at some level in most community health promotion programs. In addition, the substantial track record of the field of marketing, from which social marketing draws heavily, provides further justification for its inclusion. Social marketing approaches are utilized widely in health promotion and these approaches are built on the large knowledge base of more general business marketing. Social marketing is the extension of marketing principles to social and health issues (Kotler & Roberto, 1989; Novelli, 1990; Wallack, Dorfman, Jernigan, & Themba, 1993). Kotler and Roberto defined it as "a social-change management technology involving the design, implementation, and control of programs aimed at increasing the acceptability of a social idea or practice" (p. 24). The marketing context—comprised of product, price, promotion, position, and place—forms the overarching organizing structure for a marketing approach. The adoption of a social marketing approach requires the interventionist to study and attend carefully to the context (marketplace) and the needs of the target population (consumer) so that tailored interventions are designed and delivered. Social marketing is based on two general assumptions: (a) Programs/messages should be designed on the basis of the perceived needs and expectation of consumers, and (b) successful programs are those that achieve a successful exchange between message sender and receiver (Kotler & Roberto, 1989; Novelli, 1990).

Community Development

Community development (or community organization) refers to the study of or intervention around the natural organization of persons and institutions in community systems. A key goal of community development is the stimulation and coalescing of community resources and expertise (Bracht & Kingsbury, 1990). Bracht and Kingsbury defined community organization as "a planned process to activate a community to use its own social structures and any available resources (internal or external) to accomplish community goals, decided primarily by community representatives and consistent with local values" (p. 67). Comprehensive planning and community diagnosis/analysis, a key dimension of many public health intervention models, is a prerequisite to successful community intervention (Farquhar et al., 1990; Haglund & Tillgren, 1988; Winett, 1995; Winett et al., 1989). There are three critical dimensions at the core of successful community development: multisectoral inclusion, organizational linkages, and enabling and support.

Multisectoral inclusion refers to the involvement and subsequent active participation of diverse community members and organizational constituencies in planning, implementing, and evaluating community health programs (Chavis & Newbrough, 1986; Chavis & Wandersman, 1990; Wandersman, Chavis, & Stucky, 1983). There is a substantial literature documenting the importance of inclusion and participation in determining a program's success and long-term viability (Bracht & Tsouros, 1990; Goodman, Burdine, Meehan, & McLeroy, 1993). Coalitions have become popular vehicles for enhancing community inclusion and participation. More empirical research needs to be conducted on inclusion strategies and tactics. In particular, it is important to understand better how coalitions operate, how they maintain their viability, how best to utilize local human and material resources, and the processes through which they improve the impact of community interventions.

The Pawtucket Heart Health Program (PHHP) was guided by community development underpinnings through its emphasis on recruiting and developing a strong lay leadership program and associated community networks at both individual and organizational levels (Carleton et al., 1995; Lefebvre et al., 1987; Lefebvre, Lasater, Assaf, & Carleton, 1988). This network consists of recipients of intervention as well as agents of communication about CVD prevention. PHHP was also guided by aspects of social cognitive theory in that attention was directed at increasing self-efficacy of individuals (see earlier discussion) and collective efficacy (i.e., group beliefs that networks or organizational can lower CVD risk status in the community; Lefebvre et al., 1988).

Organizational linkages refer to communication, coordination, and collaboration among multiple community sectors. Community groups that promote open and honest communication, have formal and informal mechanisms for exchanging information regularly, and agree on a common purpose have the essential building blocks for mounting a successful community health program. Coordination refers to interorganizational planning, objective setting, and health services delivery. By definition, comprehensive community health programs require diverse community organizations and constituencies to coordinate efforts. Significant barriers to coordination include territoriality, competition, ineffective communication, and lack of resources. Collaboration is the most complex function faced by community groups because it requires multiple constituencies to work for jointly determined goals and objectives.

A community's ability to determine its own "health" is the core principle underlying enabling and support. An *enabling approach* will change the typical hierarchical relationship between researchers (giving direction) and community groups (taking direction). A theoretical perspective that overlaps with enabling and support function of community development is empowerment and thus this is reviewed next.

Empowerment

There is a small but growing literature on empowerment, as is evidenced by publication of an entire issue of the *American Journal of Community Psychology* on this subject in 1992. The empowerment literature examines the processes and effects of individual, organizational, and community empowerment, with *empowerment* defined as efforts at these multiple levels of analysis to exert control and gain mastery over salient issues. Empowerment can also be defined by the absence or low levels of normlessness, powerlessness, social isolation, and helplessness (Chapman, 1994; Wallerstein, 1992;

Zimmerman, 1990b; Zimmerman, Israel, Schulz & Checkoway, 1992). Wallerstein (1992) considered empowerment as "a social action process that promotes participation of people, organizations, and communities towards the goals of increased individual and community control, political efficacy, improved quality of community life, and social justice" (p. 198). Participation, control, and critical awareness are essential aspects of empowerment. At the individual level of analysis, these factors include a belief in people's ability to exert control, their involvement in decision making, and their understanding of causal agents. At the organizational level of analysis these factors refer to settings that provide individuals with opportunities to exert control and to organizational effectiveness in service delivery and the policy process. At the community level of analysis, these factors refer to the contexts in which organizations and individuals interact to enhance community living and to insure that their communities address local needs and concerns.

According to Zimmerman (in press), "Empowerment theory connects individual well-being with the larger social and political environment, and suggests that people need opportunities to become active in community decision-making in order to improve their sense of empowerment" (p. 31). Empowering communities provide opportunities for individuals and groups in the community to exert control and influence (i.e., shape the community agenda, participate in community decision making, have access to community resources). Empowered communities can be characterized as providing community members with opportunities to participate actively in the community by addressing community problems and utilizing community resources.

There are several key concepts underlying empowerment theory: environmental awareness, control, participation, and community connectedness. Environmental awareness includes understanding the factors that impede or facilitate goal attainment, as well as strategies to overcome barriers through resource utilization. It also includes an understanding of the causal agents underlying a problem or issue (Zimmerman, 1990a; Zimmerman et al., 1992). Perceived and real control is perhaps the core construct underlying empowerment. The importance of encouraging broad participation has generated consensus in health promotion networks (Green, 1986). Green (1986) pointed out that "the principle holds that the practice of health education depends for its success on involving people in defining their own needs, setting their own priorities, controlling their own solutions, and evaluating their own progress" (pp. 211–212). Perspectives complementary to empowerment (i.e., those that focus on power, choice, self-determination, control over destiny) are found in theories or constructs such as powerlessness, learned helplessness, competent community, health locus of control, and self-efficacy (Bandura, 1986; Iscoe, 1974; Seligman, 1975; Zimmerman, 1990b).

There are four general categories of empowering competencies in community interventions: diagnosing, organizing, issue framing, and taking action (hereafter referred to as the "Just DO IT" framework): *Diagnosing* is the ability to understand the root causes of a problem or issue at multiple levels of analysis and to identify the barriers to and facilitators of alternative solutions. This competency requires a commitment to diligent investigation, reconnaissance, and detailed issue analysis. *Organizing* is the ability to work with various community constituencies on an issue of mutual interest, to resolve interpersonal conflicts, work as part of a team, and put the agenda of the group ahead of any personal agenda. *Issue framing* presents an issue in such a way that it generates interest, concern, and desire to take action among targeted constituencies. *Taking action* is the ability to determine which action(s) are appropriate to the issue and situation at hand (i.e., the costs and benefits) and the skill in implementing the action(s) effectively.

Mass Media

It is unlikely that a large scale community intervention can be successful without mass media involvement (Flora & Cassidy, 1990; Green & McAlister, 1984). Although the media can affect awareness, interest (or motivation), trial attempts (or experimentation), and adoption of behavior (Green & McAlister, 1984), there is strong evidence that media approaches alone are more likely to influence cognitive factors such as awareness and motivation than health-related behavior. The media are important in setting the public agenda about health issues (i.e., what people think about, how issues are framed). Thus, the media can create and reinforce public awareness about an issue, contribute to its salience, serve as a cue to action, and reinforce action that is taken. Media campaigns have the advantage that they can effectively reach opinion leaders. In turn, opinion leaders who adopt innovations into their own lives can promote broader adoption among others whom they influence through modeling and persuasion.

Effective media campaigns have used multiple and diverse channels and formats (Farquhar et al., 1990; Flora & Farquhar, 1988). For television, this includes free speech messages, public service announcements, paid advertisements, editorials, news stories, news series, public affairs programs, talk shows, magazine programs, live remote broadcasts, specials produced by a station, acquisitions aired by a station, and community calendars. For newspaper, this includes paid advertisements, letters to the editor, editorials, guest opinions, spot news coverage, multipart news coverage, feature stories (in news, business, sports, lifestyle, feature columns), and community calendars. For radio, this includes live copy public service announcements, preproduced public service announcements, paid editorials, news stories, news series, talk shows, call-in tips, live remote broadcasts, and community calendars. Less utilized channels are also important. These include the internet, cable television, neighborhood newspapers, organizational newsletters, trade magazines, videos in medical offices and other settings, films at community events, direct mail, billboards, grocery bag advertising, monthly bill inserts, paycheck inserts, placemats, telephone book advertisements, bumper stickers, public transit advertisements, and sponsorship of community events. Soliciting cosponsorship and funding of interventions from local community organizations is a media strategy that utilizes principles of community development.

The Stanford Five City Project (FCP), and its predecessor, the Three Community Study (TCS), are widely recognized as models for the effective use of media in community intervention (Farquhar et al., 1983, 1990; Flora & Farquhar, 1988; Maccoby & D. G. Altman, 1988), although the Stanford studies also were heavily influenced by community development, diffusion of innovations, and social cognitive theories. The Stanford projects employed media professionals, both academic and frontline, to shape the message content and channels through which to best reach the community. A social marketing perspective (Kotler & Roberto, 1989; Novelli, 1990) guided their efforts. A diverse array of heart healthy messages were delivered continuously through mass media, social networks (e.g., physicians, teachers, parks and recreation staff), lifepath points (e.g., grocery stores, restaurants, banks, libraries), worksites, schools, and households (Flora & Farquhar, 1988).

INTERVENTION STRATEGIES

An often asked question is, "What approaches to community intervention work?" Whereas on the surface, this is a legitimate question, it may be the wrong question. Thus, before this chapter attempts to answer this question, an important caveat should be stated. As others have noted, it may be more instructive to analyze how interventions work (in what settings, at what times, and with whom) than to address whether an intervention does or does not work (D. G. Altman, 1986; Hornik, 1980). Because interventions "work" differently in different contexts, knowing whether an intervention worked in one place is of marginal value. Instead, addressing the mechanisms underlying the outcomes achieved is the most important information to obtain. This perspective is consistent with the ecological roots reviewed previously.

That said, some conclusions are offered from the literature. First, the best individual-level interventions are not very effective. A cynical, if not honest, response to the question about what works is, "not enough." A cursory evaluation of published studies on the efficacy of interventions as diverse as tobacco use, body weight, nutrition, practice of unsafe sexual behaviors, injury-prone behavior, use of sunscreen, medication-taking, environmental protection, and so on, leads to the conclusion that not enough is known about preventing disease and promoting health. Indeed, the best interventions achieve changes in a small proportion of the target population, many of whom were motivated to make a change in the first place. Furthermore, many changes achieved in the short term are not sustained over the medium and long term. Because there is publication bias favoring interventions with positive effects, it can be assumed that taken together, the true effectiveness of all interventions in a particular health area is lower than published studies.

With that as a backdrop, it is suggested that community interventions with the following characteristics are likely to achieve desired changes more times than not:

Utilize data-based planning and feedback systems (epidemiological, public opinion, strategic) as the driving force behind the development and refinement of interventions.

Involve the target population in some aspects of intervention planning, implementation, and evaluation.

Develop clearly articulated, highly focused, agreed-on goals and objectives and stick to them, all the while maintaining flexibility at the tactical (programmatic) level.

Emphasize passive prevention approaches whenever possible so that people are protected automatically rather than having to engage in an active behavior.

Change the social norms around which individual behavior occurs.

Target the root causes of problems, especially those at the sociocultural environment.

Consider community intervention strategies that take into account the resources available (i.e., ends being adjusted to the means). Taking on too much given the available resources, a tradition for health educators, is a recipe for failure.

Consider the timing and location of intervention in design and implementation.

As noted by Green and McAlister, large scale intervention, compared to targeted intervention, typically requires more planning and coordination and attention to the diffusion of innovations (Green & McAlister, 1984). Both types of intervention, however, are enhanced by the active participation of individuals and organizations affected by the issue addressed (Green & McAlister, 1984). A predominant theme in community intervention is the need for comprehensive intervention at multiple levels in the community (Cheadle et al., 1993; Elder et al., 1993; Mittelmark et al., 1993; Stokols, 1992, 1996). More recently, this discussion has expanded to include policy approaches to intervention, both within the community and from outside the community.

LEVEL OF INTERVENTION

Health problems or issues can be defined in numerous ways and the way an issue is defined has a direct bearing on the type of intervention (Winett, 1995; Winett et al., 1989). In the case of dietary behavior, for example, the problem of people eating a diet too high in fat can be attributed to the behavior of individuals who eat too much fat, to restaurants or food producers who do not provide healthy options for consumers, to advertisers who mislead consumers about the healthfulness of their products, and to agricultural or economic policy that affects the profitability of growing or manufacturing certain foods. In theory, a community intervention to reduce dietary fat intake would ideally approach the problem comprehensively by targeting the multiple influences on dietary behavior. Similarly, the causes of gun violence can be considered from multiple perspectives. Ownership of firearms can be framed as a constitutional right of self-protection or as the primary cause of a public health epidemic. The well-known sound bite, "guns don't kill people, people kill people," illustrates how the definition of an issue can influence subsequent interventions. Available interventions for reducing gun violence include passage of laws requiring a waiting period for gun ownership and/or the possession of a gun permit, gun owner education programs, laws limiting the type of guns and ammunition allowed to be purchased, grassroots action (e.g., "take back our streets" marches) to convey community norms, and family education to encourage safe use and storage of weapons.

Green asserted that the community level of analysis should be the "center of gravity" for health promotion (Green & Kreuter, 1990):

> Governments can formulate policies, provide leadership, allocate funding, and generate data for health promotion. ... Individuals can govern their own behavior and control the determinants of their own health up to a point. ... But the decisions on priorities and strategies for social change affecting the more complicated lifestyle issues can best be made collectively as close to the homes and workplaces of those affected as possible. (p. 322)

Although, in practice, health promotion is implemented through multiple levels (from the individual through policy), the community level is key to building a comprehensive strategy to promote health and prevent disease among the population at-large.

In simple terms, then, a community approach can be distinguished from a clinical or individual approach by the outlook taken to disease etiology and prevention (Rose, 1992). For example, community health psychologists, reflecting on heart disease in their community, might ask, "Why do so many people in my community have premature heart attacks?" In contrast, clinical psychologists practicing in the community might ask, "Why did this patient have a heart attack?" As Rose noted, these two perspectives, although complementary from the larger perspective of heart disease prevention and treatment, actually focus on different aspects of disease etiology and prevention. The public health, or community, approach is concerned primarily with incidence rates (i.e., new cases of a disease or health condition) and prevalence rates (i.e., total number of cases of a disease or health condition) and in methods to change the behavior and environments that contribute to disease incidence and prevalence. The clinical approach is concerned primarily with disease etiology among individuals and targeted methods to reduce risk or treat disease among these individuals. According to Rose (1992), "The individual strategy is a rescue operation for individuals in need, whereas the population strategy is a radical attempt to deal with the underlying causes" (p. 312). Thus, the importance of community intervention is often based on the assumption that greater improvement in health can be obtained by small changes in the behaviors (or environments) of large numbers of people than by large changes among a small number of people at high risk (Altman, 1995a).

The Policy Level Approach to Intervention

The implementation of policy is a key area where intervention strategies can have a dramatic effect on community health. In the 1990s, there has been increased attention to the linking community intervention with health policy (E. R. Brown, 1991; Brownson, Koffman, Novotny, Hughes, & Eriksen, 1995; Glanz et al., 1995; King et al., 1995; Schmid, Pratt, & Howze, 1995; Schwartz, Goodman, & Steckler, 1995; Steckler, Dawson, Goodman, & Epstein, 1987). In fact, scholars in health education rarely wrote about policy approaches until the late 1970s and early 1980s (Mico, 1978; Milio, 1981; Steckler & Dawson, 1982; Steckler et al., 1987) and there is even less attention to this topic in the health psychology literature. Historically, many of the advances in public health had at the roots policy change (Schmid et al., 1995). Notable successes include policies around food preparation, sanitation, waste disposal, refrigeration, sewage treatment, and water purification (Rosen, 1993). In health psychology, policy approaches have not been central to the field, although a small, but increasing, number of psychologists are encouraging the field to expand along these lines (Ewart, 1991; Leviton, 1996; Winett, 1995; Winett et al., 1989).

Policies can be oriented to active prevention (i.e., policies that require individuals to take action in order to be protected) or passive prevention (i.e., policies that protect individuals without the individual engaging in a health protective behavior). In the case of interventions to reduce motor vehicle fatalities, for example, active strategies might include driver education around safe driving habits or seatbelt education programs. Passive strategies—including engineering roads to be safer (e.g., quality of surfacing, signs, curves, etc.), providing airbags in all automobiles, installing automatic seatbelt restraints, enforcing DWI laws through roadside checks and increased police funding, and designing cars better able to withstand impact—contributed to the 50% reduction per mile driven over the last 25 years (Schmid et al., 1995).

From the perspective of dietary behavior to prevent CVD, the tradition of intervention is to persuade individuals to change their eating habits. Indeed, at first glance, eating is the epitome of individual behavior. Although interventions directed at individual behavior are certainly worthwhile, Glanz and colleagues (1995) articulated a series of policy interventions that would complement an individual focus. Nutrition-related policy interventions might include regulations requiring labeling of food products and point-of-purchase advertising to facilitate informed consumer choice, expanding the accessibility of healthy food products to make it easier for individuals interested in purchasing healthy food products to readily obtain these products, requiring that institutional providers of food (e.g., schools, nursing homes, hospitals) make healthy food items accessible, educational policies that ensure that health professionals (particularly physicians and nurses) have adequate training in nutrition, and policies that provide monetary incentives for food producers and consumers to purchase healthy food choices (e.g., through taxation, price supports, coupons, tax incentives).

Along similar lines, King and colleagues (1995) presented a range of policy and environmental intervention options to promote physical activity, a behavior with strong relations to a variety of acute and chronic mental and physical health conditions. These included restricting downtown city districts to foot or bicycle traffic only, zoning parking lots to facilitate both convenience and physical activity, designing buildings that make stairs safe and readily accessible for routine use, and building communities that allow for walking and biking between residential, school, and commercial areas. There also are legislative and regulatory mechanisms to promote physical activity (King et al., 1995), including: reduce liability costs for physical activity centers through better certification, equipment/facilities, and training; develop zoning regulations that protect open spaces and areas for exercise (e.g., bike or walking paths, greenways, par courses), provide tax incentives for nonmechanized consumer products or recreational products that require physical activity; establish incentive systems for walk/bike-to-work/shop programs; require enhanced physical education curriculum in schools; and encourage workplaces to facilitate opportunities for physical activity through flex time, on-site facilities, or discounts with off-site facilities.

Public opinion surveys find broad-based support for public policies to promote health and prevent disease (Jeffery et al., 1990). Some people, however, make the mistake that such data and health policy are highly associated. Indeed, advocacy is often more important than the "facts" in garnering support for and ultimately influencing health policy (D. G. Altman, Balcazar, Fawcett, Seekins, & Young, 1994; Chapman, 1994; Wallack et al., 1993). Data are usually necessary for health policy change, but they are not usually sufficient. Furthermore, the person(s) who disseminates the data is often as important as the data.

Thus, community interventions are popular because they have the potential to improve health above and beyond what can be achieved by individual approaches alone. Indeed, part of the rationale underlying the efficacy of community intervention is the belief that changing the community at-large is a more cost-effective means to achieving societal health goals then reaching individuals one person at a time. Also, community interventions have the potential advantage of delivering beneficial programs both to those who explicitly desire assistance as well as to those who could benefit from intervention but who do not know if they could benefit or who do not have access through more traditional service delivery mechanisms.

RESULTS OF KEY COMMUNITY INTERVENTION TRIALS

Community interventions have been employed in a variety of substantive areas, although those targeting cardiovascular disease prevention and substance abuse have been widely recognized as model programs (Cardiovascular Disease Plan Steering Committee, 1994; Elder et al., 1993; Farquhar et al., 1990; Haglund & Tillgren, 1988; Maccoby & D. G. Altman, 1988; Puska et al., 1985; Shea & Basch, 1990). Wagennar, Murray, Wolfson, Forster, and Finnegan (1994) tested a community activation model to reduce underage drinking, a problem that is so widespread that 64% of high school seniors report alcohol consumption within the last 30 days (L. D. Johnston, O'Malley, & Bachman, 1991). T. Rogers, Feighery, Tenacati, Butler, and Weiner (1995) described community mobilization and media strategies in California to counteract the influence of $6.03 billion tobacco companies spent nationally on product marketing.

The emphasis on cardiovascular disease (CVD) is in part due to the fact that CVD is the leading cause of death in the United States, causing over 720,000 deaths in 1990 and that many risk factors are behavioral in origin (McGinnis, 1994). Many risk factors for heart disease (e.g., tobacco, nutrition, obesity, physical activity, hypertension) are associated with the second and third causes of death, cancer (over 550,000 deaths each year) and cerebrovascular diseases (over 144,000 deaths). Other preventable causes of death among the top 10 include unintentional injuries (over 92,000 deaths), chronic lung disease (over 86,000 deaths), diabetes (over 47,000 deaths), and AIDS (over 25,000 deaths; McGinnis, 1994). On the cost side, the proportion of the Gross National Product spent on health care has increased from 6% in 1960 to over 14% today. Some of costs are associated with preventable, premature disease. For example, a typical coronary artery bypass graft costs over $30,000 and typical treatment for lung cancer costs about $29,000 (Department of Health and Human Services, 1991). Thus, to improve the health of the population, individuals must be encouraged to practice healthier behaviors, design environments that facilitate the practice of these behaviors, and pass/enforce public policies that reinforce healthy choices. Community interventions represent a key approach to achieving these goals.

Results from large community intervention trials to promote health and prevent disease have been mixed (Susser, 1995). In light of earlier comments about the importance of understanding the contextual underpinnings of how programs work, however, these trials have generated important data that will be instrumental in helping guide future community interventions. In addition, the fact that policy approaches to health promotion are relatively new tools in the armamentarium of interventions, the large community intervention trials described here did not generally employ policy as primary intervention strategies and tactics. If these programs were begun in the current era of health promotion/disease prevention, it is likely that policy intervention would take central stage (Brownson et al., 1995; Glanz et al., 1995; King et al., 1995; Schwartz et al., 1995; Speers & Schmid, 1995). A few key community intervention trials are reviewed later.

The Community Trial for Smoking Cessation (COMMIT), a 4-year study in 22 communities in the United States and Canada (11 treatment communities, 11 comparison communities), found small, but significant, treatment effects in cohort analyses for light-to-moderate smokers but no treatment effects for heavy smokers (the COMMIT Research Group, 1995a, 1995b; Fisher, 1995). No treatment effects were found in cross-sectional analyses on overall smoking prevalence (The COMMIT Research Group, 1995b). Although the effects among light-to-moderate in the cohort analysis were small from a clinical cessation perspective (quit rates were .306 in treatment and .275 in comparison communities), taken across the 11 treatment communities, the results had public health significance: Three thousand more smokers in treatment communities compared to comparison communities quit smoking.

Similarly, results on adult cigarette smoking in the six community Minnesota Heart Health Program (MHHP) found short-term effects favoring treatment communities but long-term effects were limited to women in the cross-sectional (vs. longitudinal) sample (Lando et al., 1995). Although MHHP interventions were comprehensive (e.g., cessation contests, classes, self-help materials, telephone counseling, home correspondence courses), little attention was given to policy or environmental tobacco interventions.

Another large CVD community-based risk reduction study, the Pawtucket Heart Health Program (PHHP), was evaluated in two communities over a 8.5-year period (Carleton et al., 1995). The effects found were similar to those found in the MHHP already described. That is, with the exception of inconsistent treatment effects for body mass index and overall CVD risk, there were no effects attributable to the intervention (Carleton et al., 1995).

In contrast, CVD risk factor findings from the Stanford Five-City Project (FCP) and in its predecessor, the Stanford Three Community Study, generally reveal treatment effects favoring treatment (Farquhar et al., 1983, 1990; Maccoby & D. G. Altman, 1988; Meyer, Nash, McAlister, Maccoby, & Farquhar, 1980). The treatment was multifaceted, including mass media, extensive community organization, health professional delivered services, school- and worksite-based intervention, and environmental supports. Over a 5-year period of intervention in the FCP, analyses revealed effects favoring treatment communities for CVD knowledge, smoking, and blood pressure, with smaller changes in pulse rate and cholesterol level (Farquhar et al., 1990). All-cause mortality risk reduction also favored treatment communities at the majority of timepoints for both longitudinal and cross-sectional analyses. Excluding research costs, Farquhar et al. estimated that it cost about $4 per capita to deliver the intervention each year.

Likewise, 10-year findings from the North Karelia Project in Finland found that CHD mortality reductions were 22% in the treatment community, 12% in the comparison community, and 11% in Finland as a whole (excluding the treatment community; Puska, Nissinen, Salonen, & Toumilehto, 1983; Puska et al., 1985). In contrast, CVD risk factor findings from the MHHP were not as promising (Luepker et al., 1994). In essence, although MHHP treatment communities showed declines in relevant risk factors, these declines were just as evident in comparison communities (i.e., the intervention did no better than the secular trend). Because there is evidence that the specific interventions employed in the MHHP were effective, the investigators concluded that failure to find treatment effects was probably due to inadequate penetration in the community such that the proportion of the population exposed to intervention was sufficient to exceed the secular trend (Luepker et al., 1994). Luepker et al. concluded, "What we now recognize is that it is far easier to change the risk profiles of the people who participate in those programs than to engage a large enough fraction of the community to change risk profiles of the entire community" (p. 1392).

The Stanford team articulated this difficulty in a different way (Fortmann et al., 1995). They noted that each year in the FCP, each adult in treatment communities was exposed to about 100 educational messages, delivered over 5 hours. Of these 5 educational hours, about 1 hour was from radio and television. In contrast, the average American is exposed each year to 35,000 advertisements (or 292 hours of advertising). Clearly, community health programs will always be underresourced with respect to the effects of broader secular influence.

In addition to the daunting amount of advertising that health promotion programs must overcome, the programs themselves are underresourced. The Stanford, Pawtucket, and Minnesota studies had annual budgets that exceed what many community organizations have available. In addition, the research studies were conducted by highly trained professionals and community leaders. In order to test community approaches with more modest means, the U.S. Centers for Disease Control and Prevention funded a series of studies focused on reducing cardiovascular disease. One of these community mobilization efforts, which received $2.2 million over 5 years and operated through a state and local health department, produced mixed results, having a favorable intervention effect on cholesterol and smoking but not on other risk factors for cardiovascular disease. In addition, the project influenced levels of community awareness of risk and fostered greater cooperation among community health agencies (Goodman et al., 1995). The Planned Approach to Community Health (PATCH), a community mobilization initiative also funded by CDC, is an even more modest effort that provides communities with $5,000 per year on average, and with most work being implemented by volunteers. PATCH reports modest, but in some cases, promising results especially in mobilizing community members (Buckner, Miner, Dreuter, & Wilson, 1992; Goodman, Steckler, Hoover, & Schwartz, 1993).

Taken together, the results of these large trials leave room for optimism and pessimism. On the one hand, there is little question that broad-based community interventions can be implemented in diverse communities with fidelity and effectiveness. Whether these interventions can penetrate broadly and deeply enough to produce community-wide change above and beyond secular trends is less certain. In addition, there is little evidence that specific interventions, or even types of interventions, are essential to success. Rather, because there are complex interactions between community characteristics and the health problems targeted, a "one-size-fits-all" orientation to intervention is certain to be problematic.

THE PROCESS OF INTERVENTION

This chapter does not provide an exhaustive discussion on the logistics of designing and implementing a community intervention. Other publications make this contribution (Bracht et al., 1994; Bracht & Kingsbury, 1990; M. Johnston, 1988;

Mittelmark et al., 1993; Wallack & Wallerstein, 1986). Rather, an overview is provided that helps to define community intervention among other interventions that promote health and prevent disease. The overview that follows discusses processes by which interventionists enter communities, develop community relationships, evaluate outcomes, and sustain programs.

Gaining Community Entree

Community health promotion may best be understood as a staged, sequential, and developmental process that begins with the skillful entree into a community, including the diagnosis of community structures, needs, capacities, and history. Kahn (1970), a pioneer of modern approaches to community entree based on labor organizing experiences in the South, maintained that community organizing is a technique and discipline—and not a mystique. This maxim sets a tone for community entree as an intervention strategy that is planned and well-orchestrated. The first step in the entree process is discerning who has political power and social influence, and what relations different sectors of the community have with sources of local influence. The CSAP partnership (see Fig. 36.1) used multisectorial committees, in part, in recognition that each committee represented community "stakeholders" of power and influence. R. B. Warren and D. I. Warren (1977), who focused on neighborhood development, provided a list of elements to consider prior to entree, including defining the boundaries of the neighborhood, identifying businesses, homes, and areas for recreation, and cultivating key informants to get a sense of the local history and current issues of importance. Such explorations prior to active involvement in communities enable the expert to choose appropriate tactics in making contact with community gatekeepers. Well-developed approaches with gatekeepers can legitimize the community health promotion specialist's entree into the community. Eng and Blanchard (1991) provided a step-by-step approach to community diagnosis, using environmental health as a case study, and described how health promotion initiatives can be derailed when the experts' initial contacts were with individuals who did not hold widespread credibility in a rural Southern community. As a result, subsequent efforts to gain entree into the community were not successful. This provides a cautionary tale illustrating the important of an accurate diagnosis of community structure and especially gatekeepers.

In community health promotion, needs assessment is a frequently used approach to facilitate entree (Green & Kreuter, 1991). Usually, the assessment combines data collection methods to determine the needs most important to both target populations and funding agencies. For example, the CSAP needs assessment (see Fig. 36.1) combined demographic information about the number of youth in the community, with social indexes including the number of youth suspended from school or arrested due to illegal substance use, survey methods that identified levels of community awareness and concern regarding youth ATOD use, group interviews to gain a richer and deeper understanding of community concerns, and resource inventories of services available.

The Planned Approach to Community Health (PATCH), developed at the Centers for Disease Control and Prevention, also typifies this technique (U.S. Department of Health and Human Services, 1995). Overall, the PATCH approach consists of five phases: mobilizing the community, collecting and organizing data, choosing health priorities, developing a comprehensive intervention plan, and evaluating the intervention. Phase I mobilization involves compiling demographic profiles and other information regarding the makeup of the community. Phase 2 is a needs assessment that consists of mortality and morbidity indicators, coupled with perceptions of need from community leaders. These types of data form the basis for prioritizing and addressing the needs expressed in the assessment. Because needs will differ across these groups and across different methods of data collection, integrating perspectives is critical (McKillip, 1987) and convergent analysis is an often-used technique for this purpose. Convergent analysis is the sequencing of data produced by each method to assure that community groups and funders have a logically presented and full picture of the data on which to base planning decisions. McKillip (1987) provided a rich and distinct approach to gathering and integrating needs assessment data.

Reliance on needs assessment may be insufficient in mobilizing communities to participate effectively. For instance, in a critique of the PATCH approach, Goodman and colleagues (1993) noted that assessments based on health status and needs perceived by the community do not identify the capacities present in communities to effectively address needs. As a result, PATCH projects may accurately reflect need, but may not suggest what community assets are present to implement community health promotion strategies effectively. Marti-Costa and Serrano-Garcia (1983) echoed critiques of needs that are based primarily on health status indicators and community leader perceptions, noting that such assessments rarely involve grassroots community members and thus do not contribute to developing community capacity. In reaction to this criticism, recent approaches to entree include the mapping of community capacities. For instance, Kretzmann and McKnight (1993) provided inventories for mapping the capacities of individuals that includes skills, levels of community interests, and involvement in community activities. They also provided maps of associations that may be present in neighborhoods that can offer opportunities for residents to meet.

Cultivating Citizen Participation

An important result of skillful entree is the health promotion specialist's cultivation of trust among community constituencies who are most concerned and/or affected by a presenting health issue. Webster's dictionary defines trust as the "total confidence in the integrity, ability, and good character of another." The definition suggests that trust engenders the absence of perceived harm. The entree process, if well-organized and based on an accurate understanding of community dynamics, enables the community health promotion specialist to be sensitive to community concerns and to approach community members in a way that produces trust. Often, the health promotion specialist will have to overcome citizen reservations in order to gain their support.

In the CSAP partnership, the formation of committees was often hampered by competition or "turf" guarding among organization members. Organizations within a community may compete for the same resources and this may limit cooperation. The ability for organizations to put aside such fears for the greater community good that concerted action can bring is often facilitated by an individual who is trusted by all parties. The specialist tries to cultivate participation among various community constituencies through an organized recruitment approach that is calculated to raise awareness of the importance of the health promotion initiative, and to instill a concern for the issue. Most importantly, participation is likely to result when concern is internalized and community members feel a personal responsibility to participate (Parham, Goodman, Steckler, Schmid, & Koch, 1993).

Goodman, D. W. Smith, Dawson, and Steckler (1991) identified five phases for recruiting participants in complex health promotion initiatives that consist of establishing legitimacy for the community development effort and credibility of the community health promotion specialist; anticipating questions from community members regarding the nature of that effort; overcoming initial skepticism and resistance that members have about becoming involved; addressing community questions about the logistics involved in participating; and convincing the community of the benefits to be derived. Several studies indicate that strategies directed at increasing perceived benefits and reducing attendant costs tend to sustain participation (Wandersman & Alderman, 1993; Wandersman, Florin, Friedmann, & Meier, 1987). Perceived high costs can also result in the untimely termination of community health programs (Goodman & Steckler, 1987–1988), whereas perceived benefits can increase the likelihood that programs are sustained (Bracht et al., 1994; Goodman & Steckler, 1989a, 1989b; Prestby, Wandersman, Florin, Rich, & Chavis, 1990). Frequently, cited benefits and incentives include those that achieve the organization's goals that are perceived as important and enhance group identity and status (Knoke & Woods, 1981; Rich, Edelstein, Hallman, & Wandersman, 1995; Wandersman et al., 1987).

Planning and Implementing Community Initiatives

To foster effective participation, health promotion specialists facilitate the participants' abilities to plan, organize, and implement effective community actions. Thus, aiding community groups in planning initiatives is an important intervention in community health promotion. Butterfoss and colleagues (Butterfoss, Goodman, Wandersman, Valois, & Chinman, 1996) described the evolution of a Plan Quality Index developed for the partnerships in Fig. 36.1 that, at first, was used by professional evaluators to rate the adequacy of the plans. Because community groups objected to such ratings, the index was transformed into a narrative that provided the community with guidance for making the plan more effective and for effectively implementing it. Such interventions are important, as the level of community participation does not seem to correlate with the plan quality or degree to which the plan is implemented (Butterfoss, Goodman, & Wandersman, 1996).

Empowerment As Means and End in Community Health Promotion

Citizen initiatives in community health promotion often entail influencing governmental, health, social, and welfare organizations to be responsive to community concerns. Consequently, the health promotion specialist may facilitate the development of community power. Empowerment is "a process by which individuals, communities and organizations gain mastery over their lives" (Rappaport, 1984). Citizen participation can be empowering (McMillan, Florin, Stevenson, Kerman, & Mitchell, 1995) and, for many communities, empowerment can be an end in itself (Rich et al., 1995). But, once empowered, communities may seek to influence the types of services and policies that affect the community (Zimmerman, 1995). Interventions that promote empowerment among participants have been reported as effective in improving birth outcomes for homeless women (Ovrebo, Ryan, Jackson, & Hutchinson, 1994), influencing governmental policy (Wang & Burris, 1994), producing modest (and mixed) results in increasing community competence (Eng & Parker, 1994), and increasing awareness and concern of the adverse consequences of excessive drinking among Native American teenagers (Wallerstein & Bernstein, 1988).

Community Coalitions, Mediating Social Structures, and Other Strategic Alliances

For community members to become empowered, their participation in a larger organized effort often is necessary (Speer & Hughey, 1995). A community coalition exemplifies the "empowering" process, because coalition members pool their individual resources to develop a critical mass in leveraging community change (C. Brown, 1984; Butterfoss et al., 1993). The CSAP partnership depicted in Fig. 36.1 is an example of a coalition that can empower citizen action. McMillan and colleagues (1995) demonstrated that such coalitions are empowering of members when they perceive that important benefits result from participating, that the group climate is supportive of members, that the group is highly committed to the work, and that the group has a strong identification with its community. McMillan et al. suggested that group interventions be directed at these variables. Guides to coalitions are beginning to proliferate and thus the health promotion specialist may be assisted by checklists and worksheets for coalition development (C. Brown, 1984; Kaye, 1990).

Community coalitions, like the CSAP partnership, may be classified as "mediating social structures," or "institutions standing between the individual in his private life and the large institutions of public life" (Berger & Neuhaus, 1977). McLeroy and colleagues (1988) noted that mediating structures are important components of a community and, besides community coalitions, include family, informal social networks, churches, voluntary associations, and neighborhoods.

Several studies illustrate the effectiveness of mediating structures as points of intervention. For instance, the strategic use of mediating structures (individuals or organizations) proved effective for enlisting participation and increasing social support (Eng & Young, 1992), and in connecting community residents to health programs. Lay health advisors can increase access to health services among disenfranchised groups like migrant workers (Watkins et al., 1994), among pregnant women who are poor, rural, and isolated (Goodman, 1992), and between local health agencies and churches in African American communities (Eng & Hatch, 1991). Other studies describe how linking agents influence the process of support for the institutionalization of health promotion programs in organizations (Goodman & Steckler, 1989a, 1989b; Penha-Walton & Pichert, 1993). The partnership depicted in Fig. 36.1 served as a mediating structure by linking committees representing parents and youth with important institutions like the police. Such linkages facilitated community-wide campaigns like the CSAP "Red Ribbon" campaign, where youth in cooperation with the police place red ribbons on highway overpasses to reinforce awareness to not drink and drive and police work with youth to see whether stores would sell alcohol or tobacco to minors.

Coalitions are one type of strategic alliance that may be nurtured by the community health promotion specialist. Others include networks, consortia, leadership councils, and citizen panels (Bracht & Gleason, 1990). Regardless of its form, strategic alliances generally share certain characteristics. Typically, they work well when members gain access to new information, ideas, materials, and other resources; when duplication of services and competition is minimized and consensus decision making is maximized; when the potential for each member to maximize power and influence is achieved; and when responsibility for addressing complex or controversial issues is shared across member organizations. Strategic alliances are forestalled when members' resources are diverted unduly to the alliance, when the alliance focuses on issues that are not of core concern to members, or when the alliance delays in taking action due to a slow and cumbersome process for reaching consensus (Alter & Hage, 1993; Butterfoss et al., 1993).

Because strategic alliances are hard to cultivate and maintain, technical assistance can be contoured to facilitate ongoing development among member groups (Florin, Mitchell, & Stevenson, 1993). For example, Gray (1989) outlined three stages of the collaborative process: problem setting for developing a common definition of the problem, identification of stakeholders, and a commitment to collaborate; direction setting for setting the agenda, exploring options, establishing ground rules, organizing subgroups, and reaching agreement; and implementation for building external support, establishing structures to sustain collective activities, and monitoring the agreement. Others propose a three-stage model of network development as a continuum from informal to formal linkages (Alter & Hage, 1993). The three stages include exchange or obligational networks composed of loosely linked organizations devoted to resource exchange with few joint activities and that are maintained by individuals who coordinate and integrate tasks across organizations; action or promotional networks of organizations that share and pool resources to accomplish concerted action, but whose interorganizational activities tend to be peripheral to member organizations' goals; and systemic networks of organizations that have formal links that are long term to abet the joint production of goods or services.

The literature on voluntary community-based organizations and the institutionalization of community health promotion programs identify organizational characteristics and operations that are indicators of organizational competency (Goodman, McLeroy, Steckler & Hoyle, 1993; Goodman & Steckler, 1987–1988, 1989a, 1989b; Goodman, Wandersman, Chinman, Imm, & Morrissey, 1996). Among the organizational characteristics and operations that are likely to play a role are: formalization of rules and procedures for managing the coalition; well-established internal communication patterns; a variety of leadership roles; ability to access and exchange resources; procedures for conflict resolution; active recruitment and training of members who are representative of community agencies and constituencies; and participatory decision making. Keeping coalition members participating actively benefits from provision of incentives. Viable coalitions do a better job of accessing resources external to the organization. Finally, coalitions that evaluate their mission, goals, objectives, and activities regularly are more efficacious than coalitions that are not privy to such self-evaluation data. Organizations that achieve high levels of each of these processes and outcomes are more likely to create a favorable organizational climate, such as greater group cohesiveness, which in turn has been shown to be related to greater satisfaction, participation, and performance (Florin & Wandersman, 1990). Likewise, there is a body of research illustrating that citizen participation in the research and intervention process not only has the potential to improve the quality of life for communities and individuals but it can also increase the quality of data collected by researchers.

EVALUATION OF COMMUNITY INTERVENTIONS

There is a substantial literature on evaluating community intervention (D. G. Altman, 1986; Blackburn et al., 1983; Blake et al., 1987; Carleton et al., 1995; Cowen, 1978; Fawcett et al., 1995; Goodman & Steckler, 1989a; Group, 1995; Jackson, Altman, Howard-Pitney, & Farquhar, 1989; Kelly, 1988; Levine et al., 1993; Luepker et al., 1994; Pirie, 1990; Wandersman et al., 1983; Winkelstein & Marmot, 1981). A systematic review of this literature is beyond the scope of this chapter, although there is reasonably strong evidence that interventions in community settings can be effective in changing individual health behavior and environmental supports that promote health. Most of these interventions employ multilevel intervention approaches, but it is not possible to disentangle the effects of the different approaches.

Evaluations of large scale community intervention trials face several key evaluation challenges (Fortmann et al., 1995). Validity threats include compensatory rivalry of comparison communities, compensatory equalization of treatments, resentful demoralization of comparison communities, between-city variation on baseline risk factors even after census matching, and diffusion or imitation of treatment in comparison communities. Also, there are several critical choices about the design that need to be considered. These include whether to evaluate specific effects of individual interventions, synergistic effects of entire interventions, or effects of complementary interventions. In recent years, evaluators of community interventions have developed highly refined systems of process monitoring (Fawcett et al., 1995; Goodman et al., 1996).

With respect to monitoring and evaluation of community health promotion initiatives, it is often the case that community groups do not have the expertise and financial resources to monitor progress and results. Consequently, community development experts have begun to develop monitoring and evaluation systems that can be implemented in collaboration with nonprofessionals. A goal of such evaluations is the transfer of expertise to the community members to build capacity and to empower community groups to implement self-monitoring and evaluation of community health promotion initiatives. Approaches that establish partnerships with community members and build monitoring and evaluation skills may be viewed as a type of capacity building intervention. Recent notable examples of such approaches to promote physical and mental health include Prevention Plus III (Linney & Wandersman, 1991, 1996), a four-step approach to identifying program goals, processes, outcomes, and impacts applicable to most community-based programs, and FORECAST (Formative Evaluation, Consultation, and Systems Technique), a technique that is used to help community groups monitor the development of community initiatives and make systemic adjustments to assure that the initiative evolve according to plan (Goodman & Wandersman, 1994). Fawcett et al. (1994) and Francisco, Paine, and Fawcett (1993) developed a complementary system that uses "Tracking of Actions" logs to monitor the vital community processes that may indicate whether the community is on track in producing desirable community changes. The log data are graphed cumulatively from month to month so that trends in effort can be assessed over time; community groups use the graph to fine tune the community intervention.

Both longitudinal (cohort) and cross-sectional (independent) surveys have been utilized as core outcome evaluation data collection tools. Cohort designs have the advantage that they allow for controlling baseline levels, studying stable population groups, analyzing change processes, increased statistical power, and studying changes based on intervention exposure and individual covariates. Disadvantages of cohort designs include out-migration, selective dropout, and testing effects. In contrast, the advantages of cross-sectional designs are that data are collected from a representative of entire community and data are not affected by drop-outs or by prior participation. Disadvantages of cross-sectional designs include lower statistical power, midstudy in-migration and thus reduced intervention exposure, expense and greater difficulty in accounting for individual characteristics.

In reviewing the community-based literature as a whole, Fortmann et al. (1995) concluded that "health education in various forms, as well as social policies and economic conditions, causes risk factor changes. The most important questions now address how communities change and how interventions can be designed to enhance most effectively these changes in healthful directions" (p. 582).

RESEARCHER AND COMMUNITY RELATIONSHIPS

At the root of community intervention is the relation between interveners and communities. There is a long history of strained relations, different priorities, and poor communication between communities and interventionists (D. G. Altman, 1995b; Wandersman et al., 1983). Some of the key issues that affect the relation between researchers and communities working on health, as well as other topics, revolve around the following themes (D. G. Altman, 1995b): (a) ownership and control; (b) research versus service delivery; (c) time orientation; (d) ensuring program integrity; (e) overcoming the status quo; (f) gaining broad-based support; (g) reliance on experts and being an expert; (h) funding priorities versus community priorities; and (i) competition for existing resources. Ideally, researchers and community representatives who are engaged in collaborative projects to promote community health offer each other new ideas and perspectives in a mutually beneficial way. Historically, however, barriers have prevented researchers from carrying out their "public trust" with communities and a variety of "town-gown" tensions have become commonplace. This is unfortunate because researchers and communities have resources that are mutually beneficial (D. G. Altman, 1995b). Indeed, projects that include significant and meaningful citizen participation can create strong linkages between the community and interventionists and improve on the design and implementation of effective interventions (Chavis, Stucky, & Wandersman, 1983; Marentette & Kurji, 1988). Sustaining community health interventions (also referred to as institutionalization or incorporation) has presented itself to psychologists and policymakers with as yet little evidence that it is a high priority. Institutionalization is predicated on building community and organizational supports for programs (Goodman & Steckler, 1989b) and increasing community and practitioner competence in addressing community health issues (Eng & Young, 1992). Strategies (Steckler & Goodman, 1989) and measures (Goodman et al., 1993) for program institutionalization exist and community programs can benefit by building institutionalization into their planning and assessments.

Lewin (1951) coined the term "action research" to describe theoretically based research that made a difference in the real world. Many community interventions were implicitly influenced by an action research perspective. In the Minnesota Heart Health Program, for example, three quarters of the programs initiated by the researchers were continued by local community groups (Bracht & Gleason, 1990; Murray, 1986). In the Stanford Five City Project, allocation of resources to the communities, ongoing technical assistance and training, and encouragement of local community program development, resulted in the community building a permanent infrastructure to support chronic disease prevention and the adoption by numerous community groups of specific programs and programmatic strategies initiated under the research grant (D. G. Altman, 1995b; Farquhar et al., 1990; Fortmann et al., 1995). Indeed, over half of the larger programs initiated by the Stanford group were maintained by community groups for at least a few years after the research program ended (Fortmann et al., 1995). Furthermore, the Stanford group alone has distributed over one million copies of educational materials used in the study to other researchers, educators, worksites, and other community-based organizations. In a community intervention to reduce CVD in a low socioeconomic status section of New York City, Shea and colleagues concluded that it is feasible to deliver a broad-based community intervention in a disadvantaged community. Programs originally developed in an academic health center can be transferred to a community-run organization, however, without ongoing resources, community organizations in poor communities are unlikely to be able to sustain programs (Shea, Basch, Wechsler & Lantigua, 1996).

The conflicts between researchers and communities can be understood from a dialectical perspective. A dialectic is partly defined by the opposition of two forces (Altman, Vinsel & Brown, 1981; Rappaport, 1977), although these forces are aspects of a unity with each force partly defining the other. For the researcher concerned with sustaining interventions, a dialectical tension exists between maintaining control over the interventions and allowing the community to assume control. Similarly, there are dialectical tensions for the community between the desire for autonomy and the community's dependence on researchers for their expertise and for taking action immediately versus waiting until evidence for intervention efficacy emerges. These dialectical tensions affect the extent to which interventions are sustained. Without recognizing and coping with these tensions, sustaining community interventions will be difficult to achieve.

We suggest that it is time once again for health psychology to confront the issue of how its research makes a difference to communities (Altman, 1995b). This issue has both practical and empirical ramifications. The practical ramifications relate to social relevance and utility of science. Scientists, however, must believe that participating in community interventions will also result in more valid empirical research and theory. In psychology, a number of distinguished scientists have commented on these relationships. Bevan (1970), for example, noted:

> It is tragic that so many academicians—including many of us in psychology—whose fields of expertness give them a legitimate interest in the substance of such problems are so ignorant of what is going on in the real world beyond the campus gates. ... Indeed, in the very least, such ignorance is a denial of the responsibilities of enlightened citizenship. (p. 445)

One of the problems that has prevented psychologists from being more active in community interventions is the age old conflict between theory and action. Indeed, there are some psychologists with whom we have interacted who believe that community intervention is inconsistent with a psychological approach. Lewin (1951) commented on similar tensions some years ago:

> Many psychologists working today in an applied field are keenly aware of the need for close cooperation between theoretical and applied psychology. This can be accomplished in psychology, as it has been accomplished in physics, if the theorist does not look toward applied problems with highbrow aversion or with a fear of social problems, and if the applied psychologist realizes that there is nothing so practical as a good theory. (p. 169)

A psychological perspective could bring value to community interventions and involvement in community interventions would bring value to psychologists. Thus, health psychologists have much to offer to community interventionists, but they must be willing to apply their knowledge and expertise in the community laboratory. Unfortunately, many psychology students and many psychology training programs do not view the community at-large as an appropriate setting for psychological intervention. As the next generation of psychologists is trained, they are well-advised to follow the advice of Miller (1969), a 20th-century leader in psychology:

> Our responsibility is less to assume the role of experts and try to apply psychology ourselves than to give it away to the people who really need it—and that includes everyone. The practice of valid psychology by nonpsychologists will inevitably change people's conception of themselves and what they can do. When we have accomplished that, we will really have caused a psychological revolution. (p. 1071)

CONCLUSIONS

This chapter has reviewed the theoretical, conceptual, empirical, and logistical underpinnings of community intervention. As a strategy, the popularity of community intervention has grown substantially in recent decades. As others have noted (Thompson & Kinne, 1990): "The increasing focus on 'community' in health promotion is due, at least in part, to growing recognition that behavior is greatly influenced by the environment in which people live. Proponents of community approaches to behavioral change recognize that local values, norms, and behavior patterns have a significant effect on shaping an individual's attitudes and behaviors" (p. 45). The basis for social and community interventions extends from at least two lines of reasoning, one philosophical and one practical. On philosophical grounds, the principals of democracy are the ideological girders for social approaches to health education. Steckler and colleagues (1987) maintained that health education practice is founded on democracy as a political philosophy and citizen participation is sine qua non as a professional principle. This professional orientation extends from Nyswander (1967), who was most concerned with social participation in an open society, and Steuart (Steuart & Kark, 1993), who maintained that "health education is rooted in the recognition that the culture of a community has a deep and abiding influence on its health ... [and] is socially oriented in its interpretations of the epidemiology of health and disease" (p. S-29). From the standpoint of democratic principles, the most effective health education strategy is one that raises the levels of awareness and concerns for groups at health risk and enables them to devise their own strategies to reduce risk, strategies that are valid culturally and contextually. On practical grounds, change in health behavior and status is more likely to occur when the social and cultural context is altered to support pro-health options.

REFERENCES

Ajzen, I., & Fishbein, M. (1980). *Understanding attitudes and predicting social behavior.* Englewood Cliffs, NJ: Prentice-Hall.

Alter, C., & Hage, J. (1993). *Organizations working together.* Newbury Park, CA: Sage.

Altman, D. G. (1986). A framework for evaluating community-based heart disease prevention programs. *Social Science and Medicine, 22,* 479–487.

Altman, D. G. (1995a). Strategies for community health intervention: Promises, paradoxes, pitfalls. *Psychosomatic Medicine, 57,* 226–233.

Altman, D. G. (1995b). Sustaining interventions in community systems: On the relationship between researchers and communities. *Health Psychology, 14*(6), 526–536.

Altman, D. G., Balcazar, F. E., Fawcett, S. B., Seekins, T., & Young, J. Q. (1994). *Public health advocacy: Creating community change to improve health.* Palo Alto, CA: Stanford Health Promotion Resource Center.

Altman, I., Vinsel, A., & Brown, B. B. (1981). Dialectic conceptions in social psychology: An application to social penetration and privacy regulation. In L. Berkowitz (Ed.), *Advances in experimental social psychology* (Vol. 14, pp. 108–160). New York: Academic.

Bandura, A. (1986). *Social foundations of thought and action: A social cognitive theory.* Englewood Cliffs, NJ: Prentice-Hall.

Bandura, A. (1997). *Self-efficacy: The exercise of control.* New York: Freeman.

Bennis, W. G., Benne, K. D., & Chin, R. (1969). *The planning of change* (Vol. 2). New York: Holt, Rinehart & Winston.

Berger, P. L., & Neuhaus, R. J. (1977). Mediating structures and the dilemmas of the welfare state. In *To empower people: The role of mediating structures in public policy* (pp. 1–8). Washington, DC: American Enterprise Institute for Public Policy Research.

Bevan, W. (1970). Psychology, the university, and the real world around us. *American Psychologist, 25,* 442–449.

Binder, A., Stokols, D., & Catalano, R. (1975). Social ecology: An emerging multidiscipline. *Journal of Environmental Education, 7,* 32–43.

Blackburn, H., Luepker, R., Kline, F. G., Bracht, N., Carlaw, R., Jacobs, D., Mittelmark, M., Stauffer, L., & Taylor, H. L. (1983). The Minnesota Heart Health Program: A research and demonstration project in cardiovascular disease prevention. In J. Matarrazzo, S. Weiss, J. Herd, N. Miller, & S. Weiss (Eds.), *Behavioral health: A handbook of health enhancement and disease prevention* (pp. 1171–1178). New York: Wiley.

Blake, S. M., Jeffery, R. W., Finnegan, J. R., Crow, R. S., Pirie, P. L., Ringhofer, K. R., Fruetel, J. R., Caspersen, C. J., & Mittelmark, M. B. (1987). Process evaluation of a community-based physical activity campaign: The Minnesota Heart Health Program experience. *Health Education Research, 2,* 115–121.

Bloom, M. (1996). *Primary prevention practices.* Thousand Oaks, CA: Sage.

Bracht, N., Finnegan, J. R., Rissel, C., Weisbrod, R., Gleason, J., Corbett, J., & Veblen-Mortenson, S. (1994). Community ownership and program continuation following a health demonstration project. *Health Education Research, 9*(2), 243–255.

Bracht, N., & Gleason, J. (1990). Strategies and structures for citizen participation. In N. Bracht (Ed.), *Health promotion at the community level* (pp. 109–124). Newbury Park, CA: Sage.

Bracht, N., & Kingsbury, L. (1990). Community organization principles in health promotion: A five stage model. In N. Bracht (Ed.), *Health promotion at the community level* (pp. 66–88). Newbury Park, CA: Sage.

Bracht, N., & Tsouros, A. (1990). Principles and strategies of effective community participation. *Health Promotion International, 5*(3), 199–208.

Bronfenbrenner, U. (1977). Toward an experimental ecology of human development. *American Psychologist, 32*(7), 513–531.

Brown, C. (1984). *The art of coalition building: A guide for community leaders.* New York: The American Jewish Committee.

Brown, E. R. (1991). Community action for health promotion: A strategy to empower individuals and communities. *International Journal of Health Services, 21*(3), 441–456.

Brownson, R. C., Koffman, D. M., Novotny, T. E., Hughes, R. G., & Eriksen, M. P. (1995). Environmental and policy interventions to control tobacco use and prevent cardiovascular disease. *Health Education Quarterly, 22*(4), 478–498.

Buckner, W., Miner, K., Dreuter, M., & Wilson, M. (1992). PATCH: Community health promotion: The agenda for the '90s. *Journal of Health Education, 23*(3).

Butterfoss, F. D., Goodman, R. M., & Wandersman, A. (1993). Community coalitions for health promotion and disease prevention. *Health Education Research, 8*(3), 315–330.

Butterfoss, F. D., Goodman, R. M., & Wandersman, A. (1996). Community coalitions for prevention and health promotion: Factors predicting satisfaction, participation and planning. *Health Education Quarterly, 23*(1), 65–79.

Butterfoss, F. D., Goodman, R. M., Wandersman, A., Valois, R. F., & Chinman, M. (1996). The plan quality index: An empowerment evaluation tool for measuring and improving the quality of plans. In D. Fetterman, S. Kaftarian, & A. Wandersman (Eds.), *Empowerment evaluation: knowledge and tools for self-assessment and accountability* (pp. 304–331). Newbury Park, CA: Sage.

Cardiovascular Disease Plan Steering Committee. (1994). *Preventing death and disability from cardiovascular diseases: A state-based plan for action.* Association of State and Territorial Health Officials.

Carleton, R. A., Lasater, T. M., Assaf, A. R., Feldman, H. A., & McKinlay, S. (1995). The Pawtucket Heart Health Program: Community changes in cardiovascular risk factors and projected disease risk. *American Journal of Public Health, 85*(6), 777–785.

Chapman, S. (1994). *The fight for public health: Principles and practice of media advocacy.* London: British Medical Journal Books.

Chavis, D. M., & Newbrough, J. R. (1986). The meaning of "community" in community psychology. *Journal of Community Psychology, 14*(4), 335–340.

Chavis, D. M., & Wandersman, A. (1990). Sense of community in the urban environment: A catalyst for participation and community development. *American Journal of Community Psychology, 18*(1), 55–81.

Chavis, D., Stucky, P., & Wandersman, A. (1983). Returning basic research to the community: A relationship between scientist and citizen. *American Psychologist*(4), 424–434.

Cheadle, A., Psaty, B. M., Diehr, P., Koepsell, T., Wagner, E., Wickizer, T., & Curry, S. (1993). An empirical exploration of a conceptual model for community-based health promotion. *International Quarterly of Community Health Education, 13*(4), 329–363.

The COMMIT Research Group. (1995a). Community intervention trial for smoking cessation (COMMIT): 1. Cohort results from a four-year community intervention. *American Journal of Public Health, 85*(2), 183–192.

The COMMIT Research Group. (1995b). Community intervention trial for smoking cessation (COMMIT): Changes in adult cigarette smoking prevalence. *American Journal of Public Health, 85*(2), 193–200.

Cowen, E. L. (1978). Some problems in community program evaluation research. *Journal of Consulting and Clinical Psychology, 46,* 792–805.

Davis, D. J. (1991). A systems approach to the prevention of alcohol and other drug problems. *Family Resource Coalition, 10,* 3.

Department of Health and Human Services. (1991). *Healthy people 2000: National health promotion and disease prevention objectives* (91–50212). Washington, DC: Department of Health and Human Services.

DiClemente, C. C., & Prochaska, J. O. (1985). Processes and sxtages of change: Coping and competence in smoking behavior change. In S. Shiffman & T. A. Wills (Eds.), *Coping and substance abuse* (pp. 319–343). New York: Academic Press.

DuRant, R. H., Escobedo, L. H., & Heath, G. W. (1995). The relationship between anabolic steroid use, strength training, and multiple drug use among adolescents in the United States. *Pediatrics, 96,* 268–272.

Elder, J. P., Schmid, T. L., Dower, P., & Hedlund, S. (1993). Community heart health programs: Components, rationale, and strategies for effective interventions. *Journal of Public Health Policy, 4,* 463–479.

Eng, E., & Blanchard, L. (1991). Action-oriented community diagnosis: A health education tool. *International Quarterly of Community Health Education, 11*(2), 93–110.

Eng, E., & Hatch, J. W. (1991). Networking between agencies and Black churches: The lay health advisor model. *Prevention in human services, 10*(1), 123–146.

Eng, E., & Parker, E. (1994). Measuring community competence in the Mississippi Delta: the interface between program evaluation and empowerment. *Health Education Quarterly, 21*(2), 199–220.

Eng, E., & Young, R. (1992). Lay health advisors as community change agents. *Family and Community Health, 15*(1), 24–40.

Ewart, C. K. (1991). Social action theory for a public health psychology. *American Psychologist, 46,* 931–946.

Farquhar, J. W., Fortmann, S. P., Flora, J. A., Taylor, C. B., Haskell, W. L., Williams, P. T., Maccoby, N., & Wood, P. D. (1990). Effects of communitywide education on cardiovascular disease risk factors: The Stanford Five-City Project. *Journal of the American Medical Association, 264,* 359–365.

Farquhar, J. W., Fortmann, S. P., Wood, P. D., & Haskell, W. L. (1983). Community studies of cardiovascular disease prevention. In N. Kaplan & J. Stamler (Eds.), *Prevention of coronary heart disease* (pp. 170–181). Philadelphia: Saunders.

Fawcett, S. B., Harris, K. J., Paine-Andrews, A. L., Lewis, R., Richter, K., Harris, K. J., Williams, E. L., Berkley, J. Y., Schuyltz, J. A., Fisher, J. L., & Lopez, C. M. (1994). *Work group evaluation handbook: Evaluating and supporting community initiatives for health and development.* Lawrence: University of Kansas, Work Group on Health Promotion & Community Development.

Fawcett, S. B., Sterling, T. D., Paine-Andrews, A., Harris, K. J., Francisco, V. T., Richter, K. P., Lewis, R. K., & Schmid, T. L. (1995). *Evaluating community efforts to prevent cardiovascular diseases.* Atlanta: Centers for Disease Control and Prevention, National Center for Chronic Disease Prevention and Health Promotion.

Fisher, E. B. (1995). Editorial: The results of the COMMIT trial. *American Journal of Public Health, 85*(2), 159–160.

Flora, J. A., & Cassidy, D. (1990). Roles of media in community-based health promotion. In N. Bracht (Ed.), *Health promotion at the community level* (pp. 143–157). Newbury Park, CA: Sage.

Flora, J. A., & Farquhar, J. W. (1988). Methods of message design: Experiences from the Stanford Five City Project. *Scandinavian Journal of Primary Health Care* (Suppl. 1), 39–47.

Florin, P., Mitchell, R., & Stevenson, J. (1993). Identifying technical assistance needs in community coalitions: A developmental approach. *Health Education Research, 8,* 417–432.

Florin, P., & Wandersman, A. (1990). An introduction to citizen participation, voluntary organizations, and community development: Insights for empowerment through research. *American Journal of Community Psychology, 18*(1), 41–54.

Fortmann, S. P., Flora, J. A., Winkleby, M. A., Schooler, C., Taylor, C. B., & Farquhar, J. W. (1995). Community intervention trials: Reflections on the Stanford Five-City Project experience. *American Journal of Epidemiology, 142*(6), 576–586.

Francisco, V. T., Paine, A. L., & Fawcett, S. B. (1993). A methodology for monitoring and evaluating community health coalitions. *Health education research: theory and practice, 8,* 403–416.

Freudenberg, N. (1984–1985). Training health educators for social change. *International Quarterly of Community Health Education, 5,* 37–52.

Glanz, K., Lankenau, B., Foerster, S., Temple, S., Mullis, R., & Schmid, T. (1995). Environmental and policy approaches to cardiovascular disease prevention through nutrition: Opportunities for state and local action. *Health Education Quarterly, 22*(4), 512–527.

Goodman, R. M. (1992). *Final evaluation report: The Marlboro County prenatal caring project.* Washington, DC: The Children's Defense Fund.

Goodman, R. M., Burdine, J. N., Meehan, E., & McLeroy, K. R. (1993). Community Coalitions for health promotion. *Health Education Research, 8*(3), theme issue.

Goodman, R. M., McLeroy, K. R., Steckler, A., & Hoyle, R. H. (1993). Development of level of institutionalization (LoIn) scales for health promotion. *Health Education Quarterly, 20*(2), 161–178.

Goodman, R. M., Smith, D. W., Dawson, L., & Steckler, A. (1991). Recruiting school districts into a dissemination study. *Health Education Research, 6*(3), 373–385.

Goodman, R. M., & Steckler, A. (1987–1988). The life and death of a health promotion program: A institutionalization case study. *International quarterly of community health education, 8*(1), 5–21.

Goodman, R. M., & Steckler, A. (1989a). A framework for assessing program institutionalization. *Knowledge in Society: The International Journal of Knowledge Transfer, 2*(1), 57–71.

Goodman, R. M., & Steckler, A. (1989b). A model for the institutionalization of health promotion programs. *Family and Community Health, 11*(4), 63–78.

Goodman, R. M., Steckler, A., Hoover, S., & Schwartz, R. (1993). A critique of contemporary community health promotion approaches: Maine—a multiple case study. *American Journal of Health Promotion, 7*(3), 208–220.

Goodman, R. M., & Wandersman, A. (1994). FORECAST: A formative approach to evaluating the CSAP community partnerships. *Journal of Community Psychology* (CSAP special issue), 6–25.

Goodman, R. M., Wandersman, A., Chinman, M., Imm, P., & Morrissey, E. (1996). An ecological assessment of community-based interventions for prevention and health promotion: Approaches to measuring community coalitions. *American Journal of Community Psychology, 24*(1), 33–61.

Goodman, R. M., Wheeler, F. C., & Lee, P. R. (1995). Evaluation of the heart to heart project: lessons from a community-based chronic disease prevention project. *American Journal of Health Promotion, 9*(6), 443–455.

Gray, B. (1989). *Collaborating: Finding common ground for multi-party problems.* San Francisco: Jossey-Bass.

Green, L. W. (1986). The theory of participation: A qualitative analysis of its expression in national and international health policies. *Advances in Health Education and Health Promotion, 1*(A), 211–236.

Green, L. W., & Kreuter, M. W. (1990). Health promotion as a public health strategy for the 1990's. *Annual Review of Public Health, 11,* 319–334.

Green, L. W., & Kreuter, M. W. (1991). *Health promotion planning: An educational and environmental approach.* Mountain View, CA: Mayfield.

Green, L. W., & McAlister, A. L. (1984). Macro-intervention to support health behavior: Some theoretical perspectives and practical reflections. *Health Education Quarterly, 11*(3), 322–339.

Group, T.C.R. (1995). Community intervention trial for smoking cessation (COMMIT): I. Cohort results form a four-year community intervention. *American Journal of Public Health, 85*(2), 183–192.

Haglund, B.J.A., & Tillgren, P. (Eds.). (1988). *Community intervention strategies.* Uppsala, Sweden: Almqvist & Wiksell Tryckeri.

Hawkins, D., & Catalano, R. (1992). *Communities that care: Action for drug abuse prevention.* San Francisco: Jossey-Bass.

Hornik, R. C. (1980). Shedding some light on evaluation's myths. *Development Communication Report, 29.*

Iscoe, I. (1974). Community psychology and the competent community. *American Psychologist, 8,* 607–613.

Iscoe, I. (1982). Toward a viable community health psychology: Caveats from the experiences of the community mental health movement. *American Psychologist, 37*(8), 961–965.

Iscoe, I., & Harris, L. C. (1984). Social and community interventions. *Annual Review of Psychology, 35,* 333–360.

Jackson, C., Altman, D. G., Howard-Pitney, B. A., & Farquhar, J. W. (1989). Evaluating community level health promotion and disease prevention interventions. *New Directions for Program Evaluation, 43,* 19–32.

Jeffery, R. W., Forster, J. L., Schmid, T. L., McBride, C. M., Rooney, B. L., & Pirie, P. L. (1990). Community attitudes toward public policies to control alcohol, tobacco and high-fat consumption. *American Journal of Preventive Medicine, 6*(1), 12–19.

Johnston, L. D., O'Malley, P.M.P., & Bachman, J. D. (1991). *Drug use among American high school seniors, college students and young adults, 1975–1990* (DHHS Pub No. ADM 91–1813). Rockville, MD: U.S. Department of Health and Human Services, National Institute on Drug Abuse.

Johnston, M. (1988). Appendix 1: Development of a community health programme. *Scandinavian Journal of Primary Health Care* (Suppl. 1), 119–129.

Kahn, S. (1970). *How people get power.* New York: McGraw-Hill.

Kaye, G. (1990). A community organizer's perspective on citizen participation research and the researcher–practitioner partnership. *American Journal of Community Psychology, 18*(1), 151–157.

Kelly, J. G. (1966). Ecological constraints on mental health services. *American Psychologist, 21,* 535–539.

Kelly, J. G. (1968). Toward an ecological conception of preventive interventions. In J.W.J. Carter (Ed.), *Research contributions from psychology to community mental health* (pp. 75–99). New York: Behavioral Publications.

Kelly, J. G. (1988). *A guide to conducting prevention research in the community.* New York: Haworth.

King, A. C., Jeffery, R. W., Fridinger, F., Dusenbury, L., Provence, S., Hedlund, S. A., & Spangler, K. (1995). Environmental and policy approaches to cardiovascular disease prevention through physical activity: Issues and opportunities. *Health Education Quarterly, 22*(4), 499–511.

Kinne, S., Thompson, B., Chrisman, N. J., & Hanley, J. R. (1989). Community organization to enhance the delivery of preventive health services. *American Journal of Preventive Medicine, 5*(4), 225–229.

Knoke, D., & Woods, J. (1981). *Organized for action: commitment in voluntary associations.* New Brunswick, NJ: Rutgers University Press.

Kotler, P., & Roberto, E. L. (1989). *Social marketing: Strategies for changing public behavior.* New York: The Free Press.

Kretzmann, J. P., & McKnight, J. L. (1993). *Building communities from the inside out: a path toward finding and mobilizing a community's assets.* Chicago: ACTA Publications.

Lando, H. A., Pechacek, T. F., Pirie, P. L., Murray, D. M., Mittelmark, M. B., Lichtenstein, E., Nothwehr, F., & Gray, C. (1995). Changes in adult cigarette smoking in the Minnesota Heart Health Program. *American Journal of Public Health, 85*(2), 201–208.

Lefebvre, R. C., Lasater, T., Carleton, R. A., & Peterson, G. (1987). Theory and delivery of health programming in the community: The Pawtucket Heart Health Program. *Preventive Medicine, 16,* 80–95.

Lefebvre, R. C., Lasater, T. M., Assaf, A. R., & Carleton, R. A. (1988). Pawtucket Heart Health Program: The process of stimulating community change. *Scandinavian Journal of Primary Health Care* (Suppl. 1), 31–37.

Levine, M., Toro, P. A., & Perkins, D. V. (1993). Social and community interventions. *Annual Review of Psychology, 44,* 525–558.

Leviton, L. C. (1996). Integrating psychology and public health. *American Psychologist, 51*(1), 42–51.

Lewin, K. (1951). *Field theory in social science.* New York: Harper & Row.

Linney, J. A., & Wandersman, A. (1991). *Prevention plus III: A four-step guide to useful program assessment.* Rockville, MD: U.S. Department of Health and Human Services, Office for Substance Abuse Prevention.

Linney, J. A., & Wandersman, A. (1996). Empowering community groups with evaluation skills: The Prevention Plus III Model. In D. Fetterman, S. Kaftarian, & A. Wandersman (Eds.), *Empowerment evaluation: Knowledge and tools for self-assessment and accountability* (pp. 259–276). Newbury Park, CA: Sage.

Luepker, R. V., Murray, D. M., Jacobs, D. R., Mittelmark, M. B., Bracht, N., Carlaw, R., Crow, R., Elmer, P., Finnegan, J., Folson, A. R., Grimm, R., Hannan, P. J., Jeffrey, R., Lando, H., McGovern, P., Mullis, R., Perry, C. L., Pechacek, R., Pirie, P., Sprafka, J. M., Weisbrod, R., & Blackburn, H. (1994). Community education for cardiovascular disease prevention: Risk factor changes in the Minnesota Heart Health Program. *American Journal of Public Health, 84*(9), 1383–1393.

Maccoby, N., & Altman, D. G. (1988). Disease prevention in communities: The Stanford Heart Disease Prevention Program. In R. Price, E. L. Cowen, R. P. Lorion, & J. Ramos-McKay (Eds.), *14 Ounces of Prevention* (pp. 165–174). Washington, DC: American Psychological Association.

Marentette, M., & Kurji, K. (1988). Community development: Use of a multi-service system in Nova Scotia. *Canadian Journal of Public Health, 79,* 458–459.

Marti-Costa, S., & Serrano-Garcia, I. (1983). Needs assessment and community development: An ideological perspective. *Prevention in Human Services, 2*(4), 75–88.

McAlister, A. L. (1991). Population behavior change: A theory-based approach. *Journal of Public Health Policy, Winter,* 345–361.

McGinnis, M. (1994). The role of behavioral research in national health policy. In S. Blumenthal, K. Matthews, & S. Weiss (Eds.), *New research frontiers in behavioral medicine: Proceedings of the national conference* (pp. 217–222). Washington, DC: NIH Publications.

McGwire, W. J. (1981). Theoretical foundations of campaigns. In R. E. Rice & W. J. Paisley, (Eds.), *Public Communication Campaigns* (pp. 67–83). Beverly Hills, CA: Sage.

McKillip, J. (1987). *Needs analysis: Tools for human services and education.* Newbury Park, CA: Sage.

McKnight, J. L. (1987). Regenerating community. *Social Policy, Winter,* 54–58.

McLeroy, K. R., Bibeau, D., Steckler, A., & Glanz, K. (1988). An ecological perspective on health promotion programs. *Health Education Quarterly, 15*(4), 351–377.

McMillan, B., Florin, P., Stevenson, J., Kerman, B., & Mitchell, R. E. (1995). Empowerment praxis in community coalitions. *American Journal of community psychology, 23*(5), 699–727.

Meyer, A. J., Nash, J. D., McAlister, A. L., Maccoby, N., & Farquhar, J. W. (1980). Skills training in a cardiovascular health education campaign. *Journal of Consulting and Clinical Psychology, 48*(2), 129–142.

Mico, P. R. (1978). An introduction to policy for health educators. *Health Education Monographs, 6* (Suppl. 1), 7–17.

Milio, N. (1981). *Promoting health through public policy.* Philadelphia: Davis.

Miller, G. A. (1969). Psychology as a means of promoting human welfare. *American Psychologist, 24,* 1063–1075.

Mills, R. C., & Kelly, J. G. (1972). Cultural adaptation and ecological analogies: Analysis of three Mexican villages. In S. E. Golann & C. Eisdorfer (Eds.), *Handbook of community mental health.* New York: Appleton-Century-Crofts.

Minkler, M. (1990). Improving health through community organization. In K. Glanz, F. M. Lewis, & B. K. Rimer (Eds.), *Health behavior and health education: Theory, research, and practice* (pp. 257–287). San Francisco: Jossey-Bass.

Mittelmark, M. B., Hunt, M. K., Heath, G. W., & Schmid, T. L. (1993). Realistic outcomes: Lessons from community-based research and demonstration programs for the prevention of cardiovascular disease. *Journal of Public Health Policy, 4,* 437–462.

Moos, R. H. (1979). Social ecological perspectives on health. In G. C. Stone, F. Cohen, & N. E. Adler (Eds.), *Health psychology: A handbook* (pp. 523–547). San Francisco: Jossey-Bass.

Murray, D. M. (1986). Dissemination of community health promotion programs: The Fargo–Moorhead Heart Health Program. *Journal of School Health, 56*(9), 375–381.

Novelli, W. D. (1990). Applying social marketing to health promotion and disease prevention. In K. Glanz, F. M. Lewis, & B. K. Rimer (Eds.), *Health behavior and health education: Theory, research, and practice* (pp. 342–369). San Francisco: Jossey- Bass.

Nyswander, D. (1967). The open society: Its implications for health educators. *Health Education Monographs, 1,* 3–13.

Ovrebo, B., Ryan, M., Jackson, K., & Hutchinson, K. (1994). The homeless prenatal program: A model for empowering homeless pregnant women. *Health Education Quarterly, 21*(2), 187–198.

Parham, D., Goodman, R. M., Steckler, A., Schmid, J., & Koch, G. (1993). Adoption of health education: Tobacco prevention curricula in North Carolina school districts. *Family and Community Health, 16*(3), 54–64.

Penha-Walton, M.L.I., & Pichert, J. W. (1993). Institutionalizing patient education programs. *Journal of Nurse Administrators, 23*(6), 36–41.

Pirie, P. L. (1990). Evaluating health promotion programs: Basic questions and approaches. In N. Bracht (Ed.), *Health promotion at the community level* (pp. 201–208). Newbury Park, CA: Sage.

Prestby, J. E., Wandersman, A., Florin, P., Rich, R., & Chavis, D. (1990). Benefits, costs, incentive management and participation in voluntary organizations: A means to understanding and promoting empowerment. *American Journal of Community Psychology, 18*(1), 117–149.

Prochaska, J. O., & DiClemente, C. C. (1983). Stages and processes of self-change of smoking: Toward an integrative model of change. *Journal of Consulting and clinical Psychology, 51,* 390–395.

Prochaska, J. O., & DiClemente, C. C. (1984). *The transtheoretical approach: Crossing traditional boundaries of therapy.* Homewood, IL: Dow Jones Irwin.

Prochaska, J. O., Velicer, W. F., DiClemente, C. C., Guadgnoli, E., & Rossi, J. S. (1990). Patterns of change: Dynamic typology applied to smoking cessation. *Multivariate Behavioral Research, 25,* 587–611.

Puska, P. (1984). Community-based prevention of cardiovascular disease: The North Karelia Project. In J. D. Matarazzo, S. M. Weiss, J. A. Herd, N. E. Miller, & S. M. Weiss (Eds.), *Behavioral health: A handbook of health enhancement and disease prevention* (pp. 1140–1147). New York: Wiley.

Puska, P., Nissinen, A., Salonen, J. T., & Toumilehto, J. (1983). Ten years of the North Karelia Project: Results with community-based prevention of coronary heart disease. *Scandanavian Journal of Social Medicine, 11,* 65–68.

Puska, P., Nissinen, A., Tuomilehto, J., Salonen, J. T., Koskela, K., McAlister, A., Kottke, T. E., Maccoby, N., & Farquhar, J. W. (1985). The community-based strategy to prevent coronary heart disease: Conclusions from the ten years of the North Karelia Project. In L. Breslow, I. B. Lave, & J. Fielding (Eds.), *Annual review of public health* (Vol. 6, pp. 147–193). Palo Alto, CA: Annual Reviews.

Rappaport, J. (1977). *Community psychology: Values, research, and action.* New York: Holt, Rinehart & Winston.

Rappaport, J. (1984). Studies in empowerment: Introduction to the issue. *Prevention in Human Services, 3,* 1–7.

Revenson, T. A. (1990). All other things are not equal: An ecological approach to personality and disease. In H. S. Friedman (Ed.), *Personality and disease* (pp. 65–94). New York: Wiley.

Revenson, T. A., & Schiaffino, K. M. (2000). Community-based health interventions. In J. Rappaport & E. Seidman (Eds.), *Handbook of community psychology* (pp. 471–493). New York: Kluwer Academic/Plenum.

Rich, R. C., Edelstein, M., Hallman, W. K., & Wandersman, A. (1995). Citizen participation and empowerment: The case of local environmental hazards. *American Journal of Community Psychology, 23*(5), 657–676.

Rogers, E. M. (1983). *Diffusion of innovations* (3rd ed.). New York: The Free Press.

Rogers, T., Feighery, E. C., Tenacati, E. M., Butler, J. L., & Weiner, L. (1995). Community mobilization to reduce point-of-purchase advertising of tobacco products. *Health Education Quarterly, 22*(4), 427–442.

Rose, J. (1992). Strategies of prevention: The individual and the population. In M. Marmot & P. Elliott (Eds.), *Coronary heart disease epidemiology: From aetiology to public health* (pp. 311–324). Oxford, England: Oxford University Press.

Rosen, G. (1993). *A history of public health.* Baltimore: Johns Hopkins University Press.

Rosenstock, I. M. (1974). Historical origins of the Health Belief Model. *Health Education Monographs, 2,* 328–335.

Sarason, S. (1983). Psychology and public policy: Missed opportunity. In R. D. Felner, L. A. Jason, J. N. Moritsugu, & S. S. Farber (Eds.), *Preventive psychology: Theory, research and practice* (pp. 245–250). New York: Pergamon.

Schmid, T. L., Pratt, M., & Howze, E. (1995). Policy as intervention: Environmental and policy approaches to the prevention of cardiovascular disease. *American Journal of Public Health, 85*(9), 1207–1211.

Schwartz, R., Goodman, R., & Steckler, A. (1995). Policy advocacy interventions for health promotion and education: Advancing the state of practice. *Health Education Quarterly, 22*(4), 421–426.

Seligman, M.E.P. (1975). *Helplessness: On depression, development, and death.* San Francisco: Freeman.

Shea, S., & Basch, C. E. (1990). A review of five major community-based cardiovascular disease prevention programs: Part 1. Rationale, design, and theoretical framework. *American Journal of Health Promotion, 4,* 203–213.

Shea, S., Basch, C. E., Wechsler, H., & Lantigua, R. (1996). The Washington Heights–Inwood Healthy Heart Program: A 6–year report from a disadvantaged urban setting. *American Journal of Public Health, 86*(2), 166–171.

Speer, P. W., & Hughey, J. (1995). Community organizing: An ecological route to empowerment and power. *American Journal of Community Psychology, 23*(5), 729–748.

Speers, M. A., & Schmid, T. L. (1995). Policy and environmental interventions for the prevention and control of cardiovascular diseases. *Health Education Quarterly, 22*(4), 476–477.

Steckler, A. (1989). Interview: Godfrey M. Hochbaum, Ph.D. *Family and Community Health, 12*(3), 72–74.

Steckler, A., Allegrante, J., Altman, D., Brown, R., Burdine, J., Goodman, R. M., & Jorgenson, C. (1995). Health education intervention strategies: Recommendations for future research. *Health Education Quarterly, 22,* 307–329.

Steckler, A., & Dawson, L. (1982). The role of health education in public policy development. *Health Education Quarterly, 9*(4), 275–292.

Steckler, A., Dawson, L., Goodman, R. M., & Epstein, N. (1987). Policy advocacy: Three emerging roles for health education. *Advances in Health Education and Health Promotion, 2,* 5–27.

Steckler, A., & Goodman, R. M. (1989). How to institutionalize health promotion programs. *American Journal of Health Promotion, 3*(4), 34–44.

Steuart, G. W., & Kark, S. L. (1993). A practice of social medicine: A South African team's experiences in different African communities. *Heath Education Quarterly, 1,* S29–S47.

Stokols, D. (1992). Establishing and maintaining healthy environments: Toward a social ecology of health promotion. *American Psychologist, 47*(1), 6–22.

Stokols, D. (1996). Translating social ecological theory into guidelines for community health promotion. *American Journal of Health Promotion, 10*(4), 282–298.

Susser, M. (1995). Editorial: The tribulations of trials—Intervention in communities. *American Journal of Public Health, 85*(2), 156–158.

Thompson, B., & Kinne, S. (1990). Social change theory: Applications to community health. In N. Bracht (Ed.), *Health promotion at the community level* (pp. 45–65). Newbury Park, CA: Sage.

Trickett, E. J. (1987). Community interventions and health psychology: An ecologically-oriented approach. In G. C. Stone, S. M. Weiss, J. D. Matarazzo, N. E. Miller, J. Rodin, & e. al. (Eds.), *Health psychology: A discipline and a profession* (pp. 151–163). Chicago: University of Chicago Press.

Trickett, E. F. (1996). A future for community psychology: The contexts of diversity and the diversity of contexts. *American Journal of Community Psychology, 24*(2), 209–229.

Trickett, E. J., Kelly, J. G., & Todd, D. M. (1972). The social environment of the high school: Guidelines for individual change and organizational redevelopment. In S. E. Golann & C. Eisdorfer (Eds.), *Handbook of community mental health* (pp. 331–406). New York: Appleton-Century-Crofts.

U.S. Department of Health and Human Services. (1995). *Planned approach to community health: Guide for the local coordinator.* Atlanta: Centers for Disease Control and Prevention; National Center for Chronic Disease Prevention and Health Promotion.

Vincent, T. A., & Trickett, E. J. (1983). Preventive interventions and the human context: Ecological approaches to environmental assessment and change. In R. Felner, L. Jason, J. Morifsugu, & S. Farber (Eds.), *Preventive psychology: Theory, research and practice* (pp. 67–86). New York: Pergamon.

Wagennar, A. C., Murray, D. M., Wolfson, M., Forster, J. L., & Finnegan, J. R. (1994). Communities mobilizing for change on alcohol: Design of a randomized community trail. *Journal of Community Psychology,* 79–101.

Wallack, L., Dorfman, L., Jernigan, D., & Themba, M. (1993). *Media advocacy and public health: Power for prevention.* Newbury Park, CA: Sage.

Wallack, L., & Wallerstein, N. (1986). Health education and prevention: Designing community initiatives. *International Quarterly of Community Health Education, 7,* 319–342.

Wallerstein, N. (1992). Powerlessness, empowerment, and health: Implications for health promotion programs. *American Journal of Health Promotion*(6), 197–205.

Wallerstein, N., & Bernstein, E. (1988). Empowerment education: Freire's ideas adapted to health education. *Health Education Quarterly, 15*(4), 379–394.

Wandersman, A., & Alderman, J. (1993). Incentives, barriers and training of volunteers for the American Cancer Society: A staff perspective. *Review of Public Personnel Administration, 13*(1), 67–76.

Wandersman, A., Chavis, D., & Stucky, P. (1983). Involving citizens in research. In R. Kidd & M. Saks (Eds.), *Advances in applied social psychology* (Vol. 2, pp. 189–212). Hillsdale, NJ: Lawrence Erlbaum Associates.

Wandersman, A., Florin, P., Friedmann, R., & Meier, R. (1987). Who participates, who does not, and why? An analysis of voluntary neighborhood organizations in the United States and Israel. *Sociological Forum, 2*(3), 534–555.

Wang, C., & Burris, M. A. (1994). Empowerment through photo novella: Portraits of participation. *Health Education Quarterly, 21*(2), 171–186.

Warren, R. B., & Warren, D. I. (1977). How to diagnose a neighborhood? In *The neighborhood organizer's handbook* (pp. 167–168, 173–196). Notre Dame: University of Notre Dame Press.

Watkins, E. L., Harlan, C., Eng, E., Gansky, S. A., Gehan, D., & Larson, K. (1994). Assessing the effectiveness of lay health advisors with migrant farmworkers. *Family and Community Health, 16*(4), 72–87.

Wicker, A. W. (1979). *An introduction to ecological psychology.* Monterey, CA: Brooks-Cole.

Winett, R. A. (1995). A framework for health promotion and disease prevention programs. *American Psychologist, 50*(5), 341–350.

Winett, R., King, A. C., & Altman, D. G. (1989). *Health psychology and public health: An integrative perspective.* New York: Pergamon.

Winkelstein, W., & Marmot, M. (1981). Primary prevention of ischemic heart disease: Evaluation of community interventions. *Annual Review of Public Health, 2,* 253–276.

Zimmerman, M. A. (1990a). Taking aim on empowerment research: On the distinction between individual and psychological conceptions. *American Journal of Community Psychology, 18*(1), 169–177.

Zimmerman, M. A. (1990b). Toward a theory of learned helplessness: A structural analysis of participation and empowerment. *Journal of Research in Personality, 24,* 71–86.

Zimmerman, M. A. (1995). Psychological empowerment: Issues and illustrations. *American Journal of Community Psychology, 23*(5), 581–599.

Zimmerman, M. A. (in press). Empowerment theory: Psychological, organizational, and community levels of analysis. In J. Rappaport & E. Seidman (Eds.), *Handbook of community psychology.* New York: Plenum.

Zimmerman, M. A., Israel, B. A., Schulz, A., & Checkoway, B. (1992). Further explorations in empowerment theory: An empirical analysis of psychological empowerment. *American Journal of Community Psychology, 20*(6), 707–727.

Zimmerman, M. A., & Rappaport, J. (1988). Citizen participation, perceived control, and psychological empowerment. *American Journal of Community Psychology, 16,* 725–749.

37

Citizen Participation and Health: Toward a Psychology of Improving Health Through Individual, Organizational, and Community Involvement

Frances Butterfoss
Center for Pediatric Research

Abraham Wandersman
University of South Carolina

Robert M. Goodman
Tulane University School of Public Health and Tropical Medicine

Never doubt that a small, thoughtful group of committed citizens can change the world. Indeed, it is the only thing that ever has.

—Margaret Mead

How can citizen participation affect health? What can psychology contribute to this field? This chapter uses a case example of a community coalition to illustrate the powerful forces that shape citizen participation and how that participation can be mobilized to build a community's capacity and competence in achieving meaningful health outcomes. In this case, the Consortium for the Immunization of Norfolk's Children (CINCH) had the potential or capacity and developed the competence to engage in effective research, planning, action, and evaluation. Although immunization has been the cornerstone of traditional medical practices tracing back to the smallpox immunization paradigm, CINCH used a nontraditional citizen participation approach to improve childhood immunization rates. By encouraging citizens to develop comprehensive and effective strategies that were carefully implemented, CINCH delivered results. Community volunteers and health and human service professionals from the public, private, and military sectors proved their competence by increasing childhood immunization rates 17% in Norfolk, Virginia. Using the case study, the chapter shows how psychological theories from personality, social, organizational, and community psychology can help advance the understanding and strategic use of community partnerships. Finally, it overviews major issues in participation at the individual, organizational, and community levels that focus on developing community capacity and competence to improve health outcomes.

CITIZEN PARTICIPATION

Citizen participation is defined as "a process in which individuals take part in decision making in the institutions, programs, and environments that affect them" (Heller, Price, Reinharz, Riger, & Wandersman, 1984, p. 339; see Churchman, 1987, for definitions of participation in different disciplines). Participation offers the potential to make schools, neighborhoods, institutions, environments, and services responsive to individuals and families.

Citizen participation results in multiple benefits, including: (1) improved quality of the environment, program, or plan because the people who are involved in implementation or usage have special knowledge that contributes to quality; (2) increased feelings of control over the environment and development of programs, plans, or environments that better fit with people's needs and values; (3) increased feelings of helpfulness and responsibility; and (4) decreased feelings of alienation and anonymity (see Wandersman, 1979).

Citizen participation can take place at multiple levels: individual, organization, and community participation. For many years, the individual model of participation in the health field has been guided by an expert medical model exemplified by the doctor–patient relationship. In a provocative book *The Silent World of Doctor and Patient,* J. Katz (1984) described the patients' rights to decision making and centered his arguments around a concept of psychological autonomy and psychological capacities (e.g., reflection and choice) of the patient to decision making. Recently, medical education has developed techniques and trained physicians to provide patients with responsible choices in decision making.

Similar changes in health models are taking place at the community level. The medical model of public health is currently being complemented by citizen participation in making decisions about community health. According to social ecological models of health and health promotion (e.g., Stokols, Allen, & Bellingham, 1996), the health of individuals is inextricably linked to the health of communities. The Healthy Cities/Healthy Communities movement defines a healthy city or community as "one that is continually creating and improving those physical and social environments and strengthening those community resources which enable people to mutually support each other in performing all the functions of life and achieving their maximum potential" (Hancock & Duhl, 1986, in Hancock, 1993, p. 7). A major vehicle for developing a healthy community is a type of citizen participation organization called a *community coalition.*

COMMUNITY COALITIONS DEFINED

The development of partnerships of community agencies, institutions, and concerned citizens to combat chronic health conditions is gaining popularity as an intervention aimed at strengthening the social fabric. A community coalition is a particular partnership that is defined as "an organization of individuals representing diverse organizations, factions, or constituencies who agree to work together in order to achieve a common goal" (Feighery & Rogers, 1989, p. 1). These diverse interest groups "combine their human and material resources to effect a specific change the members are unable to bring about independently' (Brown, 1984, p. 3).

Currently, hundreds of millions of dollars are being invested in partnership development as a prevention and health promotion intervention. Examples include "Community Partnerships" funded by the Center for Substance Abuse Prevention (CSAP); "Fighting Back" substance abuse programs funded by the Robert Wood Johnson Foundation; SAFE KIDS partnerships to prevent childhood injuries, supported by Johnson and Johnson; COMMIT and ASSIST community tobacco control programs funded by the National Cancer Institute and the National Institutes of Health; PATCH cardiovascular health promotion program granted by the U.S. Centers for Disease Control and Prevention; and Native American health promotion efforts sponsored by the U.S. Office of Minority Health.

A coalition approach to improve childhood immunization rates is appropriate given that underimmunization is a multifaceted challenge to health that must be solved by involving and strengthening multiple levels and sectors of our communities (Bernier, 1994; McLeroy, Bibeau, Steckler & Glanz, 1988; Orenstein, Atkinson, Mason, & Bernier, 1991). Even though *Healthy People 2000* set national goals to fully immunize at least 90% of children by age 2, this goal is still unrealized (Public Health Service, 1991). Depending on the state of residence, from 13% to 37% of 2-year-old children in the United States remain underimmunized and the picture is worse in urban areas (Centers for Disease Control and Prevention, 1996; Zell, Dietz, Stevenson, Cochi, & Bruce, 1994). The measles epidemic of 1989–1991 and the resurgence of pertussis prompted the Centers for Disease Control and Prevention (CDC) to provide resources to develop and implement plans to reduce morbidity and to improve availability and access to childhood immunization services (Centers for Disease Control and Prevention, 1993; National Vaccine Advisory Committee, 1991). Coalitions were a vehicle to accomplish these aims.

Research indicates that coalitions follow predictable stages from formation to institutionalization (Butterfoss, Goodman, & Wandersman, 1993). Figure 37.1 illustrates the model used to evaluate several local community partnerships for alcohol, tobacco, and other drug (ATOD) abuse prevention funded by CSAP. This model of coalitions is applicable to other public health problems.

The formation stage occurs at the initiation of funding. The agency granted the funding (lead agency) convenes an ad hoc committee of local community leaders. The ad hoc committee nominates influential citizens to serve on committees representing health care, business, education, religion, criminal justice, neighborhood organizations, the media, and other sectors of the community. Training on prevention goals, issues, and tasks takes place. The implementation stage occurs as each of the committees conducts a needs assessment to determine the extent and nature of its constituents' concerns and resources in regard to alcohol, tobacco, and other drug abuse. The needs assessment consists of secondary data as well as written questionnaires, town meetings, and interviews that are developed and conducted by the committees, with input from the staff and the evaluation team. Implementation continues, with committees using the results of the needs assessment to develop a community-wide intervention plan. The maintenance stage consists of the monitoring and upkeep of the committees and their planned activities. The outcome stage consists of the impacts that result from the deployment of community-wide strategies. The series of activities of community mobilization (needs assessment, planning, and implementation of programs and activities) are aimed at ameliorating the risk factors listed in Fig. 37.1 and therefore facilitating positive outcomes.

Table 37.1 uses the same model to show CINCH's development with its stages and time frames, as well as the competencies developed and tasks accomplished during each stage. The stages are sequential, but overlap of tasks occurs between stages. CINCH is a dynamic organization, and it recycled through tasks of formation, implementation, and maintenance as new members were recruited and strategies were revised or added. Within each stage, the capabilities that were brought to the effort and the competencies that were developed are discussed. Using needs assessment, problem solving, and decision making, members planned, implemented, and evaluated strategies to educate parents and providers and improve service delivery.

THE CONSORTIUM FOR THE IMMUNIZATION OF NORFOLK'S CHILDREN (CINCH)

Background

In 1992, the National Immunization Program of the Centers for Disease Control and Prevention (CDC) established Norfolk as a site to demonstrate how a community coalition could

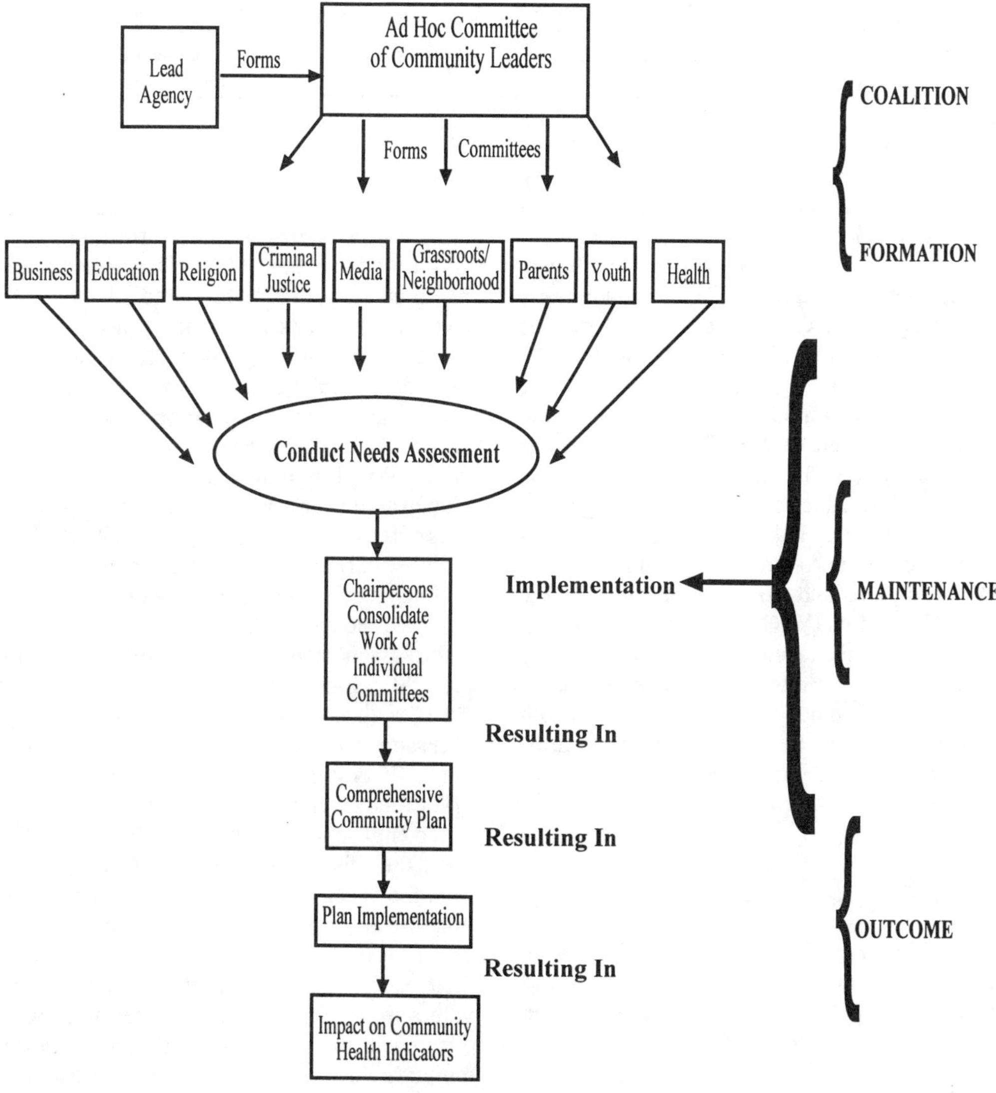

FIG. 37.1. Overview of the development of a community coalition.

TABLE 37.1
CINCH Development: Competencies Developed and Tasks Accomplished

Stage/Duration	Competency Developed	Tasks Accomplished
Formation		Identify community problem
(6 months)		Recruit members Create mission, rules, roles Collaborate Train on goals and issues
Implementation	Skills	Assess needs
(12 months)	Participation Leadership Community Values	Collect, analyze, and feedback data Develop plan
Maintenance	Resources	Initiate and monitor strategies
(12 months)	Social Networks Critical Reflection	Support and evaluate coalition group process
Outcome	Sense of Community	Begin to accomplish goals
(> 12 months)	Power	Progress toward results or impacts from community-wide strategies

improve immunization rates for children under age 2. Norfolk was selected because of its low immunization rate, ethnic diversity, and mix of public, private, and military health care systems. The coalition was based in the Center for Pediatric Research, a joint program of Children's Hospital of The King's Daughters and Eastern Virginia Medical School.

Norfolk is located in eastern Virginia, or Tidewater, where many health indicators lag behind the state average by up to 10%. According to the 1990 census, Norfolk has a population of 261,229, a birth cohort of 5,561, and an ethnic distribution of 57% White, 39% African American, and 4% other groups. The median household income is below $20,000, approximately 20% are enrolled in the Aid to Families of Dependent Children (AFDC) program, and 40% are enrolled in the Women, Infants, and Children (WIC) program. Children receive care from a combination of private, public, and military health services. Free immunizations are available to all children, regardless of family income, through five public health clinics, two hospital-based outpatient clinics, and three military sites. But, according to 1993 retrospective school-enterer data, only 46% of 2-year-olds were up to date on basic immunizations.

Year 1: Formation to Implementation

CINCH was founded in 1993. The coalition was built with consideration that it would have an inclusive membership and engage in comprehensive planning, action, and evaluation (Butterfoss et al., 1993; Kaye & Wolff, 1995). The staff helped members conceive CINCH as a competent organization—one that promoted excellence in regard to its participants, structures, and processes.

Careful consideration was given to recruiting and maintaining diverse representation from organizations that were committed to action. The staff recruited a core group of organizations who, in turn, recruited others to total 55 representatives from service organizations; academic, civic, and religious institutions; public, private, and military health care providers; and ordinary citizens. Members from various grassroots and professional organizations provided diversity according to age, occupation, ethnicity, and religion. This group of willing individuals had the capacity to mobilize for citizen action, and potential leaders stepped forward. The success of the coalition was closely related to the effectiveness of member participation and leadership.

Each member brought individual skills to the coalition and assessed the costs and benefits of participation in the overall effort. Each member also represented an organization that brought resources to the table. Members were relied on for skills, such as planning, teaching, mobilizing volunteers, and accessing the media. Member organizations contributed financially or in-kind to implement program strategies because grant funds were earmarked only for research.

To engage the membership, CINCH staff provided training about the effectiveness, efficacy, and importance of immunization, the vaccine schedule, current literature about barriers to immunization, and reasons why a coalition approach might be effective in dealing with underimmunization. Members did their part by infusing a sense of community and community values into the new coalition. They were willing to put aside differences in order to share responsibility for all of the community's children. Relying on new knowledge and core values, the coalition developed its mission which was to: (1) establish dialogue within the local community regarding immunization of preschool children; (2) determine the causes of underutilization of health services and poor vaccine coverage among local preschool children; (3) form recommendations and mobilize the community to implement solutions to improve the health and immunization status of Norfolk's children; (4) evaluate the effectiveness of interventions and make revisions in strategies, as needed; and (5) share experiences and recommendations from the CINCH project with other communities. Again, this common mission and commitment to community improvement helped members overcome barriers that commonly stall new coalitions, such as lack of direction or turf battles and competition (Butterfoss, Goodman, & Wandersman, 1996; Kaye & Wolff, 1995).

Next, members focused on organizational structure and functioning. They developed written rules of operation, criteria for membership, and roles for members, leaders, and staff.

Staff provided administrative support to members by preparing draft documents, agendas, minutes, rosters, meeting reminders, and mailings. They helped leaders set agendas, run effective meetings, and plan strategies that promoted member retention. CINCH developed work groups with complementary missions, yet each work group focused on specific tasks and populations. Members elected chairs and vice-chairs for each group and for the coalition at large. Early successes included the development of a logo, slogan, and brochure for visibility and recruitment.

Throughout this stage, members developed skills that would later be combined into effective action. They learned to work toward a common purpose and to rely on each others' talents and resources. Members were valued for their contributions to the overall effort and not for their positions or the power of their organizations. Consequently, members excluded titles from nametags and discussions and used a "one vote per organization" rule for decision making. As previously competitive organizations learned the value of collaborating to accomplish tasks, the level of trust improved.

Year 2: Implementation

The implementation stage of CINCH focused on needs assessment, data collection, analysis and feedback, and plan development. First, the work groups assisted in a needs assessment to diagnose local causes of underimmunization. CINCH members participated in all phases of the needs assessment by planning or facilitating existing and primary data collection. Parent focus groups, patient exit interviews, and health care provider surveys were planned and conducted by work groups (Butterfoss, Morrow, et al., 1998; Houseman, Butterfoss, Morrow, & Rosenthal, 1997). A household survey established that underimmunization was found in all socioeconomic groups and among all types of health care services, with only 49% of children up to date on their immunizations by age 2 (Morrow et al., 1998). Staff were responsible for entering, analyzing, and presenting data to the coalition for feedback.

Based on the data, CINCH developed a 2-year strategic immunization plan that focused on parent and provider education and support for at-risk families, thereby increasing access to immunizations and improving immunization delivery. Staff conducted workshops for work group members about the process of developing a quality action plan. Once trained, each work group used the data to identify a prioritized set of needs related to their target group (e.g., parents, providers). Then, goals, objectives, and strategies were developed to address each identified community need. The groups considered the strengths of their community and the resources they could draw on to implement various strategies. Linkages among appropriate community agencies were identified and evaluation of strategy effectiveness was planned.

After each group finalized its plan, coalition leaders coalesced the four individual plans into one overall plan that was presented at a community press conference. The intrinsic conflict and negotiation involved in this process cemented relationships among group leaders and strengthened internal support for the plan. The planning process resulted in the creation of a steering committee of leaders that met regularly to share coalition successes and challenges. Members also learned that planning is a continuous process and eventually concerned themselves with details such as developing strategy time lines, management plans, and budgets.

Year 3: Maintenance

The maintenance stage involved initiating new strategies and monitoring others. Work groups often collaborated on strategies and responsibilities overlapped between groups. Two work groups even merged to streamline their operations. Some activities were initiated and finished during the maintenance stage, and others were not achieved until the outcome stage. Each implemented strategy had a built-in evaluation component where members were taught to ask themselves whether the strategy was based on community need, was implemented as planned, and could be improved. Work group action plans were revised annually.

CDC funding restrictions prompted CINCH to develop community support for its activities and increased the likelihood of sustaining its efforts beyond the grant period. Private foundation funding enabled the coalition to hire an outreach coordinator, conduct a media campaign, and implement key strategies. In-kind contributions from CINCH members included the health department printing posters, flyers, and brochures; the medical school arranging satellite teleconferences; and community merchants contributing parent incentives.

During the maintenance stage of any coalition, membership and commitment may waiver with the realization that accomplishing goals takes time. To keep members involved, CINCH participated in health fairs, marches, and other visible community health efforts. Leaders were attuned to the need to retain members and maximize their participation. Attention was given to written reminders and phone calls about meetings and follow-up with members who missed meetings. Meetings were evaluated and members completed surveys to measure satisfaction and participation and to define areas for improvement. General membership meetings provided opportunities to cultivate and renew relationships and to celebrate incremental achievements.

Year 4: Outcome and Institutionalization

CINCH accomplished some of its more difficult strategies such as WIC linkage, physician practice assessment and feedback, hospital birth reminder systems, and legislative action during the outcome stage. Members not only had the ability to direct the course of community events, but wielded that power to influence some of the larger institutions such as hospitals and the state legislature. In 1996, members voted to broaden CINCH's geographic scope to include members from six other cities in the region and to expand its mission to address other child health issues in addition to immunization. The coalition also obtained funding to hire a coordinator and secretary. A new needs assessment work group identified, collected, and presented data related to regional child health problems. By this time, members could articulate what the greater community needed and valued. These values and data led CINCH to select perinatal health issues (infant mortality, low birth weight, lack of prenatal care) as its expanded mission under the name of the *C*onsortium for *In*fant and *C*hild *H*ealth.

CINCH has had an impact on the Norfolk community. The coalition effectively implemented 61 of 79 planned strategies (77%). Although any change in immunization levels for 2-year-olds cannot be attributed to CINCH alone, rates rose from 49% in 1993 to 66% in 1996 (Morrow et al., 1998). Higher rates were reported among hospital clinics and military providers.

CINCH's success has fostered new state contracts and federal grants that promote environmental change. The skills and experience gained from CINCH prompted a contractual agreement between CINCH's lead agency and the state health department to develop, manage, and evaluate a state immunization coalition, Project Immunize Virginia (PIV). PIV used CINCH as a model to bring together public and private partners to advocate for improved levels of immunization. Through PIV, CINCH members help other localities develop community partnerships to improve immunization rates for children. CINCH members and staff also provide technical assistance to other local partnership efforts that deal with drug and alcohol abuse, teen pregnancy, child abuse and neglect, and school health. CINCH collaborates with projects focused on case management, community policing, neighborhood improvement, and urban planning.

Under a grant from the Association of Teachers of Preventive Medicine, the Coalition Training Institute was established in Norfolk in 1995. The Institute models the CINCH process to train key health agency staff responsible for development and implementation of immunization coalitions in 88 state, territorial, and urban sites (Butterfoss, Webster, Morrow, & J. Rosenthal, 1998). CINCH members showcase what their coalition did to improve immunization rates and share lessons learned. By articulating these "lessons learned" in a way that could help others, members were empowered beyond original expectations.

Evaluation of CINCH was accomplished through member surveys, content analysis of minutes and evaluation of meetings (Butterfoss, Morrow, et al., 1998). Surveys showed that 86% of CINCH members were satisfied with the work of the coalition, 70% stated they had great influence in decision making, 90% agreed that communication was productive and positive, and 93% were satisfied with the group environment. Ninety-four percent reported that staff were competent or highly competent and 75% reported that members were competent or highly competent. Finally, 97% agreed that the action plan reflected the needs assessment and would be effective, and 87% were certain that CINCH would improve immunization rates.

Average attendance over 130 meetings was 59%, which was considered acceptable by coalition research (Prestby & Wandersman, 1985). Content analysis of meetings showed that activities were balanced among tasks of member orientation, needs assessment, planning coalition structure and functions, information sharing, development of products or services, revision of coalition structures, and evaluation. Leaders and members also completed Meeting Effectiveness Inventories (MEIs) after all meetings to determine factors that contributed to success (Goodman & Wandersman, 1994). Out of a 5-point scale, with 1 being ineffective and 5 being highly effective, work group meetings were rated at 4.4 (88%) and general meetings at 4.6 (92%). After completing the MEI, leaders and staff debriefed about how to address barriers and promote meeting effectiveness. Recommendations focused on improving attendance, tardiness, agendas, participation, leadership, and grassroots representation.

In summary, during the outcome stage, CINCH members were empowered by their participation to change how immunizations were understood, accessed, and delivered to the target population; implemented an effective action plan; obtained funding; expanded by region and mission; and advocated for legislative change.

LESSONS LEARNED FROM COALITION PRACTICE AND RESEARCH

Coalitions have their share of difficulties, and they need resources to develop and time to build collaborative relationships. However, once coalitions are established, they may be able to create and sustain more effective strategies than traditional public health institutions can do alone. Several observations from the CINCH experience may be helpful for other health promotion coalition efforts.

First, CINCH's experience proved that whereas every member brought concern for children, not all had the skills needed to be effective. Through training and practice in leadership, meeting effectiveness, needs assessment, and planning, coalition members developed skills that improved their participation and could be generalized to other civic areas. Involving community members early in needs assessment and planning helps empower them to implement planned strategies (Kaye & Wolff, 1995; Butterfoss, Goodman, & Wandersman, 1996; Butterfoss, Morrow, et al., 1998). Involving citizens in solving real problems develops a competent community.

Second, CINCH made good use of its volunteers. Training, clear roles, and ongoing contact with participating institutions were essential for member retention. Member involvement was bolstered by achievement of objectives and positive results. A clear vision of leadership and a commitment to a quality process kept members interested. Leaders were sensitive to member needs by allowing varying levels of participation during each coalition stage. They reduced burnout and maximized resources by recognizing that some members are better planners, whereas others are better doers. CINCH also made good use of each member's linkage with others. Members constantly recruited others who represented the target population or who could provide resources. New recruits stimulated creativity and renewed effort among founding members.

Third, CINCH promoted partnerships with citizens and groups in neighboring cities. When personal agendas are put aside, resources may be effectively pooled. Work group members invited health department and hospital directors, as well as counterparts from professional and voluntary agencies in neighboring cities, to join them at the table. Communities often collaborate with other communities regarding issues such as water and land use or transportation, but collaborating to promote health and prevent disease is a newer concept. Experience proved that a regional health promotion partnership could build relationships for the future.

TOWARD A PSYCHOLOGY OF CITIZEN PARTICIPATION IN COMMUNITY COALITIONS: A MULTIPLE LEVEL APPROACH

At the individual, organizational and community level, there is both a *potential* for citizens to participate and *actual* citizen participation. This section organizes an understanding of participation, based on a framework described in Table 37.1.

The Individual Level of Participation

A major puzzle in the citizen participation literature is "If participation is such a good thing, why don't more people participate?" Despite the desirable outcomes proposed as consequences of participation and exemplified in actual coalitions like CINCH, relatively few people participate in government-initiated efforts, grassroots groups, or community partnerships (e.g., ISA Associates, 1994, Langton, 1978; Verba & Nie, 1972; R. Warren, 1963). The literature pertinent to individual characteristics and participation can be divided into demographic research and personality or social psychological research.

Demographic variables (e.g., age, race, and sex) have been used in political science, sociology, and psychological studies to predict participation, however, they tend to predict relatively little variance. Two studies that used multiple demographic variables to predict participation predicted 9% of the variance or less (Edwards & White, 1980; Vassar, 1978).

Personality and social psychological variables offer interesting opportunities to understanding and predicting participation. For example, many psychologists agree that a complex interaction exists between the characteristics of the person and the environment that produces and sustains behavior. For this reason, an individual is likely to participate in only a few of the many organizations available. The organization(s) chosen are selected on the basis of the individual's own characteristics (e.g., needs, values, and personality) and the characteristics of the organization (e.g., purposes, efficacy, location).

Potential Levels of Participation. Mischel (1973, 1977) suggested five cognitive social learning variables as potentially useful in conceptualizing how personal qualities influence the impact of situations and how people generate distinct patterns of behavior in interaction with the conditions of their life. Florin and Wandersman (1984) operationalized the cognitive social learning variables to predict participation in community settings. The five cognitive social learning variables are now called skills, view of the situation, expectations, values, and personal standards (Wandersman, Florin, Chavis, Rich, & Prestby, 1985). The set of cognitive social learning variables was compared with a larger set of traditional demographic and personality trait variables for ability to discriminate members from nonmembers, and they accounted for more of the variance in participation.

Based on a review of the literature, Widmer (1984) concluded that many of the studies on why citizens participate say little about the motives and benefits of participation and focus instead on the characteristics of who participates. One approach to the issue of why people participate is represented by the political economy theory (e.g., Moe, 1980; Olson, 1965; Rich, 1980), which suggests that a social exchange takes place in organizations in which participants will invest their energy in the organization only if they expect to receive some benefits. This can be related to social exchange theory in psychology. (See Chinman & Wandersman, 1999, for a detailed review of costs, benefits, and incentives in community organizations).

Actual Levels of Participation. Wandersman, Florin, Friedmann, and Meier (1987) investigated the benefits and costs of participation in their cross-cultural study. They found two benefit (helping others and personal gains) and two cost factors (opportunity costs and organizational frustration). Absolute ratings suggested that both members and nonmembers agree that the greatest benefits are in making a contribution and helping others rather than in self-interest or personal gains. Regarding costs, nonmembers perceived more costs than members reported. In the CINCH coalition, only 9% of members reported costs and the top cost reported was the amount of time spent in consortium work. In fact, low costs of participation were associated with member satisfaction and commitment.

In the Block Booster Project (a study of 29 block associations), Prestby, Wandersman, Florin, Rich, and Chavis (1990) found that the most active participants reported receiving significantly more social/communal benefits and personal benefits than less active participants, with personal benefits best distinguishing the most active participants. They proposed that personal benefits, such as learning new skills, are likely to be exclusive to the high level participants because they are contingent on participation. Regarding costs and participation, Prestby et al. found that the least active participants reported experiencing significantly more social and/or organizational costs than the active participants. In sum, social exchange and political economy theory were supported as the participation level and the amount and type of costs were significantly and negatively associated with level of participation.

Taken as a whole, the social psychological and cost/benefit results lend empirical support to Henig's (1982) three-step model of mobilization wherein individuals perceive a condition, evaluate it as important to their well-being, and calculate that something can be done about it. This points to the importance of understanding more fully the processes through which an individual engages in a decision to participate in a particular organization.

Researchers have compared the benefits of members at different activity levels. Prestby et al. (1990) asked leaders and members which benefits they received. In general, the most active members and leaders reported experiencing more total benefits and more personal and social/communal benefits than the less active members. In relation to costs, Prestby et al. found that the least active members experienced significantly more total costs and more social/organizational costs than members of all other activity levels. Participation in partnership committees was predicted by higher benefits and lower costs (Butterfoss, Goodman, & Wandersman, 1996). Chinman and Wandersman (1999) detailed results in this area.

The Organizational Level of Participation

Like any organization, a coalition needs resources, structure, activities, and accomplishments in order to survive. These are the essential elements of an open systems framework, so named because it is open to and interacts with the environment (D. Katz & Kahn 1978). The framework proposes that organizations can be seen as mechanisms for processing resources obtained from the environment into products that affect that environment. Using Katz and Kahn's work as a departure point, Prestby and Wandersman (1985) developed a framework of organizational viability suggesting that there are four components of organizational functioning: resource acquisition, maintenance subsystem (organizational structure), production subsystem (actions or activities), and external goal attainment (accomplishments). This section draws on an application of this framework to partnerships (Wandersman, Goodman, & Butterfoss, 1997).

Resource Acquisition. In reference to Table 37.1, potential at the organizational level is represented by resources brought to the organization by its members and those recruited from external sources. A partnership's membership is its primary asset. Several variables related to the members have been associated with organizational maintenance (Prestby & Wandersman 1985), including the size of the membership, depth of members' attachment to the mission, and members' personal and political efficacy. As illustrated in CINCH, each member brings a different set of resources and skills to the partnership. The effective implementation and maintenance of a partnership require not only motivated and involved members, but also members with the skills or capacity to participate in a partnership and to gain legitimacy (Gray, 1985).

Partnerships also benefit by linking with external resources, especially those concerned with policy, planning, and services (Butterfoss et al., 1993). CINCH illustrated how external resources such as elected officials, government agencies, religious and civic groups, neighborhood and community development associations, and foundations were vital. In this and other coalitions, such resources provide expertise, meeting facilities, mailing lists, referrals, additional personnel for special projects, grant funding, loans or donations, equipment, supplies, and cosponsorship of events (Chavis, Florin, Rich, & Wandersman, 1987; Prestby & Wandersman, 1985).

Access to local communities is an important link for many partnerships (Roberts-DeGennaro, 1986), particularly those concerned with health promotion. Such partnerships often benefit by linking with individuals and organizations active in community affairs. For instance, Prestby and Wandersman's (1985) study of block associations demonstrated that those that endured tended to have strong linkages with local community organizers and with other neighborhood associations.

Partnership Structure and Functioning. The maintenance subsystem of the open systems framework involves organizational structure and functioning, which is the aspect of the partnership that obtains the resources and organizes the members. If partnerships are to be viable, they must be able to set goals, administer rewards, and mediate between members' individuals needs and the task requirements of the organization. Examples of organizational structure and function include leadership, formalized rules, roles, and procedures, decision-making and problem resolution processes, and organizational climate.

Strong central leadership is an important ingredient in the implementation and maintenance of partnership activities (Butterfoss et al., 1993). Regardless of size, partnerships tend to have a few core leaders who dominate partnership activities such as the Steering Committee in CINCH (Roberts-DeGennaro, 1986). When these leaders are attentive to and supportive of individual member concerns and are competent in negotiation, garnering of resources, problem solving, and conflict resolution, the partnership tends to be more cohesive in reaching peripheral members and in maintaining partnership operations (Brown, 1984).

Formalization is the degree to which rules, roles, and procedures are precisely defined. Examples of formalization, used by coalitions like CINCH, include written memoranda of understanding, bylaws, policy, and procedures manuals; clearly defined roles; mission statements, goals, and objectives; and regular reorientation to the purposes, goals, roles, and procedures of collaboration (Butterfoss et al., 1993; Goodman & Steckler, 1989). Formalization often results in the routinization or persistent implementation of the partnership's operations. The more routinized operations become, the more likely it is that they will be sustained (Goodman & Steckler, 1989).

The influence that participants have in making decisions is vital to a partnership. Prestby and Wandersman (1985) found that active block associations in the Neighborhood Participation Project were more likely to use a democratic decision-making process, whereas inactive associations used an autocratic or mixed democratic/autocratic process. The Block Booster project (Chavis et al., 1987) reported that active block association members felt they had a greater influence in deciding on the policies and actions of the group than did inactive block association members. Active block associations used consensus and formalized decision making procedures more often and were more decentralized than inactive block associations. In a 1993 CINCH survey, members reported either that they had a great degree of influence (74%) or some influence (26%) in determining policies and actions of the consortium.

Mizrahi and B. Rosenthal (1992) argued that conflict is an inherent characteristic of partnerships. It may arise between the partnership and its targets for social change or among partnership partners concerning issues such as leadership, goals, benefits, contributions, and representation. Mizrahi and Rosenthal identified four "dynamic tensions" that account for conflict in partnerships: (1) the mixed loyalties of members to their own organizations and to the partnership, (2) the autonomy a partnership requires and the accountability it has to its member organizations, (3) the lack of clarity about the partnership's purpose as either a means for specific change or a model for sustained interorganizational cooperation, and (4) the diversity of interests of its members. Eighty-two percent of CINCH members (1993 survey) reported that when conflict arose, they were able to resolve it effectively.

Organizational climate assesses members' perceptions of the "personality" of an organization. Moos (1986) assessed organizational climate on 10 subscales: cohesion, leader support, expression, independence, task orientation, self-discovery, anger and aggression, order and organization, leader control, and innovation. Giamartino and Wandersman (1983) used the Group Environment Scale to examine the relation of 10 social climate dimensions to member's satisfaction, enjoyment, and time involvement. Using aggregate data from 172 members of 17 block associations, they found that the average level of members' satisfaction and enjoyment was significantly related to three social climate dimensions. Members were more satisfied and enjoyed their involvement more in associations that were perceived to have higher levels of "team spirit" and comraderie among members (cohesiveness), have higher degrees of structure and formalization of activities (order and organization, and have leaders who actively directed the group and enforced rules (leader control). Importantly, no significant relations were found between any of the social climate dimensions and the average activity level of members in the organization (time spent on organizational activities in the previous 2 months). Butterfoss, Goodman, and Wandersman (1996) found that social climate characteristics (e.g., leader support, leader control) were related to satisfaction with the work, participation in the partnership, and costs and benefits. Using a 12-item social climate scale (1993 CINCH survey), 96% of members reported a positive group climate that was significantly associated with satisfaction and commitment.

The Community Level of Participation

At the community level, partnerships function as an amalgam of individuals, organizations, and interest groups. They join together in common purpose, but retain primary allegiance to their individual pursuits and interests. Unlike capacity building at the organizational level where the focus is on intra-organizational issues (Goodman, Steckler, & Alciati, 1997), capacity building at the community level is primarily concerned with building interorganizational linkages and promoting harmony (Kegler, Steckler, McLeroy, & Malek, 1998). For partnerships to operate successfully at the community level, they must, for the common good, overcome the centrifugal forces that propel members to self-interest. Partnerships that successfully overcome individualistic or divisive tendencies may be considered competent in addressing community issues of common concern. To be competent, a community partnership must have certain capacities to operate effectively.

Capacity and competence can be distinguished as a potential versus an active state. Capacity reflects a community's potential for addressing pressing health issues, whereas competence signifies how well capacity is applied. Many of the elements that signify organizational effectiveness also are attributes of community capacity and competence. According to a recent symposium convened by the Division of Chronic Disease Control and Community Intervention of the CDC, capacity consists of at least the following characteristics: participation and leadership, skills, resources, social and interorganizational networks, sense of community, community power, community values, and critical reflection (Goodman et al., 1997). The competent community not only has capacity in each of these areas, but is also able to apply each with confidence.

Participation and Leadership. Participation and leadership are two important and related dimensions of community capacity. As previously noted, organizational effectiveness is enhanced by active citizen participation. Leaders encourage participation by mobilizing citizen action forming what Steuart (1985) called a "unit of solution." Participation is basic to capacity because involvement of individual community members in local events must occur if capacity is to develop. Competence, on the other hand, is characteristic of how effectively citizen action is employed. Similarly, capacity is reflected in the emergence of leaders who form the core group of a partnership. The leadership is responsible for assuring cohesion among partnership members. The literature suggests that competent leadership is a reflection of effective leadership and decision-making style (Knoke & Wood, 1981; Mayer & Blake, 1981; R. B. Warren & D. I. Warren, 1977).

Skills. One virtue of partnerships is that members bring different skills to the partnership that results in synergy among the partnership's constituents. The diverse skills that members bring are a reflection of capacity. The integrated application of skills reflects competence. As in CINCH, different members may have skills in planning community events, lobbying, and gaining media attention. But, unless community members are competent in combining these skills into effective action, the capabilities of members are not joined in a competent manner. In rendering a skill base into competent community action, partnership members must recognize the political arena in which the community must operate, coordinate member action, and assess how best to apply skills for maximum political effect.

Resources. Members of community partnerships also bring an assortment of complementary resources. These resources may be office and meeting space, equipment and supplies, property, money, knowledge, or skills and abilities. Such resources represent capacity for enhancing the partnership's operations. Competence is reflected in the application of the resources to effective community action. For instance, the CINCH partnership was interested in a community initiative to combat underimmunization. The resources necessary included a range of organizations that not only could provide in-kind support such as meeting space, but also could combine their resources in an effective manner. Often organizations must overcome turf issues for the actual coordination of effective community action. When resources are plentiful, but their coordination by a partnership is inadequate, then the community evidences capacity without competence.

Social and Interorganizational Networks. Having extensive social and interorganizational networks can enhance community capacity to address health concerns. In evaluating a community's social networks, structural characteristics, such as size or number of linkages can be considered to reflect a community's potential to act in concert. Network competence is demonstrated through the quality of interactions among network connections such as the frequency and intensity of contacts, and the benefits that members receive from their network ties, such as emotional or tangible support and access to social contacts (Israel, 1982). Without effective interaction, networks are like telephone lines that are connected nationwide (capacity), but produce many busy signals, line overloads, and static (competence). Therefore, competent partnership networks not only have capacity to extend to many organizations and individuals in a community, but also assure that the interactions are mutually supportive and synergistic. In fact, research demonstrates that the extent of regular contacts among community members can foster cooperation (Putnam, 1993).

Sense of Community. A strong sense of community—caring and sharing among the people in a community—enables collective action to address local concerns and produce desired changes (Iscoe, 1974; Newbrough & Chavis, 1986). A strong sense of community represents capacity. When sense of community results in active relationships characterized by respect, generosity, and service to others, then community connectedness is competently used (McMillan & Chavis, 1986). Members of a competent community develop more than a sense of connection to community, but use community affiliation as a means of connecting with other community members to form active partnerships for community development. The ability to extend sense of community from one issue to another may also reflect on its competence. For example, a partnership like CINCH that forms to promote childhood immunizations may develop competent strategies to that end, but may or may not be competent in extending the partnership's activities to reduce infant mortality.

Community Power. When a strong sense of community develops, capacity exists and the community is predisposed to form partnerships around issues of shared concern. Where leaders and members are skillful in using resources, then community capacity is competently employed to increase its base of power and influence. Community power may be defined as the ability to create or resist change that matters to people who share common turf, interests, or experiences. Power is energy, and like energy may be potential (capacity) or actual (competence). A partnership by its nature forms a critical mass of members who together are able to influence change in ways that individual members alone cannot. Thus, the partnership represents potential power and has capacity to influence community direction. The way in which the partnership wields its power potential is a characteristic of competence. The term *win–lose relationships* characterizes power as limited and as a basis for control over others (Deutsch, 1973). By contrast, *win–win relationships* characterizes power as less limited and based on mutual respect, generosity, and service to others (Wallerstein, 1992). In the ideal, competent partnership action achieves win–win results. However, this is not always possible. For instance, if confronted by a turf battle with competing immunization service providers, win–lose relationships are a likely result. A partnership that can turn such confrontations into win–win situations—say, the ability to influence hospitals to collaborate in supporting a community-wide immunization awareness project—demonstrates competence in the wielding of power.

Community Values. Community capacity is not a value-free or objective term, but embodies expectations of norms, standards, and desired attributes. Community initiatives are embedded in the life and meaning of particular communities. Thus, a partnership that can articulate its core values develops capacity to act on what it believes. The way communities develop consensus about their values is an issue of competence. Community partnerships often reflect a range of values that exist in a community, creating the possibility of sharp conflicts on basic values that influence community health, such as the right of parents to home school their children and not immunize them. Diversity of values can enrich a community partnership, thus building its capacity. But diversity also may lead to conflict among the different cultural, racial, and social groups. The ability of community partnerships to reach a value consensus in implementing its initiatives is a sign of competence. This is especially critical in community coalitions, which have multiple points of view from which to draw an organizational base.

Critical Reflection. The ability of a community partnership to reach consensus around values is predicated on its capacity to engage in critical reflection, to reflect on the assumptions underlying community ideas and actions, and to contemplate alternative ways of thinking and living (Brookfield, 1987). Critical reflection includes the ability to reason logically and scrutinize arguments for ambiguity (Ennis, 1962). The ability to reason logically is a first step. The second is to put forth logical reflection so that community members gain an understanding of forces in their environment to enable them to act to promote both individual and social changes (Israel, Checkoway, Schulz, & Zimmerman, 1994; Wallerstein & Bernstein, 1994). The translation of reflection to reasoned action reflects the partnership's movement from the capacity to reflect to competently applying the lessons learned from introspection. A notable example of this process is *conscientization,* a term coined by Freire. People make the connections between themselves and the broader social context: when they reflect on their own roles in society, when they understand the history and conditions of a social problem, and when they believe they can participate in collective change (Freire, 1970). The ability, willingness, and belief in critical reflection represents a partnership's potential or capacity to act out of introspection. Capacity translates to competence when critical reflection is transformed into action based on insight. The involvement of CINCH members in training other coalition members at the Institute clearly illustrates that they have developed competency in critical reflection. By defining the challenges they faced in immunizing their children and developing innovative ways to address them, members transformed the way they related to health and human service institutions.

CONCLUSIONS

CINCH is a sustainable partnership that improved quality of life through education, advocacy, and empowerment. Throughout the project, members experienced the coalition as a unique opportunity for participation, organizational growth, and leadership. CINCH provided a positive group experience and exemplified the capacity of citizens and institutions to create dynamic, broad-based competent partnerships. This coalition model is generalizable to any locale where citizens seek to solve problems by drawing on their strengths. Promoting public health through coalitions is a community development approach that makes positive outcomes feasible.

REFERENCES

Bernier, R. (1994). Toward a more population-based approach to immunization: fostering private- and public-sector collaboration. *American Journal of Health Promotion, 84,* 1567–1568.

Brookfield, S. D. (1987). *Developing critical thinker: Challenging adults to explore alternative ways of thinking and acting* (1st ed.). San Francisco, CA: Jossey-Bass.

Brown, C. (1984). *The art of coalition building: A guide for community leaders.* New York: The American Jewish Committee.

Butterfoss, F. D., Goodman, R. M., & Wandersman, A. (1993). Community coalitions for health promotion and disease prevention. *Health Education Research: Theory and Practice, 8*(3), 315–330.

Butterfoss, F. D., Goodman, R. M., & Wandersman, A. (1996). Community coalitions for prevention and health promotion: Factors predicting satisfaction, participation and planning. *Health Education Quarterly, 23*(1), 65–79.

Butterfoss, F. D., Goodman, R. M., Wandersman, A., Valois, R., & Chinman, M. (1996). The Plan Quality Index: An empowerment evaluation tool for measuring and improving the quality of plans. In D. Fetterman, S. Kaftarian, & A. Wandersman (Eds.), *Empowerment evaluation: Knowledge and tools for self-assessment and accountability* (pp. 304–331). Thousand Oaks, CA: Sage.

Butterfoss, F. D., Morrow, A. L., Rosenthal, J., Dini, E., Crews, R. C., Webster, J. D., & Louis P. (1998). CINCH: An urban coalition for empowerment and action. *Health Education and Behavior, 25*(2), 212–225.

Butterfoss, F. D., Webster, J. D., Morrow, A. L., & Rosenthal, J. (1998). Coalitions that work: Training for public health professionals. *Journal of Public Health Management and Practice, 4*(6), 84–92.

Centers for Disease Control and Prevention. (1993). Resurgence of pertussis—United States. *MMWR, 42,* 952–953, 959–960.

Centers for Disease Control and Prevention. (1996). National, state and urban area vaccination coverage levels among children aged 19–35 months—United States, April 1994–March 1995. *MMWR, 45*(7), 145–150.

Chavis, D., Florin, P., Rich, R., & Wandersman, A. (1987). *The role of block association in crime control and community development: The Block Booster Project.* Report to the Ford Foundation.

Chinman, M., & Wandersman, A. (1999). The benefits and costs of volunteering in community organizations: Review and practical implications. *Nonprofit and Voluntary Sector Quarterly, 28*(1), 46–64.

Churchman, A. (1987). Can resident participation in neighborhood rehabilitation programs succeed? Israel's Project Renewal through a comparative perspective. In I. Altman & A. Wandersman (Eds.), *Neighborhood and community environments* (pp. 113–162). New York: Plenum.

Deutsch, M. (1973). *The resolution of conflict: Constructive and destructive processes.* New Haven, CT: Yale University Press.

Edwards, J. N., & White, R. P. (1980). Predictors of social participation: Apparent or real? *Journal of Voluntary Action Research, 9,* 60–73.

Ennis, R. H. (1962). A concept of critical thinking. *Harvard Educational Review, 32*(1), 81–111.

Feighery, E., & Rogers, T. (1989). *Building and maintaining effective coalitions* (Published as guide no. 12 in the series How-To Guides on Community Health Promotion). Palo Alto, CA: Stanford Health Promotion Resource Center.

Florin, P., & Wandersman, A. (1984). Cognitive social learning variables and participation in community development. *American Journal of Community Psychology, 12,* 689–708.

Freire, P. (1970). *Pedagogy of the oppressed.* New York: Seabury Press.

Giamartino, G., & Wandersman, A. (1983). Organizational climate correlates of viable urban block organizations. *American Journal of Community Psychology, 11,* 529–541.

Goodman, R. M., Speers, M. A., McLeroy, K., Fawcett, S., Kegler, M., Parker, E., Smith, S., Sterling, T., & Wallerstein, N. (1998). Identifying and defining the dimensions of community capacity to provide a basis for measurement. *Health Education and Behavior, 25*(3), 258–278.

Goodman, R. M., & Steckler, A. (1989). A model for the institutionalization of health promotion programs. *Family and Community Health, 11,* 63–78.

Goodman, R. M., Steckler, A., & Alciati, M. (1997). A process evaluation of the National Cancer Institute's Databased Intervention Research (DBIR) Program: A study of capacity building. *Health Education Research, 12*(2), 181–197.

Goodman, R. M., & Wandersman, A. (1994). FORECAST: A formative approach to evaluating community coalitions and community-based initiatives. *Journal of Community Psychology* (CSAP Special Issue), 6–25.

Goodman, R. M., Wandersman, A., Chinman, M., Imm, P., & Morrissey, E. (1996). An ecological assessment of community-based interventions for prevention and health promotion: Approaches to measuring coalitions. *American Journal of Community Psychology, 24*(1).

Gray, B. (1985). Conditions facilitating interorganizational collaboration. *Human Relations, 38*(10), 911–936.

Hancock, T. (1993). The evolution, impact and significance of the Healthy Cities/Healthy Communities movement. *Journal of Public Health Policy* (Spring), 5–18.

Heller, K., Price, R., Reinharz, S., Riger, S., & Wandersman, A. (1984). *Psychology and community change* (2nd ed.). Homewood, IL: Dorsey.

Henig, J. (1982). *Neighborhood mobilization: Redevelopment and response.* New Brunswick, NJ: Rutgers University Press.

Houseman, C., Butterfoss, F. D., Morrow, A. L., & Rosenthal, J. (1997). Focus groups among public, military and private sector mothers: Insights to improve the immunization process. *Journal of Public Health Nursing, 14*(4), 235–243.

ISA Associates. (1994). *National Evaluation of the Community Partnership Demonstration Program: Third Annual Report.* Rockville, MD: Center for Substance Abuse Prevention, U. S. Department of Health and Human Services.

Iscoe, I. (1974). Community psychology and the competent community. *American Psychologist, 29,* 607–613.

Israel, B. A. (1982). Social networks and health status: Linking theory research and practice. *Patient Counseling and Health Education, 4*(2), 65–79.

Israel, B. A., Checkoway, B., Schulz, A., & Zimmerman, M. (1994). Health education and community empowerment: Conceptualizing and measuring perceptions of individual organizational and community control. *Health Education Quarterly, 21*(2), 149–170.

Katz, D., & Kahn, R. L. (1978). *The social psychology of organizations* (2nd ed.). New York: Wiley.

Katz, J. (1984). *The silent world of doctor and patient.* New York: The Free Press.

Kaye, G., & Wolff, T. (1995). From the ground up: *A workbook on coalition building and community development.* Amherst, MA: AHEC Community Partners.

Kegler, K. C., Steckler, A., McLeroy, K., & Malek, S. H. (1998). Factors that contribute to effective community health promotion coalitions: A study of 10 Project ASSIST coalitions in North Carolina. *Health Education and Behavior, 25*(3), 338–353.

Knoke, D., & Wood, J. R. (1981). *Organizing for action: Commitment in voluntary associations.* New Brunswick, NJ: Rutgers University Press.

Langton, S. (Ed.). (1978). *Citizen participation in America.* Lexington, MA: Heath.

Mayer, N. S. & Blake, J. L. (1981). *Keys to the growth of neighborhood development organizations.* Washington, DC: The Urban Institute.

McLeroy, K., Bibeau, D., Steckler, A., & Glanz, K. (1988). An ecological perspective on health promotion programs. *Health Education Quarterly, 15,* 351–377.

McMillan, D. W., & Chavis, D. M. (1986). Sense of community: A definition and theory. *Journal of Community Psychology, 14,* 6–23.

Mischel, W. (1973). Toward a cognitive social learning reconceptualization of personality. *Psychological Review, 80,* 252–283.

Mischel, W. (1977). The interaction of person and situation. In D. Magnusson & N. S. Endler (Eds.), *Personality at the crossroads: Current issues in interactional psychology* (pp. 333–352). Hillsdale, NJ: Lawrence Erlbaum Associates.

Mizrahi, T., & Rosenthal, B. (1992). Managing dynamic tensions in social change coalitions. In T. Mizrahi & J. D. Morrison (Eds.), *Community organization and social administration: Advances, trends and emerging principles.* New York: Haworth Press.

Moe, T. M. (1980). *The organization of interests: Incentives and the internal dynamics of political interest groups.* Chicago: University of Chicago Press.

Moos, R. (1986). *Group environment scale manual* (2nd ed.). Palo Alto, CA: Consulting Psychologists Press.

Morrow, A. L., Rosenthal, J., Lakkis, H., Bowers, J. C., Butterfoss, F. D., Crews, R. C., & Sirotkin, B. (1998). A population-based study of risk factors for under-immunization among urban Virginia children served by public, private and military health care systems. *Pediatrics, 101*(2), E5.

National Vaccine Advisory Committee. (1991). The measles epidemic: The problems, barriers and recommendations. *Journal of the American Medical Association, 266,* 1547–1552.

Newbrough, J. R., & Chavis, D. M., (Eds.). (1986). Psychological sense of community II: Research and applications. *Journal of Community Psychology, 14*(4).

Olson, M. (1965). *The logic of collective action.* Cambridge, MA: Harvard University Press.

Orenstein, W. A., Atkinson, W., Mason, D., & Bernier, R. H. (1991). Barriers to vaccinating preschool children. *Journal of Health Care Poor Underserved, 1*(3), 315–330.

Prestby, J., & Wandersman, A. (1985). An empirical exploration of a framework of organizational viability: Maintaining block organizations. *Journal of Applied Behavioral Science, 21,* 287–305.

Prestby, J., Wandersman, A., Florin, P., Rich, R., & Chavis, D. (1990). Benefits, costs, incentive management and participation in voluntary organizations: A means to understanding and promoting empowerment. *American Journal of Community Psychology, 18,* 111–149.

Public Health Service. (1991). *Healthy People 2000: National Health Promotion and Disease Prevention Objectives* (DHHS Publication No. PHS91-50213). Washington, DC: U. S. Department of Health and Human Services.

Putnam, R. (1993). *Making democracy work.* Princeton, NJ: Princeton University Press.

Rich, R. C. (1980). The dynamics of leadership in neighborhood organizations. *Social Science Quarterly, 60,* 570–587.

Roberts-DeGennaro, M. (1986). Factors contributing to coalition maintenance. *Journal of Sociology and Social Welfare,* 248–264.

Steuart, G. (1985). Social and behavioral change strategies. *Health Education Quarterly, Supplement, 1,* S113–S115.

Stokols, D., Allen, J., & Bellingham, R. (1996). The social ecology of health promotion: Implications for research and practice. *American Journal of Health Promotion, 10*(4), 247–251.

Vassar, S. (1978). *Community participation in a metropolitan area: An analysis of the characteristics of participants.* Unpublished doctoral dissertation, University of Illinois, Chicago.

Verba, S., & Nie, N. H. (1972). *Participation America.* New York: Harper & Row.

Wallerstein. N. (1992). Powerlessness empowerment and health: Implications for health promotion programs. *Health Promotion, 6,* 197–205.

Wallerstein, N., & Bernstein, E. (Eds). (1994). Community empowerment participatory education and health. *Health Education Quarterly, 21*(2)(3).

Wandersman, A. (1979). User participation in planning environments: A conceptual framework. *Environment and Behavior, 11,* 465–482.

Wandersman, A., Florin, P., Chavis, D., Rich, R., & Prestby, J. (1985). Getting together and getting things done. *Psychology Today,* November, 64–71.

Wandersman, A., Florin, P., Friedmann, R., & Meier, R. (1987). Who participates, who does not, and why? An analysis of voluntary neighborhood associations in the United States and Israel. *Sociological Forum, 2,* 534–555.

Wandersman, A., Goodman, R., & Butterfoss, F. (1997). Understanding coalitions and how they operate: An "open systems" framework. In M. Minkler (Ed.), *Community organizing and community building for health* (pp. 261–277). New Brunswick, NJ: Rutgers University Press.

Warren, R. (1963). *The community in America.* Chicago: Rand McNally.

Warren, R. B., & Warren, D. I. (1977). *The neighborhood organizer's handbook.* South Bend, IN: University of Notre Dame Press.

Widmer, C. (1984). *An incentive model of citizen participation applied to a study of human service agency boards of directors.* Unpublished doctoral dissertation, Cornell University.

Zell, E. R., Dietz, V., Stevenson, J., Cochi, S., & Bruce, R. (1994). Low vaccination levels of U. S. pre-school and school-aged children. *Journal of the American Medical Association, 271,* 833–914.

38

The Effects of Physical Activity on Physical and Psychological Health

Wayne T. Phillips
Arizona State University

Michaela Kiernan

Abby C. King
Stanford University School of Medicine

Orandum est sit ut mens sana in corpore sano
(Our prayer is for a healthy mind in a healthy body)
—Juvenal (60–130 AD)

The concept of a body–mind connection has survived since its origination with the early Greek philosophers. Although few people even today would disagree with the sentiments expressed in the aforementioned quotation, it is apparent that both physical and mental health in the United States are at suboptimal levels as physical effort becomes less and less a necessary requisite for everyday living. Today the majority of the U.S. population is essentially sedentary, reporting little or no exercise of even low to moderate intensity (Centers for Disease Control and Prevention, 1991) . The links between such inactivity and the incidence of coronary heart disease (CHD), as well as other chronic disease states, have been well established with both epidemiological and clinical studies (Bouchard, Shephard, & Stephens, 1994; Bouchard, Shephard, Stephens, Sutton, & McPherson, 1990). Impaired psychological health is also a pandemic problem in the United States, with an estimated 8 to 20 million people (3%–8% of the population) suffering from an affective or depressive disorder (D. R. Brown, 1990; Hatfield & Landers, 1987). As many as 25% of the U.S. population suffer from mild to moderate depression, anxiety and/or other indicators of emotional disorders (President's Commission on Mental Health, 1978). These figures have been represented as "the tip of the iceberg," because the majority of individuals with such conditions rarely seek treatment (D. R. Brown, 1990, p. 607). Additionally, more than 40% of the adult population are reported as experiencing adverse health effects from stress (U.S. Department of Health and Human Services, 1991).

The financial and social costs of such levels of physical and psychological ill health are now beginning to be addressed (Shephard, 1990) and are considerable, albeit complex and extremely difficult to quantify. Although no costs specifically attributed to physical inactivity have been published, Klarman (1964) estimated that the direct costs to the U.S. economy from all forms of cardiovascular disease in 1962 was $3.1 billion, with a further sum of from $3 to $5 billion estimated for secondary costs such as loss of production, pain, and family distress. Considering that physical inactivity has been shown to be an independent risk factor for coronary heart disease (National Institutes of Health, 1995), and no more than 25% of the population meets the current physical activity–cardiovascular health recommendations (Haskell, 1995), a substantial portion of the Klarman (1964) costs could logically be attributed to physical inactivity. In 1980 the cost of mental health care in the United States was estimated at between $19.4 and $24 billion (C. A. Taube & Barrett, 1986). A decade later, this figure had escalated to approximately $148 billion per year with about half of these costs represented by nonsevere levels of mental/emotional disorders like depression and anxiety (National Advisory Mental Health Council, 1993).

The aerobics and running boom of the 1970s and 1980s brought the health benefits of exercise into high profile, and today an increasing amount of available scientific information has been accompanied by an ever-growing media focus on the desirability of physical activity and exercise from fitness and health perspectives. Despite this attention and the apparent public acceptance of the mental and physical benefits of exercise, only a relatively small percentage of the population is reported to be active on a regular basis (Casperson & Merritt, 1992; Merritt & Casperson, 1992; U.S. Department of Health and Human Services, 1991).

This chapter begins by reviewing the role of physical activity in a number of important physical and psychological health outcomes. The physical health outcomes discussed focus on cardiovascular disease morbidity and mortality, cardiovascular risk factors, and cancer. The psychological health outcomes discussed focus predominantly on depression, anxiety, and physiological "reactivity," that is, the psychobiological responses to acute and chronic stressful challenges. It also briefly reviews a number of putative mechanisms for such responses. Finally, it concludes with an overview of the rationale behind newly issued recommendations for physical activity and health, their implications for physical activity participation and adherence, and the unique challenges in terms of interpretation and implementation. Given the increasing concern for the high economic and health costs of physical inactivity, it is critical to examine how the more recent inclusive emphasis on diverse types of physical activity could be expected to affect the determinants of long-term physical activity participation, as well as the design of future clinical and community-level physical activity programs.

DEFINITION OF TERMS

With the increasing attention and investigation of its health benefits, there has been a gradual shifting of emphasis toward behaviorally oriented definitions of physical activity rather than defining such activity solely in terms of work performed or force produced (Knutsson, Lewenhaupt-Olsson, & Thorsen, 1973). This view of physical activity as a behavior has necessitated the development of new terms, or the revision of existing ones (Haskell, 1994b). This chapter focuses predominantly on the following behaviorally oriented terms.

Physical Activity

This is defined as any bodily movement produced by the contraction of skeletal muscle that increases energy expenditure above the basal level (Caspersen, Powell, & Christenson, 1985; Surgeon General's Report, 1996)

Exercise

Although the term *exercise* has been used synonymously with *physical activity,* it is more accurately categorized as a subset of physical activity, and defined as activity that is planned structured, repetitive, and purposeful with the objective of improving one or more aspects of physical fitness (Caspersen et al., 1985; Surgeon General's Report, 1996).

Fitness

This has been defined as a set of attributes (or "components") that people have or are able to achieve, relating to their ability to perform physical work (Caspersen et al., 1985). In behavioral terms, this can be defined as the ability to carry out daily tasks with vigor and alertness without undue fatigue, and with ample energy to enjoy leisure time pursuits and to meet unforeseen challenges. The components of fitness are considered to be cardiorespiratory endurance (often termed *aerobic fitness*), muscular strength, muscular endurance, muscular power, speed, flexibility, agility, balance, reaction time, and body composition. The definition of fitness has been further subdivided to differentiate those components considered to contribute more to health versus those considered to contribute more to skill or performance (Corbin & Lindsey, 1993).

Health-Related Fitness. This consists of cardiovascular fitness, muscular strength, muscular endurance, flexibility, and body composition.

Performance (or Skill) Related Fitness. This consists of speed, power, agility, balance, and reaction time.

Aerobic Fitness. This term is considered separately here because it is used in many studies as a measure of exercise capacity or exercise training. Aerobic fitness is defined by the body's capacity to take in, transport, and utilize oxygen, and is most accurately measured during a graded exercise test on a treadmill or stationary cycle. The amount of oxygen (O_2) a person's body uses ("takes up") is referred to as "oxygen uptake" and is commonly expressed as "VO_2" (volume of oxygen). The amount of oxygen able to be taken up by an individual at maximum effort (i.e., during a graded exercise test) is referred to as "maximum oxygen uptake" and is expressed as "VO_{2max}." This is generally accepted as the best measure of the functional limit of the cardiovascular system and is regarded as the gold standard index of cardiorespiratory fitness.

Psychological Health

This term, which has also been used synonymously with "mental health," has had a wide interpretation in the literature. Indeed, the diversity of definitions prompted one reviewer to note that psychological health was defined as "whatever an investigator has identified as being the psychological dependent measure in his/her investigation" (McAuley & Rudolph, 1995,

p. 69). The space limitations imposed by this chapter preclude a comprehensive coverage of such wide-ranging operational definitions. This review addresses the constructs most commonly investigated and focuses primarily on the amelioration of negative aspects of mental health such as depression, anxiety, and psychophysiological responses (i.e., stress reactivity).

PHYSICAL ACTIVITY AND PHYSICAL HEALTH

Physical Activity and All-Cause and Cause-Specific Mortality

Substantial data now exist demonstrating that higher levels of physical activity (Berlin & Colditz, 1990; Leon, Connett, Jacobs, & Rauramaa, 1987; Morris, Clayton, Everitt, Semmence, & Burgess, 1990; Paffenbarger, Hyde, Wing, & Hsieh, 1986; Powell, Thompson, Caspersen, & Ford, 1987; Shaper & Wannamethee, 1991) and endurance fitness (Blair et al., 1989; Ekelund et al., 1988; Sandvik et al., 1993) are significantly associated with reduced all-cause and selected cause-specific mortality rates, and with some increase in life expectancy (Paffenbarger et al., 1986; Pekkanen et al., 1987). Unfortunately, due to logistical constraints, no randomized clinical trial of adequate size or duration has been conducted to test the causality of this hypothesis, but the results of many observational studies are consistent with the interpretation that a more physically active lifestyle independently contributes to reduced mortality and increased longevity (Blair, Kohl, Gordon, & Paffenbarger, 1992; Powell et al., 1987).

It appears that if middle-aged men have been habitually active or become active, then they are more likely to reach old age than if they remain sedentary (Paffenbarger et al., 1993; Pekkanen et al., 1987). Men from age 35 to 39 who are assumed to have sedentary jobs, but who expend more than 2,000 kcal per week during leisure time (achievable with regular moderate intensity activity), have a life expectancy 2.51 years longer than similar men who expend less than 500 kcal per week (Paffenbarger et al., 1986). At age 55 to 59, this difference decreased to 2.02 years, and at age 65 to 69, there was a decrease to 1.35 years. Given that the average life expectancy of American men at age 65 was approximately 15.1 years in 1990 (National Center for Health Statistics, 1993), the more physically active man at age 65 would appear to have increased his life expectancy by approximately 9% over his sedentary counterpart. The data from Paffenbarger and colleagues are similar to those reported for Finnish men living in rural areas (Pekkanen et al., 1987). In that study, the adjusted gain in life expectancy for middle-aged men with high levels of physical activity was 2.1 years.

Other studies of men tend to support these results of increased longevity for more active persons together with significantly lower age-specific or age-adjusted all-cause mortality rates for more active versus sedentary men (Leon et al., 1987; Morris et al., 1990; Shaper & Wannamthee, 1991) The increased longevity attributed to a more physically active lifestyle is likely caused by the effect of physical activity on reducing mortality due to coronary artery disease (Berlin & Colditz, 1990; Lakka et al., 1994; Powell, Thompson, Caspersen, & Ford, 1987) and Type II diabetes mellitus (Manson et al., 1992). Other possible contributors to a lower mortality rate, particularly in older physically active persons, include a reduced incidence of stroke (Wannamethee & Shaper, 1992), hypertension (Reaven, Barrett-Connor, & Edelstein, 1991) and some forms of cancers (Kohl, LaPorte, & Blair, 1988). Very few data are available on sufficiently large samples of women to address the issue of increased longevity as a result of increased physical activity or physical fitness, but the evidence shows lower all-cause and cause-specific mortality rates for more physically active and fit younger and older women and is consistent with data reported for men (Blair et al., 1989).

Physical Activity and Cardiovascular Disease

Studies examining the relation between physical activity and cardiovascular disease have been thoroughly reviewed (Powell et al., 1987). Consisting primarily of large epidemiological studies, this review carefully identified methodologically sound studies such as those that excluded people at baseline who could have been inactive due to the presence of subclinical disease. The review reported a consistent inverse association between physical activity and incidence of CHD, particularly in studies with stronger methodological designs. More recent reviews (Berlin & Colditz, 1990; Blair, 1994) have supported these findings and recent position statements (Fletcher et al., 1992; Pate et al., 1995) have stated that physical inactivity is now considered to be an independent risk factor for the development of cardiovascular disease.

The *physical activity–health paradigm,* with its emphasis on moderate physical activity levels, was developed principally from the qualitative examination of these large scale epidemiological studies (Haskell, 1994b; Pate et al., 1995). Although a quantitative examination of this literature has been published (Berlin & Colditz, 1990), the authors of this meta-analysis did not report relative risk statistics between sedentary and moderately active people, the comparison critical to the physical activity–health paradigm. The majority of these studies have demonstrated that highly active or fit people are at lower disease risk than sedentary or moderately active or fit people (Ekelund et al., 1988; Morris et al., 1990; Sandvik et al., 1993), whereas other studies have shown that highly active or fit people are at similar levels of risk to those who are moderately active or fit (Blair et al., 1989; Leon et al., 1987). However, across almost all the studies, those people who are at least moderately active are at lower risk for cardiovascular disease than people who are sedentary or inactive.

Coronary Heart Disease Morbidity

There are substantially more data linking physical activity or physical fitness to all-cause and CHD-related mortality than to the prevalence of morbidity due to most diseases in younger or older persons. For example, in the past there has not been good documentation that a high level of physical activity reduces the incidence of nonfatal manifestations of CHD, including nonfatal myocardial infarction and angina pectoris. In several studies where higher levels of activity are associated with lower CHD mortality, there was no association between activity status and nonfatal manifestations of CHD (Morris, Heady, Raffle, Roberts, & Parks, 1953; Shapiro et al., 1969). Recently Lakka and colleagues (1994) reported an inverse relation between both level of physical activity and maximal oxygen uptake and acute myocardial infarction. Data are not reported separately for nonfatal and fatal events, probably because there were only 42 myocardial infarctions over 4.9 years of follow-up in 1,166 men free of CHD at baseline. The apparent difference in the association between physical activity and CHD mortality versus morbidity could be due to true biological differences in acquiring the disease as compared to dying from it, or to the known difficulty of collecting accurate morbidity data for many chronic diseases, including CHD, in population-based studies.

Data from secondary prevention or cardiac rehabilitation studies support the possibility that physical activity may be more associated with risk of dying from CHD than with nonfatal clinical manifestations. In a meta-analysis of the effects of exercise-based cardiac rehabilitation programs on cardiac morbidity and mortality, there was a 25% lower CHD mortality rate in the rehabilitation program participants but a somewhat (nonsignificant) higher prevalence of nonfatal myocardial infarction and angina pectoris (Oldridge, Guyatt, Fisher, & Rimm, 1988). Similar results evaluating a larger number of exercise-based rehabilitation programs were reported by O'Conner, Boving, and Yusuf (1989). Also, autopsy studies have observed no difference in the magnitude of coronary atherosclerosis in men who were classified as inactive or active by their major occupation, but there was less myocardial damage in the more active men (Morris & Crawford, 1958). Physical activity could reduce CHD mortality without affecting morbidity by favorably altering the "triggering event" for acute myocardial infarction or cardiac arrest. Recent data indicate that the primary triggering event for many myocardial infarctions is the acute rupture of atherosclerotic lesions and the rapid closure of the artery lumen due to platelet aggregation and cell proliferation (Fuster, L. Badimon, J. J. Badimon, & Chesebro, 1992). It could be that physical activity reduces either the risk of lesion rupture, platelet aggregation, or cell proliferation, thus reducing CHD mortality but not the development of atherosclerosis, which may be more related to the development of nonfatal clinical manifestations of myocardial ischemia.

Although the epidemiological evidence just reviewed is supportive of the importance of physical activity on CHD, the independent role of physical activity as a cardiovascular disease risk factor currently remains understudied in comparison to other CHD risk factors, such as hypertension or smoking. A timely issue in the area of physical activity (as well as for other risk factors) is the need for more studies examining populations other than White, middle-class males.

Physical Activity and Cardiovascular Disease Risk Factors

No randomized controlled studies of adequate methodological design have yet evaluated the effects of increasing physical activity or fitness on the primary prevention of cardiovascular disease (Haskell, 1995). However, a substantial amount of data reports positive effects on physical activity on the more intermediate endpoints of risk factors for cardiovascular disease.

Hypertension Hypertension has been identified as an independent risk factor for cardiovascular disease (Caspersen & Heath, 1993; Fries, 1976; Gordon, Sorlie, & Kannel, 1976; M. L. Pollock & Wilmore, 1990). Based on a considerable number of well controlled studies, the American College of Sports Medicine (ACSM) recently issued a position statement concerning the potential benefits of physical activity for primary prevention and treatment of hypertension (ACSM, 1993). Conclusions regarding the benefit of physical activity for primary prevention were based on evidence from both animal studies and large scale epidemiological studies, and generally supported the hypothesis that participation in endurance exercise training reduced risk of hypertension. For instance, the incidence of hypertension in male Harvard alumni who engaged in vigorous sports was 35% lower over a 6 to 10 year follow-up period as compared to inactive men (Paffenbarger et al., 1993). Similarly, the incidence of hypertension in physically fit men and women at the Cooper Institute for Aerobics Research in Dallas was 52% lower during a 4-year follow-up period as compared to unfit men and women (Blair, Goodyear, Gibbons, & Cooper, 1984).

Although it appears that vigorous physical activity is associated with lower incidence of hypertension, evidence that the types of activities espoused in the physical activity–health paradigm (i.e., moderate intensity physical activity) are associated with lower incidence is still evolving. Data from a large scale epidemiological study of University of Pennsylvania alumni demonstrated that although the incidence of hypertension was lower for individuals who had engaged in vigorous sports after college, the incidence was not lower for individuals who engaged in light to moderate activity after college (Paffenbarger, Jung, Leung, & Hyde, 1991). However, recent data from experimental studies using rats genetically predisposed to hypertension support the importance of moderate intensity exercise. Specifically, these studies demonstrated that animals trained at moderate intensity exercise had lower blood pressures than untrained animals (Tipton, 1991), whereas animals trained at vigorous intensity exercise had similar (and high) blood pressures relative to untrained animals (Tipton, Sebastian, Overton, Woodman, & Williams, 1983; Tomanek, Gisofi, Bauer, & Palmer, 1988). In these studies, moderate intensity exercise training attenuated an age-related increase in blood pressure rather than actually reducing blood pressure below initial levels (Tipton, 1991). If these experimental results using rats predisposed to hypertension are found to generalize to humans, then the attenuation of an age-related increase in blood pressure would still result in a lower incidence of hypertension. In support of this, a comprehensive review of the effects of endurance exercise training on blood pressure (Fagard & Tipton, 1994) found that hypertensive patients participating in endurance exercise training generally experienced a reduction in systolic and diastolic blood pressure of approximately 9 mm Hg. Borderline hypertensive patients and normotensive persons generally experienced a 6 mm Hg and 3 mm Hg reduction in systolic and diastolic pressures, respectively (Fagard & Tipton, 1994). This magnitude of blood pressure reduction in response to endurance exercise training has also been reported for men and women age 60 and older in some (Coconie et al., 1991; Hagberg, Montain, Martin, & Ehsani, 1989), although not all (Blumenthal, Siegel, & Appelbaum, 1991), randomized clinical trials.

Although the human and animal data are initially compelling, as with the literature examining physical activity and cardiovascular disease morbidity and mortality, more studies examining the primary prevention benefits of moderate as well as more vigorous physical activity for lowering blood pressure are needed with populations of women, ethnic groups other than non-Hispanic Whites, and a range of age groups.

Physical Activity and Other Chronic Diseases

Although the leading cause of death in the United States remains cardiovascular disease, age-adjusted death rates from CHD have been decreasing, whereas those of certain forms of cancer have been increasing (Lee, 1994). A growing literature suggests a strong inverse relation between physical activity and overall cancer mortality rates. However, because types of cancer (e.g., breast, colon) are thought to have different origins and biological mechanisms (Sternfield, 1992), site specific cancer in women and men is reviewed.

Breast Cancer. It has been reported that vigorous, or even moderate, physical training can interrupt the menstrual cycle and may inhibit carcinogenisis in the breast secondary to the reduction of cumulative exposure to estrogen and progesterone (Thune, Brenn, Lund, & Gaard, 1997). Research in this area has been equivocal, however, with studies reporting both positive (Frisch, Wyshak, Albright, Schiff, & Jones, 1985; Thune et al., 1997), negative (Dorgan et al., 1994), and no associations (Paffenbarger, Hyde, & Wing, 1987) between physical activity and cancer. Frisch et al. (1985) first reported a lower prevalence of breast cancer among former college athletes as compared to nonathletes in a cohort of more than 5,000 living alumni. Thune et al. (1997) reported that greater leisure time activity was associated with reduced risk of breast cancer after adjustment for age, body mass index, height, parity, and country of residence. In regularly exercising women, the risk was found to be lower in premenopausal and younger women, and with higher levels of occupational physical activity. In contrast to this, Paffenbarger, Hyde, and Wing (1987) did not find any association of breast cancer with participation in sports during early college years. Although a nonsignificant inverse trend for self-reported physical activity and postmenopausal breast cancer was reported by Albanes and colleagues for participants of the First National Health and Nutrition Examination Survey (Albanes, Blair, & P. R. Taylor, 1989), this same study also reported a suggested increased risk of premenopausal breast cancer in more active women. This latter finding was also reported by Dorgan et al. in the Framingham Heart Study (Dorgan et al., 1994). The authors found an increasing gradient of risk for breast cancer with increasing physical activity. Gammon et al. recently conducted a critical review of the physical activity and breast cancer risk literature (Gammon, John, & Britton, 1998). Evaluating each study for coherence, validity, and bias, the authors reported that the majority of epidemiological studies suggested that higher occupational and leisure time physical activity may be associated with a reduced risk of breast cancer, with the latter reporting a range of from 12% to 60% reduction in risk. The data were not sufficient to establish any dose–response relations or any critical effects of frequency, intensity, or duration. However, most of the reported physical activity was at least of moderate intensity. To further elucidate the role of physical activity, future studies should focus on more prospective or retrospective cohort designs and utilize more reliable methods of physical activity assessment.

Colon Cancer. Consistent relations have also been found between levels of occupational physical activity and lower incidence of colon cancer (Sternfield, 1992). The few epidemiological studies that have examined recreational physical activity have primarily assessed only exercise-related behaviors (e.g., hiking, sports, etc.), making it difficult to determine whether the more inclusive types of activities currently recommended (i.e., diverse types of moderate intensity activities of daily living, household chores, etc.) are associated with a lower incidence of colon cancer. For instance, assessment tools used in such research have often included a one-item closed response question about the amount of exercise for recreation (Albanes et al., 1989) or the amount of time per day spent in more vigorous physical activities such as swimming, biking, or dancing (Wu, Paganini-Hill, Ross, & Henderson, 1987). One study that measured a full range of activities (e.g., stair climbing, city blocks walked, and active sports) demonstrated that Harvard alumni who engaged in moderate (1,000–2,500 kcals) and high (> 2,500 kcals) levels of activity at two timepoints after college were at lower risk for developing colon cancer (Lee, Paffenbarger, & Hsieh, 1991). Men who only engaged in those levels of activity at one timepoint were not at lower risk. Clearly, the development of appropriate physical activity assessment tools is a critical priority for future research across disease outcomes. Indeed, future tools will need to assess the types of moderate-intensity physical activities that are routine in many women's lives, such as child care and household tasks (King & Kiernan, 1997).

PHYSICAL ACTIVITY AND PSYCHOLOGICAL HEALTH

Psychological, or mental, health is a multifaceted condition made up of both positive and negative dimensions. However, in a situation comparable to early views of health as simply the absence of disease, the majority of studies investigating the effects of physical activity on psychological function have generally represented mental health in terms of the absence, or reduction, of negative affect. This section reviews the existing literature on the role of physical activity in the prevention or reduction of negative affect (depression, anxiety, and physiologic reactivity).

Caplan (1964) operationalized the preventative aspects of physical activity as either (a) *primary prevention:* Can physical activity protect against the onset of mental health problems "by counteracting harmful circumstances before they have a chance to produce illness?" (Caplan, 1964, p. 23); (b) *secondary prevention:* Can physical activity improve or prevent the worsening of mild to moderate symptoms of mental health problems before they have a chance to turn into those requiring tertiary intervention?; and (c) *tertiary prevention:* Can physical activity serve as a treatment for already existing clinical mental health problems. The following sections briefly review the literature on these three aspects of prevention with regard specifically to depression and anxiety.

PHYSICAL ACTIVITY AND DEPRESSION

Clinical depression affects from 2% to 5% of the U.S. population per year (Kessler et al., 1994), and makes up approximately 6% to 8% of general medical practices (Katon & Schulberg, 1992). This situation, in conjunction with drug therapy that has been the treatment of choice for depressive symptoms, has significant financial implications for individual and national health care costs. Depressed individuals typically spend 1.5 times more on health care costs than nondepressed individuals and, if undergoing drug therapy, spend up to 3 times more on outpatient pharmacy costs than non-drug-treated individuals (Simon, VonKorff, & Barlow, 1995). There has been recent attention on exercise as an alternative therapy to more traditional drug treatments (Martinsen, 1990; Surgeon General's Report, 1996).

Primary Prevention

Epidemiological Studies. No longitudinal studies of adequate methodological design have yet been conducted to test the hypothesis that physical activity protects against the onset of depression, but associations between these two variables may be investigated by examining evidence from epidemiological studies. These consistently report that physical activity is associated with reduced symptoms of depression. Stephens (1988) carried out an extensive analysis of data from four large databases, two from the United States (i.e., the National Survey of Personal Health Practices and Consequences and the National Health and Nutrition Examination Survey) and two from Canada (i.e., the Canadian Health Survey and the Canadian Fitness Survey). Stephens found that physical activity was positively associated with general well-being, lower levels of anxiety and depression, and positive mood. This relation was particularly strong for women and persons over age 40. The results of the Stephens (1988) study were generally consistent across all four populations and were considered to be very robust due to the diverse nature of the four study populations, the time over which such measures were taken (10 years), and the fact that four different measures of physical activity and six different mental health constructs were employed. Other epidemiological studies have reported similar reductions in depressive symptoms (J. D. Brown & Lawton, 1986; Camacho, Roberts, Lazarus, Kaplan, & R. D. Cohen, 1991; Farmer, Locke, Moscicki, Dannenberg, Larson, & Radloff, 1988; Fredrick, Frerichs, & Clark, 1988; Lobstein, Mosbacher, & Ismail, 1983; Paffenbarger, Lee, & Leung, 1994; Ross & Hayes, 1988; Stephens & Craig, 1990), although only two of these (Camacho et al., 1991; Farmer et al., 1988) are prospective in nature.

Farmer et al. (1988), using data from the National Health and Nutrition Examination Survey, found that baseline recreational activity was an independent predictor of depression at 8-year follow-up in White women, but not White men, who were not depressed at baseline. This relation persisted after adjustment for age, chronic conditions, education, employment, income, and length of follow-up. Similar results were found by Camacho et al. (1991) in a prospective study using data from the Alameda County Study. Among subjects who were not depressed at baseline, those who reported low physical activity levels at the 1974 follow-up were at significantly greater risk (OR = 4.32, 95% CI 3.17–5.62) for depressive symptoms than those who reported high physical activity (OR = 1). This relation changed little after adjustment for a number of covariates (i.e., physical health, socioeconomic status, life events, social support, and other health habits). The authors also found that increases in physical activity levels between baseline and 1974 significantly reduced the incidence of subsequent depressive symptoms in the 1983 follow-up, although this significance was not retained following adjustment for the covariates listed previously. The greatest change in adjusted odds ratio occurred when going from high to low activity. The prospective nature of these two latter studies provide somewhat stronger evidence for an activity–depression association than do the cross-sectional studies cited earlier.

Only one study could be found that investigated, a priori the preventative effects of physical activity on depression. In a longitudinal study, Gotestam and Stiles (1990) examined Norwegian soldiers exposed to a highly stressful life situation. Those who were actively engaged in sports were significantly less depressed 12 weeks after exposure to the stressful situation as compared to those who were inactive.

Secondary and Tertiary Prevention

Intervention Studies. Although exercise is generally believed to make you "feel good," the scientific evidence in support of a causal role for exercise remains somewhat speculative. Despite the fact that the mental health and exercise literature has been noted to be "voluminous" (Sime, 1987), it has been described by at least two major authorities as lacking in reliable, sound research methods (D. R. Brown, 1990; Morgan, 1994). A number of literature reviews on exercise and depression already exist in both narrative (Dunn & Dishman,

1991; Martinsen, 1990; Morgan, 1994; Raglin, 1990; C. B. Taylor, Sallis, & Needle, 1985) and meta-analysis (Kugler, Seelback, & Kruskemper, 1994; McDonald & Hodgdon, 1991; North, McCullagh, & Tran, 1990) formats. In general, the majority of these reviews found that exercise exerted a positive effect on depression in both clinical and nonclinical populations. The existing reviews on physical activity and depression have reiterated the methodological shortcomings of this particular body of literature. These have included the use of inadequate sample sizes; lack of random assignment to groups; an absence of placebo or control groups; and use of nonblinded methodological designs (D. R. Brown, 1990). Morgan (1994), in a comprehensive and explicit critique of methodological shortcomings in the physical activity and depression literature, called for scientists to pay much closer attention to design issues in order to avoid what he termed the "Garbage in Garbage out" syndrome (p. 861).

Although early studies of physical activity and depression focused almost exclusively on clinical populations (Morgan, 1969), the more recent literature has reported intervention studies investigating the preventative effects of physical activity not only in the clinically depressed, but in nonclinical symptomatic as well as healthy populations. The physical activity intervention has usually consisted of different forms of aerobic exercise, with a much smaller number utilizing anaerobic programs principally of strength training. The majority of such studies have been, with few exceptions (King, C. B. Taylor, & Haskell, 1993), of relatively short duration (6–12 weeks). These studies have generally reported positive results in groups with diagnosed clinical depression and those with depressive symptoms (D. R. Brown, 1990; Morgan, 1994; Tables 38.1 and 38.2). The principal self-report instrument used in such studies was the Beck Depression Inventory (BDI; Beck, Ward, Mendelson, Mock, & Erbaugh, 1961). Healthy populations have been the least studied, and although early studies reported equivocal results, more recent studies have generally reported little or no effect of physical activity on depression or depressive symptoms (Table 38.3).

Time Series Studies. One of the earliest scientific studies to investigate the effects of physical activity on depression in noninstitutionalized healthy individuals was conducted by Morgan, Roberts, Brand, and Feinerman (1970). In this quasi-experimental study, 140 men from age 22 to 62 volunteered to participate in one of eight physical activity groups of running, swimming, cycling, or circuit training at an intensity of approximately 85% of predicted maximal heart rate for 2 to 3 days per week for 6 weeks. Depression was measured by the Zung Depression Scale (Zung, 1965). Mean baseline scores for all groups were within the normal range for this scale and were unchanged after the intervention. However, a subgroup of 11 of these exercisers scored above 53 on the Zung Depression Scale, indicating depressive symptoms of clinical significance (Zung, 1965). When the change scores of this subgroup were analyzed, a significant decrease in depression scores was revealed, and because these subjects were spread across all groups, this decrease appeared to be independent of mode or frequency of exercise. Although the methodology of this study is open to criticism (no random selection or assignment to groups), it represented one of the first indications that physical activity could be effective in alleviating symptoms of mild to moderate depression, but had little effect in "normal" populations. Other early studies have used similar methodological designs in moderately and clinically depressed populations. Sime (1987) reported the positive effects of a multiple baseline time series design intervention in 15 subjects with moderately elevated scores on the Beck Depression Inventory at baseline ($M = 14.2 \pm 1.0$). Subjects were used as their own control during a graduated exercise program on a cycle ergometer conducted four times per week for 10 weeks. Significant reductions in BDI scores were found at both 6-month and 21-month follow-up. Doyne et al. (1983) also utilized a time series design in four female inpatients initially diagnosed with major depressive disorder according to the Research Diagnostic Criteria (RDC; Spitzer, Endicott, & Robins, 1978) and the Schedule for Affective Disorders and Schizophrenia (SADS; Endicott & Spitzer, 1978). Following a 6-week aerobic training program, significant decreases in depression, as measured by the Beck Depression Inventory and the Depressed Adjective Checklist (DACL; Lubin, 1965), were reported and maintained at 3-month follow-up.

Since that time, the use of comparative group designs has become the norm in investigating the effect of physical activity on depression. In view of the general agreement in the literature on the lack of methodological rigor of many of these studies (D. R. Brown, 1990; Morgan, 1994), the remainder of this section focuses on published studies with either a randomized or a randomized controlled design.

Randomized Studies Focusing on Aerobic Exercise. Although the majority of reviews generally report positive effects of physical activity on depression, the number of randomized or randomized controlled trials reported in the literature is limited (Tables 38.1–38.4). Martinson, Medhus, and Sandvik (1985), in a randomized controlled trial of inpatients with major depressive disorder, randomly assigned subjects to an aerobic exercise or an occupational therapy group designated as "control." Significant postintervention differences were reported in depression scores between the aerobic exercise and occupational therapy groups. However, both groups were also reported as receiving psychotherapy during the intervention period, which calls into question the validity of the control group and somewhat blurs the independent effect of the aerobic exercise intervention. Greist, Klein, Eischens, Gurman, and Morgan (1979) randomly assigned 28 males and females diagnosed with Minor Depressive Disorder to one of three interventions (aerobic exercise, short-term psychotherapy, and long-term psychotherapy). All interventions were reported as reducing depression scores. No formal statistical analysis was presented in this study, and the randomization procedure was not strictly maintained throughout the intervention period, thus making interpretation of results difficult. Bosscher (1993) randomly assigned 24 women inpatients matched for depression scores to either a three times per week running group, or a usual care group. The authors reported significant reductions in depres-

TABLE 38.1

Physical Activity (Aerobic Exercise) Effects on Diagnosed Clinical Depression in Adult Men and Women—Intervention Studies

Author	Subjects	Diagnostic Tool	Assessment Tool	Intervention	Study Period	Result
Randomized Controlled Trials						
Netz et al. (1994)	17 M & F psychogeriatric depressed inpatients	GDS	GDS	AE (Seated, 3*wk) SOC (3*wk)	8 weeks	Sig. reduced DEP in AE and SOC Sig. greater reduction in AE vs. SOC
Martinson et al. (1985)	49 M & F inpatients with MjDD	DSM–III	BDI	AE (3*week) OT ('Control', 3*wk) Note: Both groups also received psychotherapy	6–9 weeks	Sig. reduced DEP in AE vs. OT
Randomized Trials						
Bosscher (1993)	24 depressed M & F inpatients	ZDS	ZDS	AE (3* week) UC (3*wk)	8 weeks	Sig. reduced DEP in AE vs. UC
Sexton et al. (1989)	52 M & F inpatients with MmDD	DSM–III	BDI	Lo–AE (Walking 3*wk) Hi–AE (Jogging 3*wk)	8 weeks	Sig. reduced DEP in both groups No diffs between groups
Klein et al. (1985)	74 M & F subjects with MjDD or MnDD	DSSCL–90	DSSCL–90	AE (2* week) M/R (1* week) GT (1* wk)	12 weeks	Sig. reduced DEP in all groups No diffs between groups
Greist et al. (1979)	28 M & F with MnDD	DSSCL–90	DSSCL–90	AE (3–4* week) S-T psychotherapy (1*wk) L-T psychotherapy (1*wk)	10 weeks	Reduced DEP in all groups No apparent diffs between groups but no statistical analysis presented

Note: BDI = Beck Depression Inventory; HRSD = Hamilton Rating Scale for Depression; ZDS = Zung Self-Rating Depression Scale; RDC = Research Diagnostic Criteria; DACL = Depression Adjective Check List; DSSCL–90 = Depression Subscale of Symptom Check List–90; DSM–III = Diagnostic and Statistical Manual of Mental Disorders, 3rd Edition; MADRS = Montgomery and Asberg Depression Rating Scale; CES–D = Center for Epidemiological Studies–Depression Scale; POMS = Profile of Mood States; MjDD = Major Depressive Disorder; MnDD = Minor Depressive Disorder; GT = Group Therapy; S-T = Short-Term; L-T = Long Term; AE = Aerobic Exercise; RT = Resistance Training; BB = BodyBuilding; RT + F = Resistance Training plus Flexibility; CT = Circuit Training; AE–Hi = High intensity aerobic exercise; AE–Lo = Low intensity aerobic exercise; Home = Home-based exercise; Group = Group/Class-based exercise; OT = Occupational Therapy; M/R = Meditation/Relaxation; UC = Usual Care; C = Control Group; WLC = Wait List Control Group; SOC = Socialization Control Group; NRC = Nonrandomized Control Group; PARS = Phobic Avoidance Rating Scale; CPRS = Comprehensive Psychopathological Rating Scale; ACS = Agoraphobic Cognitions Scale (Martinsen, Hoffart, & Solberg, 1989).

TABLE 38.2
Physical Activity (Aerobic Exercise) Effects on Depressive Symptoms in Adult Men and Women—Intervention Studies

Author	Subjects	Assessment Tool	Intervention	Study Period	Results
Randomized Controlled Trials					
McCann & Holmes (1984)	41 undergraduate females (> 11 on BDI, mean 15)	BDI	AE (3*wk) PR (3*wk) C	10 weeks	Sig. reduced DEP in AE vs. PR and C No diffs between PR and C
McNeil et al. (1991)	30 elderly men and women (BDI range 12–24)	BDI	AE (3*wk) SOC (2*wk) WLC	6 weeks	Sig. reduced DEP in EA and SOC vs. WLC No diffs between EA and SOC
Brown et al. (1978)	Male and female high school and college students	ZDS	AE (3*wk) C	10 weeks	Sig. reductions in DEP vs. control
Randomized Trials					
Fremont & Craighead (1987)	49 men and women (BDI range 9–30)	BDI	AE (3*wk) COG (1* week) AE + COG	10 weeks	Sig. reduced DEP in all groups vs. baseline No diffs between groups

sion scores for the running versus the usual care group. However, the usual care group consisted of mixed sports activities such as field hockey, soccer, volley ball, trampolining, and gymnastic activities—some of which also involved a major running component.

Randomized Studies Focusing on Anaerobic Exercise. The majority of studies investigating physical activity effects on depression have utilized aerobic exercise (D. R. Brown, 1990; Morgan, 1994; Surgeon General's Report, 1996) or aerobic fitness training (Folkins & Sime, 1981) as the physical activity intervention. However, the relatively few studies using nonaerobic physical activity, or comparing aerobic exercise to anaerobic exercise (Table 38.4), suggest that increases in aerobic fitness are not necessary to elicit such benefits (Doyne et al., 1987; Martinsen, Hoffart, & Solberg, 1989; Martinsen, Sandvik, & Kolbjornsrud, 1989; Sexton, Maere, & Dahl, 1989; Stein & Motta, 1992). The strongest evidence to date on the beneficial effects of nonaerobic exercise was reported recently by Singh, Clements, and Fiaterone (1997). Thirty-two community living men and women subjects from age 60 to 84 and diagnosed with major or minor depressive disorder using *DSM–IV* criteria (American Psychiatric Association, 1994) were randomly allocated to either a progressive resistance training or an attention-control group. The progressive resistance group trained at 80% of a one repetition maximum (the maximum amount of weight they could lift in a single effort), three times per week for 10 weeks. The control group consisted of an interactive health education program of lectures and videos followed by discussion. Depression was measured by the Beck Depression Inventory and the Hamilton Rating Scale for Depression. Following the 10-week intervention program, depression was significantly reduced in the progressive resistance training group as compared to control. This is the first randomized controlled trial to directly compare the effects on depression of a high intensity resistance training program with a nonexercise control group.

Randomized Studies With Healthy Populations. The effect of physical activity interventions on depressive symptoms in healthy individuals who score in the normal range for depressive symptoms has also been little studied. Results from early studies were equivocal, reporting both positive effects (Berger & Owen, 1983; Blumenthal, Williams, Needles, & Wallace, 1982; Folkins, 1976) and no effect (Folkins, Lynch, & Gardner, 1972; McPherson, Paivio, Yuhasz, Rechnitzer, & Lefcoe, 1965; Morgan et al., 1970; Naughton, Bruhn, & Lategola, 1968) on depression. Such differences, however, could be attributed to the methodological shortcomings mentioned earlier (Morgan, 1994), because most of these studies employed a nonrandomized design, or lacked an appropriate control group. Recent studies in healthy populations using a randomized controlled design (Table 38.3) generally report no changes in depressive symptoms following physical activity interventions of up to 1 year.

TABLE 38.3

Physical Activity (Aerobic Exercise) Effects on Depression in Healthy Adults—Intervention Studies

Author	Subjects	Assessment Tool	Intervention	Study Period	Result
Randomized Controlled Trials					
Brown et al. (1995)	135 Community living M & F (Range 40–69 years)	POMS	Mod–AE (3*wk) Lo–AE (3*wk) Lo–AE+RR (3*wk) TCC (3*wk) C	16 weeks	No change in DEP scores Note: In F a tendancy (P < .0525) was reported for a group * time interaction in the DEP subscale of POMS No diffs were found for individual groups vs. C
Netz et al. (1994)	17 geriatric rehabilitation patients (Mean 78 years)	GDS	AE (Seated, 3*wk) SOC (3*wk)	8 weeks	No change in DEP scores
King et al. (1993)	357 Community living M & F (Range 50–65 years)	BDI	AE–Hi (Group, 3*wk) AE–Hi Home (3*wk) AE–Lo Home (3*wk) C	12 months	No change in DEP scores
Emery & Gatz (1990)	48 Older M & F (Mean 72 years)	CES–D	AE (3*wk) SA (3*wk) WLC	12 weeks	No change in DEP scores
Blumenthal (1989)	101 Older M & F (Mean 67 years)	CES–D SCL–90	AE (3*wk) Yoga (2–3*wk) WLC	12 weeks	Sig. reduced DEP for M in AE vs. Yoga and WLC Sig. reduced psych symptoms on SCL–90 for AE and Yoga vs. WLC
Randomized Trials					
Perri & Templer (1984)	42 Older M & F (Mean 65 years)	ZDS	AE (3*wk) NRC	14 weeks	Sig. greater reduction in DEP for AE vs. NRC

TABLE 38.4

Physical Activity (Aerobic Versus Anaerobic Exercise) Effects on Depression in Adult Men and Women—Intervention Studies

Author/Date	Study Type	Subjects	Diagnostic Tool	Assessment Tool	Intervention	Study Period	Result
Subjects with clinical depression							
Singh et al. (1997)	RCT	32 elderly community living M & F with MjDD and MnDD	DSM–IV	BDI HRSD	RT (3*wk) C	10 weeks	Sig. reduced DEP in RT vs. C
Doyne et al. (1987)	RCT	40 F outpatients with MjDD and MnDD	RDC	BDI DACL HRSD	AE (4*wk) RT (4*wk) WLC	8 wks	Sig. reduced DEP in AE and RT vs. WLC No diffs between AE and RT
Pelham et al. (1993)	RT	10 M & F with MjDD	DSM–III	BDI	AE (4*wk) RT (4*wk)	12 wks	Sig. reduced DEP from baseline for AE No change in RT
Martinsen et al. 1989	RT	99 M & F inpatients with MjDD	DSM–III	BDI MADRS	AE (3*wk) RT/FLX (3*wk)	8 wks	Sig. reduced DEP for both groups No diffs between groups
Subjects with depressive symptoms							
Mutrie (1988)	RC T	24 S's with BDI > 11	None	BDI	AE (3*wk) RT (3*wk) WLC	4	Sig. reduced DEP for AE vs WLC N/S reduced DEP for RT vs. WLC
Palmer (1995)	RT	45 M & F substance abuse rehab inpatients with elevated CES–D scores	None	CES–D	AE (3*wk) CT (3*wk) BB (3*wk)	4 weeks	Sig. reduced DEP for BB vs. baseline
Healthy subjects							
Dustman et al. (1984)	RCT	43 older M & F (Mean 60.1 years)	None	BDI ZDS	AE (3*wk) RT + F NRC	12 wks	No changes in DEP scores
Stein & Motta (1992)	RCT	89 healthy M &F undergraduates	None	BDI DACL	AE RT C	7 wks	Sig. reduced DEP in AE and RT vs. C No diffs between AE and RT

Summary

Recent randomized and randomized, controlled clinical trials support the hypothesis that physical activity interventions of at least 8 weeks can significantly and beneficially impact depression in clinically depressed and nonclinical, symptomatic adult men and women. Longer duration and higher intensity interventions appear to be more effective than lower intensity shorter durations. The benefits of such interventions are not confined to aerobic exercise, but have also been reported for nonaerobic exercise such as high intensity running, moderate and high intensity resistance training, flexibility training, and yoga (Table 38.4). Although results of early studies investigating the effect of physical activity on depressive symptoms in healthy populations reported equivocal results, recent studies generally report that groups who score within the normal range of depression scores before a physical activity intervention will score within the normal range after intervention. Whereas the majority of reviews generally report beneficial effects of physical activity on depression, the relatively small number of randomized controlled studies published to date, and the methodological flaws present in a number of these, indicate that a causal effect of physical activity on depression, although tenable, still awaits more solid confirmatory evidence.

PHYSICAL ACTIVITY AND ANXIETY

Approximately 7.3% of the adult U.S. population suffers from an anxiety-related disorder necessitating treatment of some kind (Regier et al., 1988). High levels of stress-related emotions, including anxiety, are common even among otherwise healthy individuals (S. Cohen, Tyrell, & A. P. Smith, 1991). Anxiety is associated with a negative form of self-appraisal typified by worry, self-doubt, and apprehension (Landers & Petruzzello, 1994). Anxiety has been described by some authors (Franks, 1994, p. 3) as a form of "environmental stress" which usually arises when the physiological and psychological responses exceed the requirements of the new environment, although Landers (1998, p. 123) has stated that such a definition does not allow differentiation between healthy and unhealthy forms of stress. Anxiety is typically measured by questionnaire instruments that assess either *trait anxiety,* which is the general predisposition to respond with high levels of anxiety across many different situations, or *state anxiety,* which is the particular level of anxiety at a given moment. Although these two subcomponents of anxiety are often assessed separately (Spielberger, Gorsuch, Lushene, Vagg, & Jacobs, 1983), they have been shown to possess a considerable amount of overlap (R. E. Smith, 1989).

Primary Prevention

Epidemiological Studies. As with the depression literature, no primary prevention studies have been conducted on physical activity and anxiety, although the epidemiological literature consistently reports associations between these two variables (Ross & Hayes, 1988; Stephens, 1988; Stephens & Craig, 1990). Stephens (1988), in a secondary analysis of a large cross-sectional study of two Canadian surveys ($n = 23{,}791$ and 22,250) and two U.S. surveys ($n = 3{,}025$ and 6,913), reported that physical activity was associated with fewer symptoms of anxiety. Such associations, as with the depression data already reported, were strongest among women and persons age 40 or older. Ross and Hayes (1988), in a statewide telephone survey ($n = 401$), reported that adults who participated in regular exercise, sports, or other types of leisure time physical activity reported fewer symptoms of anxiety as compared to low active or inactive individuals. In contrast to the findings of Stephens (1988), these associations were similar across both age and gender.

Secondary and Tertiary Prevention

The literature reporting the effects of physical activity on anxiety is even more extensive than that of the physical activity and depression literature. Since the 1950s more than 50 reviews have been published on this topic (Gauvin & Spence, 1996). Although the great majority of these have been written in the form of a "narrative" review, in recent years this traditional format has increasingly been replaced by the "meta-analysis." This form of review enables results of different studies to be integrated (Glass, 1978) and expressed in a common unit—the "effect size" (calculated by subtracting the mean of the treatment group from the mean of the comparison group and dividing this difference by the pooled standard deviation). This allows results of studies to be combined, thus greatly increasing statistical power. In this approach a quantification of total results is also possible, providing a more objective estimate of the magnitude of an exercise treatment or intervention. Since 1991 six meta-analyses have been published in the area of exercise and anxiety (Calfas & W. C. Taylor, 1994; Kugler, Seelbach, & Kruskemper, 1994; Landers & Petruzzello, 1994; Long & van Stavel, 1995; McDonald & Hodgdon, 1991; Petruzzello, Landers, Hatfield, Kubitz, & Salazar, 1991), one of which focused exclusively on adolescents (Calfas & W. C. Taylor, 1994). In common with the depression literature, much of the research in the anxiety area has also been reported as applying relatively weak methodology that may confound the validity of the results (D. R. Brown, 1990; Gauvin & Spence, 1996), in particular that reported effects could be related to behavioral artifacts (Morgan, 1997; Raglin, 1997). Landers (1998), however, argued against this position stating that, because the effects of physical activity on anxiety reported in the meta-analytical studies are independent of both operational measures and scientific quality of study, the plausibility of this theory is severely limited.

Time Series Studies. In a similar fashion to the depression and physical activity literature, early studies on physical activity and anxiety also consisted of time series studies to investigate potential links between the two. Morgan (1986), reporting on a series of six early studies, investigated the effect of different formats of exercise on state anxiety in predominantly male groups of subjects. In the first of these studies, no anxiety-related effect was found in a group of healthy young adult men and women assigned to one of three conditions: rest, a 17-minute mile at 0% treadmill grade, and a 17-minute mile at 5% treadmill grade. The authors suggested that light to moderate intensity exercise may not be sufficient to elicit any changes in state anxiety. It may also be that, in common with the depression literature, physical activity has no effect on anxiety in healthy persons who score within the normal range for state anxiety. No baseline levels of state anxiety are reported in this study. In the next two studies, the State–Trait Anxiety Inventory was administered before and after a 20- to 30-minute bout of vigorous aerobic exercise. Both studies reported significant decreases in post-exercise state anxiety. In Studies 4 and 5 in this series, adult men were asked to run and walk to exhaustion at 80% of their VO_{2max} on two separate days. State anxiety was reported as increasing during the first half of the exercise bouts, plateauing for the second half, and significantly decreasing as compared to baseline levels immediately following exercise. In the final study in this series, Bahrke and Morgan (1978) randomly assigned 75 adult males to either treadmill walking at 70% VO_{2max}, meditation using Benson's relaxation response (Benson, 1975) or quiet rest. All three groups reported a significant decrease in state anxiety and no differences were found between groups. This experiment led to the formulation of the "Time out" or "distraction" hypothesis of anxiety reduction, which is discussed in more detail later. Further support for this theory was implied in a later study (Raglin & Morgan, 1987) comparing the effects of exercise and quiet rest on the state anxiety of normotensive (Experiment 1) and pharmocologically controlled hypertensive males (Experiment 2) in two separate but linked studies. Blood pressure and state anxiety were assessed prior to and at intervals following the exercise intervention, which consisted of jogging, cycling, or a variety of sports activities. Both mode and intensity of exercise were self-selected in order to maximize ecological validity. Quiet rest consisted of a 40-minute session in a sound-proofed chamber. Blood pressure and anxiety levels were reduced in both experiments for both quiet rest and exercise, with no differences between groups. However, the authors noted qualitative differences in the pattern of response to the two interventions. The quiet rest condition led to a faster but smaller reduction in the postexercise systolic blood pressure as compared to the exercise condition. However, this effect lasted only 2 to 3 minutes following termination of the rest condition, whereas the blood pressure reductions following the exercise condition remained lower during an hourly assessment for 3 hours of follow-up.

Narrative and Meta-Analysis Reviews. Since the association between exercise and anxiety has been extensively addressed in a number of recent excellent and comprehensive reviews, this section presents an overview of these reviews and a summary and analysis of their reported results.

As indicated by results of recent randomized trials (Table 38.5), the narrative and meta-analytical reviews cited overwhelmingly conclude that physical activity and/or fitness is related to anxiety. For example, Landers and Petruzzella (1994) analyzed the results of 27 narrative reviews conducted between 1960 and 1991 and found that 81% of these studies concluded that physical activity or fitness was related to anxiety reduction following exercise, and 19% found that most of the findings were supportive of an exercise-related reduction in anxiety. Not one of the narrative reviews concluded that there was no relationship. All six of the published meta-analyses reported positive anxiolitic effects of exercise with the magnitude of effect ranging from "small" to "moderate." This was consistent for trait and state anxiety as well as for age, gender, and the mental health status of subjects (Landers, 1998).

Although the majority of the narrative reviews conclude that exercise of higher intensities (70%–80% of VO_{2max}) is necessary to elicit anxiolytic effects, the meta-analytical reviews are not supportive of this claim. No consistent dose–response relationship has been found in these analyses; indeed, exercise at varying intensities and durations has been reported as producing similar significant reductions in anxiety following both acute and chronic exercise (Landers, 1998).

Summary

Exercise is generally reported as having a beneficial anxiolitic effect on subjects of all ages and mental health states. The greatest anxiolitic effects appear to result from aerobic rather than anaerobic exercise and when the length of the exercise training is more than 15 weeks. The law of initial values also appears to apply because subjects who have either lower levels of fitness, or higher levels of anxiety, appear to benefit the most from exercise programs. Exercise-induced reductions in anxiety appear to last between 4 to 6 hours postexercise, after which time anxiety returns to pre-exercise levels (Landers, 1997). More studies are needed to clarify dose–response relationships between intensity and duration of exercise. Current evidence is supportive of the claim that exercise, similar to other known anxiety reducing treatments such as relaxation training, has been consistently related to the relief of symptoms of anxiety.

STRESS REACTIVITY

Signs and symptoms of stress may manifest themselves through increased physiological (e.g. increased muscle tension; DeVreis, 1987), cardiovascular (Claytor, Cox, Howley, K. A. Lawler, & J. E. Lawler, 1988; Obrist, 1981), and/or biochemical (Sinyor, Schwartz, Peronnet, Brisson, & Seraganian, 1983) responses, as well as through changes in self-reported psychological stress states (Landers & Petruzzello, 1994; Morgan & Goldston, 1987; Spielberger et al., 1983). It has been pointed out by some authors that many of these physical and biochemical responses parallel those resulting from exercise (Obrist, 1981; Shulhan, Scher, & Furedy, 1986). This has led to a body of research investigating the interrelationships between physiological and psychological variables and how exercise and/or fitness may mediate such interactions. One related area of research has investigated the role of fitness in attenuating the physiological response ("reactivity") to psychosocial stressors of various kinds.

TABLE 38.5
Physical activity training effectss on state and trait anxiety - Randomized studies

Author	Subjects	Diagnostic Tool	Assessment Tool	Intervention	Study Period	Result
Blumenthal et al. (1989) (RCT)	101 healthy M & F (Mean age 67 yrs)	SCL–90	STAI–S STAI–T	AE (3*wk) Yoga (2–3*wk) WLC	12 weeks	No change in ST–Anx or TR–Anx at 12 weeks or at 12- and 46-month follow-up
Altchiler & Motta (1994) (RT)	43 healthy M & F (Mean age 32 yrs)	N/A	STAI–S STAI–T	Lo–AE (3*wk) CAL (3*wk)	8 weeks	No change in pre-exercise ST–Anx Sig. reduced post exercise ST–Anx for single AE sessions but not for CAL Posttest ST–Anx reduction sig. greater for AE vs. CAL Sig. posttest reduction in TR–Anx for AE
King et al. (1993) (RCT)	357 healthy M & F (50–65 yrs)	N/A	TMAS	AE–Hi (Group, 3*wk) AE–Hi Home (3*wk) AE–Lo Home (3*wk) C	12 months	Sig. reductions in Anx for AE vs. C No diffs in Anx between AE groups
Sexton et al. (1989) (RT)	52 M & F symptomatic neurotic inpatients (19–60 yrs)	DSM–III	STAI–S STAI–T	Lo–AE (Walking 3*wk) Hi–AE (Jogging 3*wk)	8 weeks	Sig. reduced ST–Anx and TR–Anx in both groups No diffs between groups
Martinsen et al. (1989) (RT)	79 M & F in pts with Anx disorders (Mean age 39 yrs)	DSM–III	PARS CPRS ACS	AE (3*Wk) RT + S + R (3*Wk)	8 weeks	Sig. reduced Anx on all 3 measures in both groups No diffs between groups
Blumenthal et al. (1982) (CT)	16 healthy M & F adults (25–61 yrs)	N/A	POMS STAI–S STAI–T	AE (3*Wk) MC	10 weeks	Sig. reduced ST–Anx and TR–Anx in AE vs. MC
Sinyor et al. (1986) (RCT)	38 healthy M (20–30 years)	N/A	STAI–S	AE (4*wk) RT (3*wk) WLC	10 weeks	Sig. reduction in STAI–S in all groups No diffs between groups

The reactivity literature is not extensive in comparison to that for anxiety or depression. For example, a recent meta-analysis in this area reported a total of 34 studies in a 10-year period between 1977 and 1987, only 20 of which were published articles. However, the reactivity and exercise literature is characterized by the use of a wide range and variety of psychosocial stressors and a wide range and variety of reactivity outcomes. The psychosocial stressors can be classified generally into five main categories: passive psychological stressors, such as watching a disturbing film; active psychological stressors, such as the Stroop test (Stroop, 1935) or a mental arithmetic or memory task; passive physical stressors, such as a cold pressor task; active physical stressors, such as exercise or grip strength testing; and various psychomotor tasks consisting of permutations of the first four categories (e.g., Stroop test combined with a physical response such as moving a lever). The reactivity outcomes reported have included cardiovascular (systolic blood pressure, diastolic blood pressure, and heart rate), biochemical (norepinephrine, epinephrine, endorphins), physiological (skin conductance, skin temperature, and electromyographic measures), and subjective (state and trait anxiety, mood) measures. These reactivity outcomes have been measured before, during, and after the administration of psychosocial stressors, resulting in a large number of possible permutations of dependent and independent variables. This, in combination with the lack of replication in the extant literature, makes comparisons across studies difficult. It is also probably true to say that most of the large number of reactivity responses are reported as being unaffected by exercise, although not uniformly so. This section focuses predominantly on cardiovascular and catecholamine outcomes, which are two of the most commonly reported measures in this area of research.

Cardiovascular and Catecholamine Reactivity

The "training effect" of exercise on cardiovascular and catecholamine parameters, and their concomitant benefits to physical health, are now well established (National Institutes of Health, 1995). In light of this and the cardiovascular and catecholamine responses to psychosocial stressors already mentioned, recent research has investigated whether cardiovascular fitness could also elicit a "psychological training effect," particularly because heightened cardiovascular and catacholamine reactivity to psychological stress has been linked with the development of cardiovascular disease processes (Beere, Glagov, & Zarsins, 1984; Manuck, Kaplan, & Clarkson, 1983). Two questions follow: Is stress reactivity as measured by these two outcome variables attenuated in fit versus unfit persons? and, can the reactivity of unfit persons be attenuated following a program of regular fitness training?

Is Reactivity Attenuated in Fit Versus Unfit Persons? Cross-sectional data on this question remain equivocal, with a number of studies reporting fitness-related effects but no effects on reactivity. Hull, Young, and Zeigler (1984), in a relatively complex study, investigated the reactivity of four groups of subjects categorized with low, intermediate, high, and very high fitness according to their total time to voluntary exhaustion on a treadmill during a Bruce protocol. Cardiovascular reactivity was assessed during and after passive and active psychological stressors and passive and active physiological stressors. All stressors significantly increased cardiovascular responses, but there were no fitness-related differences in reactivity except for a lower diastolic blood pressure response to the viewing of the film and to the Stroop test. Although there were fitness-related differences in norepinephrine and epinephrine during the exercise stressor, there were no differences reported during the other three stressors. Claytor et al. (1988) also found no differences in either cardiovascular, catecholamine, or cold pressor test reactivity between high and low fit male college students following administration of four different psychosocial stressors. In an interesting deviation from conventional approaches to this subject, the authors reported initially screening subjects according to their heart rate reactivity to the reaction time-shock avoidance test, and subsequently assessed the VO_{2max} of the six highest and six lowest reactors. No differences in VO_{2max} were found between groups, although a significant association between reactivity and reported history of family hypertension was found. In a more recent study involving two randomly assigned groups of competitive sportsmen and inactive men, Steptoe, Kearsley, and Walters (1993) also found no fitness-related cardiovascular reactivity to a mental arithmetic and a public speaking task following either 20 minutes of exercise at high, moderate, or light intensity. This study also analyzed cardiac baroreflex sensitivity, a little reported measure of cardiovascular function. This variable was found to be much higher (i.e., more sensitive) at baseline in the active versus the inactive group, and was inhibited in both groups during the mental arithmetic task. However, as with other cardiovascular outcome measures in this study, no differences in reactivity were found between groups. Other studies have similarly reported no fitness-related differences in cardiovascular reactivity to a variety of psychosocial tasks, including easy and hard mental arithmetic tasks (Dorheim et al., 1984; Szabo, T. G. Brown, Gauvin, & Seraganian, 1993), reaction time, and cold pressor tasks (deGeus, Lorenz, & vanDoornan, 1993; Dorheim et al., 1984; Plante & Kospocvitz, 1987).

In contrast to the aforementioned studies, other authors have noted fitness-related reactivity differences to particular cardiovascular and/or catecholamine outcome measures. Holmes and Roth (1985) divided 20 undergraduate females into low and high fit groups according to their estimated aerobic power following a submaximal cycle ergometer test. No catecholamine measures were taken in this study, but heart rate reactivity and subjective arousal were assessed during the administration of a mildly stressful memory task. High fit subjects evinced a smaller heart rate response to this task than low fit subjects, although there were no differences in subjective arousal. Other authors (Cantor, Zillman, & Day, 1978; J. P. Cox, Evans, & Jamieson, 1979; Light, Obrist, James, & Strogatz, 1987; Sinyor et al., 1983; VanDoornan & DeGeus, 1989) have also reported similar fitness-related differences in heart rate reactivity, although these differences were obtained following, but not during, the application of the stressor. Claytor (1991) reported findings that suggest a fitness-related difference in cardiovascular reactivity according to the degree of familiarization to the stressor. In a series of studies comparing high versus low fit college-age males, the authors reported no differences in cardiovascular and catecholamine reactivity to novel psychosocial stressors. However, with repeated exposure to these tasks, fit individuals exhibited an attenuated mean arterial pressure and cardiac output responses. Sothmann, Horn, Hart, and Gustafson (1987) also investigated the cardiovascular reactivity to a well-learned stressor in a fit versus an unfit group. The stressor consisted of a modified version of the Stroop color-word conflict test immediately followed by the administration of nine scrambled anagrams with a time limited performance requirement. Two practice sessions were needed to establish familiarity with the anagram challenge (i.e., no differences in total reaction time). During the performance of the well-learned task, the authors found, in contrast to Claytor (1991), no differences in heart rate reactivity between the groups, but reported a lower norepinephrine response in the fit versus the unfit group. This suggests a fitness-related attenuation of sympathetic nervous system during psychosocial stress. However, a major limitation to this study was that no reactivity measurements of the novel presentation of this vigilance task are reported. Using an electrocardiographic index of sympathetic nervous system activity, Shulhan et al. (1986) also investigated the reactivity of fit versus unfit men categorized according to their performance on the Canadian Home Fitness Step Test (1986). No fitness-related differences in heart rate reactivity were noted during a hard and easy mental arithmetic task, but the authors reported a greater attenuation of electrocardiographic T-wave amplitude in the low versus the high fit group during the hard trials. The authors considered T-wave amplitude as being an "adequate though not perfect" index of cardiac sympathetic nervous system activity, although some controversy is attached to this notion (Schwartz & Weiss, 1983). Shulhan et al. suggested that sympathetic cardiac reactivity during the performance of a psychosocial stressor is attenuated by enhanced aerobic fitness. This is in contrast to the results of Claytor (1991), who found no differences in sympathetic nervous system reactivity between fit and unfit subjects as judged by catecholamine levels.

The central ethos of the reactivity literature is that of "high reactivity = high risk," and of fitness as modifying this risk by reducing reactivity. Paradoxically, however, deGeus et al. (1993) reported an association between high fitness and higher reactivity. In this study, the authors found that heart rate reactivity tended to be higher for all stressors in the more fit subjects and was significantly higher in the memory search task. Similarly, systolic blood pressure reactivity was higher in fitter subjects and there was a significant positive correlation between VO_{2max} and systolic blood pressure reactivity to the tone avoidance and memory search tasks, a relation in the opposite direction to conventional expectations. These relations were unchanged (and in some cases strengthened), even after adjustment for the lower baseline levels of the fitter subjects. Diastolic blood pressure reactivity was also higher in fitter subjects for these same two tasks, although no significance level is reported. It would be tempting to dismiss this result as an experimental artifact except that such a finding is not unique in the reactivity literature. For example, Lake, Suarez, and Schneiderman (1985) reported that fit Type A males demonstrated higher blood pressure reactivity than their unfit counterparts only during competitive card games that also included harassment. A number of other studies have also reported results that do not fit the accepted concept of "high reactivity equals high risk" (Ahern, Gorkin, & Anderson, 1990; Kjaer & Galbo, 1988; Kvetnansky, 1980; Siegrist, 1990). Ahern et al. (1990) reported results suggesting that low rather than high reactivity to a psychomotor stressor (a video game) was predictive of cardiac arrest. Additionally, Siegrist (1990) reported that chronic occupational stress in blue collar workers was associated with reduced rather than increased cardiovascular reactivity to a mental arithmetic test presented at the end of a working day.

Although deGeus et al. (1993) found that fitness level was associated with higher cardiovascular reactivity, they found no training effects on these outcome measures in the same group of subjects even after an 8-month period. The authors, however, noted that some absolute measures of cardiovascular function (heart rate and diastolic blood pressure) were significantly improved following training and stated that such overall improvements "amply compensate" in health risk terms for the lack of improvement in cardiovascular reactivity. In a hypothesis contrary to conventional thinking on reactivity, the authors suggested that stress and exercise may independently exert separate and opposite effects on health.

Can the Reactivity of Unfit Persons Be Attenuated Following a Program of Regular Fitness Training?

The literature on aerobic training effects on reactivity is not extensive, but is equally as equivocal as that of the cross-sectional studies. Of the nine randomized controlled trials reviewed here, three report no posttraining differences in reactivity, five report posttraining reductions in reactivity and one recent study reports increases in posttraining reactivity to a variety of active and passive psychological and physical stressors.

Sinyor, Golden, Steinert, & Seraganian (1986) randomly assigned 38 healthy males to either aerobic exercise weight lifting or a wait list control. Training was conducted 3 to 4 times per week for 12 weeks. Pre- and posttest measures of fitness were assessed via a submaximal treadmill test based on time taken to attain 85% of maximal heart rate. Pre- and posttest anxiety were assessed using the Spielberger State–Trait Anxiety Inventory (Spielberger et al., 1983), and three psychosocial stressors were administered (a mental arithmetic task with exposure to white noise, a quiz, and the Stroop color-word task). Although significant differences in fitness were found in the aerobic versus the weight lifting and control groups, no group differences were found for any of the psychosocial stressors. In a similar study design, Roskies, Seraganian, & Oseasohn (1986) also reported no posttraining group differences in cardiovascular reactivity in 107 Type A men randomly assigned to aerobic training, strength training, or a stress management control group. For these two previous studies, the lack of an adequate fitness measure could have contributed to the nonsignificant findings because fitness was estimated in the Sinyor et al. study and no fitness protocol was reported for the Roskies et al. study. Additionally, in both of these studies, strength training was used as one of the comparison groups, and this activity has been reported by some as a potent modulator of cardiovascular and sympathetic nervous system function even though aerobic fitness may remain unchanged (R. Cox, Claytor, & Howley, 1989). Because strength training is a component of fitness (see definitions earlier), and may exert a nonneutral effect on reactivity, it may not be an appropriate condition for a control group. In a longer term study, Albright, King, Taylor, and Haskell (1992) randomly assigned a group of healthy middle-aged men to a 6-month moderate intensity walking program or a nonexercise control. No group differences were found in cardiovascular reactivity following posttraining presentation of a mental arithmetic task. In a nonrandomized controlled trial, Cleroux, Peronnet, & deChamplain (1985) also reported no cardiovascular (heart rate) reactivity differences to playing a video game following 20 weeks of aerobic training. As in the Sinyor and Roskies studies, fitness in this study was also estimated from heart rate responses to a submaximal exercise bout rather than from the more precise measure of VO_{2max} via a graded treadmill exercise test.

In contrast to these studies a series of investigations by Blumenthal and associates (Blumenthal et al., 1988, 1990, 1991) report posttraining differences in response to a mental arithmetic, speech, and a cold pressor task. In the two earlier studies, a group of Type A men were randomly assigned to either aerobic training or a weight training control group. In the first of these studies (Blumenthal et al., 1988), heart rate and double product (the product of heart rate and systolic blood pressure) were reduced during and following the presentation of the mental arithmetic task, and systolic blood pressure was reduced during recovery. In the second study (Blumenthal et al., 1990) systolic blood pressure, diastolic blood pressure, double product, and heart rate were all reduced during the presentation of the mental arithmetic task. A similar protocol used in the third study (Blumenthal et al., 1991), however, yielded mixed results. Two different psychosocial stressors were used (a public speaking task and a cold pressor test) in a group of 46 postmenopausal women. The aerobically trained women demonstrated lower posttraining responses in blood pressure, whereas the resistance trained women showed significant differences in recovery heart rate. Interestingly, all of the Blumenthal studies utilized strength training as a control group and the aerobic fitness groups all showed posttraining reactivity differences versus the strength training, despite the evidence cited indicating that strength training may also effect reactivity.

Relevance of Reactivity Studies to the Stress of Daily Living It is important to note that all of the experiments have utilized very short-term psychosocial stressors and the ecological validity of such interventions remains to be established. Logically, cardiovascular reactivity to real-life stressors should provide more relevant data on the etiology of cardiovascular disease (Pollack, 1994). For example, 24-hour ambulatory blood pressure has been proposed as a more reliable and accurate predictor of cardiovascular disease risk than the conventional doctor's office measurement (Weber, D.H.G. Smith, Neutel, & Cheung, 1991). A limited number of studies have assessed to what extent laboratory-based cardiovascular reactivity reflects "field-based" reactivity. A full discussion of this topic is outside the scope of this chapter and is addressed only briefly here.

The laboratory–field comparison literature has not, in general, reported significant relations either for heart rate or blood pressure (M. H. Pollack, 1994). It has been suggested (Manuck, Kasprowicz & Muldoon, 1990; Pickering & Gerin, 1990; Pollak, 1994) that such relations may have been obscured by methodological problems such as not controlling for baseline measures (M. H. Pollak, 1991), daily variations in lifestyle physical activity (Van Egeren & Sparrow, 1990), or comparisons with insufficiently stressful daily life periods (Manuck et al., 1990). M. H. Pollak (1994) attempted to address these three issues in a single experiment involving 26 male medical students. Subjects participated in one laboratory session and two 24-hour daily life monitoring days. One of the daily life monitoring days was spent in the classroom listening to lectures and the other day was spent participating in a clinical rotation in a general practice outpatient department. During both of these days, heart rate and physical activity were continuously monitored and stored, and later downloaded for analysis, using a solid state ambulatory monitor (Vitalog Instrument Co.). During the laboratory sessions, subjects were subjected to a series of stressors beginning with a 15-minute pretask baseline rest period. This was followed by a 5-minute reaction time task, a video game, and a mental arithmetic task. After controlling for baseline measures of heart rate and for daily physical activity level, heart rate levels were found to be significantly higher during clinic days as compared to classroom days. Additionally, heart rate responses to the laboratory tasks correlated significantly with clinic heart rate but not with lecture attendance heart rate. These findings indicate that laboratory-induced differences in heart rate responses generalize only to certain daily life settings. Individual differences in heart rate reactivity during daily life appears to depend on the nature of the daily life situation or on subjective or behavioral response in the daily life situation.

Summary

The adverse health consequences of higher sustained stress in daily life are now well established (Kobusa, Maddi, & Kahn, 1982; McEwen & Stellar, 1993; Spielberger, 1987). Heightened cardiovascular and catecholamine response to stress ("reactivity") has been linked with the development of cardiovascular disease process (Beere et al., 1984; McEwen & Stellar, 1993). Exercise has been proposed as a "stress inoculator," that is, as a means of reducing the responsivity to psychosocial stressors and thus, in turn, cardiovascular risk.

Evidence to support the hypotheses that exercise evokes a psychological training effect, however, is still equivocal. Methodological problems beset most of the published studies and replication studies are still rare. As an example, although aerobic fitness is one of the prime independent variables of concern in the reactivity literature, it has not been assessed consistently across studies. Fitness testing protocols have included self-report, step tests of different kinds, heart rate and blood pressure responses to submaximal bike and treadmill tests, or maximal time on treadmill at an absolute work load. Few studies investigating reactivity between fit and unfit groups have used maximal treadmill testing as a fitness measure. Additional points of methodological concern include no or inappropriate control groups, and lack of adjustment of baseline variables such as heart rate and BP, which would generally be lower for fit versus unfit subjects. The familiarity of the stressor should also be accounted for because differences in reactivity have been reported according to whether the stressor is novel or well practiced (Claytor, 1991; Sothmann et al., 1987). Existing research suggests that links between exercise, fitness, and cardiovascular reactivity may be tenable, but as yet too few consistent and reliable studies have been conducted to assert causality. More randomized controlled training studies utilizing direct measures of VO_2 are needed, together with greater emphasis on replication of findings.

MECHANISMS

A wide range of hypotheses have been proposed to explain the mechanisms by which exercise may improve aspects of mental health. For example, Gleser and Mendelberg (1990) listed five physiological and eight psychologically based hypotheses. Most of these mechanisms remain speculative, however, with little support from the scientific literature. Because no conclusive evidence has differentiated any one mechanism or group of mechanisms, this section focuses on those hypotheses that appear to be the most tenable and/or have received the most attention in the literature.

The Monoamine Hypothesis

This hypothesis proposes that improvements in psychological health are associated with changes in levels of the major neurotransmitters of the brain, principally the biogenic amines, both catecholamines (norepinepherine, epinephrine and dopamine) and indolamines (serotonin). Early evidence of the role of the amines came from pharmacological studies of psychoactive drugs known to alter affective states, but that were also found to produce changes in the brain amines of experimental animals (Schildkraut, Orsulak, Schatzberg, & Rosenbaum, 1983). In humans, because catecholamines are not able to pass the blood–brain barrier, changes in monamines have been assessed by measuring the metabolite of norepinephrine (3-methoxy-4hydroxyphenylethylene glycol or MHPG) in either urine, plasma, or cerebrospinal fluid. It is assumed in these studies that increased MHPG reflects increased brain (central) noradrenergic responses. Studies of the effects of physical activity on MHPG have not yielded consistent results either in depressed or normal subjects. Ebert, Post, and Goodwin (1972) assessed MHPG levels in six depressive patients following a day spent watching TV and reading as compared to an activity day consisting of outdoor walks, stair climbing, and table tennis. MHPG assessed from two 12-hour postsession urine collections were significantly greater following the activity day. DeLeon-Jones, Maas, Dekirmenjian, and Sanchez (1975), however, found no differences in MHPG levels between agitated subjects, exhibiting persistent pacing as compared to retarded patients exhibiting minimal physical movement. Other studies with depressed patients have reported both increases (Beckman, Ebert, Post, & Goodwin, 1979; Muscettola, Potter, Pickor, & Goodwin, 1984; Post, Kotin, & Goodwin, 1973) and no differences (Sweeney, Leckman, Maas, Hattox, & Heninger, 1980; Taube, Kerstein, Sweeney, Heninger, & Maas, 1978) in MHPG between acute physical activity of various kinds compared to an inactive period. These inconsistent results may be due in part to methodological problems and inconsistencies. Sample sizes were small, and the levels of physical activity used were very low and not well quantified or standardized. In addition, different types of depression were present in the same treatment group Sweeney et al. (1980), for example, assigned unipolar, bipolar, and schizophrenic patients to the same treatment group.

A small number of studies have examined the effect of acute exercise in nondepressed individuals (Chodakowska, Wocial, Skorka, Nazar, & Chwalbinska-Moneta, 1980; Goode, Sekermenjian, Meltzer, & Maas, 1973; Howlett & Jenner, 1978; Peyrin & Pequignot, 1983; Tang, Stancer, Takahashi, Shephard, & Warsh, 1981). Interpretation and comparison of results of these studies, however, are made difficult by the variety of designs utilized, which included treadmill walking at low and high intensity, bicycling at low and high intensity, a 5-minute step test and maximal isometric exercise over a range of muscle groups. Goode et al. (1973), comparing rest, isometric exercise, and bicycling, and Tang et al. (1981) comparing rest, treadmill walking, and bicycling, assessed plasma as well as urinary MHPG. Both studies found significant increases in plasma but not urinary MHPG. Other studies (Howlett & Jenner, 1978; Peyrin & Pequignot, 1983) found significant differences in subfractions of MHPG, but no differences in total MHPG.

No studies on the acute effects of exercise have been published, although in a series of studies with nondepressed subjects Sothmann and colleagues (Sothmann & Ismail, 1984, 1985; Sothmann, Ismail, & Chodzko-Zajko, 1984) reported no differences in MHPG levels between fitness groups based on VO_{2max}. However, Lobstein et al. (1983) reported an inverse relation between VO_2 peak and self-rated depression.

Summary

The monoamine hypothesis continues to be a promising focus of research attention from a neurobiological perspective of psychological health, particularly in the study of depression. No definite conclusions can be drawn from the existing research, however, due to the wide variation in study methodology, exercise quantification, and patient diagnosis.

The Endorphin Hypothesis

Endorphins (from "endogenous morphine") are one of the three classifications of endogenous opiates so far identified, the other two being "enkephalins" and "dynorphins." A number of studies conducted in animals and humans have shown significant increases in endorphins during and following exercise and a reported morphinelike effect—that is, an ability to reduce the sensation of pain and even produce a state of euphoria (Morgan, 1985; Ransford, 1982). Exercise has also long been known to produce a "feel good" effect, so a small number studies (Mandell, 1979; Pargman & Baker, 1980; Sachs, 1984) combined with considerable media coverage led to the development of what became virtually an urban legend—the "runners high." Despite the prevalence of this belief, however, scientific evidence supporting the role of endorphin/exercise connection to psychological health remains, at best, inconclusive.

In humans, the effects of exercise on endorphins has been conducted using two distinct approaches: (a) measurement of plasma levels of endorphins either with or without self-report of mood changes postexercise (Carr et al., 1981; Farrell, Gates, Maksud, & Morgan, 1982; Grossman et al., 1984), and (b) manipulation of endorphin levels by the administration of naloxone, an endogenous opiate receptor blocker (Farrell et al., 1986; Haier, Quaid, & Mills, 1981; Janal, Colt, Clark, & Glusman, 1984; Markoff, Ryan, & Young, 1982).

Carr et al. (1981) investigated effects of acute and chronic exercise on levels of endorphins in a group of women during stationary cycling. Significant increases in endorphin levels were found at power outputs between 70 and 100 Watts, and training was also reported as increasing this response. This work is frequently cited in support of exercise-induced endorphin secretion, but has been criticized by several authors on methodological deficiencies (Morgan, 1985). Farrell (1985), in a review of endorphin responses to exercise, listed 11 studies in humans reporting increases in post-run levels of endorphins of up to five times that of pre-run levels.

In studies investigating the correlations between exercise, endorphins, and mood changes, Farrell et al. (1982) assessed changes in plasma endorphin in six well-trained endurance athletes following treadmill running at 60%, 80% VO_{2max}, and a self-selected pace (M = 75% VO_{2max}). The "right now" profile of mood states (POMS) was completed before and 5 to 10 minutes following each run, and perceived exertion via the Borg scale (Borg, 1970) was elicited every 5 minutes during all runs. Endorphin levels increased for each of the running conditions but, contrary to expectation, the greatest increase in endorphins occurred during the 60% condition, which produced the lowest Borg score. Farrell, Gates, Morgan, and Pert (1983) also investigated endorphin responses in male and female athletes immediately following a 10-mile road race. POMS was completed before and after the race and blood was drawn immediately following. Anxiety decreased by almost 50% ($p < .05$) and plasma endorphins increased by 17.6%, although this was not significant. The large standard deviations in this study speak to a large interindividual variation in endorphin activity. In a third study, Farrell et al. (1986) investigated the effects of endorphins on postexercise tension and mood in eight males prior to 30 minutes of stationary biking at 70% of a previously determined VO_{2max}. The POMS was administered pre- and postexercise and prior to exercise subjects were given either a placebo or 50 mg of Naltrexone. Tension and mood enhancement were significantly increased for both placebo and naltrexone conditions, and this was interpreted by the authors as negating the effects of endorphins on exercise-induced mood changes.

Summary

The evidence surrounding the endorphin hypothesis is equivocal, able to be rejected or accepted depending on the series of investigators that are cited (Morgan, 1985). Although tenable, further investigation of this hypothesis is needed with more standardized methodology to allow for study comparisons and replication.

The Distraction Hypothesis

This hypothesis proposes that it is the distraction from stressful stimuli (or taking a "time out") provided by an exercise session, rather than the exercise per se, that elicits the improved affect associated with exercise. This hypothesis was first proposed by Bahrke and Morgan (1978), who randomly assigned 75 adult males to an exercise, meditation, or distraction group. The exercise group walked on a treadmill at 70% of VO_{2max}, the meditation group practiced Benson's relaxation response (Benson, 1975), whereas the distraction group rested quietly while seated in an easy chair in a sound-filtered room. All three groups experienced reductions in state anxiety with no differences between groups. A later study reported similar results, but found that anxiety reductions elicited by exercise persisted for a longer time than those elicited by distraction (Raglin & Morgan, 1987). In a recent meta-analysis, Petruzzello et al. (1991) found conflicting support for this hypothesis. For state anxiety, both exercise and cognitively based distraction therapies were equally effective in reducing anxiety. However, for trait anxiety, exercise had greater anxiolitic effects. This review also reported not only that exercise-related anxiolytic benefits lasted longer postexercise than cognitively based therapies, but that the long-term effects of such effects were also greater.

Summary

These results suggest that the distraction hypothesis, although tenable, cannot be regarded as the sole reason for postexercise reductions in anxiety.

The Thermogenic Hypothesis

This hypothesis proposes that elevations in body temperature will produce therapeutic effects. Early anecdotal evidence in support of this theory comes from Scandinavian countries who have traditionally used sauna for its alleged health benefits. More objective evidence has reported that whole body warming techniques such as sauna or warm showers reduces somatic tension (deVries, Beckman, Huber, & Deickmeir, 1968) and self-reported state anxiety levels (Raglin & Morgan, 1985). Animal studies have reported a significant effect of whole body and direct brain warming on central and peripheral neuron activity (deVries et al., 1968). Gamma motor activity is inversely related to hypothalamic temperature (Von Euler & Soderberg, 1957), which contributes significantly to tonic muscle activity (deVries, Wiswell, Bulbulian, & Moritani, 1981). Deep body temperature is increased in proportion to the intensity of exercise (Haight & Keatinge, 1973), and decreased muscle tension has been reported following both exercise and a sauna bath (deVries et al., 1981). The anxiolitic benefits of exercise, therefore, may be due to a reduction in muscle tension secondary to an elevation in body temperature. However, one of the few studies that has measured body temperature concurrently with exercise (Reeves, Levinson, Justesen, & Lubin, 1985) conflicts with this theory. The authors measured body temperature directly during exercise with subjects wearing vapor barrier and thermogenic clothing. Following 20 minutes of jumping jacks, push ups, running in place, and stationary stair stepping, body temperature increased by 1.2° C. This increase in body temperature was accompanied by an increase in anxiety. A control group (exercise with no insulating clothing) showed no temperature increases. In this study, however, no attempt was made to control for the effects of clothing on body temperature.

Summary

More study designs using simultaneous measures of exercise, body temperature, and affect are needed to confirm or deny the tenabililty of this hypothesis.

PHYSICAL ACTIVITY: NEW GUIDELINES

Prevalence of Physical Activity and Sedentary Behavior

Despite the plethora of physical and psychological benefits described, the majority of the U.S. population (Centers for Disease Control and Prevention, 1991; Surgeon General's Report, 1996; U.S. Department of Health and Human Services, 1991) and other developed nations remain essentially sedentary (Stephens & Thomas, 1994). Data from several countries in which national physical activity surveys have been conducted indicate that only about 15% of the adult population engage in vigorous physical exercise according to American College of Sports Medicine (ACSM) guidelines, with the percentage of adults who are sedentary ranging from 15% to 40% (Phillips, Pruitt, & King, 1996). Indeed, in the United States, some 30% of adults are reported as being sedentary (Casperson & Merritt, 1992; Merritt & Casperson, 1992).

Part of the reason for this low level of activity has been attributed to a history of associating "health" with "fitness" and a misperception that exercise-mediated health benefits can only be elicited with vigorous, sustained activity that is aerobic in nature. Such perceptions have been fostered by long-standing exercise guidelines (ACSM, 1978) based on the improvement of cardiovascular or cardiorespiratory fitness, and an inference that such guidelines also pertained to health (Haskell, 1994b). Recently, however, recommendations from several authoritative sources (Pate et al., 1995; Surgeon General's Report, 1996; U.S. Department of Health and Human Services, 1991) have significantly influenced traditional beliefs about the amount, intensity, and frequency of exercise necessary to elicit physical and psychological benefits. Guidelines from these authorities emphasize the importance of moderate intensity, intermittent physical activity, as well as the more traditional "fitness" activities, and suggest that the performance of more moderate intensity physical activities of daily living (ADL) may provide significant health benefits for persons who are initially sedentary. This dramatic shift to a "lifestyle activity" approach (Phillips et al., 1996) should have important implications for exercise participation and adherence by making health-related physical activity far more accessible to people of all ages.

From "Exercise Training–Fitness" to "Physical Activity–Health"

Data supportive of the health benefits of moderate intensity activities were evident from early epidemiological studies published even earlier than the 1978 ACSM guidelines (Morris & Crawford, 1958; Morris et al., 1953; Morris, Kagan, Pattison, Gardner, & Raffle, 1966). These studies reported beneficial effects of activities such as gardening, walking the dog, and stair climbing, but such "everyday" physical activities received little attention until some 20 to 30 years later, when interest gradually spread to exercises other than fitness training (Haskell, 1994b). In 1990 (ACSM, 1990) and again in 1998 (ACSM, 1998), the ACSM updated its 1978 position statement on exercise, and although the recommendations still focused predominantly on cardiovascular fitness, its authors recognized that the quantity and quality of exercise needed to obtain health-related benefits may differ from what was recommended for fitness benefits.

A major step toward promoting the concept of moderate intensity physical activity occurred in the following year when the U.S. Department of Health and Human Services published a comprehensive set of Health Promotion and Disease Prevention Objectives for the nation entitled *Healthy People 2000* (U.S. Department of Health and Human Services, 1991). Two of the eight health promotion topics identified were physical activity and fitness and mental health and mental disorders. The physical activity recommendations provided research justification for the stated objectives of reducing risk of cardiovascular disease via low, moderate, and vigorous physical activity in the general population (Objectives 1.3–1.7, pp. 97–101). The mental health recommendations included exercise as a related objective and proposed it as a potential mediator of stress-related disorders (Objective 6.5, pp. 214–215).

These general objectives laid the groundwork for more specific recommendations related to physical activity, and in February 1995 an expert panel (Pate et al., 1995) coordinated by the Centers for Disease Control and Prevention (CDC) and the American College of Sports Medicine (ACSM) published the following recommendation: "Every U.S. adult should accumulate 30 minutes or more of moderate-intensity physical activity on most, preferably all, days of the week."

This new recommendation differs from those previously published, which were based on an "exercise training-fitness" model advocating vigorous physical exercise (ACSM, 1978, 1990, 1998). The CDC/ACSM guidelines embraces a "physical activity–health" paradigm, which uniquely incorporates moderate intensity and intermittent physical activity (Table 38.6). Such a paradigm shift broadens the focus on health-related physical activity in four major areas.

First, the types and dose of physical activity thought to produce health benefits are more inclusive. Distinctions have been made between physical activity and exercise, as defined at the beginning of this chapter. In the physical activity–health paradigm, it is assumed that health benefits can be gained from participation in diverse types of moderate intensity physical activity. This is supported by studies reporting reduced coronary heart disease mortality and all-cause mortality rates among individuals who regularly engage in moderate physical activity (Blair et al., 1989; Leon et al., 1987; Morris et al., 1990; Paffenbarger et al., 1986; Shapiro et al., 1969). Most of the beneficial activities reported approximated an intensity of 4 to 7 kcal•min^{-1} and included activities such as brisk walking, house cleaning, and lawn/garden care. Additional evidence comes from intervention studies (Duncan, Gordon, & Scott, 1991; Jennings, Nelson, Nestel, Esler, Korner, Burton, & Bazelmans, 1986; Nelson, Jennings, Elser, & Kover, 1986). For example, a 24-week moderate intensity (6.4 km•hr^{-1}) walking program with initially sedentary women was equally effective in increasing high density lipoprotein cholesterol (HDL-c) levels when compared to an equidistant but more vigorous (8.0 km•hr^{-1}) walking program (Duncan et al., 1991). This suggests that health benefits derived from physical activity may be linked to exercise volume as well as exercise intensity.

Second, a unique aspect of the new paradigm is the concept that health benefits may be gained from multiple daily sessions of physical activity, as well as from one continuous daily session. Epidemiological research (Leon et al., 1987; Paffenbarger et al., 1986) identified activities associated with health benefits such as gardening, raking the lawn, and home repair. It is likely that many of these activities are performed in a discontinuous, rather than continuous, manner. In one intervention study (DeBusk, Stenestrand, Sheehan, & Haskell, 1990), 40 men approximately 50 years old were randomly assigned to one of two aerobic activity groups, the first performing moderate intensity physical activity for 30 minutes daily, and the second performing three 10-minute sessions of moderate physical activity daily. After 8 weeks of training, both groups demonstrated significant improvements in maximal oxygen uptake and exercise treadmill test duration. In addition, heart rate at submaximal workloads significantly decreased in both groups. These latter studies and others (Ebisu, 1985; Morris et al., 1990; Paffenbarger et al., 1993) support the contention that health benefits associated with improved fitness and increased physical activity are also possible with shorter, intermittent activity.

Third, the segment of the population most likely to benefit from the paradigm is increased. The new paradigm focuses on mobilizing the large segment of the population that is sedentary to become moderately active rather encouraging the small percentage of already active people to become highly active. This is because the gain in health benefits resulting from the increase in physical activity is hypothesized to be exponentially related to initial activity level, such that sedentary people who increase their physical activity to recommended moderate levels appear to achieve the greatest gain in physical health benefits (Fig. 38.1).

Fourth, the new guidelines assume that physical activity may affect a vast array of health outcomes. It is conceivable

TABLE 38.6
A Comparison of American College of Sports Medicine Position Statement 1998 with CDC/ACSM Physical Activity Recommendations

Activity Characteristics	ACSM Exercise Recommendations for Cardiorespiratory Fitness in Healthy Adults (ACSM, 1998) (Exercise Training–Fitness Model)	CDC/ACSM Physical Activity Recommendations (Pate et al., 1995) (Physical Activity–Health Paradigm)
Frequency	3–5 days per week	4–7 ("Most, preferably all") days of the week
Intensity	55/65%–90% of maximum heart rate or 40/50%–85% maximum oxygen uptake reserve Lower intensities most applicable to unfit individuals	"Moderate" (3–6 METs or 4–7 kcal/min)
Duration	20–60 min of continuous aerobic activity Intermittent activity with bouts of at least 10 min is appropriate	Accumulation of ≥ 30 min of daily activity in bouts of at least 10 min
Type	Any activity that uses large muscle groups, can be maintained continuously, and is aerobic in nature (e.g., walking, running, cycling, swimming)	Any activity that can be performed at an intensity similar to that of brisk walking

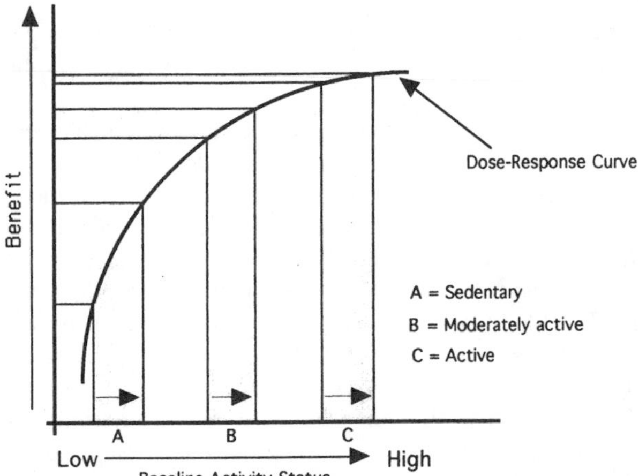

FIG. 38.1. Theoretical dose–response curve demonstrating that the magnitude of increased benefit for any given increase in activity is greater for less active persons. Note: Persons exercising vigorously who increase their level of activity (Level C) accrue only small increases in health benefit. However, they elicit the greatest *absolute* health benefits compared to those performing lower intensity activity (Levels A and B). From "Health Consequences of Physical Activity: Understanding and Challenges Regarding Dose–Response" by W. L. Haskell, 1994, *Medicine and Science in Sports and Exercise, 26,* pp. 649–660.

that the mechanisms underlying the relationship between physical activity and health may include those other than increased physical fitness. Indeed, because increased physical fitness may not be the causal mechanism affecting all health outcomes, the prevailing assumption that a "training" response is necessary (i.e., one that increases physical fitness) has been challenged. Health outcomes may in fact be affected by acute bouts of physical activity, repeated acute bouts of activity, chronic (i.e., training) bouts, or interactions between acute and chronic bouts (Haskell, 1994a; Rejeski, 1994). This issue is addressed in more detail later.

Exercise Participation and Adherence

The history of low participation in leisure time activities has been partly attributed to the vigorous nature of prior recommendations (Haskell, 1994a; Pate et al., 1995; Phillips et al., 1996). The new guidelines serve as more realistic goals for the sedentary adult who wishes to adopt health-related lifestyle activity. Attempting to accrue more moderate intensity physical activity throughout the day may improve adherence to both exercise and weight loss prescriptions (Jakicic, Wing, Butler, & Robertson, 1995). Although there are advantages to these broader and lower intensity guidelines, they may also paradoxically present some unique challenges for those involved with their effective dissemination and interpretation. Such challenges include overcoming the inertia of an exercise history generated by more than two decades of "conventional wisdom" that emphasized only the exercise training–fitness model. As a result, there may be a credibility gap to bridge in promoting moderate exercise or customary daily activities as important health-related behaviors. It will be important, therefore, for exercise professionals and lay public to recognize that the new recommendations complement, rather than replace previous guidelines.

The definition of "moderate activity" must also be clarified, because this is of paramount importance in the setting and achievement of goals. Although higher intensity activities are often relatively easy to recognize, "moderate intensity" activity is typically more difficult to identify, particularly given the influences of individual differences in perception of work effort. Additionally, many adults routinely engage in household chores, or take an occasional walk to the corner store, albeit at an intensity that may be more appropriately termed "light" rather than "moderate." Emphasis on such commonly performed physical activities may lead to a belief that one is already active enough and that further increases in activity are unnecessary. For example, being "too busy" is frequently cited as a barrier to being physically active (Dishman, 1990). It would indeed be a shame if "busy-ness" was mistakenly interpreted as health-related activity! The fact remains that most adults are not active enough and would benefit from an increase in physical activity (Surgeon General's Report, 1996; U.S. Department of Health and Human Services, 1991).

Practical Applications of the New Physical Activity Guidelines

In practical terms, the sedentary adult who wishes to become more active need not embark on a vigorous exercise program to realize health benefits. Suggested physical activity scenarios include: a brisk 10-minute walk in the morning, at lunch time, and after work; a brisk walk to the mail box, raking leaves, and stationary cycling while reading or watching television; or general house cleaning, actively playing with children, and home gardening that requires large muscle group involvement (i.e., raking and digging rather than pruning). The accumulated duration of these activities should be gradually increased toward 30 minutes per day. The key to obtaining positive health results will be to perform these activities at an intensity that at least approximates brisk walking. Because health benefits accrue in a dose–response fashion (Fig. 38.1), adults who currently engage in vigorous activity for 20 to 30 minutes or longer should continue to do so. Furthermore, the importance of muscular strength and flexibility should also not be overlooked. A growing body of data (Haskell & Phillips, 1995; Phillips & Haskell, 1995; Province et al., 1995) indicates that maintenance and/or improvement of these two components of fitness is associated with improved daily functioning and thus critical to a healthy aging process.

Implementation of Recommendations

Creative solutions will be needed to implement these recommendations for the population, including how physical activity prescriptions are administered and followed, whether the physical activity is performed in a class or home situation, and how effective is the physical activity-oriented approach as compared to the more traditional fitness-oriented approach.

King (1991) demonstrated that exercise adherence is generally better when individuals can participate in physical activity at home rather than in a class situation. Dunn et al. (1998) also reported a study comparing a "lifestyle" approach to physical activity (based on Surgeon General's Report recommendation of accumulating at least 30 minutes of daily moderate intensity physical activity) with that of a more conventional "exercise" regimen (based on ACSM fitness guidelines). In the first 6 months of a year-long randomized trial, both interventions were reported as being equally effective in increasing physical activity and physical fitness in previously sedentary men and women.

Effective implementation of these national guidelines will also require interventions and involvement at levels beyond the personal and interpersonal approaches that to date have characterized much of the nation's efforts (King, 1991). In accordance with the approach adopted by *Healthy People 2000* (U.S. Department of Health and Human Services, 1991), the authors of the CDC/ACSM guidelines issued a "call to action" aimed at increasing the joint cooperation and involvement of public health agencies, corporations, schools, communities, and health professionals, as well as individuals and families. Examples of the types of physical activity programs that could be delivered across four hierarchical levels of intervention are illustrated in Table 38.7. Within these levels, the utility of a developmental or life-span strategy should also be stressed, that is, one that takes account of life periods and transitions that may markedly affect physical activity behaviors (Table 38.8).

SUMMARY

From a public health veiwpoint, the well-publicized and well-accepted links between fitness and health appear to have been both blessing and curse over last two decades. Whereas a majority of the population would undoubtedly agree that exercise is "good for me," it has become apparent that this is not enough to motivate people to commence and/or continue a regular fitness-based program. At least part of this has been attributed to an assumption that improvement of health was inextricably linked to improvement of fitness and the vigorous intensity exercise needed to improve fitness. The extensive research base underpinning the recommendations of the Surgeon General's Report on Physical Activity and Health has provided sufficient initial evidence to assert not only that physical and mental health benefits may be elicited with physical activity or exercise that is of far lower intensity than recommended by previous guidelines, but that such benefits may also be elicited by accumulating shorter bouts of physical activity or exercise throughout the day. This has resulted in what has been termed a "paradigm shift" from an "exercise training–fitness model" to a "physical activity–health paradigm." From a public health perspective, the fact that a wide range of mental and physical benefits may be elicited by commonly performed activities of daily living will bring far greater accessibility to, and hopefully increased participation in, health-related activity for the sedentary majority of the United States. This is an exciting new prospect for practitioners and health educators alike. Early reports on recent intervention studies incorporating this new paradigm

TABLE 38.7
Examples of Physical Activity Programs by Level of Intervention, Channel, Target, and Strategy

Level of Intervention	Channel	Target	Strategy
Personal	Face-to-face: Physician's office; health clinics; health spas and clubs. Mediated/not face to face: Telephone, mail (feedback systems, correspondence courses; self-help kits and booklets)	Patients, clients	Information on risk, health benefits; counselor support; personal monitoring and feedback; problem solving (relapse prevention)
Interpersonal	Classes: Telephone/mail systems; health spas and clubs; peer-led groups.	Patients, healthy individuals, families, peers	Information; peer, family, and counselor support; group affiliation; personal or public monitoring and feedback; group problem solving.
Organizational /Environmental	Schools; worksite; neighborhoods; community facilities (e.g., par course, walk/bike paths), churches, community organizations; sites for activities of daily living (public stairs; shopping malls, parking lots).	Student body; all employees; local residents; social norms or milieu	Curricula; point-of-choice education and prompts; organizational support; public feedback; incentives
Institutional /Legislative	Policies; laws; regulations	Broad spectrum of community or population	Standardization of exercise-related curricula; insurance incentives for regular exercisers; flexible work time to permit exercise; monetary incentives for the development of adequate public facilities for exercise; Surgeon General's report on physical activity and health

Note: These four levels are not mutually exclusive—a "mix" of strategies is most likely to have the greatest effect on targeted subgroups within a community. From "Community Intervention for Physical Activity and Fitness" by A. C. King, 1991, *Exercise and Sports Science Reviews, 19*, p. 247.

TABLE 38.8

Features and Examples of Physical Activity Programs for Several Major Lifestyle Developmental Milestones

Milestone (Critical Period)	Specific Features	Goals/Strategies
Adolescence	Rapid physical and emotional changes Increased concern with appearance and weight Need for independence Short-term perspective Increased peer influence	Exercise as part of a program of healthy weight regulation (both sexes) Noncompetitive activities that are fun, varied Emphasis on independence, choice Focus on proximal outcomes (e.g., body image, stress management) Peer involvement, support
Initial Work Entry	Increased time and scheduling constraints Short-term perspective Employer demands	Choice of activities that are convenient, enjoyable Focus on proximal outcomes Involvement of worksite (environmental prompts, incentives) Realistic goal-setting/injury prevention Coeducational noncompetitive activities
Parenting	Increased family demands and time constraints Family- directed focus Postpartum effects on weight, mood	Emphasis on benefits to self and family (e.g., stress management, wt. control, well-being Activities appropriate with children (e.g., walking) Flexible, convenient, personalized regimen Inclusion of activities of daily living Neighborhood involvement, focus Family-based public monitoring, goal-setting Availability of child-related services (child care)
Retirement Age	Increased time availability and flexibility Longer term perspective on health Increased health concerns, "readiness" Caregiving duties, responsibilities (parents, spouse, children, or grandchildren)	Identification of current and previous enjoyable activities Matching of activities to current health status Emphasis on mild and moderate intensity activities, including activities of daily living Use of "life path point" information and prompts Emphasis on activities engendering independence Garnering support of family members, peers Availability of necessary services (e.g., caretaking services for significant others)

Note: From "Community Intervention for Physical Activity and Fitness" by A. C. King, 1991, *Exercise and Sports Science Reviews, 19,* p. 250.

have reported favorable improvements in various health-related measures comparable to that of the more traditional fitness-based approach. However, more widespread acceptance and adoption of the new paradigm will depend on the involvement of public health agencies, educational and corporate institutions, and communities. Finally, if a lifestyle approach to health-related physical activity is to be established, it will require the development and adoption of strategies taking account of transitional life periods that may affect physical activities and behaviors.

REFERENCES

Ahern, D. K., Gorkin, L., & Anderson, J. L. (1990). Biobehavioral variables and morality or cardiac arrest in the Cardiac Arrhythmia Pilot Study (CAPS). *American Journal of Cardiology, 66,* 59–62.

Albanes, D., Blair, A., & Taylor, P. R. (1989). Physical activity and risk of cancer in the NHANES I population. *American Journal of Public Health, 79,* 744–750.

Albright, C. L., King, A. C., Taylor, C. B., & Haskell, W. L. (1992). Effect of a six-month aerobic exercise training program on cardiovascular responsivity in healthy middle-aged adults. *Journal of Psychosomatic Research, 36,* 25–36.

Altchiler, L., & Motta, R. (1994). Effects of aerobic and nonaerobic exercise on anxiety, absenteeism, and job satisfaction. *Journal of Clinical Psychology, 50,* 829–840.

American College of Sports Medicine. (1978). The recommended quantity and quality of exercise for developing and maintaining fitness in healthy adults. *Medicine and Science in Sports and Exercise, 10,* vii–x.

American College of Sports Medicine. (1990). The recommended quality and quantity of exercise for developing and maintaining fitness in healthy adults. *Medicine and Science in Sports and Exercise, 22,* 265–274.

American College of Sports Medicine. (1993). Physical activity, physical fitness, and hypertension. *Medicine and Science in Sport and Exercise, 25,* i–x.

American College of Sports Medicine. (1998). The recommended quantity and quality of exercise for maintaining cardiorespiratory and muscular fitness, and flexibility in healthy adults. *Medicine and Science in Sports and Exercise, 30,* 975–991.

American Psychiatric Association. (1994). *Diagnostic and Statistical Manual of Mental Disorders* (4th ed.). Washington, DC: American Psychiatric Association.

Bahrke, M. S., & Morgan, W. P. (1978). Anxiety reduction following exercise and meditation. *Cognitive Therapy and Research, 2,* 232–333.

Beck, A. T., Ward, C. H., Mendelson, M., Mock, J., & Erbaugh, J. (1961). An inventory for measuring depression. *Archives of General Psychiatry, 4,* 561–571.

Beckman, H., Ebert, M. H., Post, R., & Goodwin, E. K. (1979). Effects of moderate exercise on urinary MHPG in depressed patients. *Pharmakopsychiatry, 12,* 351–356.

Beere, P. A., Glagov, S., & Zarsins, C. K. (1984). Retarding effect of lowered heart rate on coronary atherosclerosis. *Science, 226,* 180–182.

Benson, H. (1975). *The relaxation response.* New York: Morrow.

Berger, B. G., & Owen, D. R. (1983). Mood alterations with swimming—swimmers really do "feel better." *Psychsomatic Medicine, 45,* 425–433.

Berlin, J. A., & Colditz, G. A. (1990). A meta-analysis of physical activity in the prevention of coronary heart disease. *American Journal of Epidemiology, 132,* 612–628.

Blair, S. N. (1994). Physical activity, fitness, and coronary heart disease. In C. Bouchard, R. J. Shephard, & T. Stephens (Eds.), *Physical activity, fitness, and health: International proceedings and consensus statement* (pp. 579–590). Champaign, IL: Human Kinetics.

Blair, S. N., Goodyear, N. N., Gibbons, L. W., & Cooper, H. (1984). Physical fitness and incidence of hypertension in healthy normotensive men and women. *Journal of the American Medical Association, 266,* 2098–2104.

Blair, S. N., Kohl, H. W., Gordon, N. F., & Paffenbarger, R. S. (1992). How much physical activity is good for health? *Annual Review of Public Health, 13,* 99–126.

Blair, S. N., Kohl, H. W., Paffenbarger, R. S., Clark, D. G., Cooper, K. H., & Gibbons, L. W. (1989). Physical fitness and all-cause mortality: A prospective study in healthy men and women. *Journal of the American Medical Association, 262,* 2395–2401.

Blumenthal, J. A., Emery, C. F., Madden, D. J., George, L. K., Coleman, R. E., Riddle, M. W., McKee, D. C., Reasoner, J., & Williams, R. S. (1989). Cardiovascular and behavioral effects of aerobic exercise training in healthy older individuals. *Journals of Gerontology, 44,* M147–M157.

Blumenthal, J. A., Emery, C. F., Walsh, M. A., Cox, D. R., Kuhn, C. M., Williams, R. B., & Williams, S. (1988). Exercise training in healthy Type A middle-aged men: Effects on behavioral and cardiovascular responses. *Psychosomatic Medicine, 50,* 418–433.

Blumenthal, J. A., Fredrikson, M., Kuhn, C. M., Ulmer, R., Walsh-Riddle, M., & Appelbaum, M. (1990). Aerobic exercise reduces levels of cardiovascular and sympathoadrenal responses to mental stress in subjects without prior evidence of mycardial ischemia. *American Journal of Cardiology, 65,* 93–98.

Blumenthal, J. A., Siegel, W. C., & Appelbaum, M. (1991). Failure of exercise to reduce blood pressure in patients with mild hypertension. *Journal of the American Medical Association, 266,* 2098–2104.

Blumenthal, J. A., Williams, R. S., Needles, T. L., & Wallace, A. G. (1982). Psychological changes accompany aerobic exercise in healthy middle-aged adults. *Psychosomatic Medicine, 44,* 529–536.

Borg, G. (1970). Perceived exertion as an indicator of somatic stress. *Scandinavian Journal of Rehabiliation Medicine, 2,* 92–98.

Bosscher, R. J. (1993). Running and mixed physical exercises with depressed psychiatric patients. *International Journal of Sport Psychology, 24,* 70–184.

Bouchard, C., Shephard, R. J., & Stephens, T. (1994). *Physical activity, fitness, and health: International proceedings and consensus statement.* Champaign, IL: Human Kinetics.

Bouchard, C., Shephard, R. J., Stephens, T., Sutton, J. R., & McPherson, B. D. (Eds.). (1990). *Exercise, fitness and health: A consensus of current knowledge.* Champaign, IL: Human Kinetics.

Brown, D. R. (1990). Exercise and mental health. In C. Bouchard, R. J. Shephard, T. Stephens, J. R. Sutton, & B. D. McPherson (Eds.), *Exercise, fitness and mental health* (pp. 607–626). Champaign, IL: Human Kinetics.

Brown, D. R., Wang, Y., Ward, A., Ebbeling, C. B., Fortlage, L., Puleo, E., Benson, H., & Rippe, J. M. (1995). Chronic psychological effects of exercise and exercise plus cognitive strategies. *Medicine and Science in Sports and Exercise, 27,* 765–775.

Brown, J. D., & Lawton, M. (1986). Stress and well-being in adolescence: The moderating role of physical exercise. *Journal of Human Stress, 12,* 125–131.

Brown, R. S., Ramivez, D. E., & Taub, J. M. (1978). The prescription of exercise for depression. *The Physician and Sports Medicine, 6,* 34–49.

Calfas, K. J., & Taylor, W. C. (1994). Effects of physical activity on psychological variables in adolescents. *Pediatric Exercise Science, 6,* 406–423.

Camacho, T. C., Roberts, R. E., Lazarus, N. B., Kaplan, G. A., & Cohen, R. D. (1991). Physical activity and depression: Evidence from the Almeda County Study. *American Journal of Epidemiology, 134,* 220–231.

Canadian Standardized Test of Fitness (CSTF). (1986). *Operations manual* (3rd ed.). Ottawa: Fitness and Amateur Sport Canada.

Cantor, J. R., Zillman, D., & Day, K. D. (1978). Relationship between cardiorespiratory fitness and physiological responses to films. *Perceptual and Motor Skills, 46,* 1123–1130.

Caplan, G. (1964). *Principles of preventive psychology.* New York: Basic Books.

Carr, D. B., Bullen, B. A., Skrinar, G. S., Arnold, M. A., Rosenblatt, M., Beitins, I. Z., Martins, J. B., & McArthur, J. W. (1981). Physical conditioning facilitates the exercise-induced secretion of beta-endorphine and beta-lipoprotein in women. *New England Journal of Medicine, 305,* 560–562.

Caspersen, C. J., & Heath, G. W. (1993). The risk factor concept of coronary heart disease. In J. L. Durstine, A. C. King, P. L. Painter, J. L. Roitman, & L. D. Zwiren (Eds.), *Resource manual for guidelines for exercise testing and prescription* (pp. 151–167). Philadelphia: Lea & Febiger.

Casperson, C. J., & Merritt, R. K. (1992). Trends in physical activity patterns among older adults: The behavioural risk factor surveillance system, 1986–1990. *Medicine and Science in Sports and Exercise, 24* (Abstract), S26.

Caspersen, C. J., Powell, K. E., & Christenson, G. M. (1985). Physical activity, exercise, and physical fitness: Definitions and distinctions for health related research. *Public Health Reports, 100,* 126–131.

Centers for Disease Control and Prevention. (1991). Prevalence of sedentary lifestyle–behavioral risk factor surveillance system, United States, 1991. *Morbidity and Mortality Weekly Reports, 42,* 576–579.

Chodakowska, J., Wocial, B., Skorka, B., Nazar, K., & Chwalbinska-Moneta, J. (1980). Plasma and urinary catecholamines and metabolites during physical exercise in essential hypertension. *Acta Physiologica Polonica, 31,* 623–630.

Claytor, R. P. (1991). Stress reactivity: Hemodynamic adjustments in trained and untrained humans. *Medicine and Science in Sports and Exercise, 23,* 873–881.

Claytor, R. P., Cox, R. H., Howley, E. T., Lawler, K. A., & Lawler, J. E. (1988). Aerobic power and cardiovascular response to stress. *Journal of Applied Physiology, 65,* 1416–1423.

Cleroux, J. F., Peronnet, F., & deChamplain, J. (1985). Sympathetic induces during psychological and physical stumuli before and after training. *Physiology and Behavior, 35,* 271–275.

Coconie, C. C., Graves, J. E., Pollock, M. L., Phillips, M. I., Summers, C., & Hagberg, J. M. (1991). Effect of exercise training on blood pressure in 70– to 79–yr-old men and women. *Medicine and Science in Sports and Exercise, 23,* 505–511.

Cohen, S., Tyrell, D.S.J., & Smith, A. P. (1991). Psychological stress and susceptibility to the common cold. *New England Journal of Medicine, 325,* 606–612.

Corbin, C. B., & Lindsey, R. (1993). *Fitness for life.* Glenville, IL: Scott, Foresman.

Cox, J. P., Evans, J. F., & Jamieson, J. L. (1979). Aerobic power and tonic heart rate responses to psychosocial stressors. *Personality and Social Psychology Bulletin, 5,* 160–163.

Cox, R., Claytor, R., & Howley, E. (1989). Heart rate and plasma catecholamine responses to high intensity weight training. *Medicine and Science in Sports and Exercise, 21* (Suppl.), S3.

DeBusk, R. F., Stenestrand, U., Sheehan, M., & Haskell, W. L. (1990). Training effects of long versus short bouts of exercise in healthy subjects. *American Journal of Cardiology, 65,* 1010–1013.

deGeus, E.J.C., Lorenz, J. P., & vanDoornan, L.J.P. (1993). Regular exercise and aerobic fitness in relation to psychological make-up and psychological stress activity. *Psychosomatic Medicine, 55,* 347–363.

DeLeon-Jones, F., Maas, J. W., Dekirmenjian, H., & Sanchez, J. (1975). Diagnostic subgroups of affective disorders and their urinary excretion of catacholamine metabolites. *American Journal of Psychiatry, 132,* 1141–1148.

deVreis, H. A. (1987). Tension reduction with exercise. In W. P. Morgan & S. E. Goldston (Eds.), *Exercise and mental health* (pp. 99–104). Washington, DC: Hemisphere.

deVries, H. A., Beckman, P., Huber, H., & Deickmeir, L. (1968). Electromyographic evaluation of the effects of sauna on the neuromuscular system. *Journal of Sports Medicine and Physical Fitness, 8,* 1–11.

deVries, H. A., Wiswell, R. A., Bulbulian, H., & Moritani, T. (1981). Tranquilizer effects of exercise. *American Journal of Physical Medicine, 60,* 57–66.

Dishman, R. K. (1990). Determinants of participation in activity. In C. Bouchard, R. J. Shephard, T. Stephens, J. R. Sutton, & B. D. McPherson (Eds.), *Exercise, fitness, and health: A consensus of current knowledge* (pp. 75–101). Champaign, IL: Human Kinetics.

Dorgan, J. F., Brown, C., Barrett, M., Splansky, G. L., Kreger, B. E., D'Agastino, R. B., Albanes, D., & Schatzkin, A. (1994). Physical activity and risk of breast cancer in the Framingham heart study. *American Journal of Epidemiology, 139,* 662–669.

Dorheim, T., H., R., McKinney, M., Todd, G., Mellion, M., Buell, J., & Eliot, R. (1984). Cardiovascular responses of marathoners to mental challenge. *Journal of Cardiac Rehabilitation, 4,* 435–444.

Doyne, E. J., Chambless, D. L., & Beutler, L. E. (1983). Aerobic exercise as a treatment for depression in women. *Behavior Therapy, 14,* 434–440.

Doyne, E. J., Ossip-Klein, D. J., Bowman, E. D., Osborn, K. M., McDougall-Wilson, I. B., & Neimeyer, R. A. (1987). Running vs. weight lifting in the treatment of depression. *Journal of Consulting and Clinical Psychology, 1987,* 748–754.

Duncan, J. J., Gordon, N. F., & Scott, C. B. (1991). Women walking for health and fitness. How much is enough? *Journal of the American Medical Association, 266,* 3295–3299.

Dunn, A. L., & Dishman, R. K. (1991). Exercise and the neurobiology of depression. In J. O. Holloszy (Ed.), *Exercise and sports science reviews* (pp. 41–99). Baltimore: Williams & Wilkins.

Dunn, A. L., Garcia, M. E., Marcus, B. H., Kampert, J. B., Kohl, H. W., & Blair, S. N. (1998). Six-month physical activity and fitness changes in Project ACTIVE, a randomized trial. *Medicine and Science in Sports and Exercise, 30,* 1076–1083.

Dustman, R., Ruhling, R., & Russell, E. (1984). Aerobic exercise training and improved neuropsychological function of older individuals. *Neurobiology of Aging, 5,* 35–42.

Ebert, M. H., Post, R. M., & Goodwin, F. K. (1972). Effects of physical activity on urinary MHPG excretion in normal subjects. *Lancet, 11,* 766.

Ebisu, T. (1985). Splitting the distance of endurance running: On cardiovascular endurance and blood lipids. *Japanese Journal of Physical Education, 30,* 37–43.

Ekelund, L. G., Haskell, W. L., Johnson, J. L., Whaley, F. S., Criqui, M. H., & Sheps, D. S. (1988). Physical fitness as a predictor of cardiovascular mortality in asymptomatic North American men. *New England Journal of Medicine, 319,* 1379–1384.

Emery, C. F., & Gatz, M. (1990). Psychological and cognitive effects of an exercise program for community-residing older adults. *The Gerontologist, 30,* 184–188.

Endicott, J., & Spitzer, R. L. (1978). A diagnostic interview: The Schedule for Affective Disorders and Schizophrenia. *Archives of General Psychiatry, 35,* 837–844.

Fagard, R. H., & Tipton, C. M. (1994). Physical activity, fitness and hypertension. In C. Bouchard, R. J. Shephard, & T. Stephens (Eds.), *International consensus symposium on physical activity, fitness and health* (pp. 633–655.). Champaign, IL: Human Kinetics.

Farmer, M. E., Locke, B. Z., Moscicki, E. K., Dannenberg, A. L., Larson, D. B., & Radloff, L. S. (1988). Physical activity and depressive symptoms: The NHANES I Epidemiologic Follow-up Study. *American Journal of Epidemiology, 128,* 1340–1351.

Farrell, P. A. (1985). Exercise and endorphins—male responses. *Medicine and Science in Sports and Exercise, 17,* 89–93.

Farrell, P. A., Gates, W. K., Maksud, M. G., & Morgan, W. P. (1982). Increases in plasma beta-endorphin/beta-lipotropin immuno-reactivity after treadmill running in humans. *Journal of Applied Physiology, 52,* 1245–1249.

Farrell, P. A., Gates, W. K., Morgan, W. P., & Pert, C. B. (1983). Plasma leucine enkephalin-like radiorecepter activity and tension-anxiety before and after competitive running in humans. In H. G. Knutgen, J. A. Vogel, & J. Poortmans (Eds.), *Biochemistry of exercise* (pp. 637–644). Champaign, IL: Human Kinetics.

Farrell, P. A., Gustafson, A. B., Garthwaite, T. L., Kalkhoff, R. K., Cowley, A. W., & Morgan, W. P. (1986). Influence of endogenous opioids on the response of selected hormones to exercise in man. *Journal of Applied Physiology, 61,* 1051–1057.

Fletcher, G. F., Blair, S. N., Blumenthal, J., Caspersen, C., Chaitman, B., Epstein, S., Falls, H., Froelicher, E. S. S., Froelicher, V. F., & Pina, I. L. (1992). Statement on exercise. Benefits and recommendations for physical activity programs for all Americans. A statement for health professionals by the Committee on Exercise and Cardiac Rehabilitation of the Council on Clinical Cardiology, American Heart Association. *Circulation, 86,* 340–344.

Folkins, C. H. (1976). Effects of physical training on mood. *Journal of Clinical Psychology, 32,* 385–388.

Folkins, C. H., Lynch, S., & Gardner, M. M. (1972). Psychological fitness as a function of physical fitness. *Archives of Physical Medicine and Rehabilitation, 53,* 503–508.

Folkins, C. H., & Sime, W. E. (1981). Physical fitness training and mental health. *American Psychology, 13,* 373–389.

Franks, B. D. (1994). What is stress? *Quest, 46,* 1–7.

Fredrick, T., Frerichs, R. R., & Clark, V. A. (1988). Personal health habits and symptoms of depression at the community level. *Preventive Medicine, 17,* 173–182.

Fremont, J., & Craighead, L. W. (1987). Aerobic exercise and cognitive therapy in the treatment of dysphoric moods. *Cognitive Therapy Research, 2,* 241–251.

Fries, E. (1976). Salt volume and the prevention of hypertension. *Circulation, 53,* 589–594.

Frisch, R. E., Wyshak, G., Albright, N. L., Schiff, I., & Jones, K. P. (1985). Lower incidence of breast cancer and cancers of the reproductive system among former college athletes compared to non-athletes. *British Journal of Cancer, 52,* 885–891.

Fuster, V., Badimon, L., Badimon, J. J., & Chesebro, J. H. (1992). The pathogenesis of coronary artery disease and the acute coronary syndromes. *New England Journal of Medicine, 326,* 241–250.

Gammon, M. D., John, E. M., & Britton, J. A. (1998). Recreational and occupational physical activities and risk of breast cancer. *Journal of the National Cancer Institute, 90,* 100–117.

Gauvin, L., & Spence, J. C. (1996). Physical activity and psychological wellbeing: Knowledge base, current issues and caveats. *Nutrition Reviews, 54,* S53–S65.

Glass, G. V. (1978). Integrating findings: The meta-analysis of research. *Reviews of Research in Education, 5,* 351–379.

Gleser, J., & Mendelberg, H. (1990). Exercise and sport in mental health: A review of the literature. *Israeli Journal of Psychiatry and Related Sciences, 2,* 99–112.

Goode, D. J., Sekermenjian, H., Meltzer, H. Y., & Maas, J. W. (1973). Relation of exercise to MHPG excretion in normal subjects. *Archives of General Psychiatry, 29,* 391–396.

Gordon, T., Sorlie, P., & Kannel, W. B. (1976). Problems in the assessment of blood pressure. The Framingham Study. *International Journal of Epidemiology, 5,* 327–331.

Gotestam, K. G., & Stiles, T. C. (1990, November). *Physical exercise and cognitive vulnerability: A longitudinal study.* Paper presented at the annual meeting of the Association for the Advancement of Behavior Therapy, San Francisco.

Greist, J. H., Klein, M. H., Eischens, R. R., Gurman, A. S., & Morgan, W. J. (1979). Running as treatment for depression. *Comprehensive Psychiatry, 29,* 41–54.

Grossman, A., Bouloux, P., Price, P., Drury, P. L., Lam, K. S. L., Turner, T., Thomas, J., Besser, G. M., & Sutton, J. (1984). The role of opioid pepides in the hormonal responses to acute exercise in man. *Clinical Science, 67,* 483–491.

Hagberg, J. M., Montain, S. J., Martin, W. H., & Ehsani, A. A. (1989). Effects of exercise training on 60- 69-year-olds with essential hypertension. *American Journal of Cardiology, 64,* 348–353.

Haier, R. J., Quaid, K., & Mills, J.S.C. (1981). Naloxone alters pain perception after jogging. *Psychiatric Research, 5,* 231–232.

Haight, J.S.J., & Keatinge, W. R. (1973). Elevation in set point for body temperature regulation after prolonged exercise. *Journal of Physiology, 229,* 77–85.

Haskell, W. L. (1994a). Dose-response issues from a biological perspective. In C. Bouchard, R. J. Shephard, & T. Stephens (Eds.), *Physical activity, fitness, and health: International proceedings and consensus statement* (pp. 1030–1039). Champaign, IL: Human Kinetics.

Haskell, W. L. (1994b). Health consequences of physical activity: Understanding and challenges regarding dose–response. *Medicine and Science in Sports and Exercise, 26,* 649–660.

Haskell, W. L. (1995, December). *Physical activity, lifestyle and health in America.* Paper presented at the NIH Consensus Development Conference on Physical Activity and Cardiovascular Health, Bethesda, MD.

Haskell, W. L., & Phillips, W. T. (1995). Exercise training fitness health and longevity. In C. Gisolfi, D. Lamb, & E. Nadel (Eds.), *Exercise in older adults* (Vol. 8, pp. 11–47). Carmel, IN: Cooper.

Hatfield, B. D., & Landers, D. M. (1987). Psychophysiology in exercise and sport research: An overview. In P. K. (Ed.), *Exercise and sports science reviews* (Vol. 15, pp. 351–387). New York: Macmillan.

Holmes, D. S., & Roth, D. L. (1985). Association of aerobic fitness with pulse rate and subjective responses to psychological stress. *Psychophysiology, 22,* 525–529.

Howlett, D. R., & Jenner, F. A. (1978). Studies relating to the clinical significance of urinary 3-methoxy-4-hydroxyphenylethylene glycol. *British Journal of Psychiatry, 132,* 49–54.

Hull, E. M., Young, S. H., & Ziegler, M. G. (1984). Aerobic fitness affects cardiovascular and catecholamine responses to stressors. *Psychophysiology, 21,* 353–360.

Jakicic, J. M., Wing, R. R., Butler, B. A., & Robertson, R. J. (1995). Prescribing exercise in multiple short bouts versus one continuous bout: Effects on adherence, cardiorespiratory fitness, and weight loss in overweight women. *International Journal of Obesity, 19,* 893–901.

Janal, M. N., Colt, E. W. D., Clark, W. C., & Glusman, M. (1984). Pain sensitivity, mood and plasma endocrine levels in man following long-distance running: Effects of naloxone. *Pain, 19,* 13–15.

Jennings, G., Nelson, L., Nestel, P., Esler, M., Korner, P. Burton, D, & Bazelmans, J. (1986). The effect of changes in physical activity on major cardiovascular risk factors, hemodynamics, sympathetic function, and glucose utilization in man: A controlled study of four levels of activity. *Circulation, 73,* 30–40.

Katon, W., & Schulberg, H. (1992). Epidemiology of depression in primary care. *General Hospital Psychiatry, 14,* 237–247.

Kessler, R. C., McGonagle, K. A., Zhao, S., Nelson, C. B., Hughes, M., Eshelman, S., Wittchen, H. U., & Kendler, K. S. (1994). Lifetime and 12–month prevalence of *DSM–III–R* psychiatric disorders in the United States: Results from the National Co-morbidity Survey. *Archives of General Psychiatry, 51,* 8–19.

King, A. C. (1991). Community intervention for promotion of physical activity and fitness. In J. O. Holloszy (Ed.), *Exercise and sports science reviews* (Vol. 19, pp. 211–259). Baltimore, MD: Williams & Wilkins.

King, A. C., & Kiernan, M. (1997). Physical activity and women's health: Issues and future directions. In S. J. Gallant, G. P. Keita, & R. Royak-Schaler (Eds.), *Health care for women: Psychological, social, and behavioral influences* (pp. 133–146). Washington, DC: American Psychological Association.

King, A. C., Taylor, C. B., & Haskell, W. L. (1993). Effects of differing intensities and formats of 12 months of exercise training on psychological outcomes in older adults. *Health Psychology, 12,* 292–300.

Kjaer, M., & Galbo, H. (1988). Effects of physical training on the capacity to secrete epinephrine. *Journal of Applied Physiology, 64,* 11–16.

Klarman, H. E. (1964). Economics of health. In D. W. Clark & B. MacMahon (Eds.), *Preventive and community medicine* (2nd ed., pp. 603–615). Boston: Little, Brown.

Klein, M. H., Greist, J. H., Gurman, A. S., Neimeyev, R. A., Lesser, D. P., Busuell, N. J., & Smith, R. E. (1985). A comparative outcome study of group psychotherapy vs exercise treatments for depression. *International Journal of Mental Health, 13,* 148–177.

Knutsson, E., Lewenhaupt-Olsson, E., & Thorsen, M. (1973). Physical work capacity and physical conditioning in paraplegic patients. *Paraplegia, 11,* 205–216.

Kobusa, S., Maddi, S., & Kahn, S. (1982). Hardiness and health: A prospective study. *Journal of Personality and Social Psychology, 42,* 168–177.

Kohl, H. W., LaPorte, R. E., & Blair, S. N. (1988). Physical activity and cancer: An epidemiological perspective. *Sports Medicine, 6,* 222–237.

Kugler, J., Seelbach, H., & Kruskemper, G. M. (1994). Effects of rehabilitation exercise programmes on anxiety and depression in coronary patients: A meta-analysis. *British Journal of Clinical Psychology, 33,* 401–410.

Kugler, J., Seelback, H., & Kryskemper, G. M. (1994). Effects of rehabilitation exercise programs on anxiety and depression in coronary patients: A meta-analysis. *British Journal of Clinical Psychology, 33,* 401–410.

Kvetnansky, R. (1980). Recent progress in catecholamines under stress. In E. Usdin, R. Kvetnansky, & I. Kopin (Eds.), *Catecholamines and stress* (pp. 1–7). Oxford, England: Pergamon.

Lake, B. W., Suarez, E. C., & Schneiderman, N. (1985). The Type A behavior pattern, physical fitness, and psychophysiological reactivity. *Health Psychology, 4,* 169–187.

Lakka, T. A., Venalainen, J. M., Rauramaa, R., Salonen, R., Tuomilehto, J., & Salonen, J. T. (1994). Relation of leisure-time physical activity and cardiorespiratory fitness to the risk of acute myocardial infarction in men. *New England Journal of Medicine, 330,* 1549–1554.

Landers, D. M. (1994). Performance, stress and health: Overall reaction. *Quest, 46,* 123–135.

Landers, D. M. (1998). Exercise and Mental Health. *Exercise Science: Journal of the Korea Exercise Science Academy, 7,* 131–146.

Landers, D. M. (1998,). *Exercise and mental health.* Paper presented at the fifth annual Pacific Rim Conference on Exercise Science and Sports Medicine, Chosum University, Kwang-ju, Korea.

Landers, D. M., & Petruzzello, S. J. (1994). Physical activity, fitness and anxiety. In C. Bouchard, R. J. Shephard, & T. Stephens (Eds.), *Physical activity, fitness and health. International proceedings and consensus statement* (pp. 868–882). Champaign, IL: Human Kinetics.

Lazarus, R. S., & Cohen, J. P. (1977). Environmental stress. In I. Altman & J. F. Wohlwill (Eds.), *Human behavior and the environment: Current theory and research.* New York: Plenum.

Lee, I.-M. (1994). Physical activity, fitness and cancer. In C. Bouchard, R. J. Shephard, T. Stephens, J. R. Sutton, & B. D. McPherson (Eds.), *Exercise, fitness and health. A consensus of current knowledge* (pp. 814–831). Champaign, IL: Human Kinetics.

Lee, I. M., Paffenbarger, R. S., & Hsieh, C. C. (1991). Physical activity and risk of developing colorectal cancer among college alumni. *Journal of the National Cancer Institute, 83,* 1334–1339.

Leon, A. S., Connett, J., Jacobs, D. R., & Rauramaa, R. (1987). Leisure time physical activity levels and risk of coronary heart disease and death: The Multiple Risk Factor Intervention Trial. *Journal of the American Medical Association, 258,* 2388–2395.

Light, K. C., Obrist, P. A., James, S. A., & Strogatz, D. S. (1987). Cardiovascular responses to stress: II. Relationships to aerobic exercise patterns. *Psychophysiology, 24,* 79–86.

Lobstein, D. D., Mosbacher, B. J., & Ismail, A. H. (1983). Depression as a powerful discriminator between physically active and sedentary middle aged men. *Journal of Psychosomatic Research, 27,* 69–76.

Long, B. C., & van Stavel, R. (1995). Effects of exercise training on anxiety: A meta-analysis. *Journal of Applied Sport Psychology, 7,* 167–189.

Lubin, B. (1965). Adjective check list for the measurement of depression. *Archives of General Psychiatry, 12,* 47–62.

Mandell, A. J. (1979). The *second* second wind. *Psychiatric Annals, 9,* 49–56.

Manson, J. E., Nathan, D. M., Krolewski, A. S., Stampfer, M. J., Willett, W. C., & Hennkens, C. H. (1992). A prospective study of exercise and incidence of diabetes among US male physicians. *Journal of the American Medical Association, 268,* 63–67.

Manuck, S. B., Kaplan, J. R., & Clarkson, T. B. (1983). Behaviorally induced heart rate reactivity and atherosclerosis in cynomolgus monkeys. *Psychosomatic Medicine, 45,* 95–108.

Manuck, S. B., Kasprowicz, A. L., & Muldoon, M. F. (1990). Behaviorally-evoked cardiovascular reactivity and hypertension: Conceptual issues and potential associations. *Annals of Behavioral Medicine, 12,* 17–29.

Markoff, R. A., Ryan, P., & Young, T. (1982). Endorphin and mood changes in long distance running. *Medicine and Science in Sports and Exercise, 14,* 11–15.

Martinsen, E. W. (1990). Benefits of exercise for the treatment of depression. *Sports Medicine, 9,* 380–389.

Martinsen, E. W., Hoffart, A., & Solberg, O. (1989). Comparing aerobic and nonaerobic forms of exercise in the treatment of clinical depression: A randomized trial. *Comprehensive Psychiatry.*

Martinsen, E. W., Medhus, A., & Sandvik, L. (1985). Effects of aerobic exercise on depression: A controlled study. *British Medical Journal, 291,* 109.

Martinsen, E. W., Sandvik, L., & Kolbjornsrud, O. B. (1989). Aerobic exercise in the treatment of nonpsychotic mental disorders. *Norwegian Journal of Psychiatry, 43,* 411–415.

McAuley, E., & Rudolph, D. (1995). Physical activity, aging and psychological well-being. *Journal of Aging and Physical Activity, 3,* 67–96.

McCann, I. L., & Holmes, D. S. (1984). Influence of aerobic exercise on depression: A controlled study. *Journal of Personality and Social Psychology, 46,* 1142–1147.

McDonald, D. G., & Hodgdon, J. A. (1991). *The psychological effects of aerobic fitness training: Research and theory.* New York: Springer-Verlag.

McEwen, B. S., & Stellar, E. (1993). Stress and the individual: Mechanisms leading to disease. *Archives of Internal Medicine, 153,* 2093–2101.

McNeil, J. K., LeBlanc, E. M., & Joyner, M. (1991). The effect of exercise on depressive symptoms in the moderately depressed elderly. *Psychology and Aging, 6,* 487–488.

McPherson, B. D., Paivio, A., Yuhasz, M., Rechnitzer, P., & Lefcoe, N. (1965). Psychological effects of an exercise program for post-infarct and normal adult men. *Journal of Sports Medicine and Physical Fitness, 8,* 95–102.

Merritt, R. K., & Casperson, C. J. (1992). Trends in physical activity patterns among young adults. The behavioral risk factor surveillance system. *Medicine and Science in Sports and Exercise, 24 (Abstract),* S26.

Morgan, W. P. (1969). Physical fitness and emotional health. *American Corrective Therapy Journal, 23,* 124–127.

Morgan, W. P. (1985). Affective benificence of physical activity. *Medicine and Science in Sports and Exercise, 17,* 94–100.

Morgan, W. P. (1986). Reduction of State anxiety following acute physical activity. In W. P. Morgan & S. E. Goldston (Eds.), *Exercise and mental health* (pp. 105–109). Washington, DC: Hemisphere.

Morgan, W. P. (1994). Physical activity, fitness and depression. In C. Bouchard, R. J. Shephard, & T. Stephens (Eds.), *Physical activity, fitness and health* (pp. 851–867). Champaign, IL: Human Kinetics.

Morgan, W. P. (1997). Methodological considerations. In W. P. Morgan (Ed.), *Physical activity and mental health* (pp. 3–32). Washington, DC: Taylor & Francis.

Morgan, W. P., & Goldston, S. E. (Eds.). (1987). *Exercise and mental health.* Washington, DC: Hemisphere.

Morgan, W. P., Roberts, J. A., Brand, F. R., & Feinerman, A. D. (1970). Psychologic effect of chronic physical activity. *Medicine and Science in Sports and Exercise, 2,* 213–217.

Morris, J. N., Clayton, D. G., Everitt, M. G., Semmence, A. M., & Burgess, E. H. (1990). Exercise in leisure time: Coronary heart attack and death rates. *British Heart Journal, 63,* 325–334.

Morris, J. N., & Crawford, M. D. (1958). Coronary heart disease and physical activity of work: Evidence of a national necropsy survey. *British Medical Journal, 5111,* 1485–1496.

Morris, J. N., Heady, J. A., Raffle, P.A.B., Roberts, C. G., & Parks, J. W. (1953). Coronary heart disease and physical activity of work. *Lancet, 2,* 1053–1057.

Morris, J. N., Kagan, A., Pattison, D. C., Gardner, M., & Raffle, P.A.B. (1966). Incidence and prediction of ischaemic heart disease in London busmen. *Lancet, 2,* 552–559.

Muscettola, G., Potter, W. Z., Pickor, D., & Goodwin, F. K. (1984). Urinary 3-methoxy-4-hydroxyphenylglycol and major affective disorders. *Archives of General Psychiatry, 41,* 337–342.

Mutrie, N. (1988). Exercise as a treatment for moderate depression in the UK health service. *Sport, Health, Psychology and Exercise Symposium Proceedings* (pp. 96–105). London: The Sports Council and Health Education Authority.

National Advisory Mental Health Council. (1993). Health care reform for Americans with severe mental illnesses: Report of the National Advisory Mental Health Council. *American Journal of Psychiatry, 150,* 1447–1465.

National Center for Health Statistics. (1993). Monthly Vital Statistics Report. Advance Report of Final Mortality Statistics, 1990. *National Center for Health Statistics, 41*(7).

National Institutes of Health. (1995). *NIH Consensus Development Conference on Physical Activity and Cardiovascular Health.* Bethesda, MA: National Institutes of Health.

Naughton, J., Bruhn, J. G., & Lategola, M. T. (1968). Effects of physical training on physiologic and behavioral characteristics of cardiac patients. *Archives of Physical Medicine and Rehabilitation, 49,* 131–137.

Nelson, L., Jennings, G. L., Elser, M. D., & Kover, P. I. (1986). Effects of changing levels of physical activity on blood pressure and hemodynamics in essential hypertension. *Lancet, 8505,* 473–476.

Netz, Y., Yaretzki, A., Salganik, I., Jacob, T., Finkeltov, B., & Argov, E. (1994). The effect of supervised physical activity on cognitive and affective state of geriatric and psychogeriatric in-patients. *Clinical Gerontologist, 15,* 47–56.

North, T. C., McCullagh, P., & Tran, Z. V. (1990). Effect of exercise on depression. In K. B. Pandolf (Ed.), *Exercise and sports science reviews* (Vol. 18, pp. 379–415). Baltimore: Williams & Wilkins.

O'Conner, G. T., Boving, J. E., & Yusuf, S. (1989). An overview of randomized trials of rehabilitation with exercise after myocardial infarction. *Circulation, 80.*

Obrist, P. A. (1981). *Cardiovascular psychophysiology: A perspective.* New York: Plenum.

Oldridge, N. B., Guyatt, G. H., Fisher, M. E., & Rimm, A. A. (1988). Cardiac rehabilitation after myocardial infarction: Combined exercise of randomized clinical trials. *Journal of the American Medical Association, 260,* 945–950.

Paffenbarger, R. S., Hyde, R. T., & Wing, A. L. (1987). Physical activity and incidence of cancer in diverse populations: A preliminary report. *American Journal of Clinical Nutrition, 45,* 312–317.

Paffenbarger, R. S., Hyde, R. T., Wing, A. L., & Hsieh, C.-C. (1986). Physical activity, all-cause mortality, and longevity of college alumni. *New England Journal of Medicine, 314,* 605–613.

Paffenbarger, R. S., Hyde, R. T., Wing, A. L., Lee, I., Jung, D. L., & Kampert, J. B. (1993). The association of changes in physical-activity level and other lifestyle characteristics with mortality among men. *New England Journal of Medicine, 328,* 538–545.

Paffenbarger, R. S., Jung, D. L., Leung, R. W., & Hyde, R. T. (1991). Physical activity and hypertension: An epidemilogical view. *Annals of Medicine, 23,* 319–327.

Paffenbarger, R. S., Lee, I. M., & Leung, R. (1994). Physical activity and personal characteristics associated with depression and suicide in American college men. *Acta Psychiatrica Scandinavica* (Suppl. 377), 16–22.

Palmer, L. K. (1995). Effects of a walking program on attributional style, depression, and self-esteem in women. *Perceptual and Motor Skills, 81,* 891–898.

Pargman, D., & Baker, M. C. (1980). Running high: Enkephalin addicted. *Journal of Drug Issues, 10,* 341–349.

Pate, R. R., Pratt, M., Blair, S. N., Haskell, W. L., Macera, C. A., Bouchard, C., Buchner, D., Ettinger, W., Heath, G. W., King, A. C., Kriska, A., Leon, A. S., Marcus, B. H., Morris, J., Paffenbarger, R. S., Patrick, K., Pollock, M. L., Rippe, J. M., Sallis, J., & Wilmore, J. H. (1995). Physical activity and public health: A recommendation from the Centers for Disease Control and the American College of Sports Medicine. *Journal of the American Medical Association, 273,* 402–407.

Pekkanen, J., Marti, B., Nissinen, A., Tuomilehto, J., Punsar, S., & Karvonen, M. (1987). Reduction of premature mortality by high physical activity: 20–year follow-up of middle-aged Finnish men. *Lancet, 1136,* 1473–1477.

Pelham, T. W., Campagna, P. D., Ritvo, P. G., & Birnie, W. A. (1993). The effects of exercise therapy on clients in a psychiatric rehabilitation program. *Psychosocial Rehabilitation Journal, 16,* 75–84.

Perri, S., & Templer, D. (1984). The effects of an aerobic exercise program on psychological variables in older adults. *International Journal of Aging and Human Development, 20,* 167–172.

Petruzzello, S. J., Landers, D. M., Hatfield, B. D., Kubitz, K. A., & Salazar, W. (1991). A meta-analysis on the anxiety-reducing effects of acute and chronic exercise: Outcomes and mechanisms. *Sports Medicine, 11,* 143–182.

Peyrin, L., & Pequignot, J. M. (1983). Free and conjugated 3-methoxy-4-hydroxyphenylglycol in human urine: Peripheral origin of the glucuronide. *Psychopharmacology, 79,* 16–20.

Phillips, W. T., & Haskell, W. L. (1995). "Muscular fitness"—Easing the burden of disability in elderly adults. *Journal of Aging and Physical Activity, 3,* 261–289.

Phillips, W. T., Pruitt, L. A., & King., A. C. (1996). Life style activity: Current recommendations. *Sports Medicine, 22,* 1–7.

Pickering, T. G., & Gerin, W. (1990). Cardiovascular reactivity in the laboratory and the role of behavioral factors in hypertension: A critical review. *Annals of Behavioral Medicine*(12).

Plante, T. G., & Kospocvitz, D. (1987). The influence of aerobic exercise on physiological stress reactivity. *Psychophysiology, 24,* 670–677.

Pollak, M. H. (1991). Heart rate reactivity to laboratory tasks and ambulatory heart rate in daily life. *Psychosomatic Medicine, 53,* 25–35.

Pollak, M. H. (1994). Heart rate reactivity to laboratory tasks and in two daily life settings. *Psychosomatic Medicine, 56,* 271–276.

Pollock, M. L., & Wilmore, J. H. (1990). *Exercise in health and disease* (2nd ed.). Philadelphia: Saunders.

Post, R. M., Kotin, J., & Goodwin, F. K. (1973). Psychomotor activity and cerebrospinal fluid amine metabolites in affective illness. *American Journal of Psychiatry, 130,* 67–72.

Powell, K. E., Thompson, P. D., Caspersen, C. J., & Ford, E. S. (1987). Physical activity and the incidence of coronary heart disease. *Annual Review of Public Health, 8,* 253–287.

President's Commission on Mental Health. (1978). *Report to the president* (Stock No. 040-000-00390-8). Washington, DC: U.S. Government Printing Office.

Province, M. A., Hadley, E. C., Hornbrook, M. C., Lipsitz, L. L., Miller, J. P., Mulrow, C. D., Ory, M. G., Sattin, R. W., Tinnetti, M. E., & Wolf, S. L. (1995). The effects of exercise on falls in elderly patients. *Journal of the American Medical Association, 273,* 1341–1347.

Raglin, J. S. (1990). Exercise and mental health: Beneficial and detrimental effects. *Sports Medicine, 6,* 323–329.

Raglin, J. S. (1997). Anxiolytic effects of physical activity. In W. P. Morgan (Ed.), *Physical activity and mental health* (pp. 107–128). Washington, DC: Taylor & Francis.

Raglin, J. S., & Morgan, W. P. (1985). Influence of vigorous activity on mood state. *Behavior Therapist, 8,* 179–183.

Raglin, J. S., & Morgan, W. P. (1987). Influence of exercise and quiet rest on state anxiety and blood pressure. *Medicine and Science in Sports and Exercise, 19,* 456–463.

Ransford, C. P. (1982). A role for amines in the antidepressant effect of exercise: A review. *Medicine and Science in Sports and Exercise, 14,* 1–10.

Reaven, P. D., Barrett-Connor, E., & Edelstein, S. (1991). Relation between leisure-time physical activity and blood pressure in older women. *Circulation, 83,* 559–565.

Reeves, D. L., Levinson, D. M., Justesen, D. R., & Lubin, B. (1985). Endogenous hyperthermia in normal human subjects: Experimental study of emotional states (II). *International Journal of Psychosomatics, 32,* 18–23.

Regier, D. A., Boyd, J. H., Burke, J. D., Rae, D. S., Myers, J. K., Kramer, M., Robbins, L. N., George, L. K., Karno, M., & Locke, B. Z. (1988). One-month prevalence of mental disorders in the United States. *Archives of General Psychiatry, 45,* 977–986.

Rejeski, J. (1994). Dose–response issues from a phychosocial perspective. In C. Bouchard, R. J. Shephard, & T. Stephens (Eds.), *Physical activity, fitness, and health: International proceedings and consensus statement* (pp. 1040–1055). Champaign, IL: Human Kinetics.

Roskies, E., Seraganian, P., & Oseasohn, R. (1986). The Montreal Type A intervention project: Major findings. *Health Psychology, 5,* 45–69.

Ross, C. E., & Hayes, D. (1988). Exercise and psychologic well-being in the community. *American Journal of Epidemiology, 127,* 762–761.

Sachs, M. J. (1984). The runner's high. In M. L. Sachs & G. W. Buffone (Eds.), *Running as therapy: An integrated approach* (pp. 273–287). Lincoln: University of Nebraska Press.

Sandvik, L., Erikssen, J., Thaulow, E., Erikssen, G., Mundal, R., & Rodhal, K. (1993). Physical fitness as a predictor of mortality among healthy, middle-aged Norwegien men. *New England Journal of Medicine, 328,* 533–537.

Schildkraut, J. J., Orsulak, P. J., Schatzberg, A. F., & Rosenbaum, A. H. (1983). Relationship between psychiatric diagnostic groups of depressive disorders and MHPG. In J. W. Maas (Ed.), *MHPG: Basic mechanisms and psychpathology* (pp. 129–144). New York: Academic Press.

Schwartz, P. J., & Weiss, T. (1983). T-Wave amplitude as an index of cardiac sympathetic activity: A misleading concept. *Psychphysiology, 20,* 696–701.

Sexton, H., Maere, A., & Dahl, N. H. (1989). Exercise intensity and reduction in neurotic symptoms. *Acta Psychiatrica Scandinavica, 80,* 231–235.

Shaper, A. G., & Wannamethee, G. (1991). Physical activity and ischaemic heart disease in middle aged British men. *British Heart Journal, 66,* 384–394.

Shapiro, S., Weinblatt, E., Frank, C. W., & Sager, R. V. (1969). Incidence of coronary heart disease in a population insured for medical care (hip). *American Journal of Public Health, 59* (Suppl.), 1.

Shephard, R. J. (1990). Costs and benefits of an exercising versus a nonexercising society. In C. Bouchard, R. J. Shephard, T. Stephens, J. R. Sutton, & B. D. McPherson (Eds.), *Exercise, fitness and health: A consensus of current knowledge* (pp. 49–60). Champaign, IL: Human Kinetics.

Shulhan, D., Scher, H., & Furedy, J. J. (1986). Phasic cardiac reactivity to psychological stress as a function of aerobic fitness levels. *Psychophysiology, 23,* 562–566.

Siegrist, J. (1990). Occupational stress and cardiovascular reactivity in blue-collar workers. *Work and Stress, 4,* 295–304.

Sime, W. E. (1987). Exercise in the prevention and treatment of depression. In W. P. Morgan & S. E. Goldston (Eds.), *Exercise and mental health* (pp. 145–152). Washington, DC: Hemisphere.

Simon, G. E., VonKorff, M., & Barlow, W. (1995). Health care costs of primary care patients with recognized depression. *Archives of General Psychiatry, 52,* 850–856.

Singh, N. A., Clements, K. M., & Fiatarone, M. A. (1997). A randomized controlled trial of progressive resistance training in depressed elders. *Journal of Gerontology, 52A,* M27–M35.

Sinyor, D., Golden, M., Steinert, Y., & Seraganian, P. (1986). Experimental manipulation of aerobic fitness and the response to psychosocial stress: Heart rate and self-reported measures. *Psychosomatic Research, 48,* 324–337.

Sinyor, D., Schwartz, S. G., Peronnet, F., Brisson, G., & Seraganian, P. (1983). Aerobic fitness level and reactivity to psychological stress: Physiological, biochemical, and subjective measures. *Psychosomatic Medicine, 45,* 205–217.

Smith, R. E. (1989). Conceptual and statistical issues in research involving multidimensional anxiety scales. *Journal of Sport and Exercise Psychology, 11,* 452–457.

Sothmann, M. S., Horn, T. S., Hart, B. A., & Gustafson, A. B. (1987). Comparison of discrete cardiovascular fitness groups on plasma catecholamine and selected behavioral responses to psychological stress. *Psychophysiology, 24,* 47–54.

Sothmann, M. S., & Ismail, A. H. (1984). Relationships between urinary catecholomine metabolites, particularly MHPG, and selected personality and physical fitness characteristics in normal subjects. *Psychosomatic Medicine, 46,* 523–533.

Sothmann, M. S., & Ismail, A. H. (1985). Factor analytic derivation of the MHPG/NM ratio: Implications for studying the link between physical fitness and depression. *Biological Psychiatry, 20,* 570–583.

Sothmann, M. S., Ismail, A. H., & Chodzko-Zajko, W. J. (1984). Influence of catecholamine activity on the hierarchical relationships among physical fitness conditions and selected personality characteristics. *Journal of Clinical Psychology, 40,* 1308–1317.

Spielberger, C. D. (1987). Stress, emotions and health. In W. P. Morgan & S. E. Goldman (Eds.), *Exercise and mental health* (pp. 11–16). Washington, DC: Hemisphere.

Spielberger, C. D., Gorsuch, R. L., Lushene, R. E., Vagg, P. R., & Jacobs, G. A. (1983). *Manual for the state–trait inventory of STAI (Form Y).* Pala Alto, CA: Consulting Psychologists Press.

Spitzer, R. L., Endicott, J., & Robins, E. (1978). Research diagnostic criteria: Rationale and reliability. *Archives of General Psychiatry, 35,* 773–782.

Stein, P. N., & Motta, R. W. (1992). Effects of aerobic and nonaerobic exercise on depression and self-concept. *Perceptual and Motor Skills, 74,* 79–89.

Stephens, T. (1988). Physical activity and mental health in the United States and Canada: Evidence from four population surveys. *Preventive Medicine, 17,* 35–47.

Stephens, T., & Craig, C. L. (1990). *The well-being of Canadians: Highlights of the 1988 Campbell's survey.* Ottawa: Canadian Fitness and Lifestyle Research Institute.

Stephens, T., & Thomas, C. J. (1994). The demography of physical activity. In C. Bouchard, R. J. Shephard, & T. Stephens (Eds.), *Physical activity, fitness, and health: International proceedings and consensus statement* (pp. 204–213). Champaign, IL: Human Kinetics.

Steptoe, A., Kearsley, N., & Walters, N. (1993). Cardiovascular activity during mental stress following vigorous exercise in sportsmen and inactive men. *Psychophysiology, 30,* 245–252.

Sternfield, B. (1992). Cancer and the protective effect of physical activity: The epidemiological evidence. *Medicine and Science in Sports and Exercise, 24,* 1195–1209.

Stroop, J. P. (1935). Studies of interference in serial verbal reactions. *Journal of Experimental Psychology, 18,* 643–662.

Surgeon General's Report. (1996). *Physical activity and health.* U.S. Department of Health and Human Services.

Sweeney, D. R., Leckman, J. F., Maas, J. W., Hattox, S., & Heninger, G. R. (1980). Plasma free and conjugated MGPG in psychiatric patients. *Archives of General Psychiatry, 35,* 1100–1103.

Szabo, A., Brown, T. G., Gauvin, L., & Seraganian, P. (1993). Aerobic fitness does not influence directly heart rate reactivity to mental stress. *Acta Physioligica Hungaria, 81,* 229–237.

Tang, S. W., Stancer, H. C., Takahashi, S., Shephard, R. J., & Warsh, J. J. (1981). Controlled exercise elevates plasma but not urinary MHPG and VMA. *Psychiatry Research, 4,* 13–20.

Taube, C. A., & Barrett, S. A. (Eds.). (1986). *Mental health, United States 1985.* Rockville, MD: U.S. Department of Health and Human Services (NIMH).

Taube, S. L., Kerstein, L. S., Sweeney, D. R., Heninger, G. R., & Maas, J. W. (1978). Urinary 3-methoxy-4-hydroxyphenylglycol and psychiatric diagnosis. *American Journal of Psychiatry, 135,* 78–81.

Taylor, C. B., Sallis, J. F., & Needle, R. (1985). The relationship of physical activity and exercise to mental health. *Public Health Reports, 100,* 195–202.

Thune, I., Brenn, T., Lund, E., & Gaard, M. (1997). Physical activity and the risk of breast cancer. *New England Journal of Medicine, 336,* 1269–1275.

Tipton, C. M. (1991). Exercise,training and hypertension: An update. In J. O. Holloszy (Ed.), *Exercise and sports science reviews* (Vol. 19, pp. 447–505). Baltimore: Waverly.

Tipton, C. M., Sebastian, L. A., Overton, J. M., Woodman, C. R., & Williams, S. B. (1983). Influences of exercise intensity, age, and medication on resting systolic blood pressure of SHR populations. *Journal of Applied Physiology, 64,* 1179–1185.

Tomanek, R. J., Gisofi, C. V., Bauer, C. A., & Palmer, P. J. (1988). Coronary vasodilator reserve, capillarity and mitochondria in trained hypertensive rats. *Journal of Applied Physiology, 64,* 1179–1185.

U.S. Department of Health and Human Services, U. (1991). *Healthy People 2000: National health promotion and disease prevention objectives* (DHHS Publication PHS 91-50212). Washington, DC: Public Health Service.

Van Egeren, L. F., & Sparrow, A. W. (1990). Ambulatory monitoring to assess real-life cardiovascular reactivity in Type A and Type B subjects. *Psychosomatic Medicine, 52,* 297–306.

VanDoornan, L.J.P., & DeGeus, E.J.C. (1989). Aerobic fitness and the cardiovascular response to stress. *Psychophysiology, 26,* 17–28.

Von Euler, C., & Soderberg, V. (1957). The influence of hypothalamic thermoreceptive structures on the electroencephalogram and gamma motor activity. *EEG Clinical Neurophysiology, 9,* 391–408.

Wannamethee, G., & Shaper, A. G. (1992). Physical activity and stroke in British middle-aged men. *British Medical Journal, 304,* 597–601.

Weber, M. A., Smith, D.H.G., Neutel, J. M., & Cheung, D. G. (1991). Applications of ambulatory blood pressure monitoring in clinical practice. *Clinical Chemistry, 37,* 1880–1884.

Wu, A. H., Paganini-Hill, A., Ross, R. K., & Henderson, B. E. (1987). Alcohol, physical activity and other risk factors for colorectal cancer: A prospective study. *British Journal of Cancer, 55,* 678–694.

Zung, W. W. K. (1965). Self-rating depression scale. *Archives of General Psychiatry, 12,* 63–70.

III

Applications to the Study of Disease

39

Hostility (and Other Psychosocial Risk Factors): Effects on Health and the Potential for Successful Behavioral Approaches to Prevention and Treatment

Redford B. Williams
Duke University Medical Center

There was a time, not very long ago, when behavioral medicine researchers studying the effects of psychosocial factors on health and disease gathered themselves into guilds—not unlike those medieval guilds of armorers, goldsmiths, cobblers, and the like—each specializing in a rather narrow area of inquiry. In the early 1970s, for example, the Type A Behavior Pattern (TABP) guild was powerful and prominent at national meetings and in the research literature. By the early 1980s, however, the TABP guild was in decline, with negative studies leading to the formation of the hostility guild, the membership of which was drawn largely from the old TABP guild.

The hostility guild extended its hegemony in the 1980s (easily documented by a Medline search for papers with "hostility" in the keyword list), but it was soon under challenge from other guilds (i.e., the depression guild, the social support guild, the job strain guild), all with members who seemed to be engaged in a zero-sum game: There's only a limited amount of psychosocial risk factor "capital" available, and to the extent your risk factor is up, mine is down. This competition among psychosocial risk factor guilds led to a kind of internecine warfare, with engagements taking the form of statements like, "It's not hostility that's responsible for increased coronary risk; it's the low social support among hostile people that's really doing the damage."

I participated in this warfare, often with gusto, on both the giving and receiving ends of the zero-sum debate—often defending my favorite risk factor, hostility, against the encroachments of those carrying the banner of depression, social support, or job strain. It was not a very satisfying endeavor, however, when I so often found myself at odds with other investigators who were not only good friends but also respected colleagues. By nature a lumper rather than a splitter, I began in the early 1990s to search for some means of reconciling, in my own mind if nowhere else, the competing factions. The initial phase of this search culminated in my 1993 presidential address to the American Psychosomatic Society (R. B. Williams, 1994), in which I hypothesized that the clustering of health damaging behavioral (smoking, high alcohol consumption, and dysregulated eating) and biological (increased sympathetic and HPA axis function, decreased parasympathetic function, and dysregulated immune system function) characteristics in persons with high hostility levels is mediated by reduced serotonergic function in the central nervous system.

The major advance here was to move away from the spurious notion that risk characteristics act independently of each other—"Is it hostility or the increased smoking (or sympathetic excess, higher cholesterol, etc.)?" Instead, I was beginning to realize, researchers need to look at the joint effects of clusters of risk characteristics, and try to understand why risk characteristics show this tendency to co-occur. This insight was facilitated by G. Kaplan's (1995) description of the compounded effects on mortality of combinations of psychosocial risk factors—for example, in the Kuopio study where mortality was doubled when one or two psychosocial risk factors were present, but quadrupled when three were present.

Another insight came when I was invited by Johannes Siegrist to attend a satellite meeting in Utrecht before the 1994 Amsterdam International Congress of Behavioral Medicine. There I encountered Michael Marmot and learned about his pioneering research (Marmot et al., 1991) documenting the health damaging impact of lower socioeconomic status (SES) in British civil servants working in Whitehall. When recalling earlier research (Barefoot et al., 1991; Matthews, Kelsey, Meilahn, Kuller, & Wing, 1989) showing increased levels of psychosocial risk factors in lower SES groups, I was inspired to extend my earlier hypothesis (R. B. Williams, 1994) that the clustering of biobehavioral risk factors in hostile persons might be driven by reduced levels of CNS serotonergic function. This shift in my thinking was also influenced by realizing that the same biobehavioral risk factors found in hostile persons also tend to cluster in persons with the other psychosocial risk factors (e.g., smoking in persons with depression), as well as new findings from my own research showing that psychosocial risk factors themselves also cluster in the same persons (R. B. Williams et al., 1997).

The time had come to move away from the guild approach to psychosocial risk factors and look at the big picture. Now, rather than focusing on the single psychosocial risk factor of hostility and mechanisms responsible for its impact on health and disease, it is my view that there is a need to focus on the clustering of psychosocial risk factors, especially in lower SES groups, the biobehavioral mechanisms whereby such clusters damage health, and the possible utility of psychosocial and behavioral interventions in both primary and secondary prevention. This chapter reviews the current state of affairs in each of these areas.

PSYCHOSOCIAL RISK FACTORS: EPIDEMIOLOGIC EVIDENCE

Initial findings of an association between higher scores on the Cook and Medley Ho scale on the Minnesota Multiphasic Personality Inventory (MMPI) and coronary atherosclerosis severity in a cross-sectional study (R. B. Williams, Haney, Lee, Blumenthal, & Kong, 1980) and coronary heart disease (CHD) incidence and all-cause mortality in two prospective studies (Barefoot, Dahlstrom, & R. B. Williams, 1983; Shekelle, Gale, Ostfeld, & Paul, 1983) spawned a very large body of research on the role of hostility as a psychosocial risk factor. This research, recently reviewed by Miller, Smith, Turner, Guijarro, and Hallet (1996), has documented that the psychological characteristic of hostility, as measured with a wide array of instruments, is a risk factor, not only for CHD but for virtually any physical illness. It has become increasingly clear, however, that hostility is not the only psychosocial characteristic that is "coronary prone," or health damaging in the broader sense.

Thus, *depression,* whether construed as a subsyndromal predisposition or a clinical disorder, has been shown to predispose to increased risk of CHD (Anda et al., 1993) or all-cause mortality (Barefoot & Schroll, 1997) in healthy people, as well as the risk of dying in post-MI patients (Frasure-Smith, Lesperance, & Talajic, 1994). Similarly, *social isolation* (or low social support) predicts increased risk of CHD and all-cause mortality (House, Landis, & Umberson, 1988), as well as a poor prognosis in CHD patients (R. B. Williams et al., 1992). *Job stress,* whether defined as high strain (high demands/low control) or effort–reward imbalance, has also been shown to increase risk of CHD (Bosma, Peter, Siegrist, & Marmot, 1998) in healthy people, although an impact on prognosis in CHD patients has not been confirmed (Hlatky et al., 1995). *Lower SES* also predisposes to increased risk of CHD and all-cause mortality in healthy people (Adler, Boyce, Chesney, Folkman, & Syme, 1993) and a poorer prognosis in CHD patients (R. B. Williams et al., 1992).

It is now evident that these psychosocial risk factors do not occur in isolation from one another, but tend to cluster in the same individuals and groups. Thus, working women who report high job strain are characterized by increased levels of hostility, anger, depression, anxiety, and social isolation (R. B. Williams et al., 1997). And when psychosocial risk factors do co-occur, their impact on mortality is compounded (Kaplan, 1995). A specific example of this dynamic interaction among psychosocial risk factors comes from a recent study that found a larger impact of an intense episode of anger on risk of having a myocardial infarction in lower as compared to higher SES individuals (Mittelman, Maclure, Nachnani, Sherwood, & Muller, 1997).

It is becoming increasingly evident that lower SES, rather than being simply one among a list of other psychosocial risk factors, may be, in fact, a "master" risk factor that contributes to increased levels of the other risk factors. As already noted, both psychosocial risk factors and risky health behaviors are increased in lower SES groups (Barefoot et al., 1991; Matthews et al., 1989). Whereas health behaviors like smoking, alcohol consumption, obesity, and sedentary lifestyle are all increased among lower SES individuals, these risky health behaviors account for no more than from 12% to 13% of the predictive effect of lower SES on mortality in a nationally representative sample containing both men and women (Lantz et al., 1998). However, when a broader set of risk factors, including representatives from behavioral, biological, and psychosocial domains are controlled for, the SES gradient in all-cause mortality becomes nonsignificant (Lynch, G. A., Kaplan, R. D., & Salonen, 1997), suggesting that SES effects on health are mediated by factors in these three domains.

This epidemiological evidence leads to the conclusion that hostility and other psychosocial risk factors do not occur in isolation from one another, but tend to cluster in the same individuals. Moreover, lower SES appears to be a driver of increased levels of the other psychosocial risk factors, perhaps even acting through them, somehow, to increase risk of developing a wide range of diseases. Pathogenesis is something that happens at the level of cells and molecules. Psychosocial risk factors do not themselves act directly on cells and molecules, however. There must be mediators between the psychosocial domain and the cellular/molecular domain.

PSYCHOSOCIAL RISK FACTORS: BIOBEHAVIORAL MECHANISMS

Both hostility and depression are associated with alterations in autonomic balance and HPA axis function that could account for at least some of their health-damaging effects. When anger is induced in laboratory studies (T. W. Smith & Allred, 1989; Suarez, Kuhn, Schanberg, R. B. Williams, & Zimmerman, 1998; Suarez & R. B. Williams, 1989), for example, persons who score high on the same hostility scale that predicts increased risk of CHD and all-cause mortality exhibit larger sympathetic nervous system (SNS)-mediated cardiovascular responses than low scorers. Hostile persons also show increased SNS activation during everyday life, as documented by larger increases in daytime urinary epinephrine excretion (Suarez, R. B. Williams, Peoples, Kuhn, & Schanberg, 1991) and down regulation of lymphocyte beta adrenergic receptors (Shiller et al., 1997). Veith and coworkers (1994) documented increased SNS outflow in patients with major depression.

There is also evidence that parasympathetic (PNS) function is reduced in both hostile and depressed persons. Laboratory research (Fukudo et al., 1992) has shown decreased PNS antagonism of SNS effects on myocardial function in high hostile subjects. Both hostility (Sloan et al., 1994) and depression (Carney et al., 1988) are associated with decreased PNS function during ambulatory ECG monitoring.

Increased and dysregulated HPA axis function has long been a known accompaniment of depression (Holsboer, van Bardeleben, Gerken, Stallag, & Muller, 1984). Persons with hostile personality have also been found in recent research to exhibit increased HPA activation, both in ambulatory (Pope & T. W. Smith, 1991) and laboratory (Suarez et al., 1998) conditions.

Biologic changes similar to those documented in depressed and hostile persons are also present in persons who are socially isolated and/or exposed to high demand/low control jobs or life situations. Increased urinary catecholamine excretion has been found (Fleming, Baum, Gisriel, & Gatchel, 1982), for example, in persons reporting low social support. Persons in high strain jobs exhibit (Schnall et al., 1990) increased ambulatory blood pressure and increased left ventricular mass index—both likely the result of chronically increased SNS function. Working women with young children living in the home—clearly a high demand/low control situation!—show greater 24-hour urinary cortisol excretion than working women without children at home (Luecken et al., 1997).

Psychosocial risk factors are also associated with increased behavioral/physical risk factor levels. Two large-scale studies, one prospective (Siegler, Peterson, Barefoot, & R. B. Williams, 1992) and one cross-sectional (Scherwitz et al., 1992), and each involving over 5,000 subjects, found hostility to be associated with increased cigarette smoking, alcohol consumption, body mass index, 24-hour caloric intake, and cholesterol/HDL ratio. Hostility has also been found to predict increased incidence of hypertension (Barefoot, Dahlstrom, & Williams, 1983). Increased smoking (Glassman et al., 1990) and alcohol consumption (Hartka et al., 1991) are also well-documented in depression. Persons with low social support are less likely to succeed in smoking cessation (Mermelstein, S. Cohen, Lichtenstein, Baer, & Kamarck, 1986) or to adhere to a prescribed medical regimen (C. A. Williams et al., 1985).

How do the increased behavioral/physical risk factors, altered SNS/PNS balance, and increased HPA function among persons with psychosocial risk factors actually contribute to the development of CHD and other major diseases? Previous attempts (J. R. Kaplan, Petterson, Manuck, & Olsson, 1991) to answer this question have focused on the biological plausibility of these biobehavioral characteristics as contributors to possible pathogenic mechanisms—for example, via excessive cardiovascular arousals that promote atherogenesis via mechanical injury of arterial endothelium. Endothelial injury is only part of the story, however. An emerging consensus (Ross, 1993) sees chemical mediators like oxidatively modified low density lipoprotein (LDL) as modifying the cellular and molecular biology of the monocyte/macrophage system in ways that are critically involved in the events leading to the development of the atherosclerotic plaque. To understand how epidemiological associations between psychosocial factors and increased risk of major illnesses like CHD are mediated, it is necessary to identify the direct linkages between biobehavioral characteristics like increased SNS activity, smoking, and increased lipid levels and those events at the cellular and molecular levels that facilitate processes like atherogenesis and tumorigenesis that are responsible ultimately for the development of diseases like CHD and cancer.

Adams (1994) proposed that the search for such linkages can profitably focus on the effects of biobehavioral factors on the cellular and molecular biology of the monocyte/macrophage system. The combination of increased smoking and elevated lipids (including LDL) observed in hostile persons is likely to result in elevated circulating levels of oxidized LDL—recognized (Ross, 1993) as a key promotor of atherogenesis. Oxidized LDL causes a wide array of changes in murine macrophage gene expression and functions that are consistent with a phenotype—suppression of certain immediate early inflammatory genes and decreased macrophage mediated killing of tumor cells (Thai, J. G. Lewis, R. B. Williams, Johnson, & Adams, 1995)—that has the potential (Adams, 1994) to facilitate both atherogenesis and tumorigenesis. Ligation in vitro of the macrophage beta adrenergic receptor—a likely occurrence among hostile, depressed, and socially isolated persons, given their increased SNS function—appears to stimulate a similar phenotype (Adams, 1994). Based on these observations, Adams (1994) proposed that stress (e.g., associated with psychosocial risk factors) could potentiate the effects of oxidized lipids on monocyte/macrophage gene expression and functions involved in both atherogenesis and tumorigenesis. Preliminary support for this hypothesis comes from human studies in the laboratory showing both anger (Suarez, Sasaki, J. G. Lewis, R. B. Williams, & Adams, 1996) and pharmacologically induced alterations in autonomic balance (R. B. Williams et al., 1998) to be associated with differential effects on monocyte gene expression in high as contrasted to low hostile persons.

I have dealt at some length with the monocyte/macrophage system because I believe it is a key area where specific data indicate a strong heuristic potential for extending to the cellular and molecular levels an understanding of mechanisms whereby psychosocial factors increase risk of disease. Prior research in psychoneuroimmunology is also helping to to identify cellular/molecular mechanisms. Thus, studies showing decreased immune function in association with depression (Evans et al., 1992) and high demand/low control life situations (Kiecolt-Glaser & Glaser, 1992) provide further evidence of cellular mechanisms whereby the biologic and behavioral/physical accompaniments of psychosocial risk factors could affect health.

The foregoing review leads to this synthesis: Psychosocial risk factors do not themselves lead directly to increased risk of disease and death. Rather, their health damaging effects are probably mediated by the behavioral/physical and biological characteristics that co-occur with the psychosocial risk factors. These biobehavioral characteristics are the proximate contributors to pathophysiology, via an altered internal biochemical milieu that changes monocyte/macrophage gene expression and functions in ways that promote, at the cellular/molecular levels, the pathophysiological events (like atherogenesis and tumorigenesis) that are ultimately responsible for the development of life threatening diseases.

This scenario in no way minimizes the impact of *direct* pathogens—genetic predispositions (e.g., oncogenes), environmental toxins/carcinogens, infectious agents, and the like—on pathogenesis. Rather, it sees biobehavioral factors associated with psychosocial risk factors as contributing to disease by affecting the cellular and molecular processes whereby the body copes with these direct pathogens. An example of such an effect on cellular/molecular processes is preliminary observations of differential alterations in monocyte functions following behavioral and pharmacologic manipulations in high versus low hostile persons (Suarez et al., 1996; R. B. Williams et al., 1998).

In contrast to the progress just reviewed regarding the "downstream" biological mechanisms whereby low SES and other psychosocial risk factors contribute to pathogenesis, as Kaplan (1995) noted, relatively little attention has been given to the factors involved in the development of psychosocial (and associated biobehavioral) risk factors. To explore this issue, a developmental and neurobiological perspective must be taken.

Some time ago, a review of the extensive evidence linking a wide range of biological and behavioral characteristics to variations in brain serotonergic function led to the heuristic hypothesis (R. B. Williams, 1994) that the clustering of health-damaging biobehavioral characteristics observed in hostile persons (and persons with the other psychosocial risk factors that tend to cluster with hostility) is mediated by decreased function of the neurotransmitter serotonin in the brain. Research showing that children in lower SES groups hear fewer positive communications from their parents from birth to age 3 (Hart & Risley, 1995), and research showing that, compared to mother-reared monkeys, rhesus monkeys who are reared in peer groups from birth to age 6 months exhibit biobehavioral alterations that appear to be mediated by reduced brain serotonergic function (Higley, Suomi & Linnoila, 1992; Higley et al., 1993), have led to the expansion and extension of this hypothesis as follows: Reduced brain serotonergic function resulting from the experience of relatively harsh and adverse circumstances in early childhood is one important factor contributing to the clustering of health damaging psychosocial and biobehavioral characteristics in lower SES groups (R. B. Williams, 1998).

The foregoing review leads to these conclusions:

> Hostility, depression, social isolation, stress at work (high job strain, effort–reward imbalance), and lower SES have been shown in prospective epidemiological studies to increase risk of developing CHD as well as a broad range of other medical illnesses in healthy populations.
>
> In patients with clinical evidence of CHD, depression, social isolation, and lower SES have also been shown to confer a poorer prognosis.
>
> A wide range of potentially health damaging behaviors and biological characteristics have been found in persons with psychosocial risk factors and are the likely mediators of the increased disease risk observed in such persons and groups.
>
> Reduced brain serotonergic function, known to be influenced by both genetic and environmental factors, is an attractive candidate to account for the clustering of biobehavioral and psychosocial risk factors in certain individuals and groups (i.e., lower SES).

The purpose of doing the research leading to these conclusions is, ultimately, to be able to use the knowledge gained to develop effective interventions to ameliorate the health damaging effects of psychosocial risk factors and accompanying biobehavioral characteristics. Here also, there has been encouraging progress in recent years, especially with interventions aimed at improving prognosis in patients with disease already present.

PSYCHOSOCIAL RISK FACTORS: POTENTIAL FOR SUCCESSFUL PREVENTION AND TREATMENT

Group-based behavioral interventions targeting psychosocial factors have already been shown to improve prognosis in both CHD (Friedman et al., 1986; Blumenthal, Jiang, Babyak, et al., 1997) and cancer (F. I. Fawzy et al., 1993; Spiegel, Bloom, Kraemer, & Gottheil, 1989). Based on these encouraging observations, albeit with small sample sizes, R. B. Williams and Chesney (1993) asserted that enough is already known about the impact of psychosocial factors on prognosis in established CHD to proceed with randomized clinical trials of behavioral interventions aimed at reducing the mortality associated with depression and social isolation in CHD patients. The National Heart, Lung, and Blood Institute is currently supporting just such a trial—the ENRICHD study, the first large-scale, multicenter randomized clinical trial of a psychosocial intervention in any major illness (Blumenthal et al., 1997).

Another application for behavioral interventions is in patients with chronic medical conditions that, although not necessarily life threatening, are associated with much suffering and costly use of medical diagnostic and treatment services. In the Hawaii Medicaid study, Cummings, Pallak, Dorken, and Henke (1991) conducted a randomized clinical trial in which patients who were high utilizers of medical services were randomly assigned to three groups: no mental health treatment, traditional one-on-one psychotherapy for up to 50 sessions over a year, or a highly structured group-based intervention consisting of no more than 8 sessions of training in various coping skills. Compared to the other two groups, both of which showed increased medical costs during the year following randomization, the patients randomized to the structured group intervention showed a decrease of from 15% to 20% in costs for medical-surgical services.

These encouraging early intervention studies—especially when considered in the light of the extensive progress, reviewed earlier in this chapter, toward documenting the health damaging impact of psychosocial risk factors and the intervening biobehavioral mechanisms—make for considerable optimism that behavioral medicine and health psychology are on the threshold of an exciting new era. In this new era there will be an application of the knowledge and technology that emerges from the research reviewed herein in the day-to-day clinical care of patients with the widest conceivable range of medical disorders. As this technology transfer proceeds, there will be a time in the not distant future when behavioral interventions will be incorporated into the care of patients with heart disease and cancer with the expectation that both quality and quantity of life will be increased.

During this same time frame, the development of behavioral interventions will lead to decreased suffering and costs among patients in primary care medical settings, whether or not a chronic medical condition is present. In the more distant future, similar approaches will be developed and applied in a wide range of *primary prevention* programs, designed to keep healthy people well. After all, it is far more efficient and less costly to cut off toxic pollution at its source than it is to remove the pollutants from the water far downstream!

For this exciting potential to be fully realized, however, it will take more than the best of our research and good intentions. Until digitalis leaf was packaged into tablets with a more or less standard dose of digitalis glycosides for patients with the "dropsy" (congestive heart failure), the pharmacological promise contained in Sir William Withering's 18th-century observations of the potential benefits of the foxglove plant could not be realized. Thus, it will be essential for health psychologists and others working in the field of behavioral medicine to package behavioral interventions into products that can be delivered in a standardized fashion with reasonable expectation that similar benefits will be achieved across settings and deliverers. Such products will be entities that can be bought and sold, leading to the development—analogous to the genesis of the pharmaceutical industry 200 years ago in the work leading to development of standardized digitalis leaf preparations—of a new "behavioro-tech" industry that will be essential to ensure that research is transferred to and regularly used in clinical practice.

It is already possible to discern key elements in the successful intervention programs described here:

Group settings are more efficient than one-on-one approaches, enable patients to learn from one another, and serve as a powerful source of social support.

Proven principles of *cognitive behavior therapy* and *behavior therapy,* along with *social skills training* enable patients to gain hands-on practice in the use of skills they can use to handle the stressful situations and resulting negative emotions they need to face in the here and now.

Treatment is limited to a fixed number of sessions, often no more than six to eight, during which each skill to be mastered is presented in a manualized, protocol-driven format that enables patients to learn to practice and apply the skill to actual problems they are currently encountering at work, home or play.

R. B. Williams and V. P. Williams (1993) developed a behavioral intervention program incorporating these elements that was aimed at reducing the impact of hostility and anger on health. This program has been refined to develop the "LifeSkills" system (V. P. Williams & R. B. Williams, 1997), a six-session workshop that targets not only hostility/anger but the other established psychosocial risk factors as well. Moreover, it aims to prevent stressful situations from occurring in the first place by providing training in skills that will enhance emotional competencies and the quality of interpersonal relationships. Rather than approaching people as broken and in need of fixing, the LifeSkills system takes a wellness focus based on the message that people can benefit from learning and practicing skills that will improve their ability to cope and introduce a more positive focus into their life and relationships. The LifeSkills Workshop trains people to use two sets of skills:

Learn to understand yourself and others by:

- Increasing your awareness of thoughts and feelings
- Evaluating and managing negative thoughts and feelings
- Communicating effectively using speaking and listening skills
- Empathizing with others

Learn to act effectively by:

- Using problem solving when it is the situation that bothers you
- Practicing assertion when it is another person's behavior
- Keeping acceptance as an option when it will cause no one harm
- Increasing the positives in your life and relationships

Not unlike colleagues in basic biomedical sciences who partner with their academic institutions to form private corporations—"biotech spinoffs"—to facilitate technology transfer with respect to research findings in cellular and molecular biology, Virginia Williams and I have formed a "behavioro-tech" spinoff company, Williams LifeSkills, Inc., to further develop and market the LifeSkills system to both medical and corporate, as well as individual, buyers. Our corporate strategy is based on the premise, growing out of the research already reviewed, that psychosocial factors increase risk and costs of medical illness and that well-designed and implemented behavioral intervention packages have the potential to reduce these risks and costs. Preliminary analyses of data from corporate settings show significant decreases in hostility/anger, depression, and social isolation in persons following participation in the LifeSkills Workshop.

There has been one randomized clinical trial (Gidron, Davidson, & Bata, 1999) that used a group hostility-control intervention based on the earlier *Anger Kills* model and found decreases in both self-report and behaviorally assessed hostility levels, as well as diastolic blood pressure that were sustained over a 2-month follow-up period in post-MI patients randomized to the intervention as compared to patients receiving usual care. Although small in scale, this trial provides, along with the other clinical trials described earlier, encouraging evidence that structured group-based behavioral interventions that teach a set of key coping skills have real potential to improve prognosis once major illness is present. Only time will tell, but it is likely that such interventions have a role in primary prevention as well.

CONCLUSIONS

It is now possible to look back over the past quarter century and reflect with some pride on the accomplishments of behavioral medicine and health psychology during this exciting period. We are no longer gathered into guilds, each jealously defending its own particular psychosocial risk factor against the encroachments of other, competing guilds. Instead, we now realize that the psychosocial risk factors being studied separately do not occur in isolation from one another and associated biobehavioral characteristics, but tend to cluster in the same individuals and groups. It appears that, like the Vichy inspector played by Claude Raines in *Casablanca,* we have rounded up "the usual suspects" and find they belong to the same gang.

There has also been considerable progress toward identifying the biological and behavioral pathways whereby these psychosocial risk factors (including combinations of them, which are common) actually participate in the etiology is medical disease. We are just beginning to use the new tools of cellular and molecular biology in this endeavor. However, there are already exciting portents that we will be able to identify not only the basic mechanisms whereby clusters of psychosocial and biobehavioral risk characteristics participate in pathogenesis, but also the basic neurobiological mechanisms responsible for the clustering in the first place.

Finally, and most exciting and satisfying of all, in the not-too-distant future it appears increasingly likely that we will be able to apply what we have learned to reduce human suffering and disease and, at the same time, enhance well-being and quality of life.

ACKNOWLEDGMENTS

Preparation of this chapter was supported in part by grants P01-HL36587 and R01-HL44998 from the National Heart, Lung, and Blood Institute; grants 5P60-AG11268 and P02-AG12058 from the National Institute on Aging; grant K01-MH70482 from the National Institute of Mental Health; the Duke Clinical Research Unit grant M01-RR30; and research support from the Fetzer Institute and the John D. and Catherine T. McArthur Foundation.

REFERENCES

Adams, D. O. (1994). Molecular biology of macrophage activation: A pathway whereby psychosocial factors can potentially affect health. *Psychosomatic Medicine, 56,* 316–327.

Adler, N. E., Boyce, T., Chesney, M. A., Folkman, S., & Syme, S. L. (1993). Socioeconomic inequalities in health: No easy solution. *Journal of the American Medical Association, 269,* 3140–3145.

Anda, R., Williamson, D., Jones, D., Macera, C., Eaker, E., Glassman, A., & Marks, J. (1993). Depressed affect, hopelessness, and the risk of ischemic heart disease in a cohort of U.S. adults. *Epidemiology,4,* 285–294.

Barefoot, J. C., Dahlstrom, W. G., & Williams, R. B. (1983). Hostility, CHD incidence, and total mortality: A 25-year follow-up study of 255 physicians. *Psychosomatic Medicine, 45,* 59–63.

Barefoot, J. C., Helms, M. J., Mark, D. M., Blumenthal, J. A., Califf, R. M., Haney, T. L., O'Connor, C. M., Siegler, I. C., & Williams, R. B. (1996). Depression and long term mortality risk in patients with coronary artery disease. *American Journal of Cardiology, 78,* 613–617.

Barefoot, J. C., Peterson, B. L., Dahlstrom, W. G., Siegler, I. C., Anderson, N. B., & Williams, Jr., R. B. (1991). Hostility patterns and health implications: Correlates of Cook–Medley Hostility scale scores in a national survey. *Health Psychology, 10*(1), 18–24.

Barefoot, J. C., & Schroll, M. (1997). Symptoms of depression, acute myocardial infarction and total mortality in a community sample. *Circulation, 93,* 1976–1980.

Blumenthal, J. A., Jiang, W., Babyak, M. A., Krantz, D. S., Frid, D. J., Coleman, R. E., Waugh, R., Hanson, M., Appelbaum, M., O'Conner, C., & Morris, J. J. (1997). Stress management and exercise training in cardiac patients with myocardial ischemia. *Archives of Internal Medicine, 157,* 2213–2223.

Blumenthal, J. A., O'Connor, C., Hinderliter, A., Fath, K., Hegde, S. B., Miller, G., Puma, J., Sessions, W., Sheps, D., Zakhary, B., & Williams, R. B. (1997). Psychosocial factors and coronary disease. A National Multicenter Clinical Trial (ENRICHD) with a North Carolina focus. *North Carolina Medical Journal, 58,* 802–808.

Bosma, H., Peter, R., Siegrist, J., & Marmot, M. (1998). Two alternative job stress models and the risk of coronary heart disease. *American Journal of Public Health, 88,* 68–74.

Carney, R. M., Rich, M., deVelde, A., Saini, J., Clark, K., & Freedland, K. E. (1988). The relationship between heart rate, heart rate variability and depression in patients with coronary artery disease. *Journal of Psychosomatic Research, 32,* 159–164.

Cummings, N. A., Dorken, H., Pallak, M. S., & Henke, C. (1991). The impact of psychological intervention on health care costs and utilization. *HCFA Contract Report # 11-C-98334419.*

Evans, D. L., Folds, J. D., Pettito, J. M., Golden, R. N., Pedersen, C. A., Corrigan, M., Gilmore, J. H., Silva, S. G., Quade, D., & Ozer, H. (1992). Circulating natural killer cell phenotypes in men and women with major depression: Relation to cytotoxic activity and severity of depression. *Archives of General Psychiatry, 49,* 388–395.

Fawzy, F. I, Fawzy, N. W., Hyun, C. S., Elashoff R., Guthrie, D., Fahey, J. L., & Morton D. L. (1993). Malignant melanoma: Effects of an early structured psychiatric intervention, coping, and affective state on recurrence and survival 6 years later. *Archives of General Psychiatry,50,* 681–689.

Frasure-Smith, N., Lesperance, F., & Talajic, M. (1994). Post-myocardial infarction depression and 18–month prognosis. *Circulation, 90,* I614.

Fleming, R., Baum, A., Gisriel, M. M., & Gatchel, R. J. (1982). Mediating influences of social support on stress at Three Mile Island. *Journal of Human Stress, 8,* 14–22.

Friedman, M., Thoresen, C. E., Gill, J. J., Ulmer, D., Powell, L. H., Price, V. A., Brown, B., Thompson, L., Rabin, D. D., & Breall, W. S., et al., (1986). Alteration of Type A behavior and its effect on cardiac recurrences in post myocardial infarction patients: Summary results of the Recurrent Coronary Prevention Project. *American Heart Journal, 112,* 653–665.

Fukudo, S., Lane, J. D., Anderson, N. B., Kuhn, C. M., Schanberg, S. M., McCown, N., Muranaka, M., Suzuki, J., & Williams, R. B. (1992). Accentuated vagal antagonism of beta adrenergic effects on ventricular repolarization: Differential responses between Type A and Type B men. *Circulation, 85,* 2045–2053.

Gidron, Y., Davidson, K., & Bata, I. (1999). The short-term effects of a hostility-reduction intervention in CHD patients. *Health Psychology, 18,* 416–420.

Glassman, A. H., Helzer, J. E., Covey, L. S., Cottler, L. B., Stetner, F., Tipp, J. E., Johnson, J. (1990). Smoking, smoking cessation, and major depression. *Journal of the American Medical Association, 264,* 1546–1549

Hart, T., & Risley, T. R. (1995). *Meaningful differences in the everday experience of young American children.* Baltimore, MD: Paul H. Brookes.

Hartka, E., Johnstone, B., Leino, E. V., Motoyoshi, M., Temple, M. T., & Fillmore, K. M. (1991). A meta-analysis of depressive symptomatology and alcohol consumption over time. *British Journal of Addiction, 86,* 1283–1298.

Higley, J. D., Suomi, S. J., & Linnoila, M. (1992). A longitudinal assessment of CSF monoamine metabolites and plasma cortisol concentrations in young rhesus monkeys. *Biological Psychiatry, 32,* 127–145.

Higley, J. D., Thompson, W. W., Champoux, M., Goldman, D., Hasert M. F., & Kraemer, G. W. (1993). Paternal and maternal genetic and environmental contributions to cerebrospinal fluid monoamine metabolites in Rhesus monkeys (*Macaca mulatta*). *Archives of General Psychiatry, 50,* 615–623.

Hlatky, M. A., Lam, L. C., Lee, K. L., Clapp-Channing, N. E., Williams, R. B., Pryor, D. B., Califf, R. M., & Mark, D. B. (1995). Job strain and the prevalence and outcome of coronary artery disease. *Circulation, 92,* 327–333.

Holsboer, F., van Bardeleben, U., Gerken, A., Stallag, K., & Muller, O. A. (1984). Blunted corticotrophin and normal response to human corticotrophin-releasing factor in depression. *New England Journal of Medicine, 311,* 1127.

House, J. S., Landis, K. R., & Umberson, D. (1988). Social relationships and health. *Science, 241,* 540–545.

Kaplan, G. A. (1995). Where do shared pathways lead? Some reflections on a research agenda. *Psychsomatic Medicine, 57,* 208–212.

Kaplan, J. R., Petterson, K., Manuck, S. B., & Olsson, G. (1991). Role of sympathoadrenal medullary activation in the initiation and progression of atherosclerosis. *Circulation, 94*(Suppl. 6), VI23–VI32.

Kiecolt-Glaser, J. K., & Glaser, R. (1992). Psychoneuroimmunology: Can psychological interventions modulate immunity? *Journal of Consulting Clinical Psychology, 60,* 1–6.

Lantz, P. M., House, J. S., Lepkowski, J. M., Williams, D. R., Mero, R. P., & Chen, J. (1998). Socioeconomic factors, health behaviors, and mortality: Results from a nationally represenative prospective study of US adults. *Journal of the American Medical Association, 279,* 1703–1708.

Luecken, L. J., Suarez, E. C., Kuhn, C. M., Barefoot, J. C., Blumenthal, J. A., Siegler, I. C., & Williams, R.B. (1997). Stress and employed women: I. Impact of marital status and children at home on neurohormone output and home strain. *Psychosomatic Medicine, 59,* 352–359.

Lynch, J. W., Kaplan, G. A., & Salonen, J. T. (1997). Why do poor people behave poorly? Variation in adult health behaviours and psychosocial characteristics by stages of the socioeconomic lifecourse. *Social Science in Medicine, 44,* 809–819.

Marmot, M. G., Smith, G. D, Stansfield, S., Patel, C., North, F., Head, J., White, I., Brunner, E., & Feeney, A. (1991). Health inequalities among British civil servants. The Whitehall II study. *Lancet, 337,* 1387–1393.

Matthews, K. A, Kelsey, S. F., Meilahn, E. N., Kuller, L. H., & Wing, R. R. (1989). Educational attainment and behavioral and biologic risk factors for coronary heart disease in middle-aged women. *American Journal of Epidemiology, 129,* 1132–1144.

Mermelstein, R., Cohen, S., Lichtenstein, E., Baer, J. S., & Kamarck, T. (1986). Social support and smoking cessation and maintenance. *Journal of Consulting and Clinical Psychology, 54,* 447–453.

Miller, T. Q., Smith, T. W., Turner, C. W., Guijarro, M. L., & Hallet, A. J. (1996). A meta-analytic review of research on hostility and physical health. *Psychological Bulletin, 119,* 322–348.

Mittelman, M. A., Maclure, M., Nachnani, M., Sherwood, J. B., & Muller, J. E. (1997). Educational attainment, anger, and the risk of triggering myocardial infarction onset. *Archives of Internal Medicine, 157,* 769–775.

Pope, M. K., & Smith, T. W. (1991). Cortisol excretion in high and low cynically hostile men. *Psychosomatic Medicine, 53,* 386–392.

Ross, R. (1993). The pathogenesis of atherosclerosis: A perspective for the 1990s. *Nature, 362,* 801–805.

Scherwitz, K. W., Perkins, L. L., Chesney, M. A., Hughes, G. H., Sidney, S., & Manolio, T. A. (1992). Hostility and health behaviors in young adults: The CARDIA study. Coronary artery risk development in young adults study. *American Journal of Epidemiology, 136,* 136–145.

Schnall, P., Pieper, C., Schwartz, J. E., Karasek, R. A., Schlussel, Y., Devereux, R. B., Ganau, A., Alderman, M., Warren, K., & Pickering, T.G. (1990). The relationship between job strain, workplace diastolic blood pressure, and life ventricular mass index: Results of a case-control study. *Journal of the American Medical Association, 263,* 1971–1972.

Shekelle, R. B., Gale, M., Ostfeld, A. M., & Paul, O. (1983). Hostility, risk of coronary disease, and mortality. *Psychosomatic Medicine, 45,* 219–228.

Shiller, A. M., Suarez, E. C., Kuhn, C. M., Schanberg, S. M., Williams, Jr., R. B., & Zimmermann, E. A. (1997). The relationship between hostility and beta-adrenergic receptor physiology in healthy young males. *Psychosomatic Medicine, 59,* 481–487.

Siegler, I. C., Peterson, B. L., Barefoot, J. C., & Williams, R. B. (1992). Hostility during late adolescence predicts coronary risk factors at midlife. *American Journal of Epidemiology, 136*(2), 146–154.

Spiegel, D., Bloom, J. R., Kraemer, H. C., & Gottheil, E. (1989). Effect of psychosocial treatment on survival of patients with metastatic breast cancer. *Lancet, 2,* 888–890.

Sloan, R. P., Shapiro, P. A., Bigger, J. T., Jr., Bagiella, E., Steinman, R. C., & Gorman, J. M. (1994). Cardiovascular autonomic control and hostility in healthy subject. *American Journal of Cardiology, 74,* 298–300

Smith, T. W., & Allred, K. D. (1989). Blood pressure reactivity during social interaction in high and low cynical hostile men. *Journal of Behavorial Medicine, 11,* 135–143.

Suarez, E. C., Kuhn, C. M., Schanberg, S. M., Williams, R. B., & Zimmermann, E. A. (1998). Neuroendocrine, cardiovascular, and emotional responses of hostile men: The role of interpersonal challenge. *Psychosomatic Medicine, 60,* 78–88.

Suarez, E. C., Sasaki, M., Lewis, J. G., Williams, R. B., & Adams, D. O. (1996, March). *Anger increases expression of interleukin-1 on monocytes in hostile women.* Paper presented at annual meeting of the American Psychosomatic Society, Williamsburg, VA.

Suarez, E. C., & Williams, R. B. (1989). Situational determinants of cardiovascular and emotional reactivity in high and low hostile men. *Psychosomatic Medicine, 51,* 404–418.

Suarez, E. C., Williams, R. B., Peoples, M. C., Kuhn, C. M., & Schanberg, S. M. (1991, October). *Hostility-related differences in urinary excretion rates of catecholamines.* Paper presented at the annual meeting of the Society for Psychophysiological Research, Chicago, IL.

Thai, S-F., Lewis, J. G., Williams, R. B., Johnson, S. P., & Adams, D. O. (1995). Effects of oxidized LDL on mononuclear phagocytes: Inhibition of induction of four inflammatory cytokine gene RNAs, release of NO, and cytolysis of tumor cells. *Journal of Leukocyte Biology, 57,* 427–433.

Veith, R. C., Lewis, N., Linares, O. A., Barnes, R. F., Raskind, M. A., Villacres, E. C., Murburg, M. M., Ashleigh, E. A., Castillo, S., Peskind, E. R., Pascualy M., & Halter, J. B. (1994). Sympathetic nervous system activity in major depression: Basal and desipramine-induced alterations in plasma norepinephrine kinetics. *Archives of General Psychiatry, 51,* 411–422.

Williams, C. A., Beresford, S. A., James, S. A., LaCroix, A. Z., Strogatz, D. S., Wagner, E. H., Kleinbaum, D. G., Cutchin, L. M., & Ibrahim, M. A. (1985). The Edgecombe County High Blood Pressure Control Program: III. Social support, social stressors, and treatment dropout. *American Journal of Public Health, 75,* 483–486.

Williams, R. B. (1994). Neurobiology, cellular and molecular biology, and psychosomatic medicine. *Psychosomatic Medicine, 56,* 308–315.

Williams, R. B. (1998). Lower socioeconomic status and increased mortality. Early childhood roots and the potential for successful interventions. *Journal of the American Medical Association, 279,* 1745–1746.

Williams, R. B., Barefoot, J. C., Blumenthal, J. A., Helms, M. J., Luecken, L., Pieper, C. F., Siegler, I. C., & Suarez, E. C. (1997). Psychosocial correlates of job strain in a sample of working women. *Archives of General Psychiatry, 54,* 543–548.

Williams, R. B., Barefoot, J. C., Califf, R. M., Haney, T. L., Saunders, W. B., Pryor, D. B., Hlatky, M. A., Siegler, I. C., & Mark, D. B. (1992). Prognostic importance of social and economic resources among medically treated patients with angiographically documented coronary artery disease. *Journal of the American Medical Association, 267,* 520–524.

Williams, R. B., & Chesney, M. A. (1993). Psychosocial factors and prognosis in established coronary artery disease. The need for research on interventions. *Journal of the American Medical Association, 270,* 1860–1861.

Williams, R. B., Haney, T. L., Lee, K. L., Blumenthal, J. A., & Kong, Y. (1980). Type A behavior, hostility, and coronary atherosclerosis. *Psychosomatic Medicine, 42*(6), 539–549.

Williams, R. B., Sasaki, M., Lewis, J. G., Kuhn, C. M., Schanberg, S. M., Suarez, E. C., Feaganes, J. R., & Adams, D. O. (1998). Differential responsivity of monocyte cytokine and adhesion proteins in high and low hostile human: A pilot study. *International Journal of Behavioral Medicine, 4*(3), 264–272.

Williams, R. B., & Williams, U. P. (1993). *Anger Kills.* New York: Times Books.

Williams, U. P., & Williams, R. B. (1997). *LifeSkills.* New York: Times Books.

40

Stress and Silent Ischemia

Willem J. Kop
Uniformed Services University of the Health Sciences
John S. Gottdiener
St. Francis Hospital, Roslyn, NY
David S. Krantz
Uniformed Services University of the Health Sciences

Evidence indicates that both chronic (Appels, 1990; Friedman & Rosenman, 1959; Kop, 1997; Williams et al., 1980) and acute (Krantz, Kop, Santiago, & Gottdiener, 1996) psychologically stressful circumstances can promote coronary artery disease (CAD) progression and its clinical manifestations such as chest pain, myocardial infarction, and sudden cardiac death. Current models of the effects of mental and physical stress on the heart suggest that behaviorally induced autonomic nervous system activation can produce clinical cardiovascular events at several levels: by promoting atherosclerosis and subsequent plaque formation in the coronary artery wall; by directly triggering disturbances in cardiac rhythm (arrhythmias) through alterations of the neural activation of the heart; and by producing intermediate pathologic or pathophysiologic processes causing ischemia in patients with CAD (Krantz et al., 1996b). This chapter addresses the third level, that is, mental and physical triggers of cardiac ischemia.

The characteristic symptom of coronary artery disease is stress-induced anginal pain. Angina is a consequence of myocardial ischemia, which may develop when the oxygen supply to the heart does not meet cardiac oxygen demand (Krantz et al., 1996b). Myocardial ischemia is commonly manifest in patients with CAD. However, many cardiac ischemic episodes are asymptomatic, or "silent" (Deanfield et al., 1983; Krantz et al., 1994; Nabel, Rocco, Barry, Campbell, & Selwyn, 1987). The absence of symptoms may interfere with patients' recognition of impending cardiac events as well as the accuracy with which symptoms are described to medical professionals (Kenyon, Ketterer, Gheorghiade, & Goldstein, 1992; Theisen et al., 1995). Moreover, the incidence of painless and undetected acute myocardial infarction is estimated to be approximately 10% (Kannel & Abbott, 1984). This chapter focuses on silent ischemia during episodes of mental stress in laboratory settings and activities of daily life and addresses possible biobehavioral mechanisms that may explain stress-induced silent ischemia. Specifically, it describes: the prevalence of mental stress-induced myocardial ischemia in the laboratory; the characteristics of (silent) ischemia in field studies; possible mechanisms for the onset of ischemia with mental stress and its characteristic absence of cardiac symptoms; and the predictive value of silent ischemia for adverse prognosis in patients with CAD.

MENTAL STRESS-INDUCED SILENT ISCHEMIA: LABORATORY STUDIES

Myocardial ischemia is a consequence of an imbalance between cardiac demand (the workload of the heart) and coronary blood supply (the delivery of oxygenated blood to the heart via the coronary arteries). As is discussed later, mental and physical stress may increase cardiac demand by increasing heart rate and blood pressure; and, in addition, other evidence indicates that mental stress may also reduce coronary blood supply to the heart. Thus, mental stress may cause cardiac ischemia because it unfavorably effects the balance between cardiac demand and supply (Krantz et al., 1996b; Rozanski et al., 1988). Cardiac ischemia triggered by mental stress is generally transient and asymptomatic. Ischemia may, in rare circumstances, occur in the absence of atherosclerotic coronary disease; this often reflects cardiac pathology including aortic stenosis, cardiomyopathy, congenital abnormalities, and syndrome X (i.e., impaired perfusion of the coronary resistance vessels). This review of stress-induced ischemia is limited to patients with established CAD.

Myocardial ischemia can be objectified utilizing several procedures that are increasingly sensitive to detect cardiac changes indicative of cardiac ischemia (Fig. 40.1). For the purpose of this chapter, these procedures can broadly be divided into the electrocardiogram (ECG), and echocardiographic and/or radionuclide techniques to assess cardiac function and perfusion.

Electrocardiographic Measures of Ischemia

Because the cardiac muscle is electrically active, electrocardiographic recordings can be made to measure beat-by-beat electrical polarization and recovery of the cardiac muscle cells. Ischemia prolongs the duration of recovery, and the ischemic area is repolarized last (Braunwald, 1988). Ischemia during exercise testing and activities of daily life can be assessed using shifts in the ST-segment of the ECG, where a depression of > 0.10 mV for a duration of more than 1 minute is the critical index for diagnosis of ischemia (Fig. 40.2). To document episodes of ischemia during the activities of daily life, ambulatory Holter monitors have been developed that record continuous ECGs for 24 hours on tape.

Wall Motion Abnormalities, Decrease in Ejection Fraction, and Perfusion Defects

Under normal circumstances, the left ventricle of the heart muscle contracts in a rhythmic, coordinated pattern and ejects blood into the aorta to produce a pulsatile maintenance of systemic blood pressure. However, when the heart muscle becomes ischemic, this contraction pattern may become uneven. The occurrence of unevenness of left ventricular contraction pattern is referred to as *wall motion abnormalities*. In the absence of cardiac muscle damage due to prior myocardial infarction, these wall motion abnormalities are generally not present in resting conditions, but can be induced by procedures that increase cardiac demand, such as exercise testing. Stress-induced wall motion abnormalities occur at the specific regions where ischemia occurs. To objectify stress-induced wall motion abnormalities, baseline measures of cardiac wall motion are compared to wall motion during a stress task. Both echocardiographic and radionuclide techniques are available to detect changes in cardiac function and determine inducibility of cardiac ischemia.

A measure of stress-induced ischemia that is related to the pump function of the heart uses a < 5% increase in *ejection fraction* as diagnostic criterium. Normally, when cardiac demand is elevated, the ejection fraction (the relative output of the heart during systole) increases. However, if the heart becomes ischemic, this increase does not occur. Normal values for baseline ejection fractions range from 50% to 75%. Inducibility of ischemia during exercise is suspected when the increase in ejection fraction from baseline is less than 5%. Similar criteria (a 5% drop in ejection fraction) have been used to detect mental stress ischemia (Ironson et al., 1992), al-

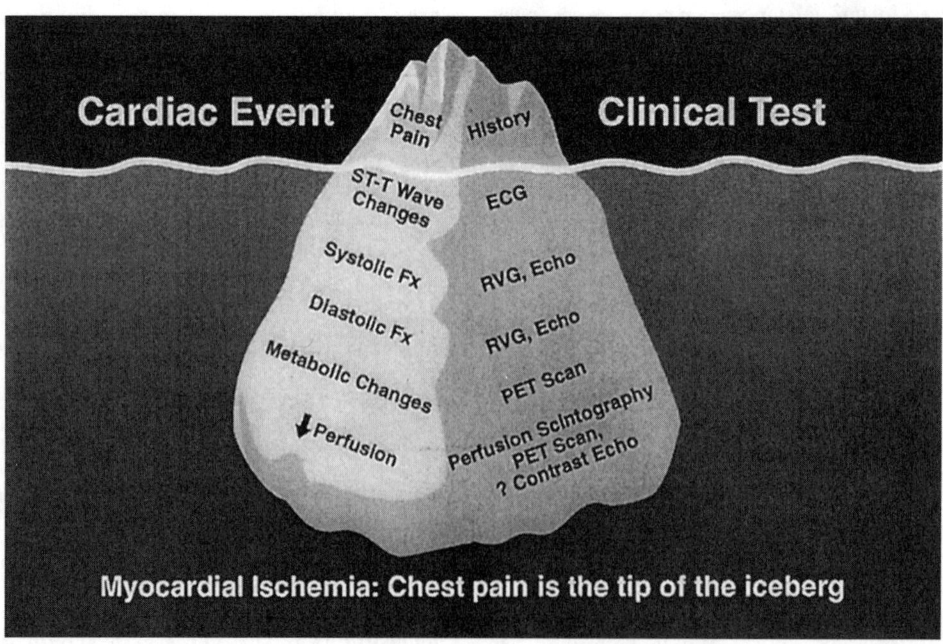

FIG. 40.1. Chest pain reflects only the top of the iceberg of underlying cardiac disease. New cardiological tests are becoming increasingly sensitive in the detection of ischemic coronary artery disease.

A

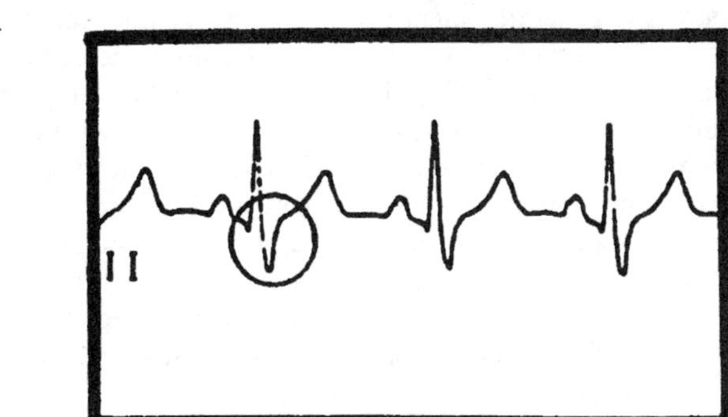

B

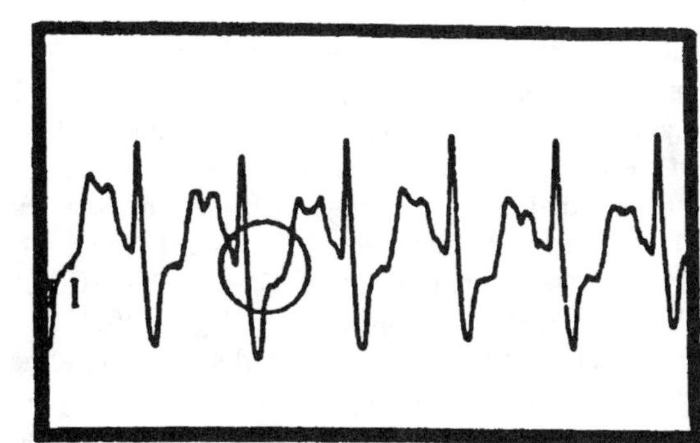

FIG. 40.2. Characteristic electrocardiographic (ECG) pattern indicative of stress-induced ischemia. A. The baseline ECG shows a rhythm of 80 beats/min and the ST segment is marked by the circle. B. ST segment depression, which is indicative of stress-induced ischemia, can occur when cardiac demand increases (160 beats/min).

though recent studies indicate that a steeper decrease (8%) in ejection fraction is required to optimally determine ischemia with mental stress (Becker et al., 1996; Goldberg et al., 1996).

Alternatively, positron emission tomographic techniques can be used to objectify unevenness in the cardiac blood *perfusion* and stress-induced changes thereof. Deanfield and colleagues demonstrated that most (93 out of 95) episodes of ST segment depression during exercise co-occurred with cardiac perfusion deficits (Deanfield et al., 1984). As is discussed later, the correspondence between radionuclide and ECG measures of ischemia is less consistent with mental stress (Rozanski et al., 1988) and cold pressor (Deanfield et al., 1987).

The most commonly used clinical assessment methods for inducible cardiac ischemia, however, are infrequently used in mental stress studies. Generally, exercise or pharmacologically induced ischemia is assessed using echocardiographic or myocardial perfusion single-photon emission computed tomographic (SPECT) studies. SPECT studies may involve thallium and/or technetium (Tc) 99m methoxy isobutyl isonitrile (sestamibi) isotopes. Evidence regarding the prevalence and severity of mental stress-induced ischemia using these standard assessment techniques (Giubbini et al., 1991; Gottdiener et al., 1994) has revealed similar results as studies using radionuclide ventriculography and PET scanning.

Prevalence of Silent Ischemia During Physical Exercise and Laboratory Mental Stress Tasks

Some of the early studies examining the effects of mental stress on myocardial ischemia have found stress-induced ST segment depression (Schiffer, Hartley, Schulman, & Abelmann, 1976; Taggart, Carruthers, & Somerville, 1973; Taggart, Gibbons, & Somerville, 1969). Later studies repeatedly demonstrated, however, that ST segment depression with mental stress is uncommon (Blumenthal et al., 1995; Rozanski et al., 1988; Specchia et al., 1984) and occurs in less than 20% of patients with stable CAD. ST depression during mental stress is especially rare in patients who do not have ST depression during physical exercise testing (Specchia et al., 1984).

As noted earlier, more sensitive methods are now being used in mental stress studies to detect cardiac ischemia, such as echocardiography, radionuclide ventriculography, and positron emission tomography. Indeed, these sensitive measures are indispensable if researchers are to reliably investigate mental stress-induced ischemia. One of the earliest studies in this area was performed by Deanfield and colleagues (Deanfield, Shea, & Kensett, 1984). Utilizing positron emission tomography, mental arithmetic caused ischemia in 12 of 16 (75%) CAD patients. In a study by Rozanski et al. (1988), ischemia was assessed using radionuclide ventriculography during a series of mental stress tasks (mental arithmetic, public speaking, and Stroop color-word test) and exercise testing. Of the 29 patients who had exercise-induced wall motion abnormalities, 21 (71%) had ischemia during mental stress. It was further noted that the speech task was the most potent trigger of ischemia. This finding is consistent with the observation of Ironson et al. (1992) where a speech task, specifically aimed to the recall of an anger provoking event, produced a steeper decrease in ejection fraction than either arithmetic with harassment or a nonanger speech task. Similar results have been reported by Gottdiener and colleagues (1994). These investigators further showed that there was a relation between the severity of exercise stress-induced left ventricular dysfunction and the extent to which mental tasks triggered ischemia, suggesting that mental stress-induced ischemia may in part reflect the severity of underlying CAD. La Veau et al. (1989) and Burg et al. (1993) showed that the onset of ischemia occurs rapidly on the start of mental stress (< 2 min). There are also studies using radionuclide techniques in more ambulatory settings in which it has been found that mental stress can trigger ischemia (Breisblatt et al., 1988; Legault, Langer, Armstrong, & Freeman, 1995) with an overall prevalence ranging from 30% to 70%, whereas ST segment depression was generally not observed.

Chest pain accompanies mental stress-induced ischemia at a very low prevalence (< 10%), whereas estimates of exercise-induced chest pain range from 35% to 70%. Various explanations have been offered for this phenomenon, which is discussed in more detail later. In brief, it has been suggested that silent ischemia is less severe and occurs at lower cardiac demand than symptomatic cardiac ischemia and, in addition, that psychological factors and stress-induced changes in endogenous opioids, such as beta-endorphin, may mediate the relation between mental stress ischemia and chest pain (Deedwania, 1995).

Some evidence suggests that apparently paradoxical reductions in ejection fraction may occur, especially in healthy women, with no angiographic evidence of CAD (Becker et al., 1996). Moreover, even with ischemia of some portion of the left ventricle, compensating increases in contraction of nonischemic segments may serve to maintain or increase ejection fraction with stress. Therefore, the validity of mental stress-induced ischemia can be improved when changes in wall motion or myocardial perfusion are used, rather than either a drop in ejection fraction that would reveal false positives, or ST segment depression that would yield false negative findings.

Psychological Factors Associated With the Inducibility of Laboratory Mental Stress-Induced Ischemia

Based on the evidence that psychological traits such as the Type A behavior pattern, trait anger, and hostility are associated with an increased risk of myocardial infarction and sudden cardiac death (Friedman & Rosenman, 1959; Williams et al., 1980) and these traits are related to increased cardiovascular reactivity (Krantz et al., 1996b), research has examined whether this psychological profile affects the threshold for inducibility of ischemia with mental stress. In a group of 30 patients with coronary artery disease, Burg et al. demonstrated lower anger control and elevated hostility, aggressive responding during the Type A interview, and trait anger in patients with mental stress-induced ischemia ($N = 15$) as compared to nonischemic patients. Of note, the ischemic patients did not score higher on measures of anxiety or neuroticism than nonischemic patients, indicating that the antagonistic behavioral style is specific for a lower threshold for mental stress-induced ischemia. Moreover, no differences in hemodynamic response between ischemic versus nonischemic patients were found, which may suggest that the differences between high hostile patients versus patients without this profile may result from differences in stress-induced changes in coronary supply.

One study found that hostility was associated with more severe ischemia in women and middle-aged men (Helmers et al., 1993). In addition, the combination of both hostility and defensiveness was associated with more severe ischemia during laboratory tasks and demonstrated more frequent episodes of ischemia during the activities of daily life (Helmers et al., 1995). This study indicates that psychological traits, other than hostility may modulate the relation between mental stress and inducibility of cardiac ischemia.

In summary, mental stress tasks may cause ischemia in 30% to 70% of patients with stable CAD. Ischemia with mental stress is generally silent and is commonly not accompanied by ST segment depression. Thus, sensitive measures of cardiac ischemia—such as alterations in wall motion, pump function, or cardiac perfusion—are needed to assess the ischemic effects of mental stress tasks in the laboratory. In addition, if patients do not have ischemia during provocative physical exercise testing, then the likelihood of ischemia with mental stress is small. Hostility is a psychological trait that may potentiate the effects of mental stress on ischemia by increased cardiovascular reactivity and/or exaggerated emotional responses to mental challenges.

MENTAL AND PHYSICAL TRIGGERS OF SILENT ISCHEMIA DURING ACTIVITIES OF DAILY LIFE

Using a methodology involving both ambulatory ECG monitors and structured diary assessments, episodes of ambulatory ischemia can be cross-tabulated with activities and symptoms that co-occur with these ischemic events. Several studies have indicated that mental stress can function as a trigger of ischemia during the activities of daily life. The majority of ambulatory ischemic episodes (> 75%) are silent (Cecchi et al., 1983; Gabbay et al., 1996; Schang & Pepine, 1977). For example, Schang and Pepine (1977) demonstrated that most ischemic events occur at relatively low levels of physical activity, such as slow walking or sitting. In addition, the heart rate at which ambulatory ischemic events occur is reported to be significantly lower than the ischemic heart rate of diagnostic exercise testing (Andrews et al., 1993; Mulcahy et al., 1989). These relatively low ambulatory ischemic heart rates may in part reflect peculiarities of the standard treadmill exercise test, where cardiac demand is increased much faster than what is generally observed during daily monitoring (Panza, Diodati, Callahan, Epstein, & Quyyumi, 1992). It is nonetheless accepted that the majority of ambulatory ischemic events occur at relatively low cardiac demand and are often symptomatically silent; a result that parallels the characteristics of mental stress-induced ischemia in the laboratory.

To examine specific mental and physical activities that trigger ambulatory ischemia, patients' activity ratings during ischemia have been correlated with concomitant ischemia. This procedure is especially worthwhile from a methodological perspective, because most ischemic events are asymptomatic, thereby preventing symptom-based report bias. In a study of patients who were "uncertain" while waiting for the result of their diagnostic coronary angiography, Freeman and colleagues (Freeman, Nixon, Sallabank, & Reavely, 1987) found that ischemia was more prevalent than in a nonstressed control period. Moreover, ambulatory ischemia was related to the extent of perceived distress and elevation of catecholamine levels. Several other studies have used structured diary systems to examine the relation between activities of daily life as triggers of ischemia.

Barry and colleagues (1988) asked patients to complete a diary page each time their activities changed and rate them as either "rest," "usual," or "stress." Most episodes of ischemia occurred at "usual" levels of activity. However, by definition, activities that are labeled as "usual" are engaged in most frequently during daily life. Therefore, the duration of ischemia was divided by the total time spent in each activity category. When correcting for the duration of activities, a graded relation was found such that more intense physical and/or mental activities were associated with more ischemia.

In a similar study in 63 patients with CAD, using a more sophisticated diary system, Gabbay et al. (1996) confirmed that ambulatory ischemia occurred at relatively sedentary activities. Of note was that ischemia occurred in 5% of the time spent in either high physical or high mental activity, as compared to 0.2% of the low activity control episodes (Fig. 40.3). Of the emotions assessed (anger, anxiety, tension, happiness, depression), "anger" was a significant trigger of ischemic events. In addition, among smokers, it was found that ischemia occurred more than five times as often while patients were smoking than when they were not. Although coffee and alcohol consumption were related to ischemia as well, these associations disappeared after adjusting for concomitant smoking.

It is well-documented that cardiac events have an increased incidence in the early morning hours (6 AM to 9 AM). Similar to the pattern of occurrence of clinical manifestations of CAD, there is a circadian rhythm of transient ischemia. In an elegant experiment, Parker et al. (1994) demonstrated that the increases in activity after waking up contribute considerably to the early morning peak of ambulatory ischemia. When patients were instructed to stay in bed until noon, a corresponding delay in the "morning" peak of ischemia was observed. A recent study (Krantz et al., 1996a) showed that physical and mental triggers of ischemia are more potent in the first 6 hours after waking up. In addition, there appears to be an additional underlying endogenous circadian variation in vulnerability for ischemia, independent of patients' activities.

The aforementioned studies lead to the following conclusions: (a) ischemia during the activities of daily life is generally silent (75%–95%); (b) ambulatory ischemia occurs most frequently during patients' usual activities, but when adjusting for the duration of activities, a graded relation is observed between the level of both physical and mental stressors and the likelihood of subsequent ischemia; (c) the ambulatory ischemic heart rate is often lower than with standard treadmill exercise testing. It has furthermore been shown that symptomatic ischemic events are more common during physical than during mental activities (Krantz et al., 1994). The evaluation of triggers of ambulatory ischemia are somewhat limited by the reliance on diaries. Patients generally complete diaries with a frequency of 2 to 3 assessments per hour awake. Because mental and physical activities are proximate triggers of ischemic events, this relatively low rate of assessment might be too infrequent, and therefore underestimate the importance of these triggers. Laboratory procedures are more adequate in this respect, but lack the opportunity to examine real-life stressors. Recent studies have nonetheless demonstrated correspondence between laboratory and field assessments of mental stress-induced ischemia.

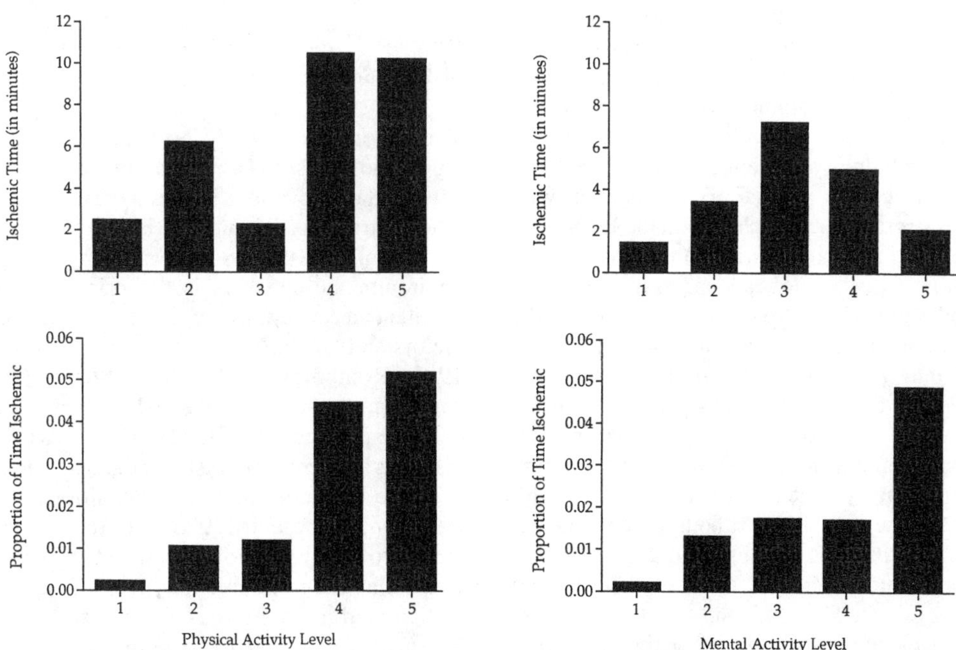

FIG. 40.3. Relation between increasing levels of physical (left panel) and mental (right panel) activity during the activities of daily life and duration of ambulatory ischemia. The upper two panels show the ischemic time unadjusted for the time spent in that specific activity level, the lower panels show the time-adjusted ischemic duration. Adapted from "Triggers of Myocardial Ischemia During Daily Life in Patients With Coronary Artery Disease: Physical and Mental Activities, Anger and Smoking" by F. H. Gabbay et al., 1996, *Journal of the American College of Cardiology, 27,* 585–592.

Correspondence Between Laboratory and Field Assessments of Ischemia

To examine the relation between ischemia during mental stress in the laboratory with ischemia during the activities of daily life, Blumenthal and colleagues (Blumenthal et al., 1995) studied 132 patients with stable CAD in both settings. Mental stress-induced ischemia (during either arithmetic, speech, mirror trace, or the Type A interview) was observed in 45 patients (34%), and ambulatory ischemia occurred in 58 patients (44%). Mental stress-induced ischemia was significantly more present in patients with ambulatory ischemia (26/58; 45%) than in patients without ambulatory ischemia (19/74; 26%). Results with laboratory exercise showed that exercise-induced wall motion abnormalities were unrelated to ambulatory ischemia, whereas exercise-induced ST depression during exercise was significantly associated with ischemia during daily life. To further validate that emotions and mental activities are independent triggers of cardiac ischemia, the authors demonstrated that ambulatory ischemia occurred three times as often in patients with mental stress-induced ischemia in the laboratory, while statistically controlling for the presence of exercise-induced ST segment depression. Similar associations between laboratory mental stress-induced ischemia for ambulatory ischemia were demonstrated by Legoult et al. (1995).

In an earlier study, Gottdiener et al. (1994) reported ambulatory ischemia in 24 out of 45 (53%) CAD patients. Laboratory–field comparisons were possible in 41 patients, of whom 19 (46%) displayed ambulatory ischemia. In contrast to the previously described findings of Blumenthal, no overall association was found between ambulatory ischemia and the presence of mental stress-induced ischemia in the laboratory (10/19; 53%), as compared to patients who did not have ambulatory ischemia (12/22; 55%). However, when the analyses were restricted to ambulatory ischemic episodes that occurred at low physical activity, it was found that patients with evidence of mental stress-induced ischemia in the laboratory had longer (22.9 ± 24.5 min) and more (23) ischemic events than patients without an ischemic response to mental stress (2.4 ± 3.5 min and 8 episodes, respectively). Moreover, the heart rate during ambulatory ischemia was lower (105 ± 15 beats/min) in patients with mental stress-induced ischemia, than in patients lacking this response (114 ± 21 beats/min).

Another laboratory–field study indicated that mental stress-induced increases in heart rate but not blood pressure are predictive of ambulatory ischemia (Krittayaphong, Light, Biles, Ballenger, & Sheps, 1995). Although ischemia occurred in 50% of the 18 patients, the authors did not report its association with ambulatory ischemia. Other methodological problems regarding this study include the small sample size and use of anti-ischemic medication in some of the subjects.

In summary, ischemia during the activities of daily life can be observed with ambulatory ECG monitoring and occurs in 30% to 50% of patients with stable CAD. Typically these ischemic episodes are asymptomatic (approximately 85%) and occur at relatively low heart rates. These characteristics of ambulatory ischemia are similar to the cardiac effects of mental stress in laboratory settings. There is some evidence that mental stress-induced ischemia in the laboratory is a better predictor of ambulatory ischemia than exercise-induced ischemia, especially if these ambulatory episodes occur at low cardiac demand. However, these laboratory–field associations are somewhat limited by the restrictions regarding patient inclusion. That is to say, it has generally been required that patients meet the criteria of a prior diagnostic exercise test indicative of inducibility of ischemia, which makes exercise–mental stress comparisons a complicated issue. The well-documented observation that mental stress-induced ischemia occurs at relatively low cardiac demand and generally occurs without cardiac symptoms, has lead to specific studies regarding possible biobehavioral mechanisms that may account for this phenomenon. These mechanisms are discussed next.

PATHOPHYSIOLOGICAL MECHANISMS OF STRESS-INDUCED SILENT ISCHEMIA

In order to explain the occurrence of silent ischemia, studies have examined factors that affect cardiac demand as well as factors that might impair coronary supply. In addition, several explanations have been purported to specifically account for the absence of symptoms during stress-induced ischemia, including the severity of ischemia itself, increases in endogenous β-endorphins with mental stress, and psychological factors. The following sections address the issues of cardiac demand and supply and mediators of ischemic pain perception.

Increased Cardiac Demand; Effects of Hemodynamic Reactivity

The response to acute psychological challenges most often includes the release of catecholamines and corticosteroids, with concomitant elevations in blood pressure, heart rate, and cardiac contractility (Krantz & Manuck, 1984). This has lead to the assumption that an increased physiological response to environmental stressors is the primary pathophysiological mechanism accounting for the relation between psychosocial factors and CAD (Engebretson & Matthews, 1992; Lepore, 1995; Rumboldt et al., 1993; Suarez, Williams, Kuhn, Zimmerman, & Schanberg, 1991). Increased reactivity may enhance progression of CAD even at early stages of atherosclerosis by increasing vascular damage due to elevated blood pressure and arterial lipid deposition (Fuster, Badimon, Badimon, & Chesebro, 1992). At a later stage of coronary atherosclerosis, which is of relevance for this chapter, increased catecholamine responses may result in episodes of transient ischemia due to increased cardiac demand (Krantz & Manuck, 1984; blood pressure and heart rate) and/or impaired coronary supply related to coronary constriction (Muller, Abela, Nesto, & Tofler, 1994) and increased tendency toward blood clot formation (Markovitz & Matthews, 1991).

Although mental stress can elicit significant hemodynamic responses, the increase in heart rate during mental stress is relatively small compared to exercise testing, whereas blood pressure elevations in CAD patients are comparable to those observed with exercise (Blumenthal et al., 1995; Rozanski et al., 1988). The systolic blood pressure response is probably the main determinant of the cardiac demand component of mental stress-induced ischemia in the laboratory (Blumenthal et al., 1995). Note also that ischemia in itself may cause elevations of heart rate and blood pressure. However, hemodynamic elevations precede rather than follow ischemia. In addition, because ischemia with mental stress is generally silent, it is not likely that symptom-mediated elevation of autonomic nervous system activity is a confounding factor in the observed relation between stress-induced increases in cardiac demand and inducibility of ischemia.

Decreased Coronary Supply; Endothelial Dysfunction and Modifying Risk Factors

Because ischemia triggered by mental stress develops at lower cardiac demand than exercise-induced ischemia, it has been suggested that impaired coronary supply is a crucial factor in this process. Yeung and colleagues (Yeung et al., 1991) demonstrated that mental stress during cardiac catheterization can produce paradoxical coronary constriction in patients with CAD (Fig. 40.4). Other studies since then have confirmed this observation (Boltwood et al., 1993; Lacy et al., 1995), although negative findings have been reported as well (Dakak, Quyyumi, Eisenhofer, Goldstein, & Cannon, 1995; L'Abbate, Simonetti, Carpeggiani, & Michelassi, 1991).

The study by Yeung et al. (1991) found a linear relation between the coronary effects of mental stress and the response to intracoronary acetylcholine ($r = 0.58$). This suggests impaired coronary endothelial function as a pathophysiological mechanism for stress-induced coronary constriction (Fuster et al., 1992; Krantz et al., 1996b; Muller et al., 1994). Moreover, mental stress and acetylcholine administration have been shown to reduce coronary diameter in normal coronary arteries of patients with CAD risk factors, such as hypertension and elevated cholesterol (Kuhn et al., 1991; Vita et al., 1990, 1992). Preliminary evidence is available showing that mental stress-induced coronary constriction in smooth arteries is more severe in male coronary patients with hypertension and/or elevated LDL cholesterol (Gottdiener et al., 1997). Stress-induced factors that affect endothelial function may include circulating catecholamines (Fuster et al., 1992) and possibly vagal withdrawal. Vagal withdrawal has been shown to precede silent myocardial ischemia during daily life (Goseki, Matsubara, Takahashi, Takeuchi, & Ibukiyama, 1994; Kop et al., 1995; Verdino et al., 1995), and in dogs it has been demonstrated that pharmacological or surgical blockade of cardiac vagal innervation results in coronary constriction (Kovach, Gottdiener, & Verrier, 1995).

Therefore, mental stress may cause (silent) ischemia by in part reducing coronary supply. This process results from endothelial dysfunction and is most likely mediated by CAD risk factors and sympathovagal activation of the heart.

Physical and Psychological Factors Accounting for the Absence of Pain During Myocardial Ischemia

In many medical conditions, visceral pain is a very poor self-warning system for pathophysiological abnormalities. Mechanisms of cardiac pain perception have been disappointingly elusive (Malliani, 1986). There are no nerve endings in the myocardium that have a specific function in mediating pain perception. The uncoupling of cardiac ischemia and symptomatology has been documented by Krantz et al. (1994). Using Holter monitoring and structured diary techniques, 85% of the ischemic episodes were found to be silent. Moreover, as shown in Fig. 40.5, 66% of the reports of typical chest pain were not accompanied by ischemia. Furthermore, ischemia during physical activity was significantly more often symptomatic than ischemia occurring at high mental activity. Table 40.1 summarizes factors that have been found to be associated with the absence of anginal symptoms during cardiac ischemia.

Evidence has indicated that ischemia is less severe in asymptomatic episodes (Dellborg, Emanuelsson, & Swedberg, 1993; Hecht, DeBord, Sotomayor, Shaw, & Ryan, 1994; Hendler, Greyson, Robinson, & Freeman, 1992; Klein, Chao, Berman, & Rozanski, 1994; Marwick, 1995; Nihoyannopoulos, Marsonis, Joshi, Athanassopoulos, & Oakley, 1995). In part, the less severe ischemia could result from the effects of collateral coronary flow that may act as a natural bypass (Dellborg et al., 1993), or by more cardiac tis-

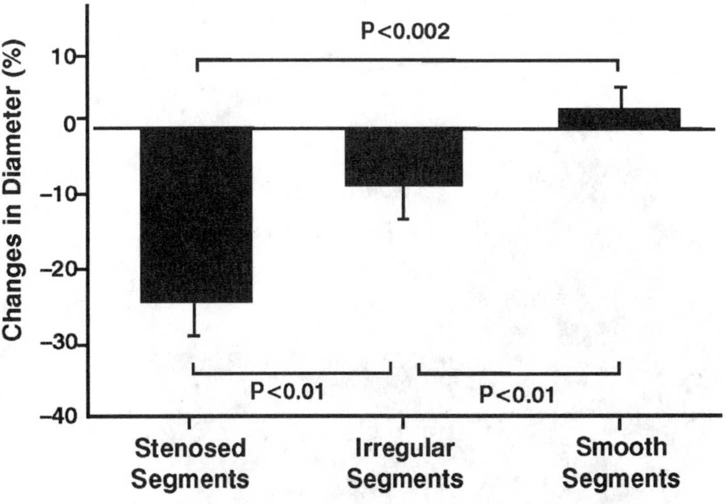

FIG. 40.4. Effects of mental stress on coronary diameter in stenosed segments, irregular segments, and smooth segments. Stenosed segments constricted significantly more (–24%) than irregular (–9%) and nondiseased (3%) segments. Adapted from "The Effect of Atherosclerosis on the Vasomotor Response of Coronary Arteries to Mental Stress" by Yeung et al., 1991, *New England Journal of Medicine, 325,* 1551–1556.

sue damage at rest as reflected by previous transmural (Q-wave) myocardial infarction (Titus & Sherman, 1991). It should be noted, however, that less severe ischemia during silent episodes has not been confirmed in several studies (Deanfield et al., 1984; Gasperetti, Burwell, & Beller, 1990; Light et al., 1991; Torosian, Lumley, Pickard, & Ketterer, 1997). Other studies have shown that cardiac demand is lower during asymptomatic ischemia (Deanfield et al., 1983; Schang & Pepine, 1977), but this is not an unchallenged position either (Carboni, Lahiri, Cashman, & Raftery, 1987). In addition, effective pharmacological treatment of documented ischemia is not necessarily accompanied by a reduction of anginal complaints (Borzak et al., 1993), which further supports the imperfect association between symptoms and underlying biological processes.

A second mechanism involves gradual decreases in autonomous nervous system functioning, which may result in impaired pain perception. Autonomic nervous system dysfunction may explain the increased prevalence of silent ischemia in diabetic patients due to peripheral neuropathy (Hikita et al., 1993; Langer, Freeman, Josse, Steiner, & Armstrong, 1991) and in the elderly (Ambepitiya, Roberts, Ranjadayalan, & Tallis, 1994).

Thirdly, it has been reported that patients with silent ischemia are characterized by a generalized higher threshold for pain stimuli (Droste & Roskamm, 1983). Light, Sheps, and colleagues demonstrated that mental stress may increase plasma β-endorphin concentrations (Light et al., 1991; Sheps et al., 1995), thereby increasing the pain-sensitivity threshold. The importance of endogenous opioids is further supported by studies examining the effects of coronary angioplasty. This invasive procedure is used to remove obstructive coronary blockages by inflating a small balloon at the site of coronary obstruction, temporarily causing ischemia due to complete occlusion of a major coronary artery. Even in the setting of such a strong ischemic stimulus, approximately 30% of the patients remain free of symptoms (Dellborg et al., 1993; Falcone et al., 1993; Titus & Sherman, 1991). Higher plasma endorphin levels have been reported in patients without symptoms during angioplasty, whereas no difference in the severity or duration of ischemia has been noted between symptomatic and silent patients (Falcone et al., 1993). Biomedical predictors of "silent" ischemia may therefore include: lower cardiac demand and less severe ischemia; higher pain threshold due to autonomic nervous system dysfunction; and elevated endorphin levels. Nonetheless, the medical and biological predictors of absence of symptoms have as yet not revealed a consistent pattern of results and leaves room for psychological investigations regarding the nature of silent ischemia.

Recently, patterns of brain activity in symptomatic versus asymptomatic cardiac ischemia have been investigated using positron emission tomography (PET) studies assessing changes in cerebral blood flow (Rosen et al., 1996). Ischemia was induced using dobutamine, a β1-agonist that does not pass the blood–brain barrier. Ischemia resulted in increased

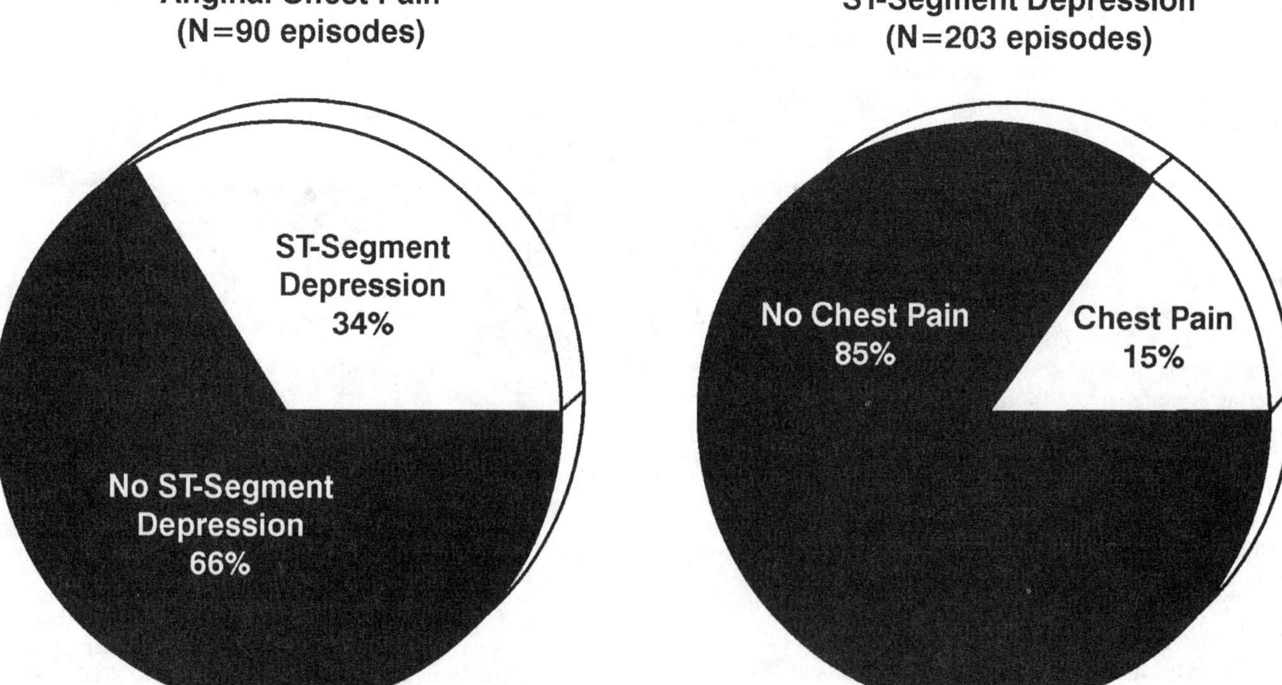

FIG. 40.5. Association of cardiac ischemia (ST segment depression) and anginal pain. Thirty-one of 90 reports of chest pain (34%) were accompanied by ischemia (left), whereas only 31 of the 203 ischemic episodes were associated with chest pain (15%). Adapted from "Triggers of Angina and ST-Segment Depression in Ambulatory Patients With Coronary Artery Disease: Evidence for an Uncoupling of Angina and Ischemia, by Krantz et al., 1994, *American Heart Journal, 128,* 703–712.

activation of the brain stem, thalamus, and left hippocampal gyrus. Moreover, sustained alterations in brain activity were noted in the thalamus and dorsal frontal cortex until 13 minutes postischemia. Patients with painful ischemia ($N = 9$) displayed much more extended cerebral activation than patients with silent ischemia ($N = 9$), specifically in the ventral cyngulate and dorsal frontal regions. Rosen et al. hypothesized that "gating" at the thalamic level may account for the altered central nervous system processing of cardiac ischemia. Alternatively, the perception of pain may induce cortical activation, and this study does not allow the differentiation of cause and effect of painful ischemia and concomitant cerebral activation.

Among the psychological factors that have been reported to predict the absence of ischemic symptoms is the observation that lower levels of depression are variably associated with silent ischemia (Davies et al., 1993; Light et al., 1991). In one study (Light et al., 1991) examining 45 CAD patients with ST depression during exercise testing, it was found that low scores on the Minnesota Multiphasic Personality Inventory (MMPI) depression subscale was associated with a lower frequency of anginal symptoms (28%) as compared to patients who had high depression scores (54%). Interestingly, these results were congruent with exercise-induced β-endorphins response, which was significantly higher in the nondepressed patients. Some evidence indicates that the Type A behavior pattern (Keefe, Castell, & Blumenthal, 1986; Siegel et al., 1989) and anger control (Torosian et al., 1997) are related to silent ischemia, but this has not been confirmed in other studies (Davies et al., 1993; Light et al., 1991). Type A behavior may be related to the denial of physical and mental complaints. Denial has been found to predict absence of symptoms during ischemia (Freedland et al., 1991) and may be the general factor that accounts for the evidence supporting various symptom-based psychological constructs, such as low symptom awareness (Freedland et al., 1991), undercomplaining (Davies et al., 1993), and certain components of alexithymia (Torosian et al., 1997). In this respect, it is of relevance that alexithymia is related to myocardial infarction without symptoms and a delay in hospitalization for myocardial infarction (Kenyon et al., 1992; Theisen et al., 1995). This is in contrast, however, to the contention that alexithymia relates to symptom overreporting. To summarize, although the literature on psychological predictors of silent ischemia is still far from consistent, some evidence suggests that silent ischemia is related to lower depression scores and a tendency toward denial of symptoms.

TABLE 40.1
Possible Mediators Responsible for the Absence of Symptoms During Episodes of Myocardial Ischemia

Cardiovascular factors

- Low cardiac demand (mental stress, ambulatory ischemia)
- Ischemia less severe
- Collateral coronary flow
- Prior Q-wave infarction
- Peripheral Claudication
- Anti-anginal medication

Factors Affecting Autonomous and Central Nervous System Function

- Diabetes mellitus
- Age
- Inhibition of autonomic input at thalamic level

General Pain Threshold

- Elevated a-endorphins
- Stress-induced decrease in sensitivity

Psychological Factors

- Low depression
- Denial of symptoms

PREDICTIVE VALUE OF SILENT AND MENTAL STRESS-INDUCED ISCHEMIA FOR FUTURE CARDIAC EVENTS

The prognostic importance of painless ischemia will be dependent on the method used for its detection. In general, most studies indicate that ischemic episodes during the activities of daily life are associated with an adverse risk of myocardial infarction and cardiac death, as is the presence of exercise-induced ischemia (e.g., Jain, Burg, Soufer, & Zaret, 1995; Pepine et al., 1994; Rocco et al., 1988). However, the presence or absence of ischemic pain has not added to the prediction of long-term outcome (Jain et al., 1995). For example, in a study of 406 post- MI patients, ambulatory ischemia was predictive of recurrent MI and unstable angina, independent of presence of anginal pain, physical exercise stress test results, cardiac function, and other clinical predictors.

Evidence accumulates that ischemia elicited by mental stress during laboratory tasks is predictive of adverse outcome (Jain et al., 1995; Jiang et al., 1996; Krantz et al., 1999). In a 2-year follow-up study in 30 patients with exercise inducible ischemia and coronary disease (Jain et al., 1995), mental stress was administered using the arithmetic task with harassment. Fifteen patients developed transient wall motion abnormalities with mental stress of whom 10 (67%) suffered a cardiac event during follow-up, as compared to 4 of 15 (27%) patients without mental stress-induced ischemia. In addition to the small sample size, this study is limited by the continued use of cardiac medication during mental stress testing and the use of suboptimal cardiac endpoints during follow-up such as episodes of unstable angina.

In a more recent study, Jiang et al. followed 126 patients with coronary disease for an average duration of 2 years and recorded the incidence of cardiac death, myocardial infarction, and coronary revascularization (Jiang et al., 1996). Ischemia was provoked in 67% of the patients using a series of five mental tasks. The investigators found that new cardiac events occurred in 27.4% of the patients with mental stress-induced ischemia, as compared to 11.9% of patients who did not develop ischemia during mental stress (Fig. 40.6). The most potent mental stress predictor of adverse outcome was the arithmetic task (OR = 3.9; $p < .001$). Exercise-induced ST segment depression was a marginally significant predictor of new events (OR = 1.8; $p = .07$), whereas ambulatory ischemia was unrelated to outcome. A recent follow-up study was consistent with this finding and showed that mental stress-induced ischemia was associated with a greater than twofold risk for an adverse long-term outcome. No such associations were found with exercise-induced ischemia (Krantz et al., in press).

At present it is not known whether the prognostic value of ischemia induced by mental stress reflects its association with ambulatory measures of ischemia, the severity of underlying CAD, or other cardiovascular risk factors. It is undoubtedly important to combine research from both behavioral and medical disciplines to explain the absence of symptoms during cardiac ischemia and to clarify the prognostic value of silent ischemia for future cardiac events.

CONCLUSIONS

Mental stress is a potent trigger of cardiac ischemia in patients with coronary artery disease. Characteristic of mental stress-induced ischemia is the absence of symptoms such as chest pain and the lower cardiac demand at onset of ischemia. This has lead to the hypothesis that impaired cardiac blood supply following paradoxical stress-induced constriction of the coronary arteries is a crucial factor in ischemia triggered by mental stress. Future studies are needed to examine whether psychological factors such as hostility are associated with increased coronary constriction to mental stress.

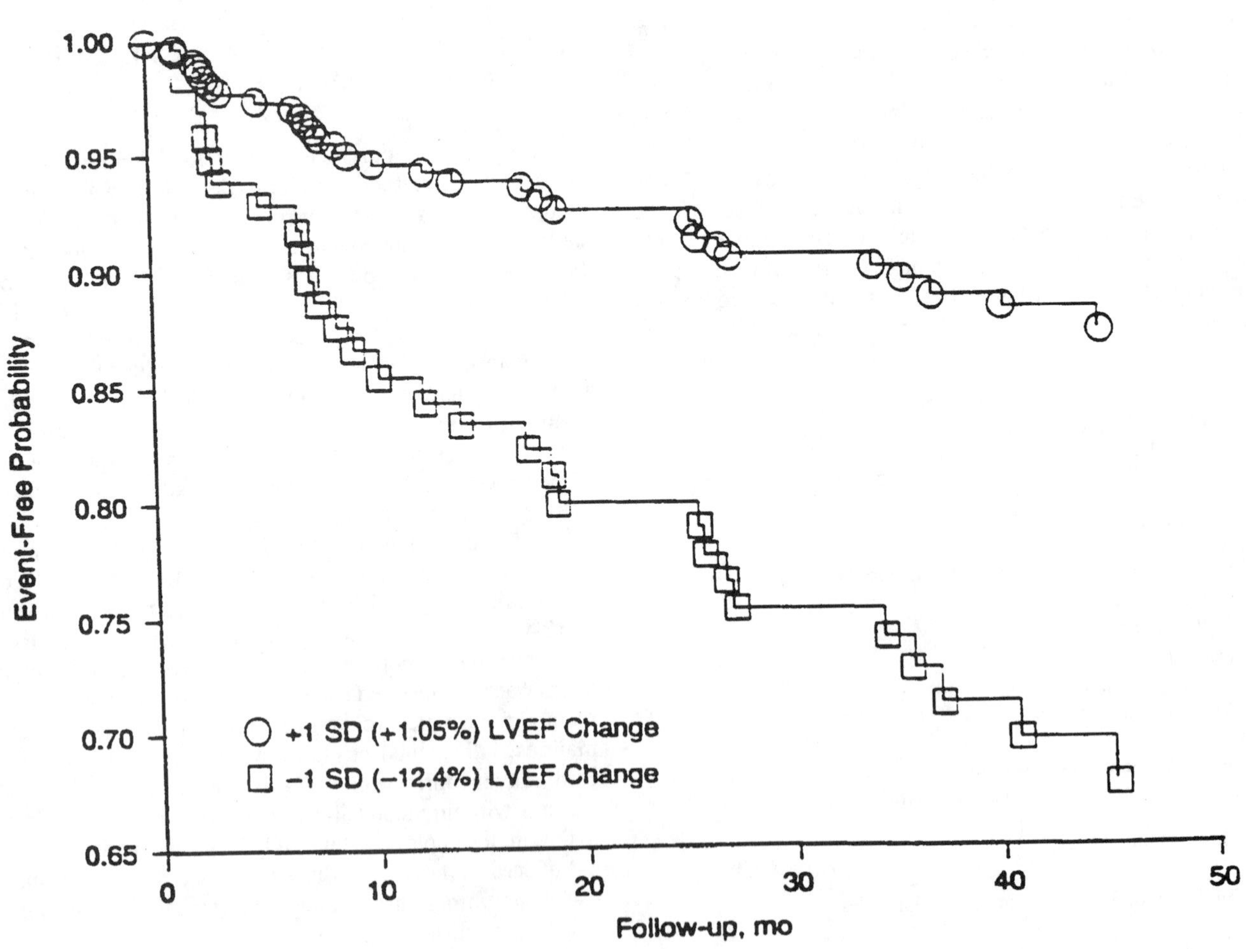

FIG. 40.6. Probability of an event-free survival as related to mental stress-induced ischemia. Patients who had less than 1 standard deviation decrease in ejection fraction (−12.4%) with mental stress had an adjusted relative risk of 2.4 ($p = .02$) for an adverse outcome during follow-up compared to patients with a > 1 standard deviation increase in ejection fraction (+1%) with mental stress. Adapted from "Mental Stress-Induced Myocardial Ischemia and Cardiac Events" by Jiang et al., 1996, *Journal of the American Medical Association, 275,* 1651–1656.

An important and unresolved issue is the dissociation between chest pain and cardiac ischemia. Possible mechanisms of asymptomatic ischemia have been discussed, including cardiovascular factors such as lower cardiac demand and lesser severity of ischemia, the autonomous nervous system function, elevated endogenous opioids, and psychological factors such as lower depression scores and denial of symptoms. In addition, possible differences in cerebral processing may account for altered perception of pain in cardiac ischemia. Large studies will be needed to determine the individual and interactive contributions of biologic and psychological factors in silent ischemia.

Finally, a series of studies are now available in support of the predictive value of mental stress-induced ischemia for future cardiac events in patients with established coronary artery disease. Most studies were restricted to patients with a prior positive exercise test for ischemia. This limits the possibility to disentangle the predictive value of ischemia induced by mental versus physical stress. In addition, further research is needed to clarify the biobehavioral mechanisms accounting for the higher incidence of adverse events in patients with ischemia during mental stress in the laboratory. It could be that patients with mental stress-induced ischemia have a worse cardiac condition to start with, but it is also conceivable that increased cardiovascular reactivity and a higher prevalence of ischemic episodes during the activities of daily life account for the predictive value of mental stress ischemia. Given the specific hemodynamic characteristics of mental stress-induced ischemia, pharmacological treatments targeted to counteract coronary vasoconstriction combined with psychological interventions directed at reducing anger, hostility, and depressive symptoms may ultimately prove beneficial in the treatment of patients with coronary artery disease.

ACKNOWLEDGMENTS

The research presented in this chapter was made possible by grants from the National Institutes of Health (HL47337, HL58638), the USUHS (RO7233), and the Dutch Heart Foundation (94-098).

The opinions and assertions expressed herein are those of the author and should not be construed as reflecting those of the USUHS or of the U.S. Department of Defense.

REFERENCES

Ambepitiya, G., Roberts, M., Ranjadayalan, K., & Tallis, R. (1994). Silent exertional myocardial ischemia in the elderly: A quantitative analysis of anginal perceptual threshold and the influence of autonomic function. *Journal of the American Geriatric Society, 42*(7), 732–737.

Andrews, T. C., Fenton, T., Toyosaki, N., Glasser, S. P., Young, P. M., MacCallum, G., Gibson, R. S., Shook, T. L., & Stone, P. H. (1993). Subsets of ambulatory myocardial ischemia based on heart rate activity. Circadian distribution and response to anti-ischemic medication. The Angina and Silent Ischemia Study Group (ASIS). *Circulation, 88,* 92–100.

Appels, A. (1990). Mental precursors of myocardial infarction . *British Journal of Psychiatry, 156,* 465–471.

Barry, J., Selwyn, A. P., Nabel, E. G., Rocco, M. B., Mead, K., Campbell, S., & Rebecca, G. (1988). Frequency of ST-segment depression produced by mental stress in stable angina pectoris from coronary artery disease. *American Journal of Cardiology, 61,* 989–993.

Becker, L. C., Pepine, C. J., Bonsall, R., Cohen, J. D., Goldberg, A. D., Coghlan, C., Stone, P. H., Forman, S., Knatternud, G., Sheps, D. S., & Kaufmann, P. G. (1996). Left ventricular, peripheral vascular, and neurohormonal responses to mental stress in normal middle-aged men and women: Reference group for the psychophysiological investigations of myocardial ischemia (PIMI) study. *Circulation, 94,* 2768–2777.

Blumenthal, J. A., Jiang, W., Waugh, R. A., Frid, D. J., Morris, J. J., Coleman, R. E., Hanson, M., Babyak, M., Thyrum, E. T., & Krantz, D. S. (1995). Mental stress-induced ischemia in the laboratory and ambulatory ischemia during daily life. Association and hemodynamic features. *Circulation, 92*(8), 2102–2108.

Boltwood, M. D., Taylor, C. B., Burke, M. B., Grogin, H., & Giacomini, J. (1993). Anger report predicts coronary artery vasomotor response to mental stress in atherosclerotic segments. *American Journal of Cardiology, 72*(18), 1361–1365.

Borzak, S., Fenton, T., Glasser, S. P., Shook, T. L., MacCallum, G., Young, P. M., & Stone, P. H. (1993). Discordance between effects of anti-ischemic therapy on ambulatory ischemia, exercise performance and anginal symptoms in patients with stable angina pectoris. The Angina and Silent Ischemia Study Group (ASIS). *Journal of the American College of Cardiology, 21*(7), 1605–1611.

Braunwald, E. (1988). *Heart disease.* Philadelphia: Saunders.

Breisblatt, W. M., Weiland, F. L., McLain, J. R., Tomlinson, G. C., Burns, M. J., & Spaccavento, L. J. (1988). Usefulness of ambulatory radionuclide monitoring of left ventricular function early after acute myocardial infarction for predicting residual myocardial ischemia. *American Journal of Cardiology, 62*(16), 1005–1010.

Burg, M. M., Jain, D., Soufer, R., Kerns, R. D., & Zaret, B. L. (1993). Role of behavioral and psychological factors in mental stress-induced silent left ventricular dysfunction in coronary artery disease. *Journal of the American College of Cardiology, 22*(2), 440–448.

Carboni, G. P., Lahiri, A., Cashman, P. M., & Raftery, E. B. (1987). Ambulatory heart rate and ST-segment depression during painful and silent myocardial ischemia in chronic stable angina pectoris. *American Journal of Cardiology, 59*(12), 1029–1034.

Cecchi, A., Dovellini, E., Marchi, F., Pucci, P., Santoro, G., & Fazzini, P. (1983). Silent myocardial ischemia during ambulatory electrocardiographic monitoring in patients with effort angina. *Journal of the American College of Cardiology, 1,* 934–939.

Dakak, N., Quyyumi, A. A., Eisenhofer, G., Goldstein, D. S., & Cannon, R. O., III. (1995). Sympathetically mediated effects of mental stress on the cardiac microcirculation of patients with coronary artery disease. *American Journal of Cardiology, 76*(3), 125–130.

Davies, R. F., Linden, W., Habibi, H., Klinke, W. P., Nadeau, C., Phaneuf, D. C., Lepage, S., Dessain, P., & Buttars, J. A. (1993). Relative importance of psychologic traits and severity of ischemia in causing angina during treadmill exercise. Canadian Amlodipine/Atenolol in Silent Ischemia Study (CASIS) Investigators. *Journal of the American College of Cardiology, 21*(2), 331–336.

Deanfield, J. E., Maseri, A., Selwyn, A. P., Ribeiro, P., Chierchia, S., Krikler, S., & Morgan, M. (1983). Myocardial ischaemia during daily life in patients with stable angina: Its relation to symptoms and heart rate changes. *The Lancet, 2*(8353), 753–758.

Deanfield, J. E., Shea, M., & Kensett, M. (1984). Silent ischemia due to mental stress. *The Lancet, 2,* 1001–1005.

Deanfield, J. E., Shea, M., Ribiero, P., de Landsheere, C. M., Wilson, R. A., Horlock, P., & Selwyn, A. P. (1984). Transient ST-segment depression as a marker of myocardial ischemia during daily life. *American Journal of Cardiology, 54*(10), 1195–1200.

Deanfield, J. E., Shea, M., Ribiero, P., de Landsheere, C. M., Wilson, R. A., Horlock, P., & Selwyn, A. P. (1987). Asymptomatic myocardial ischemia following cold provocation. *American Heart Journal, 114*(3), 469–476.

Deedwania, P. C. (1995). Mental stress, pain perception and risk of silent ischemia. *Journal of the American College of Cardiology, 25*(7), 1504–1506.

Dellborg, M., Emanuelsson, H., & Swedberg, K. (1993). Silent myocardial ischemia during coronary angioplasty. *Cardiology, 82*(5), 325–334.

Droste, C., & Roskamm, H. (1983). Experimental pain measurement in patients with asymptomatic myocardial ischemia. *Journal of the American College of Cardiology, 1*(3), 940–945.

Engebretson, T. O., & Matthews, K. A. (1992). Dimensions of hostility in men, women, and boys: Relationships to personality and cardiovascular responses to stress. *Psychosomatic Medicine, 54*(3), 311–323.

Falcone, C., Guasti, L., Ochan, M., Codega, S., Tortorici, M., Angoli, L., Bergamaschi, R., & Montemartini, C. (1993). Beta-endorphins during coronary angioplasty in patients with silent or symptomatic myocardial ischemia. *Journal of the American College of Cardiology, 22*(6), 1614–1620.

Freedland, K. E., Carney, R. M., Krone, R. J., Smith, L. J., Rich, M. W., Eisenkramer, G., & Fischer, K. C. (1991). Psychological factors in silent myocardial ischemia. *Psychosomatic Medicine, 53*(1), 13–24.

Freeman, L., Nixon, P., Sallabank, P., & Reavely, D. (1987). Psychological stress and silent myocardial ischemia. *American Heart Journal, 114,* 477–482.

Friedman, M., & Rosenman, R. (1959). Association of specific overt behavior pattern with blood and cardiovascular findings: blood cholesterol level, blood clotting time, incidence of arcis senilis and clinical coronary artery disease. *Journal of the American Medical Association, 169,* 1286–1296.

Fuster, V., Badimon, L., Badimon, J. J., & Chesebro, J. H. (1992). The pathogenesis of coronary artery disease and the acute coronary syndromes (1). *New England Journal of Medicine, 326,* 242–250.

Gabbay, F. H., Krantz, D. S., Kop, W. J., Hedges, S. M., Klein, J., Gottdiener, J. S., & Rozanski, A. (1996). Triggers of myocardial ischemia during daily life in patients with coronary artery disease: Physical and mental activities, anger and smoking. *Journal of the American College of Cardiology, 27,* 585–592.

Gasperetti, C. M., Burwell, L. R., & Beller, G. A. (1990). Prevalence of and variables associated with silent myocardial ischemia on exercise thallium-201 stress testing. *Journal of the American College of Cardiology, 16*(1), 115–123.

Giubbini, R., Galli, M., Campini, R., Bosimini, E., Bencivelli, W., & Tavazzi, L. (1991). Effects of mental stress on myocardial perfusion in patients with ischemic heart disease. *Circulation, 83,* II100–II107.

Goldberg, A. D., Becker, L. C., Bonsall, R., Cohen, J. D., Ketterer, M. W., Kaufmann, P. G., Krantz, D. S., Light, K. C., McMahon, R. P., Noreuil, T., Pepine, C. J., Raczynski, J., Stone, P. H., Strother, D., Taylor, H., & Sheps, D. S. (1996). Ischemic, hemodynamic, and neurohormonal responses to mental and exercise stress. Experience from the Psychophysiological Investigations of Myocardial Ischemia Study (PIMI). *Circulation, 94*(10), 2402–2409.

Goseki, Y., Matsubara, T., Takahashi, N., Takeuchi, T., & Ibukiyama, C. (1994). Heart rate variability before the occurrence of silent myocardial ischemia during ambulatory monitoring. *American Journal of Cardiology, 73*(12), 845–849.

Gottdiener, J. S., Howell, R. H., Kop, W. J., Lu, D., Papademetriou, V., Popma, J. J., Ferguson, M., Vernalis, M., & Krantz, D. S. (1997). Serum lipids and hypertension potentiate coronary vasoconstriction with mental stress . *Journal of the American College of Cardiology, 29,* 524A

Gottdiener, J. S., Krantz, D. S., Howell, R. H., Hecht, G. M., Klein, J., Falconer, J. J., & Rozanski, A. (1994). Induction of silent myocardial ischemia with mental stress testing: Relation to the triggers of ischemia during daily life activities and to ischemic functional severity. *Journal of the American College of Cardiology, 24*(7), 1645–1651.

Hecht, H. S., DeBord, L., Sotomayor, N., Shaw, R., & Ryan, C. (1994). Truly silent ischemia and the relationship of chest pain and ST segment changes to the amount of ischemic myocardium: Evaluation by supine bicycle stress echocardiography. *Journal of the American College of Cardiology, 23*(2), 369–376.

Helmers, K. F., Krantz, D. S., Bairey-Merz, C. N., Kop, W. J., Gottdiener, J. S., & Rozanski, A. (1995). Defensive hostility: Relationship to multiple markers of cardiac ischemia in patients with coronary disease. *Health Psychology, 14,* 202–209.

Helmers, K. F., Krantz, D. S., Howell, R. H., Klein, J., Bairey, C. N., & Rozanski, A. (1993). Hostility and myocardial ischemia in coronary artery disease patients: evaluation by gender and ischemic index . *Psychosomatic Medicine, 55*(1), 29–36.

Hendler, A. L., Greyson, N. D., Robinson, M. G., & Freeman, M. R. (1992). Patients with symptomatic ischemia have larger thallium perfusion abnormalities and more adverse prognosis than patients with silent ischemia. *Canadian Journal of Cardiology, 8*(8), 814–818.

Hikita, H., Kurita, A., Takase, B., Nagayoshi, H., Uehata, A., Nishioka, T., Mitani, H., Mizuno, K., & Nakamura, H. (1993). Usefulness of plasma beta-endorphin level, pain threshold and autonomic function in assessing silent myocardial ischemia in patients with and without diabetes mellitus. *American Journal of Cardiology, 72*(2), 140–143.

Ironson, G., Taylor, C. B., Boltwood, M., Bartzokis, T., Dennis, C., Chesney, M., Spitzer, S., & Segall, G. M. (1992). Effects of anger on left ventricular ejection fraction in coronary artery disease. *American Journal of Cardiology, 70*(3), 281–285.

Jain, D., Burg, M., Soufer, R., & Zaret, B. L. (1995). Prognostic implications of mental stress-induced silent left ventricular dysfunction in patients with stable angina pectoris. *American Journal of Cardiology, 76*(1), 31–35.

Jiang, W., Babyak, M., Krantz, D. S., Waugh, R. A., Coleman, E. R., Hanson, M. M., Fird, D. J., McNulty, S., Morris, J. J., O'Connor, C. M., & Blumenthal, J. A. (1996). Mental stress-induced myocardial ischemia and cardiac events. *Journal of the American Medical Association, 275,* 1651–1656.

Kannel, W. B., & Abbott, R. D. (1984). Incidence and prognosis of unrecognized myocardial infarction. an update on the Framingham study. *New England Journal of Medicine, 311*(18), 1144–1147.

Keefe, F. J., Castell, P. J., & Blumenthal, J. A. (1986). Angina pectoris in Type a and Type b cardiac patients. *Pain, 27*(2), 211–218.

Kenyon, L. W., Ketterer, M. W., Gheorghiade, M., & Goldstein, S. (1992). Delay in response to acute myocardial infarction. *Circulation, 85*(6), 2333

Klein, J., Chao, S. Y., Berman, D. S., & Rozanski, A. (1994). Is "silent" myocardial ischemia really as severe as symptomatic ischemia? The analytical effect of patient selection biases. *Circulation, 89*(5), 1958–1966.

Kop, W. J. (1997). Acute and chronic psychological risk factors for coronary syndromes: Moderating effects of coronary artery disease severity. *Journal of Psychosomatic Research, 43,* 167–181.

Kop, W. J., Gottdiener, J. S., Verdino, R., Howell, R. H., Haddad, A. H., & Krantz, D. S. (1995). Relation of mental stress and vagal withdrawal to silent ischemia during the activities of daily life. *Circulation, 94,* I-676

Kovach, J. A., Gottdiener, J. S., & Verrier, R. L. (1995). Vagal modulation of epicardial coronary artery size in dogs. A two-dimensional intravascular ultrasound study. *Circulation, 92,* 2291–2298.

Krantz, D. S., Hedges, S. M., Gabbay, F. H., Klein, J., Falconer, J. J., Merz, C. N., Gottdiener, J. S., Lutz, H., & Rozanski, A. (1994). Triggers of angina and ST-segment depression in ambulatory patients with coronary artery disease: Evidence for an uncoupling of angina and ischemia. *American Heart Journal, 128*(4), 703–712.

Krantz, D. S., Kop, W. J., Gabbay, F., Rozanski, A., Barnard, M., Klein, J., Pardo, Y., & Gottdiener, J. S. (1996a). Circadian variation of ambulatory ischemia: Triggering by daily activities and evidence for an endogenous circadian component. *Circulation, 93,* 1364–1371.

Krantz, D. S., Kop, W. J., Santiago, H. T., & Gottdiener, J. S. (1996b). Mental stress as a trigger of myocardial ischemia and infarction. *Cardiology Clinics, 14*(2), 271–287.

Krantz, D. S., & Manuck, S. B. (1984). Acute psychophysiologic reactivity and risk or cardiovascular disease: A review and methodologic critique. *Psychological Bulletin, 96,* 435–464.

Krantz, D. S., Santiago, H. T., Kop, W. J., Bairey-Merz, C. N., Rozanski, A., & Gottdiener, J. S. (1999). Prognostic value of mental stress testing in coronary artery disease. *American Journal of Cardiology.*

Krittayaphong, R., Light, K. C., Biles, P. L., Ballenger, M. N., & Sheps, D. S. (1995). Increased heart rate response to laboratory-induced mental stress predicts frequency and duration of daily life ambulatory myocardial ischemia in patients with coronary artery disease. *American Journal of Cardiology, 76*(10), 657–660.

Kuhn, F. E., Mohler, E. R., Satler, L. F., Reagan, K., Lu, D. Y., & Rackley, C. E. (1991). Effects of high-density lipoprotein on acetylcholine-induced coronary vasoreactivity. *American Journal of Cardiology, 68*(15), 1425–1430.

L'Abbate, A., Simonetti, I., Carpeggiani, C., & Michelassi, C. (1991). Coronary dynamics and mental arithmetic stress in humans. *Circulation, 83,* II94–II99.

Lacy, C. R., Contrada, R. J., Robbins, M. L., Tannenbaum, A. K., Moreyra, A. E., Chelton, S., & Kostis, J. B. (1995). Coronary vasoconstriction induced by mental stress (simulated public speaking). *American Journal of Cardiology, 75*(7), 503–505.

Langer, A., Freeman, M. R., Josse, R. G., Steiner, G., & Armstrong, P. W. (1991). Detection of silent myocardial ischemia in diabetes mellitus. *American Journal of Cardiology, 67*(13), 1073–1078.

La Veau, P. J., Rozanski, A., Krantz, D. S., Cornell, C. E., Cattanach, L., Zaret, B. L., & Wackers, F. J. (1989). Transient left ventricular dysfunction during provocative mental stress in patients with coronary artery disease. *American Heart Journal, 118*(1), 1–8.

Legault, S. E., Langer, A., Armstrong, P. W., & Freeman, M. R. (1995). Usefulness of ischemic response to mental stress in predicting silent myocardial ischemia during ambulatory monitoring. *American Journal of Cardiology, 75*(15), 1007–1011.

Lepore, S. J. (1995). Cynicism, social support, and cardiovascular reactivity. *Health Psychology, 14*(3), 210–216.

Light, K. C., Herbst, M. C., Bragdon, E. E., Hinderliter, A. L., Koch, G. G., Davis, M. R., & Sheps, D. S. (1991). Depression and Type A behavior pattern in patients with coronary artery disease: Relationships to painful versus silent myocardial ischemia and beta-endorphin responses during exercise. *Psychosomatic Medicine, 53*(6), 669–683.

Malliani, A. (1986). The elusive link between transient myocardial ischemia and pain. *Circulation, 73*(2), 201–204.

Markovitz, J. H., & Matthews, K. A. (1991). Platelets and coronary heart disease: Potential psychophysiologic mechanisms. *Psychosomatic Medicine, 53,* 643–668.

Marwick, T. H. (1995). Is silent ischemia painless because it is mild? *Journal of the American College of Cardiology, 25*(7), 1513–1515.

Mulcahy, D., Keegan, J., Sparrow, J., Park, A., Wright, C., & Fox, K. (1989). Ischemia in the ambulatory setting—the total ischemic burden: Relation to exercise testing and investigative and therapeutic implications. *Journal of the American College of Cardiology, 14*(5), 1166–1172.

Muller, J. E., Abela, G. S., Nesto, R. W., & Tofler, G. H. (1994). Triggers, acute risk factors and vulnerable plaques: The lexicon of a new frontier. *Journal of the American College of Cardiology, 23*(3), 809–813.

Nabel, E. G., Rocco, M. B., Barry, J., Campbell, S., & Selwyn, A. P. (1987). Asymptomatic ischemia in patients with coronary artery disease. *Journal of the American Medical Association, 257*(14), 1923–1928.

Nihoyannopoulos, P., Marsonis, A., Joshi, J., Athanassopoulos, G., & Oakley, C. M. (1995). Magnitude of myocardial dysfunction is greater in painful than in painless myocardial ischemia: An exercise echocardiographic study. *Journal of the American College of Cardiology, 25*(7), 1507–1512.

Panza, J. A., Diodati, J. G., Callahan, T. S., Epstein, S. E., & Quyyumi, A. A. (1992). Role of increases in heart rate in determining the occurrence and frequency of myocardial ischemia during daily life in patients with stable coronary artery disease. *Journal of the American College of Cardiology, 20*(5), 1092–1098.

Parker, J. D., Testa, M. A., Jimenez, A. H., Tofler, G. H., Muller, J. E., Parker, J. O., & Stone, P. H. (1994). Morning increase in ambulatory ischemia in patients with stable coronary artery disease. Importance of physical activity and increased cardiac demand. *Circulation, 89*(2), 604–614.

Pepine, C. J., Geller, N. L., Knatterud, G. L., Bourassa, M. G., Chaitman, B. R., Davies, R. F., Day, P., Deanfield, J. E., Goldberg, A. D., McMahon, R. P., Mueller, H., Ouyang, P. Pratt, C., Proschan, M., Rogers, W. J., Selwyn, A. P., Sharaf, B., Sopko, G., Stone, P. H., & Conti, R. (1994). The asymptomatic cardiac ischemia pilot (acip) study: Design of a randomized clinical trial, baseline data and implications for a long-term outcome trial. *Journal of the American College of Cardiology, 24*(1), 1–10.

Rocco, M. B., Nabel, E. G., Campbell, S., Goldman, L., Barry, J., Mead, K., & Selwyn, A. P. (1988). Prognostic importance of myocardial ischemia detected by ambulatory monitoring in patients with stable coronary artery disease. *Circulation, 78,* 877–884.

Rosen, S. D., Paulesu, E., Nihoyannopoulos, P., Tousoulis, D., Frackowiak, R. S., Frith, C. D., Jones, T., & Camici, P. G. (1996). Silent ischemia as a central problem: Regional brain activation compared in silent and painful myocardial ischemia. *Annals of Internal Medicine, 124*(11), 939–949.

Rozanski, A., Bairey, C. N., Krantz, D. S., Friedman, J., Resser, K. J., Morell, M., Hilton Chalfen, S., Hestrin, L., Bietendorf, J., & Berman, D. S. (1988). Mental stress and the induction of silent myocardial ischemia in patients with coronary artery disease. *New England Journal of Medicine, 318,* 1005–1012.

Rumboldt, Z., Giunio, L., Miric, D., Polic, S., Bozic, I., & Tonkic, A. (1993). *The Lancet, 341*(8850), 965–966.

Santiago, H. T., Kop, W. J., Bairey-Merz, C. N., Rozanski, A., Gottdiener, J. S., & Krantz, D. S. (1996). The prognostic value of mental stress-induced ischemia and cardiovascular reactivity: 3 year follow-up. *Psychosomatic Medicine, 59,* 68.

Schang, S. J., & Pepine, C. (1977). Transient asymptomatic ST segment depression during daily activity. *American Journal of Cardiology, 39,* 396–402.

Schiffer, F., Hartley, L. H., Schulman, C. L., & Abelmann, W. H. (1976). The quiz electrocardiogram: A new diagnostic and research technique for evaluating the relation between emotional stress and ischemic heart disease. *American Journal of Cardiology, 37*(1), 41–47.

Sheps, D. S., Ballenger, M. N., De Gent, G. E., Krittayaphong, R., Dittman, E., Maixner, W., McCartney, W., Golden, R. N., Koch, G., & Light, K. C. (1995). Psychophysical responses to a speech stressor: Correlation of plasma beta-endorphin levels at rest and after psychological stress with thermally measured pain threshold in patients with coronary artery disease. *Journal of the American College of Cardiology, 25*(7), 1499–1503.

Siegel, W. C., Mark, D. B., Hlatky, M. A., Harrell, F. E., Pryor, D. B., Barefoot, J. C., & Williams, R. B. (1989). Clinical correlates and prognostic significance of Type a behavior and silent myocardial ischemia on the treadmill. *American Journal of Cardiology, 64*(19), 1280–1283.

Specchia, G., De Servi, S., Falcone, C., Gavazzi, A., Angoli, L., Bramucci, E., Ardissino, D., & Mussini, A. (1984). Mental arithmetic stress testing in patients with coronary artery disease. *American Heart Journal, 108*(1), 56–63.

Suarez, E. C., Williams, R. B., Kuhn, C. M., Zimmerman, E. H., & Schanberg, S. M. (1991). Biobehavioral basis of coronary-prone behavior in middle-age men. Part II: Serum cholesterol, the Type A behavior pattern, and hostility as interactive modulators of physiological reactivity. *Psychosomatic Medicine, 53*(5), 528–537.

Taggart, P., Carruthers, M., & Somerville, W. (1973). Electrocardiogram, plasma catecholamines and lipids, and their modification by oxyprenolol when speaking before an audience. *The Lancet, 2*(825), 341–346.

Taggart, P., Gibbons, D., & Somerville, W. (1969). Some effects of motor-car driving on the normal and abnormal heart. *British Medical Journal, 4*(676), 130–134.

Theisen, M. E., MacNeill, S. E., Lumley, M. A., Ketterer, M. W., Goldberg, A. D., & Borzak, S. (1995). Psychosocial factors related to unrecognized acute myocardial infarction. *American Journal of Cardiology, 75*(17), 1211–1213.

Titus, B. G., & Sherman, C. T. (1991). Asymptomatic myocardial ischemia during percutaneous transluminal coronary angioplasty and importance of prior Q-wave infarction and diabetes mellitus. *American Journal of Cardiology, 68*(8), 735–739.

Torosian, T., Lumley, M. A., Pickard, S. D., & Ketterer, M. W. (1997). Silent versus symptomatic myocardial ischemia: The role of psychological and medical factors. *Health Psychology, 16*(2), 123–130.

Verdino, R. J., Gottdiener, J. S., O'Leary, S., Howell, R., Kop, W. J., & Krantz, D. S. (1995). Altered heart rate variability precedes ischemia (abstract). *Journal of the American College of Cardiology,* (2b), 312A.

Vita, J. A., Treasure, C. B., Nabel, E. G., McLenachan, J. M., Fish, R. D., Yeung, A. C., Vekshtein, V. I., Selwyn, A. P., & Ganz, P. (1990). Coronary vasomotor response to acetylcholine relates to risk factors for coronary artery disease. *Circulation, 81*(2), 491–497.

Vita, J. A., Treasure, C. B., Yeung, A. C., Vekshtein, V. I., Fantasia, G. M., Fish, R. D., Ganz, P., & Selwyn, A. P. (1992). Patients with evidence of coronary endothelial dysfunction as assessed by acetylcholine infusion demonstrate marked increase in sensitivity to constrictor effects of catecholamines. *Circulation, 85*(4), 1390–1397.

Williams, R. B., Haney, T. L., Lee, K. L., Kong, Y. H., Blumenthal, J. A., & Whalen, R. E. (1980). Type A behavior, hostility, and coronary atherosclerosis. *Psychosomatic Medicine,* 539–549.

Yeung, A. C., Vekshtein, V. I., Krantz, D. S., Vita, J. A., Ryan, T. J., & Ganz, P. (1991). The effect of atherosclerosis on the vasomotor response of coronary arteries to mental stress. *New England Journal of Medicine, 325,* 1551–1556.

41

Stress, Immunity, and Susceptibility to Infectious Disease

Anna L. Marsland
University of Pittsburgh Cancer Institute

Elizabeth A. Bachen
University of California, San Francisco

Sheldon Cohen
Carnegie Mellon University

Stephen B. Manuck
University of Pittsburgh

Psychoneuroimmunology is the study of relations between behavioral factors, the central nervous system, the immune system, and health. To date, the human literature within this field has focused on a working model that stressful life events impact immune function, which in turn modifies host resistance to immune-related disease (S. Cohen & Herbert, 1996). Upper respiratory infections (URI) have served as the primary disease model in this literature and recent prospective studies support popular belief and provide compelling evidence that stressful life events and psychological distress predict biologically verified infectious illness (S. Cohen et al., 1998; S. Cohen, Tyrrell, & A. P. Smith, 1991, 1993; Stone et al., 1992). To date, however, the mechanism(s) of this effect remains unclear. Although there is substantial evidence that stress is associated with changes in immune function (Herbert & S. Cohen, 1993), the implications of stress-induced immune changes for susceptibility to disease have not been established. This chapter provides an overview of the human literature in psychoneuroimmunology, exploring evidence linking stress to immune function and susceptibility to infectious disease. Particular attention is given to individual differences in the magnitude of stress-related changes in immunity as one plausible explanation for variability in susceptibility to infectious pathogens.

STRESS AND SUSCEPTIBILITY TO INFECTIOUS DISEASE

There is consistent evidence that persons under stress report more symptoms of URI, and that stress results in greater health care utilization for URI (S. Cohen & Williamson, 1991). For example, Stone, Reed, and Neale (1987) found that for 79 couples followed over 3 months, daily life events rated as undesirable increased 3 to 4 days prior to the onset of self-reported symptoms of URI. However, whereas self-reported symptoms of URI may tap underlying pathology, it is also possible that they reflect a biased interpretation of physical sensations without underlying illness. This possibility is supported by studies in which effects of stress are observed on symptom reporting, but not verified disease (S. Cohen & Williamson, 1991).

In support of a relation between stress and increased susceptibility to URI, epidemiological studies in which the presence of pathology was verified by physician diagnosis or biological methods, have found that major stressful life events, chronic family conflict, and disruptive daily events increase risk for upper respiratory disease (Graham, Douglas, & Ryan, 1986; Meyer & Haggerty, 1962; Turner Cobb & Steptoe, 1996). For example, Meyer and Haggerty followed 100 members of sixteen families for a 12-month period. Daily life events that disrupted family and personal life were four times more likely to precede than to follow new streptococcal and nonstreptococcal infections (as diagnosed by throat cultures and blood antibody levels) and associated symptomatology. Similarly, Turner Cobb and Steptoe (1996) found that among 107 adults followed for 15 weeks, individuals who developed clinically verified URI ($n = 29$) endorsed higher levels of life event stress than individuals who remained healthy. In another study, individuals who perceived their families as being more "chaotic" or "rigid" were found to be at greater risk of verified influenza B infection than individuals who described their families as more "balanced" (Clover, Abell, Becker, Crawford, & Ramsey, 1989). However, community studies like these do not control for the possible effects of stressful life events on exposure to infectious agents. Indeed, increased incidence of infection in these studies may be attributable to stress-induced increases in exposure to infectious agents rather than to stress-induced immunosuppression.

More recent studies provide control for exposure by experimentally inoculating healthy individuals with common cold or flu viruses (viral challenge studies). Here, volunteers are assessed for degree of stress and then experimentally exposed to a cold or influenza virus or placebo. They are then kept in quarantine and monitored for the development of infection and illness. Early viral inoculation studies were limited by a range of methodological weaknesses, including insufficient sample sizes and lack of control for factors known to influence susceptibility to viral infection (including preexisting antibodies to the infectious agent and age). Furthermore, the possible role of stress-elicited changes in health practices, such as smoking and alcohol consumption, was not considered. These limitations may account for initial failures to find consistent relations between stress and susceptibility to URI (S. Cohen & Williamson, 1991). In contrast, recent viral challenge studies have included multiple controls for factors known to be independently associated with susceptibility to viral infection (S. Cohen et al., 1991, 1993, 1998; Stone et al., 1992). These studies consistently find an association between stress and susceptibility to URI. For example, among 394 healthy adults, stressful life events, perceptions of current stress, and negative affect all predicted the probability of developing a biologically verified cold, with greater stress related linearly to susceptibility (S. Cohen et al., 1991, 1993). This dose–response relation was found across five different URI viruses. In addition, recent research suggests that the longer the duration of stressful life events, the greater the risk of becoming infected (S. Cohen et al., 1998). A large number of control factors (including, age, sex, allergic status, body weight, season, and virus-specific antibody status before challenge) have not been able to explain the increased risk for colds among persons reporting greater stress. Smoking, alcohol consumption, diet, exercise, and sleep quality have also failed to account for the relation between stress and illness in these studies (S. Cohen et al., 1991). Similar results have been independently replicated by Stone et al. (1992).

In addition to episode onset, severity of infectious disease appears to be influenced by stress. For example, S. Cohen et al. (1995) found that negative mood measured prior to viral exposure was related to colds and influenza of greater severity, as determined by the amount of mucus produced over the course of illness. In sum, recent well-controlled studies corroborate prospective studies of community samples in indicating that psychological stress is associated with increased susceptibility to upper respiratory disease. In addition, there is consistent evidence for increased symptom reporting under stress.

MECHANISMS THAT MAY LINK STRESS TO DISEASE

A number of potential pathways exist through which an association between stress and infectious pathology might occur, including behavioral and immune mechanisms. In the first case, psychosocial factors could directly or indirectly influence health through changes in health-related behaviors. For example, poor nutritional status, smoking, drug and alcohol intake, lack of exercise, and poor sleep have all been shown to compromise immune status and health (Irwin, Lacher, & Caldwell, 1992; Kiecolt-Glaser & Glaser, 1988; Kronfol et al., 1989; Kusaka, Kondou, & Morimoto, 1992). However, as noted earlier, these behavioral factors do not account for much of the variability among individuals in infectious disease susceptibility. Hence, other mechanisms must also be operating.

The influence of stress on the immune system is considered the primary biological pathway through which stress can influence infectious pathology. Numerous neurochemicals released during stress are associated with modulation of immune function, including catecholamines (epinephrine and norepinephrine), corticosteroids, and opiates (e.g., Darko, Irwin, Risch, & Gillin, 1992; Herberman & Ortaldo, 1981; Irwin et al., 1992). In addition, direct anatomical links exist between the central nervous and immune systems, as evidenced by sympathetic and parasympathetic innervation of lymphoid organs (Felten & Olschowka, 1987; Livnat, Felten, Carlson, Bellinger, & Felten, 1985). Moreover, immune cells, which migrate between lymphoid organs and the peripheral bloodstream, have receptors for a variety of hormones and neurotransmitters that are released during stress (see Plaut, 1987). Thus, there is extensive evidence for direct anatomical and functional links between the central nervous and immune systems, providing a biological pathway for the influences of stress on susceptibility to infectious disease.

To date, the only study to examine whether the immune system mediates the association of chronic stressors and colds found little evidence for the role of either numbers of circulating white blood cell populations or NK cell activity (S. Cohen et al., 1998). However, the immune response to viral pathogens involves a complex cascade of events. Researchers measuring immune function in humans are limited to a few basic markers that provide a poor overall estimate of the body's ability to resist disease. Hence, it remains likely that other immune components operate as pathways in the link between stress and susceptibility to disease. The remainder of this chapter focuses on evidence that stress is accompanied by changes in immune function, which may in turn render the individual more susceptible to infectious disease. First, however, a brief overview of measures of immune function is offered.

MEASUREMENTS OF IMMUNOCOMPETENCE

The immune system is a highly complex, interactive network and there is no single, adequate measure of its status (Cunnick, Lysle, Armfield, & Rabin, 1988). Human studies are limited to quantitative and functional assessments of immune parameters sampled from peripheral blood and saliva. These tests include assessment of the numbers and functional abilities of various subgroups of immune cells. In enumerative assays, the various populations of leukocytes are identified and counted by staining the unique surface molecules of each cell type with specific fluorescent reagents. Using this technique, the percentages or absolute numbers of circulating T-lymphocytes (and their subsets), B lymphocytes, macrophages, and NK cells can be determined.

With respect to functional assessments, lymphocyte proliferation assays are commonly used in human research. In this assay, leukocytes are incubated with experimental antigens called mitogens that nonspecifically stimulate T or B lymphocytes to divide. The rate of resultant proliferation is taken as a measure of immunocompetence, with greater cell division reflecting a more effective immune response. Commonly used mitogens include phytohemagglutinin (PHA) and concanavalin A (Con A), which stimulate the proliferation of T lymphocytes, and pokeweed mitogen (PWM), which activates T and B lymphocytes. Natural killer cell cytotoxicity is also frequently measured. NK cells are a subset of lymphoid cells with the ability to spontaneously kill some human tumor and virally infected cells. The ability of NK cells to destroy tumor cells (NK cell activity) is most commonly assessed by a chromium release assay. Enhanced NK cell activity may also be measured by incubating NK cells with stimulatory cytokines, such as interleukin-2 (IL-2) or gamma-interferon (IFN-g). The ability of these cytokines to increase NK cell activity is then compared to cytotoxicity levels found in unstimulated samples. Finally, in vitro assays are also used to measure cytokine concentrations in the circulation or the production of cytokines by lymphocytes and monocytes following stimulation with mitogens.

In contrast to these laboratory measures, other indices of immunocompetence are performed in vivo, assessing immune function in the living organism. One such measure is antibody production in response to inoculation with an antigen (e.g., vaccination with recombinant hepatitis B vaccine or keyhold limpet hemocyanin). Here, individuals ingest or are inoculated with an antigen and the amount of antibody produced in response to that specific antigen is quantified in serum. Certain antibody responses (e.g., salivary immunoglobulin A) can also be measured in saliva. In general, greater antibody response is thought to reflect better immunocompetence; however, elevated antibody levels to latent herpes virus may reflect a weakened ability of the immune system to keep such viruses in check. Therefore, higher antibody levels to herpes viruses (e.g., Epstein–Barr virus) are often interpreted as indicating poorer immunocompetence (Kiecolt-Glaser & Glaser, 1987).

CHRONIC STRESSORS AND IMMUNITY

Several reviews (Bachen, Marsland, Manuck, & S. Cohen, 1998; Kiecolt-Glaser & Glaser, 1991; O'Leary, 1990) and a meta-analysis of the literature on stress and immunity in humans (Herbert & S. Cohen, 1993) conclude that naturalistic stress (as measured by both self-report and objective life events) is reliably associated with modulation of functional and enumerative aspects of the immune system. The most consistent functional alterations include reduced NK cell activity and lymphocyte proliferation to PHA and Con A, and increased antibody levels to latent herpes viruses, suggesting decreases in the competence of the immune system to control latent virus activity. In terms of enumerative parameters, chronic stress is associated with decreases in percentages or absolute numbers of circulating B cells, T cells, T-helper cells, T suppressor/cytotoxic cells and NK cells. Stress has also been associated with decreases in total serum IgM (Herbert & S. Cohen, 1993) and in the concentration of total salivary IgA (Evans, Bristow, Hucklebridge, Clow, & Walters, 1993).

To date, the majority of studies in this literature has examined the influence of naturally occurring stressors on immune function. Numerous life event stressors and environmental demands have been associated with immune changes, including job stress (Arnetz et al., 1987), long-term unemployment (Arnetz et al., 1987; Dorian et al., 1985), loss of an intimate relationship due to death (Kemeny et al., 1995; Schleifer, Keller, Camerino, Thornton, & Stein, 1983) or separation/divorce (Kennedy, Kiecolt-Glaser, & Glaser, 1988), caring for a relative with Alzheimer's disease (Kiecolt-Glaser, Glaser, Shuttleworth, Dyer, Ogrocki, & Speicher, 1987), marital conflict (Kiecolt-Glaser et al., 1997), and natural disasters, such as earthquakes (Soloman, Segerstrom, Grohr, Kemeny, & Fahey, 1997) and hurricanes (Ironson et al., 1997), missile attacks during the 1991 Persian Gulf War (Weiss et al., 1996) and residing near a damaged nuclear power plant (McKinnon, Weisse, Reynolds, Bowles, & Baum, 1989). Interestingly, there is also evidence that alterations in immunity may persist (i.e., fail to habituate) with prolonged stressor exposure (e.g., Baum, 1990; Kiecolt-Glaser & Glaser, 1991; Kiecolt-Glaser, Glaser, et al., 1987).

Naturalistic Stressors

One stressor that has been associated consistently with altered immunity is the loss of a close personal relationship from either death or divorce. Early studies demonstrated that lymphocyte proliferative responses among bereaved subjects were lower after the death of a loved one than during the pre-bereavement period (Schleifer et al., 1983), and were also lower than in nonbereaved controls (Bartrop, Lazarus, Luckhurst, Kiloh, & Penny, 1977). In these studies, immunologic alterations persisted from 2 to 14 months after the loss. Recent studies support these findings (e.g., Goodkin et al., 1996; Kemeny et al., 1995) and also demonstrate that the degree of immune change associated with bereavement may be related to the severity of concomitant depressed mood. For example, Irwin, Daniels, T. L. Smith, Bloom, and Weiner (1987) found that levels of depression among a group of bereaved women correlated inversely with NK cell activity (r = .89). Similarly, M. W. Linn, B. S. Linn, and Jensen (1984) found reduced lymphocyte proliferation to PHA in bereaved spouses, but only among those who also had depressive symptomatology.

Loss of a relationship from separation or divorce has also been associated reliably with immune alterations. In this regard, Kiecolt-Glaser, Fisher, et al. (1987) found decreased proliferative responses to PHA, higher antibodies to Epstein–Barr virus, and lower percentages of circulating NK and T-helper cells among 16 recently separated or divorced women than among a matched group of married women. Similarly, in a study of 32 men, individuals who had been separated or divorced for up to 3 years had higher antibody levels to latent viruses than matched, married controls (Kiecolt-Glaser et al., 1988). Other studies have demonstrated that poorer marital quality among married couples is related to greater distress, loneliness, and latent virus antibody response. For example, in a study of newlyweds, couples who expressed greater hostility during a discussion of marital problems showed the most pronounced suppression of immune function, as measured by natural killer cell activity and proliferative responses to PHA and Con A over a 24-hour period, and by higher antibody titers to latent Epstein–Barr virus. Similar findings were reported recently in a study of 31 older couples who had been married an average of 42 years. Here, men and women who showed greater suppression of lymphocyte proliferative response and higher antibodies to latent Epstein–Barr virus displayed more negative behavior during conflict, and described their usual marital disagreements as more negative, than individuals who showed better immune responses (Kiecolt-Glaser et al., 1997).

Several studies have also examined immune responses to the stress associated with caring for a family member with Alzheimer's disease (AD). Here, it has been demonstrated that caregivers frequently suffer higher levels of depression, more frequent health complaints, and decreased life satisfaction, due to the stressfulness of the caregiving experience (Light & Lebowitz, 1989; S. H. Zarit, Orr, & J. M. Zarit, 1985). Kiecolt-Glaser and colleagues published a series of studies examining immunologic alterations associated with caregiving for a family member with AD. To date, results indicate changes in several cellular immune components supportive of immunosuppression, including lower percentages of total lymphocytes and T-helper subsets, lower in vitro interleukin-1B responses to lipopolysaccharide stimulation, poorer NK cell response to stimulatory cytokines (IFN-γ and IL-2), and higher antibody titers to Epstein–Barr virus (Esterling, Kiecolt-Glaser, Bodnar, & Glaser, 1994). Interestingly, caregivers also showed slower healing of a 3.5 mm punch biopsy wound (Kiecolt-Glaser, Marucha, Malarkey, Mercado, & Glaser, 1995), making it possible that the decreases in immune function observed among caregivers leads to an impairment in wound healing. Taken together, then, there is a large body of evidence demonstrating that chronic naturalistic stressors, such as loss due to death or divorce, marital conflict, or caring for a relative with AD, modulate immune function.

Examination Stress

Numerous studies in the PNI literature have employed a quasi-experimental design, examining immune changes from before to after a naturally occuring event. Probably best known in this literature are the series of studies by Kiecolt-Glaser, Glaser and colleagues (e.g., Kiecolt-Glaser et al., 1986; Kiecolt-Glaser, Garner, Speicher, Penn, & Glaser, 1984) examining immune responses of medical students to examination stress. Compared to measures taken at less stressful times (e.g., just following a vacation), students demonstrate modulation of a number of immune components during examinations, including decreases in the total number of circulating T lymphocytes and NK cells, and in lymphocyte response to mitogen stimulation, lowered gamma interferon production and reduced NK cell activity (Dobbin, Harth, McCain, Martin, & Cousin, 1991; Glaser, Kiecolt-Glaser, Stout, Tarr, Speicher, Holliday, 1985; Glaser, Rice, Speicher, Stout, & Kiecolt-Glaser, 1986; Kiecolt-Glaser, & Glaser, 1987). During exams, students have also shown increased levels of circulating antibodies to Epstein Barr and other herpes viruses (Glaser et al., 1993; Glaser, Kiecolt-Glaser, Speicher, & Holliday, 1985) and slower healing of a punch biopsy wound (Kiecolt-Glaser, Page, Marucha, MacCallum, & Glaser, 1998).

Vaccination Responses

Other investigations have explored the impact of perceived stress on the ability to produce antibodies (develop immunity) to novel antigens. These in vivo immune measures may provide a more proximate mechanism of stress–infectious disease associations because they are directly related to host resistance. Results of early retrospective studies examining relations between life event stressors and antibody response to influenza viruses are inconclusive, possibly due to the memory distortion and bias inherent in recalling stressful events. For example, Green, Betts, and Ochitill (1978) found that higher perceived life change stress, during the 12 months preceding inoculation with an influenza virus, was associated with a lower antibody response; however, others reported no significant relations (Locke & Heisel, 1977; Locke, Hurst, & Heisel, 1979). Results of prospective studies are more consistent, indicating that higher levels of perceived stress around the time of influenza vaccination are associated with lower antibody responses (Bovbjerg, Manne, & Gross, 1990; Locke et al., 1979).

One limitation of using a common live virus, such as influenza vaccine, to examine development of immunity is the likelihood that individuals have already been exposed to the virus. Consequently, antibody response is influenced by factors such as preexisting antibody levels, the amount of time since prior sensitization, and ongoing environmental exposure. In order to avoid these potential confounds, more recent prospective studies have examined antibody responses to novel antigens, to which the individual has not had prior exposure. Once again, results suggest that an individual's psychological "state" around the time of antigen challenge and antibody formation may influence their level of antibody response. For example, Snyder, Roghmann, and Sigal (1993) demonstrated that 3 weeks after inoculation with keyhold limpet hemocyanin (KLH), individuals reporting more psychological distress and "bad" life events mounted a lower lymphocyte proliferation response to KLH than individuals who reported "good" life events and social support. Similarly, Stone et al. (1994) had volunteers ingest a capsule containing an innocuous novel antigen daily for 12 weeks. During this period, volunteers also completed daily diaries, recording positive and negative daily events, and gave daily saliva samples to assess secretory immunoglobulin A (sIgA), an antibody to the novel antigen. Once again, more desirable daily events were associated with greater, and more undesirable events with less, antibody to the novel antigen.

Other research has explored the impact of perceived stress on antibody response to hepatitis B vaccination. To date, these studies have yielded inconsistent findings. Glaser et al. (1992) followed medical students who received each of three hepatitis B inoculations during an examination period. Those individuals who mounted an adequate immune response to the first dose of vaccine (25% of sample) reported less stress and anxiety to subsequent examinations than those who did not seroconvert until later. However, there was no prospective relation between perceived stress and antibody response to the first vaccination in the series. In another study, Jabaaij et al. (1993) demonstrated that greater perceived stress around the time of the initial vaccination was associated with lower final antibody levels, as assessed after a series of three vaccinations. In contrast, Petry, Weems, and Livingstone (1991) found a positive relation between negatively perceived stress, irascibility, depression, and anxiety and peak antibody titers.

Reasons for contradictory findings across studies are unclear. Comparisons are made difficult by variability in study design, including psychological constructs measured, and timing of psychological and immune measurements. In regard to the latter, it is possible that psychological stress influences antibody response to hepatitis B vaccination in a time-dependent fashion, with stress having a greater impact in the earlier phases of the immune response around the time of initial antibody formation. In support of this possibility, Jabaaij et al. (1993) demonstrated that whereas psychological distress at the time of the initial vaccination was associated with lower peak antibody responses following a complete vaccination series, levels of distress around the time of the final booster vaccination were unrelated to the final immune response. Other studies measuring stress later in the antibody response also failed to find an association or found opposite effects (Marsland et al., in press; Petry et al., 1991). In sum, there is consistent evidence that high levels of perceived stress around the time of antigen challenge are associated with a decreased in vivo immune response. It remains to be determined whether a reduction in the magnitude of antibody response to vaccinations translates into increased susceptibility to infection; however, it has been demonstrated that individuals who mount lower antibody responses lose their protective status more quickly (Hollinger, 1989).

Individual Differences in Immune Responses to Naturalistic Stress

Not all individuals demonstrate immune changes following stressful life events. Indeed, there is marked variability among individuals in the magnitude of their immune responses to stress. In this regard, it is suggested that negative events only have an impact on immune function when they lead to negative affect or psychological distress. It is proposed that such distress is elicited when persons perceive that demands imposed by life events exceed their ability to cope (Lazarus & Folkman, 1984). In support of this model, a recent meta-analysis of the literature concluded that depressed mood states in clinical and nonclinical samples modulate various immune components, as evidenced by a down regulation of NK cell activity, lowered proliferative response of lymphocytes to the mitogens PHA, Con A, and PWM, and decreases in the total numbers of circulating lymphocytes, NK and B cells, and T-cell subpopulations (Herbert & S. Cohen, 1993). Furthermore, a number of studies have demonstrated that level of perceived distress moderates the impact of life event stress on immune function. For example, Locke and colleagues (1984) found that among students who reported high levels of life-change stress, those with many psychological symptoms of distress, including anxiety and depression, had lower NK cell activity than similarly stressed peers with few symptoms. Thus, there is some consensus that psychosocial adaptation to stress modulates immune function, with poor coping and emotional distress being associated with greater changes in immune components.

Interindividual variability in the magnitude of immune responses to stress may also be attributable to psychosocial buffers (e.g., interpersonal resources) that modulate the negative impact of adverse life events. For example, perceived inadequacy of interpersonal relationships, as measured by self-report, is related to distress and diminished immune function among medical students taking examinations (e.g., Kiecolt-Glaser & Glaser, 1991), caregivers of relatives with AD (Kiecolt-Glaser, Glaser et al., 1987), and psychiatric inpatients on the day of admission (Kiecolt-Glaser et al., 1984). There is also evidence that supportive interpersonal relationships buffer the adverse impact of negative life events on immune function (Kennedy et al., 1988). For example, Baron, Cutrona, Hicklin, Russell, and Lubaroff (1990) found that social support was associated with higher NK cell activity and greater proliferative responses to PHA (but not Con A) among 23 women whose husbands were being treated for urological cancer. Similarly, Glaser et al. (1992) showed that, when compared with individuals reporting low levels of social support, medical students with more support mounted greater antibody responses to hepatitis B vaccination. In sum, although few studies examine individual differences in immune response to naturalistic stressors, there is some evidence that psychosocial adaptation modulates immune function, with distress (as measured by symptoms of anxiety or depression) being associated with greater immunosuppression.

Intervention Studies

Related to the stress-buffering hypothesis, studies have also examined whether interventions designed to lower emotional distress also reduce or prevent stress-related changes in immunity. These studies have used a diverse array of psychological interventions, including stress management training, relaxation, hypnosis, cognitive-behavioral strategies, exercise, and coping skills training. In general, results are consistent with improved immune function, or an amelioration of stress-related changes (Kiecolt-Glaser & Glaser, 1992). For example, Kiecolt-Glaser et al. (1985) demonstrated increases in NK cell activity and decreases in HSV antibody titers following progressive relaxation training in a group of older adults. One of the most widely cited studies in this literature evaluated the effects of a six-session group intervention for patients with malignant melanoma (R. I. Fawzy et al., 1993). When compared with patients who received routine medical care, the intervention, comprised of psychological support and training in relaxation, stress management, problem-solving and coping skills, effectively enhanced coping and reduced psychological distress, and was associated with an increase in the percentage of NK cells and NK cell activity, and a decrease in the percentage of T-helper cells. Other studies suggest that the down regulation of immune components known to accompany notification of positive HIV antibody status can be attenuated by aerobic exercise training (La Perriere et al., 1990, 1991) or by cognitive-behavioral stress management intervention (Antoni et al., 1991). However, not all findings are consistent. An 8-week stress reduction intervention was not associated with changes in immunological measures in HIV-seropositive men when compared with waiting list controls (Coates, McKusick, Kuno, & Stites, 1989). Similarly, Kiecolt-Glaser et al. (1986) found that a hypnotic/relaxation intervention did not attenuate the decline in NK cell activity associated with examination stress in medical students. Despite thse negative findings, the majority of studies in this literature suggest that interventions designed to manage or reduce stress are associated with improved immune function or an amelioration of stress-related changes in immunity. Again, however, the health significance of these positive, but relatively small, immunologic changes remains unknown.

Persistence of Immunological Changes

Many studies suggest that chronic naturalistic stressors are capable of evoking psychological and immunological changes that continue long after a stressful event has ended. For example, extended stress responses were found in former caregivers of AD relatives who had died at least 2 years earlier (Esterling et al., 1994). Similar ongoing responses were observed among residents of Three-Mile Island (TMI) more than 6 years after the nuclear plant accident occurred. In comparison to a group of demographically similar controls, many TMI-area residents continued to exhibit heightened levels of distress, elevated 24- hour urinary catecholamine excretion, increased latent herpes virus antibodies, and diminished numbers of B lymphocytes, T-suppressor/cytotoxic lymphocytes, and NK cells (Baum, 1990; McKinnon et al., 1989). These differences were not attributable to health behavior, because the two groups did not differ on diet, smoking, health, medications, or substance abuse.

It is unclear why stress-elicited changes in immune function persist over prolonged periods of time. As previously discussed (see Bachen et al., 1998), one possibility is that stressful life events may initiate a series of other related stressors, such as financial difficulties or social isolation, as well as behavioral or mood changes that could perpetuate immune alterations (Kasl, 1984; Kiecolt-Glaser & Glaser, 1988; Stone, Marco, Cruise, Cox, & Neal, 1996). In addition, cognitions, such as intrusive thoughts or images, may be important in sustaining stress reactions even when the initiating event no longer exists (Baum, 1990; Baum, L. Cohen, & Hall, 1993). For example, McKinnon et al. (1989) found that intrusive thoughts or imagery about the TMI accident and its health effects were related to elevated anxiety and immunologic changes in TMI-area residents. Similarly, intrusive thoughts about upcoming stressful events, such as a medical school examination (Workman & LaVia, 1987) or waiting for HIV test results (Antoni et al., 1990), have been shown to be related to poorer proliferative responses to PHA.

SUMMARY OF NATURALISTIC STRESS

In sum, it is well established that naturalistic stress modulates both functional and enumerative aspects of immunity. The most consistent alterations suggest that stress may suppress immune function over protracted intervals during particularly intense or prolonged stressors. Despite these central tendencies, not all individuals demonstrate immune changes following stressful life events. Indeed, there is marked variability among individuals in the magnitude of immune responses to stress. This interindividual variability has been attributed to a number of psychosocial buffers, including interpersonal resources and coping skills, which are thought to modulate the negative impact of adverse life events. To date, it remains unclear how stress may contribute to changes in the immune system. Potential pathways include the impact of stress on health practices (e.g., changes in diet, exercise or sleep) and/or the stress-induced activation of more physiological pathways (e.g., neuroendocrine parameters). Few naturalistic investigations have examined relations between health practices, neuroendocrine factors, and immune measures during stress (Herbert & S. Cohen, 1993). However, recent studies indicate that sleep disturbances may play an important role in the modulation of immune function during naturalistic stress. For example, Ironson et al. (1997) found evidence that the onset of sleep problems following Hurricance Andrew partially mediated the relation between posttraumatic stress symptoms and lowered NK cell activity in a community sample affected by this disaster. Such findings are consistent with earlier reports that partial sleep deprivation is associated with reduced NK cell activity in humans (Irwin et al., 1992, 1994).

LABORATORY STRESSORS AND IMMUNITY

In order to examine whether psychological stress, independent of concomitant changes in health behaviors, alters immune components, investigators have recently begun to examine the effects of acute laboratory stress on immune functioning in healthy individuals. These controlled, experimental studies also provide a means to explore neuroendocrine pathways associated with stress and immunity. Findings from these studies reveal significant immunologic alterations following exposure to a range of standardized, short-term laboratory stressors that are generally perceived by subjects as aversive, demanding, or interpersonally challenging. Stressors employed in these studies include mental arithmetic, unsolvable puzzles, evaluative speech tasks, electric shocks and/or loud noise, marital discussions involving conflict and disturbing films depicting combat surgery (for a review, see Kiecolt-Glaser, Cacioppo, Malarkey, & Glaser, 1992). In contrast to some of the less common naturalistic stressors (e.g., bereavement or caring for a relative with AD), some of these challenges may more accurately characterize everyday hassles, and thus account for more observed interindividual variability in immune response to stress and susceptibility to disease.

The immediate effects of short-term laboratory challenge on immune function are not entirely consistent with longer term changes seen following chronic forms of naturalistic stress. In contrast to the chronic stress literature, acute stressors are usually associated with a transient increase in the number of circulating T-suppressor/cytotoxic lymphocytes and NK cells (Bachen et al., 1992; Brosschot, Benschop, Godaert, Heijen, & Ballieux, 1992; Herbert et al., 1994; Manuck, S. Cohen, Rabin, Muldoon, & Bachen, 1991; Marsland et al., 1995; Naliboff et al., 1991; Zakowski, McCallister, Deal, & Baum, 1992). Decreases in the ratio of T-helper to T-suppressor lymphocytes (CD4:CD8 ratio) have also been reported (Bachen et al., 1992; Brosschot et al., 1992; Landmann et al., 1984). Less consistent findings include alterations in the number of T-helper and B-cell populations (Bachen et al., 1992; Caggiula et al., 1995; Gerritsen, Heijnen, Wiegant, Bermond, & Frijda, 1996; Marsland et al., 1995).

With regard to functional measures, both chronic naturalistic and acute laboratory stress have been associated with reduced lymphocyte mitogenesis on exposure to PHA, Con A, and PWM (Bachen et al., 1992; Caggiula et al., 1995; Gerritsen et al., 1996; Manuck et al., 1991; Marsland et al., 1995; Weisse et al., 1990; Zakowski, L. Cohen, Hall, Wollman, & Baum, 1994); however, not all results are consistent (Brosschot et al., 1992; Zakowski et al., 1994). In contrast to the decreases associated with chronic stress, a growing number of studies suggest that NK cell activity is increased following acute challenge (Cacioppo, 1994; Naliboff et al., 1991; but not Sieber, Rodin, Larson, Ortega, & Cummings, 1992). Indeed, recent evidence suggests that the NK cell response to stress is biphasic, with an immediate increase in activity, followed by a later decrease to below baseline levels (Delahanty et al., 1996; Schedlowski et al., 1993).

Immune responses to acute stress appear to be rapid and short lasting, occurring as early as 5 minutes after stressor onset (Herbert et al., 1994) and returning to baseline levels within 15 minutes, in the case of cell subset redistribution (Brosschot et al., 1992). Changes in functional measures have been shown to last longer, with reductions in lymphocyte proliferation remaining for at least 90 minutes after challenge (Weisse et al., 1990; Zakowski et al., 1992); elevations in NK cell activity may persist for at least 1 hour (Gerritsen et al., 1996). Studies that include both sexes demonstrate that immune responses to acute stress are similar among men and women (Herbert et al., 1994).

How the transient immune responses seen following discrete acute stress relate to those associated with chronic naturalistic stress is unknown. However, it is hypothesized that alternative physiological mechanisms may account for these differential effects (Herbert & S. Cohen, 1993). In the case of acute psychological stress, research findings suggest that immune responses are largely mediated by activation of the sympathetic nervous system. For example, it has been demonstrated that immune outcomes assessed after a laboratory stressor covary with the magnitude of sympathetic activation elicited under the same stimulus conditions (Landmann et al., 1984; Manuck et al., 1991; Zakowski et al., 1992). Pharmacological studies also indicate that the administration of physiological doses of sympathetic stimulants (e.g., exogenous catecholamines or isoproterenol) invokes functional modulations of cellular immunity that are similar to those seen during mental stress (Crary et al., 1983; van Tits et al., 1990). Finally, the speed of the immune reactions to acute stress makes it unlikely that other, slower responding hormones (e.g., cortisol) mediate these effects. Indeed, two studies have demonstrated immune changes in the absence of concomitant changes in cortisol levels (Manuck et al., 1991; Zakowski et al., 1992).

More direct evidence for sympathetic mediation derives from the observation that stress-related immune responses are blocked by adrenergic receptor inhibition (Bachen et al., 1995; Benshop et al., 1994). Indeed, it has been demonstrated that administration of an adrenergic inhibitor prevents stress-induced alterations in a variety of immune parameters, including proliferative responses to PHA and Con A, NK cell number and activity, and the ratio of T-helper to T-suppressor/cytotoxic cells (Bachen et al., 1995; Benschop et al., 1995).

The exact mechanism of sympathetic-immune mediation remains unclear. Recent evidence suggests that activation of the sympathetic nervous system may influence the immune system by both active and passive processes (Marsland et al., 1997). Under stress, an increase in arterial blood pressure driven by activation of the sympathetic nervous system causes fluid to filter out of circulation into extravascular spaces, leading to a passive increase in the concentration of all nondiffusible constituents of blood, including lymphocytes (C. Jern, Wadenvik, Mark, Hallgren, & S. Jern, 1989). It is possible to mathematically correct changes in lymphocyte subtype numbers to determine the degree to which the passive concentration of blood constituents accounts for changes in circulating cell numbers. By using this arithmetic correction, it has been shown that increases in the concentration of circulating T-suppressor/cytotoxic and NK cells following acute stress are partly, but not wholly, attributable to hemoconcentration (Marsland et al., 1997). Interestingly, an active decrease in the circulating numbers of T-helper and B lymphocytes during stress was also revealed, but only when hemoconcentration was taken into account. This raises the possibility that there is a stress-induced decrease in these cell subtypes, which is frequently masked by a simultaneous reduction in plasma volume.

The observation that hemoconcentration only partly accounts for acute rises in T-suppressor/cytotoxic and NK cell numbers suggests that more active mechanisms of immune response must also be implicated (see Bachen et al., 1995, 1998, for further discussion). In this regard, it is thought that alterations in adhesion molecules on cell surfaces may enable these cell populations to be mobilized into circulation from the endothelium of blood vessels. Recent studies indicate that catecholamines prevent the adherence of human NK cells to endothelial tissue in vitro (Benshop, Oostveen, Heijen, & Ballieux, 1993). It has also been demonstrated that acute psychological stress alters the expression of surface adhesion molecules on lymphocytes (Mills & Dimsdale, 1996). Finally, changes in mitogen-stimulated lymphocyte proliferation may, in part, reflect sympathetically mediated impairments of IL-2 production by T-helper lymphocytes (Heilig, Irwin, Grewal, & Sercarz, 1993) and decreased antigen-presentation by macrophages (Heilig et al., 1993).

In contrast to the rapid, short-lived immune responses associated with acute stress, exposure to more chronic stressors leads to relatively stable shifts in the baseline levels of immune measures (Herbert & S. Cohen, 1993). Here, it is likely that more prolonged secretion of stress hormones induces more stable changes in neuroendocrine pathways, such as modification of receptor density and sensitivity (Chrousos & Gold, 1992; Herbert & S. Cohen, 1993). Alternatively, the more delayed release of other hormones (e.g., cortisol, ACTH, and B-endorphin) may account for differential effects. In this regard, Goodkin et al. (1996) reported that plasma cortisol levels correlated inversely with proliferative response to PHA. Similarly, Antoni and colleagues (1990) found that anxiety levels and intrusive thoughts were associated with higher plasma cortisol levels and lower proliferative responses to PHA among individuals who were awaiting the results of HIV testing. Mechanisms aside, there is recent evidence that immune responses to acute and chronic stress may be related, with individuals who report higher levels of life event stress and daily hassles mounting greater immunologic responses to acute stress (Brosschot et al., 1994; Pike et al., 1997).

Although it is now well established that acute and chronic stress are associated with both functional and enumerative aspects of immunity, an examination of response variability reveals that individuals differ substantially in the magnitude of their immunologic reactivity to stress (Kiecolt-Glaser et al., 1992; Manuck et al., 1991; Naliboff et al., 1991), with many individuals exhibiting little or no response (Glaser, Kiecolt-Glaser, Stout et al., 1985; Manuck et al., 1991; Schleifer et al., 1983). It is suggested that these differences reflect variability among individuals in the magnitude of their sympathetic responsivity to stress, an aspect of individual difference that has been demonstrated to be relatively stable over time (Dimsdale, Young, Moore, & Struss, 1987). Recent findings provide initial evidence that interindividual variability of behaviorally evoked immune reactivity is also reproducible on retesting, and may therefore denote a stable dimension of individual differences (Marsland et al., 1995; Mills, Haeri, & Dimsdale, 1995). In these studies, the stability of cellular immune reactions to a laboratory stressor was assessed on two occasions, separated by a 2- or 6-week interval. Significant test–retest correlations were observed for the magnitude of change in proliferative response to PHA (but not Con A), numbers of T-suppressor/cytotoxic and NK cells, and the ratio of T-helper to T-suppressor/cytotoxic cells (*r*s ranged from .40–.60; Marsland et al., 1995; Mills et al., 1995). Similarly, another study has demonstrated that individuals who mount greater heart rate responses (an index of sympathetic arousal) to a speech task show greater increases in NK cell activity when exposed to a mental arithmetic task on a different day than do persons exhibiting low heart rate responses under the same stimulus conditions (Sgoutas-Emch et al., 1994). Taken together, these findings suggest that individuals vary consistently in the magnitude of their cellular immune reactivity to acute stress.

The existence of such dispositional characteristics makes it conceivable that exaggerated immune responsivity to behavioral challenge may be implicated in the pathogenesis of immune-related disease, such as host resistance to infection (S. Cohen & Manuck, 1995). One possibility is that individuals who show exaggerated immune responses to laboratory stressors exhibit similarly exaggerated reactions to everyday hassles (e.g., work demands and time pressures), rendering them more immunocompromised and hence more susceptible to infectious disease. To date, one published study has explored whether individual differences in immune reactivity moderate associations between psychological stress and infectious illness (Boyce et al., 1995). Boyce and colleagues found that children (age 3–5) showing the largest stress-induced increases in circulating numbers of B cells and in lymphocyte proliferation to PWM were at greatest risk for developing upper respiratory infections in response to a naturalistic stressor. However, interpretation of these effects is unclear because the interaction between immune reactivity and stress, as a predictor of infection, was attributable in large part to an unexpectedly lower incidence of disease for high reactive children not exposed to naturalistic stress (S. Cohen & Manuck, 1995). Moreover, previous studies involving adults have not found reliable increases in circulating B cell numbers or proliferative response to PWM following stress. Although intriguing, further replications of these findings are needed, not only with children, but using adult samples as well.

Marsland, S. Cohen, Rabin, and Manuck (in press) further explored whether individual differences in immune reactivity are germane to susceptibility to infectious disease. This study examined whether immune reactivity predicted antibody response to recombinant hepatitis B vaccination, an in vivo measure of host resistance to viral infection. For this purpose, 84 healthy graduate students who tested negative for prior exposure to hepatitis B virus were administered the standard series of three hepatitis B vaccinations. The first two vaccinations were given 6 weeks apart, with a follow-up booster dose administered 6 months following the first shot. Five months after the first dose, each subject completed a battery of stress measures and a blood sample was drawn to assess hepatitis B surface antibody levels. Four to 6 weeks following completion of the vaccination series, subjects returned to the laboratory to perform an acute laboratory stress protocol, measuring immunologic responses to an evaluative speech task. Findings demonstrated that, when compared with high antibody responders, subjects who mounted lower antibody responses to hepatitis B vaccination following the first two doses displayed greater stress-induced suppression of immune function, as measured by proliferative response to PHA, but not Con A or PWM. As such, this study lends some support to the hypothesis that individual differences in the magnitude of stress-induced suppression of immune function may have clinical significance, being related to an in vivo immune response relevant for protection against infection. Consistent with other studies measuring the impact of stress later in the antibody response (Jabaaij et al., 1993; Snyder et al., 1993; Stone et al., 1994), no association was found between stress and antibody response.

At present, the clinical significance of the observed differences in magnitude of antibody response among the high and low responders is unknown. This study was conducted using young, healthy participants and a vaccination protocol designed to produce maximal immunity to hepatitis B in greater than 90% of individuals. Hence, the majority of subjects show an antibody titer that is considered to be protective against hepatitis B infection by the end of the vaccination series. However, it is known that individuals who mount lower antibody responses to hepatitis B vaccination lose their protective status more quickly (Horowitz, Ershler, McKinney, & Battiola, 1988). Hence, subjects who showed greater immune reactivity following acute stress might be expected to have a decreased duration of immunity to hepatitis B than individuals who are less immunoreactive. It is also possible that individual differences in reactivity would have a greater impact on vaccination response among less healthy populations (e.g., elderly or very young persons) or those who already have compromised immune function (e.g., individuals with HIV or cancer).

In sum, some initial evidence is provided that individual differences in the magnitude of immune responses to acute laboratory challenge are related to an in vivo measure of immune competence. However, prospective studies employing measures of individual difference as predictors of disease outcome are required in order to show that individuals who show greater suppression of immune function following stress are more vulnerable to infectious disease.

CONCLUSIONS

In support of popular belief, there is now substantial evidence for the role of psychological stress in susceptibility to upper respiratory infectious disease (e.g., S. Cohen et al., 1991; Stone et al., 1992). One possible mediator of this relation is the modulation of immune function, thereby influencing host susceptibility to infectious pathogens. In this regard, it is well established that both major stressful experiences (e.g., bereavement or natural disasters) and more minor stressors (e.g., arguing with a spouse, acute laboratory challenge) are associated with changes in immune function. However, it remains unclear whether associations between psychological factors and infectious disease are attributable to stress-induced changes in immunity. Indeed, the clinical significance of relatively small immunologic alterations has not been established. Many associations between stress and health or between stress and the immune system may be attributable to concomitant changes in health behaviors. Recent studies conducted in laboratory settings, however, provide evidence that the sympathetic nervous system mediates some immunologic changes during acute challenge stress. It has also been demonstrated that individuals differ substantially in the magnitude of their immunologic responsivity to stress, with recent evidence suggesting that these response tendencies may reflect stable attributes of individuals. Hence, it is conceivable that there is a meaningful distribution of differences in immunologic reactivity that may form a physiological basis for differences in susceptibility to infection.

Future research in psychoneuroimmunology needs to focus on whether the type or magnitude of stress-related immune modulation influences host resistance to disease, especially in light of the fact that immune responses of stressed persons generally fall within normal ranges (Rabin, S. Cohen, Ganguli, Lysle, & Cunnick, 1989). Indeed, it has been suggested that substantial fluctuations in immune function can be tolerated without producing increased susceptibility to disease (S. Cohen, 1988). The role of the immune system in susceptibility to infectious disease needs to be addressed with prospective studies, measuring psychosocial parameters and immune mediators relevant for the disease under study, controlling for health behavior, and documenting disease outcomes.

REFERENCES

Antoni, M. H., August, S., LaPerriere, A., Baggett, H. L., Klimas, N., Ironson, G., Schneiderman, N., & Fletcher, M. A. (1990). Psychological and neuroendocrine measures related to functional immune changes in anticipation of HIV-1 serostatus notification. *Psychosomatic Medicine, 52,* 496–510

Antoni, M. H., Baggett, L., Ironson, G., LaPerriere, A., August, S., Klimas, N., Schneiderman, N., & Fletcher, M. A. (1991). Cognitive-behavioral stress management intervention buffers distress responses and immunologic changes following notification of HIV-1 seropositivity. *Journal of Consulting and Clinical Psychology, 59,* 906–915.

Arnetz, B. B., Wasserman, J., Petrii, B., Brenner, S. O., Levi, L., Eneroth, P., Salovaara, H., Hjelm, R., Salovaara, L., Theorell, T.,

& Petterson, I. L. (1987). Immune function in unemployed women. *Psychosomatic Medicine, 49,* 3–12.

Bachen, E. A., Manuck, S. B., Cohen, S., Muldoon, M. F., Raible, R., Herbert, T. B., & Rabin, B. S. (1995). Adrenergic blockade ameliorates cellular immune responses to mental stress in humans. *Psychosomatic Medicine, 57,* 366–372

Bachen, E. A., Manuck, S. B., Marsland, A. L., Cohen, S., Malkoff, S. B., Muldoon, M. F., & Rabin, B. S. (1992). Lymphocyte subset and cellular immune responses to a brief experimental stressor. *Psychosomatic Medicine, 54,* 673–679.

Bachen, E. A., Marsland, A. L., Manuck, S. B., & Cohen, S. (1998). Immunomodulation: Psychological stress and immune competence. In T. F. Kresina (Ed.), *Handbook of immune modulating agents* (pp. 145–159). New York: Marcel Dekker.

Baron, R. S., Cutrona, C. E., Hicklin, D., Russell, D. W., & Lubaroff, D. M. (1990). Social support and immune function among spouses of cancer patients. *Journal of Personality and Social Psychology, 59,* 344–352.

Bartrop, R., Lazarus, L., Luckhurst, E., Kiloh, L. G., & Penny, R. (1977). Depressed lymphocyte function after bereavement. *Lancet, 1,* 834–836.

Baum, A. (1990). Stress, intrusive imagery, and chronic distress. *Health Psychology, 9,* 653–675.

Baum, A., Cohen, L., & Hall, M. (1993). Control and intrusive memories as possible determinants of chronic stress. *Psychosomatic Medicine, 55,* 274–286.

Benschop, R. J., Nieuwenhui, E. E., Tromp, E. A., Godaert, G. L., Ballieux, R. E., & van Doornen, L. J. (1994). Effects of b-adrenergic blockade on immunologic and cardiovascular changes induced by mental stress. *Circulation, 89,* 762–769.

Benschop, R. J., Oostveen, F. G., Heijnen, C. J., & Ballieux, R. E. (1993). B_2–adrenergic stimulation causes detachment of natural killer cells from cultured endothelium. *European Journal of Immunology, 23,* 3242–3247.

Bovbjerg, D. H., Manne, S. L., & Gross, P. A. (1990). Immune response to influenza vaccine is related to psychological state following exams. *Psychosomatic Medicine, 52,* 229

Boyce, W. T., Chesney, M., Alkon, A., Tschann, J. M., Adams, S., Chesterman, B., Cohen, F., Kaiser, P., Folkman, S., & Wara, D. (1995). Psychobiological reactivity to stress and childhood respiratory illnesses: Results of two prospective studies. *Psychosomatic Medicine, 57,* 411–422.

Brosschot, J. F., Benschop, R. J., Godaert, G. L., Heijnen, C. J., & Ballieux, R. E. (1992). Effects of experimental psychological stress on distribution and function of peripheral blood cells. *Psychosomatic Medicine, 54,* 394–406.

Brosschot, J. F., Benschop, R. J., Godaert, G.L.R., Olff, M., De Smet, M., Heijen, C. J., & Ballieux, R. E. (1994). Influence of life stress on immunological reactivity to mild psychological stress. *Psychosomatic Medicine, 56,* 216–224.

Cacioppo, J. T. (1994). Social neuroscience: Autonomic, neuroendocrine, and immune responses to stress. *Psychophysiology, 31,* 113–128.

Caggiula, A. R., McAllister, C. G., Matthews, K. A., Berga, S. L., Owens, J. F., & Millers, A. L. (1995). Psychological stress and immunological responsiveness in normally cycling, follicular-stage women. *Journal of Neuroimmunology, 59,* 103–111.

Chrousos, G. P., & Gold, P. W. (1992). The concepts of stress and stress disorders: Overview of physical and behavioral homeostasis. *Journal of the American Medical Association, 267,* 1244–1252.

Clover, R. D., Abell, T., Becker, L. A., Crawford, S., & Ramsey, C. N. (1989). Family functioning and stress as predictors of influenza B infection. *Journal of Family Practice, 28,* 193–213.

Coates, T. J., McKusick, L., Kuno, R., & Stites, D. P. (1989). Stress reduction training changed number of sexual partners but not immune function in men with HIV. *Americal Journal of Public Health, 79,* 885–887.

Cohen, S. (1988). Psychosocial models of the role of social support in the etiology of physical disease. *Health Psychology, 7,* 269–297.

Cohen, S., Doyle, W. J., Skoner, D. P., Fireman, P., Gwaltney, J. M., Jr., & Newsom, J. T. (1995). State and trait negative affect as predictors of objective and subjective symptoms of respiratory viral infections. *Journal of Personality and Social Psychology, 68,* 159–169.

Cohen, S., Doyle, W. J., Skoner, D. P., Frank, E., Rabin, B. S., & Gwaltney, Jr., J. M. (1998). Types of stressors that increase susceptibility to the common cold in healthy adults. *Health Psychology, 17,* 214–223.

Cohen, S., & Herbert, T. B. (1996). Health Psychology: Psychological factors and physical disease from the perspective of human psychoneuroimmunology. *Annual Review of Psychology, 47,* 113–142.

Cohen, S., & Manuck, S. B. (1995). Stress, reactivity, and disease. *Psychosomatic Medicine, 57,* 423–426.

Cohen, S., Tyrrell, D.A.J., & Smith, A. P. (1991). Psychological stress and susceptibility to the common cold. *New England Journal of Medicine, 325,* 606–612

Cohen, S., Tyrrell, D.A.J., & Smith, A. P. (1993). Negative life events, perceived stress, negative affect, and susceptibility to the common cold. *Journal of Personality and Social Psychology, 64,* 131–140.

Cohen, S., & Williamson, G. M. (1991). Stress and infectious disease in humans. *Psychological Bulletin, 109,* 5–24

Crary, B., Hauser, S. L., Borysenko, M., Kutz, I., Hoban, C., Ault, K. A., Weiner, H. L., & Benson, H. (1983). Epinephrine-induced changes in the distribution of lymphocyte subsets in peripheral blood of humans. *Journal of Immunology, 131,* 1178–1181.

Cunnick, J. E., Lysle, D. T., Armfield, A., & Rabin, B. S. (1988). Shock-induced modulation of lymphocyte responsiveness and natural killer cell activity: Differential effects of induction. *Brain, Behavior and Immunity, 2,* 102–113.

Darko, D. F., Irwin, M. R., Risch, S. C., & Gillin, J. C. (1992). Plasma beta-endorphin and natural killer cell activity in major depression: A preliminary study. *Psychiatry Research, 43,* 111–119.

Delahanty, D. L., Liegey Dougall, A., Schmitz, J. B., Hawken, L., Trakowski, J. H., Jenkins, F. J., & Baum, A. (1996). Time course of natural killer cell activity and lymphocyte proliferation in response to two acute stressors in healthy men. *Health Psychology, 15,* 48–55

Dimsdale, J. E., Young, D., Moore, R., & Struss, W. (1987). Do plasma norepinephrine levels reflect behavioral stress? *Psychosomatic Medicine, 49,* 375–382

Dobbin, J. P., Harth, M., McCain, G. A., Martin, R. A., & Cousin, K. (1991). Cytokine production and lymphocyte transformation during stress. *Brain, Behavior, and Immunity, 5,* 339–348.

Dorian, B., Garfinkel, P., Keystone, E., Gorczyinski, R., Darby, P., & Garner, D. (1985). Occupational stress and immunity. *Psychosomatic Medicine, 47*(Abstract), 77.

Esterling, B. A., Kiecolt-Glaser, J. K., Bodnar, J. C., & Glaser, R. (1994). Chronic stress, social support, and persistent alterations in the natural killer cell response to cytokines in older adults. *Health Psychology, 13,* 291–298.

Evans, P., Bristow, M., Hucklebridge, F., Clow, A., & Walters, N. (1993). The relationship between secretory immunity, mood and life events. *British Journal of Clinical Psychology, 32,* 227–236.

Fawzy, R. I., Fawzy, N. W., Hyun, C. S., Elashoff, R., Guthrie, D., Fahey, J. L., & Morton, D. L. (1993). Malignant melanoma: Effects of an early structured psychiatric intervention, coping, and affective state on recurrence and survival 6 years later. *Archives of General Psychiatry, 50,* 681–689.

Felten, S. Y., & Olschowka, J. (1987). Noradrenergic sympathetic innervation of the spleen: II. Tyrosine hydroxylase (TH)-positive nerve terminals for synaptic like contacts on lymphocytes in the splenic white pulp. *Journal of Neuroscience Research, 18,* 37–48.

Gerritsen, W., Heijnen, C. J., Wiegant, V. M., Bermond, B., & Frijda, N. H. (1996). Experimental social fear: Immunological, hormonal, and autonomic concomitants. *Psychosomatic Medicine, 58,* 273–286.

Glaser, R., Kiecolt-Glaser, J. K., Bonneau, R. H., Malarkey, W., Kennedy, S., & Hughes, J. (1992). Stress-induced modulation of the immune response to recombinant hepatitis B vaccine. *Psychosomatic Medicine, 54,* 22–29.

Glaser, R., Kiecolt-Glaser, J. K., Speicher, C. E., & Holliday, J. E. (1985). Stress, loneliness, and changes in herpes virus latency. *Journal of Behavioral Medicine, 8,* 249–260.

Glaser, R., Kiecolt-Glaser, J. K., Stout, J. C., Tarr, K. L., Speicher, C. E., & Holliday, J. E. (1985). Stress-related impairments in cellular immunity. *Psychiatry Research, 16,* 233–239.

Glaser, R., Pearson, G. R., Bonneau, R. H., Esterling, B. A., Atkinson, C., & Kiecolt-Glaser, J. K. (1993). Stress and the memory T-cell response to the Epstein–Barr virus in healthy medical students. *Health Psychology, 12,* 435–442.

Glaser, R., Rice, J., Speicher, C. E., Stout, J. C., & Kiecolt-Glaser, J. K. (1986). Stress depresses interferon production by leukocytes concomitant with a decrease in natural killer cell activity. *Behavioral Neuroscience, 100,* 675–678.

Goodkin, K., Feaster, D. J., Tuttle, R., Blaney, N. T., Kumar, M., Baum, M. K., Shapshak, P., & Fletcher, M. A. (1996). Bereavement is associated with time-dependent decrements in cellular immune function in asymptomatic human immunodeficiency virus type-1 seropositive homosexual men. *Clinical Diagnostics and Laboratory Immunology, 3,* 109–118.

Graham, N.M.H., Douglas, R. B., & Ryan, P. (1986) Stress and acute respiratory infection. *American Journal of Epidemiology, 124,* 389.

Green, W. A., Betts, R. F., & Ochitill, H. N. (1978). Psychosocial factors and immunity: Preliminary report. *Psychosomatic Medicine, 40,* 87.

Heilig, M., Irwin, M., Grewal, I., & Sercarz, E. (1993). Sympathetic regulation of T-helper cell function. *Brain, Behavior and Immunity, 7,* 154–163

Herberman, R. B., & Ortaldo, J. R. (1981). Natural killer cells: Their role in defense against disease. *Science, 214,* 24.

Herbert, T. B., & Cohen, S. (1993). Stress and immunity in humans: A meta-analytic review. *Psychosomatic Medicine, 55,* 364–379.

Herbert, T. B., Cohen, S., Marsland, A. L., Bachen, E. A., Rabin, B. S., Muldoon, M. F., & Manuck, S. B. (1994). Cardiovascular reactivity and the course of immune response to an acute psychological stressor. *Psychosomatic Medicine, 56,* 337–344.

Hollinger, F. B. (1989). Factors influencing the immune response to hepatitis B vaccine, booster dose guidelines, and vaccine protocol recommendations. *American Journal of Medicine, 87*(Suppl.), 3A, 36S–40S.

Horowitz, M. M., Ershler, W. B., McKinney, W. P., & Battiola, R. J. (1988). Duration of immunity after hepatitis B vaccination: Efficacy of low-dose booster vaccine. *Annals of Internal Medicine, 108,* 185–189.

Ironson, G., Wyningo, C., Schneiderman, N., Baum, A., Rodriguez, M., Greenwood, D., Benight, C., Antoni, M., LaPerriere, A., Huang, H., Klimas, N., & Fletcher, M. (1997). Posttraumatic stress symptoms, intrusive thoughts, loss, and immune function after hurricane Andrew. *Psychosomatic Medicine, 59,* 128–141.

Irwin, M., Daniels, M., Smith, T. L., Bloom, E., & Weiner, H. (1987). Impaired natural killer cell activity during bereavement. *Brain, Behavior and Immunity, 1,* 98–104.

Irwin, M., Lacher, U., & Caldwell, C. (1992). Depression and reduced natural killer cytotoxicity: A longitudinal study of depressed patients and control subjects. *Psychological Medicine, 22,* 1045–1050.

Irwin, M., Mascovich, A., Gillin, J., Willoughby, R., Pike, J., & Smith, T. (1994). Partial sleep deprivation reduces natural killer cell activity in humans. *Psychosomatic Medicine, 65,* 493–498.

Jabaaij, L., Grosheide, P. M., Heijtink, R. A., Duivenvoorden, H. J., Ballieux, R. E., & Vingerhoets, A.J.J.M. (1993). Influence of perceived psychological stress and distress on antibody response to low dose rDNA hepatitis B vaccine. *Journal of Psychosomatic Research, 37,* 361–369.

Jern, C., Wadenvik, H., Mark, H., Hallgren, J., & Jern, S. (1989). Haematological changes during acute mental stress. *British Journal of Haematology, 71,* 153–156.

Kasl, S. V. (1984). *Health Care and Human Behavior.* A. Steptoe & A. Mathews (Eds.), London: Academic Press.

Kemeny, M. E., Weiner, H., Duran, R., Taylor, S. E., Visscher, B., & Fahey, J. L. (1995). Immune system changes after the death of a partner in HIV-positive gay men. *Psychosomatic Medicine, 57,* 547–554.

Kennedy, S., Kiecolt-Glaser, J. K., & Glaser, R. (1988). Immunological consequences of acute and chronic stressors: Mediating role of interpersonal relationships. *British Journal of Medical Psychology, 61,* 77–85.

Kiecolt-Glaser, J. K., Cacioppo, J. T., Malarkey, W. B., & Glaser, R. (1992). Acute psychological stressors and short-term immune changes: What, why, for whom, and what extent? *Psychosomatic Medicine, 54,* 680–685.

Kiecolt-Glaser, J. K., Fisher, L. D., Ogrocki, P., Stout, J. C., Speicher, C. E., & Glaser, R. (1987). Marital quality, marital disruption, and immune function. *Psychosomatic Medicine, 49,* 13–34.

Kiecolt-Glaser, J. K., Garner, W., Speicher, C. E., Penn, G., & Glaser, R. (1984). Psychosocial modifiers of immunocompetence in medical students. *Psychosomatic Medicine, 46,* 7–11

Kiecolt-Glaser, J. K., & Glaser, R. (1987). Psychosocial moderators of immune function. *Annals of Behavioral Medicine, 9,* 16–20.

Kiecolt-Glaser, J. K., & Glaser, R. (1988). Methodological issues in behavioral immunology research with humans. *Brain, Behavior and Immunity, 2,* 67–78

Kiecolt-Glaser, J. K., & Glaser, R. (1991). Stress and immune function in humans. In R. Ader, D. L. Felten, & N. Cohen (Eds.), *Psychoneuroimmunology* (pp. 849–867). Orlando, FL: Academic Press.

Kiecolt-Glaser, J. K., & Glaser, R. (1992). Psychoneuroimmunology: Can psychological interventions modulate immunity? *Journal of Clinical and Consulting Psychology, 60,* 569–575.

Kiecolt-Glaser, J. K., Glaser, R., Cacioppo, J. T., MacCallum, R. C., Snydersmith, M., Kim, C., & Malarkey, W. B. (1997). Marital conflict in older adults: Endocrinological and immunological correlates. *Psychosomatic Medicine, 59,* 339–349.

Kiecolt-Glaser, J. K., Glaser, R., Shuttleworth, E., Dyer, C., Ogrocki, P., & Speicher, C. E. (1987). Chronic stress and immunity in family caregivers of Alzheimer's disease victims. *Psychosomatic Medicine, 49,* 523–535.

Kiecolt-Glaser, J. K., Glaser, R., Strain, E. C., Stout, J. C., Tarr, K. L., Holliday, J. E., & Speicher, C. E. (1986). Modulation of cellular immunity in medical students. *Journal of Behavioral Medicine, 9,* 5–21.

Kiecolt-Glaser, J. K., Glaser, R., Williger, D., Stout, J., Messick, G., Sheppard, S., Ricker, D., Romisher, S. C., Briner, W., Bonnell, G., & Donnerberg, R. (1985). Psychosocial enhancement of immunocompetence in a geriatric population. *Health Psychology, 4,* 25–41.

Kiecolt-Glaser, J. K., Kennedy, S., Malkoff, S., Fisher, L., Speicher, C. E., & Glaser, R. (1988). Marital discord and immunity in males. *Psychosomatic Medicine, 50,* 213–229.

Kiecolt-Glaser, J. K., Marucha, P. T., Malarkey, W. B., Mercado, A. M., & Glaser, R. (1995). Slowing of wound healing by psychological stress. *Lancet, 346,* 1194–1196.

Kiecolt-Glaser, J. K., Page, G. G., Marucha, P. T., MacCallum, R. C., & Glaser, R. (1998). Psychological influences on surgical recovery. *American Psychologist, 53,* 1209–1218.

Kronfol, Z., Nair, M., Goodson, J., Goel, K., Haskett, R., & Schwartz, S. (1989). Natural killer cell activity in depressive illness: A preliminary report. *Biological Psychiatry, 26,* 753–756.

Kusaka, Y., Kondou, H., & Morimoto, K. (1992). Healthy lifestyles are associated with higher natural killer cell activity. *Preventative Medicine, 21,* 602–615.

Landmann, R. M., Muller, F. B., Perini, C., Wesp, M., Erne, P., & Buhler, F. R. (1984). Changes in immunoregulatory cells induced by psychological and physical stress: Relationship to plasma catecholamines. *Clinical and Experimental Immunology, 58,* 127–135

La Perriere, A. R., Antoni, M. H., Schneiderman, N., Ironson, G., Klimas, N., Caralis, P., & Fletcher, M. A. (1990). Exercise intervention attenuates emotional distress and natural killer cell decrements following notification of positive serologic status for HIV-1. *Biofeedback and Self-Regulation, 15,* 229–242.

La Perriere, A. R., Fletcher, M. A., Antoni, M. H., Ironson, G., Klimas, N., & Schneiderman, N. (1991). Aerobic exercise training in an AIDS risk group. *International Journal of Sports Medicine, 12,* S53–S57.

Lazarus, R. S., & Folkman, S. (1984). *Stress, appraisal, and coping.* New York: Springer.

Light, E., & Lebowitz, B. D. (1989). *Alzheimer's disease treatment and family stress: Directions for research.* Rockville, MD: National Institute of Mental Health.

Linn, M. W., Linn, B. S., & Jensen, J. (1984). Stressful events, dysphoric mood, and immune responsiveness. *Psychology Reports, 54,* 219–222.

Livnat, S., Felten, S. Y., Carlson, S. L., Bellinger, D. L., & Felten, D. L. (1985). Involvement of peripheral and central catecholamine systems in neural-immune interactions. *Journal of Neuroimmunology, 10,* 5–30.

Locke, S. E., & Heisel, J. S. (1977). The influence of stress and emotions on human immunity. *Biofeedback and Self-Regulation, 2,* 320.

Locke, S. E., Hurst, M. W., Heisel, J. S. (1979). *The influence of stress and other psychosocial factors on human immunity.* Paper presented at the annual meeting of the American Psychosomatic Society, Dallas, TX.

Locke, S. E., Kraus, L., Leserman, J., Hurst, M. W., Heisel, J. S., & Williams, R. M. (1984). Life changes stress, psychiatric symptoms, and natural killer cell activity. *Psychosomatic Medicine, 46,* 411–453.

Manuck, S. B., Cohen, S., Rabin, B. S., Muldoon, M. F., & Bachen, E. A. (1991). Individual differences in cellular immune response to stress. *Psychological Science, 2,* 111–115.

Marsland, A. L., Cohen, S., Rabin, B. S., & Manuck, S. B. (in press). The influence of stress, trait negative affect, and acute immune reactivity on antibody response to hepatitis B vaccination. *Health Psychology.*

Marsland, A. L., Herbert, T. B., Muldoon, M. F., Bachen, E. A., Patterson, S., Cohen, S., Rabin, B., & Manuck, S. B. (1997). Lymphocyte subset redistribution during acute laboratory stress in young adults: Mediating effects of hemoconcentration. *Health Psychology, 16,* 1–8.

Marsland, A. L., Manuck, S. B., Fazzari, T. V., Stewart, C. J., & Rabin, B. S. (1995). Stability of individual differences in cellular immune responses to acute psychological stress. *Psychosomatic Medicine, 57,* 295–298.

McKinnon, W., Weisse, C. S., Reynolds, C. P., Bowles, C. A., & Baum, A. (1989). Chronic stress, leukocyte subpopulations, and humoral response to latent viruses. *Health Psychology, 8,* 389–402

Meyer, R. J., & Haggerty, R. J. (1962). Streptoccocal infections in families. *Pediatrics, 29,* 539–549.

Mills, P. J., & Dimsdale, J. E. (1996). The effects of acute psychologic stress on cellular adhesion molecules. *Journal of Psychosomatic Research, 41,* 49–53.

Mills, P. J., Haeri, S. L., & Dimsdale, J. E. (1995). Temporal stability of acute stressor-induced changes in cellular immunity. *International Journal of Psychophysiology, 19,* 287–290.

Naliboff, B. D., Benton, D., Soloman, G. F., Morley, J. E., Fahey, J. L., Bloom, E. T., Makinodan, T., & Gilmore, S. L. (1991). Immunological changes in young and old adults during brief laboratory stress. *Psychosomatic Medicine, 53,* 121–132.

O'Leary, A. (1990). Stress, emotion and human immune function. *Psychological Bulletin, 108,* 363–382

Petry, L. J., Weems, L. B., & Livingstone, J. N. (1991). Relationship of stress, distress, and the immunologic response to a recombinant hepatitis B vaccine. *Journal of Family Practice, 32,* 481–486.

Pike, J. K., Smith, T. L., Hauger, R. L., Nicassio, P. M., Patterson, T. L., McClintick, J., Costlow, C., & Irwin, M. R. (1997). Chronic life stress alters sympathetic, neuroendocrine, and immune responsivity to an acute psychological stressor in humans. *Psychosomatic Medicine, 59,* 447–457.

Plaut, M. (1987). Lymphocyte hormone receptors. *Annual Review of Immunology, 5,* 621–669.

Rabin, B. S., Cohen, S., Ganguli, R., Lysle, D. T., & Cunnick, J. E. (1989). Bidirectional interaction between the central nervous and the immune system. *Critical Reviews in Immunology, 9,* 279–312.

Schedlowski, M., Jacobs, R., Stratmann, G., Richter, S., Hadicke, A., Tewes, U., Wagner, T. O., & Schmidt, R. E. (1993). Changes of natural killer cells during acute psychological stress. *Journal of Clinical Immunology, 13,* 119–126.

Schleifer, S. J., Keller, S. E., Camerino, M., Thornton, J. C., & Stein, M. (1983). Suppression of lymphocyte stimulation following bereavement. *Journal of American Medical Association, 250,* 374–377.

Sgoutas-Emch, S. A., Cacioppo, J. T., Uchino, B. N., Malarkey, W., Pearl, D., Kiecolt-Glaser, J. K., & Glaser, R. (1994). The effects of an acute psychological stressor on cardiovascular, endocrine, and cellular immune response: A prospective study of individuals high and low in heart rate reactivity. *Psychophysiology, 31,* 264–271.

Sieber, W. J., Rodin, J., Larson, L., Ortega, S., & Cummings, N. (1992). Modulation of human natural killer cell activity by exposure to uncontrollable stress. *Brain, Behavior, and Immunity, 6,* 141–156.

Snyder, B. K., Roghmann, K. J., & Sigal, L. H. (1993). Stress and psychosocial factors: Effects on primary cellular immune response. *Journal of Behavioral Medicine, 16,* 143–161.

Soloman, G. F., Segerstrom, S. C., Grohr, P., Kemeny, M., & Fahey, J. (1997). Shaking up immunity: Psychological and immunologic changes after a natural disaster. *Psychosomatic Medicine, 59,* 114–127.

Stone, A. A., Bovbjerg, D. H., Neale, J. M., Napoli, A., Valdimarsdottir, H., Cox, D., Hayden, F. G., & Gwaltney, J. M. (1992). Development of common cold symptoms following experimental rhinovirus infection is related to prior stressful life events. *Behavioral Medicine,* fall, 115–120.

Stone, A. A., Marco, C. A., Cruise, C. E., Cox, D. S., & Neale, J. M. (1996). International *Journal of Behavioral Medicine, 3,* 1–10

Stone, A. A., Neale, J. M., Cox, D. S., Napoli, H., Valdimarsdottir, H., & Kennedy-Moore, E. (1994). Daily events are associated with a secretory immune response to an oral antigen in men. *Health Psychology, 13,* 440–446.

Stone, A. A., Reed, B. R., & Neale, J. M. (1987). Changes in daily event frequency precede episodes of physical symptoms. *Journal of Human Stress,* 70–74.

Turner Cobb, J. M., & Steptoe, A. (1996). Psychosocial stress and susceptibility to upper respiratory tract illness in an adult population sample. *Psychosomatic Medicine, 58,* 404–412.

van Tits, L.J.H., Michel, M. C., Grosse-wide, H., Happel, M., Eigler, F. W., Soliman, A., & Brodde, O. E. (1990). Catecholamines increase lymphocyte beta-2 adrenergic receptors via a beta adrenergic, spleen-dependent process. *American Journal of Physiology, 258,* E191–202.

Weiss, D. W., Hirt, R., Tarcic, N., Berzon, Y., Ben-Zur, H., Breznitz, S., Glaser, B., Grover, N. B., Baras, M., & O'Dorisio, T. M. (1996). Studies in psychoneuroimmunology: psychological, immunological, and neuroendocrinological parameters in Israeli civilians during and after a period of Scud missile attacks. *Behavioral Medicine, 22,* 5–14.

Weisse, C. S., Pato, C. N., McAllister, C. G., Littman, R., Breier, A., Paul, S. M., & Baum, A. (1990). Differential effects of controllable and uncontrollable acute stress on lymphocyte proliferation and leukocyte percentages in humans. *Brain, Behavior, and Immunity, 4,* 339–351.

Workman, E. A., & LaVia, (1987). T-lymphocyte polyclonal proliferation: Effects of stress and stress response style on medical students taking national board examinations. *Clinical Immunology and Immunopathology, 43,* 308–313.

Zakowski, S. G., Cohen, L., Hall, M. H., Wollman, K., & Baum, A. (1994). Differential effects of active and passive laboratory stressors on immune function in healthy men. *International Journal of Behavioral Medicine, 1,* 163–184.

Zakowski, S. G., McAllister, C. G., Deal, M., & Baum, A. (1992). Stress, reactivity, and immune function in healthy men. *Health Psychology, 11,* 223–232.

Zarit, S. H., Orr, N. K., & Zarit, J. M. (1985). *The hidden victims of Alzheimer's disease: Families under stress.* New York: New York University Press.

42

Nonpharmacological Treatment of Hypertension

Alvin P. Shapiro
University of Pittsburgh School of Medicine

The health benefit from lowering blood pressure in hypertensive patients has been a major clinical research accomplishment of the last four decades. In the late 1940s and 1950s, the efforts were primarily diagnostic and therapy was limited to reassurance, hope, and prayer. Pharmacological studies at that time were concerned with evaluating acute effects of potent drugs such as the ganglionic blocking agents and the veratrum alkaloids and their applications to therapy were limited because of their potent side effects. High blood pressure reduction, with such drastic measures as fever therapy and sympathectomy, were employed in some severe situations as well as nitrates, orally and parenterally. Clinics did follow hypertensive patients closely and were impressed by the variability of blood pressure and by the value of supportive therapy—mainly reassurance, hospitalization, and lifestyle changes—in reducing blood pressure and even occasionally reversing or delaying consequences of the disease. Reiser, Rosenbaum, and Ferris (1951), in fact, reported a small group of patients in whom malignant hypertension was ameliorated in this fashion, at least for a brief period of time. Nonpharmacological therapy was the order of the day, by default, because specific drugs to treat hypertension were not available. Indeed, it was preferable to speak of the drugs that began to emerge in the 1950s as "hypotensive" agents and not as "antihypertensive" drugs.

Pharmacological therapy of malignant hypertension did make progress in the 1950s with the advent of combinations of long acting ganglionic blocking agents, the vasodilator drug hydralazine, and the diuretics of the thiazide genre. With these agents, the malignant phase of the disease could be reverted to a more benign course, but their use in the more modest forms of hypertension and in those with mild disease was inhibited by their disturbing side effects, which interfered in many ways with patient comfort and lifestyle. Orthostatic symptoms, difficulty in urination, constipation, headaches, impotence—both libidinous and erectile failure—were all very real problems in their use. And, although these could be tolerated in patients with the malignant and most severe phases of hypertension, it was difficult to justify their administration in the asymptomatic mild hypertensive. There was uncertainty as to whether life expectancy was shortened even in the individual with modest degrees of hypertension (i.e., diastolics of 100 to 115 mm Hg) and it was generally felt that with mild hypertension (i.e., diastolics of 90 to 105 mm Hg) who constituted about two thirds of the hypertensive population, the risk of death and even of significant morbidity was minimal. Accordingly, it was justifiable to view this approach with reassurance and supportive therapy, often accompanied by admonitions for weight control and a low salt diet as a method of management. These measures did result in significant lowering of blood pressure, as shown for example in studies from the 1951 group in Cincinnati (Reiser et al., 1951). Beyond the supportive therapy that was offered to patients, there were reports of significant lowering of blood pressure with more extensive psychotherapy, including psychoanalysis. These now historic events illustrate that the idea of treating hypertension with behavioral techniques is not a new concept, but rather one that physicians relied on before the advent of current pharmacological treatment.

Research has come full circle over the last 30 years. Pharmacological therapy first showed its value in the nonmalignant hypertensive in the reports of Freis and his coworkers. Their classic study on a relatively small group of male veterans in the 1960s treated patients with reserpine, thiazides, and hydralazine. The patients were divided into three groups, depending on their blood pressure levels; levels were defined as severe, moderate, and mild. A definite diminution in deaths and morbidity primarily from cerebrovascular events was demonstrated in the first two of these groups—namely those with BPs of over 115 mm Hg and those with levels from 105 to 115 mm Hg—but it was still unclear whether an appreciable impact was made on the mild group (with BPs of 90 to 105 mm Hg; Veteran's Administration Cooperative Study Group on Antihypertensive Agents, 1967, 1970, 1972). It remained for the Hypertension Detection and Followup Program (HDFP), a study conducted in 14 centers throughout the United States, to establish the value of treatment in the mild group. The HDFP enlisted and studied a population of 10,000 patients, recruited directly by house-to-house surveys in selected census tracts who were treated and followed for a minimum of 5 years; it began in the early 1970s and was reported in 1979 (HDFP Cooperative Group, 1979a, 1979b). The design of the study was relatively simple: The patients were randomly divided into two groups, one of which received special care (SC) in clinics especially established for the purpose of goal oriented, intensive care. Patients were followed closely with medications added as necessary to achieve diastolic blood pressures of 90 mm Hg or at least 10 mm Hg below their baseline. The medication used was reserpine—and later propranolol-thiazides, hydralazine, methyl dopa, and guanethidine sulfate, added stepwise to achieve the aforementioned goal. The other group of patients were assigned to regular care (RC), meaning they were turned over to their regular source of treatment, usually from their community physicians, but were seen yearly by the investigators for evaluation and follow-up. The majority of the RC patients also received some therapy from their regular source, but it was not of the intensity or goal orientation of the SC group. Although it was not considered ethical or appropriate to have a placebo group, it was recognized that the RC group would have less intense treatment because, particularly for the mild hypertensives, this was the *Zeitgeist* during this period of time.

The results were impressive. The primary endpoint was overall mortality and there was a greater than 16% decrease in deaths in the SC group. This difference was most marked in the so-called mild hypertensive patients. In fact, the differences were less in the moderate and severe patients, a fact that was interpreted as meaning that the physicians caring for the RC patients were more convinced of the need for aggressive therapy in their more severe hypertensives than they were of the need for therapy in the milder forms of the disorder. The major cause of death prevented, as in the Freis study, was cerebrovascular event. Evidence for prevention of death from cardiac causes was much less convincing, in spite of the fact that hypertension is considered a significant risk factor in cardiac, particularly coronary atherosclerotic, disease. The meaning of this failure to demonstrate a decrease in coronary artery disease (CAD) mortality created a storm of controversy that remains to this day. It has been blamed on poor choice of drugs (although at the time of this study only the ones used were pharmacologically available), electrolyte abnormalities, exaggeration of lipid risk factors, and the additional genetic/environmental/behavioral influences on atherosclerotic coronary artery disease, as contrasted to cerebrovascular disease. The difference is not due to drug factors, but to the fact that the connection between hypertension and CAD is not as direct as it is between cerebrovascular disease, particularly cerebral hemorrhage and hypertension.

These data, along with subsequent clinical trials, have firmly established that treatment of hypertension with present-day pharmacological agents has a significant impact on morbidity and mortality of the disease. Consequently, the development, evaluation, and marketing of drugs to treat hypertension has become a major industry whose goal is treatment for most all hypertensive subjects who number some 15% to 20% of the population. At the same time, however, the "pathopharmacology" of these drugs has posed a considerable problem and has led, as mentioned earlier, full circle to a reconsideration of nonpharmacological means of treatment, particularly in the milder degrees of hypertension. The problem of side effects of drugs is of course not insurmountable; in the aforementioned HDFP study, for example, although about a third of patients reported difficulties with one or another of the drugs they were receiving, only 9% had to be dropped from the program. The rest were successfully transferred to other drugs. Nevertheless, the problem has served as an impetus and a challenge to advocates of behavioral therapies and dietary and lifestyle change as alternative methods of treatment.

Under the heading of dietary changes in management, control of weight and reduction of sodium intake constitute the two major approaches. Calcium and potassium supplementation to the diet have had their advocates. Smoking cessation, alcohol restriction, and physical exercise have been scrutinized as lifestyle changes that can influence blood pressure. Avoidance of daily stress by change in occupation, environment, climatic extremes, spouse and associates, and so on all have had a long history of being offered as gratuitous advice to patients by friends, family, and indeed by physicians and other health care providers. Control of these factors requires knowledge of the social and cultural forces that influence them as well as the development of techniques to put them into effect, and in this respect behavioral manipulation, defined in a broad way, is essential. But the specific behavioral therapies which have been utilized to lower blood pressure have more direct psychological origins. They include psychotherapy, environmental modification, suggestion, placebo administration, relaxation, and biofeedback. The background, utilization, and outcomes are discussed for each of these. First, however, some discussion of the dietary and life changes is in order.

SODIUM INTAKE

Diet is strongly influenced by social and cultural factors and accordingly is affected by behavior. Most important to the consideration of hypertension is sodium intake. In fact, Denton (1965) argued that the salt-seeking behavior of humans has had a major evolutionary impact. Some of the most potent adaptations in humans are directed at sodium control and the phylogenetic development of the renin-angiotensin system (RAS) primarily relates to sodium conservation. Salt is essential to human life, yet its intake can vary from as low as 1 mequiv/day to as high as 400 and perhaps 800 mequiv/day, while the person maintains normal health and function. Sodium intake has been considered a significant factor in the pathogenesis of hypertension for many years and this chapter does not cover this literature in any detail. However, some of the epidemiological data concerning the effects of sodium are pertinent to the social, cultural, and behavioral influences on hypertension, which are within the agenda here. Studies of various cultural groups have indicated that sodium intake in close, primitive societies correlates with differences in levels of blood pressure among such societies. Sodium intake in the most primitive tribes is quite low, as is the prevalence of hypertension within them. Cassel (1974) and Henry (1988) discussed the process of acculturation in terms of the stress that particular societies experience, but Page, Damon, and Moellering (1974) suggested that this process of acculturation is also associated with increased sodium intake, which plays an equally important role in their development of hypertension.

The sodium intake of civilized people (150–200 mequiv/day) can be considered high and "unnatural," because primitive groups often subsist adequately even in hot climates with intakes of less than 40 mequiv/day. Older studies of the Yanamano Indians of South America have been particularly revealing in this regard; their sodium intake averages 5 mequiv/day and there is literally no hypertension among them and they do not show the blood pressure rise that occurs with aging. It is of interest, in view of what was said earlier about the evolutionary development of the RAS as a sodium conserving mechanism, that the Yanamanos maintain their low blood pressures in spite of peripheral renin activities (PRA) that are two to three times normal values (Oliver, Cohen, & Neal, 1975).

In regard to sodium conservation as an evolutionary development, an interesting theory has been put forward by Grim to possibly explain the higher prevalence of hypertension among Blacks in the United States (Wilson & Grim, 1991). He argued that Blacks from the interior of equatorial Africa had developed more potent sodium conservation mechanisms than those from coastal areas and they survived the rigors of the slave trade to a greater extent during the long sea voyages that brought them to this country. Deaths on the slave ships were massive and most were due to sodium-depleting causes (e.g., malnutrition, diarrhea, heat, fever, etc.). Thus the Blacks in the United States constitute the major descendants of this sodium conserving group, retaining sodium more avidly, having now a higher predilection to hypertension, and responding more dramatically to sodium restriction and diuretic therapy. Whether such a genetic selection could have taken place in the brief period of the past several hundred years is a matter of speculation, but it is an interesting hypothesis that is perhaps amenable to further investigation.

The evidence that a decrease in sodium intake in the diet will lower blood pressure in man derives mainly from the effectiveness of the diuretics and from the results of drastic sodium restriction with such regimens as the Kempner rice diets of years ago, in which sodium intake was decreased to approximately 10 mequiv/day. Direct evidence is less available concerning lesser degrees of sodium restriction, on the order of from 75 to 100 mequiv/day that could be achieved by avoidance of added salt and well-known high sodium foods, which can have a measurable effect on blood pressure in man. A study by Parijs, Joossens, Van der Linden, Verstreken, & Amery (1973) demonstrated that a reduction from the usual 200 mequiv/day to approximately 100 lowered blood pressure about 10/5 mm Hg and supplemented the effect of diuretics. Similarly, T. Morgan et al. (1978) demonstrated a diastolic decline averaging 7.3 mm Hg in a group of patients with a sodium intake reduction reflected in urinary sodium decrease from approximately 191 mequiv to only an average of 157 mequiv/day. There was a wide variation in the success in reducing sodium intake in Morgan's patients; those with values approaching 100 mequiv/day had the better blood pressure results. These results occurred and persisted over a 2-year period. A study of interest by Singer et al. (1995) relates to the additive effect of lowering sodium on the hypotensive effect of an ACE inhibitor. These investigators showed that modest reduction of sodium intake (from 206 mequiv/day to 109 mequiv/day) was equally effective as hydrochlorothiazide in improving blood pressure control.

Luft, Bloch, Weyman, Murray, and Weinberger (1978) derived the reverse data—namely, that in healthy people put on progressively high intakes of sodium starting at low levels and rising to as high as 800 mequiv/day—blood pressure will show a proportional rise. This certainly would be expected from animal data like those of Menely and Dahl, who showed this phenomenon in numerous experiments over the years (Menely & Ball, 1958; Dahl, 1961). Quite striking, however, in terms of Dahl's data on genetic differences in salt sensitive and resistant rats, studies of increased sodium intake reported by Kawasaki, Delea, Bartter, and H. Smith (1978) noted that mild hypertensive patients divided themselves into groups who were quite sensitive to salt intake and others who were considerably less sensitive.

What does all of this mean as a behavioral or cultural risk factor for hypertension? First, nobody really understands people's craving for excessive salt intake beyond their physiologic need and their ability to conserve it. It seems at least in part to be a learned habit. There is evidence that infants have little or no taste for salt, a fact that has finally persuaded some baby food manufacturers to remove sodium from baby food products because they primarily were adding it for the "tasting mothers" rather than the "consuming infants." Avoidance of salt can be learned (or perhaps salt taste can be "unlearned"), as has been the experience in treating hypertensives; anecdotally, patients who observe this behavior for a significant period of time develop a sensitive sodium taste threshold and can taste salt in situations where others do not.

On the other hand, however, there seems to be some evidence that there is an increased salt avidity in hypertensives. The question "Do you salt your food before you taste it?" is said to be answered in the positive by hypertensive patients, although there is no adequately controlled study of this phenomenon that includes normotensives. Interestingly, Langford, Watson, and Thomas, (1977) showed that patients put on diuretics can develop an increased salt intake if they are not closely watched in this regard. This is reminiscent of old observations that demonstrated that sodium-depleted rats (e.g., after adrenalectomy) preferentially will consume saline containing fluid when offered, rather than water alone.

These data suggest that man has developed a powerful tool to maintain the sodium content and concentration in his body at adequate levels for maintenance of life, and this has played a significant evolutionary role in development from marine to terrestrial animals. This mechanism may have evolved in man under certain environmental circumstances as per Grim's hypothesis. Because of cooking and preserving habits and other cultural influences on taste in modern society, people currently consume considerably more sodium than they need for their vital body functions and it is probable that this increase in sodium intake, at least in particularly prone individuals, plays a significant role in predisposition and perpetuation of hypertension.

Reduction of sodium intake to a more physiologic amount (e.g., 100 mequiv/day or about 4 to 5 grams of salt) would require major social and cultural behavioral changes. Until there is better information concerning variability of salt sensitivity, such a mass attempt at reeducation of the public, particularly in view of other dietary onslaughts on a hopeful but skeptical public, would be ill-advised. Freis (1976) suggested editorially that reduction of salt intake to low levels would "wipe out hypertension in several generations," but his statement at the most is a "provocative suggestion" rather than a pragmatic proposal. Nevertheless, the aforementioned decisions to remove sodium from baby food, and current labeling of food contents are encouraging examples of such cultural progress.

Although reduction of sodium intake is not easily achieved in normal persons, there is not enough data for its use in first step management of the hypertensive patient. Diminished intake becomes an important part of the nonpharmacological approach to the management of hypertension and is a behaviorally oriented therapy (Jacob, Wing, & A. P. Shapiro, 1987). In addition to being an important first step in the management of the hypertensive, it continues to apply when the patient is then put on a diuretic, because reduction of sodium intake does result in a lesser incidence of the development of hypokalemia from the diuretic.

WEIGHT MANAGEMENT

Obesity is a social and cultural phenomenon that has been clearly demonstrated to play a role in the predisposition and perpetuation of hypertension. It is not known why the prevalence of hypertension is greater in the obese individual, but much evidence has accumulated that weight reduction does reduce blood pressure. In fact, clinical experience finds it difficult to effectively lower blood pressure in the hypertensive patient who remains obese. Both epidemiological studies as well as clinical trials have established this relation, and many of these observations are cited and reviewed by Jacob et al. (1987). One mechanism that has been suggested for this relation is that the obese person has perforce an increased sodium intake, but several studies have controlled this factor and shown that weight loss without sodium reduction does lower blood pressure. Other studies have derived data indicating that drug therapy can be reduced and blood pressure control maintained with weight loss and some have provided data relating actual kilograms of weight loss to mm Hg of blood pressure decline achieved. Examples are the study by L. E. Ramsay, M. H. Ramsay, Hettiaracchi, Davies, and Winchester (1978) in which a fall of 2.5/1.5 mm Hg was noted with every kilogram of weight decline, and that by Stamler et al. (1980) on the Chicago Coronary Prevention Evaluation Program (CPEP) in which one kilogram of weight loss was associated with a 2.5/1.8 mm Hg decline. Such data give credence to the encouragement doctors often give patients that they will lower their blood pressure "one mm Hg for every pound they lose." In the CPEP study, the weight loss and blood pressure decline were maintained for the 5-year duration of the study in those patients who did not drop out of the program.

Most studies and treatments of obesity in the hypertensive patient have relied on nutrition-education interventions, involving the keeping of diaries of food intake along with review of these data and provision of caloric and nutritional advice. Behavioral strategies have been employed to a lesser extent, so that there is a need for their further study and application in the obese hypertensive.

Another aspect of the relation of obesity to hypertension is the so-called sleep-apnea syndrome. Unlike the usual "dipping" of blood pressure that occurs during sleep in most hypertensive patients, an undefined number of obese individuals suffer from periods of airway obstruction during sleep characterized by marked snoring, apnea, anoxia, and elevation of blood pressure. This syndrome has been associated with an increased incidence of strokes and coronary events in such individuals, although the exact prevalance of either the syndrome or its complications is not evident. Nevertheless, relief of the syndrome by weight loss as well as mechanical nighttime breathing aids and even airway surgery has been noted to improve hypertension and its control (Fletcher, 1995). This aspect of obesity and its relation to hypertension, cerebrovascular events, and heart disease requires further clinical application.

OTHER DIETARY INTERVENTIONS

An extensive literature exists of a variety of dietary interventions that have been advocated to treat and/or prevent hypertension. The most interest is in potassium intake, calcium intake, and vegetarianism. Reviews of these attempts and outcomes are available and no further discussion is offered here, except to mention them for the purpose of completeness. Suffice it to say from my own examination of the literature and clinical experience, I do not particularly use any of these modalities in treating my patients. In a recent report, Sachs et al. (1995) showed that no appreciable effects on blood pressure were noted in hypertensive patients treated with combinations of potassium, calcium, and magnesium.

PHYSICAL EXERCISE

Exercise has been advocated as a method of controlling blood pressure long before it was adopted in the behavioral field. The use of behavioral principles has moved it away from the coaches and fitness experts into the realm of nonpharmacological therapies. Cardiovascular fitness training is of particular pertinence to the management of hypertension. This literature has been reviewed recently (Jacob et al., 1987) and it has been noted that although aerobic exercise may result in modest reduction of blood pressure in most published studies, significant methodological limitations tend to minimize the value of the data. Thus, there is often an absence of no-treatment control groups and the lack of adequate documentation of intermediate variables such as maximal oxygen uptake as a measure of achieved fitness, and the possibility that weight loss is a compounding factor.

The persistence of an exercise effect has been studied by several investigators, who have found a tendency for the lowered levels to increase to baseline levels after discontinuation and a lack of relation to intensity of the exercise. Conflicting predictors of response have been noted, that is, low renin values predicted favorable results in one study and high catecholamines were predictive of diminished response in another. Most clinicians warn against the use of isometric exercise in hypertensive patients. Weight lifting, for instance, can cause sharp peaks in blood pressure that are considered potentially dangerous. Such exercise is ill-advised, for older individuals, although the effects in younger patients have not been impressive.

To summarize, the effects of exercise have not been evaluated with clinical trials methodology. It is likely, however, that small, at least transient, declines can be achieved with improved cardiovascular fitness achieved through aerobic exercise (and in our own patients we advocate this lifestyle addition). Most people are increasingly sedentary and when they become aware that they have an elevated blood pressure, their first reaction is often to "take it easy," thus further encouraging inactivity. Patients need to be made aware that exercise is not harmful to their blood pressure, cardiovascular fitness is improved, weight loss is helped, and the exercise need not be of an intense nature. Over the years, we have taken care of many adolescents and young people with modest elevations of blood pressure, who after secondary causes of their hypertension or significant congenital cardiac disease have been ruled out, have participated in strenuous sports activities (including football, basketball, running, skiing) without ill effects. To be sure, controlled clinical trials are sparse, and compliance over a long time, as with diet, is a problem in this lifetime disease, but it is a simple nonpharmacological change in lifestyle and it is strongly advocated in patient management, albeit not to the exclusion of pharmacological modalities as needed.

BEHAVIORAL THERAPIES

As mentioned earlier, behavioral methods of treatment have a long history that probably stems from the fact that observers of blood pressure have always noted the variability and reactivity of the pressure under many circumstances—both spontaneously and seemingly induced by whatever is being done to the patient. Attempts to manipulate blood pressure behaviorally have been classified in six categories.

Psychotherapy

Traditional verbal psychotherapy as a method of treating hypertension arose from two concepts. First, because anxiety seemed to elevate blood pressure, its relief by psychotherapy should then lower it. This straightforward relation requires simple techniques, for example reassurance and supportive psychotherapy. Second, insofar as the hypertensive individual may not be able to handle aggressive and hostile impulses—as suggested by Alexander, Binger, and Dunbar, among others—psychodynamic analytics therapy might lead to resolution of these conflicts and hence lowering of blood pressure.

Historically, verbal reassurance has played an important role in the management of hypertension. In fact, current attempts at creating public and individual concern about hypertension contrast sharply to attitudes clinicians tried to develop in hypertensive patients before the development of current pharmacologic agents. Patients were reassured and discouraged from worrying about blood pressure levels, based on data that the actual level of blood pressure on any one occasion did not reflect the true status and severity of the ailment or correlate with symptoms; that blood pressure levels were variable and reactive to many stimuli; and that prognosis was often unpredictable and patients might function for many years without disability despite elevated blood pressures. Patients were not encouraged to take their own blood pressure, ask their physicians its level, or keep personal records of it. The development of a "manometer neurosis" was a matter of concern; reassurance and supportive psychotherapy often with a mild sedative, such as phenobarbital, were mainstays of treatment. Environmental manipulation—such as job change, rest periods, change of domicile, or domestic arrangements—was frequently recommended. Such treatment, which can be referred to as "a pill and a prayer," was in fact all that was available for the mild and moderate hypertensive, with such therapies as severe sodium restriction and sympathectomy considered as drastic and reserved for patients with severe and progressive disease as defined by end-organ damage rather than blood pressure levels per se.

Two specific studies, one of supportive psychotherapy, the other of analytic therapy, deserve comment in this historical context. The first of these is a study by Reiser et al. done by the Cincinnati group in the early 1950s (Reiser et al., 1951), before the "pharmacological explosion"; hence, this sample of 230 patients received no specific drug therapy. A supportive therapeutic relationship was maintained in 98 of these patients for a minimum of 2 years. Significantly improved blood pressure levels (falls of 20/10 to 40/20 mm Hg) occurred in from 22% to 58% of these patients, the degree of impact depending on which of three levels of intensity of supportive psychotherapy they received. Treatment ranged from simple reassurance to superficial insight therapy and was administered by internists, albeit a group with special interest and training in psychosomatic illness. Of further note, from 17% to 40% showed improvement in physical findings, whereas 60% reported symptomatic improvement. Seventeen percent of the 98 patients died, with an average survival of 20 months, but the deaths related to the amount of target-organ damage with which they first presented, rather than to the levels of their blood pressure. Duration of these salutary effects on blood pressure and other findings was not established in this study. Even at the time, and certainly retrospectively, these outcomes were not impressive in terms of controlling the disease, but they do provide a background indicating that levels of blood pressure can decline and some improvement can ensue without specific therapy and thus they do speak to the natural history of hypertension.

A second, pertinent study was that by Moses, Daniels, and Nickerson (1956), which consisted of only 10 patients, but followed closely in psychoanalytic therapy for up to 6 years. Two of the patients discontinued therapy, but the other eight showed significant improvement with reduction of pressure to normal (in four with mild hypertension) and to a "borderline level" in two of the remaining four. One patient with an accelerated phase of his hypertension reverted to a benign state with the aid of potent drugs that became available during his course. Moses did not think that as a therapeutic modality, psychoanalysis had a role in the treatment of hypertension per se, being limited by its length, the age and intelligence of the patient, the severity of the psychiatric process, and the degree of reversibility of the somatic state. In the few patients who improved, major reconstructive changes in personality had to be achieved to accomplish the somatic results. There was never any advocacy or enthusiasm about further attempts to utilize psychoanalysis in the treatment of hypertension, but again Moses' work remains as an indication that blood pressure lowering of significance can occur during the course of hypertension, again without specific pharmacologic intervention.

The status of psychotherapy as a therapy for hypertension can thus be summarized from the data already described, and subsequent reviews as follows:

1. Declines in blood pressure of up to 20–40/10–30 mm Hg may be achieved and maintained over several years of continued therapy, although subject to "escape" with imposed stress.
2. Patients need to be seen regularly by an experienced therapist, but for supportive therapy it is appropriate and preferable that the therapist be the patient's internist or general physician. For psychoanalytic therapy, an analyst who is "comfortable" with somatic illness is necessary.
3. Supportive therapy is always indicated, especially when drugs are used, because it augments compliance. Any successful provider–patient relationship can offer this basic support.
4. Analytic therapy is highly selective, and the patient's suitability and psychiatric need independent of hypertension determines its use. It is expensive and time consuming.
5. Psychotherapy as treatment clearly has not proceeded beyond a few brief uncontrolled clinical trials, but has a long history of anecdotal experience and pragmatic application.

Environmental Manipulation

Environmental manipulation and modification to lower blood pressure is based on the hypothesis that stressful stimuli arising in the patients' environment adversely affect their blood pressure. Considerable epidemiologic evidence that environment influences blood pressure levels is available. Urban populations generally have higher pressures than rural populations. Cultural change, adjustment to a new environment, socioeconomic status, and type of job all have been implicated as affecting blood pressure. Anecdotal examples of improvement with change of environment, job, or home can be provided by most clinicians, and such change is probably recommended to patients frequently without controlled follow-up. However, controlled studies in which change of environment as a therapy has been tested are not available. There are references in the Soviet literature to the use of rest therapy and job adaptation, but with little data (Simonson & Brozek, 1959).

Data are available concerning certain types of acute changes in environment. For instance, hospitalization generally has a predictable, although variable in degree, effect on blood pressure. In 33 hospitalized hypertensive patients receiving no specific pharmacologic therapy, a maximum fall of mean blood pressure of 25.4 ± 19.8 (standard deviation) mm Hg was reported, with this maximum occurring 10 ± 5 days after admission to the hospital (A. P. Shapiro, 1956). Moutsos, Sapira, Scheib, and A. P. Shapiro (1967) showed that the placebo effect in six hospitalized patients whose mean blood pressure fell an average of 20 mm Hg was largely the effect of withdrawal from environmental stress. This hospital effect might also relate to the extinction of a conditioned pressor response to blood pressure measurement.

The long-term consequences of hospitalization and other environmental changes are not known. Combining hospitalization with pharmacologic agents is additive and in accelerated hypertension can be an important therapeutic maneuver. Although most patients with benign hypertension can be managed as outpatients, hospitalization is justified when environmental stress causes progressive difficulty in blood pressure control. Hospitalization can have a "negative" effect when conflict between patient and physician or other hospital personnel develops or when problems at home or on the job are potentiated by the patient's hospitalization (A. P. Shapiro, 1959). Similarly, any environmental manipulation carries the risk of failing to reduce stress and hence could further exacerbate the blood pressure problem.

To summarize, with the exception of hospitalization, environmental manipulation as a therapy for hypertension primarily has the status of biobehavioral speculation based on epidemiologic data in animal models (Henry & Cassel, 1969).

PLACEBO AND SUGGESTION

The effects of placebos usually have been discussed in regard to their role in evaluating drug therapy. Placebo effects are not treatment modalities, but require understanding because they can confound the results achieved by specific therapies, both pharmacologic and nonpharmacologic. The placebo has been defined as any therapy for component of therapy that is used for its nonspecific psychologic and physiologic effect but has no specific pharmacologic impact on the condition being treated (A. K. Shapiro, 1968). Study of the placebo effect in hypertension has contributed to knowledge of the phenomenon, but especially it has related to the development of clinical pharmacology and new drug evaluation (Smith & Melmon, 1972).

Placebo effects are variable and not always reproducible, the dose–response relations are difficult to identify, and the response is not a necessary consequence of the intent of the treatment. The mechanisms by which the physiologic effects occur are complex and diverse. However, that placebo effects are viewed as nonspecific is a consequence of current deficiencies in understanding the relations of the multiple factors involved. These factors fall within one of three general categories (Liberman, 1962, A. K. Shapiro, 1968, 1971): (a) patient variables—attitudes toward the physician, the treatment, and the illness; levels of anxiety and expectation, education, and past experience with illness; (b) physician variables—credibility, enthusiasm, authority, empathy, and sympathy; and (c) situational variables—location and form of treatment, interactions with staff and family, content and meaning of instructions and suggestions.

Several conclusions may be drawn from current analyses of the placebo effect. First, attempts to define an identifiable "placebo reactive" personality have generally failed (Beecher, 1959; A. K. Shapiro, 1971). Second, placebo effects can also adversely affect the clinical course of the patient because side effects, with both subjective and objective symptoms and signs, can be observed with placebo use (Beecher, 1959; A. P. Shapiro, 1956; A. P. Shapiro, Myers, Reiser, & Ferris, 1954; Uhlenhuth et al., 1959; Wolf, 1959). Third, deception is not essential to placebo action, except in the special case of "blind" drug trials. Fourth, the doctor (provider)–patient relationship is the agency of the placebo effect (Adler & Hammett, 1973).

Magnitude of Placebo and Suggestion Effects on Blood Pressure

Placebo factors include various psychological influences and manipulations that may be associated with systematic directional shifts in blood pressure (Alexander, 1939; Reiser et al., 1951; A. P. Shapiro, 1956; Wolf et al., 1955). Blood pressure changes in most studies are in the same range of magnitude as those described with behavioral procedures discussed elsewhere in this chapter (about 5–25 mm Hg, systolic or diastolic).

The salutary effect of a sustained therapeutic relation in the hypertensive patient has been mentioned earlier. The converse effect, an adverse response to a negative change in the physician's attitudes and enthusiasm—which partially negated the effect of both the placebo and the antihypertensive drug under study (A. P. Shapiro et al., 1954), despite a double-blind experimental design—also has been described. Wolf and colleagues (1955) and Pickering (1968) likewise noted a potent role for the doctor–patient relationship as an adjunct or deterrent to pharmacotherapy.

Certain variables that cannot be easily separated from placebo effects are relevant to the procedures already described. The first appearance of a patient at treatment site often has a pressor effect, probably related to apprehension. Accommodation to the situation results in a relative decline in blood pressure, appearing to be improvement. The use of placebo as an "antihypertensive" medication may or may not result in lower blood pressure; this outcome depends on physician attitudes, severity of hypertension, and whether comparison is made with initial visits, nontreatment periods, or hospitalization (Freis, 1960; Jacob & A. P. Shapiro, 1994; Pickering, 1968; D. Shapiro, Schwartz, & Tursky, 1972; A. P. Shapiro & Teng, 1957).

An older, but classic, study of suggestion by Goldring and associates (1956) of 31 outpatients shows the effect of intensive reassurance combined with visual exposure to a dramatic but innocuous device, which subjects were informed was a "therapeutic electron gun." Blood pressures fell an average of 20/14 mm Hg; in eight of the patients diastolic blood pressure fell below 90 mm Hg, an average diastolic fall of 2S mm Hg. Although the effect lasted only several weeks and a precise experimental design was lacking, these data have special pertinence to biofeedback, relaxation, and psychotherapy studies. Similarly, numerous stimuli may result in acute blood pressure elevations in normotensive and hypertensive persons, for example, stressful interviews (Wolf et al., 1955), the amount of interpersonal interaction (Williams, Kimball, & Williard, 1972), forced perception of conflict (Sapira, Scheib, Moriarty, & A. P. Shapiro, 1971), psychodrama involving assertiveness or hostility (Kalis, Harris, & Sokolow, 1957), and frustrating or demanding verbal and mental tasks (Brod, Fencl, Hejl, & Jirka, 1959; A. P. Shapiro, 1961). Removal of the noxious stimulus in these situations results in a return of pressures to baseline that might be interpreted as resulting from a specific therapeutic intervention.

Suggestion as a therapeutic factor also has been shown in experiments involving direct verbal instruction to control blood pressure without biofeedback or meditation with appropriate directional changes of 15/10 mm Hg (Redmond, Gaylor, McDonald, & A. P. Shapiro, 1974; A. P. Shapiro, Redmond, McDonald, & Gaylor, 1975). In some studies of voluntary control of blood pressure, instruction appears crucial to responses (Brener, 1974; Brener & Kleinman, 1970; Redmond et al., 1974; D. Shapiro, Schwartz, & Tursky, 1972), and in most studies involving hypertensive persons, awareness of the task required (i.e., to lower blood pressure) occurs either explicitly or is surmised by the patient. Such awareness of therapeutic intent clearly influences the response to medications (Knowles & Lucas, 1960; Sternbach, 1964) and will facilitate voluntary control of other autonomic responses (Bergman & Johnson, 1972; Blanchard et al., 1974) posing a further problem in evaluating the specificity of behavioral therapies.

Evaluation of Placebo Effects

Placebo influences produce a summation of social, attitudinal, and environmental factors that affect the blood pressure levels of hypertensive patients. Awareness of these factors has led to the design of elaborate control procedures for evaluating antihypertensive drugs, and such procedures are equally necessary for the rational assessment of nonpharmacologic therapies. Although the placebo effect is potent, it is not proposed as a planned therapeutic approach to the management of hypertension in the present era of pharmacological and nonpharmacological therapies, but its impact on the patient and on evaluation of therapy must be continually recognized. Similarly, suggestion per se will influence outcome, although it has little if any lasting value.

BIOFEEDBACK

As stated by Miller (1974), biofeedback is the "use of modern instrumentation to give better moment-to-moment information about a specific physiologic process that is under the control of the nervous system but not clearly or accurately perceived. In the terminology of 'servo systems,' such information has been called feedback. Such information about a biologic process is called biofeedback" (p. 684). With the aid of this information, it is possible to develop some control over a physiologic process.

Historically, responses innervated by the autonomic nervous system were considered "involuntary" and not modified by trial-and-error learning (also termed instrumental, or operant, conditioning). However, it is now documented that when animals or humans are provided with feedback for different physiologic processes and are given appropriate incentives for controlling the responses, they can learn to self-regulate functions such as heart rate, blood pressure, blood flow, skin temperature, sweat gland activity, and gastric and intestinal processes (Miller, 1969; D. Shapiro & Schwartz, 1972).

Neither the peripheral nor central mechanisms involved in the self-regulation of blood pressure are clearly known. Changes in muscle tension and respiration may be contributing factors, but they are not the sole mechanisms. Differential control of heart rate and blood pressure can be achieved depending of the specific type of biofeedback. For instance, in studies by Schwartz (Schwartz, 1974) and D. Shapiro and coworkers (D. Shapiro, Tursky, Gershown, & Stern, 1969; D. Shapiro, Tursky, & Schwartz, 1970a, 1970b), normotensive subjects learned to change either heart rate or systolic blood pressure, or both, simultaneously, and in either direction, with different kinds of biofeedback aimed at the patterns in which these different physiologic changes were recurring. Importantly, simultaneous changes in blood pressure and heart rate also may occur if subjects are given specific instructions to control these functions, and they will draw on various cognitive and somatic strategies to produce more complex physiologic patterns. Because blood pressure is the outcome of the relation between cardiac output and peripheral resistance, then depending on the type of biofeedback and instructions used, changes in heart rate, stroke volume, and peripheral resistance may be differentially involved, with the exact details of each needing specification. In addition, biofeedback for other potentially relevant physiologic responses, such as muscle tension (electromyography), sweat gland activity (galvanic skin response), and skin temperature theoretically may aid in lowering blood pressure (Schwartz, 1973; D. Shapiro, Mainardi, & Surwit, 1976)

Biofeedback methods use diverse techniques. Most effective are constant pressure cuff systems with which binary (yes/no) feedback for increase or decrease of blood pressure at each beat can be given. The system is usually more reliable for systolic pressure than for diastolic pressure. More intermittent biofeedback procedures based on a standard cuff system obviously cannot be used to recognize rapid changes in blood pressure but may aid patients to self-monitor or regulate pressure both in the laboratory and at home. Ambulatory indirect monitors can be adapted for such use. Various types of "rewards" are used for lowering blood pressure or achieving objectives, but praise and support from family and therapist along with the patient's desire for self-regulation are major incentives in the process. The magnitude of blood pressure decline with biofeedback has been reviewed in numerous publications, and has not appreciably changed from what was described in a review of the then existing data (A. P. Shapiro, Schwartz, Ferguson, Redmond, & Weiss, 1977); it is usually modest and generally does not exceed approximately 20/10 mm Hg. How permanent such effects are and their value in the long-term for chronic hypertension is discussed in more detail in the next section.

RELAXATION THERAPY

Relaxation therapy is a form of stress management and has a long history. Practitioners of certain Eastern disciplines and religions, notably Zen and Yoga, for hundreds of years have reported the ability to control autonomically regulated functions. Consideration of biofeedback methods in the treatment of hypertension reawakened interest in these older methods of relaxation and led to a number of new and perhaps simpler techniques. As with biofeedback, the revision of traditional opinion that the autonomic nervous system is beyond conscious control encouraged this progress.

Relaxation methods, although differing in specifics and focus, seek to elicit calmness and a hypometabolic state. The response is associated with decreased sympathetic arousal and heightened activity in the supraoptic and preoptic areas of the anterior hypothalamus (Beary, Benson, & Klemchuk, 1974; Hess, 1957). This integrated state of lowered sympathetic activity might be expected to lower blood pressure, because essential hypertensive subjects show a reactive pressor response to stimuli and the sympathetic nervous system is the major mediator of this response (Abboud, 1976; Benson, 1975; Benson, Beary, & Carol, 1974).

Several specific relaxation methods have been proposed for the treatment of hypertension. Several publications (Schwartz et al., 1979; A. P. Shapiro et al., 1977) are summarized here:

1. Progressive relaxation (Jacobsonian): a technique directed at relaxation of major skeletal muscle groups.
2. Autogenic training: standard "autosuggestive" exercises for inducing altered physiologic and mental states.
3. Hypnotic relaxation: hypnosis and posthypnotic suggestion to induce physiologic and mental relaxation.
4. Zen meditation: methods of meditation involving passive concentration on respiration and a logical exercise (koans) to elicit the relaxation response.
5. Hatha yoga: relaxation is elicited through bodily postures and exercises (asanas), breath control (pranayana), and meditation (dhyana).
6. Transcendental meditation: a cognitive technique derived from Vedic practices in which individuals assume a comfortable position, breath peacefully, close the eyes, and repeat a "mantra" (a Sanskrit word for sound) as each breath is exhaled.
7. Relaxation response: a simplified and standardized meditative technique developed by Benson and coworkers based on transcendental meditation and Zen and specifically directed to relaxation, but tailored more to Western culture.

None of the previous methods were specifically devised for treatment of hypertension. All claim nonspecific benefits for lifestyle and "well-being," as well as their potential for hypotensive effects. The abbreviated descriptions fail to do justice to the emphasis and contextual variables that give each method its particular character. Benefits from each technique are enhanced by a trained clinician or teacher, who initiates and instructs the patient, gives encouragement and corrective feedback, and follows progress and compliance.

The magnitude of effects with relaxation and stress management techniques are modest and increasingly less impressive. Following the initial enthusiasm for their use, the effects have been shown to be relatively transient and not particularly evident outside of the laboratory, as for instance when ambulatory, day-long monitoring is performed. Effects on endpoints other than blood pressure have not been achieved, with the possible exception of studies by Patel (1975; Patel & North, 1975), who showed effects lasting up to 12 months associated with decrease in drug requirements and in a few patients a decline in morbidity, but her studies have not been repeated or confirmed by other investigators. An interesting observation by Stone and DeLeo (1976) did show some decline in plasma renin activity and components of the catecholamine system that were cited as evidence of decrease in adrenergic activity along with blood pressure, but whether cause or effect remains unanswered. Relaxation effects are also not easily distinguished from those due to sleep, particularly because some studies show EEG patterns of sleep during transcendental meditation, for instance. Recent studies by Chesney, Black, Swan, and Ward (1987) and Agras, Taylor, Kraemer, Southam, and Schneider (1987) have been discouraging in terms of the specificity of relaxation as a therapeutic modality in that they failed to show a long-term advantage of behavioral therapy over blood pressure monitoring in the research clinic. In both trials, there was a progressive decline in blood pressure in the control groups during monitoring in the clinic or work site. These studies emphasize the need to monitor for a period of time, before adding relaxation, a fact that has been well-known to the clinical pharmacologist evaluating drugs.

Concerns and doubts about the specificity of relaxation and other behavioral therapies have been summarized in a review questioning whether the effects of stress management really represent just regression to the mean and related factors (Jacob & A. P. Shapiro, 1994). As results of better designed studies have accumulated, the clinical effects appear less convincing. Larger blood pressure declines tend to be reported in studies that do not include adequate baseline assessments. Habituation to a new environment, as may occur in a subject attending a new clinic, treatment program, or provider plays a role in eliciting blood pressure decline as does the development of a therapeutic relationship with the physician or other provider. Differential effects in habituation between control and treatment groups may occur as related to waiting periods before therapy is started. Drop-out rates may differ; in some studies, drop-out rates are higher in the behavioral treatment patients than in controls or even in drug studies. Certainly, compliance is a major problem in behavioral studies, particularly when such treatments require home practice by the patient. Carryover effects into the environment are also questionable. In a study comparing drugs and relaxation with measurements done at different sites, the most favorable results were seen on blood pressure changes within a relaxation session; conversely, no relaxation effect was noted on automated ambulatory monitoring outside of the therapist's laboratory or in the hypertension clinic when seen by the patient's usual physician (Jacob et al., 1992).

These findings are consistent with the notion that relaxation produces a state opposite to that of "stress." In effect, whereas stress produces a transient presser response, relaxation induces a transient depressor response. The situational specificity of the relaxation effect suggests that it is similar to the placebo response (Jacob et al., 1986). Gould et al., using intra-arterial ambulatory monitoring, observed that the placebo effect was limited to the clinic setting, while active drug effects were also observed in other environments (Gould, Mann, Davies, Altman, & Raferty, 1987). There does not seem to be any studies on relaxation therapy that have noted significant declines during ambulatory monitoring.

Self-quieting maneuvers may be acquired by subjects in any therapeutic study and are particularly pertinent in evaluating outcomes in behavioral studies. Thus patients may "learn" quickly to "sit still" when blood pressure is being measured and this ability may be different between treated and control groups.

SUMMARY OF OUTCOMES OF BEHAVIORAL THERAPIES

Over many years of clinical and research involvement with the management of hypertension much thought has been given to the use of behavioral techniques, and most have been practiced at one time or another. In fact, as mentioned previously, such methods were all that were available in the "early days." Certain usages, such as reassurance and resistance to panic (both on the part of the patient as well as the doctor) when finding an unusually high pressure, have remained a part of the therapeutic armamentarium in the present era of specific and effective drug therapy. Our interests in biofeedback and relaxation treatments were primarily research-oriented and from our own work and from review of the contributions of many others, we have come to certain conclusions. Relaxation and biofeedback have provided further evidence of the reactivity and variability of blood pressure in the hypertensive patient. Just as stress studies have clearly delineated the pressor response as a feature of blood pressure control, which may cause detrimental consequences in the predisposition, precipitation, and perpetuation of hypertensive disease, the behavioral therapies have established the existence of a depressor response, which may in the short-term occasionally have ameliorative consequences, at least on blood pressure alone. As such, the lowering of blood pressure by relaxation is an epiphenomenon. It is the converse of the well-established pressor response, involving varied depressor mechanisms—autonomic nervous system, hormonal and local—of considerable interest in understanding blood pressure control, but of minimal clinical significance in the long-term management of hypertension. Similar conclusions regarding the effectiveness of cognitive behavioral therapies have been reached in a recent meta-analysis reported by Eisenberg et al. (1993). On the other hand, a report by Schneider et al. (1995) on a favorable short-term outcome from transcendental meditation amd progressive muscle relaxation in a group of older African Americans is worthwhile to note and may have further application.

ACKNOWLEDGMENT

This article is adapted from chapter 6 in Hypertension and Stress: A Unified Concept, by Lawrence Erlbaum Associates, Inc., Mahwah, NJ.

REFERENCES

Abboud, F. M. (1976). Relaxation, autonomic control, and hypertension [editorial]. *New England Journal of Medicine, 294,* 107–109.

Adler, H. M., & Hammett, V. O. (1973). The doctor–patient relationship revisited. An analysis of the placebo effect. *Annals of Internal Medicine, 78,* 595–598.

Agras, W. S., Taylor, C. B., Kraemer, H. C., Southam, M. A., & Schneider, J. A. (1987). Relaxation training for essential hypertension at the worksite: II. The poorly controlled hypertensive. *Psychosomatic Medicine, 49,* 264–273.

Alexander, F. (1939). Emotional factors in essential hypertension. *Psychosomatic Medicine, 1,* 173–179.

Beary, J. F., Benson, H., & Klemchuk, H. P. (1974) A simple physiologic technique which elicits the hypometabolic changes of the relaxation response. *Psychomatic Medicine, 36,* 115–120.

Beecher, H. K. (1959). Placebos and the evaluation of the subjective response. In S. O. Waife & A. P. Shapiro (Eds.), *The clinical evaluation of new drugs* (pp. 62–75). New York: Hoeber- Harper.

Benson, H. (1975). *The relaxation response.* New York: Morrow.

Benson, H., Beary, J. F., & Carol, M. P. (1974). The relaxation response. *Psychiatry, 37,* 37–46.

Bergman, J. S., & Johnson, H. J. (1972). Sources of information which affect training and raising of heart rate. *Psychophysiology, 9,* 30–39.

Blanchard, E. B., Scott, R. W., Young, L. D., & Edmunson, E. D. (1974). Effect of knowledge of response on the self-control of heart rate. *Psychophysiology, 11*(3), 251–264.

Brener, J. (1974). A general model of voluntary control applied to the phenomena of learned cardiovascular change. In P. A. Obrist, A. H. Black, & J. Brener (Eds.), *Cardiovascular psychophysiology* (pp. 365–391). Chicago: Aldine.

Brener, J., & Kleinman, R. A. (1970). Learned control of decreases in systolic blood pressure. *Nature, 226,* 1063–1064.

Brod, J., Fencl, V., Hejl, Z., & Jirka, J. (1959). Circulatory changes underlying blood pressure elevation during acute emotional stress. *Clinical Science, 18,* 269–279.

Cassel, J. (1974). Hypertension and cardiovascular disease in migrants: A potential source of clues. *International Journal of Epidemiology, 3,* 204–206.

Chesney, M. A., Black, G. W., Swan, G. E., & Ward, M. M. (1987). Relaxation training for essential hypertension at the worksite: I. The untreated hypertensive. *Psychosomatic Medicine, 49,* 250–263.

Dahl, L. K. (1961). Effects of chronic excess salt feeding: Induction of self-sustaining hypertension in rats. *Journal of Experimental Medicine, 114,* 231–236.

Denton, D. A. (1965). Evolutionary aspects of the emergence of aldosterone secretion and salt appetite. *Physiology Review, 45,* 245–293.

Eisenberg, D. M., Delbanco, T. L., Berkey, C. S., Kaptchuk, T. J., Kupelnick, B., Kuhl, J., & Chalmers, T. C. (1993). Cognitive behavioral techniques for hypertension: Are they effective? *Annals of Internal Medicine, 118,* 964–972.

Fletcher, F. C. (1995). The relationship between systemic hypertension and obstructive sleep apnea: Facts and theory. *American Journal of Medicine, 98,* 118–128.

Freis, E. D. (Chairman). VAH Cooperative Study Group. (1960). A double blind control study of anti-hypertensive agents. *Archives of Internal Medicine, 106,* 133–148.

Freis, E. D. (1976). Salt, volume and the prevention of hypertension. *Circulation, 53,* 589–595.

Goldring, W., Chasis, H., Schreiner, G. F., et al. (1956). Reassurance in the management of benign hypertensive disease. *Circulation, 14,* 260–264.

Gould, B. P., Mann, S., Davies, A. B., Altman, D. G., & Raferty, E. B. (1987). Does placebo lower blood pressure? *Health Psychology, 6,* 399–416.

HDFP Cooperative Group. (1979a). Five year findings of the Hypertension Detection and Followup Program: I. Reduction in mortality of persons with high blood pressure, including mild hypertension. *Journal of the American Medical Association, 242,* 2562–2571.

HDFP Cooperative Group. (1979b). Five year findings of the Hypertension Detection and Followup Program: II. Mortality by race, sex, and age. *Journal of the American Medical Association, 242,* 2572–2577.

Henry, J. P. (1988). Stress, salt, and hypertension. *Social Science and Medicine, 26,* 293–302.

Henry, J. P., & Cassel, J. C. (1969). Psychosocial factors in essential hypertension; epidemiologic and animal experimental evidence. *American Journal of Epidemiology, 90,* 171–180.

Hess, W. R. (1957). *Functional organization of the diencephalon.* New York: Grune & Stratton.

Jacob, R. G., & Shapiro, A. P. (1994). Is the effect of stress management on blood pressure just regression to the mean? *Hemeostatis, 35,* 113–119.

Jacob, R. G., Shapiro, A. P., O'Hara, P., Portser, S., Kruger, A., Gatsonis, C., & Ding, Y. (1992). Relaxation therapy for hypertension: Setting specific effects. *Psychosomatic Medicine, 54,* 87–101.

Jacob, R. G., Shapiro, A. P., Reeves, R. A., Johnson, A. M., McDonald, R. H., Jr., & Coburn, P. C. (1986). Relaxation therapy for hypertension: Comparison of effects with concomitant placebo, diuretic, and beta blocker. *Archives of Internal Medicine, 146,* 2335–2340.

Jacob, R. G., Wing, R., & Shapiro, A. P. (1987). The behavioral treatment of hypertension: Long-term effects. *Behavior Therapy, 18,* 325–352.

Kalis, B. L., Harris, R. E., & Sokolow, M. (1957). Response to psychological stress in patients with essential hypertension. *American Heart Journal, 53,* 572–578.

Kawasaki, T., Delea, C. S., Bartter, F. C., & Smith, H. (1978). The effect of high sodium and low sodium intakes on blood pressure and other related variables in human subjects with idiopathic hypertension. *American Journal of Medicine, 64,* 293–298.

Knowles, J. B., & Lucas, C. J. (1960). Experimental studies of the placebo response. *Journal of Mental Science, 106,* 231–240.

Langford, H. G., Watson, R. L., & Thomas, J. G. (1977). Salt intake and the treatment of hypertension. *American Heart Journal, 93,* 531–532.

Liberman, R. (1962). An analysis of the placebo phenomena. *Journal of Chronic Disease, 15,* 761–783.

Luft, F., Bloch, R., Weyman, A., Murray, A., & Weinberger, M. (1978). Cardiovascular responses to extremes of salt intake in man. *Clinical Research, 26,* 365A.

Menely, G. R., & Ball, C.O.T. (1958). Experimental epidemiology of chronic sodium chloride toxicity and the protective effect of potassium chloride. *American Journal of Medicine, 25,* 713–725.

Miller, N. E. (1969). Learning of visceral and glandular responses. *Science, 163,* 434–445.

Miller, N. E. (1974). Biofeedback: Evaluation of a new technique [editorial]. *New England Journal of Medicine, 290,* 684–685.

Morgan, T., Adam, W., Gillies, A., Wilson, M., Morgan, G., & Carney, S. (1978). Hypertension treated by salt restriction. *Lancet, 1,* 227–230.

Moses, L., Daniels, G. E., & Nickerson, J. L. (1956). Psychogenic factors in essential hypertension. *Psychosomatic Medicine, 18,* 471–485.

Moutsos, S. E., Sapira, J. D., Scheib, E. T., & Shapiro, A. P. (1967). An analysis of the placebo effect hospitalized hypertensive patients. *Clinical Pharmacology Therapy, 8,* 676–683.

Oliver, W. J., Cohen, E. L., & Neal, J. V. (1975). Blood pressure, sodium intake, and sodium related hormones in the Yanomano Indians. *Circulation, 52,* 146–151.

Page, L. B., Damon, A., & Moellering, R. C. (1974). Antecedents of cardiovascular disease in six Solomon Island societies. *Circulation, 49,* 2232–2246.

Parijs, J., Joossens, J. V., Van der Linden, L., Verstreken, G., & Amery, A.K.P.C. (1973). Moderate sodium restriction and diuretics in the treatment of hypertension. *American Heart Journal, 85,* 22–34.

Patel, C. H. (1975). Twelve-month follow-up of yoga and biofeedback in the management of hypertension. *Lancet, 1,* 62–64.

Patel, C. H., & North, W. R. (1975). Randomized control trial of yoga and biofeedback in management of hypertension. *Lancet, 2,* 93–95.

Pickering, G. W. (1968). *High blood pressure* (2nd ed.). London: Churchill.

Ramsay, L. E., Ramsay, M. H., Hettiaracchi, J., Davies, D. L., & Winchester, J. (1978). Weight reduction in a blood pressure clinic. *British Medical Journal, 2,* 244–245.

Redmond, D. P., Gaylor, M. S., McDonald, R. H., Jr., & Shapiro, A. P. (1974). Blood pressure and heart rate response to verbal instructions and relaxation in hypertension. *Psychosomatic Medicine, 36,* 285.

Reiser, M.F., Brust, A. A., Shapiro, A. P., Baker, H. M., Ransohoff, W., & Ferris, E. B. (1951). Life situations, emotions, and the course of patients with arterial hypertension. *Psychosomatic Medicine, 13,* 133–139.

Reiser, M.F., Rosenbaum, M., & Ferris, E.B. (1951). Psychologic mechanisms in malignant hypertension. *Psychosomatic Medicine, 13,* 147–159.

Sachs, R. G., Brown, L. E., Appel, L., Borhani, N., Evans, D., & Whetton, P. (1995). Combinations of potassium, calcium, and magnesium supplements in hypertension. *Hypertension, 26,* 950–956.

Sapira, J. D., Scheib, E. T., Moriarty, R., & Shapiro, A. P. (1971). Difference in perception between hypertensive and normotensive populations. *Psychosomatic Medicine, 33,* 239–250.

Schneider, R. H., Staggers, R., Alexander, C. N., Sheppartd, W., Rainforth, M., Kondwani, K., Smith, S., & King, C. G. (1995). A randomized controlled trial of stress reduction for hypertension in older African Americans. *Hypertension, 26,* 820–827.

Schwartz, G. E. (1973). Biofeedback as therapy: Some theoretical and practical issues. *American Psychologist, 28,* 666–673.

Schwartz, G. E. (1974). Toward a theory of voluntary control of response patterns in the cardiovascular system. In P. A. Obrist, A. H. Black, & J. Brener (Eds.), *Cardiovascular psychophysiology* (pp. 406–441). Chicago: Aldine.

Schwartz, G. E., Shapiro, A. P., Redmond, D. P., Ferguson, D.C.E., Ragland, D. R., & Weiss, S. M. (1979). Behavioral medicine approaches to hypertension: An integrative analysis of theory and research. *Journal of Behavioral Medicine, 2,* 311–363.

Shapiro, A. K. (1968). Semantics of the placebo. *Psychiatric Quarterly, 42,* 653–695.

Shapiro, A. K. (1971). Placebo effects in medicine, psychotherapy, and psychoanalysis. In A. E. Bergin & S. L. Garfield (Eds.), *Handbook on psychotherapy and behavioral change* (pp. 439–473). New York: Aldine.

Shapiro, A. P. (1956). Consideration of the multiple variables involved in the evaluation of hypotensive agents. *Journal of the American Medical Association, 160,* 30–39.

Shapiro, A. P. (1959). Cardiovascular disorders. In S. O. Waife & A. P. Shapiro (Eds.), *Clinical evaluation of new drugs* (pp. 135–152). New York: Hoeber-Harper.

Shapiro, A. P. (1961). An experimental study of comparative responses of blood pressure to noxious stimuli. *Journal of Chronic Disease, 13,* 293–311.

Shapiro, A. P., Myers, T., Reiser, M. F., & Ferris, E. B. (1954). Comparison of blood pressure response to veriloid with that to the doctor–patient relationship. *Psychosomatic Medicine, 15,* 478–488.

Shapiro, A. P., Redmond, D. P., McDonald, R. H., Jr., & Gaylor, M. (1975). Relationships of perception, cognition, suggestion and operant conditioning in essential hypertension. In *Hormones, homeostasis and the brain: Progress in brain research* (Vol. 42, pp. 299–312). Amsterdam: Elsevier Scientific.

Shapiro, A. P., Schwartz, G. E., Ferguson, D. C. E., Redmond, D. P., & Weiss, S. M. (1977). Behavioral methods in the treatment of hypertension. *Annals of Internal Medicine, 86,* 626–636.

Shapiro, A. P., & Teng, H. C. (1957). Technique of controlled drug assay illustrated by a comparative study of Rauwolfia serpentina, phenobarbital, and placebo in the hypertensive patient. *New England Journal of Medicine, 256,* 970–995.

Shapiro, D., Mainardi, J. A., & Surwit, R. S. (1976). Biofeedback and self-regulation in essential hypertension. In G. E. Schwartz & J. Beatty (Eds.), *Biofeedback; theory and research* (pp. 313–347). Academic Press.

Shapiro, D., & Schwartz, G. E. (1972). Biofeedback and visceral learning: Clinical applications. *Seminal Psychiatry, 4,* 171–184.

Shapiro, D., Schwartz, G. E., & Tursky, B. (1972). Control of diastolic blood pressure in man by feedback and reinforcement. *Psychophysiology, 9,* 296–304.

Shapiro, D., Tursky, B., Gershown, E., & Stern, M. (1969). Effects of feedback and reinforcement on the control of human systolic blood pressure. *Science, 163,* 588–589.

Shapiro, D., Tursky, V., & Schwartz, G. E. (1970a). Control of blood pressure in man by operant conditioning. *Circulation Research, 26(Suppl. 1),* 1–27–1–32.

Shapiro, D., Tursky, B., & Schwartz, G. E. (1970b). Differentiation of heart rate and blood pressure in man by operant conditioning. *Psychosomatic Medicine, 32,* 417–423.

Simonson, E., & Brozek, J. (1959). Russian research in arterial hypertension. *Annals of Internal Medicine, 50,* 129–193.

Singer, D.R.J., Markandu, N. D., Capuccio, F. P., Miller, M. A., Sagnella, G. A., & MacGregor, G. A. (1995). Reduction of salt intake during converting enzyme inhibitor treatment compared with addition of a thiazide. *Hypertension, 25,* 1042–1044.

Smith, W. M., & Melmon, K. L. (1972). Drug choice in disease. In K. L. Melmon & H. F. Morelli (Eds.), *Clinical pharmacology* (pp. 3–20). New York: Macmillan.

Stamler, J., Farinaro, E., Mojonnier, L. M., Hall, Y., Moss, D., & Stamler, R. (1980). Prevention and control of hypertension by nutritional-hygienic means. *Journal of the American Medical Association, 243,* 1819–1823.

Sternbach, R. A. (1964). The effects of instructional sets on autonomic responsivity. *Psychophysiology, 1,* 67–72.

Stone, R. A., & DeLeo, J. (1976). Psychotherapeutic control of hypertension. *New England Journal of Medicine, 294,* 80–84.

Uhlenhuth, E. H., Cantor, A., Neustadt, J. D., et al. (1959). The symptomatic relief of anxiety with meprobamate, phenobarbital and placebo. *American Journal of Psychiatry, 115,* 905–910.

Veteran's Administration Cooperative Study Group on Antihypertensive Agents. (1967). I. Results in patients with diastolic blood pressures of 115 through 129 mm Hg. *Journal of the American Medical Association, 202,* 1028–1034.

Veteran's Administration Cooperative Study Group on Antihypertensive Agents. (1970). II. Effects of treatment on morbidity in hypertension: Results in patients with diastolic blood pressures averaging 90 through 114 mm Hg. *Journal of the American Medical Association, 213,* 1143–1152.

Veteran's Administration Cooperative Study Group on Antihypertensive Agents. (1972). III. Influence of age, diastolic pressure, and prior cardiovascular disease: Further analysis of side effects. *Circulation, 45,* 991–1004.

Williams, R. B., Kimball, C. P., & Williard, H. N. (1972). The influence of interpersonal interaction in diastolic blood pressure. *Psychosomatic Medicine, 34,* 194–198.

Wilson, T. W., & Grim, C. E. (1991). Biohistory of slavery and blood pressure differences in Blacks today: An hypothesis. *Hypertension, 17*(Suppl. 1), I122–I128.

Wolf, S. (1959). The pharmacology of placebos. *Pharmacological Review, 11,* 629–704.

Wolf, S., Cardon, P. V., Shepard, E. M., & Wolff, H. G. (1955). *Life stress and essential hypertension. A study of circulatory adjustments in man.* Baltimore: Williams & Wilkins.

43

Cancer

Barbara L. Andersen
Deanna M. Golden-Kreutz
Ohio State University
Vicki DiLillo
University of Alabama, Birmingham

The human cost of cancer is staggering. Each year in the United States over 1.4 million individuals are diagnosed and another half million people—one person every 90 seconds—die of the disease (Parker, Tong, Bolden, & Wingo, 1997). Although much of the increase in cancer incidence and mortality over the years appears to be related to advances in early detection as well as the general aging of the population (age is a risk factor; Garfinkel, 1994), Cunningham (1997) noted cancer death rates may now be trending downward (i.e., drop of 1%–3%) in the United States.

Cancers vary in their prevalence and mortality. Tables 43.1 and 43.2 display data from the United States on the incidence and death rates by specific sites and genders. These data indicate, for example, that the most common diagnoses are breast cancer for women and prostate cancer for men, but that lung cancer is the number one killer for both sexes (Parker et al., 1997). There is, however, variability across countries. For example, age-adjusted death rates per 100,000 population across sites and gender from 1990 to 1993 ranged from a high of 385 in Hungary to a low of 139 in Albania; the rate for the United States was 276 (see Tables 43.3 and 43.4; Parker et al., 1997). In short, cancer is a significant medical problem that affects the health status of millions of people worldwide.

Research on the psychological, social, and behavioral aspects of oncology began in the early 1950s, however, the knowledge base has significantly expanded during the last 20 years. In particular, research has clarified relations between psychological responses (e.g., personality, mood, coping style, relationships), social factors (e.g., presence/absence of partner, size of social network, level of social support), and behavioral variables (e.g., compliance with treatment, diet, exercise). Contemporary research incorporates these variables and biologic systems (e.g., immune and endocrine) to examine and test their effects on disease course (see F. I. Fawzy et al., 1993, for an example; see Andersen, Kiecolt-Glaser, & Glaser, 1994, for a discussion).

A brief overview of the biobehavioral aspects of cancer is provided. The chapter begins with a conceptual framework, the biobehavioral model of adjustment to the cancer stressor. Then, descriptive research findings are reviewed within a cancer-relevant time line—from symptom discovery to survivorship or recurrence and death. Aside from reviewing the relevant clinical and empirical data, specific psychological intervention studies are discussed that are designed to reduce stress and enhance coping and adjustment.

A BIOBEHAVIORAL MODEL OF CANCER STRESS AND DISEASE COURSE

The stability of many cancer mortality rates, particularly those with the highest incidence such as lung and breast, makes it imperative that new, innovative steps be taken to improve survival and enhance quality of life. Concurrently, it has become noteworthy to the medical community that psychological interventions result in significant improvements in quality of life (see Andersen, 1992, for a review). Further, both qualitative (e.g., Maier, Wakins, & Fleshner, 1994) and quantitative (e.g., Herbert & Cohen, 1993) summaries of the

TABLE 43.1
1997 Estimates of Cancer Incidence by Site and Gender for the 5 Leading Sites

Cancer Incidence			
Male (Total est. 785,800)		**Female (Total est. 506,000)**	
Site	**Number(%)**	**Site**	**Number(%)**
Prostate	334,500(43%)	Breast	180,200(30%)
Lung	98,300(13%)	Colon/Rectum	79,800(13%)
Colon/Rectum	48,100(8%)	Lung	50,900(11%)
Bladder	39,500(5%)	Uterus	34,900(6%)
Lymphoma	30,300(4%)	Ovary	26,800(4%)

Note: Adapted from Parker, Tong, Bolden, and Wingo (1997).

TABLE 43.2
1997 Estimates of Cancer Mortality by Site and Gender for the 5 Leading Sites

Cancer Mortality			
Male (Total est. 294,100)		**Female (Total est. 265,900)**	
Site	**Number (%)**	**Site**	**Number (%)**
Lung	94,400 (32%)	Lung	66,000 (25%)
Prostate	41,800 (14%)	Breast	43,900 (17%)
Colon/Rectum	27,000 (9%)	Colon/Rectum	27,900 (10%)
Pancreas	13,500 (5%)	Pancreas	14,600 (5%)
Lymphoma	12,400 (4%)	Ovary	14,200 (5%)

Note: Adapted from Parker, Tong, Bolden, and Wingo (1997).

TABLE 43.3
Age-Adjusted Death Rates in Adult Males Per 100,000 for Selected Countries and Disease Sites for 1990–1993

Country	All Sites	Colon/Rectum	Lung	Prostate	Stomach
United States	165.3 (27)	16.5	57.1	17.5	5.0
Hungary	258.7 (1)	38.0	81.6	15.8	23.4
Poland	204.2 (8)	15.4	71.3	9.9	21.6
Italy	189.2 (15)	15.3	57.0	11.6	16.9
New Zealand	170.6 (21)	26.4	42.6	19.0	9.0
Finland	149.9 (31)	12.4	46.1	18.3	11.5
Israel	116.9 (43)	15.3	25.7	9.2	8.7
Mexico	81.6 (48)	3.3	15.9	10.6	9.9

Note: Figures in parentheses are in order of rank based on data from 48 countries during the years 1990–1993. Adapted from Parker, Tong, Bolden, and Wingo (1997).

TABLE 43.4
Age-Adjusted Death Rates in Adult Females Per 100,000 for Selected Countries and Disease Sites for 1990–1993

Country	All Sites	Breast	Colon/Rectum	Lung	Stomach
United States	111.1 (8)	22.0	11.2	25.6	2.3
Denmark	138.7 (1)	27.2	17.2	24.8	3.9
Austria	105.6 (16)	21.8	13.7	9.3	7.8
Russian Fed.	99.9 (21)	14.9	12.3	7.3	16.9
Argentina	96.4 (27)	21.3	9.2	6.0	4.8
France	86.5 (36)	19.7	10.1	5.2	3.3
Japan	75.2 (43)	6.6	9.8	8.1	14.2
Albania	42.7 (48)	5.2	2.2	5.0	6.3

Note: Figures in parentheses are in order of rank based on data from 48 countries during the years 1990–1993. Adapted from Parker, Tong, Bolden, and Wingo (1997).

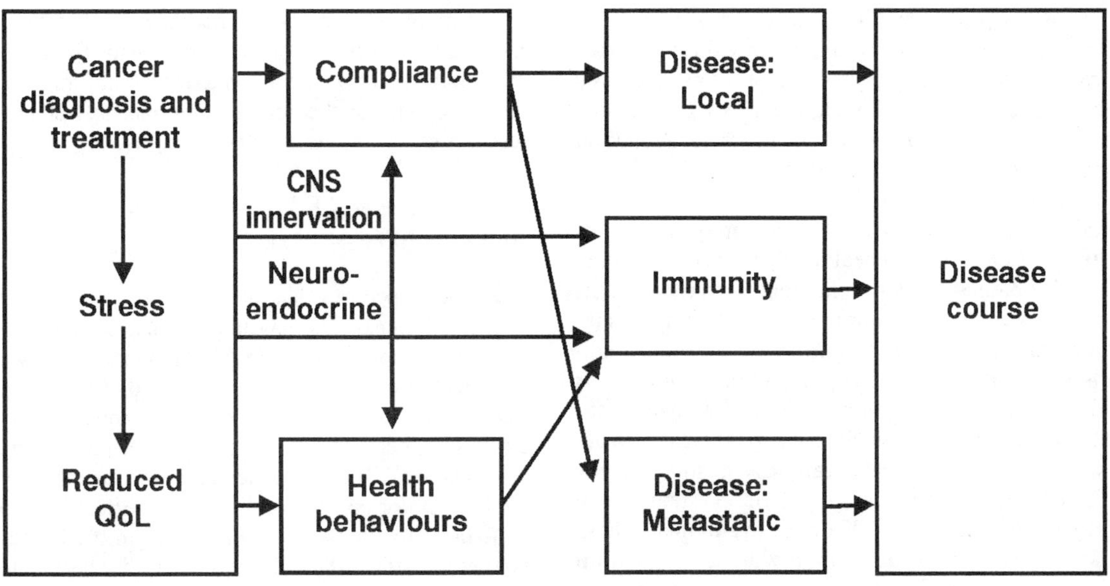

FIG. 43.1 Theoretical model. A biobehavioral model of the psychological, behavioral, and biologic pathways from cancer stressors to disease course (CNS = Central Nervous System). From Andersen, Kiecolt-Glaser, and Glaser (1994).

psychoneuroimmunology (PNI) literature conclude that psychological distress and stressors (i.e., negative life events, both acute and chronic) are reliably associated with changes—down regulation—in immunity. Thus, addressing the mental health needs of those with cancer will have important quality of life benefits, and the biologic or health consequences of psychological interventions are being tested as well. Figure 43.1 provides a representation of a model of the psychological and behavioral factors and biologic mechanisms by which disease or health outcomes might be influenced. The rationale and empirical support for this novel viewpoint are detailed in the following paragraphs.

Stress and Quality Of Life

The model first considers the occurrence of stress and lowered quality of life that come with diagnosis and treatment. These are objective, negative events, and whereas negative events do not always produce stress and lowered quality of life, data from many studies document severe, *acute stress* at diagnosis (e.g., Andersen, Anderson, & deProsse, 1989a). It is also the case that lengthy cancer treatments and disruptions in major life areas occur, producing *chronic stress.* Emotional distress, in combination with the other life disruptions, can result in a stable, but lower, quality of life. Other permanent sequelae, such as sexual problems and/or sterility, may impact intimate relationships and social support. Unemployment, underemployment, job discrimination, and difficulty in obtaining health insurance can also become chronic stressors.

Health Behaviors

Important adverse heath behavior sequelae (see arrow from cancer stress and lowered quality of life to health behaviors in Fig. 43.1), an increase in negative behaviors and/or a decrease in positive ones, can occur. There are many circumstances that can result in negative health behaviors. Individuals who are depressed and/or anxious are more likely to self-medicate with alcohol and other drugs, and then alcohol abuse can potentiate distress. Distressed individuals often have appetite disturbances or dietary changes that are manifest by eating less often or eating meals of lower nutritional value. Although there are individual differences in behavioral changes of this type, women may be at greater risk. Distressed individuals may report sleep disturbances, such as early morning awakening, sleep onset insomnia, and middle night insomnia. Cigarette smoking and caffeine use, which often increase during periods of stress, can intensify the physiologic effects of psychosocial stress, such as increasing catecholamine release. Conversely, individuals who are stressed may not begin or abandon their previous positive health behaviors, such as engaging in regular physical activity.

The model suggests that health behaviors may, in turn, affect immunity (see arrow from health behaviors to immunity in Fig. 43.1). Problematic health behaviors can have direct as well as interactive effects on immunity. For example, substance abuse has direct effects on immunity, as well as indirect effects via alterations in nutrition, and poor nutrition is associated with a variety of immunological impairments. Conversely, there is growing evidence that positive health behaviors, such as physical activity, can have positive consequences for both the immune and endocrine systems, even among individuals with chronic diseases. In summary, these lines of data suggest that distressed individuals tend toward negative health behaviors that may potentiate their stress and, concurrently, exert down regulating immune effects. Furthermore, positive health behaviors, such as exercise, may have the converse effect.

The model suggests that health behaviors may be directly related to disease progression (see arrow from health behaviors to disease: metastatic in Fig. 43.1). Considering all the health behaviors already noted, the strongest case can be made for the importance of nutrition and diet in breast cancer. A variety of data links nutrition/dietary factors and risk for breast cancer, such as epidemiological data of varied cancer rates corresponding with population differences in body fat, animal models linking high fat diets and tumor growth, and correlations between rates of obesity and the increase of breast cancer incidence. More germane to the model are data suggesting that increased fat intake, obesity at diagnosis, and weight gain may be related to recurrence and survival. Alternatively, some suggest that fiber, rather than fat, is the critical dietary factor, in that fiber is postulated to modify serum estrogen levels by increased fecal excretion of estrogens. Taken together, these data suggest that behavioral factors relevant to nutrition, fat/fiber balance, and energy expenditure (vis-à-vis weight gain) may be relevant to disease progression in breast cancer.

Compliance

The second behavioral factor noted in the model is treatment (non)compliance (see arrow from stress/quality of life to compliance in Fig. 43.1). Compliance problems cross a wide range of diseases, therapies, and individual patient characteristics. In cancer, some patients become discouraged and fail to complete treatment. A general implication of such behaviors is the invalidation of clinical trials, but a specific implication for individual patients is that their survival may be compromised if an inadequate dosage of therapy is received. That is, dosage reductions can compromise their survival when a lower intensity of cancer therapy results in differential (i.e., lower) survival rates. The model presumes that a range of compliance behaviors may be relevant, as different treatments may produce different behavioral difficulties. The model suggests that poor compliance can affect either local or metastatic control of the disease or both, and the route selected depends on the treatment regimen as well as the characteristics of an individual's noncompliance.

The Interaction Of Health Behaviors And Compliance

The model specifies that the processes governing compliance and health behaviors may interact (see double-headed arrow between compliance and health behaviors in Fig. 43.1) or even be synergistic. That is, those who are compliant with treatment may expect better health outcomes and, thus, comply with diet, exercise, sleep, and so on or other behaviors indicative of "good health." It is also noteworthy that changes in health behaviors and/or compliance have been offered as post hoc explanations for the survival difference in the Spiegel, Bloom, Kraemer, and Gottheil (1989) report (discussed later).

Biological Pathways

Stress sets into motion important biological effects involving the autonomic, endocrine, and immune systems (Uchino, Cacioppo, & Kiecolt-Glaser, 1996). Stress may be routed to the immune system by the central nervous system (CNS) via activation of the sympathetic nervous system or through neuroendocrine-immune pathways (i.e., the release of hormones; see Fig. 43.1). In the latter case, a variety of hormones released under stress have been implicated in immune modulation (e.g., catecholamines, cortisol, prolactin, and growth hormone).

Without any stress pathway (effect) to immunity, there is evidence for the importance of the immune responses in host resistance against cancer progression, and hence the arrows going in both directions from immunity to local and metastatic disease. Experts in the immunology/cancer area (e.g., Whiteside & Herberman, 1994) cite the following important findings with regard to the specific importance of NK (natural killer) cell activity: (a) Patients with a variety of solid malignancies and large tumor burdens have diminished NK cell activity in the blood; (b) low NK cell activity in cancer patients is significantly associated with the development of distant metastases; and (c) in patients treated for metastatic disease, the survival time without metastasis correlates with NK cell activity.

In considering these mechanisms, a central issue is whether an immune response can be affected by stress, and if it can, whether or not the magnitude of the effect has any biologic significance. Both time-limited (acute), as well as chronic, stressors can produce immunologic changes in relatively healthy individuals. Some of the largest effects, usually found in NK cell assays, are found for lengthy stressors and/or those that have interpersonal components (Herbert & Cohen, 1993, for review). Many of the qualities of chronic stressors (continued emotional distress, disrupted life tasks—e.g., employment—and social relationships) are associated with decrements in quality of life reported by cancer patients.

This relation between stress and immunity has been tested by Andersen and colleagues (1998). Women ($N = 116$) diagnosed and surgically treated for Stage II (70%) or III (30%) invasive breast cancer were studied. Prior to beginning adjuvant therapy, all women completed a validated questionnaire assessing stress about the cancer experience (Impact of Event Scale) and provided a 60 cc blood sample. A panel of NK cell and T-cell assays were conducted: (a) NK cell lysis; (b) the response of NK cells to recombinant gamma interferon (rIFN-g) and recombinant interleukin-2 (rIL-2); (c) blastogenic response of peripheral blood leukocytes (PBLs) to phytohemagglutinin A (PHA) and concanavalin A (ConA) and the proliferative response of PBLs to a monoclonal antibody (MAb) to the T-cell receptor (T3). Multiple regression models were used to test the contribution of psychological stress in predicting immune function. All regression equations controlled for variables that might also be expected to exert short- or long-term effects on these responses, such as age, stage of disease, and length of time of surgical recovery, and ruled out other potentially confounding variables (e.g., nutritional status) that might also be influential. These controls reduced the plausibly of alternative, rival hypotheses for the findings. Significant effects were found and replicated between and within assays, including the following: stress significantly ($p < .05$) predicted NK cell lysis; stress significantly ($p < .01$) predicted the response of NK cells to rIFN-g, replicated across 4 effector:target dilution ratios; stress significantly predicted the response of PBLs to ConA ($p < .05$) and PHA ($p < .05$), and the proliferative response to the T3 MAb ($p < .05$). The cells from 62% of the sample did not respond to rIL-2, but stress was not a factor in predicting the response for the remainder of the sample (38%). The data show that the physiologic effects of stress inhibited a panel of cellular immune responses, including cancer-relevant NK cell cytotoxicity and T-cell responses.

Disease Course

Are there adverse health (illness) consequences of stress? There are few data on this important issue, and the majority come from healthy (but stressed) adults. One of the more compelling studies is Cohen, Tyrrell, and Smith's (1991) experiment with healthy volunteers. Subjects were inoculated with either a cold virus or a placebo. Analyses revealed that rates of both respiratory infection and clinical colds increased in a dose–response manner with increases in psychological stress across five different strains of cold viruses. Data from the Kiecolt-Glaser/Glaser laboratories (Kiecolt-Glaser, Marucha, Malarkey, Mercado, & Glaser, 1995) show that Alzheimer's caregivers had slower healing of a wound (punch biopsy) than matched community controls. These relations remain to be studied with cancer patients, but this experimental data from stressed but otherwise healthy samples suggest the covariation of stress and selected health outcomes.

SPECIFIC PSYCHOLOGICAL, SOCIAL, AND BEHAVIORAL RESPONSES: FROM SYMPTOMS TO DISEASE OUTCOMES

Symptom Appearance

In view of the magnitude of the cancer problem and the potential for life threat, it is puzzling that some individuals delay in seeking medical treatment for symptoms, yet delay is a surprisingly common circumstance. Whether the time lag occurs when seeing a physician for symptoms, being diagnosed with a medical condition, or beginning treatment for the condition, all individuals, and even some physicians, can be "delayers."

One model of delay is that proposed by Andersen, Cacioppo, and Roberts (1995), in which delay is conceptualized as a series of stages, including appraisal, illness, behavioral, and scheduling delays. Each stage is governed by a distinct set of decisional and appraisal processes (see Fig. 43.2). Appraisal delay—delay surrounding interpretation of the importance and meaning of the symptoms—appears to be the most psychologically important and has been found, not surprisingly, to account for the bulk of the delay in seeking a cancer diagnosis. In a study of recently diagnosed women with cancer, the appraisal interval was approximately 80% of the total delay for women with gynecologic cancer, whereas for women with breast symptoms, a site with a narrower range of symptom diversity, the interval accounted for 60% of the delay (Andersen et al., 1995).

The finding of the appraisal period as being inordinately lengthy for cancer patients is consistent with the clinical presentation of this disease. First, the development of malignancy and the appearance of cancer symptoms are oftentimes protracted, and a complex and changing symptom picture can be typical, unlike the presentation of many other serious medical problems (e.g., myocardial infarction; see Matthews, Siegel, Kuller, Thompson, & Varat, 1983). Symptoms can also vary with the site and extent of the disease. For example, ovarian cancer has varied presentations—pelvic cramping, low back pain, pain or bleeding with intercourse, urinary frequency irregularities, among others. Moreover, as the disease progresses regionally or systemically, it can involve other bodily systems and the symptom picture can then change

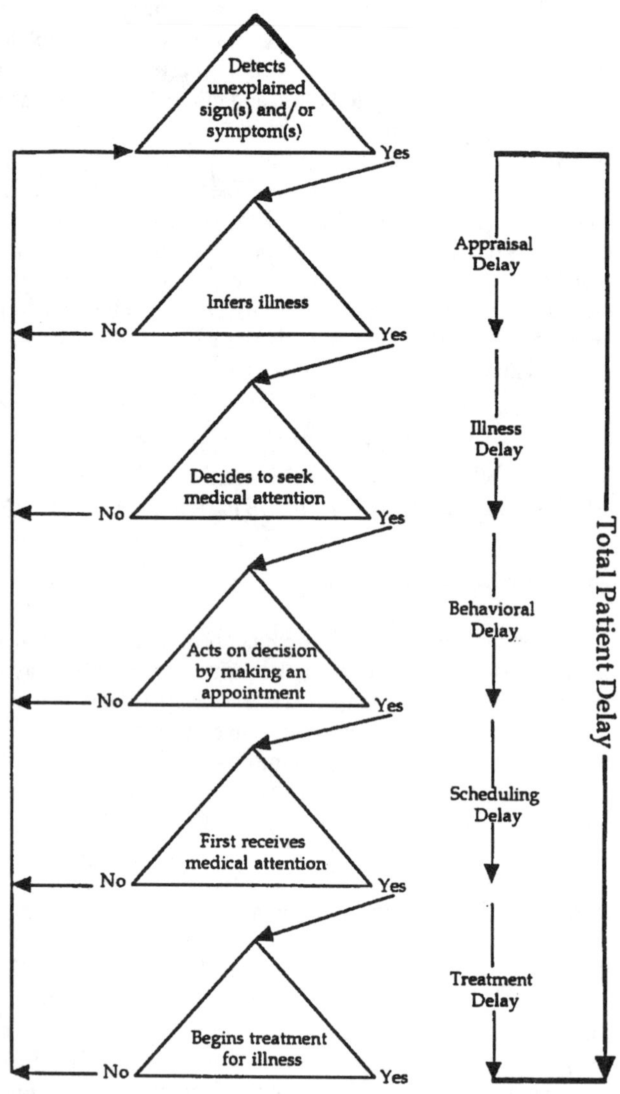

FIG. 43.2 Delay in seeking a cancer diagnosis: Delay stages and psychophysiological comparison processes. From Andersen, Cacioppo, and Roberts (1995).

from specific or localized complaints (e.g., vaginal discharge/bleeding) to diffuse ones (e.g., loss of appetite, nausea, "flu" symptoms). Finally, whereas cancer is a life threatening disease, it is a low probability one for many individuals. Thus, the appraisal process may lengthen as people think it unlikely that their symptoms would indicate a condition as serious as cancer.

Briefly considering the other stages, illness delay is defined as the number of days elapsing from the time individuals conclude they are ill to the day they decide to seek medical help. At this time individuals must decide, for example, whether to seek assistance from others (e.g., physician, others with a similar condition) or to self-treat the illness. After this, the delay is spent in making two remaining decisions. One is the delay between the decision to seek medical attention and acting on this decision by making an appointment (e.g., behavioral delay). The other is the time that elapses between the person making an appointment and the first receipt of medical attention (e.g., scheduling delay). Economic factors such as affordability, social factors such as family influence, and cognitive factors such as the extent to which the decision to seek medical help is based on issue-relevant thinking, are more likely to modulate the delay time between a decision to seek and an action to receive medical care (behavioral delay). In contrast, both patient characteristics (such as the manner in which the person describes their concerns and symptoms) or medical environment characteristics (such as a physician's appointment backlog), which are not under an individual's control, may modulate the delay incurred when scheduling an appointment. Therefore, shortening delay to seeking a diagnosis once symptom/sign awareness has occurred (tertiary prevention) would improve survival as early detection is linked to improved survival rates for many sites (e.g., cervix, breast, colon, prostate).

Coping style is another factor that appears to be associated with a woman's perception of a breast mass as problematic. Styra, Sakinofsky, Mahoney, Colapinto, and Currie (1993) examined coping strategies employed by women attending a clinic for examination of an undiagnosed breast mass. Women were classified as "identifiers" or "nonidentifiers," based on their perception of the breast lump as problematic (i.e., women who perceived the mass as problematic were termed "identifiers," whereas those women who did not were "nonidentifiers"). Seventy-four percent of the women were classified as nonidentifiers. This group employed more than three times the number of avoidant coping mechanisms than did identifiers. Interestingly, time of delay to seeking definitive diagnosis of the mass was comparable for identifiers and nonidentifiers. Although this study did not examine the relationship between coping style and length of appraisal delay per se, it does raise the question of a potential association between the variables.

Diagnosis

Weisman and Worden (1976) noted that the diagnosis of cancer produces an "existential plight," meaning that the news brings shock, disbelief, and emotional turmoil. Today, it is known that individuals can even become alarmed at the time of medical screening, long before a cancer diagnosis is suggested (Wardle & Pope, 1992), and it may be the fear of the risk for disease that may deter individuals from involvement in screening and/or monitoring programs (Lerman et al., 1991, 1996).

Perhaps because of these natural, difficult reactions, decades ago there were concerns by the medical community about communicating a diagnosis of "cancer." Those times, however, are long since past in the United States as well as most Western countries. Patients, including children, are now told details of the disease and treatments. In addition to the moral, ethical, and legal reasons for such disclosure

(Woodard & Pamies, 1992), there are beneficial effects of coping successfully with extreme stressors (Taylor, 1983). Follow-up studies of childhood leukemia survivors, for example, have pointed toward more favorable long-term adjustment for children when they learn of their diagnosis early, whether directly, accidentally, or through their own efforts, in comparison to children who learn later (Slavin, O'Malley, Koocher, & Foster, 1982). Further, the manner in which the information is disclosed is important. For example, it has been suggested that a patient's tendency to cope with stress by seeking out or avoiding information influences satisfaction with medical communication, and an individual's information-seeking style should be considered when providing information about diagnosis and treatment (Steptoe, Sutcliffe, Allen, & Coombes, 1991). Additionally, physicians who communicate hope have, in turn, patients who are more hopeful and who report more favorable emotional adjustment (Sardell & Trierweiler, 1993).

Empirical reports have clarified the specific emotions—sadness (depression), fear (anxiety), and confusion—that can characterize this period. It is not surprising that depressive symptoms are the most common affective problem. In general, greater depressive symptomatology is more common for those patients in active treatment rather than those on follow-up, receiving palliative rather than curative treatment, with pain or other distressing symptoms rather than not, or those with a history of affective disorder, alcoholism, or other stressors (poor social support; e.g., Bukberg, Penman, & Holland, 1984; Holland, 1989; Pettingale, Burgess, & Greer, 1988). Whereas it has been estimated that approximately 50% of cancer patients meet the American Psychiatric Association's criteria for a formal psychiatric disorder, the clear majority of these diagnoses represent adjustment disorders (i.e., emotional and/or behavioral problems related to a known transient stressor—cancer; Derogatis et al., 1983; see Tope, Ahles, & Silberfarb, 1993, for a review). Specific clinical diagnoses for depression and anxiety are 13% and 4%, respectively (Derogatis et al., 1983).

One factor that has been found to moderate distress is dispositional optimism. A number of studies have documented beneficial effects of optimism on general psychological and physical well-being in a wide range of patient populations (for a review, see Scheier & Carver, 1992). With respect to cancer patients specifically, Carver and colleagues determined that optimism versus pessimism predicts adjustment to early stage breast cancer over several time points, with pessimists faring worse than their more optimistic counterparts in terms of subjective well-being, satisfaction with sex life, and occurrence of intrusive thoughts (Carver et al., 1994). They suggested that dispositional pessimism may serve as a marker of vulnerability to poor adjustment in the period of time surrounding treatment for early stage breast cancer.

Importantly, the clinical problem of diagnostic and treatment-related distress can be alleviated through psychological interventions (see Andersen, 1992, and Speigel, 1996, for reviews). A comprehensive example of such an effort is the study by F. I. Fawzy and colleagues (1990a, 1990b). They attempted to reduce distress and enhance immune functioning in newly diagnosed melanoma patients via a structured group support intervention that included health education, illness-related problem solving, relaxation training, and group support. The format was weekly group treatment for six sessions. Eighty patients with early stage melanoma participated and were randomized to intervention or control conditions. The posttreatment analyses indicated that the intervention subjects reported significantly more vigor, but there were no other emotional distress differences. By 6 months, emotional distress had improved for the intervention subjects with significantly lower depression, confusion, and fatigue, and higher vigor. Coping data indicated that the intervention subjects reported significantly more use of active behavioral strategies by treatment's end, a pattern that continued with the addition of active cognitive strategies by 6 months. Regarding the immunologic findings, at 6 months there was a significant difference in groups with better immunologic status for the intervention subjects. These data are impressive in that they suggest that improvements in psychological status and coping are associated with changes (up regulation) in immune responses.

Improvements such as these in mood and coping are all the more impressive because they are often achieved with brief, cost-effective interventions (e.g., 10 therapy hours with delivery in a group format; Andersen, 1992). Studies that have provided follow-up data also suggest some consolidation of intervention effects across time (upward of 6 months posttreatment), with lowered emotional distress, enhanced coping, and improved sexual functioning (e.g., Capone, Good, Westie, & Jacobson, 1980).

Treatment

A certain component of the emotional distress occurring at diagnosis is due to the anticipation of treatment. Primary cancer therapies are surgery and/or radiotherapy, with chemotherapy or hormonal therapy (e.g., tamoxifen) used as primary or adjuvant treatment. Bone marrow treatment, once reserved for metastatic disease is now being used in combination as a primary therapy not only for hemotologic malignancies, but for solid tumors (e.g., breast, ovary) as well. Regardless of the protocol, however, all treatments are preceded or followed by physical examinations, tumor surveys, and/or laboratory studies. Thus, the diagnostic period can be prolonged, and the receipt of therapy can represent multiple medical stressors for the individual.

As is discussed later, the data are consistent in their portrayal of more distress (particularly fear and anxiety), slower rates of emotional recovery, and, perhaps, higher rates of other behavioral difficulties (e.g., food aversions, continued fatigue and malaise) in cancer patients in comparison to individuals undergoing noncancer-related medical treatment. The emotional crisis that characterizes the diagnostic period lessens as time passes, and longitudinal studies find that as treatments end and recovery begins there is an emotional rebound (e.g., Andersen, Anderson, & deProsse, 1989b; Bloom, 1987; Edgar, Rosberger, & Nowlis, 1992). This lowering of emotional distress over time is found even for patients undergoing radical treatment requiring major adjustments (e.g., radical neck dissection with laryngectomy; Manuel, Roth, Keefe, & Brantley, 1987).

There have been few investigations of cancer surgery or radiotherapy per se, but there are numerous descriptive and intervention studies of the reactions of healthy individuals undergoing surgery or other difficult medical procedures for benign conditions. In both literatures, the studies are consistent in their portrayal of high levels of self-reported preoperative or pretreatment anxiety predicting higher postoperative anxiety and longer recovery periods (e.g., decreased time out of bed, increased pain reports). What may distinguish cancer surgery patients are higher overall levels of distress and slower rates of emotional recovery (Gottesman & Lewis, 1982). The scenario for radiotherapy patients is similar. But as a course of radiotherapy can be lengthy (e.g., 4–6 weeks), heightened anxiety at the termination of treatment can also occur (e.g., Andersen & Tewfik, 1985). This unexpected increase in distress has been found clinically, and may be apt to occur at the completion of active treatment, when patients face being "on their own" and may experience heightened fears of recurrence.

Psychological and behavioral efforts to reduce patients' treatment anxiety have been incorporated into patterns of routine care. Such efforts include procedural information (e.g., the way the surgery or radiotherapy is done), sensory information on the actual physical sensations of the surgery or preparatory events, behavioral coping instructions, cognitive coping interventions, relaxation, hypnosis, and emotion-focused interventions (e.g., Wallace, Priestman, Dunn, & Priestman, 1993). Such efforts produce benefits on a broad band of outcomes—ratings of negative affect and pain, amount of pain medication, length of stay, behavioral recovery, and physiological indices (Johnston & Vogele, 1993).

Considerable research has been conducted on the psychological/behavioral aspects of coping with chemotherapy. Over a decade of research has revealed that many cancer patients will develop nausea and/or vomiting in response to cytotoxic treatments (Morrow & Hickok, 1993). However, antiemetic drug treatments have dramatically reduced the incidence of such problems. Behavioral treatments for these problems have included hypnosis, progressive muscle relaxation with guided imagery, systematic desensitization, cognitive distraction, and biofeedback. (e.g., Burish & Jenkins, 1992; Redd, 1993; Vasterling, Jenkins, Tope, & Burish, 1993). Effective preventive care, with or without behavioral strategies, can reduce the likelihood of classically conditioned anticipatory reactions (i.e., nausea and vomiting becoming associated with previously neutral events such as going to the hospital, sitting in the waiting room).

Bone Marrow Transplantation (BMT)

Over the past two decades, BMT has evolved from an experimental procedure performed only when conventional therapies have failed (e.g., recurrent breast cancer) to a therapy tested as a first line therapy in clinical trials (Baker, Curbow, & Wingard, 1991). Initially used only for those with lymphohematopoietic malignancies or disorders characterized by bone marrow failure (e.g., leukemia, Hodgkin's disease, and non-Hodgkin's lymphoma; Wingard, Curbow, Baker, & Piantadosi, 1991), BMT is now being tested with a variety of solid tumors for which the risk of recurrence is high (e.g., neuroblastomas, germ cell tumors, and cancers of the breast and ovary). The rapid acceptance and expanded use of this toxic modality is no less than dramatic, particularly as an adjuvant treatment for breast cancer patients.

BMT is a complex and potentially fatal treatment. The target of the treatment, the bone marrow, is destroyed with high dose chemotherapy, with or without subsequent whole body irradiation. The bone marrow to be transplanted comes from either a donor (allogenic BMT) or from the patients themselves (autologous BMT) after it has been removed and treated. Although allogenic BMT has a role, its expansion is limited by the need for a suitable donor and the subsequent risk of graft versus host disease for the patient. In the case of autologous BMT, a variety of ex vivo procedures are used to destroy the malignant cells in the patient's marrow prior to reinfusion, including treatment with cytotoxic drugs, exposure to monoclonal antibodies that will attack tumor associated antigens, or harvesting and introducing stem cells (cells from peripheral blood).

Patients (and their families) are faced with a number of stressors: a life threatening illness, location of a suitable donor (for allogeneic transplants; Alby, 1991; Patenaude, 1990), a toxic treatment, and common but potentially fatal side effects (e.g., liver failure). There are also many acute side effects (e.g., hair loss, mouth and gastrointestinal mucositis, infertility, skin breakdown, infection, pneumonia). Hospitalization can be prolonged (e.g., 3–6 weeks) and it is generally spent in isolation (Alby, 1991; Baker et al., 1991; Winer & Sutton, 1994). Of course, in the end, the treatment can fail and the disease can persist or rapidly recur (Patenaude, 1990; Winer & Sutton, 1994). The many difficulties—toxicity, uncertainty, illness and isolation, dependency, constant need for care, financial strain—all communicate to patients that they have little or no control and can result in loneliness, anxiety, and/or depression (Alby, 1991; Altmaier, Gingrich, & Fyfe, 1991). In attempting to cope, patients may be demanding or, conversely, withdrawn (H. N. Brown & Kelly, 1976; Patenaude, 1990). Psychological efforts have focused on providing support to patients, their families, and staff, maximizing control for patients (e.g., making choices about the hospital environment whenever possible; Patenaude, 1990). For example, BMT rooms are often equipped with televisions/radios and free weights or stationary bicycles so that patients might exercise to feel stronger and less fatigued. Additionally, patients are encouraged to bring personal items from home (e.g., pictures, photographs) to decorate their rooms. Finally, as might be expected, increased medical complications, age, distance from home, and poorer pretransplant psychosocial adjustment are variables associated with the need for more intensive psychological consultation (Futterman, Wellisch, Bond, & Carr, 1991).

Treatment Morbidity

Although there are many disease/treatment-related complications, behavioral efforts have focused on three specific ones. First, a primary side effect of cancer treatment is fatigue (Pickard-Holley, 1991), which is the most commonly reported symptom of people that have been diagnosed with and treated for cancer, especially those receiving radio- and/or chemotherapy (Nail & King, 1987; Smets, Garssen, Schuster-Uitterhoeve, & deHaes, 1993). Fatigue and associated symptoms (feeling tired, a lack of energy, sleepy, confused) have been related to other cancer morbidities (e.g., decreased quality of life) and poor treatment compliance (e.g., stopping treatments). Despite being a common experience for patients, few studies have been conducted to delineate the underlying mechanisms and correlates of fatigue (see Smets et al., 1993, and Winningham et al., 1994, for reviews). Irvine, Vincent, Bubela, Thompson, and Graydon (1991), for example, noted that research has not demonstrated consistent relations among fatigue, sleeplessness, psychological distress (e.g., negative mood/depression) and a possible biological correlate (e.g., anemia). However, it appears that fatigue does reduce overall daily functioning. It is important for patients and researchers to document fatigue as distinct from depression, and that fatigue is an expected side effect of treatment rather than a sign of disease.

Psychological and behavioral interventions for fatigue have focused on alleviating or increasing tolerance to fatigue through preparatory information on side effects and activity/rest cycle recommendations (e.g., naps in the afternoon; Nail & King, 1987; Smets et al.,1993), as well as other activity (e.g. exercise; Winningham, 1991), coping efforts (e.g., planning and scheduling activities, decreasing nonessential activities, relying on others for assistance as needed; Rhodes, Watson, & Hanson, 1988), and interventions aimed at improving/maintaining nutritional status (Kalman & Villani, 1997).

Second, appetite and weight changes (either loss or gain) can represent different problems for patients based on their diagnosis and treatments. Appetite and weight loss are significant clinical problems for those cancer patients susceptible to tumor-induced metabolism or taste changes, having tumor-related obstructions (often diagnosed as primary cachexia/anorexia), or receiving gastrointestinal-toxic chemotherapy or abdominal radiotherapy (secondary cachexia/anorexia). Importantly, malnutrition is associated with increased morbidity and mortality (Knox, 1991). Food aversions learned in connection with chemotherapy may affect up to 50% of the aforementioned patients. These conditioned aversions are rapidly acquired (usually after 1 to 3 treatments) and maintained after long delays (e.g., 48 hours between food intake and aversive drug-induced reactions such as nausea; Jacobson & Schwartz, 1993). Whereas food aversions may not involve appetite or weight loss per se, patients may unknowingly develop aversions to their favorite foods and this can in turn affect their daily routine and perceived quality of life (Jacobson & Schwartz, 1993; Knox, 1991).

Researchers have recently begun to investigate morbidity related to weight gain in breast cancer patients. The mechanisms of such weight gain have yet to be clearly elucidated (Demark-Wahnefried, Rimer, & Winer, 1997), but it appears that this phenomenon may be more pronounced in women receiving hormonal therapy and/or chemotherapy, than in women receiving surgery or surgery plus radiation (Demark, Winer, & Rimer, 1993). It is clear that treatment-related weight gain is subjectively distressing to many breast cancer patients, and may result in decreased quality of life (Knobf, Mullen, Xistris, & Moritz, 1983; Prozanto et al., 1990). Furthermore, it has been suggested that weight gain during therapy for breast cancer may be associated with increased recurrence and decreased survival (Camoriano et al., 1990, Chlebowski et al., 1991; Cruz, Muss, Brockschmidt, & Evans, 1990; Donegan, Hartz, & Rimm, 1978). Given the potential psychosocial and physical morbidities associated with weight gain in breast cancer patients, it seems relevant to more clearly elucidate the mechanisms behind, and consequences of, this common occurrence.

Third, much of the current literature regarding compliance has focused on early detection/screening practices of patients, especially in regards to breast (i.e., mammography utilization), prostate, skin, and colorectal cancers. However, compliance with treatment remains important, as the expectation and/or experience of unpleasant side effects (such as those described here) can diminish a patient's quality of life. Furthermore, such side effects can at times be so discouraging or annoying that a patient may be reluctant to continue treatment or even want to prematurely terminate (Morrow & Hickok, 1993; Richardson, Marks, & Levine, 1988). When patients are noncompliant, the dosage of treatment may be reduced, which can in turn lower the cure rate. Noncompliance with treatment has been related to increased emotional distress (e.g., Gilbar & De-Nour, 1989; Richardson et al., 1988), increased hostility and guilt (Ayres et al., 1994) severity of treatment side effects (e.g., nausea and vomiting; Lewis, Linet, & Abeloff, 1983; Richardson et al., 1988), lower income (Lebovits et al., 1990), and being an adolescent patient (Tebbi, 1993). Even when patients are responsible for self-administration of therapy, such as taking their chemotherapy at home in order to reduce the number of hospital visits, their noncompliance may continue. One report of multidrug therapy with adults with hematologic malignancies indicated that self-reports (vs. sera reports) overestimated compliance by a factor of two (Richardson et al., 1987). In short, noncompliance is a behavioral problem that can directly impact the effectiveness of cancer therapy.

Psychological interventions to improve patient compliance have focused on a variety of techniques, including appointment reminders, clearly written and specific treatment communications (Anderson & Kirk, 1982), home visits, and medication-taking shaping interventions (Richardson et al., 1987). Additionally, hospital-based interventions such as offering a tour of the oncology clinic, videotape presentations about the therapy, discussion/question sessions, and take-home information (Burish, Snyder, & Jenkins, 1991; Nail & King, 1987; Rainey, 1985) have been employed as well. Burish et al. (1991) and others (e.g., Nail & King, 1987; Rainey, 1985) suggested that preparatory information can improve coping with treatment.

Importantly, psychological interventions can reduce distress during and immediately following cancer treatments. The findings from two illustrative studies are presented. Cain, Kohorn, Quinlan, Latimer, and Schwartz (1986), for example, compared individual and group therapy formats with 72 women with gynecologic cancer. The intervention was comprised of eight components, including discussion of the causes of cancer at diagnosis, impact of the treatment(s) on body image and sexuality, relaxation training, emphasis on good dietary and exercise patterns, communication difficulties with medical staff and friends/family, and setting goals for the future to cope with uncertainty and fears of recurrence. Posttreatment analyses indicated all groups improved with time, however anxiety was significantly lower for the individual therapy subjects only. Gains for the intervention subjects were more impressive with the 6-month follow-up data when there were no differences between the intervention formats, but both groups reported less depression and anxiety and better psychosocial adjustment than the no treatment control group. Thus, the brief intervention, delivered either in an individual or group format, appeared to be immediately effective, with gains enhanced during the early recovery months.

Edgar et al. (1992) provided a psychosocial intervention to 205 patients who were randomized into two groups: One group received the intervention soon after entering the study and the other group after a wait of 4 months. The majority (n = 159) of patients had been diagnosed with breast, colon, lung, uterine, or head and neck cancers. The intervention (comprised of 5 1-hour sessions) focused on coping skills and included problem solving, goal setting, cognitive reappraisal, relaxation training, and at 4-month intervals, workshops on health care information and available resources. Whereas coping improved over the year for all patients, the later intervention group experienced lower levels of distress sooner than the group who had received the intervention earlier. Edgar et al. (1992) suggested that the delay in intervention may have been beneficial because it afforded patients the time to reduce feelings of being overwhelmed and they were, therefore, more ready to participate in the intervention. These and related data (e.g., Forester, Kornfield, & Fleiss, 1985; see Andersen, 1992, for a review) attest to the significant distress that occurs when patients are in the midst of coping with diagnosis and treatment. Importantly, impressive gains can be achieved by the end of the intervention and often these positive gains are stronger with follow-up.

Recovery and Long-Term Survival

The most important cancer endpoints have been treatment response rates, length of disease-free interval, and survival. Yet, as the prognosis for some sites has improved, there has been increased attention to quality of life, particularly for long-term survivors of cancer. The term *survivor* typically refers to individuals surviving at least 5 years, as the probability of late recurrence declines significantly after that time for most sites. As individuals recover and resume their life patterns, there may be residual emotional distress, with some difficulties requiring continued coping. Each of these circumstances is discussed, and examples are provided of both emotional and physical challenges that may confront the cancer survivor.

An investigation by Dunkel-Schetter, Feinstein, Taylor, and Falke (1992) sheds light on the strategies cancer patients use as they recover and resume their life activities. They studied coping patterns of 603 cancer patients. Patient diagnoses included breast cancer, gastrointestinal, circulatory or lymph, gynecological, and respiratory cancers. The timing of the assessment ranged from initial diagnosis to more than 5 years posttreatment. Five coping patterns were identified: seeking or using social support, focusing on positive aspects, distancing, cognitive escape-avoidance (e.g., fantasizing or wishful thinking with fatalistic thoughts of poor outcomes), and behavioral escape-avoidance (e.g., social withdrawal, drug use). All patients used multiple coping strategies, but distancing was the most common. Unique patterns were also found for subgroups. For example, individuals who viewed cancer as more stressful tended to use less adaptive strategies, such as cognitive and behavioral escape-avoidance, whereas patients reporting less distress relied on more adaptive strategies, such as seeking or using social support, focusing on the positive, and distancing themselves from the cancer experience. Data such as these might be considered when tailoring psychological interventions to patient subgroups (e.g., identifying patients likely to use drugs/alcohol to cope).

Lingering emotional distress from the "trauma" of a cancer diagnosis, treatment, and more generally life threat is similar to the distress experienced by individuals who have experienced other traumatic events (e.g., natural disasters, physical assault; Alter et al., 1996). In fact, the residual distress from the diagnosis and treatment of a life threatening illness/disorder (e.g., cardiac arrest, burns, cancer) is now included as one of the circumstances that may precipitate Posttraumatic Stress Disorder (PTSD), a disorder characterized by intrusive thoughts, avoidant behavior, and hyperarousal surrounding the traumatic event (*DSM–IV*, American Psychiatric Association, 1994). Much of the existing PTSD research has been conducted with pediatric cancer patients and their parents (e.g., Butler, Rizzi, & Handwerger, 1996; Kazak et al., 1997; Stuber, Christakis, Houskamp, & Kazak, 1996). However, it is known that adults undergoing BMT for acute leukemia (Lesko, Ostroff, Mumma, Mashberg, & Holland, 1992) and survivors of Hodgkin's disease (Cella & Tross, 1986) report higher levels of PTSD symptoms than healthy controls. Although it is unlikely that such a diagnosis would be made for the "average" cancer patient, Cordova and colleagues (1995) documented PTSD rates in a breast cancer sample ranging from 5% to 10%, and suggested that this may be comparable, if not an underestimate, to other cancer survivor populations. Risk factors for cancer-related PTSD may include undergoing the most difficult of treatment regimens (e.g., BMT), having treatments with life altering and/or disfiguring effects (e.g., limb amputations, pelvic exenteration, laryngectomies), having a history of anxiety disorder and/or being exposed to previous traumatic events, and reporting a lower quality of life (e.g., Green, 1990; Irvine, B. Brown, Crooks, Roberts, & Browne, 1991).

Second, some cancer survivors may need to cope with the expected but nevertheless troubling sequelae, which may be a consequence of the disease or treatment and be permanent. For example, coping with altered cognitive and physical abilities (e.g., changes in memory and attention due to chemotherapy/radiation or loss of natural speech following laryngectomy); and/or changes in organ functions (e.g., infertility) may require adjustment that demands new behaviors or emotions. Others may have to cope with losses (e.g., a sexual relationship that does not include intercourse). Third, late side effects of cancer treatment, for example, a bowel dysfunction that is traced to pelvic radiotherapy, can occur and change health status as well as impact mood and coping.

Despite these possibilities, longitudinal data indicate that if the disease is controlled, by 1 year posttreatment the severe distress of diagnosis will have dissipated and emotions will have stabilized. The first longitudinal studies conducted in the United Kingdom for breast cancer patients indicated that by 12 (Maguire et al., 1978) and 24 months (Morris, Greer, & White, 1977), approximately 20% of the patients had problems with moderate to severe depression in comparison to 8% of benign disease comparison subjects. However, more recent controlled longitudinal studies of breast (Bloom, 1987; Vinokur, Threatt, Caplan, & Zimmerman, 1989), gynecologic (Andersen et al.,1989b), and Hodgkin's disease and non-Hodgkin's lymphoma (Devlen, Maguire, Phillips, Crowther, & Chambers, 1987) patients conducted in the United States and other countries (e.g., the Netherlands; de Haes, van Oostrom, & Welvaart, 1986) have indicated no differences between the levels of emotional distress of individuals with cancer and either benign disease or healthy comparison subjects. The consistency of findings is important because it represents replications across site and; to some degree, treatment toxicity. Thus, the remaining discussion is prefaced by noting that global adjustment problems do not occur for the majority of cancer survivors; a more likely scenario is the occurrence of specific problem areas.

An exception to this positive trajectory may be the circumstances of BMT survivors, who generally experience a somewhat slower recovery (Syrajala, Chapko, Vitaliano, Cummings, & Sullivan, 1993). Comparison of BMT survivors and other cancer patients on maintenance chemotherapy indicated that psychological functioning was satisfactory for both groups when assessed 3 to 4 years postdiagnosis (Altmaier et al., 1991). However, when BMT patients were assessed sooner (2–4 years posttreatment), they reported poorer physical functioning, greater impaired personal functioning (e.g., need for self-care assistance), and more sexual difficulties than individuals on maintenance chemotherapy (Altmaier et al., 1991). Also, data do suggest a risk of neuropsychological impairment from BMT procedures. Andrykowski (1992) found impairments in memory and higher cognitive processing, which may be a sequelae of BMT per se, or due to cancer treatments prior to BMT (e.g., cranial radiation, intrathecal chemotherapy). The many difficult aspects of BMT already noted (e.g., intensive chemotherapy, possible whole body irradiation, long recovery time, isolation) may also contribute to this slowed and more problematic recovery (see Winer & Sutton, 1994; or Andrykowski, 1994, for a review).

One life area that undergoes disruption for cancer survivors is sexuality. All cancer patients with solid tumors (approximately 85% of adult patients) and many treated for hemotologic malignancies are vulnerable to sexual dysfunction. Across sites, estimates range from 10% (e.g., breast cancer patients treated with lumpectomy), 70% to 90% (e.g., women with vulva cancer treated with modified radical vulvectomy), to 100% (e.g., men with prostate cancer treated with radical prostatectomy), with the distribution skewed toward greater levels of disruption; among the hematologic malignancies, estimates are in the range of 20% (Andersen & Lamb, 1995). Although it is clear that the sexual problems are psychologically distressing, disease and treatment sequelae are the primary reasons for the sexual problems (e.g., nerve dissection during prostatectomy, gynecologic complications with long-term adjuvant tamoxifen therapy for breast cancer, Wolf & Jordan, 1992; female androgen deficiency syndrome from cytotoxic agents and/or bilateral salpingo-oophorectomies, Kaplan & Owett, 1993). Consistent with this etiology, longitudinal studies indicate that if sexual problems develop, they do so as soon as intercourse resumes, and if untreated, they are unlikely to resolve (see Andersen & Elliott, 1994, for a discussion).

Even with disease and cancer treatments producing significant disruption, there also appear to be important individual differences in the magnitude of the difficulty. Moreover, a specific aspect—sexual self schema (self-concept)—appears to predict specific risk for sexual morbidity. Sexual self schema is a cognitive view about sexual aspects of oneself; it is derived from past experience, manifest in current experience, and it guides the processing of sexually relevant social information (Andersen & Cyranowski, 1994). For women, the concept includes two positive aspects (an inclination to experience romantic/passionate emotions and a behavioral openness to sexual experiences and/or relationships) and a negative aspect (embarrassment and/or conservatism), which appears to deter sexual expression. For men, there are three positive aspects; an inclination to experience romantic/passionate emotions, a view of the self as aggressive and powerful, and an open-minded, liberal attitude (Andersen, Cyranowski, & Espindle, 1999). Individual differences can play a powerful role in predicting sexual behaviors and responses (Andersen & Cyranowski, 1995). Cognitive representations of sexuality represent a novel and important aspect, and tests of their predictive utility for sexual morbidity are confirmatory. For example, the role of sexual schema in predicting risk for sexual morbidity following gynecologic cancer was tested by Andersen, Woods, and Copeland (1997). It was hypothesized that women with a negative sexual self-concept, in contrast to women with a positive sexual self-concept, would be at greatest risk for sexual difficulty. Negative sexual schema women would be expected to have more difficulties because they are, in general, less romantic/passionate in their emotions, less open to sexual experiences, and more likely to have negative feelings about their sexuality. The researchers assessed 62 women who were currently disease free but who received treatment from 6 months to 5 years previously for Stage I–II disease. Comparison subjects included 68 women seeking routine gynecologic care. Analysis of the quality of life data replicated earlier prospective longitudinal findings (Andersen et al., 1989a). That is, there were no differences between the groups in the areas of mental health (emotional distress, depression) or social functioning, and, in contrast, the cancer survivors reported lower levels of sexual behavior, sexual responsiveness, and global evaluations. Sexual self schema accounted for a significant and large portion of the variance (26%) in the prediction of current sexual responsiveness (e.g., desire, excitement, orgasm, and resolution), as well as significant variance in the prediction of sexual behavior. Thus, sexual self schema appears to be an important individual difference variable in the prediction of sexual morbidity.

Despite the emotional distress and, for some, accompanying sexual disruption that couples experience, data from the controlled longitudinal studies previously discussed indicate that the majority of marriages remain intact and satisfactory. These data are consistent with early prospective studies showing that, when health problems arise for newly married couples, they are not among those problems precipitant to divorce (Bentler & Newcomb, 1978). However, multicenter studies have indicated that young survivors of childhood cancers are significantly less likely to marry, and once married they may be at greater risk for subfertility (Byrne et al., 1985; Teeter, G. E. Holmes, F. F. Holmes, & Baker, 1987).

Still, families are not immune to the cancer experience (see Baider, Cooper, & De-Nour, 1996, for a review), and the kin's distress may approach that of the patient's (Cassileth et al., 1985). Family strain appears to be affected by illness variables (e.g., prognosis, stage/duration of illness, caregiving demands, patient's distress), family variables (e.g., age and gender of family members, socioeconomic status, other family stressors), and relational variables (e.g., quality of marriage, marital communication, family stage, and social support; see Sales, Schulz, & Biegel, 1992, for a review). Those couples in which the wife/mother has cancer and young children are still in the home may be at heightened risk for relationship difficulties (Vess, Moreland, & Schwebel, 1985). In addition, Ell, Nishimoto, Mantell, and Hamovitch (1988) found that those kin who were functioning poorly (e.g., less adequate emotional support from close others, and greater stress unrelated to cancer) when the patient was diagnosed or who lost personal and social resources during the patient's treatment and recovery also, not surprisingly, functioned poorly at follow-up. In sum, a subset of partners and family members appear to be at psychosocial risk. For a review of strategies that have been used to assist spouses of cancer patients cope with stress over the illness course, see Northouse and Peters-Golden (1993).

There have been few interventions targeted for cancer survivors per se, but one such study was that by C. F. Telch and M. J. Telch (1986). They compared the effectiveness of coping skills instruction versus supportive therapy for a heterogeneous sample of cancer patients with "clear evidence of psychological distress." Both interventions were offered in a group format. The emotional distress data indicated that the coping skills group improved significantly across all measures, the support group improved on the anxiety and depression only, but the no treatment control worsened and reported significantly more mood distress, indicating differential effectiveness for cognitive behavioral/coping interventions.

Recurrence and Death

Cancer recurrence is devastating; the magnitude of distress is even greater than that found with the initial diagnosis (Mahon, Cella, & Donovan, 1990; Thompson, Andersen, & DePetrillo, 1992), and studies contrasting cancer patients showing no evidence of disease with those receiving palliative treatment (e.g., Cassileth et al., 1985) have reported the greatest distress for those with disseminated disease (Bloom, 1987). In fact, cancer recurrence has been conceptualized as a "traumatic event" with the potential to induce stress response symptoms such as intrusive thoughts, behavior aimed at avoiding cancer-related stimuli, and hyperarousal (Cella, Mahon, & Donovan, 1990). Patients recently told of their cancer recurrence reported being less hopeful, more discouraged, having increased thoughts of death and dying, as well as feelings of guilt/regret about their previous treatment decisions. In one study (Mahon et al., 1990), 45% of the patients indicated that they perceived their recurrence as "punishment," and so difficult decisions (e.g., beginning a regimen that offers little chance for cure and also has toxic side effects vs. no treatment) are made in a context of extreme emotional distress and perhaps physical debilitation from symptoms (e.g., shortness of breath with lung disease, pain from bone metastases). Yet, important emotional gains can be achieved during terminal stages (M. W. Linn, B. S. Linn, & Harris, 1982) and children and adolescents, as well as adults, can make independent decisions about the continuation of therapy when death is imminent (Nitschke et al., 1982).

Psychological interventions offered to terminal patients appear to have the effect of enhancing their quality of life. Spiegel and colleagues (Spiegel, Bloom, & Yalom, 1981; Spiegel & Bloom, 1983), for example, studied a group support intervention that included discussion of death and dying, family problems, communication problems with physicians, and living fully with terminal breast cancer. A random half of the intervention subjects were also offered self-hypnosis for pain problems (Spiegel & Bloom, 1983), which was incorporated into the support group format. Eighty-six women, 50 intervention and 36 no treatment control, participated. Analyses indicated that the intervention group reported significantly fewer phobic responses and lower anxiety, fatigue, and confusion and higher vigor than the controls. These differences were evident at all assessments, but the magnitude increased from 4 to 12 months. Women receiving hypnosis within the group support intervention reported no change in their pain sensations during the year, whereas pain sensations significantly increased for the other women in group support who did not receive hypnosis. The most startling data from this project was reported in a survival analysis: Controlling for initial disease stage, days of radiotherapy, or use of androgen or steroid treatments, the analysis indicated a survival time difference (18 months longer) favoring the intervention participants.

Finally, there are two frequent complications of disseminated disease: delirium and pain. Delirium is the second most commonly diagnosed psychiatric disorder in cancer patients and is characterized by acute perceptual and behavioral disturbances such as impairment of attention, orientation, and memory (Tope et al., 1993). Massie, Holland, and Glass (1983) found that approximatley 75% of patients with metastatic cancer meet criteria for delirium as compared to 8% of all cancer patients. Delirium in cancer patients can be caused by a number of factors, including treatment side effects (e.g, type/dosage of chemotherapy), medications (e.g., narcotics), disease progression (e.g, brain metastases), and other treatment and/or disease-related complications (e.g, metabolic and endocrine disorders; see Tope et al., 1993, for a review). Whereas delirium is a reversible brain disorder, it is often misunderstood and underdiagnosed by medical personnel, with symptoms often being attributed to depression and anxiety (Levine, Silberfarb, & Lipowski, 1978).

Although it might be one of the first symptoms of cancer or be present when disease is localized, pain is more common and less controllable for those with metastatic disease (Ahles, Ruckdeschel, & Blanchard, 1984). Eighty percent of patients with recurrent cancer report moderate to severe pain, as compared to 40% of earlier stage patients (see Ashburn & Lipman, 1993, for a review). The major cause of cancer pain, accounting for roughly 70% of the cases, is due to direct tumor involvement (e.g., nearby metastatic bone disease, nerve compression), and the remainder is usually due to medical therapy (e.g., postoperative pain, radiation-induced pain). Thus, the pain experienced by cancer patients can be any combination of acute malignant pain, chronic malignant pain, and/or chronic nonmalignant pain (Ashburn & Lipman, 1993).

With this variable presentation, it is important that a pain assessment be completed before and during treatment for pain control (Ashburn & Lipman, 1993; Coyle, Adlehardt, Foley, & Portenoy, 1990). Besides pain-specific qualities and diagnostic/treatment considerations, other factors are also important in assessing the patient's experience of pain. For instance, pain is associated with depression, anxiety, and delirium (Massie & Holland, 1992), and may increase suicidal ideation (Coyle et al., 1990). If pain worsens or is difficult to control, then quality of life deteriorates and emotional distress increases (Massie & Holland, 1992), physical mobility may decline (Ashburn & Lipman, 1993), and social interactions may suffer (Strang & Qvarner, 1990). It is striking that inadequately controlled pain has been cited as a primary reason for requests of physician-assisted suicide among cancer patients (Foley, 1991, 1995; Seale & Addington-Hall, 1994).

The most difficult circumstance of pain control is when chronic pain accompanies disease progression. Treatment combinations of antitumor therapy, anesthetic blocks, and behavioral approaches are considered. When palliative therapy is of little use and/or brings further debilitation, psychological interventions may provide support and pain control and, secondarily, treat pain sequelae (e.g., sleep disturbances, reduced appetite, irritability).

CONCLUSIONS

Significant progress has been made in understanding the psychological, social, and behavioral aspects of cancer. More is known about the psychological processes and reactions to the diagnosis and treatment of cancer than is known about any other chronic illness. Breast cancer patients (see Glanz & Lerman, 1992, for a review), have been well studied, but other disease sites, men, and children are becoming more commonly studied. Future research will test the generalizability of these descriptive data and formulate general principles of adjustment to illness. While providing estimates of the magnitude of quality of life problems, these data can be used for models that predict which patients might be at greatest risk for adjustment difficulties (see Andersen, 1996, for a discussion). The latter is an important step toward designing interventions tailored to the difficulties and circumstances of cancer patients. The mental health community emphasizes the need to reduce stress and prevent deteriorations in quality of life for those with cancer. The importance of such efforts is underscored by three contextual factors. First, the stability of many cancer mortality rates (particularly those with the highest incidence such as lung and breast) makes it imperative that new, innovative treatments be developed to improve survival rates. Second, research has demonstrated that psychological interventions result in significant improvements in quality of life (see Andersen, 1992, for a review). Third, both qualitative (Maier et al., 1994) and quantitative (Herbert & Cohen, 1993) summaries of the psychoneuroimmunology (PNI) literature conclude that psychological distress and stressors (e.g., negative life events, both acute and chronic) are reliably associated with changes—down regulation—in immunity. Thus, addressing the mental health needs of those with cancer will have important quality of life benefits and the possibility is raised of positive biologic (or health) consequences as well. Finally, the biobehavioral model offered here provides a theoretical framework for examining questions of the interaction of psychological, behavioral, and biological variables in disease course.

REFERENCES

Ahles, T. A., Ruckdeschel, J. C., & Blanchard, E. B. (1984). Cancer related pain: I. Prevalence in an outpatient setting as a function of stage of disease and type of cancer. *Journal of Psychosomatic Research, 28,* 115–119.

Alby, N. (1991). Leukaemia: Bone marrow transplantation. In M. Watson (Ed.), *Cancer patient care: Psychosocial treatment methods* (pp. 281–288). Cambridge, England: BPS Books.

Alter, C. L., Pelcovitz, D., Axelrod, A, Goldenberg, B., Harris, H., Meyers, B., Grobois, B., Mandel, F., Septimus, A., & Kaplan, S. (1996). Identification of PTSD in cancer survivors. *Psychsomatics, 37,* 137–143.

Altmaier, E. M., Gingrich, R. D., & Fyfe, M. A. (1991). Two-year adjustment of bone marrow transplant survivors. *Bone Marrow Transplantation, 7,* 311–316.

American Psychiatric Association. (1994). *Diagnostic and statistical manual of mental disorders* (4th ed., Rev.). Washington, DC: American Psychiatric Association.

Andersen, B. L. (1992). Psychological interventions for cancer patients to enhance the quality of life. *Journal of Consulting and Clinical Psychology, 60,* 552–568.

Andersen, B. L. (1996). Predicting, understanding, and treating the sexual difficulties of gynecologic cancer survivors. *Cancer Control, 3,* 27–33.

Andersen, B. L., Anderson, B., & deProsse, C. (1989a). Controlled prospective longitudinal study of women with cancer: I. Sexual functioning outcomes. *Journal of Consulting and Clinical Psychology, 57,* 683–691.

Andersen, B. L., Anderson, B., & deProsse, C. (1989b). Controlled prospective longitudinal study of women with cancer: II. Psychological outcomes. *Journal of Consulting and Clinical Psychology, 57,* 692–697.

Andersen, B. L., Cacioppo, J. T., & Roberts, D. C. (1995). Delay in seeking a cancer diagnosis: Delay stages and psychophysiological comparison processes. *British Journal of Social Psychology, 34,* 33–52.

Andersen, B. L., & Cyranowski, J. C. (1994). Women's sexual self schema. *Journal of Personality and Social Psychology, 67,* 1079–1100.

Andersen, B. L., & Cyranowski, J. C. (1995). Women's sexuality: Behaviors, responses, and individual differences. *Journal of Consulting and Clinical Psychology, 63,* 891–906.

Andersen, B. L., & Elliott, M. L. (1994). Female cancer survivors: Appreciating their sexual concerns. *Canadian Journal of Human Sexuality, 3,* 107–122.

Andersen, B. L., Cyranowski, J. C., & Espindle, D. M. (1999). Men's sexual self schema. *Journal of Personality and Social Psychology, 76*(4), 645–661.

Andersen, B. L., Farrar, W. B., Golden-Kreutz, D., Kutz, L. A., MacCallum, R., Courtney, M. E., & Glaser, R. (1998). Stress and immune responses following surgical treatment for regional breast cancer. *Journal of the National Cancer Institute, 90*(1), 30–36.

Andersen, B. L., Kiecolt-Glaser, J. K., & Glaser, R. (1994). A biobehavioral model of cancer stress and disease course. *American Psychologist, 49,* 389–404.

Andersen, B. L., & Lamb, M. A. (1995). Sexuality and cancer. In A. I. Holleb, D. Fink, & G. P. Murphy (Eds.), *Clinical Oncology* (2nd ed., pp. 699–713). Atlanta, GA: American Cancer Society.

Andersen, B. L., & Tewfik, H. H. (1985). Psychological reactions to radiation therapy: Reconsideration of the adaptive aspects of anxiety. *Journal of Personality and Social Psychology, 48,* 1024–1032.

Andersen, B. L., Woods, X. A., & Copeland, L. J. (1997). Sexual self schema and sexual morbidity among gynecologic cancer survivors. *Journal of Consulting and Clinical Psychology, 65,* 221–229.

Anderson, R. J., & Kirk, L. M. (1982). Methods of improving patient compliance in chronic disease states. *Archives of Internal Medicine, 142,* 1673–1675.

Andrykowski, M. A. (1992). Neuropsychologic impairment in adult bone marrow transplant candidates. *Cancer, 70,* 2288–2297.

Andrykowski, M. A. (1994). Psychosocial factors in bone marrow transplantation: A review and recommendations for research. *Bone Marrow Transplantation, 13,* 357–375.

Ashburn, M. A., & Lipman, A. G. (1993). Management of pain in the cancer patient. *Anesthesia Analog, 76,* 402–416.

Ayres, A., Hoon, P. W., Franzoni, J. B., Matheny, K. B., Cotanch, P. H., & Takayanagi, S. (1994). Influence of mood and adjustment to cancer on compliance with chemotherapy among breast cancer patients. *Journal of Psychosomatic Research, 38,* 393–402.

Baider, L., Cooper, C., & De-Nour, A. K. (1996). *Cancer and the family.* London: Wiley.

Baker, F., Curbow, B., & Wingard, J. (1991). Role retention and quality of life or bone marrow transplant survivors. *Social Science Medicine, 32,* 697–704.

Bentler, P. M., & Newcomb, M. D. (1978). Longitudinal study of marital success and failure. *Journal of Consulting and Clinical Psychology, 46,* 1053–1070.

Bloom, J. R. (1987). Psychological response to mastectomy. *Cancer, 59,* 189–196.

Brown, H. N., & Kelly, M. J. (1976). Stages of bone marrow transplantation: A psychiatric perspective. *Psychsomatic Medicine, 38,* 439–446.

Burish, T. G., & Jenkins, R. A. (1992). Effectiveness of biofeedback and relaxation training in reducing the side effects of cancer chemotherapy. *Health Psychology, 11,* 17–23.

Burish, T. G., Snyder, S. L., & Jenkins, R. A. (1991). Preparing patients for cancer chemotherapy: Effect of coping preparation and relaxation interventions. *Journal of Consulting and Clinical Psychology, 39,* 518–525.

Butler, R. W., Rizzi, L. P., & Handwerger, B. A. (1996). Brief report: The assessment of Posttraumatic Stress Disorder in pediatric cancer patients and survivors. *Journal of Pediatric Psychology, 21,* 499–594.

Bukberg, J., Penman, D., & Holland, J. C. (1984). Depression in hospitalized cancer patients. *Psychosomatic Medicine, 436,* 199–212.

Byrne, J., Mulvihill, J. J., Myers, M. H., Abbott, S. C., Connelly, R. R., Hanson, M. R., Hassinger, D. D., Naughton, M. D., Austin, D. F., Gurgin, V. A., Holmes, F. F., Homes, G. F., Latourette, H. B., Weyer, P. J., Meigs, J. W., Teta, M. J., Strong, L. C., & Cook, J. A. (1985). Risk of infertility among survivors of childhood and adolescent cancer. *American Journal of Human Genetics, 37,* 24–48.

Cain, E. N., Kohorn, E. I., Quinlan, D. M., Latimer, K., & Schwartz, P. E. (1986). Psychosocial benefits of a cancer support group. *Cancer, 57,* 183–189.

Camoriano, J. K., Loprinzi, C. L., Ingle, J. N., Therneau, T., Krook, J., & Veeder, M. (1990). Weight gain in women treated with adjuvant therapy or observed following mastectomy for node-posotove breast cancer. *Journal of Clinical Oncology, 8,* 1327–1334.

Capone, M. A., Good, R. S., Westie, K. S., & Jacobson, A. F. (1980). Psychosocial rehabilitation of gynecologic oncology patients. *Archives of Physical Medicine and Rehabilitation, 61,* 128–132.

Carver, C. S., Pozo-Kaderman, C., Harris, S. D., Noriega, V., Scheier, M. F., Robinson, D. S., Ketcham, A. S., Moffat, F. L., & Clark, K. C. (1994). Optimism versus pessimism predicts the quality of women's adjustment to early stage breast cancer. *Cancer, 73,* 1213–1220.

Cassileth, B. R, Lunk, E. J., Strouse, T. B., Miller, D. S., Brown, L., & Cross, P. A. (1985). A psychological analysis of cancer patients and their next-of-kin. *Cancer, 55,* 72–76.

Cella, D. F., Mahon, S. M., & Donovan, M. I. (1990). Cancer recurrence as a traumatic event. *Behavioral Medicine, 16*(1), 15–22.

Cella, D. F., & Tross, S. (1986). Psychological adjustment to survival from Hodgkin's disease. *Journal of Consulting and Clinical Psychology, 54,* 616–622.

Chlebowski, R. T., Rose, D., Buzzard, I. M., Blackburn, G., Insull, W., Grosvenor, M., Elashoff, R., & Wynder, E. (1991). Adjuvant dietary fat intake reducation in postmenopausal breast cancer patient management. *Breast Cancer Research and Treatment, 20,* 73–84.

Cohen, S., Tyrrell, D. A., & Smith, A. P. (1991). Psychological stress and susceptibility to the common cold. *New England Journal of Medicine, 325,* 606–612.

Cordova, M. J., Andrykowski, M. A., Kenady, D. E., McGrath, P. C., Sloan, D. A., & Redd, W. H. (1995). Frequency and correlates of posttraumatic-stress-disorder-like symptoms after treatment for breast cancer. *Journal of Consulting and Clinical Psychology, 63,* 981–986.

Coyle, N., Adelhardt, J., Foley, K. M., & Portenoy, R. K. (1990). Character of terminal illness in the advanced cancer patient: Pain and other symptoms during the last four weeks of life. *Journal of Pain and Symptom Management, 5,* 83–93.

Cruz, J. M., Muss, H. B., Brockschmidt, J. K., Evans, G. (1990). Weight changes in women with metastatic breast cancer treated with megestrol acetate: A comparison of standard versus high-dose therapy. *Seminars in Oncology, 17,* 63–67.

Cunningham, M. (1997). Giving life to numbers. *CA—A Cancer Journal for Clinicians, 47,* 3–4.

deHaes, J. C., van Oostrom, M. A., & Welvaart, K. (1986). The effect of radical and conserving surgery on quality of life of early breast cancer patients. *European Journal of Surgical Oncology, 12,* 337–342.

Demark-Wahnefried, W., Rimer, B. K., & Winer, E. P. (1997). Weight gain in women diagnosed with breast cancer. *Journal of the American Dietetic Association, 97,* 519–529.

Demark, W., Winer, E. P, & Rimer, B. K. (1993). Why women gain weight with adjuvant chemotherapy. *Journal of Clinical Oncology, 11,* 1418–1429.

Derogatis, L. R., Morrow, G. R., Fetting, J., Penman, D., Piasetsky, S., Schmale, A. M., Henricho, M., & Carnicke, C. L. (1983). The prevalence of psychiatric disorders among cancer patients. *Journal of the American Medical Association, 249,* 751–757.

Devlen, J., Maguire, P., Phillips, P., Crowther, D., & Chambers, H. (1987). Psychological problems associated with diagnosis and treatment of lymphomas: I. Retrospective study and II: Prospective study. *British Medical Journal, 295,* 953–957.

Donegan, W. L., Hartz, A. J., & Rimm, A. A. (1978). The association of body weight and recurrent cancer of the breast. *Cancer, 41,* 1590–1594.

Dunkel-Schetter, C., Feinstein, L. G., Taylor, S. E., & Falke, R. L. (1992). Patterns of coping with cancer. *Health Psychology, 11,* 79–87.

Edgar, L., Rosberger, Z., & Nowlis, D. (1992). Coping with cancer during the first year after diagnosis: Assessment and intervention. *Cancer, 69,* 817–828.

Ell, K., Nishimoto, R, Mantell, J., & Hamovitch, M. (1988). Longitudinal analysis of psychological adaptation among family members of patients with cancer. *Journal of Psychosomatic Research, 32,* 429–438.

Fawzy, F. I., Cousins, N., Fawzy, N., Kemeny, M. E., Elashoff, R., & Morton, D. (1990a). A structured psychiatric intervention for cancer patients: I. Changes over time in methods of coping and affective disturbance. *Archives of General Psychiatry, 47,* 720–725.

Fawzy, F. I., Fawzy, N., Hyun, C. S., Guthrie, D., Fahey, J. L., & Morton, D. (1993). Maliganant melanoma: Effects of an early structured psychiatric intervention, coping, and effective state on recurrence and survival six years later. *Archives of General Psychiatry, 50,* 681–689.

Fawzy, F. I., Kemeny, M. E., Fawzy, N., Elashoff, R., Morton, D., Cousins, N., & Fahey, J. L. (1990b). A structured psychiatric intervention for cancer patients: II. Changes over time in immunological measures. *Archives of General Psychiatry, 47,* 729–735.

Foley, K. M. (1991). Misconceptions and controversies regarding the use of opioids in cancer pain. *Anti-Cancer Drugs, 6*(Suppl. 3), 4–13.

Foley, K. M. (1995). The relationship of pain and symptoms management to patient requests for physician-assisted suicide. *Journal of Pain and Symptom Management, 6,* 289–297.

Forester, B., Kornfeld, D. S., & Fleiss, J. (1985). Psychotherapy during radiotherapy: Effects on emotional and physical distress. *American Journal of Psychiatry, 142,* 22–27.

Futterman, A. D., Wellisch, D. K., Bond, G., & Carr, C. R. (1991). The psychosocial levels system: A new rating scale to identify and assess emotional difficulties during bone marrow transplantation. *Psychosomatics, 32,* 177–186.

Garfinkel, L. (1994). Evaluating cancer statistics. *CA—A Cancer Journal for Clinicians, 44,* 5–6.

Gilbar, O., & De-Nour, A. K. (1989). Adjustment to illness and dropout of chemotherapy. *Journal of Psychosomatic Research, 33,* 1–5.

Glanz, K., & Lerman, C. (1992). Psychosocial impact of breast cancer: A critical review. *Annals of Behavioral Medicine, 14*(3), 204–212.

Gottesman, D., & Lewis, M. (1982). Differences in crisis reactions among cancer and surgery patients. *Journal of Consulting and Clinical Psychology, 50,* 381–388.

Green, B. L. (1990). Defining trauma: Terminology and generic stressor dimensions. *Journal of Applied Social Psychology, 20,* 1632–1642.

Herbert, T. B., & Cohen, S. (1993). Depression and immunity: A meta-analytic review. *Psychological Bulletin, 113,* 472–486.

Holland, J. C. (1989). Anxiety and cancer: The patient and the family. *Journal of Clinical Psychiatry, 50,* 20–25.

Irvine, D., Brown, B., Crooks, D., Roberts, J., & Browne, G. (1991). Psychosocial adjustment in women with breast cancer. *Cancer, 67,* 1097–1117.

Irvine, D. M., Vincent, L., Bubela, N., Thompson, L., & Graydon, J.(1991). A critical appraisal of the research literature investigating fatigue in the individual with cancer. *Cancer Nursing, 14,* 88–199.

Jacobsen, P. B., & Schwartz, M. D. (1993). Food aversions during cancer therapy: Incidence, etiology, and prevention. *Oncology, 7,* 139–143.

Johnston, M., & Vogele, C. (1993). Benefits of psychological preparation for surgery: A meta-analysis. *Annals of Behavioral Medicine, 15,* 245–256.

Kalman, D., & Villani, X. (1997). Nutritional aspects of cancer-related fatigue. *American Dietetic Association, 97,* 650–654.

Kaplan, H. S., & Owett, T. (1993). The female androgen deficiency syndrome. *Journal of Sex & Marital Therapy, 19,* 3–24.

Kazak, A. E., Barakat, L. P., Meeske, K., Dimitri, C., Meadows, A. T., Casey, R., Penati, B., & Stuber, M. L. (1997). Posttraumatic stress, family functioning, and social support in survivor of childhood leukemia and their mothers and fathers. *Journal of Consulting and Clinical Psychology, 65,* 120–129.

Kiecolt-Glaser, J. K., Marucha, P. T., Malarkey, W. B., & Mercado, A. M. & Glaser, R. (1995). Slowing of wound healing by psychological stress. *Lancet, 346,* 1194–1196.

Knobf, M. K., Mullen, J. C., Xistris, D., & Moritz, P. A. (1983). Weight gain in women with breast cancer receiving adjuvant chemotherapy. *Oncology Nursing Forum, 10,* 28–34.

Knox, L. S. (1991). Maintaining nutritional status in persons with cancer. In *Cancer nursing: Maintaining nutritional status in persons with cancer* (pp. 1–11). Atlanta, GA: American Cancer Society.

Lebovits, A. H., Strain, J. J., Schleifer, S. J., Tanaka, J. S., Bhardwaj, S., & Messe, M. R. (1990). Patient noncompliance with self-administration chemotherapy. *Cancer, 65,* 17–22.

Lesko, L. M., Ostroff, J. S., Mumma, G. H., Mashberg, D. E., & Holland, L. C. (1992). Long-term psychological adjustments of acute leukemia survivors: Impact of bone marrow transplantation versus conventional chemotherapy. *Psychosomatic Medicine, 54,* 30–47.

Lerman, C., Miller, S. M., Scarborough, R., Hanjani, P., Nolte, S., & Smith, D. (1991). Adverse psychologic consequences of positive cytologic cervical screening. *American Journal of Obstetrics and Gynecology, 165,* 658–662.

Lerman, C., Schwartz, M. D., Miller, S. M., Daly, M., Sands, C., & Rimer, B. K. (1996). A randomized trial of breast cancer risk counseling: Interacting effects of counseling, educational level, and coping style. *Health Psychology, 15,* 75–83.

Levine, P. M., Silberfarb, P. M., & Lipowski, Z. J. (1978). Mental disorders in cancer patients: A study of 100 psychiatric referrals. *Cancer, 43,* 1385–1391.

Lewis, C., Linet, M. S., & Abeloff, M. D. (1983). Compliance with cancer therapy by patients and physicians. *American Journal of Medicine, 74,* 673–678.

Linn, M. W., Linn, B. S., & Harris, R. (1982). Effects of counseling for late stage cancer patients. *Cancer, 49,* 1048–1055.

Maguire, G. P., Lee, E. G., Bevington, D. J., Kuchemann, C. S., Crabtree, R. J., & Cornell, C. E. (1978). Psychiatric problems in the first year after mastectomy. *British Medical Journal, 1,* 963–965.

Mahon, S. M., Cella, D. F., & Donovan, M. I. (1990). Psychosocial adjustment to recurrent cancer. *Oncology Nursing Forum, 17,* 47–54.

Maier, S. F., Wakins, L. R., & Fleshner, M. (1994). Psychoneuroimmunology: The interface between behavior, brain, and immunity. *American Psychologist, 49,* 1004–1017.

Manuel, G. M., Roth, S., Keefe, F. J., & Brantley, B. A. (1987). Coping with cancer. *Journal of Human Stress,* 149–158.

Massie, M. J., & Holland, J. C. (1992). The cancer patient with pain: Psychiatric complications and their management. *Journal of Pain and Symptom Management, 7,* 99–109.

Massie, M. J., Holland, J. C., & Glass, E. (1983). Delirium in terminally ill cancer patients. *American Journal of Psychiatry, 140,* 1048–1050.

Matthews, K. A., Siegel, J. M., Kuller, L. H., Thompson, M., & Varat, M. (1983). Determinants of decision to seek medical treatment by patients with acute myocardial infarction symptoms. *Journal of Personality and Social Psychology, 44,* 1144–1156.

Morris, T., Greer, H. S., & White, P. (1977). Psychological and social adjustment to mastectomy: A two-year follow-up study. *Cancer, 40,* 2381–2387.

Morrow, G. R., & Hickok, J. T. (1993). Behavioral treatment of chemotherapy-induced nausea and vomiting. *Oncology, 7,* 83–89.

Nail, L. M., & King, K. B. (1987). Fatigue. *Seminars in Oncology Nursing, 3,* 257–262.

Nitschke, R., Humphrey, G. B., Sexauer, C. L., Catron, B., Wunder, S., & Jay, S. (1982). Therapeutic choices made by patients with end-stage cancer. *Journal of Pediatrics, 101,* 471–476.

Northouse, L. L., & Peters-Golden, H. (1993). Cancer and the family: Strategies to assist spouses. *Seminars in Oncology Nursing, 9,* 74–82.

Parker, S., Tong, T., Bolden, S., & Wingo, P. (1997). Cancer statistics, 1997. *CA—A Cancer Journal for Clinicians, 47,* 5–27.

Patenaude, A. F. (1990). Psychological impact of bone marrow transplantation: Current perspectives. *Yale Journal of Biology and Medicine, 63,* 515–519.

Pettingale, K. W., Burgess, C., & Greer, S. (1988). Psychological response to cancer diagnosis: I. Correlations with prognostic variables. *Journal of Psychosomatic Research, 32,* 255–261.

Pickard-Holley, S. (1991). Fatigue in cancer patients. *Cancer Nursing, 14,* 13–19.

Prozanto, P., Brema, F., Amorosa, D., Bertelli, G., Conte, P. F., Martini, M. C., Pastorino, G., & Rooso, R. (1990). Megestrol acetate: Phase II study of a single daily administration in advanced breast cancer. *Breast Cancer Research and Treatment, 17,* 51–54.

Rainey, L. C. (1985). Effects of preparatory education for radiation oncology patients. *Cancer, 56,* 1056–1061.

Redd, W. H. (1993). The Morrow/Hickok article reviewed: Behavioral treatment of chemotherapy-induced nausea and vomiting. *Oncology, 7,* 94–95.

Rhodes, V. A., Watson, P. M., & Hanson, B. M. (1988). Patients' descriptions of the influence of tiredness and weakness on self-care abilities. *Cancer Nursing, 11,* 186–194.

Richardson, J. L., Marks, G., Johnson, C. A., Graham, J. W., Chan, K. K., Selser, J. N., Kishbaugh, C., Barranday, Y., & Levine, A. M. (1987). Path model of multidimensional compliance with cancer therapy. *Health Psychology, 6,* 183–207.

Richardson, J. L., Marks, G., & Levine, A. (1988). The influence of symptoms of disease and side effects of treatment on compliance with cancer therapy. *Journal of Clinical Oncology, 6,* 1746–1752.

Sales, E., Schulz, R., & Biegel, D. (1992). Predictors of strain in families of cancer patients: A review of the literature. *Journal of Psychosocial Oncology, 10,* 1–26.

Sardell, A. N., & Trierweiler, S. J. (1993). Disclosing the cancer diagnosis. *Cancer, 72,* 3355–3365.

Scheier, M. F., & Carver, C. S. (1992). Effects of optimism on psychological and physical well-being: Theoretical overview and empirical update. *Congitive Therapy and Research, 16,* 201–228.

Seale, C., & Addington-Hall, J. (1994). Euthanasia: Why people want to die earlier. *Social Science and Medicine, 39,* 647–654.

Slavin, L. A., O'Malley, J. E., Koocher, G. P., & Foster, D. J.(1982). Communication of the cancer diagnosis to pediatric patients: Impact on long-term adjustment. *American Journal of Psychiatry, 139,* 179–183.

Smets, E. M., Garssen, B., Schuster-Uitterhoeve, A. L., & deHaes, J. C. (1993). Fatigue in cancer patients. *British Journal of Cancer, 68,* 220–224.

Speigel, D. (1996). Cancer and depression. *British Journal of Psychiatry, 168,* 109–116.

Speigel, D., & Bloom, J. R. (1983). Group therapy and hypnosis reduce metastatic breast carcinoma pain. *Psychosomatic Medicine, 45,* 333–339.

Speigel, D., Bloom, J. R., Kraemer, H. C., & Gottheil, E. (1989). Effect of psychosocial treatment on survival of patients with metastatic breast cancer. *Lancet,* October 14, 888–891.

Speigel, D., Bloom, J. R., & Yalom, I. (1981). Group support for patients with metastatic cancer: A randomized outcome study. *Archives of General Psychiatry, 38,* 527–533.

Steptoe, A., Sutcliffe, I., Allen, B., & Coombes, C. (1991). Satisfaction with communication, medical knowledge, and coping style in patients with metastatic cancer. *Social Science in Medicine, 32*(6), 627–632.

Strang, P., & Qvarner, H. (1990). Cancer-related pain and its influence on quality of life. *Anticancer Research, 10,* 109–112.

Stuber, M., Christakis, D., Houskamp, B., & Kazak, A. E. (1996). Posttraumatic symptoms in childhood leukemia survivors and their parents. *Psychosomatics, 37,* 254–261.

Styra, R., Sakinofsky, I., Mahoney, L., Colapinto, N. D., & Currie, D. J., (1993). Coping styles in identifiers and nonidentifiers of a breast lump as a problem. *Psychosomatics, 34*(1), 53–60.

Syrjala, K. L., Chapko, M. K., Vitaliano, P. P., Cummings, C., & Sullivan, K. M. (1993). Recovery after allogeneic marrow transplantation: Prospective study of predictors of long-term physical and psychosocial functioning. *Bone Marrow Transplantation, 11,* 319–327.

Taylor, S. E., (1983). Adjustment to threatening events: A theory of cognitive adaptation. *American Psychologist, 38,* 1161–1173.

Tebbi, C. K. (1993). Treament compliance in childhood and adolescence. *Cancer, 71*(Suppl. 10), 3441–3449.

Teeter, M. A., Holmes, G. E., Holmes, F. F., & Baker, A. B. (1987). Decisions about marriage and family among survivors of childhood cancer. *Journal of Psychosocial Oncology, 5,* 59–68.

Telch, C. F., & Telch, M. J. (1986). Group coping skills instruction and supportive group therapy for cancer patients: A comparison of strategies. *Journal of Consulting and Clinical Psychology, 54,* 802–808.

Thompson, L., Andersen, B. L., & DePetrillo, D. (1992). The psychological processes of recovery from gynecologic cancer. In M. Coppleson, P. Morrow, & M. Tattersall (Eds.), *Gynecologic Oncology* (2nd ed., pp. 1499–1506). Edinburgh: Churchill Livingstone.

Tope, D. A., Ahles, T. A., Silberfarb, P. M. (1993). Psycho-Oncology: Psychological well-being as one component of quality of life. *Psychotherapy and Psychosomatics, 60,* 129–147.

Uchino, B. N., Cacioppo, J. T., & Kiecolt-Glaser, J. K. (1996). The relationship between social support and physiolocial processes: A review with emphasis on underlying mechanisms and implications for health. *Psychological Bulletin, 119,* 488–531.

Vasterling, J., Jenkins, R. A., Tope, D. M., & Burish, T. G. (1993). Cognitive distraction and relaxation training for the control of side effects due to cancer chemotherapy. *Journal of Behavioral Medicine, 16,* 65–80.

Vess, J. D., Moreland, J. R., & Schwebel, A. I. (1985). A followup study of role functioning and the psychosocial environment of families of cancer patients. *Journal of Psychosocial Oncology, 3,* 1–14.

Vinokur, A. D., Threatt, B. A., Caplan, R. D, & Zimmerman, B. L. (1989). Physical and psychosocial functioning and adjustment to breast cancer: Long-term follow-up of a screening population. *Cancer, 63,* 394–405.

Wallace, L. M., Priestman, S. G., Dunn, J. A., & Priestman, T. J. (1993). The quality of life of early breast cancer patients treated by two different radiotherapy regimens. *Clinical Oncology, 5,* 228–233.

Wardle, J., & Pope, R. (1992). The psychological costs of screening for cancer. *Journal of Psychosomatic Research, 36,* 609–624.

Weisman, A. D., & Worden, J. W. (1976). The existential plight in cancer: Significance of the first 100 days. *International Journal of Psychiatry in Medicine, 7,* 1–15.

Whiteside, T. L., & Herberman, R. B. (1994). Role of human natural killer cells in health and disease. *Clinical and Diagnostic Laboratory Immunology,. 1,* 125–133.

Winer, E. P., & Sutton, L. M. (1994). Quality of life after bone marrow transplantation. *Oncology, 8,* 19–31.

Wingard, J. R., Curbow, B., Baker, F., & Piantadosi, S. (1991). Health, functional status, and employment of adult survivors of bone marrow transplantation. *Annals of Internal Medicine, 114,* 113–118.

Winningham, M. L. (1991). Walking program for people with cancer. Getting Started. *Cancer Nursing, 14,* 270–276.

Winningham, M. L., Nail, L. M., Burke, M. B., Brophy, L., Cimprich, B., Jones, L. S., Pickard-Holley, S., Rhodes, V., St. Pierre, B., Beck, S., Glass, E. C., Mock, V. L., Mooney, K. H., & Piper, B. (1994). Fatigue and the cancer experience: The State of the Knowledge. *Oncology Nursing Forum, 21,* 23–36.

Wolf, D. M., & Jordan, V. C. (1992). Gynecologic complications associated with long-term adjuvant tamoxifen therapy for breast cancer. *Gynecologic Oncology, 45,* 118–128.

Woodard, L. J., & Pamies, R. J. (1992). The disclosure of the diagnosis of cancer. *Primary Care, 19,* 657–663.

44

Subjective Risk and Health Protective Behavior: Cancer Screening and Cancer Prevention

Leona S. Aiken
Mary A. Gerend
Arizona State University
Kristina M. Jackson
University of Missouri

This chapter explores the role of perceived risk in health protective behavior. Cancer serves as the context of the presentation; the discussion employs the literature on cancer screening and prevention to highlight theory and findings on the perception of risk in relation to health behavior. The origins of perceived risk, its role in health behavior models, and the linkages between perceived risk and behavior are explored. In models of health behavior, perceived risk for disease is the motivational engine for health protective action. This chapter is intended to serve two purposes: to provide both a broad picture of the literature on risk perception in health psychology and to characterize research on perceived risk for cancer as a putative determinant of cancer screening and preventive behavior.

CHAPTER OVERVIEW

The chapter first addresses the role of perceived susceptibility in models of health behavior. It then turns to perceived risk as a construct, its measurement, its observed relation to objective risk for cancer, and its determinants. It next explores the relation of perceived susceptibility and cancer distress to cancer screening and cancer preventive behavior. Here it considers not only the susceptibility–behavior link, but also explores other variables that may moderate or even mitigate the impact of perceived susceptibility on specific cancer protective behaviors. The chapter then considers interventions to increase screening and preventive behavior that involve the perceived susceptibility construct. The emphasis is on the use of mediational analysis to assess the direct and indirect impact of perceived susceptibility on screening and preventive behavior. Finally, it explores a number of issues that arise in consideration of how perceived susceptibility impacts health protective behavior.

CANCER PREVALENCE

Cancer is a feared disease of high prevalence. By age 59, over 8% of men and 9% of women will have developed an invasive cancer; from birth to death, these percentages rise to 47% of men and 38% of women (Landis, Murray, Bolden, & Wingo, 1998). Cancer is the second leading cause of death (23% of all deaths) behind heart disease (32%) among adults in the United States. In all, 1.23 million new cases of cancer and over 564,800 cancer deaths are expected in the United States in 1998 (Landis et al., 1998).

SCREENING AND PREVENTIVE RECOMMENDATIONS

The public is inundated with information about cancer and with recommendations for cancer screening and prevention.

As of 1998, the American Cancer Society recommended extensive cancer screening (American Cancer Society, 1998). Screening recommendations include an annual mammogram for women age 40 and older; colon and rectal screening with fecal occult blood test (FOBT) annually, plus flexible sigmoidoscopy every 5 years for men and women over age 50; annual prostate-specific antigen (PSA) blood test and digital rectal examination (DRE) for men age 50 and older; annual pelvic examinations for all women age 18 and older, with annual Pap tests until at least three negative Pap tests have been achieved, and then less frequent Pap tests; and endometrial screening for women at high risk for uterine cancer (American Cancer Society, 1998). Regular self-examinations are also recommended, including skin self-examination (American Academy of Dermatology, 1994; National Cancer Institute, 1995), breast self-examination (BSE) for all women beginning at age 20 (American Cancer Society, 1998), and testicular self-examination for men (National Cancer Institute, 1992). (See also the screening recommendations of the U.S. Preventive Services Task Force, 1996.) Beyond screening are recommendations for cancer prevention through lifestyle modification, including skin protection (American Cancer Society, 1997b) and diet (American Cancer Society, 1996).

SCREENING UTILIZATION IN THE UNITED STATES

According to the National Health Interview Surveys of 1987, 1992, and 1994, a population-based national survey of 40,000 households (American Cancer Society, 1997a; National Center for Health Statistics, 1996), the percentage of women age 50 and over who have had a mammogram in the past 2 years rose from 25% to 56% between 1987 and 1994. These rates were similar for Black and Hispanic women (56% and 50%, respectively, in 1994, up from 19% and 18%, respectively, in 1987), although rates lagged for low income women (38% in 1994) and those with less than a high school education (42%). Rates for Pap test utilization (within the past 3 years) achieved 77% in 1994 (74% for Hispanic women), again lagging behind for low education women (62%). As of 1992, about a third of the population had had one of three colorectal screening tests, DRE within the past year, FOBT within the past 2 years, or a sigmoidoscopy at least once.

OPENLY AIRED CANCER DEBATES

Epidemiological findings make the news, and the public hears a relentless array, often contradictory, of associations between behaviors and cancer (Taubes, 1995). Medical debates about the efficacy of screening for mortality reduction are publicly aired (Aiken, Jackson, & Lapin, 1998). The debate on the efficacy of mammography screening for women under age 50 raged in the public media for most of this decade (Aiken et al., 1998). Prostate screening currently is occasioning considerable debate, along the lines of the previous mammography debate (Albertsen, 1996; E. S. Wolfe & W. W. Wolfe, 1997). Increasingly, laypersons are asked by their physicians to decide whether they wish to be screened, with the argument that patient choice must be preserved (Woolf & Lawrence, 1997). Issues concerning appropriate screening are aired against a backdrop of economic constraints posed by the health care industry.

CLASSES OF CANCER PROTECTIVE BEHAVIORS

For the exploration of perceived risk and behavior, cancer protective behaviors must be divided into two broad categories—screening for early detection versus prevention. Screening behaviors may further be divided into those that are medically based (e.g., mammography) versus those that involve self-examination (e.g., BSE). This distinction is important because the barriers to screening are expected to be very different for the two categories. These barriers may interact with or obscure the role of perceived risk. A similar argument can be made for specific preventive behaviors. Although the discussion draws on literature on a variety of cancers, medically based screening is exemplified with mammography, self-screening with BSE, and preventive behavior with skin protection.

PERCEIVED RISK IN MODELS OF HEALTH BEHAVIOR

This section is devoted to an overview of the role of perceived risk in models of health protective behavior. Health psychology is rich in models of the putative determinants of health protective behavior. At the core of essentially all these models is the concept of *perceived risk*—the extent to which individuals believe that they are subject to a health threat (Becker, 1990; Gerrard, Gibbons, & Bushman, 1996; Kowalewski, Henson, & Longshore, 1997; van der Pligt, 1998; Weinstein, 1993).

Health psychology draws on a theoretically based literature in risk perception and its determinants (Kahneman & Tversky, 1973; Kasperson et al., 1988; Slovic, 1987; Tversky & Kahneman, 1974). Formal models of risk (Kasperson et al., 1988) postulate that risk is a joint function of the probability of occurrence of a negative event, and the magnitude of its consequences; risk is the product of these factors.

Literature applying perceptions of risk to health behavior is less precise. The term *perceived risk,* as well as the terms *perceived susceptibility* and *perceived vulnerability* are used interchangeably for measures of the subjective likelihood of contracting a disease, absent any consideration of severity. Consistent with application in health, the terms *perceived risk, perceived susceptibility,* and *perceived vulnerability* are used here to refer to subjective estimates of the likelihood of personally contracting a disease, and not the combination of likelihood and consequences. *Perceived severity* is used here to refer to perceptions of disease consequences independent of likelihood.

According to Weinstein (1993), models of health behavior assume that the motivation for health protective behavior stems from anticipation of some negative health outcome coupled with hope of avoiding the outcome. Anticipation of a negative outcome involves foremost the perception that one is personally susceptible to some disease; for strong health motivation to be achieved, this perception must be coupled with the anticipation that the disease consequences are severe (Weinstein, 1993).

Our particular interest in this chapter is the linkage of perceived susceptibility to health protective behavior. A theoretical context for this linkage is provided by consideration of the way in which perceived susceptibility is used in models of health protective behavior. Three widely applicable models of health behavior, the health belief model (HBM; Becker & Maiman, 1975; Rosenstock, 1966; 1974a, 1974b, 1990), protection motivation theory (PMT; Prentice-Dunn & Rogers, 1986; Rogers, 1975, 1983), and the precaution adoption process model (PAPM; Weinstein, 1988) employ the perceived susceptibility construct as a driving force in health protective behavior. Perceived risk appears as well in the transtheoretical model of change (TTM; Prochaska, DiClemente, & Norcross, 1992), and the recently proposed cognitive-social health information processing (C-SHIP) model (S. M. Miller, Shoda, & Hurley, 1996). Perceived risk is also implicit in the theory of reasoned action (TRA; Ajzen & Fishbein, 1980; Fishbein & Ajzen, 1975) and its extension, the theory of planned behavior (Ajzen, 1991), as well as subjective expected utility theory (Ronis, 1992; Weinstein, 1993), as they are applied to health behavior.

Although perceived susceptibility is consistently cast as the motivating engine for health protective behavior, the specific role of perceived susceptibility and assumptions about how it combines with other constructs vary in informative ways across models. A brief characterization of the role of the perceived susceptibility construct in several well-established models of health behavior and the newer C-SHIP model is provided. A characterization of the complete health models is beyond the scope of this chapter; Conner and Norman (1996); Glanz, Lewis, and Rimer (1990); Weinstein (1993); and Weinstein, Rothman, and Sutton (1998) provided explications of these and other models; Conner and Norman (1996) provided extensive reviews of literature employing these models as well. Curry and Emmons (1994) provided a thorough summary of applications of the HBM, TRA, and the TTM to breast cancer screening.

Perceived Susceptibility as Motivator: Health Belief Model

The health belief model (HBM) traces its origins to problems encountered in the U.S. Public Health Service nearly half a century ago—problems of failures of *asymptomatic* individuals to undergo screening tests or to engage in preventive health behaviors (Rosenstock, 1966, 1974a; 1990). Ironically, the health belief model is still being applied to the same issues, which are abundant in the area of cancer prevention and early detection. The HBM states that individuals will undertake a health action to the extent that they believe themselves to be susceptible to a health threat (*perceived susceptibility*), believe that the consequences of the disease are serious (*perceived severity or seriousness*), believe that the proposed health action will offer protection against the health threat (*perceived benefits*), and believe that barriers to performing the health action can be overcome (*perceived barriers*). Finally, individuals must receive some trigger, or cue, in order to act (*cue to action*). Interestingly, in current interventions to increase cancer screening, a reminder letter (a cue to action) is a common component (e.g., Bastani, Marcus, Maxwell, Das, & Yan, 1994). Physicians' recommendations for screening have been conceptualized as a cue to action as well (Fox, Siu, & Stein, 1994).

Perceived susceptibility is, in a sense, the centerpiece of the HBM. There are two aspects to perceived susceptibility: the individuals' belief that contracting a disease is a realistic possibility for themselves, and the individuals' belief that they may have the disease in the complete absence of symptoms (Rosenstock, 1990). Failure to utilize cancer screening tests may be attributed to a lack of belief that pathology can exist in the absence of symptoms (Rosenstock, 1990). Perceived susceptibility and perceived severity combine to form perceived threat, a determinant of the likelihood of adopting a health action; this combination closely reflects the formal definition of risk (Kasperson et al., 1988) provided earlier. The HBM is silent on the nature of the combinatorial rules for the constructs; in most applications of the health belief model, simple additive effects of the constructs have been explored. The interplay of perceived threat with perceived benefits is important for cancer screening, in that high risk individuals, although they perceive heightened vulnerability, may avoid seeking screening if they believe that cancer treatment cannot save them (e.g., Lerman & M. D. Schwartz, 1993, for breast cancer; M. D. Schwartz, Lerman, Daly, et al., 1995, for ovarian cancer). Ronis (1992) suggested a combinatorial rule for HBM constructs in which perceived susceptibility and severity are necessary precursors to the perception of benefits of health action, a characterization on which we draw in our later discussion of interventions.

The health belief model has made sustained contributions as a heuristic for the study of psychosocial correlates of preventive health behavior. (See reviews by Harrison, Mullen, & Green, 1992; Janz & Becker, 1984; and Sheeran & Abraham, 1996.) Typically, the perceived barriers construct has been the strongest correlate of lack of protective behavior, whereas perceived susceptibility has typically exhibited low to moderate positive correlations with protective behavior.

Whereas perceived susceptibility is expected to combine with perceived severity to motivate health protective behavior, perceived severity by itself rarely correlates with preventive behavior or screening behavior (Janz & Becker, 1984; Harrison et al., 1992). This is certainly true for cancer research: Perceived severity has failed to show predictive utility and has not been amenable to change via intervention, as cancer apparently is seen as uniformly serious (Champion, 1994; Curry & Emmons, 1994; Rimer, 1990; but see Ronis & Harel, 1989, for an exception). Researchers often forgo the measurement of perceived severity in characterizing the HBM for cancer-related behavior (e.g., Hyman, Baker, Ephraim, Moadel, & Philip, 1994; Vernon, Myers, & Tilley, 1997). Thus, perceived susceptibility by itself, rather than the combination of susceptibility and severity, is de facto characterized as the motivating force for cancer protective behavior.

Fear Arousing Communication, Perceived Susceptibility, and Behavior: Protection Motivation Theory

Perceived susceptibility also plays a central role as a motivator of health protective behavior in PMT, a model that arose from consideration of the impact of fear arousing communication on the adoption of health protective behavior (Beck & Frankel, 1981; Rogers, 1975). As in the HBM, perceptions of susceptibility and severity that resulted from fear communications were expected to combine with perceptions of the existence of an effective health protective behavior to arouse *protection motivation*, which in turn led to intentions to adopt the protective health behavior (Rogers, 1975). In the revised form of PMT (Rogers, 1983; Prentice-Dunn & Rogers, 1986), a special motivating role for perceived susceptibility coupled with perceived severity was provided, that of lowering the probability of a maladaptive response (e.g., delay in seeking treatment for suspected cancer symptoms, persistence in behaviors that put one at increased cancer risk). Rippetoe and Rogers (1987) applied PMT to an experimental investigation of breast self-examination.

How Perceptions of Susceptibility Accrue: The Precaution Adoption Process Model

Models of health behavior assume that in order for perceived susceptibility to act as a motivational force, perceptions of susceptibility must be personal (i.e., individuals must feel that they, themselves, are vulnerable). Weinstein (1988) proposed the precaution adoption process (PAPM) as a stage model of the adoption of health behavior. In general, stage models (Weinstein et al., 1998) characterize individuals as falling into a series of ordered categories with regard to adoption of a health behavior. In PAPM, these stages move from lack of awareness of the health issue (Stage 1) through health behavior maintenance (Stage 7). Consistent with this stage structure, beliefs about perceived susceptibility are assumed to develop in a series of cumulative stages. First, individuals are assumed to become aware of a health hazard (awareness), then to believe in the likelihood of the hazard for others (general susceptibility), and finally to acknowledge their own personal vulnerability (personal susceptibility). Personal susceptibility is assumed to be critical in the decision to take precautionary action (Weinstein et al., 1998). Assessment of discrepancies between general susceptibility versus personal susceptibility has uncovered optimistic biases (Weinstein, 1980) about people's vulnerability; these biases are discussed later. The PAPM has been applied to home testing for radon gas, which is an environmental cancer threat (Weinstein & Sandman, 1992).

The Growth of Perceived Susceptibility and the Process of Adopting Health Behaviors: Transtheoretical Model of Change

The TTM, as the PAPM, is a stage model of health behavior adoption (Prochaska et al., 1992). Progress through the first two stages is hypothesized to be driven by the growth of awareness of perceived susceptibility from *precontemplation,* during which the individual has no sense of vulnerability to a health threat, to *contemplation,* in which there is an awareness of one's own vulnerability to a health threat but no commitment to health action. Although the transtheoretical model was initially applied to smoking cessation as a cancer preventive action, the model has now been applied to cancer screening as well. For example, Lipkus, Rimer, and Strigo (1996), Rakowski et al. (1992), and Siegler, Feaganes, and Rimer (1995) applied this model to mammography screening.

Cognitive-Social Health Information Processing

The C-SHIP model (S. M. Miller et al., 1996) is a comprehensive model of the genesis and maintenance of health-protective behavior, initially expounded in the context of the complex sustained behavior of breast self-examination (BSE). The model considers five classes of determinants of health behavior that incorporate both cognitions and affect. Among these, two classes address issues of perceived susceptibility: *health-relevant encodings,* including health risks and vulnerabilities, plus attentional strategies for gathering versus avoiding health relevant information; and *health beliefs and expectancies,* including how vulnerabilities, such as genetic predisposition, impact subjective likelihood of disease development. The model specifies how information about objective risk and resultant perceptions of susceptibility interact with emotions associated with receiving health information, with health goals, and with self-regulation in producing health behaviors. That the model addresses the interplay of emotion with cognitions about people's vulnerability is important for an understanding of cancer screening behavior among high risk individuals; this issue is discussed later.

Perceived Susceptibility as a Predisposing Factor in Complex Hybrid Models of Health Behavior Adoption

Within this decade, a number of authors have proposed extensive integrative frameworks of the putative determinants of health protective behavior, which have been employed in the design of interventions to increase health behavior. Four such frameworks are summarized in Curry and Emmons (1994). Each framework specifies a complex causal chain of variables that ultimately leads to health behavior. Most important for our consideration is the fact that perceived susceptibility is included as a predisposing factor for health behavior adoption early in the causal chain, a factor that may facilitate overcoming barriers to the health protective behavior (McBride, Curry, Taplin, Anderman, & Grothaus, 1993) and lead to receptiveness to health promotion interventions (the PRECEDE-PROCEED model of Green & Kreuter, 1991).

Summary: Perceived Susceptibility as a Predisposing Factor for Health Behavior Adoption

Not surprisingly, models of health behavior have matured and increased in complexity. Early models have been augmented with new variables, for example, the addition of self-efficacy for health behavior to both the HBM (Rosenstock, Strecher, & Becker, 1988) and PMT (Rogers, 1983). New stage models have viewed health behavior adoption as dynamic, in part driven by perceived susceptibility. The interplay of susceptibility cognitions with emotion has been elucidated. Hybrid models have incorporated a complex network of environmental and medical system variables along with individual cognitions, including perceived susceptibility. The evolution of these models has clarified the role of perceived susceptibility as a potentially powerful predisposing factor at the outset of the process of adoption of health behaviors, a factor that motivates this process of adoption. Drawing on this evolution of health behavior models, we conceptualize perceived susceptibility to disease as a *distal construct in a mediational chain* of constructs that eventuates in protective health behavior.

PERCEIVED SUSCEPTIBILITY: MEASUREMENT AND DETERMINANTS

This section first considers approaches to the measurement of perceived susceptibility. It then reviews comparisons of objective risk for cancer with subjective risk, raising the question of whether individuals overestimate or underestimate their cancer risk relative to objective risk. Finally, it explores the putative determinants of perceived susceptibility, drawing on both a broad literature on determinants of risk, and a cancer-specific literature.

Measurement of Perceived Susceptibility

Alternative approaches to the measurement of perceived susceptibility lead to varying pictures of personal perceptions of risk for developing cancer. Two broad classes of measures are *absolute measures,* in which personal ratings are made without reference to any outside group, and *comparative measures,* in which personal perceived susceptibility is compared to susceptibility in some normative group (Weinstein & Klein, 1996).

Absolute Measures

Rating Scales. Among absolute measures, typical rating scales ask individuals for Likert scale judgments of their likelihood of developing cancer—for example, "What do you think are the chances that you personally will get breast cancer someday" (5-point scale; Bastani, Marcus, & Hollatz-Brown, 1991). These are the most commonly used measures of perceived susceptibility, employed both in studies of the psychosocial correlates of health protective behavior and in evaluations of interventions.

Numerical Estimates. Numerical estimates of the chance of contracting cancer are also taken as absolute indicators of perceived susceptibility—for example, "Risk of developing breast cancer in the next 10 years" (< 1%, 1–5%, 6–10%, 11–20% or > 20%; Dolan, Lee, & McDermott, 1997). Perceived risk has also been measured with rate judgments —for example, "the number of women out of 1000 whom you think would develop breast cancer in the next 10 years" (Black, Nease, & Tosteson, 1995; see also L. M. Schwartz, Woloshin, Black, & Welch, 1997). Such measures have enjoyed relatively limited application, most often in studies comparing perceived to objective risk.

Comparative Risk

Direct comparative risk is measured with some form of the following question: "What do you believe are your chances of getting (disease) compared to other (men/women) your own age?", with typical responses of "a lot lower, somewhat lower, about the same, somewhat higher, and a lot higher." This measure has been applied to cancer in general (Kreuter & Strecher, 1995); lung cancer, skin cancer, and cancer in general (Weinstein, 1987); breast cancer (e.g., Aiken, Fenaughty, West, Johnson, & Luckett, 1995); and colorectal cancer (e.g., Blalock, DeVellis, Afifi, & Sandler, 1990). *Indirect comparative risk* is assessed by having individuals rate the perceived likelihood of developing the disease for themselves and for others on separate scales; the difference between these two ratings reflects comparative risk (Weinstein & Klein, 1996).

Measure of comparative risk are sometimes used in combination with absolute rating scales in the formation of multi-item susceptibility measures. However, the two most common applications of comparative risk items have been in research on optimistic bias (e.g., Weinstein, 1980) and in studies of individual attributions of risk (e.g., Aiken et al., 1995). Direct comparative risk items provide risk estimates only in relation to others; thus, the specification of the comparison group is critical. An individual who felt quite vulnerable to a disease, when measured on an absolute rating scale, might nonetheless feel less at risk than more unfortunate others (Klein & Weinstein, 1997), yielding a comparative rating of relatively low comparative risk.

Perceived Susceptibility Versus Cancer Worry and Cancer Distress

Perceived susceptibility has been distinguished from more emotional aspects of vulnerability in studies of cancer-related health behaviors, consistent with the C-SHIP model. Items such as "Thinking about breast cancer makes me feel upset and frightened" (McCaul, Schroeder, & Reid, 1996) have been used to characterize cancer *worry,* as distinct from perceived susceptibility. Sjöberg (1998) argued that worry versus perceived risk reflect emotional versus cognitive reactions to threat, respectively. The two variables are weakly correlated (e.g., $r = .20$; McCaul et al., 1996) and form independent factors in the measurement of predictors of colorectal cancer screening adherence (Vernon et al., 1997). In addition to worry, fear of cancer and cancer treatment (Berman & Wandersman, 1992; Salazar & de Moor, 1995), cancer anxiety (Gram & Slenker, 1992), and morbid concern about breast cancer (Irwig et al., 1991) also have been included in research. A growing literature on breast and ovarian cancer screening among high risk women (e.g., Audrain et al., 1998; M. D. Schwartz, Taylor, et al., 1999) has employed such measures of cancer-specific distress.

Perceived Vulnerability to Cancer and Objective Risk

Comparisons of Objective and Subjective Risk

A number of approaches have been taken to the comparison of objective with subjective risk for cancer. Objective risk measures are of two types. First are rates of risk in the *population* (e.g., the percent of women in the population ever contracting breast cancer). Second are risk estimates derived for specific *individuals,* based on their particular status on known risk factors; derivation of these latter estimates employs epidemiological models of risk. Subjective measures are numerical estimates of risk, or rating scale measures of absolute or comparative risk.

Population Estimates. When determined from actual versus estimated population rates, community samples overestimate their probability of developing and dying of cancer (e.g., Helzlsouer, Ford, Hayward, Midzenski, & Perry, 1994, for cancer in general; Ward, Hughes, Hirst, & Winchester, 1997, for prostate cancer).

Epidemiological Estimates and Individual Assessments. Individuals' risk estimates based on epidemiological models have been compared with their own subjective numerical risk estimates. The Gail model (Gail et al., 1989), a five-factor epidemiological model of breast cancer risk among Caucasian women, predicts risk for breast cancer among women who obtain annual mammograms. Risk factors include number of first-degree relatives (mother or sisters) with breast cancer, age at menarche, age at first live birth, number of previous biopsies and chronological age. Using this model, Black et al. (1995) and Dolan et al. (1997) found that women grossly overestimate their chances of developing breast cancer, for example, by a factor of 20 in women under age 50 (Black et al., 1995). Subjective and objective estimates correlate moderately (for example, $r = .46$ for breast cancer in a sample of women under age 50; Siegler et al., 1995).

Those at heightened cancer risk due to their being first-degree relatives (FDRs) of individuals with cancer also overestimate their personal risk. More than 60% of FDRs greatly overestimated their lifetime risk of breast cancer as compared to Gail estimates (Lerman et al., 1995). Among FDRs, specific Gail model risk components were found to be unrelated to numerical ratings (0%–100%) of the chance of getting breast cancer someday (Daly et al., 1996).

Comparative Risk Ratings Versus Epidemiological Estimates. A number of investigations have compared an epidemiological estimate of risk with a direct measure of comparative risk. Such studies provide a very different picture of the relation of objective to subjective risk, depending on the disease. Individuals are optimistic (i.e., underestimate their risk) for heart attack within the next 10 years (Avis, Smith, & McKinlay, 1989; Kreuter & Strecher, 1995), but overestimate their risk of cancer in this time frame, with almost half of individuals showing pessimistic bias (Kreuter & Strecher, 1995).

Comparative Risk and Unrealistic Optimism

While people overestimate their absolute risk of contracting cancer, studies of comparative risk suggest that individuals exhibit *unrealistic optimism* or *optimistic bias* (Weinstein, 1980, 1987; Weinstein & Klein, 1996); that is, they believe they are less likely to contract specific cancers than are others their own age. This bias has been demonstrated for breast cancer (Aiken et al., 1995), skin cancer (A. J. Miller, Ashton, McHoskey, & Gimbel, 1990), and colorectal cancer (Blalock et al., 1990; Lipkus, Rimer, Lyna, et al., 1996), as well as brain cancer, leukaemia, and lung cancer (Lek & Bishop, 1995). In contrast, comparative judgments of "cancer in general" do not yield optimistic bias (Weinstein, 1980, 1984), even when "cancer in general" and specific cancers are rated by the same sample (Weinstein, 1982, 1987). FDRs of women with breast cancer accurately estimate their comparative risk as high when asked to compare their risk to women without a family history of breast cancer (Audrain et al., 1995; Lerman, Kash, & Stefanek, 1994). However, when asked to compare their risk to others their own age, with family history unspecified, a substantial portion of FDRs incorrectly rate their risk as lower than average (Aiken et al., 1995; Blalock et al., 1990).

Whereas much effort has been made to untangle the sources of optimistic bias and risk perceptions in general, the behavioral implications of the optimistic bias for protective behavior are unclear (van der Pligt, 1998; Weinstein & Klein, 1996), and have not been addressed in the context of cancer. Van der Pligt (1996) argued that comparative risk appraisal may not be a determinant of health behavior and does not contribute to the prediction of health behavior beyond perceived vulnerability.

Determinants of Perceived Risk for Cancer

Two literatures inform the question of the determinants of perceived risk for cancer. The first, cancer-specific literature examines individuals' rationales for their ratings of their own risk of cancer relative to others their own age, following a methodology first employed by Weinstein (1984). The second is a broader literature on the determinants of risk.

Determinants of Comparative Risk for Cancer

Weinstein (1984) coded the reasons generated by individuals for their comparative risk judgments into five categories:

actions and behavior patterns, heredity, physiology or physical attributes, environment, and psychological attributes. For cancer in general, breast cancer (Aiken et al., 1995; Lipkus, Rimer, & Strigo, 1996; Salazar, 1994), and colorectal cancer (Blalock et al., 1990; Lipkus, Rimer, Lyna, et al., 1996), personal lifestyle-related actions were seen as decreasing risk (e.g., proper diet, exercise). For lung cancer, personal actions (smoking) were seen as increasing risk (Lek & Bishop, 1995). Across cancers, attributions for heredity were that the absence of disease in the family reduced risk below average. In contrast, women who believed their risk to be above average for breast cancer mentioned heredity most often as the determining factor (Aiken et al., 1995; McCaul & O'Donnell, 1998; Savage & Clarke, 1996). Of interest is that FDRs of colorectal cancer patients rarely mentioned heredity as increasing their risk, even after they had been informed they were at increased risk due to their sibling's cancer (Blalock et al., 1990). These results taken together suggest that individuals believe they have some control over whether they get cancer through their own actions. However, there is lack of understanding of the role of heredity in cancer. Absence of family history is viewed as highly protective, even though most cancers are not associated with family history. At the same time, a family history of cancer may not lead to perceptions of increased risk.

General Determinants of Perceived Risk

Van der Pligt (1996, 1998) summarized an extensive literature on the determinants of perceived risk. Classes of determinants include cognitive heuristics, disease characteristics, personal motivations, and personality and information-processing strategies (Gerend, 1998). (See Fischhoff, Bostrom, & Quadrel, 1993, for a discussion of risk perception and communication.)

Cognitive Heuristics. Individuals rely on cognitive heuristics in estimating uncertain events (Kahneman & Tversky, 1973; Tversky & Kahneman, 1973, 1974), and these heuristics may underlie inaccurate perceptions of risk in the health domain. The *availability heuristic* (Tversky & Kahneman, 1973) indicates that individuals base frequency estimates on the salience of the event in question, or the ease with which the event comes to mind. Personal experience with other individuals who have cancer (Wardle, 1995), coupled with the extensive media coverage of cancer, may contribute to the observed overestimates of cancer risk (Slovic, Fischhoff, & Lichtenstein, 1979; van der Pligt, 1998). The *representativeness heuristic* (Kahneman & Tversky, 1973) indicates that individuals base likelihood estimates for a hypothetical event (e.g., a personal diagnosis of breast cancer) on their similarity to events with comparable characteristics (e.g., the individual's similarity to others diagnosed with breast cancer).

Characteristics of the Health Threat. Bias in perceptions of comparative risk has been hypothesized to depend on disease characteristics (Weinstein, 1984, 1987; Weinstein & Klein, 1996). Harris (1996) and Weinstein (1987) provided support for a direct relation between the perceived controllability or preventability of a disease and optimistic bias concerning risk; that is, the more controllable or preventable a disease was perceived to be, the greater the optimistic bias. Evidence of a relation of optimistic bias with disease heritability is lacking (Weinstein, 1982). The "absent/exempt" principle (e.g., "If I haven't gotten the disease by now, I won't get it"; Weinstein, 1987) is associated with lower perceived risk with increasing age (e.g., Aiken, West, Woodward, & Reno, 1994, for breast cancer), although cancer incidence increases with age.

Maintenance of Self-Esteem. Optimistic biases for perceived personal risk have in part been attributed to a motivation to protect oneself from feelings of distress or anxiety about future negative events (e.g., Perloff, 1983). This protection may accrue from downward social comparisons, that is, comparisons of one's own risk with the risk of others who are actually more vulnerable (Klein, 1996; Klein & Weinstein, 1997; Perloff & Fetzer, 1986).

Personality Characteristics and Modes of Information Processing. A variety of personality dimensions have been associated with perceived risk. Among them are monitoring blunting (M. D. Schwartz, Lerman, S. Miller, Daly, & Masny, 1995), psychological defense (Dziokonski & Weber, 1977; Paulhus, Fridhandler, & Hayes, 1997), anxiety (MacLeod, Williams, & Berekian, 1991), and neuroticism (Darvill & Johnson, 1991). This may explain linkages noted between personality factors and breast screening behavior (Siegler et al., 1995) reviewed by Siegler and Costa (1994).

PERCEIVED SUSCEPTIBILITY AND CANCER RELATED BEHAVIOR

This section considers the relations of perceived susceptibility to both screening for early detection of cancer and cancer preventive behavior. A critical issue for health psychology is the implication of perceptions of susceptibility for protective behavior. As we have already indicated, we conceptualize perceived susceptibility to disease as a distal construct in a mediational chain of constructs that eventuates in health behavior. Relations of perceived susceptibility to behavior are likely to be complex, to be mediated, moderated, or nullified by other determinants of the particular behavior in question, determinants that are explored in the discussion of perceived susceptibility and protective behavior. Given space limitations, this chapter does not provide a comprehensive review, but it does reference and summarize existing reviews and highlight important themes (see Royak-Schaler, Stanton, & Danoff-Burg, 1997, for related work).

Perceived Susceptibility, Distress, and Screening

Accuracy of Self-Report of Screening Behavior

Studies of screening behavior often rely on self-report of screening. Several reports suggest approximately 95% accuracy for self-reports of having had a mammogram when compared to clinic records (Aiken, West, Woodward, Reno, & Reynolds, 1994; Degnan et al., 1992; Etzi, Lane, & Grimson, 1994; King, Rimer, Trock, Balshem, & Engstrom, 1990; Rimer et al., 1992). Correct recollection of whether a mammogram occurred within the past year or 2 years appears somewhat lower (73% accuracy; Degnan et al., 1992). Self-report accuracy is lower for screening tests that occur during the course of physician examination, for example, 61% verification of Pap smears against laboratory records (Bowman, Sanson-Fisher, & Redman, 1997), and very low verification rates for digital rectal examination (DRE) and fecal occult blood test (FOBT) against medical charts (Lipkus, Rimer, Lyna et al., 1996). Finally, self-reports of breast self-examination (BSE) may overestimate actual performance (Alagna, Morokoff, Bevett, & Reddy, 1987).

Perceived Susceptibility and Mammography Screening

McCaul, Branstetter, Schroeder, and Glasgow (1996) provided an extensive meta-analysis of the relation between breast cancer risk and mammography screening. The weighted average correlation between family history and screening was $r = .27$, with only one article reporting a nonsignificant negative correlation. For perceived vulnerability and screening, the average weighted correlation was a somewhat lower, $r = .16$, with a stronger relationship evidenced in cross-sectional ($r = .19$) than in prospective designs ($r = .10$). Higher screening likelihood was noted among women who had breast problems, $r = .30$. Worry about breast cancer was positively associated with screening, $r = .14$. The positive relation of perceived susceptibility to screening has been confirmed in more recent studies (Cole, Bryant, McDermott, Sorrell, & Flynn, 1997; Lauver, Nabholz, Scott, & Tak, 1997; Lipkus, Rimer, & Strigo, 1996). Perceived susceptibility is not a proxy for family history, and predicts screening compliance above and beyond family history (Aiken, West, Woodward, & Reno, 1994).

As we have argued, the relation of perceived susceptibility to screening has been found to be moderated by other psychosocial variables. Aiken, West, Woodward, and Reno (1994) found that susceptibility related to compliance with mammography screening only when perceived barriers to screening were low; under high perceived barriers, no such relation was observed.

Medical System and Demographic Determinants of Screening. A growing literature in the public health domain provides documentation of medical system determinants of the use of medically based cancer screening tests. The impact of health care coverage (e.g., Potosky, Breen, Graubard, & Parsons, 1998) and, moreover, continuity of care, (e.g., O'Malley, Mandelblatt, Gold, Cagney, & Kerner, 1997), have been documented. This literature further reflects the impact of demographic variables on screening utilization, among them race (e.g., Frazier, Jiles, & Mayberry, 1996; Paskett, Rushing, D'Agostino, & Tatum, 1997; Pearlman, Rakowski, Ehrich, & Clark, 1996), acculturation among minority women (Kaplan et al., 1996), and age (Caplan & Haynes, 1996; M. E. Costanza, 1992) in interaction with race (Fox & Roetzheim, 1994). These variables set limits on the impact of psychosocial variables on screening utilization.

Perceived Susceptibility and Breast Self-Examination (BSE)

Evaluation of the relation of perceived vulnerability to BSE performance takes into account not only the frequency of BSE performance relative to the recommended monthly schedule (American Cancer Society, 1998), but also the adequacy of BSE performance (see review by Zapka & Mamon, 1986). S. M. Miller et al. (1996), Savage and Clarke (1996), and Aiken et al. (1995) all pointed out the mixture of positive and null results for the relation of perceived vulnerability to BSE frequency. When relations of vulnerability to BSE frequency are found, they are modest, ranging from .14 to .25 (S. M. Miller et al., 1996). The balanced mix of positive and null results yields a lower average correlation across studies. Interestingly, perceived susceptibility relates to thoroughness and accuracy of BSE performance (Fletcher, Morgan, O'Malley, Earp, & Degnan, 1989; Wyper, 1990). However, across studies, the perceived barriers construct (including such factors as large breast size, difficulty of performing BSE, lack of expertise in BSE; Salazar, 1994) dominates as the strongest predictor of BSE frequency within the HBM framework, with correlations approaching –.5 (Wyper, 1990). Strong barriers may override perceptions of susceptibility in influencing performance versus nonperformance of BSE.

Self-Efficacy and Screening. As would be expected for a self-screening behavior, self- efficacy or self-confidence in the ability to adequately perform BSE is correlated strongly with BSE frequency (e.g., Alagna et al., 1987; Champion, 1991; Rutledge & Davis, 1988; Sortet & Banks, 1997; see reviews by S. M. Miller et al., 1996, and Salazar, 1994). This relation has been found both retrospectively and prospectively. Similarly, the importance of self-efficacy has also been demonstrated for testicular self-examination (Brubaker & Wickersham, 1990).

Fear, Worry, Cancer Distress, and Screening Behavior

In both the general population and in FDRs of individuals with cancer, fear of cancer, worry about cancer, and cancer distress have been associated with both insufficient and excessive screening, thus providing a plethora of conflicting results across studies.

General Population. McCaul and colleagues (McCaul, Reid, Rathge, & Martinson, 1996; McCaul, Schroeder, & Reid, 1996) found a positive relation of breast cancer worry to mammography screening in the general population, as did Ward et al. (1997) for prostate cancer. However, in an inner-city population, an inverted U-shaped relation was observed: Moderate worry about breast cancer was associated with greater attendance at a first mammography screening than was either extreme (Sutton, Bickler, Sancho-Aldridge, & Saidi, 1994). The same inverted U-shaped relation was observed between BSE frequency and breast cancer worries (Lerman et al., 1991). Among older low income Mexican American women, fear of and fatalism about cancer were associated with lower Pap smear rates (Suarez, Roche, Nichols, & Simpson, 1997). Worry appears to serve as a barrier to mammography among African American women (Friedmanet al., 1995). Again in a sample with a substantial inner-city component, Bastani et al. (1994) reported a strong negative association between fear of finding breast cancer and screening. This brief sampling of articles suggests possible demographic differences in the relation of emotional aspects of cancer threat on screening, with cancer worry adversely affecting screening among inner-city, low income, and minority individuals; these findings, however, are not universal.

High Risk Individuals. A conflicting pattern of results is also observed for high risk individuals, FDRs of individuals with cancer. Ovarian cancer worries among FDRs have been positively associated with screening (M. D. Schwartz, Lerman, Daly, et al., 1995). In contrast, high breast cancer distress (i.e., extreme worry, intrusive thoughts about breast cancer) among FDRs is associated with reduced screening (Lerman et al., 1993; see also Kash, Holland, Halper, & D. G. Miller, 1992; Lerman et al., 1994), although the opposite has also been found (Stefanek & Wilcox, 1991). Interestingly, distress has been associated with either excessive or insufficient BSE (Epstein et al., 1997; Lerman et al., 1994). Cancer distress among FDRs of women with breast and ovarian cancer is associated with high perceived risk of cancer and low perceived control over cancer development (Audrain et al., in press).

Conflicting Findings and the Elusive Inverted U-Shaped Function

In the now classic fear communication literature, Janis and Feshbach (1953) argued that fear served as a positive motivator for protective behavior up to some critical level of fear. Above that critical fear level, avoidance of the threat was expected to replace protective behavior, yielding an inverted U-shaped relation between level of fear and behavior.

Resolving Conflicting Findings. Lerman and M. D. Schwartz (1993) used the notion of an inverted U-shaped relation to highlight an important issue in resolving conflicting literature on the relations of worry and distress to cancer screening—the range and level of distress represented among participants in any individual study. If it is assumed for a moment that an inverted U-shaped relation of distress to screening exists, then all relations (positive, inverted U, negative, or no relation) are possible as segments of the distress continuum are sampled. The resolution of conflicting study outcomes may lie in the segment of the distress continuum represented in any study. The McCaul, Reid, et al. (1996) meta-analysis showed only monotonic increasing relations of both susceptibility and cancer worry to behavior. However, the meta-analysis did not include articles in which avoidance of screening by FDRs of breast cancer victims was associated with high cancer distress, discussed further later (e.g., Kash et al., 1992; Lerman et al., 1994). In samples from the general population—samples such as those of McCaul, Reid, et al. (1996)—it is possible that there are insufficient very high distress cases for a curvilinear relation to be manifested and/or detected statistically.

Distress Versus Perceived Susceptibility. Support for the inverted U-shaped relation is found when emotional distress and not the more cognitive assessment of perceived susceptibility serves as the predictor of cancer screening behavior. Perhaps the inverted U-shaped relation of risk to behavior has been sought in the wrong variable, that is, in perceived susceptibility rather than cancer distress. (See Hailey, 1991, for consideration of an inverted U-shaped relation of distress to screening among FDRs of women with breast cancer.)

Modifying Perceived Susceptibility and Cancer Distress Through Training

High Risk Women. As already described, FDRs of women with cancer typically exhibit excessive perceived risk and associated high cancer distress, apparently leading to failure to follow screening recommendations (i.e., either excessive or insufficient screening) and even to requests for prophylactic surgery (Lerman et al., 1995). Interventions to reduce perceived susceptibility among FDRs have sometimes been successful (Alexander, Ross, Sumner, Nease, & Littenberg, 1995) . However, women with high cancer distress benefit less from such susceptibility focused interventions, suggesting that both cancer distress and inaccurate perceptions of risk must be simultaneously addressed (Lerman et al., 1995). Reductions in cancer distress have been achieved through individual counseling (Lerman et al., 1996; Schwartz, Lerman, et al., 1998). An important issue is whether clarifying that perceived risk is overestimated will lead to underutilization of mammography screening (M. D. Schwartz, Rimer, Daly, Sands, & Lerman, 1998).

General Population. The extent to which subjective risk estimates can be made more accurate through intervention has also been explored in the general population (Weinstein & Klein, 1995), where perceived risk typically exceeds objective risk. Kreuter and Strecher (1995) reported increased accuracy in perceived risk (i.e., decreased perceived risk) for cancer in the general population following an educational intervention. Lipkus, Biradavolu, Fenn, Keller, and Rimer (1998) explored strategies for increasing accuracy of risk perceptions for cancer.

Repeated Screening

An important question is whether screening behaviors are sustained over time among asymptomatic women. Ronis, Yates, and Kirscht (1989) argued that the factors that lead to initiation of a behavior do not sustain the behavior, and that habits, rather than attitudinal variables, determine repeated behavior. Similar arguments were made by S. M. Miller et al. (1996) in the context of BSE performance.

Correlations of perceived susceptibility with repeated mammography screening are not reliably observed, with positive associations noted by Lerman, Rimer, Trock, Balshem, and Engstrom (1990) and Fenaughty, Aiken, and West (1993), but no association noted by Marshall (1994), Cockburn, Schofield, White, Hill, and Russell (1997), and Orton et al. (1991). Anxiety about mammography appears to be negatively related to repeated screening (Lerman et al., 1990).

Medical System and Demographic Determinants of Repeated Screening. A host of demographic and medical system variables relate to repeated screening, just as with mammography compliance taken at any single point in time. Younger age, physician recommendation, having had regular clinical breast examinations by a physician, and family breast cancer history are positively associated with repeated mammography screening (Hitchcock, Steckevicz, & Thompson, 1995; Lerman et al., 1990; Zapka, Stoddard, Maul, & Costanza, 1991). Failure of asymptomatic women to return for a second mammogram at a regular interval is associated with negative experiences with the initial mammogram, among them pain, embarrassment, and unpleasant interaction with clinic staff (Marshall, 1994; Orton et al., 1991). Again, it appears that many variables operate on repeated screening that weaken the potential impact of perceptions of susceptibility.

Sequelae of Abnormal Screening Tests and Discovery of Symptoms

Two related literatures highlight the reciprocal nature between screening and perceived vulnerability and cancer distress. The first literature, which addresses the impact of abnormal screening tests on psychological functioning, was reviewed by Paskett and Rimer (1995). This literature shows clear negative psychological effects of abnormal Pap smear and mammography test results, including heightened cancer distress, with varying levels of follow-up screening (from 20% to 95% across studies). The second literature, on delay in seeking treatment following the self-identification of a possible cancer symptom (e.g., a breast lump), was reviewed by Facione (1993). This literature characterizes the myriad fears engendered by discovery of cancer symptoms and their association with delay in seeking treatment.

Preventive Behavior: Sun Protection

Although the focus is primarily on screening, this section touches on cancer prevention, with a consideration of perceived vulnerability as a correlate of sun protection. The incidence of deadly melanoma has risen 4% per year since 1973. Skin protection through limiting sun exposure and sunscreen use is recommended (American Cancer Society, 1998). (However, there is now significant controversy as to the efficacy of sunscreen for protection against melanoma; Facelmann & Wu, 1998).

Sun protection against skin cancer poses four related issues. First, because intensive sun exposure between age 10 and 24 is associated with melanoma development (Holman et al., 1986), adolescents must adopt sun protection. Second, sun exposure early in life is associated with much later development of skin cancer, thus raising the issue for health psychology of how to induce behavior change against *distal* risk. Third, normative influences play heavily in tanning: A suntan is perceived as healthy (e.g., Hill et al., 1992; Mermelstein & Riesenberg, 1992) and attractive (A. J. Miller et al., 1990). Fourth, parents must play an active role in their children's skin protection (Rodrigue, 1996).

Objective risk based on skin type (Fitzpatrick, 1988) is associated with perceived susceptibility to skin cancer (Clarke, Williams, & Arthey, 1997; Jackson, 1997; Webb, Friedman, Luce, Weinberg, & Cooper, 1996). Arthey and Clarke (1995) provided a review of the psychological literature on suntanning and sun protection. Positive associations between perceived susceptibility and sun protection have been noted among high school students (Mermelstein & Riesenberg, 1992; Wichstrom, 1994), university students (Cody & Lee, 1990), the general U.S. population (Hall, May, Lew, Koh, & Nadel, 1997), and parents protecting their children (Lescano & Rodrigue, 1997), but such relations are not uniformly observed. In fact, a negative relation has been found between sun protection and perceived risk among individuals with chronically high sun exposure (Carmel, Shani, & Rosenberg, 1996). Elevated perceptions of susceptibility in this case appear to result from past high risk behavior. A similar relation has been observed in the HIV/AIDS literature; those who have engaged in high risk sexual behavior subsequently report high perceived vulnerability to HIV/AIDS (Gerrard et al., 1996). Manipulations of perceived susceptibility in interventions have resulted in increased intentions for sun protection (e.g., Cody & Lee, 1990; Mahler, Fitzpatrick, Parker, & Lapin, 1997).

Normative Influences. Normative influences (Pratt & Borland, 1994; Wichstrom, 1994), particularly for appearance (A. J. Miller et al., 1990), have shown reliable relations with sun tanning versus sun protective behavior, particularly among adolescents. Self-presentation (impression management) may well lead to health risks (Leary, Tchividjian, & Kraxberger, 1994); suntanning exemplifies this phenomenon. Recent interventions (e.g., Jones & Leary, 1994; Prentice-Dunn, Jones, & Floyd, 1997) also highlight the impact of appearance concerns. These powerful normative influences, which are much less often considered in relation to screening behaviors such as mammography (but see Montano & Taplin, 1991), highlight the unique forces, in addition to perceived vulnerability, that influence particular cancer-specific behaviors.

INTERVENTIONS TO INCREASE SCREENING

This section addresses interventions to increase cancer screening, and, more specifically, attempts to link manipulations of perceived susceptibility to increased screening. Experimental interventions provide the vehicle for untangling the causal impact of putative determinants such as perceived vulnerability on cancer protective behavior. The use of mediational analysis to assess the extent of direct and indirect impact of manipulations of perceived susceptibility on screening outcomes is also highlighed. Comprehensive summaries of interventions to increase cancer screening have been provided by Rimer (1994) for mammography screening and by Snell and Buck (1996) for breast, cervical, and colorectal cancer.

From the perspective of health psychology, theory-based interventions that employ models such as the HBM to design program components are most of interest, because they permit the linking of changes in constructs in the model (e.g., perceived susceptibility) to changes in screening behaviors. A number of mammography screening interventions have included components designed to increase perceived vulnerability to breast cancer (Aiken, West, Woodward, Reno, & Reynolds, 1994; Champion, 1994; Curry, Taplin, Anderman, Barlow, & McBride, 1993; Rimer et al., 1992; Skinner, Strecher, & Hospers, 1994; Zapka et al., 1993). In some studies, the perceived susceptibility component was only one small part of a large complex intervention, and no attempt was made to establish a direct linkage from this component to behavioral outcomes (Champion, 1994; Rimer et al., 1992; Zapka et al., 1993). In contrast, Curry et al. (1993) showed that providing tailored personal objective risk information to FDRs of breast cancer victims increased screening; Skinner et al. (1994) showed a similar impact of tailored messages in a community sample.

Mediational Analysis of Intervention Impacts

Aiken, West, Woodward, Reno, and Reynolds (1994) implemented an HBM-based mammography intervention, with individual program components that targeted each of the four HBM constructs: perceived susceptibility, severity, benefits, and barriers. *Mediational analysis,* a statistical procedure that establishes linkages among chains of variables, was used to test the linkages from an intervention through intermediate *mediators* (the HBM components) to mammography compliance (West & Aiken, 1997). This mediational analysis is presented here because of our strong conviction (West & Aiken, 1997) that mediational analysis provides important insights into the way in which theoretical constructs influence behavior. To date, mediational analysis has been used productively in both mental health and substance abuse research, as well as in several areas of basic psychological research.

Requirements for Mediational Analysis. In order to test the theory of an intervention through mediational analysis, the following are required: a specified theoretical model on which the program will be built, a measurement instrument that provides distinct measures of each construct in the model that will serve as a mediator, a translation of each construct of the model into a distinct component of the intervention, assessment of postintervention levels on each of the constructs targeted in the model in an experimental versus control group (with adequate statistical control of pretest levels), and measurement of the outcome. West and Aiken (1997) summarized the conditions that must be met in order to demonstrate that a putative mediator (here, perceived susceptibility) produced change in the outcome (here, mammography screening), as specified by Judd and Kenny (1981), Baron and Kenny (1986), and MacKinnon (1994).

The Mediational Role of Susceptibility in Intervention

In the intervention, the HBM was amended by assessing intentions for screening at immediate posttest as well as actual compliance 3 months following the intervention. Mediational paths were established from perceived susceptibility and perceived benefits to intentions, as was a strong link from intentions to subsequent screening. The role of perceived susceptibility in the causal chain from intervention through compliance is of interest here. The model of the impact of HBM constructs on outcomes is illustrated in Fig. 44.1. It differs from typical characterizations of the HBM in that the four HBM constructs are not treated as coequal predictors of outcome. Rather, following Ronis (1992), a model was specified in which perceived susceptibility and perceived severity were antecedents of perceived benefits, under the assumption that a woman would not perceive the benefits of mammography screening unless she felt threatened (perceived susceptibility plus severity) by breast cancer. Again following Ronis (1992), it was specified that the effect of perceived susceptibility on outcome would be mediated through perceived benefits, that is, that the effect of susceptibility would be an *indirect effect* through benefits, in the following causal sequence:

$$\text{Intervention} \rightarrow \text{Susceptibility} \rightarrow \text{Benefits} \rightarrow \text{Intentions.}$$

This mediational chain was confirmed. In addition, a *direct path* from susceptibility to intentions was confirmed, that is,

$$\text{Intervention} \rightarrow \text{Susceptibility} \rightarrow \text{Intentions.}$$

The size of the indirect effect of susceptibility, over and above the direct effect, was substantial.

The full details of the mediational analysis, including explorations of possible roles for perceived susceptibility, are provided in West and Aiken (1997). What is critical here is a conception of perceived susceptibility at the outset of a causal chain that flows through other constructs. Examining only the direct effects of susceptibility on intentions or behavior may obscure the role of perceived susceptibility in the behavioral compliance process, potentially leading to underestimates of the total effect of perceived susceptibility on behavior.

Some research on screening and preventive behavior omits considerations of perceived susceptibility and examines variables that are conceptually downstream of perceived suscepti-

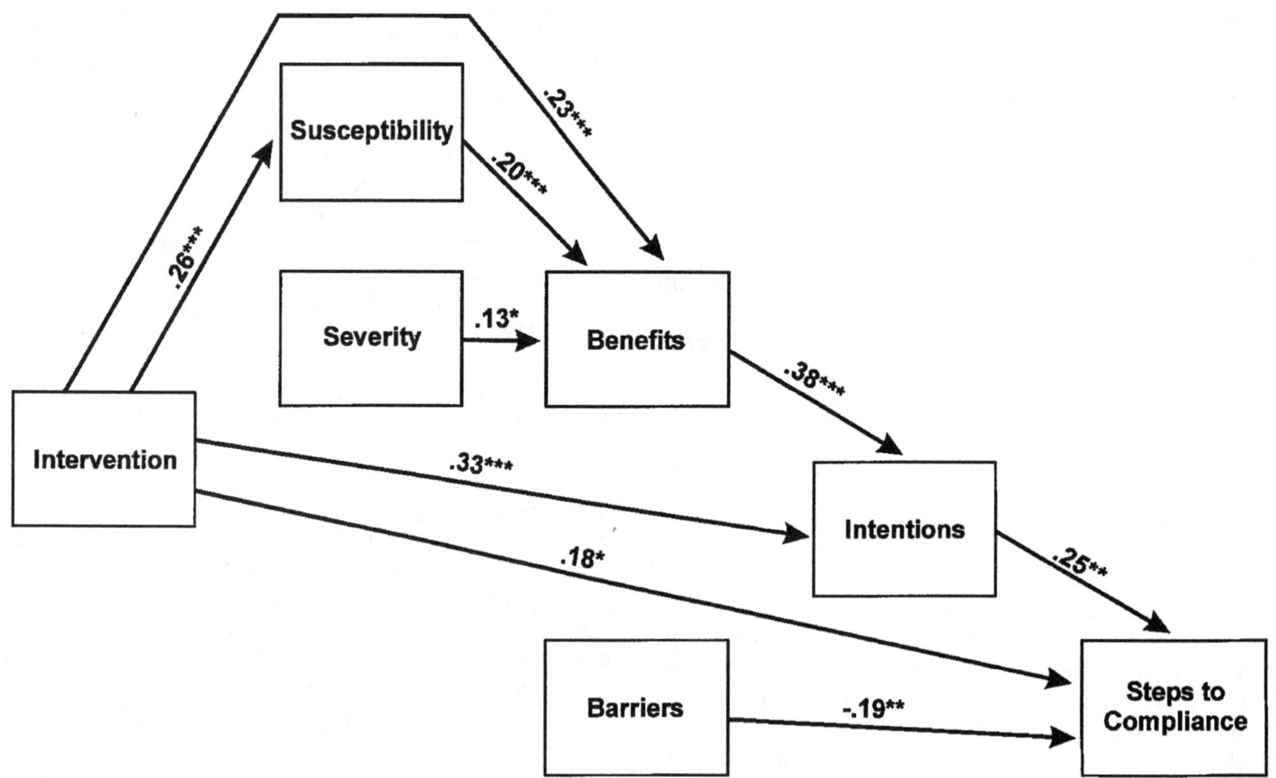

FIG. 44.1. Mediational analysis of the impact of a health belief model (HBM) based intervention on compliance with mammography screening recommendations. The indirect mediational path from intervention to perceived susceptibility through perceived benefits to intentions for screening illustrates how perceived susceptibility serves as an apparent precursor to benefits in the HBM. For paths, $*p < .05$, $**p < .01$, $***p < .001$. From "Increasing Screening Mammography in Asymptomatic Women: Evaluation of a Second-Generation, Theory-Based Program" by L. S. Aiken, S. G. West, C. K. Woodward, R. R. Reno, and K. D. Reynolds, 1994, *Health Psychology, 13,* p. 534. Copyright © 1994 by the American Psychological Association. Reprinted with permission.

bility in the causal chain from perceived susceptibility to behavior. For example, Rakowski (Rakowski et al., 1992, 1997; Rakowski, Fulton, & Feldman, 1993) focused on the impact of *decisional balance,* or the balance between perceived pros and cons of mammography on screening uptake. Such a focus on downstream variables (here analogous to benefits of and barriers to screening) does not diminish the role of perceived susceptibility earlier in the causal process.

ISSUES IN CHARACTERIZING THE ROLE OF PERCEIVED VULNERABILITY IN CANCER-RELATED BEHAVIOR

A number of issues have arisen in the course of this consideration of the impact of perceived vulnerability on cancer protective behavior. These have included the impact of perceived vulnerability versus cancer fear, worry, and distress on screening behavior; the existence of an inverted U-shaped relation between cancer distress and protective behavior; the difference in determinants of medically based versus self-implemented screening; and the place of perceived vulnerability in mediational chains of putative determinants of cancer-related behavior.

To these issues the following are added: the level of numeracy in the lay public, defined as "facility with basic probability and numerical concepts" (L. M. Schwartz et al., 1997), and the ability of lay individuals to understand and produce risk estimates; public understanding of screening tests and the impact of confusion between early detection and prevention; the difference in relation of perceived vulnerability to screening versus preventive health action over time; the impact of the complementary relation among screening behaviors (e.g., BSE versus mammography) on the observed link between vulnerability and screening; the role of conditional versus unconditional threat in accounting for cancer-related behavior; the impact of message framing on the link from risk to behavior; the existence of moderators of the relation of perceived vulnerability to cancer related behavior, including demographics, level of risk, personality, and barriers to behavior; and the need for experimental intervention as well as psychosocial research, coupled with mediational analysis, to understand the role of individual constructs in cancer protective behavior.

Numeracy

One critical issue that has only very recently been broached in the context of cancer screening is the *numeracy* of the lay public, a parallel in the quantitative domain to literacy. Although individuals' numerical estimates of perceived risk for cancer are interpreted as meaningfully reflecting perceived vulnerability, the competency of the lay public in understanding and using probability estimates or rates has not been considered. More numerate women exhibit smaller overestimates of the probability of developing and dying of breast cancer, as well as of the absolute mortality risk reduction attributable to mammography (Black et al., 1995), and are better able to apprehend information about mortality reduction attributable to mammography (L. M. Schwartz et al., 1997). Consideration of numeracy is critical in risk-related research (Fischhoff et al., 1993), as well as in medical settings, where individuals are asked to make their own medical decisions with regard to screening and treatment based on probability and rate information (L.M. Schwartz et al., 1997).

Humans as Intuitive Statisticians. Over three decades ago, a literature developed in applications of Bayesian decision theory in psychology (Edwards, Lindman, & Savage, 1963), which examined the ways in which individuals estimate the probability of events and revise their probability estimates based on new information. Two principles emerged that may help to explain biases in the lay public's understanding of risk for cancer. First, people appeared to overestimate low probabilities and underestimate high probabilities (Mueller & Edmonds, 1967; see also Lichtenstein, Slovic, Fischhoff, Layman, & Combs, 1978). This may partially explain the overestimates of rates of specific cancers, which are low percentage wise, on a cancer by cancer basis (American Cancer Society, 1998). Second, people are conservative in revising their estimates of probabilities in the face of new information (Phillips & Edwards, 1966), which may partially account for failures of training to eradicate biases in perceived risk.

Public Understanding of Screening Tests, and Detection Versus Prevention

The public historically has exhibited a lack of understanding of screening tests for asymptomatic individuals. Both Rimer, Keintz, Kessler, Engstrom, and Rosan (1989) and Zapka, Stoddard, M. D. Costanza, and Greene (1989) reported that women believed mammograms were unnecessary in the absence of breast symptoms (see review by Vernon, Laville, & Jackson, 1990). Recall that in the original HBM formulation, perceived vulnerability in the absence of symptoms was seen as requisite for health behavior (Rosenstock, 1990). Public belief that screening tests are unnecessary for asymptomatic individuals persists (Cockburn, Redman, Hill, & Henry, 1995).

Aiken et al. (1995) and Barnard and Nicholson (1997) also found confusion between screening for cancer detection versus cancer prevention. Cancer detection aims at finding existing cancers in an early, treatable state, whereas prevention aims to avoid cancer development. Women, failing to distinguish early detection from prevention, mistakenly attributed their lower perceived personal risk for contracting breast cancer to the fact that they receive regular mammograms. From an intervention perspective, correcting this misconception ironically may result in decreased screening rates. Even with these misconceptions, there is apparently understanding of and acceptance of the fact that screening tests may result in both false negative and false positive outcomes (Aiken et al., 1998; Cockburn et al., 1995).

Temporal Factors in the Perceived Risk–Behavior Linkage

For both prevention and detection, the cross-sectional relation of perceived risk to behavior changes in complex ways as health innovations diffuse over time (Weinstein & Nicolich, 1993). When a health protective behavior is first introduced, those who perceive themselves at the highest risk for the health threat may self-select the behavior, occasioning a strong positive correlation between perceived risk and behavior. If the behavior is screening, then perceived vulnerability to the occurrence of the disease should not diminish as the behavior is adopted, because screening is not, of course, preventive. In fact, perceived severity may diminish if people come to believe in the benefits of early detection for cancer survival. However, as a screening innovation is adopted broadly by the medical profession and increasing numbers of individuals are screened, the pool of screened individuals will contain individuals at lower perceived risk, thus diluting the correlation of perceived risk and screening. For preventive behavior, the initial self-selection of high risk individuals may again result in substantial positive correlations between perceived risk and behavior. However, should the disease risk be mitigated or substantially lessened by the preventive behavior, then, in time, a negative correlation may be observed between perceived risk and behavior—those who reliably engage in the behavior may correctly perceive themselves to be at lower risk. (See Aiken et al., 1995, for a consideration of temporal factors in perceived and objective risk as related to mammography screening, and Gerrard et al., 1996, for a critical discussion of these relations in the HIV/AIDS context.)

Complementary Screening Tests

Multiple screening tests for the same cancer (e.g., BSE and mammography) may be considered by some individuals to be complementary (i.e., a woman might opt for regular BSE and forego mammography). If so, this would weaken the relation of psychosocial variables to each behavior taken separately. BSE frequency and mammography compliance appear to be uncorrelated (Aiken et al., 1995). Perceived vulnerability might better predict a breast screening index crediting either mammography or BSE, but this possibility has not been explored empirically. Similar arguments can be made for FOBT, sigmoidoscopy, and DRE for colorectal cancer, and PSA and DRE for prostate screening.

Conditional Health Threat

Perceptions of susceptibility to cancer or its severity are in part governed by beliefs about personal actions that mitigate or increase cancer risk. Ronis (1992) characterized *conditional health threat* as the perception of threat under some behavior specification, that is, if the individual were to take a specific protective health action versus to take no health action (see also Rogers, 1983). Ronis (1992) and van der Pligt (1998) argued that the measurement of conditional health threat would provide better understanding of protective health behavior because such conditional measures untangle the influence of current protective behavior on perceived vulnerability. Weinstein and Nicolich (1993) theorized that the discrepancy in level of perceived risk associated with participation versus nonparticipation in a health protective behavior reflected perceived effectiveness of the health precaution.

It is proposed that the components of conditional health threat—that is, conditional susceptibility versus conditional severity—will have differential associations with preventive versus screening behavior. For preventive behavior, high perceived susceptibility given inaction coupled with high perceived benefits of the health action is expected to produce preventive behavior, with a subsequent reduction in perceived susceptibility. For screening, the matter is different because susceptibility is not reduced by screening; rather, the argument for screening is that consequences (severity) of cancer will be reduced with early detection, so that the appropriate conditional characterizations of perceived severity are "severity if treated early" versus "severity if treated late" (Ronis & Harel, 1989). Ronis and Harel (1989) applied this dual conception of perceived severity to BSE performance and showed a link of these severity measures, but not conditional susceptibility, to BSE, yielding new insight into the potential role of perceived severity in screening. Jackson (1997) applied conditional perceived susceptibility and severity to skin cancer preventive behaviors and found the opposite effect—that conditional measures of perceived susceptibility, but not severity, predicted skin protection. Measures of conditional threat may provide help to clarify the links of perceived susceptibility and severity to cancer protective behaviors.

Message Framing, the Understanding of Risk, and Health Protective Behavior

The impact of perceptions of risk on decisions concerning health behavior is strongly affected by the manner in which risks are framed. As specified in prospect theory (Kahneman & Tversky, 1979), individuals respond differently to information presented as gains (e.g., the number of breast cancer deaths averted by regular mammography screening) versus as losses (e.g., the number of breast cancer deaths associated with failures to be screened). Thus considerations of perceived risk in relation to cancer-related behavior must take into account message framing as a moderator of the perceived risk–behavior link. Rothman and Salovey (1997) provided an extensive review of the impact of message framing on health behavior. Meyerowitz and Chaiken (1987), Rothman, Salovey, Antone, Keough, and Martin (1993), and Banks et al. (1995) provided examples of the impact of message framing on BSE, skin protection, and mammography utilization, respectively.

Moderators of the Role of Perceived Susceptibility

Variables like demographics, personality, and barriers to health action may moderate (change) the relation of perceived vulnerability to protective health behavior. High perceived barriers nullified the effect of susceptibility on mammography compliance (Aiken, West, Woodward, & Reno, 1994). Conscientiousness as a personality trait moderated the relation of cancer distress to mammography screening among FDRs of breast cancer victims (Schwartz, Taylor, et al., 1999). Moderation of the perceived susceptibility–behavior link by demographic, medical system, personality, and other psychosocial variables should be explored.

Mediational Chains and Experimental Intervention Research

Our conception of perceived susceptibility is that it stands at the outset of a causal chain that flows through other constructs to health behavior. Consideration of mediational chains from perceived susceptibility through other variables to behavior is critical for advancing an understanding of the way health behaviors accrue. To reiterate, examination of both the direct effect and the indirect effects of susceptibility through other variables on behavior is required to estimate accurately the total effect of perceived susceptibility on health protective behavior.

The understanding of whether, how, and to what extent individual variables such as perceived susceptibility operate in determining health protective behavior is best advanced through the evaluation of model-based interventions, with research structured so that mediational analysis of the effects of putative determinants of behavior can be accomplished (West & Aiken, 1997). A distinguishing feature of psychology as a discipline is the strength in theory and experimentation. Thus, health psychologists may entertain a special role in health behavior research, providing careful theory testing in controlled settings, and the refinement of models of health behavior on a strong empirical base.

REFERENCES

Aiken, L. S., Fenaughty, A. M., West, S. G., Johnson, J. J., & Luckett, T. L. (1995). Perceived determinants of risk for breast cancer and the relations among objective risk, perceived risk, and screening behavior over time. *Women's Health: Research on Gender, Behavior, and Policy, 1,* 27–50.

Aiken, L. S., Jackson, K. M., & Lapin, A. (1998). Mammography screening for women under 50: Women's response to medical controversy and changing practice guidelines. *Women's Health: Research on Gender, Behavior, and Policy, 4,* 169–197.

Aiken, L. S., West, S. G., Woodward, C. K., & Reno, R. R.(1994) Health beliefs and compliance with mammography-screening recommendations in asymptomatic women. *Health Psychology, 13,* 122–129.

Aiken, L. S., West, S. G., Woodward, C. K., Reno, R. R., & Reynolds, K. D. (1994). Increasing screening mammography in asymptomatic women: Evaluation of a second-generation, theory-based program. *Health Psychology, 13,* 526–538.

Ajzen, I. (1991). The theory of planned behavior. *Organizational behavior and human decision processes, 50,* 179–211.

Ajzen, I., & Fishbein, M. (1980). *Understanding attitudes and predicting social behavior.* Englewood Cliffs, NJ: Prentice-Hall.

Alagna, S. W., Morokoff, P. J., Bevett, J. M., & Reddy, D. M. (1987). Performance of breast self-examination by women at high risk for breast cancer. *Women and Health, 12,* 29–46.

Albertsen, P. C. (1996). Screening for prostate cancer is neither appropriate nor cost-effective. *The Urologic Clinics of North America, 23,* 521–530.

Alexander, N. E., Ross, J., Sumner, W., Nease, R. F., & Littenberg, B. (1995). The effect of an educational intervention on the perceived risk of breast cancer. *Journal of General Internal Medicine, 11,* 92–97.

American Academy of Dermatology (1994). *Skin cancer: An undeclared epidemic.* Schaumburg, IL: American Academy of Dermatology.

American Cancer Society (1996). Advisory Committee on Diet, Nutrition, and Cancer Prevention. Guidelines on diet, nutrition, and cancer prevention: Reducing the risk of cancer with health food choices and physical activity. *CA—A Cancer Journal for Clinicians, 46,* 325–341.

American Cancer Society (1997a). *Cancer risk report: Prevention and Control, 1997.* Atlanta, GA: American Cancer Society.

American Cancer Society (1997b). *Facts on skin cancer.* Atlanta, GA: American Cancer Society.

American Cancer Society (1998). *Cancer facts and figures, 1998.* Atlanta, GA: American Cancer Society.

Arthey, S., & Clarke, V. A. (1995). Suntanning and sun protection: A review of the psychological literature. *Social Science and Medicine, 40,* 265–274.

Audrain, J., Lerman, C., Rimer, B., Cella, D., Steffans, R., Gomez-Caminero, A., & the High Risk Breast Cancer Consortium. (1995). Awareness of heightened breast cancer risk among first-degree relatives of recently diagnosed breast cancer patients. *Cancer Epidemiology, Biomarkers & Prevention, 4,* 561–565.

Audrain, J., Schwartz, M. D., Lerman, C., Hughes, C., Peshkin, B. N, & Biesecker, B. (1998). Psychological distress in women seeking genetic counseling for breast-ovarian cancer risk: The contributions of personality and appraisal. *Annals of Behavioral Medicine.*

Avis, N. E., Smith, K. W., & McKinlay, J. B. (1989). Accuracy of perceptions of heart attack risk: What influences perceptions and can they be changed. *American Journal of Public Health, 79,* 1608–1612.

Banks, S. M., Salovey, P., Greener, S., Rothman, A. J., Moyer, A., Beauvais, J., & Epel, E. (1995). The effects of message framing on mammography utilization. *Health Psychology, 14,* 178–184.

Barnard, N. D., & Nicholson, A. (1997). Beliefs about dietary factors in breast cancer prevention among American women, 1991 to 1995. *Preventive Medicine, 26,* 109–113.

Baron, R. M., & Kenny, D. A. (1986). The moderator-mediator variable distinction in social psychological research: Conceptual, strategic, and statistical considerations. *Journal of Personality and Social Psychology, 51,* 1173–1182.

Bastani, R., Marcus, A. C., & Hollatz-Brown, A. (1991). Screening mammography rates and barriers to use: A Los Angeles Survey. *Preventive Medicine, 20,* 350–363.

Bastani, R., Marcus, A. C., Maxwell, A. E., Das, I. P., & Yan, K. X. (1994) Evaluation of an intervention to increase mammography screening in Los Angeles. *Preventive Medicine, 23,* 83–90.

Beck, K. H., & Frankel, A. (1981). A conceptualization of threat communications and protective health behavior. *Social Psychology Quarterly, 44,* 204–217.

Becker, M. (1990). Theoretical models of adherence and strategies for improving adherence. In S. A. Shumaker, E. G. Schron, J. K. Ockene, C. T. Parker, J. L. Probstfield, & J. M. Wolle (Eds.), *The handbook of health behavior change* (pp. 5–43). New York: Springer.

Becker, M. H., & Maiman, L. A. (1975). Sociobehavioral determinants of compliance with health and medical care recommendations. *Medical Care, 8,* 10–24.

Berman, S. H., & Wandersman, A. (1992). Measuring fear of cancer: The fear of cancer index. *Psychology and Health, 7,* 187–200.

Black, W. C., Nease, R. F., Jr., & Tosteson, A.N.A. (1995). Perceptions of breast cancer risk and screening effectiveness in women younger than 50 years of age. *Journal of the National Cancer Institute, 87,* 720–731.

Blalock, S. J., DeVellis, B. M., Afifi, R. A., & Sandler, R. S. (1990). Risk perceptions and participation in colorectal cancer screening. *Health Psychology, 9,* 792–806.

Bowman, J. A., Sanson-Fisher, R., & Redman, S. (1997). The accuracy of self-reported Pap smear utilization. *Social Science and Medicine, 44,* 969–976.

Brubaker, R. G., & Wickersham, D. (1990). Encouraging the practice of testicular self-examination: A field application of the theory of reasoned action. *Health Psychology, 9,* 154–163.

Caplan, L. S., & Haynes, S. G. (1996). Breast cancer screening in older women. *Public Health Review, 24,* 193–204.

Carmel, S., Shani, E., & Rosenberg, L. (1996). Skin cancer protective behaviors among the elderly: Explaining their response to a health education program using the health belief model. *Educational Gerontology, 22,* 651–668.

Champion, V. L. (1991). The relationship of selected variables to breast cancer detection behaviors in women 35 and older. *Oncology Nursing Forum, 18,* 733–739.

Champion, V. L. (1994). Strategies to increase mammography utilization. *Medical Care, 32,* 118–129.

Clarke, V. A., Williams, T., & Arthey, S. (1997). Skin type and optimistic bias in relation to the sun protection and suntanning behaviors of young adults. *Journal of Behavioral Medicine, 20,* 207–222.

Cockburn, J., Redman, S., Hill, D., & Henry, E. (1995). Public understanding of medical screening. *Journal of Medical Screening, 2,* 224–227.

Cockburn, J., Schofield, P., White, V., Hill, D., & Russell, I. (1997). Predictors of returning for second round screening at a population based mammographic screening programme in Melbourne, Australia. *Journal of Epidemiology and Community Health, 51,* 62–66.

Cody, R., & Lee, C. (1990). Behaviors, beliefs, and intentions in skin cancer prevention. *Journal of Behavioral Medicine, 13,* 373–389.

Cole, S. R., Bryant, C. A., McDermott, R. J., Sorrell, C., & Flynn, M. (1997). Beliefs and mammography screening. *American Journal of Preventive Medicine, 13,* 439–443.

Conner, M., & Norman, P. (Eds.). (1996). *Predicting health behavior: Research and practice with social cognition models.* Buckingham, England: Open University Press.

Costanza, M. E. (1992). Breast cancer screening in older women: Synopsis of a forum. *Cancer, Supplement, 69,* 1925–1931.

Curry, S. J., & Emmons, K. M. (1994). Theoretical models for predicting and improving compliance with breast cancer screening. *Annals of Behavioral Medicine, 16,* 302–316.

Curry, S. J., Taplin, S. H., Anderman, C., Barlow, W. E., & McBride, C. (1993). A randomized trial of the impact of risk assessment and feedback on participation in mammography screening. *Preventive Medicine, 22,* 350–360.

Daly, M. B., Lerman, C. L., Ross, E., Schwartz, M. D., Sands, C. B., & Masny, A. (1996). Gail model breast cancer risk components are poor predictors of risk perception and screening behavior. *Breast Cancer Research and Treatment, 41,* 59–70.

Darvill, T. J., & Johnson, R. C. (1991). Optimism and perceived control of life events as related to personality. *Personality and Individual Differences, 12,* 951–954.

Degnan, D., Harris, R., Ranney, J., Quade, D., Earp, J. L., & Gonzalez, J. (1992). Measuring the use of mammography: Two methods compared. *American Journal of Public Health, 82,* 1386–1388.

Dolan, N. C., Lee, A. M., & McDermott, M. M. (1997). Age-related differences in breast carcinoma knowledge, beliefs, and perceived risk among women visiting an academic general medical practice. *Cancer, 50,* 413–420.

Dziokonski, W., & Weber. S. J. (1977). Repression-sensitization, perceived vulnerability, and the fear appeal communication. *Journal of Social Psychology, 102,* 105–112.

Edwards, W., Lindman, H., & Savage, L. H. (1963). Bayesian statistical inference for psychological research. *Psychological Review, 70,* 193–242.

Epstein, S. A., Lin, T. H., Audrain, J., Stefanek, M., Rimer, B., Lerman, C., & the High-Risk Breast Cancer Consortium. (1997). Excessive breast-self examination among first-degree relatives of newly diagnosed breast cancer patients. *Psychosomatics, 38,* 253–261.

Etzi, S., Lane, D. S., & Grimson, R. (1994). Use of mammography vans by low-income women: The accuracy of self-reports. *American Journal of Public Health, 84,* 107–109.

Facelmann, K., & Wu, C. (1998). Melanoma madness: The scientific flap over sunscreens and skin cancer. *Science News, 153,* 360–361, 363, 365.

Facione, N. C. (1993). Delay versus help seeking for breast cancer symptoms: A critical review of the literature on patient and provider delay. *Social Science and Medicine, 12,* 1521–1534.

Fenaughty, A. M., Aiken, L. S., & West, S. G. (1993, April). *Psychosocial correlates of repeated mammography screening.* Paper presented at the meeting of Western Psychological Association, Phoenix, AZ.

Fischhoff, B., Bostrom, A., & Quadrel, M. J. (1993). Risk perception and communication. *Annual Review of Public Health, 14,* 183–203.

Fishbein, M., & Ajzen, I. (1975). *Belief, attitude, intention, and behavior: An introduction to theory and research.* Reading, MA: Addison Wesley.

Fitzpatrick, T. B. (1988). The validity and practicality of sun-reactive skin Types 1 through 6. *Archives of Dermatology, 124,* 869–871.

Fletcher, S. W., Morgan, T. M., O'Malley, M. S., Earp, J. L., & Degnan, D. (1989). Is breast self-examination predicted by knowledge, attitudes, beliefs, or sociodemographic characteristics. *American Journal of Preventive Medicine, 5,* 207–215.

Fox, S. A., & Roetzheim, R. G. (1994). Screening mammography and older Hispanic women: Current status and issues. *Cancer, Supplement, 74,* 2029–2033.

Fox, S. A., Siu, A. L., & Stein, J. A. (1994). The importance of physician communication on breast cancer screening of older women. *Archives of Internal Medicine, 154,* 2058–2068.

Frazier, E. L., Jiles, R. B., & Mayberry, R. (1996). Use of screening mammography and clinical breast examinations among Black, Hispanic, and White women. *Preventive Medicine, 25*(2), 118–125.

Friedman, L. C., Webb, J. A., Weinberg, A. D., Lane, M., Cooper, H. P., & Woodruff, A. (1995). Breast cancer screening: racial/ethnic differences in behaviors and beliefs. *Journal of Cancer Education, 10,* 213–216.

Gail, M. H., Brinton, L. A., Byar, D. P., Corle, D. K., Green, S. B., Schairer, C., & Mulvihill, J. J. (1989). Projecting individualized probabilities of developing breast cancer for White females who are being examined annually. *Journal of the National Cancer Institute, 81,* 1879–1886.

Gerend, M. A. (1998). *Perceived susceptibility to disease: Understanding perceptions of risk for diseases of aging in older women.* Unpublished manuscript, Arizona State University.

Gerrard, M., Gibbons, F. X., & Bushman, B. J. (1996). Relationship between perceived vulnerability to HIV and precautionary sexual behavior. *Psychological Bulletin, 119,* 390–409.

Glanz, K., Lewis, F., & Rimer, B. (Eds.). (1990). *Health behavior and health education: Theory, research, and practice.* San Francisco: Jossey-Bass.

Gram, I. T., & Slenker, S. E. (1992). Cancer anxiety and attitudes toward mammography among screening attenders, nonattenders, and women never invited. *American Journal of Public Health, 82,* 249–251.

Green, L. W., & Kreuter, M. W. (1991). *Healthy promotion planning: An educational and environmental approach* (2nd ed.). Mountain View, CA: Mayfield.

Hailey, B. J. (1991). Family history of breast cancer and screening behavior: An inverted U-shaped curve? *Medical Hypotheses, 36,* 397–403.

Hall, H. I., May, D. S., Lew, R. A., Koh, H. K., & Nadel, M. (1997). Sun protection behaviors of the U. S. White population. *Preventive Medicine, 26,* 401–407.

Harris, P. (1996). Sufficient grounds for optimism?: The relationship between perceived controllability and optimistic bias. *Journal of Social and Clinical Psychology, 15,* 9–52.

Harrison, J. A., Mullen, P. D., & Green, L. W. (1992). A meta-analysis of studies of the health belief model with adults. *Health Education Research, 7,* 107–116.

Helzlsouer, K. J., Ford, D. E., Hayward, R.S.A., Midzenski, M., & Perry, H. (1994). Perceived risk of cancer and practice of cancer prevention behaviors among employees in an oncology center. *Preventive Medicine, 23,* 302–308.

Hill, D., White, V., Marks, R., Theobald, T., Borland, R., & Roy, C. (1992). Melanoma prevention: Behavioral and nonbehavioral factors in sunburn among an Australian urban population. *Preventive Medicine, 21,* 654–669.

Hitchcock, J. L., Steckevicz, M. J., & Thompson, W. D. (1995). Screening mammography: Factors associated with adherence to recommended age/frequency guidelines. *Women's Health: Research on Gender, Behavior, and Policy, 1,* 221–235.

Holman, C.D.J., Armstrong, B. K., Heenan, P. J. Blackwell, J. B., Cummings, F. J., English, J.D.R., Holland, S., Kelsall, G. R., Matz, L. R., & Rouse, I. L. (1986). The causes of melanoma: Results from the West Australian Lions Melanoma Project. *Recent Results in Cancer Research, 102,* 18–37.

Hyman, R. B., Baker, S., Ephraim, R., Moadel, A., & Philip, J. (1994). Health belief variables as predictors of screening mammography utilization. *Journal of Behavioral Medicine, 17,* 391–406.

Irwig, L, Cockburn, J., Turnbull, D., Simpson, J. M., Mock, P., & Tattersal, M. (1991). Women's perceptions of screening mammography. *Australian Journal of Public Health, 15,* 24–32.

Jackson, K. M. (1997). *Psychosocial model and intervention to encourage sun protective behavior.* Unpublished doctoral dissertation, Arizona State University.

Janis, I. L., & Feshbach, S. (1953). Effects of fear-arousing communications. *Journal of Abnormal and Social Psychology, 48,* 78–92.

Janz, N. K., & Becker, M. H. (1984). The health belief model: A decade later. *Health Education Quarterly, 11,* 1–47.

Jones, J. L., & Leary, M. R. (1994). Effects of appearance-based admonitions against sun exposure on tanning intentions in young adults. *Health Psychology, 13,* 86–90.

Judd, C. M., & Kenny, D. (1981). *Estimating the effects of social interventions.* New York: Cambridge University Press.

Kahneman, D., & Tversky, A. (1973). On the psychology of prediction. *Psychological Review, 80,* 237–251.

Kahneman, D., & Tversky, A. (1979). Prospect theory: An analysis of decision under risk. *Econometrica, 47,* 263–291.

Kaplan, R. M., Navarro, A. M., Castro, F. G., Elder, J. P., Mishra, S. I., Hubbell, A., Chrvala, C., Flores, E., Ramirez, A., Fernandez-Esquer, M. E., & Ruiz, E. (1996). Increased use of mammography among Hispanic women: Baseline results from the NCI Cooperative Group on Cancer Prevention in Hispanic Communities. *American Journal of Preventive Medicine, 12,* 467–471.

Kash, K. M., Holland, J. C., Halper, M. S., & Miller, D. G. (1992). Psychological distress and surveillance behaviors of women with a family history of breast cancer. *Journal of the National Cancer Institute, 84,* 24–30.

Kasperson, R. E., Renn, O., Slovic, P., Brown, H. S., Emel, J., Goble, R., Kasperson, J. X., & Ratick, S. (1988). The social amplification of risk: A conceptual framework. *Risk Analysis, 8,* 177–187.

King, E. S., Rimer, B. K., Trock, B., Balshem, A., & Engstrom, P. (1990). How valid are mammography self-reports. *American Journal of Public Health, 80,* 1386–1388.

Klein, W. M. (1996). Maintaining self-serving social comparisons: Attenuating the perceived significance of risk-increasing behaviors. *Journal of Social and Clinical Psychology, 15,* 120–142.

Klein, W. M. & Weinstein, N. D. (1997). Social comparison and unrealistic optimism about personal risk. In B. Buunk & F. X. Gibbons (Eds.), *Health, coping, and social comparison* (pp. 25–61). Hillsdale, NJ: Lawrence Erlbaum Associates.

Kowalewski, M. R., Henson, K. D., & Longshore, D. (1997). Rethinking perceived risk and health behavior: A critical review of HIV prevention research. *Health Education and Behavior, 24,* 313–325.

Kreuter, M. W., & Strecher, V. J. (1995). Changing inaccurate perceptions of health risks: Results from a randomized trial. *Health Psychology, 14,* 56–63.

Landis, S. H., Murray, T., Bolden, S., & Wingo, P. A. (1998). Cancer statistics, 1998. *CA—A Cancer Journal for Clinicians. 48,* 6–29.

Lauver, D., Nabholz, S., Scott, K., & Tak, Y. (1997). Testing theoretical explanations of mammography use. *Nursing Research, 16,* 32–39.

Leary, M. R., Tchividjian, L. R., & Kraxberger, B. E. (1994). Self-presentation can be hazardous to your health: Impression management and health risk. *Health Psychology, 13,* 461–470.

Lek, Y., & Bishop, G. D. (1995). Perceived vulnerability to illness threats: The role of disease type, risk factor perception and attributions. *Psychology and Health, 10,* 205–217.

Lerman, C., Daly, M., Sands, C., Balshem, A., Lustbader, E., Heggan, T., Goldstein, L., James, J., & Engstrom, P. (1993). Mammography adherence and psychological distress among women at risk for breast cancer. *Journal of the National Cancer Institute, 85,* 1074–1080.

Lerman, C., Kash, K., & Stefanek, M. (1994). Younger women at increased risk for breast cancer: Perceived risk, psychological well-being, and surveillance behavior. *Journal of the National Cancer Institute Monographs, 16,* 171–176.

Lerman, C., Lustbader, E., Rimer, B., Daly, M., Miller, S., Sands, C., & Balshem, A. (1995). Effects of individualized breast cancer risk counseling: A randomized trial. *Journal of the National Cancer Institute, 87,* 286–292.

Lerman, C., Rimer, B., Trock, B., Balshem, A., & Engstrom, P. F. (1990). Factors associated with repeat adherence to breast cancer screening. *Preventive Medicine, 19,* 279–290.

Lerman, C., & Schwartz, M. D. (1993). Adherence and psychological adjustment among women at high risk for breast cancer. *Breast Cancer Research and Treatment, 28,* 145–155.

Lerman, C., Schwartz, M. D., Miller, S. M., Daly, M., Sands, C., & Rimer, B. K. (1996). A randomized trial of breast cancer risk counseling: Interacting effects of counseling, educational level, and coping style. *Health Psychology, 15,* 75–83.

Lerman, C., Trock, B., Rimer, B. K., Jepson, C., Brody, D., & Boyce, A. (1991) Psychological side effects of breast cancer screening. *Health Psychology, 10,* 259–267.

Lescano, C. M., & Rodrigue, J. R. (1997). Skin cancer prevention behaviors among parents of young children. *Children's Health Care, 26,* 107–114.

Lichtenstein, S., Slovic, P., Fischhoff, B., Layman, M., & Combs, B. (1978) Judged frequency of lethal events. *Journal of Experimental Psychology: Human Learning and Memory, 4,* 551–578.

Lipkus, I. M., Biradavolu, M., Fenn, K., Keller, P., & Rimer, B. (1998). *Testing different formats for informing women of their breast cancer risk: Implications for risk communication in mammography screening.* Unpublished manuscript, Duke University Medical Center.

Lipkus, I. M., Rimer, B. K., Lyna, P. R., Pradhan, A. A., Conaway, M., & Woods-Powell, C. T. (1996). Colorectal screening patterns and perceptions of risk among African-American users of community health center. *Journal of Community Health, 21,* 409–427.

Lipkus, I. M., Rimer, B. K., & Strigo, T. S. (1996). Relationships among objective and subjective risk for breast cancer and mammography stages of change. *Cancer Epidemiology, Biomarkers and Prevention, 5,* 1005–1011.

MacKinnon, D. P. (1994). Analysis of mediating variables in prevention and intervention studies. In A. Cazares & L. Beatty (Eds.), *Scientific methods for prevention intervention research* (NIDA Monograph No. 139, pp. 127–153). Rockville, MD: National Institute on Drug Abuse.

MacLeod, A. K., Williams, J.M.G., & Berekian, D. A. (1991). Worry is reasonable. The role of explanations in pessimism about future personal events. *Journal of Abnormal Psychology, 100,* 478–486.

Mahler, H.I.M., Fitzpatrick, B., Parker, P., & Lapin, A. (1997). The relative effects of a health-based versus an appearance-based intervention designed to increase sunscreen use. *American Journal of Health Promotion, 11,* 426–429.

Marshall, G. (1994). A comparative study of re-attenders and non-re-attenders for second triennial National Breast Screening Programme appointments. *Journal of Public Health Medicine, 16,* 79–86.

McBride, C. M., Curry, S. J., Taplin, S., Anderman, C., & Grothaus, L. (1993). Exploring environmental barriers to participation in mammography screening in an HMO. *Cancer Epidemiology, Biomarkers, and Prevention, 2,* 599–605.

McCaul, K. D., Branstetter, A. D., Schroeder, D. M., & Glasgow, R. E. (1996). What is the relationship between breast cancer risk and mammography screening? A meta-analytic review. *Health Psychology, 15,* 423–429.

McCaul, K. D., & O'Donnell, S. M. (1998). Naive beliefs about breast cancer risk. *Women's Health: Research in Gender, Behavior, and Policy, 4,* 93–101.

McCaul, K. D., Reid, P. A., Rathge, R. W., & Martinson, B. (1996). Does concern about breast cancer inhibit or promote breast cancer screening. *Basic and Applied Social Psychology, 18,* 183–194.

McCaul, K. D., Schroeder, D. M., & Reid, P. A. (1996). Breast cancer worry and screening: Some prospective data. *Health Psychology, 15,* 430–433.

Mermelstein, R. J., & Riesenberg, L. A. (1992). Changing knowledge and attitudes about skin cancer risk factors in adolescents. *Health Psychology, 11,* 371–376.

Meyerowitz, B. E., & Chaiken, S. (1987). The effect of message framing on breast self-examination attitudes, intentions, and behavior. *Journal of Personality and Social Psychology, 52,* 500–510.

Miller, A. J., Ashton, W. A., McHoskey, J. W., & Gimbel, J. (1990). What price attractiveness? Stereotype and risk factors in suntanning behavior. *Journal of Applied Social Psychology, 20,* 1272–1300.

Miller, S. M., Shoda, Y., & Hurley, K. (1996). Applying cognitive-social theory to health-protective behavior: Breast self-examination in cancer screening. *Psychological Bulletin, 119,* 70–94.

Montano, D. E., & Taplin, S. H. (1991). A test of an expanded theory of reasoned action to predict mammography participation. *Social Science and Medicine, 6,* 733–741.

Mueller, M. R., & Edmonds, E. M. (1967). Effects of information about environmental probability. *Psychonomic Science, 7,* 339–340.

National Cancer Institute. (1992). *What you need to know about testicular cancer.* Bethesda, MD: The National Cancer Institute.

National Cancer Institute. (1995). *What you need to know about skin cancer.* Bethesda, MD: The National Cancer Institute.

National Center for Health Statistics. (1996). *Healthy People 2000 Review, 1995–1996.* Hyattsville, MD: Public Health Service.

O'Malley, A. S., Mandelblatt, J., Gold, K., Cagney, K. A., & Kerner, J. (1997). Continuity of care and the use of breast and cervical cancer screening services in a multiethnic community. *Archives of Internal Medicine, 157,* 1462–1470.

Orton, M., Fitzpatrick, R., Fuller, A., Mant, D., Mlynek, C., & Thorogood, M. (1991). Factors affecting women's response to an invitation to attend for a second breast cancer screening examination. *British Journal of General Practice, 41,* 320–323.

Paskett, E. D., & Rimer, B. K. (1995). Psychological effects of abnormal Pap tests and mammograms: A review. *Journal of Women's Health, 4,* 73–82.

Paskett, E. D., Rushing, J., D'Agostino, R., Jr., & Tatum, C. (1997). Cancer screening behaviors of low-income women: The impact of race. *Women's Health: Research on Gender, Behavior, and Policy. 3,* 203–226.

Paulhus, D. P., Fridhandler, B., & Hayes, S. (1997). Psychological defense: Contemporary theory and research. In R. Hogan, J. Johnson, & S. Briggs (Eds.), *Handbook of personality* (pp. 543–579). San Diego: Academic Press.

Pearlman, D. M., Rakowski, W., Ehrich, B., & Clark, M. A. (1996). Breast cancer practices among Black, Hispanic, and White women: Reassessing differences. *American Journal of Preventive Medicine, 12,* 327–337.

Perloff, L. S. (1983). Perceptions of vulnerability to victimization. *Journal of Social Issues, 39,* 41–61.

Perloff, L. S., & Fetzer, B. K. (1986). Self–other judgments and perceived vulnerability to victimization. *Journal of Personality and Social Psychology, 50,* 502–510.

Phillips, L. D., & Edwards, W. (1966). Conservatism in a simple probability inference task. *Journal of Experimental Psychology, 72,* 346–354.

Potosky, A. L., Breen, N., Graubard, B. I., & Parsons, P.E. (1998). The association between health coverage and the use of cancer screening tests. Results from the 1992 National Health Interview Survey. *Medical Care, 36,* 257–270.

Pratt, K., & Borland, R. (1994). Predictors of sun protection among adolescents at the beach. *Australian Psychologist, 29,* 135–139.

Prentice-Dunn, S., Jones, J. L., & Floyd, D. L. (1997) Persuasive appeals and the reduction of skin cancer risk: The roles of appearance concern, perceived benefits of a tan, and efficacy information. *Journal of Applied Social Psychology, 27,* 1041–1047.

Prentice-Dunn, S., & Rogers, R. W. (1986). Protection motivation theory and preventive health: Beyond the health belief model. *Health Education Research,* 1(3), 153–161.

Prochaska, J. O., DiClemente, C. C., & Norcross, J. C. (1992). In search of how people change: Applications to addictive behaviors. *American Psychologist, 47,* 1102–1114.

Rakowski, W., Andersen, M. R., Stoddard, A. M., Urban, N., Rimer, B. K., Lane, D. S., Fox, S. A., & Costanza, M. E. (1997). Confirmatory analysis of opinions regarding the pros and cons of mammography. *Health Psychology, 16,* 433–441.

Rakowski, W., Dube, C. E., Marcus, B. H., Prochaska, J. O., Velicer, W. F., & Abrams, D. B. (1992). Assessing elements of women's decisions about mammography. *Health Psychology, 11(2),* 111–118.

Rakowski, W., Fulton, J. P., & Feldman, J. P. (1993). Women's decision making about mammography: A replication of the relationship between stages of adoption and decisional balance. *Health Psychology, 12,* 209–214.

Rimer, B. K. (1990). Perspectives on intrapersonal theories in health education and health behavior. In K. Glanz, F. M. Lewis, & B. K. Rimer (Eds.), *Health behavior and health education* (pp. 140–157). San Francisco: Jossey-Bass.

Rimer, B. K. (1994). Mammography use in the U.S.: Trends and the impact of interventions. *Annals of Behavioral Medicine, 16,* 317–326.

Rimer, B. K., Keintz, M. K., Kessler, H. B., Engstrom, P. F., & Rosan, J. R. (1989). Why women resist screening mammography: Patient related barriers. *Radiology, 172,* 243–246.

Rimer, B. K., Resch, N., King, E., Ross, E., Lerman, C., Boyce, A., Kessler, H., & Engstrom, P. (1992). Multistage health education program to increase mammography screening among women ages 65 and older. *Public Health Reports, 107,* 369–380.

Rippetoe, P. A., & Rogers, R. W. (1987). Effects of components of protection motivation theory on adaptive and maladaptive coping with a health threat. *Journal of Personality and Social Psychology, 52,* 596–604.

Rodrigue, J. R. (1996). Promoting healthier behaviors, attitudes, and beliefs toward sun exposure in parents of young children. *Journal of Consulting and Clinical Psychology, 64,* 1431–1436.

Rogers, R. W. (1975). A protection motivation theory of fear appeals and attitude change. *Journal of Psychology, 91,* 93–114.

Rogers, R. W. (1983). A protection motivation theory of fear appeals and attitude change: A revised theory of protection motivation. In J. R. Cacioppo & R. E. Petty (Eds.), *Social psychology: A sourcebook* (pp. 153–176). New York: Guilford.

Ronis, D. L. (1992). Conditional health threats: Health beliefs, decisions, and behaviors among adults. *Health Psychology, 11,* 127–134.

Ronis, D. L., & Harel, Y. (1989). Health beliefs and beast examination behaviors: Analysis of linear structural relations. *Psychology and Health, 3,* 259–285.

Ronis, D. L., Yates, J. F., & Kirscht, J. P. (1989). Attitudes, decisions, and habits as determinants of repeated behavior. In A. R. Pratkanis, S. J. Breckler, & A. G. Greenwald (Eds.), *Attitude structure and function* (pp. 213–239). Hillsdale, NJ: Lawrence Erlbaum Associates.

Rosenstock, I. M. (1966). Why people use health services. *Milbank Memorial Fund Quarterly, 44,* 94–124.

Rosenstock, I. M. (1974a). Historical origins of the health belief model. *Health Education Monographs, 2,* 328–335.

Rosenstock, I. M. (1974b). The health belief model and preventive health behavior. *Health Education Monographs, 2,* 354–386.

Rosenstock, I. M. (1990). Explaining health behavior through expectancies. In K. Glanz, F. M. Lewis, & B. K. Rimer (Eds.), *Health behavior and health education* (pp. 140–157). San Francisco: Jossey-Bass.

Rosenstock, I. M., Strecher, V. J., & Becker, M. J. (1988). Social learning theory and the health belief model. *Health Education Quarterly, 15,* 175–183.

Rothman, A. J., & Salovey, P. (1997). Shaping perceptions to motivate healthy behavior: The role of message framing. *Psychological Bulletin, 121,* 3–19.

Rothman, A. J., Salovey, P., Antone, C., Keough, K., & Martin, C. D. (1993). The influence of message framing on intentions to perform health behaviors. *Journal of Experimental Social Psychology, 29,* 408–423.

Royak-Schaler, R., Stanton, A. L., & Danoff-Burg, S. (1997). Breast cancer: Psychological factors influencing risk perception, screening, diagnosis, and treatment. In S. J. Gallant, G. P. Keita, & R. Royak-Schaler (Eds.), *Health care for women: Psychological, social, and behavioral influences* (pp. 295–314). Washington, DC: APA Books.

Rutledge, D. N., & Davis, G. T. (1988). Breast self-examination compliance and the health belief model. *Oncology Nursing Forum, 15,* 175–179.

Salazar, M. K. (1994). Breast self-examination beliefs: A descriptive study. *Public Health Nursing, 11,* 49–56.

Salazar, M. K., & de Moor, C. (1995). An evaluation of mammography beliefs using a decision model. *Health Education Quarterly, 22,* 110–126.

Savage, S. A., & Clarke, V. A. (1996). Factors associated with screening mammography and breast self-examination intentions. *Health Education Research, 11,* 409–421.

Schwartz, L. M., Woloshin, S., Black, W. C., & Welch, H. G. (1997). The role of numeracy in understanding the benefit of screening mammography. *Annals of Internal Medicine, 127,* 966–972.

Schwartz, M. D., Lerman, C., Audrain, J., Cella, D., Rimer, B., Stefanek, M., Garber, J., Lin, T. H., & Vogel, V. (1998). The impact of a brief problem-solving training intervention for relatives of recently diagnosed breast cancer patients. *Annals of Behavioral Medicine, 20,* 7–12.

Schwartz, M. D., Lerman, C., Daly, M., Audrain, J., Masny, A., & Griffith, K. (1995). Utilization of ovarian cancer screening by women at increased risk. *Cancer Epidemiology, Biomarkers, & Prevention, 4,* 269–373.

Schwartz, M. D., Lerman, C., Miller, S., Daly, M., & Masny, A. (1995). Coping disposition, perceived risk, and psychological distress among women at increased risk for ovarian cancer. *Health Psychology, 14*(3), 232–235.

Schwartz, M. D., Rimer, B. K., Daly, M., Sands, C., & Lerman, C. (1998). *A randomized trial of breast cancer risk counseling: The impact upon self-reported mammography utilization.* Unpublished manuscript, Georgetown University Medical Center.

Schwartz, M. D., Taylor, K. L., Willard, K., Siegel, J., Lamdan, R., & Moran, K. (1999). Distress, personality, and mammography utilization among women with a family history of breast cancer. *Health Psychology, 18,* 327–332.

Sheeran, P., & Abraham, C. (1996). The health belief model. In M. C. Conner & P. Norman (Eds.), *Predicting health behavior* (pp. 23–61). Buckingham, England: Open University Press.

Siegler, I. C., & Costa, P. T. (1994). Personality and breast cancer screening behaviors. *Annals of Behavioral Medicine, 16,* 347–351.

Siegler, I. C., Feaganes, J. R., & Rimer, B. K. (1995). Predictors of adoption of mammography in women under age 50. *Health Psychology, 14,* 274–278.

Sjöberg, L. (1998). Worry and risk perception. *Risk Analysis, 18,* 85–93.

Skinner, C. S., Strecher, V. J., & Hospers, H. (1994). Physician recommendations for mammography: Do tailored messages make a difference? *American Journal of Public Health, 84,* 43–49.

Slovic, P. (1987). Perception of risk. *Science, 236,* 280–290.

Slovic, P., Fischhoff, B., & Lichtenstein, S. (1979). Rating the risks. *Environment, 21,* 14–20, 36–39.

Snell, J. L., & Buck, E. L. (1996). Increasing cancer screening: A meta-analysis. *Preventive Medicine, 25,* 702–707.

Sortet, J. P., & Banks, S. R. (1997). Health beliefs of rural Appalachian women and the practice of breast self-examination. *Cancer Nursing, 20,* 231–245.

Stefanek, M. E., & Wilcox, P. (1991). First degree relatives of breast cancer patients: Screening practices and provision of risk information. *Cancer Detection and Prevention, 15,* 379–384.

Suarez, L., Roche, R. A., Nichols, D., & Simpson, D. M. (1997). Knowledge, behavior, and fears concerning breast and cervical cancer among older low-income Mexican-American women. *American Journal of Preventive Medicine, 13,* 137–142.

Sutton, S., Bickler, G., Sancho-Aldridge, J., & Saidi, G. (1994). Prospective study of predictors of attendance for breast screening in inner London. *Journal of Epidemiology and Community Health, 48,* 65–73.

Taubes, G. (1995). Epidemiology faces its limits. *Science, 259,* 164–169.

Tversky, A., & Kahneman, D. (1973). Availability: A heuristic for judging frequency and probability. *Cognitive Psychology, 5,* 207–232.

Tversky, A., & Kahneman, D. (1974). Judgment under uncertainty: Heuristics and biases. *Science, 184,* 1124–1131.

U.S. Preventive Services Task Force. (1996). *Guide to clinical preventive services* (2nd ed.). Baltimore: Williams & Wilkins.

Van der Pligt, J. (1996). Risk perception and self-protective behavior. *European Psychologist, 1,* 34–43.

Van der Pligt, J. (1998). Perceived risk and vulnerability as predictors of precautionary behavior. *British Journal of Health Psychology, 3,* 1–14.

Vernon, S. W., Laville, E. A., & Jackson, G. L. (1990). Participation in breast screening programs: A review. *Social Science and Medicine, 30,* 1107–1118.

Vernon, S. W., Myers, R. E., & Tilley, B. C. (1997). Development and validation of an instrument to measure factors related to colorectal cancer screening adherence. *Cancer Epidemiology, Biomarkers, and Prevention 6,* 825–832.

Ward, J. E., Hughes, A. M., Hirst, G. H., & Winchester, L. (1997). Mens' estimates of prostate cancer risk and self-reported rates of screening. *Medical Journal of Australia, 167,* 240–241.

Wardle, J. (1995). Women at risk for ovarian cancer. *Journal of the National Cancer Institute Monographs, 17,* 81–85.

Webb, J. A., Friedman, L. C., Luce, S. B., Weinberg, A. D., & Cooper, P. (1996). Demographic, psychosocial, and objective risk factors related to perceived risk of skin cancer. *Journal of Cancer Education, 11,* 174–177.

Weinstein, N. D. (1980). Unrealistic optimism about future life events. (1980). *Journal of Personality and Social Psychology, 39,* 806–820.

Weinstein, N. D. (1982). Unrealistic optimism about susceptibility to health problems. *Journal of Behavioral Medicine, 5,* 441–460.

Weinstein, N. D. (1984). Why it won't happen to me: Perceptions of risk factors and susceptibility. *Health Psychology, 3,* 431–457.

Weinstein, N. D. (1987). Unrealistic optimism about susceptibility to health problems: Conclusions from a community-wide sample. *Journal of Behavioral Medicine, 10,* 481–500.

Weinstein, N. D. (1988). The precaution adoption process. *Health Psychology, 7,* 355–386.

Weinstein, N. D. (1993). Testing four competing theories of health-protective behavior. *Health Psychology, 12,* 324–333.

Weinstein, N. D., & Klein, W. M. (1995). Resistance of personal risk perceptions to debiasing interventions. *Health Psychology, 14,* 132–140.

Weinstein, N. D., & Klein, W. M. (1996). Unrealistic optimism: Present and future. *Journal of Social and Clinical Psychology, 15,* 1–8.

Weinstein, N. D. & Nicolich, M. (1993). Correct and incorrect interpretations of correlations between risk perceptions and risk behaviors. *Health Psychology, 12,* 235–245.

Weinstein, N. D., Rothman, A. J., & Sutton, S. R. (1998). Stage theories of health behavior: Conceptual and methodological issues. *Health Psychology, 17,* 290–299.

Weinstein, N. D., & Sandman, P. M. (1992). A model of the precaution adoption process: Evidence from home radon testing. *Health Psychology, 11,* 170–180.

West, S. G., & Aiken, L. S. (1997). Toward understanding individual effects in multicomponent prevention programs: Design and analysis strategies. In K. J. Bryant, M. Windle, & S. G. West (Eds.), *The science of prevention: Methodological advances from alcohol and substance abuse research* (pp. 167–209). Washington, DC: American Psychological Association.

Wichstrom, L. (1994). Predictors of Norwegian adolescents' sunbathing and use of sun screen. *Health Psychology, 13,* 412–420.

Wolfe, E. S., & Wolfe, W. W. (1997). Discussion of the controversies associated with prostate cancer screening. *Journal of the Royal Society of Health, 117,* 151–155.

Woolf, S. H., & Lawrence, R. S. (1997). Preserving scientific debate and patient choice: Lessons from the consensus panel on mammography screening. *Journal of the American Medical Association, 278,* 2105–2108.

Wyper, M. A. (1990). Breast self-examination and the health belief model: Variations on a theme. *Research in Nursing and Health, 13,* 421–428.

Zapka, J. G., Costanza, M. E., Harris, D. R., Hosmer, D., Stoddard, A., Barth, R., & Gaw, V. (1993). Impact of a breast cancer screening community intervention. *Preventive Medicine, 22,* 34–53.

Zapka, J. G., & Mamon, J. A. (1986). Breast self-examination by young women: Characteristics associated with proficiency. *American Journal of Preventive Medicine, 2,* 70–78.

Zapka, J. G., Stoddard, A. M., Costanza, M. D., & Greene, H. L.(1989). Breast cancer screening by mammography: Utilization and associated factors. *American Journal of Public Health, 79,* 1499–1502.

Zapka, J. G., Stoddard, A., Maul, L., & Costanza, M. E. (1991). Interval adherence to mammography screening guidelines. *Medical Care, 29,* 697–707.

45

Stress and Breast Cancer

Douglas L. Delahanty
Kent State University

Andrew Baum
University of Pittsburgh Cancer Institute

A major theme in research on health and behavior has been the impact of stress on the pathophysiology of disease and development of systemic dysfunction. Stress appears to be a major factor in the etiology of cardiovascular disease, AIDS, and several other chronic and/or life threatening illnesses. For disease states produced by years of slowly developing pathogenic conditions, this means identifying stressors and processes experienced over very long periods of time. This daunting task has made conclusions about stress and disease in humans tentative, and this literature requires cautious reading and interpretation. Nevertheless, research has produced suggestive evidence of the role of stress in a wide array of disease processes, including cancer. A growing area of investigation concerns stress as an etiological factor in breast cancer.

Each year, more than 184,000 American women are diagnosed with breast cancer, and 45,000 die from the disease (Parker, Tong, Bolden, & Wingo, 1996). Breast cancer is the most common cancer among women and is second only to lung cancer in mortality rates (Henderson, 1995). As with many cancers, until recently, relatively little was known about its etiology and progression. Researchers now know that some breast cancer is attributable to heritable genetic polymorphisms, some appears to be associated with lifetime estrogen exposure, and some to other major known risk factors (e.g., weight, age). There is also considerable variability of disease course among patients (Henderson, 1995) and the reasons for this variability are not well understood. Researchers have increasingly turned to psychological or behavioral variables to explain cases in which response to treatment and/or treatment outcomes vary (Andersen, 1994; Fox, 1983; Jensen, 1991).

Studies of the effects of stress on the development and promotion of breast cancer have produced variable results, with some researchers noting an association between stress and cancer outcomes (C. L. Cooper, R. Cooper, & Faragher, 1989; Funch & Marshall, 1983; Ramirez et al., 1989). Other investigations have not found associations between stress and disease outcomes (Cassileth, Lusk, D. S. Miller, Brown, & C. Miller, 1985; Greer & Morris, 1975; T. J. Priestman, S. G. Priestman, & Bradshaw, 1985). This chapter reviews the findings and limitations of studies examining the link between stress and breast cancer, concentrating on the extent to which stress and psychological factors contribute to the etiology and progression of breast cancer in women. Mechanisms through which stress may influence breast cancer are also discussed. This discussion does not review the larger literatures on stress and coping; these issues have been discussed elsewhere in this volume (see chap. 17).

THE EFFECTS OF STRESS ON BREAST CANCER

The term *cancer* refers to a heterogeneous group of more than 100 specific types of cancer that are characterized by dysregulated and rapid cell growth and the potential for invasive or metastatic growth. Types of cancer vary considerably with regard to risk factors, etiology, disease course, and treatment. Depending on the site of the original tumor, its size, or whether it has metastasized, different cancers follow different courses and some appear to be related to stress. Some cancers are extremely aggressive, follow a very predictable disease course, and appear to progress inexorably as a function of biological factors (Levy & Wise, 1987). Others, including breast cancer, follow more variable disease courses, appear to be less exclusively affected by tumor biology, and appear to be affected by other factors. Investigators and clinicians have argued that the unexplained variance in the course of breast cancer may be due to psychosocial factors, and the impact of factors like stress on disease course has been examined at virtually every stage of breast cancer. The popular press has focused primarily on studies finding positive relations between psychosocial variables and breast cancer, and many popular books and magazine articles have instructed cancer patients that they can overcome cancer with their thoughts or by reducing distress (LeShan, 1977; Siegel, 1986). Methodological limitations alone suggest caution in interpreting such bold claims, and consequences of such lessons are also evident. If cancer patients believe they caused their cancer themselves or that they can prevent it from progressing, they may blame themselves, becoming depressed and less responsive to treatment and exacerbating their disease (Sapolsky, 1994). Scientific evidence of a direct link between psychological factors and cancer onset and progression lags far behind these popular assertions (Fox, 1983; Levenson & Bemis, 1991).

Available data are drawn from several sources, most notably animal studies of experimentally applied stress on tumor growth or rejection and from correlational studies of human cancer patients and naturalistic stressors. As might be expected, evidence of an association between stress and cancer is more dramatic in animal studies than in human investigations.

Animal Research

Animal models allow for highly controlled studies under laboratory conditions and have provided important information about the relations between stress and cancer (e.g., Justice, 1985; Riley, Fitzmaurice, & Spackman, 1981; Sklar & Anisman, 1980). Interestingly, this research has produced findings suggesting both exacerbation and inhibition of tumor growth and metastasis as a function of stress (Ben-Eliyahu, Yirmiya, Liebeskind, Taylor, & Gale, 1991; Newberry, Frankie, Beatty, Maloney, & Gilchrist, 1972). This highlights the complex nature of the stress–cancer relation, and has led to the examination of differences in methodology among studies to explain the different findings. Several factors appear to determine outcomes in these studies, most notably the timing of tumor initiation and the organism being studied.

Type of Cancer and Timing of Tumor Induction. In animals, viral tumors and mammary tumor viruses appear to be more responsive to stress than nonviral, chemically induced tumors such as chemically induced mammary tumors (Justice, 1985). The reverse appears to be true in humans; nonviral tumors have been more affected by stress, whereas viral tumors tend to follow a fairly nonmodifiable course (Levy & Wise, 1987). In animals, viral tumors also appear to be more immunoresponsive than nonviral tumors, and the stress-induced enhancement of these tumors might be due to stress-induced immunomodulation (Justice, 1985).

The timing of tumor induction and stress exposure appears to be very important in interpreting these studies (Justice, 1985; Riley, 1981). Stress applied after introduction of tumors appears to decrease immune defenses and enhance tumor growth, but stress experienced before induction has the opposite effect. Forced swimming decreased NK activity against mammary tumors in Fischer 344 rats in an in vitro assay and led to significantly more lung metastases in stressed animals (Ben-eliyahu et al., 1991). In another study, rotation stress administered 4 to 6 days after tumor implantation resulted in immunosuppression and rapid tumor growth, and was associated with higher mortality than when stress was administered 3 days before implantation (Riley, 1981). Administering stress before implantation resulted in immunoenhancement and suppression of tumor growth.

This finding can be explained if the importance of adaptation and rebound of bodily systems following resolution or termination of a stressor is considered. For example, Monjan and Collector (1977) found that stress-induced immunosuppression is often followed by a rebound increase in number or efficacy of cells after the stressor has been terminated or adaptation is acheived. This would result in a transient increase in immune function prior to settling back to "baseline" levels. For animals who were stressed after implantation, tumor growth may have been enhanced by suppression of host defenses by stress experienced while tumors were growing. For animals who experienced stress first, tumors may have been implanted into a rebounding, enhanced host defense.

Species, Strain, and Previous Experience. Findings in the animal literature also differ across species and across different strains of the same species (Sklar & Anisman, 1980). For example, stress differentially effects neurochemical and hormonal levels in different strains of mice and rats, and this can have opposite effects on disease progression (Ray & Barrett, 1975; Wahlsten, 1978). In addition, social conditions (housing) and previous stress history have been shown to play a role in determining the effects of stress on cancer progression (Sklar & Anisman, 1980). Group-housed mice have smaller stress-induced catecholamine changes than do mice raised in isolation (Blanc et al., 1980; B. L. Welch & A. S. Welch, 1970), and mice raised in isolation develop mammary tumors earlier than do group-reared mice (Henry, Stephens, & Watson, 1975).

Prior stress exposure can also affect subsequent stressful experiences. Anisman and Sklar (1979) exposed mice to a set of 60 shocks that resulted in a depletion of hypothalamic norepinephrine (NE; Anisman & Sklar, 1979). Subsequent exposure to 10 shocks resulted in no NE depletion in mice not previously exposed to shock, but a large depletion in those that were previously exposed, suggesting that previous stress exposure may sensitize an animal to subsequent stressful experiences. Early life stress experience has also been found to affect later ability to resist tumor development (Seligman & Visintainer, 1985). At 27 days old, rats were exposed to either escapable shock, inescapable shock, or no shock. The escapable and inescapable shock groups were yoked so that the animals received the same amount of shock. When the rats were 90 days old, they were injected with sarcoma tumor cells and were reassigned to the three conditions in such a way that nine groups of every combination of early and later stress experience were formed. Results indicated that early escapable shock experience was associated with better tumor rejection in both adult shock conditions. Exposure to early inescapable shock was associated with poorer rejection of tumors in both the escapable and inescapable adult conditions. These studies suggest, despite equivocal data, that stress affects the growth of tumors. They also highlight the importance of control and adaptation as determinants of stress and cancer progression. Further, this research suggests the possibility of sensitization of stress-related responses and raises questions about the conditions necessary for more protective habituation of responses to occur. In addition, animal research has clearly identified the immune system as a potential mechanism underlying stress-related cancer progression (Sikora & James, 1991).

Animal research has been useful in many ways, permitting accelerated views of cancer etiology, experimental manipulation of tumor induction, and facilitating identification of potential mechanisms of stress-related influences on cancer etiology. However, findings in the animal literature often apply to only one strain of animal, and generalization of these findings to a more heterogeneous population may be inappropriate (Redd & Jacobsen, 1988). In addition, the level of carcinogen to which the animals are exposed, or the dose with which they are injected, is typically much higher than humans would experience (Redd & Jacobsen, 1988). As noted, viral tumors appear more sensitive to psychological factors in animals, but human cancers that are the most modifiable by psychological influences are more often nonviral (Levy & Wise, 1987). Finally, it may be unwarranted to assume that using injected or induced tumors parallels "spontaneous" breast cancer in humans (Levy, 1985). However, the animal literature suggests there is a link between stress and tumor growth/rejection, and that psychological variables can affect disease course. The next section examines the relation between stress and cancer in humans.

Stress and Breast Cancer in Humans

The broad physiological, behavioral, cognitive, and emotional changes associated with stress could affect breast cancer at several different levels. First, stress may have direct effects on immune defenses and on the tumor itself that may enhance tumor growth or metastases. Stress can also increase drug, alcohol, or tobacco use, result in poorer diets, poorer sleep, and less exercise, and inhibit screening, prevention, and early detection. These behaviors may have further effects on immunity (Friedman, Klein, & Specter, 1991; Grunberg & Baum, 1985; Irwin, Smith, & Gillin, 1992; MacGregor, 1986). Stress may also decrease the likelihood of a woman engaging in breast self-examination or having regular mammograms, which may lead to a delay in seeking treatment and a worse prognosis if subsequent diagnosis is first made at a later stage of disease. Lerman and colleagues (1993) found that people who are experiencing stress are less likely to adhere to their doctor's suggestions, prescriptions, or orders. However, evidence linking stress directly to the onset of cancer is weak and methodological problems suggest caution when interpreting the findings of studies examining the effects of stress on breast cancer onset.

Retrospective studies of stress and the onset of breast cancer have also produced variable results, with some studies reporting that stress is associated with initial appearance of disease (Becker, 1979; Forsen, 1991), some finding that stress protects against cancer onset (T. J. Priestman et al., 1985), and some finding no relation between stress and cancer diagnosis (Schonfield, 1975; Snell & Graham, 1971). Obvious mismatches between the time frame inherent in cancer development and the periods that can be monitored for stress are responsible for some of these mixed results, particularly in retrospective studies. There are limits to accurate recall of stress or stressors and most studies limit measurement to periods within a few years of diagnosis. Other studies have examined women during their postoperative disease-free interval following surgery for breast cancer (Barraclough et al., 1992; Ramirez et al., 1989) and have also produced mixed results. Although these studies evaluate stress effects on disease progression, they are relevant because they examine recurrence following a disease-free interval. Ramirez et al. (1989) found that severely threatening life events and difficulties were significantly associated with the first recurrence of breast cancer (relative risk = 5.67). However, in a similar study, the opposite was found (Barraclough et al., 1992). After adjusting for age and axillary lymph node involvement, the relative risk of recurrence associated with severe life events during the year before surgery was .43, suggesting that psychosocial stress did not contribute to the relapse of breast cancer.

Retrospective studies of stressful life events and breast cancer development have been criticized for a number of reasons. C. L. Cooper, R. D. Cooper, and Faragher (1986a) discussed several limitations of these studies, including the small numbers of participants and lack of or improper control groups that are often found in these studies. Other than limits on recall, however, the most serious limitation of these studies is the fact that the participants knew their diagnosis prior to participating in the research. Knowledge of disease status could influence the way patients recall past stressful experiences. Those individuals experiencing stress because they have just been diagnosed with a life threatening disease may be more likely to report or recall life stress prior to diagnosis than women not experiencing the stress of diagnosis.

To correct for influences due to patients knowing their diagnoses prior to participation in studies, investigators have used limited prospective designs in which participants were interviewed prior to learning their diagnoses. These studies revealed that, although the number of stressful life events reported was comparable among patients diagnosed with breast cancer and those with benign lesions or healthy breasts, perceived severity of stressful events differed among the groups (C. L. Cooper, R.F.D. Cooper, & Faragher, 1986b, 1989; C. L. Cooper & Faragher, 1993; Edwards et al., 1990; Geyer, 1993; Muslin, Gyarfas, & Pieper, 1969). In general, more severe events were reported by women subsequently diagnosed with breast cancer than by women in control groups (C. L. Cooper et al., 1986b, 1989). Coping may be important in this observed association. A higher proportion of women diagnosed with breast cancer reported suppressing emotions (especially anger) than those with benign disease (Greer & Morris, 1975; Wirsching, Stierlin, Hoffmann, Weber, & Wirsching, 1982). Some of these studies have not found such effects (e.g., Schonfield, 1975). However, eliminating retrospective recall after diagnosis appears to have produced stronger evidence of a stress–cancer link.

Although results of life events research in breast cancer onset are sometimes inconsistent, many studies have reported positive relations between stressful experiences and subsequent breast cancer diagnosis. However, these studies must be interpreted cautiously, even when retrospective biases have been avoided. Brown (1981) argued that respondent-based measures of recent life events are largely inaccurate and subject to bias, and investigator-based interviews should be used in life event research. Perhaps more damaging to the previous findings are timing issues involved in the onset of breast cancer. Breast cancer is a relatively slow developing disease (Henderson, 1995). From the time cancerous cells appear, it may take 10 years before a tumor is detectable. Recent life event studies typically ask about life events occuring between 2 and 5 years preceding diagnosis. This suggests that researchers are not measuring stressful events that occur prior to cancer onset, but instead are measuring events that occur prior to diagnosis that may be associated with the progression of disease (i.e., the speed and extent of tumor growth). These problems have led many investigators to conclude there is no demonstrable relation between stress and the onset of breast cancer (Hilakivi-Clarke, Rowland, Clarke, & Lippman, 1993; A. B. Jensen, 1991; Levenson & Bemis, 1991).

Stress and Breast Cancer Progression

Although the evidence for a relation between stressful experiences and onset of breast cancer is weak, research examining the effects of stress on the progression of breast cancer is more promising. In part this is because of the uncertainty about the events causing and characterizing initial development of tumors. Initiation of disease is characterized by a series of mutagenic events in which cell mechanics are altered and restraints against uncontrolled growth are eliminated. Progression, on the other hand, refers to the development and course of the disease. Research on the onset of breast cancer suffers from the difficulty of not knowing exactly when onset occurs, and promotion and development of disease before discovery are similarly diffuse. However, consideration of progression of disease after detection and diagnosis bears the benefit of a clearer time frame. The stage of breast cancer can be determined at diagnosis and progression is readily measured. Abundant anecdotal evidence suggests that psychological factors can impact breast cancer progression. For instance, two patients can present with identical tumor types, identical stage at diagnosis, and identical treatment histories and still have vastly different disease outcomes. It is thought that some of this variance in outcome may be due to psychosocial factors such as stress.

Stressors Experienced by Breast Cancer Patients. There are many stressors that face women diagnosed with breast cancer, including the fear of possible death, the stress of informing family members, and the stress associated with being informed that their life is going to drastically change. Disruption, social stigmatization, side effects of treatment, and other stressors more specific to the disease and treatment are also pertinent. These stressors occur in the context of a disrupted family and other ongoing sources of stress. The majority of studies that are discussed here examine responses to the stress of screening and diagnosis. However, treatment can also be extremely stressful. The initial choice between a full mastectomy versus breast conservation surgery can be a difficult decision, and women choosing breast conservation surgery have been found to have more short-term psychological symptoms than those choosing a mastectomy (Levy et al., 1992). Anticipation of surgery as well as surgery itself can be extremely stressful, and it has been shown to decrease NK cell activity for as long as 24 hours postsurgery, just when physicians would want NK activity to be at its highest (Massie & Holland, 1991; Pollock, Lotzova, & Stanford, 1991). Further, the toxic side effects of chemotherapy can be so aversive that some patients believe they are worse than the cancer itself. An extensive literature has examined the effects of these diagnostic and treatment stressors on breast cancer progression, and has implicated a number of factors as moderators of the relation between stress and cancer progression.

Moderators of Stress and Breast Cancer Progression. In addition to being the primary risk factor for breast cancer, age has also been examined as a potential moderator of the relation between stress and cancer progression. Younger and older women may respond differently to a diagnosis of breast cancer. Younger patients perceive breast cancer to be a greater threat to their lives than older patients, and younger patients are rated as being in marginally poorer mental health following diagnosis (Funch & Marshall, 1983; Vinokur, Threatt, Vinokur-Kaplan, & Satariano, 1990). In addition, an interaction between disease severity and age has been found, indicating that younger patients with later stage disease experienced more deterioration of mental health and well-being in the first year postdiagnosis than did similarly impaired older women (Vinokur et al., 1990). Although older age was associated with use of more medications and greater limitation in activity, it was also associated with better mental health and well-being (Vinokur, Threatt, Caplan, & Zimmerman, 1989). Age also interacted with severity of disease such that younger patients with more severe disease had significantly greater difficulty adjusting to their illness than equally ill older women.

Personality and coping style also appear to moderate the relation between stress and cancer. The Type C personality has been proposed to describe a set of personality characteristics commonly seen in individuals diagnosed with malignant melanoma (Temoshok & Fox, 1984). Subsequently, Type C or the cancer prone personality was extended to refer to behaviors and characteristics common to victims of all cancers (Temoshok, 1987). Type C individuals express the opposite personality style of Type A individuals studied in research on cardiovascular disease (e.g., Glass, 1977). Type C individuals are cooperative, unassertive, patient, compliant, and likely to suppress their emotions. Although Type C individuals make very good patients, these characteristics have been consistently linked to poorer outcome in breast cancer patients (M. R. Jensen, 1987; Temoshok, 1987).

M. R. Jensen (1987) examined 52 women with a history of breast cancer and 34 healthy controls to determine what percentage of the variance in cancer progression could be accounted for by psychological variables. All patients were aware of their diagnoses when they filled out a variety of questionnaires designed to measure coping and personality variables, and rate of neoplastic growth and spread over an average of 2 years was examined. After controlling for disease stage at diagnosis, age, total length of disease course, and blood chemistry, neoplastic spread was found to be positively associated with a repressive personality style, suppression of emotion, helplessness-hopelessness, chronic stress, and comforting daydreaming. These psychological variables alone accounted for 44% of the variance in outcomes (higher levels were associated with greater neoplastic spread), whereas medical variables alone accounted for only 23% of the variance in disease progression.

Hostility appears to affect progression of breast cancer by itself, although results are mixed as to the direction of the relation. Two studies have found that patients who report lower levels of hostility have shorter survival times than those who report higher levels of hostility (Derogatis, Abeloff, & Melisaratos, 1979; Stavraky et al., 1968). Short-term survivors reported higher levels of positive mood, and treating oncologists perceived short-term survivors as being better adjusted to their illnesses. On the other hand, long-term survivors reported higher levels of hostility, as well as higher anxiety, alienation, dysphoric mood, and overall symptomatology, suggesting again that individuals who did not suppress emotions had longer overall and disease-free survival times. Long-term survivors also reported significantly more negative attitudes toward their physicians, again suggesting that "good" patients (i.e., more compliant, quiet, noncomplaining patients) may have faster cancer progression (Derogatis et al., 1979). In contrast, a study of 133 recently diagnosed breast cancer patients found that low anger was a significant predictor of survival 4 years later (Hislop, Waxler, Coldman, Elwood, & Kan, 1987), and Stanton and Snider (1993) found that cancer and benign diagnosis patients did not differ in mood, coping, or appraisal.

Optimism has been examined as an intervening variable in stress–cancer research as well. Having an optimistic outlook has been associated with less distress (Carver et al., 1993). Researchers met with patients 1 day before surgery, 10 days after surgery, and at 3-, 6-, and 12-month follow-ups. Optimistic outlook was inversely related to distress at each time point. In addition, use of acceptance (accepting the reality of the situation) before surgery predicted less postsurgical distress. The use of humor at the 3-month follow-up also predicted less distress at the 6-month follow-up, and denial and disengagement 3 months after surgery predicted higher levels of distress at the 6-month follow-up. However, no indices of disease state or progression were measured, so the effects of coping style on progression of breast cancer were not observed. Extrapolating from studies examining personality variables and progression, it might be predicted that optimism and humor would be associated with less distress and poorer prognosis.

In a series of studies, Greer, Morris, and Pettingale prospectively followed early stage breast cancer patients and measured outcomes in 5-year intervals. Five-year recurrence-free survival was significantly more common in patients who had responded to their diagnoses with denial and a "fighting spirit" versus those who responded with stoic acceptance or feelings of helplessness/hopelessness (Greer, Morris, & Pettingale, 1979). Denial, in this study, referred to a pattern of response in which patients rejected or minimized any evidence of their disease and the seriousness of their disease. Fighting spirit, on the other hand, referred to those who planned to do everything possible to conquer or beat their cancer. Therefore, fighting spirit is similar to the more active, hostile responses reported as leading to better prognoses in the previously mentioned studies. Ten and 15-year follow-up revealed that initial psychological response to diagnosis continued to predict outcome as long as 15 years postdiagnosis (Greer, Morris, Pettingale, & Haybittle, 1990; Pettingale, Morris, Greer, & Haybittle, 1985). It is important to note that this study has been criticized for not controlling for stage of disease, and the results should be interpreted with caution. However, analyses that controlled for this revealed that psychological responses to diagnosis were not related to clinical stage (Greer, 1991).

In a replication of these studies, Dean and Surtees (1989) found that after controlling for age, tumor size, histological node status, treatment, marital status, and menopausal status, women who responded with this kind of denial were significantly more likely to be recurrence-free at follow-up relative to those employing other coping strategies. However, there were no differences in outcome between those responding with a fighting spirit and those responding with stoic acceptance or helplessness-hopelessness. In addition, women who were diagnosed with a psychiatric illness prior to surgery were significantly less likely to have a recurrence at follow-up. This finding is similar to those of Derogatis et al. (1979) and Jensen (1987), who found that women reporting more anxiety and negative mood had a better prognosis.

Not all studies examining personality variables have found a relation between personal predispositions and breast cancer progression (Buddeberg et al., 1991; Cassileth et al., 1985; Jamison, Burish, & Wallston, 1987). Many of these negative studies examined samples composed entirely or predominantly of patients with advanced cancer. A possible explanation for the differences in results may be that personality variables influence earlier stages of breast cancer, but once the disease has progressed past a certain stage, the influences of personality may recede or be overwhelmed by other factors.

As these data suggest, one of the most controversial issues in breast cancer patients is the use of denial in coping with diagnosis. Studies examining the use of denial report contradictory results, with some studies finding that denial is associated with lower levels of distress and better prognosis (e.g., Dean & Surtees, 1989; Greer et al., 1979; Watson, Greer, Blake, & Shrapnell, 1984) and others finding that use of denial predicts higher distress and poorer outcome (e.g., Carver et al., 1993; C. L. Cooper & Faragher, 1993). However, studies that find a relation between denial and lower stress or better prognosis typically assess denial prior to or immediately following knowledge of disease state (Watson et al., 1984). For example, recently diagnosed breast cancer patients who denied the seriousness of their diagnoses reported significantly less mood disturbance during the time between diagnosis and surgery than did women who did not use denial (Dean & Surtees, 1989; Greer et al., 1979). In addition, the use of denial was not associated with length of delay in seeking treatment (Watson et al., 1984). However, studies examining the use of denial at later times following diagnosis tend to report negative effects of denial (Carver et al., 1993). Overall, it appears that initial use of denial, after screening but prior to diagnosis, may lead to decreased distress and better prognosis in breast cancer patients. However, later use of denial may be a poor coping strategy that could lead to faster disease progression.

Social support and perceived social support have also received attention as potential moderators of the relation between stress and breast cancer progression. Funch and Marshall (1983) found that marital status and number of friends and relatives were not related to survival, but organizational involvement was, indicating that women who reported being involved in more organizations had significantly longer survival. A series of studies found that social support was a factor in the effects of stress on cancer-related immune activity (Levy, Herberman, Lippman, & d'Angelo, 1987; Levy, Herberman, Maluish, Schlien, & Lippman, 1985; Levy et al., 1990). Levels of social support predicted natural killer (NK) cell activity and NK measures were linked to indices of progression (Levy et al., 1987). Other studies have found that NK cell activity has been associated with longer disease-free survival time (Pross & Lotzova, 1993). Coping through seeking social support has also been associated with more positive mood after diagnosis (Stanton & Snider, 1993), and breast cancer patients who engage in expressive activities (involving social interaction) and extroversion have significantly longer survival and disease-free survival times than women who do not report these activities (Hislop et al., 1987). Some researchers have not found evidence of social support affecting breast cancer (Edwards et al., 1990; Roberts, Cox, Shannon, & Wells, 1994). However, the majority of studies have found that social support is associated with higher levels of cancer-related immune indices and better prognosis (e.g., Helgeson & Cohen, 1996).

Summary and Conclusions. Overall, the evidence for a relation between stress and progression of breast cancer is suggestive but far from definitive. Literature reviews have concluded that cancer progression, rather than onset, may be influenced by psychosocial factors (Levenson & Bemis, 1991), and Fox (1983) suggested that if psychosocial factors have any influence on cancer it is prognostic rather than etiologic. The variables that seem most likely to influence the effects of stress on progression include the use of denial, social support, and personality characteristics consistent with the Type C personality. Initial use of denial seems to predict less subsequent distress and better prognosis, whereas patients with higher levels of social support tend to have better outcomes. In addition, those who are "good patients" (those individuals who are cooperative, unassertive, patient, and compliant) tend to have worse prognoses, whereas the "bad patients" (those who are hostile, anxious, uncooperative, and impatient) have longer disease-free and overall survival times.

THE EFFECTS OF STRESS REDUCTION

One of the best ways to study stress and cancer progression is to reduce stress in some patients and look at differences in disease and treatment outcomes later on. Psychosocial interventions have produced dramatic differences in subsequent mortality in late stage metastatic breast cancer patients (Spiegel, Bloom, Kraemer, & Gottheil, 1989). In this key study, patients attending weekly supportive group therapy meetings lived an average of 36.6 months following onset of the intervention and control patients who received routine oncological care averaged 18.9 months. Although confounding variables were controlled for in analyses, it is important to note that, despite randomization, participants in the intervention group were marginally different from controls in initial stage of disease. In addition, the intervention group received more radiation treatment than controls.

Fawzy and colleagues examined cancer patients with malignant melanoma. Although participants were not breast cancer patients, this study is important here because it examined the immune system as a potential mechanism through which interventions may influence subsequent morbidity and mortality. Following a 6-week group intervention consisting of health education, stress management, enhancement of problem-solving skills, and psychological support, the intervention group reported higher vigor and greater use of active-behavioral coping than controls (Fawzy, Cousins, et al., 1990). At a 6-month follow-up, the intervention participants continued to report higher vigor as well as significantly lower depression, fatigue, confusion, and mood disturbance than controls (F. I. Fawzy et al., 1993). In addition, intervention subjects continued to use more active coping strategies than controls.

Patients were also examined for differences in immunological measures (F. I. Fawzy, Kemeny, et al., 1990). Immediately following the intervention, no immune differences were found between the groups. However, at the 6-month follow-up, the intervention group had significantly increased percentages of NK cells and significantly higher interferon alpha-stimulated NK cell activity relative to controls. Changes in immune parameters were correlated with changes in reported mood; the larger the decrease in self-reported depression and anxiety, the larger the increase in NK cell cytotoxicity. In a 6-year follow-up, intervention patients were more likely to have survived than were controls (F. I. Fawzy et al., 1993).

A number of other studies have examined the efficacy of stress-reducing psychosocial interventions in treating adult victims of a variety of cancers (for reviews see Andersen, 1992; Meyer & Mark, 1995). Gruber, Hall, Hersh, and Dubois (1988) administered guided imagery, relaxation training, and biofeedback to cancer patients monthly over a 1-year period. Patients were instructed to practice these techniques twice daily, and immune levels and activity were measured at each monthly session. Results showed that levels, lymphocyte proliferation to Con A and PHA, NK activity, erythrocyte-rosette formation, IL-2 production, and levels of IgG and IgM were enhanced by the intervention relative to baseline (Gruber et al., 1988, 1993).

The large number of studies examining stress reducing interventions in treating cancer patients is reflected in a number of review articles and meta-analyses that have evaluated the effectiveness of various interventions (Andersen, 1992; Helgeson & Cohen, 1996; Meyer & Mark, 1995; Posluszny, Hyman, & Baum, 1998; Sims, 1987). Although results have been mixed, relaxation training appears to be an effective component of interventions to the extent to which patients comply with practicing at home (Sims, 1987). Building social support, self-esteem, and other psychosocial moderators interventions have been effective in increasing quality of life in victims of a variety of cancers in varying stages of disease (Andersen, 1992; Helgeson & Cohen, 1996; Helgeson, Cohen, Schultz, & Yasko, 1999). Further, a recent meta-analysis of randomized psychosocial interventions in adult cancer patients found moderate effect sizes (ranging from .19–.28) of the intervention on emotional and functional adjustment as well as disease-related symptoms (Meyer & Mark, 1995).

MEDIATING EFFECTS OF THE IMMUNE SYSTEM

The possible role of stress-induced immunosuppression on the etiology and progression of breast cancer has been mentioned several times in this chapter. There is some promising evidence that stress may act through the immune system to affect breast cancer progression (Baltrusch, Stangel, & Titze, 1991; Levy & Wise, 1987; Sikora & James, 1991). However, very few studies have examined distress, immune activity, and disease course together, so the role of immune activity in the stress and breast cancer relation is often inferred from what is known about the relation between stress and immune activity and studies of immune activity in cancer patients.

Stress-related changes in T- and NK cell numbers and activity have been widely reported (Bachen et al., 1992; Goodkin et al., 1996; Manuck, Cohen, Rabin, Muldoon, & Bachen, 1991, Sieber et al., 1992; Zakowski, McAllister, Deal, & Baum, 1992). In addition, studies comparing women with breast cancer to healthy women find that women with breast cancer typically have lower levels of these immune measures (Keller, Joachim, Pearse, & Siletti, 1976; Nemoto et al., 1974). Lower levels of immune activity have been associated with decreased survival times and shorter time to recurrence (Akimoto et al., 1986; Hacene et al., 1986; Ownby et al., 1983; Pross & Lotzova, 1993). Recently, cancer-related distress in breast cancer patients was found to predict lower NK activity and lower T-cell response to mitogenic challenge (Andersen et al., 1998).

Levy and her colleagues (1985) were among the first to systematically assess immune system activity or a factor in studies of stress and breast cancer. They found that patients who had low levels of NK activity were rated as more well-adjusted to their disease than patients with higher NK activity. In addition, patients with high NK activity had significantly fewer positive nodes than those with low NK activity. These results parallel those of studies examining personality effects on progression; "good" patients tended to fare worse than "bad" patients. However, immune measures were taken following surgery so it is impossible to determine whether having more positive axillary nodes led to decreased NK activity or whether decreased NK activity led to more positive nodes. In a 3-month follow-up, NK activity remained significantly lower in those patients with positive nodes as compared to those with negative nodes (Levy et al., 1987).

CONCLUSIONS AND FUTURE DIRECTIONS

The literature on the effects of stress on breast cancer development is typical of literatures on other complicated real-world issues. Inconsistences in the findings of these studies are often attributable to confounding variables that are difficult to control and to small or nonrepresentative samples. Control groups and time frames for measurement are often less than ideal or optimal. There have been few prospective studies examining baseline biopsychosocial measures prior to diagnosis and following participants through subsequent diagnosis of breast cancer, measuring progression, recurrence, and mortality. A prospective study of this nature would involve a substantial investment of time and money and it may be more realistic to study high risk populations beginning before patients know their diagnoses. Most studies compare women diagnosed with cancer to those diagnosed with benign disease. However, the presence of a breast lump may influence or alter the way in which a women may recall life events or answer other questionnaires, suggesting that a healthy control group also should be examined. Confounding variables need to be controlled when possible, and those that cannot should be measured to allow their influence to be corrected statistically. Perhaps most importantly, stage of disease needs to be controlled, because stress may influence breast cancer progression differently at different stages of disease.

Despite the volume of research on stress and breast cancer, a number of questions remain unanswered. The effects of stress on progression of breast cancer need to be clarified. It appears that stress can affect progression, because patients who report higher levels of distress exhibit earlier recurrence and shorter survival than those reporting lower levels of distress. However, research has also indicated that patients who complain the most, and who appear least well-adjusted to their disease, have the best prognoses. As suppression of emotion is characteristic of patients with poorer prognoses, it is difficult to interpret whether individuals reporting low levels of distress are suppressing their emotions or are actually not experiencing distress. For this reason it is important to take multiple measures of stress (self-report, other-report, and physiological), as well as measures of personality and coping behaviors, to determine if patients are prone to suppressing emotions. The role of the immune system and specific immune indices in mediating the effects of stress on breast cancer progression also needs to be examined in greater detail. Although the link between stress and immune changes has been shown repeatedly, the link between stress-related immune activity and disease has not been consistently found, and mediational analyses are needed to determine if stress does affect breast cancer progression through its influence on immune cells.

Finally, although initial findings appear very promising, the efficacy of stress-reducing interventions is still untested and the understanding of mechanisms indulging their effects is still poor. Replication of studies finding less recurrence and lower mortality in patients undergoing interventions and verification of theoretically predicted moderators are necessary before endorsing these interventions. It is unknown what type of patient is most likely to benefit from interventions, whether the effectiveness of these interventions differs depending on patient's stage of disease, and what qualities of the interventions are most beneficial (i.e., content, frequency, and/or length of intevention). However, they provide a plausible and attractive mechanism explaining some of the effects of stress on cancer. Future intervention studies need to address these questions to determine the most effective and economical way to treat breast cancer patients.

REFERENCES

Akimoto, M., Ishii, H., Nakajima, Y., Iwasaki, H., Tan, M., Abe, R., & Kasai, M. (1986). Assessment of host immune response in breast cancer patients. *Cancer Detection and Prevention, 9,* 311–317.

Andersen, B. L. (1992). Psychological interventions for cancer patients to enhance the quality of life. *Journal of Consulting and Clinical Psychology, 60,* 552–568.

Andersen, B. L. (1994). Surviving cancer. *Cancer, 74,* 1484–1495.

Andersen, B. L., Farrar, W. B., Golden-Kreutz, D., Kutz, L. A., MacCallum, R., Courtney, B. E., & Glaser, R. (1998). Stress and immune responses after surgical treatment for regional breast cancer. *Journal of the National Cancer Institute, 90,* 30–36.

Anisman, H., & Sklar, L. S. (1979). Catecholamine depletion in mice upon reexposure to stress: Mediation of the escape deficits produced by inescapable shock. *Journal of Comparative and Physiological Psychology, 93,* 610–625.

Bachen, E. A., Manuck, S. B., Marsland, A. L., Cohen, S., Malkoff, S. B., Muldoon, M. F., & Rabin, B. S. (1992). Lymphocyte subset and cellular immune responses to a brief experimental stressor. *Psychosomatic Medicine, 54,* 673–679.

Baltrusch, H. J., Stangel, W., & Titze, I. (1991). Stress, cancer and immunity. New developments in biopsychosocial and psychoneuroimmunologic research. *Acta Neurologica, 13,* 315–327.

Barraclough, J., Pinder, P., Cruddas, M., Osmond, C., Taylor, I., & Perry, M. (1992). Life events and breast cancer prognosis. *British Medical Journal, 304,* 1078–1081.

Becker, H. (1979). Psychodynamic aspects of breast cancer: Differences in younger and older patients. *Psychotherapy and Psychosomatics, 32,* 287–296.

Ben-Eliyahu, S., Yirmiya, R., Liebeskind, J. C., Taylor, A. N., & Gale, R. P. (1991). Stress increases metastatic spread of a mammary tumor in rats: Evidence for mediation by the immune system. *Brain, Behavior, and Immunity, 5,* 193–205.

Blanc, G., Hervé, D., Simon, H., Lisoprawski, A., Glowinski, J., & Tassin, J. P. (1980). Response to stress of mesocortico-frontal dopaminergic neurones in rats after long-term isolation. *Nature, 284,* 265–267.

Brown, G. W. (1981). Life events, psychiatric disorder and physical illness. *Journal of Psychosomatic Research, 25,* 461–473.

Buddeberg, C., Wolf, C., Sieber, M., Riehl-Emde, A., Bergant, A., Steiner, R., Landolt-Ritter, C., & Richter, D. (1991). Coping strategies and course of disease of breast cancer patients. *Psychotherapy and Psychosomatics, 55,* 151–157.

Carver, C. S., Pozo, C., Harris, S. D., Noriega, V., Scheier, M. F., Robinson, D. S., Ketcham, A. S., Moffat, Jr., F. L., & Clark, K. C. (1993). How coping mediates the effect of optimism on distress: A study of women with early stage breast cancer. *Journal of Personality and Social Psychology, 65,* 375–390.

Cassileth, B. R., Lusk, E. J., Miller, D. S., Brown, L. L., & Miller, C. (1985). Psychosocial correlates of survival in advanced malignant disease? *New England Journal of Medicine, 312,* 1551–1555.

Cooper, C. L., Cooper, R. D., & Faragher, E. B. (1986a). Psychosocial stress as a precursor to breast cancer: A review. *Current Psychological Research & Reviews, 5,* 268–280.

Cooper, C. L., Cooper, R. D., & Faragher, E. B. (1986b). A prospective study of the relationship between breast cancer and life events, type A behaviour, social support and coping skills. *Stress Medicine, 2,* 271–277.

Cooper, C. L., Cooper, R., & Faragher, E. B. (1989). Incidence and perception of psychosocial stress: The relationship with breast cancer. *Psychological Medicine, 19,* 415–422.

Cooper, C. L., & Faragher, E. B. (1993). Psychosocial stress and breast cancer: The inter-relationship between stress events, coping strategies and personality. *Psychological Medicine, 23,* 653–662.

Dean, C., & Surtees, P. G. (1989). Do psychological factors predict survival in breast cancer? *Journal of Psychosomatic Research, 33,* 561–569.

Derogatis, L. R., Abeloff, M. D., & Melisaratos, N. (1979). Psychological coping mechanisms and survival time in metastatic breast cancer. *Journal of the American Medical Association, 242,* 1504–1508.

Edwards, J. R., Cooper, C. L., Pearl, S. G., de Paredes, E. S., O'Leary, T., & Wilhelm, M. C. (1990). The relationship between psychosocial factors and breast cancer: Some unexpected results. *Behavioral Medicine,* 5–14.

Fawzy, F. I., Cousins, N., Fawzy, N. W., Kemeny, M. E., Elashoff, R., & Morton, D. (1990). A structured psychiatric intervention for cancer patients: I. Changes over time in methods of coping and affective disturbance. *Archives of General Psychiatry, 47,* 720–725.

Fawzy, F. I., Fawzy, N. W., Hyun, C. S., Elashoff, R., Guthrie, D., Fahey, J. L., & Morton, D. L. (1993). Malignant melanoma: Effects of an early structured psychiatric intervention, coping, and affective state on recurrence and survival 6 years later. *Archives of General Psychiatry, 50,* 681–689.

Fawzy, F. I., Kemeny, M. E., Fawzy, N. W., Elashoff, R., Morton, D., Cousins, N., & Fahey, J. L. (1990). A structured psychiatric intervention for cancer patients: II. Changes over time in immunological measures. *Archives of General Psychiatry, 47,* 729–735.

Forsen, A. (1991). Psychosocial stress as a risk for breast cancer. *Psychotherapy and Psychosomatics, 55,* 176–185.

Fox, B. H. (1983). Current theory of psychogenic effects on cancer incidence and prognosis. *Journal of Psychosocial Oncology, 1,* 17–31.

Friedman, H., Klein, T., & Specter, S. (1991). Immunosuppression by marijuana and components. In R. Ader, D. L. Felten, & N. Cohen (Eds.), *Psychoneuroimmunology* (pp. 931–953). San Diego, CA: Academic Press.

Funch, D. P., & Marshall, J. (1983). The role of stress, social support and age in survival from breast cancer. *Journal of Psychosomatic Research, 27,* 77–83.

Geyer, S. (1993). Life events, chronic difficulties and vulnerability factors preceding breast cancer. *Social Science and Medicine, 37,* 1545–1555.

Glass, D. C. (1977). *Behavior patterns, stress and coronary disease.* Hillsdale, NJ: Lawrence Erlbaum Associates.

Goodkin, K., Feaster, D. J., Tuttle, R., Blaney, N. T., Kumar, M., Baum, M. K., Shapshak, P., & Fletcher, M. A. (1996). Bereavement is associated with time-dependent decrements in cellular immune function in asymptomatic human immunodeficiency virus Type 1–seropositive homosexual men. *Clinical and Diagnostic Laboratory Immunology, 3,* 109–118.

Greer, S. (1991). Psychological response to cancer and survival. *Psychological Medicine, 21,* 43–49.

Greer, S., & Morris, T. (1975). Psychological attributes of women who develop breast cancer: A controlled study. *Journal of Psychosomatic Research, 19,* 147–153.

Greer, S., Morris, T., & Pettingale, K. W. (1979). Psychological response to breast cancer: Effect on outcome. *Lancet, 2,* 785–787.

Greer, S., Morris, T., Pettingale, K. W., & Haybittle, J. L. (1990). Psychological response to breast cancer and 15–year outcome. *Lancet, 335,* 49–50.

Gruber, B. L., Hall, N. R., Hersh, S. P., & Dubois, P. (1988). Immune system and psychological changes in metastatic cancer patients using relaxation and guided imagery: A pilot study. *Scandinavian Journal of Behaviour Therapy, 17,* 25–46.

Gruber, B. L., Hersh, S. P., Hall, N.R.S., Waletzky, L. R., Kunz, J. F., Carpenter, J. K., Kverno, K. S., & Weisse, S. M. (1993). Immunological responses of breast cancer patients to behavioral interventions. *Biofeedback and Self-Regulation, 18,* 1–22.

Grunberg, N. E., & Baum, A. (1985). Biological commonalities of stress and substance abuse. In S. Shiffman & T. A. Wills (Eds.), *Coping and substance use* (pp. 25–62). San Diego, CA: Academic Press.

Hacene, K., Desplaces, A., Brunet, M., Lidereau, R., Bourguignat, A., & Oglobinne, J. (1986). Competitive prognostic value of clinicopathologic and bioimmunological factors in primary breast cancer. *Cancer, 57,* 245–250.

Helgeson, V. S., & Cohen, S. (1996). Social support and adjustment to cancer: Reconciling descriptive, correlational, and intervention research. *Health Psychology, 15*(2), 135–148.

Helgeson, V. S., Cohen, S., Schulz, R. & Yasko, J. (1999). Educationa and peer discussion group interventions and adjustment to breast cancer. *Archives of General Psychiatry, 56*(4), 340–347.

Henderson, I. C. (1995). Breast cancer. In G. P. Murphy, W. Lawrence, Jr., & R. E. Lenhard, Jr. (Eds.), *American Cancer Society textbook of clinical oncology* (pp. 198–219). Atlanta: The American Cancer Society.

Henry, J. P., Stephens, P. M., & Watson, F.M.C. (1975). Force breeding, social disorder and mammary tumor formation in CBA/USC mouse colonies: A pilot study. *Psychosomatic Medicine, 37,* 277–283.

Hilakivi-Clarke, L., Rowland, J., Clarke, R., & Lippman, M. E. (1993). Psychosocial factors in the development and progression of breast cancer. *Breast Cancer Research and Treatment, 29,* 141–160.

Hislop, T. G., Waxler, N. E., Coldman, A. J., Elwood, J. M., & Kan, L. (1987). The prognostic significance of psychosocial factors in women with breast cancer. *Journal of Chronic Diseases, 40,* 729–735.

Irwin, M., Smith, T. L., & Gillin, J. C. (1992). Electroencephalographic sleep and natural killer activity in depressed patients and control subjects. *Psychosomatic Medicine, 54,* 10–21.

Jamison, R. B., Burish, T. G., & Wallston, K. A. (1987). Psychogenic factors in predicting survival of breast cancer patients. *Journal of Clinical Oncology, 5,* 768–772.

Jensen, A. B. (1991). Psychosocial factors in breast cancer and their possible impact upon prognosis. *Cancer Treatment Reviews, 18,* 191–210.

Jensen, M. R. (1987). Psychobiological factors predicting the course of breast cancer. *Journal of Personality, 55,* 317–342.

Justice, A. (1985). Review of the effects of stress on cancer in laboratory animals: Importance of time of stress application and type of tumor. *Psychological Bulletin, 98,* 108–138.

Keller, S. E., Joachim, H. L., Pearse, R., & Siletti, D. M. (1976). Decreased T lymphocytes in patients with mammary cancer. *American Journal of Clinical Pathology, 65,* 445.

LeShan, L. (1977). *You can fight for your life.* New York: M. Evans.

Lerman, C., Daly, M., Sands, C., Balshem, A., Lustbader, E., Heggan, T., Goldstein, L., James, J., & Engstrom, P. (1993). Mammography adherence and psychological distress among women at risk for breast cancer. *Journal of the National Cancer Institute, 85,* 1074–1080.

Levenson, J. L., & Bemis, C. (1991). The role of psychological factors in cancer onset and progression. *Psychosomatics, 32,* 124–132.

Levy, S., Herberman, R., Lippman, M., & d'Angelo, T. (1987). Correlation of stress factors with sustained depression of natural killer cell activity and predicted prognosis in patients with breast cancer. *Journal of Clinical Oncology, 5,* 348–353.

Levy, S. M. (1985). *Behavior and cancer.* San Francisco, CA: Jossey-Bass.

Levy, S. M., Haynes, L. T., Herberman, R. B., Lee, J., McFeeley, S., & Kirkwood, J. (1992). Mastectomy versus breast conservation surgery: Mental health effects at long-term follow-up. *Health Psychology, 11,* 349–354.

Levy, S. M., Herberman, R. B., Maluish, A. M., Schlien, B., & Lippman, M. (1985). Prognostic risk assessment in primary breast cancer by behavioral and immunological parameters. *Health Psychology, 4,* 99–113.

Levy, S. M., Herberman, R. B., Whiteside, T., Sanzo, K., Lee, J., & Kirkwood, J. (1990). Perceived social support and tumor estrogen/progesterone receptor status as predictors of natural killer cell activity in breast cancer patients. *Psychosomatic Medicine, 52,* 73–85.

Levy, S. M., & Wise, B. D. (1987). Psychosocial risk factors, natural immunity, and cancer progression: Implications for intervention. *Current Psychological Research and Reviews, 6,* 229–243.

MacGregor, R. R. (1986). Alcohol and immune defense. *Journal of the American Medical Association, 256,* 14774–1479.

Manuck, S. B., Cohen, S., Rabin, B. S., Muldoon, M. F., & Bachen, E. A. (1991). Individual differences in cellular immune response to stress. *Psychological Science, 2,* 111–115.

Massie, M. J., & Holland, J. C. (1991). Psychological reactions to breast cancer in the pre- and post-surgical treatment period. *Seminars in Surgical Oncology, 7,* 320–325.

Meyer, T. J., & Mark, M. M. (1995). Effects of psychosocial interventions with adult cancer patients: A meta-analysis of randomized experiments. *Health Psychology, 14,* 101–108.

Monjan, A. A., & Collector, M. I. (1977). *Science, 196,* 307.

Muslin, H. L., Gyarfas, K., & Pieper, W. J. (1969). Separation experience and cancer of the breast. *Annual New York Academy of Science Journal, 125,* 802–806.

Nemoto, T., Han, T., Minowada, J., Angkor, V., Chamberlain, W. A., & Dad, T. L. (1974). Cell-mediated immune status of breast cancer patients: Evaluation by skin tests, lymphocyte stimulation and counts of rosette forming cells. *Journal of the National Cancer Institute, 53,* 641–646.

Newberry, B. H., Frankie, G., Beatty, P. A., Maloney, B. D., & Gilchrist, J. C. (1972). Shock stress and DMBA-induced mammary tumors. *Psychosomatic Medicine, 34,* 295–303.

Ownby, H. E., Roi, L. D., Isenberg, R. R., Brennan, M. J., & the Breast Cancer Prognostic Study Associates. (1983). Peripheral lymphocyte and eosinophil counts as indicators of prognosis in primary breast cancer. *Cancer, 52,* 126–130.

Parker, S. L., Tong, T., Bolden, S., & Wingo, P. A. (1996). Cancer statistics, 1996. *CA—A Cancer Journal for Clinicians, 46,* 5–27.

Pettingale, K. W., Morris, T., Greer, S., & Haybittle, J. L. (1985). Mental attitudes to cancer: An additional prognostic factor. *Lancet, 1,* 750.

Pollock, R. E., Lotzova, E., & Stanford, S. D. (1991). Mechanism of surgical stress impairment of human perioperative natural killer cell cytotoxicity. *Archives of Surgery, 126,* 338–342.

Posluszny, D., Hyman, K., & Baum, A. (1998). Group interventions in cancer: The benefits of social support and education of patient adjustment. *Theory and Research on Small Groups, 5,* 87–105.

Priestman, T. J., Priestman, S. G., & Bradshaw, C. (1985). Stress and breast cancer. *British Journal of Cancer, 51,* 493–498.

Pross, H. F., & Lotzova, E. (1993). Role of natural killer cells in cancer. *Natural Immunity, 12,* 279–292.

Ramirez, A. J., Craig, T.K.J., Watson, J. P., Fentiman, I. S., North, W.R.S., & Rubens, R. D. (1989). Stress and relapse of breast cancer. *British Medical Journal, 298,* 291–293.

Ray, O. S., & Barrett, R. J. (1975). Behavioral, pharmacological, and biochemical analysis of genetic differences in rats. *Behavioral Biology, 15,* 391–417.

Redd, W. H., & Jacobsen, P. B. (1988). Emotions and cancer: New perspectives on an old question. *Cancer, 62,* 1871–1879.

Riley, V. (1981). Psychoneuroendocrine influences on immunocompetence and neoplasia. *Science, 212,* 1100–1109.

Riley, V., Fitzmaurice, M. A., & Spackman, D. H. (1981). Psychoneuroimmunologic factors in neoplasia: Studies in animals. In R. Ader (Ed.), *Psychoneuroimmunology* (pp. 31–102). New York: Academic Press.

Roberts, C. S., Cox, C. E., Shannon, V. J., & Wells, N. L. (1994). A closer look at social support as a moderator of stress in breast cancer. *Health & Social Work, 19,* 157–164.

Sapolsky, R. M. (1994). *Why zebras don't get ulcers: A guide to stress, stress-related diseases, and coping.* New York: Freeman.

Schonfield, J. (1975). Psychological and life-experience differences between Israeli women with benign and cancerous breast lesions. *Journal of Psychosomatic Research, 19,* 229–234.

Seligman, M.E.P., & Visintainer, M. A. (1985). Tumor rejection and early experience of uncontrollable shock in the rat. In F. R. Brush & J. B. Overmier (Eds.), *Affect conditioning and cognition: Essays on the determinants of behavior* (pp. 203–210). Hillsdale, NJ: Lawrence Erlbaum Associates.

Sieber, W. J., Rodin, J., Larson, L., Ortega, S., Cummings, N., Levy, S., Whiteside, T., & Herberman, R. (1992). Modulation of human natural killer cell activity by exposure to uncontrollable stress. *Brain, Behavior and Immunity, 6,* 141–156.

Siegel, B. S. (1986). *Love, medicine, and miracles.* New York: Harper & Row.

Sikora, K., & James, N. (1991). Immune modulation and cancer. *British Medical Bulletin, 47,* 209–226.

Sims, S.E.R. (1987). Relaxation training as a technique for helping patients cope with the experience of cancer: A selective review of the literature. *Journal of Advanced Nursing, 12,* 583–591.

Sklar, L. S., & Anisman, H. (1980). Social stress influences tumor growth. *Psychosomatic Medicine, 42,* 347–365.

Snell, L., & Graham, S. (1971). Social trauma as related to cancer of the breast. *British Journal of Cancer, 25,* 721–734.

Spiegel, D., Bloom, J. R., Kraemer, H. C., & Gottheil, E. (1989). Effect of psychosocial treatment on survival of patients with metastatic breast cancer. *The Lancet, 2,* 888–891.

Stanton, A. L., & Snider, P. R. (1993). Coping with a breast cancer diagnosis: A prospective study. *Health Psychology, 12,* 16–23.

Stavraky, K. M., et al. (1968). Psychological factors in the outcome of human cancer. *Journal of Psychosomatic Research, 12*(4), 251–259.

Temoshok, L. (1987). Personality, coping style, emotion and cancer: Towards an integrative model. *Cancer Surveys, 6,* 545–567.

Temoshok, L., & Fox, B. H. (1984). Coping styles and other psychosocial factors related to medical status and to prognosis in patients with cutaneous malignant melanoma. In B. H. Fox & B. H. Newberry (Eds.), *Impact of psychoendocrine systems in cancer and immunity* (pp. 258–287). Toronto: Hogrefe.

Vinokur, A. D., Threatt, B. A., Caplan, R. D., & Zimmerman, B. L. (1989). Physical and Psychosocial functioning and adjustment to breast cancer. *Cancer, 63,* 394–405.

Vinokur, A. D., Threatt, B. A., Vinokur-Kaplan, D., & Satariano, W. A. (1990). The process of recovery from breast cancer for younger and older patients. *Cancer, 65,* 1242–1254.

Wahlsten, D. (1978). Behavioral genetics and animal learning. In H. Anisman & G. Bignami (Eds.), *Psychopharmacology of aversively motivated behavior* (pp. 63–118). New York: Plenum.

Watson, M., Greer, S., Blake, S., & Shrapnell, K. (1984). Reaction to a diagnosis of breast cancer: Relationship between denial, delay and rates of psychological morbidity. *Cancer, 53,* 2008–2012.

Welch, B. L., & Welch, A. S. (1970). Control of brain catecholamines and serotonin during acute stress and after d-amphetamine by natural inhibition of monoamine oxidase: An hypothesis. In E. Costa & S. Garattini (Eds.), *Amphetamines and related compounds* (pp. 415–445). New York: Raven.

Wirsching, M., Stierlin, H., Hoffman, F., Weber, G., & Wirsching, B. (1982). Psychological identification of breast cancer patients before biopsy. *Journal of Psychosomatic Research, 26,* 1–10.

Zakowski, S. G., McAllister, C. G., Deal, M., & Baum, A. (1992). Stress, reactivity, and immune function in healthy men. *Health Psychology, 11,* 223–232.

46

Behavioral Intervention in Comprehensive Cancer Care

William H. Redd
Ruttenberg Cancer Center, Mount Sinai Medical Center

Paul Jacobsen
Moffitt Cancer Center & Research Institute

Cancer and its treatment adversely affect almost every aspect of a person's life. Indeed, there are few things more dreaded than being diagnosed with cancer. Although severe psychiatric reactions are relatively infrequent among cancer patients, significant adjustment problems and disorders are common. Indeed, over one-half of those treated for the disease experience fear, pain, insomnia, and related anxiety disorders (Derogatis, Morrow, & Fetting, 1983). A major advance in efforts to reduce such cancer-related distress has been the application of behavioral principles.

In this chapter, we discuss the application of behavioral principles in the design of psychosocial interventions with adult and pediatric cancer patients. The chapter is presented in four distinct sections. The first section reviews basic principles of behavioral intervention in the context of cancer treatment. The aim of that overview is to lay the foundation for the discussion of specific interventions. The second and third sections examine behavioral intervention with adults and children, respectively. It is important to note that the foci of clinical research with each of these two groups are quite different, each reflecting the problems that are encountered most frequently. Intervention research with adult patients has focused on symptom control and psychological adjustment, whereas the pediatric work has been broader. That work has examined methods to reduce pain and distress as well as issues surrounding treatment compliance and parents' impact on children's adjustment. These differences are reflected in the specific organization used in the adult and pediatric sections. The final section of the chapter considers future directions for clinical research.

OVERVIEW

The cognitive-behavioral perspective is based on the postulate that patient reactions to cancer and its treatment are a function of the context (i.e., social setting) under which the individual is diagnosed and treated, the social contingencies that operate, as well as his/her prior history and his/her individual strengths and weaknesses. Cognitive factors (e.g., beliefs, attitudes, and expectations) are also seen as playing a role (Turk, Meichenbaum, & Genest, 1983). Each of these factors is considered in the design and implementation of psychosocial interventions. The aim of such cognitive-behavioral intervention (the term that is most frequently used to identify this approach to clinical care) is to identify and then modify those factors (i.e., social contingencies, thoughts, feelings, and behaviors) that contribute to the development and maintenance of symptom. As the name implies, the cognitive-behavioral perspective incorporates both behavioral and cognitive approaches to psychosocial change. Reflecting its behavioral origins, the cognitive-behavioral perspective uses techniques for behavior change derived from the principles of operant conditioning (Skinner, 1953) and respondent conditioning (Pavlov, 1927).

To maximize therapeutic effectiveness, cognitive-behavioral interventions often combine several cognitive and behavioral change techniques into a "package." Standardized multi-component intervention packages have been developed for a range of purposes including the management of stress reactions (Meichenbaum, 1985) and chronic pain (Turk, Meichenbaum, & Genest, 1983) and the treatment of anxiety disorders (Barlow & Cerny, 1988). When the patient is a child, parents are often included in the intervention as coaches. In such pediatric interventions, parents typically function as change agents as they play a role in both the development and maintenance of the child's symptom behavior.

The contribution of cognitive-behavioral approaches to comprehensive care in adults and children is increasingly well recognized by various professional groups. A recent survey of cancer center health care providers revealed that cognitive-behavioral interventions were among the most widely offered psychosocial services (Coluzzi, Grant, Doroshow, Rhiner, Ferrell, & Rivera, 1995). This widespread use of such intervention strategies can be attributed to several factors. First, and perhaps most important, cognitive-behavioral interventions have been shown to be effective in reducing emotional distress and controlling physical symptoms in cancer patients (Meyer & Mark, 1995). Second, the interventions can usually be administered in a brief period of time and thus are well suited for use in oncology where rapid control of aversive symptoms may be necessary. Third, the interventions can be easily tailored to deal with the unique symptom control problems and quality of life issues that cancer patients experience. Fourth, the interventions are readily accepted by patients because of the emphasis that is placed on increasing the patient's sense of personal control and self-efficacy. Cognitive-behavioral intervention strategies place great importance on the normalization of patient adjustment.

INTERVENTION WITH ADULTS

We focus on three areas in oncology where cognitive-behavioral interventions have had a major impact on care of adult cancer patients. They are relief of pain, control of aversive reactions to chemotherapy administration, and enhancement of emotional well-being. Summaries of controlled randomized trials of the effectiveness of cognitive-behavioral intervention with adults are provided in Tables 46.1, 46.2, and 46.3.

Pain

Relaxation training is often recommended, either alone or as an adjunct to pharmacotherapy, in the management of cancer pain (Cobb, 1984). Despite considerable anecdotal evidence of the efficacy of relaxation training for cancer-related pain (Ahles, 1987; Millard, 1993), an extensive literature search uncovered only one study that used a controlled randomized design to directly examine the effectiveness of this technique (Sloman, Brown, Aldana, & Chee, 1994; see Table 46.1). In this study, researchers examined the effects of an intervention that combined progressive muscle relaxation with "mental imagery" on patients' reports of pain and their use of analgesic medications. Hospitalized patients with cancer pain were randomly assigned to a no intervention condition or to conditions in which relaxation training was provided either by audiotape or by a nurse. Compared to the control group, patients who received either audio taped instruction or live instruction reported significantly less pain and used fewer non-opioid analgesics. Although this study requires replication, it provides preliminary evidence of the effectiveness of relaxation training in alleviating cancer-related pain.

As with relaxation training, there is considerable anecdotal evidence in support of the use of hypnosis to relieve cancer-related pain (Hilgard, 1975; Margolis, 1985). However, evidence based on randomized studies is extremely limited. Spiegel and colleagues (1989) conducted one of the few controlled investigations of the efficacy of hypnosis in relieving cancer-related pain. In this study, women with metastatic breast cancer were randomly assigned to a no intervention condition or to group therapy. Patients assigned to the group therapy condition were then nonrandomly assigned to groups that either did or did not include instruction in hypnosis for pain control. Results indicated that, compared to patients in the control condition, patients who received group therapy reported less severe pain and less suffering over a one-year period. Additional analyses indicated that patients who received group therapy and hypnosis experienced less pain than patients who received group therapy alone. Although these findings support the use of hypnosis for relief of pain related to metastatic disease, they require replication for at least two reasons. First, the assignment to self-hypnosis in this study was not based on random assignment. Second, since many subjects died before the one year follow-up, the outcome analyses required extensive use of statistical corrections for missing data. Future studies could best deal with this issue by examining the efficacy of hypnosis over shorter time intervals.

Multicomponent cognitive-behavioral interventions have repeatedly been demonstrated to be effective in the treatment of chronic nonmalignant pain (Keefe, Dunsmore, & Burnett, 1992). Turk and Rennert (1981) were among the first to describe a multicomponent cognitive-behavioral intervention specifically designed to relieve cancer-related pain. Their approach involved education about the contribution of beliefs, attitudes, and emotions to the experience of pain as well as training in the use of both behavioral and cognitive techniques (e.g., relaxation, imagery, attention diversion, problem solving) for coping with pain. Clinical reports suggest that multicomponent cognitive-behavioral interventions are effective against cancer-related pain (Fishman & Loscalzo, 1987; Loscalzo & Jacobsen, 1990). However, the first controlled study to evaluate this approach yielded equivocal results. In this study (Syrjala, Cummings, & Donaldson, 1992), patients receiving chemotherapy before bone marrow transplantation were randomized to one of four conditions: (1) cognitive-behavioral coping skills training; (2) hypnosis training; (3) attentional control; or (4) no treatment control. Of principal interest was the impact of the interventions on the severity of chemotherapy-induced oral mucositis pain. Results indicated that patients who underwent hypnosis training, but not cognitive-behavioral training, experienced less pain than controls.

The authors of this study caution, however, that the numerous components included in the two cognitive-behavioral training sessions (relaxation training, cognitive restructuring, development of coping self-statements, and psychoeducation about symptoms and side effects) may have exceeded what patients could learn in such a short time. In a subsequent study (Syrjala, Donaldson, Davis, Kippes, & Carr, 1995), the same investigators tested a refined version of the cognitive-behavioral intervention in which the number of skills taught was reduced. Once again, patients receiving chemotherapy before bone marrow transplantation were randomized to one of four conditions: (1) cognitive-behavioral coping skills training; (2) relaxation training only; (3) nonspecific therapist support; or (4) no treatment control. Results of this subsequent study confirmed predictions that patients who received the cognitive-behavioral intervention or relaxation training alone would report less pain than patients in the other two groups. It should be noted, however, that an expected additive benefit of cognitive-behavioral skills training beyond relaxation training alone was not observed.

Aversion Reactions to Chemotherapy

The use of cognitive-behavioral interventions with chemotherapy patients initially focused on the clinical problem of anticipatory nausea and vomiting (ANV). In the early 1980s, a series of clinical reports described patients who had previously received emetogenic chemotherapy and who became nauseated and/or vomited in anticipation of subsequent treatments (Redd & Andresen, 1981; Nesse, Carli, Curtis, & Kleinman, 1980). In addition to describing this phenomenon, the authors of these clinical reports hypothesized that anticipatory reactions in chemotherapy patients were examples of classically conditioned responses. Similar to conditioned vomiting responses that could be experimentally induced in laboratory animals (Skinner, 1953), cancer patients appeared to develop ANV when previously neutral stimuli (e.g., the sights, sounds, and smells of the treatment environment) acquired nausea/emesis eliciting properties due to repeated association with chemotherapy administration and its aversive aftereffects. Based on this respondent conditioning conceptualization, several researchers investigated the efficacy of cognitive-behavioral interventions for controlling ANV. Three interventions were found to be effective in the first round of controlled clinical trials: hypnosis (Redd, Andresen, & Minagawa, 1982), progressive muscle relaxation training combined with guided imagery (Burish & Lyles, 1981; Lyles et al., 1982) and systematic desensitization (Morrow & Morrell, 1982; see Table 46.2). In the study of hypnosis, changes in anticipatory vomiting were shown to correspond in the expected direction with the introduction, withdrawal, and reintroduction of hypnosis-induced relaxation. In the studies of relaxation training and systematic desensitization, patients with ANV who were randomly assigned to the cognitive-behavioral intervention subsequently experienced less anticipatory nausea and/or vomiting than patients randomly assigned to either no treatment or attention control conditions.

In the studies cited, the cognitive-behavioral interventions were delivered to chemotherapy patients by specially trained mental health professionals. At least one study has investigated whether the potential availability of these interventions could be increased by training oncology personnel in the use of cognitive-behavioral techniques. In this study (Morrow, Asbury, Hammon, Dobkin, Caruso, & Pandya, 1992), patients with ANV were randomly assigned to receive no treatment or to receive systematic desensitization from either a clinical psychologist, an oncologist, or an oncology nurse trained in the technique. Results indicated that patients in each intervention condition experienced significant declines in anticipatory nausea relative to patients who received no treatment. Moreover, there were no differences in the magnitude of the therapeutic effects based on whether the intervention was delivered by a psychologist, a physician, or a nurse.

The means by which relaxation training and systematic desensitization reduce ANV have been the subject of considerable debate (Carey & Burish, 1988; Jacobsen & Redd, 1988). Speculation among researchers (Carey & Burish, 1988; Jacobsen & Redd, 1988) has centered around two possible mechanisms of action: physiological relaxation and cognitive distraction. The relaxing effects of these interventions may serve to inhibit the muscular contractions in the gastrointestinal tract involved in nausea and vomiting. Alternatively, the cognitive demands of these interventions could serve to direct attention away from sensations of nausea or from stimuli that have acquired nausea-eliciting properties. To isolate the possible role of distraction in ANV control, one study (Vasterling, Jenkins, Tope, & Burish, 1993) evaluated an intervention that has both distraction and relaxation components (progressive muscle relaxation training) as well as an intervention that has a distraction component but no relaxation component (video game playing). Compared to a no treatment control condition, patients in both intervention conditions experienced significantly less anticipatory nausea. Moreover, the two interventions did not differ in their effectiveness. Thus, results suggest that control of ANV can be achieved by distraction alone.

Other research has examined whether cognitive-behavioral interventions conducted before the start of chemotherapy are effective in preventing or postponing development of ANV. Two studies that examined this issue (Burish, Carey, Krozely, & Greco, 1987; Lerman et al., 1990) yielded mixed results. In both studies, patients scheduled to begin chemotherapy were randomly assigned to receive either progressive muscle relaxation and guided imagery or no intervention before the start of treatment. One study (Burish, Carey, Krozely, & Greco, 1987) found that by the fourth infusion (i.e., after several "conditioning trials") patients in the no intervention condition were experiencing significantly more anticipatory nausea and anticipatory anxiety than patients in the intervention condition. The same study also found that patients in the intervention condition experienced significantly less nausea, vomiting, and anxiety after chemotherapy than patients in the no intervention condition. The other study (Lerman et al., 1990) found no significant group differences in anticipatory nausea when it was assessed at the third infusion. However,

Table 46.1

Summary of Controlled Randomized Studies of Cognitive Behavioral Interventions to Relieve Cancer-Related Pain

STUDY	PARTICIPANTS		INTERVENTION								OUTCOMES				
	Diagnosis	Females /Males	Control groups (n)	Experimental groups (n)	Format	# & length of sessions	C-B components				Coping	Emot well-Being	Phys well-Being	Functioning	Phys arousal
							Coping	Relax	Hyp-nosis	Guided Imagery					
Sloman et al., (1994)	Mixed	F=19 M=48	No tx (20)	#1 (20) #2 (20)	Indiv Indiv	4 sessions (adm. by audiotape) 4 sessions (adm. by nurse)		x x		x x			+ +		
Speigel & Bloom, (1989)	Breast	F=54	No tx (24)	#1 (30)	Group	52 sessions, 90 mins			x				+		
Syrjala et al., (1992)	Hematologic malignancy or lymphoma	F=19 M= 26	No tx (10) Attn (12)	#1 (11) #2 (12)	Indiv Indiv	2 sessions, 90 mins 2 sessions, 90 mins	x	x	x	x		+ 0	+ 0		
Syrjal et al. (1995)	Leukemia or lymphoma	F=41 M=53	No tx (?) Attn (?)	#1 (?) #2(?)	Indiv Indiv	12 sessions 12 sessions	x	x x		x x			+ +		

x = Component included in intervention
+ = Significant improvement relative to controls
0 = Nonsignificant improvement relative to controls

Table 46.2

Summary of Controlled Randomized Studies of Cognitive - Behavioral Interventions to Relieve Aversive Reactions to Chemotherapy

STUDY	PARTICIPANTS		INTERVENTION								OUTCOMES				
	Diagnosis	Females /Males	Control groups (n)	Experimental groups (n)	Format	# & length of sessions	C-B components				Coping	Emot well-Being	Phys well-Being	Func-tioning	Phys arousal
							Prep info	Coping	Relax	Distr					
Burish & Lyles (1981)	Mixed	F=14 M=2	No tx (8)	#1 (8)	Indiv	5 sessions			x			+	+		-
Lyles et al., (1982)	Mixed	F=31 M=19	No tx (18) Attn (14)	#1 (18)	Indiv	5 sessions			x			+	+		-
Morrow & Morrell (1982)	Mixed	F=42 M=18	No tx (20) Attn (20)	#1 (20)	Indiv	2 sessions, 1 hour			x				+		
Morrow et al. (1992)	Mixed	?	No tx (14)	#1 (29) #2(29)	Indiv Indiv	2 sessions, 1 hour (adm. by oncology staff) 2 sessions, 1 hour (adm. by psychologist)			x x				+ +		
Vasterling et al. (1993)	Mixed	F=39 M=21	No tx (20)	#1 (20) #2 (2)	Indiv Indiv	5 sessions 5 sessions			x	 x		+ +	+ +		- -
Burish et al. (1987)	Mixed	?	No tx (12)	#1 (12)	Indiv	6-8 sessions			x			+	+		-
Lerman et al. (1990)	Mixed	F=32 M=16	No tx (23)	#1 (25)	Indiv	1 session, 30 mins			x			0	+		
Burish et al. (1991)	Mixed	F=29 M=31	Attn (15)	#1 (15) #2 (15) #3 (15)	Indiv Indiv Indiv	1 session, 90 min 4 sessions 5 sessions	x x	x x	 x x			+ + 0	+ 0 +	+ 0 0	

x = Component included in intervention
+ = Significant improvement relative to controls
0 = Nonsignificant improvement relative to controls

patients in the intervention condition did experience significantly less nausea after chemotherapy than patients in the no intervention condition.

Although findings regarding ANV prevention are inconclusive, both studies suggest that cognitive-behavioral interventions conducted before the start of chemotherapy may have other beneficial effects. Specifically, these interventions may serve to limit posttreatment nausea and vomiting and reduce treatment-related emotional distress. In one of the few controlled studies designed specifically to address this issue (Burish, Snyder, & Jenkins, 1991), patients about to begin chemotherapy were randomly assigned to one of four intervention conditions: relaxation training, coping preparation, relaxation training and coping preparation, or no treatment. Relaxation training consisted of instruction in progressive muscle relaxation immediately before the first infusion. Coping preparation consisted of four components: (1) a tour of the oncology clinic that provided patients with procedural information as well as concrete sensory information regarding chemotherapy administration; (2) a videotape presentation of a patient modeling successful coping with chemotherapy treatment; (3) a discussion and question and answer session that offered patients an opportunity to express feelings and concerns and to receive suggestions on how to cope with treatment and its side effects; and (4) a booklet that patients could use to review previously presented information. This 90-minute intervention was conducted on a day prior to the first chemotherapy administration. Findings indicated that the coping preparation yielded a number of beneficial effects. Compared to patients in the no treatment condition, patients who received coping preparation reported less anticipatory nausea, posttreatment vomiting, and depression. Moreover, among patients working outside the home, those who underwent the coping preparation reported less interference associated with cancer and its treatment on their ability to work. The benefits of relaxation training were less extensive, and the addition of relaxation training to coping preparation did not yield additional benefits. Findings from this study suggest that brief training in coping skills before the start of treatment may be an effective means of improving quality of life during chemotherapy.

Emotional Well-Being

The use of multi-component cognitive-behavioral interventions to improve well-being in cancer patients has been the subject of considerable attention in recent years. This interest can be attributed, in part, to evidence suggesting that psychosocial interventions designed to improve emotional and physical well-being in cancer patients may also improve survival (F. I. Fawzy, N. W. Fawzy, & Kemeny, 1990; Spiegel, Bloom, Kraemer, & Gottheil, 1989). Interest in this area has also been stimulated by the increased recognition of the importance of quality of life (a construct that includes both emotional and physical well-being) as an endpoint in cancer treatment (Cella, 1993; Osoba, 1994). Although there is considerable enthusiasm for the use of cognitive-behavioral interventions to improve emotional well-being, a review of the literature indicates that only a handful of studies have evaluated these interventions using controlled randomized designs (see Table 46.3).

Worden and Weisman were among the first to develop and evaluate cognitive-behavioral interventions to reduce distress and improve well-being in cancer patients. In a landmark study (Worden & Weisman, 1984), these investigators evaluated two interventions designed to promote coping and adaptation among newly diagnosed patients. Both interventions focused on the development of problem-solving skills. In the first approach, the therapist focused on the specific problems the patient was currently facing. In the second approach, the therapist focused more on the development of general problem-solving skills and discussed the solution of common problems faced by cancer patients. The second approach also included training in progressive muscle relaxation. Participants in the study were newly diagnosed cancer patients who were identified as being at high risk for psychological distress using well-defined criteria. These individuals were randomized to one of the two intervention conditions and their responses were compared to those of a nonrandomized control group. Results indicated that patients in both intervention groups experienced less psychological distress at follow-up than controls. Despite its methodological limitations (i.e., the lack of a nonrandomized control group), this study has had an enormous impact on the field of psychosocial oncology. Elements of this intervention have been incorporated into several other multi-component interventions that have been clinically validated and are described later.

Building on the work of Worden and Weisman (1984), Heinrich and Schag (1985) evaluated a stress and activity management program designed for cancer patients and their spouses. In multi-couple groups, participants were taught specific problem solving skills, received training in relaxation and information about coping with cancer and its treatment, and were encouraged to engage in physical exercise and to increase positively valued activities. The responses of couples randomized to this program were compared with those of couples randomized to standard care. Contrary to predictions, patients who received stress and activity management training did not demonstrate better psychosocial adjustment or activity levels than patients who received standard care.

Other studies that have evaluated similar cognitive-behavioral interventions have obtained different results. Telch and Telch (1986) examined the impact on quality of life of a group-administered program of coping skills training. The program consisted of five modules that covered: (1) relaxation and stress management; (2) communication and assertion; (3) problem solving and constructive thinking; (4) feelings management; and (5) pleasant activity planning. The effects of this intervention were tested by randomly assigning cancer patients to receive group coping skills instruction, supportive group therapy, or no treatment. Results indicated that, immediately following the 6-week intervention, patients who underwent coping skills training were less emotionally distressed and reported fewer problems than patients in the other two conditions.

Table 46.3

Summary of Controlled Randomized Studies of Cognitive-Behavioral Interventions to Improve Emotional Well-Being

STUDY	PARTICIPANTS		INTERVENTION								OUTCOMES		
	Diagnosis	Females/ Males	Control groups (n)	Experimental groups (n)	Format	# length of sessions	C-B Components				Coping	Emotional Well Being	Functioning
							Info	Coping/ Problem Solving	Relax	Activity Planning			
Heinrich & Schag (1985)	Mixed	?	No tx (25)	#1 (26)	Group Group	6 sessions, 2 hours	x	x	x	x		0	
Telch & Telch (1986)	Mixed	F=27 M=14	No tx (14)	#1 (13) #2 (14)	Group Group	6 sessions, 90 mins 6 sessions, 90 mins		x	x	x	+ +	+ +	
Fawzy et al. (1990)	Melanoma	F=35 M=31	No tx (28)	#1 (38)	Group	6 sessions, 90 mins	x	x	x		+	+	
Greer et al. (1992)	Mixed	F=32 M=124	No tx (84)	#1 (72)	Indiv	6 sessions, 1 hour		x	x	x		+	
Cain et al. (1986)	Gynecologic	F=80	Std Care (29)	#1 (21) #2 (22)	Indiv Group	8 sessions 8 sessions		x x	x x	x x		+ +	+ +

x = Component included in intervention
+ = Significant improvement relative to controls
0 = Nonsignificant improvement relative to controls

A study by Fawzy and colleagues (1990) has provided additional evidence that cognitive-behavioral interventions are effective in promoting adaptive coping and reducing emotional distress. In this study, patients with early stage melanoma were randomly assigned to a no treatment control condition or to a group administered program that included: health education, problem-solving skills training modeled after the work of Worden and Weisman (1984), stress management training, and psychological support. At a 6-month follow-up, the intervention group was found to be experiencing less emotional distress and to be using more active coping methods than the control group.

Greer and colleagues (1992) tested an individually administered cognitive-behavioral intervention designed to improve emotional well-being. The intervention, referred to as "adjuvant psychological therapy," has multiple components including coping skills training, cognitive restructuring, and progressive muscle relaxation training. In a controlled outcome study designed to evaluate the effectiveness of this intervention, cancer patients who met specific criteria for psychological morbidity were randomized to receive either adjuvant psychological therapy or no treatment. At a 4-month follow-up, patients who had received the cognitive-behavioral intervention were found to be experiencing less emotional distress than patients who received no treatment. These effects remained evident at a 12-month follow-up (Moorey et al., 1994).

At least one study has directly compared individual versus group administered forms of cognitive-behavioral interventions to promote emotional well-being. In this study (Cain, Kohorn, Quinlan, Latimer, & Schwartz, 1986), women with gynecologic cancer were randomized to either individual or group forms of "thematic counseling" or no treatment. Both the individual and group interventions included the following components: psychoeducation about cancer and its treatment, relaxation training, development of problem-solving skills, and discussion of diet and exercise. Data collected at a 6-month follow-up indicated that women who received thematic counseling either as individuals or in groups were less emotionally distressed and had made a better adjustment to their illness than women in the control group. Women who received thematic counseling also report better sexual functioning and greater participation in leisure activities. Thus, there does not appear to be any difference in efficacy associated with the format (i.e., group vs. individual) of cognitive-behavioral intervention.

INTERVENTION WITH CHILDREN

The importance of behavioral intervention in pediatric oncology is appreciated by most pediatric oncologists and nurse specialists. Clear evidence of this recognition is the recommendation made by the World Health Organization Consensus Conference for childhood cancer. That group endorsed behavioral procedures as the treatment of choice for pain associated with invasive medical procedures (Zeltzer et al., 1990). Interest in behavioral intervention has grown steadily as medical treatment regimes for children have become more aggressive and thereby more painful for the patient. Behavioral research in pediatric oncology has focused on the application of specific behavioral procedures to increase treatment compliance and reduce child suffering.

Intervention With Specific Adjustment/Psychosocial Problems

Problems that have been studied include: distress during invasive diagnostic and treatment procedures, treatment side effects, and social and academic reintegration. Under each problem we discuss how specific behavioral procedures have been applied, and results from clinical trials of their efficacy.

Bone marrow aspiration and lumbar puncture are used in both the diagnosis and treatment of patients. Bone marrow aspiration is a diagnostic procedure in which a needle is inserted into a bone, usually in the lower back, in order to extract marrow. This procedure is used to diagnose leukemia and other cancers, to determine if the cancer has metastasized, and to evaluate chemotherapy effectiveness (Gambino, 1989). It is extremely painful and often requires physical restraint of the child to complete the procedure if inadequate local anesthesia or sedation are used. Lumbar puncture involves the insertion of a needle into the spinal canal and the removal of spinal fluid. It is used to diagnose infections, brain hemorrhage, tumors, or other obstructions (Gambino, 1989). Like bone marrow aspiration, many children become anxious and uncooperative during lumbar puncture.

Unfortunately, in many cases both of these procedures must be administered repeatedly, creating for some children, near phobic reactions. Depending on the child's age and cognitive understanding of the procedure, bone marrow aspiration sometimes resembles torture to the child (Katz, Kellerman, & Siegel, 1980). Because of the anxiety and pain caused by such invasive treatments and many children's limited understanding of why treatment is necessary, young patients often become noncompliant and actively resist these procedures. Indeed, from 38% to 84% do not cope well during bone marrow aspiration and lumbar puncture (Ellis & Spanos, 1994).

Pharmacological interventions can reduce pain and anxiety during bone marrow aspiration and lumbar puncture, but many clinicians try to limit their use due to feared long-term neurological side effects. In addition, some children report that sedation makes them feel out of control (Ellis & Spanos, 1994), further supporting the use of behavioral interventions in lieu of, or in addition to pharmacological intervention.

Although hypnosis has been used for over a century, most of the research regarding its effectiveness is anecdotal or based on case reports (Carey & Burish, 1988; Ellis & Spanos, 1994; Manne & Andersen, 1991; Rape & Bush, 1994; Zeltzer & LeBaron, 1986). Despite imprecision in definitions, a general lack of standardized interventions, and few controlled studies, hypnosis has been found to be effective in alleviating distress associated with a number of cancer treatment procedures. (Systematic studies of behavioral interventions with pediatric oncology patients undergoing bone marrow aspiration and lumbar puncture are reviewed in Table 46.4).

In a pioneering study, Hilgard and LeBaron (1984) found that hypnosis reduced distress during bone marrow aspiration in a group of 6- to 19-year-old patients. After one hypnosis treatment session, patients experienced a 30% reduction in self-reported pain. Treatment effects were found to vary by patients' level of hypnotizability, with more hypnotizable patients experiencing greater reductions in pain and anxiety.

In a more methodologically rigorous, randomized controlled study, Kuttner, Bowman, and Teasdale (1988) investigated the relative efficacy of imaginative involvement/hypnosis as compared to both distraction and standard care. Participants were 3- to 10-year-old children identified by medical staff as having difficulty tolerating bone marrow aspirations. After one intervention session, imaginative involvement/hypnosis was determined to be better (in terms of reduction in distress) than standard care.

Multimodal Strategies With Bone Marrow Aspiration and Lumbar Puncture

Jay and her colleagues have developed a comprehensive intervention package that employs a range of techniques to reduce the pain and suffering of pediatric oncology patients during medical procedures (Jay, Elliott, Katz, & Siegel, 1987; Jay, Elliott, Ozolins, Olson, & Pruitt, 1985; Jay, Elliott, Woody, & Siegel, 1991). Their intervention package incudes various strategies such as breathing exercises, reinforcement in the form of a trophy (a prize) for lying still and doing the breathing exercises, emotive imagery, behavioral rehearsal, and modeling. Although there have been other multimodal intervention packages for reducing distress associated with lumbar puncture (e.g., Chen, Zeltzer, Craske, & Katz, 1999; McGrath & de Veber, 1986), the intervention developed by Jay and colleagues has been the most thoroughly evaluated. In a series of studies, Jay and colleagues found their intervention to be effective in reducing procedural stress for children with cancer and their parents (Jay & Elliott, 1990; Jay, Elliott, Katz, & Siegel, 1987; Jay, Elliott, Woody, & Siegel, 1991).

Medical procedures are not only potentially distressing for the children who experience them, but may also cause distress for the parents who watch their children undergo these invasive procedures. Because some parents become distressed when their children undergo medical procedures and parents influence the distress experienced by their children (Jay, Ozolins, Elliott, & Caldwell, 1983), Jay and Elliot (1990) designed and evaluated the efficacy of a multimodal intervention for parents. Parents were assigned to either accompany their child as he or she received one of two child-focused interventions or received stress inoculation training themselves. The stress inoculation program employed by Jay and Elliot (1990) included three components: modeling and education; positive self-statements; and relaxation training combined with suggestions for coping. As compared to parents in the child focused conditions, parents in the stress inoculation group reported lower state and trait anxiety and higher positive self-statements.

The work of Jay and her colleagues indicated that a multimodal intervention is effective in reducing children's distress during bone marrow aspiration and lumbar puncture (Jay, Elliott, Katz, & Siegel, 1987; Jay, Elliott, Ozolins, Olson, & Pruitt, 1985; Jay, Elliott, Woody, & Siegel, 1991). In addition, their multimodal intervention was found to be more effective than a pharmacological intervention or an attention control condition in reduction of children's behavioral distress and pain during bone marrow aspiration (Jay, Elliott, Katz, & Siegel, 1987). Adding a pharmacological treatment to the psychological intervention did not enhance the effect of the psychological intervention in reducing children's bone marrow aspiration and lumbar puncture distress (Jay, Elliott, Woody, & Siegel, 1991). Finally, an intervention for parents based on a stress inoculation training model was found to reduce parents' distress associated with their child's medical procedure (Jay & Elliott, 1990). It is important to point out that these studies did not address which aspects of the multimodal intervention package were most effective nor which components were effective for which children. The question, "Which intervention, and for whom?", needs to be addressed.

Venipuncture is frequently used for diagnostic blood tests, transfusions, bone marrow aspiration, lumbar puncture, and chemotherapy. Up to 77% of children find venipuncture distressing (Jacobsen et al., 1990). Children's apprehension concerning venipuncture can lead to muscle rigidity, making the procedure more difficult (and painful) to perform. The recent development of a local anesthetics, EMLA, may make the entire procedure less painful, thereby diminishing the need for behavioral intervention with venipuncture. However, until EMLA is more widely assessed in randomized clinical trials with children, behavioral interventions remain an important treatment option for distress associated with venipuncture. (Systematic studies of behavioral interventions with pediatric oncology patients undergoing venipuncture are reviewed in Table 46.4).

Building on the work of Dahlquist and colleagues (1985), Manne and colleagues (Manne et al., 1990; Manne, Bakeman, Jacobsen, Gorfinkle, & Redd, 1994) have obtained strong support for the efficacy of behavioral interventions in reducing distress associated with venipuncture. Their three session intervention package involves both the child and the parent and includes a combination of distraction, paced breathing, and reinforcement for the children, and instructions in behavioral coaching for the parents. During venipuncture, the child is distracted by using a party blower while the parent coaches. The parent counts out loud to pace the child's breathing into the blower and encourages the child to use it. Positive reinforcement consists of the child "winning" stickers for holding their hand still while the venipuncture is performed and for using the party blower. In randomized controlled studies, Manne and her colleagues have found that these behavioral interventions effectively reduce distress during venipuncture (1990, 1994). Particularly important for clinicians is that they demonstrated that this cost effective (e.g., use of a party blower and parent coaching) intervention reduced both children's and parents' distress. There are, however, several remaining questions, including which behavioral strategy is most ef-

Table 46.4
Behavioral Interventions for Pediatric Oncology Patients

Medical Procedure/ Authors	Sample	Research Design	Intervention	Variables	Major Results/Significant Findings
BMA Hilgard & LeBaron (1982)	N=24, 6-19 years old "chiefly forms of leukemia"; 24 had 1 intervention session, 19 had 2 or more	Baseline-posttest	Hypnosis (e.g., imaginative involvement through story telling)	Self-reported Pain (scale of 0-10 or FACES). Observer-rated Pain & Anx (scale of 0-10). Hypnotizability (Stanford Hypnotic Clinical Scale for Children; SHCSC).	1. After 1 session reduction in: self-report pain, observer rated pain, and observer rated anxiety. 2. High hypnotizablility associated w/greater decreases in pain & anxiety. 3. Additive effects of session 2 not sig. 4. Overall, the higher initial distress (pain and anxiety), the greater the likelihood of patients to participate in the intervention.
BMA & LP Zeltzer & LeBaron (1982)	N=33, 6-17 years old; 28 L, 3 NHL, 2 Neural Tumors	Repeated -Measures Factorial	Hypnosis (e.g., imagery, fantasy & deep breathing) vs. Nonhypnotic behavioral techniques (e.g., distraction & deep breathing)	Self-reported Pain & Anx (scale of 1-5). Observer-rated Pain & Anx (scale of 1-5).	1. BMA pain decreased in both groups, greater reductions in hypnosis group. 2. BMA anxiety reduced in hypnosis group. 3. LP pain decreased in hypnosis group. 4. LP anxiety reduced in both groups.
BMA & LP & Chemotherapy Injection Kellerman et al. (1983)	N=16, mean age 14.0 years, SD+ 1.6, 8 ALL, 3 AML, 2 HD & Ewing's sarcoma, 1 NHL, 1 Neurobl, 1 Osteogenic sarcoma	Baseline-posttest	Hypnosis (e.g., fantasy and relaxation)	Self-reported Anx & Discomfort (scale of 1-5). Trait Anx (State-Trait Anxiety Inventory; STAI). Self-Esteem (Rosenberg Self-Esteem Scale; RSES). Health Locus of Control (HLOC) . Illness Impact (II).	1. Reductions in anxiety & discomfort. 2. Reduction in Trait Anx.
BMA Katz et al. (1987)	N=36, 6-12 years old; 36 ALL	Repeated-measures factorial	Hypnosis (e.g., imagery, muscle relaxation, suggestion for mastery, and reentering hypnosis) vs. Nondirected Play	Observer-rated Procedural Distress (Procedural Behavioral Rating Scale-revised; PBRS-r). Nurses rating of child's Anx (scale 1-5). Self-reported Fear (FACES 1-7) & Pain (scale 0-100). Therapist rating of rapport & responsiveness to hypnosis (scale 1-5).	1. Self-rated pain & fear decreased after intervention in both groups. 2. Children who were rated as responding to the hypnosis training tended to report less fear and pain during procedure.
BMA Kuttner et al. (1988)	N=48, 3-10 years old; 48 had ALL or AML. 48 had 1 intervention session, 30 had 2nd session	Repeated-measures factorial	Hypnosis /Imaginative Involvement (e.g., imagery & direct suggestions for analgesia) vs. Distraction (e.g., younger children instructed in bubble blowing and older children in deep breathing) vs. Standard Medical Practice (control group)	Observer-rated Procedural Distress (PBRS-r). Observer-rated Anx (1-5). Observer rated Pain (1-5). Self-reported Pain & Anx (FACES 1-5).	1. At 1st intervention session, younger children (3-6 years old), who received hypnosis treatment had lower observer rated distress as compared to the other 2 groups. 2. For older children (7-10 years old) both interventions resulted in less observer rated pain and anxiety vs. the control group. 3. At 2nd intervention session, all 3 groups showed reductions in distress, pain, and anxiety, and medical staff were observed using distraction with the control group.

BMA & LP Wall & Womack (1989)	N=20, 5-18 years old; no information on cancer diagnosis	Repeated-measures factorial	Hypnosis (e.g. imagery & relaxation) & Procedural Information vs. Active Cognitive Strategy (e.g. distraction techniques) & Procedural Information	Self-reported Anticipatory Anx, Procedural Anx, & Procedural Pain (scale 1-20). State Anx (STAI). McGill Pain Questionnaire (MPQ; for 12+ year old patients). Hypnotizability (SHCSC). Level of imaginative involvement (scale 1-4). Observer- rated Procedural Pain and Anx (scale 1-20). Heart rate. Peripheral temp. (in finger).	1. Reductions in self-reported and observer rated pain in both groups. 2. Observer rated anxiety decreased in both groups.
LP McGrath & deVeber (1986)	N=14, 3-11 years old; AML or ALL	Baseline-posttest	Information, distraction, "hypnotic-like" suggestions for analgesia, imagery, relaxation, and modification of children's expectations of fear, anxiety, or pain.	Parent & Nurses rated Anx (not at all anxious to extremely anxious), Pain (no pain to intense pain), Behavioral Distress (e.g., crying), & Relaxed Behaviors (e.g., playing, remaining calm). Self-reported pain, and strength and unpleasantness of pain (FACES). Children were interviewed extensively about the procedure (e.g., about their perceived ability to control their pain & about their pain coping strategies).	1. Reductions in anxiety, pain, and distress behaviors. 2. Reductions in anxiety and pain at three-month, and six month follow ups.
LP Chen et al. (1999)	N = 50, 3-18 years old leukemia	Baseline-posttest	Memory-based intervention (memory reframing)	Self-reported anxiety and pain; (VAS); behavioral observation; physiologic measures (blood pressure and heart rate); medical chart review	1.Reduction in distress
BMA Jay et al. (1987)	N=56, 3-13 years old; 56 L	Repeated-measures counterbalanced	Multimodal, see Jay et al.(Jay, S.M., Elliott, C.H., Ozolins, M., Olson, R.A., & Pruitt, S.D. 1985) vs. Valium vs. Minimal treatment-attention control	Observer-rated Behavioral Distress (OSBD). Self-reported Pain (scale 0-100). Pulse Rate. Blood Pressure.	1. Reductions in observer rated distress, self-report of pain, and pulse rates in the behavior therapy condition as compared to the attention control condition. 2. Reductions represent 18% less behavioral distress, and 25% less self-reported pain in the behavioral treatment as compared to the attention control condition. 3. Reductions in diastolic blood pressure in the Valium condition as compared to the attention control condition.

continued on next page

Medical Procedure /Authors	Sample	Research Design	Intervention	Variables	Major Results/Significant Findings
BMA&LP Jay & Elliott (1990)	N =72 parents of L or Lymph patients 3-12 years old	Repeated-measures factorial	Stress Inoculation (e.g., filmed modeling & education, self-statement training, muscle relaxation & imagery) vs. Child focused Intervention (accompanying child in a multimodal condition or multimodal & Valium condition)	Observer-rated Parent Behavior (Parent Behavior Scale; PBS). State & Trait Anx (STAI). Pulse Rate. Blood Pressure. Self-reported Anx & Coping Difficulty. Self-statements (Self-Statement Inventory for Medical Procedures; SSIMP).	1. Lower state & trait anxiety, & higher positive self-statement scores were found for parents in the stress inoculation condition as compared to parents in the child-focused condition.
BMA&LP Jay et al. (1991)	N=83, 3.5-12 years old; 83 L or Lymph	Repeated-measures factorial	Multimodal, see Jay et al.(Jay, S.M., Elliott, C.H., Ozolins, M., Olson, R.A., & Pruitt, S.D. 1985) vs. Multimodal & Valium	Observer -rated behavioral distress (OSBD). Self-rated Pain and Fear (FACES 1-5). Pulse Rate.	1. Reductions in behavioral distress, pain ratings, and heart rate found for both groups. 2. Although not sig., reduction in behavioral distress was greater in the multimodal intervention vs. multimodal and Valium.
VP Dahlquist et al. (1985)	N=3, 11-13 years old; 3 Lymph or Osteosarcoma	Baseline-posttest	Multimodal (e.g., muscle relaxation, positive coping statements & positive reenforcement)	Observer-rated behavioral distress (OSBD). Parent- rated Child's Distress. Medical personnel-rated Child's Distress. Self-reported Distress (Scale 1-7).	1. 46% - 68% reduction in observer rated distress. 2. 9% - 22% reduction in medical personnel rated distress. 3. 0% - 67 % reduction in self-rated distress.
VP Manne et al. (1990)	N=23, 3-9 years old; 1 Neurobl, 13 L, 5 Embryonic rhabdomyosarcoma 1 Wilm's tumor, 1 Congenital immune disorder, 1 Eosnogranuloma	Repeated-measures factorial	Multimodal involves both the child and the parent (e.g. distraction, paced breathing, and reinforcement for the child, and instruction in behavioral coaching for the parents) vs. Attention control	Observer-rated Procedural Distress (modified PBRS). Self-reported Pain & Fear (FACES). Parents' self-report of their Anx and their child's Pain. Nurses report of Needle Insertion Difficulty, his/her Own Distress, and the Child's Distress (5 point scales).	1. Decreased observed child's distress, parents' rating of child's pain, and parents' own anxiety only in the intervention group. 2. Intervention was associated with reductions of physical restraint.
VP Manne et al. (1994)	N=35, 3-8 years old; 19 AL, 5 Neurobl, 2 Wilm's tumor, 2 Glioma, 2 Kostman's syndrome, 1 Embryonic Rhab-domyosarcoma, 1 HD, 2 Wiscott Aldrich syndrome, 1 Hepatoblastoma	Repeated-measures factorial	Multimodal, see Manne et al.(Manne, S.L., Redd, W.H., Jacobsen, P.B., Gorfinkle K, Schorr O, & Rapkin B. 1990) & IV Nurses Coaching of parents to coach the child vs. Multimodal without Nurses Coaching	Observer-rated Child's Distress (e.g., pain or fear, procedure noncompliance), Child's Coping (e.g., non-procedure-related activity), and Parents' Coping (scale developed by authors based in part on CAMPIS). Child's Use of Intervention Procedure. Parents' Coaching Behaviors and Parents' Praise. Nurses Coaching of Parent, Coaching of Child, and Praise.	1. Most parents and children used the intervention, and intervention use was associated with less child crying. 2. Specific directions by parents predicted the child's use of the intervention more strongly than global encouragement. 3. Nurses in the no coach condition were instructed to not coach parents, but parents in the no nurse coaching condition were coached by the nurses. 4. Nurses in both conditions were instructed not to coach children directly, but most did. 5. Children who were older and less distressed during procedure preparation were more likely to accept the intervention.

Medical Procedure /Authors	Sample	Research Design	Intervention	Variables	Major Results/Significant Findings
Chemotherapy Zeltzer, Kellerman, Ellenberg, & Dash (1983)	N=8 (3 additional participants rejected hypnosis & 1 participant didn't display chemotherapy-related symptoms) , 10-20 years old; 4 HD, 2 ANLL, 1 Neurobl, 1 Ependymoma 1 Astrocytoma, 1 Ovarian carcinoma, 1 Brain stem astrocytoma, & 1 Osteogenic sarcoma	Baseline-posttest	Hypnosis (e.g., symptom specific suggestions during imagery for "notice the cool, clean air and taste the snow", and posthypnotic suggestions for relaxation and reentering a hypnotic state)	Self-reported frequency, duration, and intensity of emesis episode (scale 1-10). Trait Anx (STAI). Self-esteem (RSES). Health Locus of Control (HLOC).Illness Impact (II). Observer-rated (parents & nurses) frequency, duration, and intensity of emesis episode (scale 1-10).	1. Reductions in self-reported frequency on emesis ranging from 19%-100%. 2. Duration of emesis was reduced in six of the eight participants. 3. Reductions in trait Anx 6 months post-intervention. 4. Four of the five participants who had taken an antiemetic (chlorpromazine) discontinued its use.
Chemotherapy Zeltzer, LeBaron & Zeltzer (1984)	N=19, 6-17 years old; 11 L, 3 Lymph, 5 Bone Tumors	Repeated-Measures Factorial	Hypnosis (e.g., imagery, and posthypnotic suggestion to have a good appetite) vs. Supportive Counseling (e.g. distraction, deep breathing, and instruction to avoid thinking about his/her symptoms)	Self-reported Nausea, Vomiting, and extent of Bother caused by these symptoms (scale of 0-10). Parent-rated Child's Nausea, Vomiting, and Bother (scale 0-10). Hypnotizability (SHCSC).	1. Reductions in nausea, vomiting, and bother in both groups. No differences between intervention groups. 2. Hypnotizability was not related to symptom reduction in the hypnosis group.
Chemotherapy LeBaron & Zeltzer (1984)	N= 8, 10-17 years old; 5 L, 1 Lymph, 2 Bone tumors	Baseline-posttest	Hypnosis, Distraction (e g., playing games), Relaxation, Reassurance & Information	Self-reported Nausea, Vomiting, and extent of Bother and Disruption of Activities caused by these symptoms (scale of 0-10). Parent-rated Child's Nausea, Vomiting, Bother, and Disruption of Actives (scale 0-10).	1. Reductions in nausea, vomiting, bother, and disruption of activities.
Chemotherapy Cotanch et al. (1985)	N=12, 10-18 years old; 8 Sarcomas, 1Testicular Seminoma, 1 Neurobl, 2 ALL	Repeated-Measures Factorial	Hypnosis (e.g., imagery, fantasy, suggestions for safety, feeling thirst) vs. Standard Procedure Control Group (e.g., comfort, deep breathing, and distraction)	Self-reported Nausea & Vomiting (e.g., severity 0-100). Nurse-rated Nausea & Vomiting (e.g., duration, amount of vomiting). Psychophysical Scaling of Child's Severity & Intensity of Nausea (adapted Pain Perception Profile, PPP). Oral Intake.	1. Reduction in frequency, amount, severity and duration of vomiting in the hypnosis group. 2. Children in the hypnosis group reported being "less bothered" by chemotherapy. 3. Children in the hypnosis group tended ($p = .071$) to have greater oral intake 24 hours post-infusion.

continued on next page

Medical Procedure /Authors	Sample	Research Design	Intervention	Variables	Major Results/Significant Findings
Chemotherapy Kolko & Rickard-Figueroa (1985)	N=3, 11-17 years old; 3 ALL	Combined Multiple-baseline & ABAB withdrawal	Distraction (i.e. played video games)	Self-reported Anticipatory Distress (24 hr. Symptom Checklist e.g., bit nails, insomnia). Self-reported & Observer-rated distress due to side-effects (e.g., distress, scale 0-4 due to dizziness, nausea). State Anx (STAI). Observer-rated distress (modified PBRS).	1. Reductions in anticipatory symptoms and state anxiety with video game use. The effect was replicated on the withdrawal and reintroduction of video game use. 2. Reductions in observer-rated distress with video game use. The effect was replicated on the withdrawal and reintroduction of video game use. 3. The introduction and withdrawal of video games produced changes (reductions and exacerbations) in postchemotherapy side effects.
Chemotherapy Redd et al (1987)	Study 1: N=26, 9-20 years old; 7L, 6 Lymph, 11 Sarcoma, 1 Teratoma, 1 Brain Tumor Study 2: N=15 of initial 26, 9-18 years old; 6 L, 4 Lymph, 1 Brain Tumor, 4 Sarcoma	Study 1: Repeated-Measures Factorial Study 2: Combined ABAB withdrawal & Repeated Measures	Distraction (played video games) vs. Control (no attempts to limit or change children's behavior)	Study 1: Self-reported Nausea (no nausea to nausea as bad as it could be). Observer - rated Nausea-related Behaviors. Study 2: Self-reported Nausea (same format as Study 1). Self-reported Anx (no anxiety to anxiety as bad as it could be). Pulse Rate. Blood Pressure.	Study 1: 1. Reductions in nausea for the intervention group. 69% of the children who played video games reported a sizable decrease in nausea vs. 23% of the children in the control group reported a similar decrease. Study 2: 1. The introduction and withdrawal of the opportunity to play video games produced changes (reduction and exacerbation, respectively) in nausea. 2. In one instance (of nine comparisons) a physiological measure changed significantly, video game playing was associated with an increase in physiological arousal (i.e. increase in systolic blood pressure). 3. Contrast groups (based on the use of antimetics) indicated that the group receiving antimetics tended to rate their nausea as more severe and to report greater changes in nausea with the withdrawal and introduction of video games.
Chemotherapy Zeltzer et al. (1991)	N=54, 5-17 years old;20 L, 34 Solid Tumor	Repeated-measures factorial	Hypnosis (e.g., fantasy, suggestions for feeling good, security, feeling hungry and wanting to socialize) vs. Active Cognitive Distraction /Relaxation (e.g. counting dots on a father's tie, deep breathing), vs. Equal amount of therapist attention (control group)	Self-reported Anticipatory Nausea & Vomiting (yes or no). Self-reported and Parent-reported Postchemotherapy Side-Effects (e.g., severity in terms of duration of nausea and vomiting on a scale from 0 - 10). Distress (indicated by how much chemotherapy bothered the child. Functional Disfunction (e.g., days of disruption of school and social activities).	1. Shorter duration of nausea in both intervention groups vs. the control group. 2. Shorter duration of vomiting in the hypnosis vs. control group. 3. In general, side-effects for the hypnosis group improved over time, for the active cognitive distraction/relaxation group side-effects improved slightly or stayed the same, and for the control group they got worse. 4. Functional disfunction (e.g., in school, social, eating and sleeping) was determined by emetic potential of chemotherapy and total symptom score was predicted by emetic potential and prophylactic antimetics.

Chemotherapy Jacknow et al. (1994)	N=20, 6-18 years old; 5 L, 8 HL, 7 Solid Tumors	Repeated-measures factorial	Hypnosis (e.g., imaginative involvement, suggestions for feeling safe and well, for turning off the vomiting-control center in the brain) & p.r.n. antiemetics vs. Equal amount of therapist attention & Standard Antiemetic Regimen (control group)	Self-reported Nausea (five faces). Vomiting (frequency scale 0-9). Practice of Hypnosis (for the intervention group). Antiemetic Medication Use (from medical records).	1. The hypnosis group used less p.r.n. medication. 2. At 1 to 2 months postdiagnosis, the hypnosis group experienced less anticipatory nausea, but no significant differences were found at 4-6 months postdiagnosis.
Social Reintegration Varni, Katz, Colegrove & Dolgin (1993)	N=64, 5-13 years old; 36 ALL, 7 HD, 2 NHL, 3 Wilm's tumor, 3 Neurobl, 4 Rhabdomyo-sarcoma, 1 Osteogenic sarcoma, 1 Ewing's sarcoma, 2 Brain tumor, 5 Other	Repeated-measures factorial	Multimodal Behavioral (e.g., modeling and cue-controlled relaxation) & Standard Intervention vs. Standard Intervention	Self-reported depression (CDI), anxiety (STAIC), general self-esteem (SPPC), and perceived social support (SSSC). Parent-reported behavioral and emotional problems and social competence (CBCL).	1. Nine moths post-intervention the Behavioral Intervention group displayed fewer behavioral problems, experienced increased school competence, and reported greater social and emotional support from classmates and teachers compared to pre-intervention. No such differences were found in the Standard Intervention group.

Table 4 Abbreviations

Disease

L =Leukemia
AL =Acute leukemia
ALL =Acute lymphocytic leukemia
AML =Acute myelogenous leukemia
ANLL =Acute nonlymphocytic leukemia
HD =Hodgkin's disease
Lymph =Lymphoma
Neurobl =Neuroblastoma
NHL =Non-Hodgkin's lymphoma

Procedures

BMA=Bone Marrow Aspiration
LP= Lumbar Puncture
VP=Venipuncture

Measures

Anx=Anxiety
CAMPIS=Child-Adult Medical Procedure Interaction Scale [Blount et al.]
CDI =Children's Depression Inventory [Kovacs]
CBCL=Child behavior Checklist [Achenbach]
FACES= Faces Scale, a set of face drawings [LeBaron & Zeltzer, Katz et al.]
HLOC=Health Locus of Control Scale [Wallston et al.]
II=Illness Impact [Zeltzer et al.]
MPQ=McGill Pain Questionnaire [Melzack]
OSBD=Observation Scale of Behavioral Distress [Jay et al.]
PBRS=Procedural Behavior Rating Scale [Katz]
PBRS-r=Procedural Behavior Rating Scale-Revised [Katz et al.]
PBS=Parent Behavior Scale [Jay & Woody]
SHCSC=Stanford Hypnotic Clinical Scale of Children [Morgan & Hilgard]
SSIMP=Self-Statement Inventory for Medical Procedures [Jay & Elliott]
SSSC=Social Support Scale for Children [Harter]
SPPC=Self-Perception Profile for Children [Harter]
STAI=State-Trait Anxiety Inventory [Spielberger]
STAIC=State-Trait Anxiety Inventory for Children [Spielberger]
RSES=Rosenberg Self-Esteem Scale [Rosenberg]

Adapted from DuHamel, K. N., Vickberg, S.M.J., & Redd, W. H. (1998). Behavioral interventions pediatric oncology. In J. Holland, W. Breitbart, P. Jacobsen, M. Lederberg, M. Loscalzo, M. J. Massie, & R. McCorkle (Eds.), *Handbook of psycho-oncology: Psychological care of the patient with cancer* (pp. 161-172). New York: Oxford.

fective for reducing venipuncture distress, an intervention package such as that developed by Manne and colleagues or an intervention such as those used with bone marrow aspiration and lumbar puncture, which also included hypnosis.

Treatment side effects can be severe with pediatric patients. In addition to pain and anxiety associated with medical procedures, patients often have problems related to treatment side effects. Aggressive treatments using multimodal therapy such as surgery, radiation, and chemotherapy can lead to a variety of aversive side effects. With several chemotherapeutic agents and radiation, patients often experience fatigue, diarrhea, hair loss, and post-treatment nausea. The most common side effects associated with cancer chemotherapy are nausea, vomiting, and dysphoria. After repeated chemotherapy treatments some patients develop anticipatory nausea, that is, they become nauseated in anticipation of treatment. Like the conditioned reflex of Pavlov's dogs (Pavlov, 1927), the patient's nausea in response to conditioned stimuli, such as the site of the clinic, can be as intense as unconditioned responses elicited by actual treatment (Redd, Andresen, & Minagawa, 1982). Although the prevalence of nausea and vomiting reported in the literature varies, up to 71.2% of children receiving chemotherapy have been reported to have nausea during chemotherapy, and up to 76% of children have been reported to have anticipatory nausea (Dolgin, Katz, McGinty, & Siegel, 1985; Hockenberry-Eaton & Benner, 1990; Jacknow, Tschann, Link, & Boyce, 1994; Zeltzer, Dolgin, LeBaron, & LeBaron, 1991). In addition, up to 43% of children have been reported to have anticipatory vomiting (Zeltzer, Dolgin, S. LeBaron, & C. LeBaron, 1991). Although antiemetic medications have had some success in treating nausea and vomiting during chemotherapy, they are not effective for anticipatory symptoms. Further, antiemetic use can result in multiple side effects such as headache and extrapyramidal reactions (Jacknow, Tschann, Link, & Boyce, 1994). In young children, severe nausea and vomiting can also lead to dehydration, electrolyte imbalance, and weight loss (Hockenberry-Eaton & Benner, 1990). Compounding the issues surrounding side effects and quality of life, some patients' treatment can be so aversive that they become noncompliant with treatment regimes, leading to increased morbidity and mortality (Burish, Carey, Krozely, & Greco, 1987).

Hypnosis and/or distraction for control of nausea and vomiting has received considerable clinical and research attention. Most of the studies have focused on adult cancer patients. Behavioral methods studied with children have been generally limited to hypnosis and/or distraction and most involve a single participant, not comparisons of intervention groups (Carey & Burish, 1988). (Systematic studies of behavioral interventions for treatment side effects with pediatric oncology patients are reviewed in Table 46.3).

In a group of 10- to 17-year-old patients, LeBaron and Zeltzer (1984) assessed the efficacy of a behavioral intervention for reducing nausea and vomiting during chemotherapy. The behavioral intervention package included directing the child's attention away from thoughts about the chemotherapy by playing games, focusing on a object in the room, telling stories, and using muscle relaxation. Reassurance and information were also provided. The results indicated that after the intervention, there were reductions in children's disruption of activities, nausea, vomiting, and the difficulties these symptoms caused. However, the lack of a control group makes the benefits of the behavioral strategies over nonspecific factors, such as reassurance or simply the passage of time, difficult to evaluate. Despite this study limitation, this classic study provided preliminary results suggesting that a behavioral intervention package was effective in reducing treatment side effects.

Cognitive/attentional distraction through video game playing to control anticipatory nausea in a group of 9- to 20-year-old cancer patients was assessed in two studies conducted by Redd and colleagues (Redd et al., 1987). In both studies there was a marked (up to 69%) reduction in nausea. In a subsequent study Zeltzer et al. (1991) investigated the relative efficacy of a hypnosis intervention as compared to a nonhypnotic distraction/relaxation intervention, and a standard control group in children 5 to 17 years of age. Their results suggested that hypnosis was superior to the nonhypnotic distraction/relaxation intervention in reducing chemotherapy side effects.

A recent study by Jacknow and colleagues (1994) evaluated the efficacy of hypnosis to control nausea and antiemetics in a group of 6- to 18-year-old newly diagnosed cancer patients. Not only did the children in the hypnosis group experience less anticipatory nausea then those in the standard care comparison group, they also used less antiemetic medication that was prescribed to be taken as they felt it was needed. The results also indicated the need to maintain active patient intervention throughout the child's treatment course. Beneficial effects were observed at 1 and 2 month post hypnotic intervention, but not at 6 months.

It is difficult to draw clear conclusions regarding the relative efficacy of hypnosis versus distraction in the control of chemotherapy side effects in children. The problem is that the procedures (i.e., counting the dots on their father's tie and completing arithmetic problems) used by Zelter and colleagues (1991) may be far less effective for distracting children than the video games procedures used by Redd and colleagues (1987). Further research is needed to define the parameters of hypnosis, cognitive/attention distraction, and relaxation training in the control of treatment side effects.

Post-treatment adjustment has received increased attention during the last five years. Indeed, in addition to coping with the distress associated with medical procedures and treatment side effects, children with cancer must confront other challenges, such as re-entering the school environment after diagnosis. Returning to school and resuming normal interactions with peers is an important process for the child who has been diagnosed with cancer. Based on the notion that an early return to school can "normalize" the child's life in the midst of coping with cancer, thus promoting optimal rehabilitation, several authors have recommended re-entry into the school environment as soon as possible for pediatric cancer patients (Deasy-Spinetta & Spinetta, 1980; Katz, Dolgin, & Varni, 1990; Lansky, Cairns, & Zwartjes, 1983). In addition to normalizing life and encouraging rehabilitation, a prompt return to school can provide opportunities for social support (from peers and teachers) and exposure to socialization processes typically experienced by school-aged children. Such access to social support and socialization experiences may be crucial for proper adjustment. Indeed, positive peer relationships and perceived social support are associated with several positive corollaries, such as increased stress resistance, improved academic achievement, decreased levels of behavioral problems, and pro-social behaviors in general (Green, Forehand, Beck, & Vosk, 1980; Varni, Katz, Colegrove, & Dolgin, 1993).

Clinical researchers have only recently begun to explore the use of multimodal interventions to promote post-treatment adjustment. Varni and his colleagues (1993) assessed the relative efficacy of a social skills training intervention as compared to a standard school reintegration program with 5 to 13 year old children with cancer. Both groups received the Standard Intervention, which included: (1) education for patients, parents, school and medical staff emphasizing the importance of an early return to school; (2) school conferences and classroom presentations intended to demystify the cancer experience for both teachers and classmates; and (3) regular follow-ups with patients, parents, teachers, classmates, and medical staff. The Behavioral Intervention Group also received the multimodal social skills training (e.g., modeling and cue-controlled relaxation), while the Standard Care Intervention Group spent equal time in individual play interaction with the research assistant. Results indicate that nine months after completing the intervention, pediatric cancer patients in the Behavioral Intervention condition experienced fewer behavioral problems and increased school competence (as reported by their parents). In addition, these children reported experiencing greater emotional and social support from their classmates and teachers after completing the multimodal intervention. Children receiving standard care did not experience these positive changes. Results of this initial study are quite important as they indicate that behavioral techniques are useful tools for teaching social skills and that the acquisition of such skills has a positive effect on pediatric adjustment.

FUTURE DIRECTIONS

The clinical research reviewed in this chapter clearly indicates the utility of behavioral interventions to reduce the pain and suffering of cancer patients. Hypnosis, distraction, and multimodal interventions have been found to effectively reduce distress associated with medical procedures, and hypnosis and distraction were found to reduce treatment side effects. In addition, a multimodal behavioral intervention has been effectively used to improve adjustment and overall quality of life.

It is always difficult to predict future advances in clinical research. However, there are a number of important new trends. The first is the shift towards greater sophistication in research methodology. For example, the earlier studies generally lacked appropriate comparison groups, making the effect of the specific intervention as compared to nonspecific factors or time difficult to assess. More recent studies have included standard care comparison groups, in addition to two treatment groups, making examination of the mechanisms underlying treatment effectiveness possible (e.g., comparing distraction through hypnosis with distraction through focusing on objects in the room). Second, there has been increased interest in training family members and other health care providers to provide behavioral interventions in the hope of adding to the benefits of interventions provided by trained professionals. Third, behavioral interventions are also being applied to new areas outside of symptom management, for example, to facilitate school reintegration. In addition, there is recent work involving the application of both behavioral interventions and cognitive remediation for neuropsychological (attention difficulties) deficits (Butler, 1996).

There also are new problem areas currently being identified that may benefit from application of behavioral interventions, such as other medical procedures (e.g., bone marrow transplant; BMT), cancer related fatigue, and symptoms of posttraumatic stress disorder (PTSD), such as night terrors. There has been research documenting that BMT is a stressful experience for oncology patients and their families, and that BMT may be associated with PTSD (Lee, Cohen, Stuber, & Nader, 1994; Smith, Redd, DuHamel, Vickberg, & Ricketts, 1999; Stuber, Nader, Yasuda, Pynoos, & Cohen, 1991). In addition, PTSD and fatigue have been documented in adult cancer survivors (Alter et al., 1996; Piper, 1996), and behavioral interventions are being used to help adults cope with these difficulties (Piper, 1994; Shalev, Bonne, & Eth, 1996). Cancer survivors with PTSD symptoms and/or fatigue, may also benefit from behavioral intervention to reduce these difficulties; this is an area for future research.

One of the main thrusts of future work may well be the application of behavioral theory and research to prevent adjustment problems. For example, how can chemotherapy be given so as to reduce the development of aversive side effects, such as food aversions? We do not mean to suggest that behavioral interventions are a panacea for all the challenges faced by oncology patients. Nor are we suggesting that behavioral interventions be used exclusively, but rather as adjunctive treatments to other biological and psychosocial interventions. Indeed, there are limits to the application of behavioral principles, such as challenges to family adaptation. As noted by Ostroff and Steinglass (1996), there are challenges experienced by most families of children with cancer, such as the family's need to change and adjust to the different stages of the child's illness (e.g., from illness-focus during acute phase to post-treatment readjustment). These areas of potential difficulty faced by families of cancer patients are outside the realm of behavioral interventions and may be more effectively treated by family therapy interventions designed specifically to address them (Ostroff & Steinglass, 1996). In addition, there are many factors (i.e., cultural influences) that may contribute to the patient's and their families adjustment, or lack thereof, which are also outside the realm of behavioral principles.

Given the limits in theory and application, it is clear that behavioral researchers and clinicians have made a significant contribution to our understanding of patients' responses to cancer diagnosis, treatment, and rehabilitation, and to the design of effective methods for reducing pediatric patients' distress. The strength of the work that has been conducted leads one to expect important advances in the future.

REFERENCES

Ahles, T. A. (1987). Psychological techniques for the management of cancer-related pain. In D. B. McGuire & C. H. Yarbro (Eds.), *Cancer pain management* (pp. 245–258). Orlando, FL: Grune and Stratton.

Alter, C. L., Pelcovitz, D., Axelrod, A., Goldenberg, B., Harris, H., Meyers, B., Grobois, B., Mandel, F., Septimus, A., & Kaplan, S. (1996). Identification of PTSD in cancer survivors. *Psychosomatics, 37,* 137–143.

Barlow, D. H., & Cerny, J. A. (1988). *Psychological treatment of panic.* New York: Guilford.

Burish, T. G., Carey, M. P., Krozely, M. G., & Greco, A. (1987). Conditioned side effects induced by cancer chemotherapy: Prevention through behavioral treatment. *Journal of Consulting and Clinical Psychology, 55,* 42–48.

Burish, T. G., & Lyles, J. N. (1981). Effectiveness of relaxation training in reducing adverse reactions to cancer chemotherapy. *Journal of Behavioral Medicine, 4,* 65–78.

Burish, T. G., Snyder, S. L., & Jenkins, R. A. (1991). Preparing patients for cancer chemotherapy: Effect of coping preparation and relaxation interventions. *Journal of Consulting and Clinical Psychology, 59,* 518–525.

Butler, R. (1996). Cognitive remediation of attentional deficits and non-verbal learning disabilities following childhood CNS disease. *Journal of the International Neuropsychology Abstracts,* 2(1), 18.

Cain, E. N., Kohorn, E. I., Quinlan, D. M., Latimer, K., & Schwartz, P. E. (1986). Psychosocial benefits of a cancer support group. *Cancer, 57,* 183–189.

Carey, M. P., & Burish, T. G. (1988). Etiology and treatment of the psychological side effects associated with cancer chemotherapy. A critical review and discussion. *Psychological Bulletin, 104,* 307–325.

Cella, D. F. (1993). Quality of life as an outcome of cancer treatment. In S. L. Groenwald, M. Goodman, M. H. Frogge, & C. H. Yargro (Eds.), *Cancer nursing: Principles and practice.* Boston: Jones and Bartlett.

Chen, E., Zeltzer, K., Craske, M. G., & Katz, E. R. (1999). Alteration of memory in the reduction of children's distress repeated aversive medical procedures. *Journal of Consulting and Clinical Psychology, 67,* 481–490.

Cobb, S. C. (1984). Teaching relaxation techniques to cancer patients. *Cancer Nursing, 7,* 157–162.

Coluzzi, P. H., Grant, M., Doroshow, J. H., Rhiner, M., Ferrell, B., & Rivera, L. (1995). Survey of the provision of supportive care services at National Cancer Institute-designated cancer centers. *Journal of Clinical Oncology, 13,* 756–764.

Cotanch, P., Hockenberry, M., & Herman, S. (1985). Self-hypnosis antiemetic therapy in children receiving chemotherapy. *Oncolgy Nursing Forum, 12*(4), 41–46.

Dahlquist, L. M., Gil, K. M., Armstrong, D., Ginsberg, A., & Jones, B. (1985). Behavioral management of children's distress during chemotherapy. *Journal of Behavior Therapy and Experimental Psychiatry, 16,* 325–329.

Deasy-Spinetta, P., & Spinetta, J. J. (1980). The child with cancer in school: Teacher's appraisal. *American Journal of Pediatric Hematology/Oncology, 2,* 89–94.

Derogatis, L. R., Morrow, G. R., & Fetting, J. (1983). The prevalence of psychiatric disorders among cancer patients. *Journal of the American Medical Association, 249,* 751–757.

Dolgin, M. J., Katz, E. R., McGinty, K., & Siegel, S. E. (1985). Anticipatory nausea and vomiting in pediatric cancer patients. *Pediatrics, 75,* 547–552.

DuHamel, K. N., Vickberg, S.M.J., & Redd, W. H. (1998). Behavioral interventions pediatric oncology. In J. Holland, W. Breitbart, P. Jacobsen, M. Lederberg, M. Loscalzo, M. J. Massie, & R. McCorkle (Eds.), *Handbook of psycho-oncology: Psychological care of the patient with cancer* (pp. 161–172). New York: Oxford.

Ellis, J. A., & Spanos, N. P. (1994). Cognitive-behavioral interventions for children's distress during bone marrow aspirations and lumbar punctures: A critical review. *Journal of Pain and Symptom Management, 9*(2), 96–108.

Fawzy, F. I., Fawzy, N. W., & Kemeny, M. E. (1990). A structured psychiatric intervention for cancer patients. I. Changes over time in methods of coping and affective disturbance. *Archives of General Psychiatry, 47,* 720–725.

Fishman, B., & Loscalzo, M. (1987). Cognitive-behavioral interventions in management of cancer pain: Principles and applications. *Medical Clinics of North America, 71,* 271–287.

Gambino, S. R. (1989). Diagnostic tests and procedures. In D. F. Tapley, T. Q. Morris, L. P. Rowland, R. J. Weiss, G. J. Subak-Sharpe, & D. M. Goetz (Eds.), *The Columbia University college of physicians and surgeons complete home medical guide.* New York: Crown.

Green, K. D., Forehand, R., Beck, S. J., & Vosk, B. (1980). An assessment of the relationship among measures of children's social competence and children's academic achievement. *Child Development, 51,* 1149–1156.

Greer, S., Moorey, S., & Baruch, J.D.R. (1992). Adjuvant psychological therapy for patients with cancer: a prospective randomised trial. *BMJ, 304,* 675–680.

Heinrich, R. L., & Schag, C. C. (1985). Stress and activity management: Group treatment for cancer patients and spouses. *Journal of Consulting and Clinical Psychology, 53,* 439–446.

Hilgard, E. R. (1975). *Hypnosis in the relief of pain.* Los Altos, CA: William Kaufman.

Hilgard, J. R., & LeBaron, S. (1982). Relief of anxiety and pain in children and adolescents with cancer: Quantitative measures and clinical observation. *International Journal of Clinical and Experimental Hypnosis, 4,* 417–442.

Hilgard, J. R., & LeBaron, S. (1984). *Hypnotherapy of Pain in Children with Cancer.* Los Altos, California: William Kaufmann.

Hockenberry-Eaton, M., & Benner, A. (1990). Patterns of nausea and vomiting in children: Nursing assessment and intervention. *Oncology Nursing Forum, 17*(4), 575–584.

Jacknow, D. S., Tschann, J. M., Link, M. P., & Boyce, W. T. (1994). Hypnosis in the prevention of chemotherapy-related nausea and vomiting in children: A prospective study. *Journal of Developmental and Behavioral Pediatrics, 15,* 258–264.

Jacobsen, P. B., & Redd, W. H. (1988). The development and management of chemotherapy-related anticipatory nausea and vomiting. *Cancer Investigation, 6,* 329–336.

Jacobsen, P. B., Manne, S. L., Gorfinkle K, Schorr O, Rapkin B, & Redd, W. H. (1990). Analysis of child and parent behavior during painful medical procedures. *Health Psychology, 9(5),* 559–576.

Jay, S. M., & Elliott, C. H. (1990). A stress inoculation program for parents whose children are undergoing painful medical procedures. *Journal of Consulting and Clinical Psychology, 58*(6), 799–804.

Jay, S. M., Elliott, C. H., Katz, E., & Siegel, S. E. (1987). Cognitive-behavioral and pharmacological interventions for children's distress during painful medical procedures. *Journal of Consulting and Clinical Psychology, 55,* 860–865.

Jay, S. M., Elliott, C. H., Ozolins, M., Olson, R. A., & Pruitt, S. D. (1985). Behavioral management of children's distress during painful medical procedures. *Behavior Research and Therapy, 23,* 513–520.

Jay, S. M., Elliott, C. H., Woody, P. D., & Siegel, S. (1991). An investigation of cognitive-behavior therapy combined with oral Valium for children undergoing painful medical procedures. *Health Psychology, 10*(5), 317–322.

Jay, S. M., Ozolins, M., Elliott, C., & Caldwell, S. (1983). Assessment of children's distress during painful medical procedures. *Journal of Health Psychology, 2,* 133–147.

Katz, E. R., Dolgin, M. J., & Varni, J. W. (1990). Cancer in Children and Adolescents. In A. M. Gross & R. S. Drabman (Eds.), *Handbook of clinical behavioral pediatrics* (pp. 129–146). New York: Plenum.

Katz, E. R., Kellerman, J., & Ellenberg, L. (1987). Hypnosis in the reduction of acute pain and distress in children with cancer. *Journal of Pediatric Psychology, 12*(3), 379–394.

Katz, E. R., Kellerman, J., & Siegel, S. E. (1980). Behavioral distress in children with cancer undergoing medical procedures: Developmental considerations. *Journal of Consulting and Clinical Psychology, 3,* 356–365.

Keefe, F. J., Dunsmore J., & Burnett R. (1992). Behavioral and cognitive-behavioral approaches to chronic pain: Recent advances and future directions. *Journal of Consulting and Clinical Psychology, ,* 528–536.

Kellerman, J., Zeltzer, L., Ellenberg, L., & Dash, J. (1983). Hypnosis for the reduction of acute pain and anxiety associated with medical procedures. *Journal of Adolescent Health Care, 4,* 85–90.

Kolko, D. J., & Rickard-Figueroa, J. L. (1985). Effects of video games on the adverse corollaries of chemotherapy in pediatric oncology patients:A single-case analysis. *Journal of Consulting and Clinical Psychology, 53,* 223–228.

Kuttner, L., Bowman, M., & Teasdale, M. (1988). Psychological treatment of distress, pain, and anxiety for young children with cancer. *Journal of Developmental and Behavioral Pediatrics, 9*(6), 374–382.

Lansky, S. B., Cairns, N. U., & Zwartjes, W. (1983). School attendance among children with cancer: A report from two centers. *Journal of Psychosocial Oncology, 1,* 72–82.

LeBaron, S., & Zeltzer, L. K. (1984). Behavioral intervention for reducing chemotherapy-related nausea and vomiting in adolescents with cancer. *Journal of Adolescent Health Care, 5,* 178–182.

Lee, M. L., Cohen, S. E., Stuber, M. L., & Nader, K. (1994). Parent-Child interactions with pediatric bone marrow transplant patients. *Journal of Psychosocial Oncology, 12*(4), 43–59.

Lerman, C., Rimer, B., Blumberg, B., Cristinzio, S., Engstrom, P. F., MacElwee, N., & Seay, J. (1990). Effects of coping style and relaxation on cancer chemotherapy side effects and emotional responses. *Cancer Nursing, 13,* 308–315.

Loscalzo, M., & Jacobsen, P. B. (1990). Practical behavioral approaches to the effective management of pain and distress. *Journal of Psychosocial Oncology, 8,* 139–169.

Lyles, J. M., Burish, T. G., Krzely, M. G., Oldham, R. K., Masters, J. C., Hollon, S. D., & Rimm, D. C. (1982). Efficacy of relaxation training and guided imagery in reducing the aversiveness of cancer chemotherapy. *Journal of Consulting and Clincal Psychology, 50,* 509–524.

Manne, S., & Andersen, B. (1991). Pain and pain-related distress in pediatric cancer patients. In J. Bush & S. Harkins (Eds.), *Pain in children: Clinical and research issues from a developmental perspective.* New York: Springer-Verlag.

Manne, S., Bakeman, R., Jacobsen, P., Gorfinkle, K., & Redd, W. H. (1994). An analysis of an intervention to reduce children's distress during venipuncture. *Health Psychology, 13,* 556–566.

Manne, S. L., Redd, W. H., Jacobsen, P. B., Gorfinkle, K., Schorr, O., & Rapkin, B. (1990). Behavioral intervention to reduce child and parent distress during venipuncture. *Journal of Consulting and Clinical Psychology, 58,* 565–572.

Margolis, C. G. (1985). Hypnotic interventions for pain management. *International Journal of Psychosomatics, 32,* 12–19.

McGrath, P. A., & de Veber, L. L. (1986). The management of acute pain evoked by medical procedures in children with cancer. *Journal of Pain and Symptom Management, 1,* 145–150.

Meichenbaum, D. (1985). *Stress inoculation training.* Elmsford, New York: Pergamon.

Meyer, T. J., & Mark, M. M. (1995). Effects of psychosocial interventions with adult cancer patients: A meta-analysis of randomized experiments. *Health Psychology, 14,* 101–108.

Millard, R. W. (1993). Behavioral assessment of pain and behavioral pain management. In Patt, R. B. (Ed.), *Cancer Pain.* (pp. 85–97). Philadelphia: Lippincott.

Moorey, S., Greer, S., Watson, M., Baruch, J.D.R., Robertson, B. M., Mason, A., Rowden, L., Runmore, R., Law, M., & Bliss, J. M. (1994). Adjuvant psychological therapy for patients with cancer: Outcome at one year. *Psycho-Oncology, 3,* 39–46.

Morrow, G. R., Asbury, R., Hammon, S., Dobkin, P., Caruso, L., & Pandya, K. (1992). Comparing the effectiveness of behavioral treatment for chemotherapy-induced nausea and vomiting when administered by oncologists, oncology nurses, and clinical psychologists. *Health Psychology, 11,* 250–256.

Morrow, G. R., & Morrell B. S. (1982). Behavioral treatment for the anticipatory nausea and vomiting induced by cancer chemotherapy. *New England Journal of Medicine, 207,* 1476–1480.

Nesse, R. M., Carli, T., Curtis, G. G., & Kleinman, P. D. (1980). Pre-treatment nausea in cancer chemotherapy: A conditioned response? *Psychosomatic Medicine, 42,* 33–36.

Osoba, D. (1994). Lessons learned from measuring health-related quality of life in oncology. *Journal of Clinical Oncology, 12,* 608–616.

Ostroff, J., & Steinglass, P. (1996). Psychosocial adaptation following treatment: A family systems perspective on childhood cancer survivorship. In L. Baider, C. L. Cooper, & A. Kaplan De-Nour (Eds.), *Cancer and the family.* New York: Wiley.

Pavlov, I. P. (1927). *Conditioned refexes: An investigation of pysiological activity of the cerebral cortex (Lecture III).* Oxford, England: Oxford University Press.

Piper, B. F. (1994). Hints on how to combat fatigue. In M. Dollinger, E. H. Rosenbaum, & G. Cable (Eds.), *Everyone's guide to cancer therapy.* Kansas City: Somerville House.

Piper, B. F. (1996). Measuring fatigue. In M. Stromborg & S. Olson (Eds.), *Instruments for clinical research in health care.* Philadelphia: Saunders.

Rape, R. N., & Bush, J. P. (1994). Psychological preparation for pediatric oncology patients undergoing painful procedures: A methodological critique of the research. *Children's Health Care, 23*(1), 51–67.

Redd, W. H., & Andresen, G. V. (1981). Conditioned aversion in cancer patients. *The Behavior Therapist, 4,* 3–4.

Redd, W. H., Andresen, G. V., & Minagawa, R. Y. (1982). Hypnotic control of anticipatory emesis in patients receiving cancer chemotherapy. *Journal of Consulting and Clinical Psychology, 50,* 14–19.

Redd, W. H., Jacobsen, P. B., Die-Trill, M., Dermatis, H., McEvoy, M., & Holland, J. C. (1987). Cognitive/attentional distraction in the control of conditioned nausea in pediatric cancer patients receiving chemotherapy. *Journal of Consulting & Clinical Psychology, 55,* 391–395.

Shalev, A. Y., Bonne, O., & Eth, S. (1996). Treatment of Posttraumatic Stress Disorder: A review. *Psychosomatic Medicine, 58,* 165–182.

Skinner, B. F. (1953). *Science and human behavior.* New York: Macmillan.

Sloman, R., Brown, P., Aldana, E., & Chee, E. (1994). The use of relaxation for the promotion of comfort and pain relief in persons with advanced cancer. *Contemporary Nurse, 3,* 6–12.

Smith, M. Y., Redd, W., DuHamel, K. N., Vickberg, S. J., & Ricketts, P. (1999). Validation of the posttraumatic stress disorder checklist-civilian in survivors of bone marrow transplantation. *Journal of Traumatic Stress, 12*(3), 485–499.

Spiegel, D., Bloom, H. C., Kraemer, J. R., & Gottheil, E. (1989). Effect of psychosocial treatment on survival of patients with metastatic breast cancer. *The Lancet, 2,* (8668), 888–901.

Spiegel, D., & Bloom, J. R. (1983). Group therapy and hypnosis reduce metastatic breast carcinoma pain. *Psychosomatic Medicine, 45,* 333–339.

Stuber, M. L., Nader, K., Yasuda, P., Pynoos, R. S., & Cohen, S. (1991). Stress responses after pediatric bone marrow transplantation: Preliminary results of a prospective longitudinal study. *Journal of the American Academy of Child and Adolescent Psychiatry, 30*(6), 952–957.

Syrjala, K. L., Cummings, C., & Donaldson, G. (1992). Hypnosis or cognitive-behavioral training for the reduction of pain and nausea during cancer treatment: A controlled clinical trial. *Pain, 48,* 137–146.

Syrjala, K. L., Donaldson, G. W., Davis, M. W., Kippes M. E., & Carr, J. E. (1995). Relaxation and imagery and cognitive-behavioral training reduce pain during cancer treatment: A controlled clinical trial. *Pain, 63,* 189–198.

Telch, C. F., & Telch, M. J. (1986). Group coping skills instruction and supportive group therapy for cancer patients: a comparison of strategies. *Journal of Consulting and Clinical Psychology, 54*(6), 802–808.

Turk, D. C., Meichenbaum, D., & Genest, M. (1983). *Pain and behavioral medicine: A cognitive-behavioral perspective.* New York: Guilford.

Turk, D. C., & Rennert, K. (1981). Pain and the terminally ill cancer patient: a cognitive-social learning perspective. In H. J. Sobel (Ed.), *Behavior therapy in terminal care: A humanistic approach.* Cambridge, MA: Ballinger.

Varni, J. W., Katz, E. R., Colegrove, R. J., & Dolgin, M. (1993). The impact of social skills training on the adjustment of children with newly diagnosed cancer. *Journal of Pediatric Psychology, 18,* 751–767.

Vasterling, J., Jenkins, R. A., Tope, D. M., & Burish, T. G. (1993). Cognitive distraction and relaxation training for the control of side effects due to cancer chemotherapy. *Journal of Behavioral Medicine, 16,* 65–80.

Wall, V. J., & Womack, W. (1989). Hypnotic versus active cognitive strategies for alleviation of procedural distress in pediatric oncology patients. *American Journal of Clinical Hypnosis, 31*(3), 181–190.

Worden, J. W., & Weisman, A. (1984). Preventive psychosocial intervention with newly diagnosed cancer patients. *General Hospital Psychiatry, 6,* 243–249.

Zeltzer, L. K., Altman, A., Cohen, D., LeBaron, S., Munuksela, E. L., & Schechter, N. L. (1990). Report of the subcommittee on the management of pain associated with procedures in children with cancer. *Pediatrics, 86,* 826–831.

Zeltzer, L. K., Dolgin, M. J., LeBaron, S., & LeBaron, C. (1991). A randomized, controlled study of behavioral intervention for chemotherapy distress in children with cancer. *Pediatrics, 88,* 34–42.

Zeltzer, L., Kellerman, J., Ellenberg, L., & Dash, J. (1983). Hypnosis for reduction of vomiting associated with chemotherapy and disease in adolescents with cancer. *Journal of Adolescent Health Care, 4,* 77–84.

Zeltzer, L., & LeBaron, S. (1982). Hypnosis and nonhypnotic techniques for reduction of pain and anxiety during painful procedures in children and adolescents with cancer. *Journal of Pediatrics, 101,* 1032–1035.

Zeltzer, L., & LeBaron, S. (1986). The hypnotic treatment of children in pain. *Advances in Developmental and Behavioral Pediatrics, 7,* 197–234.

Zeltzer, L. K., LeBaron, S., & Zeltzer, P. (1984). The effectiveness of behavioral intervention for reducing nausea and vomiting in children receiving chemotherapy. *Journal of Clinical Oncology, 2*(6), 683–689.

47

Frontiers in the Behavioral Epidemiology of HIV/STDs

Joseph A. Catania

Diane Binson

M. Margaret Dolcini

Judith Tedlie Moskowitz

Ariane van der Straten

University of California, San Francisco

This chapter discusses the field of HIV/STD behavioral epidemiology with a special emphasis on heterosexual adults.[1] We have limited our review of the extensive HIV-behavioral epidemiological literature to include an in-depth examination of the following topic areas considered pivotal to understanding the spread of HIV/STDs. The topic areas, including sexual mixing and networks, mapping risk behavior, and the conceptualization of the several dimensions related to sexual relationships, parallel the following general aims (listed later) of the field (Catania & Binson, 1992; Catania et al., 1993; Dolcini, Coates, Catania, Kegeles, & Hauck, 1995): (a) prevention behaviors and beliefs (mapping studies), and assessment of how these change over time; (b) identification of social vectors related to the spread and prevention of HIV/STDs (e.g., how people within a particular social stratum sexually interact with other social strata); and (c) development of explanatory models for understanding onset, maintenance, and change in the patterns of behavior related to HIV/STD transmission. In short, the primary goals of behavioral epidemiology are to predict potential routes of future disease spread, target population segments for prevention, and generate an understanding of the causes of safe and unsafe behaviors.

Prior work on the first two aims includes research on the geography of disease spread (e.g., Golub, Gorr, & Gould, 1993; Wallace, 1991, 1994), studies on the risk behaviors of travelers (e.g., Choi, Catania, Coates, Hyung, & Hearst, 1992), research on sexual networks (e.g., Service & Blower, 1995), and at the population level, investigations of the size and characteristics of at risk populations with respect to HIV testing, condom use, and risk practices (e.g., Catania, Binson, et al., 1995; Catania, Stone, Binson, & Dolcini, 1995).

There have been a number of national and urban surveys on aspects of the behavioral epidemiology of HIV infection for representative samples of adults (e.g., Catania, Coates, & Kegeles, 1994; Catania, Coates, Kegeles, Thompson-Fullilove, et al., 1992; Catania, Coates, Kegeles, Ekstrand, et al., 1989; Catania et al., 1993; Choi, Catania, & Dolcini, 1994; Dolcini et al., 1993; Grinstead, Faigeles, Binson, & Eversley, 1993; Hingson et al., 1989; Kanouse et al., 1991; Keeter & Bradford, 1988; Kost & Forrest, 1992; Laumann, Gagnon, Michael, & Michaels, 1994; Leigh, Temple, & Trocki, 1993; Marín, Gomez, & Hearst, 1993; Peterson, Catania, Dolcini, & Faigeles, 1993; Sabogal, Pierce, Pollack,

[1]To better understand how HIV may spread, the sociobehavioral pathways that other STDs follow must also be recognized. Therefore, it is of primary importance to consider other STDs when investigating the routes of HIV infection.

Faigeles, & Catania, 1993; Tanfer, Grady, Klepinger, & Billy, 1993). Prior surveys have sampled young and middle-aged adults, but recent work has explored the behavioral epidemiology of HIV disease among late middle-aged and elderly individuals who, since 1984, have annually comprised some 10% of the AIDS cases (Stall & Catania, 1994). Regardless of the age groups studied, the bulk of this prior work has been on mapping the distribution of risk behavior and prevention practices and examining their antecedents. Few studies have focused on issues of sexual networks and sexual mixing. Mapping and sexual mixing are two of the three central topics of this chapter.

The third section discusses the varied theoretical perspectives that guide the research that specifically examines the antecedents of risk behavior, behavior change, and maintenance of healthy sexual practice. Despite the apparent diversity of theoretical models concerning risky sexual behavior, they are, in fact, remarkably similar in terms of their focus on the assessment of the individual rather than the sexual relationship or dyad. In order to explore this critical gap in HIV behavioral-epidemiological research, the discussion is centered on the relational aspects of sexual risk behavior, and previously unpublished data on sexual roles, sexual communication, power structures, and relationship cohesion are presented.

In brief, the chapter provides an overview of the epidemiology of HIV and other STDs among heterosexual adults, discusses the topic of sexual mixing, and presents recent research findings in this area. The second section is devoted to the presentation of recent findings on mapping HIV-related risk behaviors and prevention practices among heterosexual adults. The last section discusses a proposed model of sexual relationships, and provides data relevant to this model.

SEXUAL MIXING

Epidemiology of HIV (and Other STDs)

Intravenous drug users and gay and bisexual men continue to be the groups most affected by HIV disease (Centers for Disease Control, 1994), and there is recent evidence that the prevention gains evidenced in the 1980s among gay cohorts of that time have not translated to the younger gay cohorts (D. H. Osmond et al., 1994). It is also important to recognize that new infections among heterosexuals are growing. For some time, heterosexual spread through sexual routes appeared to be chiefly due to sexual contact with partners in other high risk groups (bisexual, IDU, transfusion recipients). However, since 1992, the number of AIDS cases that have been attributed to heterosexual contact with a heterosexual partner not considered to be at high risk have increased to either match or even surpass the number of heterosexuals infected by high risk partners (see Fig. 47.1).

The following demographic breakdown describes heterosexual groups that currently appear to be at the greatest risk for HIV/STD infection. In general, African American and Latin

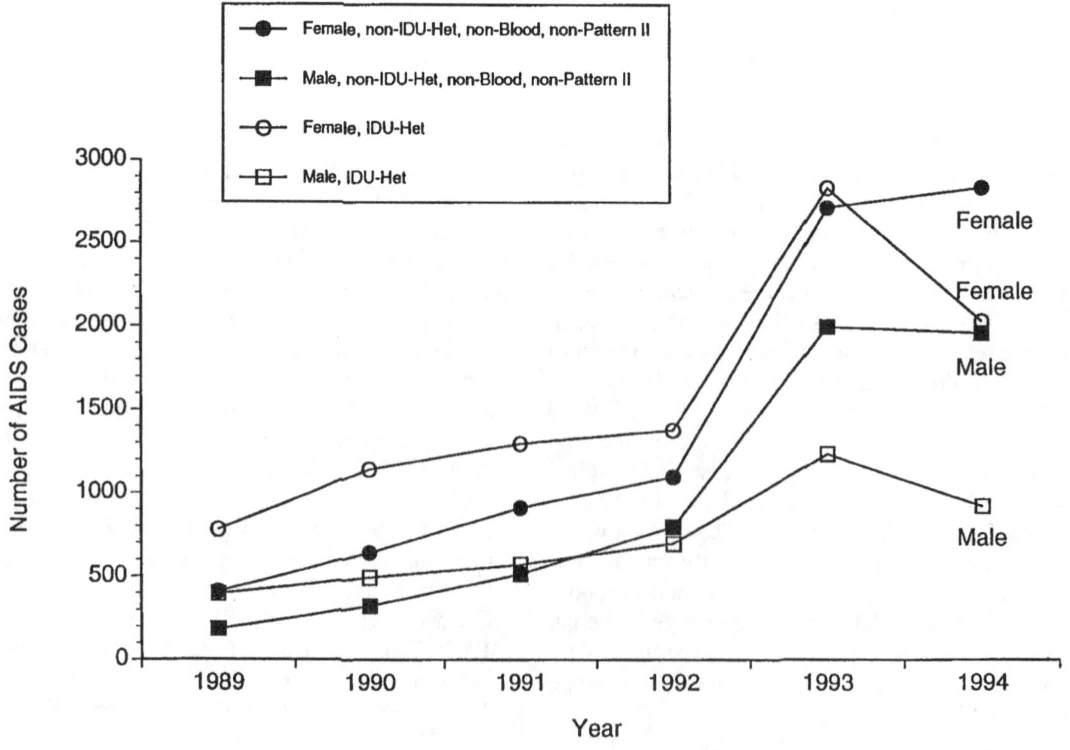

FIG. 47.1. Heterosexual contact (IDU, non-IDU, Blood, Pattern II) AIDS cases 1989–1994, ages 13 and older. Source of data: Centers for Disease Control.

women show the highest rates of new HIV/STD infections (Centers for Disease Control, 1994). However, both the AIDS data and recent behavior surveys now indicate that young adults are the largest and probably highest risk group. Young adults are in a developmental stage associated with extensive dating. Consequently, they are more likely to engage in increased sexual activity with a wider range of partners than at any other point in their adult life cycle (Binson, Dolcini, Pollack, & Catania, 1993; Dolcini et al., 1993; Siegel et al., 1992).

Other STDs that are cofactors for HIV, and are serious problems in their own right, are highly prevalent among heterosexuals. Siegel et al. (1992) reported biological data for a probability sample of White, African American, and Hispanic unmarried heterosexuals from age 20 to 44 indicating that, among women, 35% of Whites, 39% of Hispanics, and 55% of African Americans were positive for genital herpes; for men, the estimates are 26%, 20%, and 32%, respectively. The rate of Chlamydia infection has (per 100,000) doubled from 1987 to 1991 (from 91.4 to 197.5) (Webster, Greenspan, Nakashima, & Johnson, 1993), and has been found across a wide spectrum of populations (including Whites, African Americans, urban and rural populations, and low and high education groups; Ferris & Litaker, 1993; A. H. Herold et al., 1993; Holmes et al., 1993; Leka, Patrick, & Benenson, 1990). These alarming statistics make us keenly aware that there are large and active pathways for HIV to travel throughout segments of the heterosexual population.

Sexual Mixing

The degree to which HIV will spread along the biological pathways created by other STDs will depend on the extent of sexual mixing (in addition to relevant biological factors). Sexual mixing, which has been found to have a central influence on HIV/STD transmission rates (Anderson, 1991; Garnett & Anderson, 1993), is defined as the extent to which people engage in sexual activities with sexual partners from other sexual networks (dissortative mixing), and the extent to which they interact sexually with partners from their own network (assortative mixing; Gupta, Anderson, & May, 1989). Sexual networks are keys to understanding sexual mixing (Laumann et al., 1994).

The basic idea of a sexual network is quite simple. If, for example, Person A is having sex with Person C, and Person B is having sex with Person A, then Persons A, B, and C are all members of the same sexual network. STDs are spread, according to current perspectives, when members of a "core group" transmit infection to other network members. A core group is defined as one that, by virtue of its behavior, is disproportionately responsible for the spread of an STD in a given community (e.g., Aral & Holmes, 1984; Garnett & Anderson, 1993; Potterat, 1992). For instance, commercial sex workers in some communities might be conceptualized as a core group.

However, an emphasis on core groups as a key concept is problematic for the following reasons. First, the concept of a core group places a few vaguely defined social groups at the center of HIV/STD spread. Although this approach may have had utility when dealing with STDs that are concentrated in distinct geographic or social clusterings of the population, it does not provide much guidance for understanding the social pathways that lead to STD/HIV spread across diverse social segments. The core group concept is particularly limited when dealing with highly prevalent STDs with a wide geographic and social distribution (e.g., HSV-2 and Chlamydia; H. Miller, personal communication, 1995; N. Padian, personal communication, 1995). With a highly prevalent STD, a large number of sexual networks may contribute to disease spread in relation to the degree of infection in each network and the extent of sexual mixing within and between networks. Thus, rather than simply specifying core groups, it is possible to go a step further within network theory and specify a range of network contributions to disease spread.

A modification to the core group concept is proposed that assumes the degree of infection often varies across sexual networks. In other words, some networks would have a high prevalence of an STD(s), others moderate levels, whereas others may have no STDs whatsoever. STD spread within a network may produce local or "small" epidemics, but community, regional, or national spread will depend in large part on the extent to which other networks become infected, and the amount of contact that takes place between networks. In conceptualizing the network population that mixes across sexual networks, the term "heavy mixer" (disassortative mixers) has been proposed to describe people who sexually mix across multiple networks, "light mixers" who only rarely stray outside their own network, and "nonmixers" who stay completely within their own network.

Heavy mixers, as a group, may have a high prevalence of STDs, but they do not necessarily have to originate from the same sexual network or social segment. Thus, some heavy mixers may reside, for the most part, in networks with a low prevalence of STDs but through their diverse extra network contacts, they may subsequently contract an STD. That is, people who have multiple sexual partners from multiple networks are more likely to encounter a network with a high STD prevalence, to become infected, and to transport an STD back to their current "home" network (i.e., the network they interact with most frequently). In general, heavy mixers form an important link in the spread of HIV and other STDs from infected networks to non- or less infected sexual networks. For prevention purposes, it would be useful to identify the social psychological characteristics of networks with a high prevalence of STDs and of heavy mixers; these data could then be used to more effectively target particular networks and heavy mixers.

Sexual Patterns

Very few studies have been conducted that provide a broad perspective on sexual networks and mixing patterns. The research examining sexual networks has generally been based on tracing studies, which are subject to substantial bias. In the case of tracing studies, investigators begin with an infected sample from a public health STD clinic, and then attempt to trace the sexual contacts of the infected individuals, their partners, and sometimes the partners of the partners (Garnett & Anderson,

1993; Klovdahl et al., 1994; Ramstedt, Giesecke, Forssman, & Granath, 1991; Woodhouse et al., 1994). Garnett and Anderson (1993) noted that the primary difficulty with tracing studies is that they contain self-selection biases related to the geographic service areas of public STD clinics, and the following additional biases: underreporting of STDs by private physicians, and the fact that those seeking care at public clinics or private practices are a nonrandom subsample of those who are infected (e.g., infected people may not seek treatment because they are asymptomatic or because the symptoms abate). Therefore, tracing studies do not provide a representative picture of sexual networks or patterns of mixing in the general population. To adequately describe segments of the population that mix across different social strata, a representative sample of the community, under investigation for HIV/STD spread, is mandatory.

Although, the mate selection research may provide some guides to the study of sexual networks, this literature has generally limited its attention to the selection of marital or primary sexual partners (e.g., see reviews by Buss, 1988; Buss & Schmitt, 1993; Feingold, 1992; Perper, 1989). Patterns of selection may be different for primary and secondary partners (e.g., Buss & Schmitt, 1993). Empirical data supporting this position found that the social class of infected respondents was predictive of choice of primary partner, but not of secondary partners (Ramstedt et al., 1991). Although the mate selection literature does not provide an exhaustive guide to the types of patterns that might be expected among people with multiple sexual partners, this work does provide a starting point. Investigators of friendship networks and mate selection have defined networks in terms of social characteristics (e.g., race, age, social class, education), geographic location (e.g., a city, neighborhood, a public bar), and value systems (Laumann et al., 1994; Verbrugge, 1977; Yamaguchi, 1990), and have generally found that people form primary relationships and friendships with similar others (i.e., homophily).

An investigation of sexual networks examined age and ethnic mixing by analyzing data gathered from unmarried heterosexuals who participated in the AMEN survey (AIDS in Multiethnic Neighborhoods survey; a household probability survey in San Francisco; Catania, Binson, & Stone, 1996). A mixing typology (nonmixers, light mixers, heavy mixers) was derived, the validity of this typology with respect to biological indices of genital herpes was examined, and social and psychological characteristics of people evidencing sexual mixing across different age and racial/ethnic groups were identified. Heavy mixing was defined as engaging in sex with two or more partners outside one's own social stratum in the past year. Age mixing (i.e., engaging in sex with people outside your own age group) may be a particularly important element in STD transmission. For an STD to be maintained in the population it must be propagated from older generations to each new generation entering the sociosexual phase of life (typically beginning during adolescence and reaching a zenith in the 20s). In a closed social system (i.e., no STDs entering from outside the system), the STDs unique to the older group will die out with the eventual deaths of the group members, as long as none of the members engaged in sex with younger cohorts.

Race and ethnicity are also important network-mixing features because they provide barriers to forming relationships. Different racial and ethnic groups may be separated by geography, language, social class, social customs, and prejudice. When racial/ethnic barriers are strong, it would be expected that sexual mixing and, to some degree, particular STDs would be well contained. However, as these barriers break down and more sexual mixing occurs, it could then be assumed that there would be a greater increase in the transmission of STDs across racial/ethnic lines. What is particularly unclear, however, is the extent to which members of different racial/ethnic groups mix with other ethnic/racial groups.

It was found that heavy age and ethnic mixers were significantly more likely than light/nonmixers to evidence genital herpes, even after controlling for numbers of sexual partners, race, age, gender, education, neighborhood of residence. Thus, mixing accounts for variation in STD prevalence above that accounted for by the usual set of STD risk factors. In addition, ethnic and age mixing reflect different mixing patterns (i.e., heavy age mixers are not redundant with heavy ethnic mixers). In general, light and heavy mixers tended to be similar with respect to condom use, attitudes toward condoms, perceived risk for HIV, and in misconceptions concerning routes of HIV transmission. Thus, heavy mixers are not cognizant, or at least not concerned, about their greater risk for HIV/STDs. Also, people having a history of IDU and incarceration were more likely to be heavy age mixers, but not heavy ethnic mixers. Thus, heavy age and ethnic mixing comprise individuals from the same types of high risk social groups. With regard to age mixing, the IDU-jail findings have important targeting and epidemiological implications. IDUs and incarcerated people are easier to target because they often come into contact with social institutions (corrections officers, the police, methadone treatment centers). Epidemiologically, both populations tend to have high levels of HIV and other STDs, and therefore are major conduits for the spread of these diseases to other social strata.

Originally, it was hypothesized that male heavy mixers would be more likely than female heavy mixers to be represented among those with a history of incarceration or drug use, but the study was unable to find any gender differences with respect to age mixing. Significant variation in ethnic mixing was exclusively related to the group of individuals who endorsed the "other" ethnic category (i.e., comprised of Asians, Pacific Islanders, American Indians, and others). Hispanics and African Americans relative to Whites (reference group) did not contribute significantly to this pool of heavy mixers. Apparently, members of the "other" ethnic groups have greater social license to interact sexually with partners from Hispanic, White, or African American groups, whereas the latter three groups seem less willing to engage in interracial sex. Lastly, mixing patterns did not yield substantial variations by gender. These latter results seem somewhat atypical when compared to other urban centers throughout the United States, and may reflect sexual mixing norms unique to San Francisco.

Mixing By City Size and Demographic Group

A recent survey has examined sexual network and mixing issues in a national probability sample of heterosexual adults from age 18 to 49 (Laumann et al., 1994). This data set has been analyzed using our mixing typology to focus on race (restricted to White, African American, Hispanic), which is the most reliably reported variable compared to other common demographics (e.g., partner's income, education, religion). Because the spread of HIV/STDs beyond current high risk groups may be primarily driven by people who have unprotected sex with multiple sexual partners, the analysis was constrained to people with two or more sexual partners. Numerous studies have indicated that having even two partners in the past year will increase the odds of contracting STDs. Furthermore, the bulk of HIV/STD risk factors (e.g., unprotected sex with multiple sexual partners) and AIDS/STD cases occur among young adults, minority populations, and in major urban areas.

The prevalence of heavy (race) mixing among respondents with multiple sexual partners in the past year was highest for the largest urban centers (18%), and decreased with city size (medium cities (12%), suburbs of medium cities (9%), and small cities/rural areas (10%). The 18% figure for all large size cities is somewhat lower than that observed in San Francisco. The relatively high number of unmarried people with multiple sexual partners (25%) from San Francisco reflects perhaps a greater diversity in racial groups or an acceptance of cross-race dating that would be more typical of a liberal urban setting such as San Francisco.

With regard to gender, race, and age group, the national data indicate that for respondents with multiple sexual partners, women are more likely than men to be heavy mixers (14% vs. 11%, $p < .05$)[2] that Hispanic males (59% vs. 17% African Americans, 5% Whites, $p < .05$), and females (33% vs. 4% African Americans, 15% Whites, $p < .05$) are more likely than other males or females to be heavy mixers, with African American males and White females reporting moderate levels of heavy mixing. These patterns vary somewhat by age group. Young adult (age 18–29) Hispanic males and females report the most heavy mixing (79% and 36%, respectively), with moderate levels reported by African American males and White females (23% and 20%, respectively). The overall pattern is similar for those in their 30s, with missing cells making other age comparisons by race and gender impractical. However, the overall age pattern reveals a decline of heavy mixing related to an increase in age across gender (e.g., 19%, 10%, and 10%, respectively, for female respondents age 18–29, 30–39, 40–49, $p < .05$; and 12%, 11%, and 8%, respectively, for male respondents age 18–29, 30–39, 40–49, $p < .05$). In both gender groups, there were insufficient numbers to compute figures for those from age 50 to 59. Apparently, norms for age-appropriate partners influence the age mixing patterns of both men and women.

In brief, an analysis of the Laumann et al. national data in conjunction with the AMEN study's San Francisco data indicated that people in large urban centers evidence the greatest degree of sexual mixing. This observation may vary somewhat for different age, gender, and race groups. The mixing data indicate some interesting patterns with regard to race and gender that need to be further explored, but the present data suggest that the cross-racial spread of HIV/STDs may be propagated across social groups to a larger extent by Hispanic males and White females, particularly in large urban settings. This does not preclude spread within racial groups. For instance, among African Americans there may be considerable within-group transmission of STDs and HIV, and indeed prevalence levels of AIDS and STDs have been found to be relatively high among young adult African Americans. Lastly, although the heavy mixers analyses defines mixing as "out group" sexual contacts based on demographic characteristics, in fact, some of these "out group" sexual contacts may reside exclusively within one's own network. It is not possible to separate assortative from dissortative mixing; a full network tracing study would ultimately be needed to accomplish this task.

[2]All statistical tests are based on chi-square analyses.

MAPPING AT RISK POPULATIONS OVER TIME

Although it is important to study the social and behavioral dynamics of sexual networks and mixing, it is also important to describe the various segments of the heterosexual population that are at risk for HIV, estimate the size of these populations, and investigate the population dynamics of at risk groups. One issue that has not been extensively investigated, is how rapidly people move into or out of the at risk population over time. The relevance of this turnover may depend on the following factors: the degree of infectivity and susceptibility to infection associated with a particular pathogen, size of the sexual networks, degree of mixing, number of contacts, and type of sexual contacts. If an infectious agent is highly contagious (e.g., an STD with a high probability of transmission on any given sexual encounter) and the population of at risk people is turning over rapidly, then many people might be expected to become infected over a very short period of time. Similarly, a pathogen with a low rate of transmission that enters a population with a low turnover rate (i.e., at risk people stay at risk for long periods of time) may also lead, over a longer time span, to a widely spread disease. Some STDs have low rates of partner–partner transmission, particularly for penis-in-vagina sexual activity.[3] In order to more fully understand the ways these infections may spread, more must be known about the disbursement of sexual net-

[3]Although some reports have obtained low HIV infectivity rates for vaginal intercourse, there is considerable variability in rates both within and across studies (de Vincenzi, 1994; Haverkos & Battjes, 1992; Jacquez, Koopman, Simon, & Longini, 1994; Padian, Shiboski, & Jewell, 1991; Phillips & Johnson, 1992). Heterosexual transmission of HIV has occurred after only a few sexual contacts and has failed to occur after hundreds of contacts (Auerbach, Wypijewska, & Brodie, 1994) and per contact female-to-male infectivity rates across studies have ranged from .0001 to .06 (Jacquez et al., 1994). Recent work sheds light on these anomalies in indicating that infectivity may vary with stage of HIV disease progression (Jacquez et al., 1994). Infectivity is high following initial infection, reduces dramatically during the asymptomatic period, and then rebounds during the symptomatic stage. Thus, average infectivity rates may not be meaningful.

works across different sociogeographic areas (e.g., neighborhoods, urban centers, inter-city).

Recent Mapping Data: National AIDS Behavioral Survey

Although ideally it would be useful to conduct mapping studies in conjunction with information obtained on sexual networks, at the present time such data are not available. Thus, mapping work has proceeded on the more general level, and has largely consisted of examining large population segments and variations in prevention practices, along with risk factors in various subsegments. In recent attempts to map changes in HIV/STD-relevant risk factors, condom use, and HIV antibody testing for a national probability sample of heterosexual adults, no appreciable reduction was found, over an approximate 1-year span, in the prevalence of HIV-related sexual risk factors nationally or in major urban centers (Catania et al., 1995). However, this seemingly stable population is actually very dynamic in that the annual turnover rate is approximately 38% for the segment of the high risk population that has multiple sexual partners. Thus, over a 1-year period, 38% of the at risk population moves to a no risk status, whereas another 38% of previously no risk people acquire some level of risk for HIV or other STDs. Movement into and out of the "at risk pool" may be facilitated by a host of factors, including such things as changes in marital/relationship status, partner availability, illness, and concerns about HIV/STDs. Although the process of partnering through legal marriage or cohabitation insures some degree of risk reduction, this reduction may at times be illusory. It has actually been found that heterosexuals with a history of risk factors for HIV seldom obtain testing prior to cohabiting or marriage, and do not regularly use condoms following establishment of the relationship (Catania, Coates, & Kegeles, 1996). Further, married people reporting extramarital sexual partners are typically the least likely to use condoms or obtain HIV testing (Choi et al., 1994).

CURRENT MODELS OF HIV/STD PREVENTION PRACTICES

The third major topic area in behavioral epidemiology concerns research on the antecedents of risk behaviors, and behavior change and maintenance. An enormous amount of research focusing on the antecedents of HIV-related risk behaviors and prevention practices has been conducted on a wide variety of populations. Guiding this work in the sexual area are a number of models and theoretical formulations, including Cognitive Social Learning Theory (Bandura, 1986), Script Theory (Gagnon, 1990; Miller, Bettencourt, DeBro, & Hoffman, 1993), Self-efficacy models (Mahoney, Thombs, & Ford, 1995), Theory of Reasoned Action (Terry, Gallois, & McCamish, 1993), Health Belief Model (Mahoney et al., 1995), Perceived Risk models (Weinstein, 1989), Protection Motivation Theory (e.g., Black, Stanton, Whitehead, & Galbraith, 1993), Stage Models (Bowen & Trotter, 1995; Boyer & Kegeles, 1991; Breakwell, Millward & Fife-Schaw, 1994; Catania, Coates, Kegeles, et al., 1989; Catania, Coates, & Kegeles, 1996; Catania, Kegeles, & Coates, 1990; J. D. Fisher, W. A. Fisher, Williams, & Malloy, 1994; Grimley, Prochaska, Velicer, & Prochaska, 1995; Grimley, Riley, Bellis, & Prochaska, 1993; Kowalewski, Longshore, & Anglin, 1994; Malow, Corrigan, Cunningham, West, & Pena, 1993; Prochaska, Redding, Harlow, Rossi, & Velicer, 1994), Interpersonal Communication Models (Cupach & Metts, 1991; Edgar, Hammond, & Freimuth, 1989; Freimuth, Hammond, Edgar, McDonald, & Fink, 1992), and a synthesis of these models/theories with concepts from developmental psychology (Boyer & Kegeles, 1991; Catania, Coates, Kegeles, et al., 1989; Catania et al., 1990; Catania, Coates, & Kegeles, 1994), diffusion theory (Rogers, 1982), social network theory (Dolcini et al., 1995), gender-related social role models (Amaro, 1995), social support and help-seeking models (Boyer & Kegeles, 1991; Breakwell et al., 1994; Catania, Coates, Kegeles, et al., 1989; Catania et al., 1990; Catania, Coates, & Kegeles, 1996; Kowalewski et al., 1994; Malow et al., 1993), and stress and coping models (Folkman, Chesney, Pollack, & Phillips, 1992).

In the tradition of American psychology and sociology, there is considerable emphasis placed on the effects of cognitions and social norms related to AIDS-relevant sexual behaviors. Some perspectives focus on a small select set of beliefs, norms, and behaviors (e.g., TRA, HBM, SEM), and are concerned with the individual. This focus on individuals may be more appropriate for understanding the health risks associated with solitary activities like cigarette smoking and alcohol consumption rather than interpersonal sexual behavior. In addition, many models do not address behavior change processes and, in fact, some cases incorrectly describe sexual behavior change as an instantaneous, all-or-none phenomenon. However, a number of models or theories of sexual health either explicitly (e.g., stage models; Boyer & Kegeles, 1991; Catania, Coates, Kegeles, et al., 1989; Catania et al., 1990; Catania, Coates, & Kegeles, 1996; Prochaska et al., 1994) or implicitly[4] include consideration of change processes in the form of stages that divide the process into meaningful units. Stage models of change are heuristic in value and have a long history of utility in developmental psychology and sociology. Change processes are important to consider at both the individual and dyadic levels, because changes in sexual behavior typically require two people, with possibly different expectations and beliefs, to cooperate in making these changes. These stages may be investigated individually (e.g., Breakwell et al., 1994) or as multistage models (e.g., Catania, Coates, & Kegeles, 1996). Stage models are most useful when there is a normative or modal pattern of change (e.g., Catania et al., 1990; Freimuth et al., 1992) that, in turn, aids in delineating individuals or couples who deviate from this pattern.

In an effort to overcome the limitations of any single model or theory attempting to understand sexual behavior, a number of models have been based on heuristic amalgamations derived from a combination of existing theoretical perspectives. For instance, the AIDS Risk Reduction Model combines aspects of

[4]For example, although cognitive social learning theory does not explicitly make use of stage concepts, it can be implied from assertions, such as Bandura's (1994) comment, that commitment to behavior change almost uniformly precedes adoption of the behavior.

perceived risk models, attribution theory, self-efficacy models, cost–benefit analysis, social support and help seeking models, interpersonal negotiation models, and developmentally based stage theory to aid in understanding the process of behavior change in the sexual context (Catania, Binson, & Stone, 1996; Catania, Coates, Kegeles, et al., 1989; Catania et al., 1990, 1991; Catania, Coates, Golden, et al., 1994; Catania, Coates, & Kegeles, 1994). The unique aspect of this model is its movement from an initial consideration of the individual to consideration of the sexual dyad, all set within the broader social psychological context of support networks and reference group norms. Other approaches to understanding sexual health are being developed (J. D. Fisher et al., 1994), but the utility of these models over prior models remains to be demonstrated. Some models contain conceptual gaps. For instance, the Transtheoretical Model (Grimley et al., 1993; 1995; Prochaska et al., 1994) hypothesizes that the change process begins with problem recognition, but neglects to mention the causal attributions that may dictate the type of preventive behavior individuals may choose (e.g., believing one is at risk for HIV due to mosquito bites might lead to purchasing mosquito repellent rather than condoms). Furthermore, the Transtheoretical Model emphasizes interpersonal control issues, but is somewhat vague on other interpersonal issues that are relevant in the sexual context, such as interpersonal negotiation skills and coping with a partner's rejection (Boyer & Kegeles, 1991; Catania, Coates, & Kegeles, 1994; J. D. Fisher et al., 1994; Freimuth et al., 1992; Miller et al., 1993).

Sexual Relationships

To some extent, however, conceptual limitations at the interpersonal level plague most models of sexual health, although some models examine interpersonal skills (Boyer & Kegeles, 1991; Breakwell et al., 1994; Catania, Coates, Kegeles, et al., 1989; Catania et al., 1990; Catania, Coates, & Kegeles, 1996; J. D. Fisher et al., 1994; Freimuth et al., 1992; Malow et al., 1993; Miller et al., 1993). Prior work has demonstrated the importance of interpersonal situations by showing that condom use varies for people with risk factors for HIV/STDs, depending on the type of relationship (casual or committed; for review see Catania, Coates, & Kegeles, 1996; Dolcini et al., 1993), and by showing that the antecedents of condom use related to these two types of relationships vary as well (Catania, Coates, & Kegeles, 1994). Understanding the interpersonal factors in HIV/STD risk behaviors and prevention practices is crucial. Models that do not include interpersonal components are at best incomplete, and may lead to prevention programs that cannot be expected to have a strong impact. In the area of adolescent AIDS prevention programs, for instance, programs based solely on cognitive models have been typically ineffective, as compared to approaches that also emphasize interpersonal skills and problem solving (J. Fisher & W. Fisher, 1992; Kirby, Barth, Leland, & Fetro, 1991).

Despite recent work that includes consideration of the sexual dyad, and a small corpus of theories that highlight the importance of interpersonal dynamics (e.g., Cognitive Social Learning Theory, Script Theory), it is difficult to make predictions regarding specific sexual situations. For instance, it is not possible to derive from the existing models or theories a set of hypotheses that would predict the consistently observed differences in condom use with secondary versus primary sexual partners, nor would these models predict that people who have extramarital sexual activity are highly unlikely to use condoms with their extramarital partners (Catania et al., 1993; Catania, Coates, & Kegeles, 1994; Choi et al., 1994). Whereas the current models are conceptually elegant, and offer post hoc explanations, they may fall short in predicting behavior in real-life relationships.

This is not to say that the literature has completely ignored social considerations. However, in terms of interpersonal factors, the major focus of the empirical literature, to date, has been on interactive elements of sexual relationships (e.g., the effects of sexual communication, negotiation, and assertiveness skills on prevention practices; Catania, Coates, & Kegeles, 1994). These studies have produced only a very limited understanding of the way interpersonal variables may change across sexual situations, and have not provided much information on their antecedents and expression within different social groups.

Despite the paucity of work on sexual relationships, there is, however, a rich body of literature in the area of family and marital relationships that may be useful to understanding sexual relationships and health (Boss, Doherty, LaRossa, Schumm, & Steinmetz, 1993). The model proposed is based on six major "relational" elements of import in understanding how relationships function, adapt, and reach decisions. These elements include relationship roles, interactive processes, conflict issues, relationship cohesion and flexibility, and emotional factors. Each of these elements has a pivotal role in various models or theories of close interpersonal relationships, and are supported by data from studies of marital relationships and families.

A Relational Model

Although in marital relationships relationship roles often involve issues concerning expectations for husbands and wives (Rodgers & White, 1993), the use of the concept of relationship roles is restricted here to that of sexual roles. The concept of a sexual role has application to a broad set of relationships, including first-time sexual encounters, casual sexual relationships, as well as relationships at varying stages of greater interpersonal commitment and involvement, (e.g., steady dating, engaged, married). Thus, the concept of sexual roles should reflect the varied and changing roles that men and women occupy in their sexual relationship(s) over time. Sexual roles are generally defined then as norm-governed expectations that men and women have regarding appropriate behavior in a given sexual encounter. To a large extent these roles are expected to be gender specific, reflecting gender role differences with respect to sexual conduct, and to be patterned by normative scripts for appropriate sequences of sexual activity (e.g., kissing and petting precede coitus, men initiate increasing levels of sexual intimacy). However, sexual roles alone do not a relationship make, and couples often have to negotiate variations in sexual practices, condom use, and actively problem solve sexual difficulties that arise. Interactive processes, which are key to marital theories (Fitzpatrick & Ritchie, 1993), are also proposed to be a central element governing the interaction between sexual partners. These processes may include modes of communication (verbal, nonverbal), listening skills, content issues (e.g., substantive vs. affective communication) and qualitative dimensions that reflect, for instance, assertiveness, combativeness, and gentleness.

Sexual roles and interactive processes are important for guiding sexual behavior across a wide variety of sexual relationships (from one-time contacts to ongoing relationships), but there are a number of other potential socioemotional dimensions that effect intimate relationships, and are important to the decisions people may make about their sexual practices and, consequently, their sexual health. Because people may enter into a sexual relationship with different expectations and motives, there is often, but not universally, an element of conflict between partners. For instance, one person may feel things are moving too quickly toward intercourse, or one partner may want to use condoms whereas the other will not. Conflict theories have had a long history in the study of marital and family relationships (Farrington & Chertok, 1993), and this work can be applied to the study of sexual relationships. In particular, issues of power are central to most social conflict theories, and are often considered to be important elements in sexual relationships (Amaro, 1995). Sexual relationships, however, should not be characterized solely as power struggles. They also involve other strong emotional components (e.g., lust, physical attraction, and love) that may influence the decisions couples make about sexual health practices. For instance, some people may forgo condoms because they were so attracted to a new partner that they did not want to "turn them off" by suggesting they might have a disease.

Intimate relationships also can be characterized in terms of their degree of cohesiveness and flexibility (Doherty & Baptiste, 1993). The degree of commitment that partners have to each other and the boundaries they place on their sexual relationship define the degree of cohesion in the sexual relationship. For example, a sexual relationship may be characterized at one extreme in terms of mutual monogamy and at the other extreme in terms of mutual nonmonogamy; the boundaries of the sexual relationship will determine the degree of extra-relationship sex that partners may engage in. Cohesiveness may be virtually absent in the one-time casual sexual encounter as compared to the marital dyad where the presumption of fidelity is often adhered to. Lastly, flexibility is important to sexual relationships. If sexual partners are highly flexible in their approach to their sexual relationship, then they are able to modify their sexual roles, introduce innovations into the relationship (e.g., condom use), and adapt to the changing demands on that relationship. Flexibility in relationships will enable partners to more easily achieve a healthy and enjoyable sex life.

The six elements of the sexual relationship described previously are hypothesized as a set of factors that will directly impact sexual health risks in a given relationship.[5] However, these six elements do not exist in isolation from other social, environmental, situational, and developmental contexts. For instance, Amaro (1995) noted the importance of considering social or cultural contexts related to ethnicity/race in considering gender differences in sexuality. Situational contexts also must be considered, and may for example involve variations in mood and drug use across sexual encounters. People and relationships have histories that form a developmental context for considering the sexual relationship. Developmental contexts may include personality differences or similarities brought by partners into the sexual encounter that reflect differences in developmental histories (e.g., differences in sexual guilt, personal sexual history). Developmental context may also include changes in the relationship (e.g., changes in trust, commitment, nurturance, mutuality, and meaning), and the interplay between individual and relationship change (e.g., changes in self-concept that influence a person's assertiveness in the relationship). Sexual relationships also occur in different social environmental contexts that may be more or less supportive of healthy sexual practices. For example, the world of the intravenous drug user or the crack addict would provide another contextual element to consider within the rubric of external forces that influence the six key elements of the sexual relationship outlined earlier.

A number of investigators have noted the lack of research on various elements in the model already outlined (e.g., gender differences; Amaro, 1995). Further, the significance of power differentials and role-related behavior patterns in sexual relationships (i.e., scripts) has received attention on a theoretical level, but has not been actively researched (Abraham & Sheeran, 1994; Amaro, 1995). Relationship cohesion issues have not been extended to considerations of sexual relationships and sexual health. Lastly, sexual communication has been studied (Catania, McDermott, & Pollack, 1984), but variations in communication skills across social groups have not been adequately described. The antecedents of good sexual communication skills are still unknown.

The next sections concern aspects of four of the model elements described earlier. Based on data from the National AIDS Behavioral Survey (Catania, Coates, Stall, et al., 1992; Catania et al., 1995), Judith Moskowitz examined gender differences in perceptions of sexual self-regulation and sexual resistance in the developmental context formed by changes in the sexual relationship over time. Ariane van der Straten discusses the importance of sexual communication, and presents data from Wave 2 of the National AIDS Behavioral Survey (Catania, Coates, Stall, et al., 1992; Catania et al., 1995) on the distribution of health protective sexual communication skills (HPSC) across social strata, and examines preliminary evidence on the antecedents of HPSC. Diane Binson, based on qualitative studies of heterosexual men and women, discusses issues of power in sexual relationships. Lastly, M. Margaret Dolcini explores personal and interpersonal differences between relationships that differ in their emphasis on sexual fidelity.

[5]This description of the model is not intended to explicate the full range of relations among this set of relational variables.

Sexual Roles: Gender Differences and Developmental Context

For heterosexuals, traditional sexual roles and scripts provide sexual partners with a simple set of behavioral expectations that govern what men and women are "supposed" to do in their sexual encounters. Not surprisingly, many investigators believe that gender differences in sexual attitudes, beliefs, and behaviors touch at the very heart of heterosexual interactions (for review see Amaro, 1995). There are well-documented gender differences in sexual beliefs, attitudes, and behaviors that rival or exceed the magnitude of gender differences in verbal ability, mathematics performance, and aggressive behavior (Oliver & Hyde, 1993). Men tend to have more liberal sexual attitudes, an earlier age of first sexual intercourse, and more extensive sexual experience than women (E. S. Herold & Mewhinney, 1993; Kim, Marmor, Dubin, & Wolfe, 1993; Laumann et al., 1994; Leitenberg, Detzer, & Srebnik, 1993; Oliver & Hyde, 1993; Trocki, 1992). Gender differences in sexual beliefs and behavior have important implications for sexual health. For instance, if a man and a woman in a sexual dyad have vastly different attitudes toward condom use, the likelihood of the partners coming to some agreement on safer sexual behavior is probably low. Therefore, the study of gender differences in sexual behaviors is extremely important in determining whether individuals in a dyad will engage in safe sexual behavior.

Although other investigators have pointed out the importance of gender differences in sexual relationships and considered how sociocultural context interacts with gender issues (Amaro, 1995), prior models have not entertained the possibility that developmental factors may influence the extent to which gender roles and stereotypes may affect sexual encounters. Relationships evolve and change with time, and the effects of such changes have been postulated to account for the striking differences observed in condom use with secondary relationships when compared with primary relationships (Catania, Coates, & Kegeles, 1994). Developmental considerations may help to explain the fluctuation in the impact that gender differences have on the sexual relationship over time. Based on prior work (Deaux & Major, 1987), it is proposed that gender differences are of most concern in the early stages of relationships, because there has been less time to learn about the intrinsic qualities of one's sexual partner. The tendency would be to view the person in terms of stereotypic beliefs. As information about that person increases with subsequent interactions, these stereotypic beliefs may be expected to break down. Thus, in sexual relationships, the operation of gender stereotypes may be expected to peak early in the sexual relationship, but to wane over the course of time (Holland, Ramazanoglu, Scott, Sharpe, & Thompson, 1991).

Gender Differences: National AIDS Behavioral Survey Findings

The possibility that gender differences are dependent on the developmental context of the relationship was examined. Specifically, the study looked at the possibility that the strength of sexual beliefs and behaviors as a function of gender is dependent on the length of time the respondent has been in the relationship. The present analyses are based on data from the second wave of the NABS (Catania, Coates, Stall, et al., 1992; Catania et al., 1995). Two variables were examined within relationships of different length. The two variables reflect elements of the sexual relationship that might be expected to have significant gender-stereotypic components early in relationships but that may change over time. Following traditional sexual scripts and/or gender stereotypes, men are expected to be more likely than women to initiate sexual activity, and to be successful in regulating the sexual relationship to obtain desired outcomes. Women, in this traditional script, are more passive about initiating sex, and less assertive in getting what they want when they do have sex. These expected gender differences were examined in respondents with primary sexual relationships of varying length. Although cross-sectional data are not ideal for studying intrarelationship change, they do provide a means for modeling developmental changes in that the information obtained on interrelationship gender differences most likely reflects an underlying normative pattern of intrarelationship change. Thus, the magnitude of the gender differences in four groups of respondents was compared: respondents who had been with their partners for a year or less, respondents who had been with their partner for 2 to 5 years, those who had been with their partners for 6 to 10 years, and respondents with partners for 11 years or more.

Initiating Sex. Respondents were asked if "When you have sex you are usually the one who makes the first move? (agree–disagree scale)." It was hypothesized that men would be more likely to agree with this statement than women and the gender difference would be especially large in relationships of shorter duration. Based on an analysis of variance model, it was found that of respondents with a primary sexual partner (N = 3,057), there were significant gender difference in initiation (p = .001) with males being more likely to report initiation. However, the extent of the gender difference did not change as a function of length of relationship. Thus, gender-related role differences in expectations for initiation apparently do not change as a result of an increase in partner contact.

Sexual Self-Regulation. The sexual self-regulation scale was used to assess respondents' perceptions of their ability to regulate the sexual encounter so as to achieve positive outcomes (Catania et al., 1984). As noted previously, traditional gender stereotypes would dictate that women would be reluctant to achieve sexual satisfaction through assertive means (i.e., it is the male's responsibility to satisfy his partner). This stereotype may be operating at its peak early on in a relationship, but as the relationship matures, and the female partner becomes more comfortable with and knowledgeable about her male partner, she may become more assertive in meeting her sexual needs. The data partially support this hypothesis. An analysis of variance confirms the predicted interaction between gender and length of current relationship on sexual self-regulation. However, although women in short duration relationships (< 1 year) had lower self-regulation scores than their male counterparts (*N* = 666), this difference was not significant. Nevertheless, gender differences were apparent for respondents in relationships of longer duration. For respondents who had been with their partners from 2 to 5 years (*N* = 846), women were significantly higher than men on sexual self-regulation. At 6 to 10 years (*N* = 652), women were still higher, although the difference did not reach statistical significance. At 11 years or more (*N* = 820), women were again significantly higher than men on sexual self-regulation. The pattern of means for male and female respondents within each length of relationship group is illustrated in Fig. 47.2, and suggest that women's perceptions of their ability to regulate the sexual relationship increased with relationship length.

These analyses are preliminary, but they do suggest that some role-related gender differences are not influenced by developmental context and others apparently are affected. Thus, some sexual role-related behaviors, such as initiating the sexual encounter, may be resistant or slow to change. Understanding which role-related behaviors are difficult to change is important to efforts aimed at motivating couples to achieve healthy sexual practices. The ability to regulate the sexual relationship may be of particular import to efforts to use condoms. As research has demonstrated, some women may be at a disadvantage in this regard, especially early on in a new sexual relationship. The data have not yet been examined with respect to race and age, but it might be expected that some minority women and older women may have more difficulty with being sexually assertive (M. T. Fullilove, R. E. Fullilove, Haynes, K. & Gross, 1990; Marín, Tschann, Gomez, & Kegeles, 1993; M. W. Osmond et al., 1993; Sabogal, Perez-Stable, Otero-Sabogal, & Hiatt, 1995).

In order to further pursue the idea that gender differences in sexual attitudes, behaviors, and safer sex strategies are modified by relationship development, longitudinal designs must be used in order to study couples throughout all phases of their relationships (e.g., Blumstein & Schwartz, 1983; Howard, Blumstein, & Schwartz, 1986; Peplau, Rubin, & Hill, 1977).

Some have argued that psychologists should discontinue the study of gender differences on the grounds that gender studies perpetuate differences between the genders, along with sex discrimination (Baumeister, 1988; McHugh, Koeske, & Frieze, 1986). However, gender differences in the sexual behavior of individuals involved in a sexual encounter play a fundamental role in the manifestation of safer sexual behaviors, and for this reason alone they cannot be ignored. Without the continued study of the gender differences, and the ways in which these differences are expressed within various contexts, a vital source of information would be missed that could be extremely beneficial in designing more effective sexual risk interventions.

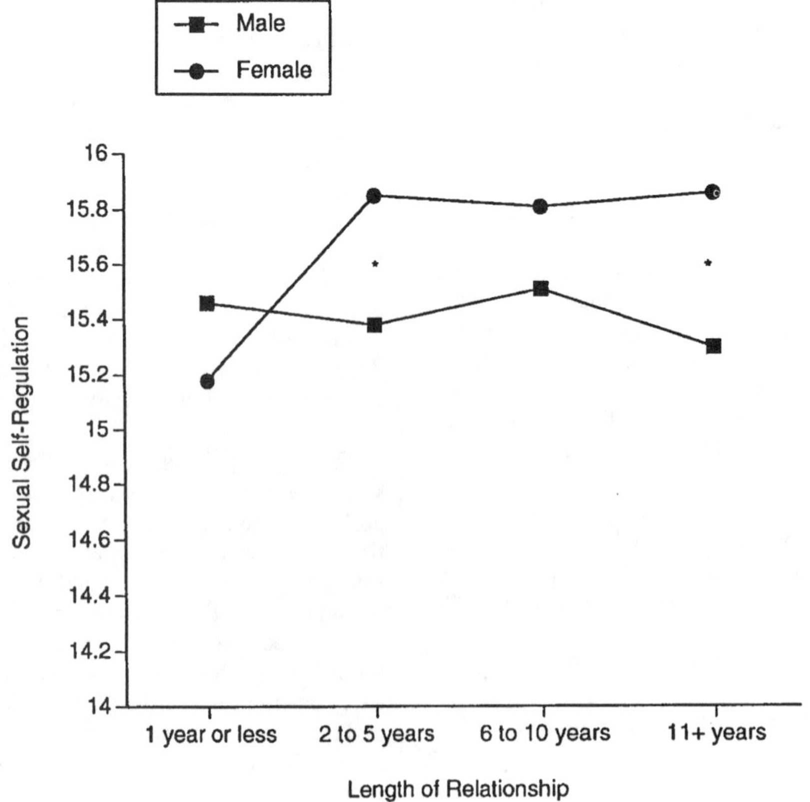

FIG. 47.2. Sexual self-regulation. *Difference is statistically significant.

Sexual Communication and Sexual Health

Interactive processes are extremely important for understanding sexual relationships. By virtue of the cooperative and interpersonal nature of most sexual activities, communication is an integral component of sex. In interpersonal relationships, the quality of the communication and the quality of the relationship are closely linked. Good sexual communication skills are important both for sexual and relationship satisfaction (Cupach & Metts, 1991; Snyder & Berg, 1983; Zimmer, 1983).

Although all aspects of interpersonal communication (e.g. process, style, and content) are likely to influence sexual behavior, this discussion is limited to the topic of communication content, specifically related to new relationships. The content of sexual communications is likely to be somewhat different for new versus committed relationships, thus it is important to consider the developmental context of the sexual communication process (Cupach & Metts, 1991; Galligan & Terry, 1993; Wight, 1992; Wingood, Hunter-Gamble, & DiClemente, 1993). Individuals in a new relationship may have little knowledge of their partner's sexual history and views on safer sex precisely when need for discussion and negotiation of sexual issues is at its zenith (Metts & Fitzpatrick, 1992). Thus, new relationships represent both a critical time for safer sex communication, and a "window of opportunity" for developing interventions aimed at changing behavior. However, discussions regarding sexual matters are not easy to conduct. In new or developing relationships, where there is a great deal of uncertainty about commitment and expectations, concerns about self-presentation, partner selection, and the relationship may take precedence over longer term health concerns. Furthermore, many heterosexuals do not discuss condoms with their partner if another contraceptive method is used, because they associate condoms primarily with birth control (Edgar, Freimuth, Hammond, McDonald, & Fink, 1992; Gold, Karmiloff-Smith, Skinner, & Morton, 1992). The use of sexual communication for health purposes is further complicated because indirectness and ambiguity are strategically used in sexual encounters both for erotic purpose and to avoid rejection (Adelman, 1992b; Cupach & Metts, 1991). In addition, sexual communication is sometimes coded and nonverbal, and explicit discussion about safer sex may be an open acknowledgment of sexual intentions, which may seem contrary to normative sexual scripts. Nevertheless, many people do communicate about sexual health matters early in their relationships (Catania, Coates, & Kegeles, 1994; see Table 47.1).

Health Related Sexual Communication

We have used the term *health protective sexual communication* (HPSC) to describe communication content that pertains to HIV, STDs, and birth control. HPSC is an important interpersonal element in HIV prevention. Prior work provides strong evidence for the link between HPSC and safer sexual practices (Catania, Coates, & Kegeles, 1994), and reciprocally, a lack of communication has been associated with unprotected sex and other negative outcomes such as unintended pregnancies (Campbell & Barnlund, 1977; Edgar et al., 1992; Gold et al., 1992). It was previously found that people with high levels of HPSC are nearly four times more likely to use condoms than those at moderate to low levels (Catania, Coates, & Kegeles, 1994). Furthermore, the relation between HPSC and condom use holds across diverse populations even after controlling for psychosocial and behavioral factors in multivariate models (Catania, Coates, Greenblatt, et al., 1989; Catania, Coates, Kegeles, et al., 1992; Catania, Coates, Golden, et al., 1994; Centers for Disease Control, 1990; Choi, Wermuth, & Sorensen, 1990; DiClemente, 1991; Edgar et al., 1992; Freimuth et al., 1992; Mays & Cochran, 1993). Lastly, interventions that improve interpersonal communication have beneficial effects on condom use (Kelly et al., 1994; Wenger, Linn, Epstein, & Shapiro, 1991).

HPSC may facilitate safer sex practice in a number of ways. First, HPSC may facilitate the translation of shared intentions into action (e.g., mutual intention to use condoms). Second, HPSC may act as a reminder of HIV and influence the saliency of safer sex concerns over other sexual desires. Third, HPSC may have a persuasive function, for example, by changing the mind of an unmotivated person. Whereas cooperation may be obtained in order to please the partner, or out of fear of punishment, HPSC may in fact reduce uncertainties regarding safe sex behavior, and increase social support by allowing an expression of support, perhaps even encouragement, for safer sex. Finally, HPSC may reinforce subjective norms about condom use, which in turn facilitates the enactment of the behavior.

Correlates of Health Protective Sexual Communication

Despite robust findings linking HPSC and safer sex behavior, little is known about the antecedents of HPSC in the context of new relationships (Basen-Engquist, 1992; Catania, Coates, & Kegeles, 1994; Cupach & Metts, 1991; Edgar et al., 1992; Galligan & Terry, 1993). Preliminary findings are presented on an analysis of demographic and psychosocial correlates of HPSC from a national sample of heterosexuals who, in the past year, had sex with a new (for that year) person.[6]

A number of potential antecedents of HPSC were examined. Of primary importance are variables in the sexual domain. These include perceived sexual self-regulation with regard to the sexual dyad as a whole, and to sexual health matters such as use of condoms, sexual assertiveness skills, and comfort with the possibility of displeasing the partner. These are central elements in negotiating safer sex. Indeed, changing sexual behavior is an interpersonal process that requires confident and assertive people to regulate their sexual interactions, to cope with the embarrassment over discussing sexual matters, as well as overcoming concerns about potential negative consequences of such discussions (Bandura, 1994; Basen-Engquist, 1992; Edgar, 1992; Edgar et al., 1992; Freimuth et al., 1992; Galligan & Terry, 1993). Gender was examined as a proxy for relationship-related role variables,

[6]A summary of the psychosocial measures can be obtained from the first author.

and the following contextual variables were assessed. These include situational (alcohol and drug use during sex), sociocultural (race, education), and developmental context variables (marital status, age, risk expectancies/labeling, sexual guilt, commitment to use condoms, testing and prevention histories; note that commitment and risk expectancies are viewed here as outcomes of individual developmental histories concerning past risk practices, experiences with STDs, and sex-related health scares).

The hypothesized correlates of HPSC were examined in a multivariate model (final $R^2 = .31$; data not shown).[7] The results indicate that respondents with higher HPSC scores were more likely to have greater sexual self-regulation skills (ΔR^2 at entry = .015, $p < .001$; final $\beta = .083$) and condom regulation skills (ΔR^2 at entry = .138, $p < .001$; final b: ability to use a condom = .133, ability to have condom available = .154; persuasive ability = –.002), to be more able to resist unwanted sexual advances (ΔR^2 at entry = .04, $p < .001$; final $\beta = .119$), but were not more or less likely to be concerned about issues of social impression management with regard to voicing desires to use condoms with a new partner.

In terms of developmental contextual variables, higher HPSC scores were associated with a history of being tested for HIV (ΔR^2 at entry = .007, $p < .05$; final $\beta = .08$). Success and failure with HIV-preventive experience may then shape motivations to communicate about such matters (e.g., experience with preventive behaviors may increase self-confidence in one's ability to communicate about safer sex matters to new sexual partners). The multivariate analyses did not show significant differences in HPSC by marital status[8] (see Table 47.1). Age, however, did correlate with HPSC (see Table 47.1; ΔR^2 at entry = .007, $p < .05$; final β: ages 18–29 = .169, 30–39 = .109), with younger respondents from age 18 to 29 being more likely to report HPSC. This may reflect historical differences in comfort with discussing sexual matters or age differences in perceptions of the need to discuss such matters (e.g., greater concern by the young regarding STDs, HIV). Sexual guilt, commitment to use condoms, and perceived HIV risk were also unrelated to HPSC. However, perceived STD risk was significant (ΔR^2 at entry = .005, $p < .05$; final β = –.079). The STD-related perceived risk findings are counterintuitive, and may reflect the causal problems associated with concurrent assessments of perceived risk and sexual communication. Thus, people who have communicated about condoms are more likely to have used them, and therefore perceive themselves to be at low risk (Weinstein & Nicolich, 1993). Perceived susceptibility to HIV was not associated with HPSC, indicating that in this population STDs may be perceived as a bigger threat than HIV, or alternatively, that people feel they have little control over their ability to protect themselves against AIDS. Researchers are continuing to explore possible mediating factors (e.g., gender, ethnicity) with regard to the developmental contextual correlates of HPSC.

In terms of situational variables, respondents who reported having used alcohol before sex were less likely to have communicated with their partner (ΔR^2 at entry = .007, $p < .01$; final β = –.065). Thus, substance use in conjunction with sex may negatively impact motivation or ability to discuss safer sexual matters (Freimuth et al., 1992; Gold et al., 1992; Wight, 1992).

Other sociocultural and relationship variables were represented in the present model by social demographic variables that are assumed to be proxies for other underlying sociocultural processes. Table 47.1 further illustrates how HPSC skills differ by social demographic variables. There was correspondence between the univariate analyses in Table 47.1 and the multivariate modeling of these variables after controlling for all other correlates. Higher HSPC was related to being female (ΔR^2 at entry = .03, $p < .001$; final $\beta = .206$) and to being non- White (ΔR^2 at entry = .007, $p < .05$; final b: White = –.089, Hispanic = –.057). As discussed previously, women are more likely than men to talk about intimate matters (Amaro, 1995; Herold & Mewhinney, 1993; Peplau, 1983; Tolhuizen, 1989). Also, condom use is a different behavior for men than it is for women. Men may choose not to talk about condoms, but simply wear one, whereas women must communicate their desire to use a condom to their partner (Edgar et al., 1992). With regard to communication proficiency, ethnic differences revealed interesting findings. In particular, when considering proficient communicators (see Table 47.1; table note), African Americans are more likely to be highly proficient communicators (40%) as compared to Whites and Latinos (29%–30%). This parallels attitudinal data indicating that African Americans may generally be more comfortable about sexual matters (Belcastro, 1985).

What Are We Talking About?

Although sexual communication is considered to be a key sexual relationship variable of central importance for sexual health, not all studies support this view. A few studies have found no association between discussion and use of condoms (Basen-Engquist, 1992; Cline, Freeman, & Johnson, 1990; Cline, Johnson, & Freeman, 1992). Thus, high levels of sex talk is no guarantee that safe sex behavior will occur, as discussion can be used as a substitute rather than an antecedent to condom use. Indeed, sex communication may even have negative effects on HIV prevention, if it promotes ineffective precautions or creates an enhanced but inappropriate sense of trust and safety between partners (Cline et al., 1990; Cochran & Mays, 1990; Mays & Cochran, 1993). Also, to avoid personal relationship threats inherent, for some, in the discussion of sexual practices, many people may talk about AIDS in a general manner rather than discuss AIDS as it relates to their own relationships (Cline et al., 1992; Perlmutter-Bowen & Michal-Johnson, 1989; Wingood et al., 1993). Such general talk is unlikely to have any effect on safer sex practice. Indeed,

[7]Results presented here (change in R^2 at entry, p value and final b coefficients) refer to a main effects model only. Various gender and race interactions are currently being explored, but are not discussed in this chapter.

[8]The presence of a significant association between HPSC and marital status might be obscured in this sample because the new sexual partners toward which HPSC is directed are probably a mixture of primary and secondary partners (61% of the sample had two or more sexual partners in the past year).

TABLE 47.1
Health Protective Sexual Communication by Sociodemographic Characteristics for Heterosexual Adults in Dating Relationships (N = 837)

Sociodemographic Characteristics	N	HPSC Mean (SD)	Proficient Communicators (%)
Gender			
Male	441	20.9 (6.8)[a]***	21[b]***
Female	396	25.6 (7.3)	47
Age Group			
18–29	440	23.6 (7.2)[c]**	37[d]*
30–39	284	23.1 (7.5)	32
40–49	113	21.2 (7.9)	27
Ethnicity			
White	392	22.3 (7.3)[c]***	30[b]*
African American	323	24.4 (7.3)	40
Hispanic	122	22.4 (7.7)	29
Education			
< 12 years	86	23.6 (8.1)[c]	36[d]
12 years	209	23.3 (7.8)	37
> 12 years	542	23.0 (7.3)	32
Marital Status			
Married	56	21.8 (8.0)[c]†	30[b]
Cohabitinge	67	25.02 (7.1)	42
SDWf	248	23.3 (7.5)	35
Never Married	466	22.9 (7.3)	32
Total sample	**837**	**23.1(7.4) range: 10–40**	**34%**

Note: Prior work has indicated that the relation of HPSC to condom use was not linear across the scale scores, and respondents in the upper one third of scores were substantially more likely to use condoms than those in either the middle or lower thirds (Catania et al., 1994b). Column two then describes proficient communicators by dichotomizing the dependent variable [the top one third higher scores (scores 27–40 = proficient communicators) versus medium to low scores (scores 10–26 = lower communicators)]. The present preliminary analyses are based on Wave II (1992) of the National AIDS Behavioral Survey, a probability telephone survey of HIV-relevant sexual behavior in the United States. Methodological details on the surveys are described elsewhere (Catania et al., 1992b). The present analysis is based on a sample of 837 respondents (a combination of a national and a high risk city sample) who reported having had sex with at least one new sexual partner in the past 12 months, were heterosexual (defined as respondents with all sexual partners of the opposite gender in the past 5 years), age 18 to 49, and who completed the HSPC 10-item scale. Asians, Native Americans, and Pacific Islanders were excluded because they were not adequately represented for analysis purposes ($n = 24$).
[a] t test for mean difference
[b] chi-square test of heterogeneity
[c] One way ANOVA F test
[d] Mantel–Haenszel test for linear association
[e] Cohabiting = Living with main sexual partner, but not married
[f] SDW = Separated, Divorced, Widowed
† $p < .1$
* $p < .05$
** $p < .01$
*** $p < .001$

prior work suggests that to be effective, HPSC must be specific, intentional, and persuasive. Thus, it is important to consider what is being said specifically, and not simply conclude that because people are talking about "sex" or "AIDS" it will yield clear decisions or any decisions at all with respect to sexual health.

The art of sexual communication is not a simple matter. As studies indicate, people who are more assertive, more self-confident, better able to express their feelings and needs in the sexual arena, and have a history of taking preventive actions (e.g., were tested for HIV) are more proficient communicators. Moreover, communication may need to be integrated into the sexual repertoire and scripts in a way that does not detract from the quality of the sexual relationship. Many people find it difficult to discuss health-related sexual matters without disrupting the flow of the love-making process. Thus, many qualitative issues that have not yet been explored (e.g., timing, tact, and listening skills) may be of primary importance in learning how to discuss safe sexual practices. Finally, health protective sexual communication is likely to remain conflict laden, as long as the seemingly contradictory values related to sex remain. Sexual values such as ambiguity and explicitness, romanticism and health, trust and risk, intimacy and protection may perpetuate the difficulties surrounding discussions and decisions about safe sex (Adelman, 1991; Holland et al., 1992; Wight, 1992). With the emergence of AIDS and other STDs, new paradigms should be developed to capture the interpersonal quality of sexual encounters (Adelman, 1991, 1992a). For example, if safe sex is viewed as an adversarial process, effective negotiators may require assertiveness skills and power to obtain compliance. Alternatively, if safe sex is thought of as part of a "conversation" (Davies, Hickson, Weatherburn, & Hunt, 1993), as a "step" or movement in a dance, then it may require qualities such as imagination, adaptability, interpersonal, and nurturing skills to become a proficient communicator.

Power Dynamics in Sexual Encounters

When people come together to have sex, they are also coming together for a number of reasons that reflect social and emotional issues. Love, nurturance, altruism, and perceived attractiveness are all positive emotional elements that play themselves out in this intimate social situation. However, the process of coming together may also place partners at odds with one another. Power issues in the sexual relationship are key elements in the nature and potential resolution of these conflicts. The effects of gender differences with regard to power are particularly obvious in the sexual relationship. This section explores the issue of power dynamics in the arena of sexual health decision making.

In the context of AIDS, women are told they should protect themselves when having penetrative sex, even though men control the means of protection. To argue that women are free to choose the most rational form of protection ignores the nature of systematic inequalities in the social relationships between women and men, and the nature of social arrangements that systematically privilege male sexuality and desire (Holland, Ramazanoglu, Scott, Sharpe, & Thompson, 1990a; Holland, Ramazanoglu, Sharpe, & Thompson, 1994). This is not to say, however, that gender-specific obstacles to safer sex practice are the sole responsibility of men, as many of these obstacles are rooted in women's conception and acceptance of gender roles and sexuality.

The Continuation of Male Privilege

The changes brought about by women's changing position in society have not altered, for the most part, the deeply internalized sexual scripts of male dominance and female passivity that frame heterosexual encounters (Siann, 1994). For adolescent men, the message is to have sex, and for adolescent women, the message is to avoid it. In all types of coupled relationships, Blumstein and Schwartz (1983) found that men continued to stress the need for dominance and women stressed the need not for submission, but a reluctance to dominate, and a desire for closer emotional relationships. Men are still expected to be assertive in dating and sexual relationships. They are expected to ask women out, propose marriage, and make sexual advances (Blumstein & Schwartz, 1983; Peplau, 1984). However, situations in which women dominate or in which both partners mutually decide the nature of their sexual encounters are certainly not unusual. It is important to better understand the ways in which the characteristics of each partner (e.g., age, education, social class), the nature of the relationship, and the situational context in which sex occurs condition the level and nature of power dynamics in sexual encounters.

Women's Participation in the Reprodution of Male Privilege

One important research direction that needs to be pursued is the examination of the ways in which society socially constructs women to participate in their own domination. Women often are described in terms of, and encouraged to develop, personal psychological characteristics that are pleasing to men (Amaro, 1995). These characteristics form a certain familiar cluster: submissiveness, passivity, docility, dependency, lack of initiative, and the inability to act, to decide, or to think. Asking women to place their own needs (e.g., condom use) ahead of the needs of their male partner would contradict aspects of feminine identity. In a study of women in late adolescence, Holland and her colleagues (Holland, Ramazanoglu, Scott, Sharpe & Thompson, 1990b) found that male power in heterosexual encounters was both embraced and resisted by young women in the course of negotiating sex (Holland et al., 1990a). Their reluctance to insist on condoms stemmed from an unwillingness to hurt men's feelings, and the fear that the assertion of their own needs would upset their male partners. Even in relationships defined in terms of love and trust, sexual safety was often a contradictory practice. Young women tended to silence their own thoughts and feelings for the sake of the relationship, especially when their thoughts and feelings threatened to be disruptive (Brown & Gilligan, 1992).

There are also situations in which women use aspects of gender roles to facilitate safer sex practices, but in the process, reinforce these stereotypes. For example, A. Kline, E. Kline, and Oken (1992) found that one strategy African American and Hispanic women (IDUs or the partners of IDUs) used to persuade their partners to use condoms was to focus on the male role as "protector of the family," in effect reinforcing the male role as the one in control. In Sobo's (1993) description of the experiences and understandings of heterosexual relationships of low income African American women, it was clear that practicing unsafe sex was one way to deny that one's sexual partner was unfaithful. Using a condom was seen as a signal of infidelity in their relationship, and fostered an image of their partner they did not want portrayed in their social world. However, the unintended consequence of idealizing and romanticizing such relationships indirectly reinforced the script of monogamy for women, but not for men.

The Decline of the Double Standard

One of the trends over the last 20 to 25 years has been the decline in age of first intercourse for women (Tanfer & Schoorl, 1992; Zelnik, Kantner, & Ford, 1981). A second trend is the increase in age of first marriage for both men and women and an increase in sexual relationships outside of marriage (Binson et al., 1993). One way of thinking about these trends is that they are possibly reflecting a decline in the double standard and an increase in equality between men and women. A closer inspection, however, reveals a more complicated situation. Recent work by Laumann and his colleagues (1994) found that 90% of the men and only 70% of women reported wanting sex when they had sex the first time. Besides the fact that fewer women actually wanted sex initially, the reasons they gave for engaging in sex for the first time are particularly interesting. Women were twice as likely than men to report they had sex because of affection for their partner (48% for women; 25% for men). Of those who indicated they did not want but were not forced to have sex, 10% of the men and 38% of the women indicated they had sex because of affection for their partner. In addition, younger women were more likely than older women to report not wanting their first experience of vaginal intercourse to occur when it did (Laumann et al., 1994). It appears that although more women are having sex at younger ages, fewer women engage in sex because they want to. Holland et al. (1990a) also found that for many young English women, sex was not a particularly pleasurable experience. Women valued the social relationship, not the sexual relationship. What are some of the reasons young women who do not want to have sex, willingly engage in it? What are the consequences to their sexual health? To explore this question, the data are examined from six focus groups that were part of a research project designed to investigate various dimensions of power in the context of sexual interactions among young men and women.[9] Each of the focus group sessions lasted from 2½ to

[9]This study was supported with a grant from the American Foundation for AIDS Research (no. 02285-16-RG).

3 hours. There were between 8 and 12 participants in each group, four groups of women and two groups of men. Participants were between age 18 and 25, noncollege educated, African American, White, and Hispanic. All were sexually active and had two or more partners in the last year.

Scripting Theory

One approach to the analysis of power issues in sexual relationships involves analyzing these interactions in terms of sexual scripts, particularly cultural scripts that tend to define and reinforce male domination. Sexual scripting theory (Gagnon, 1990; Gagnon & Simon, 1973; Simon & Gagnon, 1986, 1987) addresses the structure of sexual encounters: with whom people have sex, when and where they should have sex, what they should do sexually, and why they should do sexual things. Scripts operate at three levels: cultural, interpersonal, and intrapsychic. Cultural scenarios are instructional guides that exist at the level of collective life. Interpersonal scripts operate at the level of social interaction and the acceptance and use of such scripts are the basis for continued patterns of structured social behavior. Intrapsychic scripts represent the content of mental life. In part, they are the result of cultural scenarios and the demands of interaction, and in part, they are independent of them. This section focuses on cultural scripts that reinforce male domination in heterosexual scenarios, and the ways in which young women both embrace and reject their sexual script.

One study's findings, which involved the lack of discussion between men and women regarding sex and/or risk protection, has a direct bearing on the context of power dynamics. Much of their sexual activity appears to be guided by unstated, implicitly accepted *cultural scenarios.* In interviews with men, it became clear that using protection was the antithesis of sex as they defined it. That is, sex was "supposed to be" spontaneous, not planned. Even though they often have sex in mind when dating, they felt any discussion of sex would destroy the element of spontaneity. This has implications, of course, in terms of condom use. In particular, men felt they could not look prepared because sex has to at least look spontaneous: "If you've got it [condom] right there, she's going to think, oh, you just knew this was going to happen, you just knew that you were going to get this [sex]."

Submission and Resistance

One reason women gave for having sex, even when they did not want to, was the belief that it was something they had to do to keep a boyfriend, because it was what they thought relationships were all about. When they were in their teens, they felt they would receive love if they had sex. Sex was a means of obtaining approval from men. Many of these women felt that relationships were supposed to be this way, and it was part of what was expected of them as women. These accounts of their personal experiences echo the sexual script for women. That is, cultural scripts organized sexual situations for these young women in such a way that they were not expected to exert control. Instead, the scripts legitimized submissiveness as the appropriate behavior in those situations. The following descriptions exemplify the powerful influence of the submissive script on women's sexual beliefs and expectations:

> Our whole relationship was based on it (sex), and if I wanted to keep him as my boyfriend, I had to have sex with him on a regular basis. There was a lot of pressure there. A lot of pressure. ... You guys are saying the pressure's on, and that's the truth, but at the time, I thought that's what it's all about. I said, all right, I'm going to be miserable forever. That's it, sex is not going to be good, and if I'm going to have any kind of relationship at all, this is part of the equation. That's sad. I know that now.

Or, as one of the younger woman stated:

> If I could change one thing, it would be not to get too involved and too trusting, because they [men] end up hurting you in the end. ... I don't regret having my baby or having sex, because *it's all a part of growing* (emphasis added).

Women interviewed attempted to empower themselves through control of their appearance. They talked about making themselves alluring through their dress in order to entice a man into having sex with them. At other times they would use this pressure as a way to gain control over sexual encounters, as a *form of resistance.* For example, one woman discussed "dismissing" men after having sex with them, telling them to leave immediately. That is, rather than withholding sex, she withheld "romance." She used this strategy as a way to make men more interested in future sexual encounters. It was her way of getting her sex partners to want to have sex with her, even though she was not particularly interested in having sex. It was her way, perhaps, of gaining control over her feelings of powerlessness. She felt she was "calling the shots." It has often been stated that in past generations women were the regulators of sex. Now, it appears, women do not regulate whether or not sex takes place, but instead they regulate what sex means. One aspect of their insurgency resides perhaps in resisting the cultural script that organizes and interprets the meaning of sex for women as attachment or commitment to the men in their lives.

Another strategy women used to resist male control of the sexual context was through the use of drugs and/or alcohol. Studies indicate that alcohol or drugs are used in sexual encounters to reduce sexual inhibitions, to make individuals feel free to pursue their amorous feelings. People also use alcohol as an excuse to have sex in situations where they really want to have sex, but find it difficult to admit that they do, to themselves (or their partners). Some young women, however, discussed alcohol use as a *form of resistance.* That is, alcohol and/or drugs was used to get through a sexual encounter they did not want. This was a premeditated action. They knew they did not want to have sex. They used alcohol to get through it, to numb themselves—it was a passive way to resist in the process of complying. This kind of passive resistance allowed them to control the subjective meaning of particular sexual encounters, even though objectively, they were complying with what their boyfriends wanted. He may have "thought he knew what was going on," but she was in control from her perspective. Using drugs and/or alcohol was a way to do what they thought was expected of them (cultural script), to use sex as a way of getting male approval, as "a way to be loved," but to deny the powerlessness involved. Ultimately, neither partner was in control, and sex in these contexts was frequently unprotected.

The Erosion and Permanence of the Sexual Domination of Women

The introduction of the "pill" in the late 1950s set the conditions for an upheaval in the sexual balance of power between men and women. Women who came of age in 1960s were the first generation of women to have access to reliable birth control, they were the first generation of young women in large numbers to have the option of approaching sex as recreation so that they were not burdened with pregnancy or the constraints of a relationship. In the age of "free love," the double standard that afforded men permission and encouragement to experiment sexually and disapproved of women who acted in a similar manner was challenged. Although there may be an increasing egalitarianism between men and women, reflected in the greater societal indifference to the double standard, consider whether the disappearance, or at least easing, of the double standard is, in every aspect, a wonderful development for women. In the past 30 years, there have been changes in the sexual script in heterosexual relationships, yet the fundamental sexual and social inequality between men and women remain. The sexual context has changed, the rules of the game have changed. The relaxing of the double standard is a positive and potentially liberating change. It has increased the number of options open to women. However, as recent research in this area has shown, sex is still embedded in a gendered system: Sex is something that young men want and "getting it" is basically an unvarnished good for men; for young women, sex is often associated with fear and danger. Whereas women are open to sexual encounters with men, they also are much more likely than men to be forced to do something sexually that they did not want to do (Choi, Binson, Adelson, & Catania, 1998; Laumann et al., 1994). For many women, close, personal relationships veil the reality of sexual coercion, as many were forced to do something sexual by someone they trusted and knew well (Laumann et al., 1994; Muehlenhard & McCoy, 1991).

Research on Sexual Power Dynamics

Studying the distribution of power in heterosexual encounters requires asking questions about the construction of sexual meaning (Schneider & Gould, 1987). Where does meaning come from? Do women have the power to define sexual vocabularies and to create their own meaning? These questions are critical for a more complete understanding of the ways by which safer sex practices are incorporated into interpersonal scripts. What strategies do women (and men) use to ensure safer sex practices with their sexual partners? In what ways do the images of what it means to be a man and what it means to be a women reinforce the domination of women in heterosexual encounters? The development of a model of sexual risk behaviors that considers women's social status needs to include variables that reflect a woman's power in a specific relationship and her adherence to traditional roles (Amaro, 1995). Future work needs to extend these research efforts to include the sexual dyad, to investigate the ways in which power dynamics are socially encouraged and individually resisted, and to grapple with strategies that confront the foundation of the social inequality of women. This research will help to empower women and men to negotiate gratifying sexual lives.

Sexual Boundaries

Another important element in the sexual relationships is the boundaries placed on sexual activity with others. Relationship boundaries are determined either implicitly or explicitly by the individuals in the relationship. In sexual relationships, these boundaries concern people's beliefs about monogamy and nonmonogamy. In monogamous relationships, neither partner has other sexual partners, whereas in nonmonagamous relationships, one or both partners has sex with individuals outside the relationship. Nonmonogamous relationships tend to come about via two pathways. In some instances, there is mutual consent to having an open relationship in which one or both partners may have extra relational sexual partners. In other instances, there is no explicit agreement about the acceptability of having other partners, but one or both individuals has sex with others. These latter relationships are referred to as semi-closed.

Relationships in which there are outside sexual partners carry potential health risks; prior work suggests that men are more likely than women to have extra relational sex (Choi et al., 1994; Grinstead et al., 1993). In fact, it has been observed that many women are at risk for HIV and other STDs due to the behavior of their main sexual partner, although they themselves do not engage in risky behaviors (Dolcini & Catania, 1995; Grinstead et al., 1993). Here the focus is on women with a risky male sexual partner (WWRP). These women are often portrayed as less powerful individuals unable to protect themselves for a variety of personal, social, and/or economic reasons (Amaro, 1995; Worth, 1989). Although power issues are indeed important in sexual relationships, focusing on subgroups of WWRPs is expected to reveal a more complex picture. Women in open relationships will be expected to differ from those in semi-closed, but risky relationships.

Defining WWRPS: Open Versus Semi-Closed Relationships

Drawing from the NABS II (Catania et al., 1995), a group of 209 women from age 18 to 49, who had risky male sexual partners, was identified. A risky male partner was identified as someone who had multiple partners or who had used IV drugs in the past 5 years. Within the sample addressed here, all of the male partners had multiple partners. Each WWRP indicated whether she and her partner had a relationship in which both partners agreed that having outside sexual relationships was acceptable.[10] One third of women indicated they had an open relationship. Women in open versus semi-closed relationships were compared on a number of demographic, contextual, behavioral, and attitudinal variables in order to characterize these two subgroups.

Demographic and Contextual Characteristics: Open Relationships

It was found that WWRPs in open relationships were more highly educated ($p = .001$)[11] and tended to have higher incomes ($p = .09$).[12] Education has been associated with a greater departure from traditional sex roles and norms and behavioral differences have been found between low and highly educated women (Dolcini et al., 1993). There were no ethnic differences between those in open and semi-closed relationships, despite having an ethnically mixed sample of women (42% White, 39% African American, 15% Hispanic, 4% other). Open relationships tended to be shorter than semi-closed relationships (3.8 years vs. 6.4, $p < .001$).[13] Differences in relationship length may reflect difficulties in maintaining open relationships and the constant negotiation necessary to accommodate outside sexual partners. Because all of the male partners and over half of the females in open relationships had other partners, all of the women in the sample in open relationships had to deal with these issues. Given the complexities of maintaining multiple sexual relationships, it is not surprising that only a small minority of those in open relationships were living in the same household as their male partner (4%). In contrast, almost half of those in semi-closed relationships lived in the same household. Moreover, it was found that almost a fourth of those in open relationships lived in a different city than their main partner. This situation has important implications for the geographic spread of STDs. Another factor that was expected to differ between these two groups was the presence of children in the home. It was surprising to find that there were no differences between the two groups in this regard; approximately half of all women had children living with them.

HIV/STD Related Attitudes and Behaviors

Individuals who have extra-relational sex partners can reduce their risks by engaging in health protective behaviors. There was speculation that those in open relationships would recognize the greater risks associated with their chosen lifestyle and would engage in more protective behaviors. Neither of these was true. There were no differences in perceptions of personal risk for HIV or STDs between women in open versus semi-closed relationships. Likewise, there were no differences in condom use, and overall condom use for the sample was low (23% WWRPs always used condoms). Thus, whether the relationship was open or semi-closed, these women tended not to acknowledge their risk for HIV/STDs and were not engaging in high levels of protective behaviors.

It has been speculated that bisexuals are at greater risk for HIV/STD transmission, and in fact may be a "bridge" for disease transmission from one group to another (Chu, Peterman, Doll, Buehler, & Curran, 1992). Sexual orientation was examined within the sample of WWRPs, and found that those in open relationships were far more likely to report that either they or their male partner had same gender sexual partners (females: 7 vs. 1%, $p = .02$; males: 5 vs. < 1%, $p = .07$).[14] In addition to being a marker for potentially greater disease transmission, being bisexual or having a partner who is bisexual may also reflect more liberal sexual attitudes.

Aside from sexual activity, the other primary behavior involved in the transmission of HIV is IV drug use. According to the WWRPs, one quarter of their male partners had a history of using IV drugs. Women in open relationships were far less likely to report having a partner who used IV drugs compared to women in semi-closed relationships (10% vs. 34%, $p < .001$).[15] Thus, a significant proportion of women in semi-closed relationships have the potential to be exposed to HIV through multiple sources as a function of their partner's behavior.

Psychosexual Variables

We have seen substantial differences between WWRPs in open versus semi-closed relationships on a number of characteristics. Yet, little is known about why some women are in open relationships. One speculation is that there are philosophical reasons for choosing this type of relationship. Consistent with this notion are our findings that women in open relationships were less guilty about sex ($p = .04$)[16] and held more liberal attitudes about sex (i.e., extramarital sex, premarital sex; $p < .001$)[17] than those in semi-closed relationships. Another possibility is that open relationships develop as a function of troubled sexual partnerships. That is, one or both partners have sexual problems and engage in extra relational sex as a way to obtain sexual satisfaction. Although the WWRPs as a whole report more sexual problems than a group of matched control women (Dolcini & Catania, 1995), no differences were found between women in open versus semi-closed relationships with regard to sexual problems.

In keeping with the notion that extra relational sex takes place by the male in semi-closed relationships due to his

[10]The question used to determine open versus closed relationship is: "Some couples have open sexual relationships. In this type of relationship partners openly agree that one or both of them can have sex with people outside their relationship. Do you have this kind of sexual relationship with your main sexual partner?"

[11]Chi-square

[12]Chi-square

[13]*t* test, Mann–Whitney U

[14]Chi-square

[15]Chi-square

[16]*t* test, Mann–Whitney U

[17]*t* test, Mann–Whitney U

greater power, other variables were examined that might reflect imbalances in power within the relationship to see if these differed by type of relationship. The two groups of women did not differ in their ability to resist sexual encounters, to regulate the sexual relationship, or in their ability to initiate sex in the relationship. As a whole, WWRPs report less ability to regulate their sexual relationships as compared to controls, but do not differ on the other variables (Dolcini & Catania, 1995). So, there may be less control in general for WWRPs, but having a power differential does not differentiate those in open versus semi-closed relationships. The findings suggest that it is possible for people in egalitarian relationships to negotiate either a monogamous or a nonmonogamous relationship depending on their philosophical orientation.

In summary, evidence was found for two types of sexual relationships in which one or both partners were having extra-relational sex and important differences were found between women in open versus semi-closed relationships. Those in open relationships were more educated, were less likely to live with their partner, and were in relationships of shorter duration. They also held more liberal sexual attitudes, were less guilty about sex, and were more likely to be bisexual as compared to women in semi-closed relationships. Taken together, these findings suggest strong philosophical differences between women in these two groups and point to the need to examine subgroups within at risk populations, such as WWRPs.

CONCLUSIONS

This chapter has discussed emergent areas in the behavioral epidemiology of HIV, including work on sexual mixing, mapping at risk populations, and sexual relationships. Thus, it has moved from a macrolevel of analysis that examines the connections between disparate sexual dyads to a microlevel that concerns the basic unit in the transmission of sexual diseases, the sexual dyad. It is important, however, to not forget the individual in this process. Change begins with individuals, is behaviorally enacted in the bounds of the sexual dyad, and modifications within dyads produce changes in the sexual network dynamics of STD/HIV transmission.

In studying the sexual relationship, there are numerous problems that have confronted investigators in research on marital and family relationships. How do researchers conceptualize, assesses, and analyze dyadic or couple information? Current approaches to studying sexual relationships are often more like a tug-o-war than a dance. Issues of altruism, mutuality, and negotiation are not being adequately addressed in the literature.

In addition, this is a culture that often views penises and vaginas as an enemy from which people need protection. Sex negative cultures are not good bases for developing healthy sexual lives. How such cultural variables influence sexual relationships is an important issue that deserves more attention than it is currently receiving. This brief look at this issue illustrates that even basic skills, such as sexual communication, vary as a result of ethnicity. Thus, ethnic-cultural issues may contribute to the development of sexual communication skills. However, it was also found that males and females are consistently different from each other in sexual communication skills across ethnic groups. Consequently, any developmental differences that occur across ethnic groups also take place in a larger cultural context that universally produces gender differences in sexual skill development. These types of analyses, however, are still in their infancy. Researchers are far from reaching the goal of identifying the cultural institutions and related beliefs and values that shape the differences observed across grossly classified demographic variables.

Research on sexual networks is still in its infancy, and there are difficulties with existing work that relies on the egocentric method of network identification. Ideally, researchers would want to begin with probability samples of a population and trace all of the sample member's sexual partners over a period of time, then conduct interviews with each partner. At this juncture, it is unclear how successful they would be in accomplishing tracing procedures occurring outside the context of the legal imperatives of public health agencies. Further, they do not know how deep they would need to trace in order to have an accurate picture of the size and density of sexual networks. Do they need to interview the respondents' partners, the partners' partners, and so on? Where can researchers stop the tracing process and still have an adequate picture?

Although some of this discussion of sexual mixing falls into the purview of mathematical modeling of HIV/STDs, health psychologists are of central importance in generating the behavioral data that modelers will employ. Health psychologists may also make other contributions in this area. Researchers need to know more about how to conceptualize sexual mixing patterns if they are to describe the degree of mixing among and between heterosexual population segments with multiple sexual partners, and the geographic distribution of their population. The spread of HIV/STDs nationally not only depends on the degree of mixing across and within social strata (and other behavioral and biological conditions), but, as noted previously, also depends on the "sexual avenues" connecting cities, suburbs, and rural areas (Golub et al., 1993; Wallace, 1991, 1994). What are the social and behavioral rules that govern these network structures and mixing patterns? These complexities, in addition to the unknown contributions of HIV co-factors with a high prevalence among heterosexuals (e.g., HSV-2, chlamydia; Laga et al., 1993; Siegel et al., 1992; Webster et al., 1993), strike a cautionary note to the view that heterosexual spread will not occur because of low average infectivity rates (e.g., Laumann et al., 1994). In addition, the unknowns about the population dynamics of HIV, and the continued increase in heterosexually transmitted cases, suggest that the prudent action at this juncture is to assume that at-risk heterosexuals should be the target of prevention programs promoting condom use, HIV testing, and other prevention practices; if nothing else, they may well avoid contracting one of the 15 or more other STDs currently infecting the U.S. heterosexual population.

To date, the epidemiological mapping data indicate that adult heterosexuals at risk for HIV and other STDs represent a fluid, dynamic population. Estimating changes in the size, turnover, and prevention practices of this population segment remains an important challenge. There is a need for a series of surveys in this area to assess the reliability of past findings, and to regularly monitor how the general U.S. population is responding to HIV and other STD prevention programs.

In summary, this chapter has reviewed literature on sexual mixing and networks, and has presented new data showing that the degree of sexual mixing differs by urban setting, gender, age, and ethnic group. Recent mapping studies illustrate the fluid nature of at risk populations. This fluidity complicates the ability to predict STD/HIV disease spread. It has touched on the many social and psychological models currently being used to study sexual behaviors relevant to HIV disease, and noted some general common deficiencies in these models. A particular deficiency is the lack of work on the sexual relationship. Finally, the chapter has presented the elements of a model for understanding sexual relationships and followed this with data on four aspects of sexual relationships that are of significance for sexual health: gender differences, sexual communication, power, and relationship boundaries.

ACKNOWLEDGMENTS

This work was supported in part by grants to the first author from the National Institute on Mental Health and National Institute on Aging (MH48642, MH48638, MH43892, MH51523).

REFERENCES

Abraham, C. S., & Sheeran, P. (1994). Modelling and modifying young heterosexuals' HIV-preventive behaviour: A review of theories, findings, and educational implications. *Patient Education & Counseling, 23,* 173–186.

Adelman, M. B. (1991). Play and incongruity: Framing safe-sex talk. *Health Communication, 3,* 139–155.

Adelman, M. B. (1992a). Health passions: Safer sex as play. In M. A. Fitzpatrick, T. Edgar, & V. S. Freimuth (Eds.), *AIDS: A common perspective* (pp. 69–89). Hillsdale, NJ: Lawrence Erlbaum Associates.

Adelman, M. B. (1992b). Sustaining passion: Eroticism and safe-sex talk. *Archives of Sexual Behavior, 21,* 481–494.

Amaro, H. (1995). Love, sex, and power: Considering women's realities in HIV prevention. *American Psychologist, 50,* 437–447.

Anderson, R. (1991). The transmission dynamics of sexually transmitted diseases: The behavioral component. In J. Wasserheit, S. Aral, & K. Holmes (Eds.), *Research issues in human behavior and sexually transmitted diseases in the AIDS era* (pp. 38–60). Washington, DC: American Society for Microbiology.

Aral, S. O., & Holmes, K. K. (1984). Epidemiology of sexually transmitted diseases. In K. K. Holmes, P. Mardh, P. F. Sparling, & P. J. Weisner (Eds.), *Sexually transmitted diseases* (pp. 126–141). New York: McGraw-Hill.

Auerbach, J. D., Wypijewska, C., & Brodie, K. H. (Eds.). (1994). *AIDS and behavior: An integrated approach.* Washington, DC: National Academy Press.

Bandura, A. (1986). *Social foundations of thought and action: A social cognitive theory.* Englewood Cliffs, NJ: Prentice-Hall.

Bandura, A. (1994). A social cognitive approach to the exercise of control over AIDS infection. In R. J. Diclemente & J. L. Peterson (Eds.), *Preventing AIDS: Theories and methods of behavioral interventions* (pp. 89–115). New York: Plenum.

Basen-Engquist, K. (1992). Psychosocial predictors of "safer sex" behaviors in young adults. *AIDS Education and Prevention, 4,* 120–134.

Baumeister, R. F. (1988). Should we stop studying sex differences altogether? *American Psychologist, 43,* 1092–1095.

Belcastro, P. A. (1985). Sexual behavior differences between Black and White students. *Journal of Sex Research, 21,* 56–67.

Binson, D., Dolcini, M. M., Pollack, L. M., & Catania, J. A. (1993). Multiple sex partners among young adults: The National AIDS Behavioral Surveys (NABS). *Family Planning Perspectives, 25,* 268.

Black, M., Stanton, B., Whitehead, T. L., & Galbraith, J. (1993). *Planning theory-based intervention research: The reduction of AIDS-risk behavior in adolescents.* Unpublished manuscript.

Blumstein, P., & Schwartz, P. (1983). *American couples: Money, work, sex.* New York: Morrow.

Boss, P. G., Doherty, W. J., LaRossa, R., Schumm, W. R., & Steinmetz, S. K. (Eds.). (1993). *Sourcebook of family theories and methods: A contextual approach.* New York: Plenum.

Bowen, A. M., & Trotter, II, R. (1995). HIV risk in intravenous drug users and crack cocaine smokers: Predicting stage of change for condom use. *Journal of Consulting and Clinical Psychology, 63,* 238–248.

Boyer, C. B., & Kegeles, S. M. (1991). AIDS risk and prevention among adolescents. *Social Science and Medicine, 33,* 11–23.

Breakwell, G. M., Millward, L. J., & Fife-Schaw, C. (1994). Commitment to "safer" sex as a predictor of condom use among 16–20 year olds. *Journal of Applied Social Psychology, 24,* 189–217.

Brown, L., & Gilligan, C. (1992). *Meeting at the crossroads: Women's psychology and girls' development.* Cambridge, MA: Harvard University Press.

Buss, D. M. (1988). The evolution of human intrasexual competition: Tactics of mate attraction. *Journal of Personality and Social Psychology, 54,* 616–628.

Buss, D. M., & Schmitt, D. P. (1993). Sexual strategies theory: An evolutionary perspective on human mating. *Psychological Review, 2,* 204–232.

Campbell, B. K., & Barnlund, D. C. (1977). Communication style: A clue to unplanned pregnancy. *Medical Care, 15,* 181–186.

Catania, J. A., & Binson, D. (1992). *Behavioral epidemiology of HIV-related sexual behavior: Report to the NIMH.* San Francisco: University of California.

Catania, J. A., Binson, D., Dolcini, M. M., Stall, R., Choi, K.-H., Pollack, L. M., Hudes, E. S., Canchola, J., Phillips, K., Moskowitz, J. T., & Coates, T. J. (1995). Risk factors for HIV and other sexually transmitted diseases and prevention practices among US heterosexual adults: Changes from 1990–1992. *American Journal of Public Health, 85.*

Catania, J. A., Binson, D., & Stone, V. (1996). The relationship of sexual mixing across age and racial groups to herpes simplex virus-2 among unmarried heterosexuals with multiple sexual partners. *Health Psychology, 15*(5), 362–370.

Catania, J. A., Coates, T. J., Golden, E., Dolcini, M. M., Peterson, J., Kegeles, S., Siegel, D., & Fullilove, M. (1994). Correlates of condom use among Black, Hispanic, and White heterosexuals in San Francisco: The AMEN Longitudinal Survey. *AIDS Education and Prevention, 6*(1), 12–26.

Catania, J. A., Coates, T. J., Greenblatt, R., Dolcini, M. M., Kegeles, S. M., Puckett, S., Corman, M., & Miller, J. (1989). Predictors of condom use and multiple-partnered sex among sexually-active adolescent women: Health interventions. *Journal of Sex Research, 26,* 514–524.

Catania, J. A., Coates, T. J., & Kegeles, S. (1994). A test of the AIDS risk reduction model: Psychosocial correlates of condom use in the AMEN cohort survey. *Health Psychology, 13,* 548–555.

Catania, J. A., Coates, T. J., Kegeles, S. M., Ekstrand, M., Guydish, J., & Bye, L. (1989). Implications of the AIDS risk reduction model for the gay community: The importance of perceived sexual enjoyment and help-seeking behaviors. In V. Mays, G. Albee, & S. Schneider (Eds.), *Primary prevention of AIDS: Psychological approaches* (pp. 242–261). Newbury Park, CA: Sage.

Catania, J. A., Coates, T. J., Kegeles, S., Thompson-Fullilove, M., Peterson, J., Marin, B., Siegel, D., & Hulley, S. (1992). Condom use in multi-ethnic neighborhoods of San Francisco: The population-based AMEN (AIDS in Multi-Ethnic Neighborhoods) study. *American Journal of Public Health, 82,* 284–287.

Catania, J. A., Coates, T. J., Peterson, J., Dolcini, M. M., Kegeles, S., Siegel, D., Golden, E., & Fullilove, M. (1993). Changes in condom use among Black, Hispanic, and White heterosexuals in San Francisco: The AMEN cohort survey. *Journal of Sex Research, 30,* 121–128.

Catania, J. A., Coates, T. J., Stall, R. D., Bye, L., Kegeles, S. M., Capell, F., Henne, J., McKusick, L., Morin, S., Turner, H., & Pollack, L. (1991). Changes in condom use among homosexual men in San Francisco. *Health Psychology, 10,* 190–199.

Catania, J. A., Coates, T. J., Stall, R., Turner, H., Peterson, J., Hearst, N., Dolcini, M., Hudes, E., Gagnon, J., Wiley, J., & Groves, R. (1992). Prevalence of AIDS-related risk factors and condom use in the United States. *Science, 258,* 1101–1106.

Catania, J. A., Kegeles, S. M., & Coates, T. J. (1990). Towards an understanding of risk behavior: An AIDS risk reduction model (ARRM). *Health Education Quarterly, 17,* 381–399.

Catania, J. A., McDermott, L., & Pollack, L. (1984). Assessment of locus of control: Situational specificity in the sexual context. *Journal of Sex Research, 20,* 310–324.

Catania, J. A., Stone, V., Binson, D., & Dolcini, M. M. (1995). Changes in condom use among heterosexuals in Wave 3 of the AMEN survey. *Journal of Sex Research, 32*(3), 193–200.

Centers for Disease Control. (1990). Heterosexual behaviors and factors that influence condom use among patients attending a sexually transmitted disease clinic - San Francisco. *Morbidity and Mortality Weekly Report, 39,* 685–689.

Centers for Disease Control. (1994). *HIV/AIDS surveillance report.* U.S. Department of Health and Human Services.

Choi, K.-H., Binson, D., Adelson, M., & Catania, J. A. (1998). Sexual harassment, sexual coercion, sexual dysfunction, and HIV risk among U.S. adults 18–49 years. *AIDS & Behavior, 2,* 33–40.

Choi, K., Catania, J. A., Coates, T. J., Hyung, L. D., & Hearst, N. (1992). International travel and AIDS risk in South Korea. *AIDS, 6,* 1555–1557.

Choi, K., Catania, J. A., & Dolcini, M. M. (1994). Extramarital sex and AIDS risk among U.S. adults in 1990: Results from the national AIDS behavioral surveys. *American Journal of Public Health, 84,* 2003–2007.

Choi, K., Wermuth, L., & Sorensen, J. (1990). Predictors of condom use among women sexual partners of intravenous drug users. In *Proceedings of the Sixth International Conference on AIDS, 2,* p. 271.

Chu, S. Y., Peterman, T. A., Doll, L. A., Buehler, J. W., & Curran, J. W. (1992). AIDS in bisexual men in the United States: Epidemiology and transmission to women. *American Journal of Public Health, 82,* 220–224.

Cline, R. W., Freeman, K. E., & Johnson, S. J. (1990). Talk among sexual partners about AIDS: Factors differentiating those who talk from those who do not. *Communication Research, 17,* 792–808.

Cline, R. W., Johnson, S. J., & Freeman, K. E. (1992). Talk among sexual partners about AIDS: Interpersonal communication for risk reduction or risk enhancement? *Health Communication, 4,* 39–56.

Cochran, S. D., & Mays, V. M. (1990). Sex, lies, and HIV. *New England Journal of Medicine, 322,* 774–775.

Cupach, W., & Metts, S. (1991). Sexuality and communication use in close relationships. In K. McKinney & S. Sprecher (Eds.), *Sexuality in close relationships* (pp. 93–110). Hillsdale, NJ: Lawrence Erlbaum Associates.

Davies, P. M., Hickson, F.C.I., Weatherburn, P., & Hunt, A. J. (1993). Theorizing sex. In P. M. Davies, F.C.I. Hickson, P. Weatherburn, & A. J. Hunt (Eds.), *Sex, gay men, and AIDS* (pp. 45–60). London: Falmer.

Deaux, K., & Major, B. (1987). Putting gender into context: An interactive model of gender-related behavior. *Psychological Review, 94,* 369–389.

de Vincenzi, I. (1994). A longitudinal study of human immunodeficiency virus transmission by heterosexual partners. *New England Journal of Medicine, 331,* 341–346.

DiClemente, R. J. (1991). Predictors of HIV-preventive sexual behavior in a high-risk adolescent population: The influence of perceived peer norms and sexual communication on incarcerated adolescents' consistent use of condoms. *Journal of Adolescent Health, 12,* 385–390.

Doherty, W. J., & Baptiste, Jr., D. A. (1993). Theories emerging from family therapy. In P. G. Boss, W. J. Doherty, R. LaRossa, W. R. Schumm, & S. K. Steinmetz (Eds.), *Sourcebook of family theories and methods: A contextual approach* (pp. 505–524). New York: Plenum.

Dolcini, M. M., & Catania, J. A. (1995, March). *Psychosocial profiles of women with risky sexual partners: The National AIDS Behavioral Surveys.* Paper presented at the meeting of the Society of Behavioral Medicine, San Diego.

Dolcini, M. M., Catania, J. A., Coates, T. J., Stall, R., Hudes, E. S., Gagnon, J. H., & Pollack, L. M. (1993). Demographic characteristics of heterosexuals with multiple partners: The national AIDS behavioral surveys (NABS). *Family Planning Perspectives, 25,* 208–214.

Dolcini, M. M., Coates, T. J., Catania, J. A., Kegeles, S. M., & Hauck, W. W. (1995). Multiple sexual partnerships and their psychosocial correlates: The population-based AIDS in Multiethnic Neighborhoods (AMEN) Study. *Health Psychology, 14,* 22–31.

Edgar, T. (1992). A compliance-based approach to the study of condom use. In T. Edgar, M. Fitzpatrick, & V. Freimuth (Eds.), *AIDS: A communication perspective* (pp. 47–68). Hillsdale, NJ: Lawrence Erlbaum Associates.

Edgar, T., Freimuth, V. S., Hammond, S. L., McDonald, D. A., & Fink, E. L. (1992). Strategic sexual communication: Condom use resistance and response. *Health Communication, 4,* 83–1104.

Edgar, T., Hammond, S., & Freimuth, V. (1989). The role of mass media and interpersonal communication in promoting AIDS-related behavioral change. *AIDS and Public Policy Journal, 4,* 3–9.

Farrington, K., & Chertok, E. (1993). Social conflict theories of the family. In P. G. Boss, W. J. Doherty, R. LaRossa, W. R. Schumm, & S. K. Steinmetz (Eds.), *Sourcebook of family theories and methods: A contextual approach* (pp. 357–381). New York: Plenum.

Feingold, A. (1992). Gender differences in mate selection preferences: A test of the parental investment model. *Psychological Bulletin, 112,* 125–139.

Ferris, D. G., & Litaker, M. (1993). Chlamydial cervical infections in rural and urban pregnant women. *Southern Medical Journal, 86,* 611–614.

Fisher, J., & Fisher, W. (1992). Changing AIDS-risk behavior. *Psychological Bulletin, 111,* 455–674.

Fisher, J. D., Fisher, W. A., Williams, S. S., & Malloy, T. E. (1994). Empirical tests of an information-motivation-behavioral skills model of AIDS-preventive behavior with gay men and heterosexual university students. *Health Psychology, 13,* 238–250.

Fitzpatrick, M. A., & Ritchie, L. D. (1993). Communication theory and the family. In P. G. Boss, W. J. Doherty, R. LaRossa, W. R. Schumm, & S. K. Steinmetz (Eds.), *Sourcebook of family theories and methods: A contextual approach* (pp. 565–585). New York: Plenum.

Folkman, S., Chesney, M. A., Pollack, L., & Phillips, C. (1992). Stress, coping, and high-risk sexual behavior. *Health Psychology, 11,* 218–222.

Freimuth, V. S., Hammond, S. L., Edgar, T., McDonald, D. A., & Fink, E. L. (1992). Factors explaining intent, discussion and use of condoms in first time sexual encounters. *Health Education Research, 7,* 203–215.

Fullilove, M. T., Fullilove, R. E., Haynes, K., & Gross, S. (1990). Black women and AIDS prevention: A view towards understanding the gender rules. *Journal of Sex Research, 27,* 47–64.

Gagnon, J. (1990). The explicit and implicit use of the scripting perspective in sex research. *Annual Review of Sex Research, 1,* 1–43.

Gagnon, J. H., & Simon, W. (1973). *Sexual conduct: The social sources of human sexuality.* Chicago: Aldine.

Galligan, R. F., & Terry, D. J. (1993). Romantic ideals, fear of negative implications, and the practice of safe sex. *Journal of Applied Social Psychology, 23,* 1685–1711.

Garnett, G. P., & Anderson, R. M. (1993). Contact tracing and the estimation of sexual mixing patterns: The epidemiology of gonococcal infections. *Sexually Transmitted Diseases, 20,* 181–191.

Gold, R. S., Karmiloff-Smith, A., Skinner, M. J., & Morton, J. (1992). Situational factors and thought processes associated with unprotected intercourse in heterosexual students. *AIDS Care, 4,* 305–323.

Golub, A., Gorr, W. L., & Gould, P. (1993). Spatial diffusion of the HIV/AIDS epidemic: Modeling implications and case study of AIDS incidence in Ohio. *Geographical Analysis, 25,* 85–100.

Grimley, D. M., Prochaska, J. O., Velicer, W. F., & Prochaska, G. E. (1995). Contraceptive and condom use adoption and maintenance: A stage paradigm approach. *Health Education Quarterly, 22,* 20–35.

Grimley, D. M., Riley, G. E., Bellis, J. M., & Prochaska, J. O. (1993). Assessing the stages of decision-making for contraceptive use for the prevention of pregnancy, sexually transmitted diseases, and acquired immunodeficiency syndrome. *Health Education Quarterly, 20,* 455–470.

Grinstead, O. A., Faigeles, B., Binson, D., & Eversley, R. (1993). Sexual risk for human immunodeficiency virus infection among women in high-risk cities. *Family Planning Perspectives, 25,* 252–256, 277.

Gupta, S., Anderson, R., & May, R. (1989). Networks of sexual contacts: Implications for the pattern of spread of HIV. *AIDS, 3,* 807–817.

Haverkos, H. W., & Battjes, R. J. (1992). Female-to-male transmission of HIV [letter]. *Journal of the American Medical Association, 268,* 1855.

Herold, A. H., Woodard, L. J., Roetzheim, R. G., Pamies, R. J., Young, D. L., & Micceri, T. (1993). Seasonality of chlamydia trachomatis genital infections in university women. *Journal of American College Health, 42,* 117–120.

Herold, E. S., & Mewhinney, D.M.K. (1993). Gender differences in casual sex and AIDS prevention: A survey of dating bars. *Journal of Sex Research, 30,* 36–42.

Hingson, R., Strunin, L., Craven, D., Mofenson, L., Mangione, T., Berlin, B., Amaro, H., & Lamb, G. (1989). Survey of AIDS knowledge and related behavior changes among Massachusetts adults. *Preventive Medicine, 18,* 806–816.

Holland, J., Ramazanoglu, C., Scott, S., Sharpe, S., & Thompson, R. (1990a). *Don't die of ignorance—I nearly died of embarassment: Condoms in context, WRAP Paper 2.* London: Tufnell.

Holland, J., Ramazanoglu, C., Scott, S., Sharpe, S., & Thompson, R. (1991). Between embarassment and trust: Young women and the diversity of condom use. In P. Aggleton, P. Davies, & G. Hart (Eds.), *AIDS: Responses, intervention, and care* (pp. 127–149). Basingstoke: Falmer Press.

Holland, J., Ramazanoglu, C., Scott, S., Sharpe, S., & Thompson, R. (1992). Risk, power, and the possibility of pleasure: Young women and safer sex. *AIDS Care, 4,* 273–283.

Holland, J., Ramazanoglu, C., Sharpe, S., & Thompson, R. (1994). Achieving masculine sexuality: Young men's strategies for managing vulnerability. In L. Doyal, J. Naidoo, & T. Wilton (Eds.), *AIDS: Setting a feminist agenda* (pp. 122–148). London: Taylor & Francis.

Holland, J., Ramazanoglu, S. S., Scott, S., Sharpe, S., & Thompson, R. (1990b). Sex, gender, and power: Young women's sexuality in the shadow of AIDS. *Sociology of Health and Illness, 12,* 337–350.

Holmes, M. D., Safyer, S. M., Bickell, N. A., Vermund, S. H., Hanff, P. A., & Phillips, R. S. (1993). Chlamydial cervical infection in jailed women. *Americal Journal of Public Health, 83,* 551–555.

Howard, J. A., Blumstein, P., & Schwartz, P. (1986). Sex, power, and influence tactics in intimate relationships. *Journal of Personality and Social Psychology, 51,* 102–109.

Jacquez, J. A., Koopman, J. S., Simon, C. P., & Longini, I. M. (1994). Role of the primary infection in edipemics of HIV infection in gay cohorts. *Journal of Acquired Immune Deficiency Syndromes, 7,* 1169–1184.

Kanouse, D., Berry, S., Gorman, E., Yano, E., Carson, S., & Abrahamse, A. (1991). *AIDS-related knowledge, attitudes, beliefs, and behaviors in Los Angeles County.* Santa Monica, CA: Rand.

Keeter, S., & Bradford, J. (1988). Knowledge of AIDS and related behavior change among unmarried adults in a low-prevalence city. *American Journal of Preventive Medicine, 4*(3), 146–152.

Kelly, J. A., Murphy, D. A., Washington, C. D., Wilson, T. S., Koob, J., Davis, D. R., Ledzmea, G., & Davantes, B. (1994). The effects of HIV/AIDS intervention groups for high-risk women in urban clinics. *American Journal of Public Health, 84,* 1918–1922.

Kim, M. Y., Marmor, M., Dubin, N., & Wolfe, H. (1993). HIV risk-related sexual behaviors in New York City: Associations with race, sex, and intravenous drug use. *AIDS, 7,* 409–414.

Kirby, D., Barth, R. P., Leland, N., & Fetro, J. V. (1991). Reducing the risk: Impact of a new curriculum on sexual risk taking. *Family Planning Perspectives, 23,* 253–263.

Kline, A., Kline, E., & Oken, E. (1992). Minority women and sexual choice in the age of AIDS. *Social Science Medicine, 34,* 447–457.

Klovdahl, A. S., Potterat, J. J., Woodhouse, D. E., Muth, J. B., Muth, S. Q., & Darrow, W. W. (1994). Social networks and infectious disease: The Colorado Springs Study. *Social Science and Medicine, 38,* 79–88.

Kost, K., & Forrest, J. (1992). American women's sexual behavior and exposure to risk of sexually transmitted diseases. *Family Planning Perspectives, 24,* 244–254.

Kowalewski, M. R., Longshore, D., & Anglin, M. D. (1994). The AIDS risk reduction model: Examining intentions to use condoms among injection drug users. *Journal of Applied Social Psychology, 24,* 2002–2027.

Laga, M., Manoka, A., Kivuvu, M., Malele, B., Tuliza, M., Nzila, N., Goeman, J., Behets, F., Batter, V., Alary, M., Heyward, W. L., Ryder, R. W., & Piot, P. (1993). Non-ulcerative sexually transmitted diseases as risk factors for HIV-1 transmission in women: Results from a cohort study. *AIDS, 7,* 95–102.

Laumann, E. O., Gagnon, J. H., Michael, R. T., & Michaels, S. (1994). *The social organization of sexuality: Sexual practices in the United States.* Chicago: University of Chicago Press.

Leigh, B. C., Temple, M. T., & Trocki, K. F. (1993). The sexual behavior of US adults: Results from a national survey. *American Journal of Public Health, 83,* 1400–1408.

Leitenberg, H., Detzer, M. J., & Srebnik, D. (1993). Gender differences in masturbation and the relation of masturbation experience in preadolescence and/or early adolescence to sexual behavior and sexual adjustment in young adulthood. *Archives of Sexual Behavior, 22,* 87–98.

Leka, T. W., Patrick, K., & Benenson, A. S. (1990). Chlamydia trachomatis urethritis in university men: Risk factors and rates. *Journal of the American Board of Family Practice, 3*(2), 81–86.

Mahoney, C. A., Thombs, D. L., & Ford, O. J. (1995). Health belief and self-efficacy models: Their utility in explaining college student condom use. *AIDS Education and Prevention, 7,* 32–49.

Malow, R. M., Corrigan, S. A., Cunningham, S. C., West, J. A., & Pena, J. M. (1993). Psychosocial factors associated with condom use among African-American drug abusers in treatment. *AIDS Education and Prevention, 5,* 244–253.

Marín, B., Gomez, C. A., & Hearst, N. (1993). Multiple heterosexual partners and condom use among Hispanics and non-Hispanic Whites. *Family Planning Perspectives, 25,* 170–174.

Marín, B. V., Tschann, J. M., Gomez, C. A., & Kegeles, S. M. (1993). Acculturation and gender differences in sexual attitudes and behaviors: Hispanic vs. non-Hispanic White unmarried adults. *American Journal of Public Health, 83,* 1759–1761.

Mays, V. M., & Cochran, S. D. (1993). Ethnic and gender differences in beliefs about sex partner questionning to reduce HIV risk. *Journal of Adolescent Research, 8,* 77–88.

McHugh, M. C., Koeske, R. D., & Frieze, I. H. (1986). Issues to consider in conducting non-sexist psychological research: A guide for researchers. *American Psychologist, 41,* 879–890.

Metts, S., & Fitzpatrick, M. (1992). Thinking about safer sex: The risky business of 'know your partner' advice. In T. Edgar, M. Fitzpatrick, & V. Freimuth (Eds.), *AIDS: A communication perspective* (pp. 1–20). Hillsdale, NJ: Lawrence Erlbaum Associates.

Miller, L. C., Bettencourt, B. A., DeBro, S. C., & Hoffman, V. (1993). Negotiating safer sex: Interpersonal dynamics. In J. B. Pryor & G. D. Reeder (Eds.), *The social psychology of HIV infection* (pp. 85–126). Hillsdale, NJ: Lawrence Erlbaum Associates.

Muehlenhard, C., & McCoy, M. (1991). Double standard double blind—the sexual double standard and women's communication about sex. *Psychology of Women Quarterly, 15,* 447–461.

Oliver, M. B., & Hyde, J. S. (1993). Gender differences in sexuality: A meta-analysis. *Psychological Bulletin, 114,* 29–51.

Osmond, D. H., Page, K., Wiley, J., Garrett, K., Sheppard, H., Moss, A., Schrager, L., & Winkelstein, W. (1994). HIV infection in homosexual and bisexual men 18–29 years of age: The San Francisco Young Men's Health Study. *American Journal of Public Health, 84,* 1933–1937.

Osmond, M. W., Wambach, K. G., Harrison, D. F., Byers, J., Levine, P., Imershein, A., & Quadagno, D. M. (1993). The multiple jeopardy of race, class, and gender for AIDS risk among women. *Gender and Society, 7,* 99–120.

Padian, N. S., Shiboski, S. C., & Jewell, N. P. (1991). Female-to-male transmission of human immunodeficiency virus. *Journal of the American Medical Association, 266,* 1664–1667.

Peplau, L. A. (1983). Roles and gender. In H. Kelley, E. Berscheid, A. Christensen, J. J. Harvey, T. L. Huston, G. Levinger, E. McClintock, L. A. Peplau, & D. R. Peteron (Eds.), *Close relationships* (pp. 220–264). New York: Freeman.

Peplau, L. A. (1984). Power in dating and marriage. In J. Freedman (Ed.), *Women: A feminist perspective* (4th ed., pp. 121–137). Mountain View, CA: Mayfield.

Peplau, L. A., Rubin, Z., & Hill, C. T. (1977). Sexual intimacy in dating relationships. *Journal of Social Issues, 33,* 86–109.

Perlmutter-Bowen, S., & Michal-Johnson, P. (1989). The crisis of communicating in relationships: Confronting the threat of AIDS. *AIDS & Public Policy Journal, 4,* 10–19.

Perper, T. (1989). Theories and observations on sexual selection and female choice in human beings. *Medical Anthropology, 11,* 409–454.

Peterson, J., Catania, J., Dolcini, M., & Faigeles, B. (1993). Multiple sexual partners and condom use among African Americans in high risk cities of the United States: The National AIDS Behavioral Surveys (NABS). *Family Planning Perspectives, 25,* 263.

Phillips, A., & Johnson, A. (1992). Female-to-male transmission of HIV [letter]. *Journal of the American Medical Association, 268,* 1855–1856.

Potterat, J. J. (1992). Socio-geographic space' and sexually tramsmissible diseases in the 1990s. *Today's Life Science,* pp. 16–22, 31.

Prochaska, J. O., Redding, C. A., Harlow, L. L., Rossi, J. S., & Velicer, W. F. (1994). The transtheoretical model of change and HIV prevention: A review. *Health Education Quarterly, 21,* 471–486.

Ramstedt, K., Giesecke, J., Forssman, L., & Granath, F. (1991). Choice of sexual partner according to the rate of partner change and social class of the partners. *International Journal of STD & AIDS, 2,* 428–431.

Rodgers, R. H., & White, J. M. (1993). Family development theory. In P. G. Boss, W. J. Doherty, R. LaRossa, W. R. Schumm, & S. K. Steinmetz (Eds.), *Sourcebook of family theories and methods: A contextual approach* (pp. 225–254). New York: Plenum.

Rogers, E. M. (1982). *Diffusion of innovations* (3rd ed.). New York: The Free Press.

Sabogal, F., Perez-Stable, E. J., Otero-Sabogal, R., & Hiatt, R. A. (1995). Gender, ethnic, and acculturation differences in sexual behavior: Hispanic and non-Hispanic White adults. *Hispanic Journal of Behavioral Sciences, 17,* 139–159.

Sabogal, F., Pierce, R., Pollack, L., Faigeles, B., & Catania, J. (1993). Multiple sex partners among Hispanics in the United States: The National AIDS Behavioral Surveys (NABS). *Family Planning Perspectives, 25,* 257.

Schneider, B. E., & Gould, M. (1987). Female sexuality: Looking back into the future. In B. B. Hess & M. M. Ferree (Eds.), *Analyzing gender: A handbook of social science research* (pp. 120–153). Newbury Park: Sage.

Service, S. K., & Blower, S. M. (1995). HIV transmission in sexual networks: An empirical analysis. *The Proceedings of the Royal Society: Biological Science, 260,* 237–244.

Siann, G. (1994). *Gender, sex, and sexuality.* London: Taylor & Francis.

Siegel, D., Golden, E., Washington, A., Morse, S., Fullilove, M., Catania, J., Marin, B., & Hulley, S. (1992). Prevalence and correlates of herpes simplex infections: The population-based AMEN study. *Journal of the American Medical Association, 286,* 1702–1708.

Simon, W., & Gagnon, J. (1986). Sexual scripts: Permanence and change. *Archives of Sexual Behavior, 15,* 97–120.

Simon, W., & Gagnon, J. (1987). A sexual scripts approach. In J. H. Geer & W. O'Donohue (Eds.), *Theories of human sexuality* (pp. 363–383). New York: Plenum.

Snyder, D. K., & Berg, P. (1983). Determinants of sexual dissatisfaction in sexually distressed couples. *Archives of Sexual Behavior, 12,* 237–246.

Sobo, E. J. (1993). Inner-city women and AIDS: The psycho-social benefits of unsafe sex. *Culture, Medicine, and Psychiatry, 17,* 455–485.

Stall, R., & Catania, J. A. (1994). AIDS risk behaviors among late middle-aged and elderly Americans: The National AIDS Behavioral Surveys (NABS). *Archives of Internal Medicine, 154,* 57–63.

Tanfer, K., Grady, W. R., Klepinger, D. H., & Billy, J.O.G. (1993). Condom use among U.S. men, 1991. *Family Planning Perspectives, 25,* 61–66.

Tanfer, K., & Schoorl, J. (1992). Premarital sexual careers and partner change. *Archives of Sexual Behavior, 21,* 25–68.

Terry, D. H., Gallois, C., & McCamish, M. (Eds.). (1993). *The theory of reasoned action.* New York: Pergamon.

Tolhuizen, J. (1989). Communication strategies for intensifying dating relationships: Identification, use, and structure. *Journal of Social and Personal Relationships, 6,* 413–434.

Trocki, K. F. (1992). Patterns of sexuality and risky sexuality in the general population of a California county. *Journal of Sex Research, 29,* 85–94.

Verbrugge, L. M. (1977). The structure of adult friendship choices. *Social Forces, 56*(2), 576–597.

Wallace, R. (1991). Traveling waves of HIV infection on a low dimensional "socio-geographic" network. *Social Science Medicine, 32,* 847–852.

Wallace, R. (1994). A fractal model of HIV transmission on complex socio-geographic networks. Part 2: Spread from a ghettoized "core group" into a "general population." *Environment and Planning, 26,* 767–778.

Webster, L., Greenspan, J. R., Nakashima, A. K., & Johnson, R. E. (1993). An evaluation of surveillance for chlamydia trachomatis infections in the United States, 1987–1991. *Morbidity and Mortality Weeklly Report, 42*(SS-3), 21–27.

Weinstein, N. (1989). Perceptions of personal susceptibility to harm. In V. Mays, G. Albee, & J. Jones (Eds.), *Psychological approaches to the prevention of AIDS* (pp. 142–167). Beverly Hills, CA: Sage.

Weinstein, N. D., & Nicolich, M. (1993). Correct and incorrect interpretations of correlations between risk perceptions and risk behaviors. *Health Psychology, 12,* 235–245.

Wenger, N. S., Linn, L. S., Epstein, M., & Shapiro, M. F. (1991). Reduction of high-risk sexual behavior among heterosexuals undergoing HIV antibody testing: A randomized clinical trial. *American Journal of Public Health, 81,* 1580–1585.

Wight, D. (1992). Impediments to safer heterosexual sex: A review of research with young people. *AIDS Care, 4,* 11–23.

Wingood, G. M., Hunter-Gamble, D., & DiClemente, R. J. (1993). A pilot study of sexual communication and negotiation among young African American women: Implications for HIV prevention. *Journal of Black Psychology, 19,* 190–203.

Woodhouse, D. E., Rothenberg, R. B., Potterat, J. J., Darrow, W. W., Muth, S. Q., Klovdahl, A. S., Zimmerman, H. P., Rogers, H. L., Maldonado, T. S., Muth, J. B., & Reynolds, J. U. (1994). Mapping a social network of heterosexuals at high risk for HIV infection. *AIDS, 8,* 1331–1336.

Worth, D. (1989). Sexual decision-making and AIDS: Why condom promotion among vulnerable women is likely to fail. *Studies in Family Planning, 20*(6), 297–307.

Yamaguchi, K. (1990). Homophily and social distance in the choice of multiple friends. *Journal of the American Statistical Association, 85*(410), 356–366.

Zelnik, M., Kantner, J., & Ford, K. (1981). *Sex and pregnancy in adolescence.* Beverly Hills, CA: Sage.

Zimmer, D. (1983). Interaction patterns and communication skills in sexually distressed, maritally distressed and normal couples. *Journal of Sex and Marital Therapy, 9,* 251–255.

48

HIV Disease in Ethnic Minorities: Implications of Racial/Ethnic Differences in Disease Susceptibility and Drug Dosage Response for HIV Infection and Treatment

Vickie M. Mays
University of California, Los Angeles

Bennett T. So
University of North Carolina School of Medicine

Susan D. Cochran and Roger Detels
UCLA School of Public Health

Rotem Benjamin, Erica Allen, and Susan Kwon
University of California, Los Angeles

AIDS was originally considered a disease of the gay population (Mays & Cochran, 1987). In particular, AIDS was viewed as a White gay male disease (Cochran & Mays, 1988; Mays & Cochran, 1995). However, increasingly over the years, both the highest incidence and greatest numbers of new cases of HIV infection in the United States are within ethnic minority populations, especially among African Americans and Hispanics (Karon et al., 1996; Rosenberg & Biggar, 1998). A recent study examining the prevalence of HIV infection found that the estimated rate in White males was from 3.3 to 4.9 per 1,000, but from 16.8 to 22.5 among Black males and from 9.0 to 13.0 among Hispanic males (Karon et al., 1996). Similar patterns were found for women, with estimates of from 1.7 to 2.6, 10.6 to 14.2, and 5.6 to 8.2 for Whites, Blacks, and Hispanics, respectively. Using data from 1995, Rosenberg and Biggar (1998) showed that HIV incidence attributable to heterosexual contact is striking in its pattern among successive birth cohorts of ethnic minorities. They found that Black women have the highest incidence of infection attributable to heterosexual contact, with estimates that 1 in every 1,000 20-year-old Black women become HIV infected via heterosexual sexual routes. This compares to estimates that 1 in 2,800 similar aged Hispanic women and 1 in 15,000 White women suffer similar fates. Concurrently, the incidence of HIV infection is greater among young ethnic minority men than in White men in every transmission route, including male-to-male sexual transmission (Rosenberg & Biggar, 1998). Here, the incidence of AIDS cases attributable to male-to-male sexual contact is four times higher in Black men and two times higher in Hispanic men when compared to

White men. This discrepancy in risk is expected to widen as the incidence and numbers of new cases of HIV infection in White gay men declines (Fahey & Flemming, 1997).

In the meantime, AIDS-related research continues in the hope of finding new drugs for the treatment of AIDS and HIV infection. But the implication of these accelerating trends, shifting a greater illness burden into ethnic minority communities, presents a new challenge for researchers. Much research continues to be conducted using White male subjects. Blacks, who earlier in the history of AIDS clinical trials represented 34% of all AIDS cases (Fahey & Flemming, 1997), previously made up only 7% of the subjects in National Institute of Health (NIH) HIV/AIDS studies (Ready, 1988). Similarly, Hispanics represented 17% of AIDS cases, but were only 9% of the NIH research subjects. There are many complicated reasons for the low participation of ethnic minorities in HIV-related clinical drug and vaccine trials ranging from debatable scientific decisions to politics (El-Sadr & Capps, 1992; "Getting Cancer Patients Into Clinical Trials," 1991; Mays, 1998, 1999; Mays & Cochran, 1999). But despite this, there is growing evidence in various areas of medicine that racial/ethnic differences in disease susceptibility and drug response do exist (Pollack, Safari, & DuPont, 1983; Winchester, Chen, Rose, Selby, & Borkowsky, 1995; Zhou, Koshakji, Silberstein, Wilkinson, & Wood, 1989; Zhou, Shay, & Wood, 1993). Failure to consider these differences while attempting to develop new methods of treatment, or even possibly a cure, could have significant public health implications, particularly for ethnic minority Americans. In the hopes of encouraging consideration of these issues more fully, this chapter reviews here the existing evidence for HIV-relevant racial differences in disease susceptibility and drug dosage response.

GENETIC RACIAL DIFFERENCES RELATED TO HUMAN LEUKOCYTE ANTIGENS

A particularly useful area to consider in identifying possible racial/ethnic differences in HIV infection and disease is in distribution of Human Leukocyte Antigens (HLA) because of their relation to immune function. HLA molecules have a significant function in initiating the immune response through processing and presenting foreign antigens to T-cells, which then triggers clearance of the virus from the body. Racial variations in the genes encoding HLA Class I and II molecules have an effect on antigen presentation and may influence the host immune response. These tissue type antigens are used by the T-cells of the immune system to distinguish host cells from foreign cells (i.e., the self from the nonself). Every individual has a unique combination of HLA molecules on chromosome 6 called the major histocompatibility complex (MHC). HLA-A, HLA-B, and HLA-C are encoded by Class I genes, whereas HLA-DR, HLA-DQ, and HLA-DP regions are encoded by Class II genes. The Class II regions determine the selection of various cell membrane associated glycoproteins that serve numerous functions in the regulation of the T-cell immune response of the body (Callender & Dunston, 1987). A subset of T-cells kill viral infected cells, but ironically HIV also attacks a subset of the population called the CD4+ cells. Studying specific racial variations in the Class II region may further elucidate the role they play in the T-cell mediated immune system response to HIV infection.

Because the use of HLA typing is common for the determination of the histocompatibility of tissues for transplantation, research in this area has led to the discovery of HLA determinants associated with particular racial groups. These determinants are polymorphic, resulting in differences between races in the frequency of the alleles (gene variants) at the various HLA loci. For example, in a sample drawn in Washington, DC, HLA-A23 and A30 were four times more likely to be found in Blacks than in Caucasians (Dunston, Henry, Christian, M. D. Ofosu, & Callendar, 1989). Also, B45, Bw58, Bw53, Bw70, Cw7, DRw13, and DRw8 were also more likely to be found in Blacks. Further, unique HLA specificities are seen in the Black population. For instance, Aw34, Aw36, A19v, and Bw42 appear to be unique to Blacks (Callender & Dunston, 1987; Dunston, Hurley, Hartz, & Johnson, 1989).

Although a majority of previous HLA research focused on racial differences only between the Black and White population, presently DNA technology allows further identification of specific HLA alleles, suggesting HLA relatedness and differences with other racial groups. Osborne and Mason (1993) designed an HLA haplotype frequency table consisting of HLA alleles common to the U.S. Hispanic population. They reported similarities and differences in HLA A/B haplotypes among Hispanic Americans of both Caribbean and Mexican ancestry. They also reported that HLA A19/B12, A25/B12, A1/B17, A2;A34/B38, and A1;A3/B40 are common in Mexican Americans, whereas A9/B12, A19/B12, A29/B12, A2/B16, A28/B17, A19/B44, A24/B40 are shown to be common in Caribbean Hispanics. For example, HLA A28/B17 is 24 times more likely to be found in Hispanic Americans of Caribbean origin than in those of Mexican ancestry (Osborne & Mason, 1993).

Investigation of HLA Class II alleles in South American Indians show specific HLA haplotypes among those of Brazilian and Argentinean background (Cerna et al., 1993). In a study of three Argentinean tribes (Eastern Toba, Western Toba Pilaga, and Mataco Wiehi) and Xvantes from Central Brazil, the most common HLA allele was DPB1*0402 (Cerna et al., 1993). However, Brazilians display four DR groups: DRB1*0404, DRB1*0407, DRB1*0802, and DRB1*1402. Frequent alleles at the DRB1 locus in Argentineans were shown to include DRB1*04, DRB1*0802, and DRB1*14.

Modern genetic studies of HLA genes have made possible comparisons between Ashkenazi Jews from Eastern and Central Europe and Non-Ashkenazi Jews from Mediterranean and Asian Countries (Martinez-Laso, Gomez-Casado, Morales, & Martinez-Quiles, 1996). Common alleles found in both Jewish groups are DRB1*07, DRB1*0402, DRB1*1104, DRB1*0102. Allelic differences within the Jewish population can be illustrated in the frequency of alleles at the DR13 loci. For example, DRB1*1301 is more common in Ashkenazi than in non-Ashkenazi Jews. Furthermore, DRB1*1301 is six times more likely to be present in non-Ashkenazi Jews of Mediterranean ancestry in this subgroup (Martinez-Laso et al., 1996).

These disparate results suggest significant biological differences in HLA between races. Given the important role of HLA in immune-related disease, these racial differences may play an important, but understudied, role in HIV and may subtly influence outcomes of research directed at disease susceptibility and drug dosage response in HIV/AIDS. Studying ethnic differences in HIV disease may lead to important insights in the varied role of the viral immune response and identify new approaches for therapeutic research.

It is already known that each individual has a unique distribution of HLA alleles, and specific HLA haplotype combinations are found more frequently in different ethnic groups. Studies have also shown that with particular combinations of HLA haplotypes, the chances for long-term survival with HIV and AIDS is improved (Kaslow et al., 1990; Louie, Newman, & King, 1991; Steel et al., 1988). Yet, most of these studies have been done using data gathered from gay White men, who represent only a portion of those living with HIV and AIDS (Louie et al., 1991). In one study conducted by Louie et al. (1991) of gay White men living in 19 census tracts having the highest risk for AIDS in San Francisco, results showed that those who carried HLA DRB1* 1101, 1104, and 1201 had the worst disease outcome. The presence of DRB1* 0101 (DR1), HLA A* 2401 (A24), HLA B* (B35), and HLA C* 0401 (C4) was associated with an increased rate of progression to AIDS, whereas those with the alleles HLA DRB1* 0701 and 0702 had a slower CD4 cell decline as well as slower progression to AIDS (Louie et al., 1991). Within the study, a comparison was made between those who were symptomatic and those who were asymptomatic. The HLA alleles DRB1* 0702 and DQA1* 0201 were more frequent among HIV+ asymptomatic men compared to HIV+ men who were symptomatic. Therefore, the presence of these alleles may confer a protection against the progression of AIDS. This study also showed that CD4+ cell counts declined faster in those with the HLA allele DQA1* 0101 present, thus resulting in the more rapid progression of AIDS. The presence of the HLA combination A1-B8-DR3 was also associated with rapid CD4 cell decline (Louie et al., 1991).

Other studies of African Americans and Caucasians offer further support for the role of HLA differences and HIV/AIDS disease progression. In the heterosexual population, HLA distribution is associated with the severity of HIV infection, and the likelihood of developing AIDS. HLAs found more frequently among HIV+ African Americans are A31(19), B35, Cw6, Cw7, DR11, DR12, DQ1, and DQ3, when compared to controls. Among the Caucasian HIV+ participants, A28, A66, B48, Cw7, Cw8, DR10, DR5, DQ1, and DQ7 are associated with HIV infection. Although some haplotypes are common in the two groups, Cw4 and DR6 were more common among uninfected African Americans (M. N. Brackin et al., 1995). Thus, Cw4 and DR6 may provide protective resistance to HIV infection. On the other hand, A69(28)-B40 and B12-DR14(6) were associated with rapid progression in African Americans. In Caucasians, A28-B17-DR9 and DQ2 were associated with rapid progression, and A30(19)-B67 with slow progression. Studies of other ethnic groups reveal associations with different alleles of the same genes (Louie et al., 1991).

Studies have also reported other HLA associations with susceptibility to HIV-1 infection as well as to disease progression. It was shown that susceptibility to infection with HIV-1 among both African Americans and Caucasians may be influenced by HLA-DQB1 alleles (Achord, Lewis, M. N. Brackin, & Cruse, 1997). Using molecular methods, Achord and colleagues (1997) found a significantly higher frequency of DQB1*0605 in HIV-1 positive African Americans as compared to HIV-1 negative African American controls. DQB1*0602 was associated with HIV-1 infection in Caucasians. Although no HLA-DQB1 marker was found to be protective against HIV-1 infection in African Americans, HLA-DQB1*0603 was found to be protective in Caucasians. These results demonstrated that different HLA molecules may be associated with HIV-1 infection or protection from infection in Caucasians and African Americans (Achord et al., 1996). Possible HLA associations with HIV-1 disease progression between different ethnic groups was also examined. HLA allele frequencies among slow progressors were compared to those of rapid progressors, stratified by race. HIV-1 infected African Americans positive for the DQB1*0602 allele exhibited slower disease progression. Kaplan–Meier survival analysis showed a mean survival time of 71.3 months for those patients without the allele as compared to 117.8 months for the African American patients who had this allele. No marker was found to be associated with rapid disease progression in African Americans. In the HIV-1 infected Caucasian group, the DQB1*0302 allele was more common in rapid progressors. Patients positive for the DQB1*0302 allele had a mean survival time of 47.5 months as compared to 70.7 months for patients without the allele as shown by the Kaplan–Meier survival analysis (Achord et al., 1997).

Numerous studies have investigated the role HLA plays in response to HIV-1. It has been shown that MHC Class II DRB1 alleles of the infant influence transmission of HIV-1 from an infected mother during gestation and delivery and the association may be influenced by ethnicity (Winchester et al., 1995). Winchester et al. (1995) found a higher frequency of the DRB1*03011 HLA allele in the infected White infants born to HIV-1 positive mothers and a higher frequency of DRB1*1501 in the uninfected group. Also demonstrated was a higher prevalence of DR13 alleles, including DRB1*1301, 1302, and 1303 among the African American and Hispanic infants studied. The DRB1 13 alleles are associated with an enhanced immune response to a specific HIV peptide and to resistance to HIV infection. The frequency of the DRB 13 alleles varied with racial ethnicity. Among the African American infants, 29% of uninfected infants were positive for these alleles, in comparison to 0% of HIV-infected infants (Winchester et al., 1995). The association of specific HLA molecules with HIV-1 susceptibility was further examined in Italian children. The DRB1*1301 allele was also found to be more frequent among infected Italian infants as compared to uninfected Italian infants born to HIV-1 positive mothers (Greggio et al., 1993; Scorza Smeraldi, et al., 1986).

In another study by Just et al. (1992), an association of HLA genotypes and susceptibility to HIV perinatal infection was found among Black infants born to HIV positive mothers. Results of this study showed the HLA DQA1*0102 allele provided a protective role whereas the allele DPB1*0101 was associated more with risk of infection. The uninfected infants had a higher prevalence of the DQA1*0102 allele than the infected infants (65% vs. 43%). Whereas the DPB1*0101 was more commonly detected among the infected infants (66%) than among the uninfected infants (43%). Additionally, infants who lack the allele DQA1*0102 and have a specific amino acid sequence of -asp-glu-ala-val- at HLA-DPB1 positions #84-87 have a stronger association with HIV infection than those infants with the specified amino acid sequence of DPB1 and the DQA1*0102 allele. Results of the study also show that the infants most protected from HIV infection, had a different sequence of amino acids at positions #84-87 of the DPB1 gene locus other than -asp-glu-ala-val-, and may or may not have had the DQA1*0102 allele.

In a study (Kilpatrick, Hague, Yap, & Mok, 1991) conducted on Scottish infants born to HIV+ mothers, the frequency of HLA DR3 was three times higher in the HIV+ infants (i.e., 13% as compared with 30%). The low rate of HIV+ infants may be due to the haplotype combination they found for this group. A3-B7-DR2 was found only in the infants who were not HIV infected, perhaps offering some form of protection. The study also confirmed the results of other studies using White samples, which indicated that A1-B8-DR3 may be associated with susceptibility (Just et al., 1992; Kilpatrick et al., 1991; Yanase et al., 1986).

These studies based on infants of different ethnic backgrounds, combined with previous studies examined, hint at the possible relevance of differences in the HLA make up of different racial groups in HIV disease. Furthermore, HLA loci have also been shown to play a role in several other diseases. For example, HLA typing of Class II region reveals significant differences between African Americans with and without Grave's disease (M. H. Ofosu et al., 1996).

HLA loci are important factors in graft survival in kidney transplantation. It has been shown that the chance of graft survival increases when DRw6 allele matched in kidney transplantation (Callendar & Dunston, 1987). For kidney transplantation, in particular, race seems to have a major role in the outcome of the operation. In 1987, Blacks accounted for 12% of the U.S. population, but made up 27% of the patients with end-stage renal disease. Racial differences in ABO blood groups and MHC antigens make organ matches extremely difficult, especially because only 8% of donors are Black (Kasiske et al., 1991). For blood types O, A, B, and AB, the distribution in the White population is 45%, 40%, 11%, and 4%, respectively. On the other hand, the Black distribution is 49%, 27%, 20%, and 4%, respectively. Whereas ABO typing must be matched in the first place for tissue transplantation, exact MHC matching of HLAs is not always possible because the majority of donated kidneys are from Caucasians. Because of frequent mismatching, long-term survival of grafts is significantly lower for Blacks than for Whites (Kasiske et al., 1991). In general, when recipients had no HLA mismatches, they suffered fewer rejections and required less cyclosporine, which is the steroid administered to enhance graft survival (Callender & Dunston, 1987). Newer studies suggest that when equivalent Black and White kidney recipients are chosen and a cyclosporine regimen is followed, patient and graft survival are the same in Blacks and Whites (Friedman, 1991). Although accessibility of health services and everyday life and economic struggles that act as barriers in facilitating necessary daily health regimes may contribute to graft loss in poor Blacks (especially within the inner city), the effects of racially determined HLA typings still play a significant role in graft survival.

Sickle cell disease is another area in which—in this instance transfusion-related immune response—there is an association with several HLA specificities. Sickle cell disease patients commonly undergo blood transfusions in the treatment of their illness. Studies show that after receiving a transfusion, patients with HLA-B35 are six times more likely to produce antibodies against the transfused cells (alloimmunization) than patients without this antigen (Alarif, Castro, M. Ofosu, Dunston, & Scott, 1986). In addition, a lower incidence of alloantibodies has been associated with the presence of HLA-DR3 and of A28 and B15 (M. D. Ofosu, Saunders, Dunston, Castro, & Alarif, 1986). These associations, given the racial differences in HLA typing, indicate that Blacks may be more susceptible to alloimmunization due to transfusions received in the treatment of sickle cell disease. Indeed, in one study among Blacks, a 30% alloimmunization rate was found, whereas Whites had a 5% rate despite receiving greater numbers of transfusions (Vichinsky et al., 1990). Because Blacks comprise a low proportion of blood donors (the donor population being mainly White), differences in the antigen mismatching between donors and recipients among African Americans may account for the resulting differences in alloimmunization frequency.

Association between HLA haplotypes and susceptibility to insulin dependent (Type 1) diabetes mellitus (IDDM) has also been studied. Specifically, it has been shown that the HLA-DQ region plays a role in IDDM susceptibility (Fletcher et al., 1988; Ronningen et al., 1993). In general, among Caucasians, DR3 is almost always associated with DQw2, whereas among Blacks, DR3 may be associated with two phenotypes, DQw2 or DQw-. In a study of Black IDDM patients and Black non-IDDM controls, the haplotype DR3-DQw2 was found in all IDDM patients, whereas DR3-DQw-, common in the control group, was not found in the IDDM patients (Dunston et al., 1989). The DR3-DQw2 haplotype, therefore, seems to be a marker for insulin dependence in the Black diabetes patients studied, whereas DR3-DQw- is more likely to be associated with resistance to IDDM. Because IDDM is more prevalent among Black Americans than Black Africans, and DR3-DQw2 (found in nearly all Caucasians) is associated with susceptibility to IDDM, it is possible that the susceptibility genes for IDDM were introduced into the Black American population due to the admixture of Caucasian genes (Dunston et al., 1989).

Further studies also indicate genetic differences in the susceptibility and resistance to IDDM in the Mexican American population. Although the incidence of IDDM among Native Americans is low, the incidence in Non-Hispanic Whites is 15/100,000 year and 9.5/100,000 year in Mexican Americans (Eisenbarth, 1986). This pattern is consistent with the lower prevalence of the European derived HLA-DR3 haplotype in the Mexican American population, which has HLA haplotypes derived from the Native American and Hispanic Caucasian admixture heritages. Furthermore, HLA-DR3 and DR4 linkage to specific HLA DQB1 alleles influences risk of IDDM (Sanjeevi et al., 1993). Recent studies show that the Mexican population contains a variety of different DR4-DRB1 alleles (Erlich et al., 1993). Namely, there are 9 different DRB1 alleles, and 16 different DRBQ haplotypes. The risk of IDDM in this population varies from highly susceptible to protective based on the DRB1 allele present. High risk haplotypes—DRB1*0402, DQA1*0301, DRB1*0405, and DQB1*0302—are of European origin. Specifically, DRB1*0405 is common in Spain and may illustrate the Hispanic Caucasian descent in the Mexican American population. Lower rates of IDDM in Mexican American controls corresponds to Native American ancestry.

Race has also been found to be a major contributor to the prevalence of diabetic nephropathy. In inner-city Blacks (e.g., from Brooklyn), Hispanics, and Native American Indians, the prevalence of non-insulin-dependent diabetes (NIDDM) is much higher than in non-Hispanic Whites (Friedman, 1991). Within these diabetic groups, there also seems to be a genetic predisposition to increased risk for diabetic nephropathy as compared to Caucasians. This disposition is associated with a genetic risk for hypertension. The rate of erythrocyte lithium-sodium countertransport is a marker for hypertension, and this rate is increased in those who develop nephropathy. In addition to this genetically inherited trait, end-stage renal disease (ESRD) due to diabetic nephropathy is caused mainly by NIDDM. Because Blacks, Hispanics, and American Indians suffer from NIDDM to a much greater extent than Whites, they also suffer from a higher prevalence of diabetic ESRD (Friedman, 1991).

Mixing of genes between races from interracial matings has led to changes in susceptibility. For example, following the introduction of Caucasian genes into the Pima Indian population, the prevalence of NIDDM has decreased commensurate with the decreasing prevalence of the Gm 3;0 5,13,14 haplotype, which is a risk factor for NIDDM (Friedman, 1991). Thus, as a function of the dilution of the genes associated with NIDDM susceptibility, the prevalence of NIDDM has decreased accordingly. Therefore, interracial mating is an important factor to consider when examining ethnic differences in disease susceptibility. As previously discussed, the distribution of HLA alleles are different among different racial groups. Thus, acquisition of genes from parents of differing ethnic backgrounds influences biologically based responses and outcomes to disease.

HLA specificities also play a role in the susceptibility to human T-cell leukemia virus Type I (HTLV-I). In the HTLV-I endemic area of Kyushu, Japan, HLA-DQw3 is associated with HTLV-I infection that is associated with T-cell leukemia (ATL). Ninety one percent of the ATL patients had increased frequencies of HLA A26 and B39, as compared to HTLV-1 infected individuals without ATL. Thus, these alleles may be associated with predisposition to developing ATL in the course of HTLV-I infection (Uno, Kawato, Matsuoka, & Tsuda, 1988; White et al., 1996). Different alleles were observed in Black and Caribbean ATL patients in which frequencies of A36, B18, and Class II HLA-DR53 were higher (White et al., 1996).

Ethnic differences have been observed in age of onset and severity of myasthenia gravis between Chinese and Caucasians. Chinese patients were found to have less severe cases and display an earlier occurrence of this disease than Whites. Among Chinese patients, there is a strong correlation of Bw46 and DR9 with myasthenia gravis (Chen, Chiu, & Hsieh, 1993). Furthermore, the frequency of the Bw46DR9 combination was found to be increased in Chinese juvenile patients with onset before age 20 and decreased thereafter (20% $\geq$ 20 and 60% $\leq$ 20). However, A1, B8, and DR3 are correlated with myasthenia gravis in Whites over age 40. Also, specific HLA combinations are associated with myasthenia gravis in other ethnic groups: HLA-DR8 and DR3 in Whites; A1, B8, and DR5 in American Blacks; and DR9 and DRw8 in Japanese.

HIV-associated diseases also show racial differences. In a study of patients with renal disease due to HIV-1 infection, known as HIV-1 associated nephropathy (HIVN), Black HIV-infected patients were more likely than Whites to develop HIVN (Bourgoignie, Ortiz-Interian, Grenn, & Roth, 1989). Moreover, whereas the majority of HIV-infected patients are White, most HIVN patients are Black. Even after taking IV drug use into account, HIVN occurs 10 times more often in Blacks. Furthermore, the predilection for HIVN cannot be attributed to differences in age, duration of disease, or to the presence of other major opportunistic infections. This suggests a strong possibility that genetic factors are responsible for the higher frequency of HIVN among Blacks (Bourgoignie et al., 1989).

Investigations have demonstrated that non-HLA genetic factors also influence susceptibility to HIV infection and the pathogenesis of AIDS. The vast majority of people are susceptible to infection with HIV. However, rare individuals remain uninfected by HIV-1 despite multiple sexual contacts with subjects known to be HIV-1 infected (Detels et al., 1996; Liu et al., 1996). In mid-1996, a naturally occurring 32-bp deletion mutation (delta 32 allele) in the chemokine receptor gene CCR5 was found in subjects who remain uninfected despite repeated, extensive exposure to HIV-1 (O'Brien et al., 1998). Before the discovery of the role of chemokine receptor genes in HIV infection, only HLA genetic factors were thought to affect susceptibility of HIV infection. Studies have since identified molecular co-receptors that HIV uses in conjunction with CD4 cell entry. The macrophage-tropic, or M-tropic HIV strains use CD4 and a chemokine receptor gene called CCR5, whereas the protein CXCR4 is an entry coreceptor for T lymphocytes-tropic (T-tropic) HIV strains only (O'Brien & Goedert, 1998). Several studies confirmed the protective role of homozygosity for a 32 base pair (Δ32) deletion in the CCR5 gene to HIV-1 infection. Rare individuals homozygous for this ΔCCR5 allele appear to be protected from HIV-1 infection despite repeated exposure to HIV-1 through unprotected sex with HIV-1 positive partners (Liu et al., 1996). It has been shown that genotype frequencies of the ΔCCR5 allele vary markedly across different ethnic groups. Among Caucasians in North America or Europe, about 1% are ΔCCR5 homozygous. Homozygous ΔCCR5 is rarely found in non-Caucasians. Heterozygosity of the ΔCCR5 allele is found in approximately 10% to 20% of Caucasians, approximately 6% of African Americans, 7% of Hispanics, 13% of Native Americans, and 1% or less of Asians (Dean et al., 1996; McNicholl, D. K. Smith, Qari, & Hodge, 1997; Zimmerman et al., 1997).

Similarly, Smith et al. (1997) reported that homozygosity for the ΔCCR5 was not uncommon among exposed but uninfected individuals (1%–5%), but extremely rare among infected individuals (< .1%) (Dean et al., 1996; Huang et al., 1996). The different frequency of the homozygous ΔCCR5 allele between Caucasian HIV-positive homosexual men (0%), and in highly exposed seronegative (4.5%), provides further support for the protective role of the ΔCCR5 allele (Zimmerman et al., 1997).

Whereas individuals homozygous for the ΔCCR5 allele appear to be resistant to infection, it has been shown that heterozygosity may delay the progression to AIDS in infected individuals. Infected individuals heterozygous for the ΔCCR5 experienced a delay in the onset of AIDS of approximately 2 to 4 years, as compared to individuals with the normal CCR5 gene, in several large AIDS cohort studies (Dean et al., 1996; Huang et al., 1996; M. W. Smith et al., 1997). The long-term nonprogressors of the homosexual cohorts showed more than twice the percentage of heterozygotes compared with rapid progressors (Dean et al., 1996). The data suggest that heterozygosity for the ΔCCR5 allele does not affect susceptibility to infection, but rather it may postpone progression to AIDS among those already infected. Population studies have estimated the frequency of ΔCCR5 at approximately 15% among North American or European Caucasians, but have not found any cases of ΔCCR5 among Black populations with the exception of African Americans in the United States. A global distribution of the ΔCCR5 allele shows the highest allele frequency recorded in the Ashkenazi Jewish population, 20.9%, descendants of ancient Israel and east European people, a frequency of from 2% to 5% throughout Europe and a general absence in sub-Saharan Africa peoples (Martinson, Chapman, Rees, Liu, & Clegg, 1997). In a study of the urban Brazilian population, comprised of Europeans, Asiatics, Arabians, Africans, and Native Amerindians, the frequency of the mutant allele in this population was 35%, but no homozygous ΔCCR5 individual has been discovered so far (Passos & Picanc, 1998). Differences in prevalence of the ΔCCR5 allele continue to be examined among different ethnic groups. A study of the CCR5 gene among 377 Puerto Ricans showed 94.2% nondeletion homozygote (normal CCR5 gene), 5.8% ΔCCR5 allele heterozygotes, and 0% ΔCCR5 allele homozygote (Gonzales et al., 1998). Thus, Puerto Ricans appear to resemble the U.S. Hispanic population, whose genotype frequencies were 93.3% nondeletion homozygote and 6.7% ΔCCR5 allele heterozygotes. In comparison, a study of U.S. Caucasians found 77.4% nondeletion homozygote, and 22.6% ΔCCR5, whereas African Americans exhibited 97.7% nondeletion homozygote and 2.3% ΔCCR5 allele heterozygotes (Gonzalez et al., 1998; Zimmerman et al., 1997). These findings underscore the possible importance of differential population distributions of the ΔCCR5 allele in HIV-1 infection and progression.

Recent investigations reveal that the ΔCCR5 allele is not the only genetic determinant of HIV-1 prognosis. A CCR2-64I mutation allele was discovered at a frequency of from 10% to 15% among Caucasians and African Americans (M. W. Smith et al., 1997). It was shown that CCR2-64I does not influence infection by HIV-1, but delays progression to AIDS. HIV-1 infected individuals carrying the CCR2-64I allele progressed to AIDS from 2 to 4 years later than those HIV-1 infected individuals carrying the normal CCR2 allele. Unlike the different frequency of the ΔCCR5 allele among different ethnic groups, the CCR2-64I allele mutation was found in every ethnic group tested: 98% in Caucasians, 15.1% in African Americans, 17.2% in Hispanics, and 25% in Asians. The frequency of the CCR2-64I allele was consistently lower among those who progressed rapidly to AIDS than in the nonprogressor or slow group with delayed onset of AIDS for more than 6 to 12.5 years following infection (M. W. Smith et al., 1997).

Another genetic determinant discovered to be associated with the slower progression to AIDS, not HIV infection, is homozygosity for a mutation in the 3' untranslated region of the SDF-1 gene (Winkler et al., 1998). The SDF-1 is the specific chemokine ligand for the chemokine receptor CXCR4, a coreceptor with CD4 for T-tropic HIV (HIV-1). It is postulated that the mutant allele (SDF1-3'A) blocks or down regulates CXCR4, effectively blocking infection by the T-tropic HIV-1 strain often present late in the course of HIV infection. Winkler et al. (1998) found different frequencies of the SDF1-3'A allele among different ethnic groups. Among Caucasians tested, the prevalence was 21.1%, among Hispanics 16%, among African Americans 5.7%, and among Asians 25.7%. In a study of 2,857 patients, there was a marked delay in progression to AIDS for those individuals homozygous for the SDF1-3'A allele. It was also found that the delay in progression associated with the SDF1-3'A allele was twice as long as the delay associated with ΔCCR5 or CCR2-64I alleles (Winkler et al., 1998). In another study, the ethnic diversity of the SDF1-3'A allele was reported to vary widely among the different populations (Su, Chakraborty, Jin, Xiao, & Lu, 1998). The frequency of the allele ranged from 2.9% in the African populations to 71.4% in the New Guinean population. Individuals homozygous for this allele were not found among the African populations studied, but were found among populations in North America, Europe, Asia, and Oceania. The frequency of the SDF1-3'A allele was lowest in Africa (2.9%–9.1%) and higher in American Indians, Europeans, and Asians (12.2%–36.6%). The prevalence of the allele was highest among two New Guinean highlander populations (66.7%–71.4%). The frequency of homozygotes for this allele was also highest among the two New Guinean highlander populations (39.6%–47.6%). The global range of the SDF1-3'A allele and its genotype among various ethnic groups, and its role in delaying the onset of AIDS provides opportunities for exploring potential genetic-based therapeutic interventions (Su et al., 1998; Winkler et al., 1998).

Recent investigations have identified an allele that speeds up the development of AIDS. Martin et al. (1998) showed that individuals who are homozygous for the promoter allele CCR5P1, which influences the CCR5 gene, progress to AIDS more rapidly than those with other alleles of the CCR5 gene. The CCR5P1 directs the synthesis of other receptors that the virus uses for entry in to the CD4+ cell. Thus, the virus can replicate more rapidly, causing the individual to develop symptoms of AIDS several years earlier than those not homozygous for the CCR5P1 allele. In a study conducted by Martin et al. (1998), the frequency of individuals homozygous for the CCR5P1 gene was 12.7% among Caucasians and 6.7% among African Americans. Homozygous Caucasian cohorts exhibited a rapid progression to AIDS, but the African American homozygous cohort failed to show accelerated progression to AIDS (Martin et al., 1998). Apparently, not everyone who is homozygous for the CCR5P1 will progress quickly to AIDS. Nevertheless, approximately 10% to 17% of those patients who develop AIDS within 3.5 years of being infected are homozygous for the CCR5P1 gene, whereas others not homozygous for the CCR5P1 gene may stay symptom-free for 15 or more years.

OTHER RACIAL DIFFERENCES IN DISEASE

In another study of racial differences, inmates in two large prisons were assessed and retested for conversion of the tuberculin test to positive (Stead, Senner, Reddick, & Lofgren, 1990). The rate of conversion was twice as high for Blacks as for Whites, although all the inmates were exposed to the same environmental factors. The study raises the possibility that the reason for the high TB test conversion may be attributable to racially determined genetic differences.

Racial differences have also been observed in lipoprotein and cardiovascular abnormalities among renal disease patients (Burrell et al., 1991). In general, Blacks have lower total cholesterol (TC) concentrations, higher high density lipoprotein-cholesterol (HDL-C) concentrations, a lower TC/HDL-C ratio, a higher apolipoprotein (apo) A-I concentration, lower apo B concentration, and a higher A-I/B ratio than Whites (Burrell et al., 1991). This better lipid profile is significant in terms of heart disease and end-stage renal disease (ESRD). Racial disparity is also apparent in the levels of lipoprotein a, Lp(a). Lp(a) is strongly associated with coronary heart disease. Serum Lp(a) levels exceeding 25mg/dl are twice as likely to lead to myocardial infarction (Harris-Hooker & Sanford, 1994). Interestingly, Blacks are shown to have twice as much serum Lp(a) than Whites, yet there was no rise in the CHD mortality in Black participants studied (Harris-Hooker & Sanford, 1994). Overall, these findings may indicate that the reduced incidence of coronary disease and mortality in Black ESRD patients, despite increased incidence of hypertension overall, may be due to the genetically favorable lipid profile of Blacks (Burrell et al., 1991). The outcome of mortality and morbidity of cardiovascular disease in African Americans is influenced by a number of other factors ranging from lack of preventive health services to racism in health care.

For over 50 years, racial differences have also been recognized in hypertensive patients (Adams, 1932). Epidemiological evidence has demonstrated clearly that some Blacks experience higher rates of elevated blood pressure during childhood (Voors, Foster, Frerichs, Webber, & Berenson, 1976) and adulthood (Hypertension Detection and Follow-Up Program Cooperative Group, 1977; Roberts & Maurer, 1981) and higher rates of target organ damage (Saunders, 1985, 1987). The significantly reduced renin levels in Blacks, as compared to Whites, is considered to be the pathophysiologic mechanism underlying differences among White and Black hypertensive patients. Although there is certainly some evidence that environmental factors may contribute to differences in the prevalence of morbidity and mortality from hypertension between Blacks and Whites, there is also an abundance of evidence of genetic differences with associated hormonal and physiologic aberrations (Saunders, 1987; Voors et al., 1976).

HTLV infection, hypertension, tuberculosis, diabetic nephropathy, and HIV-1 associated nephropathy are not the only diseases with racially different susceptibilities. They serve, however, as examples of diseases for which environmental and lifestyle factors are not sufficient to account for the observed ethnic/racial differences in frequency and morbidity. Therefore, genetic factors are a likely candidate for causal influence. Elucidation of the biologic mechanisms associated with genetic differences would confirm their role. For example, the elucidation of the CCR5 receptor in attachment of HIV to CD4+ cells provides a biologic confirmation of genetic determinants that covary with race.

ARE THERE BIOLOGICALLY BASED DIFFERENCES IN DISEASE SUSCEPTIBILITY ACROSS GEOGRAPHICAL SPACE?

The recent discovery of the ΔCCR5 allele and its differing frequency among different ethnic groups prompted numerous studies of the global distribution of the ΔCCR5 deletion allele. As we remarked earlier, an extensive population survey conducted by Martinson et al. (1997) found geographical differences in distribution. An additional study of the frequency of the ΔCCR5 allele across Eurasia revealed a range of from 0% to 14%, affirming the previous study of a north to south gradient in allele frequency and its near absence in East Asian, Middle Eastern and American Indian populations (Stephens et al., 1998). The highest allele frequency in North Europe is among the Swedes. Among the Mediterranean population the frequency is from 5% to 14%, among Greeks 4.4%, and among the Saudi and East Asian populations 0%. The data show high ΔCCR5 allele frequency among northern European Caucasians (Central Asian groups such as Tatars, Tuvinians, Kazakhs, Uzbeks, Uigurs and Azerbaijanis), and an absence among the Lebanese, Georgians, Saudis, Koreans, Chinese, and American Indians (Stephens et al., 1998). Yudin et al.

(1998) examined the allele distribution across the Russian part of Eurasia and found a 10.4% to 22.2% frequency among the West Siberian populations (whose descendants typically are from European parts of Russia). In contrast, very low frequencies of the ΔCCR5 allele were found among the Far Eastern and Native East Siberian populations.

The uneven distribution of the ΔCCR5 allele across geographic regions and racial groups has generated discussions about the rate of HIV transmission or the speed of the disease progression in different racial groups. Certain populations carrying the ΔCCR5 allele may have an increased survival advantage in the HIV epidemic, whereas those lacking the gene variant may have a higher prevalence of HIV infection and a more rapid disease progression. African Americans, having a lower prevalence of the ΔCCR5 allele, are at greater risk for HIV infection than Caucasians in the United States, when known risk factors were controlled. The global pattern of the ΔCCR5 allele and its associated effect on HIV infection and disease progression calls for closer investigations (McNichol et al., 1997).

Human T-cell Leukemia Virus (HTLV-1) may also be an important cofactor in HIV disease progression. Coinfection with HTLV-1 is thought to increase the rate of development to an AIDS state (Cohen, Sande, & Volberding, 1995). Several studies have been conducted on the seroprevalence of HTLV-I in different regions of the world. From their data, different areas of the world have been found to be endemic areas of HTLV-I. In addition to areas in Japan and the Caribbean already discussed, Levine et al. (1988) found a new high risk population in a group of Native Americans from southern Florida. In addition to this group, other areas of the United States have been shown to be HTLV-I endemic areas. Williams et al. (1988) found HTLV-I seropositivity to be high in the southeastern and southwestern United States. Robert-Guroff et al. (1985) also found a high prevalence in Eskimo populations in the Arctic.

Besides these areas of relatively high seroprevalence in North America, HTLV-I has been found in South America, particularly in southwestern Colombia (Maloney, Ramirez, Levin, & Blattner, 1989) and Venezuela (Merino et al., 1984). These results have implications for possible racial differences because in all of these studies, the HTLV-I antibody appeared to be less prevalent in Whites than in non-Whites. In addition, Levine et al. (1988) observed varying percentages of HTLV-I positive patients with non-Hodgkin's lymphoma (from < 5% in the Middle East, Asia, and Europe, to 84% in nonendemic areas of Japan). They attributed this variability to either different strains of HTLV-I or other retroviruses or to differences in the genetic susceptibility of the hosts.

IMMUNOLOGIC EVIDENCE FOR RACIAL DIFFERENCES IN HIV DISEASE

Racial differences have been found in the expression of HIV antigen p24 (HIV-Ag). HIV-Ag is used as a marker for the clinical progression of HIV infection. In HIV positive individuals, p24 prevalence increases with increasing immunodeficiency, as measured by T-cell counts. Chaisson et al. (1991) confirmed a racial difference in the prevalence of HIV p24-Ag between Blacks and Whites (18% vs. 38%). Further, anti-p24 antibodies were detected in higher proportions of Blacks (84% vs. 65%), and Blacks had higher mean immunoglobulin levels than Whites. These results may indicate that Blacks have a more sustained humoral response to HIV infection than Whites. Similar results were found in a comparative study with AIDS patients from Uganda, Kenya, and the United Kingdom. As opposed to patients from the United Kingdom, there was no significant reduction in p24 antibodies among East African asymptomatic and AIDS patients and p24 antigenemia occurred more frequently in UK individuals (65%) (Kaleebu et al., 1991).

In a study of HIV infected injecting drug users (IDU) conducted by Gorter, Vranizan, Osmond, and Moss (1992), racial and sex differences were found in the presence of the HIV marker p24 antigenemia. Black females were much less likely to have the p24 antigenemia than Black males or White males and females. Of the cohort studied, only 1% of the Black IDU women tested positive for the p24 antigen, whereas 14% of Black men, 12% of White men, and 20% of the White women were p24 antigen-positive. The low prevalence of the HIV p24 antigenemia in Black females however, does not necessarily mean a slower progression to AIDS than Whites or Black men. Results of this study should be considered in studying HIV in ethnic minority women.

There are also other reports of important immunological differences among subpopulations that may have clinical implications (Gorter et al., 1992). In an investigation by Lucey and colleagues (1992), Blacks had significantly higher IgG and IgA levels than Whites. This observation suggests that racial differences in humoral immunity may underlie the observed racial differences in HIV antibody levels and HIV antigenemia.

A study done on malaria by Hill et al. (1991) supports the hypothesis that extraordinary polymorphism of major histocompatibility complex genes has evolved primarily through natural selection by infectious pathogens. This theory of pathogen driven MHC diversity requires that individuals of different MHC types should differ in their susceptibility to at least some major infectious pathogens. In fact, the study showed that the presence of HLA Bw53 and either the HLA haplotype DRB1* 1302 or DQB1*O501 provides the same protection as the sickle cell variant. Interestingly enough, these HLA combinations are common among West Africans (40%), but almost completely absent from Whites and Asians (0%–1%). This study suggests that malaria has influenced the evolution of polymorphic MHC genes in humans. The study opens doors into a new way of thinking. It is now possible to ask the question of whether or not HIV and AIDS are having any similar effects (Hill et al., 1991).

As suggested by the malaria study, individuals of different MHC types should differ in their susceptibility to at least some major infectious pathogens. Unfortunately, no convincing associations between HLA polymorphism and susceptibility to commonly fatal infectious diseases have yet been identified, in contrast to well-known associations between HLA and many autoimmune diseases (Hill et al., 1991).

Specific HLA combinations have been found to increase or to decrease the progression of AIDS. If each ethnic group has its own patterns of HLA combinations, then more extensive research needs to be done in order to isolate HLA or loci influencing disease progression within specific ethnic populations.

Of course, no one population is completely ethnically distinct from another, thus the high prevalence of HTLV-I and especially HTLV-II in Native American populations is particularly interesting due to the mixing of the Native American gene pool. In the United States, the Native American Indian and Black populations have intermingled, resulting in the introduction of Black genes into the Native American population. Of course, the converse is equally true. That is, a Native American predisposition could have been introduced into the American Black population. Cross-racial studies between American Blacks, American Indians, and African Blacks would further elucidate this possibility. This intermingling is useful for studies of genetic susceptibilities. Further, it cannot necessarily be assumed that all members within a particular racial/ethnic group are genetically homogeneous.

RACIAL DIFFERENCES IN DRUG RESPONSE

Racial factors play a role in drug response as well. For example, Asians have been shown to require lower dosages of a wide variety of psychotropic drugs, including neuroleptics, tricyclics, lithium, and benzodiazepines (Lin, Poland, & Lesser, 1986). Similarly, Blacks and Hispanics also require lower clinical dosages of tricyclics. Racial differences in the metabolism and sensitivity to the drug were found between Asians and Caucasians (Zhou, Adedoyin, & Wood, 1992).

Pharmacokinetic effects can vary depending on the efficiency and extent to which a given drug is metabolized. Metabolism of drugs can be measured by observing the blood concentration of the drug as a function of drug dosage. Differences in drug sensitivity are shown by observing the effects of varying drug dosages. By looking at both of these effects, researchers have determined some of the reasons behind the racial differences in drug response (Zhou et al., 1992). For example, the effects of propranolol, a beta-blocker, were examined in Chinese and American White subjects (Zhou et al., 1989). It is already known that the dosages of propranolol prescribed in China are significantly lower than those prescribed in the United States and Europe. Zhou et al. (1989) concluded that Chinese males have a greater sensitivity to propranolol based on genetic racial differences mediating the effects of the drug on heart rate and blood pressure. Whereas the actual mechanism of the increased sensitivity in Chinese is unknown, they suggest that differences in the beta-receptor sites on the heart are partly responsible. In addition, the Chinese subjects demonstrated a dissimilar metabolism of propranolol as compared to the Caucasian subjects. Chinese males were able to metabolize propranolol two times faster than Caucasians by means of ring oxidation and conjugation. As a result, Asians had lower plasma concentrations of the drug at any given dosage (Zhou et al., 1989). The twofold higher clearance of propranolol in Asians further accentuates the sensitivity differences observed in that Asians still showed a greater response to propranolol at a given dosage, even though the drug was broken down at a greater rate in Asians than in Whites.

Zhou, Shay, and Wood (1993) studied the differences in plasma binding of propranolol between Caucasian and Chinese men. Chinese men not only have higher concentrations of unbound propranolol, but the ratio of unbound (–) to (+)–propranolol was greater in Chinese men than in Caucasian men. A larger concentration of unbound propranolol may contribute to their heightened sensitivity to the effects of propranolol.

Differences in the effects of propranolol in Black and Caucasian men have also been documented. In one study (J. A. Johnson, 1993), Black men were less sensitive to 1-propranolol than Caucasian men (Johnson & Burlew, 1992). Beta-receptors possessed a greater affinity for propranolol in Caucasian men, hence producing a greater sensitivity to beta-blockade. It was also noted that in order to occupy 92.5% of the beta-receptors, Black males needed seven times more propranolol than White males.

J. A. Johnson, Burlew, and Stiles (1995) observed that Caucasian males were more sensitive to the chronotropic effects of isoproterenol, a beta-agonist, than Black males. Black men needed twice the amount of isoproterenol than Caucasian men to attain the same response.

Ethnic differences in parasympathetic response have also been of concern to researchers. Equal doses of atropine, which induces parasympathetic blockade, were administered to eight American-born Caucasian men and Chinese men (Zhou et al., 1992). The heart rates of the Chinese participants had a significantly greater increase than those of the Caucasian participants. The plasma atropine concentration was also measured and used to correct the increase in heart rate in both groups. The Chinese men had a 2.8 fold higher heart rate for each nanogram per milliliter of plasma atropine in comparison to the Caucasian men. In addition to these findings, researchers observed that the Chinese men had a significantly higher heart rate reduction than the Caucasian men when propranolol was given along with atropine (Zhou et al., 1992). Apparently, Chinese men are much more sensitive to the effects of atropine than Caucasian men (Zhou et al., 1992). These results also support previous research described earlier that Chinese men are more sensitive to propranolol (Zhou et al., 1989).

Much research has focused on racial differences in the effects of haloperidol, a commonly used neuroleptic drug (Lin, Poland, et al., 1988). Haloperidol is a stimulator of prolactin secretion. In studies of Asians and Caucasians, Caucasians had lower plasma concentrations of haloperidol and a lower prolactin response than did the Asians subjects (Lin, Poland, et al., 1988). Even after controlling for variations in body surface area, the difference in drug response remained significant. Because researchers found no distinctions in the responses of foreign-born and American-born Asians, differences in lifestyles do not appear to be a significant factor in this aspect of drug response. Instead, the differential drug responses are likely due to genetic differences between Asians and Caucasians (Lin, Poland, et al., 1988). Lin et al. (1989) further observed in schizophrenic patients that the racial difference in drug response was mainly due to pharmacodynamic factors. With fixed dosages, Asian patients had slightly greater serum concentrations of haloperidol and greater extra pyramidal symptoms. With variable dosages, Asian patients again required lower dosages for an optimal clinical response (Lin et al., 1989). As in their previous study, body surface area was controlled. Therefore, the lower dosages required for Asians appear to be due to increased sensitivity to haloperidol.

Building on these findings, Chang et al. (1991) discovered that in patients with schizophrenia, Chinese patients had higher haloperidol plasma levels than non-Chinese patients, which included Caucasians, Hispanics, and Blacks. In addition, this study examined "reduced haloperidol," the alcohol metabolite produced by the reduction of haloperidol at the benzylic ketone. The ratios of "reduced haloperidol" to haloperidol were lower in the Chinese patients than the non-Chinese patients. This suggests racially influenced differential rates in the metabolism of haloperidol.

Racial differences have also been observed in studies of anxiolytic medications. For example, studies with the benzodiazepine-like drug, alprazolam, also show that racial differences in pharmacokinetic effects exist between Asians and Caucasians (Lin, Lau, et al., 1988). Because of this, Asians require lower clinical dosages of alprazolam than Caucasians (Lin, Lau, et al., 1988). To what extent this is due to differences in behavioral factors, such as diet, is unknown, but evidence for genetic factors were strongly suggested. Zhang, Reviriego, Lou, Sjeoqvist, and Bertilsson (1990) found interethnic differences in the metabolism of diazepam, an anxiolytic sedative. In their study, Chinese subjects metabolized diazepam at a much slower rate than Caucasian subjects, suggesting that those of Chinese descent may require lower doses of diazepam. Finally, Caraco, Tateishi, and Wood (1995) discovered that their Chinese subjects possessed a slower metabolism of diazepam than the Caucasian subjects. They also observed ethnic differences in omeprazole's inhibitory effect on the metabolism of diazepam. After taking omeprazole, diazepam clearance was similar in both the Caucasian and Chinese participants. However, the area under the concentration time curve (AUC) for diazepam's metabolite, desmethyldiazepam, was significantly lower in the Caucasian group than in the Chinese group. Thus, it appears that not only do Chinese men metabolize diazepam at a slower rate than Caucasian men, but the effect of omeprazole among Chinese men is greatly reduced as compared to Caucasian men.

Lithium is another psychiatric medication that has been examined for possible racial differences in drug effects. In one study (Strickland, Lin, Fu, Anderson, & Zheng, 1995), African American and Caucasian bipolar patients displayed different drug-related responses. Specifically, African Americans evidenced much higher red blood cell lithium concentrations and a much higher lithium ratio when compared to Caucasians. They also experienced a greater number of side effects. The results hint that African Americans may require lower dosages of lithium than Caucasians.

Although studies on racial differences in the effects of psychotropic medication has clearly demonstrated possible differences with relevance to dosing regimens, research in other major diseases is less developed with the exception of treatment of hypertension. Racial differences between Blacks and Whites in the prevalence and the sequelae of hypertension also have important therapeutic implications. Evidence that Blacks are relatively unresponsive to antihypertensive therapy is inconclusive. On the contrary, there is significant evidence that when pharmacologic interventions are combined with other environmental measures, Blacks benefit more (Hypertension Detection and Follow-up Program Cooperative Group, 1979a, 1979b). There is also strong evidence that in monodrug therapy, the optimal drugs to achieve effective control in Blacks are different from those likely to be successful in Whites (Cubeddu et al., 1986; Saunders, 1985).

Evidence for other race-related differences in treatment of hypertension also exists. For example, the pharmacokinetics of nifedipine, a dihydropyridine calcium channel blocker, differs among racial groups. Ahsan et al. (1993) discovered that Asians, South Asians in particular, had higher plasma concentrations of nifedipine after a standard dose than Caucasians. Also, the area under the plasma concentration time curve (AUC) was twice as high in Asians as in Caucasians. Sowunmi, Rashid, Akinyinka, and Renwick (1995) observed that South Asians as well as Nigerians had a significantly higher AUC and higher plasma concentrations than Caucasians. The difference of nifedipine metabolism between the three populations suggests differential bioavailability and/or differential systematic clearance.

IMPLICATIONS FOR HIV/AIDS RESEARCH

From the disparate evidence presented, it is clear that racial differences exist for disease susceptibility and drug response. In many cases, increased susceptibility or resistance to a disease is associated with known racial differences in HLA specificities, CCR5, CCR2, SDF1, and the recently discovered CCR5P1 gene (Martin et al., 1998). With the recent discoveries of these host genes, new genetic therapeutic approaches may be designed to target the specific gene variant among individuals (McNicholl et al., 1997). Furthermore, different races can have varying responses to drugs. These responses are determined by differences in absorption, metabolism, or excretion (pharmacokinetic effects) or by differences in drug sensitivity (pharmacodynamic effects) that are influenced by genetic factors (Lin, Lau, et al., 1988; Lin, Poland, et al., 1988). Because of these biologically determined differences in disease susceptibility and drug response, the importance of cross-racial factors when conducting studies of disease and developing pharmacologic interventions needs to be taken into consideration.

The multigenetic influence on HIV-1 infection and progression to AIDS, and its difference in prevalence among ethnic groups, provides a basis for therapeutic opportunities. The studies presented here that show varying frequencies of the host genes among ethnic populations provide sufficient support for the importance of considering the patient's racial genetic profile in developing appropriate therapeutic strategies. Accordingly, any research conducted must take into account cross-racial factors so that what is known about the course of the disease in any given population can be elucidated accurately.

The only mechanism by which to achieve this is through the inclusion of an ethnically representative subject population in clinical trials of HIV/AIDS drugs. This would help ensure that a particular drug in standard recommended dosage has the desired therapeutic effect in one racial group as it does in another. Without cross-racial data, the results of trials on one race may not necessarily be applicable to another race. AIDS researchers must be sensitive to these issues to prevent the approval of HIV- related therapies that may not have the same efficacy or safety profile in populations outside the gay White male community. An example of one such study, Study ACTG 116-B/117, was reviewed by the Food and Drug Administration a few years back. This study was sponsored by the National Institute on Allergies and Infectious Diseases, the leading governmental agency conducting AIDS research in the United States (Japour et al., 1995), and was designed to compare the efficacy and toxicity of didanosine (ddI) and zidovudine (ZDV or AZT) in the treatment of primary HIV infection in patients who tolerated previously more than 16 weeks of ZDV. The investigators concluded, based on information from 913 participants who were randomized at the time of analysis, ddI appeared to be more effective than ZDV in delaying time to first new AIDS-defining event or death in the study population. This benefit was seen in the subgroup of patients who entered the study with AIDS-related complex (ARC) or asymptomatic disease, but not in those with AIDS. The composition of this study population was 96% male, 82% White, and 79% from the homosexual/bisexual risk behavior group. The biological and genetic composition of this group, more homogenous than the general HIV infected population, may capitalize unknowingly on finding effects that may be influenced by unmeasured factors, thus overestimating the effectiveness of this treatment when widely applied. Although no studies have shown these findings to be detrimental, nonetheless it is important that findings from studies that lack diversity be approached cautiously as proven treatment plans for those who were not participants in the study. Further research should be conducted to determine whether results from such studies are equally effective in the populations not a part of the study.

Admittedly, the challenges of recruiting and retaining some subpopulations, especially the socially and economically disenfranchised, may be difficult, expensive and require considerable investment of time and resources (El-Sadr & Capps, 1992; Mays, 1998, 1999; Mays & Cochran, 1999). Nonetheless, by including more representative samples of the affected populations of a particular disease, more accurate and useful information can be gained. This is especially important in the development of effective HIV-related drug treatments as trends of incidence of HIV infection indicates a rise in new cases within ethnic minority groups who in the past have been the least likely to be recruited into studies.

Yet, despite 15 years of research in the quest for a cure or control of HIV/AIDS, HIV clinical studies, drug treatment, and drug and vaccine development study methodology is only in its infancy when it comes to ensuring adequate study participation by ethnic/minorities (Mays, 1998, 1999; Mays & Cochran, 1990, 1999). This is because of a variety of complicated reasons (Mays, 1998, 1999; Mays & Cochran, 1999; Stone, Mauch, Steger, Janas, & Craven, 1997). But there are also a number of steps that can be taken to increase the likelihood of advancement of scientific knowledge in the area of biomedical research on HIV-related disease susceptibility, disease progression and pharmacologic interventions for ethnic minority groups.

The following steps are recommended: First and foremost, leadership by the federal government is critical in directing the research agenda to focus on possible racial/ethnic differences in susceptibility to infection, disease progression, and clinical and drug treatment options and strategies. This could be accomplished through the following:

1. A request by the President to the federal agencies and the Surgeon General to ensure that all clinical, vaccine, drug development, and drug treatment research scientifically demonstrates effectiveness across ethnic/racial groups.
2. Development of a mechanism (collaborative workgroups, advisory boards, or citizen consultants of experts on HIV and ethnic minorities drawn from senior researchers with strong research publication records, senior policy advisors and clinicians with long histories of working with minority populations) under the combined auspices of Office of AIDS Research (OAR), Office of Minority Health (OMH) and NIH with the charge to identify the gaps in the current NIH, OAR, and private-sector research portfolios; recommend new directions for biomedical research within NIH and OAR that would ensure better science on HIV-related racial/ethnic differences in genetic and immunologic aspects of HIV disease susceptibility, disease progression, and clinical and drug treatment strategies and options; and review the international HIV research portfolio to determine possible ethnic/racial difference research studies that could answer specific scientific questions.
3. A convening of a conference on biomedical research on racial/ethnic minorities with a series of commissioned papers. Publish and disseminate papers, develop regional and national data sharing collaborations, and provide seed funding for collaborators to engage in data analyses on issues identified as high priority by the conference.
4. Development of funding opportunities (RFAs, RFPs) targeting gaps in the biomedical research portfolio on racial/ethnic differences in HIV infection, disease progression/nonprogression, drug treatment, and clinical and drug development response.
5. Creation of a cooperative agreement for funding for collection of biological data from racial/ethnic minorities who are HIV seronegative high risk, HIV seropositive, and diagnosed with AIDS in order to develop a specimen repository, under the scientific direction of a multiethnic senior research team. This repository

could be made accessible nationally to investigators who submit proposals to the senior multiethnic research team that maintains oversight.

6. Building on previous federal initiatives designed to increase the number of ethnic minority principal investigators, development of a RFA for three funding cycles within NIAID targeting basic genetic, immunologic, vaccine, and treatment research on racial/ethnic differences under the leadership of senior/tenured minority principal investigators.
7. Development of review guidelines for NIH review committees that address not only inclusion of minorities but the inclusion of specific scientific hypotheses that explore racial/ethnic differences in genetic and immunologic responses to HIV infection, disease progression/nonprogression, response to drug development, and clinical and drug treatment strategies and options.

Whereas leadership by the federal government is essential and necessary to accelerating the science of racial/ethnic differences in susceptibility for HIV infection, disease progression/nonprogression and responses to vaccine candidates and clinical and drug treatment strategies and options, there are others who can exert leadership in this domain. For example:

1. Medical journal editors should require that when minorities are participants in studies, evidence be provided that there are no differences from nonminorities if their data are not presented separately or in comparison to nonminorities or between ethnic groups. Analyses by race/ethnicity should be required unless there is a statistical case for foregoing such procedures.
2. Researchers must take seriously the task of mastering the scientific literature on HIV in ethnic minorities in order to develop testable hypotheses that can advance the field on ethnic/racial differences in the cause and treatment of HIV infection and disease. Many investigators will find that increased attention to this body of data will not only assist in advancing science but better equip them to design racially/ethnic diverse studies and maintain study cohorts.

Finally, although the authors could envision a number of additional recommendations to urge HIV research or biomedical research on racial/ethnic differences, none is as compelling as urging mechanisms to ensure that scientific findings are translated into prevention, intervention, and treatment strategies that reach the community. Without creating mechanisms by which the findings actually reach and benefit the population being focused on, researchers lose credibility with the community and fail to achieve the fundamental purpose of science, that is, to improve the lives of others.

ACKNOWLEDGMENTS

The terms, *Black* and *African American,* are often used interchangeably in the literature. Some present-day African Americans are descended from Africans brought to this country more than a 150 years ago. However over time there has been admixture in which African Americans share a mixed biological heritage with Native Americans, Whites, and other racially distinct populations. There are also a number of groups that within research studies are designated Black but maintain some genetic distinctions in their admixture from African Americans such as Haitians, Belizeans, or Black Puerto Ricans. In studies, the designation of Blacks or African Americans may vary in which biological heritage groups are included. Therefore, throughout this chapter the term adopted by the original author of the work being reviewed is used in order to remain true to their designation of the population.

This work was supported by grants from the National Institute of Mental Health and the National Institute on Allergy and Infectious Diseases (R01MH42584, R01MH44345, R01AI38216) and an NIMH Scientist Development Award (K21MH00878) to the third author. We thank Mary Carrington, Lovell Jones, David Carlisle, and Karol Watson for their assistance, although we assume all responsibility for the contents of the chapter.

REFERENCES

Achord, A. P., Lewis, R. E., Brackin, M. N., Henderson, H., & Cruse, J. M. (1996). HIV-1 disease association with HLA-DQ antigens in African Americans and Caucasians. *Pathobiology, 64,* 204–208.

Achord, A. P., Lewis, R. E., Brackin, M. N., & Cruse, J. M. (1997). HLA-DQB1 markers associated with human immunodeficiency virus Type I disease progression. *Pathobiology, 65,* 210–215.

Adams, J. M. (1932). Some racial differences in blood pressures and morbidity in groups of White and colored workmen. *American Journal of the Medical Sciences, 184,* 342–350.

Ahsan, C. H., Renwick, A. G., Waller, D. G., Challenor, V. F., George, C. F., & Amanullah, M. (1993). The influence of dose and ethnic origins on the pharmacokinetics of nifedipine. *Clinical Pharmacology and Therapeutics, 54*(3), 329–338.

Alarif, L., Castro, O., Ofosu, M., Dunston, G., & Scott, R. B. (1986). HLA-B35 is associated with red cell alloimmunization in sickle cell disease. *Clinical Immunology and Immunopathology, 38,* 178–183.

Bourgoignie, J. J., Oritz-Interian, C., Green, D. F., & Roth, D. (1989). Race, a cofactor in HIV-1–associated nephropathy. *Transplantation Proceedings, 6,* 3899–3901.

Brackin, M. N., Lewis, R. E., Brackin, B. T., Achord, A., Henderson, H., Crawford, M., & Cruse, J. M. (1995). Progression of HIV infection is associated with HLA-DQ antigens in Caucasians and African Americans. *Pathobiology, 62,* 22–41.

Brown, C., Kline, R., Atibu, L., Francis, H., Ryder, R., & Quinn, T. C. (1991). Prevalence of HIV-1 p24 antigenemia in African and North American populations and correlation with clinical status. *AIDS, 5,* 89–92.

Brown, S. R., Lane, J. R., Wagner, K. F., Zhou, S., Chung, R., Ray, K. L., Blatt, S. P., & Burke, D. S. (1995). Rates of p24 antigenemia and viral isolation in comparable White and Black HIV-infected subjects. *AIDS, 9,* 325–328.

Burrell, D. E., Antignani, A., Goldwasser P., Mittman, N., Fein, P. A., Slater, P. A., Gan, A., & Avram, M. M. (1991). Lipid abnormailites in Black renal patients. *Lipid, 91,* 192–196.

Callender, C. O., & Dunston, G. M. (1987, February/March). Kidney transplantation: A dilemma for Black Americans. *Renal Life,* 11.

Caraco, Y., Tateishi, T., & Wood, A. J. (1995). Interethnic difference in omeprazole's inhibition of diazepam metabolism. *Clinical Pharmacology and Therapeutics, 58,* 62–72.

Cerna, M., Falco, M., Friedman, H., Raimondi, E., Maccagno, A., Fernandez-Vina, M., & Statsny, P. (1993). Differences in HLA Class II alleles of isolated South American Indian populations from Brazil and Argentina. *Human Immunology, 37,* 213–220.

Chaisson, R. E., Fuchs, E., Stanton, D. L., Quinn, T. C., Hendricksen, C., Bartlett, J. G., & Farzadegan, H. (1991). Racial heterogeneity of HIV antigenemia in people with HIV infection. *AIDS, 5*(2), 177–180.

Chang, W. H., Jann, M. W., Hwu, H. G., Chen, T. Y., Lin, S. K., Wang, J. M., Ereshefsky, L., Saklad, S. R., Richards, A. L., & Lam, Y.W.F. (1991). Ethnic comparisons of haloperidol and reduced haloperidol plasma levels: Taiwan Chinese patients versus American non-Chinese. *Journal of Formosan Medical Association, 90*(6), 572–578.

Chen, W. H., Chiu, H. C., & Hsieh, R. P. (1993). Association of HLA-Bw46DR9 combination with juvenile myasthenia gravis in Chinese. *Journal of Neurology, Neurosurgery, and Psychiatry, 56,* 382–385.

Cochran, S. D., & Mays, V. M. (1988). Epidemiologic and sociocultural factors in the transmission of HIV infection in Black gay and bisexual men. In M. Shernoff & W. A. Scott (Eds.), *The sourcebook of lesbian/gay health care* (2nd ed., pp. 202–211). Washington, DC: National Gay and Lesbian Health Foundation.

Cohen, P. T., Sande, M. A., & Volberding, P. A. (Eds.). (1994). *The AIDS knowledge base: A textbook on HIV disease from the San Francisco General Hospital* (2nd ed.). Boston: Little, Brown.

Cubeddu, L. X., Aranda, J., Singh, B., Klein, M., Brachfeld, J., Freis, E., Roman, J., & Eades, T. (1986). A comparison of verapamil and propranolol for the initial treatment of hypertension—racial differences in response. *Journal of the American Medical Association, 256*(16), 2214–2221.

Dean, M., Carrington, M., Winkler, C., Huttley, G. A., Smith, M. W., Allikmets, R., Goedert, J. J., Buchbinder, S. P., Vittinghoff, E., Gomperts, E., Donfield, S., Vlahov, D., Kaslow, R., Saah, A., Rinaldon, C., Detels, R., Hemophilia Growth and Development Study, Multicenter AIDS Cohort Study, Multicenter Hemophilia Cohort Study, San Francisco City Cohort, ALIVE Study, & O'Brien, S. J. (1996). Genetic restriction of HIV-1 infection and progression to AIDS by a deletion allele of the CKR5 structural gene. *Science, 273,* 1856–1861.

Detels, R., Mann, D., Carrington, M., Hennessey, K., Wu, Z., Hirji, K. F., Wiley, D., Visscher, B. R., & Giorgi, J. V. (1996). Resistance to HIV infection may be genetically mediated. *AIDS, 10,* 102–104.

Dunston, G. M., Henry, L. W., Christian, J., Ofosu, M. D., & Callendar, C. O. (1989). HLA-DR3, DQ heterogeneity in American Blacks is associated with susceptibility and resistance to insulin dependent diabetes mellitus. *Transplant Proceedings, 21,* 653–655.

Dunston, G. M., Hurley, C. K., Hartzman, R. J., & Johnson, A. H. (1987). Unique HLA-D region heterogeneity in American Blacks. *Transplantation Proceedings, 19,* 870–871.

Eisenbarth, G. S. (1986). Type I diabetes mellitus. A chronic autoimmune disease. *New England Journal of Medicine, 314,* 1360–1368.

El-Sadr, W., & Capps, L. (1992). The challenge of minority recruitment in clinical trials for AIDS. *Journal of the American Medical Association, 267,* 954–957.

Erlich, H. A., Zielder, A., Chang, J., Shaw, S., Raffel, L. J., Klitz, W., Costin, G., Pressman, S., Bugamwan, T., et al. (1993). HLA Class II alleles and susceptibility and resistance to insulin dependent diabetes mellitus in Mexican-American families. *Nature Genetics, 3,* 358–364.

Fahey, J. L., & Flemmig, D. S. (1997). *AIDS-HIV reference guide for medical professionals* (4th ed.). Baltimore: Willliams & Wilkins.

Fletcher, J., Mijovic, C., Odugbesan, O., Jenking, D., Bradwell, A. R., & Barnett, A.Q.H. (1988). Trans-racial studies implicate HLA-DQ as a component of genetic susceptibiliity to Type 1 (insulin-dependent) diabetes. *Diabetologia, 31,* 864–870.

Friedman, E. A. (1991). Diabetic nephropathy in the inner city. *New York State Journal of Medicine, 91,* 203–207.

Getting cancer patients into clinical trials. (1991, May 21). *Washington Post,* Vol. 7, 21.

Gonzales, S., Tirado, G., Revueltta, G., Yamamura, Y., Lu, Y., Nerurkar, V. R., & Yanagihara, R. (1998). CCR5 chemokine receptor genotype frequencies among Puerto Rican HIV-1–seropositive individuals. *Boletin Asociacion Medica de Puerto Rico, 90,* 12–15.

Gorter, R. W., Vranizan, K. M., Osmond, D. H., & Moss, A. R. (1992). Differences in laboratory values in HIV Infection by sex, race, and risk group. *AIDS, 6,* 1341–1347.

Greggio, N. A., Cameran, M., Giaquinto, C., Zacchello, F., Korolvuk, D., & Colizzi, V. (1993). DNA HLA-DRB1 analysis in children of positive mothers and estimated risk of vertical HIV transmission. *Disease Markers, 11,* 29–35.

Harris-Hooker, S., & Sanford, G. L. (1994). Lipids, lipoproteins, and coronary heart disease in minority populations. *Atherosclerosis, 108,* 83–104.

Hill, A. V. S., Allsopp, C. E. M., Kwiatkowski, D., Anstey, N. M., Twumasi, P., Rowe, P. A., Bennett, S., Brewster, D., McMichael, A. J., & Greenwood, B. M. (1991). Common West African HLA antigens are associated with protection from severe malaria. *Nature, 352,* 595–600.

Huang, Y., Paxton, W. A., Wolinsky, S. M., Neumann, A., Zhang, L., He, T., Kang, S., Ceradini, D., Jin, Z., Yazdanbakhsh, K., Kunstman, K., Erickson, D., Dragon, E., Landau, N. R., Phair, J., Ho, D. D., & Koup, R. A. (1996). The role of mutant CCR5 allele in HIV-1 transmission and disease progression. *Nature Medicine, 2,* 1240–1243.

Hypertension Detection and Follow-up Program Cooperative Group. (1977). Race, education, and prevalence of hypertension. *American Journal of Epidemiology, 106,* 351–361.

Hypertension Detection and Follow-up Program Cooperative Group. (1979a). Five-year findings of the hypertension detection and follow-up program: I. Reduction in mortality of persons with high blood pressure, including mild hypertension. *Journal of the American Medical Association, 242,* 2562–2571.

Hypertension Detection and Follow-up Program Cooperative Group. (1979b). Five-year findings of the hypertension detection and follow-up program: II. Mortality by race, sex, and age. *Journal of the American Medical Association, 242,* 2572–2577.

Japour, A. J., Welles, S., D'Aquila, R. T., Johnson, V. A., Richman, D. D., Coombs, R. W., Reichelderfer, P. S., Kahn, J. O., Crumpacker, C. S., & Kuritzkes, D. R. (1995). Prevalence and clinical signficance of zidovudine resistance mutations in human immunodeficiency virus isolated from patients after long-term zidovudine treatment. AIDS Clinical Trials Group 116B/117 Study Team and the Virology Committee Resistance Working Group. *Journal of Infectious Diseases, 171,* 5, 1172–1179.

Johnson, J. A. (1993). Racial differences in lymphocyte beta-receptor sensitivity to propranolol. *Life Sciences, 53,* 297–304.

Johnson, J. A., & Burlew, B. S. (1992). Racial differences in propranolol pharmacokinetics. *Clinical Pharmacology and Therapeutics, 51,* 495–500.

Johnson, J. A., Burlew, B. S., & Stiles, R. W. (1995). Racial Differences in beta-adrenoceptor-mediated responsiveness. *Journal of Cardiovascular Pharmacology, 25,* 90–96.

Just, J., Louie, L., Abrams, E., Nicholas, S. W., Wara, D., Stein, Z., & King, M. C. (1992). Genetic risk factors for perinatally acquired HIV-1 infection. *Pediatric and Perinatal Epidemiology, 6,* 215–224.

Kaleebu, P., Cheingson-Popov, R., Callow, D., Katabira, E., Mubiru, F., Biryahwaho, B., Sempala, S., Gilks, C., Brindle, R., Were, J. B., et al. (1991). Comparative humoral responses to HIV-1 p24gag and gp120env in subjects from East Africa and the UK. *AIDS, 5,* 1015–1019.

Karon, J. M., Rosenberg, P. S., McQuillan, G., Khare, M., Gwinn, M., & Petersen, L. R. (1996). Prevalence of HIV Infection in the United States, 1984 to 1992. *Journal of the American Medical Association, 276*(2), 126–131.

Kasiske, B. L., Neylan, J. F., Riggio, R. R., Danovitch, G. M., Kahna, L., Alexander, S. K., & White, M. G. (1991). The effect of race on access and outcome in transplantation. *New England Journal of Medicine, 324,* 302–307.

Kaslow, R. A., Duquesnoy, R., Vanraden, M., Kingsley, L., Marrari, M., Friedman, H., Su, S., Saah, A. J., Detels, R., Phair, J., et al. (1990). A1, Cw7, B8, DR3 HLA antigen with rapid decline of T-helper lymphocytes in HIV-1 infection. *Lancet, 335,* 927–930.

Kilpatrick, D. C., Hague, R. A., Yap, P. L., & Mok, J. Y. (1991). HLA antigen frequencies in children born to HIV-infected mothers. *Disease Markers, 9,* 21–26.

Levine, P. H., Blattner, W. A., Clark, J., Tarone, R., Maloney, E. M., Murphy, E. M., Gallo, R. C., Robert-Guroff, M., & Saxinger, W. C. (1988). Geographical distribution of HTLV-I and identification of a new high risk population. *International Journal of Cancer, 42,* 7–12.

Lin, K. M., Lau, J. K., Smith, R., Phillips, P., Antal, E., & Poland, R. E. (1988). Comparison of alprazolam plasma levels in normal Asian and Caucasian male volunteers. *Psychopharmacology, 96,* 365–369.

Lin, K. M., Poland, R. E., Lau, J. K., & Rubin, R. T. (1988). Haloperidol and prolactin concentrations in Asians and Caucasians. *Journal of Clinical Psychopharmacolgy, 8,* 195–201.

Lin, K. M., Poland, R. E., & Lesser, I. M. (1986). Ethnicity and psychopharmacology. *Culture, Medicine, and Psychiatry, 10,* 151–165.

Lin, K. M., Poland, R. E., Nuccio, L., Matsuda, K., Hathuc, N., Su, T. P., & Fu, P. (1989). A longitudinal assessment of haloperidol doses and serum concentrations in Asian and Caucasian schizophrenic patients. *American Journal of Psychiatry, 146,* 1307–1311.

Liu, R., Paxton, W. A., Choe, S., Ceradini, D., Martin, S. R., Horuk, R., MacDonald, M. E., Stuhlmann, H., Koup, R. A., & Landa, N. R. (1996). Homozygous defect in HIV-1 coreceptor accounts for resistance of some multiply-exposed individuals to HIV-1 infection. *Cell, 86,* 367–377.

Louie, L. G., Newman, B., & King, M. C. (1991). Influence of host genotype on progression to AIDS among HIV-infected men. *Journal of Acquired Immune Deficiency Syndromes, 4,* 814–818.

Lucey, D. R., Hendrix, C. W., Andrzejewski, C., Melcher, G. P., Butzin, C. A., Henry, R., Wians, F. J., Jr., & Boswell, R. N. (1992). Comparison by race of total serum IgG, IgA, and IgM with CD4+ T-cell counts in North American persons infected with human immunodeficiency virus type 1. *Journal of Acquired Immune Deficiency Syndromes, 5,* 325–332.

Maloney, E. M., Ramirez, H., Levin, A., & Blattner, W. A. (1989). A survey of the human T-cell lymphotropic virus type I (HTLV-I) in southwestern Colombia. *International Journal of Cancer, 44,* 419–423.

Martin, M. P., Dean, M., Smith, M. W., Winkler, C., Gerrard, B., Michael, N. L., Lee, B., Doms, R. W., Margolick, J., Buchbinder, S., et al. (1998). Genetic acceleration of AIDS progression by a promoter variant of CCR5. *Science, 282,* 1907–1911.

Martinez-Laso, J., Gomez-Casado, E., Morales, P., Martinez-Quiles, N. (1996). HLA-DR and DQ polymorphism in Ashkenazi and non-Ashkenazi Jews: Comparison with other Mediterraneans. *Tissue Antigens, 47,* 63–71.

Martinson, J. J., Chapman, N. H., Rees, D. C., Liu, Y. T., & Clegg, J. B. (1997). Global distribution of the CCR5 gene 32-basepair deletion. *Nature Genetics, 16,* 100–103.

Mays, V. M. (1998). The shifting demographics of the epidemic: How to design studies to reflect current and future affected populations. In *Clinical AIDS Research: The Present Status and Future Outlook.* Proceedings of the Public Responsibility in Medicine & Research (PRIM&R) Brown University AIDS Program and Tufts University School of Medicine, Boston, MA.

Mays, V. M. (1999). Methods for increasing recruitment and retention of ethnic minorities in health research through addressing ethical concerns. *Proceedings of the Health Survey Methodology Conference.* Washington, DC: USDHHS.

Mays, V. M., & Cochran, S. D. (1987). Acquired immunodeficiency syndrome and Black Americans: Special psychosocial issues. *Public Health Reports, 102*(2), 224–231.

Mays, V. M., & Cochran, S. D. (1990). Methodological issues in the assessment and prediction of AIDS risk-related sexual behaviors among Black Americans. In B. Voeller, J. Reinisch, & M. Gottlieb (Eds.), *AIDS and sex: An integrated biomedical and biobehavioral approach* (pp. 97–120). New York: Oxford University Press.

Mays, V. M., & Cochran, S. D. (1995). HIV/AIDS in the African American community: Changing concerns, changing behaviors. In M. Stein & A. Baum (Eds.), *Chronic diseases* (pp. 259–272). New York: Lawrence Erlbaum Associates.

Mays, V. M., & Cochran, S. D. (1999). Methods for increasing relevance of telephone and field-survey research to community needs. *Proceedings of the National Center for Health Statistics National Conference on Health Statistics.* Washington, DC: USDHHS.

McNicholl, J. M., Smith, D. K., Qari, S. H., & Hodge, T. (1997). Host genes and HIV: The role of the chemokine receptor gene CCR5 and its allele (Δ32 CCR5). *Emerging Infectious Diseases, 3,* 261–271.

Merino, F., Robert-Guroff, M., Clark, J., Biondo-Bracho, M., Blattner, W. A., & Gallo, R. C. (1984). Natural antibodies to human T cell leukemia/lymphoma virus in healthy Venezuelan populations. *International Journal of Cancer, 34,* 501–506.

Murphy, E. L., Hanchard, B., Figueroa, J. P., Gibbs, W. N., Lofters, W. S., Campbell, M., Goedert, J. J., & Blattner, W. A. (1989). Modeling the risk of adult T-cell leukemia/lymphoma in persons infected with human T-lymphotropic virus Type I. *International Journal of Cancer, 43T,* 250–253.

O'Brien, T. R., & Goedert, J. J. (1998). Chemokine receptors and genetic variability. *Journal of the American Medical Association, 279,* 317–318.

O'Brien, R. R., Padian, N. S., Hodge, T., Goedert, J. J., O'Brien, S. J., & Carrington, M. (1998). CCR-5 genotype and sexual transmission of HIV-1. *AIDS, 12*(4), 444–445.

Ofosu, M. D., Saunders, D. A., Dunston, G. M., Castro, O., & Alarif, L. (1986). Association of HLA and autoantibody in transfused sickle cell disease patients. *American Journal of Hematology, 22,* 27–33.

Ofosu, M. H., Dunston, G., Henry, L., Ware, D., Cheatham, W., Brembridge, A., Brown, C., & Alarif, L. (1996). HLA-DQ3 is associated with Graves' disease in African Americans. *Immunological Investigations, 25,* 103–110.

Osborne, L., & Mason, J. (1993). HLA A/B haplotype frequencies among U. S. Hispanic and African-American Populations. *Human Genetics, 91,* 326–332.

Passos, Jr., G.A.S., & Picanc, V. P. (1998). Frequency of the ΔCCR5 deletion allele in the urban Brazilian population. *Immunology Letter, 61,* 205–207.

Pollack, M. S., Safai, B., & DuPont, B. (1983). HLA-DR5 and DR2 are susceptibility factors for Acquired Immunodeficiency Syndrome with Kaposi's Sarcoma in different ethnic subpopulations. *Disease Markers, 1,* 135–139.

Ready, T. (1988). Too Few Minorities in AIDS tests, critics say, Scientist "ignoring" Blacks Hispanics, women. *Washington Watch,* 1.

Robert-Guroff, M., Clark, J., Lanier, A. P., Beckman, G., Melbye, M., Ebbesen, P., Blattner, W. A., & Gallo, R. C. (1985). Prevalence of HTLV-I in Arctic regions. *International Journal of Cancer, 36,* 651–655.

Roberts, J., & Maurer, K. (1981). National Center for Health Statistics. Hypertension in adults 25–74 years of age, United States, 1971–1975. *Vital and health statistics* (Series 11, No. 211. DHHS Publication PHS 81-1671). Washington, DC: U.S. Government Printing Office.

Ronningen, K. S., Spurkland, A., Tait, B. D., et al. (1993). HLA class II association in insulin-dependent diabetes mellitus among Blacks, Caucasoids and Japanese. In K. Tsuji, M. Aizawa, & T. Sasazuki (Eds.), *HLA 1991* (pp. 713–722). Oxford, England: Oxford University Press.

Rosenberg, P. S., & Biggar, R. J. (1998). Trends in HIV Incidence among young adults in the United States. *Journal of the American Medical Association, 279*(23), 1894–1899.

Sanjeevi, C., Zeilder, A., Shaw, S., Rotter, J., Nepom, T., Costin, G., Raffel, L., Eastman, S., Kockum, I., Wassmuth, R., et al. (1993). Analysis of HLA-DQA1 and -DQB1 genes in Mexican Americans with insulin-dependent diabetes mellitus. *Tissue Antigens, 42,* 72–77.

Saunders, E. (1987). Hypertension in Blacks. *Medical Clinics of North America, 71,* 1013–1029.

Saunders, E. (1985). Special techniques for management in Blacks. In W. D. Hall, E. Saunders, & N. B. Shulman (Eds.), *Hypertension in Blacks: Epidemiology, pathophysiology, and treatment* (pp. 209–228). Chicago: Year Book.

Scorza Smeraldi, R., Fabio, G., Lazzarin, A., Eisera, N. B., Moroni, M., & Zanussi, C. (1986). Susceptibility to Acquired Immunodeficiency Syndrome in Italian patients with Human-Immunodeficiency-virus infection. *The Lancet, 2,* 1187–1189.

Smith, M. W., Dean, M., Carrington, M., Winkler, C., Huttley, G. A., Lomb, D. A., Goedert, J. J., O'Brien, T. R., Jacobson, L. P., Kaslow, R., et al. (1997). Contrasting genetic influence of CCR2 and CCR5 variants on HIV-1 infection and disease progression. *Science, 277,* 959–965.

Sowinski, K. M., Burlew, B. S., & Johnson, J. A. (1995). Racial differences in sensitivity to the negative chronotropic effects of propranolol in healthy men. *Clinical Pharmacology and Therapeutics, 57,* 678–683.

Sowunmi, A., Rashid, T. J., Akinyinka, O. O., & Renwick, A. G. (1995). Ethnic differences in nifedipine kinetics: Comparisons between Nigerians, Caucasians and South Asians. *British Journal of Clinical Pharmacology, 40,* 489–493.

Stead, W. W., Senner, J. W., Reddick, W. T., & Lofgren, J. P. (1990). Racial differences in susceptibility to infection by Mycobacterium tuberculosis. *New England Journal of Medicine, 322,* 422–427.

Steel, C. M., Ludlam, C. A., Beatson, D., Peutherer, J. F., Cuthbert, R. J., Simmonds, P., Morrison, H., & Jones, M. (1988). HLA haplotype A1 B8 DR3 as a risk factor for HIV-related disease. *Lancet, 1,* 1185–1188.

Stephens, J. C., Reich, D. E., Goldstein, D. B., Shin, H. D., Smith, M. W., Carrington, M., Winkler, C., Huttley, G. A., Allikmets, R., Schriml, L., et al. (1998). Dating the origin of the CCR5-Δ32 AIDS-resistance allele by the coalescence of haplotypes. *American Journal of Human Genetics, 62,* 1507–1515.

Stone, V. E., Mauch, M. Y., Steger, K., Janas, S. F., & Craven, D. E. (1997). Race, gender, drug use and participation in AIDS Clinical trials. *Journal of General Internal Medicine, 12,* 150–157.

Strickland, T. L., Lin, K. M., Fu, P., Anderson, D., & Zheng, Y. (1995). Comparison of lithium ratio between African-American and Caucasian bipolar patients. *Biological Psychiatry, 37,* 325–330.

Su, B., Chakraborty, R., Jin, L., Xiao, J., & Lu, D. (1998). An HIV-resistant allele is exceptionally frequent in New Guinean Highlanders. *Journal of the American Medical Association, 280,* 1830.

Uno, H., Kawano, K., Matsuoka, H., & Tsuda, K. (1988). HLA and adult T cell leukemia: HLA-linked genes controlling susceptibility to human T cell leukemia virus Type I. *Clinical and Experimental Immunology,* 71, 211–216.

Vichinsky, E. P., Earles, A. Johnson, R. A., Hoag, M. S., Williams, A., & Lubin, B. (1990). Alloimmunization in sickle cell anemia and transfusion of racially unmatched blood. *New England Journal of Medicine, 322,* 1617–1621.

Voors, A. W., Foster, T. A., Frerichs, R. R., Webber, l. S., & Berenson, G. S. (1976). Studies of blood pressure in children, ages 5–14 years, in a biracial community: The Bogalusa Heart Study. *Circulation, 54,* 319–327.

White, J. D., Johnson, J. A., Nam, J. M., Cranston, B., Hanchard, B., Waldmann, T. A., & Manns, A. (1996). Distribution of Human Leukocyte Antigens in a population of Black patients with Human T-cell Lymphotrophic Virus Type I-Associated Adult T-cell Leukemia/Lymphoma. *Cancer Epidemiology, Biomarkers & Prevention, 5,* 873–875.

Williams, A. E., Fang, C. T., Slamon, D. J., Poiesz, B. J., Sandler, S. G., Darr, W. F., II, Shulman, G., McGowan, E. I., Douglas, D. K., Bowman, R. J., et al. (1988). Seroprevalence and epidemiological correlates of HTLV-I infection in U. S. blood donors. *Science, 240,* 643–646.

Winchester, R., Chen, Y., Rose, S., Selby, J., & Borkowsky, W. (1995). Major Histocompatibility complex class II DR allelels DRB1*1501 and those encoding HLA-DR13 are preferentially associated with a diminution in maternally transmitted human immunodeficiency virus 1 infection in different ethnic groups: Determination by an automated sequence-based typing method. *Proceedings of the National Academy Sciences in the United States of America, 92,* 12374–12378.

Winkler, C., Modi, W., Smith, M. W., Nelson, G. W., Wu, X., Carrington, M., Dean, M., Honjo, T., Tashiro, K., Yabe, D., et al. (1998). Genetic restriction of AIDS pathogenesis by an SDF-1 chemokine gene variant. *Science, 279,* 389–392.

Yanase, Y., Tango, T., Okumura, K., Tada, T., & Kawasaki, T. (1986). Lymphocyte subsets identified by monoclonal antibodies in healthy children. *Pediatric Research, 20,* 1147–1151.

Yudin, N. S., Vinogradov, S. V., Potapova, T. A., Naykova, T. M., Sitnikova, V. V., Kulikov, I. V., Khasnulin, V. I., Konchuk, C., Vloschinskii, P. E., Ivanov, S. V. et al.(1998) Distribution of CCR5–delta 32 gene deletion across the Russian part of Eurasia. *Human Genetics, 102,* 695–698.

Zhang, Y. A., Reviriego, J., Lou, Y. O., Sjeoqvist, F., & Bertilsson, L. (1990). Diazepam metabolism in native Chinese poor and extensive hydroxylators of S-mephenytoin: Interethnic differences in comparison with White subjects. *Clinical Pharmacology and Therapeutics, 48*(5), 496–502.

Zhou, H. H., Adedoyin, A., & Wood, A. (1992). Differing effect of atropine on heart rate in Chinese and White subjects. *Clinical Pharmacology and Therapeutics, 52* (2), 120–124.

Zhou, H. H., Koshakji, R. P., Silberstein, D. J., Wilkinson, G. R., & Wood, A.J.J. (1989). Racial differences in drug response: Altered sensitivity to and clearance of propranolol in men of Chinese descent as compared with American Whites. *New England Journal of Medicine, 320,* 565–570.

Zhou, H. H., Shay, S. D., & Wood, A.J.J. (1993). Contribution of differences in plasma binding of propranolol to ethnic differences in sensitivity. *Chinese Medical Journal, 106* (12), 898–902.

Zimmerman, P. A., Buckler-White, A., Alkhatib, G., Spalding, T., Kubofcik, J., Combadiere, C., Weissman, D., Cohen, O., Rubbert, A., Lam, G., et al. (1997). Inherited resistance to HIV-1 conferred by an inactivating mutation in CC chemokine receptor 5: Studies in populations with contrasting clinical phenotypes, defined racial background, and quantified risk. *Molecular Medicine, 3,* 23–36.

49

Women and AIDS: A Contextual Analysis

Jeannette R. Ickovics
Beatrice Thayaparan
Kathleen A. Ethier
Yale University

An estimated 33.6 million adults are now infected with the human immunodeficiency virus (HIV; UNAIDS, 1999). With 16,000 people becoming infected daily, as many as 40 million people will be infected with HIV by the turn of the century. Women account for 44% of all estimated HIV infections worldwide, and the proportion of women infected is rapidly increasing in every geographic region. At the present rate of infection, the numbers of women and men infected will be equal by the year 2000. Currently, the ratio of female-to-male AIDS cases varies dramatically by region; in sub-Saharan Africa the ratio is 1:1, in the Carribean the ratio is 1:3, in South and Southeast Asia the ratio is 1:4, and in Europe, the Middle East, North America and Latin America the ratio is 1:5 (UNAIDS, 1998).

The AIDS epidemic has undergone profound demographic changes within the United States. In 1981, when AIDS was first identified, it was considered a disease of men who have sex with men; indeed, at that time, the syndrome was called "gay-related immunodeficiency disease (GRID)" (Centers for Disease Control and Prevention [CDC], 1981). In 1985, only 6.5% of newly diagnosed cases of AIDS were among women (CDC, 1986). Thirteen years later, this percentage has more than tripled to 23% (CDC, 1998a). Through 1998, 109,311 women in the United States have been diagnosed with AIDS; more than one half have died from AIDS-related causes. Nationally, AIDS is the third leading cause of death among young women from age 25 to 44. In some U.S. cities along the eastern seaboard (e.g., Miami, New York, Newark), AIDS is the leading cause of death among women in this age group. Although AIDS-related deaths decreased 13% overall in 1996, deaths among women with AIDS increased 3% (CDC, 1997).

Epidemiological data on the numbers of those infected with HIV (as opposed to diagnosed with AIDS) is scarce; however, some studies suggest that an even greater proportion of women are infected than is reflected in the data on reported AIDS cases. For instance, 27% of HIV cases through 1998 were among women, as compared to 16% of all AIDS cases (CDC, 1998a). In a study of nearly 2,000 patients in Los Angeles County, California, women were 3.4 times more likely to be diagnosed with HIV than AIDS (Sorvillo et al., 1995). Thus, new patterns of HIV transmission are not necessarily reflected by the standard AIDS surveillance techniques.

There are two main routes of HIV transmission among women. These include the sharing of needles by injection drug users (IDUs) and heterosexual sex. Heterosexual intercourse is the main route of HIV infection among women globally, accounting for three quarters of all AIDS cases. However, in the U.S., only 39% of cumulative AIDS cases are documented as having been caused though heterosexual transmission, whereas 43% of all women with AIDS have a history of injection drug use (CDC, 1998a). The epidemiology appears to be shifting: Among *new* AIDS cases in the U.S. the number attributed to heterosexual contact exceeds the number attributed to injection drug use.

Women are more likely than men to be infected with HIV through heterosexual sex for biological, epidemiological, and social reasons (World Health Organization [WHO], 1993). Male-to- female transmission of HIV is estimated to be eight times more likely than female-to-male transmission (Padian, Shiboski, Glass, & Vittinghoff, 1997). As the receptive sexual partner in heterosexual activity, women are more at risk for HIV and other sexually transmitted diseases for anatomical reasons; the mucosal tissue lining the walls of the vagina is fragile and prone to injury. HIV found in seminal fluids and in sperm cells of seropositive men pose a great risk to their heterosexual partners (Royce, Sena, Cates, & Cohen, 1997). Heterosexual women are also at greater risk epidemiologically by virtue of sheer numbers: More men are infected with HIV, so the probability of having a seropositive partner is greater for women than for men. Finally, in many cultures women are expected to be sexually and socially subordinate to men; in such sociocultural environments, women may have limited power to protect themselves from HIV.

Risky sexual behavior does not exist in a vacuum, and as such must be examined within its developmental, social, and psychological contexts. Health psychology can contribute to the understanding of these contexts and the roles they play in disease transmission and progression. This chapter reviews the current empirical findings regarding women and HIV within an ecological perspective (Revenson, 1990). An ecological perspective considers characteristics of both the individual and the environment, including the dynamic pattern of interaction between them. This chapter is not intended to be an exhaustive review, rather it is an attempt to elucidate the complex sociocultural, interpersonal, temporal, and situational contexts that have an impact on women's risk for HIV infection. It also focuses on factors that have a potential impact on disease progression, coping and adjustment, and access to health care for women with or at risk for HIV.

In addition to addressing issues specific to women *infected* with HIV, it also considers women *affected* by the disease. Women are members of communities devastated by HIV, such as the explosive epidemics in sub-Saharan Africa, Southeast Asia, and in U.S. cities like San Francisco, Los Angeles, New York, Newark, New Haven, and Miami. These women are not necessarily infected themselves; however, they are directly affected by their roles as lovers, caretakers, or friends of those with HIV and AIDS. Subsequently, they may also be at risk for HIV infection.

AN ECOLOGICAL PERSPECTIVE

Biologists first used ecological approaches to describe the interdependence of plant and animal life in the same environmental habitat. Psychologists have articulated theoretical and empirical considerations of the interaction between the person and the environment for more than 60 years (Bronfenbrenner, 1977; Lewin, 1951/1972; Murray, 1938). As applied to health psychology, an ecological approach emphasizes that health is a result of a reciprocal and bidirectional association between individuals and the social contexts in which they live. These social contexts include individual relationships as well as the broader social, political, and cultural contexts of health behaviors and health outcomes. The ecological approach has been applied to analyses of the association between personality and disease (Revenson, 1990) and the role of sociodemographic factors on psychophysiological responses such as heart rate and blood pressure (Anderson & McNeilly, 1991). The advantage of this approach is the recognition of the interdependence of individuals and their social contexts, and the complex associations among factors that influence health and health behaviors.

Following this conceptual model, this chapter examines four contextual domains that may influence HIV transmission and progression patterns for women at risk for HIV and those already infected: sociocultural, interpersonal, temporal, and situational contexts. The issues considered in each context are not meant to be mutually exclusive; there is overlap, as illustrated in Fig. 49.1.

SOCIOCULTURAL CONTEXT

Sociocultural factors—particularly culture and social class—have long been associated with health outcomes and health behaviors, such as differences in patients' symptom reports (Zborowski, 1958), differences in physicians' evaluation of such reports (Revenson, 1990), health seeking behavior, and adherence to prescribed treatment regimens (Kirscht, 1983; Matthews, Kelsey, Meilahn, Kuller, & Wing, 1989). These sociocultural factors may result in different cognitive models of illness and health care services as well as perceived or actual barriers to health care utilization (Revenson, 1990).

The study of women and HIV illustrates how sociocultural influences can impose a profound impact on women's health in particular (Amaro, 1995; de Bruyn, 1992; Fee & Krieger, 1993; Gay & Underwood, 1991; Gollub, 1999; Gupta & Weiss, 1993; Ickovics & Rodin, 1992; Krieger & Margo, 1990; Zierler & Krieger, 1997). These factors may determine whether preventive services are sought or whether women receive treatment for other sexually transmitted diseases that place them at increased risk for HIV transmission. Moreover, varying perceptions of and access to the medical system may have implications for women already infected with HIV. Access to antiretroviral drugs to slow the replication of HIV, as well as prophylaxis and treatment for opportunistic infections can extend life and enhance its quality for people infected with HIV. The cultural and economic conditions in which women live must be considered to understand fully the factors that put women at increased risk for contracting HIV, and the impact on the health and health care of those infected.

Cultural Factors Influencing HIV Prevention and Treatment

Norms are imparted through socialization—a process that gives individuals the knowledge, motivation, and skills to participate in their particular community; socialization provides information through social comparison processes and information exchange (Fischer, 1988; Latkin et al., 1995; Stryker & Statham, 1985). These norms regulate attitudes and behaviors, and social sanctions can result from deviation from these norms. In terms of their impact on HIV transmission, culturally determined values can influence perceptions of HIV, attitudes toward high risk behavior, norms of behavior, and the potential for behavior changes (Jemmott, Catan, Nyamathi & Anastasia, 1995). *Sex roles,* the gender-related

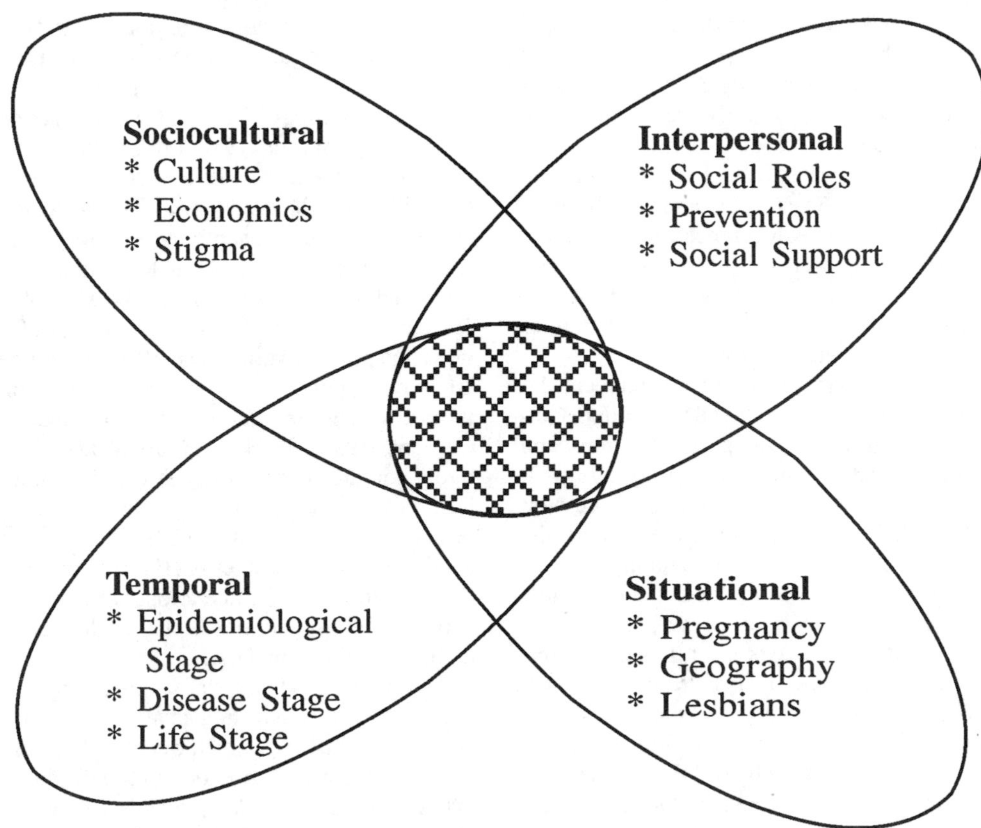

FIG. 49.1. Women and AIDS: A contextual analysis. Figure adapted from Revenson (1990).

roles determined by cultural norms regarding social interaction (Spence, Deaux, & Helmreich, 1985), can have an impact on HIV risk behavior. Even though societal endorsement of gender equality is common in the developed world, there is still resistance to the breakdown of sex roles. Individuals are pressured to conform, and may be differentially exposed to HIV-related risks as a function of their ascribed roles.

In many cases, social structures act to maintain the inequality of social relationships between men and women, which may adversely impact on women's risk for HIV. For instance, Amaro (1995) suggested that boys who have traditional views toward masculinity are more likely when they are older to have multiple sexual partners, to not know their partners very well, to not use condoms consistently, and to believe that contraception is a woman's responsibility. A woman's subordinate role increases her vulnerability to HIV because it may disable her from engaging in prevention practice, may lead her to participate in behaviors that place her at greater risk for HIV, or may increase the likelihood of sexual abuse or rape (de Bruyn, 1992; Gay & Underwood, 1991). Forced sexual intercourse is often violent and may produce bleeding; vaginal tissue can rupture during sexual intercourse, thereby increasing the ability of HIV to penetrate into the bloodstream (Piot et al., 1988).

The impact of culturally determined gender roles on sexuality and the negotiation of safer sex has been largely ignored, yet this may be one of the most important variables in predicting HIV transmission (Amaro, 1995). For example, despite the dangers inherent in unprotected anal intercourse (Kimball, Gonzalez, & Zacarias, 1991), in some cultures anal sex is considered an effective contraceptive and a viable way to preserve a woman's virginity (Parker, 1987). To enhance sensation during vaginal intercourse, some women use intravaginal irritants such as herbs and hydroxides to dry the vaginal mucosa. Although this practice is believed to enhance the pleasure of sexual intercourse, the resulting abrasions to the woman's vagina increase her susceptibility to HIV and other STDs. These behaviors, which place women at higher risk for HIV transmission, result directly from cultural norms that place men in a more powerful position than women, leaving women less able to protect themselves.

Social roles and the accompanying attitudes toward sexuality, health, and health care are transmitted through cultural and religious norms. The impact of these norms on HIV transmission may partially explain racial and ethnic differences in HIV seroprevalence. In the United States, a disproportionate number of Hispanic and Black women are infected.[1] Al-

[1]Following the Centers for Disease Control and Prevention, the broad terms *Hispanic* and *Black* are used. Hispanic refers to the ethnicity of individuals of Spanish descent often from Central and South American countries; race may be White or Black. Black refers to the race of persons of African or African American descent, as well as many from Caribbean countries.

though Hispanics and Blacks account for 10.3% and 12.6% of the individuals within the population (U.S. Bureau of the Census, 1997), among women with AIDS, 20.2% are Hispanic and 56.7% are Black (CDC, 1998a). Recent analyses indicate that Hispanic women are at seven times greater risk for AIDS than white woman (Klevens, Diaz, Fleming, Mays, & Frey, 1999). There is no reason to expect that race and ethnicity, per se, is responsible for these differences. Race and ethnicity serve as proxies for aspects of culture, religion, and social class that each have direct consequences for a woman's sexual behavior and her ability to prevent HIV infection, as well as her attitudes toward treatment for HIV.

For example, Black women may face cultural and social demands that increase their susceptibility to HIV infection. Cultural values emphasize family structure, gender relations, and social and economic survival; and these must be considered in the context of sexism, racism and economic oppression (Jemmott et al., 1995; Tesh, 1988). It has been argued that the sex ratio imbalance in African American communities may create a conflict for Black women: With fewer men available for intimate relationships, these opportunities are highly valued (Bennett, 1995; Worth, 1990). Moreover, this gender imbalance reinforces an existing power disparity favoring men when the desire for relationships exceeds the supply of potential partners (Guttentag & Secord, 1993). According to Mays and Cochran (1988), women may be fearful that the demand for safe sex will drive away a man; demands for condom use may be misinterpreted as lack of trust or suspicion, and may lead to accusations that the woman is sexually promiscuous, perhaps resulting in verbal or physical hostility.

Within the Latino culture, *machismo* is an attempt to institutionalize male dominance and female subordination (Barker & Loewenstein, 1997; Low et al., 1993; Torres, 1998). The tradition of *marianismo* also reinforces the inequality between men and women, relating women's nature to that of the Virgin Mary, which highlights the importance of motherhood as a primary role and focuses on deference and subordination to a greater power (Livingston, 1992). In a culture where a woman's social identity and acceptability is determined by her fertility, any contraception may pose a threat to her status in society (Kimball et al., 1991; Smyke, 1991). Such socialization can result in a feeling of powerlessness among adult women in their relationships with men (Gay & Underwood, 1991). *Simpatía* is another cultural script that emphasizes harmonious interpersonal relationships, and has been shown to be more prevalent among Latinos than Anglos (Marín, 1989; Triandis, Marín, Lisansky, & Betancourt, 1984). Some assert that it is "unacceptable" for a Hispanic woman to tell her husband to stop risky behavior or to use a condom in part because it could create conflict (Ehrhardt, 1988; Worth, 1990). Anecdotal accounts indicate that a woman's request to use a condom may be misinterpreted as a suspicion that she is already infected or an accusation of her partner's infidelity (de Bruyn, 1992). Moreover, Catholicism as the predominant religion in Latin America forbids the use of birth control. Indeed, Latinas are less likely to report using contraception (Marin, Tschann, Gomez, & Kegeles, 1993; Moscher & Bachrach, 1986).

Throughout the world, religious institutions like churches, temples, synagogues, and mosques serve as a foundation for a community's values. Religious guidelines regarding sexuality and birth control have a strong impact on members of a community (Worth, 1990). If condom use is discouraged, then women are faced with a social pressure that may increase their risk for HIV infection.[2] For instance, for both Catholics and Moslems, contraceptive use is forbidden. In a study of nearly 300 Moslem women in Kuwait, only 1% reported current condom use (Al-Gallaf, Al-Wazzan, Al-Namash, Shah, & Behbehani, 1995). In recent prevention efforts, United Nations and other governmental officials have begun to educate Islamic religious leaders so that they in turn would educate their communities about the importance of condom use (Simons, 1996). In Uganda, the Ministry of Health has actively sought the help of both Catholic and Muslim church leaders to campaign for safe sex by sponsoring workshops on reproductive health. Muslim leaders agreed to allow use of condoms when a partner is HIV seropositive. The Ugandan Catholic leaders continue to oppose condom use; they have chosen to advise families to change their behaviors and to remain faithful in marriages.

Culture may also have an impact on women's choices about HIV treatment. In a small study of women with HIV, Hispanic and Black women were two times more likely to delay entry into health care following a diagnosis with HIV than White women (Ickovics, Forsyth, Ethier, Harris, & Rodin, 1996). In the United States, the Black community has had a long history of distrust of public health services and research, fueled by the legacy of the Tuskegee syphilis study and a history of sterilization of women of color without their knowledge or consent (Auerbach, Wypijewska, & Brodie, 1994). Thus, they may be less inclined to seek traditional health care and may prefer alternative medical practices.

Throughout the world, there are deep cultural histories of the use of traditional healing practices. Complementary medicine is often less invasive than Western medical practices, relying on herbal remedies, botanicals, and healing rituals (Worth, 1990). In some traditions, healers are viewed as ministers of religions like Voodoo or Santeria. Recently, some conventional doctors have begun to promote the integration of both Western medicine and folk healing. These doctors claim that the combination of both traditions are better for patients because it promotes trust and respect, and encourages patients to work with their doctors to alleviate symptoms (Belluck, 1996). As a result, donor organizations and African governments have increasingly been interested in involving traditional healers in HIV/AIDS prevention initiatives (Green, Zokwe, & Dupree, 1995).

Cultural, racial, and ethnic stereotypes and expectations are generally well articulated. However, there are few studies that

[2]It is also important to note that some religious organizations have played a central role in the fight against AIDS by advocating HIV-related service and developing counseling programs and peer support groups (Crawford et al., 1992; Jenkins, 1995). Religious organizations that promote abstinence or sex only between married partners also may decrease the numbers of partners and reduce risk.

provide empirical evidence to support these statements. Fernandez (1995) emphasized that some of these stereotypes are outdated, and broad generalizations about racial or ethnic groups have been derived in part from clinical samples that do not account for important cultural mediators such as education, social class, and geography. It is also important to note that the incidence of HIV varies not only among Whites, Blacks, and Hispanics, but within sub-groups based on nationality, education, social class, and residence in rural versus urban settings (Menendez at al., 1990; Selik, Castro, Pappaioanou, & Buehler, 1989; Worth, 1990). This suggests that subcultures within larger racial or ethnic groups impact HIV transmission. For example, the prevalence of AIDS among Puerto Rican born Hispanics is seven times greater than the prevalence of AIDS among Mexican-born Hispanics (Selik et al., 1989). Similarly, there may be differences among Blacks based on background and country of origin (e.g., Africa, United States, Caribbean, Haiti; Jemmott et al., 1995). Thus, it is important to move the focus away from particular racial and ethnic groups per se, to gain a broader understanding of how culture works to prevent women from achieving social and economic equality within their particular communities.

Social Class and Its Influence on HIV Prevention and Treatment

Imbalances in economic situations, and subsequently in power, equality and control, have an adverse impact on women's health. Women are significantly more likely than men to be poor (U.S. Bureau of the Census, 1997). Individuals of lower social class have higher rates of morbidity and mortality from nearly all illnesses (Adler et al. 1994; Adler, Boyce, Chesney, Folkman, & Syme, 1992; Lantz et al., 1999; Pincus & Callahan, 1985; Pincus, Callahan, & Burkhauser, 1987; Rogot, 1992). The association between social class and health is said to be one of the most enduring relations in social science (Mechanic, 1994). The impact of social class on health can begin in childhood and have long-term consequences for adults' health (Williams, 1990). The disparity in health status between economic strata is found globally, and appears to vary linearly as a function of class inequalities within a given society (Adler et al., 1992).

Limited access to health care is one reason given for the social class differential in health outcomes. Poor women may also be at increased risk because they are more likely to engage in health damaging behaviors, such as excessive alcohol and drug use. Individuals of lower social classes have been shown to experience a greater number of undesirable life events (McLeod & Kessler, 1990) as well as higher levels of chronic and enduring stress (Turner, Wheaton, & Lloyd, 1995) as compared to individuals of higher social classes. In addition to differences in stress exposure, the impact of stress varies with social class. Compared to those of higher social classes, individuals of lower social classes experience greater distress when under comparable levels of stress (Kessler, 1979). Several studies also have shown that social class is related to the use of certain coping strategies in response to stress. Compared to those with less education and income, individuals in higher social classes are more likely to use active coping and less likely to use avoidant coping to manage stress (Aspinwall & Taylor, 1992; Billings & Moos, 1981).

When women are poor, they are not in a position to protect themselves from HIV. Women who are financially dependent on a husband or sexual partner may believe they have no choice but to comply with his demands (Gay & Underwood, 1991). This observation led Jonathan Mann, former director of the World Health Organization/ Global Program on AIDS, to call for the "economic emancipation" of women to prevent the further spread of HIV. The need for economic equity predates HIV. However, the neglect of the legal, medical, and social rights of women has been highlighted by the HIV pandemic. Poverty may increase a woman's vulnerability to HIV because of three conditions that it creates: lower levels of education, inadequate employment opportunities possibly resulting in commercial sex work, and the lack of adequate health care facilities (Gay & Underwood, 1991).

A condition that coexists with poverty is limited educational opportunities. When there are few educational facilities, these resources are less accessible to women. This results in lower literacy rates, thus restricting women's access to anti-HIV campaigns that rely on printed materials such as posters and pamphlets (de Bruyn, 1992). Women in impoverished environments also have less access to radio or television, and hence may remain disconnected from these communication lines.

The lack of funds for basic needs such as food and housing, is an acute reality for many women in developing and industrialized countries. Some women engage in commercial sex work to obtain money to meet such basic needs that take precedence over the perceived risk of HIV (Smyke, 1991). For example, in Thailand, one million women have joined the sex industry, explaining in part Thailand's high incidence of HIV infection (Lurie, Hintzen, & Lowe, 1995). Visiting prostitutes is common practice among local men in many Asian countries, and with the booming business of sex tourism, there is never a lack of clientele. These encounters reinforce the subordinate and economically inferior position of women.

Ironically, Lurie and his colleagues (1995) suggested that economic development programs such as structural adjustment programs, have often facilitated HIV transmission. Economic development in developing countries has led to currency devaluation, higher prices for goods, decreased availability of loans, income and consumption tax increases, reductions in government spending on health and social services for the local population, and increases in the number of migrant workers. All of these factors result in increased poverty, and in urban settings increased drug use and commercial sex work. As a result of being far from home (and as part of the cultural milieu), male migrant workers often use the sexual services of prostitutes. HIV transmission may occur between sex worker and client in the cities, then men can infect their wives or sex partners on returning home to rural villages, and subsequently their children. Women in rural areas of developing nations remain dependent on their male partners for economic support. This economic inequity combined with the cultural expectation of sexual subordination facilitates the spread of HIV.

HIV can be classified as a preventable disease, and therefore could be better controlled if adequate resources were available (Livingston, 1992). In developing countries, antiretroviral therapies are simply unaffordable, diagnostic facilities are not always available (Mann et al., 1992), and physicians often do not have proper training to handle the epidemic with regard to basic medical care or psychosocial needs of women (Ha & Ickovics, 1996). Even though there are more resources available in industrialized countries, many women still do not receive appropriate care and treatment for HIV-related disease (Shapiro et al., 1999; Solomon et al., 1999; Worth, 1990). HIV-specific primary care, gynecological care, drug treatment, and pediatric services must be integrated to facilitate access to health care services among persons with HIV (Smith et al., 1997).

It is difficult to disentangle culture from socioeconomic factors, when examining issues for women and HIV in the U.S. Poverty rates among Hispanics and Blacks are 29% and 33%, respectively, with a poverty rate of 11% among Whites (Williams & Collins, 1995). It has been argued that Hispanics and Blacks are less concerned with HIV risk because they face more immediate concerns such as food, shelter, and clothing, as well as more stressful life events that demand their immediate attention (Amaro, 1995; Mays & Cochran, 1988). Although this makes intuitive sense, there are limited data to support this empirically. In recent studies, social class has been shown to be a more important health indicator than race. Adjustment for social class may eliminate or reduce signs of racial disparity in health. Social class differences have persisted, even after controlling for race in reports of general poor health (Navarro, 1990), violent deaths (Greenberg & Schneider, 1994), illegal drug use (Lillie-Blanton, Anthony, & Schuster, 1993) and HIV risk behavior (Ickovics, et al., 2000). Williams and Collins (1995) suggested that failing to adjust for social class in studies of health can reinforce racial prejudices and stereotypes, diverting both public attention and research funding from the underlying social factors that are responsible for the pattern of risk distribution.

INTERPERSONAL CONTEXT

In this contextual analysis of women and HIV, the importance of interpersonal relationships cannot be over-stated. Because HIV is an infectious disease, it is by definition transmitted within an interpersonal network, (i.e. sexual relations or shared needles). Interpersonal relationships can be categorized as instrumental, supportive, disruptive, burdensome, or neutral (Latkin et al., 1994). The nature of women's interpersonal relationships can have important consequences for their HIV risk behavior and treatment for those diagnosed with HIV. This section considers theory and empirical findings relevant to interpersonal relationships with a focus on heterosexual and drug-using peer relationships, as well as social support for women infected by HIV and those who may be affected as loved ones and caretakers of the ill. (A discussion of women who have sex with women is presented later).

Heterosexual Relationships

The key factors in determining the risk of sexual transmission of HIV are the frequency and type of sexual activity (R. M. Anderson, 1992; Piot et al., 1988). Heterosexual intercourse with an infected partner is the primary mode of transmission for women with HIV throughout the world. Transmission occurs within the context of a sexually intimate, interpersonal relationship. Relationship involvement has been shown to be an important predictor of both the initiation and maintenance of safer sexual behavior among heterosexual women (Morrill, Ickovics, Golubchikov, Beren, & Rodin, 1996). Decisions around safer sexual behavior occur not only within the context of a single relationship, but also within patterns of sexual relationships that individuals have developed over time and possibly with multiple partners. Past unprotected intercourse is often the best predictor of future unprotected intercourse (Dublin, Rosenberg, & Goedert, 1992).

Women accommodate their sexual behavior depending on the nature of their relationship with their partner. Women in more involved relationships are significantly more likely to have unprotected intercourse (Catania et al., 1992; Hobfoll, Jackson, Lavin, Britton, & Shepherd, 1993; Morrill et al., 1996; Stark, Tesselaar, Fleming, O'Connell & Armstrong, 1996). Kippax and colleagues (Kippax, Crawford, Davis, Rodden, & Dowsett, 1993; Kippax et al., 1997) refer to unprotected intercourse in the context of certain relationship arrangements as "negotiated safety"—a strategy that depends on accurate knowledge of both partners' serostatus as well as honesty and trust in the relationship. Others (Ekstrand, 1992), however, warn that anything less than complete monogamy between two seronegative partners carries some risk of HIV transmission; therefore, condoms should always be used to maximize prevention. As failsafe as this approach may sound ("no unprotected intercourse, no risk"), it clearly does not reflect current practices observed for heterosexual women.

Some women having unprotected intercourse in a committed relationship are actually at increased risk for contracting HIV in part because assessments of partner risk often are inaccurate (Kalichman & Hunter, 1992). Sexual relationships outside of a primary relationship are often not disclosed, especially when these relationships are between two men (Carballo-Dieguez & Dolezal, 1996; Mason, Marks, Simoni, Ruiz & Richardson, 1995). In one study, three quarters of men who had both male and female partners had not disclosed their sexual activity with other men to their female partners, and nearly two thirds had not modified their sexual behavior to protect their female partners from HIV (Kalichman, Roffman, Picciano, & Bolan, 1997). Studies of these men and their relationships with female and male partners suggest that many lead "dual lives," keeping their homosexual interests and activities secret from their female partners. Nearly one quarter of bisexual men who died of AIDS were married to women at the time of their death (Chu, Peterman, Doll, Buehler, & Durran, 1992).

Future research must continue to examine the nature of relationships and the interpersonal context of decision making for heterosexual women. It is important to recognize the complexity of individual choice and human intimacy—including communication, partner attitudes, relative control, and power—which can be even more important in determining HIV risk behavior than individual factors (Morrill, 1994).

Drug-Related Relationships

Women who use injection drugs are at great risk for HIV because of the potential for transmission through needle sharing as well as unprotected sexual activity with an HIV-infected partner. The majority of women who inject drugs have sexual partners who also inject drugs; most are sexually active and few consistently use condoms (Weissman & Brown, 1995). Use of drugs (particularly crack cocaine) and use of alcohol and drugs before sex have been associated with a greater number of sexual partners, more unprotected intercourse, and a greater likelihood of prostitution (Chaisson et al., 1991; R. Fullilove, M. Fullilove, Bowser & Gross, 1990; McCoy & Inciardi, 1993).

Studies of the social relationships of injection drug users (IDUs) indicate that male partners play a critical role in women's drug use. Men are often the initiators of drug using activity, play a role in the progression of drug use, and are involved in women's drug-related criminal activities such as commercial sex work (Anglin, Hser, & McGlothlin, 1987; el-Bassel, Cooper, Chen, & Schilling, 1998; Hser, Anglin, & McGlothlin, 1987; Rosenbaumm, 1981; Weeks et al., 1998; Worth & Rodriguez, 1987). Having a male partner who uses drugs places adolescent girls at greater risk of using drugs themselves (Amaro, Zuckerman, & Cabral, 1989). One quarter of women using the New Haven, Connecticut needle exchange program began injecting before age 18, and 39% have been injecting for over 10 years (Heimer, Kaplan, O'Keefe, Khoshnood, & Altice, 1994).

For women, drug use is closely tied to relationships with male partners. For men, drug using activity is initiated primarily through a same-sex friend. The differential contexts determining drug use also have implications for addiction and disengagement from drug use. In a study of women enrolled in methadone treatment, drug use and HIV permeated sexual, familial, and household relationships (Pivnick, Jacobson, Eric, Doll, & Drucker, 1994). More than one half of the women who lived with a sexual partner reported that their partners were currently using drugs. Almost one third of the study participants' siblings were drug users; and 70% of the women had at least one sibling who also used drugs. These data lend credence to the notion that HIV and drug use are not individual problems, but interpersonal ones.

Women who use drugs face a number of challenges to risk reduction and HIV prevention. They are likely to have a significant history of sexual, other physical or psychological abuse; feelings of powerlessness, psychological distress, and depression; lack of consistent social support and resources; and lack of accessible drug treatment (for review see Weissman & Brown, 1995). These women are at extremely high risk for HIV transmission. Although social norms among drug users have changed as a result of the HIV epidemic, making it less "acceptable" to share needles (Des Jarlais & Friedman, 1994; Selwyn, Feiner, Cox, Lipshutz, & Cohen, 1987), most women who inject drugs report some needle sharing, often with a sexual partner (Weissman & Brown, 1995).

Finally, individuals actively using drugs are more likely to engage in antisocial behaviors, such as theft or other criminal acts to get money for drugs. These behaviors can lead to the withdrawal of drug users from mainstream society, whereby they retreat to a "drug subculture" or network, comprised of other drug users (Faulpel, 1991). Limiting contact with the members of one's drug network can reduce the frequency of drug-use. Moreover, network-oriented interventions to discourage HIV risk behaviors, such as needle sharing may be useful (Latkin et al., 1995). Unfortunately, women have had less access to needle exchange and drug treatment programs than their male counterparts; programs are notably limited for women with children and those who are pregnant (Ethier, Ickovics, & Rodin, 1996; Heimer et al., 1994). In addition to structural barriers, there may be psychological barriers to prevention; avoidant coping has been associated with increased drug use (Nyamathi, Stein, & Brecht, 1995).

Social Support: Prevention, Adjustment, Disclosure and Stigma

Social support and its association with health has received considerable research attention over the past decade. Individuals with a high degree of social support are less likely to be adversely affected by stressful situations and become ill. Moreover, if an individual does become ill, social support facilitates coping and recovery, and has a positive impact on immune function (Cohen, 1988; Cohen & Williamson, 1991; Uchino, Cacioppo, & Kiecolt-Glaser, 1996).

When the interpersonal context of women and HIV is considered, social support is a key factor, particularly when considering prevention and adjustment to a diagnosis with HIV. A woman's ability to alter high risk behavior may be connected to her social support network. Women who have more social support are less likely to appraise the conditions of their lives as threatening and more likely to use active coping techniques (Nyamathi, Wayment & Dunkel-Schetter, 1993); active coping in turn has been related to less risky sexual behavior (Nyamathi et al., 1993, 1995).

In general, women report higher levels of social support and benefit more from support than men (Hobfoll, 1986). Unfortunately, due to the nature of HIV transmission, some of the people in an infected woman's support network may be infected themselves. Wofsy (1987) suggested that women with HIV may feel profoundly isolated. Many women with HIV will not seek support or services even if available; they report being fearful of being identified with HIV due to possible stigmatization and rejection by family members or friends (Chung & Magraw, 1992; Hackl, Somlai, Kelly, & Kalichman, 1997; Lea, 1994). There can be a sense of shame and self-denigration, especially for women who are mothers. These women worry about the harm to their children, directly (through maternal transmission) or indirectly (through abandonment by death or the stigma of having an HIV-infected parent (Geballe, Grvendel, & Andiman, 1995).

Women as Caretakers

Women often provide support to family members living with HIV/AIDS. HIV results in cyclical bouts with illness, usually becoming more severe and debilitating over time. Because HIV is a chronic disease, developing over the course of from 10 to 12 years, many health care problems are managed at home, where a primary caregiver has a critical role in assisting the ill person to sustain physical and psychological well-being (Folkman, Chesney, Cooke, Boccellari & Collette, 1994; Wight, LeBlanc, & Aneshensel, 1998). Folkman and her colleagues (1994) highlighted how caregiving partners of people with HIV can differ in important ways from traditional caregivers. People with HIV and their primary caregivers tend to be young and middle-aged, so they often lack the life experience and lessons that they could draw on to assist in difficult circumstances. Primary caretakers of persons with HIV may be infected themselves or be at risk for infection, whereas traditionally, caregivers usually do not have the same disease as the person for whom they are caring. Finally, because HIV is a stigmatized disease, the caregivers themselves often feel stigmatized; this can result in depression, anxiety, stress, isolation, frustration, and emotional and physical exhaustion (American Association of Retired Persons [AARP], 1994). Greater illness severity and longer duration of caregiving have a negative effect on the caregivers' own health status (Wight et al., 1998).

Sometimes, the caregiver herself has HIV and is caring for her infected partner and/or infected children. HIV-positive caregivers report more caregiver burden (e.g., disruptions with work, community activities, finances, and personal goals) than HIV-negative caregivers (Folkman et al., 1994). Parental care-giving issues (e.g., protecting children from indirect stigma) often are immediate and primary concerns of women living with HIV/AIDS.

The broad impact of the HIV epidemic on a family needs to be further investigated. HIV infection is a multigenerational disease directly affecting mothers and offspring, and indirectly affecting many others. At the end of the year 1999, it was estimated that 11.2 million children worldwide lost their mothers to HIV disease, including approximately 70,000 children and adolescents in the United States (UNAIDS, 1999). In the United States in 1991, it was estimated that 13% of children and 9% of adolescents whose mothers died of all causes were children of women who died of AIDS-related diseases (Michaels & Levine, 1992); no doubt these proportions have risen during the past decade. Grandmothers most often become the guardians of these orphans; other sources of care include other family members, foster families, or institutional care (Geballe et al., 1995; Michaels & Levine, 1992).

Women who care for family members are often socially "invisible," operating within a private household and without the benefits of using community-based health care services (Schiller, 1993). This isolation is unfortunate, as many people with HIV and their caretakers could benefit from tangible sources of support: specific information about HIV services and health care, access to support groups, welfare services and legal advice, material assistance with basic needs like food, shelter, and medicine. Emotional support and palliative care may be critical as individuals progress with HIV disease. Caregivers who are themselves HIV-positive may need special support to help cope with this double burden.

TEMPORAL CONTEXT

The cliché "timing is everything" is particularly relevant to the discussion of women and HIV disease. This section examines three temporal considerations: the time during an individual's developmental life stage when she becomes infected, the natural progression of HIV disease over time, and the temporal changes of the epidemic itself (i.e., the changing epidemiology of HIV). Although research has focused on the changing epidemiology of HIV, other research endeavors that focus on the natural history of disease among women and the degree to which temporal factors might influence psychological adaptation to disease and/or health outcomes have been limited. Typically, the effects of disease severity, patient age, and time of infection are statistically controlled, rather than examined (Revenson, 1990).

Developmental Life Stage

HIV risk and the consequences of HIV transmission change as a function of developmental and life course events. Biological age, stages of development, life events, and the evolution of romantic and family relationships can influence both the determinants and consequences of HIV risk.

Among children with AIDS, nearly all acquired HIV through perinatal transmission (CDC, 1998a). HIV can be transmitted from mother to child during pregnancy (Rouzioux et al., 1993), delivery (Burgard et al., 1992; Goedert, Duliege, Amos, Felton, & Biggar, 1991), and through breast feeding (Datta et al., 1994; Van de Perre et al., 1991). Without any therapeutic interventions during pregnancy, HIV transmission rates from mother to child are approximately 15% to 30% in the United States and approach 50% in developing countries (Davis et al., 1995; Husson et al., 1995; Kumar, Uduman, & Khurranna, 1995). In one of the most dramatic breakthroughs in prevention since the beginning of the epidemic, transmission rates were lowered 67% (from 24.0% to 8.3% transmission) with the use of the drug zidovudine (also known as ZDV or AZT) during pregnancy, labor and delivery, and for the child six weeks post-partum (Conner et al., 1994). Transmission is determined primarily by maternal factors such as advanced disease state, low CD4+ cell count, and increased HIV-1 RNA viral load (Dickover et al., 1996). In addition, features of labor and delivery—such as fetal exposure to maternal blood, premature rupture of membrane, and type of delivery (vaginal vs. cesarean)—influence transmission (Boyer et al., 1994; Moodley, Bobat, Coutsoudis & Coovadia, 1994; Landesman et al., 1996). (See also section on *Situational Context, Pregnancy, Parenthood and HIV Testing.*)

In addition to profoundly difficult physical health problems, children and their caretakers may be faced with compounding factors such as developmental and cognitive delays and emotional difficulties for young children who cannot understand or cope with their own illness at home, in school, or other social settings. The social environments of many children with HIV also are challenged by poverty. Special services for HIV-infected youth and their families are essential (Huba & Melchior, 1999).

Among adolescents and young adults, AIDS rates are rising rapidly. Approximately 7000 young people, aged 15 to 24, get infected with HIV throughout the world each day (UNAIDS, 1999). Extremely high HIV seroprevalence rates have been documented in teenage women attending antenatal clinics throughout Africa (Rwandan HIV Seroprevalence Study Group, 1989; Ryder et al. 1989; Wade et al., 1992; Wilkins et al., 1989).

Since 1990, the number of AIDS cases among U.S. teenagers has more than tripled. Twenty-five percent of new HIV infections in the United States are estimated to occur among those between age 13 and 20 (Office of National AIDS Policy, 1996). Two young people become infected with HIV every hour of every day; of these, more than one third are female. HIV prevalence among young women has increased 36% to 45%; in contrast prevalence among young men is stable or declining (Rosenberg & Bigger, 1998). Young heterosexual women represent a next wave of the epidemic; those most at risk include young women from northern inner cities, those who use crack cocaine, those who have multiple sex partners, and those who have prevalent STDs (Holmberg, 1996; Rosenberg & Bigger, 1998; Wortley & Fleming, 1997). High rates of gonorrhea, chlamydia, and syphilis are associated with the rapidly rising rates of AIDS among adolescents and young adults (Hein, Dell, Futterman, Rotheram-Borus, & Shaffer, 1995; Laga et al., 1990; Plummer et al., 1991). Three million STDs per year are reported in the United States among teens 15 to 19 years old (CDC, 1998c; Kaiser Family Foundation, 1998). Adolescent females have higher STD rates than any age and gender group (Berman & Hein, 1999). Women with other STDs have a risk of contracting HIV, if exposed, that is 3 to 50 times that of an uninfected person (St. Louis, Wasserheit, & Gayle, 1997). Despite these risks, only 8% of young women believe that they are personally at risk of getting an STD (Kaiser Family Foundation, 1998). A young woman's interpersonal relationships can have a profound impact on her STD and HIV risk behaviors (see section on *Interpersonal Context*); if she is powerless in a relationship, then she is less able to negotiate condom use.

Behavioral, psychological and social factors place adolescents at high risk for HIV transmission: sexual experimentation, initiation of high risk behavior (including drug use), a sense of invulnerability and immortality, less well-developed cognitive and social processes, and less access to age-appropriate social and medical services (Ickovics & Rodin, 1992; Moss, 1994). While sexual experience and reports of multiple sexual partners declined among adolescent males from 1991 to 1997, there was no significant decrease among adolescent females (CDC, 1998c). In national studies of American high school students, from 62% to 76% reported having had sexual intercourse by age 18 (CDC, 1998c; Laumann, Gagnon, Michael, & Michaels, 1996). Sexually active adolescents often engage in sex with high risk partners, have multiple sexual partners, and use condoms inconsistently, if at all, (DiClemente et al., 1992; Durbin et al., 1993; Kann et al., 1996; Millstein & Moscicki, 1995; Morris, Harrison, Knox, Tromanhauser, & Marquis, 1995; Orr & Langefeld, 1993; Rickman et al., 1994; Rotheram-Borus, Meyer-Bahlburg, & Koopman, 1992). Nearly 20% of sexually active teenagers have had four or more different sexual partners (Kann et al., 1996). Up to two thirds of sexually active adolescents report no use or ineffective use of contraception (Clark, Zabin, & Hardy, 1984; Harris, 1986). It is critical to learn more about HIV and STD risk within the context of adolescent pregnancy, where young women not only fail to protect themselves, but may actively seek pregnancy (Merrick, 1995) leaving them vulnerable to other risks associated with unprotected sex.

Resistance to explicit sex education in schools has created a structural barrier for prevention among American youth (DiClemente, 1998; Jemmott, Jemmott & Fong, 1998; National Institutes of Health, 1997). It is important to remember, however, that those most at risk include gay youth, runaways or homeless youth, those who have lost a parent to AIDS, and illiterate adolescents. Growing up in communities touched by HIV—whether urban centers, suburban neighborhoods, or rural towns—adolescents may feel a great sense of fear and hopelessness about any attempt to stop the spread of disease.

Young adult women (age 25–40) continue to be one of the fastest growing groups newly diagnosed with AIDS and dying of AIDS-related complications in the United States and globally. Decisions around childbearing have major implications for HIV risk, and these are considered primary reproductive years. On the one hand, women who are actively seeking pregnancy are at risk for HIV because they are having unprotected sex. On the other hand, in an effort to prevent pregnancy, women may unwittingly put themselves at risk for HIV and other STDs. Currently available contraceptives have differential effects on reducing the risks of unintended pregnancy and STDs. Hormonal contraception, which is most effective at reducing risk for pregnancy, is least effective at reducing risk for STDs, resulting in a "contraceptive trade-off dilemma" (Cates, 1996). New methods of contraception, such as long-acting injectable depot medroxyprogesterone acetate (Depo Provera) and implantable levonorgestrel (Norplant), are extremely effective at preventing pregnancy; however, they provide no protection against HIV and other STDs. Further, the more effective the chosen contraceptives are for preventing pregnancy, the less likely individuals are to use condoms to prevent STDs (Polaneczky, Slap, & Forke, 1994; Santelli, Davis, & Celantano, 1995; Weisman, Plichta, & Nathanson, 1991). Overall, condoms are the best single contraceptive method for preventing both pregnancy and STDs; more behavioral research is necessary to identify the determinants of condom use for protection against pregnancy versus disease.

The partners of midlife and older heterosexual women rarely use condoms. Indeed, unprotected sex becomes more common with the onset of menopause and diminished pregnancy-related concerns (AARP, 1994). Biological changes such as decreased vaginal lubrication and the thinning of the vaginal walls may also place postmenopausal women at increased risk for HIV transmission. Research focused on substance use among midlife and older women and their partners has been limited, but some do use injection drugs. If and when HIV infection does occur, older women find that social support is especially limited (AARP, 1994).

Eighteen percent of women with AIDS in the United States are over age 40 when diagnosed with AIDS (CDC, 1998a). However, health care providers often do not recognize HIV risk behavior for their female patients in midlife. Women diagnosed with HIV at age 50 or older are more likely than younger women to have never used a condom prior to their HIV diagnosis and are more likely to be diagnosed with HIV while hospitalized (i.e., already symptomatic; Schable, Chu & Diaz, 1996). It is estimated that among Americans age 50 or older, the prevalence of having at least one risk factor for HIV infection is 10% (Stall & Catania, 1994). Lack of knowlege about HIV interventions and their own risk of infection place older women at risk for HIV (Yates, Stellato, Johannes & Avis, 1999; Zablotsky, 1998). Older patients may also experience difficulty adjusting to disease and accessing health care and social support due to their limited educational experience and social isolation (Schable et al., 1996). Finally, therapeutics used to treat or prophylax against HIV-related disease have not been tested for drug interactions among some of the most common drugs that midlife and older women may be taking, such as hormone replacement therapy, and medications for hypertension, hypercholesteremia, or depression.

HIV seems to accelerate the entire developmental life cycle. What individuals would normally experience over the course of decades is experienced over the course of years: death of friends and loved ones, loss of physical and sexual functioning, deterioration in cognition and memory, and the effects of aging on their bodily appearance. Life events that occur "off time" with regard to the normative life cycle are considered more stressful—particularly when events are premature, allowing no time for anticipatory coping or planning (Revenson, 1990). Selwyn (1996) articulated the anomalies in the usual pattern of the family life cycle, in which death crowds out life, and inflicts a cruel and painful destruction of the family, across multiple generations.

Disease Stage/Natural History and Progression

For women and men, the basic biological processes that accompany HIV are likely to operate in the same way (Fauci, Pantaleo, Stanley, & Weissman, 1996); however, sex differences in the clinical manifestations of HIV are prevalent. Anemia, irregular menses, mucocutaneous candidiasis, vaginitis, genital herpes, dysplasia, and cervical cancer are common in HIV-positive women (Korn & Abercrombie, 1997; Massad et al., 1999; Sun et al., 1997). Most sex differences in disease manifestation have been documented in areas in which women and men differ fundamentally (i.e., gynecological complications); however, these manifestations were not fully realized as symptomatic of progression to AIDS for women until years into the AIDS epidemic. In areas where there has been no clear documentation of differences between men and women (e.g., neurological complications), it is unknown whether this is a result of null findings or due to the lack of information on women and HIV available in research (Fox-Tierney, Ickovics, Ceretta, & Ethier, 1999).

Evidence regarding sex differences in the clinical course of HIV disease and survival rates have been inconsistent. Many recent studies do not report sex differences in the rate of clinical progression (Chaisson, Keruly, & Moore, 1995; Cu-Uvin et al., 1996; Smith & Moore, 1995). However, Farzadegan et al. (1998) found that women with the same viral load as men had a 1.6 times greater risk of AIDS, indicating perhaps that disease progression for women is more rapid than for men.

The HIV Epidemiology Research Study (HERS) was one of the first prospective cohorts designed to study the impact of HIV on women's health (Smith et al., 1997). It demonstrated an increased prevalence of vaginal and oral yeast infections, oral lesions, and human papilloma virus (HPV) among women with HIV compared to their HIV-negative counterparts. Extremely high levels of depression, and social and emotional stress were reported by women with HIV as well as by the uninfected, at-risk women (Moore et al., 1999). Moreover, early findings indicated that many women with HIV did not receive adequate medical care, despite scientific advances in the realm of HIV treatment (Smith et al., 1997).

There has been tremendous progress in the clinical care for people with HIV. Persons infected with HIV are living longer and the quality of life has improved. Clinical care has become more complex as effective treatments are developed, including combination antiretroviral therapies and prophylaxis to prevent disease complications. A critical breakthrough in effective treatments was established with the development of a new class of drugs called *protease inhibitors* that reduce viral replication of HIV (Deeks, Smith, Holodniy, & Kahn, 1997). Critical issues still remain with regard to the widespread use of these drugs; among the most important issues are cost and strict patient adherence so that viral resistance does not occur. In the United States, women have had significantly less access to quality care, including less access to therapeutic drugs (Shapiro, et al., 1999; Solomon, et al., 1999). In the developing world, basic therapeutic agents are still unavailable, let alone more sophisticated medications—for women or men.

Epidemiological Changes in HIV

The dynamic quality of the HIV epidemic has been documented both globally and in the United States; epidemiologic patterns indicate changes that are detrimental to women. For example in Thailand, as in other Asian countries, the epidemic has progressed from injection drug users to commercial sex workers, their male clients, and, finally to other sexual partners of these men (e.g., wives), and their children.

In the United States and European countries, the epidemiological waves have been different. HIV was first diagnosed among men who have sex with men (CDC, 1981). The view of HIV as a "homosexual disease" had an indirect but serious impact on women with HIV, in part because early research on HIV focused almost exclusively on men (Ickovics & Rodin,

1992). Women who contracted HIV in the early years were misdiagnosed or were diagnosed late because they were not considered at risk.

The "second wave" of the epidemic was characterized as a disease of drug users and prostitutes (Miller, Turner, & Moses, 1990; Treichler, 1988). Identifying commercial sex workers as a potential source of transmission resulted in a stereotype that treated women as "vectors" of disease (Livingston, 1992). Consequently, female sex workers were often blamed for the spread of the disease. In Brazil, groups of sex workers (usually all female) infected with HIV have been arrested and/or deported to rural areas (de Bruyn, 1992). Ironically, no cultural stigma was attached to their male clients (Bergman, 1988).

In its initial diagnoses, biomedical research identified "risk groups" in its evaluation of AIDS-infected populations. This categorization often stigmatized the target groups and the associated populations. The linkage of "unacceptable" behaviors (i.e., sex and drug use) and a deadly disease created a hostile climate for HIV-positive individuals (de Bruyn, 1992; Livingston, 1992). To avoid problems associated with stigmatization, the public focus must be shifted toward identifying "risk practices." HIV is a disease whose reproduction depends on individuals' behaviors, not personal attributes. Understanding the changing epidemiology and the temporal context of HIV disease is critical so that informed decisions can be made about prevention and treatment for those with HIV and those most at risk of infection. With the movement from the broad perspective of the epidemic back to considering the lives of individuals affected, the unique life situations surrounding each individual touched by HIV must be recognized.

SITUATIONAL CONTEXT

This final context considered as part of the ecological approach to HIV disease comprises factors that are specific to an individual or to a group of persons. A given situation may limit or enhance the possible responses of an individual. In this section, women infected or at risk for HIV and possible situations that may uniquely or differentially affect them are considered. Specifically, pregnancy, parenthood, and HIV testing, women in sexual relations with other women, and women living in rural environments are addressed.

Pregnancy, Parenthood, and HIV Testing

Currently, more than 80% of women with AIDS are of childbearing age (CDC, 1998a). Personal and literary accounts emphasize the importance of motherhood in the lives of many women. Some women seek to get pregnant after they find out that they have HIV, because they want to leave "something or someone behind." Others find out that they are HIV positive when they are pregnant. The choice to keep the child and the risk of the child being HIV-infected may be a source of great stress. In addition, permanency planning for children (i.e., caretaking and legal arrangements for the children after the death of the parents) is an immediate concern (Geballe et al., 1995).

Findings from an AIDS clinical trial (i.e., ACTG 076) demonstrated that zidovudine (ZDV) can prevent mother-to-child HIV transmission. These data indicated that the risk of vertical transmission can be reduced by two thirds—from 25% to 8%—when zidovudine is taken during pregnancy, administered during delivery, and taken by the newborn for 6 weeks postpartum (Conner et al., 1994). The release of these findings has been associated with an increase in ZDV use during pregnancy and a decline in HIV transmission from mothers to infants (Cooper et al., 1994; Lindegren et al., 1999). There is still limited understanding about the mechanism through which ZDV exerts its protection. In addition, it is critical to understand why ZDV fails to prevent perinatal transmission in some cases. High maternal HIV-1 RNA level is one of the strongest predictor of perinatal transmission risk (Dickover et al., 1996; Mofenson et al., 1999); ZDV reduced maternal viral load prior to delivery, which significantly decreased the probability of HIV transmission from mother to child. Obstetrical factors are also important predictors of transmission (Landesman et al., 1996).

Following the release of these critically important findings, the U.S. Public Health Service developed practice guidelines for the use of ZDV to reduce vertical transmission and for the implementation of universal counseling and voluntary HIV testing of pregnant women (CDC, 1995). In 1999, the Institute of Medicine went further, recommending *routine* prenatal testing of all pregnant women (Stoto, Almario, & McCormick, 1999). Guideline objectives are to increase HIV testing rates (i.e., toward 100%) so that pregnant women with HIV can be diagnosed and treated, thus reducing perinatal transmission.

Although prenatal HIV testing may diagnose seropositive women who did not know their HIV status, questions remain about the linkage to services for these women and their children. Access to these services are necessary if women with HIV are to be offered prophylactic Zidovudine therapy to prevent vertical transmission, and to receive care for their own HIV-related medical conditions. Earlier studies suggest that women diagnosed with HIV during pregnancy were more likely to delay seeking health care (Ickovics et al., 1996), or fail to obtain regular HIV-related care for themselves altogether (Butz et al., 1993). Many women with HIV also have reported health care discrimination, restricting access to services (Lester, Partridge, Chesney, & Cooke, 1995). Finally, primary prevention must also be a priority: insuring that women get the information and skills they need to protect themselves from HIV transmission—*before* they get pregnant.

The value of an HIV diagnosis during pregnancy via routine prenatal testing is emphasized by recent evidence that indicates that elective caesarian-section (Anonymous, 1999), single dose nevirapine (Guay et al., 1999; Musoke et al., 1999), and abbreviated regimens of zidovudine prophylaxis (Shaffer et al., 1999; Shapiro et al., 1999; Wade et al., 1998) can reduce risk of perinatal transmission. Identifying women with HIV during pregnancy provides an important opportunity to optimize the health care of women and children, reduce the risk of vertical transmission, and enable women to make informed reproductive and healthcare choices.

Women Who Have Sex With Women: Affected and Infected by the AIDS Epidemic

The role of lesbians and bisexual women in the HIV epidemic has been characterized almost exclusively as one of activists and care givers (Corea, 1992; Rieder & Ruppelt, 1988). Lesbians and bisexual women have been strong advocates through local community agencies and nonprofit organizations—visible on the front lines of the political battles to make treatment, services, and clinical trials more readily available and more affordable. They have been important partners in effective community mobilization for gay men and for women with HIV-related disease. As members of the gay community, women who have sex with women often have been the providers of emotional, physical, and financial support to their gay male friends. They are likely to have experienced multiple AIDS-related losses of friends and loved ones. As such, their psychosocial needs must also be considered in any review of the impact of the HIV epidemic on women.

It is also important to acknowledge that women who have sex with women (WSW) are infected with HIV. The earliest case report of likely female-to-female transmission of HIV appeared in 1984 (Sabatini, Patel, & Hirschman, 1984). A woman with AIDS reported that she had only had sex with women and did not have any other risks for HIV infection (e.g., no injection drug use, no blood transfusion). Additional cases were documented because the individuals presented for medical care (Sabatini et al., 1984; Marmor et al., 1986; Monzon & Capellan, 1987; Rich et al., 1993) or were participating in HIV-related research on another topic (Perry, Jacobsberg, & Fogel, 1989); no systematic recruitment or sampling strategies were used.

Other existing research studies including women with HIV (e.g., HIV/AIDS surveillance, blood donor studies) have not provided evidence of female-to-female transmission (Castro et al., 1988; Chu, Beuhler, Fleming, & Berfelman, 1990). The restrictiveness of these categories used to determine infection source (i.e., women's HIV transmission is classified as having occurred through heterosexual sex or injection drug use if they have had sex with at-risk men or injected drugs since 1978) may underestimate transmission that actually occurred through sex between women. In addition, much of the sexual risk behavior data in the HIV/AIDS reporting systems are inconsistent and/or missing, particularly information concerning sexual contact with women (Kennedy, Scarlett, Duerr, & Chu, 1995; Morrow, 1995).

Women who have sex with women have exposure to vaginal secretions, blood, and menstrual fluids that may place them at risk for HIV. HIV has been detected in cervical and vaginal secretions (Belec, Georges, Steenman, & Martin, 1989; Clemetson et al., 1993; Henin et al., 1993; Van de Perr, DeClerq, & Coniaux-Leclerc, 1988; Vogt, Witt, & Craven, 1986, 1987; Wofsy et al., 1986; Zorr, Schafer, & Dilger, 1994). In their account of possible female-to-female transmission, Marmor et al. (1986) reported that the sexual contact between the women included oral and digital vaginal contact, oral-anal contact, contact during menses, and vaginal bleeding as a result of sexual contact. A growing body of literature suggests that other sexually transmitted infections, such as herpes simplex, human papilloma virus (HPV), bacterial vaginosis, trichomoniasis, and gonorrhea can be transmitted between women sexually (Berger et al., 1995; Edwards & Thin, 1990; Ferris, Batish, Wright, Cushing, & Scott, 1996; Kellock & O'Mahony, 1996; O'Hanlan & Crum, 1996).

A lack of knowledge about the sexual behaviors of HIV-infected women has led to misperceptions about the transmission risk among women who have sex with women. Among a group of HIV infected women recruited because of a history of injecting drug use and HIV-related sexual risk behaviors, 18% reported ever having sex with a woman and 6% reported sex with a woman in the past 6 months (Moore et al., 1996). Other researchers have reported that substantial proportions of STD clinic patients and drug users reported sex with women and/or bisexual or lesbian self identity (Bevier, Chiasson, Heffernan, & Castro, 1995; Deren et al., 1996). Given rates of same sex behavior by HIV-infected women and the lack of prevention guidelines for this group of women, female-to-female transmission may be a more significant public health risk than was previously thought.

Behavioral research suggests that women who have sex with women may engage in other behaviors that put them at risk for HIV (Gomez, 1995; Stevens, 1993). Among HIV-infected and high risk women, women with female partners may engage in more drug using and sexual HIV risk behaviors than women who only have sex with men (Bevier et al., 1995; Deren et al., 1996; Friedman et al., 1995; Harris et al., 1993; Moore et al., 1996).

Women who have sex with women who would like to practice safer sex also face obstacles. Products used for protection against HIV and other STDs include latex gloves and dental dams, items traditionally used in medical settings. Because these are not designed for, or marketed and packaged for sexual use, they are difficult to obtain and often expensive (Stevens, 1994). In addition, they may not provide adequate protection against infection (e.g., dental dams are often too small).

Finally, there is often tension between a focus on the specific prevention needs of lesbians and bisexual women *versus* the need for prevention programs to target the *behaviors* that put women at risk (rather than a particular sexual orientation). Few prevention programs have been designed to address the sexual issues of women having sex with other women; there has been a scarcity of information on acceptable safer sex activities and safer sex materials, communication skills within the context of a lesbian relationship, and personal risk appraisal as it pertains to the sexual relationship between women (Morrow, 1995). Investigators must acknowledge the diversity of behavior within sexual self-definition, creating behavior-based messages that are widely applicable, while gaining an understanding of the unique prevention issues pertaining to women who have sex with women.

Geography Is Destiny: Coping With HIV in Urban Versus Rural Settings

Another important situational context for women with HIV is their geographic location. In an urban environment, women are more likely to be infected or at high risk for HIV transmission. Because HIV first hit the urban centers in the United States, it is likely that women in the cities are also more likely to be affected by AIDS-related losses. In a community-based study of women in a medium-sized city, 72% reported knowing at least one person who had died of AIDS; 30% knew four or more people who had died of AIDS including family members and close friends (Ickovics, Druley, Morrill, Grigorenko, & Rodin, 1998). Access to health care, risk of social isolation, and stigma are also important issues for women with HIV in urban areas.

HIV has also hit the U.S. heartland. People are becoming infected in rural areas throughout this country. The greatest proportionate increases in the U.S. epidemic are occurring in the south and midwest (CDC, 1996). In addition, individuals who moved to urban centers and became infected there, are returning home to families of origin for care as their disease progresses (Cohn et al., 1994). Distance often compounds issues of access to health care in numerous ways: availability of transportation; cost and time needed to travel to a clinic, including taking time off from work for routine medical visits and arranging for child care; lack of a supportive community to assist with daily needs, social support, or medical attention. Although the stigma for HIV- positive women is great everywhere, it may be greater in rural areas due to fear of identification and isolation. Furthermore, because the number of HIV cases in rural areas is limited, understanding and compassion about HIV/AIDS may be more limited as well.

In 1996, it was estimated that 23,000 people with AIDS lived in rural regions of the United States (Shernoff, 1996). The escalating numbers of patients with HIV resulted in increased demands for medical care, and these medical facilities were unstable before the HIV epidemic. Many rural communities still have had limited contact with the HIV epidemic, resulting in fewer opportunities to develop social services and medical treatment services for persons with HIV and their family members. Long distances to medical facilities and the reluctance of medical personnel to provide care to persons with HIV are significant barriers to medical care in rural areas (Gunter, 1988; Heckman, et al., 1998). Coordinated care (e.g., primary HIV care, gynecological care, drug treatment, mental health services) may be particularly difficult to obtain in rural areas. Lack of employment opportunities, unsupportive work environments, and a shortage of mental health professionals were identified as significant barriers for persons with HIV in smaller communities (Heckman et al., 1998).

Increases in HIV seroprevalence rates in rural regions in Africa also have been documented (Boerma, Urassa, Senkoro, Klokke, & Ngweshemi, 1999; Kane et al., 1993; Mulder, Nunn, Wagner, Kamali, & Kengeya-Kayondo, 1994). Increased seroprevalance in rural regions is due in part to seasonal migration for employment in urban areas as well as sexual mixing within these small geographic rural areas (Boerma et al., 1999; Kane et al., 1993; Lurie et al., 1995). Despite the profound magnitude of the HIV epidemic in Africa and the spread of HIV into the countryside, there has been limited attention to HIV disease in rural Africa. In a study of 482 people in rural Senegal, it was surprising to learn that 29% of the men and 13% of the women had never even heard of AIDS (Lagarde, Pison, & Enel, 1996). Awareness and access to adequate health care must increase.

To address HIV disease among women in rural communities, we must strengthen and supplement informal networks of family members, neighbors, and civic and religious organizations, as well as increase the availability of more formal sources of support and health care for persons with HIV and their families (Shernoff, 1996). Tartaglia (1996) focused on the importance of religious institutions, suggesting that churches are historically and functionally among the most influential of rural institutions. Special efforts are required to overcome the challenges in rural communities where diversity and anonymity are outside the norm (Anderson & Shaw, 1994). The development of satellite health clinics (Heckman et al., 1998) and telephone-linked support groups (where telephones are available) have been suggested as ways of bringing services to individuals where they live (Rounds, Galinsky, & Stevens, 1991).

CROSS-CUTTING THEMES AND CONCLUDING COMMENTS

An ecological perspective provides an excellent heuristic within which to frame a discussion about women with HIV and those at risk. This model allows for an examination of a wide array of factors—broadening the discourse to consider women within the social contexts of their lives. The determinants (e.g., sexual and drug-using behavior) and consequences (e.g., coping with diagnosis, caretaking, access to treatment) are embedded within sociocultural, interpersonal, and temporal and situational contexts. In this final section, the implications of this ecological approach for prevention, treatment, research and policy in the arena of women and HIV are considered. The section concludes with the role that health psychology can play in this evolving epidemic.

Prevention

Thus far, there is no available cure for AIDS and no medical vaccine to prevent the acquisition of HIV. Primary prevention is the only "magic bullet"; condoms and abstinence are the only ways of decreasing risk of HIV through sexual transmission (Elias & Coggins, 1996). The economic and social reasons discussed earlier make this approach difficult for many women (See section on *Sociocultural Context*). Inexpensive, effective and acceptable female controlled barrier methods, virucides and microbicides must be developed and distributed to provide more options for safer sex (Gollub, 1995; Elias & Coggins, 1996). Recently, the female condom has been introduced as a method for STD prevention; if used consistently and correctly, the risk of STD transmission is reduced by 97% in each act of intercourse. Methods that offer protection, but not contraception would be particularly useful in those cultures where a woman's status is determined by her fertility.

Prevention interventions that are both gender specific and culturally sensitive must be emphasized to promote health enhancing behaviors and reduce health damaging behaviors. Health professionals must be trained in "cultural competency" to best meet their clients' diverse educational and linguistic backgrounds as well as their emotional and practical support needs (de Bruyn, 1992; Livingston, 1992; Smyke, 1991). There is a critical need to balance concern for cultural sensitivity with direct attention and candid discussions of sexual behavior and drug use—considered "off limits" in nearly every culture. Moreover, women must be empowered with assertion and negotiation skills to enhance their ability for noncoercive decision making (Livingston, 1992). Until women can have more complete control of their lives, HIV infection will continue to be the outcome of their social, physical, and economic subordination. And for women who are in control but still engaging in risky behavior, they must be educated about the likelihood of HIV infection and methods of prevention.

Although a complete description of prevention interventions is beyond the scope of this chapter, it is important to note that many targeted HIV prevention programs have included women (for reviews see Exner, Seal, & Ehrhardt, 1997; Ickovics & Yoshikawa, 1998). Programs have focused on preventing high risk sexual and drug using behavior among pregnant women (Hobfoll, Jackson, Lavin, Britton, & Shepherd, 1994), poor women in urban housing developments (Sikemma et al., 2000), women in primary health care clinics (Kelly et al., 1994; Shain et al., 1999), and adolescents (St. Lawrence et al., 1995). These studies and others have provided evidence for the effectiveness of cognitive behavioral group interventions (see for reviews Kalichman, Carey & Johnson, 1996; Kelly et al., 1997).

Finally, with regard to prevention—early adolescence may represent a "critical window" for establishing low risk behaviors (Barone et al., 1996; NIH, 1997). It is well documented that behavior change is difficult to promote and maintain. Teaching safer sex to children and adolescents before they become sexually active may make it more likely that safer sexual behavior is initiated and sustained. In a report to the President, the Office of National AIDS Policy (1996) called for immediate and direct action to reduce HIV among adolescents in part by implementing intensive HIV education and prevention programs in schools, religious organizations, and community groups. This must be done to prevent the continued spread of HIV among adolescents, despite political and moral arguments to the contrary.

Treatment

The clinical complications of HIV-related illness place a huge strain on medical and social services in both the public and private sectors, and in countries throughout the world (CDC, 1996). There have been few other occasions in scientific history that clinicians and investigators have been compelled to move so rapidly from "the bench to the bedside." Recently, there have been several breakthroughs in the treatment of disease with protease inhibitors and combination antiretroviral therapies. However, questions persist about how these scientific breakthroughs will affect the health care and quality of life of average women infected with HIV. (See section on *Temporal Context, Disease Stage/Natural History and Progression*).

Women who are infected with HIV should have access to the broadest range of treatment options. Unfortunately, given high rates of poverty, that is not always the case, especially in the developing world. In the United States, women are more likely than men to receive their health care through the social service system; ease of access and the quality of care received by people who rely on Medicaid and Medicare has not been uniformly good (Bastian et al., 1993). With the broad expansion of managed care, federal welfare reform, and cuts in health and social service benefits in many states, health care for women with HIV may become even more scarce and difficult to obtain.

Treatment for HIV during pregnancy has become a particularly challenging issue. Although zidovudine is the only medication approved as safe and effective for the prevention of vertical transmission, it is considered "suboptimal treatment" when used by itself to treat adult HIV-related disease (CDC, 1998b). Physicians are prescribing combination therapy for pregnant women; however, it is unclear which strategy is best for both mother and child because the clinical trials have not yet been completed. Women should receive information on the benefits and risks of all drugs during pregnancy to enable them to make fully informed decisions. Information must be given in culturally, linguistically, and age-appropriate language. Women's reproductive decisions must not jeopardize on-going care. Voluntary HIV testing should be available to all women so that they can make informed decisions about maintaining or terminating a pregnancy.

Women with HIV need coordinated care including primary care, specialized services for HIV-related illness, gynecological services, psychological, social and legal services, case management for assistance with obtaining entitlements, family support, drug treatment, and coordinated access to pediatric and adult medical services if they have children. All of these supplemental services require a commitment to provide funding for comprehensive care. Due to continued epidemic spread and longer survival following diagnosis, the numbers of women living with HIV continues to expand; their medical, social, legal and other needs grow more complex.

Finally, identification and treatment of other sexually transmitted diseases is a critical point for intervention. In a randomized controlled study in Tanzania, Grosskurth et al. (1995) randomly assigned six communities to enhanced services for the diagnosis and treatment of STDs, and six matched communities were provided no enhanced services. Although there was no significant change in self-reported sexual behavior, there was a 40% reduction in HIV incidence among individuals in the intervention communities. This indicates the importance of integrated treatment services, and is the first study of its kind to indicate the effectiveness of community treatment interventions to slow the spread of the HIV epidemic.

Research

Traditional theories of behavior change have provided a good foundation for HIV prevention research (e.g., Health Belief Model: Rosenstock, 1974; Theory of Reasoned Action: Azjen & Fishbein, 1977; Social Cognitive Learning Theory: Bandura, 1977). However, as the HIV epidemic has moved forward, it became clear that these models were limited. They were originally formulated for domains other than sexuality and drug use, and it was assumed that the behavior in question is under individual, volitional control. Traditionally, the interpersonal and situational processes and competing predictors of risk have not been taken into consideration (see for review, Auerbach et al., 1994). However, some theoretical adaptions have occurred, and these have provided important frameworks for new and ongoing HIV research (e.g., AIDS Risk Reduction Model: Catania, Kegeles, & Coates, 1990; Diffusion Theory: as adapted by Kelly, 1997).

The ecological model described in this chapter provides a broad approach, incorporating sociocultural, interpersonal, temporal and situational factors that may influence risk behavior or response to disease. It appears that investigators are trying to encompass a broad range of factors in new theoretical models; whereas this adequately reflects the complexity of behavior, it makes it difficult to test in a specific research study. Revenson (1990) suggested at least two reasons why context has generally been ignored in health research: It may be difficult to specify which aspects of social context may be important for an individual or a group; and, typically, investigators seek to eliminate threats to validity by ruling out the effects of "extraneous" variables, eliminating unwanted sources of variance.

Theoretical approaches in the realm of HIV and AIDS continue to evolve, and research agendas have moved forward, with or without a theoretical foundation. Investigators have called for research (in general) that integrates basic biological, epidemiological, psychological, and social factors to better understand transmission of HIV through sex and drug use (e.g., Auerbach et al., 1994; Coates, Temoshok & Mandel, 1984; Ickovics & Rodin, 1992; Kelly & Kalichman, 1995; NIH, 1997). Structural factors—such as class, race/ethnicity, gender relations, and community—that increase risk for HIV, affect progression of disease, and provide points of intervention have also been highlighted.

In terms of conducting research, methodological challenges persist, such as the reliance on self-reported behavior, development of adequate measures of risk behaviors and their predictors, longitudinal follow-up of study participants, and the generalizability of results from one study sample to the population (i.e., diverse populations such as homeless women, users of community health clinics or drug treatment programs, school-based or out-of-school adolescents; Catania, Gibson, Chitwood, & Coates, 1990). Given the complexities of HIV, research should be interdisciplinary and include multiple methodologies for data collection (e.g., quantitative, qualitative, ethnographic, objective health indicators).

To gain a real understanding of how HIV affects women, biologically, psychologically, and socially, women must be included in research (Rodin & Ickovics, 1990). Moreover, research on women and HIV must not be driven by past trends, but rather by important scientific issues and opportunities in the present and future of the epidemic. An important focus may be on distinctive patterns of behaviors and social conditions among specific subgroups of women; targeted prevention interventions could then follow. In the second decade of the AIDS pandemic, it is surprising that research on women with HIV and those most at risk continues to be limited. A cadre of researchers has been mobilized, however, and as we enter the next decade, understanding of factors affecting the lives of both women and men should be enhanced.

Policy

> AIDS is a preventable disease, and the behavior placing the public health at greatest risk may be occurring in legislative and other decision making bodies. (NIH, 1997)

An independent, nongovernment consensus panel convened by the National Institutes of Health (1997) called on government and policy leaders at all levels to reverse policies that place the public at risk and to take the lead in implementing proven, lifesaving public health strategies. This panel strongly endorsed the use of needle exchange programs, youth education on safer sex, and better availability of drug abuse treatment to diminish the spread of HIV. The panel highlighted the government leadership and policy changes in AIDS-stricken countries such as Thailand and Uganda as models of how public policy can effectively reduce the spread of AIDS, saving lives and reducing the costs of the epidemic.

Because AIDS is primarily a sexually transmitted disease, it strikes adolescents, young adults, and people in early middle age; these are the very people on whom society relies for production and reproduction. Lost productivity has social and economic consequences for schools, hospitals, factories, and governments. In countries that are not yet industrialized or are in the process of industrializing, AIDS threatens economic development itself (United Nations, 1999).

There has been increased awareness of policy issues that affect women with HIV/AIDS and those most at risk; however, current public policy has not always been developed in their best interest (Ethier et al., 1996). Public policies can influence research funding, treatment access, and cost, and social protection against bias and discrimination. In general, women with HIV and those most at risk have not had a strong advocacy group to work on their behalf to change public policy to better address their needs. Current rates of HIV and projections for the future indicate that women throughout the world will be affected increasingly by the AIDS pandemic in the years to come. The impact of this pandemic cannot be measured solely by counting the number of people infected or ill. For every person infected with HIV, there are countless others who are affected by the impact of the disease as family members, neighbors, colleagues, and friends. Priorities for prevention, treatment, and research must be established at many levels (e.g., local, regional, national, international), and those in positions of power (or those with access to the powerful others) must insure that these priorities are addressed in a systematic and comprehensive fashion.

The Role of Health Psychology in the Understanding of Women and HIV

Women with HIV and those at risk for HIV do not represent a homogenous group. However, all may have to confront issues unique to women such as power differentials in intimate relationships, the need for treatment of gynecological complications of HIV, and issues with regard to pregnancy, reproductive decision making, and parenthood. Health psychology and behavioral medicine can play an important role in enhancing understanding of the problems faced by women infected with HIV and those most at risk.

Matarazzo (1980) described the field as broadly addressing: the promotion and maintenance of health, the prevention and treatment of illness, the identification of etiologic and diagnostic correlates of health, illness and related dysfunction, and the improvement of the health care system and health policy formation. The complexities of HIV—as highlighted by the ecological approach that takes into consideration sociocultural, interpersonal, temporal, and situational contexts—are best addressed through interdisciplinary investigations and clinical practice. This is a challenging domain, and researchers must rise to the challenge through scientific excellence as well as the courage and compassion required to address the needs of women with HIV, those most at risk, their family members and loved ones.

REFERENCES

Adler, N. E., Boyce, T., Chesney, M., Cohen, S., Folkman, S., Kahn, R. L., & Syme, S. (1994). Socioeconomic status and health: The challenge of the gradient. *American Psychologist, 49,* 15–24.

Adler, N. E., Boyce, T., Chesney, M., Folkman, S., & Syme, S. L. (1992). Socioeconomic inequalities and health: No easy solution. *Journal of the American Medical Association, 269,* 3140–3145.

Al-Gallaf, K., Al-Wazzan, H., Al-Namash, H., Shah, N. M., & Bahbehani, J. (1995). Ethnic differences in contraceptive use in Kuwait: A clinic-based study. *Social Science and Medicine, 41,* 1023–1031.

Amaro, H. (1995). Love, sex and power: Considering women's realities in HIV prevention. *American Psychologist, 50,* 437–447.

Amaro, H., Zuckerman, B., & Cabral, H. (1989). Drug use among adolescent mothers: Profile of risk. *Pediatrics, 84,* 144–151.

American Association of Retired Persons. (1994). *Midlife & Older Women and HIV/AIDS: Report on the seminar.* Washington, DC: AARP.

Anderson, D., & Shaw, S. (1994). Starting a support group for families and partners of people with HIV/AIDS in a rural setting. *Social Work, 39,* 135–138.

Anderson, R. M. (1992). Some aspects of sexual behavior and the potential demographic impact of AIDS in developing countries. *Social Science and Medicine, 34,* 271–280.

Anderson, N. B., & McNeilly, M. (1991). Age, gender and ethnicity as variables psychophysiological assessment: Sociodemographics in context. *Psychological Assessment: A Journal of Consulting and Clinical Psychology, 3,* 376–384.

Anglin, M. D., Hser, Y. I., & McGlothin, W. H. (1987). Sex differences in addict careers. Becoming addicted. *American Journal of Drug and Alcohol Abuse, 13,* 59–71.

Anonymous. (1999). Elective caesarean-section versus vaginal delivery in prevention of vertical HIV-1 transmission: A randomized clinical trial. The European Mode of Delivery Collaboration. *Lancet,* 353:1035–9.

Aspinwall, L. G., & Taylor, S. E. (1992). Modeling cognitive adaptation: A longitudinal investigation of the impact of individual differences and coping on college adjustment and performance. *Journal of Personality and Social Psychology, 63,* 989–1003.

Auerbach J. D., Wypijewska C., & Brodie H. K. H. (Eds.). (1994). *AIDS and behavior: An integrated approach.* Washington, DC: National Academy Press.

Azjen, I., & Fishbein, M. (1977). Attitude-behavior relations: A theoretical analysis and review of empirical research. *Psychological Bulletin, 84,* 888–918.

Bandura, A. (1977). Self-efficacy: Toward a unifying theory of behavioral change. *Psychological Review, 84,* 191–215.

Barker, G., & Loewenstein, I. (1997). Where the boys are: Attitudes related to masculinity, fatherhood, and violence toward women among low-income adolescent and young adult mailes in Rio de Janeiro, Brazil. *Youth and Society, 29,* 166–196.

Barone, C., Ickovics, J., Ayers, T., Katz, S., Voyce, C., & Weissberg, R. (1996). High-risk behavior among young urban students. *Family Planning Perspectives, 28,* 69–74.

Bastian, L., Bennett, C., Adams, J., Waskins, H., Divine, G., & Edlin, B. (1993). Difference between men and women with HIV-related pneumocystis carinii pneumonia: Experience from 3,070 cases in New York City in 1987. *Journal of Acquired Immune Deficiency Syndromes, 6,* 617–623.

Belec, L., Georges, A. J., Steenman, G., & Martin, P. M. V. (1989). Antibodies to human immunodeficiency virus in vaginal secretions of heterosexual women. *Journal of Infectious Disease, 160,* 385–391.

Belluck, P. (1996, May 9). Mingling two worlds of medicine. *New York Times.*

Bennett, C. E. (1995). The Black population in the United States: March 1994 and 1993. *US Bureau of the Census, Current Population Reports,* P20–480. Washington, DC: U.S. Government Printing Office.

Berger, F. J., Kolton, S., Zenilman, J. M., Cummings, M., Feldman, J., & McCormack, W. M. (1005). Bacterial vaginosis in lesbians: A sexually transmitted idsease. *Clinical Infectious Diseases, 21,* 1402–1405.

Bergman. (1988). AIDS and prostitution. *Journal of Marshall Law Review, 21,* 777, 791.

Berman, S. M., & Hein, K. (1999). Adolescent and STDs. In K. K. Holmes, et al. (Eds.), *Sexually transmitted diseases* (3rd ed., pp. 129–142). New York: McGraw-Hill.

Bevier, P., Chiasson, M., Heffernan, R., & Castro, K. (1995). Women at a sexually transmitted disease clinic who reported same-sex contact: Their HIV seroprevalance and risk behaviors. *American Journal of Public Health, 85,* 1336–1367.

Billings, A. G., & Moos, R. H. (1981). The role of coping responses and social resources in attenuating the stress of life events. *Journal of Behavioral Medicine, 4,* 157–189.

Boerma, J. T., Urassa, M., Senkoro, K., Klokke, A., & Nqweshemi, J. Z. (1999). Spread of HIV infection in rural area of Tanzania. *AIDS, 13*(10), 1233–1240.

Boyer, P. J., Dillon, M., Navaie, M., Deveikis, A., Keller, M., & Bryson, Y. J. (1994). Factors predictive of maternal-fetal transmission of HIV-1. Preliminary analysis of zidovudine given during pregnancy and/or delivery. *Journal of the American Medical Association, 271,* 1925–1930.

Bronfenbrenner, U. (1977). Doing your own thing—our undoing. *Child Psychiatry & Human Development, 8,* 3–10.

Burgard, M., Mayaux, M. J., Blanche, S., Ferroni, A., Guihard-Moscato, M. L., Allemon, M. C., Ciraru-Vigneron, N., Firtion, G., Floch, C., Guillot, F., Lachassine, E., Vial, M., Griscelli, C., Rouzioux, C., & The HIV Infection in Newborns French Collaborative Study Group. (1992). The use of viral culture and p24 antigen testing to diagnose human immunodeficiency virus infection in neonates. *New England Journal of Medicine, 327,* 1192–1197.

Butz, A. M., Hutton, N., Joyner, M., Vogelhut, J., Greenberg-Friedman, D., Schreibeis, D., & Anderson, J. R. (1993). HIV-infected women and infants: Social and health factors impending utilization of health care. *Journal of Nurse-Midwifery, 38,* 103–109.

Carballo-Dieguez, A., & Dolezal, C. (1996). HIV risk behavior and obstacles to condom use among Puerto Rican men in New York City who have sex with men. *American Journal of Public Health, 86,* 1619–1622.

Castro, K. G., Lifson, A. R., White, C. R., Bush, T. J., Chamberland, M. E., Lekatsas, A. M., Jaffe, H. W. (1988). Investigations of AIDS patients with no previously identified risk factors. *Journal of the American Medical Association, 259,* 1338–1342.

Catania, J., Coates, R., Stall, R., Turner, H., Peterson, J., Hearst, N., Dolcini, M., Hudes, E., Gagnon, J., Wiley, J., & Groves, R. (1992). Prevalence of AIDS-related risk factors and condom use in the United States. *Science, 258,* 1101–1106.

Catania, J. A., Gibson, D. R., Chitwood, D. D., & Coates, T. J. (1990). Methodological problems in AIDS behavioral research: Influences on measurement error and participation bias in studies of sexual behavior. *Psychological Bulletin, 108,* 339–362.

Catania, J. A., Kegeles, S. M., & Coates, T. J. (1990). Towards an understanding of risk behavior: An AIDS risk reduction model (AARM). *Health Education Quarterly, 17,* 53–72.

Cates, W., Jr. (1996). Contraception, unintended pregnancies, and sexually transmitted diseases: Why isn't a simple solution possible? *American Journal of Epidemiology, 143,* 311–318.

Centers for Disease Control and Prevention. (1981). Kaposi's sarcoma and *Pneumocystis pneumonia* among heterosexual men: New York City and California. *Morbidity and Mortality Weekly Report, 30,* 305–308.

Centers for Disease Control and Prevention. (1986). *HIV/AIDS Surveillance Report. Year-end Edition, 1985.* Atlanta, GA: CDC.

Centers for Disease Control and Prevention. (1995). US Public Health Service recommendations for human immunodeficiency virus counseling and voluntary testing for pregnant women. *MWWR,* 44(RR- 7), 1–15.

Centers for Disease Control and Prevention. (1996). Statistical Projections/Trends. Document # 320210.

Centers for Disease Control and Prevention. (1997). Update: Trends in AIDS incidence, deaths, and prevalence—United States, 1996. *Morbidity and Mortality Weekly Report, 46,* 165–173.

Centers for Disease Control and Prevention. (1998a). *HIV/AIDS Surveillance Report. Year-end Edition, 1998.* Atlanta, GA: CDC.

Centers for Disease Control and Prevention. (1998b). Public Health Service task force recommendations for the use of antiretroviral drugs in pregnant women infected with HIV-1 for maternal health and for reducing perinatal HIV-1 transmission in the United States. *Morbidity and Mortality Weekly Report, 47* (No. RR-2). [See updates at http://www.hivatis.org]

Centers for Disease Control and Prevention. (1998c). Trends in sexual risk behaviors among high school students—United States, 1991–1997. *Morbidity and Mortality Weekly Report, 47,* 749–752.

Chaisson, R., Bachetti, P., Osmond, D., Brodie, B., Sande, M., & Moss, A. (1991). Cocaine use and HIV infection in intravenous drug users in San Francisco. *Journal of the American Medical Association, 261,* 501–505.

Chaisson, R. E., Keruly, J. C., & Moore, R. D. (1995). Race, sex, drug use, and progression of human immunodeficiency virus disease. *New England Journal of Medicine, 333,* 751–756.

Chu, S., Peterman, T., Doll, L., Buehler, J., & Durran, J. (1992). AIDS in bisexual men in the United States: Epidemiology and transmission to women. *American Journal of Public Health, 82,* 220–224.

Chu, S. Y., Buehler, J. W., Fleming, P. L., & Berkelman, R. L. (1990). Epidemiology of reported cases of AIDS in lesbians, United States 1980–1989. *American Journal of Public Health, 80,* 1380–1381.

Chung, J., & Magraw, M. (1992). A group approach to psychosocial issues faced by HIV-positive women. *Hospital and Community Psychiatry, 43,* 891–894.

Clark, S. D., Zabin, L. S., & Hardy, J. B. (1984). Sex, contraception and parenthood: Experience and attitudes among urban Black young men. *Family Planning Perspectives, 16,* 77–82.

Clemetson, D. B. A., Moss, G. B., Willerford, D. M., Hensel, M., Emonyi, W., Holmes, K. K., Plummer, F., Ndinya-Achola, J., Roberts, P. L., Hillier, S., & Kreiss, J. K. (1993). Detection of HIV DNA in cervical and vaginal secretions: prevalence and correlates among women in Nairobi, Kenya. *Journal of the American Medical Association, 269,* 2860–2864.

Coates, T. J., Temoshok, L., & Mandel, J. (1984). Psychosocial research is essential to understanding and treating AIDS. *American Psychologist, 39,* 1309–1314.

Cohen, S. (1988). Psychological models of the role of social support in the etiology of physical disease. *Health Psychology, 7,* 269–297.

Cohen, S., & Williamson, G. M. (1991). Stress and infectious disease in humans. *Psychological Bulletin, 109,* 5–24.

Cohn, S. E., Klein, J. D., Mohr, J. E., et al. (1994). Geography of AIDS: Patterns of urban and rural migration. *Southern Medical Journal, 87,* 599–606.

Connor, E. M., Sperling, R. S., Gelber, R., Kiselev, P., Scott, G., O'Sullivan, M. J., VanDyke, R., Bey, M., Shearer, W., Jacobson, R. L., et al. (1994). Reduction of maternal-infant transmission of human immunodeficiency virus type 1 with zidovudine treatment. *New England Journal of Medicine, 331,* 1173–1180.

Corea, G. (1992). *The invisible epidemic: The story of women and AIDS.* New York: Harper Collins.

Cu-Uvin, S., Flanigan, T., Rich, J., Mileno, M., Meyer, K., & Carpenter, C. (1996). Human immunodeficiency virus infection and acquired immunodeficiency syndrome among North American women. *American Journal of Medicine, 101,* 316–322.

Datta, P., Embree, J. E., Kreiss, J. K., Ndinya-Achola, J. O., Braddick, M., Temmerman, M., Nagelkerke, N. J., Maitha, G., Holmes, K. K., Piot, P., et al. (1994). Mother-to-child transmission of human immunodeficiency virus type 1: Report from the Nairobi Study. *Journal of Infectious Diseases, 170,* 1134–1140.

Davis, S. F., Byers, R. H., Jr., Lindegren, M. L., Caldwell, M. B., Karon, J. M., & Gwinn, M. (1995). Prevalence and incidence of vertically acquired HIV infection in the United States. *Journal of the American Medical Association, 274,* 952–955.

de Bruyn, M. (1992). Women and AIDS in developing countries. *Social Science and Medicine, 34,* 249–262.

Deeks S. G., Smith M., Holodniy M., & Kahn J. O. (1997). Protease inhibitors: A review for clinicians. *Journal of the American Medical Association, 227,* 145–153.

Deren, S., Goldstein, M., Williams, M., Stark, M., Estrada, A., Friedman, S. R., Young, R. M., Needle, R., Tortu, S., Saunders, L., Beardsley, M., Jose, B., McCoy, V. (1996). Sexual orientation, HIV risk behavior, and serostatus in multisite sample of drug-injecting and crack-using women. *Women's Health: Research on Gender, Behavior and policy, 2,* 35–47.

Des Jarlais, D., & Friedman, S. (1994). AIDS and the use of injected drugs. *Scientific American, 270,* 75–80.

Dickover, R., Garratty, E., Herman, S., Sim, M., Plaeger, S., Boyer, P., Keller, M., Deveikis, A., Stieham, E., & Bryson, Y. (1996). Identification of levels of maternal HIV-1 RNA associated with risk of perinatal transmission. *Journal of the American Medical Association, 275,* 599–605.

DiClemente, R. J. (1998). Preventing sexually transmitted infections among adolescents: A clash of ideology and science. *Journal of the American Medical Association, 279,* 1574–1575.

DiClemente, R. J., Durbin, M., Siegel, D., Krasnovsky, F., Lazarus, N., & Comacho, T. (1992). The determinants of condom use among junior high school students in a minority, inner-city school district. *Pediatrics, 89,* 197–202.

Durbin, M., DiClemente, R. J., Siegel, D., Krasnovsky, F., Lazarus, N., & Comacho, T. (1993). Factors associated with multiple sex partners among junior high school students. *Journal of Adolescent Health, 14,* 202–207.

Dublin, S., Rosenberg, P., & Goedert, J. (1992). Patterns and predictors of high-risk sexual behavior in female partners of HIV infected men with hemophilia. *AIDS, 6,* 475–482.

Edwards, A., & Thin, R. N. (1990). Sexually transmitted diseases in lesbians. International *Journal of STD and AIDS, 1,* 178–181.

Ehrhardt, A. (1988, January 29–20). *Implications of sexual and contraceptive practices/attitudes for prevention of heterosexual transmission in men in heterosexual relationships.* Paper presented at the NIDA Technical Review Meeting.

Ekstrand, M. (1992). Safer sex maintenance among gay men: Are we making any progress? *AIDS, 6,* 875–887.

el-Bassel, N. Cooper, D. K., Chen, D. R., & Schilling, R. F. (1998). Personal social networks and HIV status among women on methadone. *AIDS Care, 10*(6), 735–749.

Elias, C. J., & Coggins, C. (1996). Female-controlled methods to prevent sexual transmission of HIV. *AIDS, 10,* S43–S51.

Ethier, K., Ickovics J., & Rodin J. (1996). For whose benefit? Women, AIDS, and public policy. In A. O'Leary & L. Jemmott (Eds.), *Women and AIDS: The emerging epidemic.* New York: Plenum.

Exner, T. M., Seal, D. W., & Ehrhardt, A. A. (1997). A review of HIV interventions for at-risk women. *AIDS and Behavior, 1,* 93–124.

Farzadegan, H., Hoover, D. R., Astemborski, J., Lyles, C. M., Margolick, J. B., Markham, R. B., Quinn, T. C., & Vlahov, D. (1998). Sex differences in HIV-1 viral load and progression to AIDS. *Lancet,* 352:1510–4.

Fauci, A. S., Pantaleo, G., Stanley, S., & Weissman, D. (1996). Immunopathogenic mechanisms for HIV infection. *Annals of Internal Medicine, 124,* 654–663.

Faulpel, C. (1991). *Shooting dope: Career patterns of hard-core heroin users.* Gainsville: University of Florida Press.

Fee, E., & Krieger, N. (1993). Understanding AIDS: Historical interpretations and the limits of biomedical individualism. *American Journal of Public Health, 83,* 1477–1486.

Ferris, D. G., Batish, S., Wright, T. C., Cushing, C., & Scott, E. H. (1996). A neglected lesbian health concern: Cervical neoplasia. *Journal of Family Practice, 43*(6), 581–584.

Fernandez, I. (1995). Latinas and AIDS: Challenges to prevention efforts. In A. O'Leary & L. Jemmott (Eds.), *Women and AIDS: Primary prevention.* New York: Plenum.

Fisher, J. (1988). Possible effects of reference group-based social influence on AIDS risk behavior and AIDS prevention. *American Psychologist, 43,* 914–920.

Folkman, S., Chesney, M., Cooke, M., Boccellari, A., & Collette, L. (1994). Caregiver burden in HIV-positive and HIV-negative partners of men with AIDS. *Journal of Consulting and Clinical Psychology, 62,* 746–756.

Fox-Tierney, R., Ickovics, J., Cerreta, C., & Ethier, K. (1997). Women and HIV/AIDS-related neurological and neuropsychological research: Potential gender differences remain understudied.

Friedman, S. R., Jose, B., Deren, S., DesJarlais, D. C., Neaigus, A., & Consortium, N. A. (1995). Risk factors for Human Immunodeficiency Virus seroconversion among out-of-treatment drug injectors in high and low seroprevalence cities. *American Journal of Epidemiology, 142,* 864–874.

Fullilove, R., Fullilove, M., Bowser, B., & Goss, S. (1990). Risk of sexually transmitted disease among black crack users in Oakland and San Francisco, Calif. *Journal of the American Medical Association, 263,* 851–855.

Gay, J., & Underwood, U. (1991). Women in danger: A call for action. *The World's Women 1970–1990. Trends and Statistics.* United Nations: National Council for International Health.

Geballe, S., Grvendel, J., & Andiman, W. (Eds.). (1995). *Forgotten children of the AIDS epidemic.* New Haven, CT: Yale University Press.

Goedert, J. J., Duliege, A. M., Amos, C. I., Felton, S., & Biggar, R. J. (1991). High risk of HIV-1 infection for first-born twins. *Lancet, 338,* 1471–1475.

Gollub, E. L. (1995) . Women-centered prevention techniques and technologies. In A. O'Leary & L. S. Jemmott (Eds.), *Women at risk: Issues in the primary prevention of AIDS* (pp. 43–82). New York: Plenum.

Gollub, E. L. (1999). Human Rights is a US problem, too: The case of women and HIV. *American Journal of Public Health, 89*(10), 1479–1482.

Gomez, C. A. (1995). Lesbians at risk for HIV: The unresolved debate. In G. D. Herek (Ed.), *Contemporary perspectives on lesbians and gay psychology: Vol 2, AIDS. Identity and community* (pp. 19–31). Thousand Oaks, CA: Sage.

Green, E. C., Zokwe, B., & Dupree, J. P. (1995). The experience of an AIDS prevention program focused on South African traditional healers. *Social Science and Medicine, 40,* 503–515.

Greenberg, M., & Schneider, D. (1994). Violence in American cities: Young Black males is the answer, but what was the question. *Social Science and Medicine, 39,* 179–187.

Grosskurth, H., Mosha, F., Todd, J., et al. (1995). Impact of improved treatment of sexually transmitted diseases on HIV infection in rural Tanzania: Randomized controlled trial. *Lancet, 346,* 530–536.

Guay, L. A., Musoke, P., Fleming, T., et al. (1999). Intrapartum and neonatal single-dose Nevirapine compared with Zidovudine for prevention of mother-to-child-transmission of HIV-1 in Kampala Uganda: HIVNET 012 Randomized trial. *Lancet, 354,* 795.

Gunter, P. (1988). Rural gay men and lesbians: In need of services and understanding. In M. Shernoff & W. Scott (Eds.), *The sourcebook on lesbian/gay health care.* Washington, DC: The National Lesbian/Gay Health Foundation.

Gupta, G., & Weiss, E. (1993). Women's lives and sex: Implications for AIDS prevention. *Culture, Medicine and Psychiatry, 17,* 399–412.

Guttentag, M., & Secord, PF. (1993). *Too many women?* Beverly Hills, CA: Sage.

Ha, T., & Ickovics, J. (1996). Confronting the emerging AIDS epidemic in Vietnam: Social context and preliminary data on physicians preparedness. *AIDS, 10,* 1180–1181.

Hackl, K. L., Somlai, A. M., Kelly, J. A., & Kalichman, S. C. (1997). Women living with HIV/AIDS: The dual challenge of being patient and caregiver. *Health & Social Work, 22,* 53–62.

Harris, I. B. (1986). Investing in young children. *Zero to Three, 7,* 15–16.

Harris, N. V., Thiede, H., McGough, J. P., & Gordon, D. (1993). Risk factors for HIV infection among injection drug users: Results of blinded surveys in drug treatment centers, King County, Washington 1988–1991. *Journal of Acquired Immune Deficiency Syndromes, 6,* 1275–1282.

Heckman, T. G., Somlai, A. M., Peters, J., Walker, J., Otto-Salaj, L., Galdabini, C. A., & Kelly, J. A. (1998). Barriers to care among persons living with HIV/AIDS in urban and rural areas. *AIDS Care, 10*(3), 365–75.

Heimer, R., Kaplan, E. H., O'Keefe, E., Khoshnood, K., & Altice, F. (1994). Three years of needle exchange in New Haven: What have we learned? *AIDS & Public Policy Journal, 9,* 59–74.

Hein, K., Dell, R., Futterman, D., Rotheram-Borus, M. J., & Shaffer, N. (1995). Comparison of HIV+ and HIV–adolescents: Risk factors and psychosocial determinants. *Pediatrics, 95,* 96–104.

Henin, Y., Mandelbrot, L., Henrion, R., Pradinaud, R., Couland, J.P.K., & Montagnier, L. (1993). Virus excretion in the cervicovaginal secretions of pregnant and nonpregnant HIV-infected women. *Journal of Acquired Immune Deficiency Syndromes, 1,* 72–75.

Hobfoll, S. E. (1986). *Stress, social support and women.* Washington, DC: Hemisphere.

Hobfoll, S. E., Jackson, A., Lavin, J., Britton, P., & Shepard, J. (1993). Safer sex, knowledge, behavior and attitudes of inner city women. *Health Psychology, 12,* 481–488.

Hobfoll, S. E., Jackson, A. P., Lavin, J., Britton, P. J., & Shepard, J. B. (1994). Reducing inner-city women's AIDS risk activities: A study of single pregnant women. *Health Psychology, 13,* 397–403.

Holmberg, S. D. (1996). The estimated prevalence and incidence of HIV in 96 large U. S. metropolitan areas. *American Journal of Public Health, 86,* 642–654.

Hser, Y. I., Anglin, M. D., & McGlothin, W. (1987). Sex differences in addict careers: 1. Initiation of use. *American Journal of Drug and Alcohol Abuse, 13,* 33–57.

Huba, G. J., & Melchior, L. A. (1998). A model for adolescent-targeted HIV/AIDS services: conclusions from 10 adolescent-targeted projects funded by the Special Projects of National Significance Program of the Health Resources and Services Administration. *Journal of Adolescent Health, 23,* 11–27.

Husson, R., Lan, Y., Kojima, E., Venzon, D., Mitsuya, H., & McIntosh, K. (1995). Vertical transmission of human immunodeficiency virus Type 1: Autologous neutralizing antibody, virus loads and virus phenotype. *Journal of Pediatrics, 126,* 865–871.

Ickovics, J. R., Beren, S., Grigorenko, E., Druley, J., Morrill, A., & Rodin, J. (2000). *Pathways of risk: Disaggregating race and class as predictors of women's high-risk sexual behavior.* Manuscript submitted for publication.

Ickovics, J., Druley, J., Morrill, A., Grigorenko, E., & Rodin, J. (1998). "A grief observed": Women's experience of HIV-related illness and death. *Journal of Consulting and Clinical Psychology, 66,* 958–966.

Ickovics J. R., Forsyth, B., Ethier, K. A., Harris, P., & Rodin, J. (1996). Delayed entry into health care for women with HIV: Implications of time of diagnosis for early medical intervention. *AIDS Patient Care, 10,* 21–24.

Ickovics, J., Morrill, A., Beren, S., Walsh, U., & Rodin, J. (1994). Limited effects of HIV counseling and testing for women: A prospective study of behavioral and psychological consequences. *Journal of the American Medical Association, 272,* 443–448.

Ickovics, J. R., & Rodin, J. (1992). Women and AIDS in the United States: Epidemiology, natural history, and mediating mechanisms. *Health Psychology, 11,* 1–16.

Ickovics, J. R., & Yoshikawa, H. (1998). Preventive interventions to reduce heterosexual HIV risk for women: current persepctives, future directions. *AIDS, 12*(S), S197–S207.

Jemmott, L. S., Catan, V., Nyamathi, A., & Anastasia, J. (1995). African American women and HIV-risk reduction issues. In A. O'Leary & L. S. Jemmott (Eds.), *Women at risk: Issues in the primary prevention of AIDS* (pp. 131–157). New York: Plenum.

Jemmott, J. B., III., Jemmott, L. S., & Fong, G. T. (1998). Abstinence and safer sex HIV risk-reduction intervention for African American adolescents. *Journal of the American Medical Association, 279*(19), 1529–36.

Kaiser Family Foundation. (1998). *Sexually transmitted diseases in America: How many cases and at what cost?* American Social Health Association.

Kalichman, S., Hunter, T., & Kelly. (1992). The disclosure of celebrity HIV infection: Its effects on public attitudes. *American Journal of Public Health, 82,* 1374–1376.

Kalichman, S. C., Carey, M. P., & Johnson, B. T. (1996). Prevention of sexually transmitted HIV infection: A meta-analytic review of the behavioral outcome literature. *Annals of Behavioral Medicine, 18,* 6–15.

Kalichman, S. C., Roffman, R. A., Picciano, J. F., & Bolan, M. (1997). Sexual relationships, sexual behavior, and HIV infection: HIV-seropositive gay and bisexual men seeking prevention services. *Professional Psychology Research & Practice, 28*(4), 355–360.

Kane, F., Alary, M., Ndoye, I., Coll, A. M., M'boup, S., Gueye, A., Kanki, P. J., & Joly, J. R. (1993). Temporary expatriation is related to HIV-1 infection in rural Senegal. *AIDS, 7,* 1261–1265.

Kann, L., Warren, C., Harris, W., Collins, J., Williams, B., Ross, J., & Kolbe, L. (1995). Youth risk behavior surveillance—United States. *MMWR CDC Surveillance Summaries, 45,* 1–84.

Kellock, D. J., & O'Mahoney, C. P. (1996). Sexually acquired metronidazole-resistant trichomonas in a lesbian couple. *Genitourinary Medicine, 72,* 60–61.

Kelly, J. A., & Kalichman, S. C. (1995). Increased attention to human sexuality can improve HIV-AIDS prevention efforts: key research issues and directions. *Journal of Consulting and Clinical Psychology, 63,* 907–918.

Kelly, J. A., Murphy, D. A., Sikkema, K. J., McAuliffe, T. L., Roffman, R. A., Solomon, L. J., Winett, R. A., & Kalichman, S. C. (1997). Randomized, controlled, community-level HIV-prevention intervention for sexual-risk behavior among homosexual men in US cities: Community HIV prevention research collaborative. *Lancet, 350,* 1500–1505.

Kelly, J. A., Murphy, D. A., Sikkema, K. J., & Kalichman, S. C. (1993). Psychological interventions to prevent HIV infection are urgently needed. New priorities for behavioral research in the second decade of AIDS. *American Psychologist, 48,* 1023–1034.

Kelly, J. A., Murphy, D. A., Washington, C. D., Wilson, T. S., Koob, J. J., Davis, D. R., Ledzema, G., & Davantes, B. (1994). The effects of HIV/AIDS intervention groups for high-risk women in urban clinics. *American Journal of Public Health, 84,* 1918–1922.

Kennedy, M., Scarlett, M., Duerr, A., & Chu, S. (1995). Assessing HIV risk among women who have sex with women: Scientific and communication issues. *Journal of the American Medical Women's Association, 50,* 103–107.

Kessler, R. C. (1979). Stress, social status and psychological distress. *Journal of Health and Social Behavior, 20,* 259–272.

Kippax, S., Crawford, J., Davis, M., Rodden, P., & Dowsett, G. (1993). Sustaining safe sex: A longitudinal study of a sample of homosexual men. *AIDS, 7,* 257–263.

Kippax, S., Noble, J., Prestage, G., Crawford, J. M., Campbell, D., Baxter, D., & Cooper, D. (1997). Sexual negioation in the AIDS era. *AIDS, 11,* 191–197.

Kirscht, J. P. (1983). Preventative health behavior: A review of research and issues. *Health Psychology, 2,* 277–301.

Kimball, A. M., Gonzalez, R., & Zacarias F. (1991). AIDS among women in Latin America and the Caribbean. *Bulletin of PAHO, 25,* 367–373.

Klevens, R. M., Diaz, T., Fleming, P. L., Mays, M. A., & Frey, R. (1999). Trends in AIDS among Hispanics in the United States. *American Journal of Public Health, 89*(7), 1104–1106.

Korn, A. P., & Abercrombie, P. D. (1997). Gynecology and family planning care for the woman infected with HIV. *Obstetrics & Gynecology Clinics of North America, 24*(4), 855–872.

Krieger, N., & Margo, G. (1990). AIDS: The politics of survival: Introduction. *International Journal of Health Services, 20,* 583–588.

Kumar, R., Uduman, S., & Khurranna, A. (1995). Impact of maternal HIV-1 infection on perinatal outcome. *International Journal of Gynecology and Obstetrics, 49,* 137–143.

Laga, M., Nzila, N., Manoka, A. T., Malele, M., Bush, T. J., Behets, F., Heyward, W. L., Piot, P., & Ryder, R. (1990). *Non ulcerative sexually transmitted diseases (STD) as risk factors for HIV infection.* Paper presented at the Sixth International AIDS Conference, San Francisco.

Lagarde, E., Pison, G., & Enel, C. (1996). Knowledge, attitudes and perception of AIDS in rural Senegal: Relationship to sexual behavior and behavior change. *AIDS, 10,* 327–334.

Landesman, S., Kalish, L., Burns, D., Minkoff, H., Fox, H., Zorrilla, C., Garcia, P., Fowler, M., Mofenson, L., & Tuomala, R. (1996). Obstetrical factors and the transmission of human immunodeficiency virus type 1 from mother to child. *New England Journal of Medicine, 334,* 1617–1623.

Lantz, P. M., House, J. S., Lepkowski, J. M., Williams, D. R., Mero, R. P., & Chen, J. (1999). Socioeconomic factors, health behaviors, and mortality: Results from a nationally representative prospective study of US adults. *Journal of the American Medical Association, 279,* 1703–1708.

Latkin, C., Mandell, W., Oziemkowska, M., Celentano, D., Vlahov, D., Ensminger, M., & Knowlton, A. (1995). Using social network analysis to study patterns of drug use among urban drug users at high risk for HIV/AIDS. *Drug and Alcohol Dependence, 38,* 1–9.

Laumann, E. O., Gagnon, J. H., Michael, R. T., & Michaels, S. (1996). *The social organization of sexuality: Sexual practices in the United States.* Chicago: University of Chicago Press.

Lea, A. (1994). Women with HIV and their burden of caring. *Health Care for Women International, 15,* 489–501.

Lemp, G. F., Jone, M., Kellogg, T. A., Nieri, G. N., Anderson, L., Withum, D., & Katz, M. (1995). HIV seroprevalence and risk behaviors among lesbians and bisexual women in San Francisco and Berkeley, CA. *American Journal of Public Health, 85,* 1549–1552.

Lester, P, Partridge J. C., Chesney, & M. A., Cooke, M. (1995). The consequences of a positive prenatal HIV antibody test for women. *Journal of AIDS & Human Retrovirology, 10,* 341–349.

Lever, J. (1995). Lesbian sex survey. *Advocate,* 23–30.

Lewin, K. (1951/1972). *Field theory for the behavioral sciences.* Chicago: University of Chicago Press (Midway Reprints).

Lillie-Blanton, M., Anthony, J. C., & Schuster. C. R. (1993). Probing the meaning of racial/ethnic group comparisons in crack cocaine smoking. *Journal of the American Medical Association, 269,* 993–997.

Lindegren, M. L., Byers, R. H. Jr., Thomas, P., Davis, S. F., Caldwell, B., Rogers, M., Gwinn, M., Ward, & J. W., Fleming, P. L. (1999). Trends in perinatal transmission of HIV/AIDS in the United States. *Journal of the American Medical Association, 282*(6), 531–538.

Livingston, I. L. (1992). AIDS/HIV crisis in developing countries: The need for greater understanding and innovative health promotion approaches. *Journal of the National Medical Association, 84,* 755–770.

Low, N., et al. (1993). AIDS in Nicaragua: Epidemiological, political, and sociocultural perspectives. *International Journal of Health Services, 23,* 685–702.

Lurie P., Hintzen P., & Lowe R. A. (1995). Socioeconomic obstacles to HIV prevention and treatment in developing countries: The roles of the International Monetary Fund and the World Bank. *AIDS, 9,* 539–546.

Mann, J., Tarantola, D. J., & Netter, T. W. (Eds.). (1992). *AIDS in the World: The Global AIDS Policy Coalition.* Cambridge, MA: Harvard University Press.

Marín, G. (1989). AIDS prevention among Hispanics: Needs, risk behaviors and cultural values. *Public Health Reports, 104,* 411–415.

Marin, B. V., Tschann, J. M., Gomez, C. A., & Kegeles, S. M. (1993). Acculturation and gender differences in sexual attitudes and behaviors: Hispanic vs. non-Hispanic white unmarried adults. *American Journal of Public Health, 83,* 1759–1761.

Marmor, M., Weiss, L. R., Lyden, M., Weiss, S. H., Saxinger, W. C., Spira, T. J., & Feorino, P. M. (1986). Possible female-to-female transmission of human immunodeficiency virus. *Annals of Internal Medicine, 105,* 969.

Mason, H., Marks, G., Simoni, J., Ruiz, M., & Richardson, J. (1995). Culturally sanctioned secrets? Latino men's nondisclosure of HIV infection to family, friends and lovers. *Health Psychology, 14,* 6–12.

Massad, L. S., Riester, K. A., Anastos, K. M., Fruchter, R. G., Palefsky, J. M., Burk, R. D., Burns, D., Greenblatt, R. M., Muderspach, L. I., Miotti, P. (1999). Prevalence and predictors of squamous cell abnormalities in Papanicolaou smears from women infected with HIV-1: Women's Interagency HIV Study Group. *Journal of Acquired Immune Deficiency Syndromes, 21*(1), 33–41.

Matarazzo, J. (1980). Behavioral health and behavioral medicine: Frontiers for a new health psychology. *American Psychologist, 35,* 807–817.

Matthews, K. A., Kelsey, S. F., Meilahn, E. N., Kuller, L. H., & Wing, R. R. (1989). Educational attainment and behavioral and biological risk factors for coronary heart disease in middle-aged women. *American Journal of Epidemiology, 129,* 1132–1144.

Mays, V., & Cochran, S. (1988). Issues in the perception of AIDS risk and risk reduction activities by Black and Hispanic/Latino women. *American Psychologist, 43,* 949–957.

McCoy, H. V., & Inciardi, J. A. (1993). Women and AIDS: Social determinants of sex-related activities. *Women and Health, 20,* 69–86.

McLeod, J. D., & Kessler, R. C. (1990). Socioeconomic status differences in vulnerability to undesirable life events. *Journal of Health and Social Behavior, 31,* 162–172.

Mechanic, D. (1994). Socioeconomic status and health. In D. Mechanic (Ed.), *Inescapable decisions: The imperatives of health reform* (pp. 137–150). New Brunswick, NJ: Transaction.

Menendez, B. S., Drucker, E., Vermund S. H., Castano, R. R., Perez-Agosto, R. R., Parga, F., & Blum, S. (1990). AIDS mortality among Puerto Rican and other Hispanics in New York City. *Journal of Acquired Immunodeficiency Syndrome, 3,* 644–648.

Merrick, E. (1995). Adolescent childbearing as career "choice": Perspective from an ecological context. *Journal of Counseling and Development, 73,* 288–293.

Michaels, D., & Levine, C. (1992). Estimates of the number of motherless youth orphaned by AIDS in the United States. *Journal of the American Medical Association, 268,* 3456.

Miller, H. G., Turner, C. F., & Moses, L. (Eds.). (1990). *AIDS: The second decade.* Washington, DC: National Academy Press.

Millstein, S. G., & Moscicki, A. B. (1995). Sexually-transmitted disease in female adolescents: Effects of psychosocial factors and high risk behaviors. *Journal of Adolescent Health, 17,* 83–90.

Mofenson, L. M., Lambert, J. S., Stiehm, E. R., Bethel, J., Meyer, W. A., 3rd, Whitehouse, J., Moye, J., Jr., Reichelderfer, P., Harris, D. R., Fowler, M. G., Mathieson, & B. J., Nemo, G. J. (1999). Risk factors for perinatal transmission of human immunodeficiency virus Type 1 in women treated with zidovudine: Pediatric AIDS Clinical Trials Group Study. *New England Journal of Medicine, 341*(6), 385–393.

Monzon, O. T., & Capellan, J.M.B. (1987). Female-to-female transmission of HIV. *Lancet, 2,* 40–41.

Moodley, D., Bobat, R., Coutsoudis, A., & Coovadia, H. (1994). Caesarean section and vertical transmission of HIV-1. *Lancet, 344,* 338.

Moore, J., Warren, D., Zierler, S., Schuman, P., Solomon, L., Schoenbaum, E., & Kennedy, M. (1996). Characteristics of HIV-infected lesbian and bisexual women in four urban centers. *Women's Health: Research on Gender, Behavior, and Policy, 2,* 49–60.

Moore, J., Schuman, P., Schoenbaum, E., Boland, B., Solomon, L., & Smith, D. (1999). Severe adverse life events and depressive symptoms among women with or at risk for HIV infection in four cities in the United States. *AIDS, 13,* 2459–2468.

Morrill, A. (1994). *Women and heterosexual relationships: An interpersonal model of HIV risk.* Unpublished doctoral dissertation, Boston College, Boston, MA.

Morrill, A. C., Ickovics, J. R., Golubchikov, V., Beren, S. E., & Rodin, J. (1996). Safer sex: Predictors of behavioral maintenance and change for heterosexual women. *Journal of Consulting and Clinical Psychology.*

Morris, R. E., Harrison, E. A., Knox, G. W., Tromanhauser, E., & Marquis, D. K. (1995). Health risk behavioural survey from 39 juvenile correctional facilities in the United States. *Journal of Adolescent Health, 17,* 334–344.

Morrow, K. M. (1995). In A. O'Leary & L. S. Jemmott (Eds.), *Women at risk: Issues in the primary prevention of AIDS.* New York: Plenum.

Morrow, K. M., Fuqua, R. W., & Meinhold, P. M. (1994). *Self- reported HIV risk behaviors and serostatus in lesbian and bisexual women.* Paper presented at the Convention of the American Psychological Association: Psychosocial and Behavioral Factors in Women's Health: Creating an Agenda for the 21st Century.

Morrow, K. M., Meinhold, P. M., & Fuqua, R. W. (1994). *Incidence of HIV-related risk behaviors and seropositivity in lesbian/bisexual women's communities.* Paper presented at the 15th Anniversary Convention of the Society of Behavioral Medicine, Boston, MA.

Moscher, W., & Bachrach, C. (1986). *Contraceptive use* (Publication No. 86-1988). Hyattsville, MD: National Center for Health Statistics.

Moss, N. (1994). Behavioral risks for HIV in adolescents. *Acta Paediatrica, 400*(Suppl.), 81–87.

Mulder, D., Nunn, A., Wagner, H., Kamali, A., & Kengeya-Kayondo, J. (1994). HIV-1 incidence and HIV-1 associated mortality in a rural Ugandan population cohort. *AIDS, 8,* 97–92.

Murray, J. K. (1938). *Explorations in personality.* New York: Oxford University Press.

National Institutes of Health (1997; February 11–13). *National Institutes of Health Consensus Development Statement: Interventions to prevent HIV risk behaviors, 15*(2), 1–41, Rockville, MD.

Musoke, P, Guay, L. A., Bagenda, D, Mirochnick, M., Nakabiito, C., Fleming, T., Elliott, T., Horton, S., Dransfield, K., Pav, J. W., Murarka, A., Allen, M., Fowler, M. G., Mofenson, L., Hom, D., Mmiro, F., & Jackson, J. B. (1999). A phase I/II study of the safety and pharmacokinetics of nevirapine in HIV-1 infected pregnanct Ugandan women and their neonates (HIVNET 006). *AIDS, 13,* 479–486.

Navarro, V. (1990). Race or class versus race and class: Mortality differentials in the United States. *Lancet, 336,* 1238–1240.

Nyamathi, A., Wayment, H., & Dunkel-Schetter, C. (1993). Psychosocial correlates of emotional distress and risk behavior in Black women at risk for HIV infection. *Anxiety Stress and Coping, 6,* 133–148.

Nyamathi, A., Stein, J., & Brecht, M. (1995). Psychosocial predictors of AIDS risk behavior and drug use behavior in homeless and drug addicted women of color. *Health Psychology, 14,* 265–273.

Office of National AIDS Policy (1996). *Youth & HIV/AIDS: An American agenda: A report to the President.* Washington, DC: The White House.

O'Hanlan, K. (1993). *Lesbians in health research.* Paper presented at the Scientific Conference on Recruitment and Retention of Women in Health Research, Stanford, CA.

O'Hanlan, D. A., & Crum, C. P. (1996). Human papillomavirus-associates cervical intraepithelial neoplasia following lesbian sex. *Obstetrics and Gynecology, 88,* 702–703.

Orr, D. P., & Langefeld, C. D. (1993). Factors associated with condom use by sexually active male adolescents at risk for sexually transmitted disease. *Pediatrics, 91,* 873–879.

Padian, N. S., Shiboski, S., & Jewell, N. (1990). The effect of the number of exposures on the risk of heterosexual HIV transmission. *Journal of Infectious Disease, 161,* 883–887.

Padian, N. S., Shiboski, S., Glass, S., & Vittinghoff, E. (1997). Heterosexual transmission of HIV in Northern California: Results from a 10 year study. *American Journal of Epidemiology, 146,* 350–357.

Parker, R. (1987). Acquired immunodeficiency syndrome in urban Brazil. *Medical Anthropology Quarterly,* 155–165.

Perry, S., Jacobsberg, L., & Fogel, K. (1989). Orogenital transmission of human immunodefiency virus. *Annal of Internal Medicine, 111,* 951.

Pincus, T., & Callahan, L. F. (1985). Formal education as a marker for increased mortality and morbidity in rheumatoid arthritis. *Journal of Chronic Disease, 38,* 973–984.

Pincus, T., Callahan, L. F., & Burkhauser, R. V. (1987). Most chronic disease are reported more frequently by individuals with fewer than 12 years of formal education in the age 18–64 U. S. population. *Journal of Chronic Disease, 40,* 865–874.

Piot, P., et al. (1988). AIDS: An international perspective. *Science, 239,* 573–579.

Pivnick, A., Jacobson, A., Eric, K., Doll, L., & Drucker, E. (1994). AIDS, HIV infection, and illicit drug use within inner-city families and social networks. *American Journal of Public Health, 84,* 271–273.

Plumb, M., Schaper, P., & Escoffier, J. (1996). *Oral sex review: HIV transmission risk of cunnilingus.* New York: Office of Gay and Lesbian Concerns.

Plummer, F. A., Simonsen, J. N., Cameron, D. W., Ndinya-Achola, J. O., Kreiss, J. K., Gakinya, M. N., Waiyaki, P., Cheang, M., Piot, P., & Romald, A. R. (1991). Co-factors in male-to-female transmission of HIV. *Journal of Infectious Diseases, 163,* 133–139.

Polaneczky, M., Slap, G., & Forke, C. (1994). The use of levonorgestrel implants (Norplant) for contraception in adolescent mothers. *New England Journal of Medicine, 331,* 1201–1206.

Revenson, T. (1990). All other things are not equal: An ecological approach to personality and disease. In H. S. Friedman (Ed.), *Personality and disease* (pp. 65–94). New York: Wiley.

Rich, J. D., Buck, A., Toumala, R. E., & Kanzajian, P. H. (1993). Transmission of human immunodeficiency virus infection presumed to have occurred via female homosexual contact. *Clinical Infectious Disease, 17,* 1003–1005.

Rickman, R. L., Lodico, M., DiClemente, R. J., Morris, R., Baker, C., & Huscroft, S. (1994). Sexual communication is associated with condom use by sexually active incarcerated adolescents. *Journal of Adolescent Health, 15,* 383–388.

Rieder, I., & Ruppelt, P. (Eds.). (1988). *AIDS: The women.* San Francisco: Cleis Press.

Rodin, J., & Ickovics, J. R. (1990). Women's health: Review and research agenda as we approach the 21st century. *American Psychologist, 45,* 1018–1034.

Rogot, E. (1992). *A mortality study of 1.3 million persons by demographic, social, and economic factors: 1979–1985 follow-up: U.S. National longitudinal mortality study.* Bethesda, MD: National Institute of Health, National Health, Lung, and Blood Institute.

Rosenbaum, M. (1981). *Women on heroin.* New Brunswick, NJ: Rutgers University Press.

Rosenberg, P. S., & Biggar, R. J. (1998). Trends in HIV incidence among young adults in the United States. *Journal of the American Medical Association, 279*(23), 1894–1899.

Rosenstock, I. (1974). The health belief model and preventive health behavior. *Health Education Monographs, 2,* 328–335.

Rotheram-Borus, M. J., Meyer-Bahlburg, H. F. L., & Koopman, C. (1992). Lifetime sexual behaviors among runaway males and females. *Journal of Sex Research, 29,* 15–29.

Rounds, K., Galinsky, M., & Stevens, L. (1991). Linking people with AIDS in rural communities: The telephone group. *Social Work, 36,* 13–18.

Rouzioux, C., Costagliola, D., Burgard, M., Blanche, S., Mayaux, M. J., Griscelli, C., & Valleron, A. J. (1993). Timing of mother-to-child HIV-1 transmission depends on maternal status. *AIDS, 7*(Suppl. 2), S49–S52.

Royce, R. A., Sena, A., Cates, W., & Cohen, M. S. (1997). Sexual Transmission of HIV. *New England Journal of Medicine,* 1072–1078.

Rwandan HIV Seropositive Study Group. (1989). Nationwide community-based serological survey of HIV-1 and other human retrovirus infections in a Central African country. *Lancet, I,* 941–943.

Ryder, R. W., Nsa, W., Hassig, S. E., Behets, F., Rayfield, M., & Bayende, E., et al. (1989). Perinatal transmission of the human immunodeficiency virus: One year follow-up of 475 infants born to seropositive women in Zaire. *New England Journal of Medicine, 320,* 1637–1642.

Sabatini, M. T., Patel, K., & Hirschman, R. (1984). Kaposi's sarcoma and T-cell lymphoma in an immunodeficient woman: A case report. *AIDS Research, 1,* 135–137.

Santelli, J., Davis, M., & Celantano, D. (1995). Combined use of condoms with other contraceptive methods among inner-city Baltimore women. *Family Planning Perspectives, 27,* 74–78.

Schable, B., Chu, S. Y., & Diaz, T. (1996). Characteristics of women 50 years of age or older with heterosexually acquired AIDS. *American Journal of Public Health, 86,* 1616–1618.

Schiller, N. (1993). The invisible women: Caregiving and the construction of AIDS health services. *Culture, Medicine and Psychiatry, 17,* 487–512.

Selik, R. M., Castro, K., Pappaioanou, M., & Buchler, J. (1989). Birthplace and the risk of AIDS among Hispanics in the United States. *American Journal of Public Health, 79,* 836–839.

Selwyn, P. A. (1996). Before their time: A clinician's reflections on death and AIDS. In H. Spiro, & M. Kernan, et al. (Eds.), *Facing death.* New Haven, CT: Yale University Press.

Selwyn, P., Feiner, C., Cox, C., Lipshutz, C., & Cohen, R. (1987). Knowledge about AIDS and high risk behavior among injection drug users in New York City. *AIDS, 1,* 247–254.

Shaffer, N., Chuachoowong, R, Mock, P. A., Bhadrakom, C. Siriwasin, W., Young, N. L., chotpitayasunondh, T, Chearskul, S., Roongpisuthipong, A., Chinayon, P., Karon, J., Mastro, T. D., & Simonds, R. J. (1999). Short-course Zidovudine for perinatal HIV-1 transmission in Bangkok, Thailand: A randomized controlled trial. *Lancet, 353,* 773.

Shain, R. N., Piper, J. M., Newton, E. R., Perdue, S. T., Ramos, R., Champion, J. D., & Guerra, F. A. (1999). A randomized, controlled trial of a behavioral intervention to prevent sexually transmitted disease among minority women. *New England Journal of Medicine, 340*(2), 93–100.

Shapiro, D, E., Sperling, R. S., & Coombs, R. W. (1999). Effect of Zidovudine on perinatal HIV-1 transmission and maternal viral load. *Lancet, 354,* 156.

Shapiro, M. F., Morton, S. C., McCaffrey, D. F., Senterfitt, J. W., Fleishman, J. A., Perlman, J. F., Athey, L. A., Keesey, J. W., Goldman, D. P., Berry, S. H., & Bozzette, S. A. (1999). Variations in the care of HIV-infected adults in the United States: Results from the HIV Cost and Services Utilization Study. *Journal of the American Medical Association, 281*(24), 2305–2315.

Shernoff, M. (1996). Returning with AIDS: Supporting rural emigrants. *FOCUS: A Guide to AIDS Research and Counseling, 11,* 4.

Sikkema, K. J., Kelly, J. A., Winett, R. A., Solomon, L. J., Cargill, V. A., Roffman, R. A., McAuliffe, T. L., Heckman, T. G., Anderson, E. A., Wagstaff, D. A., Norman, A. D., Perry, M. J., Crumble, D. A., & Mercer, M. G., (2000). Outcomes of a randomized community-level HIV prevention intervention for women living in 18 low-income housing developments. *American Journal of Public Health, 90,* 57–63.

Simons, M. (1996, June 7). HIV is still spreading rapidly, U.N. says. *The New York Times.*

Smith, D. K., & Moore, J. S. (1995). Epidemiology, manifestations, and treatment of HIV infection in women. In A. O'Leary & L. S. Jemmott (Eds.), *Women at risk: Issues in the primary prevention of AIDS* (pp. 1–32). New York: Plenum.

Smith, D. K., Warren, D. L., Viahov, D., Shcuman, P., Stein, M. D., Greeberg, B. L., & Homberg, S. D. (1997). Design and baseline particpant characteristics of the human immunodefiency virus epidemiology research (HER) study: A prospective cohort study of human immunodeficiency virus infection in US women. *American Journal of Epidemiology, 146,* 1–12.

Smyke, P. (1991). *Women and health.* New Jersey: Zed Books.

Solomon, L., Stein, M., Flynn, C., Schuman, P., Schoenbaum, E., Moore, J., Holmberg, S., & Graham, N. M. (1998). Health services use by urban women with or at risk for HIV-1 infection: The HIV Epidemiology Research Study (HERS). *Journal of Acquired Immune Deficiency Syndromes (JAIDS), 17*(3), 253–261.

Sorvillo F., Kerndt P., Cheng K., Beall G., Turner P., Beer V., & Kovacs A. (1995). Emerging patterns of HIV transmission: The value of alternative surveillance methods. *AIDS, 9,* 625–629.

Spence, J. T., Deaux, K., & Helmreich, R. L. (1985). Sex roles in contemporary American society. In G. Lindzey & E. Aronson (Eds.), *Handbook of social psychology* (Vol. 2, pp. 149–178). New York: Random House.

Stevens, P. E. (1993). *HIV risk reduction for three subgroups of lesbian and bisexual women in San Francisco. (Year One project evaluation report).* San Francisco: Lyon-Martin Women's Health services.

St. Lawrence, J. (1993). African-American adolescents' knowledge, health-related attitudes, sexual behavior, and contraceptive decisions: Implications for the prevention of adolescent HIV infection. *Journal of Consulting and Clinical Psychology, 61,* 104–112.

St. Louis, M., Wasserheit, J., & Gayle, H. (1997). Janus considers the HIV pandemic: Harnessing recent advances to enhance AIDS prevention. *American Journal of Public Health, 87,* 10–12.

Stall, R., & Catania, J. (1994). AIDS risk behaviors among late middle-aged and elderly Americans. *Archives of Internal Medicine, 154,* 57–63.

Stark, M., Tesselaar, H., Fleming, D., O'Connell, A., & Armstrong, K. (1996). Contraceptive method and condom use among women at risk for HIV infection and other sexually transmitted diseases—Selected U.S. sites, 1993–1994. *Morbidity and Mortality Weekly Report, 45,* 820–823.

Stoto, M. A., Almario, D. A., & McCormic, M. C. (1999). Reducing the odds: Preventing perinatal transmission of HIV in the United States. Washington, DC: Institute of Medicine, National Academy Press.

Stryker, S., & Statham, A. (1985). Symbolic interaction and role theory. In G. Lindzey & E. Aronson (Eds.), *Handbook of social psychology, I* (pp. 311–378). New York: Random House.

Sun, X. W., Kuhn, L., Ellerbrock, T. V., Chiasson, M. A., Bush, T. J., & Wright, T. C. Jr. (1997). Human papillomavirus infection in women infected with the human immunodeficiency virus. *New England Journal of Medicine, 337*(19), 1343–1349.

Tartaglia, A. (1996). AIDS and the rural church. *FOCUS: A Guide to AIDS Research and Counseling, 11,* 5.

Tesh, S. (1988). *Hidden arguments, political ideology and disease prevention policy.* New Brunswick, NJ: Rutgers University Press.

Torres, J. B. (1998). Masculinity and gender roles among Puerto Rican men: Machismo on the U.S. mainland. *American Journal of Orthopsychiatry, 78,* 16–26.

Treichler, P. A. (1988). AIDS, gender and biomedical discourse. In E. Fee & D. Fox (Eds.), *AIDS: The burden of history.* Berkeley: University of California Press.

Triandis, H., Marin, G., & Lisansky, J. B. (1984). Simpatia as a cultural script for Hispanics. *Journal of Personality and Social Psychology, 47,* 1363–1375.

Turner, R. J., Wheaton, B., & Lloyd, D. A. (1995). The epidemiology of social stress. *American Sociological Review, 60,* 104–125.

Uchino, B., Cacioppo, J., & Kiecolt-Glaser, J. (1996). The relationship between social support and physiological processes: A review with emphasis on underlying mechanisms and implications for health. *Psychological Bulletin, 3,* 488–531.

UNAIDS. (1999, December). *AIDS epidemic update: December 1999.* Geneva, Switzerland: UNAIDS/World Health Organization.

United Nations, Department of Economic and Social Affairs of the United Nations Secretariat. (1999). *The demographic impact of HIV/AIDS.* New York: United Nations.

U.S. Bureau of the Census. (1995). *Statistical abstract of the United States 1995.* Washington, DC: U.S. Department of Commerce.

U.S. Bureau of the Census. (1997). *1997 Statistical abstract of the United States.* Washington, DC: U.S. Department of Commerce.

Van de Perr, P., De Clerq, A., & Coniaux-Leclerc, J. (1988). Detection of HIV p17 antigen in lymphocytes but not epithelial cells from cervicovaginal secretions of women seropositive for HIV: Implications for heterosexual transmission of the virus. *Genitourin Medicine, 1,* 30–33.

Van de Perre, P., Simonon, A., Msellati, P., Hitimana, D. G., Vaira, D., Bazubagira, A., Van Goethem, C., Stevens, A. M., Karita, E., Sondag-Thull, D., et al. (1991). Postnatal transmission of human immunodeficiency virus Type 1 from mother to infant. A prospective cohort study in Kigali, Rwanda. *New England Journal of Medicine, 325,* 593–598.

Vogt, M. W., Witt, D. J., & Craven, D. E. (1986). Isolation of HTLV-III/LAV from cervical secretions of women at risk for AIDS. *Lancet, 8480,* 525–527.

Vogt, M. W., Witt, D. J., & Craven, D. E. (1987). Isolation patterns of the human immunodeficiency virus from cervical secretions during the menstrual cycle of women at risk for acquired immunodefiency syndrome. *Annals of Internal Medicine, 3,* 380–382.

Wade, A., Dieng-Sang, A., & Diall, A. A., et al. (1992). Epidemiologic trends of HIV-1 and HIV-2 infection in an HIV-2 endemic area: The Senegalese experience 1989–1991. Abstract No. WeC 1067. *The Eighth International Conference on AIDS,* Amsterdam, The Netherlands.

Wade, N. A., Birkhead, G. S., Warren, B. L., Charbonneau, T. T., French, P. T., Wang, L., Baum, J. B., Tesoriero, J. M., & Savicki, R. (1998). Abbreviated regimens of zidovudine prophylaxis and perinatal transmission of the human immunodeficiency virus. *New England Journal of Medicine, 339,* 1409–1414.

Weeks, M. R., Singer, M., Himmelgreen, D. A., Richmond, P., Grier, M., & Radda, K. (1998). Drug use patterns of substance abusing women: Gender and ethnic differences in an AIDS prevention program. *Drugs & Society, 13*(1–2), 35–61.

Weisman, C., Plichta, S., & Nathanson, C. (1991). Consistency of condom use for disease prevention among adolescent users of oral contraception. *Family Planning Perspectives, 23,* 71–74.

Weissman, G., & Brown, V. (1995). Drug-using women and HIV: Risk-reduction and prevention issues. In A. O'Leary & L. Jemmott (Eds.), *Women at risk: Issues in the primary prevention of AIDS.* New York: Plenum.

Wight, R. G., LeBlanc, A. J., & Aneshensel, C. S. (1998). AIDS Caregiving and health among midlife and older women. *Health Psychology, 17,* 130–137.

Wilkins, H. A., Alonson, P., Balden, S., & et al. (1989). Knowledge of AIDS, use of condoms and results of counseling subjects asymptomatic HIV-2 infection in the Gambia. *AIDS Care, 1,* 247–256.

Williams, D. R. (1990). Socioeconomic differentials in health: A review and redirection. *Social Psychology Quarterly, 53,* 81–99.

Williams, D. R., & Collins, C. (1995). U. S. Socioeconomic and racial differences in health: Patterns and explanations. *Annual Review of Sociology, 21,* 349–386.

Wofsy, C. (1987). Human immunodeficiency virus in women. *Journal of the American Medical Association, 257,* 2074–2076.

Wofsy, C., Cohen, J. S., Hauer, L. B., Padian, N. S., Michaelis, B. A., Evans, L. A., & Levy, J. A. (1986). Isolation of AIDS-associated retrovirus from genital secretions of women with antibodies to the virus. *Lancet, 1*(8480), 527–529.

World Health Organization. (1993, September). *13 million HIV positive women by 2000.* (Press Release WHO/69).

Worth, D. (1990). Minority women and AIDS: Culture, race, and gender. In D. A. Feldman (Ed.), *Culture and AIDS.* New York: Praeger.

Worth, D., & Rodriguez, R. (1987). Latina women and AIDS. *Radical America, 20,* 63.

Wortley, P. M., & Fleming, P. L. (1997). AIDS in women in the United States. Recent trends. *Journal of the American Medical Association, 278,* 911–916.

Yates, M. E., Stellato, R. K., Johannes, C. B., & Avis, N. E. (1999). The importance of AIDS-related knowledge for mid-life and older women. *AIDS Education & Prevention, 11*(3), 224–231.

Zablotsky, D. L. (1998). Overlooked, ignored and forgotten: Older women at risk for HIV infection and AIDS. *Research on Aging, 20,* 760–75.

Zborowski, M. (1958). Cultural components in response to pain. In E. G. Jaco (Ed.), *Patients, physicians and illness* (pp. 256–268). New York: The Free Press.

Zierler, S., & Krieger, N. (1997). Reframing women's risk: Social inequalities and HIV infection. *Annual Review of Public Health, 18,* 401–436.

Zorr, B., Schafer, A. P., & Dilger, I. (1994). HIV-I detection in endocervical swabs and mode of HIV-1 infection. *Lancet, 343,* 852.

50

Living With HIV Disease

Sheryl L. Catz
Jeffrey A. Kelly
Medical College of Wisconsin

The first cases of AIDS were identified in the United States nearly two decades ago. Many characteristics of AIDS quickly set the disease apart from other illnesses. One was the early association of AIDS with casual sex, and with homosexual behavior in particular. Initially and briefly known as "gay-related infectious disease" (GRID), AIDS appeared as a disease carrying unique stigma related to homosexuality, drug use, and other lifestyle issues that elicit social disapproval. Although other sexually transmitted diseases (STDs) have long been known, few are as fatal and there is little modern precedent—other than syphilis in the era before antibiotics—for a debilitating, incurable, fatal sexually transmitted infection. Especially in the AIDS epidemic's early years, there were widespread fears (bordering at times on hysteria) concerning possible disease transmission during everyday social contact. Although much has changed in public understanding of AIDS and in attitudes toward persons with the disease, these changes are not universal and AIDS still carries considerable stigma.

There has also been a steady progression in scientific and medical knowledge about AIDS and in progress toward more effective treatments for the disease. Two of the early benchmarks in this progression were the identification of human immunodeficiency virus (HIV) infection as the agent responsible for the illness and a reconceptualization of the disease process away from its focus on AIDS alone and toward a larger spectrum of HIV-related conditions. As the pathogenesis of HIV-related disease became better known, treatment advances have also occurred and, in recent years, have dramatically advanced. Although AIDS continues to take many lives, new treatments hold out the promise of longer and healthier life for some persons with HIV disease.

Kobayashi (1997) pointed out that the psychosocial and coping issues that confront people living with HIV/AIDS have changed throughout the history of the disease, in large part related to the evolution of treatments for HIV/AIDS. From a point early in the AIDS epidemic when the disease was seen as invariably fatal and effective treatment did not exist, HIV medical care has evolved to the point where both patients and health care providers can now approach disease management from at least a guardedly optimistic perspective. These treatment advances have also influenced the psychological coping issues faced by persons living with HIV. Psychological interventions remain critical for helping patients cope with the ramifications of HIV disease and benefiting from new treatments, as they have throughout the history of AIDS. However, and in parallel with HIV medical care advances, the psychological needs of persons with HIV are different than earlier in the AIDS epidemic.

This chapter describes psychological issues raised by HIV treatment advances. This discussion focuses on mental health and health behavior aspects of HIV disease, and on the interplay between medical advances and psychological care needs. Attention is especially focused in four areas: potential adjustment and coping challenges faced by persons living with HIV in this era of new HIV medical advances, issues related to patient adherence to new HIV treatment regimens, sexual or drug use risk behavior among HIV-seropositive and seronegative persons, and the emerging nature of HIV as a serious, chronic, but often manageable disease.

PSYCHOLOGICAL AND COPING CHALLENGES FACING PERSONS WITH HIV IN AN ERA OF NEW TREATMENTS

Although HIV was known to be the agent responsible for AIDS since the early 1980s, little was understood about the nature of the virus and there were at first no effective treatments for HIV disease. Prophylactic and palliative care were available to manage some AIDS-related opportunistic diseases, but no medical interventions were able to directly target the underlying HIV infection responsible for those diseases. Psychosocial research on AIDS in the early 1980s often found—not surprisingly—evidence of pervasive depression, suicidality, and adjustment disorders among predominantly young persons diagnosed with a debilitating, fatal, frightening, and highly stigmatized disease (e.g., Dilley, Ochitill, Perl, & Volberding, 1985; Perry & Tross, 1984). In this early era, one technological advance with important psychosocial ramifications was the availability of antibody tests beginning in 1985. From a medical standpoint, the ability to identify persons with HIV who had not yet developed AIDS opened new opportunities for their participation in clinical drug trials. On a societal level, increased compassion and activism followed the knowledge that HIV could not be transmitted through casual contact (Kobayashi, 1997). Given the limited treatment options at that time, a central question facing many at-risk individuals was whether or not to get "tested." Knowing their serostatus might help prevent the spread of HIV to others, but did little to protect individuals from facing what was often feared to be a "death sentence." Because most cases of HIV infection and AIDS occurred within the gay community and among injection drug users' (IDUs) social networks, the coping resources of persons in these communities were also often taxed by their experiences with multiple AIDS-related deaths (Martin & Dean, 1993).

Following the development in 1987 of the first antiviral medication, zidovudine (AZT), HIV prognoses and treatments were viewed somewhat more hopefully (Rabkin, Williams, Neugebauer, Remien, & Goetz, 1990). Mental health research at the time also began to identify more complex patterns of coping and adjustment to HIV disease (Folkman, Chesney, Pollack, & Coates, 1993; Hays, Turner, & Coates, 1992) and more individual variation in how persons psychologically adapted to their illness (Williams, Rabkin, Remien, Gorman, & Ehrhardt, 1991). However, this initial hopefulness was followed by disillusionment as the long-term benefits of available antiviral therapies like AZT alone came into doubt. Despite these concerns, research indicated that whereas some individuals experienced considerable levels of psychological distress, many people living with HIV disease coped relatively well with their illness and often maintained hope for their long-term health outlook (Rabkin et al., 1997).

Throughout the late 1980s and early 1990s, perceptions of physical and emotional well-being among people living with HIV seemed closely tied to results from laboratory markers of disease progression that measure changes in immune function (i.e., CD4 lymphocyte counts). For example, a CD4 count falling below 200 became an important psychological turning point because this laboratory value served as the immunological benchmark for defining an AIDS diagnosis (CDC, 1992). Willingness to initiate or continue treatment was often influenced by a person's ability to tolerate drug side effects and beliefs concerning whether the benefits of available treatments outweighed their deleterious effects on quality of life (Nannis, Temoshok, Smith, & Jenkins, 1993).

New HIV Treatments and Technology

Basic science research has shown that the viral replication cycle is characterized by very rapid proliferation of HIV, with up to10,000 billion particles produced and destroyed daily (Ho et al., 1995). Because HIV replicates so rapidly, it can quickly mutate to become drug resistant. Improved understanding of these viral dynamics led to the development of new treatment tools. By 1996, several major medical advances would profoundly alter the nature of clinical HIV care. Diagnostic markers became available to quantify disease status by directly measuring levels of "viral load" (HIV RNA) in blood plasma. These assays provided important information about the progression of viral replication that complemented available CD4 markers of immune functioning. Shortly thereafter, a potent class of medications called protease inhibitors were developed and combined with other new or existing antiretrovirals that together targeted HIV at multiple points in its replication cycle. Combinations of highly active antiretroviral therapies (HAART) quickly came into widespread clinical use (Carpenter et al., 1998). HAART regimens are typically triple drug combinations which include a protease inhibitor (i.e., indinivir, saquinavir, nelfinavir, ritonavir) and two nucleoside analogues (i.e., zidovudine, lamivudine, stavudine, zalcitabine, didanosine). When combined, three (or sometimes even more) of these drugs slow viral replication, reduce viral load, and diminish the development of resistant viral strains. HAART regimens have changed the face of AIDS care because they are capable of suppressing plasma viral load to undetectable levels, increasing CD4 levels, improving clinical outcomes, and decreasing AIDS-related mortality (Carpenter et al., 1998; Deeks, Smith, Holodniy, & Kahn, 1997; Hammer et al., 1997). For the first time in the history of HIV disease, medical care providers have potent antiviral medications and methods to directly monitor their effectiveness in suppressing viral replication.

Emerging Psychological Adjustment Issues

The advent of powerful new combination treatments for HIV has raised a host of new issues related to social and psychological coping with HIV disease. One set of issues involves whether, how well, and for how long patients derive benefits from the new regimens. Different treatment outcomes and disease course trajectories may create very different sets of adjustment issues. Many people who were seriously ill experience significant improvements in health after beginning HAART. For some, this reversal of HIV disease progression is well-sustained. However, other patients are unable to tolerate or absorb the medications and must quickly stop HAART or switch to different regimens (Carpenter et al., 1998). Still others experience treatment failure following an initial period of earlier treatment response. People with HIV who begin HAART regimens while they still have relatively good immune functioning are most likely to have a favorable virological response to treatment (Fatkenheuer et al., 1997). However, some asymptomatic individuals experience iatrogenic effects of HAART that negatively impact quality of life. Different life issues, medical decisions, and coping responses may arise in each of these situations.

Shortly after they were introduced in the United States, protease inhibitors were widely publicized as "near cures" for HIV disease. Many people living with HIV respond to HAART with dramatic and well-sustained improvements in health and well-being. This phenomenon has been described by some as providing a chance for persons with HIV to lead a "second life" (Rabkin & Ferrando, 1997). How persons re-adapt from a focus on early death from AIDS to the prospect—but not the guarantee—of longer life is not yet known. To date, there has been little research describing psychosocial adjustment among persons for whom viral replication is successfully suppressed. However, stressful life events and new decisions may accompany the experience of having such a "second lease" on life (Kelly, Otto-Salaj, Sikkema, Pinkerton, & Bloom, 1998; Klein, 1998; Rabkin & Ferrando, 1997). For example, questions about when and whether individuals should return to work, or begin or end relationships, are likely consequences of the health reversals that may follow successful treatment. In addition to enhancing their quality of life, improvements in functioning may also create stress. It can be difficult for persons to make a rapid transition from anticipating declining health and death to holding a more optimistic health outlook that requires planning long into the future. For example, some persons with HIV or AIDS have traded their life insurance policies for cash or incurred debts in the expectation of an early death. Others who qualified for disability entitlements or Medicaid assistance after leaving work or lost personal assets may have difficulty regaining economic self-sufficiency. The high costs of HIV medications—often $10,000 to $15,000 per year—can lead to challenging dilemmas when eligibility for medication entitlements due to disability may be lost through a return to employment, but when employment income is insufficient to pay for the medications needed to remain healthy.

In addition to economic stressors, other sources of social stress can emerge during shifts from relatively poor to good health. Grief responses may be exacerbated or rekindled by "survivor's guilt" when individuals escape the fate of partners and friends who died of AIDS-related complications earlier in the epidemic. Improved health and feedback about lower viral load may also precipitate changes in current living situations and relationships. Previous decisions to live near better medical services or with family members who could function as caretakers may need to be re-examined. The scope of life goals is likely to alter, necessitating new decisions about changing careers, resuming education, or reproduction options. Expectations of living a longer life or the possibility that new medications might reduce HIV infectivity could, for instance, lead to increased choices to have children. Life change, whether positive or negative, can be stressful. It is not yet clear to what extent HAART-related life changes create adjustment difficulties for persons with HIV disease or the way best to facilitate smooth transitions.

There are also direct ways in which HAART regimens may diminish rather than enhance quality of life. Some of the common side effects associated with protease inhibitors include nausea, diarrhea, fatigue, and headaches. Difficulty tolerating medication or following complex and frequent dosing schedules may interfere with activities of daily life. Meal times, travel, and work or leisure activities often need to be carefully coordinated with times when various pills must be taken or when side effects are most likely to impair functioning. Recent research with persons taking these regimens suggests that many patients are very concerned that medication taking has too much become a central focus of their lives (Stone et al., 1998).

As protease inhibitor use in clinical settings has increased, it has become evident that many persons living with HIV disease (up to 50% in some studies) do not respond well or do not maintain viral suppression responses to the new regimens (e.g., Deeks, Loftus, Cohen, Chin, & Grant, 1997). This raises an important question of how these individuals cope when they learn that they themselves did not get an opportunity for a "second life." Rabkin and Ferrando (1997), Kelly, Otto-Salaj, et al. (1998), and others have raised the possibility that HAART treatment failure could precipitate considerable psychological distress, pessimism, and coping problems. This is particularly so because, unlike the common disappointment with earlier treatments, failure of HAART regimens takes place in the context of media reports of "miraculous" new treatments or personal contacts with others who have experienced dramatic health gains. On a societal level, this raises the concern that there will be a "re-marginalization of the dying" in terms of HIV service provision and public policy, and increased opportunities for HIV discrimination (Klein, 1998).

At the individual level, personal perceptions and explanations of treatment outcomes can play a large role in determining psychological responses to HAART. Because strict medication adherence is necessary for treatment success, individuals who do not respond well to HAART regimens may make an attribution that they have failed the regimen rather than that the regimen has failed for them, thus reacting with guilt, low self-esteem, or depression. Such self-blame and discouragement may be especially salient when treatment failure follows a period of initial treatment success. Alternatively, persons who observe others doing well on a HAART regimen but are themselves unable to tolerate the regimen may experience negative situational attributions, hopelessness, anger, or mistrust of medical advances. In either case, uncertainties and realistic fears that future antiretrovirals will also not work are likely to color the perceptions of persons who experience failure of HAART regimens (Rabkin & Ferrando, 1997).

ADHERENCE: BEHAVIORAL INFLUENCES ON MEDICAL OUTCOMES

Although coping is generally viewed as a mental health issue, the ways in which individuals cope with HIV disease and with antiretroviral treatments also carry implications for two important areas of their health behavior: treatment adherence and transmission risk practices. Less adaptive coping and greater affective distress have been associated with greater problems adhering to HIV treatment regimens (Singh et al., 1996). HIV-infected persons experiencing high levels of psychological distress may also be more likely to display patterns of continued unprotected sexual activity (Kelly, Murphy, Bahr, Koob, et al., 1993). This suggests that interventions for emotionally distressed persons living with HIV disease may carry not only psychological benefits, but also public health and medical treatment outcome benefits.

The goal of successful antiretroviral therapy is to achieve maximal sustained viral suppression (Carpenter et al., 1998). Clinical benefits may result from even partial viral suppression. However, near-total suppression of HIV viral load is necessary in order to minimize the development of drug resistant viral strains. Virological failure of HAART is characterized by the development of multidrug resistance and a resumption of rapid viral replication. Cross-resistance may occur within classes of antiretroviral medications, so failure of one HAART regimen is likely to make success with subsequent regimens less likely. Durable viral suppression in response to combination antiretroviral therapy is the medical outcome of most critical importance for the long-term success of HIV care. For that reason, it is critical that patients adhere fully, immediately, and continously with HAART regimens. Failure to do so can render the regimen ineffective and lead to drug resistance that reduces the likely success of future treatment.

Adherence in medication taking behavior has been linked to medical outcomes in several studies (Hecht, Colfax, Swanson, & Chesney, 1998; Montaner et al., 1998). In one clinical study of persons with HIV infection taking protease inhibitors at a San Francisco hospital, those who reported high levels of medication adherence were over four times more likely than those who reported medication nonadherence to achieve an optimal level of viral suppression (Hecht, Colfax, et al., 1998). An association between less than perfect protease inhibitor adherence and failure to sustain maximal viral suppression has also been demonstrated in a large clinical drug trial (Montaner et al., 1998). Thus, even short "drug holidays" or occasional missed doses of protease inhibitors may be sufficient to facilitate the emergence of drug resistance and treatment failure (Katzenstein, 1997). Even more so than for past HIV treatments or for drug regimens used to treat many other chronic diseases, therapeutic efficacy of HAART is greatly determined by treatment adherence.

Treatment Adherence Issues

Medication adherence has become a prominent behavioral issue in HIV care. The urgency of improving antiretroviral medication adherence has been widely acknowledged by the HIV medical community, with the importance of adherence formally recognized in antiretroviral treatment guidelines (Carpenter et al., 1998). In a national survey of physicians and patients, Gallant and Block (1998) found that 89% of HIV care providers rated treatment adherence as a serious problem. Of 359 patients on combination therapy regimens interviewed, 43% reported lapses in antiretroviral adherence during the previous week and 26% said they had not adhered to the regimen in the past day. Both physicians and patients in the study described regimen complexity as an important reason for nonadherence. Furthermore, the necessity for following regimens strictly over time was especially problematic, with the length of self-initiated drug holidays reported to increase with longer durations of treatment (Gallant & Block, 1998).

Such findings are not surprising given the tremendous behavioral burden associated with combination therapy. HAART regimens are extremely complex; regimens requiring 20 to 30 pills taken daily are not uncommon. HIV treatments are now expected to be chronic and lifelong in their duration. Because taking HAART necessitates maintaining such complicated medication taking habits over extended time periods, adherence problems are likely to be the rule rather than the exception. Since the objective of HAART regimens is often to prevent onset of HIV disease in persons who are infected, they can be construed as chronic preventive regimens. Such preventive interventions may be particularly likely to produce nonadherence. The general chronic illness literature shows that only about one half of patients adhere to interventions that are preventative or long term (Podell, 1975; Rosenstock, 1975). As many as 80% of patients may be partially nonadherent at some time during the course of any chronic illness (Dunbar-Jacob, Burke, & Puczynski, 1995). In general, patients are less likely to adhere to complex regimens (Agras, 1989) or regimens that include multiple medications (Blackwell, 1992). All of these are characteristics of HIV HAART regimens.

In addition to regimen characteristics, several factors investigated in the context of other chronic illnesses are relevant to HIV medication adherence (Ickovics & Meisler, 1997). These include characteristics of the disease, provider, and patient. Adherence may vary with differences in disease severity, although adherence problems have been observed among those who are seriously ill as well as those who are asymptomatic. Research with other diseases has also established a link between medical provider characteristics and patient behavior. The quality of provider/patient interactions, communication styles, and clinic environment factors can impact adherence (DiMatteo et al., 1993). Psychosocial factors, including greater social support and less psychological distress, have also been associated with adherence across a variety of chronic illnesses. However, reliable predictors of nonadherence at the level of individual patient characteristics have been difficult to identify. Nonadherence can occur among individuals of all ages, social classes, and ethnic groups (DiMatteo & DiNicola, 1982). In short, every person managing a chronic disease is at some risk for treatment adherence problems. This means that interventions to improve adherence require an identification of specific barriers to adherence throughout the course of treatment.

Much may also be learned about relevant barriers from investigations of adherence to previous HIV treatments. Before the development of HAART, a number of studies examined adherence to AZT monotherapy (Eldred, Wu, Chaisson, & Moore, 1998; Muma, Ross, Parcel, & Pollard, 1995; Singh et al., 1996; Smith, Rapkin, Morrison, & Kammerman, 1997). There is evidence that provider relationships and psychosocial factors (including social support, coping, and depression) contribute to AZT treatment adherence among persons with HIV (Morse et al., 1991; Mostashari, Riley, Selwyn, & Altice, 1998; Shelton et al., 1993; Singh et al., 1996). For example, patient perceptions of physician communication style and the presence of good emotional supports were found to be positively associated with antiretroviral adherence in a study undertaken with incarcerated women (Mostashari et al., 1998). One important longitudinal investigation of antiretroviral adherence conducted in a veteran's hospital suggested that treatment adherent patients with HIV disease had lower levels of depression and more adaptive coping than those who were not adherent (Singh et al., 1996). Another common finding among many early investigations of antiretroviral adherence involves the importance of patient beliefs. Even for relatively simple regimens like AZT monotherapy, patient beliefs in their ability to adhere to antiretroviral therapy have been related to higher rates of adherence (Eldred et al., 1998). Furthermore, patient beliefs concerning the efficacy or personal benefits of antiretrovirals appear to influence medication adherence. The perceived ability of AZT to improve health, to prolong life, or to provide protection from AIDS-related illness has been linked to medication taking patterns and to treatment drop-out (Aversa & Kimberlin, 1996; Geletko, Ballard, & Mathews, 1995; Muma et al., 1995; Samet et al., 1992; Smith et al., 1997). Perception that the benefits of treatment outweigh its limitations and drawbacks were also especially important influences on adherence to AZT regimens (Geletko et al., 1995; Muma et al., 1995; Nannis et al., 1993). It is likely that similar factors will prove relevant for understanding adherence to new HAART treatments as well.

Due to the powerful impact of adherence on treatment outcomes, effective behavioral interventions to promote HAART regimen adherence are urgently needed. The development of these interventions will require an identification of factors that influence adherence to combination therapies. It will also require the refinement of adherence assessment methodologies. Accurate measurement of patients' adherence to medication regimens has proven extremely challenging in the behavioral medicine field. These measurement issues are difficult even for regimens that require only once-a-day dosing of single medications. Because HAART regimens involve many more daily doses of multiple medications, assessment of adherence to new HIV therapies is complex. No gold standard exists for assessing treatment adherence. Consequently, the strongest way to measure adherence behavior is through a multimethod approach in which an array of complementary assessment techniques is used. Outcome measures that may prove useful for determining the effectiveness of behavioral interventions to promote HAART adherence include patient self-report instruments, self-monitoring techniques, electronic dose monitoring instruments, prescription refill data, pill counts, clinic appointment keeping records, serum assays of medication levels, and clinical markers expected to coincide with regimen adherence. Each of these methods has both benefits and drawbacks. For instance, self-reports of adherence are relatively inexpensive and efficient to administer, but are indirect measures that consistently tend to overestimate good adherence. On the other hand, electronic monitoring of medication container opening behavior can overestimate poor adherence when pill bottles are opened less often or at different times than pills are actually taken. Electronic monitoring systems may also be costly and relatively inconvenient for patients to use. Biological, as well as behavioral, indices of adherence can reflect a great deal of measurement error. Direct assays of medication levels are expensive and often unavailable, are susceptible to inaccuracies due to individual variations in bioavailability, and tend to measure information only about the most recent dose taken rather than overall levels of adherence. Caution must also be used when interpreting biological markers, such as CD4 counts or viral load values, as evidence of medication adherence. Although biological markers are objective measures of medical outcome, changes in these indices also reflect factors other than adherence such as pretreatment disease severity and history of resistance to previously prescribed medications.

In spite of the continuing need for more advanced measurement technologies and more complete modeling of adherence predictors, the clinical demand for interventions promoting antiretroviral adherence has been so pressing since the development of protease inhibitors that a variety of interventions are being attempted by care providers. The development of HIV treatment adherence interventions can be informed by previous research. However, relatively few empirically validated adherence interventions are to be found even in the general, non-HIV treatment literature (see Dunbar-Jacob et al., 1995; Haynes, McKibbon, & Kanani, 1996, for reviews). Of the randomized, controlled intervention studies of long-term medication adherence that have been conducted, only those including very complex and intensive interventions have demonstrated effects on adherence (e.g., Bailey et al., 1990; Haynes et al., 1976; Logan, Milne, Achber, Cambell, & Haynes, 1979; Saunders, Irwig, Gear, & Ramushu, 1991). No studies to date have shown maintenance effects, and none have indicated which intervention components are most effective. Nonetheless, a number of adherence promoting strategies have been suggested by the literature. These generally include enhancing the use of social support resources, increasing self-efficacy regarding the ability to follow treatment plans, improving patient education about the expected positive and negative consequences of medication regimens, modifying the treatment environment to minimize barriers to keeping appointments or refilling prescriptions, enhancing patient–provider relationships by promoting trust and good communication skills, and employing basic behavioral techniques. These techniques include goal setting and behavioral contracting, self-monitoring and self-reinforcement, social reinforcement, the provision of behavioral or medical outcome feedback, the use of environmental reminders or specially organized medication dispensers, and the tailoring of regimen dosing schedules to fit daily routines.

Interventions for promoting adherence to HIV medications can build on such strategies. The need for effective strategies to improve adherence to HAART regimens is perhaps one of the greatest challenges faced by behavioral scientists in this new era of HIV treatment. It is a challenge that must be met with innovation and multidisciplinary cooperation. Controlled trials of adherence interventions at the level of the service system, provider, and patient must be undertaken. It is essential that interventions be developed that maximize the involvement of patients in the management of their own care, and foster collaborative, problem-solving approaches to the initiation and maintenance of adherence to HAART. Successful medication adherence carries significant health benefits for individuals living with HIV, as well as public health benefits by reducing the possibility of new infections with drug-resistant HIV strains.

HIV TRANSMISSION RISK BEHAVIOR

Past research on the effects of HIV serostatus knowledge on sexual risk behavior has shown that most persons aware of their HIV-positive status reduce or avoid engaging in activities that could transmit infection to others (Cleary et al., 1991; Higgins et al., 1991). On the other hand, these studies also indicate that a substantial minority of HIV-seropositive persons have difficulty in consistently refraining from unprotected sexual behavior. Approximately one third of young gay or bisexual seropositive men in a San Francisco cohort reported they had recently engaged in unprotected anal intercourse (Lemp et al., 1994), with similar levels of unprotected sex reported in samples of HIV-infected injection drug users (Rhodes, Donoghoe, Hunter, & Stimson, 1993; Singh et al., 1993) and cohorts of gay men (Robins et al., 1994). Factors that differentiate HIV-seropositive persons who do from those who do not engage in unprotected sexual activities following awareness of their serostatus include levels of psychological distress (Kelly, Murphy, Bahr, Koob, Brasfield et al., 1993), coexisting substance use patterns (Kalichman, Kelly, & Rompa, 1997; Robins et al., 1994), relationship characteristics and comfort in disclosing HIV serostatus to sexual relationship partners (Remien, Carballo-Dieguez, & Wagner, 1995), and psychological controls related to sex (Centers for Disease Control and Prevention, 1996). Persons most likely to report continued patterns of risky activities are those with high levels of current psychological distress, poor coping, concurrent substance use problems, difficulty in disclosing their serostatus, limited social supports, and poor levels of sexual self-control. One randomized outcome study found that a small group intervention that improved coping skills and social supports for depressed persons living with HIV produced not only changes in mental health indicators but also reductions in levels of subsequent unprotected sexual behavior (Kelly, Murphy, Bahr, Kalichman, et al., 1993). This suggests that if people are assisted in effectively coping with their HIV disease, they are also more likely to be able to successfully self-manage risk in their sexual lives.

The availability of combination antiretroviral therapies for the treatment of HIV disease, media heralding of HIV treatment advances as "near cures" or cause for "great hope" in the conquest of AIDS, and optimism due to a reduction in death rates from AIDS may be influencing public perceptions concerning the severity of AIDS and perceptions about the need to maintain safer sex. Dilley, Woods, and McFarland (1997) found evidence of diminishing concerns about becoming HIV-infected among some gay men in San Francisco. Kelly, Hoffmann, et al. (1998), in a community sample survey of gay and bisexual men in the midwest, found that AIDS was still perceived as a serious threat among most men. However, 13% felt that AIDS is a less serious threat than it was in the past and nearly 20% of HIV-positive men on combination therapy regimens said they personally practice safe-sex less often since HIV medical treatments have advanced. Whether similar perceptions of diminished AIDS severity are occurring among heterosexual men, women, adolescents, or IDUs has not yet been examined.

It is possible—but not yet well-established in vivo—that at least some individuals with undetectable plasma HIV viral load levels may have lower HIV transmission infectivity (Vernazza et al., 1997). However, persons who have been nonadherent with HAART regimens or those who have not responded well to the treatments can develop HIV strains that are resistant to antiretroviral medications. Transmission of drug-resistant virus to sexual or needle-sharing partners is a potentially serious concern because individuals who contract drug-resistant HIV are unlikely to benefit optimally from currently available treatments. There is evidence that sexual transmission of multidrug-resistant viral strains has already taken place (Hecht, Grant, et al., 1998; Imrie et al., 1997).

Traditionally, HIV prevention efforts have been construed primarily from the perspective of encouraging HIV-seronegative persons to remain uninfected. HIV-seropositive persons have been seen primarily as in need of care services, not prevention efforts. Although these needs remain, the changing nature of the HIV epidemic and the populations now most threatened by it call for a broader perspective. Given that persons at greatest risk for contracting HIV are younger, more disenfranchised, and more disadvantaged than ever before, effective HIV prevention for high risk seronegative populations will increasingly also need to include services such as substance use, social, and youth services. While persons living with HIV will continue to require a variety of care services, some will also require ongoing behavior change encouragement, support, and counseling. In this context, it will be important for service providers to remain cognizant that persons living with HIV continue to be sexual beings and may require ongoing support in areas such as serostatus disclosure to potential partners, avoiding high risk practices, and handling situations that could otherwise result in risky sexual or drug use activities. As persons with HIV live longer and healthier lives, the challenges of maintaining these behavior changes will be greater and more sustained.

HIV AS A CHRONIC DISEASE

Since very early in the HIV epidemic, there has always been the hope—articulated throughout the years in the health care provider community, the AIDS activist community, and the community of persons living with HIV—that HIV infection might someday become a serious, chronic, but manageable, disease. Advances in medical treatment are bringing this hope closer to reality. It is still too early to declare success in making HIV disease manageable; too many patients still do not derive or maintain benefit from even the newest antiretroviral combinations, and the history of HIV disease is one with many treatment hopes that did not prove durable. Nonetheless, the potential outlook for many persons living with HIV is brighter than it has ever been before. To a large extent, psychological and behavioral medicine interventions will play a key role in determining whether this potentially hopeful outlook will endure. The effective treatment of persons living with HIV will require that difficult problems be addressed. These include promoting adherence to difficult medical regimens that are remarkably unforgiving of lapses; assisting patients in coping with successes, failures, and uncertainty in their health outlook; and encouraging the avoidance of transmission risk behavior among both seropositive and seronegative persons.

When AIDS first appeared, many aspects of the disease were startling because they were new. HIV/AIDS continues to remain, in many respects, a unique disease by virtue of its stigmatized public perception, sexually transmitted infectious characteristics, concentration within certain communities and social networks, and the coping challenges that confront persons with HIV. To a very great extent, American society has not yet come to terms with the types of policies—including improved sexual education for young people, ensuring ready access to condoms, and needle exchange for out-of-treatment IDUs—that will prove essential for stopping the epidemic. However, medical aspects of HIV disease and, more specifically, the roles for health psychologists to contribute to HIV prevention and care are coming to resemble the psychological profession's role in other chronic disease areas. What has been learned about promoting treatment adherence in diseases such as hypertension, diabetes, and other illnesses can be applied to the newer problem of HIV treatment adherence. Lessons learned in helping people cope with serious chronic diseases with uncertain long-term outlooks such as cancer can provide a framework for assisting patients with HIV to cope with similar uncertainties. Behavioral medicine paradigms and principles useful in other health behavior areas can guide efforts related to HIV. What is learned in the HIV/AIDS behavioral medicine area can, in turn, contribute to efforts to assist persons with diseases other than AIDS. There is not a need to reinvent the wheel of behavioral medicine knowledge for health behavior problems experienced by persons with HIV. However, there is a need to make the wheel turn faster given the urgencies of this disease.

Finally, the challenges created by AIDS will continue to evolve. There have already been important changes in the demography of the American HIV epidemic. Persons contracting HIV are younger, poorer, more disenfranchised, and more estranged from traditional health and mental health service systems than ever before. Substance abuse has become even more closely intertwined with HIV risk than in the past, and groups now most vulnerable to HIV disease (including drug-involved and impoverished women, young and ethnic minority men who have sex with men, IDUs, and the homeless) are populations highly underrepresented in the behavioral medicine field. For all of these vulnerable groups, coping, mental health, treatment adherence, and transmission risk avoidance efforts are likely to be exceptionally difficult. They will require that health psychologists develop new culturally tailored approaches, service delivery mechanisms, and—perhaps—sensitivities. Ultimately, meeting these challenges will also expand and benefit this field.

ACKNOWLEDGMENTS

Preparation of this chapter was supported by center grant P30-MH52776 from the National Institute of Mental Health (NIMH) and from Office of AIDS Research (OAR) and NIMH grant R01-MH54935.

REFERENCES

Agras, S. (1989). Understanding adherence to the medical regimen: The scope of the problem and a theoretical perspective. *Arthritis Care and Research, 2,* S2–S7.

Aversa, S. L., & Kimberlin, C. (1996). Psychosocial aspects of antiretroviral medication use among HIV patients. *Patient Education and Counseling, 29,* 207–219.

Bailey, W. C., Richards, J. M., Brooks, C. M., Soong, S. J., Windsor, R. A., & Manzella, B. A. (1990). A randomized trial to improve self-management practices of adults with asthma. *Archives of Internal Medicine, 150,* 1664–1668.

Blackwell, B. (1992). Compliance. *Psychotherapy and Psychosomatics, 58,* 161–169.

Carpenter, C.C.J., Fischl, M. A., Hammer, S. M., Hirsch, M. S., Jacobsen, D. M., Katzenstein, D. A., Montaner., J.S.G., Richman, D. D., Saag, M. S., Schooley, R. T., Thompson, M. A., Vella, S., Yeni, P. G., & Volberding, P. A. (1998). Antiretroviral therapy for HIV infection in 1998: Updated recommendations of the International AIDS Society—USA panel. *Journal of the American Medical Association, 280,* 78–86.

Centers for Disease Control and Prevention. (1992). 1993 revised classification system for HIV infection and expanded surveillance case definition for AIDS among adolescents and adults. *Morbidity and Mortality Weekly Report, 41*(RR-17), 1–19.

Centers for Disease Control and Prevention. (1996). Continued sexual risk behavior among HIV-seropositive, drug using men—Atlanta; Washington, DC; and San Juan, Puerto Rico, 1993. *Morbidity and Mortality Weekly Report, 45,* 151–152.

Cleary, P. D., Van, N., Rogers, T., Singer, E., Shipton-Levy, R., Steilen, M., Stuart, A., Avorn, J., & Pindyck, J. (1991). Behavior changes after notification of HIV infection. *American Journal of Public Health, 81,* 1586–1590.

Deeks, S. G., Loftus, R., Cohen, P., Chin, S., & Grant, R. (1997, September). Incidence and predictors of virological failure of indinavir and/or ritonavir in an urban health clinic (Abstract

LB-02). In program and abstracts of the 37th Interscience Conference on Antimicrobial Agents and Chemotherapy, Toronto, Ontario.

Deeks, S. G., Smith, M., Holodniy, M., & Kahn, J. O. (1997). HIV-1 protease inhibitors: A review for clinicians. *Journal of the American Medical Association, 277,* 145–153.

Dilley, J., Ochitill, H., Perl, M., & Volberding, P. (1985). Findings in psychiatric consultations with patients with acquired immune deficiency syndrome. *American Journal of Psychiatry, 142,* 82–86.

Dilley, J. W., Woods, W. J., & McFarland, W. (1997). Are advances in treatment changing views about high-risk sex? *New England Journal of Medicine, 337,* 501–502.

DiMatteo, M., & DiNicola, D. D. (1982). *Achieving patient compliance.* New York: Pergamon.

DiMatteo, M. R., Sherbourne, C. D., Hays, R. D., Ordway, L., Kravitz, R. L., McGlynn, E. A., Kaplan, S., & Rogers, W. H. (1993). Physicians' characteristics influence patients' adherence to medical treatment: Results from the Medical Outcomes Study. *Health Psychology, 12,* 93–102.

Dunbar-Jacob, J., Burke, L. E., & Puczynski, S. (1995). Clinical assessment and management of adherence to medical regimens. In P. M. Nicassio & T. W. Smith (Eds.), *Managing chronic illness: A biopsychosocial perspective* (pp. 313–349). Washington, DC: American Psychological Association.

Eldred, L. J., Wu., A. W., Chaisson, R. E., & Moore, R. D. (1998). Adherence to antiretroviral and pneumocystis prophylaxis in HIV disease. *Journal of Acquired Immune Deficiency Syndromes and Human Retrovirology, 18,* 117–125.

Fatkenheuer, G., Theisen, A., Rockstroh, J., Grabow, T., Wicke, C., Becker, K., Wieland, U., Pfister,H., Reiser, M., Hegener, P., Franzen, C., Schwenk, A., & Salzberger, B. (1997). Virological treatment failure of protease inhibitor therapy in an unselected cohort of HIV-infected patients. *AIDS, 11,* F113–F116.

Folkman, S., Chesney, M. A., Pollack, L., & Coates, T. J. (1993). Stress, control, coping and depressive mood in human immunodeficiency virus-positive and -negative gay men in San Francisco. *Journal of Nervous and Mental Disease, 181,* 409–416.

Gallant, J. E., & Block, D. S. (1998). Adherence to antiretroviral regimens in HIV-infected patients: Results of a survey among physicians and patients. *Journal of the International Association of Physicians in AIDS Care, 4,* 32–35.

Geletko, S. M., Ballard, C. R., & Mathews, W. C. (1995). Health beliefs and discontinuation of zidovudine therapy. *American Journal of Health-System Pharmacists, 52,* 505–507.

Hammer, S. M., Squires, K. E., Hughes, M. D., Grimes, J. M., Demeter, L. M., Currier, J. S., Eron, J. J., Feinberg, J. E., Balfour, H. H., Peyton, L. R., Chodakewitz, J. A., & Fischl, M. A. (1997). A controlled trial of two nucleoside analogues plus indinavir in persons with human immunodeficiency virus Infections and CD4 cell counts of 200 per cubic millimeter or less. *New England Journal of Medicine, 337,* 725–733.

Hays, R. B., Turner, H., & Coates, T. J. (1992). Social support, AIDS-related symptoms, and depression among gay men. *Journal of Consulting and Clinical Psychology, 60,* 463–469.

Haynes, R. B., McKibbon, K. A., & Kanani, R. (1996). Systematic review of randomized trials of interventions to assist patients follow prescriptions for medications. *Lancet, 348,* 383–386.

Haynes, R. B., Sackett, D. I., Gibson, E. S., Taylor, D. W., Hackett, B. C., Roberts, R. S., & Johnson, A. L. (1976). Improvement of medication compliance in uncontrolled hypertension. *Lancet, 1,* 1265–1268.

Hecht, F., Colfax, G., Swanson, M., & Chesney, M. A. (1998). Adherence and effectiveness of protease inhibitors in clinical practice (Abstract 151). In program and abstracts of the 5th conference on Retroviruses and Opportunistic Infections, Chicago.

Hecht, F. M., Grant, R. M., Petropoulus, C. J., Dillon, B., Chesney, M. A., Tian, H., Hellman, N. S., Brandapalli, N. I., Diglio, L., Branson, B., & Kahn, J. O. (1998). Sexual transmission of an HIV-1 variant resistant to multiple reverse-transcriptase and protease inhibitors. *New England Journal of Medicine, 339,* 307–311.

Higgins, D. L., Galavotti, C., O'Reilly, K. R., Schnell, D. J., Moore, M., Rugg, D. L., & Johnson, R. (1991). Evidence for the effects of HIV antibody counseling and testing on risk behavior. *Journal of the American Medical Association, 266,* 2419–2429.

Ho, D. D., Neumann, A. V., Perelson, A. S., Chen, W., Leonard, J. M., & Markowitz, M. (1995). Rapid turnover of plasma virions and CD4 lymphocytes in HIV-1 infection. *Nature, 373,* 123–126.

Ickovics, J. R., & Meisler, A. W. (1997). Adherence in AIDS clinical trials: A framework for clinical research and clinical care. *Journal of Clinical Epidemiology, 50,* 385–391.

Imrie, A., Beveridge, A., Genn, W., Vizzard, J., Cooper, D. A., & the Sydney Primary HIV Infection Study Group. (1997). Transmission of human immunodeficiency virus type 1 resistant to nevirapine and zidovudine. *Journal of Infectious Disease, 175,* 1502–1506.

Kalichman, S. C., Kelly, J. A., & Rompa, D. R. (1997). Continued high-risk sex among HIV seropositive gay and bisexual men seeking HIV prevention services. *Health Psychology, 16,* 369–373.

Katzenstein, D. A. (1997). Adherence as a particular issue with protease inhibitors. *Journal of the Association of Nurses in AIDS Care, 8,* 10–17.

Kelly, J. A., Hoffmann, R. G., Rompa, D. R., & Gray, M. (1998). Protease inhibitor combination therapies and perceptions of gay men regarding AIDS severity and the need to maintain safer sex. *AIDS, 12,* F91–F95.

Kelly, J. A., Murphy, D. A., Bahr, G. R., Kalichman, S. C., Morgan, M. G., Koob, J. J., Stevenson, L. Y., Bernstein, M. B., & Brasfield, T. L. (1993). Outcomes of cognitive-behavioral and support group brief therapies for depressed HIV-infected persons. *American Journal of Psychiatry, 150,* 1679–1686.

Kelly, J. A., Murphy, D. A., Bahr, G. R., Koob, J. J., Morgan, M. G., Kalichman, S. C., Stevenson, L. Y., Brasfield, T. L., Bernstein, B. M., & St. Lawrence, J. S. (1993). Factors associated with severity of depression and high-risk sexual behavior among persons diagnosed with HIV infection. *Health Psychology, 12,* 215–219.

Kelly, J. A., Otto-Salaj, L. L, Sikkema, K. J., Pinkerton, S. D., & Bloom, F. R. (1998). Implications of HIV treatment advances for behavioral research on AIDS: Protease inhibitors and new challenges in HIV secondary prevention. *Health Psychology, 17,* 310–319.

Klein, S. J. (1998, June). *New emotional and psychosocial issues for patients and providers in the era of HAART.* Paper presented at the meeting of the 12th World AIDS Conference, Geneva, Switzerland.

Kobayashi, J. S. (1997). The evolution of adjustment issues in HIV/AIDS. *Bulletin of the Menninger Clinic, 61,* 146–188.

Lemp, G. F., Hirozawa, A. M., Givertz, D., Nieri, G. N., Anderson, L., Lindegren, M. L., Janssen, R. S., & Katz, M. (1994). Seroprevalence of HIV and risk behaviors among young homosexual and bisexual men. *Journal of the American Medical Association, 272,* 449–454.

Logan, A. G., Milne, B. J., Achber, C., Cambell, W. P., & Haynes, R. B. (1979). Work site treatment of hypertension by specially trained nurses: A controlled trial. *Lancet, 2,* 1175–1178.

Martin, J. L., & Dean, L. (1993). Effects of AIDS-related bereavement and HIV-related illness on psychological distress among gay men: A 7–year longitudinal study, 1985–1991. *Journal of Consulting and Clinical Psychology, 61,* 94–103.

Montaner, J. S., Reiss, P., Cooper, D., Vella, S., Harris, M., Conway, B., et al. (1998). A randomized, double-blind trial comparing combinations of nevirapine, didanosine, and zidovudine for HIV-infected patients. *Journal of the American Medical Association, 279,* 930–937.

Morse, E. V., Simon, P. M., Coburn, M., Hyslop, N., Greenspan, D., & Balson, P. M. (1991). Determinants of subject compliance within an experimental anti-HIV drug protocol. *Social Science and Medicine, 32,* 1161–1167.

Mostashari, F., Riley, E., Selwyn, P., & Altice, F. L. (1998). Acceptance and adherence with antiretroviral therapy among HIV-infected women in a correctional facility. *Journal of Acquired Immune Deficiency Syndromes and Human Retrovirology, 18,* 341–348.

Muma, R. D., Ross, M. W., Parcel, G. S., & Pollard, R. B. (1995). Zidovudine adherence among individuals with HIV infection. *AIDS Care, 7,* 439–447.

Nannis, E. D., Temoshok, L. R., Smith, M., & Jenkins, R. A. (1993). Perceptions of AZT: Implications for adherence to medical regimens. *Journal of Applied Biobehavioral Research, 1,* 39–54.

Perry, S. W., & Tross, S. (1984). Psychiatric problems of AIDS inpatients at the New York hospital: Preliminary report. *Public Health Reports, 99,* 200–205.

Podell, R. N. (1975). *Physician's guide to adherence in hypertension.* West Point, PA: Merck.

Rabkin, J. G., & Ferrando, S. (1997). A "second life" agenda. *Archives of General Psychiatry, 54,* 1049–1053.

Rabkin, J. G., Goetz, R. R., Remien, R. H., Williams, J. B., Todak, G., & Gorman, J. M. (1997). Stability of mood despite HIV illness progression in a group of homosexual men. *American Journal of Psychiatry, 154,* 231–238.

Rabkin, J. G., Williams, J. B., Neugebauer, R., Remien, R., & Goetz, R. (1990). Maintenance of hope in HIV-spectrum homosexual men. *American Journal of Psychiatry, 147,* 1322–1326.

Remien, R. H., Carballo-Dieguez, A., & Wagner, G. (1995). Intimacy and sexual risk behavior in serodiscordance male couples. *AIDS Care, 7,* 429–438.

Rhodes, T. J., Donoghoe, M. C., Hunter, G., & Stimson, G. (1993). Continued risk behavior among HIV positive drug injectors in London: Implications for intervention. *Addiction, 88,* 1553–1560.

Robins, A. G., Dew, M. A., Davidson, S., Penkower, L., Becker, J. T., & Kingsley, L. (1994). Psychosocial factors associated with risky sexual behavior among HIV-seropositive gay men. *AIDS Education and Prevention, 6,* 483–492.

Rosenstock, I. M. (1975). Patient's compliance with health regimens. *Journal of the American Medical Association, 234,* 402–403.

Samet, J. H., Libman, H., Steger, K. A., Dhawan, R. V., Chen, J., Shevitz, A. H., Dewees-Dunk, R., Levenson, S., Kufe, D., & Craven, D. E. (1992). Compliance with zidovudine therapy in patients infected with Human Immunodeficiency Virus, Type 1: A cross-sectional study in a municipal hospital clinic. *American Journal of Medicine, 92,* 495–502.

Saunders, L. D., Irwig, L. M., Gear, J. S., & Ramushu, D. L. (1991). A randomized controlled trial of compliance improving strategies in Soweto hypertensives. *Medical Care, 29,* 669–678.

Shelton, D., Marconi, K., Pounds, M., Scopetta, M., O'Sullivan, M. J., & Szapocznik, J. (1993). Medical adherence among prenatal, HIV seropositive, African-American women: Family issues. *Family Systems Medicine, 11,* 343–356.

Singh, B. K., Koman, J. J., Catan, V., Souply, K., Birkel, R., & Golaszewski, T. (1993). Sexual risk behavior among injection drug-using human immunodeficiency virus positive clients. *International Journal of the Addictions, 28,* 735–747.

Singh, N., Squier, C., Sivek, C., Wagener, M., Hong Nguyen, M., & Yu, V. L. (1996). Determinants of compliance with antiretroviral therapy in patients with human immunodeficiency virus: Prospective assessment with implications for enhancing compliance. *AIDS Care, 8,* 261–269.

Smith, M. Y., Rapkin, B. D., Morrison, A., & Kammerman, S. (1997). Zidovudine adherence in persons with AIDS: The relation of patient beliefs about medication to self-termination of therapy. *Journal of General Internal Medicine, 12,* 216–223.

Stone, V. E., Clarke, J., Lovell, J., Steger, K. A., Hirschhorn, L. R., Boswell, S., Monroe, A. D., Stein, M. D., Tyree, T. J., & Mayer, K. H. (1998). HIV/AIDS patients' perspectives on adhering to regimens containing protease inhibitors. *Journal of General Internal Medicine, 13,* 586–593.

Vernazza, P. L., Gilliam, B. L., Dyer, J., Fiscus, S. A., Eron, J. J., Frank, A. C., & Cohen, M. S. (1997). Quantification of HIV in semen: Correlation with antiviral treatment and immune status. *AIDS, 11,* 987–993.

Williams, J. B. , Rabkin, J. G., Remien, R. H., Gorman, J. M., & Ehrhardt, A. A. (1991). Multidisciplinary baseline assessment of homosexual men with and without human immunodeficiency virus infection. *Archives of General Psychiatry, 48,* 124–130.

51

Cultural Diversity and Health Psychology

Hope Landrine
Elizabeth A. Klonoff
San Diego State University / University of California-San Diego Joint Doctoral Program in Clinical Psychology

Two social factors that play a role in everyone's health (Bubker et al., 1989) are the nature and quality of their jobs/work environments (J. V. Johnson & Johannson, 1991; Karasek & Theorell, 1990; Sauter, Hurrell, & Cooper, 1989; Schor, 1991), and their socioeconomic (SES) status (Marmot, Kogevinas, & Elston, 1987; Schnall, Landsbergis, & Baker, 1994). Because U.S. minority groups tend to occupy low status jobs characterized by high job strain and low job control and stability, the nature of their work undoubtedly contributes to their differential morbidity and mortality (Amick, Levine, Tarlov, & Walsh, 1995). Likewise, because many minorities live in poverty (Amick et al., 1995), low SES also plays a role in minority excess morbidity and mortality through a variety of mechanisms (Baquet, Horm, Gibbs, & Greenwald, 1991; Coulehan, 1992; Hampton, 1992; Marmot & Theorell, 1988). These include low access to medical care (Blendon, Aiken, Freeman, & Corey, 1989) and high exposure to stress (King & Williams, 1995), air pollution (Brajer & Hall, 1992), toxic waste sites in their neighborhoods (Commission for Racial Justice, 1987), and carcinogens at work (Gottlieb & Husen, 1982; Samet, Kutvrit, Waxweiler, & Key, 1984).

Although these factors (along with low education) have been demonstrated to play a significant role in the health status of minorities, they nonetheless remain social rather than cultural variables. Social variables are parts (aspects), processes (mechanisms for maintaining), and products (results) of social stratification that may or may not be valued by, and are beyond the control of Whites and minorities alike (Landrine, Klonoff, Alcaraz, Scott, & Wilkins, 1995). Cultural variables, on the other hand, are factors that are purposefully transmitted to successive generations through socialization because they are valued (Landrine, 1992; Landrine & Klonoff, 1996a; Landrine, Klonoff, & Brown-Collins, 1992). Manuscripts on culture and minority health abound, but almost always focus on social variables and fail to mention any cultural factors. Poverty, low education, and unemployment, however, never have been aspects of anyone's culture.

Alternatively, other research on culture and minority health rightly ignores social variables as such to focus instead on the role of acculturation. These studies have found that acculturation contributes significantly to the variance in minority health behavior and morbidity irrespective of the minority group in question. For example, studies have found that acculturation plays a role in weight and dieting among Japanese (Furukawa, 1994) and Chinese (Schultz, Spindler, & Josephson, 1994) Americans, and in chronic disease among Cambodian Americans (Palinkas & Pickwell, 1995). For Mexican Americans, acculturation has been demonstrated to play a role in hypertension (Espino, 1990); AIDS risk and knowledge of AIDS transmission (Epstein, Dusenbury, Botvin, & Diaz, 1994); cancer knowledge and risk reduction behaviors (Balcazar, Castro, & Krull, 1995); compliance with medical treatments (Pachter, Susan, & Weller, 1993); cigarette smoking among children, adolescents (Landrine, Richardson, Klonoff, & Flay, 1994), and adults (G. Marin, B. V. Marin, Otero-Sabogal, Sabogal, & Perez-Stable, 1989; G. Marin, Perez-Stable, & B. V. Marin, 1989); use of health services (Wells, Golding, & Hough, 1989); dietary patterns (Gardner, Winkleby, & Viteri, 1995); salt consumption and exercise frequency (Vega et al., 1987); and chronic disease morbidity (Balcazar et al., 1995). For African Americans, studies of acculturation and health have only just begun because the African American Acculturation Scale (AAAS; Landrine & Klonoff, 1994a, 1996a) is a recent instrument. Nonetheless, studies using the AAAS similarly have found that levels of acculturation among African Americans play a role in hypertension (Landrine & Klonoff, 1996a); smoking (Klonoff & Landrine, 1996, 1999a; Landrine & Klonoff, 1996a); knowledge of AIDS transmission (Klonoff & Landrine, 1997a); coping styles and psychiatric symptoms (Landrine & Klonoff, 1996a); alcohol use (Klonoff & Landrine, in press); and frequency of experiencing racial discrimination (Landrine & Klonoff, 1996a, 1996b), with racial discrimination also contributing uniquely to the variance in smoking and hypertension.

Such studies are an important step in the direction of focusing on cultural rather than social variables and thereby bringing cultural diversity to health psychology, but they are nonetheless troubling. This is because these studies demonstrate that the extent to which minorities participate in their own indigenous culture versus that of the dominant White society (levels of acculturation) plays a role in minority health, but they simultaneously rarely reveal precisely *what it is* about the indigenous culture that accounts for the acculturation effect. Acculturation, after all, is merely a psychometric abstraction, like a first principle component. As such, it summarizes and represents the plethora of indigenous cultural beliefs and practices adhered to by traditional, half-adhered to by bicultural, and rejected by highly acculturated minorities. Like other mathematical abstractions in psychology, however, acculturation has been reified (i.e., *mistaken for a cultural variable or entity itself*). The cultural beliefs, values, and practices that constitute the *r*s in the correlation matrix and the independent variables of scientific relevance have been largely forgotten. Acculturation, however, like poverty and low education, similarly is not an aspect of anyone's culture; it is not a value, belief, ritual, or practice purposefully transmitted to successive generations.

Hence, research on cultural diversity and health, whether it focuses on social variables or on a reified abstraction, never addresses culture insofar as it never highlights the specific cultural independent variables that contribute to minority health behavior, morbidity, and mortality. Culture then seems "an incredibly well-kept secret in psychology" (Shweder & LeVine, 1984), something everyone whispers about, but never exposes or confronts. Because culture is such a well-kept secret, it is easy to assume that minority health beliefs and practices could not possibly differ so much from those of biomedicine that they necessitate significant changes in the content and process of delivering interventions and care to minority populations, let alone contradict health psychology's findings and knowledge. This chapter challenges that assumption by presenting those neglected, hidden health beliefs and practices.

The information presented here is a brief summary of decades of research in medical anthropology, where the health beliefs and practices of American minority groups (and of people in other cultures across the globe) have been thoroughly analyzed—but their role in subsequent health behavior has not. Hence, all biomedical, empirical studies (in preventive medicine, public health, etc.) on the role of these beliefs and practices in health behavior, morbidity, and mortality also are discussed, but the number of these, relative to the anthropological ones, is small. Nonetheless, this chapter assumes that all of the health beliefs and practices of minorities play a significant role in their health whether or not this has been demonstrated empirically to be the case. That assumption is logical because acculturation has been shown to play a significant role in the health behavior, morbidity, and mortality of all minority groups, and the health beliefs and practices described here are the "why" and the "how" of that ubiquitous, acculturation effect. Thus, this chapter does not address the role of acculturation in minority health, but instead focuses on the factors beneath that variable. Likewise, it devotes little time to rates of specific diseases, or to data on health damaging behaviors among minorities because that information is available elsewhere (e.g., Amick et al., 1995; Harwood, 1981; Polednak, 1989; Ruzicka & Kaye, 1989; Spector, 1996). Instead, it presents only a brief paragraph on the major health problems of each minority group and then turns to neglected cultural variables relevant to that group's health. Similarly, it ignores social variables such as poverty (not because they are unimportant but) because they are not cultural variables. The exception is that the chapter briefly addresses the role of current and historical racism in minority health. Although discrimination against minorities is a social variable, the ubiquitous distrust of Whites that it has produced is a cultural variable, that is, a set of attitudes regarding Whites and White health professionals that is purposefully taught to successive generations and impacts minority help seeking and compliance with treatment.

First, the chapter summarizes the health beliefs and practices of each of the four major American minority groups (Latinos, Asians, African Americans, and Native Americans, respectively). Because these four categories represent literally thousands of ethnic/cultural and language groups, far more are omitted than are included, and generalizations are made that should be understood as unavoidable rather than as stereotyping. In each case, however, the description is meant to apply only to the traditional (orthodox, prototypical) members of the cultures in question, with the understanding that bicultural and acculturated members of these cultures deviate from them, yielding subsequent intracultural heterogeneity in beliefs and practices. Next, a brief summary is provided that highlights the similarities among the four major cultural groups and arrives at a preliminary model of the proximal and distal social and cultural variables in minority health that can be used to organize future research. Finally, the implications of the findings are discussed and specific conclusions and suggestions are presented for research and practice in a more culturally diverse and sensitive health psychology.

LATINO AMERICANS

The term *Latino* is used to refer to a culturally heterogeneous population of Americans with Spanish surnames, including those with Mexican, Puerto Rican, Cuban, Central American, and South American heritage. Because all of these groups cannot be discussed here, the focus is on Mexican Americans, who, as is demonstrated here, are by and large prototypical of the Latino population as a whole.

Health Problems of Latinos

The leading causes of death among Latinos are summarized in Table 51.1 by gender, along with the leading causes of death among other minority groups. As shown, the major health problems of Latinos include high rates of heart disease, injuries, neoplasms, cerebrovascular disease, diabetes, and AIDS (U.S. Department of Health & Human Services [DHHS], 1996).

General Cultural Factors Influencing Health Behavior

Racism and Distrust of Whites. Among the many cultural factors influencing Latino health behavior is a distrust of Whites that is a response to "centuries of colonial domination, oppression, and exploitation by Anglo-American society" (Ginorio, Gutierrez, Cauce, & Acosta, 1995, p. 241). This anti-Latino racism has ranged from U.S. appropriation of lands belonging to Mexico, to contemporary job and housing discrimination, to violence against Mexican, Central, and South American citizens, new immigrants, and refugees (Ginorio et al., 1995). Its effects on Latino help seeking, although rarely addressed, cannot be overestimated (Atkinson, Morten, & Sue, 1993; Ginorio et al., 1995). Research on the role of distrust of Whites in Latino delay in seeking and compliance with treatment is needed, and may reveal that such distrust contributes to the data in Table 51.1.

Mexican American Beliefs About Illness

Like the other sociocentric[1] cultures to be discussed here, Mexican Americans view health holistically, drawing few distinctions between mind and body, between religion and medicine, or among physical, emotional, spiritual, and social processes (Clark, 1970; Farge, 1977; Rubel, 1960; Schreiber & Homiak, 1981; Spector, 1996). Harmony, or balance, among all of these is understood as the definition of health, and imbalance, or disruptions of harmony, as the foundation of illness. The three major causes of illness (disharmony) recognized in Mexican American folk medicine (or *ethnomedicine,* the medical knowledge of a culture) are strong emotions, imbalance of a variety of naturalistic variables, and supernatural factors, in sharp contrast to the etiological constructs of biomedicine (Baca, 1969; Castro, Furth, & Karlow, 1984; Currier, 1966; De la Cancela & Martinez, 1983; Spector, 1996). Traditional and acculturated Mexican Americans alike endorse these three causal attributions for illness. For traditional Mexican Americans, such folk medical beliefs persist in pure form and may constitute the entirety of their medical knowledge. For more acculturated Mexican Americans, these beliefs persist in one of two ways: For some, the beliefs coexist alongside biomedical concepts in a compartmentalized system of dual beliefs (Castro et al., 1984; Farge, 1977; Spicer, 1977), whereas for others folk medical beliefs are integrated with those of biomedicine, with biomedical causes of illness (e.g., viruses) viewed as explaining the "how," and cultural causes explaining the "why" of disease, such that the latter remain more important (Farge, 1977; Spector, 1996; Spicer, 1977).

Emotions. Emotions are viewed as the principal cause of illness and occupy a status in Mexican American folk medicine analogous to the position of micro-organisms in biomedicine. The amount or dosage of specific emotions, along with the nature and seriousness of the diseases produced by them, are highly differentiated, with emotions ranked in terms of their pathogenicity; the latter is a function of the tendency of a specific emotion to persist (in an individual over time) rather than of its pleasantness or aversiveness (Clark, 1970; Fabrega, 1974; Spector, 1996). Anger, envy, and worry are particularly pathogenic because they tend to persist, and hence these emotions occupy a place of prominence in the folk etiological beliefs of traditional and acculturated Mexican Americans alike (Castro et al., 1984), as well as in the ethnomedicine of other Latino cultures (including those of Puerto Ricans, Cubans, and Central and South Americans; Harwood, 1981; Klein, 1978; Spector, 1979, 1996; Spicer, 1977). Emotions are viewed as inevitable, but as forces that should be discharged quickly (in talk or action) to maintain emotional homeostasis and a relatively flat affective presentation; illness is understood as produced when the body carries an excessive load of emotions. Given the pathogenicity of affect, interpersonal relations have disease implications. Family arguments, separations, frightening (traumatic) experiences, unemployment, and other social and interpersonal factors are viewed as distal causes of disease because of the emotions (proximal cause) they elicit. Relationships then are key variables not only in the cause but also in the cure and prevention of disease, and maintaining interpersonal harmony thereby occupies a place of prominence in minority beliefs about health promotion and disease prevention. As will be shown, the latter view characterizes the prevention beliefs of all sociocentric cultures.

In addition to reflecting emotional states and interpersonal relations, disease also is understood as the result of the imbalance of naturalistic factors such as hot and cold. Although anger, envy, worry, and fright are understood as the

[1]Throughout this chapter, the cultures of minority groups are referred to as *sociocentric cultures,* an anthropological term meant to distinguish them from the individualistic or *egocentric cultures* of White Western Europeans and Americans (Fabrega, 1974; Shweder & LeVine, 1984). These two types of cultures differ in their fundamental assumptions about the nature of the person and of the person–environment relation. The former endorse mind/body, self/other, and person/environment holism, whereas the latter endorse dualism in each of those domains. These beliefs, in turn, sculpt cultural differences in health beliefs and practices. The many differences between egocentric and sociocentric cultures will become clear in the chapter.

TABLE 51.1
The 10 Leading Causes of Death in 1993 by Gender and Ethnicity

		Men					Women				
Cause	Overall	White	Black	Native American	Asian	Hispanic	White	Black	Native American	Asian	Hispanic
Diseases of heart	1	1	1	1	1	1	1	1	1	2	1
Malignant neoplasms	2	2	2	3	2	2	2	2	2	1	2
Cerebrovascular disease	3	3	6	7	3	6	3	3	5	3	3
COPD	4	4	8	10	6		4	10	3	4	7
Unintentional injuries	5	5	5	2	4	3	6	5	8	7	5
Pneumonia and influenza	6	6	7	6	5	10	5	6	7	5	6
Diabetes Mellitus	7	9	9	8	9	9	7	4	4	6	4
HIV	8	8	4		10	4		7			9
Suicide	9	7		5	8	8			10	8	
Homicide/legal intervention	10		3	9	7	5	9			10	
Liver disease/cirrhosis		10		4		7		6	6		
Perinatal conditions			10					8			8
Atherosclerosis							8				
Nephritis/nephrotic syndrome							9		9		
Septicemia							10				
Congenital anomalies										9	10

Note: Adapted from U.S. Department of Health and Human Services (1996). *Health United States 1995*. DHHS Pub. No. (PHS) 96-1232. Hyattsville, MD: Public Health Service, Centers for Disease Control and Prevention, National Center for Health Statistics.

major proximal causes of disease in all Latino cultures, the balance of hot and cold is understood as playing an additional, powerful role in health (Baca, 1969; Castro et al., 1984; Clark, 1970; Kay & Yoder, 1987; Spector, 1979, 1996; Steffenson & Colker, 1982).

The Ubiquitous Hot/Cold Theory of Disease. Beliefs regarding the balance of hot and cold are an important aspect of the folk medical beliefs of all Latino cultures (Currier, 1966; Farge, 1977; Messer, 1987; Rubel, 1960), including those of Mexicans, Puerto Ricans (Fabrega, 1974; Harwood, 1971, 1981), Guatemalans (Cosminsky, 1975, 1977; Logan & Morrill, 1979; Weller, 1983), and Cubans (and others) in their homelands as well as in the United States (Spector, 1979, 1996). Indeed hot/cold theory also has been found in Asia (Leslie, 1976; Poyneer, 1983; Tran, 1980), Morocco (Greenwood, 1981), Malaysia (Laderman, 1987; Pool, 1987), Africa (Horton, 1967; Namboze, 1983), China (Gould-Martin, 1978), India/southeast Asia (Armarasingham, 1980; Khare & Ishvara, 1986; Nichter, 1987), and Korea (Kendall, 1987), as well as among the American members of these cultural groups (Harwood, 1981; Gould-Martin, 1978; Spector, 1979, 1996). Likewise, hot/cold beliefs even have been found among isolated cultures such as some South American Indian tribes (Colson & de Armellada, 1983; Messer, 1987). Hence, the imbalance of hot and cold may be the (non-White) world's most common causal attribution for illness.

The precise origin of the hot/cold theory of disease and how it became so widespread remain topics of debate among medical anthropologists and historians. Beliefs about the balancing of opposites or "humors" appear to have arisen independently and simultaneously in ancient Greece, India, and China, and then to have spread through trade and conquest (Laderman, 1987; Messer, 1987), with 16th-century Spanish humoral theory (a derivation of earlier Hippocratic theory) spread in this manner to the many conquered lands that became Latin America. Evidence suggests, however, that some version of hot/cold theory arose independently in all sociocentric cultures, and that the hot/cold theories of conquerors and traders were accepted simply because they were consistent with these preexisting, indigenous beliefs (Laderman, 1987). This is clearly the case for the Aztec, Maya, and Zapotec (Messer, 1987), and for the Akawaio, Pemon, and other isolated, South American Indian tribes who speak neither English nor Spanish and could not have borrowed these ideas from Spanish and other Old World countries during the conquest (Colson & de Armellada, 1983). Theoretically, the belief that changes in heat or cold produces disease could arise independently in all sociocentric cultures because these cultures regard the line between person and environment as a thin, semi-permeable membrane (Landrine, 1992) that permits changes in the environment to cause changes in the mind and body (Fabrega, 1974; Landrine, 1992).

The sociocentric hot/cold theory of disease posits that the healthy body is the result of the balance or equilibrium between the contrasting qualities of "hot" and "cold." Illness is seen as resulting from disequilibrium after internal or external exposure to excessive amounts of "heat" or "cold" and hence is treated by restoring that balance. Hot and cold are not simply temperatures, but also are qualities of individuals, medicines, emotions, foods, places, symptoms, diseases, health interventions, cures, and objects, all of which are categorized as such in folk medicine. Water, "cold" (in terms of temperature or spice) foods, and air are ordinary sources of "cold" and must be neutralized by eating "hot" foods, using *emplastos calientes* (hot poultices), or drinking hot drinks to avoid development of symptoms and illnesses classified as "cold" (Clark, 1970; Currier, 1966; Farge, 1977; Harwood, 1971, 1981; Kay & Yoder, 1987; Spector, 1996). Likewise, strong emotions, exposure to the sun, and "hot" foods are mundane sources of heat requiring cure (restoration of balance) through eating "cold" foods or medicines, use of *emplastos frios* (cold poultices), or rubbing the body with a raw egg (a "cold" treatment and common Latino folk cure called "sweeping") to avoid developing hot symptoms. Hence, traditional Mexican and other Latino Americans will not comply with medications or interventions that they classify as "hot" if they also classify their illness as such, and instead only comply with treatments understood to be the opposite of the symptoms (Harwood, 1981). In addition, as already mentioned, Mexican American folk medicine also attributes illness to wind, drafts, or air ("mal aire," bad air). These are typically linked to the hot/cold theory of disease as a type of "cold" (night air in particular) that can enter the body through its various cavities and result in illness. As will be seen, Native, African, and Asian Americans (in particular) also attribute illness to wind/air. Recent empirical studies have confirmed etiological beliefs regarding hot/cold and air/drafts even among acculturated, minority college students (Landrine & Klonoff, 1994b).

In summary, all Latino cultures view health as harmony within the body, between people, and between people and environmental and spiritual realms. Consequently, disruptions in relationships, violations of behavioral and moral taboos (creating disharmony), and disruptions in emotions or in the environment are all seen as causing diseases that are simultaneously physical, psychiatric, social, and moral in nature. This holism characterizes all sociocentric cultures (internationally as well as within the United States), such that imbalance and disharmony are central to Asian, African, and Native American beliefs about illness as well. Likewise, all sociocentric cultures lack the mind/body dualism of biomedicine and thereby draw no lines between emotional versus physical symptoms, nor do they classify disease into those two broad categories. Hence, across minority cultures in the United States and around the globe, people presenting depression expect to be asked about their diets and exercise patterns, and those presenting pain expect to be asked about their morals, emotions, and relationships (Harwood, 1981). This ubiquitous mind/body holism plays a role in the equally ubiquitous biomedical misconception of minorities as "somatisizers." One cannot, of course, "somatisize" (move events from the mind to the body side of the dualism) in the absence of the dualism on which the Western construct of somatization rests. Hence, such holism also plays a role in Latino dissatisfaction with health care providers interested only in symptoms related to one side of the dualism (Schreiber & Homiak, 1981) and in Asian American confusion regarding the dualist classification of care providers (Hare, 1993; Hoang & Erickson, 1985; Poyneer, 1983).

Mexican American Folk Disorders

Just as the medical knowledge of relatively powerless ethnic groups (within the United States and around the world) is called "folk medicine" to distinguish it from ("real") biomedicine, so too the cures developed by these groups are called "folk cures"; the healers of these groups are called "folk healers"; and disorders specific to these groups are called "folk disorders." Folk disorders, or culture bound syndromes, then are diseases (reliable, observed constellations of symptoms) exhibited only by a specific ethnic/cultural group (Simons & Hughes, 1985).[2] The folk disorders and folk cures of Mexican Americans and of other minorities have received

[2]Some have argued that the use of the adjective "folk" to qualify the medical knowledge and diseases of Others is inherently racist. This is because the term privileges the knowledge and illness experience of White Western Europeans/Americans while dismissing those of all other ethnic groups by relegating them to the lesser "folk" (i.e., superstition) domain (Baer, Singer, & Johnson, 1986; Pachter et al., 1993). Importantly, the term *folk illness* in particular seems little more than a "means of excluding the illness experience of a minority group from resources available to others" by denying it legitimacy (Patcher et al., 1992, p. 286). Hence, folk disorders (among minorities within the United States and around the world) are not possible diagnoses in any diagnostic system (the DSM, or the ICD), and receive little biomedical research attention or efforts to find cures for them despite their prevalence and the fact that minorities do die from them. This "unwillingness to seriously respond to an illness experience outside of the biomedical paradigm," despite the morbidity and mortality associated with folk disorders, persists because it serves Western biomedicine's efforts to "enforce its hegemonic position as the 'broker' of health and health care" (Patcher et al., 1992, p. 286). Of course, a wide diversity of White Western (European and American) ostensible illnesses, such as infantile colic (Sampson, 1989), hypoglycemia (Hunt et al., 1990; Klonoff & Biglan, 1987), premenstrual syndrome (Ruble, 1977), and menopausal "hot flashes" (MacPherson, 1981; McCrea, 1983), along with White Western magical disease causes such as "stress" (Young, 1980) qualify as folk disorders and folk etiological concepts (respectively) insofar as they are endorsed and exhibited almost exclusively by this ethnic/cultural group. Indeed, because these disorders and this etiological factor ("stress") have "no standardized diagnostic criteria [and] consist primarily of subjective symptoms [that] resolve in a relatively brief period" (Sampson, 1989, p. 583), they are more prototypically "folk" (i.e., superstition, bogus, or psychosomatic) than are any of the folk illnesses of minority groups.

little attention from biomedicine (health psychology included) despite their prevalence and persistence, and so are addressed briefly here. It should be noted, however, that the exception to this neglect is folk cures that cause minority illness or death, for these have received considerable attention from mainstream health scientists. The inordinate attention paid to toxic/lethal minority folk cures is reasonable from a public health perspective. However, when that attention is viewed in the context of the total neglect of folk disorders and of helpful cures, it also may be a means for biomedicine to address cultural diversity while simultaneously reinforcing the cultural hierarchies purportedly challenged by that focus. This chapter assumes that (1) folk disorders represent "real" biomedical diseases that have yet to be identified because of ethnocentric neglect by biomedicine (Simons & Hughes, 1985); that (2) folk cures are more or less effective treatments (whose mechanism of effect is currently unknown); and that (3) this accounts for the prevalence and persistence of both in many cultures for many centuries.

The major folk disorders of Mexican Americans are summarized next, and demonstrated to hold for other Latino cultures within the United States and around the globe as well; this is followed by a discussion of Latino folk healers and cures.

Caida de la mollera ("fallen fontanelle") is a disorder restricted to infants of both sexes and characterized by inability to suck the breast or bottle, persistent fever and diarrhea, inordinate restlessness and crying, and vomiting. Mexican American folk medicine argues that *caida* occurs when the mollera (the fontanelle of the parietal or frontal bone of the cranium) falls and leaves a "soft spot" as a result of an infant fall from some height or suddenly withdrawing the nipple from the infant's mouth during breast feeding. The fallen fontanelle, according to folk theory, results in a downward projection of the palate that inhibits the infant's ability to ingest food and causes the symptoms observed (Rubel, 1993; Rubel, O'Nell, & Ardon, 1984; Trotter, 1985a, 1991; Trotter, Ortiz de Montellano, & Logan, 1989). *Caida* has been recognized in all Latino cultures for many centuries, including Spain, Mexico, and Central and South America (Baca, 1969; Currier, 1966; Ingham, 1970; Spicer, 1977; Trotter, 1991). The brief biomedical attention devoted to *caida* has led to the conclusion that it is the Latino folk name for dehydration among infants in which, however, cause and effect have been reversed in folk understandings. Specifically, Latinos, observing the loss of subcutaneous fluid over the fontanelle (a result of dehydration caused by infant diarrhea) seem to have mistaken this effect (depressed fontanelle and the exaggeration of palatal rugae) as the cause of the symptoms observed (Simons & Hughes, 1985; Trotter et al., 1989). Enteric diseases, with ensuing diarrhea and dehydration among infants, are common in Latino cultures across the globe and within the United States (Simons & Hughes, 1985; Trotter et al., 1989).

Empacho ("indigestion infection") is a disorder afflicting children and adults of both sexes and characterized by lack of appetite, stomachache, intestinal pain and cramping, diarrhea, abdominal swelling, and vomiting. In folk medicine, the disorder is said to be due to a poorly digested piece of food becoming lodged in the intestines because the food was toxic (e.g., unrefrigerated dairy products), or because the person was socially obligated to eat when not hungry (an emotional cause; Rubel, 1960). *Empacho* has been recognized by a diversity of Latino cultures for centuries and is a common complaint among Mexicans (Baer & Ackerman, 1988), Mexican Americans (Martin, Martinez, Leon, Richardson, & Acosta, 1985; Rubel, 1993; Rubel et al., 1984; Trotter, 1985b, 1991), Guatemalans (Weller et al., 1991), and Puerto Ricans (Harwood, 1981), and occasionally results in death. Typical folk cures for *empacho* include drinking teas and massage of the stomach and intestines (Trotter, 1981a) by a Mexican (*curandera*), Puerto Rican (*santiguador*), or Guatemalan (*sobador*) folk healer. Other common folk treatments for empacho are toxic and detailed later here. The brief biomedical attention devoted to empacho has concluded that it is an enteric disease secondary to eating foods that are not fully cooked and/or to allergy to milk products (Patcher et al., 1992).

Mal ojo (the "evil eye") can afflict anyone of any age or gender (although more common among women), and is characterized by the sudden onset of a plethora of somatic and psychiatric symptoms, including severe headache, anxiety, depression, crying, insomnia, and rashes. According to folk theory, it is caused by the envious or admiring gaze of a strong person at a weaker one, with the emotion-laden stare subjecting the victim to disease provoking, excessive affect. If not treated, it is said to advance to a fatal stage (*ojo pasado*) characterized by uncontrollable coughing, vomiting, and eventual death. Hence, when the symptoms of *mal ojo* appear, victims immediately retrace their steps in an effort to locate the person who caused the symptoms. This person then touches the victim to rupture the effect of *mal ojo* by symbolically atoning for and taking back the emotion (Baca, 1969; Clark, 1970; Schreiber & Homiak, 1981; Trotter, 1981a, 1991). *Mal ojo* has been recognized in a variety of Latino cultures for many centuries, has been associated with deaths, and is one of the folk disorders believed to necessitate the intervention of a *curandera,* a Mexican folk healer (Babb, 1981; Trotter, 1981a; Trotter & Chavira, 1981; G.H.D. Smith, 1995). Although no biomedical studies of *mal ojo* were found, several reviews indicate that belief in this disorder spans many cultures, as demonstrated later here.

Susto ("fright" or "soul loss") is the best- known of the Latino culture-bound syndromes and has been found among Mexicans and Central and South Americans in their homelands, as well as among the American members of these minority groups (Clark, 1970; Klein, 1978; Martin et al., 1985; Rubel et al., 1984; Rubel, 1960, 1993; Trotter, 1981a, 1982, 1985a, 1991). As is shown here, Asian/American and Native American cultures also recognize a disorder called fright or soul loss that has symptoms and a folk etiology matching that of Latino *susto,* such that "magical fright" may be the single most common folk disorder in the (non-White) world. *Susto* can afflict people of any age or gender (but is more common among women and children), and according to Latino folk medical theory, is caused by a frightening or traumatic experience (i.e., excessive emotion). Common precipitating experiences include being deserted by a husband, being physically assaulted, and the death of or serious injury to a loved one.

The trauma of this frightening experience is said to cause the soul to become dislodged from the body (leaving the individual immobilized and helpless), with this soul loss manifested in a sudden onset of anxiety, fatigue, muscular weakness, severe appetite loss, fever, vertigo, and nausea. Additional symptoms depend on the stage of the disorder, and include stomachache, diarrhea, and vomiting (in early stages, *susto nuevo* or *tripa ida*); languor, anorexia nervosa, inability to urinate, and lack of motivation to do everyday tasks (in middle stages, *asustado*); and wasting away until an early, untimely death in advanced stages (*susto pasado* or *mal de delgadito*). Little biomedical attention has been devoted to *susto* despite the deaths associated with it. Some (Rubel et al., 1984) have suggested that it is a form of hysteria. Others (Bolton, 1981) have suggested that it is severe hypoglycemia (because, in addition to the folk cure "sweeping," *susto* is treated by ingesting sugar), or vitamin B deficiency coupled with anemia (Trotter, 1982). There is little evidence for these hypotheses given the absence of biomedical investigations of patients with *susto.*

Mal puesto ("bewitchment," or evil hex or curse) is the belief in witches (*brujas*) or sorcerers (*brujos*) and in their ability to curse or hex someone (manifested in illness). It has been found in all Latino cultures across the globe and within the United States (Clark, 1970; Harwood, 1981; Ingham, 1970; Kay & Yoder, 1977; Rubel, 1960, 1987; Schreiber & Homiak, 1981; G.H.D. Smith, 1995; Trotter & Chavira, 1981), as well as among the many other cultural groups discussed here. In Latino cultures, the symptoms of being hexed or bewitched (*embrujada*) include exhibitionism, psychotic symptoms, and screaming and crying (in conjunction with any host of physical symptoms). No biomedical studies of *mal puesto* were found.

Other Mexican and Latino American folk disorders that have received less attention from medical anthropologists are: *bilis,* an anxiety disorder due to upsetting emotional experiences; *latido,* a folk name for anorexia nervosa; *chipil,* an emotional disturbance in infants; and *pasmo,* a postpartum illness afflicting women who violate the restrictions (e.g., no intercourse, baths, spicy foods) associated with the *la dieta* or *la cuarentena* (the 40-day period of convalescence following delivery), and manifested in swelling, septicemia, and other serious symptoms. Latido and late stages of susto are identical to anorexia nervosa; the well-known low prevalence of that eating disorder among minority women (Landrine, 1995) may be an artifact of biomedicine's refusal to recognize folk disorders.

Frequency of Folk Disorders. The prevalence of the aforementioned folk disorders among Mexican and other Latino Americans is unclear because studies report inconsistent results and employ populations from different geographical regions. For example, Trotter (1982), in a study of 198 current ailments reported to him by a small group of subjects, found that 3% of these were folk disorders (with susto the most common). Alternatively, Rivera's (1988) review of the literature revealed that 95% of Latinos reported experiencing at least one episode of a folk illness in their lifetimes, whereas H. W. Martin et al. (1985) found a differing prevalence rate that differed from both of these. Likewise, because treatment from *curanderas* (folk healers) is sought exclusively for folk disorders (*empacho, mal ojo,* and *susto* in particular; see G.H.D. Smith, 1995), rates of utilization of *curanderas* are an indirect measure of prevalence of folk disorders. Accordingly, Rivera's (1988) review found *curanderas* consulted by 5% (of northern) to 23% of (southern) California Mexican Americans, and by 32% to 80% of Mexican Americans in other geographical regions. The studies of Trotter (1991) and others suggest that almost all Mexican Americans, irrespective of level of acculturation, are aware of the folk disorders and readily admit knowing someone who suffers from one, but may deny experiencing a folk disorder themselves.

Mexican American Folk Healers

The Mexican American community has a wide variety of folk healers (Anderson, 1970; Babb, 1981; Ingham, 1970; Schreiber & Homiak, 1981; G.H.D. Smith, 1995; Trotter, 1985a; Trotter & Chavira, 1981; Weaver, 1973) who have counterparts in all other Latino American communities. These indigenous therapists include (but are not limited to) the following:

Yerberos ("herbalists") are men or women who specialize in the herbal home remedies used by laypeople to treat biomedical and folk illness, and have long been an important health resource in Mexican and other Latino American neighborhoods. Although there are no data on the frequency with which they are consulted, the ubiquitous use of herbal home remedies reported in all ethnographic studies (Maduro, 1983; Trotter, 1981a, 1981b) suggests that they are a mainstay of the Latino folk health care system.

Parteras (women) are midwives (who often are both folk and former biomedical practitioners) specializing in the delivery of infants. They are particularly common and deliver the majority of the babies in the Rio Grande Valley of Texas and other parts of the borderland states, as well as in other Latino and in African American communities (Babb, 1981).

Sobadoras (women) are masseuses who use massage and prayer to treat muscular pains, joint dislocation, *caida,* and *empacho,* and may use spiritual cures as well (Babb, 1981).

Señoras ("wise women") are older women specializing in the treatment of folk disorders (particularly those afflicting infants), who also sometimes act as midwives (Babb, 1981).

Espiritualistas ("spiritualists") treat biomedical disorders (with prominent psychiatric symptoms) and folk disorders through a combination of massage, herbal remedies, prayer, trance, and spirit mediumship. The latter magico-religious practices distinguish them from other healers, and they have counterparts in Puerto Rican, Cuban, and African American communities (Anderson, 1970; Babb, 1981; Ingham, 1970; Laguerre, 1981; Schreiber & Homiak, 1981; G.H.D. Smith, 1995)

Curanderas are the most common and most frequently studied of the Latino folk healers because their system of healing (called *curanderismo*) is ancient, diverse, and well-established (Rivera & Wanderer, 1986; Kiev, 1968; Maduro, 1983; G.H.D. Smith, 1995; Torres, 1983; Trotter, 1980; Trotter & Chavira, 1981). *Curanderas* (usually women) can be found in every urban center, and often (and increasingly) have a sophisticated knowledge of biomedicine that they use in conjunction with folk cures (Applewhite, 1995; De la Cancela & Martinez, 1983; Mayers, 1992; G.H.D. Smith, 1995). For example, Dona Elena Avila, a *curandera* practicing in New Mexico, has graduate degrees in nursing, and was the clinical coordinator of UCLA's Neuropsychiatric Institute and Director of Maternal–Child Nursing at Thomason Hospital in El Paso (G.H.D. Smith, 1995). She is widely known for integrating the interventions of biomedical nursing with those of *curanderismo*. The modern *curandera's* consulting room thus contains indigenous herbs, palm leaves, crosses, and poultices, as well as medical instruments, hypodermic needles, and antibiotics. Classic *curanderismo* includes at least 1,100 folk cures (Anderson, 1970, detailed 1,135 of these) that range from herbal remedies to inhalation and sweating therapies, to prayers, incantations, and magico-religious rituals. *Curanderas* are consulted primarily for treatment of folk disorders, but also are sought for treatment of chronic illness in children, and for recalcitrant, socially disruptive symptoms in adults (depression, alcohol and drug abuse, impotence).

Estimates of the frequency of consulting *curanderas* vary widely with methodology employed. In face-to-face interviews conducted by Latinos, rates range from 23% to 80% (Rivera, 1988), depending on the questions asked, geographical region, and the decade in which the study was conducted. Alternatively, in the more impersonal methodology used in the Hispanic Health and Nutrition Examination Survey (HHANES; Higgenbotham, Trevino, & Ray, 1990), only 4.2% of Mexican Americans reported seeking assistance from a *curandera* (or other folk healer) in the past year. Although still a considerable utilization rate, this may be lower than the true rate because HHANES assessed only past-year (vs. lifetime) use of *curanderas*, and used an impersonal procedure in a culture that values highly personal contact (Atkinson et al., 1993). Likewise, when use of folk healers is examined by assessing home use by lay people of cures typically recommended by *curanderas* and herbalists, rates are again extremely high and range from 50% to 95% (Applewhite, 1995; De la Cancela & Martinez, 1983; Mayers, 1992; Trotter, 1980, 1981a, 1981b).

Mexican American Folk Cures

Discussion of the diversity of folk cures used by Mexican and other Latino Americans is beyond the scope of this chapter. The reader is referred to Anderson (1970) for an overview of 1,135 cures, and to the major studies on curanderas for other cures and healing rituals (Kiev, 1968; Maduro, 1983; Rivera & Wanderer, 1986; G.H.D. Smith, 1995; Torres, 1983; Trotter, 1980; Trotter & Chavira, 1981). The most common cures include massage, changes in diet, social support, teas, herbal remedies, rest, saunas, and prayers (conducted conjointly), as well as "sweeping." In the latter, a whole, unbroken, raw egg ("cold") is rubbed on the patient's body (or is placed in water under the patient's bed) to absorb the "heat." Crosses made from palm leaves are used along with prayers that are said in threes throughout the cure; massage, herbal teas, herbal remedies, and a salve made from chili powder and olive oil are used as well, along with discussion of the patient's interpersonal relationships. Sweeping is used in all other Latino American cultures as well.

Toxic Herbal Remedies for Empacho. Although there are few studies assessing the pharmacological efficacy of the herbal remedies used in Latino American folk cures, those that exist suggest that all of these herbs contain potent, chemically active ingredients that therefore can be effective treatments for fever, pain, and the like, or can be lethal (Trotter, 1985a). Most attention has been devoted to those that are toxic or lethal, and specifically to the toxic/lethal herbal remedies found in the medicine cabinets of most Mexican American households. Two of these toxic/lethal remedies used for the treatment of *empacho* are *greta* (lead oxide) and *azarcon* (lead tetroxide); both are available throughout Mexican American communities in *yerberias* (herb shops) and consist of 89% and 93% elemental lead, respectively. Many cases (case studies) of lead poisoning (among children in particular) as a result of these remedies have been reported among Mexican Americans (Baer & Ackerman, 1988; Baer, de Alba, Cueto, Ackerman, & Davidson, 1989; Centers for Disease Control, 1981, 1983b; Trotter, 1985a, 1985b). However, no systematic studies of the frequency of use of these lead-based remedies have been conducted. Hence the role this folk cure (undiagnosed, low-level lead poisoning) plays in Mexican American physical and mental health and in intellectual deficits among Mexican American children remains unknown. Although Trotter (a medical anthropologist) identified several other toxic herbs in the medicine cabinets of Mexican Americans, such as *asoque* (containing mercury) and *anil* (laundry bluing, containing toxic aniline dye), no studies have been conducted on these. The need for research on Mexican American effective and toxic folk cures is clear.

Finally, several studies suggest that Latino American knowledge of folk medical theories, folk cures, and folk healers plays a role in their help seeking, health behavior, and compliance with treatment (e.g., Applewhite, 1995; H. W. Martin et al., 1985; Mayers, 1992; Nall & Speilberg, 1967; Schreiber & Homiak, 1981; Spector, 1979, 1996). This is supported by the many studies of the health behavior impact of levels of acculturation among Mexican Americans cited in the Introduction here.

Puerto Rican Americans

Numerous studies indicate that Puerto Rican health beliefs, practices and folk cures are similar to those already detailed for Mexican Americans, including the predominance of the hot/cold theory of disease, notions of health as symbolic balance, and the attribution of illness to wind/drafts and witches or evil spirits (Harwood, 1971, 1981). Belief in the disease causing effects of evil spirits and other supernatural forces and entities is far stronger and more prevalent among this group than among Mexican Americans however, with 30-40% of normal and 90% of psychiatric patient Puerto Ricans seeking cures from spirit mediums for physical and psychiatric symptoms believed to be so caused (Harwood, 1971, 1977, 1981). This no doubt represents the strong influence of African cultures on the island: Unlike Mexican-Americans, but similar to African Americans and to people from Afro-Caribbean cultures (e.g., Cubans, Haitians), Puerto Ricans hold spiritist beliefs that dominate their concepts of illness, and they participate in healing cults/religions such as *mesa blanca* and *santeria* as a result. Details of these magico-spiritist religions/healing cults cannot be discussed here but are detailed elsewhere (Harwood, 1977, 1981; Paulino, 1995); they are similar to voodoo, however (Paulino, 1995), which is discussed in the African American section. To be noted here is that many Puerto Ricans firmly believe that each individual has a guardian angel (present from birth), and each person is influenced by it as well as by the numerous disembodied spirits of deceased and divine beings, all of whom play an active role in determining life events and health and disease. The activity of these spirits, whether acting on their own or in conjunction with witches and sorcerers, is understood as the sole proximal cause of all disease, with all other (Latino and biomedical) causes viewed as distal and secondary.

Mal ojo and *empacho* are recognized as folk disorders by Puerto Ricans, and both are commonly found among this group as well (Harwood, 1981). However, other folk disorders specific to Puerto Ricans also have been identified. These include "states" of the blood, such *sangre gruesa* (thick blood) and *sangre debil* (weak blood). These etiological concepts and folk disorders are common among African American and Afro-Caribbean cultures (Laguerre, 1981) and so are discussed in the section on African Americans. The other (and most well-known) Puerto Rican folk disorder is the *ataque de nervios* (attack of the nerves, or "worry"), which is so common and well researched that it is often called the "Puerto Rican Syndrome" (Harwood, 1981). This disorder can be exhibited by anyone (but is common among women after a traumatic experience), and consists of anxiety, depression, shouting, screaming, tearing one's clothing, and tonic and clonic convulsions, all viewed as socially acceptable responses to trauma (Harwood, 1981). This syndrome is similar to Latino *susto* (Rubel, 1993), and nearly identical to African American, Central American, and Afro-Caribbean "worry," or "worriation," as discussed later here. Finally, three types of indigenous healers are recognized in the Puerto Rican community: spiritists, herbalists, and *curanderas*. The treatment provided by these healers is identical to that provided by their counterparts in Mexican American and other Latino communities, with the exception of the spiritists whose interventions are more mystical and similar to those of voodoo priests.

ASIAN AMERICANS

The term *Asian* refers to Americans whose cultural background/ethnicity is Chinese, Indian, Japanese, Korean, Sinhalese, Pakistani, Filipino, and southeast Asian, where the latter term refers to Vietnamese, Cambodian, Thai, and Laotian (including the Mein, Hmong, Kha, Yao and other hill tribes of Laos). Because the health beliefs and practices of all of these ethnic groups cannot be covered in a single chapter, the focus is on a few groups who can be regarded as prototypical and representative of others; this is the reason for the focus on the Chinese, whose folk medical system has shaped those of many other Asian groups.

Studies of Health Problems of Asian Americans

The major health problems confronting Asian Americans (Table 51.1) are heart disease, cancer, cerebrovascular disease, chronic obstructive pulmonary disease (COPD), diabetes, pneumonia, and influenza (USDHHS, 1996). The major health problems of southeast Asian refugees are high rates of hepatitis B, tuberculosis, anemia, and intestinal parasites (Catanzaro & Moser, 1982; Hoang & Erickson, 1982), along with depression (Root, 1995; Westermeyer, Vang, & Neider, 1983) secondary to witnessing war and torture, and to separation from family left in southeast Asia (Root, 1995).

General Cultural Factors Influencing Health Behavior

Three of the many global, cultural factors that influence the health behavior of Asian Americans are racism and distrust of Whites, fear of shame, and language barriers and indigenous health schema.

Racism and Distrust of Whites. Like the other ethnic groups discussed here, Asian Americans have long been the victims of White racism and exploitation, much of it legitimated in laws such as the 1882 Chinese Exclusion Act, the 1908 Gentleman's Agreement, the 1917 Barred Zone Act, the 1922 Cable Act, 1945 War Brides Act, the 1964–1965 Immigration Act, and the 1979 Refugee Act. These laws systematically excluded dark-skinned Asians; outlawed miscegenation; permitted only men to immigrate in order to serve as cheap, manual laborers; or allowed only women to immigrate who were then sold (75% of Chinese women in California at the turn of the century) as sexual slaves to White American men (Root, 1995). Other examples of anti-Asian racism include violence and discrimination against the Japanese in the 1930s and 1940s (culminating in their internment in camps); current neglect of the many needs of the Hmong despite their dedicated service to the Central Intelligence Agency (CIA) during the Vietnam war (Adler, 1995); and ongoing discrimination (in housing and other services) and violence against Asians because they are viewed (since the 1970s) as responsible for America's economic woes (Atkinson et al., 1993; Root, 1995). The 1986 Civil Rights

Commission Report on Anti-Asian Activities revealed repeated cases of the murder of Asian Americans by Whites who blame Asians for their unemployment, as well as ongoing vandalism, job discrimination, and assault (Atkinson et al., 1993). This historical and current social context of White violence and racism has been neglected, but it nonetheless may play a role in Asian American reticence to seek help from White health care providers, with subsequent dangerous delays in seeking treatment. The role of anti-Asian racism and violence in smoking, alcohol use, and other health problems among Asian Americans has never been investigated.

Shaming Practices and the Fear of Shame. All sociocentric cultures understand individuals as existing only by virtue of and in relation to others, rather than as independent, encapsulated selves. People are understood as members of families (as husbands, mothers, daughters, and sons) first and as individuals second (rather than the other way around as in egocentric cultures). Indeed, in many sociocentric cultures, people are viewed as synonymous with such family roles and it is not believed that there is an individual lurking behind a role that he or she may be uncomfortable occupying (Landrine, 1992; P. Lewis & E. Lewis, 1984; Marsella, DeVos, & Hsu, 1985). Hence, in all sociocentric cultures, interdependence, mutual obligation, and reciprocity characterize interpersonal relationships; the needs of the family have priority over those of the individual; and maintaining interpersonal harmony is highly valued. In Asian cultures, these sociocentric attitudes and values (regarding mutual obligation in particular) do not simply influence or characterize, but instead dominate the emotional, cognitive, and behavioral life of traditional members (Atkinson et al., 1993; P. Lewis & E. Lewis, 1984; Marsella et al., 1985; D. Sue & D. W. Sue, 1993).

In Asian cultures, people are understood as owing an eternal, bottomless debt to their parents for bringing them into the world and caring for them as a child. Such a debt can never be repaid and is akin to an infinite bank loan whose collateral is the offspring's existence. Hence, offspring are eternally obligated to pay only the interest (that continues to accrue) on this loan in lieu of the principal. These interest payments consist of obedience, respect, achievement, and behavior that conforms to social norms, and are understood as a minor request (as the very least an individual can do) in light of the principal. When Asians violate social or moral norms, they incur shame (*tiu lien*) or "loss of lien" (loss of face). To violate social norms and incur loss of lien is analogous to refusing to pay even the interest on a generous, unpayable loan from parents. The response of parents and the community to such behavior is much like a bank's would be in a similar situation: The person's social credit—the presumption of trust, confidence, dignity, and respect—is revoked by parents, and the person's social credit rating destroyed throughout the community, making it impossible for loans (social support, respect, trust, confidence) to be secured elsewhere.

Thus, to incur shame and be subjected to shaming practices means that the person who violated a norm is treated by their families and the entire community as a pariah (i.e., a despised outcast who is condemned, distrusted, avoided, mocked, and rejected by all). All social, family, and community support (along with acknowledgment of the person's existence) are immediately withdrawn, and no one trusts the person's words or deeds any longer. Individuals are left alone with their mistakes etched like a scarlet letter on the forehead, while the community points and stares in disdain, and then turns its back. Simultaneously, aspersions are cast on the parents: Just as individuals would doubt the good judgment of a bank that gave loans to unemployed, unreliable people who had no means or intention of repaying them, so too parents are regarded as poor moral guides, and hence as unreliable people (who cannot be trusted) themselves when their offspring incur shame. This practice of shaming seems cruel only if the context of reciprocity is ignored. When a community is based on reciprocity, it is imperative that each person attempt to repay what they have received; an individual who takes but fails to reciprocate even so little as appropriate conduct and conformity threatens the foundation that undergirds the social structure and must be punished lest the presumptive trust that is community weaken and crumble. It is then not surprising that no fear is greater among traditional Asians then that of incurring shame and shaming practices; the behavioral conformity seen among many traditional Asians makes sense in this context.

Because symptoms of all types are understood as shameful, fear of loss of lien inhibits both help seeking and the disclosure of symptoms when help is finally sought. Symptoms are understood as shameful for two reasons. The first is that symptoms are understood as at least in part reflecting violations of taboos, and hence, their mere presence raises questions about the morals of self and family. In addition and more importantly, having symptoms (being ill) means that individuals will need to be cared for by their family and indeed, might be a burden on them. Illness thereby increases their obligations—increases what they owe to an intolerable, impossible level of debt from which they have no hope of ever being free—and so is more shameful still. To disclose illness to health care providers or researchers is to disclose this state of poverty and debt, and is thus a means of incurring further shame. Such beliefs are held by Chinese (Gould-Martin & Ngin, 1981; Spector, 1996), Japanese (Norbeck & Lock, 1987), and many southeast Asian cultural groups (Barney, 1980; Hoang & Erickson, 1985). Consequently, traditional members of many Asian American cultures fail to disclose the nature and history of their symptoms and problematic health behaviors for fear of incurring shame (Gould-Martin & Ngin, 1981; Hoang & Erickson, 1985; Norbeck & Lock, 1987; Tran, 1980). Assurances regarding confidentiality do not lessen this reticence to disclose or lessen the patient's fear of loss of lien through such disclosures (Hoang & Erickson, 1982, 1985). Health professionals then face patients who have sought help but are reluctant to disclose why, and researchers face subjects who will not answer questions or who simply deny all symptoms and problematic health behaviors. For many southeast Asians (unlike Chinese) the fear of shame also leads to delaying help seeking as long as possible (Hoang & Erickson, 1982, 1985; Muecke, 1983a, 1983b; Strand & Jones, 1983; Tran, 1980). How can diagnosis, treatment, or research be achieved when people will not describe their symptoms? Essentially, traditional Asians expect health professionals to discern their problems by making statements about the person's possible problem, and then attending to the person's *nonverbal* (rather than verbal) responses (Gould-Martin & Ngin, 1981; Tran, 1980); this allows traditional Asians to disclose physical and psychiatric symptoms viewed as shameful without actually disclosing them.

Language and Indigenous Schema. Even when traditional people (from southeast Asian cultures in particular) reluctantly disclose their symptoms, the validity of these self-reports must remain suspect because of indigenous health schema and culturally specific uses of medical terminology that violate the understandings of biomedicine. Vietnamese and Hmong may disclose feeling "hot," for example, but this refers to hot–cold beliefs or malaise rather than to fever (Cheon-Klessig, Camilleri, McElmurry, & Ohlson, 1988; Hoang & Erickson, 1985). Other traditional southeast Asians might state they have hepatitis and mean by this only that they have itching, because hepatitis is understood as a liver disease that causes itching (Hoang & Erickson, 1982, 1985; Muecke, 1983a,1983b). Alternatively, because Hmong folk understandings of the liver are analogous to American folk understandings of the heart (as the seat of emotion), Hmong complaints of "liver pain" are actually reports of depression, equivalent to reporting a "broken heart" (Cheon-Klessig et al., 1988). Still other traditional southeast Asians might disclose kidney trouble, and mean by this that they are impotent or have some other sexual dysfunction, because the kidney is understood as the location of sexuality (Hoang & Erickson, 1985). Hence, both language differences and the presence of indigenous health schema are cultural factors that influence health behavior of traditional Asian Americans. These may lead biomedical practitioners and researchers to misinterpret people's reports, and can lead Asian patients to misinterpret the practitioner's words as well. Biomedical information provided to minority patients is processed through indigenous health schema, and can be misunderstood and inaccurately recalled when it cannot be assimilated into preexisting health beliefs (Steffenson & Colker, 1982). This can result in unwitting noncompliance, namely, noncompliance due to the inability to integrate and recall directives (Steffenson & Colker, 1982).

With these general cultural factors affecting health behavior outlined, the discussion turns to the health beliefs, practices, folk disorders, and indigenous folk remedies of a variety of Asian American cultures.

Chinese Americans

Beliefs About Health and Illness

Chinese American concepts of health are based on the philosophy and teachings of Tao (604 BC). According to these doctrines, harmony with the universe and its forces is the essence of health, and illness is construed as imbalance or disharmony. Specifically, health is understood as the result of the balance of the two opposing, complementary forces (called ethers) of Yin and Yang. Yin and Yang work together with six other variables to determine health and illness: the hot/cold polarity, poison, blood, Chi, wind, and the seven emotions. These seven variables are understood as the only causes of illness (Gould-Martin & Ngin, 1981; Hare, 1993; Kaptchuk, 1983; Maciocia, 1989; Spector, 1979, 1996).

Yin and Yang. Yin and Yang are understood as opposite forces that comprise the universe and each person. Yin is viewed as negative energy, coldness, wetness, darkness, and femaleness, and is believed to store strength, conserve energy, and restore physical vitality. The inside and the front of the body are construed as Yin, as are diseases of the winter and spring. Yang is viewed as positive energy or force, lightness, warmth, dryness, fullness, and maleness. The surfaces of the body and the back are construed as Yang, as are diseases of the summer and fall. When Yin and Yang are in balance, the person is healthy. Disruption in this balance or harmony is viewed as the sole proximal cause of any and all diseases and pain. Internal (e.g., aging, personality, fatigue, poor diet, lifestyle) and external (e.g., other people, the weather, micro-organisms) factors are understood as additional causes of disease, but as distal (indirect) causes that play a role by altering Yin or Yang (Gould-Martin, 1978; Gould-Martin & Ngin, 1981; Ludman & Newman, 1984). Whereas these concepts at first appear inscrutable at best, they are analogous to biomedical constructs. Specifically, Yin might be thought of as analogous to the parasympathetic and Yang to the sympathetic nervous system. Stress and viruses then disrupt the balance of these, and the ensuing imbalance has health implications and consequences.

Wind refers literally to the wind, as well as to any draft. Symptoms and illnesses understood as caused by wind are those whose names rhyme with the Chinese word for wind; such problems are treated by bed rest (Gould-Martin & Ngin, 1981; Spector, 1996). Wind (like the other causes here) is understood as a distal cause of illness that alters the fundamental balance of Yin and Yang (proximal cause). *Hot/cold* beliefs have been found in all sociocentric cultures, Chinese (B. Chang, 1974; Gould-Martin, 1978), and all southern Asian cultures included. For example, these beliefs figure prominently in the health schema of the ayurvedic (Indian) folk medicine that dominates India, Sri Lanka, and all of southern Asia (Kapferer, 1983; Khare & Ishvara, 1986; Nichter, 1980, 1987). For Chinese and Chinese Americans, as for other sociocentric cultures, hot and cold are properties of illnesses, foods, treatments, and medications, and it is believed that these must be balanced and regulated to maintain health (see Gould-Martin & Ngin, 1981, for Chinese American classification of symptoms, food, and cures as hot, cold, or wind). For Chinese and Chinese Americans, however, hot and cold are understood as subsumed by the Yin–Yang polarity. *Poison* refers to any symptom entailing swelling, pus, or itching, and is understood as the distal cause of such conditions. Symptoms and illnesses attributed to poison are treated by cold treatments and foods. *Blood* refers literally to blood, and *Chi* to a mythical energy or force understood as the "breath of life," and as flowing through a system of pathways called *me-*

ridians that are viewed as analogous to blood vessels and capillaries. Chi is construed as blocked when severe illness or chronic pain appears, and treatment consists of freeing the flow of Chi through acupuncture or acupressure; the sole raison d' etre of the latter two well-known treatments is to manipulate the flow of Chi (Kaptchuk, 1983; Maciocia, 1989).

Finally, *the seven emotions* (joy, anger, worry, contemplation, grief, apprehension, and fright) are understood as important distal causes of illness insofar as full, direct expression of emotion disrupts social harmony, and such disruptions are disease provoking. Hence, many have been taught that it is inappropriate to display emotion (and particularly, to complain) in the direct ways recognized in the West, leading Chinese and other Asian Americans to be misunderstood as emotionally flat. Chinese and other traditional Asian Americans have learned a full array of complex, rich, and subtle ways to express emotion and to complain, however, and these are nonverbal rather than verbal. It is (often erroneously) assumed by traditional Asians that outsiders can "read" these nonverbal complaints. Hence, health professionals are assumed to be trained in reading nonverbal behavior, and therefore are expected to know what is wrong with patients, how much pain they experience, and the treatment they desire simply by looking at them. Verbal complaints and descriptions of symptoms by patients or research subjects thereby are brief or even absent. In addition, because emotions are viewed as disease provoking, traditional Chinese physicians use psychological interventions (along with physical ones) for physical symptoms. Psychotherapy then is not recognized as a separate treatment to be sought from a specialist (but instead understood as part of all treatment) and the Western system of dualistic healers is regarded as confusing (Hare, 1993). This increases the tendency of traditional Asians to bring psychological complaints to those treating their physical problems, resulting in their being viewed as "somatisizers" (Gould-Martin & Ngin, 1981; Hare, 1993).

Chinese Folk Disorders

Fright refers to a folk illness characterized by listlessness, fever, crying, and lack of appetite. It is common among children and understood as the result of the soul getting lost after a frightening experience. It is treated with the "Protect-infant pill" (*po-yin taan*), crushed pearl powder, and other folk remedies that are readily available in Chinese grocery stores and herb shops (Gould-Martin & Ngin, 1981; Spector, 1996). The symptoms and epidemiology of this folk disorder are remarkably similar to Latino *caida* and thus raise questions regarding the possible role of enteric disease, diarrhea, and dehydration for Chinese children as well; that possibility has never been investigated.

The evil eye is a folk disorder widely recognized throughout Asia (including China, India, and southeast Asia), as well as in Africa and Mediterranean cultures (Pasquale, 1984). In each of these cultures, beliefs about this folk disorder, the role of gaze and envy, and the symptoms associated with the folk disorder match those reported by Latinos (as detailed earlier here). Beliefs in the evil eye are common among traditional American members of these diverse cultural groups (Harwood, 1981).

Chinese Health Attitudes

Traditional Chinese Americans view the body as a gift from their parents rather than as a personal possession, and feel obligated to their parents and families to maintain their health. Because illness is shameful (as discussed earlier), traditional Chinese Americans seek preventative care and seek assistance for symptoms early (Gould-Martin & Ngin, 1981), whereas traditional southeast Asian Americans delay seeking help for the same reasons (Hoang & Erickson, 1982, 1985). Paradoxically, however, traditional Chinese Americans may not disclose their symptoms or medical histories because they expect health professionals to intuit the problem as described earlier. Hence, traditional Asians distrust long diagnostic interviews and tests and view the need for these as a sign of the health professional's or researcher's incompetence (Gould-Martin & Ngin, 1981; Leslie, 1969, 1976). Likewise, the interpersonal norm of *jang* requires silence, modesty, and avoidance of speaking about oneself, and similarly leads to a quiet waiting for the professional to intuit problems. Other health attitudes of traditional Asians include the expectation that family members will be included in all phases of a treatment viewed as their responsibility, and that health professionals will conduct themselves in a polite, authoritative, and distant manner. Making jokes or being warm and friendly are viewed as inappropriate, result in lack of confidence in the treatment and treatment provider, and hence in lack of compliance (Gould-Martin & Ngin, 1981). Taking medication is aversive for traditional Chinese Americans and hence, medications tend to be taken only until symptoms are relieved and then discontinued. If symptoms are not obvious (e.g., in hypertension) medications probably never will be taken. Translating pharmacological and behavioral interventions into terms consistent with folk understanding (e.g., the restoration of balance, the unblocking of Chi) may be necessary to achieve compliance with any type of treatment, including behavioral interventions (Gould-Martin & Ngin, 1981).

Asian American Folk Cures

In the Chinatowns of U.S. cities, indigenous healers known simply as "Chinese Doctors" are readily available and consulted for care instead of, or conjointly with, seeking treatment from biomedical practitioners (Chan & J. K. Chang, 1976; Hare, 1993). The "Chinese doctor" takes a holistic approach to health, and uses acupuncture, teas, rest, massage, acupressure, and/or moxibustion (use of heat) to restore health (Hare, 1993). In addition, there are several culturally specific folk treatments (particularly for pain) that are commonly used by the layperson and folk healer alike throughout the Chinese American community. These interventions are also practiced by the laity and folk healers of a variety of other Asian American groups as well, including the Hmong, Mien, Lao, Cambodian, and Vietnamese. Only the four most common of these treatments are summarized here.

Coining (Cao gio). The term *cao gio* literally means "to scratch the wind," and is a treatment for symptoms understood as caused by wind or "bad wind" in the body. Such symptoms include cold, cough, pain, vomiting, and headaches. Coining entails applying a menthol oil or ointment to the painful or symptomatic area, and then rubbing a coin vigorously over that spot. The coining is usually between the ribs on the front and back of the body, as well as along the trachea, the inner aspect of both upper arms, and/or along the sides of the spine because these are the areas associated with "wind" (breathing). The procedure leaves reddish-purple scars on the coined spots and these are taken as verification that "bad wind" was the cause of the symptoms. The procedure is uncomfortable and results in long-standing but superficial, ecchymotic spots on the coined areas in a pattern resembling strap marks, such that it appears that the person has been whipped (Ashworth, 1993; Buchwald et al., 1992; Gilman et al., 1992; McClenon, 1993; Yeatman et al., 1976, 1980). Coining is used particularly on children who have upper respiratory infections, and its scars are commonly misunderstood as signs of child abuse (Ashworth, 1993; Yeatman et al., 1980). Asian Americans are often charged with child abuse for using a folk treatment that is (for them) analogous to a White American treating a child's cold with chicken soup and tea. Some of these intercultural misunderstandings have had tragic consequences, including a case in which a Vietnamese father was falsely accused and then convicted and imprisoned for child abuse because of coining: He then committed suicide because of the shame of his conviction and imprisonment (Ashworth, 1993). Coining is used by Vietnamese, Hmong, Mien, Lao, Cambodian, and Chinese.

Burning (Poua). Burning is a treatment based on the Chinese theory of moxibustion, a set of principles that attribute certain symptoms to excess cold; the purpose of burning is to apply heat and thereby restore the balance of hot and cold that is seen as essential to health. Originally, parts of the moxa herb were used, but today any weedlike grass is used. This is peeled and allowed to dry; then the tip is dipped in heated oil, ignited, applied to the skin in the area requiring treatment, and held there until clear, obvious burns have been achieved. Laotians and Cambodians may use yarn, and Thai may use lit cigarettes instead of weeds for burning treatment. The area burned is contingent on the site and nature of the symptoms. Joints are typically burned on listless infants, the forehead burned for other symptoms, and the buttocks and fingers burned for enuresis and temper tantrums, respectively. In other cases, burns are scattered about the body of an adult, in a pattern following the meridians. The treatment is extremely painful and is the intervention of last resort. Because this treatment results in serious burns across the body, is it likely to be misinterpreted as a sign of spousal or child abuse, whether or not cigarettes are used to burn (Ashworth, 1993; Buchwald et al., 1992; Gilman et al., 1992; Justice et al., 1992; McClenon, 1993; Yeatman et al., 1976, 1980). Burning is used by Vietnamese, Hmong, Mien, Lao, Cambodian, and Chinese.

Cupping (Ventouse). This (originally French) folk treatment is practiced by a variety of Asian cultural groups, and its precise form varies from group to group. The underlying principle across groups is to create a vacuum inside a cup by igniting alcohol-soaked cotton inside the cup. When the flame extinguishes, the cup is immediately applied to the skin of the painful or symptomatic site. Suction is created, and the skin is pulled up into the mouth of the cup. The cup remains in place for 15 to 20 minutes, or until the suction can be easily released. The treatment is extremely painful. The suction is believed to exude the noxious/poisonous elements or substances by "cupping the poison," or "cupping the bad wind." It is believed that the greater the bruising that results from this treatment, the more serious the underlying disorder. Cupping leaves circular, ecchymotic, and painful burn marks in vertical rows of two to four cup marks on both sides of the chest, abdomen, and back, or, one single cup mark on the forehead. Cupping is used to treat pain of any type, particularly among adolescents and adults. This treatment is used by Vietnamese, Hmong, Mien, Lao, Cambodian, and Chinese in particular, and tends to be misunderstood as abuse (Ashworth, 1993; Buchwald et al., 1992; Gilman et al., 1992; McClenon, 1993; Yeatman et al., 1976, 1980).

Pinching (Bot gio). In this treatment, tiger balm (a mentholated ointment) is massaged into the area before the skin is pinched. For some Asian groups (e.g., Hmong), the area is pinched and then pricked with a needle until blood is drawn. Pinching (in all its varieties) is believed to exude "bad wind" and/or poisonous elements. It results in nonsymmetri- cal scars and bruises that may be found anywhere on the body, but are particularly likely to be found between the eyes, along the trachea, in a necklace pattern around the base of the neck, and along the spine. Pinching is used to treat pain, exhaustion, cough, lack of appetite, fever, and minor illnesses. It is an extremely common practice among the Hmong, Mien, Vietnamese, and Cambodian (Ashworth, 1993; Gilman et al., 1992; McClenon, 1993; Tran, 1980; Yeatman et al., 1976, 1980).

Korean Americans

The health beliefs and healing practices detailed earlier have been found among Koreans and Korean Americans (Choe & Lee, 1975; Kendall, 1987; P. C. Kim & Pak, 1983; Y. K. Kim & Sich, 1977; Lee, 1966; Roh, 1970; Sich, 1981), whose ethnomedicine is a derivation of traditional Chinese medicine. Several folk disorders specific to Korean Americans also have been identified (Pang, 1994). These include *Hwabyung* (a form of depression with marked somatic symptoms), *Han* (a form of depression with extreme guilt), and *Shinggyongshaeyak* (a somata-psychic syndrome resembling what biomedicine once called "neurasthenia"). These folk disorders, like the health beliefs and practices detailed thus far, have received no attention from researchers in health psychology, and are ignored by biomedicine (i.e., medicine, public health) as well.

Southeast Asian Americans

The general Asian cultural factors affecting health behavior outlined earlier in this section hold for traditional southeast Asians. Norms regarding silence, prohibitions against speaking about oneself, obligation to parents and family, and fear of loss of lien all play a role in health behavior (Barney, 1980; Poyneer, 1983; Tran, 1980; Uba, 1992; Westermeyer et al., 1983). The health beliefs of southeast Asian Americans are diverse and depend primarily on religion, and secondarily on whether the person has adopted Chinese or ayurvedic (traditional Hindu) health schema. On the whole, however, all of these folk understandings attribute illness to the interplay of supernatural and physical forces, and draw no distinctions between religious and medical beliefs (Westermeyer, 1988). The four major religions in question are as follows.

Buddhism is the belief that life is suffering (including pain and disease), that all suffering stems from desire, and that disease is to be eliminated by eliminating desire (through meditation and other spiritual means). Symptoms thereby are inherently shameful manifestations of desire; seeking treatment for pain or other symptoms is delayed, or treatment (though sought) will not be followed (Hoang & Erickson, 1982, 1985; Westermeyer, 1988).

Confucianism, on the other hand, is a set of behavioral guidelines and ethics entailing respect for and obedience to social hierarchies, and the worship of ancestors. Its health implications are that believers expect health professionals (who represent an extremely high status group) to behave in a superior, authoritarian manner, and tend to comply precisely with all treatment recommended by these superiors (Hoang & Erickson, 1985; Muecke, 1983a, 1983b).

Taoism is the belief in TAO, the creative principle that organizes the universe; all things progress naturally toward perfection and harmony (toward TAO) and hence no steps should be taken to interfere with this. Seeking treatment for symptoms violates this because it is an active step taken (an "unnatural action") to alter the natural progress of events. Hence, seeking treatment is delayed; treatment, if sought, is refused or passively accepted but (covertly) not complied with; and surgery, invasive diagnostic procedures, and even the drawing of blood are prohibited.

Animism is common among Laotian hill tribes (Hmong, Yao), and is the belief that gods, demons, and evil spirits are the only proximal cause of illness, which therefore is to be treated by an indigenous healer, or a shaman. "String-tying" is one health practice associated with these beliefs, and consists of tying a black string around an individual's wrist or waist to communicate with deceased ancestors and prevent or cure illness (Erickson & Hoang, 1980; Hoang & Erickson, 1982, 1985; Muecke, 1983a).

Each of these very different systems of religious beliefs not only has obvious implications for health behavior but is also a system of health beliefs; each entails the view that balance and harmony are synonymous with health, and that curing consists of reestablishing those (Poyneer, 1983). In addition to these views, southeast Asian Americans may have adopted global, Indochinese folk medical schema (a derivation of traditional Chinese medicine), or the folk medical beliefs of ayurvedic (traditional Indian) medicine. The former recognizes natural (wind, diet), supernatural (gods, demons, evil spirits, spells) and metaphysical (the balance of Yin, Yang, hot and cold) causes of illness (Cheon-Klessig et al., 1988; Tran, 1980). Ayurveda, on the other hand, is the medicine of Hindu culture, and stems from Sanskrit texts of the first through eighth centuries (Fleischman, 1976–1977). It consists of the belief that the cause of all disease is imbalance among the three vital essences or *dosha* (*kapha,* or phlegm; *pitta,* or bile; and *vayu,* or wind), with the sole cause of this imbalance being an unhealthy diet. Changes in diet and use of herbal remedies are the only cures recognized as valid by followers of ayurveda and the only cures used by a vaid (ayurvedic healer) to restore health (Ghandi, 1965).

Three attitudes hold across these systems of health beliefs and religions, and are more or less prototypical of southeast Asians irrespective of specific culture: (1) Surgery is unacceptable because it mutilates the body and the soul is understood as attached to various body parts (Cheon-Klessig et al., 1988; Hoang & Erickson, 1982, 1985). (2) Traditional healers are sought and folk remedies (described previously) used prior to seeking help from practitioners of biomedicine (Buchwald et al., 1992; Cheon-Klessig et al., 1988; Gilman et al., 1992; McClenon, 1993) by approximately 70% of these populations, with subsequently low health service utilization until late stages of disease when symptoms are extreme (Barney, 1980; Cheon-Klessig et al., 1988; Strand & Jones, 1983; Westermeyer et al., 1983). And, (3) appointments for treatment, waiting to see professionals, and preventive care are regarded as confusing, nonsensical "foreign" concepts (Hoang & Erickson, 1985; Tran, 1980).

Laotian/Hmong Folk Cures. The folk remedies detailed earlier (e.g., cupping, burning, etc.) are used by traditional southeast Asian Americans. In addition, however, Laotian Americans (Hmong, in particular) frequently use two other folk remedies as well, and both have major health implications. The first (and the most common folk remedy for pain among Hmong Americans) is an herbal medicine that is inhaled or smoked and contains large quantities of opium—something its users may not know and that accounts for its effectiveness (Rubio, Ekins, Singh, & Dowis, 1987; R. M. Smith & Nelsen, 1991; Westermeyer, 1974, 1988). Opium remains the major cash crop for the Hmong in Laos (where it once was legal to grow; Barney, 1980; Westermeyer, 1982), and many still routinely smoke opium for health purposes freely and openly in the streets of Laos (Westermeyer, 1974, 1982, 1988). Hence, use of an opium herbal remedy has a long cultural history and so continues among refugees in the United States. It has resulted in frequent opium addiction, serious health problems, and prosecution (for receiving packages from overseas containing crude solid opium) among Laotian Americans (Cheon-Klessig et al., 1988; Logue, 1983; Westermeyer, 1974, 1988). To complicate matters, southeast Asian refugees, understanding that Americans use aspirin and acetaminophen for pain, now tend to mix these with the opium remedy. This toxic combination results in deaths among Hmong American children in particular (Cheon-Klessig et al., 1988; Logue, 1983; Rubio et al., 1987; R. M. Smith & Nelsen, 1991; Westermeyer, 1974, 1988). The percentage of southeast Asian patients whose symptoms are related to undisclosed, chronic opium use is unknown.

The second folk remedy used by Hmong (and Thai) refugees is a set of herbs for curing illness believed to be caused by various evil spirits. These herbs include *Tshuaj Rog, Tauj Dub, Ntiv, Nkoj Liab, Niam Tij,* and others, are dispensed by Hmong American shamans (*Txi neng*) in herb shops, and are as common in Hmong and Thai American medicine cabinets as are aspirin for most Americans. Although most of these herbs have yet to be fully analyzed, a few of them have been demonstrated to contain arsenic and lead. Consequently, like Mexican Americans (Centers for Disease Control, 1981, 1983a), cases of lead poisoning due to folk remedies are frequent among southeast Asian American children (Centers for Disease Control, 1983b).

Sudden Death Hmong Folk Disorder. "Nightmare" is a prevalent Hmong folk disorder and is the only Asian folk disorder to receive attention from biomedicine, no doubt because it is *the leading cause of death* among Hmong men. Nightmare consists of awakening from sleep with a feeling of extreme fear and panic; followed by total or partial paralysis and a sensation of pressure in the chest; the feeling or perception of an alien being (animal, human, or spirit) in the room; and culminating in sudden, unexplained death (Adler, 1995; Holtan, Carlson, Egbert, Mielke, & Thao, 1984; Parrish, 1988). This folk disorder has come to be known as *Sudden Unexplained Nocturnal Death Syndrome* (SUNDS) by biomedicine. Deaths from SUNDS are frequent: In 1981 to 1982, the death rate for 25- to 44-year-old male Hmong from this syndrome was equal to the sum of the rates of the five leading causes of death in all non-Hmong U.S. men of the same age (Holtan et al., 1984). Nightmare is not influenced by religion (traditional Asian vs. Christian), and was frequent in Laos prior to immigration but did not lead to any deaths in the native country (Adler, 1995). From 74% to 97% of Hmong believe this disorder to be caused by the nocturnal visit of an evil spirit who presses the life out of the victim (Adler, 1995; Holtan et al., 1984). Such beliefs are consistent with the Hmong view that every household and environment (e.g., the water, the fields, the mountains) is replete with spirits (Cheon-Klessig et al., 1988) who determine events, including health and disease. Hmong also believe that the failure to engage in traditional rituals (as they did in Laos) accounts for the disorder's new ability to kill (Adler, 1995). Although men and women suffer from nightmare attacks, virtually all the deaths have been among men (Adler, 1995). A similar folk disorder appearing at night, causing sudden death and known as "nightmare," was recognized by the ancient Greeks and Romans, and is currently recognized by the French (who call it *cauchemar*), Germans (*Alpdruck*), Mexicans (*pesadilla*), and Poles (Holtan et al., 1984).

AFRICAN AMERICANS

This section refers to a heterogeneous population of Americans who descended from African slaves,[3] who themselves descended from the indigenous peoples of western Africa. Although the term *African American* encompasses African, Haitian, West Indian, and other Caribbean Americans, the data reported here are based on those traditionally construed as American "Blacks" in U.S. racial classification schema (Landrine & Klonoff, 1996a), rather than those of Caribbean ancestry.

Studies of the Health Problems of African Americans

The leading causes of death among African Americans are shown in Table 51.1. The major health problems of African Americans include the highest (age-adjusted) rates of cancer and cancer mortality of all ethnic groups (Baquet & Gibbs, 1992; Baquet et al., 1991; USDHHS, 1987, 1995); high rates of diabetes (USDHHS, 1995; Klonoff, Landrine, & Scott, 1995); prevalent hypertension (estimated at up to 34% of the population); excess cardiovascular disease (USDHHS, 1987; Rivo, Kofie, Schwartz, Levy, & Tuckson, 1989); prevalent obesity (Burke et al., 1992; Kumanyika, 1987, 1994; Neser, Thomas, Semenya, Thomas, & Gillum, 1986); and high rates of AIDS (USDHHS, 1995, 1996). These health problems are in part the result of three problematic health behaviors among Blacks: high rates of cigarette smoking among adults (Centers for Disease Control, 1988; Fiore et al., 1989; Novotny, Warner, Kendrick, & Remington, 1988) coupled with low rates of quitting smoking (Orleans et al., 1989; Royce et al., 1993); poor diets and nutrition (Block & Subar, 1992; Gerber et al., 1991; Kant, Block, Schatzkin, Ziegler, & Nestle, 1991; Serdula et al., 1995); and lack of exercise (Burke et al., 1992; C. E. Lewis, Raczynski, Heath, Levinson, & Cutter, 1993). These three problematic health behaviors transcend social class, occupation, and education. Hence, although health psychology and related disciplines readily attribute the problematic health behaviors and excess morbidity of African Americans to such social factors, those factors cannot alone account for the data, and neglected cultural variables therefore also must be involved (Hildreth & Saunders, 1992; Landrine & Klonoff, 1996a).

General Cultural Factors Influencing Health Behavior

Racism and Distrust of Whites. That Blacks have experienced profound racism historically and continue to experience it currently is well-known (Bell, 1992; Dovidio &

[3]Although all African Americans descended from indigenous Africans, not all descended from slaves, because not all Blacks in the United States during the colonial era were slaves. At any time, 15% were free. Indeed, American Blacks represent three distinct genetic populations with vastly different precolonial and colonial era histories (Sowell, 1978, 1994); this point is discussed further later.

Gaertner, 1986; Landrine et al., 1995). Such racism persists as a factor in the daily lives of Blacks whether at work (Idson & Price, 1992; Krieger, 1990), leisure (Cose, 1993), or when seeking health care (Harrison, 1994), and its frequency and impact cannot be exaggerated. For example, a scale was constructed to measure the frequency and appraisal of racism in Blacks' lives (Landrine & Klonoff, 1996a, 1996b). Racism was operationalized as a set of specific racist acts or *racist events* (e.g., being called a "nigger," being followed by the police or store security guards) that are analogous to the generic stressful life events and hassles that dominate stress research. Studies using our Schedule of Racist Events (SRE; Landrine & Klonoff, 1996a, 1996b) revealed that 98% of Blacks reported experiencing some type of racist event in the past year irrespective of their gender, age, education, and socioeconomic status. The frequency of racist events experienced also predicted smoking (Landrine & Klonoff, 1996a, 1996b) and hypertension (Krieger, 1990) among Blacks better than all status variables combined.

Foremost among the global, cultural factors that play a role in Black health and health behavior is a profound, ubiquitous distrust of Whites that is a response to this racism (Jones, 1993; Landrine & Klonoff, 1996a, 1996b). That distrust is taught to successive generations, and so is a cultural variable (Helms, 1990; Landrine & Klonoff, 1994a, 1996a; Thompson, 1994). Black distrust of Whites is legion and thus has been measured through a variety of scales including the *Cultural Mistrust Inventory* (Terrell & Terrell, 1981), and the *Cultural Mistrust Subscale* of the African American Acculturation Scale (see Landrine & Klonoff, 1996a, for a review of both). In several investigations, it was found that African American's distrust of Whites transcends their social class and education, and plays a role in anxiety, somatic, and depressive symptoms, as well as in prevalence rates of hypertension and cigarette smoking, with all of these higher for Blacks high in cultural mistrust (Klonoff et al., 1996; Landrine & Klonoff, 1996a,1996b). Likewise, others have found that Black acceptance of health information provided by Whites is mediated by such cultural mistrust (Kalichman, Kelly, Hunter, Murphy, & Tyler, 1993; Mays & Cochran, 1988).

Although traditional Blacks distrust Whites as a whole, they distrust White health professionals in particular and even more so, and distrust information on and interventions regarding AIDS provided by such professionals most of all (Jones, 1993). Health workers/researchers have repeatedly found that many Blacks believe that HIV is an artificially created virus, and that AIDS prevention programs are a ruse for infecting Blacks with it as part of a larger, genocidal conspiracy to annihilate the Black population (Jones, 1993). Surveys in 1990 and 1992 (Jones, 1993) consistently report such attitudes, along with a rejection of AIDS treatment and prevention programs (Jones, 1993). AIDS blood tests and donating blood are viewed by 54% of Blacks as a mechanism for purposefully infecting them with HIV; AZT is viewed as a poison meant to eliminate Blacks; the encouraged use of condoms is perceived as a plot to decrease Black births; and the distribution of clean needles to addicts is seen as an effort to increase substance abuse in the Black community (Jones, 1993). *Tony Brown's Journal,* a popular and influential Black discussion program on PBS (Public Broadcasting System), and articles in the *Los Angeles Sentinel* (the largest, West coast Black newspaper) and *Essence* (a national Black magazine) have all repeated the view that the HIV virus and AIDS prevention programs are the genocidal conspiracy of White health scientists (Jones, 1993). Consequently, for example, in 1988, a federal AIDS prevention program in Washington, DC had to be halted because Blacks refused to submit to household blood tests, and Black city officials similarly suspected that the program was a (disguised) genocidal experiment (Jones, 1993).

Blacks' specific distrust of White health professionals and of the AIDS-related information they provide are both a response to a single racist event in history, namely, the Tuskegee Syphilis Study. This experiment is rarely mentioned in health psychology articles, undergraduate or graduate texts, and is virtually absent from health psychology articles about Blacks and AIDS, thereby implying that health psychologists may not be aware of it. The Black (and the gay) community, however, is aware of it, and that knowledge has shaped Black health behavior and attitudes (e.g., above) more profoundly than any other event.[4] Because the importance of the Tuskegee experiment to current Black health behavior cannot be overestimated, a summary of it is provided here based on Thomas and Quinn (1991), Jones (1981, 1993), Silver (1988), and Brandt (1988); the reader is referred to Jones (1981, 1993) for the details of the experiment.

The Tuskegee Syphilis Experiment, 1932–1972. In 1928, the Public Health Service (PHS) had recently completed a study of the prevalence of syphilis in rural, southern Blacks and found a rate of 25%.[5] As part of this syphilis-control demonstration project, the PHS also provided free treatment for the Blacks they tested to prove that Blacks could be treated successfully for the disease with the two drugs of the time (arsphenamine and mercury). With this successful demonstration project in hand, the PHS proposed a new project to the Julius Rosenwald Fund (a Chicago-based group dedicated to improving the health of Blacks) to expand the project throughout Black communities in the south. The Rosenwald Fund supported that project, knowing that Blacks would trust

[4]Indeed, the Tuskegee experiment also initially determined the gay community's attitudes about AIDS; gays explicitly mentioned the experiment as the reason for their initial belief that HIV was a virus constructed by the federal government to annihilate the gay population (Jones, 1993).

[5]Whether all of these Blacks had syphilis or had lupus misdiagnosed as syphilis, is a reasonable question to raise. This is because lupus (an incurable, autoimmune disorder of unknown cause) is extremely prevalent in Black women (but not men). Its symptoms include sores similar to those seen in syphilis, and its auto-antibodies frequently lead to false positive syphilis test results even today (see Klonoff & Landrine, 1997b). Hence, when both men and women were tested by the PHS, rates of (ostensible) syphilis were 25%, 35%, and 40%; but, when the PHS later tested only Black men (such that the diagnosis of syphilis probably was accurate) rates of syphilis were 15%. That the Black community of the 1930s was replete with syphilis remains as a "fact" in this historical literature and one that warrants critical reassessment.

the PHS and would participate in light of the prior (1928) PHS work in Black communities. Hence, from 1929 to 1931, Black women and men throughout the south were again recruited to participate in a syphilis control project, and were tested for syphilis, with positive test results found for 35% to 40% of the population. The procedures used to recruit Blacks and gain their trust and cooperation were the most culturally tailored to date. They included recruitment through Black churches and conducting the blood tests in those churches; enlisting the assistance of Black church leaders who encouraged Blacks to participate; gaining the cooperation and participation of local agencies; enlisting the assistance of the Tuskegee Institute (a prestigious, Black institute); using local Black medical staff from Tuskegee to do the testing; getting Blacks released from work (without loss of income or job) to be tested; providing food and a free physical exam; and having a Black nurse from the community establish a relationship with each subject and provide each with transportation to the testing site.

Finally, the PHS took the additional culturally sensitive step of translating syphilis into the language of Black folk medicine to facilitate cooperation. Because Blacks believed (since slavery) that various "states" of one's blood ("high," "low," and "bad" blood) played an etiological role in all illness, syphilis was described to them as a type of "bad blood"—it was presented in a manner consistent with their indigenous health schema.

Hence, Blacks were told by local Black religious and other leaders that "government doctors" wanted to test and treat them for "bad blood." Given the source of the message, convenience of testing sites, and the incentives entailed, Blacks cooperated fully and enthusiastically. Blacks were never told, however, that the "bad blood" in question was a highly contagious, serious disease that was transmitted sexually and from mother to fetus. Given that they would be treated for syphilis, explaining exactly what it was in terms other than "bad blood" seemed unnecessary to the PHS.

When the testing phase was complete and the need for treatment established, the next step was to initiate treatment (which at the time was an expensive, 1-year course of two drugs for each infected person). However, this did not occur because the PHS lost their funding. The Depression decimated the Rosenwald Fund that had supported the project; without its financial support, the PHS could not conduct the treatment phase. The PHS was no more satisfied with this outcome than anyone who loses a grant would be, and wanted to salvage something publishable from the years of identifying and testing Blacks, and of establishing a successful, grassroots network for doing so. Thus, they decided to conduct a study on *untreated* syphilis in Black men that has come to be known as the Tuskegee Syphilis Experiment. The PHS believed and hoped that if it could demonstrate that the disease was as damaging to Blacks as it was to Whites, funding for treating Blacks could be secured in the future.

Hence, in 1932, the elaborate network and culturally sensitive procedures (detailed previously) for recruiting Blacks were used again to recruit a new sample of 600 Black men (only) for research purposes. The men were divided into 399 with syphilis and 201 healthy controls, and the plan was to compare them over a course of 9 months. The PHS told the new sample (like prior ones) that they would be tested and treated for "bad blood," again with no explanation regarding the transmission of syphilis. Importantly, however, this time the PHS was lying insofar as no treatment was planned or would be forthcoming. Many men were given some treatment for fear that if they did not experience some relief, they would cease participation in the project. The treatment provided was purposefully less than half of the dose of the two drugs needed to cure syphilis. Neither the subjects nor the Tuskegee Institute was told the true purpose of the study.

When the initial 9-month period was over, the PHS did not want to relinquish the project because it viewed the Blacks as an enormous opportunity to study the long-term manifestations of untreated syphilis. The rationale for the study changed from empirically demonstrating the need to provide better health care for poor Blacks, to exploiting those Blacks for research and publication purposes. Thus, the study continued for the next 40 years, ending in 1972 only because the press discovered and exposed it. For that 40-year period, numerous foundations, government agencies, and universities colluded in the project by sending staff to examine the men and publish articles about their irreversible cardiovascular and neurologic damage, or by assisting in keeping the project a secret from the general public. Penicillin was discovered in the 1940s to be a cheap, effective cure for syphilis (one that the PHS readily could afford), leaving the PHS with little justification for failing to treat the men. But, meetings were held in the 1940s at which it was concluded by the PHS and others that the experiment not only had to continue but had to continue "to endpoint" (until each man died) because the data from the men's autopsies would make an "invaluable," "incomparable" scientific monograph. Hence, penicillin was withheld from the men for 30 years. Between the 1940s and 1970s, all of the men had heard about penicillin and believed it could cure their "bad blood." To stop them from seeking penicillin elsewhere, the PHS convinced the men that it not only would not cure but might kill them, and then took extra steps to isolate the men from other sources of biomedical information and care. This included assuring that no local hospital or clinic (these provided with the men's names) would treat them. Indeed, numerous federal, state, and local agencies conspired repeatedly to assure that these men never received treatment. This included agreements with the government and war departments to assure that the men either were not drafted for World War II (because all draftees were treated with penicillin) or, if drafted, would not receive treatment and would not serve. Other agencies and public officials conspired to keep the men's untimely deaths from cardiovascular complications a secret from the public, and arranged death certificates for that purpose.

For the 40 years of the project, the Tuskegee men were subjected to annual, barbaric (i.e., rushed and without anesthesia) lumbar punctures (along with X-rays) for research purposes only, and were told that these were shots of medicine to cure them. As a result of these repeated, poorly conducted lumbar punctures, some men died and others developed irreversible headaches or paralysis. Scientific articles on the men's severe neurologic and other symptoms, as well as on their brief life spans (relative to healthy Blacks) appeared throughout journals in the 1940s, 1950s, and 1960s and did not hide the nature of the protocol. Nonetheless, physicians, scientists, and editors who read these articles did not object to the study, despite its obvious immorality and the current civil rights movement. Just one person, Peter Buxton, tried many times to stop the experiment, and failing to do so, finally revealed it to the press. When the story appeared in the July 25, 1972, issue of the *Washington Star,* almost all of the Tuskegee men had died painfully and prematurely. The response to the study was outrage among Blacks, Whites, scientists, physicians, Congress, and the White House. Congressional investigations and hearings were convened in 1972 and 1973 (at which the few surviving men spoke) and these shaped future federal guidelines (i.e., current ones) for the treatment of human subjects in research—requiring, first and foremost, that subjects give full, informed consent to participate. In 1974, a $10 million out-of-court settlement was reached between the U.S. government and the Tuskegee survivors and their heirs. It paid each $5,000 to $37,500 in exchange for promises to file no further action. Most of these funds were returned to the U.S. government in 1977–1978 because heirs had failed to come forward within the 3 years stipulated by the settlement. Finally, in 1997, President Bill Clinton publically apologized to the Black community for the Tuskegee Experiment.

The Legacy of Tuskegee. In the Black communities around the nation, the story of the Tuskegee study is told to each generation, accurately or (equally often) inaccurately, as a study in which Blacks were purposefully infected with syphilis in order to study them (Jones, 1993). Although the latter inaccurate story is the basis for the Black belief that their community was purposefully infected with HIV for research purposes, accurate knowledge of the study has had equally negative consequences. For Blacks, the study is far more than an example of racism. Rather, it is also understood as proof that White health scientists (particularly those with federal funds) and the federal government are involved in conspiracies against Blacks in which lies are told to Blacks about their diseases and health; Blacks are denied available treatment and allowed to die; Black churches and leaders are not told the truth and are used to further White genocidal ends; and Blacks are used for publication purposes (Jones, 1993; Thomas & Quinn, 1991). In the context of Tuskegee, current Black distrust and rejection of White health scientists, of information about AIDS, and of AIDS prevention programs is understandable, particularly because 1972 was not that long ago. Indeed, efforts to culturally tailor AIDS prevention programs for the Black community are especially likely to raise the specter of Tuskegee, because such strategies (e.g., involving Black health care providers and conducting the project through churches) are identical to those used to fool Blacks in the past. Thus, Black leaders (e.g., from the Nation of Islam; see Thomas & Quinn, 1991) respond to AIDS prevention programs with suspicion and ask how Blacks can know that current efforts are not Tuskegee again (Jones, 1993; Thomas & Quinn, 1991). This suggests that what health psychology researchers often assume to be a Black lack of knowledge about AIDS transmission and risk factors (Kalichman, Hunter, & Kelly, 1992) can instead be a conscious rejection of biomedical evidence in favor of genocidal theories by both uneducated and highly educated (including physicians) Blacks alike (Jones, 1993; Klonoff et al., 1996). Although many ethnic groups (e.g., Latinos; see Klonoff et al., 1996) believe that AIDS can be contracted by donating blood or by having a blood test, such beliefs among Blacks arose in an historical context that lends them a different meaning, namely, distrust (rather than lack) of information.

Hence, suspicions about AIDS are one example of the legacy of the Tuskegee Experiment. Indeed, a recent study (Klonoff & Landrine, 1999b) found that one in four Blacks currently believe that the HIV virus was created by the federal government to annihilate the Black population. These beliefs were more common among Black men (the subjects of the Tuskegee Study) than among women. These AIDS conspiracy views were predicted by high (rather than low) education and by frequent experiences with racism. This suggests that such views represent the rejection of biomedical information by educated Blacks in favor of conspiracy theories that are consistent with their knowledge of history and their experiences in a racist world.

A second example of the legacy of Tuskegee is that much of the Black community firmly believes that the easy availability of drugs (crack cocaine in particular) in their communities is the result of those drugs being distributed there by the federal government as part of a (continuing) genocidal conspiracy (Jones, 1993). Hence, well-known Black delays in seeking and noncompliance with treatment, as well as failure to alter unhealthy lifestyles, may all be at least in part a function of similar generalizations from Tuskegee and subsequent distrust and rejection of health information provided by Whites. It does not make sense, for example, that Blacks, irrespective of education, seem to know as little about the dangerous consequences of cigarette smoking (Klesges et al., 1988; Martin, Cummings, & Coates, 1990) as they ostensibly know about AIDS prevention. This apparent lack of health-related information on a variety of topics even among Blacks with college degrees can only be explained as a rejection of such information as a result of Tuskegee, and hence as the sad legacy of that study (Klonoff et al., 1996).

With the importance of Black distrust of Whites and the Tuskegee study outlined as global cultural factors influencing Black health behavior, the next section focuses on specific cultural health beliefs and practices.

Beliefs About Illness

The health beliefs and practices of traditional African Americans are by and large derivations of those of the west Africans who came to the United States as slaves (Baer, 1985; Bailey, 1987, 1991; Brandon, 1991; Goodson, 1987; Hall & Bourne, 1973; Hill, 1973; Hill & Matthews, 1981; Holloway, 1991; Jacques, 1976; W. Jordan, 1975, 1979; Laguerre, 1987; Mulira, 1991; Sexton, 1992; Snow, 1974, 1977, 1978, 1983; Watson, 1984). These beliefs have been influenced minimally by European American beliefs, but strongly by Native Americans beliefs because indigenous Indians and slaves had many contacts throughout the colonial era (e.g., Native Americans provided sanctuary for runaway slaves and the two groups established cooperative, free communities). Prior to the civil war, the health of slaves was maintained primarily by slave owners out of self-interest (Jackson, 1981) and secondarily by slave women healers who used African remedies (Goodson, 1987; Holloway, 1991; Landrine & Klonoff, 1996a). With the end of the war and the emancipation of the slaves, biomedical services were denied to the freed Blacks (Charatz-Litt, 1992; Cooke, 1984; Goodson, 1987; Jackson, 1981; Jacques, 1976; Spector, 1996). Consequently, west African health beliefs, cures, and traditional healers were all that remained, and the latter became solely responsible for Black health care during Reconstruction (Cooke, 1984; Tallant, 1946). At that point, a folk system of medical beliefs and practices (dominated by west African herbalism and voodoo, and colored by Native American practices) crystallized, and became the African American ethnomedicine that continues among contemporary, traditional Blacks (Hill & Matthews, 1981; Holloway, 1991; Jackson, 1981; Jordan, 1975, 1979; Sexton, 1992). Discrimination against Blacks by biomedicine, as patients (Harrison, 1994; Hildreth & Saunders, 1992; Morias, 1967) and professionals (e.g., Black physicians were not allowed to be members of the American Medical Association until 1965, see Charatz-Litt, 1992) in part accounts for the strength and persistence of Black folk medicine.

West African cultures view people as fundamentally a spirit and a process rather than as a material entity, and have no word for "religion" because all things are essentially spiritual and religious (Mbiti, 1975). So too, traditional African Americans view people not as matter but as a spirit or soul (Barrett, 1974; Holloway, 1991; Jules-Roseta, 1980), and hence view all people and things as connected to and influencing all others on a spiritual or mystical plane (Bailey, 1991). Few distinctions are drawn among mind, body, spirit, and nature, or between religion and medicine, and health-related beliefs and practices are infused with a spirituality that is even more pronounced than that of the other sociocentric cultures described here (Jackson, 1981; Warner, 1977; Watson, 1984). Hence, Blacks classify illness as natural (consistent with the spirit, plan, and laws of God, nature and the universe) or unnatural (inconsistent with the foregoing), with these two types of illness having different symptoms, causes, and cures (Bailey, 1991; Flaskerud & Rush, 1989). This system of classification of illness is the most common one used by contemporary traditional African Americans (Bailey, 1991) and persists as the dominant nosology in the west African cultures from which African Americans descended (Holloway, 1991).

Natural Illnesses. Illnesses classified as natural are those viewed as subject to the laws of God and nature, and so are understood as normal and predictable (Snow, 1974, 1977, 1978, 1983). All illnesses that have mild or acute, nonfrightening, time-limited symptoms that can be prevented and easily cured are classified as natural (Bailey, 1991). These illnesses are believed to be the (proximal) result of lack of balance or harmony, whether they are understood as due (distally) to forces of nature, or to punishment for sin. Forces of nature believed to cause natural illness include exposure to cold or heat; impurities that enter the body through air, food, or water; improper diet and lack of moderation in habits (Flaskerud & Rush, 1989; Hill & Matthews, 1981; S. M. Johnson & Snow, 1982); and various cycles and phases of life, the moon, the tides, and the planets (Cooke, 1984), all of which effect only the exposed person. Illness that is construed as punishment for sin (breach of taboo), on the other hand, can befall the sinners or their relatives, and children in particular. Because natural illnesses are part of God's plan, they are understood as curable, with those due to forces of nature treated by biomedicine and prayer, and those understood as due to sin relieved only through prayer and assistance of religious or spiritual experts (Snow, 1974, 1978).

Unnatural Illnesses. All remaining illnesses (those whose symptoms are fatal, incurable, progressive, frightening and confusing, extreme, bizarre, or psychiatric) are classified as unnatural. These illnesses are understood as the result of malevolent forces and supernatural entities that disrupt the harmony and balance of the universe and thereby interrupt God's plan (Snow, 1974, 1983). Etiological agents include evil or Satan (Snow, 1983; Warner, 1977); ghosts, other spirits, and possession by these (Holloway, 1991); and hexes, curses, and spells due to witchcraft or voodoo (Cooke, 1984; W. Jordan, 1975, 1979; Laguerre, 1987; Mulira, 1991; Snow, 1983; Paulino, 1995; Warner, 1977). Treatment of unnatural illnesses necessitates the use of not only spiritual remedies such as prayer and laying on of hands, but of magico-religious, traditional remedies such as charms, herbs, special teas, and salves, and use of root doctors or voodoo healers, with biomedical interventions deemed ineffective. Microscopic disease causing agents (e.g., viruses) are understood by traditional African Americans as causes of illness as well, but as merely the "how" rather than the "why" of illness (Spector, 1996). Recent surveys of African American adults who were diverse in education, social class, and geographical region of residence support the aforementioned literature. For example, recent studies found a strong belief in the healing power of prayer; a tendency to seek health care from ministers (primarily) or root doctors (voodooists); classifying illness as natural versus unnatural; and attributing illness to supernatural causes among traditional Blacks but not among Whites (Landrine & Klonoff, 1994a, 1994b, 1996a). Likewise, in a survey of African Americans in Detroit, Bailey (1991) found use of the dichotomous nosology and its causal attributions for illness. Thus, the primary (proximal) causes of illness recognized by traditional African Americans are natural (cold, poor diet) and supernatural (God's punishment, effects of evil) factors, with the latter given more weight.

African American Folk Healers and Healing Practices

Like other sociocentric cultures, traditional African Americans view the ability to heal as a sacred gift, and healers as blessed or highly spiritual people (Baer, 1981, 1985; Hall &

Bourne, 1973; Hill & Matthews, 1981; Sexton, 1992; Watson, 1984). The diversity of indigenous healers (e.g., ministers, spiritual leaders, folk doctors, grannies, midwives, advisors, prophets, and root or voodoo doctors) recognized are categorized into three broad types (Baer, 1981, 1985). The first are those who learned healing from elders or received training in biomedicine, and hence can only heal simple, natural illnesses caused by forces of nature. The second type received the "gift of healing" from God through a religious experience and can heal all natural illness irrespective of cause. The third and most powerful healers are those understood as born with the "power of curing" (a sign of which was present at their birth), who are hence capable of curing natural and unnatural illness (Baer, 1981; Snow, 1974; Watson, 1984). Of these many folk healers and healing practices, space here permits a discussion of only four specifically African American (rather than Afro-Caribbean) ones: ministers, midwives, herbalists, and voodoo practitioners.

- *Ministers* are consulted for advice and healing for a diversity of problems, including psychiatric and physical symptoms and interpersonal crises. They provide social support, information, prayer, and guidance, and play a powerful role in the health decisions and behaviors of many traditional Blacks (Hill & Matthews, 1981; Landrine & Klonoff, 1996a; and Watson, 1984, in particular).
- *Midwives* are the most common traditional folk healers in the Black community. This is because the practice of midwifery is an ancient African tradition (the word *midwife* is the English translation of the Congo word "healing-woman") and was introduced to the United States by the slaves. Midwifery was one of the few African healing practices that slave owners allowed slave women to perform, such that the tradition continues in the Black community (Holloway, 1991). Midwives are consulted for advice on pregnancy, childbirth, and gynecological issues, and deliver infants (Bailey, 1991; Hill & Matthews, 1981).
- *Herbalists* use a set of herbal remedies derived originally from the botanical knowledge of slave women (Goodson, 1987; Mitchell, 1978), crystallized during Reconstruction (Cooke, 1984; J. J. Jackson, 1981). Whereas the prevalence of herbalists remains unclear, their existence does not insofar as a variety of herbalists have shops throughout the urban and rural Black communities around the nation (Baer, 1985; Bailey, 1991; Goodson, 1987; Jacques, 1976; W. Jordan, 1979; Mitchell, 1978) and are regularly consulted for care. The treatment of herbalists consists of recommending that people decrease the salt and fat in their diets and decrease their stress, along with ingesting an herbal remedy (Bailey, 1991). The most common herbal remedies used include sassafras tea, dandelion and valerian root, epsom salt, garlic tablets, vinegar, and lemon juice (Bailey, 1991), along with cream of tartar, leaf tea, catnip tea, jimson weed, huckleberry, holly, goat's milk, cattle blood, and other herbs (see Mitchell, 1978; Payne-Jackson & Lee, 1993; and Boyd, Shimp, & Hackney, 1984, for detailed lists of herbs and their therapeutic purposes). Many of these remedies (e.g., ingesting astringent substances to control diabetes; see Bailey, 1991) are based on underlying concepts of restoring symbolic balance (between, in this example, "bitter" and "sugar" [diabetes, "sweet"]). Others are based on the view that "flushing" "impurities" from the body through the use of herbs restores balance and health, and still others are meant to restore balance to ethnomedical entities such as "high," "low," "thin," and "weak" blood. Importantly, herbalists are typically consulted to prevent, control, or cure the diabetes and hypertension that are prevalent among Blacks, with biomedical treatments ignored by the Blacks in question. For example, Bailey (1991) found that, when told by a physician that they had hypertension, 62.7% of poor, Detroit Blacks did nothing about it (did not comply with biomedical treatment), and an additional 26.5% consulted an herbalist for care instead of complying with biomedical treatment. Belief in Black folk medicine clearly impacts help seeking and other heath-related behavior (Bailey, 1987).

Toxic Herbal Remedies. Like the arsenic-, lead-, and opium-based herbal remedies of Latino and Hmong Americans, only those few African American folk cures that have caused serious illness or death have received scientific attention. Foremost among these is sassafras tea, a drink made from the root bark of the sassafras tree. The use of sassafras in drinks and of sassafras leaves as poultices originated among the slaves and Navajo of the colonial era (Vogel, 1970), whose cures were often adopted by Whites (e.g., the African practice of midwifery and of inoculations) because they were effective. Sassafras leaves then became so popular that they were used throughout the nation through the 1950s to control bleeding, and were the main ingredient in tea and root beer (Haines, 1991; Hand, 1980). The use of sassafras ceased in 1960 when the Food and Drug Administration demonstrated that safrol (the active chemical constituent) was toxic and caused ataxia, hypothermia, hypertension, liver cancer, and other symptoms. Sassafras nonetheless is sold in Black herbalists' shops, and is one of the most frequently used herbal remedies (Bailey, 1991) among Blacks, with occasional toxic consequences (Haines, 1991). The role of this folk remedy in prevalent hypertension and liver disease among African Americans has never been investigated.

- Voodoo. Although the number of people who still practice *voodoo* in the United States is unclear, it is clear that voodoo practitioners (called "root doctors," or conjurers) and their followers persist (W. Jordan 1975, 1979; Laguerre, 1987; Matthews, 1987; Mitchell, 1978; Mulira, 1991; Sexton, 1992; Simpson, 1978; Spector, 1996; Tingling, 1967), and are quite prevalent in specific communities (e.g., New Orleans and the Sea Islands of Georgia and the Carolinas). Voodoo (often called "root work") came to the United States in the late 1600s with the slaves from west Africa who had belonged to an African religion that worshipped a god they called *Vodu* (pronounced voodoo) simply because the Dahomean (west African) word *vodu* means god, spirit, or deity (Mulira, 1991; Simpson, 1978; Tallant, 1946). In the states, Whites quickly came to call the slave deity, the religious/healing sect, its members, priests, and rites and practices voodoo (Tallant, 1946). The term *hoodoo* simultaneously emerged among Whites to refer to the negative practice (i.e., to harm others) of voodoo (Mitchell, 1978; Mulira, 1991), and both terms (voodoo and hoodoo) came to dominate in 1947. Because voodoo was a religion that slaves would not relinquish and purposefully transmitted to successive generations of thousands of Blacks (Simpson, 1978), the World Order of Congregational Churches recognized voodoo as a bona fide religion in 1945 (Mulira, 1991; Simpson, 1978); this increased its acceptance among nonbelievers and may or may not have increased its followers (Mulira, 1991). Voodoo is a prevalent religion today in Trinidad, Brazil, and Haiti, as well as in the specific U.S. geographical regions already mentioned (Mulira, 1991).

Voodoo as practiced by contemporary, traditional African Americans is a set of health and healing practices with three components. The first is mystical and entails manipulating universal energy, contacting spirits, conjuring, hexing, and casting spells through a variety of rituals and dances for the benefit of the ill person who has sought help. The second is psychological and entails providing social and emotional support, and reaffirmation of faith and community for the ill person, along with songs and intense prayer. The third component is herbal folk medicine, that is, the use of botanical roots for cures (hence, practitioners are sometimes called root doctors and voodoo rites called rootwork). In voodoo rootwork, however, the herbs used extend well beyond those identified previously, and include ancient cures such as blackroot, kidney weed, and the "life-everlasting-plant" (believed to prolong life and act as a charm against illness), which are combined with rituals, charms, concoctions, dances, prayers, songs, and pieces of wood joined together in specific patterns and believed to possess magical power (Matthews, 1987; Mitchell, 1978; Mulira, 1991). Because those who use the life everlasting plant (in conjunction with prayer) in particular tend to be free of illness and to live to an extremely old age, it is the most common folk remedy used by Blacks, Native Americans, and Whites of the Sea Islands (Holloway, 1991). In addition, *gris-gris,* the symbols of voodoo, are often used to prevent illness. Powders and oils (often colored in symbolic ways) that are highly and pleasantly scented are often used as good *gris-gris,* whereas oils and powders with vile odors serve as bad *gris-gris.* A variety of colored candles are also used, with the color of the candle signifying the intention of the ritual (Mitchell, 1978; Mulira, 1991; Spector, 1996). One component of voodoo, that of putting a "fix", hex, or curse on another, is well-known because several unexplained deaths have been associated with this practice (Meador, 1992; Mulira, 1991; Spector, 1996); it is believed that no one survives a voodoo hex and that there are no rituals or cures that can reverse it.

Santeria is an additional, separate health/healing and religious cult among African and Cuban Americans (Harwood, 1977; Holloway, 1991; Paulino, 1995; Sandoval, 1977). This Afro-Caribbean religion arose among the west African slaves who were imported to Cuba in the 1700s to cultivate tobacco and sugar. It consists of a combination of west African (Yoruba) and Spanish-Catholic beliefs, and includes beliefs in reincarnation; use of African magical and occult techniques, including herbal medicine, spells, hexes, curses, and witches; beliefs and practices from Latino espiritism and Hispanic humoral medicine; and the frequent (well-known, controversial) use of animal sacrifices and animal blood for religious and health purposes (Brandon, 1991). Although a discussion of this religion/healing cult is beyond the confines of this chapter, it should be noted that Santeria has many followers in the United States. Although the majority of these are Cubans, substantial percentages are African American, Puerto Rican, and European American (Brandon, 1991). Santeria is an important, Afro-Caribbean religion/healing tradition whose many health beliefs, indigenous healers, and healing practices are used by some unknown (but substantial) percentage of American minorities (Brandon, 1991).

Healing Practices and Health Beliefs of Black Muslims. Although Islam is one of the fastest growing religions in the United States, few studies have investigated the impact of Muslim health care beliefs and practices. There are many different Muslim sects, and many Islamic cultures (Kemp, 1996). Some of the sects (e.g., the Nation of Islam) are comprised entirely of African Americans (7% of Blacks are Muslims), and others (e.g., the Sunni and the Shiite) consist of Arab, non-Arab middle Eastern, African, African American, Asian, or Anglo members. Health beliefs and practices common to these diverse sects include the Islamic diet, which is kosher in the traditional sense of that term. Thus, eating from dishes or with utensils that have had contact with forbidden foods is prohibited, and forbidden foods include pork products and beans. Consequently, many foods conceptualized as traditional African American "soul foods" (e.g., black-eyed peas with ham, ham hocks, pork ribs, pork chops) are not allowed; this yields an enormous (religious) diversity in African American dietary practices that is largely ignored in national nutritional studies (Spector, 1996). Because of these dietary restrictions, Black Muslim inpatients refuse to eat, eat only foods brought in by family members, or require a vegetarian diet with which health care providers must comply (Kemp, 1996). Likewise, diabetic Black Muslims will refuse to take insulin manufactured from pork pancreas (a common source of insulin). One important Muslim ritual is the fast of Ramadan, a 30-day period during which adult Muslims fast from sunup to sundown. During this time, no meat is eaten and only one meal per day (in the evening) is consumed. Some Muslims interpret the fast to mean abstinence from all food, water, and medicine for the 30 days, whereas others allow water and/or medicine only during the day (Kemp, 1996). Consequently, prescriptions will not be taken as prescribed or at all during this period.

African American Folk Disorders

A diversity of folk disorders and ethnomedical entities among African Americans have been identified and include clots, tedders, gas, ear noises, states of blood, falling out, and worriation, to name a few. Because a discussion of all of these is beyond the scope of this chapter, the discussion focuses briefly on states of blood, falling out, and worriation.

States of Blood. In Black folk medicine, blood is believed to take on a variety of "states" (e.g., bad, bruised, high, low, thin, thick, and weak blood) that are manifested in or cause illness (Bailey, 1987, 1991; Jackson, 1981; Weidman, 1979). For example, *bruised blood* is believed to be darker than normal, unable to circulate, the result of injury, and to be a cause of illness. *High blood,* on the other hand, refers to blood believed to collect in high spots of the body (e.g., the head) due to poor diet and stress, and manifested in dizziness and episodes of falling-out; many Blacks equate high blood pressure with this folk disorder and that, in part, explains their tendency to use folk herbal and other remedies for hypertension. Similarly, *low blood* refers to a folk condition in which a person is believed to lack enough blood (due to poor diet) and is seen as the cause of weakness and malaise. Finally, *bad blood* is a folk condition that originally referred to blood contaminated by toxins or by supernatural forces and thereby causing serious illness; after the Tuskegee study, however, the term came to mean (and currently means) blood contaminated by syphilis.

These notions regarding states of blood are west African in origin and are found in a diversity of African and Afro-Caribbean cultures, including among Cubans, Puerto Ricans (as mentioned previously), and others. Thus for example, Haitians (in the United States and Haiti) recognize a diversity of similar states of blood, including *san cle* (thin blood) and *san febl* (weak blood), which are both believed to cause psychiatric symptoms; *san epe* (thick blood believed to be the cause of hypertension); *san jon* (yellow) and *san noa* (dark) blood, which are both believed to cause incurable disease; and *move san* (bad) and *san gate* (spoiled) blood, which are due to venereal disease and magical fright, respectively. U.S. Haitians also believe that blood turns to water as a result of excess alcohol use, and that this in turn causes tuberculosis (Harwood, 1981). Likewise, Haitian Americans recognize a folk disorder called *gaz,* which is similar to African American concepts of "gas" and Asian concepts of "wind" in which (cold) air or wind is believed to enter the body and cause symptoms at the point of entry: Wind/gas entering the ears is believed to be the cause of headaches and mouth pain; wind/gas in the legs is seen as the cause of rheumatism; wind/gas entering the stomach is seen as the cause of abdominal, intestinal, and back pain, and so on.

Falling Out. This folk disorder is confined almost exclusively to women and seen primarily in Blacks, and secondarily in Cubans and other Afro-Caribbeans (e.g., Haitians, Bahamians). Although Blacks constitute 17% to 22% of the population, they account for at least 50% of cases of falling out (Lefley, 1979a,1979b; Weidman, 1979). In falling out, an individual whose medical history is negative for drug or alcohol use, seizure disorder, head injury, cardiovascular disease, diabetes, or abnormal blood pressure, and who currently does not appear to be under great stress, suddenly and inexplicably loses consciousness and consequently either falls out of her chair (hence the term) or simply drops where she stood. The period of unconsciousness is brief (1–10 minutes), and the individual returns to normal consciousness without fatigue, amnesia, or other seizure-related signs. The cause of this folk disorder is unknown and little biomedical research has been conducted on it (save a few case studies that used the Draw-A-Person and Rorschach tests to attribute it to hysteria), despite its prevalence among African Americans. This folk disorder is so common that it has given rise to the Black colloquialism "to fall out" (e.g., "I fell out" or "We fell out"), meaning to laugh so hysterically that one falls out of a chair and rolls on the floor (Landrine & Klonoff, 1996a).

Worriation. Worriation (the name used by Blacks), or nerves (*ataque de nervios,* the name used by Latinos), is a folk disorder specific to Black, Latino (Mexican, Central American, and especially Puerto Rican), and some Afro-Caribbean women (Camino, 1989). An enormous number of studies have been published on this folk disorder and emphasize its symptoms (e.g., Hill, 1988; Hill & Matthews, 1981; Nations, Camino, & Walker, 1988), and epidemiology (e.g., Davis & Whittin, 1988). Its symptoms are those of severe anxiety disorders (e.g., anxiety, panic attacks) and include marked somatic complaints. Some of the somatic symptoms (e.g., vague aches and pains, dizziness, heart racing, "jittery" stomach) are seen in anxiety disorders, whereas others (e.g., sudden rashes on and itching of the feet) may not be, and are presented frequently enough to raise questions about the ostensible psychiatric nature of this disorder. Although women exhibiting this disorder typically attribute it to excess stress or worry (hence the name), the cause has not been identified. Underlying endocrinological disorders (e.g., thyroid or adrenal dysfunctions) and lupus, both of which are exacerbated by stress and manifested in anxiety and rashes, are possibilities (see Klonoff & Landrine, 1997b) that have yet to be investigated.

NATIVE AMERICANS

The term *Native American* is used to refer to a culturally heterogeneous and geographically dispersed population that descended from the indigenous peoples of North America. The Native American population has been categorized in a variety of ways, including classification into 365 state-recognized tribes, 200 tribal language groups, and 511 distinct cultural/political groups recognized by the federal government (U.S. Bureau of the Census, 1983; LaFromboise, 1993). Because data on this plethora of groups cannot be summarized here, the focus is on the health beliefs and practices of Navajo and Crow tribes as more or less prototypical of the Native American population as a whole. There has been a great deal of contact among (and consolidation of) Native American tribes, resulting in overlap in health beliefs and practices that render the Navajo and Crow examples here representative of the population as a whole.

Studies of Health Problems of Native Americans

Major overview studies of Native American health are provided by Manson (1982), Manson and Dinges (1988), and Sievers and Fisher (1981). The major health problems of Native Americans are high rates of obesity and diabetes (Nelson et al., 1988; Petitt, Baird, Aleck, Bennett, & Knowler, 1983; Savage & Bennett, 1992; Sievers & Fisher, 1981); heart and cardiovascular disease (Coulehan, 1992; R. F. Gillum, 1988; R. F. Gillum, B. S. Gillum, & N. Smith, 1984); gall bladder disease and cancers of the gall bladder and biliary tract (Boss, Lanier, Dohan, & Bender, 1982; Hampton, 1992; Morris, Buechley, Key, & Morgan, 1978; Weiss, Ferrell, Hanis, & Styne, 1984); alcohol abuse (LaFromboise et al., 1995; May, 1982; Greig, P. S. Walker, & R. D. Walker, 1992; Weibel-Orlando, 1984); fetal alcohol syndrome (May, 1992); cirrhosis (USDHHS, 1996); depression and suicide (LaFromboise et al., 1995; Red Horse, 1992; Shore & Manson, 1981); and cervical and lung cancer (S. W. Jordan & Key, 1981; Gottlieb & Husen, 1982; Lanier & Knutson, 1986). High lung cancer rates are due to increased cigarette smoking and to working in uranium mines. The leading causes of death among Native Americans are shown in Table 51.1.

General Cultural Factors Influencing Health Behavior

Two of the many global cultural factors that influence the health behavior of Native Americans are racism and distrust of Whites, and the belief in noninterference.

Racism and Distrust of Whites. All of the ethnic groups discussed in this chapter have experienced profound White racism, oppression, and exploitation, which form a larger historical and social context from which health behavior, morbidity, and mortality are not readily separated. For Native Americans, this racism has taken the form of confiscation of tribal lands; slaughter and extermination on a scale equivalent to attempted genocide; and treaties formed but then broken by the U.S. government, culminating in the relegation of Native Americans to impoverished Indian reservations that are both ghettos and internment camps (LaFromboise, 1993). This history, coupled with the continuing "missionary zeal" of White professionals (who wish to rescue the "backward" Indians from their ways) have led to a deep distrust of White health professionals (LaFromboise, 1993). Isolated incidents of Whites who were trusted and then violated that trust (e.g., the White teacher who from 1979 to 1988 molested 94 Native American children at a reservation school) only increase that distrust and increase Indian reticence to seek help from any outsider (LaFromboise, 1993). The role of this history and social context in Native American health status and help seeking has yet to be fully investigated; it must be suspected, however, that it contributes significantly to Native American high rates of depression, suicide, and alcohol abuse.

Noninterference. Whether Native American cultures are characterized by the goal of living an artful (Acoma), peaceful (Hopi), or beautiful (Navajo) life, all are devoted to achieving and maintaining tranquility, cooperation, unselfishness, giving, kindness, respect and appreciation for all life forms, and communion with the land and nature from which people cannot be separated (Bryan, 1985; Hoxie, 1989; LaFromboise et al., 1995; Witherspoon, 1970, 1973, 1975). The profound significance of appreciating and respecting all living things and regarding all life forms as sacred cannot be overstated, and is manifested in a noninterventionist philosophy. This is the belief that people should leave things alone out of respect and appreciation for who and what they are; that deep affection consists of not intervening, disturbing, manipulating, or changing; that those who truly regard others and the planet as inherently priceless will "mind their own business" and let things be. Although this philosophy and these values have obvious benefits, there are negative implications as well. For example, this live-and-let-live philosophy is manifested in a laissez faire approach to the weaning and toilet training of children, as well as in a high tolerance for physical and psychiatric symptoms in others, with subsequent delays seeking treatment (Dinges, Trimble, Manson, & Pasquale, 1986). When coupled with the reticence to seek treatment from outsiders because of a social and historical context of White racism and missionary zeal, the delays in help seeking can be serious (Dinges et al., 1986; LaFromboise, 1993).

With these two general factors in mind, the next sections review the evidence on Native American health beliefs and practices, and highlight the Navajo and Crow as prototypical examples.

Navajo Indians

The Navajo are the largest Native American tribe (Deuschle, 1986), and are more likely than other tribes to be urban, with 54% of Navajo residing in major cities (Taylor, 1988). Along with the increasing urbanization of the Navajo, there has been a corresponding steady decline in urban, traditional Native American health care centers in the past two decades, leading Navajo to appear increasingly in biomedical settings for care (Campbell, 1989), and hence to be the Native Americans most likely to be encountered.

Beliefs About Illness

Like the other sociocentric cultures discussed here, the Navajo view health holistically, and hence do not draw distinctions between physical, spiritual, and social entities, or between religion and medicine (Avery, 1991; Deuschle, 1986; Kunitz & Levy, 1981). Harmony, or balance, among the physical, spiritual, and social faces of reality are understood as the foundation of health, and imbalance in these is central to illness. Disruptions in balance and harmony, along with the influence of a diversity of natural and supernatural forces, are the only causes of illness recognized by traditional members. In the Navajo language, there are no words for or concepts relating to microscopic disease-causing agents (Frisbie, 1987; Kunitz, 1981; Kunitz & Levy, 1981; Sorrell & B. A. Smith, 1993). The major proximal causes of illness recognized are violation of a behavioral taboo, witchcraft, soul loss and spirit intrusion, ghosts, and natural phenomena (thunder, lightening, animals), the set of which are sometimes called the negative values (Adair & Deuschle, 1970; Avery, 1991; Deuschle, 1986; Frisbie, 1987; Kunitz, 1981; Kunitz & Levy, 1981; Sorrell & B. A. Smith, 1993).

Breach of Taboo. Some form of breach of taboo is the most frequent and most powerful cause of illness recognized, and is believed to play a role in all illness irrespective of other causes. The two types of breach of taboo are engaging in prohibited acts (e.g., incest), and contact with taboo, dangerous (disease-producing) objects; such breaches then cause illness through several complex causal chains. For example, sibling incest is understood as the cause of generalized seizure disorder, but may or may not be assumed to have been committed by children with that disorder. This is because grand mal seizure disorder also is called "Moth sickness" due to the belief that the moth is the principal etiological agent. According to folk beliefs, the original incest between siblings was committed by the Butterfly People in the mythic past who twisted and convulsed like moths in a flame. By virtue of the belief that "like causes like" (that causes and their effects are similar), people who exhibit convulsions are understood as behaving like a moth and hence as suffering from "Moth sickness," whether or not they engaged in sibling incest. Similarly, it is believed that a witch can cause people to touch a moth or make the people "wild," such that they act like a moth; these people will eventually commit sibling incest and develop grand mal seizure disorder. Hence, although breach of taboo is understood as the cause of convulsions, the path from breach to symptom may be complex and indirect. Indeed, Navajo believe that one major cause of illness in adults is a breach of taboo committed by their mothers when pregnant with them (Avery, 1991; Deuschle, 1986; Frisbie, 1987; Kunitz, 1981; Kunitz & Levy, 1981).

Witchcraft. Witchcraft is understood as another common cause of illness and takes three forms: witchery, frenzy witchcraft, and sorcery. *Witchery* is the primary form of witchcraft among the Navajo and is mentioned in their creation myths. Witches always are associated with the dead (taboo dangerous objects) and with incest (taboo behavior), and hence witchery entails a breach of taboo. To become a witch, a person must kill a relative (a sibling usually) and eat part of that person's body; witches are also said to live in incestuous unions. Witches work their evil by touching their intended victim with a powder made from the flesh of corpses (thereby bringing the victim into contact with a disease provoking taboo object), and by transforming themselves into animals and manipulating their victim's behavior; hence, witches cause disease by manipulating their victims into breaching a taboo. *Sorcery* is similar to witchery, but sorcerers use their victims nails, hair, or other excreta to cause disease. Because these bits of the victim are understood as possessing the victim's characteristics and as a proxy for the person, things done to them are believed to happen to the person. These bits of the victim are exposed to dangerous (etiologic) taboo objects (e.g., lightening, graves), thereby forcing the victim to unwittingly breach a taboo and become ill. Finally, *frenzy witchcraft* entails ingesting the datura plant, which contains scopolamine and hyoscyamine and produces hallucinations and other psychiatric symptoms that are summarized by the folk term "frenzy." This form of witchcraft is used to manipulate women so that they can be seduced and manipulate men into gambling away their savings; in all cases, the victim unwittingly breaches a taboo during the frenzy and hence becomes ill (Adair & Deuschle, 1970; Deuschle, 1986; Kunitz, 1981; Kunitz & Levy, 1981).

Soul Loss A person's soul, or "wind" (*honich'ih,* Holy-Spirit-Wind; see Haile, 1943, and McNeley, 1973), is understood as entering the body immediately after birth and departing to the afterworld at death; at both of these points the wind-soul is understood as only loosely attached to the body and so able to detach readily without disease implications. Thus, ghosts of dead elderly or infants have no health implications, whereas ghosts of those who died when the wind-soul was firmly attached to the body are believed to cause disease in others. This concept is somewhat similar to the loss of soul discussed for other ethnic groups previously here. *Spirit Intrusion* refers to the possession of a person's wind-soul by an evil supernatural spirit; this is said to be manifested in disease. *Ghosts and evil spirits* also are believed to cause illness (the ghosts of departed relatives in particular). Finally, *natural phenomena* understood as disease provoking include whirlwinds, water, hail, animals, and lightning. Lightning is considered particularly pathogenic and includes all things that are slender or move in a zigzag pattern like lightning (e.g., snakes, arrows). A diversity of animals are believed to cause disease, including bear, coyote, snake, ant, moth, insects, certain reptiles, and all fish (Adair & Deuschle, 1970; Kunitz, 1981; Kunitz & Levy, 1981).

Indigenous Healers and Healing Practices

Traditional Navajo religion focuses on maintaining harmony and tranquility among people, the supernatural, and the earth. Because illness is understood as disharmony, religion and religious rituals are health oriented, and there is no distinction between religion and medicine. Although there is considerable religious diversity among the Navajo, the Native American Church (peyote-ism) dominates. This religion began among the Comanche Indians in the 1930s, and then spread to an enormous number of other tribes (other Plains Indians as well as tribes of the prairies and Rocky Mountains; Kunitz, 1981; Kunitz & Levy, 1981). The brevity (one night vs. the traditional eight nights) and ensuing low cost of the healing ceremonies of the Native American Church (relative to the lengthy, expensive traditional ceremonies of most tribes, including the Navajo) account for its birth during the Depression and its continued expansion and popularity. The healing practices of the Native American Church entail far more than ingesting peyote, and include reintegration of the symptomatic individual into the community, ritualized group confession, atonement, social support, advice, prayer, and caring.

As indicated by earlier examples, all sociocentric cultures draw few if any distinctions between religion and medicine. Importantly, however, this means that health beliefs and healing rituals are sacred and consecrated. Hence, whereas other ideas may change, health beliefs and practices remain stable, and little incorporation of biomedical concepts occurs despite education and acculturation (Adair & Deuschle, 1970; Deuschle, 1986; Kunitz, 1981; Kunitz & Levy, 1981). For example, although Navajo recognize that some diseases are contagious, their own system of folk medical beliefs does not include any etiologic agents that could cause a contagious disease (Adair & Deuschle, 1970). Likewise, many Navajo have contact with biomedical views through the Indian Health Service (IHS)[6] and many increasingly select mainstream health careers (Haller & Aitken, 1992). Nonetheless, biomedical beliefs are understood but not adopted; they are viewed (and respected because all knowledge is respected) as White knowledge and beliefs that are good for White people, whereas Navajo knowledge and beliefs are good for Navajo. Thus, Adair and Deuschle (1970) and Medicine (1981) found no evidence of incorporation of biomedical views or curing techniques among Navajo ceremonialists, despite the long presence and influence of the IHS. Biomedical services are used by Navajo because of the belief that only White medicine can relive the symptoms of certain (usually infectious) diseases. Biomedical interventions and drugs are understood, however, as merely alleviating the symptoms, rather than as truly curing the underlying cause of disease; the underlying cause is understood as detailed earlier and only cured by a traditional ceremony (Adair & Deuschle, 1970; Kunitz & Levy, 1981).

Traditional healers play a prominent role in all Native American cultures (e.g., Jilek, 1974a, 1974b; Sandner, 1978, 1979) and are known as medicine men and women, witch-doctors, shamans, or native healers, as well as by indigenous labels such as *angakok* (Eskimo) and *wiscaca waka* (Lakota). Navajo traditional healers (or ceremonialists) perform healing ceremonies called sings (Sandner, 1978, 1979). These are sacred, curative rituals that aim to restore harmony (to treat the underlying problem) rather than to remove symptoms per se (Frisbie, 1987), and require from 6 to 10 years to learn (Kunitz & Levy, 1981). A sing entails prayers, chants, and social support. Practices of medicine men and women include diagnosing the cause of disharmony and then restoring it through a combination of sings, herbal remedies, massage and other physical manipulations, sand paintings, and dancing rituals (Avery, 1991; Deuschle, 1986; Kunitz, 1981; Kunitz & Levy, 1981; Sandner, 1979). Diseases and corresponding sings are named and classified in terms of the etiologic agent understood to be the cause of the problem. Thus, symptoms understood as caused by evil are healed with the Evil Way chant, whereas those caused by wind or lightning are healed with the Wind and Shooting (Lightning) Way chants, respectively. There are many of these sings, each for a specific physical or psychiatric symptom, including the Night Way, Plume Way, Earth and Beauty Ways; the Life Way and Flint Way (for injuries and chronic physical disorders); and the Coyote Way, Hand Trembling Way, Frenzy Witchcraft Way, Moth Way, Mountain Top Way, and Twirling Way. These are used prior to and conjointly with biomedical services.

Traditional healers and ceremonialists from neighboring tribes (e.g., Hopi) often are invited to participate in Navajo healing rituals (Kunitz, 1981; Kunitz & Levy, 1981). Such cooperation among a diversity of tribes, along with participation in the transtribal Native American Church, in part accounts for the similarities in the health beliefs and practices of many Native American tribes. In addition, the 1934 Indian Reorganization Act permitted reservation peoples to reorganize for the purpose of self-government, and led to the formation of large, cooperative, consolidated reservation-based groups composed of several tribes. Although these cultural/political groups are now referred to as tribes, they are not tribes in the traditional sense. Examples of consolidated tribes include the Kiowa-Comanche-Apache, Cheyenne-Arapaho, and the Northwest Affiliated Tribes (Deloria, 1983). Such overlap and cooperation has resulted in similarities in health beliefs and practices. Although the health beliefs and practices of the Sioux (composed of 15 distinct tribes), Chippewa (composed of 19 distinct tribes), Potawatomi (composed of 4 distinct tribes), Crow, and Navajo are not identical (and there is considerable variance within each of these groups as well), the underlying principles, values, spiritual nature, and healing caring practices of Navajo and Crow health systems are representative of others. Navajo ceremonialists, like the traditional healers of many cultures discussed thus far, are older, wise people whose power to heal is understood as magical and/or sacred in origin. This power permits the indigenous healers of many cultures, the Navajo ceremonialist included, to make an immediate diagnosis simply by looking at the patient. Hence, long diagnostic interviews and testing are unusual and cast aspersions on the competence of biomedical practitioners (Kunitz & Levy, 1981).

There are almost no studies of the extent to which Navajo comply with biomedical treatment (Kunitz, 1981; Kunitz & Levy, 1981), although there are several indicating that incorporating Navajo beliefs and practices increases compliance (Atteneave, 1974; Deuschle, 1986; Fleming, 1983; Frisbie, 1987; Jilek, 1971; Manson, 1982; Manson & Dinges, 1988; Sorrell & B. A. Smith, 1993). For example, in some settings, medicine men have been permitted to perform sings in patients' rooms with the family attending (Frisbie, 1987), and in

[6]The IHS is the major federal agency charged with providing health care to Indians (*forever*) in exchange for Indian lands captured or surrendered to the U.S. government in treaty agreements throughout the late 1800s and early 1900s. Originally administered by the war department, the IHS was transferred to the Department of the Interior's Bureau of Indian Affairs, and then was established in 1955 as a division of the PHS. General medical and surgical services have been provided by the IHS since its inception, and mental health services were added in 1965. The IHS is the major provider of health services for all Native Americans irrespective of residence (cities vs. reservations), directly or indirectly through subcontractors.

others traditional and biomedical healing rituals have been used conjointly, with patient compliance and rate of recovery enhanced in both cases (Deuschle, 1986). Similarly, Frisbie (1987) discussed many successful ways in which Native American health practices and beliefs have been accommodated by biomedical settings, including establishing a Native Science Healing Room (designed by two singers) at the Gallup, New Mexico, Medical Center. Less dramatic efforts that nonetheless increase compliance include assuring patients that blood and urine samples will not be used for witchcraft, describing how such samples will be disposed of, and having medicine men bless both in- and outpatient facilities to ward off the ghost infections that result from prior deaths in or associated with the setting (Sorrell & B. A. Smith, 1993). Evidence also suggests that Navajo will not comply with treatment without consent of family and permission of the elder woman (Navajo are matriarchal) who makes treatment decisions for tribe members (Deuschle, 1986; Sorrell & Smith, 1993).

Thus, unlike the many other cultural groups discussed here, Native American indigenous healers and healing ceremonies (from a diversity of tribes) have been treated with (a modicum of) respect by biomedical practitioners, and efforts have been made to integrate these into mainstream care in order to increase patient compliance and recovery (Atteneave, 1974; Fleming, 1983; Haller & Aitken, 1992; Jilek, 1971; Manson, 1982; Manson & Dinges, 1988). Physicians, psychotherapists, and nurses often attend traditional healing ceremonies and medicine men are invited to participate fully in case conferences and treatment planning and delivery (Atteneave, 1974; Bergman, 1971, 1973a, 1973b; Haller & Aitken, 1992; Jilek, 1971; Manson, 1982; Manson & Dinges, 1988). Indeed, two schools designed to train biomedical practitioners in Native American healing have been established and funded by the federal government (Bergman, 1971, 1973a, 1973b) for mental health professionals. Some (e.g., LaFromboise, 1993) have attributed these unique cooperative efforts to the 1978 American Indian Religious Freedom Act (PL 95-134), which guarantees these ceremonies the same protection granted to other religions under the constitution. However, many of the healing cults of other minorities (e.g., African American *voodoo*) have been recognized as religions and churches since the 1940s (Simpson, 1978; Tallant, 1946) and yet their traditional healers are rarely similarly integrated into biomedical settings and services or afforded respect as experts. The difference may be that White Americans have hostile attitudes and feelings of cultural superiority where people of African and Latino descent are concerned, but have romantic fantasies and mythical beliefs about Native Americans that render them alone an attractive, desirable, exotic-primitive minority group (Deloria, 1983). Native American scholar Vine Deloria Jr. (1983) argued that such fantasies, along with considerable guilt about the historical treatment of Native Americans, account for the common tendency of Whites to claim Indian ancestors (e.g., that there is an "Indian princess" in their family line). Such fantasies account for the respect afforded to Native American healers as well: Whites do not proudly proclaim fantasized, Black or Mexican ancestors, and White health professionals similarly have exhibited little interest in consulting with indigenous healers of these cultures (Landrine & Klonoff, 1996a).

Crow Indians

Health Beliefs, Practices, and Healers. Like the other cultures discussed here, Crow Indian health beliefs are characterized by holism and hence entail no distinctions among physical, spiritual, and social realities; all entities, processes, and phenomena are intimately connected, might be understood as faces of a single unified process or reality, and thus are in a sense one (Frey, 1987; Hoxie, 1989). Harmony, tranquility, and balance among these various faces of reality is understood as health, and disharmony or imbalance as illness (Bryan, 1985; Buehler, 1992; Frey, 1987; Hoxie, 1989; Vogel, 1970). In addition to such imbalances, illness is understood as caused by evil spirits and other supernatural factors, natural phenomena, and by witches. Crow beliefs about the causes of illness are similar to Navajo beliefs and to those of many other Native American tribes. Rituals, ceremonies, and sacred objects are the major healing practices used by Crow Indians to prevent and cure illness, and entail chants and prayers in a manner similar to those of Navajo and other tribes. There are four major Crow rituals/ceremonies:

Sun dances consists of fasting, praying, and dancing for 3 to 4 days to heal illness or injury, and are conducted conjointly with treatment from a medicine woman/man who uses sacred objects (usually a sacred eagle feather fan).

Prayer rituals are used for prevention and healing, and are conducted by a family member under the guidance of a medicine woman/man or clan aunt/ uncle.

Smudging rituals are part of the prayer rituals in which sacred herbs are burned to ward off the malevolent spirits understood to cause illness; this practice is particularly common when hospitalization occurs and is conducted in the hospital.

Sweat baths (sauna) are used by Crow and by many other Plains Indian tribes for healing and preventing illness (Bryan, 1985; Buehler, 1992; Frey, 1987; Hoxie, 1989; Vogel, 1970).

Sacred objects used for preventing and healing illness and injury include amulets, tobacco, peyote, and various herbs. For example, herbs such as cedar and sage, are used in Smudging Rituals and also are hung over doorways to prevent illness by warding off malevolent spirits. Tobacco smoke is used in Sun Dances, and peyote is ingested during other sacred rituals. Among the diversity of amulets, the most common is the umbilical cord pouch, a small, leather pouch in which one's own umbilical cord is stored to protect oneself from illness and to assist individuals in finding their true life path; umbilical cord pouches are worn by traditional and transitional (bicultural) Crow alike (Bryan, 1985; Buehler, 1992; Frey, 1987; Hoxie, 1989; Vogel, 1970).

Crow indigenous healers are spiritual/religious leaders who are understood as possessing a sacred, magical power to prevent and heal specific illnesses, and clan aunts and uncles also maintain the health of clan members. The clan is the major social unit of Crow culture, with each person being a member of one of eight matrilineal clans. Each clan has one or more clan aunts/uncles who provide "spiritual mediation" (a combination of Prayer Rituals and Sun Dances) to achieve recovery from illness and solve social and other problems. These cultural healers and healing practices are consulted and used prior to seeking help from biomedical practitioners (Buehler, 1992). Even those who label themselves as transitional (bicultural) or modern (acculturated) Indians use traditional healing and healers conjointly with biomedicine (Frey, 1987) because traditional healing is sacred and cannot be rejected anymore than religion can be rejected. These healers, along with the Crow population, represent many different religions. Individual Crow may belong to one of several Christian denominations as well as one of the many Crow Churches (such as the Tobacco Society and Sun Dance Religion), or they may belong to the Native American Church. Each of these churches has its own additional, highly specific health beliefs and practices, although all such beliefs entail attributing illness to imbalance/disharmony and to the actions of malevolent spirits and supernatural entities. Although it is clear that Crow (and other Indian tribes) use the biomedical services provided by the IHS, we found no data on their compliance with treatment.

SUMMARY

Similarities Among Minority Groups

Table 51.2 provides a summary comparison of the major health beliefs and practices of American minorities that were detailed in this chapter. As shown, there is remarkable similarity among minority groups in their holistic assumptions, definitions of health, causal attributions for illness, folk disorders, and types of healing provided by indigenous healers, with some of these factors being identical. These striking similarities are not coincidences, but rather they reflect the worldview of sociocentric cultures.

As noted here, across the globe and across cultural groups within the United States, two distinct worldviews (or metaphors we live by) can be identified. The first is the (mind/body, self/other, and person/environment) holism of sociocentric cultures, and the second is the dualism of more egocentric (individualistic) White Western cultures. When holism is the basic assumption of a culture, it is necessarily the case that balance is emphasized, and that maintaining emotional, bodily, interpersonal, spiritual, and universal harmony (homeostasis) is viewed as essential to health. Likewise, in the context of holism, the boundaries between body and the world are so thin that natural and supernatural entities and forces readily traverse it. Thus, there is necessarily a high degree of interaction between body and others, body and the environment, body and mind, and body and spiritual/universal forces. Consequently, such factors, along with interpersonal relations, gain primacy as etiological agents. Thus, the hot/cold theory of disease, and a belief in the etiological significance of spirits, natural and supernatural entities, interpersonal relations and of emotions hold across sociocentric cultures, and disease has social and moral implications. This holism stands in stark contrast to White Western dualism in which the body is understood as separate from the mind, others, the environment, and the gods/universe. In the context of such dualism, disease is primarily understood as the unidirectional invasion of alien forces that break through defenses to attack the body as nation-state. Thus, the many differences between the cultures of minorities and that of the dominant group in our society where health beliefs, practices, and behavior are concerned are predictable from the framework of holistic versus dualist worldviews.

Of particular importance is the difference in the etiological significance of emotions in these two worldviews. In sociocentric cultures, emotions are viewed as integrated with bodily and social processes, and indeed in many cultures are viewed as localized to specific regions of the body. Hence, physical events (diseases) have emotional and interpersonal implications (and vice versa). Alternatively, in the West, even within the "new holism" of contemporary health psychology, emotions are still nonetheless basically understood as psychological processes that can be readily distinguished from bodily and environmental events. Hence, although it is increasingly believed that emotional and interpersonal events can have physical implications, disease nonetheless is understood as a physical (rather than a moral, spiritual, and social) event (Fabrega, 1974; White & Marsella, 1982). Thus, minorities—but not Whites—view illness as shameful because of its moral/spiritual implications, and as a family rather than as an individual event. This difference between the true holism of sociocentric cultures and the pseudo-holism (beneath which dualism persists) of Western biomedicine becomes problematic when those who participate in holism are treated by those who participate in dualism (Fabrega, 1974; Hare, 1993).

A Preliminary Theoretical Model of Minority Health

The information presented in this chapter (and the striking similarities among minority groups) suggest a tentative, theoretical model of the role of cultural variables in minority health, depicted in Fig. 51.1. As noted in the Introduction, social status variables such as poverty and low education obviously play a role in the health status and behavior of minorities and so are included in the model, but as distal predictors only. Distal predictors are variables that the set stage (are necessary) for but are not sufficient to predict morbidity, mortality, or health behavior; such variables act indirectly as a diathesis. Hence, for example, although poverty plays a role in high rates of cigarette smoking, obesity, hypertension, and failure to exercise among Blacks, these health problems also persist irrespective of social class, education, and occupation, such that status variables alone do not account for them. Poverty and low levels of education are then distal predictors that play an indirect role in the health status, behaviors, and problems in question and account for only a small percentage of the variance. These social status factors play a role in minority health primarily through their ability to predict access to

TABLE 51.2
Similarities in Health Beliefs and Practices of American Minority Cultures

	Puerto Ricans	Mexicans & Other Latinos	Southeast Asians	Chinese & Other Asians	African Americans	Afro-Caribbeans	Native Americans
Basic Assumption	Mind/body & person /environment holism	Mind/body & person /environment holism	Mind/body & person /environment holism	Mind/body & person /environment holism	Mind/body & person /environment holism	Mind/body & person /environment holism	Mind/body & person /environment holism
Definition of Health	Balance & harmony	Balance & harmony	Balance & harmony	Balance & harmony	Harmony	Balance & harmony	Harmony
Major Proximal Causes of Illness	Supernatural factors	Emotions	Supernatural factors	Natural factors	Natural & supernatural factors	Supernatural factors	Breach of taboo (supernatural)
Other Proximal Causes	Natural factors & emotions	Natural factors	Natural factors & emotions	Emotions	Supernatural factors & emotions	Supernatural factors	Supernatural factors
Distal Causes Recognized	Supernatural factors	Supernatural factors	Supernatural factors	Supernatural	Biomedical factors	Natural factors	Natural factors
Very Distal Causes	Biomedical factors	Biomedical factors	Biomedical factors	Biomedical factors	Supernatural factors	Biomedical factors	Biomedical factors
Folk Disorders	Fright/soul loss Worry Evil eye Empacho States of blood Possession Hex/curse	Fright/soul loss Worry Evil eye Empacho Caida Hex/curse	Fright/soul loss Evil eye Nightmare (SUNDS) Possession Hex/curse	Fright/soul loss Evil Eye	Worry Falling out States of blood Possession/trance Hex/curse	Worry Falling out States of blood Possession/trance Hex/curse	Soul loss Possession Hex/curse

Indigenous Healers	Spiritualists Herbalists Curanderas Pateras (midwives)	Herbalists Curanderas Pateras (midwives) Spiritualists	Chinese doctors Vaids Herbalists	Chinese doctors Herbalists	Ministers Herbalists Midwives Voodooists	Spiritualists Herbalists Midwives Voodooists	Ceremonialists
Folk Cures	Magical rituals Tea, herbs Prayer Diet/rest Physical manipulation	Tea, herbs Prayer Diet/rest Physical manipulation Magic rituals	Magical rituals Diet change Tea, herbs Meditation	Tea, herbs Diet/rest Physical manipulation (acupuncture, acupressure) Meditation	Prayer Tea, herbs Diet/rest Magical rituals	Magical rituals Tea/herbs Diet/rest Prayer	Magical rituals Herbs Diet/rest Prayer/chants Physical manipulation
Expectations of Care providers	Charismatic Intuits problem Warm, personal	Charismatic Intuits problem Warm, personal	Charismatic Intuits problem Formal, polite	Charismatic Intuits problem Formal, polite	Charismatic Intuits problem Warm, personal	Charismatic Intuits problem Warm, personal	Charismatic Intuits problem Warm, personal
Cultural Factors Affecting Health Behavior	Distrust of Whites Language	Distrust of Whites Language	Distrust of Whites Fear of shame Language	Distrust of Whites Fear of shame Language	Distrust of Whites Dialect	Distrust of Whites Language	Distrust of Whites Noninterference Language

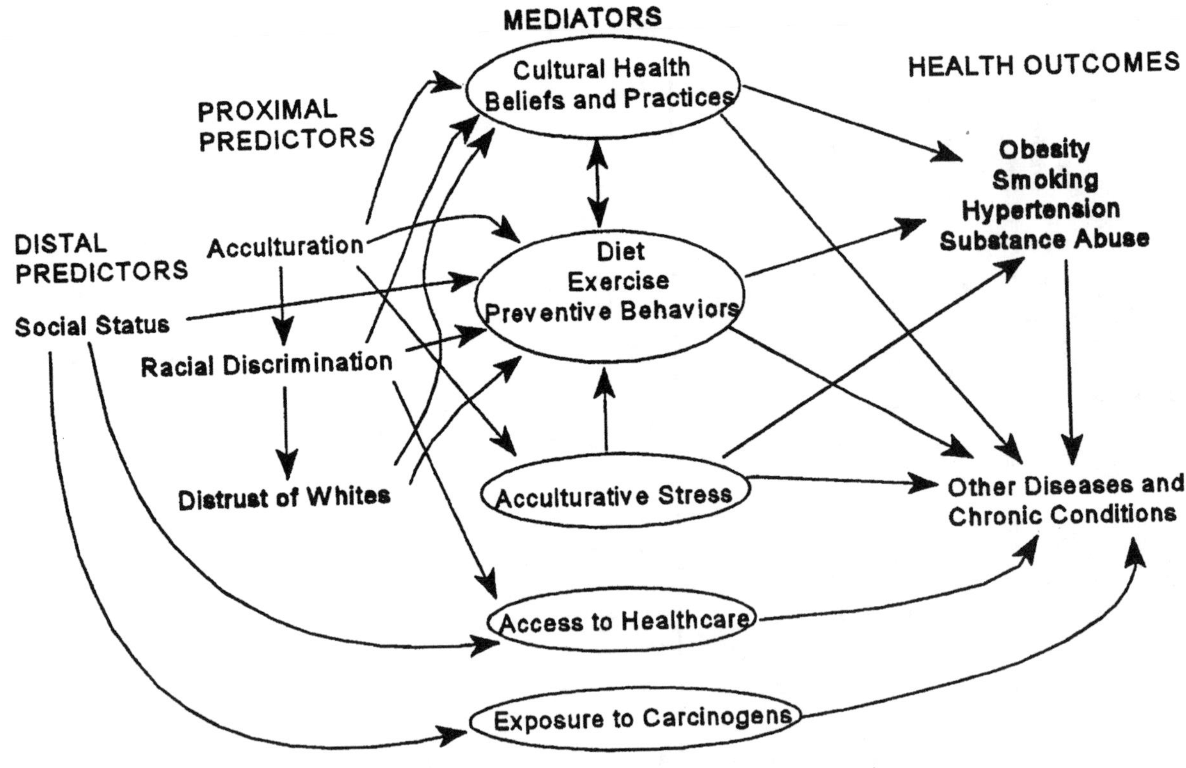

FIG. 51.1. Theoretical model of variables in minority health.

health care and exposure to carcinogens, and do not predict health beliefs and practices.

Proximal predictors, on the other hand, are variables that directly influence health behavior, morbidity, and mortality, and account for the majority of the variance in those. In the tentative model (based on this review), the proximal predictors are discrimination, distrust of Whites, and levels of acculturation. Theoretically, discrimination plays a role in minority health in two ways. First, racist discrimination against minorities may limit their access to care and alter the nature and type of care they receive. In addition, discrimination predicts the extent to which minorities distrust Whites and the health information and programs they provide. This, in turn, in part predicts health beliefs and practices, participation in prevention programs, and other important (mediator) variables. Levels of acculturation also play a role insofar as they predict the degree of participation in the many health beliefs and practices of the ethnomedical systems detailed here. The cultural health beliefs and practices in question then are important (moderator variables and) predictors of health behavior. The three proximal predictors are theoretically related insofar as there is less discrimination against acculturated minorities (who are more similar, culturally, to Whites) than against their traditional counterparts (as was demonstrated empirically; Landrine & Klonoff, 1996a); in turn, discrimination is related to the degree of distrust of Whites and the health information and programs they provide. This model is only a tentative one, and is provided in an effort to bring coherence to the various factors that impact minority health, and in the effort to place neglected cultural variables in the center of that picture. This model can be used to form specific empirical hypotheses that may better predict minority health behavior and lead to insights regarding tailoring prevention and treatment programs for minorities.

CONCLUSIONS

Landrine and Klonoff (1992) argued that White Western health schema entail the assumption that only health experts have knowledge of illness and of curing. Consequently,

> it is often assumed that the curing relationship is one in which a community of experts brings information and health care to a lay community for which both are lacking. Western cultural concepts of "delivering" and "providing" "service" and "care" to "recipients" and "target populations" who may not "comply" with "treatment regimens" highlight the [Western] representation of the victim of illness as a knowledgeless, empty container into whom both reified illness and reified cures are poured. (Landrine & Klonoff, 1992, p. 268)

It was argued that this null hypothesis view of minorities is incorrect because minorities, instead, are participants in living, complex, dynamic cultures, each of which has its own, centuries-old system of folk medicine. This chapter has provided a mere glimpse of those systems of ethnomedicine to demonstrate that minorities have—not nothing, but—a wealth of health information, beliefs, practices, services, and care within their own communities. It then seems self-evident that the interventions of health psychology and related disciplines must be adapted to fit within these preexisting, indigenous cultural frameworks if they are to be successful. This is particularly because these preexisting systems of ethnomedicine cannot be dismissed, because they are neither trivial, limited to a few members of the culture, nor limited to conceptualizing and treating folk disorders. Rather, they are alive and dynamic in the sense that they continually adapt to and incorporate new biomedical diseases and cures to render them coherent for the culture's members. Thus, for example, Haitian Americans have incorporated AIDS into their preexisting health framework, and understand the disease as a punishment for taboo behavior, most likely to appear in those who have a diathesis of "bad blood" (Farmer, 1990; Hippolyte, 1993). Likewise, Latinos (*curanderas,* in particular) also have incorporated AIDS into their ethnomedical understandings. Although AIDS is understood as caused by a virus that can be transmitted sexually and perinatally (the "how"), it also is believed to be caused by evil spirits (the "why"), and to occur among those who have a diathesis of exposure to mal aire and a chronic imbalance of hot/cold (the "why"; Flaskerud & Cavillo, 1991; Rivera, 1990). Similarly, African Americans have incorporated AIDS into their preexisting ethnomedicine, and, although they likewise understand its viral etiology (the "how"), they nonetheless view it as an "unnatural illness" strongly tied to taboo behavior and punishment for it (the "why"; see Flaskerud & Rush, 1989). Systems of ethnomedicine are alive, dynamic, and highly adaptable to biomedicine, and biomedicine must become similarly dynamic and adapt to ethnomedicine.

Research Suggestions

Racism. This review indicates that racism plays a role in minority health, and warrants serious scientific attention. Racist discrimination may play a direct role as a culturally specific stressor that impacts smoking, alcohol use, diet and other health-related behaviors as well as immunological functions, just as other stressors do. The Schedule of Racist Events (SRE; Landrine & Klonoff, 1996a, 1996b) can be used to investigate the role of racist events in Black health, and may serve as a model for future scales to assess racist discrimination and its health impact for other minority groups. Investigations of the frequency and prevalence of racist events in the lives of all minorities, and of their role in health behavior and morbidity, are obviously long overdue. Studies of how minorities cope with racist discrimination are also needed insofar as coping may mediate the racist stress–symptom relationship.

Studies of the role of ethnic discrimination in minority health are important not only because of the variance that such discrimination no doubt accounts for, but for an additional reason as well, namely: Ethnicity is more than a marker for culture and history. It is also a marker for a plethora of social, contextual, and structural inequalities, deprivations, and processes strongly related to health. To fully elucidate the factors underlying differential morbidity and mortality by ethnicity, studies must address this social aspect of ethnicity along with the cultural dimension. The role of long neglected cultural variables in the health of minorities should and indeed must be examined, but "in the context of families embedded in a wider societal context conditioned by federal policies that enable or constrain public health programs and community development" (Harrison, 1994, p. 93). To focus solely on cultural variables is to deny "that health and health care are situated in a wider social context structured and constrained by principles of racial [and ethnic] hierarchy and forces of racism" (Harrison, 1994, p. 93). The danger in focusing on the role of cultural factors in the health of any ethnic-minority group is that research may take a "victim-blaming" turn (Hoff, 1994) in which the consequences of ethnic stratification, deprivation, and exploitation are erroneously attributed to the "culture" or the cultural "lifestyle" of politically and economically subordinate groups. "Victim-blaming is alive and well" in health psychology and related disciplines (Hoff, 1994, p. 96), but can be combated by focusing on both the social and the cultural dimensions of ethnicity via examining culture within the context of ethnic stratification, prejudice, and discrimination.

Distrust of Whites. Likewise, investigations of the role of distrust of Whites (secondary to historical and current racism) also are needed. This review indicates that all minorities distrust Whites to some extent. This distrust no doubt plays a role in seeking and complying with treatment provided or recommended by Whites, as well as in acceptance and trust of health information (and associated prevention programs), and willingness to participate in research and interventions. These studies are particularly needed for Blacks in light of the evidence presented here on the legacy of Tuskegee. Like studies of the impact of racism, investigations of minority distrust of Whites are long overdue, and the absence of both can only be explained as a function of the culture of health psychology and health psychologists.

Health Beliefs. Systematic studies of the prevalence among each minority group of the health beliefs detailed here are badly needed. The extent to which the health beliefs are endorsed, the extent and manner in which they are integrated with biomedical understandings, and the relationship between ethnomedical beliefs and status variables must be understood before the health implications of the beliefs can be carefully examined. Then, the relationship between ethnomedical beliefs and health behavior must be systematically investigated; the latter studies can use any major theoretical model of the belief–behavior relationship (e.g., the health belief model, the theory of reasoned action). What is clear in this chapter is that health psychology's knowledge of people's health beliefs (based on studies of Whites) applies to Whites alone, and bears no resemblance to the beliefs held by American minorities.

Generalizations from studies based on Whites clearly are inappropriate. New instruments are needed to investigate the causal attributions of sociocentric people, and new models of the health beliefs–behavior relationship may be needed as well given the vast differences between holistic and dualistic worldviews.

Folk Healers/Health Practices. Systematic studies of the prevalence among each minority group of the diversity of folk healers detailed here are needed, along with careful examination of the extent to which minorities frequent indigenous healers for care. Presence of and contact with indigenous healers appears to play a role (in some studies cited here) in minority compliance with treatment and so must be assessed.

Folk Cures. Similarly, studies of the nature of the cures used and recommended by indigenous healers are needed, and the extent to which minorities comply with these versus biomedical cures must be assessed. Investigations of the effectiveness of these cures are badly needed and may shed light on their persistence in minority communities. The extent to which minorities experience symptom relief after ingesting herbs and attending prayer meetings cannot be ignored given how frequently these treatments are sought. Likewise, however, studies of the frequency of use of toxic/lethal folk remedies are needed to prevent unnecessary health problems and deaths among minorities, children in particular. The undisclosed chronic use of toxic/lethal folk remedies may play a role in symptoms presented and in recalcitrant health problems among minorities, and must be investigated to better understand minority morbidity and mortality.

Folk Disorders. Analysis of the prevalence, epidemiological distribution, symptoms, and stages of folk disorders is needed. These disorders have been reported reliably by minorities for centuries, and neglect of them cannot be justified. Studies are needed that identify the nature of the underlying dysfunction entailed in these disorders, and no doubt will find that each corresponds to a known (in all probability) or unknown "real" pathogenic process. *Susto, mal ojo, ataque de nervios,* and worriation, for example, may represent a form of posttraumatic stress disorder, or underlying endocrine dysfunction, and other folk disorders appear to correspond to enteric pathology no doubt secondary to the poor living conditions of many impoverished minorities. Investigations of SUNDS are obviously needed, given that it is the leading cause of death for Hmong men. To continue to ignore reliable constellations of symptoms from which many people suffer or die simply because they are exhibited solely by minorities and violate current disease nosologies can only be regarded as racist.

Practice/Intervention Suggestions

Health education, promotion, and intervention programs must be tailored in a manner that renders them consistent with the folk medicine and folk medical beliefs of each minority group, African Americans included. Unlike other minorities, African Americans alone have been regarded as a cultureless "race" (a genetically distinct group) despite their genetic variability (Landrine & Klonoff, 1996a; Sowell, 1978, 1994). Hence, health-related research on and interventions for them have focused on social variables (such as poverty) and on biological factors presumably correlated with ostensible race. Consequently, African Americans have received more research attention from health psychology[7] than all other cultural minorities, but simultaneously and paradoxically also have received the least attention to cultural factors in their health. Numerous references have been provided in the section on African Americans to highlight that they have as much of a culture as any other minority group. Their culture clearly includes a long-standing system of ethnomedicine that must be addressed by health psychology. Continuing to ignore minority health beliefs and practices (as most of medicine and virtually all of health psychology do; see Klonoff et al., 1995) by attributing their differences and lack of compliance to their lack of education or poverty cannot continue. Such responses to diversity are racist insofar as they render differences deficits, and are Procrustean efforts to render minorities more or less "White," despite the cultural limbs lost. Efforts to include, rather than dismiss, diversity might use the following guidelines:

1. Culturally specific health concepts can be readily included in treatment suggestions and programs by adding them to biomedical directives. Nothing is lost by suggesting that people engage in the health rituals (prayer, teas, rest) that they intend to engage in anyway, but the biomedical intervention will be perceived as more legitimate because it meets the patient's expectations. Translating interventions into the language of ethnomedicine also may be beneficial. Again, nothing is lost by suggesting that antihypertensive medications (for example) lower blood pressure and unblock chi (for the Chinese), decrease the "heat" in the body (for Latinos), or maintain balance and homeostasis (for all minority groups).
2. Likewise, family members may need to be included in treatment planning and delivery. It may be beneficial to discuss and present health problems as a family issue necessitating action on the family's part. This strategy can be used not only with individual patients, but also in community health promotion and disease prevention programs. Strategies that give control and responsibility for the intervention to family, community, or religious leaders may be similarly useful.
3. Finally, indigenous healers can be incorporated into practice and communitywide interventions as an integral aspect of the intervention.

Each of the previous suggestions is consistent with successful strategies that have been used with traditional Native

[7]We operationalize this as number of articles published in *Health Psychology* 1982–1992, see Klonoff et al. (1995) for an empirical analysis of this by race/ethnicity.

Americans. These strategies have not been applied to other minority groups despite their clear, empirically demonstrated success with Native Americans; adopting these as a general approach to minority groups seems appropriate. When the intervention is for a community, these strategies are likely to be successful because at least some community members will be traditional and endorse ethnomedicine. When the recipient of the intervention is an individual patient, however, the success of these strategies is contingent on assessment of the extent to which that minority patient is traditional and therefore endorses ethnomedical beliefs and concepts. Harwood (1981) suggested asking the following questions as a means for assessing this with individual patients:

What do you think has caused your problem?
Why do you think it started when it did?
What do you think your sickness does to you? How does it work?
How bad (severe) do you think your illness is? Do you think it will last a long time, or will be better soon in your opinion?
What kind of treatment would you like to have?
What are the most important results you hope to get from treatment?
What are the chief problems your illness has caused you?
What do you fear most about your sickness? (p. 29)

If patients' answers suggest that they are not traditional in their health beliefs, then the strategies suggested here are not necessary.

The previous suggestions are only a few of the many changes in the content and process of delivering interventions to minorities that are needed. Other changes are contingent on the specific ethnic minority group to whom services are to be delivered, and may require new assessment procedures to (for example) address fears of loss of lien and reticence to disclose symptoms. Each of these recommended strategies is, in a sense, simple insofar as it is readily accommodated by standard, biomedical practice. Simultaneously, however, culturally tailoring programs to minorities in the ways outlined here is not as simple as it might at first seem. This is because the biomedical view of what an illness is (a reified entity housed within an individual) and the sociocentric, holistic concept of illness (a process located everywhere but manifested in an individual) are diametrically opposed understandings. Biomedical health education and disease prevention programs, no matter how culturally tailored and sensitive, necessarily reflect and communicate their underlying, dualistic assumptions, and these are destructive to minority cultural life. As Fabrega (1974) put it:

> the spread of modern medicine should be seen, not as a process that simply erodes and takes the place of native views and practices, but rather as a pervasive undermining (with consequent disarticulation) of established modes of thinking, feeling, and behaving. In [sociocentric cultures] conceptions about disease, indeed experiences of and with disease, are isomorphic with those that articulate one's personal identity and also give meaning to social relations. What is more, all of these form the fabric of what we may term "medical care." It is not surprising, then, that the intrusion of Western medicine into such a setting brings with it more than decreased infant mortality and rates of infectious diseases; it brings with it the destruction of the previously mentioned unity in social relations, body and self. Insofar as it operates through specialized occupational and suboccupational groups (nurses, internists, psychiatrists, surgeons, etc.), medicine tends to segmentalize the person in various ways. Each of these groups has a perspective that is organized by separate premises, obligations, and explanations, all of which are in conflict with native understandings. Problems are somewhat arbitrarily divided into "mental" versus "physical," "social" versus "medical," "Natural" versus "superstitious," thereby producing disarticulations. In other words, what to [sociocentric people] is a single crisis having broad ramifications is in this new system or view a heterogeneous collection of "problems," each of which has a separate cause and locus. In this process of differentiation and specialization, Western medicine ... fragments and undermines the native cultural system. (pp. 246–247)

The difficult task faced by health psychology and related disciplines in this increasingly multicultural society then is not so much that of culturally tailoring interventions for minorities, nor even of creating cooperative systems of care that include both biomedical and indigenous healers and cures. Rather, it is to do so without disrupting the holism that undergirds minority understandings of health, and also provides the web that ties people to each other, and to their environment and their gods. Holism is not a view about health, but rather is a view of life and the universe that is merely reflected in health beliefs and practices. It is holism as a metaphor people live by that we must take care to protect.

ACKNOWLEDGMENTS

Supported by funds provided by the California Tobacco-Related Disease Research Program Grant Numbers 6RT-0081 and 8RT-0013, and by the California Department of Health Services, Tobacco Control Section Grant Number 94-20962.

REFERENCES

Adair, J., & Deuschle, K. W. (1970). *The People's health: Medicine and anthropology in a Navajo community.* New York: Appleton-Century-Crofts.

Adler, S. R. (1995). Refugee stress and folk belief: Hmong sudden deaths. *Social Science and Medicine, 40*(12), 1623–1629.

Amick, B. C., Levine, S., Tarlov, A. R., & Walsh, D. C. (1995). *Society and health.* New York: Oxford University Press.

Anderson, J. Q. (1970). *Texas folk medicine: 1,133 cures, remedies, preventatives and health practices.* Austin TX: Encino Press.

Applewhite, S. L. (1995). Curanderismo: Demystifying the health beliefs and practices of elderly Mexican Americans. *Health & Social Work, 20,* 247–253.

Armarasingham, L. R. (1980). Movement among healers in Sri Lanka. *Culture, Medicine, and Psychiatry, 4,* 553–557.

Ashworth, M. (1993). Child abuse, true or false? *The Practitioner, 237,* 108–109.

Atkinson, D. R., Morten, G., & Sue, D. W. (1993). *Counseling American Minorities* (3rd ed., pp. 199–210). Wisconsin: Brown/Brown & Benchmark.

Atteneave, C. (1974). Medicine men and psychiatrists in the Indian Health Service. *Psychiatric Annals, 4,* 49–55.

Avery, C. Z. (1991). Native American medicine: Traditional healing. *Journal of the American Medical Association, 256,* 2271–2273.

Babb, J. (1981). *Border healing woman.* Austin, TX: University of Texas Press.

Baca, J. (1969). Some health beliefs of the Spanish-speaking. *American Journal of Nursing, 69,* 2172–2176.

Baer, H. A. (1981). Prophets and advisors in Black spiritual churches: Therapy, palliative or opiate? *Culture, Medicine and Psychiatry, 5*(2), 145–170.

Baer, H. (1985). Toward a systematic typology of Black folk healers. *Phylon, 43,* 327–343.

Baer, H., & Ackerman, A. (1988). Toxic Mexican folk remedies for the treatment of empacho: The case of Azarcon, Greta, & Albayalde. *Journal of Ethnopharmacology, 24,* 31–39.

Baer, H., de Alba, G., Cueto, L. M., Ackerman, A., & Davidson. S. (1989). Lead based remedies for empacho: Patterns and consequences. *Social Science & Medicine, 29,* 1373–1379.

Baer, H., Singer, A. M., & Johnson, J. (1986). Toward a critical medical anthropology. *Social Science & Medicine, 23,* 95–98.

Bailey, E. J. (1987). Sociocultural factors and health care seeking among Black Americans. *Journal of the National Medical Association, 79,* 389–392.

Bailey, E. J. (1991). *Urban African American health care.* New York: University Press of America.

Balcazar, H., Castro, F. G., & Krull, J. L. (1995). Cancer risk reduction in Mexican-American women: The role of acculturation, education, and health risk factors. *Health Education Quarterly, 22*(1), 61–66.

Baquet, C. R., & Gibbs, T. (1992). Cancer and Black Americans. In R. L. Braithwaite & S. E. Taylor (Eds.), *Health issues in the Black community* (pp. 106–120). San Francisco, CA: Jossey- Bass.

Baquet, C. R., Horm, J. W., Gibbs, T., & Greenwald, P. (1991). Socioeconomic factors and cancer incidence among Blacks and Whites. *Journal of the National Cancer Institute, 83,* 551–557.

Barney, G. L. (1980). *The Hmong of Northern Laos.* Arlington, VA: National Indochinese Clearinghouse (Indochinese Refugee Education Series, No. 16).

Barrett, L. E. (1974). *Soul-force: African heritage in Afro- American religion.* Garden City, NY: Anchor.

Bell, D. (1992). *Faces at the bottom of the well: The permanence of racism.* New York: Basic Books.

Bergman, R. (1971). The importance of psychic medicine: Training Navajo medicine men. *National Institute of Mental Health Program Reports, 5,* 20–43.

Bergman, R. (1973a). Navajo medicine and psychoanalysis. *Human Behavior, 2,* 8–15.

Bergman, R. (1973b). A school of medicine men. *American Journal of Psychiatry, 130,* 663–666.

Blendon, R., Aiken, L., Freeman, H., & Corey, C. (1989). Access to medical care for Black and White Americans. *Journal of the American Medical Association, 261,* 278–281.

Block, G., & Subar, A. F. (1992). Estimates of nutrient intake from a food frequency questionnaire: The 1987 National Health Interview Survey. *Journal of the American Dietetic Association, 92*(8), 969–977.

Bolton, R. (1981). Susto, hostility, and hypoglycemia. *Ethnology, 19,* 261–276.

Boss, L. P., Lanier, A. P., Dohan, P. H., & Bender, T. R. (1982). Cancer of the gall bladder and biliary tract in Alaska Natives. *Journal of the National Cancer Institute, 69,* 1005–1007.

Boyd, E., Shimp, L., & Hackney, M. (1984). *Home remedies and the Black elderly: A reference manual for health care providers.* Ann Arbor, MI: University of Michigan.

Brajer, V., & Hall, J. V. (1992). Recent evidence on the distribution of air pollution effects. *Contemporary Policy Issues, 10,* 63–71.

Brandon, G. (1991). Sacrificial practices in Santeria, an African-Cuban religion in the United States. In J. E. Holloway (Ed.), *Africanisms in American culture* (pp. 119–147). Bloomington: Indiana University Press.

Brandt, A. (1988). AIDS: From social history to social policy. In, E. Fee & D. Fox (Eds.), *AIDS: The burdens of history* (pp. 147–171). Berkeley, CA: University of California Press.

Bryan, W. (1985). *Montana's Indians.* Helena, MT: Montana Magazine.

Bubker, J. P., Comby, D. S., & Kehrer, B. H. (1989). *Pathways to health: The role of social factors.* Menlo Park, CA: Kaiser.

Buchwald, D., Panwala, S., & Hooton, T. M. (1992). Use of traditional health practices by Southeast Asians refugees in a primary care clinic. *Western Journal of Medicine, 156,* 507–511.

Buehler, J. (1992). Traditional Crow Indian health beliefs. *Journal of Holistic Nursing, 10,* 18–33.

Burke, G. L., Savage, P. J., Manolio, T. A., Sprafka, J. M., Wagenknecht, L. E., Sidney, S., Perkins, L. L., Liu, K., & Jacobs, D. R., Jr. (1992). Correlates of obesity in young Black and White women: The CARDIA study. *American Journal of Public Health, 82,* 1621–1625.

Camino, L. A. (1989). Nerves, worriation, and Black women. *Health Care for Women International, 10,* 295–314.

Campbell, G. R. (1989). The changing dimension of Native American health. *American Indian Culture and Research Journal, 13,* 1–20.

Castro, F. G., Furth, P., & Karlow, H. (1984). The health beliefs of Mexican, Mexican-American, and Anglo American women. *Hispanic Journal of the Behavioral Sciences, 6,* 365–383.

Catanzaro, A., & Moser, R. J. (1982). Health status of refugees from Vietnam, Laos, and Cambodia. *Journal of the American Medical Association, 247,* 1303–1308.

Centers for Disease Control (1981). Use of lead tetroxide as a folk remedy for gastrointestinal illness. *MMWR, 32,* 546–547.

Centers for Disease Control. (1983a). Folk remedy-associated lead poisoning in Hmong children—Minnesota. *MMWR, 32,* 555–556.

Centers for Disease Control. (1983b). Lead poisoning from Mexican folk remedies. *MMWR, 32,* 554–555.

Centers for Disease Control. (1988). Cigarette smoking among adults—United States. *MMWR, 40,* 757–759, 765.

Chan, C. W., & Chang, J. K. (1976). The role of Chinese medicine in New York City's Chinatown. *American Journal of Chinese Medicine, 4,* 31–45, 129–146.

Chang, B. (1974). Some dietary beliefs in Chinese folk culture. *American Dietetic Association Journal, 65,* 436–38.

Charatz-Litt, C. (1992). A chronicle of racism: The effects of the White medical community on Black health. *Journal of the National Medical Association, 84*(8), 717–725.

Cheon-Klessig, Y., Camilleri, D., McElmurry, B., & Ohlson, V. (1988). Folk medicine in the health practice of Hmong refugees. *Western Journal of Nursing Research, 10,* 647–660.

Choe, Y. T., & Lee, S. H. (1975). *Acupuncture and moxibustion points.* Seoul: Ko Moon Sa.

Clark, M. (1970). *Health in the Mexican-American culture.* Berkeley, CA: University of California Press.

Colson, A. B., & de Armellada, C. (1983). An amerindian derivation for Latin American creole illnesses and their treatment. *Social Science & Medicine, 17,* 1229–1248.

Commission for Racial Justice. (1987). *Toxic wastes and race in the United States: A national report on the racial and socioeconomic characteristics of communities with hazardous waste sites.* New York: United Church of Christ.

Cooke, M. A. (1984). *The health of Blacks during reconstruction, 1862–1870.* Ann Arbor, MI: University Microfilms.

Cose, E. (1993). *The rage of the privileged class.* New York: Harper-Collins.

Cosminsky, S. (1975). Changing food and medical beliefs and practices in a Guatemalan community. *Ecology of Food & Nutrition, 4,* 183–191.

Cosminsky, S. (1977). Alimento and fresco: Nutritional concepts and their implications for health care. *Human Organization, 36,* 203–207.

Coulehan, J. L. (1992). Epidemiology of cardiovascular disease in American Indians. In E. W. Haller & L. P. Aitken (Eds.), *Mashkiki, old medicine nourishing the new: American Indians and Alaska Natives in biomedical research careers* (pp. 29–50). New York: University Press of America.

Currier, R. L. (1966). The hot–cold syndrome and symbolic balance in Mexican and Spanish-American folk medicine. *Ethnology, 5,* 251–263.

Davis, D. L., & Whittin, R. (1988). Medical and popular traditions of nerves. *Social Science and Medicine, 18,* 1209–1221.

De la Cancela, V., & Martinez, I. Z. (1983). An analysis of culturalism in Latino mental health: Folk medicine as a case in point. *Hispanic Journal of the Behavioral Sciences, 5,* 251–274.

Deloria, V., Jr. (1983). Indians today: The real and the unreal. In D. R. Atkinson, G. Morten, & D. W. Sue (Eds.), *Counseling American minorities* (2nd ed., pp. 47–76). Dubuque, IA: William C. Brown.

Deuschle, K. W. (1986). Cross-cultural medicine: The Navajo Indians as an exemplar. *Daedalus, 115,* 175–184.

Dinges, N. G., Trimble, J. E., Manson, S. M., & Pasquale, F. L. (1986). Counseling and psychotherapy with American Indians and Alaska Natives. In A. J. Marsella & P. B. Pedersen (Eds.), *Cross- cultural counseling and psychotherapy* (pp. 243–277). New York: Pergamon.

Dovidio, J. F., & Gaertner, S. (1986). *Prejudice, discrimination, and racism.* Orlando, FL: Academic Press.

Epstein, J. A., Dusenbury, L., Botvin, G. J., & Diaz, T. (1994). Acculturation, belief about AIDS and AIDS education among New York City Hispanic parents. *Hispanic Journal of Behavioral Science, 16*(3), 342–354.

Erickson, R. V., & Hoang, G. N. (1980). Health problems among Indochinese refugees. *American Journal of Public Health, 70,* 1003–1006.

Espino, D. V. (1990). Hypertension and acculturation in elderly Mexican Americans: Results from the 1982–1984 Hispanic HANES. *Journal of Gerontology, 45*(6), 309.

Fabrega, H. (1974). *Disease and social behavior.* Cambridge, MA: MIT Press.

Farge, E. J. (1977). A review of findings from three generations of Chicano health care behavior. *Social Science Quarterly, 58,* 407–411.

Farmer, P. (1990). Sending sickness: Sorcery, politics, and changing concepts of AIDS in rural Haiti. *Medical Anthropology Quarterly, 4,* 6–27.

Fiore, M. C., Novotny, T. E., Pierce, J. P., Hatziandreau, E. J., Patel, K. M., & Davis, R. M. (1989). Trends in cigarette smoking in the United States—the changing influence of gender and race. *Journal of the American Medical Association, 261,* 49–55.

Flaskerud, J. H., & Calvillo, E. R. (1991). Beliefs about AIDS, health and illness among low-income Latina women. *Research in Nursing & Health, 14,* 431–438.

Flaskerud, J. H., & Rush, C. (1989). AIDS and traditional health beliefs and practices of Black women. *Nursing Research, 38,* 210–215.

Fleischman, P. (1976–1977). Ayurveda. *International Journal of Social Psychiatry, 22*(4), 282–287.

Fleming, C. M. (1983). The emergence of culture-based mental health services for Native Americans. *Listening Post, 4,* 17–19.

Frey, R. (1987). *The world of the Crow Indians.* Norman, OK: University of Oklahoma Press.

Frisbie, C. J. (1987). *Navajo medicine bundles or jish.* Albuquerque: University of New Mexico Press.

Furukawa, T. (1994). Weight changes and eating attitudes of Japanese adolescents under acculturative stresses. *International Journal of Eating Disorders, 15*(1), 71–74.

Gardner, C., Winkleby, M. A., & Viteri, F. E. (1995). Dietary intake patterns and acculturation levels of Hispanic immigrant men: A pilot study. *Hispanic Journal of Behavioral Sciences, 17*(3), 347–350.

Gerber, A. M., James, S. A., Ammerman, A. S., Keenan, N. L., Garrett, J. M., Strogatz, D. S., & Haines, P. S. (1991). Socioeconomic status and electrolyte intake in Black adults: The Pitt County Study. *American Journal of Public Health, 81*(12), 1608–1612.

Ghandi, M. K. (1965). *Nature cure.* Bombay: Pearl.

Gillum, R. F. (1988). Ischemic heart disease mortality in American Indians. *American Heart Journal, 115,* 1141–1144.

Gillum, R. F., Gillum, B. S., & Smith, N. (1984). Cardiovascular risk factors among urban American Indians. *American Heart Journal, 107,* 756–776.

Gilman, S. C., Justice, J., Saepharn, K., & Charles, G. (1992). Use of traditional and modern health services by Laotian refugees. *Western Journal of Medicine, 157,* 310–315.

Ginorio, A. B., Gutierrez, L., Cauce, A. M., & Acosta, M. (1995). Psychological issues for Latinas. In H. Landrine (Ed.)., *Bringing cultural diversity to feminist psychology* (pp. 241–263). Washington, DC: APA.

Goodson, M. (1987). Medical-botanical contributions of African slave women to American medicine. *Western Journal of Black Studies, 2,* 198–203.

Gottlieb, L. S., & Husen, L. A. (1982). Lung cancer among Navajo uranium miners. *Chest, 81,* 449–452.

Gould-Martin, K. (1978). Hot, cold, clean, poison and dirt: Chinese folk medical categories. *Social Science and Medicine, 12,* 39–46.

Gould-Martin, K., & Ngin, C. (1981). Chinese Americans. In A. Harwood (Ed.), *Ethnicity and medical care* (pp. 130–210). Cambridge, MA: Harvard University Press.

Greenwood, B. (1981). Cold or spirits? Choice and ambiguity in Morocco's pluralistic medical system. *Social Science & Medicine, 15,* 219–222.

Greig, L. M., Walker, P. S., & Walker, R. D. (1992). American Indian alcohol use and abuse: Patterns and epidemiology. In E. W. Haller & L. P. Aitken (Eds.), *Mashkiki, old medicine nourishing the new: American Indians and Alaska Natives in Biomedical Research Careers* (pp. 55–60). New York: University Press of America.

Haile, B. (1943). Soul concepts of the Navajo. *Annali Lateranensi, 7,* 59–94.

Haines, J. D., Jr. (1991). Sassafras tea and diaphoresis. *Postgraduate Medicine, 4,* 75–76.

Hall, A. L., & Bourne, P. G. (1973). Indigenous therapists in a Black urban community. *Archives of General Psychiatry, 28,* 137–142.
Haller, E. W., & Aitken, L. P. (1992). *Mashkiki, old medicine nourishing the new: American Indians and Alaska Natives in Biomedical Research Careers.* New York: University Press of America.
Hampton, J. W. (1992). Cancer death rate rises among Native Americans with assimilation and as more live longer. In E. W. Haller & L. P. Aitken (Eds.), *Mashkiki, old medicine nourishing the new: American Indians and Alaska Natives in biomedical research careers* (pp. 119–123). New York: University Press of America.
Hand, W. (1980). *Magical medicine: The folkloric component of medicine in the folk belief, custom and ritual of the peoples of Europe and America.* Berekely: University of California Press.
Hare, M. L. (1993). The emergence of an urban, U.S. Chinese medicine. *Medical Anthropology Quaterly, 7*(1), 30–49.
Harrison, F. (1994). Racial and gender inequalities in health and health care. *Medical Anthropology Quarterly, 8,* 90–95.
Harwood, A. (1971). The hot–cold theory of disease: Implications for treatment of Puerto Rican patients. *Journal of the American Medical Association, 216,* 1153–1158.
Harwood, A. (1977). *Rx: Spiritist as needed.* New York: Wiley.
Harwood, A. (1981). *Ethnicity and medical care.* Cambridge, MA: Harvard University Press.
Helms, J. (1990). *Black and White racial identity.* New York: Greenwood.
Higgenbotham, J. C., Trevino, F. M., & Ray, L. A. (1990). Utilization of curanderos by Mexican Americans: Prevalence and predictors, findings from HHANES 1982–1984. *American Journal of Public Health, 80*(Suppl.), 32–35.
Hildreth, C. J., & Saunders, E. (1992). Heart disease, stroke, and hypertension in Blacks. In R. L. Braithwaite & S. E. Taylor (Eds.), *Health issues in the Black community* (pp. 90–105). San Francisco, CA: Jossey-Bass.
Hill, C. E. (1973). Black healing practices in the rural south. *Journal of Popular Culture, 6,* 829–853.
Hill, C. E. (1988). *Community and health systems in the rural American south.* Boulder, CO: Westview.
Hill, C. E., & Matthews, H. (1981). Traditional health beliefs and practices among southern rural Blacks. In M. Black & J. S. Reed (Eds.), *Perspectives on the American South* (pp. 307–332). New York: Gordon and Breach Science Publishers.
Hippolyte, R. K. (1993). *Cultural beliefs affecting AIDS education in the Haitian community.* Office of Services to Special Populations, New York City Department of Mental Health, May 7, 1993, pp. 1–31.
Hoang, G. N., & Erickson, R. V. (1982). Guidelines for providing medical care for southeast Asian refugees. *Journal of the American Medical Association, 248,* 710–714.
Hoang, G. N., & Erickson, R. V. (1985). Cultural barriers to effective medical care among Indochinese patients. *Annual Review of Medicine, 36,* 229–239.
Hoff, L. A. (1994). Comments on race, gender, and class bias in nursing. *Medical Anthropology Quarterly, 8,* 96–99.
Holloway, J. E. (1991). *Africanisms in American culture.* Bloomington: Indiana University Press.
Holtan, N., Carlson, D., Egbert, J., Mielke, R., & Thao, T. C. (1984). *Final report of the SUNDS planning project.* St. Paul, MI: St. Paul-Ramsey Medical Center.
Horton, R. (1967). African traditional thought and Western science. *Africa, 37,* 50–55.
Hoxie, F. E. (1989). *The Crow.* New York: Chelsea House.
Hunt, L. M., Browner, C. H., & Jordan, B. (1990). Hypoglycemia: Portrait of an illness construct in everyday use. *Medical Anthropology Quarterly, 8,* 191–210.
Idson, T. L., & Price, H. F. (1992). Analysis of wage differentials by gender and ethnicity in the public sector. *Review of Black Political Economy, 20,* 75–97.
Ingham, J. M. (1970). On Mexican folk medicine. *American Anthropologist, 72,* 76–87.
Jackson, J. J. (1981). Urban Black Americans. In A. Harwood (Ed.), *Ethnicity and medical care* (pp. 37–129). Cambridge, MA: Harvard University Press.
Jacques, G. (1976). Cultural health traditions: A Black perspective. In M. Branch & P. Paxton (Eds.), *Providing safe nursing care for ethnic people of color.* New York: Appleton- Century Crofts.
Jilek, W. (1971). From crazy witchdoctor to auxiliary psychotherapist: The changing image of the medicine man. *Psychiatria Clinica, 4,* 200–220.
Jilek, W. (1974a). Indian healing power: Indigenous therapeutic practices in the Pacific Northwest. *Psychiatric Annals, 9,* 351–358.
Jilek, W. (1974b). Witchdoctors succeed where doctors fail. *Canadian Psychiatric Association Journal, 9,* 341–349.
Johnson, J. V., & Johannson, G. (1991). *The psychosocial work environment and health.* Amityville, New York: Baywood.
Johnson, S. M., & Snow, L. F. (1982). Assessment of reproductive knowledge in an inner-city clinic. *Social Science and Medicine, 16,* 1657–1662.
Jones, J. H. (1981). *Bad blood: The Tuskegee Syphilis Experiment, a tragedy of race and medicine.* New York: The Free Press.
Jones, J. H. (1993). *Bad blood: The Tuskegee Syphilis Experiment, New and expanded edition.* New York: The Free Press.
Jordan, S. W., & Key, C. R. (1981). Carcinoma of the cervix in southwestern American Indians. *Cancer, 47,* 2523–2532.
Jordan, W. (1975). Voodoo medicine. In R. Williams (Ed.), *Textbook of Black-related diseases* (pp. 716–738). New York: McGraw-Hill.
Jordan, W. (1979). The roots and practice of voodoo medicine. *Urban Health, 8,* 38–41.
Jules-Roseta, B. (1980). Creative spirituality from Africa to America: Cross-cultural influences in contemporary religious forms. *Western Journal of Black Studies, 4,* 273–285.
Kalichman, S. C., Kelly, J., Hunter, T. L., Murphy, D. A., & Tyler, R. (1993). Culturally-tailored HIV-AIDS risk-reduction messages targeted to African-American urban women. *Journal of Consulting and Clinical Psychology, 91,* 291–295.
Kalichman, S. C., Hunter, S., & Kelly, J. A. (1992). Perceptions of AIDS susceptibility among minority and non-minority women at risk for HIV infection. *Journal of Consulting and Clinical Psychology, 60,* 725–632.
Kant, A. K., Block, G., Schatzkin, A., Ziegler, R. G., & Nestle, M. (1991). Dietary diversity in the US population, NHANES II, 1976–1980. *Journal of the American Dietetic Association, 91*(12), 1526–1531.
Kapferer, B. (1983). *A celebration of demons: Exorcism and the aesthetics of healing in Sri Lanka.* Bloomington: University of Indiana Press.
Kaptchuk, T. J. (1983). *The web that has no weaver: Understanding Chinese medicine.* New York: Congdon & Weed.
Karasek, R., & Theorell, T. (1990). *Healthy work: Stress, productivity and the reconstruction of working life.* New York: Basic Books.
Kay, M., & Yoder, M. (1987). Hot and cold in women's ethnotherapeutics: The American-Mexican west. *Social Science and Medicine, 25*(4), 347–355.
Kemp, C. (1996). Islamic cultures: Health-care beliefs and practices. *American Journal of Health Behavior, 20*(3), 83–89.

Kendall, L. (1987). Cold wombs in balmy Honolulu: Ethnogynecology among Korean immigrants. *Social Science and Medicine, 25,* 367–376.

Khare, R., & Ishvara, K. (1986). *Modes of food classification in South Asia.* South Carolina: Carolina Academic Press.

Kiev, A. (1968). *Curanderismo.* New York: The Free Press.

Kim, P. C., & Pak, I. K. (1983). *Handbook of Oriental medicine.* Seoul: Tonga Toso.

Kim, Y. K., & Sich, D. (1977). A study on traditional healing techniques and illness behavior in a rural Korean township. *Anthropological Study, Seoul, 3,* 75–108.

King, G., & Williams, D. R. (1995). Race and health: A multidimensional approach to African American health. In B. C. Amick, S. Levine, A. R. Tarlov, & D. C. Walsh (Eds.), *Society and health* (pp. 93–130). New York: Oxford University Press.

Klein, J. (1978). Susto: The anthropological study of diseases of adaptation. *Social Science and Medicine, 12,* 23–28.

Klesges, R. C., Somes, G., Pacale, R. W., Klesges, L. M., Murphy, M., Brown, K., & Williams, E. (1988). Knowledge and beliefs regarding the consequences of cigarette smoking and their relationships to smoking status in a biracial sample. *Health Psychology, 7,* 387–401.

Klonoff, E. A., & Biglan, A. (1987). "Hypoglycemic" anxiety: The role of reinforcement in psychophysiological disorders. *Behavior Modification, 11,* 102–113.

Klonoff, E. A., & Landrine, H. (1996). Acculturation and cigarette smoking among African-American adults. *Journal of Behavioral Medicine, 19*(5), 501–514.

Klonoff, E. A., & Landrine, H. (1997a). Distrust of Whites, acculturation, and AIDS knowledge among African-Americans. *Journal of Black Psychology, 23,* 50–57.

Klonoff, E. A., & Landrine, H. (1997b). *Preventing misdiagnosis of women: A guide to physical disorders with psychiatric symptoms.* Thousand Oaks, CA: Sage.

Klonoff, E. A., & Landrine, H. (1999a). Acculturation and cigarette smoking among African-Americans: Replication and implications for prevention and cessation programs. *Journal of Behavioral Medicine, 22*(2), 195–204.

Klonoff, E. A., & Landrine, H. (1999b). Do Blacks believe that HIV/AIDS is a government conspiracy against them? *Preventive Medicine, 28,* 451–457.

Klonoff, E. A., & Landrine, H. (in press). Acculturation and alcohol use among Blacks. *Western Journal of Black Studies.*

Klonoff, E. A., Landrine, H., & Scott, J. (1995). Double jeopardy: Ethnicity, gender and health. In H. Landrine (Ed.), *Bringing cultural diversity to feminist psychology* (pp. 335–360). Washington, DC: American Psychological Association.

Krieger, N. (1990). Racial and gender discrimination: Risk factors for high blood pressure? *Social Science and Medicine, 30,* 1273–1281.

Kumanyika, S. (1987). Obesity in Black women. *Epidemiology Review, 9,* 31–50.

Kumanyika, S. K. (1994). Obesity in minority populations: An epidemiologic assessment. *Obesity Research, 2*(2), 166–182.

Kunitz, S. J. (1981). Health care on the Navajo reservation. *Social Science and Medicine, 15A,* 183–191.

Kunitz, S. J., & Levy, J. E. (1981). Navajos. In A. Harwood (Ed.), *Ethnicity and medical care* (pp. 337–396). Cambridge, MA: Harvard University Press.

Laderman, C. (1987). Destructive heat and cooling prayer: Malay humoralism in pregnancy, childbirth, and the postpartum period. *Social Science and Medicine, 25,* 357–365.

LaFromboise, T. D. (1993). American Indian mental health policy. In D. R. Atkinson, G. Morten, & D. W. Sue (Eds.), *Counseling American minorities: A cross-cultural perspective* (4th ed., pp. 123–144). Madison, WI: Brown & Benchmark.

LaFromboise, T., Choney, S. B., James, A., & Running Wolf, P. R. (1995). American Indian women and psychology. In H. Landrine (Ed.), *Bringing cultural diversity to feminist psychology.* Washington, DC: American Psychological Association.

Laguerre, M. (1981). Haitian Americans. In A. Harwood (Ed.), *Ethnicity and medical care* (pp. 172–210). Cambridge, MA: Harvard University Press.

Laguerre, M. (1987). *Afro-Caribbean folk medicine.* South Hadley, MA: Bergin & Garvey.

Landrine, H. (1992). Clinical implications of cultural differences: The Referential v. Indexical Self. *Clinical Psychology Review, 12,* 401–415.

Landrine, H. (1995). *Bringing cultural diversity to feminist psychology.* Washington, DC: APA.

Landrine, H., & Klonoff, E. A. (1992). Culture and health-related schema. *Health Psychology, 11*(4), 267–276.

Landrine, H., & Klonoff, E. A. (1994a). The African American Acculturation Scale. *Journal of Black Psychology, 20,* 104–127.

Landrine, H., & Klonoff, E. A. (1994b). Cultural diversity in causal attributions for illness: The role of the supernatural. *Journal of Behavioral Medicine, 17,* 181–193.

Landrine, H., & Klonoff, E. A. (1996a). *African American acculturation: Deconstructing race and reviving culture.* Thousand Oaks, CA: Sage.

Landrine, H., & Klonoff, E. A. (1996b). The Schedule of Racist Events: A measure of racial discrimination and a study of its negative physical and mental health consequences. *Journal of Black Psychology, 22,* 144–168.

Landrine, H., Klonoff, E. A., Alcaraz, R., Scott, J., & Wilkins, P. (1995). Multiple variables in discrimination. In B. Lott & D. Maluso (Eds.), *The social psychology of interpersonal discrimination* (pp. 183–224). New York: Guilford.

Landrine, H., Klonoff, E. A., & Brown-Collins, A. (1992). Cultural diversity and methodology in feminist psychology. *Psychology of Women Quarterly, 16,* 145–163.

Landrine, H., Richardson, J. R., Klonoff, E. A., & Flay, B. (1994). Cultural diversity in the predictors of adolescent cigarette smoking. *Journal of Behavioral Medicine, 17,* 1–15.

Lanier, A. P., & Knutson, L. R. (1986). Cancer in Alaska Natives: A 15 year summary. *Alaska Medicine, 28,* 37–41.

Lee, S. (1966). *Korean folk medicine.* Seoul: Seoul National University Monograph Series 3, Seoul National University Publishing Center.

Lefley, H. P. (1979a). Female cases of falling out. *Social Science and Medicine, 13B,* 115–116.

Lefley, H. P. (1979b). Prevalence of potential falling-out cases among the Black, Latin, and non-Latin White populations of the city of Miami. *Social Science and Medicine, 13B,* 113–114.

Leslie, C. (1969). Modern India's ancient medicine. *Transaction,* June, 46–55.

Leslie, C. (1976). *Asian medical systems.* Berkeley: University of California Press.

Lewis, P., & Lewis, E. (1984). *People's of the golden triangle.* New York: Thames & Hudson.

Lewis, C. E., Raczynski, J. M., Heath, G. W., Levinson, R., & Cutter, G. R. (1993). Physical activity of public housing residents in Birmingham, Alabama. *American Journal of Public Health, 83*(7), 1016–1020.

Logan, M., & Morrill, W. (1979). Humoral medicine and informant variability: An analysis of acculturation and cognitive change among Guatemalan villagers. *Anthropos, 74,* 785–802.

Logue, P. (1983). Living among the Hmong in a refugee camp: Shamans, herbalists, and modern medicine. *World Vision, 6,* 6–9.

Ludman, E. K., & Newman, J. M. (1984). Yin and yang in the health-related food practices of three Chinese groups. *Journal of Nutrition Education, 16,* 4–7.

Maciocia, G. (1989). *The foundations of Chinese medicine: A comprehensive text for acupuncturists and herbalists.* New York: Churchill Livingstone.

MacPherson, K. I. (1981). Menopause as disease. *Advances in Nursing Science, 3,* 95–113.

Maduro, R. (1983). Curanderismo and Latino views of disease and curing. *Western Journal of Medicine, 139,* 868–874.

Manson, S. M. (1982). *New directions in prevention among American Indian and Alaska Native communities.* Portland, OR: Oregon Health Sciences University.

Manson, S. M., & Dinges, N. G. (1988). *Behavioral health issues among American Indians and Alaska Natives: Explorations on the frontiers of biobehavioral science.* Denver: University of Colorado Health Sciences Center.

Marin, G., Marin, B. V., Otero-Sabogal, R., Sabogal, F., & Perez-Stable, E. J., (1989a). The role of acculturation in the attitudes, norms, and expectancies of Hispanic smokers. *Journal of Cross-Cultural Psychology, 20*(4), 399–415.

Marin, G., Perez-Stable, E. J., & Marin, B. V. (1989b). Cigarette smoking among San Francisco Hispanics. *American Journal of Public Health, 79,* 196–198.

Marmot, M., & Theorell, T. (1988). Social class and cardiovascular disease: The contribution of work. *International Journal of Health Services, 18,* 659–674.

Marmot, M., Kogevinas, M., & Elston, M. (1987). Social-economic status and disease. *Annual Review of Public Health, 8,* 11–135.

Marsella, A. J., DeVos, G., & Hsu, F.L.K. (1985). *Culture and self: Asian and Western perspectives.* New York: Tavistock.

Martin, H. W., Martinez, C., Leon, R., Richardson, C., & Acosta, V. R. (1985). Folk illnesses reported to physicians in the Lower Rio Grande Valley. *Ethnology, 24,* 229–236.

Martin, R., Cummings, S., & Coates, T. (1990). Ethnicity and smoking: Differences in White, Black, and Asian medical patients who smoke. *American Journal of Preventive Medicine, 6,* 194–199.

Matthews, H. (1987). Rootwork. *Southern Medical Journal, 80,* 885–891.

May, P. A. (1982b). Susceptibility to substance abuse among American Indians. *Research Monograph No. 41.* Rockville, MD: National Institute on Drug Abuse.

May, P. A. (1992a). Fetal alcohol syndrome and American Indians. In E. W. Haller & L. P. Aitken (Eds.), *Mashkiki, old medicine nourishing the new: American Indians and Alaska Natives in biomedical research careers* (pp. 61–68). New York: University Press of America.

Mayers, R. S. (1992). Use of folk medicine by elderly Mexican American women. In B. L. Kail (Ed.), *Special problems in noncompliance among elderly women of color* (pp.121–133). Lewiston, New York: Edwin Mellen.

Mays, V. M., & Cochran, S. (1988). Issues in the perception of AIDS risk and risk reduction activities by Black and Hispanic/Latina women. *American Psychologist, 43,* 949–957.

Mbiti, J. S. (1975). *African religions and philosophies.* Garden City, New York: Anchor.

McClenon, J. (1993). The experiential foundations of shamanic healing. *Journal of Medical Philosophy, 18,* 107–127.

McCrea, F. (1983). The politics of menopause. *Social Problems, 31,* 111–123.

McNeley, J. (1973). *The Navajo Wind theory of life and behavior.* Unpublished doctoral dissertation, University of Hawaii.

Meador, C. K. (1992). Hex death: Voodoo magic or persuasion? *Southern Medical Journal, 85,* 244–247.

Medicine, B. (1981). Native American resistance to integration: Contemporary confrontations and religious revitalization. *Plains Anthropologist, 94,* 277–286.

Messer, E. (1987). The hot and cold in Mesoamerican indigenous and Hispanized thought. *Social Science and Medicine, 25*(4), 339–346.

Mitchell, F. (1978). *Hoodoo medicine: Sea Islands herbal remedies.* Berkeley, CA: Reed & Cannon.

Morias, H. M. (1967). *The history of the Negro in medicine.* New York: Publishers Co.

Morris, D. L., Buechley, R. W., Key, C. R., & Morgan, M. V. (1978). Gall bladder disease and gall bladder cancer among American Indians in tri-cultural New Mexico. *Cancer, 42,* 2472–2477.

Muecke, M. A. (1983a). Caring for southeast Asian refugee patients in the U.S.A. *American Journal of Public Health, 73,* 431–438.

Muecke, M. A. (1983b). In search of healers: Southeast Asian refugees in the American health care system. *Cross Cultural Medicine, 139,* 835–840.

Mulira, J. G. (1991). The case of voodoo in New Orleans. In J. E. Holloway (Ed.), *Africanisms in American culture* (pp. 34–68). Bloomington: Indiana University Press.

Namboze, J. M. (1983). Health and culture in African society. *Social Science and Medicine, 17,* 2041–2043.

Nall, F. C., & Speilberg, J. (1967). Sociocultural factors in the response of Mexican Americans to medical treatment. *Journal of Health & Social Behavior, 8,* 299–308.

Nations, M. K., Camino, L. A., & Walker, F. B. (1988). "Nerves": A folk idiom for anxiety and depression? *Social Science and Medicine, 26,* 1245–1259.

Nelson, R. G., Newman, J. M., Knowler, W. C., Sievers, M. L., Kunzelman, C. L., Petitt, D. J., Moffet, C. D., Teutsch, S. M., & Bennett, P. H. (1988). Incidence of end-stage renal disease in Type 2 diabetes mellitus in Pima Indians. *Diabetologia, 28,* 264–268.

Neser, W. B., Thomas, J., Semenya, K., Thomas, D. J., & Gillum, R. F. (1986). Obesity and hypertension in a longitudinal study of Black physicians: The Meharry Cohort Study. *Journal of Chronic Disease, 39,* 105–113.

Nichter, M. (1980). The layperson's perception of medicine as perspective into the utilization of multiple therapy systems in the Indian context. *Social Science and Medicine, 14B,* 225–230.

Nichter, M. (1987). Cultural dimensions of hot, cold and sema in Sinhalese health culture. *Social Science and Medicine, 25* (4), 377–387.

Norbeck, E., & Lock, M. (1987). *Health, illness and medical care in Japan.* Honolulu: University of Hawaii Press.

Novotny, T. E., Warner, K. E., Kendrick, J. S., & Remington, P. L. (1988). Smoking by Blacks and Whites: Socioeconomic and demographic differences. *American Journal Public Health, 78,* 1187–1189.

Orleans, C. T., Schoenbach, V. J., Salmon, M. A., Strecher, V. J., Kalsbeek, W., Quade, D., Brooks, E. F., Konrad, T. R., Blackmon, C., & Watts, C. D. (1989). A survey of smoking and quitting patterns among Black Americans. *American Journal of Public Health, 79,* 176–181.

Pachter, L. M., Susan, D. O., & Weller, C. (1993). Acculturation and compliance with medical therapy. *Journal of Developmental and Behavioral Pediatrics, 14*(3), 163–168.

Palinkas, L. A., & Pickwell, S. M. (1995). Acculturation as a risk factor for chronic disease among Cambodian refugees in the United States. *Social Science and Medicine, 40*(12), 1643.

Pang, K.Y.C. (1994). Understanding depression among elderly Korean immigrants through their folk illnesses. *Medical Anthropology Quarterly, 8,* 209–216.

Parish, R. G. (1988). Death in the night: Mysterious syndrome in Asian refugees. In E. Berstein & L. Tomchuck (Ed.), *1989 medical health annual* (pp. 286–290). Chicago: Encyclopedia Britannica.

Pasquale, E. A. (1984). The evil eye. *Home Healthcare Nurse,* May–June, 32–35.

Patcher, L. M., Bernstein, B., & Osorio, A. (1992). Clinical implications of a folk illness: Empacho in mainland Puerto Ricans. *Medical Anthropology, 13,* 285–299.

Paulino, A. (1995). Spiritism, Santeria, Brujeria and voodooism: A comparative view of indigenous healing systems. *Journal of Teaching in Social Work, 12,* 105–124.

Payne-Jackson, A., & Lee, J. (1993). *Folk wisdom and mother wit.* Westport, CT: Greenwood.

Petitt, D. J., Baird, H. R., Aleck, K. A., Bennett, P. H., & Knowler, W. C. (1983). Excessive obesity in offspring of Pima Indian women with diabetes during pregnancy. *New England Journal of Medicine, 308,* 242–245.

Polednak, A. P. (1989). *Racial and ethnic differences in disease.* New York: Oxford University Press.

Pool, R. (1987). Hot and cold as an explanatory model: The example of Bharuch District in Gujarat, India. *Social Science & Medicine, 25,* 389–399.

Poyneer, S. V. (1983). Cultural aspects influencing health care delivery to southeast Asian refugees. *Public Health, 16,* 10–12.

Red Horse, J. G. (1992). Treatment and prevention of suicide among American Indians. In E. W. Haller & L. P. Aitken (Eds.), *Mashkiki, old medicine nourishing the new: American Indians and Alaska Natives in biomedical research careers* (pp. 67–79). New York: University Press of America.

Rivera, G. (1988). Hispanic folk medicine utilization in Colorado. *Social Science Research, 72,* 237–240.

Rivera, G. (1990). AIDS and Mexican folk medicine. *Social Science Research, 75,* 3–7.

Rivera, G., & Wanderer, J. J. (1986). Curanderismo and childhood illness. *Social Science Journal, 23,* 361–363.

Rivo, M. L., Kofie, V., Schwartz, E., Levy, M. E., & Tuckson, R. V. (1989). Comparisons of Black and White smoking-attributable mortality, morbidity, and economic costs in the District of Columbia. *Journal of the National Medical Assocation, 81,* 1125–1130.

Roh, J. Y. (1970). *Guidance of traditional medicine in Korea.* Seoul: Kyung Hee University.

Root, M.P.P. (1995). The psychology of Asian American women. In H. Landrine (Ed.), *Bringing cultural diversity to feminist psychology* (pp. 265–301). Washington, DC: American Psychological Association.

Royce, J. M., Hymowitz, N., Corbett, K., Hartwell, T. D., & Orlandi, M. A. for the COMMIT Research Group (1993). Smoking cessation factors among African Americans and Whites. *American Journal of Public Health, 83,* 220–226.

Rubel, A. (1960). Concepts of disease in Mexican-American culture. *American Anthropologist, 62,* 795–814.

Rubel, A. (1993). The study of Latino folk illness. *Medical Anthropology, 15,* 209–213.

Rubel, A., O'Nell, C. W., & Ardon, R. C. (1984). *Susto: A folk illness.* Berkeley: University of California Press.

Rubio, E., Ekins, B., Singh, P., & Dowis, J. (1987). Hmong opiate folk remedy toxicity in three infants. *Veterinary and Human Toxicology, 29*(4), 323–325.

Ruble, D. (1977). Premenstrual symptoms: A reinterpretation. *Science, 197,* 291–293.

Ruzicka, L., & Kaye, P. (1989). *Differential mortality.* New York: Oxford University Press.

Samet, J. M., Kutvrit, D. M., Waxweiler, R. J., & Key, C. R. (1984). Uranium mining and lung cancer in Navajo men. *New England Journal of Medicine, 310,* 1481–1484.

Sampson, H. A. (1989). Infantile colic and food allergy: Fact or fiction? *Journal of Pediatrics, 115,* 583–584.

Sandner, D. F. (1978). Navajo medicine. *Human Nature, 1,* 54–62.

Sandner, D. F. (1979). *Navajo symbols of healing.* New York: Harcourt, Brace, Jovanovich.

Sandoval, M. C. (1977). Santeria: Afrocuban concepts of disease and its treatment. *Journal of Operational Psychiatry, 8,* 52–63.

Sauter, S. L., Hurrell, J. J., & Cooper, C. L. (1989). *Job control and worker health.* London: Wiley.

Savage, P. J., & Bennett, P. H. (1992). Obesity and diabetes in American Indians and their inter-relationship among the Pima Indians of Arizona. In E. W. Haller & L. P. Aitken (Eds.), *Mashkiki, old medicine nourishing the new: American Indians and Alaska Natives in biomedical research careers* (pp. 95–105). New York: University Press of America.

Schnall, P. L., Landsbergis, P. A., & Baker, D. (1994). Job strain and cardiovascular disease. *Annual Review of Public Health, 15,* 381–411.

Serdula, M. K., Coates, R. J., Byers, T., Simoes, E., Mokdad, A. H., & Subar, A. F. (1995). Fruit and vegetable intake among adults in 16 states: results of a brief telephone survey. *American Journal of Public Health, 85*(2), 236–239.

Schor, J. B. (1991). *The overworked American.* New York: Basic Books.

Schreiber, J. M., & Homiak, J. P. (1981). Mexican Americans. In A. Harwood (Ed.), *Ethnicity and medical care* (pp. 264–336). Cambridge, MA: Harvard University Press.

Schultz, J. D., Spindler, A. A., & Josephson, R. V. (1994). Diet and acculturation in Chinese women. *Journal of Nutrition Education, 26*(6), 266–268.

Sexton, R. (1992). Cajun and Creole treaters: Magico-religious folk healing in French Louisiana. *Western Folklore, 51,* 237–248.

Shore, J. H., & Manson, S. M. (1981). Cross-cultural studies of depression among American Indians and Alaska Natives. *White Cloud Journal, 2,* 5–12.

Shweder, R. , & LeVine, R. A. (1984). *Culture theory.* Cambridge, England: Cambridge University Press.

Sich, D. (1981). Traditional concepts and customs on pregnancy, birth, and the postpartum period in rural Korea. *Social Science and Medicine, 15B,* 65–69.

Sievers, M. L., & Fisher, J. R. (1981). Diseases of North American Indians. In A. R. Rothschild (Ed.), *Biocultural aspects of disease* (pp.191–252). New York: Academic Press.

Silver, G. (1988). AIDS: The infamous Tuskegee study. *American Journal of Public Health, 78,* 1500–1501.

Simons, R. C., & Hughes, C. C. (1985). *The culture-bound syndromes.* Dordrecht, Holland: D. Reidel.

Simpson, G. E. (1978). *Black religions in the New World.* New York: Columbia University Press.

Smith, G.H.D. (1995). Curanderismo: Mexican folk healing. *Journal of Big Bend Studies, 7,* 217–227.

Smith, R. M., & Nelsen, L. A. (1991). Hmong folk remedies: Limited acetylation of opium by aspirin and acetaminophen. *Journal of Forensic Sciences, 36,* 280–287.

Snow, L. F. (1974). Folk medical beliefs and their implications for the care of patients. *Annals of Internal Medicine, 81,* 82–96.

Snow, L. F. (1977). Popular medicine in a Black neighborhood. In E. H. Spicer (Ed.), *Ethnic medicine in the southwest* (pp. 19–95). Tucson: University of Arizona Press.

Snow, L. F. (1978). Sorcerers, saints, and charlatans: Black folk healers in urban America. *Culture, Medicine and Psychiatry, 2,* 69–106.

Snow, L. F. (1983). Traditional health beliefs and practices among lower class Black Americans. *Western Journal of Medicine, 139,* 820–828.

Sorrell, M. S., & Smith, B. A. (1993). Navajo beliefs: Implications for health professionals. *Journal of Health Education, 24,* 336–338.

Sowell, T. (1978). Three Black histories. In T. Sowell (Ed.), *American ethnic groups* (pp. 7–64). New York: Urban Institute.

Sowell, T. (1994). *Race and culture: A world view.* New York: Basic Books.

Spector, R. E. (1979). *Cultural diversity in health and illness.* New York: Appleton Century Crofts.

Spector, R. E. (1996). *Cultural diversity in health and illness* (2nd ed.). New York: Appleton Century Crofts.

Spicer, E. H. (1977). *Ethnic medicine in the southwest.* Tucson: University of Arizona Press.

Steffensen, M. A., & Colker, L. (1982). Intercultural misunderstanding about health care: Recall of descriptions of illness and treatment. *Social Science & Medicine,16,* 1949–1954.

Strand, P. J., & Jones, W. (1983). Health service utilization by Indochinese refugees. *Medical Care, 21,* 1089–1096.

Sue, D., & Sue, D. W. (1993). Ethnic identity: Cultural factors in the psychological development of Asians in America. In D. R. Atkinson, G. Morten, & D. W. Sue (Eds.), *Counseling American minorities* (3rd ed., pp. 199–210). Wisconsin: Brown/Brown & Benchmark.

Tallant, R. (1946). *Voodoo in New Orleans.* New York: Macmillan.

Taylor, T. L. (1988). Health problems and use of services at two urban American Indian clinics. *Public Health Reports, 103,* 88–95.

Terrell, F., & Terrell, S. L. (1981). An inventory to measure cultural mistrust among Blacks. *Western Journal of Black Studies, 5,* 180–184.

Thomas, S. B., & Quinn, S. C. (1991). The Tuskegee Syphilis Study 1932 to 1972: Implications for HIV education and AIDS risk education programs in the Black community. *American Journal of Public Health, 81*(11), 1498–1504.

Thompson, V. L. (1994). Socialization to race. *Journal of Black Psychology, 20,* 175–188.

Tingling, D. C. (1967). Voodoo, root work and medicine. *Psychosomatic Medicine, 29,* 483–491.

Torres, E. (1983). *The folk healer: The Mexican American tradition of curanderismo.* Kingsville, TX: Nieves.

Tran, T. M. (1980). *Indochinese patients: Cultural aspects of the medical and psychiatric care of Indochinese refugees.* Washington, DC: Action for Southeast Asians.

Trotter, R. T. (1980). Curanderismo: An emic theoretical perspective of Mexican American folk medicine. *Medical Anthropology, 4,* 423–487.

Trotter, R. T. (1981a). Folk remedies as indicators of common illnesses. *Journal of Ethnopharmacology, 4,* 207–221.

Trotter, R. T. (1981b). Remedios caseros: Mexican American home remedies and community health problems. *Social Science & Medicine, 15B,* 107–114.

Trotter, R. T. (1982). Susto: The context of community morbidity patterns. *Ethnology, 21,* 205–216.

Trotter, R. T. (1985a). Folk medicine in the southwest: Myths and medical facts. *Postgraduate Medicine, 78,* 167–179.

Trotter, R. T. (1985b). Greta and azarcon: A survey of episodic lead poisoning from a folk remedy. *Human Organization, 44,* 64–72.

Trotter, R. T. (1991). A survey of four illnesses and their relationship to intracultural variation in a Mexican American community. *American Anthropologist, 93,* 115–125.

Trotter, R. T., & Chavira, J. A. (1981). *Curanderismo: Mexican American folk healing.* Athens: University of Georgia Press.

Trotter, R. T., Ortiz de Montellano, B., & Logan, M. H. (1989). Fallen fontanelle in the American southwest: Its origins, epidemiology, and possible organic causes. *Medical Anthropology, 10,* 211–221.

U.S. Bureau of the Census. (1983). *1980 census of the population.* Washington, DC: U.S. Bureau of the Census.

U.S. Department of Health and Human Services. (1987). *Report of the Secretary's Task Force on Black and Minority Health: Vol. I. Executive summary.* Washington, DC: U.S. Dept. Health and Human Services.

U.S. Department of Health and Human Services. (1995). *Health United States, 1994* (DHHS Publication No. PHS 95-1232). Hyattsville, MD: Public Health Service, Centers for Disease Control.

U.S. Department of Health and Human Services. (1996). *Health United States, 1995* (DHHS Publication No. PHS 96-1232). Hyattsville, MD: Public Health Service, Centers for Disease Control.

Vega, W., Sallis, J., Patterson, T., Rupp, J., Atkins, C., & Nader, P. R. (1987). Assessing knowledge of cardiovascular health-related diet and exercise behaviors in Anglo- and Mexican-Americans. *Preventive Medicine, 16,* 696–709.

Vogel, V. J. (1970). *American Indian Medicine.* Norman, OK: University of Oklahoma Press.

Warner, R. (1977). Witchcraft and soul loss: Implications for community psychiatry. *Hospital and Community Psychiatry, 28,* 686–690.

Watson, W. (1984). *Black folk healing: The therapeutic significance of faith.* New Brunswick, NJ: Transaction Books.

Weaver, J. L. (1973). Mexican American health care behavior. *Social Science Quarterly, 54,* 85– 102.

Weibel-Orlando, J. (1984). Substance abuse among American Indian youth. *Journal of Drug Issues, Spring,* 331–335.

Weidman, H. H. (1979). Falling out. *Social Science and Medicine, 13B,* 95–112.

Weiss, K. M., Ferrell, R. E., Hanis, C. L., & Styne, P. N. (1984). Genetics and epidemiology of gall bladder disease in new world native peoples. *American Journal of Human Genetic, 36,* 1259–1278.

Weller, S. C. (1983). New data on intercultural variability: The hot–cold concept of medicine and illness. *Human Organization, 42,* 249–257.

Weller, S. C., Ruebush, T. K., & Klein, R. E. (1991). An epidemiological description of a folk illness: A study of empacho in Guatemala. *Medical Anthropology, 13,* 19–31.

Wells, K. B., Golding, J. M., & Hough, R. L. (1989). Acculturation and the probability of use of health services by Mexican Americans. *Health Services Research, 24*(2), 237.

Westermeyer, J. (1974). Opium smoking in Laos. *American Journal of Psychiatry, 131*(2), 165–170.

Westermeyer, J. (1982). *Poppies, pipes, and people: Opium and its use in Laos.* Berkeley: University of California Press.

Westermeyer, J. (1988). Folk medicine in Laos: A comparison between two ethnic groups. *Social Science and Medicine, 27,* 769–778.

Westermeyer, J., Vang, T. F., & Neider, J. (1983). Refugees who do and do not seek psychiatric care: An analysis of premigratory and postmigratory characteristics. *Journal of Nervous and Mental Disease, 171,* 86–91.

White, G. M., & Marsella, A. J. (1982). Introduction. In A. J. Marsella & G. M. White (Eds.), *Cultural conceptions of mental health and therapy* (pp. 1–38). Boston, MA: D. Reidal Publishing Company.

Witherspoon, G. (1970). A new look at Navajo social organization. *American Anthropologist, 72,* 55–65.

Witherspoon, G. (1973). Sheep in Navajo culture and social organization. *American Anthropologist, 75,* 1441–1447.

Witherspoon, G. (1975). *Navajo kinship and marriage.* Chicago: University of Chicago Press.

Yeatman, G. W., & Dang, V. V. (1980). Cao Gio (coin rubbing). Vietnamese attitudes toward health care. *Journal of the American Medical Association, 244,* 2748–2749.

Yeatman, G. W., Shaw, C., Barlow., M. J., & Barlett, G. (1976). Pseudobattering in Vietnamese children. *Pediatrics, 58,* 616–618.

Young, A. (1980). The discourse on stress and the reproduction of conventional knowledge. *Social Science and Medicine, 14B,* 133–146.

Author Index

A

Aagesen, C. A., 575, *578*
Aalberg, V., 454, *455*
Aaronson, L. S., 509, *511*
Abbas, A. K., 108, *113*
Abbey, A., 290, 294, *306*, 560, 561, 562, *568*, *569*
Abbot, J., 544, 549, *554*
Abbott, R., 155, *170*
Abbott, R. A., 67, 71, *82*, 179, *193*, 395, *402*
Abbott, R. D., 669, *680*
Abbott, S. C., 720, *722*
Abboud, F. M., 704, *706*
Abe, R., 753, *754*
Abel, E. L., 290, *307*
Abel, M. M., 434, *439*
Abela, G. S., 674, 675, *681*
Abeles, M., 391, *399*
Abeles, N., 472, *476*
Abell, T., 684, *692*
Abell, T. D., 508, 509. *517*
Abelmann, W. H., 671, *682*
Abeloff, M. D., 717, *724*, 751, *754*
Abelson, R. P., 30, *41*
Aber, J. L., 442, *446*
Abercrombie, P. D., 826, *836*
Abey-Wikrama, I., 374, *379*
Abi-Mansour, P., 286, *314*
Abma, J., 559, 560, *569*
Abraham, C., 729, *745*
Abraham, C. S., 784, *795*
Abrahamse, A., 777, *797*
Abram, S. E., 128, *133*
Abrams, B., 503, *511*
Abrams, D. B., 68, *78*, 269, *277*, 302, *307*, 524, 528, *532*, *536*
Abrams, E., 804, *814*
Abramson, L. Y., 180, *189*, *190*
A'Brook, M. F., 374, *379*
Acevedo, M. C., 146, *168*
Achber, C., 576, *579*, 849, *852*
Acheson, K. J., 267, *278*
Achord, A., 803, *812*
Achord, A. P., 803, *812*
Ackerman, A., 860, 862, *888*
Ackerson, L., 451, 452, *456*
Acosta, M., 857, *889*
Acosta, V. R., 860, 861, 862, *892*
Acquas, E., 252, *258*
Acredelo, C., 34, *45*
Acri, J. B., 255, 256, 257, *258*
Adair, J., 878, 879, *887*
Adam, G., 87, 89, *93*
Adam, W., 699, *707*
Adami, H., 288, *307*
Adami, H. O., 520, *535*
Adams, A., 122, 125, *136*
Adams, C. A., 367, 370, *379*
Adams, D. O., 663, 664, *666*, *668*
Adams, J., *474*, 830, *832*
Adams, J. D., 100, *102*
Adams, J. M., 807, *812*
Adams, M. M., 496, *514*, 500, 508, *511*
Adams, S., 328, *332*, 690, *692*
Adams, S. H., 66, *78*
Adams, S. L., 301, *307*
Adams-Campbell, L. L., 432, 433, *437*
Adcock, R. A., 326, 327, *334*
Addington-Hall, J., *721*, *724*
Adedoyin, A., 809, *816*
Adelhardt, J., *721*, *723*
Adelman, M. B., 787, 789, *795*
Adelmann, P. K., 353, *360*
Adelson, M., 792, *796*
Ader, R., 105, 108, 109, 111, *113*, *114*
Adler, D., 178, *191*
Adler, D. A., 285, *309*
Adler, H. M., 703, *706*
Adler, N., 60, *78*, 158, 160, *162*, 356, *360*
Adler, N. E., 139, *172*, 463, *465*, 498, *516*, 566, *568*, *569*, 662, *666*, 821, *832*
Adler, R., 444, *447*
Adler, S. R., 863, 869, *887*
Affleck, G., 29, 37, *41*, *46*, 54, 55, *56*, *57*, 180, *193*, 204, *205*, *208*, 219, *229*, 330, *331*, 391, 395, 396, 397, 398, *399*, *403*, 561, 562, 564, *570*
Affonso, D. D., 497, *511*
Afifi, R. A., *532*, *533*, 731, 732, 733, *741*
Ager, J. W., 290, *311*, 506, 509, *514*
Ager, J., 290, *307*
Agras, S., 266, *278*, 848, *851*
Agras, W. S., 266, *278*, 705, *706*
Agustsdottir, S., 178, *192*
Ahern, D. K., 124, *134*, 153, 154, *162*, *165*, 642, *650*
Ahern, D. L., 122, 125, *136*
Ahlbom, A., 68, *81*
Ahles, T. A., 715, *721*, *725*, 758, *774*
Ahlquist, D. A., 531, *532*
Ahmed, F., 496, *511*, 523, *532*
Ahmed, S., 574, *580*
Ahmed, S. S., 286, *318*
Ahn, D. K., 576, *580*
Ahsan, C. H., 810, *812*
AIDS Community Demonstration Projects, *16*
Aiello, J., 368, *382*
Aiello, J. R., 352, *360*, 368, 369, 370, *379*, *383*
Aiken, L., 855, *888*
Aiken, L. S., 212, *229*, 729, 731, 732, 733, 734, 736, 737, 738, 739, *740*, *741*, *742*, *746*
Aikens, J. E., 330, *331*
Aikens, K. S., 330, *331*
Ainslie, G. W., 90, *93*
Ainsworth, M. D. S., 354, *360*
Aitken, L. P., 879, 880, *890*
Aitken, M. L., 571, 576, *579*
Ajani, U. A., 286, 294, *307*
Ajzen, I., 4, 5, 11, 12, *16*, 19, 39, *41*, *43*, 53, *56*, 196, *205*, 462, *465*, *466*, 566, *569*, 574, *577*, *578*, 595, *607*, 729, *741*, *742*
Akers, L., 525, *537*
Akimoto, M., 753, *754*
Akin, M., 471, *475*
Akinyinka, O. O., 810, *815*
Alagna, S. W., 734, *741*
Alarif, L., 804, *812*, *814*
Alary, M., 794, *798*, 829, *835*
Albanes, D., 631, *650*, *652*
Albarede, J. L., 216, *230*
Albert, C. M., 286, 294, *307*
Albert, M. S., 289, *311*
Albertsen, P. C., 728, *741*
Albrecht, A. E., 269, *277*, 524 *536*
Albrecht, S. A., 506, 509, *511*
Albrecht, T. L., 393, *399*
Albright, C. L., 642, *650*
Albright, N. L., 631, *652*
Alby, N., 716, *721*
Alcarez, R., 855, 870, *891*
Alciati, M., 621, *624*
Aldana, E., 758, 760, *776*
Alderfer, M. A., 32, 33, *47*, 155, *172*
Alderman, M., 663, *667*
Aldwin, C. M., 32, *46*, 153, 155, *169*, *171*, 324, *332*, 504, *511*
Aleck, K. A., 877, *893*

Alegefi, S., 373, *380*
Alexander, C., 158, *168*
Alexander, C. N., *706*, *707*
Alexander, C. S., 224, *233*, 506, *518*
Alexander, F., 92, *93*, 139, 152, 156, 157, *162*, 703, *706*
Alexander, F. G., 65, 66, *78*
Alexander, G. R., 499, *511*
Alexander, J., 290, *317*
Alexander, J. F., 149, *171*
Alexander, N. E., 735, *741*
Alexander, S. K., 804, *814*
Alfrey, H., 547, *557*
Al-Gallaf, K., 820, *832*
Algera, G., 436, *440*
Algert, S., 269, *275*
Alha, A., 290, *311*
Alkhatib, G., 806, *816*
Alkon, A., 328, *332*, 690, *692*
Allegrante, J., 525, *532*, 593, *611*
Allemon, M. C., 824, *833*
Allen, B., 715, *724*
Allen, B. P., 460, *466*
Allen, J., 614, *624*
Allen, K., 371, *381*
Allen, M., 827, *837*
Allen, S., 269, *278*, 397, *401*, 523, 524, *537*
Allen, W. R., 432, *438*
Allie, S. M., 419, 420, 424
Allikmets, R., 806, 807, *813*, *815*
Allison, K., *189*, *190*, 442, *447*
Allison, K. A., 444, *447*
Allison, K. W., 444, *446*
Allison, S. T., 196, *206*
Allolio, B., 503, *517*
Allport, F. H., 198, *205*
Allport, G. W., 60, *78*, 140, *162*, 179, *190*
Allred, K. D., 148, 149, 150, 151, 152, 155, 158, *162*, *171*, 178, 179, 184, *190*, 663, *668*
Allsopp, C. E. M., 808, *813*
Almada, S. J., 66, *78*, 153, *162*
Almario, D. A., 827, *839*
Alnaes, R., 285, *307*
Al-Namash, H., 820, *832*
Aloisi, R., 330, *331*
Alonson, P., 825, *839*
Alonzo, A. A., 28, *41*
Alpert, B. S., 431, *440*
Alpert, J. S., 153, *169*
Alpert, N., 345, *348*
Alsalili, M., 563, *569*
Altchiler, L., 640, *650*
Alter, C., 604, *607*
Alter, C. L., 718, *721*, 773, *774*
Alterman, A. I., 299, 301, *306*, *307*, *317*
Altice, F., 823, *835*
Altice, F. L., 849, *853*
Altmaier, E. M., 716, 719, *721*
Altman, A., 764, *776*
Altman, D., 593, *611*
Altman, D. G., 591, 595, 596, 598, 599, 600, 604, 605, 606, *607*, *609*, *611*, 705, *706*
Altman, I., 370, *379*, 606, *607*
Alvarado, J. P., 502, *514*
Alvarez, W., 145, *166*
Al-Wazzan, H., 820, *832*
Amanullah, M., 810, *812*
Amaro, H., 290, *307*, 431, *438*, 503, 506, *518*, 545, 548, *554*, 777, 782, 784, 785, 788, 790, 792, *795*, *797*, 818, 819, 822, 823, *832*
Amateau, L. M., 221, *231*
Ambepitiya, G., 676, *679*
Ambrosioni, E., 434, *437*
American Academy of Dermatology, 727, *741*
American Academy of Pediatrics Committee on Substance Abuse and Committee on Children with Disabilities, 289, *307*
American Association of Retired Persons, 825, 826, *832*
American Association of Retired Persons and the Travelers Foundation, 478, *489*
American Cancer Society, 530, *532*, 727, 728, 734, 736, 739, *741*
American College of Obstetrics and Gynecology, 550, *554*
American College of Sports Medicine, 526, *532*, 630, 646, 647, *650*
American Diabetes Association, 330, *332*
American Medical Association, 542, 544, 548, *554*
American Psychiatric Association, 119, *133*, 281, 284, *307*, 325, *332*, 635, *650*, 718, *722*
Amery, A. K. P. C., 699, *707*
Amick, B. C., 855, 856, *887*
Amiel-Tison, C., 496, 503, *511*
Amling, C. L., 470, *474*
Ammerman, A. S., 287, *317*, 521, 522, *533*, *535*, 869, *889*
Amorosa, D., 717, *724*
Amos, C. I., 824, *834*
An, Z. X., 270, *277*
Anand, R., 251, 252, *260*
Ananda, S., 256, *260*
Anastasia, J., 818, 820, 821, *835*
Anastos, K. M., 826, *836*
Ances, I. G., 269, *278*
Anda, R., 153, 156, *162*, 662, *666*
Anda, R. F., 268, *279*, 290, *307*, 523, *539*
Anderman, C., 519, 530, *536*, 730, 737, *742*, *743*
Ander-Peciva, S., 215, *233*
Andersen, B., 764, *775*
Andersen, B. L., 24, *41*, 390, 398, *399*, 709, 711, 712, 713, 714, 715, 716, 718, 719, 720, *721*, *722*, *725*, 747, 753, *754*
Andersen, M. R., 738, *744*
Andersen, R. E., 272, 273, *279*
Anderson, B., 390, *399*, 711, 715, 719, 720, *722*
Anderson, B. J., 293, *313*, 441, *446*, *447*
Anderson, C. A., 180, *190*
Anderson, D., 810, *815*, 829, *832*
Anderson, D. L., 63, *80*
Anderson, E., 543, 545, 550, *556*
Anderson, E. S., 830, *838*
Anderson, G. L., 521, *538*
Anderson, H. R., 497, 498, 506, 509, *512*, *515*, *517*
Anderson, J., 182, *193*
Anderson, J. L., 28, 40, *41*, 153, *162*, 642, *650*
Anderson, J. Q., 861, 862, *887*
Anderson, J. R., 68, *79*, 827, *833*
Anderson, K., 521, *535*
Anderson, K. M., 571, 576, *579*
Anderson, L., 388, *399*, 850, *852*
Anderson, M., 432, 435, *440*
Anderson, N. B., 77, *78*143, 148, *162*, *171*, 188, *193*, 431, 432, 433, 435, 436, *437*, *439*, 662, 663, *666*, *667*, 818, *832*
Anderson, N. J., 498, 506, *516*
Anderson, P., 444, *447*
Anderson, R., 779, *795*, *797*
Anderson, R. J., 717, *722*
Anderson, R. M., 779, 780, *797*, 822, *832*
Anderson, R. W., 73, *83*
Anderson, S. J., 327, *333*
Anderssen, N., 526, 527, *532*
Anderssen, S. A., 270, *278*
Andiman, W., 823, 824, 827, *834*
Ando, K., 250, *261*
Ando, Y., 371, *379*, *384*
Andrasik, F., 123, *134*
Andres, J. M., 453, *456*
Andres, R., 469, *476*
Andres, R. L., 503, *511*
Andresen, G. V., 759, 772, *775*
Andreski, P., 283, 284, *308*
Andrews, F. M., 560, 561, 562, *568*, *569*
Andrews, J., 305, *307*
Andrews, J. A., 525, *537*
Andrews, K., 304, 305, *312*
Andrews, M., 343, *346*
Andrews, T. C., 672, *679*
Andrykowski, M. A., 25, *41*, 388, *400*, 452, 453, *455*, 718, 719, *722*, *723*
Andrzejewski, C., 808, *814*
Aneshensel, C. S., 25, *41*, 478, 481, 483, *489*, 824, *839*
Angel, M., 140, 158, *162*
Angel, R., 393, *399*, 436, *437*
Angelakos, E. T., 434, *438*
Angell, K., 340, *346*
Angkor, V., 753, *756*
Anglin, M. D., 782, *797*, 823, *832*, *835*
Angoli, L., 671, 676, *680*, *682*
Anisman, H., 111, *115*, 748, *754*, *756*
Annas, G. J., 531, *533*
Annent, J., 96, *102*
Annunziato, B., 221, *231*
Ansell, D., 531, *532*, *536*
Anson, O., 177, *190*
Anstey, N. M., 808, *813*
Antal, E., 810, *814*
Anthenelli, R. M., 289, 297, *307*
Anthony, E. J., 185, *190*
Anthony, J. C., 283, 284, 285, 300, *312*, 822, *836*
Antick, J., 297, *316*
Antick, J. R., 297, *316*
Antignani, A., 807, *812*
Anton, R. F., 299, *312*
Antone, C., *740*, *745*
Antoni, M., 325, 326, 328, *334*, 342, *346*, 685, 688, *693*
Antoni, M. H., 63, 74, *80*, 245, 246, 340, 342, 343, *346*, *347*, 388, 395, 398, *401*, 688, 690, *691*, *694*
Antonova, K., 372, *379*
Antonovsky, A., 176, 177, 184, 185, *190*
Antonucci, T. C., 485, *489*
Anttila, R., 454, *455*
Anwar, R., 543, 544, *556*
Anwar, R. A. H., 549, *556*
Aotaki-Phenice, L., 367, *381*
Apajasalo, M., 454, *455*
Aparicio-Pages, M. N., 329, *332*
Apospori, E., 462, *468*
Appel, L., 700, *707*
Appel, W. H., 575, *580*
Appelbaum, M., 146, *163*, 631, 642, *651*, 664, 665, *666*
Appels, A., 49, *57*, 669, *679*
Applewhite, S. L., 862, *887*
Appleyard, D., 369, *379*
Aral, S. O., 779, *795*
Aranda, J., 810, *813*
Arbisi, P., 64, *79*
Arbuckle, T. Y., 289, *312*
Archer, R., 219, *230*
Archie, C., 509, *512*
Ardissino, D., 671, *682*
Ardon, R. C., 860, 861, *893*
Arenberg, D., 469, *476*
Argov, E., 636, *655*

Arguelles, A. E., 372, 373, *383*
Arky, R. A., 265, *276*, 471, *475*
Armarasingham, L. R., 858, *888*
Armfield, A., 685, *692*
Armistead, L., 222, *230*
Armor, D. A., 564, *570*
Armour, J. A., 88, *93*
Armsden, G. C., 325, *336*
Armstead, C., 431, *437*
Armstead, C. A., 77, *78*, 143, *162*, 432, 433, 436, *437*, *439*
Armstrong, B. K., 736, *742*
Armstrong, D., 765, 768, *774*
Armstrong, K., 822, *839*
Armstrong, M. A., 281, 286, 287, 288, 290, *312*
Armstrong, P. W., 671, 674, 676, *681*
Armstrong, W., 340, *347*
Arndt, D., 374, *383*
Arnetz, B. B., 685, *691*
Arnold, D., 272, *278*
Arnold, M. A., 645, *651*
Arnow, P. M., 366, *379*
Arntz, A., 121, 123, *133*, *136*
Arntzen, A., 496, *512*
Arö, S., 216, *231*
Arshad, S., 451, *455*
Arthey, S., 736, *741*
Ary, D., 461, 462, *465*
Ary, D. V., 305, *307*
Asbury, R., 759, 761, *775*
Asch, S., 196, *205*
Ascherio, A., 153, *167*
Aseltine, R. H., 407, *411*, 508, *517*
Asendorpf, J. B., 73, *78*, 142, 157, *162*
Ashburn, M. A., *721*, *722*
Ashforth, B. E., 417, 425
Ashihara, T., 434, *440*
Ashkanazi, G. S., 583, 584, *589*
Ashleigh, E. A., 325, *335*, 663, *668*
Ashley, J. M., 526, *535*
Ashley, M. J., 286, *307*
Ashton, H., 250, *258*
Ashton, W. A., 732, 736, *744*
Ashworth, D. R., 867, *888*
Aspinwall, L., 155, 156, *172*
Aspinwall, L. G., 179, *190*, *193*, 391, 394, 395, *402*, 504, *512*, 821, *832*
Assaf, A., 528, *533*
Assaf, A. R., 593, 596, 601, 604, *607*, *609*
Assmann, S. F., 481, *491*
Astemborski, J., 826, *834*
Astroff, S., 70, *82*
Atchley, R. C., 469, *475*
Ateinza, A. A., 482, *491*, *492*
Athanassopoulos, G., 675, *681*
Athey, L. A., 822, 826, *838*
Atkins, C., 855, *894*
Atkins, C. J., 576, *577*
Atkins, J., 196, *207*
Atkinson, C., 686, *693*
Atkinson, D. R., 857, 862, 863, 864, *888*
Atkinson, J. H., 122, 125, 126, 130, *136*
Atkinson, L., 286, *315*
Atkinson, L. M., 286, 287, *315*
Atkinson, W., 614, *624*
Atrash, H. K., 499, *517*
Atteneave, C., 879, 880, *888*
Audrain, J., 526, *536*, 729, 732, 735, *741*, *742*, *745*
Auerbach, J. D., 781, *795*, 820, 831, *832*
Augenstein, D. G., 373, *384*
Augenstein, J. S., 373, *384*
August, S., 688, 690, *691*
Ault, K. A., 689, *692*
Austin, D. F., 288, *308*, 720, *722*
Austin, G. A., 40, *42*
Avendano, M., 27, 36, *43*
Averill, J. R., 49, *56*, 124, *133*, 151, *162*
Aversa, S. L., 849, *851*
Avery, C. Z., 877, 878, 879, *888*
Avery, S., 562, *569*
Avis, N. E., 732, *741*, 826, *839*
Avorn, J., 850, *851*
Avram, M. M., 807, *812*
Ax, A. F., 72, *78*
Ax, A. R., 139, 152, *162*
Axelrod, A., 718, *721*, 773, *774*
Axelrod, J., 502, *512*
Ayanian, J. Z., 473, *474*
Ayers, T., 830, *832*
Ayres, A., 72, *78*, 717, *722*
Azariah, R., 177, 180, *190*
Azjen, I., 831, *832*

B

Baba, S., 287, *317*
Baba, V. V., 321, 326, 327, *332*
Babb, J., 860, 861, *888*
Babisch, W., 371, 373, *379*, *381*, *382*
Babor, T. F., 285, *313*, *316*, 405, 410, *411*
Babyak, M., 329, *334*, 671, 674, 675, 677, *679*, *680*
Babyak, M. A., 150, 152, 159, *166*, 664, 665, *666*
Baca, J., 857, 858, 860, *888*
Bacal, C., 472, *475*
Bachen, E. A., 327, 328, *332*, *333*, *335*, 685, 688, 689, 690, *692*, *693*, *694*, 753, *754*, *755*
Bacher, B., 252, *258*
Bachetti, P., 823, *833*
Bachman, J. D., 600, *609*
Bachman, J. G., 459, 460, 461, 464, *465*, *467*
Bachrach, C., 820, *837*
Bachrach, C. A., 560, *570*
Back, K., 196, *206*
Back, K. W., 202, *206*
Backus, C. A., 183, *193*
Baddeley, A. D., 409, *413*
Badimon, J. J., 630, *653*, 674, 675, *680*
Badimon, L., 630, *653*, 674, 675, *680*
Badura, B., 396, *403*
Baer, H., 859, 862, 872, 873, 874, *888*
Baer, H. A., 873, 874, *888*
Baer, J. S., 223, *232*, 305, *306*, *307*, *313*, 663, *667*
Baer, R. D., 27, *47*
Baertschi, P., 267, *278*
Bagchi, B. K., 95, *102*
Bagenda, D., 827, *837*
Baggett, H. L., 688, 690, *691*
Bagiella, E., 663, *668*
Bagley, C., 67, *81*
Bagley, S. P., 436, *437*
Bahbehani, J., 820, *832*
Bahkre, M. S., 639, 645, *650*
Bahnson, J., 531, *534*
Bahr, G. R., 848, 850, *852*
Baider, L., 325, 326, *332*, 720, *722*
Bailey, E. J., 872, 873, 874, 876, *888*
Bailey, J. M., 150, *168*
Bailey, S., 576, *579*
Bailey, W. C., 576, *577*, 849, *851*
Bain, C., 523, *539*
Baird, H. R., 877, *893*
Bairey, C. N., 670, 671, 672, 675, *680*, *681*
Bairey, N., 150, *166*
Bairey-Merz, C. N., 672, 677, 678, *680*, *681*, *682*
Bak, S. M., 550, *555*
Bakeman, R., 188, *192*, 765, 768, *775*
Baker, A. B., 720, *725*
Baker, C., 825, *838*
Baker, D., 68, *81*, 855, *893*
Baker, F., 522, *538*, 716, *722*, *725*
Baker, H. M., 703, *707*
Baker, L. C., 508, 509, *517*
Baker, M. C., 645, *655*
Baker, N. J., 549, *554*
Baker, S., 729, *742*
Baker, T. B., 405, 410, *411*
Bakketeig, L. S., 496, *512*
Balcazar, F. E., 600, *607*
Balcazar, H., 521, *532*, 855, 856, *888*
Baldassare, M., 367, 368, 369, *379*
Balden, S., 825, *839*
Baldwin, M., 152, *171*
Balfour, D. J. K., 251, 252, *258*
Balfour, H. H., 846, *852*
Bali, L., 255, *258*
Ball, C. O. T., 699, *707*
Ball, D. M., 295, *307*
Ballard, C. R., 849, *852*
Ballard, T. J., 500, 508, *512*, *514*
Ballenger, M. N., 674, 676, *681*, *682*
Ballieux, R. E., 687, 689, 690, *691*, *692*, *693*
Balogh, S., 74, *78*
Balshem, A., 519, 531, *537*, 732, 734, 735, 736, *743*, 749, *755*
Balshem, A. M., 531, *532*, *537*
Balson, P. M., 849, *853*
Baltes, M. M., 38, *41*, 488, *489*
Baltes, P. B., 38, *41*, 470, *474*
Baltrusch, H. J., 327, *332*, 753, *754*
Banav, N., 471, *475*
Band, D. A., 562, *569*
Bandini, L. G., 267, *275*
Bandura, A., 4, 13, *16*, 19, 24, 39, *41*, 53, *56*, 62, 65, *78*, *84*, *102*, 122, 124, 125, 126, 127, 130, *133*, 142, 144, 145, 151, *162*, 182, 186, *190*, 235, 236, 237, 238, 239, 240, 241, 242, 243, 244, 245, *246*, *247*, 328, *336*, 461, 464, *465*, 485, 486, *489*, 574, 576, *577*, 595, 597, *607*, 782, 787, *795*, 831, *832*
Bane, A. L., 461, *466*
Banerjee, S., 222, *230*, 304, *307*
Bangert-Drowns, R., 344, *348*
Banki, C. J., 299, *307*
Banks, S. M., *740*, *741*
Banks, S. R., 734, *745*
Banuazizi, A., 186, *191*
Baptiste, D. A., Jr., 784, *796*
Baptiste, S., 123, *134*
Baquet, C. R., 523, *538*, 855, 869, *888*
Barakat, B., 499, *516*
Barakat, L. P., 718, *723*
Baram, D., 563, *569*
Baranowski, T., 268, *278*
Baraona, M., 288, *310*
Baras, M., 685, *695*
Barbaree, H. E., 123, 130, *135*
Barber, L. T., 523, *538*
Barber, T., 88, 89, *93*, *94*, 126, *133*
Barber, T. X., 89, *93*, *94*
Barchas, J. D., 126, *133*
Barclay, C. R., 406, 407, 408, *411*
Barclay, L. C., 152, *167*
Bardos, G., 89, *93*
Barefoot, J., 61, 66, 75, 76, *78*
Barefoot, J. C., 64, 65, 66, *78*, *81*, 148, 149, 150, 153, 154, *162*, *163*, *166*, *173*, 217, *233*, 662, 663, *666*, *667*, *668*, 677, *682*

Barerra, M., Jr., 222, *229*
Barger, S. D., 19, 23, 26, 27, *42*, 157, *163*
Barker, G., 820, *832*
Barker, N. D., 429, *438*
Barker, S., 374, *382*
Barlett, G., 867, *895*
Barling, J., 482, *489*
Barlow, C. E., 525, *533*
Barlow, D., 197, *207*
Barlow, D. H., 758, *774*
Barlow, G., 146, *171*
Barlow, M. J., 867, *895*
Barlow, W., 632, *656*
Barlow, W. E., 737, *742*
Barnard, C. N., 576, *579*
Barnard, M., 673, *681*
Barnard, N. D., 576, *577*, 739, *741*
Barnes, G. M., 222, *230*, 300, 301, 304, *307*, 357, *360*
Barnes, R. F., 663, *668*
Barnet, B., 503, *512*
Barnett, A. Q. H., 804, *813*
Barnett, P. A., 144, *163*
Barney, G. L., 864, 868, *888*
Barnlund, D. C., 787, *795*
Barnum, R., 292, *309*
Baron, J. A., 290, *312*
Baron, R. A., 356, *360*
Baron, R. M., 144, *163*, 212, *229*, 367, 370, *379*, 737, *741*
Baron, R. S., 227, *229*, 328, *332*, 687, *692*
Barone, C., 830, *832*
Barone, D. F., 238, *246*
Barr, H. M., 289, 290, *317*
Barraclough, J., 749, *754*
Barranday, Y., 717, *724*
Barrera, M., 304, 305, *308*, 505, *512*
Barrett, D. C., 154, *163*, 268, *278*
Barrett, J. E., 256, *259*
Barrett, J. J., 480, *490*
Barrett, L. E., 873, *888*
Barrett, M., 631, *652*
Barrett, R .J., 748, *756*
Barrett, S. A., 628, *657*
Barrett-Connor, E., 520, 530, *533*, *534*, 629, *656*
Barrett-Connor, E. L., 471, *474*
Barron, W. M., 503, *512*
Barros, F., 225, *233*
Barrranday, Y., 219, *232*
Barry, J., 669, 672, 677, *679*, *681*
Barry, M. J., 407, *411*
Barsevick, A., 394, *401*
Barsky, A. J., 27, *41*
Barth, R., 737, *746*
Barth, R. P., 504, *512*, 783, *797*
Bartholow, B. D., 300, 301, *316*
Bartlett, E. E., 524, *539*
Bartlett, J. G., 808, *813*
Bartlett, S. J., 272, 273, *276*, *279*
Bartolucci, A. A., 478, *490*
Barton, C., 575, *580*
Bartone, P. T., 178, *190*
Bartrop, R., 686, *692*
Bartter, F. C., 699, *707*
Bartus, S., 571, 575, 576, *580*
Bartzokis, T., 150, *167*, 670, 671, *680*
Baruch, J. D. R., 763, 764, *774*, *775*
Basch, C. E., 591, 595, 600, 606, *611*
Basen-Engquist, R. F., 787, 788, *795*
Basham, R. B., 160, *170*
Basit, A., 419, 424
Basmajian, J. V., 91, *93*, 97, *102*
Bass, C., 153, *163*
Bass, D. M., 481, 482, *489*
Bass, E. B., 548, *556*
Bass, J. W., 576, *577*
Bassett, J. R., 434, 435, *437*, *438*
Bast, L. P., 462, *467*
Bastani, R., 524, *535*, 729, 731, 735, *741*
Bastian, L., 830, *832*
Bastian, L. A., 471, 472, *474*, *475*
Bata, I., *162*, *165*, *666*, *667*
Batchelor, C., 433, *440*
Bates, M. E., 301, *307*
Bates, W., 300, *315*
Batish, S., 828, *834*
Battarbee, H. D., 434, *438*
Batter, V., 794, *798*
Battiola, R. J., *691*, *693*
Battjes, R., 463, *465*
Battjes, R. J., 781, *797*
Bauchner, H., 503, 506, *518*
Baucom, D., *489*, *491*
Bauer, C. A., 630, *657*
Baum, A., 50, *56*, 68, 69, *78*, 97, 100, *102*, 146, *166*, 226, *230*, 245, *246*, 256, *259*, 321, 323, 324, 325, 326, 327, 328, 329, *332*, *333*, *334*, *336*, *337*, 367, 368, 369, 370, 374, 376, *379*, *381*, *385*, 433, 434, 435, *437*, *438*, *440*, 663, *667*, 684, 685, 688, 689, *692*, *693*, *695*, 749, 753, *755*, *756*
Baum, D. J., 444, *447*
Baum, J. B., 827, *839*
Baum, M. K., 686, 690, *693*, 753, *755*
Bauman, K. E., 302, *307*
Baumann, L., 22, 23, 28, *41*
Baumann, L. J., 36, *41*
Baumeister, R. F., 786, *795*
Baumert, P. W., Jr., *455*
Baumgarten, M., 481, *491*
Baumgartner, H., 371, 373, *382*
Baxelmans, J., 647, *653*
Baxter, D., 822, *835*
Baxter, J. E., 267, 272, 273, *277*, *279*
Bayende, E., 825, *838*
Bayless, C., 527, *536*
Bazubagira, A., 824, *839*
Bazzare, T. L., 526, *533*
Beach, S. R., 154, *165*, 483, *489*
Beadnell, B., 497, 498, *516*
Beal, W. E., 341, 343
Beall, G., 817, *838*
Beall, S. K., 157, *169*, 340, 341, 342, 343, *347*
Beardsley, M., 828, *833*
Beare, D., 290, *315*
Beary, J. F., 704, *706*
Beatson, D., 803, *815*
Beattie, G., 345, *347*
Beattie, M., 224, *232*
Beatty, P. A., 748, *756*
Beaulieu, C., 125, *134*
Beaupaire, J., 563, 565, *570*
Beaupre, P., *489*, *491*
Beauvais, J., *740*, *741*
Beck, A. T., 480,*489*, 633, *650*
Beck, K. H., 730, *741*
Beck, N. C., 584, *589*
Beck, S., 717, *725*
Beck, S. J., 773, *774*
Becker, C., 436, *438*
Becker, D., 266, *279*
Becker, F., 377, *379*
Becker, G., 561, *570*
Becker, H., 749, *754*
Becker, J., 290, *317*
Becker, J. T., 850, *853*
Becker, K., 847, *852*
Becker, L. A., 684, *692*
Becker, L. C., 329, *334*, 671, 672, *679*, *680*
Becker, M., 239, 243, *246*, 730, *741*
Becker, M. D., 36, *41*
Becker, M. H., 4, *16*, 19, 39, *41*, *43*, 53, *57*, 388, *399*, 574, *578*, 729, *741*, *743*
Becker, M. J., 731, *745*
Becker, U., 286, *310*
Beckham, J., 154, *162*
Beckham, J. C., 120, 125, *134*, *135*
Beckman, G., 808, *815*
Beckman, H., 644, *650*
Beckman, P., 646, *652*
Bedrick, J., 301, *307*
Beebe, G. W., 329, *334*
Beecher, H. K., 131, *133*, 703, *706*
Beer, V., 817, *838*
Beere, P. A., 641, 643, *650*
Beernstein, L., 288, *308*
Beeson, L., 520, *535*
Beevers, D. G., 287, 289, *311*, *313*
Begg, D., 300, 301, *308*
Begleiter, H., 296, *307*, *315*
Beh, H. C., 371, 372, *380*
Behets, F., 794, *798*, 825, *836*, *838*
Behrman, R. E., 499, *517*
Beilin, L. J.. 287, *315*, 521, 522, *534*
Beitins, I. Z., 645, *651*
Beitman, B. D., 283, 300, *312*
Beitner-Johnson, D., 252, *258*
Bekemeier, B., 544, *555*
Belamker, R. H., 297, *314*
Belanger, A. J., 266, *277*
Belcastro, P. A., 788, *795*
Belec, L., 828, *832*
Belisle, M., 576, *577*
Belizan, J. M., 225, *233*
Belknap, J. K., 298, *309*
Bell, C. S., 463, *465*
Bell, D., 869, *888*
Bell, I. R., 65, *78*
Bell, P., 366, *379*
Bell, R. M., 461, *465*, *466*
Bellack, A. S., 10, *16*, 284, 285, *314*
Bellavance, F., 481, *491*
Belle, D., 209, *229*, 435, *437*
Beller, G. A., 676, *680*
Bellinger, D. L., 684, *694*
Bellingham, R., 614, *624*
Bellis, J. M., 782, 783, *797*
Belluck, P., 820, *832*
Belsher, G.,327, *332*
Belsky, D. H., 505, *517*
Bem, D. J., 142, 151, 160, *163*
Bemis, C., 748, 750, 752, *755*
Bencivelli, W., 671, *680*
Bender, B., 451, 452, *456*
Bender, T. R., 877, *888*
Benedict, S., 526, *532*
Ben-Eliyahu, S., 326, *332*, *336*, 748, *754*
Benenson, A. S., 779, *798*
Benes, K. A., 441, *447*
Bengtson, V. L., 225, *233*
Benight, C., 685, 688, *693*
Benight, C. C., 245, *246*, 325, 326, 328, *334*
Benjamin, B., 366, *380*
Benjamin, L., 152, *171*
Benjamin, L. S., 152, 160, 161, *163*
Benne, K. D., 591, *607*
Benner, A., 772, *774*
Bennet, P. H., 296, *313*
Bennett, C., 830, *832*
Bennett, C. E., 820, *832*

Bennett, C. L., *474*
Bennett, L. A., 304, 305, *307, 318*
Bennett, P., 398, *399*
Bennett, P. H., 266, 270, *277, 278*, 877, *892, 893*
Bennett, S., 808, *813*
Bennett, T. L., 505, *513*
Bennett-Johnson, S., 19, *43*
Bennis, W. G., 591, *607*
Benotsch, E. G., 150, *163*
Benotsch, E., 343, *346*
Benschop, R. J., 689, 690, *692*
Bensenberg, M., 462, *467*
Benson, H., 92, *93*, 100, *102*, 150, 158, *167, 168*, 636, 639, 645, *651*, 689, *692*, 704, *706*
Benson, V., 477, *489*
Benthin, A. C., 196, *206*
Bentler, P. M., 196, *207*, 222, *232, 233*, 292, 302, *317*, 357, 358, *360*, 720, *722*
Bentley, A. F., 188, *190*
Bentley, G., 121, *135*
Benton, D., 689, 690, *694*
Ben-Zur, H., 685, *695*
Berekian, D. A., 733, *743*
Beren, S., 822, *835*
Beren, S. E., 179, 183, *192*, 822, *837*
Berendes, H. W., 499, *512*
Berenson, A. B., 504, *518*
Berenson, G. S., 807, *815*
Berenstein, V., 65, *83*
Beresford, S. A., 663, *668*
Berfari, R., 145, *166*
Berg, B. J., 560, *569*
Berg, J., 572, *577*
Berg, P., 787, *799*
Berga, S. L., 328, *332*, 689, *692*
Bergamaschi, R., 676, *680*
Bergant, A., 751, *754*
Bergbower, K., 180, *190*
Berger, B. G., 635, *651*
Berger, B. J., 828, *832*
Berger, M., 369, *379*
Berger, P. L., 603, *607*
Berger, R. S., 327, *335*
Berglund, M., 289, *307*
Bergman, B. A., 368, *379*
Bergman, J. S., 704, *706*
Bergman, R., 880, *888*
Bergman-Losman, B., 356, *360*
Bergner, M., 473, *474*
Bergstralh, E. J., 470, *474*
Berk, B. C., 329, *336*
Berk, R. A., 541, *554*
Berk, S. F., 541, *554*
Berkanovic, E., 23, 34, *41*, 226, *232*
Berkelman, R. L., 828, *833*
Berkey, C. S., *706*
Berkley, J. Y., 605, *608*
Berkman, L., 210, 214, 215, *229*, 286, *317*
Berkman, L. F., 160, *163*, 217, 226, 228, *229, 233*
Berkowitz, G. S., 500, *512*
Berkowitz, R., 575, *579*
Berkowitz, R. I., 272, 273, *279*
Berlin, B., 777, *797*
Berlin, B. M., 462, *467*
Berlin, J. A., 629, *651*
Berman, B. A., 524, *535*
Berman, D. S., 670, 671, 675, *680, 681*
Berman, E. R., 267, *277*
Berman, L. B., 473, *475*
Berman, S. H., 732, *741*
Berman, S. M., 825, *832*
Bermond, B., 689, *693*
Bernal, G. A. A., 121, *134*
Bernard, L. C., 184, *190*
Bernard, S. L., 486, *491*
Bernard, T. M., 22, *44*
Berndt, S., 575, *577*
Bernholz, C. D., 575, *578*
Bernier, R., 614, *623*
Bernier, R. H., 614, *624*
Bernstein, A. B., 530, *535*
Bernstein, B., 859, 860, *893*
Bernstein, E., 603, *611, 623, 625*
Bernstein, I. H., 242, 243, *246*
Bernstein, L., 289, 290, *315, 318*, 525, *532*
Bernstein, M. B., 848, 850, *852*
Berntorp, E., 221, 227, *233*
Berntsen, D., 325, *332*
Berrios, D. C., 542, 544, 545, 548, *554*
Berry, C. C., 434, *438*
Berry, D., 340, *346*
Berry, D. S., 356, *360*
Berry, J. W., 483, *490*
Berry, S., 777, *797*
Berry, S. D., 389, *402*, 473, *476*
Berry, S. H., 822, 826, *838*
Berscheid, E., 505, *512*
Bertagni, P., 506, *518*
Bertelli, G., 717, *724*
Berthiaume, M., 505, 506, *512*
Berthoff, M. A., 487, *491*
Bertilsson, L., 810, *815*
Bertolet, B., 329, *334*
Bertolucci, D., 293, *318*
Berton, K., 71, *83*
Berzon, Y., 685, *695*
Besedovsky, H. O., 112, *113*
Besser, G. M., 645, *653*
Best, J. A., 461, 464, *465, 466*
Bethea, C. L., 502, *517*
Bethel, J., 827, *837*
Bettencourt, B. A., 782, 783, *798*
Bettiker, R. L., 252, *260*
Betts, R. F., 686, *693*
Betz, A. L., 405, 406, 409, *413*
Betz, N. E., 184, *193*
Beutler, L. E., 119, *133*, 633, *652*
Bevan, W., 606, *607*
Beveridge, A., 850, *852*
Bevett, J. M., 734, *741*
Bevier, P., 828, *832*
Bevington, D. J., 719, *724*
Bey, M., 824, 827, *833*
Beyer, A., 373, *379*
Bhadrakom, C., 827, *838*
Bhagat, R. S., 419, 420, 424
Bhardwaj, S., 717, *724*
Bhopal, R. S., 293, *318*
Biassoni, R., 328, *335*
Bibeau, D., 528, *536*, 593, 603, *610*, 614, *624*
Bibeau, G., 420, 424
Bickell, N. A., 779, *797*
Bickler, G., 735, *745*
Bickman, L., 369, *379*
Bidder, G. B., 88, 89, *94*
Biedermann, H. J., 124, 129, *133*
Biegel, D., 720, *724*
Biegler. M., 499, *513*
Bieliauskas, L. A., 329, *336*
Bienenstock, J., *113, 114*
Bierman, E. L., 469, *475*
Bierut, L. J., 295, *311*
Biesecker, B., 732, 735, *741*
Bietendorf, J., 670, 671, 675, *681*
Biggar, R. J., 801, *815*, 824, 825, *834, 838*
Bigger, J. T., Jr., 663, *668*
Biglan, A., 461, 462, *465*, 859, *891*
Bijlsma, J. W. J., 393, *400*
Bijur, P. E., 292, *307*
Bild, D., 526, 527, *532*
Bild, D. E., 520, 527, 528, *535, 538*
Biles, P. L., 674, *681*
Billings, A. G., 217, 223, *229*, 292, *314, 455, 456*, 821, *832*
Billings, J., 148, *171*, 340, *347*
Billings, R., 124, *135*
Billy, J. O. G., 778, *799*
Binder, A., 591, 593, *607*
Bindman, A., 552, *556*
Binik, Y. M., 398, *400*
Binson, D., 777, 779, 780, 782, 783, 784, 785, 790, 792, *795, 796, 797*
Biondi, M., 321, 328, *332*
Biondo-Bracho, M., 808, *814*
Biradavolu, M., 735, *743*
Birbaumer, N., 121, 126, 128, 129, *134*
Birch, L. L., 267, *275, 277*
Birenbaum, L., 394, *401*
Birge, S. J., 525, *536*
Birk, L., 96, *102*
Birkel, L., 528, *535*
Birkel, R., 850, *853*
Birkeland, K. I., 270, *278*
Birkhead, G. S., 827, *839*
Birnbaum, D., 27, 32, *46*
Birnie, W. A., 637, *655*
Biryahwaho, B., 808, *814*
Bish, A., 565, *569*
Bishop, G. D., 26, *41*, 732, 733, *743*
Bishop, M., 397, *402*
Bisits, A., 502, *515*
Bjarnason, N. H., 471, *474*
Bjorgvinsdottir, L., 496, *514*
Bjornson-Benson, W. M., 523, *537*
Bjorntorp, P., 265, *278*
Black, A. H., 90, *93*
Black, D., 472, *475*
Black, D. R., 274, *276*
Black, G., 152, 159, *166*
Black, G. W., 149, 152, 158, 159, *166*, 705, *706*
Black, J. D. W., 291, *314*
Black, M., 782, *795*
Black, W., 528, 531, *534*
Black, W. C., 731, 732, 738, 739, *741, 745*
Blackburn, G., 717, *722*
Blackburn, G. L., 266, *277*, 526, *535*
Blackburn, H., 593, 601, 604, *607, 609*
Blackhall, L., 550, *555*
Blackmon, C., 869, *892*
Blackmore, C. A., 499, *517*
Blackmore-Prince, C., 500, *512*
Blackwell, B., 848, *851*
Blackwell, J. B., 736, *742*
Blair, A., 631, *650*
Blair, E., 272, *279*, 406, 407, 408, *411*, 524, *537*
Blair, S., 145, *166*
Blair, S. H., 145, *163*
Blair, S. N., 266, *276*, 525, 526, 527, 528, *533, 535, 537*, 573, *579*, 629, 630, 647, *651*, 629, 646, 647, 648, 649, *652, 653, 655*
Blake, J. L., 621, *624*
Blake, S., 752, *756*
Blake, S. M., 604, *607*
Blakelock, E. H., Jr., 435, *438*
Blalock, J. E., 111, *113*
Blalock, S. J., 204, *205*, 393, 397, *399, 400*, 532, *533*, 731, 732, 739, *741*
Blanc, G., 748, *754*
Blanchard, C. G., 393, *399*

Blanchard, E. B., 100, *102*, 123, *133*, 704, *706*, *721*
Blanchard, J. J., 284, 285, *314*
Blanchard, L., 602, *608*
Blanche, S., 824, *833*, *838*
Bland, J. M., 497, 498, *512*, *517*
Blane, H. T., 292, 300, 302, *307*, *313*, *314*
Blaney, N. T., 686, 690, *693*, 753, *755*
Blaney, P., 156, *172*
Blansjaar, B. A., 289, *307*
Blasband, D., 508, *513*
Blasband, D. E., 486, *490*
Blaschke, T. F, 571, *580*
Blascovich, J., 239, *246*
Blass, J. P., 469, *475*
Blattner, W. A., 808, *814*, *815*
Blazer, D., 226, *233*
Blazer, D. G., 153, *171*, 215, *229*, 471, *475*, *476*
Blechman, E. A., *162*, *163*, 223, *234*, 441, *446*, 469, *474*
Bleecker, E. R., 90, 91, *93*
Blehar, M. C., 354, *360*
Bleich, A., 325, *334*
Blendon, R., 855, *888*
Bliss, J. M., 764, *775*
Bliss, R. E., 523, 524, *534*
Bloch, R., 434, *439*, 699, *707*
Bloch, S., 444, *447*
Block, A. R., 120, *133*
Block, D. R., 524, *537*
Block, D. S., 848, *852*
Block, G., 520, *533*, 869, *888*, *890*
Block, J., 140, 159, *163*
Blois, M., 340, *348*
Blomgren, H., 110, *114*
Blomkvist, V., 221, 227, *233*
Blondel, B., 506, 508, *512*
Bloom, B. R., 571, *577*
Bloom, E., 686, *693*
Bloom, E. T., 689, 690, *694*
Bloom, F. E., 252, *260*, 297, *315*
Bloom, F. R., 847, *852*
Bloom, H. C., 758, 762, *776*
Bloom, J., 218, 219, 223, *232*, *233*, 340, *348*
Bloom, J. R., 122, 124, *136*, 664, *668*, 713, 719, 720, *722*, *724*, 752, *756*, 760, *776*
Bloom, M., 595, *607*
Bloomgarden, Z. T., 330, *332*
Blose, J. O., 291, *311*
Blot, W. J., 287, 288, *307*
Blow, F. C., 153, *165*, 285, *308*
Blower, S. M., 777, *798*
Blum, D., 29, *46*
Blum, K., 296, *308*
Blum, S., 821, *836*
Blumberg, B., 759, 761, *775*
Blume, S., 292, *316*
Blumenthal, J., 150, *166*, 629, *652*
Blumenthal, J. A., 72, 74, *78*, *84*, 146, 148, 149, 153, *162*, *163*, *165*, *170*, 329, *334*, 576, *579*, 631, 635, 640, 642, *651*, 662, 663, 664, 665, *666*, *667*, *668*, 669, 671, 672, 674, 675, 677, *679*, *680*, *682*
Blumenthal, S. J., 522, 523, *533*
Blumer, D., 119, *133*
Blumhagen, D., 23, 35, 37, *41*
Blumstein, P., 786, 790, *795*, *797*
Blute, M. L., 470, *474*
Bluthe, R. M., 112, *114*
Bly, S., 374, *379*
Blythe, B. J., 461, *466*, *467*
Boardley, D. J., 520, *533*
Bobat, R., 824, *837*
Bobik, A., 74, *80*
Boccellari, A., 824, *834*
Boccuti, L., 451, *456*
Bock, B., 503, *512*
Bodnar, J. C., 227, *230*, 328, *333*, 481, 482, *490*, 686, 688, *692*
Boeke, S., 393, *400*
Boerma, J. T., 829, *832*
Boffetta, P., 286, 287, *308*
Bogdan, G. F., 525, *537*
Bogdanov, M., 252, *260*
Boggs, S. R., 454, *456*
Bogic, L.V., 500, *512*
Bohman, M., 295, 296, 297, 300, 301, *308*, 217
Bohus, B., 326, *332*
Boileau, B., 453, *457*
Boisoneau, D., 325, *336*
Boivin, J., 296, *314*, 560, *569*
Bolan, G., *16*
Bolan, M., 822, *835*
Boland, B., 389, 398, *401*, 826, *837*
Bolden, S., 709, 710, 711, *724*, 727, *743*, 747, *756*
Boldizar, J. P., 444, *447*
Boles, S. M., 522, 528, *534*
Bolger, N., 61, 70, *78*, *79*, 144, 154, *163*, 188, *190*, 393, 394, 395, *399*, 504, *512*
Bolme, P., 90, *93*
Bolton, P. A., 325, *336*
Bolton, R., 861, *888*
Boltwood, M., 150, *167*, 670, 671, *680*
Boltwood, M. D., 675, *679*
Bond, A., 504, *518*
Bond, G., 716, *724*
Bonduelle, D., 575, *580*
Boneh-Kristal, E., 373, *383*
Bonen, A., 527, *538*
Bonge, D., 542, *555*
Bonica, J. J., 117, 118, *133*
Bonne, O., 773, *776*
Bonneau, R. H., 328, *333*, 686, 687, *693*
Bonneh, D. Y., 177, *190*
Bonnell, G., 688, *693*
Bonomi, A., 22, *42*
Bononi, P., 272, *277*
Bonsall, R., 329, *334*, 671, 672, *679*, *680*
Bookstein, F. L., 289, 290, *317*
Bookwala, J., 156, *170*, 480, 481, 482, *489*, *492*
Boon, C., 340, *348*
Booth, A., 366, 367, 368, 369, *379*, *380*
Booth, B. M., 285, *308*
Booth, R., 342, 343, *347*
Booth-Kewley, S., 75, 76, *80*, 142, 154, 155, 158, *163*, *165*, 340, *347*
Borcherding, S., 126, *134*
Borch-Johnsen, K., 286, *310*
Borg, G., 645, *651*
Borgeat, F., 124, *133*, 505, 506, *512*
Borghetti, A., 373, *380*
Borghi, C., 436, *437*
Borhani, N., 145, 148, *166*, *171*, 700, *707*
Borkowsky, W., 802, 803, *815*
Borland, R., 183, *190*, 736, *742*, *744*
Bornstein, M. H., 503, *512*
Bornstein, R. A., 388, *402*
Borrelli, B., 503, *512*
Bortner, R. W., 66, *82*, 149, *168*
Borum, M. L., *532*, *533*
Borysenko, J., 158, *167*
Borysenko, M., 158, *167*, 689, *692*
Borzak, S., 669, 676, 677, *679*, *682*
Bosi, E., 330, *332*
Bosimini, E., 671, *680*
Bosma, H., 662, *666*
Bosmajian, L., 548, *557*
Boss, L. P., 877, *888*
Boss, M., 432, *440*
Boss, P. G., 783, *795*
Bosscher, R. J., 633, *651*
Bosse, R., 145, 155, *168*, *169*
Bostrom, A., 733, 739, *742*
Bostwick, D. G., 470, *474*
Boswell, R. N., 808, *814*
Boswell, S., 847, *853*
Botchin, M. B., 151, 152, 159, *167*
Botha, J. R., 575, *579*
Bottoms, S. F., 496, *515*
Botvin, G. J., 461, 462, 463, 464, *465*, *467*, 855, *889*
Bouchard, C., 265, 266, *276*, *277*, 525, 526, *533*, *537*, 573, *579*, 627, 629, 646, 647, 648, *651*, *655*
Bouchard, T. J., Jr., 140, 146, *163*
Boucsein, W., 373, *383*
Bouloux, P., 645, *653*
Bouman, D. E., 584, *590*
Bourassa, M. G., 677, *681*
Bourg, E., 148, *162*, *165*
Bourgoignie, J. J., 805, *812*
Bourguignat, A., 753, *755*
Bourne, P. G., 872, 874, *890*
Boutros, N. N., 126, *134*
Boutwell, W. B., 528, *532*
Bouza, A., 548, *554*
Bovbjerg, D., 109, 110, *113*, *114*
Bovbjerg, D. H., 24, 25, *41*, *45*, 89, *93*, 110, *114*, 326, 328, *336*, 683, 684, 686, *691*, *692*, *694*
Bovbjerg, R. R., *474*, *475*
Bovbjerg, V. E., 576, *577*
Boving, J. E., 630, *655*
Bowden, B., 326, *336*
Bowen, A., 504, *518*
Bowen, A. M., 782, *795*
Bowen, D. J., 254, 255, *258*, *259*, 470, 472, *475*, 521, 522, *533*
Bowen, K. M., 109, *114*
Bower, G. H., 30, *41*
Bowers, B. J., 299, *318*
Bowers, J. C., 617, 618, *624*
Bowers, M., 547, *557*
Bowers, P. M., 292, 302, *314*
Bowes, G., 576, *580*
Bowes, W. A., 502, *514*
Bowker, L., 548, *554*
Bowlby, J., 340, *346*, 354, *360*
Bowles, C. A., 685, 688, 684
Bowman, B. J., 177, *190*
Bowman, E. D., 635, 637, *652*
Bowman, J. A., 734, *741*
Bowman, M., 765, 766, *775*
Bowman, R .J., 808, *815*
Bowman, S. R., 479, *490*
Bowry, P., 451, 452, *456*
Bowser, B., 823, *834*
Boxer, A., 561, *569*
Boxer, A. S., 564, *569*
Boyce, A., 530, *536*, 734, 735, 737, *743*, *744*
Boyce, T., 662, *666*, 821, *832*
Boyce, W. T., 328, *332*, 367, *380*, 506, *512*, 690, *692*, 771, 772, *774*
Boyd, E., 874, *888*
Boyd, J. H., 638, *656*
Boyd, J. R., 574, *577*
Boyd, S. T., 576, *579*
Boyer, C. B., 782, 783, *795*
Boyer, J., 290, *317*
Boyer, P., 827, *833*
Boyer, P. J., 824, *832*
Boyes-Braem, P., 23, *46*

Boykin, A., 243, *246*
Boyko, O. B., 471, *474*
Boylan, R., 34, *45*
Boyle, S., 73, *83*
Bozarth, M. A., 252, *258*
Bozic, I., 674, *681*
Bozzette, S. A., 822, 826, *838*
Brachfeld, J., 810, *813*
Bracht, N., 528, *536*, 591, 593, 595, 596, 601, 603, 604, 605, *607*, *609*
Brackin, B. T., 803, *812*
Brackin, M. N., 803, *812*
Bradbeer, C. S., 154, *172*
Bradburn, N. M., 406, 408, 409, 410, *412*, *413*
Bradbury, T. N., 154, *164*, 508, *516*
Braddick, M., 824, *833*
Bradford, J., 777, *797*
Bradford, R., 452, 453, *456*
Bradizza, C. M., 301, *313*
Bradley, C. F., 506, *518*
Bradley, R. H., 369, 378, *380*
Bradshaw, C., 747, 749, *756*
Bradwell, A. R., 804, *813*
Brady, J. V., 89, *94*
Brady, K. T., 284, *308*
Braff, D., 255, *258*
Braff, D. L., 255, *261*
Bragdon, E. E., 676, 677, *681*
Braithwaite, V. A., 222, *232*
Brajer, V., 855, *888*
Brambilla, D. J., 432, 433, *437*
Bramucci, E., 671, *682*
Branas, C. C., 290, *316*
Branch, P., 499, *517*
Brand, F. R., 633, 635, *654*
Brand, R., 340, *347*
Brand, R. J., 148, *170*, 215, *231*
Brandapalli, N. I., 850, *852*
Brandenberger, G., 373, *380*
Brandon, G., 872, 875, *888*
Brandon, T. H., 405, 410, *411*
Brandt, A., 870, *888*
Brannick, M., 302, *315*
Brannock, J. C., 297, *316*
Brannon, J., 22, *42*
Brano-Driehorst, S., 153, *166*
Branson, B., 850, *852*
Branstetter, A. D., 734, *743*
Brantley, B. A., 716, *724*
Brantley, P., 340, *346*
Brasfield, T. L., 10, *16*, 848, 850, *852*
Braunwald, E., 670, *679*
Bravo, E. L., 503, *512*
Brawley, L., 243, *246*
Brazy, J. E., 499, *518*
Breakwell, G. M., 782, 783, *795*
Breall, W., 148, *162*, *165*
Breast Cancer Prognostic Study Associates, 753, *756*
Brebner, J., 355, *360*
Brecht, M., 823, *837*
Breed, W., 305, *318*
Breen, N., 528, 530, *533*, 734, *744*
Breier, A., 689, *695*
Breinl, S., 373, *383*
Breisblatt, W. M., 671, *679*
Brema, F., 717, *724*
Brembridge, A., 804, *814*
Brener, J., 88, *93*, 703, *706*
Brenn, T., 631, *657*
Brennan, J. J., 471, *475*
Brennan, M. J., 753, *756*
Brennan, P. L., 223, *229*, 394, 397, *401*
Brenner, G. F., 219, *232*
Brenner, S. O., 685, *691*
Brent, E. E., 297, 300, 301, *316*
Breslau, N., 283, 284, 301, *308*, *312*
Breslow, J. L., 286, *310*
Breslow, M. J., 472, *475*
Bresnahan, K., 503, *512*
Bret-Dibat, J. L., 112, *114*
Brett, G., 366, *380*
Brewer, D. D., 327, *332*
Brewer, W., 129, *133*
Brewer, W. F., 406, *412*
Brewster, D., 808, *813*
Brezinka, V., 395, *399*
Breznitz, S., 685, *695*
Bricker, M. C., 497, 498, 509, *516*
Brickman, A. L., 327, *332*
Bridges, M. W., 155, 157, *170*, 184, *193*, 391, *402*, 585, *590*
Brief, A. P., 64, *79*, 354, 355, 356, *360*, *361*
Brief, D. J., 576, *577*, *579*
Briggs, A. H., 296, *308*
Briggs, S. R., 154, *163*
Brill, P. L., 418, 424
Brindle, R., 808, *814*
Briner, W., 688, *693*
Brinsden, P. R., 562, *569*
Brinton, L. A., 530, *534*, 732, *742*
Brisson, G., 639, 641, *656*
Bristow, M., 685, *692*
Brittingham, G. L., 32, *45*, 486, 488, *490*
Britton, J. A., 631, *653*
Britton, P., 822, *835*
Britton, P. J., 830, *835*
Broadhead, W. E., 225, *229*
Broadhead, W. G., 546, *557*
Broakmeyer, R., 472, *475*
Brock, D. M., 355, *362*
Brockschmidt, J. K., 717, *723*
Brod, J., 703, *706*
Brodaty, H., 471, *475*
Brodde, O. E., 689, *695*
Broderick, J., *411*, *412*
Broderick, J. B., 406, 407, *411*, *413*
Brodie, B., 823, *833*
Brodie, K. H., 781, *795*
Brodie, M. J., 576, *579*
Brody, D., 735, *743*
Brody, E., 480, *491*
Brody, E. M., 36, *41*
Brodzinsky, D. M., *568*, *569*
Bronfenbrenner, U., 442, *447*, 593, *607*, 818, *833*
Brook, D. W., 222, *229*
Brook, J. S., 222, *229*
Brooke, O. G., 497, *512*
Brookfield, S. D., *623*
Brooks, C. M., 576, *577*, 849, *851*
Brooks, E. F., 869, *892*
Brooks, M. M., 395, *402*
Brooks, P. M., *331*, *335*
Brooks-Gunn, J., 442, *447*, 496, 501, 503, *512*, *515*
Brophy, L., 717, *725*
Brosschot, J., 342, 343, *348*
Brosschot, J. F., 689, 690, *692*
Brostoff, J., 108, *114*
Brough, D. I., 497, 498, 510, *513*
Broughton, R., 141, *173*
Brower, K. J., 285, *308*
Brown, B., 327, *334*, 718, *723*
Brown, B. B., 606, *607*
Brown, C., 250, *258*, 429, *437*, 603, *607*, 614, 620, *623*, 631, *652*, 804, *814*
Brown, D., 454, *456*
Brown, D. R., 523, *532*, 627, 632, 633, 635, 636, 638, *651*
Brown, E. F., 285, *315*
Brown, E. R., 599, *607*
Brown, G. K., 25, 29, *42*, 125, 126, 129, *133*, *134*, 219, *229*
Brown, G. W., 322, *332*, 407, *412*, 501, *512*, 750, *754*
Brown, H. N., 716, *722*
Brown, H. S., 728, 729, *743*
Brown, J., 373, *380*, 405, 410, *411*
Brown, J. D., 65, *83*, 197, *208*, 390, *402*, 525, *536*, 564, *570*, 585, *590*, 632, *651*
Brown, J. L., 442, *446*
Brown, K., 285, *308*, 432, *439*, 523, *536*, 872, *891*
Brown, K. J., 255, 256, *258*
Brown, K. S., 461, 464, *465*, *466*
Brown, K. W., 356, *360*
Brown, L., 720, *722*, 790, *795*
Brown, L. E., 700, *707*
Brown, L. L., 157, *163*, 218, *229*, 389, 398, *399*, 747, 751, *754*
Brown, M. L., 531, *533*
Brown, N. R., 409, *412*
Brown, P., 758, 760, *776*
Brown, P. J., 283, 284, *308*
Brown, R., 109, 112, *114*, 593, *611*
Brown, R. A., 285, *308*
Brown, R. S., 635, *651*
Brown, S., 65, *84*, 243, 245, *246*, *247*, 328, *336*, 340, *347*
Brown, S. A., 283, 297, 301, *308*, *310*, *316*, 327, *332*
Brown, S. L., 478, 483, *490*
Brown, T. G., 641, *657*
Brown, T. N., 432, *439*
Brown, V., 823, *839*
Brown-Collins, A., 855, *891*
Browne, A, 541, 542, 543, *554*, *556*
Browne, G., 327, *334*, 718, *723*
Brownell, K., 266, *276*
Brownell, K. D., 50, *56*, 183, *190*, 266, 270, *276*, *277*, 469, *474*, 521, *533*
Browner, C. H., 859, *890*
Browning, S. R., 287, *317*, 435, *440*
Brownley, K. A., 435, *439*
Brownson, R. C., 599, 600, *607*
Brozek, J., 702, *708*
Brubaker, R. G., 734, *741*
Bruce, D., 406, *412*
Bruce, F. C., 508, *514*
Bruce, M. L., 488, *492*
Bruce, R., 614, *625*
Bruhis, S., 371, 372, *383*
Bruhn, J. G., 635, *655*
Bruner, J., 187, *190*
Bruner, J. S., 40, *42*
Brunet, M., 753, *755*
Brunner, E., 662, *667*
Brunzell, J. D., 267, *276*
Bruschi, G., 373, *380*
Brush, L. D., 541, *554*
Brust, A. A., 703, *707*
Brutsaert, D. L., 154, *165*
Bryan, E. S., 302, *307*
Bryan, W., 877, 880, *888*
Bryant, C. A., 734, *741*
Bryant, H. U., 109, *114*
Bryant-Greenwood, G. D., 500, *512*
Bryson, Y., 827, *833*
Bryson, Y. J., 824, *832*
Bubb, J., *446*, *447*
Bubela, N., 717, *723*
Bubker, J. P., 855, *888*
Buchanan, C. M. 443, *447*

Buchanan, G., 67, *79*, 356, *362*
Buchbinder, S., 807, 810, *814*
Buchbinder, S. P., 806, *813*
Buchholz, K., 434, *438*
Bucholz, K., 296, *315*
Bucholz, K. K., 295, *311*
Buchner, D., 526, *537*, 573, *579*, 629, 646, 647, 648, *655*
Buchsbaum, M., 297, *314*
Buchwald, D., 867, 868, *888*
Buck, A., 828, *837*
Buck, E. L., 737, *745*
Buck, K. J., 298, *309*
Buckelew, S. P., 581, 582, 583, *589*
Buckenmeyer, P., 272, 273, *279*
Buckle, S., 220, *230*
Buckler-White, A., 806, *816*
Buckley, C. E., 469, *474*
Buckley, J., 39, *45*
Buckner, W., 601, *607*
Bucquet, H., 216, *230*
Buddeberg, C., 751, *754*
Budner, N., 473, *476*
Buechley, R. W., 877, *892*
Buehler, J., 821, 822, *833*, *838*, 880, 881, *888*
Buehler, J. W., 793, *796*, 828, *833*
Buell, J., 641, *652*
Buerkle. L., 496, *516*
Buescher, P. A., 500, *516*
Bugamwan, T., 805, *813*
Buhler, F. R., 157, *169*, 689, *694*
Buhrfeind, E. D., 342, 343, *348*
Buican, B., 419, 424
Buis, M., 523, 524, *536*
Buka, S. L., 444, *448*
Bukberg, J., 715, *722*
Bulbulian, H., 646, *652*
Bulcroft, R. A., 394, *402*, 488, *492*
Bull, D. F., 112, *114*
Bullard, R. D., 432, *437*
Bullen, B. A., 645, *651*
Bullinger, M., 373, 374, 375, 378, *381*
Bullock, L., 543, 545, *554*, *556*
Bulman, R. J., 583, *589*
Bunker, C., *279*
Bunnell, B. N., 257, *260*
Burack, J. H., 154, *163*
Burchfiel, C. M., 286, *310*
Burchill, S., 154, 155, 156, *164*
Burchinal, M., 445, *447*
Burdine, J., 593, *611*
Burdine, J. N., 596, *608*
Bureau of Labor Statistics, 352, *360*, 541, 542, 543, *554*, *555*
Burell, G., 398, *399*
Burg, M., 530, 531, *533*, 677, *680*
Burg, M. A., 531, *536*
Burg, M. M., 150, *163*, 486, *489*, 671, *679*
Burgard, M., 824, *833*, *838*
Burge, D., 154, *164*
Burge, S., 551, *555*
Burger, C., 576, *579*
Burger, P. C., 469, *474*
Burgess, C., 715, *724*
Burgess, E. D., 220, *230*
Burgess, E. H., 629, 647, *654*
Burgess, E. S., 285, *308*
Burgess, P., 325, *333*
Burghen, G. A., 220, *231*
Burgio, K. L., 90, 91, 92, *93*
Buring, J. E., 286, *310*, 520, 522, *537*
Burish, T. G., 50, *58*, 329, *334*, 716, 717, *722*, *725*, 751, *755*, 759, 761, 762, 764, 772, *774*, *775*, *776*
Burk, R. D., 826, *836*
Burke, G. L., 520, *538*, 869, *888*
Burke, J. D., 638, *656*
Burke, L., 574, *577*
Burke, L. E., 572, 573, 574, 575, *577*, *578*, 848, 849, *852*
Burke, M. B., 675, *679*
Burke, M. D., 717, *725*
Burke, M. J., 354, 355 356, *360*
Burke, R. J., 417, 419, 421, 424, 426
Burke, V., 521, 522, *534*
Burkhauser, R. V., 821, *837*
Burlew, B. S., 809, *813*
Burn, P., 266, *276*
Burnam, A., 282, 284, *311*
Burnam, M. A., 547, *555*
Burnett, R., 120, *135*, 758, *775*
Burnett, R. E., 326, 327, *334*
Burns, D., 824, 826, 827, *836*
Burns, D. M., 522, *538*
Burns, E. A., 25, *44*
Burns, J. M., 572, *577*
Burns, M. J., 671, *679*
Burrell, D. E., 807, *812*
Burris, M. A., 603, *611*
Burt, C. D. B., 408, 409, 410, *412*
Burt, V. L., 429, *437*
Burton, D., 647, *653*
Burton, J. R., 92, *94*
Burton, L., 444, *446*, 480, *492*
Burton, L. C., 481, 482, *489*
Burton, L. M., *189*, *190*, 441, 442, 444, *447*, *448*
Burton, L. R., 272, 273, *277*, *279*
Burton, S., 406, 407, 408, *411*
Burwell, L. R., 676, *680*
Busch, T. L., 520, *533*
Busch-Rossnagel, N. A., 506, *518*
Bush, J. P., 764, *775*
Bush, T. J., 825, 826, 828, *833*, *836*, *839*
Bushman, B. J., 728, 736, 739, *742*
Buske-Kirschbaum, A., 109, 110, *114*
Buss, A. H., 66, 75, *79*
Buss, D. M., 62, 69, *79*, 142, 144, *163*, 780, *795*
Busse, E. W., 469, *474*
Busse, R., 32, *46*
Busuell, N. J., 634, *653*
Butcher, A. H., 64, *79*
Butler, B. A., 266, 270, 272, 273, 274, *277*, *278*, *279*, 648, *653*
Butler, J. L., 600, *610*
Butler, R., 125, *134*, 773, *774*
Butler, R. W., 718, *722*
Butler, T., 291, *311*
Butler, W. T., 565, *569*
Buttars, J. A., 677, *679*
Butterfoss, F., 620, *625*
Butterfoss, F. D., 592, 603, 604, *607*, 614, 616, 617, 618, 620, 621, *623*, *624*
Buttner, E. H., 417, 425
Butz, A. M., 827, *833*
Butzin, C. A., 808, *814*
Buunk, B., 36, *42*
Buunk, B. P., 196, 204, *206*, 397, *399*, 417, 426
Buysse, D. J., 146, *166*
Buzzard, I. M., 717, *722*
Byar, D. P., 732, *742*
Bye, L., 777, 782, 783, *796*
Byers, J., 786, *798*
Byers, R. H., *16*
Byers, R. H., Jr., 824, 827, *833*, *836*
Byers, S. O., 435, *438*
Byers, T., 266, 270, *278*, *279*, 521, 523, *537*, *539*, 869, *893*
Bykov, K. M., 87, 89, *93*
Bylsma, W., 196, 204, *207*
Bylund, D. B., 297, 303, *316*
Byosiere, P., 355, 358, *361*, 415, 420, 425
Byrne, B. M., 417, 424
Byrne, J., 720, *722*

C

Cabral, H., 290, *307*, 503, 506, *512*, *518*, 545, 548, *554*, 823, *832*
Cacciola, J. S., 301, *307*
Cacioppo, J., 823, *839*
Cacioppo, J. T., 72, *81*, 160, *172*, 203, *206*, 226, 227, *233*, 324, 328, *332*, *336*, 355, 357, *363*, 393, 394, *403*, 685, 686, 689, 690, *692*, *693*, *694*, 712, 713, 714, *722*, *725*
Cadoni, C., 252, *258*
Cadoret, R. J., 295, 296, *308*
Caetano, R., 282, 290, *308*
Cafasso, L., 480, *491*
Caggiula, A., 328, *332*
Caggiula, A. R., 250, *258*, 689, *692*
Cagney, K. A., 734, *744*
Cain E. N., 718, *722*, 763, 764, *774*
Caine, K., 297, *316*
Caine, S. B., 255, *261*
Cairncross, K. D., 434, *437*
Cairns, D., 120, *134*
Cairns, N. U., 772, *775*
Calderon, A., 367, *385*
Caldwell, B., 369, *380*, 827, *836*
Caldwell, C., 684, 689, *693*
Caldwell, D. S., 120, 125, *134*, *135*, *489*, *491*
Caldwell, M. B., 824, *833*
Caldwell, S., 765, *775*
Calesnick, L. E., 370, *379*
Calfas, K., 527, *539*
Calfas, K. J., 398, *399*, 527, *533*, *536*, 638, *651*
Calhoun, D. A., 431, 433, *437*, *438*
Calhoun, J. B., 368, *380*
Calhoun, K. S., 547, 548, *556*
Calhoun, L. G., 183, *193*
Califf, R. M., 153, *162*, 217, *233*, 662, *667*, *668*
Callahan, L. F., 55, *56*, 177, *190*, 821, *837*
Callahan, T. S., 672, *681*
Callan, V. J., 564, *569*
Callaway, E., 109, *115*, 255, *258*
Calle, E. E., 530, 531, *533*
Callendar, C. O., 802, 804, *812*, *813*
Callow, D., 808, *814*
Calvillo, E. R., 885, *889*
Camac, C., 300, *318*
Camacho, T., 146, *167*
Camacho, T. C., 55, *57*, 632, *651*
Camara, W. J., 350, *362*
Cambell, W. P., 849, *852*
Cameran, M., 803, *813*
Camerino, M., 685, 686, 690, *694*
Cameron, A., 186, *191*
Cameron, A. E., 219, *231*
Cameron, C., 397, *402*
Cameron, C. L., 390, 397, 398, *402*
Cameron, D. W., 825, *837*
Cameron, J., 245, *246*
Cameron, L., 201, 202, *206*
Cameron, L. C., 22, 26, 27, 28, 30, 31, 32, 33, 34, *42*
Cameron, L. D., 19, 22, 23, 28, 38, *41*, *44*
Cameron, O., 330, *332*
Cameron, P., 371, *380*
Cameron, R. P., 498, *512*
Camici, P. G., 669, 676, *681*

Camilleri, D., 865, 868, 869, *888*
Camino, L. A., 876, *888*, *892*
Camli, O., 369, *385*
Camoriano, J. K., 717, *722*
Camp, D. E., 523, *533*
Campagna, P. D., 637, *655*
Campbell, B. K., 787, *795*
Campbell, D., 822, *835*
Campbell, D. T., 52, *56*, 143, *164*
Campbell, G. R., 877, *888*
Campbell, J., 367, 370, *383*, *385*, 549, *555*
Campbell, J. C., 542, 543, 544, *555*
Campbell, M. K., 522, *533*
Campbell, R. T., 480, 481, *491*
Campbell, S., 672, 677, *679*, *681*
Campbell, S. M., 251, 256, *260*, 263, *277*, 520, *536*, 562, *569*
Campbell, T., 150, *169*
Campbell, W. P., 576, *579*
Campbell, W. S., 289, *315*
Campfield, L. A., 266, *276*
Campini, R., 671, *680*
Campion, S. L., 285, *315*
Canadian Centre for Justice Statistics, 544, *555*
Canadian Standardized Test of Fitness, 642, *651*
Canchola, J., 777, 782, 792
Candib, L., 551, *555*
Cane, D. G., 152, *165*
Cannon, R. O., III., 675, *679*
Cannon, W. B., 67, 75, *79*, 87, 88, *93*, 139, *163*, 321, 322, 326, *332*
Cantor, A., 703, *708*
Cantor, J. R., 641, *651*
Cantor, M. H., 507, *512*
Cantor, N., 76, *79*, 140, 141, 142, 144, 159, *163*
Cantrell, R., 373, *380*
Cao, H. B., 270, *277*
Capell, F., 783, *796*
Capellan, J. M. B., 828, *837*
Caplan, B., 584, *589*
Caplan, G., 340, *346*, 632, *651*
Caplan, L. S., 530, *533*, *536*, 734, *741*
Caplan, M., *162*, *163*
Caplan, R., 304, 305, *310*
Caplan, R. D., 719, *725*, 750, *756*
Capone, M. A., 715, *722*
Capone, R. J., 153, 154, *162*, *165*
Cappell, H., 302, 303, *308*
Capps, L., 802, 811, *813*
Capuccio, F. P., 699, *708*
Caraco, Y., 810, *813*
Caralis, P., 688, *694*
Carballo-Dieguez, A., *832*, 850, *853*
Carboni, G. P., 676, *679*
Cardinali, D. P. 328, *333*
Cardiovascular Disease Plan Steering Committee, 600, *607*
Cardon, P. V., 703, *708*
Carey, K. B., 301, 302, *308*, *313*
Carey, M. P., 177, *191*, 759, 761, 764, 772, *774*, 830, *835*
Cargill, V., 830, *838*
Carl, F., 528, *535*
Carlaw, R., 528, *536*, 593, 601, 604, *607*, *609*
Carlestam, G., 371, 373, *380*
Carleton, R., 528, *533*
Carleton, R. A., 183, *192*, 593, 595, 596, 601, 604, *607*, *609*
Carli, T., 759, *775*
Carlos, M. L., 506, *514*
Carlson, D., 869, *890*
Carlson, K. J., 407, *411*, 497, *512*
Carlson, R., 179, *190*
Carlson, S., 152, 158, *171*
Carlson, S. L., 684, *694*
Carmargo, C. A., Jr., 287, *308*
Carmel, S., 177, *190*, 736, *741*
Carmelli, D., 66, *79*, 158, 159, *172*
Carmody, T. P., 252, *258*, 573, *577*
Carmona, A., 88, *94*
Carnahan, S., 367, *385*
Carney, K., 576, *580*
Carney, R. M., 38, *42*, 64, 67, 74, *79*, *80*, 153, 154, 155, *163*, 663, *666*, 677, *680*
Carney, S., 699, *707*
Carnicke, C. L., 715, *723*
Carnickle, C. L. M., 388, *400*
Carol, M. P., 704, *706*
Carp, C., 371, *380*
Carpeggiani, C., 675, *681*
Carpenter, C., 826, *833*
Carpenter, C. B., 108, *114*
Carpenter, C. C. J., 846, 847, 848, *851*
Carpenter, J. K., 753, *755*
Carpenter, P. J., 452, *456*
Carr, C. R., 716, *723*
Carr, D. B., 645, *651*
Carr, J. E., 759, 760, *776*
Carr, K., 296, *315*
Carr, S., 28, *44*
Carr, T., 367, *384*
Carr, T. S., 370, *380*
Carrere, S., 367, 368, 378, *381*
Carrieri, V. L., 506, *516*
Carrington, M., 805, 806, 807, *813*, *815*
Carroll, D., 398, *399*, 433, *438*
Carroll, E. M., 325, *333*
Carroll, K., 523, *538*
Carroll, R. G., 434, *439*
Carruthers, M., 671, *682*
Carson, R. C., 140, *163*
Carson, S., 777, *797*
Carstensen, L. L., 38, *42*
Carter, B. D., 453, *456*
Carter, N. L., 371, 372, *380*
Carter, R., 527, *536*
Cartwright, L., 372, *380*
Cartwright, L. K., 66, *79*
Cartwright, S., 355, *360*
Caruso, L., 759, 761, *775*
Carver, C., 156, *172*
Carver, C. S., 20, 21, 22, 31, 40, *42*, 61, 64. 67. 69, 70, 71, 76, 77, *79*, *82*, 142, 153, 154, 155, 156, *163*, *170*, 179, 181, 184, *190*, *192*, *193*, 340, 343, *347*, 356, *362*, 391, 395, 397, *399*, *402*, 433, 435, *438*, 504, 505, *512*, 585, *590*, 715, *722*, *724*, 751, 752, *754*
Cascio, W. F., 352, 353, *360*
Cascione, R., 389, 397, 398, *399*
Casey, K. L., 127, 131, *133*, *135*
Casey, P. H., 369, 378, *380*
Casey, R., 718, *724*
Cash, T. F., 28, *45*
Cashman, P. M., 676, *679*
Casper, L. M., 506, *512*
Caspersen, C., 629, *652*
Caspersen, C. J., 525, 526, *533*, *537*, 604, *607*, 628, 629, 630, 646, *651*, *654*, *655*
Caspi, A., 142, 151, 160, *163*, 300, 301, *308*
Cassel, C. K., 531, *533*
Cassel, J., 368, *380*, 500, 505, 509, *516*, 699, 702, *706*
Cassem, N. H., 22, *43*
Cassidy, D., 595, 597, *608*
Cassidy, J. T., 584, *589*
Cassileth, B. R., 156, *163*, 218, *229*, 389, 398, *399*, 720, *722*, 747, 751, *754*
CAST Investigators, 395, *402*
Castano, R. R., 821, *836*
Castell, P. J., 677, *680*
Castelli, W. P., 153, *165*, 265, *276*
Castellon, C., 180, *192*
Castillo, S., 146, *168*, 291, 293, *318*, 663, *668*
Castle, S., 481, *490*
Castro, F. G., 521, *532*, 734, *743*, 855, 856, 857, 858, *888*
Castro, K., 821, 828, *832*, *838*
Castro, K. G., 828, *833*
Castro, L., 330, *337*
Castro, O., 804, *812*, *814*
Castro, W. L., *331*, *337*
Catalano, R., 591, 593, *607*, *609*
Catalano, R. F., 285, 301, 304, *308*, *311*, 327, *332*
Cataldo, M. F., 452, 454, *456*
Catan, V., 818, 820, 821, *835*, 850, *853*
Catania, J., 778, 779, 794, *798*, 822, 826, *833*, *839*
Catania, J. A., 777, 778, 779, 780, 782, 783, 784, 785, 787, 789, 790, 792, 793, *795*, *796*, *798*, *799*, 831, *833*
Catanzaro, A., 863, *888*
Cates, D. S., 152, 158, 159, *166*
Cates, W., 818, *838*
Cates, W., Jr., 825, *833*
Cates, W. J., 565, *569*
Cathey, M., 473, *476*
Catlett, A. T., 499, *518*
Catley, D., *411*, *413*
Catron, B., 720, *724*
Cattanach, L., 671, *681*
Cauce, A. M., 506, *512*, 857, *889*
Cauley, J. A., 527, *536*
Causey, D., 221, *230*
Cavatorta, A., 373, *380*
Caveny, J. L., 520, *538*
Cayton, T., 149, *162*
CDC AIDS Community Demonstration Projects Research Group, *16*
Cecchi, A., 672, *679*
Celano, M., 451, *456*
Celantano, D., 818, 822, 823, 825, *836*, *838*
Celentano D. D., 117, *136*, 224, *233*, 506, *518*
Cella, D., 732, 735, *741*, *745*
Cella, D. F., 22, *42*, 388, *401*, 718, 720, *722*, *724*, 762, *774*
Center on Addiction and Substance Abuse at Columbia University, 291, *308*
Centers for Disease Control, 778, 779, 787, *796*, 862, 869, *888*
Centers for Disease Control and Prevention, 428, *438*, 526, 527, *533*, 566, *569*, 614, *623*, 627, 646, *651*, 817, 820, 824, 825, 826, 827, 830, *833*, 846, 850, *851*
Ceradini, D., 805, 806, *813*, *814*
Cerna, M., 802, *813*
Cerny, J. A., 758, *774*
Cerreta, C., 826, *834*
Cervone, D., 59, *79*
Cesana, G. C., 373, *380*
Chaffin, M., 292, *312*
Chaikelson, J. S., 289, *307*
Chaiken, S., 65, *83*, *740*, *744*
Chaisson, R., 823, *833*
Chaisson, R. E., 808, *813*, 826, *833*, 849, *852*
Chait, A., 272, *277*
Chaitman, B., 329, *334*, 629, *652*
Chaitman, B. R., 677, *681*
Chakraborty, R., 266, *278*, 806, 807, *815*
Chaliki, H., 27, *42*
Challenor, V. F., 810, *812*
Chalmers, B., 497, *512*

Chalmers, I., 508, *513*
Chalmers, T. C., *706*
Chamberlain, K., 177, 180, *190*
Chamberlain, W. A., 753, *756*
Chamberland, M. E., 828, *833*
Chamberlin, R., 508, *516*
Chambers, H., 719, *723*
Chambers, L., 65, *81*, 150, *168*
Chambless, D. L., *162*, *163*, 633, *652*
Champion, D., 196, *207*
Champion, J. D., 830, *838*
Champion, V., 531, *533*
Champion, V. L., 530, *533*, 729, 734, 737, *741*
Champoux, M., 664, *667*
Chan, C. W., 866, *888*
Chan, K. K., 219, *232*, 717, *724*
Chan, L. S., 575, *579*
Chan, R. W., 567, *569*
Chandra, A., 559, 560, *569*
Chandra, V., 217, *229*
Chaney, J. M., 327, *335*, 584, *589*
Chang, B., 865, *888*
Chang, G., 299, *306*, *314*
Chang, J., 805, *813*
Chang, J. K., 866, *888*
Chang, L. C., 563, *570*
Chang, P., 373, *385*
Chang, P. P., 154, *165*
Chang, Q., 329, 330, *335*
Chang, W. H., 810, *813*
Chao, S. Y., 675, *680*
Chape, C., 433, *438*
Chapelsky, D., 522, *535*
Chapko, M. K., 719, *725*
Chapman, H. A., 498, 510, *512*
Chapman, N. H., 806, 807, *814*
Chapman, N. J., 482, *491*
Chapman, R., 158, *167*
Chapman, S., 596, 600, *607*
Chaput, F., *455*, *456*
Charatz-Litt, C., 873, *888*
Charbonneau, T. T., 827, *839*
Charles, G., 867, 868, *889*
Charles, M. A., 270, *278*
Charleton, M., 375, *384*
Charlop, M. H., 452, *456*
Charlson, M. E., 407, *412*
Charney, D., 255, *260*
Chase, G. A., 463, *468*
Chasis, H., 703, *706*
Chassin, L., 197, *206*, 222, *229*, 297, 300, 301, 304, 305, *307*, *308*, 209, *313*, *314*, *315*, 462, *467*
Chastain, R., 344, *347*
Chastain, R. L., 124, *135*
Chaudhary, B. S., 217, *233*
Chaudry, N., 442, *446*
Chauhan, P., 531, *536*
Chaves, J. F., 125, *136*
Chavez, A., 226, *230*
Chavira, J. A., 860, 861, 862, *894*
Chavis, D., 596, 603, 604, 605, *608*, *610*, *611*, 619, 620, 621, 622, *623*, *624*, *625*
Chavis, D. M., 596, *607*
Chawla, S., 226, *230*, 435, *438*
Cheadle, A., 598, *608*
Cheang, M., 825, *837*
Chearskul, S., 827, *838*
Cheatham, W., 804, *814*
Checkoway, B., 597, *612*, *623*, *624*
Chedzko-Zajko, W. J., 644, *656*
Chee, E., 758, 760, *776*
Chee, M., 72, *81*
Chefer, S. I., 91, *93*
Cheingson-Popov, R., 808, *814*
Chelton, S., 675, *681*
Chen, D. R., 823, *834*
Chen, E., 531, *532*, *536*, 765, 767, *774*
Chen, J., 662, *667*, 821, *836*, 849, *853*
Chen, P. Y., 354, *360*
Chen, T. Y., 810, *813*
Chen, W., 846, *852*
Chen, W. H., 805, *813*
Chen, X., 486, 487, 488, *492*
Chen, Y., 802, 803, *815*
Cheng, K., 817, *838*
Chenoweth, J., 527, *536*
Chenowith, R. L., 302, *307*
Cheon-Klessig, Y., 865, 868, 869, *888*
Cherek, D. R., 374, *380*
Chermack, S. T., 290, *317*
Chernigovsky, V. N., 87, 89, *93*
Cherniss, C., 416, 421, 424
Cherpitel, C. J., 290, 304, *308*
Chertok, E., 784, *796*
Chesebro, J. H., 630, *653*, 674, 675, *680*
Chesher, G., 289, *312*
Chesney, A. P., 432, 435, *438*
Chesney, M., 144, 150, *167*, *168*, *170*, 328, *332*, 396, 398, *400*, 670, 671, *680*, 690, *692*, 821, 824, *832*, *834*
Chesney, M. A., 149, 152, 158, 159, *166*, 389, *399*, 519, 520, *533*, 662, 663, 664, *666*, *667*, *668*, 705, *706*, 782, *797*, 827, *836*, 846, 848, 850, *852*
Chester, R., 553, *555*
Chester, T. J., 366, *382*
Chesterman, B., 328, *332*, 690, *692*
Chestnut, D. E., 421, 426
Chettur, V., 144, *168*
Cheung, D. G., 643, *657*
Cheung, P., 177, *190*
Cheung, R., 575, *577*
Chevalley, C., 572, *580*
Chiang, H., 373, *385*
Chiasson, M., 828, *832*
Chiasson, M. A., 826, *839*
Chicz-DeMet, A., 502, 503, *518*
Chierchia, S., 669, 676, *679*
Chilman, C. S., 506, *512*
Chin, R., 591, *607*
Chin, S., 847, *851*
Chinayon, P., 827, *838*
Ching, P. I. Y. H., 268, *276*
Chinman, M., 603, 604, 605, *607*, *609*, 619, 620, *623*
Chiodi, A., 502, *513*
Chiodo, G., 549, 550, 552, *557*
Chipperfield, B., 297, *317*
Chir, B., 374, *382*, 525, *537*
Chiriboga, D. A., 151, *169*
Chitwood, D. D., 831, *833*
Chiu, D., 286, *310*
Chiu, H. C., 805, *813*
Chlebowski, R. T., 717, *722*
Cho, N. H., 270, *278*
Chodakewitz, J. A., 846, *852*
Chodakowska, J., 644, *651*
Choe, S., 805, 806, *814*
Choe, Y. T., 867, *888*
Choi, K., 777, 782, 783, 792, *796*
Choi, K.–H., 792, *796*
Choney, S. B., 877, *891*
Chotpitayasunondh, T., 827, *838*
Chou, C. P., 357, 358, *360*
Chou, P., 282, *310*
Chou, S. P., 286, 288, *308*, *310*
Chrestman, K., 553, *555*
Chrisman, N. J., 19, *42*, 591, *609*
Chrismon, J. H., 523, *535*
Christakis, D., 718, *724*
Christensen, A., 152, *171*, 343, *346*, 562, *570*
Christensen, A. J., 55, *56*, 150, *163*, 220, 221, *229*
Christensen, M. F., 122, *134*
Christenson, G. M., 628, *651*
Christian, J., 368, *380*, 802, 804, *813*
Christian, J. C., 436, *438*
Christiansen, B. A., 301, 302, *308*, *310*, *317*
Christiansen, C., 471, *474*
Christodoulou, G. N., 575, *579*
Chrousos, G. P., 502, *512*, 690, *692*
Chrvala, C., 734, *743*
Chu, J., 523, *538*
Chu, S., 822, 828, *833*, *835*
Chu, S. Y., 793, *796*, 826, 828, *833*, *838*
Chuachoowong, R., 827, *838*
Chumlea, W., 374, *384*
Chung, J., 823, *833*
Churchman, A., 614, *623*
Chwalbinska-Moneta, J., 644, *651*
Ciarnello, R., 297, *314*
Cibils, L. A., 225, *234*
Cicchetti, D., 442, *447*
Ciccione, D. S., 126, *134*
Ciccone, E., 328, *335*
Cigala, F., 373, *380*
Cimprich, B., 717, *725*
Cioffi, D., 23, *42*, 124, 129, *134*, 146, 154, *163*
Ciotti, P., 566, *570*
Ciraru-Vigneron, N., 824, *833*
Clancy, R. L., 109, *114*
Clancy, S., 125, 130, *136*
Clapp-Channing, N. E., 662, *667*
Clark, C. L., 282, *308*
Clark, D., 417, 419, 425
Clark, D. A., 388, *399*
Clark, D. C., 575, *578*, *579*
Clark, D. G., 629, 645, *651*
Clark, D. M., 33, *42*
Clark, H., 155, *170*, 179, 184, *192*
Clark, J., 808, *814*, *815*
Clark, K., 74, *79*, 663, *666*
Clark, K. C., 64, *79*, 156, *163*, 395, 397, *399*, 715, *722*, 751, 752, *754*
Clark, L., 340, *346*
Clark, L. A., 75, *84*, 152, 153, 155, *164*, *172*, 283, *308*, 354, 355, 356, *363*
Clark, M., 202, *206*, 857, 858, 859, 860, 861, *889*
Clark, M. A., 734, *744*
Clark, M. S., 25, *42*, 145, *163*, 210, *229*
Clark, N., 19, *42*
Clark, N. M., 388, *399*
Clark, R., 431, 432, *437*, *439*
Clark, S., 272, *277*
Clark, S. D., 825, *833*
Clark, S. L., 484, 487, 488, *490*
Clark, V. A., 632, *652*
Clark, W. B., 282, *314*
Clark, W. C., 645, *653*
Clarke, J., 847, *853*
Clarke, P. B. S., 250, *258*
Clarke, R., 750, *755*
Clarke, V. A., 733, 734, 736, *741*, *745*
Clarkson, R. B., 62, *82*
Clarkson, T. B., 641, *654*
Classen, C., 340, *346*
Classification of American Indian race on birth and death certificates—California and Montana, 429, *438*
Clay, D. L., 584, *589*
Clayton, D. G., 629, 647, *654*
Claytor, R., 643, *652*
Claytor, R. P., 639, 641, 642, 644, *651*

Cleary, P. D., *205*, *207*, 393, *399*, 850, *851*
Cleary, S. D., 211, 212, 213, 222, *234*, 305, *318*
Clegg, C. W., 358, *363*
Clegg, J. B., 806, 807, *814*
Cleghorn, F., 10, *16*
Clements, K. M., 635, 637, *656*
Clements, P. J., *56*, *58*
Clemetson, D. B. A., 828, *833*
Clemmey, P. A., 38, *42*
Cleroux, J. F., 642, *651*
Cleven, K., 398, *401*
Clevidence, B. A., 289, *315*
Clifford, C., 272, *276*, 470, 472, *475*
Clifford, E., 506, *512*
Cline, R. W., 788, 789, *796*
Clipp, E. C., 479, 480, 481, 482, *493*
Cliver, S. P., 499, 501, *514*
Clonger, C. R., 296, *315*
Cloninger, C. R., 285, 295, 296, 299, 300, 301, *308*, *313*
Close, N., 429, *438*
Clover, R. D., 684, *692*
Clow, A., 685, *692*
Coakley, E. H., 523, 524, *535*
Coates, R., 822, *832*
Coates, R. J., 270, *278*, 521, *537*, 869, *893*
Coates, T., 293, *317*, 398, *400*, 872, *892*
Coates, T. J., 396, *400*, 462, *467*, 507, *514*, 688, *692*, 777, 779, 782, 783, 784, 785, 787, 789, 792, 793, *795*, *796*, 831, *833*, 846, *852*
Coatsworth, J. D., 326, *336*
Coatu, S., 371, *380*
Cobb, J., 22, *43*
Cobb, S., 226, *231*
Cobb, S. C., 758, *774*
Coben, J. H., 544, *555*
Coble, H. M., 210, *229*
Coburn, M., 849, *853*
Coburn, P. C., 705, *707*
Coccaro, E. F., 151, *164*
Cochi, S., 614, *625*
Cochran, S., 820, 822, *836*, 870, *892*
Cochran, S. D., 787, 788, 789, *796*, *798*, 801, 811, *813*, *814*
Cockburn, J., 183, *190*, 530, *533*, 732, 736, 739, *741*, *742*
Coconie, C. C., 631, *651*
Codega, S., 676, *680*
Cody, R., 736, *741*
Coe, C. L., 76, *83*
Coen, K. M., 250, *258*
Coffey, C. E., 471, *474*
Cogan, R., 509, *514*
Coggins, C., 829, *834*
Coghlan, C., 671, 672, *679*
Coghlan, J. P., 434, *440*
Cohan, C. L., 154, *164*
Cohen, A., 371, *380*
Cohen, C., 366, *385*
Cohen, D., 764, *776*
Cohen, E. L., 699, *707*
Cohen, F., 139, 142, 143, 144, 145, 146, *164*, *172*, 176, *190*, 328, *332*, 690, *692*
Cohen, G., 408, 409, 410, *412*
Cohen, H. J., 531, *533*
Cohen, J., 143, *164*, 212, *229*, 285, *308*
Cohen, J. B., 296, *308*
Cohen, J. D., 329, *334*, 671, 672, *679*, *680*
Cohen, J. S., 828, *839*
Cohen, L., 50, *56*, 68, *78*, 324, 327, 328, *332*, *336*, 688, *692*, *695*
Cohen, L. H., 183, *192*
Cohen, L. J., 397, *402*, 504, *517*, 505, *516*
Cohen, L. R., 183, *190*
Cohen, M. J., 297, *316*
Cohen, M. S., 818, *838*, 850, *853*
Cohen, N., 105, 108, 109, 111, *113*, *114*, 522, *538*
Cohen, O., 806, *816*
Cohen, P., 212, 222, *229*, 285, *308*, 847, *851*
Cohen, P. T., 808, *813*
Cohen, R., 216, *233*, 286, *312*, 823, *838*
Cohen, R. D., 55, *57*, 156, *165*, 215, *231*, 632, *651*
Cohen, S., 28, 33, 34, *42*, 60, 67, 74, 77, *79*, *80*, 140, 143, 144, 152, 154, 160, *164*, *166*, 188, *192*, 209, 210, 211, 217, 218, 219, 223, 226, *229*, *230*, *231*, *232*, 321, 322, 324, 326, 327, 328, *332*, *333*, *335*, 340, *346*, 354, 355, 356, *360*, 366, 370, 373, 374, 375, 378, *380*, *381*, 393, 394, *399*, *400*, 453, *457*, 478, 479, 485, *490*, 500, 502, 505, 507, *512*, *514*, 524, *533*, 638, *651*, 663, *667*, 683, 684, 685, 687, 688, 689, 690, *691*, *692*, *693*, *694*, 709, 713, *721*, *723*, 752, 753, *754*, *755*, 773, *776*, 821, 823, *832*, *833*
Cohen, S. E., 773, *775*
Cohen, S. J., 436, *439*
Cohler, B. J., 187, *190*
Cohn, B. A., 471, *474*
Cohn, S. E., 829, *833*
Coie, J., 445, *447*
Coker, A. L., 520, *533*
Col, N. F., 472, *474*
Colapinto, N. D., 714, *725*
Colcher, I. S., 576, *577*
Colder, C. R., 300, *308*
Colder, M., 342, 343, *347*
Colditz, G. A., 153, *167*, 265, 268, *276*, *277*, *279*, 286, 287, 290, *310*, *311*, *318*, 471, 472, *474*, *475*, 520, 523, 524, *535*, *539*, 629, *651*
Coldman, A. J., 218, *231*, 329, *333*, 751, 752, *755*
Cole, C., 441, 445, *447*
Cole, M. G., 575, *577*
Cole, P. V., 250, *260*
Cole, R., 508, *516*
Cole, S. R., 734, *741*
Cole, S. W., 157, *164*, 344, *346*, 393, *399*
Colegrove, R. J., 771, 773, *776*
Coleman, D. H., 292, *308*
Coleman, E. A., 530, *533*
Coleman, E. R., 677, *680*
Coleman, J. S., 442, *447*
Coleman, R. E., 329, *334*, 640, *651*, 664, 665, *666*, 671, 674, 675, *679*
Colfax, G., 848, *852*
Colizzi, V., 803, *813*
Colker, L., 858, 865, *894*
Coll, A. M., 829, *835*
Collado, S., 432, 435, *440*
Collector, M. I., 748, *756*
Collette, J., 366, 368, *380*, *385*
Collette, L., 824, *834*
Collie, J., 119, *134*
Colligan, D., 176, *191*, 340, *347*
Colligan, M., 201, *206*
Collins, A., 564, *569*
Collins, A. C., 251, 256, *258*, *260*
Collins, B. A., 499, 501, *513*
Collins, B. E., 51, 52, *56*, *57*
Collins, C., 72, *80*, 397, *402*, 822, *839*
Collins, F., 256, *259*
Collins, G., 266, *276*
Collins, J., 825, *835*
Collins, J. J., 292, 294, *308*, *309*
Collins, J. J., Jr, 292, *310*
Collins, J. W., 499, *511*, *513*
Collins, J. W., Jr., 496, *512*
Collins, K. S., 530, *533*
Collins, L. M., 461, *466*
Collins, N., 496, 498, 500, 506, 507, 510, *514*, *516*, *518*
Collins, N. L., 224, *230*, 496, 506, 507, *513*
Collins, P., 64, *79*
Collins, R., 432, *440*
Collins, R. L., 196, 204, *206*
Colson, A. B., 858, 859
Colt, E. W. D., 645, *653*
Colten, M. E., 223, *233*
Coluzzi, P. H., 758, *774*
Colvin, C. R., 140, *165*
Colvin, D., 74, *82*
Comacho, T., 825, *833*, *834*
Combadiere, C., 806, *816*
Combe, C., 522, *538*
Combs, B., 739, *743*
Combs, C., 24, *45*
Comby, D. S., 855, *888*
Commission for Racial Justice, 855, *889*
COMMIT Research Group, 525, *533*, 600, *608*
Compas, B. E., 397, *400*, 504, *513*
Compton, W. M., 283, *309*
Conaway, M., 732, 733, 734, *743*
Conaway, M. R., 530, *536*
Condib, D., 92, *93*
Condiotte, M. M., 53, *56*
Coniaux-Leclerc, J., 828, *839*
Conill, A. M., 272, *276*
Conley, J., 497, 506, 507, *514*
Conneally, P. M., 296, *315*
Connelly, C. E., 575, *577*
Connelly, R. R., 720, *722*
Conner, M., 729, *741*
Connett, J., 526, *536*, 629, 647, *654*
Connett, J. E., 523, *537*
Connolly, J. F., 343, *347*
Connolly, K. J., 561, 562, *569*
Connor, E. M., 824, 827, *833*
Connor, J., 397, *400*
Connors, G. J., 301, *309*
Conrad, D. W., 371, *380*
Conroy, R. M., 74, *80*
Consortium, N. A., 828, *834*
Conte, P. F., 717, *724*
Conti, R., 677, *681*
Contrada, R. J., 62, 64, 65, 66, 68, 69, 71, 72, 73, 75, *79*, *82*, *84*, 139, 142, 144, 145, 146, 149, 150, 151, 157, 158, *164*, *166*, *169*, 179, 187, *190*, 675, *681*
Converse, S. A., 26, *41*
Conway, B., 848, *853*
Conway, M., 407, *412*
Conway, T. L., 326, *332*
Conwell, I. M., 502, 503, *514*
Cook, A., 388, *399*
Cook, E. F., 471, *475*
Cook, E. T., *162*, *166*
Cook, J. A., 720, *722*
Cook, N. R., 286, 294, *307*
Cook, P. J., 291, *309*
Cook, R., 565, *569*
Cook, T. D., 143, *164*
Cook, T. G., 301, *307*
Cook, W., 73, *79*, 149, 157, *164*
Cooke, I. D., 561, 562, *569*
Cooke, M., 824, 827, *834*, *836*
Cooke, M. A., 873, 874, *889*
Cool, V. A., 454, *456*
Coombes, C., 715, *724*
Coombs, R. W., 811, *813*, 827, *838*
Cooney, N. L, 285, *313*
Coons, H., 22, 29, 34, 38, *44*
Cooper, C., 326, 327, *332*, 720, *722*

Cooper, C. L., 350, 351, 355, 356, 357, 359, *360*, 747, 749, 750, 752, *754*, 855, *893*
Cooper, D., 574, *579*, 822, *835*, 848, *853*
Cooper, D. A., 850, *852*
Cooper, D. K., 823, *834*
Cooper, D. K. C., 576, *579*
Cooper, H., 629, 630, 647, *651*
Cooper, H. P., 735, *742*
Cooper, K. H., 145, *163*, 526, *533*
Cooper, M. L., 211, 223, *232*, 287, 301, 302, *309*, *316*, 358, *360*
Cooper, P., 736, *745*
Cooper, R., 747, 749, 750, *754*
Cooper, R. D., 749, 750, *754*
Cooper, R. S., 427, *439*
Cooper, T., 148, *164*
Cooper, T. B., 151, *164*
Cooper-Patrick, L., 154, *165*
Coovadia, H., 824, *837*
Copeland, L. J., 390, 398, *399*, 719, *722*
Copp, L. A., 120, *137*
Copper, R. L., 499, 501, *513*, *514*
Coppotelli, H., 223, *230*
Corbett, J., 595, 601, 603, *607*
Corbett, K., 869, *893*
Corbett, M., 432, *439*
Corbin, C. B., 628, *651*
Corcoran, J. R., 583, 584, *589*
Corder, L., 477, *491*
Cordes, C. L., 417, 418, 424
Cordilia, A., 294, *309*
Cordova, M. J., 388, *400*, 718, *723*
Corea, G., 828, *833*
Corey, C., 855, *888*
Coriell, M., 210, *229*
Corle, D. K., 732, *742*
Corman, M., 787, *795*
Corneil, D. W., 355, *360*
Cornell, C. E., 671, *681*, 719, *724*
Corning, A. F., 177, 185, *191*
Cornoni-Huntley, J., 286, *316*
Corona, D. F., 506, *515*
Coroni-Huntley, J. C., 436, *438*
Corrada, M., 472, *475*
Correa, A., 188, *192*
Correia, C. J., 302, *308*
Corrigall, W. A., 250, 252, *258*, *260*
Corrigan, M., 664, *667*
Corrigan, P. W., 419, 424
Corrigan, S. A., 526, 527, *534*, *535*, 782, 783, *798*
Corti, B., 521, 522, *534*
Corty, E., 197, *206*, 462, *467*
Coryell, W., 152, *166*, 285, *318*
Cose, E., 870, *889*
Cosier, R. A., 353, *361*
Cosmi. E. V., 502, *513*
Cosminsky, S., 858, *889*
Costa, F. V., 434, *437*
Costa, P., 66, 76, *82*, 152, *173*
Costa, P. T., 32, *42*, 61, 66, *78*, *82*, 140, 149, 154, *164*, *168*, *173*, 329, *337*, 394, 395, *400*, 469, *476*, 548, *557*, 733, *745*
Costa, P. T., Jr., 62, 64, 65, 66, *83*, 140, 142, 145, 147, 149, 153, 154, 158, 159, 160, *164*, *168*, *172*, 202, *206*, 354, *362*, 469, *476*
Costagliola, D., 824, *838*
Costanza, M. D., 739, *746*
Costello, C. G., 327, *332*, 561, *570*
Costello, E., 265, *279*
Costin, G., 805, *813*, *815*
Costlow, C., 690, *694*
Cotanch, P., 769, *774*
Cotanch, P. H., 72, *78*, 717, *722*
Cotrell, V., 484, *490*
Cotroneo, P., 499, 501, *513*
Cottington, E., 372, *385*
Cottington, E. M., 373, *380*
Cottler, L. B., 283, *309*, 663, *667*
Cotton, N. S., 295, *309*
Cotton, P., 552, *555*
Cottrell, N. B., 202, *206*
Couchman, G. M., 471, *474*
Couland, J. P. K., 828, *835*
Coulehan, J. L., 855, 877, *889*
Council on Ethical and Judicial Affairs, American Medical Association, 548, 552, *555*
Council on Scientific Affairs, 550, *555*
Council on Scientific Affairs, American Medical Association, *489*, *490*
Council, J. R., 124, *134*
Courneya, K., 527, *536*
Courtney, B. E., 753, *754*
Courtney, M. E., 713, *722*
Cousin, K., 686, *692*
Cousins, N., 218, *230*, 715, *723*, 752, *754*
Coussons, R. T., 574, *577*
Coussons-Read, M. E., 109, *114*
Coustan, D., 504, *518*
Coutinho, R., *511*, *513*
Coutsoudis, A., 824, *837*
Covey, L. S., 663, *667*
Covington, T. R., 574, *577*
Coward, R. T., 487, *491*
Cowen, E. L., 604, *608*
Cowley, A. W., 645, *652*
Cox, B. M., 250, *258*
Cox, C., 823, *838*
Cox, C. E., 752, *756*
Cox, D., 36, *41*, *43*, 326, 328, *336*, 473, *474*, 683, 684, *691*, *694*
Cox, D. J., 23, *43*, 123, *135*, 389, 398, *400*
Cox, D. R., 642, *651*
Cox, D. S., 687, 688, *691*, *695*
Cox, J. P., 641, *652*
Cox, R., 643, *652*
Cox, R. H., 639, 641, *651*
Cox, S., 503, *515*
Cox, V., 366, 367, *383*
Cox, V. C., 366, 367, 368, *380*, *384*
Cox, W. M., 301, 302, *309*
Coyle, J. T., 299, *317*
Coyle, N., *721*, *723*
Coyne, J., 145, *166*
Coyne, J. C., 67, 68, 69, 75, *79*, *81*, 152, 154, 156, *164*, 188, *190*, 394, 397, 398, *400*, 487, 488, *489*, *490*, 509, *513*
Coyne, L., 157, *164*
Crabb, D. W., 288, *309*
Crabbe, J. C., 296, 298, *309*, *313*
Crabtree, R. J., 719, *724*
Craib, K. J., 471, *475*
Craig, C. L., 632, 638, *656*
Craig, K., 129, 130, *136*
Craig, K. D., 122, *134*
Craig, K. J., 324, 325, 326, *332*, *333*
Craig, T. K. J., 329, *335*, 747, 749, *756*
Craighead, L. W., 635, *652*
Craigmyle, N., 90, *93*
Cramer, D., 523, *539*
Cramer, J. A., 573, 574, 575, *577*
Cramer, J. C., 506, 508, *513*
Crandall, C. S., 196, *206*
Crandon, A. J., 497, *513*
Crane, R. J., 66, 71, 73, *83*
Crano, W. D., 196, *206*
Cranston, B., 805, *815*
Crary, B., 689, *692*
Craske, M. G., 765, 767, *776*
Craven, D., 777, *797*
Craven, D. E., 811, *815*, 828, *839*, 849, *853*
Craven, J. L., 219, *231*
Crawford, C. A., 462, *467*
Crawford, D., 526, *533*
Crawford, D. W., 526, *535*
Crawford, J., 822, *835*
Crawford, J. M., 822, *835*
Crawford, M., 803, *812*
Crawford, M. D., 630, 646, *654*
Crawford, S., 684, *692*
Creamer, M., 325, *333*
Creamer, V. A., 297, *308*
Creasy, R. K., 503, *516*
Creighton, P. A., 531, *533*
Crenshaw, K., *554*, *555*
Crespin, H. A., 372, 373, *383*
Crestani, F., 112, *115*
Crews, R. C., 617, 618, *623*
Crews, T. M., 300, 301, *316*
Crick, N. R., 151, *164*
Crimmins, E. M., 477, *490*
Cripps, A. W., 109, *114*
Criqui, M. H., 63, *80*, 143, 153, 155, 156, 158, 159, 160, *165*, *168*, 395, *400*, 629, *652*
Crisson, J. E., 120, *134*, *135*
Cristinzio, C. S., 530, *537*
Cristinzio, S., 759, 761, *775*
Critchlow, B., 293, *309*
Crocker, M. F., 119, 124, 130, *134*
Crockett, S. J., 522, *533*
Croft, J. B., 435, *440*, 519, *536*
Crofton, C., 394, *402*
Cronkite, R., 217, *232*
Croog, S. H., 72, *81*
Crook, J., 123, *136*
Crooks, D., 327, *334*, 718, *723*
Crooks, V. C., 52, *57*
Crose, C., 296, *315*
Cross, D. G., 217, *230*
Cross, J., 432, 433, *437*
Cross, P. A., 389, 398, *399*, 720, *722*
Crouch, M., 24, 37, 38, *44*
Crow, R., 593, 601, 604, *609*
Crow, R. S., 604, *607*
Crowe, L. C., 293, *309*
Crowe, R. R., 296, *315*
Crown, J. P., 110, *114*
Crowne, D., 156, *164*, 719, *723*
Crowne, D. P., 73, *79*
Crowther, J. H., 498, *512*
Croyle, R. T., 19, 20, 22, 23, 26, 27, 30, 32, 33, *42*, *46*, 157, *163*, 202, *206*
Cruddas, M., 749, *754*
Cruise, C. E., *411*, *412*, 688, *695*
Cruise, L. J., 406, 410, *413*
Crum, C. P., 828, *837*
Crum, R. M., 283, 284, 285, 300, *312*
Crumble, D. A., 830, *838*
Crump, C. E., 528, *533*
Crumpacker, C. S., 811, *813*
Cruse, J. M., 803, *812*
Cruz, J. M., 717, *723*
Cruzen, D., 396, *403*
Csikszentmihalyi, M., 356, *360*, 410, *412*
Cubeddu, L. X., 810, *813*
Cuesdan, L., 371, *380*
Cueto, L. M., 862, *888*
Culver, C., 344, *347*
Cumming, R. G., 290, *309*
Cummings, C., 719, *725*, 758, 760, *776*

Cummings, E. M., 151, *164*
Cummings, F. J., 736, *742*
Cummings, J. L., 25, *42*
Cummings, M., 828, *832*
Cummings, M. A., 63, *80*
Cummings, N., 328, *336*, 374, *384*, 689, *694*, 753, *756*
Cummings, N. A., 665, *667*
Cummings, S., 872, *892*
Cummings, S. R., 408, *412*
Cummins, R. W., 109, *115*
Cunnick, J. E., 111, *114*, 685, *691*, *692*, *694*
Cunningham, M., 709, *723*
Cunningham, S. C., 782, 783, *798*
Cupach, W., 782, 787, *796*
Curb, J. D., 286, *316*
Curbow, B., 716, *722*, *725*
Curio, I., 371, 373, *382*
Curran, J. W., 793, *796*
Curran, P. J., 300, 301, 304, 305, *308*, *309*, *314*
Currie, D M., 581, *589*
Currie, D. J., 714, *725*
Currie, V. E., 110, *114*
Currier, J. S., 846, *852*
Currier, R. L., 857, 858, 859, 860, *889*
Curry, S., 521, 524, *533*, *538*, 598, *608*
Curry, S. J., 519, 522, 524, 525, 530, *533*, *534*, *536*, 729, 730, 737, *742*, *743*
Curti, R., 373, *380*
Curtis, A. B., 435, *440*
Curtis, G. C., 324, *335*
Curtis, G. G., 759, *775*
Cushing, C., 828, *834*
Cutchin, L. M., 663, *668*
Cuthbert, B., 31, *43*
Cuthbert, R. J., 803, *815*
Cutler, J. A., 429, *437*
Cutrona, C., 225, *230*
Cutrona, C. E., 211, 227, *229*, *230*, 328, *332*, 394, *400*, 507, 508, *513*, 687, *692*
Cutter, G., 523, 524, *538*, *539*
Cutter, G. R., 499, 501, *514*, 527, *536*, 869, *891*
Cutter, H. S. G., 301, *309*
Cu-Uvin, S., 826, *833*
Cyfieco, A., 373, *380*
Cygan, R., 543, 546, *555*
Cyr, H. N., 267, *275*
Cyranowski, J. C., 719, *722*
Cyr-Provost, M., 126, *134*
Czajka, J. A., 343, *346*
Czajkowski, S. M., 63, *79*, 393, *402*

D

D'Agostino, R. B., 266, *277*, 631, *652*
D'Andrade, R. G., 26, *42*
D'Angelo, T., 329, *334*
d'Avernas, J. R., 461, *465*, *466*
D'Costa, A., 66, *83*
D'Eon, J. L., 125, *136*
Dad, T. L., 753, *756*
Dadds, M. R., 217, 221, *230*, *232*, 391, *401*
D'Agostino, R., Jr., 734, *744*
Dahl, L. K., 434, *438*, 699, *706*
Dahl, N. H., 635, 640, *656*
Dahlquist, L. M., 765, 768, *774*
Dahlstrom, G., 61, 66, 75, 76, *78*
Dahlstrom, W. G., 149, 150, *162*, 662, 663, *666*
Daikoku, N., 499, *516*
Dakak, N., 675, *679*
Dakof, G. A., 196, 204, *206*, 218, *230*, 509, *513*
Daldrup, R., 119, *133*
Dalen, J. E., 153, *169*
Daley, S. E., 154, *164*
Daling, J., 523, *534*
Daling, J. R., 523, *538*
Daly, M. B., 732, *742*
Daly, M., 64, *83*, 394, *401*, 714, *724*, 729, 732, 733, 735, *743*, *745*, 749, *755*
Damarin, F., 125, *134*
Dame, A., 66, *79*
Damon, A., 699, *707*
Dan, C. M., 330, *334*
Dana, G. S., 525, *537*
Dang, V. V., 867, *895*
d'Angelo, T., 752, *755*
Daniel, S., 563, *569*
Daniels, G. E., 702, *707*
Daniels, M., 686, *693*
Danne, T., 330, *333*
Dannenberg, A. L., 632, *652*
Danoff-Burg, S., 390, 397, 398, *402*, 561, *570*, 733, *745*
Danovitch, G. M., 804, *814*
Dantzer, R., 112, *114*, *115*
D'Aquila, R. T., 811, *813*
Darby, P., 685, *692*
Dark, K. A., 109, *115*
Darke, L. L., 546, *556*
Darkes, J., 302, *306*, *309*, *310*
Darko, D. F., 684, *692*
Darley, J., 195, 196, *206*
Darley, J. M., 25, 29, *42*
Darne, B., 287, *312*
Darr, W. F., II., 808, *815*
Darrow, W. W., 780, *797*, *799*
Darvill, T. J., 733, *742*
Das, A., 499, 501, *513*
Das, I. P., 729, 735, *741*
Dash, J., 766, 769, *775*, *776*
Datillo, A. M., 527, *534*
Datillo, J., 527, *534*
D'Atri, D. A., 367, *380*
Datta, P., 824, *833*
Dattore, P. J., 157, *164*
Daubman, K. A., 486, *490*
Daum, C., 371, *382*
Davantes, B., 787, *797*, 830, *835*
Davenport, A., 291, 293, *318*
Davenport, Y. B., 575, *577*
Davey-Smith, G., 433, *438*
David, H., 505, 506, *512*
David, J. P., 150, *172*, 184, 187, *193*
David, R. J., 499, *511*, *513*
Davidson, E. A. F., 154, *172*
Davidson, K., *162*, *165*, 180, *190*, *666*, *667*
Davidson, L., 367, *381*
Davidson, L. M., 324, *332*, 434, 435, *438*
Davidson, R. J., 61, 69, 71, 73, 76, *79*, *84*, 157, 158, *163*, *168*
Davidson, S., 850, *853*, 862, *888*
Davidson-Katz, K., 585, *590*
Davies, A. B., 705, *706*
Davies, B., 327, *335*
Davies, D. L., 700, *707*
Davies, J., 502, *515*
Davies, P., 287, *313*
Davies, P. M., 789, *796*
Davies, P. T., 151, *164*
Davies, R. F., 677, *679*, *681*
Daviglus, M. L., 66, *78*
Davila, J., 154, *164*
Davis, A. A., 506, *513*
Davis, C. E., 576, *578*
Davis, C. L., *113*, *114*
Davis, D. D., *162*, *166*
Davis, D. J., 592, *608*
Davis, D. L., 876, *889*
Davis, D. R., 304, 305, *310*, 787, *797*, 830, *835*
Davis, E., 566, *569*
Davis, G. C., 283, *308*
Davis, G. T., 734, *745*
Davis, H., 431, 433, *438*, *440*
Davis, K., 74, *83*
Davis, L., 480, 481, *491*
Davis, M., 255, *258*, 822, 825, *835*, *838*
Davis, M. D., 146, *164*
Davis, M. R., 676, 677, *681*
Davis, M. W., 759, 760, *776*
Davis, N. A., 531, *534*
Davis, P. J., 151, *164*
Davis, R. M., 869, *889*
Davis, R. O., 499, 501, *514*
Davis, S. F., 824, 827, *833*, *836*
Davis-Hearn, M., 460, 464, *467*
Davison, G. C., 101, *102*
Davison, K., 340, *346*
Davison, K. P., 342, 343, *347*
Davison, R. J., 156, 157, *172*
Dawson, D. A., 282, 295, *309*, *310*, 528, 530, *534*
Dawson, E., 119, *135*
Dawson, L., 599, 603, 606, *608*, *611*
Day, K. D., 641, *651*
Day, P., 677, *681*
Day, R. D., 372, *385*
Dayton, G., 523, *534*
de Alba, G., 862, *888*
de Armellada, C., 858, 859, *889*
de Bruyn, M., 818, 819, 820, 821, 827, 830, *833*
de Castro, J. M., 521, *534*
De Clerq, A., 828, *839*
de Flores, T., 63, *80*
De Gent, G. E., 676, *682*
de Groot, M., 441, 445, *447*
De Jong, J., 74, *82*
De Kloet, E. R., 112, *115*
De la Cancela, V., 857, 862, *889*
de Monchaux, C., 322, *336*
de Moor, C., 464, *466*, 732, *745*
de Paredes, E. S., 749, 752, *754*
De Potter, B., 395, *400*
de Ridder, D. T. D., 390, 391, 394, 397, *401*, *402*
de Ruiter, A. J. H., 326, *332*
De Servi, S., 671, *682*
De Smet, M., 690, *692*
de Turk, P., 499, *513*
de Veber, L. L., 765, 767, *775*
de Vincenzi, I., 781, *796*
de Wit, H., 297, *309*
Deal, M., 328, *337*, 689, *695*, 753, *756*
Dean, C., 329, *333*, 751, 752, *754*
Dean, H. A., 548, *556*
Dean, L., 846, *852*
Dean, L. M., 367, 368, *380*, *381*
Dean, M., 806, 807, 810, *813*, *814*, *815*
Deanfield, J. E., 669, 671, 676, 677, *679*, *680*, *681*
Dearwater, S. R., 544, *555*
Deary, I. J., 152, *172*
Deasy-Spinetta, P., 772, *774*
Deaux, K., 785, *796*, 819, *838*
DeAvila, M. E., 181, *192*
DeBakey, S. F., 282, 286, *317*, *318*
DeBord, K. A., 291, *318*
DeBord, L., 675, *680*
DeBranski, C., 269, *278*
DeBro, S. C., 782, 783, *798*
Debusk, R., 527, *535*
DeBusk, R. F., 273, *277*, 576, *579*, *580*, 647, *652*

deChamplain, J., 642, *651*
DeChant, H. K., 548, *556*
DeClemente, R. J., 787, *796*
DeCuir-Whalley, S., 452, 454, *456*
Deedwania, P. C., 672, *680*
Deeg, D. H. J., 469, *474*
Deeks, S. G., 826, *833*, 846, 847, *851*, *852*
Deffenbacher, J. L., *162*, *164*
DeFrank, R. S., 501, *515*
DeFries, J. C., 296, *315*
DeFriese, G. H., 486, *491*
Defronzo, R. A., 254, *260*
DeGeest, S., 572, 575, 576, *577*
DeGenova, M. K., 63, 64, *79*
deGeus, E. J. C., 641, 642, *652*, *657*
DeGiovanni, J., 436, *440*
Degnan, D., 734, *742*
DeGood, D. E., 123, 129, *136*
DeGruy, F. C., 225, *229*
deGues, A., 576, *580*
Dehaene, P., 290, *317*
deHaes, J. C., 717, 719, *723*, *724*
Deickmeir, L., 646, *652*
Deis, A., 286, *310*
DeJoseph, J. F., 508, 509, *516*
DeJoy, D. M., 375, *385*
Dekirmenjian, H., 644, *652*
Dekker, G. A., 499, 505, *516*
Del Boca, F. K., 285, 302, *310*, *313*, 405, 410, *411*
Del Rey, A., 112, *113*
Delahanty, D. L., 325, 326, 327, 328, *332*, *333*, 689, *692*
DeLalla, F., 571, *577*
Delamater, A. M., 441, *446*, *447*
deLandsheere, C. M., 671, *680*
Delaney, R., 397, *401*
Delbanco, T. L., *706*
Delea, C. S., 699, *707*
DeLeo, J., 705, *708*
DeLeon-Jones, F., 644, *652*
Deliakis, J., 575, *578*
DeLisa, J. A., 581, 586, *589*, *590*
Dell, R., 825, *835*
Dellborg, M., 675, 676. *680*
Delmas, P. D., 471, *474*
DeLongis, A., 504, *513*
Deloria, V., Jr., 879, 880, *889*
Demark, W., 717, *723*
Demark-Wahnefried, W., 717, *723*
Demas, P., 327, *333*
Dembroski, T. M., 63, 66, 72, 73, 76, 77, *79*, *82*, 140, 149, *164*, *165*, *168*, 460, 461, *466*
Demeter, L. M., 846, *852*
Dempsey, S. J., 22, *42*
Deneau, G. A., 250, *258*
Denham, M. J., 575, *577*
Denicoff, K. D., *113*, *114*
Denious, J., 543, 553, *556*
Dennis, C., 150, *167*, 670, 671, *680*
Dennis, D. A., 301, *318*
Denollet, J., 153, *165*, 395, *400*
De-Nour, A. K., 325, 326, *332*, 717, 720, *722*
Dent, C. W., 461, *466*
Denton, D. A., 434, *440*, 698, *706*
Denyes, M. J., 444, *447*
DePalma, N., 297, *312*
Department of Health and Human Services, 592, 600, *608*
DePaulo, B. M., 214, 222, *234*, 486, 488, *490*
DePetrillo, D., 720, *725*
deProsse, C., 390, *399*, 711, 715, 719, 720, *722*
Depue, R. A., 64, *79*
Derby, C., 525, *539*
Deren, S., 828, *833*, *834*
DeRijk, R. H., 112, *115*
DeRisi, D. T., 370, *379*
Dermatis, H., 770, 772, *775*
Derogatis, L. R., 388, *400*, 548, *556*, 715, *723*, 751, *754*, 757, *774*
Des Jarlais, D., 823, *833*
Des Jarlais, D. C., 828, *834*
Desai, N., 91, *93*
DeSavino, P., 345, *346*
Deshmukh, A. A., 575, *577*
DeSouza, E. B, 502, *513*
Desplaces, A., 753, *755*
Despres, J., 265, *277*
Despres, J. P., 265, 266, *276*
Dessain, P., 677, *679*
Deszca, E., 419, 424
Detels, R., 803, 805, 806, *813*, *814*
Deter, H. C., 434, *438*
Detre, T., 148, *164*
Detzer, M. J., 785, *798*
Deuschle, K. W., 877, 878, 879, 880, *887*, *889*
Deuser, W. E., 180, *190*
Deutsch, M., 197, *206*, 622, *623*
Deveikas, A., 827, 824, *832*, *833*
DeVellis, B., 239, 243, *246*
DeVellis, B. M., 204, *205*, 389, 393, 397, *399*, *400*, 522, *532*, *533*, 731, 732, 733, *741*
DeVellis, R., 52, *58*, 181, *193*
DeVellis, R. F., 53, 55, *56*, 204, *205*, 236, 242, *246*, *247*, 521, 522, *533*, *535*
Devereux, R. B., 663, *667*
DeVincent, C., 504, 505, *515*
Devins, G. M., 220, *230*, 395, 398, *400*, *401*
DeVito, C. A., 290, *314*
Devlen, J., 719, *723*
Devlin, M., 266, *278*
DeVos, G., 864, *892*
deVreis, H. A., 639, 646, *652*
DeVries, M., 405, 406, 410, *413*
Devsa, S. S., 530, *534*
Dew, M. A., 850, *853*
Dewees-Dunk, R., 849, *853*
Dewey, J., 188, *190*
DeWhite, W., 531, *536*
Dhawan, R. V., 849, *853*
Di Chiara, G., 252, *258*
Di Clemente, R., 340, *348*
Di Padova, C., 288, *310*
Diall, A. A., 825, *839*
Diamant, J., 435, *438*
Diamond, E., 72, 73, *79*
Dias, L., 497, *513*
Diaz, T., 820, 826, *838*, 855, *889*
DiBona, G. F., 434, *439*
DiCara, L. V., 88, 89, *93*, *94*
Dicker, R. C., 546, *556*
Dickins, J., 575, *577*
Dickover, R., 827, *833*
Dickson, B. E., 523, *534*
Dickson, N., 300, 301, *308*
DiClemente, C., 522, *538*
DiClemente, C. C., 5, *17*, 20, *45*, 243, *246*, 461, *465*, 521, 522, *534*, 593, *608*, *610*, 729, 730, *744*
DiClemente, R. J., 787, 788, 789, *799*, 825, *833*, *834*, *838*
Diefenbach, M., 23, 26, 32, *42*
Diefenbach, M. A., 239, *246*
Diehl, A. M., 289, *314*
Diehl, M., 574, *579*
Diehr, P., 598, *608*
Dienel, D., 373, *382*
Diener, C., 356, *360*
Diener, E., 75, *79*, 356, *360*, *362*, 389, *400*, 406, *413*
Dieng-Sang, A., 825, *839*
Dienstbier, R., 376, *380*
Dienstfrey, H., 340, *346*
Dietrich, R. A., 300, *309*
Die-Trill, M., 770, 772, *775*
Dietz, A. T., 525, *537*
Dietz, V., 614, *625*
Dietz, W. H., 265, 268, 267, *275*, *276*
DiFranceisco, W., 305, *310*, *318*
Digenio, A. G., 73, *79*
Diglio, L., 850, *852*
Digman, J. M., 140, *165*
Dignan, M., 531, *534*
Dijkstra, I., 112, *114*
Dilger, I., 828, *839*
Dill, C. A., 462, *466*
Dill, L., 548, *556*
Dilley, J., 846, *852*
Dilley, J. W., 850, *852*
Dillon, B., 850, *852*
Dillon, K. M., 179, *190*
Dillon, M., 824, *832*
Dilworth-Anderson, P., 436, *437*
DiMartino, V., 326, 327, *334*
DiMatteo, M., 848, *852*
DiMatteo, M. R., 848, *852*
Dimeff, L. A., *306*, *313*
Dimitri, C., 718, *723*
Dimond, M., 34, *46*
Dimsdale, J. E., 65, *79*, 434, *438*, 690, *692*, *694*
Ding, Y., 705, *707*
Dinges, N. G., 877, 879, 880, *889*, *892*
Dini, E., 617, 618, *623*
DiNicola, D. D., 848, *852*
Dinoff, B., 397, *402*
Dinwiddie, S. H., 295, *311*
Diodati, J. G., 672, *681*
DiPaola, M., 119, *137*
DiPietro J., 503, *514*
DiPietro, J. A., 502, *513*
DiPietro, L., 454, *456*
DiPlacido, J., 188, *190*
Dishion, T. J., 222, *230*
Dishman, R. K., 525, 526, 527, 528, *534*, *535*, 632, 648, *652*
Dittman, E., 676, *682*
Ditto, P. H., 25, 29, *42*, 202, *206*
Divine, G., *474*, 830, *832*
Dixon, R. A., 442, *447*
Dixon, T., 148, *162*, *165*
Djang, W. T., 471, *474*
D'Lugoff, B. C., 92, *93*
Dobbin, J. P., 686, *692*
Dobbins, C., 49, 53, *58*, 182, *193*
Dobbins, C. J., 54, *57*, 219, *233*
Dobbs, S. M., 575, *577*
Dobkin, P., 759, 761, *775*
Dobson, A. J., 286, *313*
Dodd, M. J., 120, *137*
Dodge, K., 61, 66, 75, 76, *78*
Dodge, K. A., 149, 151, *162*, *164*, *168*
Dohan, P. H., 877, *888*
Doherty, W. J., 783, 784, *795*, *796*
Dohrenwend, B. S., 183, *190*
Dolan, N. C., 731, 732, *742*
Dolce, J. J., 124, 130, *134*, 524, *537*
Dolcini, M., 778, *798*, 822, *832*
Dolcini, M. M., 777, 779, 782, 783, 784, 785, 787, 789, 790, 792, 793, *795*, *796*
Dolecek, T. A. 576, *577*
Doleys, D. M., 119, 124, 130, *134*

Dolezal, C., 822, *832*
Dolgin, M., 771, 773, *776*
Dolgin, M. J., 770, 772, *774*, *775*, *776*
Dolgoy, L., 150, *169*
Dolhert, N., 289, 290, *318*
Dolinsky, Z. S., 285, *316*
Doll, L., 822, 823, *833*, *837*
Doll, L. A., 793, *796*
Doll, L. S., 327, *333*
Doll, R., 286, 288, *309*, *317*
Doll, S. R., 520, *534*
Dombrowski, M., 92, *93*
Dominguez, B., 343, *346*
Domino, J. V., 547, *555*
Dompeling, E., 575, *577*
Doms, R. W., 807, 810, *814*
Donaldson, G., 758, 760, *776*
Donaldson, G. W., 759, 760, *776*
Donegan, W. L., 717, *723*
Donfield, S., 806, *813*
Donnelly, D. A., 340, 343, *346*
Donnerberg, R., 688, *693*
Donny, E. C., 250, *258*
Donoghoe, M. C., 850, *853*
Donovan, D. M., 283, *313*
Donovan, J., 222, *230*
Donovan, M. I., 720, *722*, *724*
Dooley, B. B., 370, *380*
Dorfman, L., 596, 600, *611*
Dorgan, J. F., 631, *652*
Dorheim, T. H. R., 641, *652*
Dorian, B., 326, *333*, 685, *692*
Doriaswamy, P. S., 471, *474*
Dorkin, H., 665, *667*
Dorn, L. D., 502, *513*
Doroshow, J. H., 758, *774*
Dougall A. L., 324, 325, 326, 327, 328, *332*, *333*
Dougherty, J., 394, *401*
Dougherty, T. W., 417, 418, 424
Douglas, D. K., 808, *815*
Douglas, E. B., 146, *168*
Douglas, J. M., *16*
Douglas, R. B., 684, *693*
Dovellini, E., 672, *679*
Dovidio, J. F., 869, *889*
Dowdall, G. W., 289, 291, 293, *318*
Dowdy, A. A., 576, *577*
Dower, P., 591, 598, 600, *608*
Dowis, J., 868, 869, *893*
Dowling, H., 267, *277*
Downe-Wamboldt, B., 330, *335*
Downey, G., 69, *79*
Downey, J., 564, *569*
Downey, K., 301, *312*
Downham, M. A. P. S., 366, *384*
Downs, R., 471, *475*
Downs, W. R., 292, *314*
Dowsett, G., 822, *835*
Doyle, W. J., 28, 33, *42*, 60, *79*, 154, 160, *164*, 322, 326, 328, *332*, 683, 684, *692*
Doyne, E. J., 633, 635, 637, *652*
Dracup, K., 22, *42*, 154, *169*, 330, *335*
Dragon, E., 806, *813*
Dragonas, T., 506, *518*
Dransfield, K., 827, *837*
Draper, M., 471, *474*
Drapkin, R. G., *275*, *276*
Drescher, V. M., 88, 89, *94*
Dressler, W. W., 226, *230*, 433, 436, *438*
Dreuter, M., 601, *607*
Drewnowski, A., 267, *276*
Driver, J. L., 576, *579*
Drossman, D. A., 546, 547, *555*
Droste, C., 124, *134*, 676, *680*
Drotar, D., 449, *456*
Drucker, E., 821, 823, *836*, *837*
Druley, J., 822, 829, *835*
Druley, J. A., 395, *400*, 487, *491*
Drury, P. L., 645, *653*
Dryfoos, J., 463, *466*
Dubbert, P., 525, 526, 527, *534*, *536*
Dubbert, P. M., 526, 527, 528, *535*, *536*
Dube, M. F., 250, *258*
Dubin, N., 785, *797*
Dublin, S., 822, *834*
DuBois, D. L., 222, *230*
Dubois, P., 753, *755*
Dubow, E. F., 221, *230*
Dubrow, N., *455*, *456*
Ducette, J., 178, *191*
Duchene, A. G., 576, *577*
Duelberg, S., 526, *534*
Duerr, A., 828, *835*
Duffy, J., 269, *276*, 524, *535*
Duffy, M. E., 178, *192*
Dufour, M., 282, 285, *309*, *310*
Dufour, M. C., 282, 288, *310*, *314*, *318*
Dufton, B. D., 125, *134*
Dugan, B. B., 576, *580*
Dugan, J. W., 127, *135*
Duggan, A. K., 503, *512*
Dugoni, B. L., 143, 148, 158, *169*
DuHamel, K., 222, *234*
DuHamel, K. N., 771, 773, *774*, *776*
Duits, A. A., 393, *400*
Duivenvoorden, H. J., 389, 392, 395, 398, *401*, *403*, 687, *691*, *693*
Duliege, A. M., 824, *834*
Dumas, J. E., *162*, *163*
Dumont, K., 188, *192*
Dunbar, F., 92, *93*
Dunbar, H. F., 139, 152, 156
Dunbar, J., 572, 574, *577*
Dunbar-Jacob, J., 571, 572, 573, 574, 575, *577*, *578*, *580*, 848, 849, *852*
Dunbar-Jacob, J. M., 573, 574, *580*
Duncan, G. J., 442, *447*
Duncan, J. J., 647, *652*
Duncan, S. C., 304, 305, *309*
Duncan, T. E., 304, 305, *309*
Dundore, D., 121 *134*
Dungan, S., 453, *457*
Dunkel-Schetter, C., 63, 69, *79*, 218, 224, *230*, *232*, 389, 394, *400*, 486, *490*, 496, 498, 500, 501, 502, 503, 504, 505, 506, 507, 508, 510, *513*, *514*, *515*, *516*, *517*, *518*, 718, *723*, 823, *837*
Dunmeyer, S., 282, *315*
Dunn, A. L., 632, 649, *652*
Dunn, D. S., 584, 585, *589*
Dunn, J. A., 716, *725*
Dunn, N. J., 302, *309*
Dunne, M. P., 295, *311*
Dunning, E. J., 573, 574, *577*, *578*
Dunsmore, J., 120, *135*, 758, *775*
Dunston, G., 804, *812*, *814*
Dunston, G. M., 802, 804, *812*, *813*
Dupon, M., 575, *578*
DuPont, B., 802, *815*
Dupree, J. P., 820, *834*
Duquesnoy, R., 803, *814*
Dura, J. R., 227, *229*, *231*
Duran, R., 685, 686, *693*
DuRant, R. H., 592, *608*
Durbin, M., 825, *833*, *834*
Durel, L. A., 61, *81*, 146, 149, *167*, 433, 435, *438*
Durkin, T. M., *113*, *114*
Durran, J., 822, *833*
Durup, J., 417, 419, 425
Dusenbury, L., 525, *535*, 599, 600, *609*, 855, *889*
Dussault, G., 420, 424
Dussault, J., 266, *276*
Dustman, R., 637, *652*
Dutton, D. B., 23, *45*
Dutton, J. E., 352, *362*
Dvorak, R., 441, 445, *447*
Dweck, C. S., 444, *447*
Dworkin, B. R., 90, *93*, *94*
Dworkin, S. I., 90, *93*
Dwyer, J., 64, 74, *81*, 180, *191*
Dwyer, J. H., 461, *467*
Dwyer, K., 572, 573, 574, *577*, *578*
Dwyer, K. A., 159, *171*, 391, 394, *402*
Dwyer, K. M., 461, *466*
Dyck, D. G., 112, *114*
Dyer, A. R., 66, *78*, 287, *313*, *317*
Dyer, C., 685, 687, *693*
Dyer, C. S., 327, 328, *334*
Dyer, J., 850, *853*
Dyer, J. R., 576, *577*
Dyke, S., 270, *279*
Dykema, J., 180, *190*
Dykman, B. M., 180, *189*
Dykstra, L. A., 109, *114*
Dysart, J. M., 431, *438*
Dziokonski, W., 733, *742*

E

Eades, T., 810, *813*
Eaker, E., 153, 156, *162*, 662, *666*
Eaker, E. D., 153, *165*
Earles, A., 804, *815*
Earls, F., 442, 443, 445, *448*
Earls, F. J., 444, *448*
Early, J. L., 526, *533*
Earnest, A., 203, *206*
Earp, J., 153, *172*
Earp, J. A., 521, *535*
Earp, J. L., 528, *533*, 734, *742*
Easterling, D., 24, *45*
Easterling, D. V., 22, 25, 26, 27, 29, 31, 34, 38, *42*, *44*, *45*
Eastman, S., 805, *815*
Eaves, L. J., 295, *312*, 326, *334*
Ebanks, C. M., *455*, *456*
Ebbeling, C. B., 636, *651*
Ebbesen, P., 808, *815*
Ebert, M. H., 644, *650*, *652*
Ebisu, T., 647, *652*
Ebrahim, S., 526, 527, *534*
Eccles, J., 443, *447*
Eckenrode, J., 34, *42*, 508, *516*
Eckhardt, L., 464, *466*
Eckman, M. H., 472, *474*
Economic and Social Council, 542, *555*
Eddy, D. M., 530, *534*
Edelmann, R. J., 561, 562, *569*
Edelstein, M., 603, *610*
Edelstein, S., 629, *656*
Edelstein, S. L., 471, *474*
Edenberg, H. J., 296, *307*, *315*
Edgar, L., 715, 718, *723*
Edgar, T., 782, 783, 787, 788, *796*, *797*
Edgecomb, J. L., 153, *165*
Edgemon, I. P., 434, *439*
Edlin, B., 830, *832*
Edlin, B. R., *474*

Edmonds, D., 576, *578*
Edmonds, E. M., 739, *744*
Edmonds, L., 371, *381*
Edmundson, E., 460, 461, *466*
Edmunson, E. D., 704, *706*
Edwards, A., 828, *834*
Edwards, C., 196, *207*, 464, *466*
Edwards, D., 343, *346*
Edwards, D. L., 150, *163*
Edwards, E. A., 368, *381*
Edwards, J. N., 368, 369, *379*,*381*, 619, *623*
Edwards, J. R., 351, 354, 355, 356, *360*, 749, 752, *754*
Edwards, K., 340, *347*
Edwards, K. R., 498, *513*
Edwards, W., 739, *742*, *744*
Efird, C. M., 508, *514*
Egami, H., 289, *311*
Egbert, J., 869, *890*
Egeland, B., 496, *513*
Ehlers, A., 33, *42*
Ehlers, C. L., 297, *309*
Ehnholm, C., 290, *317*
Ehrhardt, A., 820, *834*
Ehrhardt A. A., 830, *83*, 846, *8534*
Ehrich, B., 734, *744*
Ehrlich, J., 183, *191*
Ehsani, A. A., 631, *653*
Eich, E., 407, *412*
Eigler, F. W., 689, *695*
Eikelboom, R., 111, *114*
Eimas, P. D., 23, *46*
Eischens, R. R., 633, *653*
Eisdorfer, C., 469, *474*, 478, *490*
Eisen, S. A., 38, *42*, 74, *79*, 325, *333*, *336*
Eisenbarth, G. S., 805, *813*
Eisenberg, D. M., *706*
Eisenberg, N., 151, *169*
Eisenhofer, G., 675, *679*
Eisenkramer, G., 64, *80*, 677, *680*
Eisenstat, S. A., 497, *512*
Eisera, N. B., 803, *815*
Eisler, R. M., 10, *16*
Ekbom, A., 288, *307*
Ekelund, L. G., 629, *652*
Ekins, B., 868, 869, *893*
Ekman, P., 75, *79*, 149, *170*
Ekstrand, M., 777, 782, 783, *796*, 822, *834*
Elarth, A. M., 571, 576, *579*
Elashoff, R., 218, *230*, 664, *667*, 688, *692*, 715, 717, *722*, *723*, 752, *754*
Elashoff, R. M., 526, *535*
el-Bassel, N., 823, *834*
Elbourne, D., 505, 508, *513*
Elder, G. H., 142, 151, 160, *163*
Elder, G. H., Jr., 442, *447*
Elder, J. P., 464, *466*, 591, 598, 600, *608*, 734, *743*
Elder, N., 499, 501, *513*
Elders, J., 462, *466*
Eldred, L. J., 849, *852*
Eliakim, M., 366, *385*
Elias, C. J., 829, *834*
Elias, J. W., 469, *474*
Elias, M. F., 153, *165*, 469, *474*
Elias, P. K., 469, *474*
Elie, R., 124, *133*
Eliot, R., 641, *652*
Ell, K., 218, *230*, 329, *333*, 389, *400*, 720, *723*
Ellard, J. H., 394, *400*
Ellen, J. E., 565, 566, *569*, *570*
Ellenberg, L., 766, 769, *775*, *776*
Ellerbrock, T. V., 826, *839*
Ellickson, P. L., 461, *465*, *466*
Elliot, T., 827, *837*
Elliot, V. E., 254, *260*
Elliott, B. A., 542, 543, 544, 546, *555*
Elliott, C. H., 765, 767, 768, *774*, *775*
Elliott, D. S., 442, *447*
Elliott, E., 287, *317*
Elliott, G. R., 478, *490*
Elliott, M. L., 719, *722*
Elliott, P., 287, *317*
Elliott, S. A., 497, 498, 510, *513*
Elliott, T., 586, 587, *590*
Elliott, T. R., 583, 584, 585, 586, *589*
Ellis, A. P., 397, *402*
Ellis, J. A., 764, *774*
Ellman, G., 109, *115*
Ellsworth, P., 340, *347*
Elmer, P., 593, 601, 604, *609*
Elmer, P. J., 287, *317*
El-Sadr, W., 802, 811, *813*
Elser, M. D., 647, *655*
Elston, M., 855, *892*
Elting, E., 72, *80*
Elwood, J. M., 218, *231*, 329, *333*, 751, 752, *755*
Elwood, P., 371, 373, *379*, *381*
Ely, D., 434, *440*
Ely, D. L., 226, *230*
Emanuel, I., *511*, *513*
Emanuele, M. A., 289, *309*
Emanuele, N. V., 289, *309*
Emanuelsson, H., 675, 676. *680*
Embree, J. E., 824, *833*
Emel, J., 728, 729, *743*
Emery, C. F., 636, 640, 642, *651*, *652*
Emkey, R., 471, *475*
Emlen, A. C., 482, *491*
Emley. G., 374, *382*
Emmanual, J. 330, *331*, *337*
Emmons, K., 522, *538*
Emmons, K. M., 729, 730, *742*
Emmons, R. A., 63, 66, *81*, 187, *190*
Emonyi, W., 828, *833*
Enders, I., 330, *333*
Endicott, J., 633, *652*, *656*
Endres, R. K., 575, *580*
Enel, C., 829, *836*
Eneroth, P., 685, *691*
Eng, A., 461, 462, *465*
Eng, E., 602, 603, 604, 605, *608*, *611*
Eng, T. R., 565, *569*
Engebretson, T. O., 73, 77, *79*, *83*, 674, *680*
Engel, B. T., 88, 89, 90, 91, 92, *93*, *94*
Engel, G. L., 61, *80*, 119, *134*
Engle, D., 119, *133*
Engle, P. L., 406, 410, *412*
English, J. D. R., 736, *742*
Engstrom, K., 499, *516*
Engstrom, P., 734, 735, 737, *743*, *744*, 749, *755*
Engstrom, P. F., 519, 530, 531, *532*, *537*, 736, 739, *743*, *744*, 759, 761, *775*
Ennis, R. H., 622, *623*
Enqvist, B., 327, *333*
Ensminger, M., 818, 822, 823, *836*
Ensminger, M. E., 463, *468*
Epel, E., *740*, *741*
Ephraim, R., 729, *742*
Epley, S. W., 202, *206*
Epping-Jordan, J. E., 397, *400*
Epse, K., 406, *412*
Epstein, A. M., 473, *474*
Epstein, J. A., 855, *889*
Epstein, L., 19, *43*, 256, *259*
Epstein, L. H., 265, 266, 270, 272, 273, 274, *276*, *279*, 523, 524, 526 *533*, *534*, *537*
Epstein, M., 787, *799*
Epstein, N., 599, 606, *611*
Epstein, S., 28, 29, *42*, *43*, 629, *652*
Epstein, S. A., 735, *742*
Epstein, S. E., 672, *681*
Epstein, Y., 368, *382*
Epstein, Y. M., 367, 368, 370, *379*, *381*, *383*
Erbaugh, J., 480, *489*, 633, *650*
Erdman, R. A. M., 393, *400*
Ereshefsky, L., 810, *813*
Erfurt, J., 528, *535*
Erfurt, J. C., 433, *438*
Eric, K., 823, *837*
Ericksen, K. P., 293, *309*
Erickson, A., 464, *466*
Erickson, B., 203, 204, *207*
Erickson, D., 806, *813*
Erickson, D. J., 283, 284, 301, 302, 304, *309*, *312*, *316*, *318*
Erickson, J., 371, *381*
Erickson, M., 462, *466*
Erickson, P., 473, *475*
Erickson, R. V., 859, 863, 864, 865, 866, 868, *889*, *890*
Eriksen, M. P., 599, 600, *607*
Erikssen, G., 629, *656*
Erikssen, J., 629, *656*
Erkkila, K., 454, *455*
Erkkola, R. U., 503, *518*
Erlich, H. A., 805, *813*
Erne, P., 689, *694*
Ernest, J. M., 496, 500, *516*
Ernst, D., 216, 217, *233*
Ernster, V., 472, *475*
Ernster, V. L., 471, 472, *475*, *476*
Eron, J. J., 846, 850, *852*, *853*
Ershler, W. B., *691*, *693*
Ershoff, D. H., 524, 525, *534*
Ertama, L., 290, *311*
Escobedo, L. H., 592, *608*
Escudero, M., 368, *383*
Eshleman, S., 283, *312*, 632, *653*
Esler, M., 74, *80*, 647, *653*
Esparza, J., 266, *278*
Espindle, D. M., 719, *722*
Espino, D. V., 855, *889*
Esposito, J., 408, *412*
Esquifino, A. I., 328, *333*
Essen, J., 366, 367, *381*
Esterling, B., 340, 342, 343, *346*, *347*
Esterling, B. A., 63, 74, *80*, 227, *230*, 328, *333*, 481, 482, *490*, 686, 688, *692*, *693*
Estes, M. A., 398, *402*
Estes, N. C., 398, *402*
Esteve, L. G., 63, *80*
Estrada, A., 828, *833*
Eth, S., 773, *776*
Ethier, K., 823, 826, 831, *834*
Ettema, J. H., 371, 372, *383*
Ettinger, B., 472, *475*
Ettinger, W., 526, *537*, 573, *579*, 629, 646, 647, 648, *655*
Ettinger, W. H., Jr., 469, *475*
Etzi, S., 734, *742*
Eury, S. E., 254, 255, *258*, *259*
Evans, A. M., 531, *533*
Evans, A. S., 328, *334*
Evans, D., 700, *707*
Evans, D. A., 286, 289, *311*, *316*
Evans, D. L., 664, *667*
Evans, D. M., 285, 302, *308*, *309*
Evans, G., 717, *723*
Evans, G. W., 366, 367, 368, 369, 370, 371, 373, 374, 375, 376, 377, 378, *380*, *381*, *382*, *385*, 393, *401*

Evans, J., 435, *440*
Evans, J. F., 641, *652*
Evans, J. G., 469, *475*
Evans, L. A., 828, *839*
Evans, P., 685, *692*
Evans, R. I., 459, 460, 461, 462, 463, *466*
Everaerd, W., 342, 343, *348*
Everhart, D., 124, *135*
Everitt, M. G., 629, 647, *654*
Evers, A. W. M., 393, *400*
Eversley, R., 777, 792, *797*
Everson, D., 523, *534*
Everson, S. A., 156, 157, *165*, 473, *475*
Ewart, C., 153, *162*
Ewart, C. K., 76, *80*, 160, *165*, 239, 243, 244, 245, *246*, 599, *608*
Exner, T. M., 830, *834*
Exon, J. H., 110, *114*
Exton, M. S., 112, *114*
Eysenck, H. J., 61, *80*
Eysenck, S., 177, *191*
Ezer, A., 509, *514*

F

Fabbri, R., 566, *570*
Fabio, G., 803, *815*
Fabrega, H., 857, 858, 859, 881, *887*, *889*
Facelmann, K., 736, *742*
Facione, N. C., 22, 26, 28, 30, *43*, 736, *742*
Faden, R., 550, *555*
Faden, R. R., 544, *556*
Fagard, R. H., 631, *652*
Fagerhaugh, S., 122, *134*
Fahey, J., 157, *164*, 481, *490*, 685, *694*
Fahey, J. L., 156, *170*, 218, *230*, 393, *399*, 664, *667*, 685, 686, 688, 689, 690, *692*, *693*, *694*, 709, 715, *723*, 752, *754*, 802, *813*
Faigeles, B., 777, 778, 792, *797*, *798*
Fairburn, C., 327, *335*
Fairhurst, S. K., 243, *246*, 461, *465*
Falco, M., 802, *813*
Falcone, C., 671, 676, *680*, *682*
Falconer, J. J., 669, 671, 673, 675, 676, *680*, *681*
Falk, A., 215, *230*
Falke, R. L., 63, 69, *79*, 718, *723*
Falkner, B., 434, *438*
Faller, C., 461, *465*
Fallon, P., 548, *556*
Falls, H., 629, *652*
Fals-Stewart, W., 285, *309*
Falzoi, M., 373, *380*
Famularo, R., 292, *309*
Fang, C. T., 808, *815*
Fant, R. V., 523, *534*
Fantasia, G. M., 675, *682*
Faraday, M. M., 254, 255, 256, 257, *259*
Faragher, E. B., 747, 749, 750, 752, *754*
Farber, E. A., 496, *513*
Farge, E. J., 857, 858, 859
Farinaro, E., 700, *708*
Farinati, F., 288, *314*
Farley, R., 432, *438*
Farmer, A., *532*, *535*
Farmer, J. E., 584, *590*
Farmer, M. E., 283, 284, 301, *315*, 632, *652*
Farmer, P., 25, *43*, 885, *889*
Farnot, U., 225, *233*
Farnum, J. E., 498, *518*
Farquhar, J., 528, *534*
Farquhar, J. W., 266, 268, *277*, *278*, 591, 593, 595, 596, 597, 598, 600, 601, 604, 605, 606, *608*, *609*, *610*
Farran, C. J., 480, 481, *491*
Farrand, M. E., 576, *577*
Farrar, W. B., 713, *722*, 753, *754*
Farrell, M. P., 222, *230*, 304, *307*
Farrell, P. A., 645, *652*
Farrington, K., 784, *796*
Farzadegan, H., 808, *813*, 826, *834*
Fasoli, M., 288, *312*
Fass, R. J., 388, *402*
Fath, K., 665, *666*
Fatkenheuer, G., 847, *852*
Fauci, A. S., 826, *834*
Faulpel, C., 823, *834*
Faust, J., 452, *456*
Fava, G. A., 66, *80*
Favagehi, M., 326, 327, *335*
Fawcett, J., 575, *578*, *579*
Fawcett, S. B., 600, 604, 605, *607*, *608*
Fawzy, F. I., 218, *230*, 664, *667*, 709, 715, *723*, 752, *754*, 761, 763, 764, *774*
Fawzy, N., 709, 715, *723*
Fawzy, N. W., 218, *230*, 664, *667*, 688, *692*, 752, *754*, 761, 763, 764, *774*
Fawzy, R. I., 688, *692*
Fazzari, T. V., 689, 690, *694*
Fazzini, P., 672, *679*
Feaganes, J. R., 63, *83*, 530, *538*, 664, *668*, 730, 732, 733, *745*
Feaster, D. J., 686, 690, *693*, 753, *755*
Feder, S. I., 524, *536*
Fee, E., 818, *834*
Feeney, A., 291, *313*, 662, *667*
Feeney, J. A., 63, *80*
Feeny, D. H., 473, *475*
Feighery, E., 614, *623*
Feighery, E. C., 600, *610*
Feigin, M., 509, *514*
Fein, P. A., 807, *812*
Feinberg, J. E., 846, *852*
Feiner, C., 823, *838*
Feinerman, A. D., *633*, *635*, *654*
Feingold, A., 780, *796*
Feinleib, M., 67, *80*, 142, 147, *166*, 216, *232*, 265, *276*
Feinstein, A. R., 473, *475*
Feinstein, L. G., 63, 69, *79*, 486, *490*, 508, *513*, 718, *723*
Feldman, H., 528, *533*
Feldman, H. A., 593, 596, 601, 604, *607*
Feldman, J., 289, 290, *317*, 828, *832*
Feldman, J. P., 738, *744*
Feldman, P., 496, 505, 506, 507, 510, *513*, *517*
Feldstein, M., 450, *457*
Fell, J. C., 293, *309*
Felner, R. D., 222, *230*, 506, *512*
Felten, D., 684, *694*
Felten, D. L., 105, *113*
Felten, S. Y., 684, *693*, *694*
Felton, B. J., 29, *43*, 392, 393, *400*, *402*
Felton, S., 824, *834*
Felts, W. R., 117, *135*
Fenaughty, A. M., 731, 732, 733, 734, 736, 739, *740*, *742*
Fencl, V., 703, *706*
Feng, Z., 521, 522, *536*, *538*
Fenn, K., 735, *743*
Fennell, R. S., 453, 454, *456*
Fentiman, I. S., 329, *335*, 747, 749, *756*
Fenton, L. R., 452, *456*
Fenton, T., 292, *309*, 672, 676, *679*
Feorino, P. M., 828, *836*
Ferguson, D. C. E., 704, 705, *707*
Ferguson, M., 675, *680*
Ferketich, S. L., 497, 498, *516*
Fernandez, E., 126, *133*, *134*
Fernandez, I., 821, *834*
Fernandez-Esquer, M. E., 734, *743*
Fernandez-Vina, M., 802, *813*
Fernberg, P. M., 352, *360*
Ferrando, S., 847, *853*
Ferrannini, E., 254, *260*
Ferrario, C. M., 573, *578*
Ferrario, M., 373, *380*
Ferre, C. D., 499, *517*
Ferrell, B., 758, *774*
Ferrell, R. E., 877, *894*
Ferrence, R., 286, *307*
Ferris, D. G., 779, *796*, 828, *834*
Ferris, E. B., 697, 701, 703, *707*
Ferroni, A., 824, *833*
Fertig, J., 250, *260*
Feshbach, S., 459, 460, *467*, 735, *743*
Festinger, L. 36, *43*, 195, 196, 200, *206*, 462, *466*
Fetro, J. V., 783, *797*
Fett, S. L., 544, 547, 548, *557*
Fetting, J., 388, *400*, 715, *723*, 757, *774*
Fetzer, B. K., 733, *744*
Feuer, E. J., 530, *533*
Feussner, J. R., 530, 531, *539*
Feyerabend, C., 250, *260*
Fiaterone, M. A., 635, 637, *656*
Fibel, B., 155, *165*
Fidel, J., 366, *385*
Fiegal, K. M., 263, *277*
Field, B. J., 220, *231*
Fields, H. L., 131
Fienberg, S. E., 405, *412*
Fife-Schaw, C., 782, 783, *795*
Fifield, H., 219, *229*
Fifield, J., 29, *41*, 54, 55, *56*, 204, *205*, 396, *399*
Figiel, G. S., 471, *474*
Filer, M., 211, 221, *234*
Filewich, R. J., 90, *93*
Fillmore, K. M., 663, *667*
Finch, C. E., 469, *475*
Fincham, F. D., 154, *165*
Findlay, R. C., 372, *385*
Findley, J. D., 89, *94*
Fine, M., 186, *191*
Fine, M. J., 178, *191*
Fineburg, N. S., 436, *439*
Fink, E. L., 782, 783, 787, 788, *796*, *797*
Finkelhor, D., 542, 543, *555*
Finkeltov, B., 636, *655*
Finkle, A., 371, *381*
Finn, P. R., 298, 300, 303, *309*
Finn, S. E., 150, *168*
Finnegan, J., 593, 601, 604, *609*
Finnegan, J. R., 595, 600, 601, 603, 604, *607*, *611*
Finnegan, L. P., 470, 472, *476*
Finney, J., 217, *232*
Fiore, M. C., 869, *889*
Fird, D. J., 677, *680*
Fireman, P., 33, *42*, 154, *164*, 684, *692*
Firestone, L. L., 299, *311*
First, W., 564, *569*
Firtion, G., 824, *833*
Fischer, E., 292, *312*
Fischer, K., 327, *333*
Fischer, K. C., 64, *80*, 677, *680*
Fischer, R. L., 498, *518*
Fischhoff, B., 733, 739, *742*, *743*, *745*
Fischl, M. A., 846, 847, 848, *851*, *852*
Fiscus, S. A., 850, *853*
Fish, R. D., 675, *682*
Fishbein, H. A., 576, *578*
Fishbein, M., 4, 5, 11, 12, *16*, 19, 39, *43*, 196, *205*, 462, 463, *466*, 574, *578*, 595, *607*, 729, *741*, *742*, 831, *832*

Fisher, E. B., 71, *84*, *446*, *447*, 600, *608*
Fisher, E. B., Jr., 151, *172*
Fisher, G., 429, 433, *440*
Fisher, J., 783, *797*, 818, *834*
Fisher, J. A., 267, *275*
Fisher, J. D., 486, *490*, *491*, 782, 783, *797*
Fisher, J. G., 91, *94*, 96, *103*
Fisher, J. L., 605, *608*
Fisher, J. R., 877, *893*
Fisher, L., 327, 328, *334*, 686, *694*
Fisher, L. A., 302, *307*
Fisher, L. D., 68, *81*, 327, 328, *334*, 686, *693*
Fisher, M. E., 630, *655*
Fisher, N. M., 525, *534*
Fisher, W., 783, *797*
Fisher, W. A., 782, 783, *797*
Fishman, B., 154, *169*, 758, *774*
Fiske, S. T., 30, *41*
Fisler, R., 345, *348*
Fitzgerald, H. E., 301, *318*
Fitzgerald, L. F., 541, 542, 543, *556*
Fitzmaurice, M. A., 748, *756*
Fitzpatrick, B., 736, *742*, *743*
Fitzpatrick, D. F., 74, *78*
Fitzpatrick, K. M., 444, *447*
Fitzpatrick, M., 787, *798*
Fitzpatrick, M. A., 784, *797*
Fitzpatrick, R., 219, *230*, 473, *474*, *532*, *535*, 736, *744*
Fixler, D., 454, *457*
Flack, J. M., 431, *438*, 573, *578*
Flamigni, C., 566, *570*
Flanagan, C., 443, *447*
Flanders, D., 266, *279*
Flanders, W. D., 530, 531, *533*
Flanigan, T., 826, *833*
Flannery, G. J., 177, *190*
Flannery, G. R., 108, *115*
Flannery, R. B., 177, *190*
Flareau, B. J., 531, *537*
Flaskerud, J. H., 873, 885, *889*
Flay, B., 855, *891*
Flay, B. R., 303, *309*, 459, 460, 461, *465*, *466*, *467*
Flegal, K. M., 520, *536*
Fleischman, P., 868, *889*
Fleisher, C. L., 487, *491*
Fleishman, J. A., 397, *400*, 504, *513*, 822, 826, *838*
Fleiss, J., 718, *723*
Fleissner, K., 480, 481, 482, *492*
Fleming, C. B., 327, *332*
Fleming, C. M., 879, 880, *889*
Fleming, D., 822, *839*
Fleming, I., 367, 368, 370,*381*, 433, 434, 435, *438*
Fleming, P. L., 820, 825, 827, 828, *833*, *836*, *839*
Fleming, R., 226, *230*, 434, 435, *438*, 663, *667*
Fleming, T., 827, *834*, *837*
Flemmig, D. S., 802, *813*
Fleshner, M., 112, *114*, 709, *721*, *724*
Fletcher, A., 473, *474*
Fletcher, A. P., 573, *578*
Fletcher, B., 31, *46*, 74, *83*, 397, *402*
Fletcher, F. C., 700, *706*
Fletcher, G. F., 629, *652*
Fletcher, J., 804, *813*
Fletcher, M., 685, 688, *693*
Fletcher, M. A., 245, *246*, 325, 326, 328, *334*, 340, 342, 343, *347*, 388, 395, 398, *401*, 686, 688, 690, *691*, *693*, *694*, 753, *755*
Fletcher, S. W., 519, 528, 531, *534*, *535*, 575, *578*, 734, *742*
Flett, G. L., 394, 395, *400*
Flexner, C., 471, *474*
Flitcraft, A., 542, 543, 544, 545, 548, 549, 550, 551, *555*, *557*
Floch, C., 824, *833*
Floor, E., 158, *168*
Flor, H., 118, 120, 122, 123, 124, 125, 126, 127, 128, 129, 130, *134*, *136*
Flora, J., 268, *278*, 528, *534*
Flora, J. A., 593, 595, 596, 597, 598, 600, 601, 604, 605, 606, *608*
Flores, C. M., 252, *259*
Flores, E., 734, *743*
Flores, K. S., 498, *513*
Flores, L., *56*, *58*
Florian, V., 178, 179, 184, *190*, 354, *362*
Florin, P., 503, *517*, 603, 604, *608*, *610*, *611*, 619, 620, 621, *623*, *624*, *625*
Flory, J. D., 156, *170*
Floyd, D. L., 736, *744*
Floyd, R. L., 524, *534*
Flynn, B. S., 525, *537*
Flynn, C., 822, 826, *838*
Flynn, M., 734, *741*
Foa, E., 340, 342, 343, 345, *346*, *347*
Foartmann, S., 528, *534*
Foege, W. H., 286, 290, *313*
Foerster, S., 522, *535*, 599, 600, *608*
Foester, E., 576, *578*
Fogarty, D. G., 330, *334*
Fogel, B., 397, *400*, 504, *513*
Fogel, K., 828, *837*
Fogelman, K., 366, 367, *381*
Folds, J. D., 664, *667*
Foley, K. M., *721*, *723*
Folger, R., 354, *363*
Folgering, H., 575, *577*
Folk, F., 373, *380*
Folkins, C. H., 635, *652*
Folkman, S., 20, 25, 31, 40, *43*, *44*. 50, *56*, 61, 62, 68, 69, *81*, 142, 144, *168*, 181, 188, *191*, *192*, 240, *246*., 322, 324, 328, *332*, *334*, 389, 390, 391, 396, 397, 398, *399*, *400*, *401*, 450, *456*, 478, *491*, 501, 504, 505, *513*, *515*, 561, *569*, 662, *666*, 687, 690, *692*, *694*, 782, *797*, 821, 824, *832*, *834*, 846, *852*
Folkow, B., 434, *438*, *440*
Follansbee, D., 441, *447*
Follenius, M., 373, *380*
Follette, W. C., 576, *577*, *579*
Follick, M. J., 122, 124, 125, *134*, *136*, 153, 154, *162*, *165*
Folsom, A. R., 265, *277*, 287, *317*, 520, *535*, 593, 601, 604, *609*
Fondacaro, K. M., 504, *513*
Fondacaro, M. R., 224, *230*
Fong, G. T., 825, *835*
Fontana, A., 397, *401*
Foote, A., 528, *535*
Forbes, D., 499, *513*
Ford, D. E., 154, *165*, 732, *742*
Ford, D. L. Jr., 419, 420, 424
Ford, E. S., 629, *655*
Ford, G. R., 480, 484, *490*
Ford, K., 790, *799*
Ford, M., 146, *171*
Ford, O. J., 782, *798*
Fordyce, W. E., 119, 121, 128, *134*
Forehand, R., 222, *230*, 773, *774*
Forester, B., 718, *723*
Forette, B., 472, *474*
Foreyt, J. P., 526, *535*
Forgas, J. P., 31, *43*
Forke, C., 825, *837*
Forman, A., 434, *440*
Forman, S., 329, *334*, 671, 672, *679*
Formica, R., 202, *208*
Foroud, T., 296, *315*
Forrest, J., 777, *797*
Forsen, A., 329, *333*, 749, *755*
Forssman, L., 780, *798*
Forster, J. L., 268, 271, *276*, *277*, 600, *609*, *611*
Forsthoff, C. A., 22, 28, *43*
Forthofer, R., 268, *278*
Forti, B., 285, *315*
Fortlage, L., 636, *651*
Fortmann, S. P., 268, *278*, 591, 593, 595, 596, 597, 598, 600, 601, 604, 605, 606, *608*
Foruzani, H. H., 375, *385*
Foster, D. J., 715, *724*
Foster, G., 406, *413*
Foster, G. D., 266, 271, 272, 273, *276*, *278*, *279*
Foster, M., 393, *399*
Foster, T. A., 807, *815*
Foulkes, L. M., 454, *456*
Fournier, G., 266, *276*
Fowkes, F. G. R., 152, *172*
Fowler, C. J., 297, *310*
Fowler, F. J., 407, *411*
Fowler, M., 824, 827, *836*
Fowler, M. G., 827, *837*
Fowles, H., 111, *114*
Fox, A., 289, *312*
Fox, B. H., 67, *80*, 139, *172*, 329, *333*, 747, 748, 750, 752, *755*, *756*
Fox, C. S., 472, *475*
Fox, D., 187, *190*
Fox, H., 824, 827, *836*
Fox, K., 672, *681*
Fox, R. C., 416, 425
Fox, S. A., 530, *534*, 729, 734, 738, *742*, *744*
Fox-Tierney, R., 826, *834*
Foy, D. W., 325, *333*
Fozard, J. L., 469, *474*
Frackowiak, R. S., 676, *681*
Frame, P. S., 531, *533*
Francheschi, S., 288, *312*
Franchini, L., 373, *380*
Francis, M. E., 342, 345, *346*, *347*
Francisco, V. T., 604, 605, *608*
Frank, A. C., 850, *853*
Frank, C. W., 630, 647, *656*
Frank, E., 28, *42*, 322, 326, 328, *332*, *489*, *492*, 683, 684, *692*
Frank, R. G., 581, 582, 583, 584, 586, 588, *589*, *590*
Frankel, A., 730, *741*
Frankenhaeuser, M., 356, *360*, 367, 371, *381*, *383*, *384*
Frankie, G., 748, *756*
Franks, B. D., 638, *652*
Franks, M. M., 481, 482, 483, *490*, *491*, *492*
Franks, P., 153, *167*
Frank-Stromborg, M., 54, *57*
Franz, C. E., 187, *190*
Franz, R., 397, *402*
Franzen, C., 847, *852*
Franzoni, J. B., 72, *78*, 717, *722*
Fraser, A. M., *511*, *517*
Fraser, D. W., 366, *382*
Fraser, G. F., 520, *535*
Frasure-Smith, N., 67, *80*, 154, *165*, 327, 329, 330, *333*, 662, *667*
Fratiglioni, L., 480, *490*
Fraumeni, J. F., 288, *308*, 530, *534*
Frautchi, N., 149, *166*
Frayne, S., 543, 546, *555*
Frazier, E. L., 734, *742*
Frazier, L. D., 479, *490*
Frazier, W., 542, 543, 544, 545, 548, 549, 550, 551, *557*

Frederiksen, L. W., 576, *579*
Frederikson, M., 110, *114*
Frederikson, N., 356, *360*
Fredman, L., 215, *233*, 483, 484, *492*
Fredrick, T., 632, *652*
Fredrikson, M., 146, *163*, 436, *438*, 642, *651*
Freedland, K., 154, 155, *163*, 329, *334*
Freedland, K. E., 38, *42*, 67, 74, *79*, 153, *163*, 663, *666*, 677, *680*
Freedman, D. S., 270, *278*
Freedman, J. L., 366, 368, *381*
Freedman, R. R., 91, 92, *93*
Freeman, E. W., 561, 564, *569*
Freeman, G., 255, *260*
Freeman, H., 855, *888*
Freeman, H. L., 366, *381*
Freeman, K. E., 788, 789, *796*
Freeman, L., 672, *680*
Freeman, M. R., 671, 674, 675. 676, *680*, *681*
Freidson, E., 200, *206*
Freimuth, V. S., 782, 783, 787, 788, *796*, *797*
Freire, P., *623*
Freis, E., 810, *813*
Freis, E. D., 700, 703, *706*
Fremont, J., 635, *652*
Fremouw, W. J., 125, 126, *134*
French, C., 462, *465*
French, J. R. P., Jr., 12, *16*
French, P. T., 827, *839*
French, S. A., 267, 268, 272, *277*, 520, 521, 523, *534*, *535*, *536*
French, S. N., 269, *277*
French, T. M., 92, *93*
Frenz, A., 177, *191*
Frerichs, R. R., 25, *41*, 632, *652*, 807, *815*
Freud, S., 139, *165*
Freudenberg, N., 591, *608*
Freudenberger, H. J., 420, 424
Freund, K. M., 550, *555*
Frey, M. A., 444, *447*
Frey, R., 820, *836*, 880, 881, *889*
Frezza, M., 288, *310*
Friberg, P., 434, *440*
Frid, D. J., 329, *334*, 664, 665, *666*, 671, 674, 675, *679*
Fridhandler, B., 733, *744*
Fridinger, F., 525, *535*
Fridinger, R., 599, 600, *609*
Fried, L. E., 290, *307*, 545, 548, *554*
Fried, L. P., 520, *533*
Fried, Y., 369, *383*
Friedhoff, A. J., 183, *191*
Friedlander, L., *532*, *538*
Friedman, A., 452, *456*
Friedman, E. A., 804, 805, *813*
Friedman, E., 375, *381*
Friedman, G. D., 281, 286, 287, 294, *312*, 531, *537*, 574, *579*
Friedman, H. S., 59, 61, 63, 75, 76, *80*, 140, 142, 143, 153, 154, 155, 156, 158, 159, 160, *165*, *168*, 340, 343, *347*, 395, *400*
Friedman, H., 156, *169*, 749, *755*, 802, 803, *813*, *814*
Friedman, J., 374, *381*, 670, 671, 675, *681*
Friedman, L., 548, 550, *555*
Friedman, L. C., 735, 736, *742*, *745*
Friedman, L. S., 394, *402*, 488, *492*
Friedman, M., 139, 147, 148, *162*, *165*, 435, *438*, 664, *667*, 669, 672, *680*
Friedman, R., 150, *169*, 573, *580*
Friedman, R. B., 574, *579*
Friedman, S., 823, *833*
Friedman, S. R., 828, *833*, *834*
Friedman, W. J., 408, 409, *412*
Friedmann, R., 603, *611*
Friedmann, R., 619, *625*
Friedrich, G., 371, 373, *385*
Friend, K. E., 197, 198, *206*
Friend, R., 64, *83*, 394, *400*
Fries, E., 429, *438*, 521, 522, *533*, 630, *652*
Fries, H., 523, *537*
Fries, J., 473, *475*
Fries, J. F., 395, *401*
Friese, M., 150, *169*
Frieze, I. H., 542, 543, *555*, 786, *798*
Frijda, N. H., 689, *693*
Frisbie, C. J., 878, 879, 880, *889*
Frisbie, W. P., 499, *513*
Frisch, R. E., 631, *652*
Frith, C. D., 676, *681*
Fritz, H. L., 219, *231*
Froelich, J. C., 298, 299, *310*
Froelicher, E. S. S., 629, *652*
Froelicher, V. F., 629, *652*
Frohlich, E. D., 431, *438*
Frohm, K. D., 149, 150, *171*
Fromme, H., 373, *379*
Fromme, K., 301, *310*
Frone, M. R., 211, 223, *232*, 287, 301, 302, *309*, *316*, 357, 358, *360*
Froom, P., 373, *383*
Frost, F., 429, *438*
Fruchter, R. G., 826, *836*
Fruetel, J. R., 604, *607*
Fruhstorfer, B., 371, 373, *381*
Fry, P. S., 179, *191*
Fry, R., 546, *555*
Fu, P., 809, 810, *814*, *815*
Fuchs, C. S., 286, *310*
Fuchs, E., 808, *813*
Fuchs, R., 235, *246*
Fujimoto, W., 429, *438*
Fujita, F., 75, *79*
Fukudo, S., 663, *667*
Fulkerson, J. A., 523, *534*
Fuller, A., 736, *744*
Fuller, T. D., 368, *381*
Fullerton, C. S., 326, *333*
Fullerton, J. T., 530, *534*
Fullilove, M., 777, 779, 783, 787, 789, 794, *795*, *796*, *798*, 823, *834*
Fullilove, M. T., 786, *797*
Fullilove, R., 823, *834*
Fullilove, R. E., 786, *797*
Fulton, J. P., 738, *744*
Funch, D. P., 218, *230*, 329, *333*, 747, 750, 752, *755*
Funder, D. C., 140, *165*, *167*
Funk, S., 158, *165*
Funk, S. C., 178, 183, 184, *191*, 354, *360*
Funkenstein, D. H., 72, *80*
Fuqua, R. W., 830, *838*
Furedy, J. J., 639, 642, *656*
Furst, C. J., 110, *114*
Furstenberg, F., 463, *467*
Furstenberg, F. F., 442, 444, *446*, *447*
Furth, P., 857, 858, *888*
Furukawa, T., 855, *889*
Fuster, V., 630, *653*, 674, 675, *680*
Futterman, A. D., 716, *723*
Futterman, D., 825, *835*
Fydrich, T., 118, *134*
Fyfe, M. A., 716, 719, *721*

G

Gaard, M., 631, *657*
Gaarder, K. R., 92, *93*
Gaas, E., 101, *102*
Gabbay, F. H., 150, *165*, 669, 672, 673, 675, 676, *680*, *681*
Gabe, J., 368, 378, *381*
Gabriele, T., 369, *379*
Gabrielli, W. F., 297, 298, *315*
Gabrielli, W. F., Jr., 297, *310*
Gaebel, W., 575, *578*
Gaertner, S., 870, *889*
Gaes, G., 368, *384*
Gaffney, D. K., 251, 256, *260*
Gagnon, J., 782, 784, 785, 789, 791, *796*, *797*, *798*, *799*, 822, *832*
Gagnon, J. H., 777, 779, 780, 781, 783, 785, 790, 791, 792, 793, 794, *796*, *797*, *798*, 825, *836*
Gail, M. H., 732, *742*
Gaines, C. L., 574, *579*
Gaines, R., 510, *514*
Gainey, R. R., 327, *332*
Gakinya, M. N., 825, *837*
Galanter, E., 21, *45*
Galasso, M., 502, *517*
Galavotti, C., 850, *852*
Galbo, H., 642, *653*
Galbraith, J., 782, *795*
Galbraith, M. E., 396, *403*
Galdabini, C. A., 829, *835*
Gale, M., 66, 72, *83*, 148, 149, *171*, 662, *667*
Gale, R., 326, *332*
Gale, R. P., 748, *754*
Galinsky, M., 829, *838*
Gallagher, P., 226, *230*
Gallant, J. E., 848, *852*
Galle, O. R., 369, 378, *381*
Galli, M., 671, *680*
Galligan, G. P., 787, *797*
Gallison, C., 461, *465*
Gallo, L. C., 141, 143, 150, 151, 152, 158, 161, *165*, *171*
Gallo, R. C., 808, *814*, *815*
Gallois, C., 782, *799*
Gambino, S. R., 764, *774*
Gambling, S., 584, *589*
Gambone, J., 550, *555*
Gambone, J. C., 546, 547, *556*
Gammon, M. D., 631, *653*
Gan, A., 807, *812*
Ganau, A., 663, *667*
Ganguli, R., *691*, *694*
Ganley, R. M., 326, *333*
Gano, D., 125, 126, *134*
Gansky, S. A., 604, *611*
Ganster, D. C., 355, 356, 359, *360*
Gantt, D. L., 210, *229*
Ganz, P., 675, *682*
Ganz, P. A., 388, *401*
Gapstur, S. M., 265, *277*
Garabino, J., *455*, *456*
Garber, J., 735, *745*
Garcia, M. E., 649, *652*
Garcia, P., 824, 827, *836*
Garcia, S., 142, *166*
Gard, M., 74, *79*
Gardell, B., 350, *360*, *361*
Gardener, S. H., 498, *515*
Gardner, C., 855, *889*
Gardner, G. T., 375, *381*
Gardner, M., 646, *655*
Gardner, M. M., 635, *652*
Gardner, P. S., 366, *384*
Gardner, R. W., 429, *438*
Garfin, S. R., 122, 125, 126, 130, *136*
Garfinkel, L., 286, 287, *308*, 709, *723*

Garfinkel, P., 685, *692*
Garfinkel, P. E., 326, *333*
Garite, T. J., 501, 502, 510, *514*, *518*
Garland, M., 549, 550, 552, *557*
Garmezy, N., 185, *191*
Garner, D., 685, *692*
Garner, W., 686, 687, *693*
Garner, W. R., 27, *43*
Garnett, G. P., 779, 780, *797*
Garratty, E., 827, *833*
Garrett, J. M., 435, *440*, 869, *889*
Garrett, K., 778, *798*
Garrisson, R. J., 265, *276*
Garron, D. C., 119, *135*, 329, *336*
Garssen, B., 717, *724*
Garthwaite, T. L., 645, *652*
Garvey, A. J., 523, 524, *534*
Garwick, A. W., 445, *448*
Gary, H. E., Jr., 432, 435, *438*
Gary, L. E., 523, *532*
Gasparini, A., 369, *381*
Gasperetti, C. M., 676, *680*
Gastfriend, D. R., 299, *317*
Gastorf, J. W., 195, *206*
Gatchel, R. J., 64, *80*, 96, 97, 100, 101, *102*, 226, *230*, 370, *379*, 434, 435, *437*, 663, *667*
Gates, E., 567, *569*
Gates, W. K., 645, *652*
Gatsonis, C., 705, *707*
Gattoni, F., 374, *381*
Gattioni, F. E. G., 374, *379*
Gatz, M., 646, *652*
Gauci, M., 109, *114*
Gauthier, J., 126, 127, *133*
Gauvin, L., 638, 641, *653*, *657*
Gavazzi, A., 671, *682*
Gaw, V., 737, *746*
Gawltney, J. M., 326, 328, *336*
Gawltney, J. M., Jr. 322, 326, 328, *332*
Gay, J., 818, 819, 820, 821, *834*
Gaykema, R. P. A., 112, *114*
Gayle, H., 825, *838*
Gaylor, M., 120, *133*
Gaylor, M. S., 703, *707*
Gazendam, B., 124, *136*
Gaziano, J. M., 286, 294, *307*, *310*
Gazmararian, J. A., 496, 500, 508, *512*, *514*, *517*
Gear, J. S., 849, *853*
Geary, M., *489*, *492*
Geballe, S., 823, 824, 827, *834*
Gebretsadik, T., 472, *475*
Gebski, V. J., 523, 524, *535*
Geenen, R., 393, *400*
Geer, J. H., 101, *102*
Gehan, D., 604, *611*
Gehlbach, S. H., 225, *229*
Geil, R., 367, 368, *381*
Geist, R. F., 544, *555*
Gelb, A. B., 66, *79*
Gelber, R., 824, 827, *833*
Gelberman, R., 576, *580*
Gelernter, C. S., 284, *314*
Gelernter, J., 296, *314*
Gelernter, S., 303, *312*
Geletko, S. M., 849, *852*
Gelfand, A. N., 546, 547, 548, *557*
Geller, M., 451, *456*
Geller, N. L., 677, *681*
Geller, R., 451, *456*
Gelles, R. J., 541, 543, 548, 553, *555*, *557*
Gellman, M. D., 226, *233*
Genant, H. K., 471, *475*
Genazzani, A. R., 503, *517*
Genest, M., 122, 126, 128, 129, *136*, 757, 758, *776*
Genn, W., 850, *852*
Gentile, A., 288, *312*
Gentry, W. D., 121, *134*, 432, 435, *438*
George, C. F., 810, *812*
George, J. M., 64, *79*, 354, 355, 356, *360*, *361*
George, L. K., 469, 471, *474*, *475*, *476*, 479, 480, 481, 482, 483, *490*, *493*, 638, 640, *651*, *656*
George, W. H., 293, 294, 302, *309*, *310*
Georges, A. J., 828, *832*
Gerace, T., 148, *171*
Gerard, H., 197, *206*
Gerard, H. B., 196, *206*
Gerber, A. M., 287, *317*, 869, *889*
Gerend, M. A., 733, *742*
Gerin, W., 226, *230*, 432, 435, *438*, *440*, 643, *655*
Gerken, A., 663, *667*
Gerkman, L. F., 153, *171*
German, P. S., 481, 482, *489*
Germanson, T., 284, *315*
Gerrard, B., 807, 810, *814*
Gerrard, M., 196, 204, *206*, 305, *310*, 728, 736, 739, *742*
Gerritsen, W., 689, *693*
Gershown, E., 704, *708*
Gershuny, B. S., 292, 304, *316*
Gerzanich, V., 251, 252, *260*
Gest, S. D., 185, *191*
Getz, J. G., 463, *466*
Geyer, M., 255, *258*
Geyer, M. A., 255, *261*
Geyer, S., 749, *755*
Ghandi, M. K., 868, *889*
Ghanta, V. K., 109, 110, *115*
Gheorghiade, M., 669, 677, *680*
Ghosh, S., 576, *580*
Giacomini, J., 675, *679*
Giamartino, G., 621, *623*
Giaquinto, C., 803, *813*
Gibberd, R. W., 291, *318*
Gibbons, A., 571, *578*
Gibbons, D., 671, *682*
Gibbons, F. X., 36, *42*, 196, 204, *206*, 305, *310*, 397, *399*, 728, 736, 739, *742*
Gibbons, J., 432, 433, *437*
Gibbons, L. W., 145, *163*, 629, 630, 647, *651*
Gibbons, R. D., 575, *578*
Gibbons, S., 373, *381*
Gibbs, M. S., 325, *333*
Gibbs, P. S., 434, *440*
Gibbs, T., 855, 869, *888*
Giblin, P. T., 506, 509, *514*
Gibofsky, A., 219, *232*, 394, *402*, 487, *492*
Gibson, D. R., 831, *833*
Gibson, E. S., 572, 575, 576, *578*, 849, *852*
Gibson, R. S., 672, *679*
Gidron, Y., *162*, *165*, 343, *347*, *666*, *667*
Gidycz, C. A., 294, *312*
Giele, J. Z., 482, *490*
Gielen, A., 550, *555*
Gielen, A. C., 544, *556*
Gierlings, R. E. H., 120, 122, *136*
Giesecke, J., 780, *798*
Gil, A., 462, *468*
Gil, K. M., 120, 122, 125, 126, *134*, *135*, *136*, 765, 768, *774*
Gilbar, O., 717, *723*
Gilbert, M. A., 463, *466*
Gilchrest, L. D., 461, 463, *467*
Gilchrist, J. C., 748, *756*
Gilewski, T. A., 25, *41*, 110, *114*
Gilks, C., 808, *814*
Gill, J., 291, *310*
Gill, J. J., 148, *162*, *163*, 664, *667*
Gill, J. S., 287, *313*
Gill, T. M., 473, *475*
Giller, E. L., 325, *334*, *335*, *336*
Giller, E. L., Jr., 325, *336*
Gilliam, B. L., 850, *853*
Gilliam, W. J., 89, *94*
Gillies, A., 699, *707*
Gilligan, C., 790, *795*
Gillin, J., 689, *693*
Gillin, J. C., 684, *692*, 749, *755*
Gillis, M. M., *162*, *163*
Gillmore, M. R., 304, *308*
Gillum, B. S., 877, *889*
Gillum, R. F., 869, 877, *889*, *892*
Gilman, S. C., 867, 868, *889*
Gilmore, J. H., 664, *667*
Gilmore, S. L., 689, 690, *694*
Gilson, B., *532*, *538*
Gimbel, J., 732, 736, *744*
Gin, N. E., 543, 546, *555*
Gingrich, R. D., 716, 719, *721*
Ginorio, A. B., 857, *889*
Ginsberg, A., 765, 768, *774*
Ginzel, K. H., 251, *259*
Giordani, M. F., 434, *437*
Giorgi, J. V., 805, *813*
Giorgino, K. B., 397, *399*
Giovani, G., 462, *466*
Giovannucci, E., 153, *167*, 286, 287, *310*, *311*
Giovino, G. A., 523, 524, *534*, *539*
Giraldi, T., 327, *337*
Girdler, S. S., 432, 435, *438*, *439*
Gisofi, C. V., 630, *657*
Gisriel, M. M., 226, *230*, 663, *667*
Gittleman, D. F., 546, 547, *557*
Giubbini, R., 671, *680*
Giunio, L., 674, *681*
Given, B., 575, *578*
Given, C. W., 575, *578*
Givertz, D., 850, *852*
Gladden, R. M., 184, *191*
Glagov, S., 641, 643, *650*
Glaister, C., 572, 574, *577*, *578*
Glancy, C. J., 73, *80*
Glanz, K., 521, 522, 528, *534*, *536*, *538*, 573, *578*, 593, 599, 600, 603, *608*, *610*, 614, *624*, *721*, *723*, 729, *742*
Glaser, B., 685, *695*
Glaser, F. B., 284, *315*
Glaser, R., 68, 72, 74, *81*, *82*, 100, *103*, *113*, *114*, 144, 154, 157, *167*, *169*, 227, *230*, 326, 327, 328, 329, *333*, *334*, 342, *347*, 398, *399*, *400*, 481, 482, *490*, *491*, 664, *667*, 684, 685, 686, 687, 688, 689, 690, *692*, *693*, *694*, 709, 711, 713, *722*, *723*, 753, *754*
Glaser, R. G., 227, *229*, *231*
Glasgow, M. S., 92, *93*
Glasgow, R., 461, *465*
Glasgow, R. E., 441, *447*, 522, 528, *534*, 734, *743*
Glass, B., 436, *438*
Glass, D. C., 62, 66, 71, 72, *80*, *82*, *84*, 143, 148, 149, 151, *165*, *167*, *168*, 324, 326, *333*, 370, 371, 375, 376, *381*, 751, *755*
Glass, E., *721*, *724*
Glass, E. C., 717, *725*
Glass, G., 344, *348*
Glass, G. V., 339, *347*, *348*, 638, *653*
Glass, I., 575, *579*
Glass, N., 544, *555*
Glass, R., 566, *570*
Glass, S., 818, *837*

Glasse, L., 531, *533*
Glasser, S. P., 672, 676, *679*
Glassman, A., 153, 156, *162*, 662, *666*
Glassman, A. H., 663, *667*
Glassman, J., 406, *413*
Glazer, G., 510, *514*
Glazer, H. I., 31, *46*
Gleason, J., 595, 601, 603, 604, *607*
Gledhill-Hoyt, J., 289, 291, 293, *318*
Gleiberman, L., 305, *310*, *318*
Gleser, J., 644, *653*
Gleser, L. J., 274, *276*
Glick, I., 255, *258*
Glick, S. D., 250, *259*
Glicksman, A., 478, 483, *491*
Glover, V., 502, *514*
Glowinski, J., 748, *754*
Gluck, H., 546, 547, *555*
Gluck, J. P., 581, 582, *589*
Glue, P., 300, *310*
Glueck, C. J., 576, *578*
Glueckauf, R. L., 480, *492*
Glusman, M., 645, *653*
Glynn, R. J., 286, *315*
Glynn, T. J., 459, 460, 463, *467*, 523, *538*
Gnys, M., 327, *336*
Goate, A., 296, *315*
Goble, L., 141, *171*
Goble, R., 728, 729, *743*
Godaert, G. L., 689, 690, *692*
Godbey, C., 526, *535*
Godbey, G., 526, *533*
Godoy, J. F., 372, *385*
Goduka, I., 367, *381*
Goedert, J., 822, *834*
Goedert, J. J., 805, 806, *813*, *814*, *815*, 824, *834*
Goehler, L. E., 112, *114*
Goel, K., 684, *694*
Goeman, J., 794, *798*
Goethals, G., 195, *208*
Goethals, G. R., 195, 196, *206*
Goetz, R., 846, *853*
Goetz, R. R., 846, *853*
Goland, R. S., 502, 503, *514*
Golbeck, A., 464, *466*
Golbus, M. S., 497, *518*
Gold, D. P., 289, *307*
Gold, K., 734, *744*
Gold, M., 340, *348*
Gold, M. S., 252, *259*
Gold, P.W., 502, *512*, 690, *692*
Gold, R. S., 787, 788, *797*
Goldberg, A. D., 329, *334*, 669, 671, 672, 677, *679*, *680*, *681*, *682*
Goldberg, D. E., 156, 157, *165*
Goldberg, D. M., 250, *259*
Goldberg, J., 325, *333*, *336*, 415, 422, 424, 425, 574, *579*
Goldberg, J. D., 217, *233*
Goldberg, L. D., 329, *334*
Goldberg, R., 217, *229*
Goldberg, R. J., 472, *474*
Goldberg, S. R., 250, *259*
Goldbert, R. J., 286, *310*
Goldblatt, P. O., 329, *334*
Goldbohm, A., 520, *535*
Goldbohm, R. A., 287, *317*
Golden, B. R., 410, *412*
Golden, E., 777, 779, 783, 787, 789, 794, *795*, *796*, *798*
Golden, M., 640, 642, *656*
Golden, R. N., 664, *667*, 676, *682*
Goldenberg, B., 718, *721*, 773, *774*
Goldenberg, R. L., 499, 501, *513*, *514*
Goldenhar, L. M., 357, *361*
Golden-Kreutz, D., 713, *722*, 753, *754*
Goldfarb, T. L., 250, *259*
Goldfried, M. R., *102*
Goldhaber, S. Z., 286, *310*
Golding, J., 506, *518*
Golding, J. M., 547, *555*, 855, *894*
Goldman, A. I., 460, 464, *467*
Goldman, D., 296, *310*, *313*, 553, *555*, 664, *667*
Goldman, D. P., 822, 826, *838*
Goldman, L., 471, *475*, 677, *681*
Goldman, M. S., 292, 301, 302, *306*, *308*, *309*, *310*, *314*, *315*, *317*
Goldman, S., 272, *276*
Goldring, W., 703, *706*
Goldstein, A., 250, *258*
Goldstein, D. E., 584, *589*, 807, *815*
Goldstein, D. S., 434, *438*, 675, *679*
Goldstein, I. B., 73, 76, 77, *81*, 150, *167*
Goldstein, L., 735, *743*, 749, *755*
Goldstein, M., 527, *536*, 828, *833*
Goldstein, M. S., 226, *232*
Goldstein, R., 27, 36, *43*
Goldstein, R. F., 499, *518*
Goldstein, S., 669, 677, *680*
Goldstein, S. J., 521, *534*
Goldston, S. E., 639, *654*
Goldwasser, P., 807, *812*
Golembiewski, R. T., 417, 419, 425
Goleszewski, T., 850, *853*
Goli, V., 122, 126, *136*
Gollub, E. L., 818, 829, *834*
Golombok, S., 565, 567, *569*
Golub, A., 777, 794, *797*
Golubchikov, V., 822, *837*
Golubchikov, V. V., 179, 183, *192*
Gomberg, E. S. L., 285, 301, 303, *318*
Gomez, C. A., 777, 785, *798*, 820, 828, *834*, *836*
Gomez, R., 502, *517*
Gomez-Caminero, A., 732, *741*
Gomez-Casado, E., 802, *814*
Gomperts, E., 806, *813*
Gonder-Frederick, L., 36, *41*, *43*, 123, *135*, 389, 398, *400*
Gonder-Frederick, L. A., 23, *43*
Gondoli, D. M., 292, 302, *314*
Gonin, R., 366, *385*
Gonzales, D., 523, *537*
Gonzales, S., 806, *813*
Gonzalez, J., 734, *742*
Gonzalez, R., 819, 820, *835*
Gonzalez, S., 445, *448*
Gonzalez, V., 245, *246*
Good, B. J., 25, *43*
Good, R. S., 715, *722*
Goodard, M., 374, *379*
Goode, D. J., 644, *653*
Goode, K. T., 484, *490*
Goode, P. S., 92, *93*
Goodenow, C., 219, *230*
Gooding, W., 266, *279*
Goodkin, K., 398, *401*, 686, 690, *693*, 753, *755*
Goodman, L. A., 541, 542, 543, *556*
Goodman, M., 150, *165*
Goodman, R., 620, *625*
Goodman, R. M., 592, 593, 594, 596, 599, 600, 601, 602, 603, 604, 605, 606, *607*, *608*, *609*, *610*, *611*, 614, 616, 617, 618, 620, 621, *623*, *624*
Goodnow, J. A., 40, *42*
Goodson, J., 684, *694*
Goodson, M., 872, 873, 874, *889*
Goodstadt, M. S., 460, *467*
Goodstein, R. K.37, *43*
Goodwin, D. W., 295, 298, *310*, *315*
Goodwin, E. K., 644, *650*
Goodwin, F. K, 283, 284, 301, *315*, 644, *652*, *655*
Goodwin, J. M., 227, *233*
Goodwin, J. S., 218, 227, *230*, *233*, 329, *333*
Goodyear, N. N., 630, *651*
Goolsby, J. R., 353, *362*
Gora-Maslak, G., 296, *313*
Gorbach, S., 272, *276*
Gorczyinski, R., 685, *692*
Gorczynski, R. M., 109, 112, *114*
Gorden, G., 432, 433, *437*
Gorder, D. D., 576, *577*
Gordon, A. J., 224, *230*
Gordon, A. S., 222, *229*
Gordon, D., 828, *834*
Gordon, D. J., 576, *578*
Gordon, E. E. I., 29, *45*
Gordon, J. R., 274, *277*
Gordon, L., 366, *380*, 574, *578*
Gordon, L. U., 478, *490*, 500, *512*
Gordon, M., 574, *579*
Gordon, N. F., 629, 647, *651*, *652*
Gordon, P., 368, *383*
Gordon, T., 630, *653*
Gore, S., 34, *42*, 473, *474*
Gorelick, P. B, 287, 299, *310*
Gorenflo, D. W., 196, *206*
Gorfinkle, K., 765, 768, *774*, *775*
Gori, F., 502, *513*
Gorin, A. A., *411*, *413*
Gorkin, L., 153, 154, *162*, *165*, 573, *578*, 642, 550
Gorman, E., 777, *797*
Gorman, J. M., 663, *668*, 846, *853*
Gorny, H., 371, *384*
Gorr, W. L., 777, 794, *797*
Gorsuch, R. L., 498, *514*, 638, 639, 642, *656*
Gorter, R. W., 808, *813*
Gortmaker, S. L., 265, 268, *276*
Goseki, Y., 675, *680*
Goss, G., 496, *515*
Goss, S., 823, *834*
Gossard, D., 126, 127, *133*
Götestam, K. G., 121, *135*, 632, *653*
Gotham, H. J., 284, 302, *316*
Gotlib, I. H., 75, *79*, 180, *191*
Gotlib, J. H., 152, *165*
Gotlieb, S., 499, 501, *514*
Gottdiener, J., 150, 157, *165*, *166*
Gottdiener, J. S., 63, 64, 73, 76, 77, *80*, 669, 670, 671, 672, 673, 675, 676, 677, 678, *680*, *681*, *682*
Gottesman, D., 715, *722*
Gottheil, E., 218, 219, *233*, 340, *348*, 664, *668*, 713, *724*, 752, *756*, 758, 762, *776*
Gottlieb, B. H., 188, *190*, 397, *400*, 505, *514*
Gottlieb, L. S., 855, 877, *889*
Gottlieb, N. H., 527, *534*
Gottlieb, S. E., 453, *456*
Gottlieb, S. H., 89, *93*
Gottman, J. M., 75, *80*
Gould, B. P., 705, *706*
Gould, D., 454, *457*
Gould, K., 340, *347*
Gould, M., 792, *798*
Gould, P., 777, 794, *797*
Gould-Martin, K., 858, 864, 865, 866, *889*
Gournic, S. J., 294, *310*
Gove, W. R., 367, 368, 369, 378, *381*
Gowan, D., 453, *456*
Gowing, M. K., 349, *362*

Grabill, C. M., 498, *512*
Grabow, T., 847, *852*
Gracey, D., 521, 522, *534*
Gradman, A., 397, *401*
Grady, D., 472, *475*, 542, 544, 545, 548, *554*
Grady, K., *162*, *163*
Grady, K. E., 219, *230*
Grady, W. R., 778, *799*
Graeven, D. B., 371, *381*
Graf, P., 374, *381*
Graff-Radford, S. B., 407, *412*
Grafstrom, M., 480, *490*
Graham, A. V., 509, *517*
Graham, F. K., 255, *259*
Graham, J. W., 196, 197, 200, *206*, 219, *232*, 460, *467*, 717, *724*
Graham, M. A., 487, *492*
Graham, N. M., 822, 826, *838*
Graham, N. M. H., 327, *335*, 684, *693*
Graham, R. M., 434, *438*
Graham, S., 287, *317*, 520, *535*, 749, *756*
Graham, T. W., 436, *438*
Graham-Pole, J., 453, *456*
Grahl, C., 571, *578*
Gram, I. T., 732, *742*
Gramling, S. E., 526, *535*
Gramzow, R., 152, *172*
Granath, F., 780, *798*
Grand, A., 216, *230*
Grandits, G. A., 149, *164*
Grandjean, E., 374, *381*
Grannemann, B. D., 152, *167*
Granstrom, P. A., 575, *578*
Grant, A., 508, *516*
Grant, B. F., 282, 286, 288, 295, *309*, *310*
Grant, C. H., 393, *399*
Grant, I., 327, *332*, 482, *493*
Grant, L., 552, *555*
Grant, M., 758, *774*
Grant, M. C., 530, *538*
Grant, R., 847, *851*
Grant, R. M., 850, *852*
Grassi, L., 327, *333*
Grau, R., 127, *135*
Graubard, B. I., 734, *744*
Gravenstein, S., 481, *491*
Graves, J. E., 631, *651*
Gray, B., 604, *609*, 620, *624*
Gray, C., 525, *536*, 601, *609*
Gray, G., 22, *42*
Gray, I. C., 119, *137*
Gray, J., *532*, *538*
Gray, J. A., 252, *259*, *260*
Gray, M., 850, *852*
Gray, R., 286, *309*
Gray, W. D., 23, *46*
Graydon, J., 717, *723*
Graziano, S., *16*
Graziano, W. G., 160, *166*
Grazier, K., 117, *134*
Grebb, J. A., 252, *260*
Greco, A., 759, 761, 772, *774*
Greden, J., *489*, *490*
Greeberg, B. L., 822, 826, *838*
Greeley, J., 289, 302, 303, *308*, *310*, *312*
Green, B. L., 325, *333*, 357, *361*, 718, *723*
Green, C. J., 156, *169*
Green, C. R., 250, *258*
Green, D. F., 805, *812*
Green, E. C., 820, *834*
Green, K. D., 773, *774*
Green, L., 186, *191*, 519, 521, *534*
Green, L. W., 526, 527, *533*, *534*, 576, *579*, 591, 595, 597, 599, 602, *609*, 729, 730, *742*
Green, O. C., 270, *278*
Green, P., 197, 199, *207*
Green, S. B., 732, *742*
Green, W. A., 686, *693*
Greenbaum, D. S., 548, *557*
Greenbaum, P. E., 301, 302, *317*
Greenbaum, R. B., 548, *557*
Greenberg, A. H., 112, *114*
Greenberg, E. R., 525, *537*
Greenberg, J. S., 481, *491*
Greenberg, M., 822, *834*
Greenberg, M. A., 325, *333*, 341, 342, 343, 344, *347*
Greenberg, M. T., *162*, *166*, 221, *230*
Greenberg, R. S., 288, *308*
Greenberg-Friedman, D., 827, *833*
Greenblatt, R., 787, *795*
Greenblatt, R. M., 826, *836*
Greene, D., 196, 197, *207*
Greene, H. L., 739, *746*
Greene, T., 366, *379*
Greener, S., *740*, *741*
Greenfield, S., 389, *402*, 473, *476*
Greenfield, T., 290, *308*
Greeno, K., 481, 484, *493*
Greenspan, D., 849, *853*
Greenspan, J. R., 779, 794, *799*
Greenwald, P., 855, 869, *888*
Greenwood, B. M., 808, *813*
Greenwood, B., 858, *889*
Greenwood, D., 325, 326, 328, *334*, 685, 688, *693*
Greenwood, M. R. C., 267, *276*
Greer, H. S., 719, *724*
Greer, S., 67, *80*, *82*, 329, *333*, 715, *724*, 747, 750, 751, 752, *755*, *756*, 763, 764, *774*, *775*
Greggio, N. A., 803, *813*
Gregory, M. C., 55, *56*, 220, 221, *229*
Greig, L. M., 877, *889*
Greist, J. H., 633, 634, *653*
Greminger, P., 576, *578*
Greulich, R. C., 469, *476*
Grewal, I., 690, *693*
Grey, A., 542, 543, 544, 545, 548, 551, *557*
Greyson, N. D., 675, *680*
Grier, M., 823, *839*
Griffen, L. M., 367, 370, *379*
Griffith, K., 729, 735, *745*
Griffith, L. S., 220, *231*
Griffith, P., 152, *166*
Griffiths, R. R., 250, *259*
Griffitt, W., 369, *381*
Grignolo, A., 434, *438*
Grigorenko, E., 822, 829, *835*
Grillon, C., 255, *260*
Grilo, C. M., *275*, *276*
Grim, C., 434, *439*
Grim, C. E., 434, 436, *438*, *439*, 699, *708*
Grimes, J. M., 846, *852*
Grimley, D. M., 782, 783, *797*
Grimm, L. G., 152, *173*
Grimm, R., 373, *383*, 593, 601, 604, *609*
Grimson, R., 530, *536*, 734, *742*
Grindstaff, C. F., 224, *233*, 506, 509, *518*
Grinstead, O. A., 777, 792, *797*
Griscelli, C., 824, *833*, *838*
Grisso, J. A., 290, *310*, 543, 545, *555*
Gritz, E. R., 269, *276*, 524, *535*
Grizzle, J., 528, *532*
Grober, J. S., *162*, *163*
Grobois, B., 718, *721*, 773, *774*
Grochowicz, P. M., 109, *114*
Groeneveld, H., 73, *79*
Groenman, N. H., 120, *137*
Grogin, H., 675, *679*
Grohr, P., 685, *694*
Gronbaek, M., 286, *310*
Grosclaude, P., 216, *230*
Grosheide, P. M., 687, *691*, *693*
Gross, A., 290, *312*
Gross, J., 340, *347*
Gross, J. J., 63, *80*
Gross, P. A., 686, *692*
Gross, S., 786, *797*
Grossarth-Maticek, R., 67, *80*, 157, *166*
Grosse-wide, H., 689, *695*
Grosskurth H., 830, *834*
Grossman, A., 645, *653*
Grossman, L., 303, *313*, 461, *466*
Grossman, P., 154, *172*
Grosvenor, M., 717, *722*
Grota, L. J., *113*
Groth, H., 576, *578*
Grothaus, L., 519, 530, *536*, 730, *743*
Grothaus, L. C., 524, *533*, 524
Group, T. C. R., 604, *609*
Grover, N. B., 685, *695*
Groves, R., 784, 785, 789, *796*, 822, *832*
Grube, J. W., 305, *306*, *310*, *314*, *318*
Gruber, B. L., 753, *755*
Gruber, J. E., 497, 506, 507, *514*
Gruen, G., 378, *385*
Gruen, R. J., 183, *191*, 504, *513*
Grunberg, N., 376, *379*
Grunberg, N. E., 252, 254, 255, 256, 257, *258*, *259*, *260*, *261*, 326, *333*, 749, *755*
Grvendel, J., 823, 824, 827, *834*
Gryskiewicz, N., 417, 425
Grzesiak, R. C., 126, *134*
Guadgnoli, E., 593, *610*
Guasti, L., 676, *680*
Guay, L. A., 827, *834*, *837*
Guccione, M., 154, *168*
Gudmundsson, S., 496, *514*
Guenther-Grey, C., *16*
Guerra, F. A., 830, *838*
Guerra, N., *162*, *172*
Gueye, A., 829, *835*
Guihard-Moscato, M. L., 824, *833*
Guijarro, M. L., 140, 150, 151, 158, *169*, 662, *667*
Guillot, F., 824, *833*
Guinn, S. L., 353, *361*
Guiry, E., 74, *80*
Guitart, X., 252, *258*
Gullberg, B., 221, 227, *232*
Gullette, E., 150, *166*
Gump, B., 156, *170*
Gunderson, E. K. E., 367, *380*
Gunman, A. S., 633, 634, *653*
Gunnarsson, G., 496, *514*
Gunter, P., 829, *834*
Günther, T., 371, *382*
Gupta, D. K., 588,*590*
Gupta, G., 818, *834*
Gupta, S., 779, *797*
Gur, E., 325, *334*
Guralnik, J., 216, *233*
Gurevich, M., 65, *81*
Gurgin, V. A., 720, *722*
Gurung R. A. R., 505, 506, 507, 510, *514*, *517*
Gustafson, A. B., 642, 644, 645, *652*, *656*
Gustafson, K. E., 499, *518*
Guthrie, D., 218, *230*, 664, *667*, 688, *692*, 709, *723*, 752, *754*

Guthrie, T. J., 461, *466*
Gutierres, S. E., 357, *361*
Gutierrez, J. L. A., 326, *336*
Gutierrez, L., 857, *889*
Gutin, B., 525, *532*
Gutmann, M., 19, 22, 23, 28, 36, 38, *44*, *45*
Guttentag, M., 820, *834*
Guyatt, G. H., 473, *475*, 630, *655*
Guydish, J., 777, 782, 783, *796*
Guy-Grand, B., 265, *278*
Guyll, M., 150, *166*
Guyton, A. C. 329, 330, *331*, *333*
Guze, S. B., 295, *310*
Gwaltney, J. M., 60, *79*, 154, 160, *164*, 683, 684, *691*, *694*
Gwaltney, J. M., Jr., 28, 33, *42*, 683, 684, *692*
Gwinn, M., 801, *814*, 824, 827, *833*, *836*
Gwinn, M. L., 288, *310*
Gwyther, L. P., 483, *490*
Gyarfas, K., 749, *756*

H

Ha, T., 822, *834*
Haan, N., 69, *80*
Haber, J. D., 547, *555*
Haber, R., 552, *556*
Habibi, H., 677, *679*
Hacene, K., 753, *755*
Hackett, B. C., 849, *852*
Hackett, T. P., 22, *43*
Hackl, K. L., 823, *834*
Hackman, J. R., 421, 425
Hackney, M., 874, *888*
Haddad, A. H., 675, *681*
Hadden, W., 429, 433, *440*
Hade, B., 124, *133*
Hädicke, A., 328, 329, *336*, 689, *694*
Hadley, E. C., 648, *655*
Haefner, D. P., 36, *41*
Haeri, S. L., 690, *694*
Hagberg, J. M., 631, *651*, *653*
Hage, J., 604, *607*
Hage, J. N., 375, *384*
Haggerty, K., 327, *332*
Haggerty, R. J., 684, *694*
Hagglund, K. J., 584, *589*
Haglund, B. J. A., 596, 600, *609*
Hague, R. A., 804, *814*
Hahn, K. W., 126, *133*
Hahn, R. A., 429, *438*
Hahn, R. C., 328, *333*
Haier, R. J., 645, *653*
Haight, J. S. J., 646, *653*
Haile, B., 878, *889*
Hailey, B. J., 72, *81*, 145, *168*, 388, *401*, 735, *742*
Haines, A. P., 153, *166*
Haines, J. D., Jr., 874, *889*
Haines, M., 306, *310*, 367, *380*
Haines, P. S., 287, *317*, 869, *889*
Hair, E. C., 160, *166*
Hakes, T. B., 110, *114*
Hale, C., 395, *402*
Hale, W. D., 155, *165*
Hale, W. E., 145, *169*
Haley, L., 502, *514*
Haley, N., 523, *538*
Haley, N. J., 523, *535*
Haley, W. E., 478, 480, 483, *490*
Haley, W. T., 484, *490*
Hall, R. P., 432, 435, *438*
Hall, A., 210, *231*
Hall, A. L., 872, 873, *890*
Hall, C., 391, *399*
Hall, E., 286, *309*
Hall, H. F., 122, 125, 126, 130, *136*
Hall, H. I., 736, *742*
Hall, J. V., 855, *888*
Hall, M., 50, *56*, 68, *78*, 146, *166*, 324, *332*, 688, *692*
Hall, M. H., 327, 328, *336*, 689, *695*
Hall, N. R., 753, *755*
Hall, N. R. S., 753, *755*
Hall, S. M., 224, *231*, 269, *276*, 524, *535*
Hall, W. J., 27, *42*
Hall, Y., 700, *708*
Haller, D. L., 504, *514*
Haller, E. W., 879, 880, *890*
Hallet, A. J., 140, 150, 151, 158, *169*, 662, *667*
Hallgren, J., 689, *693*
Hallman, W. K., 603, *610*
Halloran, M. M., 289, *309*
Hallstrom, A., 153, *162*
Halman, L. J., 560, 561, 562, *568*, *569*
Halper, M. S., 735, *743*
Halpern, D., 369, 374, 378, *381*
Halpern, J., 66, *79*
Halpern, P. L., 375, *384*
Halter, J. B., 469, *475*, 663, *668*
Hamaker, S., 356, *363*
Hamberger, K., 550, *555*
Hamberger, L. K., 542, *555*
Hambleton, R. K., 243, *246*
Hamburger, M., 389, 398, *401*
Hames, C. G., 434, 436, *438*
Hamilton, C. J., 292, *310*
Hamilton, G., 573, *580*
Hamilton, M., 480, *490*
Hamilton-Leaks, J., 506, *513*
Hammen, C., 154, *164*, *166*
Hammer, S. M., 846, 847, 848, *851*, *852*
Hammersley, R., 407, 410, *412*
Hammersley, R. H., 405, *413*
Hammett, V. O., 703, *706*
Hammon, S., 759, 761, *775*
Hammond, S., 782, *796*
Hammond, S. L., 782, 783, 787, 788, *796*, *797*
Hamovitch, M., 218, *230*, 329, *333*, 720, *723*
Hampson, S. E., 36, *43*
Hampton, J. W., 855, 877, *890*
Hampton, R. L., 543, 553, *555*
Han, T., 753, *756*
Hanchard, B., 805, *815*
Hancock, T., 614, *624*
Hand, D., 374, *382*
Hand, D. J., 374, *385*
Hand, W., 874, *890*
Handwerger, B. A., 718, *722*
Haney, T. L., 72, *84*, 148, 149, 153, *162*, *163*, *165*, *166*, 217, *233*, 662, *668*, 669, 672, *682*
Haney, T., 154, *162*, 436, *437*
Hanff, P. A., 779, *797*
Hanis, C., 266, *278*
Hanis, C. L., 877, *894*
Hanisch, R., 525, *532*
Hanjani, P., 714, *724*
Hankinson, S. E., 265, *277*, 286, *310*, 472, *474*
Hanley, J. A., 100, *103*
Hanley, J. R., 591, *609*
Hanna, E. Z., 286, *310*
Hannan, P. J., 593, 601, 604, *609*
Hanneke, C. R., 543, *555*, *557*
Hanpeter, J. A., 74, *79*
Hans, P., 548, 550, *555*
Hansdottir, I., *56*, *58*
Hanselka, L. L., 460, 461, *466*
Hansell, P. L. L., 504, *514*
Hansen, C. H., 157, *166*
Hansen, D., 501, *516*
Hansen, D. H., 270, *278*, 576, *580*
Hansen, J. S., 356, *360*
Hansen, R. D., 157, *166*
Hansen, S., 88, *93*
Hansen, W. B., 196, 197, 200, *206*, 460, 461, 463, *466*, *467*
Hansom, J., 546, *557*
Hanson, B. L., 223, *231*
Hanson, B. M., 717, *724*
Hanson, B. S., 215, 221, 224, 226, 227, *230*, *231*, *232*
Hanson, C. L., 220, *231*
Hanson, H. M., 250, *259*
Hanson, M., 664, 665, *666*, 671, 674, 675, *679*
Hanson, M. M., 329, *334*, 677, *680*
Hanson, M. R., 717, 720, *722*, *724*
Hanson, R. L., 296, *313*
Happel, M., 689, *695*
Harber, K., 33[illegible] *347*
Harbin, T. J., 148, *166*
Harburg, E., 304, 305, *310*, *318*, 432, 433, 435, *438*
Harden, P. W., 297, *311*
Hardin, J. M., 92, *93*
Hardy, D., 196, *207*
Hardy, J. B., 825, *833*
Hardy, J. D., 150, *166*
Hardy, K. J., 434, *440*
Hare, J., 453, *456*
Hare, M. L., 859, 865, 866, 881, *890*
Harel, Y., 729, *740*, *745*
Harford, T. C.. 282, 288, 289, 295, *309*, *310*, *314*
Hargreaves, W., 65, *82*
Harkness, A. R., 152, 155, *172*
Harkness, L., 325, *334*, *335*
Harlan, C., 604, *611*
Harlan, L. C., 530, *535*
Harlan, W. R., 470, 472, *476*
Harlass, F. E., 500, *511*
Harlem Study Team, 531, *536*
Harlow, L. L., 782, 783, *798*
Harold, G. T., 154, *165*
Harre, R., *189*, *192*
Harrell, F. E., 148, *162*, 677, *682*
Harrell, J. P., 432, *439*, *440*
Harrell, L. E., 480, *490*
Harrington, H. L., 300, 301, *308*
Harris T. O., 322, *332*
Harris, A. H., 89, *94*
Harris, D. H., 366, *379*
Harris, D. R., 737, *746*, 827, *837*
Harris, E. L., 149, *168*
Harris, H., 718, *721*, 773, *774*
Harris, I. B., 825, *834*
Harris, J. R., 266, *278*
Harris, K. J., 604, 605, *608*
Harris, L. C., 591, *609*
Harris, M., 848, *853*
Harris, N. V., 828, *834*
Harris, P., 733, *742*
Harris, R. E., 703, *707*
Harris, R. P., 531, *535*
Harris, R., 528, 531, *534*, 720, *724*, 734, *742*
Harris, S. D., 64, *79*, 156, *163*, 395, 397, *399*, 715, *722*, 751, 752, *754*
Harris, S. S., 526, *533*
Harris, T., 407, *412*, 471, *475*, 501, *512*
Harris, W., 825, *835*
Harris, W. H., 432, *438*
Harris-Hooker, S., 807, *813*
Harrison, D. F., 786, *798*
Harrison, E. A., 825, *837*

Harrison, F., 870, 873, 885, *890*
Harrison, J. A., 729, *742*
Harrop, J. W., 548, *555*
Harrop-Griffiths, J., 546, *557*
Hart, B., 369, *381*
Hart, B. A., 642, 644, *656*
Hart, B. L., 25, *43*
Hart, C. L., 286, *311*
Hart, T., 664, *667*
Harth, M., 686, *692*
Hartka, E., 663, *667*
Hartley, L. H., 671, *682*
Hartman, K. A., 22, *44*
Hartman, V. L., 327, *335*
Hartmannn, J., 297, 303, *316*
Hartnett, S. A., 435, *439*
Harts, J., 298, 299, *310*
Hartwell, S. L., 220, *231*
Hartwell, T. D., 869, *893*
Hartz, A. J., 717, *723*
Hartzman, R. J., 802, *813*
Haruta, K., 373, *383*
Harvey, C. M., 531, *534*
Harvey, J., 272, 273, *277, 279*
Harvey, J. H., 184, 187, *193*
Harvey, M. G., 353, *361*
Harvey, S., 291, *311*
Harvey, S. M., 327, *333*
Harvie, P., 416, 417, 419, 422, 423, 425
Harwood, A., 856, 857, 858, 859, 860, 861, 863, 866, 875, 876, *887, 890*
Hasert M. F., 664, *667*
Hashtroudi, S., 408, *412*
Hasin, D., 266, *278*
Haskell, W., 526, 527, 528, *532, 534, 535*
Haskell, W. L., 273, *277*, 520, 526, *533, 537, 539*, 573, 576, *579, 580*, 591, 593, 595, 596, 597, 598, 600, 601, 606, *608*, 627, 628, 629, 630, 633, 636, 640, 642, 646, 647, 648, *650, 652, 653, 655*
Haskett, R., 684, *694*
Hasselblad, V., 472, *475*
Hassen, R., 368, *381*
Hassig, S. E., 825, *838*
Hassinger, D. D., 720, *722*
Hastie, R., 406, *412*
Hastings, T., 327, *333*
Hatch, J. P., 91, *94*, 96, 101, *102, 103*, 126, *134*
Hatch, J. W., 604, *608*
Hatch, M., 501, *514*
Hatch, M. C., 509, *514*
Hatchett, L., 394, *400*
Hatfield, B. D., 627, 638, 645, *653, 655*
Hatfield, E., 203, *206*
Hatfield-Timajchy, K., 499, *517*
Hathuc, N., 809, 810, *814*
Hatsukami, D., 253, *259*, 269, *278*, 523, 524, *535, 537, 538*
Hatton, D. C., 272, *277*
Hattori, H., 371, *379*
Hattox, S., 644, *657*
Hatziandreau, E. J., 869, *889*
Hauck, W. W., 777, 782, *796*
Hauenstein, L. S., 433, *438*
Hauer, L. B., 828, *839*
Hauge, C., 285, *317*
Haugen, S. E., 353, *361*
Hauger, R. L., 151, *164*, 690, *694*
Hauser, S. L., 689, *692*
Hauser, S. T., 441, 443, 445, *447, 448*
Haut, A. E., 583, *589*
Havas, S., 429, *438*, 522, *535*
Havassey, B. E., 224, *231*
Haverkos, H. W., 781, *797*
Haviland, M. G., 63, *80*
Havis, J., 461, *466*
Hawashi, P., 435, *440*
Hawken, L., 327, 328, *333*, 689, *692*
Hawkins, D., 593, *609*
Hawkins, J. D., 285, 301, 304, *308, 311*
Hawkins, R. B., 576, *578*
Hawkins, S. A., 406, *412*
Hawthorne, V. M., 286, *311*
Hayashida, M., 299, *306, 317*
Haybittle, J. L., 67, *80*, 751, *755, 756*
Hayden, F. G., 326, 328, *336*, 683, 684, *691, 694*
Hayes, D., 632, 638, *656*
Hayes, S., 733, *744*
Haynes, K., 786, *797*
Haynes, L. T., 750, *755*
Haynes, R. B., 272, *277*, 572, 575, 576, *578, 579*, 849, *852*
Haynes, S., 530, *533*
Haynes, S. G., 67, *80*, 142, 147, *166*, 734, *741*
Hays, D. M., 506, *512*
Hays, J. C., 471, *475, 476*
Hays, R. B., 507, *514*, 846, *852*
Hays, R. D., 389, *402*, 473, *476*, 848, *852*
Hayward, M. C., 326, *333*
Hayward, R. S. A., 732, *742*
Hazan, C., 354, *361*
Hazuda, H. P., 160, *166*
Hazzard, W. R., 469, *475*
HDFP Cooperative Group, 698, *706*
He, T., 806, *813*
Head, J., 291, *313*, 366, 367, *381*, 662, *667*
Heady, J. A., 630, 646, *654*
Heagarty, M. C., 496, 503, *515*
Healthy People 2000, 526, *535*
Hearn, M. D., 150, *166*
Hearn, M. T., 562, 563, *570*
Hearst, N., 777, 784, 785, 789, *796, 798*, 822, *832*
Heath, A. C., 295, *311, 312*, 325, *334, 336*
Heath, C., 266, *279*
Heath, C. W., Jr., 286, 288, *317*
Heath, G., 527, *536*
Heath, G. W., 526, 527, *536, 537*, 573, *579*, 592, 593, 594, 598, 602, *608, 610*, 629, 630, 646, 647, 648, *651, 655*, 869, *891*
Heath, K. V., 471, *475*
Heatherington, E. M., 160, *169*
Heaton, T. B., 559, *569*
Hebel, J. R., 524, *537*
Heber, D., 526, *535*
Hebert, J., 522, *538*
Hebert, J. R., 521, *536*
Hebert, L. E., 289, *311*
Hecht, F., 848, *852*
Hecht, F. M., 850, *852*
Hecht, G. M., 671, *680*
Hecht, H. S., 675, *680*
Heck, E., 481, *490*
Hecker, M. H. L., 149, *166*
Hecker, M. L., 152, 158, 159, *166*
Heckhausen, J., 585, *590*
Heckman, T. G., 829, 830, *835, 838*
Hedegaard, M., 497, 501, *514*
Hedges, L. V., 409, *412*
Hedges, S., 150, *165*
Hedges, S. M., 159, *167*, 669, 672, 673, 675, 676, *680, 681*
Hediger, M. L., 269, *278*, 498, 505, *517, 518*
Hedlund, S., 591, 598, 600, *608*
Hedlund, S. A., 525, *535*, 599, 600, *609*
Hedman, M., 356, *360*
Heenan, P. J., 736, *742*
Heffernan, R., 828, *832*
Hegan, T., 394, *400*
Hegde, S. B., 665, *667*
Hegener, P., 847, *852*
Heggan, T., 735, *743*, 749, *755*
Heiden, L., 125, 126, *134*
Heidrich, S. M., 22, 28, *43*
Heien, D. M., 282, *311*
Heijnen, C. J., 326, *332*, 689, 690, *693, 692*
Heijtink, R. A., 687, *691, 693*
Heikkila, K., 72, *81*
Heilbronn, M., 119, *133*
Heilemann, M. S., 496, *515*
Heilig, M., 690, *693*
Heim, C. R., 50, *57*
Heiman, R. J., 186, *191*
Heimberg, R., 197, *207*
Heim-Duthoy, K. L., 575, *579*
Heimendinger, J., 521, 522, 528, *532, 534, 535, 536, 538*
Heimer, R., 823, *835*
Hein, K., 825, *832, 835*
Heini, A. F., 263, *276*
Heinold, J. W., 523, 524, *534*
Heinrich, R. L., 762, 763, *774*
Heins, H. C., 508, *514*
Heirich, M., 528, *535*
Heise, L. L., 542, 543, *555, 556*
Heisel, J. S., 686, 687, *694*
Heishman, S. J., 255, *259*
Heisler, J., 523, *538*
Heisler, J. A., 324, *332*
Heiss, G., 153, *171*
Hejl, Z., 703, *706*
Held, P. J., *474, 475*
Helder, L., 24, *46*
Helfand, M., 496, 499, *518*
Helgeson, V. S., 54, *57*, 63, *80*, 204, *206*, 217, 218, 219, *231*, 393, 394, 396, *400, 401*, 507, *514*, 752, 753, *755*
Hellberg, D., 523, *535*
Heller, B., 340, *348*
Heller, K., 224, *230*, 486, 487, 488, *492*, 614, *624*
Hellerstedt, W., 523, 524, *535, 537*
Hellerstedt, W. L., 269, 272, 273, 274, *277, 278, 279*
Hellhammer, D., 109, 110, *114*
Hellhammer, D. H., *411, 412, 413*
Hellman, L., 158, *167*
Hellman, N. S., 850, *852*
Helmers, K. F., 63, 64, 66, 73, 76, 77, *80*, 150, 157, *166*, 672, *680*
Helmkamp, J., 372, *385*
Helmreich, R. L., 819, *838*
Helms, J., 870, *890*
Helms, M., 120, *134, 135, 489, 491*
Helms, M. J., 662, *668*
Helms, M. S., 153, *162*
Helquist, M., 10, *16*
Helton, A., 543, 545, 550, *556*
Helzer, J. E., 282, 283, 284, 285, *311*, 663, *667*
Helzlsouer, K. J., 732, *742*
Hemmick, R. M., 393, *399*
Hemmingsen, R., 501, *516*
Hemophilia Growth and Development Study, 806, *813*
Hemphill, P., 327, *333*
Hemsell, D. L., 545, *556*
Henderson, A. H., 461, 462, *466, 467*
Henderson, B. E., 290, *315*, 525, *532*, 631, *657*
Henderson, C., 292, *316*, 508, *516*
Henderson, C. R., 508, *516*
Henderson, H., 803, *812*
Henderson, I. C., 747, 750, *755*

Henderson, J. M., *455*
Henderson, K. A., 527, *535*
Henderson, M. M., 272, *276*, 521, 522, *535*, *538*
Henderson, V. W., 472, *475*
Henderson, W. G., 325, *333*
Hendler, A. L., 675, *680*
Hendrick, R. E., 528, *538*
Hendricks, S. E., 74, *78*
Hendricksen, C., 808, *813*
Hendriks, H. F., 286, *311*
Hendrix, C. W., 808, *814*
Hendrix, W. H., 419, 425
Henggeler, S. W., 220, *231*
Henig, J., 620, *624*
Henin, Y., 828, *835*
Heninger, G. R., 644, *657*
Henke, C., 665, *667*
Henke, C. J., 65, *82*
Henley, J., 286, 288, *317*
Henne, J., 783, *796*
Henneborn, W. J., 509, *514*
Hennekens, C., 472, *474*
Hennekens, C. E., 286, 294, *307*
Hennekens, C. H., 265, *276*, *277*, *279*, 286, 287, *310*, *315*, *316*, *318*, 471, *475*, 520, 522, 523, *537*, *539*
Hennessey, J. F., 564, *569*
Hennessey, K., 805, *813*
Henningfield, J. E., 250, 255, *259*, 523, *534*
Hennkens, C. H., 629, *654*
Hennrikus, D. J., 268, 274, *276*, 291, *318*
Henricho, M., 715, *723*
Henrichs, R., 388, *400*
Henriksen, T. B., 497, 501, *514*
Henrion, R., 828, *835*
Henry, D., 434, *440*
Henry, D. P., 434, *439*, *440*
Henry, E., 739, *741*
Henry, J. P., 63, *80*, 434, *439*, 699, 702, *706*, 748, *755*
Henry, L., 804, *814*
Henry, L. W., 802, 804, *813*
Henry, R., 808, *814*
Henry, R. C., 548, *557*
Henry, W. P., 151, 152, *166*
Hense, H. W., 373, *382*
Hensel, H., 371, 373, *382*
Hensel, M., 828, *833*
Henson, K. D., 728, *743*
Herberg, A. J., 252, *260*
Herberman, H. B., 326, *333*
Herberman, R., 329, *334*, 374, *384*, 752, 753, *755*, *756*
Herberman, R. B., 227, *231*, 329, *334*, *335*, 684, *693*, 713, *725*, 750, 752, 753, *755*
Herbert, M., 155, 156, *172*, 179, *193*, 395, *402*
Herbert, T. B., 67, 74, 77, *80*, 144, 154, *166*, 226, *229*, 326, 327, 328, *332*, *333*, 356, *360*, 394, *400*, 486, *490*, 502, *514*, 683, 685, 687, 688, 689, 690, *692*, *693*, *694*, 709, 713, *721*, *723*
Herbert, T., 140, *164*
Herbert, T. L., 508, *513*
Herbold, M., 373, *382*
Herbst, J., 152, *173*
Herbst, M. C., 676, 677, *681*
Herd, D., 282, *311*
Herd, J. A., 139, 153, *162*, *172*
Herlong, H. F., 289, *314*
Herman, A. A., 496, *512*
Herman, C. P., 195, *207*, 146, *170*
Herman, E., 123, *134*
Herman, L., 441, 445, *447*
Herman, S., 549, *556*, 769, *774*, 827, *833*
Hermann, J., 112, *114*
Hermans, H. J. M., 187, *191*
Hermansen, L., 295, *310*
Hernandez, J. T., 292, *311*, 546, 547, *557*
Hernandez, M., 506, *518*
Hernandez-Avila, M., 290, *311*
Herold, A. H., 779, *797*
Herold, E. S., 785, 788, *797*
Herren, T., 463, *467*
Herrera, J. A., 499, 502, *514*
Herrick, S. E., 584, 585, *589*
Herridge, C., 374, *382*
Herridge, C. F., 374, *379*
Herrmann, C., 153, *166*
Hersen, M., 10, *16*
Hersh, S. P., 753, *755*
Herskowitz, R. D., 441, *447*
Hertz-Picciotto, I., 528, *533*
Hervé, D., 748, *754*
Hervig, L. K., 140, 143, 155, 160, *168*
Herzberg, D. S., 154, *164*
Herzog, A., 366, 369, *383*
Herzog, A. N., 366, 369, *383*
Herzog, A. R., 472, *475*
Herzog, C., 470, *476*
Heshka, S., 267, *277*, 366, 367, 368, *381*, *382*
Heskinen, E. 66, *82*
Hess, M. J., 353, *361*
Hess, W. R., 704, *706*
Hesselbrock, M. N., 284, 285, *311*
Hesselbrock, V., 283, 285, 296, *307*, *311*, *315*, *316*
Hesselbrock, V. M., 297, *312*
Hessling, R. M., 196, *206*
Hestrin, L., 670, 671, 675, *681*
Heth, C. D., 245, *246*
Hetherington, E. M., 296, *315*
Hetherington, M. M., 267, *276*
Hettiaracchi, J., 700, *707*
Heurtin-Roberts, S., 37, *43*
Hewett, J. E., 584, *589*
Hewitt, J. K., 146, *172*
Hewitt, P. L., 394, 395, *400*
Heyden, S., 436, *438*
Heyman, P., 88, 89, *94*
Heymsfield, S. B., 267, *277*, 526, *535*
Heyneman, N. E., 125, 126, *134*
Heyward, W. L., 794, *798*, 825, *836*
Hiatt, R. A., 786, *798*
Hibberd, A. D., 109, *114*
Hickcox, M., 327, *336*, 406, 410, *413*
Hickey, A., 22, *45*
Hickey, D., 509, *516*
Hickie, I., 471, *475*
Hicklin, D., 227, *229*, 328, *332*, 687, *692*
Hickman, J., 149, *172*
Hickok, J. T., 716, 717, *724*
Hicks, D., 553, *556*
Hickson, F. C. I., 789, *796*
Hide, S., 451, *455*
Hierholzer, J. C., 366, *379*
Hiernaux, J., 436, *439*
Higbee, J., 366, *379*
Higbee, K. L., 459, *467*
Higgenbotham, J. C., 862, *890*
Higgens, P., 55, *57*
Higginbottom, S. F., 482, *489*
Higgins, D. L., 850, *852*
Higgins, E. T., 65, 74, *80*, *83*
Higgins, M., 429, *437*
Higgins, P., 330, *331*, 391, 395, 398, *399*
Higgins, S. T., 253, *259*
High-Risk Breast Cancer Consortium, 732, 735, *741*, *742*
Highton, J., *331*, *336*
Higley, J. D., 664, *667*
Higuchi, S., 288, *314*
Hikita, H., 676, *680*
Hilakivi-Clarke, L., 750, *755*
Hildreth, C. J., 869, 873, *890*
Hilgard, E. R., 758, *774*
Hilgard, J. R., 765, 766, *774*
Hill, A. V. S., 808, *813*
Hill, C., 496, *516*
Hill, C. E., 872, 873, 874, 876, *890*
Hill, C. T., 786, *798*
Hill, D., 530, *533*, 736, 739, *741*, *742*
Hill, D. J., 183, *190*
Hill, D. R., 62, *79*
Hill, E. M., 285, *308*
Hill, F. A., 88, *94*
Hill, H. A., 523, 524, *535*
Hill, J., 519, *537*
Hill, J. O., 272, *275*, *277*, *278*
Hill, P. C., 461, 462, *466*
Hill, S., 195, *208*
Hillard, P., 550, *556*
Hillard, T. C., 471, *475*
Hill-Barlow, D., 152, *172*
Hillier, S., 828, *833*
Hilton Chalfen, S., 670, 671, 675, *681*
Hilton, S. C., 502, *513*
Hilton, W. F., 72, *80*
Hilyer, J. C., 527, *536*
Himmelgreen, D. A., 823, *839*
Hindelang, R. D., 63, *79*
Hinderliter, A., 665, *666*
Hinderliter, A. L., 432, 435, *438*, *439*, 676, 677, *681*
Hingson, R., 290, 293, *311*, *317*, 777, *797*
Hingston, R. W., 462, *467*
Hinkley, C., 225, *231*, 496, 509, *515*
Hinrichsen, G. A., 392, *400*, 480, *490*
Hinshaw, S. P., 326, *336*
Hintzen, P., 821, 829, *836*
Hippolyte, R. K., 885, *890*
Hiramatsu, K., 371, *382*
Hiramoto, R. N., 109, 110, *115*
Hirji, K. F., 805, *813*
Hirokawa, A., 373, *383*
Hiroto, D., 375, *382*
Hiroto, D. S., 375, *382*
Hirozawa, A. M., 850, *852*
Hirsch, C., 480, *492*
Hirsch, C. H., 481, 482, *489*
Hirsch, M. S., 846, 847, 848, *851*
Hirschhorn, L. R., 847, *853*
Hirschi, T., 442, *447*
Hirschman, R., 828, *838*
Hirshfeld, R., 152, *166*
Hirshman, R. S., 146, *168*
Hirst, G. H., 732, 734, *745*
Hirst, S., 530, *533*
Hirt, R., 685, *695*
Hislop, T. G., 218, *231*, *233*, 329, *333*, 751, 752, *755*
Hitchcock, J. L., 523, 524, *534*, 736, *742*
Hitchcock, P. J., 4, *16*
Hitimana, D. G., 824, *839*
HIV Infection in Newborns French Collaborative Study Group, 824, *833*
Hjelm, R., 685, *691*
Hjemdahl, P., 503, *516*
Hjemdalh, P., 62, *82*
Hjermann, I., 270, *278*
Hlatky, M. A., 148, *162*, 217, *233*, 662, *667*, *668*, 677, *682*
Ho, D. D., 806, *813*, 846, *852*
Ho, S. C., 216, *231*

Hoag, M. S., 804, *815*
Hoang, G. N., 859, 863, 864, 865, 866, 868, *889*, *890*
Hoban, C., 689, *692*
Hobbs, S. A., 453, 454, *456*
Hobel, C., 506, 507, *514*
Hobel, C. J., 502, 510, *514*, *517*
Hobfall, S. E., 54, *56*, 69, *80*, *229*, *233*, 322, *333*, 393, *400*, 498, 506, 509, 510, *512*, *514*, *515*, 822, 823, 830, *835*
Hochbaum, G., 19, *43*
Hochberg, M.C., 117, *135*
Hochschild, A. R., 353, *361*
Hockenberry, M., 769, *774*
Hockenberry-Eaton, M., 772, *774*
Hockstein, G., 461, *466*
Hodgdon, J. A., 633, 638, *654*
Hodge, T., 805, 806, 808, 810, *814*
Hodges, H., 252, *259*
Hodgson, D. M., 502, *513*
Hoehn-Saric, R., 154, *166*
Hoerr, N. L., 92, *94*
Hoff, L. A., 885, *890*
Hoffart, A., 634, 635, *654*
Hoffman, C., 581, *590*
Hoffman, D., 523, *535*
Hoffman, F., 750, *756*
Hoffman, H., 301, *311*
Hoffman, H. J., 499, 501, *514*
Hoffman, J., 245, *247*, 330, *337*
Hoffman, J. M., *331*, *337*
Hoffman, J. T., 584, 585, *589*
Hoffman, R. G., 850, *852*
Hoffman, S., 290, *310*, 509, *514*
Hoffman, V., 782, 783, *798*
Hoffmann, R. G., III, 453, *4456*
Hogan, D. P., 506, *512*
Hogg, R. S., 471, *475*
Hogston, P., 547, *556*
Hogue, C. J., 499, *517*
Holaday, B., 442, *447*
Holahan, C. J., 154, *170*, 394, 397, *401*, 504, *514*
Holahan, C. K., 394, 397, *401*
Holbrook, T. L., 117, *134*
Holcomb, S., 272, *277*
Holden, E. W., 452, *456*
Holden, G., 182, *191*
Holder, H. D., 291, *311*
Hole, D. J., 286, *311*
Holland, J., 785, 789, 790, *797*
Holland, J. C., 63, *79*, 110, *114*, 715, 718, *721*, *722*, *723*, *724*, 735, *743*, 750, *756*, 770, 772, *775*
Holland, S., 736, *742*
Hollatz-Brown, A., 731, *741*
Hollenberg, J., 292, *312*
Holliday, J. E., 686, 688, 690, *693*
Hollinger, F. B., 687, *693*
Hollingsworth, D. R., 269, *275*
Hollis, J. F., 216, 217, *233*, 522, 528, *534*
Hollon, S. D., *162*, *166*, 461, *467*, 759, 761, *775*
Holloway, J. E., 872, 873, 874, 875, *890*
Hollt, V., 252, *258*
Holm, L., 546, *557*
Holman, C. D. J., 736, *742*
Holman, H. R., 124, 127, *135*
Holman, J. M., 55, *56*, 220, 221, *229*
Holmberg, C., 454, *455*
Holmberg, L., 287, 288, *307*, *317*
Holmberg, S., 822, 826, *838*
Holmberg, S. D., 822, 825, 826, *835*, *838*
Holme, I., 270, *278*
Holmes, D. S., 635, 641, *653*, *654*
Holmes, F. F., 720, *722*, *725*
Holmes, G. E., 720, *725*
Holmes, J., 572, *578*
Holmes, J. H., 496, 503, *515*, 543, 545, *555*
Holmes, K. K., 779, *795*, 824, 828, *833*
Holmes, M. D., 779, *797*
Holmes, P. E., 419, 424
Holmes, S. J., 304, *311*
Holmes, T. H., 68, *80*, 322, *333*
Holodniy M., 826, *833*, 846, *852*
Holroyd, K. A., 123, *134*, 145, *166*, 397, *403*
Holsboer, F., 112, *115*, 663, *667*
Holt, P., 178, *191*
Holtan, N., 869, *890*
Hom, D., 827, *837*
Homanics, G. E., 299, *311*
Homes, G. F., 720, *722*
Homiak, J. P., 857, 859, 860, 861, 862, *893*
Hommer, D. W., 325, *335*
Hong Nguyen, M., 848, 849, *853*
Hong, G., 368, 372, *383*
Honigfeld, G., 101, *103*
Honjo, T., 806, 807, *815*
Honkanen, R., 290, *311*
Hons, R. B., 220, *230*
Hood, D., 462, *465*
Hood, H. V., 10, *16*
Hooker, K., 25, *43*, 479, *490*
Hoon, P. W., 72, *78*, 717, *722*
Hooton, T. M., 867, 868, *888*
Hoover, C. W., 123, *135*
Hoover, D. R., 154, *168*, 826, *834*
Hoover, S., 594, 601, 602, *608*
Hopp, H. P., 521, 522, *533*
Hopper, C., 367, *384*
Hopper, C. H., 370, *380*
Hops, H., 304, 305, *307*, *309*, 394, *402*, 488, *492*
Horan, M. J., 429, *437*
Horgan, D., 497, *514*
Horlock, P., 671, *680*
Horm, J., 521, *535*
Horm, J. W., 855, 869, *888*
Horn, T. S., 642, 644, *656*
Hornbrook, M. C., 648, *655*
Horne, R., 24, *43*
Hornik, R. C., 23, *47*, 598, *609*
Horowitz, A., 478, *489*, *490*
Horowitz, M. J., 145, *166*, 325, *334*, 397, *401*
Horowitz, M. M., *691*, *693*
Hortnagl, J., 373, *383*
Horton, C., 125, *136*
Horton, R., 858, *890*
Horton, S., 827, *837*
Horuk, R., 805, 806, *814*
Horvath, T., 374, *381*
Horwatt, K., 434, *439*
Horwitz, R. I., 217, *229*
Horwitz, S. M., 454, *456*
Hosmer, D., 737, *746*
Hospers, H., 737, *745*
Hough, R. L., 855, *894*
Houle, M., 562, *570*
Houlihan, J., 441, *447*
House, J. S., 210, 214, 215, *231*, 355, *361*, 472, *475*, 505, *514*, 662, *667*, 821, *836*
House, P., 196, 197, *207*
Houseman, C., 617, *624*
Houseworth, S. J., 149, *166*, 432, 436, *4*
Houskamp, B., 718, *724*
Houston, B. K., 72, 73, *80*, *81*, 144, 150, 151, 152, 158, 159, *165*, *166*, *170*, *171*, 178, *191*, 354, *360*
Hovell, M., 464, *466*
Hovell, M. F., 150, *170*
Hovener, G., 330, *333*
Hovey, M., 550, *555*
Howard, B. V., 270, *277*
Howard, J., 531, *535*
Howard, J. A., 786, *797*
Howard-Pitney, B. A., 604, *609*
Howe, G., 441, *448*
Howe, G. R., 287, *317*, 520, *535*
Howe, G. W., 160, *169*
Howell, D. C., 398, *400*
Howell, R., 150, *166*, 675, *682*
Howell, R. H., 671, 672, 675, *680*, *681*
Howes, L. G., 287, *311*
Howland, J., 290, *311*
Howlett, D. R., 644, *653*
Howley, E., 643, *652*
Howley, E. T., 639, 641, *651*
Howze, E., 599, *611*
Hoxie, F. E., 877, 880, *890*
Hoxworth, T., *16*
Hoyle, R. H., 604, 605, *608*
Hryshko, A., 221, *230*
Hser, Y. I., 823, *832*, *835*
Hsieh, C.-C., 629, 631, 647, *654*, *655*
Hsieh, R. P., 805, *813*
Hsing, A. W., 288, *307*
Hsu, F. L. K., 864, *892*
Hu, Y. H., 270, *277*
Hu, Z. X., 270, *277*
Huang, H., 325, 326, 328, *334*, 685, 688, *693*
Huang, J., 373, *385*
Huang, K. E., 563, *569*
Huang, Y., 806, *813*
Huba, G. J., 25, *41*, 825, *835*
Hubbard, J. J., 185, *191*
Hubbell, A., 734, *743*
Hubbell, F. A., 543, 546, *555*
Huber, G. P., 410, *412*
Huber, H., 646, *652*
Huber-Smith, M. J., 324, *335*
Hubert, H. B., 265, *276*
Hucklebridge, F., 685, *692*
Hudes, E., 777, 782, 784, 785, 789, 792, *795*, *796*, 822, *832*
Hudes, E. S., 777, 779, 783, 793, *796*
Hudis, C. A., 25, *41*, 110, *114*
Hudlin, M., 548, 550, *555*
Hudson, S., 24, *44*
Hug, R., 73, 76, 77, *81*, 150, *167*
Huggins, G., 499, *516*
Hughes, A. M., 732, 734, *745*
Hughes, C., 732, 735, *741*
Hughes, C. C., 859, 860, *893*
Hughes, G. H., 483,*490*, 663, *667*
Hughes, G., 150, *170*, 523, *538*
Hughes, J., 328, *333*, 523, *538*, 687, *693*
Hughes, J. R., 253, *259*
Hughes, M., 283, *312*, 367, 368, 369, 378, *381*, 632, *653*
Hughes, M. D., 846, *852*
Hughes, R. G., 599, 600, *607*
Hughey, J., 603, *611*
Huizinga, D., 442, *447*
Hulka, J. F., 546, 547, *557*
Hull, C. L., 251, *260*
Hull, D., 571, 575, 576, *580*
Hull, E. M., 641, *653*
Hull, J. G., 354, *361*
Hulley, S., 145, 148, *166*, *171*, 777, 779, 787, 794, *796*, *798*
Hultsch, D. F., 469, *475*
Humphrey, G. B., 720, *724*
Huncharek, M. D., 290, *314*

Hunt, A. J., 789, *796*
Hunt, D. E., 443, 444, *447*
Hunt, J. R., 470, 472, *475*
Hunt, L. M., 859, *890*
Hunt, M. K., 522, *538*, 593, 594, 598, 602, *610*
Hunt, S., 146, *171*, 330, *331*
Hunt, T., 322, *336*
Hunt, W. C., 218, *230*, 329, *333*
Hunter, C. Y., *511*, *517*
Hunter, D. J., 265, *277*, 286, 287, *310*, *317*, 472, *474*, 520, *535*
Hunter, G., 290, *312*, 850, *853*
Hunter, S., 872, *890*
Hunter, T., 822, *835*
Hunter, T. L., 870, *890*
Hunter, W., *532*, *535*
Hunter-Gamble, D., 787, 788, 789, *799*
Hurd, P. D., 462, *467*
Hurley, C. K., 802, *813*
Hurley, K., 20, 28, 31, *45*, 68, 74, *78*, *82*, 729, 730, 734, 736, *744*
Hurlich, M., 522, *538*
Hurrell, J. J., 855, *893*
Hurrell, J. J., Jr., 350, 351, 352, 355, 357, 358, 359, *361*, *362*, 415, 426
Hurst, M. W., 686, 687, *694*
Hurtado, A., 499, *514*
Hurwicz, M., 23, 34, *41*, 226, *232*
Hurwitz, B. E., 435, *440*
Husband, A. J., 105, 109, 111, 112, *114*
Huscroft, S., 825, *838*
Husen, L. A., 855, 877, *889*
Hussey, J. R., 520, *533*
Husson, R., 824, *835*
Hussong, A. M., 300, *308*
Husten, C. G., 523, *535*
Huster, W. J., 471, *474*
Hutchins, E., 503, *514*
Hutchinson, K., 603, *610*
Hutchinson, R., 374, *382*
Hutchison, S., 184, *190*
Hutt, C., 368, *382*
Huttenlocher, J., 409, *412*
Huttley, G. A., 806, 807, *813*, *815*
Hutton, N., 827, *833*
Huyser, B., *331*, *334*
Hwang, H. B., 299, *311*
Hwu, H. G., 810, *813*
Hyde, J. S., 785, *798*
Hyde, R. T., 525, 526, *537*, 629, 630, 631, 647, *655*
Hygge, S., 373, 374, 375, 378, *381*
Hyman, D., 368, 370, *383*
Hyman, K., 753, *756*
Hyman, M. D., 574, *578*
Hyman, R. B., 729, *742*
Hymowitz, N., 869, *893*
Hypertension Detection and Follow-up Program Cooperative Group, 807, 810, *813*
Hyslop, N., 849, *853*
Hyson, A. S., 127, *135*
Hyun, C. S., 218, *230*, 664, *667*, 688, *692*, 709, *723*, 752, *754*

I

Ianni, P., 91, 92, *93*
Ianotti, R., 449, *456*
Iatesta, M., *16*
Ibrahim, M., 663, *668*
Ibukiyama, C., 675, *680*
Ickes, W., 142, *166*
Ickovics, J., 822, 823, 826, 829, 830, 831, *832*, *834*, *835*
Ickovics, J. R., 179, 183, 185, *192*, 389, 398, *401*, 818, 820, 822, 825, 826, 827, 830, 831, *835*, *837*, *838*, 848, *852*
Ida, Y., 289, *311*
Idler, E. L., 146, *166*
Idson, T. L., 870, *890*
Ilgen, D. R., 415, 425
Imaizumi, T., 434, *440*
Imanishi, K., 287, *317*
Imber-Black, E., *568*, *569*
Imershein, A., 786, *798*
Imeson, J. D., 153, *166*
Imm, P., 604, 605, *609*
Imrie, A., 850, *852*
Inciardi, J. A, 823, *836*
Ingersoll, K. S., 504, *514*
Ingersoll-Dayton, B., 482, *491*
Ingham, I., 202, *206*
Ingham, J. M., 860, 861, *890*
Ingle, J. N., 717, *722*
Ingraham, L. H., 178, *190*
Ingram, D. D., 153, *167*
Ingram, K. M., 177, 185, *191*
Ingram, R. E., 155, *167*, 398, *399*
Inkster, M., 395, *402*
Inoki, R., 250, *258*
Inoue, K., 77, *81*
Institute of Medicine, 267, *276*
Insull, W., 272, *276*, 521, *535*, 717, *722*
Insull, W., Jr., 574, *578*
Inui, T., 552, *557*
Inui, T. S., 576, *580*
Ionescu-Tirgoviste, C., 330, *334*
Iritani, B., 304, *308*
Ironson, G., 150, *167*, 245, *246*, 325, 326, 328, *334*, 388, 395, 398, *400*, *401*, 670, 671, *680*, 685, 688, 690, *691*, *693*, *694*
Ironson, G. H., 226, *233*
Irvine, D., 327, *334*, 718, *723*
Irvine, D. M., 717, *723*
Irving, L. M., 182, *193*, 398, *402*
Irwig, L., 732, *742*
Irwig, L. M., 849, *853*
Irwin, C. E., 26, 37, *45*, 463, *465*, 566, *569*
Irwin, C. E., Jr., 454, *456*
Irwin, M., 283, *316*, 684, 686, 689, 690, *693*, 749, *755*
Irwin, M. R., 684, 690, *692*, *694*
ISA Associates, 619, *624*
Isaac, N., 550, *556*
Isacsson, J. T., 215, 221, 224, 226, *231*
Isacsson, S.-O., 215, *230*
Iscoe, I., 591, 597, *609*, 622, *624*
Isenberg, R. R., 753, *756*
Ishii, E. K., 372, *385*
Ishii, H., 753, *754*
Ishvara, K., 858, 865, *891*
Ising, H., 371, 373, 374, *379*, *382*, 283
Ising, H. R., 373, *381*
Ismail, A. H., 632, 644, *654*, *656*
Isohanni, M., 304, *311*
Israel, B. A., 597, *612*, 622, *623*, *624*
Istvan, J., 501, *514*
Itil, T. M., 297, *310*
Ito, A., 371, *382*
Ittelson, W. H., 369, *384*
Iulian, M., 330, *334*
Ivanov, S. V., 807, *815*
Iverius, P. H., 267, *276*
Ivery, D., 270, *278*
Ivester, C. A., 250, *259*
Iwasaki, H., 753, *754*
Izard, C. E., 75, *81*

J

Jaakkola, M., 288, *311*
Jabaaij, L., 687, *691*, *693*
Jabaij, L., 110, *114*
Jabobson, A. M., 441, *447*
Jackman, G., 74, *80*
Jacknow, D. S., 771, 772, *774*
Jackson, A., 822, *835*
Jackson, A. P., 830, *835*
Jackson, C., 604, *609*
Jackson, D., 432, 435, *440*
Jackson, D. N., 480, *492*
Jackson, E. L., 526, *533*, *535*
Jackson, G., 526, *535*
Jackson, G. L., 739, *745*
Jackson, I. M. D., 289, *311*
Jackson, J. B., 827, *837*
Jackson, J. J., 873, 874, 876, *890*
Jackson, J. S., 432, 435, *437*, *439*, 485, *489*
Jackson, K., 603, *610*
Jackson, K. M., 728, 736, 739, *740*, *743*
Jackson, R. L., 31, *45*
Jackson, S., 480, 483, *489*, *492*
Jackson, S. E., 358, *360*, 416, 417, 418, 419, 425
Jackson, T., 200, *207*
Jacob, M. C., 567, *569*
Jacob, R. G., 700, 703, 705, *707*
Jacob, T., 151, 154, *167*, *168*, 222, *232*, 304, 305, *311*, 636, *655*
Jacobs, D., 148, *171*, 523, 526, 527, 528, *532*, *536*, *538*, 604, *607*
Jacobs, D. R., 462, *467*, 527, *538*, 593, 601, 604, *609*, 629, 647, *654*
Jacobs, D. R., Jr., 869, *888*
Jacobs, G. A., 66, 71, 73, *83*, 435, *439*, 638, 639, 642, *656*
Jacobs, R., 328, 329, *336*, 689, *694*
Jacobs, S., 471, *475*
Jacobs, S. C., 150, *169*
Jacobsberg, L., 154, *169*, 828, *837*
Jacobsen, D. M., 846, 847, 848, *851*
Jacobsen, P., 765, 768, *775*
Jacobsen, P. B., 24, 25, *41*, *45*, 89, *93*, 717, *723*, 749, *756*, 758, 759, 765, 768, 770, 772, *774*, *775*
Jacobson, A., 823, *837*
Jacobson, A. F., 715, *722*
Jacobson, A. M., 441, 443, 445, *447*, *448*
Jacobson, C. K., 559, *569*
Jacobson, E., 97, *103*
Jacobson, J. A., 366, *382*
Jacobson, J. L., 290, *311*
Jacobson, L., 297, *315*
Jacobson, L. P., 806, *815*
Jacobson, P. B., 110, *114*
Jacobson, R. L., 824, 827, *833*
Jacobson, S. W., 290, *311*
Jacoby, C., *162*, *163*
Jacques, G., 872, 873, 874, *890*
Jacquez, J. A., 781, *797*
Jaeger, B., 407, *412*
Jaferi, G., 286, *318*
Jaffe, A. J., 299, *306*, *314*
Jaffe, A. S., 38, *42*, 74, *79*, 154, 155, *163*
Jaffe, D. T., 359, *361*
Jaffe, H. W., 828, *833*
Jagadeeswaran, P., 296, *308*
Jahanshahi, M., 120, *135*
Jain, D., 150, *163*, 671, 677, *679*, *680*
Jain, U., 368, *382*
Jakicic, J. M., 266, 270, 273, 274, *277*, *278*, *279*, 648, *653*

Jamal, M., 321, 326, 327, *332*
James, A., 877, *891*
James, J., 735, *743*, 749, *755*
James, N., 749, 753, *756*
James, S. A., 64, 71, *81*, 188, *191*, 287, *317*, 433, 435, 436, *438*, *439*, *440*, 499, *516*, 641, *654*, 663, *668*, 869, *889*
James, W., 88, *94*
Jamieson, J. L., 641, *652*
Jamison, K. R., 36, *43*
Jamison, R. B., 329, *334*, 751, *755*
Jamner, L. D., 73, 74, 76, 77, *81*, 126, *134*, 150, 157, *167*
Janal, M. N., 645, *653*
Janas, S. F., 811, *815*
Janca, A., 283, *309*
Janet, P., 345, *347*
Janeway, C. A., Jr., 330, *334*
Janigian, A. S., 487, *492*
Janis, I. L., 459, 460, *467*, 735, *743*
Jann, M. W., 810, *813*
Jansen, G., 371, *382*
Jansen, J. B. M. J., 329, *332*
Jansen, M. A., 67, *81*
Jansen-McWilliams, L., 157, *168*
Janssen, R. S., 850, *852*
Janz, N. K., 4, *16*, 19, 39, *43*, 388, *399*, 574, *578*, 729, *743*
Janzon, L., 215, 221, 224, 226, *231*
Japour, A. J., 811, *813*
Jarrett, L., 32, 33, *47*, 155, *172*
Jarvik, M., 253, *261*
Jarvik, M. E., 250, 256, *259*, *260*
Jasinski, D. R., 250, *259*
Jasnoski, M. L., 65, *78*
Jatulis, D., 268, *278*
Java, R., 408, 409, 410, *412*
Jawad, A., 274, *279*
Jay, S., 720, *724*
Jay, S. M., 765, 767, 768, *774*, *775*
Jeffrey, R., 593, 601, 604, *609*
Jeffery, R. W., 267, 268, 269, 270, 271, 272, 273, 274, *276*, *277*, *278*, *279*, 520, 521, 523, 524, 525, *535*, *536*, *537*, *539*, 599, 600, 604, *607*, *609*
Jeffries, S., 496, *516*
Jemelka, R., 547, *557*
Jemelka, R. P., 546, 547, *557*
Jemmo, H. J. B., III, 825, *835*
Jemmot, J., 502, *514*
Jemmot, J. B., 66, 76, *81*, 158, *168*
Jemmott, J. B., III, 22, 25, 29, *4,2* 158, *167*, 202, *206*
Jemmott, L. S., 818, 820, 821, 825, *835*
Jemos, J. J., 575, *579*
Jenking, D., 804, *813*
Jenkins, C. D., 66, 72, 73, 76, *81*, *82*, 147, *167*
Jenkins, F. J., 328, 324, 325, 326, 327, 328, *332*, *333*, *334*, 689, *692*
Jenkins, L., 374, *382*, *385*
Jenkins, R., 291, *311*
Jenkins, R. A., 716, 717, *722*, *725*, 759, 761, 762, *774*, *776*, 846, 849, *853*
Jenkins, S. R., 420, 425
Jenkins, T., 502, *514*
Jenkins, W., 431, *438*
Jenner, F. A., 644, *653*
Jennette, B., 587, *590*
Jennings, G., 647, *653*
Jennings, G. L., 647, *655*
Jennings, J. R., 77, *81*, 142, 144, 154, *163*, *167*, 327, 329, *334*, 433, 435, *439*, 473, *475*
Jennison, K. M., 223, *231*
Jensen, A. B., 747, 750, *755*
Jensen, G., 286, *310*
Jensen, J., 686, *694*
Jensen, M. P., 122, 124, 129, 130, *134*, 394, *402*, 488, *492*
Jensen, M. R., 155, 156, 157, *167*, 751, *755*
Jensen-Campbell, L. A., 160, *166*
Jepson, C., 531, *532*, *537*, 735, *743*
Jequier, E., 267, *278*
Jern, C., 689, *693*
Jern, S., 689, *693*
Jernigan, D., 596, 600, *611*
Jerone, C., 112, *115*
Jerusalem, M., 182, *191*
Jessor, R., 222, *230*, 301, 303, *311*, 462, *467*
Jessor, S. L., 301, 303, *311*, 462, *467*
Jewell, N. P., 781, *798*
Jewitt, D. E., 286, *315*
Jiang, W., 329, *334*, 664, 665, *666*, 671, 674, 675, 677, *679*, *680*
Jiang, X. G., 270, *277*
Jiang, Y. Y., 270, *277*
Jick, D. T., 359, *361*
Jilek, W., 879, 880, *890*
Jiles, R. B., 734, *742*
Jimenez, A. H., 673, *681*
Jin, L., 806, 807, *815*
Jin, Z., 806, *813*
Jirka, J., 703, *706*
Joachim, H. L., 753, *755*
Jobe, J. B., 405, 407, 408, 410, *412*, *413*
Jodar, I., 63, *80*
Joffe, A., 503, *512*
Johannes, C. B., 826, *839*
Johannson, G., 855, *890*
Johansson, J. E., 87, *94*
John, E. M., 631, *653*
John, J. K., 575, *580*
John, O. P., 140, 152, *167*, *168*
Johnson, A., 781, *798*
Johnson, A. H., 802, *813*
Johnson, A. L., 572, 575, 576, *578*, 849, *852*
Johnson, A. M., 705, *707*
Johnson, B. T., 830, *835*
Johnson, C., 303, *312*
Johnson, C. A., 219, *232*, 460, 461, 462, 464, *466*, *467*, 526, *535*, 717, *724*
Johnson, C. C., 150, *170*
Johnson, C. H., 508, *512*
Johnson, C. L., 263, *277*, 520, *536*
Johnson, D. M., 23, *46*
Johnson, D. R., 366, *380*
Johnson, D. S., 398, *400*
Johnson, E. H., 66, 71, 73, *83*, 433, 435, *439*
Johnson, E. J., 25, *43*
Johnson, F., 499, 501, *513*
Johnson, H. J., 704, *706*
Johnson, J., 663, *667*, 859, *888*
Johnson, J. A., 805, 809, *813*, *815*
Johnson, J. C., 584, *589*
Johnson, J. E., 26, 40, *43*
Johnson, J. J., 731, 732, 733, 734, 739, *740*
Johnson, J. L., 629, *652*
Johnson, J. V., 215, *232*, 350, *362*, 855, *890*
Johnson, K. A., 473, *476*
Johnson, M. A., 472, *475*
Johnson, M. K., 408, *412*
Johnson, M. M. P., 542, 543, 544, 546, *555*
Johnson, R., 544, 549, *554*, 850, *852*
Johnson, R. A., 804, *815*
Johnson, R. C., 733, *742*
Johnson, R. E., 779, 794, *799*
Johnson, S. B., *446*, *447*, 449, *456*
Johnson, S. J., 788, 789, *796*
Johnson, S. L., 154, *167*, 267, *277*
Johnson, S. M., 873, *890*
Johnson, S. P., 663, *668*
Johnson, T. R., 502, *513*
Johnson, V., 300, *312*
Johnson, V. A., 811, *813*
Johnston, D., 464, *466*
Johnston, F. E., 265, *279*
Johnston, J. C., 121, *136*
Johnston, J. J., 524, *537*
Johnston, L. D., 459, 460, 461, 464, *465*, *467*, 601, *609*
Johnston, M., 600, *609*
Johnstone, B., 663, *667*
Joiner, T. E., 154, *170*
Joly, J. R., 829, *835*
Jonas, B. S., 153, *167*
Jones, B., 765, 768, *774*
Jones, D., 153, 156, *162*, 473, *474*, 662, *666*
Jones, D. R., 329, *334*, 432, *439*
Jones, F. N., 371, *382*
Jones, G., 340, *346*
Jones, J. H., 870, 872, *890*
Jones, J. K., 573, *578*
Jones, J. L., 736, *743*, *744*
Jones, K. L., 503, *511*
Jones, K. P., 631, *652*
Jones, L. L., 486, *493*
Jones, L. S., 717, *725*
Jones, M., 563, *570*, 803, *815*
Jones, M. C., 300, 301, *311*
Jones, M. L., 546, *557*
Jones, M. R., 498, *513*
Jones, N. L., 473, *475*
Jones, P., 499, 501, *513*
Jones, S., 20, 21, *44*, 460, *467*
Jones, S. M., 442, *446*
Jones, T., 676, *681*
Jones, W., 864, 868, *894*
Jono, R. T., 73, *81*
Jonsson, H., 221, 227, *233*
Joossens, J. V., 699, *707*
Joplin, J. R., 354, *362*
Jordan, B., 859, *890*
Jordan, S. W., 877, *890*
Jordan, V. C., 719, *725*
Jordan, W., 872, 873, 874, *890*
Jorgensen, R. S., 177, *191*
Jorgenson, C., 593, *611*
Jose, B., 828, *833*, *834*
Joseph, H., 160, *169*
Joseph, J. G., 4, *16*
Joseph, M. H., 252, *260*
Josephs, R. A., 303, *317*
Josephson, R. V., 855, *893*
Joshi, J., 675, *681*
Josse, R. G., 676, *681*
Joyce, C. R. B., 22, *45*
Joyner, M., 635, *654*, 827, *833*
Judd, C. M., 212, *232*, 737, *743*
Judd, J. T., 289, *315*
Judd, L. L., 283, 284, 301, *315*
Judge, J., 525, *539*
Jules-Roseta, B., 873, *890*
Julius, S., 431, *439*
Julkunen, J., 157, *165*
June, L., 255, *261*
Juneau, M., 576, *580*
Jung, D. L., 629, 630, 647, *655*
Jurich, J. A., 63, 64, *79*
Jussim, L., 66, 76, *79*, 149, *164*
Just, J., 804, *814*
Justesen, D. R., 646, *656*

Justice, A., 748, *755*
Justice, A. C., 471, *475*
Justice, J., 867, 868, *889*
Jutras, S., 480, *490*
Jylhä, M., 216, *231*

K

Kadden, R. M., 285, *313*
Kaell, A. T., 406, 407, *411*, *412*, *413*
Kagan, A., 646, *655*
Kagan, J., 65, *78*, 344, *347*
Kagawa-Singer, M., 436, *440*
Kahana, B., 325, *336*, 484, *490*
Kahana, E., 484, *490*
Kahill, S., 419, 425
Kahn, H. S., 268, *279*
Kahn, J. O., 811, *813*, 826, *833*, 846, 850, *852*
Kahn, R. L., 349, 350, 351, 355, 358, *361*, *362*, 415, 420, 425, 620, *624*, 821, *832*
Kahn, S., 177, 178, 185, *191*, 353, *361*, 602, *609*, 643, *653*
Kahn, W., 574, *579*
Kahna, L., 804, *814*
Kahneman, D., 197, *206*, 407, 408, *413*, 728, 733, *740*, *743*, *745*
Kahnemann, D., 38, 40, *43*
Kaiser Family Foundation, 825, *835*
Kaiser, M. K., 486, 488, *490*
Kaiser, P., 328, *332*, 690, *692*
Kaitila, I., 454, *455*
Kalaher, S., 124, *136*
Kalarchian, M. A., 273, *276*
Kaleebu, P., 808, *814*
Kalichman, S., 822, *835*
Kalichman, S. C., 3, *16*, 823, 830, 831, *834*, *835*, 848, 850, *852*, 870, 872, *890*
Kalil, K. M., 497, 506, 507, *514*
Kalil, R. S. N., 575, *579*
Kalin, N. H., 157, *163*
Kalincinski, I., 373, *384*
Kalis, B. L., 703, *707*
Kalish, L., 824, 827, *836*
Kalkhoff, R. K., 645, *652*
Kalman, D., 717, *723*
Kalsbeek, W., 869, *892*
Kalsbeek, W. D., 435, *439*, 486, *491*
Kalstrom, G. E., 434, *440*
Kamada, T., 77, *81*
Kamali, A., 829, *837*
Kamarck, T., 223, *232*, 327, 329, *334*, 473, *475*, 500, *512*, 663, *667*
Kamarck, T. W., 77, *81* 142, 144, 154, *167*, 226, *231*, 433, 435, *438*
Kamb, M. L., *16*
Kame, V. D., 525, *534*
Kamen-Siegel, L., 64, 74, *81*, 180, *191*
Kames, L. D., 546, *556*
Kamin, L. J., 436, *439*
Kaminsky, B., 153, *166*
Kamiya, J., 88, 89, *93*, *94*
Kammeier, M. L., 301, *311*
Kammerman, S., 849, *853*
Kampert, J. B., 629, 630, 647, 649, *652*, *655*
Kan, L., 218, *231*, *233*, 329, *333*, 751, 752, *755*
Kanani, R., 849, *852*
Kanazir, D. T., 67, *80*
Kandel, D., 462, *467*
Kandel, D. B., 196, *206*, 303, 304, 305, *311*, *312*
Kanders, B. S., 266, *277*, 526, *535*
Kane, F., 829, *835*
Kane, R. A., 469, *475*
Kanetsky, P., 531, *536*
Kanfer, F. H., 4, 5, 13, *16*, 19, *43*
Kanfer, R., 4, *16*
Kang, S., 806, *813*
Kanki, P. J., 829, *835*
Kann, L., 825, *835*
Kannel, W. B., 67, *80*, 142, 147, 153, *166*, *168*, 471, *475*, 630, *653*, 669, *680*
Kanner, A. D., 68, *81*
Kano, M. J., 267, 272, *278*
Kanouse, D., 777, *797*
Kant, A. K., 869, *890*
Kant, G. J., 257, *260*
Kantner, J., 790, *799*
Kanuha, V., 542, *556*
Kanzajian, P. H., 828, *837*
Kapferer, B., 865, *890*
Kapiro, J., 72, *81*
Kaplan, B. H., 153, *171*, 215, 225, *229*, *233*, 436, *438*, 500, 505, 509, *516*, 523, 524, *535*
Kaplan, B. J., 498, 510, *514*
Kaplan, D., 301, *310*
Kaplan, E. H., 823, *835*
Kaplan, G., 55, *57*, 66, 76, *82*, 146, 153, 154, 156, 157, *165*, *167*, 215, 216, 218, *231*, *232*, *233*, 328, *334*, 473, *475*, 632, *651*, 662, 664, *667*
Kaplan, G., 286, *312*, 473, *475*
Kaplan, G. D., 51, *57*, 181, *193*, 236, *247*
Kaplan, H. B., 303, *312*
Kaplan, H. I., 252, *260*
Kaplan, H. S., 719, *723*
Kaplan, J. R., 62, 72, *82*, 143, 151, 152, 154, 158, 159, *164*, *167*, *168*, 641, *654*, 663, *667*
Kaplan, R. F., 297, *312*
Kaplan, R. M., 150, *170*, 220, *231*, 327, *334*, 387, 398, *399*, *401*, 470, 472, *475*, 576, *577*, 734, *743*
Kaplan, S., 718, *721*, 773, *774*, 848, *852*
Kaprio, J., 66, *82*
Kaptchuk, T. J., *706*, 865, 866, *890*
Karagodina, I. L., 373, *382*
Karan, L., 252, *260*
Karas, R. H., 472, *474*
Karasek, R., 68, *81*, 855, *890*
Karasek, R. A., 350, 351, 358, *361*, *363*, 663, *667*
Kardaun, J. W. P. F., 469, *474*
Karita, E., 824, *839*
Kark, S. L., *607*, *611*
Karlin, R., 368, *382*
Karlin, R. A., 368, 370, *379*, *383*
Karlovac, M., 366, 370
Karlow, H., 857, 858
Karlsson, C., 371, 373, *380*
Karmiloff-Smith, A., 787, 788, *797*
Karno, M., 638, *656*
Karoly, P., 63, *81*, 122, 124, 130, *134*, 391, *399*
Karon, J., 827, *838*
Karon, J. M., 801, *814*, 824, *833*
Karoum, F., 74, *82*
Karper, L. P., 255, *260*
Karsdorf, G., 373, *382*
Karvonen, M., 629, *655*
Kasai, M., 753, *754*
Kase, N., 566, *570*
Kash, K., 732, 735, *743*
Kash, K. M., 735, *743*
Kashani, J. H., 583, 584, 588, *589*, *590*
Kashani, S. R., 583, 588, *589*, *590*
Kasiske, B. L., 575, *579*, 804, *814*
Kasl, S. V., 22, 36, *41*, *43*, 146, *166*, 226, *231*, 328, *334*, 480, *489*, *491*, *493*, 688, *693*
Kaslow, R., 806, *813*, *815*
Kaslow, R. A., 803, *814*
Kasperson, J. X., 728, 729, *743*
Kasperson, R. E., 728, 729, *743*
Kasprowicz, A. L., 643, *654*
Kasprzyk, D., 239, *246*
Kass, M. A., 574, *579*
Kass, N., 544, 550, *555*, *556*
Kassel, J. D., 327, *336*
Kasser, V. G., 486, *490*
Katabira, E., 808, *814*
Katahn, M., 272, *278*
Katayama, Y., 287, *317*
Kato, P. M., 357, *361*, 393, *401*
Kato, S., 250, *261*
Katon, W., 548, *556*, 632, *653*
Katon, W. J., 546, 547, 548, *557*
Katz, D., 620, *624*
Katz, E., 765, 767, *774*
Katz, E. R., 764, 765, 766, 767, 771, 772, 773, *774*, *775*, *776*
Katz, J., 614, *624*
Katz, M., 850, *852*
Katz, M. R., 389, 395, *401*
Katz, P. P., 330, *334*
Katz, S., 830, *832*
Katz, V. L., 502, *514*
Katzenstein, D. A., 846, 847, 848, *851*, *852*
Katzung, B. G., 327, *334*
Kauffmann, R. H., 398, *401*
Kaufman, J. E., 480, 481, *491*
Kaufman, P. G., 77, *83*
Kaufman, R. J., 110, *114*
Kaufmann, P. G., 329, *334*, 671, 672, *679*, *680*
Kaus, C., 25, *43*
Kavoussi, R. J., 151, *164*
Kawachi, I., 153, *167*, 523, 524, *535*
Kawaguchi, A., 287, *317*
Kawano, K., 805, *815*
Kawas, C., 472, *475*
Kawasaki, T., 699, *707*, 804, *815*
Kay, D. R., 584, *589*
Kay, M., 858, 859, 861, *890*
Kay, T., 526, *535*
Kayamori, Y., 287, *317*
Kaye, G., 603, *609*, 616, 617, 618, *624*
Kaye, M. A., 27, 28, *43*
Kaye, P., 856, *893*
Kaye, S. A., 265, *277*
Kayman, S., 268, *278*
Kazak, A. E., 718, *723*, *724*
Keane, A., 178, *191*
Kearsley, N., 641, *656*
Keating, J., 370, 376, *384*
Keatinge, W. R., 646, *653*
Keefe, F. J., 120, 122, 124, 125, 126, *134*, *135*, *136*, *137*, *489*, *491*, 530, *536*, 576, *579*, 677, *680*, 716, *724*, 758, *775*
Keefe, S. E., 506, *514*
Keegan, J., 672, *681*
Keehn, R. J., 329, *334*
Keeler, E. B., 282, *313*
Keenan, N. L, 287, *317*., 435, *440*, 869, *889*
Keener, J. J., 284, 285, *311*
Keesey, J. W., 822, 826, *838*
Keeter, S., 777, *797*
Kegeles, S., 777, 782, 783, 785, 787, 789, *795*, *796*
Kegeles, S. M., 463, *465*, 566, *569*, 777, 782, 783, 785, *795*, *796*, *798*, 820, 831, *833*, *836*
Kegler, K. C., 621, *624*
Kehoe, K., 72, *80*
Kehrer, B. H., 855, *888*
Keil, U., 373, *382*
Keinan, G., 509, *514*, *515*

Keintz, M. K., 530, *537*, 739, *744*
Keita, G. P., 357, *361*, 541, 542, 543, 553, *556*
Keith, S. J., 283, 284, 301, *315*
Kellar, K. J., 251, 252, *259*, *260*
Kellcrova, E., 373, *384*
Kelleher, K., 292, *312*
Kelleher, K. J., 369, 378, *380*
Kellen, J. C., 395, *402*
Keller, H. B., 530, *537*
Keller, J., 429, *438*
Keller, M., 152, *166*, 824, 827, *832*, *833*
Keller, M. L., 28, 38, *45*
Keller, P., 735, *743*
Keller, S. E., 685, 686, 690, *694*, 753, *755*
Kellerman, J., 764, 766, 769, *775*, *776*
Kellett, J., 366, *382*
Kelley, C. L., 405, *412*
Kelley, J. E., 397, *401*
Kelley, K. W., 112, *114*
Kelley, M. R., 289, *309*
Kellock, D. J., 828, *835*
Kelloway, E. K., 482, *489*
Kelly, G., 19, *43*, 141, *167*
Kelly, J., 870, *890*
Kelly, J. A., 3, 10, *16*, 398, *401*, 787, *797*, 823, 829, 830, 831, *834*, *835*, *838*, 847, 848, 850, *852*, 872, *890*
Kelly, J. G., 593, 604, *609*, *610*, *611*
Kelly, K., *113*
Kelly, K. E., 150, *166*
Kelly, M. J., 716, *724*
Kelly, S., 373, 375, *380*
Kelman, G. R., 291, *318*
Kelman, S., 282, *315*
Kelsall, G. R., 736, *742*
Kelsey, J. L., 117, *134*, *135*, 290, *310*
Kelsey, K. S., 521, *535*
Kelsey, S. F., 662, *667*, 818, *836*
Keltikangas-Jarvinen, L., 63, *81*
Keltner, D., 340, *347*
Kemeny, M., 156, *170*, 505, 506, *517*, 685, *694*
Kemeny, M. E., 54, *57*, 64, 67, *82*, 155, 156, 157, *164*, *170*, *172*, 179, *193*, 218, *230*, 393, 395, *399*, *402*, 685, 686, *693*, 715, *723*, 752, *754*, 761, 763, 764, *774*
Kemeny, M. W., 344, *346*
Kemeny, N., 394, *401*
Kemmann, E., 560, 562, 564, *569*
Kemp, C., 875, *890*
Kemp, S., 408, 409, 410, *412*
Kemp, V. H., 498, *517*
Kempen, H. J. G., 187, *191*
Kempton, T., 222, *230*
Kenady, D. E., 388, *400*, 718, *723*
Kendall, A., 272, *277*
Kendall, L., 858, 867, *891*
Kendall, P. C., 155, *162*, *167*, *172*, 266, *276*, 461, *467*
Kendler, K. S., 160, *167*, 295, *312*, 326, *334*, 632, *653*
Kendrick, D. T., 140, *167*
Kendrick, J. S., 524, 525, *535*, *537*, 869, *892*
Kengeya-Kayondo, J., 829, *837*
Kennard, B. D., 454, *457*
Kennedy, M., 112, *114*, 828, *835*, *837*
Kennedy, S., 327, 328, *333*, *334*, 685, 686, 687, *693*, *694*
Kennedy-Moore, E., 87, *691*, *695*
Kennell, J., 225, *231*, *233*, 496, 509, *515*, *517*
Kenney, D. A., 144, *163*
Kenning, M., 452, *456*
Kenny, D., 737, *743*
Kenny, D. A., 212, *229*, 737, *741*
Kensett, M., 671, 676, *680*
Kent, C., *16*
Kent, S., 112, *114*
Kenyon, K., 151, *168*, 222, *232*
Kenyon, L. W., 669, 677, *680*
Keopke, D., 464, *466*
Keough, K., *740*, *745*
Kercher, K., 483, *492*
Kerckhoff, A. C., 201, *206*
Kerin, J. F., 563, *570*
Kerlikowske, K., 472, *475*
Kerman, B., 603, *610*
Kern, D. E., 548, *556*
Kerndt, P., 817, *838*
Kerner, J., 734, *744*
Kernis, M. H., 152, *167*
Kerns, R., 397, *401*
Kerns, R. D., 120, *134*, *136*, 150, *163*, 387, 394, *401*, 486, 488, *491*, *492*, 671, *679*
Kersell, M. W., 461, *465*, *466*
Kerstein, L. S., 644, *657*
Keruly, J. C., 826, *833*
Kesnaiemi, A., 72, *81*
Kessel, S., 499, *512*
Kessler, H., 734, 737, *744*
Kessler, H. B., 739, *744*
Kessler, L., 528, 530, *533*
Kessler, L. G., 530, *535*
Kessler, R., 521, *538*
Kessler, R. C., 4, *16*, 283, 284, 285, 295, 300, *312*, 326, *334*, 357, *361*, 366, *380*, 472, *475*, 478, *489*, *490*, 500, 508, *512*, *517*, 632, *653*, 821, *835*, *836*, 435, 436, *439*
Kesteloot, H., 287, *313*
Ketcham, A. S., 64, *79*, 156, *163*, 395, 397, *399*, 715, *722*, 751, 752, *754*
Ketterer, M. W., 329, *334*, 669, 671, 676, 677, *680*, *682*
Kewman, D. G., 585, 586, *590*
Key, C. R., 218, *230*, 329, *333*, 855, 877, *890*, *892*, *893*
Key, M. K., 498, *514*
Keyes, S., *568*, *569*
Keys, C., 367, *385*
Keyserling, T. C., 521, *535*
Keystone, E., 685, *692*
Khan, J. A., 217, *230*
Khare, M., 801, *814*
Khare, R., 858, 865, *891*
Khasnulin, V. I., 807, *815*
Khoshaba, D. M., 184, *191*
Khoshnood, K., 823, *835*
Khurranna, A., 824, *836*
Kidd, S., 408, *412*
Kidder, D. P., 574, *579*
Kiecolt-Glaser, J., *113*, *114*, 342, *347*, 482, *493*, 823, *839*
Kiecolt-Glaser, J. K., 100, *103*, 144, 151, 154, 157, 160, *167*, *169*, *172*, 226, 227, *233*, 227, *229*, *230*, *231*, 324, 326, 327, 328, 329, *333*, *334*, *335*, *336*, 355, 357, *363*, 393, 394, 398, *399*, *400*, *403*., 481, 482, 484, *490*, *491*, *492*, 664, *667*, 68, 72, 74, *81*, *82*, 684, 685, 686, 687, 688, 689, 690, *692*, *693*, *694*, 709, 711, 713, *722*, *725*
Kiernan, M., 631, *653*
Kieser, M., 67, *81*
Kiesler, D. J., 140, 141, 142, 144, 151, 160, 161, *167*, *172*
Kiev, A., 862, *891*
Kihlstrom, J. F., 159, *163*
Kilbey, M. M., 284, 301, *308*, *312*
Kilbourn, K., 245, *246*
Killen, J., 461, 464, *467*
Killen, J. D., 464, *468*
Killingsworth, C., 496, 505, 506, *513*
Kiloh, L. G., 686, *692*
Kilpatrick, D. C., 804, *814*
Kim, C., 685, 686, *693*
Kim, M. Y., 785, *797*
Kim, P. C., 867, *891*
Kim, S., 326, *336*
Kim, Y. K., 867, *891*
Kimball, A. M., 819, 820, *835*
Kimball, C. P., 703, *708*
Kimberlin, C., 849, *851*
Kimerling, R., 547, 548, *556*
Kimmel, H. D., 88, *94*
Kinalska, I., 373, *384*
Kinder, D. R., 30, *41*
Kindlon, D. J., 444, *448*
Kindy, P., 552, *557*
King, A., 527, 528, *535*
King, A. C., 273, *277*, 524, 526, 527, *536*, 525, 526, 527, 528, *533*, *535*, *537*, 573, 576, *579*, 591, 595, 596, 598, 599, 600, *609*, *611*, 629, 631, 633, 636, 640, 642, 646, 647, 648, 649, *650*, *653*, *655*
King, C. G., *706*, *707*
King, D. S., 65, *78*
King, E., 530, *536*, *537*, 734, 737, *744*
King, E. S., 734, *743*
King, G., 855, *891*
King, J. E., 50, *57*, *58*
King, K. B., 217, *231*, 717, *724*
King, L. A., 63, 66, *81*
King, M., 525, *539*
King, M. C., 803, 804, *814*
King, M. G., 105, 109, 111, 112, *114*
King, T., 503, *512*
Kingsbury, L., 591, 595, 596, 601, 605, *607*
Kingsley, L., 803, *814*, 850, *853*
Kington, R. S., 427, *439*
Kinne, S., 522, *538*, 591, 593, 606, *609*, *611*
Kinney, J. M., 483, 486, *491*, *492*
Kinney, R. K., 64, *80*
Kinney, R. P., 472, *475*
Kinscherff, R., 292, *309*
Kiolbasa, T. A., 330, *331*
Kippax, S., 822, *835*
Kippes M. E., 759, 760, *776*
Kirby, D., 463, *467*, 783, *797*
Kircher, J. C., 157, 158, *163*, *171*
Kirk, L. M., 717, *722*
Kirk, S., 397, *402*
Kirk, S. B., 390, *402*
Kirkeeide, R., 340, *347*
Kirkland, F., 125, 126, *134*
Kirkland, J., 227, *231*
Kirkley, B. G., 521, *535*
Kirkwood, J., 329, *335*, 750, 752, *755*
Kirschbaum, C., 109, 110, *114*, *411*, *412*, *413*
Kirscht, J., 223, *231*
Kirscht, J. L., 576, *579*
Kirscht, J. P., 4, *16*, 36, *41*, 576, *579*, 736, *745*, 818, *835*
Kirsh, L. B., 444, *446*
Kirson, D., 30, *46*
Kiselev, P., 824, 827, *833*
Kishbaugh, C., 219, *232*, 717, *724*
Kitayama, S., 186, *191*
Kitson, G. C., 509, *517*
Kittel, F., 395, *399*
Kitzman, H., 508, *516*
Kivlahan, D. R., *306*, *313*
Kivuvu, M., 794, *798*
Kjaer, M., 642, *653*
Klag, M. J., 154, *165*
Klappach, H., 373, *384*
Klarman, H. E., 627, 628, *653*

Klatsky, A. L., 294, *310*, *312*
Klaus, M., 225, *231*, *233*, 496, 509, *515*, *517*
Kleban, M. H., 36, *41*, 478, 480, 483, *491*
Klebanoff, M. A., 500, *515*
Klebanov, P. K., 442, *447*
Kleiber, D., 527, *534*
Klein, B., 435, *440*
Klein, J., 63, 64, 73, 76, 77, 89, 150, 157, *165*, *166*, 669, 671, 672, 673, 675, 676, *680*, *681*, 857, 860, *891*
Klein, J. D., 829, *833*
Klein, J. L., 289, *307*
Klein, K. R., 273, *276*
Klein, M., 810, *813*
Klein, M. H., 633, 634, *653*
Klein, M. W., 731, 733, *743*
Klein, R. E., 860, *894*
Klein, R. S., 327, *333*
Klein, S. J., 847, *852*
Klein, T., 749, *755*
Klein, W. M., 731, 732, 733, 735, *743*, *746*
Kleinbaum, D. G., 153, *171*, 215, *233*, 433, 435, *439*, 523, 524, *535*, 663, *668*
Kleinman, A., 19, *43*, 62, *81*, 117, *135*, 548, *556*
Kleinman, J. C., 523, *539*
Kleinman, P. D., 759, *775*
Kleinman, R. A., 703, *706*
Klem, M. L., 268, 270, *275*, *277*, *278*, 576, *580*
Klemchuk, H. P., 704, *706*
Klepinger, D. H., 778, *799*
Klerman, G., 152, *166*
Klerman, G. L., 27, *41*
Klesges, L. M., 254, *260*, 872, *891*
Klesges, R. C., 254, *260*, 269, *276*, *277*, 470, 472, *475*, 523, *533*, *536*, 872, *891*
Klevens, R. M., 820, *836*
Kliewer, D., 453, *456*
Klimas, N., 325, 326, 328, *334*, 398, *401*, 685, 688, 690, *691*, *693*, *694*
Klimukhin, A. A., 373, *382*
Kline, A., 790, *797*
Kline, C. L., 124, *134*
Kline, E. M., 88, 89, *94*
Kline, E., 790, *797*
Kline, F. G., 604, *607*
Kline, G., 526, *538*
Klineberg, R. J., 290, *309*
Klinger, E., 302, *309*
Klinke, W. P., 677, *679*
Klitz, W., 805, *813*
Klock, S., 562, 564, *570*
Klohn, L. S., 22, 24, 33, *43*
Klohnen, E. C., 159, *167*
Klokke, A., 829, *832*
Klonoff, E. A., 393, *401*, 855, 856, 859, 869, 870, 871, 872, 873, 874, 876, 880, 884, 885, 886, *891*
Klopovich, P. M., 575, *579*
Klosterhalfen, S. 109, *114*
Klosterhalfen, W., 109, *114*
Klovdahl, A. S., 780, *797*, *799*
Kluft, C., 286, *311*
Kmetz, C., 66, *79*
Knapp, J. E., 156, *170*
Knapp, P., 343, *347*
Knatternud, G., 671, 672, *679*
Knatterud, G. L., 329, *334*, 677, *681*
Knight, B. P., 531, *535*
Knight, R. G., *331*, *336*
Knipschild, P., 371, 373, 374, *382*
Knobf, M. K., 717, *723*
Knoke, D., 603, *609*, 621, *624*
Knoke, J., 572, *577*
Knop, J., 297, 298, *315*
Knopf, R. F., 324, *335*
Knopf, S., 250, *258*
Knopp, R. H., 576, *577*, *579*
Knott, V. J., 523, *536*
Knouse, S. B., 506, *515*
Knowler, W. C., 270, *278*, 296, *313*, 877, *892*, *893*
Knowles, J. B., 703, *707*
Knowles, J. H., 37, *43*
Knowlton, A., 818, 822, 823, *836*
Knox, G. W., 825, *837*
Knox, L. S., 717, *723*
Knox, S. S., 226, *231*
Knusden, L., 216, *233*
Knutson, L. R., 877, *891*
Knutsson, E., 628, *653*
Koarwlny, K., *455*, *456*
Kobasa, S. C., 61, 70, *81*, 142, 144, 158, *167*, 177, 178, 179, 185, *191*, 353, *361*
Kobayashi, J. S., 845, 846, *852*
Kobusa, S., 643, *653*
Koch, G., 603, *610*, 676, *682*
Koch, G. G., 486, *491*, 676, 677, *681*
Kockum, I., 805, *815*
Koelega, H., 376, *382*
Koepke, J. P., 434, 435, *438*, *439*
Koepsell, T., 598, *608*
Koepsell, T. D., 576, *580*
Koeske, R., 266, 273, *276*, *279*
Koeske, R. D., 786, *798*
Koestner, R., 184, *191*
Koffka, K., 253, *260*
Koffman, D. M., 599, 600, *607*
Kofie, V., 869, *893*
Kofler, W., 373, *383*
Kofler, W. W., 373, *383*
Kogevinas, M., 855, *892*
Koh, H. K., 736, *742*
Kohl, H. W., 145, *163*, 525, *533*, 629, 647, 649, *651*, *652*, *653*
Köhler, W., 253, *260*
Kohlmann, C. W., 73, *81*
Kohn, P. M., 65, *81*
Kohorn E. I., 718, *722*, 763, 764, *774*
Kohrt, W. M., 525, *536*
Koiranen, M., 304, *311*
Koivula, T., 288, *311*
Kojima, E., 824, *835*
Kok, F. J., 287, *318*
Kolb, K. J., 352, *360*
Kolbe, L., 454, *456*, 825, *835*
Kolbjornsrud, O. B., 635, 637, 640, *654*
Kolko, D. J., 770, *775*
Kolman, C. J., 289, *314*
Kolman, M. L., 576, *580*
Kolodner, K., 548, *556*
Kolodner, K. B., 76, *80*
Kolonel, L.. N., 218, *231*
Kolton, S., 828, *832*
Koman, J. J., 850, *853*
Komaromy, M., 552, *556*
Kompier, M. A., 326, 327, *334*
Kompier, M. A. J., 358, *361*
Konarska, M., 434, *439*
Konchuk, C., 807, *815*
Kondou, H., 684, *694*
Kondwani, K., *706*, *707*
Kong, Y., 662, *668*
Kong, Y. H., 669, 672, *682*
Konig, J., 67, *81*
Kono, S., 287, *317*
Konopka, B., 528, *535*
Konrad, T. R., 486, *491*, 869, *892*
Koob, G. F., 252, *260*, 830, *835*, 850, *852*
Koob, J., 787, *797*
Koocher, G. P., 715, *724*
Koolen, M. I., 434, *439*
Koolhaas, J. M., 326, *332*
Koopman, C., 340, *346*, 825, *838*
Koopman, J. S., 366, *382*, 781, *797*
Kooyers, K. J., 274, *276*
Kop, W., 150, 157, *165*, *166*, 472, *475*
Kop, W. J., 63, 64, 73, 76, 77, *80*, 669, 670, 672, 673, 675, 677, *680*, *681*, *682*
Koplan, J., 526, *533*
Koplan, J. P., 531, *534*
Koplow, D. A., 119, *135*
Kordonouri, O., 330, *333*
Korecki. R., 373, *384*
Korn, A. P., 826, *836*
Korner, P., 647, *653*
Kornfeld, D., 153, *162*
Kornfeld, D. S., 718, *723*
Kornguth, P. J., 530, *536*
Kornzweig, N. D., 30, *43*
Korolvuk, D., 803, *813*
Korpi, E. R., 299, *312*
Koshakji, R. P., 802, 809, *816*
Koshar, J. H., 496, *515*
Koskela, K., 600, 601, *610*
Koskenvou, M., 66, 72, *81*, *82*
Koskinen, P., 286, *312*
Kosloski, K., 483, 484, *491*, *492*
Kospocvitz, D., 641, *655*
Koss, M. P., 294, *312*, 541, 542, 543, 546, 547, 548, 553, *555*, *556*, *557*
Koss, P. G., 543, 546, 547, 548, *556*, *557*
Kost, K., 777, *797*
Kosten, T. R., 325, *334*, *335*
Kostis, J. B., 675, *681*
Koszarny, Z., 371, 374, *382*
Kotarba, J. A., 120, *135*
Kotin, J., 644, *655*
Kotler, P., 596, 598, *609*
Kotler, P. L., 146, *167*
Kottke, T. E., 600, 601, *610*
Koup, R. A., 805, 806, *813*, *814*
Koushki, P. A., 197, 198, *206*
Kovach, J., 283, *312*
Kovach, J. A., 675, *681*
Kovacs, A., 817, *838*
Kovar, P., 525, *532*
Kovatchev, B., 36, *41*, *43*
Kover, P. I., 647, *655*
Kovess, V., 285, *317*
Kowachi, I., 286, *310*
Kowalewski, M. R., 728, *743*, 782, *797*
Kozak, L. J., 429, 433, *440*
Kozak, M., *346*, *347*
Koziol-McLain, J., 544, 549, *554*
Kozlowski, L., 519, *537*
Kozlowski, L. T., 146, *170*, 250, *260*
Kozma, C., 528, *533*
Kraaimaat, F. W., 393, *400*
Kraemer, G. W., 664, *667*
Kraemer, H., 340, *348*
Kraemer, H. C., 273, *277*, 576, *580*, 664, *668*, 705, *706*, 713, *724*, 752, *756*
Kraemer, J. R., 758, 762, *776*
Krailo, M., 219, *232*, 576, *580*
Krakoff, L. R., 72, *80*
Kramer, B. J., 478, 483, *491*
Kramer, F. M., 271, *277*
Kramer, H., 218, 219, *233*
Kramer, M., 268, *276*, 638, *656*
Kramer, M. S., 496, 501, *515*

Kramer, N., 445, *448*
Kramer, R. A., *455*, *456*
Krank, M. D., 111, *114*
Krantz, D., 97, 100, *102*
Krantz, D. S., 50, *57*, 61, 62, 63, 64, 66, 67, 73, 76, 77, *79*, *80*, *81*, 143, 146, 149, 150, 157, 159, *165*, *166*, *167*, 329, *334*, 366, 373, 374, 375, 376, 378, *380*, *382*, 431, *439*, 664, 665, *666*, 669, 670, 671, 672, 673, 674, 675, 676, 677, 678, *679*, *680*, *681*, *682*
Kranzler, H. R., 285, 299, *312*, *314*
Krasnegor, N., 449, *456*
Krasnegor, N. A., 19, *43*
Krasnovsky, F., 825, *833*, *834*
Kraus, L., 158, *167*, 687, *694*
Krause, J. S., 586, *590*
Krause, N., 211, 225, *231*, 357, *361*, 487, *491*
Kravitz, R. L., 848, *852*
Kraxberger, B. E., 736, *743*
Krebs-Smith, S. M., 521, *538*
Kreger, B. E., 266, *277*, 631, *652*
Kreiger, N., 290, *312*
Kreiss, J. K., 824, 825, 828, *833*, *837*
Kremen, A. M., 159, *163*
Kremer, E. F., 120, *133*
Krenz, C., 482, *493*
Kretzmann, J. P., 602, *609*
Kreuger, L. W., 74, *79*
Kreuter, M., 519, 521, *534*
Kreuter, M. W., 591, 599, 602, *609*, 730, 731, 732, 735, *742*, *743*
Krieger, N., 185, *191*, 432, *439*, 818, *834*, *836*, 870, *891*
Krier, M., 222, *230*
Krikler, S., 669, 676, *679*
Kris-Etherton, P., 272, *277*
Krishnan, K. R. R., 471, *474*, *475*, *476*
Krishnan, R., 154, *172*
Kriska, A., 526, *537*, 573, *579*, 629, 646, 647, 648, *655*
Kriska, A. M., 527, *536*
Kristal, A., 522, *538*
Kristal, A. R., 521, 522, *533*, *534*, *536*, *538*
Kristt, D. A., 92, *94*
Krittayaphong, R., 674, 676, *681*, *682*
Kritz-Silverstein, D., 530, *534*
Krogh, A., 87, *94*
Krohne, H. W., 24, *43*, 73, *81*
Krolewski, A. S., 330, *334*, 471, *475*, 629, *654*
Krone, R. J., 64, *80*, 677, *680*
Kronenberger, W. G., 453, *456*
Kronfol, Z., 684, *694*
Krook, J., 717, *722*
Krozely, M. G., 759, 761, 772, *774*
Kruczek, T., 452, *456*
Krueger, G. P., 326, 327, *334*
Krueger, J., 197, *206*
Kruger, A., 705, *707*
Kruger, M., 290, *307*
Krull, J. L., 521, *532*, 855, 856, *888*
Kruppa, B., 371, *379*
Kruskemper, G. M., 633, 638, *653*
Kruus, L., 24, *45*
Krystal, J., 255, *260*
Kryter, K., 371, 372, 374, *382*
Krzely, M. G., 759, 761, *775*
Kubitz, K. A., 638, 645, *655*
Kubofcik, J., 806, *816*
Kubzansky, L. D., 153, *167*
Kuchemann, C. S., 719, *724*
Kuchibatla, M., 432, 435, *440*
Kuczmarski, R. J., 263, *277*, 520, *536*
Kuehnel, R. H., 272, 273, *279*
Kufe, D., 849, *853*
Kugler, J., 633, 638, *653*
Kuhar, M. J., 252, *260*
Kuhl, J., *706*
Kuhlman, D. M., 300, *318*
Kuhn, C. M., 146, 149, 150, *163*, *172*, *173*, 642, *651*, 663, 664, *667*, *668*, 674, *682*
Kuhn, F. E., 675, *681*
Kuhn, L., 826, *839*
Kulik, J. A., 36, 37, *43*, 202, 203, *206*, *207*, 217, *231*
Kulikov, I. V., 807, *815*
Kuller, L., 372, 373, *380*, *385*
Kuller, L. H., 22, 33, *45*, 153, 157, *167*, 265, 268, 269, 270, *277*, *278*, *279*, 372, *385*, 576, *580*, 662, *667*, 714, *724*, 818, *836*
Kumanyika, S., 869, *891*
Kumanyika, S., K., 436, *440*
Kumar, M., 63, 74, *80*, 245, *246*, 342, 343, *346*, *347*, 398, *401*, 686, 690, *693*, 753, *755*
Kumar, R., 250, *258*, 824, *836*
Kumashiro, M., 77, *81*
Kummel, E., 119, *137*
Kunitz, S., 431, *438*
Kunitz, S. J., 877, 878, 879, *891*
Kuno, R., 688, *692*
Kunstman, K., 806, *813*
Kuntz, A., 85, *94*
Kunz, J. F., 753, *755*
Kunzelman, C. L., 877, *892*
Kuo, W. H., 185, *191*
Kuosmanen, P., 290, *311*
Kupari, M., 286, *312*
Kupelnick, B, *706*
Kupersmidt, J. B., 445, *447*
Kupfer, D. J., 146, *166*, 266, *279*
Kuppermann, M., 567, *569*
Kurita, A., 676, *680*
Kuritzkes, D. R., 811, *813*
Kurji, K., 605, *609*
Kurppa, K., 371, *383*
Kurth, C. L., 267, *276*
Kurz, D., 549, 551, *556*
Kurzon, M., 292, *307*
Kusaka, Y., 684, *694*
Kusche, C. A., *162*, *166*
Kushi, L. H., 520, *535*
Kushner, M. G., 283, 300, 301, *312*
Kusnecov, A. W., 105, 109, 111, *114*
Kusulas, J. W., 140, 143, 155, 160, *168*
Kusumakar, V., 325, *336*
Kuttner, L., 765, 766, *775*
Kutvrit, D. M., 855, *893*
Kutz, I., 689, *692*
Kutz, L. A., 713, *722*, 753, *754*
Kverno, K. S., 753, *755*
Kvetnansky, R., 642, *654*
Kwiatkowski, D., 808, *813*
Kwoh, C. K., 572, 574, 575, *577*, *578*

L

L'Abbate, A., 675, *681*
La Perriere, A. R., 688, *694*
La Vasque, M. E., 254, *260*
La Veau, P. J., 671, *681*
La Vecchia, C., 288, 290, *312*
Laakso, R., *331*, *335*
Laaksonen, H., 66, *82*
Labarthe, D., 429, *437*
Labouvie, E. W., 301, *307*
Labouvie, W. W., 300, *312*
Lacey, L., 523, 524, 531, *532*, *536*
Lachassine, E., 824, *833*
Lacher, U., 684, 689, *693*
Lack, E. R., 70, *82*
Lackland, D., 526, *538*
LaCroix, A. Z., 286, *316*, 435, *439*, 663, *668*
Lacroix, J. M., 22, 27, 36, *43*, *46*
Lacy, C. R., 675, *681*
Laderman, C., 858, *891*
Ladwig, K. H., 67, *81*
Lafreniere, K., 65, *81*
Laga, M., 794, *798*, 825, *836*
Lagarde, E., 829, *836*
Laguerre, M., 861, 863, 872, 873, 874, *891*
Lahiri, A., 676, *679*
Lakatta, E. G., 469, *476*
Lake, B. W., 642, *654*
Lakey, B., 160, *167*, *169*, 368, 369, *382*, 509, *517*
Lakin, P., 531, *536*
Lakka, T. A., 629, 630, *654*
Lakkis, H., 617, 618, *624*
Lam, G., 806, *816*
Lam, K. S. L., 645, *653*
Lam, L. C., 662, *667*
Lam, Y. W. F., 810, *813*
Lamb, G., 777, *797*
Lamb, M. A., 719, *722*
Lamb, R., 219, *230*
Lambert, C. E., 178, *191*
Lambert, J. S., 827, *837*
Lambert, V. A., 178, *191*
Lambertz, M., 88. *94*
Lamdan, R., 732, *740*, *745*
Lamers, C. B. H. W., 329, *332*
Lamnin, A. D., 340, 343, *347*
Lan, Y., 824, *835*
Land, G. H., 506, *517*
Landa, N. R., 805, 806, *814*
Landau, N. R., 806, *813*
Landers, D. M., 627, 638, 639, 645, *653*, *654*, *655*
Landesman, S., 824, 827, *836*
Landis, K. R., 215, *231*, 355, *361*, 662, *667*
Landis, S. H., 727, *743*
Landmann, R. M., 689, *694*
Lando, H., 204, *206*, 269, *278*, 523, 524, 525, *535*, *536*, *537*, 593, 601, 604, *609*
Lando, H. A., 525, *536*, 601, *609*
Landolt-Ritter, C., 751, *754*
Landrine, H., 393, *401*, 855, 856, 859, 861, 864, 869, 870, 871, 872, 873, 874, 876, 880, 884, 885, 886, *891*
Landsbergis, P. A., 355, 359, *361*, 421, 425, 855, *893*
Landsverk, J., 23, 34, *41*
Lane, D., 530, 531, *533*
Lane, D. S., 530, 531, *536*, 734, 738, *742*, *744*
Lane, J. D., 326, 327, *334*, 436, *437*, 663, *667*
Lane, M., 735, *742*
Lane, M. J., 519, *536*
Lane, M. K., 560, 562, 564, *569*
Lang, A. R., 301, 303, *312*
Lang, C. A., 531, *537*
Lang, P., 31, *43*
Lang, P. J., 95, *103*
Lang, T., 287, *312*
Lange, A., 342, 343, *348*
Langefeld, C. D., 825, *837*
Langenberg, P., 483, 484, *492*
Langer, A., 225, *233*, 671, 674, 676, *681*
Langer, E., 376, *382*
Langer, E. J., 49, 50, *56*
Langer, R. D., 470, 472, *475*
Langford, H. G., 700, *707*
Langhorst, P., 88, *94*

Langinvanio, H., 72, *81*
Langley, J., 300, 301, *308*
Langley, J. N., 87, 88, *94*
Langlie, J. K., 146, *167*
Langlois, J. A., 290, *314*
Langton, S., 619, *624*
Lanier, A. P., 808, *815*, 877, *888*, *891*
Lankenau, B., 599, 600, *608*
Lansky, S. B., 772, *775*
Lantican, L. S. M., 506, *515*
Lantigua, R., 606, *611*
Lantz, P. M., 662, *667*, 821, *836*
Lanza, A. F., 219, *231*, 398, *401*
Lanza, R. P., 576, *579*
Lanzetta, J. T., 122, *136*
LaPann, K., 290, *310*
LaPerriere, A., 325, 326, 328, *334*, 685, 688, 690, *691*, *693*
Lapides, J., 90, *94*
Lapin, A., 728, 736, 739, *740*, *743*
Lapinski, H., 500, *512*
Laporte, R. E., 527, *536*, 629, *653*
Larimer, M., 305, *307*
Larimer, M. E., *306*, *313*
Larner, M., 367, *385*
LaRossa, R., 783, *795*
Larouche, L. M., 124, *133*, 420, 424
Larsen, D. L., 182, *193*
Larsen, F. J., 575, *579*
Larsen, R. J., 389, *400*
Larsen, S. F., 405, 406, 409, *412*, *413*
Larson, D., 344, *347*
Larson, D. B., 632, *652*
Larson, K., 604, *611*
Larson, L., 328, *336*, 374, *384*, 689, *694*, 753, *756*
Larson, R., 410, *412*
Larsson, B., 215, *233*
Larsson, G., 177, *191*
Lasater, T., 528, *533*, 595, 596, *609*
Lasater, T. M., 183, *192*, 460, *466*, 593, 596, 601, 604, *607*, *609*
Lasser, N., 148, *171*
Latané, B., 195, *207*
Lategola, M. T., 635, *655*
Latimer K., 718, *722*, 763, 764, *774*
Latinga, L. J., 153, *167*
Latkin, C., 818, 822, 823, *836*
Latourette, H. B., 720, *722*
Lau, J. K., 809, 810, *814*
Lau, R. R., 22, *44*, 52, 53, *56*, 145, *167*
Lauber, A., 374, *381*
Laumann, E. O., 777, 779, 780, 781, 785, 790, 792, 794, *798*, 825, *836*
Launier, R., 19, 24, *44*
Lauver, D., 734, *743*
Laveist, T., 433, *439*
Laventurier, M. F., 575, *579*
LaVia, M. F., 688, *695*
Laville, E. A., 739, *745*
Lavin, A., 184, *190*
Lavin, J., 498, *512*, 822, 830, *835*
Lavoie, J. P., 480, *490*
Lavoie, K., 150, *169*
Lavori, P., 152, *166*, 445, *447*
Law, M., 764, *775*
Lawler, B. K., 122, *134*
Lawler, J. E., 434, *439*, 639, 641, *651*
Lawler, K. A., 185, *193*, 432, 433, 435, *437*, *439*, 639, 641, *651*
Lawrence, A. M., 289, *309*
Lawrence, R. C., 117, *135*
Lawrence, R. H., 481, *491*
Lawrence, R. S., 728, *746*
Lawson, E. J., 503, *515*
Lawson, K., 126, *135*, 371, *382*
Lawson, L., 429, *440*
Lawton, M., 632, *651*
Lawton, M. P., 478, 480, 483, 484, *491*
Layde, P. M., 288, *310*
Layman, M., 739, *743*
Lazarus, L., 686, *692*
Lazarus, N., 286, *312*, 825, *833*, *834*
Lazarus, N. B., 632, *651*
Lazarus, R., 450, *456*
Lazarus, R. S., 19, 20, 24, 25, 26, 31, 40, *44*, 50, *56*, 61, 62, 66, 68, 69, 75, *81*, 142, 144, *168*, 181, 184, 188, *191*, 240, *246*, 322, 324, *334*, 390, 391, 396, 397, *400*, *402*, 478, *491*, 501, 504, 505, *513*, *515*, 561, *569*, 687, *694*
Lazorick, S., 500, 508, *512*
Lazzarin, A., 803, *815*
Le Moal, M., 112, *115*
Lea, A., 823, *836*
Leach, L. R., 584, *590*
Leap, T. L., 419, 425
Leary, M. R., 736, *743*
Leary, T., 140, *168*
Leavitt, F., 119, *135*
LeBaron, C., 764, 770, 772, *776*
LeBaron, S., 764, 765, 766, 768, 770, 772, *774*, *775*, *776*
Lebedun, M., 202, *207*
LeBlanc, A. J., 824, *839*
LeBlanc, E. M., 635, *654*
Lebovits, A. H., 717, *724*
Lebovits, B. Z., 139, *169*
Lebowitz, B. D., 686, *694*
Lecci, L., 63, *81*
Leckman, J. F., 644, *657*
Lederman, E., 502, *515*
Lederman, R. P., 501, 502, 505, *515*
Lederman, S. A., 499, *517*
Ledoux, J., 29, *44*
Ledzmea, G., 787, *797*, 830, *835*
Lee, A. J., 152, *172*
Lee, A. M., 731, 732, *742*
Lee, B., 807, 810, *814*
Lee, C., 736, *741*
Lee, D., 72, *81*, 330, *331*, *337*
Lee, D. J., 408, 409, *413*
Lee, E. G., 719, *724*
Lee, G. R., 487, *491*
Lee, H., 289, 291, 293, *318*
Lee, I., 629, 630, 647, *655*
Lee, I. M., 290, *314*
Lee, I.-M., 631, 632, *654*, *655*
Lee, J., 227, *231*, 329, *334*, *335*, 521, *538*, 750, 752, *755*, 874, *893*
Lee, J. W., 432, *440*
Lee, K. A., 496, *515*
Lee, K. L., 72, *84*, 662, *667*, *668*, 669, 672, *682*
Lee, M. L., 773, *775*
Lee, N. C., 288, *310*, 523, *536*, 546, *556*
Lee, P. R., 526, *536*, 594, 601, *609*
Lee, R. T., 417, 425
Lee, S., 867, *891*
Lee, S. H., 867, *888*
Lee, V., 345, *347*
Lee, W. W., 524, *537*
Leedham, B., 564, *569*
Lees, R. E., 371, *382*
Lefcoe, N., 635, *654*
Lefebre, R. C., 179, *193*
Lefebure, R., 155, *170*
Lefebve, R. C., 67, 71, *82*
Lefebvre, M. F., 125, *135*
Lefebvre, R. C., 395, *402*, 595, 596, *609*
Leff, J., 575, *579*
Lefley, H. P., 553, *556*, 876, *891*
LeFromboise, T. D., 876, 877, 880, *891*
Leftcourt, H. M., 585, *590*
Legault, S. E., 671, 674, *681*
Lehman, D., 339, *347*, 487, *490*
Lehnert, H., 109, 110, *114*
Lehrer, P., 367, *381*
Leiblum, S. R., 560, 562, 563, 564, *569*
Leibowitz, R., 397, *402*
Leibring, E., 153, *166*
Leifer, M., 497, *515*
Leigh, B. C., 222, *231*, 293, 301, *312*, 777, *798*
Leigh, H., 74, *81*, 157, *167*
Leigh, J. P., 395, *401*
Leigh, P., 473, *475*
Leiker, M., 72, *81*, 145, *168*
Leino, E. V., 663, *667*
Leisen, J. C. C., 397, *401*
Leitch, C. J., 221, *230*
Leitenberg, H., 785, *798*
Leiter, M. P., 415, 416, 417, 418, 419, 420, 421, 422, 424, 425, 426
Lek, Y., 732, 733, *743*
Leka, T. W., 779, *798*
Lekander, M., 110, *114*
Lekatsas, A. M., 828, *833*
Leland, N., 783, *797*
LeMarchand, L., 218, *231*
Lemerise, E. A., 151, *168*
Lemieux, A. M., 76, *83*
Lemieux, S., 265, *277*
Lemke, J. H., 146, *166*
Lemon, J., 289, *312*
Lemp, G. F., 850, *852*
Lenkner, L. A., 372, *385*
Lenox, K., 445, *447*
Lenox, R. H., 257, *260*
Lense, L., 473, *476*
Lenthem, J., 121, *135*
Lentz, A., *16*
Lenz, J. W., 65, *81*, 150, *168*
Leon, A., 64, *79*, 526, *536*
Leon, A. S., 153, *171*, 526, *537*, 573, *579*, 629, 646, 647, 648, *654*, *655*
Leon, G. R., 150, *168*, 523, *534*
Leon, R., 860, 861, 862, *892*
Leonard, J. M., 846, *852*
Leonard, K. E., 292, 300, 302, *307*, *313*, *314*, *315*
Leonard, K., 304, 305, *311*
Leonard, K. L., 432, *440*
Leonard, L. L., 290, *317*
Leonard, P., 74, *80*
Leo-Summers, L., 217, *229*
Lepage, S., 677, *679*
Leparsky, E. A., 496, *517*
Lepisto, E. M., 432, *439*
Lepkowski, J. M., 662, *667*, 821, *836*
Lepore, S., 339, *347*
Lepore, S. J., 150, *168*, 226, *231*, 365, 368, 369, 370, 375, 376, 377, 378, *381*, *382*, 393, 394, *401*, 501, *515*, 674, *681*
Lercher, P., 372, 373, *383*
Lerer, B., 325, *334*
Lerman, C., 30, *42*, 64, *83*, 394, *401*, 519, 530, 531, *532*, *536*, *537*, 714, *721*, *723*, *724*, 729, 732, 733, 734, 735, 736, 737, *740*, *741*, *742*, *743*, *744*, *745*, 749, *755*, 759, 761, *775*
Lerman, C. L., 732, *742*
Lerman, M., 54, *56*

Lerner, M. J., 584, *590*
Lerner, R. M., 442, *447*
Lerner, S. E., 470, *474*
Lernmark, A., 330, *336*
Lerrmakers, E. A., 273, *278*
Lescano, C. M., 736, *743*
Leserman, J., 546, 547, *555*, 687, *694*
LeShan, L., 748, *755*
Lesko, L. M., 110, *114*, 718, *724*
Leslie, C., 858, 866, *891*
Lesperance, F., 67, *80*, 154, *165*, 327, 329, 330, *333*, 662, *667*
Lesser, D. P., 634, *653*
Lesser, I. M., 809, *814*
Lester, P., 827, *836*
Letizia, K. A., 271, 272, *276*, *278*
Letourneau, P. K., 220,*230*
Leu, D., 286, *312*
Leukefeld, C. G., 459, 460, 463, *467*
Leung, R., 290, *314*
Leung, R. W., 630, 632, *655*
Leupker, R. V., 150, *166*
Levengood, R. A., 325, *336*
Levenkron, J. C., 27, *42*
Levenson, A., 177, *190*
Levenson, H., 52, *57*
Levenson, J. L., 748, 750, 752, *755*
Levenson, M. R., 32, *46*, 65, *81*
Levenson, R. W., 63, 75, *80*, 298, 303, *313*, *316*
Levenson, S., 849, *853*
Leventhal, E. A., 22, 24, 25, 28, 30, 31, 32, 34, 37, 38, 40, *42*, *44*, *45*, 68, *79*, 201, 202, *206*
Leventhal, H., 19, 20, 21, 22, 23, 24, 25, 26, 27, 28, 29, 30, 31, 32, 33, 34, 36, 37, 38, 40, *41*, *42*, *44*, *45*, 65, 68, 69. 71. 75. *79*, *81*, *83*, 122, 124, 129, 130, *135*, 139, 144, 145, 146, 151, *164*, *168*, 187, *190*, 200, 201, 202, *206*, *207*, 390, 391, 396, 397, *401*, 460, *467*, 574, *579*
Levesque, J. M., 576, *577*
Levi, F., 290, *312*
Levi, L., 352, *362*, 371, 373, *380*, 685, *691*
Levin, A., 808, *814*
Levin, H., 565, *570*
Levin, J. B., 562, *570*
Levin, J. S., 501, 510, *515*
Levine, A., 396, *403*
Levine, A. M., 219, *232*, 576, *580*, 717, *724*
Levine, B., 574, *578*
Levine, C., 824, *836*
Levine, D. M., 226, *231*, 576, *579*
Levine, E. G., 478, 483, *490*
Levine, H. M., 160, *170*
Levine, J., 397, *401*
Levine, M., 591, 604, *609*
Levine, P., 786, *798*
Levine, P. H., 808, *814*
Levine, P. M., *721*, *724*
LeVine, R. A., 856, 857, *893*
Levine, S., 65, 72, *81*, *84*, 245, *247*, 328, *336*, 855, 856, *887*
Levinson, D. M., 646, *656*
Levinson, H., 350, 351, *361*
Levinson, R., 527, *536*, 869, *891*
Leviton, L. C., 599, *609*
Levitsky, D. A., 272, *277*
Levitsky, D. K., 327, 329, *336*
Levitz, M. D., 464, *466*
Levkoff, S. E., *205*, *207*
Levy, A., 366, 368, *381*
Levy, J., 431, *438*
Levy, J. A., 828, *839*
Levy, J. E., 877, 878, 879, *891*
Levy, L., 366, 369, *383*
Levy, M., 433, *440*
Levy, M. E., 869, *893*
Levy, P. S., 287, *316*
Levy, R., 148, *162*, *165*, 226, *230*
Levy, S., 67, *81*, 329, *334*, 374, *384*, 752, 753, *755*, *756*
Levy, S. M., 227, *231*, 325, 329, *334*, *335*, 748, 749, 750, 753, *755*
Lew, E. A., 265, *278*
Lew, R. A., 736, *742*
Lewenhaupt-Olsson, E., 628, *653*
Lewin, I., 498, *517*
Lewin, K., 19, 40, *44*, 196, *207*, 591, 605, 606, *609*, 818, *836*
Lewinsohn, P. M., 25, 29, *47*
Lewis, C., 716, 717, *723*, *724*
Lewis, C. E., 285, *313*, 520, 527, *536*, *538*, 869, *891*
Lewis, D., 160, *167*
Lewis, E., 864, *891*
Lewis, F., 729, *742*
Lewis, J. G., 663, 664, *668*
Lewis, L. W., 90, *94*
Lewis, M. J., 531, *534*
Lewis, N., 663, *668*
Lewis, P., 864, *891*
Lewis, R., 605, *608*
Lewis, R. E., 803, *812*
Lewis, R. K., 604, 605, *608*
Lewontin, R. C., 436, *439*
Lex, B. W., 436, *440*
Li, C. C., 436, *440*
Li, G. W., 270, *277*
Li, L. W., 481, *491*
Li, T. K., 296, 297, 298, 299, *307*, *310*, *311*, *313*, *315*
Li, Z., 546, 547, *555*
Lian, J. F., 573, *578*
Liang, J., 216, 223, *233*
Liao, Y., 427, *439*
Liberman, R., 703, *707*
Libman, H., 849, *853*
Libretti, A., 373, *380*
Lichtenstein, E., 53, *56*, 223, *232*, 460, 461, *465*, *466*, 522, 524, 525, *533*, *536*, *537*, *538*, 601, *609*, 663, *667*
Lichtenstein, M. J., 576, *579*
Lichtenstein, P., 62, *82*
Lichtenstein, S., 733, 739, *743*, *745*
Lichtman, A. H., 108, *113*
Lichtman, R., 196, 204, *208*
Lichtman, R. R., 396, *403*
Lichtman, S. W., 267, *277*
Lidereau, R., 753, *755*
Lieber, C. S., 288, *310*, *313*
Lieberman, J. R., 506, *514*
Liebeskind, J., 326, *332*
Liebeskind, J. C., 748, *754*
Liebling, B., 146, *170*
Liebschutz, J. M., 547, *556*
Lief, H. I., 416, 425
Liegey Dougall, A., 689, *692*
Liem, J. H., 186, *191*
Liem, R., 186, *191*
Lifson, A. R., 828, *833*
Light, B. G., 444, *447*
Light, E., 686, *694*
Light, K. C., 432, 434, 435, *438*, *439*, 641, *654*, 671, 674, 676, 677, *680*, *681*, *682*
Light, R., 369, *383*
Lillie-Blanton, M., 433, *439*, 822, *836*
Lilly, G., 546, *557*
Limandri, B., 549, 550, 552, *557*
Limon, J. P., 141, 151, 152, 158, *171*
Lin, E. H., 74, *82*, 156, *168*
Lin, J., 270, *277*
Lin, K. M., 809, 810, *814*, *815*
Lin, S. K., 810, *813*
Lin, T. H., 735, *742*, *745*
Linares, O. A., 663, *668*
Linberg, N., 154, *164*
Linde, B., 503, *516*
Lindegren, M. L., 824, 827, *833*, *836*, 850, *852*
Lindell, S. E., 215, 221, 224, 226, *231*
Linden, W., 65, *81*, 150, 157, *168*, 677, *679*
Lindgren, P., 523, *537*
Lindhard, J., 87, *94*
Lindheimer, M. D., 503, *512*
Lindman, H., 739, *742*
Lindsay, D. S., 408, *412*
Lindsay, R., 32, 33, *47*, 155, *172*
Lindsey, A. M., 506, *516*
Lindsey, R., 628, *651*
Lindsley, D. B., 95, *103*
Lindstrom, J., 251, 252, *260*
Linet, M. S., 717, *724*
Lingle, D. D., 472, *475*
Link, K. E., 64, *79*
Link, M. P., 771, 772, *774*
Linn, B. S., *205*, *207*, 686, *694*, 720, *724*
Linn, E., 22, *42*
Linn, L. S., 787, *799*
Linn, M. W., *205*, 107, 686, *694*, 720, *724*
Linnan, L., 521, 522, *534*
Linney, J. A., 605, *609*
Linnoila, M., 74, *82*, 290, 299, *311*, *316*, 664, *667*
Linssen, A. C. G., 124, *136*
Lintell, M., 369, *379*
Linton, M. A., 294, *314*
Linton, S., 121, *135*
Linton, S. J., 121, *135*, 407, *412*
Lip, G. Y. H., 576, *579*
Lipello, A., 573, 574, *578*
Lipetz, P. D., 329, *334*
Lipid Research Clinics Program, 573, *579*
Lipkus, I. M., 64, 65, *81*, 149, *162*, 730, 732, 733, 734, 735, *743*
Lipman, A. G., *721*, *722*
Lipnick, R., 523, *539*
Lipowski, Z., 550, *556*
Lipowski, Z. J., *721*, *724*
Lippel, K., 420, 424
Lippman, M., 67, *81*, 329, *334*, 752, 753, *755*
Lippman, M. E., 750, *755*
Lipsey, M., 344, *347*
Lipshutz, C., 823, *838*
Lipsitz, L. L., 648, *655*
Lipton, R. B., 117, *136*
Lisansky, J. B., 820, *839*
Lising, A. A., 583, *589*
Liskow, B. I., 285, *315*
Lisman, S. A., 303, *317*
Lisoprawski, A., 748, *754*
Lissner, L., 266, 272, *276*, *277*
Listwak, S. J., *113*, *114*
Litaker, M., 779, *796*
Litt, I. F., *474*, *475*
Litt, M. D., 124, *135*, 285, *313*, 562, 564, *570*
Littenberg, B., 735, *741*
Little, B. R., 187, *191*
Littlefield, C., 453, *456*
Littlefield, C. H., 219, *231*
Littler, W. A., 436, *440*
Littman, R., 374, *385*, 689, *695*
Litvak, S. B., 126, *136*
Litwak, E., 507, *515*
Liu, K., 869, *888*

Liu, P. A., 270, *277*
Liu, R., 805, 806, *814*
Liu, S. C., 329, *336*
Liu, W., 436, *437*
Liu, X., 216, 223, *233*
Liu, Y. T., 806, 807, *814*
Livingston, I. L., 226, *231*, 820, 822, 827, 830, *836*
Livingstone, J. N., 687, *694*
Livnat, S., 684, *694*
Llabre, M., 553, *556*
Llabre, M. M., 226, *233*, 433, 435, *438*, *440*
Lloyd, D. A., 821, *839*
Loader, S., 27, *42*
Lobel, K., 552, *556*
Lobel, M., 196, 204, *208*, 224, *232*, 390, 397, *403*, 496, 497, 498, 500, 501, 503, 504, 505, 506, 507, 510, *513*, *516*, *518*, 561, *569*
Lobo, R. A., 561, 566, *570*
Lobstein, D. D., 632, *654*
Locher, J. L., 92, *93*
Lochman, J., 445, *447*
Lock, M., 864, *892*
Locke, B. Z., 283, 284, 301, *315*, 632, 638, *652*, *656*
Locke, S., 176, *191*, 502, *514*
Locke, S. E., 158, *167*, 340, *347*, 686, 687, *694*
Lockhart, L. L., 543, *556*
Locklear, V. S., 463, *467*
Lockwood, C. J., 502, 503, *515*
Lodico, M., 825, 828
Loeb, M., 375, *383*, *384*
Loebel, M., 224, *230*
Loehlin, J. C., 296, *315*
Loewenstein, I., 820, *832*
Lof, K., 288, *311*
Lofback, K., 576, *577*
Lofgren, J. P., 807, *815*
Loftus, E. F., 405, 407, 408, 409, 410, *412*
Loftus, R., 847, *851*
Logan, A. G., 576, *579*, 849, *852*
Logan, M., 858, *891*
Logan, M. H., 860, *894*
Logan-Young, W., 27, *42*
LoGerfo, J. P., 576, *580*
Logsdon, R. G., 484, *489*, *491*, *492*
Logue, P., 868, 869, *891*
Lohman, T. G., 263, *277*
Lohmeier, T. E., 434, *439*
Lohr, J. M., 542, *555*
Lomb, D. A., 806, *815*
Long, B., 527, *539*
Long, B. C., 638, *654*
Long, B. J., 527, *533*, *536*
Long, J. C., 296, *313*
Longabaugh, R., 224, *232*
Longcope, C., 289, *315*
Longini, I. M., 781, *797*
Longnecker, M. P., 287, *313*, *316*, 525, *537*
Longshore, D., 728, *743*, 782, *797*
Lonnqvist, J., 290, *317*
Loosen, P. T., 157, *163*
Lopatka, C., 121, *136*
Loper, R. G., 301, *311*
Lopez, A. D., 286, 288, *317*, 473, *475*
Lopez, A. G., 326, *336*
Lopez, C. M., 605, *608*
Lopez, F. G., 354, *361*
Lopez, J., 553, *555*
Loprinzi, C. L., 717, *722*
Lord, L., 443, *447*
Lorenz, J. P., 641, 642, *652*
Lorig, K., 124, 127, *135*, 245, *246*, 388, *399*
Loscalzo, M., 758, *774*, *775*
Loseke, D. R., 541, *554*
Lotze, M. T., *113*, *114*
Lotzova, E., 750, 752, 753, *756*
Lou, H. C., 501, *516*
Lou, Y. O., 810, *815*
Louie, D., 524, *534*
Louie, L., 804, *814*
Louie, L. G., 803, *814*
Louis, P., 617, 618, *623*
Lounsbury, P., 29, *45*
Love, E. J., 526, *538*
Love, R., 25, 27, 32, 33, *42*, *44*
Love, R. R., 22, 24, 25, 29, 34, 38, *44*, *45*
Loveless, P., 549, 550, 552, *557*
Lovell, J., 847, *853*
Lovell, M., 572, *577*
Lovett, S. M., 497, *511*
Lovinger, D. M., 299, *313*
Low, N., 820, *836*
Lowe, R. A., 821, 829, *836*
Lowenstein, G., 463, *467*
Lowenstein, S. R., 544, 549, *554*
Lowry, P., 502, *515*
Lowry, P. N., 366, *384*
Lowy, M. T., 325, *336*
Lox, C., 527, *536*
Lu, D., 675, *680*, 806, 807, *815*
Lu, D. Y., 675, *681*
Lu, I. L., 504, *514*
Lu, Y., 806, *813*
Lubar, J. F., 91, *94*
Lubaroff, D., 343, *346*
Lubaroff, D. M., 227, *229*, 328, *332*, 687, *692*
Lubin, B., 498, *515*, 633, 646, *654*, *656*, 804, *815*
Lucas, C. J., 703, *707*
Lucas, E. A., 251, *259*
Lucas, J., 471, *475*
Luce, S. B., 736, *745*
Lucey, D. R., 808, *814*
Luchins, D., 419, 424
Luchterhand, C., 22, 29, 34, 38, *44*
Luciana, M., 64, *79*
Lucke, J. F., 73, *80*
Luckett, T. L., 731, 732, 733, 734, 739, *740*
Luckhurst, E., 686, *692*
Ludford, J. P., 459, 460, 463, *467*
Ludlam, C. A., 803, *815*
Ludman, E. K., 865, *892*
Ludwig, W. W., *275*, *278*
Luecken, L., 662, *668*
Luecken, L. J., 663, *667*
Luepker, R., 528, *536*, 604, *607*
Luepker, R. V., 460, 462, 464, *467*, 593, 601, 604, *609*
Luft, F., 434, *439*, *440*, 699, *707*
Luft, F. C., 434, 436, *438*, *439*, *440*
Luker, K., 463, *467*
Lumeng, L., 298, 299, *310*, *311*, *313*
Lumey, L. H., *511*, *515*
Lumley, M. A., 397, *401*, 669, 676, 677, *682*
Lumpkin, J. B., 406, 410, *412*
Lund, E., 631, *657*
Lundberg, U., 356, *360*, 367, 368, 371, *381*, *383*, *384*
Lunell, N. O., 503, *516*
Lunk, E. J., 720, *722*
Lupien, P., 266, *276*
Lupien, P. J., 265, *276*
Luria, A. R., 95, *103*
Lurie, P., 821, 829, *836*
Lushene R., 72, 73, 76, 77, *79*
Lushene, R. E., 638, 639, 642, *656*
Lusk, E. J., 156, *163*, 218, *229*, 389, 398, *399*, 747, 751, *754*
Lustbader, E., 732, 735, *743*, 749, *755*
Lustman, P. J., 67, *79*, 220, *231*, 388, *401*
Lutgendorf, S. K., 343, *347*, 398, *401*
Luthe, W., 97, *103*
Lutz, H., 669, 673, 675, 676, *681*
Lutz, L. J., 575, *580*
Lutzenberger, W., 126, *134*
Luzi, G., 502, *513*
Lydiard, R. B., 284, *308*
Lye, D., 223, *233*
Lyerla, M. S., 291, *315*
Lykes, B. B., 186, *191*
Lyketsos, C. G., 154, *168*
Lykken, D., 356, *361*
Lykouras, E. P., 575, *579*
Lyles, C. M., 826, *834*
Lyles, J. M., 759, 761, *775*
Lyles, J. N., 759, 761, *774*
Lylkken, D. T., 140, 146, *163*
Lyna, P. R., 523, *538*, 732, 733, 734, *743*
Lynch, C. F., 471, *475*
Lynch, J. W., 662, *667*
Lynch, M., 442, *447*
Lynch, S., 635, *652*
Lyness, S. A., 72, *81*
Lyons, M. J., 325, *336*
Lyons-Ruth, K., 151, *168*
Lysle, D. T., 109, 111, *114*, 685, *691*, *692*, *694*

M

M'boup, S., 829, *835*
Ma, X., 325, *336*
Maas, J. W., 644, *652*, *653*, *657*
Mabe, N., 290, *317*
MacArthur, J. W., 645, *651*
Maccagno, A., 802, *813*
MacCallum, G., 672, 676, *679*
MacCallum, R., 713, *722*, 753, *754*
MacCallum, R. C., 484, *492*, 685, 686, *693*, *694*
Maccoby, N., 461, 464, *467*, *468*, 528, *534*, 591, 593, 595, 596, 597, 598, 600, 601, 606, *608*, *609*, *610*
MacDermid, S. M., 63, 64, *79*
MacDonald, L. D., 506, 509, *515*
MacDonald, M. E., 805, 806, *814*
MacDougall, J., 66, 76, *82*
MacDougall, J. M., 72, 73, 76, 77, *79*, 146, 149, *164*, *165*, *168*
MacElwee, N., 759, 761, *775*
Macera, C., 153, 156, *162*, 662, *666*
Macera, C. A., 519, 526, *536*, *537*, 573, *579*, 629, 646, 647, 648, *655*
MacEwen, K. E., 482, *489*
MacGregor, G. A., 699, *708*
MacGregor, R. R., 749, *755*
Maciocia, G., 865, 866, *892*
MacIver, D., 443, *447*
Mack, D. A., 351, *361*
Mackay, P. W., 283, *313*
MacKenzie, C., 525, *532*
MacKinnon, D. P., 461, 463, *467*, 737, *743*
Mackintosh, E., 370, *384*
Mackintosh, J., 366, *383*
MacLean, C., 326, *334*
MacLean, C. R. K., 327, 329, *336*
MacLeod, A. K., 733, *743*
Maclure, M., 150, *169*, 286, 287, 290, *313*, 662, *667*
MacMahon, S., 287, *313*
MacMurray, J. P., 63, *80*
MacNaughton, K., 453, *456*
MacNeill, S. E., 669, 677, *682*
MacPherson, K. I., 859, *892*

MacQueen, G. M., 111, *113*, *114*
Macquiling, K., 549, *556*
Macrae, S., 112, *114*
Madans, J., 523, *539*
Madden, D. J., 640, *651*
Madden, P. A., 295, *311*
Madden, P. A. F., 295, *311*
Maddi, S., 353, 354, *361*, 643, *653*
Maddi, S. R., 177, 178, 184, 185, *191*, 353, *361*
Maddock, J. M., 297, *314*
Maddox, G. L., 146, *168*, 469, *474*, *475*
Maddux, J. E., 54, *57*, 235, 238, 243, *246*
Madhok, R., 293, *313*
Maduro, R., 861, 862, *892*
Maenner, G., 289, 291, 293, *318*
Maere, A., 635, 640, *656*
Maes, S., 390, 391, 397, *401*
Magee, W. J., 357, *361*
Mager, D., 283, *309*
Magnani, B., 434, *437*
Magnani, L. E., 178, *191*
Magnes, L., 297, *307*
Magnus, P., 496, *512*
Magovern, G., 155, *170*
Magovern, G. J., 67, 71, *82*, 179, *193*
Magovern, G. J., Sr., 395, *402*
Magraw, M., 823, *833*
Magrini, O., 566, *570*
Maguire, G. P., 719, *724*
Maguire, P., 719, *723*
Maheswaran, R., 287, *313*
Mahler, H. I. M., 36, 37, *43*, 217, *231*, 736, *743*
Mahler, H. L., 202, 203, *206*, *207*
Mahon, S. M., 720, *722*, *724*
Mahoney, C. A., 782, *798*
Mahoney, L., 714, *725*
Mahoney, M. A., 463, *468*
Mahurin, K., 73, *80*
Maibach, E., 235, 237, 239, 240, 241, 243, *246*
Maides, S. A., 181, *193*, 236, *247*, 51, 55, *57*, *58*
Maier, C., 575, *577*
Maier, L. A., 110, *114*
Maier, S., 585, *590*
Maier, S. F., 31, *45*, 112, *114*, 127, *135*, 180, *192*, 444, *448*, 709, *721*, *724*
Maiman, L., 36, *41*
Maiman, L. A., 729, *741*
Main, C. J., 119, *137*
Mainardi, J. A., 704, *708*
Maislin, G., 290, *310*
Maisonneuve, I. M., 250, *259*
Maisto, S. A., 297, *314*
Maisto, S. L., 301, *313*
Maitha, G., 824, *833*
Maiuro, R. D., 325, *336*
Maixner, W., 676, *682*
Majerovitz, S. D., 219, *232*, 394, *402*, 487, *492*
Major, B., 196, 204, *207*, 785, *796*
Makela, A., 454, *455*
Makepeace, J. M., 541, 542, *556*
Makinodan, T., 689, 690, *694*
Maksud, M. G., 645, *652*
Malarkey, S. B., 481, *491*
Malarkey, W., 328, *333*, 687, 690, *693*, *694*
Malarkey, W. B., 72, *81*, 326, 327, *334*, 481, *491*, 685, 686, 689, 690, *693*, *694*, 713, *723*
Malatesta, C., 344, *347*
Malcarne, V. L., *56*, *58*, 504, *513*
Maldonado, T. S., 780, *799*
Male, D. K., 108, *114*
Malec, J. F., 588, *590*
Malek, S. H., 621, *624*
Malele, B., 794, *798*
Malele, M., 825, *836*
Malinow, M. R., 573, *577*
Maliza, C., 329, *336*
Malkoff, S., 327, 328, *334*, 686, *694*
Malkoff, S. B., 327, *332*, 689, *692*, 753, *754*
Malliani, A., 675, *681*
Mallinckrodt, B., 210, *229*
Mallotte, C. K., *16*
Malloy, P., 224, *232*
Malloy, T. E., 782, 783, *797*
Maloney, B. D., 748, *756*
Maloney, E. M., 808, *814*
Malow, R. M., 782, 783, *798*
Maluish, A. M., 329, *334*, 752, 753, *755*
Mamon, J. A., 734, *746*
Mancuso, C. A., 407, *412*
Mandarino, J. V., 327, 329, *336*
Mandel, D. R., 367, 370, *379*
Mandel, F., 718, *721*, 773, *774*
Mandel, H., 25, *45*
Mandel, J., 831, *833*
Mandelblatt, J., 531, *536*, 734, *744*
Mandelbrot, L., 828, *835*
Mandell, A. J., 645, *654*
Mandell, W., 818, 822, 823, *836*
Mandin, H., 220, *230*
Manfredi, C., 523, 524, *536*
Mangan, C. E., 24, *45*
Mangelsdorff, A. D., 354, *362*
Mangione, T., 777, *797*
Manion, L., 497, 498, 509, *516*
Mann, D., 805, *813*
Mann, J., 220, *230*, 327, *335*
Mann, L. M., 297, 301, *308*, *313*
Mann, S., 705, *706*
Mann, T., 357, *361*, 393, *401*
Manne, S., 219, *232*, 388, 395, 398, *402*, *403*, 764, 765, 768, *775*
Manne, S. L., 25, *41*, 110, *114*, 394, *401*, 686, *692*, 765, 768, *774*, *775*
Manning, M. M., 124, *135*
Manning, W. G., 282, *313*
Manns, A., 805, *815*
Mannucci, E., 72, *80*
Manoka, A., 794, *798*
Manoka, A. T., 825, *836*
Manolio, T., 523, *538*
Manolio, T. A., 663, *667*, 869, *888*
Manson, J. E., 265, *276*, *277*, *279*, 286, 294, *307*, *310*, 471, 472, *474*, *475*, 520, 522, *536*, *537*, *539*, 629, *654*
Manson, S. M., 877, 879, 880, *889*, *892*, *893*
Mant, D., *532*, *535*, 736, *744*
Mantell, J., 218, *230*, 329, *333*, 720, *723*
Manton, K. G., 477, *491*
Mantonakis, J. E., 575, *579*
Manuck, S., 376, *382*, 473, *475*
Manuck, S. B., 62, 67, 72, 77, *81*. *82*, 140, 143, 144, 151, 152, 154, 158, 159, *163*, *164*, *167*, *168* 327, 328, *332*, *333*, *335*, 431, 432, 433, 435, *439*, *440*, 641, 643, *654*, 663, *667*, 674, *681*, 685, 688, 689, 690, *691*, *692*, *693*, *694*, 753, *754*
Manuel, G. M., 716, *724*
Manzella, B., 524, *539*
Manzella, B. A., 576, *577*, 849, *851*
Mao, H.-Y., 72, *81*
Maoz, B., 177, *190*
Mara, G., 373, *380*
Marano, M. A., 477, *489*
Maranto, G., 566, *570*
Marburger, W., 409, 410, *412*
Marchbanks, P. A., 523, *536*
Marchi, F., 672, *679*
Marco, C., *205*, *207*
Marco, C. A., 148, *172*, 406, 410, *413*, 688, *695*
Marconi, K., 849, *853*
Marcovina, S. M., 482, *493*
Marcus, A. C., 729, 731, 735, *741*
Marcus, B. H., 269, *277*, 503, *512*, 524, 526, 527, 528, *533*, *535*, *536*, *537*, 573, *579*, 629, 646, 647, 648, 649, *652*, *655*
Marcus, H., 25, *45*
Marcus, H. R., 186, *191*
Marcus, M., 266, 272, *278*, *279*
Marcus, M. D., 266, 272, 274, *277*, *278*, *279*
Marek, T., 417, 418, 426
Marentette, M., 605, *609*
Margalit, M., 177, *191*
Margo, G., 818, *836*
Margolick, J., 807, 810, *814*
Margolick, J. B., 826, *834*
Margolis, C. G., 758, *775*
Margolis, K. L., 571, *579*
Margulies, S., 340, 342, 343, *347*
Mariana, C., 330, *334*
Mariani, J., 211, 221, *234*
Marin, B., 777, 779, 787, 794, *796*, *798*
Marín, B. V., 785, *798*, 820, *836*, 850, *892*
Marin, G., 820, *836*, *839*, 850, *892*
Marin, N. F., 297, *314*
Mark, D. B., 153, *162*, 217, *233*, 662, *667*, *668*, 677, *682*
Mark, H., 689, *693*
Mark, M., 340, 344, *347*
Mark, M. M., 398, *401*, 753, *756*, 758, *775*
Markandu, N. D., 699, *708*
Markert, B., 373, *382*
Markham, R. B., 826, *834*
Markides, K. S., 428, 436, *439*, *440*
Markoff, R. A., 645, *654*
Markovitz, J. H., 144, 153, *168*, 326, 329, *335*, 674, *681*
Markowitz, M., 846, *852*
Marks, E., 158, *168*
Marks, G., 196, 197, 200, *206*, 219, *232*, 717, *724*, 822, *836*
Marks, J., 153, 156, *162*, 662, *666*
Marks, J. S., 500, 508, *512*, *514*
Marks, M. J., 251, 256, *258*, *260*
Marks, R., 736, *742*
Marksides, K. S., 151, *169*
Marlatt, G. A., 274, *277*, 301, *306*, *313*, *317*
Marlowe, D., 73, *79*, 156, *164*
Marmor, M., 785, *797*, 828, *836*
Marmot, M. G., 287, 291, *313*, 433, *438*, 662, *666*
Marmot, M., 287, *317*, 604, *611*, 662, *666*, 855, *892*
Maronde, R. F., 575, *579*
Maroto, J. J., 179, *193*
Marquis, D. K., 825, *837*
Marrari, M., 803, *814*
Marsal, K., 496, 503, *514*, *517*
Marschall, D. E., 152, *172*
Marsella, A. J., 353, *362*, 368, *383*, 864, 881, *892*, *894*
Marsh, G. R., 469, *474*
Marshall, G., 736, *743*
Marshall, G. N., 52, 53, 54, *57*, 140, 143, 155, 160, *168*
Marshall, J., *113*, *114*, 218, *230*, 329, *333*, 747, 750, 752, *755*
Marshall, J. R., 287, *317*, 520, *535*
Marshall, R., 367, *385*
Marshall, S., 444, *446*
Marsland, A. L., 72, *82*, 154, 158, 159, *168*, 327, 328, *332*, *333*, 685, 688, 689, 690, *691*, *692*, *693*, *694*, 753, *754*

Marsonis, A., 675, *681*
Marston, M. V., 459, *467*
Marteau, T. M., 444, *447*
Marti, B., 629, *655*
Marti-Costa, S., 602, *610*
Martier, S., 290, *307*
Martier, S. S., 290, *307*
Martin, A. D., 273, *278*
Martin, B., 27, 36, *43*
Martin, B. J., 572, *577*
Martin, C. D., *740, 745*
Martin, E. D., 300, *313*
Martin, G., 394, *401*
Martin, G. M., 581, *589*
Martin, H. W., 860, 861, 862, *892*
Martin, J., 368, 369, 376, *381*, 526, *536*, 563, *569*
Martin, J. L., 846, *852*
Martin, K., 453, *456*
Martin, L. M., 530, 531, *533*
Martin, L. R., 61, *80*, 143, 153, 155, 160, *165*, *168*, *169*, 395, *400*
Martin, M., 355, *360*, 574, *579*
Martin, M. P., 807, 810, *814*
Martin, N., 100, *103*
Martin, N. G., 295, *311*
Martin, P., 432, 435, *440*, 472, *475*
Martin, P. M. V., 828, *832*
Martin, P. R., 125, 126, *135*
Martin, R., 29, *45*, 150, *172*, 195, 200, 201, *205*, *207*, *208*, 872, *892*
Martin, R. A., 686, *692*
Martin, S. R., 805, 806, *814*
Martin, S. S., 486, *493*
Martin, W. H., 631, *653*
Martinez, C., 860, 861, 862, *892*
Martinez, G., 343, *346*
Martinez, I. Z., 857, 862, *889*
Martinez, J. E., 502, *514*
Martinez, M., 504, *515*
Martinez, S., 120, *134*, *135*
Martinez-Laso, J., 802, *814*
Martinez-Quiles, N., 802, *814*
Martini, M. C., 717, *724*
Martino, A. M., 251, *260*
Martins, J. B., 645, *651*
Martinsen, E. W., 632, 633, 634, 635, 637, 640, *654*
Martinson, B., 731, 734, 735, *744*
Martinson, J. J., 806, 807, *814*
Martire, L. M., 482, 483, 487, *491*
Marucha, P. T., 326, 327, 329, *334*, *335*, 481, *491*, 686, *694*, 713, *723*
Marwick, T. H., 675, *681*
Marxer, F., 68, *81*
Maschke, C., 373, 374, *383*
Mascovich, A., 689, *693*
Maseri, A., 669, 676, *679*
Mashberg, D. E., 718, *724*
Maslach, C., 415, 416, 417, 418, 419, 420, 422, 424, 425, 426
Maslonek, K. A., 111, *114*
Masny, A., 64, *83*, 729, 732, 733, 735, *742*, *745*
Mason, A., 764, *775*
Mason, D., 614, *624*
Mason, H., 822, *836*
Mason, J., 325, *336*, 802, *814*
Mason, J. O., 571, *579*
Mason, J. W., 68, 75, *82*, 321, 322, 324, 325, *334*, *335*, *336*
Mason, P. J., 452, *456*
Massad, L. S., 826, *836*
Massey, S., 186, *191*
Massie, E., 345, *346*
Massie, M. J., *721*, *724*, 750, *756*
Masten, A. S., 185, *191*
Masters, J. C., 759, 761, *775*
Mastro, T. D., 827, *838*
Mastroianni, L. J., 561, *569*
Mata, A., 226, *230*
Matarazzo, J., *832*, *836*
Matarazzo, J. D., 573, *577*
Matheny, A. P., Jr., 454, *456*
Matheny, K. B., 72, *78*, 717, *722*
Mathews, R., 376, *384*
Mathews, W. C., 849, *852*
Mathieson, B. J., 827, *837*
Mathiowetz, N. A., 408, *412*
Matseoane, S., 531, *536*
Matsubara, T., 675, *680*
Matsuda, K., 809, 810, *814*
Matsuoka, H., 805, *815*
Matt, K. S., 330, *331*, *337*
Matthews, D. E., 267, *277*
Matthews, H., 872, 873, 874, 875, 876, *890*, *892*
Matthews, J. T., 573, *578*
Matthews, K., 60, 62, *78*, *82*, 146, 153, 158, 160, *162*, *164*, *168*, 356, *360*, 372, *385*, 449, *456*
Matthews, K. A., 22, 33, *45*, 61, 66, 67, 70, 71, 73, *79*, *82*, 142, 148, 149, 151, 155, 156, 157, 159, *168*, *170*, *173*, 179, *193*, 222, *232*, 265, 269, *277*, *279*, 326, 328, 329, *332*, *335*, 372, 373, *380*, *385*, 395, *402*, 436, *438*, 469, 470, 472, *475*, 503, *515*, 662, *667*, 674, *680*, *681*, 689, *692*, 714, *724*, 818, *836*
Mattson, R. H., 573, 574, 575, *577*, *579*
Matuszek, P. A. C., 357, *362*
Matyas, T. A., 120, *136*
Matz, L. R., 736, *742*
Mauch, M. Y., 811, *815*
Maul, L., 736, *746*
Maurer, K., 807, *815*
Maurer, L., 548, *554*
Maurice, J., 65, *81*, 150, *168*
Maxwell, A. E., 729, 735, *741*
Maxwell, L., 378, *383*
Maxwell, L. E., 369, *381*
Maxwell, S. E., 461, *466*
May, D. S., 736, *742*
May, P. A., 877, *892*
May, R., 779, *797*
Mayaux, M. J., 824, *833*, *838*
Mayberry, L. J., 497, *511*
Mayberry, R., 734, *742*
Maycock, V. A., 254, *259*
Mayer, J. D., 159, *168*
Mayer, K. H., 847, *853*
Mayer, N. S., 621, *624*
Mayers, R. S., 862, *892*
Mayerson, S. E., 63, *79*
Mayes, M., 91, *93*
Mayle, J. E., 548, *557*
Maynard, K. E., 149, *166*
Mayne, T. J., 343, 345, *346*, *347*
Mayo, K., 527, *536*
Mayou, R., 327, *335*
Mays, M. A., 820, *836*
Mays, V., 820, 822, *836*
Mays, V. M., 787, 788, 789, *796*, *798*, 801, 802, 811, *813*, *814*, 870, *892*
Maziarka, S., 371, 374, *382*
Mazor, M., 502, *517*
Mbiti, J. S., 873, *892*
McAdams, D. P., 142, *168*, 187, *190*, *191*
McAdoo, W. G., *275*, *278*
McAfee, M. P., 294, *310*
McAlister, A., *16*, 461, 464, *466*, *467*, 600, 601, *610*
McAlister, A. L., 461, 464, *467*, *468*, 591, 595, 597, 598, 601, *609*, *610*
McAllister, C., 374, *385*
McAllister, C. G., 328, *332*, *337*, 689, *692*, *695*, 753, *756*
McAnarney, E. R., 496, 501, *515*
McArdle, S., 367, *381*, 434, *438*
McAuley, E., 527, *536*, 628, *654*
McAuliffe, T. L., 830, 831, *835*
McAvay, G. J., 486, 488, *491*, *492*
McBride, C., 524, *535*, 737, *742*
McBride, C. M., 269, *278*, 519, 523, 524, 525, 530, *534*, *536*, *537*, 600, *609*, 730, *743*, *744*
McBride, W. J., 298, 299, *313*
McCabe, J., 527, *538*
McCabe, P., 398, *401*
McCaffrey, D. F., 822, 826, *838*
McCain, G., 366, 367, 368, *380*, *383*, *384*
McCain, G. A., 686, *692*
McCall, M., 572, 574, *577*, *578*
McCallum, A., 293, *313*
McCallum, D. M., 145, 158, *172*, 179, *193*
McCallum, R., 368, 372, *383*
McCamish, M., 782, *799*
McCann, B. S., 576, *577*, *579*
McCann, D. S., 324, *335*
McCann, I. L., 635, *654*
McCarron, D. A., 272, *277*
McCarter, R., 429, *438*
McCarthy, B. J., 508, *514*
McCarthy, D., 369, *383*
McCartney, K., 62, *82*
McCartney, W., 676, *682*
McCarty, R., 434, *439*
McCaul, K. D., 731, 733, 734, 735, *743*
McCauley, J., 543, 548, *555*, *556*
McClearn, G. E., 62, *82*, 266, *278*, 296, *313*
McClelland, D., 158, *167*
McClelland, D. C., 158, *167*, 182, 184, *191*
McClelland, G. H., 212, *232*
McClenon, J., 867, 868, *892*
McCleod, D. R., 154, *166*
McClintick, J., 690, *694*
McClure, C. M., 95, *103*
McCord, J., 305, *313*
McCormack, W. M., 828, *832*
McCormick, M. C., 496, 499, 503, *515*, 827, *839*
McCown, N., 663, *667*
McCoy, H. V., 823, *836*
McCoy, M., 792, *798*
McCoy, V., 828, *833*
McCracken, S. G., 297, *309*
McCrae, R., 202, *206*
McCrae, R. R., 61, *82*, 140, 142, 145, 147, 149, 152, 153, 154, 160, *164*, *168*, *173*, 329, *337*, 354, *362*, 394, 395, *400*
McCranie, E. W., 178, *191*
McCrea, F., 859, *892*
McCreary, C., 119, *135*
McCright, J., 566, *569*
McCroskery, J. H., 153, *167*
McCubbin, J. A., 503, *515*
McCullagh, P., 633, *655*
McCulloch, J. A., 119, *137*
McCurley, J., 270, 273, *276*
McCurry, S. M., *489*, *492*
McCusker, J., 481, *491*
McDaniels, S. M., 109, *115*
McDermott, A., 520, *535*
McDermott, L., 784, 785, *796*
McDermott, M. M., 731, 732, *742*
McDermott, R. J., 734, *741*

McDonald, C., 289, *318*
McDonald, D. A., 782, 783, 787, 788, *796*, *797*
McDonald, D. G., 633, 638, *654*
McDonald, K. B., 506, 508, *513*
McDonald, N., 374, *383*
McDonald, P. G., 435, *440*
McDonald, R. H., Jr., 703, 705, *707*
McDougall-Wilson, I. B., 635, 637, *652*
McDowell, B. J., 92, *93*
McDuffie, F. C., 117, *135*
McElduff, P., 286, *313*
McElmurry, B., 865, 868, 869, *888*
McElroy, M., 66, *79*
McEvoy, L. T., 282, 283, 284, *311*
McEvoy, M., 770, 772, *775*
McEwan, K. L., 561, *570*
McEwan, R. T., 293, *313*
McEwen, B. S., 321, 328, *335*, 502, 510, *515*, 643, *654*
McFall, M. E., 283, *313*
McFarland, C., 198, *207*
McFarland, W., 850, *852*
McFarlane, A., 345, *347*
McFarlane, A. C., *331*, *335*
McFarlane, J., 508, *515*, *516*, 543, 545, 550, *554*, *556*
McFeeley, S., 750, *755*
McGarvey, S., 504, *518*
McGee, D., 216, *232*
McGee, H. M., 22, *45*
McGhee, W. H., 63, *80*
McGhie, A., 124, 129, *133*
McGill, D. B., 531, *532*
McGinnis, J. M., 286, 290, *313*, 526, *536*
McGinnis, M., 600, *610*
McGinty, K., 772, *774*
McGlashen, N., 366, *383*
McGlothin, W., 823, *835*
McGlothin, W. H., 823, *832*
McGlynn, E. A., 389, *402*, 473, *476*, 848, *852*
McGonagle, K. A., 283, *312*, 632, *653*
McGonigle, M., 152, *171*
McGonigle, M. M., 150, 151, *168*
McGough, J. P., 828, *834*
McGovern, P., 593, 601, 604, *609*
McGovern, P. G., 204, *206*
McGovern-Gorchov, P., 530, *536*
McGowan, E. I., 808, *815*
McGowan, J. A., 470, 472, *476*
McGowan, M. B., 586, *590*
McGowen, A. K., 291, *318*
McGrath, P. A., 765, 767, *775*
McGrath, P. C., 388, *400*, 718, *723*
McGrath, S., 225, *231*, 496, 509, *515*
McGue, M., 140, 146, *163*, 295, 296, 298, 299, *313*
McGuigan, K., 461, *465*, *466*
McGuire, M., 575, *578*, *579*
McGuire, M. T., *275*, *277*
McGuire, W., 595, *610*
McGuire, W. J., 461, *467*
McHoskey, J. W., 732, 736, *744*
McHugh, M. C., 786, *798*
McHugh, T. A., 217, *230*
McIntosh, K., 824, *835*
McIntosh, L. J., 496, *515*
McIntyre, C. W., 356, *363*
McKay, G., 211, *229*
McKay, H., 442, *448*
McKay, J. R., 182, *191*, 301, *307*
McKee, D. C., 640, *651*
McKelby, J., 343, *346*
McKelvey, L., 150, 152, 160, *162*, *163*
McKenney, J. M., 575, *579*
McKenzie, S., 523, *534*
McKibbon, K. A., 849, *852*
McKillip, J. L., 602, *610*
McKinlay, J. B., 23, *45*, 225, *232*, 732, *741*
McKinlay, P., 366, *383*
McKinlay, S., 528, *533*, 593, 596, 601, 604, *607*
McKinlay, S. M., 432, 433, *437*
McKinney, M., 564, *569*, 641, *652*
McKinney, W. P., *691*, *693*
McKinnon, W., 685, 688, 684
McKnight, J. L., 591, 602, *609*, *610*
McKusick, L., 293, *317*, 398, *400*, 462, *467*, 688, *692*, 783, *796*
McLain, J. R., 671, *679*
McLanahan, S., 340, *347*
McLaughlin, C., 369, *379*
McLaughlin, J. K., 288, *307*, *308*
McLean, A., 572, *577*
McLean, J., 374, *379*
McLean, M., 502, *515*
McLean, S., 576, *579*
McLeay, R. A., 436, *440*
McLeer, S. V., 543, 544, 549, *556*
McLenachan, J. M., 675, *682*
McLeod, J. D., 821, *836*
McLeod, R. S., 531, *538*
McLeroy, K., 614, 621, *624*
McLeroy, K. R., 528, *536*, 593, 596, 603, 604, 605, *608*, *610*
McLerran, D. F., 521, 522, *534*
McLoughlin, E., 544, *555*
McLoyd, V. C., 432, *439*
McMahon, C., 565, *570*
McMahon, C. E., 139, *168*
McMahon, M., 272, *277*
McMahon, R. P., 329, *334*, 671, 677, *680*, *681*
McMichael, A. J., 808, *813*
McMillan, B., 603, *610*
McMillan, D. W., 622, *624*
McMillen, D. L., 293, *313*
McMillen, R., 344, *348*
McNally, R. J., 326, 327, *335*
McNamara, G., 213, 222, 223, *234*
McNamara, P. M., 265, *276*
McNaney-Flint, H., 471, *475*
McNeil, D., 289, *318*
McNeil, D. W., 301, *307*
McNeil, J. K., 635, *654*
McNeilly, M., 432, 435, *440*, 818, *832*
McNeilly, M. D., 431, 432, *437*, *439*
McNeley, J., 878, *892*
McNicholl, J. M., 806, 808, 810, *814*
McNulty, S., 329, *334*, 677, *680*
McPherson, B. D., 627, 635, *651*, *654*
McPherson, J. M., 369, 378, *381*
McQuillan, G., 801, *814*
McQuillin, J., 366, *384*
McRae, R. R., 32, *42*
Mead, K., 672, 677, *679*, *681*
Mead, L. A., 154, *165*
Meade, T. W., 153, *166*
Meador, C. K., 875, *892*
Meadows, A. T., 718, *723*
Meaher, R. B., 156, *169*
Means, B., 406, 407, 408, 409, *412*
Meares, H., 222, *230*
Meares, R., 374, *381*
Mears, B., 218, *233*
Mechanic, D., 34, 35, *45*, *46*, 69, *82*, 117, *135*, 146, *169*, 195, 200, *207*, 393, 394, *401*, 821, *836*
Medhus, A., 633, *654*
Mediansky, L., 218, *230*, 329, *333*
Medicine, B., 879, *892*
Medley, D., 73, *79*, 149, 157, *164*
Mednick, S. A., 297, 298, *310*, *315*
MedPac, 582, *590*
Medsger, T. A., 117, *135*
Meecham, W. C., 374, *383*
Meehan, E., 596, *608*
Meek, P. S., 298, 303, *313*
Meeske, K., 718, *723*
Mefford, I. N., 126, *133*
Mehta, S., 327, *335*
Mehta, V., 510, *514*
Meichenbaum, D., 122, 126, 128, 129, *136*, 757, 758, *775*, *776*
Meier, A., 269, *278*
Meier, A. M., 499, 501, *513*
Meier, H., 374, *381*
Meier, L. J., 243, *246*
Meier, R., 603, *611*, 619, *625*
Meigs, J. W., 720, *722*
Meijer, H., 371, *382*
Meikle, A. W., 471, *475*
Meilahn, E. N., 153, *168*, 265, 270, *278*, *279*, 576, *580*, 662, *667*, 818, *836*
Meilman, H., 150, *165*
Meilman, P. W., 291, 293, *313*, *315*
Meis, P., 496, *516*
Meis, P. J., 500, *515*, *516*
Meisenheimer, J. R., II., 353, *361*
Meisler, A. W., 848, *852*
Mela, D. J., 267, *277*
Melamed, B., 31, *43*
Melamed, B. G., 219, *232*, 449, *456*
Melamed, S., 371, 372, 373, *383*
Melanson, P. M., 330, *335*
Melbye, M., 808, *815*
Melcher, G. P., 808, *814*
Melchert, H., 372, *382*
Melchior, L. A., 825, *835*
Melin, B., 356, 260
Melin, L., 121, *135*, 407, *412*
Melisaratos, N., 751, *754*
Mellion, M., 641, *652*
Mellman, T. A., 326, *335*
Mello, N. K., 289, *313*
Melmon, K. L., 703, *708*
Melton, J., 544, 547, 548, *557*
Meltzer, D. W., 574, *579*
Meltzer, H. Y., 644, *653*
Melzack, R., 27, *45*, 118, 127, 128, 131, *133*, *135*
Mendelberg, H., 644, *653*
Mendelson, J. H., 289, *313*
Mendelson, M., 480, *489*, 633, *650*
Mendes de Leon, C. F., 72, *81*, 327, 330, *335*
Mendez, V. M., 343, *346*
Mendola, R., 55, *57*, 561, 562, *570*
Meneely, G. R., 434, *438*
Menely, G. R., 699, *707*
Menendez, B. S., 821, *836*
Menon, G., 406, 407, *412*
Menton, K. G., 366, 367, *383*
Merbaum, M., *102*
Mercado, A. M., 326, 327, *334*, 481, *491*, 686, *694*, 713, *723*
Mercer, M. B., 830, *838*
Mercer, R. T., 497, 498, *516*
Mercy, J. A., 542, *556*
Meredith, K., 119, *133*
Meredith, L. S., 473, *476*
Merigan, T. C., 571, *580*
Merikangas, K. R., 284, 295, *314*
Merino, F., 808, *814*
Mermelstein, R., 223, *232*, 500, *512*, 663, *667*
Mermelstein, R. J., 736, *744*

Mero, R. P., 472, *475*, 662, *667*, 821, *836*
Merrick, E., 825, *836*
Merrill, J., 463, *467*
Merritt, R. K., 526, *533*, 628, 646, *651*, *654*
Merriwether-DeVries, C., 444, *446*
Merskey, H., 117, *133*, *135*
Merton, R. K., 351, *362*
Mertz, C., 150, 157, *166*
Mervis, C. B., 23, *46*
Merz, C. N., 669, 673, 675, 676, *681*
Merz, C. N. B., 63, 64, 73, 76, 77, *80*
Meshefedjian, G., 481, *491*
Messe, M. R., 717, *724*
Messer, E., 858, *892*
Messerschmidt, P. M., 292, 294, *309*
Messick, D. M., 196, *206*
Messick, G., 100, *103*, 688, *693*
Metter, E., 472, *475*
Metts, S., 782, 787, *796*, *798*
Metz, J. A., 272, *277*
Metzger, B. E., 270, *278*
Metzger, L. S., 287, *315*
Metzler, C. W., 462, *465*
Metzner, H. L., 210, 214, 215, *231*
Mewhinney, D. M. K., 785, 788, *797*
Meyer, A. J., 601, *610*
Meyer, B., 498, *513*
Meyer, D., 19, 22, 23, 28, 36, 38, *44*, *45*, 68, *81*, 158, *167*, 200, *207*, 574, *579*
Meyer, D. F., 326, *335*
Meyer, I. H., 185, 188, *191*
Meyer, K., 826, *833*
Meyer, P. A., 519, *536*
Meyer, R. E., 284, 285, 299, *306*, *311*, *314*, *316*
Meyer, R. J., 684, *694*
Meyer, T., 340, 344, *347*
Meyer, T. J., 398, *401*, 753, *756*, 758, *775*
Meyer, W. A., III, 827, *837*
Meyer-Bahlburg, H. F. L., 825, *838*
Meyerhoff, J. L., 257, *260*
Meyerowitz, B., 564, *569*
Meyerowitz, B. E., *740*, *744*
Meyers, A. M., 575, *579*
Meyers, A. R., 290, *308*
Meyers, A. W., 254, *260*, 269, *276*, 269, *277*
Meyers, B., 718, *721*, 773, *774*
Meza, M. A., 343, *346*
Mezey, E., 289, *314*
Mezey, M. D., 469, *475*
Miaskiewicz, S., 272, *279*
Micceri, T., 779, *797*
Micciolo, R., 506, *518*
Michael, N. L., 807, 810, *814*
Michael, R. T., 777, 779, 780, 781, 785, 790, 792, 794, *798*, 825, *836*
Michaelis, B. A., 828, *839*
Michaels, D., 824, *836*
Michaels, S., 777, 779, 780, 781, 785, 790, 792, 794, *798*, 825, *836*
Michalak, R., 373, *383*
Michal-Johnson, P., 788, 789, *798*
Michel, M. C., 689, *695*
Michela, J. L., 351, *361*
Michelassi, C., 675, *681*
Michielutte, R., 500, *516*, 531, *534*
Michnich, M. E., *532*, *538*
Mico, P. R., 599, *610*
Midanik, L. T., 177, *191*, 282, *314*
Middlestadt, S. E., 4, 10, *16*
Midgley, C. 443, *447*
Midzenski, M., 732, *742*
Mielke, R., 869, *890*
Mihalek, R. M., 299, *311*
Mijovic, C., 804, *813*
Mikawa, K., 287, *317*
Mikulincer, M., 178, 179, 184, *190*, *229*, *233*, 354, *362*
Milanesi, L., 366, *383*
Milas, N. C., 576, *577*
Milburn, A. K., 546, 547, *556*, *557*
Milech, D., 125, 126, *135*
Mileno, M., 826, *833*
Milgrom, H., 451, 452, *456*
Milio, N., 591, 599, *610*
Millar, K., 21, *45*
Millar, L. K., 500, *512*
Millar, M. G., 21, *45*
Millard, R.W., 758, *775*
Miller, A. B., 287, *317*, 520, *535*
Miller, A. J., 732, 736, *744*
Miller, A. L., 328, *332*
Miller, B., 480, 481, 482, 483, *491*
Miller, B. A., 292, 293, 294, *314*, *318*
Miller, B. H., 483, *491*
Miller, C., 218, *229*, 747, 751, *754*
Miller, C. A., 499, *516*
Miller, D. G., 735, *743*
Miller, D. S., 156, *163*, 218, *229*, 389, 398, *399*, 720, *722*, 747, 751, *754*
Miller, D. T., 198, 199, 200, *207*
Miller, G., 665, *666*
Miller, G. A., 21, *45*, 606, *610*
Miller, H. G., 463, *467*, 827, *836*
Miller, I. W., 285, *308*
Miller, J., 787, *795*
Miller, J. P., 648, *655*
Miller, J. Z., 434, 436, *438*, *439*
Miller, L .C., 782, 783, *798*
Miller, L. S., 282, *315*
Miller, M. A., 699, *708*
Miller, M. C., 506, *516*
Miller, M. H., 200, *207*
Miller, N., 524, 525, *535*
Miller, N. E., 31, *46*, 704, *707*, 88, 89, 90, *93*, *94*
Miller, N. S., 252, *259*
Miller, P., 202, *206*, 221, *233*
Miller, P. A., 151, *169*
Miller, P. M., 10, *16*, 292, 301, *314*
Miller, R. L., 36, *46*, 195, 203, 204, *207*, 339, *348*
Miller, S., 732, 733, 735, *743*, *745*
Miller, S. B., 63, *82*, 150, *169*
Miller, S. M., 20, 24, 28, 31, *45*, 64, 68, 70, 74, *78*, *82*, *83*, 124, *135*, 239, *246*, 714, *724*, 729, 730, 734, 735, 736, *743*, *744*
Miller, T. Q., 66, 76, *82*, 140, 143, 148, 150, 151, 158, *169*, 662, *667*
Miller, T. R., 290, *316*
Miller, W. T., 571, 576, *579*
Miller, Y., 285, 301, *311*
Millers, A. L., 689, *692*
Millingen, K. S., 576, *579*
Millner, L., 531, *532*, *537*
Millon, T., 156, *169*
Mills, J., 373, *383*
Mills, J. S. C., 645, *653*
Mills, P. J., 690, *694*
Mills, R. C., 593, *610*
Mills, T., 50, *57*
Millstein, S., 449, *456*
Millstein, S. G., 26, 37, *45*, 565, *570*, 825, *836*
Millward, L. J., 782, 783, *795*
Milne, B. J., 563, *570*, 576, *579*, 849, *852*
Milner, D., 226, *230*, 435, *438*
Milofsky, E. S., 300, *317*
Minagawa, R. Y., 759, 772, *775*
Mineka, S., 152, 155, *164*
Miner, K., 601, *607*
Miner, L. L., 251, 256, *258*
Mingari, M. C., 328, *335*
Mingay, D. J., 405, 406, 407, 408, 410, *412*, *413*
Minkler, M., 591, *610*
Minkoff, H., 824, 827, *836*
Minor, M. A., 525, *536*
Minowada, J., 753, *756*
Miotti, P., 826, *836*
Miranda, J., 65, *82*
Miric, D., 674, *681*
Mirochnick, M., 827, *837*
Mirsky, A. F., 289, 290, *317*
Mischel, W., 28, *45*, 59, 61, 62, 76, 77, *82*, *83*, 141, 142, 144, 159, *169*, 188, *192*, 619, *624*
Mishra, S. I., 734, *743*
Mitani, H., 676, *680*
Mitchell, D., 120, *134*, *135*
Mitchell, F., 874, 875, *892*
Mitchell, J., 266, *278*
Mitchell, M., 546, 547, *555*
Mitchell, M. C., 289, *314*
Mitchell, R., 604, *608*
Mitchell, R. E., 368, 369, *383*, 603, *610*
Mitchell, S. N., 252, *260*
Mitlak, B. H., 471, *474*
Mitsuya, H., 824, *835*
Mittelman, M. A., 662, *667*
Mittelmark, M., 480, *492*, 528, *536*, 604, *607*
Mittelmark, M. B., 460, 461, *466*, *467*, 525, *536*, 593, 594, 598, 601, 602, 604, *607*, *609*, *610*
Mittendorf, R., 525, *537*
Mittleman, M. A., 150, *169*
Mittlemark, M., 148, *171*
Mittman, N., 807, *812*
Mitz, L. F., 357, *361*
Mixon, M., 431, *438*
Miyake, S., 77, *81*
Miyasato, K., 250, *259*
Mizener, D., 124,*135*
Mizrahi, T., 621, *624*
Mizuno, K., 676, *680*
Mlynek, C., 736, *744*
Mmiro, F., 827, *837*
Moadel, A., 729, *742*
Moch-Sibony, A., 375, *383*
Mock, J., 480, *489*, 633, *650*
Mock, P., 732, *742*
Mock, P. A., 827, *838*
Mock, V. L., 717, *725*
Modi, W., 806, 807, *815*
Moe, T. M., 619, *624*
Moellering, R. C., 699, *707*
Moertel, C. G., 531, *532*
Moestrup, T., 221, 227, *232*
Moeykens, B., 291, 293, *318*
Mofenson, L., 777, *797*, 824, 827, *836*, *837*
Mofenson, L. M., 827, *837*
Moffat, F. L., 156, *163*, 395, 397, *399*, 715, *722*
Moffat, F. L., Jr., 64, *79*, 751, 752, *754*
Moffet, C. D., 877, *892*
Moffitt, T. E., 300, 301, *308*
Mohler, E. R., 675, *681*
Mohr, J. E., 829, *833*
Moilanen, I., 304, *311*
Moinpour, C. M., 388, *401*
Mojonnier, L. M., 700, *708*
Mok, J. Y., 804, *814*
Mokdad, A. H., 521, *537*, 869, *893*
Molema, J., 575, *577*
Moletteire, C., 124, 130, *134*
Molfese, V. J., 497, 498, 509, *516*
Molgaard, C., 464, *466*

Molin, J., 496, *514*
Molina, B. S. G., 301, 304, 305, *308*, *314*
Molinek, F. R., Jr., 473, *476*
Moll, J., 290, *317*
Molleman, E., 204, *207*
Molnar, C., 345, *346*, *347*
Monaco, J. H., 286, 288, *317*
Monahan, D. J., 479, *490*
Monga, M., 503, *516*
Monga, T. N., 124, 129, *133*
Monjan, A. A., 748, *756*
Monou, H., 77, *81*
Monroe, A. D., 847, *853*
Montagnier, L., 828, *835*
Montague-Clouse, J., 285, *317*
Montain, S. J., 631, *653*
Montaner, J. S., 471, *475*, 848, *853*
Montaner, J. S. G., 846, 847, 848, *851*
Montano, D., 497, *516*
Montano, D. E., 239, *246*, 736, *744*
Montebugnoli, L., 434, *437*
Montemartini, C., 676, *680*
Montgomery, A., 296, *308*
Montgomery, A. A., 483, *491*
Montgomery, A. M. J., 252, *260*
Montgomery, R. J., 478, *491*
Montgomery, R. J. V., 484, *491*
Montgomery, S. B., 4, *16*
Monzon, O. T., 828, *837*
Moodley, D., 824, *837*
Mooney, K. H., 717, *725*
Moore, B. S., 375, *384*
Moore, D. E., 523, *534*
Moore, E., 296, *313*
Moore, J., 389, 398, *401*, 822, 826, 828, *837*, *838*
Moore, J. S., 826, *838*
Moore, M., 850, *852*
Moore, M. J., 291, *309*
Moore, M. L., 496, 500, *516*
Moore, P., 202, 203, *206*, *207*
Moore, P. J., 126, *134*, 498, *516*
Moore, R., 690, *692*
Moore, R. D., 226, *231*, 327, *335*, 826, *833*, 849, *852*
Moorey, S., 763, 764, *774*, *775*
Moorjani, S., 265, 266, *276*
Moos, R., 449, *456*, 621, *624*
Moos, R. H., 217, 223, *229*, *232*, 292, *314*, 388, 390, 394, 397, *401*, *455*, *456*, 504, *514*, 593, *610*, 821, *832*
Mor, V., 531, *533*
Morales, P., 802, *814*
Moran, G., 150, *165*
Moran, K., 732, *740*, *744*
Moran, S. L. V., 375, *383*
Morbidity and Mortality Weekly Report (MMWR), 528, *537*, 549, 550, *556*
Morch, H., 421, 426
Moreland, J. R., 720, *725*
Morell, M., 670, 671, 675, *681*
Morell, R. W., 574, *579*
Moretta, A., 328, *335*
Moretta, L., 328, *335*
Moreyra, A. E., 675, *681*
Morgan, C., 255, *260*
Morgan, G., 699, *707*
Morgan, M. G., 848, 850, *852*
Morgan, M., 669, 676, *679*
Morgan, M. V., 877, *892*
Morgan, M., 305, *314*
Morgan, T., 699, *707*
Morgan, T. M., 734, *742*
Morgan, W. J., 633, *653*
Morgan, W. P., 632, 633, 635, 638, 639, 641, 645, *650*, *652*, *654*, *656*
Morgenstern, H., 454, *456*
Moriarty, R., 703, *707*
Morias, H. M., 873, *892*
Morimoto, K., 684, *694*
Morin, S., 783, *796*
Morisky, D. E., 576, *579*
Moritani, T., 646, *652*
Moritz, D. J., 480, *491*
Moritz, P. A., 717, *723*
Morley, J. E., 689, 690, *694*
Morokoff, P. J., 734, *741*
Moroni, M., 803, *815*
Morrell B. S., 759, 761, *775*
Morrill, A., 822, 823, 829, *835*, *837*
Morrill, A. C., 179, 183, *192*, 822, *837*
Morrill, W., 858, *891*
Morris, C. D., 272, *277*
Morris, D. L., 877, *892*
Morris, E. W., 119, *137*
Morris, J., 524, 526, *537*, *539*, 573, *579*, 629, 646, 647, 648, *655*
Morris, J. J., 329, *334*, 664, 665, *666*, 671, 674, 675, 677, *679*, *680*
Morris, J. N., 629, 630, 646, 647, *654*, *655*
Morris, M., 186, *191*, 395, *402*
Morris, M. A., 330, *335*
Morris, R., 825, *838*
Morris, R. C., Jr., 434, *440*
Morris, R. E., 825, *837*
Morris, T., 67, *80*, *82*, 329, *333*, 719, *724*, 747, 750, 751, 752, *755*, *756*
Morrison, A., 472, *475*, 849, *853*
Morrison, C., 152, 158, *171*
Morrison, C. L., 454, *456*
Morrison, D. M., 304, *308*, 463, *467*
Morrison, H., 803, *815*
Morris-Prather, C. E., 432, *439*, *440*
Morrissey, E., 604, 605, *609*
Morrow, A. L., 617, 618, *623*, *624*
Morrow, C., 453, *456*
Morrow, D., 574, *579*
Morrow, G. R., 388, *400*, 715, *723*, 757, 759, 761, *774*, *775*
Morrow, J., 505, *516*
Morrow, K. A., 562, *570*
Morrow, K. M., 828, *837*
Morrow, L., 67, *81*
Morse, D. E., 254, 255, 256, *258*, *259*, *260*
Morse, E. V., 849, *853*
Morse, S., 779, 794, *798*
Morten, G., 857, 862, 863, 864, *888*
Mortensen, O., 122, *134*
Mortola, J., 471, *475*
Morton, B. R., 250, *259*
Morton, D., 218, *230*, 709, 715, *723*, 752, *754*
Morton, D. L., 218, *230*, 664, *667*, 688, *692*, 752, *754*
Morton, J., 787, 788, *797*
Morton, S. C., 822, 826, *838*
Morton-Williams, J., 374, *385*
Mosbach, P. A., 30, 31, *44*
Mosbacher, B. J., 632, *654*
Moscher, W., 820, *837*
Moscicki, A. B., 825, *836*
Moscicki, E. K., 632, *652*
Moser, D. K., 22, *42*, 154, *169*, 330, *335*
Moser, R. J., 863, *888*
Moses, H. D., 301, *318*
Moses, L., 702, *707*, 827, *836*
Moses, L. E., 463, *467*
Mosha, F., 830, *834*
Mosher, W. D., 530, *539*, 559, 560, *569*, *570*
Mosier, K., 419, 420, 425, 426
Moskowitz, D. S., 140, *169*, 356, *360*
Moskowitz, J. T., 390, *400*, 777, 782, 792
Moskowitz, M., 272, *276*
Moss, A., 778, *798*, 823, *833*
Moss, A. R., 808, *813*
Moss, D., 700, *708*
Moss, G. B., 828, *833*
Moss, H. B., 297, *314*
Moss, M., 478, 483, *491*
Moss, N., 825, *837*
Mosskov, J. I., 371, 372, *383*
Moss-Morris, R., 39, *45*
Mostardi, R. A., 226, *230*
Mostashari, F., 849, *853*
Motoyoshi, M., 663, *667*
Motta, R., 640, *650*
Motta, R. W., 635, 637, *656*
Mougey, E. H., 257, *260*
Moum, T., 496, *512*
Mourant, A. E., 436, *440*
Moushmoush, B., 286, *314*
Moutsos, S. E., 702, *707*
Moye, J., Jr., 827, *837*
Moyer, A., 392, *401*, *740*, *741*
Moynihan, J. A., *113*
Mroczek, D. K., 153, 155, *169*, *171*
Msellati, P., 824, *839*
Mubiru, F., 808, *814*
Mudar, P., 301, 302, *309*
Mudd, S. A., 285, *308*
Muderspach, L. I., 826, *836*
Muechler, E., 563, *569*
Muecke, M. A., 864, 865, 868, *892*
Muehlenhard, C., 792, *798*
Muehlenhard, C. L., 294, *314*
Mueller, H., 677, *681*
Mueller, M. R., 739, *744*
Mueller, T. I., 285, *308*
Muenz, L. R., 67, *81*
Mueser, K. T., 284, 285, *314*
Muirhead, J., 564, *569*
Mujais, S. K., 503, *512*
Mukasa, H., 289, *311*
Mulcahy, D., 672, *681*
Mulcahy, R., 74, *80*
Mulder, C. L., 398, *401*
Mulder, D., 820, *837*
Muldoon, M. F., 327, 328, *332*, *333*, *335*, 573, 574, *578*, 643, *654*, 689, 690, *692*, *693*, *694*, *753*, *754*, *755*
Mulira, J. G., 872, 873, 874, 875, *892*
Mullahy, J., 291, *314*
Mullan, J. T., 478, 481, 483, 484, *489*, *491*, *492*
Mullen, B., 196, *207*
Mullen, J. C., 717, *723*
Mullen, M., 272, 273, *277*
Mullen, P. D., 524, 525, *534*, 729, *742*
Müller, C., 286, *310*
Muller, F. B., 157, *169*, 689, *694*
Muller, J. E., 150, *169*, 662, *667*, 673, 674, 675, *681*
Muller, O. A., 663, *667*
Muller, R., 374, *381*
Mullins, L. L., 327, *335*
Mullis, R., 593, 599, 600, 601, 604, *608*, *609*
Mullooly, J. P., 216, 217, *233*
Mulrow, C. D., 648, *655*
Mulrow, C., 576, *579*
Mulry, R. .P., 150, *169*
Multicenter AIDS Cohort Study, 806, *813*
Multicenter Hemophilia Cohort Study, 806, *813*
Mulvey, K. P., 547, *556*
Mulvihill, J. J., 720, *722*, 732, *742*

Muma, R. D., 849, *853*
Mumford, E., 339, *347*
Mumma, G. H., 718, *724*
Mundal, R., 629, *656*
Mundfrom, D. J., 369, 378, *380*
Munoz, H., 502, *517*
Munoz, R. F., 65, *82*
Munroe, R. H., 369, *383*
Munroe, R. L., 369, *383*
Munroe, W. P., 575, *579*
Munuksela, E. L., 764, *776*
Munzenrider, R., 417, 419, 425
Muranaka, M., 663, *667*
Murarka, A., 827, *837*
Murata, P. F., 530, *534*
Murburg, M. M., 325, *335*, 663, *667*
Murch, R. L., 183, *192*
Murdoch, D., 294, *314*
Murphy, B., 183, *190*
Murphy, D. A., 3, *16*, 235, 237, 239, 241, 243, *246*, 398, *401*, 787, *797*, 830, 831, *835*, 848, 850, *852*, 870, *890*
Murphy, D. L., 297, *314*
Murphy, E. M., 808, *814*
Murphy, G. E., 291, *314*
Murphy, J. K., 431, *440*
Murphy, J. M., 298, 299, *313*
Murphy, L., 201, *206*
Murphy, L. M. B., 330, *335*
Murphy, L. R., 352, 358, 359, *361*, *362*, 415, 426
Murphy, M., 872, *891*
Murray, A., 699, *707*
Murray, C., 565, *569*
Murray, C. J. L., 572, *577*
Murray, C. L. G., 473, *475*
Murray, D., 150, *168*, 460, 461, *466*, 528, *536*
Murray, D. M., 150, *166*, 460, 464, *467*, 525, *536*, 593, 600, 601, 604, 605, *609*, *610*, *611*
Murray, E., 342, *347*
Murray, E. J., 340, 343, *346*, *347*
Murray, H. A., 60, *82*
Murray, J. K., 818, *837*
Murray, M. A., 219, *231*
Murray, R., 369, *383*
Murray, R. H., 434, *439*
Murray, R. M., 295, *307*
Murray, R. P., 523, 524, *537*
Murray, T., 727, *743*
Murrell, S. A., 225, *232*
Musante, L., 66, 76, *82*, 146, *168*
Muscat, J. E., 290, *314*
Muscettola, G., 644, *655*
Muslin, H. L., 749, *756*
Musoke, P., 827, *834*, *837*
Muss, H. B., 717, *723*
Mussini, A., 671, *682*
Must, A., 265, 268, *276*
Muth, J. B., 780, *797*, *799*
Muth, J. L., 28, *45*
Muth, S. Q., 780, *797*, *799*
Mutinga, M. L., 433, *437*
Mutrie, N., 637, *655*
Mutschler, P. H., 482, *490*
Myburgh, J. A., 575, *579*
Myers, D. G., 356, *362*
Myers, G. C., 366, 367, *383*
Myers, H., 431, 432, 435, *437*
Myers, H. F., 357, *362*, 436, *440*
Myers, J. K., 638, *656*
Myers, M. H., 720, *722*
Myers, R. E., 502, *516*, 531, *532*, *537*, 729, 731, *745*
Myers, T., 703, *707*
Myrsten, A., 356, *360*

N

Nabel, E. G., 669, 672, 675, 677, *679*, *681*, *682*
Nabholz, S., 734, *743*
Nabke, C., 289, *312*
Naccarato, R., 288, *314*
Nachman, G., 546, 547, *555*
Nachnani, M., 662, *667*
Nachtigall, R. D., 561, *570*
Nadeau, A., 265, 266, *276*
Nadeau, C., 677, *679*
Nadel, M., 736, *742*
Nader, K., 453, *457*, 773, *775*, *776*
Nader, P. R., 855, *894*
Nadler, A., 486, *490*, *491*
Nagayoshi, H., 676, *680*
Nagelkerke, N. J., 824, *833*
Nagoshi, C. T., 297, 298, 301, *314*, *318*
Nah, G., 544, *555*
Nail, L. M., 717, *724*, *725*
Nair, M., 684, *694*
Nair, P. P., 289, *315*
Nakabiito, C., 827, *837*
Nakajima, Y., 753, *754*
Nakamura, H., 676, *680*
Nakamura, K., 287, 289, *311*, *317*
Nakamura, M., 434, *440*
Nakamura, R. K., 250, *260*
Nakashima, A. K., 779, 794, *799*
Nakashima, T., 251, *260*
Nakasone, T., 371, *382*
Nakayama, H., 251, *260*
Nakazawa, Y., 289, *311*
Naliboff, B., 546, *556*
Naliboff, B. D., 689, 690, *694*
Nall, F. C., 862, *892*
Nam, J. M., 805, *815*
Namboze, J. M., 858, *892*
Nance, N. W., 508, *514*
Nanda, K., 471, 472, *474*, *475*
Nanni, C., 396, *403*
Nannis, E. D., 846, 849, *853*
Napoli, A., 326, 328, *336*, 683, 684, 687, *691*, *694*
Nappi, C., 503, *517*
Nasar, J. L., 375, *385*
Nash, J. D., 601, *610*
Nash, J. M.. 118, *136*
Nasrallah, H. A., 388, *402*
Natelson, B. H., 329, 330, *335*
Nathan, D. M., 629, *654*
Nathan, P., 125, 126, *135*
Nathan, P. E., 285, 300, 301, *314*
Nathan, P. W., 128, *135*
Nathanson, C., 825, *839*
Nathanson, C. A., 463, *468*
National Academy of Sciences Institute of Medicine, 269, *277*
National Advisory Mental Health Council, 628, *655*
National Alliance for Caregiving and the American Association of Retired Persons, 478, 482, 483, *491*
National Cancer Institute, 471, *475*, 727, *744*
National Center for Health Statistics, 117, *135*, 393, *401*, 427, 428, 429, 430, *440*, 629, *655*, 728, *744*
National Institute on Aging, 470, *475*
National Institute on Alcohol Abuse and Alcoholism, 282, 283, 284, 286, 287, 288, 289, 290, 294, 296, 297, 299, 300, *314*
National Institutes of Health, 471, *475*, 525, 526, 527, *537*, 627, 641, *655*, 825, 830, 831, *837*
National Research Council, 462, *467*
National Task Force on the Prevention and Treatment of Obesity, 274, *277*
National Vaccine Advisory Committee, 614, *624*
National Victim Center, 549, *556*
Nations, M. K., 876, *892*
Naughton, J., 635, *655*
Naughton, M. D., 720, *722*
Navaie, M., 824, *832*
Navarro, A. M., 734, *743*, 822, *837*
Nayagam, A. T., 154, *172*
Nayfield, S. G., 388, *401*
Naykova, T. M., 807, *815*
Naylor, S. K., 434, *439*
Nazar, K., 644, *651*
NCI Breast Cancer Screening Consortium Members, 530, *533*
Ndinya-Achola, J., 828, *833*
Ndinya-Achola, J. O., 824, 825, *833*, *837*
Ndoye, I., 829, *835*
Neaigus, A., 828, *834*
Neal, J. V., 699, *707*
Neal, M. B., 482, *491*
Neale, A.V., 218, *232*, 329, *335*
Neale, J., 340, *348*
Neale, J. M., 24, *46*, 324, 326, 328, *336*, 683, 684, 687, 688, *691*, *694*, *695*
Neale, M. C., 295, *312*, 326, *334*
Nealey, J. B., 158, *171*
Nease, R. F., 735, *741*
Nease, R. F., Jr., 731, 732, 739, *741*
Neaton, J., 148, *171*
Nebes, R. D., 469, *474*
Needle, R., 633, *657*, 828, *833*
Needles, D. J., 180, *189*
Needles, T. L., 74, *78*, 635, 640, *651*
Negri, E., 288, 290, *312*
Neider, J., 863, 868, *894*
Neidhart, B., 373, *383*
Neighbors, B., 222, *230*
Neighbors, H. W., 435, 436, *439*
Neimeyer, R. A., 635, 637, *652*
Neimeyev, R. A., 634, *653*
Nelsen, L. A., 868, 869, *893*
Nelson, C. B., 283, 284, 285, 300, *312*, 357, *361*, 632, *653*
Nelson, D. E., 290, *314*
Nelson, D. L., 349, 351, 352, 354, 355, 357, *362*
Nelson, G. W., 806, 807, *815*
Nelson, J. C., 63, *80*
Nelson, J. J., 576, *578*
Nelson, L., 647, *653*, *655*
Nelson, R. G., 270, *278*, 877, *892*
Nelson, W. T., 250, *258*
Nemeroff, C. B., 471, *474*
Nemo, G. J., 827, *837*
Nemoto, T., 753, *756*
Nepom, T., 805, *815*
Nerenz, D., 19, 20, 22, 24, 25, *44*, *45*, 68, *81*, 200, *207*, 574, *579*
Nerenz, D. R., 25, 38, *45*, 122, 129, *135*, 391, 396, *401*
Nerlove, S. B., 26, *42*
Nerurkar, V. R., 806, *813*
Neser, W. B., 869, *892*
Nespor, S. M., 254, 257, *259*, *260*
Nesse, R. M., 324, *335*, 759, *775*
Nesselroade, J. R., 62, *82*, 470, *474*
Nestle, M., 869, *890*
Nestler, E. J., 252, *258*, *260*
Nesto, R. W., 674, 675, *681*
Neter, E., 498, *516*
Netto, C. A., 252, *259*
Netz, Y., 636, *655*
Netzer, J. K., 487, *491*

Neugebauer, R., 846, *853*
Neuhaus, R. J., 603, *607*
Neumann, A., 806, *813*
Neumann, A. V., 846, *852*
Neumann, E., *489*
Neus, H., 371, 372, 373, *383*, *385*
Neustadt, J. D., 703, *708*
Neutel, J. M., 643, *657*
Nevitt, M. C., 408, *412*
Newberry, B. H., 748, *756*
Newbrough, J. R., 596, *607*, 622, *624*
Newcomb, M. D., 160, *169*, 196, *207*, 222, 224, *232*, *233*, 293, 302, *317*, 720, *722*
Newcomb, P., 472, *475*
Newcomb, P. A., 525, *537*
Newhouse, J. P., 282, *313*
Newlin, D., 303, *313*
Newlin, D. B., 297, 298, *314*
Newman, B., 803, *814*
Newman, J., 303, *313*
Newman, J. M., 865, 877, *892*
Newman, M., 325, *334*
Newman, S., 219, *230*
Newmann, J., *474*, *475*
Newnham, J., 499, *516*
Newsom, J., 480, *492*
Newsom, J. T., 33, *42*, 60, *79*, 154, *164*, 481, 482, 484, 487, 488, *489*, *491*, *493*, 684, *692*
Newstrom, J. W., 358, *362*
Newton, C., 391, *399*
Newton, C. R., 123, 130, *135*, 562, 563, *570*
Newton, E. R., 830, *838*
Newton, T., 72, *81*
Newton, T. L., 64, 66, 71, 73, 75, *82*, 151, 157, *169*
Neylan, J. F., 804, *814*
Nezu, A.M., *275*, *278*
Ng, R., 393, *399*
Ngin, C., 864, 865, 866, *889*
Ngu, L., 141, *171*
Ngu, L. Q., 141, 151, 152, 158, *171*
Niaura, R., 154, *165*
Niaura, R. S., 68, *78*, 269, *277*, 302, *307*, 524, *536*
Niaz, M. A., 576, *580*
Nicassio, P. M., 38, *42*, 55, *57*, 126, 129, *133*, 219, *229*, 690, *694*
Nicaud, V., 287, *312*
Nichol, K. L, 571, *579*
Nicholas, J. J., 588, *590*
Nicholas, S. W., 804, *814*
Nichols, D., 735, *745*
Nicholson, A., 739, *741*
Nicholson, P. W., 575, *577*
Nichter, M., 858, 865, *892*
Nickel, E. J., 285, *315*
Nickerson, J. L., 702, *707*
Nicolich, M., 739, *746*, 788, *799*
Nicolopoulos, V., 521, *538*
Nicosia, G., 368, 370, *379*, *383*
Nides, M. A., 523, *537*
Nie, N. H., 619, *625*
Niederman, J. C., 328, *334*
Niedzwiecki, D., 110, *114*
Nielsen, H. J., 285, *317*
Nieri, G. N., 850, *852*
Nieuwenhui, E. E., 689, *692*
Nigam, A., 406, *412*
Nihoyannopoulos, P., 675, 676, *681*
Nikoomanesh, P., 91, *93*
Nillius, S. J., 523, *537*
Nilsson, H.. 434, *440*
Nilsson, S., 523, *535*
Nilsson, S., 88, *94*
Nim, J., 501, *516*
Nisbett, R., 40, *45*
Nisbett, R. E., 8, *16*
Nisell, H., 503, *516*
Nishi, S., 366, 369, 284
Nishimoto, R., 218, *230*, 329, *333*, 720, *723*
Nishioka, T., 676, *680*
Nisker, J., 563, *569*
Nissinen, A., 600, 601, *610*, 629, *655*
Nitschke, R., 720, *724*
Nixon, P., 672, *680*
Noble, E., 296, *308*
Noble, J., 282, *310*, 822, *835*
Noblitt, R., 460, *466*
Nochajski, T. H., 292, 302, *314*
Noel, N., 224, *232*
Noelker, L. S., 481, 482, *489*
Noell, J., 462, *465*
Nogami, H., 296, *308*
Nolan, C. M., 571, 576, *579*
Nolan, J. C., 471, *475*
Nolen-Hoeksema, S., 340, *347*, 505, *516*
Noll, R. B., 454, *456*
Nolte, S., 714, *724*
Nomura, A. M. Y., 218, *231*
Nonas, C., 266, *278*
Noonan, A. E., 483, *491*
Noonan, D. L., 305, *318*
Norbeck, E., 864, *892*
Norbeck, J. S., 498, 506, 507, 508, 509, *516*
Norburn, J. E. K., 486, *491*
Norcross, J. C., 20, *45*, 729, 730, *744*
Nordback, I., 288, *311*
Nordentoft, M., 501, *516*
Norell, S. E., 574, *579*
Noreuil, T., 671, *680*
Norgren, R., 112, *115*
Noriega, V., 64, *79*, 156, *163*, 395, 397, *399*, 715, *722*, 751, 752, *754*
Norman, A. D., 830, *838*
Norman, G., 123, *136*, 499, 501, *513*
Norman, P., 729, *741*
Norris, F. H., 146, 156, *163*, *169*
Norris, V. K., 486, *492*
Norris, V. R., 483, *491*
Norsen, L. H., 217, *231*
North, F., 291, *313*, 662, *667*
North, R. B., 128, *135*
North, T. C., 633, *655*
North, W. R., 705, *707*
North, W. R. S., 329, *335*, 747, 749, *756*
Northam, E., 444, *447*
Northouse, A. L., 218, *232*
Northouse, L. L., 720, *724*
Northover, J., *532*, *535*
Norton, J. A., 503, *515*
Norton, L., 25, *41*, 110, *114*
Norusis, M., 148, *171*
Nosanchuk, T. A., 203, 204, *207*
Notelovitz, M., 273, *278*
Nothwehr, F., 525, *536*, 601, *609*
Nott, K. H., 154, *172*, 221, *232*
Nouwen, A., 123, *135*
Novaco, R., 366, 367, 370, *383*, *385*
Novak, D. A., 453, *456*
Novelli, W. D., 596, 598, *610*
Novikov, S. V., 573, *578*
Novotny, J., 90, *93*
Novotny, T. E., 599, 600, *607*, 869, *889*, *892*
Novy, M. J., 502, *517*
Nowak, J., 325, *336*
Nowalk, M. P., 266, *279*
Nowlin, J. B., 149, *163*, 469, *474*
Nowlis, D., 715, 718, *723*
Nqweshemi, J. Z., 829, *832*
Nsa, W., 825, *838*
Nuccio, L., 809, 810, *814*
Nuckolls, K. B., 500, 505, 509, *516*
Nunley, J., 120, *134*, *135*
Nunn, A., 829, *837*
Nunnally, J. C., 242, 243, *246*
Nurius, P., 25, *45*
Nurminen, T., 371, *383*
Nurnberger, J. I., 296, 297, *307*, *315*
Nurnberger, J. I., Jr., 575, *577*
Nussbaum, G., 325, *336*
Nutt, D., 300, *310*
Nuttall, P., 483, *492*
Nyamathi, A., 818, 820, 821, 823, *835*, *837*
Nyamathi, A. M., 177, *192*
Nyswander, D., 591, 606, *610*
Nzila, N., 794, *798*, 825, *836*

O

O'Boyle, C. A., 22, *45*
O'Brien, A. T., 480, 481, 482, *492*
O'Brien, J., 574, *578*
O'Brien, L. A., 290, *310*
O'Brien, S. J., 805, 806, *813*, *814*
O'Brien, T. R., 805, 806, *814*, *815*
O'Conner, C., 30, *46*
O'Conner, G. T., 630, *655*
O'Connor, C., 664, 665, *666*
O'Connor, C. M., 153, *162*, 329, *334*, 677, *680*
O'Donnell, D., 575, *579*
O'Donoghue, V., 256, 257, *259*
O'Dorisio, T. M., 685, *695*
O'Hanlan, K. A., 828, *837*
O'Hara, N. M., 268, *278*
O'Hara, P., 524, *537*, 705, *707*
O'Keefe, E., 823, *835*
O'Keeffe, J. L., 147, 150, 151, 155, *171*
O'Leary, A., 53, *57*, 65, 69, 75, *79*, *84*, 124, 126, 127, *133*, *135*, 139, 144, 145, 146, 151, *164*, *169*, 182, 183, 185, 187, *192*, *190*, 243, 245, *246*, *247*, 326, 327, 328, 329, *335*, *336*, 685, *694*
O'Leary, S., 675, *682*
O'Mahoney, C. P., 828, *835*
O'Malley, K., 22, *45*
O'Malley, M. S., 531, *535*
O'Malley, P. M., 459, 460, 461, 464, *465*, *467*
O'Malley, P. M. P., 600, *609*
O'Neill-Wagner, P., 367, *380*
O'Nell, C. W., 860, 861, *893*
O'Reilly, K., *16*
O'Reilly, K. R., 850, *852*
O'Shaughnessy, M. V., 471, *475*
O'Sullivan, M. J., 824, 827, *833*, 849, *853*
Oakley, A., 505, 508, 509, *513*, *516*
Oakley, C. M., 675, *681*
Obeidallah, D. A., *189*, *190*, 442, 443, 444, *447*, *448*
Oberman, A., 526, 527, *532*
O'Brien, C. P., 299, *306*, *317*
Obrist, P. A., 153, *171*, 434, 435, *438*, *439*, 639, 641, *654*, *655*
O'Campo, P., 544, 550, *555*, *556*
Occupational Safety and Health Act of 1970, 350, *362*
Ochan, M., 676, *680*
Ochitill, H., 846, *852*
Ochitill, H. N., 686, *693*
Ochs, L., 462, *465*
Ockene, I. S., 153, *169*
Ockenfels, M. C., *411*, *412*, *413*
O'Connell, A., 822, *839*

O'Connor, S., 297, *312*
Odell, P. M., 266, *277*
Oden, A., 217, *233*
O'Donnell, S. M., 733, *744*
Odugbesan, O., 804, *813*
Oehler, J. M., 499, *518*
Oei, T., 302, *310*
O'Farrell, T. J., 301, *309*
Offenbacher, E., 267, *277*
Offermann, L. R., 349, *362*
Office of National AIDS Policy, 825, 830, *837*
Office of Technology Assessment, U. S. Congress, 560, 565, *570*
Offord, K. P., 525, *538*
Ofosu, M., 804, *812*
Ofosu, M. D., 802, 804, *813*, *814*
Ofosu, M. H., 804, *814*
Ogata, E. S., 270, *278*
Ogawa, S., 373, *383*
Ogden, E., 95, *103*
Ogilvie, D. R., 187, *192*
Oglevie, D. M., 142, *169*
Oglobinne, J., 753, *755*
Ogrocki, P., 68, *81*, 327, 328, *334*, 685, 686, 687, *693*
Ogus, E. D., 420, 426
O'Hara, M. W., 498, 506, 510, *516*, 546, *557*
O'Heeron, R. C., *346*, *347*
Ohlig, W., 367, *385*
Ohlson, V., 865, 868, 869, *888*
Oja, H., 304, *311*
Oka, R., 527, *535*
O'Keeffe, M. K., 324, *332*
Oken, E., 790, *797*
Okifuji, A., 573, 574, *580*
Okuda, H., 251, *260*
Okumura, K., 804, *815*
Okun, M. A., 330, *331*, *337*
Oldenski, R. J., 531, *537*
Oldham, G., 369, *383*
Oldham, R. K., 759, 761, *775*
Oldridge, N. B., 527, 528, *535*, 572, 573, *579*, 630, *655*
Olds, D. L., 508, *516*
O'Leary, T., 749, 752, *754*
Olefsky, J., 266, *277*
Olff, M., 690, *692*
Olfson, M., *455*, *456*
Oliver, M. B., 785, *798*
Oliver, W. J., 699, *707*
O'Loughlin, J. L., 296, *314*
Olschavsky, R. W., 462, *467*
Olschowka, J., 684, *693*
Olshavsky, R., 197, *206*
Olson, H. C., 289, 290, *317*
Olson, J. M., 195, *207*
Olson, M., 619, *624*
Olson, R. A., 452, *456*, 765, *775*
Olsson, G., 62, *82*, 663, *667*
Olszewski, D., 375, *384*
Olvera, Y., 343, *346*
Omae, T., 297, *317*
O'Malley, A. S., 734, *744*
O'Malley, J. E., 715, *724*
O'Malley, M. S., 734, *742*
O'Malley, S. S., 297, 299, *306*, *314*
O'Meara, T., 371, *381*
Omowale, N., 432, *439*
O'Neal, P., 300, *315*
Onesti, G., 434, *438*
Ong, E. L. C., 154, *172*
Oostveen, F. G., 690, *692*
Oparil, S., 272, *277*, 431, 433, *437*
Ordin, D. L., 350, 352, *362*
Ordway, L., 848, *852*
O'Reilley, C. A., 110, *114*
Oreland, L., 297, *310*, *315*, *317*
Orenstein, W. A., 614, *624*
Oritz-Interian, C., 805, *812*
Orive, R., 196, *206*
Orlandi, M. A., 463, 464, *467*, 869, *893*
Orleans, C. T., 223, *230*, 519, 523, 524, *535*, *537*, 869, *892*
Orme, T., 292, *314*
Ormel, J., 49, *57*, 367, 368, *381*
Orne, M. T., 88, *94*
Ornish, D., 340, *347*, 576, *577*
Oro'-Beutler, M. E., 119, *133*
Orodenker, S. Z., 482, *490*
Orr, D. P., 825, *837*
Orr, E., 178, 183, *192*
Orr, N. K., 686, *695*
Orr, R. K., 472, *474*
Orr, S. T., 499, *516*
Orsulak, P. J., 644, *656*
Ortaldo, J. R., 684, *693*
Ortega, S., 328, *336*, 374, *384*, 689, *694*, 753, *756*
Orth, D. N., 157, *163*
Orth-Gomer, K., 160, *169*, 215, 216, *232*
Ortiz de Montellano, B., 860, *894*
Ortiz, G. A., 372, 373, *383*
Orton, M., 736, *744*
Ory, H. W., 546, *556*
Ory, M. G., 486, *491*, 648, *655*
Osada, Y., 373, *383*
Osborn, K. M., 635, 637, *652*
Osborne, L., 802, *814*
Osborne, L. N., 154, *165*
Oseasohn, R., 100, *103*, 642, *656*
Osguthorpe, J., 373, *383*
Osguthorpe, N., 373, *383*
Osler, W., 139, *169*
Osman, L., 452, *456*
Osmond, C., 749, *754*
Osmond, D., 823, *833*
Osmond, D. H., 778, *798*, 808, *813*
Osmond, M. W., 786, *798*
Osoba, D., 762, *775*
Osol, A., 92, *94*
Osorio, A., 859, 860, *893*
Osowiecki, D., 397, *400*
Ossip-Klein, D. J., 635, 637, *652*
Ostergren, P.-O., 215, 221, 227, *230*, *232*
Osterweis, M., 117, *135*
Ostfeld, A. M., 66, 72, *83*, 139, 149, 153, 154, *169*, *171*, 329, *336*, 480, *491*, 662, *667*
Ostroff, J., 773, *775*
Ostroff, J. S., 718, *724*
Ostroff, R. B., 325, *334*, *335*
Ostrow, D., 293, *314*
Ostrow, D. G., 4, *16*, 462, *467*
Otero-Sabogal, R., 786, *798*, 850, *892*
Ottman, W., 373, *383*
Otto-Salaj, L., 829, *835*
Otto-Salaj, L. L., 847, *852*
Oudshoorn, N., 373, 374, *382*
Ouellette, S., 353, 354, *362*
Ouellette, S. C., 176, 177, 178, 179, 184, 185, 186, 187, 188, *191*, *192*
Ouellette Kobasa, S. C., 179, 184, 186, *192*
Ouellette, V. L., 574, 575, *577*
Ouyang, P., 677, *681*
Overpeck, M. D., 292, *307*
Overton, J. M., 630, *657*
Ovrebo, B., 603, *610*
Owen, D. R., 635, *651*
Owens, J., 155, *170*
Owens, J. F., 67, 71, *82*, 155, 156, 157, *168*, *170*, 179, *193*, 269, *277*, 328, *332*, 395, *402*, 689, *692*
Owett, T., 719, *723*
Ownby, H. E., 753, *756*
Oyama, O. N., 298, 303, *313*
Ozawa, H., 287, *317*
Ozer, D. J., 155, *169*
Ozer, E., 416, 425
Ozer, E. M., 390, *400*, 519, 520, *533*
Ozer, H., 664, *667*
Oziemkowska, M., 818, 822, 823, *836*
Ozolins, M., 765, *775*

P

Paarlberg, K. M., 499, 505, *516*
Pabreza, L. A., 252, *259*
Pacale, R. W., 872, *891*
Pace, T. M., 327, *335*
Pachacek, T. F., 464, *467*
Pachter, L. M., 19, 27, *45*, *47*, 855, 859, *892*
Packard, B. A., 520, *537*
Padayachee, N., 73, *79*
Padeh, B., 498, *517*
Padian, N. S., 781, *798*, 805, *814*, 818, 828, *837*, *839*
Padilla, A. M., 506, *514*
Paffenbarger, R. S., 145, *163*, *169*, 525, 526, *533*, *537*, 573, *579*, 629, 630, 631, 632, 637, 646, 647, 648, *651*, *654*, *655*
Paffenbarger, R. S., Jr., 290, *314*, 527, 528, *535*
Pagana, K. D., 178, *192*
Paganini-Hill, A., 290, *315*, 472, *475*, 631, *657*
Pagano, F., 20, 21, 30, *44*
Page, G. G., 686, *694*
Page, K., 778, *798*
Page, L. B., 699, *707*
Pagel, M. D., 497, *516*
Paige, S. R., 74, *78*
Paine, A. L., 605, *608*
Paine-Andrews, A., 604, 605, *608*
Paine-Andrews, A. L., 605, *608*
Pais, J., 285, *313*
Paivio, A., 635, *654*
Pak, I. K., 867, *891*
Pakenham, K. I., 221, *232*, 391, *401*
Palatano, A. L., 27, 40, *45*
Palefsky, J. M., 826, *836*
Palermo, A., 373, *380*
Paley, B., 154, *164*
Palfrey, J. S., 444, *448*
Palinkas, L. A., 527, *536*, 855, *892*
Pallak, M. S., 665, *667*
Pallonen, U., 464, *467*
Palmer, D., 154, *172*
Palmer, D. G., *331*, *336*
Palmer, J. R., 287, *315*
Palmer, L. K., 637, *655*
Palmer, P. J., 630, *657*
Palmer, R. H., 574, *578*
Palmer, S., 188, *192*
Palmer, S. C., 32, 33, *47*, 155, *172*
Palmeri, D., 571, 575, 576, *580*
Palmore, E. B., 469, *474*
Palombo, R., 522, *538*
Palsane, M. N., 367, 368, 369, 370, 376, *381*
Pambianco, G., 527, *536*
Pamies, R. J., 715, *725*, 779, *797*
Pamuk, E., 266, *279*
Pamuk, E. R., 496, *514*
Pan, X. R., 270, *277*
Pandina, R. J., 300, *312*

Pandya, K., 759, 761, *775*
Paneth, N. S., 499, *516*
Pang, K. Y. C., 867, *893*
Pang, M. G., 293, *313*
Pantaleo, G., 826, *834*
Panwala, S., 867, 868, *888*
Panza, J. A., 672, *681*
Paolucci, G., 373, *384*
Papademetriou, V., 675, *680*
Pappaioanou, M., 821, *838*
Pappas, G., 429, 433, *440*
Para, M. F., 388, *402*
Parazzini, F., 288, *312*
Parcel, G. S., 268, *278*, 849, *853*
Pardo, Y., 673, *681*
Parga, F., 821, *836*
Pargman, D., 645, *655*
Parham, D., 603, *610*
Parijs, J., 699, *707*
Park, A., 672, *681*
Park, C. L., 183, *192*, 390, *400*, 498, 505, *516*
Park, D. C., 574, *579*
Park, M., 499, *517*
Parker, B., 508, *515*, *516*, 543, 545, *556*
Parker, D. A., 289, *314*
Parker, D. L., 286, 290, *316*
Parker, E., 603, *608*
Parker, E. S., 289, *314*
Parker, J., 563, *569*
Parker, J. C., *331*, *334*
Parker, J. D., 673, *681*
Parker, J. O., 673, *681*
Parker, P., 736, *743*
Parker, R., 819, *837*
Parker, S., 709, 710, 711, *724*
Parker, S. L., 747, *756*
Parkes, C. M., 340, *347*
Parks, E. B., 63, *79*
Parks, J. J., 419, 424
Parks, J. W., 630, 646, *654*
Parks, K. A., 294, *314*
Parmelee, P. A., 484, *491*
Parrish, J. M., 452, *456*
Parrish, K. M., 288, *314*
Parrish, R. G., 869, *893*
Parrott, A. C., 256, *260*
Parsons, O. A., 288, 289, *314*, *315*
Parsons, P. E., 734, *744*
Partridge, J. C., 827, *836*
Pasagian-Macaulay, A., 270, *278*
Pasagian-Macaulay, A. P., 576, *580*
Pascale, R. W., 272, *277*, 523, *536*
Pasch, L. A., 508, *516*, 565, *568*, *570*
Pascualy, M., 663, *668*
Pasino, J., 120, *134*
Paskett, E. D., 734, 736, *744*
Pasquale, E. A., 866, *893*
Pasquale, F. L., 877, *889*
Passchier, J., 393, *400*, 499, 505, *516*
Passos, G. A. S., Jr., 806, *815*
Pastorino, G., 717, *724*
Patcher, L. M., 859, 860, *893*
Pate, R. R., 526, *537*, 573, *579*, 629, 646, 647, 648, *655*
Patel, C., 662, *667*
Patel, C. H., 705, *707*
Patel, K., 828, *838*
Patel, K. M., 869, *889*
Patel, U. A., 250, *260*
Patenaude, A. F., 716, *724*
Pato, C., 374, *385*
Pato, C. N., 689, *695*
Patrick, D. L., 473, *475*
Patrick, K., 526, 527, *533*, *536*, *537*, *539*, 573, *579*, 629, 646, 647, 648, *655*, 779, *798*
Patrick-Miller, L., 25, 32, 33, *42*, *44*, *45*
Patterson, B., 520, *533*
Patterson, B. H., 521, *538*
Patterson, C. J., 445, *447*, 567, *569*
Patterson, G. R., 151, *169*, 222, *230*
Patterson, J. C., 149, *162*
Patterson, J. M., 445, *448*
Patterson, R. E., 521, 522, *534*, *536*
Patterson, S., 689, 690, *694*
Patterson, T., 855, *894*
Patterson, T. L., 327, *332*, *334*, 690, *694*
Pattison, D. C., 646, *655*
Pattison, P., 325, *333*
Patton, D., 119, *134*
Patton, D. M., 63, 64, *79*
Paty, J., 406, 410, *413*
Paty, J. A., 327, *336*
Pauker, S. G., 472, *474*
Pauker, S. J., 531, *533*
Paul, L. C., 220, *230*
Paul, O., 66, 72, *83*, 139, 149, *169*, *171*, 329, *336*, 662, *667*
Paul, S., 374, *385*, 497, *511*
Paul, S. M., 689, *695*
Paulesu, E., 676, *681*
Paulhus, D. L., 157, *168*, *169*
Paulhus, D. P., 733, *744*
Paulino, A., 863, 873, 875, *893*
Paulson, R. J., 561, 566, *570*
Paulus, P. B., 366, 367, 368, 369, 376, *380*, *383*, *384*
Pauly, M. V., *474*, *475*
Pav, D., 330, *331*
Pav, J. W., 827, *837*
Pavlov, I., 253, *260*
Pavlov, I. P., 757, 772, *775*
Pawlicka, E., 373, *384*
Pawtucket Heart Health Program Writing Group, 528, *533*
Paxton, W. A., 805, 806, *813*, *814*
Payne, R. L., 357, *360*
Payne-Jackson, A., 874, *893*
Pbert, L. A., 179, *193*
Peacock, J. L., 497, 498, 506, 509, *512*, *515*, *517*
Pearce, K. L., 92, *94*
Pearl, D., 690, *694*
Pearl, S. G., 749, 752, *754*
Pearlin, L. I., 54, *57*, 478, 481, 482, 483, 484, *489*, *491*, *492*, 504, *517*
Pearlman, D. M., 734, *744*
Pearse, R., 753, *755*
Pearson, G. R., 686, *693*
Pechacek, R., 593, 601, 604, *609*
Pechacek, T., 462, *467*
Pechacek, T. F., 523, 525, *536*, *538*, 601, *609*
Peck, J. R., 64, *83*, 125, *136*
Pedersen, C. A., 664, *667*
Pedersen, N. L., 62, *82*, 266, *278*
Pederson, W., 301, *315*
Peebles, R. J., 117, *135*
Peeke, H. V. S, 109, *115*
Peirce, R. S., 211, 223, *232*
Pekkanen, J., 290, *317*., 629, *655*
Pelcovitz, D., 718, *721*, 773, *774*
Pelham, T. W., 637, *655*
Pelham, W. E., 303, *312*
Pena, A. S., 329, *332*
Pena, J. M., 782, 783, *798*
Pena, M., 265, *279*
Penati, B., 718, *723*
Pender, N. J., 54, *57*
Pendergast, D. R., 525, *534*
Peng, X., 251, 252, *260*
Penha-Walton, M. L. I., 604, *610*
Penick, E. C., 285, *315*
Penkower, D., 345, *346*
Penkower, L., 850, *853*
Penman, D., 388, *400*, 715, *722*, *723*
Penn, G., 686, 687, *693*
Pennebaker, J., 201, *206*, 340, *346*, *347*, 397, *403*
Pennebaker, J. W., 28, 32, 34, 36, *45*, *46*, 62, 68, 74, 76, *82*, *84*, 122, 123, *135*, 142, 146, 147, 153, 154, 157, 158, *169*, *172*, 200, *207*, 339, 340, 341, 342, 343, 344, 345, *346*, *347*, *348*, 354, *363*
Penney, L., 562, *570*
Pennington, L. L., 257, *260*
Pennington, P., 184, *190*
Penny, R., 686, *692*
Pentz, M. A., 461, 463, *467*
Peoples, M. C., 663, *668*
Peoples-Sheps, M. D., 508, *517*
Pepine, C., 672, 676, *682*
Pepine, C. J., 329, *334*, 671, 672, *679*, *680*, *681*
Peplau, L. A., 562, *569*, 786, 788, 790, *798*
Pequignot, J. M., 644, *655*
Percival, L., 375, *384*
Perdue, M., *113*, *114*
Perdue, S. T., 830, *838*
Perelson, A. S., 846, *852*
Perez, G. R., 504, *517*
Perez, S. L., 343, *346*
Perez-Agosto, R. R., 821, *836*
Perez-Febles, A., 444, *446*
Perez-Stable, E. J., 65, *82*, 786, *798*, 850, *892*
Peri, T., 343, *347*
Perini, C., 157, *169*, 689, *694*
Perissin, L., 327, *337*
Perkin, M. R., 498, *517*
Perkins, D. V., 591, 604, *609*
Perkins, K. A., 269, *278*, 523, 524, *537*
Perkins, L., 150, *170*
Perkins, L. L., 520, *538*, 663, *667*, 869, *888*
Perl, M., 846, *852*
Perlick, D., 250, 256, *260*
Perlman, J. F., 822, 826, *838*
Perlmutter-Bowen, S., 788, 789, *798*
Perloff, L. S., 733, *744*
Pernanen, K., 294, *315*
Peronnet, F., 639, 641, 642, *651*, *656*
Perper, T., 780, *798*
Perri, M. G., 273, *275*, *278*
Perri, S., 636, *655*
Perrin, J. M., 265, *276*
Perrine, M. W., 290, *308*
Perris, C., 297, *315*
Perris, H., 297, *315*
Perry, C., 460, 461, 462, 464, *466*, *467*
Perry, C. L., 461, 464, *465*, *468*, 523, *534*, 593, 601, 604, *609*
Perry, H., 732, *742*
Perry, M., 66, 75, *79*, 749, *754*
Perry, M. J., 830, *838*
Perry, S., 154, *16*, 828, *8379*
Perry, S. W., 846, *853*
Persico, A. M., 296, *317*
Persoons, J. H. A., 112, *115*
Persson, I., 288, *307*
Persson, L., 221, 227, *232*
Pert, C. B., 645, *652*
Pervin, L. A., 59, 60, *82*
Pescosolido, B. A., 23, *45*
Peshkin, B. N., 732, 735, *741*
Peskind, E. R., 663, *668*
Pestone, M., 267, *277*

Peter, R., 662, *666*
Peterman, T., 822, *833*
Peterman, T. A., *16*, 793, *796*
Peters, J., 829, *835*
Peters, M. D., 30, *41*
Peters, M. L., 120, 122, *136*
Peters, T. J., 286, 287, *315*
Petersen, A. C., 502, *513*
Petersen, L. R., 801, *814*
Petersen, R., 508, *517*
Peters-Golden, H., 720, *724*
Peterson, B., 61, 66, 75, 76, *78*, 154, *162*
Peterson, B. L., 148, 149, *162*, *163*, 662, 663, *666*, *668*
Peterson, C., 67, 70, 74, 77, *82*, 155, 156, *168*, *169*, 180, 181, 183, *190*, *192*, 356, *362*, 585, *590*
Peterson, E., 283, *308*
Peterson, E. A., 373, *384*
Peterson, F. J., 272, *276*
Peterson, G., 595, 596, *609*
Peterson, G. M., 576, *579*
Peterson, H. B., 523, *536*
Peterson, J., 777, 783, 784, 785, 787, 789, *795*, *796*, *798*, 822, *832*
Peterson, J. B., 289, *315*
Peterson, J. L., 188, *192*
Peterson, K., 268, *276*
Peterson, L., 292, 304, *316*, 367, *385*, 454, *456*
Peterson, L. S., 559, 560, *569*
Peterson, M., 525, *532*
Peterson, R. A., 449, *456*
Petitt, D. J., 877, *892*, *893*
Petitti, D., 472, *475*
Petitti, D. B., 328, *333*, 472, *475*, 574, *579*
Petitto, J., 72, 73, 76, 77, *79*
Peto, R., 286, 288, *309*, *317*
Petraglia, F., 503, *517*
Petraitis, J., 303, *309*
Petrie, K., 177, 180, *190*
Petrie, K. J., 20, 39, *45*, 342, 343, *347*
Petrii, B., 685, *691*
Petropoulus, C. J., 850, *852*
Petruzzello, S. J., 638, 645, *655*
Petry, L. J., 687, *694*
Petterson, I. L., 685, *692*
Petterson, K., 663, *667*
Pettersson, R., 523, *537*
Pettigrew, A. G., 496, 503, *511*
Pettingale, K. W., 62, 67, *80*, *82*, 329, *333*, 715, *724*, 751, 752, *755*, *756*
Pettito, J. M., 664, *667*
Pettitt, D. J., 270, *278*
Petty, F., 285, *308*
Peutherer, J. F., 803, *815*
Peveler, R., 327, *335*
Peyrin, L., 644, *655*
Peyton, L. R., 846, *852*
Pfaff, H., 396, *403*
Pfeiffer, C., 29, *41*, 54, 55, *56*, 204, *205*, 219, *229*, 396, *399*
Pfister, H., 847, *852*
Pflieger, K., 431, *438*
Phair, J., 803, 806, *813*, *814*
Phaneuf, D. C., 677, *679*
Phares, E. J., 51, *57*
Phifer, J. F., 225, *232*
Philbert, R. A., 471, *475*
Philip, J., 729, *742*
Philipps, L. H., 498, 510, *516*
Philips, H. C., 120, 121, 124, 129, *135*
Phillips, A., 781, *798*
Phillips, C., 531, *532*, *536*, 782, *797*
Phillips, J., 522, *538*
Phillips, K., 451, *456*, 777, 782, 792
Phillips, L. D., 739, *744*
Phillips, M. I., 631, *651*
Phillips, N., 224, *233*, 506, 509, *518*
Phillips, P., 719, *723*, 810, *814*
Phillips, R. S., 779, *797*
Phillips, T. C., 298, *309*
Phillips, W. T., 646, 648, *653*, *655*
Phipps, S., 452, 454, *456*
Piantadosi, S., 716, *725*
Piasetsky, S., 388, *400*, 715, *723*
Picanc, V. P., 806, *815*
Picciano, J. F., 822, *835*
Piccinino, L. J., 559, 560, *569*
Pichert, J. W., 604, *610*
Pick, D., 417, 426
Pick, J., 85, 87, *94*
Pickar, D., 74, *82*
Pickard, S. D., 676, 677, *682*
Pickard-Holley, S., 717, *724*, *725*
Pickens, R., 250, *259*, 523, *538*
Pickering, G. W., 703, *707*
Pickering, R., 282, *310*
Pickering, T., 435, *437*
Pickering, T. G., 90, *93*, 226, *230*, 355, 359, *361*, 435, *438*, 643, *655*, 663, *667*
Pickor, D., 644, *655*
Pickwell, S. M., 855, *892*
Pickworth, W. B., 523, *534*
Pieper, C., 226, *230*, 431, 432, 435, *437*, *439*, *440*, 663, *667*
Pieper, C. F., 351, *361*, 662, *668*
Pieper, W. J., 749, *756*
Pierce, C. A., 585, 586, *590*
Pierce, G. R., 160, *169*, *170*, 209, *232*, *233*, 355, *362*, 393, *401*, 509, *517*
Pierce, J. L., 358, *362*
Pierce, J. P., 869, *889*
Pierce, R., 778, *798*
Pierce, W. D., 245, *246*
Pierson, R. N., 265, *279*
Pietzcker, A., 575, *578*
Pihko, H., 454, *455*
Pihl, R. O., 289, 294, 297, 298, 300, 303, *309*, *311*, *314*, *315*
Pike, J., 689, *693*
Pike, J. K., 690, *694*
Piliusik, M., 34, *45*
Pillemer, K., 483, 486, *492*
Pillow, D. R., 304, 305, *308*
Pilowsky, I., 119, *135*
Pimm, T. J., 29, *45*
Pina, I. L., 629, *652*
Pinault, S., 266, *276*
Pincus, T., 177, *190*, 821, *837*
Pinder, P., 749, *754*
Pindyck, J., 850, *851*
Pinkerton, S. D., 847, *852*
Pinn, V. W., 470, 472, *475*
Pinsky, J., 153. *165*
Pinto, B., 503, *512*
Pinto, B. M., 526, 527, *536*
Piot, P., 794, *798*, 819, 822, 824, 825, *833*, *836*, *837*
Piotrkowski, C. S., 350, *362*
Piotrowski, N. A., 243, *246*
Piper, B., 717, *725*
Piper, B. F., 773, *775*
Piper, J. M., 830, *838*
Pirie, P., 460, 464, *467*, 524, *535*, 593, 601, 604, *609*
Pirie, P. L., 269, *278*, 523,524, 525, *536*, *537*, 600, 601, 604, *607*, *609*, *610*
Pirola, R. C., 289, *318*
Pisani, V. D., 575, *578*, *579*
Pisarska, K., 267, *277*
Pison, G., 829, *836*
Pi-Sunyer, F. X., 265, 268, 272, *277*, *278*
Pittman, D. J., 282, *310*
Pivnick, A., 823, *837*
Pivonka, E., 521, *538*
Plaeger, S., 827, *833*
Plant, J. S., 369, *384*
Plante, T. G., 641, *655*
Plantinga, P., 265, *279*
Plaut, M., 684, *694*
Plichta, S., 463, *468*, 825, *839*
Pliska, M., 549, *555*
Plomin, R., 62, *82*, 160, *169*, 296, *313*, *315*
Plumlee, L. A., 89, *94*
Plummer, F., 828, *833*
Plummer, F. A., 825, *837*
Pober, J. S., 108, *113*
Podd, L., 325, *335*
Podell, R. N., 848, *853*
Podrid, P. J., 329, *335*
Podsakoff, P., 358, *363*
Pogue-Geile, M., 77, *81*
Pohorecky, L. A., 31, *46*, 302, *315*
Poiesz, B. J., 808, *815*
Poirier, S., 552, *557*
Polacca, M., 553, *555*
Poland, M. L., 506, 509, *514*
Poland, R. E., 809, 810, *814*
Polaneczky, M., 825, *837*
Polatin, P. B., 64, *80*
Poldrugo, F., 285, *315*
Polednak, A., 530, 531, *533*
Polednak, A. P., 531, *536*, 856, *893*
Polen, M. R., 177, *191*
Polic, S., 674, *681*
Polich, J., 297, *315*
Polin, G., 576, *580*
Pollack, L., 396, *400*, 778, 782, 783, 784, 785, *796*, *797*, *798*, 846, *852*
Pollack, L. M., 777, 779, 782, 783, 790, 792, 793, *795*, *796*
Pollack, M. S., 802, *815*
Pollak, M. H., 642, 643, *655*
Pollard, R. B., 849, *853*
Polley, B. A., 269, *278*
Pollitzer, W. S., 436, *440*
Pollock, M. L., 526, *537*, 573, *579*, 629, 630, 631, 646, 647, 648, *651*, *655*
Pollock, R. E., 750, *756*
Pollock, S. E., 178, *192*
Pollock, V. E., 297, *310*, *315*
Pomerleau, O. F., 250, *260*
Pond, E. F., 498, *517*
Ponsford, J. L., 588, *590*
Pool, R., 858, *893*
Poole, D., 367, *381*
Poon, L. W., 472, *475*
Pope, C. R., 216, 217, *233*
Pope, M. K., 149, 150, 151, 155, *169*, *170*, *171*, 180, *193*, 663, *667*
Pope, R., 714, *725*
Pope, S. K., 369, 378. *380*
Pope-Cordle, J., 272, *278*
Popiel, D., 449, *456*
Popke, E. J., 255, 256, *258*
Popma, J. J., 675, *680*
Popp, K. A., 254, *259*
Poppen, J., 371, *381*
Porcu, E., 566, *570*
Porjesz, B., 296, *307*
Porte, D., 254, *261*

Portenoy, R. K., *721*, *723*
Porter, L., *411*, *412*
Porter, L. A., 217, *231*
Porter, L. E., 406, 407, *411*, *413*
Porter, L. S., 398, *401*, 406, 410, *411*, *413*
Porter, T. F., *511*, *517*
Portnoy, S., 453, *456*
Porto, M., 501, 502, 503, 510, *518*
Ports, T., 340, *347*
Portser, S., 705, *707*
Posavac, E. J., 143, 148, 158, *169*
Pose, S. V., 225, *234*
Posluszny, D., 753, *756*
Posluszny, D. M., 66, *80*
Post, E., 287, *316*
Post, R., 644, *650*
Post, R. M., 644, *652*, *655*
Potapova, T. A., 807, *815*
Potosky, A. L., 734, *744*
Potter, J. D., 265, *277*, 287, *317*, 472, *475*
Potter, P., 330, *337*
Potter, P. T., *331*, *335*, *337*
Potter, W. Z., 644, *655*
Potterat, J. J., 779, 780, *797*, *798*, *799*
Potthoff, J. G., 154, *170*
Potts, M. K., 226, *232*
Pouliot, M. C., 265, *276*
Poulton, J. F., 180, *193*
Poulton, J. L., 155, *171*
Pounds, M., 849, *853*
Pous, J., 216, *230*
Poustka, F., 371, 373, *382*, *384*
Powch, I. G., 150, *170*
Powell, B. J., 285, *315*
Powell, K. E., 525, 526, 527, 528, *533*, *535*, *537*, 628, 629, *651*, *655*
Powell, L. H., 148, 151, *162*, *165*, *170*
Power, D. J., 410, *412*
Power, M. J., 221, *232*
Powers, S. I., 441, 442, *448*
Powers, S. W., 454, *456*
Powley, T. L., 86, 87, *94*
Poyneer, S. V., 858, 859, 868, *893*
Pozo, C., 64, *79*, 156, *163*, 395, 397, *399*, 751, 752, *754*
Pozo-Kaderman, C., 715, *722*
Pozzato, G., 288, *310*
Pradhan, A. A., 732, 733, 734, *743*
Pradinaud, R., 828, *835*
Pratt, C., 677, *681*
Pratt, K., 736, *744*
Pratt, M., 526, 527, *533*, *537*, 573, *579*, 599, *611*, 629, 646, 647, 648, *655*
Prechtl, J. C., 86, 87, *94*
Preedy, V. R., 286, 287, *315*
Prentice, D. A., 198, 199, 200, *207*
Prentice, R. L., 272, *276*, 521, *535*
Prentice-Dunn, S., 729, 730, 736, *744*
President's Commission on Mental Health, 627, *655*
Presley, C. A., 291, *315*
Pressman, S., 805, *813*
Presson, C., 197, *206*
Presson, C. C., 462, *467*
Prestage, G., 822, *835*
Prestby, J., 618, 619, 620, 621, *624*, *625*
Prestby, J. E., 603, *610*
Preston-Martin, S., 288, *308*
Prevey, M. L., 574, 575, *577*
Pribram, K. H., 21, *45*
Price, C., 367, *380*
Price, D. D., 128, *136*
Price, H. F., 870, *890*
Price, K. P., 96, *102*
Price, P., 645, *653*
Price, R., 614, *624*
Price, V. A., 148, 151, *162*, *165*, *170*
Priestman, S. G., 716, *725*, 747, 749, *756*
Priestman, T. J., 716, *725*, 747, 749, *756*
Prigerson, H. G., 146, *166*
Prihoda, T. J., 126, *134*
Prilleltensky, I., 187, 188, *190*, *192*
Primavera, J., 506, *512*
Primomo, J., 218, *232*
Prineas, R. J., 265, *277*
Prinz, R. J., *162*, *163*
Pritchard, C. W., 503, *517*
Prkachin, K., 180, *190*
Probart, C., 521, 522, *536*, *538*
Probstfield, J., 575, *578*
Prochaska, G. E., 782, 783, *797*
Prochaska, J. O., 5, *17*, 20, *45*, 461, *465*, 593, *608*, *610*, 729, 730, *744*, 782, 783, *797*, *798*
Prohaska, T., 485, *492*
Prohaska, T. R., 28, 38, *45*, 146, *168*
Prohaska, V., 409, *412*
Project RESPECT Study Group, *16*
Proniewska, W., 373, *384*
Pronk, N., 273, 274, *279*
Pronk, N. P., 273, *278*
Proschan, M., 677, *681*
Proshansky, H., 369, *384*
Pross, H. F., 752, 753, *756*
Provence, S., 525, *535*, 599, 600, *609*
Province, M. A., 648, *655*
Prozanto, P., 717, *724*
Prud'homme, D., 265, 266, *276*, *277*
Pruitt, L. A., 646, 648, *655*
Pruitt, S. D., 765, *775*
Pruyn, J., 204, *207*
Pryds, O., 501, *516*
Pryor, D. B., 148, *162*, 217, *233*, 662, *667*, *668*, 677, *682*
Przybeck, T. R., 284, 285, *311*
Psaty, B. M., 576, *580*, 598, *608*
Ptacek, J., 406, *412*
Ptacek, J. T., 64, *83*
Public Health Service, 614, *624*
Pucci, P., 672, *679*
Puckett, S., 787, *795*
Puczunski, S., 572, 573, *578*, 848, 849, *852*
Puddey, I. B., 287, *315*
Pugh, U. M., 367, *380*
Pugsley, S. O., 473, *475*
Pukkala, E., 156, *165*
Puleo, E., 636, *651*
Pulles, M. P. J., 371, 389
Pullum, S. G., 499, *513*
Puma, J., 665, *666*
Punsar, S., 629, *655*
Pupkin, M., 499, *516*
Puska, P., 215, *231*, 290, *317*, 595, 600, 601, *610*
Putnam, R., 622, *624*
Pylypuk, A., 367, *382*
Pynoos, R. S., *229*, *232*, 453, *457*, 773, *776*

Q

Qari, S. H., 806, 808, 810, *814*
Quadagno, D. M., 786, *798*
Quade, D., 664, *667*, 734, *742*, 869, *892*
Quadrel, M. J., 733, 739, *742*
Quaid, K., 645, *653*
Qualls, S. H., 473, *476*
Quamma, J. P., *162*, *166*
Queen, S., 433, *440*
Quesenberry, C. P., Jr., 531, *537*
Quick, J. C., 349, 350, 351, 352, 354, 355, 356, 357, *361*, *362*
Quick, J. D., 349, 350, 351, 352, 355, 356, *361*, *362*
Quigley, B. M., 292, *315*
Quigley, J., 150, *165*
Quigley, L. A., *306*, *313*
Quinlan, D. M., 718, *722*, 763, 764, *774*
Quinlan, J. J., 299, *311*
Quinlan, P. E., *113*, *114*
Quinn, N. R., 26, *42*
Quinn, P. C., 23, *46*
Quinn, R. P., 349, 350, 351, *361*
Quinn, R. W., 366, *384*
Quinn, S. C., 870, 872, *894*
Quinn, T. C., 808, *813*, 826, *834*
Quinn, V. P., 524, 525, *534*
Quittner, A. L., 480, *492*
Quyyami, A. A., 672, 675, *679*, *681*
Qvarner, H., *721*, *724*

R

Rabin, B. S., 28, *42*, 105, 111, *114*, 160, *164*, 322, 326, 327, 328, *332*, *333*, *335*, 683, 684, 685, 689, 690, *691*, *692*, *693*, *694*, 753, *754*, *755*
Rabkin, J. G., 144, *170*, 846, 847, *853*
Raboy, B., 567, *569*
Rachman, S., 40, *46*, 121, *136*
Rackley, C. E., 675, *681*
Raczynski, J., 329, *334*, 671, *680*
Raczynski, J. M., 144, *168*, 527, *536*, 869, *891*
Radda, K., 823, *839*
Radder, J., 373, *384*
Radloff, L. S., 355, *362*, 480, *492*, 632, *652*
Rae, D. S., 283, 284, 301, *315*, 638, *656*
Raether, C., 267, 272, 273, *277*
Raferty, E. B., 705, *706*
Raffel, L., 805, *815*
Raffel, L. J., 805, *813*
Raffety, B., 406, *412*
Raffle, P. A. B., 630, 646, *654*, *655*
Raftery, E. B., 676, *679*
Ragland, D. R., 148, 152, 159, *166*, *170*, 705, *707*
Raglin, J. S., 633, 638, 639, 641, 645, *655*, *656*
Rahaim, J. E., 267, *276*
Rahe, R., 326, *332*
Rahe, R. H., 68, *80*, 322, 323, 328, *333*, *335*
Rahman, M. A., 254, 255, 256, *259*
Rai, R. M., 373, *384*
Raible, R., 328, *332*, 689, 690, *692*
Raiciu, M., 371, *380*
Raikes, A., 542, 543, *555*
Raikkonen, K., 63, *81*, 156, *170*
Raimondi, E., 802, *813*
Raines, B. E., 460, 461, 462, 463, *466*
Rainey, L. C., 717, *724*
Rainforth, M., *706*, *707*
Raj, P. P., 117, *136*
Rajagopal, D., 480, *491*
Rajan, L., 508, 509, *516*
Rajapark, D. C., 441, *447*
Rajkumar, S., 575, *580*
Rakin, D., 148, *162*, *165*
Rakos, R. F., 523, *537*
Rakowski, W., 183, *192*, 388, *399*
Rakowski, W., 734, 738, *744*
Ramazanoglu, C., 785, 789, 790, *797*
Ramirez, A., 734, *743*
Ramirez, A. J., 329, *335*, 747, 749, *756*

Ramirez, H., 808, *814*
Ramirez, M., 185, *191*, 480, *490*
Ramivez, D. E., 635, *651*
Ramm, D., 469, *474*
Ramos, L. L., 553, *556*
Ramos, R., 830, *838*
Ramsay, L. E., 700, *707*
Ramsay, M. H., 700, *707*
Ramsey, C. N., 508, 509, *517*, 684, *692*
Ramsey, D. L., 435, *439*
Ramsey, R., 499, 501, *513*
Ramstedt, K., 780, *798*
Ramushu, D. L., 849, *853*
Rand, C., 451, 452, *456*, 573, *580*
Rand, C. S., 574, *580*
Randall, B. L., 576, *577*
Ranjadayalan, K., 676, *679*
Rankin, J., 286, *307*
Rankin, L. I., 434, *439*, *440*
Rankin, M., 506, 509, *511*
Ranney, J., 734, *742*
Ransford, C. P., 645, *656*
Ransohoff, D. F., 531, *537*
Ransohoff, W., 703, *707*
Ransom, L. J., 177, *191*
Rantakari, K., 454, *455*
Rao, V. P., 471, *474*
Rape, R. N., 764, *775*
Rapkin B., 765, 768, *774*, *775*
Rapkin, A. J., 546, *556*
Rapkin, B. D., 188, *192*, 849, *853*
Rapozzi, V., 327, *337*
Rappaport, B. S., 452, *456*
Rappaport, J., 593, 594, 595, 603, 606, *610*, *612*
Rapson, R. L., 203, *206*
Rashid, T. J., 810, *815*
Raska, K., 65, *84*, 245, *247*, 328, *336*
Rasker, J. J., 575, *580*
Raskin, G., 292, 302, 304, *316*
Raskind, M. A., 663, *668*
Rasmussen, V., 285, *317*
Rastam, L., 226, *231*
Rastogi, S. S., 576, *580*
Ratcliffe, S. D., 575, *580*
Rather, B. C., 302, *315*
Rathge, R. W., 731, 734, 735, *744*
Ratick, S., 728, 729, *743*
Rau, M. T., 226, *229*, *233*, 478, *492*
Rauch, J., 461, *466*
Rauch, S., 345, *348*
Raudenbush, S. W., 442, 443, 444, 445, *448*
Rauh, V. A., 499, *517*
Rauma, D., 541, *554*
Rauramaa, R., 526, *536*, 629, 630, 647, *654*
Rautonen, J., 454, *455*
Raven, B. H., 12, *16*
Ravoux, A. C., 471, *474*
Ravussin, E., 266, 267, *278*
Rawlings, J. S., 500, *511*
Ray, L. A., 151, *169*, 862, *890*
Ray, O. S., 748, *756*
Raye, C. L., 408, *412*
Rayfield, M., 825, *838*
Raygada, M., 254, 257, *259*, *260*
Raynaud, J. M., 575, *578*
Raynor, W. J., 329, *336*
Ray-Prenger, C., 297, 303, *316*
Read, J. A., 500, 503, *511*, *515*
Read, J. D., 405, *413*
Reading, A. E., 563, *570*
Ready, T., 802, *815*
Reagan, K., 675, *681*
Reasoner, J., 640, *651*
Reavely, D., 672, *680*
Reaven, G. M., 266, *277*
Reaven, P. D., 629, *656*
Rebecca, G., 672, *679*
Rebel, M., 563, *569*
Rebentisch, E., 371, 373, *382*, *383*
Rebuffe-Scrive, M., 265, *278*
Rechlin, L. R., 481, 482, *489*
Rechnitzer, P., 635, *654*
Rectanus, E., 367, *381*, 434, *438*
Red Horse, J. G., 877, *893*
Redd, W., 773, *776*
Redd, W. H., 24, 25, *41*, *45*, 89, *93*, 110, *114*, 388, 393, *400*, *401*, 716, 718, *723*, *724*, 749, *756*, 759, 765, 768, 770, 771, 772, *774*, *775*
Reddick, W.T., 807, *815*
Redding, C. A., 782, 783, *798*
Reddy, D. M., 734, *741*
Reddy, M. N., 523, *535*
Redelemeir, D., 407, *413*
Redinbaugh, E. M., 484, *492*
Redman, S., 291, *318*, 734, 739, *741*
Redmond, D. P., 703, 704, 705, *707*
Redmond, G., 372, *385*
Redwine, L., 245, *246*
Reeb, K. G., 509, *517*
Reed, B. D., 575, *580*
Reed, B. R., 324, 328, *336*, 683, *695*
Reed, B., 340, *348*
Reed, D., 216, *232*
Reed, D. M., 286, *310*
Reed, G. M., 54, *57*, 64, 67, *82*, 156, *170*
Reed, M. L., 117, *136*
Reed, T., 436, *440*
Reeder, S., 23, *41*
Rees, D. C., 806, 807, *814*
Rees, M. B., 52, *56*
Reese, H. W., 470, *474*
Reese, Y., 524, *539*
Reesor, K. A., 126, 129, 130, *135*, *136*
Reeves, D. L., 646, *656*
Reeves, J. L., 407, *412*
Reeves, R. A., 705, *707*
Reeves, R. S., 526, *535*
Regan, T. J., 286, *318*
Regen, H., 497, *516*
Regier, D. A., 282, 283, 284, 301, *315*, 638, *656*
Rehm, L. P., 155, *170*
Rehnqvist, N., 62, *82*
Reich, D. E., 807, *815*
Reich, J. W., 245, *247*, 395, 398, *402*, 487, 488, *492*, *493*
Reich, P., 108, *114*
Reich, T., 296, *307*, *315*
Reichelderfer, P., 827, *837*
Reichelderfer, P. S., 811, *813*
Reichman, B. S., 110, *114*
Reichman, M. E., 289, *315*
Reid, A., 389, 398, *401*
Reid, G., 221, *230*
Reid, J. B., 222, *230*
Reid, J. C., 588, *590*
Reid, P. A., 731, 734, 735, *744*
Reid, R. D., 366, *385*
Reifman, A., 217, *232*, 393, *402*
Reinhart, M. A., 548, *557*
Reinharz, S., 614, *624*
Reinsch, S., 576, *577*
Reis, H. T., 217, *231*, 505, *512*
Reis-Bergan, M., 305, *310*
Reise, S. P., 158, *165*
Reiser, M., 847, *852*
Reiser, M. F., 703, *707*
Reisin, E., 37, *43*
Reisine, S. T., 219, *230*
Reisine, T. D., 502, *512*
Reiss, D., 160, *169*, 296, 305, *307*, *315*, 441, 445, *448*
Reiss, P., 848, *853*
Reister, K. A., 826, *836*
Reiter, R., 550, *555*
Reiter, R. C., 546, 547, *556*, *557*
Rejeski, J., 648, *656*
Relton, J. K., 112, *114*
Relyea, G., 523, *533*
Remien, R., 846, 850, *853*
Remington, P. L., 268, *279*, 290, *307*, 869, *892*
Renn, O., 728, 729, *743*
Renner, J., 255, *261*
Rennert, K., 758, *776*
Reno, R. R., 733, 734, 737, 738, *740*, *741*
Renwick, A. G., 810, *812*, *815*
Renzetti, C., 542, *556*
Repetti, R. L., 393, *403*
Report of the Secretary's Task Force on Black and Minority Health, 431, *440*
Resch, M., 394, *401*
Resch, N., 530, *536*, 734, 737, *744*
Rescorla, R. A., 30, *46*
Resnick, H., 325, *336*
Resnick, H. S., 325, *333*
Resnick, L. M., 272, *277*
Resnick, R. J., 452, *456*
Resnick, S., 472, *475*
Resnik, S., 367, *385*
Resser, K. J., 670, 671, 675, *681*
Retzlaff, B. M., 576, *577*
Reuman, D., 443, *447*
Revenson, T., 818, 824, 826, 831, *837*
Revenson, T. A., 29, *43*, *46*, 62, *82*, 142, 144, 160, 161, *170*, 219, *231*, *232*, 324, *332*, 387, 392, 393, 394, 397, 398, *400*, *401*, *402*, 487, 488, *492*, 504, *511*, 566, *570*, 591, 593, *610*
Reviriego, J., 810, *815*
Revueltta, G., 806, *813*
Reynolds, A., 145, *166*
Reynolds, C. F., 146, *166*, *489*, *492*
Reynolds, C. P., 685, 688, 684
Reynolds, E. H., 575, *580*
Reynolds, J. U., 780, *799*
Reynolds, K., 522, *535*
Reynolds, K. D., 734, 737, 738, *741*
Reynolds, P., 153, 154, *167*, 218, *232*, 328, *334*
Reynolds, R. V., 397, *403*
Reynolds, S. L., 477, *490*
Reynolds, S., 283, *308*
Reznick, J. S., 344, *347*
Rhiner, M., 758, *774*
Rhoads, D. L., 223, *232*
Rhoads, G. K., 353, *362*
Rhode, P., 25, 29, *47*
Rhodes, F. M., *16*
Rhodes, J. E., 506, 508, *513*, *517*
Rhodes, M., 73, *80*
Rhodes, T. J., 850, *853*
Rhodes, V. A., 717, *724*, *725*
Rhodewalt, F., 142, 147, 148, 149, 150, 151, 152, 155, *170*, 178, 180, 188, *192*, *193*
Ribeiro, E. B., 252, *260*
Ribeiro, P., 669, 671, 676, *679*, *680*
Ricco, M., 373, *380*
Rice, A. P., 153, *165*
Rice, D., 581, *590*
Rice, D. P., 282, 286, 290, *315*, *316*
Rice, J., 297, *307*, 325, *336*, 686, *693*

Rice, J. P., 296, *307*, *315*
Rice, R. R., 388, *402*
Rich, A. R., 178, *192*
Rich, J., 826, *833*
Rich, J. D., 828, *837*
Rich, M., 154, 155, *163*, 663, *666*
Rich, M. A., 220, 221, *229*
Rich, M. W., 38, *42*, 64, 74, *79*, 153, *163*, 677, *680*
Rich, R. C., 603, *610*, 619, *624*
Rich, R., 603, *610*, 619, 620, 621, *623*, *624*, *625*
Rich, V. L., 178, *192*
Richard, J., 575, *580*
Richard, J. M., Jr., 576, *577*
Richard, K., 122, *136*
Richards, A. L., 810, *813*
Richards, G. E., 270, *278*
Richards, J. M., 341, 343, *348*, 849, *851*
Richards, J. S., 585, 586, 587, *590*
Richards, L., 471, *475*
Richards, T. J., 327, *336*
Richardsen, A. M., 421, 426
Richardson, C., 860, 861, 862, *892*
Richardson, D. W., 153, *162*
Richardson, J., 822, *836*
Richardson, J. L., 219, *232*, 576, *580*, 717, *724*
Richardson, J. R., 855, *891*
Richardson, P. J., 286, 287, *315*
Rich-Edwards, J. W., 520, 522, *537*
Richman, D. D., 811, *813*, 846, 847, 848, *851*
Richmond, P., 823, *839*
Richter, D., 751, *754*
Richter, K., 605, *608*
Richter, K. P., 604, 605, *608*
Richter, M., 111, *115*
Richter, S., 328, 329, *336*, 689, *694*
Rickard-Figueroa, J. L., 770, *775*
Rickels, K., 561, *569*
Ricker, D., 688, *693*
Ricker, J., 587, 588, *590*
Ricketts, P., 773, *776*
Rickman, R. L., 825, *838*
Rickwood, D. J., 222, *232*
Riddle, M. W., 640, *651*
Ridker, P. M., 286, *315*
Riedel, S. E., 483, 484, *492*
Rieder, I., 828, *838*
Riedlinger, W. F., 436, *440*
Riehl-Emde, A., 751, *754*
Rieker, P. P., 453, *457*
Ries, R. K., 548, *556*
Riesco, N., 63, *80*
Riesenberg, L. A., 736, *744*
Riesenmy, K. D., 285, *315*
Rietmeijer, C. A., *16*
Rigby, A. S., 509, *516*
Riger, S., 614, *624*
Riggio, R. R., 804, *814*
Riggs, D., 345, *346*, *347*
Rijks, T. I., 187, *191*
Riley, E., 849, *853*
Riley, G. E., 782, 783, *797*
Riley, K., 484, *490*
Riley, V., 748, *756*
Rimé, B., 339, 342, 343, *348*
Rimer, B., 729, 732, 735, 736, *741*, *742*, *743*, *745*, 759, 761, *775*
Rimer, B. K., 63, *83*, 519, 523, 524, 528, 530, 531, *534*, *536*, *537*, *538*, 714, 717, *723*, *724*, 729, 730, 732, 733, 734, 735, 736, 737, 738, 739, *743*, *744*, *745*
Rimm, A. A., 630, *655*, 717, *723*
Rimm, D. C., 126, *136*, 759, 761, *775*
Rimm, E. B., 153, *167*, 268, *276*
Rimmer, J., 292, *314*
Rimon, R., *331*, *335*
Rinaldon, C., 806, *813*
Ringhofer, K. R., 604, *607*
Rini, C., 506, 507, 510, *517*
Rini, C. K., 496, 501
Rippe, J. A., 573, *579*
Rippe, J. M., 526, *537*, 629, 646, 647, 648, *651*, *655*
Rippetoe, P. A., 730, *744*
Rips, L. J., 408, 409, *412*
Risch, N., 296, *310*
Risch, S. C., 684, *692*
Risley, T. R., 664, *667*
Rissel, C., 595, 601, 603, *607*
Ritchie, L. D., 784, *797*
Ritchie, S. W., 486, *492*
Ritchie, T., 296, *308*
Ritenbaugh, C., 470, 472, *475*
Rittenhouse, J. D., 144, 158, *172*
Ritter, C., 54, *56*, 498, 510, *512*
Ritvo, P. G., 637, *655*
Ritz, M. C., 252, *260*
Rivera, G., 861, 862, 885, *893*
Rivera, L., 758, *774*
Rives, K., 576, *580*
Rivlin, L., 369, *384*
Rivo, M. L., 869, *893*
Rizzi, L. P., 718, *722*
Rizzo, T., 270, *278*
Robacy, P., 453, *457*
Robbins, A. S., 155, *170*, 179, 184, *192*
Robbins, C., 210, 214, 215, *231*
Robbins, L. N., 638, *656*
Robbins, M. A., 153, *165*
Robbins, M. L., 675, *681*
Robert-Guroff, M., 808, *814*, *815*
Roberto, E. L., 596, 598, *609*
Roberts, A. H., 128, *134*
Roberts, C. G., 630, 646, *654*
Roberts, C. S., 752, *756*
Roberts, D. C., 712, 714, *722*
Roberts, J., 327, *334*, 718, *723*, 807, *815*
Roberts, J. A., 633, 635, *654*
Roberts, L. E., 86, *94*
Roberts, M., 548, 550, *555*, 676, *679*
Roberts, M. A., 387, *402*
Roberts, P. L., 828, *833*
Roberts, R. E., 632, *651*
Roberts, R. H., 436, *440*
Roberts, R. S., 849, *852*
Roberts-DeGennaro, M., 620, *624*
Robertson, A., 292, *317*
Robertson, B. M., 764, *775*
Robertson, C., 120, *134*, *135*
Robertson, C. F., 576, *580*
Robertson, D., 371, *380*
Robertson, P., *568*, *569*
Robertson, R. J., 273, 274, *277*, 648, *653*
Robertson, S., 225, *231*, *233*, 496, 509, *515*, *517*
Robin, R. W., 553, *555*
Robins, A. G., 850, *853*
Robins, E., 292, *314*, 633, *656*
Robins, L. N., 282, 283, 300, 304, *311*, *315*
Robins, R. W., 296, *313*
Robins, T. G., 372, *385*
Robinson, B. S., 354, 355, *360*
Robinson, D. S., 64, *79*, 156, *163*, 395, 397, *399*, 715, *722*, 751, 752, *754*
Robinson, E., 432, 435, *440*, *489*, *491*
Robinson, E. L., 432, *439*
Robinson, J. A., 406, *413*
Robinson, J. C., 91, *93*, 463, *468*
Robinson, L. A., 254, *260*
Robinson, M. G., 675, *680*
Robinson, S. E., 330, *331*, *337*
Robison, J., 542, 543, 544, 545, 548, 551, *557*
Robitaille, C., 24, *44*
Robitaille, Y., 296, *313*
Roccella, E. J., 429, *437*
Rocco, M. B., 669, 672, 677, *679*, *681*
Roche, A., 374, *384*
Roche, R. A., 735, *745*
Rockstroh, J., 847, *852*
Rodden, P., 822, *835*
Rodgers, D., 368, *385*
Rodgers, R. H., 783, *798*
Rodhal, K., 629, *656*
Rodin, G., 389, 395, *401*
Rodin, G. M., 219, *231*
Rodin, J., 50, *56*, 64, 74, *81* 179, 183, 180, *191*, *192*, 254, *260*, 328, *336*, 370, 374, *379*, *384*, 486, 488, *491*, 503, *515*, 689, *694*, 753, *756*, 818, 820, 822, 823, 825, 826, 827, 829, 831, *834*, *835*, *837*, *838*
Rodrigue, J. R., 453, *456*, 736, *743*, *744*
Rodriguez, M., 143, 144, 152, 154, *165*, 325, 326, 328, *334*, 479, *490*, 685, 688, *693*
Rodriguez, R., 155, 156, *172*, 179, *193*, 395, *402*, 823, *839*
Roehling, P. V., 301, *315*
Roehrich, L., 302, *315*
Roehrs, T., 290, *315*
Roeper, P. R., 435, *438*
Roesch, S., 502, *514*
Roesch, S. C., 510, *517*
Roester, R., 443, *447*
Roetzheim, R. G., 734, *742*, 779, *797*
Rofe, Y., 202, 203, *207*, 498, *517*
Roffman, R. A., 822, 830, 831, *835*, *838*
Rogers, E. M., 595, *610*, 782, *798*
Rogers, F., 576, *580*
Rogers, H. J., 243, *246*
Rogers, H. L., 780, *799*
Rogers, J., *16*
Rogers, M., 827, *836*
Rogers, M. M., 508, *517*
Rogers, M. P., 108, *114*
Rogers, P., 287, *315*
Rogers, R. W., 19, 22, 24, 33, 39, *43*, *46*, 729, 730, *740*, *744*
Rogers, S. W., 252, *259*
Rogers, T., 600, *610*, 614, *623*, 850, *851*
Rogers, W. H., 389, *402*, 473, *476*, 848, *852*
Rogers, W. J., 677, *681*
Roghmann, K. J., 687, *691*, *694*
Rogosch, F., 222, *229*, 301, 304, *307*, *308*, *315*
Rogot, E., 821, *838*
Roh, J. Y., 867, *893*
Rohay, J., 572, *577*
Rohay, J. M., 573, 574, 575, *578*
Rohde, F., 10, *16*
Rohe, D. E., 586, *590*
Roi, L. D., 753, *756*
Roitt, I. M., 108, *114*
Roizen, J., 294, *315*
Rolls, B. J., 267, 272, *276*, *278*
Romald, A. R., 825, *837*
Roman, J., 810, *813*
Romano, J. M., 122, 129, 130, *134*, 394, *402*, 488, *492*
Romano, P. S., 223, *232*
Romans, M., 531, *538*
Romeril, C. S., 371, *382*
Romero, R., 502, *517*
Romieu, I., 520, *537*
Romisher, S. C., 688, *693*

Romm, E., 251, 256, *260*
Romney, A. K., 26, *42*
Romonov, K., 66, *82*
Rompa, D. R., 850, *852*
Ronamelli, A., 373, *380*
Ronis, D. L., 729, 736, 737, *740*, *744*, *745*
Ronningen, K. S., 804, *815*
Rook, K. S., 210, *232*, 486, *492*, 508, *517*
Room, R., 282, 286, *307*, *314*
Rooney, B. L., 600, *609*
Roongpisuthipong, A., 827, *838*
Roos, C., 547, *555*
Rooso, R., 717, *724*
Root, M. P., 548, *556*
Root, M. P. P., 863, *893*
Rosan, J. R., 519, 530, *537*, 739, *744*
Rosario, M., 421, 426
Rosato, E., 406, *413*
Rosberger, Z., 715, 718, *723*
Rosch, E., 23, *46*
Rose, D., 717, *722*
Rose, G., 287, *313*, *317*
Rose, I. C., 252, *260*
Rose, J., 225, *230*, 599, *610*
Rose, J. E., 250, 256, *260*
Rose, J. H., 218, *232*
Rose, K., 552, *556*
Rose, K. M., 142, *169*, 187, *192*
Rose, M. S., 526, *538*
Rose, R., 66, *82*
Rose, R. J., 72, *81*, 436, *438*
Rose, R. M., 356, *362*
Rose, S., 436, *439*, 802, 803, *815*
Rosecrans, J. A., 252, *260*
Rosella, J., 572, *578*
Rosen, G., 591, 599, *610*
Rosen, M. G., 508, *517*
Rosen, S. D., 676, *681*
Rosenbaum, A. H., 644, *656*
Rosenbaum, M., 823, *838*
Rosenberg, E. L., 149, *170*
Rosenberg, H., 223, *232*
Rosenberg, J., 285, *317*
Rosenberg, L., 287, *315*, 736, *741*
Rosenberg, P., 822, *834*
Rosenberg, P. S., 801, *814*, *815*, 825, *838*
Rosenberg, R., 120, *136*, 488, *492*
Rosenberg, S. A., *113*, *114*
Rosenberger, P. H., 388, *402*
Rosenblatt, M., 645, *651*
Rosengren, A., 153, *170*, 215, 216, *232*
Rosenman, R., 669, 672, *680*
Rosenman, R. H., 66, *79*, *82*, 139, 147, 149, *165*, *167*, *168*, *170*, 330, *335*, 435, *438*
Rosensteil, A. K., 124, 125, *136*
Rosenstock, I., 831, *838*
Rosenstock, I. M., 19, 36, 39, *41*, *46*, 53, *57*, 574, 576, *579*, *580*, 591, 595, *611*, 729, 731, 739, *745*, 848, *853*
Rosenstock, R., 239, 243, *246*
Rosenthal, B., 621, *624*
Rosenthal, J., 617, 618, *623*, *624*
Rosenthal, M., 587, 588, *590*
Rosenthal, R., 344, *348*
Rosenthal, R. A., 349, 350, 351, *361*
Rose-Rego, S. K., 480, *492*
Roskamm, H., 124, *134*, 676, *680*
Roskies, E., 100, *103*, 576, *577*, 642, *656*
Rosner, B., 265, *279*, 286, 287, 289, 290, *310*, *311*, *318*, 471, 472, *474*, *475*, 520, 523, 524, *534*, *539*
Ross, C. E., 632, 638, *656*
Ross, D., 294, *314*
Ross, E., 530, 531, *537*, 732, 734, 737, *742*, *744*
Ross, E. A., 531, *532*, *537*
Ross, E. M., 472, *474*
Ross, H. E., 283, 284, *315*
Ross, J., 735, *741*, 825, *835*
Ross, L., 8, *16*, 40, *45*, 196, 197, *207*
Ross, M., 405, 407, *412*, *413*
Ross, M. J., 327, *335*
Ross, M. W., 849, *853*
Ross, R., 663, *667*
Ross, R. K., 290, *315*, 525, *532*, 631, *657*
Ross, S. B., 297, *315*
Rossi, J. S., 461, *465*, 593, *610*
Rossi, L. S., 782, 783, *798*
Rossouw, J. E., 470, 472, *476*
Rosti, G., 327, *333*
Roth, A., 498, *515*
Roth, D., 805, *812*
Roth, D. L., 480, 484, *490*, 641, *653*
Roth, H. D., 287, *316*
Roth, R. S., 586, *590*
Roth, S. H., 330, *331*, *337*
Roth, S., *331*, *337*, 397, *402*, 504, *517*, 716, *724*
Roth, T., 290, *315*
Rothbaum, B., 345, *347*
Rothbaum, F., 396, *402*
Rothbaum, F. M., 50, *57*
Rothenberg, R. B., 531, *538*, 780, *799*
Rotheram-Borus, M. J., 825, *835*, *838*
Rothfleisch, J., 289, *315*
Rothman, A. J., 729, 730, *740*, *741*, *745*, *746*
Rotnizky, A., 265, *276*
Rotnitzky, A. G., 523, 524, *535*
Rotstein, S., 110, *114*
Rotter, J., 805, *815*
Rotter, J. B., 51, 55, *57*, 141, *170*, 236, *246*
Rotton, J., 65, *82*, 372, *384*
Roudebush, R. E., 109, *114*
Roumayah, N. E., 496, *515*
Rounds, K., 829, *838*
Rounsaville, B., 299, *306*, *314*
Rounsaville, B. J., 285, *316*
Rouse, I. L., 287, *315*, 436, *742*
Rouse, L., 525, *534*
Routh, D. K., 449, *456*
Rouzioux, C., 824, *833*, *838*
Rovekamp, A., 372, *384*
Rovelli, M., 571, 575, 576, *580*
Rovine, M., 478, 483, *491*
Rowden, L., 764, *775*
Rowe, J. W., 226, *233*
Rowe, P. A., 808, *813*
Rowell, L. B., 87, *94*
Rowland, J., 750, *755*
Rowland, L., 526, 527, *534*
Rowlands, D. B., 436, *440*
Rowley, D. L., 499, 508, *517*
Rowley, P., 27, *42*
Roy, A., 74, *82*, 299, *316*
Roy, C., 736, *742*
Royak-Schaler, R., 733, *745*
Roy-Byrne, P. P., 546, 547, *557*
Royce, J. M., 869, *893*
Royce, R. A., 818, *838*
Rozanski, A., 63, 64, 73, 76, 77, *80*, 150, 157, *165*, *166*, 669, 670, 671, 672, 673, 675, 676, 677, 678, *680*, *681*, *682*
Rozelle, R. M., 460, 461, *466*
Rozin, P., 267, *278*
Ruback, B., 367, *384*
Ruback, R. B., 370, *380*
Rubbert, A., 806, *816*
Rubel, A., 857, 858, 860, 861, 863, *893*
Rubenow, J., 454, *456*
Rubens, R. D., 329, *335*, 747, 749, *756*
Ruberman, W., 217, *233*
Rubin, D., 344, *348*
Rubin, D. C., 409, *413*
Rubin, G. L., 288, *310*, 546, *556*
Rubin, P., 501, *516*
Rubin, R. T., 809, 810, *814*
Rubin, S. C., 110, *114*
Rubin, S. M., 472, *475*
Rubin, Z., 786, *798*
Rubinfeld, A. R., 576, *580*
Rubinow, D. R., *113*, *114*
Rubio, E., 868, 869, *893*
Ruble, D., 859, *893*
Ruckdeschel, J. C., 393, *399*, *721*
Rucker, L., 543, 546, *555*
Rudd, P., 574, *580*
Ruddel, H., 373, *383*
Rudolph, D., 527, *536*, 628, *654*
Rudy, T. E., 122, 124, 127, 129, 130, *134*, *136*
Ruebush, T. K., 860, *894*
Rueff, B., 287, *312*
Ruger, U., 153, *166*
Rugg, A. J., 497, 498, 510, *513*
Rugg, D. L., 850, *852*
Ruggiero, L., 504, *518*
Rugh, J. D., 91, *94*, 96, *103*
Ruhling, R., 637, *652*
Ruiz, E., 734, *743*
Ruiz, M., 822, *836*
Rumboldt, Z., 674, *681*
Runmore, R., 764, *775*
Running Wolf, P. R., 877, *891*
Rupp, J., 855, *894*
Ruppelt, P., 828, *838*
Rusbult, C., 368, 372, *383*
Rush, C., 873, 885, *889*
Rushing, J., 734, *744*
Russek, L. G., 151, *170*
Russell, D., 211, 225, *230*, 542, 543, *556*
Russell, D. W., 227, *229*, 305, *310*, 328, *332*, 687, *692*
Russell, E., 637, *652*
Russell, I., 736, *741*
Russell, M., 109, *115*, 211, 223, *232*, 287, 292, 301, 302, *309*, *316*, 357, 358, *360*
Russell, M. A., 250, *260*
Russell, P. O., 523, 524, *534*, *537*
Russell, R. P., 576, *579*
Russell, S. F., 66, 71, 73, *83*
Russo, J., 481, 484, *493*, 546, 547, *557*
Russo, N. F., 541, 542, 543, 553, *556*
Rutan, G., 268, *279*
Rutenfranz, J., 373, *383*
Rutherford, M. J., 301, *307*
Rutledge, D. N., 734, *745*
Rutledge, J. H., 528, *538*
Rutter, M., 366, 378, *384*
Ruzek, S. L., 519, *537*
Ruzicka, L., 856, *893*
Rwandan HIV Seroprevalence Study Group, 825, *838*
Ryan, C., 675, *680*
Ryan, E. A., 330, *335*
Ryan, K. B., 461, *465*, *466*
Ryan, M., 603, *610*
Ryan, P., 645, *654*, 684, *693*
Ryan, R. M., 485, 486, *490*, *492*
Ryan, S. M., 63, *80*
Ryan, T. J., 675, *682*
Ryan, W., 186, *189*, *192*
Ryan-Wenger, N. M., 450, *456*
Rybarczyk, B., 588, *590*

Ryden, J., 548, *556*
Ryder, R., 825, *836*, *838*
Ryder, R. W., 794, *798*
Rye, P., 50, *58*
Rye, P. D., 50, *57*
Ryst, E., 326, *336*

S

Saab, A., 806, *813*
Saab, P. G., 433, 435, *438*, *440*
Saad, M. F., 270, *278*
Saadatmand, F., 523, *532*
Saag, M. S., 846, 847, 848, *851*
Saah, A. J., 803, *814*
Saah, M. I., 255, 256, *258*
Sabat, S. R., *189*, *192*
Sabatini, M. T., 828, *838*
Sabbioni, M., 24, *45*
Sabharwal, S. C., 91, *93*
Sable, M. R., 506, *517*
Sabogal, F., 778, 786, *798*, 850, *892*
Sabroe, S., 497, 501, *514*
Sacamano, J., 325, *336*
Sacchetti, D. A., 267, *277*
Sachs, M. J., 645, *656*
Sachs, R. G., 700, *707*
Sackett, D. I., 849, *852*
Sackett, D. L., 572, 575, 576, *578*
Sacks, F. M., 287, *318*
Sadeh, A., 326, *335*
Sadler, G. R., 530, *534*
Sadock, B. J., 252, *260*
Saegert, S., 369, 370, 376, *382*, *383*, *384*
Saenz, D. S., 357, *361*
Saepharn, K., 867, 868, *889*
Safai, B., 802, *815*
Safer, M., 200, *207*
Safonova, T., 496, *517*
Safyer, S. M., 779, *797*
Sagebiel, R., 340, *348*
Sager, R. V., 630, 647, *656*
Sagnella, G. A., 699, *708*
Sagrestano, L. M., 496, 505, 506, 507, 510, *513*, *517*
Sahu, S. C., 588, *590*
Saidi, G., 735, *745*
Saini, J., 74, *79*, 663, *666*
Saini, V., 329, 330, *335*
Saito, Y., 477, *490*
Sakinofsky, I., 714, *725*
Saklad, S. R., 810, *813*
Salamone, J. D., 252, *260*
Salata, R., 272, *279*
Salazar, M. K., 732, 733, 734, *745*
Salazar, W., 638, 645, *655*
Sales, E., 720, *724*
Salganik, I., 636, *655*
Salkovskis, P. M., 33, *46*
Sallabank, P., 672, *680*
Salle, H., 371, 373, *382*
Salley, A., *489*, *491*
Sallis, J., 526, 527, *537*, *539*, 573, *579*, 629, 646, 647, 648, *655*, 855, *894*
Sallis, J. F., 150, *170*, 464, *466*, 525, 526, 527, *533*, *534*, *536*, 633, *657*
Sallis, J. F., Jr., 327, *334*
Salmeron, B., 499, *514*
Salmon, M. A., 519, *537*, 869, *892*
Salonen, J. T., 66, 76, *82*, 156, 157, *165*, 215, *231*, 473, *475*, 600, 601, *610*, 629, 630, *654*, 662, *667*
Salonen, R., 156, *165*, 629, 630, *654*
Salovaara, H., 685, *691*
Salovaara, L., 685, *691*
Salovey, P., 27, 32, *46*, 119, 129, *136*, 159, *168*, *740*, *741*, *745*
Saltzman, L. E., 500, 508, *512*, *514*, 542, *556*
Salvatierra, O., Jr., *474*, *475*
Salzberger, B., 847, *852*
Samdahl, D., 527, *534*
Samelson, L., 290, *310*
Sameroff, A. J., 498, *518*
Samet, F., 548, 550, *555*
Samet, J. H., 547, *556*, 849, *853*
Samet, J. M., 218, *230*, 329, *333*, 855, *893*
Samples, F., 442, *446*
Sampson, H. A., 859, *893*
Sampson, P. D., 289, 290, *317*
Sampson, R. J., 442, 443, 445, *448*
Samuelson, C., 524, *539*
San Francisco City Cohort ALIVE Study, 806, *813*
Sanchez, J., 644, *652*
Sanchez, L. L., 282, *318*
Sanchez, M. J., 405, *412*
Sanchez, R., 550, *556*
Sanchez-Thorin, J. C., 330, *335*
Sancho-Aldridge, J., 735, *745*
Sande, K. J., 267, *276*
Sande, M., 552, *556*, 823, *833*
Sande, M. A., 808, *813*
Sandelands, L. E., 352, *362*
Sanderman, R., 49, *57*
Sanders, G., 197, *207*
Sanders, G. S., 143, 146, *172*, 200, 202, *207*
Sanders, J. D., 149, 150, 151, *171*
Sandler, I. N., 221, *233*, 509, *517*
Sandler, R. B., 527, *536*
Sandler, R. S., 522, *532*, *533*, 731, 732, 733, *741*
Sandler, S. G., 808, *815*
Sandman, C. A., 496, 501, 502, 503, 510, *517*, *518*
Sandman, P. M., 730, *746*
Sandman, P. O., 480, *490*
Sandner, D. F., 879, *893*
Sandoval, M. C., 875, *893*
Sands, C., 714, *724*, 732, 735, *743*, *745*, 749, *755*
Sands, C. B., 732, *742*
Sandvik, L., 629, 633, 635, 637, 640, *654*, *656*
Sanford, G. L., 807, *813*
Sanford, M. D., 462, *467*
Sanjeevi, C., 805, *815*
Sanne, H., 217, *233*
Sanson-Fisher, R., 734, *741*
Sanson-Fisher, R. W., 291, *318*
Santelli, J., 825, *838*
Santi, S., 464, *466*
Santiago, H. T., 669, 670, 672, 675, 677, *681*, *682*
Santoro, G., 672, *679*
Sanzo, K., 227, *231*, 329, *335*, 752, *755*
Sapira, J. D., 702, 703, *707*
Sapolsky, R. M., 748, *756*
Sarafian, B., 22, *42*
Sarason, B., 160, *170*
Sarason, B. R., 160, *169*, *170*, 209, *232*, *233*, 355, *362*, 393, *401*, 505, 509, *517*
Sarason, I. G., 160, *169*, *170*, 209, *232*, *233*, 322, *336*, 355, *362*, 393, *401*, 505, 509, *517*
Sarason, S., 591,*611*
Sardell, A. N., 715, *724*
Sargent, R. G., 520, *533*
Sarnaa, S., 72, *81*
Sarno, A. P., 500, *511*
Saron, C., 158, *168*
Sarugeri, E., 330, *332*
Sasaki, M., 664, *668*
Sasaki, S., 287, *317*
Sassaman, W. H., 95, *103*
Sassetti, M., 548, *556*
Satariano, W. A., 750, *756*
Satin, A. J., 545, *556*
Satler, L. F., 675, *681*
Sattin, R. W., 290, *314*, 648, *655*
Saucier, G., 159, *170*
Saucier, J.-F., 420, 424, 505, 506, *512*
Sauer, M. V., 561, 566, *570*
Saulter, T., 432, 435, *440*
Saunders, D., 550, 552, *555*, *556*, *557*, 563, 565, *570*
Saunders, D. A., 804, *814*
Saunders, E., 807, 810, *815*, 869, 873, *890*
Saunders, J. B., 286, *315*
Saunders, L. D., 849, *853*
Saunders, L., 828, *833*
Saunders, W. B., 217, *233*, 662, *668*
Sauter, P. J., 855, *893*
Sauter, S. L., 350, 352, *362*, 415, 426
Savage, L. H., 739, *742*
Savage, P. J., 869, 877, *888*, *893*
Savage, S. A., 733, 734, *745*
Savicki, R., 827, *839*
Savitz, D. A., 500, *512*
Saward, E. W., 37, *46*
Saxarra, H., 109, *114*
Saxinger, W. C., 808, *814*, 828, *836*
Sayette, M. A., 303, *316*
Scambler, A., 202, *207*
Scambler, G., 202, *207*
Scanlan, J., 481, 484, *493*
Scarborough, R., 714, *724*
Scarlett, M., 828, *835*
Scarr, S., 62, *82*
Schaafsma, G., 286, *311*
Schable, B., 826, *838*
Schachinger, H., 434, *438*
Schachter, S., 23, 30, 36, 37, *46* 146, *170*, 195, 196, 200, 202, *206*, *207*, 250, 256, *260*
Schaefer, C., 506, *512*
Schaefer, J. A., 388, 390, *401*
Schaefer, P., 31, 38, 40, *44*
Schaeffer, C., 68, *81*
Schaeffer, M. A., 367, 368, 370, *384*, 434, 435, *437*, *440*
Schafer, A. P., 828, *839*
Schafer, J., 285, *309*
Schaffer, D. M., 496, *517*
Schag, C. C., 762, 763, *774*
Schaie, K. W., 470, *476*
Schairer, C., 732, *742*
Schall, J. I., 269, *278*
Schanberg, S. M., 149, 150, *172*, *173*, 663, 664, *667*, *668*, 674, *682*
Schanck, R. L., 198, *207*
Schandler, S. L., 297, *316*
Schang, S. J., 672, 676, *682*
Schapiro, J. M., 571, *580*
Scharlach, A. E., 482 *492*
Schatzberg, A. F., 644, *656*
Schatzkin, A., 287, 289, *315*, *316*, 631, *652*, 869, *890*
Schaubroeck, J., 356, *360*
Schaufeli, W. B., 417, 418, 420, 425, 426
Schechter, M. D., *568*, *569*
Schechter, M. T., 471, *475*
Schechter, N. L., 764, *776*
Schechtman, K. B., 71, *84*
Schedlowski, M., 109, *114*, 328, 329, *336*, 689, *694*
Schei, B., 547, *557*
Scheib, E. T., 702, 703, *707*
Scheidt, P. C., 292, *307*
Scheier, M., 156, *170*
Scheier, M. F., 20, 21, 22, 31, 40, *42*, 61, 64, 67, 69, 70, 71, 73, 77, *79*, *82*, 142, 155, 156,

163, *170*, 179, 184, *192*, *193*, 356, *362*, 391, 395, 397, *399*, *402*, 504, 505, *512*, 585, *590*, 715, *722*, *724*, 751, 752, *754*
Scheinin, M., 503, *518*
Schell, L., 371, *384*
Schell, L. M., 371, *384*
Schemper, M., 575, *580*
Scher, H., 639, 642, *656*
Scherer, K., 69, *82*
Scherer, K. R., 25, *44*, *46*, 64, 73, *78*, *84*, 157, *162*
Scherr, P. A., 286, 289, *311*, *316*
Scherwitz, K. W., 663, *667*
Scherwitz, L., 71, *83*, 147, 150, *170*, 340, *347*
Scherwitz, L. W., 149, *166*, *576*, *577*
Scheufele, P. M., 254, 255, 256, *259*
Scheyer, R. D., 573, 574, 575, *577*
Schiaffino, K. M., 29, *46*, 219, *232*, 394, *402*, 487, 488, *492*, 591, *610*
Schiessel, R., 575, *580*
Schiff, I., 631, *652*
Schiffer, F., 671, *682*
Schildkraut, J. J., 644, *656*
Schiller, D., 267, *278*
Schiller, N., 824, *838*
Schilling, E. A., 70, *78*, 154, *163*
Schilling, R. F., 823, *834*
Schindler, C. W., 250, *261*
Schinke, S., 436, *437*, 464, *465*
Schinke, S. P., 461, 463, *466*, *467*, 504, *512*
Schkade, J., 368, *380*
Schlegel, R. P., 462, *467*
Schleifer, S. J., 685, 686, 690, *694*, 717, *724*
Schlenk, E. A., 571, 573, 574, *578*, *580*
Schlesinger, H. J., 339, *347*
Schlien, B., 329, *334*, 752, 753, *755*
Schlundt, D., 36, *41*, *43*
Schlundt, D. G., 272, *278*
Schlussel, Y., 663, *667*
Schmale, A. M., 388, *400*, 715, *723*
Schmeck, K., 373, *384*
Schmid, J., 603, *610*
Schmid, T., 599, 600, *608*
Schmid, T. L., 268, *276*, 591, 593, 594, 598, 599, 600, 602, 604, 605, *608*, *609*, *610*, *611*
Schmidlin, O., 434, *440*
Schmidt, A. J. M., 120, 121, 122, 123, *133*, *136*
Schmidt, C., 152, *173*
Schmidt, D., 370, 376, *384*
Schmidt, J. A., 142, 144, 160, 161, *172*
Schmidt, L. D., 177, 185, *191*
Schmidt, P., 67, *80*
Schmidt, R. E., 328, 329, *336*, 689, *694*
Schmidt, R. F., 128, *136*
Schmidt, T., 549, 550, 552, *557*
Schmied, L. A., 185, *193*, 435, *439*
Schmitt, D. P., 780, *795*
Schmitt, R. C., 366, 368, 369, *384*
Schmitz, J. B., 327, 328, *332*, *333*, 689, *692*
Schnall, P., 663, *667*
Schnall, P. L., 351, 355, 359, *361*, 855, *893*
Schneider, B. E., 792, *798*
Schneider, D., 822, *834*
Schneider, J. A., 705, *706*
Schneider, M., 368, 369, 376, 377, *382*
Schneider, M. S., 24, *46*, 64, *83*
Schneider, R. H., 327, 329, *336*, *706*, *707*
Schneider, S. G., 155, 156, *172*, 179, *193*, 395, *402*
Schneiderman, L., 329, *336*
Schneiderman, N., 62, 63, 74, 77, *80*, *83*, 226, *233*, 245, *246*, 325, 326, 328, *334*, 340, 342, 343, *346*, *347*, 388, 395, 398, *401*, 433, 435, *438*, *440*, 642, *654*, 685, 688, 690, 691, *693*, *694*
Schneidman, D. S., 117, *135*
Schnell, D. J., 850, *852*
Schnohr, P., 286, *310*
Schober, R., 22, *46*
Schobitz, B., 112, *115*
Schoch, W. A., 575, *578*
Schoeller, D. A., 267, *275*, *278*
Schoenbach, V. J., 215, *233*, 523, 524, *535*, 869, *892*
Schoenbaum, E., 389, 398, *401*, 822, 826, 828, *837*, *838*
Schoenbaum, E. E., 327, *333*
Schoenberg, J. B., 288, *308*
Schofield, P., 183, *190*, 736, *741*
Scholes, D., 523, *538*
Scholl, T. O., 269, *278*, 498, 505, *517*, *518*
Schonfeld, I. S., 354, 355, *362*
Schonfield, J., 749, 750, *756*
Schooler, C., 54, *57*, 504, *517*, 601, 604, 605, 606, *608*
Schooler, T. Y., 324, *332*
Schooley, R. T., 846, 847, 848, *851*
Schoorl, J., 790, *799*
Schopler, J., 368, 372, *383*
Schopp, L. H., 584, *589*
Schor, J. B., 855, *893*
Schork, A., 305, *310*, *318*
Schork, M. A., 433, *438*
Schork, N. J., 431, 435, *439*
Schorling, J. B., 523, *537*
Schorr, O., 765, 768, *774*, *775*
Schorr, S., 220, *230*
Schorr, U., 434, *438*
Schotanus, K., 112, *115*
Schott, T., 396, *403*
Schottenfeld, R. S., 299, *306*, *314*
Schoutrop, M. J. A., 342, 343, *348*
Schrager, L., 778, *798*
Schramm, W. F., 506, *517*
Schranz, D. B., 330, *336*
Schreibeis, D., 827, *833*
Schreiber, J. M., 857, 859, 860, 861, 862, *893*
Schreiner, G. F., 703, *706*
Schreurs, K. M. G., 394, *402*
Schriml, L., 807, *815*
Schroeder, A. F., 548, *556*
Schroeder, A., 378, *381*
Schroeder, D. M., 731, 734, *743*, *744*
Schroll, M., 153, *163*, 662, *666*
Schron, E. B., 395, *402*, 573, *580*
Schron, E., 153, *162*
Schuckit, M. A., 283, 289, 296, 297, 298, 300, 301, *307*, *309*, *315*, *316*, 327, *332*
Schuerman, J. A., 120, *137*
Schugens, M. M., 126, *134*
Schulberg, H., 632, *653*
Schulenberg, J., 283, 284, 285, 300, *312*
Schull, W. J., 266, *278*, 433, *438*
Schulman, C. L., 671, *682*
Schulman, P., 180, *192*
Schulman, S., 221, 227, *233*
Schulsinger, F., 266, *278*, 295, 297, 298, *310*, *315*
Schulte, H. M., 503, *517*
Schulte, W., 373, *383*
Schultz, J. D., 855, *893*
Schultz, J. H., 97, *103*
Schultz, R., 50, *57*, 155, 156, *170*
Schulz, A., 597, *612*, *623*, *624*
Schulz, L. O., 266, *278*
Schulz, R., 226, *229*, *233*, 478, 480, 481, 482, 483, 484, 487, *489*, *490*, *491*, *492*, *493*, 585, *590*, 720, *724*, 753, *755*
Schuman, P., 389, 398, *401*, 822, 826, 828, *837*, *838*
Schumm, W. R., 783, *795*
Schuster, C. R., 822, *836*
Schuster, M. M., 548, *557*
Schuster, T. L., 508, *517*
Schuster-Uitterhoeve, A. L., 717, *724*
Schutz, H. W., 575, *577*
Schuyltz, J. A., 605, *608*
Schwam, J., 452, *456*
Schwankovsky, L., 396, *403*
Schwartz, D. P., 123, 129, *136*
Schwartz, E., 869, *893*
Schwartz, G., 397, *401*
Schwartz, G. E., 59, 61, 71, 73, 74, 76, *81*, *83*, *84*, 92, *93*, 151, 156, 157, *167*, *170*, *172*, 703, 704, 705, *707*, *708*
Schwartz, H. S., 351, *362*
Schwartz, J., 30, *46*
Schwartz, J. E., 61, *80*, 143, 153, 155, 156, 158, 159, 160, *165*, *168*, 351, 355, 359, *361*, 395, *400*, 406, 410, *411*,*413*, 442, 445, *448*, 663, *667*
Schwartz, L. M., 731, 738, 739, *745*
Schwartz, M. D., 64, *83*, 714, *724*, 729, 732, 733, 735, *740*, *741*, *742*, *743*, *745*
Schwartz, M. S., 97, *103*
Schwartz, N., 406, 410, *413*
Schwartz, P., 786, 790, *795*, *797*
Schwartz, P. E., 718, *722*, 763, 764, *774*
Schwartz, P. J., 642, *656*
Schwartz, R., 74, *80*, 594, 599, 600, 601, 602, *608*, *611*
Schwartz, R. D., 251, *260*
Schwartz, R. S., 482, *493*
Schwartz, S., 684, *694*
Schwartz, S. G., 639, 641, *656*
Schwarz, D. F., 543, 545, *555*
Schwarzer, R., 53, 54, *57*, 179, 180, 182, *191*, *193*, 235, *246*, 505, 506, *517*
Schwarzmann, S. W., 571, *580*
Schwebel, A., 125, *134*
Schwebel, A. I., 720, *725*
Schweitzer, J. B., 453, 454, *456*
Schweitzer, J. W., 183, *191*
Schweizer, R., 571, 575, *580*
Schweizer, R. T., 575, 576, *580*
Schwenk, A., 847, *852*
Schwenk, T. L., 527, *536*
Scoggins, B. A., 434, *440*
Scopetta, M., 849, *853*
Scorza Smeraldi, R., 803, *815*
Scott, C. B., 647, *652*
Scott, C. S., 553, *556*
Scott, E. H., 828, *834*
Scott, E., 471, *475*
Scott, G., 824, 827, *833*
Scott, J., 855, 869, 870, 886, *891*
Scott, K., 734, *743*
Scott, M., 289, 290, *317*
Scott, R. B., 804, *812*
Scott, R. W., 704, *706*
Scott, S., 785, 789, 790, *797*
Scragg, R., 286, *316*
Scrimshaw, S. C., 496, 500, 506, 510, *518*
Scrimshaw, S. C. M., 224, *230*, *232*, 496, 501, 506, 507, *513*, *515*, *517*, *518*
Seagle, H. M., *275*, *277*
Seal, D., 575, *577*
Seal, D. W., 830, *834*
Sealand, N., 442, *447*
Seale, C., *721*, *724*
Searles, J. S., 296, 301, *307*, *316*
Sears, S. F., 273, *278*
Seay, J., 394, *401*, 759, 761, *775*
Sebastian, A., 434, *440*
Sebastian, L. A., 630, *657*

Secher, N. J., 497, 501, *514*
Sechrist, K. R., 54, *57*
Secker-Walker, R. H., 525, *537*
Secord, P. F., 820, *834*
Seegmiller, B., 496, *517*
Seekins, T., 600, *607*
Seelbach, H., 633, 638, *653*
Seeley, J. R., 25, 29, *47*
Seeman, T. E., 216, 226, *233*, 486, 488, *489*, *491*, *492*
Seeman, T., 228, *229*, 393, *403*
Sega, R., 373, *380*
Segal, B. L., 140, 146, *163*
Segal, D., 342, *347*
Segall, G. M., 150, *167*, 670, 671, *680*
Segerstrom, S. C., 156, *170*, 685, *694*
Seggie, J. L., 575, *579*
Seifert,C. M., 27, 40, *45*
Sekermenjian, H., 644, *653*
Selby, J., 802, 803, *815*
Selby, J. V., 531, *537*
Seleshi, E., 126, *134*
Seligman, M., 155, 156, *169*
Seligman, M. E., 444, *448*
Seligman, M. E. P., 25, *46*, 54, *57*, 64, 67, 74, *81*, *82*, 121, *136*, 180, 181, *190*, *191*, *192*, 356, *362*, 375, *382*, 585, *590*, 597, *611*, 748, *756*
Selik, R. M., 821, *838*
Sellers, D., 575, *578*
Sellers, S. L., 432, *439*
Selner-O'Hagan, M., 444, *448*
Selser, J. N., 223, *232*, 717, *724*
Seltzer, M. M., 481, *491*
Selwyn, A. P., 669, 671, 672, 675, 676, 677, *679*, *680*, *681*, *682*
Selwyn, P., 823, *838*, 849, *853*
Selwyn, P. A., 826, *838*
Selye, H., 67, 68, *83*, 321, 322, 323, 325, *336*, 418, 426
Semczuk, B., 371, *384*
Semenya, K., 869, *892*
Semmence, A. M., 629, 647, *654*
Sempala, S., 808, *814*
Semple, S. J., 478, 483, *491*, *492*
Sena, A., 818, *838*
Senchak, M., 292, *313*
Sender, L., 453, *456*
Senkoro, K., 829, *832*
Senner, J. W., 573, *577*, 807, *815*
Senterfitt, J. W., 822, 826, *838*
Seppanen, A., 503, *518*
Septimus, A., 718, *721*, 773, *774*
Seracchioli, R., 566, *570*
Seraganian, P., 100, *103*, 639, 640, 641, 642, *656*, *657*
Sercarz, E., 690, *693*
Serdula, M. K., 270, *278*, 521, *537*, 869, *893*
Sereika, S., 572, 573, 574, 575, *577*, *578*, *580*
Sermsri, S., 368, *381*
Serrano-Garcia, I., 602, *610*
Service, S. K., 777, *798*
Sessions, W., 665, *666*
Sethi, B. B., 575, *580*
Setterlind, S., 177, *191*
Severson, H., 461, *465*
Severson, H. H., 522, 525, 528, *534*, *537*
Sevitz, H., 575, *579*
Sexauer, C. L., 720, *724*
Sexson, S., 454, *456*
Sexson, S. B., 454, *456*
Sexton, H., 635, 640, *656*
Sexton, M., 524, *537*
Sexton, R., 872, 873, 874, *893*
Seydel, E. R., 575, *580*
Seyle, H., 139, *170*
Sgoutas-Emch, S. A., 690, *694*
Shaffer, D., 325, *336*
Shaffer, D. R., 483, *493*
Shaffer, N., 825, 827, *835*, *838*
Shah, A. S., 471, *474*
Shah, N. M., 820, *832*
Shaham, Y., 257, *260*
Shain, R. N., 830, *838*
Shakerin, L. R., 546, 547, *556*
Shalev, A. Y., 343, *347*, 773, *776*
Shan, A., 432, 435, *440*
Shanhan, S., 250, *260*
Shani, E., 736, *741*
Shanks, G. L., 124, 129, *133*
Shannon, C., 351, *361*
Shannon, J., 521, *535*
Shannon, L., 409, *413*
Shannon, V. J., 752, *756*
Shaper, A. G., 286, *318*, 629, *656*, *657*
Shapiro, A. H., 367, *384*
Shapiro, A. K., 101, *103*, 703, *707*
Shapiro, A. P., 700, 702, 703, 704, 705, *707*
Shapiro, D., 73, 76, 77, *81*, 88, 89, 92, *93*, *94*, 139, 150, *167*, *172*, 703, 704, *708*
Shapiro, D. E., 827, *838*
Shapiro, M. F., 787, *799*, 822, 826, *838*
Shapiro, P. A., 663, *668*
Shapiro, R. M., *275*, *278*
Shapiro, S., 528, 531, *534*, 576, *579*, 630, 647, *656*
Shapiro, S. H., 575, *578*
Shapshak, P., 686, 690, *693*, 753, *755*
Sharaf, B., 677, *681*
Sharma, A. M., 434, *438*
Sharp, D., 371, 373, *382*
Sharp, L. K., 342, 343, *347*
Sharpe, N., 39, *45*
Sharpe, P. A., 520, *533*
Sharpe, S., 785, 789, 790, *797*
Sharpe, T. M., 326, *336*
Shaten, J., 266, *276*
Shaver, P. R., 354, *361*
Shaver, P., 30, *46*
Shavit, N., 575, *579*
Shaw, C., 442, *448*, 867, *895*
Shaw, G. M., 496, *517*
Shaw, R., 675, *680*
Shaw, S., 805, *813*, *815*, 829, *832*
Shaw, S. M., 527, *538*
Shawaryn, M. A., 29, *46*
Shay, M. J., 153, *169*
Shay, S. D., 802, 809, *816*
Shea, M., 671, 676, *680*
Shea, S., 591, 595, 600, 606, *611*
Shearer, W., 824, 827, *833*
Shearin, E. N., 160, *170*
Shearn, D., 88, *94*
Shears, S., 296, *315*
Sheehan, M., 647, *652*
Sheehan, N. W., 483, *492*
Sheehan, P. W., 217, *230*
Sheeran, P., 729, *745*, 784, *795*
Sheffield, D., 433, *438*
Shefft, B. K., 4, 5, *16*
Shejwal, B., 367, 369, 370, *381*
Shekelle, R. B., 66, 72, *78*, *83*, 139, 148, 149, 150, 153, 154, *162*, *169*, *171*, *173*, 329, *336*, 662, *667*
Shelton, D., 849, *853*
Shelton, D. R., 219, *232*, 576, *580*
Shelton, J., 121, *134*
Shelton, R. C., *162*, *166*
Shepard, E. M., 703, *708*
Shepel, L. F., 218, *234*
Shephard, R. J., 525, *533*, 627, 644, *651*, *656*, *657*
Shepherd, J., 822, *835*
Shepherd, J. B., 830, *835*
Shepherd, R. W., 502, *517*
Sheppard, H., 778, *798*
Sheppard, S., 100, *103*, 688, *693*
Sheppard, W., *706*, *707*
Shepperd, J. A., 179, *193*
Sheps, D., 665, *666*
Sheps, D. S., 329, *334*, 629, *652*, 671, 672, 674, 676, 677, *679*, *680*, *681*, *682*
Sher, K. J., 283, 284, 291, 292, 297, 298, 300, 301, 302, 303, 304, 305, *306*, *308*, *309*, *312*, *313*, *315*, *316*, *318*
Sher, T. G., 562, *570*
Sherbourne, C. D., 473, *476*, 848, *852*
Sherer, D. M., 502, *517*
Sherer, M., 54, *57*
Sheridan, D., 549, *555*
Sheridan, J., 481, *491*
Sheridan, P. J., 296, *308*
Sherman, C. T., 676, *682*
Sherman, J., 197, *206*
Sherman, J. J., 503, *515*
Sherman, M., 150, *165*
Sherman, S. J., 462, *467*
Shernoff, M., 829, *838*
Sherrill, J. T., *489*, *492*
Sherrod, D. R., 210, *229*, 370, 375, *384*
Shervington, D. O., 523, 524, *538*
Sherwin, R., 429, *438*
Sherwood, A., 154, *172*, 435, *439*
Sherwood, J. B., 150, *169*, 662, *667*
Shevell, S. K., 408, 409, *412*
Shevitz, A. H., 849, *853*
Shewchuk, R., 586, 587, *589*, *590*
Shi, L., 287, *316*
Shiavi, R. G., 576, *579*
Shiboski, S., 818, *837*
Shiboski, S. C., 781, *798*
Shide, D. J., 267, 272, *278*
Shields, J. L., 72, 73, 76, 77, *79*
Shields, N. M., 543, *555*, *557*
Shields, S. L., 576, *579*
Shiffman, S., 77, *83*, 253, 256, *261*, *275*, *276*, 327, *336*, 406, 407, 410, *413*
Shiffman, S. S., 405, 406, 410, *413*
Shifren, K., 479, *490*
Shiller, A. M., 663, *667*
Shimp, L., 874, *888*
Shin, H. D., 807, *815*
Shinchi, K., 287, *317*
Shine, P., 371, *384*
Shinn, M., 393, *400*, 421, 426
Shiono, P. H., 499, *517*
Shipley, M., 219, *230*
Shipley, M. H., 433, *438*
Shipley, M. J., 287, *313*
Shipton-Levy, R., 850, *851*
Shirao, I., 289, *311*
Shirom, A., 417, 426
Shite, F. A., 480, *490*
Shoaib, M., 250, *261*
Shock, N., 469, *476*
Shock, N. W., 95, *103*
Shoda, Y., 20, 28, 31, *45*, 59, 61, 62, 68, 74, 76, 77, *78*, *82*, *83*, 142, 159, *169*, 188, *192*, 729, 730, 734, 736, *744*
Shoham, S. B., 54, *56*
Shontz, F. C., 157, *164*
Shook, T. L., 672, 676, *679*
Shoor, S., 124, 127, *135*

Shopland, D. R., 522, *537*
Short, J., 221,*233*
Shore, J. H., 877, *893*
Shorter, T., 496, 503, *515*
Shrager, L. R., 273, *276*
Shragg, P., 269, *275*
Shrapnell, K., 752, *756*
Shrivastava, P., 349, *362*
Shuchter, S., 340, *348*
Shukla, G. D., 588, *590*
Shulhan, D., 639, 642, *656*
Shulman, G., 808, *815*
Shulman, L. E., 117, *135*
Shultz, J. M., 286, 290, *316*
Shulz, G., 88, *94*
Shumaker, S. A., 393, 395, *402*, 470, 472, *475*
Shuster, M. M., 91, *93*
Shuttleworth, E., 685, 687, *693*
Shuttleworth, E. C., 327, 328, *334*
Shutty, M. S., 123, 129, *136*, 584, *589*
Shutz, Y., 267, *278*
Shuval, J. T., *229*, *233*
Shweder, R., 856, 857, *893*
Siani, R., 506, *518*
Siann, G., 790, *798*
Sich, D., 867, *891*, *893*
Sidney Primary HIV Infection Study Group, 850, *852*
Sidney, S., 432, *439*, 523, 526, 527, *532*, *538*, 663, *667*, 869, *888*
Sieber, M., 751, *754*
Sieber, M. F., 300, 301, *316*
Sieber, W., 374, *384*
Sieber, W. J., 328, *336*, 689, *694*, 753, *756*
Siegal, J. M., 547, *555*
Siegel, B. S., 748, *756*
Siegel, D., 777, 779, 783, 787, 789, 794, *795*, *796*, *798*, 825, *833*, *834*
Siegel, J., 732, *740*, *745*
Siegel, J. M., 22, 33, *45*, 65, *83*, 221, *230*, 714, *724*
Siegel, S., *113*, *114*, 765, 767, 768, *774*, *775*
Siegel, S. E., 764, 772, *774*, *775*
Siegel, W. C., 631, 642, *651*, 677, *682*
Siegelaub, A. B., 281, *312*
Siegenthaler, W., 576, *578*
Siegler, I. C., 63, 64, 65, 66, 72, 74, *81*, *83*, 143, 145, 148, 149, 151, 153, *162*, *163*, *171*, 217, *233*, 469, 471, 473, *474*, *475*, *476*, 530, *538*, 662, 663, *666*, *667*, *668*, 730, 732, 733, *745*
Siegman, A. W., 73, *83*, 149, *171*
Siegman, C., 52, *56*
Siegris, J., 662, *666*
Siegrist, J., 157, *166*, 351, *362*, 642, *656*
Siervogel, R., 374, *384*
Siever, L., 74, *83*
Siever, L. J., 325, *336*
Sievers, M. L., 877, *892*, *893*
Sifneos, P. E., 157, *171*
Sigal, L. H., 687, *691*, *694*
Sigvardsson, S., 295, 296, 300, 301, *308*
Siimes, M. A., 454, *455*
Sikkema, K. J., 3, *16*, 830, 831, *835*, *838*, 847, *852*
Sikora, K., 749, 753, *756*
Silberfarb, P. M., 715, *721*, *724*, *725*
Silberstein, D. J., 802, 809, *816*
Siletti, D. M., 753, *755*
Sillanaukee, P., 288, *311*
Silva, A., 343, *346*
Silva, P. A., 300, 301, *308*
Silva, R., 183, *191*
Silva, S. G., 664, *667*
Silver, G., 870, *893*
Silver, R., 339, 340, *347*, *348*
Silver, R. L., 394, *402*
Silverglade, L., 66, *83*
Silverman, B. L., 270, *278*
Silverman, M., 452, *456*
Silverstein, B., 146, *170*, 250, 256, *260*
Silverstein, M., 225, *233*, 486, 487, 488, *492*
Sim, M., 827, *833*
Simcha-Fagan, O., 442, 445, *448*
Sime, W. E., 632, 633, 635, *652*, *656*
Simel, D. L., 472, *475*
Simion, P., 330, *334*
Simkin, L., 526, *536*
Simkin, L. R., 524, *536*
Simkin-Silverman, L., 270, *278*, 576, *580*
Simmonds, P., 803, *815*
Simoes, E., 521, *537*, 869, *893*
Simon, C. P., 781, *797*
Simon, G. E., 632, *656*
Simon, H., 748, *754*
Simon, L. J., 530, *533*
Simon, N., 145, *166*
Simon, P. M., 849, *853*
Simon, W., 791, *797*, *798*, *799*
Simonds, R. J., 827, *838*
Simonetti, I., 675, *681*
Simoni, J., 822, *836*
Simoni, L. E., 575, *578*
Simonon, A., 824, *839*
Simons, M., 820, *838*
Simons, R. C., 19, *46*, 859, 860, *893*
Simonsen, J. N., 825, *837*
Simonsick, E. M., 153, *171*
Simons-Morton, B. G., 268, *278*
Simonson, E., 702, *708*
Simpson, D. M., 735, *745*
Simpson, G. E., 874, 875, 880, *893*
Simpson, J. M., 732, *742*
Simpson, R. J., Jr., 473, *476*, 521, *535*
Simpson, S., 436, *437*
Sims, C., 269, *278*
Sims, D. G., 366, *384*
Sims, S. E. R., 753, *756*
Simsek, H., 288, 289, *316*
Sinaki, M., 525, *538*
Sindelar, J. L., 291, *314*
Sinden, J., 252, *259*
Singer, A. M., 859, *888*
Singer, D. R. J., 699, *708*
Singer, E., 407, *413*, 850, *851*
Singer, G., 108, *115*
Singer, J., 367, *384*
Singer, J. E., 23, 36, *46*, 69, *78*, 195, 200, *207*, 324, 326, *333*, 370, 371, 375, *381*
Singer, J. L., 340, *348*
Singer, M., 823, *839*
Singer, P., 73, *81*
Singer, R., 20,21, *44*
Singer, R. P., 460, *467*
Singh, B., 810, *813*
Singh, B. K., 850, *853*
Singh, J., 353, *362*
Singh, M., 288, 289, *316*
Singh, N., 848, 849, *853*
Singh, N. A., 635, 637, *656*
Singh, P., 868, 869, *893*
Singh, R., 576, *580*
Singh, R. B., 576, *580*
Single, E., 286, *307*
Sinkkonen, J., 454, *455*
Sintonen, H., 454, *455*
Sinyor, D., 639, 640, 641, 642, *656*
Sipprelle, R. C., 325, *333*
Siriwasin, W., 827, *838*
Sirotkin, B., 617, 618, *623*
Sita, A., 150, *169*
Sitnikova, V. V., 807, *815*
Siu, A. L., 729, *742*
Sivek, C., 848, 849, *853*
Sivo, P. J., *162*, *163*
Sivyer, M., 109, *114*
Sjeoqvist, F., 810, *815*
Sjoberg, L., 731, *745*
Sjostrom, K., 503, *517*
Skaff, M. M., 478, 482, 484, *491*, *492*
Skelton, J. A., 19, 20, *46*
Skews, H., 74, *80*
Skibinski, K., 454, *456*
Skinner, B. F., 87, 89, *94*, 251, 253, *261*, 757, 759, *776*
Skinner, C. S., 737, *745*
Skinner, D., 453, *456*
Skinner, E. A., 324, *336*
Skinner, J. B., 301, *309*
Skinner, M. J., 787, 788, *797*
Skitka, L. J., 419, 425
Skitka, L., 420, 426
Sklar, L. S., 748, *754*, *756*
Skokan, L. A., 54, *57*
Skoner, D. P., 28, 33, *42*, 60, *79*, 154, 160, *164*, 322, 326, 328, *332*, 683, 684, *692*
Skorka, B., 644, *651*
Skowronski, J. J., 405, 406, 408, 409, *413*
Skrinar, G. S., 645, *651*
Slade, P. O., 121, *135*
Slamon, D. J., 808, *815*
Slap, G., 825, *837*
Slater, J. A., 453, *457*
Slater, M. A., 122, 125, 126, 130, *136*
Slater, P. A., 807, *812*
Slatopolsky, E., 525, *536*
Slavin, B., 576, *579*
Slavin, L. A., 715, *724*
Slenker, S. E., 530, *538*, 732, *742*
Slinkard, L., 461, 464, *467*
Slinkard, L. A., 461, *467*
Sloan, D. A., 388, *400*, 718, *723*
Sloan, R. P., 663, *668*
Slob, A., 373, *384*
Slocumb, J., 550, *557*
Sloman, R., 758, 760, *776*
Sloss, E. M., 282, *313*
Slovic, P., 728, 729, 733, 739, *743*, *745*
Slutske, W. S., 295, *311*
Smart, C. R., 528, *538*
Smart, R. G., 282, *306*, *316*
Smeriglio, V. L., 224, *233*, 506, *518*
Smets, E. M., 717, *724*
Smilga, C., 100, *103*
Smilkstein, G., 497, *516*
Smith, A. F., 408, 410, *413*
Smith, A. P., 33, *42*, 328, *332*, 638, *651*, 683, 684, *691*, *692*, 713, *723*
Smith, A., 154, *164*, 340, *346*
Smith, B., 451, 452, *456*, 576, *580*
Smith, B. A., 878, 879, 880, *894*
Smith, C. A., 52, 53, 54, *56*, *57*, *58*, 159, *171*, 182, *193*, 219, *233*, 391, 394, 395, 396, *402*, 434, *440*
Smith, C. R., 576, *579*
Smith, D., 101, *102*, 714, *724*, 826, *837*
Smith, D. A., 488, *490*, 509, *513*
Smith, D. A. F., 394, *400*
Smith, D. E., 272, *278*, 520, *538*
Smith, D. H. G., 643, *657*
Smith, D. K., 806, 808, 810, *814*, 822, 826, *838*
Smith, D. W., 603, *608*

Smith, F. J., 266, *276*
Smith, G. D., 286, *311*, 662, *667*
Smith, G. H. D., 860, 861, 862, *893*
Smith, G. P., 112, *115*
Smith, G. R., 109, *115*
Smith, G. S., 290, *316*
Smith, G. T., 292, 301, 302, *308*, *314*, *317*
Smith, H., 699, *707*
Smith, H. G., 374, *383*
Smith, J. A., III, 471, *475*
Smith, J. P., 427, *439*
Smith, K. M., 252, *260*
Smith, K. W., 732, *741*
Smith, L. J., 64, *80*, 677, *680*
Smith, M., 344, *348*, 826, *833*, 846, 849, *852*, *853*
Smith, M. A., 150, *171*
Smith, M. L., 339, *348*
Smith, M. S., 50, *58*
Smith, M. W., 806, 807, 810, *813*, *814*, *815*
Smith, M. Y., 188, *192*, 773, *776*, 849, *853*
Smith, N., 877, *889*
Smith, R., 406, *412*, 502, *515*, 550, *557*, 810, *814*
Smith, R. A., 50, *57*, 528, *538*
Smith, R. A. P., 50, *58*
Smith, R. C., 548, *557*
Smith, R. E., 64, *83*, 634, 638, *653*, *656*
Smith, R. M., 868, 869, *893*
Smith, R. T., 508, 509, *516*
Smith, S., 49, 53, *58*, 397, *401*, *706*, *707*
Smith, S. S., 296, *317*
Smith, T. L., 289, *307*, 686, 690, *693*, *694*, 749, *755*
Smith, T., 33, *46*, 689, *693*
Smith, T. W., 55, *56*, 61, 62, 64, 66, 69, 70, 71, 72, 76, *83*, 122, 125, *136*, 140, 141, 142, 143, 145, 146, 147, 148, 149, 150, 151, 152, 153, 154, 155, 157, 158, 160, 161, *162*, *163*, *165*, *166*, *169*, *170*, *171*, *173*, 178, 179, 180, 184, 187, 188, *190*, *193*, 220, 221, *229*, 662, 663, *667*, *668*
Smith, W. K., 269, *278*
Smith, W. M., 703, *708*
Smith-Warner, S. A., 287, *317*
Smoll, F. L., 64, *83*
Smyke, P., 820, 821, 830, *838*
Smyth, J., *411*, *412*
Smyth, J. M., 157, *171*, 341, 342, 343, 344 *348*, *411*, *413*
Smyth, K., 436, *440*
Smyth, K. A., 480, *492*
Snead, D. B., 525, *536*
Sneddon, I., 572, *577*
Snell, J. L., 737, *745*
Snell, L., 749, *756*
Snell, M. K., 271, *277*
Snetselaar, L., 574, *577*
Snider, P., 390, *402*
Snider, P. R., 156, *172*, 391, 395, 396, 397, 398, *402*, 504, *518*, 751, 752, *756*
Snidman, N., 344, *347*
Snoek, J. D., 349, 350, 351, *361*
Snow, B., 70, 72, *80*, *83*
Snow, D., 388, *399*
Snow, L. F., 872, 873, 874, *890*, *893*, *894*
Snow, M. H. M., 154, *172*
Snyder, B. K., 687, *691*, *694*
Snyder, C. R., 182, *193*, 238, *246*, 585, *590*
Snyder, D. K., 787, *799*
Snyder, M., 142, *166*, 375, *382*
Snyder, S., 396, *402*
Snyder, S. L., 717, *722*, 761, 762, *774*
Snyder, S. S., 50, *57*
Snydersmith, M., 685, 686, *693*
Sobal, J., 521, *538*
Sobel, J., 460, *467*
Sobel, J. L., 461, *466*
Sobel, R., 330, *331*
Sobo, E. J., 790, *799*
Sobol, A. M., 265, 268, *276*
Sobol, D. F., 461, *466*
Sobolew-Shubin, A., 396, *403*, 487, *492*
Society for Assisted Reproductive Technology/American Society of Reproductive Medicine, 560, 561, 563, *570*
Soderberg, V., 646, *657*
Soeken, K., 508, *515*, 543, 545, *556*
Soghikian, K., 177, *191*
Sokol, R. J., 290, *307*, *311*, 508, *517*
Sokolow, M., 703, *707*
Solberg, O., 634, 635, *654*
Soldatkina, S. A., 373, *382*
Soler, E., 375, *384*
Soliman, A., 689, *695*
Solinger, J. W., 123, *135*
Solky, J. A., 485, 496, *492*
Soloman, G. F., 685, 689, 690, *694*
Solomon, L., 822, 826, 828, *837*, *838*
Solomon, L. J., 525, *537*, 830, 831, *835*, *838*
Solomon, M., 441, *447*
Solomon, M. J., 531, *538*
Solomon, R., 34, *46*
Solomon, R. L., 30, *46*
Solomon, Z., *229*, *233*
Solvason, H. B., 109, 110, *115*
Somerfield, M. R., 394, 395, *400*
Somers, J. M., *306*, *313*
Somervell, P. D., 153, *171*
Somerville, W., 671, *682*
Somes, G., 872, *891*
Somlai, A. M., 823, 829, *834*, *835*
Sondag-Thull, D., 824, *839*
Sonksen, P. H., 576, *579*
Sontag, S., 186, *193*
Soong, S. J., 576, *577*, 849, *851*
Sopko, G., 677, *681*
Sorensen, G., 522, 523, 528, *532*, *538*
Sorensen, J., 787, *796*
Sorensen, T. I. A., 266, *278*, 286, *310*
Sorenson, S. B., *229*, *232*, 547, *555*
Sorlie, P., 630, *653*
Sormanti, M., 453, *457*
Sorof, J., 434, *440*
Sorrell, C., 734, *741*
Sorrell, M. S., 878, 879, 880, *894*
Sortet, J. P., 734, *745*
Sorvillo, F., 817, *838*
Sosa, R., 225, *233*, 496, 509, *517*
Sothmann, M. S., 642, 644, *656*
Sotomayor, N., 675, *680*
Soufer, R., 150, *163*, 671, 677, *679*, *680*
Soumi, S., 367, *380*
Souply, K., 850, *853*
Southam, M. A., 705, *706*
Southard, D. R., 71, *84*, 151, *172*
Southwick, S., 325, *336*
Southwick, S. M., 325, *336*
Sowell, T., 869, 886, *894*
Sowinski, P., 252, *259*
Sowunmi, A., 810, *815*
Spaccarelli, S., 326, *336*
Spaccavento, L. J., 671, *679*
Spackman, D. H., 748, *756*
Spadoni, L., 523, *534*
Spafkin, R. P., 153, *167*
Spalding, A. D., 183, *193*
Spalding, T., 806, *816*
Spangler, K., 525, *535*, 599, 600, *609*
Spanos, D., 524, *539*
Spanos, N. P., 125, *136*, 764, *774*
Sparrow, A. W., 643, *657*
Sparrow, D., 153, *167*
Sparrow, J., 672, *681*
Spealman, R. D., 250, *259*
Spear, S. F., 306, *310*
Spears, G., 177, *190*
Specchia, G., 671, *682*
Specter, S., 749, *755*
Spector, P. E., 354, *360*
Spector, R. E., 856, 857, 858, 859, 862, 864, 865, 866, 873, 874, 875, *894*
Speer, P. W., 603, *611*
Speers, M. A., 600, *611*
Speicher, C. E., 68, *81*, 227, *229*, *231*, 327, 328, 329, *334*, 685, 686, 687, 688, 690, *693*, *694*
Speigel, D., 713, 720, *724*
Speilberg, J., 862, *892*
Speizer, F. E., 265, *276*, *277*, 286, 287, 290, *310*, *311*, *317*, *318*, 471, 472, *474*, *475*, 520, 523, *535*, *539*
Spence, J. C., 638, *653*
Spence, J. D., 144, *163*
Spence, J. T., 155, *170*, 179, 184, *192*, 819, *838*
Spence, N. D., 119, *135*
Spencer, K. A., 484, *492*
Spera, S. P., 342, *348*
Sperber Nissinoff, K., 272, *279*
Sperling, R. S., 824, 827, *835*, *838*
Speroff, L., 566, *570*
Spicer, E. H., 857, 860, *894*
Spiefelhalter, D., 473, *474*
Spiegel, D., 122, 124, *136*, 218, 219, *233*, 340, *346*, *348*, 664, *668*, 752, *756*, 758, 760, 762, *776*
Spiegelman, D., 287, *317*, 520, *535*
Spielberger, C. D., 66, 71, 73, *83*, 350, *362*, 435, *439*, 497, *518*, 638, 639, 642, 643, *656*
Spiezer, F. E., 265, *279*
Spigner, C., 327, *333*
Spilich, G. J., 255, *261*
Spilker, B., 473, *476*
Spindler, A. A., 855, *893*
Spinetta, J. J., 772, *774*
Spinhoven, P., 124, *136*
Spira, T. J., 828, *836*
Spirito, A., 504, *518*
Spiro, A., 32, *46*, 153, 155, *167*, *169*, *171*
Spiro, H., 35, *45*
Spitz, A. M., 500, 508, *512*, *517*
Spitzer, R. L., 266, 268, 633, *652*, *656*
Spitzer, S. B., 226, *233*, 433, 435, *438*
Spitzer, S., 150, *167*, 670, 671, *680*
Spitznagel, E. L., 283, *309*
Splansky, G. L., 631, *652*
Spohr H. L., 289, 290, *317*
Sposari, G., 372, 373, *383*
Sprafka, J. M., 593, 601, 604, *609*, 869, *888*
Sprangers, M. A. G., 388, *402*
Springer, K., *568*, *570*
Spurkland, A., 804, *815*
Squier, C., 848, 849, *853*
Squires, K. E., 846, *852*
Srebnik, D., 785, *798*
St. Clair, P. A., 224, *233*, 506, *518*
St. John, C., 506, *518*
St. Lawrence, J., 830, *838*
St. Lawrence, J. S., 10, *16*, 848, 850, *852*
St. Louis, M., 825, *838*
St. Pierre, B., 717, *725*
Staats, H., 153, *166*
Stablein, D., 154, *165*

Stables, G., 522, *535*
Stack, C. B., 441, 442, *448*
Stack, J. A., *489*, *492*
Stacy, A., 305, *307*
Stacy, A. W., 293, 301, 302, *312*, *317*
Staffa, J. A., 573, *578*
Staggers, R., *706*, *707*
Stahl, S. M., 202, *207*
Stall, R., 222, *231*, 293, *312*, *317*, 462, *467*, 777, 778, 779, 782, 783, 792, 793, *796*, *799*, 822, 826, *832*, *839*
Stall, R. D., 154, *163*, 783, 784, 785, 789, *796*
Stallag, K. , 663, *667*
Stallard, E., 477, *491*
Stallard, T. J., 436, *440*
Stalnaker, D., 527, *535*
Stamler, J., 66, *78*, 148, *171*, 287, *313*, *317*, 436, *440*, 700, *708*
Stamler, R., 287, *313*, *317*, 436, *440*, 700, *708*
Stampfer, M. J., 153, *167*, 265, 268, *276*, *277*, *279*, 286, 287, 290, *310*, *311*, *315*, *318*, 471, 472, *474*, *475*, 520, 523, *537*, *539*, 629, *654*
Stampler, F. M., 546, *556*
Stanaszek, W. F., 574, *577*
Stancer, H. C., 644, *657*
Stanczyk, F. Z., 502, *517*
Stanford, S. D., 750, *756*
Stangel, W., 327, *332*, 753, *754*
Stanley, N., 521, 522, *534*
Stanley, S., 826, *834*
Stansfield, S., 662, *667*
Stansfield, S. A., 371, 374, *384*, *385*
Stanton, A. L., 143, 156, *171*, *172*, 390, 391, 395, 396, 397, 398, *402*, 504, *518*, 561, 562, *570*, 733, *745*, 751, 752, *756*
Stanton, B., 782, *795*
Stanton, B. A., 73, *81*
Stanton, D. L., 808, *813*
Stark, E., 542, 543, 544, 545, 548, 549, 550, 551, *557*
Stark, K., 141, *171*
Stark, M., 822, 828, *833*, *839*
Starlinger, M., 575, *580*
Starr, K., 398, *401*
Starz, T. W., 572, 574, 575, *577*, *578*
Stasiewicz, P. R., 303, *317*
Statham, A., 818, *839*
Statham, D. J., 295, *311*
Statsny, P., 802, *813*
Staufer, R. N., 117, *134*
Stauffer, L., 604, *607*
Stavraky, K. M., 751, *756*
Staw, B. M., 352, *362*
Stead, W. W., 807, *815*
Steckevicz, M. J., 736, *742*
Steckler, A., 528, *536*, 591, 593, 594, 599, 600, 601, 602, 603, 604, 605, 606, *608*, *610*, *611*, 614, 620, 621, *624*
Steel, C. M., 803, *815*
Steel, R. P., 419, 425
Steele, C. M., 303, *317*
Steen, S. N., 272, 273, *279*
Steenman, G., 828, *832*
Steer, R. A., 498, *518*
Stefanek, M., 732, 735, *742*, *743*, *745*
Stefanek, M. E., 735, *745*
Stefanick, M., 527, *535*
Stefanick, M. L., 520, *539*
Stefanski, V., 326, *336*
Steffans, R., 732, *741*
Steffens, D. C., 471, *476*
Steffensen, M. A., 858, 865, *894*
Steger, K., 811, *815*
Steger, K. A., 847, 849, *853*
Stehbens, J. A., 454, *456*
Steilen, M., 850, *851*
Stein, A. D., *511*, *515*
Stein, E., 522, *538*
Stein, J., 823, *837*
Stein, J. A., 196, *207*, 222, *233*, 530, *534*, 547, *555*, 729, *742*
Stein, M., 685, 686, 690, *694*, 822, 826, *838*
Stein, M. D., 822, 826, *838*, 847, *853*
Stein, M. J., 52, 53, 55, *56*, *57*, *58*
Stein, P. N., 635, 637, *656*
Stein, Z., 804, *814*
Steinbach, U., 216, *233*
Steinberg, A. M., *229*, *232*
Steinberg, W., 288, *317*
Steiner, G., 676, *681*
Steiner, H., 326, *336*
Steiner, R., 751, *754*
Steinert, Y., 640, 642, *656*
Steingart, R. M., 473, *476*
Steinglass, P., 292, *317*, 441, *448*, 773, *775*
Steinhausen, H. C., 289, 290, *317*
Steinman, R. C., 663, *668*
Steinmetz, S., 541, 543, *557*
Steinmetz, S. K., 783, *795*
Stellar, E., 321, 328, *335*
Stellato, R. K., 826, *839*
Steller, E., 510, *515*, 643, *654*
Stemhagen, A., 288, *308*
Stenchever, M. A., 547, *557*
Stenestrand, U., 647, *652*
Stephens, J. C., 807, *815*
Stephens, M. A. P., 481, 482, 483, 484, 487, 488, *489*, *490*, *491*, *492*
Stephens, P. M., 748, *755*
Stephens, R. E., 329, *334*
Stephens, T., 525, 527, *533*, *538*, 627, 632, 638, 646, *651*, *656*
Steptoe, A., 49, *57*, 641, *656*, 684, *695*, 715, *724*
Stergachis, A. S., 523, *538*
Sterling, T. D., 604, 605, *608*
Stern, J. S., 272, *277*
Stern, M., 704, *708*
Sternbach, R. A., 128, *134*, 703, *708*
Sternberg, J. A., 271, 272, *278*
Sternfield, B., 631, *656*
Stetner, F., 663, *667*
Stets, J. E., 542, *557*
Stetson, B., 527, *534*
Stetson, B. A., 297, *308*
Steuart, G., 621, *624*
Steuart, G. W., *607*, *611*
Stevens, A. M., 824, *839*
Stevens, J. A., 290, *314*
Stevens, L., 829, *838*
Stevens, M., 451, *455*
Stevens, P. E., 828, *838*
Stevenson, H. C., Jr., 436, *440*
Stevenson, J., 603, 604, *608*, *610*, 614, *625*
Stevenson, L. Y., 848, 850, *852*
Stevens-Simon, C., 501, *515*
Stewart, A. J., 187, *190*, *193*, 389, *402*, 473, *476*
Stewart, C. J., 689, 690, *694*
Stewart, C. M., 497, *512*
Stewart, D., 545, *557*
Stewart, J., 111, *114*, 453, *456*
Stewart, M. A., 295, 296, *308*
Stewart, M. W., *331*, *336*
Stewart, R., 371, *384*
Stewart, S. M., 454, *457*
Stewart, W. F., 117, *136*
Stice, E., 305, *309*
Stieham, E., 827, *833*
Stiehm, E. R., 827, *837*
Stierle, H., 109, 110, *114*
Stierlin, H., 750, *756*
Stigendel, L., 221, 227, *233*
Stiles, R. W., 809, *813*
Stiles, T. C., 632, *653*
Stiles, W., 154, 155, 156, *164*
Stimson, G., 850, *853*
Stinson, F. S., 282, 286, 288, 293, *310*, *314*, *317*, *318*
Stinson, J., 496, *515*
Stites, D. P., 688, *692*
Stitzel, J. A., 256, *260*
Stockbauer, J. W., 506, *517*
Stoddard, A., 522, *538*, 736, 737, *746*
Stoddard, A. M., 738, 739, *744*
Stokes, J., 266, *277*
Stokols, D., 366, 367, 370, 373, 374, 375, 378, *380*, *383*, *385*, 527, 528, *538*, 591, 593, 598, *607*, *611*, 614, *624*
Stokols, J., 367, 370, *383*, *385*
Stolerman, I. P., 252, *261*
Stoller, E., 24, *46*
Stoller, E. P., 24, *46*
Stone, A., 340, *348*
Stone, A. A., 24, *46*, 77, *83*, 182, *193*, 324, 326, 328, *336*, 341, 342, 343, 344, *347*, 398, *401*, 405, 406, 407, 410, *411*, *412*, *413*, 683, 684, 687, 688, *691*, *694*, *695*
Stone, C., 255, *258*
Stone, G. C., 139, *172*
Stone, I. C., 545, *556*
Stone, K., 292, *309*
Stone, P. A., 576, *577*
Stone, P. H., 329, *334*, 671, 672, 673, 676, 677, *679*, *680*, *681*
Stone, R. A., 705, *708*
Stone, S. V., 142, 154, 158, 159, *172*
Stone, V., 777, 780, 783, 784, 785, *795*, *796*
Stone, V. E., 811, *815*, 847, *853*
Stones, M., 340, *348*
Stoney, C. M., 77, *83*, 431, *440*
Storer, B. E., 472, *475*
Story, J., 196, *207*
Stoto, M. A., 827, *839*
Stotts, C. R., 523, *538*
Stout, J., 100, *103*, 688, *693*
Stout, J. C., 68, *81*, 327, 328, *334*, 686, 688, 690, *693*
Stout, R., 224, *232*
Stover, S. L., 586, *590*
Stoyva, J., 88, 89, *93*, *94*
Strachan, A. 575, *579*
Strack, S., 156, *172*
Strain, E. C., 686, 688, *693*
Strain, J. J., 717, *724*
Strand, F. L., 434, *437*, *440*
Strand, P. J., 864, 868, *894*
Strandberg, L. R., 575, *579*
Strang, P., *721*, *724*
Strassberg, D. L., 463, *468*
Stratmann, G., 328, 329, *336*, 689, *694*
Strauman, T. J., 65, 76, *83*
Straus, M. A., 292, *308*, 541, 542, 543, *557*
Straus, M. E., 480, *492*
Strauss, A., 22, *44*
Strawbridge, W. J., 55, *57*
Strecher, V., 239, 243, *246*
Strecher V. J., 53, *57*, 522, 523, 524, *533*, *535*, 731, 732, 735, 737, *743*, *745*, 869, *892*
Street, S., 367, 370, *384*
Streissguth, A. P., 287, 289, 290, *317*
Strickland, B. R., 51, *57*, 145, *172*
Strickland, T. L., 810, *815*

Strigo, T. S., 730, 733, 734, *743*
Stroebe, M., 343. *348*
Stroebe, W., 343, *348*
Stroebel, C., 100, *103*
Strogatz, D. S., 287, *317*, 435, *439*, *440*, 641, *654*, 663, *668*, 869, *889*
Strom, B. L., 290, *310*
Strom, T. B., 108, *114*
Strong, L. C., 720, *722*
Strong, W. B., 431, 433, *438*, *440*
Stroop, J. B., 641, *657*
Stroot, E., 301, *310*
Strother, D., 671, *680*
Strouse, T. B., 389, 398, *399*,720, *722*
Strube, M. J., 71, *83*
Struening, E. H., 144, *170*
Strunin, L., 293, *317*, 462, *467*, 777, *797*
Strupp, B. J., 272, *277*
Struss, W., 690, *692*
Stryker, S., 818, *839*
Stuart, A., 850, *851*
Stuber, M., 718, *724*
Stuber, M. L., 453, *457*, 718, *723*, 773, *775*, *776*
Stucky, P., 596, 604, 605, *608*, *611*
Stuhlmann, H., 805, 806, *814*
Stull, D. E., 483, *492*
Stults, B., 146, *171*
Stunkard, A., 266, *278*, 406, *413*
Stunkard, A. J., 183, *192*, 265, 266, 271, 272, *276*, *278*, *279*
Stutzman, D., 575, *578*
Stutzman, R. E., 90, 92, *93*
Styne, P. M., 877, *894*
Styra, R., 714, *725*
Su, B., 806, 807, *815*
Su, S., 803, *814*
Su, T. P., 809, 810, *814*
Suarez, E. C., 63, 66, *83*, 149, 150, *172*, *173*, 642, *654*, 662, 663, 664, *667*, *668*, 674, *682*
Suarez, L., 735, *745*
Subar, A. F., 521, *537*, *538*
Subar, A., 520, *533*
Subar, A. F., 869, *888*, *893*
Subramariam, G., 406, 407, *411*
Suchindran, C., 508, *517*
Suchman, E. A., 200, *207*
Sudhakar, M., 286, *318*
Sudhir, K., 434, *440*
Sudilovsky, A., 72, *81*
Sudman, S., 406, 409, 410, *413*
Sue, D., 864, *894*
Sue, D. W., 857, 862, 863, 864, *888*, *894*
Sugarman, J. R., 429, *440*
Sugg, N., 552, *557*
Sugisawa, H., 216, 223, *233*
Suissa, S., 296, *314*
Suitor, J. J., 483, 486, *492*
Sullens, C. M., 575, *577*
Sullivan, K. M., 719, *725*
Sullivan, M. J. L., 125, *136*
Sullivan, M. J., 473, *475*
Sullivan, M. L., 445, *448*
Sullivan, S. E., 524, *534*
Sullivan, S. R., 575, *579*
Sullivan-Halley, J., 525, *532*
Suls, J., 24, 31, 36, 38, *44*, *46*, 62, 65, 66, 72, 73, 74, 76, *83*, 143, 144, 148, 150, 158, *172*, 184, 187, *193*, 195, 196, 197, 199, 200, 201, 203, 204, *206*, *205*, *207*, *208*, 397, *402*
Summers, C., 631, *651*
Summers, T. P., 419, 425
Sumner, W., 735, *741*
Sun, X. W., 826, *839*
Sunaday, E., 369, *379*
Sung, H. Y., 581, *590*
Suomi, S. J., 664, *667*
Surbone, A., 110, *114*
Surbonem, A., 25, *41*
Surgeon General's Report, 628, 632, 635, 646, 648, *657*
Surtees, P.G., 329, *333*, 751, 752, *754*
Surwit, R. S., 139, 146, *172*, 330, *336*, 704, *708*
Susan, D. O., 855, 859, *892*
Susman, E. J., 502, *513*
Susman, J., 340, *347*
Susser, M., 600, *611*
Sussman, S., 461, 462, *466*, *468*
Sutcliffe, I., 715, *724*
Sutton, J., 645, *653*
Sutton, J. R., 627, *651*
Sutton, L. M., 716, 719, *725*
Sutton, R. I., 351, *362*
Sutton, R. L., 543, 545, *555*
Sutton, S., 735, *745*
Sutton, S. R., 460, *468*, 729, 730, *746*
Sutton-Tyrrell, K., 157, *168*
Suzuki, J., 663, *667*
Svärdsudd, K,. 215, *233*
Svensson, J. C., 226, *231*
Svikis, D., 523, *538*
Swain, M., 496, 499, 501, *513*, *516*
Swam, J. H., 442, *447*
Swaminathan, H., 243, *246*
Swan, G., 408, *412*
Swan, G. E., 66, *79*, 158, 159, *172*, 705, *706*
Swank, R. L., 576, *580*
Swanson, K. L., 406, *413*
Swanson, M., 848, *852*
Swedborg, K., 675, 676. *680*
Sweeney, D. R., 644, *657*
Sweet, D., 340, *348*
Sweet, R. B., 90, *94*
Swerdloff, R. S., 472, *476*
Swerdlow, N. R., 252, 255, *260*, *261*
Swianiewica, W., 373, *384*
Switlyk, P., 576, *578*
Symbaluk, D. G., 245, *246*
Syme, S., 821, *832*
Syme, S. L., 209, 210, 214, 215, 223, *229*, *230*, *231*, *232*, 355, *360*, 393, *399*, 505, *512*, 662, *666*, 821, *832*
Symister, P., 394, *400*
Synder, G. W., 272, *277*
Syrjala, K. L., 719, *725*, 758, 759, 760, *776*
Sys, S., 153, *165*
Sytniac, M., 497, 506, 507, *514*
Szabo, A., 641, *657*
Szapocznik, J., 849, *853*
Szata, W., 371, 374, *382*
Szklo, M., 217, *229*
Szymanski, J. J., 588, *590*

T

Taaid, N., 255, *261*
Taal, E., 575, *580*
Taams, M. A., 393, *400*
Tada, T., 804, *815*
Tafalla, R., 371, *381*
Tafalla, R. J., 371, *385*
Taggart, P., 671, *682*
Taguchi, F., 436, *437*
Taira, K., 371, *382*
Tait, A., 289, *318*
Tait, B. D., 804, *815*
Tak, Y., 734, *743*
Takada, K., 250, *261*
Takahashi, S., 644, *657*
Takahaski, N., 675, *680*
Takase, B., 676, *680*
Takayanagi, S., 717, *722*
Takefman, J., 560, *569*
Takeshita, A., 434, *440*
Takeuchi, T., 675, *680*
Tal, M., *489*, *490*
Talajic, M., 67, *80*, 327, 329, 330, *333*, 154, *165*, 662, *667*
Talan, M. I., 89, 91, *93*, *94*
Talbott, E., 372, 373, *380*, *385*
Talbott, E. O., 372, *385*
Tallant, R., 873, 875, 880, *894*
Talley, N. J., 544, 547, 548, *557*
Tallis, R., 676, *679*
Tam, T., 290, *308*
Tamamoto, T., 371, *382*
Tan, M., 753, *754*
Tanaka, J. S., 717, *724*
Tanda, G., 252, *258*
Tanfer, K., 778, 790, *799*
Tang, S. W., 644, *657*
Tangney, J. P., 152, *172*
Tango, T., 804, *815*
Tanis, D. C., 373, *384*
Tannenbaum, A. K., 675, *681*
Tanur, J. M., 405, *412*
Tanzy, K., 481, *490*
Taplin, S. H., 239, *246*
Taplin, S., 519, 530, *536*, 730, *743*
Taplin, S. H., 736, 737, *742*, *744*
Tarcic, N., 685, *695*
Tarlov, A. R., 855, 856, *887*
Tarnopolsky, A., 374, *382*, *385*
Tarone, R., 808, *814*
Tarr, K. L., 686, 688, 690, *693*
Tartaglia, A., 829, *839*
Tarter, R., 300, *317*
Tarter, S. K., 372, *385*
Tashima, L., 500, *512*
Tashiro, K., 806, 807, *815*
Tashkin, D. P., 523, *537*
Tasker, F., 567, *569*
Tassin, J. P., 748, *754*
Tateishi, T., 810, *813*
Tatelbaum, R., 508, *516*
Tattersal, M., 732, *742*
Tatum, C., 734, *744*
Taub, J. M., 635, *651*
Taub, K., 220, *230*
Taube, C. A., 628, *657*
Taube, S. L., 644, *657*
Taubes, G., 728, *745*
Taubman, O., 178, 179, 184, *190*
Tauscher, J., 371, *382*
Tausig, J., 561. *569*
Tausignant, M., 285, *317*
Tavazzi, L., 671, *680*
Taylor, A., 326, *332*
Taylor, A. N., 748, *754*
Taylor, C., 527, 528, *534*, *535*
Taylor, C. B., 126, 127, *133*, 150, *167*, 268, 273, *277*, *278*, 576, *579*, *580*, 593, 595, 596, 597, 598, 600, 601, 604, 605, 606, *608*, 633, 636, 640, 642, *650*, *653*, *657*, 670, 671, 675, *679*, *680*, 705, *706*

Taylor, D. W., 572, 575, 576, *578*, 849, *852*
Taylor, E., 526, *536*
Taylor, E. R., 524, *536*
Taylor, G., 527, *535*
Taylor, G. J., 66, *83*
Taylor, H., 329, *334*, 671, *680*
Taylor, H. L., 604, *607*
Taylor, I., 749, *754*
Taylor, J. A., 73, *83*, 156, *172*, 355, *362*
Taylor, J. L., 289, 290, *318*
Taylor, J. O., 289, *311*
Taylor, K. L., 24, 25, *41*, *45*, 110, *114*, 394, *401*, 732, *740*, *745*
Taylor, P. J., 561, *570*
Taylor, P. R., 289, *315*
Taylor, R. C., 255, *259*
Taylor, S., 34, *46*, 156, *170*
Taylor, S. E., 49, 54, *57*, 63, 64, 65, 67, 69, *79*, *82*, *83*, 155, 156, 157, *164*, *170*, *172*, 179, *190*, *193*, 196, 197, 204, *206*, *208*, 218, *230*, 344, *346*, 388, 390, 391, 393, 394, 395, 396, *399*, *402*, *403*, 504, 509, *512*, *513*, 564, *570*, 685, 686, *693*, 715, 718, *723*, *725*, 821, *832*
Taylor, S. L., 586, *590*
Taylor, S. P., 290, *317*
Taylor, T. L., 877, *894*
Taylor, V., 429, *438*
Taylor, W., 549, *555*
Taylor, W. C., 638, *6561*
Tazi, A., 112, *115*
Tchividjian, L. R., 736, *743*
Teasdale, G., 587, *590*
Teasdale, J. D., 40, *46*, 180, *190*
Teasdale, M., 765, 766, *775*
Teasdale, T. W., 266, *278*, 297, *315*
Tebbi, C. K., 717, *725*
Teddlie, C., 376, *385*
Tedeschi, R. G., 183, *193*
Teeter, M. A., 720, *725*
Teganeanu, S., 371, *380*
Teger, A., 369, *379*
Teitelbaum, M. A., 305, *307*, *318*
Telch, C. F., 266, *278*, 720, *725*, 762, 763, *776*
Telch, M. J., 464, *468*, 720, *725*, 762, 763, *776*
Telesky, C., 23, *41*
Tellegen, A., 75, *84*, 140, 146, *163*, 185, *191*, 356, *361*
Temmerman, M., 824, *833*
Temoshok, L., 67, 71, *83*, 340, *348*, 394, *403*, 750, 751, *756*, 831, *833*
Temoshok, L. R., 846, 849, *853*
Templar, D., 636, *655*
Temple, M. T., 663, *667*, 777, *798*
Temple, S., 599, 600, *608*
Tenacati, E. M., 600, *610*
Tenaglia, A. N., 389, 398, *399*
Teng, H. C., 703, *707*
Tennant, C., 563, 565, *570*
Tennant, C. C., 327, 330, *336*
Tennen, H., 29, 37, *41*, *46*, 54, 55, *56*, *57*, 180, *193*, 204, *205*, *208*, 219, *229*, 330, *331*, 391, 395, 396, 397, 398, *399*, *403*, 561, 562, 564, *570*
Tenner, S., 288, *317*
Tennstedt, S. L., 481, 483, *491*
Tentler, J. J., 289, *309*
Teoh, S. K., 289, *313*
Ter Kuile, M. M., 124, *136*
Terborg, J. R., 522, 528, *534*
Teri, L., 484, *489*, *491*, *492*
Terpin, M., 288, *310*
Terr, L., 345, *348*
Terra, N., 358, *363*
Terrazas, E. E., 326, *336*
Terrell, D. F., 432, *440*
Terrell, F., 870, *894*
Terrell, S. L., 870, *894*
Terry, D. H., 782, *799*
Terry, D. J., 221, *232*, 391, *401*, 787, *797*
Terry, R., 445, *447*
Tesh, S., 820, *839*
Tesoriero, J. M., 827, *839*
Tessaro, I., 523, 528, *538*
Tesselaar, H., 822, *839*
Tessler, R., 34, *46*
Testa, M., 196, 204, *207*, 292, *314*
Testa, M. A., 673, *681*
Teta, M. J., 720, *722*
Teutsch, S. M., 877, *892*
TeVelde, A., 74, *79*, 663, *666*
Tewes, U., 328, 329, *336*, 689, *694*
Tewfik, H. H., 716, *722*
Thai, S-F., 663, *668*
Thao, T. C., 869, *890*
Tharps, Q., 200, *207*
Thaulow, E., 629, *656*
Thayer, J. F., 584, *589*
Theisen, A., 847, *852*
Theisen, M. E., 669, 677, *682*
Thelin, T., 503, *517*
Themba, M., 596, 600, *611*
Theobald, T., 736, *742*
Theodos, V., 562, *570*
Theorell, T., 68, *81*, 221, 226, 227, *231*, *233*, 351, 358, *361*, *363*, 685, *691*, 855, *890*, *892*
Theriault, G., 265, 266, *276*
Theriot, S., 545, *556*
Therneau, T., 717, *722*
Thiede, H., 828, *834*
Thiering, P., 563, *570*
Thiessen, D., 368, *385*
Thin, R. N., 828, *834*
Thoennes, N., 542, 544, *557*
Thoits, P., 393, *399*
Thoits, P. A., 61, *84*, 214, 223, *233*
Thomas, A., 222, *230*
Thomas, C. J., 646, *656*
Thomas, D. J., 869, *892*
Thomas, D. L., 406, *413*
Thomas, J., 432, *439*, 645, *653*, 869, *892*
Thomas, J. G., 700, *707*
Thomas, L., 531, *536*
Thomas, M., 124, *135*, 342, 343, *347*
Thomas, P., 827, *836*
Thomas, P. D., 227, *233*
Thomas, R. L., 291, *311*
Thomas, S. B., 870, 872, *894*
Thombs, D. L., 782, *798*
Thompson, B., 522, *538*, 591, 593, 606, *609*, *611*
Thompson, C. P., 405, 406, 408, 409, *412*, *413*
Thompson, D., 370, *379*
Thompson, D. E., 368, 369, *379*
Thompson, D. J., 272, *276*
Thompson, D. L., 301, *309*
Thompson, E. L., 460, 461, *468*
Thompson, G. B., 528, 530, *534*
Thompson, L., 148, *162*, *165*, 717, 720, *723*, *725*
Thompson, M., 22, 33, *45*, 714, *724*
Thompson, M. A., 846, 847, 848, *851*
Thompson, N. J., *455*
Thompson, P. D., 269, *277*, 524, 525, *536*, *537*, 629, *655*
Thompson, P. J., 473, *475*
Thompson, R., 272, *276*, 372, 373, *380*, 461, *465*, 785, 789, 790, *797*
Thompson, R. J., 499, *518*
Thompson, R. J., Jr., 330, *335*
Thompson, R. S., 522, *532*, *538*
Thompson, S. C., 49, *57*, 124, *136*, 396, 398, *403*, 487, *492*
Thompson, S. J., 372, *385*
Thompson, V. L., 870, *894*
Thompson, W. D., 736, *742*
Thompson, W. W., 664, *667*
Thompson-Fullilove, M., 777, 787, *796*
Thomson, J. B., 297, 298, *314*
Thomson, S. J., 464, *466*
Thoresen, C. E., 148, *162*, *165*, *170*, 664, *667*
Thoreson, R. W., 562, *570*
Thorn, B. E., 122, 123, 125, 129, *134*, *137*
Thorndike, E. L., 251, *261*
Thornton, J. C., 685, 686, 690, *694*
Thorogood, M., 736, *744*
Thorpe, K. J., 506, *518*
Thorsen, M., 628, *653*
Thorson, C., 272, 273, *277*, *279*
Threatt, B. A., 719, *725*, 750, *756*
Thun, M., 266, *279*
Thun, M. J., 286, 288, *317*, 530, 531, *533*
Thune, I., 631, *657*
Thyer, B. A., 324, *335*
Thyrum, E. T., 671, 674, 675, *679*
Tian, H., 850, *852*
Tibblin, B., 215, *233*
Tibblin, G., 153, *170*, 215, *233*
Tierney, C., 153, *162*
Tietjen, A. M., 506, *518*
Tilden, V., 549, 550, 552, *557*
Tilden, V. P., 506, 507, 509, *516*, *518*
Tilders, F. J. H., 112, *114*, *115*
Tildesley, E., 305, *307*
Tilkin, J. M., 575, *578*
Tilley, B. C., 218, *232*, 329, *335*, 729, 731, *745*
Tillgren, P., 596, 600, *609*
Tilson, H. H., 473, *476*
Timmer, S. G., 223, *233*
Timmons, K., *489*, *491*
Timms, R. M., 576, *577*
Tindale, R. S., 143, 148, 158, *169*
Tingling, D. C., 874, *894*
Tinkoff, G. H., 73, *80*
Tinnetti, M. E., 648, *655*
Tipp, J., 297, *307*
Tipp, J. E., 663, *667*
Tipton, C. M., 630, 631, *652*, *657*
Tirado, G., 806, *813*
Tisak, J., 221, *230*
Tischfield, J. A., 296, *315*
Titus, B. G., 676, *682*
Titze, I., 327, *332*, 753, *754*
Tjaden, P., 542, 544, *557*
Tobin, D. L., 397, *403*
Tobin, J. D., 469, *476*
Tobin, J. N., 473, *476*
Tobin, S., *205*, *207*
Tobler, N. S., 460, *468*
Tochluk, S., 154, *164*
Todak, G., 846, *853*
Todd, D. M., 593, *611*
Todd, G., 641, *652*
Todd, J., 830, *834*
Todoroff, K. P., 496, *517*
Tofler, G. H., 150, *164*, 673, 674, 675, *681*
Tolan, P. H., *162*, *172*
Tolhuizen, J., 788, *799*

Tollefson, G. D., 285, *317*
Tollefson, N., 178, *191*
Tollefson, S. L., 285, *317*
Tomaka, J., 239, *246*
Tomanek, R. J., 630, *657*
Tomarken, A. J., 157, *163*
Tomkins, S., 69, *84*
Tomlinson, G. C., 671, *679*
Tomlinson, L., 452, 453, *456*
Tomlinson-Keasey, C., 61, *80*, 143, 153, 155, 156, 158, 159, 160, *165*, *168*, 395, *400*
Tompkins, C. A., 226, *229*, *233*, 478, 484, *492*
Tonascia, J., 217, *229*
Tong, T., 709, 710, 711, *724*, 747, *756*
Tonkic, A., 674, *681*
Tonnesen, H., 285, *317*
Toomey, T. C., 546, 547, *555*, *557*
Tope, D. A., 715, *721*, *725*
Tope, D. M., 716, *725*, 759, 761, *776*
Topf, M., 178, *193*
Torgersen, S., 285, *307*
Torjesen, P. A., 270, *278*
Toro, P. A., 591, 604, *609*
Torosian, T., 676, 677, *682*
Torres, E., 862, *894*
Torres, J. B., 820, *839*
Torres, M., 432, *439*
Torres, T., 527, *536*
Tortorici, M., 676, *680*
Tortu, S., 828, *833*
Tosi, D. J., 66, *83*
Tosteson, A. N. A., 731, 732, 739, *741*
Tota-Faucette, M. E., 122, 126, *136*
Toth, P., 432, 433, *440*
Totten, M. C., 179, *190*
Toumala, R. E., 828, *837*
Toumilehto, J., 600, 601, *610*
Touomala, R., 824, 827, *836*
Tourigny, L., 321, 326, 327, *332*
Tourtelot, E., 563, *569*
Tousoulis, D., 676, *681*
Tower, R. B., *489*, *493*
Townsend, A. L., 395, *400*, 481, 482, 483, *491*, *492*, *493*
Townsend, M., 473, *475*
Towson, S. M., 461, *465*
Toyosaki, N., 672, *679*
Trakowski, J. H., 327, 328, *333*, 689, *692*
Tran, T. M., 858, 864, 865, 867, 868, *894*
Tran, Z. V., 633, *655*
Trapnell, P. D., 140, *172*
Trask, O. J., 227, *229*, *231*
Traub, O., 329, *336*
Travers, P., 330, *334*
Traxler, M., 531, *536*
Treasure, C. B., 675, *682*
Trebow, E. A., 463, *467*
Treiber, F. A., 431, 433, *438*, *440*
Treichler, P. A., 827, *839*
Tremblay, A., 265, 266, *276*
Trembly, G., 20, 21, 24, *44*
Tremolieres, C., 373, *380*
Trent, L., 290, *315*
Trevino, F. M., 862, *890*
Trevorrow, T. R., 150, *170*
Triandis, H., 820, *839*
Triandis, H. C., 4, 13, *17*
Trickett, E. J., 593, *611*
Trier, C. S., *102*
Trierweiler, S. J., 715, *724*
Trijsburg, R. W., 389, 392, 395, *403*
Trimble, J. E., 463, *467*, 877, *889*
Tripathi, R. P., 588, *590*
Trivedi, J. K., 575, *580*
Trock, B., 519, *537*, 734, 735, 736, *743*
Trock, B. J., 531, *532*, *537*
Trocki, K. F., 293, *309*, 777, 785, *798*, *799*
Trois, R. J., 523, 524, *535*
Tromanhauser, E., 825, *837*
Tromp, E. A., 689, *692*
Tross, S., 718, *722*, 846, *853*
Trotter, F., II., 782, *795*
Trotter, R. T., 860, 861, 862, *894*
Trotter, R. T., II, 27, *47*
Troughton, E., 295, 296, *308*
Troup, J. P. G., 121, *135*
True, W. R., 325, *333*, *336*
Truelove, S., 366, *383*
Trueworthy, R. C., 575, *579*
Trull, T. J., 300, 301, *316*
Truman, B. I., 429, *438*
Tsai, G., 299, *317*
Tsai, Y., 185, *191*
Tschann, J. M., 328, *332*, 690, *692*, 771, 772, *774*, 785, *798*, 820, *836*
Tsouros, A., 595, 596, *607*
Tsuang, J. W., 289, *307*
Tsuda, K., 805, *815*
Tsujimaru, S., 289, *311*
Tsushima, M., 287, *317*
Tucker, J. S., 61, *80*, 143, 153, 155, 156, 158, 159, 160, *165*, *168*, 395, *400*
Tucker, L. A., 267, 272, *278*
Tucker, M. B., 223, *233*
Tuckson, R. V., 869, *893*
Tuliza, M., 794, *798*
Tulsky, D. S., 22, *42*
Tummon, I., 563, *569*
Tunis, S. L., 497, *518*
Tunks, E., 123, *136*
Tunstall, C. D., 269, *276*, 524, *535*
Tuomilehto, J., 156, *165*, 290, *317*, 629, 630, *654*, *655*
Tuomisto, M., 356, *360*
Tupler, L. A., 471, *475*
Turan, S., 434, *438*
Turbott, J., 74, *80*
Tureck, R., 564, *569*
Tureck, R. W., 561, *569*
Turk, D. C., 118, 119, 120, 121, 122, 123, 124, 125, 126, 127, 128, 129, 130, *133*, *134*, *136*, 488, *493*, 573, 574, *580*, 757, 758, *776*
Turk, E., 345, *346*
Turkewitz, G., 371, *382*
Turnbull, D., 732, *742*
Turnbull, J., *489*, *490*
Turner Cobb, J. M., 684, *695*
Turner, C. F., 827, *836*
Turner, C. G., 463, *467*
Turner, C. W., 55, *56*, 140, 143, 146, 148, 150, 151, 158, *169*, *171*, 220, 221, *229*, 662, *667*
Turner, H., 507, *514*, 783, 784, 785, 789, *796*, 822, *832*, 846, *852*
Turner, J., 119, *135*
Turner, J. A., 122, 125, 126, 130, *134*, *135*, *136*, 394, *402*, 488, *492*
Turner, J. J., 252, *259*
Turner, J. R., 146, *172*, 435, *439*
Turner, P., 817, *838*
Turner, R. A., 498, *516*
Turner, R. J., 224, *233*, 506, 509, *518*, 821, *839*
Turner, T., 645, *653*
Turner-Henson, A., 442, *447*, *448*
Turpin, G., 87, *94*
Tursky, B., 92, *93*, 126, *134*, 703, 704, *708*
Tuttle, R., 686, 690, *693*, 753, *755*
Tutu, C., 371, *380*
Tversky, A., 25, 29, 38, 39, 40, *43*, 197, *206*, 408, *413*, 728, 733, *740*, *743*, *745*
Twentyman, C. T., *275*, *278*
Twillman, R., 397, *402*
Twumasi, P., 808, *813*
Tyler, R., 870, *890*
Tyree, T. J., 847, *853*
Tyrell, D., 154, *164*, 340, *346*
Tyrell, D. S. J., 638, *651*
Tyroler, H. A., 153, *171*, 576, *578*
Tyrrell, D. A., 713, *723*
Tyrrell, D. A. J., 33, *42*, 328, *332*, 683, 684, *691*, *692*

U

U. S. Bureau of the Census, 876, *894*
U. S. Department of Health and Human Services, 252, 253, 254, 256, *261*, 521, 522, 523, 525, 526, 527, *538*, 573, *580*, 602, *611*, 627, 628, 646, 648, 649, *657*, 857, 863, 869, 877, *894*
U. S. General Accounting Office, 478, *493*
U. S. Preventive Services Task Force, 527, 531, *538*, 727, *745*
U. S. Bureau of the Census, 427, 428, *440*
Uchino, B., 823, *839*
Uchino, B. N., 160, *172*, 226, 227, *233*, 324, *336*, 355, 357, *363*, 393, 394, *403*, 690, *694*, 713, *725*
Uddin, S., 289, *309*
Uduman, S., 824, *836*
Uehata, A., 676, *680*
Ueshima, H., 287, *313*, *317*
Uhl, G. R., 296, *317*
Uhlenhuth, E. H., 703, *708*
Uitti, C., 506, *512*
Ulene, A., 461, *466*
Ullmann-Joy, P., 526, *535*
Ulmer, D., 148, *162*, *165*
Ulmer, R., 642, *651*
Ulmer, R. A., 146, *163*
Ulrey, L. M., 180, *192*
Ulvenstam, G., 217, *233*
Umberson, D., 215, 223, *231*, *233*, 355, *361*, 662, *667*
Umlauf, R. L., 583, 584, *589*
UNAIDS, 817, 825, *839*
Underwood, U., 818, 819, 820, 821, *834*
Ung, E., 124, *136*
Ungerer, J., 565, *570*
United Nations, 831, *839*
United States Bureau of the Census, 820, 821, *839*
United States Raytheon Company, 372, *385*
Uno, H., 805, *815*
Uomoto, J., *489*, *492*
Urassa, M., 829, *832*
Urban, N., 521, 522, *538*, 738, *744*
Urbanek, M., 296, *317*
Urdal, P., 270, *278*
Uretsky, N. B., 32, 33, *42*
Urquhart, J., 572, *580*
Urrows, S., 55, *57*, 330, *331*, 391, 395, 398, *399*
Urrutia, J., 225, *233*, 496, 509, *517*
Ursano, R. J., 178, *190*, 326, *333*

V

Vaccarino, V., 228, *229*

Vaccaro, D., 213, 222, *234*
Vagg, P. R., 638, 639, 642, *656*
Vague, J., 265, *278*
Vague, P., 265, *278*
Vaha-Eskeli, K. K., 503, *518*
Vaillant, G. E., 67, *82*, 155, *169*, 285, 300, *309*, *317*
Vaira, D., 824, *839*
Vaizey, M. J., 368, *382*
Valderrama, P., 343, *346*
Valdes, M., 63, *80*
Valdimarsdottir, H., 326, 328, *336*, 683, 684, 687, *691*, *694*
Valdimarsdottir, H. B., 182, *193*
Valencia, M. E., 266, *278*
Valentin, L., 503, *517*
Valeri, C. R., 158, *167*
Valins, S., 68, *78*, 369, 370, *379*
Valleron, A. J., 824, *838*
Valliant, G. E., 180, *192*
Valois, R. F., 603, *607*
Valoski, A., 270, 273, *276*
Valoski, A. M., 270, 273, *276*
van Bardeleben, U., 663, *667*
Van Brummelen, P., 434, *439*
Van Dam, A.-M., 112, *115*
Van de Perre, P., 824, 828, *839*
Van den Brandt, P. A., 287, *317*
Van Denburgh, M., 286, *310*
van der Hart, O., 345, *348*
van der Kolk, B., 345, *348*
van der Kolk, B. A., 31, *46*
Van der Linden, L., 699, *707*
Van der Pligt, J., 728, 732, 733, *740*, *745*
Van Dijk, J. G., 289, *307*
van Doornen, L. J., 689, *692*
Van Duyn, M. A., 522, *535*
Van Dyke, R., 824, 827, *833*
Van Eek, H., 120, *137*
Van Eerdewegh, P., 296, *315*
Van Egeren, L. F., 643, *657*
Van Geijn, H. P., 499, 505, *516*
Van Goethem, C., 824, *839*
Van Grunsven, P. M., 575, *577*
Van Horn, L. V., 576, *577*
Van Huss, E., 433, *440*
Van Itallie, T. B., 265, *278*, *279*
Van Keppel, M., 125, 126, *135*
van Knippenberg, A., 204, *207*
van Oostrom, M. A., 719, *723*
Van Schayck, C. P., 575, *577*
van Stavel, R., 638, *654*
van Tits, L. J. H., 689, *695*
Van Treuren, R. R., 354, *361*
Van Weel, C., 575, *577*
Van Yperen, N., 196, 204, *206*
Van Yperen, N. W., 417, 426
Van, N., 850, *851*
Vanalainen, J. M., 629, 630, *654*
VanCamp, S., 527, *539*
Vancouver, J. B., 548, *557*
vanden Brandt, P. A., 520, *535*
Vanderklok, M., 196, *207*
VanderZee, K., 204, *208*
Vandiver, P. A., 300, 301, *316*
Vandongen, R., 287, *315*
vanDoornan, L. J. P., 641, 642, *652*, *657*
Vang, T. F., 863, 868, *894*
Vanhove, G. F., 571, *580*
VanItallie, T. B., 520, *536*
Vannatta, K., 454, *456*
Vanraden, M., 803, *814*
van't Spijker, A., 389, 392, 395, *403*
Vara, L. S., 273, *276*
Varat, M., 22, 33, *45*, 714, *724*
Varner, M. W., *511*, *517*
Varnes, J., 528, *532*
Varni, J. W., 771, 772, 773, *775*, *776*
Vartiainen, E., 290, *317*
Vassar, S., 619, *625*
Vasterling, J., 716, *725*, 759, 761, *776*
Vaughan, D. E., 286, *315*
Vaughan, K. B., 122, *136*
Vaughan, R., 222, *234*
Vaughn, B., 496, *513*
Vaughn, C., 575, *579*
Vaux, A., 209, *233*, 393, *400*
Vavak, C. R., 72, *81*, 150, 151, *166*
Veblen-Mortenson, S., 595, 601, 603, *607*
Vedhara, K., 154, *172*
Veeder, M., 717, *722*
Veenstra, J., 286, *311*
Vega, W., 462, *468*, 855, *894*
Veitch, R., 369, *381*
Veith, R. C., 325, *335*, 663, *668*
Vekshtein, V. I., 675, *682*
Velasquez, M. M., 461, *465*
Velicer, W. F., 461, *465*, 593, *610*, 782, 783, *797*, *798*
Velie, E. M., 496, *517*
Vella, S., 846, 847, 848, *851*, *853*
Vellozzi, C. J., 531, *538*
Velthuis-te Wierik, E. J., 286, *311*
Venditti, E. M., 266, 270, *278*, *279*
Venner, R. M., 119, *137*
Venzon, D., 824, *835*
Vera, M. N., 372, *385*
Verba, S., 619, *625*
Verbrugge, L. M., 780, *799*
Verdino, R., 675, *681*
Verdino, R. J., 675, *682*
Verghese, A., 575, *580*
Verhoef, M. J., 526, *538*
Vermund, S. H., 779, *797*, 821, *836*
Vernalis, M., 675, *680*
Vernazza, P. L., 850, *853*
Verne, J., *532*, *535*
Vernon, S. W., 153, 154, *171*, 218, *232*, 329, *335*, 729, 731, 739, *745*
Veroff, J., 223, *233*
Verrier, R. L., 329, 330, *335*, 675, *681*
Verspaget, H. W., 329, *332*
Verstreken, G., 699, *707*
Vess, J. D., 720, *725*
Veteran's Administration Cooperative Study Group on Antihypertensive Agents, 698, *708*
Vetter, H., 67, *80*, 157, *166*
Vetter, W., 576, *578*
Vezina, M., 420, 424
Viahov, D., 822, 826, *838*
Vial, M., 824, *833*
Vichinsky, E. P., 804, *815*
Vickberg, S. J., 773, *776*
Vickberg, S. M. J., 771, *774*
Vickers, R. R., 140, 143, 155, 158, 160, *163*, *168*, 326, *332*
Vickers, R. R., Jr., 155, *168*
Victor, M., 289, *317*
Victora, C., 225, *233*
Vidal, J. M., 420, 424
Viegener, B. J., *275*, *278*
Vieth, A., 300, 301, *316*
Vieth, A. Z., 584, *589*
Vik, P. W., 327, *332*
Vila, J., 372, *385*
Vila, K. L., 269, *276*, 524, *535*
Villacres, E. C., 663, *668*
Villafane, C. T., 372, 373, *383*
Villani, X., 717, *723*
Villar, J., 225, *233*
Vincent, L., 717, *723*
Vincent, S. D., 546, *557*
Vincent, T. A., 593, *611*
Vincent, V. A. M., 112, *115*
Vingerhoets, A. J. J. M., 687, *691*, *693*
Vingerhoets, J. J. M., 499, 505, *516*
Vinogradov, S. V., 807, *815*
Vinokur, A. D., 393, *399*, 719, *725*, 750, *756*
Vinokur, I. L., 373, *382*
Vinokur-Kaplan, D., 750, *756*
Vinsel, A., 606, *607*
Vinson, D. C., 289, 290, *317*
Virkkunen, M., 299, *316*
Virnelli, S., 354, *361*
Virts, K. L., 272, *278*
Visco, J., 154, *165*
Visintainer, M. A., 748, *756*
Visintainer, P., 480, *492*
Visker, K. E., 250, *259*
Visot, L. R., 583, *589*
Visscher, B., 156, *170*, 685, 686, *693*
Visscher, B. R., 64, 67, *82*., 157, *164*, 344, *346*, 393, *399*, 805, *813*
Visuri, T., 290, *311*
Vita, J. A., 675, *682*
Vitaliano, P. P., 325, *336*, 469, *476*, 481, 482, 484, *493*, 719, *725*
Viteri, F. E., 226, *230*, 855, *889*
Vito, D., 464, *466*
Vittinghoff, E., 806, *813*, 818, *837*
Vizzard, J., 850, *852*
Vlaeyen, J. W. S., 120, *137*
Vlahor, D., 389, 398, *401*, 806, *813*, 818, 822, 823, 826, *834*, *836*
Vloschinskii, P. E., 807, *815*
Vogel, S. F., 469, *474*
Vogel, V., 735, *745*
Vogel, V. J., 874, 880, *894*
Vogele, C., 716, *723*
Vogel-Sprott, M., 297, *317*
Vogt, M. W., 828, *839*
Vogt, R. A., 266, 272, 273, *276*, *279*
Vogt, T. M., 216, 217, *233*
Vogulhut, J., 827, *833*
Voigt, L., 523, *534*
Vokey, J. R., 405, *413*
Vokonas, P. S., 153, *167*
Volavka, J., 297, 298, *310*, *315*
Volberding, P., 846, *852*
Volberding, P. A., 808, *813*, 846, 847, 848, *851*
Volpicelli, J. R., 299, *306*, *317*
von Eiff, A. W., 371, 373, *383*, *385*
Von Euler, C., 646, *657*
von Knorring, A.-L., 297, *317*
von Knorring, L., 297, *310*, *315*, *317*
VonKorff, M., 632, *656*
VonSternberg, T., 571, *579*
Vookles, J., 65, *83*
Voors, A. W., 807, *815*
Vorakitphokatorn, S., 368, *381*
Vosk, B., 773, *774*
Vossler, E., 571, 575, 576, *580*
Voyce, C., 830, *832*
Vranizan, K. M., 808, *813*

W

Wachs, T. D., 369, 375, 378, *385*
Wachspress, J., 473, *476*
Wachtel, P., 142, 151, *172*

Wack, J., 254, *260*
Wackers, F. J., 671, *681*
Waddell, G., 119, *137*
Wadden, T. A., 265, 266, 270, 271, 272, 273, *276*, *278*, *279*
Wade, A., 825, *839*
Wade, C., 153, *163*
Wade, N. A., 827, *839*
Wadenvik, H., 689, *693*
Wadhwa, N., 394, *400*
Wadhwa, N. K., 64, *83*
Wadhwa, P. D., 496, 501, 502, 503, 510, *511*, *517*, *518*
Wadley, V. G., 480, *490*
Wagener, M., 848, 849, *853*
Wagenknecht, L., 523, *538*
Wagenknecht, L. E., 869, *888*
Wagennar, A. C., 600, *611*
Wagner, C. C., 142, 144, 160, 161, *172*
Wagner, E., 598, *608*
Wagner, E. H., 522, 524, *533*, *534*, 576, *580*, 663, *668*
Wagner, G., 850, *853*
Wagner, H., 829, *837*
Wagner, P. E., 152, *172*
Wagner, T. O., 689, *694*
Wagner, T. O. F., 328, 329, *336*
Wagstaff, D. A., 830, *838*
Wahby, V., 325, *336*
Wahl, H. W., 485, 488, *489*
Wahlsten, D., 748, *756*
Wainwright, S. P., 454, *457*
Waiyaki, P., 825, *837*
Wakabayashi, K., 287, *317*
Wakins, L. R., 709, *721*, *724*
Walcott-McQuigg, J. A., 357, *363*
Walden, C. E., 576, *577*
Walden, T., 368, 375, *383*
Waldmann, T. A., 805, *815*
Waldron, I., 223, *233*
Waletzky, L. R., 753, *755*
Walitzer, K. S., 297, 300, 301, 303, *316*
Walker, A. J., 486, *493*
Walker, E. A., 546, 547, 548, *557*
Walker, F. B., 876, *892*
Walker, J., 829, *835*
Walker, L., 548, 549, *557*
Walker, P. S., 877, *889*
Walker, R. D., 877, *889*
Walker, S. N., 54, *57*
Walker, S. S., 431, *440*
Wall, M., 525, *537*
Wall, P. D., 118, 127, 128, 131, *135*, *137*
Wall, S., 354, *360*
Wall, T. D., 358, *363*
Wall, V. J., 767, *776*
Wallace, A. G., 74, *78*, 635, 640, *651*
Wallace, C. Y., 496, 503, *515*
Wallace, D., 144, *168*
Wallace, L. M., 716, *725*
Wallace, R., 777, 794, *799*
Wallace, R. B., 153, *171*, 286, *316*
Wallace, R. K., 327, 329, *336*
Wallack, L., 305, *306*, *310*, *318*, 596, 600, 602, *611*
Wallander, J. L., 330, *331*
Wallbott, H. G., 64, *84*
Waller, D., 226, *231*
Waller, D. A., 454, *457*
Waller, D. G., 810, *812*
Wallerstein, N., 596, 597, 602, 603, *611*, 622, *623*, *625*
Wallhagen, M. I., 55, *57*
Wallin, L., 356, *360*
Walling, M. K., 546, *557*
Wallis, L. A., *474*, *476*
Wallston, B. S., 49, 50, 51, 52, 53, 55, *57*, *58*, 181, *193*, 236, *247*
Wallston, K. A., 49, 50, 51, 52, 53, 54, 55, *56*, *57*, *58*, 126, *133*, 159, *171*, 180, 181, 182, *193*, 219, *229*, *233*, 236, *247*, 329, *334*, 391, 394, 395, *402*, 751, *755*
Wallston, K. S., 125, *134*
WALPA group members, 287, *312*
Walsh, A. G., 546, *557*
Walsh, B. T., 266, *278*
Walsh, D. C., 855, 856, *887*
Walsh, M. A., 642, *651*
Walsh, W. P., 394, *401*
Walsh-Riddle, M., 642, *651*
Walsh-Riddle, S., 146, *163*
Walters, E. E., 326, *334*
Walters, N., 641, *656*, 685, *692*
Walton, K. G., 327, 329, *336*
Waltz, M., 396, *403*
Wambach, K. G., 786, *798*
Wamboldt, M., 451, *457*
Wamboldt, M. Z., 452, *457*
Wan, C. K., 72, 73, 76, *83*, 150, *172*, 183, *193*, 197, *207*
Wanderer, J. J., 862, *893*
Wandersman, A., 592, 596, 603, 604, 605, *607*, *608*, *609*, *610*, *611*, 614, 616, 617, 618, 619, 620, 621, *623*, *624*, *625*, 732, *741*
Wang, C., 472, *476*, 603, *611*
Wang, C. H., 434, *439*
Wang, H., 156, *170*
Wang, H. Y. J., 64, 67. *82*
Wang, J., 265, *279*
Wang, J. M., 810, *813*
Wang, J. P., 270, *277*
Wang, J. X., 270, *277*
Wang, L., 827, *839*
Wang, N., 154, *165*
Wang, S. H., 469, *474*
Wang, X., 252, *258*
Wang, Y., 636, *651*
Wannamethee, G., 629, *656*, *657*
Wannamethee, S. G., 286, *318*
Wara, D., 328, *332*, 690, *692*, 804, *814*
Ward, A., 636, *651*
Ward, C. H., 71, *84*, 151, *172*, 480, *489*, 633, *650*
Ward, J. E., 732, 734, *745*
Ward, J. R., 64, *83*, 125, *136*
Ward, J. W., 827, *836*
Ward, K. D., 153, *171*
Ward, M. M., 705, *706*
Ward, R. H., *511*, *517*
Ward, S. E., 22, 28, *43*
Wardlaw, S. L., 502, 503, *514*
Wardle, J., 714, *725*, 733, *745*
Ware, D., 804, *814*
Ware, J. E., 52, 53, *56*, 389, *402*, 473, *476*
Warheit, G., 462, *468*
Warnecke, R., 523, 524, *536*
Warner, K. E., 869, *892*
Warner, L. A., 283, 284, 285, 300, *312*
Warner, R., 873, *894*
Warner, V., *455*, *456*
Warr, P. B., 420, 426
Warrack, G., 291, *307*
Warram, J. H., 330, *334*
Warren, B. L., 827, *839*
Warren, C., 825, *835*
Warren, D., 828, *837*
Warren, D. I., 602, *611*
Warren, D. L., 822, 826, *838*
Warren, K., 355, 359, *361*, 663, *667*
Warren, R., 619, *625*
Warren, R. B., 602, *611*, 621, *625*
Warren, W. B., 502, 503, *514*
Warren-Boulton, E., *446*, *447*
Warrenburg, S., 397, *401*
Warsch, J. J., 644, *657*
Warshaw, C., 551, 552, *557*
Warwick, D., 297, *307*
Washburn, A. L., 88, *93*
Washburn, R., 526, *538*
Washington Post, 802, *813*
Washington, A., 779, 794, *798*
Washington, A. E., 567, *569*
Washington, C. D., 787, *797*, 830, *835*
Waskin, H., *474*
Waskins, H., 830, *832*
Wasserheit, J., 825, *838*
Wasserman, D. A., 224, *231*
Wasserman, J., 282, *313*, 685, *691*
Wassertheil-Smoller, S., 67, *84*, 473, *476*
Wassmuth, R., 805, *815*
Waters, E., 354, *360*
Watkins, E. L., 604, *611*
Watkins, G., 374, *385*
Watkins, L. L., 154, *172*
Watkins, L. R., 112, *114*
Watkins, P. L., 71, *84*, 151, *172*
Watson, D., 23, 32, 34, 36, *45*, *46*, 62, 68, 75, 76, *84*, 142, 147, 152, 153, 154, 155, 158, *164*, *172*, 283, *313*, 340, *348*, 354, 355, 356, *363*
Watson, D. W., 250, *258*
Watson, F. M. C., 748, *755*
Watson, J. B., 251, 253, *261*
Watson, J. P., 329, *335*, 497, 498, 510, *513*, 747, 749, *756*
Watson, M., 752, *756*, 764, *775*
Watson, P. J., 101, *102*
Watson, P. M., 717, *724*
Watson, R. D., 436, *440*
Watson, R. L., 700, *707*
Watson, W., 872, 873, 874, *894*
Watts, C. D., 869, *892*
Watts, C. H., 542, 543, *555*
Watts, J. C., 20, 21, 24, 30, 31, *44*
Watts, N., 471, *475*
Waugh, R., 664, 665, *666*
Waugh, R. A., 329, *334*, 671, 674, 675, 677, *679*, *680*
Waxler, N. E., 218, *231*, 329, *333*, 751, 752, *755*
Waxler-Morrison, N., 218, *233*
Waxweiler, R. J., 855, *893*
Wayment, H., 339, *347*, 823, *837*
Wayner, E. A., 108, *115*
Waziri, R., 327, 329, *336*
Weatherburn, P., 789, *796*
Weaver, J. L., 861, *894*
Weaver, S. M., 506, *512*
Webb, G. R., 291, *318*
Webb, J. A., 735, 736, *742*, *745*
Webb, S., 366, 368, *380*
Webb, S. D., 368, *385*
Webber, L. S., 807, *815*
Weber, B., 330, *333*
Weber, G., 750, *756*
Weber, M. A., 643, *657*
Weber. S. J., 733, *742*
Webster, D. W., 305, *310*, *318*
Webster, J., 354, 355, *360*
Webster, J. D., 617, 618, *623*
Webster, L., 779, 794, *799*
Webster, L. A., 288, *310*
Wechsler, H., 289, 291, 293, *318*, 606, *611*
Weckler, L., 252, *261*

Wedel, H., 215, *232*
Weeks, M. R., 823, *839*
Weems, L. B., 687, *694*
Weene, B. A., 543, 545. *555*
Wegner, D., 397, *403*
Wehler, C. A., 265, *276*
Wehner, J. M., 299, *318*
Weibel-Orlando, J., 877, *894*
Weid, H. W., 326, *332*
Weidman, H. H., 876, *894*
Weidner, D., 503, *517*
Weigel, C., 450, *457*
Weigman, O., 575, *580*
Weiland, F. L., 671, *679*
Weinberg, A. D., 735, 736, *742*, *745*
Weinberger, D. A., 61, 71, 73, 76, *84*, 156, 157, *172*
Weinberger, J., 184, *191*
Weinberger, M., 434, *439*, *440*, 699, *707*
Weinberger, M. H., 434, 436, *438*, *439*, *440*
Weinblatt, E., 217, *233*, 630, 647, *656*
Weiner, B. H., 153, *169*
Weiner, H., 685, 686, *693*
Weiner, H. L., 689, *692*
Weiner, L., 600, *610*
Weiner, R. D., 471, *474*
Weiner, S., 503, *515*
Weingarden, K., 508, *517*
Weingartner, P. J., 560, *569*
Weinman, J., 39, *45*
Weinsier, R. L., 263, *276*
Weinstein, A., 451, *457*
Weinstein, N., 197, *208*, 782, 788, *799*
Weinstein, N. D., 728, 729, 730, 731, 732, 733, 735, 739, *743*, *746*
Weinstock, R., 272, 273, *279*
Weintraub, J. K., 31, *42*, 433, 435, *438*, 505, *512*
Weisäth, L., *229*, *233*
Weisberg, J., *489*, *491*
Weisbrod, R., 593, 595, 601, 603, 604, *607*, *609*
Weisel, H., 267, *277*
Weisman, A., 762, 764, *776*
Weisman, A. D., 714, *725*
Weisman, C., 825, *839*
Weisman, C. S., 463, *468*
Weisman, M. H., *56*, *58*
Weiss, R. S., 340, *347*
Weiss E., 818, *834*
Weiss, D. W., 685, *695*
Weiss, G. L., 182, *193*
Weiss, J. M., 31, *46*
Weiss, K. M., 877, *894*
Weiss, L., 367, 368, 370, *381*, 433, 435, *438*
Weiss, L. H., 486, *491*
Weiss, N., 523, *534*
Weiss, N. S., 523, 531, *537*, *538*
Weiss, S., 471, *475*
Weiss, S. H., 828, *836*
Weiss, S. M., 59, 77, *83*, 139, 148, *164*, *172*, 704, 705, *707*
Weiss, S. T., 153, *167*
Weiss, T., 90, 91, *94*, 642, *656*
Weissberg, R., 830, *832*
Weissberg, R. P., *162*, *163*
Weisse, C., 374, *385*
Weisse, C. S., 63, *84*, 685, 688, 689, 684, *695*
Weisse, S. M., 753, *755*
Weissfeld, L., 305, *310*
Weissman, D., 806, *816*, 826, *834*
Weissman, G., 823, *839*
Weissman, M. M., *455*, *456*
Weissman, W., 461, *465*
Weiss-Perry, B., 441, *447*
Weisz, J., 396, *402*
Weisz, J. R., 50, *57*
Welch, A., 397, *400*
Welch, A. S., 373, *385*, 748, *756*
Welch, B. L., 371, 372, 373, *385*, 748, *756*
Welch, H. G., 731, 738, 739, *745*
Welin, L., 215, *233*
Weller, A., 354, *362*
Weller, C., 855, 859, *892*
Weller, P., 10, *16*
Weller, S. C., 27, 37, *47*, 858, 860, *894*
Welles, S., 811, *813*
Wellisch, D. K., 716, *723*
Wellman, B., 210, *231*
Wellman, H. M., 408, *411*
Wells, B. L., 183, *192*, 530, *533*
Wells, E. A., 304, *308*
Wells, H. B., 500, *516*, 531, *534*
Wells, K., 389, *402*, 473, *476*
Wells, K. B., 855, *894*
Wells, N. L., 752, *756*
Wells-Parker, E., 293, *313*, 344, *348*
Welte, J. W., 287, *316*
Welvaart, K., 719, *723*
Wen, F., 157, *168*
Wendel, G. D., 545, *556*
Wener, R., 367, *385*
Wenger, M. A., 95, *102*
Wenger, N. K., 471, 472, *476*
Wenger, N. S., 787, *799*
Wenig, P., 91, 92, *93*
Wenneberg, S. R., 327, 329, *336*
Were, J. B., 808, *814*
Wergowske, G., 286, *310*
Wermuth, L., 787, *796*
Werther, G., 444, *447*
Wertlieb, D., 441, *447*, *448*, 450, *457*
Wesp, M., 689, *694*
West, C. A. C., 480, *490*
West, J. A., 782, 783, *798*
West, S., 370, *384*
West, S. G., 212, *229*, 731, 732, 733, 734, 736, 737, 738, 739, *740*, *741*, *742*, *746*
Westen, D., 141, 142, 151, *172*
Westermeyer, J., 863, 868, 869, *894*
Westfall, U. E., 574, *580*
Westie, K. S., 715, *722*
Westman, M., 178, 183, *192*, *193*, 353, *363*
Wetherall, L. D., 371, *382*
Wetle, T., *205*, *207*
Wetsteyn, J. C. F. M., 576, *580*
Wetzel, R. D., 291, *314*
Wewers, M. E., 254, *259*
Wexler, J. P., 473, *476*
Wexler, P., 576, *580*
Weyer, P. J., 720, *722*
Weyman, A., 699, *707*
Weyman, A. E., 434, *439*
Whalen, C., 471, *475*
Whalen, R. E., 72, *84*, 669, 672, *682*
Whaley, F. S., 629, *652*
Wharton, R., 292, *309*
Wheatley, K., 286, *309*
Wheaton, B., 821, *839*
Wheeler, F., 526, *538*
Wheeler, F. C., 594, 601, *609*
Wheeler, L., 195, *205*, *208*
Whelton, P., 429, *437*, 700, *707*
Whipple, R., 525, *539*
Whitaker, C. C., 388, *402*
Whitaker, P., 64, *83*
Whitcher-Alagna, S., 486, *490*
White, A. A., 405, *412*
White, C., 432, 435, *440*
White, C. C., 527, *538*
White, C. R., 828, *833*
White, E., 521, 522, *538*
White, G. M., 881, *894*
White, H. R., 300, *312*
White, I., 662, *667*
White, J. D., 805, *815*
White, J. M., 783, *798*
White, J. W., 543, *557*
White, K., 576, *580*
White, K. L., 37, *47*
White, M. G., 804, *814*
White, P., 719, *724*
White, R. P., 619, *623*
White, R. T., 406, *413*
White, V., 736, *741*, *742*
White, V. M., 530, *533*
Whitehead, T. L., 782, *795*
Whitehead, W. E., 88, 89, 90, 92, *93*, *94*, 123, *137*, 548, *557*
Whitehouse, J., 827, *837*
Whiteman, M., 222, *229*
Whiteman, M. C., 152, *172*
Whiteneck, G. G., 586, *590*
Whiteside, L., 369, 374, 378, *380*, *384*
Whiteside, T. L., 713, *725*
Whiteside, T., 227, *231*, 329, *335*, 752, 753, *755*, *756*
Whitfield, J., 531, *536*
Whitfield, J. B., 295, *311*
Whitlatch, C. J., 478, 481, 483, *489*
Whitman, S., 531, *532*, *536*
Whittin, R., 876, *889*
Whitworth, J. A., 434, *440*
Wians, F. J., Jr., 808, *814*
Wibbelsman, C., 463, *465*
Wichstrom, L., 736, *746*
Wicke, C., 847, *852*
Wicker, A. W., 595, *611*
Wickersham, D., 734, *741*
Wickizer, T., 598, *608*
Widaman, K. F., 301, *317*
Widmayer, S., 367, *385*
Widmer, C., 619, *625*
Widom, C. S., 292, *318*
Wieand, H. S., 531, *532*
Wiebe, D. J., 32, 33, *47*, 64, *84*, 145, 155, 158, *172*, *173*, 178, 179, *193*
Wiebe, J., 343, *346*
Wiebe, J. S., 150, *163*, 220, *229*
Wieczorek, W. F., 293, *318*
Wiedenfeld, S. A., 65, *84*, 245, *247*, 328, *336*
Wiegant, V. M., 689, *693*
Wieland, U., 847, *852*
Wielgosz, A. T., 153, *172*
Wiemann, C. M., 504, *518*
Wienman, J. A., 20, *45*
Wierson, M., 222, *230*
Wigal, J. K., 397, *403*
Wigfield, A., 443, *447*
Wiggins, J. S., 140, 141, 160, *172*, *173*
Wight, D., 787, 788, 789, *799*
Wight, R. G., 824, *839*
Wiklund, I., 217, *233*, 395, *402*
Wilcox, L. S., 530, *539*
Wilcox, P., 735, *745*
Wildey, M., 464, *466*
Wilenski, D., 341, *348*
Wiley, D., 805, *813*
Wiley, J., 293, *317*, 462, *467*, 778, 784, 785, 789, *798*, 822, *832*
Wilhelm, K., 471, *475*
Wilhelm, M. C., 749, 752, *754*
Wilhelmsen, J., 217, *233*

Wilhelmsen, L., 215, 216, *232, 233*
Wilhelmsson, C., 217, *233*
Wilhemsen, L., 153, *170*
Wilk, J., 272, 273, *279*
Wilkens, W., 101, *103*
Wilkie, D. J., 120, *137*
Wilkie, F. W., 469, *474*
Wilkins, H. A., 825, *839*
Wilkins, P., 855, 870, *891*
Wilkins, S., 481, *490*
Wilkinson, G. R., 802, 809, *816*
Willaims, E., *306, 313*
Willard, K., 732, *740, 745*
Willerford, D. M., 828, *833*
Willett, C., 471, *475*
Willett, J. B., 441, 445, *447*
Willett, W., 286, *310*, 520, *535*
Willett, W. C., 153, *167*, 265, 268, *276, 277, 279*, 286, 287, 290, *310, 311, 317, 318*, 472, *474*, 520, 523, *537, 539*, 629, *654*
William, J. T., 296, *315*
Williams, A., 339, *347*, 804, *815*
Williams, A. E., 808, *815*
Williams, B., 825, *835*
Williams, C. A., 663, *668*
Williams, C. L., 462, *465*
Williams, D. A., 120, 122, 123, 125, 129, *134, 135, 137*
Williams, D. L., 460, *466*
Williams, D. R., 432, 433, 436, *439, 44.*, 662, *667*, 821, 822, *836, 839*, 855, *891*
Williams, E., 872, *891*
Williams, E. L., 605, *608*
Williams, F. J., 122, 126, *136*
Williams, G. D., 282, 293, *318*
Williams, J. B., 846, *853*
Williams, J. K., 72, *82*, 154, 158, 159, *168*
Williams, J. M. G., 733, *743*
Williams, K. R., 542, 553, *554*
Williams, L., 358, *363*
Williams, M., 344, *348*, 828, *833*
Williams, M. E., 470, *476*
Williams, P., 368, 378, *381*, 528, *534*
Williams, P. G., 61, 76, *83*, 140, 143, 158, 160, *171, 173*, 178, 179, 187, *193*, 330, *336*
Williams, P. T., 520, *539*, 593, 595, 596, 597, 598, 600, 601, 606, *608*
Williams, R., 61, 66, 75, 76, *78*, 146, *171*
Williams, R. B., 64, 65, 66, 74, *78, 81*, 139, 149, 150, 153, 154, *162, 165, 166, 172, 173*, 217, *233*, 642, *651*, 661, 662, 663, 664, 665, *666, 667, 668*, 669, 672, 674, 677, *682*, 703, *708*
Williams, R. B., Jr., 63, 66, 72, *83, 84*, 146, 148, 149, 150, 151, *162, 163, 164, 172, 173*, 432, 436, *437*, 662, 663, *666, 667*
Williams, R. M., 158, *167*, 687, *694*
Williams, R. S., 74, *78*, 635, 640, *651*
Williams, S., 359, *360*, 642, *651*
Williams, S. B., 630, *657*
Williams, S. L., 126, *133*, 243, *247*
Williams, S. S., 782, 783, *797*
Williams, T., 736, *741*
Williams, V. P., 665, *668*
Williamson, D., 153, 156, *162*, 662, *666*
Williamson, D. F., 266, 268, 270, *278, 279*, 290, *307*, 523, *539*
Williamson, G., 154, *164*
Williamson, G. M., 33, 34, *42*, 321, 328, *332*, 480, 481, 483, 484, 485, *492, 493*, 500, *512*, 683, 684, *692*, 823, *833*
Williard, H. N., 703, *708*
Willig, C., 296, *315*
Williger, D., 100, *103*, 688, *693*
Willis, P. W., 434, 435, *439*
Willis, S. L., 574, *579*
Willms, J., 289, 290, *317*
Willoughby, R., 689, *693*
Wills, T. A., 36, *46*, 160, *164*, 195, 196, 204, *208*, 209, 210, 211, 212, 213, 214, 218, 221, 222, 223, 225, 228, *230, 234*, 302, 305, *318*, 324, 327, *332, 333*, 355, *360*, 393, *399*, 485, *490*
Wilmore, J. H., 526, *537*, 573, *579*, 629, 630, 646, 647, 648, *655*
Wilpers, S., 142, *162*
Wilson, C., 250, *260*
Wilson, D., 344, *347*
Wilson, D. P., 575, *580*
Wilson, J. F., 560, *569*
Wilson, J. R., 297, 298, *314*
Wilson, J. S., 289, *318*
Wilson, M., 601, *607*, 699, *707*
Wilson, M. D., 503, *512*
Wilson, R. A., 671, *680*
Wilson, T. S., 787, *797*, 830, *835*
Wilson, T. W., 699, *708*
Wilson, W. J., 442. *448*
Wimbush, F. B., 395, *402*
Winblad, B., 480, *490*
Winchester, J., 700, *707*
Winchester, L., 732, 734, *745*
Winchester, R., 802, 803, *815*
Winders, S. E., 254, 255, *259, 261*, 269, *277*
Windsor, R. A., 524, *539*, 576, *577*, 849, *851*
Winer, E. P., 716, 717, 719, *723, 725*
Winett, R., 591, 595, 596, 598, 599, *611*
Winett, R. A., 593, 596, 598, 599, *611*, 830, 831, *835, 838*
Wing, A. L., 525, 526, *537*, 629, 630, 631, 647, *655*
Wing, R., 700, *707*
Wing, R. R., 153, *168*, 265, 266, 267, 268, 269, 270, 271, 272, 273, 274, *275*, 276, 277, 278, 279., 520, *539*, 576, *580*, 648, *653*, 662, *667*, 818, *836*
Wing, S. B., 435, *439*
Wingard, D. L., 61, *80*, 143, 153, 155, 156, 158, 159, 160, *165, 168*, 395, *400*, 471, *474*
Wingard, J., 716, *722*
Wingard, J. R., 716, *725*
Wingerd, J., 367, *385*
Wingo, P., 709, 710, 711, *724*
Wingo, P. A., 727, *743*, 747, *756*
Wingood, G. M., 787, 788, 789, *799*
Winicour, P., 22, *42*
Wink, A., 373, *384*
Wink, P., 66, *79*
Winkelstein, W., 604, *611*, 778, *798*
Winkelstein, W., Jr., 471, *476*, 523, *539*
Winkleby, M. A., 527, 528, *539*, 601, 604, 605, 606, *608*, 855, *889*
Winkler, C., 806, 807, 810, *813, 814, 815*
Winn, D. M., 288, *308*
Winningham, M. L., 717, *725*
Winokur, G., 291, 295, *307, 310*, 471, *475*
Winsborough, H. H., 366, *385*
Winston, T. J., 506, *518*
Winter, R. J., 270, *278*, 576, *580*
Winters, M. A., 571, *580*
Wintgens, A., 453, *457*
Wirsching, B., 750, *756*
Wirsching, M., 750, *756*
Wirt, R., 462, *465*
Wise, B. D., 748, 749, 753, *755*
Wise, P. S., 66, *83*
Wise, R., 451, *456*
Wise, R. A., 574, *580*
Wishner, A. R., 543, 545, *555*
Wisniewski, L., 273, *276*
Wisniewski, N., 294, *312*
Wiswell, R. A., 646, *652*
Witherspoon, G., 877, *895*
Witt, D. J., 828, *839*
Wittchen, H. U., 283, *312*, 632, *653*
Witteman, J. C. M., 287, *318*
Witty, T. E., 584, 585, *589*
Wocial, B., 644, *651*
Wodak, A. D., 286, *315*
Wofsy, C., 823, 828, *839*
Wohlgemuth, W., 435, *440*
Wohlwill, J. F., 375, *385*
Wojno, W. C., 487,*491*
Wolchick, S. A., 221, *233*
Wolf, C., 751, *754*
Wolf, D. M., 719, *725*
Wolf, S., 703, *708*
Wolf, S. L., 648, *655*
Wolf, T. A., 531, *532, 537*
Wolfe, B. B., 252, *259*
Wolfe, D. M., 349, 350, 351, *361*
Wolfe, E. S., 728, *746*
Wolfe, F., 473, *476*
Wolfe, H., 785, *797*
Wolfe, J., 283, 284, *308*
Wolfe, W. W., 728, *746*
Wolff, H. G., 139, *173*, 703, *708*
Wolff, T., 616, 617, 618, *624*
Wolfsdorf, J. I., 441, 445, *447*
Wolfson, L., 525, *539*
Wolfson, M., 600, *611*
Wolin, S. J., 304, 305, *307, 318*
Wolinsky, S. M., 806, *813*
Wolitski, R. J., *16*
Wolk, A., 287, 288, *307, 317*, 520, *535*
Wollman, C. A., 393, *402*
Wollman, K., 328, *336*, 689, *695*
Wolman, B. B., 92, *94*
Woloshin, S., 731, 738, 739, *745*
Wolpe, J., 97, *103*
Wolpert, H., 441, 445, *447*
Womack, W., 767, *776*
Wonderlich, S. A., 583, 584, 588, *589, 590*
Wong, J. B., 472, *474*
Wong, J. G., 530, 531, *539*
Woo, G., 500, 506, 507, 510, *517, 518*
Wood, A., 809, *816*
Wood, A. J., 810, *813*
Wood, A. J. J., 802, 809, *816*
Wood, J. R., 621, *624*
Wood, J. V., 196, 204, *208*, 396, *403*
Wood, M. D., 291, 300, 301, 302, *312, 316, 318*
Wood, P., 528, *534*
Wood, P. D., 520, *539*, 591, 593, 595, 596, 597, 598, 600, 601, 606, *608*
Wood, P. K., 284, 291, 297, 300, 301, 302, 304, *309, 312, 316, 318*
Woodall, K. L., 151, *168, 173*, 222, *232*
Woodard, L. J., 715, *725*, 779, *797*
Woodbury, M. A., 469, *474*
Wood-Dauphinee, S., 389, *403*
Woodhouse, D. E., 780, *797, 799*
Woodman, C. R., 630, *657*
Woodruff, A., 735, *742*
Woodruff, S. I., 464, *466*
Woodruff, W. J., 546, 547, 548, *556*
Woods, J., 603, *609*
Woods, M., 272, *276*, 508, *517*
Woods, M. N., 522, *538*
Woods, N. F., 218, *232*

Woods, R., 502, *515*
Woods, S. C., 254, *261*
Woods, W., 10, *16*
Woods, W. J., 850, *852*
Woods, X. A., 390, 398, *399*, 719, *722*
Woods-Powell, C. T., 523, *538*, 732, 733, 734, *743*
Woodward, C. K., 733, 734, 737, 738, *740*, *741*
Woodward, W. R., 236, *247*
Woodworth, G., 295, 296
Woody, P. D., 765, 768, *775*
Woolf, R. B., 508, *517*
Woolf, S. H., 728, *746*
Woolfolk, R. L., 367, *381*
Woomert, A., 486, *491*
Wooten, W., 527, *536*, *539*
Wooten, W. J., 527, *533*
Worchel, S., 376, *385*
Worden, J. W., 714, *725*, 762, 764, *776*
Worden, T. J., 66, 71, 73, *83*, 435, *439*
Working Well Trial, 522, *538*
Workman, E. A., 688, *695*
World Health Organization, 583, *590*, 817, *839*
Worth, D., 792, *799*, 820, 821, 822, 823, *839*
Wortley, P. M., 825, *839*
Wortman, C., 339, *347*, *348*, 487, *490*
Wortman, C. B., 140, 143, 155, 160, *168*, 342, *347*, 394, *402*, *489*, *490*, 583, *589*
Wozny, M. A., 561, *570*
Wright, C., 672, *681*
Wright, E. J., 498, 510, *516*
Wright, J. C., 61, *83*
Wright, J. T., Jr., 575, *579*
Wright, K. M., 178, *190*
Wright, L. B., 433, *440*
Wright, L. K., 479, 480, 481, 482, *493*
Wright, R. A., 72, *84*, 144, *173*
Wright, S. F., 394, *402*, 488, *492*
Wright, T. C., 826, 828, *834*, *839*
Wright, T. L., 124, *135*
Wu, A. H., 631, *657*
Wu, A. W., 849, *852*
Wu, C., 736, *742*
Wu, C. F., 286, *318*
Wu, J. Y., 299, *311*
Wu, M., 524, *535*
Wu, T., 373, *385*
Wu, W., 296, *315*
Wu, X., 806, 807, *815*
Wu, Z., 805, *813*
Wulfert, E., 183, *193*
Wunder, S., 720, *724*
Wuorenma, J., 571, *579*
Wurster, R. D., 87, *94*
Wurtman, R. J., 252, *260*
Wyatt, R. J., 297, *314*
Wynder, E., 523, *535*, 717, *722*
Wynder, E. L., 522, *539*
Wyndham, C. H., 366, *385*
Wyningo, C., 685, 688, *693*
Wynings, C., 325, 326, 328, *334*
Wyper, M. A., 734, *746*
Wypijewska, C., 781, *795*, 820, 831, *832*
Wyshak, G., 27, *41*, 631, *652*
Wyss, J. M., 433, *437*

X

Xiao, J. Z., 270, *277*
Xiao, J., 806, 807, *815*
Xistris, D., 717, *723*
Xue, X., 550, *555*

Y

Yabe, D., 806, 807, *815*
Yaffe, S., 499, *512*
Yaffe, S. J., 19, *43*
Yali, A. M., 496, 504, 505, 510, *515*, *518*
Yalom, I., 720, *724*
Yamaguchi, K., 462, *467*, 780, *799*
Yamamoto, S. Y., 500, *512*
Yamamura, Y., 806, *813*
Yan, K. X., 729, 735, *741*
Yanagihara, R., 806, *813*
Yanagita, T., 250, *261*
Yanase, Y., 804, *815*
Yang, H. M., 471, *475*
Yang, W. Y., 270, *277*
Yano, E., 777, *797*
Yano, K., 216, *232*
Yanovski, S., 266, *278*
Yao, J. K., 297, *314*
Yap, P. L., 804, *814*
Yaple, K., 509, *516*
Yarandi, H. N., 436, *440*
Yaretzki, A., 636, *655*
Yarnall, K. S. H., 523, *538*
Yarnell, J. W. G., 366, *385*
Yarnold, P. R., 152, *173*
Yarrington, J., 444, *446*
Yasko, J., 753, *755*
Yasuda, P., 453, *457*, 773, *776*
Yates, B. C., 218, *232*
Yates, J. F., 736, *745*
Yates, M. D., 295, 296, *308*
Yates, M. E., 826, *839*
Yates, W. R., 285, *308*
Yatham, L. N., 325, *336*
Yaun, S., 287, *317*
Yazdanbakhsh, K., 806, *813*
Yeager, K., 527, 528, *535*
Yeager, K. K., 526, *533*
Yeatman, G. W., 867, *895*
Yehuda, R., 325, *336*
Yellen, S. B., 22, *42*
Yeni, P. G., 846, 847, 848, *851*
Yesavage, J. A., 289, 290, *318*
Yeung, A. C., 675, *682*
Yi, H., 293, *318*
Yi, S. I., 434, *440*
Yingling, J., 250, *259*
Yip, B., 471, *475*
Yirmiya, R., 326, *332*, 748, *754*
Yllo, K., 542, 543, *555*
Yocum, D., 330, *331*, *337*
Yoder, M., 858, 859, 861, *890*
Yoder, P. S., 23, *47*
Yodfat, Y., 366, *385*
Yong, L. C., 268, *279*
Yoshikawa, H., 830, *835*
Young, A., 859, *895*
Young, D., 527, *535*, 690, *692*
Young, D. L., 779, *797*
Young, J. L., 530, *534*
Young, J. Q., 600, *607*
Young, K., 393, *403*
Young, L. D., 397, 398, *403*, 704, *706*
Young, N. L., 827, *838*
Young, P. M., 672, 676, *679*
Young, R., 464, *466*, 604, 605, *608*
Young, R. M., 828, *833*
Young, S. H., 641, *653*
Young, T., 645, *654*
Younkin, S. L., 184, *193*
Yount, S. E., 327, *332*
Yu, E., 431, *438*
Yu, V. L., 848, 849, *853*
Yu, Z. J., 252, *261*
Yuan, S. S., 520, *535*
Yudin, N. S., 807, *815*
Yuhasz, M., 635, *654*
Yuker, H. E., 584, *590*
Yurko, K., 156, *169*
Yusuf, S., 630, *655*
Yuzpe, A A., 562, 563, *570*
Yuzpe, A., 563, *569*

Z

Zabin, L. S., 825, *833*
Zablotsky, D. L., 826, *839*
Zacarias, F., 819, 820, *835*
Zacchello, F., 803, *813*
Zachariah, R., 509, *518*
Zachary, V., 575, *580*
Zador, P. L., 290, *318*
Zahniser, S. C., 508, *514*, 524, 525, *535*
Zakhari, S., 286, *318*
Zakhary, B., 665, *666*
Zakowski, S. G., 327, 328, *336*, *337*, 689, *695*, 753, *756*
Zaks, J., 371, *380*
Zalcman, S., 111, *115*
Zambrana, R., 496, *517*
Zambrana, R. E., 496, 500, 506, 510, *518*
Zane, L. Y. S., 366, 369, *384*
Zane, N., 393, *403*
Zanettini, R., 373, *380*
Zang, E. A., 522, *539*
Zank, S., *489*
Zanna, M., 195, *207*, *208*
Zannino, L., 321, 328, *332*
Zanussi, C., 803, *815*
Zapka, J. G., 734, 736, 737, *746*
Zaret, B. L., 150, *163*, 671, *679*, *680*, *681*
Zarit, J. M., 686, *695*
Zarit, S. H., 478, 481, 483, *489*, 686, *695*
Zarrow, M., 406, *412*
Zarsins, C. K., 641, 643, *650*
Zautra, A., 219, *232*
Zautra, A. J., 245, *247*, 330, *331*, *335*, *337*, 388, 395, 398, *402*, *403*, 487, 488, *492*, *493*
Zax, M., 498, *518*
Zayas, L. H., 506, *518*
Zazove, P., 575, *580*
Zborowski, M., 818, *839*
Zedeck, S., 419, 420, 425, 426
Zeiss, A. M., 25, 29, *47*
Zeitouni, N. C., 298, *309*
Zekoski, E. M., 498, 510, *516*
Zelazo, P. D., 289, *315*
Zell, E. R., 614, *625*
Zelnik, M., 790, *799*
Zeltzer, K., 765, 767, *774*
Zeltzer, L., 764, 766, *775*, *776*
Zeltzer, L. K., 764, 769, 770, 772, *775*, *776*
Zeltzer, P., 769, *776*
Zemore, R., 218, *234*
Zenilman, J., *16*
Zenilman, J. M., 828, *832*
Zhang, H., 270, *277*
Zhang, L., 806, *813*
Zhang, Y. A., 810, *815*
Zhao, L., 305, *310*
Zhao, S., 283, *312*, 632, *653*
Zheng, G., 434, *439*

Zheng, H., 270, *277*
Zheng, Y., 810, *815*
Zhou, H. H., 802, 809, *816*
Zhu, W., 504, 505, *515*
Zich, J., 394, *403*
Ziegler, M. G., 434, *438*, 641, *653*
Ziegler, R. G., 869, *890*
Zielder, A., 805, *813*, *815*
Zierler, S., 818, 828, *837*, *839*
Zillman, D., 25, *47*, 641, *651*
Zimbardo, P., 202, *208*
Zimmer, D., 787, *799*
Zimmer-Gembeck, M. J., 496, 499, *518*
Zimmerman, B. J., 19, *42*
Zimmerman, B. L., 719, *725*, 750, *756*
Zimmerman, E. H., 674, *682*
Zimmerman, H. P., 780, *799*
Zimmerman, M. A., 595, 597, 603, *612*
Zimmerman, M., 285, *318*,322, *337*, *623*, *624*
Zimmerman, P. A., 806, *816*
Zimmerman, R., 19, 22, 23, 28, *41*, *44*, 462, *468*
Zimmermann, E., 149, *173*
Zimmermann, E. A., 150, *172*, 663, *667*, *668*
Zimmermann-Tansella, C., 506, *518*
Zinaman, M., 503, *512*
Zincke, H., 470, *474*
Zinsmeister, A. R., 544, 547, 548, *557*
Ziporyn, T., 497, *512*
Zirkel, S., 76, *79*
Zisook, S., 340, *348*
Zokwe, B., 820, *834*
Zola, I., 36, *47*
Zonderman, A., 149, *164*, 472, *475*
Zonderman, A. B., 66, *78*, 152, 153, 154, *162*, *173*, 329, *337*, 548, *557*
Zone, J. B., 178, *192*
Zorick, F., 290, *315*
Zorr, B., 828, *839*
Zorrilla, C., 824, 827, *836*
Zorzet, S., 327, *337*
Zrull, M., 224, *230*
Zucker, R. A., 285, 301, 303, 304, *318*
Zuckerman, A., 61, 70, *79*, 144, 154, *163*, 188, *190*, 394, *399*
Zuckerman, B., 290, *307*, 503, 506, *512*, *518*, 545, 548, *554*, 823, *832*
Zuckerman, D., 542, 543, 544, 545, 548, 551, *557*
Zuckerman, M., 300, *318*
Zung, W. W. K., 633, *657*
Zuniga, M. E., 506, *518*
Zuskar, D., 499, *517*
Zusman, R. M., 434, *438*
Zuspan, F. P., 225, *234*
Zwaag, R. V., 366, *384*
Zwartjes, W., 772, *775*
Zweifel, M., 298, 299, *310*
Zwi, A. B., 542, 543, *555*
Zyzanski, S. J., 147, *167*, 509, 517

Subject Index

A

Above average effect, 197
Adherence
  Dietary, 573
  Interventions, 576
  Measures of, 574, 575
  Medication, 573
  Patterns of, 572
  Predictors of, 573, 574
  Quantitative assessment of, 572
Affiliation, 202, 203
African American Acculturation Scale, 852, 866
Aging
  Age at disease onset and, 471
  Definition of normal, 470
  Depression and, 471
  Gender and, 471
  Health related quality of life and, 473
  HRT and, 472
  Period/time effects, 470, 471
AIDS and behavior change, 3
  Condom use and, 5, 6, 7, 8, 9, 10, 12, 15
AIDS risk reduction model, 782, 783
Alcohol
  Cancer and, 287
  Cognitive disorders and, 289
  Crime and, 293
  Family and, 291, 292
  Fetal effects and, 289, 290
  Heart disease and, 286
  High risk behaviors and, 292, 293
  Hormonal changes and, 289
  Hypertension and, 287
  Injury and, 290
  Liver disease and, 288
  Neurochemical mediators, 299
  Pancreatitis and, 288
  Peptic ulcer and, 288
  Role performance and, 291
  Stroke and, 287
Alcohol abuse, 281, 282
  Animal studies of, 298
  Attention-allocation model of, 303
  Behavior-genetic research
    Adoption studies, 295
    Family studies, 295
    Genetic marker studies, 296
    Twin studies, 295
    Vulnerability studies, 296, 297, 298
  Economic cost, 282
  Etiology of, 300 301, 302, 303
  Familial influences in, 304
  Mass media effects, 305
  Psychiatric diagnoses and, 283, 284, 285
  Stress response dampening model of, 303
  Tension-reduction hypothesis of, 302
Alcohol dependence, 281, 282
Anger, 65, 66, 71, 72
Antigen, 106
Appraisal, 68
Assisted reproductive technologies (ART)
  Definition of, 560
  Psychological consequences of use of, 563, 564, 565
Asthma, 451, 452
Attribution and effect on illness, 33
Attributional Style Questionnaire, 180
Autobiographical memory, 406
Autonomic nervous system, 85, 86, 87, 92

B

Behavior change
  Interventions and, 15
  Measurement techniques
    Action alternatives and, 8
    Attitude measurement , 11
    Relevant referents and, 7
    Personal characteristics and, 8
      Emotional reactions, 13
    Perceived normative pressure, 12
    Perceived outcomes and, 7
    Self-efficacy, 14
    Self standards and sanctions, 13
  Stages of change, 5
  Variables related to, 5
Behavioral medicine
  Definition of, 96
Behavioral prediction, theories of, 4, 5
Behavioral change, theories of, 4, 5
Biofeedback
  Definition of, 87, 96, 97
  Disorders, 98, 99
Body Mass Index (BMI), 263
Burnout
  Definition of, 415
  Depersonalization and, 416
  Emotional exhaustion and, 416
  Sources/outcomes of, 418
  Job-person fit and, 420, 421, 422
  Organizational health and, 423
  Reduced personal accomplishment and, 416
  Social support and, 422

C

Cancer
  Stress
    Biobehavioral model of, 709
    Biological pathways and, 713
    Bone marrow transplantation and, 716
    Compliance to treatment and, 712, 713
    Delay of treatment and, 714
    Diagnosis and, 714, 715
    Disease course and, 713
    Health behaviors and, 712
    Interventions, 717, 718, 737
    Perceived risk of, 728
    Prevalence, 727
    Quality of life and, 711
    Recovery/long-term survival and, 718, 719, 720
    Recurrence/death and, 720, 721
    Sexual dysfunction and, 719
    Treatment and, 715, 716
    Treatment morbidity and, 717
Cancer intervention
  Adult, 758, 759
  Children, 764, 765, 772
Cancer screening
  Breast cancer
    Barriers/facilitators, 528, 530
    Current status, 528
    Interventions, 531
  Cervical cancer
    Barriers/facilitators, 530
    Current status, 530
    Interventions, 532
  Colorectal cancer
    Barriers/facilitators, 531, 532
    Current status, 531

Interventions, 532
Caregiving
Beneficial effects of, 483, 484
Mental health outcomes of, 480
Physical health outcomes of, 481
Theoretical models of, 478, 479
Work/leisure activities and, 482
Care receiving
Beneficial effects of, 486
Mental health outcomes, 487
Physical health outcomes, 488
Theoretical models of, 484, 485
Center for Epidemiologic Studies depression scale, 355
Citizen participation, 614
Chronic illness
Childhood
Asthma, 451, 452
Beliefs about illness, 450
Coping and, 391, 395, 396, 397
Demographics and, 395
Environment/culture and, 393
Optimism, 395
Personality and, 394, 395
Positive adjustment to, 388
Social support and, 393, 394
Classical conditioning, 253
Closed brain injury, 587
Cognitive clarity, 202, 203
Cognitive Errors Questionnaire (CEQ), 125
Cognitive Social Health Information Processing (C-SHIP) model, 730
Commonsense model of self regulation, 20, 574
Community coalitions, 614, 615, 618
Community intervention
Community development and, 596
Ecological principles and, 594, 595
Empowerment and, 596, 603
Evaluation of, 604
Mass media and, 597
Policy and, 599
Process of, 601, 602, 603, 604
Researchers and, 605
Social cognitive theory, 595
Social ecology perspective, 593
Social marketing and, 596
Strategies of, 598
Community participation, 619, 620, 621
Community Trial for Smoking Cessation (COMMIT), 600
Condition-specific control, 52, 53
Conditioned health threat, 740
Conflict Tactics Scale (CTS), 553
Consortium for the Immunization of Norfolk's Children (CINCH), 613, 615, 616, 617, 618
Content Analysis of Verbatim Explanation Technique (CAVE), 180
Control, *see* Perceived control, Locus of control
Cook-Medley Hostility Scale, 77, 149
Coping, 181
Childhood chronic illness and, 450
Chronic illness and, 391, 395, 396, 397
Pregnancy and, 504
Transplantation and, 453
Coronary heart disease
Psychosocial factors
Biobehavioral mechanisms, 663, 664
Epidemiologic evidence, 662
Prevention and treatment, 664, 665
Counterdependence, 354
Crowding, 366, 367
Immune function and, 368
Motivation and, 370
Psychological health and, 368
Psychophyiological studies and, 368
Psychosocial resources and, 369
Cultural Mistrust Inventory, 866
Cytokines, 107, 108, 112

D

Diabetes, adolescents
Dangerous neighborhoods and, 444
Organization in community and, 442
Risk-taking behaviors and, 445
Stage-environment fit model and, 443
Diet
Barriers to change, 521
Interventions, 521
Overweight and, 520
Practices, 521
Disability, 582, 585, 586
Disclosure
Academic functioning and, 342
Affective/well being measures and, 342
Benefits of, 339, 340
Cancer research and, 340
Clinical benefits of, 344
Cognitive and linguistic changes and, 345
Employment functioning, 342
Health reports and, 341
Immune function and, 342
Inhibition and, 344
Short-term effects of, 342
Traumatic memory research and, 345
Disengagement, 65, 67, 71, 74
Domestic violence, *see* male partner violence
Double standard, 790

E

Ecological momentary assessment (EMA), 410, 411
Emotional suppression/repression, 65, 66, 67, 71, 73
Ethnicity
Health status and, 429
Hypertension and, 430, 431
Cardiovascular reactivity and, 431
Coping resources and, 435
Racial stress, 432
SNS effects and, 434
Socioecologic stress and, 433
Socioeconomic status and, 432
Sodium effects and, 434
Experience sampling method (ESM), 410, 411
Eustress, 355, 356
Explanatory style, 180

F

False consensus effect, 197
Framingham Type A Scale, 147

G

Gate control theory, 118, 127, 128
Gender differences in sexual relationships, 785
Glasgow Coma Scale, 587

H

Handicap, 583
Hardiness, 177, 178, 353
Health behavior model, 145, 146
Health belief model, 3, 4, 39, 53, 146, 151, 574, 729
Health beliefs/practices
African Americans, 865, 868, 869
Folk healers, 869, 870
Folk disorders, 872
Healing practices, 870, 871
Racism/distrust of Whites, 865
Tuskegee Syphilis Experiment, 866, 867
Voodoo, 871
Asian Americans
Language and indigenous schema, 861
Racism/distrust of Whites, 859
Shaming practices, 860
Chinese Americans, 861
Folk cures, 862, 863
Folk disorders, 862
Health attitudes, 862
Yin and Yang, 861
Latino Americans, 852, 853
Emotions, 853
Folk cures, 858
Folk disorders, 855, 856, 857
Folk healers, 857
Hot/cold theory of disease, 854
Racism/distrust of Whites, 853
Native Americans
Healers/healing practices, 874, 875, 876, 877
Racism/distrust of Whites, 873
Southeast Asian Americans
Folk cures, 864, 865
Religions, 864
Sudden Death Hmong Folk Syndrome (SUNDS), 865
Health locus of control, 51, 181, 239
Hematopoiesis, 106
HIV, 3, 157
Chronic nature of, 847
Epidemiology of, 778
Highly active antiretroviral therapies (HAART), 842, 843
Psychological adjustment with, 842
Transmission risk behavior, 846
Treatment adherence, 844, 845
Treatment of, 842
Women
Caretaking and, 824
Drug-related relationships and, 823
Heterosexual relationships and, 822
Lesbianism/bisexuality and, 828
Life stage of, 824, 825
Policy, 831
Pregnancy/parenthood and, 827
Prevention, 829, 830
Research, 831
Sociocultural influences and, 818, 819, 820
Social support and, 823
Social class and, 821
Treatment of, 830
Urban vs. rural settings and, 829
Hostility, 65, 66, 71, 72, 149, 150, 158
Hot/cold theory of disease, 854
Hypertension
Biofeedback and, 704
Environmental manipulation and, 702
Physical exercise and, 701
Placebo/suggestion and, 703, 704
Psychotherapy and, 701, 702
Relaxation therapy and, 704, 705
Sodium intake and, 698, 699
Weight management and, 700

I

Ideographic Functional Status Assessment, 188
Illness behavior model, 146, 151

Illness (Problem) representation
Attributes of, 22, 68
Adolescent transition, 37
Bidirectionality of emotion, 25
Coping, 23, 24, 27
Culture and language , 37
Emotional responses, 24, 29, 30, 31, 69
Fear, 21
Health outcomes, 39, 69
"hot" cognition, 30, 31
If-then rules, 28, 40
Interpreting somatic and social factors, 35
Later life transition, 38
Negative affect and symptoms, 26, 27
Problem solving episodes, 24, 29, 30, 31
Sharing of, 36
Social observation-comparison, 36, 37
Somatic and social factors, 35
Structure of, 23
Immune system conditioning, 105, 108
Behavioral effects of infection and, 112
Chemotherapy and, 110
Stress and, 111
Immunity
Chronic stressors and, 685, 686
Definition of, 106
Intervention studies, 688
Lab stressors and, 689, 690, 691
Measures, 685
Naturalistic stress and, 688
Impairment, 582
Infertility
Adjustment among families created by, 565
Background, 559, 560
Prevention of
Delayed childbearing, 566
Sexually transmitted diseases, 565
Psychological reactions to, 561
Stress and coping framework and, 561
Injuries in childhood, 454
Internal-External scale (I-E scale), 51
Interoceptive conditioning, 89, 90
Ischemia
EKG measures of, 670
Lab studies, 669, 673
Pathophysiological mechanisms, 674, 675, 676
Predictive value of, 677, 678
Prevalence during physical and mental tasks, 671
Psychological factors in, 672
Triggers of, 672, 673

J

Jenkins Activity Survey, 147
John Henryism, 435

L

Learned helplessness, 54
Life Events and Difficulties Schedule (LEDS), 323
Life expectancy, 428
Life Orientation Test (LOT), 77, 155, 179
Locus of control, 236
Definition of, 51, 70
Limitations, 53
Lorig's Arthritis Self-Management Program, 245

M

Male partner violence
Attitudes toward women and, 552
Chronic pain and, 547
Chronic pelvic pain and, 546
Definition of, 542
Gastrointestinal disorders and, 547
General prevalence and patterns of, 543, 544
Misdiagnosis of, 550
Personal fears and, 552
Physician involvement
Personal barriers, 551
Systematic barriers, 551
Pregnancy and, 545
Prevalence in medical care settings, 544
Protocol in medical departments regarding, 549, 550
Retraumatization and, 551
Mapping studies, 781, 782
Marlowe-Crowne Social Desirability Scale, 77, 150, 156
Maslach Burnout Inventory (MBI), 416
Mass psychogenic illness, 201, 202
Millon Behavioral Health Inventory, 156
Minnesota Heart Health Program (MHHP), 601
Multidimensional health locus of control, 181
Multidimensional health locus of control scale (MHLC scale), 52

N

National AIDS Behavioral Survey, 785
Natural Killer (NK) cells, 107, 110, 328
Negative affect, 354
Neuroticism, 152, 153, 300
Nicotine
Activity level and, 254
Attention and, 255
Body weight regulation and, 254
Effect on central nervous system, 251
Neuroendocrine system and, 252
Neurotransmitter system and, 252
Reinforcement and, 251
Self-administration, 250, 251
Stress and, 256, 257
Noise
Coping behaviors and, 374
Immune function and, 374
Methodological problems in research of, 378, 379
Motivation and, 375
Physical health and, 371
Psychological health and, 374
Psychophysiologic outcomes and, 371, 372, 373
Numeracy, 739

O

Obesity
Definition of, 263
Morbidity and mortality and, 265
Prevention of, 268
Psychosocial consequences, 266
Open brain injury, 587
Open relationships, 792, 793
Operant conditioning, 87, 89, 91, 253
Clinical application, 91
Pain behaviors and, 120
Optimism, 70, 155, 179, 751
Chronic illness and, 395
Orientation to Life Questionnaire (OLQ), 177
Outcome evaluation, 71
Overdependence, 354

P

Pain
Cognitive factors and, 122, 123
Cognitive-behavioral model, 129, 130
Coping strategies, 125, 126
Diathesis-stress model, 128, 129
Gate control theory, 118, 127, 128
Physiological processes, 130, 131, 132
Unidimensional sensory model, 118
Pain prone personality, 119
Pawtucket Heart Health Program, 596, 601
Perceived Competence Scale (PC scale), 54
Perceived control
Appraisal, 50
Definition of, 49, 101
Measurement of, 51, 54
Operationalization of, 51
Personal and situational variables, 55
Placebo effect, 101, 102
Primary vs. secondary, 50
Study of, 50, 51
Perceived health competence scale, 54
Perceived risk
Breast self examination and, 734
Comparative risk and, 732
General determinants of, 733
Mammography screening and, 734
Measurement of, 731, 732
Sun protection and, 736
Personal Views Survey, 178
Personality
As a risk factor of illness, 62, 63, 64, 65
Context, 62
Chronic illness and, 394, 395
Definition of, 60
Five factor taxonomy, 140, 141, 142, 300
Measurement
Content, 75
Content relevance, 76, 77
Structure, 76
Stress moderation models, 144
Structure of, 61, 62
Type A, 139, 147, 148, 149
Pessimistic attribution style, 70
Peyer's patches, 106
Physician Assessment and Counseling for Exercise Program (PACE), 527
Physical activity
Adherence and, 648
Anxiety and, 638, 639
Barriers/facilitators, 526, 527
Breast cancer and, 631
Cardiovascular disease and, 629
Colon cancer and, 631
Coronary heart disease morbidity, 629, 630
Definition of, 628
Depression and, 632
Distraction hypothesis and, 645
Endorphin hypothesis and, 645
Health effects, 525
Hypertension and, 630
Interventions, 527
Monoamine hypothesis and, 644
New guidelines for, 646, 647
Physical health and, 629
Prevalence, 525
Psychological health and, 631, 632
Recommendations for women, 526
Stress reactivity and, 639, 640, 642, 643
Thermogenic hypothesis and, 645, 646
Placebo effect, 101, 102, 109
Planned Approach to Community Health (PATCH), 601, 602
Pluralistic ignorance, 198
Posttraumatic Stress Disorder (PTSD), 325, 453
Power dynamics in sexual encounters, 789
Pregnancy
Coping in, 504

Depression and, 498
Fetal variables in, 499
Male partner violence and, 545
Maternal variables in, 499
Preterm delivery and, 500
Social support and, 505
Direct effects model of, 509
Functions or types of, 507
Negative aspects of, 508
Interventions and outcomes, 508
Sources or providers of, 506, 507
State anxiety and, 497
Stress and, 500, 501
Behavioral mechanisms, 503
Physiological mechanisms, 502, 503
Stress models and, 496
Prenatal Coping Inventory, 505
Precaution adoption process model, 730
Primary appraisal, 240, 391, 396
Protection motivation theory, 730
Psychophysiological technology, 77

Q

Quieting reflex, 100

R

Recall biases
Frequency rates and, 407
Reconstruction/Reproduction errors and, 407, 408
Previous experience and, 406
Reconstruction/Reproduction errors and, 406, 407
Temporal information, 408
Bounding/rounding and, 409
Duration biases, 409, 410
Telescoping and, 409
Rehabilitation
Developmental factors in, 583
History of, 581, 582
Interpersonal dynamics and, 584
Interventions
Amputation, 588
Spinal cord injury, 585, 586, 587
Traumatic brain injury, 587, 588
Psychological factors in, 583, 584
Relaxation response, 99, 100
Relaxation techniques
Autogenic training, 97, 99
Controlled breathing, 97
Muscle relaxation training, 97, 102
Repression, emotional, 65, 66, 67, 71, 73
Repressive coping, 156, 157

S

Salutogenesis, 183, 185
Schedule of Racist Events (SRE), 866, 881
Scripting theory, 791
Secondary appraisal, 240, 396
Self efficacy, 53, 54, 102, 124, 181, 182
Affect and, 238, 241
Assessment of, 242, 243
Cognition and, 238
Coping and, 240
Definition, 236, 237
Enactive mastery and, 240
Health and, 243, 244, 245
Modeling and, 241
Motivation and, 238
Selection processes and, 239
Self-confidence and, 240
Theory, 574
Self esteem, 239
Self reliance, 354
Sense of coherence, 176, 177, 184
Sensory specific satiety, 267
Sexual communication, 787, 788, 789
Sexual domination of women, 792
Sexual health, 787
Sexual mixing, 779
Sexual patterns, 779, 780, 781
Sexual roles, 783, 784, 785
Smoking
Health effects, 522, 523
Patterns, 523
Physiological effects of nicotine, 523
Smoking cessation, 253, 269
Barriers to, 521
Effect washout in interventions and, 464
Fear-based interventions, 459, 560
Information based interventions, 460
Interventions, 524
HIV risk and, 463
Life skills model, 461, 462
Social inoculation model and, 461
Synergism of risk-taking behaviors, 462
Social comparison
Chronic medical conditions and, 204, 205
Content-induced, 201
Gender and, 199
Medical care seeking behavior and, 200, 202
Theory, 36, 195, 196
Social cognitive theory, 3, 4
Social dominance behavior, 152
Social learning theory, 39, 40, 55, 122, 181, 182, 236, 237, 301, 461
Social support, 150, 160, 355, 752
Arthritis and, 219
Behavioral mechanisms and, 214
Blood pressure and, 226
Burnout and, 422
Cancer and, 218
Children and adolescents and, 221
Chronic illness and, 393, 394
Definition, 209
Diabetes and, 219, 220
Direct vs. indirect effects, 212
Disease onset and, 216
Elderly and, 216, 225
Functional measures of, 210
HIV infection and, 221
Hemodialysis and, 220, 221
Immune system and, 227
Main effect model of, 211, 212
Matching hypothesis of, 211
Mortality and, 215
Pregnancy and, 224, 225, 505, 506, 507, 508, 509
Recovery from illness and, 217
Structural measures of, 210
Substance use and, 223
Transplantation and, 453
Weight loss and, 274
Stanford Five City Project (FCP), 598, 601
Stress
Acute vs. chronic, 323
Biological theories of, 321, 322
Breast cancer
Animal research and, 748
Human research and, 749
Immune system and, 753
Progression of, 750, 751
Cancer and, 328, 329
Coping and, 68, 69
Definition of, 323
Diabetes and, 330
Disease and, 327, 684
Health and, 100
Heart disease and, 329
Immune-mediated disease and, 327, 328
Infectious illness and, 328
Personality research and, 59, 67, 69
Psychological theories, 322
Rheumatoid arthritis, 330
Susceptibility to infectious disease, 683, 684
Transplantation and, 452
Trauma and, 326
Stress response, 69, 71
Stressor exposure, 69
Stressors, 68
Structured Interview (SI), 149
Sudden Unexplained Nocturnal Death Syndrome (SUNDS), 865
Suppression, emotional, 65, 66, 67, 71, 73

T

Taylor Manifest Anxiety Scale, 156, 355
Theoretical model of minority health, 877
Theory of planned behavior, 53, 566, 574
Theory of reasoned action, 3, 4, 39, 196, 574
Theory of self-regulation, self control, 4
Theory of subjective culture and interpersonal relations, 4
Three Community Study (TCS), 598, 601
TOTE (test-operate-test-exit), 20, 21
Transplantation
Adherence to treatment and, 454
Cognitive function and, 454
Coping and, 453
Developmental considerations and, 453
Posttraumatic stress disorder, 453
Quality of life, 454
Social support and, 453
Stress and, 452, 453
Transtheoretical model of change, 730, 783
Tuskegee Syphilis Experiment, 866, 867
Type A personality, 139, 147, 148, 149

V

Very low calorie diet (VLCD), 272
Visceral afferents, 88
Visceral learning
History of, 85, 86, 87, 92
Visceral perception, 88
Voodoo, 871

W

Weight gain
Menopause, 269, 270
Pregnancy and, 269

Y

Young adults and, 268
Weight loss
Benefits, 266
Diet and, 272
Environmental/behavioral factors and, 267
Exercise and, 273
Genetics and, 266

Maintenance of, 274, 275
Social support and, 274
Work stress
Definition of, 349
Demand-control model of, 351
Effort-reward imbalance model of, 351
History of research on, 349, 350
Role stress/person-environment fit model of, 351
Preventive stress management model of, 351
Psychoanalytic theory and, 351
Work stress research
Diversity issues in, 357
Nonrecursive relationships among variables in, 357
Workplace interventions, 358, 359